Murray and Nadel's
Textbook of
Respiratory Medicine

VOLUME TWO

Murray and Nadel's
Textbook of Respiratory Medicine

Fourth Edition

Editors

Robert J. Mason, M.D.

Professor of Medicine
University of Colorado Health Sciences Center
Professor of Medicine
National Jewish Medical and Research Center
Denver, Colorado

John F. Murray, M.D., D.Sc. (Hon),
F.R.C.P.

Professor Emeritus of Medicine
University of California, San Francisco
Former Chief, Chest Service
San Francisco General Hospital
Cardiovascular Research Institute Investigator
San Francisco, California

V. Courtney Broaddus, M.D.

Professor of Medicine
University of California, San Francisco
Chief, Division of Pulmonary and Critical Care
  Medicine
San Francisco General Hospital
San Francisco, California

Jay A. Nadel, M.D., D.Sc. (Hon)

Professor of Medicine, Physiology, and Radiology
University of California, San Francisco
Cardiovascular Research Institute Investigator
San Francisco, California

ELSEVIER
SAUNDERS

ELSEVIER
SAUNDERS

The Curtis Center
170 S Independence Mall W 300E
Philadelphia, Pennsylvania 19106

TEXTBOOK OF RESPIRATORY MEDICINE

ISBN 0–7216–0327–0 (2 Volume Set)
Part number: 9997637577 (Volume 1)
Part number: 9997637569 (Volume 2)

NOTICE

Knowledge and best practice in this field are constantly changing. As new research and experience broaden our knowledge, changes in practice, treatment and drug therapy may become necessary or appropriate. Readers are advised to check the most current information provided (i) on procedures featured or (ii) by the manufacturer of each product to be administered, to verify the recommended dose or formula, the method and duration of administration, and contraindications. It is the responsibility of the practitioner, relying on their own experience and knowledge of the patient, to make diagnoses, to determine dosages and the best treatment for each individual patient, and to take all appropriate safety precautions. To the fullest extent of the law, neither the Publisher nor the Editors assumes any liability for any injury and/or damage to persons or property arising out or related to any use of the material contained in this book.

THE PUBLISHER

First edition 1988. Second edition 1994. Third edition 2000.

Library of Congress Cataloging-in-Publication Data

Murray and Nadel's textbook of respiratory medicine—4th ed. [edited by]
  Robert J. Mason, V. Courtney Broaddus, John F. Murray, Jay A. Nadel
    p. cm.
Includes bibliographical references and index.
ISBN 0–7216–0327–0
1. Respiratory organs–Diseases. I. Title: Textbook of respiratory medicine. II. Murray, John F.
(John Frederic). III. Nadel, Jay A.
RC731.T48 2005
616.2—dc22   2005042900

Acquisitions Editor: Dolores Meloni
Developmental Editor: Jennifer Shreiner

Printed in the United States of America

Last digit is the print number: 9 8 7 6 5 4 3 2 1

Working together to grow
libraries in developing countries

www.elsevier.com | www.bookaid.org | www.sabre.org

ELSEVIER BOOK AID International Sabre Foundation

We dedicate this textbook to Dr. Julius H. Comroe, Jr., who was our mentor during the formative years of our professional development. Dr. Comroe was one of the truly great academicians of his generation. He was an investigator of exceptional merit, an educator whose influence was worldwide, and a medical statesman of exemplary integrity and vision. In dedicating this book, we acknowledge especially Dr. Comroe's scholarly contributions and his commitment to the importance of basic science in the solution of clinical problems.

J.F.M.
J.A.N.
R.J.M.
V.C.B.

Contributors

Lewis Adams, Ph.D.
Head, School of Physiotherapy and Exercise Science,
Griffith University, Gold Coast Campus, Queensland,
Australia
Dyspnea

Anthony J. Alberg, Ph.D., M.P.H.
Assistant Professor, Department of Epidemiology, Johns
Hopkins University Bloomberg School of Public Health,
Baltimore, Maryland
Epidemiology of Lung Cancer

Richard K. Albert, M.D.
Professor of Medicine, University of Colorado Health
Sciences Center; Chief of Medicine, Denver Health
Medical Center, Denver, Colorado
Preoperative Evaluation

Kurt H. Albertine, Ph.D.
Course Director, Medical Gross Anatomy, and Professor,
Departments of Pediatrics, Medicine, and Neurobiology
& Anatomy, University of Utah School of Medicine, Salt
Lake City, Utah
Anatomy of the Lungs

Thomas K. Aldrich, M.D.
Professor of Medicine, and Chief, Pulmonary Medicine
Division, Albert Einstein College of Medicine; Chief,
Pulmonary Medicine Division, Montefiore Medical
Center, Bronx, New York
The Lungs and Neuromuscular Diseases

Ronald C. Balkissoon, M.D.
Associate Professor, Department of Medicine, University
of Colorado School of Medicine; Associate Professor,
Department of Medicine, National Jewish Medical and
Research Center, Denver, Colorado
Disorders of the Upper Airways

John R. Balmes, M.D.
Professor, Department of Medicine, University of
California, San Francisco; Chief, Division of Occupational
and Environmental Medicine, San Francisco General
Hospital, San Francisco, California
*Evaluation of Respiratory Impairment/Disability;
Occupational Asthma; Air Pollution*

Joan Albert Barberà, M.D.
Associate Professor, Department of Medicine, University
of Barcelona; Consultant in Pulmonary Medicine,
Hospital Clinic, Barcelona, Spain
Pulmonary Complications of Abdominal Disease

Peter J. Barnes, D.M., D.Sc., F.R.C.P.
Professor of Thoracic Medicine, National Heart and Lung
Institute; Head, Respiratory Medicine, Imperial College
London, London, United Kingdom
*General Pharmacologic Principles; Airway
Pharmacology*

Scott Barnhart, M.D., M.P.H.
Associate Dean, and Professor of Medicine and
Occupational and Environmental Health Sciences,
University of Washington; Medical Director, Harborview
Medical Center, Seattle, Washington
Evaluation of Respiratory Impairment/Disability

Fuad M. Baroody, M.D.
Associate Professor of Otolaryngology-Head and Neck
Surgery and Pediatrics, Section of Otolaryngology-Head
and Neck Surgery, University of Chicago, Chicago,
Illinois
Disorders of the Upper Airways

**Margaret R. Becklake, M.B., B.Ch., M.D.,
F.R.C.P.(Lond.)**
Professor Emeritus, Departments of Medicine and of
Epidemiology, Biostatistics and Occupational Health,
McGill University; Honorary Physician, McGill University
Health Centre, Royal Victoria Hospital Pavilion,
Montréal, Québec, Canada
Pneumoconioses

John A. Belperio, M.D.
Assistant Professor, Division of Pulmonary and Critical
Care, Department of Internal Medicine, David Geffen
School of Medicine at UCLA, Los Angeles, California
Inflammation, Injury, and Repair

Neal L. Benowitz, M.D.
Professor of Medicine, Psychiatry and Biopharmaceutical
Sciences, and Chief, Division of Clinical Pharmacology,
University of California, San Francisco; Chief, Division of
Clinical Pharmacology, San Francisco General Hospital
Medical Center, San Francisco, California
Smoking Hazards and Cessation

Paul D. Blanc, M.D., M.S.P.H.
Professor of Medicine, and Endowed Chair, Occupational and Environmental Medicine, University of California, San Francisco, San Francisco, California
Acute Pulmonary Responses to Toxic Exposures

Tracey L. Bonfield, Ph.D.
Department of Pulmonary Medicine, Cleveland Clinic, Cleveland, Ohio
Pulmonary Alveolar Proteinosis

Richard C. Boucher, M.D.
William R. Kenan Professor of Medicine, and Director, Cystic Fibrosis Center, University of North Carolina at Chapel Hill, Chapel Hill, North Carolina
Cystic Fibrosis

Homer A. Boushey, Jr., M.D.
Professor of Medicine, Department of Medicine, Director, Asthma Clinical Research Center, and Chief, Division of Allergy & Immunology, Department of Medicine, University of California, San Francisco, San Francisco, California
Asthma

Alfred A. Bove, M.D., Ph.D.
Emeritus Professor of Medicine, Temple University School of Medicine; Chief of Cardiology, Temple University School of Medicine and Temple University Hospital, Philadelphia, Pennsylvania
Diving Medicine

Alice M. Boylan, M.D.
Associate Professor of Medicine, Department of Medicine, The Medical University of South Carolina, Charleston, South Carolina
Tumors of the Pleura

T. Douglas Bradley, M.D.
Professor, Department of Medicine, and Director, Centre for Sleep Medicine and Circadian Biology, University of Toronto; Staff Physician, Toronto General Hospital, University Health Network, and Toronto Rehabilitation Institute, Toronto, Ontario, Canada
Sleep Disorders

V. Courtney Broaddus, M.D.
Professor of Medicine, University of California, San Francisco; Chief, Division of Pulmonary and Critical Care Medicine, and Associate Director, Lung Biology Center, San Francisco General Hospital, San Francisco, California
Pleural Effusion; Tumors of the Pleura

Paul G. Brunetta, M.D.
Founder, Tobacco Education Center at UCSF Mount Zion Medical Center, San Francisco; Senior Clinical Scientist and Medical Director, Genentech, Inc., South San Francisco, California
Smoking Hazards and Cessation

Esteban G. Burchard, M.D.
Assistant Professor of Medicine, Clinical Pharmacology & Biopharmaceutical Sciences, Division of Pulmonary and Critical Care, Departments of Medicine & Biopharmaceutical Sciences, University of California, San Francisco; Department of Medicine, San Francisco General Hospital, San Francisco, California
Asthma

Martha Cavazos, M.D.
Clinical Endocrinology Fellow, Department of Medicine, University of California, San Francisco, San Francisco, California
Pulmonary Complications of Endocrine Diseases

Bartolome R. Celli, M.D.
Professor of Medicine, Tufts University; Chief, Division of Pulmonary and Critical Care Medicine, Caritas St. Elizabeth's Medical Center, Boston, Massachusetts
Pulmonary Rehabilitation

Richard N. Channick, M.D.
Associate Professor of Medicine, Pulmonary and Critical Care Division, University of California, San Diego, School of Medicine, and UCSD Medical Center, La Jolla, California
Pulmonary Vasculitis and Primary Pulmonary Hypertension

Kian Fan Chung, M.D., D.Sc., F.R.C.P.
Professor of Respiratory Medicine, National Heart and Lung Institute, Imperial College; Consultant Physician, Royal Brompton and Harefield NHS Trust, London, United Kingdom
Cough

Susan Claster, M.D.
Clinical Professor of Medicine, Division of Hematology, University of California, San Francisco, San Francisco, California
Pulmonary Complications of Hematologic Disease

Franklin R. Cockerill, III, M.D.
Professor, Department of Laboratory Medicine and Pathology, Mayo College of Medicine; Chair, Division of Clinical Microbiology, Department of Laboratory Medicine and Pathology, Mayo Clinic, Rochester, Minnesota
Microbiologic Diagnosis of Lower Respiratory Tract Infection

R. Edward Coleman, M.D.
Professor of Radiology and Director of Nuclear Medicine, Duke University Medical Center, Durham, North Carolina
Nuclear Medicine Techniques

Harold R. Collard, M.D.
Instructor, Division of Pulmonary Sciences and Critical Care Medicine, University of Colorado Health Sciences Center, Denver, Colorado
Diffuse Alveolar Hemorrhage and Other Rare Infiltrative Disorders

Jean-François Cordier, M.D.
Professor of Respiratory Medicine, Claude Bernard
University; Head, Department of Respiratory Medicine,
Reference Center for Orphan Pulmonary Diseases,
Hôpital Louis Pradel, Lyon, France
Eosinophilic Lung Diseases

David B. Corry, M.D.
Associate Professor of Medicine and Immunology, Baylor
College of Medicine, Houston, Texas
Asthma

Vincent Cottin, M.D., Ph.D.
Claude Bernard University; Department of Respiratory
Medicine, Reference Center for Orphan Pulmonary
Diseases, Hôpital Louis Pradel, Lyon, France
Eosinophilic Lung Diseases

Robert L. Cowie, M.D.
Professor, Departments of Medicine and of Community
Health Sciences, University of Calgary; Respirologist,
Calgary Health Region; Director, Tuberculosis Services,
Calgary, Alberta, Canada
Pneumoconioses

Scott F. Davies, M.D.
Professor of Medicine, University of Minnesota;
Pulmonary and Critical Care Staff Physician, and Chief of
Medicine, Hennepin County Medical Center,
Minneapolis, Minnesota
Fungal Infections

Teresa De Marco, M.D., F.A.C.C.
Professor of Clinical Medicine, University of California,
San Francisco, School of Medicine; Professor of Clinical
Medicine, Director, Heart Failure and Pulmonary
Hypertension Program, and Medical Director, Heart
Transplantation, University of California, San Francisco
Medical Center, San Francisco, California
Cor Pulmonale

R. M. du Bois, M.D., M.A., F.R.C.P., F.A.C.C.P.
Professor, Department of Respiratory Medicine, Imperial
College and Royal Brompton Hospital, London, United
Kingdom
The Lungs and Connective Tissue Diseases

James Duffin, Ph.D.
Professor Emeritus, Departments of Anaesthesia and
Physiology, and Member, Institute of Biomedical
Engineering, Faculty of Applied Science and Engineering,
University of Toronto, Toronto, Ontario, Canada
Hypoventilation and Hyperventilation Syndromes

Richard M. Effros, M.D.
Clinical Professor, Department of Medicine, Harbor-
UCLA Medical Center, Torrance, California; Emeritus
Professor, Department of Medicine, Medical College of
Wisconsin, Milwaukee, Wisconsin
Acid-Base Balance

Mark D. Eisner, M.D., M.P.H.
Assistant Professor, Department of Medicine, University
of California, San Francisco, San Francisco, California
Air Pollution

Karen A. Fagan, M.D.
Associate Professor of Medicine, Cardiovascular
Pulmonary Research Laboratory, Pulmonary
Hypertension Center, Division of Pulmonary Sciences and
Critical Care Medicine, University of Colorado Health
Sciences Center, Denver, Colorado
Pulmonary Vascular Pharmacology

John V. Fahy, M.D.
Associate Professor of Medicine, Department of Medicine,
University of California, San Francisco, San Francisco,
California
Asthma

Peter F. Fedullo, M.D.
Professor of Medicine, Pulmonary and Critical Care
Division, Department of Medicine, University of
California, San Diego, and UCSD Medical Center, San
Diego, California
Pulmonary Thromboembolism

Matthew J. Fenton, Ph.D.
Professor of Medicine, Microbiology and Immunology,
University of Maryland School of Medicine, Baltimore,
Maryland
Monocytes, Macrophages, and Dendritic Cells of the Lung

Walter E. Finkbeiner, M.D., Ph.D.
Professor and Vice-Chair, Department of Pathology,
University of California, San Francisco; Chief, Anatomic
Pathology, San Francisco General Hospital, San Francisco,
California
General Features of Respiratory Pathology

Faith T. Fitzgerald, M.D.
Professor of Medicine, University of California, Davis,
School of Medicine; Faculty, Professor of Medicine, and
Physician—General Medicine, University of California,
Davis, Health System, Sacramento, California
History and Physical Examinations

Hans G. Folkesson, Ph.D.
Associate Professor, Department of Physiology and
Pharmacology, Northeastern Ohio Universities College of
Medicine, Rootstown, Ohio
Alveolar and Distal Airway Epithelial Fluid Transport

Rodney J. Folz, M.D., Ph.D.
Associate Professor of Medicine and Assistant Research
Professor of Cell Biology, Duke University Medical
Center, Durham, North Carolina
*Pulmonary Complications of Organ Transplantation
and Primary Immunodeficiencies*

Andrew P. Fontenot, M.D.
Associate Professor of Medicine and Immunology, Departments of Medicine and Immunology, University of Colorado Health Sciences Center, Denver, Colorado
Immune Recognition and Responses

Joe G. N. Garcia, M.D.
David Marine Professor of Medicine, and Chief, Division of Pulmonary and Critical Care Medicine, Johns Hopkins University School of Medicine, Baltimore, Maryland
Pulmonary Circulation and Regulation of Fluid Balance

G. F. Gebhart, Ph.D.
Professor and Head, Department of Pharmacology, Carver College of Medicine, University of Iowa, Iowa City, Iowa
Chest Pain

Matthew Bidwell Goetz, M.D.
Professor of Clinical Medicine, David Geffen School of Medicine at UCLA; Chief, Infectious Diseases, VA Greater Los Angeles Healthcare System, Los Angeles, California
Pyogenic Bacterial Pneumonia, Lung Abscess, and Empyema

Warren M. Gold, M.D.
Professor of Medicine, Department of Medicine, University of California, San Francisco; Department of Medicine, Moffitt-Long Hospitals, University of California, San Francisco, San Francisco, California
Pulmonary Function Testing; Clinical Exercise Testing

Michael B. Gotway, M.D.
Assistant Professor In-Residence, Diagnostic Radiology and Pulmonary/Critical Care Medicine, and Director, Radiology Residency Training Program, University of California, San Francisco; Chief of Radiology, San Francisco General Hospital, San Francisco, California
Radiographic Techniques

Michael K. Gould, M.D.
Assistant Professor of Medicine, Stanford School of Medicine, Stanford; Research Associate and Staff Physician, VA Palo Alto Health Care System, Palo Alto, California
Benign Tumors

James Hamrick, M.D., M.P.H.
Clinical Fellow, Division of Hematology and Oncology, Department of Medicine, University of California, San Francisco, and San Francisco General Hospital, San Francisco, California
Pulmonary Complications of Hematologic Disease

Frederick G. Hayden, M.D.
Professor of Internal Medicine and Pathology, Stuart S. Richardson Professor of Clinical Virology, Department of Internal Medicine, University of Virginia School of Medicine; Physician, Division of Infectious Diseases and International Medicine, Department of Internal Medicine, University of Virginia Medical System, Charlottesville, Virginia
Viral Infections

Peter M. Henson, B.V.M.S., Ph.D.
Professor of Pathology, Medicine, and Immunology, University of Colorado School of Medicine; Professor, Department of Pediatrics, National Jewish Medical and Research Center, Denver, Colorado
Inflammation, Injury, and Repair

Arthur C. Hill, M.D.
Associate Professor of Surgery, Division of Cardiothoracic Surgery, University of California, San Francisco, San Francisco, California
Metastatic Malignant Tumors

Nicholas S. Hill, M.D.
Professor of Medicine, Tufts University School of Medicine, Boston, Massachusetts; Chief, Division of Pulmonary, Critical Care and Sleep Medicine, Tufts-New England Medical Center, Boston, Massachusetts; Medical Director, Outpatient Pulmonary Rehabilitation, New England Sinai Hospital, Stoughton, Massachusetts
Acute Ventilatory Failure

Philip C. Hopewell, M.D.
Professor of Medicine, University of California, San Francisco; San Francisco General Hospital, San Francisco, California
Tuberculosis and Other Mycobacterial Diseases

Laurence Huang, M.D.
Associate Professor of Medicine, University of California, San Francisco; Chief, AIDS Chest Clinic, Positive Health Program, San Francisco General Hospital, San Francisco, California
Pulmonary Complications of Human Immunodeficiency Virus Infection

J. Michael B. Hughes, D.M., F.R.C.P.
Senior Research Investigator, National Heart and Lung Institute, Hammersmith Hospital Campus, Imperial College; Professor Emeritus, Department of Respiratory Medicine, Hammersmith Hospital, London, United Kingdom
Pulmonary Arteriovenous Malformations and Other Pulmonary Vascular Abnormalities; Pulmonary Complications of Heart Disease

Dallas M. Hyde, Ph.D.
Professor, Department of Anatomy, Physiology, and Cell Biology, School of Veterinary Medicine, and Director, California National Primate Research Center, University of California, Davis, Davis, California
Anatomy of the Lungs

Michael C. Iannuzzi, M.D.
Chief, Division of Pulmonary, Critical Care and Sleep Medicine, and Florette and Ernst Rosenfeld and Joseph Solomon Professor of Medicine, Department of Internal Medicine, The Mount Sinai School of Medicine, New York, New York
Genetic Approach to Lung Disease

Michael D. Iseman, M.D.
Professor of Medicine, University of Colorado Health Sciences Center, and National Jewish Medical and Research Center, Denver, Colorado
Bronchiectasis

James E. Jackson, F.R.C.R., M.R.C.P.
Honorary Senior Lecturer, Imperial College School of Medicine; Consultant Radiologist, Hammersmith Hospital, London, United Kingdom
Pulmonary Arteriovenous Malformations and Other Pulmonary Vascular Abnormalities

Susan L. Janson, D.N.Sc., R.N., N.P., F.A.A.N.
Professor, Department of Community Health Systems, and Adjunct Professor, Department of Medicine, University of California, San Francisco; Nurse Practitioner and Pulmonary Clinical Specialist, University of California, San Francisco, Medical Center, San Francisco, California
Patient Education and Compliance

James Jett, M.D.
Professor of Medicine and Consultant, Mayo Medical School, Rochester, Minnesota
Bronchogenic Carcinoma

Mani S. Kavuru, M.D.
Director, Pulmonary Function Laboratory, Department of Pulmonary and Critical Care Medicine, Cleveland Clinic Foundation, Cleveland, Ohio
Pulmonary Alveolar Proteinosis

Michael P. Keane, M.D.
Associate Professor of Medicine, Division of Pulmonary and Critical Care Medicine, David Geffen School of Medicine at UCLA, Los Angeles, California
Inflammation, Injury, and Repair

Suil Kim, M.D., Ph.D.
Assistant Professor of Medicine, University of California, San Francisco; Attending Staff, University of California, San Francisco Medical Center, San Francisco, California
Mucus Production, Secretion, and Clearance

Talmadge E. King, Jr., M.D.
Vice Chairman, Department of Medicine, and Constance B. Wofsy Distinguished Professor of Medicine, University of California, San Francisco; Chief, Medical Services, San Francisco General Hospital, San Francisco, California
Approach to Diagnosis and Management of the Idiopathic Interstitial Pneumonias; Diffuse Alveolar Hemorrhage and Other Rare Infiltrative Disorders

Michael R. Knowles, M.D.
Professor of Medicine, Division of Pulmonary/Critical Care Medicine, University of North Carolina at Chapel Hill; Division of Pulmonary/Critical Care Medicine, UNC Hospitals, Chapel Hill, North Carolina
Cystic Fibrosis

Kenneth S. Knox, M.D.
Assistant Professor of Medicine, Indiana University School of Medicine; Section Chief, Pulmonary, Critical Care, and Sleep Medicine, Richard L. Roudebush VA Medical Center, Indianapolis, Indiana
Fungal Infections

Brian L. Kotzin, M.D.
Vice President, Research and Development, Amgen, Inc., Thousand Oaks, California; Professor of Medicine and Immunology, University of Colorado Health Sciences Center, Denver, Colorado
Immune Recognition and Responses

Nikos G. Koulouris, M.D., Ph.D.
Associate Professor, Respiratory Medicine, University of Athens Medical School; Department of Respiratory Medicine, Sotiria Hospital, Athens, Greece
Respiratory System Mechanics and Energetics

Stephen E. Lapinsky, M.B., B.Ch., F.R.C.P.(C)
Associate Professor, Department of Medicine, University of Toronto; Site Director, Intensive Care Unit, Mount Sinai Hospital, Toronto, Ontario, Canada
The Lungs in Obstetric and Gynecologic Disease

Stephen C. Lazarus, M.D.
Professor of Medicine, Senior Investigator, Cardiovascular Research Institute, and Co-Director, Airway Clinical Research Center, University of California, San Francisco, San Francisco, California
Disorders of the Intrathoracic Airways

Warren L. Lee, M.D., F.R.C.P.(C)
Clinician Investigator and Clinician Scientist Program, University of Toronto; Consultant in Critical Care Medicine, Toronto Western Hospital, University Health Network, Toronto, Ontario, Canada
Hypoxemic Respiratory Failure, Including Acute Respiratory Distress Syndrome

Y. C. Gary Lee, M.B.Ch.B., Ph.D., F.R.A.C.P., F.C.C.P.
Wellcome Advanced Fellow, University College London, London; Consultant Chest Physician, Osler Chest Unit, Oxford Centre of Respiratory Medicine, Oxford, United Kingdom
Pneumothorax, Chylothorax, Hemothorax, and Fibrothorax

James F. Lewis, M.D., F.R.C.P.(C)
Professor of Medicine/Physiology/Pharmacology, University of Western Ontario; Respirologist, St. Joseph's Health Centre, London, Ontario, Canada
Pulmonary Surfactant

Richard W. Light, M.D.
Professor of Medicine, Vanderbilt University; Director, Pulmonary Disease Program, Saint Thomas Hospital, Nashville, Tennessee
Pleural Effusion; Pneumothorax, Chylothorax, Hemothorax, and Fibrothorax

Andrew H. Limper, M.D.
Professor of Medicine, and Chair, Pulmonary and Critical Care Medicine, Mayo Clinic College of Medicine, Rochester, Minnesota
Drug-Induced Pulmonary Disease

Robert Loddenkemper, M.D.
Professor of Medicine, Charité-Universitätsmedizin Berlin; Medical Director and Chief of Department of Pneumology, HELIOS-Klinikum Emil von Behring— Lungenklinik Heckeshorn, Berlin, Germany
Pleuroscopy, Thoracoscopy and Other Invasive Procedures

John M. Luce, M.D.
Professor of Medicine and Anesthesia, University of California, San Francisco; Associate Director, Medical and Surgical Intensive Care Units, San Francisco General Hospital, San Francisco, California
Care at the End of Life for Patients with Respiratory Failure

Judith A. Luce, M.D.
Clinical Professor of Medicine, University of California, San Francisco; Program Member, UCSF Comprehensive Cancer Center, San Francisco, California
Lymphoma, Lymphoproliferative Diseases, and Other Primary Malignant Tumors; Metastatic Malignant Tumors

Neil R. MacIntyre, M.D.
Professor of Medicine, Duke University; Medical Director, Respiratory Care Services, Duke University Medical Center, Durham, North Carolina
Principles of Mechanical Ventilation

Asrar B. Malik, Ph.D.
Distinguished Professor and Head, Department of Pharmacology, University of Illinois College of Medicine, Chicago, Illinois
Pulmonary Circulation and Regulation of Fluid Balance

Thomas R. Martin, M.D.
Professor and Vice Chair, Department of Medicine, University of Washington School of Medicine; Chief of Medicine, VA Puget Sound Health Care System, Seattle, Washington
Pulmonary Edema and Acute Lung Injury

Robert J. Mason, M.D.
Professor of Medicine, University of Colorado Health Sciences Center, Professor of Medicine, National Jewish Medical and Research Center, Denver, Colorado
Pulmonary Surfactant

Michael A. Matthay, M.D.
Professor, Medicine and Anesthesia, and Senior Associate, Cardiovascular Research Institute, University of California, San Francisco; Associate Director, Intensive Care Unit, and Director, Critical Care Medicine Training Program, Department of Medicine, University of California, San Francisco, Moffitt-Long Hospital, San Francisco, California
Alveolar and Distal Airway Epithelial Fluid Transport; Pulmonary Edema and Acute Lung Injury

Janet R. Maurer, M.D.
Medical Director, Transplantation, CIGNA HealthCare, Bloomfield, Connecticut
Lung Transplantation

F. Dennis McCool, M.D.
Professor of Medicine, Brown University, Providence; Chief, Pulmonary Critical Care Medicine, Memorial Hospital of Rhode Island, Pawtucket, Rhode Island
The Lungs and Chest Wall Disease

Francis X. McCormack, M.D.
Associate Professor of Medicine, Division of Pulmonary and Critical Care Medicine, and Director of Pulmonary and Critical Care, University of Cincinnati College of Medicine, Cincinnati, Ohio
Lymphangioleiomyomatosis

John A. McDonald, M.D., Ph.D.
Professor of Internal Medicine, Dean and Vice President of Health Sciences, and Dean, School of Medicine, University of Nevada School of Medicine, Reno, Nevada
Lung Growth and Development

Robert J. McKenna, Jr., M.D.
Clinical Chief, Thoracic Surgery, Cedars Sinai Medical Center, Los Angeles, California
Pleuroscopy, Thoracoscopy and Other Invasive Procedures

Ivan F. McMurtry, Ph.D.
Professor of Medicine, Cardiovascular Pulmonary Research Lab, Department of Medicine, University of Colorado Health Sciences Center, Denver, Colorado
Pulmonary Vascular Pharmacology

Timothy A. Morris, M.D.
Associate Professor of Clinical Medicine, Department of Medicine, University of California, San Diego; Director, Clinical Programs, Division of Pulmonary and Critical Care Medicine, UCSD Medical Center, San Diego, California
Pulmonary Thromboembolism

Jill Murray, M.B.B.Ch., F.F.Path.(SA), D.O.H.
Honorary Lecturer, Schools of Public Health and Pathology, University of the Witwatersrand; Principal Pathologist, National Institute for Occupational Health, Johannesburg, South Africa
Pneumoconioses

John F. Murray, M.D., D.Sc. (Hon), F.R.C.P.
Professor Emeritus of Medicine, University of California, San Francisco; Chief, Chest Service, 1966–1989, San Francisco General Hospital; Senior Staff, Cardiovascular Research Institute, San Francisco, California
History and Physical Examinations; Chest Pain

Jay A. Nadel, M.D., D.Sc. (Hon)
Professor of Medicine, Physiology, and Radiology; Director, Multidisciplinary Training Program in Lung Diseases; Cardiovascular Research Institute Investigator, University of California, San Francisco, San Francisco, California
Mucus Production, Secretion, and Clearance

Tom S. Neuman, M.D.
Professor of Medicine and Surgery, University of California, San Diego; Associate Director, Department of Emergency Medicine, and Director, Hyperbaric Medicine Center, University of California Medical Center, San Diego, California
Diving Medicine

Lee S. Newman, M.D., M.A.
Professor of Medicine and Professor of Preventive Medicine and Biometrics, University of Colorado Health Sciences Center; Head, Division of Environmental and Occupational Health Sciences, National Jewish Medical and Research Center, Denver, Colorado
Sarcoidosis

Stephen L. Nishimura, M.D.
Associate Professor, Department of Pathology, University of California, San Francisco, and San Francisco General Hospital, San Francisco, California
General Features of Respiratory Pathology

Thomas B. Nutman, M.D.
Head, Helminth Immunology Section, and Head, Clinical Parasitology Unit, National Institutes of Health, Bethesda, Maryland
Parasitic Diseases

David R. Park, M.D.
Assistant Professor, Division of Pulmonary and Critical Care Medicine, Department of Medicine, University of Washington; Medical Director, Pulmonary Diagnostic Services, Harborview Medical Center, Seattle, Washington
Tumors and Cysts of the Mediastinum; Pneumomediastinum and Mediastinitis

Edward F. Patz, Jr., M.D.
James and Alice Chen Professor of Radiology, and Professor in Pharmacology and Cancer Biology, Duke University School of Medicine, and Duke University Medical Center, Durham, North Carolina
Nuclear Medicine Techniques

Eliot A. Phillipson, M.D.
Professor, Department of Medicine, University of Toronto, Toronto, Ontario, Canada
Hypoventilation and Hyperventilation Syndromes; Sleep Disorders

David J. Pierson, M.D.
Professor of Medicine, Division of Pulmonary and Critical Care Medicine, University of Washington; Medical Director, Respiratory Care Department, Harborview Medical Center, Seattle, Washington
Acute Ventilatory Failure

Udaya B. S. Prakash, M.D.
Scripps Professor of Medicine, Mayo Clinic College of Medicine; Consultant in Pulmonary, Critical Care, and Internal Medicine, Mayo Medical Center, Rochester, Minnesota
Bronchoscopy

Elliot Rapaport, M.D., F.A.C.C.
Professor Emeritus of Medicine, University of California, San Francisco, School of Medicine; Attending Physician in Medicine (Cardiology), San Francisco General Hospital, San Francisco, California
Cor Pulmonale

Stephen I. Rennard, M.D.
Larson Professor of Medicine, Department of Internal Medicine, University of Nebraska Medical Center, Omaha, Nebraska
Chronic Bronchitis and Emphysema

David C. Rhew, M.D.
Associate Clinical Professor, David Geffen School of Medicine at UCLA; Staff Physician, Division of Infectious Diseases, Department of Medicine, VA Greater Los Angeles Healthcare System; Vice-President, Content Development, Zynx Health Incorporated, Los Angeles, California
Pyogenic Bacterial Pneumonia, Lung Abscess, and Empyema

David W. H. Riches, Ph.D.
Professor, Division of Pulmonary Sciences and Critical Care Medicine, Departments of Medicine and Immunology, University of Colorado Health Sciences Center; Professor and Division Head, Program in Cell Biology, Department of Pediatrics, National Jewish Medical and Research Center, Denver, Colorado
Monocytes, Macrophages, and Dendritic Cells of the Lung

Norman W. Rizk, M.D.
Professor of Medicine, Senior Associate Dean for Clinical Affairs, and Medical Director, Intensive Care Units, Stanford University School of Medicine, Stanford, California
Benign Tumors; The Lungs in Obstetric and Gynecologic Disease

Robert Rodriguez-Roisin, M.D., F.R.C.P.(E)
Professor of Medicine, University of Barcelona; Senior Consultant, Research Coordinator (iDiBAPS), Hospital Clinic, Barcelona, Spain
Pulmonary Complications of Abdominal Disease

Cecile S. Rose, M.D., M.P.H.
Associate Professor of Medicine, University of Colorado Health Sciences Center; Director, Occupational Lung Disease Clinic, National Jewish Medical and Research Center, Denver, Colorado
Hypersensitivity Pneumonitis

Charis Roussos, M.D.
Professor, Intensive Care and Pulmonary Medicine, University of Athens Medical School; Director, Department of Critical Care and Pulmonary Services, Evangelismos Hospital, Athens, Greece
Respiratory System Mechanics and Energetics

John M. Routes, M.D.
Associate Professor of Medicine and Immunology, Department of Medicine, Integrated Department of Immunology, University of Colorado Health Sciences Center; Associate Professor of Medicine, National Jewish Medical and Research Center, Denver, Colorado
Pulmonary Complications of Organ Transplantation and Primary Immunodeficiencies

Lewis J. Rubin, M.D.
Professor of Medicine, University of California, San Diego, School of Medicine; Director, Pulmonary Hypertension Program, UCSD Medical Center, La Jolla, California
Pulmonary Vasculitis and Primary Pulmonary Hypertension

Jonathan M. Samet, M.D.
Professor and Chairman, Department of Epidemiology, Johns Hopkins University Bloomberg School of Public Health; Director, Institute for Global Tobacco Control, Baltimore, Maryland
Epidemiology of Lung Cancer

George A. Sarosi, M.D.
Professor of Medicine, Indiana University School of Medicine; Chief of Medicine, Richard L. Roudebush VA Medical Center, Indianapolis, Indiana
Fungal Infections

Robert B. Schoene, M.D.
Professor of Medicine, and Program Director, Internal Medicine Residency, Divisions of Pulmonary and Critical Care Medicine, University of California, San Diego, La Jolla, California
High Altitude

Mary Beth Scholand, M.D.
Instructor, Pulmonary Division, Department of Internal Medicine, University of Utah; University of Utah Hospital, Salt Lake City, Utah
Lung Growth and Development

Marvin I. Schwarz, M.D.
James C. Campbell Professor of Pulmonary Medicine, and Head, Division of Pulmonary Sciences and Critical Care Medicine, University of Colorado Health Sciences Center, Denver, Colorado
Approach to Diagnosis and Management of the Idiopathic Interstitial Pneumonias; Diffuse Alveolar Hemorrhage and Other Rare Infiltrative Disorders

Matt X. G. Shao, M.D., Ph.D.
Postdoctoral Fellow, Cardiovascular Research Institute, University of California, San Francisco, San Francisco, California
Mucus Production, Secretion, and Clearance

Steven D. Shapiro, M.D.
Parker B. Francis Professor of Medicine, Harvard Medical School; Chief, Pulmonary and Critical Care, Brigham and Women's Hospital, Boston, Massachusetts
Chronic Bronchitis and Emphysema

Claire L. Shovlin, Ph.D., F.R.C.P.
Senior Lecturer, Respiratory Medicine, National Heart and Lung Institute, Imperial College; Honorary Consultant in Respiratory Medicine, Hammersmith Hospital, London, United Kingdom
Pulmonary Arteriovenous Malformations and Other Pulmonary Vascular Abnormalities

David Sidransky, M.D.
Professor, Otolaryngology-Head and Neck Surgery, Oncology, Pathology, Urology, and Cellular and Molecular Medicine, Department of Otolaryngology, Johns Hopkins University, Baltimore, Maryland
Biology of Lung Cancer

Gerard A. Silvestri, M.D., F.C.C.P.
Associate Professor of Medicine, Division of Pulmonary and Critical Care Medicine, Medical University of South Carolina, Charleston, South Carolina
Bronchogenic Carcinoma

Arthur S. Slutsky, M.D.
Professor of Medicine, Surgery and Biomedical Engineering, and Director, Interdepartmental Division of Critical Care Medicine, University of Toronto; Vice President (Research), St. Michael's Hospital, Toronto, Ontario, Canada
Hypoxemic Respiratory Failure, Including Acute Respiratory Distress Syndrome

Gordon L. Snider, M.D.
Maurice B. Strauss Professor of Medicine, Boston University School of Medicine; Chief, Medical Service, Boston VA Medical Center, Boston, Massachusetts
Chronic Bronchitis and Emphysema

H. Dirk Sostman, M.D.
Radiologist-in-Chief, Weill Cornell Medical Center, New York Presbyterian Hospital; Professor and Chair of Radiology, and Executive Vice Dean, Weill Medical College of Cornell University, New York, New York
Radiographic Techniques

John D. Stansell, M.D.
Professor of Medicine, University of California, San Francisco; Associate Chief/Medical Director, Positive Health Program, San Francisco General Hospital, San Francisco, California
Pulmonary Complications of Human Immunodeficiency Virus Infection

Robert M. Strieter, M.D.
Professor and Chief, Division of Pulmonary and Critical Care Medicine, Vice Chair, Department of Medicine, and Professor of Pathology, David Geffen School of Medicine at UCLA, Los Angeles, California
Inflammation, Injury, and Repair

Michael S. Stulbarg, M.D.*
Professor of Clinical Medicine, Chief, Chest Faculty Practice, and Associate Director, Sleep Disorders Center, University of California, San Francisco, San Francisco, California
Dyspnea

Eugene J. Sullivan, M.D.
Deputy Director, Division of Pulmonary and Allergy Drug Products, Center for Drug Evaluation and Research, U.S. Food and Drug Administration, Rockville, Maryland
Lymphangioleiomyomatosis

Erik R. Swenson, M.D.
Professor, Departments of Medicine and Physiology, University of Washington; Staff Physician, Department of Pulmonary and Critical Care Medicine, VA Puget Sound Health Care System, Seattle, Washington
High Altitude

Ira B. Tager, M.D., M.P.H.
Professor of Epidemiology, Division of Epidemiology, School of Public Health, University of California, Berkeley, Berkeley, California
Air Pollution

Takashi Takahashi, M.D., Ph.D.
Professor, Division of Molecular Carcinogenesis, Center for Neural Disease and Cancer, Nagoya University Graduate School of Medicine, Nagoya, Japan
Biology of Lung Cancer

Kawsar R. Talaat, M.D.
Clinical Fellow, Laboratory of Parasitic Diseases, National Institute of Allergy and Infectious Diseases, National Institutes of Health, Bethesda, Maryland
Parasitic Diseases

Mary Jane Thomassen, Ph.D.
Director, Cytokine Biology Laboratory, Division of Pulmonary and Critical Care Medicine, Cleveland Clinic Foundation, Cleveland, Ohio
Pulmonary Alveolar Proteinosis

Alkis Togias, M.D.
Associate Professor of Medicine, Divisions of Allergy and Clinical Immunology and Respiratory and Critical Care Medicine, Johns Hopkins University School of Medicine; Attending Physician, Department of Medicine, Johns Hopkins Hospital; Attending Physician, Department of Medicine, Johns Hopkins Bayview Medical Center, Baltimore, Maryland
Disorders of the Upper Airways

Antoni Torres, M.D.
Associate Professor, University of Barcelona; Head of Pulmonology Department, Hospital Clinic, Barcelona, Spain
Pyogenic Bacterial Pneumonia, Lung Abscess, and Empyema

John J. Treanor, M.D.
Professor of Medicine, Infectious Diseases Unit, University of Rochester School of Medicine and Dentistry, Rochester, New York
Viral Infections

Raymond Tso, M.D.
Fellow, Albert Einstein College of Medicine, and Montefiore Medical Center, Bronx, New York
The Lungs and Neuromuscular Diseases

George E. Tzelepis, M.D.
Associate Professor of Medicine, Department of Pathophysiology, University of Athens Medical School; Chief, Pulmonary Services, Laiko General Hospital, Athens, Greece
The Lungs and Chest Wall Disease

Eric Vallières, M.D., F.R.C.S.C.
Surgical Director, Lung Cancer Program, Thoracic Surgery, Swedish Cancer Institute, Seattle, Washington
Tumors and Cysts of the Mediastinum; Pneumomediastinum and Mediastinitis

Elliott Vichinsky, M.D.
Medical Director, Hematology/Oncology Programs, Children's Hospital Oakland, Oakland, California
Pulmonary Complications of Hematologic Disease

Peter D. Wagner, M.D.
Head, Division of Physiology, Department of Medicine, and Professor of Medicine and Bioengineering, University of California, San Diego, La Jolla, California
Ventilation, Blood Flow, and Gas Exchange

Yasmine S. Wasfi, M.D.
Instructor, Department of Medicine, National Jewish Medical and Research Center, and University of Colorado Health Sciences Center, Denver, Colorado
Sarcoidosis

W. Richard Webb, M.D.
Professor of Radiology, and Chief of Thoracic Imaging, University of California, San Francisco, San Francisco, California
Radiographic Techniques

*Deceased

A. U. Wells, M.D.
Professor of Respiratory Medicine, Interstitial Lung
Disease Unit, Royal Brompton Hospital, London, United
Kingdom
The Lungs and Connective Tissue Diseases

Jeffrey A. Wesson, M.D., Ph.D.
Assistant Professor, Department of Medicine, Medical
College of Wisconsin; Physician, Department of Medicine,
Nephrology Division, Zablocki VA Medical Center,
Milwaukee, Wisconsin
Acid-Base Balance

John B. West, M.D., Ph.D., D.Sc.
Professor of Medicine and Physiology, University of
California, San Diego, School of Medicine, La Jolla,
California
Ventilation, Blood Flow, and Gas Exchange

John G. Widdicombe, D.M., D.Phil., F.R.C.P.
Emeritus Professor of Physiology, University of London,
London, United Kingdom
Cough

Jeanine P. Wiener-Kronish, M.D.
Professor of Anesthesia and Medicine, Vice-Chairman,
Department of Anesthesia, and Investigator,
Cardiovascular Research Institute, University of
California, San Francisco, San Francisco, California
Preoperative Evaluation

Mary C. Williams, Ph.D.
Professor of Pulmonary Medicine, Boston University
School of Medicine, Boston, Massachusetts
Anatomy of the Lungs

Prescott G. Woodruff, M.D., M.P.H.
Assistant Professor of Medicine, Division of Pulmonary
and Critical Care Medicine, Department of Medicine,
University of California, San Francisco, San Francisco,
California
Asthma

James R. Yankaskas, M.D.
Professor of Medicine, University of North Carolina at
Chapel Hill; Co-Director, Adult Cystic Fibrosis Program,
Chapel Hill, North Carolina
Cystic Fibrosis

Joseph D. C. Yao, M.D.
Assistant Professor, Department of Laboratory Medicine
and Pathology, Mayo College of Medicine; Consultant,
Division of Clinical Microbiology, Department of
Laboratory Medicine and Pathology, Mayo Clinic,
Rochester, Minnesota
*Microbiologic Diagnosis of Lower Respiratory Tract
Infection*

Rex C. Yung, M.D.
Assistant Professor of Medicine and Oncology, Johns
Hopkins University School of Medicine; Director of
Pulmonary Oncology and Director of Bronchoscopy,
Departments of Medicine and Oncology, Johns Hopkins
Hospital, Baltimore, Maryland
Epidemiology of Lung Cancer

Spyros G. Zakynthinos, M.D., Ph.D.
Associate Professor, Intensive Care and Pulmonary
Medicine, University of Athens Medical School; Associate
Professor of Intensive Care Medicine, Department of
Critical Care and Pulmonary Services, Evangelismos
Hospital, Athens, Greece
Respiratory System Mechanics and Energetics

Noe Zamel, M.D., F.R.C.P.(C), F.C.C.P.
Professor, Department of Medicine, University of
Toronto; Pulmonologist, Department of Medicine,
Toronto General Hospital and Mount Sinai Hospital,
Toronto, Ontario, Canada
Lung Transplantation

Leslie Zimmerman, M.D.
Professor of Clinical Medicine, University of California,
San Francisco; Medical Director, Intensive Care Unit, San
Francisco Veterans Hospital, San Francisco, California
Pulmonary Complications of Endocrine Diseases

Richard L. ZuWallack, M.D.
Professor of Clinical Medicine, University of Connecticut
School of Medicine, Farmington; Associate Chief,
Pulmonary and Critical Care, St. Francis Hospital and
Medical Center, Hartford, Connecticut
Pulmonary Rehabilitation

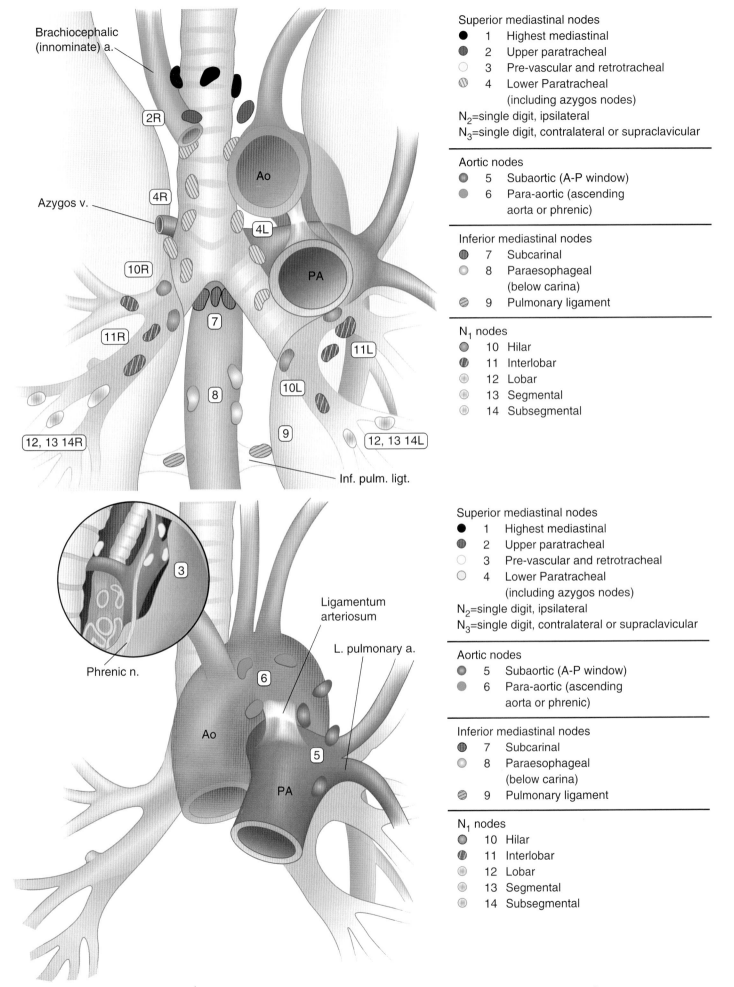

Figure 44.2 Mediastinal lymph node maps. a, artery; Ao, aorta; A-P, aortic-pulmonary; PA, pulmonary artery; v, vein.

Figure 53.22 Usual interstitial pneumonia pattern often shows a striking subpleural distribution. This low-power photomicrograph is from an area without the usual remodeling of the lung architecture with cystic (honeycomb) changes. (Courtesy of Thomas V. Colby, MD, Mayo Clinic, Scottsdale, AZ.)

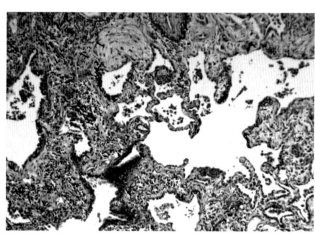

Figure 53.24 Usual interstitial pneumonia pattern. Two fibroblastic foci of loose organizing connective tissue are seen in the top center and top right of the photomicrograph adjacent to an area of dense fibrosis. (Courtesy of Thomas V. Colby, MD, Mayo Clinic, Scottsdale, AZ.)

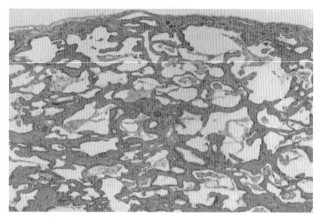

Figure 53.28 Photomicrograph of nonspecific interstitial pneumonia with a mixed cellular-fibrotic pattern. The alveolar walls are thickened by dense collagen and a few lymphocytes and plasma cells. The fibroblastic foci that are commonly found in the usual interstitial pneumonia pattern are not present in this lesion.

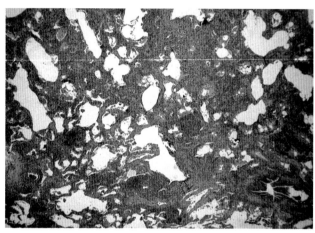

Figure 53.37 Photomicrograph of lymphocytic interstitial pneumonia showing diffuse lymphoid infiltrate that extends through the pulmonary interstitium. (Original magnification ×10.)

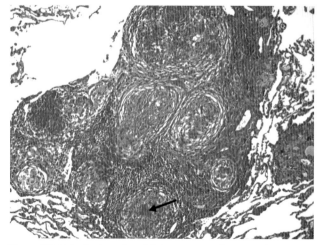

Figure 55.6 A cluster of multiple noncaseating granulomata with surrounding normal lung parenchyma. The *arrow* indicates a multinucleated giant cell within a granuloma. (Original magnification ×100.) (Courtesy of Carlyne Cool, MD, National Jewish Medical and Research Center.)

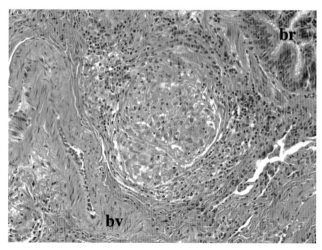

Figure 55.7 View of a well-formed noncaseating granuloma located between a blood vessel (bv) and a bronchiole (br). (Original magnification ×200.) (Courtesy of Carlyne Cool, MD, National Jewish Medical and Research Center.)

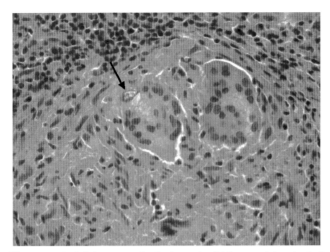

Figure 55.8 A Schaumann body (*arrow*) within a multinucleated giant cell within a sarcoid granuloma. (Original magnification ×400.) (Courtesy of Carlyne Cool, MD, National Jewish Medical and Research Center.)

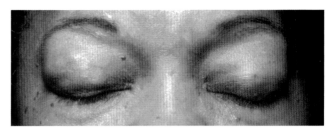

Figure 55.9 Enlargement of lacrimal glands in a sarcoidosis patient.

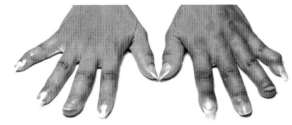

Figure 55.10 Joint and bone involvement in the hands of a sarcoidosis patient.

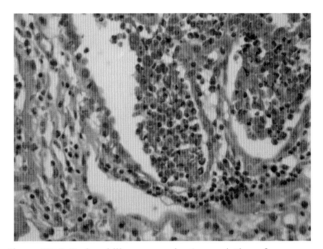

Figure 57.1 Eosinophilic pneumonia. Accumulation of eosinophils within the alveolar lumen. (Courtesy of Françoise Thivolet-Béjui, MD, Department of Pathology, Louis-Pradel Hospital and Claude Bernard University, Lyon.)

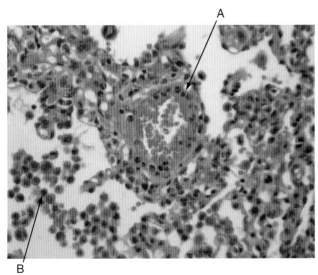

Figure 57.2 Eosinophilic pneumonia. Eosinophils infiltrate the arteriolar wall (non-necrotizing vasculitis) **(A)** and are present within the alveolar lumen **(B)**. (Courtesy of Françoise Thivolet-Béjui, MD, Department of Pathology, Louis-Pradel Hospital and Claude Bernard University, Lyon.)

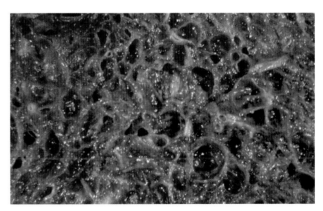

Figure 58.4 Gross specimen of lymphangioleiomyomatosis lung tissue. Extensive cystic changes are evident.

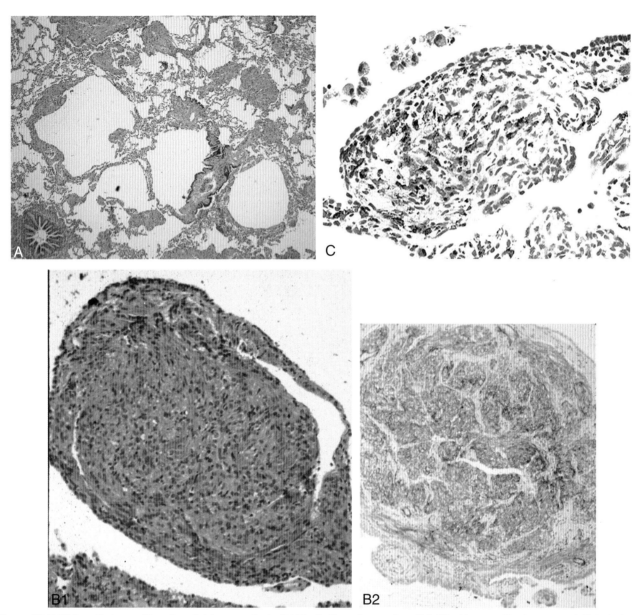

Figure 58.5 Histopathology of lymphangioleiomyomatosis (LAM). **A,** Smooth muscle cell infiltration, cystic change, and distorted pulmonary architecture characteristic of LAM. **B,** LAM nodule stained with hematoxylin and eosin (*B1*) or smooth muscle α-actin (*B2*). **C,** HMB-45 staining of LAM lung tissue.

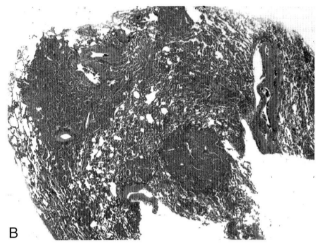

B

Figure 58.6 Radiographic and histopathologic presentation of multifocal micronodular pneumocyte hyperplasia (MMPH). **B,** Low-power view of the lung biopsy from a patient with MMPH reveals diffuse nodular proliferation of alveolar type II cells.

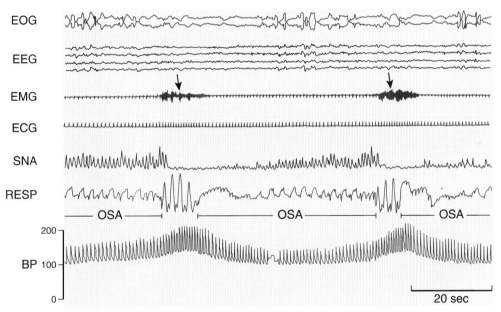

Figure 74.4 Recordings of sympathetic activity (from the peroneal nerve) and of arterial blood pressure in a patient with obstructive sleep apnea (OSA). Muscle sympathetic nerve activity (SNA) is suppressed at the beginning of the apnea but increases as arterial oxygen saturation (not shown) decreases, reaching a peak at termination of the apnea, after which it is abruptly inhibited by lung inflation. Surges in blood pressure (BP) peak shortly after peak muscle SNA and arousal from sleep (*arrows*). Other channels show the electroencephalogram (EEG), electrocardiogram (ECG), electromyogram (EMG), electro-oculogram (EOG), and respirations (RESP). (From Somers VK, Dyken ME, Clary MP, et al: Sympathetic neural mechanisms in obstructive sleep apnea. J Clin Invest 96:1897–1904, 1995.)

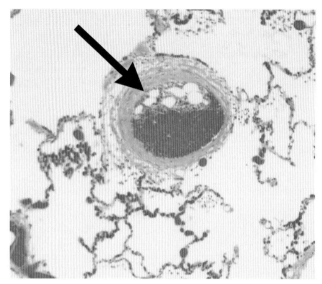

Figure 79.4 Fat emboli *(arrow)* in a pulmonary vessel of a sickle cell patient who died from acute chest syndrome.

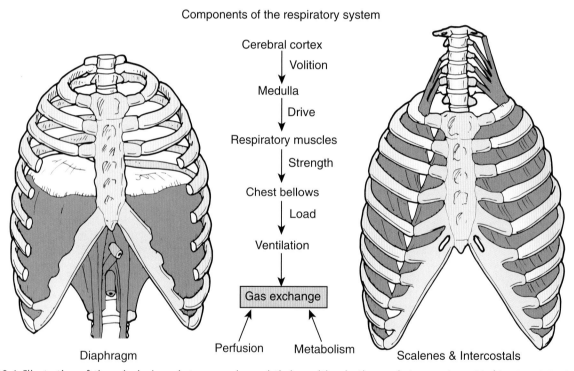

Components of the respiratory system

Cerebral cortex

Volition

Medulla

Drive

Respiratory muscles

Strength

Chest bellows

Load

Ventilation

Gas exchange

Perfusion   Metabolism

Diaphragm

Scalenes & Intercostals

Figure 82.1 Illustration of the principal respiratory muscles and their position in the respiratory system. (The drawing of the diaphragm is from Rochester DF, Arora NS, Braun NMT: Maximum contractile force of the human diaphragm muscle determined in vivo. Trans Am Clin Climatol Assoc 93:200–208, 1981; and the drawing of the scalene and intercostal muscles is from Osmond DG: Functional anatomy of the chest wall. *In* Roussos C, Macklem PT [eds]: The Thorax. New York: Marcel Dekker, 1985, pp 199–223.)

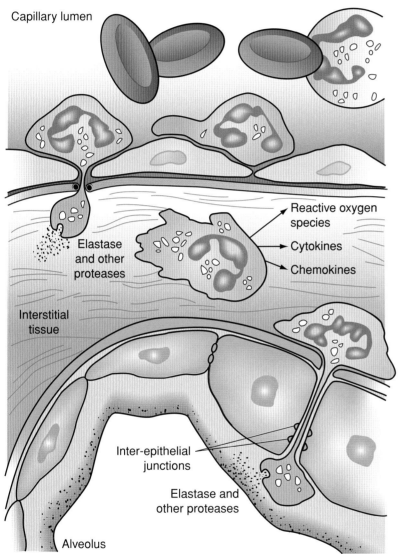

Capillary lumen

Reactive oxygen species

Cytokines

Chemokines

Elastase and other proteases

Interstitial tissue

Inter-epithelial junctions

Elastase and other proteases

Alveolus

Figure 85.2 Role of neutrophils in the pathogenesis of acute lung injury. Activated neutrophils exit the bloodstream and transmigrate across the alveolar-capillary membrane, releasing cytokines, proteases, reactive oxygen species, and other compounds. Although crucial to host defense against pathogens, the compounds secreted or released by the neutrophil have the capacity to damage the tissue of the host. (Adapted from Lee WL, Downey GP: Leukocyte elastase: Physiological functions and role in acute lung injury. A state of the art review. Am J Respir Crit Care Med 164:896–904, 2001.)

Preface to the Fourth Edition

The first edition of the *Textbook of Respiratory Medicine* was published in 1988. Its goal was to provide a well-balanced, authoritative, and fully documented book that integrated basic scientific principles with the practice of respiratory medicine—a much-needed treatise. This ambitious undertaking was widely read and well received and led, in turn, to a second edition (1994) and then to a third (2000). During this 12-year period, the field of respiratory medicine underwent incredible growth in many of its disciplines: lung cell biology, imaging and other diagnostic methods, pharmaceuticals and therapeutic interventions, and medical ethics. To accommodate this explosion of knowledge, each new edition was thoroughly reorganized and new chapters written by expert authors were added.

Since the last edition was published, the pace of progress in basic science and clinical medicine has become even faster, and completely new modalities have been added in the biotechnologic, genomic, and informational sciences. The fourth edition of the *Textbook of Respiratory Medicine* is admirably positioned to report and analyze these developments, but because of the rapidity of change, is being published after a 5-year cycle instead of the usual 6 years. As with its predecessors, the *Textbook* has been reorganized, with the addition of several new chapters plus the consolidation or removal of old ones to make room for recently acquired information and to avoid repetition. Seventy-eight new authors, with an increasingly international presence, have joined other distinguished colleagues to write about subjects ranging from positron emission tomography scanning to severe acute respiratory syndrome to video-assisted thoracoscopic surgery. To provide the necessary expertise for these chapters, we have often paired complementary coauthors: a pulmonologist with a specialist from another field, or with a thoracic surgeon, or with a basic scientist. We are deeply grateful to these dedicated authors for their outstanding contributions.

Readers should notice further changes. The headings in the printed text have been highlighted with color to improve the readability and organization of the material. All of the illustrations have been redrawn for better clarity and presentation, and new color figures have been added. As always, the book is thoroughly referenced to aid those wishing to delve further into any subject.

To stay current and relevant in this rapidly changing world, the *Textbook* will also be available as an online version, which will complement, expand, and continually update the printed edition. Online publishing allows inclusion of volumes of supplementary material and additional figures and posting of updates on key developments, as well as the easy downloading of all figures and tables for use in slide presentations. We anticipate that the online version will serve as a major resource for readers and a bridge between the printed editions of the *Textbook*.

Since the last edition, important changes have taken place at W. B. Saunders, our usual publisher, as well; Saunders has been incorporated within the international scientific publishing firm of Elsevier Inc. Our editors deserve thanks and acknowledgment for their important contributions, particularly Jennifer Shreiner, Dolores Meloni, and Todd Hummel. Copyediting and production were performed by Berta Steiner and her staff at Bermedica Production, Ltd. We also thank our local staff, Mary DeJesus, Patricia Arrandale, Shirley Pearce, and Teneke Warren for their invaluable help.

With this edition, the *Textbook* is also undergoing a transition of editorial leadership. The original founders and creators, Doctors John F. Murray and Jay A. Nadel, are shifting responsibility to the newer generation, Doctors Robert J. Mason and V. Courtney Broaddus. In recognition of their outstanding contributions, the book has been renamed *Murray and Nadel's Textbook of Respiratory Medicine*. On a personal note, we are grateful to John and Jay for their teachings and discussions at the bedside, blackboard, and laboratory. Through their guidance, we and many others learned to incorporate science in our approach to patients. We deeply thank both of them for creating this *Textbook* and entrusting us with its future.

V. Courtney Broaddus, M.D.
Robert J. Mason, M.D.

Preface to the First Edition

The rapid growth of knowledge of basic scientific principles and their application to respiratory medicine has resulted in a proliferation of monographs and texts dealing with selected aspects of pulmonary science and clinical medicine, but no single work has provided a comprehensive description of all that is currently known. The *Textbook of Respiratory Medicine* is an attempt to provide a well-balanced, authoritative, and fully documented book that integrates scientific principles with the practice of respiratory medicine. The text is sufficiently detailed and referenced to serve as the definitive source for interested students, house officers, and practitioners, both pulmonary specialists and generalists. It is written by leading experts, to guarantee that the material is authoritative and contemporary.

To deal with such an enormous amount of material, we have divided the book into three major sections. This organization should help guide interested readers from the intricacies of basic science to their application at the bedside. We begin in Part I with Scientific Principles of Respiratory Medicine. As implied, this is where the reader will find detailed information about the anatomy and development of the respiratory tract, respiratory physiology, pharmacology and pathology, and defense mechanisms and immunology. A strong foundation in these basic sciences will make possible a rational and scientific approach to the more specialized clinical material included in the subsequent sections. Part II, Manifestations and Diagnosis of Respiratory Disease, contains four chapters on the cardinal signs and symptoms of respiratory disorders and ten chapters on diagnostic evaluation, ranging from the history and physical examination to the newest and most sophisticated imaging, applied physiologic, and invasive techniques. Discrete clinical disorders are included in Part III, Clinical Respiratory Medicine. There are sections on Infectious Diseases, Obstructive Diseases, Neoplasms, Disorders of the Pulmonary Circulation, Infiltrative and Interstitial Diseases, Environmental and Occupational Disorders, Disorders of the Pleura, Disorders of the Mediastinum, Disorders in the Control of Breathing, Respiratory Manifestations of Extrapulmonary Disorders, and Respiratory Failure. All but one

of the sections dealing with a generic clinical problem begin with a chapter entitled "General Principles and Diagnostic Approach." New challenges to adult respiratory medicine have sprung up, and these are reflected in chapters on subjects such as cystic fibrosis (previously a disease only of childhood!), environmental and occupational diseases, disorders of breathing, and respiratory problems associated with unusual atmospheres (high altitude, diving). The book ends with a novel and important section on Prevention and Control.

Putting together a *Textbook* of this scope and magnitude is no easy task and involves making certain decisions that all readers may not agree with. For example, while trying to keep the length of the book as manageable as possible, we decided to permit some overlap of content. Thus, readers will find bronchodilators discussed in the chapter on airway pharmacology and again in the pertinent chapters on obstructive airway diseases. We have also welcomed differences of opinion among authors, provided the issues were clearly stated and the reasons for the author's position documented.

Our struggles were not as arduous as they might have been because we have had considerable help from many sources. First of all was the help from the 95 authors, who worked long and hard on their various contributions. The two editors worked in San Francisco, where they had the benefit of expert secretarial support from Ms. Dorothy Ladd and Mrs. Beth Cost. Special acknowledgment goes to Ms. Aja Lipavsky who, as editorial assistant, handled correspondence, proofing, permissions, and innumerable other details, and prepared the index. At W.B. Saunders in Philadelphia, the book was the brainchild of then-president John Hanley and was published with the guidance of J. Dereck Jeffers, William Lamsback, and the new president Lewis Reines. Production was supervised by Evelyn Weiman.

The long gestation of this book is over, parturition is near, and it will soon begin a life of its own. Like all expectant parents, we are concerned about how our offspring will make its way in the real world. We hope people will like it and find it useful.

John F. Murray, M.D.
Jay A. Nadel, M.D.

Contents

VOLUME TWO

Murray and Nadel's
Textbook of Respiratory Medicine

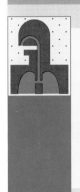

42

Biology of Lung Cancer

Takashi Takahashi, M.D., Ph.D., David Sidransky, M.D.

INTRODUCTION

Lung cancer has become the leading cause of cancer death in many industrialized countries. A better understanding of the molecular pathogenesis of this fatal disease is thus an urgent issue in order to develop better diagnostic approaches and new targeted therapies. In the development of squamous carcinoma, oncogenic triggering converts normal bronchial epithelium into hyperplastic, metaplastic and dysplastic lesions, leading to the subsequent emergence of a carcinoma in situ and then an overt squamous cell carcinoma. Adenocarcinoma is also considered to develop at least in part from a premalignant precursor lesion, atypical adenomatous hyperplasia. Molecular biologic studies have demonstrated that overt cancers carry multiple genetic and epigenetic alterations, resulting in the inactivation of tumor suppressor genes and activation of dominant oncogenes during the initiation of carcinogenesis and subsequent progression to lung cancer (Fig. 42.1).

Epidemiologic studies have demonstrated that most cases of primary lung cancer are caused by smoking. (This topic is covered extensively in Chapter 43, Epidemiology of Lung Cancer.) Converging studies support the notion that carcinogens in smoke are the main initiators of lung cancer by inducing multiple genetic alterations mainly through formation of deoxyribonucleic acid (DNA) adducts. Fingerprints of such genetic insults can be seen, for example, in the mutational spectra of *p53* and K-*ras*.[1] Proper cell cycle regulation and checkpoint functions are crucial for maintaining genomic integrity, and their abrogations are thought to contribute to genomic instability,[2] thereby playing an important role even in the early steps of cancer development. Many of the tumor suppressor genes and oncogenes altered in lung cancer are known to play a role in the regulation of cell cycle progression in either a direct or an indirect manner, and a considerable proportion of these cancer-related genes are a component of vital checkpoint mechanisms. In this chapter, we summarize recent advances in the molecular biology of lung cancer. In addition, we discuss the ways in which these molecular changes are being translated into novel diagnostic approaches with a variety of applications for the early detection and monitoring of lung cancer.

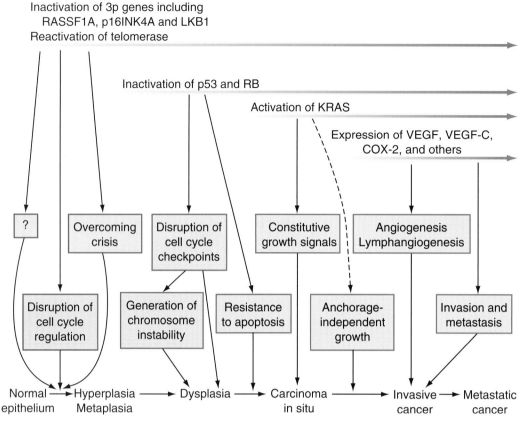

Figure 42.1 Accumulation of alterations in the multistep progression of lung carcinogenesis. Supposed biologic consequences resulting from the genetic and epigenetic alterations are indicated.

CHROMOSOMAL ALTERATIONS

Consistent chromosomal alterations are considered to be indicative of critical molecular events such as inactivation of tumor suppressor genes and activation of dominant oncogenes. It has been shown that lung cancers share similar chromosome changes, and they also possess certain histologic type-specific characteristic chromosomal alterations.[3] Loss of chromosomal arm 3p was among the first to be identified as a nonrandom genomic aberration in lung cancer. In addition to the common loss of 3p, chromosomal losses are also frequent on 4q, 5q, 8p, 10q, 13q, and 17p in small cell lung cancer (SCLC) and on 8p, 9p, 13q, and 17p in non–small cell lung cancer (NSCLC). Chromosomal gains were shown to be frequent on 3q, 5p, and 8q in SCLC and on 1q, 3q, 5p, and 8q in NSCLC.

The presence of chromosome aberrations is one of the hallmarks of neoplastic cells, and chromosome instability has been demonstrated in many human cancers, including lung cancer. Recent progress in molecular and cellular biology combined with technical developments in cytogenetics have shed light on the underlying mechanisms of this instability. Accumulating evidence suggests that failures in cell cycle checkpoint control and defects in the DNA double-strand break repair system are important in the development of chromosome instability.[3,4]

TUMOR SUPPRESSORS AND GROWTH-INHIBITORY SIGNALS

During the processes of lung carcinogenesis and progression, multiple tumor suppressor genes are inactivated. Tumor suppressor gene inactivation usually requires two events: deletion of a large chromosomal DNA segment of one allele and a smaller mutational or epigenetic inactivation of the other allele. Tumor suppressor genes are best defined as genes whose reduced function can lead to neoplastic change. A. G. Knudson, after studying the kinetics of inherited childhood tumors, first suggested that afflicted children inherited one of two mutations that were rate limiting for tumor development.[5] According to the Knudson hypothesis, an individual with an inherited predisposition to cancer inherits one normal and one mutant tumor suppressor gene from his or her parents. The tumor is more likely to occur in such an individual because only the remaining normal tumor suppressor gene must be inactivated. In contrast, a non-predisposed individual must acquire somatic mutations in both the maternal and paternal suppressor gene alleles to initiate tumor formation. This "two-hit" hypothesis provides a useful framework for considering the role of tumor suppressor inactivation in cancer development.[5]

In addition to genetic alterations and differences in gene expression, alterations in DNA methylation, an epigenetic process present in mammalian cells, are also a hallmark of

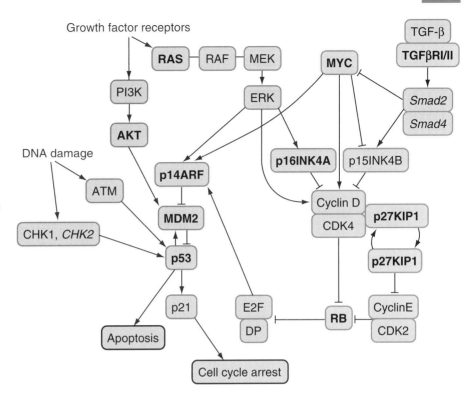

Figure 42.2 Simplified model depicting components of two major pathways, p14ARF-p53 and p16INK4A-RB, as well as other signaling pathways of oncogenes and growth factors involved in the pathogenesis of lung cancer. Components with frequent and infrequent alterations are indicated in **bold** and *italic*, respectively.

human cancer.[6] The promoter regions of many genes contain an abundance of cytosine-guanosine (CpG) dinucleotides termed *CpG islands*. With the exception of genes on the inactive X chromosome and imprinted genes, CpG islands are protected from methylation in normal cells. This protection is critical, because methylation of CpG islands is associated with loss of expression of that particular gene. We now know that the silencing of tumor suppressor genes associated with promoter hypermethylation is a common feature in human cancer, and serves as an alternative mechanism for loss of tumor suppressor gene function.

The loss of the second, heterozygous allele can be detected via various methods, and is referred to as a loss of heterozygosity. Previous cytogenetic and loss-of-heterozygosity studies have identified a number of chromosomal regions as frequent targets for chromosomal aberrations in lung cancer, providing clues to the localization of tumor suppressor genes involved in the pathogenesis of cancer. Among the suspected chromosomal regions, 9p21, 13q14, and 17p13 have consequently been shown to harbor the *p16INK4A* and *p14ARF*, retinoblastoma (*RB*), and *p53* genes, respectively. Inactivation of these genes plays a fundamental role in the pathogenesis of lung cancer. Moreover, these tumor suppressor proteins compose functional linkages by involvement of common pathways such as the p14ARF-p53 and p16INK4A-RB pathways (Fig. 42.2).

p53/MDM2/p14ARF PATHWAY

The *p53* tumor suppressor gene is often regarded as a guardian of the genome, playing a central role as a safeguard against genetic instability. Upon DNA damage, the ATM and ATR kinases are activated, resulting in the phosphorylation

and consequential activation of the p53 protein directly at Ser15 and indirectly via CHK2 or CHK1 at Ser20 (Fig. 42.3). Activated p53 transactivates a number of downstream target genes, including *p21CIP1/WAF1*, *14-3-3σ*, *BAX*, and *GADD45*.[7] Up-regulation of *p21CIP1/WAF1*[8,9] and *14-3-3σ*[10] by p53 imposes cell cycle arrest at G_1 and G_2, respectively, and activated p53 may participate directly in DNA repair through the induction of *p53R2*.[11] Alternatively, unrepairable DNA damage may lead to apoptotic cell death via p53-dependent induction of various downstream genes, including the proapoptotic *Bcl-2* family (*BAX, NOXA,* and *PUMA*),[12–14] *APAF-1*,[15] *PIG3*,[16] and *p53AIP*.[17] Phosphorylation at Ser46 of the p53 protein by HIPK2 has been suggested to play a role in the induction of apoptosis by p53 in concert with phosphorylation at other serines as described previously.[18,19] The regulation of centrosome duplication has also been linked to p53 and its effector, p21CIP1/WAF1.[20]

Since the initial report on *p53* mutations in primary lung cancer,[21] a large number of *p53* mutations have been documented. These mutations are present in approximately 90% of SCLCs and 30% to 50% of NSCLCs depending on histologic type (Table 42.1), and they are clustered at particular hotspots.[22] These hotspot codons generally harbor CpG sites, where 5-methyl-cytosine has been suggested to enhance the formation of DNA adducts at the guanine residue.[23] The resultant bulky DNA adducts, which are mainly formed by carcinogens in cigarette smoke, preferentially cause a guanine-to-thymine (G → T) transversion. Highly sensitive densitometric examination has revealed that smoking induces *p53* mutations even in bronchial epithelial cells of normal morphologic appearance.[24] In addition to a role for p53 inactivation at the early stages of lung cancer development, accumulating evidence suggests

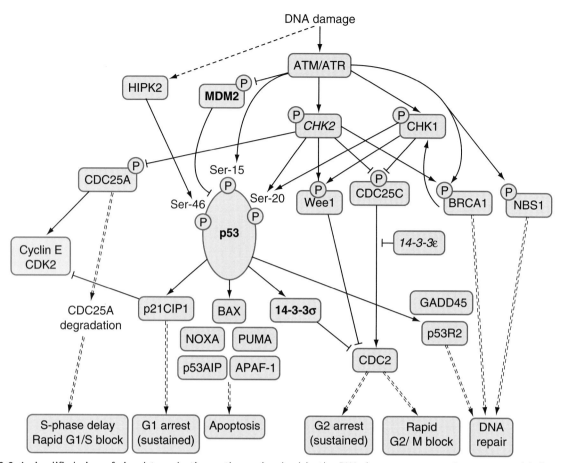

Figure 42.3 A simplified view of signal transduction pathways involved in the DNA damage response. Components with frequent and infrequent alterations are indicated in **bold** and *italic,* respectively.

Table 42.1 Selected Genetic and Epigenetic Changes in Primary Lung Cancers

| | SCLC | NSCLC | |
		Adeno	SCC
Oncogenes			
ras	*	30%	*
B-raf	*	5%	*
myc†	75%	<10%	<10%
Suppressor Genes			
p53	90%	30%	50%
RB	90%	10%	*
p16/INK4A	*	60%	80%
LKB1		30%	*
PTEN	10%	<10%	<10%
RASSF1A	100%	60%	60%

* <5%; most oncogenes are activated by point mutation or amplification, whereas tumor suppressor genes are inactivated by deletion, mutation, or promoter methylation. All numbers are approximate.
† A large number of tumors harbor overexpression without amplification.
Adeno, adenocarcinoma; NSCLC, non–small cell lung cancer; SCC, squamous cell carcinoma; SCLC, small cell lung cancer.

a possible correlation with poor prognosis after surgical treatment of lung cancers,[25] especially in stage I tumors.[26]

MDM2, a ubiquitin E3 ligase, interacts with p53 and targets the p53 protein for degradation, thereby functioning as an oncogene,[27] whereas p53 in turn up-regulates MDM2 expression, creating an autoregulatory negative feedback loop. MDM2 is also positively regulated through its phosphorylation by AKT, a downstream effector of growth factor signals.[28] Whereas amplification of *MDM2* is present in 14% of osteosarcomas,[29] *MDM2* has been reported to be over-expressed without gene amplification in 25% to 50% of NSCLCs, paradoxically in association with a favorable prognosis.[30,31] p14ARF, which is encoded by an alternative coding frame of the *p16INK4A* locus, exerts growth inhibition by inhibiting the ubiquitin E3 ligase activity of MDM2[32] and by sequestering MDM2 into the nucleolus.[33,34] It is of note that p14ARF is induced by oncogenic signals (Myc, Ras, and E2F1), suggesting the existence of a negative feedback mechanism.[35–37] Deletion of p14ARF may therefore potentiate tumor-promoting activity of these oncogenes. Although mutations specifically inactivating *p14ARF* instead of *p16INK4A* have not been found in lung cancers, loss of *p14ARF* expression has been reported in about 60% of lung cancers.[38] The concurrence of *p53* mutations and *p16/p14ARF* deletions in primary lung tumors suggests that *p53* mutation provides an additional growth advantage to that of p16/p14ARF by alteration of other pathways.[39]

RETINOBLASTOMA AND CYCLIN D KINASE INHIBITORS

The p16INK4A-RB pathway is a critical regulator of cell cycle progression. Whereas the RB protein is hypophosphorylated at G_1, it is sequentially phosphorylated by cyclin D-CDK4/6 and cyclin E-CDK2 during G_1/S transition. This modification leads to the dissociation of RB from E2F/DP heterodimers, leaving them in a transcriptionally active state. These heterodimers activate the expression of genes involved in cell proliferation and promote cell cycle progression as well as differentiation, development, and apoptosis.[40,41] p16INK4A keeps the RB protein in the hypophosphorylated form by inhibiting cyclin D-CDK4/6 activity, and consequently prevents activation of the E2F/DP heterodimers.

Alterations of RB are detected in almost all SCLCs (>90%).[42–44] This unusually high incidence of RB abnormalities is seen only in a very few types of human tumors such as SCLC and retinoblastoma. In SCLC tumor specimens, the *RB* locus in the 13q14 region almost invariably exhibits the loss of one allele and a structural alteration of the other allele of the *RB* gene, which is usually due to small deletions, nonsense mutations, and splicing abnormalities rather than missense mutations. As predicted from RB inactivation, E2F1 is frequently overexpressed in SCLC.[45] In contrast, loss of RB protein expression is rather rare in NSCLC (15% to 30%), with a higher frequency in late-stage NSCLC than in early-stage tumors, suggesting a possible association with tumor progression.[46,47] Although RB inactivation in NSCLC does not seem to correlate with time to relapse or death,[48] the combination of RB and p53 may correlate with a poor prognosis in early-stage NSCLC.[49] It is interesting that RB alterations in large cell carcinomas with neuroendocrine features were detected as frequently as in SCLC, suggesting a possible relationship between genetic alterations of the *RB* gene and neuroendocrine differentiation.[50] This notion is supported by experimental data showing that $Rb^{+/-}$ mice developed neuroendocrine tumors of various origins after long latency periods.[51] Alterations in *Rb* and *p53* appear to cooperate in tumorigenesis, as shown using mice deficient in the respective genes, perhaps because *p53* mutation may allow cells to escape from p53-dependent apoptosis induced by the inactivation of the Rb pathway.[52,53] Indeed, virtually all SCLC tumor specimens show both p53 and RB alterations.

p16INK4A, which maintains RB in its hypophosphorylated state, exerts tumor suppressor activity only in the presence of wild-type RB function. Almost 60% of primary NSCLCs were shown to inactivate p16 through point mutation, homozygous deletion, or promoter hypermethylation. Consistent with these notions, RB and p16INK4A are reciprocally inactivated in two major classes of lung cancers (i.e., SCLC and NSCLC), resulting in the inactivation of the p16INK4A-RB pathway in virtually all types of lung cancers.[54,55] It is also interesting that *p16INK4A* and *RB* are inactivated by different mechanisms, and tumor-specific epigenetic *p16INK4A* gene silencing through promoter hypermethylation is detectable exclusively in NSCLC and not in SCLC. These findings have stimulated several clinical trials using demethylation or DNA chromatin-altering agents that may reverse epigenetic gene silencing of tumor suppressor genes such as *p16INK4A*.

The other cyclin D kinase (CDK) inhibitor family is composed of p21CIP1/WAF1, p27KIP1, and p57KIP2, which have a wider spectrum of target CDK molecules. Expression levels of p27KIP1 were shown to be reduced in 70% of NSCLC tumor specimens due to increased ubiquitin-proteasome–mediated degradation and were associated with a poor prognosis.[56,57] However, no genetic alterations of the *p27KIP1* gene have been reported thus far. Interestingly, SCLC exhibits increased p27KIP1 expression,[56] which may favor survival of SCLC cells by preventing apoptosis in an unfavorable microenvironment.[58]

TUMOR SUPPRESSOR GENES AT THE 3p REGION

Allelic loss involving the short arm of chromosome 3 is one of the most frequent genetic alterations in both SCLC (>90%) and NSCLC (~70%). At least four separate consensus regions of allelic loss have been identified: 3p25–p26, 3p21–p22, 3p14, and 3p12.[59,60] In addition, recent high-resolution allelotyping indicated the presence of eight distinct sites with frequent allelic loss as defined by loss of heterozygosity.[61] It has been shown that allelic loss of 3p (and other regions such as 9p) is detectable even in histologically normal or mildly abnormal epithelium in lung cancer patients and healthy (current and former) smokers,[62,63] and that the frequency and extent of 3p allelic loss increases progressively along with increasing severity of histopathologic changes in preneoplastic/preinvasive lesions. These findings suggest that multiple tumor suppressor genes may reside on 3p and that their inactivation may occur cumulatively due to increasing instability from endogenous genetic changes or exogenous carcinogens such as those found in cigarette smoking. Thus, several genes on 3p may lead to the development and progression of lung cancer.

Several putative tumor suppressor genes have been identified in homozygously deleted 3p regions in lung cancer cell lines. Some of these regions constitute common fragile sites. Fragile sites are site-specific gaps or breaks seen on metaphase chromosomes after partial inhibition of DNA synthesis. The sites appear to be highly susceptible to DNA damage and represent unstable and highly recombinogenic DNA. The *FHIT* (*fragile histidine triad*) gene encoding a diadenosine triphosphate hydrolase was identified as a tumor suppressor gene spanning the most frequent fragile site at 3p14.2.[64,65] When introduced into cancer cells with a *FHIT* gene alteration, FHIT inhibits tumor growth by inducing apoptosis and cell cycle arrest[66,67]; mice deficient for the *Fhit* gene were shown to be highly susceptible to carcinogens.[68] In addition to structural disruptions, as expected from its location at the fragile site, epigenetic mechanism loss of FHIT expression was also reported.[69] Although specific point mutations are lacking, loss of FHIT expression was detected in virtually all SCLCs, and more frequently in squamous cell carcinoma than in adenocarcinoma.[65,70] An association between loss of FHIT expression and smoking history was also reported in both lung cancers and preneoplastic lesions.[71–73]

Allelic loss in the 3p21.3 region is among the earliest changes in lung cancer development, suggesting the presence of a tumor suppressor gene(s) important for the initiation of lung carcinogenesis.[61] Detailed analyses of the homozygously deleted regions at 3p21.3 resulted in the identification of several candidate tumor suppressor genes.[74–77] One promising candidate in this chromosome region, *RASSF1*, encodes a protein with a Ras-association domain and interestingly may mediate apoptotic and growth inhibitory signals from the *ras* oncogene. *RASSF1* frequently shows loss of expression in SCLC due to hypermethylation of its promoter region.[78–80] Introduction of exogenous *RASSF1A* inhibits cell growth and tumor formation of lung cancer cell lines.[79–81] To date, rare genetic alterations have been identified in *RASSF1* as well as in other candidate tumor suppressor genes at 3p21.3, including *BLU*, *NPR2/Gene21*, *FUS1*, *HYAL1* (*hyaluronidase*), *FUS2*, and *SEMA3B* (*semaphorin 3B*).[82] Notably, loss or reduced expression was clearly shown for *CACNA2D2* (*voltage-dependent calcium channel* α2/δ *subunit 2*), *SEMA3B*, *BLU*, and *HYAL1* in primary tumors[80]; however, it remains to be elucidated which gene or genes are playing a decisive role in lung carcinogenesis, and why so many candidate tumor suppressor genes with rare genetic changes and frequent epigenetic inactivations exist in this particular chromosome region. One possibility is that a few tumor suppressor genes on 3p conform to the classic two-hit model based on Knudson's hypothesis requiring inactivation of both alleles,[5] whereas haploinsufficiency of other genes in which one allele is still expressed in the tumor (hemizygous, or +/−, state) may result in growth advantage of affected cells.

TRANSFORMING GROWTH FACTOR-β SIGNAL PATHWAY

Transforming growth factor (TGF)-β inhibits cell proliferation of normal epithelial cells, including bronchial and peripheral lung epithelial cells, through the induction of CDK inhibitors (p15INK4B, p21CIP1, p27KIP1),[83,84] as well as partly through down-regulation of Myc.[85] TGF-β signaling is known to be impaired by the activation of the mitogen-activated protein kinase (MAPK) cascade and the nuclear factor-κB (NF-κB) pathway, implying the presence of crosstalk within these signaling pathways. Lung cancer cell lines are often unresponsive to TGF-β signaling, and expression profiling analysis has identified decreased expression of the TGF-β receptor type II gene (*TGFβRII*) as one characteristic feature present in lung cancer specimens when compared with normal lung tissues.[86] One study suggested that expression of *TGFβRII* was frequently lost in lung cancers due to an epigenetic mechanism involving histone deacetylation and altered chromatin conformation rather than aberrant hypermethylation of its promoter.[87] In contrast, genetic alterations of *TGFβRII* such as frameshift mutations, shown to be relatively frequent in colorectal cancers with the microsatellite instability phenotype, are rarely observed in lung cancers, consistent with a lack of marked microsatellite instability in lung cancer.[88] *Smad4* and *Smad2*, which mediate TGF-β signaling transmitted through TGFβRII, are occasionally mutated in lung cancers[89,90] through homozygous deletion or point mutation.

CELL CYCLE CHECKPOINTS AND DNA REPAIR MECHANISMS

Cell cycle checkpoints induce arrest or delay of cell cycle progression and provide sufficient time for DNA repair,

if possible, thereby protecting cells from propagating damaged DNA. Although the mechanisms to sense DNA damage remain to be fully understood, it has been shown that double-stranded DNA breaks activate the ATM and ATR kinases, which play central roles in the DNA damage response by phosphorylating several key molecules, including CHK1, CHK2, p53, BRCA1, and NBS1. This in turn leads to further downstream signaling and cell cycle arrest or delay at G_1, S, and G_2 (see Fig. 42.3). Frequent genetic alterations of the *p53* gene impair the G_1 checkpoint in the majority of lung cancers, and G_2 checkpoint impairment was recently shown to be frequent also in SCLC.[91] In this regard, it is of note that *CHK2* is mutated in lung cancer, albeit at a low frequency,[92] and loss of a key controller of the G_2 checkpoint gene *14-3-3σ* due to hypermethylation was recently shown to be a frequent event in SCLC.[93]

Chromosomal instability, which often results in aneuploidy, has been shown to be a common feature of lung cancer cells.[94] The mitotic spindle checkpoint, which assures properly ordered chromosome segregation by preventing cells with an unattached kinetochore from entering into mitosis, is frequently impaired in lung cancer cell lines.[95–97] Whereas defects in the mitotic spindle checkpoint are closely associated with the presence of chromosome instability in colorectal cancer,[98] there must be additional alterations in lung cancers, because there are examples of chromosome instability without mitotic spindle checkpoint impairment.[3] Other checkpoints, including prophase and postmitotic checkpoints, may be abnormal. Epigenetic inactivation of the *CHFR* prophase checkpoint gene has been reported in lung cancer[99] and *p53* alterations may also be indirectly involved in the induction of chromosomal numerical alterations, perhaps due to defects in the postmitotic checkpoint.[94]

OTHER TUMOR SUPPRESSOR GENES

The *LKB1/STK11* gene is a tumor suppressor, because germline mutations of this gene lead to the Peutz-Jeghers syndrome, a condition associated with gastrointestinal polyposis and a predisposition to cancer. A recent study discovered that *LKB1/STK11* is inactivated mainly due to nonsense mutations specifically in about one third of primary lung adenocarcinomas.[100] Moreover, loss of LKB1 protein expression due to inactivating mutations was observed in 26% of adenocarcinomas, and this loss was also detected in 5% and 21% of low- and high-grade atypical adenomatous hyperplasia lesions, respectively.[101] These findings support the notion that *LKB1* inactivation may play a role in the transition from premalignant to malignant tumor growth.

Many tyrosine and serine/threonine kinases are involved in growth-promoting pathways, and several phosphatases negatively regulate these pathways. PTEN/MMAC1 (phosphatase and tensin homolog/mutated in multiple advanced cancers 1) functions as a phosphoinositide 3-phosphatase that negatively regulates phosphatidylinositol 3-kinase (PI3K)/AKT signaling. PTEN may be involved in the induction of apoptosis due to loss of cellular attachment (anoikis) and inhibition of cell migration. Although the locus where the *PTEN/MMAC1* gene resides (10q23.3) has been shown to be lost frequently in lung cancer, somatic mutations or homozygous deletions of the *PTEN/MMAC1* gene itself are present in a relatively small subset of cell lines (~10%) and primary lung cancer specimens (0 to ~5%).[102–105]

The 11q23 region is one of the most frequent targets of chromosomal deletion in a variety of cancers and has been suggested to harbor at least two putative tumor suppressor genes.[106] *TSLC1/IGSF4* encoding an immunoglobulin superfamily member was recently cloned from a genomic fragment corresponding to 11q23.2, based on its functional competency in the suppression of tumorigenicity of human A549 and mouse Lewis lung cancer cell lines.[107] Although *TSLC1* mutations are very uncommon, expression of *TSLC1* was shown to be reduced by aberrant hypermethylation of its promoter region.[108] Another putative tumor suppressor gene at 11q23, *PPP2R1B*, encoding the β isoform of protein phosphatase 2 regulatory subunit A, was also found to be mutated in a fraction of cell lines (15%) and primary lung cancers (6%).[109] The *PPP1R3* gene residing at the 7q31 region, which encodes the protein phosphatase 1 regulatory (inhibitor) subunit 3A, was also shown to exhibit infrequent mutations in NSCLC cell lines (15%) and primary lung cancer tissues (5%).[110]

ONCOGENES AND GROWTH-PROMOTING SIGNALS

Cell proliferation is positively regulated by several growth-promoting pathways, including MAPK cascades as well as the PI3K-AKT, phospholipase C–protein kinase C (PLC-PKC), and NF-κB pathways (Fig. 42.4). A growth factor–mediated signal may diverge through a tyrosine kinase receptor into several pathways, such as the Ras-Raf-MAPK, PI3K-AKT, and PLC-PKC pathways, whereas NF-κB is convergently activated by several distinct stimuli, including growth factors, cytokines, and extracellular matrix attachment. Therefore, alteration of a single component of the growth-promoting pathways may aberrantly affect several signaling pathways, resulting in a broad range of cellular dysfunction. The elucidation of the complex divergent and convergent networks of these growth-promoting pathways should thus lead not only to a better understanding of the fundamental functional interaction between oncogenes, but also to the development of novel therapeutic approaches through manipulation of key molecules in signaling networks.

RAS GENE FAMILY

The Ras family consists of three proto-oncogene members, K-Ras (K-Ras-2), H-Ras, and N-Ras, which bind to guanosine triphosphate (GTP) in their active state, and return to an inactive guanosine diphosphate–interacting state through their intrinsic GTPase activity.[111] A single amino acid substitution at codon 12, 13, or 61 affects the GTPase activity, resulting in the accumulation of an active GTP-bound form and the constitutive activation of downstream targets, through the Raf-1/MAPK pathway. The activation of Raf-1 induces transcription of several growth-promoting genes, including those for cyclin D1, *myc*, and growth factors, mainly via the MAPK cascade.[112] Of particular note is that oncogenic *ras* mutants also induce cell cycle arrest through induction of ARF, p16INK4a, and p53 in normal fibroblast cells.[36] This may in turn explain the frequent simultaneous occurrence of K-*ras* mutations and alterations of the p16INK4A/p14ARF or p53 pathway, or both, in

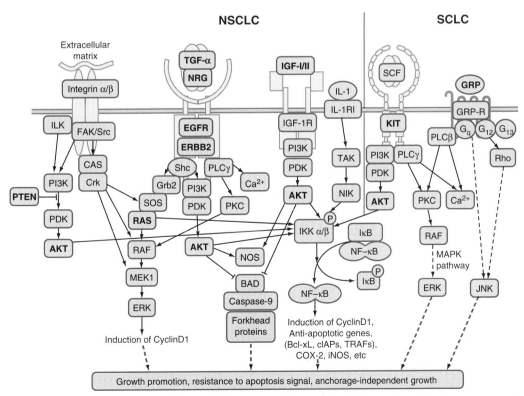

Figure 42.4 Activation of growth-promoting pathways in lung cancer. Components that are altered in lung cancer are indicated in **bold**. NSCLC, non-small cell lung cancer; SCLC, small cell lung cancer.

cancer cells, thereby averting cell cycle arrest, and suggests the occurrence of *ras* mutations in an ordered multiple-step manner during the carcinogenic process. Among the *ras* family members, the K-*ras* gene is most frequently affected (almost exclusively in adenocarcinoma), usually at codon 12.[113,114] Mutations of H-*ras* or N-*ras* are very rare (~1%) in lung cancers. In addition, K-*ras* mutations are reportedly present in 25% to 40% of atypical adenomatous hyperplasia lesions,[115,116] although there has been considerable controversy over whether K-*ras* mutations are present in premalignant or normal-appearing lung tissues.[117,118] K-*ras* mutations are predominantly $G \rightarrow T$ transversions, implying their creation through DNA adduct formation from tobacco exposure.[119] K-*ras* mutations were shown to be significantly associated with shortened survival in surgically treated patients.[117] Interestingly, K-*ras* mutations in Japanese lung adenocarcinoma cases, often occurring in nonsmokers, show a strong association with the goblet cell subtype of adenocarcinoma.[120]

B-*raf,* involved in a signaling pathway parallel to *ras,* was recently found to harbor activating mutations in primary cancers.[121] A single $G \rightarrow T$ transversion resulted in dominant oncogenic signaling in approximately 5% of primary adenocarcinomas.[122-124] As in other cancers, tumors with K-*ras* mutations generally do not harbor B-*raf* mutations, and vice versa. This inverse correlation suggests that K-*ras* and B-*raf* ultimately signal through the same pathway.

MYC ONCOGENES

Myc protein transactivates the cell cycle–regulating genes and promotes cell cycle progression probably by several mechanisms. Myc represses p15INK4B[85,125] and may downregulate the CDK inhibitor p27KIP1.[126,127] Myc induces cyclin D1/D2 expression and accumulation of the cyclin D-CDK4 complex, which in turn sequesters p21CIP1 and p27KIP1 and leads to the release of active cyclin E-CDK2 and cell cycle progression (see Fig. 42.2).[128] Recent reports based on microarray analysis showed that Myc induced the expression of cyclin D2 and CDC2, and repressed the CDK inhibitor p21CIP1.[129,130]

Gene amplification of one of the members of the *myc* family is detectable in 25% to 30% of SCLC cell lines as well as in 5% to 15% of primary tumor specimens, whereas overexpression of one of the members is detectable in virtually all SCLCs.[131-133] Thus, the vast majority of SCLCs appear to have both *p53* mutations and Myc overexpression, consistent with the notion that inactivation of the ARF/MDM2/p53 pathway is required for Myc-induced transformation.[34,134] In addition, in cell lines and primary specimens of NSCLC, overexpression of the *myc* gene without gene amplification is observed more frequently (50% to 70%) than is overexpression of Myc with gene amplification (<10%).[131,133,135-137] Overexpression without gene amplification may be explained by loss of transcriptional attenuation of the *myc* and L-*myc* genes[138] and antisense messenger ribonucleic acid expression of the N-*myc* gene.[139]

GROWTH FACTORS AND THEIR RECEPTORS

The *erb*-b family consists of four receptor-type tyrosine kinase genes, epidermal growth factor receptor (EGFR, or

erb-b), *erb*-b2 (HER-2/neu), *erb*-b3, and *erb*-b4, for which several specific ligands have been identified. The ligands epidermal growth factor (EGF), TGF-α, and amphiregulin are specific for EGFR, while neuregulins/heregulins bind to Erb-B3 or Erb-B4. Erb-B2 lacks intrinsic kinase activity and forms a heterodimer with other members of the *erb*-b family, thereby enhancing their signaling.[140] The specific interactions of these ligands and receptors stimulate several signaling pathways, such as Ras-Raf-MAPK, PI3K-AKT, and PLC-PKC, thus mediating growth-stimulating signals.[141] EGFR is overexpressed without gene amplification in a large proportion of lung cancers (70% of squamous cell cancers and 40% of adenocarcinomas).[142,143] The EGFR type III mutation (in-frame deletion within the extracellular domain), which is reportedly present in 16% of NSCLCs, was suggested to be a tumor-specific antigen potentially useful for targeting cancer cells.[144] Specific EGFR-activating somatic mutations were recently reported in NSCLCs from patients who responded to tyrosine kinase inhibitors.[145,146] These mutations were more common (~25%) in Japanese patients and those with bronchoalveolar carcinoma, providing an explanation for increased response rate in these patients. In contrast to frequent gene amplification in breast cancers, gene amplification of Erb-B2 is very rare (~3%),[147,148] but overexpression is detectable in 30% of lung cancers.[149,150] Erb-B3 overexpression was detected in 20% of NSCLCs and also showed an association with a poor prognosis.[151] Overexpression of TGF-α is present in 60% of NSCLCs, suggesting the existence of a possible autocrine/paracrine stimulatory loop in lung cancer.[142,152] High-level expression of amphiregulin was reported in over 40% of lung cancers and was also associated with a poor prognosis,[153] whereas expression of neuregulin has been found in lung cancer cell lines, not in the normal bronchial epithelial cells.[154]

Anchorage-independent growth and resistance to anoikis, the apoptosis that follows loss of cell attachment, is thought to be a common characteristic of neoplastic cells, including lung cancer, and may be important in survival of metastases. Although the activation of the Jun kinase–activator protein-1 and AKT–NF-κB pathways leads to the acquisition of such a phenotype, other alterations thus far identified in lung cancer may also be involved in the activation of these pathways. For example, autocrine secretion of members of the EGF family and overexpression of the EGF receptor are frequently observed in lung cancer, conceivably activating these pathways. Activation of PI3K signaling to AKT may also be facilitated by mutations in *PTEN* or *PP2A,* as discussed earlier. Moreover, constitutive activation of AKT is frequently detected in more than 80% of NSCLC cell lines, in turn promoting cell survival.[155]

ANGIOGENIC FACTORS

Angiogenesis is thought to play an important role in tumor progression and metastasis, and is positively and negatively regulated by many cytokines and growth factors, including vascular endothelial growth factors (VEGFs), angiopoietins (Angs), platelet-derived growth factor, basic fibroblast growth factor, interleukin-8, TGF-β, and TGF-α. Two distinct families of endothelial cell–specific receptor tyrosine kinases, the VEGF receptor (VEGFR) and TIE families, have been identified and are thought to promote angiogenesis by mediating signals elicited by binding of VEGFs and Angs, respectively.[156] Genetic alterations such as gene amplification involving VEGFs, Angs, and their respective receptors have not been reported in lung cancer, but high-level expression of VEGF is detectable in about 50% of lung cancers, and is associated with a higher microvessel density.[157,158] VEGF expression may also be induced by hypoxia in lung cancer tissues, via hypoxia inducible factor-1α (HIF-1α),[159] and may also be induced by cyclooxyge-nase-2, which has increased expression in lung cancers.[160] It remains controversial whether a high level of VEGF expression, a high microvessel density, or both correlate with a poor prognosis.[161–163] VEGF-C promotes lymphangiogene-sis through the activation of VEGFR-3–mediated signals, and is expressed in about 40% of NSCLCs.[164] Its possible involvement in lymphatic metastasis of lung cancer was further supported in experiments in a highly metastatic lung cancer cell subline.[165] Recently, frequent expression of Ang-1 and TIE2 was also reported in NSCLC.[166,167] Under-standing the control of angiogenesis offers therapeutic opportunities for "starving" tumors without the need to attack the tumor cells directly.

TELOMERASE

Telomere maintenance is a critical component of immortal-ity due to the inability of DNA polymerases to replicate the end of the chromosomal DNA. Active telomerase works in concert with inactivation of the RB or p53 pathway to produce immortality. For example, inactivation of the p16INK4A/RB pathway alone may override senescence, causing cells to continue to lose telomeric DNA and to die through p53-mediated apoptosis[168]; loss of p53 function allows premalignant cells to continue proliferating and sub-sequently reach a second barrier, called crisis, which is char-acterized by chromosomal instability, end-to-end fusions, and catastrophic cell death (Fig. 42.5). Telomerase activa-tion and subsequent stabilization of the telomeric DNA is thought to be essential for cells to escape from this crisis in order to proliferate indefinitely.[169]

Indeed, the activation of telomerase is frequently observed in lung cancers (100% of SCLCs and 80% of NSCLCs),[170] and telomerase activity was shown to correlate with cell proliferation and pathologic progression in NSCLC.[171] In addition, telomerase activity is also detectable in precancerous tissues, suggesting the early selection pres-sure for telomere maintenance. Although the precise molec-ular mechanism involved in the activation of telomerase still remains obscure, telomerase may be directly activated by Myc.[172,173] Interestingly, a gene locus that represses expres-sion of the active subunit of telomerase may be present on chromosomal arm 3p, a region commonly lost in lung cancer (see earlier).[174,175] Indeed, because of the critical role of telomerase in chromosomal integrity, there are probably various means of activating its function in cancer.

EXPRESSION SIGNATURE OF LUNG CANCERS

Recent rapid progress in microarray and mass spectrometry technologies has made it possible to analyze genome-wide expression profiles. Expression profiling sets the stage for

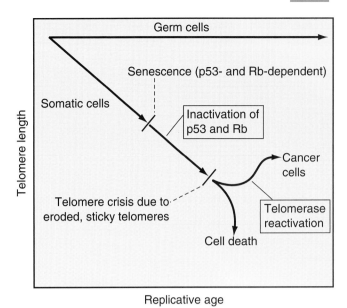

Figure 42.5 Progressive shortening (erosion) of telomere leading to cell death by crisis and the reactivation of telomerase as an important step in oncogenesis. Telomerase activation and subsequent stabilization of the telomeric DNA is thought to be essential for cells to escape from cell crisis in order to proliferate indefinitely.

identifying molecular markers that enable cancer classifica-tion and outcome prediction. Expression profiling of lung cancer has demonstrated the presence of histologic type-specific expression patterns or signatures and indicated the heterogeneity of adenocarcinoma, and a relationship of specific expression signatures with clinical outcome.[86,176–178] Recently, a metastatic signature was also identified based on the analysis of lung adenocarcinoma cases, leading to the identification of a set of genes potentially associated with metastatic capability.[179] In addition, a prediction model was constructed that correctly classified adenocarcinoma cases into high- and low-risk groups.[176,177,180]

MOLECULAR CORRELATES

As noted previously, a number of DNA alterations (gene mutation, microsatellite instability, promoter methylation, and overexpression) occur during the development of cancer and can be used as markers for cancer detection in clinical samples.[181–183] In addition, the detection of molec-ular changes present in invasive cancer may identify high-risk populations and ultimately may define molecular criteria for the diagnosis of cancer.[182,183] Over the past decade, a variety of approaches have been developed that may improve the results of conventional cancer screening by detecting these molecular markers in clinical samples. Sur-gical resection remains the most effective form of treatment for NSCLC; however, at the time of diagnosis, more than 65% of all patients will have advanced disease that is no longer amenable to curative therapy.[184] Earlier diagnosis of patients with lung cancer would increase the number of potentially resectable patients, but better detection approaches are needed.

DETECTION OF MOLECULAR ALTERATIONS IN SPUTUM OR BRONCHOALVEOLAR LAVAGE FLUID

The majority of molecular screening studies for lung cancer performed to date have focused on detecting genetic abnormalities in exfoliated cells from body fluid samples, including sputum or bronchoalveolar lavage (BAL) fluid, or in the circulating DNA found in serum or plasma (Table 42.2). K-*ras* gene mutations were one of the earliest molecular abnormalities detected in lung cancer and were among the first targets in molecular screening studies. In one approach, investigators used a polymerase chain reaction (PCR) technique that enriched for mutations to detect K-*ras* mutations in BAL fluid obtained from patients with NSCLC.[185] With this approach, mutant K-*ras* alleles were detected in the BAL fluid from 56% of patients with primary adenocarcinoma of the lung and from 31% of all patients with NSCLC.[185] K-*ras* mutations were not detected in the 30 control patients. Tumor tissue was available in 35 of 56 patients with NSCLC, and, in all cases, the K-*ras* mutation status of the BAL fluid was identical to that of the primary tumor. The sensitivity for diagnosing adenocarcinoma in this group of patients with unspecified-stage lung cancer was high, and the specificity was 100% (see Table 42.2).[185]

A similar study also reported K-*ras* mutations in 60% of NSCLC tumors and 47% of sputum samples from patients with NSCLC.[186] However, K-*ras* mutations were also detected in normal-appearing lung tissues from 60% of patients with NSCLC, in 10% of lung tissue samples from patients without cancer, and in 12.5% of sputum samples from patients with benign lesions, suggesting a less than perfect specificity of this technique for overt cancer. As the number of PCR cycles and the sensitivity of this assay increased, the specificity was compromised, limiting its value as a screening test.[186] Furthermore, K-*ras* mutations are only detected in a minority of adenocarcinomas of the lung (30% to 50% of cases), limiting their use as a marker for lung cancer.[187] Mutations of *ras* and of *p53* have also been detected in the sputum of patients with adenocarcinoma of the lung, in some cases from sputum specimens stored more than 1 year prior to clinical diagnosis. Mao and colleagues were the first to report tumor-specific mutant cells in seven of eight cytologically negative archived sputum samples obtained from patients before they were diagnosed with lung cancer.[188] In this study, a semiquantitative plaque hybridization assay was used; the plaque hybridization assay is cumbersome but able to detect 1 mutant cell against a background of 10,000 normal cells, and is limited only by the number of plaques screened.[188]

Table 42.2 Selected Trials Using Molecular Approaches to Detect Lung Cancer

Clinical Sample	Molecular Marker	Patients[a]	Controls[b]	Sensitivity (%)[c]	Specificity (%)[d]	Reference
BAL	K-ras[e]	14	30	100[e]	100[e]	185
Sputum	K-ras/p53	10	5	80	100	188
BAL	K-ras[e]	8	11	50	100	187
	p53	22	23	39	100	
	Microsatellites (15)[s]	22	14	14	83	
	p16 methylation	19	30	63	100	
Sputum	p16	9	125	100	86	190
	MGMT methylation	6	128	75	75	
BAL	CDH1	27	14	48	100	191
	p16	7	34	14	100	
	MGMT	12	29	58	100	
	APC	17	24	29	100	
	RASSF1A methylation	14	27	29	100	
BAL	Mitochondrial DNA	10	0	80	N/A	192
Plasma	Microsatellites (3)[s]	21	10	93	100	195
Serum	p16	9	13	33	100	196
	DAP-K	5	17	80	100	
	GSTP1	2	20	50	100	
	MGMT methylation	6	16	66	100	
Serum	APC methylation	85	54	47	100	197

[a] Number of cancer patients with evidence of marker in primary tumor.
[b] Number of patients without cancer and cancer patients without evidence of molecular marker in primary tumor.
[c] Sensitivity of molecular assay reported as fraction of patients with evidence of mutation or microsatellite alteration detected in body fluid. Includes only patients from whom both tumor and body fluid were analyzed.
[d] Specificity is reported as the fraction of patients with cancer and evidence of the molecular alteration in the primary tumor.
[e] Includes only patients with primary adenocarcinoma of the lung.
[s] Number of microsatellite markers used in study given in parentheses.

Microsatellite alterations represent another molecular screening tool for the detection of cancer. Investigators initially screened 100 primary cancers, including 58 lung cancers (35 SCLCs and 23 NSCLCs) with a panel of nine tri- and tetranucleotide markers, and identified microsatellite instability in 26 of the tumors, including 50% of the SCLCs and 9% of the NSCLCs.[189] In serial dilution experiments, the presence of these novel alleles (or bands) could be detected with a sensitivity of 1:200 to 1:500.[189] They also examined sputum samples collected from two patients with SCLC with markers demonstrating instability in the primary tumor. Both of these sputum samples contained the same new allele found in the tumor.[189]

To examine the sensitivity of many of these molecular screening strategies in detecting cancer in patients with potentially curable lung cancer, investigators evaluated PCR-based assays for the detection of four molecular markers frequently abnormal in NSCLC in the BAL fluid from 50 patients with resectable (stages I to IIIa) NSCLC (see Table 42.2).[187] Because most molecular markers are present only in a minority of patients with a particular malignancy, screening for multiple markers increases the likelihood that at least one particular genetic alteration will be present in the primary tumor that can be detected in cytologic fluid samples from a given patient. Twenty-eight of these 50 tumors contained a p53 mutation, and the identical mutation was detected with a plaque hybridization assay in the BAL fluid in 39% of these patients. Eight of 19 primary adenocarcinomas contained a K-ras mutation, and the identical mutation was detected with a mutation ligation assay in the BAL fluid in 50% of these patients. The p16 gene harbored promoter hypermethylation in 19 of 50 tumors, and methylated p16 alleles were detected in the BAL fluid from 63% of these patients using methylation-specific PCR. Microsatellite instability in at least 1 marker was detected, with a panel of 15 markers frequently altered in NSCLC in 23 of 50 tumors. However, the identical alteration was detected in the BAL fluid in only 14% of these patients. When all four techniques to detect mutations, methylations, or microsatellite instability were combined, at least one genetic alteration was present in the tumor in 43 patients (86%) and was found in the paired BAL sample in 23 of these 43 patients (53%).[187]

Several factors influenced the ability to detect molecular alterations in BAL fluid in this study.[187] Tumor location played a role; tumor-specific p53 mutations in BAL fluid were detected significantly more often in patients with centrally located tumors than in patients with peripheral tumors (100% vs. 29%). Tumor size also played a significant role; the p53 plaque hybridization assay detected molecular alterations more often in patients with advanced (stages IB, II, and IIIa) tumors than in limited stage IA (≤3.0 cm) tumors (59% vs. 9%). On the other hand, tumor type did not influence yield; in contrast to cytology, which is much more sensitive at detecting squamous cell cancer than adenocarcinoma, the molecular assays detected cancer cells in the BAL fluid from these two tumor types with similar frequency.[187]

More recently, with a highly sensitive nested methylation-specific PCR,[190] methylation was detected in the sputum samples of every patient with squamous cell lung cancer, sometimes up to 3 years prior to clinical diagnosis. However, aberrant methylation was also detected in 14% of cancer-free and 23% of long-term tobacco smokers. It is thus possible that this sensitive assay may detect individuals at high risk of developing squamous cell lung cancer, although this will not be known without long-term follow-up. More recently, a quantitative methylation assay showed promise in accurately distinguishing cancer cases from controls.[191] The detection of aberrant hypermethylation of cancer-related genes in the sputum shows promise as a new approach for detecting lung cancer, but long-term follow-up is essential to understand the significance of false positives with these very sensitive techniques.

Mitochondrial DNA mutations were identified in human cancer and subsequently used as a marker for molecular cancer detection. Mitochondrial DNA mutations were identified in 43% (6 of 14) of NSCLCs. Using a sensitive oligonucleotide-mismatch ligation assay, mitochondrial DNA mutations were present in 80% (8 of 10) of corresponding BAL samples from lung cancer patients.[192] Mitochondrial DNA analysis has one distinct advantage over other nuclear DNA-based methods for cancer detection.[192] Each cell contains hundreds to thousands of mitochondrial genomes, and cancer cells have an increased number of mitochondria in their cytoplasm. Moreover, mutated mitochondrial DNA appears to gain a significant replicative advantage over wild-type mitochondrial DNA, eventually becoming homoplasmic (wherein all mitochondria share the same genome). The end result is considerable amplification (20- to 200-fold) of tumor-derived mutated mitochondrial DNA.[192] Moreover, a mononucleotide repeat (D310) has recently been identified as a frequent mutational hot spot for mitochondrial DNA alterations in a variety of primary tumors, including lung cancer.[193] The identification of mitochondrial DNA mutation hot spot D310 could simplify the strategy for detecting mitochondrial DNA mutation in clinical samples. In addition, gene chip/array technologies can be applied to develop high-throughput analysis of the entire mitochondrial genome, as previously demonstrated for nuclear p53 mutations.[194]

DETECTION OF MOLECULAR ALTERATIONS IN CIRCULATING DNA

Molecular approaches have also been applied to detect tumor-specific alterations in circulating DNA. The concentration of DNA in the serum of patients with cancer is significantly higher than in cancer-free individuals and provides another potential source for noninvasive molecular detection of cancer. In one study of patients with SCLC, investigators identified microsatellite instability in 76% (16 of 21), and further demonstrated that 93% (15 of 16) of the patients with microsatellite instability in tumor DNA had similar microsatellite alterations in the corresponding plasma DNA.[195] Follow-up examinations of plasma DNA after 3 to 6 months revealed identical microsatellite alterations in three of four patients, suggesting that the circulating DNA came from the tumor.

Methylation-specific PCR has also been used to identify tumor-specific epigenetic alterations in the serum of patients with lung cancer. Investigators initially screened 22 primary NSCLCs with four candidate methylation genes, and detected aberrant methylation in 68% (15 of 22) of the primary NSCLCs in at least one of these four genes: p16, the metastasis suppressor gene *DAPK*, the detoxification gene *GSTP1*, and the DNA repair gene *MGMT*.[196] In contrast, none of the 22 corresponding normal lung tissues demonstrated aberrant methylation in any of these four genes.[196] More importantly, identical aberrant methylation was detected in the corresponding serum in 11 of these 15 patients (73%) with aberrant methylation in the primary tumors. In contrast, no patients with unmethylated tumor DNA showed methylation in their corresponding serum.[196] Recently, aberrant adenomatous polyposis coli (APC) promoter hypermethylation was detected in 95 of 99 (96%) of lung cancer tissues and provides an additional target for a serum-based screening test for lung cancer[197] using a quantitative technique. Aberrant APC gene methylation was detected in the serum or plasma in 42 of 89 (47%) of patients with lung cancer, but was not detected in 50 healthy control patients.[197] Promoter hypermethylation is an important pathway for silencing gene transcription in cancer cells. As the list of methylated genes in cancer increases in conjunction with improved high-throughput techniques, detection of gene methylation in clinical samples such as sputum, BAL fluid, and serum will be more fully explored in larger clinical trials.

Recently, protein profiling of serum or plasma using high-throughput mass spectroscopy was reported.[198] Cases and controls could be distinguished by statistical algorithms that identified key protein patterns in the spectra. At a 10% false-positive rate, serum protein patterns could detect 50% to 70% of primary tumors. Identification of common mass peaks in cancer patients should yield new protein markers. Whether use of a limited combination of individual protein markers or of a complete protein profile will provide better sensitivity, specificity, or both remains to be determined.

Promising results have been reported using several molecular detection strategies for the detection of common smoking-related cancers. These early studies have clearly demonstrated the potential improvement in sensitivity and specificity of molecular approaches in detecting cancer. However, before the introduction of these approaches into routine clinical use, further large clinical studies are clearly needed. A prospective comparison between conventional cancer detection methods and newer molecular techniques documenting improved detection rates in patients with early stage cancers is required before these approaches are adopted in routine clinical practice. In addition, broad technical improvements in molecular detection assays and high-throughput automation are pivotal for eventual clinical implementation. With the profile of the common or specific molecular changes in a particular tumor type rapidly evolving, emerging molecular detection approaches will become an important tool in cancer diagnosis and treatment.

SUMMARY

Accumulating evidence clearly indicates that key genetic and epigenetic alterations that positively or negatively regulate various cellular processes lead to the initiation and progression of lung cancer. The accumulation of these alterations confers various capabilities on lung cancer cells, including resistance to apoptosis, sustained proliferation and angio-genesis, and escape from growth-inhibitory signals and telomere shortening. As further information from the human genome sequence unfolds, accompanied by the introduction of sophisticated informatics, it is likely that a finer and more comprehensive picture of lung cancer biology will be elucidated. This knowledge will facilitate a revolution in the prevention, diagnosis, and treatment of this fatal disease.

ACKNOWLEDGMENTS

T.T. is supported in part by a Grant-in-Aid for Scientific Research on Priority Areas from the Ministry of Education, Culture, Sports, Science and Technology, and a Grant-in-Aid for the Second-Term Comprehensive Ten-Year Strategy for Cancer Control from the Ministry of Health and Welfare, Japan. D.S. is supported by the lung cancer SPORE Grant (Grant # P50CA96784) and the early detection research EDRN Grant (Grant # 5 U01 CA84986-04), both from the National Cancer Institute.

REFERENCES

1. Hollstein M, Sidransky D, Vogelstein B, Harris CC: p53 mutations in human cancers. Science 253:49–53, 1991.
2. Dasika GK, Lin SC, Zhao S, et al: DNA damage-induced cell cycle checkpoints and DNA strand break repair in development and tumorigenesis. Oncogene 18:7883–7899, 1999.
3. Balsara BR, Test JR: Chromosomal imbalances in human lung cancer. Oncogene 21:6877–6883, 2002.
4. Masuda A, Takahashi T: Chromosome instability in human lung cancers: Possible underlying mechanisms and potential consequences in the pathogenesis. Oncogene 21:6884–6897, 2002.
5. Knudson AG Jr, Hethcote HW, Brown BW: Mutation and childhood cancer: A probabilistic model for the incidence of retinoblastoma. Proc Natl Acad Sci U S A 72:5116–5120, 1975.
6. Baylin SB, Herman JG, Graff JR, et al: Alterations in DNA methylation: A fundamental aspect of neoplasia. Adv Cancer Res 72:141–196, 1998.
7. Yu J, Zhang L, Hwang PM, et al: Identification and classification of p53-regulated genes. Proc Natl Acad Sci U S A 96:14517–14522, 1999.
8. Harper JW, Adami GR, Wei N, et al: The p21 Cdk-interacting protein Cip1 is a potent inhibitor of G1 cyclin-dependent kinases. Cell 75:805–816, 1993.
9. el-Deiry WS, Tokino T, Velculescu VE, et al: WAF1, a potential mediator of p53 tumor suppression. Cell 75:817–825, 1993.
10. Hermeking H, Lengauer C, Polyak K, et al: 14-3-3 sigma is a p53-regulated inhibitor of G2/M progression. Mol Cell 1:3–11, 1997.
11. Yamaguchi T, Matsuda K, Sagiya Y, et al: p53R2-dependent pathway for DNA synthesis in a p53-regulated cell cycle checkpoint. Cancer Res 61:8256–8262, 2001.
12. Miyashita T, Reed JC: Tumor suppressor p53 is a direct transcriptional activator of the human bax gene. Cell 80:293–299, 1995.
13. Oda E, Ohki R, Murasawa H, et al: Noxa, a BH3-only member of the Bcl-2 family and candidate mediator of p53-induced apoptosis. Science 288:1053–1058, 2000.
14. Yu J, Zhang L, Hwang PM, et al: PUMA induces the rapid apoptosis of colorectal cancer cells. Mol Cell 7:673–682, 2001.

15. Robles AI, Bemmels NA, Foraker AB, Harris CC: APAF-1 is a transcriptional target of p53 in DNA damage-induced apoptosis. Cancer Res 61:6660–6664, 2001.

16. Venot C, Maratrat M, Dureuil C, et al: The requirement for the p53 proline-rich functional domain for mediation of apoptosis is correlated with specific PIG3 gene transactivation and with transcriptional repression. EMBO J 17:4668–4679, 1998.

17. Oda K, Arakawa H, Tanaka T, et al: p53AIP1, a potential mediator of p53-dependent apoptosis, and its regulation by Ser-46-phosphorylated p53. Cell 102:849–862, 2000.

18. D'Orazi G, Cecchinelli B, Bruno T, et al: Homeodomain-interacting protein kinase-2 phosphorylates p53 at Ser 46 and mediates apoptosis. Nat Cell Biol 4:11–19, 2002.

19. Hofmann TG, Moller A, Sirma H, et al: Regulation of p53 activity by its interaction with homeodomain-interacting protein kinase-2. Nat Cell Biol 4:1–10, 2002.

20. Tarapore P, Horn HF, Tokuyama Y, Fukasawa K: Direct regulation of the centrosome duplication cycle by the p53-p21Waf1/Cip1 pathway. Oncogene 20:3173–3184, 2001.

21. Takahashi T, Nau MM, Chiba I, et al: p53: A frequent target for genetic abnormalities in lung cancer. Science 246:491–494, 1989.

22. Robles AI, Linke SP, Harris CC: The p53 network in lung carcinogenesis. Oncogene 21:6898–6907, 2002.

23. Hainaut P, Pfeifer GP: Patterns of p53 G → T transversions in lung cancers reflect the primary mutagenic signature of DNA-damage by tobacco smoke. Carcinogenesis 22:367–374, 2001.

24. Hussain S, Amstad P, Raja K, et al: Mutability of p53 hotspot codons to benzo(a)pyrene diol epoxide (BPDE) and the frequency of p53 mutations in nontumorous human lung. Cancer Res 61:6350–6355, 2001.

25. Mitsudomi T, Hamajima N, Ogawa M, Takahashi T: Prognostic significance of p53 alterations in patients with non-small cell lung cancer: A meta-analysis. Clin Cancer Res 6:4055–4063, 2000.

26. Ahrendt SA, Hu Y, Buta M, et al: p53 mutations and survival in stage I non-small cell lung cancer: Results of a prospective study. J Natl Cancer Inst 95:926–927, 2003.

27. Haupt Y, Maya R, Kazaz A, Oren M: Mdm2 promotes the rapid degradation of p53. Nature 387:296–299, 1997.

28. Zhou BP, Liao Y, Xia W, et al: HER-2/neu induces p53 ubiquitination via Akt-mediated MDM2 phosphorylation. Nat Cell Biol 3:973–982, 2001.

29. Ladanyi M, Cha C, Lewis R, et al: MDM2 gene amplification in metastatic osteosarcoma. Cancer Res 53:16–18, 1993.

30. Higashiyama M, Doi O, Kodama K, et al: MDM2 gene amplification and expression in non-small-cell lung cancer: Immunohistochemical expression of its protein is a favourable prognostic marker in patients without p53 protein accumulation. Br J Cancer 75:1302–1308, 1997.

31. Ko JL, Cheng YW, Chang SL, et al: MDM2 mRNA expression is a favorable prognostic factor in non-small-cell lung cancer. Int J Cancer 89:265–270, 2000.

32. Honda R, Yasuda H: Association of p19(ARF) with Mdm2 inhibits ubiquitin ligase activity of Mdm2 for tumor suppressor p53. EMBO J 18:22–27, 1999.

33. Weber JD, Taylor LJ, Roussel MF, et al: Nucleolar Arf sequesters Mdm2 and activates p53. Nat Cell Biol 1:20–26, 1999.

34. Zhang Y, Xiong Y: Mutations in human ARF exon 2 disrupt its nucleolar localization and impair its ability to block nuclear export of MDM2 and p53. Mol Cell 3:579–591, 1999.

35. Zindy F, Eischen CM, Randle DH, et al: Myc signaling via the ARF tumor suppressor regulates p53-dependent apoptosis and immortalization. Genes Dev 12:2424–2433, 1998.

36. Palmero I, Pantoja C, Serrano M: p19ARF links the tumour suppressor p53 to Ras. Nature 395:125–126, 1998.

37. Bates S, Phillips AC, Clark PA, et al: p14ARF links the tumour suppressors RB and p53. Nature 395:124–125, 1998.

38. Sanchez-Cespedes M, Reed AL, Buta M, et al: Inactivation of the INK4A/ARF locus frequently coexists with TP53 mutations in non-small cell lung cancer. Oncogene 18:5843–5849, 1999.

39. Muller H, Bracken AP, Vernell R, et al: E2Fs regulate the expression of genes involved in differentiation, development, proliferation, and apoptosis. Genes Dev 15:267–285, 2001.

40. Ishida S, Huang E, Zuzan H, et al: Role for E2F in control of both DNA replication and mitotic functions as revealed from DNA microarray analysis. Mol Cell Biol 21:4684–4699, 2001.

41. Ren B, Cam H, Takahashi Y, et al: E2F integrates cell cycle progression with DNA repair, replication, and G_2/M checkpoints. Genes Dev 16:245–256, 2002.

42. Harbour JW, Lai SL, Whang-Peng J, et al: Abnormalities in structure and expression of the human retinoblastoma gene in SCLC. Science 241:353–357, 1988.

43. Yokota J, Akiyama T, Fung YK, et al: Altered expression of the retinoblastoma (RB) gene in small-cell carcinoma of the lung. Oncogene 3:471–475, 1988.

44. Hensel CH, Hsieh CL, Gazdar AF, et al: Altered structure and expression of the human retinoblastoma susceptibility gene in small cell lung cancer. Cancer Res 50:3067–3072, 1990.

45. Eymin B, Gazzeri S, Brambilla C, Brambilla E: Distinct pattern of E2F1 expression in human lung tumours: E2F1 is upregulated in small cell lung carcinoma. Oncogene 20:1678–1687, 2001.

46. Xu HJ, Hu SX, Cagle PT, et al: Absence of retinoblastoma protein expression in primary non-small cell lung carcinomas. Cancer Res 51:2735–2739, 1991.

47. Reissmann PT, Koga H, Takahashi R, et al: Inactivation of the retinoblastoma susceptibility gene in non-small-cell lung cancer. The Lung Cancer Study Group. Oncogene 8:1913–1919, 1993.

48. Shimizu E, Coxon A, Otterson GA, et al: RB protein status and clinical correlation from 171 cell lines representing lung cancer, extrapulmonary small cell carcinoma, and mesothelioma. Oncogene 9:2441–2448, 1994.

49. Xu HJ, Cagle PT, Hu SX, et al: Altered retinoblastoma and p53 protein status in non-small cell carcinoma of the lung: Potential synergistic effects on prognosis. Clin Cancer Res 2:1169–1176, 1996.

50. Cagle PT, el-Naggar AK, Xu HJ, et al: Differential retinoblastoma protein expression in neuroendocrine tumors of the lung: Potential diagnostic implications. Am J Pathol 150:393–400, 1997.

51. Nikitin AY, Juarez-Perez MI, Li S, et al: RB-mediated suppression of spontaneous multiple neuroendocrine neoplasia and lung metastases in Rb +/− mice. Proc Natl Acad Sci U S A 96:3916–3921, 1999.

52. Morgenbesser SD, Williams BO, Jacks T, DePinho R: A p53-dependent apoptosis produced by Rb-deficiency in the developing mouse lens. Nature 371:72–74, 1994.

53. Vogelstein B, Lane D, Levine AJ: Surfing the p53 network. Nature 408:307–310, 2000.

54. Otterson GA, Kratzke RA, Coxon A, et al: Absence of p16INK4 protein is restricted to the subset of lung cancer lines that retains wildtype RB. Oncogene 9:3375–3378, 1994.

55. Merlo A, Herman JG, Mao L, et al: 5′ CpG island methylation is associated with transcriptional silencing of the tumour suppressor p16/CDKN2/MTS1 in human cancers. Nat Med 1:686–692, 1995.

56. Yatabe Y, Masuda A, Koshikawa T, et al: p27KIP1 in human lung cancers: Differential changes in small cell and non-small cell carcinomas. Cancer Res 58:1042–1047, 1998.

57. Loda M, Cukor B, Tam SW, et al: Increased proteasome-dependent degradation of the cyclin-dependent kinase inhibitor p27 in aggressive colorectal carcinomas. Nat Med 3:231–234, 1997.

58. Masuda A, Osada H, Yatabe Y, et al: Protective function of p27(KIP1) against apoptosis in small cell lung cancer cells in unfavorable microenvironments. Am J Pathol 158:87–96, 2001.

59. Hibi K, Takahashi T, Yamakawa K, et al: Three distinct regions involved in 3p deletion in human lung cancer. Oncogene 7:445–449, 1992.

60. Latif F, Tory K, Modi WS, et al: Molecular characterization of a large homozygous deletion in the small cell lung cancer cell line U2020: A strategy for cloning the putative tumor suppressor gene. Genes Chromosomes Cancer 5:119–127, 1992.

61. Wistuba II, Behrens C, Virmani AK, et al: High resolution chromosome 3p allelotyping of human lung cancer and preneoplastic/preinvasive bronchial epithelium reveals multiple, discontinuous sites of 3p allele loss and three regions of frequent breakpoints. Cancer Res 60:1949–1960, 2000.

62. Wistuba II, Lam S, Behrens C, et al: Molecular damage in the bronchial epithelium of current and former smokers. J Natl Cancer Inst 89:1366–1373, 1997.

63. Mao L, Lee JS, Kurie JM, et al: Clonal genetic alterations in the lungs of current and former smokers. J Natl Cancer Inst 89:857–862, 1997.

64. Sozzi G, Veronese ML, Negrini M, et al: The FHIT gene 3p14.2 is abnormal in lung cancer. Cell 85:17–26, 1996.

65. Croce CM, Sozzi G, Huebner K: Role of FHIT in human cancer. J Clin Oncol 17:1618–1624, 1999.

66. Siprashvili Z, Sozzi G, Barnes LD, et al: Replacement of Fhit in cancer cells suppresses tumorigenicity. Proc Natl Acad Sci U S A 94:13771–13776, 1997.

67. Sard L, Accornero P, Tornielli S, et al: The tumor-suppressor gene FHIT is involved in the regulation of apoptosis and in cell cycle control. Proc Natl Acad Sci U S A 96:8489–8492, 1999.

68. Zanesi N, Fidanza V, Fong LY, et al: The tumor spectrum in FHIT-deficient mice. Proc Natl Acad Sci U S A 98:10250–10255, 2001.

69. Zochbauer-Muller S, Fong KM, Maitra A, et al: 5′ CpG island methylation of the FHIT gene is correlated with loss of gene expression in lung and breast cancer. Cancer Res 61:3581–3585, 2001.

70. Geradts J, Fong KM, Zimmerman PV, Minna JD: Loss of Fhit expression in non-small-cell lung cancer: Correlation with molecular genetic abnormalities and clinicopathological features. Br J Cancer 82:1191–1197, 2000.

71. Sozzi G, Sard L, De Gregorio L, et al: Association between cigarette smoking and FHIT gene alterations in lung cancer. Cancer Res 57:2121–2123, 1997.

72. Tomizawa Y, Nakajima T, Kohno T, et al: Clinicopathological significance of Fhit protein expression in stage I non-small cell lung carcinoma. Cancer Res 58:5478–5483, 1998.

73. Tseng JE, Kemp BL, Khuri FR, et al: Loss of Fhit is frequent in stage I non-small cell lung cancer and in the lungs of chronic smokers. Cancer Res 59:4798–4803, 1999.

74. Sundaresan V, Chung G, Heppell-Parton A, et al: Homozygous deletions at 3p21 in breast and lung cancer. Oncogene 17:1723–1729, 1998.

75. Xian J, Clark KJ, Fordham R, et al: Inadequate lung development and bronchial hyperplasia in mice with a targeted deletion in the Dutt1/Robo1 gene. Proc Natl Acad Sci U S A 98:15062–15066, 2001.

76. Ishikawa S, Kai M, Tamari M, et al: Sequence analysis of a 685-kb genomic region on chromosome 3p22–p21.3 that is homozygously deleted in a lung carcinoma cell line. DNA Res 4:35–43, 1997.

77. Lerman MI, Minna JD: The 630-kb lung cancer homozygous deletion region on human chromosome 3p21.3: Identification and evaluation of the resident candidate tumor suppressor genes. The International Lung Cancer Chromosome 3p21.3 Tumor Suppressor Gene Consortium. Cancer Res 60:6116–6133, 2000.

78. Dammann R, Li C, Yoon JH, et al: Epigenetic inactivation of a RAS association domain family protein from the lung tumour suppressor locus 3p21.3. Nat Genet 25:315–319, 2000.

79. Burbee DG, Forgacs E, Zochbauer-Muller S, et al: Epigenetic inactivation of RASSF1A in lung and breast cancers and malignant phenotype suppression. J Natl Cancer Inst 93:691–699, 2001.

80. Agathanggelou A, Honorio S, Macartney DP, et al: Methylation associated inactivation of RASSF1A from region 3p21.3 in lung, breast and ovarian tumours. Oncogene 20:1509–1518, 2001.

81. Dong SM, Sun DI, Benoit NE, et al: Epigenetic inactivation of RASSF1A in head and neck cancer. Clin Cancer Res 9(10 Pt 1):3635–3640, 2003.

82. Tomizawa Y, Sekido Y, Kondo M, et al: Inhibition of lung cancer cell growth and induction of apoptosis after reexpression of 3p21.3 candidate tumor suppressor gene SEMA3B. Proc Natl Acad Sci U S A 98:13954–13959, 2001.

83. Massague J, Blain SW, Lo RS: TGFβ signaling in growth control, cancer, and heritable disorders. Cell 103:295–309, 2000.

84. Miyazono K, ten Dijke P, Heldin CH: TGF-β signaling by Smad proteins. Adv Immunol 75:115–157, 2000.

85. Seoane J, Pouponnot C, Staller P, et al: TGFβ influences Myc, Miz-1 and Smad to control the CDK inhibitor p15INK4b. Nat Cell Biol 3:400–408, 2001.

86. Bhattacharjee A, Richards WG, Staunton J, et al: Classification of human lung carcinomas by mRNA expression profiling reveals distinct adenocarcinoma subclasses. Proc Natl Acad Sci U S A 98:13790–13795, 2001.

87. Osada H, Tatematsu Y, Masuda A, et al: Heterogeneous transforming growth factor (TGF)-β unresponsiveness and loss of TGF-β receptor type II expression caused by histone deacetylation in lung cancer cell lines. Cancer Res 61:8331–8339, 2001.

88. Tani M, Takenoshita S, Kohno T, et al: Infrequent mutations of the transforming growth factor β-type II receptor gene at chromosome 3p22 in human lung cancers with chromosome 3p deletions. Carcinogenesis 18:1119–1121, 1997.

89. Nagatake M, Takagi Y, Osada H, et al: Somatic in vivo alterations of the DPC4 gene at 18q21 in human lung cancers. Cancer Res 56:2718–2720, 1996.

90. Uchida K, Nagatake M, Osada H, et al: Somatic in vivo alterations of the JV18-1 gene at 18q21 in human lung cancers. Cancer Res 56:5583–5585, 1996.

91. Konishi H, Nakagawa T, Harano T, et al: Identification of frequent G_2 checkpoint impairment and a homozygous deletion of 14-3-3σ at 17p13.3 in small cell lung cancers. Cancer Res 62:271–276, 2002.

92. Haruki N, Saito H, Tatematsu Y, et al: Histological type-selective, tumor-predominant expression of a novel CHK1 isoform and infrequent in vivo somatic CHK2 mutation in small cell lung cancer. Cancer Res 60:4689–4692, 2000.

93. Osada H, Tatematsu Y, Yatabe Y, et al: Frequent and histological type-specific inactivation of 14-3-3σ in human lung cancers. Oncogene 21:2418–2424, 2002.

94. Haruki N, Harano T, Masuda A, et al: Persistent increase in chromosome instability in lung cancer: Possible indirect involvement of p53 inactivation. Am J Pathol 159:1345–1352, 2001.

95. Takahashi T, Haruki N, Nomoto S, et al: Identification of frequent impairment of the mitotic checkpoint and molecular analysis of the mitotic checkpoint genes, hsMAD2 and p55CDC, in human lung cancers. Oncogene 18:4295–4300, 1999.

96. Nomoto S, Haruki N, Takahashi T, et al: Search for in vivo somatic mutations in the mitotic checkpoint gene, hMAD1, in human lung cancers. Oncogene 18:7180–7183, 1999.

97. Sato M, Sekido Y, Horio Y, et al: Infrequent mutation of the hBUB1 and hBUBR1 genes in human lung cancer. Jpn J Cancer Res 91:504–509, 2000.

98. Cahill DP, Lengauer C, Yu J, et al: Mutations of mitotic checkpoint genes in human cancers. Nature 392:300–303, 1998.

99. Mizuno K, Osada H, Konishi H, et al: Aberrant hypermethylation of the CHFR prophase checkpoint gene in human lung cancers. Oncogene 21:2328–2333, 2002.

100. Sanchez-Cespedes M, Parrella P, Esteller M, et al: Inactivation of LKB1/STK11 is a common event in adenocarcinomas of the lung. Cancer Res 62:3659–3662, 2002.

101. Ghaffar H, Shin F, Sanchez-Cepedes M, et al: LKB1 protein expression in the evolution of glandular neoplasia of the lung. Clin Cancer Res 9:2998–3003, 2003.

102. Forgacs E, Biesterveld EJ, Sekido Y, et al: Mutation analysis of the PTEN/MMAC1 gene in lung cancer. Oncogene 17:1557–1565, 1998.

103. Yokomizo A, Tindall DJ, Drabkin H, et al: PTEN/MMAC1 mutations identified in small cell, but not in non-small cell lung cancers. Oncogene 17:475–479, 1998.

104. Kohno T, Takahashi M, Manda R, Yokota J: Inactivation of the PTEN/MMAC1/TEP1 gene in human lung cancers. Genes Chromosomes Cancer 22:152–156, 1998.

105. Okami K, Wu L, Riggins G, et al: Analysis of PTEN/MMAC1 alterations in aerodigestive tract tumors. Cancer Res 58:509–511, 1998.

106. Wang SS, Virmani A, Gazdar AF, et al: Refined mapping of two regions of loss of heterozygosity on chromosome band 11q23 in lung cancer. Genes Chromosomes Cancer 25:154–159, 1999.

107. Murakami Y, Nobukuni T, Tamura K, et al: Localization of tumor suppressor activity important in nonsmall cell lung carcinoma on chromosome 11q. Proc Natl Acad Sci U S A 95:8153–8158, 1998.

108. Kuramochi M, Fukuhara H, Nobukuni T, et al: TSLC1 is a tumor-suppressor gene in human non-small-cell lung cancer. Nat Genet 27:427–430, 2001.

109. Wang SS, Esplin ED, Li JL, et al: Alterations of the PPP2R1B gene in human lung and colon cancer. Science 282:284–287, 1998.

110. Kohno T, Takakura S, Yamada T, et al: Alterations of the PPP1R3 gene in human cancer. Cancer Res 59:4170–4174, 1999.

111. Moodie SA, Willumsen BM, Weber MJ, Wolfman A: Complexes of Ras.GTP with Raf-1 and mitogen-activated protein kinase kinase. Science 260:1658–1661, 1993.

112. Schulze A, Lehmann K, Jefferies HB, et al: Analysis of the transcriptional program induced by Raf in epithelial cells. Genes Dev 15:981–994, 2001.

113. Slebos RJ, Kibbelaar RE, Dalesio O, et al: K-ras oncogene activation as a prognostic marker in adenocarcinoma of the lung. N Engl J Med 323:561–565, 1990.

114. Mills NE, Fishman CL, Scholes J, et al: Detection of K-ras oncogene mutations in bronchoalveolar lavage fluid for lung cancer diagnosis. J Natl Cancer Inst 87:1056–1060, 1995.

115. Westra WH, Baas IO, Hruban RH, et al: J. K-ras oncogene activation in atypical alveolar hyperplasias of the human lung. Cancer Res 56:2224–2228, 1996.

116. Cooper CA, Carby FA, Bubb VJ, et al: The pattern of K-ras mutation in pulmonary adenocarcinoma defines a new pathway of tumour development in the human lung. J Pathol 181:401–404, 1997.

117. Sugio K, Kishimoto Y, Virmani AK, et al: K-ras mutations are a relatively late event in the pathogenesis of lung carcinomas. Cancer Res 54:5811–5815, 1994.

118. Urban T, Ricci S, Danel C, et al: Detection of codon 12 K-ras mutations in non-neoplastic mucosa from bronchial carina in patients with lung adenocarcinomas. Br J Cancer 82:412–417, 2000.

119. Rodenhuis S, Slebos RJ: The ras oncogenes in human lung cancer. Am Rev Respir Dis 142:S27–S30, 1990.

120. Kobayashi T, Tsuda H, Noguchi M, et al: Association of point mutation in c-Ki-ras oncogene in lung adenocarcinoma with particular reference to cytologic subtypes. Cancer 66:289–294, 1990.

121. Davies H, Bignell GR, Cox C, et al: Mutations of the BRAF gene in human cancer. Nature 417:949–954, 2002.

122. Brose MS, Volpe P, Feldman M, et al: BRAF and RAS mutations in human lung cancer and melanoma. Cancer Res 62:6997–7000, 2002.

123. Naoki K, Chen TH, Richards WG, et al: Missense mutations of the BRAF gene in human lung adenocarcinoma. Cancer Res 62:7001–7003, 2002.

124. Cohen Y, Xing M, Mambo E, et al: BRAF mutation in papillary thyroid carcinoma. J Natl Cancer Inst 95:625–627, 2003.

125. Staller P, Peukert K, Kiermaier A, et al: Repression of p15INK4b expression by Myc through association with Miz-1. Nat Cell Biol 3:392–399, 2001.

126. Spruck C, Strohmaier H, Watson M, et al: A CDK-independent function of mammalian Cks1: Targeting of SCF^{Skp2} to the CDK inhibitor p27Kip1. Mol Cell 7:639–650, 2001.

127. Ganoth D, Bornstein G, Ko TK, et al: The cell-cycle regulatory protein Cks1 is required for SCF^{Skp2}-mediated ubiquitinylation of p27. Nat Cell Biol 3:321–324, 2001.

128. Perez-Roger I, Kim SH, Griffiths B, et al: Cyclins D1 and D2 mediate myc-induced proliferation via sequestration of p27^{Kip1} and p21^{Cip1}. EMBO J 18:5310–5320, 1999.

129. Coller HA, Grandori C, Tamayo P, et al: Expression analysis with oligonucleotide microarrays reveals that MYC regulates genes involved in growth, cell cycle, signaling, and adhesion. Proc Natl Acad Sci U S A 97:3260–3265, 2000.

130. Guo QM, Malek RL, Kim S, et al: Identification of c-myc responsive genes using rat cDNA microarray. Cancer Res 60:5922–5928, 2000.

131. Little CD, Nau MM, Carney DN, et al: Amplification and expression of the c-myc oncogene in human lung cancer cell lines. Nature 306:194–196, 1983.

132. Takahashi T, Obata Y, Sekido Y, et al: Expression and amplification of myc gene family in small cell lung cancer and its relation to biological characteristics. Cancer Res 49:2683–2688, 1989.

133. Johnson B: The role of MYC, JUN, and FOS oncogenes in human lung cancer. In Pass H, Mitchell J, Johnson D, Turrisi A (eds): Lung Cancer: Principles and Practice. Philadelphia: Lippincott–Raven, 1996, pp 83–98.

134. Vonlanthen S, Heighway J, Altermatt HJ, et al: The bmi-1 oncoprotein is differentially expressed in non-small cell lung cancer and correlates with INK4A-ARF locus expression. Br J Cancer 84:1372–1376, 2001.

135. Cline MJ, Battifora H: Abnormalities of protooncogenes in non-small cell lung cancer: Correlations with tumor type and clinical characteristics. Cancer 60:2669–2674, 1987.

136. Gazzeri S, Brambilla E, Chauvin C, et al: Analysis of the activation of the myc family oncogene and of its stability over time in xenografted human lung carcinomas. Cancer Res 50:1566–1570, 1990.

137. Gazzeri S, Brambilla E, Caron de Fromentel C, et al: p53 genetic abnormalities and myc activation in human lung carcinoma. Int J Cancer 58:24–32, 1994.

138. Krystal G, Birrer M, Way J, et al: Multiple mechanisms for transcriptional regulation of the myc gene family in small-cell lung cancer. Mol Cell Biol 8:3373–3381, 1988.

139. Krystal GW, Armstrong BC, Battey JF: N-myc mRNA forms an RNA-RNA duplex with endogenous antisense transcripts. Mol Cell Biol 10:4180–4191, 1990.

140. Slichenmyer WJ, Fry DW: Anticancer therapy targeting the erbB family of receptor tyrosine kinases. Semin Oncol 28:67–79, 2001.

141. Schlessinger J: Cell signaling by receptor tyrosine kinases. Cell 103:211–225, 2000.

142. Rusch V, Baselga J, Cordon-Cardo C, et al: Differential expression of the epidermal growth factor receptor and its ligands in primary non-small cell lung cancers and adjacent benign lung. Cancer Res 53:2379–2385, 1993.

143. Rachwal WJ, Bongiorno PF, Orringer MB, et al: Expression and activation of erbB-2 and epidermal growth factor receptor in lung adenocarcinomas. Br J Cancer 72:56–64, 1995.

144. Garcia de Palazzo IE, Adams GP, Sundareshan P, et al: Expression of mutated epidermal growth factor receptor by non-small cell lung carcinomas. Cancer Res 53:3217–3220, 1993.

145. Paez JG, Janne PA, Lee JC, et al: EGFR mutations in lung cancer: Correlation with clinical response to gefitinib therapy. Science 304:1497–1500, 2004.

146. Lynch TJ, Bell DW, Sordella R, et al: Activating mutations in the epidermal growth factor receptor underlying responsiveness of non-small-cell lung cancer to gefitinib. N Engl J Med 350:2129–2139, 2004.

147. Schneider PM, Hung MC, Chiocca SM, et al: Differential expression of the c-erbB-2 gene in human small cell and non-small cell lung cancer. Cancer Res 49:4968–4971, 1989.

148. Shiraishi M, Noguchi M, Shimosato Y, Sekiya T: Amplification of protooncogenes in surgical specimens of human lung carcinomas. Cancer Res 49:6474–6479, 1989.

149. Kern JA, Schwartz DA, Nordberg JE, et al: p185neu expression in human lung adenocarcinomas predicts shortened survival. Cancer Res 50:5184–5187, 1990.

150. Weiner DB, Nordberg J, Robinson R, et al: Expression of the neu gene-encoded protein (P185neu) in human non-

151. Yi ES, Harclerode D, Gondo M, et al: High c-erbB-3 protein expression is associated with shorter survival in advanced non-small cell lung carcinomas. Mod Pathol 10:142–148, 1997.

152. Yoneda K, Boucher LD: Bronchial epithelial changes associated with small cell carcinoma of the lung. Hum Pathol 24:1180–1183, 1993.

153. Fontanini G, De Laurentiis M, Vignati S, et al: Evaluation of epidermal growth factor-related growth factors and receptors and of neoangiogenesis in completely resected stage I-IIIA non-small-cell lung cancer: Amphiregulin and microvessel count are independent prognostic indicators of survival. Clin Cancer Res 4:241–249, 1998.

154. al Moustafa AE, Alaoui-Jamali M, Paterson J, O'Connor-McCourt M: Expression of P185erbB-2, P160erbB-3, P180erbB-4, and heregulin alpha in human normal bronchial epithelial and lung cancer cell lines. Anticancer Res 19:481–486, 1999.

155. Brognard J, Clark AS, Ni Y, Dennis PA: Akt/protein kinase B is constitutively active in non-small cell lung cancer cells and promotes cellular survival and resistance to chemotherapy and radiation. Cancer Res 61:3986–3997, 2001.

156. Jones N, Iljin K, Dumont DJ, Alitalo K: Tie receptors: New modulators of angiogenic and lymphangiogenic responses. Nat Rev Mol Cell Biol 2:257–267, 2001.

157. O'Byrne KJ, Koukourakis MI, Giatromanolaki A, et al: Vascular endothelial growth factor, platelet-derived endothelial cell growth factor and angiogenesis in non-small-cell lung cancer. Br J Cancer 82:1427–1432, 2000.

158. Yuan A, Yu CJ, Chen WJ, et al: Correlation of total VEGF mRNA and protein expression with histologic type, tumor angiogenesis, patient survival and timing of relapse in non-small-cell lung cancer. Int J Cancer 89:475–483, 2000.

159. Giatromanolaki A, Koukourakis MI, Sivridis E, et al: Relation of hypoxia inducible factor 1 alpha and 2 alpha in operable non-small cell lung cancer to angiogenic/molecular profile of tumours and survival. Br J Cancer 85:881–890, 2001.

160. Hida T, Yatabe Y, Achiwa H, et al: Increased expression of cyclooxygenase 2 frequently occurs in human lung cancers, specifically in adenocarcinomas. Cancer Res 58:3761–3764, 1998.

161. Marrogi AJ, Travis WD, Welsh JA, et al: Nitric oxide synthase, cyclooxygenase 2, and vascular endothelial growth factor in the angiogenesis of non-small cell lung carcinoma. Clin Cancer Res 6:4739–4744, 2000.

162. Fontanini G, Boldrini L, Chine S, et al: Expression of vascular endothelial growth factor mRNA in non-small-cell lung carcinomas. Br J Cancer 79:363–369, 1999.

163. Decaussin M, Sartelet H, Robert C, et al: Expression of vascular endothelial growth factor (VEGF) and its two receptors (VEGF-R1-Flt1 and VEGF-R2-Flk1/KDR) in non-small cell lung carcinomas (NSCLCs): Correlation with angiogenesis and survival. J Pathol 188:369–377, 1999.

164. Kajita T, Ohta Y, Kimura K, et al: The expression of vascular endothelial growth factor C and its receptors in non-small cell lung cancer. Br J Cancer 85:255–260, 2001.

165. He Y, Kozaki K, Karpanen T, et al: Suppression of tumor lymphangiogenesis and lymph node metastasis by blocking vascular endothelial growth factor receptor 3 signaling. J Natl Cancer Inst 94:785–787, 2002.

166. Takahama M, Tsutsumi M, Tsujiuchi T, et al: Enhanced expression of Tie2, its ligand angiopoietin-1, vascular

endothelial growth factor, and CD31 in human non-small cell lung carcinomas. Clin Cancer Res 5:2506–2510, 1999.

167. Hatanaka H, Abe Y, Naruke M, et al: Significant correlation between interleukin 10 expression and vascularization through angiopoietin/TIE2 networks in non-small cell lung cancer. Clin Cancer Res 7:1287–1292, 2001.

168. Kiyono T, Foster SA, Koop JI, et al: Both Rb/p16INK4a inactivation and telomerase activity are required to immortalize human epithelial cells. Nature 396:84–88, 1998.

169. Artandi SE, DePinho RA: Mice without telomerase: What can they teach us about human cancer? Nat Med 6:852–855, 2000.

170. Hiyama K, Hiyama E, Ishioka S, et al: Telomerase activity in small-cell and non-small-cell lung cancers. J Natl Cancer Inst 87:895–902, 1995.

171. Albanell J, Lonardo F, Rusch V, et al: High telomerase activity in primary lung cancers: Association with increased cell proliferation rates and advanced pathologic stage. J Natl Cancer Inst 89:1609–1615, 1997.

172. Wang J, Xie LY, Allan S, et al: Myc activates telomerase. Genes Dev 12:1769–1774, 1998.

173. Wu KJ, Grandori C, Amacker M, et al: Direct activation of TERT transcription by c-MYC. Nat Genet 21:220–224, 1999.

174. Ohmura H, Tahara H, Suzuki M, et al: Restoration of the cellular senescence program and repression of telomerase by human chromosome 3. Jpn J Cancer Res 86:899–904, 1995.

175. Cuthbert AP, Bond J, Trott DA, et al: Telomerase repressor sequences on chromosome 3 and induction of permanent growth arrest in human breast cancer cells. J Natl Cancer Inst 91:37–45, 1999.

176. Tomida S, Koshikawa K, Yatabe Y, et al: Gene expression-based, individualized outcome prediction of surgically treated lung cancer patients. Oncogene 23:5360–5370, 2004.

177. Yanagisawa K, Shyr Y, Xu BJ, et al: Proteomic patterns of tumour subsets in non-small-cell lung cancer. Lancet 362:433–439, 2003.

178. Garber ME, Troyanskaya OG, Schluens K, et al: Diversity of gene expression in adenocarcinoma of the lung. Proc Natl Acad Sci U S A 98:13784–13789, 2001.

179. Ramaswamy S, Ross KN, Lander ES, Golub TR: A molecular signature of metastasis in primary solid tumors. Nat Genet 33:49–54, 2003.

180. Beer DG, Kardia SL, Huang CC, et al: Gene-expression profiles predict survival of patients with lung adenocarcinoma. Nat Med 8:816–824, 2002.

181. Sidransky D: Molecular markers in cancer diagnosis. J Natl Cancer Inst 17:27–29, 1995.

182. Sidransky D: Nucleic acid-based methods for the detection of cancer. Science 278:1054–1059, 1997.

183. Ahrendt SA, Sidransky D: The potential of molecular screening. Surg Oncol Clin N Am 8:641–656, 1999.

184. Naruke T, Goya T, Tsuchiya R, Suemasu K: Prognosis and survival in resected lung carcinoma based on the new international staging system. J Thorac Cardiovasc Surg 96:440–447, 1988 [published erratum appears in J Thorac Cardiovasc Surg 97:350, 1989].

185. Mills NE, Fishman CL, Scholes J, et al: Detection of K-ras oncogene mutations in bronchoalveolar lavage fluid for lung cancer diagnosis. J Natl Cancer Inst 87:1056–1060, 1995.

186. Yakubovskaya MS, Spiegelman V, Luo FC, et al: High frequency of K-ras mutations in normal appearing lung tissues and sputum of patients with lung cancer. Int J Cancer 63:810–814, 1995.

187. Ahrendt SA, Chow JT, Xu LH, et al: Molecular detection of tumor cells in bronchoalveolar lavage fluid from patients with early stage lung cancer. J Natl Cancer Inst 91:332–339, 1999.

188. Mao L, Hruban RH, Boyle JO, et al: Detection of oncogene mutations in sputum precedes diagnosis of lung cancer. Cancer Res 54:1634–1637, 1994.

189. Mao L, Lee DJ, Tockman MS, et al: Microsatellite alterations as clonal markers in the detection of human cancer. Proc Natl Acad Sci U S A 91:9871–9875, 1994.

190. Palmisano WA, Divine KK, Saccomanno G, et al: Predicting lung cancer by detecting aberrant promoter methylation in sputum. Cancer Res 60:5954–5958, 2000.

191. Topaloglu O, Hoque MO, Tokumaru Y, et al: Detection of promoter hypermethylation of multiple genes in the tumor and bronchoalveolar lavage of patients with lung cancer. Clin Cancer Res 10:2284–2288, 2004.

192. Fliss MS, Usadel H, Caballero OL, et al: Facile detection of homoplasmic mitochondrial DNA mutations in primary tumors and bodily fluids. Science 287:2017–2019, 2000.

193. Sanchez-Cespedes M, Parrella P, Nomoto S, et al: Identification of a mononucleotide repeat as a major target for mitochondrial DNA alterations in human tumors. Cancer Res 61:7015–7019, 2001.

194. Ahrendt SA, Halachmi S, Chow JT, et al: Rapid p53 sequence analysis in primary lung cancer using an oligonucleotide probe array. Proc Natl Acad Sci U S A 96:7382–7387, 1999.

195. Chen XQ, Stroun M, Magnenat JL, et al: Microsatellite alterations in plasma DNA of small cell lung cancer patients. Nat Med 2:1033–1035, 1996.

196. Esteller M, Sanchez-Cespedes M, Rosell R, et al: Detection of aberrant promoter hypermethylation of tumor suppressor genes in serum DNA from non-small cell lung cancer patients. Cancer Res 59:67–70, 1999.

197. Usadel H, Brabender J, Danenberg KD, et al: Quantitative adenomatous polyposis coli promoter methylation analysis in tumor tissue, serum, and plasma DNA of patients with lung cancer. Cancer Res 62:371–375, 2002.

198. Sidransky D, Irizarry R, Califano JA, et al: Serum protein MALDI profiling to distinguish upper aerodigestive tract cancer patients from control subjects. J Natl Cancer Inst 95:1711–1717, 2003.

43 Epidemiology of Lung Cancer

Anthony J. Alberg, Ph.D., M.P.H., Rex C. Yung, M.D., Jonathan M. Samet, M.D.

INTRODUCTION

Epidemiology comprises the scientific methods that are used to track the occurrence of disease, to identify its causes, and to assess the impact of interventions on incidence and natural history. Epidemiologic evidence is the foundation for primary and secondary disease prevention. The role of epidemiologic research in disease prevention is fully demonstrated by investigations of lung cancer over the last century.

Remarkably, at the start of the 20th century, lung cancer was considered a rare disease. However, its epidemic rise across the first decades of that century was soon identified as clinicians began to provide care for increasing numbers of patients with lung cancer and routine vital statistics documented rising mortality. Case-control and cohort studies, the epidemiologic study designs used to evaluate exposure-disease associations, causally linked smoking to lung cancer in investigations reported from the 1950s forward.[1] As we have continued to follow lung cancer incidence and mortality rates, we have readily shown that their rise and decline parallel past trends of cigarette smoking.[2] The epidemiologic evidence and the complementary biologic understanding of respiratory carcinogenesis have unassailably established the conclusion that smoking causes lung cancer. Epidemiologic findings are also relevant to patient care, as skilled clinicians weigh alternative diagnoses depending on risk factor profiles of patients.

This chapter provides a summary of the epidemiologic evidence on lung cancer. This literature is now extraordinarily large, and a comprehensive summary and synthesis of all of the evidence is not possible. Rather, we rely on summaries of the evidence prepared by expert committees and offer findings of representative and particularly informative studies. We also address issues of particular interest at present. Syntheses have been periodically carried out by expert review groups, including the committees assembled to prepare the U.S. Surgeon General's reports on smoking and health and other federal documents, and expert committees of other governments and organizations, including the United Kingdom's Royal College of Physicians and Scientific Committee on Tobacco and the World Health Organization's International Agency for Research on Cancer (IARC). The most recent reports include that prepared by IARC in 2002[3] and the 2004 report of the Surgeon General.[4] The Surgeon General's Report is supported by a comprehensive database of epidemiologic studies on lung cancer and other diseases that can be accessed at http://www.cdc.gov/tobacco/search/index.htm. The general topic of the epidemiologic aspects of lung cancer was reviewed in a 1994 monograph.[5]

A rare disease at its start, by the end of the 20th century, lung cancer had become one of the world's leading causes of preventable death.[6] Although tobacco had been widely used throughout the world for centuries, the present pandemic of lung cancer followed the introduction of manufactured cigarettes with addictive properties, which resulted in a new pattern of sustained exposure of the lung to inhaled carcinogens.[7] German scientists in Nazi Germany conducted some of the earliest research using the case-control design on the links between smoking and lung cancer.[8] By the early 1950s, epidemiologic studies in Britain and the United States using the case-control method had shown that cigarettes were strongly associated with the risk of lung cancer[9-11]; this association was corroborated by the pioneering cohort studies of British physicians, U.S. Veterans, and volunteers recruited by the American Cancer Society.[12] By 1964, the evidence was sufficient to support a conclusion by the U.S. Surgeon General that cigarette smoking caused lung cancer.[12] The Royal College of Physicians had reached the same conclusion 2 years previously.[13] Passive smoking, the involuntary inhalation of tobacco smoke by nonsmokers, has also been found to cause lung cancer.[14,15]

Although its predominant cause is now well known—tobacco smoking—there are other causes of lung cancer as well, some acting in concert with smoking to increase risk synergistically. The suspicion that radon was a cause of lung cancer in underground miners, raised early in the century, led to what was probably the first identification of an occupational respiratory carcinogen[16]; radon in indoor environments is now considered a significant cause of lung cancer.[17] The list of human occupational causes of lung cancer also includes arsenic, asbestos, chromates, chloromethyl ethers, nickel, polycyclic aromatic hydrocarbons, radon progeny, and other agents.[18] Outdoor air pollution, which includes combustion-generated carcinogens, is also considered to contribute to the lung cancer burden in urban dwellers. Indoor air contains several respiratory carcinogens, including radon, asbestos, and cigarette smoke. In some developing countries, exposure to fumes from cooking stoves and fires is associated with lung cancer risk. Beginning in the 1980s, associations of diet with lung cancer risk have been vigorously investigated with the anticipation that dietary micronutrients might be found that modify the high lung cancer risk in smokers.

Even though the epidemiology of lung cancer has been extensively investigated for over 50 years, there are still active areas of research, some quite relevant to prevention. Investigation of lung cancer and diet continues, using both observational and experimental approaches, and concern remains over the risk of indoor and outdoor pollutants, including, for example, radon and diesel emissions. There has also been a need for research to track the risks of smoking over time, because the cigarette has evolved in its design characteristics and yields of tar and nicotine, as assessed by standard protocol using a machine, have declined since the 1950s. The histologic characteristics of lung cancer in a number of developed countries, including the United States, have also changed in recent decades, so the frequency of adenocarcinoma has risen and that of squamous cell carcinoma has declined.[2] With change has also arisen an appreciation of the possible precursor roles of early pathologic lesions such as atypical adenomatous hyperplasia (AAH) and bronchioloalveolar carcinoma (BAC). There is also emerging evidence on genetic determinants of lung cancer risk. A current research approach, termed *molecular epidemiology,* melds the population and laboratory tools used to address susceptibility to environmental carcinogens. Although the evidence from the "traditional" epidemiologic approaches conclusively established the carcinogenicity of tobacco smoke, molecular epidemiology should characterize the sequence of molecular and cellular changes as a nonmalignant cell becomes malignant and the factors determining susceptibility to tobacco smoke. Biomarkers of exposure, dose, susceptibility, and genetic damage may allow epidemiologic investigations to uncover specific pathways of human lung carcinogenesis and to identify indicators for those at highest risk or with the earliest stages of disease.

PATTERNS OF OCCURRENCE

TEMPORAL TRENDS

Because of the high case-fatality rate of lung cancer, incidence and mortality rates are nearly equivalent, and

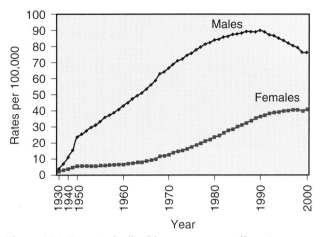

Figure 43.1 Age-standardized lung cancer mortality rates, United States: 1930–2000, age-standardized to 2000 U.S. population. (Data from Wingo PA, Cardinez CJ, Landis SH, et al: Long-term trends in cancer mortality in the United States, 1930–1998. Cancer 97:3133–3275, 2003; and National Cancer Institute and National Center for Health Statistics: Surveillance, Epidemiology, and End Results [SEER] program. U.S. Mortality Data. Bethesda, Md: National Cancer Institute, 2003. Available at http://seer.cancer.gov/mortality)

consequently routinely collected vital statistics provide a long record of the occurrence of lung cancer. We are presently amidst an epidemic of lung cancer that dates to the mid-20th century (Fig. 43.1).[19,20] Lung cancer was rare until the incidence of the disease rose sharply around 1930, culminating by mid-century with lung cancer becoming the leading cause of cancer death among men.[21] The epidemic among women followed that among men, with a sharp rise in rates from the 1960s to the present, propelling lung cancer to become the most frequent cause of female cancer mortality.[21] The epidemic among women not only occurred later, but will not peak as high as among men because smoking prevalence crested at substantially lower levels among women than among men.[2,22,23]

Examination of time trends of age-specific lung cancer mortality rates in the United States further highlights the differing epidemic patterns in men compared to women (Fig. 43.2).[22,24–27] In the older age groups, the rates continue to increase in both sexes, but the rates of increase are decelerating more significantly in men than in women.[22] The rates of lung cancer are now decreasing in the younger age groups, decreases that are more pronounced for men but also now becoming evident in women.[22] As the younger birth cohorts age, their reduced risk of lung cancer should thus translate into substantial reductions in the overall occurrence of lung cancer, reductions that will probably be more favorable for men than women. In an analysis of lung cancer mortality in the United States from 1970 to 1997, Jemal and colleagues[22] found that the rates of decrease in younger men and women, those born after 1950, were moderating, even though the decline continues. These investigators suggested that the moderation could reflect patterns of smoking initiation. In some other countries, lung cancer rates continue to rise in all age groups.

Notable shifts have taken place in the incidence rates of lung cancer by histologic type.[28] After steadily increasing in

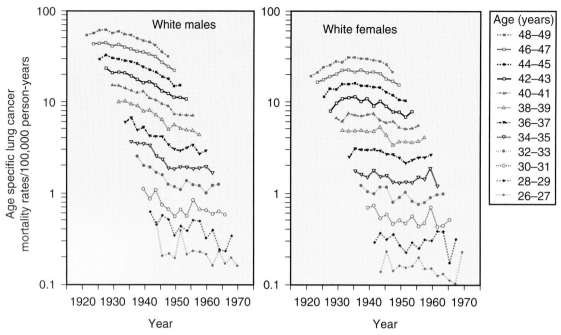

Figure 43.2 United States age-specific lung cancer mortality rates (white men and white women) by 2-year age intervals from 26 to 27 years of age through 48 to 49 years of age, plotted against birth cohort. (From Jemal A, Chu KC, Tarone RE: Recent trends in lung cancer mortality in the United States. J Natl Cancer Inst 93:277–283, 2001.)

incidence during the period 1973–1987, adenocarcinoma supplanted squamous cell carcinoma as the most frequent form of lung cancer (Table 43.1).[28] Adenocarcinoma increased markedly in all race-sex subgroups (see Table 43.1).

RACE AND ETHNICITY

Lung cancer occurrence varies by race and ethnicity. Although lung cancer incidence rates are similar among African American and white women, rates are about 50% higher among African American men than among white men.[25] The marked reduction in cigarette smoking that has occurred among African American youths[29] forecasts a possible reversal of this trend, and, if this trend persists, declines in the incidence of lung cancer among African Americans can be expected.

Lung cancer mortality rates among Hispanics, Native Americans, and Asians/Pacific Islanders are significantly lower than rates among African Americans and non-Hispanic whites.[30] Nevertheless, lung cancer occurs sufficiently often among these groups to pose a considerable public health burden.

GEOGRAPHIC PATTERNS

Lung cancer is the most commonly diagnosed cancer worldwide,[30] but its geographic distribution shows marked regional variation[31]: Age-standardized incidence rates vary over a wide range (Fig. 43.3).[32] Because of differences in cancer registration between countries, caution is needed in interpreting these data. However, this marked variation in rates cannot be explained on the basis of diagnostic practices and data quality alone. Lung cancer tends to be most

common in developed countries, particularly in North America and Europe, and less common in developing countries, particularly in Africa and South America.[33] The low rates of lung cancer in Africa[34] are comparable to U.S. rates in 1930, when rates of lung cancer were under 5 per 100,000 for both sexes.[35] In contrast, African Americans in the United States, an epicenter, now experience lung cancer incidence rates that are among the highest in the world. As the lung cancer epidemic begins to subside in the developed countries, it is on the rise in the developing world.[36]

Within countries, lung cancer incidence among men invariably outpaces that in women, by well over twofold. The international rankings of lung cancer incidence of men and women from the same countries tend to differ only slightly, so that the highest rates of lung cancer occur in the same regions of the world for both sexes.

Substantial geographic variation in lung cancer mortality rates has also been observed within countries. Trends in its regional distribution can provide clues about determinants of lung cancer. In the past, rates tended to be highest in urban areas, which led to conjecture that air pollution might be a cause of the lung cancer epidemic.[37] Subsequently, several hypotheses[38] were prompted by patterns observed in a systematic review of U.S. lung cancer mortality rates for the period 1950–1969,[39] particularly the rates among males. For example, high rates in coastal areas were postulated to reflect employment in shipyards with attendant asbestos exposure. This hypothesis was then tested in a series of population-based case-control studies that showed that employment in the shipbuilding industry was indeed associated with an excess risk of lung cancer.[40] Another shift followed in the distribution of lung cancer within the United States, with lung cancer mortality rates among white males becoming highest in the South and lower in the

Table 43.1 Age-Adjusted Incidence Rate (per 100,000) of Lung Cancer by Histologic Subtype and Time Period, SEER 1973–1977, 1978–1982, 1983–1987, and 1990–2000

Group	Subtype	1973–1977*	1978–1982*	1983–1987*	1990–2000†
Total	Total	39.5	46.8	51.4	66.9
	Squamous cell carcinoma	13.4	15.1	15.3	14.4
	Adenocarcinoma	10.5	14.2	16.7	22.1
	Small cell	5.9	8.2	9.4	9.8
	Large cell	0.0	3.9	4.9	NA
White males					
	Squamous cell carcinoma	24.3	26.8	25.5	22.3
	Adenocarcinoma	14.5	19.0	21.3	26.3
	Small cell	9.5	12.5	13.1	12.2
	Large cell	0.0	5.9	7.2	NA
White females					
	Squamous cell carcinoma	4.0	5.5	6.6	8.2
	Adenocarcinoma	6.9	10.2	12.9	19.1
	Small cell	3.4	5.5	7.1	8.9
	Large cell	0.0	2.2	3.1	NA
African American males					
	Squamous cell carcinoma	43.9	46.3	48.5	39.7
	Adenocarcinoma	18.1	27.4	32.5	36.2
	Small cell	9.5	13.3	14.0	12.7
	Large cell	0.0	8.0	10.8	NA
African American females					
	Squamous cell carcinoma	5.6	6.8	9.5	11.4
	Adenocarcinoma	6.8	10.8	13.3	18.9
	Small cell	3.6	3.9	6.0	7.2
	Large cell	0.0	2.0	3.0	NA

* Adapted from Travis WD, Travis LB, Devesa SS: Lung cancer. Cancer 75(Suppl):191–202, 1995.
† Calculated from Can Ques and SEER*Stat (available at http://seer.cancer.gov).

Northeast.[41] This fluidity in the geographic variation underscores the value of regularly monitoring lung cancer mortality patterns, as changes in the spatial distribution may signal changes in risk factor patterns.

LUNG CANCER OCCURRENCE BY HISTOLOGIC TYPE

OVERVIEW

Linking specific etiologic agents to specific histologic types of lung cancer remains a valuable, but largely elusive, goal. The interesting temporal and geographic trends in the occurrence of histologic types of lung cancer thus merit attention for the clues they may provide.

Lung cancer occurs in multiple histologic types as classified by conventional light microscopy. The four major types include squamous cell carcinoma, adenocarcinoma, large cell carcinoma, and small cell undifferentiated carcinoma; together these four types of lung cancer account for over 90% of lung cancer cases in the United States.[42] These primary bronchogenic carcinomas comprise a family of epithelial tumors that represent a subset of a larger collection of lung and pleural tumors classified most recently by the World Health Organization (WHO) in 1999.[43-45] The latest consensus classification,[46] written by the International Association for the Study of Lung Cancer (IASLC)

pathology panel, was adopted by the WHO in 2001 to provide consistent criteria for research studies.

In practice, the detailed breakdown of tumor types and variants recommended by WHO/IASLC is seldom incorporated into epidemiologic studies of lung cancer. Instead, evaluations of histology distribution tend to focus only on the four most common types noted previously. These four predominant lung cancer cell types may eventually be broken down into more refined categories based on reclassification of adenocarcinoma variants, introductions of new variants of large cell carcinoma and a new class of pleomorphic carcinoma with sarcomatous elements, and an expanded description of classes of preinvasive lung cancer lesions. A more detailed classification system could facilitate advances in understanding the relationship of specific risk factors to the etiology of specific histologic types.

Few such linkages have been made to date. An example of an exposure that increases risk for all of the major histologic types is cigarette smoking.[47-49] The dose-response relationship of increased lung cancer risk according to number of cigarettes smoked varies across the types, being steepest for small cell undifferentiated carcinoma.[47-49] A few occupational exposures, such as chloromethyl ethers and radon, seem to exhibit some specificity for small cell lung cancer.[17,42]

The most common histologic type of lung cancer diagnosed has shifted over time, from squamous cell carcinoma to adenocarcinoma. Changing patterns of diagnosis and

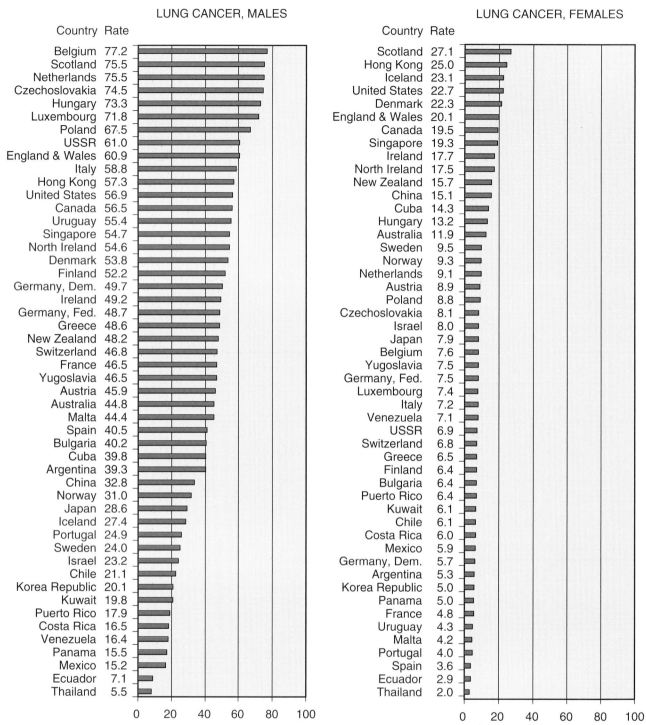

Figure 43.3 United States 1986–1988 age-adjusted death rates per 100,000 population, men and women. (From National Cancer Institute: Cancer Rates and Risks. Bethesda, Md: National Cancer Institute, 2004. Available at http://seer.cancer.gov)

classification of lung cancers could have led to these changes over time, but most observers have set aside an artifactual change.[42,50,51] Beginning in the 1970s, new techniques for the diagnosis of lung cancer became available, including the fiberoptic bronchoscope and thin-needle aspiration[52]; improved stains for mucin, the hallmark of adenocarcinoma, were also introduced. Using data from the Connecticut Tumor Registry, Thun and colleagues[52] showed that the rise in adenocarcinoma antedated these diagnostic innovations.

In the United States, during the initial decades of the smoking-caused epidemic of lung cancer, the most frequent type of lung cancer was squamous cell carcinoma, followed by small cell carcinoma. In the 1970s, a shift toward a predominance of adenocarcinoma was noted.[42,51,53] Adenocarcinoma is now the most common histologic type.[2,28] Since lung cancer incidence and mortality rates began to decline during the 1990s in men, the decline in lung cancer rates has been more rapid for squamous cell and small cell

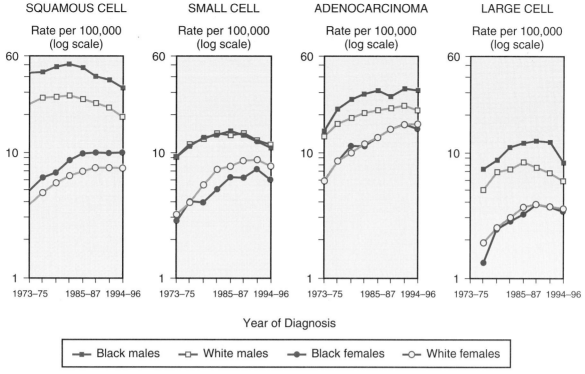

Figure 43.4 Cancer of the lung and bronchus: Surveillance, Epidemiology, and End Results (SEER) incidence rates, by histologic type, sex, race, and ethnicity, all ages, 1973–1996. (From Wingo PA, Ries LA, Giovino GA, et al: Annual report to the nation on the status of cancer, 1973–1996, with a special section on lung cancer and tobacco smoking. J Natl Cancer Inst 91:675–690, 1999.)

carcinomas than for adenocarcinoma, which is just beginning to show a lower incidence rate (Fig. 43.4).[2] In U.S. women, the overall trend of increasing lung cancer incidence rates has been more pronounced for adenocarcinoma than any other cell type.

Similar trends have been noted throughout the globe. Worldwide, adenocarcinoma tends to be the most common cell type seen in female lung cancer patients, accounting for approximately one third of all diagnoses in most regions.[54] In males, squamous cell carcinoma is still the most common cell type in some geographic regions where the lung cancer epidemic has peaked, such as Canada, Australia, and Scandinavia, but trends indicate that the overall percentage of this cell type has fallen over time to 40% or less. In the Netherlands, notable changes in cell type distribution from the period between 1989 and 1998 included a reduction in squamous cell and small cell carcinomas in men, and an increase in adenocarcinoma among women.[55] Similar trends have been noted in Australia,[56,57] Switzerland,[58] Finland,[59,60] and Italy.[61] In Japan[62–64] and Taiwan,[65] adenocarcinoma accounts for approximately one third of lung cancer diagnoses in men and two thirds in women. Some countries, such as Scotland, at first appeared to be exceptions to this pattern because squamous cell carcinoma remains the predominant cell type in both sexes.[66] But even in Scotland a similar shift is underway, as the rate of squamous cell carcinoma is now declining in all birth cohorts, whereas adenocarcinoma rates are increasing and will likely eventually surpass squamous cell rates.[66]

Hypotheses concerning the shift from squamous cell carcinoma to adenocarcinoma have focused on the potential role of changes in the characteristics of cigarettes and consequent changes in the doses and types of carcinogens inhaled.[49,67,68] Puff volume has likely increased over recent decades, with the possibility that patterns of deposition in the lung have changed, tending toward enhanced deposition of tobacco smoke in the peripheral airways and alveoli.[67] Nitrate levels in tobacco smoke have also increased due to the rise in the proportion of air-cured tobacco used in manufacturing the blended U.S. cigarette,[67] which enhances the combustion of tobacco smoke. Although more complete combustion decreases the concentrations of polycyclic aromatic hydrocarbons, the increased production of nitrogen oxides contributes to increased formation of tobacco-specific nitrosamines. An increase in dose of the potent tobacco-specific nitrosamine 4-(methylnitrosamino)-1-(3-pyridyl)-1-butanone (NNK) has been postulated as one factor leading to the increase in adenocarcinoma,[67,69] which is more consistent with changes in smoking behavior and cigarette design than with diagnostic advances.[52] NNK induces lung carcinomas, predominantly adenomas and adenocarcinomas, in mice, regardless of route of administration.[69]

Few studies can provide data to test these hypotheses because of the need for longitudinal observation of lung cancer risk in relation to the characteristics of the cigarettes smoked over time. When the risks for lung cancers of the different histologic types were compared between participants in the American Cancer Society's Cancer Prevention Study (CPS) I and CPS II, the relative risk between cigarette smoking and adenocarcinoma of the lung increased markedly in both men and women during the approximately

20-year period that separated the two studies.[52] These results suggest that the trend of increasing rates of adenocarcinoma is primarily due to changes in cigarette smoking behavior and features of cigarettes.[52]

AAH TO SMALL, FOCAL BAC TO INVASIVE ADENOCARCINOMA: A CARCINOGENIC PATHWAY

Well-developed pathways of progression from precursor lesions to clinical cancer, as seen for some cancers such as cervical and colon cancer, have been lacking for lung cancer. Evidence now suggests that lung cancer may progress in a pathway from AAH, a preinvasive lesion, to small, focal BAC, to invasive adenocarcinoma.

BAC is a subtype of adenocarcinoma. Of the small (<2 cm) peripheral lung nodules detected by rapid, low-dose, multislice-detector computed tomography (CT) scans that are proven to be stage I/II lung carcinomas, the majority have been adenocarcinomas, of which approximately 10% are BACs.[70,71] Despite its low prevalence, BAC is of interest because of its role in this sequence of progression to lung carcinogenesis that includes AAH as a precursor step. AAH is most commonly a precursor to adenocarcinoma[72,73]; it shares common chromosomal aberrations with BAC.[74]

Both AAH and BAC can appear as ground-glass opacity on CT and may be difficult to differentiate. An increased degree of heterogeneity and increased density of the ground-glass opacities on the spiral CT scan generally correlate with a higher grade of dysplasia in the AAH, and with the transition into BAC and eventual invasive adenocarcinoma, as described by the work of Noguchi and colleagues in defining histologic types A through C lesions.[75] The CT opacities that are purely ground glass encompass a pathologic transition from low- to high-grade AAH (Noguchi type A). With progression, these lesions appear to develop partially solid ground-glass opacities that may represent transformation into a BAC, with regions of collapse or fibrotic consolidation (Noguchi types B and C). These may undergo further transformation into mixed adenocarcinomas with BAC features, and eventually progress to more aggressive adenocarcinoma. These nonsolid or partially solid opacifications appear to represent a transitional range of one form of lung carcinogenesis.[75] The overall agreement between CT and pathology for pure ground-glass opacities is excellent, and the predictive value of a pure ground-glass opacity for the presence of AAH is high.[76–78]

In sum, evidence suggests that AAH may be a precursor lesion to BAC, and that small focal BACs in turn may be an intermediate step toward invasive lung adenocarcinomas. If so, this progression may constitute a carcinogenesis pathway for this one form of lung cancer. The elucidation of progression pathways such as this indicates that future assessment of patterns of lung cancer occurrence by histologic type will benefit from more detailed classification systems. Accounting for the stages along the AAH-to-BAC continuum in epidemiologic research may facilitate progress in pinpointing specific risk factors for specific histologic types. For example, advances in understanding this pathway may provide clues to the consistently higher rates of adenocarcinoma in women compared to men, because a striking female predominance is also found along the entire AAH-to-BAC continuum.[78–80]

ETIOLOGY OF LUNG CANCER

OVERVIEW

Although the causes of lung cancer are almost exclusively environmental, there is likely substantial individual variation in susceptibility to respiratory carcinogens. The risk of the disease can be conceptualized as the consequence of the interrelationship between (1) exposure to etiologic (or protective) agents and (2) individual susceptibility to these agents. The "environment" in its broadest sense may influence the risk of disease through direct exposures or indirectly by affecting the likelihood of exposure to exogenous agents. Given lung cancer's multifactorial etiology, synergistic interactions among risk factors may have substantial consequences for lung cancer risk. These interactions have typically been considered on an agent-by-agent basis, as, for example, the synergistic effect of cigarette smoking on the lung cancer risk from asbestos exposure.[81] Our emerging understanding of cancer genetics indicates the additional relevance of gene-environment interactions.

When the environment is considered more holistically, an even broader set of interactions can be proposed. For example, socioeconomic status is associated with a constellation of interacting determinants of lung cancer risk: smoking, diet, and exposures to inhaled agents in the workplace and the general environment. Lower socioeconomic status is associated with an unfavorable profile for all of these factors. Risk factor patterns at the individual and societal levels identify persons and populations at high risk and can be used to target prevention approaches toward those at greatest risk.

Given the many risk factors that have been identified for lung cancer, a practical question is the relative contribution of these factors to the overall burden of lung cancer. The "population-attributable risk" approach takes into account the magnitude of the relative risk associated with an exposure along with the likelihood of exposure in the general population. As reviewed later, population-attributable risk estimates for lung cancer indicate that, in the United States, active smoking is responsible for 90% of lung cancer; occupational exposures to carcinogens account for approximately 9% to 15%; radon causes 10% of lung cancer,[17] and outdoor air pollution perhaps 1% to 2%.[82] The contribution of nutritional factors remains to be determined, but dietary factors have been hypothesized to account for approximately 20% (range, 10% to 30%) of the lung cancer burden.[83] Because these attributable risk estimates include joint contributions of risk factors, e.g., smoking and occupation, the total percentage can exceed 100%.

ENVIRONMENTAL AND OCCUPATIONAL AGENTS

Smoking

Overview. A single etiologic agent—cigarette smoking—is by far the leading cause of lung cancer, accounting for approximately 90% of lung cancer cases in the United States and other countries where cigarette smoking is common.[84] Compared to never smokers, smokers have about a 20-fold increase in lung cancer risk at present, far higher than the risks for diseases associated with other environmental agents. In general, trends of lung cancer occurrence closely reflect patterns of smoking, but rates of occurrence lag smoking rates by about 20 years. Analyses using statistical modeling techniques show a tight association between national mortality rates and smoking.[85] The unequivocal causal association of cigarette smoking with lung cancer is one of the most thoroughly documented causal relationships in biomedical research.[4,7]

The burden of lung cancer attributable to smoking has been extensively documented. Using an attributable risk approach, the Centers for Disease Control and Prevention has documented the numbers of deaths caused in the United States by smoking-related lung cancer; for 1990, that number was 117,000.[86] The average annual number for the years 1995 to 1999 was 124,813.[87] Peto and colleagues[84] have used a different attributable risk method to quantify the burden of smoking-related deaths from lung cancer in the major developed countries. For 1990, the U.S. total was 127,000, the highest in the world, with country-specific estimates ranging down to 150 for Tajikistan. The total for the developed countries was 457,371.[84] Peto and colleagues[84] forecast a staggering future burden for China, which now has one third of the world's smokers[88]; the numbers are predicted to reach several millions by mid-century.

Cigar smoking is also an established cause of lung cancer.[89] The lung cancer risks associated with cigar smoking are substantial, but less than the risks observed for cigarette smoking due to differences in smoking frequency and depth of inhalation. The same pattern holds true for pipe smoking.[90]

Quantitative Risks. The risk of lung cancer among cigarette smokers increases with the duration of smoking and the number of cigarettes smoked per day[91] (Table 43.2). This observation has been made repeatedly in cohort and case-control studies. Risk models have been derived to estimate how lung cancer risk varies with number of cigarettes smoked, duration of smoking, and age. Such models are useful for estimating the future burden of lung cancer under various scenarios of tobacco control. In one widely cited analysis, Doll and Peto[91] proposed a quantitative model for lung cancer risk based on data from the cohort study of British physicians. This model predicted a stronger effect of duration of smoking than of amount smoked per day. Thus, a tripling of the number of cigarettes smoked per day was estimated to triple the risk, whereas a tripling of duration

of smoking was estimated to increase the risk 100-fold.[92] These quantitative dimensions of the dose-response relationship between smoking and lung cancer have implications concerning the now widespread smoking among youth. Those starting at younger ages have a greater likelihood of becoming heavier smokers and remaining smokers.[93] The exponential effect of duration of smoking on lung cancer risk markedly increases the lifetime risk for those who become regular smokers in childhood. Thus, those who initiate smoking earlier in life are most likely to develop lung cancer and most likely to do so at younger ages. Prevention approaches that delay the age of onset of smoking in a population could have substantial impact on the incidence of lung cancer by shortening the duration of smoking. In considering the likelihood of lung cancer in a particular patient, clinicians should give more weight to the duration of smoking and less to actual age.

Smoking Cessation. Cigarette smokers can benefit at any age by quitting smoking. The likelihood of developing lung cancer decreases among those who quit smoking as compared to those who continue to smoke[94,95] (Table 43.3). As the period of abstinence from smoking cigarettes increases, the risk of lung cancer decreases[94] (see Table 43.3). However, even for periods of abstinence of over 40 years, the risk of lung cancer among former smokers remains elevated compared to never smokers[94,95] (see Table 43.3). The benefits derived from smoking cessation also depend on the prior duration of smoking: For a given period of abstinence, the risk decreases with a decrease in the duration of previous smoking.[94] In general, studies have shown comparable reductions in risk following cessation regardless of sex, type of tobacco smoked, and histologic type of lung cancer.[47]

The Changing Cigarette. The composition and design of cigarettes have changed considerably since the 1950s. The marketplace has shifted from mainly unfiltered cigarettes to predominantly filtered cigarettes and to products that are labeled "light" or "mild." The filters in use in the United States are predominantly cellulose acetate, whereas charcoal filters are used extensively in Japan and some other countries.[96] In the mid-1960s, ventilation holes were added to the filter, which dilute the smoke with air drawn through them. However, smokers can readily block the holes with their fingers, which are left unblocked by the machines used to test cigarettes. There have also been substantial changes in the design of the cigarette and in the tobacco used. Reconstituted tobacco has been used increasingly since the

Table 43.2 Age-Specific Lung Cancer Mortality Rates (per 100,000) among Men and Women 60 to 69 Years of Age with Comparable Smoking Levels in the American Cancer Society's Cancer Prevention Study II (CPS-II)

Age Group	Never Smokers	Smoked 20 Cigarettes per Day for:		Smoked 40 Cigarettes per Day for:	
		30 Years	40 Years	30 Years	40 Years
Men	11.9	224.3	486.8	572.8	606.6
Women	9.8	200.8	264.4	257.7	552.8

From Thun MJ, Day-Lally C, Myers DG, et al: Trends in tobacco smoking and mortality from cigarette use in Cancer Prevention Studies I (1959–1965) and II (1982–1988). *In* Shopland DR, Burns DM, Garfinkel L, Samet JM (eds): Smoking and Tobacco Control Monograph 8: Changes in Cigarette Related Disease Risks and Their Implication for Prevention and Control, NIH Publication No. 97-4213. Bethesda, Md: National Cancer Institute, 1997, pp 305–382.

1960s, and there have been changes to the cigarette paper and additives.[96]

A concomitant shift toward lowered levels of "tar" and nicotine, as measured by a smoking machine according to a standard protocol, has occurred (Fig. 43.5). Cigarette "tar" is the label given to the condensable residue of cigarette smoke, that is, the total particulate matter of cigarette smoke deposited on the machine's filter, less the moisture and nicotine. Tar is a complex mixture that includes many chemicals that are cancer initiators or promoters.[97] Tar and nicotine yields are measured with a smoking machine according to a standardized protocol established by the Federal Trade Commission (FTC) that specifies such details as puff volume, the frequency of puffing, and the length to which the cigarette is to be smoked.[68] The protocol in use is no longer representative of typical smoking patterns.[98]

Studies using biomarkers of exposure to tobacco smoke components show little relationship of these levels with levels expected from calculations using the tar or nicotine yield as measured by the FTC's protocol.[68] These studies have been conducted both in the population context and in the laboratory setting. For example, Coultas and colleagues[99] collected both saliva for analysis for cotinine level and end-tidal breath samples for measurement of carbon monoxide level in a population sample of New Mexico Hispanics included in a respiratory health survey. The measured levels of the biomarkers were not associated with the levels expected from calculations based on the yields of tar and nicotine of the current brand and the number of cigarettes smoked. Djordjevic and colleagues[100] evaluated smoking pattern and biomarkers in the laboratory setting, contrasting smokers of medium-yield and low-yield cigarettes. The smokers had greater puff volumes and frequencies than are specified in the FTC protocol and had substantially greater intakes of tar and nicotine than implied by the brand listings. The lack of association of tar and nicotine yields with biomarker levels partially reflects compensatory changes in smoking patterns for those switching from higher to lower yield products. The compensation includes blocking of the ventilation holes, more frequent and deeper puffs, and an increase in the number of cigarettes smoked.[98]

The gradual reduction in tar yield over recent decades would be expected to have reduced smokers' exposures to carcinogens if the FTC test protocol were predictive of carcinogen doses delivered to the lung.[97] However, questions remain as to whether the FTC test method is informative with regard to lung cancer risk or risks of smoking-caused diseases more generally.[98,101] Epidemiologic studies have been carried out to assess whether the seemingly substantial changes in tar and nicotine yield, as measured by the FTC protocol, have resulted in parallel changes in the risk of smoking. Epidemiologic studies have been a key source of information on the risks of smoking cigarettes as they are actually smoked.

Table 43.3 Risk of Lung Cancer among Ex-smokers Relative to Never Smokers According to Length of Time since Smoking Cessation and Number of Cigarettes Formerly Smoked among a Cohort of U.S. Veterans

Years since Smoked	Cigarettes Smoked per Day				
	1–9	10–20	21–39	≥40	Total
<5	7.6*	12.5	20.6	26.9	16.1
5–9	3.6	5.1	11.5	13.6	7.8
10–19	2.2	4.3	6.8	7.8	5.1
20–29	1.7	3.3	3.4	5.9	3.3
30–39	0.5	2.1	2.8	4.5	2.0
≥40	1.1	1.6	1.8	2.3	1.5

* Relative risk compared to referent category of never smokers (= 1.0).

Adapted from Hrubec Z, McLaughlin JK: Former cigarette smoking and mortality among U.S. veterans: A 26-year follow-up, 1954–1980. *In* Shopland DR, Burns DM, Garfinkel L, Samet JM (eds): Changes in Cigarette-Related Disease Risks and Their Implication for Prevention and Control, NIH Publication No. 97-4213. Bethesda, Md: National Cancer Institute, 1997, pp 501–530.

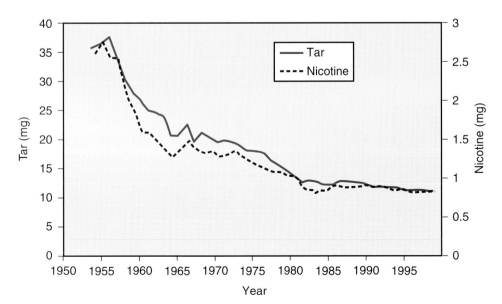

Figure 43.5 Tar and nicotine values for U.S. cigarettes as measured using the Federal Trade Commission method, 1954–1998, and weighted by actual sales to determine the content of tar and nicotine for an average cigarette smoked by the population. (From Burns DM, Benowitz NL: Public health implications of changes in cigarette design and marketing. *In* Burns DM [ed]: Smoking and Tobacco Control Monograph 13: Risks Associated with Smoking Cigarettes with Low Machine-Measured Yields of Tar and Nicotine. Bethesda, Md: National Cancer Institute, 2001, pp 1–12.)

For lung cancer, and for other diseases, two lines of epidemiologic data have been available on changes in products: The first comes from case-control studies, which compare the smoking history profiles of persons developing lung cancer over the several-year period of case accrual with those of concomitantly selected controls, and the second comes from cohort studies, which track the risk of lung cancer over time as the smoking products changed. These studies provide temporally cross-sectional assessments, but do not provide insights into the consequences of smoking one product or another across the full time period of smoking. In fact, smokers change products, and product characteristics change over time as well. Consequently, researchers cannot compare the risks of smoking one type of cigarette across decades with that of smoking another. Because of these methodologic issues, the epidemiologic data have inherent limitations.[98]

Some epidemiologic data, coming primarily from case-control studies, suggest that unfiltered cigarettes slightly increase the risk of lung cancer associated with cigarette smoking compared to filtered cigarettes (Table 43.4)[102–116] Similarly, higher tar-yield cigarettes may slightly increase the risk compared to lower tar-yield cigarettes[106,111,112,116–123] (Table 43.5). The initial evidence on cigarette type came primarily from case-control studies that compared risks in persons who had used filter-tip cigarettes to persons who had smoked nonfiltered cigarettes exclusively.[102,103] This comparison could be made among smokers in the 1960s, as there was still a substantial proportion that had not used filter cigarettes at all. For example, Bross and Gibson[102] compared lung cancer risk of filter smokers with that of nonfilter smokers among patients seen at Roswell Park Memorial Cancer Institute in Buffalo; persons were classified as filter cigarette smokers if they had used these products for at least 10 years. These initial studies indicated that filter cigarettes provided some reduction of lung cancer risk. Subsequent case-control studies that have contrasted use of either filter or lower yield products across the cumulative

Table 43.4 A Summary of Selected Studies of Lung Cancer Risk According to Type of Cigarette Smoked: Nonfiltered Relative to Filtered Cigarettes

Study	Year	Location	Results*,†	Comments
Case-Control Studies				
Bross and Gibson[102]	1968	Roswell Park, hospital-based	1.69 (1.12, 2.57)	
Wynder et al.[103]	1970	New York, hospital-based (Memorial Sloan Kettering)	1.62 (0.99, 2.65)	
Wynder and Stellman[104]	1979	U.S. multisite, hospital-based	1.9 (0.92, 1.55) [males] 1.29 (0.67, 2.47) [females]	Nonfilter usage vs. filter usage >10 yr
Wynder and Kabat[105]	1988	U.S. multisite, hospital-based	1.45 (0.79, 2.70) [males] 1.56 (0.74, 3.33) [females]	Lifetime nonfilter usage vs. Lifetime filter usage
Lubin et al.[106]	1984	Western Europe, multisite, hospital-based	1.6 (1.3, 1.8) [males] 1.8 (1.5, 2.1) 1.8 (1.3, 2.6) [females] 2.5 (1.2, 5.2)	Mixed usage Lifetime nonfilter usage Mixed usage Lifetime nonfilter usage
Pathak et al.[107]	1986	New Mexico, population-based	1.25 whites 25.0 Hispanics	Lifetime nonfilter usage
Jockel et al.[108]	1992	Germany, hospital-based	2.4 (1.2, 4.8)	All men; exclusively or partly nonfilter usage last 20 yr vs. filter usage last 20 yr
Stellman et al.[113]	1997	U.S. multisite, hospital-based	1.90 (1.31, 2.77) [males] 3.05 (1.71, 5.45) [females] 1.13 (0.79, 1.61) [males] 1.07 (0.62, 1.84) [females]	Squamous cell carcinoma, lifetime nonfilter usage vs. lifetime filter usage Adenocarcinoma, lifetime nonfilter usage vs. lifetime filter usage
Matos et al.[114]	1998	Argentina, hospital-based	2.9 (0.9, 9.2)	Mainly plain usage vs. mainly filter usage
Marugame et al.[115]	2004	Japan, hospital-based	3.24 (2.20, 4.77)	Nonfilter only or mixed usage vs. filter usage
Prospective Studies				
Hawthorne and Fry[109]	1978	West Scotland	1.20 (0.77, 1.89)	
Rimington[110]	1981	England	1.67 (1.14, 2.45)	Age-adjusted relative risk = 1.54
Garfinkel and Stellman[111]	1988	U.S. (American Cancer Society, CPS II)	1.5 (1.3, 1.8)	All women; filter for 40% of smoking relative to lifetime filter usage
Sidney et al.[112]	1993	Kaiser Permanente	1.24 (0.78, 1.89)	
Tang et al.[116]	1995	United Kingdom, combined data from four cohort studies	1.06 [males]	Plain usage vs. filter usage

* Odds ratio (and 95% confidence limits when possible) for case-control studies and relative risk (and 95% confidence limits) for prospective studies.
† The referent category of filtered cigarette smokers is equal to 1.0.

Table 43.5 A Summary of Selected Studies of Lung Cancer Risk According to Tar Exposures or Levels in Cigarettes Smoked

Study	Year	Location		Results*,† 1 (= low)	2	3	4	5
Case-Control Studies								
Joly et al.[117]	1983	Havana, Cuba, hospital-based		1.0	1.75 (1.12, 2.74)	1.62 (0.99, 2.66)		
Lubin et al.[106]	1984	W. Europe, multisite, hospital-based	Males Females	1.0 1.0	1.2	1.5 5.9	1.8 4.0	1.7 7.7
Wilcox et al.[303]	1988	New Jersey, population-based		1.0	1.62	1.96	1.89	
Kaufman et al.[119]	1989	U.S. & Canada, multisite, hospital-based		1.0	1.9 (1.0, 3.7)	3.1 (1.3, 7.1)		
Zang and Wynder[122]	1992	U.S., multisite, hospital-based	Males Females	1.0 1.0	2.6 8.3	4.4 15.1	6.2 11.6	7.3 16.3
Prospective Studies								
Hammond et al.[120]	1976	U.S. (American Cancer Society CPS-I)		1.0	1.21 (1.02, 1.45)	1.36 (1.15, 1.61)		
Higenbottam et al.[121]	1982	England (Whitehall Study)		1.0	1.15 (0.77, 1.74)	1.48 (1.0, 2.18)		
Garfinkel and Stellman[111]	1988	U.S. women (American Cancer Society CPS-II)		1.0	1.17	1.36	1.59	1.85
Sidney et al.[112]	1993	U.S. (Kaiser Permanente)		1.0	0.98 (0.66, 1.47)	0.87 (0.56, 1.37)		
Tang et al.[116]	1995	United Kingdom, combined data from four cohort studies	Males	0.75 (0.52, 1.09)	1.0			
Speizer et al.[123]	1999	U.S. (Nurses' Health Study)	Females	1.0	1.0 (0.7, 1.4)			

* Odds ratio for case-control studies and relative risk for prospective studies. 95% Confidence limits are presented when data were available.
† The exposure categories of low to high are for summary purposes only, and do not correspond to identical dosage categories.

smoking history with nonfilter or higher yield products have had generally similar findings.[101,124]

In a 1976 publication, Hammond and colleagues[120] compared mortality risks from lung cancer and other diseases by tar yield of products smoked by participants in CPS I. The follow-up interval spanned the years 1960 to 1972. Smokers were placed into three categories of products smoked: low yield (<17.6 mg/cigarette), high yield (25.8 to 35.7 mg/cigarette), and medium (intermediate between these). The standardized mortality rates for lung cancer in low- and medium-yield smokers were approximately 80% of the rate in high-yield smokers. A further analysis of tar yield using the same data set confirmed that risk for lung cancer death increased somewhat with tar yield.[125]

CPS II provides evidence on the risk of lung cancer in a cohort of about 1 million Americans followed in this analysis from 1982 to 1988. In a recent report, Harris and colleagues[126] addressed risk for lung cancer mortality in relation to the tar level of cigarette on enrollment in 1982. Those smoking the highest tar products (>22 mg) had the highest risk, after adjustment for smoking amount and for age of starting to smoke. For smokers of cigarettes with lower yields, the relative risks were similar across the range of tar levels.

Further insights have been gained by comparing the risks in the two CPS studies of the American Cancer Society; this comparison addresses whether risks have changed, comparing smokers developing disease during 1960–1972 with a similar group developing disease during the initial follow-up of CPS II, 1980–1986.[127,128] If the risk for lung cancer associated with smoking were decreasing over time, the expectation would be that risks for smokers would be less in CPS II than in CPS I. In fact, the opposite was observed; lung cancer mortality increased in male and female smokers in CPS II, compared with their male and female counterparts in CPS I (Fig. 43.6).[50] In an analysis with similar findings, Doll and colleagues[129] compared the risks of death from lung cancer and other causes during the first and second 20 years of the 40-year follow-up of the British physician cohort. Lung cancer mortality increased among smokers in the second 20 years (1971–1991), even though products smoked during this time period would have had a substantially lower tar and nicotine yield than those smoked during the first 20 years (1951–1971). For the first 20 years, the annual lung cancer mortality rate among current smokers was 264 per 100,000 and for the second 20 years it was 314 per 100,000.

Lee[124] reported a systematic review of 54 epidemiologic studies that address lung cancer risk in relation to type of cigarette. Findings were reported by filter versus nonfilter, lower tar versus higher tar, and black versus blond tobacco. A substantially reduced risk was estimated for smokers of filter versus nonfilter cigarettes, but this finding relates to cigarettes smoked decades ago. A lower reduction in relative risk, about 25%, was estimated for smokers of lower versus higher tar cigarettes.

Several expert panels have also recently reviewed the findings. The Institute of Medicine[130] carried out a

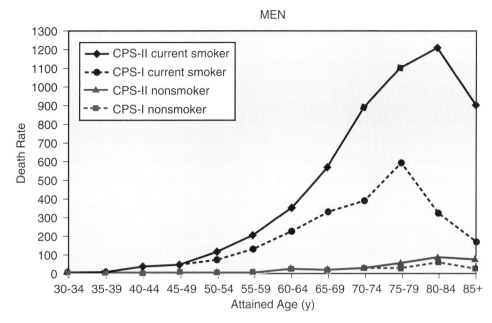

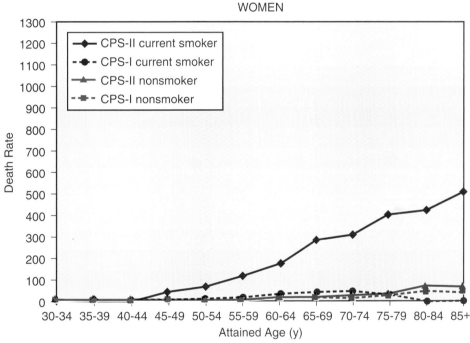

Figure 43.6 Age-specific death rates from lung cancer among current cigarette smokers and lifelong never smokers, based on smoking status at enrollment in Cancer Prevention Study (CPS) I or CPS II, according to attained age. (From Thun MJ, Day-Lally C, Myers DG, et al: Trends in tobacco smoking and mortality from cigarette use in Cancer Prevention Studies I [1959–1965] and II [1982–1988]. *In* Burns DM, Garfinkel L, Samet JM [eds]: Changes in Cigarette Related Disease Risks and Their Implication for Prevention and Control. Bethesda, Md: 1997, pp 305–382.)

comprehensive review on various harm reduction strategies for reducing the disease burden caused by smoking, including lower yield cigarettes. The Institute of Medicine report concluded that smoking lower yield products had not been shown to benefit the health of smokers.[130] This topic was also addressed in the National Cancer Institute's *Smoking and Tobacco Control Monograph 13: Risks Associated with Smoking Cigarettes with Low Machine-Measured Yields of Tar and Nicotine*.[98] This monograph provides a comprehensive review of the topic as well as new analyses of the CPS I data. The report proposes that the net consequences of having lower yield products needs consideration, along with any change in the risk of disease to smokers. If some persons start smoking or continue to smoke because they view lower yield products as having more acceptable levels

of risk, then the success of tobacco control interventions may be lessened. The report also found that compensatory changes in smoking patterns reduce any theoretical benefit of lower yield products. Overall, the report concluded that changes in cigarette design and manufacturing over the last 50 years had not benefited public health. Most recently, a Working Group convened by the IARC of the World Health Organization also reached a similar conclusion.[3]

In summary, assessing the evidence concerning the degree to which changes in the properties of cigarettes affect lung cancer risk is complex, because it requires evaluating the net effect of physical changes in the cigarette in combination with potential subsequent compensatory changes in smoking topography. Simply considering changes in the cigarette in isolation can be misleading. The studies with appropriate comparisons across time indicate that, considered in total, the changing cigarette has not led to reductions in lung cancer risk.

Passive Smoking. Passive smokers inhale a complex mixture of smoke now widely referred to as environmental tobacco smoke or secondhand smoke. Passive smoking was first considered as a possible risk factor for lung cancer in 1981 when two studies were published that described increased lung cancer risk among never-smoking women who were married to smokers. Hirayama reported the findings from a cohort study in Japan that showed that, among nonsmoking women, those whose husbands smoked cigarettes were at higher risk of lung cancer than those whose husbands were nonsmokers.[131] A case-control study in Athens reported by Trichopoulos and colleagues shortly thereafter replicated this finding.[132] Additional evidence rapidly accrued, and by 1986 two important summary reports were published. The National Research Council reviewed the epidemiologic evidence and concluded that nonsmoking spouses who were married to cigarette smokers were about 30% more likely to develop lung cancer than nonsmoking spouses married to nonsmokers, and that this relationship was biologically plausible.[133] Almost one fourth of lung cancer cases among never smokers were estimated to be attributed to exposure to passive smoking.[133] The 1986 Surgeon General's report also judged passive smoking to be a cause of lung cancer,[14] an inference corroborated by the 1992 review of the evidence and risk assessment by the U.S. Environmental Protection Agency, which classified environmental tobacco smoke as a known human (Class A) carcinogen.[15] Estimates indicate that passive smoking accounts for approximately 3000 lung cancer deaths per year in the United States.[15]

Since these conclusions were reached, several major studies have been carried out to characterize further the association of passive smoking with lung cancer, while taking into account some of the limitations of earlier studies, particularly small sample sizes, exposure misclassification, and omission of some potential confounding factors.[134,135] Various panels since 1986 have also concluded that passive smoking increases lung cancer risk, including the Scientific Committee on Tobacco and Health in the United Kingdom,[136] the California Environmental Protection Agency,[137] and the IARC of the World Health Organization.[3]

Passive smoking is more weakly associated with lung cancer than is active smoking, as expected given the lower doses of carcinogens received by the nonsmoker compared to the smoker. Because of broad societal implications, the conclusion that passive smoking causes lung cancer has generated controversy. Questions have been raised about the methodology of the epidemiologic studies, including confounding and misclassification of exposure to environmental tobacco smoke. Review groups have nonetheless concluded that the association between environmental tobacco smoke and lung cancer cannot be attributed to methodologic limitations of epidemiologic data.[3,14,15,133] Studies have been directed at the specific venues where non-smokers are exposed to tobacco smoke, including the home, workplaces, and public places. Much of the literature has focused on the increased risk associated with being married to a smoker, an exposure variable that can be readily ascertained. Meta-analyses have been conducted periodically to summarize the evidence from the epidemiologic studies. A 1997 meta-analysis by Law and colleagues[138] found an approximately 20% increased risk associated with marriage to a smoker; this excess risk appeared to be due to exposure to passive smoking, because it could not be explained by confounding or misclassification. An updating of this meta-analysis in 2003 yielded about the same estimate.[139]

Reynolds[140] summarized the evidence on workplace exposure to secondhand smoke and lung cancer risk. In general, the estimates indicate increased risk associated with exposure, although they are imprecise due to a small number of cases. There is also coherence between model-based estimates derived by combining risk estimates from studies of exposure to smoking by husbands and monitoring data from workplaces.[141]

The studies of passive smoking provide further evidence documenting the dose-response relationship between cigarette smoke and lung cancer. Even at doses far lower than those of active smoking, an increased risk is observed, suggesting that there is no threshold for tobacco carcinogenesis.[14]

Diet

The possible role of diet in modifying the risk of lung cancer has been the focus of intensive investigation, driven initially by the rationale that specific micronutrients might have anti-carcinogenic activity. The most thoroughly investigated dietary factors are also those that presently appear to have the greatest implications for prevention: fruits, vegetables, and specific antioxidant micronutrients that are commonly found in fruits and vegetables.

Research on diet and lung cancer has now been carried out for nearly 3 decades. The results of case-control and prospective cohort studies have tended to show that individuals with high dietary intake of fruits or vegetables have a lower risk of lung cancer than those with low fruit or vegetable intake.[142,142a] To understand better the basis of this protective association, fruits and vegetables have been grouped into classes and also examined individually in relation to lung cancer risk. For example, tomatoes[143-145] and cruciferous vegetables[145,146] have been associated with a reduced risk of lung cancer in a number of studies, at least for the highest-versus-lowest categories of consumption. These food-based analyses can help to clarify whether protection arises from the complex mixture that comprises fruits and vegetables or from specific biochemical constituents present in particular fruits and vegetables.

Fruits and vegetables are the major dietary source of antioxidant micronutrients. Much of the research on diet and lung cancer has been motivated by the hypothesis that diets high in antioxidant micronutrients may protect against oxidative deoxyribonucleic acid (DNA) damage and thereby protect against cancer. For example, this was one of the hypothesized roles for β-carotene,[147] the focus of now-controversial clinical trials. Two different strategies are used to evaluate the relationship of micronutrients to lung cancer risk in observational epidemiologic studies: (1) using data summarized from food-frequency questionnaires to estimate micronutrient intake and (2) drawing blood samples from study participants and assaying the concentrations of micronutrients in circulation. Studies of both dietary intake[148–151] and prediagnostic blood concentrations[152,153] suggest a protective association between carotenoids and lung cancer. The evidence for vitamin C is scant but suggestive of a protective association, whereas the data on vitamin A have yielded null findings.[142]

The protective association predicted between β-carotene and lung cancer on the basis of these observational epidemiologic studies was not confirmed in three randomized, double-blind, placebo-controlled chemoprevention trials.[154–156] In fact, two of these studies with participants at high risk for lung cancer (heavy smokers and asbestos-exposed workers) were stopped early because significantly increased risk of lung cancer was observed in the β-carotene group compared to the placebo group.[153,154,157]

The results of the randomized chemoprevention trials stand in sharp contrast to the considerable observational epidemiologic evidence favoring a protective association. The contradictory findings are not yet understood; among the potential criticisms are that the randomized trials used relatively high doses of β-carotene and that the observational epidemiologic studies may have been flawed by uncontrolled confounding or selection bias.[158] Because of the powerful role of smoking as a cause of lung cancer, disentangling the effects of other lifestyle-related factors, such as diet, from the effect of smoking may be particularly difficult. Further complicating the assessment of protection by dietary factors is the narrow range of likely effects, much smaller than the effect of smoking, and the unavoidable problem of measurement error, that is, the inevitable inaccuracy in estimating usual dietary consumption of particular foods or groups of foods. Even for dietary factors such as fruit and vegetable consumption that are fairly consistently associated with a lower risk of lung cancer, the highest exposure category is usually associated with at most a halving in the risk of lung cancer. In many instances, even after statistically adjusting for cigarette smoking, the potential residual confounding effects of smoking could thus plausibly be strong enough to account for the observed associations between dietary factors and lung cancer.

Although studies of fruits, vegetables, and micronutrients have been the centerpiece of studies of diet and lung cancer, a wide range of dietary and anthropometric factors have been investigated. For example, the results of a meta-analysis showed alcohol drinking in the highest consumption categories was associated with increased risk of lung cancer.[159] Anthropometric measures have also been studied, indicating a tendency for persons with lower body mass index to have increased lung cancer risk relative to heavier persons.[160,161] However, both alcohol drinking and low body mass index may be difficult to separate from the concomitant effects of smoking. At present, when considering the possible relationships between lung cancer and factors such as alcohol drinking and lower body mass index, cigarette smoking cannot be dismissed as a possible explanation.

Environmental Exposures

Occupational Exposures. Investigations of occupational groups who are often heavily exposed over a long time to workplace agents have provided substantial understanding of the carcinogenicity of a number of chemicals and physical agents. Among cancers that are associated with occupational exposures, cancer of the lung has perhaps the most abundant set of causes, likely reflecting the diversity of workplace exposures that can be inhaled and the potential for workers to receive substantial pulmonary doses while working in contaminated workplaces.[162] Estimates derived from case-control studies of the proportion of lung cancer that is contributed by occupational exposures—via independent or shared causal pathways—have ranged widely, but most point estimates or ranges have included values from 9% to 15%.[163–169] Although disagreement persists concerning specific estimates,[170] the message is clear: in industrialized nations, the contribution of occupational exposures to the lung cancer burden is small compared to that of cigarette smoking, but large compared to contributions of most other exposure classes. Cigarette smoking potentiates the effect of some of the known occupational lung carcinogens.[81]

Lung cancer has been observed to be associated with many workplace exposures. Workers such as coke oven workers,[171,172] who are exposed to tar and soot (which contains benzo[a]pyrene) in concentrations exceeding those present in urban air,[173] are at increased risk of lung cancer. Occupational exposures to a number of metals, including arsenic, chromium, and nickel, are also causes of lung cancer.[174] For many of the worker groups exposed to these agents, there were substantial increments in risk. However, in developed countries these hazards have largely been controlled.

For some other workplace agents, the evidence has been less clear. The results of numerous case-control and cohort studies are compatible with a weak association between exposure to diesel exhaust and the development of lung cancer.[175] Although inadequate control of cigarette smoking limits the inferences that can be drawn from many of these studies, exposure to diesel exhaust remains a likely explanation for these findings.[175] This association remains of public health concern, as the public is exposed to diesel exhaust in urban areas, and in some European countries diesel vehicles are increasingly used.[82]

The question of whether silica dust is a risk factor for lung cancer has been controversial. A twofold increase in lung cancer risk was estimated from a meta-analysis of the relationship between silicosis and lung cancer mortality.[176] Effects of smoking have not been well controlled in most of the studies.[176] The evidence for an increased risk from silica exposure, separate from an effect of silicosis, is less clear.[177,178] In 1997, the IARC did classify crystalline silica as a human carcinogen[179]; however, some still continue to question its carcinogenicity[178] and the role of silica exposure versus that of the fibrosis due to silica.[177]

Asbestos. Asbestos, a well-established occupational carcinogen, refers to several forms of fibrous, naturally occurring silicate minerals.[180,181] The epidemiologic evidence dates to the 1950s, although clinical case series had previously led to the hypothesis that asbestos causes lung cancer.[181,182] In a retrospective cohort study published in 1955, Doll observed that asbestos textile workers at a factory in the United Kingdom had a 10-fold elevation in lung cancer risk and that the risk was most heavily concentrated during the time frame before regulations were implemented to limit

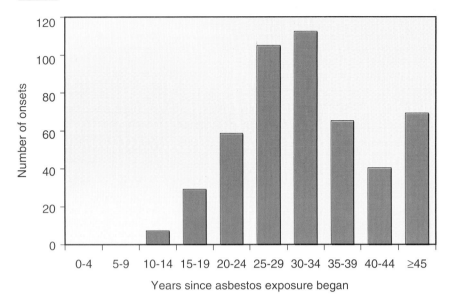

Figure 43.7 Frequency distribution of number of lung cancer cases by time since asbestos exposure began among a cohort of asbestos insulation workers. (From Selikoff IJ: Latency of asbestos disease among insulation workers in the United States and Canada. Cancer 46:2736–2740, 1980.)

asbestos dust in factories.[183] A sevenfold excess of lung cancer was subsequently observed among insulation workers in the United States.[184,185] The peak incidence occurred 30 to 35 years after the initial exposure to asbestos (Fig. 43.7).[186] The risk of lung cancer has been noted to increase with increased exposure to asbestos[187] and to be associated with each of the principal commercial forms of asbestos.[188] Whether asbestos acts directly as a carcinogen or indirectly, for example, by causing chronic inflammation that eventually leads to cancer, remains uncertain.[189,190]

Asbestos and cigarette smoking are both independent causes of lung cancer, but, in combination, they act synergistically to increase the risk of lung cancer. Controversy continues about the precise quantitative characterization of this synergy, specifically whether it meets the criteria for interaction on a multiplicative scale. This uncertainty about the quantitative nature of the joint effect of exposure to asbestos and cigarette smoke reflects limitations of the available data[3] and lack of understanding of the underlying mechanisms.[191] One widely cited study indicated a strong interaction, albeit on an additive but not on the more stringent multiplicative scale, showing the potential for greatly increased risk of lung cancer in asbestos-exposed smokers (Table 43.6).[192] Cigarette smoking may increase the lung cancer risk associated with asbestos exposure by multiple mechanisms, including altering deposition patterns in the lung and enhancing retention of asbestos fibers.[193]

Radiation. Epidemiologic studies of populations exposed to high doses of radiation show that lung cancer is one of the cancers associated with exposure to ionizing radiation. However, the risks of low-dose radiation, more relevant to contemporary workers and the general population, have proven difficult to characterize.[194,195] Assessing the cancer risk associated with low-dose radiation among humans is methodologically difficult because the signal-to-noise ratio is highly unfavorable.[196]

Two types of radiation, classified by rate of energy transfer to the tissue, are relevant to lung cancer: low linear energy transfer (LET) radiation (e.g., x-rays and γ-rays) and high-LET radiation (e.g., neutrons and radon). High-LET

Table 43.6 Summary of the Joint Relationship between Cigarette Smoking and Asbestos Exposure on the Risk of Lung Cancer Mortality: Absolute Rates and Rates Calculated Using an Additive Model and Multiplicative Model

Smoking	Mortality Rates Asbestos Exposed		Additive Model Asbestos Exposed		Multiplicative Model Asbestos Exposed	
	No	*Yes*	*No*	*Yes*	*No*	*Yes*
No	11.3*	58.4	0	47.1	1.0	5.2
Yes	122.6	601.6	111.3	590.3[†]	10.8	53.2[‡]

* Mortality rate per 100,000.
[†] Rate difference compared to referent category of no smoking and no asbestos exposure; expected value under model of no statistical interaction = 47.1 + 111.3 = 158.4. The actual mortality is higher than expected indicating an interaction on an additive scale.
[‡] Rate-ratio compared to referent category of no smoking and no asbestos exposure; expected value under model of no statistical interaction = 5.2 × 10.8 = 56.2. The actual mortality is slightly less than expected indicating no interaction on a more stringent multiplicative scale.
Adapted from Hammond EC, Selikoff IJ, Seidman H: Asbestos exposure, cigarette smoking and death rates. Ann N Y Acad Sci 330:473–490, 1979.

radiation produces ionization of relatively higher density in tissues than low-LET radiation, so in equivalent doses more biologic damage is produced by high-LET than low-LET radiation.[197] For both types of radiation, the majority of the epidemiologic evidence comes from cohorts exposed at levels substantially greater than those experienced by the general population, except for those receiving therapeutic irradiation. Risk assessment methods are then used to estimate risks to the population.

High-LET Radiation: Radon. Radon is an inert gas that is produced naturally from radium in the decay series of uranium. Two of the decay products of radon emit alpha particles that can, by virtue of their high energy and mass, cause damage to the DNA of cells of the respiratory epithelium. Epidemiologic studies of underground miners of uranium and other ores have established exposure to radon daughters as a cause of lung cancer.[17,198,199] In the underground miners exposed to radon in past centuries, very high lung cancer risks were observed; these fell for more recent workers, but the recent epidemiologic studies still show clear evidence of existing cancer risk.[17] Cigarette smoking and radon decay products synergistically influence lung cancer risk, for example, in a manner that is greater than simply adding the risks of each together.[17,199]

Radon is of broader societal interest because it is a ubiquitous indoor air pollutant, an inert gas that enters buildings from the underlying soil. On average, indoor exposures to radon for the general population are much less than those received by occupational groups such as uranium miners, although homes have been identified with concentrations as high as in underground uranium mines. However, even the lowest historical radon concentration in a uranium mine is roughly 50 to 100 times higher than in the average home.[199] Exposure to radon in indoor air is also assumed to cause lung cancer, but the magnitude of the risk is more uncertain because of the assumptions made to estimate the risk, particularly the extrapolation of findings from uranium miners to the generally lower exposures indoors. These assumptions relate to dose, dose rate, and dosimetry and also reflect the lack of information on risks of exposures of women and children. Strengthening biologic evidence supports the assumption that a single hit to a cell by an alpha particle causes permanent cellular change, an assumption leading to a nonthreshold dose-response relationship.[17]

The assumptions made by the Environmental Protection Agency and the Biological Effects of Ionizing Radiation (BEIR) IV and VI Committees of the National Research Council lead to estimates that approximately 15,000 to 20,000 lung cancer deaths per year in the United States are caused by radon.[200,201] When case-control studies are combined with meta-analysis, there is a significant association between indoor radon and lung cancer in the general population that is quantitatively comparable with risk models derived from the underground miners. This coherence lends support to extrapolating the miner data to estimate the risk of indoor radon and considering indoor radon as a public health problem that should be addressed. In the United States, the Environmental Protection Agency has called for testing of all residences and mitigation of those exceeding a guideline value.

Low-LET Radiation: X-Rays and γ-Rays. Epidemiologic data relating low-LET radiation to lung cancer stem from three principal populations: the atomic bomb survivors in Japan,[202] patients with diseases such as ankylosing spondylitis[203] or tuberculosis[204] who received multiple radiation treatments, and occupational groups in professions exposed to radiation.[205] The single, high-dose exposure of the atomic bomb survivors was associated with significant lung cancer risk.[202] Regardless of their age when the atomic bombs were dropped, the excess of lung cancer did not occur until the survivors reached older ages, when cancer usually occurs.[202]

The risks associated with exposure to lower doses of low-LET radiation have been estimated in two ways. Statistical

models have been used to extrapolate from the data on atomic bomb survivors to lower doses. Tuberculosis patients who received radiation therapy have also been studied; they were intermittently exposed to radiation. Such intermittent, low-dose exposures may be most pertinent for the general population because this exposure pattern is the most common in technologically advanced societies. Studies of tuberculosis patients suggest that, if there is any risk of lung cancer associated with this exposure pattern, it is small,[204] implying that the assumptions upon which the higher risk estimates obtained from the atomic bomb survivors data were based may not hold.[204]

Low-LET radiation therefore appears to be associated with higher lung cancer risk when exposure occurs at a higher dose rate.[204] These results contrast with those for high-LET radiation, suggesting that the two types of radiation have different dose-rate relationships.[204]

Air Pollution. During a typical day, the average adult inhales about 10,000 L of air.[206] Consequently, even the carcinogens present in the air at low concentrations are of concern as a risk factor for lung cancer. Extrapolation of the risks associated with occupational exposures to the lower concentration of carcinogens in polluted ambient air leads to the conclusion that a small proportion of lung cancer cases could be due to air pollution.[162,207,208] The role of air pollution, both outdoor and indoor, in causing lung cancer has been controversial because of potential regulatory implications.

Atmospheric Air Pollution. Carcinogens generated by combustion of fossil fuels by engines in motor vehicles, power plants, industry, and other sources include polycyclic aromatic hydrocarbons and metals such as arsenic, nickel, and chromium.[207] In considering respiratory carcinogenesis, the constituents of "air pollution" will vary by locale and over time depending on the pollution sources.[209] Consequently, epidemiologic investigations of air pollution and lung cancer have been limited by the difficulty of estimating exposure. Nevertheless, descriptive evidence is consistent with a role for air pollution in causing lung cancer. For example, urbanization and lung cancer mortality are linked.[210] However, this association could arise from differences related to urbanization in the distributions of other lung cancer risk factors, such as smoking and occupational exposures. Adjustment for these factors may considerably attenuate the effect of urban location,[211] but an urban effect persists in a number of studies.[82]

Air pollution has been assessed as a risk factor for lung cancer in epidemiologic studies of both case-control and cohort design. These studies have been reviewed in detail elsewhere.[82,212] These reviewers have found the evidence wanting because of the potential for exposure misclassification and for uncontrolled confounding, but there is biologic plausibility for outdoor air pollution to contribute to the causation of lung cancer, given the presence of carcinogens in outdoor air. If so, even a small effect could be of public health importance because of the large number of urban dwellers who are exposed.

Two prospective cohort studies[213,214] that partially address the weaknesses of earlier studies add evidence that suggests air pollution is weakly associated with the risk of lung cancer. By prospectively studying air pollution levels in relation to risk of lung cancer and by controlling for possible confounders such as age, smoking, and socioeconomic status at the individual level, these studies surmount some shortcomings noted for much previous research.[215] In a study of six U.S. cities, the adjusted risk of lung cancer mortality in the city with the highest fine particulate concentration was 1.4 times (95% confidence interval, 0.8 to 2.4) higher than in the least polluted city.[213] Using data from CPS II for 1982 to 1989, Pope and colleagues observed that, compared to the least polluted areas, residence in areas with high sulfate concentrations was associated with an increased risk of lung cancer (adjusted relative risk, 1.4; 95% confidence interval, 1.1 to 1.7) after adjustment for occupational exposures and the factors mentioned previously.[214] However, unlike in the six-cities study, fine particulate concentration was not associated with lung cancer risk.[214] In a subsequent updating of this report, follow-up was extended to 1998.[216] In this report, the risk of lung cancer associated with a 10 $\mu g/m^3$ increase in fine particles was estimated as 14%. By contrast, in the CPS I cohort, air pollution was not associated with lung cancer risk; in this study, men were stratified according to exposures in the workplace, but the study relied only on proxy, less specific measures of air pollution.[215] Some case-control studies have reported indices of air pollution to be modestly associated with elevated risks of lung cancer,[217,218] but others have reported no association.[219,220]

Another research approach to evaluate the risk of air pollution has been to investigate populations residing around point sources of pollution, such as factories and smelters. Proximity of residence to the pollution source can be used as a proxy for exposure. Many industries have been studied using this approach. Areas surrounding nonferrous smelters (which emit arsenic) have been of particular interest. An ecologic study reported by Blot and Fraumeni in 1975 suggested that excess lung cancer occurred in U.S. counties with copper, lead, or zinc smelting and refining industries.[38] The results of several subsequent case-control studies[221,222] lend support to this hypothesis by showing that the risk of lung cancer increased the nearer persons lived to nonferrous smelters, after accounting for personal cigarette smoking and employment at the smelter. Other case-control studies did not replicate this finding[223,224] but were also limited by their failure to account for smoking and employment at the smelter.

Doll and Peto,[162] in their 1981 review of the causes of cancer, estimated that perhaps 1% to 2% of lung cancer was related to air pollution. Even in light of recent findings, this appears to remain a reasonable estimate. To the extent that air pollution may contribute to the occurrence of lung cancer—and the overall epidemiologic evidence is equivocal—its contribution is minimal relative to cigarette smoking. This is to be expected, given that respiratory doses of carcinogens from active smoking are significantly greater than those received from the inhalation of atmospheric contaminants.

Indoor Air Pollution. An individual's total exposure to air pollution depends on indoor as well as outdoor exposures. Indoor air quality has large potential health implications because people may spend substantial amounts of time indoors. Indoor air pollution may stem from incoming outdoor air or originate indoors from tobacco smoking, building materials, soil gases, household products, and combustion from heating and cooking.[225] A tradeoff exists between energy efficiency and indoor air quality, as ventilation allows heated/cooled air to escape but improves indoor air quality.[226]

As discussed earlier, in more developed countries, two of the most important indoor pollutants that influence lung cancer risk in never smokers are passive smoking[14] and radon.[198] Asbestos exposure may pose a risk to building occupants, but it is estimated to be minimal.[180] Of major concern in the developing world is the indoor air contamination resulting from the use of unprocessed solid fuels, notably coal, for cooking and space heating.[227] Mumford and colleagues inferred that smoky coal was likely to be a major determinant of the geographic distribution of lung cancer in Xuan Wei, China,[228] a finding corroborated by an animal model.[229] Case-control studies conducted elsewhere in mainland China[222,230] and Taiwan[231] further implicated coal use as a risk factor for lung cancer. Another case-control study in Shanghai, where most of the homes are unheated, reported no association between use of coal and lung cancer risk.[232] Interesting evidence for a causal role of coal smoke comes from Lan and colleagues.[233] Exposure to coal burning in the preadult years was associated with lung cancer risk in a case-control study of women in Los Angeles County.[234]

HOST FACTORS

OVERVIEW

Genetic susceptibility to lung cancer has long been postulated. Environmental agents, even cigarette smoking, cause lung cancer in only a minority of exposed persons, leading to the hypothesis that susceptibility is inherently determined. Epidemiologic studies showing that a family history of lung cancer predicts increased risk further support a genetic basis for lung cancer susceptibility. This long-postulated hypothesis is now being actively addressed using the approach of molecular epidemiology. Full coverage of this topic is beyond the scope of this chapter; aspects of genetic susceptibility have been reviewed.[235–238]

Familial aggregation of lung cancer has been primarily demonstrated in case-control studies (Table 43.7).[232,239–250] In these studies, a family history of lung cancer tended to be associated with increased risk of lung cancer; most of the studies controlled for smoking, which is known to aggregate in families. In a large study in Louisiana, segregation analysis suggested that lung cancer inheritance was consistent with a mendelian codominant autosomal gene determining the early onset of disease.[251] On the other hand, the largest study of lung cancer in twins reported to date did not provide evidence indicating a genetic basis for susceptibility.[252] Follow-up of 15,924 male twin pairs in the United States did not show greater concordance between monozygotic and dizygotic twins, and death rates from lung cancer were also similar in surviving twins whose siblings died of lung cancer, whether they were monozygotic or dizygotic twins.

Table 43.7 A Summary of Selected Case-Control Studies of Lung Cancer among Persons with a Family History of Lung Cancer Compared to Those with No Family History of Lung Cancer

First Author	Year	Location	Odds Ratio*	Comment
Tokuhata[239]	1963	Buffalo, New York	2.4 (1.1, 5.2)	Adjusted for cigarette smoking, age, sex, generation
Tokuhata and Lilienfeld[240]	1964	Baltimore, Maryland	2.6 (1.4, 5.4)	Adjusted for age, sex, generation
Ooi et al.[241]	1986	Ten Louisiana parishes	2.7 (1.7, 4.2)	Adjusted for smoking, sex
Samet et al.[242]	1986	New Mexico	5.3 (2.2, 12.8) [parental]	Adjusted for cigarette smoking, age, sex, ethnicity
Gao et al.[232]	1987	Shanghai, P.R.C.	1.1 (0.6, 2.3) [parental] 3.0 (0.7, 12.5) [sibling]	Adjusted for smoking, age
Tsugane et al.[243]	1987	Tokyo, Japan	1.0 (0.3, 3.9)	Smoking and occupational exposure data collected, but not adjusted for
Horwitz et al.[244]	1988	New Haven, Connecticut	2.3 (0.6, 9.7)	Adjusted for smoking
McDuffie[245]	1991	Saskatchewan, Canada	2.0 (1.2, 3.4)	Smoking and occupational exposure data collected, but not adjusted for
Osann[246]	1991	Northern California	1.9 (0.7, 5.6)	Adjusted for cigarette smoking education, matched on age and race
Shaw et al.[247]	1991	Gulf Coast of Texas	1.7 (1.2, 2.4) [1 1st-degree relative with cancer] 2.8 (1.2, 6.6) [2 1st-degree relatives with cancer]	Adjusted for cigarette smoking, passive smoking, and number of first-degree relatives
Filho et al.[248]	1995	Sao Paulo, Brazil	3.2 (1.0, 11.1)	Smoking and occupational exposure data collected, but not adjusted for
Schwartz et al.[249]	1996	Detroit, Michigan	6.1 (1.1, 33.4)	Adjusted for smoking, occupational and medical history of each family member
Wu et al.[250]	1996	U.S., multisite	1.3 (0.9, 1.9)	Adjusted for secondhand smoke exposure

* Referent category of persons with no family history of lung cancer = 1.0 (95% confidence limits).

In a genetic epidemiology study of lung cancer in nonsmokers in Detroit, Schwartz, Yang and colleagues[249,253] have explored familial risk for lung cancer. In nonsmokers, Schwartz and colleagues[249] found an association between risk and a history of lung cancer in a first-degree relative (odds ratio, 1.4; 95% confidence interval, 0.8 to 2.5). The association was much stronger in those ages 40 to 59 years at diagnosis compared to older persons. This pattern of risk with age suggests that genetic factors may be more important at younger ages. This general finding was confirmed by a subsequent, complex segregation analysis of the same data.[253]

The evidence for aggregation and seeming susceptibility of some smokers has been viewed as a sufficient rationale for further investigation of the potential basis for lung cancer, using the new techniques of cellular and molecular biology.

RESEARCH FINDINGS ON THE GENETIC BASIS OF LUNG CANCER

With application of the new and powerful tools of modern molecular and cell biology, research findings are now characterizing the changes in cells that are caused by exposure to tobacco smoke and providing a framework for understanding the genetic and epigenetic basis of lung cancer risk. Figure 43.8, proposed by Hecht,[69] offers a general schema for the process of carcinogenesis by tobacco smoking. Viewed in the framework set by this type of model, research findings mirror the predictions of the multistage model in many respects and are enhancing understanding of the mechanisms by which smoking causes cancers of the lung and other organs. A rapidly expanding literature, based both in the laboratory and in the observational approach often referred to as "molecular epidemiology," addresses dosimetry and metabolism of tobacco carcinogens at the cellular and molecular levels, genetic determinants of susceptibility, and patterns of genetic changes in the tissues of smokers and in the cancers that the tissues develop.[69,235] Much of the research to date has been based in case-control studies that compare the genotypes of lung cancer cases with those of controls. Studies have also been carried out using cohort designs with affected and nonaffected persons sampled from the cohort and biologic samples analyzed for the markers of interest.

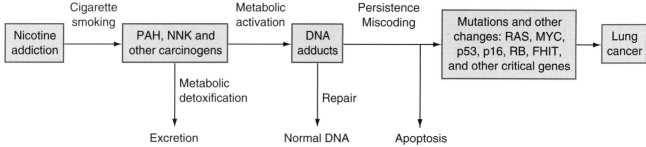

Figure 43.8 Scheme linking nicotine addiction and lung cancer via tobacco smoke carcinogens and their induction of multiple mutations in critical genes. NNK, 4-(methylnitrosamino)-1-(3-pyridyl)-1-butanone; PAH, polycyclic aromatic hydrocarbons. (From Hecht SS: Tobacco smoke carcinogens and lung cancer. J Natl Cancer Inst 91:1194–1210, 1999.)

The understanding of the epigenetic changes that may be involved in the causal pathway to lung cancer is advancing rapidly. For example, there is increasing evidence that methylation of cytosine in DNA, leading to hypermethylation of promoter regions, is frequent in most types of cancers, including lung cancer.[254] Promoter regions of many human genes have loci rich in cytosine-guanine (CpG) dinucleotides, regions referred as "CpG islands."[254,255] Hypermethylation of the CpG islands can be detected by polymerase chain reaction methods. Cells with abnormal methylation of genes have been detected in sputum before the diagnosis of lung cancer, suggesting that hypermethylation could be a useful marker for early detection.[256,257]

In a general formulation of determinants of cancer risk, the risk depends on carcinogen exposure and the factors that determine host susceptibility, including genetic predisposition.[258] For tobacco smoking and lung and other cancers, the elements of this paradigm are all topics of inquiry, using the combination of laboratory- and population-based studies indicated in the diagram in Figure 43.8. Biomarkers are central to the molecular epidemiology approach; the term refers to making measurements of indicators of exposure and dose, susceptibility, and response in biologic materials, including tissue samples, blood, urine, and saliva.[34,259] As research evolves within this paradigm, a more complete biologic understanding of the specific events underlying the multistage model, originally proposed on a conceptual basis, can be anticipated.

This framework indicates multiple points where genetically determined host characteristics might be important: carcinogen metabolism and activation, and DNA repair capacity, for example. There is a rapidly expanding literature on the molecular and cellular basis of lung cancer (for further discussion, see Chapter 42). Reviews have been published,[4,191,235,237,238,260–262] and the evidence has expanded and deepened our understanding of how smoking injures cells and causes cancer, and indicates potential approaches to identification of high-risk individuals and molecular screening.

The metabolism of toxic agents, including carcinogens, generally proceeds through two phases.[263] In phase 1, unreactive nonpolar compounds are converted, usually by oxidative reactions, to highly reactive intermediates. These intermediates are then able to form complexes with conjugating molecules in phase 2 conjugation reactions, which are usually less reactive and more easily excreted. However, the intermediate metabolite may react with other cellular components, such as DNA, before conjugation occurs. This binding to DNA may be the first step in the initiation of the carcinogenic process.[263]

Many carcinogenic compounds in tobacco smoke (e.g., polycyclic aromatic hydrocarbons) undergo metabolic activation by phase I enzymes of the cytochrome P-450 (CYP) system to form reactive intermediates that bind to DNA and cause genetic injury. Several of these enzymes have been investigated with regard to lung cancer risk, including CYP1A1 and CYP2D6. For *CYP1A1*, the current evidence suggests that two specific polymorphisms, the MspI polymorphism,[264] and a polymorphism in exon 7,[265] are associated with increased risks of lung cancer.

The enzyme CYP2D6 has been examined both for its phenotype and its genotype. This enzyme determines debrisoquine metabolism, which has been studied extensively as a phenotypic risk factor for lung cancer.[236] The initial case-control studies found that fast metabolizers had a greater lung cancer risk, consistent with the hypothesized role of rate of metabolism in determining lung cancer risk,[266] although a subsequent and larger study found no association.[267] More recent studies that have assessed genotype have generated inconsistent results,[268] with results suggesting the possibility that the *CYP2D6* metabolizer genotype may be weakly associated with increased risk of lung cancer.[269]

Glutathione S-transferase is a phase II enzyme that detoxifies reactive metabolites of polycyclic aromatic hydrocarbons. There are at least four genetically distinct classes of the glutathione S-transferases: μ, α, π, and θ. The risk estimates from a meta-analysis indicate that individuals with the *GSTM1* null genotype have higher risk of lung cancer than those with the *GSTM1* present genotype, but a pooled analysis of data from 21 case-control studies did not indicate that this susceptibility was stronger among cigarette smokers than among nonsmokers.[270] The importance of interactions between genes is highlighted when the two genotypes are studied in combination, and the *CYP1A1* Ile462Val and *GSTM1* null polymorphisms in nonsmokers indicated the combination of the two variant genotypes was associated with greater than fourfold increased likelihood of lung cancer compared to the combination of the two nonvariant genotypes.[271]

There are other candidates for determinants of susceptibility to lung cancer in smokers, including oncogenes and tumor suppressor genes and DNA repair capacity.[235] One gene of particular interest for lung cancer is *p53*, a tumor suppressor gene.[258,262] This gene has been described as "at the crossroads" for multiple cellular response pathways considered relevant to carcinogenesis.[262] The gene is frequently mutated in lung cancers: over 90% of small cell cancers and more than 50% of non–small cell cancers. The spectrum of mutations in smokers appears to be different from that in nonsmokers.[258,262] In fact, Denissenko and colleagues[272] showed binding of an activated metabolite of benzo[a]pyrene to the same p53 codons where mutations are commonly observed in lung cancers in smokers.

Substantial research has been directed at DNA repair and susceptibility in lung cancer and other tumors.[261,273] Persons with specific rare, recessive traits (e.g., xeroderma pigmentosum) have long been known to be at increased risk for cancer. DNA repair capacity has now been examined as a specific risk factor for lung cancer, with the underlying hypothesis that lesser capacity would lead to greater lung cancer risk from the multiple DNA-damaging components of tobacco smoke. Although much research remains to be done to clarify the association between variation in DNA repair capacity and lung cancer risk, the evidence to date suggests this is a promising lead.[238] With regard to DNA repair activity, a number of genes have been considered: XPA, XPD, the x-ray repair complementation group 1 and 3 (XRCC1 and XRCC3) genes, the excision repair cross complementation group 1 (ERCC1) gene, and the hoGG1 gene. One of the most extensively studied DNA repair genes to date is the nucleotide excision repair gene XPD[274,275]; the evidence to date has not yet revealed a consistent pattern of associations for any specific polymorphism.

There are a variety of assays for susceptibility to DNA damage. Individuals with a less proficient DNA repair capacity phenotype as measured by a nonspecific mutagen sensitivity assay have been shown to have an increased risk of lung cancer in some studies.[276,277]

PRESENCE OF HUMAN IMMUNODEFICIENCY VIRUS

As human immunodeficiency virus (HIV)–positive patients maintain their immune function with highly active antiretroviral therapy and live longer, evidence has emerged to indicate that HIV-positive individuals have an increased risk of lung cancer, especially non–small cell lung cancer.[278-284] In the highly active antiretroviral therapy era, a greater than twofold increase in lung cancer risk has been observed among HIV-positive men and women.[283,284]

Some aspects of the occurrence of lung cancer in HIV-positive patients are similar to patterns seen in the general population. This includes a predominance of non–small cell lung cancer,[285,286] with adenocarcinoma and squamous cell carcinoma as the two most common cell types.[284,285,287] Additionally, the increased risk of lung cancer in HIV-positive patients applies to both men and women, so the fact that the preponderance of HIV-positive patients with lung cancer are males[285] may reflect the higher prevalence of HIV infection in men compared to women. An important distinction is that HIV-positive individuals are diagnosed with lung cancer at a median age of 45 years or less,[283,284] younger than the norm.

The specific reasons for the excess lung cancer risk in HIV-positive individuals are not known, but there are several potential explanations. The elevated lung cancer risk may have little to do with HIV infection and simply be due to HIV-positive individuals having a high-risk profile for lung cancer due to high prevalence of cigarette smoking.[285,288] Alternatively, HIV infection could be a factor contributing to lung carcinogenesis. If so, potential explanations for the increased lung cancer risk could include (1) HIV acting as a viral carcinogen, (2) defective immune surveillance, and (3) recurrent opportunistic infections and parenchymal lung inflammation leading to inflammatory foci and scar carcinomas. This remains an important area for investigation, as there is presently little evidence to address these hypotheses.

PRESENCE OF ACQUIRED LUNG DISEASE

In addition to hereditary factors, increased susceptibility to lung cancer may result from underlying lung disease. Such acquired lung diseases assume two major forms: (1) those that obstruct airflow, such as chronic obstructive pulmonary disease (COPD); and (2) fibrotic disorders that restrict lung capacity, such as pneumoconioses.[289] Associations between lung cancer and both types of acquired lung disease have been noted, but, as mentioned later, this topic is complex and many issues await resolution. These questions have been debated for over 60 years.[290]

A substantial body of evidence suggests that COPD or impaired lung function is associated with the occurrence of lung cancer.[291] Cigarette smoking is the principal cause of both COPD[292] and lung cancer, being so strongly causally associated with both of these illnesses that a presumption that statistical adjustment procedures "remove" the effect of cigarette smoking may not be well founded. Thus, clarifying the relevance of COPD to the development of lung cancer awaits further proof that this association is not accounted for by cigarette smoking. The presence of COPD may indicate that the affected individual has received a greater dose of tobacco carcinogens than the typical unaffected individual. Regardless of mechanism, the presence of COPD is a clinically useful risk indicator.

Clarifying the possible relationship between pneumoconioses and lung cancer poses particularly vexing challenges. Even for asbestos exposure, which is clearly established as a potent cause of lung cancer,[188] whether lung cancer results from asbestos per se or from asbestosis remains unresolved.[189] Asbestos is likely to cause lung cancer via multiple mechanistic pathways.[293,294] For other mineral fibers, the situation is murkier. For example, determining whether silica exposure or silicosis mediates the increased lung cancer risk in silica-exposed persons has proven difficult.[295,296] The presence of silicosis is associated with an increased risk of lung cancer.[176] Understanding the basis of this association will entail isolating the independent effects of silica exposure and lung fibrosis while controlling for exposure to smoking and other lung carcinogens.[190,297]

Such differences in the pattern of associations between pneumoconioses and lung cancer emphasize that "fibrosis" is not a homogeneous exposure, but one dependent upon the properties of the specific mineral fiber or other environmental agent. Properties of the agent, such as its size, shape, and durability, and the effects of other exposures such as cigarette smoking are important considerations in assessing its potential harmfulness.[293]

GENDER

The hypothesis has been advanced that women may have a greater risk of lung cancer than men at the same level of smoking.[298] There are several methodologic issues that have clouded the interpretation of the data on this issue,[299] but the results of studies that have compared the relative risk estimates for men and women for a specific degree of smoking history demonstrate very similar associations.[300]

SUMMARY

The path to preventing lung cancer is charted by the identification of numerous exposures causally associated with lung cancer. If steps can be taken to reduce or eliminate the population's exposure to these agents, this would be expected to reduce the population's risk of lung cancer. Preventive strategies can be pursued in the public policy arena or in public health interventions directed at individual behavior. Cigarette smoking provides a useful example to illustrate the multiple levels that can form the basis of preventive strategies. In the legislative/regulatory arena, examples of tobacco control strategies include legislation that limits cigarette advertising, that reduces children's access to cigarettes, and that prohibits smoking in the workplace. Litigation against cigarette manufacturers has also proven to be a productive component of tobacco control strategies, as exemplified by the settlement between the states and the tobacco industry. Behavioral interventions to prevent children and adolescents from starting to smoke cigarettes and behavioral/pharmacologic interventions to promote smoking cessation are individual-level approaches that, if successful, could be expected to reduce the occurrence of lung cancer.

In developing lung cancer prevention strategies, certain groups warrant particular attention. Steps need to be taken toward the goal of reducing the very high lung cancer incidence rates in African American men.[301] Lung cancer is also a major women's health issue. Due to historical cigarette smoking patterns, the epidemic of lung cancer started later in women than men, but, in contrast to the situation in men, lung cancer incidence rates in women are still increasing.[302] Though lung cancer remains a critical public health problem, the decrease in the overall lung cancer burden that is presently occurring in the United States, as in much of the developed world, reflects the successes of preventive strategies. A critical global priority is to prevent the uptake of cigarette smoking in developing countries where smoking prevalence is still low, in order to prevent the increase in morbidity and mortality from lung cancer that is certain to follow an increase in smoking prevalence.

A consideration of the epidemiology of lung cancer consistently reinforces one major theme: The pandemic of lung cancer is a consequence of the tragic and widespread addiction to cigarettes throughout the world. Curtailing the pandemic of lung cancer will require preventing youths from starting to smoke cigarettes and effectively promoting smoking cessation among addicted smokers.

REFERENCES

1. White C: Research on smoking and lung cancer: A landmark in the history of chronic disease epidemiology. Yale J Biol Med 63:29–46, 1990.
2. Wingo PA, Ries LA, Giovino GA, et al: Annual report to the nation on the status of cancer, 1973–1996, with a special section on lung cancer and tobacco smoking. J Natl Cancer Inst 91:675–690, 1999.
3. International Agency for Research on Cancer: Tobacco Smoke and Involuntary Smoking, IARC Monograph 83. Lyon, France: International Agency for Research on Cancer, 2004.
4. Office of the Surgeon General and Office on Smoking and Health: The Health Consequences of Active Smoking: A Report of the Surgeon General, May 2004. Atlanta: Centers for Disease Control and Prevention, 2004.
5. Samet JM: Epidemiology of Lung Cancer. New York: Marcel Dekker, 1994.
6. Rosen G: A History of Public Health (expanded ed). Baltimore, Md: The Johns Hopkins University Press, 1993.
7. Office of the Surgeon General and Office on Smoking and Health: Reducing the Health Consequences of Smoking: 25 Years of Progress. A Report of the Surgeon General: 1989 Executive Summary, DHHS Publication No. (CDC)89–8411. Rockville, Md: U.S. Department of Health and Human Services, 1989.
8. Proctor RN: Why did the Nazis have the world's most aggressive anti-cancer campaign? Endeavour 23:76–79, 1999.
9. Doll R, Hill AB: Smoking and carcinoma of the lung. Br Med J 2:739–748, 1950.
10. Levin ML, Goldstein H, Gerhardt PR: Cancer and tobacco smoking: A preliminary report. J Am Med Assoc 143:336–338, 1950.
11. Wynder EL, Graham EA: Tobacco smoking as a possible etiologic factor in bronchiogenic carcinoma: A study of six hundred and eighty-four proved cases. J Am Med Assoc 143:329–336, 1950.
12. Surgeon General's Advisory Committee on Smoking and Health: Smoking and Health: Report of the Advisory Committee to the Surgeon General, DHEW Publication No. (PHS)64–1103. Washington, DC: U.S. Department of Health, Education and Welfare, 1964.
13. Royal College of Physicians of London: Smoking and Health: Summary of a Report of the Royal College of Physicians of London on Smoking in Relation to Cancer of the Lung and Other Diseases. London: Pitman Medical Publishing, 1962, S2–S70.
14. U.S. Surgeon-General's Office and Office on Smoking and Health: The Health Consequences of Involuntary Smoking: A Report of the Surgeon General, DHHS Publication No. (CDC)87-8398. Rockville, Md: U.S. Department of Health and Human Services, 1986.
15. Office of Health and Environmental Assessment and Office of Air and Radiation: Respiratory Health Effects of Passive Smoking: Lung Cancer and Other Disorders, Publication No. EPA/600/6-90/006F. Washington, DC: U.S. Environmental Protection Agency, 1992.
16. Samet JM: Radon and lung cancer. J Natl Cancer Inst 81:745–757, 1989.
17. National Research Council, Committee on Health Risks of Exposure to Radon, Board on Radiation Effects Research, and Commission on Life Sciences: Health Effects of Exposure to Radon (BEIR VI). Washington, DC: National Academy Press, 1998.

18. Coultas DB, Samet JM: Occupational lung cancer. Clin Chest Med 13:341–354, 1992.

19. Wingo PA, Cardinez CJ, Landis SH, et al: Long-term trends in cancer mortality in the United States, 1930–1998. Cancer 97:3133–3275, 2003.

20. National Cancer Institute and National Center for Health Statistics: Surveillance, Epidemiology, and End Results (SEER) program. U.S. Mortality Data. Bethesda, Md: National Cancer Institute, 2003. Available at http://seer.cancer.gov/mortality

21. American Cancer Society: Cancer Facts and Figures. Atlanta: American Cancer Society, 1999.

22. Jemal A, Chu KC, Tarone RE: Recent trends in lung cancer mortality in the United States. J Natl Cancer Inst 93:277–283, 2001.

23. Shopland DR: Effect of smoking on the incidence and mortality of lung cancer. In Johnson BE, Johnson DH (eds): Lung Cancer. New York: Wiley-Liss, 1995, pp 1–14.

24. Mckay FW, Hanson MR, Miller RW: Cancer mortality in the United States: 1950–1977. Natl Cancer Inst Monogr 59:1–357, 1982.

25. Ries LAG, Miller BA, Hankey BF, et al: SEER Cancer Statistics Review: 1973–1991. Bethesda, Md: National Cancer Institute, 1995.

26. Horm JW, Cicero JB: SEER Program: Cancer Incidence and Mortality in the United States, 1973–1981, NIH Publication No. 85-1837. Bethesda, Md: U.S. Department of Health and Human Services, 1984.

27. National Cancer Institute: Surveillance, Epidemiology, and End Results (SEER) Program (SEER website). Bethesda, Md: National Cancer Institute, 2001.

28. Travis WD, Travis LB, Devesa SS: Lung cancer. Cancer 75(Suppl):191–202, 1995.

29. Office of the Surgeon General: Preventing Tobacco Use Among Young People: A Report of the Surgeon General. Washington, DC: U.S. Department of Health and Human Services, 1994.

30. Coleman MP, Esteve J, Damiecki P, et al: Trends in Cancer Incidence and Mortality. Lyon, France: International Agency for Research on Cancer, 1993.

31. Gilliland FD, Samet JM: Incidence and mortality for lung cancer: Geographic, histologic, and diagnostic trends. Cancer Surv 19:175–195, 1994.

32. Harras A, Page H, and the Cancer Statistics Branch: Cancer Rates and Risks (4th ed). Bethesda, Md: National Institutes of Health, 1996.

33. Parkin DM, Pisani P, Lopez AD, et al: At least one in seven cases of cancer is caused by smoking: Global estimates for 1995. Int J Cancer 59:494–504, 1994.

34. Parkin DM, Muir CS, Whelan SL, et al: Cancer Incidence in Five Continents, Vol II. Lyon, France: International Agency for Research on Cancer, 1992.

35. Gordon T, Crittenden M, Haenszel W: Cancer mortality trends in the United States, 1930–1955. Natl Cancer Inst Monogr 6:131–350, 1961.

36. Boffetta P, Parkin DM: Cancer in developing countries. CA Cancer J Clin 44:81–91, 1994.

37. Stocks P, Campbell JM: Lung cancer death rates among non-smokers and pipe and cigarette smokers: An evaluation in relation to air pollution by benzo[a]pyrene and other substances. Br Med J 2:923–929, 1955.

38. Blot WJ, Fraumeni JF Jr: Arsenical air pollution and lung cancer. Lancet 2:142–144, 1975.

39. Mason TJ, Mckay FW: U.S. Cancer Mortality by County: 1950–1969, DHEW Publication No. (NIH)74-615. Bethesda, Md: National Cancer Institute, 1973.

40. Blot WJ, Fraumeni JF: Cancer among shipyard workers. In Peto R, Schneiderman MA (eds): Banbury Report 9: Quantification of Occupational Cancer. Cold Spring Harbor, NY: Cold Spring Harbor Laboratory, 1981.

41. Blot WJ, Fraumeni JF Jr: Changing patterns of lung cancer in the United States. Am J Epidemiol 115:664–673, 1982.

42. Churg A: Lung cancer cell type and occupational exposure. In Samet JM (ed): Lung Biology in Health and Disease. Vol 74: Epidemiology of Lung Cancer. New York: Marcel Dekker, 1994, pp 413–436.

43. World Health Organization: Histological Typing of Lung Tumours. Geneva, World Health Organization, 1981.

44. World Health Organization: The World Health Organization histological typing of lung tumors. Am J Clin Pathol 77:123–129, 1982.

45. Travis WD, Colby TV, Corrin B, et al: World Health Organization International Histological Classification of Tumours. Histological Typing of Lung and Pleural Tumours (3rd ed). New York: Springer-Verlag, 1999.

46. Brambilla E, Travis WD, Colby TV, et al: The new World Health Organization classification of lung tumours. Eur Respir J 18:1059–1068, 2001.

47. Wu-Williams AH, Samet JM: Lung cancer and cigarette smoking. In Samet JM (ed): Lung Biology in Health and Disease. Vol 74: Epidemiology of Lung Cancer, chap 4. New York: Marcel Dekker, 1994, pp 71–108.

48. Wynder EL, Covey LS: Epidemiologic patterns in lung cancer by histologic type. Eur J Cancer Clin Oncol 23:1491–1496, 1987.

49. Wynder EL, Muscat JE: The changing epidemiology of smoking and lung cancer histology. Environ Health Perspect 103(Suppl 8):143–148, 1995.

50. Thun MJ, Day-Lally C, Myers DG, et al: Trends in tobacco smoking and mortality from cigarette use in Cancer Prevention Studies I (1959–1965) and II (1982–1988). In Shopland DR, Burns DM, Garfinkel L, Samet JM (eds): Smoking and Tobacco Control Monograph 8: Changes in Cigarette Related Disease Risks and Their Implication for Prevention and Control, NIH Publication No. 97-4213. Bethesda, Md: National Cancer Institute, 1997, pp 305–382.

51. Charloux A, Quoix E, Wolkove N, et al: The increasing incidence of lung adenocarcinoma: Reality or artefact? A review of the epidemiology of lung adenocarcinoma. Int J Epidemiol 26:14–23, 1997.

52. Thun MJ, Lally CA, Flannery JT, et al: Cigarette smoking and changes in the histopathology of lung cancer. J Natl Cancer Inst 89:1580–1586, 1997.

53. Vincent RG, Pickren JW, Lane WW, et al: The changing histopathology of lung cancer: A review of 1682 cases. Cancer 39:1647–1655, 1977.

54. Janssen-Heijnen ML, Coebergh JW: Trends in incidence and prognosis of the histological subtypes of lung cancer in North America, Australia, New Zealand and Europe. Lung Cancer 31:123–137, 2001.

55. Siesling S, van Dijck JA, Visser O, et al: Trends in incidence of and mortality from cancer in The Netherlands in the period 1989–1998. Eur J Cancer 39:2521–2530, 2003.

56. Morgan LC, Grayson D, Peters HE, et al: Lung cancer in New South Wales: Current trends and the influence of age and sex. Med J Aust 172:578–582, 2000.

57. Nguyen AM, Luke CG, Roder D: Time trends in lung cancer incidence by histology in South Australia: Likely causes and public health implications. Aust N Z J Public Health 27:596–601, 2003.

58. Levi F, Franceschi S, La Vecchia C, et al: Lung carcinoma trends by histologic type in Vaud and Neuchatel, Switzerland, 1974–1994. Cancer 79:906–914, 1997.

59. Makitaro R, Paakko P, Huhti E, et al: Prospective population-based study on the survival of patients with lung cancer. Eur Respir J 19:1087–1092, 2002.

60. Makitaro R, Paakko P, Huhti E, et al: An epidemiological study of lung cancer: History and histological types in a general population in northern Finland. Eur Respir J 13:436–440, 1999.

61. Russo A, Crosignani P, Franceschi S, et al: Changes in lung cancer histological types in Varese Cancer Registry, Italy 1976–1992. Eur J Cancer 33:1643–1647, 1997.

62. Morita T: A statistical study of lung cancer in the annual of pathological autopsy cases in Japan, from 1958 to 1997, with reference to time trends of lung cancer in the world. Jpn J Cancer Res 93:15–23, 2002.

63. Yoshimi I, Ohshima A, Ajiki W, et al: A comparison of trends in the incidence rate of lung cancer by histological type in the Osaka Cancer Registry, Japan and in the Surveillance, Epidemiology and End Results Program, USA. Jpn J Clin Oncol 33:98–104, 2003.

64. Sobue T, Ajiki W, Tsukuma H, et al: Trends of lung cancer incidence by histologic type: A population-based study in Osaka, Japan. Jpn J Cancer Res 90:6–15, 1999.

65. Perng DW, Perng RP, Kuo BI, et al: The variation of cell type distribution in lung cancer: A study of 10,910 cases at a medical center in Taiwan between 1970 and 1993. Jpn J Clin Oncol 26:229–233, 1996.

66. Harkness EF, Brewster DH, Kerr KM, et al: Changing trends in incidence of lung cancer by histologic type in Scotland. Int J Cancer 102:179–183, 2002.

67. Hoffmann D, Hoffmann I: The changing cigarette, 1950–1995. J Toxicol Environ Health 50:307–364, 1997.

68. Shopland DR and the National Cancer Institute: Smoking and Tobacco Control Monograph 7: The FTC Cigarette Test Method for Determining Tar, Nicotine, and Carbon Monoxide Yields of U.S. Cigarettes. Report of the NCI Expert Committee, NIH Publication No. 96-4028. Bethesda, Md: National Institutes of Health, 1996.

69. Hecht SS: Tobacco smoke carcinogens and lung cancer. J Natl Cancer Inst 91:1194–1210, 1999.

70. Henschke CI, McCauley DI, Yankelevitz DF, et al: Early Lung Cancer Action Project: A summary of the findings on baseline screening. Oncologist 6:147–152, 2001.

71. Swensen SJ, Jett JR, Hartman TE, et al: Lung cancer screening with CT: Mayo Clinic experience. Radiology 226:756–761, 2003.

72. Chapman AD, Kerr KM: The association between atypical adenomatous hyperplasia and primary lung cancer. Br J Cancer 83:632–636, 2000.

73. Nakahara R, Yokose T, Nagai K, et al: Atypical adenomatous hyperplasia of the lung: A clinicopathological study of 118 cases including cases with multiple atypical adenomatous hyperplasia. Thorax 56:302–305, 2001.

74. Ullmann R, Bongiovanni M, Halbwedl I, et al: Is high-grade adenomatous hyperplasia an early bronchioloalveolar adenocarcinoma? J Pathol 201:371–376, 2003.

75. Noguchi M, Morikawa A, Kawasaki M, et al: Small adenocarcinoma of the lung: Histologic characteristics and prognosis. Cancer 75:2844–2852, 1995.

76. Yang ZG, Sone S, Takashima S, et al: High-resolution CT analysis of small peripheral lung adenocarcinomas revealed on screening helical CT. AJR Am J Roentgenol 176:1399–1407, 2001.

77. Kodama K, Higashiyama M, Yokouchi H, et al: Prognostic value of ground-glass opacity found in small lung adenocarcinoma on high-resolution CT scanning. Lung Cancer 33:17–25, 2001.

78. Asamura H, Suzuki K, Watanabe S, et al: A clinicopathological study of resected subcentimeter lung cancers: A favorable prognosis for ground glass opacity lesions. Ann Thorac Surg 76:1016–1022, 2003.

79. Fujimoto N, Segawa Y, Takigawa N, et al: Clinical investigation of bronchioloalveolar carcinoma: A retrospective analysis of 53 patients in a single institution. Anticancer Res 19:1369–1373, 1999.

80. Suzuki K, Asamura H, Kusumoto M, et al: "Early" peripheral lung cancer: Prognostic significance of ground glass opacity on thin-section computed tomographic scan. Ann Thorac Surg 74:1635–1639, 2002.

81. Saracci R, Boffetta P: Interactions of tobacco smoking and other causes of lung cancer. In Samet JM (ed): Lung Biology in Health and Disease. Vol 74: Epidemiology of Lung Cancer. New York: Marcel Dekker, 1994, pp 465–493.

82. Samet JM, Cohen AJ: Air pollution and lung cancer. In Holgate ST, Samet JM, Koren HS, Maynard RL (eds): Air Pollution and Health. San Diego: Academic Press, 1999, pp 841–864.

83. Willett WC: Diet, nutrition, and avoidable cancer. Environ Health Perspect 103(Suppl 8):165–170, 1995.

84. Peto R, Lopez AD, Boreham J, et al: Mortality from smoking in developed countries 1950–2000: Indirect estimates from national vital statistics. Oxford: Oxford University Press, 1994.

85. Samet JM: Lung cancer. In Greenwald P, Kramer BS, Weed DL (eds): Basic Science and Clinical Oncology. Vol 6: Cancer Prevention and Control. New York: Marcel Dekker, 1995, pp 561–584.

86. Centers for Disease Control and Prevention: Cigarette smoking: Attributable mortality and years of potential life lost, United States, 1950–1990. MMWR Morb Mortal Wkly Rep 42:37–39, 1993.

87. Centers for Disease Control and Prevention: Annual smoking-attributable mortality, years of potential life lost, and economic costs—United States, 1995–1999. MMWR Morb Mortal Wkly Rep 51:300–303, 2002.

88. Yang G, Lixin F, Tan J, et al: Smoking in China: Findings of the 1996 National Prevalence Survey. JAMA 282:1247–1253, 1999.

89. National Institutes of Health and National Cancer Institute: Smoking and Tobacco Control Monograph 9: Cigars: Health Effects and Trends, NIH Publication No. 98-4302. Bethesda, Md: U.S. Department of Health and Human Services, 1998.

90. Boffetta P, Pershagen G, Jockel KH, et al: Cigar and pipe smoking and lung cancer risk: A multicenter study from Europe. J Natl Cancer Inst 91:697–701, 1999.

91. Doll R, Peto R: Cigarette smoking and bronchial carcinoma: Dose and time relationships among regular smokers and lifelong non-smokers. J Epidemiol Community Health 32:303–313, 1978.

92. Peto R: Influence of dose and duration of smoking on lung cancer rates. IARC Sci Publ 74:23–33, 1986.

93. Office of the Surgeon General and Office on Smoking and Health: Smoking and Health: A National Status Report, DHHS Publication No. (CDC)87-8396. Atlanta: Centers for Disease Control, 1987.

94. U.S. Office of the Surgeon General and U.S. Office of Smoking and Health: The Health Benefits of Smoking Cessation: A Report of the Surgeon General, DHHS Publication No. (CDC)90-8416. Rockville, Md: U.S. Department of Health and Human Services, 1990.

95. Hrubec Z, McLaughlin JK: Former cigarette smoking and mortality among U.S. veterans: A 26-year follow-up, 1954–1980. In Shopland DR, Burns DM, Garfinkel L, Samet JM (eds): Changes in Cigarette-Related Disease Risks and Their Implication for Prevention and Control,

NIH Publication No. 97-4213. Bethesda, Md: National Cancer Institute, 1997, pp 501–530.

96. Hoffmann D, Hoffmann I, El Bayoumy K: The less harmful cigarette: A controversial issue. A tribute to Ernst L. Wynder. Chem Res Toxicol 14:767–790, 2001.

97. Office of the Assistant Secretary for Health and Surgeon General and Office on Smoking and Health: The Health Consequences of Smoking—the Changing Cigarette. A Report of the Surgeon General. Rockville, Md: U.S. Department of Health and Human Services, 1981.

98. Burns DM (ed): Smoking and Tobacco Control Monograph 13: Risks Associated with Smoking Cigarettes with Low Machine-Measured Yields of Tar and Nicotine. Bethesda, Md: National Cancer Institute, 2001.

99. Coultas DB, Howard CA, Peake GT, et al: Discrepancies between self-reported and validated cigarette smoking in a community survey of New Mexico Hispanics. Am Rev Respir Dis 88:810–814, 1988.

100. Djordjevic MV, Stellman SD, Zang E: Doses of nicotine and lung carcinogens delivered to cigarette smokers. J Natl Cancer Inst 92:106–111, 2000.

101. Samet JM: The changing cigarette and disease risk: Current status of the evidence. In Shopland DR and the National Cancer Institute: Smoking and Tobacco Control Monograph 7: The FTC Cigarette Test Method for Determining Tar, Nicotine, and Carbon Monoxide Yields of U.S. Cigarettes. Report of the NCI Expert Committee, NIH Publication No. 96-4028. Bethesda, Md: National Cancer Institute, 1996, pp 77–92.

102. Bross IDJ, Gibson R: Risks of lung cancer in smokers who switch to filter cigarettes. Am J Public Health 58:1396–1403, 1968.

103. Wynder EL, Mabuchi K, Beattie EJ Jr: The epidemiology of lung cancer: Recent trends. JAMA 213:2221–2228, 1970.

104. Wynder EL, Stellman SD: Impact of long-term filter cigarette usage on lung and larynx cancer risk: A case-control study. J Natl Cancer Inst 62:471–477, 1979.

105. Wynder EL, Kabat GC: The effect of low-yield cigarette smoking on lung cancer risk. Cancer 62:1223–1230, 1988.

106. Lubin JH, Blot WJ, Berrino F, et al: Patterns of lung cancer risk according to type of cigarette smoked. Int J Cancer 33:569–576, 1984.

107. Pathak DR, Samet JM, Humble CG, et al: Determinants of lung cancer risk in cigarette smokers in New Mexico. J Natl Cancer Inst 76:597–604, 1986.

108. Jockel KH, Ahrens W, Wichmann HE, et al: Occupational and environmental hazards associated with lung cancer. Int J Epidemiol 21:202–213, 1992.

109. Hawthorne VM, Fry JS: Smoking and health: The association between smoking behaviour, total mortality, and cardiorespiratory disease in west central Scotland. J Epidemiol Community Health 32:260–266, 1978.

110. Rimington J: The effect of filters on the incidence of lung cancer in cigarette smokers. Environ Res 24:162–166, 1981.

111. Garfinkel L, Stellman SD: Smoking and lung cancer in women: Findings in a prospective study. Cancer Res 48:6951–6955, 1988.

112. Sidney S, Tekawa IS, Friedman GD: A prospective study of cigarette tar yield and lung cancer. Cancer Causes Control 4:3–10, 1993.

113. Stellman SD, Muscat JE, Thompson S, et al: Risk of squamous cell carcinoma and adenocarcinoma of the lung in relation to lifetime filter cigarette smoking. Cancer 80:382–388, 1997.

114. Matos E, Vilensky M, Boffetta P, et al: Lung cancer and smoking: A case-control study in Buenos Aires, Argentina. Lung Cancer 21:155–163, 1998.

115. Marugame T, Sobue T, Nakayama T, et al: Filter cigarette smoking and lung cancer risk: A hospital-based case-control study in Japan. Br J Cancer 90:646–651, 2004.

116. Tang JL, Morris JK, Wald NJ, et al: Mortality in relation to tar yield of cigarettes: A prospective study of four cohorts. BMJ 311:1530–1533, 1995.

117. Joly OG, Lubin JH, Caraballoso M: Dark tobacco and lung cancer in Cuba. J Natl Cancer Inst 70:1033–1039, 1983.

118. Wilcox HB, Schoenberg JB, Mason TJ, et al: Smoking and lung cancer: Risk as a function of cigarette tar content. Prev Med 17:263–272, 1988.

119. Kaufman DW, Palmer JR, Rosenberg L, et al: Tar content of cigarettes in relation to lung cancer. Am J Epidemiol 129:703–711, 1989.

120. Hammond EC, Garfinkel L, Seidman H, et al: "Tar" and nicotine content of cigarette smoke in relation to death rates. Environ Res 12:263–274, 1976.

121. Higenbottam T, Shipley MJ, Rose G: Cigarettes, lung cancer, and coronary heart disease: The effects of inhalation and tar yield. J Epidemiol Community Health 36:113–117, 1982.

122. Zang EA, Wynder EL: Cumulative tar exposure: A new index for estimating lung cancer risk among cigarette smokers. Cancer 92:69–76, 1992.

123. Speizer FE, Colditz GA, Hunter DJ, et al: Prospective study of smoking, antioxidant intake, and lung cancer in middle-aged women (USA). Cancer Causes Control 10:475–482, 1999.

124. Lee PN: Lung cancer and type of cigarette smoked. Inhal Toxicol 13:951–976, 2001.

125. Stellman SD, Garfinkel L: Lung cancer risk is proportional to cigarette tar yield: Evidence from a prospective study. Prev Med 18:518–525, 1989.

126. Harris JE, Thun MJ, Mondul AM, et al: Cigarette tar yields in relation to mortality from lung cancer in the Cancer Prevention Study II prospective cohort, 1982–8. BMJ 328:72, 2004.

127. Public Health Service and National Cancer Institute: Changes in cigarette-related disease risks and their implication for prevention and control. Monograph 8, NIH Publication No. 97-4213. Bethesda, Md: National Cancer Institute, 1997.

128. Thun MJ, Day-Lally CA, Calle EE, et al: Excess mortality among cigarette smokers: Changes in a 20-year interval. Am J Public Health 85:1223–1230, 1995.

129. Doll R, Peto R, Wheatley K, et al: Mortality in relation to smoking: 40 years' observations on male British doctors. BMJ 309:901–911, 1994.

130. Stratton K, Shetty P, Wallace R, et al (eds): Clearing the Smoke: Assessing the Science Base for Tobacco Harm Reduction. Washington, DC: National Academy Press, 2001.

131. Hirayama T: Non-smoking wives of heavy smokers have a higher risk of lung cancer: A study from Japan. Br Med J (Clin Res Ed) 282:183–185, 1981.

132. Trichopoulos D, Kalandidi A, Sparros L, et al: Lung cancer and passive smoking. Int J Cancer 27:1–4, 1981.

133. National Research Council and Committee on Passive Smoking: Environmental Tobacco Smoke: Measuring Exposures and Assessing Health Effects. Washington, DC: National Academy Press, 1986.

134. Fontham ETH, Correa P, Reynolds P, et al: Environmental tobacco smoke and lung cancer in nonsmoking women: A multicenter study. JAMA 271:1752–1759, 1994.

135. Boffetta P, Agudo A, Ahrens W, et al: Multicenter case-control study of exposure to environmental tobacco smoke and lung cancer in Europe. J Natl Cancer Inst 90:1440–1450, 1998.

136. Scientific Committee on Tobacco and Health and Her Majesty's Stationery Office: Report of the Scientific Committee on Tobacco and Health. London: Her Majesty's Stationery Office, 1998.

137. California Environmental Protection Agency: Proposed Identification of Environmental Tobacco Smoke as a Toxic Air Contaminant. Sacramento, Ca: California Environmental Protection Agency, 2003.

138. Law MR, Morris JK, Wald NJ: Environmental tobacco smoke exposure and ischaemic heart disease: An evaluation of the evidence. BMJ 315:973–980, 1997.

139. Hackshaw A: Passive smoking: Paper does not diminish conclusion of previous reports. BMJ 327:501–502, 2003.

140. Reynolds P: Epidemiologic evidence for workplace ETS as a risk factor for lung cancer among nonsmokers: Specific risk estimates. Environ Health Perspect 107:865–877, 1999.

141. Brown KG: Lung cancer and environmental tobacco smoke: Exposure-response relationships with application to occupational risk. Environ Health Perspect 107:885–890, 1999.

142. World Cancer Research Fund and American Institute for Cancer Research: Food, Nutrition, and the Prevention of Cancer: A Global Perspective. Washington, DC: American Institute for Cancer Research, 1997.

142a. Miller AB, Altenburg HP, Bueno-de-Mesquita B, et al: Fruits and vegetables and lung cancer: Findings from the European Prospective Investigation into Cancer and Nutrition. Int J Cancer 108:269–276, 2004.

143. Bond GG, Thompson FE, Cook RR: Dietary vitamin A and lung cancer: Results of a case-control study among chemical workers. Nutr Cancer 9:109–121, 1987.

144. Brennan P, Fortes C, Butler J, et al: A multicenter case-control study of diet and lung cancer among non-smokers. Cancer Causes Control 11:49–58, 2000.

145. Hu J, Mao Y, Dryer D, et al: Risk factors for lung cancer among Canadian women who have never smoked. Cancer Detect Prev 26:129–138, 2002.

146. Neuhouser ML, Patterson RE, Thornquist MD, et al: Fruits and vegetables are associated with lower lung cancer risk only in the placebo arm of the Beta-Carotene and Retinol Efficacy Trial (CARET). Cancer Epidemiol Biomarkers Prev 12:350–358, 2003.

147. Peto R, Doll R, Buckley JD, et al: Can dietary beta-carotene materially reduce human cancer rates? Nature 290:201–208, 1981.

148. De Stefani E, Brennan P, Boffetta P, et al: Diet and adenocarcinoma of the lung: A case-control study in Uruguay. Lung Cancer 35:43–51, 2002.

149. Knekt P, Jarvinen R, Teppo L, et al: Role of various carotenoids in lung cancer prevention. J Natl Cancer Inst 91:182–184, 1999.

150. Mannisto S, Smith-Warner SA, Spiegelman D, et al: Dietary carotenoids and risk of lung cancer in a pooled analysis of seven cohort studies. Cancer Epidemiol Biomarkers Prev 13:40–48, 2004.

151. Wright ME, Mayne ST, Stolzenberg-Solomon RZ, et al: Development of a comprehensive dietary antioxidant index and application to lung cancer risk in a cohort of male smokers. Am J Epidemiol 160:68–76, 2004.

152. Comstock GW, Alberg AJ, Huang HY, et al: The risk of developing lung cancer associated with antioxidants in the blood: Ascorbic acid, carotenoids, alpha-tocopherol, selenium, and total peroxyl radical absorbing capacity. Cancer Epidemiol Biomarkers Prev 6:907–916, 1997.

153. Yuan JM, Ross RK, Chu XD, et al: Prediagnostic levels of serum beta-cryptoxanthin and retinol predict smoking-related lung cancer risk in Shanghai, China. Cancer Epidemiol Biomarkers Prev 10:767–773, 2001.

154. Alpha-Tocopherol Beta-Carotene Cancer Prevention Study Group: The effect of vitamin E and beta-carotene on the incidence of lung cancer and other cancers in male smokers. N Engl J Med 330:1029–1035, 1994.

155. Omenn GS, Goodman GE, Thornquist MD, et al: Effects of a combination of beta-carotene and vitamin A on lung cancer and cardiovascular disease. N Engl J Med 334:1150–1155, 1996.

156. Hennekens CH, Buring JE, Manson JE, et al: Lack of effect of long-term supplementation with beta-carotene on the incidence of malignant neoplasms and cardiovascular disease. N Engl J Med 334:1145–1149, 1996.

157. Omenn GS, Goodman GE, Thornquist MD, et al: Risk factors for lung cancer and for intervention effects in CARET, the Beta-Carotene and Retinol Efficacy Trial. J Natl Cancer Inst 88:1550–1559, 1996.

158. Omenn GS: Chemoprevention of lung cancer: The rise and demise of beta-carotene. Annu Rev Public Health 19:73–99, 1998.

159. Korte JE, Brennan P, Henley SJ, et al: Dose-specific meta-analysis and sensitivity analysis of the relation between alcohol consumption and lung cancer risk. Am J Epidemiol 155:496–506, 2002.

160. Knekt P, Heliovaara M, Rissanen A, et al: Leanness and lung cancer risk. Int J Cancer 49:208–213, 1991.

161. Olson JE, Yang P, Schmitz K, et al: Differential association of body mass index and fat distribution with three major histologic types of lung cancer: Evidence from a cohort of older women. Am J Epidemiol 156:606–615, 2002.

162. Doll R, Peto R: The causes of cancer: Quantitative estimates of avoidable risks of cancer in the United States today. J Natl Cancer Inst 66:1191–1308, 1981.

163. Damber LA, Larsson LG: Occupation and male lung cancer: A case-control study in northern Sweden. Br J Ind Med 44:446–453, 1987.

164. Dave SK, Edling C, Jacobsson P, et al: Occupation, smoking, and lung cancer. Br J Ind Med 45:790–792, 1988.

165. Kvale G, Bjelke E, Heuch I: Occupational exposure and lung cancer risk. Int J Cancer 37:185–193, 1986.

166. Lerchen ML, Wiggins CL, Samet JM: Lung cancer and occupation in New Mexico. J Natl Cancer Inst 79:639–645, 1987.

167. Schoenberg JB, Stemhagen A, Mason TJ, et al: Occupation and lung cancer risk among New Jersey white males. J Natl Cancer Inst 79:13–21, 1987.

168. Vineis P, Thomas T, Hayes RB, et al: Proportion of lung cancers in males, due to occupation, in different areas of the USA. Int J Cancer 42:851–856, 1988.

169. Siemiatycki J: Risk Factors for Cancer in the Workplace. Boca Raton, Fla: CRC Press, 1991.

170. Samet JM, Lerchen ML: Proportion of lung cancer caused by occupation: A critical review. In Gee BJL, Keith W, Morgan C, Brooks SM (eds): Contemporary Issues in Pulmonary Disease. Vol 2: Occupational Lung Disease. New York: Churchill Livingstone, 1984, pp 55–67.

171. Doll R, Fisher REW, Gammon EJ, et al: Mortality of gas workers with special reference to cancers of the lung and bladder, chronic bronchitis, and pneumoconiosis. Br J Ind Med 22:1–12, 1965.

172. Lloyd JW: Long-term mortality of steelworkers. V. Respiratory cancer in coke plant workers. J Occup Med 13:53–68, 1971.

173. Lawther PJ, Commins BT, Waller RE: A study of the concentrations of polycyclic aromatic hydrocarbons in gas works retort houses. Br J Ind Med 22:13–20, 1965.

174. Alberg AJ, Yung R, Strickland PT, et al: Respiratory cancer and exposure to arsenic, chromium, nickel, and polycyclic aromatic hydrocarbons. Clin Occup Environ Med 2:779–801, 2002.

175. Cohen AJ, Higgins MWP: Health effects of diesel exhaust: Epidemiology. *In* Health Effects Institute, Diesel Working Group: Diesel Exhaust: A Critical Analysis of Emissions, Exposure, and Health Effects. A Special Report of the Institute's Diesel Working Group. Cambridge, Mass: Health Effects Institute, 1995, pp 251–292.

176. Smith AH, Lopipero PA, Barroga VR: Meta-analysis of studies of lung cancer among silicotics. Epidemiology 6:617–624, 1995.

177. Checkoway H, Franzblau A: Is silicosis required for silica-associated lung cancer? Am J Ind Med 37:252–259, 2000.

178. Hessel PA, Gamble JF, Gee JB, et al: Silica, silicosis, and lung cancer: A response to a recent working group report. J Occup Environ Med 42:704–720, 2000.

179. International Agency for Research on Cancer: IARC Monographs on the Evaluation of Carcinogenic Risks to Humans. Vol 68: Silica, Some Silicates, Coal Dust and Para-aramid Fibrils. Lyon, France: International Agency for Research on Cancer, 1997.

180. Health Effects Institute, Asbestos Research Committee, and Literature Review Panel: Asbestos in Public and Commercial Buildings: A Literature Review and a Synthesis of Current Knowledge. Cambridge, Mass: Health Effects Institute, 1991.

181. Wedler HW: Asbestosis and pulmonary carcinoma (Asbestose und lungenkrebs). Bull Hyg 19:362, 1944.

182. Lynch KM, Smith WA: Pulmonary asbestosis. V. A report of bronchial carcinoma and epithelial metaplasia. Am J Cancer 36:567–573, 1939.

183. Doll R: Mortality from lung cancer in asbestos workers. Br J Ind Med 12:81–86, 1955.

184. Selikoff IJ, Churg J, Hammond EC: Asbestos exposure and neoplasia. JAMA 188:22–26, 1964.

185. Selikoff IJ, Hammond EC, Seidman H: Mortality experience of insulation workers in the United States and Canada. Ann N Y Acad Sci 330:91–116, 1979.

186. Selikoff IJ: Latency of asbestos disease among insulation workers in the United States and Canada. Cancer 46:2736–2740, 1980.

187. Newhouse ML, Berry G: Patterns of mortality in asbestos factory workers in London. Ann N Y Acad Sci 330:53–60, 1979.

188. Lemen RA, Dement JM, Wagoner JK: Epidemiology of asbestos-related diseases. Environ Health Perspect 34:1–11, 1980.

189. Browne K: Is asbestos or asbestosis the cause of the increased risk of lung cancer in asbestos workers? Br J Ind Med 43:145–149, 1986.

190. Samet JM: Does idiopathic pulmonary fibrosis increase lung cancer risk? Am J Respir Crit Care Med 161:1–2, 2000.

191. Nelson HH, Kelsey KT: The molecular epidemiology of asbestos and tobacco in lung cancer. Oncogene 21:7284–7288, 2002.

192. Hammond EC, Selikoff IJ, Seidman H: Asbestos exposure, cigarette smoking and death rates. Ann N Y Acad Sci 330:473–490, 1979.

193. Churg A, Stevens B: Enhanced retention of asbestos fibers in the airways of human smokers. Am J Resp Crit Care Med 151:1409–1413, 1995.

194. Boice JD Jr: Studies of atomic bomb survivors: Understanding radiation effects. JAMA 264:622–623, 1990.

195. Brenner DJ, Doll R, Goodhead DT, et al: Cancer risks attributable to low doses of ionizing radiation: Assessing what we really know. Proc Natl Acad Sci U S A 100:13761–13766, 2003.

196. MacMahon B: Some recent issues in low-exposure radiation epidemiology. Environ Health Perspect 81:131–135, 1989.

197. Hendee WR: Estimation of radiation risks: BEIR V and its significance for medicine. JAMA 268:620–624, 1992.

198. National Research Council and Committee on the Biological Effects of Ionizing Radiation: Health Risks of Radon and Other Internally Deposited Alpha-Emitters: BEIR IV. Washington, DC: National Academy Press, 1988.

199. Lubin JH, Boice JD Jr, Edling C, et al: Lung cancer in radon-exposed miners and estimation of risk from indoor exposure. J Natl Cancer Inst 87:817–827, 1995.

200. U.S. Environmental Protection Agency: Technical Support Document for the 1992 Citizen's Guide to Radon. Washington, DC: U.S. Environmental Protection Agency, 1992.

201. Lubin JH, Boice JD Jr, Samet JM: Errors in exposure assessment, statistical power, and the interpretation of residential radon studies. Radiat Res 144:329–341, 1995.

202. Shimizu Y, Schull WJ, Kato H: Cancer risk among atomic bomb survivors. JAMA 264:601–604, 1990.

203. Darby SC, Doll R, Gill SK, et al: Long-term mortality after a single treatment course with X-rays in patients treated for ankylosing spondylitis. Br J Cancer 55:179–190, 1987.

204. Howe GR: Lung cancer mortality between 1950 and 1987 after exposure to fractionated moderate-dose-rate ionizing radiation in the Canadian Fluoroscopy Cohort Study and a comparison with mortality in Atomic Bomb Survivors Study. Radiat Res 142:295–304, 1995.

205. Gilbert ES, Cragle DL, Wiggs LD: Updated analyses of combined mortality data for workers at the Hanford Site, Oak Ridge National Laboratory, and Rocky Flats Weapons Plant. Radiat Res 136:408–421, 1993.

206. National Research Council, Commission on Life Sciences, Board on Toxicology and Environmental Health Hazards, and Committee on the Epidemiology of Air Pollutants: Epidemiology and Air Pollution. Washington, DC: National Academy Press, 1985.

207. Friberg L, Cederlof R: Late effects of air pollution with special reference to lung cancer. Environ Health Perspect 22:45–66, 1978.

208. Doll R: Atmospheric pollution and lung cancer. Environ Health Perspect 22:23–31, 1978.

209. Pershagen G: Air pollution and cancer. *In* Vainio H, Sorsa M, McMichael AJ (eds): Complex Mixtures and Cancer Risk. Lyon, France: International Agency for Research on Cancer, 1990, pp 240–251.

210. Nasca PC, Burnett WS, Greenwald P, et al: Population density as an indicator of urban-rural differences in cancer incidence, upstate New York, 1968–1972. Am J Epidemiol 112:362–375, 1980.

211. Shannon HS, Hertzman C, Julian JA, et al: Lung cancer and air pollution in an industrial city—a geographical analysis. Can J Public Health 79:255–259, 1988.

212. Speizer FE, Samet JM: Air pollution and lung cancer. *In* Samet JM (ed): Lung Biology in Health and Disease. Vol 74: Epidemiology of Lung Cancer. New York: 1994, pp 131–150.

213. Dockery DW, Pope CA III, Xu X, et al: An association between air pollution and mortality in six U.S. cities. N Engl J Med 329:1753–1759, 1993.

214. Pope CA III, Thun MJ, Namboodiri MM, et al: Particulate air pollution as a predictor of mortality in a prospective study of U.S. adults. Am J Respir Crit Care Med 151:669–674, 1995.

215. Speizer FE: Assessment of the epidemiological data relating lung cancer to air pollution. Environ Health Perspect 47:33–42, 1983.

216. Pope CA III, Burnett RT, Thun MJ, et al: Lung cancer, cardiopulmonary mortality, and long-term exposure to fine particulate air pollution. JAMA 287:1132–1141, 2002.

217. Barbone F, Bovenzi M, Cavalleri F, et al: Air pollution and lung cancer in Trieste, Italy. Am J Epidemiol 141:1161–1169, 1995.

218. Jedrychowski W, Becher H, Wahrendorf J, et al: A case-control study of lung cancer with special reference to the effect of air pollution in Poland. J Epidemiol Community Health 44:114–120, 1990.

219. Kalandidi A, Katsouyanni K, Voropoulou N, et al: Passive smoking and diet in the etiology of lung cancer among non-smokers. Cancer Cause Cont 1:15–21, 1990.

220. Samet JM, Humble CG, Skipper BE, et al: History of residence and lung cancer risk in New Mexico. Am J Epidemiol 125:800–811, 1987.

221. Pershagen G: Lung cancer mortality among men living near an arsenic-emitting smelter. Am J Epidemiol 122:684–694, 1985.

222. Xu Z-Y, Blot WJ, Xiao HP, et al: Smoking, air pollution and the high rates of lung cancer in Shenyang, China. J Natl Cancer Inst 81:1800–1806, 1989.

223. Greaves WW, Rom WN, Lyon JL, et al: Relationship between lung cancer and distance of residence from nonferrous smelter stack effluent. Am J Ind Med 2:15–23, 1981.

224. Rom WN, Varley G, Lyon JL, et al: Lung cancer mortality among residents living near the El Paso smelter. Br J Ind Med 39:269–272, 1982.

225. Spengler JD: Sources and concentrations of indoor air pollution. *In* Samet JM, Spengler JD (eds): Indoor Air Pollution: A Health Perspective. Baltimore: Johns Hopkins University Press, 1991, pp 33–67.

226. Harrje DT: Building dynamics and indoor air quality. *In* Samet JM, Spengler JD (eds): Indoor Air Pollution: A Health Perspective. Baltimore: Johns Hopkins University Press, 1991, pp 68–81.

227. Chen BH, Hong CJ, Pandey MR, et al: Indoor air pollution in developing countries. World Health Stat Q 43:127–138, 1990.

228. Mumford JL, He XZ, Chapman RS, et al: Lung cancer and indoor air pollution in Xuan Wei, China. Science 235:217–220, 1987.

229. Mumford JL, Helmes CT, Lee XM, et al: Mouse skin tumorigenicity studies of indoor coal and wood combustion emissions from homes of residents in Xuan Wei, China with high lung cancer mortality. Carcinogenesis 11:397–403, 1990.

230. Wu-Williams AH, Dai XD, Blot W, et al: Lung cancer among women in northeast China. Br J Cancer 62:982–987, 1990.

231. Ger L-P, Hsu W-L, Chen K-T, et al: Risk factors of lung cancer by histological category in Taiwan. Anticancer Res 13:1491–1500, 1993.

232. Gao YT, Blot WJ, Zheng W, et al: Lung cancer among Chinese women. Int J Cancer 40:604–609, 1987.

233. Lan Q, Chapman RS, Schreinemachers DM, et al: Household stove improvement and risk of lung cancer in Xuanwei, China. J Natl Cancer Inst 94:826–835, 2002.

234. Wu AH, Henderson BE, Pike MC, et al: Smoking and other risk factors for lung cancer in women. J Natl Cancer Inst 74:747–751, 1985.

235. Vineis P, Caporaso N: Tobacco and cancer: Epidemiology and the laboratory. Environ Health Perspect 103:156–160, 1995.

236. Economou P, Lechner JF, Samet JM: Familial and genetic factors in the pathogenesis of lung cancer. *In* Samet JM (ed): Lung Biology in Health and Disease. Vol 74: Epidemiology of Lung Cancer. New York: 1994, pp 353–396.

237. Shields PG: Molecular epidemiology of smoking and lung cancer. Oncogene 21:6870–6876, 2002.

238. Spitz MR, Wei Q, Dong Q, et al: Genetic susceptibility to lung cancer: The role of DNA damage and repair. Cancer Epidemiol Biomarkers Prev 12:689–698, 2003.

239. Tokuhata GK, Lilienfeld AM: Familial aggregation of lung cancer among hospital patients. Public Health Rep 78:277–283, 1963.

240. Tokuhata GK: Familial factors in human lung cancer and smoking. Am J Public Health 54:24–32, 1964.

241. Ooi WL, Elston RC, Chen VW, et al: Increased familial risk for lung cancer. J Natl Cancer Inst 76:217–222, 1986.

242. Samet JM, Humble CG, Pathak DR: Personal and family history of respiratory disease and lung cancer risk. Am Rev Respir Dis 134:466–470, 1986.

243. Tsugane S, Watanabe S, Sugimura H, et al: Smoking, occupation and family history in lung cancer patients under fifty years of age. Jpn J Clin Oncol 17:309–317, 1987.

244. Horwitz RI, Smaldone LF, Viscoli CM: An ecogenetic hypothesis for lung cancer in women. Arch Intern Med 148:2609–2612, 1988.

245. McDuffie HH: Clustering of cancer in families of patients with primary lung cancer. J Clin Epidemiol 44:69–76, 1991.

246. Osann KE: Lung cancer in women: The importance of smoking, family history of cancer, and medical history of respiratory disease. Cancer Res 51:4893–4897, 1991.

247. Shaw GL, Falk RT, Pickle LW, et al: Lung cancer risk associated with cancer in relatives. J Clin Epidemiol 44:429–437, 1991.

248. Filho YW, Magaldi C, Nakao N, et al: Industrial work and lung cancer (in Spanish). Rev Saude Publica 29:166–176, 1995.

249. Schwartz AG, Yang P, Swanson GM: Familial risk of lung cancer among nonsmokers and their relatives. Am J Epidemiol 144:554–562, 1996.

250. Wu AH, Fontham ET, Reynolds P, et al: Family history of cancer and risk of lung cancer among lifetime nonsmoking women in the United States. Am J Epidemiol 143:535–542, 1996.

251. Sellers TA, Bailey-Wilson JE, Elston RC, et al: Evidence for mendelian inheritance in the pathogenesis of lung cancer. J Natl Cancer Inst 82:1272–1279, 1990.

252. Braun MM, Caporaso NE, Page WF, et al: Genetic component of lung cancer: Cohort study of twins. Lancet 344:440–443, 1994.

253. Yang P, Schwartz AG, McAllister AE, et al: Lung cancer risk in families of nonsmoking probands: Heterogeneity by age at diagnosis. Genet Epidemiol 17:253–273, 1999.

254. Jones PA, Baylin SB: The fundamental role of epigenetic events in cancer. Nat Rev Genet 3:415–428, 2002.

255. Herman JG, Baylin SB: Gene silencing in cancer in association with promoter hypermethylation. N Engl J Med 349:2042–2054, 2003.

256. Belinsky SA, Nikula KJ, Palmisano WA, et al: Aberrant methylation of $p16^{ink4a}$ is an early event in lunch cancer and a potential biomarker for early diagnosis. Proc Natl Acad Sci 95:11891–11896, 1998.

257. Palmisano WA, Divine KK, Saccomanno G, et al: Predicting lung cancer by detecting aberrant promoter methylation in sputum. Cancer Res 60:5954–5958, 2000.

258. Hussain SP, Harris CC: Molecular epidemiology of human cancer: Contribution of mutation spectra studies of tumor suppressor genes. Cancer Res 58:4023–4037, 1998.

259. International Agency for Research on Cancer: IARC Monographs on the Evaluation of the Carcinogenic Risk of Chemicals to Humans: Tobacco Smoking (Monograph 38). Lyon, France: International Agency for Research on Cancer, 1986.

206. Bergen AW, Caporaso N: Cigarette smoking. J Natl Cancer Inst 91:1365–1375, 1999.

261. Berwick M, Vineis P: Markers of DNA repair and susceptibility to cancer in humans: An epidemiologic review. J Natl Cancer Inst 92:874–897, 2000.

262. Robles AI, Linke SP, Harris CC: The p53 network in lung carcinogenesis. Oncogene 21:6898–6907, 2002.

263. Garte S, Zocchetti C, Taioli E: Gene–environment interactions in the application of biomarkers of cancer susceptibility in epidemiology. IARC Sci Publ 142:251–264, 1997.

264. Vineis P, Veglia F, Benhamou S, et al: CYP1A1 T3801 C polymorphism and lung cancer: A pooled analysis of 2451 cases and 3358 controls. Int J Cancer 104:650–657, 2003.

265. Le Marchand L, Guo C, Benhamou S, et al: Pooled analysis of the CYP1A1 exon 7 polymorphism and lung cancer (United States). Cancer Causes Control 14:339–346, 2003.

266. Amos CI, Caporaso NE, Weston A: Host factors in lung cancer risk: A review of interdisciplinary studies. Cancer Epidemiol Biomarkers Prev 1:505–513, 1992.

267. Shaw GL, Falk RT, Deslauriers J, et al: Debrisoquine metabolism and lung cancer risk. Cancer Epidemiol Biomarkers Prev 4:41–48, 1995.

268. Christensen PM, Gotzsche PC, Brosen K: The sparteine/debrisoquine (CYP2D6) oxidation polymorphism and the risk of lung cancer: A meta-analysis. Eur J Clin Pharmacol 51:389–393, 1997.

269. Rostami-Hodjegan A, Lennard MS, Woods HF, et al: Meta-analysis of studies of the CYP2D6 polymorphism in relation to lung cancer and Parkinson's disease. Pharmacogenetics 8:227–238, 1998.

270. Benhamou S, Lee WJ, Alexandrie AK, et al: Meta- and pooled analyses of the effects of glutathione S-transferase M1 polymorphisms and smoking on lung cancer risk. Carcinogenesis 23:1343–1350, 2002.

271. Hung RJ, Boffetta P, Brockmoller J, et al: CYP1A1 and GSTM1 genetic polymorphisms and lung cancer risk in Caucasian non-smokers: A pooled analysis. Carcinogenesis 24:875–882, 2003.

272. Denissenko MF, Pao A, Tang M, et al: Preferential formation of benzo[a]pyrene adducts at lung cancer mutational hotspots in P53. Science 274:430–432, 1996.

273. Goode EL, Ulrich CM, Potter JD: Polymorphisms in DNA repair genes and associations with cancer risk. Cancer Epidemiol Biomarkers Prev 11:1513–1530, 2002.

274. Gao WM, Romkes M, Day RD, et al: Association of the DNA repair gene XPD Asp312Asn polymorphism with p53 gene mutations in tobacco-related non-small cell lung cancer. Carcinogenesis 24:1671–1676, 2003.

275. Liang G, Xing D, Miao X, et al: Sequence variations in the DNA repair gene XPD and risk of lung cancer in a Chinese population. Int J Cancer 105:669–673, 2003.

276. Wei Q, Cheng L, Amos CI, et al: Repair of tobacco carcinogen-induced DNA adducts and lung cancer risk: A molecular epidemiologic study. J Natl Cancer Inst 92:1764–1772, 2000.

277. Zheng YL, Loffredo CA, Yu Z, et al: Bleomycin-induced chromosome breaks as a risk marker for lung cancer: A case-control study with population and hospital controls. Carcinogenesis 24:269–274, 2003.

278. Gabutti G, Vercelli M, De Rosa MG, et al: AIDS related neoplasms in Genoa, Italy. Eur J Epidemiol 11:609–614, 1995.

279. Johnson CC, Wilcosky T, Kvale P, et al: Cancer incidence among an HIV-infected cohort. Pulmonary Complications of HIV Infection Study Group. Am J Epidemiol 146:470–475, 1997.

280. Frisch M, Biggar RJ, Engels EA, et al: Association of cancer with AIDS-related immunosuppression in adults. JAMA 285:1736–1745, 2001.

281. Phelps RM, Smith DK, Heilig CM, et al: Cancer incidence in women with or at risk for HIV. Int J Cancer 94:753–757, 2001.

282. Herida M, Mary-Krause M, Kaphan R, et al: Incidence of non-AIDS-defining cancers before and during the highly active antiretroviral therapy era in a cohort of human immunodeficiency virus-infected patients. J Clin Oncol 21:3447–3453, 2003.

283. Bower M, Powles T, Nelson M, et al: HIV-related lung cancer in the era of highly active antiretroviral therapy. AIDS 17:371–375, 2003.

284. Powles T, Thirwell C, Newsom-Davis T, et al: Does HIV adversely influence the outcome in advanced non-small-cell lung cancer in the era of HAART? Br J Cancer 89:457–459, 2003.

285. Spina M, Sandri S, Serraino D, et al: Therapy of non-small-cell lung cancer (NSCLC) in patients with HIV infection. GICAT. Cooperative Group on AIDS and Tumors. Ann Oncol 10(Suppl 5):S87–S90, 1999.

286. Vyzula R, Remick SC: Lung cancer in patients with HIV-infection. Lung Cancer 15:325–339, 1996.

287. Tirelli U, Spina M, Sandri S, et al: Lung carcinoma in 36 patients with human immunodeficiency virus infection. The Italian Cooperative Group on AIDS and Tumors. Cancer 88:563–569, 2000.

288. Parker MS, Leveno DM, Campbell TJ, et al: AIDS-related bronchogenic carcinoma: Fact or fiction? Chest 113:154–161, 1998.

289. Cotran RS, Kumar V, Robbins SL: Robbins Pathologic Basis of Disease (5th ed). Philadelphia: WB Saunders, 1994.

290. Macklin MT, Macklin CC: Does chronic irritation cause primary carcinoma of the human lung? Arch Pathol 30:924–955, 1940.

291. Tockman MS: Other host factors and lung cancer susceptibility. In Samet JM (ed): Lung Biology in Health and Disease. Vol 74: Epidemiology of Lung Cancer. New York: 1994, pp 397–412.

292. Office of the Surgeon General and Office on Smoking and Health: The Health Consequences of Smoking—Chronic Obstructive Lung Disease: A Report of the Surgeon General. Rockville, Md: U.S. Department of Health and Human Services, 1984.

293. Barrett JC, Lamb PW, Wiseman RW: Multiple mechanisms for the carcinogenic effects of asbestos and other mineral fibers. Environ Health Perspect 81:81–89, 1989.

294. Rom WN, Travis WD, Brody AR: Cellular and molecular basis of the asbestos-related diseases. Am Rev Respir Dis 143:408–422, 1991.

295. Ng TP: Silica and lung cancer: A continuing controversy. Ann Acad Med Singapore 23:752–755, 1994.

296. Pairon JC, Brochard P, Jaurand MC, et al: Silica and lung cancer: A controversial issue. Eur Respir J 4:730–744, 1991.

297. Heppleston AG: Silica, pneumoconiosis, and carcinoma of the lung. Am J Ind Med 7:285–294, 1985.

298. Henschke CI, Miettinen OS: Women's susceptibility to tobacco carcinogens. Lung Cancer 43:1–5, 2004.

299. Perneger TV: Sex, smoking, and cancer: A reappraisal. J Natl Cancer Inst 93:1600–1602, 2001.
300. Kreuzer M, Boffetta P, Whitley E, et al: Gender differences in lung cancer risk by smoking: A multicentre case-control study in Germany and Italy. Br J Cancer 82:227–233, 2000.
301. Office of the Surgeon General: Tobacco Use among U.S. Racial/Ethnic Minority Groups: African Americans, American Indians and Alaska Natives, Asian Americans and Pacific Islanders, Hispanics: A Report of the Surgeon General. Atlanta: Centers for Disease Control, 1998.
302. Ernster VL: Impact of tobacco on women's health. *In* Samet JM, Yoon S-Y (eds): Women and the Tobacco Epidemic: Challenges for the 21st Century. Geneva: World Health Organization, 2001, pp 1–16.
303. Wilcox HB, Schoenberg JB, Mason TJ, et al: Smoking and lung cancer: Risk as a function of cigarette tar content. Prev Med 17:263–272, 1988.

44 Bronchogenic Carcinoma

Gerard A. Silvestri, M.D., F.C.C.P., James Jett, M.D.

INTRODUCTION

Lung cancer is the most common cause of cancer deaths worldwide. In the United States, lung cancer accounted for an estimated 169,400 of the 1.2 million cases of cancer and 154,900 of 555,500 cancer deaths in 2002. Although Chapter 43 is dedicated to the epidemiology of lung cancer, some of the information found therein is worth repeating. For example, added together, the number of cancer deaths from breast, colon, and prostate cancer each year would not equal the number of cancer deaths related or due to lung cancer. A common misconception among the general public is that breast cancer accounts for more cancer deaths in women. However, lung cancer will account for 25% of cancer-related deaths among women in the United States. A total of 65,700 women were expected to die from this disease in 2002. Particularly alarming is the fact that young women are the fastest rising demographic of new cigarette smokers in the United States. Many have clearly made the association between weight control and cigarette smoking. This will have effects on the prevalence of lung cancer in the decades to come.

One of the more disturbing trends in lung cancer is the explosion in rates of lung cancer in countries of the developing world. In 1985, it was estimated that there were 921,000 lung cancer deaths worldwide—an increase of 17% from 1980.[1] The International Agency for Research on Cancer in France found that the rates of lung cancer in Africa in the early 1990s were similar to those in the United States in the 1930s, at about 5 per 100,000.[2,3] By 1999, the rate of lung cancer in males of developing countries was 14 per 100,000 and on the rise, as compared to a rate of 71 per 100,000 in developed countries, which continues to decline. These rates may actually be underestimates of the true rates of lung cancer, because many cases may go undiagnosed or underreported in areas where health care is not readily available.[1] An example of how serious this problem has become is found in China, where it is estimated that nearly 800,000 Chinese men died of lung cancer in 1998.[1] At present, Chinese men smoke an average of 11 cigarettes per day, which is equivalent to the highest average rates of smoking ever seen among males in the United States. In fact, the consumption of cigarettes in China alone may surpass that of all developed countries combined.[1,4] Overall, 66.9% of Chinese men smoke. In view of such statistics, it is imperative that the medical community devotes much of its educational efforts and resources toward the elimination of cigarette smoking worldwide, which would nearly eliminate the development of lung cancer.

This chapter reviews the current strategies for the diagnosis, staging, and treatment of lung cancer. As much as possible, evidence-based review of the best currently available literature has been included. A special extended section on computed tomography (CT) screening for lung cancer is presented because the question of whether or not to screen for lung cancer on a routine basis will be one that pulmonologists will face for years to come. The reader will also come to value the role of the pulmonologist in every aspect of lung cancer care, from diagnosis to staging to caring for the complications of the disease itself and the complications of cancer treatment.

SCREENING FOR LUNG CANCER

The current position of the American Cancer Society and the U.S. Preventive Services Task Force is that there is no role for screening for lung cancer, even in high-risk individuals.[5] This position is based on the results of five randomized controlled trials that suggest that neither chest radiography nor sputum cytology satisfies the primary criterion of a beneficial screening test: reduction in lung cancer mortality.[6–8] There continues to be ongoing debate about the interpretation of these studies. One deficiency is that most of these studies did not include a "no screening" arm. Others have argued that the sample size of the studies was inadequate. The Mayo Lung Project and the Czechoslovakian studies were powered to detect a 50% reduction in lung cancer mortality in the screened group and could have missed detecting a 20% to 30% reduction.[8,9] An ongoing trial sponsored by the National Cancer Institute (Prostate, Lung, Colorectal and Ovarian Trial) is a randomized trial of chest radiography versus no screen in a low-risk population of both genders. It is powered to detect a 10% reduction in mortality due to lung cancer. Accrual to this study has been completed, but the final results will not be available for several years.

CT has been shown to be much more sensitive for detecting pulmonary nodules than the standard chest radiograph. As of 2003, there have been at least six reports of single-arm screening trials utilizing low-dose spiral CT (LD-CT), defined as a single breath-hold scan that exposes the patient to five to six times less radiation dose than a standard CT scan, with or without sputum cytology.[8,10–15] These trials have consistently shown that spiral CT detects more lung cancers than chest radiography. The study by Sone and colleagues from Japan detected 44 lung cancers with spiral CT, only 11 of which were visible by chest radiography.[11] Similarly, the New York study detected 27 lung cancers with CT, only 7 of which were visible on chest radiograph.[10] The LD-CT studies have consistently shown a high prevalence of noncalcified nodules. In general, it appears that the thinner the CT slices, the more noncalcified nodules are detected. A study from Germany with 5-mm slices detected at least one noncalcified nodule in 43% of 817 participants screened,[14] and a report from Mayo Clinic investigators observed noncalcified nodules in 51% of individuals with 5-mm slices and 3.75-mm reconstruction intervals.[13] The number of noncalcified nodules detected is increasing as centers begin to use 8- and 16-multislice detector scanners and decreasing slice thickness. In the Mayo Clinic trial, only 1.7% of the noncalcified nodules were subsequently shown to be malignant. However, all must be followed up with CT at some interval (at least yearly), which adds to the cost of screening. Studies are underway to try to determine the optimum follow-up and evaluation algorithm.

The LD-CT trials have consistently detected non–small cell lung cancer (NSCLC) as stage IA in 60% to 90% of cases, and early survival data from Japan suggest a major improvement in 5-year survival.[12] However, it is not possi-

ble to determine if this is due to lead-time bias, length-time bias, or overdiagnosis (defined as diagnosis of a cancer that would not lead to an individual's death).[16] None of the trials reported to date has had a control arm for comparison. Accordingly, it is not possible to determine if screening with LD-CT has led to a reduction in lung cancer mortality. A reduction in mortality due to NSCLC is the primary end point of the National Lung Cancer Screening Trial (NLST). This trial will randomize 50,000 high-risk participants to screening with LD-CT or chest radiography. Subjects will be screened yearly for 3 years and followed up for another 5 years. The trial is powered to detect a 20% reduction in lung cancer mortality. The NLST completed accrual in early 2004, but final results may not be available for 5 to 7 years. Until the result of the NLST is known, the American College of Chest Physician guidelines recommend that individuals should be screened with LD-CT in the context of well-designed clinical trials. They recommend against the use of single LD-CT or serial LD-CT to screen for lung cancer in individuals without symptoms or a history of cancer.[17]

PRESENTATION

Unfortunately, the symptoms of lung cancer can be nonspecific, thereby delaying the diagnoses for patients who present with this disease and leading to an advanced stage at the time of diagnosis. Approximately 40% of patients in a screened population and 98% of patients in a hospitalized population will present with symptoms.[9,18] Table 44.1 displays some of the common symptoms associated with the presentation of lung cancer. Most are nonspecific; however, some clues can be gained from the history, thus raising the clinician's suspicion that lung cancer is present. Although many smokers cough, lung cancer patients usually admit to a change in the character of their cough. The cough can increase in frequency or strength or may not be relieved with local measures. Chest pain can be present in 25% to 50% of patients at the time of presentation for evaluation for lung cancer.[18,19] The pain is generally dull in nature, tends to be persistent, remains in the same location, and is not relieved with local measures. Chest pain is usually related to involvement of the pleura but can be related to

Table 44.1 Presenting Symptoms with Bronchogenic Carcinoma

Symptoms	Percentage of Patients
Cough	45–75%
Weight loss	8–68%
Dyspnea	37–58%
Hemoptysis	27–57%
Chest pain	27–49%
Hoarseness	2–18%

From Midthun DE, Jett JR: Clinical presentation of lung cancer. In Pass HI, Mitchell JB, Johnson DH, et al (eds): Lung Cancer: Principles and Practice. Philadelphia: Lippincott–Raven, 1996, p 422.

extension into the mediastinum or chest wall. Chest pain in and of itself does not preclude the patient from consideration for surgery with curative intent. Dyspnea is frequently a complaint of patients who present with bronchogenic carcinoma, occurring in half of all new patients at presentation.[18] A partial list of the reasons for dyspnea related to lung cancer includes pulmonary embolism, superior vena cava syndrome, deconditioning, reactive airway disease, endobronchial obstruction with tumor, prior obstructive pneumonia, hemoptysis, hemorrhage, malignant pleural effusion, and extrinsic compression of the airway by tumor.

Hemoptysis in a smoker should always raise the suspicion of lung cancer. Hemoptysis can present as blood streaking of the sputum and can occur over a lengthy period of time before presentation to the physician's office because it is attributed to smoking-related bronchitis. The clinician should not be led astray if the chest radiograph is normal, because up to 5% of those with a smoking history and a normal radiograph can harbor lung cancer.[20] Because of the vascular nature of lung cancer, patients can also present with massive hemoptysis. In one series of patients with massive hemoptysis, 20% had an underlying diagnosis of lung cancer. Of those with lung cancer, 50% died from their hemoptysis, whereas of those with noncancerous causes, only 25% died of hemoptysis. Weight loss, a nonspecific symptom, in the right clinical setting should raise the suspicion of both lung cancer and metastatic disease. Weight loss alone has been correlated with an advanced presentation and poor outcome from lung cancer.

In summary, patients with lung cancer can present asymptomatically or with relatively nonspecific symptoms of underlying pulmonary disease. There are often clues in the history that should alert the clinician that lung cancer is a possibility and further investigation is warranted.

LUNG CANCER STAGING

Perhaps the most critical role of the pulmonologist in the management of lung cancer is in the diagnostic and staging evaluation of the patient. Accurately staging patients with newly diagnosed lung cancer is critical because staging dictates the patient's treatment options and predicts survival. It is intuitive that early-stage disease has a much better survival than late-stage disease. What may not be so obvious is that simple staging procedures are available to the diagnostician that can help accurately stage patients. The treatment options for lung cancer have now evolved so that treatment for patients in different stages is vastly different. For example, early-stage lung cancer (stage I and II) is a surgical disease. Locally advanced lung cancer (stage IIIA and B) is treated with a combination of chemotherapy and radiotherapy, whereas stage IV (metastatic disease) is treated with chemotherapy alone. However, there are important exceptions to these general rules that are discussed later in this chapter.

The staging of NSCLC using the tumor-node-metastasis (TNM) classification underwent revision in 1997.[21] Table 44.2 presents the revised TNM descriptors. Figure 44.1

Table 44.2 Tumor-Node-Metastasis (TNM) Descriptors

Primary Tumor (T)

TX	Primary tumor cannot be assessed, or tumor proven by the presence of malignant cells in sputum or bronchial washings but not visualized by imaging or bronchoscopy
T0	No evidence of primary tumor
Tis	Carcinoma in situ
T1	Tumor < 3 cm in greatest dimension surrounded by lung or visceral pleura without bronchoscopic evidence of invasion more proximal than the lobar bronchus (i.e., not in the main bronchus)
T2	Tumor with any of the following features of size or extent: >3 cm in greatest dimension Involves main bronchus > 2 cm distal to the carina Invades the visceral pleura Associated with atelectasis or obstructive pneumonitis that extends to the hilar region but does not involve the entire lung
T3	Tumor of any size that directly invades any of the following: chest wall (including superior sulcus tumors), diaphragm, mediastinal pleura, parietal pericardium; or tumor in the main bronchus < 2 cm distal to the carina but without involvement of the carina; or associated atelectasis or obstructive pneumonitis of the entire lung
T4	Tumor of any size that invades any of the following: mediastinum, heart, great vessels, trachea, esophagus, vertebral body, carina; or tumor with a malignant pleural or pericardial effusion or with satellite tumor nodule(s) within the primary-tumor lobe of the lung

Regional Lymph Nodes (N)

NX	Regional lymph nodes cannot be assessed
N0	No regional lymph node metastasis
N1	Metastasis to ipsilateral peribronchial and/or ipsilateral hilar lymph nodes and intrapulmonary nodes involved by direct extension of the primary tumor
N2	Metastasis to ipsilateral mediastinal and/or subcarinal lymph node(s)
N3	Metastasis to contralateral mediastinal, contralateral hilar, ipsilateral or contralateral scalene, or supraclavicular lymph node(s)

Distant Metastasis (M)

MX	Presence of distant metastasis cannot be assessed
M0	No distant metastasis
M1	Distant metastasis present

TNM STAGING OF LUNG CANCER

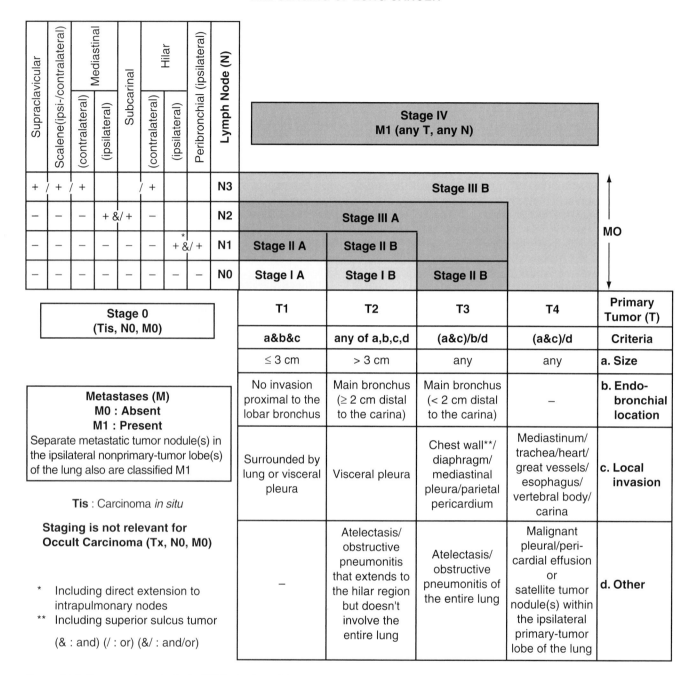

Figure 44.1 Tumor-node-metastasis (TNM) staging of lung cancer.

describes the incorporation of those descriptors into the staging systems.[21,22] Whereas the TNM staging system is applied to NSCLC, a more simplified version is employed for patients with small cell lung cancer. In this classification, patients are classified as having limited or extensive disease. Limited disease (LD) is disease that is limited to one hemithorax, and can include supraclavicular and mediastinal lymphadenopathy; extensive disease (ED) is any disease outside of the hemithorax. The implication in this classification is that LD is treated with chemotherapy and radiotherapy, whereas ED is treated with chemotherapy alone.[23]

Malignant pleural effusion can technically be categorized as LD in the staging classification for small cell lung cancer if the patient otherwise meets criteria. However, for all intents and purposes, patients with malignant pleural effusions and small cell lung cancer have the same characteristics as those with ED, and the large cooperative group trials have treated them as such.

Some important nuances to staging are described in detail later in this chapter. However, there are certain tenets of staging that must be emphasized. Prior to classifying a patient within a certain stage, the clinician should make every effort to verify any noninvasive radiologic findings with tissue confirmation of malignancy. This is particularly important in cases in which surgical resection would be precluded based on noninvasive radiologic tests. Thus, a patient who would otherwise be resectable and has a single focus of metastatic disease should have tissue confirmation of that abnormality prior to being deemed unresectable. As is pointed out later in this chapter, none of the noninvasive radiologic studies is infallible. False-positive findings in studies of the mediastinum range from 12% in positron emission tomography (PET) scans to 20% in CT scans.[24] Therefore, reliance on the scan alone to predict malignancy is simply not sufficient.

Staging can be accomplished by a number of noninvasive and invasive studies. The choice of the most appropriate study rests with the clinician and is based upon how the patient presents. Some patients may be referred for immediate surgery as both a diagnostic and a therapeutic maneuver, as in a patient with an isolated pulmonary nodule. Others may undergo no testing at all, as in a patient who is suspected of having widely metastatic disease and who has an extremely poor performance status. The next sections present a discussion of the attributes of each of the staging options available. For ease of understanding, they are divided into noninvasive and invasive techniques.

NONINVASIVE STAGING TECHNIQUES

CHEST RADIOGRAPHY

The majority of lung cancers are initially detected by plain chest radiograph. In certain situations, the plain film may be sufficient to detect spread to the mediastinum. For example, the presence of bulky lymphadenopathy in the superior or contralateral mediastinal areas may be considered adequate evidence of metastatic disease to preclude further imaging evaluation of the chest. This may be particularly true if the patient is too ill or unwilling to undergo treatment of any kind. Still, most patients should undergo CT scan of the chest unless they are so debilitated that no further evaluation or treatment is planned. The chest radiograph is simply too insensitive a measure of mediastinal lymph node involvement with lung cancer, and thus further noninvasive or invasive assessment is usually necessary.

COMPUTED TOMOGRAPHY OF THE CHEST

The vast majority of patients who present with lung cancer will undergo CT scanning of the chest. CT is helpful in defining the size, location, and characteristics of the primary mass (i.e., smooth bordered, spiculated, calcified, etc.), the presence or absence of lymphadenopathy, and, if performed through the adrenal glands, the presence of abnormalities in the liver and adrenal glands. The bony structures of the thoracic cavity can also be evaluated by chest CT.

CT of the chest is the most widely available and commonly used noninvasive modality for evaluation of the mediastinum in lung cancer. Numerous studies of CT were performed comparing clinical staging by CT to the "gold standards" of mediastinoscopy or surgery. The results demonstrated that, regardless of the lymph node size used as a threshold for defining malignant adenopathy, CT findings in isolation could not be considered as conclusive evidence that lymph nodes were malignant. In other words, in all studies there are meaningful numbers of false positives detected by CT scan. The vast majority of reports evaluating the accuracy of CT scanning for mediastinal lymph node staging have employed the administration of intravenous contrast material. Although contrast is not absolutely necessary in performing chest CT for this indication, it is useful in helping to distinguish vascular structures from lymph nodes as well as in delineating mediastinal invasion by centrally located tumors. The most widely accepted criterion for an abnormal lymph node is a short-axis lymph node diameter of 1 cm or greater on CT.

The American College of Chest Physicians recently compiled in a meta-analytic format the studies assessing the performance characteristics of CT scan for staging the mediastinum. Twenty-three studies were identified, comprising 4793 evaluable patients. The pooled sensitivity of CT scanning for staging the mediastinum was 0.60 (95% confidence interval [CI], 0.51 to 0.68) and the pooled specificity was 0.81 (95% CI, 0.74 to 0.86). The overall positive predictive value was 53% (range, 26% to 100%), and the overall negative predictive value was 82% (range, 63% to 85%).[25] CT scanning is thus an imperfect tool for staging the mediastinum. However, because CT usually guides the choice of nodes for selective node biopsy by mediastinoscopy or needle aspiration, it remains an important diagnostic tool in lung cancer. Accurate noninvasive node staging is essential in that the choice of individual nodes for sampling by nonsurgical invasive techniques including transbronchial, transthoracic, or transesophageal needle aspiration, will be directed by the findings of the CT scan. The limitation of CT-based mediastinal lymph node evaluation is evident in the fact that 5% to 15% of patients with clinical T1N0 lesions will be found to have positive lymph node involvement by surgical lymph node sampling.[26] Perhaps the most important message in evaluating the accuracy of CT scanning is that approximately 40% of all nodes deemed malignant by CT criteria are actually benign, depending on the patient population.[27] Specificity can be affected by clinical factors such as the presence of obstructive pneumonitis.[27] There is no node size that can reliably determine stage and operability. In cases in which the CT criteria for identification of a metastatic node are met, the clinician must still prove beyond reasonable doubt by biopsy or resection that the node is indeed malignant. Given the limitations of the imperfect sensitivity and specificity of CT, it is usually inappropriate to rely solely on the CT scan to determine mediastinal lymph node status. Nonetheless, CT continues to play an important and necessary role in the evaluation of patients with lung cancer and is recommended as part of the evaluation of patients who present with newly diagnosed or suspected lung cancer.[28]

CT can also be helpful in the evaluation of pleural effusion in patients with lung cancer. The CT scan can indicate the presence or absence of fluid, the contour of the pleural space, and whether or not nodules or masses are present on the pleural surface. However, the clinician should interpret these findings with caution as pleural disease can predate cancer, and the presence of pleural effusion does not guarantee that the cytology will be positive. This is an important staging issue as the finding of malignant pleural effusion in NSCLC places the patient in the T4 stage and at least stage IIIB disease. If the pleural fluid has benign cytology (e.g., fluid from prior obstructive pneumonia), then the patient may still be considered for surgical resection. To resolve this issue, recommendations have been made to perform thoracentesis with cytology on two separate occasions, followed by thoracoscopy to evaluate the pleural surface directly. If the patient remains cytology negative, then the stage and treatment offered should reflect the lower stage. CT is often inaccurate in differentiating direct tumor invasion of the visceral pleura (T2) from that of the parietal pleura or chest wall (T3). Thoracoscopy can be helpful in differentiating the extent of the primary tumor involvement into or through the pleural, but at times open thoracotomy is needed to sort out this issue. (For an in-depth discussion of the pleura in lung cancer and the use of thoracoscopy for the diagnosis and management of lung disease, see Chapters 70 and 23, respectively.)

POSITRON EMISSION TOMOGRAPHY

Perhaps the single most notable addition to the staging armamentarium for the evaluation of lung cancer is PET. This imaging modality is based on the biologic activity of neoplastic cells; PET is thus a metabolic imaging technique based on the function of a tissue rather than its anatomy. Lung cancer cells demonstrate increased cellular uptake of glucose and a higher rate of glycolysis when compared to normal cells.[29] The radiolabeled glucose analogue [18F]fluoro-2-deoxy-D-glucose undergoes the same cellular uptake as glucose, but after phosphorylation is not further metabolized and becomes trapped in cells.[30] Accumulation of the isotope can then be identified using a PET camera. Specific criteria for an abnormal PET scan are either a standard uptake value of greater than 2.5 or uptake in the lesion that is greater than the background activity of the mediastinum. It has proved useful in differentiating neoplastic from normal tissues. However, the technique is not infallible because certain non-neoplastic processes, including granulomatous and other inflammatory diseases as well as infections, may also demonstrate positive PET imaging. Furthermore, size limitations are also an issue, with the lower limit of resolution of the study being approximately 7 to 8 mm depending on the intensity of uptake of the isotope in abnormal cells.[31] One should not rely on a negative PET finding for lesions less than 1 cm on CT scan.

A burgeoning number of studies in the last several years have reported on the utility of [18F]fluoro-2-deoxy-D-glucose PET scanning in the assessment of the mediastinum in patients with lung cancer. Increasing availability of the technology now allows PET to be used widely as a diagnostic tool. It should be remembered that PET is primarily a metabolic examination and has limited anatomic resolution. It is possible for PET to identify lymph node stations, but not individual lymph nodes. CT scanning provides much more anatomic detail, but lacks the functional information provided by PET. The recent American College of Chest Physician guidelines on lung cancer combined studies with a total of 1111 evaluable patients.[25] The pooled sensitivity of PET was 0.85 (95% CI, 0.79 to 0.89) and the pooled specificity was 0.88 (95% CI, 0.82 to 0.92). The overall positive predictive value was 0.78 (range, 0.40 to 1.00) and the negative predictive value was 0.93 (range, 0.75 to 1.00). Thus, it appears that PET has both higher sensitivity and specificity for evaluation of mediastinal lymph nodes than CT scanning. This imaging technique will almost certainly assume an increasingly important role in the evaluation of patients with lung cancer. However, like CT scanning, PET can be wrong. Whereas a negative mediastinal PET may obviate the need for mediastinoscopy prior to thoracotomy, a positive mediastinal PET should not negate further evaluation or the possibility of resection. In the latter case, lymph node sampling should still be pursued, as the possibility of a false-positive PET scan cannot be ignored.

Two well-performed studies have evaluated the use of PET in the preoperative setting for lung cancer, each with compelling results.[31,32] In those studies, nearly 20% of patients were staged differently after evaluation by PET scan. Where PET scan is available, one should be obtained during the staging evaluation for lung cancer.[28] Recently introduced technology includes CT/PET fusion, a single machine that incorporates CT and PET during the same scan. This allows the clinician to obtain anatomic (CT) and functional (PET) images simultaneously. Early work suggests improvement in the number of patients correctly staged with this modality as compared to CT or PET alone.[33,34] The future of PET in lung cancer may also include its use to evaluate response to treatment.

MAGNETIC RESONANCE IMAGING

There are very few circumstances in which magnetic resonance imaging (MRI) is a useful tool in staging lung cancer. However, MRI can be useful in evaluating superior sulcus tumors, especially for possible invasion of the brachial plexus, and for evaluating vertebral invasion.

THE SEARCH FOR METASTATIC DISEASE

The purpose of extrathoracic scanning in NSCLC is usually to detect metastatic disease at common metastatic sites, such as the adrenal glands, liver, brain, and skeletal system, thereby sparing the patient fruitless surgical intervention.[35] Computed tomography of the chest, CT or MRI with contrast of the brain, and [99mTc] nuclear imaging of the skeletal system are the staging studies of choice when the clinician needs to evaluate for metastatic disease. Recently, the use of whole-body PET scans for extrathoracic staging has been introduced, and the initial studies suggest that PET can disclose non–central nervous system metastatic disease not detected by standard methods in 10% to 20% of cases.[31,32,36–38] PET appears to be at least as sensitive as isotope bone scans for detecting metastases and has fewer false-positive results.

The initial clinical evaluation may reveal abnormalities, such as abnormal symptoms, physical findings, and routine blood tests, which then lead to an expanded clinical evaluation (Table 44.3).[35] With abnormalities on these clinical evaluations, scans will be abnormal in around 50%

Table 44.3 Expanded Clinical Evaluation

Symptoms Elicited in History
Constitutional—weight loss greater than 10 lb
Musculoskeletal—focal skeletal pain
Neurologic—headaches, syncope, seizures, extremity weakness,
   recent change in mental status

Signs Found on Physical Examination
Lymphadenopathy (>1 cm)
Hoarseness, superior vena cava syndrome
Bone tenderness
Hepatomegaly (>13-cm span)
Focal neurologic signs, papilledema
Soft tissue mass

Routine Laboratory Tests
Hematocrit less than 40% in males
Hematocrit less than 35% in females
Elevated alkaline phosphatase, GGT, AST, calcium

AST, aspartate aminotransferase; GGT, γ-glutamyl transpeptidase.

of cases. Conversely, in the absence of all clinical abnormalities, the scan yield is much lower, giving rise to the recommendation that scans be omitted in this setting.[35,39-43] Advanced thoracic lesions and mediastinal lymphadenopathy are important variables, because more scan abnormalities are associated with advanced thoracic lesions.[44,45] This is particularly true for N2 disease, in which asymptomatic metastases have been documented at a higher rate than would have been expected.[44] Although several studies documented a higher incidence of brain metastases with adenocarcinomas as opposed to squamous cell cancers,[46,47] the largest single series of patients with stage I and II lung cancer found no difference.[48]

Several important caveats must be considered. First and foremost, false-positive scans can occur. Adrenal adenomas (present in 2% to 9% of the general population), hepatic cysts, degenerative joint disease, old fractures, and a variety of nonmetastatic space-occupying brain lesions are present in the general population. When clinically indicated, additional imaging studies, biopsies, or both are performed to establish the diagnosis; however, complications and costs resulting from such subsequent investigations have received little attention.[49] Another problem is that of false-negative scans—that is, metastases are present but not picked up by current scanning techniques. This was demonstrated by Pagani,[50] who found metastatic NSCLC in 12% of radiologically normal adrenal glands by percutaneous biopsy. Another difficulty is that most studies fail to specify exactly which elements comprise the prescan clinical evaluation, or use differing clinical indicators. Organ-specific findings such as headache and non–organ-specific complaints such as weight loss are both important.[40,51] Another problem is that abnormal scans in many studies were not followed up with definitive biopsy proof of metastatic disease. There are a lack of prospective randomized trials and outcome studies in the area of extrathoracic scanning. One retrospective study showed that scanning asymptomatic patients with early NSCLC did not help predict recurrences postoperatively or improve survival.[52] The only prospective randomized trial showed no statistical difference in recurrence rates or survival in a group randomized to bone scintigraphy and CT

of the head, liver, and adrenals, compared with the group assigned to CT of the chest and mediastinoscopy, followed by thoracotomy when appropriate.[53]

Adrenal and Hepatic Imaging

It is relatively common to encounter adrenal masses on routine CT scan, but many of these lesions are probably unrelated to the malignant process. A unilateral adrenal mass in a patient with NSCLC is more likely to be a metastasis than a benign lesion according to some[45,54] but not other[55,56] studies. In the presence of clinical T1N0 NSCLC, adenomas predominate,[57,58] whereas adrenal metastases are frequently associated with large intrathoracic tumors or other extrathoracic metastases.[45,59] Many studies suggest that the size of a unilateral adrenal abnormality on CT is an important predictor of metastatic spread, but this is not a universal finding.[60] Lesions larger than 3 cm are more likely to signify metastases, but benign disease is still possible.

For adrenal masses, CT, MRI, percutaneous biopsy, and even adrenalectomy can be used to help delineate benign from malignant disease. Well-defined, low-attenuation (fatty) lesions with a smooth rim on unenhanced CT are more likely to be benign adenomas,[61-63] but the CT appearance of many lesions is insufficiently distinctive.[63] Follow-up scanning with repeat CT, serial ultrasounds, or MRI (especially with chemical shift and dynamic gadolinium-enhanced techniques[64]), or 6β-iodo-^{131}I-methylnorcholesterol scanning,[65] can sometimes help with the critical distinction between metastatic disease and adenoma. Percutaneous adrenal biopsy is a relatively safe and effective means of achieving a definitive diagnosis in doubtful cases, and is especially important when the histology of the adrenal mass will dictate subsequent management.[66,67] However, this procedure may be nondiagnostic or infeasible due to anatomic constraints. When insufficient material results from a biopsy, repeat aspiration or even adrenalectomy should be considered.[60,63]

Most liver lesions are benign cysts and hemangiomas, but contrast CT (or ultrasound) is often required to establish a likely diagnosis.[26] Percutaneous biopsy can be performed when diagnostic certainty is required. One meta-analysis that specifically reviewed hepatic studies derived a pooled yield of 3% for liver metastases in asymptomatic patients with NSCLC.[49]

Brain Imaging

In most studies, the yield of CT/MRI scanning of the brain in NSCLC patients with negative clinical examinations is 0 to 10%,[45,68-73] possibly rendering the test cost-ineffective.[45] The negative predictive value of the clinical evaluation in this setting is 95% (range, 91% to 96%).

An association of positive findings between brain metastases with N2 disease in the chest and adenocarcinoma has been described.[46,69,73] The false-negative rate, wherein patients return with brain metastases within 12 months of the original scan, is reported to be 3%.[69] False-positive scans can be a problem in up to 11% of cases due to brain abscesses, gliomas, and other lesions[74]; therefore, biopsy may be essential in cases in which management is critically dependent on the histology of the brain lesion.

MRI is more sensitive than CT of the brain and picks up more lesions and smaller lesions,[75] but in some studies this has not translated into a clinically meaningful difference in terms of survival.[76] Although studies show that MRI can identify additional lesions in individual patients with metastases, there are no studies that show that MRI is better than CT in its ability to identify additional patients with metastases from lung cancer. Therefore, CT is an acceptable modality for evaluating patients for metastatic disease. However, MRI remains the preferential modality at many centers.

Bone Imaging

False-positive scan abnormalities in radionuclide bone scintigraphy are problematic because of the frequency of degenerative and traumatic skeletal damage and the difficulty in obtaining a definitive diagnosis via follow-up imaging or biopsy. The negative predictive value in this setting is 90% (95% CI, 86% to 93%) for radionuclide bone imaging with a negative clinical assessment. PET has a higher specificity for bony metastases.[77]

SUMMARY

The noninvasive clinical staging of lung cancer relies on the clinical evaluation and a number of readily available staging studies. The clinician must be wary of abnormal scans that may falsely suggest metastatic disease to the mediastinum and distant sites. Tissue confirmation by whatever means necessary is the rule rather than the exception prior to deciding on correct stage and the most appropriate treatment. The search for metastatic disease is not necessary if the patient has a normal clinical evaluation. If the patient has clinical findings indicative of metastatic disease, further evaluation is necessary, as nearly 50% of the time the patient will have metastases.[28]

INVASIVE DIAGNOSTIC AND STAGING TECHNIQUES

There are a myriad of methods that can be utilized to diagnose and stage patients with lung cancer. In certain circumstances this is accomplished with a single test. For example, a positive percutaneous biopsy of the adrenal gland performed as a first test in a patient with a lung mass will provide both a diagnosis and a stage (stage IV) simultaneously. Every effort should be made to utilize the least invasive, most accurate procedure to expedite the patient's treatment, to minimize patient discomfort and inconvenience, and to ensure that the most appropriate treatment is rendered.

SPUTUM CYTOLOGY

Sputum cytology is the least invasive method for obtaining a diagnosis of lung cancer. Its accuracy depends on the expertise of the health care team in obtaining the sample (three samples are required), the preservation technique, and the size and location of the lesion. Central lesions are more likely to yield positive cytologic results than are peripheral lesions.[78] Sputum cytology should be obtained in all patients with central lesions, who are at risk for more invasive biopsy techniques. In addition, patients with hemoptysis with or without a mass on chest radiographs should have sputum cytology obtained. The sensitivity and specificity of sputum cytology are 66% and 99%, respectively.[78]

TRANSTHORACIC NEEDLE ASPIRATION

Transthoracic needle aspiration, usually under CT or fluoroscopic guidance, is an expedient and relatively safe way to diagnose the primary tumor mass and establish a diagnosis of lung cancer. As a general rule, if a lesion is less than 3 cm in size and lateral to the mid-clavicular line, bronchoscopy would not be the diagnostic procedure of choice. Transthoracic needle aspiration should be considered under such circumstances if tissue diagnosis is necessary. One important point about transthoracic needle aspiration or other nonsurgical biopsy techniques for peripheral pulmonary lesions is that they afford no preoperative benefit, as they do not eliminate the need for surgery in most cases.[79] In the circumstance of a patient presenting with a solitary pulmonary nodule suspicious for malignancy (i.e., noncalcified, upper lobe, spiculated lesion in a long-term smoker), the diagnosis, stage, and therapy can be accomplished simultaneously with a thoracotomy and surgical resection. Thus, needle aspiration may only be essential in certain situations: patients who are poor surgical candidates for lung resection but who require tissue diagnosis prior to treatment, patients in whom a noncancerous lesion is strongly suspected, patients who request that a diagnosis of cancer be confirmed prior to considering surgery, and patients with high likelihood of metastatic disease.

One drawback of transthoracic needle aspiration is the risk of pneumothorax. Several investigations have reported a 22% to 45% risk of pneumothorax for CT-guided transthoracic needle aspiration.[80–82] Although pneumothorax may lead to hemodynamic compromise without therapeutic tube thoracostomy, in most cases of pneumothorax secondary to transthoracic needle aspiration, treatment is not required.[83] The primary factors shown to increase the risk or incidence of pneumothorax are the presence of emphysema, a smaller lesion size, and a greater depth of needle penetration from the pleural surface to the edge of the lesion.

FIBEROPTIC BRONCHOSCOPY

More than 50% of patients with advanced-stage lung cancer will have involvement of the central airways in the form of bulky endobronchial disease, extension into the airways, or extrinsic compression of the airways by the tumor or by lymphadenopathy.[84] Patients with known or suspected lung cancer may have symptoms due to endobronchial involvement that require airway inspection with bronchoscopy: shortness of breath, unilateral wheezing, hemoptysis, and cough. Endobronchial lesions can be visualized easily and biopsied through a flexible bronchoscope. The yield with three or more biopsies should approach 100%[85,86] for centrally located lesions. Endobronchial biopsies provide the highest sensitivity (0.74; range 0.48 to 0.97, 20 studies), followed by brushings (0.59; range 0.23 to 0.93, 18 studies) and washings (0.48; range 0.29 to 0.78, 12 studies).[87] Studies on the sensitivity of needle aspiration of centrally located endobronchial lesions are difficult to interpret. These studies have varied dramatically in terms of sample size and technique used. Because endobronchial biopsies or brushings provide a diagnosis in most cases, endobronchial needle aspiration is rarely performed. Overall, the sensitivity for all bronchoscopic techniques for the diagnosis of centrally located endobronchial lesions is reported as 0.88 (range 0.67 to 0.97, 30 studies).[88]

Submucosal and Peribronchial Lesions

When lung cancer presents with submucosal infiltration or extrinsic compression from peribronchial disease, endobronchial forceps biopsy has a lower yield (55%) than transbronchial needle aspiration (TBNA) (71%).[88] In these situations, normal mucosal markings are often obscured and the surface is replaced with bronchial collateral vessels and firmer surface tissue, which may have to be penetrated to reach malignant cells. In addition, peribronchial tumor may be inaccessible to biopsy forceps. Based on this architecture, TBNA can be more effective if the lesion is close enough to the tracheobronchial tree to be encountered with a 1.3- to 1.5-cm-long needle. Of note, in cases like this in which sampling error may be high, diagnostic yields may be improved by combining different methods.

Bronchoscopy for Staging Lung Cancer

Initially, the role of bronchoscopy in staging lung cancer was limited to the determination of T (tumor) status. Now, bronchoscopy has a crucial role in determining the presence of metastatic deposits of tumor in mediastinal lymph nodes, thus contributing to an accurate and a minimally invasive staging method for lung cancer.

The use of TBNA in staging lung cancer has been reported to be both sensitive and specific in diagnosing spread of cancer to lymph nodes.[89–91] The overall sensitivity of TBNA for NSCLC is 0.76 (95% CI, 0.72 to 0.79), and the specificity is 0.96 (95% CI, 0.91 to 1.00). The negative predictive value is 71% (range, 36% to 100%).[24] The standard method of performing TBNA starts with a CT scan of the chest to guide needle aspirations toward the most involved group of lymph nodes. Lesions localized by a CT scan can be accessed with bronchoscopy by measuring the number of CT slices above or below the carina (or other airway landmarks), and placing the needle the required distance above or below the landmark corresponding to that number of CT slices. When performing TBNA, the question invariably arises about the number of negative passes to perform before stopping. For various reasons such as patient comfort and safety, need for sedation, and time spent by medical staff, it is imperative to manage the time for bronchoscopy. It has recently been shown that a plateau in yield for malignancy is achieved after seven passes with the needle through a lymph node.[92] The importance of having a qualified and experienced cytopathologist on site cannot be overemphasized. Thorough interpretation by such individuals who are available for rapid on-site evaluation has been shown to enhance yield from TBNA.[93] With the assistance of these individuals, the adequacy of sampling can be rigorously assessed. All samples should contain a preponderance of lymphocytes to define true nodal sampling. Specimens without lymphocytes should be deemed unsatisfactory, and the presence of respiratory epithelium should raise concerns about contamination.

TBNA allows for minimally invasive sampling of the mediastinum and hilar lymph nodes and potentially avoids more invasive procedures such as mediastinoscopy, mediastinotomy, and open thoracotomy. There is no doubt that the combined use of TBNA and CT scan can improve not only the diagnostic but the staging evaluation of lung cancer. However, thus far, there has been wide variability in training and in usage of this helpful procedure. It is also operator dependent, with certain techniques allowing for higher yields. For an in-depth discussion of bronchoscopy, see Chapter 22.

ENDOSCOPIC ULTRASOUND

Endoscopic ultrasound (EUS) is another modality that has significantly impacted lung cancer staging, primarily due to its superior ability to sample the posterior mediastinum through the esophageal wall. Currently, EUS with fine-needle aspiration is performed using real-time ultrasound. For patients with lung cancer and posterior mediastinal adenopathy seen on chest CT scan, EUS has a sensitivity and specificity of 90% and 100%, respectively.[94,95] In patients with lung cancer who have no adenopathy seen on CT scan, EUS has been shown to sample nodes as small as 3 mm in diameter. This is useful given the high incidence of metastasis found in normal-sized lymph nodes in lung cancer.[96] Based on surgical studies, it may be possible to predict the location of mediastinal lymph node metastases at certain levels based on the location of the tumor. This relationship may influence the use of EUS in certain patients without adenopathy on chest CT scan. Lymphatic pathways favor spread to aortopulmonary window nodes from left upper lobe tumors and to subcarinal nodes from left and right lower lobe lesions.[97] EUS has been studied in patients with known lung cancer without enlarged mediastinal lymph nodes on CT, and it has detected mediastinal involvement (stage III or IV disease) in up to 42% of cases.[98]

Additionally, EUS has the advantage of being able to stage lung cancer from locations outside the mediastinum. The left lobe of the liver, a substantial part of the right lobe, and the left (but not the right) adrenal gland can be identified and sampled in 97% of patients.[99] In addition, left pleural effusions can be visualized and sampled during an EUS procedure.

MEDIASTINOSCOPY

Mediastinoscopy remains the gold standard for invasively staging the mediastinum in patients with known or suspected lung cancer. If there is mediastinal adenopathy on CT, often a surgical mediastinal procedure is performed prior to thoracotomy. Mediastinoscopy is most often used to sample lymphatics in the paratracheal (station 4), and anterior subcarinal (station 7) region (Fig. 44.2). The subcarinal area is more difficult to sample and thus has a lower yield. An extended cervical mediastinoscopy can be carried out to reach aortopulmonary and para-aortic lymph nodes (stations 5 and 6)

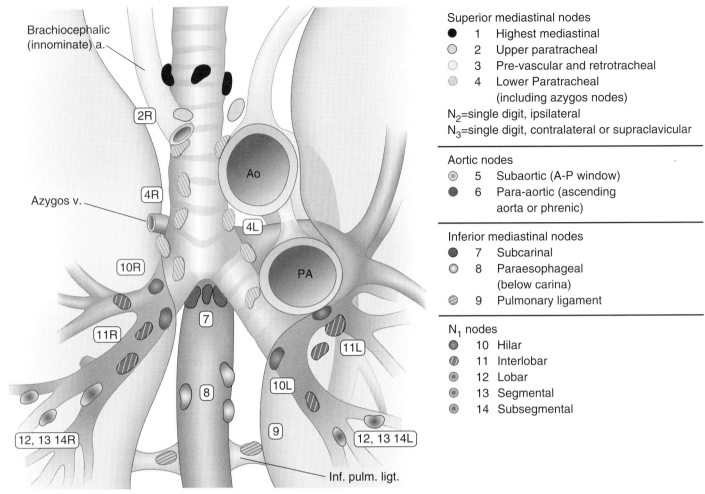

Brachiocephalic
(innominate) a.

Azygos v.

2R

4R

4L

Ao

PA

10R

7

11R

11L

12, 13 14R

8

10L

9

12, 13 14L

Inf. pulm. ligt.

Superior mediastinal nodes
- 1 Highest mediastinal
- 2 Upper paratracheal
- 3 Pre-vascular and retrotracheal
- 4 Lower Paratracheal
   (including azygos nodes)

N_2=single digit, ipsilateral
N_3=single digit, contralateral or supraclavicular

Aortic nodes
- 5 Subaortic (A-P window)
- 6 Para-aortic (ascending
   aorta or phrenic)

Inferior mediastinal nodes
- 7 Subcarinal
- 8 Paraesophageal
   (below carina)
- 9 Pulmonary ligament

N_1 nodes
- 10 Hilar
- 11 Interlobar
- 12 Lobar
- 13 Segmental
- 14 Subsegmental

Figure 44.2 Mediastinal lymph node maps. a, artery; Ao, aorta; A-P, aortic-pulmonary; PA, pulmonary artery; v, vein. *See Color Plate*
Illustration continued on opposite page

by using the same cervical incision as mediastinoscopy but dissecting into a different fascial plane. Alternatively, an anterior mediastinotomy (the so-called Chamberlain procedure) may be needed to sample lymph nodes in these aortopulmonary and para-aortic locations (stations 5 and 6) (Fig. 44.2). Overall, mediastinoscopy has a reported sensitivity of 81% to 87%, with a specificity of 100%.[101] In addition to the superior sensitivity and specificity of mediastinoscopy, it may be able to differentiate between stage IIIA and IIIB mediastinal involvement. As more is learned about lung cancer treatment, this will be important for prognosis and for potential therapy. As with any surgical procedure, mediastinoscopy has risks and limitations. It requires general anesthesia, with a morbidity of 2% and a mortality of 0.08%.[101]

TREATMENT OF LUNG CANCER

The overall 5-year survival for patients diagnosed with lung cancer is a dismal 14%.[102] This figure has not changed substantially over the past 20 years. The survival curves vary by stage, with earlier stage lung cancer patients enjoying a much better survival than do patients with later stage disease. Treatment is based on the stage of the disease and the patients' performance status at the time therapy is ini-

tiated. In general, early-stage disease is surgically managed, locally advanced disease is managed with chemotherapy and radiotherapy, and advanced disease is managed with chemotherapy with supportive care or supportive care alone. Recent trials have suggested that this paradigm may shift toward multimodality therapy (surgery, chemotherapy, and radiotherapy) in the future.[103–106] This raises the issue of how best to manage patients with newly diagnosed lung cancer through their diagnosis, staging, and therapy. The American College of Chest Physicians guideline on lung cancer recommends the use of a multidisciplinary lung cancer setting wherein patients can be evaluated by the major disciplines involved in the care of these patients, namely the pulmonologist, the thoracic surgeon, and the medical and radiation oncologists.[107] At the very least, a "tumor board" that includes the aforementioned specialties, with the addition of chest radiology, pathology, nursing, and social work, should review all new cases to ensure that patients receive optimal treatment and are considered for enrollment in clinical trials.

PROGNOSTIC FACTORS FOR LUNG CANCER

Based on an analysis of large databases in inoperable lung cancer patients, the strongest predictors of survival are good

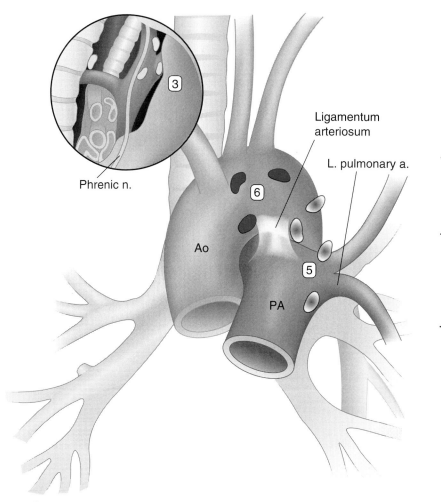

Superior mediastinal nodes
- ●   1   Highest mediastinal
- ○   2   Upper paratracheal
- ○   3   Pre-vascular and retrotracheal
- ◍   4   Lower Paratracheal (including azygos nodes)

N_2=single digit, ipsilateral
N_3=single digit, contralateral or supraclavicular

Aortic nodes
- ◉   5   Subaortic (A-P window)
- ●   6   Para-aortic (ascending aorta or phrenic)

Inferior mediastinal nodes
- ●   7   Subcarinal
- ○   8   Paraesophageal (below carina)
- ◍   9   Pulmonary ligament

N_1 nodes
- ●   10   Hilar
- ◐   11   Interlobar
- ◉   12   Lobar
- ◉   13   Segmental
- ◉   14   Subsegmental

Figure 44.2 cont'd *See Color Plate*

performance score (Karnofsky scale), lower extent of disease (stage), and absence of weight loss.[108,109] Some reports have shown female gender to be a predictor of better survival, but this is variable between studies. Performance score and the presence or absence of symptoms are predictors of outcome even with resectable early-stage disease.[110–112] Even in stage I NSCLC patients undergoing curative resection, those who were symptomatic at presentation had a worse survival compared to those who were asymptomatic.[111] Although individual reports have noted superior survival for patients with one cell type of NSCLC versus another, the general consensus in the literature is that histologic subtypes of NSCLC are not a major predictor of survival.[111–113]

In recent years, there have been numerous reports of various molecular markers and their association with outcome. Some of the best known markers include K-Ras, epithelial growth factor receptor, p53, p16, and Bcl-2. However, in many instances, the results are conflicting about the prognostic significance of these individual molecular markers.[114–116] This probably has to do, in part, with the types of cases under review and with individual laboratory variations in techniques for measuring these molecular markers. At this time, individual molecular markers are considered to be investigational and are not part of standard testing with prognostic implications for lung cancer. This

section presents a discussion of the treatment of NSCLC by stage and cell type, followed by a discussion of the treatment of small cell lung cancer (SCLC).

NON–SMALL CELL LUNG CANCER TREATMENT BY STAGE

Stage I

Stage I NSCLC is defined as a T1 (<3 cm) or T2 (>3 cm) tumor in the parenchyma of the lung, greater than 2 cm away from the carina and not invading the chest wall or parietal pleura. Stage I lung cancer does not include patients who have malignant lymph node disease or patients with metastatic disease (Fig. 44.3). Thus, the TNM classification is either T1N0M0 (stage IA) or T2N0M0 (stage IB). The differences between the two are the size of the primary tumor and the survival after surgical resection. Although stage I disease offers the best chance for long-term survival, the sad fact is that only 15% of all lung cancers present with stage I disease.[117,118]

The current treatment for stage I lung cancer is surgery. The surgical procedure of choice is a lobectomy or pneumonectomy with mediastinal lymph node sampling. It should be recognized that the patient must be a reasonable

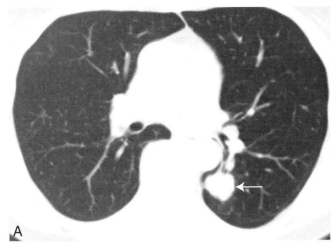

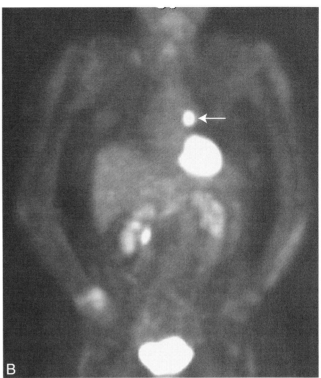

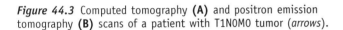

Figure 44.3 Computed tomography **(A)** and positron emission tomography **(B)** scans of a patient with T1N0M0 tumor (*arrows*).

surgical candidate. The 5-year survival for surgically resected stage IA lung cancer is 71%, whereas the survival for stage IB lung cancer is 57%.[21] Local postoperative radiation for stage I and II lung cancer, after either complete or incomplete resection of the tumor, has not been found to be of any benefit.[119] Recently, however, postoperative adjuvant chemotherapy has been shown to improve survival in one reasonably performed trial.[120] A further discussion of postoperative adjuvant therapy is presented later (see "Stage IIIA").

Some patients are surgically resectable but medically inoperable, usually because the patient does not have the pulmonary reserve to tolerate a lobectomy. These patients, particularly those with T1 tumors, may be able to tolerate a wedge resection or segmentectomy of their tumor as opposed to a lobectomy or pneumonectomy. In such cases, the local recurrence rate is higher than that of a complete resection, but the overall 5-year mortality is no different.[121] Still, whenever possible, a complete anatomic resection is preferred over a minimal resection.

Patients who are "close calls" for surgery should be thoroughly evaluated by both a pulmonologist and a thoracic surgeon prior to making a decision on operability. As previously stated, there is a difference between a patient who is resectable and a patient who is operable. Chapter 26 is devoted to the preoperative evaluation of patients with lung disease, but a brief review here is warranted. Patients with a postoperative percent predicted FEV_1 or diffusion capacity less than 40% will have a higher morbidity and mortality following lung cancer surgery. Patients with borderline values preoperatively should be referred for a differential ventilation-perfusion scan to predict postoperative function better. Where there is still question, a cardiopulmonary exercise test can be obtained. Compared to those with an oxygen consumption of greater than 20 mL/kg per minute,

who have acceptable operative risks, patients with an oxygen consumption less than 10 mL/kg per minute have both a higher predicted morbidity and mortality, and patients with an oxygen consumption between 11 and 19 mL/kg per minute have a higher morbidity but no greater mortality.[122]

For patients who either refuse surgery or are deemed medically unfit for surgery, primary radiotherapy for cure can be considered. This approach was recently evaluated in a meta-analysis of 1 randomized and 35 nonrandomized trials.[123] The studies were heterogeneous, and the 5-year cancer-specific survival ranged between 13% and 39%. The authors concluded that, even in patients with severe emphysema, radiation therapy can be tolerated if careful planning with three-dimensional conformal techniques is undertaken to minimize the radiation dose to the remaining noncancerous lung. We would recommend referral to a radiotherapist for patients who are medically inoperable for consideration of "curative" radiation therapy.

Stage II

Stage II NSCLC is defined as a T1 or T2 tumor with N1 (hilar lymph node involvement) and no distant metastasis or a T3 tumor with no nodal or distant metastasis (T3N0M0). Stage II lung cancer is further divided into stage IIA (T1N1) versus stage IIB (T2N1 tumors and T3N0 tumors). Again this distinction is made because the survival of stage IIA patients is better than the survival of patients with stage IIB.

Stage IIA lung cancer is quite uncommon, representing between 1% and 5% of patients treated in recent surgical series.[124–127] The 5-year survival for stage IIA NSCLC is between 52% and 57%.[128] Stage IIB cancer may represent up to 15% of surgically resected cases.[124,126,127] The 5-year survival for stage IIB disease is 24% to 42%.[128] For stage IIA and IIB cancer, surgical therapy is the treatment of choice. There is no benefit to postoperative radiotherapy. The value of adjuvant chemotherapy after surgery is discussed later (see "Stage IIIA"). With chest wall invasion (T3N0M0), an en bloc resection of the tumor and chest wall is the treatment of choice. A specific discussion of the evaluation and treatment of Pancoast's tumor is discussed later in the chapter.

The outcome of lung cancer surgery is improved when the surgery is performed at hospitals with a higher volume of procedures.[129] It is also important to have the surgery performed by a thoracic surgeon; when lobectomy is performed by a thoracic surgeon compared to a general surgeon, mortality is nearly halved.[130]

Stage IIIA

Stage IIIA NSCLC represents a heterogeneous group of patients with N2 disease and includes T3N1 patients (Fig. 44.4). There is substantial debate over what constitutes resectable IIIA (N2) disease. All agree that T3N1 patients are best treated with surgical resection. Some patients are found to have occult N2 metastasis at the time of thoracotomy, when a complete resection of the lymph nodes and the primary tumor is possible. These patients are best served by resecting all known disease. The area of more controversy is how best to treat patients when N2 (single or multiple station) metastases are documented prior to thoracotomy. Two small randomized prospective trials have compared surgery alone versus preoperative (neoadjuvant) chemotherapy followed by surgical resection.[103,105] Both trials observed superior survival in those who received preoperative chemotherapy. Recently, investigators have reported the preliminary results of a prospective trial that randomized patients with IIIA (N2) disease to preoperative chemoradiotherapy followed by surgical resection versus chemoradiotherapy alone (no surgery).[131] There was no difference in the median survival time or the 3-year survival (38% vs. 33%, respectively). Long-term results are pending, but it appears unlikely that surgery will add much to chemoradiotherapy for the treatment of locally advanced disease.

Postoperative (adjuvant) treatment of resected stage IIIA NSCLC has recently changed. The International Adjuvant Lung Trial randomized patients with completely resected stage I, II, and IIIA NSCLC to observation or to three or four cycles of adjuvant cisplatin-based chemotherapy.[120] Approximately 39% of all patients in the trial had stage IIIA disease. Overall, there was an absolute 4% improvement in 5-year survival (44% vs. 40%) in participants receiving adjuvant chemotherapy. Therefore, adjuvant cisplatin-based chemotherapy for three to four cycles has become the standard for resected stage IB, IIA/B, and IIIA NSCLC. However, some patients may decline adjuvant chemotherapy for such a small survival advantage when they weigh the risks versus the benefits. In contrast, adjuvant radiotherapy in the fully resected stage IIIA NSCLC patient has shown no definite improvement in survival. However, thoracic radiotherapy has been shown to significantly reduce local recurrences and should be considered in selected patients.[132]

Those individuals with bulky (>2 cm in diameter) or multistation N2 nodal metastasis comprise a less favorable subset of stage IIIA disease and are not generally considered to be operable. In the past, these patients were treated with thoracic radiotherapy alone, but their 5-year survival was only 3% to 5%. A multitude of trials have evaluated combination chemotherapy and thoracic radiotherapy versus thoracic radiotherapy alone. Three meta-analyses of these trials have all concluded that cisplatin-based chemotherapy combined with radiotherapy results in survival benefit over radiotherapy alone.[133–135] Anticipated 5-year survival with combined-modality therapy is 15% to 20%. Two recent multicenter trials have suggested that concurrent chemoradiotherapy is superior to sequential therapy with chemotherapy followed by thoracic radiotherapy.[136,137] Concurrent therapy should be reserved for those individuals with good performance scores (0 or 1) and less than 10% weight loss. Concurrent therapy is associated with a higher rate of severe esophagitis than is sequential therapy.

Stage IIIB

Stage IIIB is also a heterogeneous group and includes T4N0M0 patients. For purposes of discussion in this section, we have excluded patients with IIIB disease due to malignant pleural effusion (see "Stage IV" later). Surgery may be indicated for carefully selected T4N0-1M0 patients with or without neoadjuvant chemotherapy or neoadjuvant chemoradiotherapy (superior sulcus tumors). Individuals with T4N0-1 disease due to main carinal involvement have been treated with carinal resection with or without pulmonary resection. Carinal resection carries an operative mortality of 10% to 15% and 5-year survival of approximately 20% in carefully selected series. Patients who are T4N0 due solely to a satellite tumor nodules(s) within the primary tumor lobe have a 5-year survival of around 20% with surgery alone. There are no Phase III randomized trials to date that demonstrate that neoadjuvant chemoradiotherapy followed by surgery for stage IIIB disease results in prolonged survival compared with chemoradiotherapy alone.[138]

Patients with unresectable stage IIIB NSCLC are treated the same as those with unresectable IIIA disease. The median survival time is generally 15 to 18 months, with a 5-year survival of 10% to 20%. The randomized trials of chemoradiotherapy versus radiotherapy alone included both stage IIIA and IIIB disease participants. Combination chemotherapy with a cisplatin-based regimen and thoracic radiotherapy results in better survival than radiotherapy alone.[133–135] Trials have evaluated multiple daily fractions of thoracic radiotherapy, but there are no convincing data that hyperfractionated thoracic radiotherapy (the same total dose of radiation therapy split into two treatments in the same day) is superior to standard once-daily treatment. For stage IIIA or IIIB patients with a performance score of 0 or 1 and minimal weight loss, concurrent chemoradiotherapy is recommended.[138] Concurrent therapy appears to be associated with improved survival versus sequential therapy.[136,137]

Stage IV

Stage IIIB disease due to malignant pleural or pericardial effusion is treated the same as stage IV disease because of a similar prognosis. There are virtually no 5-year survivors with stage IV (M1) NSCLC. The goal of therapy is to try

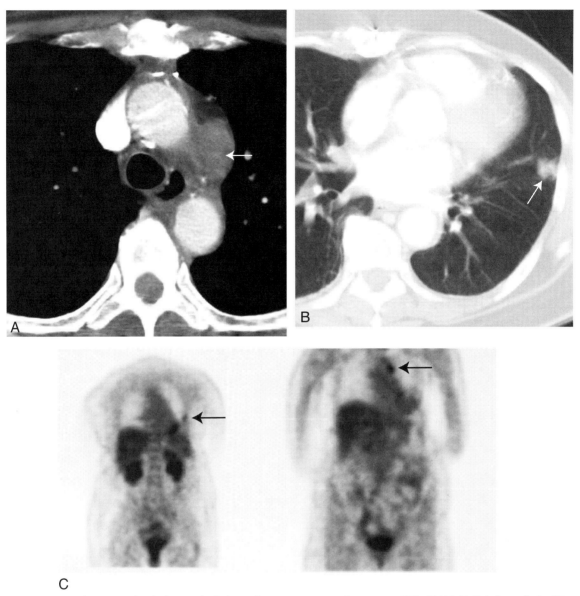

Figure 44.4 **A,** Computed tomography (CT) scan depicting primary tumor mass for a stage IIIA NSCLC (T3N1) (*arrow*). **B,** CT scan depicting enlarged aortopulmonary lymph node (*arrow*). **C,** Positron emission tomography scan with uptake in primary tumor (left image, *arrow*) and lymph node (right image, *arrow*).

to control the disease and palliate symptoms. Major response rates with current chemotherapy regimens are 10% to 30%. Patients who respond to chemotherapy may gain an additional 3 to 9 months of life on average, but eventually relapse and die of their disease. In previous trials in the 1970s and 1980s, patients were randomized to best supportive care or systemic chemotherapy. A meta-analysis evaluated eight of these randomized trials, including over 700 patients.[133] Each of these trials used a cisplatin-based chemotherapy versus supportive care. With best supportive care, the median survival time was 4 months and the 1-year survival was 15%; with chemotherapy, there was an increase in the median survival of 1.5 months and an increase in 1-year survival of 10%. In the 1990s, a number of new chemotherapy agents were introduced, including paclitaxel, docetaxel, irinotecan, vinorelbine, and gemcitabine. Phase III trials have incorporated these newer agents in combina-

tion with cisplatin or carboplatin. Trials comparing single-agent chemotherapy to a chemotherapy doublet containing a platinum compound have shown that the chemotherapy doublet is superior. Treatment with three drugs has not been shown to be superior to that with two drugs. Recent large randomized trials have tried to identify the optimum chemotherapy doublet.[139–141] Table 44.4 outlines the results of these three large randomized prospective trials. The results were uniformly similar, with response rates of 20% to 30% and median survival times of 7 to 9 months. No one platinum doublet has been shown to be superior. The chemotherapy combinations did have different toxicity profiles.

The American College of Chest Physicians guideline recommends that patients with good performance scores (0 or 1) should be considered for platinum-based chemotherapy based on the survival advantage over best supportive care.[142]

The duration of first-line therapy should be brief, consisting of three to four cycles of treatment, or fewer if there are signs of progression. Additionally, patients with good performance score who develop progressive disease should be offered second-line chemotherapy. Single-agent docetaxel has been shown to prolong survival when used in a second-line setting. Other drugs also appear to be beneficial, but have not yet received Food and Drug Administration approval for this indication.

It is generally accepted that we have hit a plateau with conventional chemotherapy for advanced NSCLC. Accordingly, there is a great deal of interest in newer agents with novel mechanisms of action (targeted therapies). The mechanisms of action of these new agents fall into the general categories of epidermal growth factor receptor inhibitors, farnesyl transferase inhibitors, cyclooxygenase-2 inhibitors, antiangiogenesis, and anti-sense molecules aimed at specific messenger ribonucleic acids.[143] To date, the only one of these agents that has received Food and Drug Administration approval for treatment of lung cancer in the United States is gefitinib (Iressa), which is an epidermal growth factor receptor tyrosine kinase inhibitor. It has been approved only for third-line treatment of relapsed NSCLC after failure with a platinum-based regimen and after docetaxel failure.[144] Many trials are underway evaluating these new agents, making this a rapidly changing area.

Table 44.5 presents an overview of treatment strategies for NSCLC.

SMALL CELL LUNG CANCER

SCLC accounts for 15% to 20% of all lung cancers. This cell type has the strongest association with cigarette smoking, and is rarely observed in a never smoker. It is the cell type most commonly associated with paraneoplastic syndromes such as the syndrome of inappropriate (excessive) antidiuretic hormone secretion (SIADH), ectopic corticotropin secretion, Lambert-Eaton myasthenic syndrome (LEMS), and sensory neuropathy.

SCLC usually presents as a centrally located mass in the hilum on chest radiograph, and may be associated with prior obstructive pneumonia. In 5% of cases or fewer, SCLC may present as a solitary pulmonary nodule/mass. SCLC is generally staged according to the old Veterans Administration Staging System, rather than the American Joint Committee on Cancer Staging system previously outlined, and classified as limited (LD) or extensive (ED) stage. LD-stage disease is confined to one hemithorax, the mediastinum, and the ipsilateral supraclavicular lymph nodes. It is disease that can be safely encompassed within one radiation portal without irradiating too much normal lung. ED stage is any disease spread beyond these sites. Malignant pleural effusion or disease extending to the contralateral supraclavicular or hilar lymph nodes is generally considered to be ED. After establishing the histologic diagnosis of SCLC, patients are usually staged with MRI of the brain, CT of the chest (through the adrenal glands), and bone scan. In the unusual

Table 44.4 Stage IV Non–Small Cell Lung Cancer Response and Survival Rate in Three Randomized Phase III Trials

Study	Regimen	RR (%)	Survival MST (mo)	Survival 1 year	Survival 2 years
Kelly et al.[139]	VC	28	8.1	36	16
	CbP	25	8.6	38	15
Schiller et al.[140]	CP	21	7.8	31	10
	GC	22	8.1	36	13
	DC	17	7.4	31	11
	CbP	17	8.1	34	11
Scagliotti et al.[141]	GC	30	9.8	38	—
	CbP	32	9.9	43	—
	VC	30	9.5	37	—

CbP, carboplatin and paclitaxel; CP, cisplatin and paclitaxel; DC, docetaxel and cisplatin; GC, gemcitabine and cisplatin; MST, median survival time; RR, response rate; VC, vinorelbine and cisplatin.

Table 44.5 Summary of Current Treatment Strategies for Non–Small Cell Lung Cancer

Stage	Surgery	Chemotherapy	Radiotherapy	Combined Chemoradiotherapy	Comments
I and II	1st line	Adjuvant—stage IB, IIA, IIB	2nd line	No	Survival improvement with adjuvant therapy (= 4%) Radiotherapy for inoperable patients
IIB (T3N0M0) Pancoast	1st line	No	No	1st line—neoadjuvant	Neoadjuvant chemoradiotherapy improves survival in this subset of stage II
IIIA	2nd line	Neoadjuvant— 2nd line	No	1st line	Combined chemoradiotherapy followed by surgery is feasible, but more data are needed to recommend routinely
IIIB (T4N0-1M0) Resectable	1st line	No	No	± Neoadjuvant— 1st line	Neoadjuvant chemoradiotherapy followed by surgery may be considered in carefully selected patients
IIIB Unresectable	No	No	No	1st line	Treatment similar to stage IIIA, stage IIIB malignant effusion is treated like stage IV
Stage IV	No	1st line	2nd line	No	Radiotherapy is used for palliation only

case of SCLC that presents as a peripheral nodule, the treatment of choice is surgical resection followed by adjuvant chemoradiotherapy. Careful preoperative staging should be performed in these individuals to rule out metastatic disease. Pre-resection mediastinoscopy should also be performed. If there are mediastinal node metastases, then surgery should be abandoned, and the patient treated with concurrent chemoradiotherapy as outlined later. Five-year survival for peripheral SCLC that is treated with surgery and adjuvant therapy is approximately 30% to 40%.

Approximately one third of patients have LD at diagnosis. LD-SCLC has a response rate of 80% to 90% with standard chemotherapy and thoracic radiotherapy, and a complete clinical response of 50% to 60%. In a meta-analysis of trials with chemotherapy alone versus combined chemotherapy and thoracic radiotherapy, survival was significantly better with combined-modality therapy. Chemotherapy usually consists of a platinum-based regimen. The two most commonly used regimens are etoposide and cisplatin or etoposide and carboplatin. Chemotherapy beyond four to six cycles has not been shown to prolong survival.

The best approach to radiotherapy for LD-SCLC is under evaluation. Two recent cooperative group trials randomized patients to once-daily versus twice-daily thoracic radiotherapy with concomitant chemotherapy.[145-147] The long-term follow up of the patients enrolled in the Eastern Cooperative Oncology Group/Radiation Therapy Oncology Group (ECOG/RTOG) trial (Table 44.6) demonstrated a superior survival at 5 years with the twice-daily radiotherapy (26% vs. 16%).[145] All patients received four cycles of etoposide and cisplatin (two cycles concurrent with radiotherapy) and thoracic radiotherapy began on day 1 with chemotherapy. However, the North Central Cancer Treatment Group trial did not demonstrate any difference in survival with twice-daily radiotherapy versus once-daily therapy (see Table 44.6).[146,147] All patients received identical chemotherapy with six cycles of etoposide and cisplatin. Radiotherapy began with cycle 4 of chemotherapy. Both trials demonstrated that the median survival time for LD-SCLC is now 18 to 20 months when patients are treated with concurrent chemoradiotherapy, and 20% to 25% of

patients will be alive at 5 years. It is unclear if twice-daily thoracic radiotherapy is superior to standard once-daily radiotherapy. Local recurrence is still a problem in over 50% of individuals with radiotherapy doses less than 50 Gy. Current trials are exploring higher doses of thoracic radiotherapy in SCLC.

ED-SCLC is treated with the same platinum-based chemotherapy doublets and has a response rate of 60% to 80%, with only 20% achieving a clinical complete remission. The median survival time for ED-SCLC is 8 to 9 months, with 10% of patients or fewer alive at 2 years.[148,149] There are virtually no 5-year survivors with ED-SCLC. Many trials have evaluated alternating non–cross-resistant chemotherapy, maintenance chemotherapy (after the initial four to six cycles), and dose intensity chemotherapy, but none of these approaches has been shown to increase survival. The standard approach to therapy of ED-SCLC is to treat with a platinum-based regimen for four to six cycles and then to observe until the patient's disease progresses, and then offer second-line chemotherapy.[145,146,148,149] A recent study from Japan compared irinotecan and cisplatin versus etoposide and cisplatin in ED-SCLC.[150] The response rate (89% vs. 67%) and survival (median survival time, 12.8 months vs. 9.4 months) were superior with the irinotecan and cisplatin regimen (2-year survival, 19.5% vs. 5.2%). Additional trials are underway to confirm or refute these results.

Prophylactic cranial irradiation (PCI) is an area of controversy. If a patient with SCLC achieves a complete remission, then there is a 50% chance of development of cranial metastasis within the next 2 years. A recent meta-analysis of seven randomized trials of PCI versus no PCI for patients in complete remission reported an observed beneficial effect after PCI, with a 5.4% increase in absolute survival (20.7% vs. 15.3%) at 3 years.[151] The major questions raised by the meta-analysis concern the optimal dose of PCI and the neuropsychological sequelae of PCI. Most, but not all, medical oncologists recommend PCI in patients who achieve a complete remission with initial therapy.

When patients relapse after initial therapy, the median survival is 3 to 4 months. There are no cures with second-line therapy. If a patient has been off treatment for 6 months or greater, then it is reasonable to use the same agents that he

Table 44.6 Small Cell Lung Cancer—Limited Disease

Trial Groups	ECOG/RTOG		NCCTG	
	Chemotherapy and Radiotherapy Once Daily	Chemotherapy and Radiotherapy Twice Daily	Chemotherapy and Radiotherapy Once Daily	Chemotherapy and Radiotherapy Twice Daily
Number of patients	176	182	133	130
Median survival time (mo)	18.6	20.3	20.5	20.4
2-yr survival	42	44	47	45
3-yr survival	—	—	34	29
5-yr survival	16	26	21	22

ECOG/RTOG, Eastern Cooperative Oncology Group/Radiation Therapy Oncology Group; NCCTG, North Central Cancer Treatment Group.
From Turrisi A III, Kim K, Blum R, et al: Twice-daily compared with once-daily thoracic radiotherapy in limited small cell lung cancer treated concurrently with cisplatin and etoposide. N Engl J Med 340:265–271, 1999.

or she received initially. If initial therapy did not include a platinum agent, then second-line therapy should be with a platinum-containing doublet. Currently, the only drug approved for second-line treatment of SCLC by the Food and Drug Administration is single-agent topotecan.[152] Other single agents such as paclitaxel or irinotecan are active, but are not yet approved by the Food and Drug Administration for second-line treatment of SCLC.

PALLIATIVE CARE

Much of this chapter is devoted to the diagnostic and treatment techniques needed to provide patients the opportunity to cure their disease. Unfortunately, most patients will eventually succumb to their disease. Although pulmonologists are adept at providing supportive care in the intensive care unit, caring for the ambulatory dying patient with lung cancer requires special consideration. There is a vast literature on ambulatory pain management, the use of interventional pulmonary techniques such as tumor ablation and stent placement to relieve malignant airway obstruction, and the use of hospice to provide end-of-life care in the home setting. With the tools now available to physicians, patients need not suffer debilitating cough, nausea, dyspnea, or pain. Pulmonologists are encouraged to provide "aggressive palliation" with the same conviction that they provide treatments for critically ill patients in the intensive care unit.[153,154]

SPECIAL CONSIDERATIONS IN LUNG CANCER

SUPERIOR SULCUS TUMORS AND PANCOAST'S SYNDROME

Pancoast's syndrome is a constellation of symptoms and signs that include shoulder and arm pain along the distribution of the eighth cranial nerve trunk and first and second thoracic nerve trunks, Horner's syndrome, and weakness and atrophy of the hand.[155–157] This most commonly is related to a local extension of an apical lung tumor located in the superior pulmonary sulcus (Pancoast's tumor). The most common cause of this symptom complex is NSCLC; however, SCLC and a number of other types of tumors and infections may rarely present in this manner.[157]

The most common initial symptom is shoulder pain, which is produced by tumor involvement of the parietal pleura, brachial plexus, vertebral bodies, and first, second, and third ribs. The pain may radiate along the upper back or shoulder into the axilla and along the distribution of the ulnar nerve. Patients are commonly treated for arthritis or bursitis of the shoulder for months before the correct diagnosis is determined. Horner's syndrome consists of ptosis, myosis, and anhydrosis, and is caused by the invasion of the paravertebral sympathetic chain and the inferior cervical (stellate) ganglion.[157] Pancoast's syndrome is present in approximately one third of patients with superior sulcus tumors reported in the literature. Weakness and atrophy of the intrinsic muscles of the hands may occur as the tumor progresses. With further extension through the intervertebral foramina, spinal compression and paraplegia may develop.

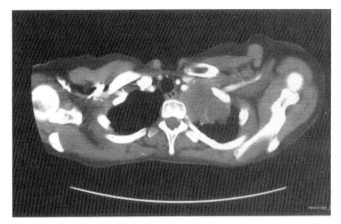

Figure 44.5 Computed tomography scan of patient with Pancoast's tumor.

The chest radiograph may show an apical tumor, although in some cases a tumor can only be identified on a CT scan of the chest. If the diagnosis is suspected, but the chest radiograph is negative, then a CT chest scan should be obtained (Fig. 44.5). CT provides additional information about the extent of the tumor, and is especially helpful in identifying other pulmonary nodules and mediastinal adenopathy. MRI of the chest is considered to be superior for evaluating patients with superior sulcus tumors because of better assessment of invasion through the pleura and subpleural fat, better evaluation of plexus involvement, and better definition of subclavian vessel involvement.[158] Magnetic resonance angiography may give the best assessment of vascular invasion of the subclavian vessels. Flexible fiberoptic bronchoscopy is frequently the first diagnostic test for apical tumors and has a diagnostic yield of approximately 50%.[159] Transthoracic needle aspiration has a very high diagnostic yield (>90%) even if the bronchoscopy is nondiagnostic.[160] Superior sulcus tumors are usually staged as T3N0M0 (stage IIB) or higher depending on size of the tumor (T3 or T4) and extent of lymph node involvement. In a large series from M. D. Anderson, 25% of patients were stage IIB, 22% were IIIA, and 53% were stage IIIB (T4 or N3).[161] Obviously, some patients are stage IV at diagnosis, but they were excluded from that report. It is estimated that one third to one half of all superior sulcus tumors have identifiable distant metastasis at diagnosis. In addition to the stage of disease and performance score, other important poor prognostic factors include weight loss, vertebral body involvement, and supraclavicular involvement. The presence of N1 or N2 nodal involvement and incomplete resections have a worse prognosis.[161,162] In patients treated for localized disease (stage IIB or IIIB), the brain is the most common site of relapse.[163]

Until recently, the most common treatment for localized superior sulcus tumors due to NSCLC was to administer preoperative radiotherapy of 30 to 50 Gy and then to resect the tumor. This resulted in 5-year survival of 25% to 35%. The current standard of practice is to perform neoadjuvant chemoradiotherapy followed by resection. This is based on results of the recent Intergroup Trial in which patients were treated with two cycles of etoposide and cisplatin chemotherapy and concurrent thoracic radiotherapy (45 Gy

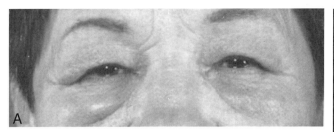

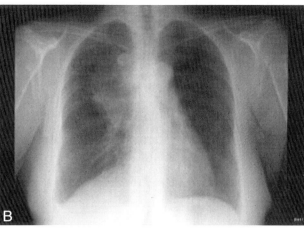

Figure 44.6 A, Facial swelling in a patient with superior vena cava (SVC) syndrome. **B,** Chest radiograph depicting right hilar mass in patient with SVC syndrome.

in 5 weeks). All patients had a negative mediastinoscopy before treatment. A pathologic complete response or minimal microscopic disease was identified in the resected specimen in 66% of patients. The overall survival at 5 years was 41%. Although the optimal regimen of treatment has not been proven, a reasonable choice is that utilized in the U.S. Intergroup Trial study.[163]

SUPERIOR VENA CAVA SYNDROME

The blockage of blood flow in the superior vena cava (SVC) results in SVC syndrome. Bronchogenic carcinoma accounts for the vast majority of these cases in older adults.[164,165] In teenagers and young adults, SVC syndrome is usually due to non-Hodgkin's lymphoma. Patients complain of dyspnea and a sensation of fullness in the head and/or lightheadedness when bending over. They may also note facial swelling. Cough, pain, and dysphagia are less frequent symptoms. Physical examination findings included dilated neck veins, a prominent venous pattern on the chest, facial edema, and a plethoric appearance (Fig. 44.6A). The chest radiograph typically shows widening of the mediastinum or a right hilar mass (Fig. 44.6B). Occasionally, it may be normal. Dilated veins on the anterior chest wall and compression of the SVC may be demonstrated with a contrast-enhanced CT scan. SVC syndrome is not generally a medical emergency. Patients should not be treated without a tissue diagnosis. Bronchoscopy or mediastinoscopy can be safely performed in the setting of SVC syndrome.[166] SVC syndrome due to SCLC is best treated with chemotherapy. Generally, after treatment, symptoms will start to resolve in 5 to 7 days because SCLC is so chemosensitive.[167] NSCLC is best treated with concurrent chemoradiotherapy (see earlier discussion of treatment of stage IIIA/IIIB NSCLC). Occasionally, surgical palliation or vascular stenting should be considered.

PARANEOPLASTIC SYNDROMES

Hormonal, neurologic, hematologic, or other remote effects of cancer not related to the direct invasion, obstruction, or metastatic effects of tumor are generally termed *paraneoplastic syndromes*. Paraneoplastic syndromes related to bronchogenic carcinoma occur in 10% to 20% of patients (Table 44.7).

MUSCULOSKELETAL EFFECTS

Clubbing of the digits may be a manifestation of lung cancer or other diseases. Clubbing may involve the fingers and toes and consists of selective enlargement of the connective tissue in the terminal phalanges. Physical findings include loss of the angle between the base of the nail bed and cuticle, rounded nails, and enlarged fingertips. Clubbing is an isolated finding and is usually asymptomatic. Nonmalignant causes of clubbing include pulmonary fibrosis, congenital heart disease, and bronchiectasis.

Hypertrophic pulmonary osteoarthropathy (HPO) is an uncommon process associated with lung cancer. HPO is characterized by painful arthropathy that usually involves the ankles, knees, wrists, and elbows and is most often symmetrical. The pain and arthropathy are caused by proliferative periostitis that involves the long bones, but may also involve metacarpal, metatarsal, and phalangeal bones. Patients may have clubbing of fingers and toes in addition to the painful arthralgias. The pathogenesis of HPO is uncertain, but it may arise from a humoral agent. For patients who smoke and have a new onset of arthralgias, HPO must be considered. A radiograph of the long bones (i.e., tibia and fibula) usually shows characteristic, periosteal new bone formation. An isotope bone scan typically demonstrates diffuse uptake by the long bones. Large cell and adenocarcinoma are the most common histologic types associated with HPO. The symptoms of HPO may resolve after thoracotomy, whether the primary cancer is resected or not. For inoperable patients, the best treatment is nonsteroidal anti-inflammatory agents.

While still a topic of debate, population-based studies from Scandinavia suggest a frequency of malignancy of 15% to 25% in patients with dermatomyositis-polymyositis.[168] The highest risk of malignancy is in the first 2 years after the diagnosis of dermatomyositis-polymyositis. A reasonable approach to cancer surveillance in these patients is a careful history and physical examination, chest radiograph, basic laboratory tests, and age-appropriate cancer screening exams. Other tests should be based on abnormalities detected during the basic evaluation.

Table 44.7 Paraneoplastic Syndromes Associated with Bronchogenic Carcinoma

System	Paraneoplastic Syndrome
Musculoskeletal	Clubbing Hypertrophic osteoarthropathy Polymyositis Osteomalacia Myopathy
Cutaneous	Dermatomyositis Acanthosis nigricans Pruritus Erythema multiforme Hyperpigmentation Urticaria Scleroderma
Endocrinologic	Cushing's syndrome Syndrome of inappropriate secretion of antidiuretic hormone Hypercalcemia Carcinoid syndrome Hyperglycemia/hypoglycemia Gynecomastia Galactorrhea Growth hormone excess Calcitonin secretion Thyroid-stimulating hormone
Neurologic	Lambert-Eaton myasthenic syndrome Peripheral neuropathy Encephalopathy Myelopathy Cerebellar degeneration Psychosis Dementia
Vascular/hematologic	Thrombophlebitis Arterial thrombosis Nonbacterial thrombotic endocarditis Thrombocytosis Polycythemia Hemolytic anemia Red cell aplasia Dysproteinemia Leukemoid reaction Eosinophilia Thrombocytopenic purpura
Miscellaneous	Cachexia Hyperuricemia Nephrotic syndrome

HEMATOLOGIC EFFECTS

Anemia frequently occurs in patients who have lung cancer and may be caused by iron deficiency, chronic disease, or bone marrow infiltration. Eosinophilia is more commonly associated with Hodgkin's disease but may occur in patients who have lung cancer. Production of various cytokines by neoplastic cells may result in eosinophilia, leukocytosis, or thrombocytosis, of which thrombocytosis is by far the most common.

The association of deep venous thrombosis and malignancy was described by Trousseau over a century ago, and lung cancer is the most common malignancy associated with Trousseau's syndrome. The causes of the hypercoagulable state remain poorly understood. One large study documented clinically significant association of idiopathic thrombosis and the subsequent development of overt cancer; however, other investigators concluded that the literature does not enable firm recommendations about whether to screen for a malignant neoplasm in patients who have unexplained venous thromboembolism.[169] Thromboembolism in the patient who has malignancy is often refractory to warfarin treatment. Treatment with low-molecular-weight heparin on a chronic basis may be effective. In a recent randomized trial, patients with cancer and deep vein thrombosis, pulmonary embolism, or both were randomized to receive low-molecular-weight heparin (dalteparin) subcutaneously once daily or oral warfarin daily for 6 months. At 6 months, the probability of recurrent thromboembolism was 9% with dalteparin treatment and 17% with warfarin, a difference that was highly significant.[170] The risks of major bleeding or any bleeding were not different in the two groups. The other advantage of low-molecular-weight heparin is that it is unnecessary to monitor the anticoagulant effect, except in some patients with renal insufficiency. A randomized trial with the oral direct thrombin inhibitor ximelagathan demonstrated that treatment for 18 months beyond the standard 6 months of anticoagulant therapy decreased the risk of developing recurrent thromboembolism versus placebo (hazard ratio, 0.16).[171] Oral ximelagathan therapy does not require anticoagulant monitoring, but further studies are needed to clarify the role of this promising drug.

HYPERCALCEMIA

Hypercalcemia in association with malignancy may arise from a bony metastasis or, less commonly, from secretion by the tumor of a parathyroid hormone–related protein (PTHrP) or other bone-resorbing cytokine. The most common cancers to cause hypercalcemia are those of the kidney, lung, breast, head, and neck, and myeloma and lymphoma. In one study of 690 consecutive lung cancers, 2.5% of cases had tumor-induced hypercalcemia.[172] Squamous cell histology is the most common cell type associated with hypercalcemia, and generally patients have advanced disease (stage III or IV) and are unresectable. Symptoms of hypercalcemia include anorexia, nausea, vomiting, constipation, lethargy, polyuria, polydipsia, and dehydration. Confusion and coma are late manifestations, as are renal failure and nephrocalcinosis. Cardiovascular effects include shortened Q–T interval, broad T wave, heart block, ventricular arrhythmia, and asystole. Individual patients may manifest any combination of these signs and symptoms in various degrees.

Hypercalcemia of malignancy that is not caused by bony metastases results from accelerated bone resorption, decreased bone deposition, or increased renal tubular reabsorption of calcium. Accelerated bone resorption is caused by activation of osteoclasts by cytokines or PTHrP in most cases. Serum parathyroid hormone levels are usually normal or low, but an elevated level of PTHrP can be detected in the serum in approximately one half of these patients.[172] Cytokines or PTHrP are secreted autonomously by the tumor. Not only does PTHrP cause renal calcium reabsorption, but also it interferes with renal mechanisms for reabsorption of sodium and water, with resultant polyuria. Polyuria and vomiting result in dehydration; decreases in glomerular filtration further aggravate the hypercalcemia.

Mild elevation of serum calcium may not require treatment, so the decision is based on the patient's symptoms. For patients who have widely metastatic and incurable malignancy, it may be most appropriate to give supportive care only and not treat the hypercalcemia. The average life expectancy in this situation is 30 to 45 days, even with aggressive treatment.[173]

Most patients who have a serum calcium of 12 to 13 mg/dL or higher are treated. The corrected serum calcium in such individuals who have low albumins is calculated by the following equation:

$$\text{Measured serum calcium} + 0.8 \times [4 \text{ g/dL} \\ (\text{or } 40 \text{ g/L}) - \text{measured serum albumin}] = \\ \text{corrected serum calcium}$$

The four basic goals of treatment are to (1) correct dehydration; (2) increase renal excretion of calcium; (3) inhibit bone resorption; and (4) treat the underlying malignancy.

Because of the polyuria, patients with hypercalcemia are volume contracted. Initial treatment is with intravenous normal saline, using 3 to 6 L per 24 hours as tolerated, with careful attention to volume status. After hydration, a loop diuretic such as furosemide or ethacrynic acid is added. Thiazide diuretics are not used because they increase calcium reabsorption in the distal tubule. Fluids and diuretics generally result in only a mild decrease of the calcium; additional treatment is needed to inhibit the accelerated bone resorption. The bisphosphonates have a high affinity for bone and inhibit osteoclast activity. Zoledronate, a newer bisphosphonate, is the most effective; the usual dose is 4 mg given intravenously over 15 minutes.[174] Normal calcium levels are achieved within 4 to 10 days in 85% of patients and last a median of 30 to 40 days. Adverse effects are generally mild and transient, and include fever, hypophosphatemia, and asymptomatic hypocalcemia. Occasional renal adverse events may occur with elevation of serum creatinine. Calcitonin inhibits bone resorption, increases renal calcium excretion, and has a rapid onset of action, but the duration of action is short lived. Calcitonin is a relatively weak agent and, when used alone, does not usually normalize the serum calcium of patients who have marked hypercalcemia. Use of calcitonin is appropriate when the calcium needs to be lowered urgently (onset of action is 4 to 6 hours) while waiting for the more effective but slower acting agents to take effect, or when relief of bony pain is desired. The effects of calcitonin and bisphosphonates are additive. Other agents such as gallium nitrate or plicamycin have been used to treat hypercalcemia, but have not generally been adopted as first-line therapies because of inconvenience of administration schedules or associated toxicities.

SYNDROME OF INAPPROPRIATE ANTIDIURETIC HORMONE SECRETION

Causes of hyponatremia include tumors, pulmonary infections, central nervous system disorders, and drugs. Approximately 10% of patients who have SCLC exhibit SIADH;

however, SCLC accounts for approximately 75% of cases of SIADH. Antidiuretic hormone (vasopressin) is secreted in the anterior hypothalamus and exerts its action on the renal collecting ducts by enhancing the flow of water from the lumen into the medullary interstitium, which results in the concentration of urine. The criteria for the diagnosis of SIADH include (1) hyponatremia associated with serum hypo-osmolality (<275 mOsm/kg), (2) inappropriately elevated urine osmolality (>200 mOsm/kg) relative to serum osmolality; (3) elevated urine sodium (>20 mEq/L); (4) clinical euvolemia without edema; and (5) normal renal (creatinine <1.5 times the upper limit of normal), adrenal, and thyroid function. The serum uric acid is usually low, and the urine osmolality–to–serum osmolality ratio is frequently greater than 2.

The severity of symptoms is related to the degree of hyponatremia and the rapidity of the fall in serum sodium. In one large series of SIADH patients, only 27% had signs or symptoms of hyponatremia despite a median sodium of 117 mEq/L (range, 101 to 129 mEq/L). Symptoms of hyponatremia include anorexia, nausea, and vomiting. With rapid onset of hyponatremia, symptoms caused by cerebral edema may include irritability, restlessness, personality changes, confusion, coma, seizures, and respiratory arrest. In minimally symptomatic or asymptomatic patients, fluid restriction of 500 to 1000 mL per 24 hours is the initial treatment of choice. If further treatment is needed, oral demeclocycline 900 to 1200 mg/day is considered. Demeclocycline induces a nephrogenic diabetes insipidus and blocks the action of antidiuretic hormone on the renal tubule, thereby increasing water excretion. The onset of action varies from a few hours to a few weeks, so this drug is not recommended for acute emergency treatment. In patients who have more severe or life-threatening symptoms (serum sodium <115 mEq/L), treatment consists of intravenous saline, supplemental potassium, and diuresis with loop diuretics such as furosemide or ethacrynic acid. With severe confusion, convulsions, or coma, it may be appropriate to treat with 300 mL of 3% saline given over 3 to 4 hours in combination with a loop diuretic (saline with no diuretic does not raise the sodium concentration). Rapid correction of the sodium may have life-threatening consequences, and caution is advised.[175] The rate of correction of the sodium is best limited to 2 mEq/L per hour, or a maximum of 20 mEq/L per day, until a level of 120 to 130 mEq/L is reached. Faster correction has been associated with the development of central pontine myelinolysis, which may result in quadriplegia, cranial nerve abnormalities that manifest as pseudobulbar palsy, alteration in mental status, and subsequent death. Accordingly, in the course of treating hyponatremia, the serum sodium must be monitored frequently to ensure that correction is not too rapid. For patients with SIADH due to SCLC, treatment with chemotherapy should be initiated as soon as possible, and is likely to result in improvement in the hyponatremia within a few weeks. After an initial response to chemotherapy, SIADH may recur when the tumor relapses.

ECTOPIC CORTICOTROPIN SYNDROME

Ectopic production of corticotropin or corticotropin-releasing hormone with associated Cushing's syndrome has been identified in patients who have SCLC, carcinoid tumor (lung, thymus, or pancreas), and neurocrest tumors such as pheochromocytoma, neuroblastoma, and medullary carcinoma of the thyroid.[176] Of those with ectopic corticotropin secretion, SCLC accounts for 75% of cases, although, of patients who have SCLC, only 1% to 2% develop Cushing's syndrome. Thus, Cushing's syndrome is seldom caused by NSCLC.

Classic features of Cushing's syndrome include truncal obesity, striae, rounded (moon) facies, dorsocervical fat pad (buffalo hump), myopathy and weakness, osteoporosis, diabetes mellitus, hypertension, and personality changes. However, the rapid growth of SCLC means that patients are more likely to present with edema, hypertension, and muscular weakness than with the classic features of Cushing's syndrome. Hypokalemic alkalosis and hyperglycemia are usually present. Patients with SCLC and Cushing's syndrome appear to have shortened survival as compared to those without the syndrome. This may be because of more frequent opportunistic infections. The best screen for Cushing's syndrome is the 24-hour urine free cortisol measurement. Elevation of cortisol production, lack of suppression with high-dose dexamethasone, and plasma corticotropin levels greater than 200 pg/mL (40 pmol/L) are highly suggestive of ectopic corticotropin as the cause of Cushing's syndrome in the absence of a pituitary adenoma (negative imaging study). The plasma level of corticotropin is elevated in many, but not all patients.

Treatment of Cushing's syndrome due to ectopic corticotropin has included adrenal enzyme inhibitors such as metyrapone, aminoglutethimide, and ketoconazole, given alone or in combination. Ketoconazole given orally at a dosage of 400 to 1200 mg/day may control hypercortisolism within a few days to weeks, but the response is variable. Dose adjustments are based on the urinary free cortisol levels. Symptomatic hypoadrenalism may result from treatment, and some authorities recommend a replacement dose of glucocorticoid when an enzyme inhibitor is started. When Cushing's syndrome arises from SCLC, it is advisable to proceed with appropriate chemotherapy and carefully watch for superimposed infections, as is necessary for any patient who is receiving high-dose corticosteroids. Cushing's syndrome related to a bronchial carcinoid or thymic carcinoid is best treated by surgical resection of the tumor.

NEUROLOGIC EFFECTS

The paraneoplastic neurologic syndromes associated with lung cancer, mostly small cell type, are quite variable. They include Lambert-Eaton myasthenia syndrome (LEMS), subacute sensory neuropathy, encephalomyelopathy, cerebellar degeneration, autonomic neuropathy, retinal degeneration, and opsoclonus.[177] The frequency of any of these neurologic syndromes in SCLC is approximately 5%, and neurologic symptoms may precede the diagnosis by months to years.[178,179] Most patients who have SCLC and an associated paraneoplastic syndrome have LD-SCLC that may or may not be obvious on initial evaluation. The tumor is often occult, and the neurologic syndrome may precede the diagnosis by months to several years. Careful radiographic evaluation of the lungs and mediastinum is indicated in a smoker who has a suspected paraneoplastic neurologic syndrome. In this

setting, even subtle abnormalities of the mediastinum require a biopsy. A positive PET scan may help identify the lesion to facilitate biopsy confirmation of the diagnosis. Many reports have suggested that patients with paraneoplastic neurologic syndromes have a better prognosis than those without the paraneoplastic syndromes with similar stage and histology.

These paraneoplastic neurologic syndromes are thought to be immune mediated, based on the identification of a number of antibodies in the serum that react with both the nervous system and the underlying cancer.[177] However, not all patients with paraneoplastic syndromes have identifiable antibodies in their serum. The literature is confusing because of different names employed by various investigators. The anti-Hu antibody is the same as antineuronal nuclear antibody type I (ANNA-1), and the anti-Ri antibody is identical to ANNA-2. Both of these antibodies, but predominantly ANNA-1, have been associated with SCLC. ANNA-1 binds to the nucleus of all neurons in the central and peripheral nervous system, including the sensory and autonomic ganglia, the myenteric plexus, and cells of the adrenal medulla. Such antibodies should not be confused with the anti–Purkinje cell antibody (anti-Yo), which is characteristically found in patients who have subacute cerebellar degeneration as a manifestation of gynecologic malignancy or breast cancer. The newly described CRMP-5 antibody, also known as anti–CV-2, has been associated with SCLC and thymomas.[177]

In a review of 162 sequential patients who had ANNA-1 (anti-Hu), 142 (88%) were proved to have cancer, 132 of whom had SCLC.[178] In 97% of these cases, the diagnosis of SCLC followed the onset of the associated neurologic syndrome, usually by less than 6 months, but in 20% the period was greater than 6 months. Of special note is that 90% of cases had disease limited to the lung or lung and mediastinum (LD-SCLC). In a report from Europe, 144 patients out of 200 with anti-Hu antibodies had a tumor in the chest. Of these, 111 were proven to be SCLC.[179] In one large series, ANNA-1 antibodies were identified in 16% of all patients with SCLC. These antibodies were associated with limited-stage disease, complete response to therapy, and longer survival as compared to patients who had SCLC and no ANNA-1 antibody. These neurologic syndromes seldom improve with treatment, so the goal is to start treatment as soon as possible, and thereby try to prevent progression of the disease process.

Less common manifestations of neurologic paraneoplastic syndromes are orthostatic hypotension and intestinal dysmotility. The gastrointestinal symptoms may present as nausea, vomiting, abdominal discomfort, or altered bowel habits suggestive of intestinal pseudo-obstruction. Many of these patients present with gastrointestinal symptoms and significant weight loss prior to the diagnosis of SCLC.

Proximal muscle weakness, hyporeflexia, and autonomic dysfunction characterize LEMS.[180,181] Cranial nerve involvement may be present and does not differentiate LEMS from myasthenia gravis. LEMS has been strongly associated with antibodies directed against P/Q-type presynaptic voltage-gated calcium channels (anti-VGCC antibodies) of peripheral cholinergic nerve terminals. These antibodies, identified in over 90% of patients with LEMS, block the normal release of acetylcholine at the neuromuscular junction. In contrast, myasthenia gravis is associated with anti–acetylcholine receptor antibodies, which are present in approximately 90% of myasthenic patients. Malignancy is present in approximately one half of patients who have LEMS, and SCLC is by far the most common malignancy. Of all patients who suffer SCLC, only 2% to 4% have LEMS. Anti-VGCC antibodies have also been identified in 25% of SCLC patients who are not affected by neurologic problems. The diagnosis of LEMS is based on characteristic electromyographic findings that show a small amplitude of the resting compound muscle action potential and facilitation with rapid, repetitive, supramaximal nerve stimulation or after brief exercise of the muscle. A single-fiber electromyogram is optimal for making the diagnosis.

LEMS is the predominant paraneoplastic neurologic syndrome that may improve with successful treatment of the associated lung cancer. The use of acetylcholinesterase inhibitors is of limited benefit in LEMS. Diaminopyridine enhances the release of acetylcholine and has been used with sustained improvement over months in the majority of patients with LEMS either with or without cancer.[182]

SUMMARY

Lung cancer is a devastating disease that currently claims more lives than breast, colon, and prostate cancer combined. Despite the poor outcome associated with this disease, the diagnostic, staging, and treatment algorithms are fairly well established and should be rigorously followed. The pulmonologist plays an important role in all aspects of lung cancer care. The pulmonologist is critical in the diagnostic and staging portions of the patients' evaluation and in the assessment of physiologic function prior to surgery. Further, the pulmonologist can add to the care of patients who have pulmonary toxicity associated with treatment and can provide palliation, both in the bronchoscopy suite and during end-of-life care. Lung cancer should be approached by a team of clinicians with expertise in all aspects of treatment to ensure the best quality care is provided to patients. Whenever possible, patients should be enrolled in clinical trials so that more information can be gained, ultimately translating into that ever-so-elusive cure for this disease.

REFERENCES

1. Liu BQ, Peto R, Chen ZM, et al: Retrospective proportional mortality study of one million deaths. BMJ 317:1411–1422, 1998.
2. Gordon T, Crittenden M, Haenszel W: Cancer mortality trends in the United States, 1930–1955. Natl Cancer Inst Monogr 6:131–350, 1961.
3. Parkin DM, Pisani P, Lopez AD, et al: At least one in seven cases of cancer is caused by smoking: Global estimates for 1995. Int J Cancer 59:494–504, 1994.
4. Yang G, Fan L, Tan J, et al: Smoking in China: Findings of the 1996 National Prevalence Survey. JAMA 282:1247–1253, 1999.
5. Smith RA, Cokkinides V, Eyre HJ: American Cancer Society guidelines for early detection of cancer. CA Cancer J Clin 53:27–43, 2003.
6. Fontana RS, Sanderson DR, Woolner LB, et al: Lung cancer screening: The Mayo program. J Occup Med 28:746–750, 1986.
7. Marcus P, Bergstralh E, Fagerstrom R, et al: Lung cancer mortality in Mayo Lung Project: Impact of extended follow up. J Natl Cancer Inst 92:1308–1316, 2000.
8. Bach P, Kelly M, Tate R, et al: Screening for lung cancer: A review of the literature. Chest 123(1 Suppl):72S–82S, 2003.
9. Fontana R, Sanderson D, Taylor W, et al: Early lung cancer detection: Results of the initial (prevalence) radiologic and cytologic screening in the Mayo Clinic Study. Am Rev Respir Dis 130:561–565, 1984.
10. Henschke C, McCauley D, Yankelevitz D, et al: Early Lung Cancer Detection Project: Overall design and findings from baseline screening. Lancet 354:99–105, 1999.
11. Sone S, Li F, Yang Z, et al: Characteristics of small lung concerns invisible on conventional chest radiography and detected by population based screening using spiral CT. Br J Radiol 73:137–145, 2000.
12. Sobue T, Moriyama N, Kaneko M, et al: Screening for lung cancer with low-dose helical computed tomography: Anti-Lung Cancer Association Project. J Clin Oncol 20:911–920, 2002.
13. Swensen S, Jett J, Sloan J, et al: Screening for lung cancer with low-dose spiral computed tomography. Am J Respir Crit Care Med 165:508–513, 2002.
14. Diederich S, Wormanns D, Semik M, et al: Screening for early lung cancer with low-dose spiral CT: Prevalence in 817 asymptomatic smokers. Radiology 222:773–781, 2002.
15. Swensen S, Jett J, Hartman T, et al: Lung cancer screening with CT: Mayo Clinic experience. Radiology 226:756–761, 2003.
16. Welch H: Finding and redefining disease. Effective Clin Pract 2:96–98, 1999.
17. Bach P, Niewwoehner D, Black W: Screening for lung cancer: The guidelines. Chest 123(1 Suppl):83S–88S, 2003.
18. Chute C, Greenberg E, Baron J, et al: Presenting conditions of 1539 population-based lung cancer patients by cell type and stage in New Hampshire and Vermont. Cancer 56:2107, 1985.
19. Hyde L, Hyde C: Clinical manifestations of lung cancer. Chest 65:299, 1974.
20. Colice GL: Detecting lung cancer as a cause of hemoptysis in a patient with a normal radiograph. Chest 111:877–884, 1997.
21. Mountain C: Revisions in the International System for Staging Lung Cancer. Chest 111:1710–1717, 1997.
22. Mountain C, Dresler C: Regional lymph node classification for lung cancer staging. Chest 111:1718–1723, 1997.
23. Darling GE: Staging of the patient with small cell lung cancer. Chest Surg Clin N Am 7:81–94, 1997.
24. Toloza E, Harpole L, Detterbeck F, et al: Invasive staging of non-small cell lung cancer: A review of the current evidence. Chest 123(1 Suppl):157S–166S, 2003.
25. Toloza E, Harpole L, McCrory DC: Non-invasive clinical staging of non-small cell lung cancer: Radiographic and clinical evaluation of intra- and extra-thoracic disease. Chest 123(1 Suppl):137S–146S, 2003.
26. American Thoracic Society and European Respiratory Society: Pretreatment evaluation of non-small cell lung cancer. Am J Respir Crit Care Med 156:320–332, 1997.
27. McLoud T, Bourgouin P, Greenberg R, et al: Bronchogenic carcinoma: Analysis of staging in the mediastinum with CT by correlative lymph node mapping and sampling. Radiology 182:319–323, 1992.
28. Silvestri GA, Tanoue LT, Margolis ML, et al: The noninvasive staging of non-small cell lung cancer: The guidelines. Chest 123(1 Suppl):147S–156S, 2003.
29. Nolop K, Rhodes C, Brudin L, et al: Glucose utilization in vivo by human pulmonary neoplasms. Cancer 60:2682–2689, 1987.

30. Wahl RI, Hitchins GD, Buchsbaum DJ, et al: ^{18}F-2-deoxy-2-fluoro-D-glucose uptake into human tumor xenografts: Feasibility studies for cancer imaging with positron-emission tomography. Cancer 67:1544–1550, 1991.

31. Pieterman RM, van Putten JWG, Meuzelaar JJ, et al: Preoperative staging of non-small-cell lung cancer with positron-emission tomography. N Engl J Med 343:254–261, 2000.

32. van Tinteren H, Hoekstra O, Smit E, et al: Effectiveness of positron emission tomography in the preoperative assessment of patients with suspected non-small cell lung cancer: The PLUS Multicentre Randomised Trial. Lancet 359:1388–1393, 2002.

33. Hany TF, Steinert HC, Goerres GW, et al: PET diagnostic accuracy: Improvement with in-line PET-CT system. Initial results. Radiology 225:575–581, 2002.

34. Antoch G, Stattaus J, Nemat AT, et al: Non-small cell lung cancer: Dual modality PET/CT in preoperative staging. Radiology 229:526–533, 2003.

35. Silvestri G, Littenberg B, Colice G: The clinical evaluation for detecting metastatic lung cancer: A meta-analysis. Am J Respir Crit Care Med 152:225–230, 1995.

36. Saunders CAB, Dussek JE, O'Doherty MJ, et al: Evaluation of fluorine-18-fluorodeoxyglucose whole body positron emission tomography imaging in the staging of lung cancer. Ann Thorac Surg 67:790–797, 1999.

37. Weder W, Schmid RA, Bruchhaus H, et al: Detection of extrathoracic metastases by positron emission tomography in lung cancer. Ann Thorac Surg 66:886–893, 1998.

38. MacManus MP, Hicks RJ, Matthews JP, et al: High rate of unsuspected distant metastases by PET in apparent stage III non-small-cell lung cancer: Implications for radical radiation therapy. Int J Radiat Oncol Biol Phys 50:287–293, 2001.

39. Hooper RG, Beechler CR, Johnson MC: Radioisotope scanning in the initial staging of bronchogenic carcinoma. Am Rev Respir Dis 118:279–286, 1978.

40. Hooper RG, Tenholder MF, Underwood GH, et al: Computed tomographic scanning in initial staging of bronchogenic carcinoma. Chest 85:774–777, 1984.

41. Turner P, Haggith JW: Preoperative radionuclide scanning in bronchogenic carcinoma. Chest 75:291–294, 1981.

42. Ramsdell JW, Peters RM, Taylor AT, et al: Multiorgan scans for staging lung cancer—correlation with clinical evaluation. J Thorac Cardiovasc Surg 73:653–659, 1977.

43. British Thoracic Society and Society of Cardiothoracic Surgeons of Great Britain and Ireland Working Party: Guidelines on the selection of patients with lung cancer for surgery. Thorax 56:89–106, 2001.

44. Grant D, Edwards D, Goldstraw P: Computed tomography of the brain, chest, and abdomen in the preoperative assessment of non-small-cell lung cancer. Thorax 43:883–886, 1988.

45. Colice G, Birkmeyer J, Black W, et al: Cost-effectiveness of head CT in patients with lung cancer without clinical evidence of metastases. Chest 108:1264–1271, 1995.

46. Tarver RD, Richmond BD, Klatte EC: Cerebral metastases from lung carcinoma: Neurological and CT correlation work in progress. Radiology 153:689–692, 1984.

47. Salvatierra A, Baamonde C, Llamas JM, et al: Extrathoracic staging of bronchogenic carcinoma. Chest 97:1052–1058, 1990.

48. Tanaka K, Kubota K, Kodama T, et al: Extrathoracic staging is not necessary for non-small cell lung cancer with clinical stage T1–2 N0. Ann Thorac Surg 68:1039–1042, 1999.

49. Hillers T, Sauve M, Guyatt G: Analysis of published studies on the detection of extrathoracic metastases in patients presumed to have operable non-small cell lung cancer. Thorax 49:14–19, 1994.

50. Pagani JJ: Non-small cell lung carcinoma adrenal metastases—computed tomography and percutaneous needle biopsy in their diagnosis. Cancer 53:1058–1060, 1984.

51. Quinn DL, Ostrow LB, Porter DK, et al: Staging of non-small cell bronchogenic carcinoma—relationship of the clinical evaluation to organ scans. Chest 89:270–275, 1986.

52. Ichinose Y, Hara N, Ohta M, et al: Preoperative examination to detect distant metastases is not advocated for asymptomatic patients with stages I and II non-small cell lung cancer—preoperative examination for lung cancer. Chest 96:1104–1109, 1989.

53. Canadian Lung Oncology Group: Investigating extrathoracic metastatic disease in patients with apparently operable lung cancer. Ann Thorac Surg 71:425–433, 2001.

54. Goerg C, Schwerk WB, Wolf M, et al: Adrenal masses in lung cancer: Sonographic diagnosis and follow-up. Eur J Cancer 28A:1400–1403, 1992.

55. Oliver T Jr, Bernardino M, Miller J, et al: Isolated adrenal masses in non-small cell bronchogenic carcinoma. Radiology 153:217–218, 1984.

56. Burt M, Heelan R, Coit D, et al: Prospective evaluation of unilateral adrenal masses in patients with operable non-small cell lung cancer: Impact of magnetic resonance imaging. J Thorac Cardiovasc Surg 107:584–588, 1994.

57. Pearlberg JL, Sandler MA, Beute GH, et al: T1N0M0 bronchogenic carcinoma: Assessment by CT. Radiology 157:187–190, 1985.

58. Heavey LR, Glazer GM, Gross BH, et al: The role of CT in staging radiographic T1N0M0 lung cancer. AJR Am J Roentgenol 146:285–290, 1986.

59. Eggesbo HB, Hansen G: Clinical impact of adrenal expansive lesions in bronchial carcinoma. Acta Radiol 37:343–347, 1996.

60. Ettinghausen SE, Burt ME: Prospective evaluation of unilateral adrenal masses in patients with operable non-small cell lung cancer. J Clin Oncol 9:1462–1466, 1991.

61. Porte HL, Ernst OJ, Delebecq T, et al: Is computed tomography guided biopsy still necessary for the diagnosis of adrenal masses in patients with resectable non-small cell lung cancer? Eur J Cardiothorac Surg 15:597–601, 1999.

62. Macari M, Rofsky NM, Naidich DP, et al: Non-small cell lung carcinoma: Usefulness of unenhanced helical CT of the adrenal glands in an unmonitored environment. Radiology 209:807–812, 1998.

63. Gillams A, Roberts CM, Shaw P, et al: The value of CT scanning and percutaneous fine needle aspiration of adrenal masses in biopsy-proven lung cancer. Clin Radiol 46:18–22, 1992.

64. Heinz-Peer G, Honigschnabi S, Schneider B, et al: Characterization of adrenal masses using MR imaging with histopathologic correlation. AJR Am J Roentgenol 173:15–22, 1999.

65. Gross MD, Shapiro B, Bouffard JA, et al: Distinguishing benign from malignant euadrenal masses. Ann Intern Med 109:613–618, 1988.

66. Nielson ME, Heaston DK, Dunnick NR, et al: Preoperative CT evaluation of adrenal glands in non-small cell bronchogenic carcinoma. AJR Am J Roentgenol 139:317–320, 1982.

67. Chapman GS, Kumar D, Redmond J, et al: Upper abdominal computerized tomography scanning in staging non-small cell lung carcinoma. Cancer 54:1541–1543, 1984.

68. Cole JFH, Thomas JE, Wilcox AB, et al: Cerebral imaging in the asymptomatic preoperative bronchogenic carcinoma patient: Is it worthwhile? Ann Thorac Surg 57:838–840, 1994.

69. Kormas P, Bradshaw J, Jeyasingham K: Preoperative computed tomography of the brain in non-small cell bronchogenic carcinoma. Thorax 47:106–108, 1992.

70. Jacobs L, Kinkel WR, Vincent RG: "Silent" brain metastasis from lung carcinoma determined by computerized tomography. Arch Neurol 77:690–693, 1977.

71. Butler AR, Leo JS, Lin JP, et al: The value of routine cranial computed tomography in neurologically intact patients with primary carcinoma of the lung. Radiology 131:339–401, 1979.

72. Mintz BJ, Turhim S, Alexander S, et al: Intracranial metastases in the initial staging of bronchogenic carcinoma. Chest 86:850–853, 1984.

73. Ferrigno D, Buccheri G: Cranial computed tomography as a part of the initial staging procedures for patients with non-small cell lung cancer. Chest 106:1025–1029, 1994.

74. Patchell R, Tibbs P, Walsh J, et al: A randomized trial of surgery in the treatment of single metastases to the brain. N Engl J Med 322:494–500, 1990.

75. Davis PC, Hudgins PA, Peterman SB, et al: Diagnosis of cerebral metastases: Double-dose delayed CT vs contrast-enhanced MR imaging. AJR Am J Roentgenol 156:1039–1046, 1991.

76. Yokio K, Kamiya N, Matsuguma H, et al: Detection of brain metastasis in potentially operable non-small cell lung cancer—a comparison of CT and MRI. Chest 115:714–719, 1999.

77. Gayed I, Vu T, Johnson M, et al: Comparison of bone and 2-deoxy-2-[^{18}F]fluoro-D-glucose positron emission tomography in the evaluation of bony metastases in lung cancer. Mol Imaging Biol 5:26–31, 2003.

78. Rivera M, Detterbeck F, Mehta A: Diagnosis of lung cancer: The guidelines. Chest 123(1 Suppl):129S–136S, 2003.

79. Torringer KG, Kern JD: The utility of fiberoptic bronchoscopy in the evaluation of solitary pulmonary nodules. Chest 104:1021–1024, 1993.

80. VanSonnenberg E, Casola G, Ho M, et al: Difficult thoracic lesions: CT-guided biopsy experience in 150 cases. Radiology 167:457–461, 1988.

81. Li H, Boiselle PM, Shepard JO: Diagnostic accuracy and safety of CT-guided percutaneous needle aspiration biopsy of the lung: Comparison of small and large pulmonary nodules. AJR Am J Roentgenol 167:105–109, 1996.

82. Kazerooni EA, Lim FT, Mikhail A, et al: Risk of pneumothorax in CT-guided transthoracic needle aspiration biopsy of the lung. Radiology 198:371–375, 1996.

83. Ost D, Fein AM, Feinsilver SH: The solitary pulmonary nodule. N Engl J Med 348:2535–2542, 2003.

84. Simoff MJ: Endobronchial management of advanced lung cancer. Cancer Control 8:337, 2001.

85. Popovich J, Kvale PA, Eichenhorn MS, et al: Diagnostic accuracy of multiple biopsies from flexible bronchoscopy: A comparison of central versus peripheral carcinoma. Am Rev Respir Dis 125:521–523, 1982.

86. Shure D, Astarita R: Bronchogenic carcinoma presenting as an endobronchial mass. Chest 83:865–867, 1983.

87. Pastis NJ, Silvestri GA: Tissue procurement: Bronchoscopic techniques. In Pass HI, Carbone DP, Johnson DH, et al (eds): Lung Cancer: Principles and Practice (3rd ed). Philadelphia: Lippincott Williams & Wilkins, 2004, in press.

88. Schreiber G, McCrory DC: Performance characteristics of different modalities for diagnosis of suspected lung cancer. Chest 123:115S–128S, 2003.

89. Wang KP, Brower R, Haponik EF, et al: Flexible transbronchial needle aspiration for staging of bronchogenic carcinoma. Chest 84:671–676, 1983.

90. Shure D, Fedullo PF: The role of transcarinal needle aspiration in the staging of bronchogenic carcinoma. Chest 86:693–696, 1984.

91. Schenk DA, Bower JH, Bryan CL, et al: Transbronchial needle aspiration staging of bronchogenic carcinoma. Am Rev Respir Dis 134:146–148, 1986.

92. Chin R, McCain TW, Lucia MA, et al: Transbronchial needle aspiration in diagnosing and staging lung cancer. Chest 166:377–381, 2002.

93. Davenport R: Rapid on-site evaluation of transbronchial aspirates. Chest 98:59–61, 1990.

94. Gress F, Savides T, Sandler A, et al: Endoscopic ultrasonography, fine needle aspiration biopsy guided by endoscopic ultrasonography and computed tomography in the preoperative staging of non-small cell lung cancer: A comparison study. Ann Intern Med 127:604–612, 1997.

95. Silvestri G, Hoffman B, Bhutani M, et al: Endoscopic ultrasound with fine-needle aspiration in the diagnosis and staging of lung cancer. Ann Thorac Surg 61:1441–1445, 1996.

96. Arita T, Kuramitsu T, Kawamura M, et al: Bronchogenic carcinoma: Incidence of metastasis to normal sized lymph nodes. Thorax 50:1267–1269, 1995.

97. Asamura H, Nakayama H, Kondo H, et al: Lobe specific extent of systematic lymph node dissection for non-small cell lung carcinomas according to a retrospective study of metastasis and prognosis. J Thorac Cardiovasc Surg 117:1102–1111, 1999.

98. Wallace M, Silvestri G, Sahai A, et al: Endoscopic ultrasound-guided fine needle aspiration for staging patients with carcinoma of the lung. Ann Thorac Surg 72:1861–1867, 2001.

99. Chang K, Erickson R, Nguyen P: Endoscopic ultrasound (EUS) and EUS-guided fine-needle aspiration of the left adrenal gland. Gastrointest Endosc 44:568–572, 1996.

100. Luke WP, Todd PF, Patterson GA, et al: Prospective evaluation of mediastinoscopy for evaluation of carcinoma of the lung. J Thorac Cardiovasc Surg 91:53–56, 1986.

101. Detterbeck FC, DeCamp MM, Kohman L, et al: Invasive staging: The guidelines. Chest 123:167S–175S, 2003.

102. American Cancer Society: Cancer Facts and Figures—1999. Atlanta: American Cancer Society, 1999.

103. Roth J, Fossella F, Komaki R, et al: A randomized trial comparing perioperative chemotherapy and surgery with surgery alone in resectable stage IIIA non-small cell lung cancer. J Natl Cancer Inst 86:673–680, 1994.

104. Roth J, Atkinson E, Fossella F, et al: Long-term follow-up of patients enrolled in a randomized trial comparing perioperative chemotherapy and surgery with surgery alone in resectable stage IIIA non-small cell lung cancer. Lung Cancer 21:1–6, 1998.

105. Rosell R, Gomez-Codina J, Camps C, et al: A randomized trial comparing preoperative chemotherapy plus surgery with surgery alone in patients with non-small cell lung cancer. N Engl J Med 330:153–158, 1994.

106. Rosell R, Gomez-Codina J, Camps C, et al: Preresectional chemotherapy in stage IIIA non-small cell lung cancer: A 7-year assessment of a randomized controlled trial. Lung Cancer 26:7–14, 1999.

107. Alberts MW, Bepler G, Hazelton T, et al: Practice organization. Chest 123:332S–337S, 2003.

108. Stanley K: Prognostic factor for survival in patients with inoperable lung cancer. J Natl Cancer Inst 65:25, 1980.

109. Pater J, Loeb M: Non-anatomic prognostic factors in carcinoma of the lung: A multivariate analysis. Cancer 50:326, 1982.

110. Sorensen J, Badsberg J: Prognostic factors in resected stage I and II adenocarcinoma of the lung. J Thorac Cardiovasc Surg 99:218, 1990.

111. Harpole DH Jr, Herndon JE II, Young WG Jr, et al: Stage I non-small cell lung cancer: A multivariate analysis of treatment methods and patterns of recurrence. Cancer 76:787–796, 1995.

112. Gail MH, Eagan RT, Feld R, et al: Prognostic factors in patients with resected stage I NSCLC: A report from the Lung Cancer Study Group. Cancer 54:1802, 1984.

113. Pairolero P, Williams D, Bergstralh E, et al: Postsurgical stage I bronchogenic carcinoma: Morbid implications of recurrent disease. Ann Thorac Surg 38:331, 1984.

114. Graziano S, Gamble G, Newman N, et al: Prognostic significance of K-ras codon 12 mutations in patients with resected stage I and II non-small cell lung cancer. J Clin Oncol 17:668–675, 1999.

115. Schiller J, Adak S, Feins R, et al: Lack of prognostic significance of p53 and K-ras mutations in primary resected non-small cell lung cancer on E4592. J Clin Oncol 19:448–457, 2001.

116. Ahrendt S, Hu Y, Buta M, et al: p53 mutations and survival in stage I non-small cell lung cancer: Results of a prospective study. J Natl Cancer Inst 95:961–970, 2003.

117. Ries LAG, Kosary CL, Hankey BF (eds): SEER Cancer Statistics Review 1973–1994: Tables and Graphs, NIH Publication No. 97-2789. Bethesda, Md: National Cancer Institute, 1997.

118. Ries LAG, Miller BA, Hankey BF, et al (eds): Cancer Statistics Review: 1973–1993, Bethesda, Md: National Cancer Institute, 1995.

119. PORT Meta-Analysis Trialists Group: Post operative radiotherapy in non-small cell lung cancer: Systemic review and meta-analysis of individual patient data from nine randomized controlled trials. Lancet 352:257–263, 1998.

120. Le Chevalier T: Results of the randomized International Adjuvant Lung Trial: Cisplatin-based chemotherapy (CT) vs no CT in 1867 patients (pts) with resected non-small cell lung cancer (NSCLC) (abstract 6). Proc Am Soc Clin Oncol 22:2, 2003.

121. Ginsburg R, Rubinstein L: A randomized comparative trial of lobectomy vs limited resection for patients with T1N0 non-small cell lung cancer. Lung Cancer 7:83–88, 1995.

122. Beckles MA, Spiro SG, Colice GL, et al: The physiologic evaluation of patients with lung cancer being considered for surgery. Chest 123(1 Suppl):105S–114S, 2003.

123. Rowell N, Williams C: Radical radiotherapy for stage I/II non-small cell lung cancer in patients not sufficiently fit for or declining surgery (medically inoperable): A systematic review. Thorax 56:628–638, 2001.

124. van Rens M, de la Riviere A, Elbers H, et al: Prognostic assessment of 2,361 patients who underwent pulmonary resection for non-small cell lung cancer, stage I, II, and III A. Chest 117:374–379, 2000.

125. Jassem J, Skokowski J, Dziadziuszko R, et al: Results of surgical treatment of non-small cell lung cancer: Validation of the new postoperative pathologic TNM classification. J Thorac Cardiovasc Surg 119:1141–1146, 2000.

126. Inoue K, Sato M, Fujimura S, et al: Prognostic assessment of 1310 patients with non-small cell lung cancer who underwent complete resection from 1980–1993. J Thorac Cardiovasc Surg 116:407–411, 1998.

127. Adebonojo S, Bowser A, Moritz D, et al: Impact of revised stage classification of lung cancer on survival: A military experience. Chest 115:1507–1513, 1999.

128. Scott WJ, Howington J, Movsas B: Treatment of stage II non-small cell lung cancer. Chest 123(1 Suppl):188S–201S, 2003.

129. Bach P, Cramer L, Schrag D, et al: The influence of hospital volume on survival after resection for lung cancer. N Engl J Med 345:181–188, 2001.

130. Silvestri G, Handy J, Lackland D, et al: Specialists achieve better outcomes than generalists for lung cancer surgery. Chest 114:675–680, 1998.

131. Albain K, Scott C, Rusch B, et al: Phase III comparison of concurrent chemotherapy plus radiotherapy (CT/RT) and CT/RT followed by surgical resection for stage IIIA(pN2) non-small cell lung cancer (NSCLC): Initial results from the Intergroup Trial 0139 (RTOG 93-09) (abstract 2497). Proc Am Soc Clin Oncol 22:621, 2003.

132. Robinson L, Wagner H Jr, Ruckdeschel J: Treatment of stage IIIa non-small cell lung cancer. Chest 123(1 Suppl):202S–220S, 2003.

133. Non-Small Cell Lung Cancer Collaborative Group: Chemotherapy in non-small cell lung cancer: A meta-analysis using updated data on individual patients from 52 randomised clinical trials. BMJ 311:899–909, 1995.

134. Marino P, Preatoni A, Cantoni A: Randomized trials of radiotherapy alone vs combined chemotherapy and radiotherapy in stages IIIA and IIIB non-small cell lung cancer. Cancer 76:593–601, 1995.

135. Pritchard R, Anthony S: Chemotherapy plus radiotherapy compared with radiotherapy alone in the treatment of locally advanced, unresectable, non-small cell lung cancer: A meta-analysis. Ann Intern Med 125:723–729, 1996.

136. Furuse K, Fukuoka M, Kawahara M, et al: Phase III study of concurrent versus sequential thoracic radiotherapy in combination with mitomycin, vindesine, and cisplatin in unresectable stage III non-small cell lung cancer. J Clin Oncol 17:2692–2699, 1999.

137. Curran W, Scott C, Langer C, et al: Long-term benefit is observed in Phase III comparison of sequential vs concurrent chemo-radiation for patients with unresectable stage III NSCLC: RTOG 9410 (abstract 2499). Proc Am Soc Clin Oncol 22:621, 2003.

138. Jett J, Scott W, Rivera M, et al: Guidelines on treatment of stage IIIB non-small cell lung cancer. Chest 123(1 Suppl):221S–225S, 2003.

139. Kelly K, Crowley J, Bunn P Jr, et al: Randomized Phase III trial of paclitaxel plus carboplatin versus vinorelbine plus cisplatin in the treatment of patients with advanced non-small cell lung cancer: A Southwest Oncology Group trial. J Clin Oncol 19:3210–3218, 2001.

140. Schiller J, Harrington D, Belani C, et al: Comparison of four chemotherapy regimens for advanced non-small cell lung cancer. N Engl J Med 346:92–98, 2002.

141. Scagliotti G, DeMarinis F, Rinaldi M, et al: Phase III randomized trial comparing three platinum-based doublets in advanced non-small cell lung cancer. J Clin Oncol 20:4285–4291, 2002.

142. Socinski M, Schell M, Peterman A, et al: Phase III trial comparing a defined duration of therapy versus continuous therapy followed by second-line therapy in advanced-stage IIIB/IV non-small cell lung cancer. J Clin Oncol 20:1335–1343, 2002.

143. Dy G, Adjei A: Novel targets for lung cancer therapy: Part I and Part II. J Clin Oncol 20:2881–2894; 3016–3028, 2002.

144. Fukuoka M, Yano S, Giaccone G, et al: Multi-institutional randomized Phase II trial of geftinib for previously treated patients with advanced non-small cell lung cancer. J Clin Oncol 21:2237–2246, 2003.

145. Turrisi A III, Kim K, Blum R, et al: Twice-daily compared with once-daily thoracic radiotherapy in limited small cell

lung cancer treated concurrently with cisplatin and etoposide. N Engl J Med 340:265–271, 1999.

146. Bonner J, Sloan J, Shanahan T, et al: Phase III comparison of twice-daily split course irradiation versus once-daily irradiation for patients with limited stage small cell lung carcinoma. J Clin Oncol 17:2681–2691, 1999.

147. Schild S, Brindle J, Geyer S, et al: Long-term results of a Phase III trial comparing once-daily radiotherapy with twice-daily radiotherapy in limited-stage small-cell lung cancer. Int J Radiat Oncol Biol Phys 59:943–951, 2004.

148. Fukuoka M, Furuse K, Saijo N, et al: Randomized trial of cyclophosphamide, doxorubicin, and vincristine versus cisplatin and etoposide versus alternation of these regimens in small cell lung cancer. J Natl Cancer Inst 83:855–861, 1991.

149. Roth B, Johnson D, Einhorn L, et al: Randomized study of cyclophosphamide, doxorubicin, and vincristine versus etoposide and cisplatin versus alternation of these two regimens in extensive small cell lung cancer: A Phase III trial of the Southeastern Cancer Study Group. J Clin Oncol 10:282–291, 1992.

150. Noda K, Nishiwaki Y, Kawahara M, et al: Irinotecan plus cisplatin compared with etoposide plus cisplatin for extensive small cell lung cancer. N Engl J Med 346:85–91, 2002.

151. Auperin A, Arriagada R, Pignon J, et al: Prophylactic cranial irradiation for patients with small cell lung cancer in complete remission. Prophylactic Cranial Irradiation Overview Collaborative Group. N Engl J Med 341:476–484, 1999.

152. von Pawel J, Schiller J, Sheperd F, et al: Topotecan versus cyclophosphamide, doxorubicin, and vincristine for the treatment of recurrent small cell lung cancer. J Clin Oncol 17:658–667, 1999.

153. Silvestri GA, Sherman C, Leong SS, et al: Caring for the dying patient with lung cancer. Chest 122:1028–1036, 2002.

154. Kvale PA, Simmoff M, Prakash UBS: Palliative care. Chest 123(1 Suppl):248S–311S, 2003.

155. Pancoast H: Importance of careful roentgen-ray investigations of apical chest tumors. J Am Med Assoc 83:1407–1411, 1924.

156. Pancoast H: Superior pulmonary sulcus tumor: Tumor characterized by pain, Horner's syndrome, destruction of bone and atrophy of hand muscles. J Am Med Assoc 99:1391–1396, 1932.

157. Arcasoy S, Jett J: Superior pulmonary sulcus tumors and Pancoast's syndrome. N Engl J Med 337:1370–1376, 1997.

158. Heelan R, Demas B, Caravelli J, et al: Superior sulcus tumors: CT and MR imaging. Radiology 170:637–641, 1989.

159. Maxfield R, Aranda C: The role of fiberoptic bronchoscopy and transbronchial biopsy in the diagnosis of Pancoast's tumor. N Y State J Med 87:326–329, 1987.

160. Walls W, Thornburg J, Naylor B: Pulmonary needle aspiration biopsy in the diagnosis of Pancoast tumors. Radiology 111:99–102, 1974.

161. Komaki R, Roth J, Walsh G, et al: Outcome predictors for 143 patients with superior sulcus tumors treated by multidisciplinary approach at the University of Texas M.D. Anderson Cancer Center. Int J Radiat Oncol Biol Phys 48:347–354, 2000.

162. Rusch V, Parekh K, Leon L: Factors determining outcome after surgical resection of T3 and T4 lung cancers of the superior sulcus. J Thorac Cardiovasc Surg 119:1147–1153, 2000.

163. Rusch V, Girouox D, Kraut M, et al: Induction chemoradiation and surgical resection of non-small cell lung carcinoma of the superior sulcus: Initial results of Southwest Oncology Group Trial 9416 (Intergroup Trial 0160). J Thorac Cardiovasc Surg 121:472–483, 2001.

164. Escalante C: Causes and management of superior vena cava syndrome. Oncology 7:61, 1993.

165. Bell D, Woods R, Levi J: Superior vena cava obstruction: A ten-year experience. Med J Aust 146:566–568, 1986.

166. Mineo T, Ambrogi V, Nofroni I, et al: Mediastinoscopy in superior vena cava syndrome: Analysis of 80 consecutive patients. Ann Thorac Surg 68:223, 1999.

167. Rowell N, Gleeson F: Steroids, radiotherapy, chemotherapy and stents for superior vena cava obstruction in carcinoma of the bronchus (Cochrane review). Cochrane Database Syst Rev 4:CD001316, 2001.

168. Sigurgeirsson B, Lindelof B, Edhag O, et al: Risk of cancer in patients with dermatomyositis or polymyositis. N Engl J Med 326:363–367, 1992.

169. Cornuz J, Pearson S, Creager M, et al: Importance of findings on the initial evaluation for cancer in patients with symptomatic idiopathic deep venous thrombosis. Ann Intern Med 125:785–793, 1996.

170. Lee A, Levine M, Baker R, et al: Low molecular weight heparin versus a coumarin for the prevention of recurrent venous thromboembolism in patients with cancer. N Engl J Med 349:146–153, 2003.

171. Schulman S, Wahlander K, Lundstrom T, et al: Secondary prevention of venous thromboembolism with oral direct thrombin inhibitory ximelagathan. N Engl J Med 349:1713–1721, 2003.

172. Takai E, Yano T, Iguchi H, et al: Tumor induced hypercalcemia and parathyroid hormone related protein in lung carcinoma. Cancer 78:1384–1387, 1996.

173. Ralston SH, Gallacher SJ, Patel U, et al: Cancer associated hypercalcemia: Morbidity and mortality. Ann Intern Med 112:499–504, 1990.

174. Major P, Lortholarhy A, Hon J, et al: Zoledronic acid is superior to pamidronate in the treatment of hypercalcemia of malignancy: A pooled analysis of two randomized controlled trials. J Clin Oncol 19:558–567, 2001.

175. Ayus J, Krothapalli R, Arieff A: Treatment of symptomatic hyponatremia and its relation to brain damage: A prospective study. N Engl J Med 317:1190–1195, 1987.

176. Orth D: Cushing's syndrome. N Engl J Med 392:791–803, 1995.

177. Darnell R, Posner J: Paraneoplastic syndromes involving the nervous system. N Engl J Med 349:1543–1554, 2003.

178. Lucchinetti C, Kimmel D, Lennon V: Paraneoplastic and oncological profiles of patients seropositive for type 1 anti-neuronal nuclear autoantibodies. Neurology 50:652–657, 1998.

179. Graus F, Keime Guibert F, Rene R, et al: Anti-Hu-associated paraneoplastic encephalomyelitis: Analysis of 200 patients. Brain 124:1138–1148, 2001.

180. Lennon V, Kryzer T, Griesmann G, et al: Calcium channel antibodies in the Lambert-Eaton syndrome and other paraneoplastic syndromes. N Engl J Med 332:1467–1474, 1995.

181. Carpentier A, Delattre J: The Lambert-Eaton myasthenic syndrome. Clin Rev Allergy Immunol 20:155–158, 2001.

182. Sanders D, Massey J, Sanders L, et al: A randomized trial of 3,4-dyaminopyridine in Lambert-Eaton myasthenic syndrome. Neurology 54:603–607, 2000.

45 Lymphoma, Lymphoproliferative Diseases, and Other Primary Malignant Tumors

Judith A. Luce, M.D.

INTRODUCTION

Although most primary malignant pulmonary tumors are classified as bronchogenic carcinomas, other types of neoplasms also occur in the lungs.[1] Lymphomas and sarcomas (cancers of presumptive mesenchymal origin) comprise the largest group of nonbronchogenic neoplasms. Carcinoid tumors, lymphoepithelial tumors, and mucoepithelial neoplasms similar to those of salivary gland origin are epithelial cancers that may occur in the lungs. The rarest of the nonbronchogenic malignancies—melanoma, pulmonary blastoma, and pulmonary tumorlets—are of obscure origin. All of these diseases share no known epidemiologic associations with bronchogenic carcinoma, and hence no preventive strategies exist. Correct diagnosis, often with special diagnostic techniques, is a key to identifying and managing these cancers. Treatment frequently differs from the approach to bronchogenic carcinoma, and curability may be greater for these cancers.

LYMPHOMAS

HODGKIN'S DISEASE

Primary Pulmonary Hodgkin's Disease

Hodgkin's disease involving the lung alone is extremely rare, having been reported only in isolated cases.[2] The disease is thought to arise in lymphoid follicles or peribronchial lymph nodes that are scattered throughout the lung. Because histologic proof requires demonstration of the pathognomonic Reed-Sternberg cell, primary pulmonary Hodgkin's disease is usually diagnosed by open (or thoracoscopic) lung biopsy.[3] Fine-needle aspiration cytology, aided by the use of special immunohistochemical stains, may also provide the diagnosis.[4] Because Hodgkin's disease so rarely involves the lung alone, defining a case requires proof of the absence of hilar or mediastinal adenopathy as well as an undisputed histologic diagnosis of Hodgkin's disease.

Primary pulmonary Hodgkin's disease has been reported more frequently in older people and in women than has Hodgkin's disease. Systemic symptoms such as fever, night sweats, and weight loss are common. The radiologic pattern may include solitary pulmonary nodules, diffuse infiltration, and cavitation; the disease is rarely bilateral and most often involves the upper lobes.

Full staging evaluation is essential in making treatment decisions for such patients. In reported cases in which the lung was the only site of disease, patients were treated with surgery and radiotherapy with apparently excellent results. When other node involvement is documented, the treatment is stage dependent, and combinations of both radiation therapy and chemotherapy are often employed. Although controversy exists over the use of chemotherapy for early-stage extranodal Hodgkin's disease, in view of the undesirability of irradiation of the lungs, chemotherapy may be the only logical choice for these rare patients.[5]

Hodgkin's Disease in Lymph Nodes with Lung Involvement

Hodgkin's disease involves the nodes of the mediastinum in approximately two thirds of all cases. Pulmonary involvement occurs in slightly more than 10% of patients and is virtually always an extension of mediastinal or hilar node involvement.[6,7] Nodular sclerosing Hodgkin's disease is the presenting histologic type in 67% to 84% of patients having thoracic involvement. Extension of the disease to the lungs may take the form of interstitial linear infiltrates, small nodules, or both (Fig. 45.1). Bulky mediastinal involvement, defined as a ratio of tumor mass diameter to internal thoracic diameter of 0.33 or more, is associated with spread to the pleura, pericardium, and chest wall. In one prospective series, interstitial or nodular lung spread was never seen without hilar node involvement, and in virtually all cases of pleural, pericardial, and chest wall involvement, bulky

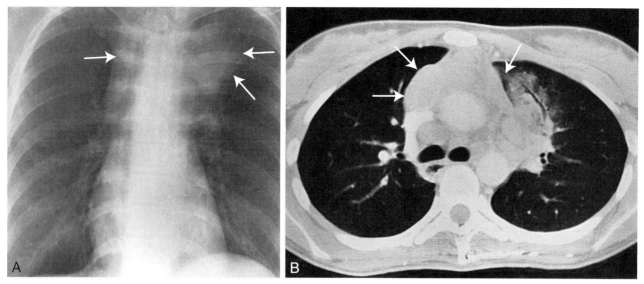

Figure 45.1 Bulky mediastinal involvement in a 35-year-old woman with nodular sclerosing Hodgkin's disease. **A,** The diameter of the anterior mediastinal mass on posterior-anterior radiograph is greater than 0.33 of the transverse inner diameter of the thorax. **B,** The computed tomographic scan demonstrates an interstitial infiltrate involving the left upper lobe adjacent to the large mass, a typical feature of pulmonary involvement by Hodgkin's disease. *Arrows* point to mass in both images.

tumor was also found in the mediastinum.[4] There are insufficient data to demonstrate that magnetic resonance imaging, positron emission tomography, gallium scanning, or other imaging methods are superior to computed tomography (CT) scanning in documenting the pulmonary extent of Hodgkin's disease.

Histologic confirmation of pulmonary extension by Hodgkin's disease may occasionally be necessary. When the disease is clearly a direct extension of known bulky involvement, such confirmation is usually not undertaken. However, patients with nodular or infiltrating pulmonary parenchymal lesions may require histologic proof before treatment is begun, especially because the differential diagnosis of such lesions includes many infectious processes.[8,9] The key Reed-Sternberg cell in the lung may be demonstrated in material from bronchial lavage,[10] bronchial brushings,[11] sputum cytology,[12] fine-needle aspiration,[13] or more formal transbronchial biopsy or thoracoscopic or open-lung biopsy. None of the reports compares techniques or provides adequate information to assess how frequently each of these methods is useful in making the proper diagnosis. The sole exception is diagnostic needle aspiration cytology: Its use in soft tissue extranodal sites, mostly pulmonary, resulted in a diagnosis of Hodgkin's disease in 15 of 18 cases.[13]

Treatment of individuals with pulmonary involvement due to Hodgkin's disease depends on the stage of disease in each patient; therefore, careful staging is necessary for all such patients. Bulky mediastinal disease of any stage is most commonly treated with a combination of chemotherapy and radiation therapy. Extension of Hodgkin's disease into the lung in a nodular or interstitial infiltrate necessitates use either of chemotherapy or of radiation therapy fields that adequately encompass the extension into the lung parenchyma; however, because radiation therapy permanently injures pulmonary parenchyma, chemotherapy is usually used first to diminish the size and extent of tumor

to spare lung from radiation. Whether the prognosis of adequately treated patients having pulmonary extranodal extension of Hodgkin's disease is worse than for patients without extension is controversial.[14,15] Long-term follow-up of the chest in patients treated for Hodgkin's disease demonstrates persistence of radiographic abnormalities, particularly paramediastinal fibrosis, that are dependent on the volume of lung included in the radiation fields, the use of bleomycin in the treatment regimen, and individual inflammatory responses to radiation therapy.[16]

Recurrent Hodgkin's Disease Involving the Lung

Because thoracic involvement is common in Hodgkin's disease, the lungs are a common site of disease recurrence. Factors predicting a high likelihood of pulmonary recurrence include advanced-stage disease at the time of diagnosis, particularly if systemic ("B") symptoms are also present; bulky mediastinal node involvement[13–15,17–19]; and incomplete or inadequate initial staging and treatment.

The radiographic pattern of pulmonary recurrence and the radiographic differential diagnosis depend on the treatment used for the primary disease. Pulmonary recurrence in patients who have received mantle irradiation is most often seen as masses at the margins of the radiotherapy fields (Fig. 45.2) or as diffuse infiltration in the pulmonary parenchyma adjacent to the field. Individuals who relapse after chemotherapy alone are likely to have recurrence in areas of prior nodal involvement, particularly if it was bulky, as well as extension into the lung.

The differential diagnosis of pulmonary recurrence in Hodgkin's disease includes infections, especially opportunistic infections, as well as pulmonary toxicity from treatment, including radiation pneumonitis and drug-induced interstitial pneumonitis.[20] Radiation pneumonitis may be present within the area of irradiated lung or diffusely throughout the lungs or may appear as a widening of the

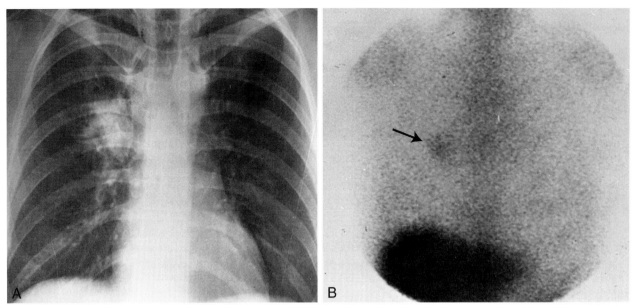

Figure 45.2 This 34-year-old man had received "mantle" radiation therapy to the thorax for nodular-sclerosing Hodgkin's disease involving the anterior mediastinum 8 years before presenting with recurrent night sweats and the right hilar mass seen in **A. B,** The gallium scan reveals isolated uptake in the same area (*arrow*). The diagnosis of recurrent Hodgkin's disease was confirmed at thoracotomy, and the patient was treated with chemotherapy.

mediastinum.[16] The time of appearance of symptoms and abnormal radiographs may be helpful: Most radiation pneumonitis develops within 8 to 12 weeks after treatment, and it is unusual for Hodgkin's disease to relapse so quickly. New masses that appear on chest radiographs years after treatment for Hodgkin's disease may not be recurrent Hodgkin's disease; non-Hodgkin's lymphoma, solid tumors such as lung cancer, and radiation-induced tumors such as sarcomas are important causes of later mortality in both adult and pediatric patients.[21,22] Other serious long-term cardiopulmonary complications of treatment are unusual.[23,24]

NON-HODGKIN'S LYMPHOMA

Non-Hodgkin's lymphoma is a term applied to a variety of lymphoid malignancies that are usually classified according to the Revised European-American Lymphoma Classification,[25] shown in Table 45.1. This classification system sorts lymphomas into categories by histology, immunophenotyping, and certain other characteristics, including chromosomal translocations. The International Prognostic Index provides risk information for patients with the most common aggressive B-cell lymphomas based on the simple criteria shown in Table 45.2.[26]

Primary pulmonary non-Hodgkin's lymphoma is rare, comprising fewer than 5% of all primary extranodal lymphomas.[26a] However, thoracic involvement in non-Hodgkin's lymphoma is quite common, with involvement in up to 40% of patients at the time of diagnosis.[27] Indolent follicular or diffuse B-cell lymphomas are the most common types among pulmonary lymphomas, and low-grade lymphoma of mucosa-associated lymphoid tissue (MALT lymphomas) is the most common indolent subtype.[28,29] Aggressive lymphomas, which may be composed of small,

large, or mixed cell types, are more likely to be localized at diagnosis and are more commonly found in other extranodal sites.[30,31] Indolent lymphomas have a long natural history, with median survival times in excess of 5 years; in contrast, aggressive lymphomas are responsive to chemotherapy and radiation therapy but have a more rapid evolution and shorter median survival times. However, only aggressive lymphomas are considered curable with current therapies.[29,32]

Primary Pulmonary Non-Hodgkin Lymphomas

The precise pathogenesis of primary pulmonary lymphomas is unknown. Virtually all pulmonary lymphomas are of B-cell origin, and most of these are the subtypes that derive from germinal center cells or post–germinal center cells.[26,31] These tumors are thought to arise in either MALT or interbronchial nodes or lymphatic channels. In the lung, bronchus-associated lymphoid tissue is sparsely distributed and usually not associated with organized lymphoid follicles.[33] When indolent lymphomas develop, they are often multicentric or diffuse in distribution, and the monoclonal cells are most often small B lymphocytes with cleaved nuclei. Benign lymphoid proliferation may present as isolated masses, as peribronchial proliferation, or as interstitial infiltration,[34] and lymphoma may develop in any of those patterns. Aggressive lymphomas may present as extensions of mediastinal nodal disease or as isolated masses within the pulmonary parenchyma, bone, or pleura; these lymphomas may either arise in situ or migrate from other lymphoid centers.

Speculation about the pathogenesis of primary pulmonary MALT lymphomas is that they are related to immune responses within the lung. The pathogenesis of MALT lymphoma in the gastrointestinal tract has been

Table 45.1 WHO/Revised European-American Lymphoma Classification

B-Cell Lymphoma
Precursor B-cell lymphomas
    B-cell lymphoblastic lymphoma/leukemia
Mature B-cell lymphomas
    B-cell chronic lymphocytic leukemia/small lymphocytic
        lymphoma
    B-cell prolymphocytic leukemia
    Lymphoplasmacytic lymphoma
    Splenic marginal zone B-cell lymphoma
    Hairy cell leukemia
    Plasma cell myeloma/plasmacytoma
    Extranodal marginal zone B-cell lymphoma of MALT type
    Mantle cell lymphoma
    Follicular lymphoma
    Nodal marginal zone B-cell lymphoma (also called
        angiocentric lymphoma)
    Diffuse large B-cell lymphoma
        Mediastinal, intravascular, primary effusion lymphomas
    Burkitt's lymphoma
        Endemic, sporadic, immunodeficiency-associated, atypical
    Plasmacytoma
    Plasma cell myeloma

T-Cell and NK-Cell Lymphomas
Precursor T-cell lymphomas
    T-lymphoblastic lymphoma/leukemia
Mature T-cell and NK-cell lymphomas
    T-cell prolymphocytic leukemia
    T-cell large granular lymphocytic leukemia
    Aggressive NK-cell leukemia
    Adult T-cell lymphoma/leukemia (HTLV-1+)
    NK/T-cell lymphoma, nasal and nasal type
    Enteropathy-type T-cell lymphoma
    Hepatosplenic (γ/δ) T-cell lymphoma
    Subcutaneous panniculitis-like T-cell lymphoma
    Mycosis fungoides
    Sézary's syndrome
    Primary cutaneous anaplastic large cell lymphoma
    Anaplastic large cell lymphoma, unspecified
    Peripheral T-cell lymphoma, unspecified
    Angioimmunoblastic T-cell lymphoma
    Anaplastic large cell lymphoma, primary systemic type

HTLV, human T-cell lymphotrophic virus; MALT, mucosa-associated lymphoid tissue; NK, natural killer; WHO, World Health Organization. From Isaacson P: Review: The current status of lymphoma classification. Br J Haematol 109:258–266, 2000.

shown to occur during *Helicobacter pylori* infection, and B cells responsive to *Helicobacter* antigens have been demonstrated. The presumption about the genesis of lymphoma is that, during proliferation of the responding B-cell pool, mutations occur that result in immortalization of a clone of B cells. The similarity of MALT lymphomas at all sites suggests that chronic antigen stimulation is the cause; what is not known about pulmonary MALTomas is what the antigen might be.[35] Indolent, small B-cell lymphomas at all sites may evolve into large cell aggressive lymphomas late in their course; this transformation is presumed to be due to further mutation of the initial B-cell clone.

As is reflected in the most recent lymphoma classification system, a number of other techniques have been applied to diagnosing and classifying lymphoma. Immunohistochemical stains may be used to identify surface immunoglobulins and surface receptors that establish B- or T-cell lineage or other surface proteins unique to lymphoid lineage cells. Because these cancers are most often monoclonal proliferations of B cells, they display unique gene rearrangements of the immunoglobulin gene loci, unique surface immunoglobulin idiotypes, and other monoclonal markers. Cytologic studies have demonstrated several characteristic gene rearrangements such as the 14:18 translocation seen in follicular lymphomas,[36] and molecular probes have been designed for detecting these genetic characteristics in small samples of cells. Making a diagnosis of non-Hodgkin's lymphoma from an extremely small sample of tissue is now possible with immunohistochemical techniques or flow cytometry. Invasive techniques such as open-lung biopsy, thoracoscopy, or transbronchial biopsy may be supplanted by transthoracic needle aspiration biopsy, bronchial lavage, or bronchial brushings.[37–39]

The signs and symptoms of non-Hodgkin's lymphoma involving the lung may be quite varied. Solitary masses may occur without symptoms. Patients with diffuse lung involvement may have cough, dyspnea, or chest pain. Lymphomas involving airways may produce cough, hemoptysis, and obstructive symptoms, including pneumonia. Systemic symptoms of lymphoma may be present: fever, night sweats, and weight loss. Patients with MALT lymphomas rarely have systemic symptoms. Patients may have other areas of extranodal lymphoma: In one series of MALT lymphomas, 25% of patients had disease in other sites, including salivary glands, bone marrow, and orbit.[30] The chest radiographic appearance is nondiagnostic: Diffuse infiltrates, reticulonodular infiltrates, small and large nodules, and effusions may be seen. The most common CT appearance in MALT lymphoma in one study was consolidation with air bronchograms, which correlated with cellular lymphocytic infiltration that expanded the interstitium and compressed adjacent alveoli.[40] Paraneoplastic signs of lymphoma may include pruritus, erythema nodosum, autoimmune phenomena, coagulopathy, hypercalcemia, and central nervous system abnormalities.

Evaluation of individuals with non-Hodgkin's lymphoma involving the lung consists of defining the intrathoracic involvement carefully and staging the patient completely. Staging evaluation includes defining all areas of nodal and extranodal disease according to the Ann Arbor classification.[41] Staging may involve biopsies of liver, bone marrow, intra-abdominal nodes, and extranodal sites. Obtaining lymph node tissue may in some cases be useful in making the distinction among the various kinds of lymphoma, provided nodal tissue is readily accessible. Laboratory evaluation should include complete blood counts, liver function tests, and determination of serum lactate dehydrogenase level. As with Hodgkin's disease, the spectrum of opportunistic infections must be carefully considered in the differential diagnosis of pulmonary infiltrates in patients having non-Hodgkin's lymphoma.

A variety of unique non-Hodgkin's lymphomas occur predominantly in the thorax. Several have unique presentations and are worthy of separate discussion. Two primary lymphomas present as large mediastinal masses: precursor T-cell lymphoblastic lymphoma/leukemia, and B-cell mediastinal lymphoma. Sixty percent of T-cell lymphoblastic

Table 45.2 International Prognostic Index for Aggressive B-Cell Non-Hodgkin's Lymphoma

Risk Factors for Patients ≤60 Years*
Ann Arbor stage (I or II vs. III or IV)
Performance status (0 or 1 vs. 2–4)
Serum lactate dehydrogenase (LDH) level (≤normal vs. >normal)

Risk Factors for All Patients
Age (≤60 vs. >60 years)
Serum LDH level (≤normal vs. >normal)
Performance status (0 or 1 vs. 2–4)
Ann Arbor stage (I or II vs. III or IV)
Extranodal involvement (≤1 site vs. >1 site)

Risk Group	Number of Risk Factors	Complete Remission (%)	Disease Free Survival		Overall Survival	
			2 year (%)	5-year (%)	2 year (%)	5-year (%)
Patients ≤60 Years Old						
Low	0	92	88	86	90	83
Low intermediate	1	78	74	66	79	69
High intermediate	2	57	62	53	59	46
High	3	46	61	58	37	32
All Patients						
Low	0–1	87	79	70	84	73
Low intermediate	2	67	66	50	66	51
High intermediate	3	55	59	49	54	43
High	4–5	44	58	40	34	26

* Risk factors in parentheses are: (low vs. high risk).
From International Non-Hodgkin's Lymphoma Prognostic Factors Project: A predictive model for aggressive non-Hodgkin's lymphoma. N Engl J Med 329:987–994, 1993.

lymphoma/leukemia involves the mediastinum. This presentation is most common in adolescent boys, usually with leukemia. It is treated with aggressive chemotherapy, often with bone marrow transplantation, and is curable for a majority of patients.[42] The B-cell disorder is rare, is usually not curable, and presents in older men and women as a primary mediastinal mass without leukemia.[43,44]

Pulmonary non-Hodgkin's lymphoma has a unique clinical course in immunosuppressed patients. Epstein-Barr virus–driven lymphoproliferative syndromes, seen in transplant patients receiving immunosuppressive drugs, mimic lymphoma in their presentation, which is usually with widespread disease.[45–47] Withdrawal of immunosuppressive medication may result in diminution of the disease, but fatalities are common. Lymphoma associated with acquired immunodeficiency syndrome (AIDS) and congenital immunodeficiency often involves extranodal sites and is virtually always intermediate or high grade in histology and B cell in origin. AIDS-associated lymphoma displays both clinical and genetic heterogeneity.[48,49] Whereas AIDS-associated lymphoma responds to radiotherapy and chemotherapy, poor tolerance of treatment and rapid relapse are the rule, and median survival is less than 1 year.[50,51]

Non-Hodgkin's lymphoma presenting as primary pleural effusion is a syndrome seen most often in patients with advanced human immunodeficiency virus (HIV) infection. Primary effusion lymphoma is a B-cell malignancy that may also involve the pericardial or peritoneal cavities, and is known to be associated with human herpesvirus 8 infection.[52] Primary effusion lymphoma is diagnosed by demonstrating malignant B cells in the pleural fluid that also stain positive for human herpesvirus 8. The prognosis of such

patients is also dependent on their survival from advanced HIV disease, as the majority of cases occur in patients having CD4 counts under 50 cells/μL.[53] Treatment consists of chemotherapy and highly active antiretroviral therapy.[54]

An older, rare disease entity, lethal midline granuloma, is now classified as a non-Hodgkin's lymphoma, extranodal natural killer T-cell lymphoma, nasal type. This rare disease entity presents in middle age with inflammatory lesions of the nasal passages and sinuses as well as the upper airways, and potential dissemination to the skin, gastrointestinal tract, testis, orbit, and central nervous system. Biopsy of the affected tissues demonstrates clonal T cells with histologic staining for CD56, the characteristic surface marker of the natural killer T cell. Local radiation therapy may control the symptoms in the airways, but both local and systemic progression is the rule. Although this disease does respond to chemotherapy, the prognosis is poor, and dissemination is usually fatal.[55]

Treatment

Treatment of non-Hodgkin's lymphoma involving the lung, as with Hodgkin's disease, depends on the stage of disease; however, in non-Hodgkin's lymphoma the classification of disease is equally important. Patients having solitary extranodal non-Hodgkin's lymphoma are acknowledged to have the same prognosis as those with nodal disease of the same stage and histologic type. Radiation therapy, chemotherapy, and biotherapies are integrated in combinations that have proven successful in randomized prospective clinical trials.

Treatment of indolent non-Hodgkin's lymphoma that does not produce significant symptoms may be delayed, because early intervention has not been shown to produce longer survival. Symptomatic patients with localized (stage I) low-grade non-Hodgkin's lymphoma may be treated with local radiotherapy or a combination of chemotherapy and radiotherapy.[56–58] Radiotherapy produces permanent pulmonary injury, so its use should be restricted to small volumes of lung. If the pulmonary involvement is diffuse, chemotherapy is the treatment of choice. A variety of agents are uniquely useful in indolent B-cell lymphomas, including adenosine deaminase inhibitors that are relatively selective for lymphoid cells and comprise the usual first-line chemotherapy. Monoclonal antibodies to B-cell antigens, particularly CD20, are useful and quite nontoxic therapies. Conventional-dose multiagent chemotherapy treatment may produce prolonged remissions but will not cure indolent lymphomas, and whether a high-dose chemotherapy approach (employing either autologous or allogeneic bone marrow rescue) is clearly more efficacious is controversial. Patients with advanced-stage (stage III or IV) indolent non-Hodgkin's lymphoma, such as MALT lymphoma, are usually candidates for chemotherapy. Treatment is started when patients are clearly symptomatic from their disease, and responses to therapy are quite common, but relapse is the rule.[59] Survival for patients with untreated early-stage indolent B-cell lymphomas is long, with median survivals in excess of 7 years; patients have shorter median survival with more advanced and symptomatic lymphomas.

Patients having aggressive non-Hodgkin's lymphomas are treated at the time of diagnosis, in keeping with the more rapid progression of these lymphomas and the potentially curative nature of therapy. Localized disease, if completely staged, may be treated successfully with radiation therapy to involved areas. Five-year survival rates of 65% were found in one study of patients with clinical stage I disease, including those with extranodal lymphoma,[60] but in a series in which all patients were totally staged, including laparotomy, the 5-year survival with local radiotherapy was 100%.[61] However, incompletely staged patients and patients having stage II disease fare poorly with only localized radiotherapy, with a survival rate of 25% or less at 5 years. Treatment with chemotherapy or combined chemotherapy and radiotherapy has clearly improved these rates: Five-year survival rates in excess of 80% are reported for patients with localized stage I or II intermediate-grade and high-grade B-cell lymphomas.[62,63] Advanced-stage intermediate-grade and high-grade non-Hodgkin's lymphomas are treated with combination chemotherapy; local radiotherapy to bulky areas of disease may be appropriate for patients whose bulky masses do not resolve entirely with chemotherapy.[64]

Non-Hodgkin's lymphoma may recur after treatment in both nodal and extranodal sites. As with Hodgkin's disease, complications of therapy and opportunistic infections must be distinguished from tumor recurrence in the lung. Recurrence is the rule in indolent lymphomas, although a long disease-free period may occur from initial treatment to recurrence, and the recurrence may be as an aggressive subtype of lymphoma. Aggressive lymphomas recur rapidly as a rule; most recurrence in diffuse large cell lymphoma, for example, occurs within the first 3 years after initial remission.

The development of pulmonary masses or infiltrates in patients who have been treated for non-Hodgkin's lymphoma may be a sign of recurrence, of opportunistic infection, of pulmonary injury due to therapy, or of new malignancy. Non-Hodgkin's lymphoma is itself a common second neoplasm following successful treatment of both childhood[65,66] and adult[67] neoplasms. Second neoplasms are increased in incidence following treatment of non-Hodgkin's lymphoma and include leukemia, bladder cancer, carcinoma of the lung, and bone sarcomas.[68] Imaging techniques may be somewhat helpful in delineating the possibilities.[16,27] Minimally invasive techniques such as fine-needle aspiration and lavage may also be useful. One series suggests that, when surgical exploration is necessary, most cases will prove to have recurrence of lymphoma rather than new primary cancers or infections.[69]

LYMPHOPROLIFERATIVE DISEASES

Disorders that are characterized by lymphoid infiltration in the lungs are numerous and varied in their manifestations. However, several of these lymphocyte-derived disorders are without obvious infectious or inflammatory cause and are commonly associated with a progressive course that terminates in a lymphoma or lymphoma-like illness. These include lymphomatoid granulomatosis, angioimmunoblastic lymphadenopathy, and other lymphoproliferative diseases, which are given various names such as pseudolymphoma and angiocentric lymphoproliferative disease. This category excludes Wegener's granulomatosis, allergic granulomatoses, sarcoidosis, and lymphocytic interstitial pneumonitis, which are described in the chapters in Section M.

Lymphoproliferative disorders of the lung have undergone reclassification because of the availability of new molecular techniques that show that many are clonal proliferations of a single lymphoid cell and are therefore really lymphomas. Revision of the concepts of how pulmonary lymphoproliferative diseases are classified has been the result of the efforts of many of the original describers of pulmonary lymphoproliferative syndromes.[70–73] Lymphoma-oriented treatment is useful in these diseases, and their termination in a therapy-resistant, often high-grade lymphoma resembles the clinical course of indolent lymphomas.

LYMPHOMATOID GRANULOMATOSIS

First described by Liebow and colleagues[74] in 1972, this angiocentric lymphoproliferative disease has always been of unknown etiology and poorly understood. Because of skin and pulmonary parenchymal involvement, the disease usually presents in adults with cough, dyspnea, and occasionally sputum production, fevers, and malaise.[75–77] Central nervous system manifestations occur in one fourth of patients and are characterized by focal deficits in an asymmetrical distribution, sometimes with seizures. Central nervous system features range from mild to very severe and have contributed to death of patients in all large series. Dermatologic involvement occurs in nearly half of patients, with patchy erythematous macular or papular areas, usually small and nonconfluent. Lesions occur most often on the extremities and may ulcerate; subcutaneous nodules can also occur.

Pulmonary involvement is almost invariably a feature of lymphomatoid granulomatosis, and the most common appearance is that of parenchymal masses, usually in the periphery and lower lobes. Extensive destruction of lung parenchyma sufficient to cause respiratory insufficiency has been reported in most series, as well as the occasional occurrence of massive hemoptysis or severe cavitary disease. Airway infiltration may also occur, usually in bronchioles, but lobar obstruction by endobronchial destructive lesions has been reported.

Other organ involvement by lymphomatoid granulomatosis is unusual. In contrast to Wegener's granulomatosis, renal involvement is rare as a clinical manifestation, but may be found at necropsy. Focal necrotic and proliferative lesions are seen, without glomerulonephritis. Hepatic involvement, although unusual, may carry a worse prognosis. Lymph node and splenic involvement is rare and does not appear to adversely affect prognosis. Also in contrast to Wegener's granulomatosis, lymphomatoid granulomatosis rarely involves the nasopharynx and upper airways.

The diagnosis of lymphomatoid granulomatosis is made histologically. This disease displays a destructive, inflammatory granulomatous angiitis, but, in contrast to Wegener's granulomatosis, the lymphoid infiltrate is composed of atypical and immature cells with abundant mitoses and a paucity of polymorphonuclear or eosinophilic leukocytes. These infiltrates have been shown to be composed of a population of B cells, usually with Epstein-Barr virus ribonucleic acid within them, and surrounding reactive T cells.[78,79] There are no characteristic laboratory values in lymphomatoid granulomatosis. In contrast to angioimmunoblastic lymphadenopathy, paraproteinemia, cytopenias, and autoimmune antibodies are uncommon.

The radiographic appearance of lymphomatoid granulomatosis is not unique. Multiple bilateral pulmonary nodules involving the lower and peripheral lung fields (Fig. 45.3) are also seen in metastases, other granulomatous diseases, and benign disorders such as eosinophilic granuloma.

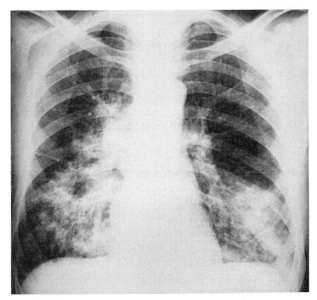

Figure 45.3 Diffuse nodular pulmonary infiltrate in a 49-year-old man with pulmonary, renal, and central nervous system abnormalities. The coalescing fluffy nodules were found to be lymphomatoid granulomatosis by biopsy. (Courtesy of Dr. G. Gamsu, University of California, San Francisco.)

Cavitation, atelectasis or lobar obstruction, large masslike lesions, and pneumothorax may be seen in lymphomatoid granulomatosis. The pulmonary lesions typically wax and wane, and some areas may regress while others are progressing. Hilar and mediastinal adenopathy is rare, as are normal chest radiographs.[80]

The pathogenesis of lymphomatoid granulomatosis is unknown. Although the disease may be associated with syndromes in which impaired immunity occurs, such as Sjögren's syndrome, chronic viral hepatitis, rheumatoid arthritis, AIDS, and renal transplantation, there has been no clear association with a specific pathogen. Although Epstein-Barr virus is frequently found in the B cells in the granulomas,[75,76] no investigator has demonstrated a causative relationship, and the virus may have infected the proliferating B cells coincidentally. Furthermore, reports that abnormal T-cell function occurs in lymphomatoid granulomatosis patients without other immune system disorders[81] suggest that lymphomatoid granulomatosis itself, or perhaps the high-grade lymphomas that frequently arise in the course of the disease, may be due to opportunistic pathogens or to an aberrant immune response to some pathogen. Both monoclonal T-cell proliferation and monoclonal B-cell proliferation have been identified late in this disease, thereby confusing the issue of pathogenesis, but suggesting the possibility of evolution to lymphoma.[82-84] The identification of primary T-cell lymphomas due to human T-cell lymphotrophic virus type 1 presenting with a syndrome much like lymphomatoid granulomatosis has further complicated the question of the pathogenesis of this disease.[85]

Treatment of lymphomatoid granulomatosis has been difficult. A significant fraction of patients have a benign disease course and may not require treatment for years or even longer. Individuals with symptomatic disease have been treated with steroids and antineoplastic drugs, predominantly low doses of cytotoxic drugs, such as cyclophosphamide, and biologics such as interferon-alpha 2B. Although the disease often responds to such measures, recurrence is frequent, and development of either refractory disease or high-grade lymphoma is common. Protracted responses to therapy may also occur, predominantly in patients having minimal disease with no central nervous system involvement. Radiotherapy works well for localized lesions,[86] but the optimum management of steroids, cytotoxic drugs, and radiotherapy remains unresolved. Lymphomatoid granulomatosis has a poor prognosis, with half or more of patients succumbing to the disease within 5 years. Its clinical course is quite heterogeneous, however, and long survivals and spontaneous remissions have been observed. The disease terminates in aggressive lymphoma in 15% to 25% of patients.

ANGIOIMMUNOBLASTIC LYMPHADENOPATHY

Angioimmunoblastic lymphadenopathy was first described by Lukes and Tindle,[87] who noted that it resembled Hodgkin's disease but without the telltale Reed-Sternberg cell. Although known initially by a wide variety of names, this syndrome has ultimately been called either angioimmunoblastic lymphadenopathy or angioimmunoblastic lymphadenopathy with dysproteinemia (AILD).[88-90] Lymphadenopathy is a constant feature of the disease. Patients are virtually always adults and often have constitutional symptoms of fever, weight loss, and fatigue. Rash occurs in nearly half, and pruritus is a common symptom. Hepatosplenomegaly and splenomegaly are common findings, and the adenopathy may occur at any or all sites. Pulmonary involvement occurs as massive adenopathy, pleural effusion, pleural thickening, or diffuse interstitial pulmonary infiltrates. Patients with AILD have a 5% to 20% likelihood of developing aggressive lymphoma; the majority who die of the disease succumb to infection, including opportunistic infections. Approximately one third of patients have a benign course, with either mild disease or spontaneous remission. Overall, however, the median survival is poor: 1.5 years.

It is the laboratory characteristics of AILD that distinguish it from other lymphoproliferative diseases. Most patients are anemic, and 40% have both clinical and laboratory evidence of autoimmune hemolytic anemia. Dysproteinemia is another hallmark feature, either with nonspecific polyclonal hyperglobulinemia, which occurs in about 70% of cases, or with hypoglobulinemia or monoclonal hyperglobulinemia, which can develop late in the disease. Leukocytosis, lymphopenia, thrombocytopenia, and eosinophilia have been reported in significant numbers of AILD patients. Autoantibodies abound: Autoimmune thrombocytopenia, aplastic anemia, and serologic evidence of other autoimmune phenomena are common. Evidence of T-cell–mediated immune defects and dysregulation is also common.[91,92]

The diagnosis of AILD may be suspected on clinical grounds, but the histologic features are necessary to finalize the diagnosis. The disease is characterized by proliferation and arborization of small blood vessels within the enlarged lymph nodes or lymphatic tissue, by effacement of normal lymph node architecture with a polymorphous inflammatory infiltrate and depletion of normal-appearing lymphocytes and germinal centers, and by the accumulation of amorphous eosinophilic material in intracellular spaces. It may resemble the histology of peripheral T-cell lymphomas, formerly called Lennert's lymphoma or Castleman's disease. Extranodal AILD may be found in bone marrow, skin, liver, lung, and rarely other internal organs. The infiltrate in such sites resembles the polymorphous appearance of Hodgkin's disease, although the Reed-Sternberg cell is absent. The appearance of the disease in HIV-infected patients is quite similar.[93] The differential diagnosis of pulmonary involvement by AILD includes infections, especially opportunistic infections. The lymphomas that occur in patients with AILD may be of any histologic type, though they are usually intermediate or high grade.[94,95]

The pathogenesis of AILD is also unknown. The association of this disease with other immune dysfunction diseases such as Sjögren's syndrome and AIDS suggests that the primary problem may be immunodysregulation. The combination of B-cell–mediated overactivity and dysregulation with T-cell underactivity is similar to the immune defects in HIV-infected individuals, many of whom also develop lymphoma. Epstein-Barr virus has also been found in lymphatic tissue of AILD patients,[96,97] but its etiologic relationship has not been established. The lymph node histology closely resembles that of patients with congenital rubella infections, and a rubella-like agent has been postulated; other infectious agents might include human T-cell lymphotrophic virus type 3, HIV, and as yet unidentified retroviruses. Clonal populations of T cells have been identified in as many as 75% of cases of AILD,[98] leading to their inclusion in the current classification schemes (see Table 45.1). B-cell and T-cell proliferation unrestrained by a malfunctioning T-cell control mechanism has been proposed as the underlying problem, which permits the ultimate development of lymphoma in AILD patients.[99]

Treatment of AILD has followed the same pattern as that of lymphomatoid granulomatosis, with the early use of steroids and cytotoxic drugs, but the need to suppress the autoimmune phenomena has led to the use of other kinds of agents. Danazol, widely prescribed for autoimmune hemolytic anemia and thrombocytopenia, has been reported to have some efficacy in AILD patients.[100] Cyclosporine has also been used,[101] as has interferon-alfa.[102,103] Lymphoma arising in AILD patients has been treated with various types of combination chemotherapy. The prognosis of AILD remains poor despite treatment.

CASTLEMAN'S DISEASE

In 1956, Castleman and colleagues[104] described a lymphoproliferative disorder, sometimes called angiofollicular lymph node hyperplasia, of unknown etiology that now bears the senior author's name. Castleman's disease tends to present two different patterns of involvement: the first type is focal, localized or unicentric, whereas the second type includes diffuse multicentric disease with systemic manifestations.[105] The lesions consist of large collections of lymphoid cells organized in loose follicles with interspersed vessels and small lymphoid cells. Unicentric Castleman's disease presents as one or more asymptomatic masses in the mediastinum or lungs in both children and adults. The masses are usually lobulated, are generally not calcified, mostly have smooth margins, and are found by CT scan to be very vascular.[106,107] These solitary masses can be diagnosed as Castleman's disease only by wide, often excisional, biopsy; smaller specimens typically yield nonspecific results.

Multicentric Castleman's disease presents more clinical challenges. In addition to the lungs and mediastinum, lesions may occur in a variety of extrathoracic sites, including the neck, retroperitoneum, pelvis, and axillary nodes. Patients often have systemic symptoms, including fever and night sweats, weight loss, fatigue, and neuropathy. Laboratory findings may include anemia, hyperglobulinemia, hypoalbuminemia, and autoimmune phenomena. Biopsies are more likely to show plasma cells than lymphocytes infiltrating among follicles. The multicentric variant has been described in patients with HIV infection and has been linked to the presence of human herpesvirus 8; human herpesvirus has also been identified in pathologic lymph nodes from patients without HIV infection.[108] The causal relationship between this virus and the disease has not been clearly defined, but the suspicion is that proliferation of B cells is actuated either by a host response to human herpesvirus infection or by genes in the virus itself. Investigators have shown that the stroma cells in Castleman's disease produce large quantities of interleukin-6[109] and that the B cells in the same masses have high levels of interleukin-6 receptors,[110] suggesting an autocrine mechanism for growth in these masses. Excess levels of interleukin-6 may also be responsible for the systemic symptoms seen in multicentric Castleman's disease.

Treatment of Castleman's disease depends on the type of disease in a given patient. The nodules of unicentric Castleman's disease are usually resected surgically, with excellent long-term results. When these lymphoid nodules are located in areas difficult to resect, they may be treated with radiation therapy. Multicentric Castleman's disease has been treated with corticosteroids, immunosuppressive therapy, cytotoxic drugs, and radiation therapy. The results of these various therapies have not been systematically reported, but in general, the more symptomatic the patient, the poorer the response and the shorter the survival; optimal treatment is unknown.[111] Anecdotal reports of patients with HIV-associated multicentric Castleman's disease suggest that highly active antiretroviral therapy for HIV may help, although there is a report of three patients with AIDS in whom symptoms of fulminant multicentric Castleman's disease developed after the initiation of highly active antiretroviral therapy.[112] Neither unicentric nor multicentric Castleman's disease progresses to lymphoma, in contrast to the other lymphoproliferative syndromes discussed in this chapter.

OTHER PRIMARY MALIGNANT TUMORS

CARCINOID AND NEUROENDOCRINE CARCINOMAS

Carcinoid tumors arising in the lungs and bronchi were first described in 1937, when they were characterized as a neoplasm distinct from bronchial adenoma. In the 1960s their microscopic features were compared with carcinoids occurring in other components of the embryonic foregut: the stomach, duodenum, gallbladder, and pancreas. Later, the electron micrographic and immunohistochemical features of these tumors were expanded. Bronchial carcinoids share neuroendocrine properties with a family of tumors thought to be derived from primitive neural crest tissue, including the gut carcinoids, amine precursor uptake and decarboxylation cells (APUDomas), pheochromocytomas, medullary carcinoma of the thyroid, and other endocrine tumors. Typical bronchial carcinoid cells are small and uniform in appearance with acidophilic cytoplasm and finely stippled chromatin. They are argyrophilic and contain neurosecretory granules on electron microscopy. They stain positively with immunohistochemical stains for neuron-specific enolase, chromogranin A, synaptophysin, serotonin, and other neurosecretory cell markers. *Neuroendocrine carcinomas*, also referred to as *atypical bronchial carcinoids*, are characterized by larger cell size and fewer characteristic nuclear and cytoplasmic features, but they retain at least some immunohistochemical stain positivity and electron micrographic features of neuroendocrine neoplasms. Both must be distinguished from other bronchial tumors and from small cell carcinoma of the lung.[113,114]

Incidence and Natural History

Bronchial carcinoids occur in a wide age range, with most clinical series showing a median age in the fifth decade of life. They are extremely rare in children but occur equally in both sexes. There are fewer than 2000 cases in the United States annually, and they represent about 2% of all primary lung tumors.[115] Bronchial carcinoids represent about 25% of all carcinoid tumors and may be slightly more common in African American males.[116] There is no known relationship to smoking or other environmental factors.

Carcinoid tumors may spread via either lymphatics or the bloodstream. The size and degree of differentiation of the primary tumor may be predictive of the likelihood of metastasis. Patterns of hematogenous spread show a predilection for the liver, bones, central nervous system, and adrenals. Serotonin-producing carcinoids are unusual in the lungs, and only about half of patients having elevated urinary serotonin metabolites also have the clinical carcinoid syndrome. Other endocrine syndromes such as Cushing's disease, inappropriate antidiuretic hormone secretion, and fever have been reported, as have rare cases associated with multiple endocrine neoplasias.[117-120]

Clinical Presentation

Central pulmonary carcinoid tumors that arise in the larger airways comprise about one half of all cases. Cough is the most common presenting symptom in such cases. Bronchial carcinoids are highly vascular tumors, and, although they originate submucosally, hemoptysis is a common presenting symptom, reported in 18% to 35% of series. Bronchial obstruction, causing stridor or wheezing, recurrent pneumonia, bronchiectasis, or lung abscess, is a common clinical feature, occurring in 15% to 25% of all patients. Weakness, weight loss, and fever are common accompanying symptoms in such patients. Systemic symptoms and local symptoms of metastasis, such as bone pain, are present in very few patients. Many patients (25% to 60%) are entirely asymptomatic, and the tumor is discovered on chest radiographs or CT scans taken for another purpose.

Diagnosis

The radiographic features of bronchial carcinoid are few, although most patients with pulmonary carcinoids have abnormal chest radiographs, due either to the tumor itself or to airway obstruction and its consequences. The tumor masses are usually not necrotic or are variable in density on plain films, and fewer than 10% have visible calcifications. CT evaluation may be useful in establishing that a pulmonary parenchymal mass has an endobronchial component[121]; in general, however, both atypical and typical bronchial carcinoids are found to be very vascular, well-defined masses, some with detectable intratumoral calcification.[122,123]

Adequate tissue for pathologic diagnosis of carcinoid or atypical carcinoid should be obtained, such as small samples from fine-needle aspiration or forceps biopsy at bronchoscopy, but this is not uniformly possible. Although these tumors are highly vascular, an increased risk of bleeding complications has not been reported in contemporary studies with flexible fiberoptic endoscopes and transbronchial biopsy. Bronchial brushings, sputum specimens, and lavage fluid are rarely worthwhile sources for tissue diagnosis. Thoracotomy and resection are frequently performed when the differential diagnosis includes a bronchogenic carcinoma.

Laboratory evaluation of patients with carcinoid tumors may include liver function tests and determination of 24-hour urine serotonin metabolites (5-hydroxyindoleacetic acid), which may be elevated in up to 25% of patients at diagnosis. Evaluation for metastatic disease may include a variety of sites: The central nervous system, adrenals, liver, and bones are the most common sites of hematogenous dissemination of bronchial carcinoid, both typical and atypical. Metastases to the hilar and mediastinal nodes may occur in carcinoid tumors, but most patients with small typical carcinoids do not require metastatic evaluation at the time of diagnosis. If the tumor is less than 2 cm in diameter, resectable, and typical in histology, the prognosis is excellent, and metastatic evaluation may not be justified.[124] However, persistent elevation of urinary 5-hydroxyindoleacetic acid or other serum hormone levels should prompt an investigation for metastatic disease.

Imaging of carcinoid tumors is performed with CT scanning and radionuclide imaging. Approximately 70% of pulmonary carcinoids are successfully imaged with radiolabeled octreotide, a somatostatin analogue that binds to somatostatin receptors on the tumor cells.[125] Positron emission tomography scanning itself is less useful, but an adaptation of such scanning using a labeled serotonin precursor, 5-hydroxytryptophan, shows some promise in pulmonary carcinoid imaging.[126]

Treatment

Surgical resection of carcinoid tumors is the only means of cure for these cancers.[126a] Because they are usually locally well defined, surgical margins may be extremely small and the risk of local recurrence low. Resection via bronchoscopy is technically possible for some tiny tumors, but in some cases resection may be incomplete.[127] If formal surgical salvage is also available, the prognosis may not be altered adversely,[127] and the procedure does offer palliation of symptoms. Tracheal carcinoids are amenable to tracheal resection or sleeve resection with good results.[128] When thoracotomy is performed and tumors are larger than 2 cm or are not well differentiated, staging by sampling the hilar and mediastinal nodes is appropriate.

Radiation therapy has a defined palliative role in the treatment of carcinoid tumors. The results from the largest reported series of patients with carcinoids of various sites suggest that, although 80% of treated patients have a partial or complete response to radiotherapy, curative therapy for gross disease is not a reasonable expectation.[129] Doses of at least 4500 to 5000 cGy are appropriate at sites where this is feasible. Prolonged symptomatic palliation may occur, especially with spinal cord metastases and osseous metastases. Hepatic and pulmonary metastases are not well treated by this therapy because of low tissue tolerance of radiation and the resulting low doses to tumor. Extrathoracic stereotactic radiosurgery (body gamma knife) is an experimental treatment modality that may prove useful in the treatment of small carcinoid tumors in patients unable to undergo thoracotomy.

Chemotherapy has a limited role in the treatment of metastatic carcinoid tumors. The most effective regimens reported contain streptozotocin, 5-fluorouracil, cyclophosphamide, dacarbazine, or doxorubicin.[130] Objective response rates are less than 40%, and combination therapy has not been formally compared with the use of single drugs. Response durations, when reported, are usually short; no trial has demonstrated a prolongation of survival compared with no treatment. Hepatic metastases, when solitary, may be treated by hepatic arterial therapy with palliative benefit.[131] The use of adjuvant chemotherapy in the treatment of resected carcinoid tumor has not been studied.

Biologic agents have recently been used with some success in the treatment of the carcinoid syndrome and metastatic carcinoid tumors. The somatostatin analogue octreotide has been shown to markedly reduce the symptoms associated with serotonin release from metastatic carcinoid tumors.[132,133] Octreotide does not predictably reduce tumor volume, nor does it produce regression of established long-term effects of serotonin, such as heart disease, but it may result in stabilization of tumor size. Tachyphylaxis may occur but can be controlled with the use of drug holidays and increased doses.[134] Interferon-alfa has been shown to produce regression in the carcinoid syndrome and, in some cases, objective tumor regression.[135,136] However, the side effects of interferon are considerably greater than those of somatostatin. Research suggests that interferon responders may be identifiable in advance, thus eliminating the toxicity to patients not likely to benefit.[137]

Bronchial carcinoids have a highly variable clinical course. The median survival in most series is more than 10 years, although aggressive metastatic disease with survival under 1 year has been reported. The best outcome is associated with small tumors, complete resection, and typical histology; such individuals have 10-year survival rates in excess of 95%.[138] Patients having systemic symptoms at diagnosis, unresectable tumors (including positive hilar lymph nodes), and male gender have a poorer outcome (10-year survival rates of 55% or less). Atypical bronchial carcinoids or neuroendocrine carcinomas are clearly associated with poorer outcome; they are more likely to have lymph node involvement at diagnosis, and even resected small tumors have a poor long-term outcome, with survival rates of 50% or less.[139,140]

MUCOEPITHELIAL MALIGNANCIES

The benign and malignant mucoepithelial malignancies include salivary gland tumors and lymphoepitheliomas originating in the lower rather than the upper airways. When these tumors occur in the nasopharynx and upper airways, they are identified by that site of origin; when they occur in the lower airways, they are referred to by their descriptive names, which are listed in Table 45.3.[141] These tumors are rare and may be confused with bronchogenic carcinoma; it is usually only when their morphology most clearly resembles salivary gland tumors that they are recognized as different.

When they present as primary pulmonary tumors, most originate in the mucosa of the large airways. Their presenting signs and symptoms are usually related to airway irritation and obstruction: cough, wheezing or stridor, hemoptysis, dyspnea, and occasionally fever or weight loss. Lymphoepitheliomas primarily present as masses on chest

Table 45.3 WHO Classification of Salivary Gland Tumors

Benign Tumors

Adenomas: pleomorphic adenoma, myoepithelioma, basal cell adenoma, Warthin's tumor (adenolymphoma), oncocytoma (oncocytic adenoma), canalicular adenoma, sebaceous adenoma

Cystadenoma: papillary and mucinous types

Carcinomas

Acinic cell carcinoma
Mucoepidermoid carcinoma
Adenoid cystic carcinoma (cylindroma)
Polymorphous low-grade adenocarcinoma
Epithelial-myoepithelial carcinoma
Basal cell adenocarcinoma
Sebaceous carcinoma
Papillary cystadenocarcinoma
Mucinous adenocarcinoma
Oncocytic carcinoma
Adenocarcinoma
Malignant myoepithelioma
Carcinoma in pleomorphic adenoma (malignant mixed tumor)

radiographs. Physical findings may be consistent with prior obstructive pneumonia, airway obstruction (either unilateral or bilateral), or signs of metastatic disease. Diagnosis may be made on chest radiograph, by contrast bronchography, or with conventional tomography or CT of the airways.[142] Bronchoscopy reveals masses within the airways, either sessile or polypoid in appearance. Bronchoscopic biopsy is usually adequate to make a diagnosis.[143] The diagnosis of lymphoepithelioma depends on recognition of the histology and on staining for the presence of Epstein-Barr virus in the tumor cells.[144]

The natural history and outcome of treatment differ for each of the varieties of this group of tumors. The adenomas have a propensity for local recurrence, and only occasionally for evolution into more malignant tumors. Pleomorphic adenoma is the most likely of this group of tumors to evolve into a higher grade carcinoma. The outcome of pleomorphic adenoma that has evolved into a carcinoma depends on the depth of the invasion of the carcinoma within the adenoma as well as the histologic type of carcinoma. When carcinosarcoma appears in a pleomorphic adenoma, the outcome is extremely poor. Occasionally Warthin's tumor develops areas of squamous metaplasia or frank neoplasia.

Of the salivary gland–like carcinomas, both cell type and histologic grade are important in long-term prognosis. Acinic cell carcinoma, polymorphous low-grade carcinoma, epithelial-myoepithelial carcinoma, and malignant myoepithelioma may all be locally invasive or recurrent, but rarely metastasize. Mucoepidermoid carcinomas have a variable outcome, depending on the histologic appearance. All adenoid cystic carcinomas must be considered to be biologically aggressive. Lymphoepithelioma has a variable natural history, but with combined treatment may actually have a better prognosis than corresponding stages of non–small cell lung carcinoma.[145,146]

Treatment depends on the local extent of the tumor and on the relative injury to the lung distal to it. Wide local excision is the preferred therapy. Salivary gland tumors, even

benign ones, have a propensity for local recurrence if not completely resected. Endobronchial therapy offers potential palliative treatment in patients unsuited for complete resection. Radiation therapy is widely reported as useful palliation for salivary gland tumors; however, case reports are scanty for its use in bronchial tumors. Radiotherapy might be considered when an attempt to resect has resulted in positive surgical margins or when regrowth has recurred after resection. For salivary gland tumors, the role of chemotherapy is palliative and should be restricted to patients having metastatic disease.[147–149] Lymphoepithelioma may be treated with combined surgery, radiation therapy, and chemotherapy with the same drugs that are used for nasopharyngeal carcinoma.[150]

SARCOMAS

Virtually any of the mesenchymal structures in and around the lungs may develop into a sarcoma, although primary sarcomas of the lung are extremely rare. Their presenting symptoms depend on the location of the tumor. Those within airways produce cough, wheezing, hemoptysis, and obstructive pneumonias; those in the pulmonary parenchyma may produce no symptoms at all until they reach a size large enough to compress the airways, irritate the pleural surface and other adjacent structures, or cause systemic symptoms; pulmonary vascular sarcomas may produce pulmonary embolism. Systemic symptoms due to pulmonary sarcomas are unusual, with occasional reports of pulmonary osteoarthropathy, fever, and hypoglycemia.

Pulmonary sarcoma has no unique radiographic features. These tumors may appear as solitary pulmonary masses and may be complicated by features such as pleural effusion, pulmonary infarction, or airway obstruction. Pathologic diagnosis is usually made with small tumor specimens, although very poorly differentiated tumors may be difficult to identify. Electron microscopy and special stains may help identify such tumors. Histologic grade is an important determinant of outcome in soft-tissue sarcomas and should be reported in all cases. Well-differentiated sarcomas of all subtypes have been reported in the lung. Diagnosis of a primary sarcoma in the lung requires careful exclusion of primary sarcoma elsewhere. For osteosarcoma, bone scan is an appropriate test. For other sarcoma cell types, CT body scanning is necessary.

Surgical resection, if complete, is curative for small, well-differentiated pulmonary sarcomas.[151] Poorly differentiated tumors are not as curable, but resection may provide some palliation and may be appropriate. Total survival rates vary from 5% to 25% or more. Unresectable or recurrent sarcomas may be treated with radiation therapy or with chemotherapy, although responses are usually brief and survival is less than 1 year.[152]

PULMONARY BLASTOMA AND CARCINOSARCOMA

Both pulmonary blastoma and carcinosarcoma are extremely rare and manifest a mixture of epithelial and mesenchymal neoplastic cells; they are often referred to as "sarcomatoid carcinomas" of the lung.[153] Pulmonary blastoma is a primitive tumor that consists of immature embryonic epithelial elements forming tubules and glands and primitive lung structures, surrounded by a malignant-appearing mesenchymal stroma.[154,155] Tumors with better differentiated mesenchymal elements or neuroendocrine cells in the stroma have also been reported and may represent part of the spectrum of this neoplasm.[156–158]

Pulmonary blastomas occur in children and adults and most commonly appear as parenchymal masses, which may be cystic or solid. They are slightly more common in women than men and are usually diagnosed by surgical resection. Resection is usually curative, especially for patients who have cystic blastomas.[159] In more aggressive tumors, late relapses and metastases occur, and the tumors are not curable. Radiation therapy may be useful for palliation, but a role for chemotherapy has not been defined.[160,161]

Carcinosarcoma is a similarly mixed tumor, but it contains malignant mature epithelium (non–small cell carcinoma) surrounded by malignant-appearing mesenchymal elements, either primitive spindle cells or more differentiated sarcoma cell types. The epithelial component is the more rapidly proliferating part of this tumor. Carcinosarcoma is reported mostly in smokers and may be caused by smoking; it is also seen mostly in middle-aged and older men.[162,163]

Carcinosarcoma is a disease that behaves much more like bronchogenic carcinoma than does pulmonary blastoma. It may present as endobronchial or parenchymal mass lesions, and metastases to lymph nodes, bones, brain, lung, and adrenals as well as local invasion are common. There is some suggestion that carcinosarcoma variants with a less-differentiated sarcomatous matrix, resembling fibrosarcoma, may have a slightly better prognosis.[164] The diagnosis may be obtained in the same manner as for bronchogenic carcinoma (see Chapter 44), and clinical evaluation for surgical resection is also performed in the same way.

Treatment of carcinosarcoma with surgical resection is preferred; palliation with radiation therapy may be appropriate in patients unsuited for surgery. Chemotherapy has a limited role, if any.[163] Palliation of metastatic disease with radiation therapy or chemotherapy is reasonable.

PULMONARY TUMORLETS

More of a medical curiosity than a clinical problem, pulmonary tumorlets are most often found at autopsy. They are tiny, often only microscopic foci of neoplastic-appearing cells that most closely resemble carcinoid tumors histologically. They are more common in diseased lungs than in healthy ones.[165–167] Classically, tumorlets are associated with inflammatory lesions in the airways, but they may also be multifocal and bilateral; when lesions exceed 0.5 cm in size, they are (arbitrarily) classified as carcinoid tumors.[168] They are only occasionally reported to have metastases,[169] and they have only rarely been reported to cause symptoms, although cases of obliterative bronchiolitis[170] and Cushing's syndrome[171] have been reported.

Tumorlets are thought to derive from normal neuroendocrine cells in the lungs. The tumorlets are argyrophilic and stain for neuron-specific enolase and other markers of neuroendocrine cells. What makes them proliferate is not understood, but they are thought to be part of the lung's inflammatory response.[172,173] Pulmonary tumorlets were

shown to have acquired novel neuroendocrine properties compared with normal pulmonary neuroendocrine cells, suggesting that the proliferation is associated with abnormal, perhaps even neoplastic features.[174] Pulmonary tumorlets remain a pathologic enigma.

OTHER TUMORS AND HEMATOLOGIC CONDITIONS

Multiple Myeloma and Waldenström's Macroglobulinemia

Multiple myeloma and Waldenström's macroglobulinemia derive from the mature, immunoglobulin (Ig)-producing B cells. Malignant plasma cells in plasmacytomas and multiple myeloma produce monoclonal IgG, IgA, or IgE; plasmacytoid small lymphocytes produce IgM in Waldenström's macroglobulinemia. Waldenström's macroglobulinemia is part of a continuum of mature B-cell lymphomas, and may be defined as a lymphoma if the magnitude of the IgM peak is small; it is usually referred to as Waldenström's macroglobulinemia when bone marrow involvement predominates or the IgM peak is in excess of 2 to 3 g/L in the serum.[175] In rare cases, each of these diseases may present as either a pulmonary parenchymal mass (called a plasmacytoma in multiple myeloma) or pleural effusion. In even rarer circumstances, these manifestations may be the first or only signs of the disease. Bone marrow involvement accompanies most cases of pulmonary involvement in these two diseases.[176,177]

Primary pulmonary involvement is frequently asymptomatic. Dyspnea is usually the first symptom of large pleural effusions. Associated symptoms may reflect the underlying systemic disease and may include fatigue, bruisability, bone pain, fever, and weight loss. Clinical signs may include adenopathy or visceromegaly in Waldenström's macroglobulinemia, petechiae or purpura, and signs of hyperviscosity such as vascular plethora, edema, or congestive heart failure.

Radiographic signs are nonspecific. The parenchymal lesions are usually poorly circumscribed masses or nodules. Lytic bone lesions may be a useful sign of multiple myeloma, although diffuse osteopenia is common to both diseases. Diagnosis may be made by needle aspiration, especially if it includes immunohistochemical staining showing a monoclonal surface immunoglobulin. The differential diagnosis includes granulomatous diseases, infection, and benign lymphoproliferative diseases. Laboratory evaluation must include demonstration of the monoclonal immunoglobulin in the tumor as well as a diligent search for systemic disease, employing bone marrow biopsy, serum and urine immunoelectrophoresis, and skeletal radiographic survey.[178,179]

True solitary plasmacytoma has a good prognosis if treated with excision or radiation therapy, but the tumor is very uncommon. It most often precedes the later development of clinically overt multiple myeloma. Patients having pleural effusion may be treated with intrapleural sclerotherapy and systemic chemotherapy. The median survival of patients with systemic disease is 3 to 4 years. Both diseases are treated with systemic chemotherapy; recent research suggests that multiple myeloma patients able to tolerate autologous bone marrow transplant benefit from this approach, with a longer disease-free interval.[180] Complications of both diseases include infections, particularly with encapsulated bacteria such as *Streptococcus pneumoniae*, and bone fractures. The latter may be treated prophylactically with parenteral aminobisphosphonates in patients with multiple myeloma, and the former with revaccination and prophylactic IgG.

Other hematologic malignancies may involve the lungs, mediastinum, and pleural space. Chronic myelogenous leukemia, especially in its late stages, may involve the pleura and may also produce focal aggregations of malignant cells, called chloromas, in a variety of soft tissues. Acute leukemias in adults may involve the pleura or present as diffuse, patchy pulmonary infiltrates. Leukemic involvement must be distinguished from infection, and the diagnosis may be made by bronchoscopy and lavage, by fine-needle aspiration, or by lung biopsy.[181]

The lung is a common target organ in patients with a variety of hematologic disorders. The reasons for this association are many: Hematologic diseases are often accompanied by inflammatory cytokine production, by altered behavior of and localization of polymorphonuclear leukocytes, and by immunosuppression. Patients with hematologic disorders are exposed to a variety of iatrogenic diseases, including injury from drugs and radiation therapy, graft-versus-host disease from allogeneic transplantation, and pulmonary toxicity from biologic agents with specific toxicity to the lung. The incidence of pulmonary toxicity of antineoplastic and anti-inflammatory drugs used in patients with hematologic disorders ranges from 3% to 30%; a variety of pathogenic mechanisms produce pulmonary toxicity. The pathogenesis of lung injury in graft-versus-host disease is poorly understood: the acute phase appears to be mediated by CD8 T cells, and the chronic phase is more characterized by infiltrating CD4 T cells. The myriad of mechanisms for the induction of pulmonary injury syndromes in hematologic disorders does not lend itself to universal treatment recommendations. Careful evaluation and treatment of underlying conditions or infections, and removal of potentially offending drugs, are keys to patient care.[182]

Primary Pulmonary Melanoma

There are only 30 cases of primary pulmonary melanoma in the literature that are well enough documented to exclude a cutaneous or ocular primary site.[183,184] The tumors in these cases were both bronchial and parenchymal, and all occurred in adults. Presenting signs are nonspecific, and an extremely careful search for a primary site or for other evidence of metastases is important before making the diagnosis of primary pulmonary melanoma.[185] Immunohistochemical staining and electron microscopy are useful confirmatory tests. The pathogenesis of primary pulmonary melanoma is not clear, but the similarity of melanoma to neuroendocrine carcinomas raises the possibility that these tumors may develop from pulmonary neuroendocrine cells. Primary pulmonary melanoma is more advanced locally at diagnosis than is cutaneous melanoma and thus more likely to recur after surgical excision. Standard treatment is surgical resection, and case reports suggest that prolonged remission of the disease is possible. Nonsurgical candidates may be palliated with radiation therapy. Newer biologic therapies and chemotherapy may be considered for individuals with recurrent or unresponsive disease.

SUMMARY

The nonbronchogenic malignancies that involve the lung are a varied group of diseases with highly variable natural histories and outcomes. The non-Hodgkin's lymphomas range from highly aggressive but curable tumors to more indolent cancers that are incurable. Pulmonary Hodgkin's disease is most often seen as a direct extension of tumor involving the hilar and mediastinal nodes and is curable with aggressive therapy, usually a combination of chemotherapy and radiotherapy. Carcinoid tumors are surgically curable if small and not atypical in appearance; larger and less differentiated tumors, especially when metastatic, have no known curative treatment. Similarly, the better differentiated mucoepithelial cancers are curable when they can be completely removed surgically; sarcomas are likewise potentially curable. Neither class of tumor is curable when metastases occur, and both have a high rate of local recurrence, even when they are low grade and indolent in nature.

This group of cancers is becoming much better defined clinically in part due to advances in their molecular characterization. Indolent inflammatory diseases can be distinguished from low-grade lymphomas by means of newer technologies, allowing for more targeted therapies for these patients. The same techniques may be used to define extranodal pulmonary involvement by other lymphomas, especially recurrent lymphomas, thereby making more appropriate treatment decisions possible with less invasive diagnostic procedures.

REFERENCES

1. Whimster WF: Lung tumors: Differentiation and classification. Pathol Annu 18:121–138, 1983.
2. Wood NL, Coltman CA: Localized primary extranodal Hodgkin's disease. Ann Intern Med 78:113–118, 1973.
3. Yousem SA, Weiss LM, Colby TV: Primary pulmonary Hodgkin's disease. Cancer 57:1217–1224, 1986.
4. Friedman M, Kim U, Shimaoka K, et al: Appraisal of aspiration cytology in management of Hodgkin's disease. Cancer 45:1653–1663, 1980.
5. Connors JM, Klimo P: Is it an E lesion or stage IV? An unsettled issue in Hodgkin's disease staging. J Clin Oncol 2:1421–1423, 1984.
6. Diehll LF, Hopper KD, Giguere J, et al: The pattern of intrathoracic Hodgkin's disease assessed by computed tomography. J Clin Oncol 9:438–443, 1991.
7. Lewis ER, Caskey CI, Fishman EK: Lymphoma of the lung: CT findings in 31 patients. AJR Am J Roentgenol 156:711–714, 1991.
8. McCloud TC, Naidich DP: Thoracic disease in the immunocompromised patient. Radiol Clin North Am 30:525–554, 1992.
9. Listinsky CM: A practical approach to the diagnosis of Hodgkin lymphoma. Am J Clin Pathol 117(Suppl):S76–S94, 2002.
10. Morales FM, Matthews JI: Diagnosis of parenchymal Hodgkin's disease using bronchoalveolar lavage. Chest 91:785–787, 1987.
11. Rubin A-HE, Ben-Shachar M, Malberger E: Cytologic diagnosis of pulmonary Hodgkin's disease via endobronchial brush preparation. Chest 96:948–949, 1989.

12. Reale FR, Varikojis D, Compton JC, et al: Cytodiagnosis of Hodgkin's disease in sputum specimens. Acta Cytol 27:258–261, 1983.

13. Friedman M, Kim U, Shimaoka K, et al: Appraisal of aspiration cytology in management of Hodgkin's disease. Cancer 45:1653–1663, 1980.

14. Torti FM, Portlock CS, Rosenberg SA, et al: Extralymphatic Hodgkin's disease: Prognosis and response to therapy. Am J Med 70:487–492, 1981.

15. Levi JA, Wiernik PH: Limited extranodal Hodgkin's disease: Unfavorable prognosis and therapeutic implications. Am J Med 63:365–372, 1977.

16. Loyer E, Fuller L, Libshitz HI, Palmer JL: Radiographic appearance of the chest following therapy for Hodgkin disease. Eur J Radiol 35:136–148, 2000.

17. Lee CKK, Bloomfield CD, Goldman AI, et al: Prognostic significance of mediastinal involvement in Hodgkin's disease treated with curative radiotherapy. Cancer 46:2403–2409, 1980.

18. Mauch P, Goodman R, Hellman S: The significance of mediastinal involvement in early stage Hodgkin's disease. Cancer 42:1039–1045, 1978.

19. Prosnitz LR, Curtis AM, Knowlton AH: Supradiaphragmatic Hodgkin's disease: Significance of large mediastinal masses. Int J Radiat Oncol Biol Phys 6:809–813, 1980.

20. Jochelson MS: The treated thorax. Radiol Clin North Am 28:763–769, 1990.

21. Tucker MA, Coleman CN, Cox RS, et al: Risk of second malignancies following Hodgkin's disease after 15 years. N Engl J Med 318:76–81, 1988.

22. Meadows AT, Obringer AC, Marrero O, et al: Second malignant neoplasms following childhood Hodgkin's disease: Treatment and splenectomy as risk factors. Med Pediatr Oncol 17:477–484, 1989.

23. Putterman C, Polliack A: Late cardiovascular and pulmonary complications of therapy in Hodgkin's disease: Report of three unusual cases, with a review of relevant literature. Leuk Lymphoma 7:109–115, 1992.

24. Allavena C, Conreoy T, Aletti P, et al: Late cardiopulmonary toxicity after treatment for Hodgkin's disease. Br J Cancer 65:908–912, 1992.

25. Isaacson P: Review: The current status of lymphoma classification. Br J Haematol 109:258–266, 2000.

26. International Non-Hodgkin's Lymphoma Prognostic Factors Project: A predictive model for aggressive non-Hodgkin's lymphoma. N Engl J Med 329:987–994, 1993.

26a. Kim JH, Lee SH, Park J, et al: Primary pulmonary non-Hodgkin's lymphoma. Jpn J Clin Oncol 34:510–514, 2004.

27. Halliday T, Baxter G: Lymphoma: Pictorial review I. Eur Radiol 13:1154–1164, 2003.

28. Cordier JF, Chailleux E, Lauque D, et al: Primary pulmonary lymphomas: A clinical study of 70 cases in non immunocompromised patients. Chest 103:201–208, 1993.

29. Kuppers R, Klein U, Hansmann ML, Rajewsky K: Cellular origin of human B-cell lymphomas. N Engl J Med 341:1520, 1999.

30. Fiche M, Capron F, Berger F, et al: Primary pulmonary non-Hodgkin's lymphomas. Histopathology 26:529–537, 1995.

31. Armitage JO, Weisenburger DD: New approach to classifying non-Hodgkin's lymphomas: Clinical features of the major histologic subtypes. J Clin Oncol 16:2780–2795, 1998.

32. Fisher RI: Overview of non-Hodgkin's lymphoma: Biology, staging, and treatment. Semin Oncol 30(2 Suppl 4):3–9, 2003.

33. Bienenstock J, Johnston N, Perey DYE: Bronchial lymphoid tissue. I. Morphologic characteristics. Lab Invest 28:686–692, 1973.

34. Kradin RL, Mark EJ: Benign lymphoid disorders of the lung, with a theory regarding their development. Hum Pathol 14:857–867, 1983.

35. Cavalli F, Isaacson P, Gascoyne RD, Zucca E: MALT lymphomas. Hematology (Am Soc Hematol Educ Program):241–258, 2001.

36. Weiss LW, Warnke RA, Sklar J, et al: Molecular analysis of the t(14;18) chromosomal translocation in malignant lymphoma. N Engl J Med 317:1185–1189, 1987.

37. Pisani RJ, Witzig TE, Li C-Y, et al: Confirmation of lymphomatous pulmonary involvement by immunophenotypic and gene rearrangement analysis of bronchoalveolar lavage fluid. Mayo Clin Proc 65:651–656, 1990.

38. Nicholson AG, Wotherspoon AC, Diss TC, et al: Pulmonary B-cell non-Hodgkin's lymphomas: The value of immunohistochemistry and gene analysis in diagnosis. Histopathology 26:395–403, 1995.

39. Zaer F, Braylan M, Zander D, et al: Multiparametric flow cytometry in the diagnosis and characterization of low-grade pulmonary mucosa-associated lymphoid tissue lymphomas. Mod Pathol 11:525–532, 1998.

40. Kinsely BL, Mastey LA, Mergo PJ, et al: Pulmonary mucosa-associated lymphoid tissue lymphoma: CT and pathologic findings. AJR Am J Roentgenol 172:1321–1326, 1999.

41. Chabner, BA, Johnson, RE, Young, RC, et al: Sequential nonsurgical and surgical staging of non-Hodgkin's lymphoma. Cancer 42:922–925, 1978.

42. Thomas DA, Kantarjian HM: Lymphoblastic lymphoma. Hematol Oncol Clin North Am 15:51–95, 2001.

43. Barth TF, Leithauser F, Moller P: Mediastinal B-cell lymphoma, a lymphoma type with several characteristics unique among diffuse large B-cell lymphomas. Ann Hematol 80(Suppl 3):B49–B53, 2001.

44. Van Besien K, Kelta M, Bahaguna P: Primary mediastinal B-cell lymphoma: A review of pathology and management. J Clin Oncol 19:1855–1864, 2001.

45. List AF, Greco FA, Vogler LB: Lymphoproliferative diseases in immunocompromised hosts: The role of Epstein-Barr virus. J Clin Oncol 5:1673–1689, 1987.

46. Young L, Alfieri C, Hennessy K, et al: Expression of Epstein-Barr virus transformation-associated genes in tissues of patients with EBV lymphoproliferative disease. N Engl J Med 321:1080–1085, 1989.

47. Purtilo DT, Strobach RS, Okano M, et al: Epstein-Barr virus-associated lymphoproliferative disorders. Lab Invest 67:5–23, 1992.

48. Northfelt DW, Kaplan LD: Clinical aspects of AIDS-related non-Hodgkin's lymphoma. Curr Opin Oncol 3:872–880, 1991.

49. Bazot M, Cadranel J, Benayoun S, et al: Primary pulmonary AIDS-related lymphoma: Radiographic and CT findings. Chest 116:1282–1286, 1999.

50. Sparano JA: Human immunodeficiency virus associated lymphoma. Curr Opin Oncol 15:372–378, 2003.

51. Levine AM: Acquired immunodeficiency syndrome-related lymphoma. Blood 80:8–20, 1992.

52. Cesarman E, Chang Y, Moore PS, et al: Kaposi's sarcoma-associated herpesvirus-like DNA sequences in AIDS-related body-cavity–based lymphomas. N Engl J Med 332:1186–1191, 1995.

53. Komanduri KV, Luce JA, McGrath MS, et al: The natural history and molecular heterogeneity of HIV-associated primary malignant lymphomatous effusions. J AIDS 13:215–226, 1996.

54. Gaidano G, Carbone A: Primary effusion lymphoma: A liquid-phase lymphoma of fluid-filled body cavities. Adv Cancer Res 80:115–146, 2001.

55. Greer JP, Kinney MC, Loughran TP Jr: T cell and NK cell lymphoproliferative disorders. Hematology (Am Soc Hematol Educ Program):259–281, 2001.

56. McLaughlin P, Fuller LM, Velasquez WS, et al: Stage I-II follicular lymphoma: Treatment results for 76 patients. Cancer 58:1596–1602, 1986.

57. Monfardini S, Banfi A, Bonnadonna G, et al: Improved five year survival after combined radiotherapy-chemotherapy for stage I–II non-Hodgkin's lymphoma. Int J Radiat Oncol Biol Phys 6:125–134, 1980.

58. Zucca D, Conconi A, Cavalli F: Treatment of extranodal lymphomas. Best Pract Res Clin Haematol 15:533–547, 2002.

59. Portlock CS, Rosenberg SA: No initial therapy for stage III and IV non-Hodgkin's lymphoma of favorable histologic types. Ann Intern Med 90:10–13, 1979.

60. Jones SE, Fuks A, Kaplan HS, et al: Non-Hodgkin's lymphomas. V. Results of radiotherapy. Cancer 32:682–691, 1973.

61. Vokes EE, Ultmann JE, Golomb HM, et al: Long-term survival of patients with localized diffuse histiocytic lymphoma. J Clin Oncol 3:1309–1313, 1985.

62. Cabanillas F, Bodey GP, Freireich EJ: Management with chemotherapy only of stage I and II malignant lymphoma of aggressive histologic types. Cancer 46:2356–2359, 1980.

63. Connors JM, Klimo P, Fairey RN, et al: Brief chemotherapy and involved field radiation therapy for limited-stage, histologically aggressive lymphoma. Ann Intern Med 107:25–30, 1987.

64. Fisher RI, Shah P: Current trends in large cell lymphoma. Leukemia 17:1948–1960, 2003.

65. Eguiguren JM, Ribiero RC, Pui CH, et al: Secondary non-Hodgkin's lymphoma after treatment for childhood cancer. Leukemia 5:908–911, 1991.

66. Meadows AT, Baum E, Bellani-Fossati F, et al: Second malignant neoplasms in children: An update from the Late Effects Study Group. J Clin Oncol 3:532–538, 1985.

67. van Leeuwen FE: Second cancers. In DeVita VT Jr, Hellman S, Rosenberg SA (eds): Cancer: Principles and Practice of Oncology (5th ed). Philadelphia: Lippincott–Raven, 1997, pp 2773–2796.

68. Travis LB, Curtis RE, Boice JD Jr, et al: Second cancers following non-Hodgkin's lymphoma. Cancer 67:2002–2009, 1991.

69. Yellin A, Pak HY, Burke JS, et al: Surgical management of lymphomas involving the chest. Ann Thorac Surg 44:363–369, 1987.

70. Colby TV, Carrington CB: Lymphoreticular tumors and infiltrates of the lung. Pathol Annu 18:27–70, 1983.

71. Churg A: Pulmonary angiitis and granulomatosis revisited. Hum Pathol 14:868–883, 1983.

72. Kennedy JL, Nathwani BN, Burke JS, et al: Pulmonary lymphomas and other pulmonary lymphoid lesions. Cancer 56:539–552, 1985.

73. Addis BJ, Hyjek E, Isaacson PG: Primary pulmonary lymphoma: A re-appraisal of its histogenesis and its relationship to pseudolymphoma and lymphoid interstitial pneumonitis. Histopathology 13:1–17, 1988.

74. Liebow AA, Carrington CRB, Friedman PJ: Lymphomatoid granulomatosis. Hum Pathol 3:457–558, 1972.

75. Katzenstein A-LA, Carrington CB, Liebow AA: Lymphomatoid granulomatosis: A clinicopathological study of 152 cases. Cancer 43:360–373, 1979.

76. Patton WF, Lynch JP III: Lymphomatoid granulomatosis: Clinicopathologic study of four cases and literature review. Medicine 61:1–12, 1982.

77. Fauci AS, Haynes BE, Costa J, et al: Lymphomatoid granulomatosis: Prospective clinical and therapeutic experience over 10 years. N Engl J Med 306:68–74, 1982.

78. Wilson WH, Kingma DW, Raffeld M, et al: Association of lymphomatoid granulomatosis with Epstein-Barr viral infection of B lymphocytes and response to interferon-alpha 2b. Blood 87:4531–4537, 1996.

79. Haque AK, Myers JL, Hudnall SD, et al: Pulmonary lymphomatoid granulomatosis in acquired immunodeficiency syndrome: Lesions with Epstein-Barr virus infection. Mod Pathol 11:347–356, 1998.

80. Frazier AA, Rosado-de-Christenson ML, Galvin JR, et al: Pulmonary angiitis and granulomatosis: Radiologic-pathologic correlation. Radiographics 18:687–710, 1998.

81. Sordillo PP, Epremian B, Koziner B, et al: Lymphomatoid granulomatosis: An analysis of clinical and immunologic characteristics. Cancer 49:2070–2076, 1982.

82. Gaulard P, Henni T, Marolleau JP, et al: Lethal midline granuloma (polymorphic reticulosis) and lymphomatoid granulomatosis: Evidence for a monoclonal T-cell lymphoproliferative disorder. Cancer 62:705–710, 1988.

83. Bleiweiss IJ, Strauchen JA: Lymphomatoid granulomatosis of the lung: Report of a case and gene rearrangement studies. Hum Pathol 19:1109–1112, 1988.

84. Jaffe ES, Wilson WH: Lymphomatoid granulomatosis: Pathogenesis, pathology, and clinical implications. Cancer Surv 30:233–248, 1997.

85. McNutt NS, Smoller BR, Kline M, et al: Angiocentric T-cell lymphoma associated with human T-cell lymphotropic virus type I infection. Arch Pathol Lab Med 114:170–175, 1990.

86. Nair BD, Joseph MG, Catton GE, et al: Radiation therapy in lymphomatoid granulomatosis. Cancer 64:821–824, 1989 [published erratum appears in Cancer 64:1795, 1989].

87. Lukes RJ, Tindle BH: Immunoblastic lymphadenopathy: A hyperimmune entity resembling Hodgkin's disease. N Engl J Med 292:1–8, 1975.

88. Frizzera G, Moran EM, Rappaport H: Angio-immunoblastic lymphadenopathy: Diagnosis and clinical course. Am J Med 59:803–818, 1975.

89. Aozasa K: Angioimmunoblastic lymphadenopathy: Review of 44 patients with emphasis on prognostic behavior. Cancer 63:1625–1629, 1989.

90. Knecht H: Angioblastic lymphadenopathy: Ten years' experience and state of current knowledge. Semin Hematol 26:208–215, 1989.

91. Neiman RS, Dervan P, Haudenschild C, et al: Angioimmunoblastic lymphadenopathy: An ultrastructural and immunologic study with review of the literature. Cancer 41:507–518, 1978.

92. Pizzolo G: Increased serum levels of soluble IL-2 receptor, CD30 and CD8 molecules, and gamma-interferon in angioimmunoblastic lymphadenopathy: Possible pathogenetic role of immunoactivation mechanisms. Br J Haematol 75:485–488, 1990.

93. Blumenfeld W: Angioimmunoblastic lymphadenopathy with dysproteinemia in homosexual men with acquired immune deficiency syndrome. Arch Pathol Lab Med 107:567–569, 1983.

94. Nathwani BN, Rappaport H, Moran EM, et al: Malignant lymphoma arising in angioimmunoblastic lymphadenopathy. Cancer 41:578–606, 1978.

95. Bluming AZ, Cohen HG, Saxon A: Angioimmunoblastic lymphadenopathy with dysproteinemia: A pathogenetic link

between physiologic lymphoid proliferation and malignant lymphoma. Am J Med 67:421–428, 1979.

96. Lipford EH Jr, Margolick JB, Longo DL, et al: Angiocentric immunoproliferative lesions: A clinicopathologic spectrum of post-thymic T cell proliferations. Blood 72:1674–1681, 1988.

97. Medeiros LJ, Jaffe ES, Chen YY, et al: Localization of Epstein-Barr viral genomes in angiocentric immunoproliferative lesions. Am J Surg Pathol 16:439–447, 1992.

98. Feller A, Griesser H, Schilling C, et al: Clonal gene rearrangement patterns correlate with immunophenotype and clinical parameters in patients with angioimmunoblastic lymphadenopathy. Am J Pathol 133:549–556, 1988.

99. Tindle B: The pathology of immunoblastic proliferations: Reaction, prelymphoma, lymphoma. Pathol Annu 26:145–186, 1991.

100. Banavali S: Danazol in treatment of angioimmunoblastic lymphadenopathy. Cancer 64:613–615, 1989.

101. Murayama T: Successful treatment of angioimmunoblastic lymphadenopathy with dysproteinemia with cyclosporin A. Cancer 69:1259–1267, 1992.

102. Schwarzmeier J: Interferon-alpha induces complete remission in angioimmunoblastic lymphadenopathy (AILD): Late development of aplastic anaemia with cytokine abnormalities. Br J Haematol 79:336–337, 1991.

103. Meuthen I: Lymphogranulomatosis X: Complete remission by low dose interferon-alpha. Br J Haematol 75:438–439, 1990.

104. Castleman B, Iverson L, Menedez VP: Localized mediastinal lymph node hyperplasia resembling thymoma. Cancer 9:822–839, 1956.

105. McCarty JJ, Vukelja SJ, Banks PM, et al: Angiofollicular lymph node hyperplasia (Castleman's disease). Cancer Treat Rev 21:291–310, 1995.

106. Onik G, Goodman P: CT of Castleman's disease. AJR Am J Roentgenol 140:691–692, 1983.

107. Fiore D, Biondetti P, Calabro F, et al: CT demonstration of bilateral Castleman tumors in the mediastinum. J Comput Assist Tomogr 7:719–720, 1983.

108. Cesarman E, Knowles DM: The role of Kaposi's sarcoma–associated herpesvirus (KSHV/HHV-8) in lymphoproliferative diseases. Semin Cancer Biol 9:165–174, 1999.

109. Emilie D, Zou W, Fior R, et al: Production and roles of IL-6, IL-10, and IL-13 in B-lymphocyte malignancies and in B-lymphocyte hyperactivity of HIV infection and autoimmunity. Methods 11:133–142, 1997.

110. Ishiyama T, Koike M, Nakamura S, et al: Interleukin-6 receptor expression in the peripheral B cells of patients with multicentric Castleman's disease. Ann Hematol 73:179–182, 1996.

111. Bowne WB, Lewis JJ, Filippa DA, et al: The management of unicentric and multicentric Castleman's disease: A report of 16 cases and a review of the literature. Cancer 85:706–717, 1999.

112. Zietz C, Bogner JR, Goebel F-D, et al: An unusual cluster of Castleman's disease during highly active antiretroviral therapy for AIDS. N Engl J Med 340:1923–1924, 1999.

113. Warren WH, Memoli VA, Gould VE: Well differentiated and small cell neuroendocrine carcinomas of the lung: Two related but distinct clinicopathologic entities. Virchows Arch Biol 55:299–310, 1988.

114. Paladugu RR, Benfield JR, Pak HY, et al: Broncho-pulmonary Kulchitsky cell carcinomas I and II—alias typical and atypical carcinoids. Cancer 55:1303–1311, 1985.

115. Kulke MH, Mayer RJ: Carcinoid tumors. N Engl J Med 340:858–868, 1999.

116. Modlin IM, Sandor A: An analysis of 8305 cases of carcinoid tumors. Cancer 79:813–829, 1997.

117. Benfield JR: Neuroendocrine neoplasms of the lung. J Thorac Cardiovasc Surg 100:628–629, 1990.

118. Harpole DH, Feldman JM, Buchanan S, et al: Bronchial carcinoid tumor: A retrospective analysis of 126 patients. Ann Thorac Surg 54:50–55, 1992.

119. Hage R, de la Riviere AB, Seldenrijk CA, et al: Update in pulmonary carcinoid tumors: a review article. Ann Surg Oncol 10:697–704, 2003.

120. Stamatis G, Freitag L, Greschuchna D: Limited and radical resection for tracheal and broncho-pulmonary carcinoid tumor: Report on 227 cases. Eur J Cardiothorac Surg 4:527–533, 1990.

121. Davis SD, Zirn JR, Govoni AF, et al: Peripheral carcinoid tumor of the lung: CT diagnosis. AJR Am J Roentgenol 155:1185–1187, 1990.

122. Naidich DP, McCauley DI, Siegelman SS: Computed tomography of bronchial adenomas. J Comput Assist Tomogr 6:725–732, 1982.

123. Zweibel BR, Austin JHM, Grimes MM: Bronchial carcinoid tumors: Assessment with CT of location and intratumoral calcification in 31 patients. Radiology 179:483–486, 1991.

124. Ducrocq X, Thomas P, Massard G, et al: Operative risk and prognostic factors of typical bronchial carcinoid tumors. Ann Thorac Surg 65:1410–1414, 1998.

125. Granberg D, Sundin A, Janson ET, et al: Octreoscan in patients with bronchial carcinoid tumours. Clin Endocrinol 59:793–799, 2003.

126. Eriksson B, Bergstrom M, Sundin A, et al: The role of PET in localization of neuroendocrine and adrenocortical tumors. Ann N Y Acad Sci 970:159–169, 2002.

126a. Cardillo G, Sera F, Di Martino M, et al: Bronchial carcinoid tumors: nodal status and long-term survival after resection. Ann Thorac Surg 77:1781–1785, 2004.

127. Van Boxem TJ, Venmans BJ, van Mourik JC, et al: Bronchoscopic treatment of intraluminal typical carcinoid: A pilot study. J Thorac Cardiovasc Surg 116:402–406, 1998.

128. Perelman MI, Koroleva N, Birjukov J, et al: Primary tracheal tumors. Semin Thorac Cardiovasc Surg 8:400–402, 1996.

129. Schupak KD, Wallner KE: The role of radiation therapy in the treatment of locally unresectable or metastatic carcinoid tumors. Int J Radiat Oncol Biol Phys 20:489–495, 1991.

130. Oberg K: The use of chemotherapy in the management of neuroendocrine tumors. Endocrinol Metab Clin North Am 22:941–952, 1993.

131. Moertel CG: An odyssey in the land of small tumors. J Clin Oncol 5:1503, 1987.

132. Janson ET, Oberg K: Long-term management of the carcinoid syndrome: Treatment with octreotide alone and in combination with alpha-interferon. Acta Oncol 32:225–229, 1993.

133. Kvols LK, Moertel CG, O'Connell MJ, et al: Treatment of the malignant carcinoid syndrome: Evaluation of a long-acting somatostatin analogue. N Engl J Med 315:663–666, 1986.

134. Mulvihill S, Pappas TN, Passaro E Jr, et al: The use of somatostatin and its analogs in the treatment of surgical disorders. Surgery 100:467–475, 1986.

135. Oberg K, Ericksson B: The role of interferon in the management of carcinoid tumors. Acta Oncol 30:519–522, 1991.

136. Filosso PL, Ruffini E, Oliaro A, et al: Long-term survival of atypical bronchial carcinoids with liver metastases, treated with octreotide. Eur J Cardiothorac Surg 21:913–917, 2002.

137. Grander D, Oberg K, Lundqvist M-L, et al: Interferon-induced enhancement of 2′,5′-oligoadenylate synthetase in mid-gut carcinoid tumors. Lancet 336:337–340, 1990.

138. Schrevens L, Vansteenkiste J, Deneffe G, et al: Clinical-radiological presentation and outcome of surgically treated pulmonary carcinoid tumours: A long-term single institution experience. Lung Cancer 43:39–45, 2004.

139. Kaplan B, Stevens CW, Allen P, et al: Outcomes and patterns of failure in bronchial carcinoid tumors. Int J Radiat Oncol Biol Phys 55:125–131, 2003.

140. Mezzetti M, Raveglia F, Panigalli T, et al: Assessment of outcomes in typical and atypical carcinoids according to latest WHO classification. Ann Thorac Surg 76:1838–1842, 2003.

141. Seifert G, Sobin LH: The World Health Organization's histological classification of salivary gland tumors: A commentary on the second edition. Cancer 70:379–385, 1992.

142. Aberle DR, Brown K, Young DA, et al: Imaging techniques in the evaluation of tracheobronchial neoplasms. Chest 99:211–215, 1991.

143. Chetty R, Forder MD, DeGroot M, et al: Muco-epidermoid and adenoid cystic carcinomas of the tracheobronchial tree. Aust N Z J Surg 61:360–362, 1991.

144. Wong MP, Chung LP, Yuen ST, et al: In situ detection of Epstein-Barr virus in non-small cell lung carcinomas. J Pathol 177:233–240, 1995.

145. Chan JK, Hui PK, Tsang WY, et al: Primary lymphoepithelioma-like carcinoma of the lung: A clinicopathological study of 11 cases. Cancer 76:413–422, 1995.

146. Chen FF, Yan JJ, Lai WW, et al: Epstein-Barr virus–associated nonsmall cell lung carcinoma: Undifferentiated "lymphoepithelioma-like" carcinoma as a distinct entity with a better prognosis. Cancer 82:2334–2342, 1998.

147. Li W, Ellerbroek NA, Libshitz HI: Primary malignant tumors of the trachea: A radiologic and clinical study. Cancer 66:894–899, 1990.

148. Grillo HC, Mathisen DJ: Primary tracheal tumors: Treatment and results. Ann Thorac Surg 49:69–77, 1990.

149. Fields JN, Rigaud G, Emami BN: Primary tumors of the trachea: Results of radiation therapy. Cancer 63:2429–2433, 1989.

150. Chan AT, Teo PM, Lam KC, et al: Multimodality treatment of primary lymphoepithelioma-like carcinoma of the lung. Cancer 83:925–929, 1998.

151. Bacha EA, Wright CD, Grillo HC, et al: Surgical treatment of primary pulmonary sarcomas. Eur J Cardiothorac Surg 15:456–460, 1999.

152. Gebauer C: The postoperative prognosis of primary pulmonary sarcomas: A review with a comparison between the histological forms and the other primary endothoracical sarcomas based on 474 cases. Scand J Thorac Cardiovasc Surg 18:251–254, 1984.

153. Wick MR, Ritter HH, Humphrey PA: Sarcomatoid carcinomas of the lung: A clinicopathologic review. Am J Clin Pathol 108:40–53, 1997.

154. Barson AJ, Jones AW, Lodge KV: Pulmonary blastoma. J Clin Pathol 21:480–485, 1968.

155. Jacobsen M, Francis D: Pulmonary blastoma. Acta Pathol Microbiol Immunol Scand [A] 88:151–160, 1980.

156. Kodama T, Koide T, Shimosato Y, et al: Six cases of well-differentiated adenocarcinoma simulating fetal lung tubules in pseudoglandular stage: Comparison with pulmonary blastoma. Am J Surg Pathol 8:735–744, 1984.

157. Nakatani Y, Dickersin R, Mark EJ: Pulmonary endodermal tumor resembling fetal lung: A clinicopathological study of five cases with immunohistochemical and ultrastructural characterization. Hum Pathol 21:1097–1107, 1990.

158. Kradin RL, Kirkham SE, Young RH, et al: Pulmonary blastoma with argyrophil cells and lacking sarcomatous features (pulmonary endodermal tumor resembling fetal lung). Am J Surg Pathol 6:165–172, 1982.

159. Priest JR, McDermott MB, Bhatia S, et al: Pleuropulmonary blastoma: A clinicopathologic study of 50 cases. Cancer 80:147–161, 1997.

160. Medbery CA III, Bibro MC, Phares JC, et al: Pulmonary blastoma: Case report and literature review of chemotherapy experience. Cancer 53:2413–2416, 1984.

161. Cutler CS, Michel RP, Yassa M, et al: Pulmonary blastoma: Case report of a patient with a 7-year remission and review of chemotherapy experience in the world literature. Cancer 82:462–467, 1998.

162. Cabarcos A, Dorronsoro MG, Beristain JL: Pulmonary carcinosarcoma: A case study and review of the literature. Br J Dis Chest 79:83–84, 1985.

163. Davis MP, Eagan RT, Weiland LH, et al: Carcinosarcoma of the lung: Mayo Clinic experience and response to chemotherapy. Mayo Clin Proc 59:598–603, 1984.

164. Ishida T, Tateishi M, Kaneko S, et al: Carcinosarcoma and spindle cell carcinoma of the lung: Clinicopathologic and immunohistochemical studies. J Thorac Cardiovasc Surg 100:844–852, 1990.

165. Whitwell F: Tumourlets of the lung. J Pathol Bacteriol 70:529–541, 1955.

166. Bonikos DS, Archibald R, Bensch KG: On the origin of the so-called tumorlets of the lung. Hum Pathol 7:461–469, 1976.

167. Ranchod M: The histogenesis and development of pulmonary tumorlets. Cancer 39:1135–1145, 1977.

168. Colby TV, Wistuba II, Gazdar A: Precursors to pulmonary neoplasia. Adv Anat Pathol 5:205–215, 1999.

169. D'Agati VD, Perzin KH: Carcinoid tumorlets of the lung with metastases to a peribronchial lymph node: Report of a case and review of the literature. Cancer 55:2472–2476, 1985.

170. Sheerin N, Harrison MK, Sheppard MN, et al: Obliterative bronchiolitis caused by multiple tumourlets and microcarcinoids successfully treated by single lung transplantation. Thorax 50:207–209, 1995.

171. Arioglu E, Doppman J, Gomes M, et al: Cushing's syndrome caused by corticotropin secretion by pulmonary tumorlets. N Engl J Med 339:883–886, 1999.

172. Gould VE, Linnoila C, Memoli VA, et al: Neuroendocrine components of the bronchopulmonary tract: Hyperplasias, dysplasias, and neoplasms. Lab Invest 49:519–537, 1983.

173. Gosney JR, Sissons MCJ, Allibone RO, et al: Pulmonary endocrine cells in chronic bronchitis and emphysema. J Pathol 157:127–133, 1989.

174. Gosney J, Green ART, Taylor W: Appropriate and inappropriate neuroendocrine products in pulmonary tumourlets. Thorax 45:679–683, 1990.

175. Owen RG, Treon SP, Al-Katib A, et al: Clinicopathological definition of Waldenstrom's macroglobulinemia: Consensus panel recommendations from the Second International Workshop on Waldenstrom's Macroglobulinemia. Semin Oncol 30:110–115, 2003.

176. Kyle RA: Subject review. Multiple myeloma: Review of 869 cases. Mayo Clin Proc 50:29–40, 1975.

177. Fudenberg HH: Waldenstrom's macroglobulinemia. In Brodsky I, Kahn SB, Moyer JH (eds): Cancer

Chemotherapy II: The Twenty-Second Hahnemann Symposium. New York: Grune & Stratton, 1972, pp 393–403.

178. Amin R: Extramedullary plasmacytoma of the lung. Cancer 56:152–156, 1985.

179. Hayes DW, Bennett WA, Heck FJ: Extramedullary lesions in multiple myeloma: Review of the literature and pathologic studies. Arch Pathol 53:262–272, 1982.

180. Anderson KC, Shaughnessy JD Jr, Barlogie B, et al: Multiple myeloma. Hematology (Am Soc Hematol Educ Program):214–240, 2002.

181. Kovalski R, Hansen-Flaschen J, Lodato RF, Pietra GG: Localized leukemic pulmonary infiltrates: Diagnosis by bronchoscopy and resolution with therapy. Chest 97:674–678, 1990.

182. Poletti V, Salvucci M, Zanchini R, et al: The lung as a target organ in patients with hematologic disorders. Haematologica 85:855–864, 2000.

183. Jennings TA, Axiotis CA, Kress Y, et al: Primary malignant melanoma of the lower respiratory tract: Report of a case and literature review. Am J Clin Pathol 94:649–655, 1990.

184. Wilson RW, Moran CA: Primary melanoma of the lung: A clinicopathologic and immunohistochemical study of eight cases. Am J Surg Pathol 21:1196–1202, 1997.

185. Cagle P, Mace ML, Fudge DM, et al: Pulmonary melanoma: Primary vs. metastatic. Chest 85:125–126, 1984.

46 Metastatic Malignant Tumors

Judith A. Luce, M.D., Arthur C. Hill, M.D.

INTRODUCTION

The lung is a common site of metastatic spread from extrapulmonary or pulmonary malignancies. Pulmonary metastases occur in 30% to 40% of all patients who have cancer. The frequency and number of these metastases are a function of both the chronology and natural history of each particular malignancy. In patients with cancer that is metastatic to lung, the presence of pulmonary metastasis may or may not contribute to clinical outcome. Autopsy studies overestimate the clinical importance of metastatic disease to the lungs because the clinical relevance of pulmonary metastasis is complex and very much related to the biologic behavior of the various cancers. For example, although as many as 40% of pancreatic carcinoma patients may have pulmonary metastases at autopsy, pulmonary metastases are rarely a clinical problem or the cause of death. Table 46.1 summarizes the approximate autopsy incidence of pulmonary metastases and their relative clinical importance in common cancers.[1,2]

PATHOGENESIS

Malignancies originating within or outside of the thorax may spread to the lungs by several routes: hematogenous, lymphogenous, direct invasion, and, perhaps, intrabronchial dissemination. The precise mechanism of pulmonary metastasis has not been fully elucidated. Research has targeted certain tumor-specific factors that allow angiogenesis, endothelial adhesion, protease production, and mediator/immune factors. Organ-specific and host-specific factors may include either permissive or defensive factors that permit or preclude tumor cell adhesion, invasion, and growth.[3,4]

HEMATOGENOUS DISSEMINATION

Cancers are capable of inducing the formation of new blood vessels, and, as a consequence of this complex process, they are capable of invading the vascular space either as single cells or as small multicellular aggregates. Cancer cells at the primary site can invade vascular structures and embolize into the systemic venous system. Once in the venous circulation, malignant cells may passively come to rest in pulmonary capillaries as microemboli or actively attach to and invade through the pulmonary capillary endothelium.[5] Animal studies with transplanted human tumors have demonstrated a broad range of capability with respect to formation of pulmonary metastases after venous injection of tumor cells.[6,7] Additionally, within a single human tumor cell line, individual clones may be identified that differ in their ability to form pulmonary metastases via the hematogenous route.[8] The balance between tumor-derived angiogenic factors and antiangiogenic factors may determine the ultimate fate of tumor cells that come to rest in the pulmonary circulation.[9,10] A combination of both tumor-related factors and pulmonary endothelial factors determines the predilection of particular cancers to form pulmonary metastases.[11] Human sarcomas, of both soft-tissue and bony origin, and certain carcinomas, such as renal cell carcinoma, gestational trophoblastic neoplasms, thyroid carcinoma, and breast and lung carcinomas, show a high frequency of spread to the lungs via hematogenous dissemination.

LYMPHOGENOUS DISSEMINATION

Malignant cells may arrive in the lungs through two routes of lymphogenous dissemination. Cancer invades lymphatic channels in a manner thought to be similar to vascular invasion. Cancer cells from involved lymph nodes near the primary site may have direct access to the larger lymphatic channels and then to the thoracic duct, superior vena cava, and finally the pulmonary vascular bed. Germ cell tumors, particularly testicular carcinoma, probably reach the lungs with characteristic high frequency via this route. Additionally, extensive mediastinal or hilar node involvement is thought to result in retrograde dissemination of malignant

Table 46.1 Frequency of Pulmonary Metastases in Cancers of Various Primary Sites

Primary Site	Autopsy Incidence (%)	Lung Only Site of Metastases (%)	Relative Risk as Major Site/Cause of Death
Lung	20–40	>10	++
Colon/rectum	20–40	9	+
Breast	60	21	+++
Prostate	15–50	18	++
Pancreas	25–40	3	+
Stomach	20–30	7	+
Liver/bile ducts	20	*	+
Esophagus	20–35	17	++
Melanoma	60–80	NA	+++
Hodgkin's disease	50–70	*	++
Non-Hodgkin's lymphoma	30–40	<10	++
Thyroid	65	N/A	+++
Head/neck	20–40	N/A	+
Gynecologic			
Ovary	10	0	+
Uterus	30–42	9	++
Cervix	20–30	14	+
Placenta, choriocarcinoma	70–100	†	++++
Renal	50–75	27	+++
Bladder	25–30	9	++
Testis (germ cell tumors)	70–80	27	+++
Soft-tissue sarcomas (adult)	40–60	N/A	+++
Pediatric			
Ewing's sarcoma	80–85	†	++++
Wilms' tumor	75–80	†	++++
Neuroblastoma	50–60	*	+
Rhabdomyosarcoma	55–60	‡	+++
Osteosarcoma	80–100	75	++++

* Extremely uncommon, less than 2%.
† Very common but consistent data not available.
‡ Depends on the primary site; varies from rare (head and neck sites) to common (trunk sites).
+, very low; ++, low; +++, moderate; ++++, high.
Data from Weiss and Gilbert[1] and De Vita et al.[2]

cells into pulmonary lymphatic channels, producing the clinical syndrome of lymphangitic metastases. This mechanism is seen most commonly in lymphomas, lung cancer, breast cancer, and other adenocarcinomas.

DIRECT INVASION

The lungs may be directly invaded by malignancies originating in the chest wall (mainly soft-tissue sarcomas), mediastinum (mainly esophageal carcinomas or primary mediastinal tumors such as thymoma, lymphoma, and germ cell tumors), abdominal viscera (especially carcinomas of the gastric cardia and liver), diaphragm, or retroperitoneum (sarcomas).

INTRABRONCHIAL DISSEMINATION

It has long been believed that malignancies that originate in the upper aerodigestive tract (the head, neck, larynx, upper esophagus, and bronchi) could spread by direct implantation from one area of the airways to another. This theory has been invoked to explain the high frequency of second carcinomas, usually squamous cell carcinomas, in individuals treated for early cancers at another upper aerodigestive tract site. This theory has been difficult to prove for a number of reasons: spread of cancer to bronchi via hematogenous dissemination has already been well documented, careful studies of individuals with early lung cancer have shown a high frequency of synchronous dysplastic or neoplastic lesions within the tracheobronchial epithelium, and techniques to show that second cancers were genetically related to the first primary tumors were lacking. However, new molecular techniques have demonstrated the genetic relationship between primary tumors and subsequent recurrences in the same primary site[12]; thus, with careful analysis by molecular techniques, this theory of intrabronchial dissemination may be either supported or contradicted.

DIAGNOSIS

SYMPTOMS

Cancer metastatic to the lung may produce a variety of symptoms. Involvement of airway mucosa may produce cough, hemoptysis, and airway obstruction with wheezing or stridor, obstructive pneumonitis, or lobar or segmental collapse and dyspnea. Bronchial metastasis is seen most commonly in breast cancer, melanoma, and other hematogenously disseminated cancers. Bronchial spread without extrapulmonary spread is rare.[13] Pulmonary parenchymal metastatic spread, via either the lymphatic or hematogenous route, often is asymptomatic. In an advanced state, parenchymal metastasis may be associated with chest tightness or fullness, dyspnea, cough, and, if the pleura is involved, pain or pleural effusion. Lymphangitic spread of cancer almost invariably causes dyspnea. When pulmonary metastases originate from mediastinal involvement, the presenting symptoms are most often caused by the mediastinal neoplasm. These symptoms include chest pressure or tightness, hoarseness due to recurrent laryngeal nerve invasion, facial and upper extremity edema, and plethora due to superior vena cava compression. Occasionally, metastasis to the lung may cause stridor due to airway compression, dysphagia from esophageal compression, or chest pain and hypotension caused by pericardial tamponade.

PHYSICAL SIGNS

The physical examination of a patient with suspected pulmonary metastases can be useful if it points to the primary site of a previously undiagnosed cancer or if it demonstrates a potential site, such as lymph nodes or other masses, to obtain a tissue diagnosis. Signs of pleural effusion, pericardial effusion, or partial or total airway obstruction are useful and should be sought. Superior vena cava syndrome is always a clinical diagnosis based on physical findings. Direct or indirect laryngoscopy may reveal or confirm vocal cord paralysis or a primary cancer in a hoarse patient with metastatic lung involvement. The physical examination of a patient with cancer metastatic to the lungs should include rectal examination, pelvic examination, and careful examination of the breasts.

RADIOGRAPHIC EVALUATION

The variety of clinical and physiologic manifestations of metastatic cancer in the lungs is mirrored in the variety of abnormalities shown by plain films of the thorax. Pleural effusions, parenchymal masses, obstructive pneumonia or lobar or segmental collapse, and hilar and mediastinal adenopathy may be seen. Lymphangitic spread is characterized by linear interstitial markings (Fig. 46.1), which radiate outward from enlarged hilar or mediastinal nodes. Lymphogenous involvement most commonly consists of small nodules, a lymphangitic appearance, or a combination of the two findings. Parenchymal metastases may have any appearance, including both smooth and ill-defined nodules or masses, cavitary masses, and, rarely, calcified masses (Figs. 46.2 and 46.3). Pneumothorax is a rare manifestation of pulmonary parenchymal metastases and must be distinguished from other benign causes of pneumothorax combined with pulmonary nodules, such as eosinophilic granuloma.

Most patients with a new appearance of multiple pulmonary nodules or lymphangitic spread already have a

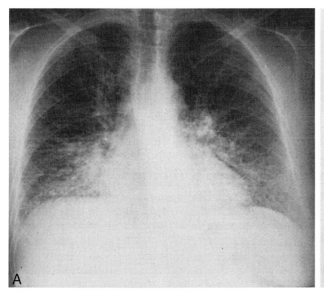 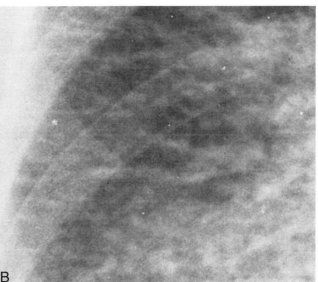

Figure 46.1 Lymphangitic dissemination of breast carcinoma in a 59-year-old woman. **A,** The posteroanterior radiograph shows widespread reticulonodular infiltrates, in addition to hilar and mediastinal adenopathy and a right mastectomy. **B,** The detail view of the right lower lobe shows the fine interstitial pattern and small nodular densities typical of lymphangitic carcinomatosis.

diagnosis of cancer. In such patients, the new radiologic finding is 70% to 80% likely to represent metastatic cancer.[14] However, the differential diagnosis of abnormal radiologic studies must be carefully considered even in patients known to have cancer, especially considering that the immunosuppression associated with cancer leads to multiple clinical sequelae.[15] The differential diagnosis of lymphangitic spread includes congestive heart failure and interstitial

inflammatory processes. Tuberculosis, septic emboli, and other infectious processes must be considered in the differential diagnosis of multiple or single parenchymal masses (Table 46.2). The effects or complications of cancer treatment (e.g., cytotoxic drugs, radiation) may also be associated with radiologic abnormalities.

Computed Tomography of the Thorax

Computed tomographic (CT) evaluation may play a role in the initial diagnosis of patients presenting with radiographic evidence of a thoracic neoplasm, either in the search for a primary site outside of the thorax or in defining the intrathoracic extent of disease. High-resolution CT may be necessary for distinguishing lymphangitic lymphoma or carcinoma from other processes such as infection or radiation change. If radiation therapy is contemplated, CT scanning is a necessary adjunct to radiation therapy treatment planning.

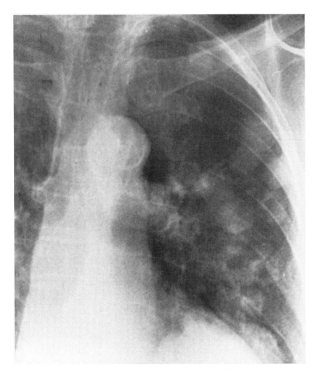

Figure 46.2 Radiograph showing cavitation of hematogenous pulmonary metastases in a 79-year-old woman with metastatic colon carcinoma. The cavities are thick walled and occasionally eccentric. The differential diagnosis includes granulomatous diseases.

Table 46.2 Differential Diagnosis of Multiple Pulmonary Nodules in Cancer Patients

Malignant Etiologies
Metastatic disease from known primary site
New primary site, solid tumor
New primary site, lymphoma or lymphoproliferative disease

Benign Etiologies
Infectious granulomas—histoplasmosis, coccidioidomycosis, tuberculosis
Pyogenic abscesses—embolic, nonembolic
Parasitic disease—paragonimiasis, hydatid cyst, filariasis
Arteriovenous malformations
Wegener's granulomatosis
Rheumatoid nodules
Sarcoidosis
Benign tumors—hamartomas, papillomatosis
Opportunistic infections—aspergillosis, nocardiosis, cryptococcosis

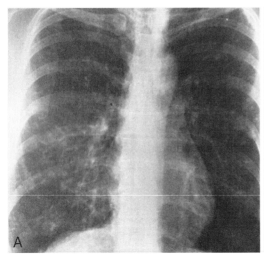
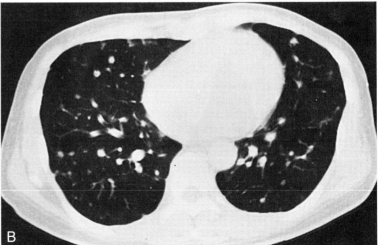

Figure 46.3 Chest radiograph of a 47-year-old woman with metastatic breast cancer showing calcification of multiple hematogenous metastases. **A,** The posteroanterior chest film shows the large number and variation of size of the metastases. **B,** The computed tomographic scan more clearly shows the density of these metastases compared with soft tissues. The differential diagnosis includes tuberculosis, fungal infections, rheumatoid arthritis, multiple hamartomas, amyloidosis, and papillomatosis.

CT imaging has been widely employed to screen for the presence of pulmonary parenchymal metastases, to evaluate patients with apparent solitary pulmonary metastasis, and to enumerate and evaluate pulmonary metastases when surgical resection is being considered. The use of CT in the evaluation of solitary pulmonary masses is discussed in Chapters 44 and 47. CT as a screening test for possible pulmonary metastases has been most widely used in the evaluation of patients with germ cell tumors, sarcomas, and melanoma. It is appropriate to use CT screening where the primary malignancy is known to cause pulmonary metastasis at high frequency, or where the presence of pulmonary metastasis may alter choice of therapy. Helical CT is capable of near 100% sensitivity for masses of 6 mm or more, about half of which prove to be malignant at subsequent excision.[16,17] Precise data on the accuracy of detection of pulmonary metastases by CT scanning when correlated with the results of surgical resection are not available for helical CT; older CT methods have both underestimated and overestimated pulmonary metastases.

Despite low specificity, the superior sensitivity of CT scan compared to plain radiography ensures that the clinical reliance on CT scanning is unlikely to change until a better test is devised. Positron emission tomography scanning as a method for detecting pulmonary metastases is not well established and is not more sensitive than CT scan for cancer metastatic to the lung. Tumors are not uniformly positive on positron emission tomography,[18] and the threshold for detection of nodules using positron emission tomography scans is approximately 1 cm. As methods for evaluating patients for surgical resection, both CT and magnetic resonance imaging (MRI) are helpful in defining unresectable metastases, with 80% to 85% specificity. Careful surgical inspection remains the most important part of the evaluation of patients whose pulmonary metastases appear to be surgically resectable by imaging procedures. CT is of little help in further defining tumor in patients with known advanced cancer. MRI offers no particular advantages over CT imaging of the thorax in the evaluation of metastatic disease at the current state of the art. This is due to unique intrinsic difficulties of the MRI modality: (1) signal loss due to cardiac pulsation and respiration, (2) artifacts caused by multiple air-tissue interfaces, and (3) low proton density. Ongoing improvements in MRI technology may reverse the relative advantage of CT over MRI in the near future.

TISSUE DIAGNOSIS

Making the diagnosis of pulmonary metastases depends on a careful clinical strategy. If the patient is not known to have cancer, the search for a primary site relies primarily on a thorough history and physical examination. Laboratory tests that are abnormal require evaluation, and site-directed laboratory screening tests, such as biochemical tumor markers for germ cell tumors, gastrointestinal malignancy, ovarian cancer, or prostate cancer, may be indicated. Imaging procedures of the thorax or other sites are performed only as indicated by the results of the history, physical examination, and laboratory tests. The role of extensive radiographic evaluation of patients with metastatic carcinoma without an obvious primary site is controversial and ultimately of little benefit to patients.[19]

If the thorax is the best available site for making a tissue diagnosis, a variety of procedures may be employed. Sputum cytology is most useful for cavitary, endobronchial, and lymphangitic metastases, although bronchoscopy with lavage or brushings may be a more sensitive procedure. Transbronchial biopsy or transthoracic needle aspiration biopsy may be employed for parenchymal masses with a high level of accuracy. Immunohistochemical staining of such specimens may be extremely useful in identifying and defining occult primary cancers, including prostate cancer, melanoma, germ cell tumors, breast cancer, and thyroid cancer. Tumor biopsy using video-assisted thoracoscopy or thoracotomy, although rarely required, can occasionally be used as part of a therapeutic strategy.

Patients with known cancer require an individualized approach to the diagnosis of pulmonary metastases. If the patient already has advanced neoplasm, the appearance of new lung findings is generally assumed to be due to metastatic disease if the radiographic or clinical differential diagnosis strongly favors metastases and the occurrence is consistent with the natural history and biologic behavior of the cancer. For example, lymphangitic carcinomatosis is common in advanced breast cancer but rare in multiple myeloma; because patients with myeloma are also significantly immunosuppressed, a detailed evaluation in such patients is indicated. If the primary cancer diagnosis is chronologically remote relative to the appearance of new pulmonary findings, if the clinical picture is inconsistent with the behavior of the known primary disease, or if the lungs are the only site of new onset of metastases, then biopsy proof of the diagnosis is indicated. Similarly, if there is clinical evidence to suggest that the pulmonary findings represent a possible second primary cancer, then tissue diagnosis is also indicated.

TREATMENT

MEDICAL THERAPY

Patients who have pulmonary metastases from otherwise curable cancers should be treated aggressively with appropriate multimodal therapy. Testicular and ovarian germ cell tumors, neuroblastoma, gestational trophoblastic neoplasms, non-Hodgkin's lymphoma, Hodgkin's disease, and osteosarcoma are included in this category. One ongoing research issue with such patients is how to proceed when curative therapy has been delivered and residual masses remain in the mediastinum or lungs. Two strategies have emerged: aggressive resection of masses that have not resolved within some specific period of time from the completion of curative therapy and an observational strategy that allows the mass to resume growing before intervention occurs. Residual masses remain after the treatment of testicular carcinomas in approximately 40% of patients who have advanced disease and negative serum tumor markers at the conclusion of treatment. At surgical excision, these masses may consist of necrotic tissue (about half), mature teratoma (about 25%), or residual carcinomas (about 25%). Long-term follow-up studies suggest that about 90% of the patients found to have mature teratoma are cured by surgery, and perhaps as many as 50% of those with residual carcinoma are also cured surgically.[20,21] Surgical guidelines are much less clear for patients with lymphoma, for whom treatment alternatives are more numerous and systemic therapy is necessary. Surgical biopsy rather than excision may be appropriate.

Unfortunately, most adults with pulmonary metastases do not have curable cancers, and palliative therapy is appropriate. For selected cancers, medical treatment may consist of chemotherapy, radiation therapy, hormonal therapy, or immunologic therapies. These may be employed with acceptable toxicity and temporary improvement, even with significant prolongation of survival in some cases. Symptom relief for untreatable patients may be aided by the selective use of radiation therapy,[22] perhaps endobronchial laser therapy,[23] or steroids. Opiates and oxygen therapy may relieve symptoms of end-stage dyspnea. Social, emotional, and physical rehabilitation support services have important roles in the care of such patients.

Nonsurgical Technologies: Radiofrequency Ablation and Stereotactic Radiosurgery

The use of high-frequency or microwave radiation, externally or internally applied, in the treatment of metastatic tumors has only recently been applied to pulmonary metastases. The aim of radiofrequency ablation (RFA) is to reduce the size of tumor masses, possibly with long-term control of growth or even cure. The potential benefits include decreased cost and morbidity compared to surgical removal, as well as treating patients who are not surgical candidates due to age, comorbidity, or extent of disease. RFA has been performed on an outpatient basis. Although many issues remain to be resolved in order to define the appropriate use of RFA, reports of large numbers of treatments and patients reveal that RFA can be safely performed. The most common complications of its use are pneumothorax, in up to 50% of patients, and bleeding, in fewer than 10% of patients. RFA produces tumor necrosis, often evolving long after the procedure. RFA may prove to be limited by the size of the tumor and to be useful only for tumors on the periphery of the lungs. Further exploration of the use of RFA in the context of clinical trials is appropriate.

Stereotactic radiosurgery is a radiation therapy methodology that involves the delivery of small doses of radiation to a specific site from a variety of angles at one time. The purpose of this technique is to deliver a large dose of radiation to a small area, and a small dose to the surrounding tissue. Stereotactic radiosurgery has been most successfully applied to the treatment of intracerebral masses, both primary tumors and metastases. By delivering the radiation from a hundred or more different points, the dose of radiation to the whole brain is minimized, and hence the injury to the brain is minimized. With the use of respiratory gating and computer-guided real-time imaging, the same technique can be employed in the treatment of masses in the thorax and abdomen, minimizing the radiation injury to critical organs such as lung and liver. Published data show that the procedure is feasible and that local control of masses may be achieved in more than 80% of patients. Stereotactic radiosurgery is experimental, but is available in an increasing number of centers, where it has been used in the treatment of pulmonary metastases in patients for whom surgery was not feasible due to underlying illness or due to the location of pulmonary masses. Long-term outcomes are not yet available.

SURGICAL THERAPY

The idea of surgical cure of pulmonary metastases is appealing and has been widely practiced in the United States and Europe for more than 100 years.[24] Despite the increasingly aggressive use of surgery for selected patients, there have been no prospective clinical trials comparing surgical with nonsurgical treatment, and most surgically treated patients still die of their malignancies.

Indications and Prognostic Factors

The indications for pulmonary metastasectomy have evolved as surgical technique has improved and the understanding of the biologic behavior of individual neoplastic disease types has expanded. As experience accumulates, improvements have occurred in patient selection, anesthetic management, intensive care unit care, nursing care, and other supportive care. In the early surgical experience, morbidity and mortality related to loss of lung parenchyma mandated that patients had to have minimal disease (few or solitary metastases) for reasonable results. However, using current operative techniques, surgeons have now extended the surgical options to include multiple metastases, bilateral disease, chest wall involvement, and metastatic involvement of vital structures (heart, great vessels, etc.). For patients with cancer metastatic to the lung, certain mandatory criteria must be met before surgical candidacy for metastasectomy can be considered[25]:

- Adequate control or cure of the primary site can be obtained.
- The patient can tolerate the planned procedure from a physiologic and functional standpoint.
- There is no evidence of extrapulmonary metastatic disease.
- There is definitive radiographic evidence that the pulmonary metastases are accessible and resectable.

An increased understanding of the factors associated with poor outcome has evolved as the use of surgery has increased. Although it was once thought that the number of metastases was a prognostic indicator, there is no evidence in the current literature that this is, in fact, the case. However, it is very clear that complete pulmonary metastasectomy is key to improved outcome. In virtually all series of patients with a variety of primary sites, the presence of unresectable or unresected pulmonary metastases is associated with a survival rate comparable to no surgery. It was once thought that an indolent natural history was an important prognostic indicator. To some extent, this is still true. Breast cancer patients with less than a 12-month interval between the initial diagnosis and the onset of pulmonary metastases have poor survival compared to patients with greater than a 36-month disease-free interval. The largest series[26–29] reveal that the disease-free interval is an important prognostic factor, but controversy remains. Cancers whose metastases commonly occur at sites other than the lungs are less likely to have favorable outcomes than are cancers such as sarcomas that metastasize almost exclusively to the lungs. Some authors have shown that the tumor doubling time predicts poor outcome if it is short, particularly shorter than 20 days; however, not all authors agree with that conclusion, particularly for osteosarcoma. Finally, a cancer that has responded well to chemotherapy is no more likely than a cancer that is refractory to chemotherapy to have a good outcome after metastasectomy, especially osteosarcoma and soft-tissue sarcoma.[28] In sum, the patients who have the longest survival intervals following metastasectomy are those who have a disease-free interval of at least a year from diagnosis, whose cancer is unlikely to spread to other sites, and whose metastases have been completely resected at surgery.

Relationship of Tumor Type to Outcome

Though the majority of adult solid tumor patients are not good candidates for metastasectomy, the surgical approach should be considered for individuals who meet the basic criteria and whose disease meets the criteria listed earlier. Whether particular types of cancer are better suited to metastasectomy is yet another source of controversy. Primary tumors whose pulmonary metastases have been successfully resected for cure, in decreasing order of success, include osteogenic and soft-tissue sarcomas; colon, rectal, uterine, cervix, and corpus tumors; head and neck, breast, testis, and salivary gland cancer; bladder and kidney tumors; and melanoma. Five-year survival rates of 20% to 30% have been found in carefully selected patients, but in none of these diseases is metastasectomy considered routine. The most aggressive procedures have been reported in colorectal cancer, in which both hepatic and pulmonary metastases have been resected in selected patients. The only clinical setting in which metastasectomy is considered relatively routine is that of osteogenic sarcoma, in which resection of pulmonary metastases (sometimes requiring several thoracotomies) is well tolerated by the relatively youthful patient population and in which the disease rarely metastasizes outside the lungs. Long-term survival after resection is frequent, and chemotherapy is relatively ineffective.

Categorization based on the characteristics of the primary tumor can guide therapy. A thorough understanding of the biologic behavior of the primary tumor should be taken into account when considering operative therapy for pulmonary metastases. Pulmonary metastasectomy has been well studied and has been found to have significant potential benefit in patients with renal cell carcinoma, colorectal carcinoma, thyroid carcinoma, and soft-tissue sarcomas. With somewhat less success, breast cancer, melanoma, and gynecologic cancer patients are potential candidates for pulmonary metastasectomy if selection criteria are met.[30,31] Head and neck cancer with pulmonary metastases can present a special and difficult dilemma: Simultaneous synchronous and metachronous tumors with similar histologic characteristics, usually squamous cell carcinoma, are common in this population, and a thorough evaluation is required to rule out a second primary tumor. Operative therapy for melanoma metastatic to the lung is controversial; however, pulmonary metastasectomy has been shown to improve survival in carefully selected patients. As Table 46.3 shows, overall surgical outcome is poor. Most patients

Table 46.3 Approximate 5-Year Survival Rates after Pulmonary Metastasectomy

Primary Site	5-Year Survival (%)
Soft-tissue sarcoma	20–35
Osteosarcoma	25–50
Melanoma	5–33
Colorectal	13–40
Testis (germ cell)	50–80
Renal	15–20
Breast	25–50
Head and neck	30

do not have prolonged survival. However, in well-selected patient subgroups, improved survival can be shown when the primary tumor is controlled and complete resection of pulmonary metastases is accomplished. Whether a randomized trial might show benefit is not known. The decision to perform metastasectomy remains a difficult one,[32,33] and, just as each tumor type has its individual characteristics, other variables must be taken into consideration: age, functional status, psychological status, and the like. Previous studies indicate that number of metastases, size of metastases, short disease-free interval, unresectable disease, and vascular invasion found in the resection specimen are unfavorable predictors of long-term survival.

As mentioned, the surgical approach to osteosarcoma metastatic to the lung has a potential role. This disease rarely metastasizes to sites other than lung and adjacent bone. Based on some very long-term survival results,[34,35] some individual investigators have advocated increased and aggressive use of thoracotomy and resection of all pulmonary metastases; furthermore, repeat thoracotomy is recommended depending on resectability and patient tolerance. A striking number of these patients later develop second malignancies,[36] consonant with genetic evidence suggesting that osteosarcoma results from the deletion of an important tumor suppressor gene. This aggressive approach has been shown by a variety of investigators to result in 5-year survival rates of 25% to 50%, but this must be viewed with some caution because of the lack of prospective trials. A recent follow-up study reported a 3-year survival of 70% in well-selected patients after excision of metastatic osteogenic sarcoma, and survival was not influenced by the number of thoracotomies (up to six) that had to be performed.[37,38]

Technical Factors

Surgical resection of pulmonary metastases requires careful planning and preparation. Before the operation, the surgeon should consider the number of tumors, their location (one lung or both lungs, anterior vs. posterior, peripheral vs. central), tumor size, local invasion, tumor response to chemotherapy, and the general condition of the patient. Thoracic CT or MRI imaging or both are necessary for proper evaluation. As was previously mentioned, the role of positron emission tomography scanning[18] for cancer metastatic to the lung is evolving, and this technique can be used to assess prognosis and direct therapy in selected patients. Bronchoscopy should precede the operation to exclude endobronchial metastasis. Mediastinoscopy should be performed if mediastinal lymphadenopathy is present on CT scan.

Once the decision has been made to perform pulmonary metastasectomy, the approach and choice of incision require an analysis of the location and extent of pulmonary metastases. The standard approach to pulmonary metastasectomy consists of thoracotomy or median sternotomy. Median sternotomy is an option if bilateral pulmonary metastases are present and the nodules are accessible from the anterior approach. If one or more nodules are inaccessible via the median sternotomy, a complete pulmonary metastasectomy can be accomplished using sequential posterolateral thoracotomy incisions or one-stage clamshell incision. Some surgeons prefer the thoracotomy instead of median sternotomy because a more thorough inspection of the lung is possible and a more careful and complete resection at the posterior and apical segments of the lung is possible. There is no significant difference in morbidity or mortality when median sternotomy is compared to thoracotomy for pulmonary metastasectomy.[39] Metastases are typically located subpleurally and may be excised using stapler, laser, electrocautery, or sharp resection followed by suture repair. Wedge resection of pulmonary metastases using staplers may result in the removal of a large portion of surrounding normal lung.[40] New laser technology is being evaluated and is reported[41] to offer advantages including decreased amount of normal lung tissue removal and possibly less morbidity (decreased air leak compared to electrocautery and stapler methods). If a metastatic pulmonary lesion is located centrally, in or near the hilum, then lobectomy, and in some cases pneumonectomy, may be the only option for complete resection.

During the operation, a conscientious effort must be made to locate and account for all of the nodules observed on the preoperative CT scan, and to palpate and remove nodules not visualized by CT scan. Direct visualization combined with palpation is the most accurate method of nodule localization. It has been suggested that wedge resection of individual nodules should be done after all nodules are marked, using a stitch, so that subsequent palpation is not obscured by previously placed staple lines. It has been reported that as many as 50 or more metastases can be removed during a single surgical procedure. As previously mentioned, anatomic lobectomy or pneumonectomy is sometimes required for complete tumor resection. The morbidity and mortality rate for pulmonary metastasectomy should be very low. Mortality in most series is less than 2%; morbid complications may occur in up to 10% of patients.[26,27] The most common complications are persistent air leak and infection. Increased rates of infection have been reported in patients having had recent chemotherapy. Respiratory failure in thoracotomy patients having had extensive prior radiotherapy and chemotherapy has been reported, especially in those who received high fractional concentrations of oxygen postoperatively.

There is considerable surgical literature supporting the use of thoracoscopy for pulmonary metastasectomy, and some nonrandomized studies[42–46] have shown results comparable to those with thoracotomy or median sternotomy. For example, in a report of 72 patients by Dowling and colleagues,[43] all lesions were successfully identified and resected using thoracoscopy. However, there are compelling data in the surgical literature that support the use of thoracotomy or median sternotomy over thoracoscopy for treatment of pulmonary metastasis. The strongest argument against thoracoscopy for pulmonary metastasis is incomplete resection due to the inaccuracy of CT in detecting all metastases that are palpable using open techniques. It has been shown that, despite the extraordinary medical advances in CT scanning, the thoracic CT scan may not demonstrate all of the pulmonary metastases that actually exist. In studies conducted in the mid-1990s, additional ipsilateral and contralateral metastases were found in as many as half of patients.[47,48] In one of these studies, a prospective trial, patients who initially underwent thoracoscopic resection for pulmonary metastases then underwent a confirmatory thoracotomy; in 10 of the 18 patients, additional malignant lesions were found, indicating a 56% failure rate of thoracic CT and thoracoscopy to detect all lesions.[47] Significantly, this study concluded that a thoracotomy is required for complete resection in the setting of pulmonary metastasis. This prospective trial was a follow-up to a retrospective review[48] in which thoracic CT was found to underestimate surgical findings in 42% of patients. In another, more recent prospective study, confirmatory thoracotomy was undertaken following thoracoscopic metastasectomy in 17 patients, 5 of whom were found to have malignancy not detected at thoracotomy, for a 29% failure of thoracoscopic metastasectomy.[49] Because most pulmonary metastases are peripherally located and because there are significant other advantages of thoracoscopy, there is a significant push by many surgeons to consider the thoracoscopic approach in all patients with cancer metastatic to the lung.

The advantages of thoracoscopy, per se, over thoracotomy are considerable. Compared with thoracotomy, thoracoscopy is associated with less chest wall trauma, chest wall deformity, and postoperative pain. In one nonrandomized study[50] of 204 patients undergoing thoracoscopic lobectomy compared to standard thoracotomy for lobectomy, it was shown that FEV_1 decreased 29% after thoracotomy compared to 15% after thoracoscopy. This same study showed that the patients treated with thoracoscopy had improved survival compared to thoracotomy-treated patients. Indirect evidence suggests that using thoracoscopy instead of thoracotomy may improve postoperative immune function by reducing the body's inflammatory response.[51] Another nonrandomized study[52] that compared thoracoscopy to thoracotomy for lung cancer patients showed a shorter length of hospital stay, an earlier return to normal activities, and improved long-term quality of life for thoracoscopy. However, to add to the complexity of assessing the utility of thoracoscopy over thoracotomy, there is one randomized study[53] comparing thoracoscopic lung biopsy ($n = 20$) to open thoracotomy ($n = 22$) in which no difference was found in pain score, postoperative spirometry values, duration of operation, and length of hospital stay.

At this time, with continual improvements both in imaging and in thoracoscopic techniques, the role of thoracoscopy in metastasectomy is evolving. Improvements in thoracoscopic technology (e.g., tactile feedback) will certainly lead to expanded use of the thoracoscopic approach for pulmonary metastatic disease in the near future. New techniques have recently been developed for small, deep lesions that have previously been difficult to biopsy by thoracoscopy. Surgeons with considerable experience using thoracoscopy for pulmonary metastasectomy report that palpation of the subpleural portion of the entire lung is feasible via the thoracoscopic ports. A new transxiphoid video-assisted approach[54] has been described in 22 patients that allows manual palpation of both lungs. This technique allowed the discovery of 12 radiologically occult nodules (8 of which were malignant) in seven patients. Four of the 22 patients were found to have unsuspected bilateral disease. Future technical advances will increase the thoracoscopic applications for cancer metastatic to the lung.

Despite the significant potential advantages of thoracoscopy for treatment of pulmonary metastasis, proper patient selection is required because there can be significant disadvantages in the use of thoracoscopy for pulmonary metastasectomy. As mentioned, the disadvantages of thoracoscopy include limited visualization, inability to palpate pulmonary lesions, and operating in a constrained space. Lesions not localized with preoperative imaging studies may not be resected. Others argue against using thoracoscopy for metastatic disease because there are studies that have shown early recurrence of cancer following thoracoscopy, although these studies were limited by small numbers of patients and short-term follow-up.[37] Although the use of thoracoscopy for diagnostic resection of metastases is widely accepted, its use for therapeutic resection is not as clearly defined and will require further evaluation with clinical trials. Therefore, the open approach is currently the best technical approach for pulmonary metastatic disease.

Extended resection for selected patients has been used in some centers for metastatic pulmonary disease. Extended resection includes chest wall resection, pneumonectomy, aortic resection followed by vascular reconstruction, and use of cardiopulmonary bypass (Fig. 46.4). Fewer than 3% of patients undergoing pulmonary metastasectomy are candidates for extended resection options. Operative mortality for extended resection has been reported to be 5%.[55,56]

SUMMARY

Regardless of their route of entry into the lungs, pulmonary metastases present a common clinical problem. Early signs and symptoms may be varied or absent. Most patients have an identified primary cancer but, for those who do not, careful history and physical examinations are useful to determine a possible primary site, and only a few laboratory tests contribute to the evaluation. Imaging studies may be very useful to find multiple pulmonary metastases not seen on conventional radiographs and to define lymphangitic or locally invasive disease. When the thorax is the only available site for obtaining tissue, a variety of techniques may be used, aided by immunohistochemical stains and in the near future by molecular techniques, to help identify the site of origin of the cancer.

Treatment of pulmonary metastases is individualized and is highly dependent on the type of cancer. Patients having

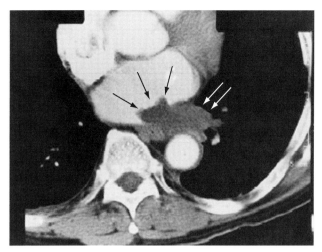

Figure 46.4 Thoracic computed tomography scan showing high-grade leiomyosarcoma metastatic to the lung with invasion into the left atrium (*black arrows*). This patient underwent pneumonectomy and partial left atrial resection. The operation required cardiopulmonary bypass. *White arrows* mark tumor in the left inferior pulmonary vein.

curable cancers are few. Treatment issues for these patients may include resection of residual disease in the lungs for diagnostic and potentially therapeutic purposes. For most patients, palliative treatment is appropriate, employing both symptomatic and anticancer therapies. Surgical resection of metastases may be advisable for highly selected patients having isolated pulmonary metastases. Metastatic sarcomas are most often approached surgically, occasionally with long-term cure of patients. The lack of prospective data limits further application of surgical treatment.

REFERENCES

1. Weiss L, Gilbert HA: Pulmonary Metastasis. Boston: GK Hall, 1978.
2. De Vita VT Jr, Hellman S, Rosenberg SA: Cancer: Principles and Practice of Oncology (3rd ed). Philadelphia: JB Lippincott, 1989.
3. Folkman J: The role of angiogenesis in tumor growth. Semin Cancer Biol 3:65–71, 1992.
4. Bogenrieder T, Herlyn M: Axis of evil: Molecular mechanisms of cancer metastasis. Oncogene 22:6524–6536, 2003.
5. Nicolson GL: Tumor and host molecules important in the organ preference of metastasis. Semin Cancer Biol 2:143–154, 1991.
6. Fidler IJ: Molecular biology of cancer: Invasion and metastasis. *In* DeVita VT Jr, Hellman S, Rosenberg SA (eds): Cancer: Principles and Practice of Oncology (5th ed). Philadelphia: Lippincott–Raven, 1997, pp 135–152.
7. Nicolson GL: Cancer metastasis: Tumor cell and host organ properties important in metastasis to specific secondary sites. Biochim Biophys Acta 948:175–224, 1988.
8. Folkman J: Angiogenesis inhibitors generated by tumors. Mol Med 1:120–122, 1995.
9. Cheng HC, Abdel-Ghany M, Elble RC, et al: Lung endothelial dipeptidyl peptidase IV promotes adhesion and metastasis of rat breast cancer cells via tumor cell surface-associated fibronectin. J Biol Chem 273:24207–24215, 1998.

10. Strieter RM, Belperio JA, Phillips RJ, Keane MP: Chemokines: Angiogenesis and metastases in lung cancer. Novartis Found Symp 256:173–184, 2004 [discussion appears in Novartis Found Symp 256:184–188, 259–269].

11. Sidransky D, Frost P, Von Eschenbach A, et al: Clonal origin of bladder cancer. N Engl J Med 326:737–740, 1992.

11a. Bandyopadhyay A, Elkahloun A, Baysa SJ, et al: Development and gene expression profiling of a metastic variant of the human breast cancer MDA-MB-435 cells. Cancer Biol Ther 4:Epub, 2005.

12. Ikezoe J, Johkoh T, Takeuchi N, et al: CT findings of endobronchial metastasis. Acta Radiol 32:455–460, 1991.

13. Felson B: Pulmonary nodules and cysts. *In* Chest Roentgenology. Philadelphia: WB Saunders, 1973, pp 314–329.

14. Viggiano RW, Swensen SJ, Rosenow EC: Evaluation and management of solitary and multiple pulmonary nodules. Clin Chest Med 13:83–95, 1992.

15. Davis SD: CT evaluation for pulmonary metastases in patients with extrathoracic malignancy. Radiology 180:1–12, 1991.

16. Diederich S, Semik MN, Lentschig MG, et al: Helical CT of pulmonary nodules in patients with extrathoracic malignancy: CT-surgical correlation. AJR Am J Roentgenol 172:353–360, 1999.

17. Wright AR, Collie DA, Williams JR, et al: Pulmonary nodules: Effect on detection of spiral CT pitch. Radiology 199:837–841, 1996.

18. Jeruslalem G, Hustinx R, Beguin Y, et al: PET scan imaging in oncology. Eur J Cancer 39:1525–1534, 2003.

19. Levine MN, Drummond MF, Labelle RJ: Cost-effectiveness in the diagnosis and treatment of carcinoma of unknown primary origin. CMAJ 133:977–978, 1985.

20. Xiao H, Liu D, Bajorin DF, et al: Medical and surgical management of pulmonary metastases from germ cell tumors. Chest Surg Clin N Am 8:131–143, 1998.

21. Jansen RL, Sylvester R, Sleyfer DT, et al: Long-term follow-up of nonseminomatous testicular cancer patients with mature teratoma or carcinoma at postchemotherapy surgery. EORTC Genitourinary Cancer Cooperative Group. Eur J Cancer 27:695–698, 1991.

22. Chetty KG, Moran EM, Sassoon CS, et al: Effect of radiation therapy on bronchial obstruction due to bronchogenic carcinoma. Chest 95:582–584, 1989.

23. Midthun DE: Endobronchial techniques in lung cancer: Options for nonsurgical care. Postgrad Med 101:169–172, 177–178, 1997.

23a. Chhajed PN, Tamm M: Radiofrequency heat ablation for lung tumors: potential applications. Med Sci Monit 9:ED5–7, 2003.

23b. Kang S, Luo R, Liao W, et al: Single group study to evaluate the feasibility and complications of radiofrequency ablation and usefulness of post treatment positron emission tomography in lung tumors. World J Surg Oncol 6:30, 2004.

23c. de Mey J, Van de Steene J, Vandenbroucke F, et al: Percutaneous placement of marking coils before stereotactic radiation therapy of malignant lung lesions. J Vasc Intervent Radiol 16:51–56, 2005.

24. Downey RJ: Surgical treatment of pulmonary metastases. Surg Oncol Clin N Am 8:341, 1999.

25. Todd TR: The surgical treatment of pulmonary metastases. Chest 112(Suppl):287S–290S, 1997.

26. International Registry of Lung Metastases: Long-term results of lung metastasectomy: Prognostic analyses based on 5206 cases. J Thorac Cardiovasc Surg 113:37–49, 1997.

27. Robert JH, Ambrogi V, Mermillod B, et al: Factors influencing long-term survival after lung metastasectomy. Ann Thorac Surg 63:777–784, 1997.

28. Lanza LA, Putnam JB Jr, Benjamin RS, et al: Response to chemotherapy does not predict survival after resection of sarcomatous pulmonary metastases. Ann Thorac Surg 51:219–224, 1991.

29. Lanza LA, Natarajan G, Roth JA, et al: Long-term survival after resection of pulmonary metastases from carcinoma of the breast. Ann Thorac Surg 54:244–248, 1992.

30. Robinson BJ, Rice TW, Strong SA, et al: Is resection of pulmonary and hepatic metastases warranted in patients with colorectal cancer? J Thorac Cardiovasc Surg 117:66–75, 1999.

31. Douglas WG, Rigual NR, Loree TR, et al: Current concepts in the management of a second malignancy of the lung in patients with head and neck cancer. Curr Opin Otolaryngol Head Neck Surg 11:86–88, 2003.

32. McIntosh R, Thatcher N: Management of the solitary metastasis. Thorax 45:909–911, 1990.

33. Moores DWO: Pulmonary metastases revisited. Ann Thorac Surg 52:178–179, 1991.

34. Beattie EJ, Harvey JC, Marcove R, et al: Results of multiple pulmonary resections for metastatic osteogenic sarcoma after two decades. J Surg Oncol 46:154–155, 1991.

35. Snyder CL, Saltzman DA, Ferrell KL, et al: A new approach to the resection of pulmonary osteosarcoma metastases. Clin Orthop Rel Res 270:247–253, 1991.

36. Burk CD, Belasco JB, O'Neill JA Jr, et al: Pulmonary metastases and bone sarcomas: Surgical removal of lesions appearing after adjuvant chemotherapy. Clin Orthop Rel Res 262:88–92, 1991.

37. Kawai A, Fukuma H, Beppu Y, et al: Pulmonary resection for metastatic soft tissue sarcomas. Clin Orthop 310:188–193, 1995.

38. Antunes M, Bernardo J, Salete M, et al: Excision of pulmonary metastases of osteogenic sarcoma of the limbs. Eur J Cardiothorac Surg 15:592–596, 1999.

39. Roth JA, Pass HI, Wesley MN, et al: Comparison of median sternotomy and thoracotomy for resection of pulmonary metastases in patients with adult soft-tissue sarcomas. Ann Thorac Surg 42:134–138, 1986.

40. Mineo TC, Ambrogi V, Tonini G, Nofroni I: Pulmonary metastasectomy: Might the type of resection affect survival? J Surg Oncol 76:47–52, 2001.

41. Rolle A, Eulerich E: Extensive multiple and lobe-sparing pulmonary resections with the Nd:YAG laser and a new wavelength of 1318 nm. Acta Chir Hung 38:115–117, 1999.

42. Dowling RD, Keenan RJ, Ferson PF, Landreneau RJ: Video-assisted thoracoscopic resection of pulmonary metastases. Ann Thorac Surg 56:772–775, 1993.

43. Dowling RD, Landreneau RJ, Miller DL: Video-assisted thoracoscopic surgery for resection of lung metastases. Chest 113(Suppl):2S–5S, 1998.

44. Landreneau FH, Mack MJ, Dowling RD, et al: The role of thoracoscopy in lung cancer management. Chest 113:68–128, 1998.

45. Henschke CI, Naidich DP, Yankelevitz DF, et al: Early Lung Cancer Action Project: Initial findings on repeat screenings. Cancer 92:153–159, 2001.

46. Lin J, Iannettoni MD: The role of thoracoscopy in the management of lung cancer. Surg Oncol 12:195–200, 2003.

47. McCormack PM, Bains MS, Begg CB, et al: Role of video-assisted thoracic surgery in the treatment of pulmonary metastases: Results of a prospective trial. Ann Thorac Surg 62:213–216, 1996.

48. McCormack PM, Ginsberg KB, Bains MS, et al: Accuracy of lung imaging in metastases with implications for the role of thoracoscopy. Ann Thorac Surg 56:863–867, 1993.

49. Mutsaerts EL, Zoetmulder FA, Meijer S, et al: Outcome of thoracoscopic pulmonary metastasectomy evaluated by confirmatory thoracotomy. Ann Thorac Surg 72:230–233, 2001.

50. Kaseda S, Aoki T, Hangai N, Shimizu K: Better pulmonary function and prognosis with video-assisted thoracic surgery than with thoracotomy. Ann Thorac Surg 70:1644–1646, 2000.

51. Leaver HA, Craig SR, Yap PL, Walker WS: Lymphocyte responses following open and minimally invasive thoracic surgery. Eur J Clin Invest 30:230–238, 2000.

52. Sugiura H, Morikawa T, Kaji M, et al: Long-term benefits for the quality of life after video-assisted thoracoscopic lobectomy in patients with lung cancer. Surg Laparosc Endosc Percut Technique 9:403–408, 1999.

53. Miller JD, Urschel JD, Cox G, et al: A randomized, controlled trial comparing thoracoscopy and limited thoracotomy for lung biopsy in interstitial lung disease. Ann Thorac Surg 70:1647–1650, 2000.

53a. Eichfeld U, Dietrich A, Ott R, Kloeppel R: Video-assisted thoracoscopic surgery for pulmonary nodules after computed tomography-guided marking with a spiral wire. Ann Thorac Surg 79:313–317, 2005.

54. Ambrogi V, Paci M, Pompeo E, Mineo TC: Transxiphoid video-assisted pulmonary metastasectomy: Relevance of helical computed tomography occult lesions. Ann Thorac Surg 70:1847–1852, 2000.

55. Boland TW, Winga ER, Kalfayan B: Chondrosarcoma: A case report with left atrial involvement and systemic embolization. J Thorac Cardiovasc Surg 74:268–272, 1977.

56. Korst RJ, Rosengart TK: Operative strategies for resection of pulmonary sarcomas extending into the left atrium. Ann Thorac Surg 67:1165–1167, 1999.

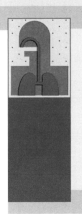

47

Benign Tumors

Michael K. Gould, M.D., Norman W. Rizk, M.D.

INTRODUCTION

Benign tumors of the lung account for fewer than 2% to 5% of primary lung tumors.[1–3] Most of these are hamartomas; other types of benign tumors are rare. In general, the etiology and pathogenesis of these uncommon conditions are poorly understood. Nomenclature is potentially confusing; benign tumors such as the granular cell myoblastoma and the sclerosing hemangioma currently are thought to be derived from neural tissue and respiratory epithelium, respectively, rather than from myocytes and endothelial cells, as the names imply. More important, some "benign" pulmonary tumors are really low-grade malignancies that may occasionally behave in a frankly malignant manner. Conversely, some malignant lung neoplasms, such as typical carcinoid tumors and slowly growing bronchioloalveolar cell carcinomas, exhibit indolent behavior that is more characteristic of a benign process. Some pulmonary lesions, although not neoplastic in the pathologic sense, mimic the clinical and radiographic features of tumors; such "pseudotumors" should be included in the differential diagnosis of benign and malignant lung tumors. In this chapter, we review common clinical manifestations of benign tumors and pseudotumors of the lung, and describe selected characteristic features of these lesions.

CLINICAL MANIFESTATIONS

The clinical picture depends primarily on the location of the lesion. Symptoms, signs, and radiographic features differ among benign tumors that arise in the trachea, the bronchi, and the lung parenchyma.

Intratracheal benign tumors may be asymptomatic but may manifest with pseudoasthmatic wheezing, stridor, cough, dyspnea, or hemoptysis. Careful examination of the tracheal air shadow by standard radiography may help detect the tumor, but confirmation by computed tomography (CT) is required.[4] Bronchoscopy is usually diagnostic and may even permit adequate tumor removal by forceps or with the aid of laser technology. However, surgical resection is usually recommended.[5,6]

Endobronchial benign tumors are frequently symptomatic, often causing partial or complete bronchial obstruction, which may result in recurrent pneumonias, bronchiectasis, unilateral wheezing, atelectasis, postobstructive pneumonitis, and postobstructive hyperinflation. Hemoptysis is occasionally noted. Standard radiography and CT may detect the obstructive consequences of the tumor rather than the tumor itself. Bronchoscopy usually reveals the location of the lesion. Because the tumor may be covered with normal mucosa, bronchial washings, brushings, and even forceps biopsy may be nondiagnostic. Transbronchial needle aspiration biopsy may provide a more suitable specimen. In some instances, the tumor can be completely removed endoscopically, but bronchotomy, sleeve resection, or even lobectomy/pneumonectomy may be required.[7,8] Although little is known about the risk of bleeding complications following biopsy of benign tracheobronchial tumors, the risk is probably less than 1.9%,[9] which was the incidence of "more than the usual amount of bleeding" in a retrospective review of almost 3100 patients who underwent bronchoscopic brushings or biopsy at a single center.[10] Although the risk is probably greatest in patients with highly vascular lesions, vascularity does not represent an absolute contraindication to biopsy.[9]

Parenchymal benign tumors of the lung are typically asymptomatic, even when large, and are customarily an unexpected finding in a chest radiograph or CT scan obtained for other purposes. A benign tumor in the lung parenchyma usually manifests radiologically as a *solitary pulmonary nodule* in an asymptomatic person. We define a solitary pulmonary nodule to be a spherical radiographic opacity that is completely surrounded by aerated lung and measures between 0.7 and 3 cm in diameter. There is no associated atelectasis, mediastinal adenopathy, or pleural effusion. Larger parenchymal mass lesions are considered malignant until proven otherwise; the diagnosis is confirmed by transthoracic needle biopsy or bronchoscopy. Because they are difficult to biopsy or characterize radiographically, smaller "subcentimeter" lesions are usually managed by observation with serial CT scans every 3 to 6 months, although the optimal interval between exams has not been determined. The prevalence of subcentimeter nodules in clinical practice may increase dramatically if lung cancer screening with low-dose spiral CT is widely adopted, but screening should not be performed routinely until its effectiveness is demonstrated in randomized, controlled trials.

Because many solitary nodules are malignant and curable, resection may be required unless benignity can be established. Although most benign nodules are granulomas, up to 10% may be benign tumors.[11]

Certain patterns of calcification almost always indicate benignity, including the central, laminated, diffuse, and "popcorn" patterns.[12] Even if the nodule is noncalcified, continued observation is justified if the lesion is "stable," that is, if there has been no increase in size during the previous 2 years.[13] However, this conventional wisdom has been challenged recently,[14,15] especially for subcentimeter nodules in which growth is difficult to detect even by repeat CT scanning. For example, in a nodule that originally measured 0.4 to 0.5 cm in diameter, even a doubling in tumor volume could be missed, because one doubling in volume corresponds to just a 26% increase in nodule diameter.[16,17] In the future, widespread adoption of computer-assisted, three-dimensional (volumetric) measurement protocols will facilitate prospective measurement of nodule growth.[18,19,19a]

Examination of the nodule by CT occasionally leads to a definitive diagnosis. CT shows the pattern of calcification more clearly than plain radiographs, and CT densitometry may identify otherwise undetectable calcification.[12,20] Most recent studies of high-resolution CT have employed criteria other than nodule density to distinguish benign from malignant nodules, but sensitivity and specificity have been variable.[21-24] As a result, although high-resolution CT can identify over 50% of all hamartomas, CT results are most often indeterminate.[25] In these cases, it is useful to estimate the probability that the nodule is malignant, either by using clinical intuition or by employing one of the quantitative models that have been developed.[26-28] One model that has undergone preliminary validation identified six independent predictors of malignancy, including three patient characteristics (age, smoking status, and prior history of an extrathoracic malignancy at least 5 years before the time of diagnosis) and three nodule characteristics (size, presence of spiculation, and upper lobe location).[28] Subsequently, this information can be employed in the decision process.[29,30] Magnetic resonance imaging has relatively little to offer in the evaluation of solitary nodules. Positron emission tomography has high sensitivity (and therefore high negative predictive value, especially when pretest probability is low) and intermediate specificity for identifying malignant lung nodules.[31] Of note, whereas most false-positive positron emission tomography results are due to granulomatous infection or inflammation, false-positive results were reported recently in two patients with benign tumors, one with a sclerosing hemangioma[32] and another with a meningioma.[33] CT with dynamic contrast enhancement represents a more widely available alternative to positron emission tomography imaging. In a recent multicenter study, the absence of nodule enhancement on CT following the administration of intravenous contrast was strongly predictive of a benign diagnosis.[34]

In patients who are good surgical candidates, management options include observation with serial chest radiographs or CT scans ("watchful waiting"), transthoracic needle biopsy (usually under CT guidance), and surgical biopsy. Although commonly applied in clinical practice, the watchful waiting strategy has never been prospectively evaluated; hence, for patients who prove to have malignant nodules, the risk of progression during the observation period from local to advanced disease has not been defined. Transthoracic needle aspiration biopsy of pulmonary nodules is sensitive for identifying malignant nodules.[35-37] In addition, this procedure identifies specific benign lesions about 50% of the time, including infectious processes and benign tumors. If the biopsy results are nondiagnostic, thoracotomy or thoracoscopy is typically indicated.[11] In most centers, the preferred surgical approach for patients with peripheral lung nodules is to perform a wedge resection via video-assisted thoracoscopic surgery, and to convert the procedure to a thoracotomy and perform a more definitive resection if the frozen section reveals malignancy.[38]

The relative merits of the various management options are still debated. Perhaps not surprisingly, a decision analysis demonstrated that the choice of strategy was a very "close call."[29] Watchful waiting was preferred when the probability of malignancy was very low (≤3%), surgery was preferred when the probability of malignancy was high (≥68%), and needle biopsy was preferred when the probability of malignancy fell between these two extremes. A more recent cost-effectiveness analysis identified similar threshold probabilities for selecting watchful waiting and surgery, and also showed that positron emission tomography imaging can efficiently guide subsequent management decisions when the probability of malignancy falls between 20% and 69%.[30] Other authors have published similar clinical algorithms that stratify patients and management recommendations according to the clinical probability of malignancy (Fig. 47.1).[11] In contrast, guidelines recently published by the American College of Chest Physicians recommend that watchful waiting and needle biopsy be reserved for patients who are nonoperable or marginally operable, and for patients who refuse surgical intervention.[38]

CLASSIFICATION

Benign tumors are customarily classified in terms of their pathologic abnormalities. The classification used in this chapter mirrors the actual clinical presentation, being based on location and on whether single or multiple lesions are detectable (Table 47.1). The clinical manifestations of benign tumors are largely dependent on whether the lesion is endobronchial or parenchymal in location.

TRACHEOBRONCHIAL BENIGN TUMORS

Recurrent Respiratory Papillomatosis

Recurrent respiratory papillomatosis (previously known as multiple laryngeal papillomatosis) is caused by human papillomavirus infection, usually from human papillomavirus types 6 or 11.[39,40] The most common neoplasm of the upper respiratory tract in young children, it may spread to the intrapulmonary tracheobronchial tree or, rarely, to the lung parenchyma after several years.[41,42] The lesions are sessile or stalked papillary growths lined with flattened squamous epithelium; they may cause hoarseness, stridor, hemoptysis,

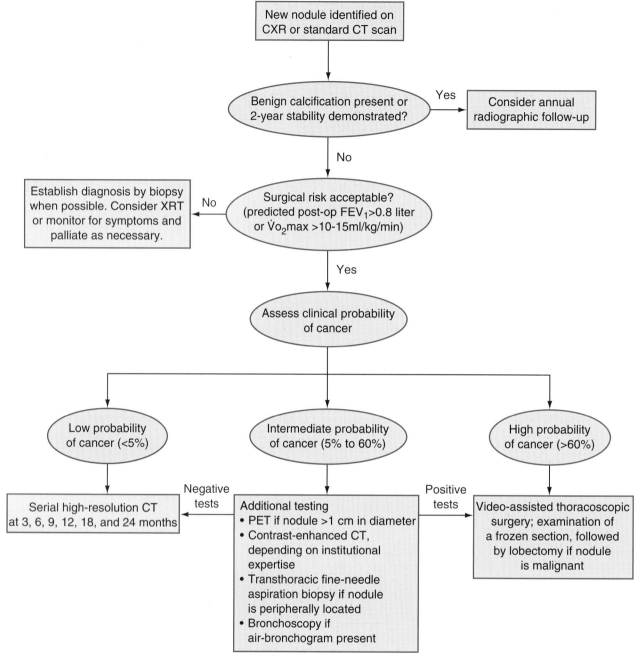

Figure 47.1 Management algorithm for patients with solitary pulmonary nodules. CT, computed tomography; CXR, chest radiograph, PET, positron emission tomography; $\dot{V}_{O_2}max$, maximal oxygen consumption; XRT, radiation therapy. (Adapted from Ost D, Fein AM, Feinsilver SH: Clinical practice: The solitary pulmonary nodule. N Engl J Med 348:2535–2542, 2003.)

asthmatic wheezing, atelectasis, and obstructive pneumonitis. In patients with parenchymal lung involvement, standard radiographs may show multiple nodular lesions that are often cavitated. The diagnosis is suggested by the history of childhood laryngeal papillomatosis and is confirmed by bronchoscopic biopsy of the lesions. The clinical course varies from spontaneous remission to rapidly progressive disease causing airway compromise. Laser vaporization of the papillomas is the mainstay of treatment, but management is challenging because lesions often recur.[43] Adjuvant therapy with interferon-alpha may be helpful in patients with severe disease.[44] Improvement following treatment with other antiviral agents[45,46] and cimetidine,[47] which, by

blocking histamine, may have immunostimulatory effects, has been reported. Malignant transformation to well-differentiated squamous cell carcinoma has been described, characteristically in young adults with long-standing papillomatosis and lower airway involvement.[48] In these cases, malignant transformation has been accompanied by increased expression of p53 and pRb proteins and reduced expression of p21[WAF1].[49–52]

Solitary Squamous Papilloma

The solitary tracheobronchial papilloma, which usually measures less than 1.5 cm in diameter, most commonly

Table 47.1 Benign Tumors and Pseudotumors of the Lung

Tracheobronchial Tumors	Solitary Parenchymal Tumors	Multiple Parenchymal Tumors	Pseudotumors
Recurrent respiratory papillomatosis	Hamartoma	Benign metastasizing leiomyoma	Tracheopathia osteochondroplastica
Solitary squamous papilloma	Sclerosing hemangioma	Multiple chondromas (Carney's triad)	Nodular sarcoidosis
Inflammatory papilloma	Papillary adenoma	Tumorlets	Nodular amyloidosis
Mucous gland adenoma	Alveolar adenoma	Chemodectomas (paraganglionomas)	Round atelectasis
Granular cell myoblastoma	Lipoma	Minute pulmonary chemodectomas	Hematoma
Endobronchial hamartoma	Leiomyoma	Hemangiomas	Lipoid pneumonia
Endobronchial lipoma	Neurofibroma		Rheumatoid granuloma
Endobronchial leiomyoma	Meningioma		Wegener's granulomatosis
	Fibroma		Loculated interlobar pleural effusion
	Clear cell (sugar) tumor		Pulmonary infarct
	Teratoma		
	Glomus tumor		
	Inflammatory pseudotumors		
	Endometrioma		
	Pseudolymphoma		

occurs in middle-aged male smokers. The tumor is usually in a lobar or segmental bronchus, manifesting clinically with hemoptysis, atelectasis, or postobstructive pneumonitis.[53] Unlike viral papillomatosis, these tumors are only occasionally associated with human papillomavirus infection.[54-56] Endoscopic removal is usually feasible. Solitary papillomas are associated with dysplasia, carcinoma in situ, or invasive carcinoma in up to one third of cases.[55]

Inflammatory Papilloma

The inflammatory tracheobronchial papilloma, usually solitary, is a polypoid mass of exuberant granulation tissue secondary to chronic irritation, such as bronchiectasis, thermal injury, and indwelling foreign bodies.[57] The usual clinical manifestation is bronchial obstruction. Treatment is local excision plus efforts to control the underlying inflammation.

Mucous Gland Adenoma

This is the only lesion that truly deserves the appellation of *bronchial adenoma*. The latter term is often misapplied to malignant tracheobronchial tumors such as the carcinoid tumor, the cylindroma (adenoid cystic carcinoma), and the mucoepidermoid carcinoma, which are discussed in Chapter 44.

The mucous gland adenoma (bronchial cystadenoma) arises in main, lobar, or segmental bronchi, often has a papillary appearance, and may cause obstructive symptoms.[58] Histologically, this tumor resembles normal tracheobronchial mucus glands; cystic spaces within the tumor are filled with mucus and lined by columnar cells. In patients with central airway obstruction, the tumor can be removed endoscopically or surgically.

Granular Cell Myoblastoma

This tumor is composed of polygonal or spindle cells with abundant granular eosinophilic cytoplasm; despite the name, it is now thought to have a neural origin, probably from Schwann cells.[59,60] The tumor can arise in many

organs, but fewer than 100 cases of bronchial origin have been reported.[61] The respiratory tract lesions are usually in the larynx or main bronchi and are multiple in 10% of cases.[62,63] The disease, which is more common in men than in women, usually becomes clinically apparent between the ages of 30 and 50 years. A rare malignant variant of the granular cell tumor is difficult to distinguish from the more common benign tumor on the basis of histologic features alone.[64]

Clinical manifestations include cough, hemoptysis, recurrent infections, and wheezing. Bronchoscopic biopsy is usually diagnostic, and bronchoscopic removal is occasionally possible. Laser therapy is sometimes helpful, but complete surgical excision is usually advisable, particularly for lesions greater than 8 mm in diameter. These tumors show a propensity for local invasiveness and may recur after limited excision.[65] In rare cases, a granular cell myoblastoma of the lung may present as a solitary pulmonary nodule.[66]

Endobronchial Hamartoma

The pathology and pathogenesis of intrapulmonary hamartomas are discussed subsequently. About 10% to 20% of all bronchopulmonary hamartomas are endobronchial in location; a literature review in 1972 listed 58 reported cases.[67] Although endobronchial tumors may cause the usual obstructive complications, they are often asymptomatic.

Endobronchial hamartomas favor central bronchi and are usually polypoid. Cartilage is present in 82% of cases but is often scanty.[68] The epithelial clefts seen in the parenchymal tumors are often missing in the endobronchial form. Bronchoscopy is usually but not always diagnostic, and the majority of cases evident bronchoscopically can be treated with rigid bronchoscopy and laser resection or ablation.[69] Resection is usually advisable for preventing or alleviating obstructive complications.

Other Mesenchymal Tumors

Several types of benign mesenchymal lung tumors that are usually parenchymal in location occasionally occur within the tracheobronchial tree, where they typically give rise to obstructive syndromes. Examples include *fibromas*,[70] which may recur after endoscopic removal; *chondromas*[71]; *neurofibromas*[72]; *glomus tumors*[73]; *inflammatory pseudotumors*[74]; and *sclerosing hemangiomas*.[74a]

The intrapulmonary *lipoma*, in contrast, is almost always endobronchial in origin.[75,76] It is believed to arise from submucosal fat in airways that contain cartilage and bronchial glands. The overwhelming preponderance of these tumors occur in the first three subdivisions of the tracheobronchial tree and hence are bronchoscopically assessable for diagnosis and treatment.[77] About 50% of pulmonary *leiomyomas*[78] are endobronchial in location and thus cause cough, expectoration, and symptoms of obstruction.

SOLITARY PARENCHYMAL TUMORS

Hamartoma

Hamartomas are the most common form of benign lung tumors, occurring in 0.2% of routine autopsies and in 0.32% of 47,000 miners.[2,3,79] They are twice as common in men as in women. About 5% to 10% of solitary pulmonary nodules are hamartomas.

Although the name suggests that hamartomas are developmental abnormalities, the current belief is that they are true neoplasms; the term *benign mesenchymoma* has been suggested.[80] Favoring tumoral status is the relatively late onset (from the late 30s, with a peak in the 60s) and a tendency to exhibit slow growth during prolonged observation. Malignant change is extremely rare,[81] and some authorities doubt that it can occur.

Microscopic examination shows a central cartilaginous area in virtually all cases,[68] with calcification in some instances. Other areas of the tumor contain myxomatous and fibroblastic tissue, often accompanied by muscular and adipose tissue, bronchial glands, and chronic inflammatory cells. Slitlike spaces or clefts lined with respiratory epithelium are commonly present, usually near the periphery of the tumor.[3] The results of cytogenetic studies indicate that only the mesenchymal component of the hamartoma is neoplastic.[82] Specific chromosomal aberrations have been described, including translocations involving chromosomes 6 and 12, and rearrangements within or close to the genes that encode the high-mobility-group proteins HMGI-C and HMGI(Y).[83,84]

The peripheral hamartoma is typically a well-circumscribed and asymptomatic nodule less than 3.0 cm in diameter, with a margin that is sharp and often lobulated. Slow growth may be detectable with serial radiographic examinations. A variety of benign tumors and congenital anomalies may occur in association with pulmonary hamartomas.[85]

Calcification is detectable in 10% to 15% of cases on plain radiographs and may show a characteristic popcorn pattern.[79,86] The presence of calcification is better seen on CT examination. High-resolution CT is diagnostic in more than 50% of hamartomas; the characteristic features (Fig. 47.2) are the combination of cartilage (with or without calcification) and focal areas of low attenuation due to fat deposits in the tumor.[25,87]

The diagnosis of peripheral hamartoma can be established by transthoracic needle aspiration biopsy in many cases,[88]

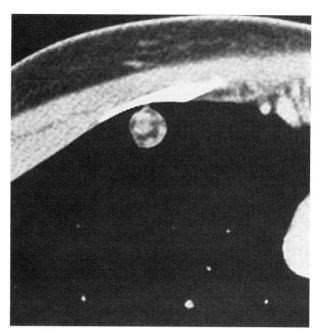

Figure 47.2 High-resolution computed tomographic image of the right lung in an asymptomatic person, showing a well-circumscribed nodule with a diameter of 1.5 cm in the subpleural position anteriorly. The nodule shows areas of increased attenuation, representing cartilage. The intranodular areas of low attenuation are fat; note the similarity to the attenuation of the subcutaneous fat. The pathologic diagnosis was a chondroid hamartoma. (Courtesy of Dr. Nestor Muller.)

and can sometimes be made by bronchoscopic transbronchial biopsy.[89] Although surgical excision is curative, it is not clear that resection is required in all or even most cases.[90] Appropriate indications for surgery might include the presence of symptoms, growth of the tumor under radiographic observation, large size of the tumor, and impingement of the mass on a vital structure.

Mesenchymal cystic hamartomas are rare tumors that may show malignant changes.[91,92] However, these lesions should be differentiated from ordinary hamartomas.

Sclerosing Hemangioma

This uncommon tumor, originally considered vascular in origin, is now generally classified as an epithelial tumor derived from type II pneumocytes.[93] Most of these tumors stain positively with pan-epithelial and pulmonary epithelium–specific immunohistochemical markers, such as epithelial membrane antigen and thyroid transcription factor-1.[94,95] The tumor usually contains several elements, including solid cellular areas, papillary structures, sclerotic regions, and dilated blood-filled spaces resembling hemangioma.[2,3,96] When a papillary pattern predominates, samples of the tumor obtained by needle biopsy or frozen section can be confused with an epithelioid hemangioendothelioma, carcinoid tumor, or well-differentiated papillary adenocarcinoma.[97,98]

The tumor is most common in middle-aged women and is usually asymptomatic.[2] The typical radiographic appearance is a well-defined homogeneous nodule that measures less than 4 cm in diameter, although a recent case report described a patient with a gigantic tumor that occupied the entire left hemithorax.[99] Lesions are multiple in a distinct minority of cases.[100,101] Although the tumor is benign, rare cases with lymph node metastasis have been reported.[102,103] Diagnosis is usually made by resection of the lesion at exploratory thoracotomy.[96]

An even more uncommon tumor that is also thought to be derived from type II cells is the *peripheral papillary adenoma*.[104] About a dozen of these tumors have been reported, including three cases that exhibited microinvasive features suggesting that this might be a tumor of uncertain malignant potential.[104] Despite their common cell of origin and clinical presentation, papillary adenomas and *alveolar adenomas* are thought to be distinct entities.[105,106]

Other Mesenchymal Tumors of Lung Parenchyma

Several types of benign tumors may arise from cells of mesenchymal origin within the lung parenchyma. Most are uncommon.

Intrapulmonary Lipoma. As mentioned, these tumors are usually endobronchial, but parenchymal tumors have been described.[107,108] The parenchymal tumor presents as a solitary nodule, and its fatty nature can be defined by the decreased attenuation noted on CT examination. They occur more commonly on the right side and in the upper lobe of the lung in middle-aged men. Resection is usually not necessary if the diagnosis can be established without surgery. *Lipoblastomas* are uncommon tumors of embryonal fat that typically affect the extremities of infants and young children. The presentation can be solitary and localized or multicentric, in which case it is called lipoblastomatosis. The first reported case of a pulmonary lipoblastoma was described recently in a 2-year-old girl.[109]

Pulmonary Leiomyoma. This tumor appears as a sharply defined, lobulated, and asymptomatic parenchymal solitary nodule in 50% of cases, occurring most commonly in middle-aged adults.[78,110] Some cases in women may actually be solitary examples of so-called *benign metastasizing leiomyoma*, which is discussed subsequently.

Neural Tumors. The parenchymal nodule of neural origin is usually a neurofibroma and occasionally a *schwannoma*.[111] Some cases are part of the syndrome of neurofibromatosis.[112,113] Intrapulmonary *meningiomas* have been described.[114–116] Because primary pulmonary meningiomas are so rare, the diagnosis should be one of exclusion after metastasis from a central nervous system primary tumor has been ruled out.[117]

Fibroma. The parenchymal fibroma is more common in men than in women and is usually asymptomatic. Some cases diagnosed as fibroma may actually represent fibrous histiocytomas[118] or leiomyomas.[2] *Desmoid tumors* are locally invasive, fibrous tumors that arise from the connective tissue sheath of skeletal muscle. Although they do not originate in the lung parenchyma, a chest wall desmoid can mimic an intrapulmonary tumor,[119] and even cause Pancoast's syndrome.[120]

Benign Clear Cell Tumor

This rare tumor presents radiographically as a well-circumscribed pulmonary nodule. Symptoms are rarely present,

and the tumors tend to first appear in adulthood. The lesion may be as large as 6 cm in diameter but is usually less than 3 cm.[121,122] The tumor is a member of the perivascular epithelioid cell (PEComa) family of tumors, which also includes angiomyolipomas, lymphangiomyomas, and lymphangioleiomyomatosis.[123]

The cells are polygonal, with abundant clear or finely vacuolated cytoplasm. Multinucleated giant cells are often present. The richness of the cytoplasm in glycogen has prompted the term *sugar tumor*. The pathologic differential diagnosis includes metastatic hypernephroma and primary clear cell carcinoma of the lung[2]; the distinction can be made with special immunochemical studies.[121] On occasion, symptomatic necrotic clear cell tumors behave as though malignant.[122] In all reported cases, the diagnosis has been established by thoracotomy or autopsy.

Teratoma

Intrapulmonary teratomas are very rare (about 65 cases have been reported worldwide), often large, and usually symptomatic.[124] Symptoms include chest pain, fever, cough, hemoptysis, and even trichoptysis.[125] The tumor is more often benign than malignant.[126] Calcification may be present, and radiologic evidence of an intratumoral tooth may be noted.

Glomus Tumor

These tumors are derived from the neuromyoarterial glomus body, a structure that is thought to play a role in temperature regulation. Pulmonary glomus tumors represent a rare manifestation of this uncommon tumor, which is found more typically in a subungual location. Fewer than a dozen cases of pulmonary glomus tumors have been reported, including two benign endobronchial tumors and a malignant glomangiosarcoma.[73,127]

Inflammatory Pseudotumors

These conditions are more inflammatory in nature than neoplastic. The specific name for each variant depends on the histology of the lesion.[2,3,128,129] In most cases, the lesions have been diagnosed and treated at thoracotomy. The diagnosis can sometimes be made by transthoracic needle aspiration biopsy; long-term follow-up with serial chest radiographs seems prudent in such cases.

Plasma Cell Granuloma. The tumor is composed of fibrous tissue and polyclonal inflammatory cells, always with large numbers of plasma cells. Because of the histology, they are sometimes referred to as inflammatory pseudotumors. Calcification and ossification are common, and amyloid degeneration may occur.[130,131] The lesion is usually a nodule that measures between 2 and 5 cm in diameter, but larger masses have been described. A relatively high proportion occur in children and adolescents. Slow growth or transformation to a lymphoma may occur, but in most cases there is no change over long observation periods.[132] As noted previously, plasma cell granulomas may present in an endobronchial location.

Plasma cell granuloma should not be confused with *plasmacytoma*, which may appear in the trachea or the lung parenchyma and is a highly malignant manifestation of multiple myeloma. The histopathology of plasmacytoma shows distinctive features of malignancy.

Fibrous Histiocytoma, Histiocytoma, and Xanthoma. These tumors consist primarily of histiocytes with eosinophilic or foamy cytoplasm and of fibroblasts and fibrous tissue in varying proportions; plasma cells are scanty. Their clinical characteristics are identical to those of plasma cell granulomas. Fibrous histiocytomas may be confused with fibromas.[118]

Pulmonary Hyalinizing Granuloma. Approximately 50 cases of this rare tumor have been reported.[133,134] The tumor contains lamellae of homogeneous hyaline material, with interspersed plasma cells and giant cells.[3] The nodule is usually 2 to 4 cm in diameter, although large lesions have been reported, and some are cavitary.[135] In many cases, multiple lesions are present, simulating metastatic tumors.[136] Associations with lymphoma,[137] *Aspergillus* infection,[138] Castleman's disease,[139] and multiple sclerosis[140] have been reported.

Pulmonary Endometrioma

Catamenial hemoptysis (hemoptysis occurring at the time of menstruation) is a rare circumstance, which is presumed to be due to intrabronchial or parenchymal endometrial tissue deposits.[141] Pulmonary endometrioma may also present as an asymptomatic solitary pulmonary nodule; the diagnosis is usually established by exploratory thoracotomy. Intrapleural endometrial deposits are much more common than bronchopulmonary lesions and may be associated with catamenial pneumothorax[142] or catamenial hemothorax.[141]

Pseudolymphoma

These large solitary nodular or irregular lung lesions are composed of a polymorphous mixture of lymphocytes, plasma cells, and histiocytes, which resembles the histologic changes in patients with lymphocytic interstitial pneumonitis. These are part of the spectrum of bronchus-associated lymphoid tissue proliferations, both benign and malignant.[143] Cough and sputum production are common. In many cases, such tumors are really low-grade lymphomas,[144] but in general, the prognosis is relatively good. (Further discussion about pulmonary lymphomas and lymphoproliferative diseases is available in Chapter 45.)

MULTIPLE PARENCHYMAL TUMORS

Many of the tumors already discussed as solitary intraparenchymal benign tumors occasionally present as multiple nodules in the lung. Such tumors include hamartomas,[145] hyalinizing granulomas, leiomyomas, and sclerosing hemangiomas.[146]

Benign Metastasizing Leiomyoma

Multiple pulmonary leiomyomas occur predominantly in women and are associated in 80% of cases with a history of prior uterine surgery for fibroid tumors.[147] Some authorities have considered these lesions to be hamartomas or

multiple primary lung tumors, but the consensus favors metastatic deposits from a uterine tumor that appears benign histologically, hence the title.[148] Cytogenetic evidence points to a clonal source.[149] When multiple tumors of this type occur in men, some authors prefer to use the term *multiple leiomyomatous hamartomas*.[150] Most patients are asymptomatic, even when the nodules are diffuse and numerous.[151] Tumors frequently express estrogen and progesterone receptors, and there is often a response to hormonal manipulation.[152] Spontaneous regression during pregnancy and menopause has also been observed.[153,154]

Multiple Chondromas (Carney's Triad)

This rare and bizarre syndrome consists of gastrointestinal stromal tumors, pulmonary chondromas, and extra-adrenal paragangliomas.[155] The different tumors may occur synchronously or in a metachronous fashion.[156] In most cases of the syndrome, only two of the three features are present. It occurs primarily in young women below the age of 30 years. Less than 10% of the patients are men. Presenting signs and symptoms are usually due to extrapulmonary manifestations of the syndrome, including iron-deficiency anemia from occult gastric bleeding, hematemesis, melena, epigastric pain, and unexplained hypertension.[157] The chondromas, which may be single or multiple, have been considered to be chondromatous hamartomas.[145] These tumors present as asymptomatic sharply circumscribed pulmonary nodules that may be calcified or even ossified (Fig. 47.3) and may show slow growth. Needle biopsy may be diagnostic.[158] In one patient with this syndrome, some of the lung nodules were metastases from the primary tumor and others were chondromas.[159] In another unusual case, a chondroma resulted in bronchial obstruction and abscess formation.[160] Although pulmonary manifestations in most cases of Carney's triad are relatively inconsequential, resection of gastrointestinal stromal tumors and paraganglionomas is necessary to prevent potentially lethal complications.

Pulmonary Tumorlets

Tumorlets are minute collections of neuroendocrine cells scattered throughout the lungs that are usually discovered as an incidental finding in postmortem or surgical material. Most commonly they are found in elderly women and are not usually detectable by radiographic studies.[161,162] Pulmonary tumorlets classically accompany inflammatory lesions in the airways but may also be multifocal and bilateral; when lesions exceed 0.5 cm in size, they are (arbitrarily) classified as carcinoid tumors.[163] Associated Cushing's syndrome has been reported.[164]

Chemodectomas (Paraganglionomas) and Minute Pulmonary Chemodectoma

Solitary intrapulmonary chemodectomas that are large enough to be detected by plain radiographs have been observed in the trachea[165] and in pulmonary parenchyma[166] in a handful of cases, including at least one patient in whom the lesions were multiple and progressive.[167] Pulmonary parenchymal tumors are typically located in close proximity to aortic arch chemoreceptors. Typical histopathology

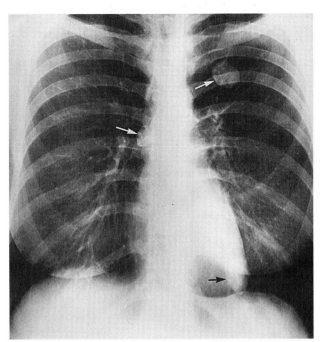

Figure 47.3 Chest radiograph of a 21-year-old woman with recurrent gastric epithelioid leiomyosarcoma, showing several well-circumscribed intrapulmonary nodules bilaterally (*arrows*). Their radiographic densities were greater than those of soft tissue but less than that of calcium. The nodule shown by the *top arrow* was in the left upper lobe and had a lobulated but sharp margin. Transthoracic needle aspiration biopsy of this nodule yielded cartilage, consistent with the diagnosis of chondroma. Mediastinal paragangliomas were discovered at a later thoracotomy. Diagnosis was pulmonary chondroma in a patient with Carney's triad.

shows tightly packed nests of round or polygonal cells surrounded by thin fibrovascular septa in a characteristic "Zelballen" (balls of cells) pattern.[168]

Multiple minute pulmonary tumors, which are 1 to 3 mm in diameter and resemble chemodectomas, have been detected as asymptomatic incidental findings in a number of cases, almost all in women.[169,170] These tumors appear to have no clinical significance. Ultrastructural studies indicate that they are not paragangliomas but more closely resemble meningothelial cells.[170] Immunohistochemical and clonal analysis suggests that at least some of these lesions may be reactive rather than neoplastic,[171] although their coexistence with pulmonary meningiomas in two cases argues otherwise.[116,172]

Hemangiomas

These rare benign vascular proliferations of infancy and childhood can be divided into two types, capillary and cavernous. Microscopically, cavernous hemangiomas contain large spaces that are filled with blood or thrombus. Capillary hemangiomas contain small, regular vascular spaces that are lined by flattened endothelium.[173] Capillary hemangiomas can be endobronchial or parenchymal, and localized or multifocal. The multifocal type should not be confused with pulmonary capillary hemangiomatosis.[174] Patients with this rare disorder present with dyspnea, hemoptysis,

and rapidly progressive pulmonary hypertension. High-resolution CT reveals areas of ground-glass attenuation with thickening of the interlobular septa and multiple poorly defined nodules. The diagnosis is typically established postmortem. Autopsy reveals abnormal proliferations of capillaries in the alveolar walls, interlobular septa, bronchiolar walls, and small blood vessels.[174,175]

PSEUDOTUMORS

Endobronchial pseudotumors include *tracheopathia osteochondroplastica*,[176–178] nodular *sarcoidosis*,[179] and tracheobronchial *amyloidosis*,[180,181] all of which may present as multiple plaques or as papillary lesions.[182] An endobronchial *mucoid pseudotumor* may have the roentgenographic appearance of a solitary nodule.[183,184]

Parenchymal pseudotumors may be solitary or multiple. *Nodular amyloidosis* of the lung presents as asymptomatic well-defined nodules that are 2 to 4 cm in diameter.[185–187] *Diffuse amyloidosis* complicating other diseases (e.g., multiple myeloma) may sometimes produce widespread infiltrates in the lung parenchyma. (The various manifestations of bronchopulmonary amyloidosis are discussed in Chapter 79.) *Round atelectasis* is usually a solitary mass but occasionally is multiple; most cases are secondary to asbestos-induced pleural disease, but occasionally it occurs secondary to trauma or silicosis. The appearance on CT is characteristic, although not always diagnostic. Classic CT features include evidence of volume loss, a juxtapleural location, associated pleural thickening, and a "comet tail" of converging bronchovascular structures that points toward the hilum.[188] Intrapulmonary *hematomas* are recognized from the trauma history and the gradual shrinkage of the mass or masses with the passage of time.

Solitary pseudotumors that mimic bronchogenic carcinoma include *paraffinoma* (or *lipoid pneumonia*), which is due to recurrent aspiration of mineral oil (the presence of nonspecific areas of consolidation with low attenuation values and a "crazy-paving" pattern should strongly suggest the diagnosis)[189,190]; intrapulmonary *rheumatoid granuloma*[191]; and a solitary mass due to *Wegener's granulomatosis*.[192] The last condition can be diagnosed with a high degree of certainty by the combination of tissue biopsy at a site of active disease and a positive test for antineutrophil cytoplasmic antibody. Necrotizing granulomas that may simulate parenchymal tumors also include *infectious granulomas* and *bronchocentric granulomatosis*.[193]

A loculated *interlobar effusion* may simulate pulmonary tumor if seen in only one projection, but the radiographic appearances on multiple views are usually diagnostic. Serial films often show that the opacity shrinks with diuretic therapy.[194] The terms *vanishing lung tumor* and *phantom tumor* have been applied to loculated effusions and hematomas that decrease in size.[195] A *pulmonary infarct* may be confused with pulmonary tumor[196,197]; this has occasionally resulted in surgical resection of old infarcts.

SUMMARY

Benign tumors of the lung are uncommon. Intratracheal and endobronchial tumors frequently give rise to symptoms of bronchial obstruction and are diagnosed (and often treated) by bronchoscopy. Parenchymal benign tumors are usually asymptomatic and are discovered serendipitously on chest radiographs. In most cases, the diagnosis is made by thoracotomy or thoracoscopy and resection, although the diagnostic usefulness of transthoracic needle biopsy is increasingly accepted. Pseudotumors may mimic benign and malignant lung tumors.

REFERENCES

1. Arrigoni MG, Woolner LB, Bernatz PE, et al: Benign tumors of the lung: A ten-year surgical experience. J Thorac Cardiovasc Surg 60:589–599, 1970.
2. Dail DH: Uncommon tumors. *In* Dail DH, Hammar SP (eds): Pulmonary Pathology (2nd ed). New York: Springer-Verlag, 1994, pp 1279–1461.
3. Churg A: Tumors of the lung. *In* Thurlbeck WM, Churg A (eds): Pathology of the Lung (2nd ed). New York: Thieme, 1995, pp 437–551.
4. McCarthy MJ, Rosado-de-Christenson ML: Tumors of the trachea. J Thorac Imaging 10:180–198, 1995.
5. Mathisen DJ: Primary tracheal tumor management. Surg Oncol Clin N Am 8:307, 1999.
6. Gaissert HA: Primary tracheal tumors. Chest Surg Clin North Am 13:247–256, 2003.
7. Wang NS, Morin J: Recurrent endobronchial soft tissue tumors. Chest 85:787–791, 1984.
8. Scott WJ: Surgical treatment of other bronchial tumors. Chest Surg Clin N Am 13:111–128, 2003.
9. Prakash UBS, Freitag L: Hemoptysis and bronchoscopy-induced hemorrhage. *In* Prakash UBS (ed): Bronchoscopy. New York: Raven Press, 1994, pp 227–251.
10. Cordasco EMJ, Mehta AC, Ahmad M: Bronchoscopically-induced bleeding: A summary of nine years' Cleveland Clinic experience and review of the literature. Chest 100:1141–1147, 1991.
11. Ost D, Fein AM, Feinsilver SH: Clinical practice: The solitary pulmonary nodule. N Engl J Med 348:2535–2542, 2003.
12. Siegelman SS, Khouri NF, Leo FP, et al: Solitary pulmonary nodules: CT assessment. Radiology 160:307–312, 1986.
13. Lillington GA: Management of solitary pulmonary nodules. Dis Mon 37:271–318, 1991.
14. Yankelevitz DF, Henschke CI: Does 2-year stability imply that pulmonary nodules are benign? AJR Am J Radiol 168:325–328, 1997.
15. Lillington GA: Solitary pulmonary nodules: New wine in old bottles. Curr Opin Pulm Med 7:242–246, 2001.
16. Collins VP, Loeffler RK, Tivey H: Observations on growth rates of human tumors. Am J Roentgenol Radium Ther Nucl Med 76:988–1000, 1956.
17. Geddes DM: The natural history of lung cancer: A review based on rates of tumor growth. Br J Dis Chest 73:1–17, 1979.
18. Yankelevitz DF, Reeves AP, Kostis WJ, et al: Small pulmonary nodules: Volumetrically determined growth rates based on CT evaluation. Radiology 217:251–256, 2000.
19. Winer-Muram HT, Jennings SG, Tarver RD, et al: Volumetric growth rate of stage I lung cancer prior to treatment: Serial CT scanning. Radiology 223:798–805, 2002.
19a. Ko JP, Naidich DP: Computer-aided diagnosis and the evaluation of lung disease. J Thorac Imaging 19:136–155, 2004.
20. Zerhouni EA, Stitik FP, Siegelman SS, et al: CT of the pulmonary nodule: A cooperative study. Radiology 160:319–327, 1986.
21. Khan A, Herman PG, Vorwerk P, et al: Solitary pulmonary nodules: Comparison of classification with standard, thin-section, and reference phantom CT. Radiology 179:477–481, 1991.
22. Zwirewich CV, Vedal S, Miller RR, et al: Solitary pulmonary nodule: High-resolution CT and radiologic-pathologic correlation. Radiology 179:469–476, 1991.
23. Takanashi N, Nobe Y, Asoh H, et al: The diagnostic accuracy of a solitary pulmonary nodule, using thin-section high resolution CT: A solitary pulmonary nodule by HRCT. Lung Cancer 13:105–112, 1995.
24. Seemann MD, Staebler A, Beinert T, et al: Usefulness of morphological characteristics for the differentiation of benign from malignant solitary pulmonary lesions using HRCT. Eur Radiol 9:409–417, 1999.
25. Siegelman SS, Khouri NF, Scott WW Jr, et al: Pulmonary hamartoma: CT findings. Radiology 160:313–317, 1986.
26. Cummings SR, Lillington GA, Richard RJ: Estimating the probability of malignancy in solitary pulmonary nodules: A bayesian approach. Am Rev Respir Dis 134:449–452, 1986.
27. Gurney JW: Determining the likelihood of malignancy in solitary pulmonary nodules with bayesian analysis. Part I. Theory. Radiology 186:405–413, 1993.
28. Swensen SJ, Silverstein MD, Ilstrup DM, et al: The probability of malignancy in solitary pulmonary nodules: Application to small radiologically indeterminate nodules. Arch Intern Med 157:849–855, 1997.
29. Cummings SR, Lillington GA, Richard RJ: Managing solitary pulmonary nodules: The choice of strategy is a "close call." Am Rev Respir Dis 134:453–460, 1986.
30. Gould MK, Sanders GD, Barnett PG, et al: Cost-effectiveness of alternative management strategies for patients with solitary pulmonary nodules. Ann Intern Med 138:724–735, 2003.
31. Gould MK, Maclean CC, Kuschner WG, et al: Accuracy of positron emission tomography (PET) for diagnosis of pulmonary nodules and mass lesions: A meta-analysis. JAMA 285:914–924, 2001.
32. Hara M, Iida A, Tohyama J, et al: FDG-PET findings in sclerosing hemangioma of the lung: A case report. Radiat Med 19:215–218, 2001.
33. Cura M, Smoak W, Dala R: Pulmonary meningioma: False-positive positron emission tomography for malignant pulmonary nodules. Clin Nucl Med 27:701–704, 2002.
34. Swensen SJ, Viggiano RW, Midthun DE, et al: Lung nodule enhancement at CT: Multicenter study. Radiology 214:73–80, 2000.
35. Santambrogio L, Nosotti M, Bellaviti N, et al: CT-guided fine-needle aspiration cytology of solitary pulmonary nodules: A prospective, randomized study of immediate cytologic evaluation. Chest 112:423–425, 1997.
36. Yankelevitz DF, Henschke CI, Koizumi JH, et al: CT-guided transthoracic needle biopsy of small solitary pulmonary nodules. Clin Imaging 21:107–110, 1997.
37. Laurent F, Latrabe V, Vergier B, et al: CT-guided transthoracic needle biopsy of pulmonary nodules smaller than 20 mm: Results with an automated 20-gauge coaxial cutting needle. Clin Radiol 55:281–287, 2000.
38. Tan BB, Flaherty KR, Kazerooni EA, et al: The solitary pulmonary nodule. Chest 123(1 Suppl):89S–96S, 2003.
39. Dickens P, Srivastava G, Loke SL, et al: Human papillomavirus 6, 11, and 16 in laryngeal papillomas. J Pathol 165:243–246, 1991.
40. Smith EM, Pignatari SS, Gray SD, et al: Human papillomavirus infection in papillomas and nondiseased

respiratory sites of patients with recurrent respiratory papillomatosis using the polymerase chain reaction. Arch Otolaryngol Head Neck Surg 119:554–557, 1993.

41. Kramer SS, Wehunt WD, Stocker JT, et al: Pulmonary manifestations of juvenile laryngotracheal papillomatosis. AJR Am J Roentgenol 144:687–694, 1985.

42. Bauman NM, Smith RJ: Recurrent respiratory papillomatosis. Pediatr Clin North Am 43:1385–1401, 1996.

43. Derkay CS, Rimell FL, Thompson JW: Recurrent respiratory papillomatosis. Head Neck 20:418–424, 1998.

44. Healy GB, Gelber RD, Trowbridge AL, et al: Treatment of recurrent respiratory papillomatosis with human leukocyte interferon: Results of a multicenter randomized clinical trial. N Engl J Med 319:401–407, 1988.

45. Armbruster C, Kreuzer A, Vorbach H, et al: Successful treatment of severe respiratory papillomatosis with intravenous cidofovir and interferon alpha-2b. Eur Respir J 17:830–831, 2001.

46. Auborn KJ: Therapy for recurrent respiratory papillomatosis. Antiviral Ther 7:1–9, 2002.

47. Harcourt JP, Worley G, Leighton SE: Cimetidine treatment for recurrent respiratory papillomatosis. Int J Pediatr Otorhinolaryngol 51:109–113, 1999.

48. Harada H, Miura K, Tsutsui Y, et al: Solitary squamous cell papilloma of the lung in a 40-year-old woman with recurrent laryngeal papillomatosis. Pathol Int 50:431–439, 2000.

49. Rady PL, Schnadig VJ, Weiss RL, et al: Malignant transformation of recurrent respiratory papillomatosis associated with integrated human papillomavirus type 11 DNA and mutation of p53. Laryngoscope 108:735–740, 1998.

50. Cook JR, Hill DA, Humphrey PA, et al: Squamous cell carcinoma arising in recurrent respiratory papillomatosis with pulmonary involvement: Emerging common pattern of clinical features and human papillomavirus serotype association. Mod Pathol 13:914–918, 2000.

51. Kotylak TB, Barrie JR, Raymond GS: Answer to Case of the Month #81: Tracheobronchial papillomatosis with spread to pulmonary parenchyma and the development of squamous cell carcinoma. Can Assoc Radiol J 52:126–128, 2001.

52. Lele SM, Pou AM, Ventura K, et al: Molecular events in the progression of recurrent respiratory papillomatosis to carcinoma. Arch Pathol Lab Med 126:1184–1188, 2002.

53. Maxwell RJ, Gibbons JR, O'Hara MD: Solitary squamous papilloma of the bronchus. Thorax 40:68–71, 1985.

54. Carey FA, Salter DM, Kerr KM, et al: An investigation into the role of human papillomavirus in endobronchial papillary squamous tumours. Respir Med 84:445–447, 1990.

55. Haselton PS: Benign lung tumors and their malignant counterparts. In Haselton PS (ed): Spencer's Pathology of the Lung (5th ed). New York: McGraw-Hill, 1996, p 881.

56. Kawaguchi T, Matumura A, Iuchi K, et al: Solitary squamous papilloma of the bronchus associated with human papilloma virus type 11. Intern Med 38:817–819, 1999.

57. Spencer H, Dail DH, Arneaud J: Non-invasive bronchial epithelial papillary tumors. Cancer 45:1486–1497, 1980.

58. England DM, Hochholzer L: Truly benign "bronchial adenoma": Report of 10 cases of mucous gland adenoma with immunohistochemical and ultrastructural findings. Am J Surg Pathol 19:887–899, 1995.

59. Deavers M, Guinee D, Koss MN, et al: Granular cell tumors of the lung: Clinicopathologic study of 20 cases. Am J Surg Pathol 19:627–635, 1995.

60. Husain M, Nguyen GK: Cytopathology of granular-cell tumor of the lung. Diagn Cytopathol 23:294–295, 2000.

61. Scala R, Naldi M, Fabianelli F, et al: Endobronchial granular cell tumour. Monaldi Arch Chest Dis 54:404–406, 1999.

62. Young CD, Gay RM: Multiple endobronchial granular cell myoblastomas discovered at bronchoscopy. Hum Pathol 15:193–194, 1984.

63. Victoria LV, Hoffman HT, Robinson RA: Granular cell tumour of the larynx. J Laryngol Otol 112:373–376, 1998.

64. Liu Z, Mira JL, Vu H: Diagnosis of malignant granular cell tumor by fine needle aspiration cytology. Acta Cytol 45:1011–1021, 2001.

65. Thomas de Montpreville V, Dulmet EM: Granular cell tumours of the lower respiratory tract. Histopathology 27:257–262, 1995.

66. Hosaka T, Suzuki S, Niikawa H, et al: A rare case of a pulmonary granular cell tumor presenting as a coin lesion. Jpn J Thorac Cardiovasc Surg 51:107–109, 2003.

67. Sibala JL: Endobronchial hamartomas. Chest 62:631–634, 1972.

68. Tomashefski JF Jr: Benign endobronchial mesenchymal tumors: Their relationship to parenchymal pulmonary hamartomas. Am J Surg Pathol 6:531–540, 1982.

69. Cosio BG, Villena V, Echave-Sustaeta J, et al: Endobronchial hamartoma. Chest 122:202–205, 2002.

70. Corona FE, Okeson GC: Endobronchial fibroma: An unusual case of segmental atelectasis. Am Rev Respir Dis 110:350–353, 1974.

71. Kiryu T, Kawaguchi S, Matsui E, et al: Multiple chondromatous hamartomas of the lung: A case report and review of the literature with special reference to Carney syndrome (see comment). Cancer 85:2557–2561, 1999.

72. Batori M, Lazzaro M, Lonardo MT, et al: A rare case of pulmonary neurofibroma: Clinical and diagnostic evaluation and surgical treatment. Eur Rev Med Pharmacol Sci 3:155–157, 1999.

73. Gaertner EM, Steinberg DM, Huber M, et al: Pulmonary and mediastinal glomus tumors—report of five cases including a pulmonary glomangiosarcoma: A clinicopathologic study with literature review. Am J Surg Pathol 24:1105–1114, 2000.

74. Buell R, Wang NS, Seemayer TA, et al: Endobronchial plasma cell granuloma (xanthomatous pseudotumor): A light and electron microscopic study. Hum Pathol 7:411–426, 1976.

74a. Devouassoux-Shisheboran M, de la Fouchardiere A, Thivolet-Bejui F, et al: Endobronchial variant of sclerosing hemangioma of the lung: histological and cytological features on endobronchial material. Mod Pathol 17:252–257, 2004.

75. Politis J, Funahashi A, Gehlsen JA, et al: Intrathoracic lipomas: Report of three cases and review of the literature with emphasis on endobronchial lipoma. J Thorac Cardiovasc Surg 77:550–556, 1979.

76. Gaerte SC, Meyer CA, Winer-Muram HT, et al: Fat-containing lesions of the chest. Radiographics 22:S61–S78, 2002.

77. Muraoka M, Oka T, Akamine S, et al: Endobronchial lipoma: Review of 64 cases reported in Japan. Chest 123:293–296, 2003.

78. White SH, Ibrahim NB, Forrester-Wood CP, et al: Leiomyomas of the lower respiratory tract. Thorax 40:306–311, 1985.

79. Gjevre JA, Myers JL, Prakash UB: Pulmonary hamartomas. Mayo Clin Proc 71:14–20, 1996.

80. van den Bosch JM, Wagenaar SS, Corrin B, et al: Mesenchymoma of the lung (so called hamartoma): A

review of 154 parenchymal and endobronchial cases. Thorax 42:790–793, 1987.

81. Basile A, Gregoris A, Antoci B, et al: Malignant change in a benign pulmonary hamartoma. Thorax 44:232–233, 1989.

82. Fletcher JA, Pinkus GS, Weidner N, et al: Lineage-restricted clonality in biphasic solid tumors. Am J Pathol 138:1199–1207, 1991.

83. Kazmierczak B, Meyer-Bolte K, Tran KH, et al: A high frequency of tumors with rearrangements of genes of the HMGI(Y) family in a series of 191 pulmonary chondroid hamartomas. Genes Chromosomes Cancer 26:125–133, 1999.

84. Tallini G, Vanni R, Manfioletti G, et al: HMGI-C and HMGI(Y) immunoreactivity correlates with cytogenetic abnormalities in lipomas, pulmonary chondroid hamartomas, endometrial polyps, and uterine leiomyomas and is compatible with rearrangement of the HMGI-C and HMGI(Y) genes. Lab Invest 80:359–369, 2000.

85. Gabrail NY, Zara BY: Pulmonary hamartoma syndrome (see comment). Chest 97:962–965, 1990.

86. Murray J, Kielkowski D, Leiman G: The prevalence and age distribution of peripheral pulmonary hamartomas in adult males. An autopsy-based study. S Afr Med J 79:247–249, 1991.

87. Potente G, Macori F, Caimi M, et al: Noncalcified pulmonary hamartomas: Computed tomography enhancement patterns with histologic correlation. J Thorac Imaging 14:101–104, 1999.

88. Hamper UM, Khouri NF, Stitik FP, et al: Pulmonary hamartoma: Diagnosis by transthoracic needle-aspiration biopsy. Radiology 155:15–18, 1985.

89. Panos RJ, Chang SW: Diagnosis of pulmonary hamartoma by bronchoscopic transbronchial biopsy. J Natl Med Assoc 81:460–463, 1989.

90. Hansen CP, Holtveg H, Francis D, et al: Pulmonary hamartoma. J Thorac Cardiovasc Surg 104:674–678, 1992.

91. Mark EJ: Mesenchymal cystic hamartoma of the lung. N Engl J Med 315:1255–1259, 1986.

92. Hedlund GL, Bisset GS 3rd, Bove KE: Malignant neoplasms arising in cystic hamartomas of the lung in childhood. Radiology 173:77–79, 1989.

93. Yousem SA, Wick MR, Singh G, et al: So-called sclerosing hemangiomas of lung: An immunohistochemical study supporting a respiratory epithelial origin. Am J Surg Pathol 12:582–590, 1988 [erratum appears in Am J Surg Pathol 13:337, 1989].

94. Illei PB, Rosai J, Klimstra DS: Expression of thyroid transcription factor-1 and other markers in sclerosing hemangioma of the lung. Arch Pathol Lab Med 125:1335–1339, 2001.

95. Nicholson AG, Magkou C, Snead D, et al: Unusual sclerosing haemangiomas and sclerosing haemangioma-like lesions, and the value of TTF-1 in making the diagnosis. Histopathology 41:404–413, 2002.

96. Sugio K, Yokoyama H, Kaneko S, et al: Sclerosing hemangioma of the lung: Radiographic and pathological study. Annals of Thoracic Surgery 53:295–300, 1992.

97. Iyoda A, Baba M, Saitoh H, et al: Imprint cytologic features of pulmonary sclerosing hemangioma: Comparison with well-differentiated papillary adenocarcinoma. Cancer 96:146–149, 2002.

98. Chan AC, Chan JK: Can pulmonary sclerosing haemangioma be accurately diagnosed by intra-operative frozen section? Histopathology 41:392–403, 2002.

99. Shibata R, Mukai M, Okada Y, et al: A case of sclerosing hemangioma of the lung presenting as a gigantic tumor occupying the left thoracic cavity. Virchows Arch 442:409–411, 2003.

100. Lee ST, Lee YC, Hsu CY, et al: Bilateral multiple sclerosing hemangiomas of the lung. Chest 101:572–573, 1992.

101. Hayashi A, Takamori S, Mitsuoka M, et al: Unilateral progressive multiple sclerosing hemangioma in a young female successfully treated by pneumonectomy: Report of a case. Int Surg 87:69–72, 2002.

102. Miyagawa-Hayashino A, Tazelaar HD, Langel DJ, et al: Pulmonary sclerosing hemangioma with lymph node metastases: Report of 4 cases. Arch Pathol Lab Med 127:321–325, 2003.

103. Kim KH, Sul HJ, Kang DY: Sclerosing hemangioma with lymph node metastasis. Yonsei Med J 44:150–154, 2003.

104. Dessy E, Braidotti P, Del Curto B, et al: Peripheral papillary tumor of type-II pneumocytes: A rare neoplasm of undetermined malignant potential. Virchows Arch 436:289–295, 2000.

105. Yousem SA, Hochholzer L: Alveolar adenoma. Hum Pathol 17:1066–1071, 1986.

106. Burke LM, Rush WI, Khoor A, et al: Alveolar adenoma: A histochemical, immunohistochemical, and ultrastructural analysis of 17 cases. Hum Path 30:158–167, 1999.

107. Hirata T, Reshad K, Itoi K, et al: Lipomas of the peripheral lung—a case report and review of the literature. Thorac Cardiovasc Surg 37:385–387, 1989.

108. Guermazi A, El Khoury M, Perret F, et al: Unusual presentations of thoracic tumors. Case 3: Parenchymal lipoma of the lung. J Clin Oncol 19:3784–3786, 2001.

109. Mathew J, Sen S, Chandi SM, et al: Pulmonary lipoblastoma: A case report. Pediatr Surg Int 17:543–544, 2001.

110. Cavazza A, Rossi G, Paci M, et al: Primary leiomyoma of the lung, with clear-cell features and admixed alveolar spaces: Description of a case presenting with pneumothorax (in Italian). Pathologica 95:108–114, 2003.

111. Bozkurt AK: Schwannoma as a cause of Pancoast's syndrome. Intern Med J 32:108–109, 2002.

112. Unger PD, Geller GA, Anderson PJ: Pulmonary lesions in a patient with neurofibromatosis. Arch Pathol Lab Med 108:654–657, 1984.

113. Margaritora S, Galetta D, Cesario A, et al: Giant neurofibroma of the chest wall. Eur J Cardiothorac Surg 21:339, 2002.

114. Flynn SD, Yousem SA: Pulmonary meningiomas: A report of two cases. Hum Pathol 22:469–474, 1991.

115. Falleni M, Roz E, Dessy E, et al: Primary intrathoracic meningioma: Histopathological, immunohistochemical and ultrastructural study of two cases. Virchows Arch 439:196–200, 2001.

116. Gomez-Aracil V, Mayayo E, Alvira R, et al: Fine needle aspiration cytology of primary pulmonary meningioma associated with minute meningotheliallike nodules: Report of a case with histologic, immunohistochemical and ultrastructural studies. Acta Cytol 46:899–903, 2002.

117. Comin CE, Caldarella A, Novelli L, et al: Primary pulmonary meningioma: Report of a case and review of the literature. Tumori 89:102–105, 2003.

118. Viguera JL, Pujol JL, Reboiras SD, et al: Fibrous histiocytoma of the lung. Thorax 31:475–479, 1976.

119. Iqbal M, Rossoff LJ, Kahn L, et al: Intrathoracic desmoid tumor mimicking primary lung neoplasm. Ann Thorac Surg 71:1698–1700, 2001.

120. Anonymous: Case records of the Massachusetts General Hospital. Weekly clinicopathological exercises. Case 18-2000: A 45-year-old woman with a thoracic mass and

Pancoast's syndrome. N Engl J Med 342:1814–1821, 2000.

121. Andrion A, Mazzucco G, Gugliotta P, et al: Benign clear cell (sugar) tumor of the lung: A light microscopic, histochemical, and ultrastructural study with a review of the literature. Cancer 56:2657–2663, 1985.

122. Gaffey MJ, Mills SE, Askin FB, et al: Clear cell tumor of the lung: A clinicopathologic, immunohistochemical, and ultrastructural study of eight cases (see comment). Am J Surg Pathol 14:248–259, 1990.

123. Govender D, Sabaratnam RM, Essa AS: Clear cell "sugar" tumor of the breast: Another extrapulmonary site and review of the literature. Am J Surg Pathol 26:670–675, 2002.

124. Groeger AM, Baldi A, Caputi M, et al: Intrapulmonary teratoma associated with thymic tissue. Anticancer Res 20:3919–3922, 2000.

125. Asano S, Hoshikawa Y, Yamane Y, et al: An intrapulmonary teratoma associated with bronchiectasia containing various kinds of primordium: A case report and review of the literature. Virchows Arch 436:384–388, 2000.

126. Morgan DE, Sanders C, McElvein RB, et al: Intrapulmonary teratoma: A case report and review of the literature. J Thorac Imaging 7:70–77, 1992.

127. Yilmaz A, Bayramgurler B, Aksoy F, et al: Pulmonary glomus tumour: A case initially diagnosed as carcinoid tumour. Respirology 7:369–371, 2002.

128. Spencer H: The pulmonary plasma cell/histiocytoma complex. Histopathology 8:903–916, 1984.

129. Cerfolio RJ, Allen MS, Nascimento AG, et al: Inflammatory pseudotumors of the lung (see comment). Ann Thorac Surg 67:933–936, 1999.

130. Bahadori M, Liebow AA: Plasma cell granulomas of the lung. Cancer 31:191–208, 1973.

131. Mandelbaum I, Brashear RE, Hull MT: Surgical treatment and course of pulmonary pseudotumor (plasma cell granuloma). J Thorac Cardiovasc Surg 82:77–82, 1981.

132. Copin MC, Gosselin BH, Ribet ME: Plasma cell granuloma of the lung: Difficulties in diagnosis and prognosis. Ann Thorac Surg 61:1477–1482, 1996.

133. Engleman P, Liebow AA, Gmelich J, et al: Pulmonary hyalinizing granuloma. Am Rev Respir Dis 115:997–1008, 1977.

134. Yousem SA, Hochholzer L: Pulmonary hyalinizing granuloma. Am J Clin Pathol 87:1–6, 1987.

135. Gans SJ, van der Elst AM, Straks W: Pulmonary hyalinizing granuloma. Eur Respir J 1:389–391, 1988.

136. Chalaoui J, Gregoire P, Sylvestre J, et al: Pulmonary hyalinizing granuloma: A cause of pulmonary nodules. Radiology 152:23–26, 1984.

137. Ren Y, Raitz EN, Lee KR, et al: Pulmonary small lymphocytic lymphoma (mucosa-associated lymphoid tissue type) associated with pulmonary hyalinizing granuloma. Chest 120:1027–1030, 2001.

138. Pinckard JK, Rosenbluth DB, Patel K, et al: Pulmonary hyalinizing granuloma associated with *Aspergillus* infection. Int J Surg Pathol 11:39–42, 2003.

139. Atagi S, Sakatani M, Akira M, et al: Pulmonary hyalinizing granuloma with Castleman's disease. Intern Med 33:689–691, 1994.

140. John PG, Rahman J, Payne CB: Pulmonary hyalinizing granuloma: An unusual association with multiple sclerosis. South Med J 88:1076–1077, 1995.

141. Joseph J, Sahn SA: Thoracic endometriosis syndrome: New observations from an analysis of 110 cases. Am J Med 100:164–170, 1996.

142. Lillington GA, Mitchell SP, Wood GA: Catamenial pneumothorax. JAMA 219:1328–1332, 1972.

143. Koss MN: Pulmonary lymphoid disorders. Semin Diagn Pathol 12:158–171, 1995.

144. Colby TV: Lymphoproliferative diseases. *In* Dail DH, Hammar SP (eds): Pulmonary Pathology (2nd ed). New York: Springer-Verlag, 1994, pp 1097–1122.

145. King TE Jr, Christopher KL, Schwarz MI: Multiple pulmonary chondromatous hamartomas. Hum Pathol 13:496–497, 1982.

146. Joshi K, Shankar SK, Gopinath N, et al: Multiple sclerosing haemangiomas of the lung. Postgrad Med J 56:50–53, 1980.

147. Lawson LM, Tiwari P, Filipenko JD: An unusual cause of an incidental lung mass. Can Respir J 10:276–277, 2003.

148. Esteban JM, Allen WM, Schaerf RH: Benign metastasizing leiomyoma of the uterus: Histologic and immunohistochemical characterization of primary and metastatic lesions. Arch Pathol Lab Med 123:960–962, 1999.

149. Tietze L, Gunther K, Horbe A, et al: Benign metastasizing leiomyoma: A cytogenetically balanced but clonal disease. Hum Pathol 31:126–128, 2000.

150. Nistal M, Hardisson D, Riestra ML: Multiple pulmonary leiomyomatous hamartomas associated with a bronchogenic cyst in a man. Arch Pathol Lab Med 127:e194–e196, 2003.

151. Abramson S, Gilkeson RC, Goldstein JD, et al: Benign metastasizing leiomyoma: Clinical, imaging, and pathologic correlation. AJR Am J Roentgenol 176:1409–1413, 2001.

152. Maredia R, Snyder BJ, Harvey LA, et al: Benign metastasizing leiomyoma in the lung. Radiographics 18:779–782, 1998.

153. Horstmann JP, Pietra GG, Harman JA, et al: Spontaneous regression of pulmonary leiomyomas during pregnancy. Cancer 39:314–321, 1977.

154. Arai T, Yasuda Y, Takaya T, et al: Natural decrease of benign metastasizing leiomyoma (see comment). Chest 117:921–922, 2000.

155. Carney JA: Gastric stromal sarcoma, pulmonary chondroma, and extra-adrenal paraganglioma (Carney triad): Natural history, adrenocortical component, and possible familial occurrence (see comment). Mayo Clinic Proc 74:543–552, 1999.

156. Scopsi L, Collini P, Muscolino G: A new observation of the Carney's triad with long follow-up period and additional tumors. Cancer Detect Prevent 23:435–443, 1999.

157. Valverde K, Henderson M, Smith CR, et al: Typical and atypical Carney's triad presenting with malignant hypertension and papilledema. J Pediatr Hematol Oncol 23:519–524, 2001.

158. Dajee A, Dajee H, Hinrichs S, et al: Pulmonary chondroma, extra-adrenal paraganglioma, and gastric leiomyosarcoma: Carney's triad. J Thorac Cardiovasc Surg 84:377–381, 1982.

159. Chahinian AP, Kirschner PA, Dikman SH, et al: Pulmonary metastatic leiomyosarcoma coexisting with pulmonary chondroma in Carney's triad. Arch Intern Med 143:1462–1464, 1983.

160. Convery RP, Grainger AJ, Bhatnagar NK, et al: Lung abscess complicating chondromas in Carney's syndrome. Eur Respir J 11:1409–1411, 1998.

161. Churg A, Warnock ML: Pulmonary tumorlet: A form of peripheral carcinoid. Cancer 37:1469–1477, 1976.

162. Miller MA, Mark GJ, Kanarek D: Multiple peripheral pulmonary carcinoids and tumorlets of carcinoid type, with restrictive and obstructive lung disease. Am J Med 65:373–378, 1978.

163. Colby TV, Wistuba II, Gazdar A: Precursors to pulmonary neoplasia. Adv Anat Pathol 5:205–215, 1998.

164. Arioglu E, Doppman J, Gomes M, et al: Cushing's syndrome caused by corticotropin secretion by pulmonary tumorlets. N Engl J Med 339:883–886, 1998.

165. Liew SH, Leong AS, Tang HM: Tracheal paraganglioma: A case report with review of the literature. Cancer 47:1387–1393, 1981.

166. Singh G, Lee RE, Brooks DH: Primary pulmonary paraganglioma: Report of a case and review of the literature. Cancer 40:2286–2289, 1977.

167. Chow SN, Seear M, Anderson R, et al: Multiple pulmonary chemodectomas in a child: Results of four different therapeutic regimens. J Pediatr Hematol Oncol 20:583–586, 1998.

168. Min KW: Diagnostic usefulness of sustentacular cells in paragangliomas: Immunocytochemical and ultrastructural investigation. Ultrastruct Pathol 22:369–376, 1998.

169. Churg AM, Warnock ML: So-called "minute pulmonary chemodectoma": A tumor not related to paragangliomas. Cancer 37:1759–1769, 1976.

170. Gaffey MJ, Mills SE, Askin FB: Minute pulmonary meningothelial-like nodules: A clinicopathologic study of so-called minute pulmonary chemodectoma. Am J Surg Pathol 12:167–175, 1988.

171. Niho S, Yokose T, Nishiwaki Y, et al: Immunohistochemical and clonal analysis of minute pulmonary meningothelial-like nodules. Hum Pathol 30:425–429, 1999.

172. Spinelli M, Claren R, Colombi R, et al: Primary pulmonary meningioma may arise from meningothelial-like nodules. Adv Clin Pathol Offic J Adriatic Soc Pathol 4:35–39, 2000.

173. Abrahams NA, Colby TV, Pearl RH, et al: Pulmonary hemangiomas of infancy and childhood: Report of two cases and review of the literature. Pediatr Dev Pathol 5:283–292, 2002.

174. Anonymous: Case records of the Massachusetts General Hospital. Weekly clinicopathological exercises. Case 38-2000: A 45-year-old woman with exertional dyspnea, hemoptysis, and pulmonary nodules. N Engl J Med 343:1788–1796, 2000.

175. Takiguchi Y, Uruma T, Hiroshima K, et al: Stable pulmonary capillary haemangiomatosis without symptomatic pulmonary hypertension. Thorax 56:815–817, 2001.

176. Anonymous: Case records of the Massachusetts General Hospital. Weekly clinicopathological exercises. Case 32-1999: A 44-year-old man with tracheal narrowing and respiratory stridor. N Engl J Med 341:1292–1299, 1999.

177. Leske V, Lazor R, Coetmeur D, et al: Tracheobronchopathia osteochondroplastica: A study of 41 patients. Medicine (Baltimore) 80:378–390, 2001.

178. Hantous-Zannad S, Sebai L, Zidi A, et al: Tracheobronchopathia osteochondroplastica presenting as a respiratory insufficiency: Diagnosis by bronchoscopy and MRI. Eur J Radiol 45:113–116, 2003.

179. Corsello BF, Lohaus GH, Funahashi A: Endobronchial mass lesion due to sarcoidosis: Complete resolution with corticosteroids. Thorax 38:157–158, 1983.

180. Chen KT: Amyloidosis presenting in the respiratory tract. Pathol Annu 24(Pt 1):253–273, 1989.

181. Yoshida T, Obara A, Yamauchi K, et al: Three cases of primary pulmonary amyloidosis. Intern Med 37:687–690, 1998.

182. Prince JS, Duhamel DR, Levin DL, et al: Nonneoplastic lesions of the tracheobronchial wall: Radiologic findings with bronchoscopic correlation. Radiographics 22:S215–S230, 2002.

183. Karasick D, Karasick S, Lally JF: Mucoid pseudotumors of the tracheobronchial tree in two cases. AJR Am J Roentgenol 132:459–460, 1979.

184. Westra D, Verbeeten B Jr: Some anatomical variants and pitfalls in computed tomography of the trachea and mainstem bronchi. I. Mucoid pseudotumors. Diagn Imaging Clin Med 54:229–239, 1985.

185. Cordier JF, Loire R, Brune J: Amyloidosis of the lower respiratory tract: Clinical and pathologic features in a series of 21 patients. Chest 90:827–831, 1986.

186. Mollers MJ, van Schaik JP, van der Putte SC: Pulmonary amyloidoma: Histologic proof yielded by transthoracic coaxial fine needle biopsy. Chest 102:1597–1598, 1992.

187. Slanetz PJ, Whitman GJ, Shepard JA, et al: Nodular pulmonary amyloidosis. AJR Am J Roentgenol 163:296, 1994.

188. O'Donovan PB, Schenk M, Lim K, et al: Evaluation of the reliability of computed tomographic criteria used in the diagnosis of round atelectasis. J Thorac Imaging 12:54–58, 1997.

189. Laurent F, Philippe JC, Vergier B, et al: Exogenous lipoid pneumonia: HRCT, MR, and pathologic findings. Eur Radiol 9:1190–1196, 1999.

190. Anonymous: Case records of the Massachusetts General Hospital. Weekly clinicopathological exercises. Case 33-1999: A 57-year-old woman with a pulmonary mass. N Engl J Med 341:1379–1385, 1999.

191. Ryu JH, Swensen SJ: Cystic and cavitary lung diseases: Focal and diffuse. Mayo Clin Proc 78:744–752, 2003.

192. Blennerhassett JB, Borrie J, Lichter I, et al: Localized pulmonary Wegener's granuloma simulating lung cancer: Report of four cases. Thorax 31:576–584, 1976.

193. Ward S, Heyneman LE, Flint JD, et al: Bronchocentric granulomatosis: Computed tomographic findings in five patients. Clin Radiol 55:296–300, 2000.

194. Haus BM, Stark P, Shofer SL, et al: Massive pulmonary pseudotumor. Chest 124:758–760, 2003.

195. Millard CE: Vanishing or phantom tumor of the lung: Localized interlobular effusion in congestive heart failure. Chest 59:675–677, 1971.

196. Miller JI, Harrison EG Jr, Bernatz PE: Surgically treated unsuspected pulmonary infarction. Ann Thorac Surg 14:181–188, 1972.

197. Louie S, Corbett MG, Lillington GA: Pseudo-pseudo-pseudotumor of the lung. Chest 88:470–471, 1985.

48 Pulmonary Thr

Peter F. Fedullo, M.

at least 10% of these episodes le
embolism; and that as many as 10
embolism—or 50,000—die each
majority of these deaths do
peutic failure. With the e
present with hemodyn
rates approach 20%
death is uncomm
firmed and ap
deaths rela
prevent
to m
f

INTRODUCTION

The one generalization about venous thromboembolism that is free from controversy is that many aspects of this disorder remain controversial. There are multiple reasons why venous thromboembolism continues to engender lively debate. Perhaps the major reason, notwithstanding the substantial advances that have been made over the past decade, is that a number of fundamental questions continue to exist regarding the pathogenesis, clinical presentation, diagnosis, and therapy of the disease.

Venous thromboembolism represents a potentially fatal disease process with a clinical presentation that is often silent or nonspecific and for which a wide range of diagnostic techniques is available, many with technical and interpretive limitations. Although estimates vary widely, the best available information suggests that at least 5 million episodes of venous thrombosis occur annually in the United States; that

...d to a pulmonary ...% of those who suffer ...year.[1,2] The overwhelming ...ot appear to arise from thera- ...ception of patients who initially ...mic impairment, in whom mortality ...to 30%, embolic recurrence is rare and ...on once the diagnosis of embolism is con- ...propriate therapy initiated.[3,4] The majority of ...ed to embolism appear to arise from a failure to ...the disease in patients at risk of it and from a failure ...ake the diagnosis in those afflicted.[1] The incidence of ...al pulmonary embolism appears to have declined over the past several decades.[5,6] However, a substantial number of patients remain at risk as a result of the demographics of an aging population and the ability of modern medicine to treat patients with chronic disease.

Contributing to the debate surrounding venous thromboembolism is the involvement of a wide range of medical disciplines in its prevention, diagnosis, and management. Thrombosis is not a discrete subspecialty. The problem of venous thromboembolism involves pulmonologists, cardiologists, hematologists, internists, specialists in vascular disease, radiologists, a range of surgical subspecialists, obstetricians, and others. Because specific prophylactic, diagnostic, and therapeutic strategies within one discipline may not necessarily be applicable to another, a perception of coherence in the clinical approach to this disease process often appears to be lacking.

During the past decade, many of the long-standing controversies surrounding the natural history, diagnosis, and therapy of venous thromboembolism have been partially or completely reconciled, resulting in substantial changes in the diagnostic and therapeutic approach to the disease. The persistence of a number of unresolved issues, and the emergence of still others, should not be a cause for clinical cynicism. In the approach to the patient with suspected venous thromboembolism, an understanding of what is unknown can prove invaluable to the decision-making process.

PATHOGENESIS AND RISK FACTORS

The triad of venous stasis, alterations in coagulation, and vascular injury identified by Virchow in 1856 as primary factors in the pathogenesis of venous thromboembolism has been supported by a considerable amount of clinical and experimental evidence. Over the past several decades, inherited and acquired abnormalities of the coagulation and fibrinolytic system, including isolated deficiencies of antithrombin III, protein C, protein S, and plasminogen as well as the presence of a lupus anticoagulant, had been described and their association with venous thromboembolism confirmed (Table 48.1).[7] Novel pathogenetic mechanisms capable of shifting the hemostatic balance toward thrombosis have been described in specific populations with an inherited predisposition to venous thromboembolic events. The term *thrombophilia* was conceived to describe familial or acquired disorders of the hemostatic mechanism that are likely to predispose to thrombosis.

The most common of these inherited predispositions, first described in 1993 by Dahlback and designated *factor V*

Table 48.1 Thromboembolic Risk Factors

Hereditary Thrombophilias
Protein C deficiency
Protein S deficiency
Antithrombin III deficiency
Factor V Leiden mutation
Prothrombin 20210 G → A variation
Hyperhomocysteinemia
Dysfibrinogenemia
Familial plasminogen deficiency

Acquired Surgical Predispositions
Major thoracic, abdominal, or neurosurgical procedures requiring general anesthesia and lasting > 30 min
Hip arthroplasty
Knee arthroplasty
Knee arthroscopy
Hip fracture
Major trauma
Open prostatectomy
Spinal cord injury

Acquired Medical Predispositions
Prior venous thromboembolism
Advanced age (particularly > 60 yr)
Malignancy
Congestive heart failure
Cerebrovascular accident
Nephrotic syndrome
Estrogen therapy
Pregnancy and the postpartum period
Obesity
Prolonged immobilization
Antiphospholipid antibody syndrome
Lupus anticoagulant
Inflammatory bowel disease
Paroxysmal nocturnal hemoglobinuria
Behçet's syndrome

Leiden mutation, is the consequence of a single point mutation on the factor V gene (adenine for guanine) resulting in activated factor V (factor Va) with diminished sensitivity to the natural anticoagulant effect of activated protein C.[8] Approximately 5% of whites in Europe and North America are heterozygous for this genetic defect; lower rates of carrier frequency have been reported among Native American, African, and Asian populations.[9,10] Although initially detected in as many as 60% of *selected* patients with venous thromboembolism, subsequent studies have detected the mutation in 10% to 20% of unselected patients.[11,12] The heterozygous state carries a 5- to 10-fold increase in lifetime risk for venous thromboembolism, whereas the risk among patients homozygous for this mutation may be increased 80-fold.[13] Factor V Leiden mutation appears to be an important risk factor for venous thromboembolism during pregnancy, in the postpartum period, and during oral contraceptive use.[14] Compared with women who do not use oral contraceptives and are not carriers of the factor V mutation, the risk of thrombosis among those with both risk factors is increased approximately 30-fold.[15]

A sequence variation in the prothrombin gene (20210G → A) was described in 1996 and is estimated to occur in approximately 2% to 4% of the population.[12,16] This mutation results in an overproduction of prothrombin, which is otherwise normal. It is associated with a three- to fourfold increased risk of lower extremity venous thrombosis and appears to act in a synergistic manner with other forms of thrombophilia in increasing both the initial and recurrent thrombosis risk.[17]

Hyperhomocyst(e)inemia has also been identified as a potential independent predisposition to venous thromboembolism. Elevation of plasma homocysteine levels may be the result of genetic abnormalities, nutritional deficiencies of vitamins (B_6, B_{12}, folate), clinical disorders (renal insufficiency, hypothyroidism, inflammatory bowel disease), or a combination of the three. Although retrospective case-control studies demonstrate an association between hyperhomocyst(e)inemia and venous thromboembolism, the results of prospective studies have not been uniform.[18,19]

The identification of these risk factors, and the likelihood that others exist, raise the possibility that screening to determine relative thromboembolic risk may be feasible in the future. However, a consensus for such an approach does not exist at the present time. Despite its prevalence in the general population, screening for factor V Leiden mutation is not advised because most patients with this abnormality will never suffer a thromboembolic event. Furthermore, the absence of this abnormality should not influence the decision to provide prophylaxis to patients at clinical risk. However, given that certain populations appear to be at considerably higher risk of thromboembolic recurrence and that prolonged anticoagulation can diminish the risk of recurrence, general recommendations for screening would include patients with a history of recurrent venous thromboembolism or with a confirmed family history of thromboembolism, a first episode of thromboembolism at an early age, spontaneous venous thrombosis, thromboses in unusual anatomic sites, arterial thrombosis, and thromboembolism associated with pregnancy or estrogen use. Whether screening should be performed prior to the initiation of oral contraceptive agents remains a matter of debate.[20,21] The relative risk of venous thromboembolism is increased approximately fourfold in users of oral contraceptives, although the increase in absolute risk is modest.[22] A policy of routine screening would deny effective contraception to a substantial number of women while preventing only a small number of deaths due to pulmonary emboli.

In most patients, even those with an identified thrombophilic state, some clinical condition associated with venous stasis, intimal injury, or both serves as the basis for the thromboembolic event.[23] Recent trials have also confirmed that the risk of venous thromboembolism in hospitalized patients is not limited to patients undergoing surgical procedures. Thromboembolic risk in patients admitted with a wide range of acute medical problems is comparable to that seen in surgical patients.[24]

Major risk factors include pelvic or lower extremity fractures, hip and knee surgery, a past history of venous thromboembolism, acute paralytic stroke or spinal injury, major traumatic injury, open prostatectomy, and abdominal or pelvic surgery for malignant disease. Other factors that enhance risk include prolonged general anesthesia, advancing age, cardiac disease, pregnancy, the postpartum period, the use of estrogen-containing compounds, malignancy, the presence of a lupus anticoagulant or antiphospholipid antibody, and prolonged immobilization.[25] It is important to recognize that these risk factors may be multiplicative.[23] Thromboembolic risk in an otherwise healthy 45-year-old individual undergoing an elective cholecystectomy is considerably less than the risk experienced by an obese 75-year-old with a history of prior venous thromboembolism undergoing the same procedure. Similarly, the patient with hip fracture or hip replacement has, by virtue of that condition alone, a 60% to 70% risk of deep venous thrombosis and a 2% to 4% risk of experiencing a fatal thromboembolic event in the absence of preventive measures. Add other risk factors, and the incidence of deep venous thrombosis—and the likelihood of a fatal complication—will be even higher. These considerations allow the development of a reasonable "risk profile" in an individual patient, a profile that should influence the use and intensity of prophylactic intervention.

NATURAL HISTORY: DEEP VENOUS THROMBOSIS

The natural history of deep venous thrombosis is now reasonably well understood.[26] Venous thrombi appear to originate either in the vicinity of a venous valve cusp, where eddy currents arise, or at the site of intimal injury. Platelet aggregation and release of mediators initiate the sequence. With local accumulation of such factors, the coagulation cascade is activated and a red fibrin thrombus develops. As thrombus extension occurs, local fibrinolytic activity is enhanced. Thus, thrombus behavior becomes a dynamic process that may result in complete dissolution, partial resolution resulting in a variable degree of intimal narrowing and valvular damage, progressive proximal extension, or embolization. If significant obstruction persists, collateral veins develop.

Extensive autopsy and clinical studies have established that some 90% of pulmonary emboli that elicit clinical attention arise from venous thrombosis in the deep veins of the lower extremities.[27] Venous thrombi capable of embolization can arise from other sites. Primary iliac or proximal femoral thrombi may develop in patients undergoing surgery involving the hip, and pelvic vein thrombosis can occur in patients undergoing pelvic or prostatic surgery. Axillosubclavian vein thrombosis may be spontaneous, resulting from congenital abnormalities of the thoracic outlet, or may be related to indwelling central venous catheters, pulmonary artery catheters, or transvenous pacing wires.[28] In patients with dilated right heart chambers or pulmonary arteries, thrombi can form at those sites and embolize distally into the branches of the pulmonary artery.

Available information also indicates that the likelihood of embolism is influenced by the location of thrombi in the veins of the lower extremity. Although the majority of thrombi form in the veins of the calf, it has been clearly demonstrated that thrombi limited to the calf veins rarely are associated with embolism.[29] However, approximately 25% of symptomatic, isolated calf thrombi when left untreated will extend to involve the proximal veins. Proximal extension into the thigh (popliteal and ileofemoral systems) poses a risk of embolization that approaches 50%.[30,31] This difference in natural history between calf-limited and proximal thrombi has several important diagnostic and therapeutic implications. First, because the vast majority of emboli arise from veins in the lower extremity, diagnostic approaches to deep venous thrombosis can be focused upon techniques that detect lower extremity thrombosis. Second, techniques that detect above-knee thrombi are of particular value whether or not they can detect calf-limited thrombi. Finally, although it is true that calf-limited thrombi rarely embolize, many have incorrectly concluded from this information that *symptomatic*, calf-limited deep venous thrombosis represents a clinically irrelevant condition. It must be emphasized that proximal extension of calf-limited thrombi may occur. Furthermore, symptomatic calf vein thrombosis appears to be subject to recurrence, albeit at a lower risk than proximal vein thrombosis.[32]

Although most above-knee thrombi represent extensions from calf thrombi, some do arise in the larger, proximal veins de novo. This occurrence appears to be restricted principally to patients with hip fracture or replacement, pelvic surgery (including prostatic resection), and other high inguinal-pelvic trauma.

At any time during this process, a portion or all of the thrombus can detach as an embolus. This risk is highest early in thrombus development before significant fibrinolysis or organization occurs. Beyond this acute phase, the long-term outlook is influenced principally by the extent of residual venous obstruction and valvular damage. If significant obstruction or valvular damage persists, downstream stasis will be present, leading to a risk of recurrent deep venous thrombosis and development of the post-phlebitic syndrome.[33]

NATURAL HISTORY: PULMONARY EMBOLISM

Pulmonary embolism is not a disease per se. It is merely a complication of venous thrombosis. Nonetheless, once it occurs, embolism can induce a series of pulmonary and cardiac effects.[34]

The pulmonary and gas-exchange consequences of embolism can be several. First, if regional pulmonary vascular obstruction is total, alveolar dead space is created. Second, with total obstruction, bronchoconstriction may occur in the lung distal to the area of obstruction as the result of alveolar hypocapnia.[35] This is probably uncommon in patients because they are free to inhale carbon dioxide–rich dead space air into the associated lung regions, and because obstruction is rarely total. Third, hyperventilation almost always occurs, the mechanism for which remains uncertain. Fourth, some degree of arterial hypoxemia often occurs.[36] One common cause of arterial hypoxemia is widening of the arteriovenous oxygen difference resulting from an acute increase in right ventricular afterload and an ensuing decline in cardiac output.[37,38] This lowering of the mixed venous oxygen content magnifies the effects of the normal venous admixture, thereby lowering the arterial PO_2. Another potential mechanism for hypoxemia is ventilation-perfusion mismatch or right-to-left shunt, either on an intrapulmonary or an intracardiac basis.[39] With embolic occlusion sufficient to increase pulmonary artery pressure, hypoxic vasoconstrictive mechanisms can be overcome, and perfusion to poorly ventilated or nonventilated lung regions may occur. On occasion, embolic events massive enough to

increase right atrial pressure may result in intracardiac right-to-left shunting through a patent foramen ovale. The final mechanism for hypoxemia relates to the fifth pulmonary consequence of embolism, loss of pulmonary surfactant.[40] Unlike the first four consequences, loss of surfactant does not occur immediately. It requires approximately 24 hours of total occlusion and lack of blood flow to develop. At that time or later, surfactant becomes depleted in the obstructed alveolar zones, resulting in atelectasis and edema. If partial thrombus resolution and reperfusion to this atelectatic region develop, hypoxemia can result.

One uncommon local consequence of pulmonary embolism is pulmonary infarction. Infarction is uncommon because the pulmonary parenchyma has three potential sources of oxygen: the pulmonary arteries, the bronchial arteries, and the airways.[41] Two of these three sources apparently must be compromised before infarction develops. Therefore, in a patient with no coexisting cardiopulmonary disease, infarction is rare. Infarction occurs in approximately 20% of patients with significant cardiac or pulmonary disease that compromises either bronchial arterial flow or airway patency. In patients with left ventricular failure, increased pulmonary venous pressure may decrease bronchial flow and infarction may result.[42]

The cardiac and hemodynamic effects of embolism are related to three factors: the degree of reduction of the cross-sectional area of the pulmonary vascular bed, the preexisting status of the cardiopulmonary system, and the physiologic consequences of both hypoxic and neurohumorally mediated vasoconstriction.[34,43–46] Obstruction of the pulmonary vascular bed by embolism acutely increases the workload on the right ventricle, a chamber ill equipped to deal with high pressure load. In patients without preexisting cardiopulmonary disease, obstruction of less than 20% of the pulmonary vascular bed results in a number of compensatory events that minimize adverse hemodynamic consequences. Recruitment and distention of pulmonary vessels occur, resulting in a normal or near-normal pulmonary artery pressure and pulmonary vascular resistance; cardiac output is maintained by increases in the right ventricular stroke volume and increases in the heart rate. As the degree of pulmonary vascular obstruction exceeds 30% to 40%, increases in pulmonary artery pressure and modest increases in right atrial pressure occur. The Frank-Starling mechanism maintains right ventricular stroke work and cardiac output. When the degree of pulmonary artery obstruction exceeds 50% to 60%, compensatory mechanisms are overcome, cardiac output begins to fall, and right atrial pressure increases dramatically. With acute obstruction beyond this amount, the right heart dilates, right ventricular wall tension increases, right ventricular ischemia may develop, the cardiac output falls, and systemic hypotension develops. In patients without prior cardiopulmonary disease, the maximal mean pulmonary artery pressure capable of being generated by the right ventricle appears to be 40 mm Hg (representing a pulmonary artery systolic pressure of approximately 70 mm Hg). The correlation between the extent of pulmonary vascular obstruction and the pulmonary vascular resistance appears to be hyperbolic, reflecting at its lower end the expansible nature of the pulmonary vascular bed and at its upper the precipitous decline in cardiac output that may occur as the right ventricle fails.[47]

The hemodynamic response to acute pulmonary embolism in patients with preexisting cardiopulmonary disease may be considerably different.[43] Unlike patients without prior cardiopulmonary disease, in whom there is a general relationship between the degree of pulmonary vascular obstruction and the level of the pulmonary artery pressure, patients with prior cardiopulmonary disease demonstrate degrees of pulmonary hypertension that are disproportionate to the degree of pulmonary vascular obstruction. As a result, severe pulmonary hypertension may develop in response to a relatively small reduction in pulmonary artery cross-sectional area. Thus, evidence of right ventricular hypertrophy (rather than right ventricular dilation) associated with a mean pulmonary artery pressure in excess of 40 mm Hg (pulmonary artery systolic pressure in excess of approximately 70 mm Hg) in a patient suspected of embolism should suggest an element of chronic pulmonary hypertension resulting from a potentially diverse group of etiologic possibilities (chronic thromboembolic pulmonary hypertension, left ventricular failure, valvular disease, right-to-left cardiac shunts, etc.).

Beyond the acute embolic event, the behavior of emboli parallels that previously described for venous thrombi; that is, they undergo resolution by fibrinolysis, by organization and recanalization, or both. The most rapid resolution of a large embolus that has been documented is 51 hours.[48] Other reports indicate that resolution is substantial during the first week and continues for 4 to 8 weeks.[49,50] The term *resolution* is used here because it is uncertain, in humans, to what degree lysis (versus organization) participates in embolic resolution. Most sequential data regarding resolution in humans are based on perfusion scan, not angiographic data. However, these data suggest that residual anatomic defects are common following embolism and, contrary to prior opinion, that complete restoration of pulmonary blood flow represents the exception rather than the rule.[51] In terms of hemodynamic resolution, it would appear that a stable pulmonary artery pressure is reached within 6 weeks.[52] How often anatomic and mild hemodynamic residuals persist is not known. What is known is that residual obstruction sufficient to cause pulmonary hypertension is rare. The clinical course and management of this small group of patients is dealt with later in this chapter.

CLINICAL PRESENTATION

The most common symptoms and physical findings of venous thrombosis include swelling, pain, erythema, and warmth. "Classic" findings such as *Homan's sign* (calf pain with flexion of the knee and dorsiflexion of the ankle), *Moses' sign* (pain with calf compression against the tibia), or a palpable cord occur infrequently and are nonspecific.

Multiple investigations have established that the clinical diagnosis of venous thrombosis is imprecise.[27,53-55] In patients with clinical signs and symptoms suggestive of venous thrombosis, 60% to 80% will not have the diagnosis established by objective testing. Furthermore, and even more disquieting, the majority of high-risk patients who are monitored and who develop deep venous thrombosis will not have signs or symptoms suggesting that diagnosis.[56] Algorithmic clinical models incorporating risk factors, symptoms, and physical signs have been demonstrated to have the ability to stratify *symptomatic* patients into risk categories, although not to a level in which clinical diagnosis, in the absence of objective testing, can be relied on exclusively to either confirm or exclude the diagnosis.[55] The differential diagnosis of deep venous thrombosis is extensive and includes cellulitis, arthritis, muscular injury or tear, neuropathy, arterial insufficiency, lymphedema, ruptured Baker's cyst, superficial thrombophlebitis, and chronic venous insufficiency.

Multiple investigations have confirmed that the diagnosis of pulmonary embolism also cannot be confirmed or excluded solely on clinical grounds.[57-59] However, recognition of the clinical signs and symptoms associated with embolism is valuable because clinical findings and clinical suspicion represent an essential first step in the diagnostic pathway. Although a somewhat arbitrary classification because presenting symptoms and signs of embolism frequently overlap, the presentation of pulmonary embolism can be categorized into one of three clinical syndromes: (1) isolated dyspnea; (2) pleuritic pain or hemoptysis; and (3) circulatory collapse.[60] Among patients without prior cardiopulmonary disease in the Prospective Investigation of Pulmonary Embolism Diagnosis (PIOPED) study, the syndrome of pleuritic pain or hemoptysis was the most common mode of presentation, occurring in approximately 60% of patients; isolated dyspnea occurred in approximately 25% and circulatory collapse occurred in 10%.

The most common presenting symptom of acute embolism is the sudden onset of dyspnea.[59-61] In various studies, this has occurred in the majority of patients. However, it must be emphasized that in PIOPED dyspnea was not present in 27% of patients ultimately proven to have embolism. Pleuritic chest pain was present in 66% of patients, whereas hemoptysis (15%) was uncommon. Other symptoms occurring in less than 50% of patients included cough (37%), leg swelling (28%), and leg pain (26%). A sense of impending doom also is reported, particularly with massive embolism. Angina also can occur with massive embolism, representing, in this circumstance, right ventricular ischemia. Syncope also may be a presenting complaint in major embolic occlusion.

The most common physical finding is unexplained tachypnea (respiratory rate ≥ 20 minute). In PIOPED, however, tachypnea was not present in approximately 30% of patients with embolism. Clinical findings noted less frequently include crackles (55%), tachycardia (30%), and an increased pulmonic component of the second heart sound (23%). Fever may develop some hours after the event and often reaches but rarely exceeds 38.3°C. As noted previously, hemoptysis may be observed; it usually is quite modest in extent, although it persists for some days. Brisk hemoptysis is rare and almost never the initial finding. With massive embolism, there may be evidence of right ventricular overload or failure, such as a right ventricular tap along the left sternal border and an accentuated pulmonary valve closure sound. If right ventricular failure occurs, there may be narrowed or fixed splitting of S_2, an S_3 and/or S_4, distended neck veins, and cyanosis. Careful examination of the legs may elicit evidence suggesting venous thrombosis. In PIOPED, clinically apparent venous thrombosis was found in only 15% of patients.

Obviously, these symptoms and signs are nonspecific. In the PIOPED study, none of the presenting symptoms was capable of discriminating between those patients with positive angiograms and those in whom the angiographic findings were negative.[60,61] Also, in terms of presenting signs, only the presence of crackles, a fourth heart sound, and an increased pulmonic component of the second heart sound could differentiate between those with positive and negative angiograms.[60,61] Furthermore, in patients with underlying cardiopulmonary disease, the presenting symptoms and signs frequently may be obscured by elements of the patient's underlying illness.[58] It is also important to recognize that the clinical presentation of embolism has been characterized in trials composed of symptomatic patients. Prospective studies of high-risk patients have established that asymptomatic emboli occur in some 40% or more of patients with proximal deep venous thrombosis.[57,62] It is likely that the frequency and severity of symptoms are influenced by the extent of embolic occlusion and the prior cardiopulmonary status of the patient. Small- or moderate-sized emboli may induce few or no symptoms in an otherwise normal individual. In patients with preexisting cardiopulmonary disease, symptoms are more common and severe.

Due to the nonspecific presentation of pulmonary embolism, the differential diagnosis is varied and extensive, especially in hospitalized patients with coexisting cardiac or pulmonary disease. Common considerations include congestive heart failure, exacerbation of chronic lung disease, postoperative atelectasis, and viral pleurisy. Emboli presenting with fever, dyspnea, and chest radiographic abnormalities easily can be confused with a bacterial pneumonia. The presence of fever and leukocytosis (rarely exceeding 15,000/μL) are uncommon but well-described accompaniments of venous thromboembolism.[63,64]

These precautionary statements regarding clinical diagnosis are not meant to suggest that the clinical presentation of venous thrombosis or pulmonary embolism cannot be used as a basis for clinical decision making. However, they are meant as a reminder that the clinical presentation of venous thromboembolism may often be atypical or subtle and should serve only to generate a suspicion of that diagnosis. A reliance on signs and symptoms that are considered "classic" prior to making the decision to proceed to confirmatory testing will ultimately lead to underdiagnosis and unnecessary mortality.

DIAGNOSIS OF VENOUS THROMBOSIS

The proper diagnostic approach to venous thromboembolism must take into account the central fact that venous thrombosis and pulmonary embolism are manifestations of the same disease process: venous thrombosis representing the source of pulmonary embolism, and pulmonary embolism representing a complication of venous thrombosis. To regard venous thrombosis and pulmonary embolism as separate diagnostic entities not only is inappropriate but also can lead to serious errors in management.

CONTRAST VENOGRAPHY

In validating any test, there must be a "gold standard." In the case of lower extremity venous thrombosis, that standard is contrast venography (Fig. 48.1). In investigative

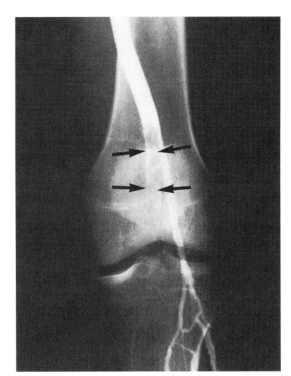

Figure 48.1 Contrast venogram disclosing a large filling defect (*arrows*) due to thrombus in the popliteal and distal superficial femoral veins. Such thrombi pose substantial embolic risk.

contexts, it is a good gold standard (as indicated later, however, that often is not the case in clinical contexts). The venogram is performed according to a specific protocol described by Rabinov and Paulin in 1972.[65] The most reliable criterion for the diagnosis of venous thrombosis is a constant intraluminal filling defect evident in two or more views. Other criteria such as nonvisualization of deep veins, venous collaterals, or nonconstant filling defects are less reliable. Under circumstances in which the proper protocol and interpretative criteria are utilized, contrast venography has high sensitivity and specificity. However, the study is not without shortcomings. As those who have seen many venograms recognize, the study is not easy to interpret, especially in patients with a prior history of venous thrombosis. Venous cannulation may often be difficult, especially in the presence of edema; expert interpretation is essential for accurate diagnosis; injection of contrast material with its associated allergic and nephropathic risks is necessary; venous thrombosis may be induced by the procedure itself; and the cost, invasive nature, and discomfort of the study make sequential studies impractical.

Due to these limitations, a number of noninvasive studies capable of being performed on a sequential basis were introduced into clinical practice. At the present time, the two most commonly validated noninvasive techniques are duplex ultrasonography and impedance plethysmography (IPG). Magnetic resonance imaging and computed tomography (CT) have proven capable of detecting thrombi, but their widespread utilization has been limited by cost, limited access, and, in the case of CT, the need for contrast administration.

DUPLEX ULTRASONOGRAPHY

Over the past decade, duplex ultrasonography, which refers to the combination of Doppler venous flow detection and real-time B-mode imaging, has assumed a central role in the noninvasive diagnosis of symptomatic lower extremity deep venous thrombosis.[66] A number of criteria are used to diagnose venous thrombosis, the most reliable of which is noncompressibility of a venous segment (Fig. 48.2). Secondary, less reliable criteria include the presence of echogenic material within the venous lumen, venous distention, and loss of phasicity, response to Valsalva's maneuver, and augmentation of spontaneous flow. The absence of an echogenic luminal mass cannot be considered useful in excluding the diagnosis of venous thrombosis because acute thrombus may not demonstrate echogenicity. Multiple studies over the past decade have demonstrated sensitivities and specificities exceeding 95% in *symptomatic* patients with proximal venous thrombosis. Although simplified compression examinations limited to the symptomatic leg or to the common femoral and popliteal veins (rather than the entire lower extremity venous system) have been suggested, the time saved with such approaches is limited, and a number of isolated superficial femoral vein or calf-limited thrombi may be overlooked.[67,68] Asymptomatic thrombi in the contralateral leg can be detected in approximately 5% to 10% of patients presenting with symptomatic acute venous thrombosis.[69,70] Although the detection of asymptomatic, contralateral thrombi has little impact on the immediate management of the patient, it may have long-term consequences when recurrence is suspected. A more prudent approach appears to be a complete examination extending from the inguinal ligament to the popliteal vein and examination of the contralateral extremity if thrombus is detected in the symptomatic leg.

Duplex ultrasonography is less accurate in the detection of symptomatic calf-limited thrombi (sensitivity approximately 70%) and in asymptomatic proximal vein thrombi (sensitivity approximately 50%), thereby limiting its utility as a screening study in high-risk populations.[71] When ultrasonography is negative in patients with suspected venous thrombosis, a strategy of serial testing has proven to be effective in detecting proximal extension.[72]

IMPEDANCE PLETHYSMOGRAPHY

IPG, an indirect technique that measures the rate of venous outflow, has been well standardized and carefully validated against contrast venography.[73] False-positive studies may result from conditions that diminish arterial inflow (congestive heart failure, shock, peripheral arterial disease) or that impede venous return (right ventricular failure, obstructive lung disease), thereby lowering the specificity of the technique. Early studies reported sensitivities of approximately 90% in symptomatic patients with proximal venous thrombosis.[73] Calf thrombi are detected in approximately 25%, a figure that reflects the lesser degree of venous obstruction in most (though not all) calf thrombi.

Recent studies of IPG accuracy have raised questions regarding the ability of IPG to detect even symptomatic proximal vein thrombosis. Reported sensitivities in these studies have been in the range of 65% to 75%.[74,75] The low sensitivity of IPG in these studies may result from its use in patients with less severe symptoms because these patients are more likely to have small, nonocclusive, or distal thrombi that IPG cannot readily detect. Supporting this premise is that fact that IPG sensitivity returns to 85% to 90% when more extensive thrombi and those that have extended into the distal superficial femoral vein are evaluated. These data support the current recommendation that a single negative IPG study should not be used to exclude venous thrombosis in a symptomatic patient. However, a strategy of serial IPG testing has been demonstrated to be useful in detecting proximal extension.[72,76] Although this strategy has proven effective, confirmatory testing with duplex ultrasonography or venography may be necessary when IPG results conflict with clinical impression, especially in patients with limited cardiopulmonary reserve, in whom embolism would be tolerated poorly.[77]

The detection of possible recurrent venous thrombosis represents a diagnostic challenge for which IPG may play a role.[78] The resolution rate for IPG-documented venous thrombosis at 6 months has been found to be 85% and at 12 months to be 95%. Therefore, reversion of IPG results from normal to abnormal in a symptomatic patient with suspected recurrent venous thrombosis provides strong evidence that recurrence has occurred. However, the utility of such an approach mandates that follow-up IPG be performed and that IPG normalization has been documented in an individual patient.

MAGNETIC RESONANCE IMAGING

Magnetic resonance imaging techniques for detecting venous thrombosis include spin-echo magnetic resonance,

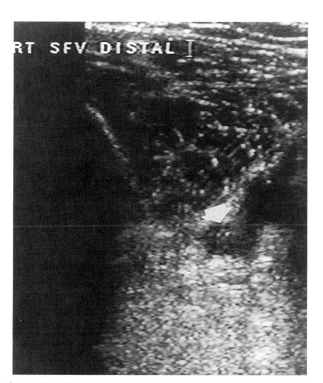

Figure 48.2 Duplex ultrasonography demonstrating a noncompressible distal superficial femoral vein containing an echogenic mass (*arrow*), consistent with venous thrombosis.

gradient-recalled-echo magnetic resonance, and magnetic resonance venography. Preliminary reports suggest that magnetic resonance imaging is at least as sensitive and specific as duplex ultrasonography.[79,80] A potential advantage of magnetic resonance imaging is that the entire length of the venous system, including the pelvic veins, can be evaluated. Disadvantages associated with magnetic resonance imaging include cost and limited access as well as the expertise required to properly perform and interpret the studies.

COMPUTED TOMOGRAPHY

The role of CT as a stand-alone test for venous thrombosis is limited. The sensitive and specificity of CT venography are comparable to ultrasonography but mandate contrast injection with its associated risks and radiation exposure. Potential advantages of CT venography include the ability to visualize the pelvic veins and vena cava. A diagnostic approach combining CT venography with CT pulmonary angiography may have a role in patients undergoing evaluation for pulmonary embolism.[81]

HEMOSTASEOLOGIC ASSAYS

The development of a rapid and accurate blood test capable of diagnosing venous thromboembolism has held special appeal and has been the subject of considerable investigative interest. A number of different serologic markers have been investigated, including D-dimer, fibrin monomer, prothrombin fragment, thrombin–antithrombin III complex, fibrinopeptide B, and fibronectin. Of these, D-dimer, alone and in combination with other noninvasive studies, has been subject to the most rigorous clinical evaluation.[82,83] D-dimer testing has proven to be highly sensitive but not specific; that is, elevated levels are present in nearly all patients with thromboembolism but also occur in a wide range of circumstances, including advancing age, pregnancy, trauma, infections, the postoperative period, inflammatory states, and malignancy. Therefore, the role of D-dimer testing is limited to one of thromboembolic exclusion. Multiple assays have been developed with sensitivities that range from 80% to almost 100%.[82,83] Highly sensitive assays such as the enzyme-linked immunosorbent assay are capable of excluding thromboembolism but are associated with such a high frequency of false-positive results as to limit their clinical utility. Less sensitive assays (e.g., latex agglutination, red cell agglutination) lack the ability to exclude thromboembolism in isolation but have been used successfully in combination with either a clinical probability estimate or a noninvasive diagnostic study. Although potentially of substantial value in diagnostic pathways, the burgeoning selection of available assays, variations in sensitivity and specificity related to the type of assay, a range of discriminate values for positivity, and lack of standardization have limited generalized application of the technique due to uncertainty among clinicians regarding the predictive value of the test they are utilizing. D-dimer testing has been utilized successfully as part of a number of different diagnostic strategies, and negative results of standardized, highly sensitive assays have proven capable of safely excluding venous thrombosis in outpatients presenting with a low or intermediate clinical likelihood of the disease.[84,85]

CLINICAL PREDICTION RULES

A major advance in the diagnostic approach to both venous thrombosis and pulmonary embolism has been a transition from a technique-oriented approach to one that utilizes bayesian analysis. In doing so, the pretest probability of the disease, calculated independently of a particular test result either through empirical means or through a standardized prediction rule, is evaluated in combination with a test's likelihood ratio (derived from the sensitivity and specificity of that test) to create a posttest probability of the disease. This posttest probability can then be utilized as a basis for clinical judgment, either excluding the disease with a certain level of probability, confirming the disease with a certain level of probability, or supporting the need for additional diagnostic testing. This approach to diagnosis has proved especially useful in an era of noninvasive testing in which results are often presented as probabilities rather than as discrete answers.

Several clinical prediction rules for venous thrombosis have been developed and validated.[86] The Wells rule, initially described in 1995 and revised in 1997 to include nine clinical features, proved capable of stratifying patients with suspected venous thrombosis into three probability categories—low, moderate, and high—in which the incidence of venous thrombosis approximates 3%, 17%, and 75%, respectively.[87] By utilizing this prediction rule in combination with lower extremity ultrasonography, the diagnosis of venous thrombosis can be safely excluded in patients with a low clinical likelihood of venous thrombosis in combination with a negative lower extremity ultrasound and confirmed in patients with a high clinical probability and a positive lower extremity ultrasound. Such an approach dramatically reduces the need for contrast venography or serial lower extremity ultrasound studies.

The Wells prediction rule was subsequently revised in 2003 to include 10 clinical characteristics capable of stratifying outpatients into clinically likely and clinically unlikely categories (Table 48.2). For outpatients falling into the clinically unlikely category, deep venous thrombosis was reliably excluded when the result of a sensitive D-dimer assay was negative, thereby limiting the need for ultrasound evaluation.[85] The ability to exclude venous thrombosis in outpatients using a clinical prediction rule and negative results of a D-dimer assay has been confirmed in other studies.[88] It should be emphasized that clinical prediction rules constructed and validated in outpatients should be viewed critically before they are applied to an inpatient population.

DIAGNOSIS OF PULMONARY EMBOLISM

There are certain parallels between the approaches to the diagnosis of pulmonary embolism and deep venous thrombosis. Perhaps the most important parallels are that clinical evidence in isolation, although capable of raising the suspicion of the disease, cannot be relied upon to confirm or exclude the diagnosis, and that the use of clinical prediction rules in combination with noninvasive testing can substantially decrease the need for invasive diagnostic testing.

Table 48.2 Wells Clinical Model for Predicting the Pretest Probability of Deep Venous Thrombosis

Clinical Characteristic	Score
Active cancer (patient receiving treatment for cancer within the previous 6 months or currently receiving palliative treatment)	1
Paralysis, paresis, or recent plaster immobilization of the lower extremities	1
Recently bedridden for 3 days or more, or major surgery within the previous 12 weeks requiring general or regional anesthesia	1
Localized tenderness along the distribution of the deep venous system	1
Entire leg swollen	1
Calf swelling at least 3 cm larger than that on the asymptomatic side (measured 10 cm below tibial tuberosity)	1
Pitting edema confined to the symptomatic leg	1
Collateral superficial veins (nonvaricose)	1
Previously documented deep venous thrombosis	1
Alternate diagnosis at least as likely as deep venous thrombosis	−2

Score	Clinical Assessment Probability
<2 points	Unlikely
2 or greater points	Likely

From Wells PS, Anderson DR, Rodger M, et al: Evaluation of D-dimer in the diagnosis of suspected deep vein thrombosis. N Engl J Med 349:1227–1235, 2003.

STANDARD LABORATORY EVALUATION

Routine laboratory studies cannot make the diagnosis of pulmonary embolism. Although none has the discriminatory power to confirm the diagnosis of embolism, they do provide valuable adjunctive information, provide support for therapeutic interventions, and may confirm the presence of an alternative diagnosis.

The majority of patients with pulmonary embolism have abnormal chest radiographs.[89] However, these abnormalities are usually subtle, nonspecific, and therefore nondiagnostic (Fig. 48.3). In the PIOPED study, the most common radiographic abnormalities were atelectasis and pulmonary infiltrates. There is some confusion about the diagnostic configuration of infiltrates due to embolism. Although usually abutting a pleural surface, these infiltrates can be of any shape, not necessarily wedge-shaped. Although pleural effusions occur in almost half of the patients, the majority of effusions are small and involve only blunting of the costophrenic angle.[90] Findings once considered specific for embolism, such as the *Westermark sign* (focal areas of avascularity), the *Hampton hump* (pleural-based, wedge-shaped density), and the *Fleischner sign* (prominence of the central pulmonary artery), have not proven to have discriminatory value. In a patient with hypoxemia or pulmonary complaints, a normal chest radiograph may be quite useful in raising the index of suspicion of embolism and by excluding confounding diagnostic options. The major roles of chest radiography in suspected pulmonary embolism, therefore, are to exclude competing diagnoses and, if ventilation-perfusion scanning is anticipated, to evaluate the pulmonary parenchyma.

Likewise, electrocardiographic findings in pulmonary embolism, although occurring frequently, are diverse and nonspecific.[91] The most common abnormalities include nonspecific tachycardia, T-wave inversion, and abnormalities of the ST segment. With more extensive occlusion, the electrocardiogram may reveal an "$S_1Q_3T_3$" pattern, a pseudoinfarction pattern (Qr in V_1), a complete or

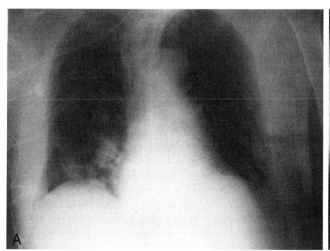
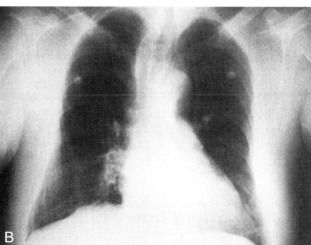

Figure 48.3 Chest radiographs in a patient with pulmonary embolism. **A,** Infiltrates caused by atelectasis with edema in the right lower lobe and in the retrocardiac area in a patient with angiographically confirmed pulmonary embolus. **B,** Two weeks later, the infiltrates have cleared.

incomplete right bundle-branch block, or right axis deviation.[92] Rhythm disturbances other than sinus tachycardia are uncommon and usually confined to patients with underlying cardiac disease.

Arterial blood gas analysis is helpful, although not definitive.[93] Arterial hypoxemia may be present, and the more massive the obstruction, the more severe the hypoxemia is likely to be. However, many other conditions also cause hypoxemia, and embolism often does not cause hypoxemia or even a widening of the alveolar-arterial PO_2 difference. Hypocapnia usually is present with embolism; hypercapnia, on the other hand, is rare. Hypercapnia appears with embolism only in patients with marked antecedent ventilatory limitation or when such limitation has been imposed because the patient is on controlled mechanical ventilation when embolism occurs.

ECHOCARDIOGRAPHY

Echocardiography may serve a valuable role in the diagnostic approach to pulmonary embolism. Under appropriate clinical circumstances, the detection of unexplained right ventricular volume or pressure overload should suggest the possibility of embolism and lead to confirmatory testing. A distinct echocardiographic pattern involving akinesia of the mid-free right ventricular wall with apical sparing has been described.[94] Properly performed *transesophageal* echocardiography has demonstrated sensitivity and specificity exceeding 90% in the detection of proximal emboli involving the pulmonary trunk and the right and left main pulmonary arteries.[95] Transesophageal echocardiography also has proven valuable in the evaluation of competing diagnostic possibilities such as right ventricular infarction, endocarditis, pericardial tamponade, and aortic dissection in patients with unexplained shock and evidence of elevated central venous pressure. The overall sensitivity

of *transthoracic* echocardiography in pulmonary embolism approximates 50%.[96] Therefore, it cannot be considered a primary diagnostic technique. Consideration can be given to its use in that subset of patients with suspected massive pulmonary embolism who are too ill for transportation or who have an absolute contraindication to the administration of a contrast agent.

More recently, echocardiography has been investigated along with other techniques as a means of stratifying risk in patients with embolism. Short-term mortality risk in pulmonary embolism is strongly related to the presence of systemic hypotension at the time of diagnosis. However, systemic hypotension represents a late and potentially fatal manifestation of right ventricular dysfunction. For this reason, transthoracic echocardiography and biochemical markers such as serum troponin or serum brain natriuretic hormone levels have been investigated as a means of evaluating right ventricular function in patients with embolism.[97–99] Preliminary studies have suggested that these techniques are capable of identifying patients with a good prognosis and may identify a subset of patients who are at risk for adverse events, including death. However, it has not been conclusively established that the potential risks of a more aggressive therapeutic approach in all such patients in the latter group, the majority of whom have a satisfactory outcome when treated with conventional therapy alone, justifies the potential benefit.[100]

VENTILATION-PERFUSION SCANNING

Despite limitations, ventilation-perfusion lung scanning is valuable if interpreted appropriately.[61] First, a negative study rules out the diagnosis of pulmonary embolism with the same degree of certainty as a negative pulmonary angiogram (Fig. 48.4) and with a higher degree of certainty than is achieved by a negative CT scan. Second, the PIOPED study

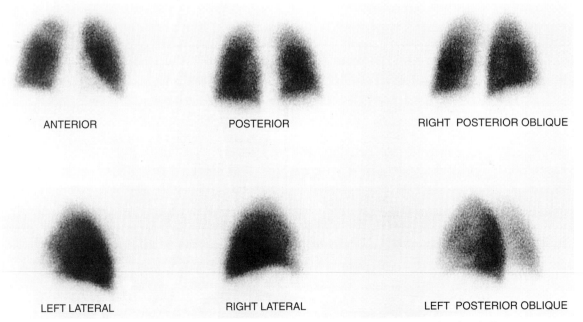

ANTERIOR   POSTERIOR   RIGHT POSTERIOR OBLIQUE

LEFT LATERAL   RIGHT LATERAL   LEFT POSTERIOR OBLIQUE

Figure 48.4 Normal six-view lung perfusion scan. This finding is capable of excluding the diagnosis of embolism.

demonstrated that a "high-probability" study (one characterized by multiple, segmental-sized, mismatched defects) is associated with embolism in approximately 87% of patients; when coupled with a high clinical probability of embolism, the positive predictive value increased to 96% (Fig. 48.5). However, the PIOPED data also provided several pieces of disquieting information: (1) the overwhelming majority of patients with suspected embolism did not have scan findings that fell into a high-probability or normal category, the only categories that can be considered definitive; (2) the majority of patients with embolism did not have a high-probability scan finding; (3) the overwhelming majority of patients without embolism did not have a normal scan; and (4) a substantial and clinically significant percentage of patients with scan findings interpreted as intermediate probability (33%) and low probability (16%) were subsequently demonstrated to have angiographic evidence of embolism.[61] It is essential that clinicians recognize that the concept of a low-probability scan is misleading and potentially dangerous because of the frequency of pulmonary embolism in patients exhibiting this scan pattern.[101]

In order to improve perfusion scan specificity, traditional interpretive criteria, including the PIOPED criteria, rely on the number and size of the perfusion defects as well as on the results of a concurrent ventilation image. The intended basis for doing so is to differentiate pulmonary vascular obstruction ("mismatched" defects) from primary parenchymal disorders that result in compensatory pulmonary vasoconstriction ("matched" defects). The Prospective Investigative Study of Acute Pulmonary Embolism Diagnosis (PISA-PED) investigators utilized a fundamentally different interpretive scheme that relied on the shape of the perfusion defects regardless of their number or size or their association with ventilation findings.[102] The results of this study suggest that embolism can be diagnosed

accurately and the need for angiography limited by perfusion results combined with an assessment of clinical likelihood in the absence of ventilation imaging. An analysis of a subset of patients from the PIOPED study came to a similar conclusion.[103]

The diagnostic approach to pulmonary embolism in patients with underlying chronic obstructive pulmonary disease remains especially problematic because the presentation of pulmonary embolism in this population may closely mimic an exacerbation of their underlying disease. Unfortunately, the value of ventilation-perfusion scanning in this population is even more limited than that in the general population in that an even higher proportion of scans fall into an indeterminate category.[104] However, among the few patients with high-probability or normal/near-normal scan findings, both the positive predictive value and negative predictive value were equivalent to that in the general population.

SPIRAL (HELICAL) COMPUTED TOMOGRAPHY

CT has represented a major advance in pulmonary embolism diagnosis. Unlike ventilation-perfusion scanning, it provides the ability to directly visualize emboli as well as to detect parenchymal abnormalities that may support the diagnosis of embolism or provide an alternative basis for the patient's complaints (Fig. 48.6). The reported sensitivity of helical CT scanning for embolism has ranged from 57% to 100%, with a specificity ranging from 78% to 100%.[105] Factors responsible for this wide divergence relate to the proximal extent of vascular obstruction that can be detected and, in part, to advances in CT technology that allow higher resolution, dramatically faster scanning times, more peripheral visualization, and less motion artifact than that provided by earlier generation scanners. Sensitivity and specificity of CT scanning for emboli involving the main and lobar pulmonary arteries exceeds 95%. Vascular involvement confined to segmental or subsegmental pulmonary vessels is associated with a decline in both sensitivity and specificity. In a recent series, the sensitivity of CT scanning for subsegmental arteries reported by two readers ranged between

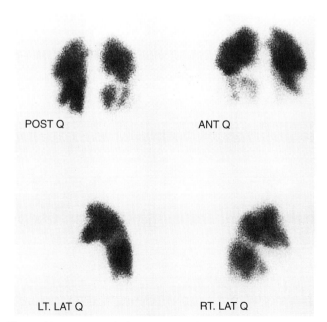

POST Q

ANT Q

LT. LAT Q

RT. LAT Q

Figure 48.5 Lung perfusion (Q) scan shows major segmental and lobar defects bilaterally. Ventilation scan and chest radiograph were normal. This pattern is strongly associated with the presence of embolism.

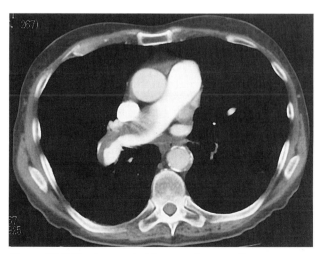

Figure 48.6 Chest computed tomography scanning demonstrating extensive embolization involving the right main, upper lobe, and lower lobe pulmonary arteries.

71% and 84% even after nonevaluable scans were excluded.[106] Isolated involvement of the subsegmental pulmonary arteries is not unusual and in various series has been demonstrated to occur in up to 30% of patients.[107,108] These findings suggest that filling defects consistent with embolism involving the main or lobar pulmonary arteries can be considered diagnostic of embolism. Defects involving the segmental and subsegmental arteries can be considered suggestive of embolism but should be supported by additional objective data. The absence of detectable filling defects reduces the likelihood of embolism but appears incapable of excluding the possibility with the same degree of certainty as a negative ventilation-perfusion scan. However, outcome studies have demonstrated that withholding anticoagulant therapy in patients with a negative CT scan coupled with a negative lower extremity ultrasound study is a safe strategy except in those patients who present with a high clinical likelihood of embolism.[109,110]

LOWER EXTREMITY VENOUS EVALUATION

Because the majority of pulmonary emboli arise from the deep veins of the lower extremities, the detection of lower extremity proximal vein thrombosis in a patient suspected of embolism, although not confirming that embolism has occurred, is strongly suggestive of that diagnosis and has an equivalent therapeutic implication. Positive ultrasound findings without symptoms or signs referable to the lower extremities should be interpreted judiciously.[111] Ultrasonography has been reported to be positive in approximately 10% to 20% of patients with suspected embolism and in 50% of patients with proven embolism.[112] Therefore, a negative ultrasound finding cannot exclude the diagnosis. CT venography as an adjunct to helical CT scanning has been investigated, and preliminary results suggest that it is capable of detecting femoropopliteal thrombosis with the same accuracy as duplex ultrasonography while also detecting pelvic and abdominal thrombosis.[81] Technical issues such as amount of contrast, image thickness, image interval, interpretive criteria, and time of scanning in relationship to contrast injection remain under investigation.

D-DIMER TESTING

The utility of D-dimer testing in pulmonary embolism diagnostic pathways is limited by the same shortfalls as those encountered in venous thrombosis pathways: that is, a low specificity that makes it most useful as an exclusionary technique in outpatients and a lack of standardization. However, studies have demonstrated that a normal D-dimer result can safely exclude embolism in patients with a low clinical probability of disease. Although preliminary data suggest that a highly sensitive assay is capable of excluding embolism at all levels of clinical probability, these results require confirmation.[113,114]

PULMONARY ANGIOGRAPHY

The studies reviewed to date are capable of excluding or confirming the diagnosis of embolism in the majority of patients with suspected embolism. Angiography should be considered in patients in whom the diagnosis has not been con-

firmed or excluded using noninvasive techniques and when it is considered unsafe to withhold anticoagulation; when cardiopulmonary instability is present; and when the results of diagnostic testing are at such odds with the clinical impression as to warrant the risk of the procedure. Like contrast venography, however, pulmonary angiography has a number of limitations as a gold standard. First, the procedure is invasive and not without risk, especially in patients with acute right ventricular failure. However, recent experience has demonstrated that the perception of risk associated with angiography outweighs the actual risk.[115] Pulmonary angiography can be performed quite safely if certain safeguards are observed and experienced personnel are involved.

Even though the risk of angiography should be nominal, the procedure has other limitations. One is accessibility: Angiography must be performed in a special facility to which the patient must be transported. In some institutions, the logistic problems involved are modest; in others they are substantial. The other limitation is interpretation. The interpretation of pulmonary angiograms is heavily influenced by three factors: the location of the thromboembolic obstruction, the quality of the images, and the experience of the interpreters. Only two angiographic findings are diagnostic of acute embolism: the filling defect and abrupt cutoff of a vessel (Fig. 48.7). Technical adequacy of the

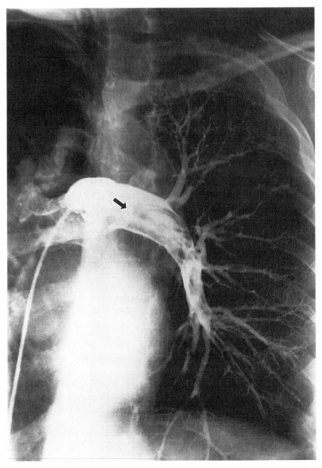

Figure 48.7 Left-sided pulmonary angiogram showing extensive filling defects within the left pulmonary artery (*arrows*) and the upper lobe, lingula, and lower lobe arteries consistent with the diagnosis of pulmonary embolism.

angiogram is critical to accurate identification of both. Flow artifacts can falsely suggest a filling defect. It is essential that good vessel opacification be obtained and that the filling defects be identified as real on a sequence of films.

Although concern about risk should not deter pulmonary angiography, there are noteworthy limitations on its performance and value. Still, it is a rather odd commentary on medical thinking that few would advise against performance of a coronary angiogram in a patient with coronary thrombosis or ischemia because of risk, yet the question of risk often deters pulmonary angiography in a patient in whom embolism is suspected. Given that the case-fatality rate of undiagnosed and untreated embolism exceeds that of myocardial infarction, it is not clear why this disparity exists; and it should not exist, given equal competence in the performance and interpretation of these two procedures.

CLINICAL PREDICTION RULES

A major advance in the diagnostic approach to embolism, as it has been in the diagnostic approach to venous thrombosis, has been the development of clinical prediction rules. A number of standardized prediction rules have been evaluated and published that range widely in their complexity. Simple, standardized prediction rules (Table 48.3) involve information that can be easily acquired even in an outpatient setting or the emergency room.[116,117] Complicated prediction rules involve an increased number of clinical variables and require expert interpretation of radiographic and electrocardiographic data.[118] Although probability assessments, whether empirical or standardized, are incapable of confirming or excluding the likelihood of pulmonary embolism with a clinically acceptable degree of certainty,

they have proven capable of stratifying patients into probability categories. By combining this derived clinical probability with the results of a noninvasive diagnostic technique, diagnostic accuracy in terms of both the confirmation and exclusion of embolism can be increased well beyond that achieved by the use of either clinical probability or the noninvasive diagnostic technique alone, and can substantially limit the number of patients who require pulmonary angiography.

In summary, an almost bewildering array of diagnostic techniques are available for patients with suspected venous thromboembolism. What the clinician at the bedside must understand and accept is that multiple approaches are possible and that a stepwise diagnostic strategy, rather than any single diagnostic technique, may be necessary to confirm or exclude the diagnosis (Fig. 48.8). Furthermore, the clinician must understand that these steps are essential and potentially lifesaving. Withholding anticoagulation in a patient who has suffered an embolic event places that patient at risk for recurrent, potentially lethal events; instituting empirical anticoagulant therapy in a patient who has not suffered an embolic event will involve unnecessary hospitalization and therapy, places the patient at risk for hemorrhagic complications, and establishes a "preexisting" condition that may adversely affect future health care costs. Finally, the clinician must understand that the use of a clinical prediction rule derived from an outpatient population might have a very different predictive value when applied to an inpatient population.

Many strategies to confirm or exclude the diagnosis of pulmonary embolism have been investigated.[117,118] Because the initiating point for the diagnostic pathway begins with clinical suspicion, the following discussion centers about that approach. Also, given substantial variations in practice that currently exist, strategies that incorporate ventilation-perfusion scanning or helical CT as the initial objective diagnostic technique are considered.

In patients in whom the clinical suspicion of embolism is considered high (greater than approximately 70% likelihood), a positive helical CT scan or a high-probability ventilation-perfusion scan result would be considered diagnostic of embolism with greater than 95 percent certainty, whereas a negative perfusion scan would exclude the diagnosis. In all other patients (non–high-probability ventilation/perfusion scan or negative CT scan), lower extremity evaluation should be undertaken. A positive study would confirm the diagnosis. In the remaining patients, several strategies are possible. Serial lower extremity evaluations could be performed. Although not confirming the absence of embolism, negative results would suggest that the likelihood of recurrence is small. Alternatively, pulmonary angiography could be performed. This latter approach is especially applicable to patients with preexisting cardiopulmonary disease, in whom the consequences of recurrence could be catastrophic.

In patients in whom the clinical suspicion of embolism is considered low (less than approximately 10% likelihood), a positive helical CT scan would be considered diagnostic of embolism and a negative perfusion scan would exclude the diagnosis. In the remaining patients, lower extremity evaluation should be undertaken. A positive study would confirm the diagnosis. For those in whom CT scanning represented the initial diagnostic procedure, outcome data

Table 48.3 Wells Clinical Model for Predicting the Pretest Probability of Pulmonary Embolism

Variable	Points Assigned
Clinical signs and symptoms of deep venous thrombosis	3.0
An alternative diagnosis is less likely than pulmonary embolism	3.0
Heart rate >100 beats/min	1.5
Immobilization or surgery in the previous 4 weeks	1.5
Previous deep venous thrombosis or pulmonary embolism	1.5
Hemoptysis	1.0
Malignancy (on treatment, treated in the last 6 months, or palliative)	1.0

Score	Clinical Assessment Probability
<2 points	Low probability
2–6 points	Intermediate probability
>6 points	High probability

From Kearon C: Diagnosis of pulmonary embolism. CMAJ 168:183–194, 2003.

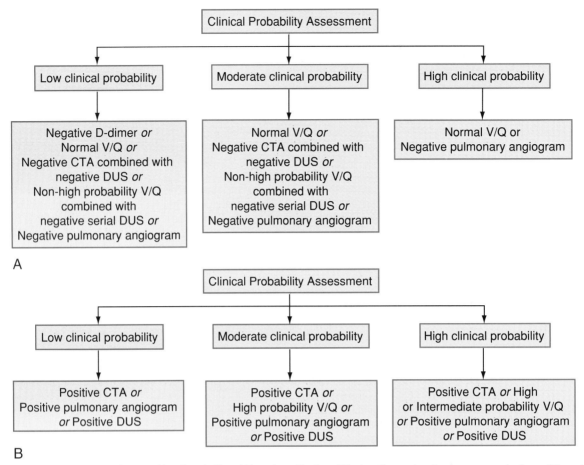

Figure 48.8 Diagnostic strategies capable of excluding **(A)** and confirming **(B)** the diagnosis of pulmonary embolism. CTA, spiral computed tomographic angiography; DUS, Doppler ultrasound; V/Q, ventilation-perfusion scan.

have demonstrated that withholding anticoagulant therapy is safe when the clinical probability of embolism is considered low and results of CT scanning and lower extremity ultrasonography are negative. For those in whom ventilation-perfusion scanning represented the initial diagnostic procedure, a low- or intermediate-probability scan result in combination with a negative lower extremity ultrasound study is sufficient to withhold anticoagulation; a high-probability scan result should be followed by additional diagnostic testing (pulmonary angiography, CT, or sequential lower extremity testing). The utility of D-dimer determinations in hospitalized patients is limited by a lack of specificity. However, a negative D-dimer result has been proven capable of safely excluding embolism in outpatients with a low probability of embolism.[113,114,119]

In patients in whom the clinical suspicion of embolism is considered moderate (approximately 10% to 70% likelihood), a high-probability ventilation-perfusion scan or a positive helical CT scan would be considered diagnostic of embolism, whereas a negative perfusion scan would exclude the diagnosis. In the remaining patients, lower extremity evaluation should be undertaken. For those in whom CT scanning represented the initial diagnostic procedure, outcome data have demonstrated that withholding of anticoagulant therapy is safe when the clinical probability of embolism is considered moderate and results of CT scanning and lower extremity ultrasonography are negative. For

those in whom ventilation-perfusion scanning represented the initial diagnostic procedure, a non–high-probability scan should be followed by additional diagnostic testing.

Special circumstances do exist that may guide the diagnostic approach. In the setting of severe, preexisting pulmonary parenchymal or airway disease, ventilation-perfusion scanning is of limited utility given the high likelihood that the scan result will be nondiagnostic. Although the positive predictive value of a high-probability scan and the negative predictive value of a normal or near-normal scan in patients with underlying lung disease are similar to that in the general population, the proportion of patients whose scans fall into a nondiagnostic category is increased substantially.[104] Under this circumstance, an approach utilizing helical CT scanning as the initial objective diagnostic study would be appropriate. The amount of contrast required for CT scanning (100 to 150 mL) poses a substantial risk of radiocontrast-induced nephropathy for patients with preexisting renal insufficiency, especially when it is associated with diabetes mellitus.[120] In such patients, a strategy utilizing duplex ultrasonography and ventilation-perfusion scanning would appear prudent, followed by selective conventional pulmonary angiography should the noninvasive techniques not yield a definitive diagnosis. Venous thromboembolism is a leading cause of maternal mortality[121]; however, given the potential risk of radiation exposure to the fetus, a diagnostic approach that limits that exposure is warranted. Therefore, duplex ultrasonography is an appropriate initial diagnostic approach. If ultrasonography is negative, the diagnostic evaluation should proceed as previously described based on the clinical assessment probability and using ventilation-perfusion scanning as the next diagnostic technique. Helical CT scanning has not been recommended as a diagnostic choice due to the risk of fetal radiation exposure, although recent data would suggest that fetal radiation exposure with CT scanning is less than that with ventilation-perfusion scanning.[122]

PREVENTION OF VENOUS THROMBOEMBOLISM

One of the most striking changes in the field of venous thromboembolism during the last two decades has been an emphasis on prevention. This emphasis is totally appropriate and, indeed, should be the cornerstone of modern management. It is clear that, if the goal is to prevent pulmonary embolism, the only effective approach is to prevent deep venous thrombosis. The basic information and tools required for developing a prophylactic strategy are now available.

To develop such a strategy, three fundamentals must be in place: (1) the population at risk must be identified; (2) the duration of the increased thromboembolic risk must be ascertained; and (3) effective, low-risk prophylactic options must be available. Populations at risk of deep venous thrombosis, and therefore of pulmonary embolism, have been identified; and such risk can, to a considerable extent, be quantified as high, moderate, or low. Furthermore, a variety of effective and safe prophylactic approaches are available. It should be emphasized that the trend toward earlier hospital discharge has been accompanied by an increased incidence of postdischarge venous thromboembolism. Thromboembolic risk does not necessarily end at the time of hospital discharge or transfer to a lower level of care.[123] In patients with an ongoing predisposition to thrombosis at the time of discharge from an acute inpatient setting, prophylaxis should be continued until the risk for venous thromboembolism has resolved.

The objective of the prophylactic strategy is to identify the degree of thromboembolic risk in the individual patient and to match the intensity of prophylaxis to that degree of risk. Although a variety of prophylactic approaches have been investigated and utilized, four approaches have proven effective: low-dose unfractionated heparin, low-molecular-weight heparin, intermittent pneumatic compression devices, and warfarin.

LOW-DOSE UNFRACTIONATED HEPARIN

Low-dose heparin has been widely studied as a prophylactic modality. Heparin, given subcutaneously in a dose of 5000 units every 8 or 12 hours, is begun as soon as the risk of deep venous thrombosis is evident and is continued until that risk has abated. This regimen has been shown to be effective in reducing the incidence of deep venous thrombosis, pulmonary embolism, and fatal pulmonary embolism in patients at low to moderate risk, such as those undergoing surgical procedures requiring general anesthesia for 30 minutes or

longer and with medical conditions requiring bed rest for several days.[124] However, this form of prophylaxis has not been optimally effective in patients whose thromboembolic risk is higher, such as those with hip fracture or hip replacement, those undergoing prostate surgery, and patients suffering major traumatic injuries.[125] Furthermore, although the bleeding risk of low-dose heparin is nominal in most patients, there are groups of patients in whom heparin administration is contraindicated, for example, those with active bleeding, hemorrhagic diathesis, and hemorrhagic stroke, and those undergoing neurologic surgery. Patients to be placed on prophylactic heparin should be screened with an initial platelet count, partial thromboplastin time, and prothrombin time. During therapy, however, monitoring of coagulation tests is not useful, as such tests do not reflect the safety or efficacy of the regimen. Monitoring of platelet counts on at least a weekly basis would appear to be a prudent option.

LOW-MOLECULAR-WEIGHT HEPARIN

Low-molecular-weight heparin preparations represent another prophylactic option. In trials that have been performed comparing the prophylactic efficacy of low-molecular-weight heparin with unfractionated heparin in general surgical and medical populations, low-molecular-weight heparin has not proven superior to unfractionated heparin, although a trend toward increasing bleeding complications associated with unfractionated heparin may exist.[126] However, this may simply represent a dose effect. Low-molecular-weight heparin preparations appear more effective than unfractionated heparin as prophylactic agents in several high-risk groups: patients undergoing hip or knee replacement, patients with spinal cord injury, patients with ischemic strokes, and patients with multiple trauma.[125,126]

PNEUMATIC COMPRESSION DEVICES

Another extensively evaluated and effective prophylactic approach in low- to moderate-risk patients is the use of mechanical leg compressive devices.[125] These devices periodically (e.g., once or twice per minute) compress the leg by an air-inflatable bladder. A variety of devices are available: thigh-length systems that provide both thigh and calf compression, calf-compressive devices, single-pulse systems, and sequential compression systems. The various compressive devices do not appear to differ in efficacy. Instead, the major determinant of efficacy appears to be strict compliance with this intervention during the period of increased thromboembolic risk.[127,128] Pneumatic compression devices appear to be as effective as unfractionated heparin in general medical, surgical, gynecologic, and urologic patients, and their use is indicated in patients in whom pharmacologic methods of prophylaxis are contraindicated.

SODIUM WARFARIN

Warfarin and other prothrombinopenic drugs, started like heparin at the onset of high risk (e.g., preoperatively), also have been shown to be effective and safe.[129] Unfortunately, use of prothrombinopenic agents has not gained wide favor as a prophylactic approach. The use of warfarin requires careful monitoring, and there is a perception among physicians that the bleeding risk associated with its use is greater than that reported in the literature. In patients undergoing hip replacement, warfarin has proven effective and has achieved general acceptance. Two regimens are widely used: small doses (1 to 2 mg) given daily for several days before surgery, with dose escalation to therapeutic range, or initiation after surgery.[130] Low-molecular-weight heparin preparations appear superior to warfarin, albeit at higher bleeding risk, in patients undergoing knee or hip replacement, with efficacy related, in part, to timing of administration.[131] It also has become evident that increased thromboembolic risk in patients undergoing hip or knee replacement can extend for 4 to 6 weeks after hospital discharge.[132] A strategy of perioperative low-molecular-weight heparin followed by extended warfarin may be appropriate.

MISCELLANEOUS AGENTS

Fondaparinux, a synthetic pentasaccharide that selectively inhibits activated factor X (factor Xa), has been demonstrated in recent trials to be effective in the prevention of venous thromboembolism in patients undergoing lower extremity orthopedic surgery.[133,134]

The oral direct thrombin inhibitors also have shown considerable promise as prophylactic agents in patients undergoing hip or knee replacement.[135] Advantages of these agents compared to existing options include oral administration and a lack of need for dose adjustments or monitoring.

There is one option available to prevent pulmonary embolism in patients at high risk who cannot be provided pharmacologic or mechanical prophylaxis. Patients with extensive trauma often fall into this category, particularly those with pelvic or lower extremity fractures and internal or intracranial bleeding. In this group, prophylactic placement of an inferior vena cava filter in selected patients provides protection against otherwise nonpreventable emboli.[136]

In summary, given the effective options available, few patients at risk for venous thrombosis cannot be protected. However, despite this awareness, surveys have demonstrated that prophylaxis is underused in populations at risk.[137,138] A number of different rationales have been proposed to account for this lack of compliance. The overstated perception of bleeding complications associated with pharmacologic methods of prophylaxis appears to remain a deterrent. Furthermore, fatal pulmonary embolism is uncommon in any individual physician's experience, thereby diminishing the perception of risk. Finally, the issue of prophylaxis is often subordinated to the compelling demands of the patient's admitting diagnosis and therapy. Whatever the reason, increased use of prophylaxis must occur if a substantial impact is to be made on the considerable and often unnecessary morbidity and mortality associated with pulmonary embolism. Not only must prophylaxis be applied, it must be applied in a manner proportionate to the patient's risk of thromboembolism.

MANAGEMENT OF VENOUS THROMBOEMBOLISM

The basic approaches to management are defined chiefly by what is known, as already described, about the patho-

genesis, pathophysiology, and natural history of venous thrombosis and pulmonary embolism.

HEPARIN

Heparin, both unfractionated and low molecular weight, remains the mainstay of therapy for venous thrombosis and for pulmonary embolism not associated with hemodynamic compromise.[139] With a strong suspicion of embolism based on clinical findings and laboratory tests, heparin therapy should be instituted immediately, without awaiting diagnostic confirmation, unless anticoagulation places the patient at significant risk.

Data suggest that physician practices in the administration of unfractionated heparin often result in levels of anticoagulation that fall below those currently recommended in the literature.[140,141] To overcome these problems, standardized protocols for heparin administration and monitoring have been recommended. A number of different intravenous heparin dosing schemes have been published, all of which have demonstrated the potential to reach a therapeutic threshold more rapidly than a nonstandardized approach.[141] The most widely utilized of these is a weight-based system that includes an 80 unit/kg intravenous bolus of heparin followed by an 18 unit/kg/hr infusion.[142] Whatever regimen is used, an activated partial thromboplastin time (aPTT) should be obtained 6 hours after the bolus dose, 6 hours after each prescribed dose adjustment, and then on a daily basis for the duration of therapy. Because maintenance of the aPTT within a rigidly defined range does not appear to increase the efficacy or safety of the drug, frequent dosage adjustments are not necessary once the dose has been stabilized within a therapeutic range. This therapeutic range of aPTT, which corresponds to heparin levels of 0.2 to 0.4 unit/mL by protamine sulfate titration or 0.3 to 0.7 unit/mL by anti–factor Xa assay, may vary substantially depending on the sensitivity of the reagent utilized and among coagulometers.[143] Therefore, unless internal validation has been performed, a target aPTT ratio of 2.0 to 3.5 should be attained. It also should be recognized that heparin requirements tend to decrease during the course of therapy, resulting in an increase in the level of the aPTT. For patients with heparin resistance (defined as the need for more than 40,000 units/day), monitoring heparin with an anti–factor Xa assay appears safe and effective and results in less escalation of the heparin dose than monitoring with the aPTT.[144]

Supporting the importance of using adequate heparin doses are data that suggest a *subtherapeutic* aPTT may be associated with an increased risk for thromboembolic recurrence, whereas a *supratherapeutic* aPTT is not associated with an increased risk of clinically important bleeding complications.[145] There is no direct evidence that the absolute dose of heparin or the level of the aPTT can predict the likelihood of bleeding. Instead, bleeding during heparin therapy appears to be related to the presence of concurrent illness such as renal disease, a history of heavy alcohol consumption, aspirin use, and prior surgical procedures or peptic ulcer disease. Failure to reach a therapeutic range within 24 hours appears to have long-term as well as short-term implications for thromboembolic recurrence. Recent data strongly suggest that patients who fail to achieve a therapeutic threshold within 24 hours have a subsequent recurrence rate significantly higher than those who do.[146]

The complexities involved in heparin administration and aPTT monitoring have been largely overcome by the introduction of low-molecular-weight heparin preparations into clinical practice.[139,147] The advantage of low-molecular-weight heparin preparations arises from their increased bioavailability and longer half-life as well as the simplicity of being administered subcutaneously once or twice daily without need for aPTT monitoring. However, clinicians must recognize that the administration of low-molecular-weight heparin may not be preferable under certain clinical circumstances. Standardized dosing is problematic in patients at the extremes of body weight; due to renal clearance of the drug, dose adjustments and monitoring with anti–factor Xa levels are necessary in patients with renal insufficiency; the anticoagulant effect of the drug cannot be monitored easily; populations exist (e.g., patients at high bleeding risk) in which a longer drug half-life is not a desirable effect; the ability of protamine sulfate to reverse the anticoagulant effect remains uncertain; and drug costs are substantially higher than with unfractionated heparin.

Clinical trials have demonstrated that the safety and efficacy of low-molecular-weight heparin preparations are comparable to unfractionated heparin in patients with venous thrombosis. Trials have also demonstrated that most patients with acute venous thrombosis can be treated safely on an outpatient basis with low-molecular-weight heparin, and that outpatient therapy can reduce total medical expenditure.[148] However, not all patients with venous thrombosis can or should be treated in an outpatient setting. Approximately 50% of patients are ineligible for outpatient therapy due to such factors as major bleeding risk, compliance problems, renal failure, significant comorbid disease, inadequate cardiopulmonary reserve, and inaccessibility for follow-up. Furthermore, embolism can occur during the early aspects of therapy in patients treated with both unfractionated and low-molecular-weight heparin preparations. Although this circumstance would not be diminished in an inpatient setting, the potential consequences of recurrence, especially in patients with preexisting cardiopulmonary disease, might be more promptly detected and managed in this setting. Even in patients who require initial inpatient management, however, the duration of hospitalization can be decreased considerably by a quick transition to outpatient therapy.

Clinical trials have demonstrated that patients with uncomplicated pulmonary embolism can be treated safely with a low-molecular-weight heparin preparation.[149,150] Data supporting the outpatient management of uncomplicated pulmonary embolism are far less robust, and definitive recommendations for this approach must await the results of future clinical trials.[151] However, preliminary data would suggest that this approach might be feasible in patients with submassive embolism, preserved right ventricular function, and a low risk of bleeding. The definitive answer to this question will likely parallel investigations evaluating the role of risk stratification approaches in pulmonary embolism.

In terms of duration of heparin therapy, studies have shown that utilizing a 5-day course of therapy in patients with proximal venous thrombosis is associated with a recurrence rate identical to that of a 10-day course.[152] This assumes, of course, that warfarin is started early and is in a therapeutic range for 2 consecutive days before heparin is discontinued, a target often difficult to achieve. It is likely that a short course of heparin therapy would be similarly effective in patients with uncomplicated pulmonary embolism. However, a longer course of therapy is advisable in patients with major pulmonary embolism or extensive iliofemoral venous thrombosis.

The major complications of unfractionated and low-molecular-weight heparins are bleeding and the development of thrombocytopenia.[153] There are no predisposing factors to heparin-associated thrombocytopenia other than a history of a previous exposure. Two types of thrombocytopenia are associated with heparin administration: an early-onset (1 to 5 days), nonimmune-mediated reduction in platelet count (type I) believed to be secondary to a direct agglutinating effect of heparin on platelets, and a late-onset (greater than 5 days), immune-mediated thrombocytopenia (type II) that may be associated with venous and arterial thrombosis. Immune-mediated thrombocytopenia can occur within a day of initiating therapy in patients who have been exposed to the drug within the prior 100 days.[154] The incidence of thrombosis with heparin-associated thrombocytopenia appears to be low, but when it occurs it is associated with considerable morbidity and mortality. Therefore, heparin should be immediately withdrawn if this diagnosis is suspected. If heparin-associated thrombocytopenia type II is confirmed by either a functional assay or immunoassay, withdrawal of heparin alone may be associated with an adverse outcome.[155] A number of options exist, including the use of direct thrombin inhibitors (lepirudin or argatroban), which do not react with heparin antibodies, or danaparoid, which appears to have a low rate of in vivo cross reactivity with heparin.[156,157] Cross reactivity between unfractionated and low-molecular-weight heparins is relatively common, and these drugs should be avoided.[158]

INFERIOR VENA CAVA FILTERS

Scientific evidence supporting the use of inferior vena cava filters is limited.[159,160] Established indications for filter placement in the therapy of venous thromboembolism include (1) protection against pulmonary embolism in patients with acute venous thromboembolism in whom conventional anticoagulation is contraindicated (recent surgery, hemorrhagic cerebrovascular accident, active bleeding, heparin associated thrombocytopenia, etc.); (2) protection against pulmonary embolism in patients with acute venous thromboembolism in whom conventional anticoagulation has proven ineffective; and, (3) protection of an already compromised pulmonary vascular bed from further thromboembolic risk (massive pulmonary embolism, chronic thromboembolic pulmonary hypertension).

Mortality from filter placement appears to be quite low regardless of what filter is used.[159] Nonfatal complications of inferior vena cava filters that occur with increased frequency include (1) complications relating to the insertion process; (2) venous thrombosis at the site of insertion; (3) filter migration; (4) filter erosion through the inferior vena cava wall; and, (5) inferior vena cava obstruction. The majority of clinically important complications appear to

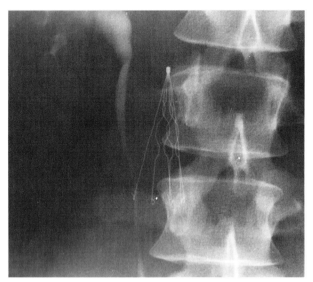

Figure 48.9 Inferior vena cava filter in place below the renal veins.

involve venous thrombosis at the insertion site and inferior vena cava obstruction.

Filter placement should not be considered as primary therapy for venous thromboembolism unless an absolute contraindication to anticoagulation exists. Although protecting the pulmonary vascular bed, filter placement does not inhibit the extension of existing venous thrombi or diminish the systemic prothrombotic state. Small thrombi can pass through patent filters or through collaterals around obstructed filters; furthermore, thrombus extension can occur through the filter itself. A recent study demonstrated that placement of a vena cava filter was capable of diminishing the incidence of early thromboembolic recurrence.[160] However, this benefit was offset by an increased long-term risk of recurrent deep venous thrombosis. Prior to filter placement, the physician must be aware that this intervention is an irrevocable one (Fig. 48.9). Given these considerations, long-term anticoagulation should be utilized following filter placement if no contraindications exist or as soon as any existing bleeding risk resolves.

MASSIVE PULMONARY EMBOLISM

The significant mortality associated with massive pulmonary embolism justifies a separate consideration of the diagnostic and therapeutic approach to this problem.[161] The definition of massive pulmonary embolism should be based on hemodynamic considerations rather than purely anatomic ones. This impression is supported by mortality statistics from the urokinase trials and others.[4,35] Although anatomically massive emboli have a greater likelihood of being associated with hemodynamic compromise, not all anatomically massive emboli lead to hemodynamic compromise. Irrespective of the degree of vascular obstruction, patients with pulmonary embolism who present with shock have a mortality rate, regardless of the type of intervention, that approaches 30%.

The therapeutic approach to the patient with hemodynamically massive pulmonary embolism should be designed to counteract the adverse physiologic consequence of pulmonary vascular obstruction whether or not that obstruction is anatomically massive. Basic care of a critically ill patient should not be overlooked while specific diagnostic and therapeutic considerations are being implemented. Oxygen should be administered to alleviate the hypoxic pulmonary vasoconstriction, which might be contributing to the pulmonary hypertension. Intubation and mechanical ventilatory support might be required to improve oxygenation and decrease metabolic demands. Although volume resuscitation has been advised, excessive preload may further distend the right ventricle and increase right ventricular wall tension, resulting in decreased coronary perfusion and right ventricular ischemia. The judicious use of inotropic support can also prove useful in increasing blood pressure, preserving right coronary artery perfusion, and supporting right ventricular function.[162] Although there is a tendency to utilize central hemodynamic monitoring in critically ill hypotensive patients, this intervention should be considered carefully in the patient with massive pulmonary embolism. A femoral approach poses the risk of dislodging residual ileofemoral thrombus, and balloon flotation poses the risk of dislodging embolic material that might be trapped within the right atrial or ventricular cavities.

Although the central goal of therapy in massive pulmonary embolism should be to relieve pulmonary vascular obstruction, the severely compromised nature of the pulmonary vascular bed makes prevention of recurrence an important secondary consideration. Therefore, assuming the requisite expertise in filter placement is available and that placement of a filter will not interfere with the primary management of the patient, placement of a filter should be considered in all patients with hemodynamically massive embolism.

THROMBOLYTIC THERAPY

The use of thrombolytic agents in acute pulmonary embolism remains controversial.[4,163] Although thrombolytic therapy does appear to accelerate the rate of thrombolysis, there is no convincing evidence to suggest that it decreases mortality, increases the ultimate extent of resolution when measured at 7 days, reduces thromboembolic recurrence rates, improves symptomatic outcome, or decreases the incidence of thromboembolic pulmonary hypertension.[164,165] The one issue about which there can be little controversy is that the use of thrombolytic agents is associated with a substantially increased risk of bleeding, including intracranial hemorrhage. Intracranial hemorrhage has occurred in 0.5% to 2% of patients treated with thrombolytic agents in trials evaluating the use of these agents in both pulmonary embolism and myocardial infarction.[164,166]

Based on these data, and assuming there is no contraindication to its use, the role of thrombolytic therapy in pulmonary embolism should be limited to those circumstances in which an accelerated rate of thrombolysis may be considered lifesaving, that is, in patients with pulmonary embolism who present with hemodynamic compromise, patients who develop hemodynamic compromise during conventional therapy with heparin, and patients with embolism associated with intracavitary right atrial or ventricular thrombi.[167,168] At the present time, the finding of right ventricular dysfunction on echocardiography in the absence of hemodynamic instability should not serve as a justification for thrombolytic therapy.[4,169,170] Approximately 40% of patients with pulmonary embolism will have echocardiographic evidence of right ventricular dysfunction. Until criteria have been established that identify a subset of patients with right ventricular dysfunction who are at risk for an adverse outcome and benefit from thrombolytic therapy, there is little basis for exposing all such patients to the considerable risk of hemorrhagic complications associated with this intervention. This is especially true given the recent advances that have occurred in heparin administration strategies.

PULMONARY EMBOLECTOMY

The role of pulmonary embolectomy in acute hemodynamically massive pulmonary embolism also remains controversial.[171,172] Patients with anatomically massive or submassive emboli who are hemodynamically compromised, who have not had a cardiac arrest, and who do not have an absolute contraindication to thrombolytic therapy should be managed initially with aggressive medical therapy, including thrombolytic therapy plus heparin. Patients in whom acute embolectomy might be considered are those with hemodynamically massive pulmonary embolism who have an absolute contraindication to anticoagulant or thrombolytic therapy, those who have suffered a cardiopulmonary arrest (although the mortality associated with embolectomy in those who have is far higher than those who have not), and those in whom aggressive medical therapy, including the use of thrombolytics, has proven ineffective.

The concept of relieving the pulmonary vascular obstruction and decreasing right ventricular afterload with a percutaneous device has been appealing. Several such devices designed to extract or fragment thrombi have been reported. Their role in massive pulmonary embolism remains investigative.[173]

POSTEMBOLIC PROPHYLAXIS

The duration of outpatient anticoagulation for patients with pulmonary embolism remains a subject of controversy.[174–177] Much of the difficulty in making definitive recommendations regarding the duration of outpatient anticoagulation results from the diverse population that is affected by the disease process. The decision to continue or withdraw therapy should be made on an individual basis and take into account factors such as the nature of the initial thromboembolic event (spontaneous or associated with a defined clinical circumstance), the type of initial event (venous thrombosis or pulmonary embolism), the presence of an ongoing predisposition (either clinical or hereditary), and possibly the persistence of residual venous thrombosis as determined by ultrasonography.[174–178]

Patients with a clearly defined initial predisposition, whose initial thromboembolic risk factors have resolved and whose ventilation-perfusion scan and noninvasive lower extremity test results have normalized, can likely be managed with a 3-month course of anticoagulation.[176]

Patients without a clearly defined initial predisposition to thromboembolism and those with persistent ventilation-perfusion scan defects or abnormal lower extremity test results should be treated for 6 months or more.[175,177] Finally, certain patients should be treated with an indefinite period of anticoagulation even though such a strategy is associated with an increased risk of hemorrhagic complications. Clinical circumstances in which indefinite periods of anticoagulation should be considered include a history of more than one episode of idiopathic venous thrombosis or pulmonary embolism; the presence of certain irreversible acquired or hereditary risk factors for venous thromboembolism (active cancer, immobilization, antiphospholipid antibody syndrome, combined thrombophilic abnormalities); the presence of extensive residual venous thrombosis or the postthrombotic syndrome; and the presence of extensive residual ventilation-perfusion scan or CT scan defects or pulmonary hypertension. Although the presence of the heterozygous factor V Leiden mutation or the prothrombin gene mutation individually does not appear to increase recurrence risk, the presence of homozygous factor V Leiden mutation or the heterozygous factor V Leiden mutation in combination with the prothrombin gene mutation does appear to be associated with an increased recurrence risk.[179]

In patients in whom anticoagulation beyond 6 months is anticipated, the use of a direct oral thrombin inhibitor that does not require prothrombin time monitoring has proven to be an effective alternative to warfarin.[180]

A standard for repeating noninvasive testing of either the lungs or deep veins of the lower extremities at the anticipated time of anticoagulant discontinuation does not exist. Although the cost implications would be substantial, such an approach would be beneficial in establishing a new baseline study that could be used for comparison in the event thromboembolic recurrence was suspected, and in identifying patients with pulmonary vascular obstruction of sufficient extent to place them at risk for the development of chronic thromboembolic pulmonary hypertension.

Regarding postembolic anticoagulant "intensity," the recommended therapeutic range for the International Normalized Ratio (INR) of prothrombin time in the majority of patients with venous thromboembolism is 2.0 to 3.0. The exception to this rule may be patients with antiphospholipid antibody syndrome, in whom an INR of 3.0 to 4.0 was considered more effective in reducing recurrence rates than an INR less than 3.0.[181] However, questions have been raised regarding the validity of this recommendation.[182] In patients with a lupus anticoagulant, in whom the baseline INR may be elevated, the INR may not reliably reflect the level of anticoagulation. In these patients, the use of tests that are insensitive to the lupus anticoagulant, such as the prothrombin-proconvertin time or chromogenic factor X assay, have been recommended.[183]

Trials evaluating the effectiveness of low-intensity anticoagulation (maintaining the INR in a range of 1.5 to 2.0) following a standard 3- to 6-month period of anticoagulation have demonstrated that such an approach is superior to placebo but is less effective than standard therapy, without an appreciable reduction in bleeding complications.[184,185]

CHRONIC THROMBOEMBOLIC PULMONARY HYPERTENSION

As already discussed, most treated pulmonary emboli resolve over some weeks, restoring the pulmonary arterial bed to normal or near-normal status. In a very small percentage of patients, estimated to represent no more than 0.1% to 0.5% of the 450,000 patients who survive a pulmonary embolic event each year in the United States, such resolution does not occur and the residual obstruction is of sufficient extent to cause persistent pulmonary hypertension.[186]

The reasons thromboembolic pulmonary hypertension develops are not clear; that is, it is not evident why this minority of patients fail to resolve their emboli. It has been found that, in approximately half of the patients, the initial diagnosis of pulmonary thromboembolism was not made, and therefore, no treatment was given.[187] Despite extensive investigation, the only identifiable thrombotic predisposition has been the presence of a lupus anticoagulant or antiphospholipid antibody syndrome in approximately 10% to 50% of patients.[188-190] The prevalence of other thrombophilic tendencies, such as antithrombin III, protein C, and protein S deficiency, does not appear to be higher than that encountered in the normal population. Preliminary evidence also suggest that the factor V Leiden mutation is no more common in patients with chronic thromboembolic pulmonary hypertension than in the general population[190]; moreover, no consistent defect in fibrinolytic activity has been identified.

The diagnosis of thromboembolic pulmonary hypertension is usually not made until the degree of pulmonary hypertension is advanced. As a result, the exact hemodynamic evolution of the disease has not been fully established.[191] The extent of pulmonary vascular obstruction appears to be a major determinant of disease initiation, with involvement of greater than 40% of the pulmonary vascular bed present in the majority of patients. Hemodynamic progression in certain patients may involve thromboembolic recurrence or in situ pulmonary artery thrombosis. However, hemodynamic progression in many patients appears to involve the development of a hypertensive pulmonary arteriopathy, similar to that encountered in other causes of secondary pulmonary hypertension.[192] This supposition is supported by several lines of evidence: a poor correlation between the extent of central anatomic obstruction and the degree of pulmonary hypertension; documented hemodynamic progression in the absence of recurrent embolic events or evidence of in situ pulmonary artery thrombosis; and histopathology demonstrating arteriopathic changes in the resistance vessels of both the involved and uninvolved pulmonary vascular system.

Survival without intervention is poor and proportional to the degree of pulmonary hypertension at the time of diagnosis. In one study, the 5-year survival rate was 30% when the mean pulmonary artery pressure exceeded 40 mm Hg and 10% when it exceeded 50 mm Hg.[193] In another study, a mean pulmonary artery pressure above 30 mm Hg appeared to serve as a threshold value portending a poor prognosis.[194]

DIAGNOSIS

Perhaps the most important aspect of dealing with this patient group is the proper approach to its recognition.

Progressive dyspnea is a complaint that is common to all patients with chronic thromboembolic pulmonary hypertension. Later in the course of the disease, exertional chest pain, near syncope or syncope, or lower extremity edema may develop.

Although a history of documented thromboembolism may not be present, many patients can provide a history consistent with an acute embolic event. They may describe an episode of "pleurisy," lower extremity "muscle strain," or prolonged, atypical "pneumonia," or they may describe a hospitalization or surgical procedure from which they never fully recovered. That an episode of venous thromboembolism was not diagnosed, or was misdiagnosed, is not surprising given recent data confirming the frequency with which venous thrombosis and pulmonary embolism are overlooked in the population at large.[195]

Diagnostic delay, particularly in the absence of an acute history of venous thromboembolism, occurs commonly. Progressive dyspnea and exercise intolerance are often attributed to coronary artery disease, cardiomyopathy, interstitial lung disease, asthma, deconditioning, or psychogenic dyspnea. Therefore, an abnormality of the pulmonary vascular bed should be considered in any patient with dyspnea in whom a definitive etiology cannot be defined. Later in the course of the disease, exertional chest pain, presyncope, or syncope may occur due to the presence of severe pulmonary hypertension and the inability of a compromised right ventricle to meet cardiac output demands.

Physical examination findings may be subtle early in the course of the illness, thereby contributing to this diagnostic delay. Prior to the development of significant right ventricular hypertrophy or overt right ventricular failure, physical examination abnormalities may be limited to a narrowing of the second heart sound or to a subtle accentuation of its pulmonic component. Late in the course of the disease, obvious findings such as a right ventricular heave, jugular venous distention, prominent a- and v-wave venous pulsations, fixed splitting of S_2, a right ventricular S_3, murmurs of tricuspid regurgitation or pulmonic insufficiency, hepatomegaly, and ascites may develop. Peripheral edema, a result of chronic lower extremity venous outflow obstruction or right ventricular failure, may be present.

A unique physical finding in certain patients with chronic thromboembolic disease is the presence of flow murmurs over the lung fields.[196] These subtle bruits, which appear to originate from turbulent flow through partially obstructed or recanalized thrombi, are high pitched and blowing in quality, heard over the lung fields rather than the precordium, accentuated during inspiration, and frequently heard only during periods of breath-holding. Their importance arises in not having been described in primary pulmonary hypertension, which represents the most common competing diagnostic possibility.

The intent of the diagnostic evaluation is to establish the presence and degree of pulmonary hypertension, to define its etiology, and, if major vessel thromboembolic disease is present, to determine whether it is accessible to surgical intervention. Findings on standard laboratory tests are nonspecific, dependent on the point in the natural history of the disease at which they are obtained, and reflective of the hemodynamic and gas-exchange consequences of the

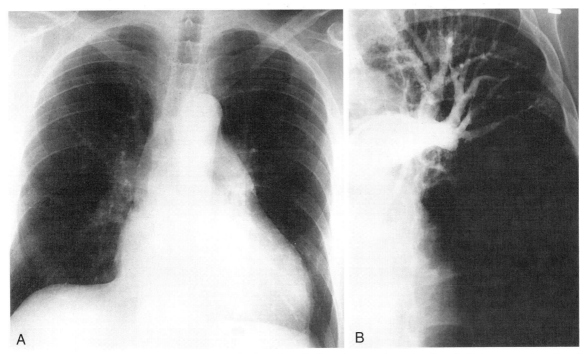

Figure 48.10 Chest radiograph in a patient with chronic thromboembolic pulmonary hypertension. **A,** Note asymmetry of central pulmonary arteries, absence of descending left pulmonary artery, left lower lobe oligemia, and peripheral density representing prior infarct. **B,** Angiogram in same patient demonstrating complete proximal occlusion of the descending left pulmonary artery.

thromboembolic obstruction and the accompanying cardiac dysfunction.

Chest radiography, although often normal, may demonstrate findings that suggest the diagnosis.[197] Enlargement of both main pulmonary arteries or asymmetry in the size of the central pulmonary arteries may be present (Fig. 48.10). Areas of hypoperfusion or hyperperfusion may be present. There also may be evidence of old pleural disease, unilaterally or bilaterally. The cardiac silhouette may reflect obvious right atrial or right ventricular enlargement; more often, right ventricular hypertrophy and enlargement are suggested only on the lateral film by encroachment on the normally empty retrosternal space.

Early in the course of the disease, electrocardiographic findings may be normal. Later in the course, electrocardiography demonstrates evidence of right ventricular hypertrophy.

Pulmonary function testing, performed to evaluate the patient's dyspnea, is often within normal limits. The majority of patients have a reduction in the single-breath diffusing capacity for carbon monoxide; however, a normal value does not exclude the diagnosis. Approximately 20% of patients demonstrate a mild to moderate restrictive defect due in part to the presence of infarct-related parenchymal scars.[198] However, the degree of spirometric defect is almost always disproportionate to the patient's gas-exchange abnormalities, symptomatic complaints, and degree of pulmonary hypertension.

In terms of gas-exchange findings, the arterial PO_2 may be within normal limits. However, the alveolar-arterial PO_2 difference is typically widened, and the majority of patients have a decline in the arterial PO_2 with exercise. Dead space ventilation is often increased at rest and worsens with

exercise. Minute ventilation is typically elevated as a result of this increased dead space ventilation.[199]

Echocardiography commonly provides the initial objective evidence that pulmonary hypertension is present. Once the diagnosis of pulmonary hypertension has been established, determination of whether it originates from abnormalities of the small, resistance vessels or from central, chronic thromboembolic obstruction is essential. Ventilation-perfusion lung scanning appears to provide an excellent, noninvasive means of distinguishing between potentially operable major vessel thromboembolic pulmonary hypertension and small vessel pulmonary hypertension.[200] In chronic thromboembolic disease, at least one (and more commonly, several) segmental or larger mismatched ventilation-perfusion defects are present. In primary pulmonary hypertension, perfusion scans either are normal or exhibit a "mottled" appearance characterized by subsegmental defects. Other disorders leading to pulmonary hypertension may be associated with segmental defects on perfusion scan, including pulmonary veno-occlusive disease, pulmonary artery sarcoma, fibrosing mediastinitis, and large vessel vasculitides.[201]

It is important to recognize that the ventilation-perfusion scan often understates the actual extent of central pulmonary vascular obstruction.[202] Channels through central obstructing lesions or partial flow around them, a result of the often complex patterns of recanalization and organization that occur following an embolic event, allow the radioisotopic agent to reach the periphery of the lung. Depending on the distribution of flow, these areas may appear normal or as relatively hypoperfused "gray zones." Therefore, ventilation-perfusion scanning, although capable of suggesting the potential presence of chronic thromboembolic obstruction, is incapable of determining the magnitude, location, or proximal extent of the disease, information critical to the question of surgical accessibility.

The role of CT scanning in the evaluation of patients with chronic thromboembolic disease remains incompletely defined. A variety of CT abnormalities have been described: chronic thromboembolic material located in an eccentric position within the central pulmonary arteries, right ventricular enlargement, dilated central pulmonary arteries, bronchial artery collateral flow, parenchymal abnormalities consistent with prior infarcts, and mosaic attenuation of the pulmonary parenchyma.[203] However, the absence of these findings does not preclude the possibility of surgically accessible chronic thromboembolic disease. Furthermore, the presence of central thrombus has been described in primary pulmonary hypertension and other chronic pulmonary disorders.[204] CT scanning is also incapable of providing essential hemodynamic data. CT is particularly useful in the evaluation of the main pulmonary arteries and of unilateral or predominantly unilateral pulmonary vascular obstruction as determined by ventilation-perfusion scanning.[203] Under these circumstances, the probability of other diagnostic possibilities such as pulmonary artery sarcoma, vasculitis, malignancy, and mediastinal fibrosis is increased. CT also has a role, along with physiologic testing, in helping to evaluate the status of the pulmonary parenchyma in patients with coexisting obstructive or restrictive lung disease.

Right-heart catheterization and pulmonary angiography are essential to designate the degree of pulmonary hypertension, to exclude competing diagnoses, and to define the surgical accessibility of the obstructing thrombotic lesions. If hemodynamic measurements at rest demonstrate only modest degrees of pulmonary hypertension, measurements should be obtained following a short period of exercise. In patients with chronic thromboembolic obstruction sufficient to abolish normal compensatory mechanisms, exercise-related increases in cardiac output will be accompanied by an almost linear elevation in pulmonary artery pressure.

The angiographic findings in chronic thromboembolic disease bear little resemblance to the sharply defined, intraluminal defects diagnostic of acute embolism.[205] Five distinct angiographic patterns have been described that correlate with the finding of organized thromboembolic material at the time of thromboendarterectomy (Fig. 48.11): (1) pouch defects; (2) pulmonary artery webs or bands; (3) intimal irregularities; (4) abrupt narrowing of the major pulmonary arteries; and (5) obstruction of lobar or segmental vessels at their point of origin, with complete absence of blood flow to pulmonary segments normally perfused by those vessels.

In certain patients, pulmonary angioscopy has proven valuable in confirming the presence of chronic thromboembolic obstruction and in determining whether it is accessible to surgical intervention.[206] The pulmonary angioscope is a fiberoptic device that allows visualization of the pulmonary arteries to the segmental level. The normal pulmonary artery has a round or oval contour with a smooth, pale, glistening appearance to the intima, and bright red blood filling the lumen (Fig. 48.12). The features of organized chronic emboli consist of roughening or pitting of the intimal surface, bands and webs across the lumen, pitted

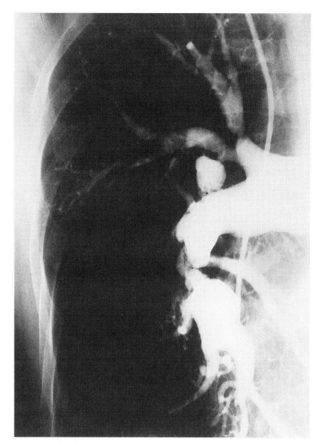

Figure 48.11 Right-sided pulmonary angiogram in a patient with chronic thromboembolic pulmonary hypertension. Many of the classic angiographic findings associated with this disease are present, including pouch defects, intimal irregularity, pulmonary artery webs with poststenotic dilation, and complete obstruction to flow of the right middle lobe and several lower lobe segmental arteries.

masses of chronic embolic material within the lumen, and partial recanalization.

Although pulmonary angiography/angioscopy usually completes the diagnostic sequence and confirms surgical accessibility, adjunctive studies may be necessary to exclude competing diagnoses. CT of the chest can be useful in determining whether a mediastinal process (e.g., fibrosing mediastinitis, malignancy) is responsible for the angiographic findings and, in selected cases, in defining the extent and accessibility of the obstructing thrombi. Arch aortography can be useful if an arteritis is being considered.[207]

The major conditions from which thromboembolic pulmonary hypertension must be distinguished include primary pulmonary hypertension and other forms of secondary pulmonary hypertension such as fibrosing mediastinitis with pulmonary arterial or venous obstruction, pulmonary hypertension associated with congenital atrial or ventricular septal defects, congenital pulmonary artery branch stenoses, pulmonary artery agenesis, tumors arising in or obstructing the central pulmonary arteries, and Takayasu's arteritis. The standard diagnostic approaches previously discussed, preferably performed at a center experienced in the management of pulmonary hypertension, are capable of excluding the majority of these competing diagnoses.

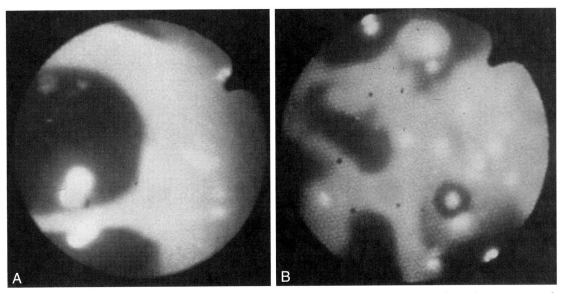

Figure 48.12 Pulmonary angioscopy. **A,** Angioscopic appearance of normal pulmonary artery. **B,** Angioscopic appearance of chronic thromboembolic pulmonary artery obstruction demonstrating multiple, recanalized channels.

Table 48.4 Published Results for Pulmonary Thromboendarterectomy since 1999

Year	Study	Location	Patients (*n*)	Preoperative PVR*	Postoperative PVR*	Mortality (%)
2000	Mares et al.[213]	Austria	33	1478 ± 107[†]	975 ± 93[†]	9.1
2000	Mares et al.[213]	Austria	14	1334 ± 135[†]	759 ± 99[†]	21.4
2000	Rubens et al.[214]	Canada	21	765 ± 372	208 ± 92	4.8
2000	D'Armini et al.[215]	Italy	33	1056 ± 344	196 ± 39[‡]	9.1
2001	Tschol et al.[216]	Germany	69	988 ± 554	324 ± 188	10.1
2001	Masuda and Nakajima[217]	Japan	50	869 ± 299[§]	344 ± 174[§]	18
2003	Hagl et al.[218]	Germany	30	873 ± 248	290 ± 117	10
2003	Jamieson et al.[209]	San Diego	500	893 ± 444	285 ± 214	4.4

* PVR, pulmonary vascular resistance in dyne-sec·cm^{-5}.
[†] Results expressed as pulmonary vascular resistance *index.*
[‡] Data in 23 patients at 3-month follow-up.
[§] 34 patients by sternotomy, 16 patients by thoracotomy.

TREATMENT

For patients suffering from chronic thromboembolic pulmonary hypertension, the decision to proceed to pulmonary thromboendarterectomy is based on both objective and subjective factors, which are carefully defined during the preoperative evaluation.[208]

Pulmonary thromboendarterectomy is considered in symptomatic patients with hemodynamic or ventilatory impairment at rest or with exercise. The mean pulmonary vascular resistance in patients undergoing surgery (Table 48.4) is typically 800 to 1000 dyne-sec·cm^{-5}, with a range of 300 to 2000 dyne-sec·cm^{-5}.[191] Patients in the lower range of pulmonary hemodynamic impairment include those with involvement limited to one main pulmonary artery, those with vigorous lifestyle expectations in whom high dead space and minute ventilatory demands are disabling, and those who live at altitude. Thromboendarterectomy is also considered in patients with normal or near-normal pulmonary hemodynamics at rest who develop significant levels of pulmonary hypertension with exercise. If surgery is deferred in patients with this hemodynamic profile, careful monitoring is recommended to detect whether progression of the pulmonary hypertension is occurring.

The location and extent of the proximal thromboembolic obstruction is the most critical determinant of operability. Occluding thrombi must involve the main, lobar, or proximal segmental arteries. Those that originate more distally are not amenable to thromboendarterectomy with current surgical techniques. In terms of extent, the anatomic and hemodynamic findings must be interpreted in concert. An acceptable postoperative hemodynamic outcome requires that the preoperative hemodynamic impairment be consistent with the magnitude of surgically accessible thromboembolic material determined by angiography or angioscopy. This determination is critical. If the major component of the preoperative hemodynamic impairment derives from surgically inaccessible disease or from the resistance conferred by a secondary, small vessel arteriopathy, residual pulmonary hypertension will be present postoperatively. Depending on the extent of the postoperative pulmonary hypertension, this outcome may be associated with adverse short-term and long-term consequences.

The only absolute contraindication to thromboendarterectomy is the presence of severe underlying lung disease, either obstructive or restrictive. Thromboendarterectomy in this population can improve the hemodynamic profile but may have little effect on the ventilatory impairment. Advanced age, severe right ventricular failure, and the presence of collateral disease influence risk assessment but do not represent absolute contraindications to the procedure if the anticipated relief of the pulmonary hypertension will improve both the quality and duration of life. Patients as young as 16 and as old as 84 years, as well as those with complex comorbid conditions, have successfully undergone the procedure.

Prior to surgery, several other essential issues must be considered. It is important that the patient be protected against embolic recurrence, both over the long term and during the high-risk perioperative period. Therefore, an inferior vena cava filter should be placed prior to surgery unless an obvious non-leg or nonpelvic source of embolism is present. For those at risk of coronary artery disease, coronary angiography is routinely performed prior to surgery, usually at the time of the right heart catheterization and pulmonary angiography. Coronary artery bypass grafting, if necessary, can be performed safely at the time of the thromboendarterectomy.[208]

Sternotomy with cardiopulmonary bypass and periods of circulatory arrest represents the procedure of choice. This approach allows access to both pulmonary arteries and assures more complete removal of the chronically obstruct-ing material.[209] A sternotomy approach also provides adequate exposure for additional procedures that need to be performed. In a recent review of 1190 patients undergoing thromboendarterectomy, 90 patients (7.6%) required such a combined procedure exclusive of solitary closure of a patent foramen ovale, which is performed in approximately 30% of thromboendarterectomy procedures.[208] The use of cardiopulmonary bypass allows periods of complete circulatory arrest, which provides a bloodless operative field essential for meticulous lobar and segmental dissections.

Thromboendarterectomy bears little resemblance to acute pulmonary embolectomy. The neointima in chronic thromboembolic disease is deceptive and is often not easily recognizable as chronic thrombus. The procedure is a true endarterectomy that requires careful dissection of chronic endothelialized material from the native intima to restore pulmonary arterial patency. Considerable experience is required by the surgical team to identify the correct operative plane and to remove the segmental-level extensions of the more proximal obstruction (Fig. 48.13). Failure to do so results in an inadequate hemodynamic outcome.

During the development of and early experience with this procedure, mortality was related to many causes. At the present time, the major causes of death have been related to reperfusion pulmonary edema and to residual postoperative pulmonary hypertension and right ventricular failure in patients in whom pulmonary thromboendarterectomy failed to achieve substantial improvement in pulmonary hemodynamics.[209]

Although an immediate improvement in pulmonary hemodynamics occurs, the postoperative course can be complex. In addition to complications common to other forms of cardiac surgery (arrhythmias, atelectasis, wound infection, pericardial effusions, delirium), patients undergoing pulmonary thromboendarterectomy often experience two unique complications capable of significantly impairing gas exchange: reperfusion pulmonary edema and pulmonary artery "steal."[210,211]

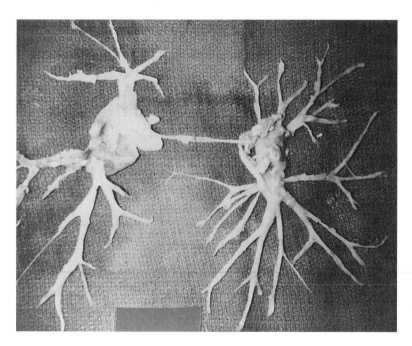

Figure 48.13 Specimen obtained at the time of pulmonary thromboendarterectomy. In addition to central thromboembolic obstruction, note multiple segmental extensions. Failure to adequately remove these distal extensions will result in an inadequate hemodynamic outcome.

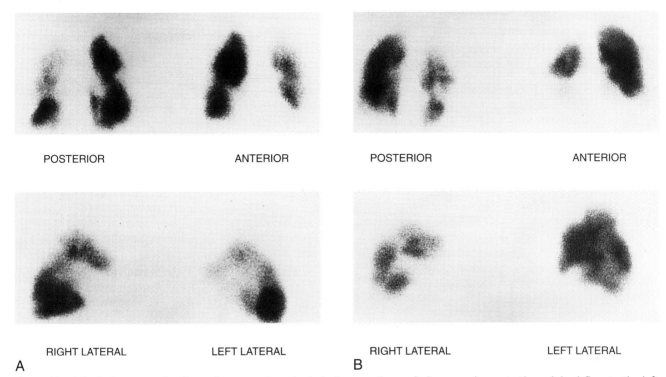

POSTERIOR ANTERIOR POSTERIOR ANTERIOR

RIGHT LATERAL LEFT LATERAL RIGHT LATERAL LEFT LATERAL

A B

Figure 48.14 Perfusion scans showing pulmonary artery steal. **A,** Preoperative perfusion scan demonstrating minimal flow to the left lung. **B,** Perfusion scan obtained in the early postoperative period demonstrating dramatic reversal of flow with vascular "steal" from right lung. Equilibration and normalization of flow over time is the rule.

Pulmonary artery steal (Fig. 48.14) represents a postoperative redistribution of pulmonary arterial blood flow away from previously well-perfused segments and into the newly endarterectomized segments. Long-term follow-up has demonstrated that pulmonary vascular steal resolves in the majority of patients.[212] Reperfusion pulmonary edema appears to represent a form of high-permeability lung injury that is limited to those areas of lung from which proximal thromboembolic obstructions have been removed (Fig. 48.15). It may appear up to 72 hours after surgery and is highly variable in severity, ranging from a mild form of edema resulting in postoperative hypoxemia to an acute, hemorrhagic, and fatal complication. When associated with pulmonary artery steal, reperfusion pulmonary edema can represent a significant challenge in terms of postoperative gas exchange. Pulmonary blood flow is directed toward edematous, noncompliant areas of lung that contribute poorly to gas exchange. Management of reperfusion edema, as with other forms of acute lung injury, is supportive until resolution occurs.

Although exact figures are not available, approximately 2500 thromboendarterectomy procedures have been performed worldwide. In reported series of patients undergoing thromboendarterectomy since 1999 (see Table 48.4), in-hospital mortality rates have ranged between 4.4% and 21.4%.[209,213-218] The specific factors affecting perioperative mortality have not been completely defined. Several studies have suggested that New York Heart Association functional class IV status, age greater than 70 years, the severity of preoperative pulmonary vascular resistance, the presence of right ventricular failure as manifested by high right atrial

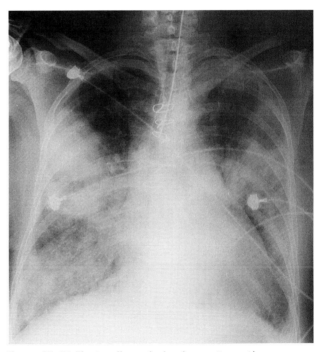

Figure 48.15 Chest radiograph showing postoperative reperfusion pulmonary edema. Only the upper lobes, from which no thromboembolic material was dissected, are spared.

pressures, details of the postoperative management, and perhaps the duration of pulmonary hypertension may adversely influence outcome. It is also reasonable to suggest that there may exist a strong relationship between volume of procedures performed and outcome, as has been demonstrated with other high-risk surgical procedures.[219] In the case of thromboendarterectomy, this may be related to consistency of patient evaluation, surgical experience, uniform delivery of postoperative care, and the presence of dedicated resources for dealing with postoperative complications. Should this prove to be the case, strong consideration could be given to performing the procedure at a limited number of referral centers.

Given what is known about the natural history of the disease and the progressive nature of the pulmonary hypertension associated with it, these findings suggest that early referral is preferable to late unless the possibility of a recent embolic event exists. Under this circumstance, a period of 6 to 8 weeks of conventional therapy is recommended to allow optimum thrombus resolution. Beyond this period of time, further improvement in the level of pulmonary hypertension cannot be achieved with medical therapy alone.[52]

Among survivors of thromboendarterectomy, restoration of pulmonary artery patency results in an immediate and dramatic hemodynamic improvement (Fig. 48.16). In published series, the mean reduction in pulmonary vascular resistance has approximated 70%, and a pulmonary vascular resistance in the range of 200 to 350 dyne-sec·cm^{-5} can be achieved (see Table 48.4). The long-term hemodynamic and symptomatic outcomes have been equally dramatic. Many patients are restored to normal activity, the majority return to class I functional status, and essentially all have improved at least one grade in the classification of cardiac disability.[220–222]

Approximately 10% to 15% of patients undergoing thromboendarterectomy will have residual levels of pulmonary hypertension following the procedure that have been associated with a negative long-term outcome. The only therapeutic alternative for patients who have undergone thromboendarterectomy with an inadequate hemodynamic outcome and for those not deemed candidates for thromboendarterectomy is lung transplantation. Preliminary results suggest that selected patients may benefit from chronic epoprostenol therapy.[223,224] Epoprostenol has been used preoperatively in patients with chronic thromboembolic pulmonary hypertension associated with severe hemodynamic impairment and has been demonstrated to improve the hemodynamic profile.[225] Whether such an approach improves outcome or decreases the incidence and severity of postoperative complications has not been determined.

OTHER FORMS OF EMBOLISM

Because the lungs receive all of the blood flow returned from the venous system, the pulmonary vascular bed serves as a "sieve" for all particulates entering the venous blood and is the first vascular bed to be exposed to any toxic substance injected intravenously. As a result of its strategic position, the pulmonary vascular bed is therefore exposed to a wide variety of potentially obstructing and injurious agents.

SCHISTOSOMIASIS

Among such agents, the most common on a worldwide basis, although not within the United States, is schistosomiasis.[226] This parasitic disorder may cause pulmonary hypertension by three mechanisms: anatomic obstruction

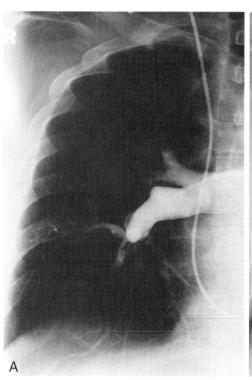
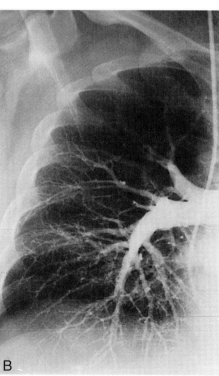

Figure 48.16 A, Preoperative pulmonary angiogram showing thromboembolic obstruction involving the right upper, middle, and lower lobe arteries. **B,** Postoperative angiogram showing normalization of flow. This angiographic improvement was accompanied by a corresponding hemodynamic improvement.

A

B

by the organism itself, an intense inflammatory vasculitic response to the components of the organism, and the development of portopulmonary hypertension. In endemic areas, schistosomal disease is the most common cause of cor pulmonale. Limited data suggest that cardiopulmonary schistosomiasis is seen most often in *Schistosoma mansoni* infection. This form of cor pulmonale does not occur in the absence of concomitant schistosomal liver disease, because the liver is always involved, usually quite extensively, before pulmonary involvement occurs. The premortem diagnosis of cardiopulmonary schistosomiasis depends on the detection of viable schistosomal ova in stool or urine along with evidence of hepatic fibrosis and pulmonary hypertension. Treatment with praziquantel can effectively eradicate schistosomal infections with minimal toxicity. However, cardiopulmonary manifestations are not likely to be reversible given the chronic fibrotic changes that have already occurred.

AIR EMBOLISM

An increasingly common form of nonthrombotic embolism in the United States is air embolism.[227] The increasing frequency of the problem reflects the wide variety of invasive surgical and medical procedures now available, the broad use of indwelling central venous catheters, the use of positive-pressure ventilation with high levels of positive end-expiratory pressure, and the frequency of thoracic and other forms of trauma. The simple inadvertent transection or disconnection of a large-bore intravenous catheter, particularly in the jugular or subclavian vein, can result in ingress of substantial quantities of air. Air bubbles enter the pulmonary vascular bed and, from there, are diffusely distributed throughout the body by way of either an intracardiac shunt or, more likely, through microvascular pulmonary shunts.

Physiologic consequences of pulmonary air embolism include an abrupt rise in pulmonary artery pressure. Noncardiogenic pulmonary edema may develop, lung compliance falls, and hypoxemia ensues. The symptoms of air embolism are variable and nonspecific, and may include alterations in sensorium, chest pain, dyspnea, or a sense of impending doom. These and other consequences appear to be due to two phenomena: actual lodgment of the bubbles in capillary beds, which interferes with nutrient supply to the affected organs; and the formation of platelet-fibrin aggregates, creating diffuse microthrombi.[228] Thrombocytopenia may be seen as a consequence of this latter event. The most serious consequences result from cerebral or coronary artery air embolism, the severity of the consequences depending upon the volume of air that gains access to the venous circulation.[227]

The best approaches to air embolism are prevention and early detection. Treatment consists of measures designed to restore blood flow and to promote reabsorption of the intravascular air. Measures designed to restore flow include patient positioning (Trendelenburg position with the left side down), removal of air through central venous catheters or direct needle aspiration, and closed-chest cardiac massage. Measures designed to increase absorption include the use of 100% oxygen and the institution of hyperbaric oxygen therapy as early as possible.[229,230] Utilizing such aggressive measures, mortality from air embolism has been dramatically reduced.

FAT EMBOLISM

Another reasonably frequent and dramatic form of nonthrombotic embolism is fat embolism.[231] A rather characteristic syndrome follows entry of neutral fat into the vascular system, consisting of the onset of dyspnea, petechiae, and mental confusion. There is a variable lag time of 24 to 48 hours in the onset of the syndrome following the inciting event.

By far the most common inciting event is traumatic fracture of marrow-containing long bones; the incidence of fat embolism rises with the number of fractures. However, orthopedic procedures and trauma to other fat-laden tissues (e.g., fatty liver) occasionally is followed by the same syndrome.

The reasons for the variability in incidence of the syndrome after apparently comparable injuries are not clear. Perhaps variations in incidence and severity relate to the amount of fat released. The pathophysiologic consequences appear to derive from two events: (1) actual vascular obstruction by neutral particles of fat and (2) the injurious effects of free fatty acids released by the action of lipases on the neutral fat.[232] The latter effect is probably the more important, causing a diffuse vasculitis with leakage from cerebral, pulmonary, and other vascular beds.[233]

The diagnosis of fat embolism syndrome is a clinical one suggested by the onset of dyspnea, neurologic abnormalities, petechiae, and fever in the proper clinical context.[234] Petechiae, typically distributed over the head, neck, anterior chest, and axillae, are present in only 20% to 50% of cases.[235] Therefore, their absence should not preclude consideration of the disease. No laboratory test is diagnostic of the syndrome.

Although a variety of treatments have been suggested (e.g., intravenous ethanol, albumin, dextran, heparin), none has proven effective. The role of corticosteroid therapy to prevent the onset of fat embolism syndrome after an inciting event remains controversial. Supportive treatment, including mechanical ventilatory support when necessary, is the primary approach, and survival is now the rule with meticulous supportive care.

AMNIOTIC FLUID EMBOLISM

Another special form of embolism is amniotic fluid embolism, a rare but unpredictable and catastrophic complication of pregnancy that represents the third leading cause of maternal mortality.[236] This disorder occurs during or after delivery when amniotic fluid gains access to uterine venous channels, and thereby to the pulmonary and general circulations. The delivery may be either spontaneous or by cesarean section; there are case reports of amniotic fluid emboli occurring during therapeutic abortion. Unexpectedly and suddenly, severe respiratory distress, cyanosis, hypotension, and, often, cardiovascular collapse occur. Although obstruction of the pulmonary vascular bed may exist, the major hemodynamic impairment appears to be related to left ventricular dysfunction.[237] Most cases develop during labor, but delayed onset of symptoms up to 48 hours after delivery has been reported.[238] Advanced maternal age, multiparity, premature placental separation, fetal death, and meconium staining of amniotic fluid are associated with increased risk of amniotic fluid embolism.

Amniotic fluid contains particulate materials that can cause pulmonary vascular obstruction, but the major pathogenetic mechanism of the syndrome remains uncertain. Amniotic fluid does have thromboplastic activity that leads to extensive fibrin deposition in the lung vasculature and, occasionally, in other organs. As a consequence of fibrin deposition, a severe consumptive coagulopathy develops, including marked hypofibrinogenemia and thrombocytopenia. Following the acute event, an enhanced fibrinolytic state often occurs.[235,239]

The diagnosis of amniotic fluid embolism is based on a compatible clinical picture, often enhanced by finding amniotic fluid components in the pulmonary circulation. The presence of squamous cells in pulmonary arterial blood, once considered pathognomonic, has proven to be a nonspecific finding.[236]

Although various forms of therapy have been suggested (e.g., antifibrinolytic agents such as aminocaproic acid, cryoprecipitate), the best approach is supportive. Even in the setting of aggressive supportive measures, however, maternal mortality is in the range of 60% to 80%, with many survivors suffering from long-term neurologic disability.

SEPTIC EMBOLISM

Septic embolism is another special disorder that, unfortunately, is also increasing in frequency owing to widespread injection drug abuse and the expanding use of indwelling intravenous catheters. Previously, septic embolism was almost exclusively a complication of septic pelvic thrombophlebitis secondary to both septic abortion and postpuerperal uterine infection. Those conditions still occur, but injection drug abuse is now by far the more common cause.[240] An increasingly common cause is iatrogenic: infections secondary to indwelling catheters inserted for a variety of diagnostic or therapeutic purposes.[241]

Microscopically, septic phlebitis consists of purulent material admixed with fibrin thrombus. Embolization from such material does occur and can result in obstruction of small pulmonary vessels, but the major consequence is pulmonary infection. Characteristically, the chest roentgenogram displays scattered pulmonary infiltrates that undergo cavitation. An increasing number of such infiltrates develop over periods of hours to a few days. Symptoms and signs include a septic temperature course, dyspnea, cough, pleuritic chest pain, and hemoptysis. Initial treatment consists of appropriate antimicrobial drugs. If an indwelling catheter is the source of the infection, it should be removed. If there is not a prompt response to this regimen, surgical isolation of the septic vein, if present, should be considered. The role of systemic anticoagulation remains uncertain. Endocarditis may complicate septic phlebitis, or mimic it, particularly in drug addicts.

OTHER EMBOLI

Because of its sieve function, the lung may also be embolized on occasion by a wide variety of other materials. Cancer cells, of course, often find their way into and adhere to the pulmonary vessels; on occasion, tumor emboli (admixtures of thrombus with cells) can occur and mimic bland embolization. Trophoblastic tissue can escape the uterus and lodge in the pulmonary circulation during evacuation of a molar pregnancy or during hysterectomy for an invasive mole. After head trauma, brain tissue has been found in the lungs; the same is true of liver cells following abdominal trauma and of bone marrow after cardiopulmonary resuscitation.

Finally, in this era of injection drug abuse, noninfectious vasculitic-thrombotic complications are being seen with increasing frequency. Particulate and irritant drug carriers (e.g., talc), and occasionally the drugs themselves, may cause vascular inflammation and secondary thrombosis.[242] More commonly, uptake of the talc into the pulmonary interstitium results in fibrosis and advanced emphysema.[243,244]

SUMMARY

Pulmonary embolism from deep venous thrombosis is an extremely important cause of morbidity and mortality. As described, a major reduction of this morbidity and mortality will occur only through the widespread use of prophylactic measures in populations at risk and through a heightened clinical suspicion and awareness of the often subtle and nonspecific presentation of the disease. Appropriate use of anticoagulants decreases the risk of further thrombosis and recurrent embolism. Despite certain unknowns, many of the long-standing controversies surrounding venous thromboembolism have been partially or completely resolved. Within the next few years, uncertainties regarding the role of CT scanning in the diagnosis of pulmonary embolism, D-dimer testing in the exclusion of venous thromboembolism, risk stratification in patients with confirmed embolism, and populations in whom outpatient management is feasible should be resolved. Physicians should be aware of these advances and begin to apply the new knowledge about the pathogenesis, natural history, diagnosis, and treatment of pulmonary embolism and, especially, of its antecedent, deep venous thrombosis.

REFERENCES

1. Dalen JE, Alpert JS: Natural history of pulmonary embolism. Prog Cardiovasc Dis 17:259–270, 1975.
2. White RH: The epidemiology of venous thromboembolism. Circulation 107(23 Suppl I):I-4–I-8, 2003.
3. Carson JL, Kelley MA, Ruff A, et al: The clinical course of pulmonary embolism. N Engl J Med 326:1240–1245, 1992.
4. Wood KE: The presence of shock defines the threshold to initiate thrombolytic therapy in patients with pulmonary embolism. Intensive Care Med 28:1537–1546, 2002.
5. Lilienfeld DE: Decreasing mortality from pulmonary embolism in the United States, 1979–1996. Int J Epidemiol 29:465–469, 2000.
6. Horlander KT, Mannino DM, Leeper KV: Pulmonary embolism mortality in the United States, 1979–1998: An analysis using multiple-cause mortality data. Arch Intern Med 163:1711–1717, 2003.
7. Macik BG, Ortel TL: Clinical and laboratory evaluation of the hypercoagulable states. Clin Chest Med 16:375–389, 1995.
8. Dahlback B, Carlsson M, Svensson PJ: Familial thrombophilia due to a previously unrecognized mechanism characterized by poor anticoagulant response to activated protein C: Prediction of a cofactor to activated protein C. Proc Natl Acad Sci U S A 90:1004–1008, 1993.

9. Ridker PM, Miletich JP, Hennekens CH, Buring JE: Ethnic distribution of factor V Leiden in 4047 men and women: Implications for venous thromboembolism screening. JAMA 277:1305–1307, 1997.

10. De Stefano V, Chiusolo P, Paciaroni K, Leone G: Epidemiology of factor V Leiden: Clinical implications. Semin Thromb Hemost 24:367–379, 1998.

11. Ridker PM, Hennekens CH, Lindpainter K, et al: Mutation in the gene coding for coagulation factor V and the risk of myocardial infarction, stroke, and venous thrombosis in apparently healthy men. N Engl J Med 332:912–917, 1995.

12. Crowther MA, Kelton JG: Congenital thrombophilic states associated with venous thrombosis: A qualitative overview and proposed classification system. Ann Intern Med 138:128–134, 2003.

13. Price DT, Ridker PM: Factor V Leiden mutation and the risks for thromboembolic disease: A clinical perspective. Ann Intern Med 127:895–903, 1997.

14. Walker ID: Thrombophilia in pregnancy. J Clin Pathol 53:573–580, 2000.

15. Vandenbroucke JP, Koster T, Briet E, et al: Increased risk of venous thrombosis in oral-contraceptive users who are carriers of factor V Leiden mutation. Lancet 334:1453–1457, 1994.

16. Poort SR, Rosendaal FR, Reitsma PH, Bertina RM: A common genetic variation in the 3′-untranslated region of the prothrombin gene is associated with elevated plasma prothrombin levels and an increase in venous thrombosis. Blood 88:3698–3703, 1996.

17. Salomon O, Steinberg DM, Zivelin A, et al: Single and combined prothrombotic factors in patients with idiopathic venous thromboembolism: Prevalence and risk assessment. Arterioscler Thromb Vasc Biol 19:511–518, 1999.

18. Ray JG: Meta-analysis of hyperhomocysteinemia as a risk factor for venous thromboembolic disease. Arch Intern Med 158:2101–2106, 1998.

19. Key NS, McGlennan RC: Hyperhomocyst(e)inemia and thrombophilia. Arch Pathol Lab Med 126:1367–1375, 2002.

20. Walker ID: Factor V Leiden: Should all women be screened prior to commencing the contraceptive pill? Blood Rev 13:8–13, 1999.

21. Seligsohn U, Lubetsky A: Genetic susceptibility to venous thrombosis. N Engl J Med 344:1222–1231, 2001.

22. Vandenbroucke JP, Koster T, Briet E, et al: Increased risk of venous thrombosis in oral contraceptive users who are carriers of factor V Leiden mutation. Lancet 344:1453–1457, 1994.

23. Anderson FA, Spencer FA: Risk factors for venous thromboembolism. Circulation 107(23 Suppl I):I-9–I-16, 2003.

24. Samama MM, Cohen AT, Darmon JY, et al: A comparison of enoxaparin with placebo for the prevention of venous thromboembolism in acutely ill medical patients. N Engl J Med 341:793–800, 1999.

25. Heit JA: Risk factors for venous thromboembolism. Clin Chest Med 24:1–12, 2003.

26. Kearon C: Natural history of venous thromboembolism. Circulation 107(23 Suppl I):I-22–I-30, 2003.

27. Sevitt S, Gallagher N: Venous thrombosis and pulmonary embolism: A clinicopathological study in injured and burned patients. Br J Surg 48:475–489, 1961.

28. Haire D: Arm vein thrombosis. Clin Chest Med 16:341–352, 1995.

29. Moser KM, LeMoine JR: Is embolic risk conditioned by location of deep venous thrombosis? Ann Intern Med 94:439–444, 1981.

30. Moser KM, Fedullo PF, Littlejohn JK, et al: Frequent asymptomatic pulmonary embolism in patients with deep venous thrombosis. JAMA 27:223–225, 1994.

31. Huisman MV, Buller HR, ten Cate J, et al: Unexpected high prevalence of silent pulmonary embolism in patients with deep venous thrombosis. Chest 95:498–502, 1989.

32. Schulman S, Rhedin A-S, Lindmarker P, et al: A comparison of six weeks with six months of oral anticoagulant therapy after a first episode of venous thromboembolism. N Engl J Med 332:1661–1665, 1995.

33. Prandoni P, Lensing AWA, Cogo A, et al: The long-term clinical course of acute deep venous thrombosis. Ann Intern Med 125:1–7, 1996.

34. Wood KE: Major pulmonary embolism: Review of a pathophysiologic approach to the golden hour of hemodynamically significant pulmonary embolism. Chest 121:877–905, 2002.

35. Severinghaus JW, Swenson EW, Finley TN, et al: Unilateral hypoventilation produced by occlusion of one pulmonary artery. J Appl Physiol 16:53–57, 1961.

36. Sergysels R: Pulmonary gas exchange abnormalities in pulmonary embolism. In Morpurgo M (ed): Lung Biology in Health and Disease. Vol 75: Pulmonary Embolism. New York: Marcel Dekker, 1994, pp 89–96.

37. Huet Y, Lemaire F, Brun-Buisson C, et al: Hypoxemia in acute pulmonary embolism. Chest 88:829–836, 1985.

38. Manier G, Castaing Y, Guenard H: Determinants of hypoxemia during the acute phase of pulmonary embolism in humans. Am Rev Respir Dis 132:332–338, 1985.

39. D'Alonzo GE, Bower JS, Dehart P, et al: The mechanisms of abnormal gas exchange in acute massive pulmonary embolism. Am Rev Respir Dis 128:170–172, 1983.

40. Cherniak V, Hodson WA, Greenfield LJ: Effect of chronic pulmonary artery ligation on pulmonary mechanics and surfactant. J Appl Physiol 21:1315–1319, 1966.

41. Shure D: The bronchial circulation in pulmonary vascular obstruction. In Butler J (ed): Lung Biology in Health and Disease. Vol 57: The Bronchial Circulation. New York: Marcel Dekker, 1992, pp 579–597.

42. Jandik J, Endrys J, Rehulová E, et al: Bronchial arteries in experimental pulmonary infarction: Angiographic and morphometric study. Cardiovasc Res 27:1076–1083, 1993.

43. McIntyre KM, Sasahara AA: Hemodynamic and ventricular response to pulmonary embolism. Prog Cardiovasc Dis 17:175–190, 1974.

44. McIntyre KM, Sasahara AA: The hemodynamic response to pulmonary embolism in patients without prior cardiopulmonary disease. Am J Cardiol 17:288–294, 1971.

45. Elliott CG: Pulmonary physiology during pulmonary embolism. Chest 101:163S–171S, 1992.

46. Smulders YM: Pathophysiology and treatment of haemodynamic instability in acute pulmonary embolism: The pivotal role of pulmonary vasoconstriction. Cardiovasc Res 48:23–33, 2000.

47. Azarian R, Wartski M, Collignon M-A, et al: Lung perfusion scans and hemodynamics in acute and chronic pulmonary embolism. J Nucl Med 38:980–983, 1997.

48. James WS, Minh VD, Minteer MA, Moser KM: Rapid resolution of pulmonary embolus in man. West J Med 128:60–64, 1978.

49. Dalen JE, Banas JS, Brooks HL: Resolution rate of acute pulmonary embolism in man. N Engl J Med 280:1194–1199, 1969.

50. Tow DE, Wagner HN Jr: Recovery of pulmonary arterial blood flow in patients with pulmonary embolism. N Engl J Med 275:1053–1059, 1967.

51. Wartski M, Collignon M-A: Incomplete recovery of lung perfusion after 3 months in patients with acute pulmonary

embolism treated with antithrombotic agents. J Nucl Med 41:1043–1048, 2000.

52. Ribeiro A, Lindmarker P, Johnsson H, et al: Pulmonary embolism: One-year follow-up with echocardiography Doppler and five-year survival analysis. Circulation 99:1325–1330, 1999.

53. Cranley JJ, Canos AJ, Sull WJ: The diagnosis of deep venous thrombosis: Fallibility of clinical symptoms and signs. Arch Surg 111:34–36, 1976.

54. Haeger K: Problems of acute deep venous thrombosis, I: The interpretation of signs and symptoms. Angiology 20:219–223, 1969.

55. Anand S, Wells PS, Hunt D, et al: Does this patient have deep venous thrombosis? JAMA 279:1094–1099, 1998 [published erratum appears in JAMA 280:328, 1988].

56. Well PS, Lensing AW, Davidson BL: Accuracy of ultrasound for the diagnosis of deep venous thrombosis in asymptomatic patients after orthopedic surgery: A meta-analysis. Ann Intern Med 122:47–53, 1995.

57. Ryu JH, Olson EJ, Pellikka PA: Clinical recognition of pulmonary embolism: Problem of unrecognized and asymptomatic cases. Mayo Clin Proc 73:873–879, 1998.

58. Goldhaber SZ, Hennekens CH, Evans DA, et al: Factors associated with the correct antemortem diagnosis of major pulmonary embolism. Am J Med 73:822–826, 1982.

59. Stein PD, Terrin ML, Hales CA, et al: Clinical, laboratory, roentgenographic, and electrocardiographic findings in patients with acute pulmonary embolism and no pre-existing cardiac or pulmonary disease. Chest 100:598–603, 1991.

60. Stein PD, Henry JW: Clinical characteristics of patients with acute pulmonary embolism stratified according to their presenting syndromes. Chest 112:974–979, 1997.

61. The PIOPED Investigators: Value of the ventilation/perfusion scan in acute pulmonary embolism: Results of the Prospective Investigation of Pulmonary Embolism Diagnosis (PIOPED). JAMA 263:2753–2759, 1990.

62. Monreal M, Ruiz J, Olazabal A, et al: Deep venous thrombosis and the risk of pulmonary embolism: A systematic study. Chest 102:677–681, 1992.

63. Afzal A, Noor HA, Gill SA, et al: Leukocytosis in pulmonary embolism. Chest 115:1329–1332, 1999.

64. Stein PD, Afzal A, Henry JW, Villareal CG: Fever in acute pulmonary embolism. Chest 117:39–42, 2000.

65. Rabinov K, Paulin S: Roentgen diagnosis of venous thrombosis in the leg. Arch Surg 104:134–144, 1972.

66. Fraser JD, Anderson DR: Deep venous thrombosis: Recent advances and optimal investigation with US. Radiology 211:9–24, 1999.

67. Pezzullo JA, Perkins AB, Cronan JJ: Symptomatic deep venous thrombosis: Diagnosis with limited compression US. Radiology 198:67–70, 1996.

68. Frederick MG, Hertzberg BS, Kliewer MA, et al: Can the US examination for lower extremity deep venous thrombosis be abbreviated? A prospective study of 755 examinations. Radiology 199:45–47, 1996.

69. Strothman G, Blebea J, Fowl RJ, Rosenthal G: Contralateral duplex scanning for deep venous thrombosis is unnecessary in patients with symptoms. J Vasc Surg 22:543–547, 1995.

70. Badgett DK, Comerota MC, Khan MN, et al: Duplex venous imaging: Role for a comprehensive lower extremity examination. Ann Vasc Surg 14:73–76, 2000.

71. Kearon C, Julian JA, Math M, et al: Noninvasive diagnosis of deep venous thrombosis. Ann Intern Med 128:663–667, 1998.

72. Heijboer H, Büller HR, Lensing AWA, et al: A comparison of real-time ultrasonography with impedance plethysmography for the diagnosis of deep-vein thrombosis in symptomatic outpatients. N Engl J Med 329:1365–1369, 1993.

73. Heijboer H, Cogo A, Buller HR, et al: Detection of deep-vein thrombosis with impedance plethysmography and real-time compression ultrasonography in hospitalized patients. Arch Intern Med 152:1901–1903, 1992.

74. Ginsberg JS, Wells PS, Hirsh J, et al: Reevaluation of the sensitivity of impedance plethysmography for the detection of proximal deep vein thrombosis. Arch Intern Med 94:439–444, 1994.

75. Wells PS, Hirsh J, Anderson DR, et al: Comparison of the accuracy of impedance plethysmography and compression ultrasonography in outpatients with clinically suspected deep vein thrombosis: A two centre paired-design prospective trial. Thromb Haemost 74:1423–1427, 1995.

76. Huisman MV, Buller HR, ten Cate JW, et al: Serial impedance plethysmography for suspected deep venous thrombosis in outpatients. N Engl J Med 314:823–828, 1986.

77. Wells PS, Hirsh J, Anderson DR, et al: A simple clinical model for the diagnosis of deep-vein thrombosis combined with impedance plethysmography: Potential for an improvement in the diagnostic process. J Intern Med 243:15–23, 1998.

78. Huisman MV, Buller HR, ten Cate JW: Utility of impedance plethysmography in the diagnosis of recurrent deep-vein thrombosis. Arch Intern Med 148:681–683, 1988.

79. Evans AJ, Sostman HD, Witty LA, et al: Detection of DVT: Prospective evaluation of MRI and sonography. J Magn Reson Imaging 1:44–51, 1996.

80. Kanne JP, Lalani TA: Role of computed tomography and magnetic resonance imaging for deep venous thrombosis and pulmonary embolism. Circulation 109 (12 Suppl 1):I15–I21, 2004.

81. Loud PA, Katz DS, Bruce DA, et al: Deep venous thrombosis with suspected pulmonary embolism: Detection with combined CT venography and pulmonary angiography. Radiology 219:498–502, 2001.

82. Kelly J, Rudd A, Lewis RG, Hunt BJ: Plasma D-dimers in the diagnosis of venous thromboembolism. Arch Intern Med 162:747–756, 2002.

83. Stein PD, Hull RD, Patel KC, et al: D-dimer for the exclusion of acute venous thrombosis and pulmonary embolism: a systematic review. Ann Intern Med 140:589–601, 2004.

84. Perrier A, Desmarais S, Miron MJ, et al: Non-invasive diagnosis of venous thromboembolism in outpatients. Lancet 353:190–195, 1999.

85. Wells PS, Anderson DR, Rodger M, et al: Evaluation of D-dimer in the diagnosis of suspected deep vein thrombosis. N Engl J Med 349:1227–1235, 2003.

86. Constans J, Boutinet C, Salmi R, et al: Comparison of four clinical prediction scores for the diagnosis of lower limb deep venous thrombosis in outpatients. Am J Med 115:436–440, 2003.

87. Wells PS, Anderson DR, Bormanis J, et al: Value of assessment of pretest probability of deep-vein thrombosis in clinical management. Lancet 350:1795–1798, 1997.

88. Schutgens RE, Ackermark P, Haas FJ, et al: Combination of a normal D-dimer concentration and a non-high pretest clinical probability score is a safe strategy to exclude deep venous thrombosis. Circulation 107:593–597, 2003.

89. Worsley DF, Alavi A, Aronchick JTT, et al: Chest radiographic findings in patients with acute pulmonary embolism: Observations from the PIOPED study. Radiology 189:133–136, 1993.

90. Stein PD, Terrin ML, Hales CA, et al: Clinical, laboratory, roentgenographic, and electrocardiographic findings in patients with acute pulmonary embolism and no pre-existing cardiac or pulmonary disease. Chest 100:598–603, 1991.

91. Stein PD, Dalen JE, McIntyre KM, et al: The electrocardiogram in acute pulmonary embolism. Prog Cardiovasc Dis 17:247–257, 1975.

92. Kucher N, Walpoth N, Wustmann K, et al: QR in V1–an ECG sign associated with right ventricular strain and adverse clinical outcome in pulmonary embolism. Eur Heart J 24:1113–1119, 2003.

93. Stein PD, Goldhaber SZ, Henry JW, Miller AC: Arterial blood gas analysis in the assessment of suspected acute pulmonary embolism. Chest 109:78–81, 1996.

94. McConnell MV, Solomon SD, Rayan ME: Regional right ventricular dysfunction detected by echocardiography in acute pulmonary embolism. Am J Cardiol 78:469–473, 1996.

95. Krivec B, Voga G, Zuran I, et al: Diagnosis and treatment of shock due to massive pulmonary embolism: Approach with transesophageal echocardiography and intrapulmonary thrombolysis. Chest 112:1310–1316, 1997.

96. Miniati M, Monti S, Pratali L, et al: Value of transthoracic echocardiography in the diagnosis of pulmonary embolism: Results of a prospective study in unselected patients. Am J Med 110:528–535, 2001.

97. Goldhaber SZ: Echocardiography in the management of pulmonary embolism. Ann Intern Med 136:691–700, 2002.

98. Konstantinides S, Geibel A, Olschewski M, et al: Importance of cardiac troponin I and T in risk stratification of patients with acute pulmonary embolism. Circulation 106:1263–1268, 2002.

99. ten Wolde M, Tulevski II, Muylder JW, et al: Brain natriuretic peptide as a predictor of adverse outcome in patients with pulmonary embolism. Circulation 107:2082–2084, 2003.

100. Hamel E, Pacouret G, Vincentelli D, et al: Thrombolysis or heparin therapy in massive pulmonary embolism with right ventricular dilation. Chest 120:120–125, 2001.

101. Hull RD, Raskob GE, Pineo GF, Brant RF: The low-probability lung scan: A need for change in nomenclature. Arch Intern Med 155:1845–1851, 1995.

102. Miniati M, Pistolesi M, Marini C, et al: Value of perfusion lung scan in the diagnosis of pulmonary embolism: Results of the Prospective Investigative Study of Acute Pulmonary Embolism Diagnosis (PISA-PED). Am J Respir Crit Care Med 154:1387–1393, 1996.

103. Stein PD, Terrin ML, Gottschalk A, et al: Value of ventilation/perfusion scans versus perfusion scans alone in acute pulmonary embolism. Am J Cardiol 69:1239–1241, 1992.

104. Hartmann IJ, Hagen PJ, Melissant CF, et al: Diagnosing acute pulmonary embolism: Effect of chronic obstructive pulmonary disease on the performance of D-dimer testing, ventilation/perfusion scintigraphy, spiral computed tomographic angiography, and conventional angiography. ANTELOPE Study Group: Advances in New Technologies Evaluating the Localization of Pulmonary Embolism. Am J Respir Crit Care Med 162:2232–2237, 2000.

105. Hiorns MP, Mayo JR: Spiral computed tomography for acute pulmonary embolism. Can Assoc Radiol J 53:258–268, 2002.

106. Ruiz Y, Caballero P, Caniego JL: Prospective comparison of helical CT with angiography in pulmonary embolism: Global and selective territory analysis. Interobserver agreement. Eur Radiol 13:823–829, 2003.

107. Oser RF, Zuckerman DA, Gutierrez FR, Brink JA: Anatomic distribution of pulmonary emboli at pulmonary angiography: Implications for cross-sectional imaging. Radiology 199:31–35, 1996.

108. Stein PD, Henry JW: Prevalence of acute pulmonary embolism in central and subsegmental pulmonary arteries and relationship to probability interpretation of ventilation/perfusion lung scans. Chest 111:1246–1248, 1997.

109. Moores LK, Jackson WL, Shorr AF, Jackson JL: Meta-analysis: Outcomes in patients with suspected pulmonary embolism managed with computed tomographic pulmonary angiography. Ann Intern Med 141:866–874, 2004.

110. Van Strijen MJL, de Monye W, Schiereck J, et al: Single-detector helical computed tomography as the primary diagnostic test in suspected pulmonary embolism: A multicenter clinical management study of 510 patients. Ann Intern Med 138:307–314, 2003.

111. Turkstra F, Kuijer PM, van Beek EJ, et al: Diagnostic utility of ultrasonography of leg veins in patients suspected of having pulmonary embolism. Ann Intern Med 126:775–781, 1997.

112. Perrier A: Diagnosis of acute pulmonary embolism: An update. Schweiz Med Wochenschr 130:254–271, 2000.

113. Marieke JHA, Kruip MD, Leclercq MGL, et al: Diagnostic strategies for excluding pulmonary embolism in clinical outcome studies: A systematic review. Ann Intern Med 138:941–951, 2003.

114. Kearon C: Diagnosis of pulmonary embolism. CMAJ 168:183–194, 2003.

115. Nilsson T, Carlsson A, Mare K: Pulmonary angiography: A safe procedure with modern contrast media and technique. Eur Radiol 8:86–89, 1998.

116. Wells PS, Anderson DR, Rodger M, et al: Derivation of a simple clinical model to categorize patients' probability of pulmonary embolism: Increasing the model's utility with the SimpliRED D-dimer. Thromb Haemost 83:416–420, 2000.

117. Wicki J, Perneger TV, Junod AF, et al: Assessing clinical probability of pulmonary embolism in the emergency ward. Arch Intern Med 161:92–97, 2001.

118. Miniati M, Monti S, Bottai M: A structured clinical model for predicting the probability of pulmonary embolism. Am J Med 114:173–179, 2003.

119. Kruip MJ, Slob MJ, Schijen JH, et al: Use of a clinical decision rule in combination with d-dimer concentration in diagnostic workup of patients with suspected pulmonary embolism: A prospective management study. Arch Intern Med 162:1631–1635, 2002.

120. Asif A, Preston RA, Roth D: Radiocontrast-induced nephropathy. Am J Ther 10:137–147, 2003.

121. Greer IA: Prevention and management of venous thromboembolism in pregnancy. Clin Chest Med 24:123–137, 2003.

122. Winer-Muram HT, Boone JM, Brown HL, et al: Pulmonary embolism in pregnant patients: Fetal radiation dose with helical CT. Radiology 224:487–492, 2002.

123. Bergqvist D, Agnelli G, Cohen AT, et al: Duration of prophylaxis against venous thromboembolism with enoxaparin after surgery for cancer. N Engl J Med 346:975–980, 2002.

124. An International Multicentre Trial: Prevention of fatal postoperative pulmonary embolism by low doses of subcutaneous heparin. Lancet 2:45–51, 1975.

125. Geerts WH, Heit JA, Clagett P, et al: Prevention of venous thromboembolism. Chest 119(Suppl):132S–175S, 2001.

126. Koch A, Ziegler S, Breitschwerdt H, Victor N: Low molecular weight heparin and unfractionated heparin in

thrombosis prophylaxis: Meta-analysis based on original patient data. Thromb Res 102:295–309, 2001.

127. Comerota AJ, Katz ML, White JV: Why does prophylaxis with external pneumatic compression for deep venous thrombosis fail? Am J Surg 164:265–269, 1992.

128. Proctor MC, Greenfield LJ, Wakefield TW, Zajkowski PJ: A clinical comparison of pneumatic compression devices: The basis for selection. J Vasc Surg 34:459–463, 2001.

129. Hirsh J, Dalen J, Anderson DR, et al: Oral anticoagulants: Mechanism of action, clinical effectiveness, and optimal therapeutic range. Chest 119(1 Suppl):8S–21S, 2001.

130. Francis CW, Marder VJ, McCollister EC, et al: Two step warfarin therapy: Prevention of postoperative venous thrombosis without excessive bleeding. JAMA 249:374–378, 1983.

131. Hull RD, Pinco GF, Stein PD, et al: Timing of initial administration of low-molecular-weight heparin prophylaxis against deep vein thrombosis in patients following elective hip arthroplasty. Arch Intern Med 161:1952–1960, 2001.

132. Planes A, Vochelle N, Darmon JY, et al: Risk of deep-venous thrombosis after hospital discharge in patients having undergone total hip replacement: Double-blind randomised comparison of enoxaparin versus placebo. Lancet 348:224–248, 1996.

133. Lassen MR, Bauer KA, Eriksson BI, et al: Postoperative fondaparinux versus preoperative enoxaparin for prevention of venous thromboembolism in elective hip-replacement surgery: A randomised double-blind comparison. Lancet 359:1715–1720, 2002.

134. Turpie AG, Bauer KA, Eriksson BI, Lassen MR: Fondaparinux vs enoxaparin for the prevention of venous thromboembolism in major orthopedic surgery: A meta-analysis of 4 randomized double-blind studies. Arch Intern Med 162:1833–1840, 2002.

135. Francis CW, Berkowitz SD, Comp PC, et al: Comparison of ximelagatran with warfarin for the prevention of venous thromboembolism after total knee replacement. N Engl J Med 349:1703–1712, 2003.

136. Girard TD, Philbrick JT, Fritz Angle J, Becker DM: Prophylactic vena cava filters for trauma patients: a systematic review of the literature. Thromb Res 112:261–267, 2003.

137. Anderson FA Jr, Wheeler HB, Goldberg RG, et al: Physician practices in the prevention of venous thromboembolism. Ann Intern Med 115:591–595, 1991.

138. Bratzler DW, Raskob GE, Murray CK, et al: Underuse of venous thromboembolism prophylaxis for general surgery patients: Physician practices in the community hospital setting. Arch Intern Med 158:1909–1912, 1998.

139. Hyers TM, Agnelli G, Hull RD, et al: Antithrombotic therapy for venous thromboembolic disease. Chest 119:176S–193S, 2001.

140. Wheeler RH, Jaquiss RD, Newman JH: Physician practices in the treatment of pulmonary embolism and deep venous thrombosis. Arch Intern Med 148:1321–1325, 1988.

141. Bernardi E, Piccioli A, Oliboni G, et al: Nomograms for the administration of unfractionated heparin in the initial treatment of acute thromboembolism—an overview. Thromb Haemost 84:22–26, 2000.

142. Raschke RA, Reilly BM, Guidry JR, et al: The weight based heparin dosing nomogram compared with a "standard care" nomogram: A randomized controlled study. Ann Intern Med 119:874–881, 1993.

143. Bates SM, Weitz JI, Johnson M, et al: Use of a fixed activated partial thromboplastin time ratio to establish a therapeutic range for unfractionated heparin. Arch Intern Med 161:385–391, 2001.

144. Levine MN, Hirsh J, Gent M, et al: A randomized trial comparing activated thromboplastin time with heparin assay in patients with acute venous thromboembolism requiring large daily doses of heparin. Arch Intern Med 154:49–56, 1994.

145. Hull RD, Raskob GE, Rosenbloom DR, et al: Optimal therapeutic level of heparin therapy in patients with venous thromboembolism. Arch Intern Med 152:1589–1595, 1992.

146. Hull RD, Raskob GE, Brant RF, et al: The importance of initial heparin treatment on long-term clinical outcomes of antithrombotic therapy: The emerging theme of delayed recurrence. Arch Intern Med 157:2317–2321, 1997.

147. Dolovich LR, Ginsberg JS, Douketis JD, et al: A meta-analysis comparing low-molecular weight heparins with unfractionated heparin in the treatment of venous thromboembolism. Arch Intern Med 160:181–188, 2000.

148. Segal JB, Bolger DT, Jenckes MW, et al: Outpatient therapy with low molecular weight heparin for the treatment of venous thromboembolism: A review of efficacy, safety, and costs. Am J Med 115:298–308, 2003.

149. Low-molecular-weight heparin in the treatment of patients with venous thromboembolism. The Columbus Investigators. N Engl J Med 337:657–662, 1997.

150. Simonneau G, Sors H, Charbonnier B, et al: A comparison of low-molecular weight heparin with unfractionated heparin for acute pulmonary embolism. N Engl J Med 337:663–669, 1997.

151. Kovacs MJ, Anderson D, Morrow B, et al: Outpatient treatment of pulmonary embolism with dalteparin. Thromb Haemost 83:209–211, 2000.

152. Hull RD, Raskob GE, Rosenbloom D, et al: Heparin for 5 days as compared with 10 days in the initial treatment of proximal venous thrombosis. N Engl J Med 322:1260–1264, 1990.

153. Chong BH: Heparin-induced thrombocytopenia. J Thromb Haemost 1:1471–1478, 2003.

154. Warkentin TE, Kelton JG: Temporal aspects of heparin-induced thrombocytopenia. N Engl J Med 344:1286–1292, 2001.

155. Wallis DE, Workman DL, Lewis BE, et al: Failure of early heparin cessation as treatment for heparin-induced thrombocytopenia. Am J Med 106:629–635, 1999.

156. Lewis BE, Wallis DE, Leya F, et al: Argatroban anticoagulation in patients with heparin-induced thrombocytopenia. Arch Intern Med 163:1849–1856, 2003.

157. Tardy-Poncet B, Mahul P, Beraud AM, et al: Failure of Organan therapy in a patient with a previous heparin-induced thrombocytopenia. Br J Haematol 90:69–70, 1995.

158. Warkentin TE, Levine MN, Hirsh J, et al: Heparin-induced thrombocytopenia in patients treated with low molecular weight heparin or unfractionated heparin. N Engl J Med 332:1330–1335, 1995.

159. Streiff MB: Vena caval filters: A comprehensive review. Blood 95:3669–3677, 2000.

160. Decousus H, Leizorovicz A, Parent F, et al: A clinical trial of vena caval filters in the prevention of pulmonary embolism in patients with proximal deep-vein thrombosis. N Engl J Med 338:409–415, 1998.

161. Tapson VF, Witty LA: Massive pulmonary embolism: Diagnostic and therapeutic strategies. Clin Chest Med 16:329–340, 1995.

162. Layish DT, Tapson VF: Pharmacologic hemodynamic support in massive pulmonary embolism. Chest 111:218–224, 1997.

163. Konstantinides S: The case for thrombolysis in acute major pulmonary embolism: Hemodynamic benefits and beyond. Intensive Care Med 28:1547–1551, 2002.

164. Dalen JE, Alpert JS, Hirsch J: Thrombolytic therapy for pulmonary embolism: Is it effective? Is it safe? When is it indicated? Arch Intern Med 157:2550–2556, 1997.

165. Konstantinides S, Geibel A, Heusel G, et al: Heparin plus alteplase compared with heparin alone in patients with submassive pulmonary embolism. N Engl J Med 347:1143–1150, 2002.

166. Meneveau N, Ming LP, Seronde MF, et al: In-hospital and long-term outcome after sub-massive and massive pulmonary embolism submitted to thrombolytic therapy. Eur Heart J 24:1447–1454, 2003.

167. Rose PS, Punjabi NM, Pearse DB: Treatment of right heart thromboemboli. Chest 121:806–814, 2002.

168. Chartier L, Bera J, Delomez M, et al: Free-floating thrombi in the right heart: Diagnosis, management, and prognostic indexes in 38 consecutive patients. Circulation 99:2779–2783, 1999.

169. Grifone S, Olivotto I, Cecchini P, et al: Short-term clinical outcome of patients with acute pulmonary embolism, normal blood pressure, and echocardiographic right ventricular dysfunction. Circulation 101:2817–2822, 2000.

170. Hamel E, Pacouret G, Vincentelli D, et al: Thrombolysis or heparin therapy in massive pulmonary embolism with right ventricular dilation. Chest 120:120–125, 2001.

171. Gray HH, Miller GAH, Paneth M: Pulmonary embolectomy: Its place in the management of pulmonary embolism. Lancet 1:1441–1445, 1988.

172. Doerge HC, Schoendube FA, Loeser H, et al: Pulmonary embolectomy: Review of a 15-year experience and role in the age of thrombolytic therapy. Eur J Cardiothorac Surg 10:952–957, 1996.

173. Uflacker R: Interventional therapy for pulmonary embolism. J Vasc Interv Radiol 12:147–164, 2001.

174. Schulman S, Sofie-Rhedin A, Lindmarker P, et al: A comparison of six weeks with six months of oral anticoagulant therapy after a first episode of venous thromboembolism. N Engl J Med 332:1661–1665, 1995.

175. Agnelli G, Prandoni P, Becattini C, et al: Extended oral anticoagulant therapy after a first episode of pulmonary embolism. Ann Intern Med 139:19–25, 2003.

176. Pinede L, Ninet J, Duhaut P, et al: Comparison of 3 and 6 months of oral anticoagulant therapy after a first episode of proximal deep vein thrombosis or pulmonary embolism and comparison of 6 and 12 weeks of therapy after isolated calf deep vein thrombosis. Circulation 103:2453–2460, 2001.

177. Agnelli G, Prandoni P, Santamaria MG, et al: Three months versus one year of oral anticoagulant therapy for idiopathic deep venous thrombosis. Warfarin Optimal Duration Italian Trial Investigators. N Engl J Med 345:165–169, 2001.

178. Prandoni P, Lensing AWA, Prins MH, et al: Residual venous thrombosis as a predictive factor of recurrent venous thromboembolism. Ann Intern Med 137:955–960, 2002.

179. De Stefano V, Martinelli I, Mannucci PM, et al: The risk of recurrent deep venous thrombosis among heterozygous carriers of both factor V Leiden and the G20210A prothrombin mutation. N Engl J Med 341:801–806, 1999.

180. Schulman S, Wahlander K, Lundstrom T, et al: Secondary prevention of venous thromboembolism with the oral direct thrombin inhibitor ximelagatran. N Engl J Med 349:1713–1721, 2003.

181. Khamashta MA, Cuadrado MJ, Jujic F, et al: The management of thrombosis in the antiphospholipid-antibody syndrome. N Engl J Med 332:993–997, 1995.

182. Crowther MA, Ginsberg JS, Julian J, et al: A comparison of two intensities of warfarin for the prevention of recurrent thrombosis in patients with the antiphospholipid antibody syndrome. N Engl J Med 349:1133–1138, 2003.

183. Moll S, Ortel TL: Monitoring warfarin therapy in patients with lupus anticoagulants. Ann Intern Med 127:177–185, 1997.

184. Ridker PM, Goldhaber SZ, Danielson E, et al: Long-term, low-intensity warfarin therapy for the prevention of recurrent venous thromboembolism. N Engl J Med 348:1425–1434, 2003.

185. Kearon C, Ginsberg JS, Kovacs MJ, et al: Comparison of low-intensity warfarin therapy with conventional-intensity warfarin therapy for long-term prevention of recurrent venous thromboembolism. N Engl J Med 349:631–639, 2003.

186. Fedullo PF, Auger WR, Kerr KM, Rubin LJ: Chronic thromboembolic pulmonary hypertension. N Engl J Med 345:1465–1472, 2001.

187. Moser KM, Auger WR, Fedullo PF: Chronic major-vessel thromboembolic pulmonary hypertension. Circulation 81:1735–1743, 1990.

188. Auger WR, Permpikul P, Moser KM: Lupus anticoagulant, heparin use, and thrombocytopenia in patients with chronic thromboembolic pulmonary hypertension: A preliminary report. Am J Med 99:392–396, 1995.

189. Wolf M, Boyer-Neumann C, Parent F, et al: Thrombotic risk factors in pulmonary hypertension. Eur Respir J 15:395–399, 2000.

190. Colorio CC, Martinuzzo ME, Forastiero RR, et al: Thrombophilic factors in chronic thromboembolic pulmonary hypertension. Blood Coagul Fibrinolysis 12:427–432, 2001.

191. Fedullo PF, Rubin LJ, Kerr KM, et al: The natural history of acute and chronic thromboembolic disease: The search for the missing link. Eur Respir J 15:435–437, 2000.

192. Moser KM, Bloor CM: Pulmonary vascular lesions occurring in patients with chronic major-vessel thromboembolic pulmonary hypertension. Chest 103:684–692, 1993.

193. Riedel M, Stanek V, Widimsky J, Prerovsky I: Longterm follow-up of patients with pulmonary thromboembolism: Late prognosis and evolution of hemodynamic and respiratory data. Chest 81:151–158, 1982.

194. Lewczuk J, Piszko P, Jagas J, et al: Prognostic factors in medically treated patients with chronic pulmonary embolism. Chest 119:818–823, 2001.

195. Meignan M, Rosso J, Gauthier H, et al: Systematic lung scans reveal a high frequency of silent pulmonary embolism in patients with proximal deep venous thrombosis. Arch Intern Med 160:159–164, 2000.

196. Auger WR, Moser KM: Pulmonary flow murmurs: A distinctive physical sign found in chronic pulmonary thromboembolic disease. Clin Res 37:145A, 1989.

197. D'Alonzo GE, Bower JS, Dantzker DR: Differentiation of patients with primary and thromboembolic pulmonary hypertension. Chest 85:457–461, 1984.

198. Morris TA, Auger WR, Ysrael MZ, et al: Parenchymal scarring is associated with restrictive spirometric defects in patients with chronic thromboembolic pulmonary hypertension. Chest 110:399–403, 1996.

199. Kapitan KS, Buchbinder M, Wagner PD, Moser KM: Mechanisms of hypoxemia in chronic thromboembolic pulmonary hypertension. Am Rev Respir Dis 139:1149–1154, 1989.

200. Fishmann AJ, Moser KM, Fedullo PF: Perfusion lung scans vs pulmonary angiography in evaluation of suspected primary pulmonary hypertension. Chest 84:679–683, 1983.

201. Bailey CL, Channick RN, Auger WR, et al: "High probability" perfusion lung scans in pulmonary venoocclusive disease. Am J Respir Crit Care Med 162:1974–1978, 2000.

202. Ryan KL, Fedullo PF, Davis GB, et al: Perfusion scan findings understate the severity of angiographic and hemodynamic compromise in chronic thromboembolic pulmonary hypertension. Chest 93:1180–1185, 1988.

203. King MA, Ysrael M, Bergin CJ: Chronic thromboembolic pulmonary hypertension: CT findings. AJR Am J Roentgenol 170:955–960, 1998.

204. Moser KM, Fedullo PF, Finkbeiner WE, Golden J: Do patients with primary pulmonary hypertension develop extensive central thrombi? Circulation 91:741–745, 1995.

205. Auger WR, Fedullo PF, Moser KM, et al: Chronic major-vessel thromboembolic pulmonary artery obstruction: Appearance at angiography. Radiology 182:393–398, 1992.

206. Shure D, Gregoratos G, Moser KM: Fiberoptic angioscopy: Role in the diagnosis of chronic pulmonary arterial obstruction. Ann Intern Med 103:844–850, 1995.

207. Kerr KM, Auger WR, Fedullo PF, et al: Large vessel pulmonary arteritis mimicking thromboembolic disease. Am J Respir Crit Care Med 152:367–373, 1995.

208. Fedullo PF, Auger WR, Kerr KM, Kim NH: Chronic thromboembolic pulmonary hypertension. Semin Respir Crit Care Med 24:273–285, 2003.

209. Jamieson SW, Kapelanski DP, Sakakibara N, et al: Pulmonary endarterectomy: Experience and lessons learned in 1,500 cases. Ann Thorac Surg 76:1457–1464, 2003.

210. Olman MA, Auger WR, Fedullo PE, et al: Pulmonary vascular steal in chronic thromboembolic pulmonary hypertension. Chest 98:1430–1434, 1990.

211. Levinson RM, Shure D, Moser KM: Reperfusion pulmonary edema after pulmonary artery thromboendarterectomy. Am Rev Respir Dis 134:1241–1245, 1986.

212. Moser KM, Metersky ML, Auger WR, et al: Resolution of vascular steal after pulmonary thromboendarterectomy. Chest 104:1441–1444, 1993.

213. Mares P, Gilbert TB, Tschernko EM, et al: Pulmonary artery thromboendarterectomy: A comparison of two different postoperative treatment strategies. Anesth Analg 90:267–273, 2000.

214. Rubens F, Wells P, Bencze S, Bourke M: Surgical treatment of chronic thromboembolic pulmonary hypertension. Can Respir J 7:49–57, 2000.

215. D'Armini AM, Cattadori B, Monterosso C, et al: Pulmonary thromboendarterectomy in patients with chronic thromboembolic pulmonary hypertension: Hemodynamic characteristics and changes. Eur J Cardiothorac Surg 18:696–702, 2000.

216. Tscholl D, Langer F, Wendler O, et al: Pulmonary thromboendarterectomy—risk factors for early survival and hemodynamic improvement. Eur J Cardiothorac Surg 19:771–776, 2001.

217. Masuda M, Nakajima N: Our experience of surgical treatment for chronic pulmonary thromboembolism. Ann Thorac Cardiovasc Surg 7:261–265, 2001.

218. Hagl C, Khaladj N, Peters T, et al: Technical advances of pulmonary thromboendarterectomy for chronic thromboembolic pulmonary hypertension. Eur J Cardiothorac Surg 23:776–781, 2003.

219. Birkmeyer JD, Siewers AE, Finlayson EV, et al: Hospital volume and surgical mortality in the United States. N Engl J Med 346:1128–1137, 2002.

220. Kramm T, Mayer E, Dahm M, et al: Long-term results after thromboendarterectomy for chronic pulmonary embolism. Eur J Cardiothorac Surg 15:579–584, 1999.

221. Archibald CJ, Auger WR, Fedullo PF, et al: Long-term outcome after pulmonary thromboendarterectomy. Am J Respir Crit Care Med 160:523–528, 1999.

222. Zoia MC, D'Armini AM, Beccaria M, et al: Pavia Thromboendarterectomy Group. Mid term effects of pulmonary thromboendarterectomy on clinical and cardiopulmonary function status. Thorax 57:608–612, 2002.

223. McLaughlin VV, Genthner DE, Panella MM, et al: Compassionate use of continuous prostacyclin in the management of secondary pulmonary hypertension: A case series. Ann Intern Med 130:740–743, 1999.

224. Ono F, Nagaya N, Okumura H, et al: Effect of orally active prostacyclin analogue on survival in patients with chronic thromboembolic pulmonary hypertension without major vessel obstruction. Chest 123:1583–1588, 2003.

225. Nagaya N, Sasaki N, Ando M, et al: Prostacyclin therapy before pulmonary thromboendarterectomy in patients with chronic thromboembolic pulmonary hypertension. Chest 123:338–343, 2003.

226. Morris W, Knauer CM: Cardiopulmonary manifestations of schistosomiasis. Semin Respir Infect 12:159–170, 1997.

227. Muth CM, Shank ES: Gas embolism. N Engl J Med 342:476–482, 2000.

228. Butler BD, Hills BA: The lung as a filter for microbubbles. J Appl Physiol 47:537–543, 1979.

229. Palmon SC, Moore LE, Lundberg J, Toung T: Venous air embolism: A review. J Clin Anesth 9:251–257, 1997.

230. Tibbles PM, Edelsberg JS: Hyperbaric-oxygen treatment. N Engl J Med 334:1642–1648, 1996.

231. Johnson MJ, Lucas GL: Fat embolism syndrome. Orthopedics 19:41–48, 1996.

232. Gossling H, Pellegrini V: Fat embolism syndrome: A review of the pathophysiology and physiological basis for treatment. Clin Orthop 165:68–82, 1982.

233. Bruecke P, Burke JF, Lam KW, et al: Pathophysiology of the pulmonary fat embolism. J Thorac Cardiovasc Surg 61:949–955, 1971.

234. Richards RR: Fat embolism syndrome. Can J Surg 40:334–349, 1997.

235. King MB, Harmon KR: Unusual forms of pulmonary embolism. Clin Chest Med 15:561–580, 1994.

236. Davies S: Amniotic fluid embolus: A review of the literature. Can J Anaesth 48:88–98, 2001.

237. Clark SL: Amniotic fluid embolism: A review. Obstet Gynecol Surg 45:360–368, 1990.

238. Clark SL: Amniotic fluid embolism. Crit Care Clin 7:877–883, 1991.

239. Clark SL, Hankins GD, Dudley DA, et al: Amniotic fluid embolism: Analysis of the national registry. Am J Obstet Gynecol 172:1158–1167, 1995.

240. Julander I: Staphylococcal septicaemia and endocarditis in 80 drug users. Scand J Infect Dis 41:49–54, 1983.

241. Clarke DE, Raffin TA: Infectious complications of indwelling long-term central venous catheters. Chest 97:966–972, 1990.

242. Robertson CH Jr, Reynolds RC, Wilson JE: Pulmonary hypertension and foreign body granulomas in intravenous drug abusers. Am J Med 61:657–662, 1976.

243. Ward S, Heyneman LE, Reittner P, et al: Talcosis associated with IV abuse of oral medications: CT findings. AJR Am J Roentgenol 174:789–793, 2000.

244. Pare JP, Cote G, Fraser RS: Long-term follow-up of drug abusers with intravenous talcosis. Am Rev Respir Dis 139:233–241, 1989.

49 Pulmonary Vasculitis and Primary Pulmonary Hypertension

Richard N. Channick, M.D., Lewis J. Rubin, M.D.

INTRODUCTION

Disorders affecting the pulmonary circulation constitute a heterogeneous group without unifying or characteristic etiologic, physiologic, or pathologic features. However, many of these diseases share a variety of clinical manifestations that are the result of the disruption of the delicate interface between the ventilation and perfusion components of gas exchange and the impact of altered pulmonary vascular dynamics on the function of the right ventricle. This chapter addresses two forms of pulmonary vascular disease: the vasculitides and primary pulmonary hypertension. Other vascular abnormalities, including pulmonary arteriovenous malformations, are described in Chapter 50.

PULMONARY VASCULITIS

The vasculitides are a heterogeneous group of disorders that are characterized by inflammation within and surrounding the blood vessel walls.[1] When the inflammation leads to destruction of the blood vessels, the process often is referred to as a necrotizing vasculitis.[2] Inflammation and necrosis of the blood vessel wall may occur as part of a primary disease process or may be secondarily associated with several other conditions. This section focuses on pulmonary vasculitis occurring as part of a primary vasculitic process.

CLASSIFICATION

Vasculitis first was identified as a distinct clinicopathologic entity in 1837 by Schönlein[3] in his description of the disease currently known as *anaphylactoid purpura*. Kussmaul and Maier,[4] in 1866, described the syndrome of *polyarteritis nodosa* in a patient with fever, muscle weakness, gastro-

intestinal symptoms, and renal disease in whom a diffuse necrotizing vasculitis was found at autopsy. Over the subsequent years, this term has been used to describe patients with a variety of vasculitides attributed to hypersensitivity reactions to drugs, infectious antigens, rheumatic diseases, and other disorders.

A number of attempts have been made to classify and organize the pulmonary vasculitides.[5-7] However, these efforts have lacked consensus because these conditions overlap considerably in clinical manifestations and morphologic features and because their causes are unknown. The American College of Rheumatology, in 1990, proposed diagnostic criteria for various vasculitides, based on a study of 807 patients who met specific criteria established for the diagnosis of several types of vasculitis.[8-16] Subjects with vasculitis secondary to underlying connective tissue diseases were excluded from this study. The recommendations from these experts were meant to provide diagnostic criteria for individual patients, not to serve as a nomenclature for vasculitis.

A subsequent International Consensus Conference that was held in Chapel Hill, North Carolina, devised a classification system for 10 different clinical entities based on the size of involved blood vessels.[17] Most experts have adopted this nomenclature in classifying vasculitides that involve the lung, with the addition of pauci-immune pulmonary capillaritis[18] and Behçet's disease[19] (Table 49.1).

EPIDEMIOLOGY

Pulmonary vasculitis is an uncommon condition despite the relative frequency of collagen vascular diseases and other conditions that may be associated with vasculitis in the general population. Even *Wegener's granulomatosis*, perhaps the best known pulmonary vasculitis, rarely is encountered

Table 49.1 Vasculitides with Significant Pulmonary Involvement

Small Vessel
Wegener's granulomatosis
Churg-Strauss syndrome
Microscopic polyangiitis
Isolated pauci-immune pulmonary capillaritis
Behçet's disease

Medium Vessel
Behçet's syndrome

Large Vessel
Giant cell (temporal) arteritis
Takayasu's arteritis
Behçet's syndrome

in clinical practice; Fauci and Wolff[20] noted that only 200 cases of this disorder had been reported up to 1967, although the true incidence probably was higher. The incidence of other pulmonary vasculitides for the most part remains unknown.

Pulmonary vasculitis can occur in persons of all ages, although anaphylactoid purpura is more common among children, and the granulomatous vasculitides usually affect patients in their fifth and sixth decades.[7] Vasculitis associated with collagen vascular disease is described most often among women, as is *necrotizing sarcoid angiitis* and granulomatosis. Conversely, Wegener's granulomatosis, *lymphomatoid granulomatosis,* and *allergic granulomatosis* and angiitis are reported most frequently in men. Familial and racial predispositions are noted primarily in patients with the collagen vascular disorders and giant cell arteritis.

PATHOLOGY

Inflammation, frequently extending through all layers of the blood vessel wall, is the hallmark of pulmonary vasculitis. With the exception of *bronchocentric granulomatosis,* this process is angiocentric because it appears to originate in the blood vessels, although surrounding tissues frequently are involved. Arteries and veins of all sizes may be involved, and capillaritis may accompany these pathologic changes in some conditions. Fibrinoid necrosis often accompanies the inflammation, as do intimal proliferation and perivascular fibrosis. Because these processes may cause obstruction of the blood vessels, pulmonary vasculitis often leads to obliterative pulmonary vascular disease. Secondary thrombosis also may contribute to vascular obstruction in this setting.

The inflammatory cells responsible for pulmonary vasculitis include neutrophils, normal and abnormal lymphocytes, eosinophils, monocytes, macrophages, histiocytes, plasma cells, multinucleated giant cells, and combinations thereof. Vasculitis is called leukocytoclastic if neutrophils predominate and granulomatous if lymphocytes predominate. However, lymphocytes may be abundant in areas of leukocytoclastic vasculitis if the process is more than 24 hours old, just as mononuclear cells, histiocytes, and multinucleated giant cells may outnumber lymphocytes in the later stages of granulomatous vasculitis.[2,21]

PATHOGENESIS AND ETIOLOGY

Despite their differences, the pulmonary vasculitides appear to share a common immunopathogenesis. Immune complexes form in the bloodstream in response to antigen load. These immune complexes localize in the blood vessel wall, are trapped along the basement membrane, and lead to activation of complement and associated chemotactic factors. Neutrophils drawn to the area of immune complex deposition release lysosomal enzymes, damaging the vessel wall and leading to fibrinoid necrosis. The end result is thrombosis and occlusion of the blood vessel. This concept is supported by several observations.[1,2,22] Leukocytoclastic vasculitis, polyarteritis nodosa, and essential mixed cryoglobulinemia may occur with illnesses such as hepatitis B infection, which are associated with immune complex deposition within blood vessel walls. Vasculitis may be a component of collagen vascular disorders, in which immunologic pathogenetic mechanisms are well accepted. Patients with vasculitis may manifest serologic abnormalities associated with immunodysfunction, including the presence of rheumatoid factor, cryoglobulinemia, hyperglobulinemia, hypocomplementemia, and circulating immune complexes. Vasculitis may be associated temporally with infections, drug ingestion, and other kinds of antigen exposure. The upper and lower airway involvement with granulomatous vasculitis in particular suggests that foreign antigens may enter the body via the respiratory tract. Finally, these and other vasculitides frequently respond to immunosuppressive or cytotoxic therapy.

Many investigators believe that pulmonary vasculitis is caused by a type III hypersensitivity reaction involving the deposition of immune complexes in blood vessels.[1] Although the antigens responsible for this process rarely have been identified, streptococcal M protein, hepatitis B surface antigen, and *Mycobacterium tuberculosis* have been found in or near the site of vascular inflammation. Immunoglobulins M, G, and A and complement breakdown products also have been localized in the blood vessels of patients with leukocytoclastic vasculitis, polyarteritis nodosa, and collagen vascular disorders.[2] How the antigens and antibodies come together is not certain; the antigens may bind to vascular basement membranes, diffuse into the blood vessels from surrounding tissues, or travel in the bloodstream. Whatever the mechanism, a significant excess of antigen over antibody is necessary to create immune complexes that are small enough to elude the reticuloendothelial system yet insoluble enough to deposit in blood vessel walls.[7]

The blood vessels also must be predisposed to accept immune complexes. Such acceptance probably involves local vasodilation and increased vascular permeability that are mediated by vasoactive amines released by platelets, mast cells, and basophils. After the immune complexes are deposited, complement activation is thought to occur by either the direct or the alternate pathway.[1] Certain complement components, such as C3a, cause further vasodilation and increased vascular permeability, whereas C5a and its breakdown product, C5a des arginine, attract neutrophils; circulating total complement and complement components are decreased. The neutrophils then are stimulated to ingest the immune complexes and to release toxic enzymes and oxygen radical species.[22]

Although this sequence can be implicated in leukocytoclastic vasculitis and polyarteritis nodosa, it may not apply to granulomatous vasculitis, in which immune complex deposition rarely is demonstrated and complement levels are increased. These facts and the characteristic histology of granulomatous vasculitis have prompted the hypothesis that cell-mediated immune events are involved in this condition. The involvement may be secondary because it follows immune complex deposition that cannot be detected. Whether such deposition occurs or not, sensitized T lymphocytes are assumed to contact antigens and either cause direct cytotoxicity or recruit mononuclear cells to the site. These mononuclear cells in turn become activated macrophages that release lysosomal enzymes. At the same time, some of the cells evolve into the histiocytes and multinucleated giant cells that participate in granuloma formation.[1]

The important role of antineutrophil cytoplasmic antibodies (ANCAs) in the pathogenesis and progression of several forms of pulmonary vasculitis has been elucidated by several investigators. Although first described in 1982,[23] the association between ANCA and Wegener's granulomatosis was first reported 3 years later.[24] Two major ANCA staining patterns have been described, cytoplasmic ANCA (c-ANCA) and perinuclear ANCA (p-ANCA). Proteinase 3 is the main target of c-ANCA, which is closely associated with Wegener's granulomatosis, and myeloperoxidase is the major autoantigenic target of p-ANCA, which can found in patients with microscopic polyangiitis, pauci-immune pulmonary capillaritis, and Churg-Strauss syndrome. In addition to targeting neutrophil proteinases, it has recently become evident that ANCA can target infection-related antigens such as bactericidal permeability-increasing protein, human lysosome-associated membrane protein 2, defensin, and azurocidin, consistent with a potential infectious role in the pathogenesis of certain vasculitides. There is recent evidence, for instance, that chronic nasal carriage of *Staphylococcus aureus* predisposes patients to relapse of systemic vasculitis,[25] further supporting the infection hypothesis. Regardless of the target antigen, it is likely that ANCA facilitates neutrophil adherence to vascular endothelial cells and thus mediates endothelial injury and transmigration of neutrophils into the perivascular space.[26,27]

SYMPTOMS

In general, systemic symptoms more commonly accompany the vasculitides that produce minimal pulmonary involvement, whereas respiratory complaints predominate among the vasculitides that primarily involve the lungs. For example, the initial manifestations of leukocytoclastic vasculitis include fever, malaise, arthralgias, and skin lesions. Symptoms referable to the skin and joints also are seen among patients with collagen vascular disorders and polyarteritis nodosa.[28] In contrast, dyspnea and cough frequently occur among patients with granulomatous vasculitis; symptoms related to the upper airways, including sinus pain and epistaxis, suggest Wegener's granulomatosis and lymphomatoid granulomatosis.[7] Hemoptysis has been reported in 12% to 40% of patients with small vessel vasculitis.[29] Evidence for pulmonary hemorrhage may be confined to a raised carbon monoxide transfer factor or

unexplained anemia. Hemorrhage in the setting of small vessel vasculitis is associated with a poor prognosis. Periodic dyspnea or a history of asthma is characteristic of allergic granulomatosis and angiitis (Churg-Strauss syndrome)[14,30]; according to a recent review of 96 patients, asthma was the most frequent manifestation at presentation.[31]

PHYSICAL FINDINGS

The physical findings generally parallel the symptoms of patients with pulmonary vasculitis. For example, purpura, bullae, and dermal ulcers may be evident in patients with leukocytoclastic vasculitis.[2] Joint deformity is suggestive of rheumatoid arthritis, whereas thickening of the skin and Raynaud's phenomenon may accompany progressive systemic sclerosis. Erosions of the nose and upper airways are characteristic of Wegener's granulomatosis and lymphomatoid granulomatosis; proptosis caused by orbital pseudotumors and sclerouveitis also are seen in the former condition.[7] Iritis and oral and genital ulcers are hallmarks of Behçet's syndrome. Peripheral nerve lesions are especially common in polyarteritis nodosa. Central nervous system lesions are described in the giant cell arteritides and other conditions.[1] Patients with eosinophilia-myalgia syndrome frequently manifest many of the features of systemic sclerosis; in addition, they may have peripheral neuropathy, myositis, and fasciitis.[32,33]

DIAGNOSIS

Despite certain characteristic presentations, the vasculitides rarely can be diagnosed solely on clinical grounds. Potentially helpful laboratory studies include the erythrocyte sedimentation rate, which usually is elevated in giant cell arteritis, and the differential white blood cell count, which is normal in most patients with vasculitis but may show an eosinophilia in patients with allergic granulomatosis and angiitis[12] or eosinophilia-myalgia syndrome.[32,33] An elevation of immunoglobulins, a decrease in total complement and complement components, and the presence of circulating immune complexes may be noted in leukocytoclastic vasculitis.[2] Determinations of rheumatoid factor levels, antinuclear antibody patterns, and ANCAs[34] are useful in the differential diagnosis of collagen vascular diseases and Wegener's granulomatosis, respectively.

Several radiologic patterns have been described in pulmonary vasculitis. Localized nodular or patchy opacities are typical of Wegener's granulomatosis, allergic angiitis and granulomatosis, necrotizing sarcoid granulomatosis, lymphomatoid granulomatosis, and bronchocentric granulomatosis.[35] Cavitation of focal nodules is commonly seen in Wegener's granulomatosis, in contrast to Churg-Strauss syndrome. More diffuse air space consolidation due to pulmonary hemorrhage and capillaritis is seen in microscopic polyangiitis, systemic lupus erythematosus, and Goodpasture's syndrome. In contrast to small vessel vasculitides, large vessel and medium vessel vasculitides such as Takayasu's arteritis and Behçet's disease may lead to radiographic evidence of pulmonary artery obstruction or aneurysms such as a lung mass, aneurysmal dilation, or consolidation due to infarction.[36,37] Large and medium vessel involvement from these disorders is often confirmed by pulmonary angiography. Pleural effusions have been reported among patients with anaphylactoid purpura, collagen vascular disease,[7] and Churg-Strauss syndrome.[38,39] Finally, visualization of the upper airways through plain roentgenograms or computed tomography often is employed in the evaluation of Wegener's granulomatosis and lymphoid granulomatosis.[22]

Hypoxemia, often in concert with hypocapnia and chronic respiratory alkalosis, is present in many patients whose lungs are involved with vasculitis.[22] Pulmonary function tests usually reveal normal or mildly reduced flow rates and lung volumes, unless obstructive or restrictive disorders coexist. Pulmonary vascular obstruction may be suggested by a decreased diffusing capacity for carbon monoxide, an increased dead space-to-tidal volume ratio, and an increased alveolar-arterial PO_2 difference at rest, which worsen during progressive exercise.[40]

Given the general lack of clinical experience with pulmonary vasculitis, a tissue biopsy may be needed for diagnosis. Skin biopsy is the preferred initial approach in patients with lesions attributable to granulomatous vasculitis, leukocytoclastic vasculitis, or polyarteritis nodosa.[2] If this approach is not helpful, upper airway biopsy may be revealing in patients suspected of having Wegener's granulomatosis or lymphomatoid granulomatosis. Renal biopsy is not recommended in patients with the former condition because granulomas usually are not present; the lungs are therefore a preferred biopsy site.[7] Transbronchial biopsy frequently is not helpful in the evaluation of pulmonary vasculitis because of the small amount of tissue obtained. As a result, many investigators recommend open lung biopsy, which now can be performed thoracoscopically.[7]

Given a specificity and sensitivity of c-ANCA of greater than 90% for active Wegener's granulomatosisis,[41] some experts believe that open lung biopsy can be avoided and a diagnosis of Wegener's granulomatosis made in the right clinical setting with c-ANCA positivity. On the other hand, positive p-ANCA can be seen in a variety of diseases, including microscopic polyangiitis, isolated pauci-immune capillaritis, and Churg-Strauss syndrome, and is therefore not specific enough to obviate the need for tissue confirmation.

TREATMENT

The mainstay of treatment for most pulmonary vasculitides is immunosuppression with corticosteroids and cyclophosphamide. Before the advent of aggressive immunosuppression, mortality from small vessel vasculitis was exceedingly high, with median survival often measured in months. Specific treatment recommendations are discussed next for each disorder.

SPECIFIC DISORDERS

As mentioned previously, this section is confined to the primary vasculitides affecting the lung that were recognized by the Chapel Hill Consensus Conference and grouped by size of vessel typically involved. Vasculitis as a secondary consequence of various systemic diseases, such as connective tissue diseases and hemorrhagic disorders, are discussed in Chapters 54 and 56, respectively.

Small Vessel Vasculitides

Wegener's Granulomatosis. Wegener,[42] in 1936, described the clinical syndrome that now bears his name and that consists chiefly of necrotizing granulomatous vasculitis of the upper and lower respiratory tract and glomerulonephritis. He considered the syndrome a variant of polyarteritis nodosa and called it "rhinogenic granuloma," with reference to the prominent nasal and paranasal involvement.[43] Although clinical attention usually is focused on the respiratory and renal lesions of Wegener's granulomatosis, the disease also may involve the eyes, ears, heart, skin, joints, and peripheral and central nervous systems.[7,43,44] The cause of Wegener's granulomatosis is unknown. However, an immunopathogenesis is supported by the finding of hypergammaglobulinemia and circulating antibodies in patients with the disorder, in addition to their dramatic response to cytotoxic therapy.[44-46]

Of the vasculitides that typically affect the lungs, Wegener's granulomatosis is the most common, comprising approximately 10% of all systemic vasculitides clinically diagnosed,[22] with an estimated prevalence of 3 per 100,000 persons in the United States.[47] Wegener's granulomatosis may affect persons of all ages but is most common in middle-aged patients, predominantly men.[7,10,46] There appears to be an overwhelming predilection for whites. Sinusitis is the most frequent presenting symptom, followed by fever, arthralgias, cough, rhinitis, hemoptysis, otitis, and ocular inflammation.[46] Upper respiratory tract involvement may include destruction of tissue and bone and secondary bacterial infection; this may lead to confusion with midline granuloma, a necrotizing and ulcerating granulomatous process usually limited to the nose and face.[48] Subglottic stenosis has been reported in 23% of patients in a National Institutes of Health series of 189 patients[49] and may require tracheotomy.[50] Pulmonary involvement is present in 85% of patients[51] and ranges from minimal to life-threatening. The chest roentgenogram is abnormal in two thirds of patients, with infiltrates occurring most frequently (63%), followed by nodules (31%), infiltrates with cavitation (8% to 10%), and nodules with cavitation (10%).[10,52-54] Bilateral abnormalities occur with nearly equal frequency as unilateral abnormalities. Atelectasis due to endobronchial obstruction and pleural disease with thickening or effusions also have been reported.[39] Lung biopsy usually reveals parenchymal necrosis, granulomatous inflammation accompanied by an infiltrate consisting of a mixture of neutrophils, lymphocytes, plasma cells, eosinophils, and histiocytes, and vasculitis with blood vessel obstruction and bland infarcts (Fig. 49.1). Capillaritis can be seen in almost one third of patients and is a significant cause of hemoptysis.[55] Less commonly, interstitial fibrosis, acute and chronic bronchiolitis, bronchiolitis obliterans, lipoid pneumonia, and tissue eosinophilia can be seen.[56]

In 1985, van der Woude and associates[24] reported a high sensitivity of ANCAs for active Wegener's granulomatosis, and suggested that ANCAs may be useful as a marker of disease activity. Although ANCA activity may be detected in other vasculitides, its presence is associated most strongly with Wegener's granulomatosis, and the cytoplasmic staining pattern is reported to be present in more than 90% of patients with untreated active disease.[57-59] The rate of

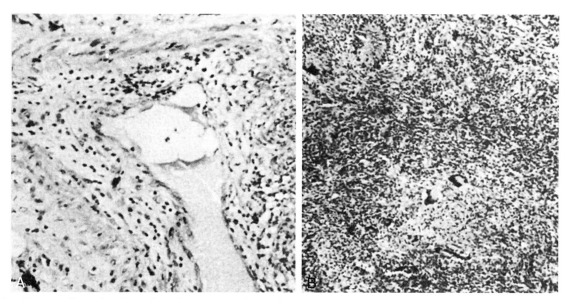

Figure 49.1 Hematoxylin and eosin stains of autopsy specimens from a patient with Wegener's granulomatosis. **A,** Angiitis in the wall of a pulmonary blood vessel. **B,** At higher power, note granulomatous inflammation with histiocytes and giant cells. (Courtesy of Martha L. Warnock, MD; from Luce JM: Vasculitis, primary pulmonary hypertension, and arteriovenous fistulas. *In* Murray JF, Nadel JA [eds]: Textbook of Respiratory Medicine. Philadelphia: WB Saunders, 1988, p 1332.)

positivity declines substantially when the disease is in remission, but the test is not sufficiently sensitive to serve as a guide to therapy.

Before the advent of combination therapy with glucocorticoids and cytotoxic drugs, average survival was 5 months. The current cytotoxic agent of choice is cyclophosphamide in a dosage of 1 to 2 mg/kg/day, either alone or in combination with lower doses of corticosteroids, continued for at least 1 year after a decline in disease activity.[60] From 75% to 90% of patients treated with this regimen experience a complete remission. A recently published study found that substitution of azathioprine at a dose of 2 mg/kg/day for cyclophosphamide did not increase the recurrence rate of patients in cyclophosphamide-induced remission and provides a less toxic alternative for long-term "maintenance" therapy.[61] Methotrexate has also been used successfully for remission maintenance.[62] The antimicrobial agent trimethoprim-sulfamethoxazole also has been reported to produce improvement or reduce the incidence of relapse in several patients.[63]

Allergic Granulomatosis and Angiitis (Churg-Strauss Syndrome). In 1951, Churg and Strauss[30] reported 13 cases of severe asthma associated with fever and hypereosinophilia. Pathologically, there were granulomatous extravascular lesions and inflammatory, granulomatous, and necrotizing vascular changes in the small arteries and veins of the lungs, heart, pancreas, spleen, kidneys, and skin. Although most of the patients had been assumed to have polyarteritis nodosa, Churg and Strauss[30] believed that the pathologic findings suggested the presence of a distinct clinical process. In 1990, the American College of Rheumatology developed six clinical criteria compatible with Churg-Strauss syndrome: asthma, eosinophilia over 10%, history of allergy, mono- or polyneuropathy, migratory/transient pulmonary infiltrates, and paranasal sinus abnormalities. When necrotizing vasculitis was confirmed on histology, the presence of

four of six criteria had a sensitivity of 85% and a specificity of 99.7%. The incidence of Churg-Strauss syndrome is 2.4 per 1 million. The cause of this disease remains unknown, but an immunologic basis is supported by the presence of elevations in immunoglobulins and circulating immune complexes in many patients.[12,64]

Churg-Strauss syndrome primarily affects middle-aged men with current or previous asthma.[31] The lungs, peripheral nerves, skin, heart, and viscera are the most commonly injured organs.[12] Renal disease is infrequent, but the prostate and lower urinary tract may be involved.[65] Lanham and colleagues[66] described three phases of the disease, which are often expressed over several years. On presentation, adult-onset asthma and allergic rhinosinusitis are typical. In the second phase, eosinophil infiltration of visceral organs such as the gastrointestinal tract and lungs occurs. Vasculitis comprises the third phase, presenting as mononeuritis multiplex, palpable purpura, cardiomyopathy, pericarditis, and focal glomerulonephritis. Cardiac involvement accounts for 50% of death from Churg-Strauss syndrome.

Diagnostic characteristics of Churg-Strauss syndrome include elevated sedimentation rate, blood eosinophilia usually exceeding 10% of the peripheral white blood cell count,[12] and anemia. p-ANCA is demonstrated in two thirds of patients. Plain chest roentgenograms most often reveal patchy infiltrative or nodular densities. One apparently distinctive radiographic finding seen on high-resolution computed tomography is the presence of bronchial wall thickening, which distinguishes Churg-Strauss syndrome from other pulmonary infiltrates with eosinophilia.[67]

Treatment has included corticosteroids, azathioprine, and cyclophosphamide. Before the availability of corticosteroids, Churg-Strauss syndrome was frequently a rapidly progressive disease. However, recent studies suggest that most patients respond favorably to therapy: None of the 20 patients reported in the American College of Rheumatology registry died as a result of the syndrome.[14] Unlike in

Wegener's granulomatosis, in Churg-Strauss syndrome cyclophosphamide has not been shown to affect mortality; although this agent may reduce the rate of relapse, this benefit is offset by an increase in lethal infections.[68] In 1998, Wechsler and associates[69] published a series of eight patients with asthma who developed Churg-Strauss syndrome after being treated with the cysteinyl leukotriene antagonist zafirlukast. In this series, development of the syndrome coincided with weaning of prednisone, suggesting that the syndrome was simply unmasked by corticosteroid tapering and not an effect of zafirlukast. Although this is a plausible hypothesis, there are case reports of the syndrome occurring in association with leukotriene antagonists in patients not receiving corticosteroids.[70]

Microscopic Polyangiitis. In 1985, Savage and colleagues[71] described 34 patients with nongranulomatous small vessel vasculitis affecting the skin and musculoskeletal system, as well as focal segmental necrotizing glomerulonephritis, and coined the term *microscopic polyarteritis*. In 1994, a consensus committee found this disorder to be a distinct clinical entity, and developed the term *microscopic polyangiitis* to acknowledge the involvement of venules and capillaries in addition to arterioles.

The average age at presentation is 50 years. Necrotizing glomerulonephritis is seen in over 80% of cases. Pulmonary capillaritis leads to alveolar hemorrhage in 30% of cases and is the cause of 25% of deaths from microscopic polyangiitis. Constitutional symptoms and vasculitic involvement of skin, nerves, joints, and gastrointestinal tract often occur. Almost half of all patients with microscopic polyangiitis have a p-ANCA staining pattern; this finding, along with the high incidence of pulmonary involvement, distinguish this entity from classic polyarteritis nodosa, a disease involving primarily medium-sized vessels.

The outcome and response to treatment in patients with microscopic polyangiitis is variable. Factors associated with poor survival include elevated serum creatinine (>1.58 mg/dL), proteinuria (>1 g/day), presence of severe gastrointestinal involvement, cardiac involvement, and central nervous system involvement, as well as the presence of alveolar hemorrhage.[72] The presence of one or more of these poor prognostic factors is considered to obligate a course of combined corticosteroids and cyclophosphamide.

Isolated Pauci-immune Pulmonary Vasculitis. In 1997, Jennings and colleagues[18] reported 29 patients with diffuse alveolar hemorrhage and biopsy-proven pulmonary capillaritis. Isolated pulmonary capillaritis was present in eight of these patients. These patients did not have ANCA or glomerular basement membrane antibodies. No patients had manifestations consistent with other forms of small vessel vasculitis, even on long-term follow-up (median 43 months). With treatment using corticosteroids, cyclophosphamide, or both, remission was the rule.

Medium Vessel Vasculitis: Behçet's Syndrome

Behçet's syndrome was described in 1937 as a symptom complex of recurrent aphthous stomatitis, genital ulceration, and uveitis.[73] It subsequently has become recognized as a systemic inflammatory disorder that also may involve the gastrointestinal tract, cardiovascular system, brain, kidneys, and lungs.[74] The underlying pathologic process is a vasculitis involving neutrophils and mononuclear cells that usually affects veins, venules, and capillaries. Immunoglobulin staining of the lesions has revealed immunoglobulin G and complement. Susceptibility to Behçet's disease has been strongly linked to the presence of the human leukocyte antigen B51 allele.[75]

Pulmonary involvement occurs in approximately 10% of patients with Behçet's syndrome and is most characterized by pulmonary artery aneurysms and often fatal episodes of hemoptysis.[76-79] The latter problem has been attributed to vasculitis of medium-sized lung vessels and to rupture of bronchial veins when intraluminal pressure is increased by thrombosis of the superior vena cava.

Although treatment experience for pulmonary involvement with Behçet's disease is limited, a recent report demonstrated significant improvement and even resolution of pulmonary artery aneurysms following treatment, typically with corticosteroids and cyclophosphamide.[80]

Hughes and Stovin,[81] in 1959, described two patients who died of massive hemoptysis due to rupture of segmented pulmonary artery aneurysms. Recurrent venous thrombosis also was detected in these patients, as was intracranial hypertension that probably was related to thrombosis of intracranial and extracranial vessels. That these abnormalities were caused by vasculitis was suggested by the finding of an inflammatory infiltrate consisting largely of lymphocytes and plasma cells in the walls of the elastic pulmonary arteries at autopsy. Neither these patients nor similar patients subsequently reported by Durieux and associates[82] and Meireles and coworkers[83] met the diagnostic criteria for Behçet's syndrome. The Hughes-Stovin syndrome therefore appears to be either a separate entity or a variant of Behçet's syndrome.

Large Vessel Vasculitis

Giant Cell Arteritis. Giant cell arteritis is a large vessel granulomatous arteritis of the aorta and its major branches. There is a predilection for the extracranial branches of the carotid artery leading to the commonly used term *temporal arteritis*. Headache, constitutional symptoms, tenderness to palpitation over the temporal artery, and polymyalgia rheumatica are the typical features of this disease. Pulmonary involvement in giant cell arteritis occurs, albeit rarely. Interstitial lung disease or multiple nodules have been described.[84] There is very limited experience on treating pulmonary complications of giant cell arteritis, but corticosteroids appear to be effective.[84]

Takayasu's Disease. In 1908, Takayasu[85] described a young woman with cataracts and arteriovenous anastomoses around the optic disks who subsequently was shown to lack pulses in her arms. Later investigators determined that the "pulseless disease" resulted from a granulomatous vasculitis involving primarily the aorta and its branches and that these lesions led to blood vessel narrowing and occlusion with aneurysm formation. These histologic changes have been reported predominantly in young Japanese women and are associated with an elevated erythrocyte sedimentation rate. Despite therapy with corticosteroids and anticoagulants, Takayasu's disease may cause blindness, cerebrovascular accidents, severe hypertension, left ventricular failure, and aortic aneurysm rupture.[16,86] Pulmonary symptoms have been reported in patients with this disorder. Pulmonary artery involvement, with or without pulmonary hypertension, has been confirmed by angiographic and autopsy studies, and pulmonary arteritis probably occurs in most patients.[16,86-88] The pulmonary artery involvement seen from Takayasu's arteritis can occur without any systemic vascular involvement and can mimic thromboembolic disease.[89,90]

PRIMARY PULMONARY HYPERTENSION

Primary pulmonary hypertension is a disease in which there is a persistent elevation of pulmonary artery pressure without demonstrable cause.[91] There is expert agreement that the definition of pulmonary hypertension, as was required for entry into the primary pulmonary hypertension registry of the National Institutes of Health,[91] is a mean pulmonary artery pressure greater than 25 mm Hg at rest or a mean pressure in excess of 30 mm Hg during exercise.

CLASSIFICATION

Primary pulmonary hypertension by definition is a diagnosis of exclusion. A classification system for pulmonary hypertensive disorders was developed at a World Health Organization conference in 1998 and further refined in 2003 at a World Symposium on pulmonary hypertension.[91a] The currently accepted classification system is shown in Table 49.2. It has been suggested that the term *primary pulmonary hypertension* be replaced with *idiopathic pulmonary arterial hypertension* to distinguish it from forms of pulmonary arterial hypertension associated with conditions such as congenital heart disease, connective tissue disease, human immunodeficiency virus (HIV) infection, drug or toxin ingestion, and portopulmonary hypertension. Primary pulmonary hypertension must also be differentiated from pulmonary hypertension related to left ventricular dysfunction (either systolic or diastolic), left-sided valvular heart disease, chronic airflow obstruction, parenchymal lung disease, severe hypoventilation, and chronic pulmonary thromboembolism. Classifying pulmonary hypertensive disorders based on clinical criteria has turned out to be the most useful method, as therapeutic options closely follow the diagnostic categories.

EPIDEMIOLOGY

Primary pulmonary hypertension first was described at autopsy by Romberg in 1891.[92] Patients with pulmonary hypertension of unknown cause were reported infrequently over the next 60 years, with only two cases identified from 10,000 consecutive autopsies at the Massachusetts General Hospital.[93] However, the condition was recognized more commonly after the advent of cardiac catheterization. Wood,[94] in 1950, detected six cases of what he called "idiopathic pulmonary hypertension" among 233 unselected British patients with presumed congenital heart disease, 152 of whom were catheterized. One year later, the term

Table 49.2 Classification of Pulmonary Hypertension Adopted by Venice World Symposium

1. Pulmonary arterial hypertension (PAH)
   Idiopathic PAH
   Familial PAH
   PAH related to:
     Connective tissue diseases
     Human immunodeficiency virus infection
     Portal hypertension
     Drugs/toxins
     Congenital heart disease
   Persistent pulmonary hypertension of the newborn
   PAH with venular/capillary involvement (pulmonary veno-occlusive disease, pulmonary capillary hemangiomatosis)

2. Pulmonary hypertension with left heart disease
   Atrial or ventricular
   Valvular

3. Pulmonary hypertension with lung disease/hypoxemia
   Chronic obstructive pulmonary disease
   Interstitial lung disease
   Sleep-disordered breathing
   Developmental abnormalities

4. Pulmonary hypertension due to chronic thrombotic and/or embolic disease
   Thromboembolic obstruction of proximal pulmonary arteries
   Thromboembolic obstruction of distal pulmonary arteries
   Nonthrombotic pulmonary emboli

5. Miscellaneous

primary pulmonary hypertension was introduced by Dresdale and associates[95] in a detailed clinical and hemodynamic study of similar patients.

Since these original studies, primary pulmonary hypertension has been reported with increased frequency. Shephard and colleagues[96] and Chapman and coworkers[97] described 14 patients with the condition in 1957; in 1958, Yu[98] reviewed the findings in 55 persons older than 12 years of age reported previously in the literature. Wolcott and colleagues[99] selected 23 cases from among Mayo Clinic patients seen from 1946 to 1965. A review of 17,901 autopsies performed on persons older than 1 year of age from 1944 to 1981 at the Johns Hopkins Hospital yielded 24 cases of primary pulmonary hypertension; this amounted to a prevalence of 0.13% of all patients.[100] The primary pulmonary hypertension registry included 187 cases collected from 32 centers between 1981 and 1985. In 1984, Rich and Brundage[101] noted that primary pulmonary hypertension was found at autopsy in approximately 1% of patients with cor pulmonale.

Primary pulmonary hypertension customarily has been considered a disease of young women. Indeed, all of Wood's[94] six patients were women between 20 and 45 years of age, as were the three patients described by Dresdale and associates.[95] An overall female-to-male ratio of 1.7:1 was found in the U.S. registry. However, primary pulmonary hypertension has been reported in both sexes within a wide age range. For example, the mean age of patients in the registry series was 36 years, with a range of 1 to 81 years. The disease appears to affect older men and women in equal numbers, although most younger patients continue to be women.

PATHOLOGY

Wood[102] in 1958 divided pulmonary hypertension into six types: *passive,* as seen with increased pulmonary venous pressure due to raised left atrial or ventricular pressure; *hyperkinetic,* caused by increased pulmonary blood flow; *obstructive,* resulting from pulmonary embolism or thrombosis; *obliterative,* manifested by a reduction of pulmonary vascular capacity; *vasoconstrictive,* brought about by functional and presumably reversible vasospasm; and *polygenic,* arising in two or more of the preceding ways. Vasoconstrictive pulmonary hypertension occurred most characteristically in response to alveolar hypoxia and usually responded to the inhalation of oxygen or the injection of acetylcholine into the pulmonary artery. Reversible vasoconstriction also was seen as an added component of the passive hypertension of mitral stenosis and the hyperkinetic hypertension caused by congenital left-to-right intracardiac shunts before the onset of Eisenmenger's syndrome. The histologic lesions observed in these reversible kinds of pulmonary hypertension consisted of medial hypertrophy of the pulmonary artery and scant intimal hyperplasia.

Also in 1958, Heath and Edwards[103] documented the pathology of hypertensive pulmonary vascular disease in a study of 67 patients with congenital heart disease and 2 patients with primary pulmonary hypertension. These investigators argued that the progression of lesions in these patients was so stereotyped as to allow division of the structural effects of pulmonary hypertension into six grades as follows: grade 1, medial hypertrophy of the pulmonary arteries and arterioles without intimal changes; grade 2, medial hypertrophy with cellular intimal proliferation; grade 3, medial hypertrophy, intimal proliferation, and intimal fibrosis; grade 4, progressive generalized vascular dilation and occlusion by intimal fibrosis and fibroelastosis; grade 5, appearance of dilation lesions, including veinlike branches of occluded pulmonary arteries, plexiform lesions, angiomatoid lesions, and cavernous lesions; and grade 6, necrotizing arteritis.

Heath and Edwards' grading system focused on the muscular pulmonary arteries 100 to 1000 μm in size. Grades 1 and 2, which were characterized by medial thickening, were comparable to the reversible vasoconstrictive phase of Wood's scheme. In grades 3 and 4, intimal changes led to progressive obstruction of the vessels, which then dilated in the presence of high pressure. Some of the dilated areas evolved into microaneurysms in which there was endothelial proliferation and the formation of in situ thrombosis; these made up the characteristic plexiform lesions. In grade 5, the dilation became rigid, and hemosiderin was extruded from vessels that either burst or allowed the diapedesis of erythrocytes. Grade 6 was seen rarely and involved perivascular neutrophilic inflammation and fibrinoid necrosis.

Heath and Edwards[103] lumped the pathology of congenital heart disease and primary pulmonary hypertension together, and a large series of patients with the latter disorder was not available until 1970. In that year, Wagenvoort and Wagenvoort[104] described the morphology of the pulmonary vessels of 150 persons in whom the diagnosis of

primary pulmonary hypertension had been made on clinical grounds. Despite their common diagnosis, the cases could be divided into several groups based on histologic analysis: chronic pulmonary thromboembolism, chronic pulmonary venous hypertension, pulmonary veno-occlusive disease, sarcoidosis, chronic bronchitis and pulmonary emphysema, pulmonary schistosomiasis, and vasoconstrictive primary pulmonary hypertension. The patients with the last disorder were the largest group, consisting of 36 men and 74 women with a mean age of 23 years and an age range of 4 days to 69 years.

The lesions that Wagenvoort and Wagenvoort[104] attributed to vasoconstrictive primary pulmonary hypertension were strikingly similar to those described earlier by Heath and Edwards[103] and Wood.[102] The earliest abnormalities were medial hypertrophy of the muscular pulmonary arteries and muscularization of the arterioles. These findings were especially prominent in children and were the only irregularities found in young infants. Although the medial thickening might be interpreted as a persistence of the high-resistance fetal circulation, it was considerably greater than that observed in infants of the same age. Less marked in children but apparent in all adults studied were intimal proliferation and laminar intimal fibrosis that gave an onion-skin appearance to the pulmonary arteries. This pattern was not seen in any patients with initially unsuspected chronic pulmonary thromboembolism and also was absent from an additional 20 patients with known thromboembolic disease.

Dilation lesions, including the plexiform variety, were observed in 77 patients with vasoconstrictive primary pulmonary hypertension and one patient with schistosomiasis (who also had *Schistosoma mansoni* ova) but was not evident in persons with chronic pulmonary thromboembolism or other disorders. Necrotizing arteritis occurred in 34 patients with chronic pulmonary thromboembolism; it never involved the veins as it does in pulmonary veno-occlusive disease. Wagenvoort and Wagenvoort[104] noted that vasculitis occurred only in persons with advanced disease and probably was a result rather than a cause of pulmonary hypertension, in contrast to the true pulmonary vasculitides. They believed that the progression of lesions in primary pulmonary hypertension was entirely consistent with a vasoconstrictive mechanism.

Subsequent investigators[105] confirmed the findings of Wagenvoort and Wagenvoort,[104] including the histologic distinctions between primary pulmonary hypertension (Fig. 49.2), chronic pulmonary thromboembolism (Fig. 49.3), and pulmonary veno-occlusive disease (Fig. 49.4).

Despite the distinct pathologic findings in primary pulmonary hypertension, there is more recent evidence that the pathologic arteriopathic changes are in fact not unique to this disease and have been reported in congenital heart disease, connective tissue disease,[106] and chronic thromboembolic disease.[107]

PATHOGENESIS AND ETIOLOGY

A dramatic change has taken place over the last several years in our thinking regarding the pathogenesis of primary pulmonary hypertension. The "paradigm" has shifted from one of vasoconstriction to one of growth and proliferation. There are several lines of evidence suggesting that primary

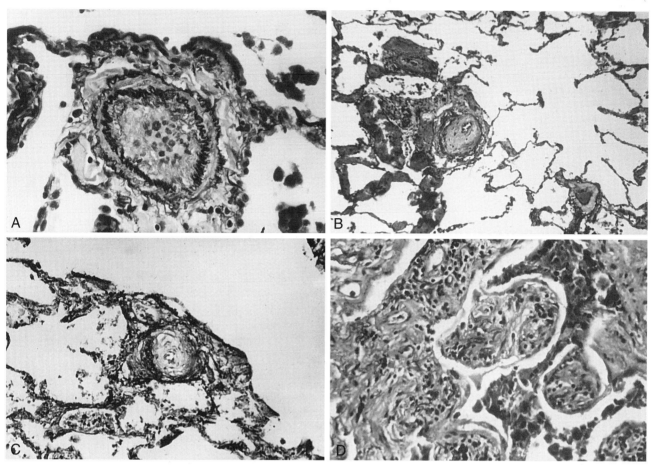

Figure 49.2 Pathologic changes of primary pulmonary hypertension. **A,** Elastic stain demonstrating medial hypertrophy and intimal proliferation. **B,** Hematoxylin and eosin stain demonstrating eccentric intimal fibrosis. **C,** Hematoxylin and eosin stain demonstrating concentric intimal fibrosis (onion-skinning). **D,** Hematoxylin and eosin stain demonstrating a plexiform lesion.

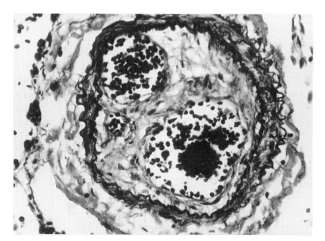

Figure 49.3 Elastic stain of lung tissue from patient with chronic pulmonary thromboembolism showing that there is little medial hypertrophy and that the organized thrombus has recanalized.

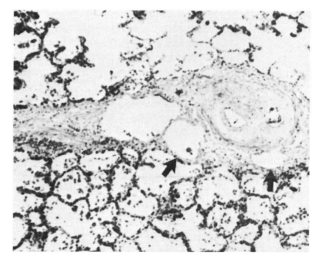

Figure 49.4 Hematoxylin and eosin stain of lung tissue from patient with pulmonary veno-occlusive disease showing occluded vein and dilated perivenous lymphatics (*arrows*). (Courtesy of Martha L. Warnock, MD; from Luce JM: Vasculitis, primary pulmonary hypertension, and arteriovenous fistulas. *In* Murray JF, Nadel JA [eds]: Textbook of Respiratory Medicine. Philadelphia: WB Saunders, 1988, p 1340.)

pulmonary hypertension develops as a result of abnormal proliferation of vascular smooth muscle cells affecting all three layers of the vessel wall and leading to intimal hyperplasia, medial hypertrophy, and adventitial proliferation. What initiates this abnormal growth is not entirely known, but there are several clues. The concept of genetic predisposition toward growth and proliferation has recently emerged. Mutations in the bone morphogenic protein receptor 2 (*BMPR2*) gene have been reported in patients with the familial form of primary pulmonary hypertension.[108] This gene contributes to the apoptotic process through a complex series of messenger proteins, as part of the transforming growth factor-β family of genes. Thus emerges the possibility that pulmonary arteriopathy is a failure of normal apoptosis. Some investigators have even referred to primary pulmonary hypertension as "cancer of the pulmonary artery."

Although this is an attractive hypothesis, the story is not that simple. For one, the presence of a *BMPR2* mutation is not always associated with the development of primary pulmonary hypertension. It is likely that another genetic or acquired insult is required to initiate the arteriopathic process. Defects in a specific voltage-gated potassium ion channel, the $K_v1.5$ channel, have been found in the pulmonary artery smooth muscle cells from patients with primary pulmonary hypertension.[109] A defect or deficiency of this channel allows excess calcium to enter the cell and thus promotes both cell contraction and growth. Overexpression of the serotonin transporter has recently been described in patients with primary pulmonary hypertension.[110] This genetic defect might lead to increased internalization of serotonin and subsequent smooth muscle cell growth. In addition to potential intrinsic genetic defects, several abnormalities in endothelial cell function have been found, many of which are likely a result of some vascular insult. An imbalance between prostacyclin and thromboxane metabolites that favors growth and proliferation has been reported in patients with primary pulmonary hypertension.[111] Similarly, a defect in the vasodilatory, antiproliferative molecule nitric oxide has been noted in the lungs of patients with pulmonary hypertension.[112] An excess in lung expression and circulating levels of the proconstrictive, pro-proliferative protein endothelin-1 has been found.[113] Whether the excess of detrimental endothelial mediators and the deficiency of "beneficial" mediators is cause or effect in primary pulmonary hypertension is not clear. Nevertheless, treatment strategies aimed at replacing the deficient (nitric oxide, prostacyclin) and blocking the overproduced (endothelin-1) substances, as is discussed later, have emerged at the forefront of the advances in this disease.

Connective Tissue Disease

Etiologies other than primary pulmonary hypertension leading to pulmonary arterial hypertension are worth discussing as they may be considerably more common than primary pulmonary hypertension itself and share many features with it. Patients with the scleroderma spectrum of diseases, most notably limited scleroderma (previously known as CREST syndrome) have been reported to have pulmonary hypertension in up to 40% of cases.[114,115] Pulmonary vascular involvement is associated with worse survival in

scleroderma.[116] Other connective tissue diseases associated with pulmonary arterial hypertension, albeit less commonly, include systemic lupus erythematosus,[117–119] mixed connective tissue disease,[120–122] and rheumatoid arthritis.[123–125]

Intracardiac Shunts

Congenital heart disease is a well-recognized "risk factor" for development of pulmonary arterial hypertension. In 1958, Wood[102] coined the term *Eisenmenger complex* to describe pulmonary hypertension at the systemic level due to high pulmonary vascular resistance, with reversed shunting through a large ventricular septal defect. Subsequently the term has been used to describe pulmonary hypertension with cyanosis and any systemic-to-pulmonary circulatory shunt. The likelihood of developing pulmonary hypertension depends on the size of the defect. However, patients with even small atrial septal defects can develop pulmonary hypertension. These patients may in fact have primary pulmonary hypertension, and the atrial septal defect merely serves as a "trigger" in a susceptible patient.

In patients with ventricular septal defects, it has been shown that 3% of patients with a defect of 1.5 cm or less will develop Eisenmenger's syndrome, whereas half of patients with a large defect will develop significant pulmonary hypertension, which also appears earlier than in atrial septal defect, often in infancy.[126] Pulmonary arterial hypertension due to true Eisenmenger's syndrome is associated with a longer natural history and apparent adequate right ventricular compensation than is the case in primary pulmonary hypertension. In addition, the intracardiac defect may actually function as a protective mechanism, providing a route for blood to reach the underfilled left ventricle.

Drugs

The effects of drugs and toxins on the human pulmonary circulation have been graphically demonstrated in the past. Between 1967 and 1970 in Switzerland, Austria, and Germany, a 20-fold increase in pulmonary hypertension was observed after the introduction of aminorex, an appetite suppressant resembling epinephrine and amphetamine.[127] The pulmonary lesions produced by this agent resembled plexogenic pulmonary arteriopathy in every respect. The case against aminorex was weakened by the facts that 20% of patients with idiopathic pulmonary hypertension in Central Europe did not take the drug, that only 1 in 1000 persons taking the drug actually developed pulmonary hypertension, and that an animal model could not be created.[128] However, the case was strengthened by the observation that the incidence of pulmonary hypertension decreased to its previous level after aminorex was withdrawn from the market. Pulmonary hypertension has been associated with another family of appetite suppressants with similar chemical structure, fenfluramine and dexfenfluramine.[129] In a case-controlled prospective study performed in Europe, the risk of developing pulmonary hypertension was increased by 20-fold in individuals who used these drugs for periods exceeding 3 months. Reversible pulmonary hypertension has been reported after discontinuation of a similar agent.[130] Interestingly, application of both aminorex and fenfluramine to pulmonary artery smooth muscle cells results in potassium channel function alterations that are similar to those observed in cells from patients with "spontaneous" primary pulmonary hypertension.[131]

In 1983, an epidemic of pulmonary hypertension was observed in Spain among people who ingested rapeseed oil contaminated with aniline and acetanilide dyes used to mark the oil as unfit for human consumption.[132] Most of the poisoned patients with pulmonary complications died of increased permeability pulmonary edema shortly after ingestion. However, several survivors manifested pulmonary hypertension during cardiac catheterization, and pathologic studies revealed medial thickening and intimal proliferation, early histologic findings of plexogenic pulmonary arteriopathy.[133] Strikingly similar findings have been observed in some patients who developed the eosinophilia-myalgia syndrome after the ingestion of contaminated L-tryptophan. Although the systemic manifestations predominated in most patients, several patients developed varying degrees of pulmonary hypertension, characterized by intimal proliferation and medial hypertrophy of small pulmonary arteries, in the absence of significant parenchymal lung disease.

Illicit drug use has been observed with increasing frequency as a cause of severe pulmonary hypertension; this may be the result of a combination of factors, including granulomatous pulmonary arteritis resulting from a reaction to talc, which commonly is used as an adulterant of parenteral drugs; obstruction of the vasculature due to other foreign material, such as cotton fibers; and the vasoconstrictive properties of some agents, such as cocaine or methamphetamine.[134]

Liver Disease

Portal hypertension is another disease associated with pulmonary arterial hypertension. Mantz and Craige[135] first described simultaneous occurrence of portal and pulmonary hypertension in a patient with portal vein thrombosis and speculated that multiple emboli emanating from portacaval anastomoses were responsible for the pulmonary hypertension. Naeye,[136] in 1960, reported six cases of coexisting portal and pulmonary hypertension and also implicated embolization from the portal vein. A subsequent large retrospective autopsy study found pulmonary hypertensive changes in 0.73% of patients with portal hypertension.[137] A more recent study in patients undergoing liver transplantation found an incidence of pulmonary hypertension of 4%.[138] The mechanism of pulmonary hypertension development in portal hypertension is not known. One hypothesis is that portosystemic shunting allows vasoactive substances, normally cleared in the liver, to reach the pulmonary vasculature. Hemodynamically, patients with portopulmonary hypertension tend to have higher cardiac outputs and lower pulmonary vascular resistance.[139] Despite more favorable hemodynamics, the mortality risk following liver transplantation has been shown to be approximately 50% in patients with even mild pulmonary hypertension (pulmonary vascular resistance >250 dyne-sec·cm^{-5}).[140]

Human Immunodeficiency Virus

The association between HIV and pulmonary arterial hypertension is well known.[141,142] In several studies, the prevalence of pulmonary hypertension in persons with HIV infection has been reported as high as 0.5%.[143] The mechanism of HIV-associated pulmonary hypertension is not known, although theories include release of cytokines and growth factors and the presence of human herpesvirus 8, a promoter of angiogenesis such as occurs in Kaposi's sarcoma. A recent report, in fact, noted the presence of human herpesvirus 8 in the cells from plexiform lesions in 10 of 16 patients with primary pulmonary hypertension.[144] Pulmonary hypertension can occur in all stages of HIV infection, including patients with no detectable viral load. There is a suggestion that many of these patients have a concomitant history of illicit injection drug use, which was noted in as many as 42% of cases.[145] Clinical and hemodynamic features of HIV-associated pulmonary hypertension are similar to those of primary pulmonary hypertension, although, in one study of 112 patients, the survival rate was lower.[146]

Sickle Cell Disease

The results of a recent Doppler echocardiographic study of 195 adults with sickle cell disease revealed that 32% had pulmonary hypertension, defined as a regurgitant jet velocity of 2.5 m/sec or higher. Increased pulmonary artery pressures were associated with both cardiovascular and renal complications and conferred a high risk of death.[147] The mechanism of vascular narrowing is probably multifactorial and includes the frequency and severity of previous pulmonary infections, fat embolism, and episodes of regional hypoxia; the magnitude of hemolysis is probably also pathogenically related through the effects of free hemoglobin and other factors that, collectively, decrease the amount of the pulmonary vasodilator nitric oxide and promote intravascular thrombosis.[148]

SYMPTOMS

Dyspnea is the cardinal symptom of primary pulmonary hypertension, occurring in more than 95% of patients in the major clinical series.[149-153] Breathlessness is the presenting symptom in 60% of patients and usually is noted first on exertion, but eventually occurs at rest. Its mechanism is probably complex: The most likely cause for the dyspnea of pulmonary hypertension is the inadequacy of cardiac output relative to metabolic requirements.[154] Reeves and Groves[155] have postulated that stretch receptors on the main pulmonary arteries also may be involved. Regardless of its mechanism, Packer[156] stressed that the severity of dyspnea does not correlate with the elevation of pulmonary artery pressure in patients with primary pulmonary hypertension.

Closely related to dyspnea are sensations of fatigue and weakness, reported by a majority of patients with primary pulmonary hypertension.[152] These sensations usually are experienced before the general disability that is present with advanced disease. They presumably reflect impaired tissue oxygenation resulting from the depressed cardiac output in patients with primary pulmonary hypertension. This impairment is usually evident during cardiac catheterization as both a low cardiac output and a decreased mixed venous PO_2.

Substernal chest pain also commonly is reported in patients with primary pulmonary hypertension.[149,150] It frequently occurs on exertion, radiates to the left shoulder or axilla, and is relieved by rest. The pain has been likened to angina pectoris and has been attributed to coronary insufficiency in the presence of increased right ventricular work and hypoxemia,[155] a concept supported by the occasional relief produced by nitroglycerin. However, pain may be present in young patients without coronary artery disease, prompting Viar and Harrison[157] to argue that the pain is caused by distention of the pulmonary artery, whose afferents enter the nervous system along the same pathways as afferents from the heart. Another plausible but unproved explanation is that the chest pain of primary pulmonary hypertension is variant angina in patients with generalized vasospastic disease.

Syncope occurs in some patients with primary pulmonary hypertension and may be its initial manifestation.[149] This symptom also is experienced first on exertion but may happen later at rest. The syncope probably is caused by a decrease in cerebral blood flow that follows an increase in pulmonary artery pressure and a decrease in cardiac output. Dresdale and associates[95] speculated that cardiac output would be especially depressed in patients with concurrent coronary insufficiency and right ventricular failure. Conversely, James[158] believed that depression of the cardiac output results primarily from bradycardia due to ischemia of the sinus node.

Another symptom associated with primary pulmonary hypertension is hemoptysis that presumably stems from microvascular aneurysms that rupture under the high pulmonary artery pressure. In addition, hoarseness may result from pressure of the enlarged main pulmonary artery on the recurrent laryngeal nerve.[159] Peripheral edema and ascites may develop after the onset of right ventricular failure.

PHYSICAL FINDINGS

Patients with early primary pulmonary hypertension may manifest no physical abnormalities. However, signs of pulmonary hypertension and a decreased cardiac output should be evident with advanced disease. As Wood[160] observed, the hands and feet of a patient with severe pulmonary hypertension are cold, the peripheral pulse is diminished, the blood pressure is likely to be low, and the pulse pressure is reduced. Signs of systemic venous hypertension should be present, including a prominent jugular venous *a* wave, which is exaggerated by abdominal compression (hepatojugular reflux) and transmitted to the liver in a presystolic hepatic pulse, and prominent *c-v* waves, which are indicative of tricuspid regurgitation. Palpation of the chest should reveal a right ventricular lift at the left sternal border that is sustained throughout the pressure-overloaded cardiac contraction, in contrast to the unsustained parasternal impulse felt in pure volume overload.

On auscultation of the chest, the second heart sound is closely split, and the second (pulmonic) component is accentuated. The valvular closure sound should increase in intensity on inspiration and may become palpable as pulmonary artery pressure rises. A systolic ejection click reflecting sudden distention of the right ventricular wall also may be heard. A murmur of tricuspid regurgitation, heard best along the left sternal border and increasing in intensity with inspiration, is heard frequently. A pulmonary regurgitant murmur may become evident after dilation of the main pulmonary artery and its valve annulus. Diastolic vibration of the aortic valve leaflet (Graham Steell's murmur) may be present along with third and fourth heart sounds. In addition to these findings, patients with right-sided heart failure usually have peripheral edema and abdominal distention due to ascites. When severe tricuspid regurgitation is present, the liver may become pulsatile.

Cyanosis occurs with variable frequency in patients with primary pulmonary hypertension and is likely to be a late phenomenon. It is most marked during exercise but also may be present at rest. Peripheral vasoconstriction and impaired oxygenation of arterial blood due to mixed venous hypoxemia resulting from the decreased cardiac output appear to be the most common mechanisms. Patients in whom right atrial pressure equals or exceeds left atrial pressure may develop severe hypoxemia and cyanosis because of opening of the foramen ovale with subsequent right-to-left shunting of blood. In addition to cyanosis, vascular plethora may be observed in hypoxemic patients with secondary polycythemia. With the exception of patients with cirrhosis and pulmonary hypertension, clubbing is not a usual manifestation of primary pulmonary hypertension. The presence of clubbing warrants a careful search for other causes of pulmonary vascular disease.

DIAGNOSIS

Although pulmonary hypertension may be appreciated on physical examination, primary pulmonary hypertension cannot be distinguished from the other causes of pulmonary hypertension by examination alone. The major entities in the differential diagnosis include those entities already discussed, plus chronic pulmonary thromboembolism (Chapter 48) and pulmonary veno-occlusive disease (described subsequently). Although the severity of pulmonary hypertension may be assessed by physical examination, laboratory evaluation is required for precise quantitation.

Laboratory Tests

Blood studies are an important part of the laboratory evaluation. The complete blood count is particularly helpful in documenting polycythemia, which is present in hypoxemic patients with primary pulmonary hypertension.[152] An even smaller number are anemic, thrombocytopenic, or both. Two reports described patients with microangiopathic hemolytic anemia and primary pulmonary hypertension, one of whom had portal hypertension as well. In both cases, intravascular fragmentation of erythrocytes and platelets was attributed to blood flow through plexiform lesions in the pulmonary circulation.[161,162] Pulmonary hypertension also has been associated with a familial platelet storage pool disease, in which platelet function was impaired and plasma levels of serotonin were elevated.[163]

Radiography

The plain chest roentgenogram is potentially useful in suggesting the presence of pulmonary hypertension and in

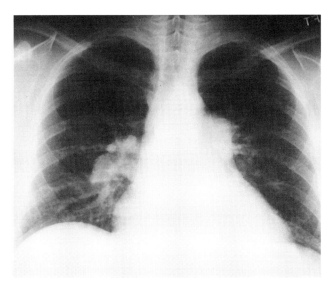

Figure 49.5 Chest roentgenogram from a patient with primary pulmonary hypertension showing the marked dilation of the main pulmonary arteries and right ventricular enlargement.

providing clues of underlying conditions such as parenchymal lung disease (Fig. 49.5). In patients with primary pulmonary hypertension, the roentgenogram characteristically reveals protrusion of the main pulmonary artery, increased width of the descending branch of the right pulmonary artery, peripheral oligemia, and an increase in the cardiothoracic ratio.

Respiratory Function Tests

Systemic arterial blood gas analysis in patients with primary pulmonary hypertension usually reveals a low PCO_2 and a normal pH, reflecting chronic respiratory alkalosis. The systemic arterial PO_2 may be normal or abnormal, but the alveolar-arterial PO_2 difference usually is increased. Several mechanisms have been proposed for the hypoxemia of patients with primary pulmonary hypertension, including diffusion impairment caused by a reduction in the number of pulmonary vessels coupled with the shortened time spent by erythrocytes in traversing the pulmonary circulation; ventilation-perfusion mismatching due to alterations in pulmonary blood flow and concomitant conditions such as bronchospasm; and right-to-left intracardiac shunting through a patent foramen ovale. Dantzker and Bower[164] demonstrated with the multiple inert gas elimination technique that the hypoxemia is caused by a combination of ventilation-perfusion mismatching, intrapulmonary shunt, and a low mixed venous PO_2 resulting from a reduced cardiac output.

Pulmonary function tests performed in patients with primary pulmonary hypertension usually reveal normal expiratory flow rates with normal or mildly reduced lung volumes.[152] The modest restrictive defect has been attributed to diminished distensibility of the pulmonary vessels.[165] The diffusing capacity for carbon monoxide often is reduced to a mild or moderate degree.[152]

Exercise testing serves to bring out physiologic abnormalities in patients with primary pulmonary hypertension if these abnormalities are not present at rest. Characteristi-

cally, patients with pulmonary hypertension achieve their target heart rate and anaerobic threshold at low levels of exercise, often accompanied by a reduction in the systemic arterial PO_2 or an increase in the alveolar-arterial PO_2 difference. The dead space-to-tidal volume ratio either fails to decrease as it should in healthy persons or actually increases during graded exercise. Submaximal exercise testing on the 6-minute walk test is extremely useful as a prognostic marker and in following patients on therapy. Six-minute walk distance has served as the primary outcome end point in several pivotal pulmonary hypertension clinical trials.

Electrocardiography

The electrocardiogram usually discloses right ventricular hypertrophy in patients with advanced primary pulmonary hypertension.[160] Electrocardiographic criteria for right ventricular hypertrophy include a QRS axis in the frontal plane that is greater than or equal to 110 degrees, an R wave in lead V_1 that is greater than 5 mm, an R-to-S ratio in lead V_1 that is greater than 1, and an R-to-S ratio in lead V_6 that is less than 1. Patients also may manifest right atrial enlargement with a symmetrical and peaked P wave in lead II that is greater than 2.5 mm in amplitude; ST segment depression and T wave inversion may be seen in the anterior chest leads. These abnormalities may not be present if pulmonary hypertension is not pronounced or if patients are young.[155]

Echocardiography

The echocardiogram may be helpful in documenting pulmonary hypertension and in ruling out conditions such as mitral valve disease and left ventricular systolic or diastolic dysfunction. Primary pulmonary hypertension has been associated in one-dimensional echocardiography with midsystolic notching, diminution of the *a* dip, prolongation of the right ventricular preejection period, increased right ventricular systolic dimensions, and midsystolic fluttering of the pulmonary valve.[166–168] Two-dimensional echocardiography helps quantitate right atrial and right ventricular size and may identify systolic flattening or diastolic bulging of the interventricular septum due to increased pulmonary artery pressure.[168] Pulmonary artery pressure can be estimated by measuring the velocity of the tricuspid regurgitant jet (TR) using the equation

$$RVSP = \left[(TR\ velocity)^2 \times 4 \right] + estimated\ CVP$$

where RVSP is right ventricular systolic pressure and CVP is the central venous pressure.[169] The precision of the pulmonary artery systolic estimate compared to right heart catheterization measurement is controversial, with studies suggesting both good and poor concordance. Intracardiac shunting may be observed after the intravenous injection of microbubbles.

Scintigraphy

Perfusion lung scanning has been used primarily to differentiate primary pulmonary hypertension from chronic pulmonary thromboembolism. Wilson and coworkers[170] scanned 21 patients with chronic obliterative pulmonary hypertension and observed three patterns: large multiple, segmental defects; multiple ill-defined defects; and no defects. The first pattern occurred exclusively among patients with documented thromboembolic disorders, whereas the third pattern was found exclusively among patients with primary pulmonary hypertension. The second pattern was attributed to disease of the small pulmonary arteries, although recurrent embolization or idiopathic hypertension could not be excluded. Later, D'Alonzo and associates[171] studied 25 patients; in all 8 patients with chronic pulmonary thromboembolism, lung scans indicated a high probability of embolic disease due to multiple segmental defects, whereas 17 patients with primary pulmonary hypertension had scans that were normal or indicated a low probability of embolism. This study suggests that lung scans are highly specific in differentiating the two conditions. If chronic thromboembolic pulmonary hypertension is suspected, pulmonary angiography or spiral computed tomography with contrast is recommended to confirm the diagnosis and assess surgical accessibility.[171a]

Cardiac Catheterization

In the evaluation of primary pulmonary hypertension, right-heart catheterization is mandatory to document the presence and severity of pulmonary hypertension, rule out cardiac causes, and determine if there is acute vasoreactivity using pharmacologic agents. Hemodynamic values, especially right atrial pressure and cardiac index, correlate closely with survival.[172] Cardiac chamber and pulmonary arterial pressures are recorded, and the wedge pressure is measured to rule out disease at the level of the left ventricle, left atrium, or large pulmonary veins. Cardiac output is measured, and from it and corresponding vascular pressures the pulmonary and systemic vascular resistances are calculated. Blood gas samples are taken to determine oxygen contents in the two circulations. These and other variables may be studied at rest or during exercise. Left-to-right intracardiac shunts may be excluded by the measurement of blood oxygen contents in the various cardiac chambers and by indicator techniques.

Cardiac catheterization in patients with primary pulmonary hypertension may reveal elevated right atrial pressure, pulmonary arterial pressures that are increased often to systemic levels, and depression of cardiac output. Pulmonary vascular resistance generally is increased, whereas systemic vascular resistance is in the normal range.[152,173] In the U.S. registry, mean values (±1 standard deviation) were as follows: right arterial pressure, 9.7 ± 6 mm Hg; pulmonary artery pressure, 60 ± 18 mm Hg; wedge pressure, 8.4 ± 4 mm Hg; cardiac index, 2.3 ± 0.9 L/min/m^2; and pulmonary vascular resistance index, 26 ± 14 mm Hg/L/min/m^2.[152] Mixed venous oxygen tensions usually are low, and the arterial-to-mixed venous oxygen content difference is increased. Approximately 20% of patients have a patent foramen ovale.

Acute vasodilator testing is performed using a short-acting agent. Commonly used drugs include inhaled nitric oxide, adenosine, and prostacyclin. Oxygen and nitrates are not adequate testing agents in patients with primary pulmonary hypertension. Criteria for defining vasoresponsiveness are discussed subsequently, but, fundamentally, acute testing is performed to identify patients who will benefit from long-term calcium channel blocker therapy.

Veno-occlusive Disease

Virtually identical hemodynamic and clinical findings may be encountered in the extremely rare disease termed *pulmonary veno-occlusive disease,* which accounts for fewer than 10% of patients with unexplained pulmonary hypertension. Like primary pulmonary hypertension, pulmonary veno-occlusive disease appears to be a morphologic rather than an etiologic entity. In addition, pulmonary veno-occlusive disease tends to afflict infants, children, and young adults, although patients older than 60 years of age have been reported. However, in the adults with veno-occlusive disease who have been reported, there is a slight male preponderance. A familial occurrence of veno-occlusive disease also has been noted. Veno-occlusive disease has been associated with viral syndromes, toxin exposure, and chemotherapy. The characteristic histologic feature of pulmonary veno-occlusive disease is obstruction of pulmonary venules and veins by intimal fibrosis; intravascular fibrous septa, which usually are considered pathognomonic of recanalized thrombi, are nearly always present.[174] These findings have led to the speculation that thrombosis is an essential pathogenetic mechanism in most cases, but the factors causing or contributing to thrombus formation are completely unknown.

Of considerable interest is the observation that narrowing or obliteration of pulmonary arteries is found in approximately half the cases of pulmonary veno-occlusive disease.[174] The morphologic appearance of the arterial lesions indicates that they also were produced by organization of intravascular thrombi and that the abnormalities were not merely secondary to pulmonary venous obstruction with attendant medial hypertrophy and arterial hypertension. These observations raise the question whether there are two variations of the same basic disorder: the classic form of pulmonary veno-occlusive disease, in which the arteries are spared, and a generalized form, in which both arteries and veins are involved.

Pulmonary veno-occlusive disease cannot be distinguished with certainty from primary pulmonary hypertension by right-heart catheterization unless the pulmonary capillary wedge pressure is elevated. Apart from the difficulties of successfully wedging a catheter in patients with pulmonary hypertension, whether the wedge pressure is elevated depends on whether the venous obstruction is in the venules or the large veins. This is because the pressure actually measured at the tip of a catheter positioned in an obstructed pulmonary artery, by either wedging or inflating a balloon, is the pressure in the next freely communicating downstream vessel. Accordingly, if venules are occluded, as is often the case in pulmonary veno-occlusive disease, the next freely communicating vessel may be a vein in which the pressure is normal. In contrast, if (large) veins are the sites of occlusion, then the pulmonary venous pressure is likely to be elevated proximally and to be detectable at catheterization. Indeed, the wedge pressure may vary in different sites within the lung in patients with veno-occlusive disease. The chest radiograph may show signs of pulmonary hypertension with prominent Kerley B lines in the absence of other signs of left-sided heart failure, and this is often the most useful clue to the diagnosis in a patient with unexplained severe pulmonary hypertension. Computed tomographic scanning may reveal interlobular septal thickening, ground-glass opacities, pleural effusions, and enlarged pulmonary arteries.[174a] The perfusion lung scan may show defects suggestive of thromboembolism but with unremarkable pulmonary angiograms.[175] In addition, patients with veno-occlusive disease may develop acute pulmonary edema in response to pharmacologic agents that reduce upstream pulmonary vascular resistance and increase cardiac output, such as prostacyclin.[176] This phenomenon probably is caused by an increase in pulmonary blood volume in the face of downstream vascular obstruction.

TREATMENT AND PROGNOSIS

A comprehensive medical approach is essential in managing patients with primary pulmonary hypertension. In particular, patients should be instructed to avoid circumstances that may increase pulmonary artery pressure and decrease cardiac output. The alveolar hypoxia of high altitude (e.g., flying in commercial aircraft) is one stimulus that may exacerbate pulmonary hypertension. Similarly, concurrent cardiopulmonary disease should be treated, oxygen should be given to hypoxemic patients, and cigarette smoking should be avoided. Indomethacin and related prostaglandin synthesis inhibitors and sympathomimetic drugs should be avoided because of their vasoconstrictive actions, as should barbiturates and other drugs that depress cardiac output.[177]

Another potentially adverse circumstance is pregnancy, which imposes an additional burden on the cardiovascular system.[178,179] Conception probably should be prevented in women with primary pulmonary hypertension, preferably without oral contraceptives, and consideration should be given to terminating pregnancies that occur. If abortion is chosen, abortifacients such as prostaglandin $F_{2\alpha}$, which may increase pulmonary artery pressure, should not be used.

Warfarin has been given to many patients with primary pulmonary hypertension because chronic pulmonary thromboembolism had not been ruled out, because in situ thrombosis was perceived as part of the pathogenesis of primary pulmonary hypertension, or because no other treatment was available. A retrospective review from the Mayo Clinic[180] suggested that anticoagulants actually may have improved survival in patients with pulmonary hypertension of unknown cause, although they often were initiated late in the course of the disease; another later study came to the same conclusion.[181] Whether the improvement was caused by alteration of the underlying lesion of plexogenic pulmonary arteriopathy, by treatment of patients who actually had chronic pulmonary thromboembolism or pulmonary veno-occlusive disease, or by preventing in situ thrombosis from becoming superimposed on these three disorders is not clear from these studies. Furthermore, the value of anticoagulation has yet to be established in a prospective randomized trial of patients with either pulmonary hypertension of unknown cause or plexogenic pulmonary arteriopathy in particular. Anticoagulation poses a potential risk, especially in persons prone to syncope or hemoptysis. If anticoagulation is contemplated in such patients, subcutaneous heparin may be considered as an alternative to warfarin. Patients with intracardiac shunting through a patent foramen ovale are at additional risk for a paradoxic embolism.

Recent advances in therapy of primary pulmonary hypertension have been dramatic and have substantively improved symptoms, exercise capacity, and survival. Four agents or classes of agents have been employed: calcium channel antagonists, intravenous epoprostenol (prostaglandin I_2), prostacyclin analogues, and endothelin receptor antagonists. Although vasodilators have been used to treat patients with primary pulmonary hypertension for many years, experience with agents such as isoproterenol,[182] phentolamine,[183] hydralazine,[184,185] diazoxide,[186] and nitrates[187] have not been encouraging. This is probably not surprising given the lack of vasoreactivity in most patients. In addition, studies of vasodilators in primary pulmonary hypertension are hampered by the lack of a meaningful physiologic end point. Most investigators focus on pulmonary vascular resistance, a variable that is calculated from pressure and flow data rather than measured directly. Pulmonary vascular resistance does indeed decline in some patients receiving vasodilators, but often this decline is caused not by a decrease in pulmonary artery pressure but by an increase in cardiac output related to tachycardia, the augmented venous return, and the recruitment of previously unused pulmonary vascular channels. Furthermore, the price paid for a decline in pulmonary vascular resistance may be a decrease in systemic vascular resistance associated with severe hypotension and an interference with hypoxic pulmonary vasoconstriction that worsens oxygenation. Conversely, pulmonary vascular resistance may be a better variable to follow than pulmonary artery pressure. Survival in patients with primary pulmonary hypertension cannot be predicted by the severity of pulmonary hypertension per se and probably is related, as is symptom relief, to increases in transpulmonary blood flow. In other words, it is now apparent that only a small percentage of patients with primary pulmonary hypertension have significant pulmonary vasoreactivity, getting back to the concept that this disease is a proliferative arteriopathy rather than a vasoconstrictive disease.

Recent data suggest that no more than 6% of patients will sustain a long-term benefit from calcium channel antagonists.[188] These patients will typically demonstrate acute reduction in pulmonary arterial pressure and pulmonary vascular resistance to near-normal during acute testing. Nifedipine, diltiazem, and amlodipine are the most commonly employed calcium channel antagonists, with amlodipine currently preferred due to its better safety profile. For the remainder of patients, vasodilator therapy is not sufficient. Moreover, calcium channel antagonist therapy may cause significant morbidity and even mortality in "nonresponders," given their effects on systemic blood pressure and negative inotropy.

Continuous intravenous infusions of prostacyclin (prostaglandin I_2, epoprostenol) have been used, either as a primary mode of treatment or as a bridge to transplantation, and produce sustained improvement in hemodynamics and exercise tolerance as well as prolonged survival.[176] Follow-up studies have confirmed the significant effect of chronic epoprostenol on survival compared to historical controls, with 5-year survival estimates of greater than 60% in treated patients,[189] a great improvement from the median survival of less than 3 years in the "pre-epoprostenol" era. Interestingly, the benefits of epoprostenol may be progressive. In one report of four patients,[190] chronic epoprostenol infusions resulted in normalization or near-normalization of pulmonary hemodynamics, allowing change to oral medications. Despite the benefits of epoprostenol, chronic use is complex and requires an indwelling central venous catheter, continuous infusion pump, and daily preparation of the medication. In addition, numerous side effects, including jaw claudication, leg and foot pain, diarrhea, rash, weight loss, and occasionally ascites occur. The complexities of dosing prostacyclin and assessing response to the therapy require a dedicated team, typically present only at large pulmonary hypertension centers.

A prostacyclin analogue, treprostinil, is available as a continuous subcutaneous infusion. This agent has been shown to improve exercise tolerance and pulmonary hemodynamics, albeit to a lesser degree than with epoprostenol.[191] The major challenge to treprostinil therapy is the sometimes debilitating pain that occurs at the site of infusion in many patients. This unfortunate adverse effect has limited the use of this agent.

The only oral agent currently approved for pulmonary hypertension in the United States is the endothelin receptor antagonist bosentan. This agent was demonstrated to improve 6-minute walk distance and functional class in two randomized, placebo-controlled trials.[192,193] A long-term follow-up study to the first trial[194] demonstrated sustained benefit in most patients. Two-year survival of a cohort of patients from the pivotal early trials with bosentan was 86%, significantly better than predicted by a National Institutes of Health formula.[194a] At an approved dose of 125 mg twice daily, the only significant adverse effect of bosentan is elevation in hepatic enzymes, which occurs in approximately 5% to 10% of patients. These abnormalities appear to be completely reversible following dose reduction or cessation.

Ongoing studies are examining other pharmacologic therapies for primary pulmonary hypertension, including phosphodiesterase-5 inhibitors, selective endothelin receptor antagonists, and the inhaled prostacyclin analogue iloprost (currently approved in Europe). In addition, the concept of combination therapy using possibly several agents working via different mechanisms is being explored.

Lung transplantation is the only therapy available for patients failing medical treatment. Successful lung transplantation, even of a single lung, leads to prompt resolution of pulmonary hypertension and a remarkable reversal of right ventricular dysfunction, a phenomenon well described following pulmonary thromboendarterectomy.[195] However, in addition to complications directly related to immunosuppression, such as opportunistic infections and graft rejection, obliterative bronchiolitis occurs with striking frequency in lung transplantation patients and can substantially compromise lung function.[196] In addition, organ availability has further limited the widespread application of this technique. (The benefits and complications of lung transplantation are discussed in detail in Chapter 89.) Given the efficacy of current medical therapy for primary pulmonary hypertension, there is no question that fewer patients require lung transplantation. Nevertheless, transplantation needs to remain an option, and attempts are underway to prioritize patients with primary pulmonary hypertension (as well as other diseases) so the "sickest" patients get the available organs first.

Survival of patients with untreated primary pulmonary hypertension is generally poor, with a median survival in the U.S. registry of 2.8 years.[152] Variables associated with poor survival included a New York Heart Association functional class III or IV, presence of Raynaud's phenomenon, elevated right atrial and mean pulmonary artery pressures, decreased cardiac index and diffusing capacity for carbon monoxide, and exercise intolerance using the 6-minute walk test.[152,172] Recent data suggest that the response to medical therapy may in fact be more important in predicting outcome than baseline factors. Specifically, a fall in total pulmonary resistance of greater than 30% and improvement in functional class to I or II following 3 months of epoprostenol were, in one study, predictive of improved long-term survival.[197]

SUMMARY

Pulmonary vasculitis is a relatively rare condition despite its association with the collagen vascular disorders and other systemic processes. It is a major component of illnesses such as the granulomatous vasculitides that affect the lungs primarily. Because of the considerable overlap among the various pulmonary vasculitides, it seems likely that they have a similar immunopathogenesis. The diagnosis of vasculitis usually is made by biopsy of involved tissues, such as the skin, upper airways, or lungs. Some, but not all, of these disorders respond to immunosuppressive or cytotoxic drugs. More specific treatment awaits an understanding of the etiology of the pulmonary vasculitides.

Primary pulmonary hypertension is a severely debilitating illness that too often is diagnosed only when it is far advanced. Mortality is related to impaired right ventricular function and is best predicted on the basis of relationships between stroke volume index and right atrial and pulmonary artery pressures. Improvements in understanding of the pathogenesis, etiologies, diagnosis, and treatment of this previously deadly disease have been striking over the last several years. Primary pulmonary hypertension is a disorder of excessive growth and proliferation of the pulmonary vascular wall, not typically a vasoconstrictive disease. Therapy is now aimed at inhibiting or reversing the proliferative changes in the vasculature and improving the ability of the right ventricle to function. These new treatments have dramatically affected, in a positive way, the lives of patients with primary pulmonary hypertension. Continued discovery of the basic pathogenetic mechanisms of primary pulmonary hypertension should lead to even more refined therapies.

REFERENCES

1. Fauci AS: The spectrum of vasculitis. Ann Intern Med 89:660–676, 1978.
2. Sams WM Jr: Necrotizing vasculitis. J Am Acad Dermatol 3:1–13, 1980.
3. Schönlein JL: Allegemeine und spezielle Pathologie und Therapie (3rd ed, Vol 2). Freiberg: Hexisan, 1837.
4. Kussmaul A, Maier K: Uber eine bisher nicht beschriebene eigenthumliche Arterienerkrankung (periarteritis nodosa)

die mit Morbus Brightii: Und rapid fortschreitender allemeiner Muskellahmung einhergeht. Dtsch Arch Klin Med 1:484–517, 1866.

5. Zeek PM: Periarteritis nodosa and other forms of necrotizing angiitis. N Engl J Med 248:764–772, 1953.

6. Liebow AA: The J. Burns Amberson lecture—pulmonary angiitis and granulomatosis. Am Rev Respir Dis 108:1–18, 1973.

7. Fulmer JD, Kaltreider B: The pulmonary vasculitides. Chest 82:615–624, 1982.

8. Bloch DA, Michel BA, Hunder GG, et al: The American College of Rheumatology 1990 criteria for the classification of vasculitis: Patients and methods. Arthritis Rheum 33:1068–1073, 1990.

9. Hunder GG, Arend WP, Bloch DA, et al: The American College of Rheumatology 1990 criteria for the classification of vasculitis: Introduction. Arthritis Rheum 33:1065–1067, 1990.

10. Leavitt RY, Fauci AS, Bloch DA, et al: The American College of Rheumatology 1990 criteria for the classification of Wegener's granulomatosis. Arthritis Rheum 33:1101–1107, 1990.

11. Lightfoot RW, Michel BA, Bloch DA, et al: The American College of Rheumatology 1990 criteria for the classification of polyarteritis nodosa. Arthritis Rheum 33:1088–1093, 1990.

12. Masi AT, Hunder GG, Lie JT, et al: The American College of Rheumatology 1990 criteria for the classification of Churg-Strauss syndrome (allergic granulomatosis and angiitis). Arthritis Rheum 33:1094–1100, 1990.

13. Mills JA, Michel BA, Bloch DA, et al: The American College of Rheumatology 1990 criteria for the classification of Henoch-Schönlein purpura. Arthritis Rheum 33:1114–1121, 1990.

14. Hunder GG, Bloch DA, Michel BA, et al: The American College of Rheumatology 1990 criteria for the classification of giant cell arteritis. Arthritis Rheum 33:1122–1128, 1990.

15. Calabrese LH, Michel BA, Bloch DA, et al: The American College of Rheumatology 1990 criteria for the classification of hypersensitivity vasculitis. Arthritis Rheum 33:1108–1113, 1990.

16. Arend WP, Michel BA, Bloch DA, et al: The American College of Rheumatology 1990 criteria for the classification of Takayasu arteritis. Arthritis Rheum 33:1129–1134, 1990.

17. Jennette JC, Falk RJ, Andrassy K, et al: Nomenclature of systemic vasculitides: Proposal of an international consensus conference. Arthritis Rheum 37:187–192, 1994.

18. Jennings CA, King TE, Tuder R, et al: Diffuse alveolar hemorrhage with underlying pauci immune pulmonary capillaritis. Am J Respir Crit Care Med 115:1101–1109, 1997.

19. Hatipoglu U, Rubinstein I: Pulmonary vasculitis: A clinical overview. Isr Med Assoc J 4:1143–1148, 2002.

20. Fauci AS, Wolff SM: Wegener's granulomatosis: Studies in eighteen patients with a review of the literature. Medicine 52:535–561, 1973.

21. Gilliam JN, Smiley JD: Cutaneous necrotizing vasculitis and related disorders. Ann Allergy 37:328–339, 1976.

22. Sullivan EJ, Hoffman GS: Pulmonary vasculitis. Clin Chest Med 19:759–776, 1998.

23. Davies D, Moran ME, Niall JF, et al: Segmental glomerulonephritis with antineutrophil antibody: Possible arbovirus aetiology. Br Med J (Clin Res Ed) 285:606, 1982.

24. van der Woude FJ, Rasmussen N, Lobatto S, et al: Autoantibodies against neutrophils and monocytes: Tool for diagnosis and marker of disease activity in Wegener's granulomatosis. Lancet 1:425–429, 1985.

25. Stegman CA, Cohen JW, Sluiter WJ: Association of chronic nasal carriage of Staphylococcus aureus and higher relapse rates in Wegener's granulomatosis. Ann Intern Med 120:12–17, 1994.

26. Falk RJ, Terrell R, Charles LA, et al: Anti-neutrophil cytoplasmic autoantibodies induce neutrophils to degranulate and produce oxygen radicals in vitro. Proc Natl Acad Sci USA 87:4115–4119, 1990.

27. Cid MC: New developments in the pathogenesis of systemic vasculitis. Current Opin Rheumatol 8:1–11, 1996.

28. Hunninghake GW, Fauci AS: Pulmonary involvement in the collagen vascular diseases. Am Rev Respir Dis 119:471–503, 1979.

29. Haworth SJ, Savage COS, Carr D, et al: Pulmonary haemorrhage complicating Wegener's granulomatosis and microscopic polyarteritis. BMJ 290:1775–1778, 1985.

30. Churg J, Strauss L: Allergic granulomatosis, allergic angiitis, and periarteritis nodosa. Am J Pathol 27:277–301, 1951.

31. Guillevin L, Cohen P, Gayraud M, et al: Churg-Strauss syndrome: Clinical study and long-term follow-up of 96 patients. Medicine 78:26–37, 1999.

32. Clauw DJ, Nashel DJ, Umhau A, et al: Tryptophan-associated eosinophilic connective tissue disease: A new clinical entity? JAMA 263:1502–1506, 1990.

33. Centers for Disease Control: Eosinophilia-myalgia syndrome: New Mexico. MMWR Morb Mortal Wkly Rep 38:756–767, 1989.

34. Rao JK, Weinberger M, Oddone EZ, et al: The role of antineutrophil cytoplasmic antibody (C-ANCA) testing in the diagnosis of Wegener's granulomatosis. Ann Intern Med 123:925–932, 1995.

35. Weisbrod GL: Pulmonary angiitis and granulomatosis: A review. Can Assoc Radiol J 40:127–134, 1989.

36. Park JH, Chung JW, Im JG, et al: Takayasu's arteritis: Evaluation of mural changes in the aorta and pulmonary artery with CT angiography. Radiology 196:86–93, 1995.

37. Ahn JM, Im JG, Ryoo JW, et al: Thoracic manifestation of Behçet syndrome: Radiographic and CT findings in nine patients. Radiology 194:199–203, 1995.

38. Erzurum SC, Underwood GA, Hamilos DL, et al: Pleural effusion in Churg-Strauss syndrome. Chest 95:1357–1359, 1989.

39. Katzenstein A, Liebow AA, Friedman PJ: Bronchocentric granulomatosis, mucoid impaction, and hypersensitivity reactions to fungi. Am Rev Respir Dis 111:497–537, 1975.

40. Wasserman K, Whipp BJ: Exercise physiology in health and disease. Am Rev Respir Dis 112:219–249, 1975.

41. Rao JK, Allen NB, Feussner JR, et al: A prospective study of antineutrophil cytoplasmic antibody (c-ANCA) and clinical criteria in diagnosing Wegener's granulomatosis. Lancet 346:926–931, 1995.

42. Wegener F: Über generalisierte, septische Gefässerkrankungen. Verh Dtsch Ges Pathol 29:202–210, 1936.

43. Godman GC, Churg J: Wegener's granulomatosis. Arch Pathol 58:533–553, 1954.

44. Howell SB, Epstein WV: Circulating immunoglobulin complexes in Wegener's granulomatosis. Am J Med 60:259–268, 1976.

45. Fahey JL, Leonard E, Churg J, et al: Wegener's granulomatosis. Am J Med 17:168–179, 1954.

46. Fauci AS, Haynes BF, Katz P, et al: Wegener's granulomatosis: Prospective clinical and therapeutic experience with patients for 21 years. Ann Intern Med 98:76–85, 1983.

47. Cotch MF, Hoffman GS, Yerg DE, et al: The epidemiology of Wegener's granulomatosis: Estimates of the five-year prevalence, annual mortality and geographic disease distribution from population based data sources. Arthritis Rheum 39:87–92, 1996.

48. Fauci AS, Johnson RE, Wolff SM: Radiation therapy of midline granuloma. Ann Intern Med 84:140–147, 1976.

49. Langford CA, Sneller MC, Hallahan CW, et al: Clinical features and therapeutic management of subglottic stenosis in patients with Wegener's granulomatosis. Arthritis Rheum 39:1754–1760, 1996.

50. Gluth MB, Shinners PA, Kasperbauer JL: Subglottic stenosis associated with Wegener's granulomatosis. Laryngoscope 113:1304–1307, 2003.

51. Hoffman GS, Kerr GS, Leavitt RY, et al: Wegener granulomatosis: An analysis of 158 patients. Ann Intern Med 116:488–498, 1992.

52. Lee KS, Kim TS, Fujimoto K, et al: Thoracic manifestation of Wegener's granulomatosis: CT findings in 30 patients. Eur Radiol 13:43–51, 2003.

53. Landman S, Burgener I: Pulmonary manifestations in Wegener's granulomatosis. AJR Am J Roentgenol 122:750–757, 1974.

54. Gohel VK, Dalinka MK, Israel HL, et al: The radiological manifestations of Wegener's granulomatosis. Br J Radiol 46:427–432, 1973.

55. Travis WD, Colby TV, Lombard C, et al: A clinicopathologic study of 34 cases of diffuse pulmonary hemorrhage with lung biopsy confirmation. Am J Surg Pathol 14:1112–1125, 1990.

56. Travis WD, Hoffman GS, Leavitt RY, et al: Surgical pathology of the lung in Wegener's granulomatosis. Am J Surg Pathol 15:315–333, 1991.

57. Specks U, Wheatley CL, McDonald TJ, et al: Anticytoplasmic autoantibodies in the diagnosis and followup of Wegener's granulomatosis. Mayo Clin Proc 64:28–36, 1989.

58. Beer DJ: ANCAs aweigh. Am Rev Respir Dis 146:1128–1130, 1992.

59. Bosch X, Font J, Mirapeix E: Antimyeloperoxidase autoantibody associated necrotizing alveolar capillaritis. Am Rev Respir Dis 146:1326–1329, 1992.

60. Fauci AS, Wolff SM, Johnson JS: Effect of cyclophosphamide upon the immune response in Wegener's granulomatosis. N Engl J Med 285:1493–1496, 1971.

61. Jayne D, Rasmussen N, Andrassy K, et al: A randomized trial of maintenance therapy for vasculitis associated with antineutrophil cytoplasmic antibodies. N Engl J Med 349:36–44, 2003.

62. Langford CA, Talar-Williams C, Barron KS, et al: A staged approach to the treatment of Wegener's granulomatosis. Arthritis Rheum 42:2666–2673, 1999.

63. Stegeman CA, Tervaert JWC, de Jong PE, et al: Trimethoprim-sulfamethoxazole (co-trimoxazole) for the prevention of relapses of Wegener's granulomatosis. N Engl J Med 335:16–20, 1996.

64. Kus J, Bergin C, Miller R, et al: Lymphocyte subpopulations in allergic granulomatosis and angiitis (Churg-Strauss syndrome). Chest 87:826–828, 1985.

65. Koss N, Monovych T, Hochholzer L: Allergic granulomatosis (Churg-Strauss syndrome): Pulmonary and renal morphologic findings. Am J Surg Pathol 5:21–28, 1981.

66. Lanham JG, Elkon KB, Pusey CD, et al: Systemic vasculitis with asthma and eosinophilia: A clinical approach to the Churg Strauss syndrome. Medicine 63:65–81, 1984.

67. Choi YH, Im J, Han BK, et al: Thoracic manifestations of Churg Strauss syndrome: Radiologic and clinical findings. Chest 117:117–124, 2000.

68. Guillevin L, Jarrousse B, Lok C, et al: Long-term follow-up after treatment of PAN and Churg Strauss angiitis with comparison of steroids, plasma exchange and cyclophosphamide to steroids and plasma exchange: A prospective randomized trial of 71 patients. J Rheumatol 18:567–574, 1991.

69. Wechsler ME, Garpestead E, Kocher Q, et al: Pulmonary infiltrates, eosinophilia and cardiomyopathy in patients with asthma receiving zafirlukast. JAMA 279:455–457, 1998.

70. Green RL, Vayonis AG: Churg Strauss syndrome after zafirlukast in two patients not receiving systemic steroid treatment. Lancet 353:725–726, 1999.

71. Savage COS, Winearis CG, Evans DJ, et al: Microscopic polyarteritis: Presentation, pathology and prognosis. Q J Med 56:467–483, 1985.

72. Gayraud M, Guillevin L, le Toumelin P, et al: Long-term follow-up of polyarteritis nodosa, microscopic polyangiitis and Churg Strauss syndrome: Analysis of four prospective trials including 278 patients. Arthritis Rheum 44:666–675, 2001.

73. Behçet H: Über rezidivierende, apthose, durch ein Virus vesursachte Geschwuse am Mund, am Auge und an den Genitalien. Dermatol Wochenschr 105:1152–1160, 1937.

74. Gamble CN, Wiesner KB, Shapiro RF, et al: The immune complex pathogenesis of glomerulonephritis and pulmonary vasculitis in Behçet's disease. Am J Med 66:1031–1039, 1979.

75. Sakane T, Takeno M, Suzuki N, et al: Behçet's disease. N Engl J Med 341:1284–1291, 1999.

76. Cadman EC, Lundberg WB, Mitchell MS: Pulmonary manifestations in Behçet syndrome. Arch Intern Med 136:944–947, 1976.

77. Petty TL, Scoggin CH, Good JT: Recurrent pneumonia in Behçet's syndrome: Roentgenographic documentation during 13 years. JAMA 238:2529–2530, 1977.

78. Raz I, Okon E, Chajek-Shaul T: Pulmonary manifestations in Behçet's syndrome. Chest 95:585–589, 1989.

79. Davies JD: Behçet's syndrome with haemoptysis and pulmonary lesions. J Pathol 109:351–356, 197.

80. Tunaci M, Ozkorkmaz B, Tunaci A, et al: CT findings of pulmonary artery aneurysms during treatment for Behçet's disease. AJR Am J Roentgenol 172:729–733, 1999.

81. Hughes JP, Stovin PG: Segmental pulmonary artery aneurysms with peripheral venous thrombosis. Br J Dis Chest 53:19–27, 1959.

82. Durieux P, Bletry O, Huchon G, et al: Multiple pulmonary arterial aneurysms in Behçet's disease and Hughes-Stovin syndrome. Am J Med 71:736–741, 1981.

83. Meireles A, Sobrinho-Simoes MA, Capucho R, et al: Hughes-Stovin syndrome with pulmonary angiitis and focal glomerulonephritis. Chest 79:598–600, 1981.

84. Kramer MR, Melzer E, Nesher G, et al: Pulmonary manifestations of temporal arteritis. Eur J Respir Dis 71:430–433, 1987.

85. Takayasu M: Case with unusual changes of the central vessels in the retina. Acta Soc Ophthalmol Jpn 12:554–557, 1908.

86. Sharma S, Kamalakar T, Rajani M, et al: The incidence and patterns of pulmonary artery involvement in Takayasu's arteritis. Clin Radiol 42:177–181, 1990.

87. Ishikawa K: Natural history and classification of occlusive thromboaortopathy (Takayasu's disease). Circulation 57:27–35, 1978.

88. Lupi-Herrera E, Sanchez-Torres G, Horwitz S, et al: Pulmonary artery involvement in Takayasu's arteritis. Chest 67:69–74, 1975.

89. Hall S, Barr W, Lie JT, et al: Takayasu arteritis: A study of 32 North American patients. Medicine 64:89–99, 1985.

90. Kerr KM, Auger WR, Fedullo PF, et al: Large vessel pulmonary arteritis mimicking chronic thromboembolic disease. Am J Respir Crit Care Med 152:367–373, 1995.

91. Rich S, Dantzker DR, Ayres SM, et al: Primary pulmonary hypertension: A national prospective study. Ann Intern Med 107:216–223, 1987.

91a. Simonneau G, Galie N, Rubin L, et al: Clinical classification of pulmonary hypertension. J Am Coll Cardiol 43:5S–12S, 2004.

92. Romberg E: Über sklerose der Lungenarterien. Dtsch Arch Klin Med 48:197–215, 1891.

93. Goodale F Jr, Thomas WA: Primary pulmonary arterial disease. Arch Pathol 58:568–575, 1954.

94. Wood P: Congenital heart disease. Br Med J 18:693–698, 1950.

95. Dresdale DT, Schultz M, Michtom RJ: Primary pulmonary hypertension. Am J Med 18:686–705, 1951.

96. Shepherd JT, Edwards JE, Burchell HB, et al: Clinical, physiological, and pathological considerations in patients with idiopathic pulmonary hypertension. Br Heart J 19:70–82, 1957.

97. Chapman DW, Abbott JP, Latson J: Primary pulmonary hypertension: Review of literature and results of cardiac catheterization in ten patients. Circulation 12:35–46, 1957.

98. Yu PN: Primary pulmonary hypertension. Ann Intern Med 49:1138–1161, 1958.

99. Walcott G, Burchell HB, Brown AL: Primary pulmonary hypertension. Am J Med 49:70–79, 1970.

100. McDonnell PJ, Toye PA, Hutchins GM: Primary pulmonary hypertension and cirrhosis: Are they related? Am Rev Respir Dis 127:437–441, 1983.

101. Rich S, Brundage BH: Primary pulmonary hypertension: Current update. JAMA 251:2252–2254, 1984.

102. Wood P: Pulmonary hypertension with special reference to the vasoconstrictive factor. Br Heart J 28:557–570, 1958.

103. Heath D, Edwards JE: The pathology of hypertensive pulmonary vascular disease: A description of six grades of structural changes in the pulmonary arteries with special reference to congenital cardiac septal defects. Circulation 18:533–547, 1958.

104. Wagenvoort CA, Wagenvoort N: Primary pulmonary hypertension: A pathologic study of the lung vessels in 156 clinically diagnosed cases. Circulation 42:1163–1184, 1970.

105. Anderson EG, Simon G, Reid L: Primary and thromboembolic pulmonary hypertension: A quantitative pathological study. J Pathol 110:273–293, 1973.

106. Jamison BM, Michel RP: Different distribution of plexiform lesions in primary and secondary pulmonary hypertension. Hum Pathol 26:987–993, 1995.

107. Moser KM, Bloor CM: Pulmonary vascular lesions occurring in patients with chronic major vessel thromboembolic pulmonary hypertension. Chest 103:685–692, 1993.

108. Deng Z, Morse JH, Slager SL, et al: Familial primary pulmonary hypertension (gene PPH1) is caused by mutations in the bone morphogenic protein receptor-II gene. Am J Hum Genet 67:737–744, 2000.

109. Yuan JX, Aldinger AM, Juhaszova M, et al: Dysfunctional voltage-gated K$^+$ channels in pulmonary artery smooth muscle cells of patients with primary pulmonary hypertension. Circulation 98:1400–1406, 1998.

110. Eddahibi S, Humbert M, Fadel E, et al: Serotonin transporter overexpression is responsible for pulmonary artery smooth muscle hyperplasia in primary pulmonary hypertension. J Clin Invest 108:1141–1150, 2001.

111. Christman BW, McPherson CD, Newman JH, et al: An imbalance between the excretion of thromboxane and prostacyclin metabolites in pulmonary hypertension. N Engl J Med 327:70–75, 1992.

112. Giaid A, Saleh D: Reduced expression of endothelial nitric oxide synthase in the lungs of patients with pulmonary hypertension. N Engl J Med 333:214–221, 1995.

113. Giaid A, Yanagisawa M, Langleben D, et al: Expression of endothelin-1 in the lungs of patients with pulmonary hypertension. N Engl J Med 328:1732–1739, 1993.

114. Schachna L, Wigley FM, Chang B, et al: Age and risk of pulmonary arterial hypertension in scleroderma. Chest 124:2098–2104, 2003.

115. Mukerjee D, St. George D, Coleiro B, et al: Prevalence and outcome in systemic sclerosis associated pulmonary arterial hypertension: Application of a registry approach. Ann Rheum Dis 62:1088–1093, 2003.

116. Lee P, Langevitz P, Alderdice CA: Mortality in systemic sclerosis (scleroderma). Q J Med 82:139–148, 1992.

117. Fayemi AO: Pulmonary vascular disease in systemic lupus erythematosus. Am J Clin Pathol 65:284–290, 1976.

118. Gross M, Esterly JR, Earle RH: Pulmonary alterations in systemic lupus erythematosus. Am Rev Respir Dis 105:572–577, 1972.

119. Matthay RA, Schwarz MI, Petty TL, et al: Pulmonary manifestations of systemic lupus erythematosus: Review of twelve cases of acute lupus pneumonitis. Medicine 54:397–409, 1974.

120. Derderian SS, Tellis CJ, Abbrecht PH, et al: Pulmonary involvement in mixed connective tissue disease. Chest 88:45–48, 1985.

121. Jones MB, Osterholm RK, Wilson RB, et al: Fatal pulmonary hypertension and resolving immune-complex glomerulonephritis in mixed connective tissue disease. Am J Med 65:855–863, 1978.

122. Wiener-Kronish JP, Solinger AM, Warnock ML, et al: Severe pulmonary involvement in mixed connective tissue disease. Am Rev Respir Dis 124:499–503, 1981.

123. Petty TL, Wilkins M: The five manifestations of rheumatoid lung. Dis Chest 49:75–82, 1966.

124. Kay JM, Banik S: Unexplained pulmonary hypertension with pulmonary arteritis in rheumatoid disease. Br J Dis Chest 71:53–59, 1977.

125. Yousem SA, Colby TV, Carrington CB: Lung biopsy in rheumatoid arthritis. Am Rev Respir Dis 131:770–777, 1985.

126. Vongpatanasin W, Brickner E, Hillis D, et al: The Eisenmenger syndrome in adults. Ann Intern Med 128:745–755, 1998.

127. Follath F, Burkart F, Schweizer W: Drug-induced pulmonary hypertension? Br Med J 1:265–266, 1971.

128. Kay JM, Smith P, Heath D: Aminorex and the pulmonary circulation. Thorax 26:262–270, 1971.

129. Abenhaim L, Moride Y, Brenot F, et al: Appetite-suppressant drugs and the risk of primary pulmonary hypertension: International Primary Pulmonary Hypertension study group. N Engl J Med 335:609–616, 1996.

130. Nall KC, Rubin LJ, Lipskind S, et al: Reversible pulmonary hypertension associated with anorexigen use. Am J Med 91:97–99, 1991.

131. Weir EK, Reeve HL, Huang JMC, et al: Anorexic agents aminorex, fenfluramine, and dexfenfluramine inhibit potassium current in rat pulmonary vascular smooth muscle and cause vasoconstriction. Circulation 94:2216–2220, 1996.

132. Garcia-Dorado D, Miller DD, Garcia EJ, et al: An epidemic of pulmonary hypertension after toxic rapeseed oil ingestion in Spain. J Am Coll Cardiol 5:1216–1222, 1983.

133. Martinez-Tello FJ, Navas-Palacios JJ, Ricoy JR: Pathology of a new toxic syndrome caused by ingestion of adulterated oil in Spain. Virchows Arch 397:261–285, 1982.

134. Schaiberger PH, Kennedy TC, Miller FC, et al: Pulmonary hypertension associated with long-term inhalation of "crank" methamphetamine. Chest 104:614–616, 1993.

135. Mantz FA, Craige E: Portal axis thrombosis with spontaneous portacaval shunt and resultant cor pulmonale. Arch Pathol 52:91–97, 1951.

136. Naeye RL: "Primary" pulmonary hypertension with coexisting portal hypertension: A retrospective study of six cases. Circulation 22:376–384, 1960.

137. Hadengue A, Benhayoun MK, Lebrec D, et al: Pulmonary hypertension complicating portal hypertension: Prevalence and relation to splanchnic hemodynamics. Gastroenterology 100:520–528, 1991.

138. Herve P, Lebrec D, Brenot F, et al: Pulmonary vascular disorders in liver disease. Eur Respir J 11:1153–1166, 1998.

139. Kuo PC, Plotkin JS, Johnson LB, et al: Distinctive clinical features of portopulmonary hypertension. Chest 112:980–986, 1997.

140. Krowka MJ, Plevak DJ, Findlay JY, et al: Pulmonary hemodynamics and perioperative cardiopulmonary-related mortality in patients with portopulmonary hypertension undergoing liver transplantation. Liver Transpl 6:443–450, 2000.

141. Coplan NL, Shimony RY, Joachim HL, et al: Primary pulmonary hypertension associated with human immunodeficiency viral infection. Am J Med 89:96–99, 1990.

142. Mette SA, Palevsky HI, Pietra GG, et al: Primary pulmonary hypertension in association with human immunodeficiency virus: A possible viral etiology for some forms of hypertensive pulmonary arteriopathy. Am Rev Respir Dis 145:1196–1200, 1992.

143. Speich R, Jenni R, Opravil M, et al: Primary pulmonary hypertension in HIV infection. Chest 100:1268–1271, 1991.

144. Cool CD, Rai PR, Yeager ME, et al: Expression of human herpesvirus 8 in primary pulmonary hypertension. N Engl J Med 349:1113–1122, 2003.

145. Mesa RA, Edell ES, Dunn WF: Human immunodeficiency virus infection and pulmonary hypertension: Two new cases and a review of 86 reported cases. Mayo Clin Proc 73:37–45, 1998.

146. Nunes H, Humbert M, Jagot J-L, et al: Hypertension arterielle pulmonaire et infection par le VIH. Sang Thromb Vaiss 10:555–562, 1998.

147. Gladwin MT, Sachdev V, Jison ML, et al: Pulmonary hypertension as a risk factor for death in patients with sickle cell disease. N Engl J Med 350:886–895, 2004.

148. Vichinsky EP: Pulmonary hypertension in sickle cell disease. N Engl J Med 350:857–859, 2004.

149. Chapman DW, Abbott JP, Latson J: Primary pulmonary hypertension: Review of literature and results of cardiac catheterization in ten patients. Circulation 12:35–46, 1957.

150. Yu PN: Primary pulmonary hypertension. Ann Intern Med 49:1138–1161, 1958.

151. Walcott G, Burchell HB, Brown AL: Primary pulmonary hypertension. Am J Med 49:70–79, 1970.

152. Rich S, Dantzker DR, Ayres SM, et al: Primary pulmonary hypertension: A national prospective study. Ann Intern Med 107:216–223, 1987.

153. Hatano S, Strasser T (eds): World Health Organization: Primary Pulmonary Hypertension. Report on a WHO Meeting. Geneva: World Health Organization, 1975.

154. Levine S, Huckabee WE: Ventilatory response to drug-induced hypermetabolism. J Appl Physiol 38:827–833, 1975.

155. Reeves JT, Groves BM: Approach to the patient with pulmonary hypertension. *In* Weir EK, Reeves JT (eds): Pulmonary Hypertension. Mt. Kisco, NY: Futura Publishing, 1984, p 144.

156. Packer M: Vasodilator therapy for primary pulmonary hypertension. Ann Intern Med 103:258–270, 1985.

157. Viar WN, Harrison TR: Chest pain in association with pulmonary hypertension: Its similarity to the pain of coronary disease. Circulation 5:1–11, 1952.

158. James TN: On the cause of syncope and sudden death in primary pulmonary hypertension. Ann Intern Med 56:252–264, 1962.

159. Brinton WD: Primary pulmonary hypertension. Br Heart J 12:305–311, 1950.

160. Wood P: Pulmonary hypertension. Br Med Bull 8:348–353, 1952.

161. Stuard ID, Heusinkveld RS, Moss AJ: Microangiopathic hemolytic anemia and thrombocytopenia in primary pulmonary hypertension. N Engl J Med 287:869–870, 1972.

162. Par PD, Chan-Yan C, Wass H, et al: Portal and pulmonary hypertension with microangiopathic hemolytic anemia. Am J Med 74:1093–1096, 1983.

163. Herve P, Drouet L, Dosquet C: Primary pulmonary hypertension in a patient with a familial platelet storage pool disease: Role of serotonin. Am J Med 89:117–120, 1990.

164. Dantzker DR, Bower JS: Mechanisms of gas exchange abnormality in patients with chronic obliterative pulmonary vascular disease. J Clin Invest 64:1050–1055, 1979.

165. Scharf SM, Feldman NT, Graboys TB, et al: Restrictive ventilatory defect in a patient with primary pulmonary hypertension. Am Rev Respir Dis 118:409–413, 1978.

166. Weyman AE, Dillon JC, Feigenbaum H, et al: Echocardiographic patterns of pulmonic valve motion with pulmonary hypertension. Circulation 50:905–910, 1974.

167. Nanda NC, Gramiak R, Robinson TI, et al: Echocardiograph evaluation of pulmonary hypertension. Circulation 50:575–581, 1974.

168. Lew W, Karliner JS: Assessment of pulmonary valve echogram in normal subjects and in patients with pulmonary arterial hypertension. Br Heart J 42:147–161, 1979.

169. Kitabatake A, Inoue M, Asao M, et el: Noninvasive evaluation of pulmonary hypertension by a pulsed Doppler technique. Circulation 68:302–309, 1983.

170. Wilson AG, Harris CN, Lavender JP, et al: Perfusion lung scanning in obliterative pulmonary hypertension. Br Heart J 35:917–930, 1973.

171. D'Alonzo G, Bower JS, Dantzker DR: Differentiation of patients with primary and thromboembolic pulmonary hypertension. Chest 85:457–462, 1984.

171a. Flipek MS, Gosselin MV: Multidetector pulmonary CT angiography: advances in the evaluation of pulmonary arterial diseases. Semin Ultrasound CT MR 25:83–98, 2004.

172. D'Alonzo GE, Barst RJ, Ayres SM, et al: Survival in patients with primary pulmonary hypertension: Results from a national prospective registry. Ann Intern Med 115:343–349, 1991.

173. Sleeper JC, Orgain ES, McIntosh HD: Primary pulmonary hypertension: Review of clinical features and pathologic physiology with a report of pulmonary hemodynamics derived from repeated catheterization. Circulation 26:1358–1369, 1962.

174. Wagenvoort CA, Wagenvoort N, Takahashi T: Pulmonary veno-occlusive disease: Involvement of pulmonary arteries and review of the literature. Hum Pathol 16:1033–1041, 1985.

174a. Resten A, Maitre S, Humbert M, et al: Pulmonary hypertension: CT of the chest in pulmonary venoocclusive disease. AJR Am J Roentgenol 183:65–70, 2004.

175. Bailey CL, Channick RN, Auger WR, et al: "High probability" perfusion lung scans in pulmonary venoocclusive disease. Am J Respir Crit Care Med 163:1974–1978, 2000.

176. Barst RJ, Rubin LJ, Long WA, et al: A comparison of continuous intravenous epoprostenol (prostacyclin) with conventional therapy for primary pulmonary hypertension. N Engl J Med 334:296–302, 1996.

177. Inkley SR, Gillespie L, Funkhouser RK: Two cases of primary pulmonary hypertension with sudden death associated with the administration of barbiturates. Ann Intern Med 43:396–406, 1955.

178. Jewett JF, Ober WB: Primary pulmonary hypertension as a cause of maternal death. Am J Obstet Gynecol 71:1335–1341, 1956.

179. Nelson DM, Main E, Crafford W, et al: Peripartum heart failure due to primary pulmonary hypertension. Obstet Gynecol 62:58S–63S, 1983.

180. Fuster V: Primary pulmonary hypertension: Natural history and the importance of thrombosis. Circulation 70:580–587, 1984.

181. Rich S, Kaufmann RN, Levy PS: The effect of high doses of calcium-channel blockers on survival in primary pulmonary hypertension. N Engl J Med 327:76–81, 1992.

182. Shettigar UR, Hultgren HN, Specter M, et al: Primary pulmonary hypertension: Favorable effect of isoproterenol. N Engl J Med 295:1414–1415, 1976.

183. Ruskin JN, Hutter AM: Primary pulmonary hypertension treated with oral phentolamine. Ann Intern Med 90:772–774, 1979.

184. Rubin LJ, Peter RH: Oral hydralazine therapy for primary pulmonary hypertension. N Engl J Med 302:69–74, 1980.

185. Lupi-Herrera E, Sandoval J, Sloane M, et al: The role of hydralazine therapy for pulmonary arterial hypertension of unknown cause. Circulation 65:645–650, 1982.

186. Klinke WP, Gilbert JAL: Diazoxide in primary pulmonary hypertension. N Engl J Med 302:91–92, 1980.

187. Pearl RG, Rosenthal MH, Schroeder JS, et al: Acute hemodynamic effects of nitroglycerin in pulmonary hypertension. Ann Intern Med 99:9–13, 1983.

188. Sitbon O, Humbert M, Ioos V, et al: Who benefits from long-term calcium-channel blocker (CCB) therapy in primary pulmonary hypertension (PPH)? Am J Respir Crit Care Med 167:A440, 2003.

189. Mclaughlin VV, Shillington A, Rich S: Survival in primary pulmonary hypertension: The impact of epoprostenol therapy. Circulation 106:1477–1482, 2002.

190. Kim NH, Channick RN, Rubin LJ: Successful withdrawal of long-term epoprostenol therapy for pulmonary arterial hypertension. Chest 124:1612–1615, 2003.

191. Simonneau G, Barst RJ, Galie N, et al: Continuous subcutaneous infusion of treprostinil, a prostacyclin analogue, in patients with pulmonary arterial hypertension: A double-blind, randomized, placebo-controlled trial. Am J Respir Crit Care Med 165:800–804, 2002.

192. Channick RN, Simonneau G, Sitbon O, et al: Effects of the dual endothelin receptor antagonist bosentan in patients with pulmonary hypertension: A randomized placebo-controlled study. Lancet 58:1119–1123, 2001.

193. Rubin LJ, Badesch DB, Barst RJ, et al: Bosentan therapy for pulmonary arterial hypertension. N Engl J Med 346:896–903, 2002.

194. Sitbon O, Badesch DB, Channick RN, et al: Effects of the dual endothelin receptor antagonist bosentan in patients with pulmonary arterial hypertension: A 1-year follow-up study. Chest 12:247–254, 2003.

194a. McLaughlin V, Sitbon O, Badesch D, et al: Survival with first-line bosantan in patients with primary pulmonary hypertension. Eur Respir J in press, 2005.

195. Moser KM, Daily PO, Peterson K, et al: Thromboendarterectomy for chronic, major vessel thromboembolic pulmonary hypertension: Immediate and long-term results in 42 patients. Ann Intern Med 107:560–565, 1987 [published erratum appears in Ann Intern Med 107:946, 1987].

196. Theodore J, Jamieson SW, Burke CM, et al: Physiologic aspects of human heart-lung transplantation: Pulmonary function status of the post-transplanted lung. Chest 86:349–357, 1984.

197. Sitbon O, Humbert M, Nunes H, et al: Long-term intravenous epoprostenol infusion in primary pulmonary hypertension: Prognostic factors and survival. J Am Coll Cardiol 40:780–788, 2002.

50 Pulmonary Arteriovenous Malformations and Other Pulmonary Vascular Abnormalities

Claire L. Shovlin, Ph.D., F.R.C.P., **James E. Jackson**, F.R.C.R., M.R.C.P., **J. Michael B. Hughes**, D.M., F.R.C.P.

INTRODUCTION

Pulmonary vascular abnormalities occur in a variety of acquired and congenital conditions. These structural defects include vascular communications that either are confined to the pulmonary circulation, as is the case with pulmonary arteriovenous malformations, or join the systemic and pulmonary circulations, as with bronchopulmonary sequestration. Aneurysmal dilations of the pulmonary artery and its branches also occur and are considered in this chapter. Although rare, these abnormalities should be diagnosed and treated, because without therapy they often become life-threatening and because successful treatment is now available for most of them.

PULMONARY ARTERIOVENOUS MALFORMATIONS

Pulmonary arteriovenous malformations (PAVMs) are abnormal vascular structures that provide a direct capillary-free communication between the pulmonary and systemic circulations. They range in size from communications within the microvasculature (telangiectases[1-3]) to large complex structures consisting of a bulbous aneurysmal sac between dilated feeding arteries and draining veins[4] (Fig. 50.1). The true anatomic shunts of PAVMs are usually distinguished from the diffusion-perfusion defects that arise in patients with intrapulmonary vascular dilations secondary to the hepatopulmonary syndrome (see Chapter 78).

Pulmonary arterial blood passing through these right-to-left (R–L) shunts cannot be oxygenated, leading to hypoxemia. In addition, the absence of a filtering capillary bed allows particulate matter to reach the systemic circulation, where it impacts in other capillary beds, including the cerebral circulation, resulting in embolic cerebrovascular accidents and brain abscesses. It is crucial for the pulmonologist to recognize that all patients with PAVMs are at risk of paradoxical emboli; also, it is wrong to assume that patients with clinically significant PAVMs will have respiratory symptoms or profound hypoxemia. Fifty percent of PAVM patients are asymptomatic (Table 50.1). In such patients, PAVMs are not benign, because these individuals remain at high risk of paradoxical embolism. The incidence of major, usually neurologic, complications approaches 50%,[5] with a 10% incidence of cerebral abscess and 27% of embolic stroke or transient ischemic attack recorded in all series.[6-17] These complications can be limited if the condition is recognized and treated with embolization using metal coils or balloons, the treatment of choice for almost all patients.

ETIOLOGY

More than 84% of PAVMs occur in individuals affected by the inherited vascular disorder hereditary hemorrhagic telangiectasia (HHT, Osler-Weber-Rendu syndrome). In one large series, 129 of 154 (84%) PAVM patients embolized at a single institution had a definite diagnosis of HHT, as defined by Shovlin et al,[18] with features of HHT absent in only 10 (6%).[19] HHT features develop with age (Table 50.2), suggesting the final proportion will be even higher.[19] Further cases of PAVMs occur as a result of surgical treatments for several forms of complex cyanotic congenital heart disease, with PAVMs developing in the lung not receiving hepatic blood from surgically generated cavopulmonary or atriopulmonary shunts.[20,21] Traumatic PAVMs are rare[22] (<0.5% in our series). Sporadic cases also occur, but many apparently sporadic cases are in fact due to underlying, undiagnosed HHT, because the diagnosis of HHT is more difficult to make than many textbooks suggest and because the majority of HHT patients worldwide are

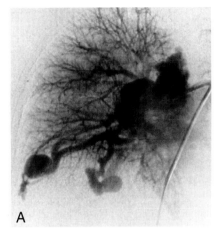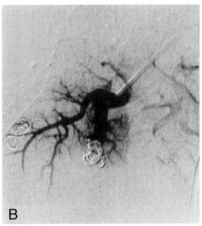

A   B

Figure 50.1 Macroscopic right lower lobe pulmonary arteriovenous malformations (PAVMs) before **(A)** and after **(B)** embolization. Note embolization coils and restored perfusion of pulmonary arterial branches in **B**. Similar PAVMs were present in the left lung. Embolization over an 18-month period reduced the right-to-left shunt from 32% (arterial So_2 78% erect) to 3% (arterial So_2 92% erect).

Table 50.1 Features of Untreated Pulmonary Arteriovenous Malformations*

	Published Series		
	Mean (%)	*Range*	*N*
Respiratory Symptoms			
Asymptomatic	50	25–58	253
Dyspnea	48	27–71	493
Chest pain	14	6–18	198
Hemoptysis	11	4–18	479
Hemothorax	<1	0–2	192
Cyanosis	30	9–73	275
Clubbing	32	6–68	267
Bruit	49	25–58	263
Embolic Phenomena			
Cerebral abscess	10	0–25	368
CVA or TIA	27	11–55	401

* All series 1948–1999 (references in text). Adapted from Shovlin CL, Letarte M: Hereditary haemorrhagic telangiectasia and pulmonary arteriovenous malformations: Issues in clinical management and review of pathogenic mechanisms. Thorax 54:714–729, 1999. CVA, cerebrovascular accident; TIA, transient ischemic attack.

probably undiagnosed. Sporadic PAVMs are usually single, and multiple PAVMs should raise particular suspicion that there is underlying HHT.[9,11,23]

Hereditary Hemorrhagic Telangiectasia

HHT is a disorder of vascular development inherited as an autosomal dominant trait. It is usually underdiagnosed because clinical appreciation of mild phenotypes is poor. The lesions associated with HHT may remain silent and unnoticed for many years, and small lesions may never be detected unless specific screening is undertaken. Careful epidemiologic studies reveal a true incidence of 1 in 5000 to 1 in 8000 in France, Denmark, and Japan,[24–26] substantially higher than early figures based on analyses of medical records. Higher prevalences are described in isolated communities.[5,24] Because PAVMs affect at least 30% of HHT patients,[27,28] the incidence of PAVMs may be estimated to be approximately 1 in 15,000 to 1 in 24,000. Several useful recent reviews are available.[29–32]

Diagnosis. Many individuals with HHT are unaware they have the disease until the family history is unmasked by the question, "Who in the family has nosebleeds?" Most patients will have nosebleeds at some stage of their life, often as children, and many meet the classic 19th-century descriptions of florid epistaxes, mucocutaneous telangiectasia and iron supplementation (or transfusion) dependence due to nasal or gastrointestinal bleeding. However, the majority of patients are minimally symptomatic and often unknown to the medical profession until a family member presents with a major complication. Even then, due to the late-onset penetrance, individuals of childbearing age may display no clinical evidence of HHT (see Table 50.2). Data suggest that, by the age of 16 years, 71% of individuals will have developed some sign of HHT, rising to over 90% by the age of 40 years.[33–35] However, these data mean that, during their childbearing years, an apparently unaffected child of an HHT patient still has a 5% to 20% chance of actually carrying the HHT disease gene.

To permit a high level of clinical suspicion without leading to overdiagnosis, recent international consensus diagnostic criteria were developed based on the four criteria of spontaneous recurrent nosebleeds, mucocutaneous telangiectasia, visceral involvement, and an affected first-degree relative.[18] These define "definite HHT" when three criteria are present; "suspected HHT" with two criteria, most commonly family history and nosebleeds; and "unlikely HHT" with one criterion, such as spontaneous nosebleeds without a family history, or a first-degree relative of an HHT patient with no signs of the disease (see Table 50.2). A crucial issue for families (and medical practitioners) is that no child of a patient with HHT can be informed that he or she does not have HHT, unless a genetic test has been performed.

Genetics and Pathogenesis. Mutations in two genes, *endoglin* and *ALK-1,* have been shown to be responsible for pure HHT, with the disease subtypes designated HHT1 and HHT2, respectively (see 29–32 for reviews). Mutations in *Smad4* result in a juvenile polyposis–HHT overlap syndrome,[36] and a further pure HHT locus has been defined recently.[36a] Confirmation that *endoglin* mutations cause HHT is available from experiments in transgenic mice, because some mice carrying one normal and one null copy

Table 50.2 Approximate Overall Frequency and Penetrance (%) of Hereditary Hemorrhagic Telangiectasia Manifestations at Various Ages

Feature	Overall Frequency	Penetrance (%)				
		0 yr	*15 yr*	*25 yr*	*45–60 yr*	*90 yr*
Epistaxes (nose bleeds)	>90	0	40	60	90	97
Mucocutaneous telangiectasia	75	0	11	30	50	75
Gastrointestinal bleeding	25	0	<1	1.5	12	25
Pulmonary AVMs (PAVMs)	>30	Majority develop around puberty				
Hepatic AVMs	20–30	Unknown				
Cerebral AVMs (CAVMs)	10–15	Unknown; some present from perinatal period				
Spinal AVMs	2	Unknown				

Penetrance figures derived from references 33–35. Other incidence data from references 27, 44, 48, 165.
AVM, arteriovenous malformation.

of the *endoglin* gene (i.e., *endoglin*[+/−] heterozygotes) display features of HHT.[37]

Endoglin and *ALK-1* encode proteins expressed on vascular endothelial cells. HHT-related gene mutations result in gene products unstable at the level of messenger ribonucleic acid or protein. Endothelial cells derived from HHT1 or HHT2 patients express approximately one half of the normal endoglin or ALK-1 levels, respectively.[38,39] It is therefore believed that, in most cases, HHT results from lack of sufficient protein for normal function. As endothelial cells derived directly from arteriovenous malformations in HHT1 patients also express half the normal levels of endoglin, these malformations do not appear to be due to an additional local loss of endoglin expression[40] due to a "second hit."

Endoglin, *ALK-1*, and *Smad4* encode proteins that mediate signaling by the transforming growth factor-β (TGF-β) superfamily. These peptide growth factors include TGF-βs, activins, and the bone morphogenetic proteins, and affect cellular growth and differentiation through signal transduction cascades from transmembrane receptor complexes (for review, see Heldin and colleagues[41]). Generally, type II TGF-β receptors bind the ligand directly, recruiting and activating type I receptors that then activate downstream cytoplasmic signaling molecules, including Smads. Receptor-associated Smads then bind into a complex with *Smad4* and translocate to the nucleus, where they modulate the expression of target genes through direct binding to deoxyribonucleic acid. ALK-1 is an endothelial-cell specific type I receptor that allows TGF-β₁ to signal through a second Smad pathway.[42] As endoglin associates with different signaling receptors and can modify TGF-β₁ signaling, it is expected that the abnormal vessels in HHT develop because of aberrant TGF-β signaling at some stage during vascular development and homeostasis. Further HHT disease gene(s) are also likely to play a part in this signaling pathway, possibly either as ligands, receptors, or downstream transducers of TGF-β family member signals.

Phenotype-Genotype Correlations. A characteristic finding is that different members of the same families display different pattern of disease. This is also observed in the mouse models, suggesting that other genetic and environmental influences modify the HHT phenotype. The presence of specific *endoglin* or *ALK-1* mutations does not allow a strong prediction of the likely course of HHT because all features of HHT can be seen in both HHT1 and HHT2.

There are data indicating that HHT1 patients with *endoglin* mutations are more at risk of certain HHT-related complications. A self-reported questionnaire study demonstrated significantly earlier age of onset for epistaxes and telangiectasia in HHT1.[43] PAVMs affect at least 30% of HHT patients.[27,28] Recent studies indicate that, in individuals who have been screened for PAVMs, the incidence in HHT2 families is up to 15%[36,44–46] compared to 30% to 40% for HHT1 families,[47] and 15% for a single HHT3 family.[36,36a] Cerebrovascular arteriovenous malformations are present in more than 10% of HHT patients in small series.[27,48] Again the frequency is thought to be higher in HHT1 families, though it was approximately 7% in two screened HHT2 populations.[44,46] HHT2 patients with *ALK-1* mutations carry the specific risk of the development of primary pulmonary hypertension indistinguishable from that seen in classic primary pulmonary hypertension families with *BMPR2* mutations,[45] and *Smad4* mutations are associated with juvenile polyposis.[36]

Cavopulmonary Shunts

In non-HHT patients, PAVMs commonly occur in patients who have undergone surgical treatments of several forms of complex cyanotic congenital heart disease, resulting in anastomoses between the superior vena cava and pulmonary arteries.[20] PAVMs associated with cavopulmonary or atriopulmonary shunts are macroscopically indistinguishable from sporadic and HHT-associated macroscopic PAVMs. Using angiography, PAVMs were detected in 31% of patients undergoing classic Glenn anastomoses after a mean follow-up of 6.8 years.[20] The only independent predictor of development of PAVMs was time after cavopulmonary shunt ($P < 0.05$), though there was a trend toward PAVMs developing more commonly in the presence of pulmonary hypertension in the contralateral lung.

The incidence of PAVMs rises substantially if microscopic arteriovenous malformations detectable by contrast echocardiography are included,[49] and microscopic arteriovenous shunting may develop within 2 hours of the procedure.[50] Some have suggested that, after superior bidirectional cavopulmonary anastomosis (BCPA), the development of functional intrapulmonary shunts (detectable by perfusion scans using technetium-99m–labeled albumin macroaggregates [^{99m}Tc-MAA]) may be universal,[51] as their 17 post-BCPA patients had shunts ranging from 11% to 64% of the cardiac output, compared to 3% to 8% in controls. (The normal adult range for this procedure would now be <2.5%.[52])

The key etiologic feature appears to be the route taken by hepatic venous effluent, because PAVMs develop in the lung that receives no or minimal hepatic venous return.[21,49] Diffuse PAVMs that developed after unintentional surgical exclusion of hepatic venous flow from the pulmonary circulation resolved after rerouting the hepatic veins to the pulmonary arteries.[53] These observations, and data from studies of the hepatopulmonary syndrome (see Chapter 78),[54] highlight the role of hepatic metabolism in influencing dilation and remodeling of the pulmonary vascular bed. Whether there will be common underlying mechanisms between PAVMS developing in the setting of cavopulmonary shunts and those developing in HHT is unclear.

PATHOPHYSIOLOGY

Anatomic Basis

Macroscopic (see Fig. 50.1) and microscopic or smaller, diffuse (Fig. 50.2) PAVMs are recognized. Dilated feeding

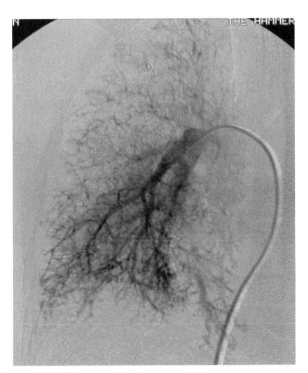

Figure 50.2 Diffuse small pulmonary arteriovenous malformations in a patient left with a right-to-left shunt greater than 30% following maximal embolization (the patient declined transplantation; arterial So_2 erect was unchanged at 78% to 79% over the next 8 years).

arteries and dilated veins are characterized by walls of varying degrees of thickness even over relatively short segments, with disorganized adventitia. Medial thinning is observed, but also prominent are areas of focal thickening with abundant elastin tissue and a varying contribution of smooth muscle cells.[2,6,40]

PAVMs only occasionally appear to develop in the pre- or perinatal period.[55-59] Screening of individuals over a period of years shows that PAVMs can develop in adult life in radiologically or physiologically normal vessels,[36,60] although it is likely that functional changes at a cellular or microscopic level predate the development of the macroscopic lesions. Once present, PAVMs tend to increase in size (see Fig. 3 in reference Shovlin and Jackson[61]), particularly during puberty, in female patients during pregnancy,[60] or in the presence of pulmonary venous hypertension secondary to mitral stenosis or left ventricular dysfunction.[62] On rare occasions, spontaneous regression has been described.[63]

Pulmonary Hemodynamics

PAVMs behave as an anatomic R–L shunt. The absence of a microvascular network of capillary vessels means that the pulmonary vascular resistance (PVR) of PAVMs is less than that of the surrounding normal lung. The effect on the overall PVR depends on the proportion of the cardiac output flowing through the shunt channels. In one study of eight PAVM patients with large R–L shunt fractions (31 ± 4% [standard error]), mean PVR and pulmonary artery pressure were 0.33 ± 0.08 mm Hg/L per minute (normal 0.5 to 1.3) and 14 ± 0.6 mm Hg (normal 12 to 16), respectively.[64] PVR was low, in spite of normal pulmonary artery pressure, because total pulmonary blood flow was high (8 ± 0.8 L/min [160% of predicted]). In more recent studies with smaller mean R–L shunt fractions (10.5% to 11.5%), mean pulmonary systolic and diastolic pressures have been in the normal range.[17,65] The occasional finding[66] of pulmonary hypertension suggests another cause, usually pulmonary thromboembolic disease, cardiac causes of a raised pulmonary venous pressure, or primary pulmonary hypertension.

Total pulmonary blood flow is high on exercise.[64] In spite of the arterial hypoxemia on exercise (arterial oxygen saturation [So_2] 74% ± 3%), tissue oxygen delivery in eight PAVM patients who achieved an oxygen consumption greater than 0.8 L/min was higher than predicted. This reflected an excessive increase in total pulmonary blood flow (142% predicted) in relation to oxygen consumption, and suggests a low systemic vascular resistance, due to either underlying disease (HHT) or hypoxemic vasodilation. The nonshunt pulmonary flow was set at the appropriate level for the metabolic demand.[64]

Right-to-Left Shunt Fraction

The anatomic R–L shunt fraction in PAVMs varies widely, up to 60%. In earlier series,[12,64,67-70] mean R–L shunts were generally higher (23% to 38%) than in later reports[17,65] (11% to 13%), in which earlier diagnosis had taken place, following more energetic screening procedures. PAVMs are more common in the lower lobes,[3,6,8,11,69] and for gravitational reasons, the PAVM shunt fraction tends to increase when patients stand up. In eight patients, the mean R–L shunt increased from 29% (±10.3% standard deviation) to 39% (±14.3%).[67] The effects on exercise depend on the change in vascular resistance through the shunt channels in relation to the change in the resistance of the normal channels: In the normal lung, PVR falls on exercise to half its value at rest, because of dilation and recruitment of vessels, predominantly those in the capillary bed. It is not known what happens to the PVR of PAVMs as overall blood flow increases on exercise; it is reasonable to suppose that for PAVMs, which lack a capillary network and are more dilated, vascular resistance will fall somewhat less than that of normal lung, and that the R–L shunt will decrease on exercise. In one study comparing the R–L shunt fraction at rest with that on maximal exercise, the shunt fraction increased (38% to 47%) in the six patients with diffuse small PAVMs (feeding vessels ≤ 2 mm in diameter and residual shunts after subsequent embolization >10%).[68] However, in the same study, the R–L shunt fraction decreased on exercise by 1% to 10% in four of six patients with larger PAVMs amenable to coil embolization, whose residual shunts were less than 10%.[68] The fall in shunt fraction on exercise in patients with the larger PAVMs suggests that these bigger sacs do not enlarge further as pulmonary vascular pressures and flow increases, and that the smaller PAVMs are more compliant.

Gas Exchange at Rest and on Exercise

Arterial PO_2 and SO_2 are inversely related to the size of the R–L shunt fraction.[71] The contribution of ventilation-perfusion mismatch to arterial hypoxemia in PAVMs is small, except in patients with significant coexistent lung disease. Calculations of the R–L shunt from arterial SO_2 measurements breathing air, often referred to as the venous admixture effect, are in good agreement with measurements of the anatomic R–L shunt,[67] confirming that the R–L shunt is the predominant cause of the arterial hypoxemia. Because of the shape of the oxygen dissociation curve, measurement of arterial PO_2 breathing air will be better at detecting small R–L shunts than pulse oximetry measurements of arterial SO_2. Nevertheless, neither measurement is specific for PAVMs, and for screening purposes other modalities need to be employed (see later section on diagnosis).

In keeping with the increased R–L shunt fraction on going from the supine to the erect position, in PAVM patients the arterial SO_2 usually falls on assuming the upright posture. This is in contrast to normal individuals, in whom

the mean fall is 0.3% (±1.5%).[52] In PAVM patients, the absolute decrease in arterial SO_2 (from supine to erect) reflects the size of the R–L shunt, being larger (~6%) for R–L shunts of greater than 20%.[17,67–69,71]

The change in arterial SO_2 from rest to exercise is more complex, depending on both the change in the shunt fraction discussed in the preceding section, and the fall in mixed venous oxygen saturation on exercise. Overall, the fall in arterial SO_2 (from rest to exercise) varies according to the resting level of SO_2 and R–L shunt, averaging 6% for mean shunts of greater than 30%,[64,68] 3% for mean shunts of 20% to 25%[17,68,69] and 1% to 2% for mean shunts of less than 12%.[17] The importance of the fall in mixed venous oxygen saturation on exercise is illustrated by a study involving 18 patients (R–L shunt at rest, 42% ± 13%),[64] in whom R–L shunt fraction and arterial SO_2 were measured simultaneously during submaximal exercise at 30 to 75 watts. The fall in arterial SO_2 (from rest to exercise) was related to the change in R–L shunt on a sliding scale from shunt decrease ($n = 6$) to shunt increase ($n = 12$). By interpolation, zero change in R–L shunt predicted a 3% fall in arterial SO_2 on exercise, reflecting the fall in mixed venous oxygen saturation on exercise.

Gas-exchange efficiency in terms of the ventilatory equivalent ($\dot{V}E/\dot{V}O_2$) is abnormally high on exercise, related to the exercise R–L shunt, and inversely to exercise arterial SO_2.[64] This high ventilatory drive on exercise is similar to that seen in patients with congenital heart disease and R–L shunts, and probably reflects shunts of both carbon dioxide and oxygen (a combined hypercapnic and hypoxemic effect). Work capacity is well preserved in PAVM patients, even when arterial SO_2 on exercise is less than 80%. There is a relationship between exercise capacity in watts (as percent predicted) and the resting R–L shunt; for mean shunts of greater than 20%[17,71] maximum power output was 65% to 75% of the predicted value, increasing to 75% to 85% of predicted for mean shunts of 10% to 15% and exceeding 90% for mean shunts of less than 10%.[17]

Pulmonary Function

Vital capacity is generally normal[17,69] but was reduced (51% to 81% of predicted) in 7 of 15 patients with large PAVMs and R–L shunts[70] (Table 50.3). There is no airflow obstruction.[17,69,70] With large R–L shunts (>20%), the carbon monoxide diffusing capacity (DL_{CO}) is often moderately reduced (71% to 78%),[12,69,70] but in the majority of patients with less R–L shunting, DL_{CO} is 90% of predicted or greater

Table 50.3 Pulmonary Function in Pulmonary Arteriovenous Malformation Series

Study	n	FEV₁		VC		FEV₁/FVC		DL_CO		DL/VA	
		Pre	Post	Pre	Post	Pre	Post	Pre	Post	Pre	Post
Chilvers et al. (1990)[70]	15		90	85				71		87	90
Pennington et al. (1992)[12]	8	106						74	73		
Dutton et al. (1995)[69]	44		89	92	93	93	89	78	79	85	90
Gupta et al. (2002)[17]	60	94	79	98	97			90	92	97	98

All values are % predicted.

(interquartile range, 76 to 100).[17] The carbon monoxide diffusing capacity per unit of alveolar volume (DL/VA) is better preserved[17,69] (see Table 50.3). Values less than 70% are unusual[70]; in a recent study, only 16 of 63 patients had values less than 90% of predicted.[17] Those with the lowest DL_{CO} and DL/VA generally had widespread and small vascular malformations. In addition, data from patients following embolization indicate that, in some patients, a vascular steal through the low-resistance PAVMs may contribute to the low diffusion values.[17]

CLINICAL FEATURES

Lack of Respiratory Symptoms

In spite of the significant hazards of untreated PAVMs, in all series between 1948 and 1999, approximately half of the patients had no respiratory symptoms[8–10,12,13,72–74] (reviewed by Shovlin and Letarte[31] and Gupta and colleagues[17]; see Table 50.1). The most common symptom is dyspnea (48% in all series; range, 27% to 71%), but this may not be appreciated until after the condition has been treated. Pleuritic chest pain of uncertain etiology occurs in up to 10% of patients. A similar percentage experience hemoptysis, which may be due to accompanying endobronchial telangiectasia. Hemorrhage into a bronchus or the pleural cavity is particularly dangerous during pregnancy.[60]

Early-Onset Strokes and Cerebral Abscess

PAVMs pose a substantial risk to patients because of the frequency of paradoxical emboli leading to cerebral abscess (10%), embolic stroke, and transient ischemic attacks in approximately 30% of patients.[6–17] Historical series of untreated patients with generally symptomatic PAVMs over periods not exceeding 15 years indicated mortality rates ranging from 4% to 22%.[7,9,23,72,75]

Pregnancy

PAVMs enlarge during pregnancy,[60,76] and there is an increased risk of pulmonary hemorrhage, which may be fatal.[60] There does not seem to be any particular risk for the fetus. Patients and their medical practitioners should be alerted to this possibility of hemoptysis, which requires urgent admission and management. Embolization in the second and third trimesters is feasible and safe; embolization therapy was undertaken safely in two North American centers between 16 and 36 weeks' gestation.[77] The estimated fetal dose of radiation as monitored by film exposures ranged from less than 50 to 220 mrad, less than half the recommended occupational exposure for a pregnant worker.[77]

DIAGNOSIS

Classic PAVM cases with large R–L shunts are easy to diagnose, with cyanosis, clubbing, a vascular bruit, and characteristic chest radiographs displaying lobulated masses and dilated feeding and draining veins. However, detection of smaller PAVMs often requires a high degree of clinical suspicion. Many patients are diagnosed as a result of a chest radiograph obtained either routinely or for nonspecific respiratory symptoms, often proven by a subsequent thoracic computed tomography (CT) scan. In other cases, PAVM screening in an at-risk population will be required in order to confirm or refute the diagnosis of PAVMs.

Available Methods

Radiology. The chest radiograph is abnormal in 60% to 90% of instances,[14,17,27,28,78] though careful scrutiny is required to detect the abnormalities, which are frequently subtle. One or more well-circumscribed lobulated masses, connected by prominent blood vessels to the hilum, may be seen (see Figs. 50.1 and 50.2). Lower lobe PAVMs, the most common, may be partially obscured by the hemidiaphragm on posteroanterior chest radiographs. PAVMs are usually multiple, with 72% of affected subjects having lesions in both lungs.[14] Three-dimensional spiral (or helical) CT is an elegant way of demonstrating the anatomy of PAVMs and their feeding vessels[79] (Fig. 50.3); the radiation burden may be minimized by the use of newer protocols and restricting exposure to a single scan (no contrast medium is required because of the natural contrast of the gas in the lung). Three-dimensional reconstructions provide impressive images[79] although these are not required for diagnosis. Where there are difficulties with interpretation of dilated and apparently vascular structures, confirmation of R–L shunting may be helpful. Magnetic resonance scanning has been less effective than CT or pulmonary angiography as small PAVMs with rapid blood flow are not visualized.[80] Magnetic resonance methodology is improving,[81,82] and because this modality provides no radiation burden, the frequency of its use will probably increase.

Measurement of the Right-to-Left Shunt. Two techniques are in common usage: (1) measurement of arterial PO_2 breathing 100% oxygen, and (2) lung and kidney scans using intravenous injection of ^{99m}Tc-MAA; both have

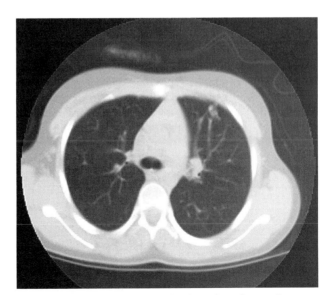

Figure 50.3 Computed tomography detection of a small pulmonary arteriovenous malformation (arterial SO_2 92% erect).

Table 50.4 Comparison of Screening Regimens and Modalities for Pulmonary Arteriovenous Malformations, with Pulmonary Angiography as the Reference Modality

Modality and Study	Number Screened	Population	Threshold Value	Sensitivity, % (Positive Likelihood)	Specificity, %	1 - Specificity, % (False Positive Likelihood)
Pa_{O_2} (100% O_2)						
Haitjema et al. (1995)[27]	36	HHT*	<575 mm Hg‡	88	75	25
Lee et al. (2003)[87]	59	HHT*	<575 mm Hg‡	95	8	92
			<500 mm Hg‡	66	64	36
Kjeldsen et al. (1999)[28]	24	HHT*	<500 mm Hg‡	100	30	70
Lee et al. (2003)[87]	29	Postembol†	<500 mm Hg‡	33	85	15
Cottin et al. (2004)[88b]	102	HHT	<535 mm Hg	62	98	2
Sa_{O_2} (Erect)						
Kjeldsen et al. (1999)[28]	24	HHT*	≤96%	71	100	0
Thompson et al. (1999)[52]	66	Postembol†	≤96%	73	35	65
			≤95%	61	75	25
^{99m}Tc-MAA Shunt						
Thompson et al. (1999)[52]	66	Postembol†	>3.5%	87	61	39
			>5.0%	68	72	28
Cottin et al. (2004)[88b]	93	HHT	Positive	71	98	2
Contrast Echo						
Lee et al. (2003)[87]	28	Postembol†	Bubbles in left heart	100	21	79
Nanthakumar et al. (2001)[78]	59	HHT*	Bubbles in left heart	94	67	33
Cottin et al. (2004)[88b]	81	HHT	Bubbles in left heart	93	53	47

* Prospective study of an HHT population.
† Small residual shunts or no shunts.
‡ 575 and 500 mm Hg represent right-to-left shunts of approximately 5% and 9%, respectively.
HHT, hereditary hemorrhagic telangiectasia; Postembol, postembolization; ^{99m}Tc-MAA, technetium-99m–labeled albumin macroaggregates. Positive, signals from renal and cerebral areas.

proved useful in monitoring outcomes after coil or balloon embolization treatment for PAVMs.[17,69,83] R–L shunt measurements confirm a diagnosis suspected on clinical grounds, and provide useful follow-up data, but they do not have sufficient sensitivity (Table 50.4) for use as a screen to exclude the presence of PAVMs.

100% Oxygen Breathing. In the classic technique, arterial PO_2 and hemoglobin concentration are measured after 100% O_2 is breathed for 15 to 20 minutes using periodic deep breaths, to wash nitrogen out of the lungs. In normal subjects, the R–L anatomic shunt is about 1% of the cardiac output, representing blood draining into the left atrium from the bronchial and coronary circulations. Normally, breathing air, the arterial PO_2 has an additional component, the "alveolar" shunt, caused by ventilation-perfusion mismatch; the combination of alveolar and anatomic shunt is called the "physiologic" shunt (about 5% of the cardiac output in normal persons, but age dependent). It is very difficult to eliminate all the nitrogen from the lung and the body tissues with 100% O_2 breathing, and a figure of 5% is usually accepted as normal for the "anatomic" R–L shunt. Rather than quoting arterial PO_2, the R–L shunt can be calculated as a percentage of the cardiac output, and it is customary to assume a value for the arteriovenous oxygen content difference of 5.0 mL per 100 mL (right heart catheterization is not performed). Recent data highlight that this arteriovenous oxygen content difference estimate is too high for the majority of PAVM patients, in whom the

A   B

Figure 50.4 Right-to-left shunt quantitation by radionuclide scans. In contrast to normal perfusion scans, the activity is not restricted to the lungs (included for reference). **A,** The renal images used for quantitation. **B,** Cerebral imaging illustrating risk of paradoxical microemboli.

measured average difference was 4.4 mL per 100 mL,[65] due to the high resting cardiac output in PAVMs.[64] As a result, this method underestimates the size of the shunt such that a 10% shunt as measured is in reality 11%.[65]

^{99m}Tc-MAA Lung and Kidney Scans. This method measures a truly anatomic shunt, rather than a physiologic estimate of the anatomic shunt. Radiolabeled human serum albumin particles (macroaggregates, 10 to 80 μ, or microspheres, 7 to 25 μ) are injected intravenously, and impact in the pulmonary arterioles. In the presence of an anatomic shunt in the heart or lungs, a fraction of the particles, proportional to shunt flow, will escape into the systemic circulation (Fig. 50.4). For a known dose of ^{99m}Tc-MAA injected, the activity over the lung fields and over the right kidney is measured by a gamma camera. Assuming 10% of the cardiac output goes to the right kidney, the R–L shunt is measured by the ratio of (right kidney counts ×10)/injected dose (the kidney:dose method), or (right kidney counts ×10)/(total lung counts + [right kidney counts ×10]) (the kidney:lung method).[68] Ideally, renal flow should be measured directly using a second tracer (kidney2:lung method), as the actual flow fraction to the right kidney deviated from the assumed 10% by ±3% absolute in one study.[65] The limits of agreement for a 100% O_2 shunt of 20% were 14% to 29% for the kidney:dose method,[71] and 5% to 35% for the kidney:lung method, compared with 12% to 28% for the kidney2:lung method.[65] However, the methods cannot be used interchangeably in follow-up of shunt size in a particular patient.[65]

Contrast Echocardiography. Contrast echocardiography is an alternative method for demonstrating intrapulmonary shunts. This method traces the circulatory transit of microbubbles generated by intravenously injected echocontrast. In intracardiac shunts, contrast passes immediately from the right to the left ventricle, whereas R–L shunting through PAVMs results in a delayed appearance of microbubbles in the left side of the circulation (left ventricle or carotid artery), within 5 to 10 cardiac cycles. The microbubble appearance can be graded on a 5-point scale, but the R–L shunt cannot be quantitated by this method.

Contrast echocardiography is considered a very sensitive method of detecting R–L shunting, and is widely used in the congenital heart disease population, particularly for detection of microscopic disease.[49,51] Initial reports in the adult HHT population suggested 100% sensitivity,[28] but false negatives are being reported[78] (see Table 50.4). Specificity may be a problem, because up to 27% of the normal population may have a patent foramen ovale,[84] and intrapulmonary shunting was demonstrated in 5% of 19 normal subjects[85] (by injection of contrast directly into the pulmonary artery, bypassing any intracardiac shunt). In a recent study, the correlation of a positive contrast echocardiography study (assessed by two blinded observers) and angiography with pulmonary venous SO_2 measurements was very poor. Contrast echocardiography was extremely sensitive, but often (6 of 11 cases) strongly positive when angiography and pulmonary venous SO_2 were negative.[85]

How to Screen Patients

The overall incidence of PAVMs in the general population is less than 0.01%, and therefore targeted screening protocols are required. Dyspnea, hemoptysis, or other clinical symptoms are not appropriate to target screening because PAVM patients are often asymptomatic, and because these symptoms occur commonly in the non-PAVM population. Suitable populations to screen would be patients with HHT (at least 30% of whom have PAVMs[27,28]), patients with cerebral abscesses, and any young patient with an embolic cerebrovascular accident, even if an apparent alternative cause is present.[86] Screening HHT patients poses particular difficulty as many individuals with HHT are unaware they have the disease until the family history is

unmasked. Even then, due to the late-onset penetrance, individuals of childbearing age may display no clinical evidence of HHT (see Table 50.2), and asymptomatic screening, or asymptomatic diagnosis via HHT mutational screening programs now available, may be warranted.

A comparison of available screening regimens is illustrated in Table 50.4. PAVM centers differ in the exact screening modalities employed, according to the particular expertise of the institution. Common to all programs are the policies of minimizing the radiation burden in an often young population, and having a sensitive screen to detect all clinically significant PAVMs. The pattern of screening has changed over the last decade as the importance of recognizing very small PAVMS has become appreciated.

Early screening studies were based upon chest radiographs, arterial SO_2/PO_2, and shunt quantitation by 100% oxygen breathing or ^{99m}Tc-MAA scans (see Table 50.4). The results for sensitivity, specificity, and false-positive rate (1 − specificity) depend on (1) the characteristics of the population being screened, and (2) the "cutoff" or threshold value chosen by the investigators. In a prospective study, those screening positively will tend to have larger R–L shunts, as in one report[28] in which the mean shunt was 19% and only one patient had a R–L shunt of less than 13%. In such studies, sensitivity or specificity could reach 100% (see Table 50.4). A posttreatment population with only small residual shunts may provide a better test of the screening modality. Within a single study,[87] altering threshold values will alter the sensitivity and false-positive detection rates, resulting in a tradeoff. The greater the sensitivity, the higher the false-positive rate (1 − specificity) (see Table 50.4). Conversely, if the threshold is set low (e.g., <500 mm Hg for 100% O_2, ≤95% for erect SO_2, >5% for ^{99m}Tc-MAA shunt), the positive likelihood of a correct diagnosis diminishes because of reduced sensitivity, even though fewer false positives will be detected (see Table 50.4).

Using these functional methods, there are no realistic cutoffs that allow adequate sensitivity to rule out clinically significant PAVMs which will be present in at least 30% of individuals in an HHT screening program, particularly as recent data indicate that patients with SaO_2 and R-L shunts in the normal range are at risk of brain abscess[88] and thromboembolic CVA.[88a] Nevertheless, physiologic measurements have a major role to play in the follow-up of individual patients. For more sensitive screening tests, the choice lies between thoracic CT scans and contrast echocardiography. Use of either test means that very few PAVMs will be missed in an HHT population. Contrast echocardiography carries no radiation burden, but all patients with positive contrast echocardiography (15 of 23, or 65%, in the study by Kjeldsen and colleagues,[28] 27 of 72, or 35% in the study by Cottin and colleagues[88b]) will need to undergo further tests with CT scans, as recommended in 88b. Thoracic CT scans have a small but significant radiation burden (approximately 4 mSv[61]), but allow careful assessment of suitability for embolization and therefore spare many patients inappropriate angiography. Some centers will use pulmonary angiography as a tool to confirm the diagnosis, but, in order to reduce the radiation burden, we prefer to restrict angiography to therapeutic embolization sessions.

TREATMENT

A "wait and see" policy is indicated only when physician and patient are fully informed of the risks of leaving PAVMs untreated, and understand that PAVMs are not benign lesions that can be safely ignored.

Successful excision of a PAVM was first reported in 1942, and surgery remained the treatment of choice until the 1980s. Surgery was never the ideal solution for the multiple PAVMs of HHT, and percutaneous transcatheter embolization, introduced in 1978,[89] is now the treatment of choice for the vast majority of patients. Steel coils have largely replaced balloons as the embolization devices of choice.[17] Considerable skill is required.

Embolization

The technique of embolization at our institution has been described previously[17] (see Fig. 50.1). Prophylactic antibiotics are administered 1 hour before the combined diagnostic and therapeutic procedure. Bilateral pulmonary arteriograms are performed in frontal and oblique projections, after measurement of the pulmonary artery pressure. The pigtail catheter used for these arteriograms is then exchanged for a Headhunter I catheter (Cordis) and embolization of the feeding vessels to the individual PAVMs is achieved with metallic coils. The majority of coils used in our institution since 1994 are mechanically detachable (Jackson Detachable Coil, William Cook Europe, Bjaeverskov, Denmark). Coils must be placed as close as possible to the neck of the malformation in an attempt to avoid occluding normal pulmonary artery branches and risking

the development of bronchial arterial collateral supply to the sac.[15] In individual patients, other techniques are required, such as packing the venous sac with coils if the anatomy of the PAVMs precludes "conventional" embolization. Treatment of particularly large and high-flow PAVMs may be achieved with coils inserted through the lumen of an occluding balloon catheter temporarily inflated to obliterate flow within the feeding vessel.[17]

In expert hands, the technique is efficacious and complications are rare, though the procedure is not without risk. Successive series highlight a learning curve (Table 50.5), and smaller series have higher complication rates.[15,90] The most common complication is transient pleurisy, particularly in those patients with peripheral PAVMs. The mechanism for this is unknown, but it appears unrelated to pulmonary infarction.[14,17] Angina, due to transient air bubble emboli, has been reduced by technical advances in later series. There are only two reports from these centers (not in the series presented) of long-term neurologic complications following paradoxical emboli.[91] The frequency of paradoxical embolism as a result of embolization should be contrasted with the natural history of untreated PAVM patients, 54% of whom experience paradoxical emboli.[17]

Physiologic Outcomes after Embolization. The effects of coil or balloon embolization on R–L shunt and gas exchange are set out in Table 50.6. Outcomes have improved with time. In recent series,[17,69] most PAVMs with feeding vessels of 3 mm or greater have been occluded, and one third of patients are left with no angiographically visible PAVMs. In the remainder, the residual shunt through

Table 50.5 Complications of Treatment in Pulmonary Arteriovenous Malformation (PAVM) Treatment Series*

Center/Reference	No. of Patients	No. of PAVMs	No. of Procedures	Total[†] Complications (%)	Angina or Cardiac (%)	Pleurisy (%)	Paradoxical Embolus (%)
Baltimore/Yale							
Pre-1983[73]	10	58	>14	35	7	14	7
1978–1987[11]	76	276	90	16	4	9	2
Pre-1994[166]	35	96	n/s	28	11	11	6
1978–1995[16‡]	45	97	47	36	2	29[‡]	4
1991–1996[167§]	82	171	n/s	27	10	15	2
Hammersmith							
1984–1990[74]	16	79	32	9	0	6	0
1987–1994[14]	53	200	102	18	3	9	3
1995–1999[17]	66	225	93	13	5	4	1[‖]
UCSF							
1986–1991[12]	8	22	n/s	50	25	25	0
France							
Pre-1991[168]	19	58	n/s	42	n/s	16	5
Netherlands							
1990–1995[13]	32	92	44	18	2	9	4.5
Denmark							
1994–1998[83]	12	20	13	31	0	15	0

* Expressed as % of procedures or, where procedures not stated (n/s), % of patients treated.
† Excluding balloon deflation.
‡ Large PAVMs (8-mm diameter).
§ Including 35 patients reported by Pollak and colleagues.[166]
‖ Early in series; has not recurred since introduction of detachable coils.

Table 50.6 Outcomes, before and after Embolization, in Pulmonary Arteriovenous Malformation Treatment Series

Center/Reference	No. of Patients	R–L Shunt (%)		SaO_2 (%)		Residual Shunt Present in (%)
		Pre	Post	Pre	Post	
Baltimore/Yale						
Pre-1983[73]	10	44	24	76–80*	82–92*	?
1978–1987[11]	76	?	?	79–83*	90–94*	?
1978–1995[16]	45	?	?	85–89*	93–97*	?
Hammersmith						
1984–1990[70]	15	33	19	86	92	?
1987–1994[14]	53	23	9	89	94	60
1994–1999[17]	66	13	6	93	96	72
San Francisco						
1986–1991[12]	8	25	13	84–88*	92–96*	?
Netherlands						
1990–1995[13]	32	16.6	7.4	91–95*	93–97*	63
Denmark						
1994–1998[83]	12	21†	13†	266 mm Hg‡	439 mm Hg‡	73

* SaO_2 derived from PaO_2 measurements via standard oxygen dissociation curve.
† Calculated from PaO_2 assuming hemoglobin 13.9 and $(Ca - C\dot{v})O_2 = 4.4$ mL per 100 mL.
‡ PaO_2 values breathing 100% oxygen.

PAVMs of 3 mm or less is less than 10%.[13,17] Although substantial improvement in oxygenation is the rule,[13,16,17] the effects on pulmonary function are small (see Table 50.6). Vital capacity and FEV_1 do not change.[17,69,71] There is a trend for the DL_{CO} and DL/VA to improve,[17,69,71] and in a recent series of 60 patients,[17] the 16 who had a low DL/VA before embolization showed significant improvement after embolization, ranging from 78% to 87% of predicted, possibly due to the elimination of a vascular steal. Exercise capacity, often relatively unimpaired before embolization, may improve in some patients,[71] and not necessarily in those in whom the DL/VA improves.[17] Arterial SO_2 at maximum exercise improves significantly, by 6% to 10% in groups with mean preembolization arterial SO_2 of less than 82%[17,69,71] and by 3% to 4% if mean preembolization arterial SO_2 is 92% or greater.[17] These data indicate that the level of arterial hypoxemia is not a major determinant of exercise capacity.

After embolization, residual shunting through untreatable (≤2 mm diameter) arterial feeding vessels is common (see Table 50.5). For example, in one series of 66 PAVM patients in whom all vessels down to 2 mm in diameter had been embolized,[40] (69%) had residual disease, a finding supported by other studies.[13,83,87]

Medical Management

Prophylactic treatment for cerebral abscess is recommended in all patients suspected of having PAVMs, and in those who have been treated for it, as the majority will have residual disease. It is good practice to give all PAVM patients antibiotic prophylaxis at least prior to dental and surgical interventions.[92–94] The British Society for Antimicrobial Chemotherapy and Dental Formulary Subcommittee has recently approved a medical alert card for PAVM patients.

Additional management issues may need to be addressed. Female patients should be advised to defer pregnancy pending formal assessment and treatment in view of the risks of PAVM growth and rupture during pregnancy,[60] and pregnancies should be managed with close liaison between obstetricians, pulmonologists, and interventional radiologists. There are no data on maneuvers to reduce thromboembolic risks, but based on the high frequency of cerebral thromboembolic complications in these patients, we suggest that options such as cessation of hormonal therapy or institution of or antiplatelet therapy should be considered on a case-by-case basis for patients experiencing transient ischemic attacks, even if there is underlying HHT.

Options If Embolization Is Not Appropriate

There are circumstances in which PAVMs cannot be treated by embolization, the most common reason being that the feeding artery is too small (<2 mm in diameter). It is doubtful that advances in transcatheter embolization techniques will permit routine embolization of feeding vessels of less than this size, and the issue arises of what to do with patients with small PAVMs not amenable to embolization.

Discrete PAVMs with Feeding Arterial Diameter of 3 mm or Less. There is a widely held belief that it is the larger PAVMs that are predominantly responsible for embolic events, and a 3-mm cutoff has become established in conventional practice, and used to define PAVMs of importance for screening purposes and efficacy of treatment.[81,82,95,96] As smaller feeding vessels have been associated with cerebral abscess (six cases ≤3 mm in our series[88]), we recommend medical prophylaxis for all patients with residual PAVMs, irrespective of the size of the feeding vessel. There may also be circumstances in which small PAVMs are single (usually non-HHT patients); in these cases thoracoscopic resection may be appropriate if embolization is not feasible.

Widespread Small PAVMs Associated with Large Right-to-Left Shunts (see Fig. 50.2). In emergency situations, pneumonectomy or lobectomy may be appropriate for these patients.[59] Lung transplantation has been undertaken in a few patients with severe hypoxemia secondary to diffuse disease (e.g., see Raynoud and colleagues[97] and Svetliza and associates[98]). However, the long-term complications of PAVMs are likely in most cases to be less than transplantation-associated morbidity. Three PAVM patients in our clinic (one male, two female) who elected not to proceed with transplantation after discussion of the risks at two different U.K. transplant centers have since remained stable over 8, 9, and 13 years, and one has had three successful pregnancies. In a retrospective series of 16 cyanosed patients with diffuse PAVMs (mean arterial PO_2 of 47 mm Hg) for whom follow-up data were available for between 0.3 and 17 years, the 2-year survival rate was 91%, four patients had successful pregnancies, and over a mean follow-up period of 6 years, 11 of the original 16 were working or studying full time.[99]

Coexistent Pulmonary Hypertension. In rare patients in whom pulmonary hypertension and PAVMs coexist, removal of a low-resistance shunt may aggravate the pulmonary hypertension.[12,13,45] As there may be unpredictable beneficial responses to embolization,[19] presumably secondary to reduced cardiac output, measurement of pulmonary artery pressures following temporary deployment of an occlusion balloon may be warranted.

SYSTEMIC-TO-PULMONARY VASCULAR COMMUNICATIONS

CLASSIFICATION

Direct communications between the systemic arterial circulation and the pulmonary circulation occurs in several situations (Table 50.7). Rare cases of traumatic systemic-to-pulmonary communications (SPCs) are a variant of type D.

Table 50.7 Causes, Pathogenesis, and Treatment of Systemic-to-Pulmonary Communications

Cause	Pathogenesis	Treatment
A. Pre- and perinatal	Persistence of fetal vasculature	Spontaneous regression
B. Congenital	Internal mammary or coronary to pulmonary artery; behaves like PDA	Vessel ligation
C. Cavopulmonary anastomosis	Exclusion of right ventricular output to the lung	Coil embolization if flow high enough
D. Acquired	Inflammatory response to lung tissue necrosis and cavitation	Bronchial artery embolization

PDA, patent ductus arteriosus.

In types A through C, the systemic arteries communicate with the pulmonary artery or its branch via the pulmonary ligament, which encloses the lung hilum; in type D, the vessels enter the lung transpleurally through dense inflammatory adhesions between the lung and the chest wall. Intralobar sequestration (see next section) is a developmental anomaly in which a systemic artery replaces a segmental pulmonary artery.

Pre- and Perinatal Systemic-to-Pulmonary Artery Collaterals

Color Doppler scanning is a sensitive technique for the detection of blood flow in small vessels in the thorax of neonates. SPCs, separate from the bronchial vessels, are seen in 66% of premature, low-birth-weight infants,[100] and are as common as a persisting patent ductus arteriosus (PDA). These SPCs arise from the proximal or distal part of the aortic arch, and may be a sign of immaturity, functioning as miniature PDAs.

The clinical outcome in these premature infants (birth weight, 1.1 ± 0.3 kg; gestational age, 28 to 29 weeks) was influenced by the presence of SPCs; 11% of infants with SPCs developed heart failure. This was treated successfully medically, except in one case in which a 2.2-mm diameter collateral from the proximal descending aorta was embolized with coils with a good result.[100] Infants with SPCs were more likely to receive treatment for PDA and for lung immaturity (steroids or surfactant). On follow-up, the number of SPCs declined with maturity, until at 1 year of age only 2 infants of the original 88 still had collaterals.

Congenital Systemic-to-Pulmonary Communications

Congenital SPCs characteristically present in the second or third decade of life with a continuous murmur like a PDA. The systemic artery is usually the internal mammary or a coronary artery. Hearne and Burbank[101] reviewed 11 cases, reported between 1947 and 1979, of communications between the right or left internal mammary artery and the right or left pulmonary artery or a lobar branch. Diagnosis was by angiography. Eight cases were considered to be congenital, two traumatic, and one neoplastic in origin. Treatment was by ligation of the vessels and resection of the lobe with the R–L shunt; the most recent cases were left untreated. Iskandrian and colleagues[102] reported 12 patients with coronary-to-pulmonary artery communications, mostly discovered accidentally during routine coronary angiography for chest pain. The SPC did not serve to "steal" blood flow from the coronary artery.

Cavopulmonary Anastomoses

SPCs are also a feature of the Fontan-Baudet[103] surgical correction for tricuspid atresia or a functionally "univentricular heart." A BCPA from the inferior vena cava to the pulmonary artery is created in these patients as a staged palliative procedure, bypassing the ventricle. In a retrospective series by McElhinney and associates,[104] BCPA was carried out at 10 months of age; 59% ($n = 76$) of patients had SPCs on follow-up catheterization at approximately 2.5 years, and 14/45 underwent coil embolization of the collateral vessels, the rationale being to unload the ventricle and prevent high flow-induced pulmonary hypertension. SPCs were more prominent in those with a pre-BCPA left-to-right shunt and, therefore, low PVR. The presence of SPCs was not associated with a poorer outcome. Note that, when the superior vena cava is anastomosed to one or the other pulmonary artery, excluding hepatic venous return, the lung on that side develops PAVMs (pulmonary artery–to–pulmonary vein communications) (see earlier in this chapter).

Adult (Acquired) Systemic-to-Pulmonary Communications

SPCs form part of the inflammatory response to the presence of necrotic lung tissue; the most frequent causes, according to Yoon and colleagues,[105] are pulmonary tuberculosis (usually chronic), aspergilloma (secondary to chronic sarcoidosis or tuberculosis), bronchiectasis including cystic fibrosis,[106] lung abscess, and cancer. Documented SPCs were usually unilateral (31 of 40 cases).[105] Overlying pleural thickening provides transpleural access for systemic vessels from the intercostal, internal mammary, thyrocervical, axillary, and inferior phrenic arteries. For more proximal disease, vascular hypertrophy and new vessel formation occurs within the bronchial circulation.

Rarely, trauma can lead to new vessel formation across an inflamed pleura. Cox and coworkers[107] reported the case of a patient with a loud bruit over the second intercostal space anteriorly, who 1 year earlier had had a pneumothorax aspirated via a tube inserted at a thoracotomy. At a subsequent thoracotomy, a large area (7.7×2.0 cm) of lung was adherent to the chest wall, which was penetrated by numerous small vessels. The lung was separated from the chest wall, and the vessels cauterized.

The most common complication is hemoptysis, which may be massive and life-threatening. Initially, protection of the airway to avoid aspiration (using the upright or semirecumbent position) is most important, followed by fluid and blood replacement and assessment of coagulation status. Bronchoscopy may help to localize the source of bleeding,[108] but in an emergency angiography takes precedence, with a view to embolization of the bleeding sites.

TREATMENT

Bronchial Artery Embolization

Selective bronchial artery angiography was introduced by Viamonte[109] in 1964, and Rémy and associates[110] reported their results on 105 patients with hemoptysis in 1977. Bronchial artery or collateral vessel embolization is carried out at angiography with particulate polyvinyl alcohol; it is a highly specialized interventional radiology technique.[111,112] In particular, transverse myelitis and paraplegia may occur if the embolic material is injected in the bronchial artery proximal to the origin of the spinal artery.

The use of "superselective" coaxial catheters (3-French gauge), with peripheral placement of the tip in a stable position distal to normal arterial branches and without reflux after injection, has made the procedure much safer[111–113] (Fig. 50.5). In 80% to 90% of cases, immediate control of hemoptysis will be achieved,[114] although 20% will rebleed in the first 6 months, and a further 50% will have significant hemoptyses on longer follow-up.

Surgery

Surgery is falling out of favor as first-line treatment for massive hemoptysis for three reasons: (1) poor condition of the patient, (2) extensive and often bilateral disease, and (3) pleural thickening that adheres the lung to the chest wall, which is traversed by extensive collateral vessels. Bronchial artery embolization is not curative, and the risk of further hemoptysis is always present. But, unlike surgery, embolization can be repeated several times. Surgery for pleuropulmonary aspergilloma is not without risk. The average perioperative mortality in 10 series was 9% (range, 0 to 23%).[115] Surgery is becoming confined to low-risk cases in which recurrent hemoptysis is a problem.

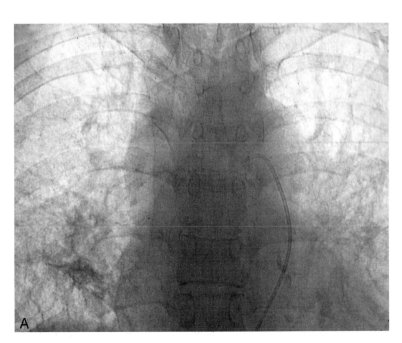

Figure 50.5 A 55-year-old woman with chronic sarcoidosis with fibrosis, cavitation, and right midzone aspergilloma, presenting with uncontrolled hemoptysis. **A,** Control film with bronchial artery catheter in place.

Figure continued on following page

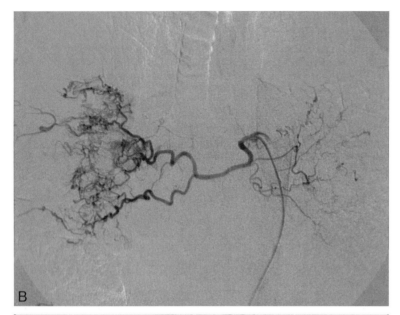

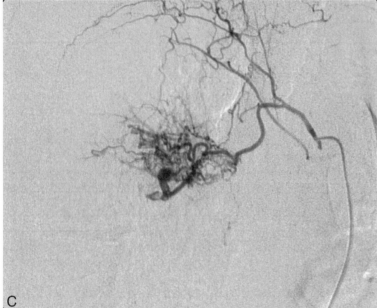

Figure 50.5 cont'd **B,** Selective contrast injection into combined right and left bronchial artery trunk with normal vessels on the left, but hypertrophied vessels on the right with abnormal vascularity over the right hilum, corresponding to the aspergilloma, and bronchial-to-pulmonary artery shunting laterally. **C,** Selective injection of right intercosto-bronchial trunk with normal intercostal arteries filling above and hypertrophied bronchial vessels below, with marked filling of large pulmonary vessels at the bottom of the image. The bronchial vessel was obliterated with a particulate polyvinyl alcohol injection.

BRONCHOPULMONARY SEQUESTRATION

CLASSIFICATION

Bronchopulmonary sequestration was first described by Pryce[116] in 1946 and defined by him as "an abnormal artery from the aorta supplying a bronchopulmonary mass or cyst which is dissociated from the normally connected bronchial tree." A distinction is made between intralobar sequestrations, which share a common visceral pleural investment with the adjacent normal lung tissue, and extralobar sequestrations, which have their own pleural lining that separates them from the remaining lung tissue (Table 50.8). In the intralobar variety the dissociation may not be complete, because airways in the sequestration may contain air, possibly exchanging via collateral channels.[117] The arterial supply is occasionally shared with the pulmonary artery, or comes from the pulmonary artery alone. The lung parenchyma is usually well differentiated, but becomes disorganized and cystic from recurrent infection.[118] Occasionally, a systemic artery supplies a lung segment with completely normal bronchial connections,[119–121] a situation better described as pulmonary artery rather than bronchopulmonary sequestration. Savic and colleagues[118] have reviewed 540 cases published in the literature up to 1979.

PATHOGENESIS

During bronchial branching (complete in humans 16 weeks after conception), the dividing buds are supplied by a capillary plexus derived from the primitive aorta; this plexus later regresses. Growth arrest locally of the pulmonary artery during bronchial division may disrupt maturation and tracheobronchial integrity, as well as leading to persistence of the blood supply from the aorta.[122] The developing lung bud lies in close proximity to the developing foregut, from

Table 50.8 Clinical and Pathophysiologic Features of Intralobar and Extralobar Pulmonary Sequestration

	Intralobar	Extralobar
Relative incidence (%)	75	25
Location	Left posterior basal segment (60%)	Left side above diaphragm (90%)
Arterial supply	Aorta >90% (thoracic 75%)	Aorta 78% (thoracic 46%)
Other foregut anomalies	14%	50%
Tracheobronchial connections	Usually absent	Always absent
Vascular resistance	Low	High
Venous drainage	Pulmonary veins	Azygos or vena cava
Age at clinical presentation	38% <10 years	60% <10 years
Infections	Common	Absent
Treatment	Surgery after careful workup of anatomy	Only required for associated abnormalities

Data from Savic B, Birtel FJ, Tholen W, et al: Lung sequestration: Report of seven cases and review of 540 published cases. Thorax 34:96–101, 1979.

which it is derived. This explains the high incidence of associated foregut anomalies[118] (see Table 50.8). Congenital cystic adenomatoid malformation accounts for 25% of all congenital lung malformations, and its association with intra- and extralobar sequestration is now well recognized.[123,124] Cases of familial pulmonary sequestration are known but rare.[121]

INTRALOBAR SEQUESTRATION

In spite of its origin from the aorta, the artery to intralobar sequestered segments is not thick-walled like a bronchial artery, but thin-walled with a wide lumen like a pulmonary artery. Input pressure is high and arterial resistance is low. Atheromatous changes are seen, as in the major pulmonary arterial vessels in pulmonary hypertension. Blood flow per unit tissue weight may be substantial. Venous drainage is into the left atrium, so the excess flow (metabolic needs being low) acts as a left-to-right shunt; occasionally, this leads to hemodynamic complications. Fabre and associates[125] described a 25-year-old man with congenital aortic valve stenosis with severe hemoptysis and congestive heart failure. His symptoms and heart failure resolved after ligation of the abnormal feeding artery and lobectomy of the sequestered segment. An unusual site of origin, the circumflex coronary artery, can lead to angina and myocardial ischemia from a steal syndrome.[126,127]

The sequestered tissue, denied normal access to the tracheobronchial tree, is prone to infection, cyst formation, and bronchiectasis with scarring. From mid-childhood onward, cough, purulent sputum production, and hemoptysis develop; a chest radiograph will reveal a solid or cystic lesion in the lower lobe, more often on the left side (Fig. 50.6). High-resolution CT scanning is a more useful diagnostic tool than bronchoscopy.[128,129] For delineation of the vascular anatomy, contrast-enhanced magnetic resonance angiography is likely to become the method of choice.[130] Surgery, even with good preoperative imaging, is not without difficulty. Nevertheless, massive and fatal hemoptysis occurring at the age of 29 years in a woman who had

been diagnosed with intralobar sequestration in childhood is an indication of the need to treat.[131]

EXTRALOBAR SEQUESTRATION

Extralobar sequestration is much less common than the intralobar variety. The location is just above the diaphragm, which is itself often abnormal with congenital herniation. Other congenital foregut abnormalities are common.[118] The clinical course is relatively benign; symptoms and age of clinical presentation are determined by the other abnormalities. The sequestered tissue is not a reservoir of infection. The feeding artery has a systemic and not a pulmonary artery structure. Its resistance is high, and blood flow is low. Extralobar sequestrations are usually asymptomatic, and are removed only as part of the treatment of associated anomalies.

PULMONARY ARTERY ANEURYSMS

CLASSIFICATION

Pulmonary artery aneurysms are a rare vascular anomaly. Bartter and colleagues,[132] in their review, defined aneurysms as "radiologically demonstrable sacs formed by the dilation of the wall of an artery, filled with blood." Dissecting aneurysms, in which blood tracks within the arterial wall following an intimal tear, are usually associated with cystic necrosis of the media of the vessel. False or pseudoaneurysms occur when all layers of the wall are breached, but the blood is contained by the surrounding tissues or by clotting. False aneurysms are a feature of a traumatic etiology (Table 50.9). If an aneurysm ruptures and is not contained in this way, bleeding into a bronchus ensues (bronchi and arteries have a common connective tissue sheath), with hemoptysis and, in fatal cases, exsanguination. Pulmonary artery aneurysms have been subdivided in Table 50.9 into those involving either the large arteries (right and left main and lobar arteries) or the medium to small pulmonary

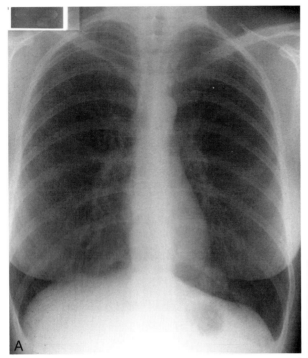

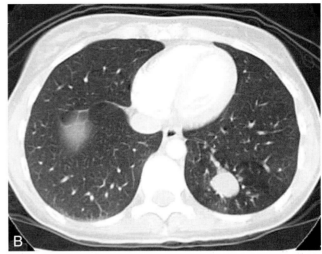

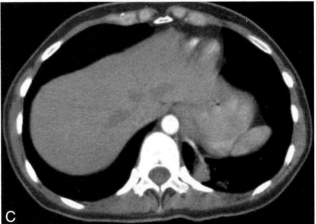

Figure 50.6 A, A 32-year-old woman whose chest radiograph shows a soft tissue mass in the left lower zone near the left heart border. **B,** Computed tomography (CT) scan showing an intrapulmonary soft tissue mass in the posterior basal segment of the left lower lobe. Note surrounding hyperinflation from collateral airflow. **C,** CT scan (mediastinal window), more caudal than **B,** with intravenous contrast enhancement showing systemic arterial supply to an intralobar sequestration.

Table 50.9 Causes, Pathogenesis, and Treatment of Pulmonary Artery Aneurysms

Cause	Pathogenesis	Treatment
Large Arteries: Dissection and False Aneurysms Predominate		
Vascular Trauma		
Congenital heart disease (e.g., PDA, ASD, VSD, pulmonary valve stenosis)	Vascular jets; aneurysms may become mycotic[169]	Surgical repair[157] Endovascular stent[158,159]
Idiopathic PHT	? Barotraumas	Dacron graft/transplant[170]
Penetrating injuries	Direct trauma[133,134]	Embolization: lobectomy[30]
Swan-Ganz (S-G) catheterization	Overinflation, spearing by catheter tip	Embolization[163]
Weakness of Arterial Wall		
Vasculitis (e.g., Behçet's syndrome)	Inflammation of vasa vasorum	Often resolves with medical therapy,[144] but may be fatal[143]
Marfan syndrome	Fibrillin deficiency: cystic medial necrosis	
Atherosclerosis	Cystic medial necrosis	
Low pressure	Dysplastic pulmonary valve; occurs in middle age[145,146]	Aneurysmorrhaphy, valve replacement[145,146]
Idiopathic		Embolization[164]
Medium and Small Pulmonary Arteries: True Aneurysms		
Infectious		
Tuberculosis	Wall replaced by granulation tissue	Embolization[161,162]
Lung abscess		
Right-sided endocarditis	Endovascular seeding Vegetations on tricuspid valve Candida from S-G catheter[151]	Antibiotics; ligation of PDA[171] Plication and lobectomy[157]
Injection drug user[91]	Endovascular seeding Tricuspid valve vegetations	Antibiotics

ASD, atrial septal defect; PDA, patent ductus arteriosus; PHT, pulmonary hypertension; VSD, ventricular septal defect.

arteries. Large artery aneurysms occur in the context of vascular trauma, endogenous or from outside the lung, or from a preexisting weakness in the arterial wall. Smaller artery aneurysms are associated with infection within the arterial wall; classically, this was due to tuberculosis. The distinction between large and medium to small vessels is by no means absolute; segmental and subsegmental arteries are common to both groups.

ETIOLOGY AND PATHOGENESIS

Vascular Trauma

Large artery aneurysms have a variety of causes, the most common of which is congenital heart disease, especially PDA[136]; pulmonary valve stenosis, atrial or ventricular septal defect, and Fallot's tetralogy are other associations. The cause is thought to be trauma to the artery wall from jets of blood ejected at high velocity by ventricular contraction. External sources of trauma include penetrating injuries such as stab wounds[133,134] and tube thoracostomy[135] or exploration at thoracotomy (Fig. 50.7). However, several reports[136-139] suggest that Swan-Ganz catheters are emerging as a common cause of trauma. Catheterization can cause a pseudo-aneurysm if the vessel wall is lacerated by the catheter tip and bleeding is contained, temporarily or permanently, by the surrounding tissues. Alternatively, a true aneurysm, with or without rupture, can develop if the catheter balloon is over-inflated in a small branch of the pulmonary artery. Kearney and Shabot,[140] in a retrospective review of 32,442 inpatients requiring catheterization from 1975 to 1991, found that catheter-induced pulmonary artery rupture occurred in 10 patients (0.03% incidence). All patients had hemoptysis. The risk factors are (1) technical, such as peripheral placement and overinflation of the balloon; and (2) pathophysiologic, the most important of which is an age greater than 60 years (pulmonary arteries are more fragile in the elderly).

Weakness of the Arterial Wall

Vascular wall weakness may predispose to aneurysm formation. This most commonly occurs in the context of vasculitis, presumably from disease of the vasa vasorum,[141] which come from the bronchial circulation. Large artery aneurysms have been reported in patients with giant cell arteritis,[142] Behçet's syndrome,[143,144] and its variant, the Hughes-Stovin syndrome.[141,143] Multiple aneurysms are a feature of Behçet's syndrome.[144] Pulmonary artery atheromatous disease, nearly always associated with pulmonary hypertension, is a cause of dissecting aneurysms; the media of the vessel shows cystic necrosis. Marfan's syndrome with fibrillin deficiency also shows cystic necrosis and dissecting pulmonary artery aneurysm formation.[132] In cystic medial necrosis, there is focal loss of elastic and muscle fibers, which are replaced by degenerate extravascular matrix; the condition is not well understood, but may represent a congenital deficiency of the arterial wall. Veldtman and associates[145] noted another more benign form called low-pressure giant pulmonary artery aneurysm, which presents in middle age; these patients have congenital deformities of the pulmonary valve with pulmonary regurgitation and right ventricular dilation. Histology of the pulmonary artery (after surgery to replace the valve and the aneurysm) showed cystic medial necrosis, but there was no dissection. The authors[145] commented on its similarity to aortic root dilation, which occurs in association with a bicuspid aortic valve. Two other cases of a similar nature were reported,[146] one of whom had an aortic root dissection.

Infection

Small artery aneurysms are generally infective (mycotic) in origin, often mycobacterial or fungal. Tuberculosis and syphilis used to be the most common causes. Before the advent of antituberculosis chemotherapy, Auerbach[147] found 45 pulmonary artery aneurysms in 1114 autopsies (a 4% incidence) of patients who died from pulmonary tuberculosis. All the aneurysms were part of a tuberculous cavity; 38 of the 45 aneurysms had ruptured, leading to death. Five of the remaining seven cases had bled prior to death. Pathologically, a large part of the arterial wall had been replaced by granulation tissue. Uncontrolled hemoptysis in chronic pulmonary tuberculosis is an indication for bronchial artery angiography and embolization (see section on systemic-to-pulmonary communications). In one case in which hemoptysis continued despite bronchial artery embolization,[148] pulmonary artery angiography showed three pseudo-aneurysms arising from an apical segmental branch of the right pulmonary artery. Two of these were embolized with coils with resolution of hemoptysis. Other in situ wall infections occur from endovascular seeding from right-sided heart valve vegetations, typically in chronic drug abusers,[149,150] but *Candida* endocarditis, introduced by a Swan-Ganz catheter, has also been described.[151]

Pregnancy

Aneurysms in a range of systemic arteries (ovarian, renal, splenic, etc.), as well as enlargement of PAVMs (see earlier), have been described in pregnancy, but a pregnancy-associated pulmonary artery aneurysm was not reported until 2001.[152] The patient, age 26 years, presented in the 19th week of pregnancy with cough, hemoptysis, and left pleuritic pain. Magnetic resonance imaging demonstrated a peripheral aneurysm arising from a peripheral artery of normal size. Left upper lobectomy was performed. The aneurysmal arterial wall showed mucoid degeneration.

DIAGNOSIS AND TREATMENT

Pulmonary artery aneurysms usually come to light in the investigation of an unusual mass on a routine chest radiograph, or during the workup for hemoptysis. Rupture may lead to massive bleeding and sudden death. Echocardiography (including transesophageal echo),[153] CT scanning,[133,144] and magnetic resonance imaging[154] are replacing angiography as first-line diagnostic investigations.

Treatment should be directed in the first instance to the underlying cause (e.g., infection, vasculitis, pulmonary hypertension, congenital heart disease). In Behçet's syndrome aneurysms may thrombose and regress,[144] but they can also have a fatal outcome.[143,155] Nevertheless, aneurysms are inherently unstable because dilation greatly increases the circumferential wall stress (S); according to the Laplace rela-

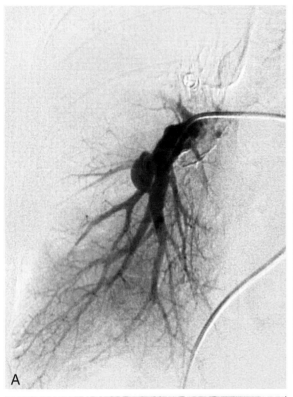

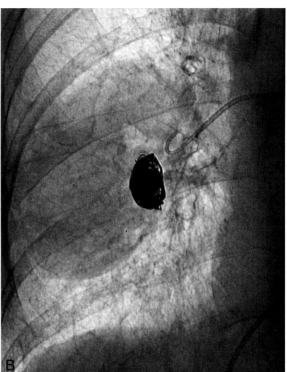

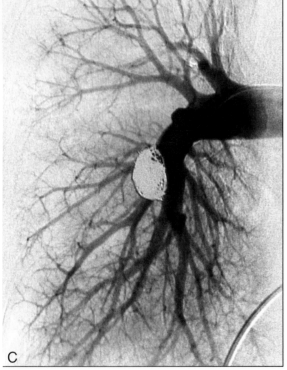

Figure 50.7 A 69-year-old woman presenting with massive hemoptysis following a thoracotomy and drainage of an empyema. **A,** Angiogram showing a traumatic oval pseudoaneurysm in the right descending pulmonary artery. **B,** No contrast injected. Aneurysmal sac is packed with coils. Note the large circular shadow in the background of a large intrapulmonary hematoma. **C,** Angiogram of the right descending pulmonary artery after packing the aneurysmal sac with steel coils. The patient recovered without further hemoptysis.

tionship, $S = Pr/t$ where P is intravascular (actually, transmural) pressure, r is the radius of the artery, and t is the thickness of the wall. As the vessel becomes larger and its wall becomes thinner, the wall stress increase is amplified; for this reason, treatment is generally recommended.

Williams and colleagues,[156] in 1971, carried out the first successful excision and repair (with a plastic prosthesis) of an aneurysm of the main pulmonary artery. The patient was a 13-year-old boy who underwent PDA ligation at 4 years of age, an enlarged pulmonary artery being noted at that time. Since then there have been many reports of successful repairs with pulmonary artery banding,[156] or excision of the aneurysm and prosthetic patch replacement.[146,157] Stents and grafts inserted endovascularly[158,159] are likely to replace open heart surgery in some instances. Embolization with steel coils, under angiographic control, is recommended for small artery aneurysms.[148,160-132] Embolization is also becoming the preferred choice for large artery aneurysms.[134,163,164]

SUMMARY

PAVMs are vascular communications that provide a direct capillary-free communication between the pulmonary and systemic circulations. PAVMs are characterized by a low PVR except in rare cases when there is coexistent pulmonary hypertension. Total pulmonary blood flow is high, and increases further on exercise. Pulmonary arterial blood passing through these R–L shunts cannot be oxygenated, leading to hypoxemia. However, 50% of PAVM patients are asymptomatic in spite of often profound hypoxemia. PAVMs are not benign, because all patients remain at high risk of paradoxical embolism leading to early-onset cerebrovascular accidents and brain abscesses, and pregnancy carries a risk of fatal pulmonary hemorrhage. Embolization using metal coils or balloons is now the treatment of choice for almost all patients.

SPCs may be either congenital or acquired. The congenital forms occur in premature infants as persistence of the fetal vasculature and regress spontaneously, or as internal mammary (or coronary) artery–to–pulmonary artery shunts mimicking a PDA but presenting in early adult life; treatment is surgical (ligation). The acquired adult type occur as part of the inflammatory response to necrotic lung tissue, occasionally with a concomitant aspergilloma. There is new vessel formation, either from the bronchial circulation or from vessels crossing from the chest wall through thickened inflamed pleura. Massive hemoptysis may occur; treatment for this medical emergency is by selective catheterization of the feeding vessels and intravascular obliteration with particulate polyvinyl alcohol.

Bronchopulmonary sequestration is a rare congenital anomaly, sometimes associated with foregut and other bronchial malformations. Isolated sequestrations present in teenagers or young adults as a soft tissue shadow on a chest radiograph or with symptoms of recurrent bronchial infection. Treatment is usually surgical.

Pulmonary artery aneurysms may affect medium-sized pulmonary arteries, in which infection, either in situ or via endovascular seeding, is the usual cause. Large pulmonary artery aneurysms are caused either by vascular trauma or by weakness of the arterial wall. Large artery aneurysms are generally false or dissecting. Treatment is by surgery or with coil embolization at angiography.

REFERENCES

1. Cooley D, McNamara D: Pulmonary telangiectasia: Report of a case proven by pulmonary biopsy. J Thorac Surg 27:614, 1954.
2. Hales M: Multiple small arteriovenous fistulas of the lungs. Am J Pathol 32:927–937, 1956.
3. Bosher L, Blake A, Byrd B: An analysis of the pathologic anatomy of pulmonary arteriovenous aneurysms with particular reference to the applicability of local excision. Surgery 45:91–104, 1959.
4. Anabtawi IA, Ellison RG, Ellison LT: Pulmonary arteriovenous aneurysms and fistulas. Ann Thorac Surg 1:277–285, 1965.
5. Westermann CJ, Rosina AF, Vries VD, Coteau PA: The prevalence and manifestations of hereditary hemorrhagic telangiectasia in the Afro-Caribbean population of the Netherlands Antilles: A family screening. Am J Med Genet 116:324–328, 2003.
6. Yater W, Finnegan J, Giffin H: Pulmonary arteriovenous fistula (varix). J Am Med Assoc 141:581–589, 1949.
7. Stringer C, Stanley A, Bates R, Summers J: Pulmonary arteriovenous fistula. Am J Surg 89:1054–1080, 1955.
8. Shumacker H, Waldhausen J: Pulmonary arteriovenous fistulas in children. Ann Surg 158:713–720, 1963.
9. Dines DE, Arms RA, Bernatz PE, Gomes MR: Pulmonary arteriovenous fistulas. Mayo Clin Proc 49:460–465, 1974.
10. Puskas J, Allen M, Moncure A, et al: Pulmonary arteriovenous malformations: Therapeutic options. Ann Thorac Surg 56:253–258, 1993.
11. White RI, Lynch-Nyhan A, Terry P, et al: Pulmonary arteriovenous malformations: Techniques and long-term outcomes of embolotherapy. Radiology 169:663–669, 1988.
12. Pennington D, Gold W, Gordon R, et al: Treatment of pulmonary arteriovenous malformations by therapeutic embolization. Am Rev Respir Dis 145:1047–1051, 1992.
13. Haitjema T, Overtoom T, Westermann C, Lammers J: Embolisation of pulmonary arteriovenous malformations: Results and follow-up in 32 patients. Thorax 50:719–723, 1995.
14. Dutton JAE, Jackson JE, Hughes JMB, et al: Pulmonary arteriovenous malformations: Results of treatment with coil embolization in 53 patients. AJR Am J Roentgenol 165:1119–1125, 1995.
15. Sagara K, Miyazono N, Inoue H, et al: Recanalization after coil embolotherapy of pulmonary arteriovenous malformations: Study of long term outcome and mechanism for recanalization. AJR Am J Roentgenol 170:727–730, 1998.
16. Lee D, White R, Egglin T, et al: Embolotherapy of large pulmonary arteriovenous malformation: Long term results. Ann Thorac Surg 64:930–940, 1997.
17. Gupta P, Mordin C, Curtiss J, et al: PAVMs: Effect of embolization on right-to-left shunt, hypoxemia and exercise tolerance in 66 patients. AJR Am J Roentgenol 179:347–355, 2002.
18. Shovlin CL, Guttmacher AE, Buscarini E, et al: Diagnostic criteria for hereditary hemorrhagic telangiectasia (Rendu-Osler-Weber syndrome). Am J Med Genet 91:66–67, 2000.
19. Shovlin CL, Jackson JE: Pulmonary arteriovenous malformations. In Peacock A, Rubin L (eds): Pulmonary Circulation (2nd ed). London: Arnold, 2004, pp 589–599.
20. Kopf G, Laks H, Stansel H, et al: Thirty-year follow-up of superior vena cava-pulmonary artery (Glenn) shunts. J Thorac Cardiovasc Surg 100:662–671, 1990.
21. Srivastava D, Preminger T, Lock JE, et al: Hepatic venous blood and the development of pulmonary arteriovenous malformations in congenital heart disease. Circulation 92:1217–1222, 1995.
22. Manganas C, Iliopoulos J, Pang L, Grant P: Traumatic pulmonary arteriovenous malformation presenting with massive hemoptysis 30 years after penetrating chest injury. Ann Thorac Surg 76:942–944, 2003.
23. Dines DE, Steward JB, Bernatz PE: Pulmonary arteriovenous fistulas. Mayo Clin Proc 58:176–181, 1983.
24. Bideau A, Brunet G, Heyer E, et al: An abnormal concentration of cases of Rendu-Osler disease in the Valserine valley of the French Jura: A genealogical and demographic study. Ann Hum Biol 19:233–247, 1992.

25. Kjeldsen AD, Vase P, Green A: Hereditary hemorrhagic telangiectasia (HHT): A population-based study of prevalence and mortality in Danish HHT patients. J Intern Med 245:31–39, 1999.

26. Dakeishi M, Shioya T, Wada Y, et al: Genetic epidemiology of hereditary haemorrhagic telangiectasia in a local community in the northern part of Japan. Hum Mutat 19:140–148, 2002.

27. Haitjema T, Disch F, Overtoom TTC, et al: Screening family members of patients with hereditary haemorrhagic telangiectasia. Am J Med 99:519–524, 1995.

28. Kjeldsen AD, Oxhøj H, Andersen PE, et al: Pulmonary arteriovenous malformations: Screening procedures and pulmonary angiography in patients with hereditary hemorrhagic telangiectasia. Chest 116:432–439, 1999.

29. Guttmacher AE, Marchuk DA, White RI: Hereditary hemorrhagic telangiectasia. N Engl J Med 333:918–924, 1995.

30. Haitjema T, Westermann CJJ, Overtoom TTC, et al: Hereditary hemorrhagic telangiectasia (Osler-Weber-Rendu syndrome)—new insights in pathogenesis, complications, and treatment. Arch Intern Med 156:714–719, 1996.

31. Shovlin CL, Letarte M: Hereditary haemorrhagic telangiectasia and pulmonary arteriovenous malformations: Issues in clinical management and review of pathogenic mechanisms. Thorax 54:714–729, 1999.

32. Begbie ME, Wallace G, Shovlin CL: Hereditary haemorrhagic telangiectasia (Osler-Weber-Rendu syndrome): A view from the 21st century. Postgrad Med J 79:18–24, 2003.

33. Plauchu H, de Chadarévian J-P, Bideau A, Robert J-M: Age-related profile of hereditary hemorrhagic telangiectasia in an epidemiologically recruited population. Am J Med Genet 32:291–297, 1989.

34. Porteous MEM, Burn J, Proctor SJ: Hereditary haemorrhagic telangiectasia: A clinical analysis. J Med Genet 29:527–530, 1992.

35. Shovlin CL, Hughes JMB, Tuddenham EGD, et al: A gene for hereditary haemorrhagic telangiectasia maps to chromosome 9q3. Nat Genet 6:205–209, 1994.

36. Gallione C, Repetto GM, Legius E, et al: A combined syndrome of juvenile polyposis and hereditary haemorrhagic telangiectasia is associated with mutations in MADH4 (SMAD4). Lancet 363:852–859, 2004.

36a. Cole S, Begbie ME, Wallace GMF, Shovlin CL: A new locus for hereditary haemorrhagic telangiectasia (HHT3). J Med Genet 2005 in press.

37. Bourdeau A, Dumont DJ, Letarte M: A murine model of hereditary hemorrhagic telangiectasia. J Clin Invest 104:1343–1351, 1999.

38. Cymerman U, Vera S, Pece-Barbara N, et al: Identification of hereditary hemorrhagic telangiectasia type I in newborns by protein expression and mutation analysis of endoglin. Pediatr Res 47:24–35, 2000.

39. Abdalla S, Pece-Barbara N, Vera S, et al: Analysis of ALK-1 and endoglin in newborns from families with hereditary hemorrhagic telangiectasia type 2. Hum Mol Genet 9:1227–1237, 2000.

40. Bourdeau A, Cymerman U, Paquet M-E, et al: Endoglin expression is reduced on normal vessels but still detectable in arteriovenous malformations of patients with hereditary haemorrhagic telangiectasia type I. Am J Pathol 156:911–923, 2000.

41. Heldin C-H, Miyazono K, ten Dijke P: TGF-β signalling from cell membrane to nucleus through SMAD proteins. Nature 390:465–471, 1997.

42. Goumans M-J, Valdimarsdottir G, Itoh S, et al: Actin receptor-like kinase (ALK) is an antagonistic mediator of lateral TGF-β/ALK5 signaling. Molecular Cell 12:817–828, 2003.

43. Berg JN, Porteous MEM, Reinhardt D, et al: Hereditary haemorrhagic telangiectasia: A questionnaire based study to delineate the different phenotypes caused by endoglin and ALK 1 mutations. J Med Genet 40:585–590, 2003.

44. McDonald J, Miller FJ, Hallam SE, et al: Clinical manifestations in a large hereditary hemorrhagic telangiectasia (HHT) type 2 kindred. Am J Med Genet 93:320–327, 2000.

45. Trembath R, Thomson J, Machado R, et al: Clinical and molecular features of pulmonary hypertension in hereditary hemorrhagic telangiectasia. N Engl J Med 345:325–334, 2001.

46. Abdalla S, Geisthoff UW, Bonneau D, et al: Visceral manifestations in hereditary hemorrhagic telangiectasia type 2. J Med Genet 40:494–502, 2003.

47. Shovlin CL, Hughes JMB, Scott J, et al: Characterization of endoglin and identification of novel mutations in hereditary hemorrhagic telangiectasia. Am J Hum Genet 61:68–79, 1997.

48. Fulbright RK, Chaloupka JC, Putman CM, et al: MR of hereditary hemorrhagic telangiectasia: Prevalence and spectrum of cerebrovascular malformations. AJNR Am J Neuroradiol 19:477–484, 1998.

49. Larsson E, Solymar L, Eriksson B, et al: Bubble contrast echocardiography in detecting pulmonary arteriovenous malformations after modified Fontan operations. Cardiol Young 11:505–511, 2001.

50. Ofoe V, Pratap U, Slavik Z: Rapid onset of intravenous shunting after surgical repair of tetralogy of Fallot with pulmonary atresia. Cardiol Young 11:236–239, 2001.

51. Vettukattil J, Slavik Z, Monro J, et al: Intrapulmonary arteriovenous shunting may be a universal phenomenon in patients with the superior cavopulmonary anastomosis. Heart 83:425–428, 2000.

52. Thompson RD, Jackson JE, Peters AM, et al: Sensitivity and specificity of radioisotope right-left shunt measurements and pulse oximetry for the early detection of pulmonary arteriovenous malformations. Chest 115:109–113, 1999.

53. Agnoletti G, Borghi A, Annecchino F, Crupi G: Regression of pulmonary venous fistulas in congenital heart disease after redirection of hepatic venous flow to the lungs. Ann Thorac Surg 72:909–911, 2001.

54. Schraufnagel D, Kay J: Structure and pathological changes in the lung vasculature in chronic liver disease. Clin Chest Med 17:1–15, 1996.

55. Higgins C, Wexler L: Clinical and angiographic features of pulmonary arteriovenous fistulas in children. Radiology 119:171–175, 1976.

56. Olgunturk R, Oguz D, Tunaoglu S, et al: Pulmonary arteriovenous malformation in the newborn. Turkish J Paediatr 43:332–337, 2001.

57. Koppen S, Korver CR, Dalinghaus M, Westermann CJ: Neonatal pulmonary arteriovenous malformation in hereditary haemorrhagic telangiectasia. Arch Dis Child Fetal Neonatal Ed 87:F226–F227, 2002.

58. Heling SK, Tennstedt C, Goldner B, Bollmann R: Prenatal diagnosis of intrapulmonary arteriovenous malformation: Sonographic and pathomorphological findings. Ultrasound Obstet Gynecol 19:514–517, 2002.

59. Ravasse P, Maragnes P, Petit T, Laloum D: Total pneumonectomy as a salvage procedure for pulmonary arteriovenous malformation in a newborn: Report of one case. J Pediatr Surg 38:254–255, 2003.

60. Shovlin CL, Winstock AR, Peters AM, et al: Medical complications of pregnancy in hereditary haemorrhagic telangiectasia. Quart J Med 88:879–887, 1995.

61. Shovlin C, Jackson J: Pulmonary arteriovenous malformations and aneurysms. *In* Gibson J, Geddes D, Costabel U, et al (eds): Respiratory Medicine (3rd ed). London: Harcourt, 2003, pp 1773–1788.

62. Chow L-C, Chow W-H, Ma K-F: Pulmonary arteriovenous malformation: Progressive enlargement with replacement of the entire right middle lobe in a patient with concomitant mitral stenosis. Med J Aust 158:632–634, 1993.

63. Vase P, Holm M, Arendrup H: Pulmonary arteriovenous fistulas in hereditary hemorrhagic telangiectasia. Acta Med Scand 218:105–109, 1985.

64. Whyte MKB, Hughes JMB, Jackson JE, et al: Cardiopulmonary response to exercise in patients with intrapulmonary vascular shunts. J Appl Physiol 75:321–328, 1993.

65. Mager J, Zanen P, Verzijbergen F, et al: Quantification of right to left shunt with ^{99m}Tc labeled albumin macroaggregates and 100% oxygen in patients with hereditary haemorrhagic telangiectasia. Clin Sci 102:127–134, 2002.

66. Sapru R, Hutchison D, Hall J: Pulmonary hypertension in patients with pulmonary arteriovenous fistulae. Br Heart J 31:559, 1968.

67. Ueki T, Hughes JMB, Peters AM, et al: Oxygen and ^{99m}Tc-MAA shunt estimations in patients with pulmonary arteriovenous malformations: Effects of changes in posture and lung volume. Thorax 49:327–331, 1994.

68. Whyte MKB, Peters AM, Hughes JMB, et al: Quantification of right to left shunt at rest and during exercise in patients with pulmonary arteriovenous malformations. Thorax 47:790–796, 1992.

69. Dutton J, Jackson J, Peters A, et al: Pulmonary arteriovenous malformations: Pathophysiology and treatment with coil embolization. AJR Am J Roentgenol 165:1119–1125, 1995.

70. Chilvers ER, Whyte MKB, Jackson JE, et al: Effect of percutaneous transcatheter embolization on pulmonary function, right-to-left shunt, and arterial oxygenation in patients with pulmonary arteriovenous malformations. Am Rev Respir Dis 142:420–425, 1990.

71. Chilvers ER, Peters AM, George P, et al: Quantification of right to left shunt through pulmonary arteriovenous malformations using ^{99}Tc^m albumin microspheres. Clin Radiol 39:611–614, 1989.

72. Sluiter-Eringa H, Orie NGM, Sluiter HJ: Pulmonary arteriovenous fistula: Diagnosis and prognosis in noncomplainant patients. Am Rev Respir Dis 100:177–188, 1969.

73. Terry P, White R, Barth K, et al: Pulmonary arteriovenous malformations: Physiologic observations and results of balloon embolization. N Engl J Med 308:1197–1200, 1983.

74. Jackson J, Whyte M, Allison D, Hughes J: Coil embolization of pulmonary arteriovenous malformations. Cor Vasa 32:191–196, 1990.

75. Gomes M, Bernatz P, Dines D: Pulmonary arteriovenous fistulas. Ann Thorac Surg 7:582–593, 1969.

76. Swinburne AJ, Fedulla AJ, Gangemi R, Mijangos JA: Hereditary telangiectasia and multiple pulmonary arteriovenous fistulas: Clinical deterioration during pregnancy. Chest 89:459–460, 1986.

77. Gershon A, Faughnan M, Chon K, et al: Transcatheter embolotherapy of maternal pulmonary arteriovenous malformations during pregnancy. Chest 119:470–477, 2001.

78. Nanthakumar K, Graham A, Robinson T, et al: Contrast echocardiography for detection of pulmonary arteriovenous malformations. Am Heart J 141:243–246, 2001.

79. Remy J, Remy-Jardin M, Wattinne L, Deffontaines C: Pulmonary arteriovenous malformations: Evaluation with CT of the chest before and after treatment. Radiology 182:809–816, 1992.

80. Gutierrez F, Glazer H, Levitt R, Moran J: NMR imaging of pulmonary arteriovenous fistulae. J Comput Assist Tomogr 8:750–752, 1984.

81. Maki D, Siegelman E, Roberts S, et al: Pulmonary arteriovenous malformations: Three dimensional gadolinium-enhanced MR-angiography—initial experience. Radiology 219:243–246, 2001.

82. Ohno Y, Hatabu H, Takenaka D, et al: Contrast-enhanced MR perfusion imaging and MR angiography: Utility for management of pulmonary arteriovenous malformations for embolotherapy. Eur J Radiol 41:136–146, 2002.

83. Andersen P, Kjeldsen A, Oxhoj H, et al: Embolotherapy for pulmonary arteriovenous malformations in patients with hereditary haemorrhagic telangiectasia. Acta Radiol 39:723–726, 1998.

84. Foster PP, Boriek AM, Butler BD, et al: Patent foramen ovale and paradoxical systemic embolism: A bibliographic review. Aviat Space Environ Med 74(6, Section II):B1–B64, 2003.

85. Feinstein J, Moore P, Rosenthal D, et al: Comparison of contrast echocardiography versus cardiac catheterization for detection of pulmonary arteriovenous malformations. Am J Cardiol 89:281–285, 2002.

86. Schussler J, Phillips S, Anwar A: Pulmonary arteriovenous fistula discovered after percutaneous patent foramen ovale closure in a 27-year-old woman. J Invasive Cardiol 15:527–529, 2003.

87. Lee WL, Graham AF, Pugas RA, et al. Contrast echocardiography remains positive after treatment of pulmonary arteriovenous malformations. Chest 123:351–358, 2003.

88. Benjamin A, Jackson J, Shovlin C: Cerebral abscess in patients with pulmonary arteriovenous malformations (Abstract). Am J Respir Crit Care Med 165:A330, 2002.

88a. Ramadan H, Begbie ME, Shovlin CL: Thromboembolic stroke in patients with pulmonary arteriovenous malformations. Thorax 59:87, 2004.

88b. Cottin V, Plauchu H, Bayle J, et al: Pulmonary arteriovenous malformations in patients with hereditary hemorrhagic telangiectasia. Am J Respir Crit Care Med 169:994–1000, 2004.

89. Porstmann W: Therapeutic embolization of arteriovenous pulmonary fistulas by catheter technique. *In* Kelop O (ed): Current Concepts in Pediatric Radiology. Berlin: Springer, 1977, pp 23–31.

90. White RI, Pollak JS: Pulmonary arteriovenous malformations: Options for management. Ann Thorac Med 57:519–521, 1994.

91. Mager HJ, Overtoom TT, Mauser HW, Westermann KJ: Early cerebral infarction after embolotherapy of a pulmonary arteriovenous malformation. J Vasc Interv Radiol 12:122–123, 2001.

92. Swanson DL, Dahl MV: Embolic abscesses in hereditary hemorrhagic telangiectasia. J Am Acad Dermatol 24:580–583, 1991.

93. Mohler ER, Monahan B, Canty MD, Flockhart DA: Cerebral abscess associated with dental procedure in hereditary haemorrhagic telangiectasia. Lancet 338:508–509, 1991.

94. Chan P: Antibiotic prophylaxis for patients with hereditary hemorrhagic telangiectasia. J Am Acad Dermatol 26:282–283, 1992.

95. Moussouttas M, Fayad P, Rosenblatt M, et al: Pulmonary arteriovenous malformations: Cerebral ischemia and neurologic manifestations. Neurology 55:959–964, 2000.

96. Khalil A, Farres M-T, Mangiapan G, et al: Pulmonary arteriovenous malformations: Diagnosis by contrast-enhanced magnetic resonance angiography. Chest 117:1399–1403, 2000.

97. Reynaud-Gaubert M, Thomas P, Gaubert J-Y, et al: Pulmonary arteriovenous malformations: Lung transplantation as a therapeutic option. Eur Respir J 14:1425–1428, 1999.

98. Svetliza G, DelaCanal A, Beveraggi E, et al: Lung transplantation in a patient with arteriovenous malformations. J Heart Lung Transplant 21:506–508, 2002.

99. Faughnan M, Lui Y, Wirth J, et al: Diffuse pulmonary arteriovenous malformations: Characteristics and prognosis. Chest 117:31–38, 2000.

100. Acherman RJ, Siassi B, Pratti-Madrid G, et al: Systemic to pulmonary collaterals in very low birth weight infants: Color Doppler detection of systemic to pulmonary connections during neonatal and early infancy period. Pediatrics 105:528–532, 2000.

101. Hearne SF, Burbank MK: Internal mammary artery-to-pulmonary artery fistulas: Case report and review of the literature. Circulation 62:1131–1135, 1980.

102. Iskandrian AS, Kimbiris D, Bemis CE, et al: Coronary artery to pulmonary artery fistulas. Am Heart J 96:605–609, 1978.

103. Fontan F, Baudet E: Surgical repair of tricuspid atresia. Thorax 26:240–248, 1971.

104. McElhinney DB, Reddy VM, Tworetzky W, et al: Incidence and implications of systemic to pulmonary collaterals after bi-directional cavopulmonary anastomosis. Ann Thorac Surg 69:1222–1228, 2000.

105. Yoon W, Kim YH, Kim JK, et al: Massive hemoptysis: Prediction of nonbronchial systemic arterial supply with chest CT. Radiology 227:232–238, 2003.

106. Brinson GM, Noone PG, Mauro MA, et al: Bronchial artery embolization for the treatment of hemoptysis in patients with cystic fibrosis. Am J Respir Crit Care Med 157:1951–1958, 1998.

107. Cox PA, Keshishian JM, Blades SB: Traumatic arteriovenous fistula of the chest wall and lung: Secondary to insertion of an intercostal catheter. J Thorac Cardiovasc Surg 54:109–112, 1967.

108. Dweik RA, Stoller JK: Role of bronchoscopy in massive hemoptysis. Clin Chest Med 20:89–105, 1999.

109. Viamonte M: Selective bronchial arteriography in man. Radiology 83:830–839, 1964.

110. Rémy J, Arnaud A, Fardou H, et al: Treatment of hemoptysis by embolization of bronchial arteries. Radiology 122:33–37, 1977.

111. Marshall TJ, Jackson JE: Vascular intervention in the thorax: Bronchial artery embolization for haemoptysis. Eur Radiol 7:1221–1227, 1997.

112. Saluja S, Henderson KJ, White RI: Embolotherapy in the bronchial and pulmonary circulations. Radiol Clin North Am 38:425–448, 2000.

113. White RI Jr: Bronchial artery embolotherapy for control of acute hemoptysis: Analysis of outcome. Chest 115:912–915, 1999.

114. Mah H, Rullon I, Mellot F, et al: Immediate and long-term results of bronchial artery embolization for life-threatening hemoptysis. Chest 115:996–1001, 1999.

115. Regnard JF, Icard P, Nicolosi M, et al: Aspergilloma: A series of 89 surgical cases. Ann Thorac Surg 69:898–903, 2000.

116. Pryce DM: Lower accessory artery with intralobular sequestration of the lung. J Pathol Bacteriol 58:457–467, 1946.

117. Suga K, Hara A, Matsumoto T, et al: Intrapulmonary bronchopulmonary sequestration: Evidence of air trapping shown by dynamic xenon-133 SPECT. Br J Radiol 74:657–661, 2001.

118. Savic B, Birtel FJ, Tholen W, et al: Lung sequestration: Report of seven cases and review of 540 published cases. Thorax 34:96–101, 1979.

119. Miyake H, Hori Y, Takeoka H, et al: Systemic arterial supply to normal basal segments of the left lung: Characteristic features on chest radiography and CT. AJR Am J Roentgenol 171:387–392, 1998.

120. Yamanaka A, Harai T, Fujimoto T, et al: Anomalous systemic arterial supply to normal basal segments of the left lower lobe. Ann Thorac Surg 72:332–338, 1999.

121. Dyer JD, Anderson JM, John PR: A familial case of pulmonary artery sequestration. Arch Dis Child 82:148–149, 2000.

122. Clements BS, Warner JO: Pulmonary sequestration and related congenital bronchopulmonary-vascular malformations: Nomenclature and classification based on anatomical and embryological considerations. Thorax 42:401–408, 1987.

123. Conran RM, Stocker JT: Extralobar sequestration with frequently associated congenital cystic adenomatoid malformation, type 2: Report of 50 cases. Pediatr Dev Pathol 2:454–463, 1999.

124. Samuel M, Burge DM: Management of antenatally diagnosed pulmonary sequestration associated with congenital cystic adenomatoid malformation. Thorax 54:701–706, 1999.

125. Fabre OH, Porte HL, Godart FR, et al: Long-term cardiovascular consequences of undiagnosed intralobar pulmonary sequestration. Ann Thorac Surg 65:1144–1146, 1998.

126. Nakayama Y, Kido M, Minami K, et al: Pulmonary sequestration with myocardial ischemia caused by vasospasm and steal. Ann Thorac Surg 70:304–305, 2000.

127. Temes RT, Talbot WA, Carrillo YM, et al: Sequestration of the lung arising from the circumflex coronary artery. Ann Thorac Surg 65:257–259, 1998.

128. Frush DP, Donnelly LF: Pulmonary sequestration spectrum: A new spin with helical CT. AJR Am J Roentgenol 169:679–682, 1997.

129. Franco J, Aliaga FJ, Domingo ML, et al: Diagnosis of pulmonary sequestration by spiral CT angiography. Thorax 53:1089–1092, 1998.

130. Au VW, Chan JK, Chan FL: Pulmonary sequestration diagnosed by contrast enhanced three-dimensional MR angiography. Br J Radiol 72:709–711, 1999.

131. Rubin EM, Garcia H, Horowitz MD, et al: Fatal massive hemoptysis secondary to intralobar sequestration. Chest 106:954–955, 1994.

132. Bartter T, Irwin RS, Nash G: Aneurysms of the pulmonary arteries. Chest 94:1065–1075, 1988.

133. Daykin EL, Irwin GAL, Harrison DA: CT demonstration of a traumatic aneurysm of the pulmonary artery. J Comput Assist Tomogr 10:323–324, 1986.

134. Savage C, Zwischenberger JB, Ventura KC, et al: Hemoptysis secondary to pulmonary pseudoaneurysm 30 years after a gunshot wound. Ann Thorac Surg 71:1021–1023, 2001.

135. Podbielski FJ, Wiesman IM, Yaghmai B, et al: Pulmonary artery pseudoaneurysm after tube thoracostomy. Ann Thorac Surg 64:1478–1480, 1997.

136. Bartter T, Irwin RS, Phillips DA, et al: Pulmonary artery pseudoaneurysm: A potential complication of pulmonary artery catheterization. Arch Intern Med 148:471–473, 1988.

137. Ray CE, Kaufman JA, Geller SC, et al: Embolization of pulmonary catheter-induced pulmonary artery pseudoaneurysms. Chest 110:1370–1373, 1996.

138. Ferretti GR, Thony F, Link KM, et al: False aneurysm of the pulmonary artery induced by a Swan-Ganz catheter: Clinical presentation and radiologic management. AJR Am J Roentgenol 167:941–945, 1996.

139. Karak P, Dimick R, Hamrick KM, et al: Immediate transcatheter embolization of Swan-Ganz catheter-induced pulmonary artery pseudoaneurysm. Chest 111:1450–1452, 1997.

140. Kearney TJ, Shabot MM: Pulmonary artery rupture associated with the Swan-Ganz catheter. Chest 108:1349–1352, 1995.

141. Hughes JP, Stovin PG: Segmental pulmonary artery aneurysms with peripheral venous thrombosis. Br J Dis Chest 53:19–27, 1959.

142. Dennison AR, Watkins PM, Gunning AJ: Simultaneous aortic and pulmonary artery aneurysms due to giant cell arteritis. Thorax 40:156–157, 1985.

143. Durieux P, Bietry D, Huchon G, et al: Multiple pulmonary artery aneurysms in Behçet's disease and Hughes-Stovin syndrome. Am J Med 71:730–741, 1981.

144. Tunaci M, Ozkorkmaz B, Tunaci A, et al: CT findings of pulmonary artery aneurysms during treatment for Behçet's disease. AJR Am J Roentgenol 172:729–733, 1999.

145. Veldtman GR, Dearani JA, Warnes CA: Low pressure giant pulmonary artery aneurysms in the adult: Natural history and management strategies. Heart 89:1067–1070, 2003.

146. Kuwaki K, Morishita K, Komatsu K, et al: Graft replacement for huge aneurysm of the main pulmonary artery. Ann Thorac Surg 70:1714–1716, 2000.

147. Auerbach O: Pathology and pathogenesis of pulmonary artery aneurysm in tuberculous cavities. Am Rev Tuberc 39:99–115, 1939.

148. Santelli ED, Katz DB, Goldschmidt AM, et al: Embolization of multiple Rasmussen aneurysms as a treatment of hemoptysis. Radiology 193:396–398, 1994.

149. Navarro C, Dickinson PCT, Kondlapoodi P, et al: Mycotic aneurysms of the pulmonary arteries in intravenous drug addicts. Am J Med 76:1124–1131, 1984.

150. McLean L, Sharma S, Maycher B: Mycotic pulmonary artery aneurysms in an intravenous drug abuser. Can Respir J 5:307–311, 1998.

151. Roush K, Scala-Barnett DM, Donabedian H, et al: Rupture of a pulmonary artery mycotic aneurysm associated with candidal endocarditis. Am J Med 84:142–144, 1988.

152. Gruber PJ, Askin FB, Heitmiller RF: Pulmonary artery aneurysm in a pregnant woman. Ann Thorac Surg 71:1023–1025, 2001.

153. Guler N, Sakarya ME, Eryonucu B, et al: Transesophageal echocardiographic detection of a pulmonary artery aneurysm complicated by thrombus. Heart Lung 32:159–161, 2003.

154. Celenk C, Celenk P, Akan H, et al: Pulmonary artery aneurysms due to Behçet's disease: MR imaging and digital subtraction findings. AJR Am J Roentgenol 172:844–845, 1999.

155. Filiz A, Dikensoy O: Lethal aneurysm formation of pulmonary arteries in a woman with Behçet's disease. Rheumatology 39:222–224, 2000.

156. Williams JE, Schiller M, Craenen J, et al: Pulmonary artery aneurysms. J Thorac Cardiovasc Surg 62:63–66, 1971.

157. Lawrenson J, Stirling J, Hewitson J: Images in cardiology: Mycotic aneurysm of the left pulmonary artery in a child with tetralogy of Fallot and *Streptococcus viridans* infective endocarditis. Heart 82:88, 1999.

158. Hannan RL, Miyaji K, Burke RP, et al: Endovascular stent graft treatment of a pulmonary artery pseudoaneurysm. Ann Thorac Surg 71:727–729, 2001.

159. Wilson N, McLeod K, Halworth D: Images in cardiology: Exclusion of a pulmonary artery aneurysm using a covered stent. Heart 83:438, 2000.

160. Cooper J, Jackson J, Walker J: False aneurysm of the pulmonary artery associated with cardiac catheterization. Br Heart J 69:188–190, 1993.

161. Remy L, Smith M, Lemaitre L, et al: Treatment of massive hemoptysis by occlusion of a Rasmussen aneurysm. AJR Am J Roentgenol 135:605–606, 1980.

162. Renie WA, Rodeheffer RJ, Mitchell S, et al: Balloon embolization of a mycotic pulmonary artery aneurysm. Am Rev Respir Dis 126:1107–1110, 1982.

163. Poplausky MR, Rozenblit G, Rundback JH, et al: Swan-Ganz catheter–induced pulmonary artery pseudoaneurysm formation: Three case reports and a review of the literature. Chest 120:2105–2111, 2001.

164. Mann P, Seriki D, Dodds PA: Embolism of an idiopathic pulmonary artery aneurysm. Heart 87:135, 2002.

165. Piantanida M, Buscarini E, Dellavecchia C, et al: Hereditary haemorrhagic telangiectasia with extensive liver involvement is not caused by either HHT1 or HHT2. J Med Genet 33:441–443, 1996.

166. Pollak J, Egglin T, Rosenblatt M, et al: Clinical results of transvenous systemic embolotherapy with a neuroradiologic detachable balloon. Radiology 191:477–482, 1994.

167. Saluja S, Sitko I, Lee DW, et al: Embolotherapy of pulmonary arteriovenous malformations with detachable balloons: Long term durability and efficacy. J Vasc Interv Radiol 10:883–889, 1999.

168. Remy-Jardin M, Wattine L, Remy J: Transcatheter occlusion of pulmonary arterial circulation and collateral supply: Failures, incidents, and complications. Radiology 180:699–705, 1991.

169. Opie C, Sandor GGS, Ashmore PG, et al: Successful palliation by pulmonary artery banding in absent pulmonary valve syndrome with aneurysmal pulmonary arteries. J Thorac Cardiovasc Surg 85:125–128, 1983.

170. Wekerle T, Klepetko W, Taghavi S, et al: Lung transplantation for primary pulmonary hypertension and giant pulmonary artery aneurysm. Ann Thorac Surg 65:825–827, 1998.

171. Lertsapcharoen P, Chottivittayatarakorn P, Benjacholamas V: Mycotic aneurysms of the pulmonary arteries. Heart 88:524, 2002.

51

Pulmonary Edema and Acute Lung Injury

Michael A. Matthay, M.D., Thomas R. Martin, M.D.

INTRODUCTION

Excessive extravascular water in the lungs (pulmonary edema) is a common clinical problem. It is always a manifestation of a serious underlying disease or disorder. Pulmonary edema can be life-threatening, but effective therapy is available to rescue patients from the deleterious consequences of disturbed lung fluid balance. The cause of the disturbance often can be identified and, in many instances, corrected. Because rational and effective therapy depends on understanding basic principles of normal and abnormal liquid and solute transport in the lungs, this chapter begins with a brief overview of the major factors that govern fluid filtration in the lungs before turning to the pathophysiology of pulmonary edema and acute lung injury. For further information, the reader is referred to the detailed description of the regulation of fluid balance in the lungs, including its anatomic basis and pharmacologic influences, that is provided in Chapter 6. This chapter emphasizes the diagnosis, treatment, and outcome of pulmonary edema and acute lung injury.

PATHOPHYSIOLOGY OF PULMONARY EDEMA AND ACUTE LUNG INJURY

Pulmonary edema occurs when fluid is filtered into the lungs faster than it can be removed. Accumulation of fluid can have serious consequences on lung function because efficient gas exchange cannot occur in fluid-filled alveoli. Lung structure relevant to edema formation and to the forces governing fluid and protein movement in the lungs has been the subject of classic and more recent reviews.[1-7]

There is always a net outward flux of fluid and protein crossing from the vascular space into the interstitium in the lungs because the balance of driving forces normally causes filtration out of the bloodstream and the microvascular

endothelium is a leaky barrier. *Leaky* is a relative term: Lung lymph flow normally is less than 0.01% of lung blood flow. Because fluid filtration in the lungs is not limited to capillaries, the term *microvascular* is used throughout this chapter to refer to the sites where fluid exchange occurs. Because of the vast surface area of the lungs, most fluid and protein exchange in the lungs occurs across the interconnecting network of capillaries embedded in the alveolar walls. Exchange can also occur across capillaries located in the interstitium at alveolar wall junctions (*corner vessels*) and across small interstitial arteries and veins. Their thick walls and small surface area probably limit fluid exchange in larger vessels in the lungs.

The essential factors that govern fluid exchange in the lungs are expressed in the Starling equation for the microvascular barrier:

$$Jv = LpS[(Pc - Pi) - \sigma d(\pi c - \pi i)]$$

where Jv is the net fluid-filtration rate (volume flow) across the microvascular barrier; Lp is the hydraulic conductivity ("permeability") of the microvascular barrier to fluid filtration (a measure of how easy it is for water to cross the barrier); S is the surface area of the barrier; Pc is the pulmonary capillary (microvascular) hydrostatic pressure; Pi is the interstitial ("perimicrovascular") hydrostatic pressure; πc is the capillary (microvascular) plasma colloid osmotic (or oncotic) pressure; πi is the interstitial (perimicrovascular) fluid osmotic pressure; and σd is the average osmotic reflection coefficient of the barrier (a measure of how effective the barrier is in hindering the passage of solutes from one side of the barrier to the other).

The microvascular hydrostatic pressure is the principal force that causes fluid filtration in the lungs. If blood were not flowing through the lungs, the opposing hydrostatic and osmotic forces on either side of the microvascular barrier would be equal, their sum would be zero, and there would be no filtration. It is the pumping action of the heart that causes blood to flow through the lungs, and the microvascular hydrostatic pressure generated in the process establishes the steady-state values of the other driving pressures and causes fluid to filter.[6,8]

According to the Starling equation, the balance between the prevailing transmural hydrostatic pressures (Pc − Pi) and the colloid osmotic pressures (πc − πi) provides the "driving force" for fluid filtration. The actual amount of filtrate that forms at any given driving force is determined by the integrity of the barrier to filtration, which is reflected in the conductivity (Lp) and reflection (σd) coefficients. The equation predicts the development of two fundamentally different kinds of pulmonary edema: the first, *increased pressure pulmonary edema,* occurs when the balance of the driving forces increases, forcing fluid across the barrier at a rate that can no longer be accommodated by lymphatic drainage; and the second, *increased permeability pulmonary edema,* occurs in the presence of acute lung injury that damages the normal barriers to fluid filtration and allows increased conductance of liquid and protein in the lungs. There also is a third type of pulmonary edema caused by impaired lymphatic drainage of filtered fluid, but this has less clinical relevance and is not discussed in detail. The lymphatic drainage of the lungs is an important means of removing filtered fluid and proteins from the perimicrovascular interstitial space.[6,8]

Because the normal microvascular barrier is leaky, the alveolar barrier must serve as the principal protection against the accumulation of alveolar edema. Fluid and protein do not normally move into alveoli, because the alveolar barrier has a low permeability even to small molecules (similar to cell membrane permeability) and because the fluid that is filtered is continuously being pumped back into the interstitium by alveolar epithelial cells,[2] drained away from the alveolar walls through the interstitium, and removed by lymphatic vessels and the lung microcirculation.

The several factors (Table 51.1) that normally protect the lungs against edema have been called *safety factors.* Under normal conditions, the lymphatic system pumps filtered fluid and protein out of the lungs as rapidly as they are formed, even when filtration of fluid and protein from the bloodstream into the interstitium is increased. Increases in fluid and protein filtration across the microvascular barrier also can be drained away from the alveolar walls down the prevailing pressure gradient into the loose peribronchovas-cular connective tissue or can be resorbed directly into blood vessels.[4] The lung lymphatics can increase their pumping capacity manyfold, particularly when the microvascular wall has been injured.[6] When the balance of driving forces is upset by higher hydrostatic pressure, the increase in filtration of water across the microvascular barrier is much larger than that in protein flux because the microvascular barrier has a low protein conductance. This results in dilution ("washdown") of interstitial protein concentration and thereby an increase in the balance of the osmotic pressure opposing the higher hydrostatic pressure (because plasma protein concentration remains high). The interstitial gel is also hydrated. Exclusion volume for protein decreases, either because of swelling or because of alteration of composition as hyaluronan is washed out from the interstitium, reducing the concentration of protein by expanding the available volume.

The osmotic safety factors work only when the microvascular barrier is normal (increased pressure edema). If the endothelial barrier is injured and its functional integrity is compromised (increased permeability edema), barrier conductance increases and the osmotic reflection coefficient decreases, making this safety factor much less effective or completely ineffective. The compliance of the interstitial space also protects the lungs against edema. Increases in interstitial volume result in only small elevations of interstitial pressure until the interstitial volume is large. This keeps the hydrostatic driving pressure across the alveolar barrier suitably low. When interstitial pressure is elevated to greater than pleural pressure, fluid flows across the visceral pleura into the pleural space, where its effects on lung function are relatively minor. Pleural fluid is drained by lymphatics in the parietal pleural and, even when pleural liquid accumulates, does not flow back from the pleural space into the lungs. The extremely low alveolar barrier solute conductance provides an osmotic force that favors absorption of water out of the air space rather than filtration of water into the air space. Fluid that does accumulate in the alveoli is pumped out by active ion transport.[2] There are several mechanisms that can up-regulate the rate of alveolar fluid clearance (see Chapter 12).

In summary, pulmonary edema results from increases in either driving pressures (increased pressure edema) or barrier conductance (increased permeability edema), or both mechanisms. What distinguishes the two types is barrier permeability, which is normal in increased pressure edema but abnormal in increased permeability edema. Fluid flow into the lungs is driven across the barrier in both types of edema by the balance of pressures.

INCREASED PRESSURE EDEMA

Increased pressure pulmonary edema (Fig. 51.1) is caused by an increase in the balance of driving forces for fluid filtration into the lungs. The essential feature of this edema is that the barriers to fluid and protein flow into the lungs are functionally intact. Increased pressure edema is often called *cardiogenic, high-pressure, hydrostatic,* or *secondary pulmonary edema* but more appropriately would be called *normal barrier pulmonary edema* because it is the barrier resistance to fluid and solute movement into the lungs that distinguishes the types of pulmonary edema.

Table 51.1 Safety Factors That Protect the Lungs against Interstitial and Alveolar Edema Accumulation

1. Lung lymphatic system
2. Resorption into blood vessels
3. Drainage into the mediastinum
4. Drainage into the pleural space
5. Extremely low alveolar epithelial barrier permeability
6. Low alveolar surface tension (surfactant)
7. Active transport by alveolar and distal airway epithelial cells

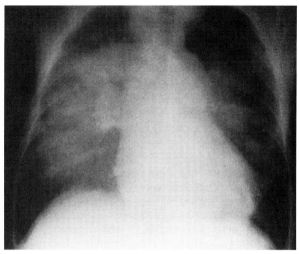

Figure 51.1 Chest roentgenogram in a patient with increased pressure pulmonary edema. The heart is enlarged, and the vascular pedicle is widened. The "butterfly" pattern of edema (infiltrates centrally distributed, close to the heart and hila) is often seen with volume overload. The patient had chronic renal failure and overhydration.

Table 51.2 Effects of Vascular Congestion and Edema on Pulmonary Function and Lung Mechanics

Vascular Congestion
Increased diffusing capacity
Increased arterial P_{O_2}
Decreased compliance
Bronchoconstriction

Interstitial Edema
Increased closing volume
Decreased maximal expiratory flow
Increased ventilation-perfusion mismatching
Decreased arterial P_{O_2}

Alveolar Flooding
Increased closing volume (air trapping)
Increased vascular resistance
Decreased lung volume (especially vital and inspiratory capacities)
Decreased compliance
Decreased diffusing capacity
Right-to-left shunting of blood (severely compromised gas exchange)

Pathophysiology

The flow of fluid and protein into the lungs increases when the sum of driving pressures is elevated. If the rate of fluid accumulation exceeds the rate at which it can be removed, increased pressure edema occurs. Because the barriers limiting fluid and protein flow into the lungs are intact, the lungs are protected against edema by the normal safety factors. Especially important is the ability to protect against increases in the principal driving pressure, lung microvascular hydrostatic pressure. Because of the microvascular barrier's low protein conductance, fluid flow increases much more than protein flow with an elevation in microvascular hydrostatic pressure. Interstitial protein concentration is diluted both by this higher fluid flow relative to protein flow and by a diminished exclusion volume for proteins as the interstitial gel is hydrated and swells. Lower interstitial protein concentration (washdown or washout of interstitial proteins) results in lower perimicrovascular osmotic pressure and thereby a greater protein osmotic pressure difference across the barrier, opposing any rise in hydrostatic pressure. In experimental animals, slightly less than 50% of an increase in hydrostatic pressure is offset by the increase in osmotic pressure difference.[8] Increased pressure edema may be slow and gradual in onset and progression because any elevation in microvascular hydrostatic pressure is attenuated by a rise in osmotic pressure difference across the microvascular barrier, owing to a decline in interstitial protein osmotic pressure.

There are limits to the ability of widening osmotic pressure difference to oppose increases in hydrostatic pressure at the microvascular barrier. Because the barrier is leaky, some protein is always carried into the interstitial space with water by convection, and washdown is limited by the barrier osmotic reflection coefficient. These factors impose limits to the decrease in interstitial protein concentration such that the maximum osmotic pressure difference able to oppose

an increase in hydrostatic pressure can at most about double, from close to 10 mm Hg to just over 20 mm Hg. This effect is also limited by the concentration of proteins in the vascular space. At low plasma protein concentrations, the capacity to oppose hydrostatic pressure increases is reduced[9] because the osmotic pressure difference across the barrier cannot be as large as normal. Lymphatic function is essential to this safety factor. Protein flow is greatly enhanced in increased pressure edema because proteins are swept into the lungs with water, and all the extravasated protein must be removed in lymph if washdown is to succeed. Lymphatic function may be compromised by an elevation in hydrostatic pressure at the outflow of the pulmonary lymphatic system into the large thoracic veins, which afford the back-pressure that must be pumped against,[10] and lymphatics in the lungs may be compressed by accumulating edema and rising pressure in the peribronchovascular connective tissue spaces. In long-standing or chronic high-pressure states (e.g., mitral stenosis), lymphatics have been said to proliferate and hypertrophy, improving the effectiveness of the lymphatic system for fluid and protein removal.[1]

The consequences of increased pressure edema on lung mechanics and gas exchange (Table 51.2) depend on how much edema accumulates.[11] Dehydration of normal subjects increases lung volumes and improves tests of ventilatory function,[12] indicating that water in the lungs affects even the normal condition. Early in the progression of edema, increases in hydrostatic pressure result in greater intrapulmonary blood volume (as vessels are recruited or distended by rising pressure), and the diffusing capacity of the lung for carbon monoxide may actually be greater than normal because pulmonary capillary blood volume is increased. Similarly, arterial P_{O_2} may also rise because ventilated units are better perfused when vascular pressures increase.[13] The small, reversible changes in airflow resistance and dynamic compliance, unaffected by vagotomy, that occur in congested lungs appear to be due to reflex bronchoconstrictor responses, but only when baseline bronchial tone is normal.[14]

When interstitial edema is present, closing volume may be increased[15] and maximum expiratory flows may be decreased. These changes were originally believed to be due to a decrease in caliber of small airways caused by compression by rising volume and pressure in the peribronchovascular connective tissue spaces. This effect would have to be in airways larger than bronchioles, because bronchioles and smaller airways do not have loose connective tissue sheaths[1] and their diameter is a function of lung volume, not transpulmonary pressure.[16] Lung compliance may be decreased in interstitial edema, but changes have been found not to be related closely to the amount of lung water[1,17]; decreased lung compliance may be due to decreased lung volume, a reflex phenomenon, or to large airway compression.[18] Arterial PO_2 may fall as a result of ventilation-perfusion mismatching, but gas exchange is not seriously compromised until the alveoli are flooded.

With alveolar flooding, lung volumes are diminished.[13] This is most marked in measurements of vital capacity, with inspiratory capacity affected more than expiratory capacity. Airways may close at higher than normal distending pressures, resulting in trapping of larger volumes of gas in the lungs.[19] Lung compliance is reduced when alveolar edema is present because lung volume is decreased.[20] Gas exchange is, of course, severely compromised when flooded alveoli are perfused (right-to-left shunt),[21] and there is an increase in wasted ventilation (ventilation of units where no gas exchange occurs).

Airflow resistance increases more with increased pressure edema than with increased permeability edema, perhaps due to effects on the bronchial circulation: Bronchial veins drain into the right atrium, so increased systemic venous pressure would result in increased bronchial venous and capillary pressures.[21] In addition to changes in airway resistance, pulmonary vascular resistance increases as edema progresses.[22] The cause of decreased pulmonary blood flow with edema is believed to be compression of alveolar wall vessels by the weight of the edema fluid. Increased resistance to blood flow in extra-alveolar vessels occurs at low lung volumes.[23] Blood flow may also be redistributed: Flow decreases at the bases as lung volume is diminished by edema.[24]

Intact red blood cells are often found in the edema fluid in increased hydrostatic pressure edema. Their presence may be due to rupture of a small number of tiny blood vessels with very high pressure, probably at the base of the lungs, where pressure is highest, and mixing of extravasated cells with edema fluid. Increased pressure edema fluid has low protein concentration, and there is no evidence that new pathways for leaking blood into the air spaces are opened up as the pressure climbs. If new pathways were created, the protein concentration of the edema fluid would increase along with the pressure. Protein concentrations in edema fluid decrease as pressure increases, indicating that proteins are effectively sieved by the barrier (passing in proportion to their size).

Light and electron microscopic examination of human and animal lung tissue in increased pressure edema shows alveolar edema and hemorrhage; thickened interstitial compartments (especially large peribronchovascular fluid cuffs)

with separated, dispersed collagen fibrils; and increased capillary surface area and volume.[25–29] More intercellular vesicles can be seen, but otherwise no detectable changes in the ultrastructure of the vascular endothelium occur, and the gap widths at intracellular junctions are not different from those in normal lungs. Electron-lucent zones (laminae rarae) may be seen in the basement membranes, particularly where the alveolar-capillary barrier is thinnest. Long-standing edema (e.g., in patients with mitral stenosis) can be associated with basement membrane thickening and increased distance between the alveoli and capillaries; increases in fibroblasts, histiocytes, and bulky strands of collagenous fibers can be seen in the interstitium. Permeability might be lowered across these widened barriers.[30] Dogs with pacing-induced chronic congestive heart failure developed a significant increase in the threshold for high-vascular-pressure edema formation (about a 50% reduction in the amount of water and protein cleared across the lung microvascular endothelial barrier at high pulmonary vascular pressures as compared with controls).[31] Morphometric analysis of the alveolar-capillary barrier showed that endothelial, interstitial, and epithelial thickness were increased compared with controls, indicating that remodeling confers an increase in the resistance to development of high-pressure–induced alveolar edema. Alveolar type II cells may be more numerous than in normal lungs, and alveolar macrophages proliferate.[29] Chronic, severe increased pressure edema may also become organized and fibrotic, may calcify, and may even result in bone formation.[32]

Mechanisms

The most common cause of increased pressure edema is elevated lung microvascular hydrostatic pressure. The sum of driving pressures might also be greater if perimicrovascular hydrostatic pressure or the osmotic pressure difference across the microvascular barrier were decreased. At the alveolar barrier, an increase in interstitial hydrostatic pressure, a decrease in alveolar hydrostatic pressure, or a decrease in osmotic pressure difference across the barrier might result in a greater sum of driving pressures. The possibilities are listed in Table 51.3.

Increased Microvascular Hydrostatic Pressure. Congestive heart failure is the most common cause of increased pressure edema. That is why increased pressure edema is often called cardiogenic even though the heart is not always

---

Table 51.3 Mechanisms of Increased Pressure Pulmonary Edema

Increased Lung Microvascular Hydrostatic Pressure
Left ventricular dysfunction
Mechanical obstruction of left atrial outflow
Volume overload
Pulmonary venous hypertension
Overperfusion
Increased lymphatic outflow pressure

Decreased Perimicrovascular Hydrostatic Pressure

Increased Alveolar Surface Tension
Inspiratory airway obstruction

primarily involved. Elevated pressures in the pulmonary microvasculature are usually due to left-sided heart failure, with elevated left atrial pressures transmitted retrograde into the pulmonary circulation. Common causes are left ventricular dysfunction (e.g., caused by acute myocardial infarction, severe coronary insufficiency, tachyarrhythmias, bradyarrhythmias, cardiomyopathies, constrictive pericarditis, aortic stenosis or regurgitation, mitral regurgitation, coarctation of the aorta, rupture of chordae tendineae or intraventricular septum, systemic hypertension) or mechanical obstruction of the left atrial outflow tract (e.g., as in mitral stenosis, left atrial myxoma). Left atrial pressure and subsequent pulmonary microvascular pressure can also be elevated by severe volume overloading in a patient with a normal or diseased heart.

An unusual cause of increased microvascular hydrostatic pressure is pulmonary venous hypertension in the absence of left ventricular or atrial disease, which can occur if the pulmonary veins are contracted (e.g., by possible muscular sphincters[33]), compressed, or obstructed (e.g., because of veno-occlusive disease or mediastinal fibrosis[34]). Bronchial venous hypertension does not appear to significantly increase fluid filtration in the lungs.[35]

Increases in fluid filtration can also be associated with increases in vascular pressure proximal to the filtration sites in the lungs. For example, pulmonary hypertension, in combination with depressed left ventricular function, has been implicated in the pathogenesis of cocaine-induced pulmonary edema.[36] Whether such increases lead to pulmonary edema depends on what happens to microvascular pressure. If high right-sided pressures are caused by increased resistance before the main site of filtration in the lungs (e.g., hypoxic pulmonary vasoconstriction of small arterial vessels,[37,38] primary pulmonary hypertension, pulmonary artery or valvular stenosis), edema does not occur. Conversely, if the lung vascular bed is only partially constricted or obstructed, or if the vascular surface area is greatly decreased (e.g., by lung resection), higher flow in perfused vessels leads to increased pressure edema[38] because microvascular pressures at the fluid exchange site are elevated in the overperfused lung. Pulmonary edema occurred in about 15% of patients after pneumonectomy and seemed to be exacerbated by administration of fresh frozen plasma,[39] probably because intravascular volume is increased by such transfusions. Any increase in blood flow through the lungs increases the pulmonary microvascular pressure at the fluid exchange sites even if the pulmonary venous pressure remains constant, because pulmonary microvascular pressure is the sum of pulmonary venous pressure plus the product of pulmonary venous resistance and blood flow.[1] High systemic venous pressure might also promote edema formation by raising the outflow pressure and thereby reducing the flow of lymph.[10]

The mechanisms of two less common causes of pulmonary edema, those occurring at high altitude and during severe neurologic insults, may involve increased microvascular hydrostatic pressure. *High-altitude pulmonary edema,*[40,41] which is also discussed in Chapter 65, appears to be caused by severe pulmonary hypertension that develops in susceptible individuals as a consequence of hypoxic vasoconstriction when the inspired PO_2 falls at altitude. Non-homogeneous obstruction of the pulmonary vascular bed

by exaggerated hypoxic vasoconstriction results in high blood flow and transmission of pressure to portions of the pulmonary vascular bed that are not protected by vasoconstriction, and pulmonary edema results from high intravascular pressure. Patients who develop high-altitude pulmonary edema have been found to have very high pulmonary arterial pressure (sometimes at systemic levels). The excessive rise in pressure precedes the development of the edema, and agents that lower pulmonary arterial pressure (e.g., oxygen, nifedipine, hydralazine, phentolamine, inhaled nitric oxide, and inhaled β_2-agonists) are effective in prevention or treatment, or both.

Postmortem edema fluid has been described as proteinaceous in high-altitude pulmonary edema, and measurements of edema fluid protein concentration have been made in two patients.[42] In one, the edema fluid–to–plasma protein concentration ratio (0.6) was in the range predicted for increased pressure edema; in the other, the ratio (0.8 in one sample, 1.1 in another) was in the range typical of increased permeability pulmonary edema. Bronchoalveolar lavage fluid of six climbers with high-altitude pulmonary edema showed a marked increase in high-molecular-weight proteins (as well as many red blood cells and alveolar macrophages).[43] Because water is resorbed from edema fluid in the alveoli much faster than protein,[44,45] the protein concentration of edema fluid increases progressively as edema resolves. The high protein concentration of postmortem high-altitude pulmonary edema and bronchoalveolar lavage fluids may be due to observations made during a time when fluid was being resorbed from, rather than added to, alveoli.

As noted earlier, overperfusion of a restricted pulmonary vascular bed, even in the absence of hypoxia, causes increased pressure edema, not increased permeability edema.[38] This can explain why some cases of high-altitude pulmonary edema are correctly classified as increased pressure pulmonary edema. Recent evidence from climbers studied at high altitude suggests that high intravascular pressures cause physical damage to vascular walls (so-called stress failure), which has been shown to occur at extreme, but sometimes transient, increases in pulmonary vascular pressures in experimental animals.[46-48] Such structural failures need not occur in large numbers to explain even severe increased permeability edema, because edema would form readily and in a quantity driven by the prevailing elevated vascular pressure.[49] The suggestion has been made that high-altitude pulmonary edema results from the stress failure of overdistended, relatively thin-walled pulmonary arteries rather than from microvascular rupture,[50] which might help explain why the prevailing vasoconstriction does not seem to offer much protection to downstream vessels, why there are no reports of gradual progression through an indolent prodrome of increased pressure edema before stress failure occurs, and why high-altitude pulmonary edema is first detected radiographically in the central lung fields surrounding large vessels rather than in the lung bases and periphery.

Plasma selectins have been measured in subjects at high altitude.[51] Levels of E-selectin were inversely related to arterial oxygen saturation in control subjects and in subjects with acute mountain sickness and with high-altitude pulmonary edema. Because endothelial cells are the only known source of E-selectin, increased plasma levels were considered to be a sign of activation or injury of endothelial cells. Plasma levels of P-selectin were not found to be elevated at high altitude.

Alternative mechanisms for the increased permeability in high-altitude pulmonary edema have been proposed. However, inflammatory responses in high-altitude pulmonary edema are probably a consequence rather than a cause of the edema.[40,52,53] The rapid reversibility of high-altitude pulmonary edema with descent to lower elevation, oxygen therapy, or pharmacologic reduction of pulmonary vascular pressure are not characteristics of acute lung injury and increased permeability pulmonary edema suspected to be caused by or related to inflammation. Also, recent work supports the conclusion that this disorder is primarily a hydrostatic type of pulmonary edema.[54]

Neurogenic pulmonary edema[55] also may be related to elevated pulmonary vascular pressures. Measurements of edema fluid protein concentration relative to plasma protein concentration in 12 patients with neurogenic pulmonary edema have been reported.[56] Seven of the patients had ratios typical of increased pressure pulmonary edema, and the other five had ratios consistent with either increased permeability pulmonary edema or with sampling during the resolution phase of increased pressure pulmonary edema (when edema fluid protein concentration rises as fluid is resorbed from the alveoli at a faster rate than protein). Measurements in eight patients had previously been reported; two of the measurements indicated increased pressure edema, and six indicated increased permeability edema or sampling during the resolution phase. Thus, half the cases of neurogenic pulmonary edema in which edema fluid protein concentration has been measured appear to involve increased pressure edema, and the fraction is perhaps even higher, depending on the timing of edema sampling.

Measurements of the alveolar-to-plasma protein concentration ratios in dogs with neurogenic pulmonary edema induced by intracisternal veratrine showed a wide range of values, indicating that both increased pressure and increased permeability mechanisms may be involved to varying degrees in that type of neurogenic pulmonary edema.[57] In other animal experiments, filtration increases in neurogenic edema[58-61] and edema following transient pulmonary hypertension[62] were attributable to increased pressure or increased vascular surface area, or both, perhaps in combination with acute lymphatic insufficiency. Animal studies can be difficult to interpret. Some models have been complicated by primary lung injury that is separate from effects on the central nervous system[63] or by evidence that vascular permeability was abnormal in control experiments[62] performed in surgically traumatized, acutely prepared animals.[64]

Both human and experimental neurogenic pulmonary edema can be associated with massive discharge of the sympathetic nervous system, resulting in systemic vasoconstriction and translocation of blood from the systemic to the pulmonary circulation, producing marked increases in pulmonary blood flow and vascular pressures. Peak pulmonary arterial pressure can reach systemic levels. Hydrostatic pressure at the fluid exchange sites in the lungs can also be elevated by catecholamine-induced left ventricular dysfunction, increased pulmonary venous resistance, and mitral valve insufficiency secondary to left ventricular dilation. Thus, as in high-altitude pulmonary edema, high

pulmonary vascular pressures could result in either increased pressure edema (from elevated microvascular hydrostatic pressure) or increased permeability edema (if pulmonary vascular pressures were high enough to cause stress failure of pulmonary vessels). Whether neurogenic pulmonary edema can occur by pressure-independent mechanisms remains controversial and unproven.[55] Some episodes of neurogenic edema may involve increased pressure; others appear to involve increased permeability. More information is needed to sort out the precise causes.

Decreased Perimicrovascular Hydrostatic Pressure. The sum of driving pressures would be greater if perimicrovascular hydrostatic pressure were diminished, thereby resulting in an increase in fluid and protein filtration at the microvascular barrier in the lungs. Pulmonary edema has been described in circumstances in which this might occur. The best clinical example is *postobstructive pulmonary edema* as a consequence of upper airway obstruction or its release, which can be caused, for example, by laryngospasm, endotracheal tube obstruction, foreign-body aspiration, epiglottitis, croup, severe acute asthma, airway compression by tumors, strangulation, or hanging. High negative intrathoracic pressures generated by inspiratory attempts against the occluded airway are transmitted to the interstitium, promoting fluid movement into the interstitium. Mechanical effects on the cardiovascular system likely contribute to this kind of edema: High negative intrathoracic pressure causes increases in cardiac preload and afterload and in pulmonary blood flow, all of which increase the microvascular pressure that drives fluid out into the interstitium. Three patients with upper airway obstruction and pulmonary edema were reported, all with low edema fluid protein concentration relative to plasma protein concentration (ratios of 0.44, 0.31, and 0.52), indicating increased pressure pulmonary edema.[65]

Aspiration of air or fluid from the pleural space with consequent reexpansion of a collapsed lung could result in a decrease in perimicrovascular hydrostatic pressure as the lung expands to fill the thorax. So-called *reexpansion pulmonary edema* has been reported in experimental animals[66,67] and in patients[68,69] after lung reexpansion, but the high edema fluid protein concentration measured in three patients[70,71] indicated that reexpansion may result in an increased permeability edema rather than an increased pressure edema. However, one recent study of protein concentration in pulmonary edema fluid from patients with reexpansion edema indicates that hydrostatic mechanisms are important.[71a] The increased permeability hypothesis was supported in studies of rabbits with experimental reexpansion edema.[72,73]

Reexpansion pulmonary edema may be a form of ischemia-reperfusion injury,[74] with the increase in lung microvascular permeability being related to restoration of blood flow, formation of oxygen free radicals, release of proinflammatory mediators, and activation of neutrophils. On reperfusion, pulmonary vascular resistance shifts more toward postcapillary venules, which elevates pressure in the microvascular vessels at the fluid exchange sites in the lungs and would aggravate edema formation across the injured barrier.[75] A patient with apparent reperfusion pulmonary edema complicating thrombolytic therapy for pulmonary embolism has been reported,[76] and reperfusion injury is probably one of the causes of the pulmonary edema that occurs in transplanted lungs.[77] Hemorrhagic and traumatic shock have also been conceived of as types of a "whole-body ischemia-reperfusion syndrome."[78]

If high alveolar surface tension were transmitted to the interstitium, perimicrovascular hydrostatic pressure would also be lowered, thereby increasing filtration across the microvascular barrier. Such an effect has been suggested by experimental findings in dog lungs.[79,80] The effect of alveolar surface tension on lung fluid balance is discussed later.

Decreased Transmural Osmotic Pressure Difference. The sum of driving pressures would be increased if the osmotic pressure difference opposing the hydrostatic pressure difference across the microvascular barrier were decreased (by lowering plasma protein concentration or by raising interstitial protein concentration), resulting in an increase in the sum of driving pressures for fluid and protein flow into the lungs. This theoretical mechanism of increased pressure edema has been the subject of study in experimental animals, with contradictory results. In some studies, hypoproteinemia was not found to increase lung microvascular liquid conductance or protein permeability.[81,82] Because the microvascular-perimicrovascular osmotic pressure gradient is generated by the microvascular hydrostatic pressure and by the barrier descriptors (conductivity and reflection coefficient), it is not possible to decrease the osmotic pressure gradient by depleting plasma proteins except transiently while a new steady state is being established. Although fluid flow would be increased temporarily, it would return to normal when a new steady state is reached, unless hydrostatic pressure or barrier characteristics were also changed. This is not to imply that protein concentrations are not important forces in lung fluid balance. Although an isolated decreased osmotic pressure gradient across the microvascular barrier cannot be sustained or be an important mechanism for increased pressure edema, the absolute concentration of protein has a profound effect on lung fluid balance when hydrostatic driving pressure is increased. When plasma osmotic pressure is low, the ability of the osmotic pressure gradient to widen in response to increased hydrostatic pressure is diminished, and edema accumulates at hydrostatic driving pressures lower than those needed to cause edema when protein concentration is normal.

Alveolar Barrier Function. The driving pressure for fluid and protein flow across the alveolar barrier would be elevated, resulting in increased pressure edema, if the interstitial hydrostatic pressure were raised or if the alveolar hydrostatic pressure or the osmotic pressure difference across the alveolar barrier were lowered. Because the osmotic pressure difference across the barrier is established by the relevant hydrostatic forces and barrier descriptors (as across the microvascular barrier), an isolated decrease in the osmotic difference could result in only a transiently increased pressure filtration until a new steady state is achieved. This transient phenomenon would not be an important mechanism for increased pressure edema in the alveolar spaces.

Interstitial hydrostatic pressure rises as interstitial edema accumulates in the lungs.[4,83] Increased interstitial hydro-

static pressure would raise the sum of driving pressures across the alveolar barrier and could drive edema formation across the alveolar or airway epithelium. The role of interstitial hydrostatic pressure in edema formation is not simple, however. Although increased interstitial hydrostatic pressure favors edema formation across the alveolar barrier, it opposes edema formation across the microvascular barrier. The relative contributions of these disparate effects have not been separated. The osmotic pressure difference across the intact alveolar barrier provides a powerful force that opposes filtration increases driven by hydrostatic pressure. Because the barrier is normally virtually impermeable even to small solutes, filtration of water would result in a decrease in alveolar osmotic pressure. A decrease of only 1 mOsm (<0.5% of the normal alveolar osmotic pressure) would balance a 19 mm Hg increase in interstitial hydrostatic pressure.

Greater pressure filtration across the alveolar barrier would also result from an increase in the sum of driving pressures if alveolar hydrostatic pressure were lowered. This is complicated by the interrelation between alveolar and interstitial hydrostatic pressures.[4,84] A drop in alveolar hydrostatic pressure, which increases the sum of driving pressures across the alveolar barrier, also results in a lowering of interstitial hydrostatic pressure, which decreases the sum of driving pressures across the alveolar barrier but increases the sum of driving pressures across the microvascular barrier. The influence of alveolar surface tension on lung fluid balance has been investigated in dogs. Administration of a detergent aerosol resulted in loss of surfactant activity, higher alveolar surface tension, lower static compliance, atelectasis, and pulmonary edema; low protein concentration in alveolar edema fluid and left-hilar afferent lymph relative to plasma protein concentration indicated that this was an increased pressure type of pulmonary edema.[85,86] Because increased pressure edema can impair surface activity of dog lung extracts[87] and isolated rabbit lungs,[88] it is possible that changes in alveolar surface tension may accelerate edema formation. However, the notion that changes in alveolar surface tension in edema lead to a self-perpetuating vicious cycle of edema formation is not borne out clinically.

The only kind of clinical pulmonary edema caused by transmural osmotic pressure differences is near drowning.[89,90] Seawater is three times more hyperosmotic (1000 mOsm) than plasma, so the volume of fluid in the air spaces after salt water aspiration increases threefold to reach osmotic equilibrium, thus markedly increasing the alveolar edema already present because of the volume of seawater itself in the alveoli. Osmotic equilibrium is reached in minutes as water is drawn from the vasculature into the alveoli by osmotic pressure.[89-91] Alveolar barrier function is not significantly compromised (unless perhaps the patient aspirates gastric contents or the seawater is contaminated or rich in particulate matter), and the alveolar edema is cleared very rapidly (50% to 60% of excess alveolar fluid is cleared in 4 hours). However, transient, minimal disturbances in endothelial barrier function may occur if cellular water loss causes cell shrinkage, thereby opening up paracellular pathways (junctions between cells) for fluid and solute movement. Freshwater near drowning proceeds in the opposite fashion: osmotic equilibrium is reached rapidly by flow of water out of the alveoli into the interstitium and bloodstream. Severe hemodilution, with hemolysis and fibrinolysis, also occurs, and the rapid water flux and hypotonicity cause severe distortion of pulmonary ultrastructure, including damage to type I and type II cells, endothelial cell swelling, basement membrane detachment, and cell disruption. Both alveolar epithelium and microvascular endothelium can thus be injured by the hypotonic fluid, leading to increased permeability pulmonary edema rather than a normal barrier type of pulmonary edema.

INCREASED PERMEABILITY EDEMA AND ACUTE LUNG INJURY

Increased permeability pulmonary edema (Fig. 51.2) is caused by an increase in liquid and protein conductance across the barriers in the lungs. The essential feature of this edema is that the integrity of the barrier to fluid and protein flow into the lung interstitium and the alveoli is altered. Increased permeability edema is sometimes called *noncardiogenic* or *primary pulmonary edema,* and the resulting clinical syndromes in humans are commonly lumped together as *acute lung injury* or the *acute respiratory distress syndrome* (ARDS).[92,93]

Pathophysiology

Accumulation of fluid and protein increases when the lung endothelial and epithelial barriers are injured. If the rate of fluid accumulation exceeds the rate at which it can be removed, increased permeability edema occurs. Because the barriers limiting fluid and protein flow into the lungs do not function normally when the lungs are injured, the lungs are not protected against edema by the usual safety factors. Although increases in fluid and protein filtration across the barriers are removed by lymphatics and drained away from

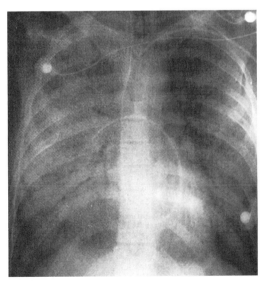

Figure 51.2 Chest roentgenogram in a patient with increased permeability pulmonary edema. The heart is not enlarged, and the vascular pedicle is of normal size. Edema is peripheral and not gravitationally distributed. Air bronchograms are present, a finding more common in increased permeability edema than in increased pressure edema. The patient had drug overdose, coma, and hypotension.

the alveolar walls as in increased pressure edema, much more fluid and protein are filtered at any given sum of driving pressures because the barriers to their flow are much less restrictive than normal. Edema formation in injured lungs is very sensitive to driving pressures.[49] Driving pressures are often increased when the lungs are injured because of the vasoconstrictive effects of inflammatory mediators such as thromboxanes, which may shift the main site of resistance to postcapillary venules, thus increasing hydrostatic pressure at the microvascular fluid exchange sites,[94] or because of effects on the heart as well as on the circulation. For example, elevated left atrial pressure, pulmonary venoconstriction, and an increase in cardiac output in sepsis can increase hydrostatic pressure at the microvascular fluid exchange sites.[95] Microvascular hydrostatic pressure in injured lungs is not related simply to pulmonary artery occlusion ("wedge") pressure, and such measurements can be misleading.

Because the barriers are leaky, protective osmotic pressure differences are lost across them; driving pressure is unopposed by osmotic pressure, and even normal hydrostatic pressure results in significant fluid and protein extravasation into interstitial and alveolar spaces. The ability of the lymphatics to pump the excess filtrate away is increased when the lungs are injured. Maximal lung lymph flow increases more when the microvascular wall has been injured than when hydrostatic pressure alone is increased (as a result of poorly understood "edema-dependent lymphatic factors"), but even this augmented lymphatic pumping capability is taxed at low driving pressures. If the epithelial barrier is injured, edema may accumulate readily in the alveoli, because most of the resistance to fluid and protein flow into the alveoli is in the epithelial barrier.[96,97] Increased permeability edema is often rapid in onset and progression because injured barriers offer much less resistance to flow and because hydrostatic driving pressure is unopposed by increases in osmotic pressure difference. Clinically, patients with increased permeability edema usually have a low intravascular hydrostatic pressure, commonly measured as a low or normal pulmonary capillary wedge pressure. In some cases, this reflects the low intravascular pressures associated with the underlying disease process (e.g., sepsis).

The consequences of increased permeability edema on lung mechanics and gas exchange depend on how much edema accumulates and how severe the causative lung injury is.[98] As with increased pressure edema, the major effects on pulmonary mechanics occur with alveolar flooding. In experimental lung injury, functional residual capacity was found to be decreased as a consequence of alveolar flooding, and this loss of ventilatable units accounted for virtually all the observed decrease in static lung compliance.[99,100] Computed tomography has provided new insights into structure-function relationships in human acute lung injury.[101,102] In the early stage of lung injury, when alveolar edema predominates, the lungs are characterized by a homogeneous alteration of vascular permeability, and edema accumulates evenly in all lung regions with a nongravitational distribution. Increased lung weight due to edema causes collapse of lung regions along the vertical axis through the transmission of hydrostatic forces (compression atelectasis, caused by the weight of edema). Thus, collapse occurs mainly in the dependent lung, where the superimposed weight from above is greatest.

Measurements of pulmonary mechanics in mechanically ventilated patients with acute lung injuries[98] showed decreased static lung compliance as a consequence of this loss of ventilatable lung. In addition, airflow resistance was increased as a result of decreased lung volume. Bronchospasm adds to the increase in airflow resistance and can be substantially reversed with bronchodilator inhalation.[103] Chest wall compliance was reduced, probably because of alterations of intrinsic mechanical properties of the chest wall by abdominal distention, chest wall edema, and pleural effusion.[98] Different respiratory mechanics and response to positive end-expiratory pressure (PEEP) during mechanical ventilation were reported in patients with ARDS originating from pulmonary disease (pneumonia, which caused consolidation) or from extrapulmonary disease (which caused edema and subsequent alveolar collapse).[104] Lung elastance was higher in pneumonia, whereas chest wall elastance and intra-abdominal pressure were higher in patients with extrapulmonary causes of their lung injuries. In pneumonia, PEEP appeared to distend normal alveoli, which are more compliant that involved alveoli, whereas in extrapulmonary causes of acute lung injury, PEEP appeared to recruit previously collapsed alveoli.

Although the effects of surface forces on decreased lung compliance in acute lung injury were believed to be small, results of experiments in isolated rabbit lungs indicated that increased permeability edema may result in more severe mechanical changes than equivalent degrees of increased pressure edema.[88] In contrast, experiments in awake sheep showed that similar degrees of pulmonary edema, regardless of the mechanism, caused similar changes in compliance and gas exchange.[21] Other experiments showed that dynamic and static lung compliance decreased early in evolving lung injury.[105] Surfactant is strongly thromboplastic, and coagulation may compound surfactant depletion when plasma proteins enter the air spaces. The injured lung may release substances that can interfere with the normal low surface tension in the alveoli,[106] and activated polymorphonuclear leukocytes (PMNs) have been shown to impair surfactant function in vitro and to degrade the major surfactant apoprotein by a combination of proteolysis and oxidant-radical–mediated mechanisms.[107] Human lung surfactant obtained by bronchoalveolar lavage of patients at risk for acute lung injury and patients with established acute lung injuries has been reported to be abnormal in chemical composition and functional activity.[108] Abnormalities also could be caused by interactions between surfactant and edema proteins, because plasma proteins (especially fibrin monomers but also fibrinogen and albumin) interfere with surfactant function. Proteinaceous edema fluid has been associated with surfactant inhibition in various experimental models.[109-111] The role of surfactant in the development and treatment of acute lung injury and the potential role for surfactant therapy are discussed in more detail later in this chapter.

As in increased pressure edema, gas exchange is severely compromised in increased permeability edema, owing both to intrapulmonary shunting of blood and to ventilation-perfusion inequalities.[112,113] The available evidence taken together does not support the concept that tissue oxygenation may be further compromised by an abnormality in the regulation of oxygen extraction, which has been hypothesized to occur in patients with acute lung injury (so-called pathologic dependency).[114,115]

New evidence indicates that patients with early acute lung injury have a marked increase in their pulmonary dead space fraction, indicating that many ventilated lung units are not well perfused, although intrapulmonary shunting may contribute also to the elevated dead space.[116] This finding explains why the minute ventilation is twice normal (approximately 12 L/min) at the onset of the acute respiratory distress syndrome. An elevated pulmonary dead space fraction has also been recently reported in pediatric patients with acute lung injury.[117]

Mechanical and gas-exchange abnormalities change with time during the course of acute lung injury. The early, exudative stage of injury, in which edema predominates, is characterized by small effective alveolar space (so-called baby lung) and true shunt; the later, proliferative stage of injury, in which fibrosis and remodeling predominate, is characterized by small and stiff lungs, with superimposed emphysema-like alterations (bullous disease), decreased alveolar ventilation, and ventilation-perfusion maldistribution rather than true shunt.

Other consequences of acute lung injury (beyond those related to edema formation) probably depend on the cause and extent of injury. Bronchoconstriction, caused by injury and mediator release, may add to mechanical and gas-exchange abnormalities. Vascular reactivity to hypoxia and other stimuli may also be altered in the injured lung's vascular bed.[118-120] Perhaps because lung metabolic function is compromised, the injured lung may add or fail to extract vasoactive substances (e.g., biogenic amines, arachidonic acid metabolites, and drugs) from the blood, and angiotensin-converting enzyme (ACE) activity may be abnormal.[121] This could have effects on the heart and the systemic circulation as well as on the pulmonary circulation. Changes in the surface of microvascular endothelial cells may lead to activation of the clotting cascade.[122] Disseminated intravascular coagulation, often associated with endotoxemia and gram-negative infections, is an ominous complication associated with thromboses, hemorrhage, and endothelial cell injury in the lungs and other organs. Abnormalities of fibrin turnover[123] and lung fibrinogen uptake[124] have been reported in acute lung injuries. There is also mounting evidence that there is a procoagulant and antifibrinolytic environment in the distal air spaces and the plasma of patients with early lung injury.[125,126] Pulmonary vascular resistance between arteries and veins also may increase as a result of morphologic alterations of the microvascular endothelium or disruption and loss of the pulmonary vascular bed.[127] If the lungs have severe structural damage, mechanical and gas-exchange abnormalities may be much greater than can be explained by edema accumulation alone.

The light and electron microscopic appearance of human[127-135] and animal[136-138] lung tissue in acute lung injury is variable. Lung morphology depends on the severity and the duration of injury and on the treatments administered rather than on the cause of injury. Exudative, proliferative, and fibrotic changes usually appear in sequence.

The earliest changes are marked by widespread alveolar and interstitial edema and hemorrhage. Injury to alveolar ducts may be particularly severe. Hyaline membranes, composed of precipitated plasma proteins, fibrin, and necrotic debris, can be seen. The alveolar epithelium may be more extensively damaged than the vascular endothelium, even if the underlying insult is blood-borne. Widespread, local areas of destruction of type I alveolar epithelial cells alternate with normal-appearing alveoli. The injured alveolar epithelium is swollen, disorganized, discontinuous, and often lifted off exposed, but usually intact, basement membranes, which are covered by hyaline membranes. Type I cells are more severely damaged than type II cells, and the thin cytoplasmic extensions of the cells far from the nucleus covering the thin side of the alveolar-capillary barrier may be most severely affected. The interstitium is widened by edema (especially in peribronchovascular cuffs) and may be choked with leukocytes, platelets, red blood cells, fibrin, and debris (especially near the alveolar walls). The thick portion of the alveolar interstitium is usually involved more than the thin portion. The microvascular endothelium is relatively preserved, usually showing little other than irregular, focal thickening as a result of cytoplasmic swelling or vacuoles and greater numbers of luminal leukocytes. Intracapillary thrombi are rare in this and subsequent phases. Large endothelial gaps are not seen, probably because they would be incompatible with even brief survival because massive edema pours across even small, focal gaps. The alveolar capillary is the usual site of injury, but some insults involve other vessels (e.g., focal gaps in arterioles less than 1 mm in diameter in air emboli–induced lung injury).

The exudative phase is followed, usually after 5 to 10 days, by a proliferative phase.[132,139] The relative contributions of the original insult, repair processes, and effects of therapies to this and subsequent phases are not well known, but some of the abnormalities that occur after the initial exudative phase seem to be related to the effects of traditional modes of mechanical ventilation that used tidal volumes between 12 and 15 mL/kg predicted body weight. In the proliferative phase, fluid has been reabsorbed from the air spaces. Fibrin may be prominent in alveoli and interstitium, and there is infiltration with inflammatory cells and fibroblasts (which may have been activated very early in the course of lung injury). The alveolar epithelium is often cuboidal, made up largely of proliferating type II cells. The air-blood barrier can be greatly thickened by interstitial and epithelial enlargement. The pulmonary vascular bed may be partially or completely disrupted, and structural alterations may greatly reduce its surface area. The proliferative phase can present clinically as an inflammatory syndrome with fever, leukocytosis, low systemic vascular resistance, diffuse alveolar infiltrates, diffuse and intense pulmonary uptake of gallium, and neutrophilia on bronchoalveolar lavage, all in the absence of any infection.[140]

A final stage may follow, often about 2 weeks after the initial insult, in which fibrotic changes of the alveolar ducts, alveoli, and interstitium predominate. Alveoli may be obliterated, alveolar walls coalesced, and functional lung units lost. The lungs may be emphysema-like, with extensive bullous changes.[132] Even severe changes at any stage may be reversible, with slow recovery toward normal lung function.

Mechanisms

Most of the conditions that have been associated with acute lung injury in humans are listed in Table 51.4. The most

Table 51.4 Clinical Disorders Associated with Acute Lung Injury

Infectious Causes
Gram-negative or gram-positive sepsis
Bacterial pneumonia
Viral pneumonia
Mycoplasmal pneumonia
Fungal pneumonia
Parasitic infections
Mycobacterial disease

Aspiration
Gastric acid
Food and other particulate matter
Fresh or sea water (near drowning)
Hydrocarbon fluids

Trauma
Lung contusion
Fat emboli
Nonthoracic trauma
Thermal injury (burns)
Blast injury (explosion, lightning)
Overdistention (mechanical ventilation)
Inhaled gases (phosgene, ammonia)

Hemodynamic Disturbances
Shock of any etiology
Anaphylaxis
High-altitude pulmonary edema
Reperfusion
Air embolism
Amniotic fluid embolism

Drugs
Heroin
Methadone
Propoxyphene
Naloxone
Cocaine
Barbiturates
Colchicine
Salicylates
Ethchlorvynol
Interleukin-2
Protamine
Hydrochlorothiazide

Hematologic Disorders
Disseminated intravascular coagulation
Incompatible blood transfusion
Rh incompatibility
Antileukocyte antibodies
Leukoagglutinin reactions
Post–cardiopulmonary bypass, pump oxygenator

Metabolic Disorders
Pancreatitis
Diabetic ketoacidosis

Neurologic Disorders
Head trauma
Grand mal seizures
Increased intracranial pressure (any cause)
Subarachnoid or intracerebral hemorrhage

Miscellaneous Disorders
Lung reexpansion
Upper airway obstruction

common causes are pneumonia, sepsis, gastric aspiration, and major trauma. The insult to the lungs occurs via either the airways or the bloodstream. The exact mechanisms by which the lungs are injured have been the subject of intense investigation in humans, animal models, and cellular systems.[93] Human studies have provided descriptive data about the events that occur in the air spaces before and after the onset of lung injury. Studies using bronchoalveolar lavage in patients before and after the onset of acute lung injury have shown that there is a major acute inflammatory response that begins before acute lung injury is clinically recognized, peaks during the first 1 to 3 days of clinically defined acute lung injury, and resolves slowly over 7 to 14 days in patients who remain intubated.[141-143] These studies have shown the complexity of the evolving inflammatory responses, which are characterized by the accumulation of acute response cytokines and their naturally occurring inhibitors, oxidants, proteinases and antiproteinases, lipid mediators, growth factors, and collagen precursors involved in the repair process.[142-152] Extensive efforts have been made to find single biologic markers that predict the onset or the outcome of acute lung injury, but these have met with only limited success.[153]

Hypotheses about mechanisms of lung injury have been tested in animal models and in vitro studies, and several reviews have summarized the findings. The existing animal models do not completely reproduce all of the aspects of acute lung injury in humans, in part because human acute lung injury evolves over a longer period of time than can be studied in the laboratory. In addition, the lungs of humans are exposed not only to the initial injurious insult, but also to the therapies that are used to treat acute lung injury, such as mechanical ventilation. Experiments with isolated cells have been useful to test specific concepts, but the complexity and redundancy of intact biologic systems is not reproduced in simplified experimental systems. Most experimental work purposely limits a study to a single causative agent; however, this turns the reality of clinical complexity into the simplicity of a single experimental pathway. Increased permeability edema in humans is likely to be caused by interactions between a number of different pathways acting in parallel or in series.

Studies in isolated organs and small animals in which hemodynamic variables are not measured can be difficult to evaluate because indices of lung injury, usually measured by the appearance of markers in lungs, lavage fluid, or perfusate, are not determined solely by the barrier function of the microvasculature. For example, when the vascular endothelium is injured, fluid and protein movement from the vascular space into the lungs is extremely sensitive to hydrostatic driving pressures and surface area for filtration,[49] and the effects of experimental interventions may be caused by changes in these parameters and not solely by changes in microvascular barrier function. The effects of microvascular driving pressures and surface area can be difficult to evaluate even in large, instrumented animals. In sheep and goats, interpretation of lung lymph fluid and protein flow changes are further complicated by contributions from lymphatics outside the lungs,[154,155] physical forces acting on lymphatics,[156] and possible intranodal modification of lymph.[157] Data from experimental animal models suggest that there are at least two broad categories of mechanisms

of acute lung injury: those that are *indirect* (i.e., requiring the participation of intermediary mechanisms, such as host defenses); and those that are *direct* (i.e., not requiring intermediary mechanisms, with injury probably occurring as a result of contact between an offending substance and lung tissue). These categories overlap because, once the lungs are injured, inflammatory responses occur, which may compound the primary mechanism of injury. Three major hypotheses about the mechanism of acute lung injury are discussed next. Each is discussed separately, but they are interrelated.

Infection. Acute lung injury develops in 20% to 45% of patients with severe sepsis.[158-160] Increased microvascular permeability to albumin has been shown to accompany human sepsis,[161] and infection and the sepsis syndrome are major causes of acute lung injury in humans.[162] Patients who develop shock in response to known or suspected infection have a particularly high incidence of acute lung injury, and the mortality of patients with acute lung injury associated with infection, the sepsis syndrome, or bacteremia is increased.[162-165] Acute lung injury also appears to predispose the lungs to infection, and delayed infection is an important cause of morbidity in patients who survive the initial lung insult.[166-169]

The mechanism by which infection and the sepsis syndrome injure the lungs is not certain.[170] It seems likely that lung injury may be related to factors other than direct damage by bacteria or other microorganisms because prognosis has not been found to be related to documented bacteremia or pneumonia.[171,172] In experimental animals, intravenous infusions of live *Pseudomonas aeruginosa*,[173] endotoxins from *Escherichia coli*,[174-176] and surgically induced peritonitis[177] all resulted in increased permeability pulmonary edema in sheep. Instillation of endotoxin into the airways of sheep also led to lung inflammation with variable degrees of lung injury.[178,179] *Pseudomonas aeruginosa* has also been reported to cause lung injury in pigs, and *E. coli* endotoxin has been reported to injure the lungs of baboons[180] and dogs[181] and to result in neutrophilic alveolitis in rats.[182] Acute lung injury caused by endotoxin in sheep is believed to be an inflammatory response mediated at least in part by PMNs and by tumor necrosis factor (TNF). Endotoxin can also affect the clotting system and metabolic functions of the lungs,[183] and it may dispose the lung to the development of pulmonary infections by increasing adherence of bacteria to endothelium.[184] However, acute lung injury in septic humans does not appear to be necessarily related to endotoxemia, because endotoxin may be undetectable or present only in low concentrations in septic patients. In one study, endotoxin was detected in plasma samples of 74% of patients believed to be at risk who subsequently developed ARDS, 64% of patients who already had ARDS, and 22% of patients believed to be at risk who did not develop ARDS.[185] Exoproducts of bacteria, such as elastase and *Pseudomonas* exoenzyme U, also have been shown to injure the lungs.[186,187]

In addition to a direct role in the pathogenesis of lung injury, bacterial products may also have an indirect role by sensitizing the lungs to the effects of mechanical stretch. Gram-negative lipopolysaccharide (LPS) causes an acute inflammatory response in the lungs of humans.[188] Bacterial LPS enhanced the responses of human alveolar macrophages to positive-pressure ventilation,[189] and pretreatment of rats with intravenous LPS enhanced cytokine production in the lungs during mechanical ventilation ex vivo.[190] In turn, mechanical ventilation with moderate or large tidal volumes increases the sensitivity of lung macrophages to LPS in vitro, and increases the expression of the LPS recognition molecule, CD14, on lung cells in vivo.[191] Endotoxin recognition pathways are increased in the lungs of patients with ARDS, and the biologic effects of LPS are amplified in the lungs of patients with lung injury.[192,193] The synergism between bacterial products and mechanical stretch suggests that interrupting these pathways could limit some forms of acute lung injury in humans.

Increased pressure edema and increased permeability edema are associated with impaired antibacterial defenses,[194,195] and bacterial infections worsen acute lung injury in dogs,[196] baboons,[197] and hamsters.[198] The cause of impaired bacterial defenses in acute lung injury is not known. Bactericidal properties of the alveolar lining material might be altered in injured or flooded lungs, and alterations in surfactant concentration and function may be important.[199] Although PMNs may be present in large numbers in the bronchoalveolar lavage fluid of patients with acute lung injury, evidence indicates the function of these PMNs is compromised.[200,201]

Inflammation. Substantial evidence implicates host defenses and inflammatory responses in the underlying mechanism of many acute lung injuries. Neutrophils, complement, and other humoral mediators of inflammation, injury, and repair are discussed in detail in Chapter 17. The neutrophil has a dual role in inflammation and lung injury. PMNs are a vital component of host defenses, and patients with severe neutropenia are at increased risk of bacterial and fungal infections. On the other hand, PMNs release toxic oxygen radicals, proteases, and other biologically active mediators that initiate inflammation. Other important cells include alveolar[202] and pulmonary intravascular macrophages,[203] and eosinophils.[204] The major mediators of the acute inflammatory response (innate immunity) are listed in Table 51.5. Normally, the pulmonary circulation contains a very large pool of marginated PMNs,[205] which must change shape to squeeze through the lung capillaries. When PMNs are activated, they stiffen and become less distensible. Such PMNs are retained for longer periods of time in the pulmonary microcirculation. Endothelial activation leads to increased expression of leukocyte adhesion molecules, providing a second mechanism to slow the transit of PMNs through the lungs.[206] Trapped PMNs respond to chemotactic gradients generated by chemokines produced by alveolar macrophages and mesenchymal cells, and migrate into the air spaces.[207] Activated PMNs generate and release toxic substances (e.g., oxygen metabolites[208] and granular constituents, such as proteases, and cationic lysosomal enzymes) that disrupt the function of the microvascular and epithelial barriers, which normally limit liquid and protein flow out of the vascular space and into the alveolar spaces, leading to increased permeability edema.

Inflammatory responses also have the potential to induce injury to lung cells by activating cell death pathways, which

Table 51.5 Possible Inflammatory Mediators of Lung Injury

Chemotactic Factors
Complement fragments
Oxidized lipids
Alveolar macrophage derived
Metabolites of arachidonic acid

Toxic Oxygen Metabolites
Superoxide anion ($O_2^- \cdot$)
Hydrogen peroxide (H_2O_2)
Hydroxyl radical ($\cdot OH$)
Peroxynitrite
Products of lipid peroxidation
Myeloperoxidase–halide–hydrogen peroxide products
    Hypohalous acid
    Halogenated amines

Inflammatory Hormones
Monokines and lymphokines (e.g., interleukins, tumor
    necrosis factor, endothelin)
Growth factors

Adhesion Molecules
Integrins
Selectins

Proteolytic Enzymes
Leukocyte granular proteases
Kallikrein

Vasoactive Substances
Metabolites of arachidonic acid
Amines
Kinins
Platelet-activating factors
Nitric oxide

Clotting Factors

lead to apoptosis.[209] Bacterial products, such as *Pseudomonas* exoenzyme U, and mechanical stretch may lead to direct cellular necrosis.[186,187] Apoptosis is mediated by a family of death receptors,[210] which include the TNF receptors and the Fas receptor. The Fas ligand (FasL) is a 45-kd peptide that is shed from the cell surface by the action of metalloproteinases such as matrilysin. Biologically active soluble FasL (sFasL) accumulates in the lungs of patients with ARDS, and induces apoptotic death of human lung epithelial cells in vitro.[211] Human sFasL induces epithelial cell death in the lungs of rabbits,[212] and a monoclonal antibody that activates membrane Fas causes alveolar wall apoptosis and fibrosis in the lungs of mice.[212,213] Apoptosis and inflammation pathways intersect, as stimulation of membrane Fas induces cytokine production in human macrophages,[214] and inflammation in the lungs of rabbits and mice.[212,215] In addition, lung injury may be able to trigger apoptosis pathways in distant organs, such as the kidney, perhaps by increasing the concentrations of circulating sFasL.[216] Thus, inflammatory responses may trigger cell death pathways, and cell death pathways triggered by sFasL can induce inflammation in the lung alveolar environment. Recent human studies implicate apoptosis in human lung injury.[217]

Direct Toxicity. Inflammation is not required for all forms of acute lung injury. ARDS occurs in neutropenic patients,[218,219] and a clinical trial using granulocyte colony-stimulating factor to increase the number and activation state of circulating neutrophils in patients with severe pneumonia was not associated with an increased incidence of ARDS.[220] Lung injuries that do not require the participation of PMNs have been reported in animal models. Examples include injuries caused by ethchlorvynol in dogs[221]; by oleic acid in isolated dog[222]; by oxygen in rats[223]; by thrombin infusions in dogs[224]; and by *E. coli* endotoxin in rabbits,[225] and by *E. coli* septicemia in baboons.[226] Important species differences exist in the mechanisms involved. For example, in some species, PMN depletion lessens the injuries caused by oleic acid,[227] thrombin infusions,[228,229] and phorbol myristate acetate.[230]

Direct lung injuries are also thought to occur in humans. Putative agents that directly injure the lungs include mechanical forces during mechanical ventilation[231,232]; toxic and corrosive chemicals and gases (e.g., hydrochloric and other acids, ozone, ammonia, chlorine, phosgene, nitrogen dioxide, the vapors of cadmium and mercury, combustion products, and oxygen, especially at high concentrations); ionizing radiation; aspiration of fresh water (near drowning) or hydrocarbon compounds (e.g., kerosine, gasoline, and dry-cleaning fluid); high temperatures (parenchymal lung burns from fires or explosions); and mechanical injuries (e.g., lung contusion from nonpenetrating chest trauma or blast injury from explosions or lightning).

Many of these injuries develop rapidly, supporting the idea that injury is caused directly by contact with the respiratory epithelium in the airways, the alveolar walls, or both. It is likely that inflammatory pathways are rapidly activated after many types of direct lung injury, as probably occurs after aspiration of gastric secretions (one of the most common causes of clinical acute lung injury). Lung injury occurs rapidly, especially to the epithelium, and is related in part to the low pH of the aspirated stomach contents (aspiration of gastric contents with pH > 2.5 is relatively benign; aspiration of gastric contents with pH < 2.5 causes severe pulmonary injury). Aspirated acid is quickly neutralized when it contacts lung tissue, but within hours, proinflammatory mediators are released and the injured lung becomes infiltrated with PMNs; then fibrin accumulates in the alveolar spaces and further structural damage is seen on histologic examination.[233] The important role of mechanical stretch is suggested by the National Institutes of Health (NIH) ARDS Network study, which tested two different tidal volume settings in patients with established ARDS.[234] Patients ventilated with lower tidal volumes had a significantly lower mortality, and this was associated with a more rapid fall in circulating concentrations of interleukin-6 than in those receiving higher tidal volumes. In an earlier study, Ranieri and associates found that a lung-protective strategy of mechanical ventilation was associated with a faster decline in inflammatory parameters in bronchoalveolar lavage fluid, suggesting that reducing stretch reduces inflammation.[203,235]

DIAGNOSIS

The diagnosis of advanced pulmonary edema, particularly when caused by heart failure, is usually easy. Unraveling the cause of other kinds of pulmonary edema may not be so straightforward, particularly in patients with increased permeability edema.

CLINICAL ASSESSMENT

Symptoms and Signs

The clinical manifestations of pulmonary edema vary with its severity and depend on the underlying pathophysiology, and the extent to which excess fluid has accumulated in the lungs. Basic initial symptoms are dyspnea, cough, and tachypnea. Wheezing may be heard and may present a problem in differential diagnosis, but patients with asthma generally do not have other symptoms and signs of congestive heart failure or pulmonary edema.[236] Patients who develop increased pressure edema may complain only of vague fatigue, mild pedal edema during the day, or exertional or paroxysmal nocturnal dyspnea. Once alveolar flooding has occurred, the diagnosis of pulmonary edema is not subtle. Patients with alveolar edema usually have severe dyspnea, tachypnea, and cough that is often productive of frothy and sometimes blood-tinged edema fluid. Crackles and rhonchi are heard over the chest, and wheezing may be present. The patient may be cyanotic if alveolar flooding has seriously compromised gas exchange. Cheyne-Stokes respiration is common in severe congestive heart failure and does not necessarily portend a poor immediate prognosis.[237]

Development of edema is often insidious in increased pressure pulmonary edema because the alveoli are protected by the normal safety factors (see Table 51.1). In contrast, in increased permeability edema, alveolar flooding usually occurs rapidly and the onset of symptoms may occur over a short period of time. Edema that occurs suddenly (or unexpectedly) sometimes is called "flash pulmonary edema."

Because pulmonary edema is always a sign of an underlying pathologic process, its cause must be identified so that effective therapy can be directed at the underlying problem producing abnormal transvascular fluid and solute flow into the lungs. Increased pressure edema is usually caused by cardiac failure and thus is usually accompanied by a history of heart disease. This can include signs and symptoms of any of the causes of chronic and acute congestive heart failure, such as coronary insufficiency, hypertension, valvular heart disease, and severe volume expansion. Elevated jugular venous pressure, cardiac enlargement, gallop rhythms, heart murmurs, arrhythmias, large tender liver, and peripheral edema suggest an underlying abnormality of cardiac function. However, pulmonary edema may be the only manifestation of silent myocardial infarction or diastolic dysfunction of the left ventricle.[238]

History and physical examination may also be helpful in differentiating increased permeability edema from increased pressure edema and in identifying a possible cause of acute lung injury. Patients with increased permeability edema usually do not have signs or symptoms of underlying cardiac disease. The cause of acute lung injury may be suggested by a history of exposure (e.g., to toxic gases or chemicals, near drowning, drug ingestion, trauma), the clinical setting (e.g., sepsis, pneumonia, emesis, seizures, pancreatitis, burns, high altitude), or the physical findings (e.g., chest trauma, long bone fractures, coma, shock). Because infection and the sepsis syndrome are major causes of acute lung injury in humans, a thorough search must be made for signs and symptoms of an infectious cause. Pulmonary and intra-abdominal sources are the most common sites of infection, and all patients should be examined carefully, with special attention being paid to abdominal, rectal, and pelvic examinations. Most patients with acute lung injury are febrile, whether or not an infection is clinically apparent.

Diagnostic Studies and Definitions

Laboratory and other diagnostic studies are helpful, but by the time many of the results are abnormal, the diagnosis is usually obvious. In the special case of pulmonary edema suspected to be caused by salt water near drowning, measurement of plasma magnesium level can help determine whether or not a patient has aspirated or swallowed seawater, or both: Severe hypermagnesemia (6.7 mg/dL; normal range, 1.6 to 2.7 mg/dL) has been reported because of the high concentration (around 125 mg/dL) of magnesium normally found in seawater.[89] Appropriate cultures for microorganisms and toxicology screens of blood and urine are useful in identifying underlying causes of acute lung injuries. Sputum or trachea aspirate examination, bronchoscopy with protected-specimen brushing, or bronchoalveolar lavage with quantitative cultures are all useful in diagnosing pneumonia in ventilated patients, even those who are being treated with antimicrobial drugs.[169,171,172,239] Lung biopsy can provide a specific diagnosis in some patients with acute lung injuries,[240,241] but the results often are not helpful because lung injuries caused by diverse underlying conditions have the same appearance and because specific therapies may not be available.

The criteria for the diagnosis of acute lung injury have been somewhat controversial. Two definitions have gained some acceptance: the expanded definition of acute lung injury[242] and the American-European Consensus Conference definition.[243]

The expanded definition of acute lung injury has four elements (Table 51.6). The first element establishes the time at which the diagnosis is made and separates the group of patients suffering from the immediate consequences of acute lung injury from those who have progressed to more indolent, chronic disease. This is an important distinction because the causes of morbidity and mortality, appropriate supportive and specific therapy, and prognosis differ between the two phases. The second element is the actual Lung Injury Score (Table 51.7), which provides an assessment of the severity of lung injury, taking into account supportive therapy, such as mechanical ventilation with PEEP and oxygen supplementation. This score is important because not all lung injuries are of equal severity and severity changes over time. The term *acute respiratory distress syndrome* is applied only to the most severe injuries (those that yield a score of >2.5); milder lung injuries, termed mild to moderate, may have a better prognosis and may differ from ARDS in other important aspects. The third element, etiology, separates the many underlying disorders that can result in acute lung injury (see Table 51.4, which is not meant to be an exhaustive or exclusive list). Multiple etiologies may be present. Finally, the fourth element, which was separated when the expanded definition of acute lung injury was first proposed, recognizes the occurrence of injury to organs other than the lungs. This is important because injury is often not limited to the lungs. Dysfunction of other organs is common,[244] and prognosis varies between isolated pulmonary and generalized systemic disorders.

The Glasgow Coma Scale is widely used to assess neurologic status. Criteria have been proposed to evaluate abnormalities in renal, cardiovascular, hepatic, gastrointestinal,

Table 51.6 Expanded Definition of Acute Lung Injury

Phase (acute or chronic)
Lung injury score (see Table 51.7)
Etiology (underlying cause or association; see Table 51.4)
Nonpulmonary organ dysfunction

Table 51.7 Components and Individual Values of the Lung Injury Score

	Value
1. Chest Roentgenogram Score	
No alveolar consolidation	0
Alveolar consolidation confined to 1 quadrant	1
Alveolar consolidation confined to 2 quadrants	2
Alveolar consolidation confined to 3 quadrants	3
Alveolar consolidation in all 4 quadrants	4
2. Hypoxemia Score	
$PaO_2/FIO_2 \geq 300$	0
PaO_2/FIO_2 225–299	1
PaO_2/FIO_2 175–224	2
PaO_2/FIO_2 100–174	3
$PaO_2/FIO_2 < 100$	4
3. PEEP Score (when ventilated)	
PEEP ≤ 5 cm H_2O	0
PEEP 6–8 cm H_2O	1
PEEP 9–11 cm H_2O	2
PEEP 12–14 cm H_2O	3
PEEP ≥ 15 cm H_2O	4
4. Respiratory System Compliance Score (when available)	
Compliance ≥ 80 mL/cm H_2O	0
Compliance 60–79 mL/cm H_2O	1
Compliance 40–59 mL/cm H_2O	2
Compliance 20–39 mL/cm H_2O	3
Compliance ≤ 19 mL/cm H_2O	4

The final value is obtained by dividing the aggregate sum by the number of components that were used	
	Score
No lung injury	0
Mild to moderate lung injury	0.1–2.5
Severe lung injury (ARDS)	>2.5

PaO_2/FIO_2, arterial oxygen tension to inspired oxygen concentration ratio; PEEP, positive end-expiratory pressure.
From Murray JF, Matthay MA, Luce JM, et al: An expanded definition of the adult respiratory distress syndrome. Am Rev Respir Dis 138:720–723, 1988.

Table 51.8 American-European Consensus Conference Definition of Acute Lung Injury and Acute Respiratory Distress Syndrome

Timing
Acute
Oxygenation (regardless of PEEP level)
PaO_2/FIO_2 ≤300 mm Hg = acute lung injury
PaO_2/FIO_2 ≤200 mm Hg = acute respiratory distress syndrome
Chest Radiograph
Bilateral infiltrates on frontal view
Pulmonary Artery Wedge Pressure
≤18 mm Hg when measured, *or*
No clinical evidence of left atrial hypertension

PaO_2/FIO_2, arterial oxygen tension to inspired oxygen concentration ratio; PEEP, positive end-expiratory pressure.

and hematologic function, all of which can complicate or coexist with acute lung injury. The Acute Physiology and Chronic Health Evaluation (APACHE) II scoring system and the Simplified Acute Physiology Score have been used to define an individual patient's overall severity of injury.[245]

The American-European Consensus Conference Definition (Table 51.8) also has four elements: (1) timing (onset must be "acute"); (2) oxygenation (arterial PO_2/FIO_2 ≤ 300 mm Hg, regardless of the level of PEEP, for the diagnosis of acute lung injury to be made, and arterial PO_2/FIO_2 ≤ 200 mm Hg, regardless of PEEP level, for the diagnosis of ARDS to be made); (3) chest radiograph (bilateral infiltrates seen on frontal view); and (4) pulmonary artery wedge pressure (≤18 mm Hg when measured, or no clinical evidence of left atrial hypertension).

The two definitions differ in the exact criteria that must be met for a diagnosis to be established, but they identify similar patients[246] and are complementary. The power of the Consensus Conference definition is that it was reached by consensus, and that it is also easy to remember. The advantages of the expanded definition are that it provides a grading system (the Lung Injury Score) whereby equally injured patients can be grouped and compared and the progress (or lack thereof) of any individual patient's course over time can be measured; that it recognizes the distinct phases of the progression of lung injuries (early vs. late disease); that it separates out the different underlying conditions that can become associated with acute lung injury (conditions in which the exact etiology and mechanism of acute lung injury may differ); and that it recognizes and requires identification of associated extrapulmonary disease (which has profound effects on mortality of patients with acute lung injuries).

Despite these clinical criteria, defining acute lung injury and ARDS is not without problems.[247] The most serious deficiency of both definitions is the failure to link the underlying pathophysiology of acute lung injury to the functional abnormalities that are at the core of the definitions (i.e., data are lacking that link any particular arterial PO_2/FIO_2 to any particular change in the structure or function of the relevant barriers in the lungs or to the degree of edema). What defines acute lung injury in a meaningful way is the altered barrier permeability of the lungs. What defines ARDS in a meaningful way is structural damage to the lung microvascular endothelial barrier, the alveolar epithelial barrier, or both. Many respiratory disorders can reach the definitions' thresholds for "diagnosis," and many acute lung injuries, especially mild ones, fail to reach them at all. For example, bacterial pneumonia may not be a different disease when it crosses some arbitrary threshold and meets criteria for acute lung injury or ARDS; venous air emboli–induced and heroin-induced pulmonary edemas are acute lung injuries, even if they fail to disturb oxygenation sufficiently to satisfy an arbitrary definition of acute lung injury or ARDS. In small numbers of patients, the Lung Injury Score has correlated with bedside measurements of lung vascular permeability[248–250] and with the extent of abnormalities on computed tomography.[251]

The Consensus Conference definition also has limitations. First, it requires that timing be acute, but it neither specifies the degree of acuity required nor accounts for the considerable heterogeneity in the course of patients with acute lung injuries, each progressing, or not progressing, at its own given pace, through exudative, proliferative, and recovery phases. Second, it requires an arbitrary pulmonary artery wedge pressure (or no clinical evidence of left atrial hypertension), but left atrial hypertension or the lack thereof is not part of the basic pathophysiology of acute lung injury. It is the pulmonary microvascular pressure that matters when the lungs are injured, and that pressure can be low, normal, or (often) elevated. However, the Consensus Conference definition is simple to apply and has facilitated enrollment of patients in clinical trials.[93]

Both definitions have been faulted for failing to allow early diagnosis and for failing to accurately predict mortality.[252,253] Regarding mortality, the relevant question about any definition is not whether it can predict who will live and who will die, but rather whether it can correctly identify and distinguish who has acute lung injury and who does not. Death is often not directly related to acute lung injury, but rather to nonpulmonary organ dysfunction, chronic liver disease, or sepsis.[253] The severity of the oxygenation defect, which is what the definitions measure, does not have major prognostic value early in the course of clinical lung injury. Finally, assessment of the accuracy of definitions[246] is difficult because there is no "gold standard" for ARDS against which the accuracy of any given definition can be measured.

Chest Radiographs

The plain chest radiograph is the most practical laboratory study available for the detection of pulmonary edema.[254–257] Disadvantages are that chest radiographs are insensitive to small changes in lung water and are only semiquantitative.[1,258] An additional limitation is that chest radiographs are not consistently helpful in distinguishing increased pressure edema from increased permeability edema.[259–261] These disadvantages are balanced by the advantages that chest radiographs are noninvasive, inexpensive, easily repeatable, readily available, and free of side effects.

Before alveolar flooding, the plain chest radiograph can show distended vascular shadows (particularly in the upper lung fields), enlargement and loss of definition of hilar structures, development of septal lines (Kerley's lines), loss of peribronchial and perivascular definition (cuffing), and perihilar haze indicating the presence of interstitial pulmonary edema. Acinar shadows, often confluent and creating irregular, patchy increases in lung density that obscure vascular markings, indicate the presence of alveolar edema. Air bronchograms may be observed in severe edema. Because the radiographic signs of interstitial and alveolar edema are determined by gas and blood volumes and their distribution in the lungs in addition to the presence of edema, the recognition and quantitation of edema are not precise, and the radiographic appearance of edema is strongly influenced by the lung volume at the time the film is made. The chest roentgenogram score is an integral part of the Lung Injury Score, but the interpretation of chest radiographs is not well standardized and significant interobserver variations have been reported.[262]

Arterial Blood Studies

Although not specific, the arterial PO_2, PCO_2, and pH are the most informative laboratory indicators of overall pulmonary function in patients with pulmonary edema. Arterial blood studies are not sensitive to early edema. Arterial PO_2 may actually rise in the earliest stages of increased pressure edema because the increase in vascular pressures distributes blood flow more uniformly to well-ventilated units. Interstitial pulmonary edema does not usually affect oxygen uptake in the lungs beyond modest hypoxemia caused by ventilation-perfusion mismatching. In contrast, alveolar flooding seriously compromises gas exchange. Hypoxemia is due to right-to-left shunting of blood resulting from perfusion of alveoli that cannot be ventilated because they are fluid filled or collapsed. Ventilation-perfusion abnormalities also contribute to the hypoxemia of edema. In two studies of groups of patients with diverse lung injuries, oxygenation appeared to depend more on the vasoconstrictive ability of the pulmonary circulation (i.e., the ability to reduce perfusion of damaged and edematous areas of the lungs) than on the amount of edema present.[263,264]

Arterial PCO_2 is often low in edema, especially in the early stages, when tachypnea results in alveolar hyperventilation. An elevated PCO_2 (more common with severe edema) indicates alveolar hypoventilation, which can be caused by underlying lung disease, increased metabolic production of carbon dioxide (perhaps related to increased work of breathing), increased wasted ventilation (ventilation of poorly perfused alveoli or airways leading to flooded, nonventilatable alveoli), or mechanical impairment caused by weak respiratory muscles.[265] Elevated PCO_2 does not necessarily indicate a poor prognosis[266] and often resolves with treatment of pulmonary edema.

Acid-base disturbances are common in increased pressure edema but often do not correlate with severity, morbidity, or mortality.[267] When edema is mild, tachypnea results in hyperventilation and consequent respiratory alkalosis (and subsequent compensating metabolic acidosis). When edema is severe or the lungs have been injured, many patients develop metabolic acidosis as a result of tissue hypoxia, increased work of breathing, intrinsic lung lactate production, or all of these.[266,268] Attempts to correct acidosis with parenteral bicarbonate administration usually are not necessary; rather, the underlying cause must be identified and treated appropriately. Respiratory acidosis caused by

alveolar hypoventilation can be treated either by noninvasive ventilation or by invasive mechanical ventilation with endotracheal intubation. Metabolic acidosis can often be corrected by alleviating hypoxemia and improving cardiac function; the possibility of underlying disease amenable to surgery (e.g., intestinal ischemia or infarction, perforation of a viscus) or pancreatitis should not be overlooked.

Pulmonary Edema Fluid Protein Concentration Measurement

When florid pulmonary edema is present, measurement of protein concentration in simultaneously collected edema fluid (suctioned through an endotracheal tube) and plasma provides a rapid, noninvasive method for distinguishing increased pressure edema from increased permeability edema.[153] Because the microvascular barrier is functionally intact in increased pressure edema, plasma proteins remain largely confined to the intravascular space, and edema fluid protein concentration is low relative to plasma protein concentration (the ratio of edema fluid to plasma protein concentration is generally <0.65). Because the microvascular barrier is injured and cannot effectively confine plasma proteins to the vascular space in increased permeability edema, edema fluid protein concentration is high relative to plasma protein concentration (ratio of edema fluid to plasma protein concentration is generally >0.75). Intermediate values (between 0.65 and 0.75) may indicate that both types of edema are present and suggest the relative contributions of each. Measurement of the ratio of edema fluid to plasma protein concentration has been shown to be a simple method for separating the types of pulmonary edema in numerous reported series of patients with pulmonary edema.[77,269-274] Three studies indicated that an increasing protein concentration in serial measurements of edema fluid in acute lung injuries was a good sign, reflecting an intact epithelial barrier and net removal of edema fluid from the alveoli.[77,273,274] Such measurements need to be correlated with the patient's clinical condition, because an increasing protein concentration in edema fluid over time might also mean that increased permeability edema was complicating what had been increased pressure edema, or that the lungs were injured more severely or more extensively as time passed.

Edema fluid can be collected by inserting a standard 14- to 18-gauge catheter through an endotracheal tube and advancing it into a wedged position in the distal air spaces (similar to the procedure for wedging a bronchoscope). Gentle suction is applied as the catheter is slowly withdrawn, and fluid is collected in a small trap. Several attempts may be needed; if no fluid can be suctioned, the clinician should try changing the patient's position. Samples grossly contaminated with airway secretions (which have a very low protein concentration, <1.0 g/dL), such as mucus, pus, and debris, should be discarded. Protein concentrations can be measured by the clinical laboratory or estimated quickly at the bedside from the protein scale of a hand-held refractometer.

Bronchoalveolar lavage has been used as a research and diagnostic tool that may also yield useful information about the cellular biochemical and microbial composition of the air space,[153,275] but lavage is not useful as a method to measure alveolar protein concentration, because the instilled saline dilutes alveolar fluid by approximately 50- to 100-fold, depending on the method that is used.[153]

Pulmonary Function Tests

With the exception of arterial blood gas analyses, by the time results of conventional tests of pulmonary function are abnormal in patients with pulmonary edema, the diagnosis is usually obvious or the patient is too sick to study. The general sequence of developing abnormalities as edema accumulates was discussed earlier in this chapter. The earliest abnormality detectable by conventional studies in increased pressure edema is a rise in diffusing capacity of the lung for carbon monoxide caused by an increase in pulmonary capillary blood volume as a result of pulmonary vascular congestion. Closing volume may be greater when interstitial edema is present, but consistent changes in routine pulmonary function tests are generally not found until the alveoli begin to flood and vital capacity begins to diminish. Because pulmonary function tests are neither sensitive nor specific in edema, provide no information for separating the two types of edema, and are difficult to perform in patients who are ill, such tests are not useful in the diagnosis of pulmonary edema.

Hemodynamic Measurements

Pulmonary vascular pressures are sometimes recommended as helpful for differentiating increased pressure edema from increased permeability edema. However, measurement of vascular pressures in the lungs is expensive and invasive, and can be associated with significant morbidity and mortality,[276–278] although one recent study reported no excess morbidity or mortality in patients with ARDS who had a pulmonary arterial catheter inserted.[279] The problems with measuring and interpreting pulmonary artery occlusion pressures have been reviewed.[277,280–282]

MEASUREMENT OF LUNG WATER AND BARRIER FUNCTION

Measurement of the amount of water in the lungs could be useful in detecting early pulmonary edema and in assessing its clinical course and response to treatment. However, no ideal technique is available. Methods in use or under investigation focus on either measurement of lung density or equilibration of tracers with water in the lungs.[1,283] Interest in such measurements assumes that accurate knowledge about lung water would be useful in diagnosis and would be beneficial in the treatment of patients with pulmonary edema. Evidence supporting this assumption is meager, and measurement of lung water remains a research method rather than a clinical tool.

Lung Density Methods

Because lung density is determined by air and blood as well as extravascular tissue and water contents, densitometric techniques are only semiquantitative, and baseline lung densities vary widely. These techniques are most useful when

a series of studies can be compared in order to estimate changes in lung water content. They are of little use in early edema because lung fluid filtration can increase greatly before lung water content actually increases. The most widely used method is the plain chest roentgenogram, because it is readily available, is relatively inexpensive, is noninvasive, and can be repeated frequently at little risk to the patient. Unfortunately, it is insensitive (lung water must increase by >30% before being recognizable) and nonspecific (other interstitial or alveolar processes produce similar radiographic shadows). More precise density measurements may be made with techniques such as transmission computed tomography,[284,285] but the problem of separating changes in gas and blood volumes from changes in water content remains. Similar information may be gathered from transthoracic γ-ray attenuation[286] or Compton scattering.[287] It might be possible to relate changes in sound speed across the lungs to lung water content,[288] but such measurements would also depend on lung volume. A theoretically related technique, transthoracic bioelectric impedance analysis, attempts to relate the resistance to an alternating electrical current passed through the thorax to the amount of water in the lungs.[289]

Nuclear magnetic resonance imaging[290] and positron emission tomography[291] techniques for measuring lung water are also under investigation. Their theoretical advantages are the noninvasive measurement of density without ionizing radiation (in the case of nuclear magnetic resonance imaging) and lack of effects of ventilation and perfusion abnormalities; their disadvantages are that the hardware for both techniques is expensive and not readily available, and the slow scanning time and cumbersome equipment are not suitable for studying seriously ill patients.

Tracer Methods

Attempts have been made to assess lung water by measuring either the rates of equilibration of a diffusible indicator and an intravascular indicator (multiple-indicator dilution technique) or the uptake of inhaled gases (soluble-gas technique). Both methods have been the subject of considerable investigation, but neither method is in clinical use. These methods are limited by the inhomogeneous distribution of the tracers and the complexity of the equipment needed to make measurements.

Multiple-Indicator Dilution Techniques. These are invasive techniques based on measuring differences in transit-time volumes between two indicators, one nondiffusible (restricted to the intravascular space) and one diffusible (able to enter the extravascular space).[292] Suitable tracers are injected into a systemic vein or the right side of the heart, and time-concentration curves are recorded from a systemic artery. Because the diffusible tracer can in theory equilibrate with a much larger volume (extravascular and intravascular volumes) than the nondiffusible tracer (intravascular volume only), the differences in concentrations of the two tracers over time after traveling through the lungs can be used to calculate both blood flow and extravascular mass (mainly water) of the lungs.

Such techniques are limited by several factors: time, which may not allow the diffusible tracer to reach areas of the lungs remote from the microvascular bed; blood flow inhomogeneities, which restrict the tracers to perfused portions of the vascular bed; inhomogeneity of water distribution in the lungs; recirculation of the indicator; measurement of mass (e.g., dry lung, blood vessels, heart) in addition to water mass; and a host of technical details concerning the appropriateness of the indicators and the methods of their injection, withdrawal, and measurement, and calculation of concentration over time. The major problems are underestimation of lung water in pulmonary edemas in which uneven distribution of blood flow develops, which occurs in most lung injuries, and insensitivity (a 50% increase in measured lung water may be significant, but edema is obvious by that time).

Two methods have been the subject of considerable research, the thermal-dye method[293] and the multiple-isotope method.[294] The thermal-dye method has come closest to clinical use, and a refinement of the method (using a fluorescent indicator) allows measurements to be made with an indwelling catheter without blood withdrawal. The major problems are underestimation of lung water, particularly when vascular perfusion inequalities exist in the lungs or large volumes of edema are present, and accuracy of measurement of thermal changes.[295] Prospective evaluations of extravascular lung water measurements by the thermal-dye method versus pulmonary artery wedge pressures to guide the hemodynamic management of critically ill patients claimed superiority of the lung-water technique[296,297]; benefit may have accrued as a result of restrained fluid therapy. The multiple-isotope method requires blood withdrawal for tracer measurement and, like the thermal-dye method, underestimates water content if there is perfusion inhomogeneity.[298] This latter method appears to provide a better estimation of lung permeability—surface area product than of lung water content.

Measurement of Barrier Function

Because transvascular fluid flow into the lungs can be abnormal long before lung water content increases, and because the two types of edema can be separated on the basis of differences in barrier function, detection of increased transvascular fluid flow into the lungs and measurement of barrier integrity might be more helpful than measurement of lung water content in edema. Clinical distinction between increased pressure edema and increased permeability edema is difficult.[299] A simple and practical method exists to evaluate barrier integrity (edema fluid protein concentration measurements, discussed earlier), and several methods have been studied to detect early edema and changes in barrier function. However, none is in routine clinical use.

DETECTION OF LUNG INJURY

Because lung injury occurs before measurements of barrier integrity or transvascular fluid flow are abnormal, methods to detect lung injury before the appearance of abnormal liquid and solute transport might be of help. Early detection of lung injury would be especially valuable if therapies were developed on the basis of the mechanisms of lung injuries.

Although tests to determine the causes of lung injuries are not available, methods such as studies of the metabolic functions of the lung and a variety of specific lung injury makers are being investigated to detect whether lungs have been injured.

Changes in Metabolic Functions of the Lung

The lungs are involved in the metabolism of a variety of biologically active substances. Because the removal and metabolism of such substances depend on endothelial cell function, alterations in metabolic function in the lungs might be sensitive early tests of endothelial cell injury. Abnormal levels, activities, or uptakes of various substances (e.g., ACE, vasoactive amines, metabolites of arachidonic acid, endothelin-1, certain drugs) have been detected when the lungs are injured. Unfortunately, the finding of normal or abnormal uptake by the lungs is neither specific nor sensitive for all acute lung injuries; metabolic functions can be influenced by drugs, cardiac output, vascular surface area, and hypoxia or hyperoxia, and serious lung injury can occur without changes in metabolic function. Although alterations in metabolic functions of the lungs are not clinically useful indicators of endothelial cell function at this time, their potential use for early detection of lung injury justifies continuing investigation.

Biologic Markers of Lung Injury

Potential markers of acute lung injury were the subject of two comprehensive reviews.[153,300] There is considerable interest in finding a simple blood, urine, or bronchoalveolar lavage test that could identify patients at risk who are destined to develop acute lung injury, or who are in the earliest stages of acute lung injury, or that could predict the outcome of patients with injured lungs. To be of clinical use, such a marker would have to be practical and inexpensive to measure as well as sensitive and specific for acute lung injury; with the exception of measurements of edema fluid protein concentration relative to plasma protein concentration (discussed earlier), none is available. There may be many reasons for the lack of progress in identifying suitable markers: many (if not most) patients cannot be enrolled into studies of early or predictive markers because they already have injured lungs when they present or injury occurs very soon after the causative insult; ARDS is not a disease, but rather a symptom complex that may result from diverse causes; injury to the lungs is often overwhelming, and subtle differences in potential markers may be missed; measurements of potential markers in biologic fluids may not reflect what is happening at the tissue and cellular levels; and there has been limited uniformity among studies in diagnostic criteria and design (e.g., suitable controls, such as patients with increased pressure pulmonary edema and severe lung disease other than acute lung injury are often not studied; measurements of putative markers are often made at a single time, rather than regularly over the course of acute lung injury). The result is that it might never be possible to find a suitable single marker. However, progress has been made in studying biologic markers that have pathogenetic and prognostic significance.

Products of complement activation were proposed as markers but were later shown to be poorly correlated with lung injury.[301,302] Measurement of circulating endotoxin was not appropriately sensitive or specific for the presence or the risk of developing lung injury. Release or activity of ACE has not been found to be sensitive or specific for acute lung injuries. Von Willebrand factor antigen was useful as a plasma marker of impending acute lung injury in septic patients, and recent work confirms that von Willebrand factor antigen levels are elevated in the edema fluid and plasma of patients with acute lung injury and correlate with poor clinical outcomes.[303] Other biochemical and inflammatory markers have been found to have some association with lung injury and mortality, including most recently surfactant protein D.[304] Elevated levels of interleukin-6 in the plasma are also associated with mortality.[234] So far at least, no simple biologic marker has been identified that can be used as elevations in cardiac enzymes are used to diagnose acute myocardial infarction.

Because PMNs are associated with the mechanism of many lung injuries, detection of their presence in the lungs, tests of their function, or measurement of their toxic metabolites might be useful. For example, increased hydrogen peroxide has been measured in the breath and urine of patients with acute lung injuries,[305,306] presumably reflecting the presence of oxygen metabolites in their injured lungs. Evidence of oxidant activity was also reported in bronchoalveolar lavage fluid.[307] Other mediators of inflammation might be appropriately considered as well. For example, TNF-α has been detected in blood[308] and bronchoalveolar lavage fluid, but an association between TNF and the development of ARDS was not found,[309] and TNF was found to be elevated in patients with severe congestive heart failure[310]; various lipoxygenase products of arachidonic acid metabolism have been detected in pulmonary edema fluid,[146] bronchoalveolar lavage fluid,[311] plasma, and urine[312]; and elastase has been detected in bronchoalveolar lavage fluid.[313-316] In addition to these possible markers, sporadic reports of abnormal substances or abnormal levels of normally occurring substances detected in fluids obtained from small groups of patients with acute lung injury are continually being reported. Often, there is overlap between levels in patients who have acute lung injuries and those who do not. The results are often of interest to illustrate the wide variety of abnormalities that can be detected when the lungs are injured and to suggest the complexity of the underlying pathophysiology.

Because acute lung injuries follow a wide variety of insults and range in severity, and because many abnormalities detected in acute lung injury are found in other severe illnesses of diverse etiology that do not involve the lungs, it seems unlikely that any single marker will be found that unequivocally identifies the risk or the presence of acute lung injury. Focus on particular subgroups of patients with common causes of injury and study of much larger groups of better diagnosed patients might be helpful. An approach that has not received much attention is investigation of the sensitivity and specificity of combinations of markers. The new field of proteomics will expand this kind of investigation and perhaps identify patterns of protein abnormalities that can be found in the plasma, edema fluid, and bronchoalveolar lavage fluid of the air spaces of the lung in ARDS.[317,318]

TREATMENT

Treatment of pulmonary edema requires adequate life support followed by specific therapy directed at the factors that led to accumulation of water in the extravascular spaces of the lungs. Rational therapy also requires a correct diagnosis and an understanding of the nature of the underlying disease state and of the strategies that might prove useful in limiting further edema accumulation and favor fluid removal from the lungs.[319]

IMMEDIATE THERAPY

Patients with alveolar edema are often severely ill and require immediate treatment for acute respiratory failure. The basic principles of treatment of hypoxemic respiratory failure are discussed in Chapters 84 and 85. Essential requirements for patients with pulmonary edema include preservation of the airway, provision of adequate ventilation, and maintenance of satisfactory oxygenation. New methods for the noninvasive measurement of blood gases have made monitoring of their oxygen saturation possible, which can be useful in assessing the adequacy of oxygen support and the effects of therapy. Blood pressure and other forms of circulatory support may also be needed.

Hydrostatic Pulmonary Edema

If the patient is not hypotensive, morphine sulfate, 5 to 10 mg, or its equivalent, should be given intravenously slowly over several minutes (rapid injection can cause pulmonary vasoconstriction and increased permeability via histamine release from the lungs). Morphine is an extremely useful drug in the treatment of cardiogenic pulmonary edema because it is a potent vasodilator as well as a central nervous system sedative, and because it does not depress myocardial contractility. Its vasodilating effects can substantially reduce pulmonary capillary pressure and may improve depressed cardiac output. The work of the heart is lessened by the vasodilating, bradycardic, and sedative effects of morphine. Cautiously administered morphine usually does not cause respiratory failure or aggravate existing carbon dioxide retention associated with acute pulmonary edema, but the patient must be closely watched if he or she is not intubated and receiving assisted ventilation. Hypotension following morphine administration indicates that too much drug was given or that the intravascular volume is lower than suspected.

If medical care is not immediately available, two historical treatments for increased pressure pulmonary edema can be lifesaving. First, rotating tourniquets can act to reduce blood volume (and thereby pulmonary perfusion pressure) by trapping blood in the extremities, away from the pulmonary circulation. Tourniquets, or blood pressure cuffs inflated to less than systolic pressure, are applied to three of the four extremities and rotated every 15 minutes. The purpose is to decrease venous return, not to stop all blood flow to the extremities. Care must be taken that the tourniquets are rotated and that venous return from any extremity is not obstructed for more than 45 minutes at a time. A study of patients with left ventricular dysfunction following myocardial infarction showed trapping of considerable blood volume in the periphery by tourniquets, but variable and sometimes unfavorable effects on left ventricular function.[320] Second, phlebotomy[321] (100 to 500 mL) can be used to reduce blood volume in acute pulmonary edema when the patient is not in shock and if drugs and supportive care are not available.

When supportive care is available, positive airway pressure, supplied by a tight-fitting face mask[322,323] or by mechanical ventilation after endotracheal intubation, performs the same function as rotating tourniquets without risking loss of limbs: High pressure in the thorax impedes venous return and traps blood volume peripherally, which has the same usually beneficial but sometimes unfavorable effects on left ventricular function as tourniquets. Positive airway pressure, mechanical ventilation, or both can also help reverse some of the physiologic disturbances that can contribute to the development of pulmonary edema: improved oxygenation can increase myocardial oxygen supply, mechanical ventilation can be of benefit to decrease the work of breathing and thus lower the work of the heart, and left ventricular afterload can be reduced when positive pleural pressure replaces the wide swings in negative pressure that occur with spontaneous ventilation.

MAJOR OPTIONS

After emergency treatment has been instituted, there are three major therapeutic options: vasodilators, diuretics, and inotropic agents. The goal of therapy with these agents is to lower the hydrostatic pressure at the filtration sites in the pulmonary vascular bed while maintaining adequate systemic delivery of oxygen. The choice of therapy is dictated by the patient's condition and the cause of the pulmonary edema.

Perhaps the most controversial topic in management is the role of bedside right-sided heart catheterization. One prospective cohort study of critically ill patients showed that flotation heart catheterization was associated with increased 30-, 60-, and 180-day mortality.[278] Subgroup analysis did not reveal any patient group for which right-sided heart catheterization was associated with improved outcome, and patients with acute respiratory failure and multiple organ system failure were at greatest hazard to do worse when a pulmonary artery catheter was placed. This was an observational study, not a randomized clinical trial, and the reasons for lack of benefit from right-sided heart catheterization were not clear: the pulmonary artery catheter might directly worsen outcome, for example, if its risks and deleterious effects outweighed any benefits; benefits might not be realized if interpretations of hemodynamic measurements were incorrect (lack of skill and knowledge is a common problem in the interpretation of such measurements); the pulmonary artery catheter might be a marker for an aggressive style of care that increases mortality; or changes in therapy in response to hemodynamic information from pulmonary artery catheters might increase mortality. The study cohort appeared to exclude the possibility that right-sided heart catheterization was used in sicker patients, thus resulting in higher mortality (the patients with and without pulmonary artery catheters were matched for severity of illness). In addition to increased mortality,

bedside flotation heart catheterization was associated with increased costs and use of resources. As a result of this observational study, the National Heart, Lung and Blood Institute (NHLBI) is sponsoring several clinical trials to assess the clinical usefulness of pulmonary artery catheterization in critically ill patients.

As already noted, measurement of vascular pressures in the lungs is expensive and invasive and can be associated with significant morbidity and mortality; the problems with measuring and interpreting pulmonary artery occlusion pressures have been reviewed. Well-designed, controlled, randomized clinical trials of the advantages versus the disadvantages of right-sided heart catheterization in critically ill patients and in patients with acute lung injuries will provide a more rational basis for the use of flotation pulmonary artery catheters in patients with pulmonary edema. In fact, one recent clinical trial reported no clinical benefit from the use of pulmonary artery catheters in surgical patients with preoperative cardiac dysfunction.[324,325] A significant increased incidence of pulmonary embolism was found in patients who had pulmonary artery catheters inserted.

The only relevant vascular pressure in any type of pulmonary edema is that at the fluid exchange sites in the lungs, and this microvascular pressure varies independently from pulmonary artery systolic and diastolic pressures and from pulmonary arterial occlusion pressure ("pulmonary capillary wedge pressure") in many experimental and clinical conditions. The distribution of vascular resistance is usually abnormal in pulmonary edema. Venous resistance is often increased. An example is sepsis, in which pulmonary artery occlusion pressure is usually normal or low, but microvascular pressure may be markedly increased. The relevant microvascular pressure in the lungs can be estimated clinically by analysis of pressure transients recorded immediately after pulmonary artery occlusion. The technique uses a ruler to find the point at which the pressure recording after balloon occlusion of the pulmonary artery catheter most obviously deviates from the rapid, immediate fall in pressure to the later, slower decrease down to the wedge pressure. This point corresponds closely to the pulmonary microvascular pressure. There are problems with subjectivity of measurements, artifacts in pressure waveforms, respiratory variations, regional differences measured in heterogeneous conditions (e.g., acute lung injuries), and measurements made in the presence of high PEEP (the pulmonary arterial pressure tracing may reflect alveolar pressure if the catheter tip is not in zone 3 conditions). The same problems plague measurements of pulmonary arterial occlusion pressures, which provide limited information about the hydrostatic pressure at the microvascular fluid exchange sites in the lungs.

Vasodilators

Vasodilators are useful pharmacologic agents for treatment of acute increased pressure pulmonary edema. Their effects occur in minutes. Through dilation of veins, vascular capacitance is increased and blood is redistributed peripherally, thereby lowering the driving pressure for fluid filtration in the lungs; through dilation of arteries, systemic vascular resistance (cardiac afterload) falls, cardiac output and stroke volume increase, and the heart works more efficiently. In addition to morphine, three classes of vasodilators may be useful in pulmonary edema: venodilators (e.g., nitrates), arteriolar dilators (e.g., phentolamine, hydralazine), and mixed dilators (e.g., nitroprusside).

Sodium nitroprusside, a direct-acting venous and arteriolar dilator, is a commonly used agent in acute pulmonary edema. Its advantages are that the effects are immediate, its half-life is short, and cardiac output is maintained by arteriolar dilation and subsequent increased cardiac stroke volume even as central blood volume is lowered (thereby reducing pressure in the pulmonary vascular bed). Its main disadvantage is that invasive hemodynamic monitoring (i.e., an arterial cannula for continuous measurement of systemic blood pressure) is required because the dose must be carefully titrated to avoid profound hypotension. Prolonged infusions can result in cyanide or thiocyanate toxicity; the earliest sign is metabolic acidosis. Arterial oxygenation can deteriorate during therapy with any vasodilator if increased pulmonary blood flow and inhibition of hypoxia-mediated pulmonary vasoconstriction result in relatively increased perfusion of a nonventilated, fluid-filled, or collapsed lung. Therapy with both nitroprusside and nitroglycerin can be complicated by methemoglobinemia, and all nitrates can precipitate increased intracranial or intraocular pressure.

Nitroprusside is usually started at 10 µg/min by intravenous infusion and increased by 5 to 10 µg every 3 to 5 minutes until the desired effect is achieved. Arterial pressure should not be allowed to fall below 60 mm Hg diastolic, and peak systolic pressure should be kept higher than 90 mm Hg. Most patients require 50 to 100 µg/min to achieve the desired effects.

Nitroglycerin and other nitrates are also direct-acting vasodilators, but their predominant effect is on the venous capacitance bed. Intravenous nitroglycerin may be particularly useful in patients with increased pressure pulmonary edema associated with acute myocardial infarction or myocardial insufficiency. Nitroglycerin consistently dilates intercoronary collateral vessels, thereby improving blood flow to ischemic or marginally perfused regions of myocardium. Nitroprusside infusion does not consistently have this effect and may actually result in a decrease in collateral blood flow to ischemic regions of the heart. Nitroglycerin may also be useful in patients with borderline hypotension; because its effects (at least at lower infusion rates) are predominantly venodilating, systemic arterial pressure can be preserved while increased venous capacitance leads to lower driving pressures for fluid filtration in the lungs. At higher doses, nitroglycerin also exerts arteriolar dilator effects similar to those of nitroprusside. The major disadvantage of intravenous nitroglycerin is that invasive hemodynamic monitoring is generally required.

Intravenous nitroglycerin infusion is started at 10 to 15 µg/min and increased 5 to 10 µg/min every 3 to 5 minutes until mean arterial pressure falls (usually by >20 mm Hg), the pulmonary vascular pressure is brought to the desired level (if it is being measured), headache becomes intolerable, or angina (if present) is relieved. Development of tachycardia during nitroglycerin infusion can indicate that cardiac filling pressures and cardiac output have fallen to low levels. Nitroprusside, which preserves cardiac output, might be a more appropriate therapeutic option under this circumstance.

Isosorbide dinitrate can also be given intravenously. In patients with severe pulmonary edema, the combination of high-dose isosorbide dinitrate plus low-dose furosemide was found to be more effective (50% fewer acute myocardial infarctions) than the combination of high-dose furosemide plus low-dose isosorbide dinitrate. The onset of action of intravenous isosorbide dinitrate is rapid (peak vasodilation at 5 minutes), but the short half-life (about half an hour) requires frequent repeat dosing when it is given by bolus injection. Usually, 3 mg is injected intravenously every 5 minutes until oxygen saturation increases, arterial blood pressure falls more than 30%, or systolic pressure is less than 90 mm Hg. The effective cumulative dose is generally around 12 mg.

Other nitrates can also be useful, especially in increased pressure pulmonary edema, if the patient is not so critically ill that urgent intravenous therapy is required. *Transdermal nitroglycerin* ointment, 0.5 to 2 inches, and oral isosorbide dinitrate, 20 to 100 mg, are effective venodilators with prolonged duration of action (3 to 5 hours). The advantage of ointment is that it can be wiped off if necessary, but both agents have the disadvantage that effects cannot be as precisely controlled as in intravenous therapy. Tolerance to the effects of transdermal nitroglycerin can develop rapidly, but can be restored after a nitrate-free interval (usually overnight).

Other vasodilators may be useful in the treatment of selected cases of acute increased pressure pulmonary edema but have not been widely used. *ACE inhibitors*, such as captopril and enalapril, act both to reduce pulmonary vascular pressure and to increase cardiac output. The ACE inhibitors have proved to be useful agents in the treatment of more indolent pulmonary edema states. However, their use is not recommended in the setting of acute myocardial infarction. A placebo-controlled, randomized, double-blind clinical trial of intravenous enalaprilat (1 mg over 2 hours) in a small number of congestive heart failure patients with acute pulmonary edema showed reduced pulmonary capillary wedge pressure, increased renal blood flow, and slightly improved oxygenation with therapy.[326]

Diuretics

Patients with symptoms of pulmonary edema may also benefit from administration of diuretic agents.[327] These drugs may exert a modest immediate effect by increasing venous capacitance and decreasing the relative perfusion of flooded alveoli (acting as vasodilators), but their principal mechanism of action is to increase sodium and water excretion by the kidneys. The resultant diuresis causes a decrease in left ventricular volume and pressure, and thereby a reduction in the pressure at the filtration sites in the lungs. The effects of therapy may be delayed for hours to days. The potent loop diuretic *furosemide*, 20 to 40 mg by slow intravenous injection, is the most useful agent in pulmonary edema. Furosemide is equally effective when administered by continuous infusion: a loading dose of 80 mg is followed by a continuous infusion at 10 to 20 mg/hr; if there is no response in an hour, the loading dose is given again and the infusion rate is doubled. Equivalent doses of other loop diuretics (bumetanide, torsemide, or ethacrynic acid) should have the same effects. Because these drugs cause excretion of substantial amounts of potassium and chloride in addition to sodium and water, their use can be associated with severe hypokalemic, hypochloremic metabolic alkalosis, and an increased tendency for development of cardiac arrhythmias if potassium balance is not carefully corrected. Oral or parenteral administration of potassium chloride is usually necessary. Potassium-sparing diuretics, such as *spironolactone*, may also be of some benefit, but the delayed onset of their relatively mild diuretic action makes them less useful than the loop diuretics in the treatment of acutely ill patients.

If the patient is hypotensive or in frank shock, diuretics are usually not of much benefit, because poor renal perfusion limits any effects they might have on the nephron. In this circumstance, continuous venovenous ultrafiltration can reduce intravascular volume even in patients who require vasopressors for blood pressure support.

If the patient has severely diseased kidneys, diuresis may not be an option. In this circumstance, continuous arteriovenous hemofiltration with or without countercurrent dialysis,[328,329] or venovenous ultrafiltration,[330] should be considered. These techniques represent considerable advances over traditional hemodialysis, which was often impossible in hemodynamically unstable patients (especially those with low cardiac output or hypotension), and peritoneal dialysis, which was both slow and poorly tolerated. Hemofiltration can be instituted, maintained, and managed successfully by well-trained intensive care unit nurses and physicians, and it is not complicated by hypotension because the circuits have small volumes, and pressures are low. Considerable fluid (up to 200 to 300 mL/hr) can be removed gradually, with the amount being titrated to the patient's cardiovascular status.

Reduction of blood volume by diuresis (or other means) may not be possible or beneficial in all patients. If the patient is hypotensive, responds to intravascular volume reduction with dramatic decreases in cardiac output and delivery of oxygen to tissues, or develops significant tachycardia, another approach to therapy must be considered in addition to, or in combination with, blood volume reduction.

Inotropic Agents

Patients with pulmonary edema who have poor cardiac output and hypotension may benefit from inotropic agents, which can be useful in managing patients with hypotension caused by cardiac pump failure, mechanical ventilation, or therapy directed at reducing thoracic blood volume. Inotropic agents increase cardiac output and therefore can lower the driving pressure for fluid filtration in the lungs by improving myocardial contractility.

Catecholamines are the most useful agents in the acute situation. Actions of these drugs are related to the magnitude of their effects on α- and β-adrenergic receptors: α stimulation results in peripheral vasoconstriction; $β_1$ stimulation results in cardiac stimulation; and $β_2$ stimulation results in vasodilation (and bronchodilation). Relatively nonselective agonists, such as norepinephrine, increase cardiac contractility, but their usefulness is somewhat limited by their tendency to raise systemic vascular resistance (which in turn limits the improvement in cardiac output) and to increase myocardial oxygen consumption because of increased heart rate and afterload. The selective β-agonist isoproterenol causes large increases in cardiac output and decreases in pulmonary capillary pressure, but its vasodilatory effects often lead to reductions in arterial pressure and increases in heart rate. The myocardium may become increasingly irritable, and myocardial ischemia can be aggravated by reduction of arterial diastolic pressure. The drugs most commonly used to provide short-term, intravenous inotropic support in acute pulmonary edema are *dopamine* (the immediate precursor in the endogenous synthesis of norepinephrine) and the synthetic catecholamine *dobutamine*.

At low doses, dopamine increases cardiac contractility, improves cardiac output without causing significant changes in heart rate or myocardial oxygen consumption, reduces systemic vascular resistance, and can directly increase renal blood flow by stimulating dopaminergic receptors, thereby increasing urine output and salt and water excretion. It is particularly useful when hypotension complicates pulmonary edema; its vasopressor activity raises systemic blood pressure while cardiac output is maintained or increased. Ventricular filling pressures are often unchanged or even raised by dopamine infusion, however, and the pressure for fluid filtration in the lungs may actually increase. Venoconstriction may aggravate this stronger force for edema accumulation in the lungs by redistributing blood volume toward the thorax. For this reason, a vasodilator (e.g., nitroglycerin and nitroprusside) may also be given in order to reverse some of the undesired vasopressor effects of dopamine. When hypotension is a major concern, a predominant venodilator (e.g., intravenous nitroglycerin, nitroglycerin ointment) can be administered with dopamine to reduce thoracic blood volume while arterial pressure is supported. Dopamine can also be used to counteract hypotension caused by nitroprusside infusions. Measurement of pulmonary vascular pressure, in addition to systemic blood pressure, may be helpful when vasodilators are also being infused. As the dose of dopamine is increased, α stimulation begins to occur along with the release of endogenous norepinephrine from nerve endings. This produces a pressor effect but also increases heart rate, ventricular irritability, and arrhythmias. Increased filling pressures in the heart also aggravate the tendency for edema formation in the lungs. Intravenous dopamine therapy is started at 2 to 5 μg/kg/min, and the dose is titrated to produce the desired effects. Doses greater than 10 to 15 μg/kg/min are usually associated with prominent α effects, and such therapy may be complicated by arteriolar vasoconstriction so intense that digital necrosis may occur. Dopamine must be infused through a large-bore, secure catheter because tissue infiltration results in necrosis from local vasoconstriction.

Dobutamine differs from dopamine in that dobutamine does not cause systemic vasoconstriction. It is primarily a positive inotropic agent but also has a mild vasodilating effect. Dobutamine increases cardiac output because it has a direct inotropic effect and because systemic vascular resistance is decreased. Filling pressures in the heart tend to fall with dobutamine infusions (rather than rise, as with dopamine), which is beneficial relative to the forces governing fluid filtration in the lungs. Dobutamine might also increase the rate of alveolar fluid clearance,[331] but the clinical relevance of this effect is also unknown. Renal blood flow tends to increase with dobutamine infusions because cardiac output improves (rather than because renal dopaminergic receptors are stimulated, as with dopamine). Dobutamine is particularly useful for the treatment of pulmonary edema due to cardiac decompensation resulting from decreased ventricular contractility.

Dobutamine infusions are started at 2 to 3 µg/kg/min, and the dose is increased every 10 to 30 minutes until the desired effects are produced. Effects may be delayed several minutes, and the maximal effect of any dose occurs after 10 minutes or more. The usual dose is 5 to 15 µg/kg/min. Side effects are common when the dose exceeds 15 µg/kg/min. Arrhythmias may occur, and tachycardia indicates the dose is too high and stroke volume is not adequate. In this circumstance, myocardial oxygen demands are excessively increased by the rapid heart rate in the presence of positive inotropy. Myocardial oxygen supply is decreased because coronary perfusion pressures are reduced and diastolic perfusion time is shortened. Dobutamine therapy is most successful when left ventricular filling pressures are kept at 18 to 20 mm Hg or higher. Dobutamine should be administered cautiously to patients with atrial fibrillation because the drug facilitates atrioventricular nodal conduction and may cause an increase in ventricular rate. Digitalis may be a more appropriate inotropic agent in that circumstance.

The lives of a limited number of patients with severe pulmonary edema refractory to immediate drug therapies might be saved by temporary mechanical support of hemodynamics (i.e., intra-aortic balloon pumps or ventricular assist devices). Extrapulmonary gas exchange,[332] or heart transplantation, lung transplantation, or both[333] (see Chapter 89), can be appropriately offered to limited number of patients, but the possibilities can be considered only if all other therapeutic options have been exhausted.

THERAPEUTIC STRATEGY

The possible therapeutic options that have been discussed are directed at the immediate treatment of patients with life-threatening pulmonary edema. Therapy must be clearly goal oriented, responsive to the underlying pathophysiology, and frequently reassessed until the patient is stable. In hydrostatic pulmonary edema, the common goal of therapy is to reduce the transudation of fluid into the lungs. Because the rate of edema formation increases exponentially with increases in pulmonary vascular pressures,[334] pressure control is crucial for successful therapy.

Increased Pressure Edema

The acute recognition and management of congestive heart failure has been the subject of comprehensive reviews.[335] With hydrostatic pulmonary edema, the goal of therapy is to reduce the hydrostatic pressure causing edema formation in the lungs. The major objective is to achieve a net negative fluid balance without adversely affecting myocardial performance. The work of the heart must be reduced as much as possible by restricting physical activity and preventing pain and anxiety, which act to increase the work of

the heart by increasing sympathetic tone. As the heart fails, cardiac performance is reflexly preserved by progressive increases in vascular volumes that act to increase cardiac stroke volume and work (the Frank-Starling mechanism). This compensatory increase in preload of the left ventricle results in pulmonary venous hypertension and raises the driving pressure for fluid filtration out of the pulmonary microcirculation. As heart failure worsens, cardiac output falls, pulmonary and systemic venous pressures rise, systemic vascular resistance increases, and edema, in the lungs and in the periphery, becomes the major manifestation of compromised cardiac function. In patients with increased pressure pulmonary edema, a reduction of vascular volume and an increase in cardiac output cause the driving pressure for edema formation to decrease. Because the normal safety factors protecting the lungs from edema driven by high filtration pressures are intact, the pressure need be lowered only to near normal. At pulmonary capillary wedge pressures less than 20 mm Hg, fluid filtration in the lungs usually should not be sufficient to cause pulmonary edema. Patients with severe cardiac failure may tolerate higher pressures (because baseline barrier permeability is lowered in the lungs and lymphatic removal capability is increased) and may require such pressures to maintain cardiac output. Therapy is directed at reducing the work the heart must perform and at increasing the heart's efficiency for the work it must do. Some patients with severe hydrostatic pulmonary edema require mechanical ventilation with positive-pressure ventilation. The resolution of alveolar edema in these patients is not simply a function of lowering lung vascular pressures; other mechanisms that augment alveolar fluid clearance are important.[336]

Most patients with acute pulmonary edema caused by cardiac failure have systolic dysfunction, but a sizable minority (around 30%) have diastolic dysfunction. Cardiac contraction is normal, but relaxation is impaired. Because the ventricle does not relax normally, end-diastolic pressure is increased, thereby increasing hydrostatic pressure in the lung microcirculation. Acute diastolic dysfunction producing pulmonary edema is now recognized as a common manifestation of acute myocardial ischemia or uncontrolled hypertension. Other causes include diabetes mellitus, aortic stenosis, infiltrative cardiomyopathies, endocardial fibroelastosis, hypothermia, septic shock, elevated thoracic pressures from mechanical ventilation, and pericardial effusion. Causal or aggravating conditions should be corrected (e.g., revascularization for coronary artery disease, control of systemic hypertension). The goal of therapy in acute diastolic dysfunction is to lower elevated filling pressures (by the cautious use of diuretics and nitrates) without significantly reducing cardiac output. These patients are prone to develop hypotension in response to diuretics and nitrates because adequate cardiac output depends on elevated filling pressures in the heart. Because systolic function is normal, positive inotropic agents do not help and can actually aggravate ischemia.

In the setting of acute increased pressure pulmonary edema, it is especially important to identify and treat correctable causes of heart failure. Acute myocardial infarction, ongoing myocardial ischemia, arrhythmias, valvular lesions, systemic hypertension, ventricular septal rupture, rheumatic or other inflammatory myocarditis, digitalis intoxication, pulmonary embolism, infection, thyrotoxicosis, or severe anemia may have caused the heart to fail and must be corrected. Cardiac patients presenting with pulmonary edema may not complain of chest pain, but most of them have significant coronary artery disease, and pulmonary edema may be the only manifestation of silent myocardial ischemia.

Increased Permeability Edema

The strategy for managing patients with acute lung injury and increased permeability pulmonary edema differs from that for patients with increased pressure pulmonary edema because the endothelial and epithelial barriers are damaged in permeability edema, whereas they are normal in high-pressure edema. The problem is not that the driving pressure for edema formation is abnormally high, but that edema forms even at low driving pressures. The goals of therapy (Table 51.9) are to treat the cause of lung injury, to provide support while the repair phase begins, to select a ventilator strategy that will not worsen the lung injury, and to reduce as much as possible the driving pressures for fluid movement across the injured barriers into the lungs.

The cause of lung injury often may not be apparent. If the cause is not obvious, it should be assumed to be infection, which is the most common treatable underlying cause of acute lung injury. Although the patient is often seriously ill, diagnostic studies must be performed to identify a possible source of infection, so that appropriate drainage and antimicrobial therapy can be instituted. Plain chest roentgenograms usually are not helpful. Abdominal sonograms and computed tomographic scans can be diagnostically useful. Sepsis from intra-abdominal infection is common and may be especially difficult to identify. Many of these infections require surgical drainage if antimicrobial drug therapy is to be effective. Because specific therapy for acute lung injury is not usually available (unless the cause is a localized infection), supportive therapy is extremely important. The initial concerns are to support ventilation and circulation. Patients with acute lung injury may be hemodynamically unstable, and ventilatory support can be complicated by hypotension or frank shock. PEEP, which may be required for adequate oxygenation, may compound the problem by impeding venous return to the heart and decreasing cardiac function.

Patients with low pulmonary capillary wedge pressures (<10 mm Hg) and systemic hypotension may require fluid resuscitation to support blood pressure and end-organ perfusion. If the patient has active, ongoing blood loss or the hemoglobin concentration is low (<7.0 g/dL), packed red blood cells are effective not only to expand intravascular volume and restore blood pressure but also to increase the oxygen-carrying capacity of the blood. Patients who are not bleeding and who have normal hemoglobin concentrations should be resuscitated with crystalloid solutions. Because the barriers restricting colloid movement from the vascular space into the lungs are not functioning normally when the lungs are injured, osmotic pressure differences favoring fluid movement into the vascular space cannot be established in the lungs; therefore, there is no advantage to fluid resuscitation with expensive colloid solutions.

Patients whose hypotension does not respond to fluid resuscitation or who have normal (>10 mm Hg) or elevated pulmonary capillary wedge pressure may require pressors or positive inotropic agents. If systemic vascular resistance is elevated, dobutamine is appropriate. For patients with septic shock, generalized vasodilation resulting in low systemic vascular resistance is the major hemodynamic abnormality.[337] Dopamine and norepinephrine, with their vasopressor properties, are often useful to support blood pressure.

Strategies to reduce pulmonary capillary wedge pressure may increase the survival of patients with acute lung injury,[338] and currently a large clinical trial is underway to test this hypothesis. Pulmonary vascular pressures can be normal, increased, or decreased in patients with acute lung injury. Injured lungs are sensitive to the driving pressure for fluid extravasation because the barriers limiting fluid and protein flow out of the bloodstream are damaged. Many clinicians believe that the goal of therapy is to maintain the lowest possible pulmonary vascular pressures that are consistent with adequate cardiac output and perfusion of vital organs. If cardiac output is adequate, no pulmonary vascular pressure is too low; edema forms readily even at normal pressure in injured lungs. Because small reductions in the driving pressure for fluid accumulation in the lungs can substantially reduce edema, therapy with drugs that lower pulmonary vascular pressures may be useful. If hypotension is a problem, blood pressure can be supported by vasopressor therapy. Some studies have demonstrated that positive fluid balance is associated with a poor outcome in patients with acute lung injury.[338,339] As noted earlier, the role of cautious volume administration and reduction of pulmonary microvascular pressure is currently being tested in a clinical trial in patients with acute lung injury.

Acute lung injury and increased permeability edema is sometimes complicated by associated volume overload or left ventricular failure. In this circumstance, wedge pressure may be modestly elevated (15 to 20 mm Hg), and the therapeutic options available for increased pressure pulmonary edema (vasodilators, diuretics, and positive inotropic agents) would appropriately be considered.

Aggressive hemodynamic and ventilatory support of critically ill patients can be detrimental if complications of therapies become more significant problems than the underlying disease itself. Strategies to increase systemic oxygen delivery

---

Table 51.9 Acute Lung Injury: Important Principles of Management

Minimize Edema Accumulation
Ensure lowest possible pulmonary microvascular pressure
Reduce vascular volume

Find and Treat Infection

Supportive Therapy
Administer oxygen
Lung-protective ventilation strategy
Optimize blood pressure and cardiac output

Do more good than harm
Avoid hypotension
Avoid volume overload
Avoid oxygen toxicity
Avoid infection

(e.g., with inotropes, intravascular fluids, and blood transfusions) or to achieve supranormal values for the cardiac index or normal values for mixed venous oxygen saturation[340] do not reduce mortality. A multicenter, randomized, controlled clinical trial of transfusion requirements in critically ill patients with euvolemia after initial treatment showed that a restrictive strategy of red cell transfusions (in which red cells were transfused if the hemoglobin concentration dropped below 7.0 g/dL and hemoglobin concentrations were maintained at 7.0 to 9.0 g/dL) was at least as effective as and was possibly superior to a liberal transfusion strategy (in which transfusions were given when the hemoglobin concentration fell below 10.0 g/dL and hemoglobin concentrations were maintained at 10.0 to 12.0 g/dL), with the possible exception of patients with active coronary ischemic syndromes, such as acute myocardial infarction and unstable angina.[341]

Lung-Protective Ventilator Strategies. In experimental animals, ventilation with high tidal volumes can increase vascular filtration pressures; produce stress fractures of microvascular endothelium, alveolar epithelium, and basement membranes; and cause lung rupture (so-called ventilation-induced lung injury).[231,342,343] The injury appears to be due to increased lung excursions at high volumes (so-called volutrauma), not high airway pressure per se, because it can be prevented by limiting thoracic motion (e.g., by placing the chest in a cast). Because the evidence from animal experiments and small clinical trials seemed compelling,[344,345] clinical studies were done to test the potential benefit of lower tidal volumes and reduced airway pressures. In a large multicenter trial, mortality was reduced from 40% to 31% with a 6-mL/kg ideal body weight tidal volume strategy that also limited plateau airway pressure to less than 30 cm H_2O.[234] In this large clinical trial of 861 patients, the small tidal volume approach also was associated with a lower incidence of nonpulmonary organ failure. The protocol for

carrying out the lung-protective ventilatory strategy is described in detail in Table 51.10. The results of this trial have transformed management of patients with acute lung injury. In fact, a follow-up clinical study has indicated that ventilation with this level of tidal volume and plateau pressure limitation used in the original NIH ARDS Network trial is associated with an overall reduction of mortality to 26%.[346] In this study, elevated levels of PEEP did not decrease mortality, but the basic lung-protective strategy was validated as effective for reducing mortality.

Interestingly, results from an Italian study showed that a low tidal volume strategy in ARDS patients attenuated the inflammatory response in both the lungs and the bloodstream, as measured by a reduction in neutrophil and cytokine concentrations in bronchoalveolar lavage fluid and a reduction in cytokines in circulating blood.[235] Other studies have confirmed that low tidal volume lung-protective ventilation is associated with reduction in inflammatory markers in the lung.[234] There is also evidence that there probably is reduction in alveolar epithelial injury based on a decline in surfactant protein D levels in the plasma of patients treated with the lung-protective ventilatory strategy.[304] More clinical and experimental work is being done to determine the mechanisms responsible for the lung-protective effect. It is clear that use of the lung protective ventilatory strategy is not associated with an adverse effect on hemodynamics or an increased need for supportive therapies, including intravenous fluids, diuretics, vasopressors, sedation, or neuromuscular blockade.[346a]

A number of adjuncts to conventional mechanical ventilation have been proposed and studied in small numbers of patients, including prone positioning extrapulmonary gas exchange (oxygenation, carbon dioxide removal, or both),[347] liquid ventilation, tracheal gas insufflation, permissive hypercapnia, and high-frequency ventilation.[348] All of these adjuncts are investigational, and their use should probably be restricted to controlled clinical trials. Reposi-

Table 51.10 National Institutes of Health ARDS Network: Lower Tidal Volume Ventilation for Acute Lung Injury/Acute Respiratory Distress Syndrome Protocol Summary

Ventilator mode	Volume assist-control
Tidal volume	≤6 mL/kg PBW*
Plateau pressure	≤30 cm H_2O
Ventilation set rate/pH goal	6–35, adjusted to achieve arterial pH ≥ 7.30 if possible
Inspiratory flow (I:E)	Adjust flow to achieve I:E = 1:1–1:3
Oxygenation goal	55 mm Hg ≤ Pao_2 ≤ 80 mm Hg *or* 88% ≤ Spo_2 ≤ 95%
FIO_2/PEEP combinations:	

FIO_2	0.3	0.4	0.4	0.5	0.5	0.6	0.7	0.7	0.7	0.8	0.9	0.9	0.9	1.0
PEEP (cm H_2O)	5	5	8	8	10	10	10	12	14	14	14	16	18	18, 22, 24

(Further increases in PEEP to 34 cm H_2O allowed but not required.)	
Weaning	Attempts to wean by pressure Support required when FIO_2/PEEP ≤ 0.40/8

* Predicted body weight:
    Male PBW = 50 + 2.3 [height (inches) −60] *or*
            50 + 0.91 [height (cm) −152.4]
   Female PBW = 45.5 + 2.3 [height (inches) −60] *or*
            45.5 + 0.91 [height (cm) −152.4]

FIO_2, fraction of inspired oxygen; I:E, ratio of the duration of inspiration to the duration expiration; Pao_2, partial pressure of oxygen in arterial blood; PEEP, positive end-expiratory pressure; Spo_2, oxyhemoglobin saturation by pulse oximetry.
From Brower RG, Ware LB, Berthiaume Y, et al: Treatment of ARDS. Chest 120:1347–1367, 2001.

tioning the patient is the simplest and least invasive of these techniques.[349] Turning patients with severe respiratory failure to the prone position can result in improved pulmonary gas exchange[350] probably as a result of increased ventilation of dorsal lung units and more favorable matching of ventilation and perfusion. Turning critically ill, mechanically ventilated patients from the supine to the prone position is not an easy task, however, and there are risks involved (e.g., extubation, kinked ventilator tubing, disconnection of catheters, hemodynamic instability, pressure sores on the face). Not all patients respond by improving their oxygenation. A recently published randomized trial showed no benefit of prone positioning for patients with acute respiratory failure, including acute lung injury.[350a]

Prevention of ventilator-associated pneumonia has been the subject of a comprehensive review and a recent meta-analysis.[329] Although a relation between gastric colonization with gram-negative bacilli and nosocomial pneumonia in intensive care unit patients has been shown,[351] selective decontamination of the digestive tract does not appear to significantly improve mortality even though respiratory tract infections are prevented.[352] The simple approach of increasing the angle of the head of the bed to 45 degrees is beneficial in reducing nosocomial infection.[353] Simple precautions, such as meticulous handwashing and removal of unnecessary catheters, should be followed.

The literature from the patients' point of view is sparse: Only a few group studies and scattered personal observations about patient experiences in intensive care units have been reported.[354] No reports of what it is like to have pulmonary edema could be found. A critical care text has sections dealing with nursing perspectives but no section on patient perspective, and both nurses and patients are slighted in this textbook. The limited information available indicates that many patients had significant amnesia for most of their intensive care unit stay and poor insight into their condition. Many survivors experience depression, which tends to diminish over a prolonged recovery time. Some experience posttraumatic stress disorder. Patient experience and longer term outcomes are important areas that only recently have been better studied.[355]

Specific Pharmacologic Therapies. Therapeutic agents that have a rational place in our incomplete understanding of the pathogenesis of acute lung injuries and that have been studied in patients with acute lung injuries and sepsis disorders include corticosteroids, ibuprofen, nitric oxide, prostaglandin E_1 (PGE_1), liposomal prostaglandins E_1 and E_2, surfactant, antiendotoxin and anti–TNF-α antibodies, platelet-activating factor receptor antagonist, interleukin-1 receptor antagonist, ketoconazole, *N*-acetylcysteine, oxothiazolidine carboxylate, and pentoxifylline. None of these agents has shown any benefit on mortality in large-scale, prospective, randomized, controlled clinical trials. There have been sporadic reports indicating that other agents might be useful. The state of clinical trials in ARDS was the subject of conference reports in 1992,[356] and in 2000,[93] which summarized the status of possible therapies and the opportunities and challenges faced in evaluating them. The establishment of the ARDS clinical trials network by the NHLBI has already fostered the conduct of large, well-

designed studies to define the efficacy and appropriate use of therapy for acute lung injury; additional trials on the value of glucocorticoids late in the evolution of ARDS have just been completed, and a study on the efficacy of reducing lung vascular pressures is underway.

Whether or not newer anti-inflammatory therapies will be useful in patients with acute lung injury remains an important question. Although inflammatory reactions can damage tissue, it is important to remember that inflammation plays an important beneficial role in the elimination of invading microorganisms. Because inflammatory pathways are redundant, blocking any one inflammatory mediator (or even multiple mediators) may have little or no effect on the overall inflammatory response. If the mechanisms of lung injury differ after various clinical events, the application of therapy directed at particular mechanisms would not be appropriate until all the underlying mechanisms are recognized. The moderate incidence of severe acute lung injury among patients admitted with high-risk diagnoses[357] complicates the problem. Finally, the timing of therapy is likely to be an important factor.

Corticosteroids. Of the possible pharmacologic agents for treatment of acute lung injuries, corticosteroids have the longest history. Despite a seemingly compelling rationale for their use in the setting of acute lung injury from sepsis, four separate, prospective, randomized, double-blind, placebo-controlled trials of high-dose methylprednisolone therapy failed to show any benefit.[358] Corticosteroid therapy did not prevent the development of acute lung injury, or decrease its incidence in patients with the sepsis syndrome. Neither did it hasten the reversal of ARDS, lower mortality, or improve respiratory function. Moreover, corticosteroids were associated with both a greater 14-day mortality rate in patients who developed acute lung injury and an increased frequency of associated infections. Corticosteroids also were ineffective in the sepsis syndrome[359] and may have caused harm. Thus, corticosteroids should not be given to patients at risk for or with developing acute lung injuries unless there is some other indication, such as a history of recent steroid therapy or another reason to suspect adrenal insufficiency. One exception may be the fat embolism syndrome. A prospective, randomized, double-blind, placebo-controlled trial of corticosteroid treatment in 64 patients with long bone fractures showed that high-dose methylprednisolone effectively prevented the development of the fat embolism syndrome,[360] and short-course corticosteroid therapy appears to be appropriate in such patients, particularly in those who developed the characteristic petechial rash.

The generally disappointing results of corticosteroid trials in acute lung injury have not discouraged investigators. Because of the diversity of underlying causes and the changing character of acute lung injuries as they progress, some investigators believe that corticosteroids might be beneficial in subsets of patients or when given at a particular time (e.g., during the proliferative phase) or for a more sustained period.[361] Results of studies of corticosteroid therapy late in the course of ARDS (so-called rescue therapy) were encouraging, and a small (24-patient), randomized, double-blind, placebo-controlled clinical trial in patients with severe ARDS whose Lung Injury Score had failed to improve by the seventh day of respiratory failure showed improvement in lung injury and other organ dysfunction scores, and reduced mortality in the treated patients.[362] An NHLBI-sponsored trial of corticosteroid therapy beginning on day 7 of ARDS has been recently completed. The results demonstrated no reduction in 60-day or 180-day hospital mortality in patients treated with corticosteroids compared to placebo.[362a]

The decision to use rescue therapy (with corticosteroids or any other drug or therapeutic maneuver) is based on the assumption that the physician knows the expected outcome, but such predictions actually are quite uncertain. One major lesson learned from the experience with corticosteroids as early treatment for acute lung injury is that no matter how compelling the rationale for their use might be based on preclinical studies, well-designed and executed large-scale clinical trials must be conducted before a promising therapy is accepted for clinical use.

Surfactant. The possibility of administering exogenous surfactant in the treatment of acute lung injury has attracted considerable attention.[363] The rationale for such therapy is based on abnormalities of surfactant composition and function that have been found in acute lung injuries and on the approval of an artificial surfactant (colfosceril [Exosurf]) for clinical use. Surfactant therapy has revolutionized the treatment of neonatal respiratory distress syndrome. Among the many possible benefits of surfactant therapy are stabilized alveoli, improved respiratory compliance, decreased work of breathing, improved gas exchange and consequently decreased need to administer toxic concentrations of oxygen, and enhanced phagocytosis and bronchial transport; these advantages plus surfactant's antibacterial and antiviral activity should reduce the possibility of lung infection. Surfactant might also inhibit the respiratory burst of PMNs and might modulate lung fibroblast and macrophage activity to decrease release of inflammatory mediators.

Results in experimental models have been mixed, but, taken as a whole, they appear to indicate that animals are not harmed by surfactant therapy and that improved gas exchange and lung compliance are reasonable possibilities. A preliminary communication indicated that colfosceril could be administered safely to ventilated patients with sepsis-induced ARDS, but no differences were found in any physiologic parameters when compared with control subjects, and a dose-dependent trend in reduction of mortality did not reach statistical significance.[364] The pilot trial was followed by a large-scale, prospective, double-blind, randomized, placebo-controlled clinical trial of aerosolized surfactant in patients with sepsis-induced ARDS.[365] This study showed no significant effect on 30-day survival, length of stay in the intensive care unit, duration of mechanical ventilation, or physiologic function. A more recent large clinical trial of recombinant surfactant protein C demonstrated no reduction in mortality or in the duration of mechanical ventilation in patients with the acute respiratory distress syndrome.[365a]

Antioxidants. Clinically, *N*-acetylcysteine has advanced farther than any other therapeutic strategy because of the hypothetical role of oxidants in the pathogenesis of acute lung injury. *N*-acetylcysteine is unique among the free-radical scavengers because it is already in widespread clinical use for acetaminophen and paracetamol overdose, condi-

tions for which it has been found to be safe and effective. It is also novel among anti-inflammatory agents being tested for human therapy because it acts selectively to quench oxygen radicals rather than globally to suppress leukocyte function. *N*-acetylcysteine appears to act both directly, by scavenging oxygen free radicals, and indirectly, by metabolism into glutathione, which is an important endogenous antioxidant.

Experimental animal studies were encouraging. Results from a randomized, double-blind pilot trial in 30 patients with acute lung injury showed that plasma and red blood cell glutathione levels were decreased in the presence of acute lung injury and could be increased by *N*-acetylcysteine administration. Improvements were shown in chest radiograph edema scores, pulmonary vascular resistance, shunt fraction, static compliance, cardiac output, oxygen delivery, and oxygen consumption.[366] Four subsequent small clinical trials in acute lung injury patients examining the effects of *N*-acetylcysteine or oxothiazolidine carboxylate (Procysteine), which also acts to augment glutathione stores, have been reported. Enthusiasm for this type of therapy has been tempered by the possibility that antioxidants could compromise defenses against infection.

Pentoxifylline. Pentoxifylline is a phosphodiesterase inhibitor that increases cyclic adenosine monophosphate in PMNs and inhibits their inflammatory function.[367] Pentoxifylline has been in clinical use for many years in the treatment of intermittent claudication, based on its purported ability to increase the flexibility of red blood cells and thereby reduce blood viscosity and increase capillary blood flow. The hypothesized role of leukocytes in acute lung injury led to studies in experimental models that have demonstrated prevention or attenuation of various acute lung injuries in several species, apparently by inhibiting PMN function.[368] However, a related compound, lisofylline, failed to show efficacy in a large Phase III NHLBI trial.[369]

Treatments for Sepsis. Two different monoclonal antibodies against endotoxin have been investigated as therapy for sepsis, the most common antecedent to acute lung injury and ARDS: HA-1A human (also known as Centoxin or nebacumab) and E5 murine (also known as Xomen).[370] The underlying rationale for therapy with these agents and the two original clinical trials that were reported have been critiqued, an economic assessment of HA-1A monoclonal antibody for gram-negative sepsis has been made, and a detailed analysis of the original trials and the questions raised about them and regarding the cost and resulting ethical dilemmas[371] was published.

In patients with sepsis and a documented gram-negative infection who were not in shock, ARDS (as defined previously in a trial of corticosteroids in patients with acute lung injury) occurred in 14% of the patients in the E5 murine trial; 60% (6 of 10) of those treated with the E5 antibody died, compared with 78% (7 of 9) of those treated with placebo. In the second E5 trial, the antibody appeared to offer some protection against development of ARDS in sepsis patients, but there was no effect on survival.[370] In the HA-1A trial, acute lung injury (ARDS as defined by the expanded definition of acute lung injury) occurred in 11% of the patients with documented gram-negative bacteremia; data on the resolution of lung injury were not published, but major complications of sepsis, which included the patients with ARDS, resolved in 62% of the treated patients, compared with 42% of those given placebo. A subsequent publication discussed the results of HA-1A therapy in the 63 septic patients with ARDS from the larger trial: The antibody did not reverse acute respiratory failure or improve long-term survival.[372]

In addition to these antiendotoxin antibodies, large-scale clinical trials in patients with sepsis syndrome treated with inhibition of TNF-α[373] and of interleukin-1[374] have been reported. Neither showed a significant difference in mortality in patients who received the inhibitors as compared with those who received placebo. No differences in the frequency of continuing or new organ system failures, such as occurs in ARDS, were found in the anti–TNF-α trial. In the interleukin-1 receptor antagonist trial, a secondary analysis of the results indicated that survival time might have been increased for patients with ARDS (28-day mortality of 44% for placebo and 34% for antibody, with the improvement occurring in the sickest patients).

On the other hand, one large clinical trial has reported efficacy of activated protein C for reducing mortality in severe sepsis. In this randomized, placebo-controlled clinical trial, mortality was reduced by 6%.[375] The most common source of severe sepsis was pneumonia, and 75% of the patients were mechanically ventilated and 75% were in shock. Because of the potential for inducing serious bleeding, patients were excluded from the trial who had a history of recent surgery, recent bleeding, severe trauma, or other factors that would increase the risk of bleeding. The mechanisms by which activated protein C works to reduce mortality are probably multifactorial. There is evidence that activated protein C reverses the procoagulant environment induced by severe sepsis and also that it has anti-inflammatory effects that may reduce cytokine-induced organ injury. Because of the relationship of organ injury in severe sepsis to the pathogenesis of acute lung injury, there is interest in the possibility that treatment such as activated protein C might be efficacious for patients with acute lung injury.[376,377] Other therapies that might inhibit coagulation and inflammation are also potentially worth testing in clinical trials. There has been some controversy regarding the results of the activated protein C trial, and some experts have recommended further trials to evaluate the efficacy of this agent, particularly because two other clinical trials using anticoagulants did not show efficacy in patients with severe sepsis.

Prostaglandin E₁ and Inhaled Nitric Oxide. Another potential pharmacologic treatment of acute lung injury was PGE_1, a vasodilator with anti-inflammatory properties. However, a 13-center, randomized, double-blind, placebo-controlled clinical trial showed no improvement in survival (mortality rate at 30 days was 60% in the treated group, 48% in the placebo group).[378] Reduction in systemic and pulmonary vascular resistance and evidence of increased oxygen availability and consumption were counterbalanced by such adverse effects as diarrhea, hypotension, fever, and cardiac arrhythmias. The trial was not designed to resolve the role of PGE_1 in patients at risk for developing acute lung injury, so the question of any prophylactic benefit was left unanswered. A smaller, independent study from one institution found PGE_1 to be an effective vasodilator, but it did not influence the development of multiple organ failure or affect

mortality of patients with acute lung injury. A secondary report from the larger trial emphasized a purported benefit of PGE_1 on oxygenation in a subset of patients, even though survival was not improved; other studies have indicated that the drug causes deterioration of pulmonary gas exchange and aggravation of arterial hypoxemia by increasing perfusion of underventilated or unventilated lung areas. Another secondary report from the trial emphasized purported beneficial effects with PGE_1 therapy on hemodynamic performance, hepatic function, and leukocyte availability, but such effects were rather subtle, and their clinical significance was not obvious.

Inhaled nitric oxide can also improve oxygenation and lower pulmonary vascular pressure in patients with ARDS, but it does not lead to a sustained improvement in oxygenation as compared with conventional therapy,[379] and it has no beneficial effects on mortality.[380,381] Use of these drugs in patients with acute lung injury is not recommended, although inhaled nitric oxide may have some value as a form of rescue therapy for ARDS patients with profound hypoxemia.

OUTCOME

RESOLUTION OF EDEMA

Until recently, much less was known about recovery from pulmonary edema than about its formation. Water (and extravasated proteins and cellular debris) must be removed from the alveoli and the interstitial spaces to restore the lungs to their normal condition. Edema could be cleared from the lungs by five routes: lymphatics, airways, blood vessels, the pleural space, and the mediastinum. Cellular debris and particulate matter must be removed from the alveoli by macrophages or must be expectorated from the airways.

The considerable advances in our understanding of the clearance of fluid and solute from the alveoli have been the subject of several reviews.[2,382–384] Active sodium chloride transport across the alveolar epithelial barrier into the interstitium drives edema fluid removal from the air spaces (see Chapter 12). The uninjured alveolar epithelium has a remarkable ability to clear fluid from the air spaces rapidly: for example, serial edema fluid protein concentration measurements relative to simultaneous plasma protein concentrations in a salt water near drowning patient showed that 50% to 60% of excess alveolar fluid in the lungs was removed over the course of just 4 hours.[89] In experimental studies in rabbits, instillation of 4 mg/kg of seawater into the lungs resulted in a 300% increase in alveolar fluid volume in less than 5 minutes from mostly pure water drawn in osmotically from the plasma by the hyperosmolar (881 ± 29 mOsm) instillate, 80% of which was cleared from the alveoli in 6 hours.[385] Equivalent volumes of iso-osmotic (292 ± 6 mOsm) saline instilled into rabbit lungs were cleared at a similar rate. In neither circumstance was there evidence of injury to the alveolar epithelial barrier, which has been found to be more resistant than the endothelial barrier to a wide range of injuries, including ischemia, alveolar and intravenous endotoxin and bacteria, intravenous oleic acid, acid aspiration, salt water aspiration, hyperoxia, intratracheal bleomycin, septic and hypovolemic shock, and rewarming after severe hypothermia. Even when mild to moderate alveolar injury occurs, the capacity to transport salt and water is often preserved; in severe injury, when the barrier is physically disrupted, the capacity to clear edema is lost, of course, and the vascular endothelium becomes the limiting barrier between the vascular and air spaces. Clinically, the capacity to remove some alveolar edema fluid (as indicated by increase in the edema fluid–to–plasma protein concentration ratio) in the first 12 hours after the development of acute lung injury is a favorable prognostic finding, associated with a mortality of only 20%; in contrast, the inability to resorb alveolar edema fluid early in the course of acute lung injury was associated with a mortality of nearly 80%.[273] The results of this earlier study were confirmed in a larger, more recent study.[274] Thus, the function of the alveolar epithelial barrier early in the course of acute lung injury may be a useful prognostic index, perhaps because it serves as a marker of the severity and extent of lung injury.

Lung Na^+,K^+-ATPase activity was increased in rats recovering from experimental thiourea-induced increased permeability pulmonary edema.[386] Alveolar fluid clearance can be increased by salmeterol in uninjured, ex vivo human lungs.[387] Experimental studies have shown that alveolar fluid clearance can be increased pharmacologically (e.g., by catecholamines), even in the presence of acute lung injury and alveolar edema,[2] raising the potential of therapy to hasten the resolution of alveolar edema.

Because clearance of protein from flooded alveoli is much slower (1% to 2% per hour) than clearance of fluid (10% to 20% per hour),[382,388] the protein left behind becomes concentrated. The rising protein concentration in the alveoli as fluid is resorbed does not affect fluid clearance, because precipitated protein exerts no osmotic pressure and the concentration of soluble macromolecules is too small to counteract the differences in ion concentration resulting from transepithelial transport. Removal of fluid from flooded alveoli may be slowed, especially when lung vascular permeability is increased, if the fluid clots. Clotting can occur because extravasation of plasma into the air spaces may lead to activation of the clotting system by surfactant or macrophage-derived procoagulants.

Fluid cleared from alveolar spaces into the alveolar interstitium can leave the lungs by flowing into the lymphatic capillaries or by moving down the prevailing pressure gradient into the loose peribronchovascular connective tissue spaces or directly into the pleural space as well. Large amounts of fluid in the air spaces may be partially cleared into peribronchovascular cuffs through the hypothesized leaky terminal-airway epithelium,[389,390] leaving alveolar fluid and solute behind to be cleared more slowly through the more impermeable alveolar epithelium.

Most of the interstitial water in pulmonary edema is in the peribronchovascular loose connective tissue spaces rather than in the alveolar walls. Because the lymphatic capillaries are arranged to drain only the alveolar wall interstitium, this route for edema removal is not significant for most interstitial water. A study in goats showed that lung lymph originated mainly from alveolar wall interstitial fluid, and the contribution of the lung lymphatic system to the clearance of interstitial edema in bronchoalveolar cuffs and interlobular septa was small. The maximum possible contribution by lung lymphatics to the clearance of interstitial edema liquid

was below 10%, and airway loss of liquid by evaporation was about twice the rate of lymphatic clearance.[391] In a study of in situ perfused sheep lungs with experimental low- and high-protein pulmonary edema, during recovery from pulmonary edema, interstitial liquid was resorbed into the circulation in inverse proportion to its protein concentration, and only a very small fraction of interstitial edema was cleared by the lung lymphatics during recovery from either type of edema.[392] Some fluid from the loose peribronchovascular interstitium may drain directly into the bloodstream by crossing the walls of blood vessels in the lungs. A study of isolated sheep lungs made edematous by raising vascular pressures showed that the primary route of edema clearance was by vascular resorption; 60% of filtered water was cleared over 3 hours, 42% by resorption into the bloodstream, and 18% by lymphatic, pleural, and mediastinal drainage.[393] Edema may also drain into the pleural space. Pleural effusions are more common in increased pressure pulmonary edema (occurring in about 25% to 50% of patients, usually on the right side if the edema is unilateral), but are present in acute lung injuries as well (occurring in about 35% of patients).[394–396] Formation and removal of pleural effusions are discussed in detail in Chapter 68. As much as 25% to 30% of pulmonary edema fluid may leave the lungs through the pleural space.[396,397] A significant portion of the interstitial edema probably follows the prevailing pressure gradient in the lungs to drain into the mediastinum, where it could be picked up by initial lymphatics.

Short-term alveolar protein clearance appears to proceed primarily by paracellular diffusion and is size dependent.[7] Most proteins are cleared intact rather than being degraded into smaller fragments (although a few specific proteins, such as vasoactive intestinal peptide and gastrin, are degraded before being cleared). An albumin-binding protein (albondin) is expressed on lung microvascular endothelial cells, and an antibody to this protein reacts with cellular proteins of alveolar epithelial cells, which also appear to have albondin-like binding sites for albumin. A polymeric immunoglobulin receptor has also been described. The significance of these receptors is unclear. The general consensus is that transcytosis (transport via vesicles) is not a major mechanism for clearing bulk quantities of albumin or other proteins from the alveolar space. Over the long term, cellular mechanisms, principally phagocytosis and catabolism by macrophages, account for most protein clearance from the alveolar space. All insoluble, precipitated proteins are removed in this way. Macrophages are also ultimately responsible for removing senescent and dead PMNs and other debris. The small ciliated surface area of the distal air spaces seems to indicate that the mucociliary route could account for only a minor fraction of alveolar protein clearance, although proteins might reach the mucociliary escalator along currents in the alveolar fluid layer. Even were this to occur, removal would be very slow (the half-time for mucociliary clearance of particles from the alveolar space is more than 4 weeks). Complete clearance of alveolar protein from pulmonary edema by any route is slow.[7]

Little is known about the mechanisms and signals that regulate endothelial barrier function or how increased endothelial permeability is returned to normal.[398] The mechanisms of resolution of lung inflammation are also poorly understood.

INCREASED PRESSURE EDEMA

The outcome of increased pressure pulmonary edema is determined by the underlying cause and the treatment that is used. Because most increased pressure pulmonary edema is caused by heart disease, outcome is largely determined by the patient's cardiac function. Patients with pulmonary edema that is uncomplicated by acute myocardial infarction can be expected to do well (mortality rate, <10%).[399] In the presence of acute myocardial infarction, the prognosis is worse. However, thrombolytic therapy and coronary angioplasty and stent placement have improved the survival of patients with pulmonary edema complicating acute myocardial infarction. Patients who recover from increased pressure pulmonary edema caused by cardiac disease require long-term outpatient management aimed at preventing recurrent episodes.

Some patients develop increased pressure pulmonary edema from noncardiac causes. Most cases are iatrogenic, being caused by massive volume overload or therapy with drugs that can affect cardiac function. This is a common cause of pulmonary edema in pregnant women, as discussed in Chapter 81. These patients can be expected to do well if the cause of the edema is removed.[400]

INCREASED PERMEABILITY EDEMA

The incidence of acute lung injury is unknown. Many authors recite the 1972 NIH speculation that there are about 150,000 new cases each year (an incidence of about 75 cases per 100,000 population per year). Some estimates indicated that the NIH figure might have been too high,[401] but the large numbers of patients enrolled in the NHLBI ARDS clinical trials since 1996 suggest that the original NIH estimate may have been reasonably accurate. A careful prospective study in King County, Washington, with demographics similar to those for the United States also suggests that the original estimate of 75 to 85 cases per 100,000 is correct.[402] The outcome of acute lung injury and resultant increased permeability pulmonary edema is determined by the underlying cause, the extent of injury, and the treatment strategy. The reported mortality rates range from 20% to 90%, but yearly ARDS mortality rates reported from a single institution in the decade between 1983 and 1993 showed a significant decrease over time that occurred in patients younger than 60 years and in those with sepsis syndrome as their risk factor for ARDS.[403] In addition, the reported mortality in major epidemiologic and therapeutic trials of ARDS in the 20 years between 1975 and 1995 decreased. The explanation may be related to use of less injurious ventilator modes, more effective treatment of infection, and better nutritional supplementation.

Acute lung injury and increased permeability pulmonary edema are often complications that occur late in the natural history of other diseases. The prognosis worsens as the number and the severity of underlying diseases increase.[93] Patients with sepsis have significantly higher mortality than patients with other clinical disorders associated with the development of acute lung injury.[93] Medical patients have a higher mortality than surgical patients. Mortality is much higher in patients with chronic liver disease[253] or histories of chronic alcohol abuse.[404] Besides damaging the liver, chronic ethanol ingestion may reduce alveolar type II cell glutathione content and impair surfactant synthesis and secretion.[405] Mortality has been reported to increase with age, but the increased mortality of older ARDS patients might be due in part to decisions to withdraw supportive care, not to the medical futility of life-sustaining therapies for older patients.[406,407] Respiratory deaths are less common than deaths from the underlying disease, from nonpulmonary organ dysfunction, or from infection. Nosocomial pneumonia is an important clinical problem in patients who have sustained acute lung injury. Patients with self-limited causes of injury (e.g., venous air emboli, fat emboli, isolated lung contusion and other trauma, massive blood transfusions, postictal pulmonary edema, heroin pulmonary edema) and those with milder degrees of edema have a greater chance of survival and often clear their edema rapidly (Fig. 51.3).

The long-term outlook for patients who survive diffuse lung injury, even if it is severe, has improved.[408-411] Most recover to have normal chest roentgenograms, no complaints of dyspnea on exertion, normal lung volumes and airflow, and normal resting and exercise arterial blood gas findings and shunt fraction. Some patients have residual airway hyperreactivity. The most common abnormality is a reduced diffusing capacity, which tends to improve gradually. Not surprisingly, patients with the most days on positive-pressure ventilation and those with the lowest static lung compliance during the course of their acute lung injuries are most likely to experience residual pulmonary impairment. Laryngotracheal stenosis, a consequence of prolonged endotracheal intubation, should be considered in patients with persistent exertional dyspnea.[412] Histologic abnormalities usually also gradually regress. Some longer term patient follow-up studies demonstrate that a significant fraction of ARDS survivors have persistent disabilities 6 to 12 months after discharge from the hospital, although this may not be specific for ARDS but rather may be a consequence of critical illness.[355]

Healing often involves some degree of fibrosis.[413,414] The fibroproliferative reaction to acute lung injury seems to begin very early in the course of acute lung injury.[150,415,416] Patients who develop fibrosis are less likely to survive than those who do not.[417] How much of this problem is due to disease and how much to treatment is not known. It may be possible to modify vigorous fibrotic reactions to lung injury, but the consequences of such therapy are unknown. It might also be possible to accelerate reconstitution of alveolar structure in injured lungs; for example, keratinocyte growth factor (fibroblast growth factor-7), which promotes alveolar epithelial hyperplasia in rodents, reduced mortality when given as pretreatment to rats exposed to hyperoxia,[418] and soluble and insoluble fibronectin increased alveolar wound healing in vitro.[419] More information about repair and healing might open new possibilities for therapy.[414,420]

Although several pharmacologic therapies for ARDS have not been effective in decreasing mortality,[93,348] the 30% reduction in mortality achieved with a lung-protective ventilatory strategy represents a major advance in understanding how to prevent ventilator-induced worsening of lung injury in these patients.[234,346]

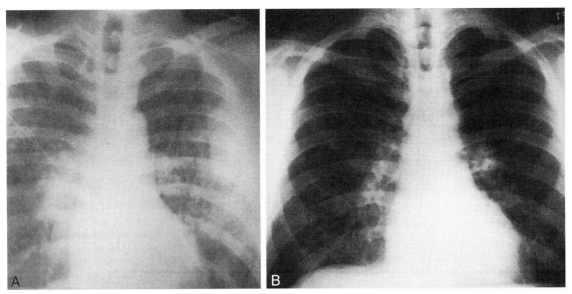

Figure 51.3 Chest roentgenograms in a patient with heroin-induced increased permeability pulmonary edema. **A,** At the time of the initial film, the heart was not enlarged, the vascular pedicle was normal, and edema was patchy, peripheral, and not gravitationally distributed. **B,** Forty-eight hours later, the chest film was normal and the patient had fully recovered. Increased permeability pulmonary edema may resolve rapidly if the initiating agent of lung injury is transient and mild, and the chronic phase of parenchymal lung injury (type II cell hyperplasia, fibrosis, connective tissue deposition, vascular remodeling) does not develop.

SUMMARY

Among the significant advances over the last 3 decades has been the acquisition of important new knowledge concerning the physiology of fluid, solute, and protein transport in healthy and diseased lungs. Pulmonary edema—the abnormal accumulation of extravascular fluid in the lung—is a pathologic state that occurs when fluid is filtered into the lungs faster than it can be removed. The many causes of pulmonary edema have been grouped into two main pathophysiologic categories: increased pressure edema that results from an increase in the hydrostatic or osmotic forces (or both) that act across the barriers that normally restrict movement of fluid and solutes in the lungs, and increased permeability edema from acute lung injury that results from a breakdown of the normal barrier properties of the endothelium or the epithelium of the lung, or both. Although these two different types of pulmonary edema share many features, they can usually be distinguished clinically and they have different treatment requirements and prognoses. This distinction is possible by careful clinical, radiologic, and physiologic evaluation. Major advances in the treatment of acute lung injury have occurred because of the successful application of lung-protective ventilatory strategies early to patients with clinical lung injury (see Table 51.10). A low tidal volume (6 mL/kg ideal body weight) coupled with a plateau pressure limit (<30 cm H_2O) is the first therapy proven to reduce mortality in patients with acute lung injury.[234,346] New insights into the pathogenesis of acute lung injury suggest that other therapies may also prove to lower mortality in this common syndrome of severe acute respiratory failure. A major development has been the ability to conduct large, prospective, randomized clinical trials sponsored by the NHLBI to test a variety of therapies that provide supportive care for patients, including mechanical ventilation, fluid therapy, and pharmacologic agents.

REFERENCES

1. Staub NC: Pulmonary edema. Physiol Rev 54:678–811, 1974.
2. Matthay MA, Folkesson HG, Clerici C: Lung epithelial fluid transport and the resolution of pulmonary edema. Physiol Rev 82:569–600, 2002.
3. Taylor A: Capillary fluid filtration: Starling forces and lymph flow. Circ Res 49:557–575, 1981.
4. Lai-Fook SJ: Mechanical factors in lung liquid distribution. Annu Rev Physiol 55:155–179, 1993.
5. Bhattacharya J: Physiological basis of pulmonary edema. *In* Matthay MA, Ingbar D (eds): Pulmonary Edema. New York: Marcel Dekker, 1998, pp 1–36.
6. Staub NC: The pathogenesis of pulmonary edema. Prog Cardiovasc Dis 23:53–80, 1980.
7. Hastings R, Folkesson HG, Matthay MA: Mechanisms of alveolar protein clearance in the intact lung. Am J Physiol Lung Cell Mol Physiol 286:L679–L689, 2004.
8. Erdmann AJ III, Vaughan TRJ, Brigham KL, et al: Effect of increased vascular pressure on lung fluid balance in unanesthetized sheep. Circ Res 37:271–284, 1975.
9. Guyton AC, Lindsey AW: Effect of elevated left atrial pressure and decreased plasma protein concentration on the development of pulmonary edema. Circ Res 7:649–657, 1959.
10. Drake RE, Dhother S, Teauge RA, et al: Lymph flow in sheep with rapid cardiac ventricular pacing. Am J Physiol 272:R1595–R1598, 1997.
11. Snapper JR: Lung mechanics in pulmonary edema. Clin Chest Med 6:393–412, 1985.
12. Javaheri S, Bosken CH, Lim SP, et al: Effects of hypohydration on lung functions in humans. Am Rev Respir Dis 135:597–599, 1987.
13. Noble W, Kay JC, Obdrzalek J: Lung mechanics in hypervolemic pulmonary edema. J Appl Physiol 49:681–687, 1975.

14. Lloyd T: Reflex effects of left heart and pulmonary vascular distension on airways of dogs. J Appl Physiol 49:620–626, 1980.

15. Lemen R, Jones JG, Graf PD, et al: Closing volume changes in alloxan-induced pulmonary edema in anesthetized dogs. J Appl Physiol 30:224–227, 1975.

16. Klingele TG, Staub NC: Terminal bronchiole diameter changes with volume in isolated, air-filled lobes of cat lung. J Appl Physiol 30:224–227, 1971.

17. Emery DL, Shown B, Batra G, et al: Changes in collateral ventilation with increased vascular pressure and edema formation. J Appl Physiol 53:70–74, 1982.

18. Ploysongsang Y, Zocchi L, Michel RP, et al: Partitioning of respiratory mechanics in pulmonary interstitial edema in dogs (abstract). Fed Proc 44:1910, 1985.

19. Hughes JMB, Rosenzweig DY: Factors affecting trapped gas volume in perfused dog lungs. J Appl Physiol 29:332–339, 1970.

20. Said S, Longacher JW, Davis RK, et al: Pulmonary gas exchange during induction of pulmonary edema in anesthetized dogs. J Appl Physiol 19:403–407, 1964.

21. Bernard GR, Pou NA, Coggeshall JW, et al: Comparison of the pulmonary dysfunction caused by cardiogenic and noncardiogenic pulmonary edema. Chest 108:798–803, 1995.

22. Bhattacharya J, Nakahara K, Staub NC: Effect of edema on pulmonary blood flow in the isolated perfused dog lung lobe. J Appl Physiol 48:444–449, 1980.

23. Murray JF: Effects of lung inflation on pulmonary arterial pressure in dogs with pulmonary edema. J Appl Physiol 45:442–450, 1978.

24. Raj JU, Bland RD, Lai-Fook SJ: Microvascular pressures measured by micropipettes in isolated edematous rabbit lungs. J Appl Physiol 60:539–545, 1986.

25. Hovig T, Nicolaysen A, Nicolaysen G: Ultrastructural studies of the alveolar-capillary barrier in isolated plasma-perfused rabbit lungs: Effects of EDTA and of increased capillary pressure. Acta Physiol Scand 82:417–431, 1971.

26. De Fouw D, Berendsen PB: Morphological changes in isolated perfused dog lungs after acute hydrostatic edema. Circ Res 43:72–82, 1978.

27. Coalson JJ, Jacques WW, Campbell GS, et al: Ultrastructure of the alveolar-capillary membrane in congenital and acquired heart disease. Arch Pathol 83:377–391, 1967.

28. Hurley J: Types of pulmonary microvascular injury. Ann N Y Acad Sci 384:269–285, 1982.

29. Bachofen H, Bachofen M, Weibel ER: Ultrastructural aspects of pulmonary edema. J Thorac Imaging 3:1–7, 1988.

30. Davies SW, Wilkinson P, Keegan J, et al: Pulmonary microvascular permeability in patients with severe mitral stenosis. Br Heart J 65:89–93, 1991.

31. Townsley M, Fu Z, Mathieu-Costello O, et al: Pulmonary microvascular permeability: Responses to high vascular pressure after induction of pacing-induced heart failure in dogs. Circ Res 77:317–325, 1995.

32. Felson B: Thoracic calcifications. Chest 56:330–343, 1969.

33. Schraufnagel DE, Patel KR: Sphincters in pulmonary veins: An anatomic study in rats. Am Rev Respir Dis 141:721–726, 1990.

34. Sande MA, Alonso DR, Smith JP, et al: Left atrial tumor presenting with hemoptysis and pulmonary infiltrates. Am Rev Respir Dis 102:258–263, 1970.

35. Charan NB, Turk GM, Hey DH: Effect of increased bronchial venous pressure on lung lymph flow. J Appl Physiol 59:1249–1253, 1985.

36. Lang SA, Maron MB: Hemodynamic basis for cocaine-induced pulmonary edema in dogs. J Appl Physiol 71:1166–1170, 1991.

37. Bland RD, Demling RH, Selinger SL, et al: Effects of alveolar hypoxia on lung fluid and protein transport in unanesthetized sheep. Circ Res 40:269–274, 1977.

38. Landolt CC, Matthay MA, Albertine KH, et al: Overperfusion, hypoxia, and increased pressure cause only hydrostatic pulmonary edema in anesthetized sheep. Circ Res 52:335–341, 1983.

39. van der Werff YD, van der Houwen HK, Heijmans PJM, et al: Postpneumonectomy pulmonary edema: A retrospective analysis of incidence and possible risk factors. Chest 111:1278–1284, 1997.

40. Bartsch P: High altitude pulmonary edema. Respiration 64:435–443, 1997.

41. Hultgren H: High-altitude pulmonary edema. In Matthay MA, Ingbar D (eds): Pulmonary Edema. New York: Marcel Dekker, 1998, pp 355–378.

42. Hackett PH, Bertman J, Rodriguez G, et al: Pulmonary edema fluid protein in high-altitude pulmonary edema. JAMA 256:36, 1986.

43. Schoene R, Swenson ER, Pizzo CJ, et al: The lung at high altitude: Bronchoalveolar lavage in acute mountain sickness and pulmonary edema. J Appl Physiol 64:2605–2613, 1988.

44. Matthay MA, Landolt CC, Staub NC: Differential liquid and protein clearance from the alveoli of anesthetized sheep. J Appl Physiol 53:96–104, 1982.

45. Matthay MA, Berthiaume Y, Staub NC: Long-term clearance of liquid and protein from the lungs of unanesthetized sheep. J Appl Physiol 59:928–934, 1985.

46. West J, Colice GL, Lee Y-J, et al: Pathogenesis of high-altitude pulmonary oedema: Direct evidence of stress failure of pulmonary capillaries. Eur Respir J 8:523–529, 1995.

47. West JB, Mathieu-Costello O: Vulnerability of pulmonary capillaries in heart disease. Circulation 92:622–631, 1995.

48. West JB, Mathieu-Costello O: Structure, strength, failure, and remodeling of the pulmonary blood-gas barrier. Annu Rev Physiol 61:543–572, 1999.

49. Huchon G, Hopewell PC, Murray JF: Interactions between permeability and hydrostatic pressure in perfused dogs' lungs. J Appl Physiol 50:905–911, 1981.

50. Jerome EH, Severinghaus JW: High-altitude pulmonary edema. N Engl J Med 334:662–663, 1996.

51. Grissom C, Zimmerman GA, Whatley RE: Endothelial selectins in acute mountain sickness and high-altitude pulmonary edema. Chest 112:1572–1578, 1997.

52. Kleger G-R, Bärtsch P, Vock P, et al: Evidence against an increase in capillary permeability in subjects exposed to high altitude. J Appl Physiol 81:1917–1923, 1996.

53. Kubo K, Hanaoka M, Hayano T, et al: Inflammatory cytokines in BAL fluid and pulmonary hemodynamics in high-altitude pulmonary edema. Respir Physiol 111:301–310, 1998.

54. Swenson E, Maggiorini M, Mongovin S, et al: Pathogenesis of high-altitude pulmonary edema: Inflammation is not an etiologic factor. JAMA 287:2228–2235, 2002.

55. Maron MB, Pilati CF: Neurogenic pulmonary edema. In Matthay MA, Ingbar D (eds): Pulmonary Edema. New York: Marcel Dekker, 1998, pp 319–354.

56. Smith WS, Matthay MA: Evidence for a hydrostatic mechanism in human neurogenic pulmonary edema. Chest 111:1326–1333, 1997.

57. Maron MB: Analysis of airway fluid protein concentration in neurogenic pulmonary edema. J Appl Physiol 62:470–476, 1987.

58. Simon R, Bayne LL, Tranbaugh RF, et al: Elevated pulmonary lymph flow and protein content during status epilepticus in sheep. J Appl Physiol 52:91–95, 1982.

59. Jones T, Townsley MI, Weidner WJ: Effects of intracranial and left atrial hypertension on lung fluid balance in sheep. J Appl Physiol 52:1324–1329, 1982.

60. van der Zee H, Neumann PH, Minnear FL, et al: Effects of transient intracranial hypertension on lung fluid and protein exchange. J Appl Physiol 54:178–184, 1983.

61. Peterson BT, Ross JC, Brigham KL: Effect of naloxone on the pulmonary vascular responses to graded levels of intracranial hypertension in anesthetized sheep. Am Rev Respir Dis 128:1024–1029, 1983.

62. Minnear FL, Barie PS, Malik AB: Effects of transient pulmonary hypertension on pulmonary vascular permeability. J Appl Physiol 55:983–989, 1983.

63. Luce JM, Huseby JS, Robertson HT: Increasing intracranial pressure with air causes air embolism, not neurogenic pulmonary edema. J Appl Physiol 50:967–970, 1981.

64. Townsley M, McClure DE, Weidner WJ: Assessment of pulmonary microvascular permeability in acutely prepared sheep. J Appl Physiol 56:857–861, 1984.

65. Kallet RH, Daniel BM, Gropper M, et al: Acute pulmonary edema following upper airway obstruction: Case reports and brief review. Respir Care 43:476–480, 1998.

66. Miller W, Toon R, Palat H, et al: Experimental pulmonary edema following re-expansion of pneumothorax. Am Rev Respir Dis 108:664–666, 1973.

67. Pavlin J, Cheney FW: Unilateral pulmonary edema in rabbits after reexpansion of collapsed lung. J Appl Physiol 46:31–35, 1979.

68. Trapnell D, Thurston JGB: Unilateral pulmonary oedema after pleural aspiration. Lancet 1:1367–1369, 1970.

69. Shaw T, Caterine JM: Recurrent re-expansion pulmonary edema. Chest 86:784–786, 1984.

70. Marland A, Glauser FL: Hemodynamic and pulmonary edema protein measurements in a case of reexpansion pulmonary edema. Chest 81:250–251, 1982.

71. Suzuki S, Tanita T, Koike K, et al: Evidence of acute inflammatory response in reexpansion pulmonary edema. Chest 101:275–276, 1992.

71a. Sue RD, Matthay MA, Ware LB: Hydrostatic mechanisms may contribute to the pathogenesis of human re-expansion pulmonary edema. Intensive Care Med 30:1921–1926, 2004.

72. Pavlin D, Nessly ML, Cheney FW: Increased pulmonary vascular permeability as a cause of re-expansion edema in rabbits. Am Rev Respir Dis 124:422–427, 1981.

73. Jackson R, Veal CF, Alexander CB, et al: Re-expansion pulmonary edema: A potential role for free radicals in its pathogenesis. Am Rev Respir Dis 137:1165–1171, 1988.

74. Heffner JE: Mechanisms underlying ischemia/reperfusion injury of the lung. In Matthay MA, Ingbar D (eds): Pulmonary Edema. New York: Marcel Dekker, 1998, pp 379–412.

75. Allison RC, Kyle J, Adkins WK, et al: Effect of ischemia reperfusion or hypoxia reoxygenation on lung vascular permeability and resistance. J Appl Physiol 69:597–603, 1990.

76. Ward BJ, Pearse DB: Reperfusion pulmonary edema after thrombolytic therapy of massive pulmonary embolism. Am Rev Respir Dis 138:1308–1311, 1988.

77. Ware L, Golder JA, Finkbeiner WE, et al: Alveolar epithelial fluid transport capacity in reperfusion lung injury after lung transplantation. Am J Respir Crit Care Med 159:980–988, 1999.

78. Modelska K, Pittet J-F: Increased-permeability edema following hemorrhagic and traumatic shock. In Matthay

MA, Ingbar D (eds): Pulmonary Edema. New York: Marcel Dekker, 1998, pp 299–318.

79. Albert RK, Lakshminarayan S, Hildebrandt J, et al: Increased surface tension favors pulmonary edema formation in anesthetized dogs' lungs. J Clin Invest 63:1015–1018, 1979.

80. Beck KC, Lai-Fook SJ: Alveolar liquid pressure in excised edematous dog lung with increased static recoil. J Appl Physiol 55:1277–1283, 1983.

81. Dodek PM, Rice TW, Bonsignore MR, et al: Effects of plasmapheresis and of hypoproteinemia on lung liquid conductance in awake sheep. Circ Res 58:269–280, 1986.

82. Parker RE, Wickersham NE, Roselli RJ, et al: Effects of hypoproteinemia on lung microvascular protein sieving and lung lymph flow. J Appl Physiol 60:1293–1299, 1986.

83. Bhattacharya J, Gropper MA, Staub NC: Interstitial fluid pressure gradient measured by micropuncture in excised dog lung. J Appl Physiol 56:271–277, 1984.

84. Lai-Fook SJ, Beck KC: Alveolar liquid pressure measured by micropipettes in isolated dog lung. J Appl Physiol 53:737–743, 1982.

85. Nieman GF, Bredenberg CE: High surface tension pulmonary edema induced by detergent aerosol. J Appl Physiol 58:129–136, 1985.

86. Bredenberg C, Nieman GF, Paskanik AM, et al: Microvascular membrane permeability in high surface tension pulmonary edema. J Appl Physiol 60:253–259, 1986.

87. Said S, Avery ME, Davis RK, et al: Pulmonary surface activity in induced pulmonary edema. J Clin Invest 44:458–464, 1965.

88. Seeger W, Wolf HRD, Stahler G, et al: Alteration of pressure-volume characteristics due to different types of edema induction in isolated rabbit lungs. Respiration 44:273–281, 1983.

89. Cohen DS, Matthay MA, Cogan MG, et al: Pulmonary edema associated with salt water near-drowning: New insights. Am Rev Respir Dis 146:794–796, 1992.

90. Folkesson HG, Effros RM: Aspiration syndromes: Acid, salt water, and fresh water. In Matthay MA, Ingbar DH (eds): Pulmonary Edema. New York: Marcel Dekker, 1998, pp 269–298.

91. Folkesson HG, Kheradmand F, Matthay MA: The effect of salt water on alveolar epithelial barrier function. Am J Respir Crit Care Med 150:1555–1563, 1995.

92. Ashbaugh DG, Bigelow DB, Petty TL, et al: Acute respiratory distress in adults. Lancet 2:319–323, 1967.

93. Ware LB, Matthay MA: The acute respiratory distress syndrome. N Engl J Med 342:1334–1349, 2000.

94. Cope DK, Grimbert F, Downey JM, et al: Pulmonary capillary pressure: A review (see comments). Crit Care Med 20:1043–1056, 1992.

95. Robbins I, Newman JH, Brigham, KL: Increased-permeability pulmonary edema from sepsis/endotoxin. In Matthay M, Ingbar, DH (eds): Pulmonary Edema. New York: Marcel Dekker, 1998, pp 203–245.

96. Gorin AB, Stewart PA: Differential permeability of endothelial and epithelial barriers to albumin flux. J Appl Physiol 47:1315–1324, 1979.

97. Montaner JSB, Tsang J, Evans KG, et al: Alveolar epithelial damage: A critical difference between high pressure and oleic acid induced low pressure pulmonary edema. J Clin Invest 77:1786–1796, 1986.

98. Pelosi P, Cereda M, Foti G, et al: Alterations of lung and chest wall mechanics in patients with acute lung injury: Effects of positive end-expiratory pressure. Am J Respir Crit Care Med 152:531–537, 1995.

99. Grossman RF, Jones JG, Murray JF: Effects of oleic acid-induced pulmonary edema on lung mechanics. J Appl Physiol 48:1045–1051, 1980.
100. Slutsky AS, Scharf SM, Brown R, et al: The effect of oleic acid-induced pulmonary edema on pulmonary and chest wall mechanics in dogs. Am Rev Respir Dis 121:91–96, 1980.
101. Gattinoni L, D'Andrea L, Pelosi P, et al: Regional effects and mechanism of positive end-expiratory pressure in early adult respiratory distress syndrome (see comments). JAMA 269:2122–2127, 1993 [published erratum appears in JAMA 270:1814, 1993].
102. Pelosi P, D'Andrea L, Vitale G, et al: Vertical gradient of regional lung inflation in adult respiratory distress syndrome. Am J Respir Crit Care Med 149:8–13, 1994.
103. Wright PE, Carmichael LC, Bernard GR: Effect of bronchodilators on lung mechanics in the acute respiratory distress syndrome (ARDS). Chest 106:1517–1523, 1994.
104. Gattinoni L, Pelosi P, Suter PM, et al: Acute respiratory distress syndrome caused by pulmonary and extrapulmonary disease: Different syndromes? Am J Respir Crit Care Med 158:3–11, 1998.
105. Byrne K, Cooper KR, Carey PD, et al: Pulmonary compliance: Early assessment of evolving lung injury after onset of sepsis. J Appl Physiol 69:2290–2295, 1990.
106. Tierney DF, Johnson RP: Altered surface tension of lung extracts and mechanics. J Appl Physiol 20:1253–1260, 1965.
107. Ryan SF, Ghassibi Y, Liau DF: Effects of activated polymorphonuclear leukocytes upon pulmonary surfactant in vitro. Am J Respir Cell Mol Biol 4:33–41, 1991.
108. Gregory TJ, Longmore WJ, Moxley MA, et al: Surfactant chemical composition and biophysical activity in acute respiratory distress syndrome. J Clin Invest 88:1976–1981, 1991.
109. Holm BA, Notter RH, Finkelstein JN: Surface property changes from interactions of albumin with natural lung surfactant and extracted lung lipids. Chem Phys Lipids 38:287–298, 1985.
110. Lewis JF, Ikegami M, Jobe AH: Altered surfactant function and metabolism in rabbits with acute lung injury. J Appl Physiol 69:2303–2310, 1990.
111. Kobayashi T, Nitta K, Ganzuka M, et al: Inactivation of exogenous surfactant by pulmonary edema fluid. Pediatr Res 29:353–356, 1991.
112. Lamy M, Fallat RJ, Koeniger E, et al: Pathologic features and mechanisms of hypoxemia in adult respiratory distress syndrome. Am Rev Respir Dis 114:267–284, 1976.
113. Dantzker DR, Brook CJ, Dehart P, et al: Ventilation-perfusion distributions in the adult respiratory distress syndrome. Am Rev Respir Dis 120:1039–1052, 1979.
114. Russell JA, Phang PT: The oxygen delivery/consumption controversy: Approaches to management of the critically ill. Am J Respir Crit Care Med 149:533–537, 1994.
115. Phang PT, Cunningham KF, Ronco JJ, et al: Mathematical coupling explains dependence of oxygen consumption on oxygen delivery in ARDS. Am J Respir Crit Care Med 150:318–323, 1994.
116. Nuckton TJ, Alonso JA, Kallet RH, et al: Pulmonary dead-space fraction as a risk factor for death in the acute respiratory distress syndrome. N Engl J Med 346:1281–1286, 2002.
117. Coss-Bu J: Dead space ventilation in critically ill children with lung injury. Chest 123:2050–2055, 2003.
118. Hill NS, Rounds S: Vascular reactivity is increased in rat lungs injured with alpha-naphthylthiourea. J Appl Physiol 54:1693–1701, 1983.
119. Hutchison AA, Ogletree ML, Snapper JR, et al: Effect of endotoxemia on hypoxic pulmonary vasoconstriction in unanesthetized sheep. J Appl Physiol 58:1463–1468, 1985.
120. Domino KB, Cheney FW, Eisenstein BL, et al: Effect of regional alveolar hypoxia on gas exchange in pulmonary edema. Am Rev Respir Dis 145:340–347, 1992.
121. Wiedemann HP, Matthay MA, Gillis CN: Pulmonary endothelial cell injury and altered lung metabolic function: Early detection of the adult respiratory distress syndrome and possible functional significance. Clin Chest Med 11:723–736, 1990.
122. Dvorak HN, Senger DR, Dvorak AM, et al: Regulation of extravascular coagulation by microvascular permeability. Science 227:1059–1061, 1985.
123. Idell S, Koenig KB, Fair DS, et al: Serial abnormalities of fibrin turnover in evolving adult respiratory distress syndrome. Am J Physiol 261:L240–L248, 1991.
124. Quinn DA, Carvalho AC, Geller E, et al: ^{99m}Tc-fibrinogen scanning in adult respiratory distress syndrome. Am Rev Respir Dis 135:100–106, 1987.
125. Ware LB, Fang X, Matthay MA: Protein C and thrombomodulin in human acute lung injury. Am J Physiol Lung Cell Mol Physiol 285:L514–L521, 2003.
126. Prabhakaran P, Ware LB, White KE, et al: Elevated levels of plasminogen activator inhibitor-1 in pulmonary edema fluid are associated with mortality in acute lung injury. Am J Physiol Lung Cell Mol Physiol 285:L20–L28, 2003.
127. Snow RL, Davies P, Pontoppidan H, et al: Pulmonary vascular remodeling in the adult respiratory distress syndrome. Am Rev Respir Dis 126:887–892, 1982.
128. Fein A, Grossman R, Jones J, et al: The value of edema fluid protein measurements in patients with pulmonary edema. Am J Med 67:32–38, 1979.
129. Bachofen M, Weibel ER: Alterations of the gas exchange apparatus in adult respiratory insufficiency associated with septicemia. Am Rev Respir Dis 116:589–615, 1977.
130. Pratt PC, Vollmer RT, Shelburne JD, et al: Pulmonary morphology in a multihospital collaborative extracorporeal membrane oxygenation project. I. Light microscopy. Am J Pathol 95:191–214, 1979.
131. National Heart, Lung and Blood Institute: Extracorporeal Support for Respiratory Insufficiency: A Collaborative Study in Response to RFP-NHLBI-73-20. Bethesda, Md: U.S. Department of Health, Education and Welfare, 1979.
132. Bachofen M, Weibel ER: Structural alterations of lung parenchyma in the adult respiratory distress syndrome. Clin Chest Med 3:35–56, 1982.
133. Albertine K: Ultrastructural abnormalities in increased-permeability pulmonary edema. Clin Chest Med 6:345–369, 1985.
134. Tomashefski JF Jr: Pulmonary pathology of the adult respiratory distress syndrome. Clin Chest Med 11:593–619, 1990.
135. Anderson WR, Thielen K: Correlative study of adult respiratory distress syndrome by light, scanning, and transmission electron microscopy. Ultrastruct Pathol 16:615–628, 1992.
136. Meyrick B, Brigham KL: Acute effects of *Escherichia coli* endotoxin on the pulmonary microcirculation of anesthetized sheep: Structure:function relationships. Lab Invest 48:458–470, 1983.
137. Schoene RB, Robertson HT, Thorning DR, et al: Pathophysiological patterns of resolution from acute oleic acid lung injury in the dog. J Appl Physiol 56:472–481, 1984.
138. Albertine K, Wiener-Kronish JP, Koike K, et al: Quantification of damage by air emboli to lung microvessels in anesthetized sheep. J Appl Physiol 57:1360–1368, 1984.

139. Meduri G, Eltorky M, Winer-Muram HT: The fibroproliferative phase of late adult respiratory distress syndrome. Semin Respir Infect 10:1184–1188, 1995.

140. Headley A, Tolley E, Meduri GU: Infections and the inflammatory response in acute respiratory distress syndrome. Chest 111:1306–1321, 1997.

141. Donnelly SC, Strieter RM, Kunkel SL, et al: Interleukin-8 and development of adult respiratory distress syndrome in at-risk patient groups (see comments). Lancet 341:643–647, 1993.

142. Goodman RB, Strieter RM, Martin DP, et al: Inflammatory cytokines in patients with persistence of the acute respiratory distress syndrome. Am J Respir Crit Care Med 154:602–611, 1996.

143. Park WY, Goodman RB, Steinberg KP, et al: Cytokine balance in the lungs of patients with acute respiratory distress syndrome. Am J Respir Crit Care Med 164:1896–1903, 2001.

144. Pugin J, Ricou B, Steinberg KP, et al: Proinflammatory activity in bronchoalveolar lavage fluids from patients with ARDS: A prominent role for interleukin-1. Am J Respir Crit Care Med 153:1850–1856, 1996.

145. Ricou B, Nicod L, Lacraz S, et al: Matrix metalloproteinases and TIMP in acute respiratory distress syndrome. Am J Respir Crit Care Med 154:346–352, 1996.

146. Ratnoff WD, Matthay MA, Wong MY, et al: Sulfidopeptide-leukotriene peptidases in pulmonary edema fluid from patients with the adult respiratory distress syndrome. J Clin Immunol 8:250–258, 1988.

147. Verghese GM, McCormick-Shannon K, Mason RJ, et al: Hepatocyte growth factor and keratinocyte growth factor in the pulmonary edema fluid of patients with acute lung injury: Biologic and clinical significance. Am J Respir Crit Care Med 158:386–394, 1998.

148. Madtes DK, Rubenfeld G, Klima LD, et al: Elevated transforming growth factor-α levels in bronchoalveolar lavage fluid from patients with acute respiratory distress syndrome. Am J Respir Crit Care Med 158:424–430, 1998.

149. Clark JG, Milberg JA, Steinberg KP, et al: Type III procollagen peptide in the adult respiratory distress syndrome: Association of increased peptide levels in bronchoalveolar lavage fluid with increased risk for death. Ann Intern Med 122:17–23, 1995.

150. Chesnutt AN, Matthay MA, Tibayan FA, et al: Early detection of type III procollagen peptide in acute lung injury: Pathogenic and prognostic significance. Am J Respir Crit Care Med 156:840–845, 1997.

151. Sittipunt C, Steinberg KP, Ruzinski JT, et al: Nitric oxide and nitrotyrosine in the lungs of patients with acute respiratory distress syndrome. Am J Respir Crit Care Med 163:503–510, 2001.

152. Zhu S, Ware LB, Geiser T, et al: Increased levels of nitrate and surfactant protein A nitration in the pulmonary edema fluid of patients with acute lung injury. Am J Respir Crit Care Med 163:166–172, 2001.

153. Pittet J-F, Mackersie RC, Martin TR, et al: Biological markers of acute lung injury: Prognostic and pathogenetic significance (State of the Art). Am J Respir Crit Care Med 155:1187–1205, 1997.

154. Koike K, Albertine KH, Staub NC: Intrathoracic sources of caudal mediastinal lymph node efferent lymph in sheep. J Appl Physiol 60:80–84, 1986.

155. Chanana AD, Joel DD: Contamination of lung lymph following standard and modified procedures in sheep. J Appl Physiol 60:809–816, 1986.

156. Laine G, Drake RE, Zavisca FG, et al: Effect of lymphatic cannula outflow height on lung microvascular permeability estimations. J Appl Physiol 57:1412–1416, 1984.

157. Adair T, Montani J-P, Guyton AC: Modification of lymph by sheep caudal mediastinal node: Effect of intranodal endotoxin. J Appl Physiol 57:1597–1601, 1984.

158. Bone RC, Fisher CJ, Clemmer TP, et al: Methylprednisolone Severe Sepsis Study Group: Early methylprednisolone treatment for septic syndrome and the adult respiratory distress syndrome. Chest 92:1032–1036, 1987.

159. Luce JM, Montgomery AB, Marks JD, et al: Ineffectiveness of high-dose methylprednisolone in preventing parenchymal lung injury and improving mortality in patients with septic shock. Am Rev Respir Dis 138:62–68, 1988.

160. Ziegler EJ, Fisher CJ, Sprung CL, et al: Treatment of gram negative bacteremia and septic shock with HA-1A human monoclonal antibody against endotoxin: A randomized, double-blind, placebo-controlled trial. N Engl J Med 324:429–436, 1991.

161. Anderson RR, Holliday RL, Driedger AA, et al: Documentation of pulmonary capillary permeability in the adult respiratory distress syndrome accompanying human sepsis. Am Rev Respir Dis 119:869–877, 1979.

162. Eisner MD, Thompson T, Hudson LD, et al: Efficacy of low tidal volume ventilation in patients with different clinical risk factors for acute lung injury and the acute respiratory distress syndrome. Am J Respir Crit Care Med 164:231–236, 2001.

163. Kaplan RL, Sahn SA, Petty TL: Incidence and outcome of the respiratory distress syndrome in gram-negative sepsis. Arch Intern Med 139:867–869, 1979.

164. Bell RC, Coalson JJ, Smith JD, et al: Multiple organ system failure and infection in adult respiratory distress syndrome. Ann Intern Med 99:293–298, 1983.

165. Torres A, Serra-Batlles J, Ferrer A, et al: Severe community-acquired pneumonia: Epidemiology and prognostic factors. Am Rev Respir Dis 144:312–318, 1991.

166. Montgomery A, Stager M, Carrico C, et al: Causes of mortality in patients with the adult respiratory distress syndrome. Am Rev Respir Dis 132:485–489, 1985.

167. Seidenfeld JJ, Pohl DF, Bell RC, et al: Incidence, site, and outcome of infections in patients with the adult respiratory distress syndrome. Am Rev Respir Dis 134:12–16, 1986.

168. Meduri GU: Host defense response and outcome in ARDS. Chest 112:1154–1158, 1997.

169. Sutherland KR, Steinberg KP, Maunder RJ, et al: Pulmonary infection during the acute respiratory distress syndrome. Am J Respir Crit Care Med 152:550–556, 1995.

170. Wiener-Kronish JP, Sawa T, Kurahashi K, et al: Pulmonary edema associated with bacterial pneumonia. *In* Matthay MA, Ingbar DH (eds): Pulmonary Edema. New York: Marcel Dekker, 1998, pp 247–267.

171. Delclaux C, Roupie E, Blot F, et al: Lower respiratory tract colonization and infection during severe acute respiratory distress syndrome: Incidence and diagnosis. Am J Respir Crit Care Med 156:1092–1098, 1997.

172. Chastre J, Trouillet JL, Vuagnat A, et al: Nosocomial pneumonia in patients with acute respiratory distress syndrome. Am J Respir Crit Care Med 157:1165–1172, 1998.

173. Brigham KL, Woolverton WC, Blake LH, et al: Increased sheep lung vascular permeability caused by *Pseudomonas* bacteremia. J Clin Invest 54:792–804, 1974.

174. Brigham KL, Bowers RE, Haynes J: Increased sheep lung vascular permeability caused by *Escherichia coli* endotoxin. Circ Res 45:292–297, 1979.

175. Traber DL, Adams T, Henriksen N, et al: Reproducibility of cardiopulmonary effects of different endotoxins in the same sheep. J Appl Physiol 54:1167–1171, 1983.

176. Gabel JC, Hansen TN, Drake RE: Effect of endotoxin on lung fluid balance in unanesthetized sheep. J Appl Physiol 56:489–494, 1984.

177. Judges D, Sharkey P, Cheung H, et al: Pulmonary microvascular fluid flux in a large animal model of sepsis: Evidence for increased pulmonary endothelial permeability accompanying surgically induced peritonitis in sheep. Surgery 99:222–234, 1986.

178. Brodgen K, Cutlip RC, Lehmkuhl HD: Response of sheep after localized deposition of lipopolysaccharide in the lung. Exp Lung Res 7:123–132, 1984.

179. Wiener-Kronish JP, Albertine KH, Matthay MA: Differential responses of the endothelial and epithelial barriers of the lung in sheep to Escherichia coli endotoxin. J Clin Invest 88:864–875, 1991.

180. Guenter CA: Role of leukocytes in the lung after endotoxin administration. Adv Exp Med Biol 23:77–85, 1971.

181. Kinnebrew PS, Parker JC, Falgout HJ, et al: Pulmonary microvascular permeability following E. coli endotoxin and hemorrhage. J Appl Physiol 52:403–409, 1982.

182. Chang JC, Lesser M: Quantification of leukocytes in bronchoalveolar lavage samples from rats after intravascular injection of endotoxin. Am Rev Respir Dis 129:72–75, 1984.

183. Heflin AC, Brigham KL: Prevention by granulocyte depletion of increased vascular permeability of sheep lung following endotoxemia. J Clin Invest 68:1253–1260, 1981.

184. Thomas PD, Hampson FW, Hunninghake GW: Bacterial adherence to human endothelial cells. J Appl Physiol 65:1372–1376, 1988.

185. Parsons PE, Worthen GS, Moore EE, et al: The association of circulating endotoxin with the development of the adult respiratory distress syndrome. Am Rev Respir Dis 140:294–301, 1989.

186. Sato H, Frank DW, Hillard CJ, et al: The mechanism of action of the Pseudomonas aeruginosa-encoded type III cytotoxin, ExoU. EMBO J 22:2959–2969, 2003.

187. Kudoh I, Wiener-Kronish JP, Hashimoto S, et al: Exoproduct secretions of Pseudomonas aeruginosa strains influence severity of alveolar epithelial injury. Am J Physiol 267:L551–L556, 1994.

188. O'Grady NP, Preas HL, Pugin J, et al: Local inflammatory responses following bronchial endotoxin instillation in humans. Am J Respir Crit Care Med 163:1591–1598, 2001.

189. Pugin J, Dunn I, Jolliet P, et al: Activation of human macrophages by mechanical ventilation in vitro. Am J Physiol Lung Cell Mol Physiol 275:L1040–L1050, 1999.

190. Tremblay L, Valenza F, Ribeiro SP, et al: Injurious ventilatory strategies increase cytokines and c-fos m-RNA expression in an isolated rat lung model. J Clin Invest 99:944–952, 1997.

191. Moriyama K, Ishizaka A, Nakamura M, et al: Enhancement of the endotoxin recognition pathway by ventilation with a large tidal volume in rabbits. Am J Physiol Lung Cell Mol Physiol 286:L1114–L1121, 2004.

192. Martin TR, Rubenfeld GD, Ruzinski JT, et al: Relationship between soluble CD14, lipopolysaccharide binding protein, and the alveolar inflammatory response in patients with acute respiratory distress syndrome. Am J Respir Crit Care Med 1515:937–944, 1997.

193. Martin TR: Recognition of bacterial endotoxin in the lungs. Am J Respir Cell Mol Biol 23:128–132, 2000.

194. LaForce F, Mullane JF, Boehme RF, et al: The effect of pulmonary edema on antibacterial defenses of the lung. J Lab Clin Med 82:634–648, 1973.

195. Mullane J, LaForce FM, Huber GL: Variations in lung water and pulmonary host defense mechanisms. Am Surg 39:630–636, 1973.

196. Esrig BC, Fulton RL: Sepsis, resuscitated hemorrhagic shock and shock lung: An experimental correlation. Am Surg 182:218–227, 1975.

197. Campbell GD, Coalson JJ, Johanson WG: The effect of bacterial superinfection on lung function after diffuse alveolar damage. Am Rev Respir Dis 129:974–978, 1984.

198. Johanson WG, Higuchi JH, Woods DE, et al: Dissemination of Pseudomonas aeruginosa during lung infection in hamsters: Role of oxygen-induced lung injury. Am Rev Respir Dis 132:358–361, 1985.

199. Wright J: Pulmonary surfactant: A front line of lung host defense. J Clin Invest 111:1453–1455, 2003.

200. Martin TR, Pistorese BP, Hudson LD, et al: The function of lung and blood neutrophils in patients with the adult respiratory distress syndrome: Implications for the pathogenesis of lung infections. Am Rev Respir Dis 144:254–262, 1991.

201. Chollet-Martin S, Jourdain B, Gilbert C, et al: Interactions between neutrophils and cytokines in blood and alveolar spaces during ARDS. Am J Respir Crit Care Med 153:594–601, 1996.

202. Sibille Y, Reynolds HY: Macrophages and polymorphonuclear neutrophils in lung defense and injury: State of the art. Am Rev Respir Dis 141:471–501, 1990.

203. Warner AE, Brain JD: The cell biology and pathogenic role of pulmonary intravascular macrophages. Am J Physiol 258:L1–L12, 1990.

204. Hoidal JR: The eosinophil and acute lung injury. Am Rev Respir Dis 142:1245–1246, 1990.

205. Hogg JC, Doerschuk CM: Leukocyte traffic in the lung. Annu Rev Physiol 57:97–114, 1995.

206. Mulligan MS, Varani J, Dame MK, et al: Role of endothelial-leukocyte adhesion molecule 1 (ELAM-1) in neutrophil-mediated lung injury in rats. J Clin Invest 88:1396–1406, 1991.

207. Albelda SM: Endothelial and epithelial cell adhesion molecules. Am J Respir Cell Mol Biol 4:195–203, 1991.

208. Weiss SJ: Tissue destruction by neutrophils. N Engl J Med 320:365–376, 1989.

209. Martin TR, Nakamura M, Matute-Bello G: The role of apoptosis in acute lung injury. Crit Care Med 31:S184–S188, 2003.

210. Kuwano K, Hara N: Signal transduction pathways of apoptosis and inflammation induced by the tumor necrosis factor receptor family. Am J Respir Cell Mol Biol 22:147–149, 2000.

211. Matute-Bello G, Liles WC, Steinberg KP, et al: Soluble Fas-ligand induces epithelial cell apoptosis in humans with acute lung injury (ARDS). J Immunol 163:2217–2225, 1999.

212. Matute-Bello G, Winn RK, Jonas M, et al: Fas (CD95) induces alveolar epithelial cell apoptosis in vivo: Implications for acute pulmonary inflammation. Am J Pathol 158:153–161, 2001.

213. Hagimoto N, Kuwano K, Miyazaki H, et al: Induction of apoptosis and pulmonary fibrosis in mice in response to ligation of Fas antigen. Am J Respir Cell Mol Biol 17:272–278, 1997.

214. Park DR, Thomsen AR, Frevert CW, et al: Fas (CD95) induces pro-inflammatory cytokine responses by human monocytes and monocyte-derived macrophages. J Immunol 170:6209–6216, 2003.

215. Matute-Bello G, Liles WC, Frevert CW, et al: Recombinant human Fas ligand induces alveolar epithelial cell apoptosis and lung injury in rabbits. Am J Physiol Lung Cell Mol Physiol 281:L328–L335, 2001.

216. Imai Y, Parodo J, Kajikawa O, et al: Injurious mechanical ventilation and end-organ epithelial cell apoptosis and organ dysfunction in an experimental model of acute respiratory distress syndrome. JAMA 289:2104–2112, 2003.

217. Albertine K, Soulier MF, Wang Z, et al: Fas and Fas ligand are up-regulated in pulmonary edema fluid and lung tissue of patients with acute lung injury and the acute respiratory distress syndrome. Am J Pathol 161:1783–1796, 2002.

218. Laufe MD, Simon RH, Flint A, et al: Adult respiratory distress syndrome in neutropenic patients. Am J Med 80:1022–1026, 1986.

219. Maunder RJ, Hackman RC, Riff E, et al: Occurrence of the adult respiratory distress syndrome in neutropenic patients. Am Rev Respir Dis 133:313–316, 1986.

220. Nelson S, Belknap SM, Carlson RW, et al: A randomized controlled trial of filgrastim as an adjunct to antibiotics for treatment of hospitalized patients with community-acquired pneumonia. J Infect Dis 178:1075–1080, 1998.

221. Fairman RP, Glauser FL, Falls R: Increases in lung lymph and albumin clearance with ethchlorvynol. J Appl Physiol 50:1151–1155, 1981.

222. Hofman WF, Ehrhart IC: Permeability edema in dog lung depleted of blood components. J Appl Physiol 57:147–153, 1984.

223. Schwartz JS, Spragg RG, Loomis WH, et al: Oleic acid causes high permeability edema in blood-free perfused rabbit lungs (abstract). Clin Res 30:74A, 1982.

224. Lindquist P, Saldeen T, Sandler H: Pulmonary damage following pulmonary microembolism in the dog: Effect of various types of treatment. Acta Clin Scand 142:15–19, 1976.

225. Gaynor E: The role of granulocytes in endotoxin-induced vascular injury. Blood 41:797–808, 1973.

226. Pingleton W, Coalson JJ, Guenter CA: Significance of leukocytes in endotoxic shock. Exp Mol Pathol 22:183–194, 1975.

227. Eiermann G, Dickey BF, Thrall RS: Polymorphonuclear leukocyte participation in acute oleic acid-induced lung injury. Am Rev Respir Dis 128:845–850, 1983.

228. Tahamont M, Malik AB: Granulocytes mediate the increase in pulmonary vascular permeability after thrombin embolism. J Appl Physiol 54:1489–1495, 1983.

229. Heath C, Lai L, Bizios R, et al: Pulmonary hemodynamic effects of antisheep serum-induced leukopenia. J Leukoc Biol 39:385–397, 1986.

230. Shasby DM, VanBenthuysen KM, Tate RM, et al: Granulocytes mediate acute edematous lung injury in rabbits and isolated rabbit lungs perfused with phorbol myristate acetate: Role of oxygen radicals. Am Rev Respir Dis 125:443–447, 1982.

231. Dreyfuss D, Saumon G: Ventilator-induced lung injury: Lessons from experimental studies. Am J Respir Crit Care Med 157:294–323, 1998.

232. Dos Santos CC, Slutsky AS: Invited review. Mechanisms of ventilator-induced lung injury: A perspective. J Appl Physiol 89:1645–1655, 2000.

233. Matthay MA, Rosen GD: Acid aspiration induced lung injury: New insights and therapeutic options. Am J Respir Crit Care Med 154:277–278, 1996.

234. The ARDS Network: Ventilation with lower tidal volumes as compared with traditional tidal volumes for acute lung injury and the acute respiratory distress syndrome. N Engl J Med 342:1301–1308, 2000.

235. Ranieri VM, Suter PM, Tortorella C, et al: Effect of mechanical ventilation on inflammatory mediators in patients with acute respiratory distress syndrome: A randomized controlled trial. JAMA 282:54–61, 1999.

236. Snashall P, Chung KF: Airway obstruction and bronchial hyperresponsiveness in left ventricular failure and mitral stenosis. Am Rev Respir Dis 144:945–956, 1991.

237. Hoffman R, Agatston A, Krieger B: Cheyne-Stokes respiration in patients recovering from acute cardiogenic pulmonary edema. Chest 97:410–412, 1990.

238. Graham SP, Vetrovec GW: Comparison of angiographic findings and demographic variables in patients with coronary artery disease presenting with acute pulmonary edema versus those presenting with chest pain. Am J Cardiol 68:1614–1618, 1991.

239. Meduri GU, Wunderink RG, Leeper KV, et al: Management of bacterial pneumonia in ventilated patients: Protected bronchoalveolar lavage as a diagnostic tool. Chest 101:500–508, 1992.

240. Warner DO, Warner MA, Divertie MB: Open lung biopsy in patients with diffuse pulmonary infiltrates and acute respiratory failure. Am Rev Respir Dis 137:90–94, 1988.

241. Patel S, Karmpaliotis D, Ayas NT, et al: The role of open-lung biopsy in ARDS. Chest 125:197–202, 2004.

242. Murray JF, Matthay MA, Luce JM, et al: An expanded definition of the adult respiratory distress syndrome. Am Rev Respir Dis 138:720–723, 1988.

243. Bernard GR, Artigas A, Brigham KL, et al: The American-European Consensus Conference of ARDS: Definitions, mechanisms, relevant outcomes, and clinical trial coordination. Am J Respir Crit Care Med 149:818–824, 1994.

244. Matuschak GM: Lung-liver interactions in sepsis and multiple organ failure syndrome. Clin Chest Med 17:83–98, 1996.

245. Knaus W, Draper EA, Wagner DP, et al: APACHE II: A severity of disease classification system. Crit Care Med 13:818–829, 1985.

246. Moss M, Goodman PL, Heinig M, et al: Establishing the relative accuracy of three new definitions of the adult respiratory distress syndrome (see comments). Crit Care Med 23:1629–1637, 1995.

247. Schuster DP: What is acute lung injury? What is ARDS? Chest 107:1721–1726, 1995.

248. Sinclair DG, Braude S, Haslam PL, et al: Pulmonary endothelial permeability in patients with severe lung injury: Clinical correlates and natural history. Chest 106:535–539, 1994.

249. Groeneveld ABJ, Raijmakers PGHM, Teule GJJ, et al: The ^{67}gallium pulmonary leak index in assessing the severity and course of the adult respiratory distress syndrome. Crit Care Med 24:1467–1472, 1996.

250. Groeneveld ABJ, Raijmakers PGHM: The ^{67}gallium-transferrin pulmonary leak index in patients at risk for the acute respiratory distress syndrome. Crit Care Med 26:685–691, 1998.

251. Owens CM, Evans TW, Keogh BF, et al: Computed tomography in established adult respiratory distress syndrome: Correlation with lung injury score. Chest 106:1815–1821, 1994.

252. Knaus WA, Sun X, Hakim RB, et al: Evaluation of definitions for adult respiratory distress syndrome. Am J Respir Crit Care Med 150:311–317, 1994.

253. Doyle RL, Szaflarski N, Modin GW, et al: Identification of patients with acute lung injury: Predictors of mortality. Am J Respir Crit Care Med 152:1818–1824, 1995.

254. Staub NC: Clinical use of lung water measurements: Report of a workshop. Chest 90:588–594, 1986.

255. Bombino M, Gattinoni L, Pesenti A, et al: The value of portable chest roentgenography in adult respiratory distress syndrome: Comparison with computed tomography. Chest 100:762–769, 1991.

256. Winer-Muram H, Rubin SA, Miniati M, et al: Guidelines for reading and interpreting chest radiographs in patients receiving mechanical ventilation. Chest 102:565S–570S, 1992.

257. Suh R, Aberle DR: Radiographic manifestations of pulmonary edema. *In* Matthay MA, Ingbar DH (eds): Pulmonary Edema. New York: Marcel Dekker, 1998, pp 85–119.

258. Coates G, Powles ACP, Morrison SC, et al: The effects of intravenous infusion of saline on lung density, lung volumes, nitrogen washout, computed tomographic scans, and chest radiographs in humans. Am Rev Respir Dis 127:91–96, 1983.

259. Aberle DR, Wiener-Kronish JP, Webb RW, et al: Hydrostatic versus increased permeability pulmonary edema: Diagnosis based on radiographic criteria in critically ill patients. Radiology 168:73–79, 1988.

260. Rocker G, Rose DH, Manhire AR, et al: The radiographic differentiation of pulmonary edema. Br J Radiol 62:582–586, 1989.

261. Thomason J, Ely EW, Chiles C, et al: Appraising pulmonary edema using supine chest roentgenograms in ventilated patients. Am J Respir Crit Care Med 157:1600–1608, 1998.

262. Rubenfeld GD, Caldwell E, Granton J, et al: Interobserver variability in applying a radiographic definition for ARDS. Chest 116:1347–1353, 1999.

263. Brigham K, Kariman K, Harris TR, et al: Correlation of oxygenation with vascular permeability-surface area but not with lung water in humans with acute respiratory failure and pulmonary edema. J Clin Invest 72:339–349, 1983.

264. Harris T, Bernard GR, Brigham KL, et al: Lung microvascular transport properties measured by multiple indicator dilution methods in patients with adult respiratory distress syndrome: A comparison between patients reversing respiratory failure and those failing to reverse. Am Rev Respir Dis 141:272–280, 1990.

265. Estenne M, Yernault J-C: The mechanism of CO_2 retention in cardiac pulmonary edema. Chest 86:936–938, 1984.

266. Aberman A, Fulop M: The metabolic and respiratory acidosis of acute pulmonary edema. Ann Intern Med 76:173–184, 1972.

267. O'Donovan R, McGowan JA, Lupinacci L, et al: Acid-base disturbances in cardiogenic pulmonary edema. Nephron 57:416–420, 1991.

268. De Backer D, Creteur J, Zhang H, et al: Lactate production by the lungs in acute lung injury. Am J Respir Crit Care Med 156:1099–1104, 1997.

269. Sprung C, Rackow EC, Fein IA, et al: The spectrum of pulmonary edema: Differentiation of cardiogenic, intermediate, and noncardiogenic forms of pulmonary edema. Am Rev Respir Dis 124:718–722, 1981.

270. Carlson RW, Schaeffer RC, Carpio M, et al: Edema fluid and coagulation changes during fulminant pulmonary edema. Chest 79:43–49, 1981.

271. Carlson R, Schaeffer RC, Michaels SG, et al: Pulmonary edema fluid: Spectrum of features in 37 patients. Circulation 60:1161–1169, 1979.

272. Sprung CL, Long WM, Marcial EH, et al: Distribution of proteins in pulmonary edema: The value of fractional concentrations. Am Rev Respir Dis 136:957–963, 1987.

273. Matthay MA, Wiener-Kronish JP: Intact epithelial barrier function is critical for the resolution of alveolar edema in humans. Am Rev Respir Dis 142:1250–1257, 1990.

274. Ware LB, Matthay MA: Alveolar fluid clearance is impaired in the majority of patients with acute lung injury and the acute respiratory distress syndrome. Am J Respir Crit Care Med 163:1376–1383, 2001.

275. Steinberg KP, Mitchell DR, Maunder RJ, et al: Safety of bronchoalveolar lavage in patients with adult respiratory distress syndrome. Am Rev Respir Dis 148:556–561, 1993.

276. Connors A, Castele RJ, Farhat NZ, et al: Complications of right heart catheterization: A prospective autopsy study. Chest 88:567–572, 1985.

277. Matthay MA, Chatterjee K: Bedside catheterization of the pulmonary artery: Risks compared with benefits. Ann Intern Med 109:826–834, 1988.

278. Connors AF, Speroff T, Dawson NV, et al: The effectiveness of right heart catheterization in the initial care of critically ill patients. JAMA 276:889–897, 1996.

279. Richard C, Warszawski J, Anguel N, et al, for the French Pulmonary Artery Catheter Study Group: Early use of the pulmonary artery catheter and outcomes in patients with shock and acute respiratory distress syndrome: A randomized controlled trial. JAMA 290:2713–2720, 2003.

280. O'Quinn R, Marini JJ: Pulmonary artery occlusion pressure: Clinical physiology, measurement, and interpretation. Am Rev Respir Dis 128:319–326, 1983.

281. Robin ED: The cult of the Swan-Ganz catheter: Overuse and abuse of pulmonary flow catheters. Ann Intern Med 103:445–449, 1985.

282. Raper R, Sibbald WJ: Misled by the wedge? The Swan-Ganz catheter and left ventricular preload. Chest 89:427–434, 1986.

283. Staub NC: The hemodynamics of pulmonary edema. Bull Eur Physiopathol Respir 22:319–322, 1986.

284. Stark P, Jasmine J: CT of pulmonary edema. Crit Rev Diagn Imaging 29:245–255, 1989.

285. Forster B, Mueller NL, Mayo JR, et al: High-resolution computed tomography of experimental hydrostatic pulmonary edema. Chest 101:1434–1437, 1992.

286. Simon D, Murray JF, Staub NC: Measurement of pulmonary edema in intact dogs by transthoracic gamma ray attenuation. J Appl Physiol 47:1228–1233, 1979.

287. Gamsu G, Kaufman L, Swann SJ, et al: Absolute lung density in experimental canine pulmonary edema. Invest Radiol 14:261–269, 1979.

288. Rice DA: Sound speed in pulmonary parenchyma. J Appl Physiol 54:304–308, 1983.

289. Nierman DM, Eisen DI, Fein ED, et al: Transthoracic bioimpedance can measure extravascular lung water in acute lung injury. J Surg Res 65:101–108, 1996.

290. Caruthers S, Paschal CB, Pou NA, et al: Regional measurements of pulmonary edema by using magnetic resonance imaging. J Appl Physiol 84:2143–2153, 1998.

291. Kaplan J, Calandrino FS, Schuster DP: A positron emission tomographic comparison of pulmonary vascular permeability during the adult respiratory distress syndrome and pneumonia. Am Rev Respir Dis 143:150–154, 1991.

292. Effros RM: Lung water measurements with the mean transit time approach. J Appl Physiol 59:673–683, 1985.

293. Böck J, Lewis FR: Clinical relevance of lung water measurement with the thermal-dye dilution technique. J Surg Res 48:254–265, 1990.

294. Chinard FP: Estimation of extravascular lung water by indicator-dilution techniques. Circ Res 37:137–145, 1975.

295. Allison R, Carlile PV, Gray BA: Thermodilution measurement of lung water. Clin Chest Med 6:439–467, 1985.

296. Eisenberg PR, Hansbrough JR, Anderson D, et al: A prospective study of lung water measurements during

patient management in an intensive care unit. Am Rev Respir Dis 136:662–668, 1987.

297. Mitchell JP, Schuller D, Calandrino FS, et al: Improved outcome based on fluid management in critically ill patients requiring pulmonary artery catheterization (see comments). Am Rev Respir Dis 145:990–998, 1992.

298. Dawson C, Bronikowski TA, Linehan JH, et al: Influence of pulmonary vasoconstriction on lung water and perfusion heterogeneity. J Appl Physiol 54:654–660, 1983.

299. Sibbald W, Cunningham DR, Chin DN: Non-cardiac or cardiac pulmonary edema? A practical approach to clinical differentiation in critically ill patients. Chest 84:452–461, 1983.

300. Connelly KG, Repine JE: Markers for predicting the development of acute respiratory distress syndrome. Annu Rev Med 48:429–445, 1997.

301. Weinberg PF, Matthay MA, Webster RO, et al: Biologically active products of complement and acute lung injury in patients with the sepsis syndrome. Am Rev Respir Dis 130:791–796, 1984.

302. Parsons PE, Giclas PC: The terminal complement complex (sC5b-9) is not specifically associated with the development of the adult respiratory distress syndrome. Am Rev Respir Dis 141:98–103, 1990.

303. Ware LB, Conner E, Matthay MA: von Willebrand factor antigen is an independent marker of poor outcome in patients with early acute lung injury. Crit Care Med 29:2325–2331, 2001.

304. Eisner M, Parsons P, Matthay MA, et al: Acute Respiratory Distress Syndrome Network: Plasma surfactant protein levels and clinical outcomes in patients with acute lung injury. Thorax 58:983–988, 2003.

305. Baldwin S, Simon RH, Grum CM, et al: Oxidant activity in expired breath of patients with adult respiratory distress syndrome. Lancet 1:11–14, 1986.

306. Sznajder J, Fraiman A, Hall JB, et al: Increased hydrogen peroxide in the expired breath of patients with acute hypoxemic respiratory failure. Chest 96:606–612, 1989.

307. Cochrane C, Spragg R, Revak SD: Pathogenesis of the adult respiratory distress syndrome: Evidence of oxidant activity in bronchoalveolar lavage fluid. J Clin Invest 71:754–761, 1983.

308. Hyers TM, Tricomi SM, Dettenmeier PA, et al: Tumor necrosis factor levels in serum and bronchoalveolar lavage fluid of patients with the adult respiratory distress syndrome. Am Rev Respir Dis 144:268–271, 1991.

309. Parsons PE, Moore FA, Moore EE, et al: Studies on the role of tumor necrosis factor in adult respiratory distress syndrome. Am Rev Respir Dis 146:694–700, 1992.

310. Levine B, Kalman J, Mayer L, et al: Elevated circulating levels of tumor necrosis factor in severe chronic heart failure. N Engl J Med 323:236–241, 1990.

311. Stephenson A, Lonigro AJ, Hyers TM, et al: Increased concentrations of leukotrienes in bronchoalveolar lavage fluid of patients with ARDS or at risk for ARDS. Am Rev Respir Dis 138:714–719, 1988.

312. Bernard GR, Korley V, Chee P, et al: Persistent generation of peptido leukotrienes in patients with the adult respiratory distress syndrome. Am Rev Respir Dis 144:263–267, 1991.

313. Lee C, Fein AM, Lippmann M, et al: Elastolytic activity in pulmonary lavage fluid from patients with adult respiratory-distress syndrome. N Engl J Med 304:192–196, 1981.

314. McGuire W, Spragg RG, Cohen AB, et al: Studies on the pathogenesis of the adult respiratory distress syndrome. J Clin Invest 69:543–553, 1982.

315. Idell S, Kucich U, Fein A, et al: Neutrophil elastase-releasing factors in bronchoalveolar lavage from patients with adult respiratory distress syndrome. Am Rev Respir Dis 132:1098–1105, 1985.

316. Wewers MD, Herzyk DJ, Gadek JE: Alveolar fluid neutrophil elastase activity in the adult respiratory distress syndrome is complexed to alpha-2-macroglobulin. J Clin Invest 82:1260–1267, 1988.

317. Hirsch J, Hansen KC, Burlingame AL, Matthay MA: Proteomics: Current techniques and potential applications to lung disease. Am J Physiol Lung Cell Mol Physiol 287:L1–L23, 2004.

318. Bowler R, Duda B, Chan ED, et al: A proteomic analysis of pulmonary edema fluid and plasma in patients with acute lung injury. Am J Physiol Lung Cell Mol Physiol 286:L1095–L1104, 2004.

319. Staub NC: Pulmonary edema: Physiologic approaches to management. Chest 74:559–564, 1978.

320. Klein H, Brodsky E, Ninio R, et al: The effect of venous occlusion with tourniquets on peripheral blood pooling and ventricular function. Chest 103:521–527, 1993.

321. Eiser A, Lieber JJ, Neff MS: Phlebotomy for pulmonary edema in dialysis patients. Clin Nephrol 47:47–49, 1997.

322. Jasmer RM, Luce JM, Matthay MA: Noninvasive positive pressure ventilation for acute respiratory failure: Underutilized or overrated? Chest 111:1672–1678, 1997.

323. Antonelli M, Conti G, Rocco M, et al: A comparison of noninvasive positive-pressure ventilation and conventional mechanical ventilation in patients with acute respiratory failure (see comments). N Engl J Med 339:429–435, 1998.

324. Sandham J, Hull RD, Brant RF, et al: A randomized, controlled trial of the use of pulmonary-artery catheters in high-risk surgical patients. N Engl J Med 348:5–14, 2003.

325. Parsons P: Progress in research on pulmonary arterial catheters. N Engl J Med 348:66–68, 2003.

326. Annane D, Bellissant E, Pussard E, et al: Placebo-controlled, randomized, double-blind study of intravenous enalaprilat efficacy and safety in acute cardiogenic pulmonary edema. Circulation 94:1316–1324, 1996.

327. Brater DC: Diuretic therapy. N Engl J Med 339:387–395, 1998.

328. Garzia F, Todor R, Scalea T: Continuous arteriovenous hemofiltration countercurrent dialysis (CAVH-D) in acute respiratory failure (ARDS). J Trauma 31:1277–1285, 1991.

329. Kollef MH: The prevention of ventilator-associated pneumonia. N Engl J Med 340:627–634, 1999.

330. Susini G, Zucchetti M, Bortone F, et al: Isolated ultrafiltration in cardiogenic pulmonary edema. Crit Care Med 18:14–17, 1990.

331. Tibayan FA, Chesnutt AN, Folkesson HG, et al: Dobutamine increases alveolar liquid clearance in ventilated rats by beta-2 receptor stimulation. Am J Respir Crit Care Med 156:438–444, 1997.

332. Kolla S, Awad SS, Rich PB, et al: Extracorporeal life support for 100 adult patients with severe respiratory failure. Ann Surg 226:544–556, 1997.

333. Grover F, Fullerton DA, Zamora MR, et al: The past, present, and future of lung transplantation. Am J Surg 173:523–533, 1997.

334. Ehrhart I, Hofman WF: Relationship of fluid filtration to lung vascular pressure during edema. J Appl Physiol 70:202–209, 1991.

335. Gheorghiade M, Cody RJ, Francis GS, et al: Current medical therapy for advanced heart failure. Am Heart J 135:S231–S248, 1998.

336. Verghese GM, Ware LB, Matthay BA, et al: Alveolar epithelial fluid transport and the resolution of clinically severe hydrostatic pulmonary edema. J Appl Physiol 87:1301–1312, 1999.

337. Wheeler AP, Bernard GR: Treating patients with severe sepsis. N Engl J Med 340:207–214, 1999.

338. Humphrey H, Hall J, Sznajder I, et al: Improved survival in ARDS patients associated with a reduction in pulmonary capillary wedge pressure (see comments). Chest 97:1176–1180, 1990.

339. Simmons RS, Berdine GG, Seidenfeld JJ, et al: Fluid balance and the adult respiratory distress syndrome. Am Rev Respir Dis 135:924–929, 1987.

340. Gattinoni L, Brazzi L, Pelosi P, et al: A trial of goal-oriented hemodynamic therapy in critically ill patients. N Engl J Med 333:1025–1032, 1995.

341. Hebert P, Wells G, Blajchman MA, et al: A multicenter, randomized, controlled clinical trial of transfusion requirements in critical care. N Engl J Med 340:409–417, 1999.

342. Webb HH, Tierney DF: Experimental pulmonary edema due to intermittent positive pressure ventilation with high inflation pressures: Protection by positive end-expiratory pressure. Am Rev Respir Dis 110:556–565, 1974.

343. Parker JC, Townsley MI, Rippe B, et al: Increased microvascular permeability in dog lungs due to high peak airway pressures. J Appl Physiol 57:1809–1816, 1984.

344. Slutsky AS, Tremblay LN: Multiple system organ failure: Is mechanical ventilation a contributing factor? Am J Respir Crit Care Med 157:1721–1725, 1998.

345. Marini JJ: Evolving concepts in the ventilatory management of acute respiratory distress syndrome. Clin Chest Med 17:555–575, 1996.

346. The Acute Respiratory Distress Syndrome Network: A trial of mechanical ventilation with higher versus lower positive end-expiratory pressures in patients with acute lung injury and acute respiratory distress syndrome. N Engl J Med 351:327–336, 2004.

346a. Cheng I, Eisner M, Thompson T, et al: Acute effects of tidal volume strategy on hemodynamics, fluid balance, and sedation in acute lung injury. Crit Care Med 2005, in press.

347. Morris AH, Wallace CJ, Menlove RL, et al: Randomized clinical trial of pressure-controlled inverse ratio ventilation and extracorporeal CO$_2$ removal for adult respiratory distress syndrome (see comments). Am J Respir Crit Care Med 149:295–305, 1994 [published erratum appears in Am J Respir Crit Care Med 149(3 Pt 1):838, 1994].

348. Brower RG, Ware LB, Berthiaume Y, et al: Treatment of ARDS. Chest 120:1347–1367, 2001.

349. Albert PK: The prone position in acute respiratory distress syndrome: Where we are, and where we do we go from here. Crit Care Med 25:1453–1454, 1997.

350. Pelosi P, Tubiolo D, Mascheroni D, et al: Effects of the prone position on respiratory mechanics and gas exchange during acute lung injury. Am J Respir Crit Care Med 157:387–393, 1998.

350a. Guerin C, Gaillard S, Lemasson S, et al: Effects of systemic prone positioning in hypoxemic acute respiratory failure: a randomized clinical trial. JAMA 292:2379–2387, 2004.

351. Heyland D, Mandell LA: Gastric colonization by gram-negative bacilli and nosocomial pneumonia in the intensive care unit: Evidence for causation. Chest 101:187–193, 1992.

352. Dematte J, Sznajder JI: Effects of selective digestive decontamination on lung injury and outcome: The verdict is not yet in. Chest 112:304–306, 1997.

353. Collard H, Saint S, Matthay MA: Prevention of ventilator-associated pneumonia: An evidence-based systematic review. Ann Intern Med 136:494–501, 2003.

354. Turner J, Briggs S, Springhorn HE, et al: Patients' recollection of intensive care unit experience. Crit Care Med 18:966–968, 1990.

355. de Perrot M, Imai Y, Volgyesi GA, et al: Effect of ventilator-induced lung injury on the development of reperfusion injury in a rat lung transplant model. J Thorac Cardiovasc Surg 124:1137–1144, 2002.

356. Petty T, Bone RC, Gee MH, et al: Contemporary clinical trials in acute respiratory distress syndrome. Chest 101:550–552, 1992.

357. Hudson LD, Milberg JA, Anardi D, et al: Clinical risks for development of the acute respiratory distress syndrome. Am J Respir Crit Care Med 151:293–301, 1995.

358. Bernard GR, Luce JM, Sprung CL, et al: High-dose corticosteroids in patients with the adult respiratory distress syndrome. N Engl J Med 317:1565–1570, 1987.

359. Slotman G, Fisher CJ, Bone RC, et al: Detrimental effects of high-dose methylprednisolone sodium succinate on serum concentrations of hepatic and renal function indicators in severe sepsis and septic shock. Crit Care Med 21:191–195, 1993.

360. Schonfeld S, Ploysongsang Y, DiLisio R, et al: Fat embolism prophylaxis with corticosteroids: A prospective study in high-risk patients. Ann Intern Med 99:438–443, 1983.

361. Hooper RG: ARDS: Inflammation, infections, and corticosteroids. Chest 100:889–890, 1991.

362. Meduri GU, Headley AS, Golden E, et al: Effect of prolonged methylprednisolone therapy in unresolving acute respiratory distress syndrome: A randomized controlled trial (see comments). JAMA 280:159–165, 1998.

362a. ARDS Network: The efficacy and safety of corticosteroids as rescue therapy for persistent acute respiratory distress syndrome. Submitted for publication, 2005.

363. Lewis JF, Jobe AH: Surfactant and the adult respiratory distress syndrome. Am Rev Respir Dis 147:218–233, 1993 [published erratum appears in Am Rev Respir Dis 147:following 1068, 1993].

364. Weg J, Balk RA, Tharratt RS, et al: Safety and potential efficacy of an aerosolized surfactant in human sepsis-induced adult respiratory distress syndrome. JAMA 272:1433–1438, 1994.

365. Anzueto A, Baughman RP, Guntupalli KK, et al: Aerosolized surfactant in adults with sepsis-induced acute respiratory distress syndrome. N Engl J Med 334:1417–1421, 1996.

365a. Spragg RG, Lewis JF, Walmrath HD, et al: Effect of recombinant surfactant protein-C based surfactant on the acute respiratory distress syndrome. N Engl J Med 351:884–892, 2004.

366. Bernard GR: N-Acetylcysteine in experimental and clinical acute lung injury. Am J Med 91:54S–59S, 1991.

367. Raffin T: Acute lung injury and pentoxifylline. Crit Care Med 18:1485–1486, 1990.

368. McDonald RJ: Pentoxifylline reduces injury to isolated lungs perfused with human neutrophils. Am Rev Respir Dis 144:1347–1350, 1991.

369. The Acute Respiratory Distress Syndrome Network: Randomized, placebo-controlled trial of lisofylline for early treatment of acute lung injury and acute respiratory distress syndrome. Crit Care Med 30:1–6, 2002.

370. Bone R, Balk RA, Fein AM, et al: A second large controlled clinical study of E5, a monoclonal antibody to endotoxin: Results of a prospective, multicenter, randomized, controlled trial. Crit Care Med 23:994–1006, 1995.

371. Luce JM: Introduction of new technology into critical care practice: A history of HA-1A human monoclonal antibody against endotoxin. Crit Care Med 21:1233–1241, 1993.

372. Bigatello L, Greene RE, Sprung CL, et al: HA-1A in septic patients with ARDS: Results from the pivotal trial. Intensive Care Med 20:328–334, 1994.

373. Abraham E, Wunderink R, Silverman H, et al: Efficacy and safety of monoclonal antibody to human tumor necrosis factor alpha in patients with sepsis syndrome: A randomized, controlled, double-blind, multicenter clinical trial. TNF-alpha MAb Sepsis Study Group. JAMA 273:934–941, 1995.

374. Fisher C, Dhainaut J-FA, Opal SM, et al: Recombinant human interleukin-1 receptor antagonist in the treatment of patients with sepsis syndrome: Results from a randomized, double-blind, placebo-controlled trial. JAMA 271:1836–1843, 1994.

375. Bernard GR, Vincent JL, Laterre PF, et al: Efficacy and safety of recombinant human activated protein C for severe sepsis. N Engl J Med 344:699–709, 2001.

376. Prabhakaran P, Ware LB, White KE, et al: Elevated levels of plasminogen activator inhibitor-1 in pulmonary edema fluid are associated with mortality in acute lung injury. Am J Physiol Lung Cell Mol Physiol 285:L20–L28, 2003.

377. Idell S: Adult respiratory distress syndrome: Do selective anticoagulants help? Am J Respir Med 1:383–391, 2002.

378. Bone RC, Slotman G, Maunder R, et al: Randomized double-blind, multicenter study of prostaglandin E$_1$ in patients with the adult respiratory distress syndrome. Prostaglandin E$_1$ Study Group (see comments). Chest 96:114–119, 1989.

379. Matthay MA, Pittet J-F, Jayr C: Just say NO to inhaled nitric oxide for the acute respiratory distress syndrome (editorial). Crit Care Med 26:1–2, 1998.

380. Dellinger RP, Zimmerman JL, Taylor RW, et al: Effects of inhaled nitric oxide in patients with acute respiratory distress syndrome: Results of a randomized phase II trial. Inhaled Nitric Oxide in ARDS Study Group (see comments). Crit Care Med 26:15–23, 1998.

381. Luhr O, Nathorst-Westfelt U, Lundin S, et al: A retrospective analysis of nitric oxide inhalation in patients with severe acute lung injury in Sweden and Norway 1991–1994. Acta Anaesth Scand 41:1238–1246, 1997.

382. Hastings RH, Grady M, Sakuma T, et al: Clearance of different-sized proteins from the alveolar space in humans and rabbits. J Appl Physiol 73:1310–1316, 1992.

383. Matalon S, O'Brodovich H: Sodium channels in alveolar epithelial cells: Molecular characterization, biophysical properties, and physiological significance. Annu Rev Physiol 61:627–661, 1999.

384. Saumon G, Basset G: Electrolyte and fluid transport across the mature alveolar epithelium. J Appl Physiol 74:1–15, 1993.

385. Folkesson HG, Kheradmand F, Matthay MA: The effect of salt water on alveolar epithelial barrier function. Am J Respir Crit Care Med 150:1555–1563, 1994.

386. Zuege D, Suzuki S, Berthiaume Y: Increase of lung sodium-potassium-ATPase activity during recovery from high-permeability pulmonary edema. Am J Physiol 271:L896–L909, 1996.

387. Sakuma T, Folkesson HG, Suzuki S, et al: Beta-adrenergic agonist stimulated alveolar fluid clearance in *ex vivo* human and rat lungs. Am J Respir Crit Care Med 155:506–512, 1997.

388. Berthiaume Y, Albertine KH, Grady M, et al: Protein clearance from the air spaces and lungs of unanesthetized sheep over 144 h. J Appl Physiol 67:1887–1897, 1989.

389. Staub NC: Alveolar flooding and clearance. Am Rev Respir Dis 127:S45–S51, 1983.

390. Conhaim RL: Airway level at which edema liquid enters the air space of isolated dog lungs. J Appl Physiol 67:2234–2242, 1989.

391. Kambara K, Longworth KE, Serikov VB, et al: Effect of interstitial edema on lung lymph flow in goats in the absence of filtration. J Appl Physiol 72:1142–1148, 1992.

392. Fukue M, Serikov VB, Jerome EH: Recovery from increased pressure or increased leakiness edema in perfused sheep lungs. J Appl Physiol 77:184–189, 1994.

393. Pearse DB, Wagner EM, Sylvester JT: Edema clearance in isolated sheep lungs. J Appl Physiol 74:126–132, 1993.

394. Wiener-Kronish JP, Broaddus VC: Interrelationship of pleural and pulmonary interstitial liquid. Annu Rev Physiol 55:209–226, 1993.

395. Wiener-Kronish JP, Matthay MA, Callen PW, et al: Relationship of pleural effusions to pulmonary hemodynamics in patients with congestive heart failure. Am Rev Respir Dis 132:1253–1256, 1985.

396. Wiener-Kronish JP, Matthay MA: Pleural effusions associated with hydrostatic and increased permeability pulmonary edema. Chest 93:852–858, 1988.

397. Broaddus VC, Wiener-Kronish JP, Staub NC: Clearance of lung edema into the pleural space of volume-loaded anesthetized sheep. J Appl Physiol 68:2623–2630, 1990.

398. Lum H, Malik AB: Regulation of vascular endothelial barrier function. Am J Physiol 267:L223–L241, 1994.

399. Wiener R, Moses HW, Richeson JF, et al: Hospital and long term survival of patients with acute pulmonary edema associated with coronary artery disease. Am J Cardiol 60:33–35, 1987.

400. DiFederico EM, Harrison M, Matthay MA: Pulmonary edema in a woman following fetal surgery. Chest 109:1114–1117, 1996.

401. Thomsen G, Morris AH: Incidence of the adult respiratory distress syndrome in the state of Utah. Am J Respir Crit Care Med 152:965–971, 1995.

402. Rubenfeld GD, Caldwell EC, Martin DM, et al: The incidence of acute lung injury (ALI) in adults in the US: Results of the King County Lung Injury Project. Am J Respir Crit Care Med 165:A219, 2002.

403. Milberg JA, Davis DR, Steinberg KP, et al: Improved survival of patients with acute respiratory distress syndrome (ARDS): 1983–1993. JAMA 273:306–309, 1995.

404. Moss M, Bucher B, Moore FA, et al: The role of chronic alcohol abuse in the development of acute respiratory distress syndrome in adults. JAMA 275:50–54, 1996.

405. Holguin F, Moss IM, Brown LAS, et al: Chronic ethanol ingestion impairs alveolar type II cell glutathione homeostasis and function and predisposes to endotoxin-mediated acute edematous lung injury in rats. J Clin Invest 101:761–768, 1998.

406. Suchyta M, Clemmer TP, Elliott CG, et al: Increased mortality of older patients with acute respiratory distress syndrome. Chest 111:1334–1339, 1997.

407. Ely E, Wheeler AP, Thompson BT, et al: Recovery rate and prognosis in older persons who develop acute lung injury and the acute respiratory distress syndrome. Ann Intern Med 136:25–36, 2002.

408. Ghio AJ, Elliott CG, Crapo RO, et al: Impairment after adult respiratory distress syndrome: An evaluation based on American Thoracic Society recommendations. Am Rev Respir Dis 139:1158–1162, 1989.

409. Elliott CG: Pulmonary sequelae in survivors of the adult respiratory distress syndrome. Clin Chest Med 11:789–800, 1990.

410. McHugh LG, Milberg JA, Whitcomb ME, et al: Recovery of function in survivors of the acute respiratory distress syndrome. Am J Respir Crit Care Med 150:90–94, 1994.

411. Hert R, Albert RK: Sequelae of the adult respiratory distress syndrome. Thorax 49:8–13, 1994.

412. Elliott CG, Rasmusson BY, Crapo RO: Upper airway obstruction following adult respiratory distress syndrome: An analysis of 30 survivors. Chest 94:526–530, 1988.

413. Bitterman PB: Pathogenesis of fibrosis in acute lung injury. Am J Med 92:39S–43S, 1992.

414. Chapman HA: Disorders of lung matrix remodeling. J Clin Invest 113:148–157, 2004.

415. Pugin J, Verghese G, Widmer MC, et al: The alveolar space is the site of intense inflammatory and profibrotic reactions in the early phase of acute respiratory distress syndrome. Crit Care Med 27:304–312, 1999.

416. Olman M, White KE, Ware LB, et al: Pulmonary edema fluid from patients with early lung injury stimulates fibroblast proliferation through IL-1beta-induced IL-6 expression. J Immunol 172:2668–2677, 2004.

417. Martin C, Papazian L, Payan M-J, et al: Pulmonary fibrosis correlates with outcome in the adult respiratory distress syndrome. Chest 107:196–200, 1995.

418. Panos RJ, Bak PM, Simonet WS, et al: Intratracheal instillation of keratinocyte growth factor decreases hyperoxia-induced mortality in rats. J Clin Invest 96:2026–2033, 1995.

419. Garat C, Kheradmand F, Albertine KH, et al: Soluble and insoluble fibronectin increases alveolar epithelial wound healing *in vitro*. Am J Physiol 271:L844–L853, 1996.

420. Matthay MA: Fibrosing alveolitis in the adult respiratory distress syndrome (editorial). Ann Intern Med 122:65–66, 1995.

52

Cor Pulmonale

Teresa De Marco, M.D., Elliot Rapaport, M.D.

INTRODUCTION

The term *cor pulmonale,* or pulmonary heart disease, has been used rather loosely for many years to describe three broad groups of patients, all of whom have pulmonary hypertension resulting in progressive right ventricular hypertrophy, right ventricular dilation, and eventual cardiac decompensation from (1) disorders that primarily affect ventilatory drive or musculoskeletal respiratory mechanics; (2) pulmonary airway, infiltrative, fibrotic, or vascular diseases; and (3) disease in which the clinical picture as it affects the lungs and pulmonary circulation is the consequence of a primary cardiovascular disorder. In 1963, an expert committee appointed by the Director General of the World Health Organization (WHO) recommended a definition based on morbid anatomy. Specifically, the committee defined chronic *cor pulmonale* as "hypertrophy of the right ventricle resulting from diseases affecting the function and/or the structure of the lung, except when these pulmonary alterations are the result of diseases that primarily affect the left side of the heart or congenital heart disease."[1] The WHO subsequently organized a major symposium on pulmonary hypertension that was held in Evian, France, in September 1998. From that meeting, attended by experts from around the world, a classification of pulmonary hypertension emerged that is generally accepted as the "gold standard" today[2] (Table 52.1). Newly introduced modifications to the classification were made at the Third World Symposium on Pulmonary Arterial Hypertension convened in Venice, Italy, in June 2003 (Table 52.2).[3] This chapter on cor pulmonale primarily deals with the group of disorders classified by this expert committee as "Pulmonary Hypertension Associated with Lung Diseases and/or Hypox-

emia." Therefore, changes in pulmonary vasculature or pulmonary function related to primary cardiovascular disease are not covered here, but are discussed in Chapter 77. We limit our discussion mainly to diseases that affect the air passages, the pulmonary vasculature, or alveolar ventilation.

PULMONARY CIRCULATION

The major pulmonary arteries normally have less medial thickening than is seen in systemic arteries, reflecting the fact that the pressures in the pulmonary arteries are approximately one fifth to one sixth of those normally found in the systemic arteries. In the systemic arteries, the ratio of medial thickness to external arterial diameter is 20% to 25%, but in the pulmonary arteries it is closer to 5%.[4] Postmortem casts of the human pulmonary arterial tree show there to be 17 branching orders, from the main pulmonary artery to the alveoli, that follow closely the branching of the bronchial tree.[5,6] The number of vessels increases by a factor of approximately three with each branching order. As these vessels branch, their overall diameter ratio remains relatively constant, ensuring that the resistance to blood flow is minimal.

Muscular branches of the pulmonary artery, vessels with a luminal diameter between 100 and 1000 μm, have circular muscle fibers capable of causing vasoconstriction. These branches also demonstrate muscle hypertrophy in patients with chronic pulmonary hypertension (Fig. 52.1). True pulmonary arterioles, comparable to systemic arterioles, are not seen normally in the pulmonary circulation. Vessels smaller than 100 μm in diameter at the terminal end of the

Table 52.1 World Health Organization Classification of Pulmonary Hypertension (1998)

Pulmonary Arterial Hypertension
Primary pulmonary hypertension
   Sporadic
   Familial
Related to:
   Collagen vascular disease
   Congenital systemic-to-pulmonary shunts
   Portal hypertension
   Human immunodeficiency virus infection
   Drugs/toxins
      Appetite suppressants
      Toxic rapeseed oil
   Persistent pulmonary hypertension of the neonate

Pulmonary Venous Hypertension
Left-sided atrial or ventricular heart disease
Left-sided valvular heart disease
Extrinsic compression of central pulmonary veins
   Fibrosing mediastinitis
   Adenopathy/tumors
Pulmonary veno-occlusive disease

Pulmonary Hypertension Associated with Disorders of the Respiratory System and/or Hypoxemia
Chronic obstructive pulmonary disease
Interstitial lung disease
Sleep-disordered breathing
Alveolar hypoventilation disorders
Chronic exposure to high altitude
Neonatal lung disease
Alveolar-capillary dysplasia

Pulmonary Hypertension due to Chronic Thrombotic and/or Embolic Disease
Thromboembolic obstruction of proximal pulmonary arteries
Obstruction of distal pulmonary arteries
   Pulmonary embolism (thrombus, tumor, ova or parasites, foreign material)
   In situ thrombosis
   Sickle cell disease

Pulmonary Hypertension due to Disorders Directly Affecting Pulmonary Vasculature
Inflammatory
   Schistosomiasis
   Sarcoidosis
   Other
Pulmonary capillary hemangiomatosis

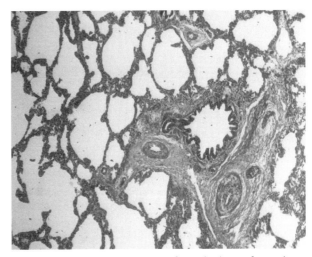

Figure 52.1 A microscopic section from the lung of a patient who had chronic pulmonary hypertension. The small branches of the pulmonary artery are seen in juxtaposition to a terminal bronchiole. There is intimal thickening and marked medial hypertrophy.

Table 52.2 Third World Symposium Diagnostic Classification of Pulmonary Hypertension (2003)

Pulmonary Arterial Hypertension (PAH)
Idiopathic (IPAH)
Familial (FPAH)
Associated with (APAH)
   Collagen vascular disease
   Congenital systemic-to-pulmonary shunts
   Portal hypertension
   HIV infection
   Drugs and toxins
   Other (thyroid disorders, glycogen storage disease, Gaucher disease, hereditary hemorrhagic telangiectasia, hemoglobinopathies, myeloproliferative disorders, splenectomy)
Associated with significant venous or capillary involvement
   Pulmonary veno-occlusive disease (PVOD)
   Pulmonary capillary hemangiomatosis (PCH)
Persistent pulmonary hypertension of the newborn

Pulmonary Hypertension with Left Heart Disease
Left-sided atrial or ventricular heart disease
Left-sided valvular heart disease

Pulmonary Hypertension associated with Lung Diseases and/or Hypoxemia
Chronic obstructive pulmonary disease
Interstitial lung disease
Sleep-disordered breathing
Alveolar hypoventilation disorders
Chronic exposure to high altitude
Developmental abnormalities

Pulmonary Hypertension due to Chronic Thrombotic and/or Embolic Disease
Thromboembolic obstruction of proximal pulmonary arteries
Thromboembolic obstruction of distal pulmonary arteries
Nonthrombotic pulmonary embolism (tumor, parasites, foreign material)

Miscellaneous
Sarcoidosis, histiocytosis X, lymphangiomatosis, compression of pulmonary vessels (adenopathy, tumor, fibrosing mediastinitis)

pulmonary arteries are usually referred to as pulmonary arterioles, but they normally have little or no medial smooth muscle. However, with chronic pulmonary hypertension, a single smooth muscle cell layer may extend longitudinally down these vessels. Therefore, pulmonary arterioles lack a true muscular media capable of reacting with vigorous vasoconstriction, but they still are capable of distending. The pulmonary vascular resistance is primarily regulated in the very small branches of the pulmonary arterial system, and these branches are the major sites of the muscularization that is seen in patients who develop pulmonary hypertension. These vessels are less distensible in response to passive increases in pressure, and they can actively vasoconstrict in the presence of hypoxia. The pulmonary capillaries do not have smooth muscle cells within their walls and therefore do not contribute to pulmonary vasoconstriction. However, they can dilate to some extent as they engorge, and numerous vessels are available for recruitment, both of which occur when pulmonary vein pressure rises. Although the pulmonary capillaries, which are literally suspended in air, cannot vasoconstrict, their diameter can decrease in response to increases in intra-alveolar or intrapleural pressure. Their caliber may also decrease if there is perivascular inflammation or interstitial transudation of fluid.

PULMONARY ARTERY PRESSURE

Pulmonary artery pressure in the normal resting recumbent adult averages 22/9 mm Hg, with a mean of 15 mm Hg. Pulmonary hypertension in the adult is said to be present when the resting pressure is higher than 30/15 mm Hg or the mean pressure is more than 25 mm Hg or 30 mm Hg with exercise. Commonly, pulmonary hypertension observed in cor pulmonale represents the net effect of a variety of different mechanisms. For example, in chronic obstructive pulmonary disease (COPD) resulting from bronchitis and emphysema, the following effects on the pulmonary circulation may be seen: reduction in the cross-sectional area of the pulmonary vasculature, reflecting anatomic loss of pulmonary capillaries as alveoli coalesce; increased pulmonary vascular resistance to pulmonary blood flow due to hypoxic pulmonary vasoconstriction, with or without additional vasoconstriction resulting from hypercapnia and vasoconstrictive and vascular remodeling mediators as a consequence of inflammation; medial hypertrophy of muscular pulmonary arteries and muscularization of the arterioles; increased resistance to pulmonary blood flow resulting from polycythemia; increased cardiac output and pulmonary blood flow from systemic arteriolar vasodilation caused by arterial hypoxemia that, in turn, raises pulmonary artery pressure; and an increase in intra-alveolar pressure with increasing lung inflation that compresses pulmonary capillaries. Pulmonary hypertension may be variable—from mild elevations with exercise that return to normal with rest; to marked elevations in pulmonary artery pressure associated with acute respiratory failure, but with restoration to the high-normal or mildly elevated range once ventilatory insufficiency is improved; to fixed severe pulmonary hypertension.

Disturbances in respiratory function ultimately affect the pulmonary circulation predominantly by production of alveolar hypoxia, regardless of whether obstructive or restrictive ventilatory insufficiency (or a combination of the two) is present, whether an abnormality in alveolar-capillary gas exchange is caused by anatomic or functional disturbances, or whether there is a ventilation-perfusion mismatch. In hypoxemia, with or without hypercapnia, pulmonary artery pressure rises out of proportion to pulmonary capillary pressure, resulting in an increase in the work of the right ventricle and its subsequent hypertrophy.

PULMONARY ARTERY WEDGE PRESSURE

The pulmonary artery wedge pressure is normally obtained during cardiac catheterization in the laboratory or at the bedside by occluding a small branch of the pulmonary

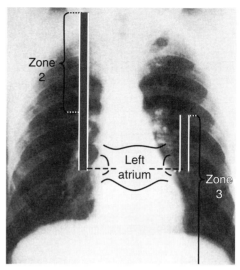

Figure 52.2 Chest radiograph showing the distribution of zones in normal human lungs in the upright position. The *solid bar* on the left shows the height "reached" by pulmonary artery pressure, and the *bar* on the right shows the height "reached" by pulmonary vein pressure; both pressures are referenced to the mid-left atrium. More of the lungs are in zone 3 than zone 2, and there is no zone 1.

artery in which the catheter is positioned, either by inflating a balloon at the end of the catheter or by wedging an end-hole catheter into the distal vessels. This extends the manometric system encompassed by the wall of the catheter, and the static column of fluid within it, to incorporate the walls of the vessel distal to the end of the catheter and the static column of blood within it (see Fig. 6.4 in Chapter 6). The extended manometric system then measures the pressure in the distal capillary-sinusoidal bed of the lung, where blood is still freely flowing (i.e., near the origin of the pulmonary venous system). Because the flow between the pulmonary capillaries and the left atrium normally is a low-resistance network, the pulmonary artery wedge pressure is usually within 1 or 2 mm Hg of left atrial pressure. Therefore, it is possible to estimate the pulmonary vascular resistance by dividing the mean pulmonary artery pressure, minus the pulmonary wedge pressure, by the cardiac output.

Although the apices of the lungs in a person who is sitting or standing are normally in West's zone 2 (Fig. 52.2), if pulmonary artery pressure decreases, zone 1 relationships may develop (for further discussion, see Chapter 6). Under these conditions, estimates of left atrial pressure from pulmonary artery wedge pressures from zone 1 regions are difficult to obtain and may be inaccurate. However, because most measurements of pulmonary artery wedge pressures are made with the patient supine and the lungs mainly in zone 3, this is ordinarily not a significant practical problem. Should it be desirable to have measurements of pulmonary vascular resistance or estimations of accurate pulmonary artery wedge pressure while the patient is sitting or standing, the pulmonary artery catheter should be wedged in the inferior portions of the lung: that is, in areas in which the vessel is below the level of the left atrium. Or, alternately, one may reasonably use total pulmonary resistance or the ratio of the mean pulmonary artery pressure to the pul-

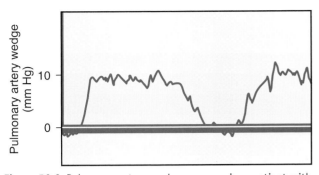

Figure 52.3 Pulmonary artery wedge pressure in a patient with chronic obstructive lung disease. Note that the wedge pressure is normal. A prominent fall in wedge pressure is observed with the onset of inspiration as intrapleural pressure falls.

monary blood flow when studying patients with pulmonary hypertension unrelated to left-sided heart events, in whom pulmonary vein pressures are presumably normal and, therefore, low. It should also be noted that the pulmonary artery wedge pressure may not reflect left atrial pressure if a patient is receiving positive-pressure ventilation. If there are wide swings in intrapleural pressure, the wedge pressure should be estimated at end-expiration and not as a mean pressure (Fig. 52.3).

PATHOPHYSIOLOGY OF THE PULMONARY CIRCULATION

Significant structural changes occur in the pulmonary circulation in patients with COPD. The presence of hypoxemia and chronic ventilatory insufficiency is associated with early evidence of intimal thickening and medial hypertrophy in the smaller branches of the pulmonary arteries.[7] Vascular smooth muscle cells are laid down longitudinally within the intima, and hypertrophy of these cells and smooth muscle cells within the media become prominent. Localized thrombosis in situ can occur, obliterating parts of the pulmonary vascular tree. Coupled with these pathologic changes is pulmonary vasoconstriction arising from the presence of alveolar hypoxemia. The structural changes together with the effects of vasoconstriction result in a significant increase in pulmonary vascular resistance. The consequence is pulmonary arterial hypertension, which in itself may further cause or worsen structural damage to the smaller branches of the pulmonary circulation, and serve as a stimulus for the development of medial hypertrophy and dilation of the larger branches of the pulmonary artery. If these developments are long-standing, prominent atherosclerotic changes may be seen in the main pulmonary artery and its major branches.[8]

As emphysema progresses, destruction of capillaries that course along alveoli that are being destroyed or coalescing into bullae further diminishes the cross-sectional area of the pulmonary vascular bed. This diminishment in area is likely to occur progressively as hyperinflation of the lungs worsens. Capillaries may also be destroyed in interstitial fibrosis or parenchymal infiltrative disease.

Early in the natural history of COPD, the resting pressure in the pulmonary artery is usually normal. It may not

be readily apparent from the vascular pressures that significant capillary destruction is taking place until almost half of the huge capillary bed is destroyed. A large capillary reserve normally exists within the lungs. For example, during exercise a normal subject may increase cardiac output severalfold with only a small rise in pulmonary perfusing pressure. Similarly, patients with an uncomplicated atrial septal defect can have a pulmonary artery pressure that is still in the normal range despite a pulmonary blood flow that is two to three times normal. Although this undoubtedly means that the cross-sectional area of the pulmonary capillary bed is increased by the distention of partially filled capillaries or recruitment of capillaries that might be closed were the flow less, it should be remembered that pulmonary vein and capillary pressures drop to right atrial levels in patients with atrial septal defect as atrial pressures equilibrate in the presence of the usual large defect. Therefore, the pulmonary artery minus pulmonary vein pressure gradient is increased despite a normal pulmonary artery pressure.

Finally, this immense capillary reserve can be demonstrated in the normal person at the time of cardiac catheterization by transient balloon occlusion of the left or right main pulmonary artery. No rise or only a small rise in the resting pulmonary artery pressure results, despite the fact that the entire cardiac output must now flow through the pulmonary circulation of one lung.[9,10] Similarly, patients after pneumonectomy often have only slightly raised resting pulmonary artery pressures following recovery from surgery.

Pulmonary parenchymal disease, particularly idiopathic pulmonary fibrosis, may produce pulmonary hypertension through disturbed gas exchange with the production of pulmonary capillary hypoxemia. This is accomplished through the reduction in pulmonary vascular distensibility by surrounding fibrotic tissue, through mismatching between the distributions of ventilation and perfusion, or directly through destruction or obliteration of a large portion of the pulmonary vascular bed. It is typical for pulmonary hypertension to be produced in patients with chronic pulmonary disease through combinations of anatomic restriction of the pulmonary vascular bed and vasoconstriction due to hypoxia, with or without hypercapnia and acidemia and vasoconstrictive, mitogenic mediators.

HYPOXIC PULMONARY VASOCONSTRICTION

Several stimuli may result in precapillary pulmonary vasoconstriction with resultant pulmonary arterial hypertension. Of these, the most potent and most important, alveolar hypoxia, may be present under a variety of circumstances. Pulmonary vasoconstriction occurs in perfectly healthy lungs. For example, the pulmonary hypertension observed in persons living at high altitudes is caused by chronic hypoxemia despite the presence of hyperventilation with resultant hypocapnia. Similarly, hypoventilation sufficient to produce alveolar hypoxia and hypercapnia, which may occur in morbidly obese patients, results in pulmonary hypertension secondary to pulmonary vasoconstriction. Other causes of primary hypoventilation, whether it arises centrally or from weakness of the muscles of respiration, may also cause pulmonary hypertension secondary to inadequate alveolar ventilation. Hypercapnia, which is primarily mediated by an increase in hydrogen ion concentration, exacerbates the pulmonary vasoconstriction that would result from a given level of alveolar hypoxia.

It is of interest to contrast the consequences of hypoxic pulmonary vasoconstriction in healthy residents who reside at high altitude with those in patients with COPD with cor pulmonale who reside at sea level. In the former case, a combination of alveolar hypoxia, hyperventilation, and hypocapnia is present. In the latter case, hypoxia is often associated with hypoventilation and hypercapnia. Subjects residing at high altitudes have an increased hematocrit and a decreased plasma volume. Their stroke volume and cardiac output tend to be low. In contrast, patients with COPD tend to have normal or increased blood volume, and their cardiac output is generally normal or even increased. Normal subjects, even those residing at very high altitudes, normally do not develop right ventricular failure despite the presence of hypoxia and pulmonary arterial hypertension; this difference suggests that acidemia and hypercapnia are important elements that contribute to impaired right ventricular function in patients with COPD.

Low alveolar PO_2 increases pulmonary artery pressure in a somewhat hyperbolic dose-response curve, with the pressure rising much more rapidly when arterial PO_2 values fall below 60 mm Hg. Nevertheless, there is still marked individual variability in the level of pulmonary artery pressure at a given high altitude; this may be explained, in part, by differences in individual sensitivity to ventilatory drive produced by hypoxia, with some persons hyperventilating more than others. However, some of the variability also lies in individual differences in pulmonary vasoconstrictor responses, which probably reflect an inherited difference in pulmonary vascular reactivity. This latter viewpoint is supported by observations of the high-altitude pulmonary hypertensive disease among cattle known as *brisket disease*.[11] When cattle native to low altitudes are exposed to high altitudes for grazing, pulmonary artery pressure climbs only moderately in some, but in others the pressure climbs steeply. Cattle with either hyporesponsive or hyperresponsive pulmonary vascular reactivity transmit these phenotypes as a genetic trait from parents to offspring.[12]

Just as it has been suggested that genetic traits may play a role in the pulmonary pressor response to the hypoxia of high altitude, one explanation for the observation that some patients with COPD develop pulmonary hypertension, whereas others do not, attributes this variability to inherited differences in the ventilatory sensitivity to hypoxia and carbon dioxide or in pulmonary vascular reactivity, or both.[13]

Most patients who develop resting pulmonary hypertension with COPD are both hypoxemic and hypercarbic; presumably, the hypercarbic patients have a low ventilatory sensitivity to carbon dioxide, because, as noted, hypoxemic residents at high altitudes hyperventilate and are hypocarbic. Therefore, it is reasoned that some patients who are born with a normal ventilatory sensitivity to carbon dioxide and hypoxia have an increased ventilatory effort in response to obstructive lung disease and, therefore, maintain relatively normal blood gases. In contrast, a patient who inherently has a low ventilatory sensitivity fails to compensate and, consequently, develops an insufficient ventilatory drive to overcome the increased airway resistance, ulti-

mately causing hypercapnia, hypoxemia, and pulmonary vasoconstriction.

The terms *pink puffers* and *blue bloaters* were applied by clinicians in the past to characterize the differences between two groups that represent extremes in the clinical-physiologic continuum of COPD. As the names imply, the pink puffers were those who were dyspneic from vigorous breathing but maintained their arterial PO_2 and PCO_2 values in a normal to near-normal range, whereas the blue bloaters were those who became cyanotic and edematous because of hypoventilation with consequent hypoxia and hypercapnia. Originally, it was postulated that these features could be explained by differences in the drive to breathe, excessive in the pink puffers and reduced in the blue bloaters. However, that theory was shattered by the results of studies that measured the drive to breathe using the $P_{0.1}$ test (see Chapter 73) in the two groups of patients: Compared with healthy subjects, drive to breathe was greatly increased in both pink puffers and blue bloaters, and there was no difference between them.[14] The more severe abnormalities in PO_2 and PCO_2 that characterize the blue bloaters are now believed to result from differences in the pattern of breathing and, probably, in intrapulmonary gas exchange.[15] However, it remains true that, in general, the more abnormal the PO_2 and PCO_2 values in patients with COPD, the more severe the pulmonary hypertension and polycythemia and the greater the likelihood of cor pulmonale.

However, the correlation between levels of arterial PO_2 and pulmonary artery pressure is not great. In a study of 120 patients with severe emphysema evaluated for entry into the National Emphysema Treatment Trial, multiple stepwise regression revealed that arterial PO_2 was not an independent predictor of mean pulmonary artery pressure; surprisingly, indices of emphysema severity and pulmonary artery pressures did not correlate either.[16] Several studies suggest that vascular remodeling is a component of early-stage COPD as evidenced by increased inflammatory cell density in the adventitia and increased thickness of the intima of pulmonary arteries in mild COPD without concomitant hypoxemia.[17,18] Furthermore, endothelial lesions have been shown to be present in cigarette smokers without chronic airflow obstruction.[19] A recent study investigated the development of pulmonary arterial hypertension in patients with moderate to severe airflow obstruction who did not meet criteria for long-term oxygen therapy and did not have resting pulmonary arterial hypertension. Seventy-six of 131 (58%) had exercise-induced pulmonary arterial hypertension. At 5 years of follow-up, 25% of the subjects had developed resting pulmonary arterial hypertension, including 32% of those who had exercise-induced pulmonary arterial hypertension at baseline.[20] These studies suggest that factors other than hypoxemia alone play a role in the development of pulmonary vasoconstriction and vascular remodeling that leads to pulmonary arterial hypertension.

RIGHT VENTRICLE

The normal right ventricle is crescent shaped and has a wall thickness less than 0.6 cm (Fig. 52.4). Its weight is usually less than 65 g in men, and less than 50 g in women.[8]

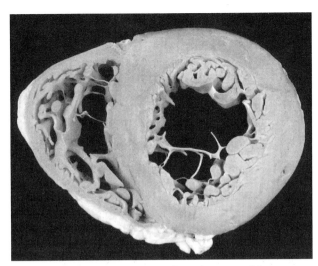

Figure 52.4 A transverse section through a normal heart illustrates a somewhat crescent-shaped right ventricular cavity, together with the presence of prominent trabeculae carneae. Note that the myocardial thickness of the normal left ventricle is considerably greater than that of the right ventricle.

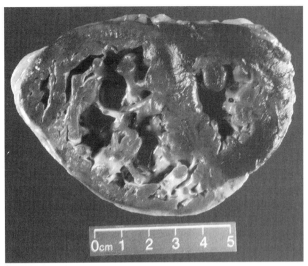

Figure 52.5 Transverse section of a heart from a patient who had severe pulmonary hypertension showing dilation of the right ventricular cavity, which has a more spherical shape than the heart shown in Figure 52.4. Marked wall thickness of the right ventricle caused by massive hypertrophy is seen. The trabeculae carneae are also hypertrophied, and endocardial sclerosis is visible on several of them. The left ventricle is relatively normal, with protrusion of the posteromedial and anterolateral papillary muscles into the cavity. The bright white patches on the lateral free wall and posterolateral septum are highlight artifacts caused by reflection of the flash during photography.

Embryologically, the right ventricle develops from two separate components: the bulbus cordis, which becomes the outflow tract, and the sinus venosus, which becomes the inflow tract. These are separated by a muscular ridge, the crista supraventricularis. Normally, the right ventricle contracts almost sequentially from inflow to outflow, thus effectively emptying its volume into the low-impedance pulmonary circulation. In the absence of cardiac disease, the right ventricle plays an almost passive role in maintaining cardiac output in accordance with the venous return and Starling's law of the heart. In fact, in congenital tricuspid atresia, early surgical approaches involved bypass of the right ventricle through anastomosis of the right atrium directly to the pulmonary artery (the so-called Fontan procedure), which resulted in perfusion of the pulmonary circulation from an elevated central venous pressure. However, it should also be noted that a damaged right ventricle with residual high central venous pressures resulting from an inferior myocardial infarction is associated with a distinctly reduced survival rate.

Because of the shape of the right ventricle, it is difficult to measure the right ventricular volume accurately by radiographic or echocardiographic techniques. In a series of 15 subjects without heart disease, right ventricular end-diastolic volume in the supine position measured by a thermodilution technique, which probably overestimates volumes, averaged 103 ± 24.4 mL/m^2.[21] With passive assumption of an upright posture by tilting, right ventricular end-diastolic volume falls due to gravitational pooling of blood within the distensible venous tree. In a separate series of eight subjects without heart disease, end-diastolic volume fell a mean of 16.3 mL/m^2 from a mean baseline of 98.1 ± 23.3 mL/m^2. This fall in end-diastolic volume causes less of an end-diastolic fiber stretch and results in a fall in stroke volume with the assumption of an upright position. At the same time, aortic baroreceptor stimulation reflexively increases heart rate by about 12 beats/min, thus compensating for an average stroke volume fall of approximately 13.3 mL/m^2; therefore, cardiac output is maintained in essentially the same range as in a recumbent patient at rest.[22]

Acute increases in right ventricular afterload result in a significant fall in stroke volume[23]; in contrast, the left ventricle can accommodate an acute increase in afterload with little change in stroke output. Chronic pulmonary hypertension with a corresponding increase in right ventricular work results in uniform hypertrophy of the right ventricle. As a result, right ventricular weight increases as right ventricular wall myocytes thicken and exhibit enlarged nuclei. Varying degrees of interstitial fibrosis occur. As the ventricle further hypertrophies, it becomes increasingly able to expel the stroke output against high pulmonary vascular resistance and maintain cardiac output. Patients have been observed with primary pulmonary hypertension or with severe mitral stenosis and pulmonary vascular disease in whom the right ventricle maintained a pulmonary artery systolic pressure significantly higher than the systemic pressure.

In patients with COPD, hypoxic vasoconstriction is associated not only with right ventricular hypertrophy but also with right ventricular dilation. The normal crescent shape of the right ventricle is progressively transformed into a more spherical structure that is better able to generate an increased stroke work (Fig. 52.5).

The increase in right ventricular work associated with pulmonary vasoconstriction, with both hypertrophy and dilation of the right ventricle, produces a significant increase in right ventricular myocardial oxygen consumption. At the same time, an increase in wall thickness tends to decrease right ventricular endocardial coronary perfusion. Furthermore, an increase in end-diastolic pressure occurs as right

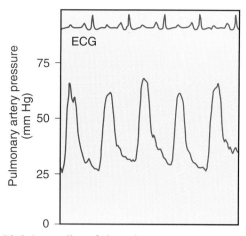

Figure 52.6 A recording of the pulmonary artery pressure at the time of cardiac catheterization in a patient with cor pulmonale and heart failure, illustrating pulsus alternans in the pulmonary artery.

ventricular stiffness increases during diastole, adding to the compromise of endocardial coronary perfusion. Taken together, these factors result in an imbalance between right ventricular myocardial oxygen demand and supply. Nevertheless, in several studies the end-diastolic pressure-volume relationship, even in the presence of resting pulmonary hypertension, suggested well-preserved right ventricular contractility in patients with COPD. It is only with the additional presence of acidemia or infection that right ventricular failure is precipitated. When chronic hypercapnia with acidosis is present in patients with alveolar hypoventilation, the ability of the right ventricle to increase its work appears to be significantly impaired, and right ventricular end-diastolic pressure increases (i.e., there is a shift to the right in the family of Starling curves). This impairment of myocardial contractility in the presence of hypercapnia probably plays a significant role in producing decompensated pulmonary heart disease in response to acute increases in arterial PCO_2 associated with exacerbations of COPD and accompanying decreases in alveolar ventilation. Recordings of right ventricular and pulmonary artery systolic pressures may show pulsus alternans similar to that often seen in left ventricular failure (Fig. 52.6). The development of right ventricular volume overload with ventricular dilation results in a decreased ejection fraction, because stroke volume tends to be maintained close to the normal range in decompensated pulmonary heart disease.[24] With exercise, patients with COPD significantly raise their right ventricular afterload, which causes further increases in right ventricular end-diastolic volume and decreases in ejection fraction. It is likely that this deterioration in hemodynamics with exercise is a major factor limiting the ability of such patients to exercise normally.

Right ventricular dilation and wall thinning result in increased right ventricular wall stress that, along with increased heart rate, leads to further increases in myocardial oxygen consumption. Increased myocardial oxygen consumption compounded by decreased myocardial perfusion as previously described results in right ventricular ischemia and worsening right ventricular function. In addition, as

pulmonary pressures rise and the right ventricle dilates, severe tricuspid regurgitation ensues, which further compromises right ventricular forward cardiac output, thereby limiting left ventricular filling. Furthermore, right ventricular dilation in the setting of an intact pericardium compromises left ventricular filling through several mechanisms. A shift of the interventricular septum toward the left ventricle and an increase in intrapericardial pressure reduce left ventricular distensibility and transmural left ventricular filling pressure, which represents the true preload of the left ventricle. As a consequence of decreased left ventricular preload, the systemic cardiac output is significantly compromised, initially with exercise and eventually even at rest. With rising right atrial pressures in patients with a patent foramen ovale, significant right-to-left atrial shunting can occur, resulting in systemic oxygen desaturation and further worsening systemic oxygen delivery.[25]

When right ventricular failure has developed and central venous pressure is elevated, when the patient stands up, neither right ventricular end-diastolic volume nor stroke volume decreases. Consequently, heart rate does not change. This lack of postural reflex compensation is attributable to failure of any incremental gravitational pooling of blood in the venous tree, because of increased plasma volume, increased tissue pressure from edema with decreasing venous distensibility, and increased venomotor tone.[22]

LEFT VENTRICLE

Controversy has existed over the years as to whether the left ventricle eventually fails when right ventricular failure results from chronic cor pulmonale. Part of the uncertainty has stemmed from the fact that the early studies of patients with cor pulmonale secondary to COPD included chiefly middle-aged or older men with a history of heavy cigarette smoking, who were likely to have coexisting coronary artery disease. Failure of the left ventricle in some of these patients may have reflected coexisting coronary artery disease rather than the natural history of decompensated pulmonary heart disease. Nevertheless, although left ventricular ejection performance is unimpaired, cardiac catheterization studies have revealed abnormal left ventricular end-diastolic pressure-volume relationships.[26] Echocardiographic studies also showed progressive impairment of left ventricular diastolic function that correlated with the severity of pulmonary hypertension.[27] It is likely that this results, in large part, from bulging of the interventricular septum from the hypertrophied and dilated right ventricle into the cavity of the left ventricle, and through ventricular interdependence exerted by pericardial constraint.[25,28] As a result, left ventricular diastolic geometry becomes distorted,[29] and filling characteristics may be altered such that a higher filling pressure is required to accomplish the same end-diastolic fiber stretch needed for a given stroke work, in accordance with Starling's law of the heart. Furthermore, measurements of pulmonary artery wedge pressure as a reflection of left heart filling pressure can be distorted because of the increase in intra-alveolar pressures, as well as the large swings in intrathoracic pressure with resultant large swings in wedge pressure tracings seen in patients with COPD (see Fig. 52.3), and increases in intrapericardial pressure. This is particularly troublesome when the patient is receiving positive end-expiratory pressure from a respirator. Pulmonary artery wedge pressures should always be estimated at end-expiration rather than attempting to measure the mean wedge pressure. Furthermore, with severe right-sided heart failure and marked elevation in right atrial pressure, coronary sinus pressure increases significantly. This can result in an increase in left ventricular wall dimension limiting left ventricular distensibility. This mechanism leading to reduced left ventricular preload appears to act independently of diastolic ventricular interaction caused by right ventricular enlargement as previously described.[30]

NEUROHORMONES

Significant neurohormonal abnormalities occur in patients with cor pulmonale. Plasma catecholamine levels generally rise in patients with decompensated pulmonary heart disease in a manner comparable to that seen in patients with heart failure secondary to primary myocardial disorders. It is clear that increased sympathetic activity is present with decompensation from cor pulmonale, resulting in high plasma levels of circulating catecholamines and stimulation of the renin-angiotensin-aldosterone systems. In the measurements by Anand and associates,[31] vasopressin actually rose to a higher level than was seen in comparable patients with failure not associated with COPD. Because cardiac output is often normal or may even be increased in decompensated pulmonary heart disease, it is likely that the decrease in systemic vascular resistance resulting from both hypercapnia and hypoxia leads to a reflex increase in circulating catecholamines and other neural hormones. Central sympathetic stimulation may also be encouraged by the direct effect of the increased PCO_2 on the central nervous system.

Recently, the neuropeptide vasoactive intestinal peptide (VIP) has been of significant interest in pulmonary hypertension. VIP primarily functions as a neurotransmitter and acts as a potent systemic and pulmonary vasodilator; it has been shown to inhibit platelet activation and vascular smooth muscle cell proliferation. These effects are mediated by stimulation of specific VIP receptors resulting in activation of the cyclic adenosine monophosphate and cyclic guanosine monophosphate (GMP) systems.[32-37] A deficiency of this neuropeptide has been found in the serum and lung tissue of patients with primary pulmonary hypertension. Chronic treatment with inhaled VIP in eight patients with primary pulmonary hypertension resulted in improved cardiopulmonary hemodynamics, exercise performance, and dyspnea.[38] The role of VIP in pulmonary hypertension associated with lung diseases or hypoxemia or both has yet to be investigated. However, given the findings described previously in primary pulmonary hypertension, VIP and its receptors represent rational and promising targets for the development of therapeutic strategies in other forms of pulmonary hypertension.

ANGIOTENSIN II

Angiotensin II is a potent vasoconstrictor of the pulmonary vascular bed. The pulmonary vasculature appears to be even more sensitive to the vasoconstrictor effects of angiotensin II than is the systemic vascular bed. This is noteworthy because increased circulating levels of angiotensin II and aldosterone are found in patients with cor pulmonale secondary to COPD who have hypoxia and hypercapnia.[39] It is likely that activation of the renin-angiotensin-aldosterone systems, together with hypoxemia, is an underlying pathophysiologic mechanism responsible for the elevation in pulmonary vascular resistance that is observed in patients with decompensated pulmonary heart disease.

A dose-response relationship of pulmonary vascular resistance to the infusion of angiotensin II has been observed in normal subjects.[40] In patients with pulmonary heart disease, lowering pulmonary vascular resistance and dropping pulmonary artery pressure is the ideal therapeutic goal. Angiotensin II inhibitors might be expected to produce this effect. They have been demonstrated to improve survival in patients with systolic heart failure caused by either coronary disease or idiopathic dilated cardiomyopathy. Could such a benefit be expected in patients whose right-sided heart failure results from COPD despite the earlier disappointing experience with vasodilators? Although such vasodilators are capable of reducing pulmonary vascular resistance, they may actually worsen hypoxemia. Increased hypoxemia can result from administration of pulmonary vasodilators because perfusion may improve in areas of impaired ventilation, thereby resulting in arterial hypoxemia as a consequence of exacerbated ventilation-perfusion mismatch. It is encouraging to note that the angiotensin-converting enzyme (ACE) inhibitor lisinopril has been demonstrated experimentally to attenuate significantly the pulmonary pressor response to hypoxic pulmonary vasoconstriction in healthy human volunteers.[41] In addition, angiotensin II receptor blockade has also been shown to produce a similar effect in hypoxic pulmonary vasoconstriction in humans.[25] However, studies performed to date have not elucidated a role for ACE inhibitors or angiotensin II receptor antagonists in the treatment of cor pulmonale.

NATRIURETIC PEPTIDES

The family of natriuretic peptides includes atrial natriuretic peptide (ANP), B-type natriuretic peptide (BNP), and C-type natriuretic peptide (CNP). Circulating ANP and BNP levels are elevated manyfold in patients with cor pulmonale, even in the absence of impaired left ventricular function.[42] Presumably, right atrial distention or overactivity in response to increased right ventricular afterload is the stimulus for their release. CNP, which appears to be normal in the usual patient with congestive heart failure of left-sided origin, is elevated in patients with cor pulmonale, although not as extensively as ANP and BNP.[43] The elevation of CNP appears to be endothelial in origin, suggesting that its stimulus for release may be either arterial hypoxemia or endothelial damage occurring in cor pulmonale. ANP, BNP, and CNP have approximately equivalent pulmonary vasorelaxant activities. Although ANPs appear to have little effect on resting vasopulmonary artery tone, they do appear to interact with the vasoactive response of hypoxic pulmonary vasoconstriction. Experimentally, they can attenuate the increased pulmonary hypertension produced by hypoxia.[44]

It has also been shown that BNP levels increase in proportion to the extent of right ventricular dysfunction in pulmonary hypertension.[45] A recent study enrolled 44 patients with right ventricular overload, 18 of whom had atrial septal defect and 26 of whom had primary pulmonary hypertension or thromboembolic pulmonary hypertension. Plasma BNP and ANP levels were measured and right heart catheterization was performed. Right and left ventricular ejection fraction, myocardial mass, and chamber volumes were determined using electron beam computed tomography. Plasma BNP and ANP levels were elevated in these patients compared to control subjects. Furthermore, the BNP-to-ANP ratios were significantly higher in patients with right ventricular pressure overload compared to volume overload. Levels of BNP correlated positively with pulmonary vascular resistance and right atrial pressure, but negatively with cardiac output and right ventricular ejection fraction. Long-term vasodilator therapy was also associated with reduced plasma BNP concentration. Another study of 60 patients with primary pulmonary hypertension, established by right heart catheterization, evaluated the long-term prognostic significance of BNP and other neurohormones.[46] On multivariate analysis, baseline plasma BNP was an independent predictor of mortality; patients with a supramedian level of baseline BNP ($\geq$150 pg/mL) had a significantly lower survival rate than those with an inframedian level ($P < 0.05$). Hence, BNP may serve as a prognostic indicator in patients with primary pulmonary hypertension. Further studies need to be performed to assess BNP's prognostic utility in cor pulmonale secondary to respiratory disorders.

Patients with cor pulmonale, who demonstrate alveolar hypoxia and elevated circulating angiotensin II levels, have a dose-related decrease in pulmonary artery pressure during an infusion of ANP.[47,48] The pulmonary pressor response to infused angiotensin II in humans appears to be significantly attenuated by BNP, but not by ANP. A similar effect is noted in response to hypoxic pulmonary pressor changes. Therefore, it is likely that BNP is the predominant natriuretic peptide modulating the response of the pulmonary vasculature to hypoxia and angiotensin II. BNP may play an important role in attenuating the pressor response that is likely to occur in humans through the actions of alveolar hypoxia and elevated angiotensin II levels. In patients with left-sided heart failure, the human recombinant BNP nesiritide has been shown to suppress endothelin and aldosterone levels, suggesting other mechanisms for the attenuating effect of this peptide on pulmonary vasoconstriction.[49] These findings suggest the possible clinical use of neutral endopeptidase inhibitors that increase circulating levels of endogenous natriuretic peptides by inhibiting their degradation.[50] Such agents might prove useful if added to ACE inhibitors and angiotensin II receptor antagonists in the management of chronic cor pulmonale characterized by alveolar hypoxia and pulmonary hypertension. However, this hypothesis has yet to be tested.

ENDOTHELIN-1

Endothelin-1 (ET-1) is a 21–amino acid peptide secreted by vascular endothelial cells in response to various stimuli, including pulsatile stretch, sheer stress, neurohormones, cytokines, growth factors, and thrombin. The secretion of ET-1 has been shown to be increased by hypoxemia in humans. The effects of ET-1 are mediated by the endothelin A (ET$_A$) and endothelin B (ET$_B$) receptors. ET$_A$ is localized on vascular smooth muscle cells and ET$_B$ is expressed on vascular smooth muscle cells, endothelial cells, and fibroblasts. The effects of ET-1 include vasoconstriction, hyperplasia, hypertrophy, fibrosis, and increased vascular permeability. Activation of ET$_B$ receptors on endothelial cells mediates release of prostacyclin (prostaglandin I$_2$) and nitric oxide (NO), which exert vasodilatory and antiproliferative effects while also inhibiting ET-1 production by endothelial cells. Furthermore, the pulmonary endothelial ET$_B$ receptors are responsible for the pulmonary clearance of up to 50% of circulating ET-1.[51]

Increased ET-1 production has been described in patients with pulmonary hypertension. Increased ET-1 levels and increased expression of receptors have been shown to be present in plexiform lesion of the lung in patients with pulmonary hypertension.[51,52] High plasma levels of ET-1 have been observed in patients with pulmonary hypertension, and this elevation correlated with disease severity and adverse prognosis.[52–56] It has been demonstrated that ET-1 concentration is elevated in the sputum and urine of patients with COPD compared to normal subjects; moreover, urinary levels increase further during COPD exacerbations.[57,58] In addition, plasma ET-1 levels have been shown to be increased in subjects who exhibit oxyhemoglobin desaturation with exercise or at night.[59,60] In another study, patients with COPD and pulmonary hypertension were shown to have elevated transpulmonary ET-1 levels.[61]

These observations suggest that ET-1 plays an important role in mediating the development or perpetuation of pulmonary hypertension in various disease states, and hence is a rational therapeutic target.

SYMPTOMS AND SIGNS

Mild pulmonary hypertension reflected in small chronic elevations in right ventricular pressure generally causes little in terms of clinical, radiologic, or electrocardiographic findings. When moderate or severe pulmonary hypertension develops (mean pulmonary artery pressure >40 mm Hg), symptoms are often those associated with the underlying pulmonary disease. Most commonly, these are dyspnea on exertion, chronic cough productive of mucoid sputum (particularly in the morning hours), variable degrees of wheezing, and noticeable occasional cyanosis; clubbing of the fingers may be present. Moderate or severe pulmonary hypertension by itself (e.g., in patients with primary pulmonary hypertension) may result in only minimal or nonspecific symptoms. In addition to exertional dyspnea and fatigue, some patients experience dizziness or even exertional syncope, attributable to the inability to increase cardiac output during exercise when significant pulmonary vascular disease and pulmonary arterial hypertension are present. Furthermore, these patients may have chest pain owing to right ventricular ischemia or stretching of the main pulmonary artery.

When resting pulmonary artery pressure is sufficiently elevated, patients may eventually reach a point at which the right ventricle cannot meet the need for increased stroke work without a significant increase in right heart filling pressures. The resultant increase in central venous pressure is associated with developing symptoms of right-sided heart failure, such as peripheral edema, right upper quadrant discomfort, nocturia, and easy fatigability. On examination, the patient often displays tachypnea, with prominent use of the accessory muscles of respiration, with arms extended holding on to the edges of the mattress, cyanosis, and neck vein distention. In COPD, pulsus paradoxus may be present. The chest may be hyperinflated. There may also be audible wheezing, particularly if the process of decompensation has been relatively acute and associated with a superimposed respiratory infection. Sinus tachycardia is often present; however, atrial and ventricular arrhythmias are also common.[62] Evidence of fluid retention may include dependent edema and some degree of ascites. The liver is enlarged and tender to palpation, and may be pulsatile, reflecting the presence of severe tricuspid insufficiency. Similarly, the neck veins are distended and, when tricuspid insufficiency is present, show a large c-v wave with rapid y descent; in addition, there may be a prominent a wave reflecting the increased force of right atrial contraction.

On examination of the chest, there may be a left parasternal systolic lift, owing to the overactivity of the enlarged right ventricle, and a thud felt over the pulmonary area as the pulmonary valve closes. The heart sounds are often difficult to hear if the patient has underlying COPD. The pulmonic component of the second heart sound (S_2) is accentuated and occurs earlier than usual, so the normal splitting may be abolished and a single loud S_2 heard. Normally not heard at the apex, the pulmonic component of S_2 may now be clearly heard. A high-pitched systolic ejection click may be heard in the second and third left intercostal spaces next to the sternum. It is often followed by a soft, localized systolic ejection murmur produced by ejection of the stroke volume into a dilated pulmonary artery. An S_3 gallop arising from the right side of the heart may be heard in the fourth and fifth interspaces immediately to the left of the sternum. A presystolic S_4 gallop may also be heard, reflecting the increased forcible contraction of the right atrium with expulsion of blood into the hypertrophied and dilated right ventricle. Often tricuspid regurgitation is present, and this results in a prominent blowing pansystolic murmur in the same location, which may increase somewhat with inspiration. When prominent pulmonary hypertension is present, a diastolic murmur of pulmonary incompetence may be heard; this murmur, known as the Graham Steell murmur, is a soft, blowing decrescendo diastolic murmur, usually well localized to the second and third left intercostal spaces next to the sternum.

Acute respiratory failure is characterized by hypoxemia and hypercapnia, or by their worsening if they are chronically present when the patient is stable, and often requires hospitalization. Dyspnea becomes intense, and the patient is usually bedridden and visibly tachypneic. Coughing is likely to be exacerbated and sputum production increased. Congestive heart failure, if not present earlier, is now clearly evident in most cases. If it was chronically present before the exacerbation of respiratory failure, it will markedly worsen. The patient may exhibit confusion, insomnia, lethargy, and marked fatigue. Fever may be present if the episode has been precipitated or aggravated by an infectious process such as community-acquired pneumonia.

CHEST RADIOGRAPH

The appearance of the chest radiograph depends in large part on the underlying cause for the presence of pulmonary hypertension. Generally, however, the main pulmonary artery segment is enlarged, together with large right and left descending pulmonary arteries. In contrast, there is abrupt tapering of the peripheral vessels, resulting in disproportionately large central pulmonary arteries and attenuated distal vessels. A right descending pulmonary artery with a diameter greater than 16 mm suggests pulmonary hypertension.[63] Enlargement of the right ventricle, which may be observed on echocardiography, is often not appreciated on the chest radiograph. If hyperinflation of the lungs is present, the overall diameter of the cardiac silhouette may not be increased, although the heart may have a globular appearance. Often some encroachment on or filling in of the retrosternal space by an enlarged right ventricle may be seen in a lateral view.

Pleural effusions are seldom seen in patients presenting with pure cor pulmonale unless coexisting left ventricular dysfunction and failure are also present. The reason is evident in the mechanisms that govern fluid formation and clearance across the pleural membranes, which were largely set forth by Staub and coworkers[64] and are illustrated in Figure 68.4 (see Chapter 68). The small amount of fluid that is normally present is filtered across the parietal pleura; removal of fluid occurs through lymphatic stomas that are also located in the parietal pleura. The visceral pleura plays little or no role in pleural fluid turnover in the normal lungs, but does serve as an important escape route for excess interstitial fluid that accumulates in the lungs during the evolution of cardiogenic pulmonary edema (see Chapter 51).

Given this analysis of the dynamics of pleural fluid exchange, pleural effusions might be expected in patients with chronic cor pulmonale and elevated right heart filling pressures, because they have increased systemic venous pressures, which must raise capillary pressures within the parietal pleura. Increased fluid transudation into the parietal pleural interstitium and then into the pleural space would be expected. Failure to find pleural effusions under these circumstances undoubtedly reflects the capacity of the parietal lymphatics to markedly increase their fluid removal capacity, by almost 20-fold. These mechanisms would appear to be substantiated by the findings of a prospective study of 37 patients admitted for congestive heart failure in which the presence of pleural effusions correlated with the values of pulmonary artery wedge pressure but not with the right atrial pressure.[65] In a subsequent retrospective study of 18 patients with long-term right atrial or pulmonary hypertension or both, but with normal pulmonary artery wedge pressures, no pleural effusions were seen.[66] However, patients have been observed with chronic cor pulmonale and acute exacerbation of cardiac decompensation resulting from a superimposed respiratory infection who demonstrate transient small pleural effusions during the acute episode. It is of interest that cattle with brisket disease accumulate transudates in the thoracic cavity as well as in the abdominal cavity and pericardial sac.[67]

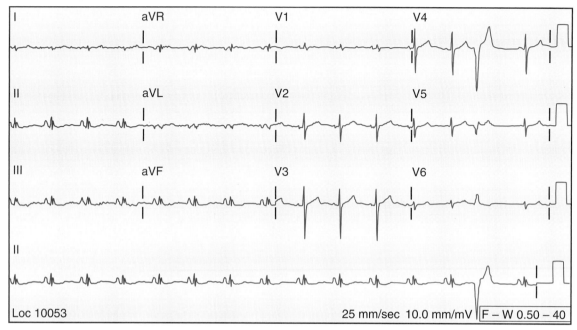

Figure 52.7 An electrocardiogram in a patient with chronic cor pulmonale reveals prominent "p pulmonale" (see text).

In summary, the parietal pleural lymphatic system appears to adjust to chronic increases in filtration rates secondary to increased systemic venous pressure, establishing a steady-state situation that prevents the formation of pleural effusions. However, if there is an acute hemodynamic change, transient filtration can clearly exceed maximum lymphatic drainage, resulting in a transudate that might take hours to days to clear before a new steady state is established.

ELECTROCARDIOGRAM

The electrocardiogram can be quite helpful in establishing the presence of chronic cor pulmonale.[68] Characteristically, the P wave has a "p pulmonale" pattern with right-axis deviation resulting in an increase in its amplitude in leads II, III, and aVF to more than 2.5 mm (Fig. 52.7). The P wave may also be tall in the right precordial leads. The QRS vector in the frontal plane often shifts to the right in cor pulmonale, and a low-voltage QRS is common if lung hyperinflation is present. Prominent S waves are seen in leads I, II, and III, probably reflecting hypertrophy of the crista supraventricularis; an incomplete right bundle-branch block pattern is also frequently observed. When pulmonary arterial hypertension is moderate or severe, the more classic findings of right ventricular hypertrophy may dominate the electrocardiogram, which exhibits tall R waves in V_1 with an R/S ratio of more than 1, and a prominent S wave in V_5 and V_6 with an R/S ratio of less than 1. The presence of electrocardiographic evidence of cor pulmonale in patients with COPD is a poor prognostic sign.[69]

ECHOCARDIOGRAPHY

Echocardiographic examination can assist the clinician in eliminating various nonpulmonary causes of secondary pulmonary hypertension, such as left ventricular failure from coronary disease or dilated congestive cardiomyopathy, aortic or mitral valve disease, and congenital heart disease with left-to-right shunt. Echocardiographic examination can also be directly useful in the evaluation of a patient with COPD. The actual level of systolic pressure in the pulmonary artery can often be estimated by continuous-wave Doppler echocardiography through analysis of the flow velocity in the presence of tricuspid regurgitation. Additionally, there is usually pulmonic insufficiency detectable by Doppler echocardiography in the presence of pulmonary hypertension; this permits estimation of the pulmonary artery diastolic pressure as well. The size of the right atrium and the right ventricle are readily determined, and the contractile state of the right ventricle can be assessed. If right heart filling pressure is increased, it may be associated with dilation of the inferior vena cava, which fails to collapse with respiratory maneuvers such as sniffing. Flattening or shift to the left of the interventricular septum suggests significant pressure overload to the right ventricle. The pulmonic velocity-time integral can be used as a surrogate measure to estimate stroke volume and be monitored serially along with the estimated pulmonary artery systolic pressure to assess response to therapy. Finally, the echocardiogram will verify that left ventricular size is normal or reduced and that left ventricular systolic function is normal in isolated cor pulmonale.

In 81 patients with severe primary pulmonary hypertension, baseline severity of the echocardiographic findings of pericardial effusion ($P = 0.003$) and indexed right atrial area ($P = 0.005$) were predictors of 12-week mortality; pericardial effusion ($P = 0.017$), indexed right atrial area ($P = 0.012$), and degree of septal shift in diastole ($P = 0.004$) were predictors of the composite end point of death or transplantation.[70] These echocardiographic abnormalities reflect the severity of right-sided heart failure; they are simple and useful predictors of adverse outcomes in this restricted patient population. Whether or not these echocardiographic parameters are of similar prognostic

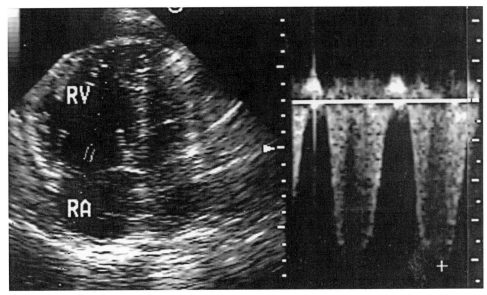

Figure 52.8 *Left,* Normal left ventricular volume is seen on this echocardiogram of a patient with chronic obstructive pulmonary disease who presented with acute severe respiratory distress. Normal contractility also was observed during recording. The right ventricle (RV) is markedly dilated (see text). *Right,* Estimation of the degree of pulmonary hypertension using continuous-wave Doppler measurement of the velocity jet from the tricuspid insufficiency that was present. A 55 mm Hg peak systolic pressure gradient between the right ventricle and right atrium (RA) was calculated, indicating moderate to severe pulmonary arterial hypertension.

utility in other causes of cor pulmonale remains to be determined.

The presence of hyperinflation of the lungs in patients with COPD often creates a technical problem that, at times, results in a less than satisfactory examination. Nevertheless, it is useful to try to interrogate cardiac structures with a transthoracic two-dimensional Doppler echocardiographic examination, because a good technician can generally obtain sufficient data to provide useful information for the clinician. There is an 80% to 85% success rate in visualizing cardiac structures adequately by echocardiography in COPD.[71] If sufficient lung hyperinflation prevents an adequate transthoracic examination, one may resort to a transesophageal echocardiogram to clarify the problem. Often patients in this situation are intubated, and a transesophageal study probe can be slipped into the esophagus with relative ease. A much better delineation of cardiac function and any cardiac pathology can be obtained by the transesophageal route than is possible with a transthoracic probe.

Figure 52.8 illustrates a Doppler echocardiographic examination in a patient with COPD who presented with severe respiratory distress. The possibility of coexisting coronary disease, which arises frequently in the older male patient, led to the question of whether the patient was in respiratory distress from pulmonary congestion secondary to left ventricular failure or the problem reflected pulmonary hypertension and ventilatory insufficiency arising from decompensated pulmonary heart disease. The figure clearly illustrates that the left ventricle was of normal size, and it was seen to have normal contractility during analog recording. By contrast, the right ventricle was moderately dilated and was observed to have a significantly decreased right ventricular systolic contractile function. Right atrial enlargement was present as well. Although tricuspid insuf-

ficiency was not a major clinical problem in this particular patient, there was sufficient tricuspid insufficiency to permit Doppler estimation of the degree of pulmonary hypertension. This is often the case when pulmonary hypertension is present. The right section of Figure 52.8 illustrates a continuous-wave Doppler jet demonstrating that a peak systolic gradient of at least 55 mm Hg was present between the right ventricle and right atrium, indicating moderate to severe pulmonary hypertension.

HEMODYNAMICS

Hemodynamic measurements in patients with decompensated pulmonary heart disease secondary to COPD are subject to error. Use of the direct Fick method to estimate cardiac output at the time of cardiac catheterization is complicated when hypoxemia is present. Hypoxemia may be caused both by shunting across the lungs, from perfusion of unventilated or poorly ventilated alveoli, and by a decrease in oxygen diffusion reflecting alveolar-capillary block from associated fibrosis, parenchymal infiltrative disease, inflammation, and/or edema. Consequently, true pulmonary blood flow, in terms of pulmonary capillary blood flow, is only approximated when systemic arterial oxygen content difference is used to calculate the arteriovenous oxygen content across the lungs. Further problems are provided by the fact that there may be difficulty in estimating oxygen consumption if the patient is receiving therapeutic oxygen.

Measurements of pulmonary blood flow by the use of indicator dilution curves such as thermodilution may also be spurious in patients with pulmonary shunting of blood and in those with very low cardiac outputs. In fact, the clinician should measure the oxygen saturation of pulmonary artery blood from the indwelling pulmonary artery catheter and verify that it is substantially lower than normal before accepting a thermodilution readout that cardiac output is markedly depressed. However, within these limitations, it would appear that cardiac output in patients with decompensated pulmonary heart disease from hypoxic pulmonary vasoconstriction is generally in the normal range or even increased due to the systemic vasodilation produced by hypoxemia; this finding contrasts with that in primary pulmonary hypertension, chronic obstructive embolic disease, mitral stenosis with pulmonary vascular disease, or decompensated heart failure caused by primary myocardial disease, in which low-output states are usually present. Hemodynamic studies in COPD patients with and without heart failure consistently show a normal cardiac output.[71,72] Measurements performed by Anand and his associates[31] in nine patients with peripheral edema due to COPD and in six patients after recovery demonstrated that patients with edema had severe salt and water retention, reduction in renal blood flow and glomerular filtration rate, and a neurohormonal activation comparable to that seen in patients with congestive heart failure due to primary myocardial disease; these occurred despite the fact that mean cardiac output was normal, as was mean pulmonary artery wedge pressure. Therefore, with an increase in arterial PO_2 and a fall in PCO_2, the patients became free from edema, with a corresponding increase in renal blood plasma flow and normalization of glomerular filtration rate.

In patients with pulmonary arterial hypertension as classified in Table 52.2, right heart catheterization is required to assess the hemodynamic severity and hence prognosis of pulmonary hypertension, to establish the pre- versus postcapillary etiology, to perform an oxygen saturation assessment across the right heart structures, to search for the presence of a congenital systemic-to-pulmonary shunt, to measure pulmonary vascular resistance, and to perform acute vasoreactivity testing to guide therapy as well as to monitor safety of treatment with calcium channel blockers.[2] It is not known if acute vasodilator therapy testing is of any utility in patients with pulmonary hypertension and cor pulmonale due to diseases of the respiratory system or hypoxemia. For a detailed description of the role of right heart catheterization and vasodilator testing in pulmonary arterial hypertension, see Chapter 49.

DIFFERENTIAL DIAGNOSIS

There are many causes of pulmonary artery hypertension, as noted in Table 52.2. At times, the underlying cause may be difficult to establish. Specific symptoms and signs of the basic disorder often help to establish the cause of pulmonary hypertension. For example, mitral stenosis noted on physical examination or by echocardiographic examination may represent the underlying cause of pulmonary hypertension. Early in the natural history of mitral stenosis, only passive pulmonary hypertension occurs; however, after prolonged elevation of left atrial and pulmonary vein pressure, pulmonary artery pressure rises out of proportion to the raised left atrial pressure from reflex pulmonary vasoconstriction. Radiographic evidence of increased interstitial markings reflecting increased lung vascular volume from high pulmonary blood flow suggests the presence of congenital

heart disease with a congenital systemic-to-pulmonary shunt. The diagnosis of idiopathic pulmonary hypertension can be made only after other causes of increased obstruction to pulmonary blood flow have been eliminated. Obstructive pulmonary vascular disease caused by appetite suppressants or other toxic substances; pulmonary hypertension associated with occasional cases of portal hypertension; silent deep venous thrombotic disease that has resulted in multiple, relatively silent pulmonary emboli with subsequent pulmonary hypertension; and pulmonary vasculitis from systemic lupus erythematosus, scleroderma, or other collagen vascular diseases are but a few examples in which the underlying cause must be sought, beginning with a careful medical history and physical examination, to explain the basis of the pulmonary hypertension.

The diagnosis of chronic cor pulmonale due to obstructive or restrictive ventilatory insufficiency is usually rapidly established because these patients either have evidence of pulmonary parenchymal disease (e.g., radiographic evidence of pulmonary infiltrative or fibrotic disease, lung hyperinflation, radiologic findings suggesting bronchiectasis), present with symptoms or physical findings that suggest underlying pulmonary disease (e.g., bronchial wheezing, history of chronic bronchitis with a chronic productive cough), or abnormalities of pulmonary function testing. Other patients present with evidence of chest wall deformities that may interfere with respiration (e.g., kyphoscoliosis). Morbid obesity may suggest the presence of the pickwickian syndrome or primary alveolar hypoventilation. Pulmonary edema on chest radiography, with dilation of the left side of the heart, indicates that COPD is not the cause, and suggests the presence of comorbid conditions affecting the left ventricle. Pulmonary edema may also occur without overt left ventricular failure in patients with acute respiratory distress syndrome (see Chapter 51).

CLASSIFICATION OF PULMONARY HYPERTENSION

In 1998, and later in 2003, the WHO convened a panel of experts to develop a treatment-oriented classification of pulmonary hypertension (see Tables 52.1 and 52.2), and to develop guidelines for diagnosis and therapy.[2,3] Pulmonary hypertension was classified into five major categories: pulmonary arterial hypertension, pulmonary hypertension with left heart disease, pulmonary hypertension associated with lung diseases and/or hypoxemia, pulmonary hypertension due to chronic thrombotic and/or embolic disease, and miscellaneous.

Table 52.3 presents an older classification of pulmonary hypertension. *Passive pulmonary arterial hypertension* results from raised pulmonary vein and capillary pressures that require the pulmonary artery perfusing pressure to rise correspondingly. In actuality, because of the distensibility of the pulmonary circulation, the mechanical rise in the distending pressure causes a diminution in the gradient between mean pulmonary artery and capillary pressures for the same degree of vasomotor tone, despite the overall rise in pulmonary artery pressure. Passive pulmonary hypertension is most frequently seen when left atrial pressure rises secondary to left ventricular failure or mitral stenosis.

Table 52.3 Classification of Pulmonary Hypertension

Passive
Left ventricular systolic pump failure
Decreased left ventricular diastolic compliance, elevated left atrial pressure
Mitral stenosis

Idiopathic

Hyperkinetic

Dietary or Ingestive Pulmonary Hypertension

Obstructive

Obliterative

Vasoconstrictive
Reflex secondary to chronic pulmonary venous or capillary hypertension
Hypoxic

Hyperkinetic pulmonary hypertension may arise when there are marked increases in pulmonary blood flow. Normally, the increased cardiac output that is seen in the so-called hyperkinetic states (e.g., severe chronic, normovolemic anemia; generalized Paget's disease; thyrotoxicosis; large arteriovenous fistula) is insufficient to significantly raise the pulmonary artery pressure. However, in congenital heart disease, with large left-to-right shunts and markedly increased pulmonary blood flow, pulmonary artery pressure may rise. Therefore, infants and young children with large ventricular septal defects may have systemic pressures in their pulmonary arteries maintained primarily by very large left-to-right shunts and resultant increased pulmonary blood flow.

Obstructive pulmonary hypertension refers to a decrease in the cross-sectional area of the pulmonary vascular bed as a result of narrowing or occlusion of distal pulmonary arterioles. This most commonly is caused by repetitive, relatively silent pulmonary emboli arising over time from (usually) unsuspected deep venous thromboses. However, it can also be seen in situations in which vasculitis of the distal pulmonary arterioles produces obstructive pulmonary vascular disease and pulmonary hypertension. Pulmonary hypertension in obstructive pulmonary vascular disease may worsen due to the development of thrombosis in situ in patients with already established pulmonary hypertension and secondary anatomic changes in the smaller branches of the pulmonary circulation. Sickle cell anemia may also be a source of such thromboses. Another cause of obliterative pulmonary vascular disease may be seen in injection drug abusers of drugs such as methylphenidate (Ritalin); the talc incorporated in the manufacturing process leads to minute repetitive embolizations. Infective endocarditis on the tricuspid valve with frequent pulmonary emboli can also produce obstructive pulmonary vascular disease.

Idiopathic or *primary pulmonary hypertension,* a relatively infrequent but serious cause of pulmonary hypertension, right ventricular hypertrophy, and eventual congestive heart failure, is discussed in detail in Chapter 49.

Dietary or *ingestive pulmonary hypertension* refers to the ingestion of any of several drugs or substances that have resulted in epidemics of pulmonary hypertension, mimicking primary pulmonary hypertension. One of the most famous of these was the Spanish toxic oil syndrome, which occurred as a result of the ingestion of rapeseed cooking oil that had been adulterated with aniline dye. A large number of children and some adults developed severe pulmonary vascular disease with hypertension as a result.[73] Ingestion of *Crotalaria* plant seeds has been used to create an animal model of pulmonary hypertension in several species.[74,75] Appetite suppressants have been associated with the development of pulmonary hypertension[76,77]; in the 1960s, aminorex fumarate, an appetite suppressant, was linked to an epidemic of pulmonary arterial hypertension in Europe, particularly Switzerland and Germany, before its toxicity was appreciated and the drug was banned from the market. This was followed by a fall in the incidence of pulmonary arterial hypertension.[77,78] Other appetite-suppressant drugs such as fenfluramine and its derivatives have been associated with an increase in cases of pulmonary arterial hypertension. In one study, exposure to the drug for longer than 3 months predicted an odds ratio of 23:1 for the development of pulmonary hypertension.[79,80]

Obliterative pulmonary hypertension results from a variety of different pulmonary parenchymal processes. It can be seen, for example, in emphysema as bullae coalesce and parts of the capillary bed of the lung are correspondingly obliterated. It may also result from diffuse pulmonary fibrosis and from a variety of parenchymal infiltrative diseases, such as sarcoidosis, advanced tuberculosis, pneumoconiosis, and scleroderma.

Vasoconstrictive pulmonary hypertension is the major cause of pulmonary hypertension that is seen in patients with chronic cor pulmonale; it is produced predominantly by alveolar hypoxia. However, patients who develop chronic pulmonary venous and pulmonary capillary hypertension, although they have obligatory passive pulmonary arterial hypertension, may develop a reflex pulmonary vasoconstriction that raises pulmonary artery pressure out of proportion to the passive elevation in pulmonary vein and capillary pressures. This is commonly seen in mitral stenosis: if unrelieved, pulmonary artery pressure climbs owing to reflex pulmonary vasoconstriction out of proportion to the rise in left atrial, pulmonary vein, and pulmonary capillary pressures. With opening of the mitral valve by balloon valvotomy or surgery and accompanying fall in left atrial pressure toward normal, the abnormalities may reverse.

A simple, mechanistic, hemodynamic classification categorizes pulmonary hypertension as follows[81]:

1. Precapillary pulmonary hypertension, which includes all diseases and disorders exclusive of congenital systemic-to-pulmonary shunts that are associated with a pulmonary capillary wedge pressure less than 15 mm Hg and pulmonary vascular resistance greater than 3 Wood units, or 240 dyne-sec·cm^{-5}.
2. Postcapillary pulmonary hypertension, which includes all left-sided cardiac lesions and pulmonary vein compression. In these disorders, the pulmonary capillary wedge pressure is greater than 15 mm Hg and leads to passive elevation of pulmonary artery pressure.
3. Mixed pulmonary hypertension, which is also defined by elevated pulmonary capillary wedge pressure, but the

degree of pulmonary arterial hypertension is in excess of the level one would expect from simple passive elevation of capillary wedge pressure alone. The pulmonary vascular resistance is 3 Wood units or greater and may be irreversible with vasodilators, suggesting that development of reactive pulmonary vasoconstriction and remodeling from chronically elevated pulmonary capillary wedge pressure has occurred; this reaction is in large part mediated by increased ET-1 activity.

4. Pulmonary hypertension resulting from high-flow states through the pulmonary circulation, as would occur with systemic-to-pulmonary shunts in which the pulmonary capillary wedge pressure is less than 15 mm Hg.[81]

TREATMENT

The goals of treatment for cor pulmonale are similar to those for treating left-sided heart failure and include relief of symptoms, improvement of functional capacity, slowing of disease progression, and reducing morbidity and mortality. These goals can be attained, in part, by addressing the major operative pathophysiologic mechanisms: hypoxemia, acidemia, pulmonary hypertension, and neurohormonal activation.[25] Certainly, treatment must be directed to the specific underlying pulmonary disorder leading to cor pulmonale (Table 52.4). In the management of chronic cor pulmonale, diet and lifestyle modifications are important. These include smoking cessation, sodium restriction, weight loss, and exercise training to improve functional performance. Structured rehabilitation programs and breathing training have been shown to be useful.[25,82] Patients with severe pulmonary arterial hypertension, especially those with a history of syncope, should avoid overexertion. In addition, pregnancy and high altitudes (>4000 feet) should also be avoided in this setting. Oral anticoagulation is considered the standard of care in patients with moderate to severe pulmonary arterial hypertension. One retrospective and one prospective trial have suggested a mortality benefit.[83,84] In the management of chronic cor pulmonale with excessive right ventricular preload, diuretic therapy is the mainstay of therapy to alleviate dyspnea, hepatic congestion, and peripheral edema. Decompression of the right ventricle with diuretics may also improve right ventricular performance by reducing its preload and wall stress. With resultant reductions in intrapericardial pressure and potential attenuation of interventricular septal shift toward the left ventricle, left ventricular filling may increase resulting in improved systemic cardiac output.

Management of patients with decompensated pulmonary heart disease must focus on improvement of the underlying pulmonary disorder if compensation is to be restored. The precipitating event for decompensation in patients with stabilized chronic cor pulmonale from either COPD or infiltrative lung disease is often an associated upper respiratory infection. Increased secretions and infection are likely to tip the balance toward further alveolar hypoxemia, hypercapnia, and acidemia, which aggravate pulmonary hypertension and worsen ventricular contractility, resulting in cardiac decompensation.

Improvement in right ventricular performance is best accomplished not only by correcting acidemia, but also by

Table 52.4 Therapeutic Strategies for Cor Pulmonale

Diet and Lifestyle
Smoking cessation
Weight loss
Sodium restriction
Judicious exercise training
Structured rehabilitation and breathing training programs
Avoidance of overexertion
Avoidance of pregnancy
Avoidance of high altitudes

Interventions
Treatment of underlying condition
  COPD (bronchodilators, corticosteroids, antibiotics, oxygen)
  Interstitial lung disease (immunosuppression, oxygen, interferon-γ [investigational])
  Sleep-disordered breathing and alveolar hypoventilation disorders (CPAP, BiPAP, surgery)
  Chronic exposure to high altitudes (return to sea level)
  Chronic thromboembolic disease (anticoagulation, inferior vena cava filters, thromboendarterectomy)
Supplemental oxygen
Pulmonary vasodilators
Anticoagulation
Diuretics
Digitalis glycosides (chronic therapy)
Nonglycoside inotropes (low-dose dobutamine or dopamine in acute severe right heart decompensation with hypoperfusion)
Lung volume-reduction surgery
Lung transplantation
Heart-lung transplantation (PAH secondary to complex congenital heart disease)
Percutaneous blade-balloon atrial septostomy (investigational)
  Severe right-sided heart failure
  Recurrent syncope

BiPAP, bilevel positive airway pressure; CPAP, continuous positive airway pressure; PAH, pulmonary artery hypertension.

reducing the afterload facing the right ventricle (i.e., reducing pulmonary artery pressure). Correction of arterial hypoxemia through the administration of an increased concentration of oxygen in inspired air lowers pulmonary artery pressure in patients with hypoxic pulmonary vasoconstriction. Improvement in alveolar ventilation with intubation and mechanical ventilation helps eliminate the acute hypercapnia and acidemia that depress myocardial contractility. Therapy with digoxin is controversial, and its effects on right ventricular function are unclear; it produces a modest increase in cardiac output in patients with pulmonary hypertension and right ventricular failure,[85] thereby increasing pulmonary blood flow and reducing right-sided heart filling pressure. However, it does not lower pulmonary artery pressure.[86] Short-term treatment with digoxin in patients with right ventricular dysfunction from pulmonary hypertension is associated with a significant reduction in circulating levels of catecholamines, and this may be a mechanism for its reported favorable hemodynamic effects in some studies.[85] It is unknown at this time if digoxin exerts beneficial effects on progression of right ventricular failure, morbidity, or survival, and therefore its use remains controversial. It must be emphasized that patients with COPD are particularly sensitive to digoxin, and close attention to dosage and electrolyte balance to prevent digitalis toxicity is necessary.

Often, an episode of acute cardiac decompensation in a patient who has chronic pulmonary hypertension due to COPD is caused by an underlying pneumonitis or superimposed bronchitis. Patchy areas of atelectasis may also play a role. Empirical antimicrobials (see Chapter 36) should be administered until cultures identify the causative organism and allow more specific treatment to be used. β_2-Agonists such as albuterol are widely accepted as standard management. Not only are they bronchodilators, but they acutely produce a fall in pulmonary artery pressure and a rise in right ventricular ejection fraction with no significant fall in arterial PO_2.[25,87] Anticholinergic drugs such as ipratropium bromide are also useful bronchodilators. Theophylline seems to lessen dyspnea and may be helpful in improving ventilation, but it has considerable toxicity. Finally, short-term corticosteroids appear useful in accelerating recovery from exacerbations of acute respiratory failure in patients with COPD and should be given as early as possible. Hypoventilation with sleep is common in patients with COPD and can contribute to nocturnal hypoxemia and hypercapnia, leading to increased pulmonary vasoconstriction. As described in Chapter 74, continuous positive airway pressure can exert beneficial effects by keeping small airways open and improving gas exchange. In patients with obstructive sleep apnea, continuous positive airway pressure is associated with improved ventricular function and survival and reduced hematocrit.[88–90]

If severe polycythemia is present, phlebotomy may be helpful, although clinicians are frequently reluctant to undertake this type of therapy today. In cattle with brisket disease, cardiac output and coronary blood flow increased without a rise in pulmonary artery pressure when phlebotomy was performed.[91] Hypoxic patients also show improvement in right ventricular ejection fraction, exercise tolerance, and neuropsychological function after phlebotomy.[25]

The role of ACE inhibitors,[92] angiotensin II receptor blockers, or aldosterone receptor blockers in chronic cor pulmonale has not been independently studied in large randomized, double-blind, clinical trials, and their potential long-term benefits are unknown.

OXYGEN THERAPY

Young adults living at high altitudes have distinctly raised pulmonary artery pressures that fall to normal if they leave to live at sea level for several years. Such observations, combined with the clinical, pathologic, and physiologic data observed in patients with COPD, emphasize the importance of hypoxia in the genesis of pulmonary hypertension. It also suggests that continuous domiciliary oxygen therapy might reduce pulmonary arterial hypertension in patients with COPD and thereby improve outcome. Controlled trials evaluating long-term oxygen administration showed improvement in survival, although they failed to demonstrate a clear and consistent reduction in pulmonary hypertension.

Two major randomized trials have been carried out. In the British Medical Research Council evaluation of long-term domiciliary oxygen in chronic hypoxic cor pulmonale, long-term oxygen administration for at least 15 hours/day

appeared to prevent further rises in pulmonary artery pressure, compared with no oxygen administration in control patients[93]; it also lessened mortality. In a National Institutes of Health study in the United States, 12 hours of nocturnal oxygen therapy was compared with continuous therapy; continuous oxygen proved distinctly more favorable, with a lessened mortality rate at 2 years.[94] Additionally, a decrease was seen in pulmonary vascular resistance, contrasted to a small rise in the group receiving only nocturnal therapy. Furthermore, oxygen therapy has been shown to relieve renal vasoconstriction and improve oxygen delivery to critical organs such as the heart and brain.[95]

Based on the results of these studies, it is clear that severely hypoxemic patients with COPD should be provided home oxygen therapy, with a goal of continuous therapy but with at least 15 hours/day of oxygen. However, it must be remembered that the acute administration of *high* concentrations of oxygen to a patient with hypoxic cor pulmonale can have adverse effects on breathing and carbon dioxide removal, particularly if the patient is already displaying alveolar hypoventilation as evidenced by hypercapnia. This is important to keep in mind when evaluating a patient's pulmonary artery hypertensive response to oxygen administration in the catheterization laboratory, and when determining the dose for use at home. Patients given domiciliary oxygen need to be observed closely when they are initially being instructed on the use of this therapy to ensure that ventilatory drive is not being substantially impaired and that arterial oxygen saturation actually rises. Further information about the long-term use of oxygen in pulmonary rehabilitation is provided in Chapter 88.

PULMONARY VASODILATORS

The recommendations for the treatment of pulmonary arterial hypertension with pulmonary vasodilators are based on studies of patients with primary pulmonary hypertension or pulmonary arterial hypertension associated with connective tissue diseases, most commonly the scleroderma spectrum of disorders. To date, no large-scale studies or guidelines have been developed with respect to vasodilator therapy for patients with pulmonary hypertension secondary to lung diseases with or without hypoxemia. Management algorithms for patients with pulmonary arterial hypertension include right heart catheterization for diagnostic as well as therapeutic indications. Protocols for vasoreactivity testing with short-acting acute vasodilators may include testing high-flow oxygen, inhaled NO up to 20 ppm, parenteral epoprostenol, or parenteral adenosine. A reduction in the pulmonary vascular resistance by more than 20% from baseline identifies a group of "responders," which comprises less than 15% of the pulmonary arterial hypertension population, but which includes those who may respond to a hemodynamically monitored trial of calcium channel blockers, such as nifedipine, diltiazem, or amlodipine. Verapamil should be avoided as it can exert substantial negative inotropic effects and worsen right ventricular function. In the treatment of primary pulmonary hypertension, high-dose calcium channel blockers have been shown to improve New York Heart Association (NYHA) functional classification and to induce echocardiographically demonstrated regression of right ventricular hypertrophy.[84]

Patients who responded to calcium channel blockade had a reported 5-year survival of 94% compared to 30% in the nonresponders.[84]

It has been far less common to evaluate and subsequently use pulmonary vasodilators as chronic therapy in patients with cor pulmonale due to COPD or diffuse parenchymal disease. Attempts to date have not significantly affected long-term function or survival. One reason is that initial acute pulmonary vasodilating responses to an agent may not persist when the agent is used chronically. For example, in a study of 53 patients with COPD and pulmonary hypertension, the decrease in pulmonary vascular resistance after initial use of the calcium antagonist nifedipine was 23% at rest and 35% during exercise. However, after an average of 13 months of treatment, the decrease in pulmonary vascular resistance was no longer significant.[96] Side effects from calcium channel blockers include worsening hypoxemia secondary to ventilation-perfusion mismatch and right-to-left shunting through a patent foramen ovale in the setting of greater reduction in systemic vascular resistance relative to pulmonary vascular resistance. Peripheral edema is also a frequent consequence of calcium channel blockade and may limit its long-term tolerance. Those patients who fail to respond to acute vasodilator testing or who have severe right ventricular failure, adverse effects with calcium channel blockers, or hypotension should be considered for treatment with oral bosentan (Tracleer), a dual endothelin receptor antagonist; subcutaneously infused treprostinil (Remodulin); or intravenously infused epoprostenol (Flolan).

Of major concern in patients with pulmonary hypertension due to lung diseases is that the pharmacologic reversal of hypoxic pulmonary vasoconstriction with vasodilators may increase pulmonary blood flow to poorly ventilated or nonventilated alveoli, with the net effect that arterial PO_2 may fall despite a drop in pulmonary artery pressure. What is frequently unappreciated is that ventilation-perfusion matching also affects carbon dioxide elimination. Minute ventilation may increase to compensate for the retention of carbon dioxide; therefore, although arterial PO_2 may fall, hypercapnia may not worsen.[97] In patients with advanced COPD, one small study reported a decrease[98] and another no change[99] in PO_2 after inhaled NO. In patients with respiratory failure from COPD, PO_2 did decrease with epoprostenol treatment.[100] However, in stable COPD patients treated with amlodipine and felodipine, there was no significant fall in PO_2.[101,102] Another practical problem limiting the use of pulmonary vasodilators is that often they also are systemic vasodilators and may result in significant hypotension. Physicians should be on the lookout for the occasional patient with pulmonary hypertension from recurrent pulmonary embolism, because of the considerable benefit from thromboendarterectomy.[103]

Endothelin Receptor Antagonists

Bosentan (Tracleer) is an orally administered competitive receptor antagonist that blocks both the ET_A and ET_B receptors. It was approved for the treatment of pulmonary arterial hypertension to improve exercise tolerance, functional capacity, and delay the time to clinical worsening in patients with WHO functional class III or IV symptoms. In a recent 12-week randomized, prospective, double-blind, placebo-controlled trial of 32 subjects with either primary pulmonary hypertension or pulmonary arterial hypertension associated with connective tissue disease, patients treated with bosentan (125 mg twice daily) improved their performance on the 6-minute walk test by a placebo-corrected treatment effect of 76 m ($P = 0.02$) and showed improvement in cardiopulmonary hemodynamics.[104] A similarly designed 16-week trial, the BREATHE-1 study, was carried out on 213 subjects with WHO classification III or IV symptoms. At 16 weeks the placebo-corrected mean improvement in 6-minute walk distance was 44 m ($P = 0.0002$) for the patients randomized to the bosentan arm. Bosentan therapy was associated with a significant improvement in WHO functional classification ($P = 0.042$) and an insignificant improvement in Borg dyspnea index score ($P = 0.059$). At 16 weeks, bosentan delayed the time to clinical deterioration. Ninety-five percent of patients on bosentan were free of adverse clinical events compared to 75% of the control patients. In a subgroup of 48 subjects who continued in the double-blind extension up to 28 weeks, 89% of those in the bosentan group compared to 63% in the placebo arm were event-free ($P = 0.0015$).[105]

Therapy with bosentan has been associated with potential liver injury, teratogenic effects, and modest reductions in hemoglobin concentration. Close monitoring of liver transaminases and hemoglobin is recommended. Pregnancy must be prevented with reliable barrier contraception as hormonal contraceptive therapy is unreliable in the presence of concomitant bosentan treatment. Monthly pregnancy tests are recommended. Side effects from bosentan include nasal congestion, pharyngitis, dyspepsia, and peripheral edema. Although bosentan has been shown to be beneficial in patients with pulmonary arterial hypertension, its role in the treatment of patients with hypertension associated with disorders of the respiratory system has yet to be determined in large-scale trials. Studies are underway to investigate its utility in pulmonary arterial hypertension due to COPD and interstitial lung disease.

The selective ET_A receptor antagonist sitaxsentan has also been subject to a recent 12-week randomized, double-blind, placebo-controlled trial in 178 subjects with NYHA functional class II, III, or IV symptoms from pulmonary arterial hypertension. Patients were randomized to placebo, sitaxsentan 100 mg, and sitaxsentan 300 mg orally once daily. The primary endpoint of peak exercise oxygen consumption was improved by +3.1%, $p < 0.01$, in the 300 mg group compared to placebo. Both the 100 mg and the 300 mg dose groups had improvement in a secondary endpoint, 6-minute walk distance of 35 and 33 meters, $p < 0.01$, respectively. Other secondary endpoints, functional class and cardiopulmonary hemodynamics significantly improved with both doses compared to placebo. Incidence of elevated aminotransferases was 0% for the 100 mg and 10% for the 300 mg dose group.[106] Thus, this investigational endothelin antagonist also shows promise, but, as with bosentan, this agent has also not been studied in pulmonary arterial hypertension associated with respiratory diseases.

Prostacyclin and Its Analogues

Prostaglandins are synthesized by the pulmonary vascular endothelium. Neonatal calves that develop severe pulmonary hypertension when exposed to chronic hypobaric hypoxia have been shown to have a relative deficit in prostaglandin production in their pulmonary arteries. This suggests that prostaglandins may play a role in the development of pulmonary hypertension by the lack of vasodilatory stimuli.[107] Normal subjects exposed acutely to high-altitude hypoxia release both vasoconstrictive and vasoactive eicosanoids, with vasoconstrictors being released initially and vasodilators being released several days later.[108] Furthermore, the medium to small pulmonary arteries of patients with primary pulmonary hypertension exhibit reduced expression of prostacyclin synthase compared with arteries from control subjects.[109]

Epoprostenol (Flolan) is a systemic and pulmonary vasodilator that also inhibits platelet aggregation, affects vascular remodeling, and opposes the effects of thromboxane A_2.[110] These effects are mediated by enhanced adenyl cyclase activity resulting in increased cyclic adenosine monophosphate in vascular smooth muscle cells and platelets. As a result of its ultrashort half-life and instability, epoprostenol use is limited to continuous intravenous infusion through a permanent indwelling central venous catheter and portable infusion pump. Side effects of the drug include flushing, headache, nausea, vomiting, diarrhea, myalgias, arthralgias, paresthesias, and jaw pain. Other adverse effects of epoprostenol therapy are consequences of the complex delivery system, including pump malfunction, catheter-related infections, and thrombosis. Based on studies in patients with pulmonary arterial hypertension, epoprostenol has been approved for the long-term treatment of patients with NYHA functional class III or IV symptoms due to primary pulmonary hypertension, pulmonary arterial hypertension associated with connective tissue disorders, or chronic thromboembolic disease. An early randomized trial in 24 patients with primary pulmonary hypertension revealed that continuous intravenous administration of epoprostenol by portable infusion pump resulted in substantial hemodynamic and symptomatic improvement over 8 weeks.[111] Barst and associates,[112] in a nonblinded study, randomly assigned 81 patients with primary pulmonary hypertension to receive either a continuous intravenous epoprostenol infusion added to conventional therapy or conventional therapy alone. The intravenous dosage, which was given chronically by infusion pump through an implanted catheter, was determined by the dosage tolerated in an earlier, short-term, dose-ranging phase of the study. By the end of 12 weeks, epoprostenol resulted in symptomatic and hemodynamic improvement, and improved survival.

More recently, a group of 69 patients with primary pulmonary hypertension were similarly given a continuous intravenous infusion of epoprostenol through an implanted catheter using a portable, battery-operated infusion pump, with an initial maximum dose titrated to symptoms or to a drop in systemic blood pressure greater than 10 mm Hg.[113] Patients were monitored up to 3 years, during which time 13 of the patients died, including 3 among 9 patients who underwent single-lung transplantation. However, 18 of the patients were monitored for 330 to 700 days and demonstrated an echocardiographically determined estimated mean fall in the right ventricular minus right atrial systolic pressure gradient from 84.1 ± 24.1 to 62.7 ± 18.2 mm Hg

($P < 0.01$). McLaughlin and colleagues[114] evaluated 27 patients with primary pulmonary hypertension who were given epoprostenol over a mean of 16.7 ± 5.2 months. By increasing the rate of infusion by an average 2.5 ng/kg/min each month, a 53% decline in pulmonary vascular resistance was achieved at the time of restudy.

Another study enrolled 111 subjects with pulmonary arterial hypertension associated with the scleroderma spectrum of connective tissue disorders. The patients were randomized to epoprostenol plus background conventional therapy versus conventional therapy alone for 12 weeks. Epoprostenol patients demonstrated an improvement in placebo-corrected median 6-minute walk distance by 99.5 m ($P < 0.003$) as well as improvements in cardiopulmonary hemodynamics and a reduction in dyspnea.[115]

All of these studies suggest the desirability of using chronic infusions of epoprostenol in patients with severe pulmonary arterial hypertension to improve exercise capacity, functional class, and survival. However, therapy with this agent is limited by its side-effect profile and complex delivery system. Hence, alternatives to epoprostenol are being sought and studies with stable prostacyclin analogues have been pursued. Large studies of epoprostenol in pulmonary arterial hypertension associated with lung diseases have not been undertaken. Because in one small study, patients with respiratory failure secondary to COPD treated with epoprostenol experienced reductions in PO_2, further studies of epoprostenol in this patient population must be performed prior to generalizing its use.[100]

Treprostinil (Remodulin) is a stable prostacyclin analogue with pharmacodynamic actions similar to epoprostenol but with a longer half-life. It can be administered via continuous subcutaneous infusion with a small pump. This agent was approved for treatment of patients with WHO classification II, III, or IV symptoms due to pulmonary arterial hypertension based on favorable results of a pivotal 12-week prospective, randomized, double-blind, placebo-controlled trial.[116] This study enrolled 470 subjects with primary pulmonary hypertension, pulmonary arterial hypertension associated with connective tissue disease, or congenital systemic-to-pulmonary shunts. Treprostinil improved exercise capacity with a between-treatment group difference in median 6-minute walk distance of 16 m ($P < 0.006$). Treprostinil improved dyspnea, quality of life, and cardiopulmonary hemodynamics. Patients who appear to tolerate higher doses of treprostinil and who have more severe disease appear to derive the most benefit from the agent. However, 85% of patients did experience infusion site pain, which required premature discontinuation of the infusion in 8% of the subjects; it is this side effect that may limit increased dosing with the agent and also its long-term usage.[116]

Investigational prostacyclin analogues that have been studied in larger trials to date include iloprost and beraprost.[117,118] Inhalational iloprost is a stable prostacyclin analogue that has been shown to selectively dilate the pulmonary arterial bed while exerting preferential vasodilation in well-ventilated lung regions. After inhalation, its vasodilatory effects last from 30 to 90 minutes. A prospective, double-blind, placebo-controlled, randomized 12-week trial enrolled 203 patients with NYHA functional class III or IV symptoms due to primary pulmonary hypertension and pulmonary arterial hypertension associated with appetite suppressant use, scleroderma, and inoperable chronic thromboembolic disease.[117] Iloprost-treated patients had improvement in the combined primary end point of 6-minute walk distance and NYHA functional class in the absence of clinical deterioration or death compared to the placebo group ($P = 0.007$). Dyspnea was also improved.[117] The oral prostacyclin analogue beraprost was also shown to improve symptoms and exercise capacity in a 12-week trial of 130 subjects with NYHA functional class II and III symptoms due to pulmonary arterial hypertension.[118] The role of these agents alone or in combination with existing, approved therapies remains to be elucidated.

Oral Phosphodiesterase V Inhibitors

Sildenafil (Viagra) is a selective inhibitor of cyclic GMP–specific phosphodiesterase type V, which is found in abundance in the smooth muscle cells of the pulmonary vascular bed. Attenuated degradation of cyclic GMP by sildenafil increases intracellular levels of this mediator, resulting in smooth muscle cell relaxation and vasodilation. When administered acutely to patients with pulmonary arterial hypertension or pulmonary hypertension in the context of lung fibrosis, sildenafil exerts potent effects on cardiopulmonary hemodynamics with significant reductions in pulmonary vascular resistance without increasing left-sided filling pressures or worsening hypoxemia.[119–123] It has also been shown to potentiate the effect of other agents such as inhaled iloprost and NO.[123,124] Chronic administration in adults and children with pulmonary hypertension appears to improve exercise distance and symptoms.[123–127] Sildenafil is well tolerated, but some subjects have experienced headache, flushing, dyspepsia, myalgias, impaired blue/green color discrimination, dizziness, hypotension, and nasal congestion. Use of sildenafil with concomitant nitrates is contraindicated due to potential life-threatening hypotension.

A large prospective, randomized, double-blind, placebo-controlled trial of 278 subjects with pulmonary arterial hypertension compared the effects of three oral doses of sildenafil (20 mg, 40 mg, and 80 mg three times daily) to placebo on exercise capacity, symptoms, and cardiopulmonary hemodynamics. Six-minute walk distance improved by 50 meters for the 80 mg 3-times daily group, 46 meters for the 40 mg 3-times daily and 45 meters for the 20 mg 3-times daily groups compared to placebo. When the sildenafil data was pooled, 35% of sildenafil-treated patients had improvement in one functional class compared to 7% of patients in the placebo arm. There was no significant difference in cardiopulmonary hemodynamics. Sildenafil was well tolerated. The most common adverse event was headache. A long-term trial with patients on the 80 mg dose is ongoing.[127a]

Nitric Oxide

NO is produced within endothelial cells by activity of the enzyme NO synthase in response to various stimuli. NO activates guanylate cyclase, which leads to increased smooth muscle cell cyclic GMP, resulting in vasodilation. In the pulmonary capillaries, inhaled NO is inactivated by binding to hemoglobin and forming nitrosylmethemoglobin. Therefore, inhaled NO specifically dilates the pulmonary vasculature and is inactivated before it reaches the systemic circulation.[128] In subjects with severe pulmonary arterial hypertension, inhaled NO at 40 ppm was shown to decrease pulmonary vascular resistance 5% to 68% from baseline with no change in systemic vascular resistance, whereas intravenous epoprostenol reduced both the pulmonary and systemic vascular resistances. Other effects of NO include suppression of smooth muscle cell proliferation and platelet aggregation.[129,130]

Inhaled NO may affect airway tone through a variety of different mechanisms. It also significantly affects pulmonary vascular tone.[131] Both pulmonary arterial and venous endothelial cells are capable of producing NO. Using a NO synthase inhibitor in 11 healthy volunteers, Stamler and colleagues[132] demonstrated that NO regulates normoxic pulmonary vascular tone. Furthermore, when volunteers were made hypoxic, inhalation of 40 ppm NO reversed pulmonary vasoconstriction without causing systemic vasodilation.[133]

Endothelial damage with impaired NO production has been proposed as contributing to both acute and chronic pulmonary hypertension.[134] In a study of pulmonary artery rings obtained from 22 patients with COPD undergoing heart-lung transplantation, impaired endothelium-dependent pulmonary artery relaxation was observed and was related to the preoperative levels of hypoxemia and hypercapnia. Additionally, reduced relaxation was significantly correlated to the degree of intimal fibromuscular thickening.[135] The inhalation of NO at 40 ppm by awake lambs reversed pulmonary hypertension caused by breathing a hypoxic gas mixture within 3 minutes.[136]

There is a reduction in the expression of NO synthase in the pulmonary arteries of patients with primary pulmonary hypertension, and the degree of expression is inversely correlated with total pulmonary resistance. Hypoxia markedly lessens NO synthase activity, decreasing NO release, and this deficiency in patients with chronic pulmonary hypertension may contribute to their increase in pulmonary vascular resistance.[137,138]

In persistent newborn pulmonary hypertension, inhaled NO has proved to be of clinical value.[139,140] Furthermore, in patients with primary pulmonary hypertension, inhaled NO has been used to predict those patients who might safely and effectively respond to calcium channel blockers. However, in patients with COPD, intermittent NO inhalations are not commonly used therapeutically, in part because of costs and practical difficulties including toxicity associated with chronic use, but also because of concern that systemic oxygenation might worsen due to increased local ventilation-perfusion mismatches, as often occurs with other vasodilators. However, NO theoretically should vasodilate only those areas it reaches as it is being inhaled, thereby increasing blood flow only to areas being ventilated and improving ventilation-perfusion match. It would seem reasonable, therefore, to test patients with severe COPD associated with acute respiratory failure (as well as patients with obliterative or primary pulmonary hypertension) for their responsiveness to this potential therapeutic agent as an acute intervention. However, at present there does not appear to be a clinically meaningful role for its chronic use.

Angiotensin-Converting Enzyme Inhibitors

Studies in rats exposed to chronic hypoxia in a barochamber and then transferred to an environment of normoxia revealed that enalapril reduced the content and concentration of collagen significantly, suggesting that partial regression of cardiac fibrosis may occur with enalapril, independent of the reduction in pressure load.[141] In another study of chronically hypoxic rats, the ACE inhibitor quinapril reduced the development of pulmonary hypertension. This was seen both early and after pulmonary hypertension was established. The degree of medial thickness in alveolar duct blood vessels was significantly reduced by quinapril treatment, and stains of vascular smooth muscle cells showed that quinapril appeared to inhibit either vascular smooth muscle cell proliferation or growth, or sometimes both.[142]

Experimental observations in normal volunteers demonstrated that the infusion of saralasin (an angiotensin II receptor blocker) not only produces pulmonary vasodilation when the renin-angiotensin system has been stimulated but also attenuates pulmonary vasoconstriction in response to acute hypoxia.[143] The results of studies in patients with chronic cor pulmonale have been inconsistent. When enalapril was added to conventional treatment in 30 patients with chronic cor pulmonale, not only was pulmonary hypertension decreased but renal vascular resistance fell, resulting in increased renal blood flow and improved glomerular filtration rate.[144] In contrast, the acute effects of captopril were studied in 15 patients with severe COPD who were recovering from right-sided heart failure. Although captopril reduced systemic arterial pressure, it failed to decrease pulmonary vascular resistance in these patients with hypoxic pulmonary hypertension, nor were there any changes in breathing frequency, minute ventilation, or pulmonary gas exchange compared with controls.[145]

Angiotensin II, type I, receptor blockade attenuates pulmonary vasoconstrictive response of acute hypoxia in normal subjects.[144] This has led to studies of the efficacy of these drugs in patients with COPD and pulmonary hypertension, but with normal left ventricular systolic function. In an acute study evaluating the response to losartan, an angiotensin II receptor blocker, after at least 1 week of therapy, nine patients with COPD had a significant reduction in both mean pulmonary artery pressure and total pulmonary vascular resistance; this was associated with a significantly lower plasma aldosterone level compared with patients receiving placebo. Although losartan produced its maximal effects 4 hours after administration, it did not alter oxygen saturation in patients with hypoxemic cor pulmonale.

The inconsistency in results with ACE inhibition may reflect the small size and short duration of the studies, as well as variations in inclusion criteria. In the study by Kiely and associates,[146] all patients had documented pulmonary vascular reactivity as assessed by a significant fall in pulmonary artery pressure in response to acute oxygen administration. It is possible that there are other patients in whom failure to demonstrate such vascular reactivity to 100% oxygen would result in a failure to demonstrate benefit from the use of an angiotensin II receptor blocker or ACE inhibitor. At present, there would appear to be no routine role for these agents in COPD. Whether ultimately there may be therapeutic value for their use in patients with cor pulmonale and pulmonary hypertension awaits the results of larger, randomized, double-blind clinical trials.

Natriuretic Peptides

In patients with COPD, infusion of ANP has been shown to reduce pulmonary artery pressure and increase the cardiac index.[147] Both ANP and BNP infusions have been shown to produce dose-related pulmonary vasodilation in patients with cor pulmonale without worsening arterial oxygen saturation or affecting systemic hemodynamics. Both agents suppress aldosterone production, and BNP has been demonstrated to suppress ET-1 levels.[49,148] There is no information to date on the long-term safety or efficacy of natriuretic peptides or neutral endopeptidase inhibitors that prevent natriuretic peptide degradation in cor pulmonale.

Nonglycoside Inotropes

In the setting of severe acute right ventricular decompensation with hypoperfusion, low-dose intravenous infusion of dopamine and dobutamine (1 to 2 µg/kg/min) may improve cardiac output, blood pressure, and renal perfusion. Oxygen and dopamine have been shown to be equipotent renal vasodilators in hypoxic COPD. Low-dose dopamine infusion (2 to 5 µg/kg/min) can increase cardiac output, reduce pulmonary vascular resistance, and improve oxygen delivery. Higher infusions of dopamine (10 µg/kg/min) have been shown to increase diaphragmatic blood flow and contraction.[149,150] Although they are effective in acute decompensated right ventricular failure, the value of these agents or of chronic oral phosphodiesterase isoform III inhibitors in chronic cor pulmonale is yet to be determined.

SURGICAL THERAPIES

The role of lung volume-reduction surgery in severe emphysema[151] is covered in Chapter 36, and lung and heart transplantation in cor pulmonale is covered in detail in Chapter 89. Lung transplantation is generally reserved for suitable candidates who continue to be highly symptomatic despite optimal medical therapy and will derive a significant improvement in quality of life from the procedure. The first-year survival from lung transplantation is approximately 65% to 70% and 5-year survival is approximately 50%, being largely limited by the development of bronchiolitis obliterans.[152]

Atrial Septostomy

Patients with primary pulmonary hypertension and a patent foramen ovale demonstrate a better survival compared to similar patients without a patent foramen ovale.[153] As a result, atrial septostomy, which involves the creation of a perforation in the atrial septum by use of a catheter-based blade, followed by graded balloon inflation across the atrial perforation, has been utilized in carefully selected patients with severe right-sided heart failure and recurrent syncope.[154,155] This technique increases the right-to-left shunt through the atrial communication, decreases right atrial pressure, and increases left ventricular filling, thereby decompressing the right ventricle and improving cardiac output. Atrial septostomy can reduce syncope and improve exercise performance. However, this procedure is limited by resultant arterial oxygen desaturation, frequent closure of the atrial septal communication, and the potential for paradoxical emboli. It is also associated with a high procedure-related mortality rate. Therefore, this investigational technique should be performed only by experienced operators when other options are not available or are inappropriate, or to serve as a bridge to lung transplantation.[156]

Percutaneous blade-balloon septostomy has not been studied in patients with cor pulmonale in association with disorders of the respiratory system. The arterial hypoxemia resulting from this procedure can be life-threatening, especially in this population, mitigating any potential beneficial effects on cardiopulmonary hemodynamics.

NATURAL HISTORY

COPD is the cause of chronic cor pulmonale in more than 80% of all cases.[157] Therefore, the natural history of cor pulmonale reflects the natural history of COPD. The American Thoracic Society reported that the death rate in 1991 from COPD was 18.6 per 100,000 persons, resulting in its ranking as the fourth leading cause of death. This represented a rise of 32.9% from 1979. In the United States, cor pulmonale accounts for approximately 80,000 deaths per year.[158]

Patients with COPD may or may not have pulmonary hypertension at rest. Furthermore, the progression of pulmonary hypertension in COPD is slow.[5] Among patients who are found to have normal pressures at rest, changes in pulmonary hemodynamics are frequently minimal over time. For example, in a group of 61 patients without initial pulmonary arterial hypertension, all of whom had arterial hypoxemia, a second cardiac catheterization on average 93.4 months later revealed an average change in mean pulmonary artery pressure from 15.5 ± 2.4 to 19.6 ± 7.0 mm Hg.[159] In a second group of 32 patients who had pulmonary hypertension on their first catheterization, there was a nonsignificant rise in mean pulmonary artery pressure, from 27.7 ± 6.0 to 31.0 ± 9.3 mm Hg, after an average delay of 60 months.[160] Hemodynamic worsening, defined as an increase of 5 mm Hg or more, occurred in approximately one third of patients and was clearly related to worsening of hypoxemia. Mortality in the group with hemodynamic worsening was significantly higher than in those with stable hemodynamics. From these observations, it is clear that pulmonary arterial hypertension in patients with COPD most closely correlates with the presence of hypoxemia, not necessarily with the extent of airflow obstruction that is present.

There has been relatively little difference in hospital survival rates among patients with acute respiratory failure in modern respiratory intensive care units compared with those managed 10 to 20 years ago, despite the significant advances in respiratory care that have emerged. The hospital survival rates in an international prospective survey of patients who were hypoxemic or hypercarbic while receiving mechanical ventilatory assistance was only 33.3%.[161] Survival rates in this heterogeneous group were higher in patients in whom acute respiratory failure was caused by pneumonia (63%) than in those with other causes. Nevertheless, the major prognostic factor was the severity of lung injury at entry, with survival as low as 18% for patients with far-advanced lung injury and 67% when acute respiratory failure was associated with less severe lung injury.

A long-term survival experience for COPD in a group who initially required hospitalization and who were in the age range of 50 to 54 years was reported from Finland.[162] Among 2727 new COPD patients, the estimated cumulative survival rate for men with COPD after 10 years was 60.1%, and for women it was 78.0%. However, the primary cause of death among patients initially hospitalized with COPD was ultimately COPD in only 22.1% of cases, with other causes such as coronary artery disease playing a prominent role. Nevertheless, it is clear that the prognosis for COPD patients in their 50s who require hospital treatment is poor.

Prognostic factors in COPD patients receiving long-term oxygen therapy have been analyzed by Oswald-Mammosser and colleagues.[163] Eighty-four patients underwent right-sided heart catheterization before institution of long-term oxygen therapy. These patients had a mean age of 63 years; they had a persistent arterial PO_2 of less than 55 mm Hg or an arterial PO_2 between 55 and 60 mm Hg and either signs of cor pulmonale or a mean pulmonary artery pressure of 25 mm Hg or greater. When actuarial survival curves were plotted with consideration of a number of variables, it was found that the 5-year survival rate for patients with an initial mean pulmonary artery pressure of 25 mm Hg or less was 62.2%, whereas it was only 36.3% in the 40 remaining patients who had initial pulmonary artery pressures higher than 25 mm Hg. Therefore, it would appear that the level of the pulmonary artery pressure at the time a patient undergoes long-term oxygen therapy is a better prognostic indicator than are such factors as FEV_1, the degree of hypoxemia, or the level of hypercapnia. It is clear that pulmonary hypertension in patients with COPD is associated with increased hospitalization[164] and higher mortality rate[165] compared to COPD patients without pulmonary hypertension. Only 33% of patients with COPD and pulmonary hypertension survive 4 years after diagnosis, compared with 64% of patients without pulmonary hypertension.[166] A mean pulmonary artery pressure of 20 to 25 mm Hg or more is associated with a poor prognosis. In one study, the 5-year survival of patients with COPD receiving long-term oxygen therapy was found to be 48%.[163]

SUMMARY

Respiratory disease can result in pulmonary hypertension, which eventually may lead to right ventricular hypertrophy, dilation, and right-sided heart failure. Many different mechanisms can contribute to pulmonary hypertension, but the most important cause is hypoxic pulmonary vasoconstriction secondary to COPD. Acute respiratory failure, with its additional burden of further hypoxemia and acidemia, may produce sudden increments in pulmonary arterial hypertension as well as impairment in right ventricular contractility, and lead to acute cardiac decompensation. Effective treatment requires attention not only to the traditional management of right-sided heart failure, but also to improvement in the underlying respiratory failure by managing any superimposed infection, improving ventilation, and administering oxygen. Chronic domiciliary oxygen therapy, after a patient recovers from acute respiratory failure, has been associated with improved survival and some relief of symptoms. Future research needs to address the therapeutic value of long-term administration of pulmonary vasodilator therapy for COPD patients with moderate to severe pulmonary hypertension using agents that have been shown to be of benefit in patients with primary pulmonary hypertension and some other forms of pulmonary arterial hypertension.

REFERENCES

1. Report of an Expert Committee. Chronic cor pulmonale: Clinical progress. Circulation 27:594, 1963.
2. Rich S, Rubin LJ, Abenhail L, et al: Executive summary from the World Symposium on Primary Pulmonary Hypertension (Evian, France, September 6–10, 1998). The World Health Organization publication via the Internet. Available at http://www.who.int/ncd/cvd/pph.html.
3. Simoneau G, Gailè N, Rubin LJ, et al: Clinical classification of pulmonary hypertension. J Am Coll Cardiol 43:5S–12S, 2004.
4. McGoon MD, Fuster V, Freeman WK, et al: Pulmonary hypertension. In Giuliani ER, Gersh BJ, McGoon MD (eds): Mayo Clinic Practice of Cardiology (3rd ed). St. Louis: Mosby, 1986, pp 1815–1836.
5. MacNee W: Pathophysiology of cor pulmonale in chronic obstructive pulmonary disease: Part one. Am J Respir Crit Care Med 150:833–852, 1994.
6. Horsfield K: Morphometry of the small pulmonary arteries in man. Circ Res 42:593–597, 1978.
7. Edwards JE: Pulmonary hypertension of cardiac and pulmonary origins: Pathologic origins. Prog Cardiovasc Dis 9:205–226, 1966.
8. Bove EK, Scott RC: The anatomy of chronic cor pulmonale secondary to intrinsic lung disease. Prog Cardiovasc Dis 9:227–238, 1966.
9. Charms BL, Brofman BL, Elder JC, et al: Unilateral pulmonary artery occlusion in man: II. Studies in patients with chronic pulmonary disease. J Thorac Cardiovasc Surg 35:316–331, 1958.
10. Widimsky J: Pressure, flow and volume changes of the lesser circulation during pulmonary artery occlusion in healthy subjects and patients with pulmonary hypertension. Prog Respir Res 5:224–236, 1970.
11. Hecht HH, Kuida H, Lange RL: Brisket disease: II. Clinical features and hemodynamic observations in altitude-dependent right heart failure in cattle. Am J Med 32:171–183, 1962.
12. Will DH, Horrell JF, Reeves JT, et al: Influence of altitude and age on pulmonary arterial pressure in cattle. Proc Soc Exp Biol Med 150:564–567, 1975.
13. Grover RF: Chronic hypoxic pulmonary hypertension. In Fishman AP (ed): The Pulmonary Circulation: Normal and Abnormal. Mechanisms, Management, and the National Registry. Philadelphia: University of Pennsylvania Press, 1990, pp 283–299.
14. Sorli J, Grassino A, Lorange G, et al: Control of breathing in patients with chronic obstructive lung disease. Clin Sci Mol Med 54:295–304, 1978.
15. Sassoon CSH, Hassell KT, Mahutte CK: Hyperoxic-induced hypercarbia in stable chronic obstructive pulmonary disease. Am Rev Respir Dis 135:907–911, 1987.
16. Scharf SM, Iqbal M, Keller C, et al: Hemodynamic characterization of patients with severe emphysema. Am J Respir Crit Care Med 166:314–322, 2002.
17. Peinado VI, Barbera JA, Abate P, et al: Inflammatory reaction in pulmonary muscular arteries of patients with mild chronic obstructive pulmonary disease. Am J Respir Crit Care Med 159:1605–1611, 1999.
18. Santos S, Peinado VI, Ramirez J, et al: Characterization of pulmonary vascular remodeling in smokers and patients with mild COPD. Eur Respir J 19:632–638, 2002.
19. Hale KA, Ewing SL, Gosnell BA, Niewoehner DE: Lung disease in long-term cigarette smokers with and without chronic air-flow obstruction. Am Rev Respir Dis 130:716–721, 1984.
20. Kessler R, Faller M, Weitzenblum E, et al: "Natural history" of pulmonary hypertension in a series of 131 patients with chronic obstructive lung disease. Am J Respir Crit Care Med 164:219–224, 2001.
21. Rapaport E, Wong M, Ferguson RE, et al: Right ventricular volumes in patients with and without heart failure. Circulation 31:531–541, 1965.
22. Rapaport E, Wong M, Escobar EE, et al: The effect of upright posture on right ventricular volumes in patients with and without heart failure. Am Heart J 71:146–152, 1966.
23. Klinger JR, Hill NS: Right ventricular dysfunction in chronic obstructive pulmonary disease. Chest 99:715–723, 1991.
24. Matthay RA, Berger HJ, Davies RA, et al: Right and left ventricular exercise performance in chronic obstructive pulmonary disease: Radionuclide assessment. Ann Intern Med 93:234–239, 1980.
25. Missov E, De Marco T: Cor pulmonale. Curr Treat Options Cardiovasc Med 2:149–158, 2000.
26. Krayenbuehl HP, Turnia J, Hess O: Left ventricular function in chronic pulmonary hypertension. Am J Cardiol 41:1150–1158, 1978.
27. Tutar E, Kaya A, Gèulec S, et al: Echocardiographic evaluation of left ventricular diastolic function in chronic cor pulmonale. Am J Cardiol 83:1414–1417, 1999.
28. Vizza CD, Lynch JP, Ochoa LL, et al: Right and left ventricular dysfunction in patients with severe pulmonary disease. Chest 113:576–583, 1998.
29. Schena M, Clini E, Errera D, et al: Echo-Doppler evaluation of left ventricular impairment in chronic cor pulmonale. Chest 109:1446–1451, 1996.
30. Watanabe J, Levine MJ, Bellotto F, et al: Effects of coronary venous pressure on left ventricular diastolic distensibility. Circ Res 67:923–932, 1990.
31. Anand IS, Chandrashekhar Y, Ferrari R, et al: Pathogenesis of congestive state in chronic obstructive pulmonary disease. Circulation 86:12–21, 1992.
32. Gunaydin S, Imai Y, Takanashi Y, et al: The effects of vasoactive intestinal peptide on monocrotaline induced pulmonary hypertensive rabbits following cardiopulmonary bypass: A comparative study with isoproterenol and nitroglycerine. Cardiovasc Surg 10:138–145, 2002.
33. Greenberg B, Rhoden K, Barnes PJ: Relaxant effects of vasoactive intestinal peptide and peptide histidine isoleucine in human and bovine pulmonary arteries. Blood Vessels 24:45–50, 1987.
34. Iwabuchi S, Ono S, Tanita T, et al: Vasoactive intestinal peptide causes nitric oxide-dependent pulmonary vasodilation in isolated rat lung. Respiration 64:54–58, 1997.

35. Soderman C, Eriksson LS, Juhlin-Dannfelt A, et al: Effect of vasoactive intestinal polypeptide (VIP) on pulmonary ventilation-perfusion relationships and central haemodynamics in healthy subjects. Clin Physiol 13:677–685, 1993.

36. Cox CP, Linden J, Said SI: VIP elevates platelet cyclic AMP (cAMP) levels and inhibits in vitro platelet activation induced by platelet-activating factor (PAF). Peptides 5:325–328, 1984.

37. Maruno K, Absood A, Said SI: VIP inhibits basal and histamine-stimulated proliferation of human airway smooth muscle cells. Am J Physiol 268:L1047–L1051, 1995.

38. Petkov V, Mosgoeller W, Ziesche R, et al: Vasoactive intestinal peptide as a new drug for treatment of primary pulmonary hypertension. J Clin Invest 111:1339–1346, 2003.

39. MacNee W: Pathophysiology of cor pulmonale in chronic obstructive pulmonary disease: Part two. Am J Respir Crit Care Med 150:1158–1168, 1994.

40. Lipworth BJ, Dagg KD: Vasoconstrictor effects of angiotensin II on the pulmonary vascular bed. Chest 105:1360–1364, 1994.

41. Cargill RI, Lipworth BJ: Lisinopril attenuates acute hypoxic pulmonary vasoconstriction in humans. Chest 109:424–429, 1996.

42. Lang CC, Coutie WJ, Struthers AD, et al: Elevated levels of brain natriuretic peptide in acute hypoxaemic chronic obstructive pulmonary disease. Clin Sci 85:529–533, 1992.

43. Cargill RI, Barr CS, Coutie WJ: C-type natriuretic peptide levels in cor pulmonale and in congestive heart failure. Thorax 49:1247–1249, 1994.

44. Zhao L, Hughes JM, Winter RJ: Effects of natriuretic peptides and neutral endopeptidase inhibition in isolated perfused rat lung. Am Rev Respir Dis 146:1198–1201, 1992.

45. Nagaya N, Nishikimi T, Okano Y, et al: Plasma brain natriuretic peptide levels increase in proportion to the extent of right ventricular dysfunction in pulmonary hypertension. J Am Coll Cardiol 31:202–208, 1998.

46. Nagaya N, Nishikimi T, Uematsu M, et al: Plasma brain natriuretic peptide as a prognostic indicator in patients with primary pulmonary hypertension. Circulation 102:865–870, 2000.

47. Adnot S, Andrivet P, Chabrier PE, et al: Atrial natriuretic factor in chronic obstructive lung disease. J Clin Invest 83:986–993, 1989.

48. Cargill RI, Lipworth BJ: Atrial natriuretic peptide and brain natriuretic peptide in cor pulmonale. Chest 110:1220–1225, 1996.

49. Aronson D, Burger AJ: Intravenous nesiritide (human B-type natriuretic peptide) reduces plasma endothelin-1 levels in patients with decompensated congestive heart failure. Am J Cardiol 90:435–438, 2002.

50. Thompson JS, Morice AH: Neutral endopeptidase inhibitors and the pulmonary circulation. Gen Pharmacol 27:581–585, 1996.

51. Dupuis J: Endothelin-receptor antagonists in pulmonary hypertension. Lancet 358:1113–1114, 2001.

52. Giaid A, Yanagisawa M, Langleben D, et al: Expression of endothelin-1 in the lungs of patients with pulmonary hypertension. N Engl J Med 328:1732–1739, 1993.

53. Stewart DJ, Levy RD, Cernacek P, Langleben D: Increased plasma endothelin-1 in pulmonary hypertension: Marker or mediator of disease? Ann Intern Med 114:464–469, 1991.

54. Morelli S, Ferri C, Polettini E, et al: Plasma endothelin-1 levels, pulmonary hypertension, and lung fibrosis in patients with systemic sclerosis. Am J Med 99:255–260, 1995.

55. Kaur S, Frishman WH, Singh I, et al: Endothelin as a therapeutic target in the treatment of cardiovascular disease. Heart Dis 3:176–188, 2001.

56. Galie N, Grigrioni F, Bacchi-Reggiani L: Relation of endothelin-1 to survival in patients with primary pulmonary hypertension. Eur J Clin Invest 26:A48, 2001.

57. Chalmers GW, Macleod KJ, Sriram S, et al: Sputum endothelin-1 is increased in cystic fibrosis and chronic obstructive pulmonary disease. Eur Respir J 13:1288–1292, 1999.

58. Sofia M, Mormile M, Faraone S, et al: Increased 24-hour endothelin-1 urinary excretion in patients with chronic obstructive pulmonary disease. Respiration 61:263–268, 1994.

59. Faller M, Kessler R, Sapin R, et al: Regulation of endothelin-1 at rest and during a short steady-state exercise in 21 COPD patients. Pulm Pharmacol Ther 11:151–157, 1998.

60. Trakada G, Marangos M, Spiropoulos K: Mechanisms of endothelin-1 elevation in chronic obstructive pulmonary disease patients with nocturnal oxyhemoglobin desaturation. Respiration 68:134–139, 2001.

61. Celik G, Karabiyikoglu G: Local and peripheral plasma endothelin-1 in pulmonary hypertension secondary to chronic obstructive pulmonary disease. Respiration 65:289–294, 1998.

62. Shih H-T, Webb CR, Conway WA: Frequency and significance of cardiac arrhythmias in chronic obstructive lung disease. Chest 94:44–48, 1988.

63. Matthay RA, Schwartz MI, Ellis JH, et al: Pulmonary artery hypertension in chronic obstructive pulmonary disease: Chest radiographic assessment. Invest Radiol 16:95–100, 1981.

64. Staub NC, Wiener-Kronish JP, Albertine KH: Transport through the pleura: Physiology of normal liquid and solute exchange in the pleural space. In Chrétien J, Bignon J, Hirsch A (eds): The Pleura in Health and Disease. New York: Marcel Dekker, 1985, pp 169–193.

65. Wiener-Kronish JP, Matthay MA, Callen PW: Relationship of pleural effusions to pulmonary hemodynamics in patients with congestive heart failure. Am Rev Respir Dis 132:1253–1256, 1985.

66. Wiener-Kronish JP, Goldstein R, Matthay RA, et al: Lack of association of pleural effusion with chronic pulmonary arterial and right atrial hypertension. Chest 92:967–970, 1987.

67. Jensen R, Pierson RE, Braddy PM, et al: Brisket disease in yearling feedlot cattle. J Am Vet Med Assoc 169:515–517, 1976.

68. Phillips RW: The electrocardiogram in cor pulmonale secondary to pulmonary emphysema: A study of 18 cases proved by autopsy. Am Heart J 56:352–371, 1958.

69. Incalzi RA, Fuso L, De Rosa M, et al: Electrocardiographic signs of chronic cor pulmonale: A negative prognostic finding in chronic obstructive pulmonary disease. Circulation 99:1600–1605, 1999.

70. Raymond RJ, Hinderliter AL, Willis PW, et al: Echocardiographic predictors of adverse outcomes in primary pulmonary hypertension. J Am Coll Cardiol 39:1214–1219, 2002.

71. Murphy ML, Dinh H, Nicholson D: Chronic cor pulmonale. Dis Mon 35:663–718, 1989.

72. Bristow JD, Morris JF, Kloster FE: Hemodynamics of cor pulmonale. Prog Cardiovasc Dis 9:239–258, 1966.

73. Lopez-Sendon J, Gomez Sanchez MAG, Mestre de Juan MJ: Pulmonary hypertension in the toxic oil syndrome. In Fishman AP (ed): The Pulmonary Circulation: Normal and Abnormal. Mechanisms, Management, and the National

Registry. Philadelphia: University of Pennsylvania Press, 1990, pp 385–395.

74. McNabb LJ, Baldwin KM: Hemodynamic and metabolic effects of exercise in *Crotalaria*-induced pulmonary hypertension in rats. J Appl Physiol Respir Environ Exercise Physiol 57:1829–1833, 1984.

75. Meyrick BO, Reid LM: *Crotalaria*-induced pulmonary hypertension: Uptake of ^{3}H-thymidine by the cells of the pulmonary circulation and alveolar walls. Am J Pathol 106:84–94, 1982.

76. Loogen F, Worth H, Schwan G, et al: Long-term follow-up of pulmonary hypertension in patients with and without anorectic drug intake. Cor Vasa 27:111–124, 1985.

77. Gurtner HP: Aminorex pulmonary hypertension. *In* Fishman AP (ed): The Pulmonary Circulation: Normal and Abnormal. Mechanisms, Management, and the National Registry. Philadelphia: University of Pennsylvania Press, 1990, pp 397–411.

78. Kay JM, Smith P, Heath D: Aminorex and the pulmonary circulation. Thorax 26:262–270, 1971.

79. Abenhaim L, Moride Y, Brenot F, et al: Appetite-suppressant drugs and the risk of primary pulmonary hypertension. International Primary Pulmonary Hypertension Study Group. N Engl J Med 335:609–616, 1996.

80. Mark EJ, Patalas ED, Chang HT, et al: Fatal pulmonary hypertension associated with short-term use of fenfluramine and phentermine. N Engl J Med 337:602–606, 1997.

81. Chatterjee K, De Marco T, Alpert J: Pulmonary hypertension: Hemodynamic diagnosis and management. Arch Intern Med 162:1925–1933, 2002.

82. Saroea HG: Chronic obstructive pulmonary disease: Major objectives of management. Postgrad Med 94:113–116, 121–122, 1993.

83. Fuster V, Steele PM, Edwards WD, et al: Primary pulmonary hypertension: Natural history and the importance of thrombosis. Circulation 70:580–587, 1984.

84. Rich S, Kaufmann E, Levy PS: The effect of high doses of calcium-channel blockers on survival in primary pulmonary hypertension. N Engl J Med 327:76–81, 1992.

85. Rich S, Seidlitz M, Dodin E, et al: The short-term effects of digoxin in patients with right ventricular dysfunction from pulmonary hypertension. Chest 114:787–792, 1998.

86. Ferrer MI, Harvey RM, Cathcart RT, et al: Some effects of digoxin upon the heart and circulation in man: Digoxin in chronic cor pulmonale. Circulation 1:161–186, 1950.

87. MacNee W, Wathen CG, Hannan WJ, et al: Effects of pirbuterol and sodium nitroprusside on pulmonary haemodynamics in hypoxic cor pulmonale. Br Med J (Clin Res Ed) 287:1169–1172, 1983.

88. He J, Kryger MH, Zorick FJ, et al: Mortality and apnea index in obstructive sleep apnea: Experience in 385 male patients. Chest 94:9–14, 1988.

89. Partinen M, Jamieson A, Guilleminault C: Long-term outcome for obstructive sleep apnea syndrome patients: Mortality. Chest 94:1200–1204, 1988.

90. Krieger J, Sforza E, Barthelmebs M, et al: Overnight decrease in hematocrit after nasal CPAP treatment in patients with OSA. Chest 97:729–730, 1990.

91. Tsagaris TJ, Sutton RB, Anderson FL: Effect of phlebotomy on coronary blood flow in calves with brisket disease. Proc Soc Exp Biol Med 142:560–563, 1973.

92. Rich S, Martinez J, Lam W, Rosen KM: Captopril as treatment for patients with pulmonary hypertension: Problem of variability in assessing chronic drug treatment. Br Heart J 48:272–277, 1982.

93. Stuart-Harris C, Flenly DC, Bishop JH, et al: Report of the Medical Research Council Working Party: Long-term domiciliary oxygen therapy in chronic cor pulmonale complicating chronic bronchitis and emphysema. Lancet 1:681–686, 1981.

94. Nocturnal Oxygen Therapy Trial Group: Continuous or nocturnal oxygen therapy in hypoxemic chronic obstructive lung disease: A clinical trial. Ann Intern Med 93:391–398, 1980.

95. Reihman DH, Farber MO, Weinberger MH, et al: Effect of hypoxemia on sodium and water excretion in chronic obstructive lung disease. Am J Med 78:87–94, 1985.

96. Gassner A, Sommer G, Fridrich L, et al: Differential therapy with calcium antagonists in pulmonary hypertension secondary to COPD. Chest 98:829–834, 1990.

97. Weinberger SE, Schwartzstein RM, Weiss JW: Hypercapnia. N Engl J Med 321:1223–1231, 1989.

98. Barbera JA, Roger N, Roca J, et al: Worsening of pulmonary gas exchange with nitric oxide inhalation in chronic obstructive pulmonary disease. Lancet 347:436–440, 1976.

99. Yoshida M, Taguchi O, Gabazza EC, et al: Combined inhalation of nitric oxide and oxygen in chronic obstructive pulmonary disease. Am J Respir Crit Care Med 155:526–529, 1997.

100. Archer SL, Mike D, Crow J, et al: A placebo-controlled trial of prostacyclin in acute respiratory failure in COPD. Chest 109:750–755, 1996.

101. Sajkov D, McEvoy RD, Cowie RJ, et al: Felodipine improves pulmonary hemodynamics in chronic obstructive pulmonary disease. Chest 103:1354–1361, 1993.

102. Sajkov D, Wang T, Frith PA, et al: A comparison of two long-acting vasoselective calcium antagonists in pulmonary hypertension secondary to COPD. Chest 111:1622–1630, 1997.

103. Archibald CJ, Auger WR, Fedullo PF, et al: Long-term outlook after pulmonary thromboendarterectomy. Am J Respir Crit Care Med 160:523–528, 1999.

104. Channick RN, Simonneau G, Sitbon O, et al: Effects of the dual endothelin-receptor antagonist bosentan in patients with pulmonary hypertension: A randomised placebo-controlled study. Lancet 358:1119–1123, 2001.

105. Rubin LJ, Badesch DB, Barst RJ, et al: Bosentan therapy for pulmonary arterial hypertension. N Engl J Med 346:896–903, 2002.

106. Barst RJ, Langleben D, Frost A, et al: Sitaxsentan therapy for pulmonary arterial hypertension. Am J Respir Crit Care Med 169:441–447, 2004.

107. Badesch DB, Orton C, Zapp LM, et al: Decreased arterial wall prostaglandin production in neonatal calves with severe chronic pulmonary hypertension. Am J Respir Cell Mol Biol 1:489–498, 1989.

108. Richalet J-P, Hornych A, Rathat C, et al: Plasma prostaglandins, leukotrienes and thromboxane in acute high altitude hypoxia. Respir Physiol 85:205–215, 1991.

109. Tuder RM, Cool CD, Geraci MW, et al: Prostacyclin synthase expression is decreased in lungs from patients with severe pulmonary hypertension. Am J Respir Crit Care Med 159:1925–1932, 1999.

110. Friedman R, Mears JG, Barst RJ: Continuous infusion of prostacyclin normalizes plasma markers of endothelial cell injury and platelet aggregation in primary pulmonary hypertension. Circulation 96:2782–2784, 1997.

111. Rubin LJ, Mendoza J, Hood M, et al: Treatment of primary pulmonary hypertension with continuous intravenous prostacyclin (epoprostenol). Ann Intern Med 112:485–491, 1990.

112. Barst RJ, Rubin LJ, Long WA, et al: A comparison of continuous intravenous epoprostenol (prostacyclin) with

conventional therapy for primary pulmonary hypertension. N Engl J Med 334:296–301, 1996.

113. Shapiro SM, Oudiz RJ, Cao T, et al: Primary pulmonary hypertension: Improved long-term effects and survival with continuous intravenous epoprostenol infusion. J Am Coll Cardiol 30:343–349, 1997.

114. McLaughlin VV, Genthner DE, Panella MM, et al: Reduction in pulmonary vascular resistance with long-term epoprostenol (prostacyclin) therapy in primary pulmonary hypertension. N Engl J Med 338:273–277, 1998.

115. Badesch DB, Tapson VF, McGoon MD, et al: Continuous intravenous epoprostenol for pulmonary hypertension due to the scleroderma spectrum of disease: A randomized, controlled trial. Ann Intern Med 132:425–434, 2000.

116. Simonneau G, Barst RJ, Galie N, et al: Continuous subcutaneous infusion of treprostinil, a prostacyclin analogue, in patients with pulmonary arterial hypertension: A double-blind, randomized, placebo-controlled trial. Am J Respir Crit Care Med 165:800–804, 2002.

117. Olschewski H, Simonneau G, Galie N, et al: Inhaled iloprost for severe pulmonary hypertension. N Engl J Med 347:322–329, 2002.

118. Galie N, Humbert M, Vachiery JL, et al: Effects of beraprost sodium, an oral prostacyclin analogue, in patients with pulmonary arterial hypertension: A randomized, double-blind, placebo-controlled trial. J Am Coll Cardiol 39:1496–1502, 2002.

119. Prasad S, Wilkinson J, Gatzoulis MA: Sildenafil in primary pulmonary hypertension. N Engl J Med 343:1342, 2000.

120. Kleinsasser A, Loeckinger A, Hoermann C, et al: Sildenafil modulates hemodynamics and pulmonary gas exchange. Am J Respir Crit Care Med 163:339–343, 2001.

121. Michelakis E, Tymchak W, Lien D, et al: Oral sildenafil is an effective and specific pulmonary vasodilator in patients with pulmonary arterial hypertension: Comparison with inhaled nitric oxide. Circulation 105:2398–2403, 2002.

122. Ghofrani HA, Wiedemann R, Rose F, et al: Sildenafil for treatment of lung fibrosis and pulmonary hypertension: A randomised controlled trial. Lancet 360:895–900, 2002.

123. Ghofrani HA, Rose F, Schermuly RT, et al: Oral sildenafil as long-term adjunct therapy to inhaled iloprost in severe pulmonary arterial hypertension. J Am Coll Cardiol 42:158–164, 2003.

124. Watanabe H, Ohashi K, Takeuchi K, et al: Sildenafil for primary and secondary pulmonary hypertension. Clin Pharmacol Ther 71:398–402, 2002.

125. Ghofrani HA, Wiedemann R, Rose F, et al: Combination therapy with oral sildenafil and inhaled iloprost for severe pulmonary hypertension. Ann Intern Med 136:515–522, 2002.

126. Erickson S, Reyes J, Bohn D, Adatia I: Sildenafil (Viagra) in childhood and neonatal pulmonary hypertension. J Am Coll Cardiol 39:402A, 2002.

127. Abrams D, Schulze-Neick I, Magee AG: Sildenafil as a selective pulmonary vasodilator in childhood primary pulmonary hypertension. Heart 84:E4, 2000.

127a. Ghofrani HA: Efficacy and safety of sildenafil citrate in pulmomonary arterial hypertension: Results of a multinational randomized, double-blind, placebo-controlled trial (sildenafil use in pulmonary arterial hypertension study SUPER-1), presented as late breaking clinical trial at CHEST 2004, 70th annual international scientific meeting of the American College of Chest Physicians, Seattle, Washington, 2004.

128. Rimar S, Gillis CN: Selective pulmonary vasodilation by inhaled nitric oxide is due to hemoglobin inactivation. Circulation 88:2884–2887, 1993.

129. Zapol WM, Rimar S, Gillis N, et al: Nitric oxide and the lung. Am J Respir Crit Care Med 149:1375–1380, 1994.

130. Nong Z, Hoylaerts M, Van Pelt N, et al: Nitric oxide inhalation inhibits platelet aggregation and platelet-mediated pulmonary thrombosis in rats. Circ Res 81:865–869, 1997.

131. Hart CM: Nitric oxide in adult lung disease. Chest 115:1407–1417, 1999.

132. Stamler JS, Singel J, Loscaizo J: Biochemistry of nitric oxide and its redox-activated forms. Science 258:1898–1902, 1992.

133. Frostell CG, Blomqvist H, Hedenstierna G, et al: Inhaled nitric oxide selectivity reverses human hypoxic pulmonary vasoconstriction without causing systemic vasodilation. Anesthesiology 78:427–435, 1993.

134. Johns RA: EDRF/Nitric oxide: The endogenous nitrovasodilator and a new cellular messenger. Anesthesiology 75:927–931, 1991.

135. Dinh-Xuan AT, Higenbotham TW, Clelland CA, et al: Impairment of endothelium-dependent pulmonary-artery relaxation in chronic obstructive lung disease. N Engl J Med 324:1539–1547, 1991.

136. Frostell C, Fratacci M-D, Wain J-C: Inhaled nitric oxide: A selective pulmonary vasodilator reversing hypoxic pulmonary vasoconstriction. Circulation 83:2038–2047, 1991.

137. Al-Ali MK, Howarth PH: Nitric oxide and the respiratory system in health and disease. Respir Med 92:702–715, 1998.

138. Dinh-Xuan AT: Endothelial modulation of pulmonary vascular tone. Eur Respir J 5:757–762, 1992.

139. Roberts JD, Polaner DM, Lang P, et al: Inhaled nitric oxide in persistent pulmonary hypertension of the newborn. Lancet 340:818–819, 1992.

140. Kinsella JP, Neish SR, Shaffer E, et al: Low-dose inhalational nitric oxide in persistent pulmonary hypertension of the newborn. Lancet 340:819–820, 1992.

141. Pelouch V, Kolar F, Ost'adal B, et al: Regression of chronic hypoxia-induced pulmonary hypertension, right ventricular hypertrophy, and fibrosis: Effect of enalapril. Cardiovasc Drugs Ther 11:177–185, 1997.

142. Nong Z, Stassen JM, Moons L, et al: Inhibition of tissue angiotensin-converting enzyme with quinapril reduces hypoxic pulmonary hypertension and pulmonary vascular remodelling. Circulation 94:1941–1947, 1996.

143. Kiely DG, Cargill RI, Lipworth BJ: Angiotensin II receptor blockade and effects on pulmonary hemodynamics and hypoxic pulmonary vasoconstriction in humans. Chest 110:698–703, 1996.

144. Mahajan SK, Sharma VK, Thakral S: Effect of enalapril on renal profile and right ventricular dimensions in chronic cor pulmonale. J Assoc Physicians India 44:323–324, 1996.

145. Zielinski J, Hawrylkiewicz I, Gorecka D, et al: Captopril effects on pulmonary and systemic hemodynamics in chronic cor pulmonale. Chest 90:562–565, 1986.

146. Kiely DG, Cargill RI, Wheeldon NM, et al: Haemodynamic and endocrine effects of type 1 angiotensin II receptor blockade in patients with hypoxaemic cor pulmonale. Cardiovasc Res 33:201–208, 1997.

147. Adnot S, Andrivet P, Chabrier PE, et al: Atrial natriuretic factor in chronic obstructive lung disease with pulmonary hypertension: Physiological correlates and response to peptide infusion. J Clin Invest 83:986–993, 1989.

148. Cargill RI, Lipworth BJ: Atrial natriuretic peptide and brain natriuretic peptide in cor pulmonale: Hemodynamic and endocrine effects. Chest 110:1220–1225, 1996.

149. Howes TQ, Deane CR, Levin GE, et al: The effects of oxygen and dopamine on renal and aortic blood flow in

chronic obstructive pulmonary disease with hypoxemia and hypercapnia. Am J Respir Crit Care Med 151:378–383, 1995.

150. Chan TY: Low-dose dopamine in severe right heart failure and chronic obstructive pulmonary disease. Ann Pharmacother 29:493–496, 1995.

151. Cooper JD, Patterson GA: Lung volume reduction surgery for severe emphysema. Semin Thorac Cardiovasc Surg 8:52–60, 1996.

152. International Society of Heart and Lung Transplantation: ISHLT Lung Transplant Registry Slides 2004. Available at http://www.ishlt.org. (Accessed on December 13, 2004.)

153. Rozkovec A, Montanes P, Oakley CM: Factors that influence the outcome of primary pulmonary hypertension. Br Heart J 55:449–458, 1986.

154. Rich S, Dodin E, McLaughlin VV: Usefulness of atrial septostomy as a treatment for primary pulmonary hypertension and guidelines for its application. Am J Cardiol 80:369–371, 1997.

155. Sandoval J, Gaspar J, Pulido T, et al: Graded balloon dilation atrial septostomy in severe primary pulmonary hypertension: A therapeutic alternative for patients nonresponsive to vasodilator treatment. J Am Coll Cardiol 32:297–304, 1998.

156. Rothman A, Beltran D, Kriett JM, et al: Graded balloon dilation atrial septostomy as a bridge to lung transplantation in pulmonary hypertension. Am Heart J 125:1763–1766, 1993.

157. Vance JW: Management of patients with cor pulmonale—acute and chronic. Prog Cardiovasc Dis 9:470–483, 1967.

158. American Thoracic Society: Standards for the diagnosis and care of patients with chronic obstructive pulmonary disease. Am J Respir Crit Care Med 152(Suppl):S77–S120, 1995.

159. Weitzenblum E, Sautegeau A, Ehrhart M, et al: Long-term course of pulmonary arterial pressure in chronic obstructive pulmonary disease. Am Rev Respir Dis 130:993–998, 1984.

160. Weitzenblum E, Loiseau A, Hirth C, et al: Course of pulmonary hemodynamics in patients with chronic obstructive pulmonary disease. Chest 75:656–662, 1979.

161. Vasilyev S, Schaap RN, Mortensen JD: Hospital survival rates of patients with acute respiratory failure in modern respiratory intensive care units. Chest 107:1083–1088, 1995.

162. Keistinen T, Tuuponen T, Kivela S-L: Survival experience of the population needing hospital treatment for asthma or COPD at age 50–54 years. Respir Med 92:568–572, 1998.

163. Oswald-Mammosser M, Weitzenblum E, Quiox E, et al: Prognostic factors in COPD patients receiving long-term oxygen therapy: Importance of pulmonary artery pressure. Chest 107:1193–1198, 1995.

164. Kessler R, Faller M, Fourgaut G, et al: Predictive factors of hospitalization for acute exacerbation in a series of 64 patients with chronic obstructive pulmonary disease. Am J Respir Crit Care Med 159:158–164, 1999.

165. Dallari R, Barozzi G, Pinelli G, et al: Predictors of survival in subjects with chronic obstructive pulmonary disease treated with long-term oxygen therapy. Respiration 61:8–13, 1994.

166. Scharf SM: Pulmonary heart disease. *In* Baum GL, Crapo JD, Celli BR (eds): Textbook of Pulmonary Heart Disease. Philadelphia: Lippincott–Raven, 1998, pp 1311–1326.

INFILTRATIVE AND INTERSTITIAL LUNG DISEASES

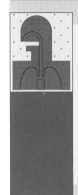

53

Approach to Diagnosis and Management of the Idiopathic Interstitial Pneumonias

Talmadge E. King, Jr., M.D., Marvin I. Schwarz, M.D.

INTRODUCTION

The term *interstitial lung disease*, in general, implies inflammatory-fibrotic infiltration of the alveolar walls (septa) resulting in profound effects on the capillary endothelium and the alveolar epithelial lining cells (Fig. 53.1). Under normal conditions, small numbers of interstitial macrophages, fibroblasts, and myofibroblasts reside within the interstitium. Other components of the interstitium include the matrix proteins of the lung, consisting of collagen-related macromolecules and the noncollagenous proteins such as fibronectin and laminin. In many of the interstitial lung diseases, interstitial fibrosis appears after injury to the gas-exchanging units. This injury increases alveolar permeability, enabling the serum contents to enter the alveolar spaces. Fibroblastic proliferation and excessive collagen deposition, the histologic hallmarks of interstitial lung disease, occur either as a direct result of the injury, as a result of an inflammatory cell response that releases proinflammatory and profibrotic cytokines, or as a consequence of the regenerative and reparative processes taking place at the epithelial and endothelial surfaces. Moreover, fibroblastic proliferation and collagen accumulation also occur within airway lumina.

Interstitial lung disease is a term describing many entities that injure the lung parenchyma, producing a disease with similar clinical, radiographic, and physiologic features. However, many interstitial lung diseases affect not only the alveolar structures but also the lumina and walls of small airways (alveolar ducts, respiratory bronchioles, and terminal bronchioles). The primary goal of the clinician is to determine if the patient does or does not have idiopathic pulmonary fibrosis (IPF)/usual interstitial pneumonia (UIP) (see later).

CLINICAL AND HISTOLOGIC CLASSIFICATION OF INTERSTITIAL LUNG DISEASE

The exact prevalence and incidence of the interstitial lung diseases are unknown. Studies suggest a prevalence of 80.9 per 100,000 for men compared to 67.2 per 100,000 for

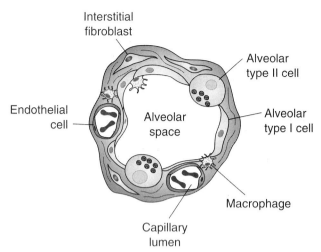

Figure 53.1 Schematic depiction of the lung parenchyma surrounding an alveolar space showing the major cells that line and lie within the interstitial space.

women. Similarly, the overall incidence of interstitial lung disease is slightly more common in men (31.5 per 100,000 per year) than women (26.1 per 100,000 per year) and increases with age. For example, among men and women 75 years of age or older, the prevalence of IPF was 250 per 100,000 and the incidence was 160 per 100,000 per year.[1]

A clinical classification of the interstitial lung diseases is shown in Table 53.1.[2] Although the diagnosis of interstitial lung disease due to occupational exposure, a medication, or a connective tissue disease may be obvious, the primary and idiopathic interstitial lung diseases are difficult to diagnose on clinical grounds alone. This chapter presents an approach for the evaluation of these patients with emphasis on the idiopathic interstitial pneumonias.

An alternative method of classification depends on the resultant histologic pattern. As seen in Figure 53.2, various injuries can produce a variety of histologic patterns, and dissimilar clinical entities listed in Table 53.1 may result in similar histologic appearances (Table 53.2).

The causes of interstitial lung diseases are daunting, but they are linked by many common features: clinical presentation, radiographic appearance, physiologic abnormalities,

---

Table 53.1 Clinical Classification of the Interstitial Lung Diseases

Connective Tissue Diseases Scleroderma Polymyositis-dermatomyositis Systemic lupus erythematosus Rheumatoid arthritis Mixed connective tissue disease Ankylosing spondylitis	Bone marrow transplantation Postinfectious Eosinophilic pneumonia Alveolar proteinosis Diffuse alveolar hemorrhage syndromes Alveolar microlithiasis Metastatic calcification

Treatment-Related or Drug-Induced Diseases
Antibiotics (nitrofurantoin, sulfasalazine)
Antiarrhythmics (amiodarone, tocainide, propranolol)
Anti-inflammatories (gold, penicillamine)
Anticonvulsants (dilantin)
Chemotherapeutic agents (mitomycin C, bleomycin, busulfan,
    cyclophosphamide, chlorambucil, methotrexate,
    azathioprine, BCNU [carmustine], procarbazine)
Therapeutic radiation
Oxygen toxicity
Narcotics
	Occupational and Environmental Diseases
	Inorganic
	  Silicosis
	  Asbestosis
	  Hard-metal pneumoconiosis
	  Coal worker's pneumoconiosis
	  Berylliosis
	  Aluminum oxide fibrosis
	  Talc pneumoconiosis
	  Siderosis (arc welder)
	  Stannosis (tin)
	Organic (Hypersensitivity Pneumonitis)
	  Bird breeder's lung
	  Farmer's lung
	  (For complete listing see Chapter 62)

Primary (Unclassified) Diseases
Sarcoidosis
Primary pulmonary Langerhans cell histiocytosis (eosinophilic
    granuloma)
Amyloidosis
Pulmonary vasculitis
Lipoid pneumonia
Lymphangitic carcinomatosis
Bronchoalveolar carcinoma
Pulmonary lymphoma
Gaucher's disease
Niemann-Pick disease
Hermansky-Pudlak syndrome
Neurofibromatosis
Lymphangioleiomyomatosis
Tuberous sclerosis
Acute respiratory distress syndrome
Acquired immunodeficiency syndrome (AIDS)
	Idiopathic Fibrotic Disorders
	Acute interstitial pneumonitis (Hamman-Rich syndrome)
	Idiopathic pulmonary fibrosis
	Familial idiopathic pulmonary fibrosis
	Desquamative interstitial pneumonitis
	Respiratory bronchiolitis
	Cryptogenic organizing pneumonia
	Nonspecific interstitial pneumonitis
	Lymphocytic interstitial pneumonia (Sjögren's syndrome,
	    connective tissue disease, AIDS, Hashimoto's thyroiditis)
	Autoimmune pulmonary fibrosis (inflammatory bowel disease,
	    primary biliary cirrhosis, idiopathic thrombocytopenic
	    purpura, autoimmune hemolytic anemia)

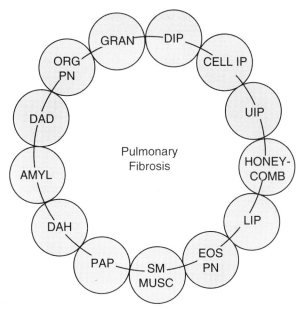

Figure 53.2 Schematic depiction showing the many different histologic patterns seen in the interstitial lung diseases that are associated with or lead to pulmonary fibrosis. AMYL, amyloidosis; CELL IP, cellular or nonspecific interstitial pneumonitis; DAD, diffuse alveolar damage; DAH, diffuse alveolar hemorrhage; DIP, desquamative interstitial pneumonia; EOS PN, eosinophilic pneumonia; GRAN, granulomatous pneumonitis; LIP, lymphocytic interstitial pneumonitis; ORG PN, organizing pneumonia; PAP, pulmonary alveolar proteinosis; SM MUSC, smooth muscle proliferation; UIP, usual interstitial pneumonitis.

and, in some instances, histologic findings. Nevertheless, a specific diagnosis can be made in many patients from the results of a careful history and certain laboratory tests. Bronchoscopy with bronchoalveolar lavage (BAL) and, often, transbronchial biopsy are useful in the diagnosis of some causes of interstitial infiltration. Thoracoscopic or open-lung biopsy is required for a definitive diagnosis of the remaining cases. Further information about many of the specific members of the interstitial disease family is found in Chapters 54 through 59 in this section. Additional discussion of other causes of interstitial lung disease is found elsewhere in the book: the pneumoconioses in Chapter 61, hypersensitivity pneumonitis in Chapter 62, and drug-induced pulmonary disease in Chapter 67.

GENERAL CLINICAL, RADIOLOGIC, AND PHYSIOLOGIC FEATURES OF INTERSTITIAL LUNG DISEASES

The hallmarks of an interstitial lung disease are progressive dyspnea and cough, an abnormal chest radiograph, and impaired pulmonary function tests.[2] However, 5% to 10% of symptomatic patients eventually diagnosed as having interstitial lung disease, at the time of presentation, have normal chest radiographs. There are also dyspneic patients with or without abnormal chest radiographs in whom routine pulmonary function tests (flows, volumes, and diffusing capacity) are normal. In this situation exercise

testing, which stresses the cardiopulmonary systems and measures gas exchange, unmasks abnormalities. Furthermore, high-resolution computed tomography (HRCT) scans and BAL can detect abnormalities in the presence of normal radiographs and physiologic tests in patients at high risk for development of interstitial lung disease, such as patients with connective tissue disease, asbestos exposure, or hypersensitivity pneumonitis and patients taking drugs known to injure the lung.

PAST HISTORY

Interstitial lung disease occurring in a patient with an established connective tissue disease is obvious; however, there are patients in whom the lung disease precedes the more typical manifestations by months to several years (see Chapter 54).

Occupational History

The occupational history is of obvious importance, and it should be detailed, because a long latency period may occasionally exist between exposure and the appearance of clinical impairment and disability. The exposure may have been of short duration but high intensity. Hypersensitivity pneumonitis, which can manifest either as recurrent acute or subacute pneumonitis or as an insidious form with slowly progressive dyspnea, must be excluded (see Chapter 62). A growing list of occupational and environmental antigens can cause granulomatous pneumonitis.

Drug History

A review of the medications used in the recent and distant past is important. Uncommonly, the lung disease may appear weeks to years after the drug has been discontinued (see Chapter 67). Aspiration (often silent) of gastric contents because of gastroesophageal reflux can lead to the insidious development of interstitial lung disease,[3,4] as can the nocturnal use of oily nose drops or use of mineral oil as a laxative.[5,6]

Smoking History

A history of tobacco use is important. More than 90% of patients with pulmonary Langerhans cell histiocytosis of the lung are smokers at the time of diagnosis; this is also true for respiratory bronchiolitis. Of patients with Goodpasture's syndrome who smoked, 100% had diffuse alveolar hemorrhage, whereas only 20% of a nonsmoking group had pulmonary disease in addition to the renal involvement.[7] Tobacco use also appears to enhance the development of interstitial fibrosis in an asbestos-exposed population. The risk of asbestosis in exposed smokers was 13 times that in a nonsmoking asbestos-exposed cohort. Hypersensitivity pneumonitis, on the other hand, infrequently appears in the active smoker. Also, the incidence of sarcoidosis is higher in nonsmokers.

Family History

Familial associations (with an autosomal dominant pattern) have been identified in cases of IPF, sarcoidosis, tuberous

Table 53.2 Histologic Patterns in the Interstitial Lung Diseases and Their Disease Associations

Type	Associations
Diffuse alveolar damage	Acute respiratory distress syndrome; drugs (cytotoxic agents, heroin, cocaine, paraquat, ethchlorvynol, aspirin); toxic gas inhalation; radiation therapy; oxygen toxicity; connective tissue disease; infections (*Legionella, Mycoplasma,* viral); acute interstitial pneumonia (Hamman-Rich syndrome)
Organizing pneumonia	Cryptogenic organizing pneumonia; organizing stage of diffuse alveolar damage; diffuse alveolar hemorrhage; drugs (amiodarone, cocaine); infections; connective tissue diseases; hypersensitivity pneumonitis; eosinophilic pneumonia; Wegener's granulomatosis
Desquamative interstitial pneumonia	Cigarette smoking; idiopathic; connective tissue diseases; primary pulmonary Langerhans cell histiocytosis; asbestosis; hard-metal pneumoconiosis (cobalt); Gaucher's disease; Niemann-Pick disease; Hermansky-Pudlak syndrome; drugs (nitrofurantoin, amiodarone)
Nonspecific interstitial pneumonitis	Idiopathic; connective tissue diseases; drugs; hypersensitivity pneumonitis; diffuse alveolar damage; infections; lymphocytic interstitial pneumonia; acquired immunodeficiency syndrome (AIDS); chronic eosinophilic pneumonia; infections; hemosiderosis; alveolar proteinosis
Usual interstitial pneumonia	Idiopathic pulmonary fibrosis; connective tissue diseases (uncommon); asbestosis; hypersensitivity pneumonitis; chronic aspiration pneumonia; chronic radiation pneumonitis; Hermansky-Pudlak syndrome; neurofibromatosis
Lymphocytic interstitial pneumonia	Idiopathic; hypogammaglobulinemia; autoimmune diseases, including Hashimoto's thyroiditis, lupus erythematosus, primary biliary cirrhosis, Sjögren's syndrome, myasthenia gravis, and chronic active hepatitis; AIDS; allogeneic bone marrow transplantation
Eosinophilic pneumonia	Idiopathic acute and chronic; tropical filarial eosinophilia; parasitic infections; allergic bronchopulmonary aspergillosis; allergic granulomatosis of Churg and Strauss; hypereosinophilic syndrome; AIDS; L-tryptophan
Alveolar proteinosis	Pulmonary alveolar proteinosis; acute silicosis; aluminum dust; AIDS; myeloproliferative disorder
Diffuse alveolar hemorrhage	
With capillaritis	Wegener's granulomatosis; microscopic polyangiitis; systemic lupus erythematosus; polymyositis; scleroderma; rheumatoid arthritis; mixed connective tissue disease; lung transplantation; drugs (retinoic acid, propylthiouracil, dilantin); Behçet's disease; cryoglobulinemia; Henoch-Schönlein purpura; pauci-immune glomerulonephritis; immune complex glomerulonephritis
Without capillaritis	Idiopathic pulmonary hemosiderosis; systemic lupus erythematosus; Goodpasture's syndrome; diffuse alveolar damage; pulmonary veno-occlusive disease; mitral stenosis; lymphangioleiomyomatosis
Amyloid deposition	Primary amyloidosis; multiple myeloma; lymphocytic interstitial pneumonia
Granuloma	Sarcoidosis; hypersensitivity pneumonitis; eosinophilic granuloma; silicosis; intravenous talcosis; berylliosis; lymphocytic interstitial pneumonia; infections
Honeycomb lung	All the entities listed above may progress to end-stage lung fibrosis, especially usual interstitial pneumonia; nonspecific interstitial pneumonia; sarcoidosis; primary pulmonary Langerhans cell histiocytosis

sclerosis, and neurofibromatosis.[8–11] Niemann-Pick disease,[12] Gaucher's disease,[13] and Hermansky-Pudlak syndrome[14,15] are inherited in an autosomal recessive fashion (see Familial Pulmonary Fibrosis later).

Gender

There are interstitial lung diseases with a sex predilection. Lymphangioleiomyomatosis occurs exclusively in women. In addition, the connective tissue diseases more commonly affect women. Occupational causes are more likely in men. However, transmission of inorganic dust, either from clothes or by living in the vicinity of a manufacturing or mining facility, has resulted in asbestosis and berylliosis in women, children, and men not employed in the industry.

SYMPTOMS

Progressive *dyspnea* is usually the most common symptom, but cough can be prominent, particularly in those patients with lymphangitic carcinomatosis in which the bronchial lymphatic channels are infiltrated. *Cough* is a prominent symptom in interstitial lung diseases that affect small airways or are bronchocentric in location, such as sarcoidosis, respiratory bronchiolitis, organizing pneumonia, pulmonary Langerhans cell granulomatosis, and hypersensitivity pneumonitis.

Substernal chest pain, an unusual complaint for most interstitial lung diseases, is frequent in sarcoidosis. *Pleuritic-type chest pain* may accompany connective tissue and drug-related interstitial lung diseases. The sudden appearance of *chest pain* due to a pneumothorax can be the presenting manifestation or complicate a preexisting eosinophilic granuloma, lymphangioleiomyomatosis, tuberous sclerosis, or neurofibromatosis. *Wheezing,* an unusual symptom in interstitial lung disease, has been reported with lymphangitic carcinomatosis, chronic eosinophilic pneumonia, respiratory bronchiolitis, and hypersensitivity pneumonitis. *Hemoptysis* is typical for the diffuse alveolar hemorrhage syndromes, lymphangioleiomyomatosis, pulmonary veno-occlusive disease, and long-standing mitral valve disease. However, alveolar hemorrhage may be present without hemoptysis. Hemoptysis occurring in a patient with an established interstitial lung disease raises the possibility of a complicating malignancy.

Symptoms in patients with interstitial lung disease are present for months to years and progress at varying rates. Several interstitial reactions are acute (days to several weeks). These are often confused with atypical pneumonias because they cause diffuse radiographic opacities and may be associated with fever. Included are acute interstitial pneumonitis (AIP; Hamman-Rich syndrome), acute eosinophilic pneumonia, some cases of hypersensitivity pneumonitis, occasionally drug-related interstitial lung diseases, some cases of organizing pneumonia, the diffuse alveolar hemorrhage syndromes, and the acute immunologic pneumonias that occur with connective tissue diseases.

PHYSICAL FINDINGS

The most typical physical finding is bibasilar inspiratory crackles. Crackles are less likely in the granulomatous diseases. Bilateral inspiratory crackles may also be present in a symptomatic patient with a negative chest radiograph. Clubbing of the digits, which in most cases indicates advanced fibrotic disease, is a common finding in patients with the idiopathic or familial forms of pulmonary fibrosis. However, the appearance of digital clubbing in a patient with an established case of interstitial lung disease could indicate an underlying bronchogenic carcinoma. With advanced fibrosis, causing chronic hypoxemia, clinical signs of pulmonary hypertension and cor pulmonale appear. Attention to potential extrapulmonary physical findings supports or suggests a specific diagnosis (Table 53.3).

RADIOGRAPHIC FEATURES

Although standard chest radiography is not as sensitive for detection of interstitial lung disease as the HRCT scan, it is the logical starting point and the most practical way of identifying and defining disease.

Plain Roentgenography

Ziskind and coworkers[16] classified the diffuse lung diseases according to the pattern on chest radiographs. They divided opacities into alveolar filling and primarily interstitial patterns. Alveolar filling is recognized by a homogeneous opacity that can be diffuse or patchy and is characterized by confluent nodules with ill-defined outer borders, air bronchograms, and obliteration or silhouetting of normal structures such as the diaphragm, heart, and intrapulmonary blood vessels (Fig. 53.3). Another feature is the acinar rosette or air alveologram, which indicates consolidation of the alveolus and small airways distal to an unobstructed terminal bronchiole (Fig. 53.4). Interstitial lung diseases that are more likely to produce this pattern are listed in Table 53.4. Several (e.g., sarcoidosis, pulmonary lymphoma) have associated hilar adenopathy. In patients with alveolar proteinosis, sparing of the lung parenchyma immediately adjacent to the diaphragm is seen. In chronic eosinophilic pneumonia, the pattern has been referred to as the radiographic negative of pulmonary edema, because the alveolar opacities are most prominent in the periphery. A similar alveolar pattern has also been reported to occur in some patients with organizing pneumonia (Fig. 53.5).

Radiographic interstitial opacities become apparent when the interstitial compartment becomes infiltrated and widened by inflammatory cells, excessive collagen, granulomatous inflammation, or smooth muscle proliferation. In other instances, malignant cells or amyloid deposits expand this compartment. These infiltrates appear as nodules, linear reticular opacities, or a combination of linear shadows and nodules (reticulonodular). Miliary nodules accompany infectious granulomas and noninfectious granulomas (e.g., sarcoidosis, eosinophilic granuloma, silicosis, and hypersensitivity pneumonitis) and some malignant diseases (e.g., melanoma, hypernephroma, and lymphoma) (Fig. 53.6). Nodules of varying size characterize the granulomatous

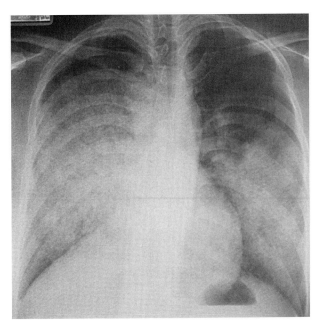

Figure 53.3 Chest radiograph showing a characteristic pattern of alveolar filling disease in a patient with diffuse alveolar hemorrhage. Note the homogeneous consolidation with obliteration of the right heart border and the pulmonary vasculature in addition to air bronchograms.

Table 53.3 Extrapulmonary Physical Findings in the Interstitial Lung Diseases

Finding	Examples
Systemic hypertension	Connective tissue disease; neurofibromatosis; some diffuse alveolar hemorrhage syndromes
Erythema nodosum	Sarcoidosis; connective tissue disease; Behçet's syndrome
Maculopapular rash	Drug-induced; amyloidosis; lipoidosis; connective tissue diseases; Gaucher's disease
Heliotrope rash	Dermatomyositis
Albinism	Hermansky-Pudlak syndrome
Discoid lupus	Systemic lupus erythematosus
Neurofibroma	von Recklinghausen's disease
Telangiectasia	Scleroderma
Raynaud's phenomenon	Connective tissue disease
Cutaneous vasculitis	Systemic vasculitides; connective tissue disease
Subcutaneous nodules	von Recklinghausen's disease; rheumatoid arthritis
Calcinosis	Dermatomyositis; scleroderma
Uveitis	Sarcoidosis; Behçet's syndrome; ankylosing spondylitis
Scleritis	Systemic vasculitis; systemic lupus erythematosus; scleroderma; sarcoidosis
Keratoconjunctivitis sicca	Lymphocytic interstitial pneumonia
Salivary gland enlargement	Sarcoidosis, lymphocytic interstitial pneumonia
Peripheral lymphadenopathy	Sarcoidosis; lymphangitic carcinomatosis; lymphocytic interstitial pneumonia; lymphoma
Hepatosplenomegaly	Sarcoidosis; eosinophilic granuloma; connective tissue disease; amyloidosis; lymphocytic interstitial pneumonia
Pericarditis	Radiation pneumonitis; connective tissue disease
Myositis	Connective tissue disease; drugs (L-tryptophan)
Bone involvement	Pulmonary Langerhans cell histiocytosis; sarcoidosis; Gaucher's disease; lymphangitic carcinomatosis
Arthritis	Connective tissue disease; systemic vasculitis; sarcoidosis
Diabetes insipidus	Pulmonary Langerhans cell histiocytosis; sarcoidosis
Glomerulonephritis	Systemic vasculitis; connective tissue disease; Goodpasture's syndrome; sarcoidosis
Nephrotic syndrome	Amyloidosis; drug-induced (gold, penicillamine); systemic lupus erythematosus
Renal mass	Lymphangioleiomyomatosis; tuberous sclerosis

lung diseases. However, linear infiltrates possibly representing an underlying cellular interstitial infiltrate are also visible.

Linear interstitial changes are seen in most interstitial lung diseases and usually in conjunction with nodular change, the so-called reticulonodular opacities (Fig. 53.7). However, there are several distinctive patterns of linear or reticular interstitial changes (Table 53.5). Short horizontal lines at the lung periphery (Kerley's B lines), representing thickened interlobular septa, are seen after obstruction of the pulmonary lymphatics (Fig. 53.8). The term *radiographic honeycomb lung* refers to a reticular pattern that correlates with the histologic "honeycombing." These small cystic structures, which are best seen in the lower and

peripheral lung zones, indicate an underlying advanced fibrotic change (Fig. 53.9).

It is typical for many interstitial lung diseases (e.g., IPF, the connective tissue diseases, asbestosis, cytotoxic drug–induced disorders) to have the greatest concentration of the reticular opacities and honeycomb changes in the lower lung zones. In fact, lower lobe volume loss and traction bronchiectasis are typical for the advanced stages of these diseases.[17] There are a group of interstitial diseases (see Table 53.5), often granulomatous, in which the radiographic changes are more prominent in the upper lung zones (Fig. 53.10).

Other radiographic features may point to a diagnosis. For example, diaphragmatic pleural calcification is indicative of

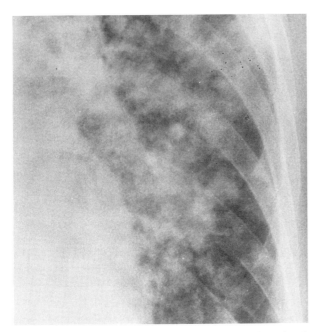

Figure 53.4 Detailed view of chest radiograph showing alveolar nodules in a patient with alveolar cell carcinoma. Note the ill-defined nodules and distal air alveolograms.

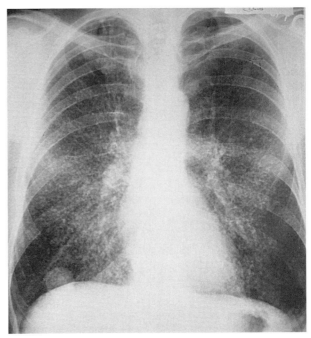

Figure 53.6 Chest radiograph showing miliary interstitial nodulation in a patient with metastatic malignant melanoma. A large mass is also present in the right lower lobe.

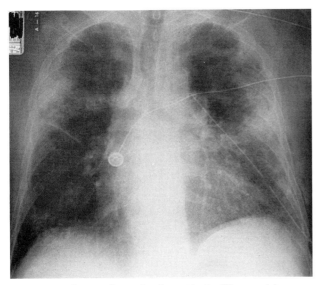

Figure 53.5 Chest radiograph of a patient with organizing pneumonia showing bilateral peripheral alveolar opacities. A similar appearance is seen in chronic eosinophilic pneumonia.

Table 53.4 Interstitial Lung Diseases Producing an Alveolar Filling Pattern on Chest Radiograph

Alveolar proteinosis (proteinaceous fluid)
Alveolar cell carcinoma (malignant cells)
Bronchioloalveolar metastases (malignant cells from pancreas, breast)
Pulmonary lymphoma (malignant lymphocytes)
Lymphocytic interstitial pneumonia (lymphoplasmacytic cells)
Alveolar sarcoid (lymphocyte-macrophage alveolitis or confluent granuloma)
Desquamative interstitial pneumonia (macrophages)
Diffuse alveolar hemorrhage (red blood cells; hemosiderin-filled macrophages)
Eosinophilic pneumonia (eosinophils, macrophages; lymphocytes)
Alveolar microlithiasis (calcium-phosphate microliths)
Bronchiolitis obliterans with organizing pneumonia (collagen)
Mineral oil aspiration (lipid-filled macrophages)
Acute hypersensitivity pneumonia (lymphoplasmacytic cells)

asbestos exposure. Pleuritis and pleural effusion may complicate the course of the connective tissue–associated interstitial lung diseases. The exception is polymyositis-dermatomyositis. Pneumothorax is often the presenting manifestation of pulmonary Langerhans cell histiocytosis or lymphangioleiomyomatosis. The majority of interstitial lung diseases result in a gradual reduction of the lung volumes. There are interstitial diseases that are bronchiolocentric, resulting in either maintenance or expansion of the lung volume (see Table 53.5). If an interstitial lung disease is superimposed on emphysema, the lung volumes often are

preserved. Chronic hypoxemia results in radiographic evidence of pulmonary hypertension.

A criticism of the alveolar-interstitial classification is that a mixed pattern is often found. For example, interstitial fibrosis may eventually be superimposed on a disease that was primarily alveolar, such as alveolar proteinosis, diffuse

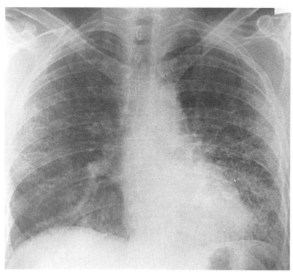

Figure 53.7 Chest radiograph showing diffuse reticulonodular opacities in a patient with idiopathic pulmonary fibrosis.

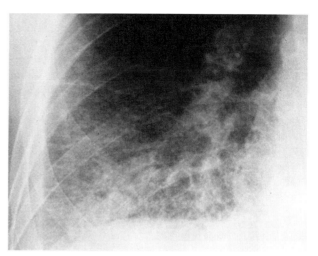

Figure 53.8 Detailed view of right lung showing Kerley's B lines and pleural effusion in a patient with lymphangitic carcinomatosis.

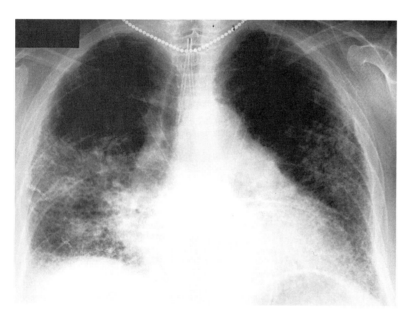

Figure 53.9 Chest radiograph showing characteristic features of honeycomb lung. A network of 2- to 3-mm cystic spaces is distributed throughout the lung fields. This patient with end-stage idiopathic pulmonary fibrosis also had pulmonary hypertension and was receiving oxygen through a transtracheal catheter.

alveolar hemorrhage, eosinophilic pneumonia, or organizing pneumonia. Sarcoidosis, a disease characterized by interstitial granuloma, can be alveolar in appearance due to either coalescence of granulomas with compression of adjacent lung or a lymphocyte-macrophage alveolitis. Dense fibrosis from any fibrotic lung disease can compress adjacent lung, producing homogeneous shadows. The appearance of alveolar opacities during the course of an interstitial lung disease may represent renewed activity of the primary disease, superimposed infection, or development of alveolar cell carcinoma or adenocarcinoma.[18,19]

Computed Tomography

Conventional chest radiographic assessment for interstitial lung disease may miss up to 10% of cases.[20] Conventional computed tomography (CT), obtained using 8- to 10-mm

slices, offers little more for the detection of radiographic-negative interstitial lung disease. HRCT, obtained with less than 3-mm slices, enables better visualization of fine parenchymal detail and therefore the detection of early air space filling or interstitial change (Fig. 53.11). In cases of suspected interstitial lung disease with negative conventional radiography, it is important to perform HRCT with prone and supine views. Dependent lung density can mask interstitial change, and vascular engorgement of the dependent portion of lung mimics septal thickening on the supine view. Abnormalities that persist on the prone view are indicative of disease.

In patients with abnormal chest radiographs, the diagnostic accuracy increases with HRCT evaluation. In cases of IPF, peripheral reticular opacities, lower zone subpleural honeycombing, and traction bronchiectasis are seen (Fig. 53.12).[21] In the connective tissue diseases, asbestosis, and

Table 53.5 Radiographic Features of the Interstitial Lung Diseases

Feature	Diseases
Upper zone–predominant disease	Radiation pneumonitis; neurofibromatosis; chronic sarcoidosis; eosinophilic granuloma; silicosis; chronic hypersensitivity pneumonitis; chronic eosinophilic pneumonia; ankylosing spondylitis; nodular rheumatoid arthritis; berylliosis; drug-induced (amiodarone, gold, BCNU [carmustine]); radiation
Increased lung volumes	Lymphangioleiomyomatosis; chronic sarcoidosis; chronic eosinophilic granuloma; chronic hypersensitivity pneumonitis; tuberous sclerosis; neurofibromatosis
Radiographic honeycomb lung	Idiopathic pulmonary fibrosis; connective tissue disease; asbestosis; drug-induced; lymphocytic interstitial pneumonia; chronic aspiration pneumonia; hemosiderosis; Hermansky-Pudlak syndrome; alveolar proteinosis
Pneumothorax	Pulmonary Langerhans cell histiocytosis; lymphangioleiomyomatosis; tuberous sclerosis; neurofibromatosis
Kerley's B lines	Lymphangitic carcinomatosis; lymphangioleiomyomatosis; left atrial hypertension (mitral valve disease, veno-occlusive disease); lymphoma; amyloidosis
Lymphadenopathy	Sarcoidosis; lymphoma; lymphangitic carcinomatosis; lymphoid interstitial pneumonia; berylliosis; amyloidosis; Gaucher's disease
Pleural disease	Lymphangitic carcinomatosis; connective tissue disease; asbestosis (pleural calcification); lymphangioleiomyomatosis (chylous effusion); drug-induced (nitrofurantoin, radiation); sarcoidosis
Eggshell calcification of lymph nodes	Silicosis; sarcoidosis; radiation

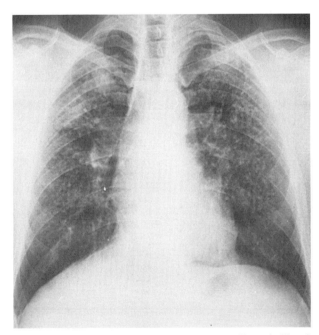

Figure 53.10 Chest radiograph showing uncomplicated silicosis. Note the nodular interstitial disease with predilection for the middle and upper lung zones.

some drug-induced interstitial lung disease, the results on HRCT, as on chest radiography, are indistinguishable from those of IPF or nonspecific interstitial pneumonia (NSIP). In scleroderma, a disease in which the prevalence rate of interstitial lung disease approaches 100% in autopsy series, HRCT detects disease in 45% to 75% of patients when conventional radiography is negative.[22,23]

In sarcoidosis, in addition to the hilar and mediastinal adenopathy, nodules deposited along bronchovascular bundles and interlobular septa, air space filling due to the lymphocyte-macrophage alveolitis, and linear densities secondary to fibrotic scarring can be seen (Fig. 53.13). In patients with hypersensitivity pneumonitis, air space–filling centrilobular nodules and linear opacities without adenopathy are present. The HRCT can be normal in symptomatic patients with biopsy-proved hypersensitivity pneumonitis.[24] In patients with pulmonary Langerhans cell histiocytosis, the combination of centrilobular nodules and cysts, most prominent in the upper lobes and occasionally accompanied by a pneumothorax, is characteristic (Fig. 53.14). In earlier pulmonary Langerhans cell histiocytosis, coalescence of the nodules produces an air space filling pattern.

In lymphangioleiomyomatosis, the HRCT is typical, revealing rounded, thin-walled cysts throughout (Fig. 53.15). A pneumothorax or pleural effusion (chylous) may accompany this change. Except for the pleural effusion, identical findings are present in tuberous sclerosis. Lymphangitic carcinomatosis produces a beaded-chain appearance of the interlobular septa that correlates with Kerley's B lines detectable by conventional radiography. In asbestos-related disease, noncalcified pleural plaques and early interstitial lung disease are often difficult to detect, and the HRCT is more sensitive than conventional chest radiography.

FUNCTIONAL ASSESSMENT

In interstitial lung disease, there are characteristic alterations of the lungs' mechanical properties and impairment of gas exchange at the alveolar-capillary interface. Assessment of ventilatory function and the mechanical properties of the

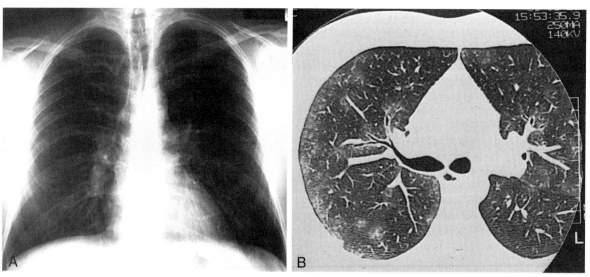

Figure 53.11 A, A normal chest radiograph from a 45-year-old man with established hypersensitivity pneumonitis. At the time, his arterial P_{O_2} while breathing room air was 48 mm Hg. **B,** A high-resolution computed tomographic image of the same patient demonstrating patchy ground-glass areas of air space filling opacities.

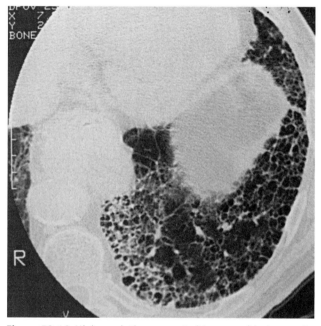

Figure 53.12 High-resolution computed tomographic image of advanced idiopathic pulmonary fibrosis showing extensive honeycomb changes.

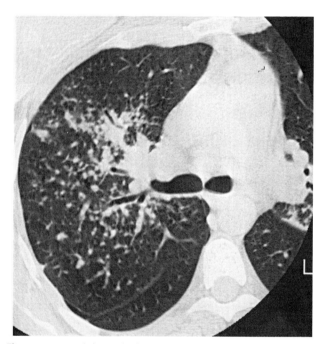

Figure 53.13 High-resolution computed tomographic image from a patient with sarcoidosis showing hilar lymphadenopathy and nodular disease as well as dense air space filling.

lungs, as well as gas exchange, particularly during exercise, are vital components of the initial evaluation of patients with suspected interstitial lung disease. In addition, serial measurements of function enable the physician to determine progression of the disease and the effects of therapeutic intervention.

Ventilatory Function

Ventilatory function tests provide an indirect index of alterations to the impedance to respiration offered by the elastic resistance to distention of the lungs and the frictional

resistance to airflow in the tracheobronchial tree. Clinically, alterations of the mechanical properties of the respiratory system are also reflected in the pattern of breathing that is adopted by the patient. These patients tend to breathe rapidly and shallowly, because a larger tidal volume would require an inordinate increase in work of breathing to overcome the greatly increased elastic resistance.

Elastic Resistance

Interstitial lung disease is associated with an increase in elastic resistance (or decreased compliance), and this can be

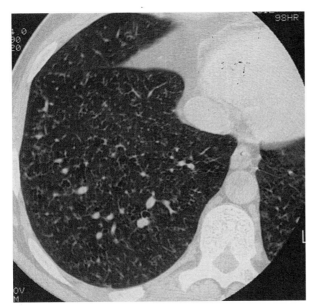

Figure 53.14 High-resolution computed tomographic image from a patient with pulmonary Langerhans cell histiocytosis showing diffuse centrilobular nodulation and cyst formation.

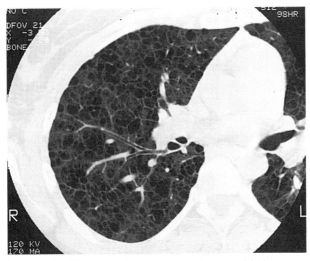

Figure 53.15 High-resolution computed tomographic image from a patient with lymphangioleiomyomatosis showing characteristic thin-walled cysts throughout the parenchyma.

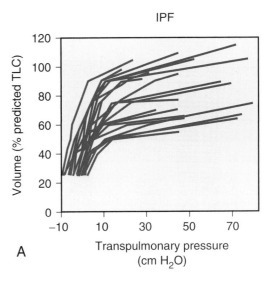

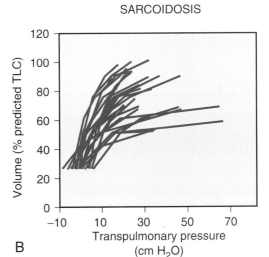

Figure 53.16 Multiple recordings showing volume-pressure characteristics in patients with idiopathic pulmonary fibrosis (IPF) **(A)** and sarcoidosis **(B)**. Note the marked variation of position and shape in both disorders. TLC, total lung capacity. (From Hanley ME, King TE Jr, Schwarz MI, et al: The impact of smoking on mechanical properties of the lungs in idiopathic pulmonary fibrosis and sarcoidosis. Am Rev Respir Dis 144:1102, 1991.)

seen in a plot of the static transpulmonary pressure (i.e., at points of no flow) at differing decrements of lung volume from total lung capacity (TLC) to residual volume. In most patients with interstitial lung disease, the plot of the volume-pressure relationship of the lungs is characteristically shifted downward and to the right, with a reduced slope (i.e., compliance is low) and a markedly increased coefficient of elastic recoil (maximum elastic recoil pressure, TLC). On the other hand, as is demonstrated in Figure 53.16, there is significant variation in the position of the volume-pressure curve in patients with IPF and sarcoidosis,[25] and the correlation between alterations of the elastic properties (and lung volume compartments) and the degree of fibrosis present is poor. This is, at least in part, a

consequence of the impact of smoking, which appears to differ in the two disorders. In patients with IPF who smoke, the volume-pressure curve is shifted upward and to the left, whereas in smokers with sarcoidosis it is shifted downward and to the right.[25]

Measurements of lung volume reflect changes in position of the volume-pressure curve of the lungs. This is because alterations of the elastic recoil of the lung or chest wall disturb the balance between the elastic forces of the lungs, which act in an expiratory direction, and those of the chest wall, which act in an inspiratory direction. In patients with interstitial lung disease the TLC, functional residual capacity, and residual volume are generally lower than expected (Fig. 53.17). A lower than expected TLC (and vital capacity) in association with a normal functional residual

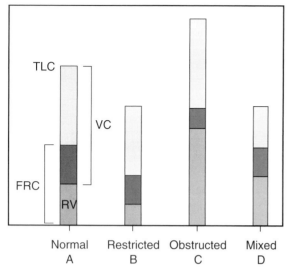

Figure 53.17 Bar graphs showing total lung capacity (TLC) and its subdivisions in healthy persons **(A)** compared with the typical abnormalities found in patients with restrictive disorders **(B)**, obstructive disorders **(C)**, and mixed disorders **(D)**. FRC, functional residual capacity; RV, residual volume; VC, vital capacity. (From Cherniack RM: Pulmonary Function Testing. Philadelphia: WB Saunders, 1992.)

capacity and a greater than expected residual volume (see Fig. 53.17) generally reflects a mixed restrictive and obstructive disorder. However, because maximum effort is necessary to determine the inspiratory capacity and the expiratory reserve volume, a less than maximal inspiration or expiration, because of either weak respiratory muscles or poor effort, leads to the same findings. Similar qualifications apply to the vital capacity, which is often used as an index of alterations of elastic resistance. In addition, as can be seen in Figure 53.17, a low vital capacity is not specific for restrictive disorders, because it is also lower than expected in patients with airflow limitation (because of an increased residual volume).

Flow Resistance

Measurement of lung volume is important when evaluating airflow resistance. This can be assessed directly from the relationship between the rate of airflow and the resistive component of the transpulmonary pressure.

In clinical practice, various indirect measures of flow resistance can be used: the FEV_1; the mean expiratory flow rate between 25% and 75% of the forced vital capacity (FVC), that is, FEF_{25-75}; the maximal expiratory flow rate ($\dot{V}max$) at a particular proportion (such as 75%, 50%, or 25%) of the FVC (from a flow-volume curve); the FEV_1/FVC ratio; or the FEV_1-to–vital capacity ratio. Low flow rates or a low FEV_1/FVC ratio (i.e., less than 70% of predicted) is believed to indicate expiratory airflow limitation. However, like airway resistance, $\dot{V}max$ values depend on the state of expansion of the airways (i.e., lung volume). The FEV_1/FVC ratio will be overestimated, and the degree of flow limitation underestimated, in the patient who does not exhale fully because of severe dyspnea or muscular weakness, pain, or poor effort.

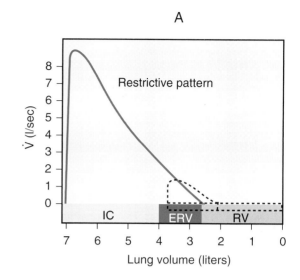

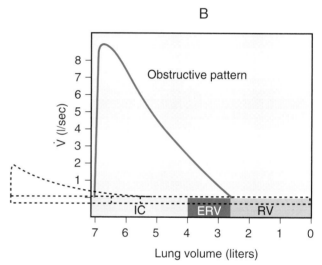

Figure 53.18 Schematic volume-flow ($\dot{V}$) curves in a healthy person (*solid line*) are compared with those in patients (*dotted lines*) with a restrictive disorder **(A)** and with an obstructive disorder **(B)**. Lung volume is reduced in the restrictive disorder, and maximum expiratory flow rates are low because they are achieved at low lung volumes. Flow rates are higher than expected at low lung volumes because the driving pressure (lung elastic recoil) is increased. ERV, expiratory residual volume; RV, residual volume. (From Cherniack RM: Pulmonary Function Testing. Philadelphia: WB Saunders, 1992.)

Airflow resistance is not generally thought to be increased in interstitial lung disease. As is seen in Figure 53.18, $\dot{V}max$ is low in interstitial lung disease, not because of an increase in flow resistance but rather because the flow rates are being achieved at low lung volumes. In fact, in uncomplicated interstitial lung disease, $\dot{V}max$ values are greater than expected at any particular lung volume (isovolume), because the lung elastic recoil pressure, which is the driving pressure for flow in the peripheral airways, is increased.[26] As a corollary, a $\dot{V}max$ lower than expected at a particular lung volume in a patient who is suffering from a restrictive disorder indicates an increase of flow resistance in the more peripheral (upstream) airways. An increase in upstream resistance has been reported in patients with IPF, extrinsic allergic alveolitis, and asbestos exposure.

Gas Exchange

Alterations of gas exchange are readily assessed by analysis of the arterial PO_2 and PCO_2 and calculation of the alveolar-arterial PO_2 difference $((A - a)PO_2)$, both at rest and during exercise.

In patients with interstitial lung disease, arterial blood analysis while at rest usually reveals hypoxemia and an increased $(A - a)PO_2$, along with hypocapnia. In addition, the diffusing capacity for carbon monoxide (DL_{CO}) is reduced, primarily because of a reduction in the alveolar-capillary surface available for gas exchange. The disturbance of gas exchange generally accompanies abnormalities in ventilatory function,[27] but gas exchange may be normal at rest in a significant number of patients. Similarly, the resting DL_{CO} may be only slightly reduced in patients who demonstrate a mild restrictive disorder or normal gas exchange while at rest, or both.

The DL_{CO} is generally greater than expected in those cases associated with recent pulmonary hemorrhage, because the red blood cells in the pulmonary alveoli take up carbon monoxide readily. Sequential measurements of the DL_{CO} within minutes may aid in the establishment of the diagnosis of alveolar hemorrhage.[28] When there is fresh blood in the alveolar spaces, each successive DL_{CO} value will be lower as the hemoglobin in the alveoli becomes saturated with carbon monoxide.

Exercise

In most patients, gas exchange is disturbed during exertion, even in those with normal gas exchange at rest. Assessment of gas exchange during exercise provides the best correlation with the severity of disease[29] and is probably the most important physiologic determination in patients with interstitial lung disease.

In general, patients with the most severe restrictive disease have the poorest exercise tolerance. As is shown in Figure 53.19, ventilation generally rises excessively during exercise and may approach the ventilatory ceiling. Characteristically, the respiratory frequency rises inordinately with increasing exercise loads because of the increased work that would be required to overcome the elastic resistance of the lungs if the tidal volume were to increase.

The excessive ventilation is frequently preferentially distributed to areas of lung that have normal compliance but diminished perfusion (i.e., high ventilation-perfusion ratio); as a result, unlike the normal response, the calculated dead space (VD) and the ratio of dead space to tidal volume (VD/VT) rise in association with rapid, shallow breathing. The increase in cardiac output with exercise and the rapid transit of blood through the pulmonary capillaries along with its redistribution in the lungs leads to a greater maldistribution of ventilation-perfusion ratios. This results in a rise in $(A - a)PO_2$ and a fall in arterial PO_2 (Fig. 53.20). Except for heavy exercise, when the transit through the circulation is exceptionally rapid, it is unlikely that a reduced ability of oxygen to diffuse across a thickened alveolar-capillary membrane plays a significant role in the hypoxemia.

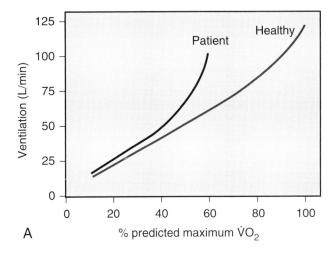

A

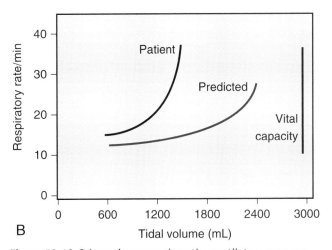

B

Figure 53.19 Schematic curves show the ventilatory response **(A)** and respiratory pattern **(B)** during increasing exercise workloads expressed as a percentage of the predicted maximum oxygen uptake ($\dot{V}O_2$) in a healthy person and in a patient with idiopathic pulmonary fibrosis. (From Cherniack RM: Pulmonary Function Testing. Philadelphia: WB Saunders, 1992.)

LABORATORY FINDINGS

Table 53.6 summarizes the results of laboratory tests that suggest or support the diagnosis of a specific interstitial lung disease.

BRONCHOALVEOLAR LAVAGE

BAL is a technique employed to sample the distal airways via the instillation of sterile saline through a wedged fiberoptic bronchoscope. After aspiration the contents, which are thought to represent the cellular, immunologic, and biochemical milieu of the alveolar structures, can be analyzed. The results of BAL for the evaluation of interstitial lung disease have been difficult to interpret because of the lack of standardized techniques for both the performance of the procedure and the subsequent analysis of the data.[30–32] Furthermore, in some of the earlier studies correlative data between lung biopsies and BAL were not obtained. Often

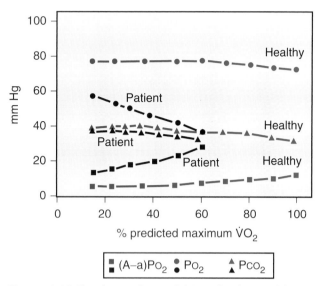

Figure 53.20 The changes in arterial P_{O_2}, alveolar-arterial P_{O_2} difference (($A - a)P_{O_2}$), and arterial P_{CO_2} during increasing exercise workloads expressed as the percentage of predicted maximum oxygen uptake ($\dot{V}_{O_2}$) in a healthy person and a patient with idiopathic pulmonary fibrosis. (From Cherniack RM: Pulmonary Function Testing. Philadelphia: WB Saunders, 1992.)

the treatment or smoking status of the patient was not considered. A multicenter publication has set forth the methods of performing and analyzing the results of BAL.[33] This study involved a large cohort of normal subjects of varying age and race who were compared with patients with documented interstitial lung disease. Smoking affects the BAL results of both normal subjects and patients by amplifying the macrophage and eosinophil populations.[33]

BAL is a useful investigative tool in many interstitial lung diseases. Cytologic analysis of BAL specimens can be diagnostic for lymphangitic carcinomatosis, alveolar cell carcinoma, and pulmonary lymphoma. If the eosinophil level exceeds 40% (normal, less than 2%), eosinophilic pneumonia is usually the cause of the diffuse pulmonary infiltration. BAL eosinophilia of a lesser degree may occur with some connective tissue diseases, IPF, or organizing pneumonia.

The finding of periodic acid–Schiff–positive lipoproteinaceous bodies in the lavage liquid was originally thought to be diagnostic for pulmonary alveolar proteinosis but has proved to be nonspecific. In cases of diffuse alveolar hemorrhage, red blood cells and hemosiderin-laden macrophages dominate the lavage specimen.

Lavage lymphocytosis (more than 35% lymphocytes) predominates in some diseases. Sarcoidosis and hypersensitivity pneumonitis are most common. Others include lymphocytic interstitial pneumonia (LIP), pulmonary lymphoma, berylliosis, and some drug-induced interstitial lung diseases. Smaller but increased percentages of lymphocytes (normal

Table 53.6 Laboratory Findings in the Interstitial Lung Diseases

Finding	Diseases
Leukopenia	Sarcoidosis; connective tissue disease; lymphoma; drug-induced
Leukocytosis	Systemic vasculitis; hypersensitivity pneumonitis; lymphoma
Eosinophilia	Eosinophilic pneumonia; sarcoidosis; systemic vasculitis; drug-induced (sulfa, methotrexate)
Thrombocytopenia	Sarcoidosis; connective tissue disease; drug-induced; Gaucher's disease; idiopathic pulmonary fibrosis
Hemolytic anemia	Connective tissue disease; sarcoidosis; lymphoma; drug-induced; idiopathic pulmonary fibrosis
Normocytic anemia	Diffuse alveolar hemorrhage syndromes; connective tissue disease; lymphangitic carcinomatosis
Urinary sediment abnormalities	Connective tissue disease; systemic vasculitis; drug-induced
Hypogammaglobulinemia	Lymphocytic interstitial pneumonia
Hypergammaglobulinemia	Connective tissue disease; sarcoidosis; systemic vasculitis; idiopathic pulmonary fibrosis; asbestosis; silicosis; lymphocytic interstitial pneumonia; lymphoma
Serum autoantibodies	Connective tissue disease; systemic vasculitis; sarcoidosis; idiopathic pulmonary fibrosis; silicosis; asbestosis; lymphocytic interstitial pneumonia
Serum immune complexes	Idiopathic pulmonary fibrosis; lymphocytic interstitial pneumonia; systemic vasculitis; connective tissue disease; eosinophilic granuloma
Serum angiotensin-converting enzyme	Sarcoidosis; hypersensitivity pneumonitis; silicosis; acute respiratory distress syndrome; Gaucher's disease
Antibasement membrane antibody	Goodpasture's syndrome
Antineutrophil cytoplasmic antibody	Systemic vasculitis

range, 15%) can be seen with these entities in addition to a number of other interstitial lung diseases, including IPF, organizing pneumonia, connective tissue diseases, and some pneumoconioses. In patients with suspected asbestos-related disease, one or more asbestos bodies per high-powered field in the BAL specimen indicate significant exposure, but this does not establish the diagnosis of asbestosis. Because of the vertical gradient of asbestos bodies recovered in the lungs of patients with asbestosis, if lavage is used to document previous asbestos exposure, samples should be obtained from a basal segment of one of the lower lobes. A diagnosis of berylliosis is confirmed when lavaged lymphocytes undergo proliferation after exposure to the mineral in vitro.

In the BAL recovered from patients with eosinophilic granuloma, all inflammatory cells are increased even though their percentages remain unchanged. Electron microscopy demonstrates increased numbers of Langerhans cells. This monocyte, which is thought to be central in the pathogenesis, has a typical pentilaminar body (Birbeck granule) in the cytoplasm, as revealed by electron microscopy. Langerhans cells have been described in other fibrotic lung diseases, but not in numbers equivalent to those of eosinophilic granuloma.[34]

Other applications of BAL include disease staging (i.e., cellular infiltrates versus fibrosis on lung biopsies) and the prediction of therapeutic responsiveness. For example, in both the connective tissue diseases and IPF, BAL lymphocytosis is associated with a cellular histology (as opposed to fibrosis) and an improved response to treatment. Furthermore, the overall survival rate in these patients is increased. On the other hand, the combination of lavage neutrophilia and eosinophilia without lymphocytosis often portends progressive unresponsive disease. In sarcoidosis, a disease that is characterized by increases in the number of T-helper (CD4+) lymphocytes in the lung, it has been suggested that clinical deterioration may be expected if the BAL lymphocyte level exceeds 28%. More recent data indicate that the level of BAL lymphocytes has no value in predicting the clinical outcome in sarcoidosis.

The assessment of potential interstitial lung disease in populations at risk is another role for BAL. For example, in patients with scleroderma and rheumatoid arthritis in whom clinical, radiologic, and physiologic evidence of interstitial lung disease is lacking, BAL studies have revealed increases in inflammatory cell populations.

TISSUE DIAGNOSIS

The final step in the evaluation of a patient with interstitial lung disease is to decide whether tissue is needed for diagnosis. As previously noted, the diagnosis of connective tissue, occupational, or drug-related interstitial lung disease is often obvious after a careful history has been taken. In cases of idiopathic and primary interstitial lung disease (see Table 53.1), the diagnosis may not be as obvious, although clinical, laboratory, and radiologic findings are often suggestive. Furthermore, the diagnosis of IPF, a commonly encountered disorder, in most situations can be established only by lung biopsy. As a matter of practicality, transbronchial biopsy can be performed during the bronchoscopy for BAL. Transbronchial biopsy is relatively safe and is often diagnostic of sarcoidosis, diffuse malignancy, alveolar pro-

teinosis, or eosinophilic pneumonia. Other entities are less frequently confirmed by this procedure. A transbronchial biopsy interpretation, which describes only inflammation, fibrosis, or both, is not evidence for IPF or any other entity listed in Table 53.1. Furthermore, even in clinically confirmed cases of connective tissue or drug-induced interstitial lung disease, several different histologic patterns may evolve (see Table 53.2), and lung biopsy is often undertaken to predict prognosis and therapeutic responsiveness, particularly if BAL and HRCT are inconclusive. If the transbronchial biopsy, clinical, and lavage data are inconclusive and the patient is not at high risk, a video thoracoscopic or open-lung biopsy should be performed. Moreover, there is a poor correlation between the results of transbronchial and open-lung biopsies unless the transbronchial biopsy yields a specific diagnosis.[35,36] Therefore, when the transbronchial biopsy is inconclusive and a definitive diagnosis is required, open or thoracoscopic lung biopsy is indicated.[37]

DIAGNOSIS AND MANAGEMENT OF THE IDIOPATHIC INTERSTITIAL PNEUMONIAS

The classification, diagnosis, and management of the idiopathic interstitial pneumonias continue to evolve.[2,38] As additional clinical and histopathologic studies are reported, it is clearer that most investigators only identify IPF as cases with the histopathologic pattern of UIP.[38,39] In addition, it is recognized that distinguishing the UIP pattern from other histopathologic patterns of idiopathic interstitial pneumonias identifies patients with differing clinical courses and prognosis. Tables 53.7 and 53.8 provide an overview of the key clinical and pathologic features of the idiopathic interstitial pneumonias.

IDIOPATHIC PULMONARY FIBROSIS

IPF (also called cryptogenic fibrosing alveolitis) is a common interstitial lung disease of unknown etiology. IPF is a well-defined clinical entity that has characteristic clinical, roentgenographic, physiologic, and pathologic manifestations. The exact prevalence of this condition is unknown, but is estimated to be 3 to 5 cases per 100,000 persons and recent studies show that it might in fact be higher and increasing in several countries.[1,40,41] The prevalence and incidence of IPF increase markedly with age.

Clinical Features

IPF occurs in middle age, usually between 50 and 70 years of age. In fact, it is quite uncommon for a patient to present before the age of 40. The typical patient presents with the insidious onset of breathlessness with exertion and a nonproductive cough. Constitutional symptoms are uncommon in lone IPF. However, weight loss, fever, fatigue, myalgias, or arthralgia is occasionally present. The onset may be heralded by a flulike illness, but this is very uncommon and its presence should suggest another diagnosis. Although patients may present with only a nonproductive cough, all patients experience dyspnea with exertion as the disease progresses. Most patients have these symptoms for months to years prior to definitive evaluation, usually around 12 to 18 months.

Table 53.7 Contrasting Pathologic Features of the Idiopathic Interstitial Pneumonias

Features	UIP	DIP	RB-ILD	AIP	NSIP	COP
Temporal appearance	Variegated	Uniform	Uniform	Uniform	Uniform	Uniform
Interstitial inflammation	Scant	Scant	Scant	Scant	Usually prominent	Usually prominent
Collagen fibrosis	Yes, patchy	Variable, diffuse	Variable, focal, mild	No	Variable, diffuse	No
Fibroblast proliferation	Fibroblast foci prominent	No	No	Diffuse	Occasional, diffuse, or rare fibroblast foci	Diffuse, fibroblastic foci
Microscopic honeycomb change	Yes	No	No	No	Rare	No
Intra-alveolar macrophage accumulation	Occasional, focal	Yes, diffuse	Peribronchiolar	No	Occasional, patchy	Foamy macrophages common
Hyaline membranes	No	No	No	Occasional, focal	No	No

AIP, acute interstitial pneumonia; COP, cryptogenic organizing pneumonia; DIP, desquamative interstitial pneumonia; NSIP, nonspecific interstitial pneumonia; RB-ILD, respiratory bronchiolitis–associated interstitial lung disease; UIP, usual interstitial pneumonia.
Adapted from Katzenstein ALA, Myers JL: Idiopathic pulmonary fibrosis: Clinical relevance of pathologic classification. Am J Respir Crit Care Med 157:1301–1315, 1998; and King TE Jr: Idiopathic interstitial pneumonia. *In* Schwarz MI, King TE Jr (eds): Interstitial Lung Diseases (4th ed). Hamilton, Ontario, Canada: BC Decker, 2003, pp 701–786.

Table 53.8 Contrasting Clinical Features of the Idiopathic Interstitial Pneumonias

Features	UIP	DIP	RB-ILD	AIP	NSIP	COP
Mean age at onset (yr)	60s	40s	40s	50s	50s	50s
Onset	Insidious	Insidious	Insidious	Acute	Subacute, insidious	Acute or subacute
History of cigarette smoking	About two thirds	Most	Most	Not known	Not known	About half
Mortality rate (mean survival)	68% (5–6 yr)	27% (12 yr)	0%	62% (1–2 mo)	11% (17 mo)	10% in 5 years
Response to steroids	Poor	Good	Good	Poor	Good	Excellent
Complete recovery possible	No	Yes	Yes	Yes	Yes	Yes (up to 70% of patients)

AIP, acute interstitial pneumonia; COP, cryptogenic organizing pneumonia; DIP, desquamative interstitial pneumonia; NSIP, nonspecific interstitial pneumonia; RB-ILD, respiratory bronchiolitis–associated interstitial lung disease; UIP, usual interstitial pneumonia.
Adapted from Katzenstein ALA, Myers JL: Idiopathic pulmonary fibrosis: Clinical relevance of pathologic classification. Am J Respir Crit Care Med 157:1301–1315, 1998; and King TE Jr: Idiopathic interstitial pneumonia. *In* Schwarz MI, King TE Jr (eds): Interstitial Lung Diseases (4th ed). Hamilton, Ontario, Canada: BC Decker, 2003, pp 701–786.

The physical examination is rarely normal. Most patients have bibasilar late inspiratory fine crackles (Velcro rales) on chest examination. Clubbing of the fingers is seen in 40% to 75% of patients and is a late finding in the disease course. Cardiac examination is usually normal except in the middle or late stages of the disease, when findings of pulmonary hypertension (i.e., augmented P_2, right-sided lift, and S_3 gallop) and cor pulmonale may become evident. Similarly, cyanosis is a late manifestation indicative of advanced disease. Spontaneous pneumothorax rarely occurs.

Blood and Serologic Studies

An elevated erythrocyte sedimentation rate, hypergamma-globulinemia, low titer-positive antinuclear antibodies (21%

of patients with lone IPF), rheumatoid factor, circulating immune complexes, and cryoimmunoglobulins have been identified in these patients.

Chest Imaging Studies

Chest Roentgenography. The most common roentgenographic abnormalities in IPF are a reticular, that is, a netlike appearance of linear or curvilinear densities. These usually appear as diffuse opacities with a predilection for the lower lung zones (Fig. 53.21; see also Fig. 53.7). A coarse reticular pattern or multiple cystic or honeycombed areas (i.e., coarse reticular pattern with translucencies measuring 0.5 to 1.0 cm in diameter) are roentgenographic findings that correlate with advanced disease and poor prognosis (see Fig.

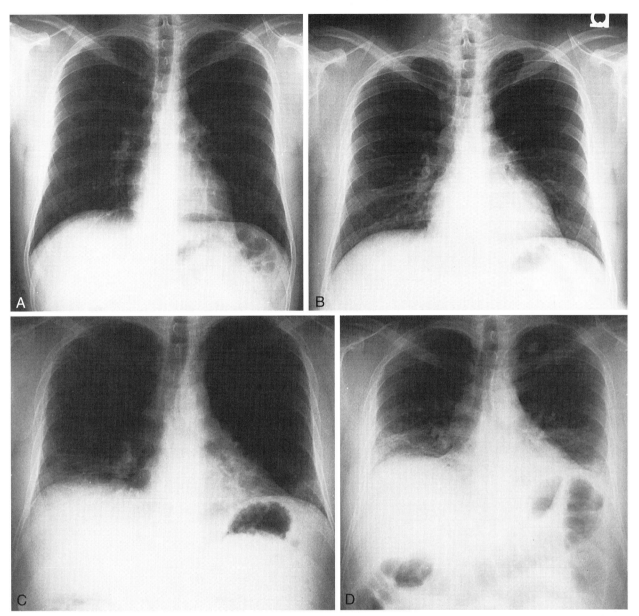

Figure 53.21 Serial chest radiographs from a patient with idiopathic pulmonary fibrosis. **A,** The posteroanterior radiograph of the chest was obtained at the time of onset of breathlessness with exercise and mild cough. The chest appears normal. **B,** The follow-up film reveals progressive loss of lung volume and bibasilar, predominantly reticular opacities. The patient had stopped regular exercise because of breathlessness with exertion. **C,** Progressive changes are evident, with severe loss of lung volume. Predominantly in the lower lung zone are seen diffuse, bilateral, coarse reticular opacities typical of the radiographic appearance of the middle to late stage of pulmonary fibrosis. **D,** Continued disease progression is evident, with honeycombing and pulmonary hypertension. Open-lung biopsy revealed usual interstitial pneumonia with extensive fibrosis and histologic honeycombing. Treatment with corticosteroids and cyclophosphamide (Cytoxan) was started, but the patient experienced a progressive decline in functional status and died 6 months after lung transplantation.

53.9). Chest roentgenographic evidence of reduced lung volumes is usually present unless there is associated obstructive airway disease.

Pleural involvement is uncommon in IPF; its presence should suggest another diagnosis, such as collagen vascular disease (especially rheumatoid arthritis or systemic lupus erythematosus), mitral valve disease, congestive heart failure, asbestosis, infection, drug-induced lung disease, or lymphangitic carcinomatosis (see Table 53.5).

Computed Tomography Scan. Increasingly, CT is being used to evaluate pulmonary parenchymal disease, especially IPF.[21,42] HRCT is useful in the differentiation of IPF from other interstitial lung diseases, the determination of the extent and severity of disease activity, and, most importantly, the detection of disease, especially in patients with normal or minimal change on plain chest roentgenograms.

HRCT findings in IPF include a marked peripheral and especially subpleural distribution of the interstitial densities. The involvement is patchy, with areas of reticulation intermingled with areas of normal tissue, and this type of involvement is often associated with cystic spaces 2 to 4 mm in diameter (see Fig. 53.12). Correlation of the HRCT findings with the histopathologic manifestations in IPF is incomplete. Early disease appears as patchy, predominantly peripheral, subpleural reticular opacities and minor degrees of honeycomb change. In more advanced disease, there is a more diffuse reticular pattern prominent in the lower lung zone associated with thickened interlobular septa and intralobular lines, often associated with honeycombing, traction bronchiectasis, and subpleural fibrosis.[17]

Identification of a relationship between pulmonary function testing and HRCT findings remains incomplete. FVC, DL_{CO}, arterial PO_2 measured at peak exercise, and oxygen desaturation during exercise are the physiologic parameters that best correlate with the global extent of disease in HRCT.[43-45] Serial HRCT scanning showed that the changes over time in the total extent of the disease were similar to those changes observed in DL_{CO} and FVC.[45]

HRCT has not replaced lung biopsy in the diagnosis and assessment of most interstitial lung diseases. Connective tissue diseases (particularly scleroderma and rheumatoid arthritis) and asbestosis may cause a similar HRCT appearance, except for the presence of parenchymal bands of fibrosis and pleural plaques in patients with asbestosis. Patients with subacute or chronic hypersensitivity pneumonitis can have similar reticular opacity or honeycombing, but often lack the bibasilar predominance seen in IPF.[46]

Studies evaluating the ability of HRCT scanning to diagnose IPF accurately have found that HRCT significantly increases the level of diagnostic confidence compared with the chest radiograph. In general, the sensitivity for a confident diagnosis is low (~48%) but the specificity is high (~95%).[47-50a] The accuracy of a confident diagnosis of IPF made on HRCT by a trained observer appears to be about 90%.[46,51-53] Less experienced observers are substantially less accurate than experienced observers.[51] A HRCT pattern highly confident of the diagnosis of IPF is associated with a very poor prognosis.[54]

Other Imaging Techniques

Gallium (^{67}Ga) Scanning. Lung scanning with radioactive gallium (^{67}Ga) is a noninvasive test for staging the "alveolitis" found in interstitial lung diseases, particularly sarcoidosis. Unfortunately, ^{67}Ga lung scanning is not recommended in the routine evaluation of IPF because it is difficult to interpret, it is not specific, and a negative scan does not exclude disease.

Ventilation-Perfusion Lung Scanning. Ventilation-perfusion lung scanning is not recommended as a routine part of the evaluation. In most parenchymal diseases, ventilation-perfusion scanning reveals an inhomogeneous reduction of blood flow, ventilation, or both. Two types of perfusion abnormalities occur in IPF: nonsegmental inhomogeneities, which are probably due to a localized loss of the capillary bed, most often in the lower lobes; and increased perfusion of the upper lung zones, resulting from pulmonary hypertension, which induces an upward shift in the gradient of capillary perfusion. Ventilation scans often reveal patchy, nonsegmental areas of decreased ventilation, reflecting regions of airway obstruction or alveolar destruction. Patchy areas of

high and low ventilation-perfusion matching usually occur, with a few areas of well-maintained ventilation-perfusion matching. These findings of mismatching of ventilation and blood flow help explain the hypoxemia and high V_D/V_T ratio found in many of these patients at rest.

Pulmonary Function Tests

The lung volumes (TLC, functional residual capacity, and residual volume) are reduced. Early on, the lung volumes may be normal, especially in patients with superimposed chronic obstructive pulmonary disease. Lung volumes are higher in smokers with IPF compared with those who have never smoked.[25]

Expiratory flow rates (FEV_1 and FVC) may be decreased because of the reduction in lung volume, but the FEV_1/FVC ratio is maintained. Because of the increased static elastic recoil found in these patients, flow rates (at any given lung volume) are often increased (see Figs. 53.16A and 53.18).

Patients with IPF are tachypneic, with rapid shallow breaths, probably because of increased work of breathing. This rapid respiratory rate presumably results from altered mechanical reflexes, caused by the increased elastic load, vagal mechanisms, or both, because no defined chemical basis for the hyperventilation has been identified (see Fig. 53.19).

The DL_{CO} is reduced, which may actually precede the loss of lung volume. The decrease in the DL_{CO} results from both a contraction of the pulmonary capillary volume and the presence of ventilation-perfusion abnormalities. The resting arterial blood gases are usually abnormal and reveal hypoxemia and respiratory alkalosis. The major cause of resting hypoxemia is ventilation-perfusion mismatching, and it is not due to either impaired oxygen diffusion, as was originally suspected, or to anatomic shunts. With exercise, the $(A - a)PO_2$ widens, and the arterial PO_2 and oxygen saturation fall. During maximal exercise, 20% to 30% of the exercise-induced widening of the $(A - a)PO_2$ may be caused by some impairment of oxygen diffusion. Importantly, the abnormalities identified at rest do not accurately predict the magnitude of the abnormalities that may be seen with exercise (see Fig. 53.20). Although these abnormalities can be assessed by oximetry, it has been demonstrated that oxygen saturation determined by this method may not yield as dramatic or significant a change as that obtained by measurement of arterial blood PO_2 and PCO_2. Exercise testing is more sensitive than assessments at rest in the detection of abnormalities in oxygen transfer. In addition, gas exchange during exercise has been demonstrated to be a sensitive parameter for following the clinical course.

During exercise, patients with IPF increase their minute ventilation primarily by increasing their respiratory frequency (see Fig. 53.19). This method of increase differs from that in normal subjects, in whom increased ventilation during mild exercise occurs by an increase in the V_T rather than respiratory rate. Thus, patients with IPF have elevated minute ventilation during exercise that is in part related to the increase in V_D ventilation. In addition, the V_D/V_T ratio is increased at rest and is maintained or decreases only slightly with exercise. Occasionally, the V_D/V_T ratio increases in interstitial lung disorders that have a prominent pulmonary vascular component, such as scleroderma or pulmonary histiocytosis X.

Pulmonary Hemodynamics

Pulmonary hypertension rarely occurs at rest but is common during exercise even in the early stages of IPF. When the vital capacity is less than 50% of predicted or the DL_{CO} is less than 45% of predicted, pulmonary hypertension at rest can be expected. In 70% of patients with advanced pulmonary fibrosis, auscultatory findings consistent with pulmonary hypertension are present. The mean pulmonary artery pressure at rest ranges between 23 to 28 mm Hg and rarely exceeds 40 mm Hg. A resting pulmonary artery pressure above 30 mm Hg is associated with a poor prognosis.

The cause of pulmonary hypertension in IPF is multifactorial, with compression and the destruction of pulmonary vessels by the interstitial infiltrative process and vasoconstriction of vessels mediated by hypoxia, acidosis, and autocoids being the most important. The pulmonary artery wedge pressure remains normal in IPF, and cor pulmonale is a late sequela. Oxygen therapy at rest and during exercise improves pulmonary hemodynamics and probably improves exercise capacity and prognosis. Few data exist on the value of vasodilator therapy in the treatment of pulmonary hypertension in the interstitial lung diseases.

Abnormalities During Sleep

Many patients with IPF, especially those with low daytime arterial oxygen saturation or a history of snoring during sleep, develop sleep disturbances that are characterized by reduced rapid-eye-movement sleep, lighter and more fragmented sleep, and hypoxemia during rapid-eye-movement sleep. Severe hypoxemia occurs in the absence of obstructive sleep apnea or changes in breathing pattern. Tachypnea persists during sleep. Identification and correction of the sleep disturbance may reduce morbidity and improve patient survival.

Histopathology

The gross appearance of the lungs in IPF reveals a distinctive nodular pleural surface, sometimes with a marked cirrhotic appearance. UIP is characterized by a heterogeneous, predominantly subpleural distribution of involvement, a pattern quite distinguishable even on low-power magnification (Fig. 53.22). There is temporal heterogeneity, with areas of end-stage fibrosis and honeycombing (thickened collagenous septa surrounding air spaces lined by bronchial epithelium) abutting areas of active proliferation of fibroblasts and myofibroblasts (Figs. 53.23 through 53.25). These discrete areas of acute fibroblastic proliferation have been termed *fibroblastic foci,* and are essential to the histopathologic diagnosis of UIP[55] (see Fig. 53.24). Katzenstein and Myers emphasized that the fibroblast focus is the earliest change in UIP.[55] There is generally minimal interstitial inflammation, and if present in significant amounts, the histopathologic diagnosis should be reconsidered. Because of this latter finding, we no longer adhere to the concept that "desquamative" interstitial pneumonia (DIP) or cellular interstitial pneumonitis (now called NSIP) is the precursor of UIP. We regard DIP and NSIP as separate and distinct entities.

Figure 53.22 Usual interstitial pneumonia pattern often shows a striking subpleural distribution. This low-power photomicrograph is from an area without the usual remodeling of the lung architecture with cystic (honeycomb) changes. (Courtesy of Thomas V. Colby, MD, Mayo Clinic, Scottsdale, AZ.) *See Color Plate*

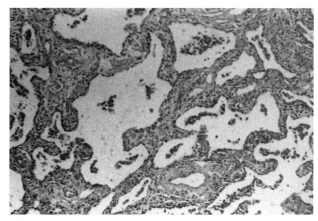

Figure 53.23 Photomicrograph of usual interstitial pneumonia showing residual lymphoplasmacytic inflammation and collagen deposition broadening alveolar walls. (Original magnification ×10.)

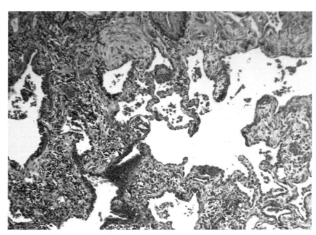

Figure 53.24 Usual interstitial pneumonia pattern. Two fibroblastic foci of loose organizing connective tissue are seen in the top center and top right of the photomicrograph adjacent to an area of dense fibrosis. (Courtesy of Thomas V. Colby, MD, Mayo Clinic, Scottsdale, AZ.) *See Color Plate*

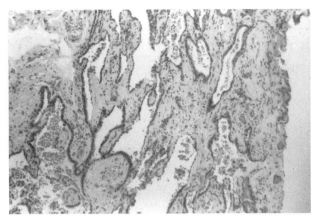

Figure 53.25 Photomicrograph of honeycomb lung in idiopathic pulmonary fibrosis. There is total disruption of the lung architecture by bands of fibrous tissue forming cystic spaces. The spaces are lined by metaplastic epithelium. (Original magnification ×10.)

Bronchogenic carcinoma (alveolar cell carcinoma, adenocarcinoma, and oat cell carcinoma) has been identified with increased frequency in advanced IPF. It is postulated that carcinoma arises from the metaplastic bronchiolar epithelium that develops in these patients. Interestingly, a number of the reported cases occurred in patients with familial IPF.

Pathogenesis

The inciting factors in the development of IPF are unknown. A widely held hypothesis is that this disorder occurs in susceptible individuals following some unknown stimulus. This inciting agent initiates a cascade of events that involves factors controlling inflammatory, immune, and fibrotic processes in the lung. Environmental, viral, immunologic, and genetic factors appear to play an important role.

Cigarette smoking is associated with the development of IPF.[56-58] More cases (72%) than controls (63%) have a history of ever smoking. The odds ratio for ever smoking was 1.6 (95% confidence interval, 1.1 to 2.4). The risk was significantly elevated for former smokers (1.9; 95% confidence interval, 1.3 to 2.9) and for smokers with 21 to 40 pack-years (2.3; 95% confidence interval, 1.3 to 3.8).[58] There was no clear exposure-response pattern with cumulative consumption of cigarettes. Infrequently, patients date the onset of their symptoms to a flulike illness. No convincing cultural, serologic, or morphologic evidence supports prior or persistent viral exposure.

An important advance in our understanding of interstitial lung disease has been the recognition that UIP appears to be a distinct pathophysiologic entity characterized by minimal inflammation and chronic fibroproliferation due to abnormal parenchymal wound healing.[59,60] This paradigm suggests that the pathologic process of UIP is the result of persistent remodeling of the lung interstitium. Multiple "microinjuries" damage and activate alveolar epithelial cells, which in turn induce an antifibrinolytic environment in the alveolar spaces, enhancing wound clot formation. Alveolar epithelial cells secrete growth factors and induce migration and proliferation of fibroblasts and differentiation into myofibroblasts. Subepithelial myofibroblasts and alveolar epithelial cells produce gelatinases that may increase basement membrane disruption and allow fibroblast-myofibroblast migration. Angiogenic factors induce neovascularization. Both intra-alveolar and interstitial myofibroblasts secrete extracellular matrix proteins, mainly collagens. An imbalance between interstitial collagenases and tissue inhibitors of metalloproteinases provokes the progressive deposition of extracellular matrix.[61] Signals responsible for myofibroblast apoptosis seem to be absent or delayed in UIP, increasing cell survival. Myofibroblasts produce angiotensinogen that, as angiotensin II, provokes alveolar epithelial cell death, further impairing re-epithelialization.[62] Although the molecular mechanisms that lead to end-stage pulmonary fibrosis in the idiopathic interstitial pneumonias are poorly understood, additional recent data suggest support for this "abnormal wound healing" hypothesis in UIP.[63-66]

The quantity and composition of pulmonary surfactant phospholipids recovered by BAL are abnormal in IPF.[67,68] McCormack and colleagues[67,68] have demonstrated that surfactant protein A is reduced in IPF and that decreases in its concentration referenced to total phospholipid (a marker of surfactant to normalize to the surface sampled by lavage and recovery) predict an adverse clinical outcome. In addition, is has been proposed that surfactant protein A and B genetic variants predispose to IPF[69] (see Familial Pulmonary Fibrosis later).

Diagnosis

The most definitive method of establishing a diagnosis is by surgical lung biopsy.[70,70a] Open or thoracoscopic lung biopsy is indicated because it provides an accurate diagnosis; it excludes neoplastic and infectious processes that occasionally mimic chronic, progressive interstitial disease; it occasionally identifies a more treatable process than originally suspected (e.g., chronic extrinsic allergic alveolitis); and it provides a better assessment of disease activity.[37,71]

Recent studies have addressed the accuracy of the combined clinical and radiographic diagnosis of IPF.[47,49] In both studies, clinicians were blinded to the results of the surgical lung biopsies, which were used as the "gold standard" for diagnosis. The clinical diagnosis of IPF had a sensitivity of 48% and a specificity of 89% compared to the histopathologic diagnosis, with a sensitivity of 62% and a specificity of 97%.[47,49] These studies argue that, when the clinical and radiographic diagnoses are consistent, IPF can be confidently diagnosed. However, they also demonstrate that this consistency is only present in about half of patients with biopsy-confirmed UIP. Furthermore, experts in the field performed these studies, and it is unclear how the outcome would vary with community physicians less familiar with these processes.

Staging of Disease Activity and Predicting Outcome

The long-term survival in IPF is distinctly poor, with only a 20% to 30% survival 5 years after the time of diagnosis. Attempts to predict who will respond to treatment have been largely disappointing. The results of several large studies have been reviewed by Mapel and colleagues.[72]

Clinical Features. Breathlessness and cough do not identify any particular histopathologic stage of disease. Cyanosis and clubbing are more common in fibrotic disease, but their presence does not exclude early inflammatory disease. Patients with a short duration of symptoms (<6 months) before therapy is started tend to achieve the greatest improvement. The type and amount of exertion required to precipitate shortness of breath have been shown to correlate with the roentgenographic profusion of diffuse reticular opacities as well as the reduction in vital capacity. Younger patients tend to have less fibrosis than do older patients, and younger patients and women survive longer than older patients and men. Current smoking (i.e., at the time of presentation) was associated with improved survival in patients with IPF,[29] whereas heavy smoking (i.e., higher number of pack-years) was associated with a worse prognosis.[29,73–75]

Serum Studies. The presence of immunologic markers, including autoantibodies, elevated sedimentation rates, circulating immune complexes, and increased serum immunoglobulins, has not been shown to influence the overall natural history of IPF.

Chest Roentgenography and High-Resolution Computed Tomography Scanning. A general pattern of evolution is seen in serial chest roentgenograms. The early changes include hazy opacities with reduction in lung volumes that progress to a reticular pattern and finally end in coarser, cystic areas of honeycombed lung. A correlation was found between chest roentgenographic profusion score and the degree of dyspnea at presentation. Patients who have fewer roentgenographic abnormalities at presentation survive longer. Unfortunately, the chest roentgenogram is not a useful monitor of the degree of inflammation present. In fact, the only roentgenographic abnormality that correlates with the histologic pattern is honeycombing. Furthermore, the roentgenogram may demonstrate no changes even while clinically apparent physiologic deterioration is occurring. Another major problem with using the chest roentgenogram to follow the disease course or to estimate the stage of disease is that there is considerable interobserver variability in the interpretation.

HRCT scanning in IPF may be useful in staging disease activity. The finding of a higher extent of ground-glass opacities and a lower extent of reticular opacities on the initial HRCT identifies those patients with IPF who are the most likely to respond to corticosteroids.[76] Unfortunately, it does not appear that the extent of honeycombing on HRCT is very useful in predicting a favorable outcome in IPF/UIP.[54]

Pulmonary Physiologic Tests. Physiologic tests are also neither sensitive nor specific for the presence of inflammation in the lung parenchyma. In fact, in patients with early disease, the routine pulmonary function tests may be normal. Reductions in the vital capacity do correlate with the degree of fibrosis present and show a relationship with the overall histologic derangements. A marked reduction in the vital capacity (<50% of predicted) is associated with pulmonary hypertension and a reduced 2-year survival. Reduction of the TLC correlates with neither the histopathologic findings nor prognosis and survival. The compliance, maximum transpulmonary pressure, and coefficient of elastic retraction of the lung correlate well with the degree of fibrosis but do not exclude the presence of cellularity.

The DL_{CO} has no correlation with the histologic stage of the disease. Patients with normal DL_{CO} values usually do not have significant gas-exchange abnormalities, whereas patients with values below 70% of predicted frequently have such changes at rest or with exercise. Survival is longer in patients with a more normal DL_{CO} (>45% of predicted value). A marked reduction of the DL_{CO} and resting hypoxemia are associated with pulmonary hypertension and decreased survival. Patients with a predominantly fibrotic process have greater abnormalities of the $(A - a)PO_2$ when compared with those with more cellular changes. Alterations in gas exchange during exercise when compared with other indices of lung function correlate best with histopathologic findings. Serial measurements of gas exchange during exercise appear to be the best predictors of responsiveness to treatment. In summary, pulmonary function testing does not correlate with histopathology, especially the degree of alveolitis present, but is nevertheless useful in establishing the presence of impairment in IPF and following its course and response to therapy. However, the severity of the initial abnormalities in FEV_1, FVC, TLC, volume of thoracic gas, residual volume, DL_{CO}, arterial PO_2, and $(A - a)PO_2$, as well as oxygen desaturation below 88% on a 6-minute walk test,[77] correlate with poorer survival.

Bronchoalveolar Lavage. It has been suggested that the BAL cellular constituents reflect the state of the pulmonary inflammatory response. Active IPF is characterized by a severalfold increase in the total number of inflammatory cells recovered from the respiratory tract. Unfortunately, many studies have failed to demonstrate a clear distinction between diseases based on the predominant cell type present in the lavage specimens. Moreover, there is no correlation between the percentage of various cell types found in the lavage fluid in patients with IPF and various clinical parameters, serum tests, or pulmonary function studies.[78,79] BAL neutrophilia and eosinophilia tend to occur in patients with more advanced fibrotic disease.

The role and value of serial BAL in assessment of the clinical progress of patients with IPF has not been adequately examined. Turner-Warwick and Haslam[80] found that, in patients with definite and sustained clinical improvement, serial lavage cell counts tended to return toward the normal. Interestingly, declines in neutrophil levels in lavage fluid tended to occur in patients who responded to prednisolone, whereas cyclophosphamide response led to a fall in eosinophil counts. Patients who failed to improve had elevated neutrophil and eosinophil counts throughout their course. On the other hand, several of the patients who did not respond appeared to have clinically stable disease and demonstrated persisting neutrophilia, which did not necessarily portend a poor prognosis.

In IPF, changes in the phosphatidylglycerol-to-phosphatidylinositol ratio are predictive of the cellularity and degree of fibrosis on histopathologic examination of open-lung biopsy specimens. In addition, patients with less depression of total phospholipids in lavage fluids improve with corticosteroid therapy, whereas those with more severe decreases in total phospholipids do not. Surfactant protein A is reduced in IPF, and decreases in its concentration referenced to total phospholipid (a marker of surfactant to normalize to the surface sampled by lavage and recovery) predict an adverse clinical outcome and poorer survival.[67,68]

Histopathology. Studies examining the relationship between outcome and histopathology have suggested that prognosis and response to therapy in IPF are determined by the extent of inflammation ("cellularity") and interstitial fibrosis on biopsy. However, this hypothesis has been challenged.[59,60,64] Until recently, no specific histologic feature, other than end-stage fibrosis and honeycombing, has been shown to correlate with treatment response or prognosis in UIP.[59,81] It has been proposed that the earliest and most characteristic manifestation of ongoing lung injury in UIP is the development of multiple fibroblastic foci.[55] We showed, in survival analyses adjusted for age, sex, and smoking history, that only the extent and severity of the fibroblastic foci were significant predictors of survival in patients with IPF.[81] A one-unit increase in the granulation/connective tissue factor was associated with a 1.74-fold greater risk of death. Other investigators have reported data supporting these findings.[82,83] Flaherty and colleagues, using a different histologic scoring system, found no relationship between fibroblastic foci and survival.[84]

Prediction Models. Investigators have attempted to identify parameters that best predict the clinical course and prognosis of IPF.[77,85-88] We showed that changes in dyspnea score, TLC, FVC, arterial Po_2, oxygen saturation, or $(A - a)Po_2$ over 6 and 12 months may be useful as surrogate end points in monitoring therapeutic efficacy in individual patients.[86]

Predictor models based on combining multiple baseline clinical, radiologic, or physiologic measurements have been derived from large groups of carefully selected patients with IPF/UIP and appear to perform well as predictors of outcome.[29,87] Our group described a modified Clinical-Radiographic-Physiologic (CRP) scoring system to predict survival in IPF.[29] Using hierarchical multivariable analysis of clinical, radiologic, and extensive physiologic variables, we developed a model that allows clinicians to make more precise prognostic estimations about patients with IPF. The model included the following parameters: age; smoking history; clubbing; extent of profusion of interstitial opacities, and presence or absence of pulmonary hypertension on the chest radiograph; percent predicted TLC; and arterial Po_2 at the end of maximal exercise. Although this baseline modified CRP score is an accurate predictor of survival in IPF, it requires both detailed radiographic analysis and exercise physiologic measurements, which are not readily available to many physicians. This may limit its utility as a predictor of survival for those in general practice.

Wells and coworkers identified a composite physiologic index (CPI) closely reflecting the morphologic extent of pulmonary fibrosis while accounting for the extent of emphysema (a finding commonly present in smokers with IPF).[87] The formula for the CPI was as follows: extent of disease on $CT = 91.0 - (0.65 \times$ percent predicted $DL_{CO}) - (0.53 \times$ percent predicted FVC$) + (0.34 \times$ percent predicted $FEV_1).$[87] The CPI correlated strongly with disease extent on CT and mortality and was more accurate than any individual pulmonary function test.[87] However, its value in clinical practice appears limited.

Clinical Course and Outcome

Once the diagnosis and the clinical severity are established, most patients require therapy because this is a potentially fatal disorder without spontaneous remission. The natural history of IPF has not been appropriately defined. Data obtained from several reports indicate that the median survival after diagnosis, with or without treatment, is 2 to 3 years. Thus, early diagnosis and treatment is important to prevent the development of irreversible fibrosis. The therapy of IPF, regardless of the agent used, requires 3 to 6 months before its effectiveness can be assessed. Few adequate randomized, controlled clinical treatment trials of sufficient numbers of patients with IPF have been performed. Consequently, conclusions drawn from the available data need to be confirmed.

Corticosteroids. Corticosteroids are the mainstay for the treatment of IPF.[72] However, the response to corticosteroid treatment in IPF is almost uniformly poor.[89,90] Most of the available data suggest that, although short-term improvement might be achieved in a minority of patients with IPF, the long-term response is poor (8% to 17%).[91-96]

Significant complications can result from corticosteroid therapy. Therefore, patients should be carefully monitored during the treatment trial. Furthermore, corticosteroid withdrawal may result in serious symptoms and morbidity, including fatigue, weakness, arthralgias, anorexia, nausea, desquamation of the skin, orthostatic dizziness and hypotension, fainting, and hypoglycemia. Careful evaluation of patients during both corticosteroid therapy and withdrawal is important. There is probably no indication for the use of corticosteroids alone in the treatment of IPF.[89,90]

Immunomodulatory and Antifibrotic Agents. Because of the often poor responsiveness of IPF to corticosteroids, immunomodulatory agents (azathioprine or cyclophosphamide alone or in combination with corticosteroids) have been tried with mixed results.[97-99]

Azathioprine. Azathioprine is a purine analogue that is slowly converted to mercaptopurine in body tissues, and it appears to act by the substitution of purines in deoxyribonucleic acid synthesis and by inhibiting adenine deaminase, which affects lymphocytes by making them ineffective, because they are so highly susceptible to adenine deaminase deficiency. In addition to cytotoxic effects, azathioprine has been reported to suppress natural killer cell activity, antibody production, and antibody-dependent cellular cytotoxicity. Azathioprine also suppresses the production of autoantibodies in animal models of autoimmune disease, although the clinical relevance of these findings remains unknown. Recent studies showed encouraging results with azathioprine and low-dose prednisone in the treatment of patients with IPF.[97]

The recommended dose for azathioprine in IPF is approximately 2 mg/kg, although the optimal dose for treating the disorder is as yet undetermined. Generally, the dose is 75 to 100 mg/day and does not exceed 150 mg/day. A trial of at least 3 to 6 months' duration is recommended to ensure an adequate opportunity for clinical response.

Significant adverse drug reactions resulting in discontinuance of azathioprine are reported in 20% to 30% of patients with rheumatoid arthritis. Fewer data are available regarding the tolerance of azathioprine in patients with IPF. Hematologic adverse effects include leukopenia, anemia, thrombocytopenia, pure red cell aplasia, and pancytopenia. Gastrointestinal complaints are the most frequent side effects, including nausea and vomiting and, less commonly, peptic ulcer disease and diarrhea. Mild elevation of hepatic enzymes has been described in approximately 5% of patients treated with azathioprine, but reports of severe hepatitis, progressive hepatic cirrhosis, and cholestasis are rare. Pulmonary complications of interstitial pneumonitis and diffuse alveolar damage have been reported in some renal transplant recipients. The carcinogenic potential of azathioprine remains to be fully defined.

Cyclophosphamide. Cyclophosphamide is a second-line drug in patients who either failed or could not tolerate corticosteroid treatment. Cyclophosphamide is an alkylating agent of the nitrogen mustard group that is absorbed orally and activated in the liver to several cytotoxic compounds. Its mode of action is the depletion of lymphocytes, thereby suppressing lymphocyte function. The recommended dose is 2 mg/kg/day given orally as a single dose, usually with oral prednisone at 0.25 mg/kg/day. We do not exceed 150 mg/day, and most patients tolerate a dose in the 100-

to 150-mg/day range. Few data are available on the length of therapy, but we believe it should be given for not less than 3 months and probably for as long as 9 to 12 months in patients experiencing stabilization or clinical improvement as documented by follow-up studies.

One side effect of cyclophosphamide therapy is leukopenia. However, careful monitoring of the blood counts allows one to adjust the dosage to an acceptable level. We generally aim to maintain a total white cell count of greater than 3000/μL or a neutrophil count greater than 1500/μL. Other possible complications include thrombocytopenia, hematuria secondary to hemorrhagic cystitis (forced fluids and frequent bladder emptying are recommended to prevent this problem), gastrointestinal symptoms (including anorexia, nausea, and vomiting), bone marrow suppression, azoospermia and amenorrhea, infection, and the development of a hematologic malignant disease.

Alternative Treatments. Recently, newer immunomodulatory or antifibrotic agents have been tried alone or in combination with corticosteroids in patients with UIP (Table 53.9).

Table 53.9 Potential New Treatments in Idiopathic Pulmonary Fibrosis (IPF)

Agent/Approach	Mechanism of Action	Comments
Molecules/Drugs Inhibiting Fibroblast Proliferation or Inducing Fibroblast Apoptosis		
Interferon gamma	Regulates macrophage functions. Inhibits fibrogenesis.	Combination of interferon gamma-1b and an oral glucocorticoid leads to improvement or stabilization of the disease in patients with idiopathic pulmonary fibrosis.[105] Shows promise for improving survival in patients with milder stages of IPF.[106] Patients with more severe disease do not appear to benefit from treatment with interferon gamma-1b.[107,108]
Pirfenidone [5-methyl-1-phenyl-2-(1H)-pyridinone]	In vitro, inhibits transforming growth factor-β–stimulated collagen synthesis, decreases the extracellular matrix, and blocks the mitogenic effect of profibrotic cytokines in adult human lung fibroblasts derived from patients with idiopathic pulmonary fibrosis. In vivo, inhibits transforming growth factor-β and platelet-derived growth factor (PDGF) gene expression. Ameliorates pulmonary fibrosis in animal models of bleomycin-induced lung injury.	Well-tolerated, slowed progression of disease, and allowed tapering of glucocorticoid and immunosuppressive therapy.[109,201] A multicenter, randomized, double-blind, placebo-controlled study was effective in stabilizing the lung function and reducing the number of patients who experienced acute exacerbation of their disease.[110]
Molecules/Drugs Inhibiting Epithelial Injury or Enhancing Repair		
N-Acetylcysteine	Prevent epithelial cell injury mediated by oxygen radicals.	Clinical studies have not shown it to be more effective than glucocorticoids.[202] Ongoing clinical trial in Europe, results pending.
Imatinib mesylate	Inhibitor of several protein-tyrosine kinases that are believed to play a role in the proliferation of tumor cells and mesenchymal cells, such as lung fibroblasts. Animal models of lung fibrosis, and histology of fibrotic human lung sections, demonstrate that PDGF is up-regulated during lung fibrogenesis. Overexpression of PDGF within the lungs of animals results in fibroproliferative pathology, and blocking PDGF signal transduction reduces lung fibrosis.	A Phase II trial is underway in the United States.
Bosentan	Endothelin A/B receptor antagonist. Improves exercise capacity, symptoms, and functional status in patients with pulmonary arterial hypertension.	Multicenter, double-blind, randomized, placebo-controlled, phase III study underway in United States, Canada, and Europe

Adapted from Selman M, King TE Jr, Pardo A: Idiopathic pulmonary fibrosis: Prevailing and evolving hypotheses about its pathogenesis and implications for therapy. Ann Intern Med 134:136–151, 2001.

Colchicine. In vitro studies suggest several mechanisms by which colchicine may interrupt the processes of collagen synthesis and deposition, and it may have anti-inflammatory effects as well. Colchicine decreases alveolar macrophage release of fibronectin and alveolar macrophage-derived growth factor, two mediators that have been implicated in alveolar inflammation. On the basis of these mechanisms of action, colchicine may have a potential therapeutic role in IPF. There are no data affirming the efficacy of colchicine as therapy for IPF.[92,100–104]

Interferon Gamma. Recent studies with interferon gamma-1b have shown promise for improving lung function and survival in patients with milder stages of IPF (FVC ≥62% of predicted or DL$_{CO}$ ≥35% of predicted, or both).[105,106,106a] In a recent, randomized trial, there was a 41% relative reduction in the risk of death in the overall treatment population, accompanied by significantly improved survival in two subgroups (i.e., treatment-adherent patients and patients with less impaired lung function).[106] These findings warrant further investigation. Patients with more severe disease do not appear to benefit from treatment with interferon gamma-1b.[107,108]

Pirfenidone. Raghu and colleagues[109] reported the results of a Phase II, open-label study evaluating pirfenidone. They found that pirfenidone was well tolerated with minimal side effects. Additionally, treatment with pirfenidone appeared to allow discontinuation or tapering of prednisone and immunosuppressive therapy without loss of lung function. A multicenter, randomized, double-blind placebo-controlled study of pirfenidone versus placebo was carried out in Japanese patients with IPF.[110] Pirfenidone was effective in stabilizing the lung function and reducing the number of patients who experienced acute exacerbation of their disease. It has been suggested that pirfenidone may slow the progression of lung impairment in patients with pulmonary fibrosis and Hermansky-Pudlak syndrome.[111]

Other Agents. A number of other immunosuppressive agents have been reported in individual cases or in small groups of patients with IPF.

Penicillamine inhibits collagen synthesis by interfering with collagen cross-linking and is a suppressor of T-cell function. Limited studies have not shown efficacy in idiopathic pulmonary fibrosis.[103,112,113]

Interferon beta-1a has been shown to reduce fibroblast migration/proliferation and inhibits collagen production by fibroblasts. Unpublished randomized clinical trials in the United States and Canada failed to show any benefit.[114,115]

Keratinocyte growth factor has been shown to induce type II pneumocytes proliferation. Administration of keratinocyte growth factor *after* the fibrotic insult has been unsuccessful in acute lung injury.[116,117]

Captopril inhibits the angiotensin-converting enzyme and completely abrogates Fas-induced apoptosis in human alveolar epithelial cells. It also has been shown to inhibit fibroblast proliferation in vitro, and reduce the fibrotic lung response in vivo. There is an ongoing trial at the National Institute of Respiratory Diseases in Mexico.[118]

Chlorambucil and *vincristine* sulfate, given alone or with corticosteroids, showed no beneficial effect.[119]

Lung Transplantation. Lung transplantation (see Chapter 89) has recently been offered to patients with IPF and holds therapeutic promise in young persons without other significant illnesses and with progressive severe disease unresponsive to other forms of treatment (Table 53.10). The American Thoracic Society has published guidelines for the selection of IPF patients who should be considered potential transplant candidates[120]:

1. Transplantation should be considered for patients who have symptomatic (including rest or exercise oxygen desaturation), progressive disease with failure to improve or maintain lung function while being treated with steroids or other immunosuppressive drug therapy.

2. If (when) pulmonary function is (becomes) abnormal, even though the patient may be minimally symptomatic, serious consideration should be given to referral to a transplant center for initial evaluation.

3. Patients are often symptomatic and have advanced disease when the vital capacity falls below 60% to 70% of predicted or the diffusing capacity (corrected for alveolar volume) falls below 50% to 60% predicted, or both.

Other Problems in Management. Clinical deterioration in patients with IPF is expected. Most patients experience

---

Table 53.10 Guidelines for Selection of Patients with Idiopathic Pulmonary Fibrosis for Lung Transplantation

General Guidelines
Severe, end-stage lung disease
  How disabled is the patient?
  Does the patient recognize the severity of the illness and the poor prognosis?
  What does the patient (and family) want?
Medical therapy ineffective
Substantial limitation in activities of daily living
Limited life expectancy (<18 months)

Relative Contraindications to Transplantation
Presence of systemic disease that may complicate postoperative management
Presence of significant psychosocial dysfunction
Presence of previous major cardiothoracic surgery
Presence of high-dose corticosteroid therapy (prednisone dose >15 mg/day)

Objective Parameters That Correlate with End-Stage Disease
Severe dyspnea
New York Heart Association functional class III or IV
  Class III: Marked limitation of physical activity, with ordinary activity resulting in fatigue, palpitation, dyspnea, or anginal pain
  Class IV: Inability to carry on any physical activity without discomfort, often with discomfort even at rest
Honeycombing or pulmonary hypertension on chest radiograph or CT scan
Severe physiologic derangement
  Total lung capacity <60%
  (A − a)PO$_2$ at rest >30
  Severe exercise desaturation or widening of the (A − a)PO$_2$ difference
  Clinical-Radiographic-Physiologic score >70

(A − a)PO$_2$, alveolar-arterial PO$_2$ difference; CT, computed tomography.
Adapted from King TE Jr: Idiopathic interstitial pneumonias. *In* Schwarz MI, King TE Jr (eds): Interstitial Lung Diseases (4th ed). Hamilton, Ontario, Canada: BC Decker, 2003, p 720.

Table 53.11 Complications of Disease or Therapy

Progressive Respiratory Failure
Mortality: 39%
Findings suggestive of disease progression are multiple and nonspecific

Bronchogenic Carcinoma
Mortality: 10%
Excess risk of 14:1 compared with general population; same histologic distribution as seen in population

Cardiovascular Disease
Mortality: 24%
Right ventricular hypertrophy, cor pulmonale due to progressive, long-standing pulmonary hypertension and right-sided heart failure
Left ventricular heart failure usually due to concurrent ischemic heart disease

Pulmonary Infection
Mortality: 2–4%
Increased incidence; glucocorticoid and cytotoxic therapy may further increase risk

Pneumothorax
Occurs less often than in other interstitial lung diseases
May be difficult to manage

Pulmonary Embolism
Mortality: 3–7%
Pulmonary angiography frequently required to make diagnosis

Adapted from Panos RJ, Mortenson RL, Niccoli SA, et al: Clinical deterioration in patients with idiopathic pulmonary fibrosis: Causes and assessment. Am J Med 88:396–404, 1990.

episodes of worsening shortness of breath, decreased exercise tolerance, or other decline in functional status during the course of their illness. Disease progression may be difficult to distinguish from disease-associated complications and adverse effects of therapy[121] (Table 53.11).

Acute Exacerbations of IPF. It is increasingly apparent that "acute exacerbations" or an "accelerated phase of rapid clinical decline" characterizes the clinical course of IPF. These episodes are defined as acute worsening (occurring over <4 weeks) involving (1) more dyspnea with the same level of exertion (sometimes associated with systemic symptoms such as fever, fatigue, and weight loss); (2) progressive hypoxemia; (3) new opacities on chest imaging studies; and (4) exclusion of infection or heart failure.[122–124] In fact, rapid progression and hospitalization because of respiratory decompensation were both independent predictors of mortality in the subsequent 3 months.[125] These episodes often represent the superimposition of another process, such as AIP, diffuse alveolar damage, diffuse alveolar hemorrhage, or organizing pneumonia. Better understanding and management of these episodes appear critical to reducing the death rate in IPF.

End-stage IPF frequently leads to incapacitating respiratory insufficiency with patients being unable to carry out activities of daily living without extreme distress. Death usually ensues because of intractable hypoxemia and respiratory failure.

FAMILIAL PULMONARY FIBROSIS

The clinical, roentgenographic, physiologic, and morphologic manifestations of familial IPF are indistinguishable from the nonfamilial form of the disease.[126] Patients usually present between the ages of 20 and 40. The younger the age at the time of presentation, the more aggressive is the disease. There may be a slight male predominance, and women tend to have a more favorable prognosis.[9,11,127] Over 68 kindreds presumed to have IPF have been reported.[11] It is estimated that familial cases account for 0.5% to 2.2% of all patients with idiopathic interstitial pneumonias, with a prevalence of 1.34 cases per 10^6 population in the United Kingdom.[9] In Finland, it was estimated that the prevalence for familial IPF was 5.9 per million population.[128] The familial form explained 3.3% to 3.7% of all Finnish cases of IPF diagnosed according to the revised American Thoracic Society/European Respiratory Society international guidelines. Geographical clustering has been noted, suggesting a recent founder effect in patients with familial IPF.[9,128]

Bitterman and coworkers reported the presence of alveolar inflammation in clinically unaffected family members of patients with familial IPF.[129] These family members had increased numbers of neutrophils and activated macrophages that released one or more neutrophil chemoattractants and growth factors for lung fibroblasts and positive ^{67}Ga lung scans. The significance of these findings is unknown, but the authors speculated that these unaffected family members might be at risk for the development of this condition.

Familial pulmonary fibrosis has been associated with multiple pathologic subsets of the idiopathic interstitial pneumonias: DIP,[130] LIP,[131] and UIP.[11] Thomas and colleagues showed that mutations in the surfactant protein C (SP-C) gene (*SFTPC*) are associated with familial DIP and NSIP and may cause type II cellular injury.[11] The mutation was not seen in control chromosomes and thus is not likely to be a polymorphism.[11] The authors hypothesized that the presence of two different pathologic diagnoses in affected relatives sharing this mutation indicates that, in this kindred, these diseases may represent pleiotropic manifestations of the same central pathogenesis.[11]

Multiple heterozygous mutations in *SFTPC* have been reported in association with children suffering from interstitial lung disease (DIP or NSIP), including familial and sporadic occurrences.[132,133] In addition, a deficiency of SP-C has been described in a small kindred suffering from a poorly defined form of interstitial pneumonitis, despite no sequence variation in *SFTPC*.[134] Taken together, these findings support a model in which misfolded pro–SP-C or SP-C can cause type II alveolar cell injury that results in interstitial lung disease.[135]

An autosomal dominant pattern of inheritance with reduced penetrance has been suggested for many examples of familial pulmonary fibrosis.[126] Linkage studies have suggested a link between the risk for familial pulmonary fibrosis and immunoglobulin γ (Gm) allotypes.[136] The finding of a significant increase in non-MM protease inhibitor phenotypes, particularly MZ, in patients with idiopathic interstitial pneumonias is additional evidence for a role for chromosome 14 in the increased susceptibility of persons to the development of pulmonary fibrosis.[137,138] There is evidence of a genetic influence in sporadic cases, including conflicting evidence of an increased presence of human leukocyte antigens HLA-B8, HLA-B12, HLA-B15, HLA-Dw6, and HLA-DR2 and a decreased incidence of HLA-Dw3 among patients with pulmonary fibrosis.[137,139–141] The strongest correlation described is that between HLA-DR3/DRw52a and the susceptibility of patients with systemic sclerosis to develop lung fibrosis.[142] Despite these findings, it remains to be determined if a definite association between a HLA locus and idiopathic interstitial pneumonias exists.

NONSPECIFIC INTERSTITIAL PNEUMONIA

NSIP originated as a histopathologic categorization reserved for surgical lung biopsies that did not demonstrate a clearly identifiable pattern.[95] The current definition of NSIP as a clinical form of idiopathic interstitial pneumonia is uncertain, as to date no distinctive clinical, radiographic, or histopathologic findings have been identified.[38] Therefore, until further definition is available, the diagnosis of NSIP should remain provisional.[38]

Clinical Features

The presentation is quite similar to other forms of idiopathic pneumonias (see Tables 53.7 and 53.8). Most patients have been middle-aged adults with a subacute onset of symptoms approximately 8 months prior to diagnosis.[95,143–146] Two thirds of the patients are women. Unlike patients with IPF, 70% are never smokers. Cough and dyspnea are present for months to years. Serologic abnormalities (antinuclear antibodies and rheumatoid factor) are common. BAL findings do not discriminate between UIP and NSIP and have no prognostic value, once the distinction between the two has been made histologically.[147]

Chest Imaging Studies

Chest Roentgenography. Chest radiographic findings show primarily lower zone reticular or hazy opacities.[95,143–145] Bilateral patchy opacities can also be seen.

Computed Tomography Scan. HRCT shows bilateral symmetrical ground-glass opacities or bilateral air space consolidation[144] (Fig. 53.26).

Pulmonary Function Tests

Pulmonary function testing shows a restrictive pattern with gas-exchange abnormalities commonly found.

Pathologic Features

The main histologic feature of NSIP is the homogeneous appearance of either inflammation or fibrosis as opposed to the heterogeneity seen in the other interstitial pneumonias. It is characterized by varying degrees of inflammation and fibrosis, with some cases having a primarily chronic inflammatory/cellular pattern ("cellular NSIP") and most cases revealing a mixed cellular-fibrotic pattern ("fibrotic NSIP")[95] (Figs. 53.27 and 53.28). Although NSIP may have significant fibrosis, it usually appears temporally uniform, and fibroblastic foci and honeycombing, if present, are rare. The temporal uniformity is distinctly different from that seen in

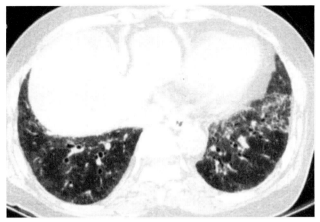

Figure 53.26 High-resolution chest computed tomographic image from a patient with nonspecific interstitial pneumonia showing bilateral, patchy, ground-glass opacities without evidence of subpleural honeycombing.

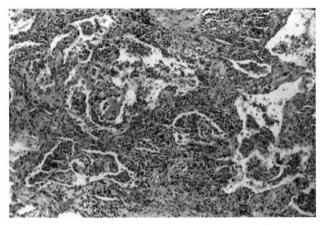

Figure 53.27 Photomicrograph of nonspecific interstitial pneumonia. Note the lymphoplasmacytic cells expanding the interstitial compartment. Alveolar macrophages are present also. (Original magnification ×10.)

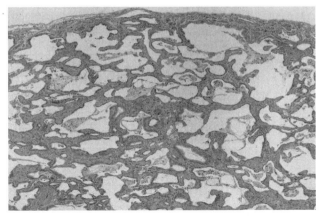

Figure 53.28 Photomicrograph of nonspecific interstitial pneumonia with a mixed cellular-fibrotic pattern. The alveolar walls are thickened by dense collagen and a few lymphocytes and plasma cells. The fibroblastic foci that are commonly found in the usual interstitial pneumonia pattern are not present in this lesion. *See Color Plate*

UIP. Fibrotic NSIP can be difficult to reliably distinguish from UIP, and there is significant interobserver variability even among expert histopathologists.[94]

Differential Diagnosis

Clinically, the most common diagnosis confused with NSIP is IPF.[95,143,144] Patients who are known to be immunocompromised are not included in this group of patients. It is extremely important that the pathologist not use "UIP" or "NSIP" to refer to any nonclassifiable interstitial pneumonia. In our experience, some of these cases represent a sampling error because of an inadequate lung biopsy. Others have an ill-defined or inadequately evaluated connective tissue disease, drug-induced interstitial lung disease, chronic hypersensitivity pneumonitis, recent acute lung injury (pneumonia or acute respiratory distress syndrome), or organizing pneumonia.[38,55,148–152] The diagnosis of NSIP pattern on surgical lung biopsy should prompt the clinician to revisit the clinical data carefully looking for these conditions.

Clinical Course and Outcome

The majority of patients with NSIP have a good prognosis, with most showing improvement after treatment with corticosteroids. Corticosteroids combined with azathioprine may be more effective than corticosteroids alone. The prognosis appears to depend on the extent of fibrosis.[55]

RESPIRATORY BRONCHIOLITIS—ASSOCIATED INTERSTITIAL LUNG DISEASE/DESQUAMATIVE INTERSTITIAL PNEUMONIA

Respiratory bronchiolitis—associated interstitial lung disease (RB-ILD) and DIP are considered together because we believe they represent different stages of the same process (see Tables 53.7 and 53.8).[152a] Also, the term *respiratory bronchiolitis—associated interstitial lung disease* is more anatomically accurate, and it conveys important pathogenetic implications compared to the older term *desquamative interstitial pneumonia*. RB-ILD is a distinct clinical syndrome found in current heavy cigarette smokers. Importantly, respiratory bronchiolitis is an accurate histologic marker of cigarette smoking, and it may be found many years after smoking ceases.[153] Also, RB/DIP-like histologic changes are exceedingly common in pulmonary Langerhans cell histiocytosis, may be sufficiently severe to cause the appearance of ground-glass attenuation on HRCT, and correlate with the cumulative exposure to cigarettes smoked.[154]

Previously, many investigators considered DIP or RB-ILD to represent an early stage of IPF. However, it is now widely viewed as a distinct clinical and pathologic entity. RB-ILD is uncommon, accounting for less than 10% of the cases of diffuse parenchymal lung disease seen by our group over the last 15 years. Because of the marked differences in clinical course and prognosis, it must be separated from other idiopathic interstitial pneumonias.

Clinical Features

RB-ILD afflicts primarily cigarette smokers in their fourth or fifth decades of life. There is a male preponderance, with men affected nearly twice as often as women. Patients with the disease commonly present with cough and dyspnea. Coarse, bibasilar end-inspiratory crepitations are frequent findings on physical examination. Finger clubbing rarely occurs in RB-ILD.[55]

Chest Imaging Studies

Chest Roentgenography. The chest roentgenogram shows less severe changes compared to IPF and may be normal in up to 20% of cases. A pattern of fine granular opacities, suggesting an acinar filling process, may be the early finding. Air bronchograms can be found when this process surrounds the airways. Most often the chest radiograph reveals diffuse, fine reticular interstitial opacities, usually with normal-appearing lung volumes. Bronchial wall thickening, prominence of peribronchovascular interstitium, small regular and irregular opacities, and small peripheral ring shadows are distinctive features of respiratory bronchiolitis. As the disease progresses, linear densities and reticulation occur. The honeycombed pattern is rare.

Computed Tomography Scan. The CT features of DIP are quite different from those of IPF, showing diffuse bronchial wall thickening, centrilobular nodules, ground-glass opacity, upper lung–predominant emphysema, and lower lung–predominant air trapping.[155] The ground-glass opacities may be diffuse or patchy, often with a peripheral predominance in the lung (Fig. 53.29).[156] Similar ground-glass opacification, without basal or peripheral predominance,

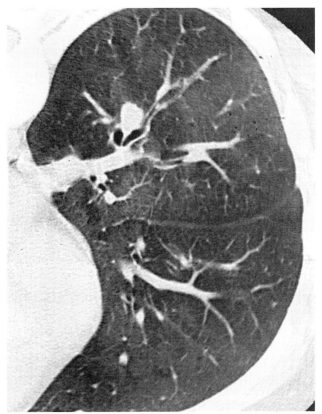

Figure 53.29 High-resolution computed tomographic image from a patient with desquamative interstitial pneumonia showing diffuse ground-glass opacities (gray-appearing areas).

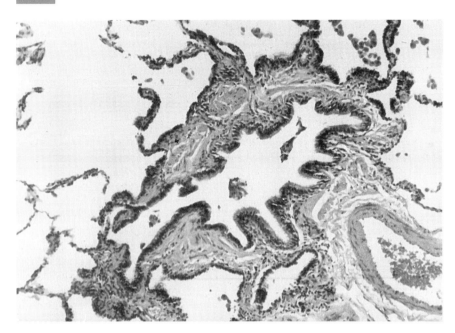

Figure 53.30 Photomicrograph of respiratory bronchiolitis showing an ectatic small airway, with thickened walls and evidence of extension of the bronchiolar metaplastic epithelium into the immediately surrounding alveoli. Intraluminal macrophages are also present within the peribronchiolar alveolar spaces.

may be found in patients with RB-ILD[157] or hypersensitivity pneumonitis.[46,158] Even on HRCT the honeycombed pattern is rarely found.[159,160]

Pulmonary Function Tests

Pulmonary function testing may be normal but usually shows mild to moderate restriction, normal or slightly reduced diffusing capacity, and mild hypoxemia. A mixed obstructive-restrictive pattern is common, although isolated increase in residual volume may be seen.

Pathologic Features

The prominent pathologic features are those of an inflammatory process involving the membranous and respiratory bronchioles, associated with the accumulation of tan-brown pigmented macrophages within respiratory bronchioles as well as neighboring alveolar ducts and alveoli.[96,161,162] The bronchiole may be ectatic with mucus stasis, and the walls are mildly thickened (Fig. 53.30). There is frequently evidence of extension of the bronchiolar metaplastic epithelium into the immediately surrounding alveoli. The pulmonary parenchyma away from the airway is usually normal or may demonstrate mild hyperinflation. These findings are sometimes so subtle as to be missed during routine evaluation, and examination of multiple sections may be required to find these abnormalities.[96]

Bedrossian and colleagues[163] coined the term *DIP-like reaction* to identify prominent intra-alveolar macrophage accumulation around space-occupying pulmonary lesions.[55] However, this DIP-like reaction is usually minimal and does not have the uniform involvement of lung parenchyma seen in RB-ILD. This DIP-like pattern can be seen in a number of other processes and is usually easily distinguished from DIP: eosinophilic granuloma, drug reactions (e.g., amiodarone), chronic alveolar hemorrhage, eosinophilic pneumonia, pneumoconioses (e.g., talcosis, hard-metal disease, asbestosis), obstructive pneumonias, and exogenous lipoid pneumonia.

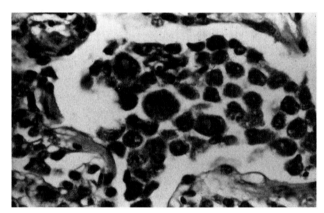

Figure 53.31 Photomicrograph of desquamative interstitial pneumonia (periodic acid–Schiff stain) showing a characteristic dense collection of macrophages filling the alveolar lumina without alveolar wall collagen. (Original magnification ×100.)

DIP is recognized by dense collections of intraluminal alveolar macrophages with little interstitial collagen (Fig. 53.31).[164] The original term is misleading in that there is no real desquamation of epithelial cells. There is simply a collection of macrophages in the air spaces.

Clinical Course and Outcome

Because there has not been a longitudinal study of a large group of subjects, the clinical course and prognosis of RB-ILD are unknown. Most studies suggest a favorable response to corticosteroids, with documented improvement in lung function and chest radiographs,[96,162] and few deaths secondary to progressive lung disease have been reported.

Patients with the DIP stage of this process also have a good prognosis. Carrington and associates[91] reported a 28% mortality after an average survival of 12 years. Other studies have shown similar results, but additional study of a larger number of subjects is needed.[96,159,160,165]

Smoking plays a major role in the pathogenesis, and smoking cessation has been associated with resolution of the symptoms and improvement in the radiographic and physiologic abnormalities. Corticosteroids may be required in refractory or recurrent cases but should not be instituted in the absence of smoking cessation.

ACUTE INTERSTITIAL PNEUMONIA

AIP is a rare fulminant form of lung injury that presents acutely (days to weeks from onset of symptoms), usually in a previously healthy individual.[166] AIP likely represents the subset of cases of idiopathic acute respiratory distress syndrome and is what Hamman and Rich described and termed "acute diffuse interstitial fibrosis"[167] (see Tables 53.7 and 53.8).

Clinical Features

Most patients are over the age of 40 years (mean age, 50 years; range, 7 to 83 years). There is no sexual predilection. A prodromal illness, lasting usually 7 to 14 days before presentation, is common. The clinical signs and symptoms include fever, cough, and shortness of breath. Routine laboratory studies are nonspecific and generally not helpful.

Chest Imaging Studies

Chest Roentgenography. Diffuse, bilateral, air space opacification is seen on chest radiograph.[168,169]

Computed Tomography Scan. CT scans show bilateral, patchy, symmetrical areas of ground-glass attenuation. Bilateral areas of air space consolidation may also be present. A predominantly subpleural distribution may be seen. Mild honeycombing, usually involving less than 10% of the lung, may be seen on CT examination. These radiographic findings are similar to those seen in acute respiratory distress syndrome.

Pulmonary Function Tests

Most patients have moderate to severe hypoxemia and develop respiratory failure. Mechanical ventilation is often required. A surgical lung biopsy is required to confirm the diagnosis of organizing diffuse alveolar damage, the histopathologic counterpart of AIP.[170]

Pathologic Features

Diffuse alveolar damage develops after an acute injury to the alveolar capillary basement membranes.[166,171,172] It is most commonly seen in the acute respiratory distress syndrome or in immunosuppressed patients who have received cytotoxic drugs or who have developed diffuse infectious pneumonias.[173,174] After the endothelial-epithelial injury, there is leakage of serum proteins and red blood cells into the alveolar spaces. The alveolar epithelium becomes necrotic and is sloughed, and the interstitium becomes edematous. Hyaline membranes, recognized as eosinophilic debris and consisting of necrotic epithelial cells, protein, and fibrin, form within alveolar spaces (Fig. 53.32). In the reparative or organizing stage of diffuse alveolar damage, there is proliferation and hyperplasia of the alveolar type II epithe-

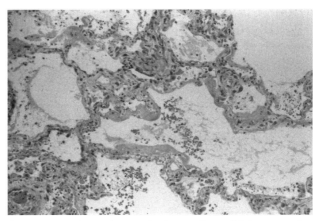

Figure 53.32 Photomicrograph of acute interstitial pneumonia showing diffuse alveolar damage. Note the hyaline membranes within alveolar spaces and edema and inflammatory cell infiltration of the alveolar wall. (Original magnification ×10.)

lial cells, which are capable of differentiating into type I cells. There is also resorption and incorporation of the hyaline membranes and alveolar exudates into the alveolar walls, associated with interstitial intraluminal fibroblast proliferation and collagen deposition. This is known as the *organizing phase* of diffuse alveolar damage. With protracted or repeated parenchymal injury, irreversible fibrosis and honeycomb lung result.[175,176]

Clinical Course and Outcome

The mortality from AIP is high (>60%), with the majority of patients dying within 3 months of presentation. However, those who recover usually have substantial recovery of lung function. We also found that a few survivors of AIP experienced recurrences and chronic, progressive interstitial lung disease.[169] It is not clear that corticosteroid therapy is effective in AIP. The main treatment is supportive care.

CRYPTOGENIC ORGANIZING PNEUMONIA

Cryptogenic organizing pneumonitis (COP) is a specific clinicopathologic syndrome characterized by a "pneumonia-like" illness, with excessive proliferation of granulation tissue within small airways and alveolar ducts, associated with chronic inflammation in the surrounding alveoli (i.e., bronchiolitis obliterans with organizing pneumonia)[38] (see Tables 53.7 and 53.8). Organizing pneumonia can be found on surgical lung biopsy in association with a number of diseases (e.g., postinfectious, drug related, connective tissue disease related, posttransplant). It is also commonly seen accompanying other histopathologic patterns (e.g., UIP). The diagnosis of COP is reserved for isolated organizing pneumonia in patients without an identifiable associated disease. The term *bronchiolitis obliterans with organizing pneumonia* historically encompassed COP but is no longer recommended for this idiopathic condition.

Clinical Features[177]

The incidence of COP is the same for both men (54%) and women (46%). The mean age at presentation is about 58 years (range, 21 to 80 years). Patients with COP are frequently very specific about the timing of their disease onset. This is because the disease onset is recent (usually <2 months) and is often dramatic, with the development of a flulike illness characterized by cough, fever, malaise, fatigue, and weight loss. Inspiratory crackles are frequently present on chest examination. Finger clubbing is rare in patients with COP.

Routine laboratory studies are nonspecific. A leukocytosis without increase in eosinophils is seen in approximately half the patients. The initial erythrocyte sedimentation rate is frequently elevated in patients with COP.

Chest Imaging Studies

Chest Roentgenography. The roentgenographic manifestations are distinctive, with bilateral, diffuse alveolar opacities in the presence of normal lung volume being characteristic.[178–180] A peripheral distribution of the infiltrates, very similar to that thought to be "virtually pathognomonic" for chronic eosinophilic pneumonia, is commonly seen in COP.[180–182] Irregular linear or nodular interstitial opacities are rarely present as the only radiographic manifestation.[183] Honeycombing is rare and is seen only as a late manifestation in the few patients with progressive disease. Other radiographic abnormalities, such as pleural effusion, pleural thickening, hyperinflation, and cavities, are rare.

Computed Tomography Scan. CT scans of the lung reveal patchy air space consolidation, small nodular opacities, and bronchial wall thickening and dilation, found most frequently in the periphery of the lung and often in the lower lung zone[18,180,183–186] (Fig. 53.33). Frequently, the CT findings are far more extensive than are expected by review of the plain chest film. The CT finding of consolidation is associated with partial or complete resolution, whereas reticular opacities are associated with persistent or progressive disease.[187]

Pulmonary Function Tests

Pulmonary function is usually impaired, with a restrictive defect being most common, although obstructive defect

(FEV$_1$/FVC ratio <70%) is found in almost one fifth of subjects with COP, mostly in current or former smokers. Gas-exchange abnormalities are extremely common, with resting and exercise arterial hypoxemia. The DL$_{CO}$ is reduced (<80% of predicted) in three fourths of the patients.

Pathologic Features

The diagnosis of COP depends on both the clinical setting and the finding of the characteristic pathologic features. Intraluminal fibrotic buds (Masson bodies) seen in respiratory bronchioles, alveolar ducts, and alveoli are the prominent feature.[188–190] Other pathologic features include foamy cells in the alveolar spaces, prominent type II cell hyperplasia, interstitial infiltrates, and fibrinous exudates.

Organizing pneumonia is recognized by the appearance in the small airways of intraluminal collections of proliferating fibroblasts that produce mucopolysaccharides and collagen. It is most prominent in the alveolar ducts but extends distally to the alveolar lumina and proximally to membranous bronchioles (Fig. 53.34). This change is accompanied by an interstitial lymphoplasmacytic infiltrate and hyperplasia of the type II epithelial cells. The organizing process, which extends into the membranous bronchioles, produces an intraluminal polypoid bronchiolitis obliterans (Fig. 53.35). Organizing pneumonia represents a common reparative response to injury occurring in a variety of interstitial lung diseases. If the injury is unresponsive to treatment, progression to irreversible fibrosis and honeycomb lung can result.

Clinical Course and Outcome

Corticosteroid therapy results in complete clinical, radiologic, and physiologic recovery in two thirds of patients. One third demonstrate recurrent or persistent disease. In general, clinical improvement is rapid, within several days or a few weeks. Occasionally recovery is quite dramatic. Relapses can occur when the corticosteroids are withdrawn, usually within 1 to 3 months. Most relapsed patients will

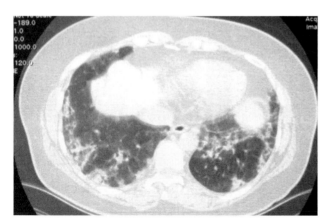

Figure 53.33 High-resolution computed tomographic image from a patient with cryptogenic organizing pneumonia showing patchy areas of consolidation and diffuse ground-glass opacities (gray-appearing areas).

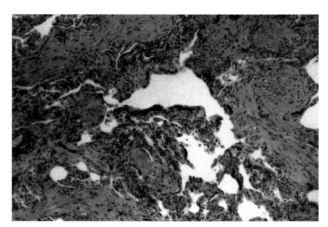

Figure 53.34 Photomicrograph indicates organizing pneumonia. Immature connective tissue and proliferating fibroblasts appearing light blue (pentachrome stain) are present in alveolar ducts and alveolar spaces, and there is an interstitial infiltrate consisting of mononuclear cells. (Original magnification ×40.)

Figure 53.35 Photomicrograph of organizing pneumonia shows a typical inflammatory polyp extending into the lumen of a terminal bronchiole. (Original magnification ×40.)

improve when re-treated with corticosteroids. Spontaneous improvement may occur over 3 to 6 months in a few patients.[178,193] Few of the patients with COP die as a result of this illness, but those prone to develop a rapidly progressive fatal form of organizing pneumonia have a clinical course similar to the "Hamman-Rich syndrome."[194] In such patients, the diagnosis is usually delayed or missed.

LYMPHOCYTIC INTERSTITIAL PNEUMONIA

LIP is an uncommon pathologic process characterized by the presence of widespread, monotonous sheets of lymphocytic infiltration in the interstitium of the lung.[195] In addition to being differentiated from IPF, it must be distinguished from lymphocytic infiltrations associated with pseudolymphoma, primary lymphomas, lymphomatoid granulomatosis, benign lymphocytic angiitis and granulomatosis, plasma cell interstitial pneumonia, and angioimmunoblastic lymphadenopathy. LIP is commonly found in association with other immunologic disorders, especially hypo- or hypergammaglobulinemic conditions and Sjögren's syndrome (Table 53.12).

Clinical Features

The clinical manifestations of LIP are dominated by those related to the underlying disease, such as Sjögren's syndrome (see Chapter 54). LIP occurs more commonly in women, usually in the fourth to sixth decade of life. It is also seen in children, particularly those with hypogammaglobulinemia or the acquired immunodeficiency syndrome. Progressive dyspnea and cough are the most common presenting symptoms, although weight loss, pleuritic pain, arthralgias, and fever also occur. Bibasilar crackles on chest examination, cyanosis, and finger clubbing are common physical findings.

Chest Imaging Studies

Chest Roentgenography. The chest roentgenogram is nonspecific, with reticular opacities being the most frequent abnormality. A mixed alveolar-interstitial pattern appears as the disease progresses, because of the coalescence of the

Table 53.12 Diseases Associated with Lymphocytic Interstitial Pneumonitis

Idiopathic Disease without Dysproteinemia
Disease with Dysproteinemia
Hypogammaglobulinemia
Monoclonal or polyclonal gammopathy
Autoimmune Diseases
Sjögren's syndrome
Chronic active hepatitis
Primary biliary cirrhosis
Myasthenia gravis
Hashimoto's thyroiditis
Pernicious anemia
Autoimmune hemolytic anemia
Systemic lupus erythematosus
Allogeneic Bone Marrow Transplantation
Acquired Immunodeficiency Syndrome
Viral Infections
Human immunodeficiency virus
Epstein-Barr virus
Human T-cell lymphotrophic virus type 1 (HTLV-1)
Miscellaneous
Tuberculosis
Celiac sprue
Dilantin
Post-*Legionella* pneumonia
Surfactant protein C deficiency

Adapted from Cosgrove GP, Fessler MB, Schwarz MI: Lymphoplasmacytic infiltrations of the lung. *In* Schwarz MI, King TE Jr (eds): Interstitial Lung Diseases (4th ed). Hamilton, Ontario, Canada: BC Decker, 2003, p 827.

opacities. Cysts, honeycombing, and pulmonary hypertension are also late manifestations.[196] Pleural effusions are infrequent and suggest a complicating lymphoma.

Computed Tomography Scan. Johkoh and coworkers showed that the main parenchymal abnormalities on the initial CT scan consisted of ground-glass attenuation, thickening of interlobular septa, centrilobular nodules, cystic air spaces, and air space consolidation[197] (Fig. 53.36). On follow-up CT, most patients improved, although several showed increased extent of disease. With the exception of cysts, the parenchymal opacities were reversible. New cysts developed in a few patients; these developed mainly in areas with centrilobular nodules on initial CT. Honeycombing was seen on follow-up CT in several patients in areas of previous air space consolidation on the initial CT.[197]

Pulmonary Function Tests

A restrictive defect is commonly seen and is often associated with a reduction in the DL_{CO} and arterial hypoxemia. A striking T-cell lymphocytosis is seen on BAL.

Pathologic Features

Open-lung biopsy is required for the diagnosis in almost all cases. The lymphocytic infiltration is usually extensive and

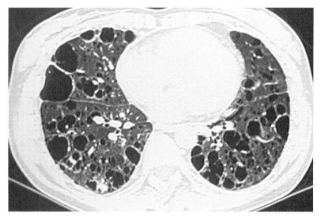

Figure 53.36 High-resolution computed tomographic image from a patient with lymphocytic interstitial pneumonia showing diffuse cysts.

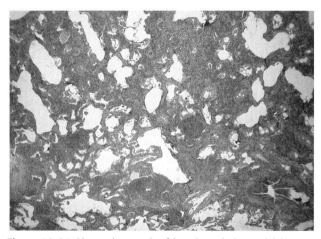

Figure 53.37 Photomicrograph of lymphocytic interstitial pneumonia showing diffuse lymphoid infiltrate that extends through the pulmonary interstitium. (Original magnification ×10.) *See Color Plate*

severe, involving the alveolar septa and peribronchiolar and perivascular interstitium (Fig. 53.37). The lymphocytes are polytypic (both B and T cells may be found), distinguishing them from the monotypic lymphocytic infiltrates characteristic of pulmonary lymphoma. The number of plasma cells and macrophages is also increased in these infiltrates. Other prominent histopathologic features include the accumulation of large interstitial reticuloendothelial cells, mononuclear cells, and giant cells forming noncaseating granulomas; the presence of perivascular and paraseptal amyloid deposition; and well-formed lymphoid germinal centers.

LIP is distinguished from DIP and NSIP by the presence of monotonous sheets of lymphocytes infiltrating the interstitium and alveolar lumina.[198] Other features include the interstitial accumulation of macrophages, noncaseating granulomas, perivascular amyloid deposits, and germinal lymphoid centers. Conversion to a low-grade pulmonary lymphoma or progression to end-stage honeycomb lung may follow.[195,199,200]

Clinical Course and Outcome

The clinical course of idiopathic LIP is unknown. In cases in which LIP is associated with another disease, the underlying disease largely determines the outcome. Marked improvement or complete resolution followed corticosteroid therapy in many case reports. Progressive pulmonary fibrosis, cor pulmonale, and death can occur despite therapy. Infection is a common complication in these patients, especially those with an associated dysproteinemia. Progression to pulmonary or systemic lymphoma occurs but appears to be quite rare.

SUMMARY

Careful histopathologic evaluation has shown the traditionally clinical diagnosis of idiopathic interstitial pneumonia to be more difficult and the findings to be more heterogeneous than was once thought. The subclassification of the idiopathic interstitial pneumonias, based on clinicopathologic criteria, has important therapeutic and prognostic implications. All patients with suspected idiopathic interstitial pneumonia should be carefully evaluated with an in-depth history and physical examination, pulmonary function testing, bronchoscopy, and HRCT scanning by physicians experienced in the care of such patients. The most important diagnosis for clinicians to establish is whether or not IPF is present. Although the clinical and radiographic diagnosis of IPF can be made confidently in some cases, patients whose diagnosis is unclear after a thorough clinical and radiographic evaluation should undergo surgical lung biopsy to establish the underlying histopathology. New insight into the pathophysiology of IPF suggests a distinctly fibroproliferative process, and antifibrotic therapies show promise. Referral for lung transplantation should be pursued early in those patients with progressive disease unresponsive to therapy. As our understanding of the pathophysiology of the idiopathic interstitial pneumonias grows, we will surely develop promising new agents that may significantly affect the morbidity and mortality of patients with these often devastating diseases.

REFERENCES

1. Coultas DB, Zumwalt RE, Black WC, Sobonya RE: The epidemiology of interstitial lung disease. Am J Respir Crit Care Med 150:967–972, 1994.
2. Schwarz MI, King TE Jr, Raghu G: Approach to the evaluation and diagnosis of interstitial lung disease. *In* Schwarz MI, King TE Jr (eds): Interstitial Lung Diseases (4th ed). Hamilton, Ontario, Canada: BC Decker, 2003, pp 1–30.
3. Mays EE, Dubois JJ, Hamilton GB: Pulmonary fibrosis associated with tracheobronchial aspiration. Chest 69:512–515, 1976.
4. Raghu G: The role of gastroesophageal reflux in idiopathic pulmonary fibrosis. Am J Med 115 Suppl 3A:60S–64S, 2003.
5. Kennedy JD, Costello P, Balikian JP, Herman PG: Exogenous lipoid pneumonia. AJR Am J Roentgenol 136:1145–1149, 1981.
6. Bandla HP, Davis SH, Hopkins NE: Lipoid pneumonia: A silent complication of mineral oil aspiration. Pediatrics 103:E19, 1999.

7. Donaghy M, Rees AJ: Cigarette smoking and lung haemorrhage in glomerulonephritis caused by autoantibodies to glomerular basement membrane. Lancet 2:1390–1393, 1983.

8. Schürmann M, Lympany PA, Reichel P, et al: Familial sarcoidosis is linked to the major histocompatibility complex region. Am J Respir Crit Care Med 162(3 Pt 1):861–864, 2000.

9. Marshall RP, Puddicombe A, Cookson WO, Laurent GJ: Adult familial cryptogenic fibrosing alveolitis in the United Kingdom. Thorax 55:143–146, 2000.

10. Verleden GM, du Bois RM, Bouros D, et al: Genetic predisposition and pathogenetic mechanisms of interstitial lung diseases of unknown origin. Eur Respir J Suppl 32:17s–29s, 2001.

11. Thomas AQ, Lane K, Phillips J 3rd, et al: Heterozygosity for a surfactant protein C gene mutation associated with usual interstitial pneumonitis and cellular nonspecific interstitial pneumonitis in one kindred. Am J Respir Crit Care Med 165:1322–1328, 2002.

12. Terry RD, Sperry WM, Brodoff B: Adult lipoidosis resembling Niemann-Pick disease. Am J Pathol 30:263–286, 1954.

13. Schneider EL, Epstein CJ, Kaback MJ, Brandes D: Severe pulmonary involvement in adult Gaucher's disease: Report of three cases and review of the literature. Am J Med 63:475–480, 1977.

14. Parker MS, Shipley W, Rosado de Christenson ML, et al: The Hermansky-Pudlak syndrome. Ann Diagn Pathol 1:99–103, 1997.

15. Anderson PD, Huizing M, Claassen DA, et al: Hermansky-Pudlak syndrome type 4 (HPS-4): Clinical and molecular characteristics. Hum Genet 113:10–17, 2003.

16. Ziskind MM, Weill H, Buechner HA, Brown M: Recognition of distinctive radiologic patterns in diffuse pulmonary disease. Arch Intern Med 114:108–112, 1964.

17. Desai SR, Wells AU, Rubens MB, et al: Traction bronchiectasis in cryptogenic fibrosing alveolitis: Associated computed tomographic features and physiological significance. Eur Radiol 13:1801–1808, 2003.

18. Muller NL, Miller RR: Computed tomography of chronic diffuse infiltrative lung disease, Part 1. Am Rev Respir Dis 142:1206–1215, 1990.

19. Muller NL, Miller RR: Computed tomography of chronic diffuse infiltrative lung disease, Part 2. Am Rev Respir Dis 142:1440–1448, 1990.

20. Epler GR, McLoud TC, Gaensler EA, et al: Normal chest roentgenograms in chronic diffuse infiltrative lung disease. N Engl J Med 298:934–939, 1978.

21. Hunninghake GW, Lynch DA, Galvin JR, et al: Radiologic findings are strongly associated with a pathologic diagnosis of usual interstitial pneumonia. Chest 124:1215–1223, 2003.

22. Schurawitzki H, Stiglbauer R, Graninger W, et al: Interstitial lung disease in progressive systemic sclerosis: High-resolution CT versus radiography. Radiology 176:755–759, 1990.

23. Harrison NK, Glanville AR, Strickland B, et al: Pulmonary involvement in systemic sclerosis: The detection of early changes by thin section CT scan, bronchoalveolar lavage and ^{99m}Tc-DTPA clearance. Respir Med 83:403–414, 1989.

24. Lynch DA, Rose C, Way DE, King TE Jr: Hypersensitivity pneumonitis: Sensitivity of high resolution CT in a population-based study. AJR Am J Roentgenol 159:469–472, 1992.

25. Hanley ME, King TE Jr, Schwarz MI, et al: The impact of smoking on mechanical properties of the lungs in idiopathic pulmonary fibrosis and sarcoidosis. Am Rev Respir Dis 144:1102–1106, 1991.

26. Cherniack RM: Pulmonary Function Testing. Philadelphia: WB Saunders, 1992.

27. Fulmer JD, Roberts WC, von Gal ER, Crystal RG: Morphologic-physiologic correlates of the severity of fibrosis and degree of cellularity in idiopathic pulmonary fibrosis. J Clin Invest 63:665–676, 1979.

28. Greening AP, Hughes JM: Serial estimations of carbon monoxide diffusing capacity in intrapulmonary haemorrhage. Clin Sci (Colch) 60:507–512, 1981.

29. King TE Jr, Tooze JA, Schwarz MI, et al: Predicting survival in idiopathic pulmonary fibrosis: Scoring system and survival model. Am J Respir Crit Care Med 164:1171–1181, 2001.

30. Costabel U, Guzman J: Bronchoalveolar lavage in interstitial lung disease. Curr Opin Pulm Med 7:255–261, 2001.

31. Costabel U, Guzman J: Bronchoalveolar lavage. *In* Schwarz MI, King TE Jr (eds): Interstitial Lung Diseases (4th ed). Hamilton, Ontario, Canada: BC Decker, 2003, pp 114–133.

32. Rottoli P, Bargagli E: Is bronchoalveolar lavage obsolete in the diagnosis of interstitial lung disease? Curr Opin Pulm Med 9:418–425, 2003.

33. BAL Cooperative Group: Bronchoalveolar lavage constituents in healthy individuals, idiopathic pulmonary fibrosis, and selected comparison groups. Am Rev Respir Dis 141:S169–S202, 1990.

34. Kawanami O, Basset F, Ferrans VJ, et al: Pulmonary Langerhans' cells in patients with fibrotic lung disorders. Lab Invest 44:227–233, 1981.

35. Gaensler EA, Carrington CB: Open biopsy for chronic diffuse infiltrative lung disease: Clinical, roentgenographic, and physiological correlations in 502 patients. Ann Thorac Surg 30:411–426, 1980.

36. Wall CP, Gaensler EA, Carrington CB, Hayes JA: Comparison of transbronchial and open biopsies in chronic infiltrative lung diseases. Am Rev Respir Dis 123:280–285, 1981.

37. Bensard DD, McIntyre RC Jr, Waring BJ, Simon JS: Comparison of video thoracoscopic lung biopsy to open lung biopsy in the diagnosis of interstitial lung disease. Chest 103:765–770, 1993.

38. Travis WD, King TE Jr (co-chairs), Bateman ED, et al: American Thoracic Society/European Respiratory Society international multidisciplinary consensus classification of the idiopathic interstitial pneumonias. Am J Respir Crit Care Med 165:277–304, 2002.

39. King TE Jr, Costabel U, Cordier J-F, et al: American Thoracic Society: Idiopathic pulmonary fibrosis: Diagnosis and treatment. International consensus statement. American Thoracic Society (ATS), and the European Respiratory Society (ERS). Am J Respir Crit Care Med 161:646–664, 2000.

40. Coultas DB: Epidemiology of idiopathic pulmonary fibrosis. Semin Respir Med 14:181–196, 1993.

41. Hubbard R, Johnston IDA, Coultas D, Britton J: Mortality rates from cryptogenic fibrosing alveolitis in seven countries. Thorax 51:711–716, 1996.

42. Wittram C, Mark EJ, McLoud TC: CT-histologic correlation of the ATS/ERS 2002 classification of idiopathic interstitial pneumonias. Radiographics 23:1057–1071, 2003.

43. Staples C, Muller N, Vedal S, et al: Usual interstitial pneumonia: Correlation of CT with clinical, functional, and radiographic findings. Radiology 162:377–381, 1987.

44. Wells AU, King AD, Rubens MB, et al: Lone cryptogenic fibrosing alveolitis: A functional-morphologic correlation based on extent of disease on thin-section computed

tomography. Am J Respir Crit Care Med 155:1367–1375, 1997.

45. Xaubet A, Agusti C, Luburich P, et al: Pulmonary function tests and CT scan in the management of idiopathic pulmonary fibrosis. Am J Respir Crit Care Med 158:431–436, 1998.

46. Lynch DA, Newell JD, Logan PM, et al: Can CT distinguish idiopathic pulmonary fibrosis from hypersensitivity pneumonitis? AJR Am J Roentgenol 165:807–811, 1995.

47. Hunninghake G, Zimmerman MB, Schwartz DA, et al: Utility of lung biopsy for the diagnosis of idiopathic pulmonary fibrosis. Am J Respir Crit Care Med 164:193–196, 2001.

48. Johkoh T, Müller NL, Cartier Y, et al: Idiopathic interstitial pneumonias: Diagnostic accuracy of thin-section CT in 129 patients. Radiology 211:555–560, 1999.

49. Raghu G, Mageto YN, Lockhart D, et al: The accuracy of the clinical diagnosis of new-onset idiopathic pulmonary fibrosis and other interstitial lung disease: A prospective study. Chest 116:1168–1174, 1999.

50. Swensen S, Aughenbaugh G, Myers J: Diffuse lung disease: Diagnostic accuracy of CT in patients undergoing surgical biopsy of the lung. Radiology 205:229–234, 1997.

50a. Aziz ZA, Wells AU, Hansell DM, et al: HRCT diagnosis of diffuse parenchymal lung disease: inter-observer variation. Thorax 59:506–511, 2004.

51. Grenier P, Valeyre D, Cluzel P, et al: Chronic diffuse interstitial lung disease: Diagnostic value of chest radiography and high-resolution CT. Radiology 179:123–132, 1991.

52. Mathieson JR, Mayo JR, Staples CA, Muller NL: Chronic diffuse infiltrative lung disease: Comparison of diagnostic accuracy of CT and chest radiography. Radiology 171:111–116, 1989.

53. Tung KT, Wells AU, Rubens MB, et al: Accuracy of the typical computed tomographic appearances of fibrosing alveolitis. Thorax 48:334–338, 1993.

54. Flaherty KR, Thwaite EL, Kazerooni EA, et al: Radiological versus histological diagnosis in UIP and NSIP: Survival implications. Thorax 58:143–148, 2003.

55. Katzenstein ALA, Myers JL: Idiopathic pulmonary fibrosis: Clinical relevance of pathologic classification. Am J Respir Crit Care Med 157:1301–1315, 1998.

56. Scott J, Johnston I, Britton J: What causes cryptogenic fibrosing alveolitis? A case-control study of environmental exposure to dust. BMJ 301:1015–1017, 1990.

57. Hubbard R, Lewis S, Richards K, et al: Occupational exposure to metal or wood dust and aetiology of cryptogenic fibrosing alveolitis. Lancet 347:284–289, 1996.

58. Baumgartner KB, Samet J, Stidley CA, et al and the Collaborating Centers: Cigarette smoking: A risk factor for idiopathic pulmonary fibrosis. Am J Respir Crit Care Med 155:242–248, 1997.

59. Selman M, King TE Jr, Pardo A: Idiopathic pulmonary fibrosis: Prevailing and evolving hypotheses about its pathogenesis and implications for therapy. Ann Intern Med 134:136–151, 2001.

60. Gauldie J: Pro-inflammatory mechanisms are a minor component of the pathogenesis of idiopathic pulmonary fibrosis. Am J Respir Crit Care Med 165:1205–1206, 2002.

61. Selman M, Ruiz V, Cabrera S, et al: TIMP-1, -2, -3, and -4 in idiopathic pulmonary fibrosis: A prevailing nondegradative lung microenvironment? Am J Physiol Lung Cell Mol Physiol 279:L562–L574, 2000.

62. Pardo A, Selman M: Idiopathic pulmonary fibrosis: New insights in its pathogenesis. Int J Biochem Cell Biol 34:1534–1538, 2002.

63. Sheppard D: Pulmonary fibrosis: A cellular overreaction or a failure of communication? J Clin Invest 107:1501–1502, 2001.

64. Gauldie J, Kolb M, Sime PJ: A new direction in the pathogenesis of idiopathic pulmonary fibrosis? Respir Res 3:1–3, 2002.

65. Zuo F, Kaminski N, Eugui E, et al: Gene expression analysis reveals matrilysin as a key regulator of pulmonary fibrosis in mice and humans. Proc Natl Acad Sci U S A 99:6292–6297, 2002.

66. Selman M, Pardo A: The epithelial/fibroblastic pathway in the pathogenesis of idiopathic pulmonary fibrosis. Am J Respir Cell Mol Biol 29(3 Suppl):S93–S97, 2003.

67. McCormack FX, King TE Jr, Voelker DR, et al: Idiopathic pulmonary fibrosis: Abnormalities in the bronchoalveolar lavage content of surfactant protein A. Am Rev Respir Dis 144:160–166, 1991.

68. McCormack FX, King TE Jr, Bucher BL, et al: Surfactant protein A predicts survival in idiopathic pulmonary fibrosis. Am J Respir Crit Care Med 152:751–159, 1995.

69. Selman M, Lin HM, Montano M, et al: Surfactant protein A and B genetic variants predispose to idiopathic pulmonary fibrosis. Hum Genet 113:542–550, 2003.

70. Raghu G: Interstitial lung disease: A diagnostic approach. Are CT scan and lung biopsy indicated in every patient? Am J Respir Crit Care Med 151:909–914, 1995.

70a. Flaherty KR, King TE Jr, Raghu G, et al: Idiopathic interstitial pneumonia: what is the effect of a multidisciplinary approach to diagnosis? Am J Respir Crit Care Med 170:904–910, 2004.

71. Ferson PF, Landreneau RJ, Dowling RD, et al: Comparison of open versus thorascopic lung biopsy for diffuse infiltrative pulmonary disease. J Thorac Cardiovasc Surgery 106:194–199, 1993.

72. Mapel DW, Samet JM, Coultas DB: Corticosteroids and the treatment of idiopathic pulmonary fibrosis: Past, present, and future. Chest 110:1058–1067, 1996.

73. Schwartz DA, Helmers RA, Galvin JR, et al: Determinants of survival in idiopathic pulmonary fibrosis. Am J Respir Crit Care Med 149:450–454, 1994.

74. Schwartz DA, Van Fossen DS, Davis CS, et al: Determinants of progression in idiopathic pulmonary fibrosis. Am J Respir Crit Care Med 149:444–449, 1994.

75. Schwartz DA, Merchant RK, Helmers RA, et al: The influence of cigarette smoking on lung function in patients with idiopathic pulmonary fibrosis. Am Rev Respir Dis 144:504–506, 1991.

76. Gay SE, Kazerooni EA, Toews GB, et al: Idiopathic pulmonary fibrosis: Predicting response to therapy and survival. Am J Respir Crit Care Med 157:1063–1072, 1998.

77. Lama VN, Flaherty KR, Toews GB, et al: Prognostic value of desaturation during a 6-minute walk test in idiopathic interstitial pneumonia. Am J Respir Crit Care Med 168:1084–1090, 2003.

78. Crystal RG, Gadek JE, Ferrans VJ, et al: Interstitial lung disease: Current concepts of pathogenesis, staging, and therapy. Am J Med 70:542–568, 1981.

79. Watters LC, Schwarz MI, Cherniack RM, et al: Idiopathic pulmonary fibrosis: Pretreatment bronchoalveolar lavage cellular constituents and their relationships with lung histopathology and clinical response to therapy. Am Rev Respir Dis 135:696–704, 1987.

80. Turner-Warwick M, Haslam PL: The value of serial bronchoalveolar lavages in assessing the clinical progress of patients with cryptogenic fibrosing alveolitis. Am Rev Respir Dis 135:26–34, 1987.

81. King TE Jr, Schwarz MI, Brown K, et al: Idiopathic pulmonary fibrosis: Relationship between histopathologic features and mortality. Am J Respir Crit Care Med 164:1025–1032, 2001.

82. Nicholson AG, Fulford LG, Colby TV, et al: The relationship between individual histologic features and disease progression in idiopathic pulmonary fibrosis. Am J Respir Crit Care Med 166:173–177, 2002.

83. Coletta EN, Pereira CA, Ferreira RG, et al: Histological data and survival in idiopathic pulmonary fibrosis. Braz J Pulmonol 29:371–378, 2003.

84. Flaherty KR, Colby TV, Travis WD, et al: Fibroblastic foci in usual interstitial pneumonia: Idiopathic versus collagen vascular disease. Am J Respir Crit Care Med 167:1410–1415, 2003.

85. Latsi PI, du Bois RM, Nicholson AG, et al: Fibrotic idiopathic interstitial pneumonia: The prognostic value of longitudinal functional trends. Am J Respir Crit Care Med 168:531–537, 2003.

86. Collard HR, King TE Jr, Bartelson BB, et al: Changes in clinical and physiologic variables predict survival in idiopathic pulmonary fibrosis. Am J Respir Crit Care Med 168:538–542, 2003.

87. Wells AU, Desai SR, Rubens MB, et al: Idiopathic pulmonary fibrosis: A composite physiologic index derived from disease extent observed by computed tomography. Am J Respir Crit Care Med 167:962–969, 2003.

88. Flaherty KR, Mumford JA, Murray S, et al: Prognostic implications of physiologic and radiographic changes in idiopathic interstitial pneumonia. Am J Respir Crit Care Med 168:543–548, 2003.

89. Collard HR, King TE Jr: Treatment of idiopathic pulmonary fibrosis: The rise and fall of corticosteroids. Am J Med 110:326–328, 2001.

90. Collard HR, Ryu JH, Douglas WW, et al: Combined corticosteroid and cyclophosphamide therapy does not alter survival in idiopathic pulmonary fibrosis. Chest 125:2169–2174, 2004.

91. Carrington CB, Gaensler EA, Coutu RE, et al: Natural history and treated course of usual and desquamative interstitial pneumonia. N Engl J Med 298:801–809, 1978.

92. Douglas WW, Ryu JH, Swensen SJ, et al: Colchicine versus prednisone in the treatment of idiopathic pulmonary fibrosis: A randomized prospective study. Members of the Lung Study Group. Am J Respir Crit Care Med 158:220–225, 1998.

93. Daniil ZD, Gilchrist FC, Nicholson AG, et al: A histologic pattern of nonspecific interstitial pneumonia is associated with a better prognosis than usual interstitial pneumonia in patients with cryptogenic fibrosing alveolitis. Am J Respir Crit Care Med 160:899–905, 1999.

94. Nicholson AG, Colby TV, Dubois RM, et al: The prognostic significance of the histologic pattern of interstitial pneumonia in patients presenting with the clinical entity of cryptogenic fibrosing alveolitis. Am J Respir Crit Care Med 162:2213–2217, 2000.

95. Katzenstein AL, Fiorelli RF: Nonspecific interstitial pneumonia/fibrosis: Histologic features and clinical significance. Am J Surg Pathol 18:136–147, 1994.

96. Yousem SA, Colby TV, Gaensler EA: Respiratory bronchiolitis-associated interstitial lung disease and its relationship to desquamative interstitial pneumonia. Mayo Clin Proc 64:1373–1380, 1989.

97. Raghu G, Depaso WJ, Cain K, et al: Azathioprine combined with prednisone in the treatment of idiopathic pulmonary fibrosis: A prospective, double-blind randomized, placebo-controlled clinical trial. Am Rev Respir Dis 144:291–296, 1991.

98. Johnson MA, Kwan S, Snell NJC, et al: Randomized controlled trial comparing prednisolone alone with cyclophosphamide and low dose prednisolone in combination in cryptogenic fibrosing alveolitis. Thorax 44:280–288, 1989.

99. Zisman DA, Lynch JP 3rd, Toews GB, et al: Cyclophosphamide in the treatment of idiopathic pulmonary fibrosis: A prospective study in patients who failed to respond to corticosteroids. Chest 117:1619–1626, 2000.

100. Peters SG, McDougall JC, Douglas WW, et al: Colchicine in the treatment of pulmonary fibrosis. Chest 103:101–104, 1993.

101. Douglas WW, Ryu JH, Bjoraker JA, et al: Colchicine versus prednisone as treatment of usual interstitial pneumonia. Mayo Clin Proc 72:201–209, 1997.

102. Douglas WW, Ryu JH, Schroeder DR: Idiopathic pulmonary fibrosis: Impact of oxygen and colchicine, prednisone, or no therapy on survival. Am J Respir Crit Care Med 161(4 Pt 1):1172–1178, 2000.

103. Selman M, Carrillo G, Salas J, et al: Colchicine, D-penicillamine, and prednisone in the treatment of idiopathic pulmonary fibrosis: a controlled clinical trial. Chest 114:507–512, 1998.

104. Addrizzo-Harris DJ, Harkin TJ, Tchou-Wong KM, et al: Mechanisms of colchicine effect in the treatment of asbestosis and idiopathic pulmonary fibrosis. Lung 180:61–72, 2002.

105. Ziesche R, Hofbauer E, Wittmann K, et al: A preliminary study of long-term treatment with interferon gamma-1b and low-dose prednisolone in patients with idiopathic pulmonary fibrosis. N Engl J Med 341:1264–1269, 1999.

106. Raghu G, Brown KK, Bradford WZ, et al: A placebo-controlled trial of interferon gamma-1b in patients with idiopathic pulmonary fibrosis. N Engl J Med 350:125–133, 2004.

106a. Strieter RM, Starko KM, Enelow RI, et al: Effects of interferon-gamma 1b on biomarker expression in patients with idiopathic pulmonary fibrosis. Am J Respir Crit Care Med 170:133–140, 2004.

107. Kalra S, Utz JP, Ryu JH: Interferon gamma-1b therapy for advanced idiopathic pulmonary fibrosis. Mayo Clin Proc 78:1082–1087, 2003.

108. Raghu G, Spada C, Otaki Y, Hayes J: IFN-gamma in the treatment of advanced IPF and fibrotic NSIP: Prospective, preliminary clinical observations in one center. Chest 120:185S, 2001.

109. Raghu G, Johnson WC, Lockhart D, Mageto Y: Treatment of idiopathic pulmonary fibrosis with a new antifibrotic agent, pirfenidone: Results of a prospective, open-label Phase II study. Am J Respir Crit Care Med 159(4 Pt 1):1061–1069, 1999.

110. Azuma A, Tsuboi E, Abe S, et al: A placebo control and double blind Phase II clinical study of pirfenidone in patients with idiopathic pulmonary fibrosis in Japan. Am J Respir Crit Care Med 165:A729, 2002.

111. Brantly ML, Troendle J, Avila N, et al: A randomized, placebo-controlled trial of oral pirfenidone for the pulmonary fibrosis of Hermansky-Pudlak syndrome. Am J Respir Crit Care Med 165:A728, 2002.

112. Meier-Sydow J, Rust M, Kronenberger H, et al: Long-term follow-up of lung function parameters in patients with idiopathic pulmonary fibrosis treated with prednisone and azathioprine or D-penicillamine. Prax Pneumol 33:680–688, 1979.

113. Meier-Sydow J, Weiss SM, Buhl R, et al: Idiopathic pulmonary fibrosis: Current clinical concepts and

challenges in management. Semin Respir Crit Care Med 15:77–96, 1994.

114. Raghu R, Bozic CR, Brown K, et al: Trial of interferon beta-1a (INFbeta-1a) in idiopathic pulmonary fibrosis (IPF): Characteristics of patients with and without surgical lung biopsy. Am J Respir Crit Care Med 161:A527, 2000.

115. Raghu R, Bozic CR, Brown K, et al: Feasibility of a trial of interferon beta-1a (IFN beta-1a) in the treatment of idiopathic pulmonary fibrosis (IPF). Am J Respir Crit Care Med 163:A707, 2001.

116. Yano T, Deterding RR, Simonet WS, et al: Keratinocyte growth factor reduces lung damage due to acid instillation in rats. Am J Respir Cell Mol Biol 15:433–442, 1996.

117. Deterding RR, Havill AM, Yano T, et al: Prevention of bleomycin-induced lung injury in rats by keratinocyte growth factor. Proc Assoc Am Physicians 109:254–268, 1997.

118. Carrillo G, Estrada A, Mejía M, et al: Inhaled beclomethasone and colchicine (IBC) versus inhaled beclomethasone, colchicine and captopril (IBCCAP) in patients with idiopathic pulmonary fibrosis (IPF). Am J Respir Crit Care Med 161:A528, 2000.

119. Meuret G, Fueter R, Gloor F: Early stage of fulminant idiopathic pulmonary fibrosis cured by intense combination therapy using cyclophosphamide, vincristine, and prednisone. Respiration 36:228–233, 1978.

120. International guidelines for the selection of lung transplant candidates. Am J Respir Crit Care Med 158:335–339, 1998.

121. Panos RJ, Mortenson R, Niccoli SA, King TE Jr: Clinical deterioration in patients with idiopathic pulmonary fibrosis: Causes and assessment. Am J Med 88:396–404, 1990.

122. Kondoh Y, Taniguchi H, Kawabata Y, et al: Acute exacerbation in idiopathic pulmonary fibrosis: Analysis of clinical and pathologic findings in three cases. Chest 103:1808–1812, 1993.

123. Hiwatari N, Shimura S, Takishima T, Shirato K: Bronchoalveolar lavage as a possible cause of acute exacerbation in idiopathic pulmonary fibrosis patients. Tohoku J Exp Med 174:379–386, 1994.

124. Akira M, Hamada H, Sakatani M, et al: CT findings during phase of accelerated deterioration in patients with idiopathic pulmonary fibrosis. AJR Am J Roentgenol 168:79–83, 1997.

125. Martinez F, Bradford W, Safrin S, et al: Rates and characteristics of death in patients with idiopathic pulmonary fibrosis (IPF). Chest 124:117S, 2003.

126. King TE Jr: Idiopathic interstitial pneumonia. In Schwarz MI, King TE Jr (eds): Interstitial Lung Diseases (4th ed). Hamilton, Ontario, Canada: BC Decker, 2003, pp 701–786.

127. Barzo P: Familial idiopathic fibrosing alveolitis. Eur J Respir Dis 66:350–352, 1985.

128. Hodgson U, Laitinen T, Tukiainen P: Nationwide prevalence of sporadic and familial idiopathic pulmonary fibrosis: Evidence of founder effect among multiplex families in Finland. Thorax 57:338–342, 2002.

129. Bitterman PB, Rennard SI, Keogh BA, et al: Familial idiopathic pulmonary fibrosis: Evidence of lung inflammation in unaffected family members. N Engl J Med 314:1343–1347, 1986.

130. Buchino JJ, Keenan WJ, Algren JT, Bove KE: Familial desquamative interstitial pneumonitis occurring in infants. Am J Med Genet Suppl 3:285–291, 1987.

131. Wright JA, Pennington JE: Familial lymphoid interstitial pneumonitis. J Pediatr 111:638, 1987.

132. Nogee LM, Dunbar AE 3rd, Wert SE, et al: A mutation in the surfactant protein C gene associated with familial

interstitial lung disease. N Engl J Med 344:573–579, 2001.

133. Nogee LM, Dunbar AE 3rd, Wert S, et al: Mutations in the surfactant protein C gene associated with interstitial lung disease. Chest 121(3 Suppl):20S–21S, 2002.

134. Amin RS, Wert SE, Baughman RP, et al: Surfactant protein deficiency in familial interstitial lung disease. J Pediatr 139:85–92, 2001.

135. Whitsett JA: Genetic basis of familial interstitial lung disease: Misfolding or function of surfactant protein C? Am J Respir Crit Care Med 165:1201–1202, 2002.

136. Musk AW, Zilko PJ, Manners P, et al: Genetic studies in familial fibrosing alveolitis: Possible linkage with immunoglobulin allotypes (Gm). Chest 89:206–210, 1986.

137. Turton CWG, Morris LM, Lawler SD, Turner-Warwick M: HLA in cryptogenic fibrosing alveolitis. Lancet 1:507–508, 1978.

138. Geddes DM, Brewerton DA, Webley M, et al: Alpha-1-antitrypsin phenotypes in fibrosing alveolitis and rheumatoid arthritis. Lancet 2:1049–1051, 1977.

139. Evans CC: HLA antigens in diffuse fibrosing alveolitis (abstract). Thorax 31:483, 1976.

140. Varpela E, Tiilikainen A, Varpela M, Tukiainen P: High prevalences of HLA-BI5 and HLA-Dw6 in patients with cryptogenic fibrosing alveolitis. Tissue Antigens 14:68–71, 1979.

141. Libby DM, Gibofsky A, Fotino M, et al: Immunogenetic and clinical findings in IPF association with the B-cell alloantigen HLA-DR2. Am Rev Respir Dis 127:618–622, 1983.

142. Briggs DC, Vaughan RW, Welsh KI, et al: Immunogenetic prediction of pulmonary fibrosis in systemic sclerosis. Lancet 338:661–662, 1991.

143. Bjoraker JA, Ryu JH, Edwin MK, et al: Prognostic significance of histopathologic subsets in idiopathic pulmonary fibrosis. Am J Respir Crit Care Med 157:199–203, 1998.

144. Park JS, Lee KS, Kim JS, et al: Nonspecific interstitial pneumonia with fibrosis: Radiographic and CT findings in seven patients. Radiology 195:645–648, 1995.

145. Park CS, Jeon JW, Park SW, et al: Nonspecific interstitial pneumonia/fibrosis: Clinical manifestations, histologic and radiologic features. Korean J Intern Med 11:122–132, 1996.

146. Drent M, du Bois RM, Poletti V: Recent advances in the diagnosis and management of nonspecific interstitial pneumonia. Curr Opin Pulm Med 9:411–417, 2003.

147. Veeraraghavan S, Latsi PI, Wells AU, et al: BAL findings in idiopathic nonspecific interstitial pneumonia and usual interstitial pneumonia. Eur Respir J 22:239–244, 2003.

148. Douglas WW, Tazelaar HD, Hartman TE, et al: Polymyositis-dermatomyositis-associated interstitial lung disease. Am J Respir Crit Care Med 164:1182–1185, 2001.

149. Kim DS, Yoo B, Lee JS, et al: The major histopathologic pattern of pulmonary fibrosis in scleroderma is nonspecific interstitial pneumonia. Sarcoidosis Vasc Diffuse Lung Dis 19:121–127, 2002.

150. Lantuejoul S, Brambilla E, Brambilla C, Devouassoux G: Statin-induced fibrotic nonspecific interstitial pneumonia. Eur Respir J 19:577–580, 2002.

151. Vourlekis JS, Schwarz MI, Cool CD, et al: Nonspecific interstitial pneumonitis as the sole histologic expression of hypersensitivity pneumonitis. Am J Med 112:490–493, 2002.

152. Arakawa H, Yamada H, Kurihara Y, et al: Nonspecific interstitial pneumonia associated with polymyositis and dermatomyositis: Serial high-resolution CT findings and functional correlation. Chest 123:1096–1103, 2003.

152a. Craig PJ, Wells AU, Doffman S, et al: Desquamative interstitial pneumonia, respiratory bronchiolitis and their relationship to smoking. Histopathology 45:275–282, 2004.

153. Fraig M, Shreesha U, Savici D, Katzenstein AL: Respiratory bronchiolitis: A clinicopathologic study in current smokers, ex-smokers, and never-smokers. Am J Surg Pathol 26:647–653, 2002.

154. Vassallo R, Jensen EA, Colby TV, et al: The overlap between respiratory bronchiolitis and desquamative interstitial pneumonia in pulmonary Langerhans cell histiocytosis: High-resolution CT, histologic, and functional correlations. Chest 124:1199–1205, 2003.

155. Park JS, Brown KK, Tuder RM, et al: Respiratory bronchiolitis associated interstitial lung disease: Radiologic features with clinical and pathologic correlation. J Comput Assist Tomogr 26:13–20, 2002.

156. Hartman TE, Primack SL, Swensen SJ, et al: Desquamative interstitial pneumonia: Thin-section CT findings in 22 patients. Radiology 187:787–790, 1993.

157. Holt RM, Schmidt RA, Godwin D, Raghu G: High resolution CT in respiratory bronchiolitis-associated interstitial lung disease. J Comput Assist Tomogr 17:46–50, 1993.

158. Silver SF, Muller NL, Miller RR, Lefcoe MS: Hypersensitivity pneumonitis: Evaluation with CT. Radiology 173:441–445, 1989.

159. Hartman TE, Primack SL, Kang EY, et al: Disease progression in usual interstitial pneumonia compared with desquamative interstitial pneumonia: Assessment with serial CT. Chest 110:378–382, 1996.

160. Akira M, Yamamoto S, Hara H, et al: Serial computed tomographic evaluation in desquamative interstitial pneumonia. Thorax 52:333–337, 1997.

161. Niewoehner D, Kleinerman J, Rice D: Pathologic changes in the peripheral airways of young cigarette smokers. N Engl J Med 291:755–758, 1974.

162. Myers JL, Veal CF, Shin MS, Katzenstein ALA: Respiratory bronchiolitis causing interstitial lung disease: A clinicopathologic study of six cases. Am Rev Respir Dis 135:880–884, 1987.

163. Bedrossian CW, Kuhn MC III, Luna MA, et al: Desquamative interstitial pneumonia-like reaction accompanying pulmonary lesions. Chest 72:166–169, 1977.

164. Liebow AA, Steer A, Billingsley JG: Desquamative interstitial pneumonia. Am J Med 39:369–404, 1965.

165. Gaensler EA, Goff AM, Prowse CM: Desquamative interstitial pneumonia. N Engl J Med 274:113–128, 1966.

166. Olson J, Colby TV, Elliott CG: Hamman-Rich syndrome revisited. Mayo Clin Proc 65:1538–1548, 1990.

167. Hamman L, Rich AR: Acute diffuse interstitial fibrosis of the lungs. Bull Johns Hopkins Hosp 74:177–212, 1944.

168. Primack SL, Hartman TE, Ikezoe J, et al: Acute interstitial pneumonia: Radiographic and CT findings in nine patients. Radiology 188:817–820, 1993.

169. Vourlekis JS, Brown KK, Cool CD, et al: Acute interstitial pneumonitis: Case series and review of the literature. Medicine 79:369–378, 2000.

170. Askin FB: Acute interstitial pneumonia: Histopathologic patterns of acute lung injury and the Hamman-Rich syndrome revisited. Radiology 188:620–621, 1993.

171. Katzenstein AL, Bloor CM, Leibow AA: Diffuse alveolar damage—the role of oxygen, shock, and related factors. A review. Am J Pathol 85:209–228, 1976.

172. Blennerhassett JB: Shock lung and diffuse alveolar damage: Pathological and pathogenetic considerations. Pathology 17:239–247, 1985.

173. Cooper JAD Jr, White DA, Matthay RA: Drug-induced pulmonary disease. Part 1: Cytotoxic drugs. Am Rev Respir Dis 133:321–340, 1986.

174. Leslie KO, Colby TV, Swensen SJ: Anatomic distribution and histopathologic patterns of interstitial lung disease. In Schwarz MI, King TE Jr (eds): Interstitial Lung Diseases (4th ed). Hamilton, Ontario, Canada: BC Decker, 2003, pp 1–30.

175. Zapol WM, Trelstad RL, Coffey JW, et al: Pulmonary fibrosis in severe acute respiratory failure. Am Rev Respir Dis 119:547–554, 1979.

176. Churg A, Golden J, Fligiel S, Hogg JC: Bronchopulmonary dysplasia in the adult. Am Rev Respir Dis 127:117–120, 1983.

177. Wright L, King TE Jr: Cryptogenic organizing pneumonia (idiopathic bronchiolitis obliterans organizing pneumonia): An update. Clin Pulm Med 4:152–158, 1997.

178. Epler GR, Colby TV, McLoud TC, et al: Bronchiolitis obliterans organizing pneumonia. N Engl J Med 312:152–158, 1985.

179. Chandler PW, Shin MS, Friedman SE, et al: Radiographic manifestations of bronchiolitis obliterans with organizing pneumonia versus usual interstitial pneumonia. AJR Am J Roentgenol 147:899–906, 1986.

180. Muller NL, Guerry-Force ML, Staples CA, et al: Differential diagnosis of bronchiolitis obliterans with organizing pneumonia and usual interstitial pneumonia: Clinical, functional, and radiologic findings. Radiology 162(1 Pt 1):151–156, 1987.

181. Davison AG, Heard BE, McAllister WAC, Turner-Warwick MEH: Cryptogenic organizing pneumonitis. Q J Med 52:382–394, 1983.

182. Bartter T, Irwin RS, Nash G, et al: Idiopathic bronchiolitis obliterans organizing pneumonia with peripheral infiltrates on chest roentgenogram. Arch Intern Med 149:273–279, 1989.

183. Oikonomou A, Hansell DM: Organizing pneumonia: The many morphological faces. Eur Radiol 12:1486–1496, 2002.

184. Nishimura K, Itoh H: Is CT useful in differentiating between BOOP and idiopathic UIP? In Harasawa M, Fukuchi Y, Morinari H (eds): Interstitial Pneumonia of Unknown Etiology. Tokyo: University of Tokyo Press, 1989, pp 317–324.

185. Muller NL, Staples CA, Miller RR: Bronchiolitis obliterans organizing pneumonia: CT features in 14 patients. AJR Am J Roentgenol 154:983–987, 1990.

186. Preidler KW, Szolar DM, Moelleken S, et al: Distribution pattern of computed tomography findings in patients with bronchiolitis obliterans organizing pneumonia. Invest Radiol 31:251–255, 1996.

187. Lee JS, Lynch DA, Sharma S, et al: Organizing pneumonia: Prognostic implication of high-resolution computed tomography features. J Comput Assist Tomogr 27:260–265, 2003.

188. Katzenstein ALA, Myers JL, Prophet DW, et al: Bronchiolitis obliterans and usual interstitial pneumonia. Am J Surg Pathol 10:373–381, 1986.

189. Guerry-Force ML, Mueller NL, Wright JL, et al: A comparison of bronchiolitis obliterans with organizing pneumonia, usual interstitial pneumonia, and small airways disease. Am Rev Respir Dis 135:705–712, 1987.

190. Myers JL, Katzenstein AL: Ultrastructural evidence of alveolar epithelial injury in idiopathic bronchiolitis obliterans-organizing pneumonia. Am J Pathol 132:102–109, 1988.

191. Kuhn C III, Boldt J, King TE Jr, et al: An immunohistochemical study of architectural remodeling and connective tissue synthesis in pulmonary fibrosis. Am Rev Respir Dis 140:1693–1703, 1989.

192. Kitaichi M: Pathologic features and the classification of interstitial pneumonia of unknown etiology. Bull Chest Dis Res Inst Kyoto Univ 23:1–18, 1990.

193. Yamamoto M, Ina Y, Kitaichi M: Bronchiolitis obliterans organizing pneumonia (BOOP): Profile in Japan. *In* Harasawa M, Fukuchi Y, Morinari H (eds): Interstitial Pneumonia of Unknown Etiology. Tokyo: University of Tokyo Press, 1989, pp 61–70.

194. Cohen AJ, King TE Jr, Downey GP: Rapidly progressive bronchiolitis obliterans with organizing pneumonia. Am J Respir Crit Care Med 149:1670–1675, 1994.

195. Koss MN, Hochholzer L, Langloss JM, et al: Lymphoid interstitial pneumonia: Clinicopathological and immunopathologic findings in 18 cases. Pathology 19:178–185, 1987.

196. Ichikawa Y, Kinoshita M, Koga T, et al: Lung cyst formation in lymphocytic interstitial pneumonia: CT features. J Comput Assist Tomogr 18:745–748, 1994.

197. Johkoh T, Ichikado K, Akira M, et al: Lymphocytic interstitial pneumonia: Follow-up CT findings in 14 patients. J Thorac Imaging 15:162–167, 2000.

198. Liebow AA, Carrington CB: Diffuse pulmonary lymphoreticular infiltrations associated with dysproteinemia. Med Clin North Am 57:809–843, 1973.

199. Turner RR, Colby TV, Doggett RS: Well differentiated lymphocytic lymphoma: A study of 47 patients with primary manifestation in the lung. Cancer 54:2088–2096, 1984.

200. Strimlan CV, Rosenow EC III, Weiland LH, Brown LR: Lymphocytic interstitial pneumonitis: A review of 13 cases. Ann Intern Med 68:616–621, 1978.

201. Nagai S, Hamada K, Shigematsu M, et al: Open-label compassionate use one year-treatment with pirfenidone to patients with chronic pulmonary fibrosis. Intern Med 41:1118–1123, 2002.

202. Behr J, Maier K, Degenkolb B, et al: Antioxidative and clinical effects of high-dose *N*-acetylcysteine in fibrosing alveolitis: Adjunctive therapy to maintenance immunosuppression. Am J Respir Crit Care Med 156:1897–1901, 1997.

54

The Lungs and Connective Tissue Diseases

R.M. du Bois, M.D., A.U. Wells, M.D.

INTRODUCTION

The lung may be involved in all connective tissue diseases.[1,1a] The involvement is often subclinical, but its true extent may be masked by exercise limitation due to musculoskeletal features of the connective tissue disease. Patterns of lung involvement vary considerably within each connective tissue disease. The differential diagnosis is made even wider by inclusion of the drug-induced pulmonary reactions (Table 54.1) and the opportunistic infections secondary to therapy for the lung disease (Table 54.2), which may present with features indistinguishable from diffuse lung disease.

It is not surprising that the lung is involved frequently in connective tissue diseases because these are systemic syndromes, but it is disappointing that little is known about the true incidence and prevalence of lung disease because of the dearth of well-controlled prospective, unselected series. Imprecision of nomenclature has also confused the issue. With this background, the aims of this chapter are to highlight the ways in which the lung may be involved in the most common connective tissue diseases and to indicate, when appropriate, the most usual pattern of lung disease for each connective tissue disease, with an emphasis on approaches to diagnosis and efficient management.

SYSTEMIC SCLEROSIS (SCLERODERMA)

The preliminary criteria for classification of systemic sclerosis (SSc) require that one major or two or more of three minor criteria be present (Table 54.3).[2] The skin changes may affect the entire extremity or the face, neck, and trunk (thorax and abdomen). Scleroderma is traditionally classified on the basis of skin disease extent. Limited disease can involve the face, but the trunk and limbs proximal to the elbows and knees are spared. Diffuse disease can involve any part of the body.

EPIDEMIOLOGY AND RISK FACTORS

The incidence of SSc is approximately 2 to 20 per 100,000 population per year, with a peak incidence in the fourth to sixth decades. The prevalence is 30 to 120 per 100,000 population, with a 3:1 to 8:1 female preponderance.[3] Mortality rates have been remarkably consistent over the years, varying from 0.9 to 1.5 per million for men and 2.1 to 3.8 per million for women in the United States. The disease occurs worldwide. Although scleroderma clusters in families with other autoimmune disease, there are very few reports of first-degree relatives having SSc. Genetic involvement in the disease has been determined by the identification of chromosomal abnormalities[4] and by studies of the major histocompatibility complex genes.[5] Although many of the early studies were serologic, more recently polymerase chain reaction technology has been employed. With this latter approach, an association between diffuse lung disease and human leukocyte antigens HLA-DR3, HLA-DR52a, HLA-DRB1*11, and HLA-DPB1*1301 has been recognized.[6]

PULMONARY MANIFESTATIONS

More is known about the pulmonary complications of SSc than any other connective tissue disease. Pulmonary

Table 54.1 Drug Toxicity: Patterns of Lung Disease That Have Been Reported as Adverse Effects of Drugs Commonly Used to Treat Connective Tissue Diseases

Pulmonary Effect	Penicillamine	Methotrexate	Gold	Cyclophosphamide	Sulfasalazine
Hypersensitivity pneumonitis		+	+		
Pulmonary infiltrate with eosinophilia		+	+		+
Interstitial pulmonary fibrosis			+	+	
Obliterative bronchiolitis	+		+		
Organizing pneumonia	+	+	+		+
Pleural effusion, thickening		+		+	+
Alveolar hemorrhage, vasculitis	+				+

Table 54.2 Immunosuppressive Therapy: Common Drugs Used in the Treatment of the Major Pulmonary Complications of Connective Tissue Diseases

Drug	Dose	Duration	Comments	Monitoring
Azathioprine	2.5 mg/kg/day Max 200 mg/day	Continuous	Maximal effect may not be evident for 6–9 months but has better adverse effect profile than cyclophosphamide. May be used long term. Starting dose 50 mg daily with monitoring full blood count in case of thiopurine methyltransferase deficiency; maintenance dose from 1 mo.	Full blood count Liver function tests
Cyclophosphamide Oral IV	2 mg/kg/day 15 mg/kg monthly for 1–6 mo	Variable Variable	Intravenous therapy for rapid induction of remission at 2–4 mg/kg/day for 3–4 days, especially for vasculitis. Pulsed IV cyclophosphamide may be given at 1- to 3-month intervals with better adverse effect profile and lower long-term cumulative dose, particularly in nonvasculitic disease. Oral cyclophosphamide may be used continuously or substituted at 3 months for azathioprine because of more favorable adverse effect profile in DLD.	Full blood count Liver function tests Urinalysis for blood
Cyclosporin A	5 mg/kg/day	Continuous	Bioavailability variable, thus blood monitoring necessary. May be used in combination with prednisolone.	Blood pressure Urea and creatinine Cyclosporin level
Methotrexate	7.5–25 mg/wk	Continuous	Little information to support use except as second-line therapy after first-line treatment. Pulmonary toxicity may be limiting.	Full blood count Liver function tests
Prednisolone	1 mg/kg/day or 20 mg alternate days	Continuous	Prednisolone used alone in high dose for cellular DLD and then titrated to control. In conjunction with immunosuppressants, the low-dose regimen is used.	Blood pressure Blood glucose Weight Bone densitometry
Methylprednisolone IV	500–1000 mg daily	3–5 days	Used for aggressive induction of remission, particularly for vasculitis or acute pneumonitis, then followed by maintenance therapy of prednisolone or prednisolone plus immunosuppressive agent.	

DLD, diffuse lung disease; IV, intravenous(ly).

involvement has emerged as the major cause of excess morbidity and mortality in SSc. The patterns of lung disease with which systemic sclerosis may present are variable and are shown in Table 54.3.

A variety of agents are known to induce SSc-like pulmonary disease, including D-penicillamine, tryptophan, bleomycin, pentazocine, and (particularly in men) the industrial agents vinyl chloride, benzene, toluene, and trichloroethylene.[7] Silica exposure increases the odds ratio of SSc, and silicosis increases the rate even further.[8] The toxic oil syndrome, first recognized in Madrid in 1981, results from ingestion of an adulterated cooking oil containing rapeseed oil denatured with aniline.[9] This provokes a scleroderma-like syndrome with pulmonary involvement. The association with silicone breast implants is unproven.

Table 54.3 Systemic Sclerosis (Scleroderma)

Criteria for Diagnosis*

Major
  Thickening of the skin of the hands
Minor
  Sclerodactyly (i.e., the changes of the major criteria but
    limited to the fingers)
  Digital pitting scars or loss of substance from the finger
    pad: depressed areas at tips of fingers or loss of digital
    pad tissue as a result of ischemia
Bibasilar pulmonary fibrosis

Lung Manifestations

Interstitial pulmonary fibrosis
Organizing pneumonia
Isolated pulmonary vascular disease
Aspiration pneumonia (secondary to esophageal dysmotility)
Chest wall restriction

* The major or two or more minor criteria required for diagnosis.

Interstitial Pulmonary Fibrosis

Pathogenesis. Of all of the lung problems in the connective tissue diseases, most is known about the pathophysiology of interstitial pulmonary fibrosis SSc. There are several distinct, but related, aspects of pathogenesis.

Predisposition. There is good evidence that individuals are predisposed genetically to develop systemic SSc, and there are emerging markers that define risks for diffuse lung disease. Class II major histocompatibility complex associations increase the risk of interstitial pulmonary fibrosis in SSc. The relative risk is increased if the anti–deoxyribonucleic acid topoisomerase (Scl-70) antibody is present. Recent studies have shown that there is an association between Scl-70 and an allele of the major histocompatibility complex *DPB1* gene. The importance of genetics to SSc is illustrated by a study of Choctaw Indians residing in southeastern Oklahoma. The prevalence of SSc in full-blooded Choctaws is roughly 1:200, which is significantly higher than that found in non–full-blooded Choctaws (1:3000) and strikingly higher than the global prevalence of SSc in other Native Americans in Oklahoma (1:10,000).[10] The genetic susceptibility probably results in injury and an immune response. It has been shown that there are highly restricted T-cell responses to epitopes of deoxyribonucleic acid topoisomerase 1, both in healthy individuals and in those with SSc. Thus, in individuals with Scl-70–responsive T-cell clones, the autoantibody may be responsible for driving the immune response. In the lung, there is an accumulation of "memory-type" CD45 Ro lymphocytes and secondary lymphoid follicles with true germinal centers within lung biopsy samples.[11] Furthermore, the T cells present within the lung express cytokines of both the T helper 1 (Th1) and T helper 2 (Th2) subsets.[12]

Inflammation Amplification. A wide variety of cytokines identified in bronchoalveolar lavage (BAL) fluid clearly contribute to the cascade of inflammation in the lungs.[13] The most striking of these are interleukin-8 (neutrophil chemoattractant and activator), tumor necrosis factor-α (an early cytokine involved in many pathologic processes), macrophage inflammatory protein-1α (important in neutrophil chemotaxis), and RANTES (regulated on activation normal T-cell expressed and secreted; important in T-cell and eosinophil recruitment and activation). It is clear, therefore, that the downstream events of the initiation result in the release of a number of proinflammatory cytokines that are responsible for further recruitment and activation of inflammatory cells at disease sites.

Fibrogenetic Factors. The hallmark of SSc in both lung and skin is the accumulation of connective tissue matrix cells and proteins.[14,15] Many factors have been studied in this regard, and a wide variety of growth factors have been identified. Perhaps the most striking of these is connective tissue growth factor, which appears to depend on transforming growth factor-β for up-regulation and has a potent effect on collagen production, as evidenced by collagen gel retraction studies.[16–18] Transforming growth factor-β is found in high amounts in the lungs of patients with SSc.[19] Endothelin (ET)-1 and coagulation cascade proteins are also present in high amounts in BAL fluid.[15,20] Fibroblasts from patients with lung disease exhibit dysregulated type I collagen biosynthesis and impaired messenger ribonucleic acid down-regulation. The balance of ET receptors (A and B) is modified in the lungs of patients with scleroderma, with a consistent decrease in ET_A and an increase in ET_B receptors.[14,21]

A number of parallel events result in the development of lung injury and subsequent fibrosis. It is simplistic to target any one of these as being the important factor, but there seems little doubt that the key cytokines in the cascade include tumor necrosis factor-α (because it occurs very early in disease and has been shown in animal models to be a pivotal factor in lung fibrosis)[22,23] and transforming growth factor-β (which colocalizes with collagen gene up-regulation and is important in connective tissue growth factor release). The balance of Th1 to Th2 cytokines is also key because, when the shift is in favor of Th2 cytokines, such as in idiopathic pulmonary fibrosis, the prognosis is worse and there is a much higher eosinophil influx into the lung, in comparison with patients with SSc, in whom the Th1/Th2 ratio is balanced and there is less eosinophil influx per unit lung involvement.[12]

Clinical Features. The prevalence of lung disease in SSc depends on the method used for detection. Dyspnea occurs in roughly 55% of patients (range, 21% to 80%).[24] Cough, a less frequently reported symptom, tends to be dry and nonproductive. Hemoptysis is rare but may complicate carcinoma or bronchial telangiectasia.[25] Pleuritic chest pain is uncommon. Pneumothorax is even less common. Chest radiographic abnormalities are present in 25% to 67% of patients, and lung function is impaired in up to 90%, although a large subset of patients have only a minor reduction in gas transfer. The lung is involved more commonly in patients with diffuse than with limited cutaneous SSc (i.e., involving skin proximal to the elbow), but the extent of skin involvement does not correlate with lung function changes. Patients are often symptom free, even with moderate pulmonary function impairment. Digital clubbing is extremely rare. Fine crackles are heard at the lung bases and are of a "Velcro" character. Pleural rub is almost never heard. Rarely, scleroderma of the chest wall may cause extrathoracic restriction. Secondary pulmonary hypertension with appropriate clinical features of right ventricular strain, raised jugular venous pressure, and ankle edema may be seen during the terminal stages of the disease.

Lung disease may be the first manifestation of SSc. A history of Raynaud's phenomenon is often helpful. Careful examination of the capillaries in the nail beds reveals the typical feature associated with scleroderma: abnormal loops associated with capillary "dropout." The presence of autoantibodies, particularly antinuclear antibodies, is helpful in suggesting a connective tissue disease etiology (Table 54.4).

Imaging. Chest radiography typically shows a reticulonodular pattern in the lung bases and periphery in early disease. There is obvious loss of volume with more extensive reticulonodular shadowing in more advanced disease. In this situation, honeycombing may be present (Fig. 54.1A).

Computed tomography (CT) has revolutionized the interpretation of the pattern and extent of disease.[26–28a] Disease is again localized to the peripheral rim, occurring earliest at the bases and posteriorly. As disease becomes more advanced, it progresses superiorly, centrally, and anteriorly. Esophageal dilation may be apparent, which can be helpful in the diagnosis if the lung disease is the first manifestation of the systemic disease (Fig. 54.1B and 1C). The pattern may be "ground glass," (reflecting either fine intralobular fibrosis or a more cellular histopathology) or an overtly fibrotic "reticular" pattern, consisting of intersecting linear abnormalities, often associated with traction bronchiectasis. Honeycomb change is present in only a minority of cases.[28a]

CT extent correlates extremely well with lung function, particularly gas transfer. Strikingly, individuals with idiopathic pulmonary fibrosis have much more hypoxia than those with SSc once the extent of disease on CT has been taken into account.[27] The extent of individual patterns (ground glass vs. reticular) is associated with the type of inflammatory cell found in BAL. More extensive reticular (consistent with more fibrosis) disease is associated with high neutrophil numbers, and this influx therefore appears to depend on disease extent regardless of disease type.[29]

Table 54.4 Autoantibodies in Connective Tissue Disease (CTD)

CTD	Autoantibody	Target	Comments
Systemic sclerosis	Anticentromere	Centromere proteins (CENP A–F)	20–40% total SSc, wide racial variation 70–80% limited cutaneous variant with pulmonary hypertension
	Scl-70	DNA topoisomerase 1	28–70% total SSc, wide racial variation; >30% diffuse cutaneous disease with ILD
	PM-Scl	—	Scleroderma-myositis overlap syndromes
	Antinucleolar	RNA polymerase-1	8–20% SSc suggests poorest 10-yr survival, renal crisis
	Ku	DNA binding proteins	Scleroderma-myositis overlap syndromes
Rheumatoid arthritis	Rheumatoid factor	IgG	Seropositive disease more frequent with pulmonary nodules.
	Antinuclear antibody	—	—
	Histone	Histone proteins	5% rheumatoid vasculitis
SLE	dsDNA	Double-stranded DNA	50–75%, strong association with nephritis
	ANA	—	90–95%
	Ro/La	RNA transcription factors	60%/20%
	Histone	Histone proteins	>90% drug-induced lupus, 20–30% primary SLE
	Sm	—	10% whites and 30% African Americans and Chinese
	Lupus anticoagulant	Phospholipid	20–30%
MCTD	U1-RNP	Small nuclear proteins	Myositis overlap syndromes (10% SSc)
	U2-RNP	—	Myositis, SLE, SSc
DM/PM	Jo-1	Histidyl tRNA synthetase	20–30% inflammatory myopathy but 50–100% when associated with diffuse fibrosing lung disease
	PL-7	Threonyl tRNA synthetase	<3% antisynthetase syndrome
	PL-12	Alanyl tRNA synthetase	<3% antisynthetase syndrome
	EJ	Glycyl tRNA synthetase	<2% antisynthetase syndrome
	OJ	Isoleucyl tRNA synthetase	<2% antisynthetase syndrome
	Mi-2	Nuclear proteins	<8% DM, associated with acute onset of classic dermatomyositis
Antiphospholipid syndrome	Anticardiolipin	Membrane phospholipids	Disease diagnosis depends on presence of clinical features
	Lupus anticoagulant		
Relapsing polychondritis	Anticartilage	Cartilage	Unknown sensitivity
	Anticollagen	Collagen	
Sjögren's syndrome	Ro (SS-A)	RNA transcription factors	40–50% primary Sjögren's syndrome (25–30% SLE)
	La (SS-B)		50% Sjögren's (10% SLE)

ANA, antinuclear antibody; CTD, connective tissue disease; DM/PM, dermatomyositis/polymyositis; DNA, deoxyribonucleic acid; dsDNA, double-stranded deoxyribonucleic acid; IgG, immunoglobulin G; ILD, interstitial lung disease; MCTD, mixed connective tissue disease; RNA, ribonucleic acid; SSc, systemic sclerosis; SLE, systemic lupus erythematosus; tRNA, transfer ribonucleic acid.

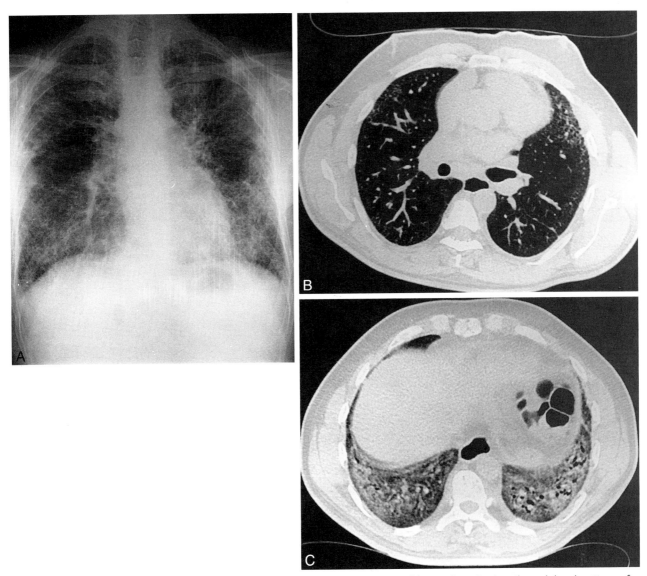

Figure 54.1 **A,** Chest radiograph from a patient with systemic sclerosis. Note the widespread predominantly peripheral pattern of reticulonodular disease. The heart borders and the diaphragm are obscured. **B,** Computed tomography (CT) scan taken at a level just below the carina in a patient with systemic sclerosis. Note the peripheral reticular pattern that in this case is more prominent anteriorly. In this patient with subtle disease, the dilated esophagus is a clue as to the true cause of the fibrosing lung disease. **C,** CT scan taken at the level of the diaphragms in a patient with more extensive interstitial pulmonary fibrosis in the context of systemic sclerosis. Note in particular the very dilated airways, indicating that the apparent ground-glass/consolidation pattern is dense fibrosis. Again, the dilated esophagus indicates that this disease is likely to be part of systemic sclerosis.

Gallium scans provide no added value. Technetium-99m–labeled diethylenetriaminepentaacetic acid clearance has been used in some medical centers to identify early disease and to predict prognosis.[30] A more rapid clearance of this isotope is indicative of a loss of epithelial cell integrity, and rapid clearance indicates uptake from the air space into the circulation. A persistently rapid clearance rate confers an increased risk of subsequent lung function deterioration, and a persistently normal clearance rate predicts lung function stability.

Lung Function Tests. The interstitial pulmonary fibrosis of SSc is characterized by a restrictive ventilatory defect of mechanical function, which results in reduced pulmonary compliance, vital capacity, and total lung capacity. Residual volume is decreased. Diffusing capacity for carbon monoxide (DL_{CO}) is reduced and may be the only abnormality in early disease. Blood gas analysis usually reveals a reduced arterial PO_2 with a normal or low arterial PCO_2. Hypoxia is usually not marked until very late in the disease process.

There have been a number of studies of rate of change of lung function in SSc.[31,32] In one study, 27 of 38 patients lost more than 30 mL of vital capacity per year (the normal rate of decline). A second study showed that vital capacity loss was greater in patients who had evidence of an active alveolitis on BAL. Rates of decline are often higher within 2 years of onset of SSc, emphasizing the importance of identifying lung disease early.

Exercise lung function testing increases ventilation-perfusion mismatching and also increases diffusion abnormalities so that hypoxia results with widening of the alveolar-arterial gradient. Minute ventilation increases generally as a consequence of increased ventilation rate rather than tidal volume. Dead space ventilation may increase on exercise, with a rise in the dead space–to–tidal volume ratio. For a given degree of lung involvement defined by CT, abnormalities on exercise gas exchange are worse in patients with idiopathic pulmonary fibrosis than in those with interstitial pulmonary fibrosis in association with SSc.

Bronchoalveolar Lavage. BAL is a useful tool for identifying alveolitis in systemic sclerosis before the onset of pulmonary symptoms.[33] A neutrophil alveolitis has been described by some authors to predict more progressive disease.[32,34,35] However, it has been shown that an increase in neutrophils reflects an increase in the extent of disease on CT, particularly the reticular pattern, and this increase is therefore likely a marker of more extensive disease rather than an independent index of progressive disease.[29]

BAL should not be used alone to determine whether treatment should be started. Many patients with apparently normal BAL findings may exhibit progressive disease. Similarly, BAL provides no added value for monitoring disease.

Biopsy. If the pattern of disease is at all atypical after review of the less invasive indices, lung biopsy is necessary. No extra information is obtained by a transbronchial biopsy, and surgical biopsy is required in this situation. Examples of circumstances in which biopsy is indicated include an unusual pattern of disease on CT, marked pleural disease, and more than 20% lymphocytes on BAL. Pathologically, the most common pattern is nonspecific interstitial pneumonia, with thickening of the alveolar walls with inflammatory cells (mononuclear cells, granulocytes, and plasma cells), connective tissue matrix cells, and proteins combined with intra-alveolar inflammation (predominantly by macrophages), type II pneumocyte proliferation, and vascular obliteration. The distribution is subpleural and basal and is maximal in posterior segments, with the macroscopic findings of the lung surface taking on a fine nodular, "cirrhotic" appearance in the early stages and honeycombing with more advanced disease.[36] This pattern differs from usual interstitial pneumonia in exhibiting a homogeneous pattern of pathology. Much less commonly, the usual interstitial pneumonia pattern of histopathology is seen. One of the hallmarks of usual interstitial pneumonia is a heterogeneous appearance, with normal alveoli seen in the same section as areas of extensive alveolar remodeling.[36a] These pathologic differences may denote disease subsets with differences in outcome. Electron microscopy shows early endothelial and epithelial cell injury, even without abnormalities on light microscopy. Autopsy studies show diffuse lung disease in up to 80% of cases and pulmonary vascular disease in up to 30%.

In some patients with a more accelerated course of disease, histopathologic examination has shown a diffuse alveolar damage pattern.[37]

Serologic Investigations. Although SSc is traditionally defined on the basis of the extent of the skin disease as outlined previously, the pattern of autoantibodies appears to be a much stronger determinant of the associated internal organ involvement.[5,38–41]

Antinuclear antibodies are found in 90% to 100% of patients with SSc (roughly 30% of normal individuals have antinuclear antibodies at a titer of 1:40). Three major autoantibodies include anticentromere, occurring in 57% of patients with limited cutaneous disease; anti-topoisomerase (Scl-70), occurring in 40% of patients with diffuse disease; and PM-Scl, occurring in a small fraction of cases in association with the polymyositis overlap syndrome. It is rare to have both Scl-70 and anticentromere antibodies. Diffuse lung disease is rare in the presence of anticentromere antibodies, and a protective role for this autoantibody has been argued but not substantiated. Interstitial pulmonary fibrosis is strongly associated with the Scl-70 antibody and with diffuse scleroderma. Limited cutaneous disease associates with vascular disease and the anticentromere antibody. Both forms of lung disease may progress to pulmonary hypertension. Other autoantibody studies that have shown associations with organ involvement include a nucleolar pattern with diffuse lung disease; the antibody B23 that recognizes this nucleolar phosphoprotein with pulmonary hypertension and is associated with the presence of the antifibrillarin antibody; and anti-Th/To antibodies with "intrinsic" pulmonary hypertension and diffuse lung disease.

Prognosis. The prognosis of interstitial pulmonary fibrosis in SSc depends on the extent of disease at presentation. Worse lung function, particularly vital capacity and DL_{CO}, indicates a poorer outcome, and similar observations have been made based on extent of disease on CT as the criterion. Several studies have shown an increased decline in lung function in patients with interstitial pulmonary fibrosis compared with normal individuals.[31,32] Although crude mortality rates are 3.9% per year for men and 2.6% per year for women, lung disease remains the most common cause of death in patients with SSc.[42] In one series of causes of death, lung disease was the most common, accounting for 21% of all deaths. There is also an increased risk of lung cancer in SSc.[43]

Treatment. There are reports of a wide variety of treatments for interstitial pulmonary fibrosis in SSc.[44,44a] Most of these include immunosuppression. However, none of these studies has been a properly controlled prospective randomized investigation. Despite this, there is a consensus in published reports of an advantage of treatment with cyclophosphamide, together with prednisolone, to improve lung function and prognosis.[45,46] Until recently, the treatment regimen used most commonly involved moderately low dosages of prednisolone at 10 mg/day or 20 mg every other day, together with cyclophosphamide at 2 mg/kg/day orally up to a maximum of 150 mg. Close scrutiny with full blood counts, liver function tests, and urine testing for evidence of hemorrhagic cystitis is needed. However, in three recent studies, including more than 60 patients, intravenous cyclophosphamide (750 to 1000 mg/m²) was administered at 2- to 4-week intervals for 6 to 12 months, with good circumstantial evidence of efficacy, as judged by CT and pulmonary function data.[47] The question of *Pneumocystis* prophylaxis is not resolved. Some medical centers use cotrimoxazole three times a week if immunosuppressive agents are being given. A recent study of interferon-α showed a greater deterioration in lung function at 1 year than with placebo.[48]

It has recently been observed that steroid therapy is associated with scleroderma renal crisis, both with high-dose therapy[49] and, more recently, with prednisolone doses of less than 10 mg daily.[50] However, confounding by severity cannot be excluded, as patients with more aggressive systemic disease are more likely to receive corticosteroids, although occasional cases of renal crisis are undoubtedly linked to high-dose corticosteroid therapy. Thus, low-dose steroid therapy remains justified as an invaluable adjunct to the treatment of lung disease, although renal function should be monitored from time to time.

End-stage lung disease has been treated with single-lung transplantation provided there is no evidence of disease activity in other organs. There appears to be no greater mortality in this group than in individuals with primary diffuse lung disease. In terminal disease that is not amenable for transplantation, consideration must be given to regular oxygen therapy, treatment of supervening heart failure, and infection.

Pulmonary Vascular Disease in Systemic Sclerosis

Unlike the other connective tissue diseases, vascular involvement in SSc is caused by concentric fibrosis of small arterioles replacing the normal intima and media, but the plexiform lesions and fibrinoid necrosis of primary pulmonary hypertension are not seen. Isolated vascular disease occurs mainly in the limited form of SSc. Associated features are those of the CREST syndrome (calcinosis, Raynaud's phenomenon, esophageal dysmotility, sclerodactyly, and telangiectasias) with prominent telangiectasia, esophageal disease, abnormal nail fold capillaries (dilated capillaries and dropout of capillary loops), and a positive anticentromere antibody. Chest radiography, CT scanning, and BAL are all normal. Lung function studies show an isolated fall in DL_{CO}. When damage to the pulmonary vascular bed is extensive (gas transfer <50% of predicted), the risk of pulmonary hypertension increases.[51] Mortality rates are increased with increasing pulmonary hypertension.[52]

Diethylenetriaminepentaacetic acid clearance measurements are usually normal in patients with pure pulmonary vascular disease in scleroderma and help to differentiate vascular disease from early diffuse disease in patients with an isolated fall in DL_{CO}.

Doppler echocardiography is a good measure of pulmonary hypertension.[53] It has been shown to correlate with measurements of pulmonary artery pressures made at right heart catheterization but is noninvasive. However, it is more inaccurate at borderline and mild levels of pulmonary hypertension. Qualitative features found on echocardiography may also suggest pulmonary hypertension in the absence of a tricuspid regurgitant jet, precluding measurement of the gradient across the tricuspid valve and thus an estimate of pulmonary artery pressure. These include right ventricular dilation and right ventricular hypertrophy.

Optimal treatment of pulmonary vascular disease in SSc has not been defined. Calcium channel antagonists may be helpful, but often the dosage required to improve pulmonary vasculature causes unacceptable drops in left-sided pressures and peripheral edema. Angiotensin-converting enzyme inhibitors can be helpful. The most promising approach at present is the use of intravenous prostacy-

clin.[54,55] Exact dosage regimens need to be validated, but in acute studies and longer term evaluation, improvements in pulmonary vascular resistance, pulmonary pressures, and, importantly, 6-minute walk distances have been shown. The oral endothelin receptor antagonist bosentan has also been shown in two studies to improve exercise capacity and hemodynamics.[56,57]

Other Pulmonary Complications

Aspiration pneumonia is extremely uncommon, particularly considering the prevalence of esophageal dysfunction in SSc. Pleural disease is uncommon. Rarely, the extent of skin tightness over the chest wall produces an extrinsic restriction of ventilation. Occasionally, the first manifestation of pulmonary parenchymal disease is organizing pneumonia. This responds well to corticosteroid therapy, as does organizing pneumonia in other contexts.

RHEUMATOID ARTHRITIS

The American Rheumatism Association revised criteria for the classification of rheumatoid arthritis (RA) require that at least four of the criteria listed in Table 54.5 be satisfied for a minimum of 6 weeks.[58]

EPIDEMIOLOGY AND RISK FACTORS

The reported incidence of RA ranges from 0.2 to 3.0/1000 person-years (<0.5/1000 person-years in most surveys), with a rising incidence with increasing age into the seventh

---

Table 54.5   Rheumatoid Arthritis

Criteria for Diagnosis*
Morning stiffness (lasting at least 1 h)
Arthritis (soft-tissue swelling or fluid) of three or more joints (PIP, MCP, wrist, elbow, knee, ankle, MTP joints)
Arthritis of hand joints (swelling of at least one wrist, MCP, or PIP joint)
Symmetrical arthritis (i.e., simultaneous arthritis of the same joints on both sides of the body)
Rheumatoid nodules
Serum rheumatoid factor positivity (at a level such that <5% of normal controls are positive)
Radiographic hand or wrist changes typical of rheumatoid arthritis

Lung Manifestations
Interstitial pulmonary fibrosis
Organizing pneumonia
Obliterative bronchiolitis
Follicular bronchiolitis
Bronchiectasis
Vasculitis
Nodules
Pleural disease
Lymphocytic interstitial pneumonia
Drug induced

* At least four criteria for a minimum of 6 weeks.
MCP, metacarpophalangeal; MTP, metatarsophalangeal; PIP, proximal interphalangeal.

decade. In adult whites, the prevalence of RA ranges from 0.5% to 2%, with a male-to-female ratio between 1:2 and 1:4. Depending on disease severity (as judged by disability scales and the need for long-term corticosteroid therapy), the age-matched mortality rate of RA is up to twofold higher than in the general population. The prevalence of RA is similar throughout the world. Evidence in support of a genetic predisposition includes familial and twin clustering and associations between RA and HLA-DRB1 alleles.[59] Hormonal factors may play a role, judging from the female preponderance of RA and a reduced incidence during pregnancy. Infectious agents and socioeconomic factors have not been shown to be etiologically important.

PULMONARY MANIFESTATIONS

Pleuropulmonary manifestations are multiple and are listed in Table 54.5.

Interstitial Pulmonary Fibrosis

The interstitial pulmonary fibrosis of RA has a male predominance (male-to-female ratio, 3:1)[60] and is histologically similar to idiopathic pulmonary fibrosis. Smoking is a risk factor for the development of overt pulmonary fibrosis in RA[61] and has also been associated with subclinical disease.[62] High titers of rheumatoid factor[61] and the presence of rheumatoid nodules[63,64] are also associated with an increased prevalence of pulmonary fibrosis in RA.

In early disease, a lymphocytic interstitial infiltrate is often the predominant abnormality,[65] and prominent peribronchiolar follicles, containing aggregates of lymphocytes with germinal centers, are often seen.[66] In long-standing disease, fibrosis predominates, often resulting in cystic changes or honeycombing. It is difficult to estimate the exact prevalence of sub-categories of interstitial pulmonary fibrosis because, in historical series, histologic descriptions of "interstitial fibrosis" have not been detailed. However, recent data suggest that non-specific interstitial pneumonia and usual interstitial pneumonia are present in significant proportions of patients with interstitial fibrosis.[66a] However, it seems that usual interstitial pneumonia is associated with a much better outcome in connective tissue disease than in an idiopathic setting.[66b] Minor pulmonary fibrosis is common in RA; in one open-lung biopsy series performed in volunteers with RA (some without clinical evidence of interstitial lung disease), pulmonary fibrosis was seen in 60% of patients.[67] Reductions in DL_{CO} are found in 40% of unselected RA patients.[68] However, radiologically overt pulmonary fibrosis is found in only 1% to 5% of RA patients (based on three large chest radiographic series).[61,63,69] In the largest prospective series reported to date, 150 consecutive patients were screened for pulmonary disease. Of these, 19% had CT evidence of interstitial fibrosis, which was often subtle; 43% of those with interstitial abnormalities also had emphysematous bullae (previous or current smoking history). Chest radiography identified abnormalities in only 14% of the whole cohort, but physiologic abnormalities were seen in 82% (gas transfer) and 14% (restrictive pattern of ventilatory defect).[70]

Severe progressive disease requiring hospitalization may be associated with cor pulmonale and respiratory failure and

has a poor prognosis, with a 5-year survival rate of less than 50%[71]; however, a large subgroup of patients have more indolent disease that progresses little during prolonged follow-up. A strong predictor of decline is a gas transfer less than 55% of predicted at presentation.[72] The most frequent symptom is exertional dyspnea, although this may be masked by a general loss of mobility due to systemic disease. The clinical picture is usually identical to that of idiopathic pulmonary fibrosis, with bilateral, predominantly basal crackles and tachypnea, cyanosis, and right heart failure in advanced disease. Finger clubbing, which is occasionally striking, is more prevalent than in other connective tissue diseases.

Organizing Pneumonia

Organizing pneumonia (bronchiolitis obliterans with organizing pneumonia) is characterized by plugs of granulation tissue in the air spaces distal to and including the terminal bronchioles, associated with lymphocytic infiltration within well-preserved bronchiolar walls and the surrounding lung interstitium. The term *bronchiolitis obliterans with organizing pneumonia* has caused confusion among clinicians,[73] stimulating the recent use of the term *proliferative bronchiolitis*.[74] Organizing pneumonia has a very different profile from the entity of bronchiolitis obliterans (also found in RA), with a clinical presentation of pneumonia (as opposed to airflow obstruction), multifocal consolidation on chest radiograph and CT, a restrictive functional defect, and a much higher chance of responsiveness to corticosteroids than bronchiolitis obliterans (with a good outcome in 15 of the first 17 reported cases) (Fig. 54.2).[75] Organizing pneumonia is more common in RA than in other connective tissue diseases (with the possible exception of polymyositis). In a series of 40 patients with RA undergoing open-lung biopsy, organizing pneumonia (6 cases) had a prevalence similar to interstitial fibrosis (5 cases),[76] although organizing pneumonia might have been overrepresented due to an acute presentation (and thus a perceived need to reach a definitive histologic diagnosis). The good prognosis generally seen in organizing pneumonia has been emphasized in the medical literature, but a minority of RA patients progress to respiratory failure and death despite treatment.

Obliterative Bronchiolitis

Obliterative bronchiolitis (OB; synonymous with bronchiolitis obliterans and constrictive bronchiolitis) (Fig. 54.3) is characterized histologically by destruction of the bronchiolar wall by granulation tissue, effacement of the lumen, and eventual replacement of the bronchiole by fibrous tissue. There is circumstantial evidence to suggest that OB may be preceded by an inflammatory exudate; prominent bronchiolar inflammation may be found in patients with the shortest symptomatic course.[77] OB in RA has now been described in numerous case reports and small series. The expression of HLA antigens B40 and DR1 is increased in OB associated with RA (but not in isolated OB).[78] In early descriptions, the hallmark of OB was a rapidly progressive, often fatal course; however, as clinician awareness of the disease was then low, patients with advanced and progressive disease

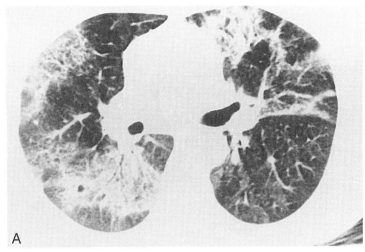

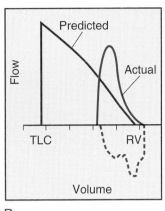

B

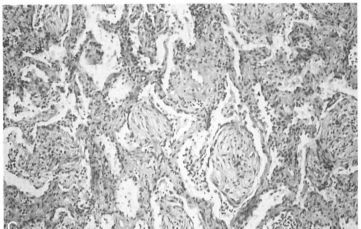

Figure 54.2 **A,** Computed tomography scan from a patient with rheumatoid arthritis and organizing pneumonia. Note the pattern of air space consolidation that is bilateral. **B,** A flow-volume loop from the same patient as in **A.** The flow-volume loop is shifted to the right by comparison with the ideal predicted loop, but the flow rates are relatively well preserved. RV, residual volume; TLC, total lung capacity. **C,** Surgical lung biopsy specimen from a patient with organizing pneumonia in the context of rheumatoid arthritis. The alveoli and respiratory bronchioles are filled with loosely packed connective tissue.

were undoubtedly overrepresented. There is great heterogeneity in the speed of progression, with some patients having indolent disease[79]; the use of CT in RA patients with suspected pulmonary complications has now identified a subgroup with occult bronchiolitis, often admixed with interstitial lung disease. The prevalence of unsuspected OB in unselected RA patients remains uncertain, with unexplained airflow obstruction identified in a significant minority (including many nonsmokers) in one study[80] but no increase in the prevalence of pulmonary function abnormalities suggestive of isolated small airway disease in two subsequent controlled series.[81,82]

Two major associations with the development of OB in RA have been reported. It is likely that secondary Sjögren's syndrome is an important predisposing factor, being associated with OB in five of six RA patients in one series[79]; the spectrum of histologic abnormalities in these cases, ranging from peribronchiolar lymphocytic infiltration to small airway destruction, was analogous to changes seen in the parotid gland in Sjögren's syndrome. As the presence or absence of Sjögren's syndrome is not documented in many case reports of OB in RA, the etiologic importance of Sjögren's syndrome remains uncertain.

More contentious is the reported association between OB and the use of penicillamine, first reported in the late 1970s.[83] After a number of case reports and small series, a significantly higher prevalence of OB was identified in RA patients who took penicillamine (3 of 133) than in other RA patients (0 of 469) in a large cohort.[77] It is possible that the development of OB and the use of penicillamine are both markers of more aggressive RA and are linked for this reason; however, OB developed less than 1 year after penicillamine was begun in 19 of the first 20 cases,[77] and thus the association is unlikely to be entirely spurious. As OB has been reported in many RA patients not taking penicillamine, it is likely that an underlying predisposition to OB in RA is unmasked by penicillamine (which disrupts collagen linkage and thus interferes with tissue repair).[84] A relationship between OB and gold therapy has been suggested[85] but is not endorsed by recent clinical experience.

Follicular Bronchiolitis

Follicular bronchiolitis (FB) is characterized by external compression of bronchioles by hyperplastic lymphoid follicles, with variable lymphocytic infiltration of the bronchiolar wall. FB is associated more commonly with RA than with other connective tissue disease[86] and is often found incidentally at lung biopsy in RA patients with interstitial pulmonary fibrosis. No causative mechanism has been identified, and it is unclear whether FB predisposes to the

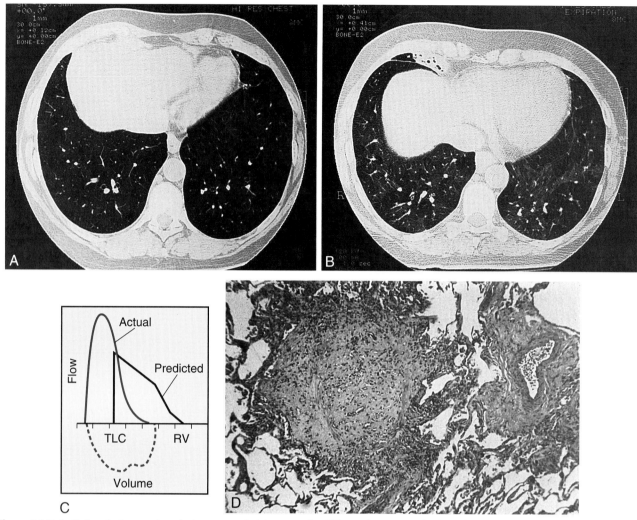

Figure 54.3 **A–C,** Inspiratory and expiratory computed tomography (CT) sections were obtained from a patient with rheumatoid arthritis with obliterative bronchiolitis. **A,** The inspiratory image is essentially normal. **B,** On the expiratory CT scan, there is extensive regional inhomogeneity, the reduced density resulting from regional vasoconstriction or regional gas trapping. **C,** A flow-volume curve from the same patient as in **A** and **B** shows marked elevation of total lung capacity (TLC) and residual volume (RV) associated with characteristic concavity of the expiratory limb, indicating airflow obstruction. **D,** Surgical lung biopsy specimen from a patient with obliterative bronchiolitis. A slitlike residual orifice is visible, but otherwise the whole of this terminal bronchiole is effaced by dense fibrous tissue. Note that the surrounding alveoli are normal.

subsequent development of OB. When found in isolation, FB simulates interstitial lung disease, with reticular or reticulonodular abnormalities on chest radiography and a pattern of functional impairment that may be restrictive or obstructive. Clinically significant isolated FB is rare in RA, but its recognition is important because a response to corticosteroid therapy, although not the rule, is much more likely than in OB; in six of the first nine reported cases, disease stabilized or regressed with treatment.[75] In a CT study of patients with histopathologically proven follicular bronchiolitis, the most prominent features were centrilobular and peribronchial nodules together with patchy ground-glass increases in attenuation in a bronchocentric distribution.[87]

Bronchiectasis

The prevalence of bronchiectasis is higher in RA than in other connective tissue diseases (Fig. 54.4). A recent liter-ature review identified 289 patients with bronchiectasis associated with RA reported since 1928; however, as respiratory symptoms preceded the systemic manifestations of RA in 90%, it is likely that chance association accounts for a high proportion of early reported cases.[88] Although associated with long-standing RA in one study,[89] bronchiectasis was found on CT in 30% of 50 RA patients with normal chest radiographs on prospective evaluation.[90] Bronchiectasis in RA is not associated with more aggressive systemic disease and is often clinically silent, with little or no sputum production and a less progressive and disabling course than in patients with idiopathic bronchiectasis.

Pulmonary Vasculitis

It is surprising that pulmonary vasculitis is reported only rarely in RA given the relatively high prevalence of systemic vasculitis in the disease. Pulmonary hypertension resulting

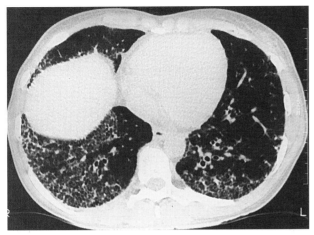

Figure 54.4 Computed tomography scan taken at the level of the diaphragm in a patient with rheumatoid arthritis. The typical reticular pattern of fibrosing alveolitis in the context of rheumatoid arthritis can be seen in the right lung. In the left lung there are similar but less advanced changes. In addition, and notably remote from the fibrotic areas, there are airways that are clearly bronchiectatic.

from pulmonary vascular disease (as opposed to extensive pulmonary fibrosis) is uncommon, although occasional cases of pulmonary vasculitis have been found at autopsy.[86] Similarly, diffuse alveolar hemorrhage is a rare complication of RA.

Pulmonary Rheumatoid Nodules

Pulmonary rheumatoid nodules may be single or multiple, are found on chest radiography in less than 1% of RA patients,[64] and are usually associated with rheumatoid nodules elsewhere in the body,[91] although they occasionally precede the development of systemic disease. Nodules are well circumscribed, with central necrotic material contained by palisading epithelioid cells and surrounded by fibrosis and lymphocytic infiltration. Nodule cavitation occasionally causes hemoptysis, and pneumothorax may result from the rupture of subpleural nodules. Diffuse infiltration by small nodules leading to respiratory failure has been reported.[92] However, nodules generally present as asymptomatic abnormalities on chest radiography and may vary in size according to underlying rheumatoid activity; thus, when solitary, their growth as judged by chest radiography may simulate malignancy.[93] Caplan's syndrome consists of the association of single or multiple nodules with coal worker's pneumoconiosis,[94] which is often trivial, in keeping with the suggestion that nodule formation results from a hypersensitivity reaction to inhaled coal dust perhaps amplified by immunologic overactivity.

Pleural Disease

Pleural disease is seen at autopsy in approximately 50% of patients,[64] and 20% give a history of pleuritic chest pain.[95] However, pleural effusions are found in less than 5%,[61,63] usually in men,[91] and are frequently asymptomatic, often being identified on routine chest radiography. In a minority, pleuritic pain and fever are prominent, and the exclu-

sion of empyema (which may be more prevalent in RA[96]) is required. Occasionally, effusions may develop acutely in association with pericarditis or exacerbations of arthritis; more typically, radiographic abnormalities are chronic, often remaining unchanged for years.[97] The fluid is an exudate, with a low glucose level (correlating poorly with serum glucose),[98] a low pH, and, usually, a predominant lymphocytosis (although a neutrophilia is occasionally found). Pleural fluid rheumatoid factor levels tend to mirror serum levels and have little independent diagnostic value.

Other Pulmonary Complications

Other pulmonary complications of RA are rare. Lymphocytic interstitial pneumonia is an occasional finding at lung biopsy[99] and responds variably to corticosteroid therapy. Apical fibrosis mimicking the lung disease of ankylosing spondylitis has been reported.[100] Extensive apical cavitation in the absence of nodules or other causes of fibrocavitary disease (including tuberculosis) has been described in a handful of cases and may follow a fulminant course.[101] Lower respiratory tract infection is increased in frequency in RA; bronchopneumonia is a common terminal event, accounting for 15% to 20% of deaths in RA patients.[102,103]

DRUG-INDUCED PULMONARY DISEASE

Drug-induced pulmonary disease is a particular problem in RA because of the widespread use of methotrexate in routine clinical practice, and it has been reported in 3% to 18% of RA patients treated with methotrexate.[104,105] In a 2-year prospective study, lung function tests and CT were used to monitor 55 patients who received methotrexate in comparison with 73 who did not. No significant differences were observed between the groups.[106] Methotrexate pneumonitis is potentially life-threatening. It presents with cough, dyspnea, fever, widespread crackles, and pulmonary infiltrates on chest radiography and CT, which may be focal or diffuse.[107] Although the presentation is sometimes explosive, more often the onset is subacute (with symptoms evolving for up to 2 months before diagnosis[107]); 50% of cases are diagnosed within 4 months of initiation of methotrexate therapy. As the clinical and radiographic features are nonspecific, methotrexate-induced lung disease should always be suspected in the treated patient presenting with progressive lung disease. Unfortunately, histologic findings are nonspecific, although prominent lymphocytic infiltration increases the probability of a methotrexate-injured lung.[108] There is conflicting evidence on whether preexisting lung disease predisposes to lung injury caused by methotrexate, but the published evidence does not suggest that functional impairment is an absolute contraindication to its use (although particular caution is warranted when pulmonary reserve is grossly compromised, and patients with previous methotrexate toxicity should not be re-treated).[107,109] Pulmonary methotrexate toxicity is associated with a mortality rate of 15% to 20%[107]; as the lymphocytic component of disease is wholly or partially reversible, immediate withdrawal of methotrexate and the early institution of steroid therapy are warranted.

Pulmonary toxicity in RA has also been documented with sulfasalazine, gold therapy, and penicillamine (discussed earlier). Pulmonary infiltrates (due to organizing pneumonia) associated with sulfasalazine occur most commonly in the upper lobes; this side effect is rare in RA, with only a handful of cases reported (most cases occurred in ulcerative colitis).[110] Pulmonary disease induced by gold takes the form of alveolar opacities adjacent to bronchovascular bundles, best demonstrated by high-resolution CT, and often associated with fever or skin rash, relatively low rheumatoid factor titers, and a BAL lymphocytosis.[111] In most patients with sulfasalazine or gold toxicity, lung disease largely regresses with withdrawal of the agent and corticosteroid therapy.

PULMONARY FUNCTION TESTS

Patterns of functional impairment in RA have been variable in unselected populations, with predominant airflow obstruction a frequent finding in one cohort,[80] but reductions in DL_{CO} ascribed to occult interstitial fibrosis in at least 40%.[68] Inconsistencies in published data can be ascribed to the confounding effects of smoking and variations in the type and severity of associated pulmonary disease. Airflow obstruction may result from bronchiectasis or OB. Interstitial pulmonary fibrosis, organizing pneumonia, and lymphocytic interstitial pneumonia give rise to restrictive defects. Pleural disease may also be restrictive but is usually distinguished by elevation of the gas transfer index (K_{CO}).

RADIOLOGIC FEATURES

In chest radiographic series of unselected patients with RA, appearances indicative of interstitial lung disease are found in 1% to 5% of cases.[61,63,69,111a] In interstitial pulmonary fibrosis, appearances are indistinguishable from idiopathic pulmonary fibrosis, with symmetrical basal interstitial opacification in limited disease and diffuse coarse reticulonodular abnormalities in extensive disease. Rheumatoid nodules are usually radiologically discrete and small, but are often multiple and may reach up to 7 cm in diameter; in Caplan's syndrome, nodules appear in crops, often grow rapidly, and may cavitate. Other chest radiographic findings in RA include focal consolidation (in organizing pneumonia, infectious pneumonia, and lung disease induced by methotrexate), hyperinflation (in OB), and pleural thickening or effusion.

The CT appearances of interstitial pulmonary fibrosis in RA are similar to those in idiopathic pulmonary fibrosis, with the most common abnormality being a reticular pattern (irregular linear opacities with cyst formation or honeycombing, typically subpleural and most extensive posteriorly and at the lung bases, except in extensive disease). Ground-glass attenuation, consisting of a patchy or diffuse increase in lung density, is likely to denote inflammatory histologic appearances or fine intralobular fibrosis, as in other fibrosing lung diseases.

The cardinal CT feature of organizing pneumonia is patchy bilateral air space consolidation (often with associated ground-glass attenuation), which is often predominantly subpleural,[112] but may have a bronchovascular distribution.[113] Small nodules (up to 1 cm in diameter) are common in organizing pneumonia; small pleural effusions and limited fibrosis (probably resulting from prolonged untreated inflammation) are occasional findings.

In bronchiolitis,[114] bronchiolar structures are occasionally visualized directly on CT as centrilobular micronodular opacities and peripheral branching structures, denoting marked thickening of the bronchiolar wall; this appearance may be most frequent in follicular bronchiolitis. In OB, areas of reduced lung density in a patchy distribution ("mosaic perfusion") are associated with a reduction in the caliber of pulmonary vessels in areas of decreased attenuation, indicative of regional hypoxic vasoconstriction in areas of severe bronchiolitis. Bronchiectasis and bronchial wall thickening on CT are common in constrictive bronchiolitis.

TREATMENT OF PULMONARY COMPLICATIONS

The treatment of pulmonary disease has usually consisted of corticosteroid therapy, with or without immunosuppressive agents. Due to small numbers, regimens have remained anecdotal. Organizing pneumonia and methotrexate pneumonitis often respond well to treatment. Regression of disease is highly variable in follicular bronchiolitis and lymphocytic interstitial pneumonia and is virtually never seen in OB. Lung function may improve in response to treatment in interstitial pulmonary fibrosis, but more often the goal is to prevent further progression of disease, especially when extensive. Anecdotal reports have suggested a response to anti–TNF-α, but others have highlighted a granulomatous lung disease adverse effect; clearly more intensive studies are needed.[114a]

SYSTEMIC LUPUS ERYTHEMATOSUS

Systemic lupus erythematosus (SLE) is an inflammatory multisystem disorder of unknown etiology with protean clinical and laboratory manifestations and a variable course and prognosis. The 1982 revised American College of Rheumatology criteria for the diagnosis of SLE require that a minimum of four of the criteria listed in Table 54.6 be satisfied (although SLE is sometimes diagnosed with fewer than four criteria).[115]

EPIDEMIOLOGY AND RISK FACTORS

SLE occurs throughout the world; the reported prevalence ranges from 12 to 50 per 100,000 population, and the incidence ranges from 1.8 to 7.6 per 100,000 population per year.[116] There is a 6-fold to 10-fold female excess, and the disease is three times more common in African Americans than in whites. The 5-year survival rate exceeds 90%, but the mortality rate is three times higher than in the general population. Support for a genetic contribution to disease includes a high prevalence in monozygotic twins, familial clustering, and associations between SLE and HLA-DR2, HLA-DR3, and the C4A null allele.[117] No infectious or other environmental factor has been shown to play a major etiologic role.

PULMONARY MANIFESTATIONS

Pleuropulmonary manifestations of SLE are listed in Table 54.6.

Diffuse Lung Disease

Diffuse lung disease on lung biopsy or at autopsy has been reported in 4%, 33%, and 70% of SLE patients.[118-120] These striking inconsistencies undoubtedly reflect major variations in the histologic diagnostic criteria: In the series with the highest prevalence, trivial interstitial thickening was categorized as "pulmonary fibrosis" but likely represented the minor residuum of infection or inflammatory complications of SLE. Only 3% of SLE patients have clinical evidence of diffuse lung disease at the onset of systemic disease, and a disease resembling interstitial pulmonary fibrosis develops during follow-up in less than 5%.[121] The clinical presentation (dyspnea, cough, predominantly basal crackles, a restrictive lung function defect or isolated reduction in DL_{CO}, basal infiltrates on chest radiography) is typical of idiopathic pulmonary fibrosis. Features not typical of idiopathic pulmonary fibrosis include variably associated pleuritic pain, a paucity of patients with morphologically extensive or functionally severe lung fibrosis, and the frequent presence of enlarged peribronchiolar lymphoid follicles at lung biopsy (although other histologic findings are indistinguishable from idiopathic pulmonary fibrosis). Partial regression of disease with corticosteroids in 9 of 14 cases in one series[122] suggests that an empirical trial of therapy is usually warranted.

Although seen in less than 2% of SLE patients, acute lupus pneumonitis is often life-threatening, with a mortality rate despite treatment of more than 50% once respiratory failure has supervened.[123] The predominant histologic feature of diffuse alveolar damage is nonspecific, and it has been argued that acute lupus pneumonitis is merely a manifestation of aspiration or bacterial infection.[118] However, well-documented striking responses to corticosteroids and immunosuppressive agents after antibiotic failure suggest strongly that the disorder is a true, albeit rare, entity. Acute lupus pneumonitis is not to be confused with organizing pneumonia ("bronchiolitis obliterans with organizing pneumonia"), discussed elsewhere in this chapter and reported in only a handful of adult patients with SLE, or with lymphocytic interstitial pneumonia, described in a small number of patients with SLE.

Table 54.6 Systemic Lupus Erythematosus

Criteria for Diagnosis*
Malar rash
Discoid rash
Photosensitivity skin rash
Oral or nasopharyngeal ulceration
Nonerosive arthritis involving two or more peripheral joints
Serositis (pleuritis or pericarditis)
Renal disorder (persistent proteinuria or cellular casts)
Neurologic disorder (unexplained seizures or psychosis)
Hematologic disorder (hemolytic anemia, leukopenia, lymphopenia, or thrombocytopenia)
Immunologic disorder (positive LE cell, anti-DNA antibody, anti-Sm antibody, false-positive syphilis serology)
Elevated antinuclear antibodies

Lung Manifestations
Acute lupus pneumonitis
Interstitial pulmonary fibrosis
Pulmonary vasculitis
Diffuse alveolar hemorrhage
Pulmonary hypertension
Shrinking lung syndrome
Antiphospholipid antibody syndrome
Organizing pneumonia
Pleural disease

* Minimum of four criteria required.

Extrapulmonary Restriction

Extrapulmonary restriction, resulting in exertional dyspnea, a restrictive functional defect, and marked decrease of DL_{CO}, is a well-recognized complication of SLE. The "shrinking lung syndrome" was first described in patients with severe restriction and a marked reduction in lung volume on chest radiography, and it is generally ascribed to diaphragmatic weakness (Fig. 54.5).[124] However, the use of sniff pressures to evaluate diaphragmatic strength may be confounded by concurrent lung restriction or airflow obstruction; in one

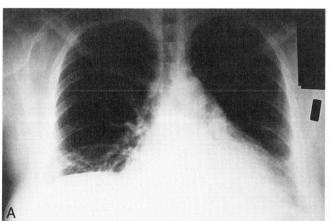
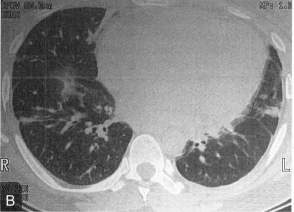

Figure 54.5 A, Chest radiograph from a patient with systemic lupus erythematosus shows marked elevation of both hemidiaphragms, in keeping with "the shrinking lung syndrome." **B,** On a computed tomography scan from the same patient as in **A,** linear abnormalities are seen that denote subsegmental atelectasis resulting from regional hypoventilation (due to diaphragmatic weakness).

study, with the use of alternative methods to evaluate diaphragmatic function, the characteristic restrictive defect was attributed to an "unspecified restriction in chest wall expansion."[125] No treatment of proven efficacy currently exists, although a handful of patients have improved in association with corticosteroid or immunosuppressive therapy. The disorder is almost always self-limited, although sometimes it is severe.

Diffuse Alveolar Hemorrhage

Although seen more frequently in SLE than in other connective tissue disorders, diffuse alveolar hemorrhage is rare in SLE. The typical presentation of acute dyspnea and extensive pulmonary infiltrates on chest radiography may mimic acute lupus pneumonitis, especially in the absence of hemoptysis. Diffuse alveolar hemorrhage is often life-threatening, with a mortality rate similar to that of acute lupus pneumonitis; however, as the two diseases are both treated empirically with corticosteroid and immunosuppressive therapy, the important differential diagnosis is opportunistic infection. Patients with SLE have underlying defects in most arms of the immune system and are at added risk of fulminant infection with the use of corticosteroids or immunosuppressive agents.[126] In this context, a misdiagnosis of acute lupus pneumonitis or diffuse alveolar hemorrhage may lead to a potentially disastrous increase in immunosuppression. Thus, the performance of BAL to exclude opportunistic infection may be crucial in SLE patients with unexplained extensive pulmonary infiltrates.

Pulmonary Hypertension

Pulmonary hypertension was once considered rare in SLE, but it is now reported with increasing frequency[127] and has a 2-year survival rate of less than 50% in severe disease. Abnormalities indicative of subclinical pulmonary hypertension are found on echocardiography in 10% of SLE patients, usually in association with Raynaud's phenomenon,[128] and thus it is likely that pulmonary hypertension results from vasoconstriction rather than pulmonary vasculitis (which is seldom identified in SLE); in autopsied patients with pulmonary hypertension, overt vasculitis is rare.

An important alternative mechanism for pulmonary hypertension is thromboembolism, which has a high prevalence in SLE, especially in patients with antiphospholipid antibodies (which cross-react with coagulation factors).[129,129a] In a 1993 study of 842 SLE patients, immunoglobulin G anticardiolipin antibodies were present more frequently than immunoglobulin M antibodies (24% vs. 13%), but both were associated with a 30% prevalence of thrombosis (as opposed to 10% in other SLE patients).[130] In view of the multiplicity of mechanisms potentially responsible for pulmonary hypertension, vasodilators, anticoagulation, and corticosteroid or immunosuppressive agents have all been advocated empirically for patients with the pulmonary vascular disease of SLE. In a small series of patients given chronic epoprostenol, measures of pulmonary hypertension, pulmonary vascular resistance, and exercise capacity all improved.[131]

Pleural Disease

Pleural disease is the most common pulmonary manifestation of SLE. Clinical or radiographic evidence of pleural involvement is seen in 20% of patients at the onset of systemic disease and occurs in at least 50% at some time[132] (with pleural abnormalities at autopsy in 50% to 100%[119,133]). Pleural disease is often asymptomatic, but pleuritic pain may be recurrent or intractable. The fluid is usually serosanguineous (but occasionally hemorrhagic) and exudative, with a neutrophilia in patients with pleurisy but a predominant lymphocytosis in chronic effusions.[132] The nonspecific histologic appearance of fibrinous pleuritis is not diagnostically useful. The identification of lupus erythematosus cells has largely fallen out of favor, as technical difficulties greatly reduce the sensitivity of the test in confirming that a pleural effusion is due to SLE.[134] The measurement of pleural fluid antinuclear antibody titers may be more diagnostically useful when the etiology of pleural disease is in doubt.[135]

SJÖGREN'S SYNDROME

Sjögren's syndrome is an autoimmune disorder characterized by lymphocytic infiltration of the lachrymal, salivary, conjunctival, and pharyngeal mucosal glands, with variable involvement of extraglandular tissue. The cardinal clinical features of keratoconjunctivitis sicca (dry eyes) and xerostomia (a dry mouth) may occur in isolation (primary Sjögren's syndrome, typically seen in women older than age 40 years) but are more often associated with connective tissue diseases such as RA, SSc, or SLE (secondary Sjögren's syndrome). Variable diagnostic criteria are used internationally; in one proposed diagnostic algorithm, sicca symptoms are mandatory, with supportive evidence including ocular signs (positive Shirmer test, rose bengal score >3), typical histologic appearances on salivary gland biopsy, antibodies to Ro (SS-A) or La (SS-B), or reduced salivary flow.[136]

EPIDEMIOLOGY AND RISK FACTORS

The reported prevalence of primary Sjögren's syndrome ranges from 0.5% to 3.0%. The etiology of the disease is unknown. There is some evidence to suggest a genetic predisposition, including familial clustering and an association with HLA-Dw2 and HLA-Dw3, but no environmental triggers have been identified.

PULMONARY MANIFESTATIONS

Pulmonary involvement is common in Sjögren's syndrome. In early series, primary and secondary Sjögren's syndromes were combined; it is likely that many of the pulmonary abnormalities seen in secondary Sjögren's syndrome were ascribed to the underlying connective tissue disease. Careful evaluation of patients with primary Sjögren's syndrome has shown that cough and dyspnea are common,[137] with objective evidence of pulmonary abnormalities in approximately one fourth of cases.[138] Lung involvement usually consists of lymphocytic infiltration similar to that seen in salivary glands and resulting in tracheobronchial disease or interstitial lung disease, depending on whether involvement is limited to secretory glandular tissue or is more widespread. However, population studies of respiratory involvement in Sjögren's syndrome have been hampered by variations in diagnostic criteria, failure to discriminate between primary and secondary Sjögren's syndrome, and failure to control for confounding features such as drug treatment and smoking. Lung manifestations include diffuse lung disease and tracheobronchial disease.

In a CT study of 35 patients, the most prevalent findings were large ± small airway disease ($n = 19$) and diffuse lung disease ($n = 12$, including 7 in whom the features were suggestive of lymphocytic interstitial pneumonia). The patterns of physiologic abnormalities were consistent with the predominant CT pattern.[139]

Diffuse Lung Disease

Although often asymptomatic, diffuse lung disease in Sjögren's syndrome may present with cough, dyspnea, crackles on auscultation, reticular or reticulonodular abnormalities on chest radiography, and a restrictive pattern of functional impairment. Interstitial involvement can be classified as pulmonary fibrosis, lymphocytic interstitial pneumonia, or lymphoma. Pulmonary fibrosis has been reported in up to 10% of patients with primary Sjögren's syndrome[140] and most frequently takes the form of fibrotic non-specific interstitial pneumonia.[140a] Although a presentation typical of extensive or progressive interstitial pulmonary fibrosis is rare, and interstitial disease in Sjögren's syndrome is often regarded as clinically insignificant, Gardiner and co-workers[140] found that patients with primary Sjögren's syndrome complaining of dyspnea (approximately 10%) have a high prevalence of histologic abnormalities (fibrosis or lymphocytic infiltration) on transbronchial biopsy.[140] A 10-year follow-up study of 30 patients showed that most patients do not develop progressive lung disease, although the total gas transfer level fell significantly in 7 cases.[141]

Lymphocytic interstitial infiltration may take the form of lymphocytic interstitial pneumonia, pseudolymphoma (extensive pulmonary lymphocytic infiltration with the formation of lymphoid follicles), or pulmonary lymphoma. Lymphocytic interstitial pneumonia, the most common

form of diffuse lung disease in Sjögren's syndrome (Fig. 54.6),[142] is characterized by a diffuse lymphocytic infiltrate, with or without histiocytes and multinucleated giant cells, most prominent around bronchioles. Pseudolymphoma, characterized by pulmonary infiltration, may regress spontaneously and often responds well to corticosteroid therapy; however, some patients progress to pulmonary lymphoma. The prevalence of lymphoma is increased 40-fold to 50-fold in Sjögren's syndrome[143]; pulmonary lymphoma has a highly variable clinical and radiographic presentation, with the spectrum of disease ranging from diffuse interstitial involvement to discrete (often perihilar) masses. It is now believed that all lymphocytic interstitial pneumonia may represent malignant disease of varying nature.

Organizing pneumonia (bronchiolitis obliterans with organizing pneumonia) has been reported in Sjögren's syndrome but occurs less frequently than in rheumatoid arthritis or polymyositis. A response to corticosteroid therapy is usual but not invariable.

Tracheobronchial Disease

Tracheobronchial disease may take the form of loss of mucous secretion in the trachea (xerotrachea), chronic bronchitis, or small airway disease. Xerotrachea occurs in up to 25% of patients with primary Sjögren's syndrome and consists of atrophy of tracheobronchial mucous glands in association with a lymphoplasmacytic infiltrate, manifesting clinically as a relentless dry cough and endobronchial inflammation at bronchoscopy.[144] It is likely that similar histologic abnormalities in bronchi and bronchioles account for an increased prevalence of bronchial hyperresponsiveness, reported in 40% to 60% of patients with primary and secondary Sjögren's syndrome.[145,146]

Subclinical bronchiolitis may be common in Sjögren's syndrome. In the interstitial lung disease of Sjögren's syndrome, lymphocytic infiltration is more prominent around small bronchioles,[147] resulting in a BAL lymphocytosis[148]; thus, it is likely that the occasional cases of isolated lymphocytic bronchiolitis, presenting with a clinical picture of chronic obstructive pulmonary disease, represent a more limited form of lymphocytic infiltration. The evaluation of airflow at low lung volumes in unselected patients with

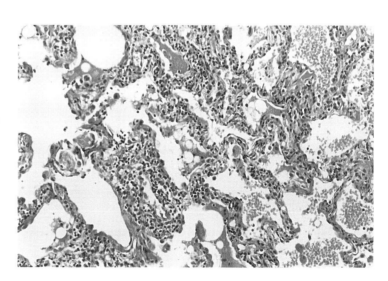

Figure 54.6 Surgical lung biopsy specimen taken from a patient with diffuse lung disease in the context of Sjögren's syndrome. Note the dense lymphocytic infiltrate within the interstitium. (Courtesy of Dr. Andrew Nicholson, Royal Brompton Hospital.)

primary and secondary Sjögren's syndrome has demonstrated a high prevalence of small airway dysfunction[137]; aerosol penetration from central airways to the lung periphery is reduced, indicating small airway obstruction.[149] These abnormalities, indicating either OB or mucous plugging, may contribute to an increased prevalence of bronchopneumonia but do not evolve into severe OB (which is not generally a feature of Sjögren's syndrome, except in occasional cases with associated RA). FB has been reported in a handful of patients with primary Sjögren's syndrome but may occur more frequently in secondary Sjögren's syndrome; in a number of reported cases of FB associated with RA, the presence of Sjögren's syndrome is not explicitly excluded. FB and diffuse bronchiolar lymphocytic infiltration may be part of the same spectrum of disease, but the relationship between the two disorders is uncertain.

POLYMYOSITIS WITH DERMATOMYOSITIS

The defining criteria for polymyositis with dermatomyositis are listed in Table 54.7. For polymyositis, a definite diagnosis is made if the first four features are present, a probable diagnosis is made if any three of the first four features are present, and a possible diagnosis is made if any two of the first four features are present. For dermatomyositis, the typical rash must be present, plus any three of the first four for a definite diagnosis, two of the first four for a probable diagnosis, and one of the first four for a possible diagnosis (Bohan and Peter criteria[150]).

The skin problems of dermatomyositis include the presence of scaly cutaneous eruptions affecting extensor surfaces of the finger joints (Gottron's tubercles) and the characteristic edema and violaceous or purplish, heliotrope rash that surrounds the eyelids. Proximal muscle weakness tends to be insidious, progressive, and painless, affecting head, neck, and limb girdles and eventually involving the muscles of the tongue and pharynx and the respiratory muscles. Pulmonary complications occur in approximately 45% of patients and are the most frequent cause of death.

EPIDEMIOLOGY AND RISK FACTORS

The inflammatory myopathies are relatively rare, affecting 2 to 10 per 100,000 population, with a female-to-male predominance of 2.5:1 and with a bimodal age distribution peaking in childhood and in the fourth to fifth decades. Dermatomyositis appears to have a higher expression of HLA-B8/DR3, HLA-B14, and HLA-B40, whereas polymyositis associates with HLA-B8/DR3 and in African Americans with HLA-B7 and HLA-DRw6.[151]

There are multiple manifestations of lung disease, as listed in Table 54.7. The presence of diffuse lung disease has been associated with two HLA haplotypes: HLA-DRB1*1302-DQA1*0102-DQB1*0604 and HLA-DRB1*0405-DQA1*03-DQB1*0401.[152] The prevalence of lung disease varies from series to series, and often the respiratory symptoms are masked by muscle fatigue. Nonetheless, pulmonary complications of the disease can be a frequent cause of death. In combined series, the prevalence of diffuse lung disease can be up to 64%. The disease may present with pulmonary symptoms, and in one recent series this was the case in 21 of 70 patients.[153]

PULMONARY MANIFESTATIONS

Diffuse Lung Disease

Diffuse lung disease is the most common problem encountered in the context of dermatomyositis with polymyositis and may occur in up to 32% of patients.[154] The pattern of diffuse lung disease often mimics that of idiopathic pulmonary fibrosis, but an acute, rapidly progressive form of acute pneumonitis can occur. Organizing pneumonia may also be the presenting feature (Fig. 54.7). The histopathologic features associated with these forms of presentation include usual interstitial pneumonia in patients with an interstitial pulmonary fibrosis pattern, diffuse alveolar damage in the acute pneumonitis, and bronchiolitis obliterans together with organizing pneumonia in those patients who have the clinical features of organizing pneumonia.[155–157] In a large series of 70 patients, Douglas and colleagues[153] reported that 82% of patients who were biopsied had the nonspecific interstitial pneumonia pattern of histopathology. More recently, it has been shown that one of the characteristic features of chronic diffuse lung disease in polymyositis with dermatomyositis is a combination of the features of organizing pneumonia and interstitial pulmonary fibrosis on high-resolution CT.[158] One recent report has described an acute presentation of pulmonary capillaritis with alveolar hemorrhage in association with polymyositis.[159]

Clinical Features. The clinical features of diffuse lung disease in polymyositis with dermatomyositis depend on the nature of the lung process. Breathlessness on exertion without wheeze is a common presenting symptom, and, if the myopathy is severe, orthopnea may be striking. Hemoptysis may occur if there is capillaritis. Pleural disease is uncommon.

Imaging. Chest radiography findings depend on lung disease. Chronic diffuse lung disease is associated with peripheral reticular nodular opacities, particularly in the lung bases as for interstitial pulmonary fibrosis. Acute pneumonitis can result in ground-glass opacification on chest radiography and alveolar hemorrhage with areas of consolidation.

CT is much more specific than radiography, highlighting the distributions of the different processes. A combination

---

Table 54.7 Polymyositis with Dermatomyositis
Criteria for Diagnosis
Symmetrical proximal muscle weakness
Muscle biopsy material showing myositis
Elevation of serum skeletal muscle enzymes
Characteristic electromyographic pattern of myositis
Typical rash of dermatomyositis
Lung Manifestations
Interstitial pulmonary fibrosis
Acute pneumonitis (with diffuse alveolar damage)
Organizing pneumonia
Aspiration pneumonia
Pulmonary vasculitis and alveolar hemorrhage
Respiratory muscle weakness

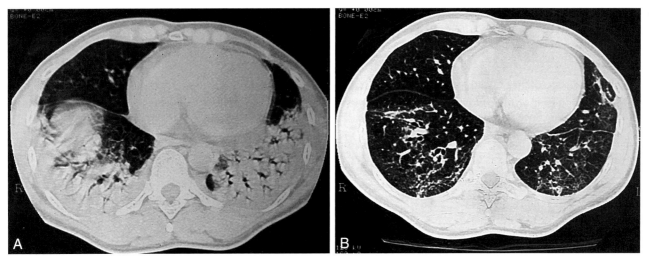

Figure 54.7 A, Computed tomography scan showing dense consolidation that denotes organizing pneumonia in a patient with polymyositis. As shown in this example, the disease tends to be most prominent posteriorly in the lower lobes. **B,** After treatment, the dense consolidation has regressed, but there is extensive residual linear opacification, representing residual fibrosis and resulting in traction bronchiectasis on the right and a restrictive functional defect.

of consolidation with a peripheral reticular pattern is highly characteristic. The consolidation may evolve into a reticular pattern.[160]

Lung function tests show a restrictive ventilatory defect with reduced gas transfer. In recent hemorrhage or marked myopathy, there may be a disproportionate preservation of the DL_{CO}. However, it must be remembered that acute hemorrhage can occur in the context of previous chronic disease, and so the DL_{CO} may be normal or subnormal but elevated from a level that was previously lower.

Dermatomyositis and polymyositis are well-recognized paraneoplastic phenomena, so it is sometimes difficult to determine which condition presented first.[161] Screening for occult carcinoma is recommended with mammography, abdominal CT, pelvic ultrasonography, and tumor markers.

Autoantibodies. Studies of autoantibodies have highlighted the association between the presence of antibodies to aminoacyl transfer ribonucleic acid (tRNA) synthetases, inflammatory myopathies, and diffuse lung disease.[162] Jo-1 (antihistidyl tRNA synthetase) is the most common, occurring in 20% to 30% of patients with inflammatory myopathy and in 50% to 100% of cases of inflammatory myopathy and diffuse lung disease, in contrast to less than 5% of patients without diffuse lung disease. A variety of novel autoantibodies have been described with affinity for other tRNA synthetase molecules: PL-12, PL-7, EJ, and OJ. These molecules help define the antisynthetase syndrome: the coexistence of myositis, diffuse lung disease, and arthritis.

In some patients, diffuse lung disease is the presenting feature. Typical CT appearances may suggest the diagnosis. In this situation, typical autoantibodies may be found, confirming a suspicion of dermatomyositis with polymyositis.

Other Pulmonary Manifestations

Aspiration pneumonia needs to be considered if there is upper airway and pharyngeal muscle weakness. The predilection for posterior segments may suggest this diagnosis.

The treatment of lung disease depends on the histopathologic pattern. Organizing pneumonia responds well to corticosteroids alone. Vasculitis may require a combination of high-dose prednisolone and immunosuppression. More chronic diffuse lung disease may respond to a combination of prednisolone and immunosuppression with cyclophosphamide or azathioprine. Some reports have shown efficacy with cyclosporine A.[163] In refractory cases, methotrexate and intravenous immunoglobulin should be considered. Occasionally, the myositis may resolve on treatment but the lung disease progresses; these cases may be very difficult to control.

MIXED CONNECTIVE TISSUE DISEASE

Mixed connective tissue disease (MCTD) is defined by the presence of features of SLE, SSc, and polymyositis (Sjögren's syndrome may also be seen) in association with high titers (>1:1600) of autoantibody directed against the extractable nuclear antigen U1-RNP.[164,165] Criteria that have been suggested for the diagnosis of MCTD include the presence of antibody to the U1 ribonuclear protein together with the clinical features of hand edema, synovitis, Raynaud's phenomenon, acrosclerosis, and myositis. At least three of these clinical features are needed in addition to the autoantibody finding. A fourth clinical feature is required if the initial three are Raynaud's phenomenon, edema, and acrosclerosis. The difference between MCTD and overlap syndrome may be semantic, but the former often presents more acutely and with greater specificity for U1-RNP. MCTD may differentiate into specific rheumatologic diseases. This differentiation may be genetically determined.[166]

The prevalence of the disease is unclear, but it is estimated at 1 in 10,000, with a 9:1 female preponderance. Pleuropulmonary complications occur in 20% to 85% of patients, but diffuse lung disease is the most common lung complication.[167] Survival is better if the diffuse lung disease is associated with U1-RNP positivity than with no U1-RNP. Pulmonary involvement, investigations, and treatment are as for the individual connective tissue diseases.

Other overlap syndromes are reported in which clinical features of more than one connective tissue disease are present in the same patient. Although MCTD tissue disease remains the most clearly definable, other overlap syndromes occur both with and without typical autoantibody association. Of the former, overlapping clinical features found in association with U2-RNP and U3-RNP and the tRNA synthetase–associated diseases (see earlier) can be considered to be part of an overlap syndrome. Antibodies to PM-Scl, KU, and U2-RNP are associated with overlaps of SSc and polymyositis.[165] Respiratory manifestations are seen in 20% to 80% of patients and diffuse lung disease is the major finding, followed by pleural disease and pulmonary hypertension.[167] In a CT study of 41 patients, the major abnormalities were ground-glass appearances in all, subpleural micronodules in 40 of 41, and nonseptal linear opacities in 32 of 41.[168] Whether these distinctly defined subsets of overlap have implications in terms of prognosis or treatment is uncertain. Treatment depends on the nature of the lung disease and is identical to the approaches used for the other connective tissue diseases.[166]

RELAPSING POLYCHONDRITIS

The diagnosis of relapsing polychondritis requires the presence of three or more of the following clinical features[169]: bilateral auricular chondritis; nonerosive, seronegative inflammatory polyarthritis; nasal chondritis; ocular inflammation; respiratory tract involvement (either upper or lower respiratory tract); cochlear with or without vestibular abnormality; and positive biopsy specimen. The presence of anticartilage antibodies may be helpful in the diagnosis.

Relapsing polychondritis is rare and is characterized by episodic painful and destructive cartilaginous inflammation. The condition affects men and women equally and has a peak incidence between 40 and 60 years of age. It is considered an autoimmune process, and autoantibodies have been found directed against cartilage and type II collagen. Diagnosis is chiefly clinical but can be confirmed at biopsy of affected cartilage, including tracheal rings.

Relapsing polychondritis is usually multifocal, affecting cartilage of the ear (85% to 94%), nose (54% to 57%) (Fig. 54.8A), upper respiratory tract (31% to 48%), and ribs. Additionally, patients frequently suffer ocular inflammation, nonerosive arthropathy (52%), and vestibulocochlear dysfunction.[169,170] It may occur in association with a wide range of other conditions, especially connective tissue disease and vasculitis. Approximately 30% of patients have a preexisting connective tissue disease.

Respiratory involvement probably accounts for around 10% of deaths in this condition. Pulmonary parenchymal disease is rare, but vasculitis may occur. Destruction and obstruction of the glottis, trachea, and bronchi lead to airway stricture, collapse, and distal infection (Fig. 54.8B and 54.8C).[171] Lung function testing shows diminution in maximal inspiratory (large, extrathoracic airways) and expiratory (smaller, intrathoracic airways) flow rates, suggesting airway collapse while static recoil pressures are preserved.

With dynamic CT scanning showing tracheal ring thickening, collapse on inspiratory maneuvers can help to localize the large airway disease.

Treatment depends on disease severity. Mild cases may be controlled with nonsteroidal anti-inflammatory drops, but troublesome relapses may require short-term high-dose corticosteroid therapy. Steroid-resistant lesions have been treated with immunosuppressive agents such as cyclophosphamide. Tracheostomy and stenting are occasionally indicated, but other surgical treatment is difficult due to the diffuse nature of involvement.[172] In one large review of 159 reported cases, three fourths of the patients required chronic corticosteroid therapy, which, in that series, decreased the frequency, duration, and severity of flare-ups but did not prevent disease progression.[173] In one study, the use of multiple, self-expandable stents via fiberoptic bronchoscopy in five patients requiring mechanical ventilation, resulted in improvement in four patients who were all able to live without mechanical ventilation for up to 20 months.[174]

BEHÇET'S SYNDROME

Behçet's syndrome occurs predominantly in the countries bordering the Mediterranean sea. Prevalence estimates approach 80 to 370 per 100,000 population in Turkey. Men and women are affected equally, and age of onset is usually in the second or third decade. There is an association between the HLA-B51 allele and, more controversially, more severely affected patients; relative risk of HLA-B51 carriers is roughly 13:1 in Turkey. Herpes simplex type 1 and streptococci have been suggested as causative agents.[175] Diagnosis requires the presence of recurrent oral ulceration occurring at least three times in a 12-month period and two of the four minor features listed in Table 54.8.[176]

Mucocutaneous ulceration is the clinical hallmark, with aphthous oral and genital ulceration seen in almost all patients. Other cutaneous features include erythema nodosum, an acneiform rash, and papular lesions of cutaneous vasculitis. Uveitis is the major cause of morbidity, but systemic vasculitis may affect all systems.

Pulmonary involvement is seen in 1% to 7% and tends to affect HLA-B51–positive younger males (<25 years) more severely. The major pulmonary manifestations are pulmonary artery aneurysms, arterial and venous thromboses,

---

Table 54.8 Behçet's Syndrome

Criteria for Diagnosis

Major (required)
  Recurrent aphthous ulceration occurring at least three times in a 12-mo period

Minor (two of four)
  Recurrent genital ulceration
  Ocular disease
  Skin lesions (erythema nodosum, skin ulcers)
  Positive pathergy test (a 2-mm erythematous papule or pustule at the prick site 48 hr after the application of a sterile hypodermic 20- to 22-gauge needle that obliquely penetrated avascular antecubital skin to a depth of 5 mm)[177]

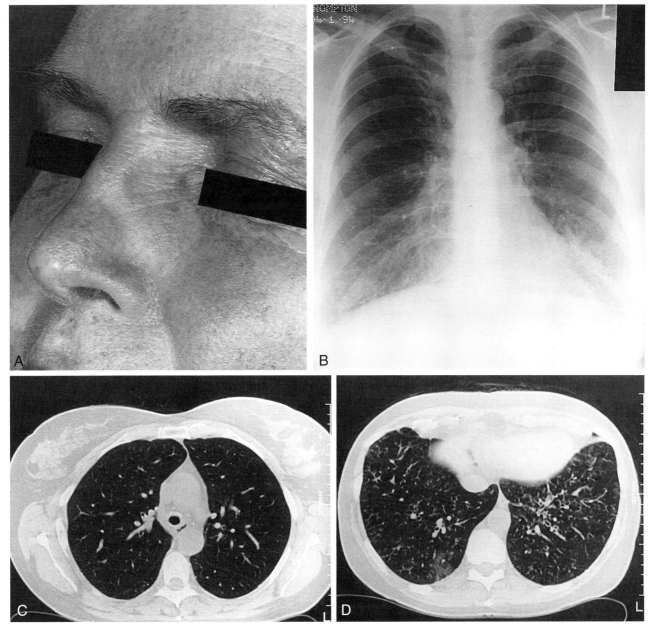

Figure 54.8 Relapsing polychondritis. **A,** Loss of cartilage in this individual's nose results in a "saddle" deformity. **B,** Chest radiograph of the same individual as in **A** demonstrating tracheal narrowing. **C,** Tracheal narrowing and thickening shown more graphically in the computed tomography scan. **D,** Thickening of the segmental bronchi is seen together with patchy attenuation ("mosaicism"), which indicates small airway involvement.

pulmonary infarction, organizing pneumonia and pleurisy.[177] Symptoms include dyspnea, chest pain, and recurrent hemoptysis that can be massive and fatal.[178]

The cardinal histologic feature is vasculitis affecting arterial and venous vessels of all sizes. Pulmonary arterial aneurysms are surrounded by inflammatory infiltrates and have thickened intima and degeneration of the elastic lamina with thrombosis. Arterial and venous thromboses, pulmonary infarcts, and, occasionally, pleural effusion also occur.[179] The radiographic abnormalities are nonspecific but may include the features of pulmonary hemorrhage, vascular occlusion, or mass lesions representing arterial aneurysm(s).[180]

Prognosis is variable. The disease course is relapsing-remitting. Pulmonary artery aneurysm carries the worst prognosis, with a 2-year survival of 70%.

Treatment is complex and depends on presentation. Steroids and immunosuppressive agents are used to control vasculitis, particularly in cases of pulmonary artery aneurysm, in which eventual regression is sometimes observed. Cyclosporine and FK506 have been successful in some patients.[177] Anticoagulants may be required for control of thrombosis, but should be used only if immunosuppression is insufficient, as there is a significant risk of hemorrhage. Pulmonary embolization and surgical resection have been reported to be successful, but surgical treatment of aneurysms can result in aneurysms at the anastomosis site.[181]

ANKYLOSING SPONDYLITIS

Ankylosing spondylitis (AS) is a seronegative spondyloarthritis developing in 0.05% to 1.5% of the general population and is associated with the major histocompatibility antigen HLA-B27.[182] The cardinal site of disease is the vertebral column, but peripheral joint arthritis is seen in approximately one third of patients, and extra-articular features include aortic regurgitation, uveitis, pulmonary disease, and extrapulmonary restriction.

Lung disease, mainly upper zone fibrosis, can occur in up to 30% of case series but fibrobullous disease is less common. In a series of 2080 patients with AS, this pattern was seen in only 1% to 2% of patients.[183] In one high-resolution CT study, limited interstitial lung disease, bronchiectasis, or paraseptal emphysema were present in the majority of patients, even when chest radiographic appearances were normal.[184] In a second study, abnormalities were seen in 15 of 21 patients, comprising thickened interlobular septa (33%), bronchial wall thickening (29%), pleuropulmonary abnormalities (29%), and linear septal thickening (29%).[185] A subclinical lymphocytic alveolitis may be evident with BAL.[186] Histologically, lung abnormalities consist of a variable mixture of lymphocytic infiltration, fibrosis, and bullous change. On chest radiography, diffuse reticulonodular infiltrates in the upper zones are usually symmetrical and are seldom extensive except in patients with severe spinal disease[187] or a long history of AS.[183] However, apical fibrosis occasionally may precede the development of extrapulmonary disease. No proven treatment exists to prevent the development of apical fibrosis; resistance to corticosteroid therapy is the rule.

Cavities may develop within distorted fibrotic apical tissue and are sometimes colonized by mycobacteria or fungi, especially *Aspergillus fumigatus,* which are isolated in up to 60% of AS patients with apical cavitation.[188] Life-threatening hemoptysis is an occasional complication of mycetoma formation within cavities and may be controllable by bronchial artery embolization; the resection of a mycetoma is a treatment of last resort due to the high prevalence of postoperative bronchopleural fistula or empyema. Advanced apical fibrosis is often associated with apical pleural thickening, but pleural disease is seldom seen adjacent to normal lung parenchyma elsewhere in the thorax. There is an increased (up to 10%) prevalence of pneumothorax in AS patients with apical fibrosis,[183] probably due to subpleural bullous degeneration in advancing disease.

Extrapulmonary restriction due to immobilization of the chest wall (costovertebral ankylosis) is an occasional complication of AS, associated with surprisingly little impairment in pulmonary function, perhaps because the diaphragm is able to make a major contribution in the presence of a high resting volume.[189]

MARFAN SYNDROME

Marfan syndrome (MS) is an autosomal dominant condition of variable penetrance affecting approximately 5 per 100,000 population. MS is characterized by abnormalities of fibrous connective tissue (due to mutations on chromosome 15), especially in the skeleton (long limbs, arachnodactyly, pectus excavatum, kyphoscoliosis), eyes (subluxation of the lens), and cardiovascular system (aortic or mitral regurgitation, aortic aneurysm). The reduced life expectancy of MS is largely attributable to cardiac complications; there is no effective treatment to reverse disease or to slow progression.

Respiratory complications can be subdivided into pulmonary and extrapulmonary abnormalities. Localized bulla formation with a predilection for the lung apex[190] is an occasional striking finding in young patients. Generalized emphysema in nonsmoking patients with MS may become evident at any age and is sometimes fatal in childhood.[191]

The high prevalence of pneumothorax in MS of 5% to 10%[192] (over 100-fold higher than in the general population) can be ascribed to the rupture of subpleural bullae; emphysema is present on chest radiography in the majority of MS patients with pneumothoraces,[192,193] which are often recurrent and bilateral. Underlying apical fibrosis has been reported in a handful of cases. Other less frequent parenchymal manifestations include congenital malformations of the middle lobes (which may be absent or rudimentary) and an increased prevalence of bronchopneumonia.[192]

Isolated pectus excavatum in MS is seldom associated with significant impairment in lung function. However, occasionally kyphoscoliosis is associated with fatal cor pulmonale.[194] It is likely that nocturnal desaturation amplifies hypoxia due to kyphoscoliosis. Increased upper airway collapsibility during sleep was recently shown to be common in MS,[195] accounting for an association between MS and obstructive sleep apnea.

SUMMARY

In connective tissue disease the lung can be involved by a wide variety of patterns of pathology affecting the trachea through the parenchyma to the pleura. Often combinations of patterns exist that flag the likelihood of connective tissue disease being the underlying problem. Some patterns of lung disease are more common in one connective tissue disease than the others. Specific pathologic entities that occur in these diseases do not generally follow the same course as their idiopathic counterparts. This chapter has aimed at making these points both in general form and also with regard to specific diseases, and also highlights predisposing factors, including genetic predisposition, and first-line treatment approaches. Increasing recognition of the pulmonary manifestations of these protean disorders is resulting in better outcomes and remains a growing field.

REFERENCES

1. Wells AU, Hansell DM, du Bois RM: Interstitial lung disease in the collagen vascular diseases. Semin Respir Med 14:333–343, 1993.
1a. Strange C, Highland KB: Interstitial lung disease in the patient who has connective tissue disease. Clin Chest Med 25:549–559, 2004.
2. Masi AT, Rodnan GP, Medsger TAJ, et al: Preliminary criteria for the classification of systemic sclerosis (scleroderma). Arthritis Rheum 23:581–590, 1980.

3. Silman AJ, Black CM, Welsh KI: Epidemiology, demographics, genetics. *In* Clements PJ, Furst DE (eds): Systemic Sclerosis. Baltimore: Williams & Wilkins, 1996, pp 23–50.

4. Artlett CM, Black CM, Briggs DC, et al: Telomere reduction in scleroderma patients: A possible cause for chromosomal instability. Br J Rheumatol 35:732–737, 1996.

5. Fanning GC, Welsh KI, Bunn C, et al: HLA associations in three mutually exclusive autoantibody subgroups in UK systemic sclerosis patients. Br J Rheumatol 37:201–207, 1998.

6. Gilchrist FC, Bunn C, Foley PJ, et al: Class II HLA associations with autoantibodies in scleroderma: A highly significant role for HLA-DP. Genes Immun 2:76–81, 2001.

7. Silver RM: Scleroderma and pseudoscleroderma: Environmental exposure. *In* Clements PJ, Furst DE (eds): Systemic Sclerosis. Baltimore: Williams & Wilkins, 1996, pp 81–98.

8. Rodnan GP, Benedek TG, Medsger TA Jr, et al: The association of progressive systemic sclerosis (scleroderma) with coal miners' pneumoconiosis and other forms of silicosis. Ann Intern Med 66:323–334, 1967.

9. Tabuenca JM: Toxic-allergic syndrome caused by ingestion of rapeseed oil denatured with aniline. Lancet 2:567–568, 1981.

10. Arnett FC, Howard RF, Tan F, et al: Increased prevalence of systemic sclerosis in a Native American tribe in Oklahoma: Association with an Amerindian HLA haplotype. Arthritis Rheum 39:1362–1370, 1996.

11. Petrek M, Pantelidis P, Southcott AM, et al: The source and role of RANTES in interstitial lung disease. Eur Respir J 10:1207–1216, 1997.

12. Majumdar S, Li D, Ansari T, et al: Different cytokine profiles in cryptogenic fibrosing alveolitis and fibrosing alveolitis associated with systemic sclerosis: A quantitative study of open lung biopsies. Eur Respir J 14:251–257, 1999.

13. Bolster MB, Ludwicka A, Sutherland SE, et al: Cytokine concentrations in bronchoalveolar lavage fluid of patients with systemic sclerosis. Arthritis Rheum 40:743–751, 1997.

14. Shi-Wen X, Denton CP, McWhirter A, et al: Scleroderma lung fibroblasts exhibit elevated and dysregulated type I collagen biosynthesis. Arthritis Rheum 40:1237–1244, 1997.

15. Cambrey AD, Harrison NK, Dawes KE, et al: Increased levels of endothelin-1 in bronchoalveolar lavage fluid from patients with systemic sclerosis contribute to fibroblast mitogenic activity in vitro. Am J Respir Cell Mol Biol 11:439–445, 1994.

16. Gauldie J, Jordana M, Cox G: Cytokines and pulmonary fibrosis. Thorax 48:931–935, 1993.

17. Xing Z, Tremblay GM, Sime PJ, et al: Overexpression of granulocyte-macrophage colony-stimulating factor induces pulmonary granulation tissue formation and fibrosis by induction of transforming growth factor-beta 1 and myofibroblast accumulation. Am J Pathol 150:59–66, 1997.

18. Sime PJ, Xing Z, Graham FL, et al: Adenovector-mediated gene transfer of active transforming growth factor-beta 1 induces prolonged severe fibrosis in rat lung. J Clin Invest 100:768–776, 1997.

19. Corrin B, Butcher D, McAnulty BJ, et al: Immunohistochemical localization of transforming growth factor-beta 1 in the lungs of patients with systemic sclerosis, cryptogenic fibrosing alveolitis and other lung disorders. Histopathology 24:145–150, 1994.

20. Gray AJ, Bishop JE, Reeves JT, et al: Partially degraded fibrin(ogen) stimulates fibroblast proliferation in vitro. Am J Respir Cell Mol Biol 12:684–690, 1995.

21. Abraham DJ, Vancheeswaran R, Dashwood MR, et al: Increased levels of endothelin-1 and differential endothelin type A and B receptor expression in scleroderma-associated fibrotic lung disease. Am J Pathol 151:831–841, 1997.

22. Piguet PF, Collart MA, Grau GE, et al: Requirement of tumour necrosis factor for development of silica-induced pulmonary fibrosis. Nature 344:245–247, 1990.

23. Piguet PF, Vesin C: Treatment by human recombinant TNF receptor of pulmonary fibrosis induced by bleomycin or silica in mice. Eur Respir J 7:515–518, 1994.

24. Alton E, Turner-Warwick M: Lung involvement in scleroderma. *In* Jayson MIV, Black CM (eds): Systemic Sclerosis: Scleroderma. London: Wiley, 1988, pp 181–205.

25. Kim JH, Follett JV, Rice JR, et al: Endobronchial telangiectases and hemoptysis in scleroderma. Am J Med 84:173–174, 1988.

26. Wells AU, Hansell DM, Rubens MB, et al: Fibrosing alveolitis in systemic sclerosis: Indices of lung function in relation to extent of disease on computed tomography. Arthritis Rheum 40:1229–1236, 1997.

27. Wells AU, Hansell DM, Rubens MB, et al: Functional impairment in lone cryptogenic fibrosing alveolitis and fibrosing alveolitis associated with systemic sclerosis: A comparison. Am J Respir Crit Care Med 155:1657–1664, 1997.

28. Wells AU, Hansell DM, Rubens MB, et al: Fibrosing alveolitis in systemic sclerosis: Bronchoalveolar lavage findings in relation to computed tomographic appearance. Am J Respir Crit Care Med 150:462–468, 1994.

28a. Desai SR, Veeraraghavan S, Hansell DM, et al: CT features of lung disease in patients with systemic sclerosis: comparison with idiopathic pulmonary fibrosis and nonspecific interstitial pneumonia. Radiology 232:560–567, 2004.

29. Wells AU, Hansell DM, Haslam PL, et al: Bronchoalveolar lavage cellularity: Lone cryptogenic fibrosing alveolitis compared with the fibrosing alveolitis of systemic sclerosis. Am J Respir Crit Care Med 157:1474–1482, 1998.

30. Wells AU, Hansell DM, Harrison NK, et al: Clearance of inhaled 99m-Tc DTPA predicts the clinical course of fibrosing alveolitis. Eur Respir J 6:797–802, 1993.

31. Schneider PD, Wise RA, Hochberg MC, et al: Serial pulmonary function in systemic sclerosis. Am J Med 73:385, 1982.

32. Silver RM, Miller KS, Kinsella MB, et al: Evaluation and management of scleroderma lung disease using bronchoalveolar lavage. Am J Med 88:470–476, 1990.

33. Wallaert B: Subclinical alveolitis in immunologic systemic disorders. Lung Suppl 168:974–983, 1990.

34. Witt C, Borges AC, John M, et al: Pulmonary involvement in diffuse cutaneous systemic sclerosis: Bronchioalveolar fluid granulocytosis predicts progression of fibrosing alveolitis. Ann Rheum Dis 58:635–640, 1999.

35. Behr J, Vogelmeier C, Beinert T, et al: Bronchoalveolar lavage for evaluation and management of scleroderma disease of the lung. Am J Respir Crit Care Med 154:400–406, 1996.

36. Bouros D, Wells AU, Nicholson AG, et al: Histopathologic subsets of fibrosing alveolitis in patients with systemic sclerosis and their relationship to outcome. Am J Respir Crit Care Med 165:1581–1586, 2002.

36a. Flaherty KR, Colby TV, Travis WD, et al: Fibroblastic foci in usual interstitial pneumonia: idiopathic versus collagen vascular disease. Am J Respir Crit Care Med 167:1410–1415, 2003.

37. Muir TE, Tazelaar HD, Colby TV, et al: Organizing diffuse alveolar damage associated with progressive systemic sclerosis. Mayo Clin Proc 72:639–642, 1997.

38. Jacobsen S, Halberg P, Ullman S, et al: A longitudinal study of pulmonary function in Danish patients with systemic sclerosis. Clin Rheumatol 16:384–390, 1997.

39. Hesselstrand R, Scheja ASGQ, Wiik A, Akesson A: The association of antinuclear antibodies with organ involvement and survival in systemic sclerosis. Rheumatology (Oxford) 42:534–540, 2003.

40. Mitri GM, Lucas M, Fertig N, et al: A comparison between anti-Th/To- and anticentromere antibody-positive systemic sclerosis patients with limited cutaneous involvement. Arthritis Rheum 48:203–209, 2003.

41. Ulanet DB, Wigley FM, Gelber AC, Rosen A: Autoantibodies against B23, a nucleolar phosphoprotein, occur in scleroderma and are associated with pulmonary hypertension. Arthritis Rheum 49:85–92, 2003.

42. Bryan C, Howard Y, Brennan P, et al: Survival following the onset of scleroderma: Results from a retrospective inception cohort study of the UK patient population. Br J Rheumatol 35:1122–1126, 1996.

43. Rosenthal AK, McLaughlin JK, Gridley G, et al: Incidence of cancer among patients with systemic sclerosis. Cancer 76:910–914, 1995.

44. Lynch JP 3rd, McCune WJ: Immunosuppressive and cytotoxic pharmacotherapy for pulmonary disorders. Am J Respir Crit Care Med 155:395–420, 1997.

44a. Dheda K, Lalloo UG, Cassim B, Mody GM: Experience with azathioprine in systemic sclerosis associated with interstitial lung disease. Clin Rheumatol 23:306–309, 2004.

45. Steen VD, Lanz JK Jr, Conte C, et al: Therapy for severe interstitial lung disease in systemic sclerosis: A retrospective study. Arthritis Rheum 37:1290–1296, 1994.

46. White B, Moore WC, Wigley FM, et al: Cyclophosphamide is associated with pulmonary function and survival benefit in patients with scleroderma and alveolitis. Ann Intern Med 132:947–954, 2000.

47. Latsi P, Wells AU: Evaluation and management of alveolitis and interstitial lung disease in scleroderma. Curr Opin Rheumatol 15:748–755, 2003.

48. Black CM, Silman AJ, Herrick AI, et al: Interferon-alpha does not improve outcome at one year in patients with diffuse cutaneous scleroderma: Results of a randomised, double-blind, placebo-controlled trial. Arthritis Rheum 42:299–305, 1999.

49. Steen VD, Medsger TA Jr: Case-control study of corticosteroids and other drugs that could precipitate or protect from the development of scleroderma renal crisis. Arthritis Rheum 41:1613–1619, 1998.

50. DeMarco PJ, Weisman MH, Seibold JR, et al: Predictors and outcomes of scleroderma renal crisis: The high-dose versus low-dose D-penicillamine in early diffuse systemic sclerosis trial. Arthritis Rheum 46:2983–2989, 2002.

51. Black CM, du Bois RM: Organ involvement: Pulmonary. *In* Clements PJ, Furst DE (eds): Systemic Sclerosis. Baltimore: Williams & Wilkins, 1996, pp 299–331.

52. MacGregor AJ, Canavan R, Knight C, et al: Pulmonary hypertension in systemic sclerosis: Risk factors for progression and consequences for survival. Rheumatology (Oxford) 40:453–459, 2003.

53. Cailes JB, Phillips GD, Wells AU, et al: Correlation of echocardiography and right heart catheter in systemic sclerosis. Am J Respir Crit Care Med 149:A43, 1994.

54. Menon N, McAlpine L, Peacock AJ, et al: The acute effects of prostacyclin on pulmonary hemodynamics in patients with pulmonary hypertension secondary to systemic sclerosis. Arthritis Rheum 41:466–469, 1998.

55. Badesch DB, Tapson VF, McGoon MD, et al: Continuous intravenous epoprostenol for pulmonary hypertension due to the scleroderma spectrum of disease: A randomized, controlled trial. Ann Intern Med 132:425–434, 2000.

56. Kuhn KP, Byrne DW, Arbogast PG, et al: Outcome in 91 consecutive patients with pulmonary arterial hypertension receiving epoprostenol. Am J Respir Crit Care Med 167:580–586, 2003.

57. Rubin LJ, Badesch DB, Barst RJ, et al: Bosentan therapy for pulmonary arterial hypertension. N Engl J Med 346:896–903, 2002.

58. Arnett FC, Edworthy SM, Bloch DA, et al: The American Rheumatism Association 1987 revised criteria for the classification of rheumatoid arthritis. Arthritis Rheum 31:315–324, 1988.

59. Nepom GT, Nepom B: Genetics of the major histocompatibility complex in rheumatoid arthritis. *In* Klippel JH, Dieppe PA (eds): Rheumatology. London: Mosby, 1998, pp 7.1–7.12.

60. Gladman DD, Anhorn KA: HLA and disease manifestations in rheumatoid arthritis—a Canadian experience. J Rheumatol 13:274–276, 1986.

61. Hyland RH, Gordon DA, Broder I, et al: A systematic controlled study of pulmonary abnormalities in rheumatoid arthritis. J Rheumatol 10:395–405, 1983.

62. Gilligan DM, O'Connor CM, Ward K, et al: Bronchoalveolar lavage in patients with mild and severe rheumatoid lung disease. Thorax 45:591–596, 1990.

63. Jurik AG, Davidsen D, Graudal H: Prevalence of pulmonary involvement in rheumatoid arthritis and its relationship to some characteristics of the patients: A radiological and clinical study. Scand J Rheumatol 11:217–224, 1982.

64. Shannon TM, Gale ME: Noncardiac manifestations of rheumatoid arthritis in the thorax. J Thorac Imaging 7:19–29, 1992.

65. Scadding JG: The lungs in rheumatoid arthritis. Proc R Soc Med 62:227–238, 1969.

66. DeHoratius RJ, Abruzzo JL, Williams RC Jr: Immunofluorescent and immunologic studies of rheumatoid lung. Arch Intern Med 129:441–446, 1972.

66a. Yoshinouchi T, Ohtsuki Y, Fujita J, et al: Nonspecific interstitial pneumonia pattern as pulmonary involvement of rheumatoid arthritis. Rheumatol Int 2005, in press.

66b. Flaherty KR, Colby TV, Travis WD, et al: Fibroblastic foci in usual interstitial pneumonia: idiopathic versus collagen vascular disease. Am J Respir Crit Care Med 167:1410–1415, 2003.

67. Cervantes-Perez C, Toro-Perez AH, Rodriguez-Jurado P: Pulmonary involvement in rheumatoid arthritis. JAMA 243:1715–1719, 1980.

68. Roschmann RA, Rothenberg RJ: Pulmonary fibrosis in rheumatoid arthritis: A review of clinical features and therapy. Semin Arthritis Rheum 16:174–185, 1987.

69. Walker WC, Wright V: Pulmonary lesions and rheumatoid arthritis. Medicine 47:501, 1968.

70. Dawson JK, Fewins HE, Desmond J, et al: Fibrosing alveolitis in patients with rheumatoid arthritis as assessed by high resolution computed tomography, chest radiography, and pulmonary function tests. Thorax 56:622–627, 2001.

71. Hakala M: Poor prognosis in patients with rheumatoid arthritis hospitalized for interstitial lung fibrosis. Chest 93:114–118, 1988.

72. Dawson JK, Fewins HE, Desmond J, et al: Predictors of progression of HRCT diagnosed fibrosing alveolitis in patients with rheumatoid arthritis. Ann Rheum Dis 61:517–521, 2002.

73. du Bois RM, Geddes DM: Obliterative bronchiolitis, cryptogenic organising pneumonitis and bronchiolitis obliterans organizing pneumonia: Three names for two different conditions. Eur Respir J 4:774–775, 1991.

74. Colby TV, Myers JL: Clinical and histologic spectrum of bronchiolitis obliterans organising pneumonia. Semin Respir Med 13:119–133, 1992.

75. Wells AU, du Bois RM: Bronchiolitis in association with connective tissue disorders. Clin Chest Med 14:655–666, 1993.

76. Yousem SA, Colby TV, Carrington CB: Lung biopsy in rheumatoid arthritis. Am Rev Respir Dis 131:770–777, 1985.

77. Wolfe F, Schurle DR, Lin JJ, et al: Upper and lower airway disease in penicillamine treated patients with rheumatoid arthritis. J Rheumatol 10:406–410, 1983.

78. Sweatman MC, Markwick JR, Charles PJ, et al: Histocompatibility antigens in adult obliterative bronchiolitis with or without rheumatoid arthritis. Dis Markers 4:19–26, 1986.

79. Begin R, Masse S, Cantin A, et al: Airway disease in a subset of nonsmoking rheumatoid patients: Characterization of the disease and evidence for an autoimmune pathogenesis. Am J Med 72:743–750, 1982.

80. Geddes DM, Webley M, Emerson PA: Airways obstruction in rheumatoid arthritis. Ann Rheum Dis 38:222–225, 1979.

81. Andonopoulos AP, Constantopoulos SH, Drosos AA, et al: Pulmonary function of nonsmoking patients with rheumatoid arthritis in the presence and absence of secondary Sjögren's syndrome: A controlled study. Respiration 53:251–258, 1988.

82. Sassoon CS, McAlpine SW, Tashkin DP, et al: Small airways function in nonsmokers with rheumatoid arthritis. Arthritis Rheum 27:1218–1226, 1984.

83. Geddes DM, Corrin B, Brewerton DA, et al: Progressive airway obliteration in adults and its association with rheumatoid disease. Q J Med 46:427–444, 1977.

84. Nimni ME, Bavetta LA: Collagen defect induced by penicillamine. Science 150:905–907, 1965.

85. Lahdensuo A, Mattila J, Vilppula A: Bronchiolitis in rheumatoid arthritis. Chest 85:705–708, 1984.

86. Yousem SA, Colby TV, Carrington CB: Follicular bronchitis/bronchiolitis. Hum Pathol 16:702–706, 1985.

87. Howling SJ, Hansell DM, Wells AU, et al: Follicular bronchiolitis: Thin-section CT and histologic findings. Radiology 212:637–642, 1999.

88. Despaux J, Polio JC, Toussirot E, et al: Rheumatoid arthritis and bronchiectasis: A retrospective study of fourteen cases. Rev Rhum Eng Ed 63:801–808, 1996.

89. Shadick NA, Fanta CH, Weinblatt ME, et al: Bronchiectasis: A late feature of severe rheumatoid arthritis. Medicine 73:161–170, 1994.

90. Perez T, Remy-Jardin M, Cortet B: Airways involvement in rheumatoid arthritis: Clinical, functional, and HRCT findings. Am J Respir Crit Care Med 157:1658–1665, 1998.

91. Kelly CA: Rheumatoid arthritis: Classical rheumatoid lung disease. Baillieres Clin Rheumatol 7:1–16, 1993.

92. Fellbaum C, Domej W, Popper H: Rheumatoid arthritis with extensive lung lesions. Thorax 44:70–71, 1989.

93. Jolles H, Moseley PL, Peterson MW: Nodular pulmonary opacities in patients with rheumatoid arthritis: A diagnostic dilemma. Chest 96:1022–1025, 1989.

94. Caplan A: Certain unusual radiological appearances in the chest of coal-miners suffering from rheumatoid arthritis. Thorax 8:29, 1953.

95. Walker WC, Wright V: Rheumatoid pleuritis. Ann Rheum Dis 26:467–474, 1967.

96. Jones FL Jr, Blodgett RC Jr: Empyema in rheumatoid pleuropulmonary disease. Ann Intern Med 74:665–671, 1971.

97. Lee PR, Sox HC, North FS, et al: Pleurisy with effusion in rheumatoid arthritis. Arch Intern Med 104:634, 1959.

98. Dodson WH, Hollingsworth JW: Pleural effusion in rheumatoid arthritis: Impaired transport of glucose. N Engl J Med 275:1337–1342, 1966.

99. Yousem SA, Colby TV, Carrington CB: Lung biopsy in rheumatoid arthritis. Am Rev Respir Dis 131:770, 1985.

100. Strohl KP, Feldman NT, Ingram RH Jr: Apical fibrobullous disease with rheumatoid arthritis. Chest 75:739–741, 1979.

101. Yue CC, Park CH, Kushner I: Apical fibrocavitary lesions of the lung in rheumatoid arthritis: Report of two cases and review of the literature. Am J Med 81:741–746, 1986.

102. Mutru O, Koota K, Isomaki H: Causes of death in autopsied RA patients. Scand J Rheumatol 5:239–240, 1976.

103. Koota K, Isomaki H, Mutru O: Death rate and causes of death in RA patients during a period of five years. Scand J Rheumatol 6:241–244, 1977.

104. St. Clair EW, Rice JR, Snyderman R: Pneumonitis complicating low-dose methotrexate therapy in rheumatoid arthritis. Arch Intern Med 145:2035–2038, 1985.

105. Alarcon GS, Kremer JM, Macaiuso M, et al: Risk factors for methotrexate-induced lung injury in patients with rheumatoid arthritis: A multicenter, case-control study. Methotrexate-Lung Study Group. Ann Intern Med 127:356–364, 1997.

106. Dawson JK, Graham DR, Desmond J, et al: Investigation of the chronic pulmonary effects of low-dose oral methotrexate in patients with rheumatoid arthritis: A prospective study incorporating HRCT scanning and pulmonary function tests. Rheumatology (Oxford) 41:262–267, 2002.

107. Kremer JM, Alarcon GS, Weinblatt ME, et al: Clinical, laboratory, radiographic, and histopathologic features of methotrexate-associated lung injury in patients with rheumatoid arthritis: A multicenter study with literature review. Arthritis Rheum 40:1829–1837, 1997.

108. Salaffi F, Manganelli P, Carotti M, et al: Methotrexate-induced pneumonitis in patients with rheumatoid arthritis and psoriatic arthritis: Report of five cases and review of the literature. Clin Rheumatol 16:296–304, 1997.

109. Cannon GW: Methotrexate pulmonary toxicity. Rheum Dis Clin North Am 23:917–937, 1997.

110. Camus P, Piard F, Ashcroft T, et al: The lung in inflammatory bowel disease. Medicine 72:151–183, 1993.

111. Tomioka R, King TE Jr: Gold-induced pulmonary disease: Clinical features, outcome, and differentiation from rheumatoid lung disease. Am J Respir Crit Care Med 155:1011–1020, 1997.

111a. Hassen Zrour S, Touzi M, Bejia I, et al: Correlations between high-resolution computed tomography of the chest and clinical function in patients with rheumatoid arthritis; Prospective study in 75 patients. Joint Bone Spine 72:41–47, 2005.

112. Alasaly K, Muller N, Ostrow DN, et al: Cryptogenic organizing pneumonia: A report of 25 cases and a review of the literature. Medicine 74:201–211, 1995.

113. Lee KS, Kullnig P, Hartman TE, et al: Cryptogenic organizing pneumonia: CT findings in 43 patients. AJR Am J Roentgenol 162:543–546, 1994.

114. Wells AU: Computed tomographic imaging of bronchiolar disorders. Curr Opin Pulm Med 4:85–92, 1998.

114a. Genovese MC, Kremer JM: Treatment of rheumatoid arthritis with etanercept. Rheum Dis Clin North Am 30:311–328, 2004.

115. Tan EM, Cohen AS, Fries JF, et al: The 1982 revised criteria for the classification of systemic lupus erythematosus. Arthritis Rheum 25:1271–1277, 1982.

116. Gladman DD, Urowitz MB: Systemic lupus erythematosus: Clinical features. *In* Klippel JH, Dieppe PA (eds): Rheumatology. London: Mosby, 1998, pp 1.1–1.17.

117. Reinersten JL, Klippel JH, Johnson AH, et al: Family studies of B lymphocyte alloantigens in systemic lupus erythematosus. J Rheumatol 9:253–262, 1982.

118. Haupt HM, Moore GW, Hutchins GM: The lung in systemic lupus erythematosus: Analysis of the pathologic changes in 120 patients. Am J Med 71:791–798, 1981.

119. Miller LR, Greenberg SD, McLarty JW: Lupus lung. Chest 88:265, 1985.

120. Gross M, Esterly JR, Earle RH: Pulmonary alterations in systemic lupus erythematosus. Am Rev Respir Dis 105:572, 1972.

121. Eisenberg H, Dubois EL, Sherwin RP, et al: Diffuse interstitial lung disease in systemic lupus erythematosus. Ann Intern Med 79:37–45, 1973.

122. Weinrib L, Sharma OP, Quismorio FP Jr: A long-term study of interstitial lung disease in systemic lupus erythematosus. Semin Arthritis Rheum 20:48–56, 1990.

123. Orens JB, Martinez FJ, Lynch JP 3rd: Pleuropulmonary manifestations of systemic lupus erythematosus. Rheum Dis Clin North Am 20:159–193, 1994.

124. Gibson CJ, Edmonds JP, Hughes GRV: Diaphragm function and lung involvement in systemic lupus erythematosus. Am J Med 63:926–932, 1977.

125. Laroche CM, Mulvey DA, Hawkins PN, et al: Diaphragm strength in the shrinking lung syndrome of systemic lupus erythematosus. Q J Med 71:429–439, 1989.

126. Nived O, Sturfelt G, Wollheim F: Systemic lupus erythematosus and infection: A controlled and prospective study including an epidemiological group. Q J Med 55:271–287, 1985.

127. Asherson RA, Oakley CM: Pulmonary hypertension and systemic lupus erythematosus. J Rheumatol 13:1–5, 1986 [published erratum appears in J Rheumatol 13:840, 1986].

128. Simonson JS, Schiller NB, Petri M, et al: Pulmonary hypertension in systemic lupus erythematosus. J Rheumatol 16:918–925, 1989.

129. Alarcon-Segovia D, Deleze M, Oria CV, et al: Antiphospholipid antibodies and the antiphospholipid syndrome in systemic lupus erythematosus: A prospective analysis of 500 consecutive patients. Medicine 68:353–365, 1989.

129a. Paran D, Fireman E, Elkayam O: Pulmonary disease in systemic lupus erythematosus and the antiphospholipid syndrome. Autoimmun Rev 3:70–75, 2004.

130. Cervera R, Khamashta MA, Font J, et al: Systemic lupus erythematosus: Clinical and immunologic patterns of disease expression in a cohort of 1,000 patients. The European Working Party on Systemic Lupus Erythematosus. Medicine 72:113–124, 1993.

131. Robbins IM, Gaine SP, Schilz R, et al: Epoprostenol for treatment of pulmonary hypertension in patients with systemic lupus erythematosus. Chest 117:14–18, 2000.

132. Good JT Jr, King TE, Antony VB, et al: Lupus pleuritis: Clinical features and pleural fluid characteristics with special reference to pleural fluid antinuclear antibodies. Chest 84:714–718, 1983.

133. Gross M, Esterly JR, Earle RH: Pulmonary alterations in systemic lupus erythematosus. Am Rev Respir Dis 105:572–577, 1972.

134. Naylor B: Cytological aspects of pleural, peritoneal and pericardial fluids from patients with systemic lupus erythematosus. Cytopathology 3:1–8, 1992.

135. Leechawengwong M, Berger HW, Sukumaran M: Diagnostic significance of antinuclear antibodies in pleural effusion. Mt Sinai J Med 46:137–139, 1979.

136. Vitali C, Bombardieri S, Moutsopoulos HM, et al: Preliminary criteria for the classification of Sjögren's syndrome: Results of a prospective concerted action supported by the European Community. Arthritis Rheum 36:340–347, 1993.

137. Papathanasiou MP, Constantopoulos SH, Tsampoulas C, et al: Reappraisal of respiratory abnormalities in primary and secondary Sjögren's syndrome: A controlled study. Chest 90:370, 1986.

138. Gardiner P: Primary Sjögren's syndrome. Baillieres Clin Rheumatol 7:59–77, 1993.

139. Taouli B, Brauner MW, Mourey I, et al: Thin-section chest CT findings of primary Sjögren's syndrome: Correlation with pulmonary function. Eur Radiol 12:1504–1511, 2002.

140. Gardiner P, Ward C, Allison A, et al: Pleuropulmonary abnormalities in primary Sjögren's syndrome. J Rheumatol 20:831–837, 1993.

140a. Ito I, Nagai S, Kitaichi M, et al: Pulmonary manifestations of primary Sjögren's syndrome: a clinical radiologic, and pathologic study. Am J Respir Crit Care Med 2005, in press.

141. Davidson BK, Kelly CA, Griffiths ID: Ten year follow up of pulmonary function in patients with primary Sjögren's syndrome. Ann Rheum Dis 59:709–712, 2000.

142. Strimlan CV, Rosenow EC, Divertie MB, et al: Pulmonary manifestations of Sjögren's syndrome. Chest 70:354, 1976.

143. Kassan SS, Thomas TL, Moutsopoulos HM, et al: Increased risk of lymphoma in sicca syndrome. Ann Intern Med 89:888–892, 1978.

144. Constantopoulos SH, Drosos AA, Maddison PJ, et al: Xerotrachea and interstitial lung disease in primary Sjögren's syndrome. Respiration 46:310–314, 1984.

145. Gudbjornsson B, Hedenstrom H, Stalenheim G, et al: Bronchial hyperresponsiveness to methacholine in patients with primary Sjögren's syndrome. Ann Rheum Dis 50:36–40, 1991.

146. La Corte R, Bajocchi G, Potena A, et al: Bronchial hyperreactivity in systemic sclerosis patients: Influence of associated Sjögren's syndrome. Ann Rheum Dis 54:636–639, 1995.

147. Liebow AA, Carrington CB: Diffuse pulmonary lymphoreticular infiltrations associated with dysproteinemia. Med Clin North Am 57:809, 1973.

148. Dalavanga YA, Constantopoulos SH, Galanopoulou V, et al: Alveolitis correlates with clinical pulmonary involvement in primary Sjögren's syndrome. Chest 99:1394–1397, 1991.

149. Fairfax AJ, Haslam PL, Pavia D, et al: Pulmonary disorders associated with Sjögren's syndrome. Q J Med 50:279–295, 1981.

150. Bohan A, Peter JB: Polymyositis and dermatomyositis (second of two parts). N Engl J Med 292:403–407, 1975.

151. Medsger TA, Oddis CV: Inflammatory muscle disease. *In* Klippel JH, Dieppe PA (eds): Rheumatology. London: Mosby, 1998, pp 13.1–13.14.

152. Horiki T, Ichikawa Y, Moriuchi J, et al: HLA class II haplotypes associated with pulmonary interstitial lesions of polymyositis/dermatomyositis in Japanese patients. Tissue Antigens 59:25–30, 2002.

153. Douglas WW, Tazelaar HD, Hartman TE, et al: Polymyositis-dermatomyositis-associated interstitial lung disease. Am J Respir Crit Care Med 164:1182–1185, 2001.

154. Schnabel A, Reuter M, Biederer J, et al: Interstitial lung disease in polymyositis and dermatomyositis: Clinical course and response to treatment. Semin Arthritis Rheum 32:273–284, 2003.

155. Nobutoh T, Kohda M, Doi Y, et al: An autopsy case of dermatomyositis with rapidly progressive diffuse alveolar damage. J Dermatol 25:32–36, 1998.

156. Fata F, Rathore R, Schiff C, et al: Bronchiolitis obliterans organizing pneumonia as the first manifestation of polymyositis. South Med J 90:227–230, 1997.

157. Shinohara T, Hidaka T, Matsuki Y, et al: Rapidly progressive interstitial lung disease associated with dermatomyositis responding to intravenous cyclophosphamide pulse therapy. Intern Med 36:519–523, 1997.

158. Mino M, Noma S, Taguchi Y, et al: Pulmonary involvement in polymyositis and dermatomyositis: Sequential evaluation with CT. AJR Am J Roentgenol 169:83–87, 1997.

159. Schwarz MI, Sutarik JM, Nick JA, et al: Pulmonary capillaritis and diffuse alveolar hemorrhage: A primary manifestation of polymyositis. Am J Respir Crit Care Med 151:2037–2040, 1995.

160. Akira M, Hara H, Sakatani M: Interstitial lung disease in association with polymyositis-dermatomyositis: Long-term follow-up CT evaluation in seven patients. Radiology 210:333–338, 1999.

161. Chow WH, Gridley G, Mellemkjaer L, et al: Cancer risk following polymyositis and dermatomyositis: A nationwide cohort study in Denmark. Cancer Causes Control 6:9–13, 1995.

162. Targoff IN: Humoral immunity in polymyositis/dermatomyositis. J Invest Dermatol 100:116S–123S, 1993.

163. Miyake S, Ohtani Y, Sawada M, et al: Usefulness of cyclosporine A on rapidly progressive interstitial pneumonia in dermatomyositis. Sarcoidosis Vasc Diffuse Lung Dis 19:128–133, 2002.

164. Amigues JM, Cantagrel A, Abbal M, et al: Comparative study of 4 diagnosis criteria sets for mixed connective tissue disease in patients with anti-RNP antibodies. Autoimmunity Group of the Hospitals of Toulouse. J Rheumatol 23:2055–2062, 1996.

165. Maddison PJ: Overlap syndromes and mixed connective tissue disease. Curr Opin Rheumatol 3:995–1000, 1991.

166. Gendi NS, Welsh KI, Van Venrooij WJ, et al: HLA type as a predictor of mixed connective tissue disease differentiation: Ten-year clinical and immunogenetic followup of 46 patients. Arthritis Rheum 38:259–266, 1995.

167. Prakash UB: Respiratory complications in mixed connective tissue disease. Clin Chest Med 19:733–746, ix, 1998.

168. Kozuka T, Johkoh T, Honda O, et al: Pulmonary involvement in mixed connective tissue disease: High-resolution CT findings in 41 patients. J Thorac Imaging 16:94–98, 2001.

169. Zeuner M, Straub RH, Rauh G, et al: Relapsing polychondritis: Clinical and immunogenetic analysis of 62 patients. J Rheumatol 24:96–101, 1997.

170. Lee-Chiong TL Jr: Pulmonary manifestations of ankylosing spondylitis and relapsing polychondritis. Clin Chest Med 19:747–757, ix, 1998.

171. Eng J, Sabanathan S: Airway complications in relapsing polychondritis. Ann Thorac Surg 51:686–692, 1991.

172. Shah R, Sabanathan S, Mearns AJ, Featherstone H: Self-expanding tracheobronchial stents in the management of major airway problems. J Cardiovasc Surg 36:343–348, 1995.

173. McAdam LP, O'Hanlan MA, Bluestone R, et al: Relapsing polychondritis: Prospective study of 23 patients and a review of the literature. Medicine 55:193–215, 1976.

174. Sarodia BD, Dasgupta A, Mehta AC: Management of airway manifestations of relapsing polychondritis: Case reports and review of literature. Chest 116:1669–1675, 1999.

175. Yazici H, Yurdakul S, Hamuryudan V: Behçet's syndrome. In Klippel JH, Dieppe PA (eds): Rheumatology. London: Mosby, 1998, pp 26.1–26.6.

176. Anonymous: Criteria for diagnosis of Behçet's disease. International Study Group for Behçet's Disease. Lancet 335:1078–1080, 1990.

177. Erkan F, Gul A, Tasali E: Pulmonary manifestations of Behçet's disease. Thorax 56:572–578, 2001.

178. Raz I, Okon E, Chajek-Shaul T: Pulmonary manifestations in Behçet's syndrome. Chest 95:585–589, 1989.

179. Tunaci A, Berkmen YM, Gokmen E: Thoracic involvement in Behçet's disease: Pathologic, clinical, and imaging features. AJR Am J Roentgenol 164:51–56, 1995.

180. Ahn JM, Im JG, Ryoo JW, et al: Thoracic manifestations of Behçet's syndrome: Radiographic and CT findings in nine patients. Radiology 194:199–203, 1995.

181. Tuzun H, Besirli K, Sayin A, et al: Management of aneurysms in Behçet's syndrome: An analysis of 24 patients. Surgery 121:150–156, 1997.

182. Schlosstein L, Terasaki PI, Bluestone R, et al: High association of an HL-A antigen, W27, with ankylosing spondylitis. N Engl J Med 288:704–706, 1973.

183. Rosenow E, Strimlan CV, Muhm JR, et al: Pleuropulmonary manifestations of ankylosing spondylitis. Mayo Clin Proc 52:641–649, 1977.

184. Casserly IP, Fenlon HM, Breatnach E, et al: Lung findings on high-resolution computed tomography in idiopathic ankylosing spondylitis—correlation with clinical findings, pulmonary function testing and plain radiography. Br J Rheumatol 36:677–682, 1997.

185. Turetschek K, Ebner W, Fleischmann D, et al: Early pulmonary involvement in ankylosing spondylitis: Assessment with thin-section CT. Clin Radiol 55:632–636, 2000.

186. Jeandel P, Bonnet D, Chouc PY, et al: Demonstration of subclinical pulmonary alveolitis in spondylarthropathies (in French). Rev Rhum Ed Fr 5:301–309, 1994.

187. Chakera TM, Howarth FH, Kendall MJ, et al: The chest radiograph in ankylosing spondylitis. Clin Radiol 26:455–459, 1975.

188. Davies D: Ankylosing spondylitis and lung fibrosis. Q J Med 41:395–417, 1972.

189. Hunninghake GW, Fauci AS: Pulmonary involvement in the collagen vascular diseases. Am Rev Respir Dis 119:471–503, 1979.

190. Turner JA, Stanley NN: Fragile lung in the Marfan syndrome. Thorax 31:771–775, 1976.

191. Dominguez R, Weisgrau RA, Santamaria M: Pulmonary hyperinflation and emphysema in infants with the Marfan syndrome. Pediatr Radiol 17:365–369, 1987.

192. Wood JR, Bellamy D, Child AH, et al: Pulmonary disease in patients with Marfan syndrome. Thorax 39:780–784, 1984.

193. Hall JR, Pyeritz RE, Dudgeon DL, et al: Pneumothorax in the Marfan syndrome: Prevalence and therapy. Ann Thorac Surg 37:500–504, 1984.

194. Wanderman KL, Goldstein MS, Faber J: Cor pulmonale secondary to severe kyphoscoliosis in Marfan's syndrome (letter). Chest 67:250–251, 1975.

195. Cistulli PA, Sullivan CE: Sleep apnea in Marfan's syndrome: Increased upper airway collapsibility during sleep. Chest 108:631–635, 1995.

55

Sarcoidosis

Yasmine Wasfi, M.D., Lee S. Newman, M.D.

INTRODUCTION

Sarcoidosis is a multisystem, inflammatory disorder characterized by noncaseating granulomas that can infiltrate almost any organ, especially the lungs. Most often occurring in early adulthood, sarcoidosis often presents with hilar lymphadenopathy, pulmonary infiltration, and eye and skin lesions. Because of its many and varied clinical manifestations, this disorder can mimic other inflammatory and infectious disorders.[1] Major targets include the lungs, lymphatics, eyes, skin, liver, bone, heart, and neurologic system. The American Thoracic Society criteria for the diagnosis of sarcoidosis include (1) the presence of a consistent clinical and radiographic picture; (2) the demonstration of noncaseating granulomas on biopsy; and (3) exclusion of other conditions that can produce similar pathology, including infections, autoimmune disorders, and inhalational diseases, as discussed later in the Differential Diagnosis section.[2]

BACKGROUND

Jonathan Hutchinson published the first description of sarcoidosis in 1877, reporting a patient who had developed multiple raised purple skin lesions over 2 years. He subsequently described several similar cases and suggested that they represented a distinct clinical entity. In 1899, Caesar Boeck reported a case of skin lesions similar to Hutchinson's and provided a name for this condition when he used the term "multiple benign sarkoid of the skin," referring to the histologic appearance that he thought resembled sarcoma. He subsequently published descriptions of similar pathology in multiple other organs, including lung and lymph nodes. The name *sarcoidosis* was derived from these descriptions.[1,2]

EPIDEMIOLOGY

Sarcoidosis occurs worldwide and affects people of both genders, all racial and ethnic backgrounds, and all ages.[1] Study of the epidemiology of sarcoidosis has been limited by the variability in patient presentation and, for many years, the absence of a clear disease definition. However, available studies demonstrate that most disease is diagnosed in adults under the age of 40, with a slight female predominance and a peak incidence in the 20- to 29-year age group. Disease can occur in children and the elderly as well. Estimated prevalence rates in the United States vary from 1 to 40 per 100,000 population. Similarly, there is a range of age-adjusted annual incidence rates in the United States, from 10.9 per 100,000 for whites to 35.5 per 100,000 for African Americans. Although similar rates have been reported in many countries, the pattern and severity of disease vary based on race, nationality, and ethnicity. The published rates likely underestimate the frequency of this disorder, because many cases may go undiagnosed or may be misdiagnosed.[1,2]

ETIOLOGY AND PATHOGENESIS

The cause of sarcoidosis remains unknown. However, there is much evidence to support the hypothesis that the disease develops when a genetically susceptible individual is exposed to a specific environmental antigen.

ENVIRONMENT

A shared environmental exposure, or possibly person-to-person transmission, is suggested by spatial and temporal clustering of cases, reports of community outbreaks, and reports of work-related risk for health care workers. Careful environmental investigation of new cases sometimes uncovers clusters of disease and may suggest sources of antigen exposures or exposures to known causes of granulomatous disease. For example, clusters of disease have been found among nurses and one group of firefighters.[3–6] A case-control study of a sarcoidosis cluster on the Isle of Man demonstrated that a significantly greater percentage of cases than controls reported previous contact with a sarcoidosis patient.[5,7,8]

Although studies such as these suggest a possible infectious etiology, no single infective agent or antigen has been consistently linked to sarcoidosis. The possibility that an infection, especially due to mycobacteria, causes sarcoidosis has been considered in multiple studies.[9,10] In addition to mycobacteria, other infectious agents have been proposed, including *Propionibacterium* species, *Rickettsia*, and viruses.[11–17] However, the published data using available tissue staining, culture, and molecular genetic methods demonstrate contradictory results. Although a specific antigen has yet to be identified, immunologic data showing skewed T-cell antigen receptor utilization in sarcoidosis patients' bronchoalveolar lavage fluid[18] strongly suggest an antigenic cause. Evidence of an up-regulated type 1 T helper (Th1) cell pattern of cytokine production (i.e., interferon-γ, interleukin-2, and tumor necrosis factor [TNF]-α) suggests that, whether or not the disease is triggered by a microbe-related antigen, the pathologic consequence is due to an overexuberant immune response, as discussed later.

A recent multicenter case-control study of the etiology of sarcoidosis (A Case Control Etiologic Study of Sarcoidosis [ACCESS]) examined 706 case-control pairs.[19] The study recruited newly diagnosed, pathology-confirmed cases, excluded cases of possible tuberculosis or chronic beryllium disease, and used random-digit telephone dialing to recruit controls matched for age, gender, race, and ethnicity from 10 centers. Questionnaires were used to obtain information about previous occupational and environmental exposures, as well as family history of sarcoidosis. The study found weak but statistically significant associations for several occupational and environmental exposures, including those potentially related to microbial bioaerosols and pesticides, but did not identify a single proximate cause of sarcoidosis. Tobacco smoking was significantly less common among sarcoidosis cases compared to controls, consistent with previous literature suggesting a protective effect.[20,21] A previous case-control study had more specifically evaluated rural exposures as potential risk factors for sarcoidosis. These investigators found that, even in multivariable models, a significant and dose-dependent association existed between exposure to wood stoves or fireplaces and the development of sarcoidosis.[22] Still another case-control investigation enrolled African American individuals with sarcoidosis and collected detailed job histories from them and from sibling controls. Several job titles and job exposures were found to be associated, both positively and negatively, with disease risk. The authors concluded that work involving exposure to metals or high humidity may place individuals at increased risk of developing sarcoidosis, but that identification of specific relevant exposures was quite difficult in the face of complex occupational exposures.[23] Other clues, including both seasonal and geographic variation in sarcoidosis risk, similarly raise questions but do not solve the riddle of etiology.[24–30] The failure of these epidemiologic studies to identify a unique relevant antigen in the face of immunologic evidence supporting the importance of exposure to antigen makes it increasingly likely that sarcoidosis occurs when susceptible individuals encounter one of a number of different environmental antigens. Briefly, the available lines of immunologic evidence suggest that sarcoidosis granulomas form as a result of (1) antigen exposure, (2) an antigen-specific cell-mediated immune response, and (3) inflammatory, or innate immune, responses that amplify and perpetuate the antigen-specific immunologic reaction. This evidence is discussed in greater detail in the Immunology section later.

GENETICS

There are several lines of evidence that support a genetic component to disease development. Although the variation in incidence, severity, and manifestations of disease among different racial and ethnic groups may be consistent with either an environmental or a genetic contribution, observations of familial clustering of disease and the presence of disease two to four times more commonly in monozygotic than in dizygotic twins clearly demonstrate the importance of genetic factors. Previous studies have shown that up to 19% of affected African American families and 5% of white families have more than one member affected.[31,32] Results of ACCESS further support these observations. An analysis of nearly 11,000 first-degree and over 17,000 second-degree relatives of the 706 cases and controls revealed an overall adjusted familial relative risk of developing sarcoidosis of 4.7 (95% confidence interval, 2.3 to 9.7). Investigations of German families with more than one affected member similarly support a genetic contribution to disease development. Specifically, evaluations of the distribution of human leukocyte antigen (HLA) and angiotensin-converting enzyme (ACE) polymorphic alleles in these families suggest an excess of specific alleles among affected first-degree relatives.[33–35] Given these observations, it is likely that multiple genes, rather than a single gene, comprise the genetic predisposition to disease.

Numerous investigators have used the candidate gene approach, which examines the potential contribution to disease risk of genetic variants with a biologically plausible role in disease pathogenesis. Based on understanding of the immunopathogenesis of sarcoidosis (see Immunology section later), the major focus has been on gene polymorphisms in the major histocompatibility complex (MHC) region of chromosome 6. To date, these studies have investigated the HLA genes (class I, or HLA-A, -B and -C; and class II, or HLA-DP, -DQ and -DR), transporter associated with antigen-processing (TAP) genes, and TNF. These studies, as well as investigations of microsatellite linkage analysis and HLA types in familial sarcoidosis,[34–36] strongly support the existence of a susceptibility locus for sarcoidosis in this region.

The majority of reported associations have been between specific HLA-DQ and -DR alleles and disease risk. In the discussion that follows, where HLA alleles are described by two names, the first is based on earlier serologic nomenclature and the second is based on more recent high-resolution genetic typing. Variants have been identified that both confer risk and appear protective. Although the associated alleles have differed by race and ethnicity, the preponderance of data across several countries, including the United States, has yielded consistent associations of sarcoidosis, as well as a more chronic disease phenotype with specific alleles of HLA-DRB1*15 and HLA-DQB1*0602. Milder disease has consistently been associated with distinct HLA-DRB1*03 alleles and HLA-DQB1*0201. Particular advances in the understanding of sarcoidosis genetics have come from a series of studies from Sweden and the United Kingdom on individuals with acute, resolving forms of disease, such as Löfgren's syndrome. This syndrome is characterized by erythema nodosum, hilar adenopathy, and joint symptoms. Berlin and colleagues[37] demonstrated that, in a Scandinavian sarcoidosis population, specific and distinct HLA-DR alleles were associated with a milder disease phenotype or with a more chronic, severe phenotype. HLA-DR17 (DRB1*03) was found nearly four times as often in patients with mild disease as in normal controls, whereas DR14 (DRB1*14) and DR15 (DRB1*15) were identified two to three times more frequently in patients with chronic disease as in normal controls. Sato and coworkers[38] performed high-resolution HLA-DQB1 typing on a large population of British and Dutch sarcoidosis patients and controls. They determined that the HLA-DQB1*0201 was strongly associated with milder disease, whereas the DQB1*0602 was associated with more severe disease. The emerging picture suggests that extended haplotypes, or multiple specific alleles on a particular chromosome, may help characterize disease risk, especially in certain subsets of clinical phenotype. Specifically, HLA-DRB1*0301/DQB1*0201 is associated with mild disease with spontaneous resolution and HLA-DRB1*1501/DQB1*0602 is associated with more severe persistent disease.[39]

Investigation of other candidate genes in the MHC region has also yielded significant associations. TAP-1 and TAP-2 are transporters critical in the processing of antigen prior to presentation through MHC class I, although some data suggest that they may play a role in delivery of antigen to the MHC class II complex as well. Evaluation of TAP-1 and TAP-2 polymorphisms in British and Polish sarcoidosis patients and controls revealed associations in each ethnic group of specific but distinct TAP-2 alleles with disease.[40] Similarly, specific polymorphic alleles in the TNF promoter have been associated with specific disease phenotypes in some studies. At least three separate studies have demonstrated a significantly increased frequency of the less common allele of the TNF -308 promoter polymorphism in patients with Löfgren's syndrome.[41-43] This allele has also been found in unexpectedly high frequencies in patients with cardiac sarcoidosis.[44] However, in two other studies, including one using a subpopulation from the ACCESS study, no difference was found in the TNF promoter -308 allele frequencies between cases and controls.[45,46] Investigation of the TNF -857 polymorphism in a British and Dutch population demonstrated an association between the less common -857T allele and sarcoidosis.[47] Taken together, these results support the existence of specific genetic variants, or more likely combinations of variants, within the MHC locus on chromosome 6 that contribute significantly to sarcoidosis disease risk.

There has also been evaluation of numerous genes outside of the MHC region with regard to their potential role in sarcoidosis susceptibility. Studies of many of these candidate genes have yielded negative or conflicting results. Of note among these is the ACE gene, selected because of the observed elevations in ACE levels in some sarcoidosis patients. This gene contains a polymorphism characterized by either the presence or absence of a particular (287-base pair) fragment within the gene. Most studies have found no association of this polymorphism with sarcoidosis. However, one case-control study in African American subjects determined that homozygosity (the absence of this fragment in both copies of the gene) was associated with sarcoidosis susceptibility, particularly in cases with a family history of sarcoidosis.[48] Several recent studies have found associations between sarcoidosis and specific alleles of polymorphisms in the interleukin (IL)-1α, the complement receptor 1, and various C-C chemokine receptor genes. The latter are of particular interest, as studies in three distinct populations (Japanese, Czech, and Dutch) have identified both strong positive and negative associations between specific polymorphic alleles and sarcoidosis.[49-51] Most recently, Spagnolo and colleagues[51] evaluated haplotypes of four polymorphisms in the C-C chemokine receptor 2 gene in a Dutch population. They determined that haplotype 2 (A at nucleotide position -6752, A at 3000, T at 3547, and T at 4385) was strongly associated with Löfgren's syndrome, even after adjusting for other known risk factors for this sarcoidosis variant, such as HLA haplotype and female sex.

In summary, the accumulated evidence strongly suggests that both environmental and genetic factors contribute to the development of sarcoidosis. The epidemiologic studies of environmental and occupational exposures have revealed numerous associations, but have failed to identify a single likely causative agent. Similarly, the investigations of potential infectious etiologies have not yielded consistent results. Therefore, as previously noted, the lack of a clear culprit antigen despite extensive investigation makes it quite likely that sarcoidosis occurs when susceptible individuals encounter one of a number of different environmental antigens. Who are these susceptible individuals? What genetic features comprise their susceptibility? The previous discussion details the findings of numerous studies that have investigated the relationship between polymorphisms in candidate genes both within and outside the MHC region of chromosome 6. As Grutters and associates[39] eloquently summarized, the emerging understanding of sarcoidosis genetics is that there are at least two disease phenotypes, mild and chronic progressive, each with a unique associated genotypic pattern. Continued investigation of the MHC genes in different sarcoidosis populations will certainly add to our understanding of these associations, the importance of extended haplotypes, and the role of linkage disequilibrium in these associations. Furthermore, as demonstrated by the C-C chemokine receptor 2 data described previously, further study of candidate genes outside of the MHC region will likely also contribute significantly to our understanding of genotype-phenotype associations in this complex disease.

IMMUNOLOGY

Sarcoidosis is mediated primarily through CD4+ T helper cells and cells derived from the mononuclear phagocytes.[52]

These cells accumulate within the affected tissue, where they become increasingly organized, and form noncaseating granulomas. Recent reviews describe in detail the current state of knowledge on the immune and inflammatory events.[53-55] The earliest manifestation of sarcoidosis is a mononuclear infiltration of the target organ, preceding granuloma formation. This infiltrative process is thought to be mediated primarily by CD4[+] T lymphocytes and mononuclear phagocytes, although other inflammatory cells (e.g., mast cells, fibroblasts) as well as epithelial and endothelial cells contribute to the nonspecific inflammatory response leading to increased tissue permeability and cell migration. The recruitment of mononuclear cells in sarcoidosis is enhanced by the production of chemokines, including RANTES (regulated on activation normal T cell expressed and secreted), monocyte chemoattractant protein-1, macrophage inflammatory protein-1α, and IL-8, all released by alveolar macrophages.[56] Additionally, there is increased expression of adhesion molecules, such as intercellular adhesion molecule-1, vascular cell adhesion molecule-1, and the selectins, which promote cell binding.[57-61]

As a consequence of chemoattractant signals, an elevated lymphocyte count and a marked increase in the CD4/CD8 T-lymphocyte ratio is observed in the affected organs of patients with active sarcoidosis. Effector cells such as dendritic cells and macrophages may function by presenting antigen to T cells and by producing proinflammatory cytokines, such as IL-12 and IL-15. IL-12 induces the differentiation of naive CD4[+] T lymphocytes into Th1 cells and promotes the release of IFN-γ. Th1 cells in sarcoidosis are antigen-activated CD4[+] T lymphocytes and produce IFN-γ and IL-2, resulting in a delayed-type hypersensitivity immune response. IL-15 acts synergistically with IL-2 and TNF-α to stimulate T-lymphocyte proliferation.

Further evidence of the critical role of CD4[+] T cells in this process comes from clinical case reports and case series of the development of sarcoidosis in patients with acquired immunodeficiency syndrome who are treated with highly active antiretroviral therapy.[62-64a] This therapy results in restoration of CD4[+] T-cell counts and, in these cases, development of a clinical syndrome of sarcoidosis as part of the immune reconstitution. Of particular interest is one case in which this occurred in the context of concomitant highly active antiretroviral therapy and IL-2 therapy, supporting not only the critical role of CD4[+] T cells, but also the importance of Th1 cytokines in the granulomatous inflammation of sarcoidosis.[65] In a subsequent case series, Morris and colleagues[66] described seven patients with human immunodeficiency virus infection and sarcoidosis, and all patients had CD4[+] T-cell counts greater than 200/μL.

Sarcoidosis antigen-specific T lymphocytes generated during the initial host response play a central role in mediating the subsequent inflammatory events within the lung. Once naive T lymphocytes are activated, they undergo clonal expansion and differentiation into effector and memory T lymphocytes. In sarcoidosis, most of the T lymphocytes appear to have been previously stimulated, likely in regional lymph nodes, and to have migrated back to the affected organ.[18] Studies of the T-lymphocyte antigen receptor (TCR) repertoire in sarcoidosis demonstrate that the disorder is initiated by an antigen-specific immune response, based on observed oligoclonal expansion of T-lymphocyte subsets bearing particular, restricted α/β TCRs. Lymphocytes bearing γ/δ TCRs are likely to play some supporting role in the pathogenesis of this disorder, although the body of evidence most strongly supports the importance of T cells that bear particular α/β TCRs on their surface.[18,67] Of note, a body of work from Sweden in patients with Löfgren's syndrome and with acute, remitting sarcoidosis demonstrated a strong association between a lung-restricted expansion of Vα2.3 CD4[+] T cells and the expression of one of two specific antigen-presenting molecules (HLA-DRB3*0101, HLA-DRB3*0301) discussed earlier.[68,69] These data suggest that the combination of a specific T-cell antigen receptor and a particular HLA antigen presentation molecule interacts with the putative sarcoidosis antigen to trigger this acute form of disease.

CD4[+] T lymphocytes from sarcoidosis patients spontaneously proliferate and release IL-2 and IFN-γ in vitro. The IL-2 stimulates further T-lymphocyte proliferation, releasing more IL-2 and IFN-γ, and is chemotactic, recruiting more T lymphocytes to the affected site. IFN-γ amplifies the immune response through its effects on multiple target cells.

The release of inflammatory cytokines serves to recruit additional peripheral blood monocytes to the affected organ, where they differentiate into exudate macrophages that show enhanced antigen-presenting capacity and release TNF-α and IL-1β, both of which promote granuloma formation. In light of potential immunotherapeutic advances, it is noteworthy that TNF-α up-regulates endothelial cell adhesion molecules involved in leukocyte binding, stimulates T-lymphocyte release of IFN-γ, and enhances T-lymphocyte proliferation, among many other potential roles in inflammation. IL-1β may be needed in granuloma formation because it stimulates exudate macrophage production of IL-8 and granulocyte-macrophage colony stimulating factor, which, in turn, promotes monocyte differentiation and resultant macrophage proliferation. The net result is an amplification loop involving antigen recognition, proinflammatory cytokine release, cell activation, recruitment, and granuloma formation. Pathogenic aspects of granuloma formation and maintenance in sarcoidosis, as compared to other granulomatous disorders, have been the subject of previous reviews.[70]

The progression from granulomatous inflammation to increasing amounts of fibrosis portends a poor prognosis. Factors leading from granuloma to fibrosis are poorly understood, but probably involve changes in local cytokine production toward a type 2 T helper cell pattern (IL-4, IL-5) and increases in growth factor expression, including transforming growth factor-β, basic fibroblast growth factor, and insulin-like growth factor-1.[71]

CLINICAL PRESENTATION: ACUTE VERSUS CHRONIC SARCOIDOSIS

The clinical presentation of sarcoidosis ranges from an incidental chest radiographic finding in an asymptomatic patient to chronic progressive organ dysfunction. Usually the disease appears between the ages of 20 and 50; however, both childhood and geriatric cases occur with some regularity. The vast majority of patients (>90%) have some form of pulmonary involvement. However, sarcoidosis may affect any organ, and therefore may present with symptoms referable to any organ. Patients may also present with nonspecific constitutional symptoms, including fatigue, fever, anorexia, and weight loss.

A distinct subgroup of sarcoidosis patients is characterized by an acute presentation, classically with Löfgren's syndrome. As previously mentioned, this syndrome, initially described by Sven Löfgren in 1946, is defined by acute erythema nodosum with bilateral hilar lymphadenopathy, fever, and polyarthritis. Symptoms are typically abrupt in onset and have a transient course. A vesicular or maculopapular rash, acute iritis, conjunctivitis, and Bell's palsy may also be features of acute disease. In a study of 579 consecutive patients with acute arthritis, Visser and colleagues[24] found that four clinical features—symmetrical ankle arthritis, symptoms for less than 2 months, age under 40, and erythema nodosum—provided a high degree of diagnostic certainty for sarcoidosis. Chest radiographs typically are normal or show significant hilar and mediastinal lymphadenopathy, without pulmonary infiltrates. Arrhythmias may occur due to acute granulomatous cardiac involvement. In general, acute disease has a higher probability of spontaneous resolution. Although relapse may occur, it is thought to be less common than in those patients with a more chronic presentation. Prognosis of patients with an acute onset of sarcoidosis is generally good.

Another subgroup of patients, often characterized by a more gradual, insidious onset, is more likely to develop chronic disease. Other risk factors for chronic disease include the presence of lupus pernio, which is a persistent, disfiguring, violaceous rash over the nose, cheeks, and ears, and the presence of multiorgan involvement at the time of diagnosis. Chronic eye involvement includes chronic uveitis, cataracts, glaucoma, or keratoconjunctivitis sicca, which can be confused with Sjögren's syndrome. Bone involvement is also much more common in chronic than acute cases, as are pulmonary infiltrates, nephrocalcinosis, and cor pulmonale. Persistence of disease and recurrence after treatment are common in the chronic form.

CLINICAL FEATURES AND DIAGNOSIS

PULMONARY SARCOIDOSIS

The lung is the most commonly involved organ in sarcoidosis, with physiologic or radiographic abnormalities, or both, demonstrable in more than 90% of patients.[2] Symptoms and physical examination findings are nonspecific. Patients may present with cough, shortness of breath and/or chest pain with crackles, wheezing, or a normal lung examination. Lung physiology is similarly nonspecific. Patients may have normal lung function, even with radiographic abnormalities, or may demonstrate restriction, obstruction, abnormal gas exchange, or a combination of these. Some studies report that the most frequent abnormalities are in the vital capacity and diffusing capacity, suggesting restrictive physiology; however, at least one study of newly diagnosed patients found airflow limitation to be the most common defect.[72] In some patients, airflow limitation may be due to endobronchial involvement, which can result

in significant local stenosis. In general, measures of gas exchange provide greater sensitivity for sarcoidosis lung impairment and response to treatment than do measures of lung volume and airflow.

The radiologic patterns in sarcoidosis are classically described by Scadding staging, which is based on the chest radiograph. However, this staging system is increasingly being supplanted by use of imaging tools that have greater sensitivity, such as spiral/thin-section computed tomography (CT). The chest radiographic stages (0 through IV) do not correspond to the chronologic progression of disease, but do correlate with likelihood of future radiographic and symptomatic disease resolution. A normal chest radiograph, or stage 0 disease, is seen in 5% to 10% of patients at presentation. Of note, in literature comparing chest radiographic to CT findings in sarcoidosis, up to one half of patients with stage 0 disease have pulmonary parenchymal abnormalities on CT scan.[73-76] In addition, 20% to 30% of these patients have physiologic abnormalities,[77] and some can demonstrate noncaseating granulomas on biopsy.[78] This group has a low likelihood of disease progression. Stage I disease (Fig. 55.1) is characterized by bilateral hilar and mediastinal lymphadenopathy, classically in the hila, right paratracheal region, and aortopulmonary window. Although the lungs appear normal radiographically in stage I disease, the majority of these patients will have diagnostic findings on transbronchial biopsies. In one study, the yield of transbronchial biopsy was 55%, compared to 70% in patients with stage II and III disease.[79] Stage I disease is the most common radiographic presentation, and the majority (55% to 90%) of these patients will demonstrate spontaneous resolution.[2] On CT scanning, stage I patients may also demonstrate adenopathy at less typical sites, such as the anterior and posterior mediastinum or axilla, as well as lymph node calcification.[76] A stage II radiograph reveals bilateral hilar or mediastinal adenopathy or both, as well as pulmonary infiltrates (Fig. 55.2). Only 40% to 70% of these patients will experience spontaneous remission.[2] The

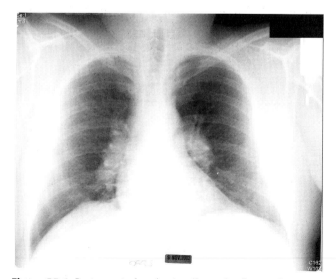

Figure 55.1 Posteroanterior chest radiograph of stage I sarcoidosis. Important features include prominent hilar lymphadenopathy and normal lungs.

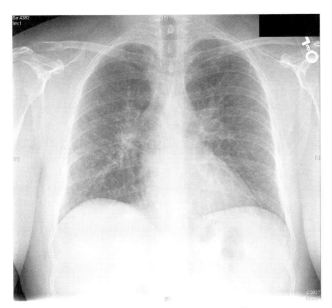

Figure 55.2 Posteroanterior chest radiograph of stage II sarcoidosis. Relevant findings include bilateral hilar lymphadenopathy and bilateral reticular and nodular interstitial infiltrates.

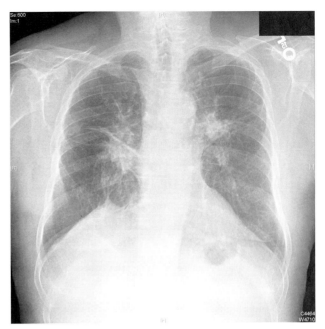

Figure 55.4 Posteroanterior chest radiograph of stage IV sarcoidosis. This image demonstrates conglomerate mass formation, upper lobe volume loss, and hilar retraction.

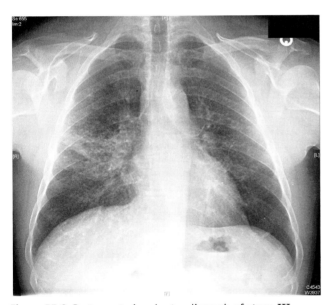

Figure 55.3 Posteroanterior chest radiograph of stage III sarcoidosis. Characteristic findings include reticular and nodular interstitial infiltrates with an upper lung predominance and the absence of lymphadenopathy.

parenchymal abnormalities may be nodular, reticular, or ground glass and tend to occur in the middle and upper lung zones. In these patients, a classic CT appearance includes 2- to 10-mm nodules in a perilymphatic distribution around the hila, along bronchovascular bundles, and in the subpleural region. Nodular coalescence may occur. A stage III radiograph (Fig. 55.3) also shows parenchymal abnormalities; however, there is no hilar or mediastinal lymphadenopathy.[76] Presentation with stage III is associated with only a 10% to 20% likelihood of spontaneous

resolution. Finally, a stage IV radiograph demonstrates fibrosis. Honeycombing is typically seen predominantly in the middle and upper lung zones, and is often associated with conglomerate mass formation, upper lobe volume loss, hilar retraction, peripheral bullae, and cystic lesions. Once fibrosis is evident, spontaneous resolution does not occur. Some of these radiographic and CT features are demonstrated in Figures 55.4 and 55.5.

A feared complication in patients with stage IV disease who develop cystic lesions is *aspergilloma*. Symptoms may include a change in cough and sputum production, accelerated dyspnea, and especially hemoptysis. Imaging studies usually show cavitation, masses, or classic mycetomas with a mass within an increasing-sized cavity. Diagnosis may be suggested by sputum cultures positive for fungi; skin tests for *Aspergillus* may be falsely negative due to the anergy displayed by sarcoidosis patients.[80,81]

Endobronchial involvement is another common presentation of pulmonary sarcoidosis. In one study, nearly half of all endobronchial biopsies demonstrated granulomatous inflammation.[82] In this group of 62 patients, positive endobronchial biopsies were associated with more progressive disease. In another study of patients with documented endobronchial disease, up to 10% had stenoses significant enough to result in an asthma-like syndrome, with airflow limitation, localized wheezing, and abnormal gas exchange.[83] Patients with endobronchial involvement have intractable cough. Airway obstruction may also result from bronchial distortion due to scarring in stage IV disease.[76]

Other pulmonary manifestations include various forms of pleural disease, including pleural effusion, pleural thickening, pleural nodules, pneumothorax, and chylothorax. Prevalence estimates for pleural involvement vary widely depending on definition and method of assessment, from less than 1% to 96%. A recent review of the literature

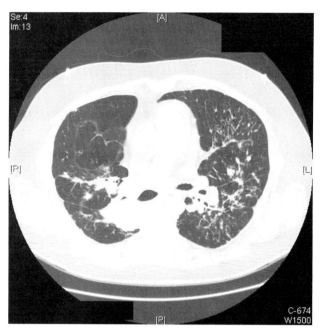

Figure 55.5 High-resolution computed tomography scan of a patient with stage IV sarcoidosis demonstrating bilateral central fibrotic (conglomerate) masses with extensive central calcification, as well as parenchymal nodular abnormalities and septal thickening.

identified 145 biopsy-proven cases of pleural involvement.[84] Among these, although radiographic stage was not always reported, pleural disease was observed in all stages of disease. The age range for all forms of pleural disease was 30 to 50 years, with an even distribution between men and women. The majority of cases (>80%) were unilateral, with the right side affected more often than the left (53% vs. 29%).[84] Pleural effusions should be diagnosed as being due to sarcoidosis only after careful exclusion of other etiologies, as one series reported that up to 40% of effusions in sarcoidosis patients may be due to other diagnoses, including reported cases of tuberculous effusion and mesothelioma.[85,86] Most effusions are small or moderate; however, three cases of massive effusion have been reported.[84,87-89] Most of the effusions are lymphocytic exudates, although several eosinophilic effusions have been reported. Effusions have been reported to resolve spontaneously, as well as with steroid therapy. Pleural thickening may be the most common sarcoid-related pleural abnormality, with CT studies reporting a prevalence of 11% to 71%.[84,90-94] High-resolution CT has enhanced the detection of pleural disease, especially for pleural nodules, which have been reported in 22% to 76% of patients.[84,95-97] Pneumothorax is a rare complication, and the relationship of the pneumothoraces to disease remains unclear. Some authors postulate that subpleural blebs (e.g., in advanced fibrocystic disease) or necrosis of subpleural granulomas cause the pneumothorax, whereas others have suggested that the occurrence is coincidental. The role of corticosteroids in treating this complication is similarly unclear.[84] Chylothorax has also been reported in nine cases, with three of these confirming the presence of lymphadenopathy or adhesions obstructing the thoracic duct.[84,98-100]

Another rare form of pulmonary involvement with sarcoidosis that deserves special mention is *necrotizing sarcoid granulomatosis*. Liebow first described this entity in 1973 in a publication that defined five idiopathic forms of pulmonary angiitis and granulomatosis.[101] These were Wegener's granulomatosis, limited Wegener's disease, lymphomatoid granulomatosis, bronchocentric granulomatosis, and necrotizing sarcoid granulomatosis. Numerous case reports and case series have since documented the existence of this distinct entity. Patients may be asymptomatic at presentation, or may have systemic symptoms, such as fever, malaise, fatigue, and weight loss; chest symptoms such as cough, chest pain, and dyspnea; or symptoms related to sites of extrathoracic involvement such as the eye or central nervous system. The typical radiographic appearance consists of solitary or multiple pulmonary nodules that often necrose and cavitate. Associated parenchymal opacification has also been described. These abnormalities are found in a distribution similar to that of sarcoidosis, subpleurally and along bronchovascular bundles, and may also be associated with lymphadenopathy. Necrotizing sarcoid granulomatosis is distinguished from sarcoidosis by the presence of cavitation on radiographic studies and the presence of necrosis and granulomatous vasculitis on histopathology, as described later. Typically the clinical course is benign and steroid-responsive; however, individual cases with severe extrathoracic involvement and initial critical illness have also been reported.[102-108]

The presence of bilateral hilar or mediastinal adenopathy (or both) in the absence of other symptoms or in the context of other features of Löfgren's syndrome is often adequate for a presumptive diagnosis of sarcoidosis. However, definitive diagnosis of intrathoracic involvement requires biopsy. It is generally recommended that patients with sarcoidosis have tissue confirmation of their diagnosis, especially if their disease is persistent or fails to fit conventional clinical patterns of multiorgan involvement, or if immunosuppressive treatment is being considered. The procedure of choice in most cases is transbronchial biopsy, which yields a diagnosis in 40% to 90% of procedures, depending on operator experience, the number of biopsies taken, and the Scadding stage.[2] Higher yields have been documented in stage II or III disease compared to stage I disease.[79] Based on this literature and our clinical experience, a minimum of six good transbronchial biopsies are needed to maximize the yield from this procedure.[109]

Endobronchial biopsies can also be diagnostic in 40% to 60% of procedures, although the yield may be even higher where mucosal abnormalities are observed.[78,110,111] Further, the addition of endobronchial to transbronchial biopsies can increase the diagnostic yield of bronchoscopy.[111-113] Other findings on bronchoscopy that support a diagnosis of sarcoidosis but are not diagnostic include bronchoalveolar lavage lymphocytosis (>10% lymphocytes) and an elevated CD4/CD8 ratio in the bronchoalveolar lavage fluid (> 2:1).[114] Two studies have demonstrated that a CD4/CD8 ratio of greater than 3.5 to 4 provides a specificity for the diagnosis of sarcoidosis of greater than 90%, but a sensitivity of only 50% to 60%.[2,114,115] However, these bronchoalveolar lavage criteria are rarely used in clinical practice. They are influenced by whether or not the patient has recently smoked (proportionately increasing the percentage of macrophages), and by the immunosuppressive treatment the

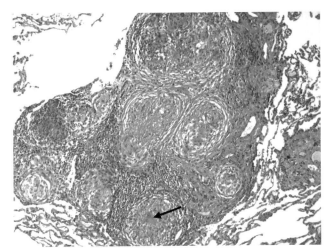

Figure 55.6 A cluster of multiple noncaseating granulomata with surrounding normal lung parenchyma. The *arrow* indicates a multinucleated giant cell within a granuloma. (Original magnification ×100.) (Courtesy of Carlyne Cool, MD, National Jewish Medical and Research Center.) *See Color Plate*

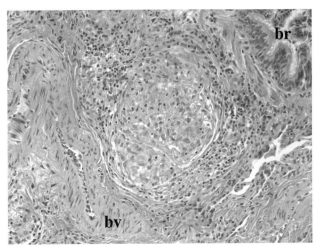

Figure 55.7 View of a well-formed noncaseating granuloma located between a blood vessel (bv) and a bronchiole (br). (Original magnification ×200.) (Courtesy of Carlyne Cool, MD, National Jewish Medical and Research Center.) *See Color Plate*

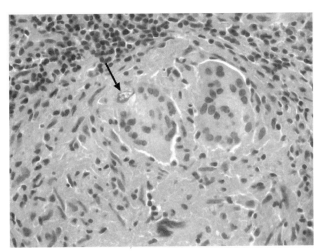

Figure 55.8 A Schaumann body (*arrow*) within a multinucleated giant cell within a sarcoid granuloma. (Original magnification ×400.) (Courtesy of Carlyne Cool, MD, National Jewish Medical and Research Center.) *See Color Plate*

patient has received (which can reduce the percentage of lymphocytes). Other supportive data may include an elevated serum ACE level, a positive gallium scan, or the presence of anergy. If bronchoscopic biopsies are nondiagnostic, other options include mediastinoscopy, video-assisted thoracoscopic lung biopsy, and open-lung biopsy. If mediastinal adenopathy is present on CT scan, then many clinicians consider mediastinoscopy to be the procedure of choice because of the need to rule out malignancies such as lymphoma. It should be noted that in some cases the tissue diagnosis can be made without a chest procedure. For example, some patients who have typical clinical and radiographic features and who have other organ involvement, such as skin nodules, sinus symptoms, or salivary gland symptoms, can have biopsies of those organs to demonstrate the presence of granulomas. In such cases, it is usually not necessary to do bronchoscopy or thoracoscopy.

The characteristic feature on lung biopsy is the noncaseating granuloma. As demonstrated in Figure 55.6, this is classically described as a well-formed, noncaseating epithelioid cell granuloma surrounded by a rim of lymphocytes and fibroblasts, with varying degrees of peripheral collagen deposition. The granulomas are found in a perilymphatic distribution, classically subpleurally and along bronchovascular bundles (Fig. 55.7). The granulomas may contain cytoplasmic inclusions within giant cells, such as asteroid bodies (star-shaped crystals consisting of microfilaments, microtubules, and other components embedded in a matrix) or Schaumann bodies (small concentric laminated calcifications composed of calcium salts, iron, and a mucopolysaccharide matrix).[116] An example of the latter is demonstrated in Figure 55.8. This appearance is typical of sarcoidosis in the lung as well as in other organs. As noted previously, the diagnosis of sarcoidosis also requires exclusion of other possible etiologies of both the clinical and pathologic presentation (see later discussion). The distinguishing histopathologic feature of necrotizing sarcoid granulomatosis is the presence of central necrosis within granulomas and a necrotizing granulomatous vasculitis. The appearance is similar to that of Wegener's granulomatosis, although the latter has a less extensive granulomatous reaction, a more severe clinical course, and positive antineutrophil cytoplasmic antibodies in most cases.[101]

EXTRAPULMONARY SARCOIDOSIS

A characteristic of sarcoidosis is the potential for the development of granulomatous inflammation in virtually any organ. Confidence in the diagnosis of sarcoidosis rises if there is involvement elsewhere, in addition to lung and thoracic lymphatics. Key characteristics of some of the more commonly affected organs are described in this section.

Ears, Nose, and Throat

There is a range of otorhinolaryngologic presentations, including salivary gland involvement sometimes resulting in severe xerostomia, otitis media, vestibular symptoms, and hearing loss. However, nasal and paranasal sinus involvement can be the most difficult to diagnose and treat properly. Presenting symptoms are usually nonspecific, including nasal congestion, postnasal drip and sinus pressure, headaches, and infections. Sometimes these will be associated with clinical features suggestive of sarcoidosis, such as lupus pernio (violaceous rash described later), nasal deformities such as saddle nose deformity, and nasal mucosal abnormalities such as friability with crusting, bleeding, and submucosal nodules. Rarely, these nodules may erode through the hard or soft palate, resulting in oral ulcerations or fistulous tracts. Other rare complications of nasal and sinus disease include epiphora (chronic tearing due to intranasal lacrimal tract outlet obstruction); anosmia (loss of the sense of smell due to direct involvement of the olfactory epithelium or obstruction of the olfactory cleft); and mass lesions with intraorbital or intracranial invasion. Even in cases with features suggestive of sarcoidosis, definitive diagnosis relies on biopsy evidence of granulomatous inflammation and exclusion of other infections and inflammatory etiologies (e.g., fungal or mycobacterial infection, Wegener's granulomatosis, rhinoscleroma).

There are a number of management strategies for sinonasal sarcoidosis, depending on disease severity. Krespi and colleagues[117] have proposed a staging system that provides some general guidelines for therapy. Stage I is defined as mild nasal disease without paranasal sinus disease. These patients can typically be managed successfully with saline nasal spray, nasal irrigation, and topical nasal steroids. Stage II is moderate disease, with involvement of both nasal and paranasal sinuses; it is typically treated with both stage I therapy and intralesional steroids. Stage III disease is characterized by severe, often irreversible, nasal and sinus disease that usually requires the therapeutic interventions of stage I and II, as well as systemic therapy. Courses of systemic antibiotics are also required for many patients who develop secondary infection related to mucus stasis or sinus ostium obstruction. Surgical interventions have traditionally been avoided due to concerns about worsening tissue destruction and inflammation; however, some recent reports suggest surgery can be performed safely and successfully in selected cases.[118] Examples of surgical indications include severe nasal obstruction that has failed to respond to medical therapy, sinus obstruction with chronic infection, and need for biopsy for diagnosis.[119]

Peripheral Lymph Nodes

Lymphadenopathy is observed most commonly in the hilar and mediastinal lymph nodes (up to 90% of patients); however, a minority of patients (5% to 30%) have peripheral lymphadenopathy.[2] The nodes are typically nontender, mobile, and located in the cervical, axillary, epitrochlear, and inguinal regions.

Heart

Cardiac sarcoidosis may occur in approximately 5% to as high as 58% of patients, with prevalence estimates varying based on the population screened and case definition.[120,121] The lack of a consistent case definition is in part due to the lack of sensitive and specific tests for this form of the disease. Electrocardiograms are abnormal in up to 50% of sarcoidosis patients, but findings are nonspecific and may include repolarization abnormalities, evidence of abnormal conduction such as intraventricular conduction delays and bundle-branch block, and arrhythmias. Rarely a transmural infarction pattern may be seen, apparently due to myocardial infiltration resulting in loss of electrical potential.[121] Echocardiograms are also frequently abnormal but seldom diagnostic. Common findings attributed to cardiac sarcoidosis include left ventricular dilation and dysfunction, regional wall motion abnormalities, wall thinning, and left atrial enlargement. Radionuclide imaging, using thallium-201, gallium-67, or technetium-99m, reveals abnormalities in patients with cardiac sarcoidosis, but its sensitivity and specificity have not been well defined.[122,123] In addition, there is case report and case series evidence of a possible role for newer technologies, such as positron emission tomography and magnetic resonance imaging (MRI), in the diagnosis and monitoring of cardiac sarcoidosis.[124–127] Finally, one highly specific but poorly sensitive test is endomyocardial biopsy. In evaluating for possible cardiac sarcoidosis, a finding of noncaseating granulomas is diagnostic, but the sensitivity of this technique in several series is low, at 25% to 50%.[128,129] Unfortunately, the diagnosis is commonly made when a patient presents with sudden death from ventricular arrhythmias or complete heart block. Supraventricular tachycardias, ventricular aneurysms, other conduction defects (e.g., first- and second-degree heart block, intraventricular conduction delay), and cardiomyopathy/congestive heart failure also occur with cardiac involvement.

Skin

Skin involvement is found in approximately 25% of sarcoidosis patients.[2] The two most classic skin lesions are erythema nodosum and lupus pernio. Erythema nodosum typically presents as raised, tender, red nodules, 1 to 2 cm in diameter, on the anterior surface of the lower legs. As described earlier, lupus pernio is a rare lesion consisting of purplish plaques typically found over the nose, cheeks, lips, and ears. It is observed more commonly in African American women and is associated with more chronic, severe disease. More common skin abnormalities include red-brown to orange macules and papules, keloids, and hyper- or hypopigmentation. With the exception of the two classic lesions, definitive evidence of skin involvement relies on biopsy demonstrating noncaseating granulomas.

Eyes

Ocular involvement occurs in 11% to 83% of sarcoidosis patients.[2] The most common presentation is uveitis, with a higher prevalence of anterior uveitis in African Americans and of posterior uveitis in whites.[130] Anterior uveitis typically presents acutely, with pain, photophobia, lacrimation, and redness, but may have a more chronic course. Posterior uveitis is typically gradual in onset and is more likely to result in visual morbidity. Conjunctival nodules are another common, although usually asymptomatic, presentation. In fact, the diagnosis of sarcoidosis can sometimes be made

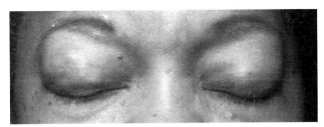

Figure 55.9 Enlargement of lacrimal glands in a sarcoidosis patient. *See Color Plate*

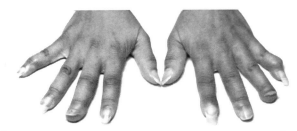

Figure 55.10 Joint and bone involvement in the hands of a sarcoidosis patient. *See Color Plate*

with conjunctival biopsy, even in patients without any ocular symptoms. Although the yield varies depending on the presence of conjunctival follicles, other ocular abnormalities, and extraocular disease, small series of conjunctival biopsies have found yields of 33% to 70%, even without evident conjunctival disease.[131–135] Although less common, lacrimal gland enlargement is a characteristic finding (Fig. 55.9). In addition to posterior uveitis, the posterior segment of the eye may be affected with vitreous hemorrhage, cataracts, glaucoma, and retinal ischemia with neovascularization. Patients with disease of the posterior segment of the eye have a higher prevalence of central nervous system involvement.[136–138] Annual ophthalmologic evaluation with slit-lamp examination is recommended to evaluate for ocular involvement. Microvascular involvement can be detected using fluorescein angiography. Vigilance for ocular involvement is extremely important, as about 10% of patients with sarcoid-associated uveitis develop blindness in at least one eye.[130,139]

Nervous System

Neurosarcoidosis has been described in both the central and peripheral nervous systems, but is clinically evident in less than 10% of patients.[2] The most common form of central nervous system involvement is meningeal infiltration and inflammation. This may manifest clinically with cranial neuropathies, hydrocephalus, headaches, and encephalopathy. Granulomatous inflammation of the cranial nerves most commonly presents as a unilateral seventh nerve palsy, but has been reported in every cranial nerve. Central lesions occur much less commonly, and often present clinically when there is pituitary involvement. Clinical syndromes include diabetes insipidus and hyperprolactinemia. Peripheral neuropathy has also been described. Diagnostic tests that may be helpful include MRI for brain lesions and leptomeningeal involvement; cerebrospinal fluid examination, which typically reveals a lymphocytic pleocytosis and elevated protein in central nervous system disease; and electrodiagnostic studies and nerve biopsy for peripheral neuropathy. Although the sensitivity and specificity of many of these studies in neurosarcoidosis is not well defined, MRI with gadolinium is the preferred imaging study for sarcoidosis patients with central nervous system symptoms, with a sensitivity in this patient population of 82%.[140,141]

Endocrine Glands

Abnormal calcium metabolism is the most common endocrine disorder in sarcoidosis. Both hypercalcemia and

hypercalciuria occur because of increased 1,25-dihydroxy-vitamin D production by activated macrophages in sarcoidal granulomas.[2,142,143] Left untreated, these abnormalities can result in the formation of renal calculi, precipitation of calcium salts in the kidney itself (nephrocalcinosis), and sometimes renal failure. Other unusual renal sequelae of sarcoidosis include interstitial nephritis and granulomatous masses.[2]

Parotid Gland

Parotid enlargement is a classic but rare disease feature. Heerfordt's syndrome, or uveoparotid fever, is characterized by parotid enlargement with fever, facial palsy, and anterior uveitis.

Liver and Spleen

Clinically apparent liver disease, such as palpable hepatomegaly or symptomatic cholestasis, is a rare complication of sarcoidosis. However, liver function test abnormalities are commonly observed.[2] Liver involvement can also be detected radiographically, with hepatomegaly or nodular lesions detected on abdominal CT or MRI.[144,145] Splenic involvement is also rarely symptomatic, but is common, as determined by studies of fine-needle aspiration biopsies.[146,147] Radiographic abnormalities (CT, MRI) are similar to those in the liver, with splenomegaly or nodular lesions observed.[144,145] Rarely, massive splenomegaly may occur and may cause thrombocytopenia or other cytopenias.[148,149]

Joints

Although arthralgias are common in patients with Löfgren's syndrome, other forms of sarcoidosis less commonly demonstrate joint involvement. Arthralgias occur in 25% to 39% of patients, but deforming arthritis is rare.[2] Between 3% and 13% of patients display bony involvement,[150] although the increasing use of MRI may increase future estimates of the frequency of osseous sarcoidosis. Classically, if the bones are involved, plain radiographs or MRI will demonstrate bone cysts in the phalanges, although virtually any bone can be affected.[150] Figure 55.10 illustrates the effects of bony involvement and arthritis in the hands of a sarcoidosis patient. Symptomatic muscle involvement, characterized by nodules, acute myositis, or chronic myopathy, is also rare; however, in systemic sarcoidosis without clinical manifestations of muscle disease, 20% to 75% of cases are found to have granulomas on muscle biopsy.[151]

Blood

Hematologic abnormalities are also seen, with as many as 40% of patients demonstrating anemia, leukopenia, lymphopenia, or a combination of these.[2] Thrombocytopenia is rare, but can be the consequence of bone marrow involvement or splenic enlargement with platelet destruction.

Other Sites

Other unusual sites of biopsy-confirmed disease have been the subject of extensive reviews, including one by Judson and colleagues[152] that defines definite, probable, and possible criteria for organ involvement. These criteria were used to describe the case population in the ACCESS study.[1,2,152]

DIFFERENTIAL DIAGNOSIS

As discussed earlier, the diagnosis of sarcoidosis is made by exclusion of other conditions. Table 55.1 summarizes the major categories of both infectious and noninfectious disorders that must be considered prior to accepting the idiopathic diagnosis. Diagnostic considerations for pulmonary granulomatous inflammation include infections with mycobacteria, bacteria, fungi, spirochetes, and protozoa. Diseases caused by occupational and environmental inhaled agents must also be considered, including hypersensitivity pneumonitis due to inhaled organic and inorganic antigens, metal-induced disorders such as chronic beryllium disease,[153] and silicosis.[154] Chronic beryllium disease is of particular interest because it is clinically, radiographically, and histopathologically indistinguishable from sarcoidosis. Chronic beryllium disease is distinguished from sarcoidosis by a history of beryllium exposure and by laboratory evidence of immunologic sensitization to beryllium using blood or lavage cells in a beryllium lymphocyte proliferation test. A recent study from Israel illustrates the need to exclude chronic beryllium disease prior to accepting a diagnosis of sarcoidosis.[155] In this study, Fireman and colleagues performed the blood beryllium lymphocyte proliferation test in 14 patients in their sarcoidosis clinic who, on repeat questioning, reported employment in industries with the potential for beryllium exposure (e.g., metal extraction, ceramics, electronics, space and atomic engineering, dental laboratories). Three of the 14 patients were found to be beryllium sensitized and were therefore diagnosed as having chronic beryllium disease. The study highlights the importance of a thorough occupational history in patients with granulomatous lung disease. In addition to the infectious

---

Table 55.1 Differential Diagnosis of Granulomatous Disease and Relevant Testing with Clinical Suspicion

Cause	Granulomatous Disease	Confirmatory Data
Infectious agents		
Mycobacteria	Tuberculosis, atypical mycobacterial infection	PPD; sputum or BAL culture
Fungi	Histoplasmosis, coccidioidomycosis	Serologic testing (histo); sputum or biopsy stains, serologies, skin tests (cocci)
Bacteria	Brucellosis	Culture (low yield); serologies
Spirochetes	Syphilis	RPR
Parasites	Leishmaniasis, toxoplasmosis	Tissue biopsy, culture, leishmanin test (leishmaniasis); serologies; BAL, lung biopsy cultures (toxoplasmosis)
Neoplasms	Carcinoma, sarcomas, malignant nasal granuloma	Full sectioning and histopathologic examination of lymph nodes
Hypersensitivity pneumonitis (HP)	Farmers' lung, bird breeder's lung, suberosis (HP secondary to moldy cork), bagassosis (HP secondary to moldy sugarcane)	Detailed history for likely exposures; examination of biopsies for other features characteristic of HP; precipitins
Metals	Chronic beryllium disease, zirconium or aluminum granulomas	Detailed history for likelihood of exposure; blood and/or BAL beryllium lymphocyte proliferation test
Silicates	Silicosis with granulomatous inflammation	Detailed history for likelihood of exposure; review of radiographic findings for features of silicosis; biopsy microanalysis for dust
Vasculitic granulomatoses and autoimmune disorders	Wegener's granulomatosis, Churg-Strauss syndrome, lymphomatoid granulomatosis, polyarteritis nodosa, bronchocentric granulomatosis, systemic lupus erythematosus, primary biliary cirrhosis, juvenile rheumatoid arthritis	Pathologic review for features of vasculitis; autoantibody studies, including c-ANCA, p-ANCA, ANA, anti-dsDNA, rheumatoid factor
Other conditions	Chronic granulomatous disease (children), Whipple's disease, lymphocytic infiltration after cancer chemotherapy, Blau syndrome, local sarcoidal reactions	

ANA, antineutrophil antibody; ANCA, antineutrophil cytoplasmic antibody; BAL, bronchoalveolar lavage; dsDNA, double-stranded deoxyribonucleic acid; PPD, purified protein derivative (of tuberculin); RPR, rapid plasma reagin test.

and exposure-related diagnoses noted previously, other diagnostic considerations include Wegener's granulomatosis and idiopathic interstitial pneumonias such as lymphocytic interstitial pneumonia.

The finding of noncaseating granulomas in lymph nodes is associated with a similarly broad differential diagnosis. Mycobacterial infection, brucellosis, toxoplasmosis, and cat-scratch disease can all cause a granulomatous lymphadenitis. Neoplasms, including Hodgkin's and non-Hodgkin's lymphoma and metastatic carcinoma, can cause lymph node enlargement and stimulate a sarcoid-like reaction. Therefore, when granulomas are identified on lymph node biopsy, the entire node must be examined histopathologically to exclude these diagnoses. Of note, nonthoracic lymph node granulomas without an identified etiology or evidence of other organ involvement are referred to as granulomatous lesions of unknown significance, and are not sufficient to make a diagnosis of sarcoidosis. The differential diagnosis of noncaseating granulomas in other organs is similar. Other specific entities that can produce noncaseating granulomas include foreign body reactions in the skin, schistosomiasis, primary biliary cirrhosis, and Crohn's disease.[1,2]

The distinction between sarcoidosis and autoimmune disorders deserves specific mention. Sarcoidosis has been associated with elevation of various autoantibodies in serum, including nonspecific elevations of rheumatoid factor and antinuclear antibodies.[156] Several researchers have suggested an association between sarcoidosis and autoimmune endocrinopathies, as well as antiphospholipid antibodies.[157-159] The putative link between sarcoidosis and autoimmunity is supported by cases of concurrent diagnoses, as well as by some of the obvious similarities in clinical presentations between sarcoidosis and the autoimmune diseases.

Although sarcoidosis is rare in children, when it does occur in preschool children, it may mimic the manifestations of juvenile rheumatoid arthritis with skin, eye, and joint involvement without lung disease. Distinction between the two entities usually requires biopsy of skin, synovium, lymph node, or liver.[160-163] In contrast, in adults, the clinical presentations of rheumatoid arthritis and sarcoidosis are quite distinct. Interestingly, the coexistence of the two diseases with biopsy verification of both has been demonstrated in numerous case reports, suggesting a possible etiologic similarity.[164-167] Sjögren's syndrome and sarcoidosis may also coexist and be difficult to distinguish, particularly when there is lung involvement.[168-172] Both diseases can present with keratoconjunctivitis sicca, parotid swelling, lung involvement, and cutaneous anergy. Some authors suggest that labial minor salivary gland biopsy or lung biopsy can distinguish between the two diseases, but even biopsy findings are sometimes inconclusive.[173,174]

EVALUATION AND MANAGEMENT

The recommended baseline evaluation and follow-up testing of sarcoidosis patients are shown in Table 55.2.[1] These recommendations are based on the major organs that are usually targeted by sarcoidosis. Other tests may be appropriate for evaluation and management, depending on the particular organs affected.

Table 55.2 Recommended Baseline and Follow-Up Clinical Evaluation for Sarcoidosis

Baseline
- Detailed history, including occupational, environmental and travel history to evaluate for exposure to known causes of granulomatous diseases (see Table 55.1).
- Physical examination with a focus on lungs, lymphatics, skin, eyes, liver, heart, nervous system, joints.
- Biopsy of an affected organ, with special stains, cultures for acid-fast bacillus and fungus to rule out infectious etiologies of granulomas.
- Chest radiography (posteroanterior and lateral)
- Full pulmonary function tests, including spirometry, lung volumes, and an assessment of gas exchange (e.g., diffusing capacity of carbon monoxide, arterial blood gases at rest and/or with exercise)
- Electrocardiogram
- Ophthalmologic examination, including slit-lamp examination.
- Laboratory evaluation, including liver function tests, renal function tests, serum calcium, and a complete blood count with differential.
- Urinalysis and 24-hour urine collection for calcium and creatinine excretion.

Other Tests
- To rule out other diagnostic possibilities (e.g., tuberculin skin test [with anergy panel], blood beryllium lymphocyte proliferation test).
- For clinical staging of organ system involvement and severity (e.g., computed tomography scan, magnetic resonance imaging, Holter monitoring, electromyogram, gallium scan)

Follow-up
Monitoring for resolution or progression:
- Track organs previously involved, using least invasive methods.
- Monitor for new involvement of common target organs annually or sooner if symptoms dictate.

As a general principle, because there is no single sensitive or specific diagnostic test for sarcoidosis, the diagnosis depends on establishing the compatible clinicopathologic picture and excluding other granulomatous diseases. Ideally, the evaluation should provide histologic confirmation of disease and negative cultures and special stains for organisms.

The clinical impact of sarcoidosis depends on the extent of granulomatous inflammation and the particular organs affected. In determining the extent and severity of disease, clinicians should use available noninvasive tools as much as possible to assess which organs are clinically involved and to assess the extent and severity of organ injury. Asymptomatic organ involvement may be missed, but is usually of mild or no clinical significance with three significant exceptions. A slit-lamp examination is recommended for all patients with suspected sarcoidosis to look for clinically undetected uveitis. Subclinical hypercalciuria, even in the absence of hypercalcemia, is associated with nephrolithiasis, and thus a baseline 24-hour urine calcium measurement is advisable. Periodic electrocardiograms should also be obtained to screen for rare, but potentially life-threatening, cardiac arrhythmias and conduction abnormalities.

A baseline complete blood count is recommended to evaluate for anemia, leukopenia, and thrombocytopenia. Serum calcium and liver enzymes may reflect organ involvement meriting treatment. Serum ACE activity is frequently elevated in sarcoidosis. This elevation is not specific, but can be of use in monitoring the progression of disease and the response to therapy unless patients are being treated with an ACE inhibitor, which will lower ACE levels.

Tests demonstrating cutaneous anergy may help suggest a diagnosis of sarcoidosis, but the anergy panel is neither sensitive nor specific. Kveim-Siltzbach skin testing—using a preparation of sarcoidosis spleen that is intradermally injected—has been used in the past to help establish a diagnosis of sarcoidosis in patients with unexplained erythema nodosum, uveitis, liver granulomas, or hypercalciuria. This is not approved for general use in the United States and is not recommended.

Given the high likelihood of pulmonary involvement at some point in the course of sarcoidosis, we recommend that the extent of lung disease be thoroughly evaluated. Typically, this would include pre- and postbronchodilator spirometry, lung volumes by body plethysmography, diffusing capacity, and, in many cases, one or more direct measures of gas exchange. These include room air arterial blood gas measurements at rest and with exercise; a fall in arterial oxygen saturation during exercise is among the most sensitive indicators of lung impairment in sarcoidosis and other forms of diffuse lung disease.[175] Baseline imaging studies, consisting at minimum of posteroanterior and lateral chest radiographs, should also be obtained. CT of the thorax using spiral and thin-section algorithms provides much greater detail of parenchymal abnormalities, including nodules, ground glass, septal lines, and adenopathy, but is not required as a baseline study.[2] Generally, patients found to have pulmonary involvement can be followed with the simplest and least invasive testing. For example, in a patient found to have a low diffusing capacity, it is often possible to follow that test, along with spirometry and chest radiographs, rather than routinely performing more invasive studies such as exercise testing with arterial blood gases.

Gallium-67 citrate scanning adds no specificity to the diagnosis of sarcoidosis, except in the case of patients with lacrimal and salivary gland involvement, in which case the so-called panda sign is observed due to increased uptake in those sites.[176] The "lambda" sign indicating hilar lymphadenopathy is also suggestive but not diagnostic.

Monitoring for disease progression, regression, or response to therapy should be customized, relying on the least invasive markers of disease activity and vital organ involvement, taking into consideration the relative sensitivity of the clinical tools available for monitoring. The clinician must remain vigilant given the tendency of this disorder to relapse and to erupt in new or previously subclinical organs.

TREATMENT

It is not known why some sarcoidosis patients recover and others progress. Even after an apparent recovery, a proportion of patients may relapse months to years later. Factors associated with worse prognosis include older age at time of diagnosis, African American race, duration of illness greater than 6 months, pulmonary infiltrates, splenomegaly, lupus pernio, and number of organs involved. A more favorable prognosis has been found in patients with acute disease who expressed HLA-DR3 and -DQ2, whether or not erythema nodosum was present.[39,68,177] It is important to recognize that the disease can spontaneously resolve without treatment. Thus, most treatment protocols incorporate a period of observation without treatment whenever possible.

CORTICOSTEROIDS

A detailed summary of current pharmacotherapy in sarcoidosis has been the subject of several recent reviews.[53,178,179] This section addresses general treatment of sarcoidosis. Oral corticosteroids remain the first-line therapy in most cases; however, there is no consensus as to when corticosteroids should be initiated.[178] Furthermore, there is some evidence, to be discussed in greater detail later, that corticosteroids might be more harmful than helpful in some instances. The use of oral corticosteroids in sarcoidosis is aimed at the relief of symptoms with intended improvement in quality of life and modulation of disease activity to prevent serious morbidity and mortality related to vital organ damage. It is debatable whether all of these goals can be achieved, especially in light of the side effects of corticosteroids.

In a systematic review, Paramothayan and Jones[178] identified all of the randomized trials of oral or inhaled corticosteroids in pulmonary sarcoidosis that included a control group. Their goal was to assess the beneficial and adverse effects of corticosteroid therapy. In synthesizing the data from eight studies that met their requirements for inclusion, the authors concluded that oral corticosteroids improved chest radiographs after 6 to 24 months of treatment and produced a small improvement in lung function and gas exchange. They found no data to suggest that systemic corticosteroid therapy alters long-term disease progression. Only two of these studies examined the efficacy of inhaled corticosteroid therapy. These demonstrated no effect on chest radiographic appearance and no consistent effects on lung function; only one study demonstrated a small improvement in symptoms.[178] In another review, Reich[180] suggested that corticosteroid-treated patients with a recent diagnosis of stage II or III sarcoidosis might derive more long-term harm than benefit, that the effect on those with disease of more intermediate duration is neutral, and that patients with chronic progressive pulmonary disease respond favorably, at least in the intermediate term. Obviously, the paucity of randomized controlled clinical trials—especially for all of the various forms of sarcoidosis organ involvement—limits the conclusions that can be drawn. A review of the American Thoracic Society consensus statement would suggest that patients with acute pulmonary sarcoidosis (stage I disease with isolated bilateral hilar adenopathy) *not* be treated because of the generally excellent outcome in the absence of therapy and the potential that corticosteroids may be detrimental if used in these acute cases.[2]

Studies examining outcome at greater than 2 years suggest no significant benefit from corticosteroid therapy in asymptomatic sarcoidosis patients with more advanced forms of pulmonary involvement.[181–185] In a British Thoracic

Society study,[186] patients not meeting the indications for immediate therapy were observed for 6 months. At that point, using a strategy of alternate assignment, they were designated either to receive long-term corticosteroid therapy or to receive corticosteroids only as indicated symptomatically. Analysis of data at 2 years suggested that the long-term therapy group experienced only mild improvements in pulmonary function, and reported numerous steroid side effects.

Based on the available literature and a survey of clinical practice in the United States and abroad, it is our general recommendation that, whenever possible, corticosteroids should not be initiated until after a period of clinical observation of 3 to 6 months, unless there is a life- or sight-threatening indication to treat immediately. Such urgent indications include eye disease that has failed to improve with topical therapy, cardiac involvement (e.g., cardiomyopathy, heart block, or serious arrhythmias), neurologic involvement (e.g., hypothalamic or pituitary dysfunction or other central nervous system involvement), hypercalcemia, hypercalciuria with associated renal insufficiency or recurrent nephrolithiasis, severe disfiguring skin lesions, severe thrombocytopenia with bleeding diathesis, progressive hepatic failure, severe incapacitating osseous or muscle involvement, and severe pulmonary involvement that is significantly impairing gas exchange. If no such urgent indications have intervened during the 3 to 6 months of observation, patients would be observed closely for pulmonary and other organ function. After these observation months, the persistence or progression of organ dysfunction would then be an indication for a trial period of treatment.

There is no consensus regarding the optimal initial dosage of corticosteroids. The American Thoracic Society consensus statement reports a usual starting dose of 20 to 40 mg of prednisone, or its equivalent, daily or on alternate days.[2] The British Thoracic Society study similarly used 30 mg of prednisolone (potency equivalent to prednisone) daily as a starting dose in both their long-term and selective therapy groups.[186] We typically start therapy at a dosage of 30 to 40 mg of prednisone daily or on alternate days, although we use higher doses (to a maximum of 60 mg daily) for severe disease, such as symptomatic cardiac involvement. Patients are seen back in the clinic 8 to 12 weeks later, at which time clinical, radiologic, physiologic, and laboratory assessments are repeated and patients are examined for side effects. Those who objectively improve on corticosteroids initiate a taper of corticosteroids to as low a dose as is tolerated without return of symptoms or organ dysfunction—usually 5 to 10 mg daily or on alternate days. The American Thoracic Society statement recommends that, for those who respond to steroids, treatment should be continued for at least 1 year. Patients who become stable on high-dose corticosteroids but who have yet to improve are maintained at the same dosage, unless they have developed significant side effects. If intolerable side effects occur, or if the disease worsens, patients are considered candidates for the addition of a second-line immunosuppressive agent. If patients suffer relapse on maintenance therapy, we reinitiate higher dose prednisone and consider second-line, steroid-sparing options.[1,2] Patients who have evidence of a clinical response to corticosteroids over the time course described earlier are reevaluated using objective measures prior to attempts to withdraw immunosuppressive medication completely. In some patients, the disease remains quiescent off all corticosteroids. Unfortunately, in others, the disease relapses, requiring that therapy be restarted for purposes of symptomatic relief and clinical control of failing organs. Even patients who are believed to have entered remission should be followed periodically, given the propensity for sarcoidosis to relapse and given the lack of available information about predictors of long-term prognosis.

OTHER IMMUNOSUPPRESSIVE AGENTS

The use of other immunosuppressive agents in sarcoidosis should be reserved for those patients who experience symptomatic disease progression despite the use of systemic corticosteroids or who require systemic therapy but cannot tolerate the side effects of steroids. In general, there has been less clinical experience and fewer published studies testing the efficacy of other immunosuppressive agents, either as single agents or as steroid-sparing agents.

Methotrexate has emerged as the preferred second-line immunosuppressive drug, especially when used as a steroid-sparing agent. There has only been one published randomized controlled trial of methotrexate in sarcoidosis.[187] The primary end point of this small study was steroid dose after 6 to 12 months; although interpretation of the results was limited by a high dropout rate, there was a suggestion of a steroid-sparing effect in this population. The largest published experience comes from Lower and Baughman,[188] who reported improvement in 33 of 50 patients treated with methotrexate for a minimum of 2 years. Those with cutaneous and musculoskeletal involvement showed the greatest response. Twenty-five of 30 patients who were also receiving corticosteroids were able to decrease corticosteroid dosage; 13 discontinued corticosteroids entirely. A follow-up report of 209 patients showed that 52% on methotrexate entered remission and 16% remained stable, with or without low-dose prednisone.[189] Other reports confirm the beneficial effects of methotrexate in cutaneous and musculoskeletal sarcoidosis.[190,191] In a study by Kaye and colleagues,[191] low-dose methotrexate (average 10 mg/wk, range 7.5 to 15 mg), when used for an average of 30 months, controlled clinical symptoms in patients with musculoskeletal involvement and helped reduce corticosteroid dose. In most studies, treatment doses of methotrexate range from 5 to 15 mg/wk, usually taken as a single or divided oral dose taken 1 day per week. Methotrexate may take up to 6 months to become effective in sarcoidosis. During this period, patients are usually maintained on corticosteroids.

Case reports on the benefits of cyclosporin A in sarcoidosis have not been supported by later larger cohort studies.[192-194] The first study to examine cyclosporin in a more rigorous fashion found that cyclosporin, administered at doses that achieved a blood level between 150 and 250 ng/mL, failed to produce clinical improvement in 20 patients who had pulmonary involvement, despite 6 months of therapy.[193] Cyclosporin was undetectable in bronchoalveolar lavage fluid, suggesting poor penetration of cyclosporin into the lung as a reason for its failure. A more recent randomized controlled trial found the combination of prednisone and cyclosporin to be no better and possibly worse than prednisone alone in treating pulmonary sarcoidosis.[194]

Despite anecdotal reports and frequent use of azathioprine, there are few published studies examining the drug's efficacy in sarcoidosis. One group reported objective improvement in 7 of 10 patients with pulmonary sarcoidosis after receiving 150 mg/day of azathioprine for 6 months.[195] Some data suggest that it may be efficacious for extrapulmonary disease,[196] although side effects often limit the acceptance of this option. Two more recent case series evaluated combined therapy with azathioprine and corticosteroids in patients with chronic pulmonary sarcoidosis. A retrospective review of 10 patients demonstrated sustained improvement in lung function in only 2 patients, but a prospective evaluation of 11 patients demonstrated symptomatic relief and improvement in lung physiology and radiographic abnormalities in 9 after an average of 20 months of therapy. Thus, azathioprine may be an effective second-line agent in some sarcoidosis patients.[197,198]

Chloroquine has proven effective in treating cutaneous manifestations of sarcoidosis,[199] hypercalcemia and hypercalciuria associated with sarcoidosis, and steroid-refractory neurosarcoidosis.[200,201] Generally, chloroquine therapy is initiated at a dosage of 500 mg/day and may be titrated up to a maximum of 1000 mg/day and decreased to a low of 250 mg/day. Because of the potential for significant ophthalmologic toxicity, hydroxychloroquine is often used instead, at a dosage of 200 to 400 mg daily. In 1967, the British Tuberculosis Association reported the first controlled trial on the use of antimalarials in sarcoidosis.[202] They observed some benefit early in attenuating symptoms of pulmonary sarcoidosis but showed little effect on disease outcome when comparing treatment and control groups at 6 months. A more recent trial examined the efficacy of chloroquine therapy in chronic pulmonary sarcoidosis.[203] During an initial run-in phase, all subjects received chloroquine therapy for 6 months and demonstrated a significant improvement in several lung physiologic parameters. During the subsequent randomization phase, subjects were assigned to receive maintenance therapy with low-dose (250 mg/day) chloroquine or to be observed off therapy. With a mean of 19.7 months of follow-up, the maintenance group demonstrated significantly slower decline in lung function and a trend toward fewer relapses. Thus, although chloroquine and hydroxychloroquine are more commonly employed for extrathoracic disease, they may have a role in pulmonary disease as well.

Cyclophosphamide is employed in selected cases of corticosteroid-refractory sarcoidosis.[204,205] It appears beneficial for both cardiac sarcoidosis and neurosarcoidosis—in the latter case, even following failure of both corticosteroid and methotrexate therapy. If used, oral cyclophosphamide is given at a dose of 1 to 2 mg/kg/day to a maximum dose of 150 mg/day. Therapy is maintained for several months before tapering. In one open-label study, the investigators used intravenous pulse cyclophosphamide therapy for the treatment of neurosarcoidosis at a dosage of 0.75 to 1.5 g monthly.[205]

Based on our present understanding of cytokine expression in sarcoidosis, it is logical to expect that anti–TNF-α therapies, either via inhibition of TNF production with thalidomide or pentoxifylline, or via direct inhibition of

TNF activity with etanercept or infliximab, should prove effective.[179] There are individual published cases and small case series data supporting the use of thalidomide in treatment of patients with several forms of cutaneous sarcoidosis, including lupus pernio.[206–210] Pentoxifylline, at high doses, improved lung function in a group of patients with mild pulmonary sarcoidosis.[211] A recent prospective, open-label study examined the treatment of sarcoidosis with etanercept, a dimeric fusion protein consisting of the extracellular binding domain of two human TNF receptors bound to the F_c portion of human IgG1.[212] This complex specifically binds TNF and inactivates it. Seventeen patients with progressive pulmonary sarcoidosis and on no other immunosuppressive agents were enrolled and followed for 3 to 12 months. The study was terminated prior to the full planned enrollment due to excessive treatment failures, defined as a deterioration in two or three of the following: lung function ($\geq$10% decline in FEV_1, forced vital capacity, total lung capacity, or diffusing capacity for carbon monoxide), dyspnea score, and chest radiograph appearance. The authors concluded that etanercept should not be further studied as a therapeutic option for patients with stage II or III pulmonary sarcoidosis. Several shortcomings of this study are worth noting. First, at baseline, all of the mean lung function values were within the normal range. Therefore, this may have been a negative study because the subjects were too healthy to experience a significant benefit from etanercept. Second, patients were not permitted to be on any other immunosuppressive therapy. Because studies in other inflammatory disorders have demonstrated efficacy of TNF blockers in conjunction with other agents, this stipulation may have doomed the study to fail from the outset. Finally, the authors conclude that the drug deserves no further investigation despite the successful responses of nearly one third of the patients studied. It is therefore still certainly possible that, for a subset of sarcoidosis patients with more significant pulmonary dysfunction and possibly on concomitant immunosuppressive therapy, this therapy will be effective. In various case reports, infliximab, a chimeric humanized monoclonal antibody that binds TNF, has been used successfully in the treatment of lupus pernio, neurosarcoidosis, and progressive cutaneous sarcoidosis.[213–216b] In one case, investigators reported clinical response in a sarcoidosis patient who presented with severe protein-losing enteropathy, hypoalbuminemia, and proximal myopathy.[217] Clinical trials are underway examining the safety and efficacy of infliximab in pulmonary and extrathoracic sarcoidosis. It is worth noting that use of anti-TNF therapies has been associated with a significantly increased risk of active tuberculosis; therefore, any patient being considered for such therapy must be screened for previously untreated or active tuberculosis.[218] If screened using purified protein derivative, other positive controls should be included because of the potential for anergy. Special stains and cultures of lung tissue and lavage can also be used to help exclude tuberculosis.

Combined regimens are coming into increasing favor as treatments for sarcoidosis, although there have been few trials. Most combination treatment regimens for sarcoidosis are corticosteroids plus a second-line agent. The corticosteroid is then slowly tapered over a 3- to 6-month period as allowed by the patient's clinical status, leaving the second drug as the main therapeutic agent. In one study, the combination of cyclosporin plus oral fluocortolone and oral methotrexate was studied in an open-label, uncontrolled trial in steroid-refractory patients.[219] All 11 patients entered remission. These preliminary results need to be confirmed with a larger, prospective, controlled trial.

In the face of immunosuppression, sarcoidosis patients are at risk of aspergilloma. The underlying goal of any therapeutic intervention for aspergilloma is the prevention of massive, life-threatening hemoptysis, which may occur in up to 26% of patients with mycetomas.[80] Unfortunately, even with identified risk factors for a poor prognosis, including the severity of underlying lung disease, immunosuppression (including corticosteroids), and underlying sarcoidosis, the likelihood of significant hemoptysis is difficult to predict. Current practice guidelines and a recent review of the literature suggest that observation, without any therapeutic intervention, is appropriate in asymptomatic patients.[80,81] However, the optimal management of those patients with mild hemoptysis or systemic symptoms, or both, and the overall utility of medical interventions are unclear. There have been no prospective, randomized, double-blind, placebo-controlled trials. However, the available evidence suggests possible utility of endobronchial or intracavitary amphotericin B and of oral itraconazole in selected patients.[80] For those who do develop massive hemoptysis, bronchial artery embolization can sometimes be used as a bridge to surgery.[80,81] Unfortunately, although surgical resection is the definitive treatment, it carries a very high morbidity and mortality, the latter ranging from 1.5 to 23%.[81] In summary, this is a challenging clinical problem with little in the way of strong evidence to guide therapeutic decisions.

LUNG TRANSPLANTATION

Patients with severe and progressive pulmonary disease despite exhaustive medical therapy may be candidates for lung transplantation. The decision regarding timing of proceeding to transplantation is a difficult one; generally, patients with severe and irreversible disease with a life expectancy of less than 3 years are considered. This assessment can be quite challenging in sarcoidosis, as a retrospective study of sarcoidosis patients awaiting transplantation demonstrates. In this study, 23 of 43 patients died while awaiting transplantation; further analysis demonstrated that elevated right atrial pressure consistent with pulmonary hypertension was the only independent predictor of mortality.[220] A recent similar retrospective cohort study examined mortality of sarcoidosis patients listed for lung transplantation throughout the United States between 1995 and 2000. Among the 405 patients for whom adequate follow-up data were available, 111, or 27.4%, died while awaiting transplantation. The mortality prediction model found an association of higher mortality with African American race, amount of supplemental oxygen needed, and mean pulmonary artery pressure.[221] These data suggest that the development of a predictive model of life expectancy to assist in deciding the time of transplantation referral, as exists for such diseases as cystic fibrosis and primary pulmonary hypertension,[222] may improve survival to transplantation in this population.

There are several other issues unique to sarcoidosis patients that must be evaluated prior to proceeding to transplantation.[222] One is the search for and treatment of other etiologies of pulmonary dysfunction, such as bronchiectasis, often found in patients with stage IV disease, and congestive heart failure. Treatment of these disorders may yield enough clinical improvement to delay the need for transplantation. The presence of severe nonpulmonary disease, especially neurologic and cardiac disease, excludes patients from consideration for lung transplantation. Heart-lung transplantation can be considered for patients with severe cardiac and pulmonary involvement.

Another potential contraindication to transplantation, particularly in patients with end-stage fibrocystic disease, is the presence of one or more mycetomas (most commonly aspergillomas). Resection of mycetomas carries a high mortality and high incidence of postoperative complications. In addition, even with the successful removal of mycetomas, concern remains regarding the presence of residual subclinical invasive or noninvasive *Aspergillus* infection or colonization that may place the patient at high risk of severe and invasive infection on posttransplantation immunosuppressive therapy.[222] One case of an end-stage sarcoidosis patient with mycetomas who died from invasive *Aspergillus* infection after heart-lung transplantation has been reported.[223] In addition, a recent review of the lung transplantation experience at one center revealed that mycetomas were present in the explanted lungs of 3% of recipients. Most of those with mycetomas had sarcoidosis (six of nine). Posttransplantation mortality was significantly increased in this population, with better survival associated with aggressive pre- and posttransplantation antifungal therapy.[224]

The decision to proceed with single- versus double-lung transplantation depends largely on the infectious issues raised previously. If individuals with bilateral bronchiectasis or bilateral mycetomas are considered for transplantation, they should undergo double-lung transplantation. However, in most end-stage sarcoidosis patients, single-lung transplantation is considered adequate.[222] Another interesting feature of transplantation in this patient population is the recurrence of sarcoidosis in lung allografts, documented in numerous reports.[225-228] This has typically been observed on surveillance transbronchial biopsies and is rarely clinically significant. Lung transplant outcomes in this population have not been well studied. Several reviews of small series of patients demonstrate survival and obliterative bronchiolitis rates comparable to those reported in transplantation for other diseases.[229-232]

SUMMARY

Sarcoidosis should be considered in any patient presenting with systemic and multiorgan symptoms, or whenever granulomatous inflammation is discovered on histology in any organ. Therapeutic advances based on an understanding of immune mechanisms will likely improve our approaches to medical management of this enigmatic condition. Further understanding derived from large, careful epidemiologic and genetic studies will also hopefully provide important clues about disease pathogenesis and, potentially, pathways to prevention of this potentially devastating illness.

REFERENCES

1. Newman LS, Rose CS, Maier LA: Sarcoidosis. N Engl J Med 336:1224–1234, 1997.
2. Statement on sarcoidosis: Joint statement of the American Thoracic Society (ATS), the European Respiratory Society (ERS) and the World Association of Sarcoidosis and Other Granulomatous Disorders (WASOG) adopted by the ATS Board of Directors and by the ERS Executive Committee, February 1999. Am J Respir Crit Care Med 160:736–755, 1999.
3. Bresnitz EA, Stolley PD, Israel HL, et al: Possible risk factors for sarcoidosis: A case-control study. Ann N Y Acad Sci 465:632–642, 1986.
4. Edmondstone WM: Sarcoidosis in nurses: Is there an association? Thorax 43:342–343, 1988.
5. Hills SE, Parkes SA, Baker SB: Epidemiology of sarcoidosis in the Isle of Man—2: Evidence for space-time clustering. Thorax 42:427–430, 1987.
6. Kern DG, Neill MA, Wrenn DS, et al: Investigation of a unique time-space cluster of sarcoidosis in firefighters. Am Rev Respir Dis 148:974–980, 1993.
7. Parkes SA, Baker SB, Bourdillon RE, et al: Incidence of sarcoidosis in the Isle of Man. Thorax 40:284–287, 1985.
8. Parkes SA, Baker SB, Bourdillon RE, et al: Epidemiology of sarcoidosis in the Isle of Man—1: A case controlled study. Thorax 42:420–426, 1987.
9. Hance AJ: The role of mycobacteria in the pathogenesis of sarcoidosis. Semin Respir Infect 13:197–205, 1998.
10. Mangiapan G, Hance AJ: Mycobacteria and sarcoidosis: An overview and summary of recent molecular biological data. Sarcoidosis 12:20–37, 1995.
11. Ishige I, Usui Y, Takemura T, et al: Quantitative PCR of mycobacterial and propionibacterial DNA in lymph nodes of Japanese patients with sarcoidosis. Lancet 354:120–123, 1999.
12. Homma JY, Abe C, Chosa H, et al: Bacteriological investigation on biopsy specimens from patients with sarcoidosis. Jpn J Exp Med 48:251–255, 1978.
13. Eishi Y, Suga M, Ishige I, et al: Quantitative analysis of mycobacterial and propionibacterial DNA in lymph nodes of Japanese and European patients with sarcoidosis. J Clin Microbiol 40:198–204, 2002.
14. Nilsson K, Pahlson C, Lukinius A, et al: Presence of Rickettsia helvetica in granulomatous tissue from patients with sarcoidosis. J Infect Dis 185:1128–1138, 2002.
15. Nagate A, Ohyashiki JH, Kasuga I, et al: Detection and quantification of human herpesvirus 6 genomes using bronchoalveolar lavage fluid in immunocompromised patients with interstitial pneumonia. Int J Mol Med 8:379–383, 2001.
16. Maeda H, Niimi T, Sato S, et al: Human herpesvirus 8 is not associated with sarcoidosis in Japanese patients. Chest 118:923–927, 2000.
17. di Gennaro G, Canzonieri V, Schioppa O, et al: Discordant HHV8 detection in a young HIV-negative patient with Kaposi's sarcoma and sarcoidosis. Clin Infect Dis 32:1100–1102, 2001.
18. Moller DR: T-cell receptor genes in sarcoidosis. Sarcoidosis Vasc Diffuse Lung Dis 15:158–164, 1998.
19. ACCESS: Design of A Case Control Etiologic Study of Sarcoidosis (ACCESS). J Clin Epidemiol 52:1173–1186, 1999.
20. Barnard JG, Rose CS, Canner MK, et al: Job and Industry Classifications Associated with Sarcoidosis in A Case Control Etiologic Study of Sarcoidosis (ACCESS). Seattle: American Thoracic Society, 2003, Vol A682.
21. Newman LS, Rose CS, Bresnitz EA, et al: A case control etiologic study of sarcoidosis: environmental and occupational risk factors. Am J Respir Crit Care Med 170:1324–1330, 2004.
22. Kajdasz DK, Lackland DT, Mohr LC, et al: A current assessment of rurally linked exposures as potential risk factors for sarcoidosis. Ann Epidemiol 11:111–117, 2001.
23. Kucera GP, Rybicki BA, Kirkey KL, et al: Occupational risk factors for sarcoidosis in African-American siblings. Chest 123:1527–1535, 2003.
24. Visser H, Vos K, Zanelli E, et al: Sarcoid arthritis: Clinical characteristics, diagnostic aspects, and risk factors. Ann Rheum Dis 61:499–504, 2002.
25. Wilsher ML: Seasonal clustering of sarcoidosis presenting with erythema nodosum. Eur Respir J 12:1197–1199, 1998.
26. Glennas A, Kvien TK, Melby K, et al: Acute sarcoid arthritis: Occurrence, seasonal onset, clinical features and outcome. Br J Rheumatol 34:45–50, 1995.
27. Bardinas F, Morera J, Fite E, et al: Seasonal clustering of sarcoidosis. Lancet 2:455–456, 1989.
28. Keller AZ: Hospital, age, racial, occupational, geographical, clinical, and survivorship characteristics in the epidemiology of sarcoidosis. Am J Epidemiol 94:222–230, 1971.
29. Siltzbach LE, James DG, Neville E, et al: Course and prognosis of sarcoidosis around the world. Am J Med 57:847–852, 1974.
30. Kajdasz DK, Judson MA, Mohr LC Jr, et al: Geographic variation in sarcoidosis in South Carolina: Its relation to socioeconomic status and health care indicators. Am J Epidemiol 150:271–278, 1999.
31. Harrington D, Major M, Rybicki BA, et al: Familial sarcoidosis: Analysis of 91 families. Sarcoidosis 11:240–243, 1994.
32. Rybicki BA, Maliarik MJ, Major M, et al: Genetics of sarcoidosis. Clin Chest Med 18:707–717, 1997.
33. Schurmann M, Reichel P, Muller-Myhsok B, et al: Angiotensin-converting enzyme (ACE) gene polymorphisms and familial occurrence of sarcoidosis. J Intern Med 249:77–83, 2001.
34. Schurmann M, Lympany PA, Reichel P, et al: Familial sarcoidosis is linked to the major histocompatibility complex region. Am J Respir Crit Care Med 162:861–864, 2000.
35. Schurmann M, Bein G, Kirsten D, et al: HLA-DQB1 and HLA-DPB1 genotypes in familial sarcoidosis. Respir Med 92:649–652, 1998.
36. Schurmann M, Reichel P, Muller-Myhsok B, et al: Results from a genome-wide search for predisposing genes in sarcoidosis. Am J Respir Crit Care Med 164:840–846, 2001.
37. Berlin M, Fogdell-Hahn A, Olerup O, et al: HLA-DR predicts the prognosis in Scandinavian patients with pulmonary sarcoidosis. Am J Respir Crit Care Med 156:1601–1605, 1997.
38. Sato H, Grutters JC, Pantelidis P, et al: HLA-DQB1*0201: A marker for good prognosis in British and Dutch patients with sarcoidosis. Am J Respir Cell Mol Biol 27:406–412, 2002.
39. Grutters JC, Sato H, Welsh KI, et al: The importance of sarcoidosis genotype to lung phenotype. Am J Respir Cell Mol Biol 29:S59–S62, 2003.
40. Foley PJ, Lympany PA, Puscinska E, et al: Analysis of MHC encoded antigen-processing genes TAP1 and TAP2 polymorphisms in sarcoidosis. Am J Respir Crit Care Med 160:1009–1014, 1999.
41. Swider C, Schnittger L, Bogunia-Kubik K, et al: TNF-alpha and HLA-DR genotyping as potential prognostic

markers in pulmonary sarcoidosis. Eur Cytokine Netw 10:143–146, 1999.

42. Labunski S, Posern G, Ludwig S, et al: Tumour necrosis factor-alpha promoter polymorphism in erythema nodosum. Acta Derm Venereol 81:18–21, 2001.

43. Seitzer U, Swider C, Stuber F, et al: Tumour necrosis factor alpha promoter gene polymorphism in sarcoidosis. Cytokine 9:787–790, 1997.

44. Takashige N, Naruse TK, Matsumori A, et al: Genetic polymorphisms at the tumour necrosis factor loci (TNFA and TNFB) in cardiac sarcoidosis. Tissue Antigens 54:191–193, 1999.

45. Pandey JP, Frederick M: TNF-alpha, IL1-beta, and immunoglobulin (GM and KM) gene polymorphisms in sarcoidosis. Hum Immunol 63:485–491, 2002.

46. Yamaguchi E, Itoh A, Hizawa N, et al: The gene polymorphism of tumor necrosis factor-beta, but not that of tumor necrosis factor-alpha, is associated with the prognosis of sarcoidosis. Chest 119:753–761, 2001.

47. Grutters JC, Sato H, Pantelidis P, et al: Increased frequency of the uncommon tumor necrosis factor -857T allele in British and Dutch patients with sarcoidosis. Am J Respir Crit Care Med 165:1119–1124, 2002.

48. Maliarik MJ, Rybicki BA, Malvitz E, et al: Angiotensin-converting enzyme gene polymorphism and risk of sarcoidosis. Am J Respir Crit Care Med 158:1566–1570, 1998.

49. Hizawa N, Yamaguchi E, Furuya K, et al: The role of the C-C chemokine receptor 2 gene polymorphism V64I (CCR2–64I) in sarcoidosis in a Japanese population. Am J Respir Crit Care Med 159:2021–2023, 1999.

50. Petrek M, Drabek J, Kolek V, et al: CC chemokine receptor gene polymorphisms in Czech patients with pulmonary sarcoidosis. Am J Respir Crit Care Med 162:1000–1003, 2000.

51. Spagnolo P, Renzoni EA, Wells AU, et al: C-C chemokine receptor 2 and sarcoidosis: Association with Lofgren's syndrome. Am J Respir Crit Care Med 168:1162–1166, 2003.

52. Hunninghake GW, Gadek JE, Kawanami O, et al: Inflammatory and immune processes in the human lung in health and disease: Evaluation by bronchoalveolar lavage. Am J Pathol 97:199–206, 1979.

53. Vourlekis JS, Sawyer RT, Newman LS: Sarcoidosis: Developments in etiology, immunology, and therapeutics. Adv Intern Med 45:209–257, 2000.

54. Agostini C, Adami F, Semenzato G: New pathogenetic insights into the sarcoid granuloma. Curr Opin Rheumatol 12:71–76, 2000.

55. Moller DR, Chen ES: What causes sarcoidosis? Curr Opin Pulm Med 8:429–434, 2002.

56. Ziegenhagen MW, Muller-Quernheim J: The cytokine network in sarcoidosis and its clinical relevance. J Intern Med 253:18–30, 2003.

57. Kim DS, Paik SH, Lim CM, et al: Value of ICAM-1 expression and soluble ICAM-1 level as a marker of activity in sarcoidosis. Chest 115:1059–1065, 1999.

58. Berlin M, Lundahl J, Skold CM, et al: The lymphocytic alveolitis in sarcoidosis is associated with increased amounts of soluble and cell-bound adhesion molecules in bronchoalveolar lavage fluid and serum. J Intern Med 244:333–340, 1998.

59. Pforte A, Schiessler A, Kressenstein S, et al: ICAM-1 expression on alveolar macrophages and in serum of sarcoidosis patients. J Clin Lab Immunol 46:125–135, 1995.

60. Dalhoff K, Bohnet S, Braun J, et al: Intercellular adhesion molecule 1 (ICAM-1) in the pathogenesis of mononuclear cell alveolitis in pulmonary sarcoidosis. Thorax 48:1140–1144, 1993.

61. Striz I, Wang YM, Kalaycioglu O, et al: Expression of alveolar macrophage adhesion molecules in pulmonary sarcoidosis. Chest 102:882–886, 1992.

62. Viani RM: Sarcoidosis and interstitial nephritis in a child with acquired immunodeficiency syndrome: Implications of immune reconstitution syndrome with an indinavir-based regimen. Pediatr Infect Dis J 21:435–438, 2002.

63. Gomez V, Smith PR, Burack J, et al: Sarcoidosis after antiretroviral therapy in a patient with acquired immunodeficiency syndrome. Clin Infect Dis 31:1278–1280, 2000.

64. Mirmirani P, Maurer TA, Herndier B, et al: Sarcoidosis in a patient with AIDS: A manifestation of immune restoration syndrome. J Am Acad Dermatol 41:285–286, 1999.

64a. Foulon G, Wislez M, Naccache JM, et al: Sarcoidosis in HIV-infected patients in the era of highly active antiretroviral therapy. Clin Infect Dis 38:418–425, 2004.

65. Blanche P, Gombert B, Rollot F, et al: Sarcoidosis in a patient with acquired immunodeficiency syndrome treated with interleukin-2. Clin Infect Dis 31:1493–1494, 2000.

66. Morris DG, Jasmer RM, Huang L, et al: Sarcoidosis following HIV infection: Evidence for CD4+ lymphocyte dependence. Chest 124:929–935, 2003.

67. Moller DR: Involvement of T cells and alterations in T cell receptors in sarcoidosis. Semin Respir Infect 13:174–183, 1998.

68. Grunewald J, Janson CH, Eklund A, et al: Restricted V alpha 2.3 gene usage by CD4+ T lymphocytes in bronchoalveolar lavage fluid from sarcoidosis patients correlates with HLA-DR3. Eur J Immunol 22:129–135, 1992.

69. Grunewald J, Wahlstrom J, Berlin M, et al: Lung restricted T cell receptor AV2S3+ CD4+ T cell expansions in sarcoidosis patients with a shared HLA-DRbeta chain conformation. Thorax 57:348–352, 2002.

70. Boros DL: Granulomatous Infections and Inflammations: Cellular and Molecular Mechanisms. Washington, DC: ASM Press, 2003.

71. Moller DR: Pulmonary fibrosis of sarcoidosis: New approaches, old ideas. Am J Respir Cell Mol Biol 29:S37–S41, 2003.

72. Harrison BD, Shaylor JM, Stokes TC, et al: Airflow limitation in sarcoidosis—a study of pulmonary function in 107 patients with newly diagnosed disease. Respir Med 85:59–64, 1991.

73. Muller NL, Kullnig P, Miller RR: The CT findings of pulmonary sarcoidosis: Analysis of 25 patients. AJR Am J Roentgenol 152:1179–1182, 1989.

74. Brauner MW, Grenier P, Mompoint D, et al: Pulmonary sarcoidosis: Evaluation with high-resolution CT. Radiology 172:467–471, 1989.

75. Lynch DA, Webb WR, Gamsu G, et al: Computed tomography in pulmonary sarcoidosis. J Comput Assist Tomogr 13:405–410, 1989.

76. Lynch DA, Newell JD, Lee JS: Imaging of Diffuse Lung Disease. Hamilton, Ontario, Canada: BC Decker, 2000.

77. McLoud TC, Epler GR, Gaensler EA, et al: A radiographic classification for sarcoidosis: Physiologic correlation. Invest Radiol 17:129–138, 1982.

78. Chapman JT, Mehta AC: Bronchoscopy in sarcoidosis: Diagnostic and therapeutic interventions. Curr Opin Pulm Med 9:402–407, 2003.

79. Koonitz CH, Joyner LR, Nelson RA: Transbronchial lung biopsy via the fiberoptic bronchoscope in sarcoidosis. Ann Intern Med 85:64–66, 1976.

80. Stevens DA, Kan VL, Judson MA, et al: Practice guidelines for diseases caused by *Aspergillus*. Infectious Diseases Society of America. Clin Infect Dis 30:696–709, 2000.

81. Soubani AO, Chandrasekar PH: The clinical spectrum of pulmonary aspergillosis. Chest 121:1988–1999, 2002.

82. Bjermer L, Thunell M, Rosenhall L, et al: Endobronchial biopsy positive sarcoidosis: Relation to bronchoalveolar lavage and course of disease. Respir Med 85:229–234, 1991.

83. Stjernberg N, Thunell M: Pulmonary function in patients with endobronchial sarcoidosis. Acta Med Scand 215:121–126, 1984.

84. Soskel NT, Sharma OP: Pleural involvement in sarcoidosis. Curr Opin Pulm Med 6:455–468, 2000.

85. Hamacher J, Losa F, Im Hof V, et al: Tuberculous pleuritis in pre-existent sarcoidosis (in German). Schweiz Med Wochenschr 121:577–582, 1991.

86. Matsuzawa K, Hamada K, Tokuyama T, et al: Photomicrographs of a pleural biopsy specimen, showing malignant mesothelioma and necrosis—malignant pleural mesothelioma in a patient with sarcoidosis (in Japanese). Nihon Kyobu Shikkan Gakkai Zasshi 35:687–691, 1997.

87. Claiborne RA, Kerby GR: Pleural sarcoidosis with massive effusion and lung entrapment. Kans Med 91:103–105, 1990.

88. Krawczyk I, Sedlaczek AM: A case of sarcoidosis with massive pleural and pericardial effusion (in Polish). Pneumonol Alergol Pol 65:81–85, 1997.

89. Schmidt RJ, Bender FH, Chang WW, et al: Sarcoidosis after renal transplantation. Transplantation 68:1420–1423, 1999.

90. Brauner MW, Grenier P, Mompoint D, et al: Pulmonary sarcoidosis: Evaluation with high-resolution CT. Radiology 172:467–471, 1989.

91. Ohmichi M, Hiraga Y, Hirasawa M: Pulmonary involvements of sarcoidosis (in Japanese). Nihon Kyobu Shikkan Gakkai Zasshi 28:48–55, 1990.

92. Kostina ZI, Ivanovskii VB, Voloshko IV, et al: Diagnosis and treatment of pleural lesions in sarcoidosis of the respiratory organs (in Russian). Probl Tuberk (7–8):21–23, 1992.

93. Ilan Y, Ben-Yehuda A, Breuer R: Pleural effusion—the presenting radiological manifestation of sarcoidosis. Isr J Med Sci 30:535–536, 1994.

94. Hashimoto M, Watanabe O, Sato K, et al: The CT findings of pulmonary sarcoidosis. Tohoku J Exp Med 179:259–266, 1996.

95. Remy-Jardin M, Beuscart R, Sault MC, et al: Subpleural micronodules in diffuse infiltrative lung diseases: Evaluation with thin-section CT scans. Radiology 177:133–139, 1990.

96. Miller BH, Rosado-de-Christenson ML, McAdams HP, et al: Thoracic sarcoidosis: Radiologic-pathologic correlation. Radiographics 15:421–437, 1995.

97. Bergin CJ, Bell DY, Coblentz CL, et al: Sarcoidosis: Correlation of pulmonary parenchymal pattern at CT with results of pulmonary function tests. Radiology 171:619–624, 1989.

98. Cappell MS, Friedman D, Mikhail N: Chyloperitoneum associated with chronic severe sarcoidosis. Am J Gastroenterol 88:99–101, 1993.

99. Jarman PR, Whyte MK, Sabroe I, et al: Sarcoidosis presenting with chylothorax. Thorax 50:1324–1325, 1995.

100. Lengyel RJ, Shanley DJ: Recurrent chylothorax associated with sarcoidosis. Hawaii Med J 54:817–818, 1995.

101. Liebow AA: The J. Burns Amberson lecture—pulmonary angiitis and granulomatosis. Am Rev Respir Dis 108:1–18, 1973.

102. Niimi H, Hartman TE, Muller NL: Necrotizing sarcoid granulomatosis: Computed tomography and pathologic findings. J Comput Assist Tomogr 19:920–923, 1995.

103. Frazier AA, Rosado-de-Christenson ML, Galvin JR, et al: Pulmonary angiitis and granulomatosis: Radiologic-pathologic correlation. Radiographics 18:687–710; quiz 727, 1998.

104. Popper HH, Klemen H, Colby TV, et al: Necrotizing sarcoid granulomatosis—is it different from nodular sarcoidosis? Pneumologie 57:268–271, 2003.

105. Dykhuizen RS, Smith CC, Kennedy MM, et al: Necrotizing sarcoid granulomatosis with extrapulmonary involvement. Eur Respir J 10:245–247, 1997.

106. Chittock DR, Joseph MG, Paterson NA, et al: Necrotizing sarcoid granulomatosis with pleural involvement: Clinical and radiographic features. Chest 106:672–676, 1994.

107. Spiteri MA, Gledhill A, Campbell D, et al: Necrotizing sarcoid granulomatosis. Br J Dis Chest 81:70–75, 1987.

108. Churg A, Carrington CB, Gupta R: Necrotizing sarcoid granulomatosis. Chest 76:406–413, 1979.

109. Gilman MJ, Wang KP: Transbronchial lung biopsy in sarcoidosis: An approach to determine the optimal number of biopsies. Am Rev Respir Dis 122:721–724, 1980.

110. Armstrong JR, Radke JR, Kvale PA, et al: Endoscopic findings in sarcoidosis: Characteristics and correlations with radiographic staging and bronchial mucosal biopsy yield. Ann Otol Rhinol Laryngol 90:339–343, 1981.

111. Bilaceroglu S, Perim K, Gunel O, et al: Combining transbronchial aspiration with endobronchial and transbronchial biopsy in sarcoidosis. Monaldi Arch Chest Dis 54:217–223, 1999.

112. Gupta D, Mahendran C, Aggarwal AN, et al: Endobronchial vis à vis transbronchial involvement on fiberoptic bronchoscopy in sarcoidosis. Sarcoidosis Vasc Diffuse Lung Dis 18:91–92, 2001.

113. Shorr AF, Torrington KG, Hnatiuk OW: Endobronchial biopsy for sarcoidosis: A prospective study. Chest 120:109–114, 2001.

114. Winterbauer RH, Lammert J, Selland M, et al: Bronchoalveolar lavage cell populations in the diagnosis of sarcoidosis. Chest 104:352–361, 1993.

115. Costabel U: Sensitivity and specificity of BAL findings in sarcoidosis. Sarcoidosis 9:211–214, 1992.

116. Travis W, Colby TV, Koss MN, et al: Non-Neoplastic Disorders of the Lower Respiratory Tract. Washington, DC: American Registry of Pathology and the Armed Forces Institute of Pathology, 2002.

117. Krespi YP, Kuriloff DB, Aner M: Sarcoidosis of the sinonasal tract: A new staging system. Otolaryngol Head Neck Surg 112:221–227, 1995.

118. Marks SC, Goodman RS: Surgical management of nasal and sinus sarcoidosis. Otolaryngol Head Neck Surg 118:856–858, 1998.

119. Tami TA: Sinonasal sarcoidosis: Diagnosis and management. Semin Respir Crit Care Med 23:549–554, 2002.

120. Sharma OP: Myocardial sarcoidosis: A wolf in sheep's clothing. Chest 106:988–990, 1994.

121. Shammas RL, Movahed A: Sarcoidosis of the heart. Clin Cardiol 16:462–472, 1993.

122. Mana J: Nuclear imaging: [67]Gallium, [201]thallium, ^{18}F-labeled fluoro-2-deoxy-D-glucose positron emission tomography. Clin Chest Med 18:799–811, 1997.

123. Eguchi M, Tsuchihashi K, Hotta D, et al: Technetium-99m sestamibi/tetrofosmin myocardial perfusion scanning in cardiac and noncardiac sarcoidosis. Cardiology 94:193–199, 2000.

124. Yamagishi H, Shirai N, Takagi M, et al: Identification of cardiac sarcoidosis with ^{13}N-NH$_3$/^{18}F-FDG PET. J Nucl Med 44:1030–1036, 2003.

125. Takeda N, Yokoyama I, Hiroi Y, et al: Positron emission tomography predicted recovery of complete A-V nodal dysfunction in a patient with cardiac sarcoidosis. Circulation 105:1144–1145, 2002.

126. Chandra M, Silverman ME, Oshinski J, et al: Diagnosis of cardiac sarcoidosis aided by MRI. Chest 110:562–565, 1996.

127. Doherty MJ, Kumar SK, Nicholson AA, et al: Cardiac sarcoidosis: The value of magnetic resonance imaging in diagnosis and assessment of response to treatment. Respir Med 92:697–699, 1998.

128. Ratner SJ, Fenoglio JJ Jr, Ursell PC: Utility of endomyocardial biopsy in the diagnosis of cardiac sarcoidosis. Chest 90:528–533, 1986.

129. Uemura A, Morimoto S, Hiramitsu S, et al: Histologic diagnostic rate of cardiac sarcoidosis: Evaluation of endomyocardial biopsies. Am Heart J 138:299–302, 1999.

130. Rothova A: Ocular involvement in sarcoidosis. Br J Ophthalmol 84:110–116, 2000.

131. Hershey JM, Pulido JS, Folberg R, et al: Non-caseating conjunctival granulomas in patients with multifocal choroiditis and panuveitis. Ophthalmology 101:596–601, 1994.

132. Spaide RF, Ward DL: Conjunctival biopsy in the diagnosis of sarcoidosis. Br J Ophthalmol 74:469–471, 1990.

133. Nichols CW, Eagle RC Jr, Yanoff M, et al: Conjunctival biopsy as an aid in the evaluation of the patient with suspected sarcoidosis. Ophthalmology 87:287–291, 1980.

134. Solomon DA, Horn BR, Byrd RB, et al: The diagnosis of sarcoidosis by conjunctival biopsy. Chest 74:271–273, 1978.

135. Khan F, Wessely Z, Chazin SR, et al: Conjunctival biopsy in sarcoidosis: A simple, safe, and specific diagnostic procedure. Ann Ophthalmol 9:671–676, 1977.

136. Stanbury RM, Graham EM, Murray PI: Sarcoidosis. Int Ophthalmol Clin 35:123–137, 1995.

137. Obenauf CD, Shaw HE, Sydnor CF, et al: Sarcoidosis and its ophthalmic manifestations. Am J Ophthalmol 86:648–655, 1978.

138. Gould H, Kaufman HE: Sarcoid of the fundus. Arch Ophthalmol 65:453–456, 1961.

139. Rothova A, Suttorp-van Schulten MS, Frits Treffers W, et al: Causes and frequency of blindness in patients with intraocular inflammatory disease. Br J Ophthalmol 80:332–336, 1996.

140. Teirstein A: Neuromuscular sarcoidosis. Semin Respir Crit Care Med 23:505–512, 2002.

141. Christoforidis GA, Spickler EM, Recio MV, et al: MR of CNS sarcoidosis: Correlation of imaging features to clinical symptoms and response to treatment. AJNR Am J Neuroradiol 20:655–669, 1999.

142. Goldstein RA, Israel HL, Becker KL, et al: The infrequency of hypercalcemia in sarcoidosis. Am J Med 51:21–30, 1971.

143. Sharma OP: Vitamin D, calcium, and sarcoidosis. Chest 109:535–539, 1996.

144. Scott GC, Berman JM, Higgins JL Jr: CT patterns of nodular hepatic and splenic sarcoidosis: A review of the literature. J Comput Assist Tomogr 21:369–372, 1997.

145. Warshauer DM, Semelka RC, Ascher SM: Nodular sarcoidosis of the liver and spleen: Appearance on MR images. J Magn Reson Imaging 4:553–557, 1994.

146. Selroos O: Fine-needle aspiration biopsy of spleen in diagnosis of sarcoidosis. Z Erkr Atmungsorgane 149:109–111, 1977.

147. Selroos O, Koivunen E: Usefulness of fine-needle aspiration biopsy of spleen in diagnosis of sarcoidosis. Chest 83:193–195, 1983.

148. Thadani U, Aber CP, Taylor JJ: Massive splenomegaly, pancytopenia and haemolytic anaemia in sarcoidosis. Acta Haematol 53:230–240, 1975.

149. Young HB, Mooney RA: Giant splenomegaly in sarcoidosis. Br J Surg 55:554–557, 1968.

150. Wilcox A, Bharadwaj P, Sharma OP: Bone sarcoidosis. Curr Opin Rheumatol 12:321–330, 2000.

151. Zisman DA SA, Lynch JP: Sarcoidosis involving the musculoskeletal system. Semin Respir Crit Care Med 23:555–570, 2002.

152. Judson MA, Baughman RP, Teirstein AS, et al: Defining organ involvement in sarcoidosis: The ACCESS proposed instrument. ACCESS Research Group. A Case Control Etiologic Study of Sarcoidosis. Sarcoidosis Vasc Diffuse Lung Dis 16:75–86, 1999.

153. Newman LS: Metals that cause sarcoidosis. Semin Respir Infect 13:212–220, 1998.

154. Safirstein BH, Klukowicz A, Miller R, et al: Granulomatous pneumonitis following exposure to the World Trade Center collapse. Chest 123:301–304, 2003.

155. Fireman E, Haimsky E, Noiderfer M, et al: Misdiagnosis of sarcoidosis in patients with chronic beryllium disease. Sarcoidosis Vasc Diffuse Lung Dis 20:144–148, 2003.

156. Weinberg I, Vasiliev L, Gotsman I: Anti-dsDNA antibodies in sarcoidosis. Semin Arthritis Rheum 29:328–331, 2000.

157. Nakamura H, Genma R, Mikami T, et al: High incidence of positive autoantibodies against thyroid peroxidase and thyroglobulin in patients with sarcoidosis. Clin Endocrinol (Oxf) 46:467–472, 1997.

158. Papadopoulos KI, Hornblad Y, Liljebladh H, et al: High frequency of endocrine autoimmunity in patients with sarcoidosis. Eur J Endocrinol 134:331–336, 1996.

159. Ina Y, Takada K, Yamamoto M, et al: Antiphospholipid antibodies: A prognostic factor in sarcoidosis? Chest 105:1179–1183, 1994.

160. Sarigol SS, Hay MH, Wyllie R: Sarcoidosis in preschool children with hepatic involvement mimicking juvenile rheumatoid arthritis. J Pediatr Gastroenterol Nutr 28:510–512, 1999.

161. Sahn EE, Hampton MT, Garen PD, et al: Preschool sarcoidosis masquerading as juvenile rheumatoid arthritis: Two case reports and a review of the literature. Pediatr Dermatol 7:208–213, 1990.

162. Ukae S, Tsutsumi H, Adachi N, et al: Preschool sarcoidosis manifesting as juvenile rheumatoid arthritis: A case report and a review of the literature of Japanese cases. Acta Paediatr Jpn 36:515–518, 1994.

163. Sakurai Y, Nakajima M, Kamisue S, et al: Preschool sarcoidosis mimicking juvenile rheumatoid arthritis: The significance of gallium scintigraphy and skin biopsy in the differential diagnosis. Acta Paediatr Jpn 39:74–78, 1997.

164. Fallahi S, Collins RD, Miller RK, et al: Coexistence of rheumatoid arthritis and sarcoidosis: Difficulties encountered in the differential diagnosis of common manifestations. J Rheumatol 11:526–529, 1984.

165. Kucera RF: A possible association of rheumatoid arthritis and sarcoidosis. Chest 95:604–606, 1989.

166. Menard O, Petit N, Gillet P, et al: Association of histologically proven rheumatoid arthritis with pulmonary sarcoidosis. Eur Respir J 8:472–473, 1995.

167. Yutani Y, Minato Y, Hirata K, et al: A rare case of sarcoidosis with rheumatoid arthritis. Osaka City Med J 41:85–89, 1995.

168. Justiniani FR: Sarcoidosis complicating primary Sjogren's syndrome. Mt Sinai J Med 56:59–61, 1989.

169. Radenne F, Tillie-Leblond I, Maurage CA, et al: Sjogren's syndrome and necrotizing sarcoid-like granulomatosis (in French). Rev Mal Respir 16:554–557, 1999.

170. Miyata M, Takase Y, Kobayashi H, et al: Primary Sjögren's syndrome complicated by sarcoidosis. Intern Med 37:174–178, 1998.

171. Lois M, Roman J, Holland W, et al: Coexisting Sjögren's syndrome and sarcoidosis in the lung. Semin Arthritis Rheum 28:31–40, 1998.

172. Gal I, Kovacs J, Zeher M: Case series: Coexistence of Sjögren's syndrome and sarcoidosis. J Rheumatol 27:2507–2510, 2000.

173. Giotaki H, Constantopoulos SH, Papadimitriou CS, et al: Labial minor salivary gland biopsy: A highly discriminatory diagnostic method between sarcoidosis and Sjögren's syndrome. Respiration 50:102–107, 1986.

174. Drosos AA, Voulgari PV, Psychos DN, et al: Sicca syndrome in patients with sarcoidosis. Rheumatol Int 18:177–180, 1999.

175. Mascolo MC, Truwit JD: Role of exercise evaluation in restrictive lung disease: New insights between March 2001 and February 2003. Curr Opin Pulm Med 9:408–410, 2003.

176. Oates E, Metherall J: Images in clinical medicine: Sarcoidosis. N Engl J Med 329:1394, 1993.

177. Grunewald J, Olerup O, Persson U, et al: T-cell receptor variable region gene usage by CD4+ and CD8+ T cells in bronchoalveolar lavage fluid and peripheral blood of sarcoidosis patients. Proc Natl Acad Sci U S A 91:4965–4969, 1994.

178. Paramothayan S, Jones PW: Corticosteroid therapy in pulmonary sarcoidosis: A systematic review. JAMA 287:1301–1307, 2002.

179. Moller DR: Treatment of sarcoidosis—from a basic science point of view. J Intern Med 253:31–40, 2003.

180. Reich JM: Adverse long-term effect of corticosteroid therapy in recent-onset sarcoidosis. Sarcoidosis Vasc Diffuse Lung Dis 20:227–234, 2003.

181. Young R: Pulmonary sarcoidosis: A prospective evaluation of glucocorticoid therapy. Ann Intern Med 7:207–212, 1970.

182. Harkleroad LE, Young RL, Savage PJ, et al: Pulmonary sarcoidosis: Long-term follow-up of the effects of steroid therapy. Chest 82:84–87, 1982.

183. Israel HL, Fouts DW, Beggs RA: A controlled trial of prednisone treatment of sarcoidosis. Am Rev Respir Dis 107:609–614, 1973.

184. Eule H, Weinecke A, Roth I, et al: The possible influence of corticosteroid therapy on the natural course of pulmonary sarcoidosis: Late results of a continuing clinical study. Ann N Y Acad Sci 465:695–701, 1986.

185. Zaki MH, Lyons HA, Leilop L, et al: Corticosteroid therapy in sarcoidosis: A five-year, controlled follow-up study. N Y State J Med 87:496–499, 1987.

186. Gibson GJ, Prescott RJ, Muers MF, et al: British Thoracic Society Sarcoidosis study: Effects of long term corticosteroid treatment. Thorax 51:238–247, 1996.

187. Baughman RP, Winget DB, Lower EE: Methotrexate is steroid sparing in acute sarcoidosis: Results of a double blind, randomized trial. Sarcoidosis Vasc Diffuse Lung Dis 17:60–66, 2000.

188. Lower EE, Baughman RP: Prolonged use of methotrexate for sarcoidosis. Arch Intern Med 155:846–851, 1995.

189. Baughman RP, Lower EE: Alternatives to corticosteroids in the treatment of sarcoidosis. Sarcoidosis Vasc Diffuse Lung Dis 14:121–130, 1997.

190. Webster GF, Razsi LK, Sanchez M, et al: Weekly low-dose methotrexate therapy for cutaneous sarcoidosis. J Am Acad Dermatol 24:451–454, 1991.

191. Kaye O, Palazzo E, Grossin M, et al: Low-dose methotrexate: An effective corticosteroid-sparing agent in the musculoskeletal manifestations of sarcoidosis. Br J Rheumatol 34:642–644, 1995.

192. Rebuck AS, Stiller CR, Braude AC, et al: Cyclosporin for pulmonary sarcoidosis. Lancet 1:1174, 1984.

193. Martinet Y, Pinkston P, Saltini C, et al: Evaluation of the in vitro and in vivo effects of cyclosporine on the lung T-lymphocyte alveolitis of active pulmonary sarcoidosis. Am Rev Respir Dis 138:1242–1248, 1988.

194. Wyser CP, van Schalkwyk EM, Alheit B, et al: Treatment of progressive pulmonary sarcoidosis with cyclosporin A: A randomized controlled trial. Am J Respir Crit Care Med 156:1371, 1997.

195. Pacheco Y, Marechal C, Marechal F, et al: Azathioprine treatment of chronic pulmonary sarcoidosis. Sarcoidosis 2:107–113, 1985.

196. Hof D: Long-term use of azathioprine as a steroid-sparing agent for chronic sarcoidosis. Am J Respir Crit Care Med 153:A870, 1996.

197. Lewis SJ, Ainslie GM, Bateman ED: Efficacy of azathioprine as second-line treatment in pulmonary sarcoidosis. Sarcoidosis Vasc Diffuse Lung Dis 16:87–92, 1999.

198. Muller-Quernheim J, Kienast K, Held M, et al: Treatment of chronic sarcoidosis with an azathioprine/prednisolone regimen. Eur Respir J 14:1117–1122, 1999.

199. Zic JA, Horowitz DH, Arzubiaga C, et al: Treatment of cutaneous sarcoidosis with chloroquine: Review of the literature. Arch Dermatol 127:1034–1040, 1991.

200. O'Leary TJ, Jones G, Yip A, et al: The effects of chloroquine on serum 1,25-dihydroxyvitamin D and calcium metabolism in sarcoidosis. N Engl J Med 315:727–730, 1986.

201. Sharma OP: Effectiveness of chloroquine and hydroxychloroquine in treating selected patients with sarcoidosis with neurological involvement. Arch Neurol 55:1248–1254, 1998.

202. British Tuberculosis Association: Chloroquine in the treatment of sarcoidosis: A report from the Research Committee of the British Tuberculosis Association. Tubercle 48:257–272, 1967.

203. Baltzan M, Mehta S, Kirkham TH, et al: Randomized trial of prolonged chloroquine therapy in advanced pulmonary sarcoidosis. Am J Respir Crit Care Med 160:192–197, 1999.

204. Demeter SL: Myocardial sarcoidosis unresponsive to steroids: Treatment with cyclophosphamide. Chest 94:202–203, 1988.

205. Lower EE, Broderick JP, Brott TG, et al: Diagnosis and management of neurological sarcoidosis. Arch Intern Med 157:1864–1868, 1997.

206. Carlesimo M, Giustini S, Rossi A, et al: Treatment of cutaneous and pulmonary sarcoidosis with thalidomide. J Am Acad Dermatol 32:866–869, 1995.

207. Rousseau L, Beylot-Barry M, Doutre MS, et al: Cutaneous sarcoidosis successfully treated with low doses of thalidomide. Arch Dermatol 134:1045–1046, 1998.

208. Lee JB, Koblenzer PS: Disfiguring cutaneous manifestation of sarcoidosis treated with thalidomide: A case report. J Am Acad Dermatol 39:835–838, 1998.

209. Oliver SJ, Kikuchi T, Krueger JG, et al: Thalidomide induces granuloma differentiation in sarcoid skin lesions associated with disease improvement. Clin Immunol 102:225–236, 2002.

210. Baughman RP, Judson MA, Teirstein AS, et al: Thalidomide for chronic sarcoidosis. Chest 122:227–232, 2002.

211. Zabel P, Entzian P, Dalhoff K, et al: Pentoxifylline in treatment of sarcoidosis. Am J Respir Crit Care Med 155:1665–1669, 1997.

212. Utz JP, Limper AH, Kalra S, et al: Etanercept for the treatment of stage II and III progressive pulmonary sarcoidosis. Chest 124:177–185, 2003.

213. Baughman RP, Lower EE: Infliximab for refractory sarcoidosis. Sarcoidosis Vasc Diffuse Lung Dis 18:70–74, 2001.

214. Petterson JA, Zochodne DW, Bell RB, et al: Refractory neurosarcoidosis responding to infliximab. Neurology 59:1660–1661, 2002.

215. Mallbris L, Ljungberg A, Hedblad MA, et al: Progressive cutaneous sarcoidosis responding to anti-tumor necrosis factor-alpha therapy. J Am Acad Dermatol 48:290–293, 2003.

216. Katz JM, Bruno MK, Winterkorn JM, et al: The pathogenesis and treatment of optic disc swelling in neurosarcoidosis: A unique therapeutic response to infliximab. Arch Neurol 60:426–430, 2003.

216a. Sollberger M, Fluri F, Baumann T, et al: Successful treatment of steroid-refractory neurosarcoidosis with infliximab. J Neurol 251:760–761, 2004.

216b. Carter JD, Valeriano J, Vasey JB, Bognar B: Refractory neurosarcoidosis: a dramatic response to infliximab. Am J Med 117:277–279, 2004.

217. Yee AM, Pochapin MB: Treatment of complicated sarcoidosis with infliximab anti-tumor necrosis factor-alpha therapy. Ann Intern Med 135:27–31, 2001.

218. Gomez-Reino JJ, Carmona L, Valverde VR, et al: Treatment of rheumatoid arthritis with tumor necrosis factor inhibitors may predispose to significant increase in tuberculosis risk: A multicenter active-surveillance report. Arthritis Rheum 48:2122–2127, 2003.

219. Pia G, Pascalis L, Aresu G, et al: Evaluation of the efficacy and toxicity of the cyclosporine A-fluocortolone-methotrexate combination in the treatment of sarcoidosis. Sarcoidosis Vasc Diffuse Lung Dis 13:146–152, 1996.

220. Arcasoy SM, Christie JD, Pochettino A, et al: Characteristics and outcomes of patients with sarcoidosis listed for lung transplantation. Chest 120:873–880, 2001.

221. Shorr AF, Davies DB, Nathan SD: Predicting mortality in patients with sarcoidosis awaiting lung transplantation. Chest 124:922–928, 2003.

222. Judson MA: Lung transplantation for pulmonary sarcoidosis. Eur Respir J 11:738–744, 1998.

223. Kanj SS, Welty-Wolf K, Madden J, et al: Fungal infections in lung and heart-lung transplant recipients: Report of 9 cases and review of the literature. Medicine (Baltimore) 75:142–156, 1996.

224. Hadjiliadis D, Sporn TA, Perfect JR, et al: Outcome of lung transplantation in patients with mycetomas. Chest 121:128–134, 2002.

225. Bjortuft O, Foerster A, Boe J, et al: Single lung transplantation as treatment for end-stage pulmonary sarcoidosis: Recurrence of sarcoidosis in two different lung allografts in one patient. J Heart Lung Transplant 13:24–29, 1994.

226. Johnson BA, Duncan SR, Ohori NP, et al: Recurrence of sarcoidosis in pulmonary allograft recipients. Am Rev Respir Dis 148:1373–1377, 1993.

227. Muller C, Briegel J, Haller M, et al: Sarcoidosis recurrence following lung transplantation. Transplantation 61:1117–1119, 1996.

228. Martinez FJ, Orens JB, Deeb M, et al: Recurrence of sarcoidosis following bilateral allogeneic lung transplantation. Chest 106:1597–1599, 1994.

229. Padilla ML, Schilero GJ, Teirstein AS: Sarcoidosis and transplantation. Sarcoidosis Vasc Diffuse Lung Dis 14:16–22, 1997.

230. Walker S, Mikhail G, Banner N, et al: Medium term results of lung transplantation for end stage pulmonary sarcoidosis. Thorax 53:281–284, 1998.

231. Nunley DR, Hattler B, Keenan RJ, et al: Lung transplantation for end-stage pulmonary sarcoidosis. Sarcoidosis Vasc Diffuse Lung Dis 16:93–100, 1999

232. Shorr AF, Helman DL, Davies DB, Nathan SD: Sarcoidosis, race, and short-term outcomes following lung transplantation. Chest 125:990–996, 2004.

56 Diffuse Alveolar Hemorrhage and Other Rare Infiltrative Disorders

Marvin I. Schwarz, M.D., Harold R. Collard, M.D., Talmadge E. King, Jr., M.D.

INTRODUCTION

Pulmonary hemorrhage usually results from conditions that are focal in either the airways or the lung parenchyma. These include bronchitis, bronchiectasis, necrotizing pneumonia, malignancy, pulmonary infarction, and arteriovenous malformations. In these conditions, either the pulmonary, or less commonly, the bronchial arteries and veins are the bleeding sources. The great majority of the alveolar structures are unaffected, although the potential for diffuse aspiration of blood exists. In addition, however, there are a group of conditions causing pulmonary hemorrhage that have adverse effects on the small pulmonary vessels (arterioles, capillaries, and venules), and these vessels are the source of bleeding. In these disorders, the majority of the alveolar capillary surface is affected, producing the syndrome known as diffuse alveolar hemorrhage (DAH).

The causes of DAH are most easily divided into those associated with the histologic entity pulmonary capillaritis and those that result from a variety of histologic processes that are not associated with this inflammatory interstitial lesion (also called "bland" DAH) (Table 56.1). This division is not absolute, as DAH associated with the connective tissue diseases and Goodpasture's syndrome has been described both with and without pulmonary capillaritis. The pathogenesis of DAH, at least for cases associated with

pulmonary capillaritis, is thought to be either immune complex mediated (e.g., systemic lupus erythematosus, Henoch-Schönlein purpura, and possibly microscopic polyangiitis and Wegener's granulomatosis), due to an antibody directed against the alveolar basement membrane (e.g., Goodpasture's syndrome), or due to direct effects of autoantibodies on the alveolar capillary endothelium (Wegener's granulomatosis and microscopic polyangiitis).[1]

DIFFUSE ALVEOLAR HEMORRHAGE

PATHOLOGY

Pulmonary capillaritis was first described by Spencer in 1957.[2] The term refers to an inflammatory lesion characterized by neutrophilic infiltration of the alveolar interstitium with subsequent fibrinoid necrosis. This in turn leads to loss of integrity of the epithelial-endothelial basement membranes and leakage of red blood cells (DAH) and neutrophils into the alveolar spaces (Figs. 56.1 and 56.2). Many of the neutrophils are undergoing a process called leukocytoclasis, and appear fragmented and pyknotic. Fragmentation of these cells leads to accumulation of nuclear dust in the lung parenchyma. Intra-alveolar hemosiderin-containing macrophages and collections of free interstitial hemosiderin appear after the acute hemorrhage. Other

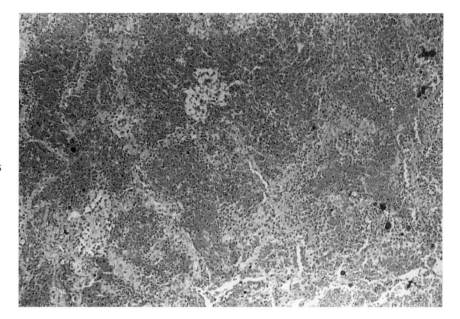

Figure 56.1 Micrograph showing diffuse alveolar hemorrhage secondary to pulmonary capillaritis. Alveolar spaces are filled with red blood cells as well as nucleated cells. The alveolar interstitium is broadened and infiltrated by neutrophils. Dark-staining hemosiderin collections can be appreciated. (Original magnification ×10.)

Table 56.1 Causes of Diffuse Alveolar Hemorrhage

With Pulmonary Capillaritis
Wegener's granulomatosis
Microscopic polyangiitis
Isolated pulmonary capillaritis
Connective tissue diseases*
Primary antiphospholipid syndrome
Mixed cryoglobulinemia
Behçet's syndrome
Henoch-Schönlein purpura
Goodpasture's syndrome*
Pauci-immune glomerulonephritis
Immune complex–associated glomerulonephritis
Drug induced (see text)
Acute lung allograft rejection

Without Pulmonary Capillaritis
Idiopathic pulmonary hemosiderosis
Systemic lupus erythematosus*
Goodpasture's syndrome*
Diffuse alveolar damage
Penicillamine
Trimellitic anhydride
Mitral stenosis
Coagulation disorders
Pulmonary veno-occlusive disease
Pulmonary capillary hemangiomatosis
Lymphangioleiomyomatosis
Tuberous sclerosis

* In systemic lupus erythematosus and Goodpasture's syndrome, diffuse alveolar hemorrhage has been reported with and without pulmonary capillaritis.

histologic features include hyperplasia of the type II alveolar epithelial lining cells, intra-alveolar organization of the DAH (organizing pneumonia), mononuclear cell infiltration of the alveolar interstitium, and small thrombi in the alveolar capillaries and venules.[3–5] In the bland form of DAH, the alveolar walls are essentially normal, and the histologic picture is that of red blood cell–filled alveoli. Other histologic processes, such as diffuse alveolar damage, pulmonary veno-occlusive disease, and lymphangioleiomyomatosis, can also be associated with DAH.

CLINICAL PRESENTATION

Cough, dyspnea, and hemoptysis are the most prominent symptoms in DAH with or without pulmonary capillaritis. Some patients complain of chest pain. However, hemoptysis is not always present when the patient is first examined and is often delayed, even when extensive intra-alveolar bleeding has occurred. In this situation, an unexplained falling hematocrit, acute diffuse pulmonary infiltration that is visible on chest radiograph, and sequential bronchoalveolar lavage revealing increasingly bloody lavagates are diagnostic. In general, the symptoms are usually of short duration, present from days to several weeks before the patient seeks medical attention. Of more importance is that, with many of the causes of DAH, the symptoms and signs are recurrent. Depending on the etiology of DAH, fever and signs and symptoms referring to a systemic vasculitis, such as cutaneous vasculitis, sinusitis, inflammatory ocular disease, arthritis, and glomerulonephritis, often accompany the pulmonary symptoms.

The chest radiograph in DAH demonstrates diffuse or focal patchy alveolar infiltration, and the computed tomography scan reveals ground-glass abnormality, confirming the presence of air space–filling disease (Figs. 56.3 and 56.4). With recurrent and chronic disease, interstitial infiltrates may appear. Radiographic interstitial infiltrates highlighted by Kerley's B lines may become apparent during resolution of the diffuse alveolar bleeding that accompanies mitral stenosis or pulmonary veno-occlusive disease. In patients with DAH in whom extrapulmonary disease is not apparent, an echocardiogram is indicated to rule out mitral valvular disease.

An iron-deficiency anemia is the rule, the white blood cell and platelet counts are usually increased, and the

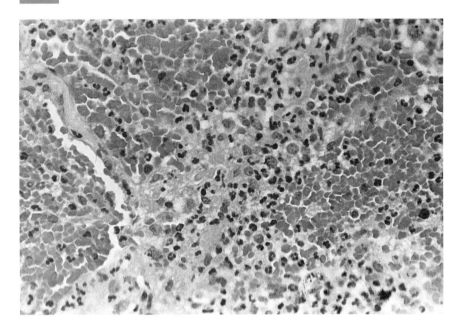

Figure 56.2 Micrograph showing diffuse alveolar hemorrhage secondary to pulmonary capillaritis. Necrotic edematous alveolar walls are infiltrated by neutrophils that often have pyknotic fragmented nuclei. The alveolar spaces are filled with red blood cells as well as neutrophils. (Original magnification ×40.)

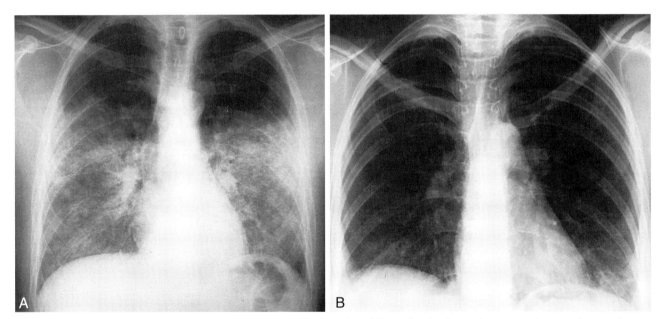

Figure 56.3 **A,** Chest radiograph showing diffuse alveolar infiltrates after diffuse alveolar hemorrhage secondary to microscopic polyangiitis. Cardiac size is normal. **B,** Chest radiograph showing patchy alveolar infiltrates due to diffuse alveolar hemorrhage in a patient with Wegener's granulomatosis.

erythrocyte sedimentation rate is elevated, particularly in cases of DAH associated with capillaritis. Bronchoalveolar lavage reveals a predominance of red blood cells and hemosiderin-containing macrophages. In DAH associated with systemic vasculitis, the connective tissue diseases, and Goodpasture's syndrome, an active urinary sediment and proteinuria, indicating glomerulonephritis, are present. Serum creatinine levels are often elevated as well. The renal histopathologic lesion is a focal segmental necrotizing glomerulonephritis with crescent formation (i.e., crescentic glomerulonephritis), a form of rapidly progressive glomerulonephritis (Fig. 56.5).

PHYSIOLOGY

Varying degrees of hypoxemia result from the ventilation-perfusion abnormalities produced by the alveolar hemorrhage, and patients often require ventilatory support. In less dramatic cases, hemoptysis is intermittent, producing patchy or focal alveolar infiltrates on the chest radiograph and little interference with gas exchange. Serial measurements of the diffusing capacity for carbon monoxide have been suggested as a sensitive indicator for active alveolar bleeding in patients with recurrent DAH.[6] An unexpected increase in the diffusing capacity is the rule in spite of the gas-exchange abnormalities and abnormal chest radiograph. This increase in diffusing capacity, attributed to the increased binding of carbon monoxide to intra-alveolar hemoglobin, occurs with acute bleeding, as hemosiderin does not bind carbon monoxide. In less obvious cases of DAH in which there is minimal or no hemoptysis, an unexpected increase in the diffusing capacity may lead to the correct initial diagnosis or to the detection of a recurrence in an established case. In several cases of recurrent DAH (especially those that follow Wegener's granulomatosis,

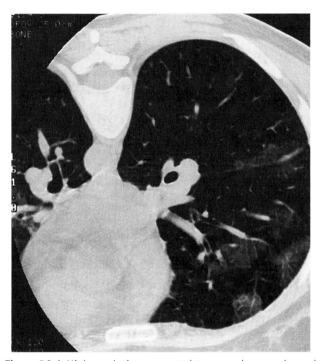

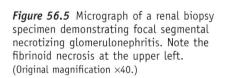

Figure 56.4 High-resolution computed tomography scan (prone) of patient in Figure 56.3B, confirming the focal nature of the alveolar hemorrhage.

microscopic polyangiitis, idiopathic pulmonary hemosiderosis [IPH], and mitral stenosis), progression to pulmonary fibrosis and restrictive ventilatory impairment have been documented.[7]

DIFFERENTIAL DIAGNOSIS

Table 56.2 summarizes the differential clinical and laboratory features of the common causes of DAH. The presence of proteinuria and an active urinary sediment (red blood cells and red blood cell casts), which for most cases of DAH heralds the underlying focal segmental necrotizing glomerulonephritis, excludes the diagnosis of IPH and isolated pulmonary capillaritis. If cutaneous lesions are present in the form of either splinter hemorrhages or palpable purpura (evidence of leukocytoclastic vasculitis), Goodpasture's syndrome can be ruled out as well. The diagnosis of Goodpasture's syndrome is confirmed by the presence of anti–glomerular basement membrane antibody (ABMA) in the serum and the linear deposition of immunoglobulin and complement in basement membranes of the kidney and lung.[8,9] Active DAH in systemic lupus erythematosus is accompanied by reduced serum complement levels as well as the presence of antinuclear and native anti–deoxyribonucleic acid antibodies in the serum. Henoch-Schönlein purpura is characterized by the formation of immunoglobulin (Ig) A immune complexes present in the circulation and also bound to tissue.[10]

Measurement of the serum antineutrophil cytoplasmic antibody (ANCA) is useful in the evaluation of vasculitis.[10a] Two types of ANCA are measured for clinical use. Cytoplasmic, or c-ANCA, is specific for the 29-kd component of the cytoplasmic granule of the neutrophil and the monocyte, producing a central granular immunofluorescent staining pattern. This granule has been identified as proteinase 3, which is an elastolytic neutral protease. Perinuclear, or p-ANCA, has specificity for the myeloperoxidase granule of the neutrophil, resulting in a perinuclear or a nuclear staining pattern.[11] The c-ANCA level is more likely to be

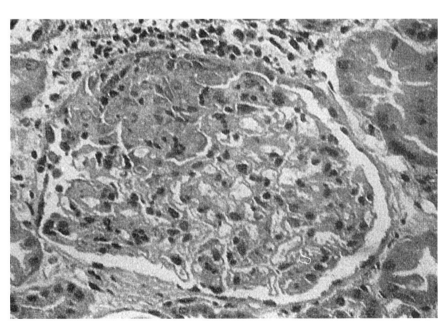

Figure 56.5 Micrograph of a renal biopsy specimen demonstrating focal segmental necrotizing glomerulonephritis. Note the fibrinoid necrosis at the upper left. (Original magnification ×40.)

Table 56.2 Clinical Differentiation of Common Diffuse Alveolar Hemorrhage Syndromes

Syndrome	Anemia	Renal Disease	Arthritis	Skin Vasculitis	ANA	RF	C_L	ABMA	ANCA	Anti-DNA Antibody	Tissue Antibody Staining
Wegener's granulomatosis	+	+	+	+	±	±	WNL	−	+ (c)	−	Granular or −
Microscopic polyangiitis	+	+	+	+	±	±	WNL	−	+ (p)	−	−
Systemic lupus erythematosus	+	+	+	±	+	+	Low	−	−	+	(Granular) immunoglobulin G
Goodpasture's syndrome	+	+	−	−	−	−	WNL	+	−	−	(Linear) immunoglobulin
Idiopathic hemosiderosis	+	−	−	−	−	−	WNL	−	−	−	−
Isolated pulmonary capillaritis	+	−	−	−	−	−	WNL	−	−	−	−
Henoch-Schönlein purpura	+	+	+	+	−	−	WNL	−	±	−	+ (granular) immunoglobulin A

ABMA, anti–basement membrane antibody; ANA, anti-nuclear antibody; ANCA, antineutrophil cytoplasmic antibody; Anti-DNA, anti–deoxyribonucleic acid antibody; C_L, complement; RF, rheumatoid factor; WNL, within normal limits.

elevated in the serum of patients with systemic vasculitis if the lungs and sinuses are involved, as in Wegener's granulomatosis, whereas p-ANCA is more likely to appear in the serum in microscopic polyangiitis, pauci-immune glomerulonephritis, and a form of isolated pulmonary capillaritis. However, there can be crossover.[12]

A positive test result for serum c-ANCA was first thought to be specific for Wegener's granulomatosis, but it also can appear in microscopic polyangiitis, although p-ANCA is more typical. p-ANCA levels are also elevated in pauci-immune glomerulonephritis, a vasculitis affecting primarily the kidneys and an occasional cause of DAH, and in two systemic vasculitides not usually associated with DAH, i.e., Churg-Strauss syndrome and polyarteritis nodosa.[13,14] Recently, it has been proposed that ANCAs are not only markers for the presence and activity of the aforementioned systemic vasculitides, but are pathogenetic.[15] They appear to induce neutrophils and mononuclear phagocytes to undergo both a respiratory burst and degranulation, which could injure the endothelium through the release of proteolytic enzymes and the generation of toxic oxygen products.

DIFFUSE ALVEOLAR HEMORRHAGE WITH CAPILLARITIS

ISOLATED PULMONARY CAPILLARITIS

Isolated pulmonary capillaritis is a small vessel vasculitis confined to the lungs and without concomitant systemic involvement.[16] There are two forms: one with serum p-ANCA positivity and the other without this positive serology.[16,17] In one series, the latter type was the most frequent cause of pulmonary capillaritis and DAH.[16] Direct immunofluorescent studies of the lung in these patients have been

negative. Although respiratory failure necessitating ventilatory support was frequent, response to corticosteroids and cyclophosphamide was good, and only one of eight patients did not survive. Recurrences appeared in two subjects. During a 4-year follow-up period, clinical or serologic evidence for a systemic vasculitis or connective tissue disease did not appear.

Isolated forms of pulmonary capillaritis causing DAH must be distinguished from IPH, which is not associated with pulmonary capillaritis, as well as lung-limited forms of Goodpasture's syndrome, the initial presentation of collagen vascular disease, antiphospholipid antibody syndrome, and mitral stenosis. All patients who present with unexplained DAH should have an echocardiogram and undergo thoracoscopic or open-lung biopsy.

WEGENER'S GRANULOMATOSIS

DAH secondary to pulmonary capillaritis can either complicate an established case of Wegener's granulomatosis or represent the initial manifestation of the disease. Pulmonary capillaritis can be the sole histologic finding, or it can occur in combination with the more typical pathologic features of Wegener's granulomatosis. Examination of open-lung biopsy specimens from 87 patients with Wegener's granulomatosis revealed a 31% incidence of capillaritis, but in only 3 patients was this an isolated finding.[5] In another series, capillaritis was present in 17% of 35 patients, but never as an isolated finding.[18] In a postmortem study of 22 patients, capillaritis was the sole histologic feature in 3 cases and occurred in conjunction with the more typical granulomatous vasculitis in 7 cases.[19] In cases in which the typical histologic features (granulomatous inflammation, small and medium vessel vasculitis, and parenchymal necrosis) and clinical presentation (sinusitis, cavitary lung lesions) are absent and only DAH with or without a cutaneous leuko-cytoclastic vasculitis or a focal segmental necrotizing glomerulitis is present, the differentiation from microscopic polyangiitis is difficult. The specific diagnosis then depends on the ANCA pattern, with c-ANCA suggesting the diagnosis of Wegener's granulomatosis. In this disease, the characteristic histologic and clinical features may appear months to years after an initial presentation of DAH and capillaritis.[8] Circulating endothelial cells have been found in patients with Wegener's granulomatosis and microscopic polyangiitis and may serve as a novel marker of active ANCA-positive vasculitis.[20]

Alveolar hemorrhage is often subclinical and recurrent in Wegener's granulomatosis (as well as microscopic polyangiitis), suggested by the presence of hemosiderin-laden macrophages on bronchoalveolar lavage. This pattern of frequently recurring DAH appears unique to the ANCA-associated vasculitides, as patients with collagen vascular disease–related DAH rarely manifest iron-positive macrophages.[21]

More than 40 cases of Wegener's granulomatosis with DAH and pulmonary capillaritis have been described. The rate of early mortality is 37%, and this mortality is most often due to acute respiratory or renal failure.[5,8,18,19,22,23] Renal disease in the form of a focal segmental necrotizing glomerulonephritis, a cutaneous leukocytoclastic vasculitis, and arthritis often accompany the DAH. Treatment with high-dose corticosteroids and cyclophosphamide is the recommended therapy and, depending on the severity of the disease, can be initially administered intravenously. Azathioprine may be substituted for cyclophosphamide after remission.[24] Recurrences with tapering of the medications are to be expected. Disease activity is monitored by measurements of erythrocyte sedimentation rates, ANCA levels, serial diffusing capacities, and microscopic urine examinations. Recurrent or persistent disease after standard therapy may respond to intravenous immunoglobulin, although the response appears transient and side-effects, including renal insufficiency, are frequent.[25] Other novel therapies, including trimethoprim-sulfamethoxazole, antilymphocyte monoclonal antibodies and tumor necrosis factor inhibitors, have been tried with some success.[26]

As previously stated, the differentiation of Wegener's granulomatosis with DAH from microscopic polyangiitis is at times difficult, because the clinical presentation, histopathologic findings, and serologic findings can be identical.[7,27] In fact, the response to treatment and the tendency for recurrences are similar. The differentiation can be established only after the development of the more typical upper airway disease and pathologic features of Wegener's granulomatosis.

MICROSCOPIC POLYANGIITIS

Microscopic polyangiitis is considered to be the small vessel variant of polyarteritis nodosa. It is a frequent cause of pulmonary capillaritis and DAH.[2,3,8,28–32] Microscopic polyangiitis is distinguishable from polyarteritis nodosa by the absence of medium-sized blood vessel involvement, the absence of asthma and systemic hypertension, and the relative sparing of the abdominal viscera. DAH has only rarely been documented as occurring with polyarteritis nodosa.[33]

The most consistent pathologic feature in microscopic polyangiitis is a focal segmental necrotizing glomerulonephritis, the renal lesion common to all systemic vasculitides. The lungs are involved by capillaritis in 20% to 30% of cases.[30,32] The alveolar hemorrhage tends to be severe and is often life-threatening. Other manifestations include fever, weight loss, cutaneous vasculitis, myalgias, arthralgias, diarrhea and gastrointestinal bleeding from mucosal vasculitis that is often visible by direct examination, peripheral neuropathy, and in a few cases sinusitis.[13,32,34] As with other vasculitides, the erythrocyte sedimentation rate is elevated, and nonspecific increases of serum rheumatoid factor and antinuclear antibody are found. Although circulating immune complexes are present in 45% of cases, tissue localization of these complexes is difficult to detect. Anti–deoxyribonucleic acid antibodies and hypocomplementemia, findings suggestive of systemic lupus erythematosus, are absent. A positive serum p-ANCA strongly supports the diagnosis. Antibodies to hepatitis B and C antigens are present in 33% of cases.[35]

Treatment consists of either oral or intravenous corticosteroids combined with cyclophosphamide or azathioprine.[24] Adjuvant treatment with plasmapheresis is recommended by some authors, but its additional efficacy is difficult to determine.[30,32] Outcome with early initiation of therapy for microscopic polyangiitis is generally good, with a 65% rate of 5-year survival. However, the presence of DAH contributes to an early mortality rate of 25%.[2,3,8,28–32] There is a tendency for recurrence with tapering of the medications. Intravenous immunoglobulin may be of use for resistant cases.[25] Factor VIIa has been used successfully in one case of massive alveolar hemorrhage with dramatic effects.[36]

The transition to pulmonary fibrosis and restrictive ventilatory impairment after recurrent DAH has been described,[7] and fibrotic lung disease has been reported as the presenting manifestation of microscopic polyangiitis.[37] There have been three cases of persistent, severe, irreversible airway dysfunction after recurrent episodes of DAH that complicated microscopic polyangiitis.[38] It is postulated that the combination of recurrent vascular obliteration from capillaritis and the release of neutral proteases and oxygen radicals from the overwhelming and recurrent burden of neutrophils causes permanent damage to the alveolar septa and results in emphysema.

CONNECTIVE TISSUE DISEASE

Rarely, DAH and glomerulonephritis occur in patients with rheumatoid arthritis,[39] scleroderma,[40] or mixed connective tissue disease. Isolated DAH and pulmonary capillaritis have also been described in polymyositis, rheumatoid arthritis, and mixed connective tissue disease.[41,42] In polymyositis, DAH was the presenting manifestation,[41] and in rheumatoid arthritis and mixed connective tissue disease, DAH and capillaritis followed the primary diagnosis (2 to 20 years).[42] The absence of a systemic vasculitis in these cases, including glomerulonephritis, was unexpected.

Among the connective tissue diseases, DAH both with and without capillaritis occurs most frequently in systemic lupus erythematosus.[8,43–45] This complication is associated with a 50% rate of mortality and is recurrent in survivors.[8,46–51] Death is caused by DAH, concurrent infection,

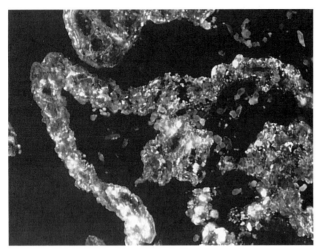

Figure 56.6 Immunofluorescence study demonstrating granular deposition of immunoglobulin G in the alveolar walls of a patient with systemic lupus erythematosus and diffuse alveolar hemorrhage secondary to pulmonary capillaritis. (Original magnification ×40.)

or another systemic complication of systemic lupus erythematosus such as renal or central nervous system disease. Histopathologic examination reveals capillaritis in most cases, but bland pulmonary hemorrhage and diffuse alveolar damage have been described.[48,52] Granular deposits of IgG and complement (C3) are found in the alveolar interstitium and within the walls of intra-alveolar blood vessels (Fig. 56.6).[43,48,50] However, immune complexes are not universally present in all cases.[49] Myers and Katzenstein[51] described four patients with systemic lupus erythematosus and massive DAH associated with pulmonary capillaritis; in two of these patients, immune complexes were demonstrated by both light and electron microscopic techniques.

It is unusual for DAH to be the initial manifestation of systemic lupus erythematosus,[47] in contrast to acute lupus pneumonitis, which is often the initial manifestation.[52] In systemic lupus erythematosus, DAH appears later in the clinical course.[8] Most patients have active lupus nephritis.[45] The onset of alveolar hemorrhage can be quite dramatic, producing severe gas-exchange abnormalities and necessitating mechanical ventilation. Reduced complement levels and increased serum titers of serum antinuclear antibodies confirm the diagnosis.

DAH must be distinguished from other causes of hemoptysis in systemic lupus erythematosus. Acute lupus pneumonitis presents with fever, cough, and dyspnea; in 50% of cases, this is the initial manifestation of systemic lupus erythematosus.[52] In addition to the diffuse alveolar infiltrates on chest radiograph that appear in both conditions, pleural and pericardial effusions are present in acute lupus pneumonitis. Although hemoptysis may accompany acute lupus pneumonitis, significant reductions of the hemoglobin are not to be expected. Histologically, acute lupus pneumonitis is an inflammatory lesion consisting of organizing pneumonia, diffuse alveolar damage, a cellular nonspecific interstitial pneumonia, and sometimes intra-alveolar hemorrhage. Other diagnostic considerations include infectious pneumonias and pulmonary infarction associated with deep venous thrombosis with or without a circulating lupus anticoagulant.[53,54]

Treatment of DAH caused by systemic lupus erythematosus includes high-dose intravenous corticosteroids as well as azathioprine or cyclophosphamide. Plasmapheresis has been combined with chemotherapy in some cases, but it probably has little or no utility.[45] Broad-spectrum antibiotic coverage is recommended because of some evidence that infection may trigger the hemorrhage.[45]

MIXED CRYOGLOBULINEMIA

Mixed cryoglobulinemia is a systemic vasculitis that is recognized by the presence of purpura, arthritis, hepatitis, and glomerulonephritis. It is thought to be an immune complex–induced disease, with most cases linked to hepatitis C (and less commonly hepatitis B) viral infection. Cutaneous vasculitis appearing as raised purpura is the clinical hallmark of this disease. Histologically, there is a perivascular polymorphonuclear infiltration with tissue extravasation and fragmentation in the dermis (leukocytoclastic vasculitis). The renal disease is a proliferative glomerulonephritis with positive granular immunofluorescence. Interstitial lung disease consisting of inflammation and fibrosis of the alveolar walls is the most common pulmonary manifestation.[55] There are only two published cases of DAH with pulmonary capillaritis that complicated mixed cryoglobulinemia.[56,57]

BEHÇET'S SYNDROME

Behçet's syndrome is a chronic relapsing illness characterized by oral and genital ulceration, iridocyclitis, thrombophlebitis, and a multisystem disease consisting of a cutaneous vasculitis, arthritis, and meningoencephalitis.[58] Immune complexes have been identified in the serum of active cases as well as in the lung and other organs.[58,59]

The lung is involved in 5% to 10% of cases of Behçet's syndrome. The pulmonary disease is typically a small vessel vasculitis affecting capillaries, venules, and arterioles. The renal disease is a focal segmental necrotizing vasculitis, as occurs in other systemic vasculitides. Immune complexes composed of IgG and complement have been identified in small pulmonary vessels in several cases.[59] In addition to alveolar hemorrhage, involvement of larger vessels can lead to aneurysms of the bronchial arteries, which can erode into bronchi, causing massive pulmonary hemorrhage and death.[60,61] Another potential cause for pulmonary hemorrhage in Behçet's syndrome is pulmonary arterial occlusion with infarction.[59] A review of 28 cases of pulmonary involvement in Behçet's syndrome emphasized several points: pulmonary complaints consisting of cough, hemoptysis, chest pain, and fever were more common in men than in women; pulmonary hemorrhage was the cause of death in 39%; and death usually occurred within 6 years of the first episode of hemoptysis. Other studies have confirmed the seriousness of this complication regardless of its cause.[60,61] Treatment consists of corticosteroids and immunosuppressive therapy.[62] Treatment with anti–tumor necrosis factor therapy has shown dramatic results in recent case reports.[63]

HENOCH-SCHÖNLEIN PURPURA

Henoch-Schönlein purpura, primarily a disease of children, also occurs in adults.[64] Adults typically present with palpable purpura (leukocytoclastic vasculitis) and glomerulonephritis.[10] The joints and gastrointestinal tract are commonly involved. Pulmonary involvement appears rare. In several large series, pulmonary disease, except for transient chest radiographic infiltrates, was not mentioned.[10] There have been proven cases of DAH with pulmonary capillaritis in patients with Henoch-Schönlein purpura.[65,65a] In one, IgA immune complexes were present in the alveolar septa.[65] It is postulated that IgA immune complexes, which are present in the serum and kidneys of these patients, are responsible for the tissue damage that results in the clinical syndrome.[66] Corticosteroids were used in both cases and are generally recommended.

GLOMERULONEPHRITIS AND ALVEOLAR HEMORRHAGE

Focal segmental necrotizing glomerulonephritis is common to all the systemic vasculitides. There are three types of isolated renal vasculitis associated with this lesion and DAH but not necessarily with other manifestations of systemic disease: (1) an immune complex–mediated glomerulonephritis, which is characterized by the granular deposition of immunoglobulin and complement in the glomerulus; (2) a pauci-immune glomerulonephritis, which does not manifest immune complexes but does demonstrate p-ANCA serology; and (3) ABMA disease (Goodpasture's syndrome), which is characterized by the presence of circulating and tissue-bound ABMA directed against the NC1 domain of the α_3 chain of type IV collagen in the lung and kidney.[12,67]

Immune complex–related crescentic glomerulonephritis is rarely accompanied by capillaritis and DAH.[4,68] Although the kidneys demonstrate granular immune deposits, immune complexes are not found in lung tissue. Pauci-immune crescentic glomerulonephritis lacks any immunoreaction product except for minimal accumulation of fibrin. In this sense, it is histologically and immunologically similar to the glomerulonephritis of microscopic polyangiitis and Wegener's granulomatosis[8] and is considered to represent a form of renal-limited vasculitis. Up to 50% of affected patients develop pulmonary capillaritis and DAH, and a smaller number develop a full-blown systemic vasculitis indistinguishable from microscopic polyangiitis. Another indication that pauci-immune crescentic glomerulonephritis represents a limited form of vasculitis is the presence of serum p-ANCA in these patients. Because clinical manifestations are often limited to the lung and kidney, it can be confused with Goodpasture's syndrome.[8,66] The two are differentiated by the absence of ABMA in the serum and by the negative findings of renal immunofluorescence studies in pauci-immune crescentic glomerulonephritis. Goodpasture's syndrome is only occasionally associated with capillaritis, more commonly presenting with bland DAH.[69] Treatment with high-dose corticosteroids plus immunosuppressive therapy with either cyclophosphamide or azathioprine is recommended.

DRUG-INDUCED ALVEOLAR HEMORRHAGE

There are many drugs that can cause alveolar hemorrhage, such as warfarin, the platelet glycoprotein IIb/IIIa inhibitors, and penicillamine.[70,70a,70b] Most are associated with bland alveolar hemorrhage due to anticoagulation, thrombocytopenia, or diffuse alveolar damage (discussed later). However, propylthiouracil, phenytoin, and mitomycin have been associated with DAH with capillaritis.[70c] DAH due to these drugs may also be associated with crescentic glomerulonephritis.

ACUTE PULMONARY ALLOGRAFT REJECTION

Pulmonary capillaritis and DAH have been reported after lung transplantation for a variety of underlying diseases.[71] The suspected acute vascular rejection can occur weeks to months after the transplantation and may be the only histopathologic manifestation of allograft rejection. This represents a serious immunologic complication that threatens survival. In addition to standard anti-inflammatory therapy with corticosteroids and cytotoxic agents, plasmapheresis may be effective.

DIFFUSE ALVEOLAR HEMORRHAGE WITHOUT CAPILLARITIS

IDIOPATHIC PULMONARY HEMOSIDEROSIS

IPH is a diagnosis of exclusion.[72,73] Efforts to rule out other causes of DAH such as mitral valve disease, systemic vasculitis, or the connective tissue diseases are essential. Clinically, this entity is characterized by recurrent DAH without renal or other systemic disease, and the histologic examination of the lung reveals bland alveolar hemorrhage with hemosiderin accumulation (Fig. 56.7).

IPH is predominantly a disease of children; however, adults, usually over 30 years of age, represent 20% of cases.[73] Disease onset occurs from 4 months to 62 years of age. Among adults, men are more often affected, and there are reports of familial cases.[74] Recurrent hemoptysis is the rule, ranging from intermittent blood-streaked sputum to life-threatening hemorrhage. Fever, cough, substernal chest pain, and fatigue secondary to iron-deficiency anemia are also reported. These symptoms do not distinguish IPH from other causes of DAH. As with other DAH etiologies, IPH can present with dyspnea and an abnormal chest radiograph but without an iron-deficiency anemia or hemoptysis. Crackles are heard, and in 20% of pediatric cases, lymphadenopathy and hepatosplenomegaly are found.[75] In chronic recurrent disease, finger clubbing, progressive dyspnea, and progressive pulmonary fibrosis appear.[73]

Pulmonary function testing reveals a restrictive ventilatory defect with an increase in the diffusing capacity for carbon monoxide during periods of active bleeding. With time and superimposition of lung parenchymal fibrosis, the diffusing capacity falls.[75] The chest radiograph reveals bilateral air space filling that is either diffuse or patchy. The alveolar infiltrates tend to resolve slowly over days to weeks, leaving a residual reticulonodular infiltrate that may persist, depending on the chronicity of the disease and the development of interstitial fibrosis. An echocardiogram is needed to rule out mitral valve disease, and a microscopic urinalysis excludes the presence of glomerulonephritis. Measurements of serum antibody, as outlined in Table 56.2, reveal the absence of associated systemic disease. However, in

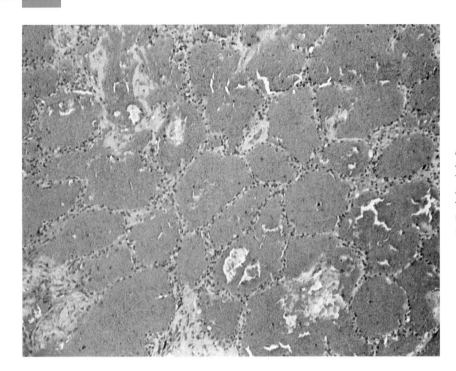

Figure 56.7 Micrograph showing bland alveolar hemorrhage in a patient with idiopathic pulmonary hemosiderosis. The alveolar walls are of normal thickness, and the apparent increase in cellularity represents type II alveolar cell hyperplasia. (Original magnification ×10.)

adult cases, lung tissue is needed to exclude the entity of isolated pulmonary capillaritis.[16] It is likely that, until the 1990s, cases of isolated pulmonary capillaritis were incorrectly diagnosed as IPH.

The pathogenesis of IPH is not understood. Some cases may be secondary to environmental exposures, such as *Stachybotrys atra*, a toxigenic fungus that has been linked to several cases of otherwise idiopathic alveolar hemorrhage.[76] Histologic examination of lung tissue reveals hyperplasia of type II alveolar epithelial cells with capillary dilation and tortuosity.[77] Erythrocytes and hemosiderin-containing macrophages fill alveolar spaces. Hemosiderin collects in the lung interstitium and is thought to be the basis for the collagen proliferation and parenchymal fibrosis that occurs in this disease.[77] The iron content of the lung is increased.[73] Pulmonary immune complexes are absent in the lung, which differentiates IPH from a rare presentation of isolated pulmonary Goodpasture's syndrome.[77]

Electron microscopic studies indicate degeneration of type I alveolar epithelial cells with exposure of their basement membranes, breaks in the continuity of the alveolar capillary basement membrane, thickening or reduplication of the membrane, separation of the basement membrane with fibrillar material found in the splits, and focal ruptures of the membrane with collagen deposition.[77–79] Although nonspecific, these findings indicate a form of diffuse alveolar injury.

Although the pathogenesis of IPH remains unclear, evidence suggests an immune disorder. Some cases have occurred in the setting of celiac disease,[80] serum IgA levels are increased in 50% of cases,[81] and there is some responsiveness to immunosuppressive therapy.[73,82] Clinical benefit and recovery from the acute hemorrhage after corticosteroid therapy have been reported, but long-term benefit is unlikely.[73,83] Azathioprine has been successful in several cases.[77,82,84] In 75% of cases, the mean length of survival is 3 to 5 years.[73,83] Adults have a better prognosis than

children. Approximately 25% of patients are free of disease after the initial episode. Another 25% are free of active disease but have persistent dyspnea and anemia, and another quarter have persistent active disease that leads to fibrosis and severe restrictive lung disease. The remainder have unresponsive disease with repeated massive hemorrhage and an early death from respiratory failure. Lung transplantation is controversial in this disease as alveolar hemorrhage has been reported to recur after bilateral lung transplantation.[85]

GOODPASTURE'S SYNDROME

Whether the case reported by Goodpasture in 1919 describes the syndrome that bears his name is questionable.[86] He described an 18-year-old man who died 6 weeks after an influenza infection and was found to have DAH, pleuritis, glomerulonephritis, splenic infarctions, and vasculitis of the small intestines. In 1965, an antibody to glomerular basement membrane (ABMA)—now identified as antibody against the NC1 domain of the α_3 chain of type IV collagen—was identified in the kidneys and lungs of some patients with DAH and glomerulonephritis.[67,87] The diagnosis of Goodpasture's syndrome, also known as ABMA disease, is reserved for cases of DAH and glomerulonephritis in which this antibody appears in the serum or is found bound to kidney and lung basement membranes in a linear manner by immunohistochemistry, or both.[8] At least 90% of patients with Goodpasture's syndrome have a circulating ABMA.[88] The higher the level, the more severe the renal disease; in general, however, the level of ABMA is not considered an accurate index of disease activity.

In 60% to 80% of cases, the lung and renal disease appear simultaneously; in 5% to 10% only the lung is affected; and in the remainder, renal disease exists by itself.[8,89,90] Men are more commonly affected (60% to 80% of patients), and the concentration of cases is greatest between the ages of 20 and 30 years.[91,92] In older cases the sex distribution is equal,[93] and the disease tends to be limited to the kidney. Interestingly, DAH is more likely to occur in patients who smoke.[93] The alveolar permeability is increased in most smokers,[94] and this is thought to be an important factor leading to the DAH in Goodpasture's syndrome. In one study, 100% of smokers with Goodpasture's syndrome developed both DAH and glomerulonephritis, and of the nonsmokers, only 20% developed DAH.[93] Also, resumption of cigarette smoking by patients with Goodpasture's syndrome who are in remission can result in recurrent episodes of DAH. Exposure to volatile hydrocarbons (e.g., petroleum products, turpentine, toluene, and pesticides) is associated with initiation, as well as exacerbations, of DAH.[69,89,90,95]

Pulmonary capillaritis is present in some cases of Goodpasture's syndrome, but the usual histologic appearance is bland pulmonary hemorrhage.[69] Alveolar wall necrosis, which is seen with systemic vasculitis, does not occur in Goodpasture's syndrome. The renal histologic findings are a focal segmental necrotizing glomerulonephritis with crescent formation. The major distinction between Goodpasture's syndrome and the other rapidly progressive glomerulonephritides is the presence of an uninterrupted linear deposition of immunoglobulin and complement along the glomerular basement membrane. Identical findings are present on alveolar basement membranes (Fig. 56.8).[96] In 5% to 10% of patients, DAH without renal disease dominates the clinical picture. However, renal biopsy still reveals the typical linear staining.[97]

It is clear that ABMA is pathogenetic; however, the stimulus for its production remains unknown. The clinical onset of Goodpasture's syndrome has been temporarily related to infection with influenza A2[98] as well as to other respiratory infections, hydrocarbon exposure, and tobacco use.[93,94] Several animal models of Goodpasture's syndrome exist.[99,100] It is interesting to note that, in some experimental models, the introduction of ABMA produces renal but not pulmonary disease. For deposition of this antibody to occur in the lung in those models, an additional injury that increases alveolar-capillary permeability is required.

The presence of histocompatibility human leukocyte antigens HLA-DRw2 and HLA-B7 (90% and 60%, respectively)

in patients with Goodpasture's syndrome indicates that susceptible individuals are predisposed to the disease.[101,102] Evidence suggests that patients with Goodpasture's syndrome and HLA-B7 and HLA-DRw2 have unusually severe renal disease and a poor prognosis.

Symptoms most often refer to the respiratory system and consist of hemoptysis, cough, and dyspnea. Fatigue caused by iron-deficiency anemia and renal failure may predominate. Microscopic hematuria and proteinuria and increases in the serum creatinine are often present, but gross hematuria and hypertension are unusual. The diffusing capacity is increased during periods of active bleeding and is considered to be a useful monitor of DAH.[103] An increase of 30% above baseline is highly suggestive of an intra-alveolar hemorrhage, and this increase may precede pulmonary symptoms or chest radiographic changes. Chest radiography may reveal patchy air space abnormalities. There are patients with Goodpasture's syndrome whose chest radiographs are abnormal but whose urinalyses and renal function test results are normal; these patients show typical linear immunofluorescence in tissue from renal biopsy.[104]

In the few patients without renal involvement, DAH responds to corticosteroids either by the oral route or by intravenous pulse dosing. However, glomerulonephritis appears resistant to the anti-inflammatory effects of corticosteroid monotherapy. Cytotoxic agents have some effect on the rapidly progressive glomerulonephritis but, again, are efficacious mainly for the control of DAH. Bilateral nephrectomy, despite initial encouraging results for the control of DAH, no longer has a role in the management of Goodpasture's syndrome. The combination of plasmapheresis, corticosteroids, and cytotoxic drugs is effective, particularly in patients who do not have oligoanuria and do not require dialysis.[105–109] Plasmapheresis (3 to 6 L daily) is generally continued for 2 weeks. Combinations of cyclophosphamide or azathioprine with corticosteroids lead to a dramatic fall in circulating ABMA, but this does not necessarily correlate with the rate of improvement in the renal and pulmonary disease.[110] With this combination therapy, even oliguric dialysis-dependent subjects responded to the point at which dialysis could be discontinued.[109] However, anuric patients do not respond to combination therapy, and dialysis and renal transplantation are then necessary.[110] Case reports of treatment of refractory, life-threatening Goodpasture's syndrome with mycophenolate mofetil and anti-CD20 monoclonal antibody have been reported with good success.[111,112]

Over time, the survival rate has improved from its historical 80% mortality at 6 months (half dying from DAH and the rest from renal insufficiency). In one study of 29 patients, the 2-year survival rate for all treated patients was approximately 50%, with the majority of the deaths occurring during the first year.[92] DAH is the usual cause of death, often being precipitated by a concomitant infection.[89] Spontaneous remissions occur in cases without clinical evidence of renal disease.[104] Oligoanuric renal failure reduces the survival rate to 50% at 6 months. Renal biopsy not only is diagnostic but also has prognostic value. In subjects in whom less than 30% of the glomeruli have undergone crescent formation with preserved renal function, there is a significant therapeutic response and improved survival. When 70% or more of glomeruli have formed crescents in conjunction

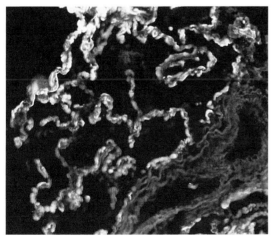

Figure 56.8 Immunofluorescence study demonstrating linear staining (immunoglobulin G) of alveolar walls in a patient with Goodpasture's syndrome. (Original magnification ×10.)

with renal insufficiency, renal failure is progressive and often unresponsive to therapy, eventually necessitating dialysis.[110]

DIFFUSE ALVEOLAR DAMAGE

Diffuse alveolar damage is the underlying histopathology of the acute respiratory distress syndrome, but it also can have a variety of other etiologies (Table 56.3).[113,114] In severe cases, red blood cells enter the alveolar space after the injury to the alveolar-capillary interface, and this can result in hemoptysis. In addition to the alveolar hemorrhage, the interstitium of the lung becomes edematous and the type I alveolar epithelial lining cells are sloughed. Even early in this process, chronic inflammation and fibroblastic proliferation of the alveolar wall are present. Hyaline membranes, which are eosinophilic-appearing debris consisting of necrotic cells, protein, and fibrin, are found adjacent to the alveolar walls. The neutrophilic influx in diffuse alveolar damage–associated DAH is not as intense as it is in pulmonary capillaritis. The chronic, or fibroproliferative, phase of diffuse alveolar damage is characterized by fibrotic nonspecific interstitial pneumonia and occasional organizing pneumonia.[115,116] Several drugs (see Chapter 67) may cause diffuse alveolar damage that, if severe, may be accompanied by DAH.

PENICILLAMINE

Ingestion of penicillamine can result in DAH and an immune complex–mediated glomerulonephritis. Glomeru-

Table 56.3 Causes of Diffuse Alveolar Damage

Drug induced
    Cytotoxic agents (bleomycin, BCNU, busulfan,
        cyclophosphamide)
    Antibiotics (nitrofurantoin)
    Analgesics (acetylsalicylic acid)
    Narcotics (heroin, methadone, crack cocaine)
    Sedatives (ethchlorvynol)
    Diuretics (hydrochlorothiazide)
    Insecticides (paraquat)

Acute respiratory distress syndrome
    Shock
    Trauma
    Oxygen toxicity
    Aspiration
    Smoke inhalation
    Ozone inhalation
    Nitrogen dioxide inhalation

Pneumonia
    Mycoplasma pneumoniae
    Legionella
    Viral
    Pneumocystis carinii

Radiation pneumonitis

Heavy metal fumes

Connective tissue diseases

Acute interstitial pneumonia (Hamman-Rich syndrome)

lar capillaries display a granular as opposed to a linear immunofluorescent pattern for IgG and the third component of complement.[117] There have been eight reports of this complication in patients receiving treatment for rheumatoid arthritis, Wilson's disease, or primary biliary cirrhosis.[117–120] In general, at least 1 g daily for a minimum of 10 months is necessary, and cases have appeared after as much as 20 years of daily treatment. All patients presented with DAH, and in one case there was no evidence of concomitant renal disease; the others had a crescentic glomerulonephritis as well.[120] Systemic involvement other than the lungs or kidneys has not been seen, which has prompted some authors to call this a drug-induced Goodpasture's syndrome.[117,118] However, the pattern of deposition of immunoglobulin in the kidney clearly differentiates this entity from Goodpasture's syndrome. Three patients recovered after a combination of immunosuppressive therapy and plasmapheresis.[118,120]

TRIMELLITIC ANHYDRIDE

Trimellitic anhydride is used for the manufacture of paints, epoxy resins, and plastics. A DAH syndrome without renal or other systemic disease reportedly occurs after the inhalation of fumes or the dry powder.[121–123] Antibodies to this compound have been identified in the serum of affected workers. A latent period of 1 to 3 months precedes the development of DAH, and this latent period supports an immunologic basis for this syndrome. With removal from exposure, which most commonly involves the spraying of this product on heated surfaces, the hemorrhage and iron-deficiency anemia resolve. Long-term physiologic impairment is not to be expected if further exposure is avoided.

MITRAL STENOSIS

Mitral stenosis must be ruled out in any individual who presents with DAH without renal disease or other systemic manifestations. Mitral stenosis can be clinically silent well into adulthood, and as a result of the pulmonary venous hypertension that develops, intermittent hemoptysis of small to moderate amounts can occur.[124] Radiographic findings consist of ground-glass abnormalities, often sparing the peripheral parenchyma, and reticular abnormalities.[125] Because DAH associated with mitral stenosis is often misdiagnosed and always recurs, a hemosiderosis-like histopathologic picture with organization of the hemorrhage and the appearance of interstitial fibrosis may appear. Massive hemoptysis may result from the rupture of engorged anastomotic bronchial varicosities that develop as a result of long-standing left atrial hypertension. Repair or replacement of the stenotic valve prevents recurrences.

COAGULATION DISORDERS

DAH can complicate hemostatic defects, but the physician must always suspect a predisposing underlying parenchymal problem, such as bronchiectasis, malignancy, systemic lupus erythematosus, mitral stenosis, or a condition that injures the alveolar capillary membrane, such as shock or sepsis. Coagulation disorders associated with DAH include disseminated intravascular coagulation,[126] idiopathic thrombocytopenic purpura,[127] thrombotic thrombocytopenic purpura,[128] acquired vitamin K deficiency,[129] and antiphospholipid antibody syndrome.[130] Occasionally, the DAH in the antiphospholipid antibody syndrome is associated with capillaritis.[131] All anticoagulant medications have been associated with DAH, including coumadin and its derivatives,[132–134] thrombolytics,[135–137] and most recently agents targeting the platelet glycoprotein IIb/IIIa.[138,139] In most iatrogenically anticoagulated patients, correction of the coagulation defect resolves the DAH.

DAH is common in patients with acute leukemia who have undergone induction chemotherapy and are thrombocytopenic.[140–143] Although thrombocytopenia is often profound and contributes to the DAH, these patients also have evidence at autopsy of diffuse alveolar damage due to chemotherapy, oxygen toxicity, or infection.

PULMONARY VENO-OCCLUSIVE DISEASE

Pulmonary veno-occlusive disease, a cause of primary pulmonary hypertension that affects all age groups, is most common in children and young adults.[144–146] The sex distribution is equal. As with other forms of pulmonary hypertension, patients with pulmonary veno-occlusive disease present with dyspnea, syncope, and physical findings suggestive of cor pulmonale.[144] Because pulmonary veno-occlusive disease is a postcapillary form of pulmonary hypertension resulting from fibrous obliteration of small veins and venules, hemoptysis, paroxysmal nocturnal dyspnea, and orthopnea occur (Fig. 56.9). Recanalization of the venous lumens suggests the possibility of previous thrombosis. The chest radiograph shows signs of pulmonary hypertension; in some cases, interstitial infiltrates with Kerley's B lines, representing alveolar septal lymphatic edema, are seen (Fig. 56.10). With significant pulmonary venous bleeding, alveolar infiltrates are superimposed. Pulmonary function studies reveal a reduced diffusing capacity for carbon monoxide with preservation of lung volumes, a physiologic picture similar to that found in other causes of primary pulmonary hypertension.

If a pulmonary artery catheter is properly placed, it reveals an elevated pulmonary capillary wedge pressure in addition to pulmonary hypertension. This helps differentiate pulmonary veno-occlusive disease–induced pulmonary hypertension from other causes of primary pulmonary hypertension.[146] Hemoptysis occurring with suspected primary pulmonary hypertension should point the clinician to a postcapillary lesion. Definitive diagnosis is achieved by lung biopsy, which demonstrates fibrous intimal obliteration of venules with acute or recanalized thrombi[145] and hemosiderosis.

Although pulmonary veno-occlusive disease occurs as a complication of chemotherapy for malignant disease[147] and of bone marrow transplantation,[148] most cases are idiopathic. The responsible chemotherapeutic agents are bleomycin and carmustine. Some idiopathic cases have autoimmune features such as Raynaud's phenomenon, arthritis, and serum autoantibodies, and cases have been described in patients with systemic lupus erythematosus. Corrin and associates[149] reported electron-dense deposits in one case. Recently, a mutation in the bone morphogenic protein receptor II gene (a gene already associated with many cases of primary pulmonary hypertension) has been identified in a patient with pulmonary veno-occlusive disease, suggesting an etiologic role.[150] Several patients have had clinical responses to azathioprine,[151] and in one patient who developed pulmonary veno-occlusive disease after bone marrow transplantation, there was resolution with corticosteroid treatment.[152] Anticoagulation is temporarily effective in some cases, as is chronic vasodilator therapy.[146,153] Vasodilator therapy has prolonged survival well beyond the expected 48 months.

PULMONARY CAPILLARY HEMANGIOMATOSIS

Pulmonary capillary hemangiomatosis is a rare cause of pulmonary hypertension associated with DAH. The DAH is

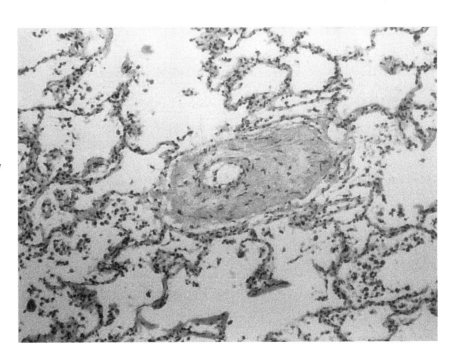

Figure 56.9 Micrograph showing a pulmonary vein in a patient with pulmonary veno-occlusive disease. Note the proliferation of collagen and the resulting luminal obliteration and partial recanalization. (Original magnification ×10.)

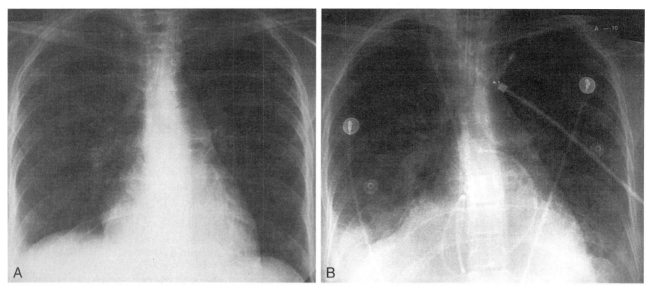

Figure 56.10 **A,** Chest radiograph of a patient with pulmonary veno-occlusive disease, demonstrating cardiomegaly, enlarged pulmonary arteries, and a prominent right ventricular airflow tract. **B,** Later chest film of the same patient, demonstrating radiographic signs of congestive heart failure. Note the alveolar infiltrates, right-sided pleural effusion, and Kerley's B lines.

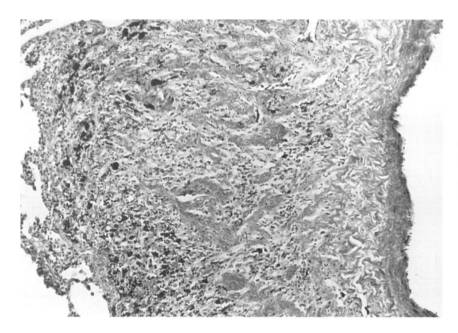

Figure 56.11 Micrograph showing pulmonary capillary hemangiomatosis. There is capillary proliferation in the wall of this large pulmonary vein. (Original magnification ×100.)

severe and recurrent.[154,155] A number of cases occurring in children and young adults have been reported. In one family, three siblings with the disorder were found. This unique histology is characterized by a proliferation of capillaries, which infiltrate the interstitium and proliferate within walls of pulmonary veins, impinging on their lumina and producing a form of pulmonary veno-occlusive disease (Fig. 56.11).[155] Patients present with symptoms of pulmonary hypertension (dyspnea, fatigue, and syncope) as well as hemoptysis.[156] The chest radiograph indicates pulmonary hypertension as well as prominent reticulonodular infiltrates. With active bleeding after rupture of this rich vascular network, alveolar infiltrates appear.

This entity must be distinguished from other causes of primary pulmonary hypertension, particularly pulmonary veno-occlusive disease, which it can mimic. Mean survival after diagnosis is usually 3 years.[156] Two reports of treatment with recombinant interferon alfa-2a suggest stabilization or improvement may occur.[156,157] Successful treatment with lung transplantation has also been reported.[156]

LYMPHANGIOLEIOMYOMATOSIS

Lymphangioleiomyomatosis (LAM) is an unusual lung disease (see Chapter 58) of premenopausal women. There is proliferation of smooth muscle in the walls of the pulmonary lymphatic vessels, which can lead to lymphatic obstruction and the formation of chylous pleural effusions. Smooth muscle also proliferates within the alveolar walls, producing an interstitial lung disease. Smooth muscle

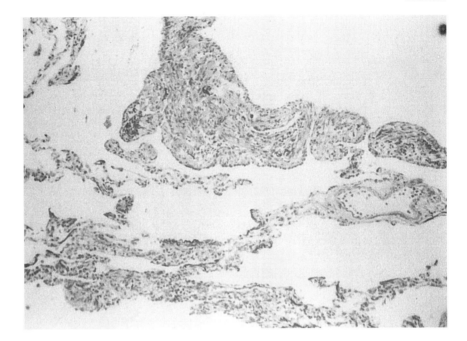

Figure 56.12 Micrograph showing lymphangioleiomyomatosis. There is smooth muscle proliferating in and broadening the alveolar walls. (Original magnification ×40.)

proliferation in the walls of bronchioles causes progressive airflow limitation, lung parenchymal cyst formation, and eventual pneumothorax (Fig. 56.12). Lastly, the myoproliferation can occlude venules and small veins, resulting in episodes of recurrent but limited alveolar hemorrhage. The abdominal lymphatic channels are sometimes involved as well, and a benign angiomyolipoma of the kidney may be present.[158–161]

Symptoms first appear in women between the ages of 17 and 47 years. Dyspnea, which eventually occurs in all affected women, may result from interstitial lung disease, a chylous pleural effusion, or obstructive lung disease. Pneumothorax causing acute dyspnea is a frequent (occurring in 40% of patients) and often recurrent complication of this disease. It is often the presenting manifestation.[158,160] Intermittent hemoptysis occurs in 40% of patients as a result of the obstruction and rupture of small pulmonary veins. The alveolar bleeding is often focal; DAH is unusual. Pathologic specimens typically demonstrate focal areas of hemorrhage and hemosiderin deposition. Involvement of the abdominal lymphatic channels, a less frequent association, can produce chylous ascites. Other rare clinical manifestations include chyluria, chylopericardium, chyloptysis, and lower extremity edema.[159,160]

The chest radiographic findings are variable. Early on, the chylous pleural effusion may dominate, or small irregular interstitial opacities representing proliferating interstitial smooth muscle bundles may produce a micronodular or miliary pattern. Septal lines (Kerley's B lines) due to the lymphatic obstruction appear, producing a coarse reticular pattern. In more advanced disease, the chest radiograph shows hyperinflation, small cystic areas that may be superimposed on a coarse reticular pattern, and sometimes a pneumothorax (Fig. 56.13). The computed tomography scan in the advanced case reveals multiple thin-walled cysts throughout the lung parenchyma (Fig. 56.14).

Although a restrictive ventilatory pattern due either to the interstitial lung disease or to the pleural effusions may be

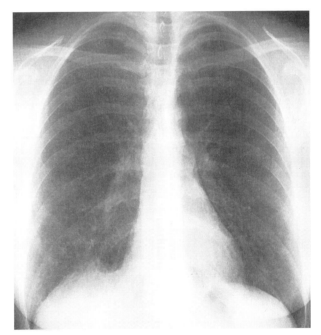

Figure 56.13 Chest radiograph showing lymphangioleiomyomatosis. Note the hyperinflation and lower zone interstitial infiltrates.

seen early on, the most frequent physiologic pattern encountered is progressive obstructive lung disease with hyperinflation and a reduced diffusing capacity for carbon monoxide. These findings are identical to those found in emphysema.[158,162] Airflow limitation in LAM is probably due to airway narrowing rather than to a loss of elastic recoil.[162]

Progress has been made in understanding the genetics of LAM.[163–165] It appears that mutations in the tumor suppressor gene tuberous sclerosis complex-2 (*TSC2*) are an important cause of sporadic cases of LAM.[164] This gene, whose product is a ubiquitously expressed protein called

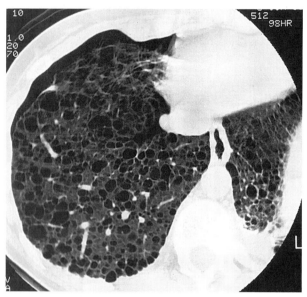

Figure 56.14 High-resolution computed tomography scan showing lymphangioleiomyomatosis. It demonstrates the network of thin-walled cysts as well as a pneumothorax.

Table 56.4 Thoracic Manifestations of Neurofibromatosis
Lung Parenchymal
Interstitial lung disease
Metastatic neural tumor
Mediastinal
Meningocele
Vagal nerve neurofibroma
Chest Wall
Subcutaneous neurofibromas
Rib notching (inferior) from intercostal neurofibroma
Kyphoscoliosis
Apical neurofibroma (Pancoast's syndrome)

tuberin, is critically important for regulating cell proliferation in smooth muscle cells.[163] A link between the abnormal *TSC2* gene and cystic lung disease has recently been suggested.[163,166]

Because LAM occurs in premenopausal women and because the disease is reported to accelerate both during pregnancy and after estrogen therapy, hormonal influences are thought to be important in its pathogenesis.[167,168] Electron microscopy of the lung in LAM reveals the proliferating smooth muscle cells to be similar to the uterine smooth muscle cells.[169] Also, a progestin receptor has been identified in the lungs of LAM subjects that is not found in the lungs of unaffected women.[170,171]

Most women die of this disease within 10 years of onset of symptoms, but the course is variable. Therapies have generally been directed toward reducing the circulating estrogen levels, and these include oral and intramuscular medroxyprogesterone, oophorectomy, tamoxifen, or various combinations of the aforementioned treatments.[168,170,172–174] Medroxyprogesterone may result in prolonged periods of disease stabilization or even physiologic improvement in some cases, especially when treatment is initiated early (e.g., in the presence of chylous effusions).[159] Unfortunately, there are no controlled studies to support the efficacy of any of these therapies; prolonged stabilization may reflect the biologic variability of individual patients rather than responsiveness to treatment. Single-lung transplantation has been successful, but recurrences of LAM have been documented.[175,176] In one study, genetic analysis of the *TCS2* mutation in LAM cells from the allograft revealed the identical mutation identified from the native lung, suggesting LAM cells may be able to migrate or metastasize.[175]

TUBEROUS SCLEROSIS

Tuberous sclerosis involving the lungs is pathologically identical to LAM and therefore has a similar clinical, radiographic, and physiologic picture. Women with tuberous sclerosis develop pulmonary disease indistinguishable from LAM. Interestingly, chylous pleural effusions are rare. In addition, treatment with antiestrogen regimens is not recommended.[177–179]

Tuberous sclerosis is a systemic disease caused by mutations in the *TSC1* and *TSC2* genes.[180] The disease typically presents with the clinical triad of mental retardation, epilepsy, and dermal angiofibroma (adenoma sebaceum).[177] Systemic manifestations include calcified cerebral and paraventricular hamartomas, renal angiomyolipomas, cardiac rhabdomyomas, and periungual fibromas. Death occurs in more than 75% of affected individuals by 20 years of age, usually from neurologic complications. Pulmonary disease is rare, appearing in 1% and only in female patients who survive to adulthood. The onset of dyspnea usually occurs during the third decade.[179] As in LAM, progressive dyspnea, recurrent spontaneous pneumothoraces, and hemoptysis are to be expected. Hemoptysis is rarely severe enough to result in the syndrome of DAH. There is no recommended treatment other than lung transplantation.

OTHER RARE INFILTRATIVE DISORDERS

NEUROFIBROMATOSIS

There are two clinically and genetically distinct forms of neurofibromatosis termed neurofibromatosis 1 and neurofibromatosis 2.[181] Lung disease is generally associated with neurofibromatosis 1, also known as von Recklinghausen's disease. Neurofibromatosis 1 is an autosomal dominant disease that is recognized by the appearance of cutaneous café au lait spots, subcutaneous neurofibromas, and the Lisch nodule in the iris.[182] The thoracic manifestations of neurofibromatosis are listed in Table 56.4. Interstitial lung disease occurs in 25% of affected patients, and dyspnea appears between the third and sixth decades.[183–186] Lower zone radiographic interstitial infiltrates are the rule, and bullous changes eventually appear in the upper zones. Physiologic testing early in the course of the disease reveals restrictive ventilatory impairment, but with time an obstructive lung disease supervenes, because the fibrotic process in the lung involves not only the interstitium but also the small airways. Scar carcinoma has been reported as a complication of neurofibromatosis.[183]

GAUCHER'S DISEASE

The infantile form of Gaucher's disease, a hereditary disorder that is most common in Ashkenazi Jews, is uniformly fatal because of central nervous system involvement. However, the adult form is relatively benign and is associated with long-term survival. It presents with hepatosplenomegaly, anemia, thrombocytopenia, long-bone erosions, and an increase in serum acid phosphatase. It is an autosomal recessive disease, the pathologic hallmark being the Gaucher cell. The Gaucher cell is a reticuloendothelial cell with a foamy cytoplasm due to the accumulation of glucocerebrosides, which results from a deficiency in glucocerebrosidase. This leads to an excessive deposition of glucocerebrosides in the reticuloendothelial system, bone marrow, central nervous system, and occasionally the lung.

Pulmonary disease occurs in adult cases.[187–189] The parenchymal disease, which consists of radiographically visible small nodules, appears during the first 3 decades of life. Pathologic examination reveals masses of glucocerebroside-filled alveolar macrophages in the alveolar spaces and infiltrating the interstitium. There are no acute or chronic inflammatory cells and there is no interstitial fibrosis. In addition to interstitial lung disease, affected patients are susceptible to lung infection. A single case of pulmonary hypertension from diffuse small vessel obstruction by these cells has been reported.[190] Although enzyme replacement (glucocerebrosidase) has therapeutic promise for many of the manifestations of Gaucher's disease, the interstitial lung disease appears unresponsive.[191]

NIEMANN-PICK DISEASE

In patients with Niemann-Pick disease, a genetically determined deficiency of sphingomyelinase causes accumulation of sphingomyelin in the cells of the reticuloendothelial and central nervous systems.[192] As in Gaucher's disease, there is an infantile form of Niemann Pick disease that is rapidly fatal. The adult form, which appears during the second and third decades, is relatively benign, presenting with hepatosplenomegaly, hemostatic defects, platelet dysfunction, and, occasionally, cerebellar ataxia. Interstitial lung disease, which appears as diffuse nodular infiltrates on the chest radiograph, is usually asymptomatic, although a mild restrictive ventilatory defect and reduced diffusing capacity have been reported.[193,194] One case of cor pulmonale in Niemann-Pick disease has been described.[193] As in Gaucher's disease, foamy alveolar macrophages are found on lung biopsy.

HERMANSKY-PUDLAK SYNDROME

Hermansky-Pudlak syndrome is an autosomal recessive disorder found in inhabitants of Puerto Rico and southern Holland.[195–198] The biochemical defect is unknown, although putatively responsible genes have been identified and several mutations have been reported.[199] In patients with this disease, there is an accumulation of a chromolipid ceroid related to lipofuscin in the reticuloendothelial system. This results in partial tyrosine-negative oculocutaneous albinism and a qualitative platelet defect. In addition,

granulomatous colitis and progressive pulmonary fibrosis occur. The interstitial lung disease is more likely to occur in women and develops during the second through fourth decades.[196] It progresses slowly and is unresponsive to treatment. It results in severe dyspnea because of the increased work of breathing and the gas-exchange abnormalities. Spirometry and measurement of lung volumes reveal restrictive lung disease. The chest radiograph shows nonspecific reticulonodular infiltrates, which progress to radiographic "honeycomb" lung and pulmonary hypertension. The histologic appearance is one of extensive interstitial fibrosis with filling of the alveolar spaces by ceroid-containing macrophages. These macrophages are identified in bronchoalveolar lavage and by subsequent staining with the Fontana-Masson silver reduction technique.[196]

PULMONARY ALVEOLAR MICROLITHIASIS

Pulmonary alveolar microlithiasis is a rare disease in which concretions collect in alveolar spaces (Fig. 56.15). The concretions are composed of calcium and phosphorus.[200,201] With time, the alveolar walls become fibrotic, and severe physiologic impairment develops.[200] There is no known cause for this condition. A systemic disorder of calcium metabolism has not been identified, nor is there evidence for common exposures or immunologic abnormalities. The serum calcium and phosphate levels are normal. Most authors believe that the responsible mechanism is an inborn error of calcium metabolism that is confined to the lung and leads to precipitation of the salts. In more than 50% of cases, a familial association, usually in siblings, is found.[200,202]

Most cases are diagnosed during the third through fifth decades. Among familial cases, women are affected more often than men, but there is an equal distribution among the sporadic cases.[202,203] Cough and dyspnea are usually reported late in the disease course and are associated with restrictive lung disease and gas-exchange impairment.[204] Expectorated microliths have been reported but are unusual.[200] With the development of interstitial fibrosis, inspiratory crackles, finger clubbing, and signs of cor pulmonale appear.[200]

The chest radiograph is characteristic and shows a diffuse bilateral calcific infiltrate with predilection for the lower lung zones. This infiltrate is alveolar, producing air bronchograms and radiographic obliteration of the heart borders, pulmonary vessels, and diaphragmatic surfaces (Fig. 56.16).[205] In the later stages, radiographic signs of pulmonary hypertension appear. The chest computed tomography scan confirms the calcified nodules and occasionally demonstrates pleural calcification.[206] The chest radiograph is often all that is needed for diagnosis, but technetium-99m bone scintigraphy or transbronchial lung biopsy can provide confirmation.[207,208]

Pulmonary function remains normal or only slightly impaired for a prolonged period after disease detection.[201] With progression and the development of fibrosis, a restrictive ventilatory defect with a reduced diffusing capacity for carbon monoxide and severe gas-exchange abnormalities develops, and respiratory failure eventually ensues. Erythrocytosis, secondary to hypoxemia, is found in the later stages of the disease.[209] Treatment is supportive. Whole-lung lavage, which is effective for pulmonary alveolar

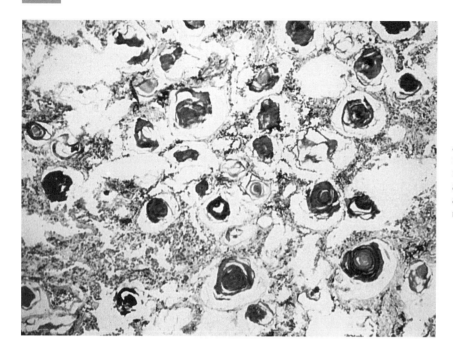

Figure 56.15 Micrograph showing alveolar microlithiasis. Intra-alveolar calcified microliths are present, and some of the alveolar walls are thickened by inflammation and collagen deposition. (Original magnification ×10.)

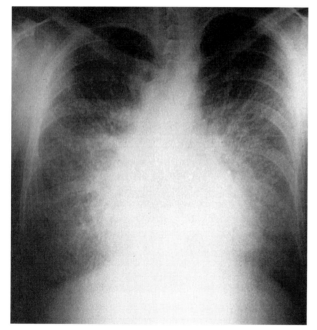

Figure 56.16 Chest radiograph showing alveolar microlithiasis. There is diffuse alveolar filling, with air bronchograms and obliteration of the heart borders.

proteinosis, has no beneficial effect.[210] Lung transplantation has been successfully performed.

SUMMARY

Diffuse alveolar hemorrhage is an uncommon but striking event that is associated with many different underlying disorders. In this chapter, the causes of DAH have been subdivided into those with and without histologic evidence of pulmonary capillaritis. Many of the disorders causing DAH appear to be immunologically mediated, either through injury to the capillary basement membrane by specific autoantibody or through deposition of immune complexes. Most conditions can be diagnosed by the presence of accompanying clinical features, laboratory abnormalities, and histologic findings, although overlap occurs. Accurate diagnosis is essential because aggressive treatment with corticosteroids, cytotoxic agents, and plasmapheresis (alone or in combination) is often helpful. This chapter has also reviewed information about other diseases that are occasionally complicated by DAH and other infiltrative lung disorders. All of these diseases are rare, and many have a genetic basis. Most are diagnosable, and treatment is available for a few.

REFERENCES

1. Schwarz MI, Brown KK: Small vessel vasculitis of the lung. Thorax 55:502–510, 2000.
2. Spencer H: Pulmonary lesions in polyarteritis nodosa. Br J Tuberc Dis Chest 51:123–130, 1957.
3. Mark EJ, Ramirez JF: Pulmonary capillaritis and hemorrhage in patients with systemic vasculitis. Arch Pathol Lab Med 109:413–418, 1985.
4. Travis WD, Colby TV, Lombard C, Carpenter HA: A clinicopathologic study of 34 cases of diffuse pulmonary hemorrhage with lung biopsy confirmation. Am J Surg Pathol 14:1112–1125, 1990.
5. Travis WD, Hoffman GS, Leavitt RY, et al: Surgical pathology of the lung in Wegener's granulomatosis: Review of 87 open lung biopsies from 67 patients. Am J Surg Pathol 15:315–333, 1991.
6. Greening AP, Hughes JM: Serial estimations of carbon monoxide diffusing capacity in intrapulmonary haemorrhage. Clin Sci (Lond) 60:507–512, 1981.
7. Nada AK, Torres VE, Ryu JH, et al: Pulmonary fibrosis as an unusual clinical manifestation of a pulmonary-renal vasculitis in elderly patients. Mayo Clin Proc 65:847–856, 1990.

8. Leatherman JW, Davies SF, Hoidal JR: Alveolar hemorrhage syndromes: Diffuse microvascular lung hemorrhage in immune and idiopathic disorders. Medicine (Baltimore) 63:343–361, 1984.

9. Beechler CR, Enquist RW, Hunt KK, et al: Immunofluorescence of transbronchial biopsies in Goodpasture's syndrome. Am Rev Respir Dis 121:869–872, 1980.

10. Roth DA, Wilz DR, Theil GB: Schonlein-Henoch syndrome in adults. Q J Med 55:145–152, 1985.

10a. Schmitt WH, van der Woude FJ: Clinical applications of antineutrophil cytoplasmic antibody testing. Curr Opin Rheumatol 16:9–17, 2004.

11. Falk RJ, Jennette JC: Anti-neutrophil cytoplasmic autoantibodies with specificity for myeloperoxidase in patients with systemic vasculitis and idiopathic necrotizing and crescentic glomerulonephritis. N Engl J Med 318:1651–1657, 1988.

12. Goeken JA: Antineutrophil cytoplasmic antibody—a useful serological marker for vasculitis. J Clin Immunol 11:161–174, 1991.

13. Guillevin L, Durand-Gasselin B, Cevallos R, et al: Microscopic polyangiitis: Clinical and laboratory findings in eighty-five patients. Arthritis Rheum 42:421–430, 1999.

14. Andrassy K, Koderisch J, Waldherr R, Rufer M: Diagnostic significance of anticytoplasmatic antibodies (ACPA/ANCA) in detection of Wegener's granulomatosis and other forms of vasculitis. Nephron 49:257–258, 1988.

15. D'Agati V: Antineutrophil cytoplasmic antibody and vasculitis: Much more than a disease marker. J Clin Invest 110:919–921, 2002.

16. Jennings CA, King TE Jr, Tuder R, et al: Diffuse alveolar hemorrhage with underlying isolated, pauciimmune pulmonary capillaritis. Am J Respir Crit Care Med 155:1101–1109, 1997.

17. Bosch X, Font J, Mirapeix E, et al: Antimyeloperoxidase autoantibody-associated necrotizing alveolar capillaritis. Am Rev Respir Dis 146:1326–1329, 1992.

18. Mark EJ, Matsubara O, Tan-Liu NS, Fienberg R: The pulmonary biopsy in the early diagnosis of Wegener's (pathergic) granulomatosis: A study based on 35 open lung biopsies. Hum Pathol 19:1065–1071, 1988.

19. Yoshikawa Y, Watanabe T: Pulmonary lesions in Wegener's granulomatosis: A clinicopathologic study of 22 autopsy cases. Hum Pathol 17:401–410, 1986.

20. Woywodt A, Streiber F, de Groot K, et al: Circulating endothelial cells as markers for ANCA-associated small-vessel vasculitis. Lancet 361:206–210, 2003.

21. Schnabel A, Reuter M, Csernok E, et al: Subclinical alveolar bleeding in pulmonary vasculitides: Correlation with indices of disease activity. Eur Respir J 14:118–124, 1999.

22. Travis WD, Carpenter HA, Lie JT: Diffuse pulmonary hemorrhage: An uncommon manifestation of Wegener's granulomatosis. Am J Surg Pathol 11:702–708, 1987.

23. Lenclud C, De Vuyst P, Dupont E, et al: Wegener's granulomatosis presenting as acute respiratory failure with anti-neutrophil-cytoplasm antibodies. Chest 96:345–347, 1989.

24. Jayne D, Rasmussen N, Andrassy K, et al: A randomized trial of maintenance therapy for vasculitis associated with antineutrophil cytoplasmic autoantibodies. N Engl J Med 349:36–44, 2003.

25. Jayne DR, Chapel H, Adu D, et al: Intravenous immunoglobulin for ANCA-associated systemic vasculitis with persistent disease activity. QJM 93:433–439, 2000.

26. Thomas-Golbanov C, Sridharan S: Novel therapies in vasculitis. Expert Opin Invest Drugs 10:1279–1289, 2001.

27. Hall JB, Wadham BM, Wood CJ, et al: Vasculitis and glomerulonephritis: A subgroup with an antineutrophil cytoplasmic antibody. Aust N Z J Med 14:277–278, 1984.

28. Thomashow BM, Felton CP, Navarro C: Diffuse intrapulmonary hemorrhage, renal failure and a systemic vasculitis: A case report and review of the literature. Am J Med 68:299–304, 1980.

29. Imoto EM, Lombard CM, Sachs DP: Pulmonary capillaritis and hemorrhage: A clue to the diagnosis of systemic necrotizing vasculitis. Chest 96:927–928, 1989.

30. Haworth SJ, Savage CO, Carr D, et al: Pulmonary haemorrhage complicating Wegener's granulomatosis and microscopic polyarteritis. Br Med J (Clin Res Ed) 290:1775–1778, 1985.

31. Zashin S, Fattor R, Fortin D: Microscopic polyarteritis: A forgotten aetiology of haemoptysis and rapidly progressive glomerulonephritis. Ann Rheum Dis 49:53–56, 1990.

32. Savage CO, Winearls CG, Evans DJ, et al: Microscopic polyarteritis: Presentation, pathology and prognosis. Q J Med 56:467–483, 1985.

33. Guo X, Gopalan R, Ugbarugba S, et al: Hepatitis B-related polyarteritis nodosa complicated by pulmonary hemorrhage. Chest 119:1608–1610, 2001.

34. Lauque D, Cadranel J, Lazor R, et al: Microscopic polyangiitis with alveolar hemorrhage: A study of 29 cases and review of the literature. Groupe d'Etudes et de Recherche sur les Maladies "Orphelines" Pulmonaires (GERM"O"P). Medicine (Baltimore) 79:222–233, 2000.

35. Bocanegra TS, Espinoza LR, Vasey FB, Germain BF: Pulmonary hemorrhage in systemic necrotizing vasculitis associated with hepatitis B. Chest 80:102–103, 1981.

36. Betensley AD, Yankaskas JR: Factor VIIa for alveolar hemorrhage in microscopic polyangiitis. Am J Respir Crit Care Med 166:1291–1292, 2002.

37. Eschun GM, Mink SN, Sharma S: Pulmonary interstitial fibrosis as a presenting manifestation in perinuclear antineutrophilic cytoplasmic antibody microscopic polyangiitis. Chest 123:297–301, 2003.

38. Schwarz MI, Mortenson RL, Colby TV, et al: Pulmonary capillaritis: The association with progressive irreversible airflow limitation and hyperinflation. Am Rev Respir Dis 148:507–511, 1993.

39. Smith B: Idiopathic pulmonary hemosiderosis and rheumatoid arthritis. Br Med J 1:1403–1404, 1966.

40. Bar J, Ehrenfeld M, Rozenman J, et al: Pulmonary-renal syndrome in systemic sclerosis. Semin Arthritis Rheum 30:403–410, 2001.

41. Schwarz MI, Sutarik JM, Nick JA, et al: Pulmonary capillaritis and diffuse alveolar hemorrhage: A primary manifestation of polymyositis. Am J Respir Crit Care Med 151:2037–2040, 1995.

42. Schwarz MI, Zamora MR, Hodges TN, et al: Isolated pulmonary capillaritis and diffuse alveolar hemorrhage in rheumatoid arthritis and mixed connective tissue disease. Chest 113:1609–1615, 1998.

43. Hughson MD, He Z, Henegar J, McMurray R: Alveolar hemorrhage and renal microangiopathy in systemic lupus erythematosus. Arch Pathol Lab Med 125:475–483, 2001.

44. Santos-Ocampo AS, Mandell BF, Fessler BJ: Alveolar hemorrhage in systemic lupus erythematosus: Presentation and management. Chest 118:1083–1090, 2000.

45. Zamora MR, Warner ML, Tuder R, Schwarz MI: Diffuse alveolar hemorrhage and systemic lupus erythematosus: Clinical presentation, histology, survival, and outcome. Medicine (Baltimore) 76:192–202, 1997.

46. Chang MY, Fang JT, Chen YC, Huang CC: Diffuse alveolar hemorrhage in systemic lupus erythematosus: A

single center retrospective study in Taiwan. Ren Fail 24:791–802, 2002.

47. Eagen JW, Memoli VA, Roberts JL, et al: Pulmonary hemorrhage in systemic lupus erythematosus. Medicine (Baltimore) 57:545–560, 1978.

48. Gertner E: Diffuse alveolar hemorrhage in the antiphospholipid syndrome: Spectrum of disease and treatment. J Rheumatol 26:805–807, 1999.

49. Desnoyers MR, Bernstein S, Cooper AG, Kopelman RI: Pulmonary hemorrhage in lupus erythematosus without evidence of an immunologic cause. Arch Intern Med 144:1398–1400, 1984.

50. Rodriguez-Iturbe B, Garcia R, Rubio L, Serrano H: Immunohistologic findings in the lung in systemic lupus erythematosus. Arch Pathol Lab Med 101:342–344, 1977.

51. Myers JL, Katzenstein AA: Microangiitis in lupus-induced pulmonary hemorrhage. Am J Clin Pathol 85:552–556, 1986.

52. Matthay RA, Schwarz MI, Petty TL, et al: Pulmonary manifestations of systemic lupus erythematosus: Review of twelve cases of acute lupus pneumonitis. Medicine (Baltimore) 54:397–409, 1975.

53. Howe HS, Boey ML, Fong KY, Feng PH: Pulmonary haemorrhage, pulmonary infarction, and the lupus anticoagulant. Ann Rheum Dis 47:869–872, 1988.

54. Alarcon-Segovia D, Deleze M, Oria CV, et al: Antiphospholipid antibodies and the antiphospholipid syndrome in systemic lupus erythematosus: A prospective analysis of 500 consecutive patients. Medicine (Baltimore) 68:353–365, 1989.

55. Bombardieri S, Paoletti P, Ferri C, et al: Lung involvement in essential mixed cryoglobulinemia. Am J Med 66:748–756, 1979.

56. Gomez-Tello V, Onoro-Canaveral JJ, de la Casa Monje RM, et al: Diffuse recidivant alveolar hemorrhage in a patient with hepatitis C virus-related mixed cryoglobulinemia. Intensive Care Med 25:319–322, 1999.

57. Ball JA, Young KR Jr: Pulmonary manifestations of Goodpasture's syndrome: Antiglomerular basement membrane disease and related disorders. Clin Chest Med 19:777–791, ix, 1998.

58. Chajek T, Fainaru M: Behcet's disease: Report of 41 cases and a review of the literature. Medicine (Baltimore) 54:179–196, 1975.

59. Gamble CN, Wiesner KB, Shapiro RF, Boyer WJ: The immune complex pathogenesis of glomerulonephritis and pulmonary vasculitis in Behcet's disease. Am J Med 66:1031–1039, 1979.

60. Raz I, Okon E, Chajek-Shaul T: Pulmonary manifestations in Behcet's syndrome. Chest 95:585–589, 1989.

61. Stricker H, Malinverni R: Multiple, large aneurysms of pulmonary arteries in Behcet's disease: Clinical remission and radiologic resolution after corticosteroid therapy. Arch Intern Med 149:925–927, 1989.

62. Yazici H, Pazarli H, Barnes CG, et al: A controlled trial of azathioprine in Behcet's syndrome. N Engl J Med 322:281–285, 1990.

63. Sfikakis PP: Behcet's disease: A new target for anti-tumour necrosis factor treatment. Ann Rheum Dis 61(Suppl 2):ii51–ii3, 2002.

64. Pillebout E, Thervet E, Hill G, et al: Henoch-Schonlein purpura in adults: Outcome and prognostic factors. J Am Soc Nephrol 13:1271–1278, 2002.

65. Kathuria S, Cheifec G: Fatal pulmonary Henoch-Schonlein syndrome. Chest 82:654–656, 1982.

65a. Nadrous HF, Yu AC, Specks U, Ryu JH: Pulmonary involvement in Henoch-Schonlein purpura. Mayo Clin Proc 79:1151–1157, 2004.

66. Kauffmann RH, Herrmann WA, Meyer CJ, et al: Circulating IgA-immune complexes in Henoch-Schonlein purpura: A longitudinal study of their relationship to disease activity and vascular deposition of IgA. Am J Med 69:859–866, 1980.

67. Butkowski R, Langeveld J, Wieslander J, et al: Localization of the Goodpasture epitope to a novel chain of basement membrane collagen. J Biol Chem 262:7874–7877, 1987.

68. Beirne GJ, Kopp WL, Zimmerman SW: Goodpasture syndrome: Dissociation from antibodies to glomerular basement membrane. Arch Intern Med 132:261–263, 1973.

69. Lombard CM, Colby TV, Elliott CG: Surgical pathology of the lung in anti-basement membrane antibody-associated Goodpasture's syndrome. Hum Pathol 20:445–451, 1989.

70. Camus P: Drug-induced infiltrative lung disease. In Schwarz MI, King TE (eds): Interstitial Lung Disease (4th ed). Hamilton, Ontario, Canada: BC Decker, 2003, pp 508–509.

70a. Erdogan D, Kocaman O, Oflaz H, Goren T: Alveolar hemorrhage associated with warfarin therapy: a case report and literature review. Int J Cardiovasc Imaging 20:155–159, 2004.

70b. Yilmaz MB, Akin Y, Biyikoglu SF, et al: Diffuse alveolar hemorrhage following administration of tirofiban in a patient with acute coronary syndrome: a fatal complication. Int J Cardiol 93:81–82, 2004.

70c. Pirot AL, Goldsmith D, Pascasio J, Beck SE: Pulmonary capillaritis with hemorrhage due to propylthiouracil therapy in a child. Pediatr Pulmonol 39:88–92, 2005.

71. Badesch DB, Zamora M, Fullerton D, et al: Pulmonary capillaritis: A possible histologic form of acute pulmonary allograft rejection. J Heart Lung Transplant 17:415–422, 1998.

72. Silverman ES, Mark EJ: Case records of the Massachusetts General Hospital. Weekly Clinicopathological Exercises. Case 36–2002: A 32-year-old man with hemoptysis of nearly three decades' duration. N Engl J Med 347:1693–1701, 2002.

73. Cohen S: Idiopathic pulmonary hemosiderosis. Am J Med Sci 317:67–74, 1999.

74. Beckerman RC, Taussig LM, Pinnas JL: Familial idiopathic pulmonary hemosiderosis. Am J Dis Child 133:609–611, 1979.

75. Bowley NB, Hughes JM, Steiner RE: The chest X-ray in pulmonary capillary haemorrhage: Correlation with carbon monoxide uptake. Clin Radiol 30:413–417, 1979.

76. Elidemir O, Colasurdo GN, Rossmann SN, Fan LL: Isolation of Stachybotrys from the lung of a child with pulmonary hemosiderosis. Pediatrics 104:964–966, 1999.

77. Yeager H Jr, Powell D, Weinberg RM, et al: Idiopathic pulmonary hemosiderosis: Ultrastructural studies and responses to azathioprine. Arch Intern Med 136:1145–1149, 1976.

78. Irwin RS, Cottrell TS, Hsu KC, et al: Idiopathic pulmonary hemosiderosis: An electron microscopic and immunofluorescent study. Chest 65:41–45, 1974.

79. Dolan CJ Jr, Srodes CH, Duffy FD: Idiopathic pulmonary hemosiderosis: Electron microscopic, immunofluorescent, and iron kinetic studies. Chest 68:577–580, 1975.

80. Wright PH, Menzies IS, Pounder RE, Keeling PW: Adult idiopathic pulmonary haemosiderosis and coeliac disease. Q J Med 50:95–102, 1981.

81. Valassi-Adam H, Rouska A, Karpouzas J: Raised IgA in idiopathic pulmonary hemosiderosis. Arch Dis Child 50:320–322, 1975.

82. Byrd RB, Gracey DR: Immunosuppressive treatment of idiopathic pulmonary hemosiderosis. JAMA 226:458–459, 1973.

83. Kjellman B, Elinder G, Garwicz S, Svan H: Idiopathic pulmonary haemosiderosis in Swedish children. Acta Paediatr Scand 73:584–588, 1984.

84. Airaghi L, Ciceri L, Giannini S, et al: Idiopathic pulmonary hemosiderosis in an adult: Favourable response to azathioprine. Monaldi Arch Chest Dis 56:211–213, 2001.

85. Calabrese F, Giacometti C, Rea F, et al: Recurrence of idiopathic pulmonary hemosiderosis in a young adult patient after bilateral single-lung transplantation. Transplantation 74:1643–1645, 2002.

86. Goodpasture E: The significance of certain pulmonary lesions in relation to the etiology of influenza. Am J Med Sci 158:863–870, 1919.

87. Hellmark T, Burkhardt H, Wieslander J: Goodpasture disease: Characterization of a single conformational epitope as the target of pathogenic autoantibodies. J Biol Chem 274:25862–25868, 1999.

88. Simpson IJ, Doak PB, Williams LC, et al: Plasma exchange in Goodpasture's syndrome. Am J Nephrol 2:301–311, 1982.

89. McPhaul JJ Jr, Mullins JD: Glomerulonephritis mediated by antibody to glomerular basement membrane: Immunological, clinical, and histopathological characteristics. J Clin Invest 57:351–361, 1976.

90. Kelly PT, Haponik EF: Goodpasture syndrome: Molecular and clinical advances. Medicine (Baltimore) 73:171–185, 1994.

91. Savage CO, Pusey CD, Bowman C, et al: Antiglomerular basement membrane antibody mediated disease in the British Isles 1980–4. Br Med J (Clin Res Ed) 292:301–304, 1986.

92. Teague CA, Doak PB, Simpson IJ, et al: Goodpasture's syndrome: An analysis of 29 cases. Kidney Int 13:492–504, 1978.

93. Donaghy M, Rees AJ: Cigarette smoking and lung haemorrhage in glomerulonephritis caused by autoantibodies to glomerular basement membrane. Lancet 2:1390–1393, 1983.

94. Jones JG, Minty BD, Lawler P, et al: Increased alveolar epithelial permeability in cigarette smokers. Lancet 1:66–68, 1980.

95. Keogh AM, Ibels LS, Allen DH, et al: Exacerbation of Goodpasture's syndrome after inadvertent exposure to hydrocarbon fumes. Br Med J (Clin Res Ed) 288:188, 1984.

96. Abboud RT, Chase WH, Ballon HS, et al: Goodpasture's syndrome: Diagnosis by transbronchial lung biopsy. Ann Intern Med 89:635–638, 1978.

97. Zimmerman SW, Varanasi UR, Hoff B: Goodpasture's syndrome with normal renal function. Am J Med 66:163–171, 1979.

98. Wilson CB, Smith RC: Goodpasture's syndrome associated with influenza A2 virus infection. Ann Intern Med 76:91–94, 1972.

99. Reynolds J, Moss J, Duda MA, et al: The evolution of crescentic nephritis and alveolar haemorrhage following induction of autoimmunity to glomerular basement membrane in an experimental model of Goodpasture's disease. J Pathol 200:118–129, 2003.

100. Nakamura A, Yuasa T, Ujike A, et al: Fcgamma receptor IIB-deficient mice develop Goodpasture's syndrome upon immunization with type IV collagen: A novel murine model for autoimmune glomerular basement membrane disease. J Exp Med 191:899–906, 2000.

101. Perl SI, Pussell BA, Charlesworth JA, et al: Goodpasture's (anti-GBM) disease and HLA-DRW2. N Engl J Med 305:463–464, 1981.

102. Rees AJ, Peters DK, Compston DA, Batchelor JR: Strong association between HLA-DRW2 and antibody-mediated Goodpasture's syndrome. Lancet 1:966–968, 1978.

103. Ewan PW, Jones HA, Rhodes CG, Hughes JM: Detection of intrapulmonary hemorrhage with carbon monoxide uptake: Application in Goodpasture's syndrome. N Engl J Med 295:1391–1396, 1976.

104. McCormack J, Kass J, Skewes M: Goodpasture's syndrome. Compr Ther 13:25–32, 1987.

105. Levy JB, Turner AN, Rees AJ, Pusey CD: Long-term outcome of anti-glomerular basement membrane antibody disease treated with plasma exchange and immunosuppression. Ann Intern Med 134:1033–1042, 2001.

106. Keller F, Offermann G, Schultze G, et al: Membrane plasma exchange in Goodpasture's syndrome. Am J Med Sci 287:32–36, 1984.

107. Fort J, Espinel E, Rodriguez JA, et al: Partial recovery of renal function in an oligoanuric patient affected with Goodpasture's syndrome after treatment with steroids, immunosuppressives and plasmapheresis. Clin Nephrol 22:211–212, 1984.

108. Johnson JP, Moore J Jr, Austin HA 3rd, et al: Therapy of anti-glomerular basement membrane antibody disease: Analysis of prognostic significance of clinical, pathologic and treatment factors. Medicine (Baltimore) 64:219–227, 1985.

109. Bygren P, Freiburghaus C, Lindholm T, et al: Goodpasture's syndrome treated with staphylococcal protein A immunoadsorption. Lancet 2:1295–1296, 1985.

110. Hind CR, Paraskevakou H, Lockwood CM, et al: Prognosis after immunosuppression of patients with crescentic nephritis requiring dialysis. Lancet 1:263–265, 1983.

111. Garcia-Canton C, Toledo A, Palomar R, et al: Goodpasture's syndrome treated with mycophenolate mofetil. Nephrol Dial Transplant 15:920–922, 2000.

112. Arzoo K, Sadeghi S, Liebman HA: Treatment of refractory antibody mediated autoimmune disorders with an anti-CD20 monoclonal antibody (rituximab). Ann Rheum Dis 61:922–924, 2002.

113. Katzenstein AL, Bloor CM, Leibow AA: Diffuse alveolar damage—the role of oxygen, shock, and related factors. A review. Am J Pathol 85:209–228, 1976.

114. Cooper JA Jr, White DA, Matthay RA: Drug-induced pulmonary disease. Part 1: Cytotoxic drugs. Am Rev Respir Dis 133:321–340, 1986.

115. Rebello G, Mason JK: Pulmonary histological appearances in fatal paraquat poisoning. Histopathology 2:53–66, 1978.

116. Tomashefski JF Jr: Pulmonary pathology of the adult respiratory distress syndrome. Clin Chest Med 11:593–619, 1990.

117. Gavaghan TE, McNaught PJ, Ralston M, Hayes JM: Penicillamine-induced "Goodpasture's syndrome": Successful treatment of a fulminant case. Aust N Z J Med 11:261–265, 1981.

118. Sternlieb I, Bennett B, Scheinberg IH: D-Penicillamine induced Goodpasture's syndrome in Wilson's disease. Ann Intern Med 82:673–676, 1975.

119. Louie S, Gamble CN, Cross CE: Penicillamine associated pulmonary hemorrhage. J Rheumatol 13:963–966, 1986.

120. Matloff DS, Kaplan MM: D-Penicillamine-induced Goodpasture's-like syndrome in primary biliary cirrhosis—successful treatment with plasmapheresis and immunosuppressives. Gastroenterology 78:1046–1049, 1980.

121. Zeiss CR, Wolkonsky P, Chacon R, et al: Syndromes in workers exposed to trimellitic anhydride: A longitudinal

clinical and immunologic study. Ann Intern Med 98:8–12, 1983.

122. Herbert FA, Orford R: Pulmonary hemorrhage and edema due to inhalation of resins containing tri-mellitic anhydride. Chest 76:546–551, 1979.

123. Ahmad D, Morgan WK, Patterson R, et al: Pulmonary haemorrhage and haemolytic anaemia due to trimellitic anhydride. Lancet 2:328–330, 1979.

124. Spence TH, Connors JC: Diffuse alveolar hemorrhage syndrome due to "silent" mitral valve regurgitation. South Med J 93:65–67, 2000.

125. Woolley K, Stark P: Pulmonary parenchymal manifestations of mitral valve disease. Radiographics 19:965–972, 1999.

126. Robboy SJ, Minna JD, Colman RW, et al: Pulmonary hemorrhage syndrome as a manifestation of disseminated intravascular coagulation: Analysis of ten cases. Chest 63:718–721, 1973.

127. Buchanan GR, Moore GC: Pulmonary hemosiderosis and immune thrombocytopenia: Initial manifestations of collagen-vascular disease. JAMA 246:861–864, 1981.

128. Martinez AJ, Maltby JD, Hurst DJ: Thrombotic thrombocytopenic purpura seen as pulmonary hemorrhage. Arch Intern Med 143:1818–1820, 1983.

129. Drent M, Wessels S, Jacobs JA, Thijssen H: Association of diffuse alveolar haemorrhage with acquired vitamin K deficiency. Respiration 67:697, 2000.

130. Wiedermann FJ, Mayr A, Schobersberger W, et al: Acute respiratory failure associated with catastrophic antiphospholipid syndrome. J Intern Med 247:723–730, 2000.

131. Espinosa G, Cervera R, Font J, Asherson RA: The lung in the antiphospholipid syndrome. Ann Rheum Dis 61:195–198, 2002.

132. Finley TN, Aronow A, Cosentino AM, Golde DW: Occult pulmonary hemorrhage in anticoagulated patients. Am Rev Respir Dis 112:23–29, 1975.

133. Barnett VT, Bergmann F, Humphrey H, Chediak J: Diffuse alveolar hemorrhage secondary to superwarfarin ingestion. Chest 102:1301–1302, 1992.

134. Papagiannis A, Smith AP, Hebden MW: Acute dyspnea, chest tightness, and anemia in a 33-year-old man. Chest 107:863–865, 1995.

135. Swanson GA, Kaeley G, Geraci SA: Diffuse pulmonary hemorrhage after streptokinase administration for acute myocardial infarction. Pharmacotherapy 17:390–394, 1997.

136. Gopalakrishnan D, Tioran T, Emanuel C, Clark VL: Diffuse pulmonary hemorrhage complicating thrombolytic therapy for acute myocardial infarction. Clin Cardiol 20:298–300, 1997.

137. Awadh N, Ronco JJ, Bernstein V, et al: Spontaneous pulmonary hemorrhage after thrombolytic therapy for acute myocardial infarction. Chest 106:1622–1624, 1994.

138. Khanlou H, Eiger G, Yazdanfar S: Abciximab and alveolar hemorrhage. N Engl J Med 339:1861–3, 1998.

139. Choi RK, Lee NH, Lim DS, et al: Pulmonary hemorrhage after percutaneous coronary intervention with abciximab therapy. Mayo Clin Proc 77:1340–1343, 2002.

140. Raanani P, Segal E, Levi I, et al: Diffuse alveolar hemorrhage in acute promyelocytic leukemia patients treated with ATRA—a manifestation of the basic disease or the treatment? Leuk Lymphoma 37:605–610, 2000.

141. Golde DW, Drew WL, Klein HZ, et al: Occult pulmonary haemorrhage in leukaemia. Br Med J 2:166–168, 1975.

142. Fireman Z, Yust I, Abramov AL: Lethal occult pulmonary hemorrhage in drug-induced thrombocytopenia. Chest 79:358–359, 1981.

143. Smith LJ, Katzenstein AL: Pathogenesis of massive pulmonary hemorrhage in acute leukemia. Arch Intern Med 142:2149–2152, 1982.

144. Wagenvoort CA, Wagenvoort N, Takahashi T: Pulmonary veno-occlusive disease: Involvement of pulmonary arteries and review of the literature. Hum Pathol 16:1033–1041, 1985.

145. Pietra GG, Edwards WD, Kay JM, et al: Histopathology of primary pulmonary hypertension: A qualitative and quantitative study of pulmonary blood vessels from 58 patients in the National Heart, Lung, and Blood Institute, Primary Pulmonary Hypertension Registry. Circulation 80:1198–1206, 1989.

146. Palevsky HI, Pietra GG, Fishman AP: Pulmonary veno-occlusive disease and its response to vasodilator agents. Am Rev Respir Dis 142:426–429, 1990.

147. Lombard CM, Churg A, Winokur S: Pulmonary veno-occlusive disease following therapy for malignant neoplasms. Chest 92:871–876, 1987.

148. Troussard X, Bernaudin JF, Cordonnier C, et al: Pulmonary veno-occlusive disease after bone marrow transplantation. Thorax 39:956–957, 1984.

149. Corrin B, Spencer H, Turner-Warwick M, et al: Pulmonary veno-occlusion—an immune complex disease? Virchows Arch A Pathol Anat Histol 364:81–91, 1974.

150. Runo JR, Vnencak-Jones CL, Prince M, et al: Pulmonary veno-occlusive disease caused by an inherited mutation in bone morphogenetic protein receptor II. Am J Respir Crit Care Med 167:889–894, 2003.

151. Sanderson JE, Spiro SG, Hendry AT, Turner-Warwick M: A case of pulmonary veno-occlusive disease responding to treatment with azathioprine. Thorax 32:140–148, 1977.

152. Hackman RC, Madtes DK, Petersen FB, Clark JG: Pulmonary venoocclusive disease following bone marrow transplantation. Transplantation 47:989–992, 1989.

153. Salzman GA, Rosa UW: Prolonged survival in pulmonary veno-occlusive disease treated with nifedipine. Chest 95:1154–1156, 1989.

154. Langleben D, Heneghan JM, Batten AP, et al: Familial pulmonary capillary hemangiomatosis resulting in primary pulmonary hypertension. Ann Intern Med 109:106–109, 1988.

155. Faber CN, Yousem SA, Dauber JH, et al: Pulmonary capillary hemangiomatosis: A report of three cases and a review of the literature. Am Rev Respir Dis 140:808–813, 1989.

156. Almagro P, Julia J, Sanjaume M, et al: Pulmonary capillary hemangiomatosis associated with primary pulmonary hypertension: Report of 2 new cases and review of 35 cases from the literature. Medicine (Baltimore) 81:417–424, 2002.

157. White CW, Sondheimer HM, Crouch EC, et al: Treatment of pulmonary hemangiomatosis with recombinant interferon alfa-2a. N Engl J Med 320:1197–1200, 1989.

158. Taylor JR, Ryu J, Colby TV, Raffin TA: Lymphangioleiomyomatosis: Clinical course in 32 patients. N Engl J Med 323:1254–1260, 1990.

159. Urban T, Lazor R, Lacronique J, et al: Pulmonary lymphangioleiomyomatosis: A study of 69 patients. Groupe d'Etudes et de Recherche sur les Maladies "Orphelines" Pulmonaires (GERM"O"P). Medicine (Baltimore) 78:321–337, 1999.

160. Johnson S: Rare diseases. 1. Lymphangioleiomyomatosis: Clinical features, management and basic mechanisms. Thorax 54:254–264, 1999.

161. Bernstein SM, Newell JD Jr, Adamczyk D, et al: How common are renal angiomyolipomas in patients with pulmonary lymphangiomyomatosis? Am J Respir Crit Care Med 152:2138–2143, 1995.

162. Burger CD, Hyatt RE, Staats BA: Pulmonary mechanics in lymphangioleiomyomatosis. Am Rev Respir Dis 143:1030–1033, 1991.

163. Krymskaya VP, Shipley JM: Lymphangioleiomyomatosis: A complex tale of serum response factor-mediated tissue inhibitor of metalloproteinase-3 regulation. Am J Respir Cell Mol Biol 28:546–550, 2003.

164. Carsillo T, Astrinidis A, Henske EP: Mutations in the tuberous sclerosis complex gene TSC2 are a cause of sporadic pulmonary lymphangioleiomyomatosis. Proc Natl Acad Sci U S A 97:6085–6090, 2000.

165. Pacheco-Rodriguez G, Kristof AS, Stevens LA, et al: Giles F. Filley Lecture: Genetics and gene expression in lymphangioleiomyomatosis. Chest 121:56S–60S, 2002.

166. Zhe X, Yang Y, Jakkaraju S, Schuger L: Tissue inhibitor of metalloproteinase-3 downregulation in lymphangioleiomyomatosis: Potential consequence of abnormal serum response factor expression. Am J Respir Cell Mol Biol 28:504–511, 2003.

167. Yano S: Exacerbation of pulmonary lymphangioleiomyomatosis by exogenous oestrogen used for infertility treatment. Thorax 57:1085–1086, 2002.

168. NHLBI Workshop Summary: Report of workshop on lymphangioleiomyomatosis. National Heart, Lung, and Blood Institute. Am J Respir Crit Care Med 159:679–683, 1999.

169. Kane PB, Lane BP, Cordice JW, Greenberg GM: Ultrastructure of the proliferating cells in pulmonary lymphangiomyomatosis. Arch Pathol Lab Med 102:618–622, 1978.

170. McCarty KS Jr, Mossler JA, McLelland R, Sieker HO: Pulmonary lymphangiomyomatosis responsive to progesterone. N Engl J Med 303:1461–1465, 1980.

171. Berger U, Khaghani A, Pomerance A, et al: Pulmonary lymphangioleiomyomatosis and steroid receptors: An immunocytochemical study. Am J Clin Pathol 93:609–614, 1990.

172. Adamson D, Heinrichs WL, Raybin DM, Raffin TA: Successful treatment of pulmonary lymphangiomyomatosis with oophorectomy and progesterone. Am Rev Respir Dis 132:916–921, 1985.

173. Svendsen TL, Viskum K, Hansborg N, et al: Pulmonary lymphangioleiomyomatosis: A case of progesterone receptor positive lymphangioleiomyomatosis treated with medroxyprogesterone, oophorectomy and tamoxifen. Br J Dis Chest 78:264–271, 1984.

174. Tomasian A, Greenberg MS, Rumerman H: Tamoxifen for lymphangioleiomyomatosis. N Engl J Med 306:745–746, 1982.

175. Karbowniczek M, Astrinidis A, Balsara BR, et al: Recurrent lymphangiomyomatosis after transplantation: Genetic analyses reveal a metastatic mechanism. Am J Respir Crit Care Med 167:976–982, 2003.

176. Bittmann I, Rolf B, Amann G, Lohrs U: Recurrence of lymphangioleiomyomatosis after single lung transplantation: New insights into pathogenesis. Hum Pathol 34:95–98, 2003.

177. Marshall D, Saul G, Sachs E: Tuberous sclerosis: A report of 16 cases in two family trees revealing genetic dominance. N Engl J Med 261:1102–1105, 1959.

178. Dwyer JM, Hickie JB, Garvan J: Pulmonary tuberous sclerosis: Report of three patients and a review of the literature. Q J Med 40:115–125, 1971.

179. Capron F, Ameille J, Leclerc P, et al: Pulmonary lymphangioleiomyomatosis and Bourneville's tuberous sclerosis with pulmonary involvement: The diffuse disease? Cancer 52:851–855, 1983.

180. Sampson JR: TSC1 and TSC2: Genes that are mutated in the human genetic disorder tuberous sclerosis. Biochem Soc Trans 31:592–596, 2003.

181. McCormack FX: Genetic basis of interstitial lung disease. In Schwarz MI, King TE (eds): Interstitial Lung Disease (4th ed). Hamilton, Ontario, Canada: BC Decker, 2003, pp 158–160.

182. Riccardi VM: Von Recklinghausen neurofibromatosis. N Engl J Med 305:1617–1627, 1981.

183. De Scheerder I, Elinck W, Van Renterghem D, et al: Desquamative interstitial pneumonia and scar cancer of the lung complicating generalised neurofibromatosis. Eur J Respir Dis 65:623–626, 1984.

184. Massaro D, Katz S: Fibrosing alveolitis: Its occurrence, roentgenographic, and pathologic features in von Recklinghausen's neurofibromatosis. Am Rev Respir Dis 93:934–942, 1966.

185. Patchefsky AS, Atkinson WG, Hoch WS, et al: Interstitial pulmonary fibrosis and von Recklinghausen's disease: An ultrastructural and immunofluorescent study. Chest 64:459–464, 1973.

186. Unger PD, Geller GA, Anderson PJ: Pulmonary lesions in a patient with neurofibromatosis. Arch Pathol Lab Med 108:654–657, 1984.

187. Fisher MR, Sider L: Diffuse reticulonodular infiltrate associated with splenomegaly. Chest 84:609–610, 1983.

188. Schneider EL, Epstein CJ, Kaback MJ, Brandes D: Severe pulmonary involvement in adult Gaucher's disease: Report of three cases and review of the literature. Am J Med 63:475–480, 1977.

189. Terry R, Sperry W, Brodoff B: Adult lipidosis resembling Niemann-Pick's disease. Am J Pathol 30:263–286, 1954.

190. Roberts W, Fredrickson D: Gaucher's disease of the lung causing severe pulmonary hypertension with associated acute recurrent pericarditis. Circulation 35:783–789, 1967.

191. Altarescu G, Hill S, Wiggs E, et al: The efficacy of enzyme replacement therapy in patients with chronic neuronopathic Gaucher's disease. J Pediatr 138:539–547, 2001.

192. Lynn R, Terry R: Lipid histochemistry and electron microscopy in adult Niemann-Pick disease. Am J Med 37:987–994, 1964.

193. Lever AM, Ryder JB: Cor pulmonale in an adult secondary to Niemann-Pick disease. Thorax 38:873–874, 1983.

194. Long RG, Lake BD, Pettit JE, et al: Adult Niemann-Pick disease: Its relationship to the syndrome of the sea-blue histiocyte. Am J Med 62:627–635, 1977.

195. Hermansky F, Pudlak P: Albinism associated with hemorrhagic diathesis and unusual pigmented reticular cells in the bone marrow: Report of two cases with histochemical studies. Blood 14:162–169, 1959.

196. White DA, Smith GJ, Cooper JA Jr, et al: Hermansky-Pudlak syndrome and interstitial lung disease: Report of a case with lavage findings. Am Rev Respir Dis 130:138–141, 1984.

197. Schinella RA, Greco MA, Garay SM, et al: Hermansky-Pudlak syndrome: A clinicopathologic study. Hum Pathol 16:366–376, 1985.

198. DePinho RA, Kaplan KL: The Hermansky-Pudlak syndrome: Report of three cases and review of pathophysiology and management considerations. Medicine (Baltimore) 64:192–202, 1985.

199. Anderson PD, Huizing M, Claassen DA, et al: Hermansky-Pudlak syndrome type 4 (HPS-4): Clinical and molecular characteristics. Hum Genet 113:10–17, 2003.

200. Prakash UB, Barham SS, Rosenow EC 3rd, et al: Pulmonary alveolar microlithiasis: A review including ultrastructural and pulmonary function studies. Mayo Clin Proc 58:290–300, 1983.

201. Miro JM, Moreno A, Coca A, et al: Pulmonary alveolar microlithiasis with an unusual radiological pattern. Br J Dis Chest 76:91–96, 1982.

202. Sosman M, Dodd G, Jones W, et al: The familial occurrence of pulmonary alveolar microlithiasis. Am J Roentgenol Radium Ther Nucl Med 77:947–1012, 1957.

203. Sears MR, Chang AR, Taylor AJ: Pulmonary alveolar microlithiasis. Thorax 26:704–711, 1971.

204. Fuleihan F, Abboud RT, Balikian J: Pulmonary alveolar microlithiasis: Lung function in five cases. Thorax 24:84–90, 1969.

205. Balikian J, Fuleihan F, Nucho C: Pulmonary alveolar microlithiasis: Report of five cases with special reference to roentgen manifestations. Am J Roentgenol Radium Ther Nucl Med 103:509–518, 1968.

206. Pant K, Shah A, Mathur RK, et al: Pulmonary alveolar microlithiasis with pleural calcification and nephrolithiasis. Chest 98:245–246, 1990.

207. Brown ML, Swee RG, Olson RJ, Bender CE: Pulmonary uptake of ^{99m}Tc diphosphonate in alveolar microlithiasis. AJR Am J Roentgenol 131:703–704, 1978.

208. Cale WF, Petsonk EL, Boyd CB: Transbronchial biopsy of pulmonary alveolar microlithiasis. Arch Intern Med 143:358–359, 1983.

209. Meyer H, Gilbert E, Kent G: A clinical review of pulmonary microlithiasis. JAMA 161:1153–1157, 1956.

210. Palombini BC, da Silva Porto N, Wallau CU, Camargo JJ: Bronchopulmonary lavage in alveolar microlithiasis. Chest 80:242–243, 1981.

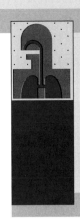

57 Eosinophilic Lung Diseases

Jean-François Cordier, M.D., Vincent Cottin, M.D., Ph.D.

INTRODUCTION

The eosinophilic lung diseases are a group of disorders (Table 57.1) characterized by the presence and presumed pathogenetic role of eosinophils in the lesional processes. They are mainly represented by the eosinophilic pneumonias, which are defined by a prominent infiltration of the lung parenchyma by eosinophils. The other eosinophilic lung diseases mainly concern the airways, as in the allergic bronchopulmonary mycoses (common asthma in which the eosinophil is considered to play an important role is not discussed in this chapter).

The eosinophil[1,2] is a polymorphonuclear leukocyte containing two types of intracytoplasmic granules. The larger granules, characterized by an electron-dense crystalloid matrix, contain the characteristic cationic proteins. The smaller amorphous granules contain arylsulfatase and acid phosphatase. The eosinophil matures in the bone marrow under the action of cytokines and especially of interleukin-5, which is involved in the differentiation of eosinophil precursors, IL-3, and granulocyte-macrophage colony-stimulating factor. The eosinophil then circulates in the blood for about 1 day before being attracted into target tissues by complex processes, including adhesion and attraction, diapedesis, and chemotaxis; there it undergoes apoptosis unless survival factors are present. Activation of the eosinophil results in degranulation with the extracellular release of the eosinophil-specific proteins, including especially major basic protein, eosinophil cationic protein, eosinophil-derived neurotoxin (also called eosinophil-protein X), and the enzymatic proteins eosinophil peroxidase

and major basic protein homologue. The finding of vacuoles in the cytoplasm of the eosinophil, and ultrastructural evidence of loss of electron density from the central core of the granules (inversion or disappearance of core density), characterize morphologically the process of degranulation. Eosinophils also release proinflammatory cytokines, arachidonic acid–derived mediators, enzymes, and reactive oxygen species. Thus, the process of eosinophil accumulation and the release of toxic substances may in itself contribute to the pathophysiology of eosinophilic disorders. Many biologic properties of the eosinophil are directed by T-helper lymphocytes, but the eosinophil interacts in many allergic or inflammatory processes with other cells, including mast cells and basophils, endothelial cells, macrophages, platelets, and fibroblasts.

The physiologic role of the eosinophil still remains unclear. It has been credited with a beneficial role in parasitic infestation, but this is now debated. Major advances have been made in recent years in the understanding of molecular and intracellular pathways regulating eosinophil priming, activation, and mediator secretion. However, a major obstacle in eosinophil research is the inability of murine eosinophils to degranulate either in vivo or in vitro, in contrast with human eosinophils, which differentially release their granule proteins after contact with different stimuli. There is in any case no doubt that the eosinophil plays a role in many inflammatory processes occurring in a variety of organs, and especially the respiratory tract. Because it has very characteristic morphology and staining properties, it is easy to detect in the tissues or biologic fluids.

Table 57.1 Classification of the Eosinophilic Lung Diseases

Eosinophilic Lung Disease of Undetermined Cause
Idiopathic eosinophilic pneumonias
    Idiopathic chronic eosinophilic pneumonia (ICEP)
    Idiopathic acute eosinophilic pneumonia (IAEP)
Churg-Strauss syndrome
Hypereosinophilic syndrome

Eosinophilic Lung Disease of Determined Cause
Eosinophilic pneumonias of parasitic origin
    Tropical eosinophilia
    Ascaris pneumonia
    Eosinophilic pneumonia in larva migrans syndrome
    Strongyloides stercoralis infection
    Eosinophilic pneumonias in other parasitic infections
Eosinophilic pneumonias of other infectious causes
Allergic bronchopulmonary aspergillosis and related syndromes
    Allergic bronchopulmonary aspergillosis
    Other allergic bronchopulmonary syndromes associated with
      fungi or yeasts
    Bronchocentric granulomatosis
Drug, toxic agents, and radiation-induced eosinophilic
    pneumonias
    Drugs (typical, occasional, or exceptional eosinophilic
      pneumonia)
    Toxic agents (toxic oil syndrome)
    Eosinophilic pneumonia induced by radiation therapy to the
      breast

**Miscellaneous Lung Diseases with Possible Associated
Eosinophilia**
Organizing pneumonia
Asthma and eosinophilic bronchitis
Idiopathic interstitial pneumonias
Langerhans cell granulomatosis
Lung transplantation
Other lung diseases with occasional eosinophilia
    Sarcoidosis
    Paraneoplastic eosinophilic pneumonia

EOSINOPHILIC PNEUMONIAS

CHARACTERISTICS

Reeder and Goodrich,[3] in 1952, published a series of cases of pulmonary "infiltration with eosinophilia," of which four were presented in detail. Two of these seem compatible with idiopathic chronic eosinophilic pneumonia (ICEP), and the other two patients probably had Churg-Strauss syndrome (CSS). Crofton and colleagues[4] published a series of 16 cases of "pulmonary eosinophilia" with a review of 450 cases from the literature, and proposed the following classification:

1. Simple pulmonary eosinophilia (Löffler's syndrome), defined by mild symptoms and transient infiltrates; the cause was mainly parasitic, but sulfonamides were mentioned as a possible cause.
2. Prolonged pulmonary eosinophilia characterized by radiographic shadows persisting for over a month; parasitic infestation and allergy were possible causes, but some cases were idiopathic.
3. Tropical eosinophilia.

4. Pulmonary eosinophilia with asthma, a rather heterogeneous category.
5. Polyarteritis nodosa.

The authors mentioned "a continuum from the simple and transient abnormalities of Löffler's syndrome to the severe and often fatal manifestations of polyarteritis nodosa." McCarthy and Pepys[5] reported 27 cases of "cryptogenic pulmonary eosinophilias" that they compared with cases of allergic bronchopulmonary aspergillosis (ABPA). Two patients with cryptogenic pulmonary eosinophilia developed systemic vasculitis.

Eosinophilic pneumonia is a pneumonia in which the eosinophils are the most prominent inflammatory cells on histopathologic examination. Other inflammatory cells, especially lymphocytes and neutrophils, are often associated, but eosinophils clearly predominate. The eosinophilic pneumonias manifest as either chronic, or acute or subacute syndromes, and in the vast majority of cases respond dramatically to corticosteroid treatment and heal without significant sequelae. In clinical practice, the eosinophilic pneumonias may be separated into two main categories: those for which a definite cause is found and those of undetermined origin (i.e., idiopathic, with the pneumonia being either solitary or included in a systemic syndrome such as CSS). A definite cause must be carefully investigated in any patient with eosinophilic pneumonia because it has practical consequences (e.g., stopping a drug responsible for iatrogenic eosinophilic pneumonia or treating a parasitic infection). When no cause is identified, the eosinophilic pneumonias may usually be included within well-characterized and individualized syndromes.

PATHOLOGY

Pathologic studies of eosinophilic pneumonia have mainly been done in patients with ICEP[6-8] that was initially diagnosed by open-lung biopsy. The pathologic features described in ICEP may be considered as the common denominator of all categories of eosinophilic pneumonias, whatever their origin. Occasional pathologic studies in eosinophilic pneumonias of determined origin have shown some additional specific features, such as a possible distinctive distribution of lesions (e.g., bronchocentric) or the presence of causal agents such as parasites or fungal hyphae.

In ICEP, the alveolar spaces are filled with eosinophils (Fig. 57.1). Macrophages are also present with some multinucleated giant cells scattered in the infiltrate; these may contain eosinophilic granules or Charcot-Leyden crystals.[6] A proteinaceous and fibrinous exudate accompanies the cellular eosinophilic infiltrate. Some eosinophilic microabscesses may be observed (foci of necrotic intra-alveolar eosinophils surrounded by macrophages or epithelioid cells with palisading arrangement). Morphologic (especially electron microscopic) as well as immunohistochemical studies have shown eosinophil degranulation within the site of eosinophilic pneumonia.[9] An associated interstitial inflammatory cellular infiltrate is invariably present, consisting of eosinophils, lymphocytes, plasma cells, and histiocytes. The global architecture of the lung remains intact, without necrosis or fibrosis.

A mild vasculitis involving both small arteries and venules is common, with perivascular cuffing and a few cells

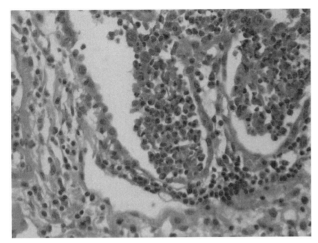

Figure 57.1 Eosinophilic pneumonia. Accumulation of eosinophils within the alveolar lumen. (Courtesy of Françoise Thivolet-Béjui, MD, Department of Pathology, Louis-Pradel Hospital and Claude Bernard University, Lyon.) *See Color Plate*

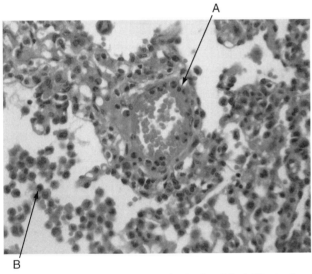

Figure 57.2 Eosinophilic pneumonia. Eosinophils infiltrate the arteriolar wall (non-necrotizing vasculitis) **(A)** and are present within the alveolar lumen **(B)**. (Courtesy of Françoise Thivolet-Béjui, MD, Department of Pathology, Louis-Pradel Hospital and Claude Bernard University, Lyon.) *See Color Plate*

infiltrating the arterial media. In simple eosinophilic pneumonia, this vasculitis is *non-necrotizing* (Fig. 57.2).

Organization of the alveolar inflammatory exudate is a rather common finding, well identified in the early reported cases of ICEP.[6] Bronchiolitis obliterans of the proliferative type may be associated. These pathologic findings suggest some possible overlap between ICEP and bronchiolitis obliterans with organizing pneumonia (OP). However, intraluminal organization of the distal air spaces is only sparse and never prominent in ICEP. Mucus plugs obstructing the small airways may be present in ICEP.[6]

The distribution of eosinophilic pneumonia is generally diffuse. However, it may be more focal in some cases, and the lesions may have an angiocentric or bronchiolocentric

distribution in some etiologic groups of eosinophilic pneumonia. The hilar lymph nodes associated with ICEP contain many eosinophils, and lymphoid hyperplasia is present.[6] In idiopathic acute eosinophilic pneumonia (IAEP), the pathologic pattern includes intra-alveolar and interstitial eosinophilic infiltrates, diffuse alveolar edema, intra-alveolar fibrinous exudates, organizing pneumonia, and non-necrotizing vasculitis.[10]

Although pathologic examination of the lung is the "gold standard" to define eosinophilic pneumonia, lung biopsy is seldom necessary in clinical practice. Transbronchial lung biopsy may show characteristic features of eosinophilic pneumonia, but the small size of the specimen usually does not allow morphologic evidence of an etiologic process. In especially complex cases, video-assisted thoracoscopic lung biopsy (which is a safe procedure) may be necessary.

DIAGNOSIS

The diagnosis of eosinophilic pneumonia requires both characteristic clinical-radiologic features (dyspnea with alveolar opacities at imaging) and the demonstration of eosinophilia (preferably in the lung, or in the peripheral blood). The eosinophilic pneumonias may manifest by different clinical-radiologic syndromes, namely Löffler's syndrome, ICEP, and IAEP.

Although it is usually safe, surgical lung biopsy in order to obtain a large piece of lung tissue is a relatively aggressive procedure. Thus, the diagnosis of eosinophilic pneumonia was and is still usually accepted when both radiographic pulmonary opacities and peripheral blood eosinophilia are present. For example, Löffler's syndrome as it occurs in ascariasis is defined by rather mild and nonspecific symptoms with cough and wheezes, transient pulmonary infiltrates, and blood eosinophilia. However, the finding of peripheral blood eosinophilia obviously does not prove that the observed pulmonary opacities correspond to eosinophilic pneumonia, and the lower limit of peripheral eosinophilia for a confident diagnosis of eosinophilic pneumonia is not established. Furthermore, in IAEP, peripheral blood eosinophilia is often absent at presentation. Diagnosing eosinophilic pneumonia solely on the finding of blood eosinophilia and pulmonary opacities therefore requires markedly elevated eosinophilia ($>1 \times 10^9/L$ and preferably $1.5 \times 10^9/L$) together with typical clinical-radiologic features.

Bronchoalveolar lavage (BAL) has become a widely accepted noninvasive surrogate of lung biopsy for the diagnosis of eosinophilic pneumonia, although no study has established a correlation between increased eosinophils at differential cell count and the finding of eosinophilic pneumonia at pathologic examination of the lung. In normal controls, BAL eosinophilia is lower than 1% of cells at differential count.[11] BAL eosinophilia of 3% or greater was found in 13.3% of a series of 1084 BAL examinations.[12] Values between 3% and 40% (and especially between 3% and 9%) were found in various conditions, including idiopathic pulmonary fibrosis, interstitial lung disease associated with connective tissue disorders, hypersensitivity pneumonitis, sarcoidosis, radiation pneumonitis, asthma, pneumoconioses, and infection. BAL eosinophilia greater than 40% was found mainly in patients with chronic eosinophilic pneumonia.

In our studies on ICEP, we chose a cutoff of 40% eosinophils or greater on BAL differential cell count for the diagnosis of ICEP.[13,14] The proposed cutoff for the diagnosis of IAEP was 25%.[15] For clinical practice, our recommendation is that a diagnosis of eosinophilic pneumonia is supported by alveolar eosinophilia when the eosinophils (1) are the predominant cell population (macrophages excepted) and (2) represent more than 25% and preferably 40% of the differential cell count.

EOSINOPHILIC LUNG DISEASE OF UNDETERMINED CAUSE

IDIOPATHIC EOSINOPHILIC PNEUMONIAS

The idiopathic eosinophilic pneumonias are described first because they represent an eosinophilic pulmonary disorder without associated manifestations specific for any etiologic agent. Idiopathic eosinophilic pneumonias may be either chronic or acute. ICEP is characterized by a progressive onset of symptoms within a few weeks with cough, increasing dyspnea, malaise, and weight loss. IAEP presents as an acute pneumonia (similar to acute lung injury or acute respiratory distress syndrome) with respiratory failure often necessitating mechanical ventilation.

Idiopathic Chronic Eosinophilic Pneumonia

Chronic eosinophilic pneumonia was individualized as a distinct entity by Carrington and colleagues,[6] who described a series of nine patients with detailed clinical, radiologic, physiologic, and pathologic data. This syndrome was further confirmed and detailed by several series[8,14,16–18] and case reports. ICEP occurs predominantly in women (with a 2:1 female-to-male ratio).[8,14] Although ICEP may occur in young people, only 6% of patients are less than 20 years old.[8,19] The incidence of ICEP peaks in the fifth decade, with a mean age of 45 years at diagnosis.[8,14] A majority of patients with ICEP are nonsmokers,[8,17] with only 4 of 62 (6.5%) smokers in our series,[14] suggesting that smoking might be protective.

A prior history of atopy is found in about half of the patients, with allergic rhinitis in 12% to 24%, drug allergy in about 10%, nasal polyps in 5% to 13%, urticaria in 10%, and eczema in 5%.[8,14] Prior asthma is present in up to two thirds of the patients.[7,8,13,14,17,18] Asthma may also occur concomitantly with the diagnosis of ICEP in 15% of patients, or develop after ICEP in 13%.[13] The presentation of ICEP is similar in asthmatics and nonasthmatics with the exception of higher total immunoglobulin (Ig) E in the former group.[13] ICEP may occur while asthmatic patients are on a desensitization program, but there is no proof that this may contribute to the development of ICEP. Asthma often gets worse after the occurrence of ICEP and requires long-term oral corticosteroid treatment.[13]

The onset of ICEP is progressive, with a mean interval between the onset of symptoms and the diagnosis of 4 months in a recent series.[14] The most common respiratory symptoms are cough, dyspnea, and chest pain.[8,14] Dyspnea is usually not severe, although the necessity for mechanical ventilation after several months of progression of disease has

occasionally been reported.[20] Hemoptysis occurs in about 10% of cases.[8,14] Wheezes at physical examination are found in one third of patients, and crackles in 38%.[8,14] Pleural effusion is uncommon and usually small when present. Upper respiratory tract symptoms of chronic rhinitis or sinusitis are present in about 20% of patients.[14] Systemic symptoms are often prominent, with fever and weight loss (10 kg or more in about 10%). Asthenia, malaise, fatigue, anorexia, weakness, and night sweats are also common.

The imaging features of ICEP are characteristic. Peripheral infiltrates on chest radiography are present in almost all cases[6,8,14,21–24] and are migratory in a quarter of the cases.[14] They usually consist of alveolar opacities with ill-defined margins, with a density varying from ground-glass to consolidation. The classic pattern of "photographic negative or reversal of the shadows usually seen in pulmonary edema" noted by Gaensler and Carrington[23] as evocative of ICEP is seen in only one fourth of patients.[8]

High-resolution computed tomography (CT) has further allowed description of the characteristic imaging features of ICEP. Whereas the opacities are bilateral in at least 50% of cases on chest radiographs, the proportion of bilateral opacities may increase up to 97.5% on high-resolution CT scans (Figs. 57.3 and 57.4).[8,14,17] The opacities predominate in the upper lobes[8,14,21] are characteristically peripheral, with generally coexisting ground-glass and consolidation opacities on high-resolution CT scans.[14,22,25] Consolidation with segmental or lobar atelectasis may be seen.[22] Septal line thickening is common.[25] Streaky or bandlike opacities parallel to the chest wall may also be present,[22] a finding also noted in cryptogenic organizing pneumonia. Upon corticosteroid treatment, consolidation and ground-glass

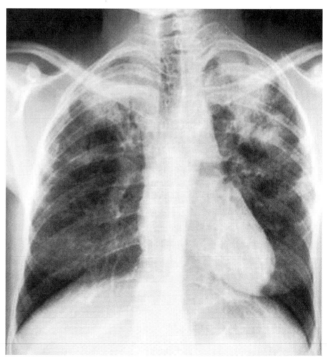

Figure 57.3 Chest radiograph of a patient with idiopathic chronic eosinophilic pneumonia showing bilateral alveolar opacities predominating in the upper lobes.

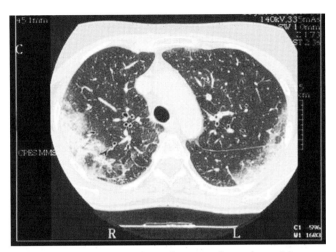

Figure 57.4 Computed tomography scan of a patient with idiopathic chronic eosinophilic pneumonia showing bilateral symmetrical peripheral alveolar opacities.

opacities rapidly show a decrease in size and extent, with possible change from consolidation to ground-glass opacities or inhomogeneous opacities, and later to streaky or bandlike opacities.[22] Cavitary lesions are extremely rare and should lead to reconsideration of the diagnosis. Small pleural effusions are present in up to 10% of cases and mediastinal lymph node enlargement in 17% of cases on high-resolution CT scans.[14]

Peripheral blood eosinophilia over 6% was present in 88% of 111 cases in the literature,[8] with a mean percentage of blood eosinophils at differential count of 26%. Because peripheral blood eosinophilia is often a diagnostic criterion of ICEP, the proportion of patients with ICEP and normal peripheral blood count is unknown. In our series (where ICEP was defined by blood eosinophilia $>1.0 \times 10^9/L$ or eosinophil percentage >40% at bronchoalveolar differential count, or both), the mean blood eosinophilia was $5.5 \times 10^9/L$, with eosinophils representing a mean of 32% of the total blood leukocyte count.[14]

Erythrocyte sedimentation rate is increased, with a mean value of about 60 mm at the first hour, and so is C-reactive protein.[8,14,17] Total blood IgE level is increased in about half of cases, and is greater than 1000 kU/L in 15%.[14] Circulating immune complexes have been reported in ICEP in about one third of patients.[14] Antinuclear antibodies may occasionally be present.[14] Markedly increased urinary eosinophil-derived neurotoxin level indicating active eosinophil degranulation is found in patients with ICEP.[26]

BAL has progressively become a major diagnostic procedure in ICEP, replacing lung biopsy. Alveolar eosinophilia is a characteristic feature in ICEP, with a mean of 58% at differential cell count.[14,27] Alveolar eosinophilia may be associated with an increased percentage of neutrophils, mast cells, and lymphocytes.[14] BAL eosinophil count drops with corticosteroid treatment.[28] Sputum eosinophilia has been reported in ICEP.[4,18] BAL eosinophils of patients with ICEP show activation features such as the release of eosinophil proteins, which are taken up by macrophages.[29] Eosinophil cationic protein and eosinophil-derived neurotoxin are increased in BAL fluid of patients with ICEP.[30] Expression

of human leukocyte antigen HLA-DR in a patient with ICEP was present on 86% of alveolar eosinophils in contrast to 7% of blood eosinophils, suggesting compartmentalization of eosinophilic activation within the lung.[31] BAL lymphocytes are characterized by an accumulation of CD4+ T cells[32] that express activation surface antigens of memory T cells (CD45RO+, CD45RA−, and CD62L−).

Manifestations outside the respiratory tract have been occasionally reported, including arthralgias, repolarization (ST-T) abnormalities on the electrocardiogram, pericarditis, altered liver function tests, eosinophilic lesions at liver biopsy, mononeuritis multiplex, diarrhea, skin nodule, immune complex vasculitis in the skin, and eosinophilic enteritis.[6,14,33] Such patients with ICEP and extrapulmonary manifestations may indeed have a disorder overlapping with systemic eosinophilic disorders, especially CSS. Furthermore, these patients often receive corticosteroid treatment, which may prevent the development of overt systemic vasculitis. In a series of ICEP patients with a high frequency of extrapulmonary signs (30%), some of which were quite evocative of CSS (especially the neurologic signs), none of the patients treated with corticosteroids developed characteristic CSS or the idiopathic hypereosinophilic syndrome on follow-up.[33] However ICEP may be a presenting feature of CSS.[34,35]

Lung function tests in ICEP show an obstructive ventilatory defect in about half the patients and a restrictive ventilatory defect in half the cases.[8,14] Hypoxemia defined by an arterial PO_2 of 75 mm Hg or less was present in 64% of patients in a series,[14] and a reduced carbon monoxide diffusing capacity, or DL_{CO} (defined as less than 80% of predicted) was present in 52%, with a reduced transfer coefficient or DL_{CO}/VA (defined as less than 80% of predicted) in only 27%. An increased alveolar-arterial oxygen gradient has been reported in 90% of cases.[8] The impaired lung function tests normalize under treatment in most patients.[8] However, a ventilatory obstructive defect may develop in some patients, especially those with a markedly increased BAL eosinophilia at initial evaluation.[36]

The natural course of untreated ICEP is not well known. Spontaneous resolution may occur,[8,14] and death resulting from ICEP seems extremely rare. The dramatic response of ICEP to corticosteroids was observed shortly after these drugs became available.[8] Symptoms improve within 1 or 2 weeks, and even within 48 hours in about 80% of cases.[14] The optimal dose of corticosteroids is not established, but the usual doses vary between 20 and 60 mg/day. Our current recommendation is to start with 0.5 mg/kg/day of prednisone. Pulmonary opacities on chest radiography clear rapidly. They disappeared within 1 week in 69% of patients in our series of patients treated with a mean initial dose of 1 mg/kg/day.[14] Almost all patients with ICEP treated by corticosteroids have a normal chest radiograph at their last follow-up visit.[14] Most patients require prolonged treatment (i.e., more than 6 months) because of relapse while decreasing or after stopping the corticosteroid treatment. In one series, recurrence occurred in 58% of cases after corticosteroids had been discontinued, and in 21% while the corticosteroids being tapered.[8] In our series, relapses occurred in half of the patients after the corticosteroids had been weaned (with a mean time between weaning and relapse of 72 weeks) or were being tapered (the mean dose of corticosteroids at the time of relapse was 11 mg/day).[14] Relapses, which may occur in the same areas of the lungs or in different areas,[14] respond very well to corticosteroid treatment. The series in which follow-up is available clearly show that most patients need prolonged corticosteroid treatment. In our series with a mean 6.2 years of follow-up, only 31% were weaned at last follow-up visit.[14] Inhaled corticosteroids may help in reducing the maintenance oral corticosteroid dose in ICEP, and relapses of ICEP are less frequent in patients with a previous history of asthma, possibly because they receive inhaled corticosteroids after stopping oral corticosteroids.[13,14]

Idiopathic Acute Eosinophilic Pneumonia

IAEP[10,15,18,37-40] differs from ICEP mainly by its acute onset, the severity of hypoxemia, the usual lack of increased blood eosinophils at presentation contrasting with a frank eosinophilic alveolitis on BAL differential cell count, and the absence of relapse after recovery. The following diagnostic criteria for IAEP have been proposed[15]: (1) acute onset (onset of any symptoms within 7 days before presentation); (2) fever; (3) bilateral infiltrates on chest radiograph; (4) severe hypoxemia (arterial PO_2 on room air ≤ 60 mm Hg, oxygen saturation on room air <90%, or alveolar-arterial oxygen gradient >40 mm Hg); (5) lung eosinophilia (BAL differential cell count with $\geq 25\%$ eosinophils or predominance of eosinophils in open-lung biopsy); and (6) no history of hypersensitivity to drugs, no historical or laboratory evidence of infection, and no other known cause of acute eosinophilic lung disease.

The average age at presentation is about 30 years in the largest series; several reported patients were 20 years old or younger, but IAEP also occurs in older patients, up to 86 years old in our series.[15,19,40] In contrast to ICEP, there is male predominance and no prior asthma history is found, although some patients may have a history of atopy.[18] Some patients had peculiar outdoor activities within the days before onset of disease, such as cave exploration, plant repotting, moving a woodpile, cleaning a smokehouse, or motocross racing in dusty conditions.[15] Four patients from our series[40] had been exposed to dust from indoor renovation work (two patients), gasoline tank cleaning, and the explosion of a tear gas bomb. One case was reported in a New York City firefighter exposed to World Trade Center dust (containing asbestos fibers, fly ash, and large-particle-size silicates, which were found in BAL cells).[41] The causative role of cigarette smoke has been discussed, as IAEP has developed soon after the initiation of smoking (especially when starting with large quantities) in some patients, and challenge with cigarette smoking was positive in some of them, but tolerance may develop in patients who resume smoking.[43-47] Whether the cigarette smoke is really a specific cause in such cases of IAEP is unknown. Given the high frequency of smoking or inhaling a variety of dusts and the rarity of IAEP, a direct causative role is unlikely. However, inhalation of smoke or of any nonspecific injurious agent may initiate or contribute to the development of IAEP in individuals intrinsically prone to develop eosinophilic reactions to nonspecific causative agents. Increased levels of $\beta(1 \rightarrow 3)$-D-glucan (a major component of the cell wall of most fungi and also one of the compo-

nents of cigarette smoke) have been reported in BAL fluid of patients with IAEP.[46]

IAEP occurs acutely in previously healthy individuals, with symptoms at presentation consisting of cough, dyspnea, fever, and chest pain. Abdominal complaints and also myalgias have been mentioned.[15] At physical examination, tachypnea and tachycardia are present, with crackles or less often wheezes on auscultation. No clinical difference has been found between patients seen in a time interval of less than 7 days or of 7 to 31 days from the first symptoms to the diagnosis of IAEP, suggesting that the diagnostic criterion of onset of any symptoms within 1 week may not be appropriate.[40] Five patients in another series also had symptom duration of longer than 7 days.[10]

Chest radiography shows bilateral infiltrates, with mixed alveolar or interstitial opacities.[15,38-40] Bilateral pleural effusion and Kerley's B lines are common.[15] Within 3 weeks the chest radiograph returns to normal,[15,38] with pleural effusions being the last abnormality to disappear.[15] At CT imaging, ground-glass opacities and air space consolidation are the most common patterns of parenchymal lesions. Poorly defined nodules and interlobular septal thickening are seen in a majority of patients; pleural effusion, present in at least two thirds of patients, is usually bilateral.[15,24,38]

White blood cell count at presentation usually shows increased leukocytosis with a predominance of neutrophils. Notably, eosinophils are only rarely higher than $0.3 \times 10^9/L$, but the eosinophil count may rise to high values during the course of disease.[15,18,40,47] Given the usual lack of initial blood eosinophilia, BAL is the key to the diagnosis of IAEP, showing an average percentage of 37% to 54% eosinophils at differential cell count.[15,40,47] After recovery, eosinophilia on BAL differential cell count may persist for several weeks.[48] We consider that the finding of eosinophilia greater than 25% on BAL differential cell count may obviate lung biopsy, at least in nonimmunocompromised patients. When pleural effusion is present, the pleural fluid differential cell count shows eosinophilia.[15,43,49] Eosinophilia was found in the sputum of six of nine patients with eosinophilic pneumonia.[18] The IgE level is raised in some patients.[49]

Hypoxemia may be severe and refractory to breathing 100% oxygen in some patients.[37,40] A majority of patients fit the definition of acute lung injury (ALI), a pulmonary disorder characterized by an acute onset, bilateral infiltrates on chest radiography, pulmonary artery wedge pressure ≤ 18 mm Hg when measured, or no evidence of left atrial hypertension, and an alveolar PO_2/FIO_2 (≤ 300 mm Hg) or the definition of acute respiratory distress syndrome (patients with ALI and with alveolar $PO_2/FIO_2 \leq 200$ mm Hg). Mechanical ventilation, either noninvasive or with intratracheal intubation, is necessary in a majority of patients.[15,40,47] In contrast, with ALI or acute respiratory distress syndrome, shock is exceptional[50,51] and extrapulmonary organ failure does not occur. FIO_2 may be decreased within a few hours of steroid treatment in many patients initially requiring oxygen.[15] When done, lung function tests have shown a mild restrictive ventilatory defect with normal FEV_1/FVC ratio and reduced DL_{CO}.[49] Alveolar-arterial oxygen gradient is increased.[15] Lung function tests performed after recovery are normal in most patients, with possible ventilatory restriction in some of them.[15,52,53]

Table 57.2 Diagnostic Criteria for Idiopathic Acute Eosinophilic Pneumonia

1. Acute onset of febrile respiratory manifestations (≤1 month duration before consultation)

2. Bilateral diffuse infiltrates on chest radiography

3. Hypoxemia, with Pao$_2$ on room air less than 60 mm Hg, and/or Pao$_2$/FIo$_2$ less than or equal to 300 mm Hg, and/or oxygen saturation on room air less than 90%

4. Lung eosinophilia, with greater than 25% eosinophils on bronchoalveolar lavage fluid differential cell count (or eosinophilic pneumonia at lung biopsy)

5. Absence of infection, or of other known causes of eosinophilic lung disease (especially exposure to drug known to induce pulmonary eosinophilia)

Adapted from references 10, 15, 40.

When performed, lung biopsy shows acute and organizing diffuse alveolar damage together with interstitial alveolar and bronchiolar infiltration by eosinophils, intra-alveolar eosinophils, and interstitial edema.[10,15,50] Recovery without corticosteroid treatment occurred in 6 of 22 patients in our series,[40] demonstrating that improvement concomitant with corticosteroid treatment cannot be considered a diagnostic criterion of IAEP. However, when a diagnosis of IAEP is made, corticosteroid treatment is usually started with intravenous methylprednisolone and later changed to oral therapy, which can be tapered over 2 to 4 weeks.[15] The response to corticosteroids occurs within 48 hours, allowing rapid weaning from the ventilator. Recovery is rapid with no significant clinical or imaging sequelae, and no relapse occurs after stopping corticosteroid treatment, in contrast with ICEP. Death is exceptional.[47]

We propose modified diagnostic criteria for IAEP (Table 57.2). Although IAEP often presents clinically like ALI or acute respiratory distress syndrome, its prognosis is much better. The key to the diagnosis is eosinophilia on BAL differential cell count, because blood eosinophilia is usually absent initially. In typical cases, we consider that lung biopsy is unnecessary, but a careful search for a cause of acute eosinophilic pneumonia is mandatory, and infectious agents must especially be sought for in BAL fluid by cultures and appropriate staining. Drug-induced AEP must also be carefully excluded.

CHURG-STRAUSS SYNDROME

Although a subgroup of patients with periarteritis (polyarteritis) nodosa and associated asthma and eosinophilia had been previously characterized, Churg and Strauss described in 1951 the eponymous syndrome, mainly from autopsied cases.[54] They described characteristic pathologic features consisting of granulomatous extravascular lesions as well as necrotizing, inflammatory, and granulomatous vascular changes, with an inflammatory exudate rich in eosinophils. The most frequent site of inflammation was the heart. In approximately half of the cases a pneumonic process was found, with an eosinophil-rich exudate mixed with giant cells in the acute stage.

In the Chapel Hill Consensus Conference on the Nomenclature of Systemic Vasculitis,[55] CSS was included in the group of small vessel vasculitides, and defined as an eosinophil-rich and granulomatous inflammation involving the respiratory tract, and necrotizing vasculitis affecting small to medium-sized vessels, and associated with asthma and eosinophilia.

The pathologic lesions of CSS currently observed[56,57] include both vasculitis (necrotizing or not, involving mainly the medium-sized pulmonary arteries) and granulomatous eosinophilic tissue infiltration. The extravascular granuloma consists of palisading histiocytes and giant cells. However, all of these features are seldom found on a single biopsy in one organ. When present, the eosinophilic pneumonia in CSS is similar to ICEP. The early (prevasculitic) phase of CSS is characterized by eosinophilic infiltration of the tissues without vasculitis (perivascular eosinophils are commonly found).

The clinical features of CSS have been well defined.[58–63] It is a very rare vasculitis, which occurs especially in adults younger than 65,[62,64] although it has occasionally been reported in children and adolescents. There is no sex predominance. The mean age of onset of vasculitis ranges from 38 to 49 years.[62,65]

Asthma, generally severe and becoming rapidly corticodependent, occurs at a mean age of about 35.[62] It usually precedes the onset of vasculitis by 3 to 9 years.[58,62,65,66] The interval between asthma and the onset of vasculitis may be much longer, or they may be contemporary.[65,66] The severity of asthma usually increases progressively until the vasculitis develops, but it may attenuate when the vasculitis flourishes and further increase when the vasculitis recedes.[62,66]

Pulmonary infiltrates represent the most typical abnormalities on chest radiography and have been reported in large series with a frequency of 37% to 72%.[58,62] The pulmonary infiltrates are usually noted at presentation, but may never develop throughout follow-up in other patients. The chest radiograph may be normal throughout the course of the disease. The pulmonary infiltrates usually consist of ill-defined opacities (Fig. 57.5), sometimes migratory, transient, and of varying density.[62,66–68] In contrast to Wegener's granulomatosis, pulmonary cavitary lesions are exceptional. Pleural effusion (usually mild) and phrenic nerve palsy may be observed. The pulmonary opacities on thin-section CT mainly consist of areas of ground-glass attenuation or air space consolidation, with peripheral predominance or random distribution (Fig. 57.6); less common findings include centrilobular nodules, bronchial wall thickening or dilation, interlobular septal thickening, hilar or mediastinal lymphadenopathy, and pleural effusion or pericardial effusion.[24,68,69] Because these abnormalities are nonspecific, a correct diagnosis of CSS was made on CT in only 44% of 111 patients with eosinophilic lung diseases.[24]

Rhinitis, present in about three quarters of cases of CSS,[62,70] is generally of the allergic type, and is often accompanied by relapsing sinusitis or polyps, or both. Paranasal sinusitis has been reported in 61% of patients.[58] Crusty rhinitis may be present. The rhinitis in CSS is distinctly much less severe than in Wegener's granulomatosis, with septal nasal perforation or nasal deformation being exceptional.

Blood eosinophilia is a major feature of CSS and usually parallels the vasculitis activity. Blood eosinophil levels are generally between 5 and $20 \times 10^9/L$, but they may reach higher values.[58,62,66] Blood eosinophilia often disappears dramatically after the initiation of corticosteroid treatment; thus, there may be an absence of eosinophilia if blood tests are not done before starting corticosteroid treatment. Eosinophilia, sometimes greater than 60%, is found on BAL differential cell count.[71] Eosinophilia (generally greater than 60% of the cells) is present in the pleural effusions.[72]

CSS is one of the pulmonary antineutrophil cytoplasmic antibody (ANCA)–associated vasculitides, together with Wegener's granulomatosis and microscopic polyangiitis.

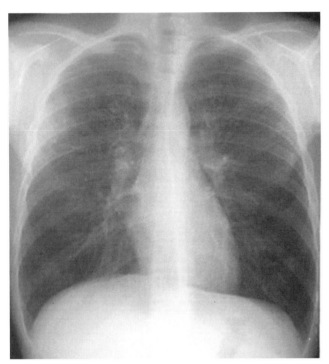

Figure 57.5 Chest radiograph of a patient with Churg-Strauss syndrome showing a right upper lobe opacity.

ANCAs have been reported in 48% to 73% of patients.[58,65] ANCAs are mainly perinuclear (p-ANCA) with myeloperoxidase specificity, and much less often cytoplasmic (c-ANCA) with proteinase-3 specificity.[58,65] IgE levels are usually markedly increased. The erythrocyte sedimentation rate is increased, and anemia is common. High levels of urinary eosinophil-derived neurotoxin have been reported, and these might represent an activity index of disease.[73]

Asthenia, weight loss, fever, arthralgias, and myalgias (all of which are unusual in simple asthma) often herald the development of the extrapulmonary manifestations of vasculitis.

Peripheral neurologic involvement mainly consists of mononeuritis multiplex, present in 77% of patients,[58] or asymmetrical polyneuropathy, whereas cranial nerve palsies and central nervous system involvement are less common. Heart damage, which may be severe and lead to death,[58,62,63,65,66] results from eosinophilic myocarditis, coronary arteritis, or both. Cardiac involvement is often insidious and asymptomatic, and thus may be recognized only when left ventricular failure and dilated cardiomyopathy have developed. Heart failure may require heart transplantation, but recurrence of eosinophilic vasculitis is possible in the transplanted heart. However, myocardial impairment as well as coronary arteritis may markedly improve with corticosteroid treatment, thus necessitating a strict cardiac evaluation in any patient with suspected CSS. Pericarditis with limited effusion is common in CSS; occasionally pericardial effusion may be more important and give rise to tamponade. In contrast with the idiopathic hypereosinophilic syndrome, endomyocardial involvement is not a common feature.

Digestive tract involvement, present in 31% of cases,[58] usually manifests as isolated abdominal pain, but intestinal or biliary tract vasculitis may be present. Other digestive manifestations include diarrhea, ulcerative colitis, gastroduodenal ulcerations, perforations (esophageal, gastric, and intestinal), digestive hemorrhage, and cholecystitis. Cutaneous lesions, present in about half of patients,[58] mainly

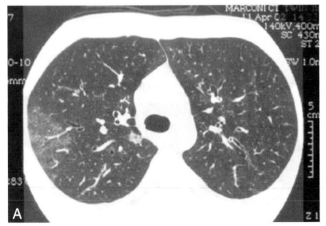

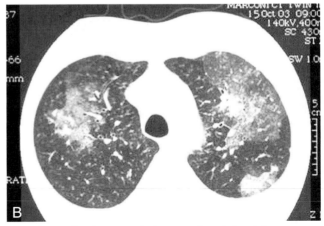

Figure 57.6 Computed tomography scan of patients with Churg-Strauss syndrome showing ground-glass opacity of the right upper lobe (**A**), and bilateral central and peripheral opacities with varying density (**B**).

consist of palpable purpura of the extremities, subcutaneous nodules (especially of the scalp and extremities), erythematous rashes, and urticaria; biopsy of the cutaneous lesions is the most common and simple procedure to obtain pathologic evidence of vasculitis. Renal involvement, present in 26% of cases, is usually mild.[58]

CSS is considered an autoimmune process involving T cells, endothelial cells, and eosinophils. Some triggering or adjuvant factors (such as vaccines or desensitization) have been suspected.[74,75] The possible role of allergy is debated, because a family history of atopy is common, and allergic rhinitis is present in many patients with CSS. Other possible triggering factors include *Aspergillus,* allergic bronchopulmonary candidiasis, *Ascaris,* bird exposure, and cocaine. Drug-induced eosinophilic vasculitis with pulmonary involvement has been reported in the past with sulfonamides used together with antiserum, and later with diflunisal,[76] macrolides,[77] and diphenylhydantoin.[78] The possible responsibility of leukotriene receptor antagonists (e.g., montelukast, zafirlukast, pranlukast) in the development of CSS has generated much debate.[65,79] Whether the association is coincidental, whether some cases of smoldering CSS flare because of reducing oral or inhaled corticosteroids and/or adding leukotriene receptor antagonists, or whether these drugs really exert a role on the pathogenesis of the vasculitis is not established at the time of writing. In any case, we consider that leukotriene receptor antagonists should be avoided in any asthma patient with eosinophilia or extrapulmonary manifestations compatible with smoldering CSS.

The diagnosis of CSS may be difficult, because the clinician is often faced with patients presenting with early and mild signs corresponding to the so-called *formes frustes* of CSS, which are more or less suppressed by corticosteroid treatment for asthma and which may later be unmasked, especially when treatment is reduced or stopped. The evolution of CSS usually proceeds through three stages: asthma and rhinitis; tissue eosinophilia (such as a pulmonary disease resembling ICEP); and then extrapulmonary eosinophilic disease with vasculitis. Diagnostic difficulties thus largely depend on the stage of disease when the patient is seen, and it is extremely important that the diagnosis of CSS be considered and established before severe organ involvement (especially cardiac) is present.

There are currently no established diagnostic criteria for CSS. Lanham and colleagues[62] proposed three diagnostic criteria: (1) asthma; (2) eosinophilia exceeding 1.5×10^9/L; and (3) systemic vasculitis of two or more extrapulmonary organs. According to the classification criteria (which are not *diagnostic* criteria, however) of the American College of Rheumatology,[80] a sensitivity of 85% and a specificity of 99.7% are obtained if four or more of the following six criteria are present in a patient with proven systemic vasculitis: asthma; eosinophilia greater than 10% at differential blood cell count; mononeuritis (including multiplex) or polyneuropathy; fluctuating infiltrates on chest radiography; bilateral maxillary sinus abnormalities; and presence of extravascular eosinophils on a biopsy comprising a vessel. However, these diagnostic and classification criteria were proposed before testing ANCAs became available; the presence of ANCAs may be considered a major diagnostic criterion. A pathologic diagnosis of CSS is desirable, but not

mandatory in most cases. The skin, nerve, and muscle are the most common sites where a pathologic diagnosis of vasculitis may be obtained.[58] Lung biopsy is seldom done. Transbronchial biopsies usually do not show vasculitis or granulomas.

The borders separating CSS from the other ANCA-associated vasculitides and the other eosinophilic syndromes are sometimes difficult to establish. An eosinophilic variant of Wegener's granulomatosis has been described.[81] Concurrent CSS and pulmonary infiltrates and temporal arteritis (either with or without giant cells, either eosinophilic or not) has been described.[82] Distinguishing between mild CSS and ICEP with minor extrathoracic symptoms may also be difficult. Some mild vasculitis (non-necrotizing) is common on pathologic examination of the lung in patients with ICEP.[6] ICEP may further progress to CSS.[34] In addition, some cases of "limited" CSS have been reported,[83] including those solely involving the lung or the heart. "Formes frustes" of CSS often consist of cases in which the disease has been controlled to a greater or lesser extent by corticosteroids given for asthma. Other cases are difficult to classify as either CSS or idiopathic hypereosinophilic syndrome. Careful clinical analysis, the presence of ANCAs, the finding of a vasculitis and granulomas on biopsy, and molecular biologic analysis (in the cases of hypereosinophilic syndrome) help in determining the final diagnosis.

Corticosteroids are clearly the mainstay of treatment of CSS, and suffice in a large number of cases.[62,84,85] An initial methylprednisolone bolus is useful in the most severe cases; then oral treatment is started, usually with 1 mg/kg/day of prednisone. Treatment is prolonged for several months with progressive reduction of doses. Relapses are common, and asthma often persists (or reappears if it had disappeared during high-dose corticosteroid treatment). Distinguishing relapse or persistence of simple asthma from relapse or persistence of vasculitis requires very precise evaluation, taking into account the levels of blood eosinophils (generally $<1 \times 10^9$ in asthma without CSS relapse). Treatment with corticosteroids alone should be reserved for patients without manifestations that could result in mortality or severe morbidity.[86] A retrospective study of patients with either polyarteritis nodosa or CSS[84] identified parameters with significant prognostic value and responsible for higher mortality: proteinuria greater than 1 g/day, renal insufficiency with serum creatinine greater than 15.8 mg/L, and gastrointestinal tract involvement. Cardiomyopathy and central nervous system involvement were associated with a relative risk of mortality of 2.2 and 1.8, respectively (not statistically significant). The addition of immunosuppressive agents to corticosteroids improved disease control, despite associated infections (which could be decreased by using bolus instead of oral cyclophosphamide administration).[87,88] Mortality was associated with disease severity, and treatment with cytotoxic agents did not prevent relapses.[89] Corticosteroid treatment alone for CSS patients without poor prognostic factors at onset is efficient, with about half of the patients achieving complete remission without relapse.[90] In patients with mild or severe relapses, or in patients with poor prognostic factors at onset, immunosuppressive treatment (such as azathioprine or cyclophosphamide) in addition to corticosteroids is warranted. Subcutaneous interferon-alpha has been successfully used mainly in CSS patients with severe disease.[91] High-dose intravenous immunoglobulins and cyclosporin have been occasionally used successfully.

The prognosis of CSS has considerably improved over time, with 79% of patients alive at 5 years.[84] In one series CSS did not appear to confer increased mortality, a rather surprising finding.[65]

HYPEREOSINOPHILIC SYNDROME

The definition of the "idiopathic" hypereosinophilic syndrome (HES) proposed by Chusid and colleagues[92] in 1975 was as follows: (1) a persistent eosinophilia greater than 1.5×10^9/L for longer than 6 months, or death before 6 months associated with the signs and symptoms of hypereosinophilic disease; (2) a lack of evidence for parasitic, allergic, or other known causes of eosinophilia; and (3) presumptive signs and symptoms of organ involvement, including hepatosplenomegaly, organic heart murmur, congestive heart failure, diffuse or focal central nervous system abnormalities, pulmonary fibrosis, fever, weight loss, and anemia. The 14 cases they reported[92] included 2 patients with "prolonged benign hypereosinophilia," 3 with eosinophilic leukemia, and 1 with possible CSS. The later published cases of idiopathic HES also proved heterogeneous, although patients with typical chronic disease shared common complications, especially cardiac involvement.

In contrast with common hypereosinophilia, which is in most cases a reactive nonclonal process (as in parasitic disorders), recent studies demonstrated that HES may result from a clonal proliferation of lymphocytes producing eosinophilopoietic chemokines, or from the clonal proliferation of the eosinophils themselves,[93–98] so that the term *idiopathic* might be abandoned in the classification of HES.[99]

The "lymphocytic variant" of HES results from the production of chemokines (especially interleukin-5) by clonal type 2 T helper lymphocytes (as demonstrated by clonal rearrangement of the T-cell receptor) bearing an aberrant immunologic phenotype (CD3−,CD4+), leading to the accumulation of eosinophils. Serum levels of IgE are elevated.[99–101] The majority of patients were recruited from dermatology clinics and had papules or urticarial plaques infiltrated by lymphocytes and eosinophils (and in some of them a cutaneous T-cell lymphoma or Sézary syndrome was ultimately present). In such cases HES may be considered as a (pre)malignant T-cell disorder.[100–102]

The "myeloproliferative variant" of HES has been recently attributed to a constitutively activated tyrosine kinase fusion protein created by fusion of FIP1L1–PDGFR-α as a consequence of an interstitial chromosomal deletion of a region in the long arm of chromosome 4 (q12) not detectable by karyotype analysis.[103,104] This fusion protein transforms hematopoietic cells and is inhibited by imatinib, a 2-phenylaminopyrimidine–based tyrosine kinase inhibitor originally used to treat chronic myelogenous leukemia. Imatinib proved effective in the treatment of chronic myeloproliferative diseases and gastrointestinal stromal tumors (also characterized by aberrant constitutively activated tyrosine kinases). Imatinib also proved effective for several months in treating HES in patients with disease refractory to corticosteroids, hydroxyurea, and interferon-alpha. Relapse occurred in one case due to a mutation in *PDGFRA*

conferring resistance to imatinib (thus demonstrating that the FIP1L1–PDGFR-α fusion protein is the target of imatinib).

The pulmonary involvement in patients with eosinophilia of clonal origin has not been studied extensively, and especially has not been examined in cases classified as one of the previously mentioned variants. However, lung or pleural involvement has been mentioned in some cases[100,101,105] in patients with clonal lymphoid proliferations. The following data are derived from older studies may therefore need reconsideration in the future.

HES is more common in men than in women (9:1), and occurs at ages between 20 and 50 years.[106] The onset is generally insidious, with eosinophilia discovered incidentally in 12% of the patients.[107] The mean eosinophil count at presentation was 20.1×10^9/L, with an average highest value of 44.4×10^9/L in one series.[108] Extremely high values of eosinophilia, in excess of 100×10^9/L, are found in some patients.[92] The main presenting symptoms are weakness and fatigue (26%), cough (24%), and dyspnea (16%).[107] Cardiovascular involvement, present in 58% of the patients,[106] is a major cause of morbidity and mortality. Fibrotic thickening of the endocardium by collagen-rich connective tissue (endomyocardial fibrosis) is characteristic of cardiac disease in HES,[107,109] which differs from the cardiac involvement seen in CSS. Endomyocardial fibrosis is preceded by an initial acute necrotic stage followed by a thrombotic process.[106] Cardiac manifestations include dyspnea, congestive heart failure, mitral regurgitation, and cardiomegaly.[107,110] Echocardiography demonstrates the classic features of HES, consisting of mural thrombus, ventricular apical obliteration, and involvement of the posterior mitral leaflet.[111] The other manifestations of HES[106] include neurologic manifestations (thromboemboli, central nervous system dysfunction, and peripheral neuropathies) and cutaneous manifestations (erythematous pruritic papules and nodules, urticaria, and angioedema).[106,112]

Pulmonary involvement is present in about 40% of patients[92,107] and includes pleural effusion, pulmonary emboli, cough, and interstitial infiltrates. Severe coughing attacks were present in 40% of the cases in one series,[108] with no other mention of bronchopulmonary disease. In another series,[110] cough was also the predominant feature, with bronchospasm and pulmonary infiltrates in 11 of 40 patients each. CT findings in five patients consisted of small nodules with or without a halo of ground-glass attenuation and focal areas of ground-glass attenuation mainly in the lung periphery.[113] CT findings are poorly specific, and a correct diagnosis was obtained in only one third of patients with the hypereosinophilic syndrome in a series of 111 patients with eosinophilic diseases.[24] Furthermore, some of the observed pulmonary imaging changes may correspond to pulmonary edema resulting from cardiac involvement, rather than genuine eosinophilic lung involvement.

Only mild eosinophilia on BAL differential cell count contrasting with high blood eosinophilia has been reported in patients with HES,[114,115] suggesting that eosinophilia may be compartmentalized in some patients with HES.

Less than half of the patients with HES respond well to corticosteroids as a first-line therapy.[110,116] Other treatments include chemotherapeutic agents (hydroxyurea, vincristine, and etoposide), cyclosporin,[106,108,116] and interferon-alpha either as monotherapy[117-120] or in association with hydroxyurea, particularly in the myeloproliferative variant.[121,122] Clearly imatinib has now become a most promising drug for a molecular targeted treatment in patients with the myeloproliferative variant of HES.

Whereas the 3-year survival was only 12% in the first published series,[92] the prognosis has improved markedly in later series, with about 70% survival at 10 years in one series,[107] and 80% survival at 5 years and 42% at 10 and 15 years in another.[110] It is fascinating that advances in gene molecular biology may result in direct clinical benefit with a better prognosis for patients with an up-to-now almost untreatable disease.

EOSINOPHILIC LUNG DISEASE OF DETERMINED CAUSE

EOSINOPHILIC PNEUMONIAS OF PARASITIC ORIGIN

Parasite infestation probably represents the most common cause of eosinophilic pneumonia in the world. Parasitic eosinophilic pneumonia in humans occurs mainly following infection by helminths (large multicellular worms) and especially nematodes (roundworms). The parasites may or may not be found at pathologic examination of the lung.

Tropical Eosinophilia

Tropical eosinophilia was first identified[123] as a syndrome characterized by severe spasmodic bronchitis, leukocytosis, and high blood eosinophilia. Patients develop a dry, hacking cough exacerbated at night (especially between 1 and 5 A.M.) and often associated with expiratory dyspnea and wheezing. Tropical pulmonary eosinophilia is one of the most common causes of cough in tropical areas with endemic filariasis.[124] Associated fever, loss of weight, and anorexia are common. Eosinophils, and sometimes Charcot-Leyden crystals, are present in the sputum. On chest radiography, disseminated bilateral opacities are present.

Tropical eosinophilia is caused by the filarial parasites *Wuchereria bancrofti* and *Brugia malayi*,[125,126] nematodes that infect more than 150 million persons in the world. The adult worms reside in the lymphatic vessels, leading to lymphatic obstruction with subsequent elephantiasis. Humans are infected by infective larvae deposited in the skin by mosquitoes. Within 6 to 12 months, the parasites develop into mature worms. First-stage larvae or microfilariae released from the fecund female's uterus circulate in the bloodstream, from where they are ingested by the mosquitoes. Human filariasis caused by *W. bancrofti* and *B. malayi* is endemic in the tropical and subtropical areas of coastal regions of Asia, the southern and western Pacific, and Africa; it is found less commonly in South and Central America.

Patients with tropical pulmonary eosinophilia do not usually have clinical features of lymphatic filariasis. Microfilariae are usually not found in the blood or the lung. The circulating microfilariae are trapped in the lung vasculature, where they release their antigenic constituents, further triggering the inflammatory pulmonary reaction. The clinical features of tropical pulmonary eosinophilia largely result from an immune response of the host to the parasites.[125,127,128]

Although blood eosinophilia is high in the early stage (less than 2 weeks) of pulmonary disease, no prominent eosinophilic infiltration is found in the lung. At this early stage, there is dense infiltration with histiocytes. Eosinophilic pneumonia occurs later (1 to 3 months), with the formation of eosinophilic abscesses and granulomatous lesions characterized by the presence of foreign-body giant cells, fibroblasts, and epithelioid cells; prominent eosinophilic infiltration is present at the periphery of the granuloma. Cases left untreated for 5 years or more eventually show pulmonary fibrosis with histiocytic infiltration.

The clinical manifestations of tropical pulmonary eosinophilia occur mainly in the second and third decades of life, with male predominance. It has been reported mostly in Indians. Tropical eosinophilia has been reported in a patient originating from India who had been living in Italy for 2 years.[129] Some patients may be misdiagnosed as having asthma, as occurred in a recent Asian immigrant to upstate New York.[130] Persisting irregular basilar opacities are present in about two thirds of patients after 1 year.[131] A "reticulonodular pattern" on chest CT has been reported in a majority of patients, with other features consisting of bronchiectasis, air trapping, and mediastinal lymphadenopathy.[132]

Blood eosinophilia is prominent, with more than 2×10^9 eosinophils per liter in all cases, and up to $60 \times 10^9/L$ in some cases.[133] IgE levels are increased.[134] Antifilarial IgG antibodies are increased, as in all patients with filariasis. BAL fluid in patients with tropical pulmonary eosinophilia shows an intense alveolitis, with a mean of 54% of eosinophils with marked degranulation.[135] Eosinophil-derived neurotoxin, a ribonuclease capable of damaging the lung epithelium, may play the most important role in the pathogenesis of pulmonary tropical eosinophilia, as suggested by selective high levels of this eosinophilic granular protein in BAL fluid.[136] In patients treated with diethylcarbamazine, BAL eosinophil counts drop within 2 weeks; blood eosinophils also decrease rapidly upon treatment.[135,137,138] Lung function tests show a restrictive ventilatory defect, with a reversible obstructive ventilatory defect and hypoxemia in about a quarter of the patients.[139,140]

Because microfilariae are not detectable in the blood, the diagnosis is made in patients with residence for several months in an endemic area by the combination of the clinical, epidemiologic, and laboratory features, including blood eosinophilia persisting for weeks with an absolute eosinophil count in the blood greater than $3 \times 10^9/L$, IgE levels exceeding 5000 kU/L, and markedly increased antifilarial IgG. Diagnosis is further supported by clinical improvement in the weeks following treatment.[126,133,141]

The current reexamined diagnostic criteria for tropical pulmonary eosinophilia include cough worse at night, residence in a filarial endemic area, eosinophil count greater than 3300 cells/μL, and clinical and hematologic response to diethylcarbamazine.[142] Diethylcarbamazine, which kills microfilariae and adult-stage worms, is the only effective drug for tropical pulmonary eosinophilia; corticosteroids in addition to diethylcarbamazine may be beneficial.[126]

Ascaris Pneumonia

Ascaris lumbricoides, a nematode or roundworm, is the most common helminth infecting humans,[143] especially children in the tropical and subtropical areas. Mature female worms in the human intestine release large numbers of eggs. The eggs expelled with stool may survive for several months or years. The disease is transmitted through food or water contaminated by human feces. The infective larvae formed within eggs develop in the small intestine, penetrate through the intestinal wall, and migrate via the venous circulation to the lungs, where they break out into the alveoli. They then migrate through the bronchi and trachea, are swallowed, and mature into adult worms in the small intestine.

Pulmonary manifestations occur during larval migration to the lungs. Pulmonary infiltrates with eosinophilia (Löffler's syndrome) may develop during the migration of the larvae of the parasite through the lung. Usually, pulmonary symptoms are mild, with cough and wheezing, transient pulmonary infiltrates, and blood eosinophilia. Transient fever is present in the majority of patients, with possible pruritic eruption at the time of respiratory symptoms. Blood eosinophilia may be as high as $22 \times 10^9/L$.[144] Symptoms spontaneously resolve in a few days, although blood eosinophilia may remain elevated for several weeks. Diagnosis may be obtained by the finding of larvae in the sputum or gastric aspirates, but is more usually made by the delayed finding of the worm or ova in the stool within 3 months of the pulmonary manifestations.[143]

Intestinal ascariasis is treated with mebendazole for 3 days, or pyrantel pamoate and albendazole.[143,145,146]

Eosinophilic Pneumonia in Larva Migrans Syndrome

Visceral larva migrans[147] is a zoonotic infection caused in humans by *Toxocara canis,* a parasite infecting many dogs and other canines. Toxocariasis occurs in all temperate and tropical areas of the world. Eggs released by female worms pass in feces of infected dogs, and the soil of public playgrounds in urban areas is therefore often contaminated with eggs of *Toxocara.* Children playing in contaminated areas may become infected, especially when they practice geophagia. Ingested eggs hatch in the intestine, migrate through the portal circulation, and invade the liver, lung, and other organs. However, in humans the development of the parasite is blocked at the larval stage.

Visceral larva migrans occurs predominantly in children, the majority of whom remain asymptomatic and undiagnosed. When symptomatic, patients can present with fever, pulmonary manifestations, seizures, or fatigue. Pulmonary manifestations occurring in about 80% of cases consist of cough, wheezes, and dyspnea; pulmonary infiltrates on chest radiography are present in approximately half the patients with pulmonary symptoms.[147,148] Severe pulmonary involvement, which occurs in about 17% of cases, may benefit from corticosteroids.[149]

Although uncommon in adults, toxocariasis is nevertheless a possible cause of pulmonary disease with eosinophilia, which may be severe[150,151] and necessitate mechanical ventilation. Patients present with fever, dyspnea, and pulmonary infiltrates on chest radiography. Wheezes or crackles are present at pulmonary auscultation. Blood eosinophilia may be present initially, or may develop only in the following days. Eosinophils are increased on BAL differential cell count. The diagnosis of toxocariasis is obtained by serologic methods, and especially by enzyme-linked immunosorbent assay. Visceral larva migrans usually requires only symptomatic treatment, the use of antihelmintics being controversial. Corticosteroids seem beneficial in cases with severe pulmonary involvement.[152]

Strongyloides stercoralis Infection

Strongyloides stercoralis is an intestinal nematode that may cause severe autoinfection in immunocompromised patients. Strongyloidiasis is widely distributed in the tropics and subtropics.[143] Human infection is acquired through the skin by contact with the soil of beaches or mud. Then larvae pass through the circulation to the lungs, where they break into alveoli, ascend the trachea, are swallowed, and reside in the small intestine, where they mature. Females deposit eggs that hatch into larvae, which pass with feces. Eosinophilia is usually present in recently infected patients, but it is often absent in disseminated disease.[153] *Strongyloides stercoralis* infection may persist for years and give rise thereafter to severe disseminated strongyloidiasis, which may affect all organs (hyperinfection syndrome), especially when immunosuppression from any cause occurs.

About 20% of hospitalized patients with strongyloidiasis have coexisting chronic lung disease.[154] Patients with chronic obstructive pulmonary disease or asthma receiving corticosteroids are therefore at risk of the hyperinfection syndrome. Löffler's syndrome occurs when larvae migrate through the lungs after acute infection. Peripheral blood eosinophilia in association with pneumonia, bronchospasm, or bronchitis and abdominal pain or diarrhea suggests strongyloidiasis in patients living, or having traveled, in endemic areas.

Massive larval infection of the lungs (hyperinfection syndrome) occurring in patients with immunosuppression manifests with fever, abdominal pain, ileus or small bowel obstruction, jaundice, or meningitis. Eosinophilia may or may not be present. Cough, wheezing, and dyspnea are associated with bilateral patchy infiltrates. Rhabditiform larvae may be recovered by BAL or bronchial washing[155,156] or in the sputum.[157]

Diagnosis of strongyloidiasis depends on the demonstration of larvae in the feces or in any secretion or tissue specimen (including sputum and BAL fluid). Immunodiagnostic assays by enzyme-linked immunosorbent assay methods may be useful for diagnosis and screening.[158] Because the risk of hyperinfection syndrome persists for years, all infected patients are treated with thiabendazole when diagnosed.[158]

Eosinophilic Pneumonias in Other Parasitic Infections

The dog hookworm *Ancylostoma braziliense,* causing cutaneous helminthiasis (creeping eruption), may produce, in 50% of cases, a typical Löffler's syndrome with transitory migratory pulmonary infiltration and peripheral eosinophilia, with almost complete absence of clinical signs or symptoms of systemic disease.[159] Pulmonary manifestations develop after the seventh day of cutaneous eruption. The human hookworms *Ancylostoma duodenale* and *Necator americanus* are other possible causes of Löffler's syndrome.

In early acute schistosomiasis (due to infection with either *Schistosoma haematobium* or *Schistosoma mansoni*), patients may develop transient multiple small pulmonary nodules on chest radiographs (best seen on CT scan) and eosinophilia.[160-162] In chronic schistosomiasis, embolization of ova in small arteries in the lungs results in granuloma formation, occlusion of pulmonary arteries, and further pulmonary hypertension. The granuloma comprises lymphocytes, eosinophils, and giant cells. A posttreatment eosinophilic pneumonitis (also called lung shift, verminous pneumonia, and reactionary Löffler-like pneumonitis) may develop.[163] It could result from parasitic antigen release following treatment.

The filarial parasite of dog, *Dirofilaria immitis* (the pulmonary fluke), may occasionally develop into adult worms in the human lung after inoculation of infective larvae by mosquitoes. It manifests mainly as solitary pulmonary nodules or masses with or without eosinophilia, but eosinophilic pulmonary infiltrates have been reported.[164,165]

Other parasites causing rare pulmonary manifestations with eosinophilia include *Paragonimus westermani*, *Trichomonas tenax*, *Capillaria aerophila*, and *Clonorchis sinensis*.

EOSINOPHILIC PNEUMONIAS OF OTHER INFECTIOUS CAUSES

Pulmonary infection with eosinophilia has been reported with the fungi *Coccidioides immitis*, *Bipolaris australiensis*, and *Bipolaris spicifera*. BAL eosinophilia has been reported in *Pneumocystis jiroveci* (formerly *carinii*) pneumonitis in patients with acquired immunodeficiency syndrome.[166] Bacterial or viral pulmonary infection (e.g., tuberculosis, brucellosis, respiratory syncytial virus infection) may occasionally be a cause of eosinophilic pneumonia.

ALLERGIC BRONCHOPULMONARY ASPERGILLOSIS AND RELATED SYNDROMES

Allergic Bronchopulmonary Aspergillosis

ABPA is distinct from the other pulmonary manifestations due to the fungus *Aspergillus*, such as invasive pulmonary aspergillosis occurring especially in immunocompromised patients, or aspergilloma developing in preexistent pulmonary cavities.[167-171] ABPA is characterized by asthma, eosinophilia, and bronchopulmonary manifestations with bronchiectasis secondary to a complex allergic and immune reaction to the presence of *Aspergillus* colonizing the airways. ABPA occurs mainly in adults with previous asthma present for several years (with a prevalence of 1% to 2%), but it is also a complication occurring in 2% to 7.8% of patients in large series of cystic fibrosis.[172,173] ABPA may be associated with allergic *Aspergillus* sinusitis,[174,175] which has been considered as a sinusal equivalent of ABPA,[175-180] resulting in a syndrome called sinobronchial allergic aspergillosis. ABPA may have an environmental (and especially occupational) dimension, as suggested by a study of workers in the bagasse-containing sites in sugarcane mills, where ABPA was diagnosed in 7% of workers who had chronic respiratory problems.[181] Interestingly, an increased prevalence of cystic fibrosis transmembrane conductance regulator gene (*CFTR*) mutations has been reported in non–cystic fibrosis patients with ABPA or sinobronchial

Table 57.3 Diagnostic Criteria for Allergic Bronchopulmonary Aspergillosis

Minimal Criteria
Asthma
Immunologic hypersensitivity to *A. fumigatus*:
　Immediate reaction to prick test
　Elevated specific immunoglobulin E
Elevated serum immunoglobulin E (usually >400 kU/L)
Central bronchiectasis*

Other Criteria
Pulmonary infiltrates on chest radiograph
Serum precipitating antibodies to *A. fumigatus*
Peripheral blood eosinophils >1 × 10⁹/L

Other Common Findings
Expectoration of mucous plugs
Presence of *Aspergillus* in sputum
Late skin reactivity to *Aspergillus* antigen

*When absent, ABPA is called ABPA-seropositive.
Adapted from Greenberger PA: Allergic bronchopulmonary aspergillosis. J Allergy Clin Immunol 110:685–692, 2002; and Greenberger PA: Allergic bronchopulmonary aspergillosis, allergic fungal sinusitis, and hypersensitivity pneumonitis. Clin Allergy Immunol 16:449–468, 2002.

allergic mycosis,[179,182] suggesting that *CFTR* mutations could be involved in the development of these conditions without overt cystic fibrosis.

ABPA results from an immune and inflammatory reaction in the bronchi and the surrounding parenchyma in response to antigens from *Aspergillus* growing in mucous plugs in the airways of asthmatics. The immunologic response of the host includes both type I hypersensitivity, mediated by IgE antibodies, and type III hypersensitivity, with the participation of IgG and IgA antibodies. Over time, the associated inflammatory reaction results in damage to the bronchial epithelium, submucosa, and adjacent pulmonary parenchyma.[183,184,184a]

The current diagnostic criteria (Table 57.3) include asthma, history of pulmonary infiltrates, proximal bronchiectasis, elevated serum IgE, and immunologic hypersensitivity to *Aspergillus fumigatus*, such as immediate reaction to prick test for *Aspergillus* antigen, precipitating antibodies against *A. fumigatus*, and elevated specific IgE against *A. fumigatus*.[185,186] There are approximately 40 antigenic components that can bind with IgE antibodies, of which 22 recombinant *Aspergillus* allergens (*Asp f* 1 to *Asp f* 22) are currently recognized.[187] Other common findings in patients with ABPA comprise the expectoration of mucous plugs, the presence of *Aspergillus* in sputum, and late skin reactivity to *Aspergillus* antigen.[185] In patients with ABPA, typical central bronchiectasis may be absent; such cases are designated ABPA-seropositive.[187] Five stages of ABPA have been distinguished: acute, remission, recurrent exacerbations, corticosteroid-dependent asthma, and fibrotic end stage.[188]

Damage to the large bronchi is a major feature of ABPA, with mucous plugs containing *Aspergillus* obstructing the airways with subsequent atelectasis and bronchial wall damage. Proximal bronchiectasis predominates in the upper lobes and is well visualized on CT scans.[189-191] In asthmatic patients, the presence of bronchiectasis affecting three or more lobes, centrilobular nodules, and mucoid impaction on CT scan are highly suggestive of ABPA[192] (Fig. 57.7);

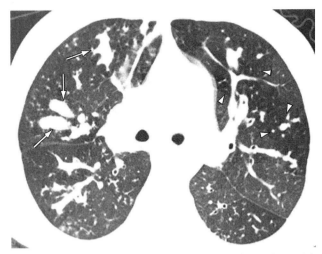

Figure 57.7 Axial computed tomography scan of a patient with allergic bronchopulmonary aspergillosis showing central bronchiectasis with mucoid impaction (*arrows*). Diffuse bilateral inhomogeneous lung opacity is present, with areas of low attenuation throughout the pulmonary parenchyma (*arrowheads*) representing mosaic perfusion resulting from a combination of large and small airway inflammation. (Courtesy of Michael B. Gotway, MD, Department of Radiology, University of California, San Francisco.)

because of its characteristic imaging presentation, the correct diagnosis of ABPA was made on CT scan in 84% of cases of ABPA in a series of patients with eosinophilic lung diseases.[24] Although surgery is seldom warranted, eosinophilic pneumonia may be found in resection specimens from patients with asthma and ABPA with chronic pulmonary consolidation.[189,193]

The acute stage of ABPA is characterized on imaging by either fleeting infiltrates due to eosinophilic pneumonia, or mucus plugging with ensuing segmental, lobar, or even whole-lung atelectasis. Fever is present. Blood eosinophilia is generally greater than 1×10^9/L. Sputum and expectorated plugs contain eosinophils and Charcot-Leyden crystals. Mucoid impaction is typically characterized by a V-shaped lesion with the vertex pointing toward the hilum, and by atelectasis.[194,195]

The treatment of ABPA mainly relies on corticosteroids during attacks, with long-term corticosteroids maintained only in patients with frequent symptomatic attacks and in patients with evidence of progressive lung damage.[196,197] Management of episodes of pulmonary consolidation may prevent the progression of ABPA to the fibrotic end stage.[198] Inhaled corticosteroids may reduce the need for long-term oral corticosteroids. Oral itraconazole is a useful adjunct to corticosteroids, allowing reduction of the doses of corticosteroids.[199,200] A double-blind, randomized, placebo-controlled study indicated that patients with corticosteroid-dependent ABPA generally benefit from concurrent itraconazole treatment; improvements included the immunologic and physiologic criteria and the corticosteroid dose, but there was no significant effect on pulmonary infiltrates.[201] Another randomized, double-blind, placebo-controlled study with itraconazole for 16 weeks in stable subjects with ABPA demonstrated that subjects receiving itraconazole had a decrease in sputum eosinophils, sputum

eosinophil cationic protein levels, serum IgE levels, and levels of serum IgG to *A. fumigatus,* and fewer exacerbations than patients receiving placebo.[202] However, itraconazole interacts with many medications and may induce adrenal insufficiency.[203,204]

Other Allergic Bronchopulmonary Syndromes Associated with Fungi or Yeasts

A similar syndrome of allergic bronchopulmonary disease may be produced by other fungi or yeasts, including *Pseudallescheria boydii, Cladosporium herbarum, Candida albicans, Stemphylium* species, *Torulopsis* species, *Curvularia lunata, Bipolaris* species, *Rhizopus* species, *Trichosporon terrestre, Fusarium vasinfectum,* and *Helminthosporium* species.

Bronchocentric Granulomatosis

Bronchocentric granulomatosis[205] is an inflammatory and destructive process beginning within the bronchiolar walls, and further extending into the surrounding parenchyma, with a peribronchiolar distribution of the lesions.[206] The granulomatous inflammatory process destroys both the mucosa and walls of the bronchioles, and the necrotic areas resulting from the destroyed bronchioles are often surrounded by palisading histiocytes. Eosinophils represent the major component of the cellular infiltrate. Scattered fungal hyphae may be demonstrated by the Grocott silver stain in some patients. A dense inflammatory infiltrate is, in most cases, present in the peribronchial tissue, but may occasionally extend more distally in the parenchyma. In asthmatic patients with bronchocentric granulomatosis, eosinophils comprise the major proportion of the infiltrate. Other possible changes include vascular inflammation and mucoid impaction.[206,207]

About half the patients with bronchocentric granulomatosis at lung pathologic examination are asthmatics who further present with fever and cough. A peripheral blood eosinophilia is common, generally greater than 1×10^9 eosinophils/L.[206,207] The radiographic features consist of masses, alveolar infiltrates or pneumonic consolidation, or reticulonodular opacities, which predominate in the upper lobes and are unilateral in a majority of patients.[208,209] Most of these patients fulfill the criteria for ABPA, and corticosteroids are effective. These patients have an excellent prognosis, although recurrences are common.[206]

Eosinophilia is usually not conspicuous when bronchocentric granulomatosis occurs in patients without asthma (an infectious cause is found in some cases).

DRUG-, TOXIC AGENT-, AND RADIATION-INDUCED EOSINOPHILIC PNEUMONIAS

More than 80 drugs have been reported to cause eosinophilic pulmonary infiltrates (Table 57.4). However, the causality has not been established in many single case reports, and thus the number of drugs that can reliably be considered as common causes of drug-induced eosinophilic pneumonia is much smaller (mainly nonsteroidal anti-inflammatory drugs or antibiotics).

Drug-induced eosinophilic lung disease may present in three main clinical settings: (1) in some patients taking a

Table 57.4 Drugs That May Cause Eosinophilic Pneumonia

Drugs with Typical Pulmonary Eosinophilia	Drugs with Exceptional Eosinophilia
Acetylsalicylic acid	Amiodarone
Captopril	Aminoglutethimide
Diclofenac	Ampicillin
Ethambutol	Beclomethasone
Fenbufen	Bicalutamide
Granulocyte-macrophage colony-stimulating factor	Bucillamine
Ibuprofen	Cephalosporins
L-Tryptophan	Chloroquine
Minocycline	Chlorpropamide
Naproxen	Clarithromycin[244]
Para-(4-)aminosalicylic acid	Clofibrate
Penicillins	Cromoglycate
Phenylbutazone	Diflunisal
Piroxicam	Erythromycin
Pyrimethamine	Fludarabine[245]
Sulindac	Furazolidone
Sulfamides/sulfonamides	Glafenine
Tolfenamic acid	Indomethacin
Trimethoprim-sulfamethoxazole	Iodinated contrast medium
	Levofloxacin
Drugs with Occasional Pulmonary Eosinophilia	Maloprim
Bleomycin	Maprotiline
Carbamazepine	Mesalazine (5-aminosalicylic acid)
Chlorpromazine	Metronidazole
Cocaine	Nalidixic acid
Desipramine	Nilutamide
Dapsone	Paracetamol
Febarbamate	Penicillamine
Gold salts	Procarbazine
Heroin	Propylthiouracil
Imipramine	Oxaliplatin[246]
Isoniazid	Ranitidine
Loxoprofen	Scotchguard
Mephenesin	Streptomycin
Methotrexate	Tenidap
Methylphedinate	Tetracycline
Nitrofurantoin	Tolazamide
Nomifensine	Tosufloxacin tosylate
Pentamidine	Trazodone
Perindopril	Troleandomycin
Phenytoin	Venlafaxine
Propranolol	
Sulfasalazine[243]	
Trimipramine	

From Cordier JF: Eosinophilic pneumonias. *In* Schwarz MI, King TE Jr (eds): Interstitial Lung Disease (4th ed). London: BC Dekker, 2003, pp 657–700.

drug for several months (or years) for the treatment of chronic disease, who progressively develop increasing dyspnea with cough and mild fever; (2) in asymptomatic patients, in whom the interstitial lung disease may be discovered by routine chest radiographs; and (3) in some patients who present with acute eosinophilic pneumonia sometimes requiring mechanical ventilation. Associated extrapulmonary iatrogenic manifestations, especially including cutaneous rashes, may be present. All the drugs taken in the weeks or months preceding the clinical syndrome must be carefully recorded in any patient presenting with eosinophilic pneumonia, including illicit drugs (cocaine, heroin), the intake of which is often denied by the patient.

Transient interstitial infiltrates with eosinophilia (Löffler's syndrome), chronic eosinophilic pneumonia, and acute eosinophilic pneumonia have all been reported as drug-induced syndromes. Systemic eosinophilic vasculitis involving the lung (and thus closely resembling CSS) has also been reported.[78,210] The regression of eosinophilic lung disease after stopping the drug is the best clue to an iatrogenic reaction. However, this may take a long time, and therefore in many reported cases corticosteroids have been given concomitantly with drug withdrawal, so that the responsibility of the drug cannot be definitely established. The only absolute proof that a drug is responsible is obtained by its reintroduction, with ensuing relapse of pneumonia. This approach may be dangerous and, thus, unethical unless no alternative treatment for a serious disease is available.

Eosinophilic drug-induced pneumonia has generally no specificity of presentation. Although in most cases patients present with pulmonary manifestations compatible with ICEP (with the exception of possible associated pleural effusion and extrapulmonary manifestations, including cutaneous rash), some patients present with the features characteristic of acute eosinophilic pneumonia. Therefore, in any case of "idiopathic" eosinophilic pneumonia an iatrogenic cause must be systematically considered.

The eosinophilia-myalgia syndrome developed in 1989 in the United States, and was subsequently proved to be related to the intake of contaminated preparations of L-tryptophan originating from a single manufacturer. Symptoms comprised respiratory manifestations (dyspnea, cough) in 67% of cases, with interstitial lung disease or infiltrates in 13% on CT scan and pulmonary hypertension on echocardiography in 4%.[211] The mean eosinophil count in this series was 4.7×10^9/L. Other symptoms observed in at least 60% of patients were myalgia, fatigue, rash, paresthesia, swelling, and muscle weakness. Diffuse interstitial infiltrates were present on chest radiography. The most conspicuous lesions at lung biopsy consisted of a small to medium-sized vessel vasculitis with mixed inflammatory cell infiltrates (primarily lymphocytes and eosinophils) involving both arteries and veins, and a chronic interstitial pneumonia consisting of lymphocytes and eosinophils. The outcome was favorable, especially in patients receiving corticosteroids.[211–213]

Ingestion of denatured cooking oil was the cause of the toxic oil syndrome that affected about 20,000 people in Spain in 1981.[214] This scleroderma-like disorder was characterized by an interstitial-alveolar pattern on chest imaging and eosinophilia during the first 4 months. In the acute phase, death was mainly due to respiratory failure, with the pathology of the pulmonary lesions consisting of vasculitis and vascular fibrosis, edema, and interstitial infiltrates of mononuclear cells and eosinophils in variable proportions. The chronic stage of disease was characterized by pulmonary hypertension, scleroderma, hepatic disease, sicca syndrome, polyneuropathy, joint contractures, and chronic pulmonary sequelae.

Chronic eosinophilic pneumonia developing after radiation therapy for breast cancer has been reported.[215] It occurred in women with a history of asthma or allergy by a median time of 3.5 months after completion of radiotherapy. Dyspnea and cough were the main presenting symptoms, with pulmonary opacities at imaging being unilateral (irradiated lung) or bilateral, and possibly migratory. All patients had blood eosinophilia of 1.0×10^9/L or greater or eosinophilia greater than 40% at BAL differential cell count, or both. Patients rapidly improved with oral corticosteroids without sequelae, but relapse occurred in some of them after treatment withdrawal. This syndrome seems similar to bronchiolitis obliterans with OP primed by radiation therapy to the breast,[216] with eosinophilic pneumonia occurring preferentially in patients with asthma or atopy.

MISCELLANEOUS LUNG DISEASES WITH ASSOCIATED EOSINOPHILIA

Blood eosinophilia or eosinophilia in BAL fluid, or both, may be present in some pulmonary disorders in which eosinophilic pneumonia is not a major finding.

ORGANIZING PNEUMONIA

OP is defined by the presence of buds composed of inflammatory cells, fibroblasts, and connective tissue within the lumina of distal air spaces. It may be secondary to various causes (such as infection or drug-induced reactions) or be cryptogenic. The typical clinical and imaging features (patchy alveolar infiltrates) of OP may closely mimic ICEP.[217] Furthermore, pathologic overlap of OP and ICEP may be encountered, with foci of OP in ICEP, and eosinophils in OP. In some cases, OP may represent the evolution of an untreated chronic eosinophilic pneumonia.[217] Eosinophilia on BAL differential cell count may be present in bronchiolitis obliterans with OP, but it is usually less than 20% on differential cell count.

ASTHMA AND EOSINOPHILIC BRONCHITIS

Infiltration of the airways by eosinophils is common in eosinophilic pneumonias, but it may occur as an isolated phenomenon. The eosinophil is considered to play a major role in the pathogenesis of asthma.[218] Eosinophilic inflammation of the airways present in the submucosa and epithelium of patients with asthma is correlated with severity of asthma.[219] Furthermore, BAL has shown mildly increased levels of eosinophils (usually less than 5%) at differential cell count in asthmatics, with the increase in eosinophils in the alveolar samples less than that in bronchial samples.[220] Interestingly, although eosinophilic infiltration of the bronchi is common in the eosinophilic pneumonias, asthma is not constant in such disorders.

Eosinophilic bronchitis (without asthma) with a high percentage of eosinophils (about 40%) in sputum is a well-recognized cause of chronic cough that is responsive to corticosteroid treatment.[221] The observed values of sputum eosinophils are often much higher in eosinophilic bronchitis than in asthma.[222] The development over time of chronic airflow obstruction in patients with eosinophilic bronchitis has been reported.[223,223a] Eosinophilic bronchitis with chronic cough induced by latex gloves has been reported in a nurse.[224]

IDIOPATHIC INTERSTITIAL PNEUMONIAS

Mildly increased levels of eosinophils may be found on BAL differential cell count in the idiopathic interstitial pneumonias (idiopathic pulmonary fibrosis, nonspecific interstitial pneumonia, cryptogenic OP). Increase of BAL eosinophils is associated with a poor clinical response to corticosteroids.[225–227] Focal eosinophilic pneumonia has been reported in cases of usual interstitial pneumonia,[228] and focal eosinophils are a minor feature of nonspecific interstitial pneumonia.[229]

LANGERHANS CELL GRANULOMATOSIS

Pulmonary Langerhans cell granulomatosis (also designated as eosinophilic granuloma or pulmonary histiocytosis X) results from the proliferation of Langerhans cells. The pulmonary pathologic lesions, consisting of nodules often assuming a stellate shape, are composed of Langerhans cells with variable numbers of eosinophils, plasma cells, and lymphocytes. Eosinophils usually present in the initial active stage of disease contribute to the "eosinophilic granuloma." Numerous in about 25% of cases, they are usually situated at the periphery of the lesions. The eosinophils are rare or absent at the chronic stage of disease.[230–234]

LUNG TRANSPLANTATION

Eosinophilic alveolitis in lung transplant recipients may be indicative of acute rejection (tissue eosinophilia is involved in rejection after renal, cardiac, hepatic, and pancreatic transplantation).[235–238] However, pulmonary eosinophilia in lung transplant recipients may also result from infectious agents such as *Aspergillus, Pseudomonas,* or coxsackievirus.[237]

OTHER LUNG DISEASES WITH OCCASIONAL EOSINOPHILIA

Sarcoidosis developed in a patient with blood eosinophilia and a previous history of asthma and eosinophilic pneumonia.[239] Pulmonary eosinophilia developed in two patients after transplantation for sarcoidosis, with bronchiolitis obliterans syndrome developing after resolution of pulmonary eosinophilia.[238] A case of ICEP overlapping with sarcoidosis and Behçet's disease has been reported.[240] Blood eosinophilia and tissue eosinophilia may be present in sarcoidosis, but are usually mild.[241]

Eosinophilic pneumonia was reported in a patient with gastric cancer producing granulocyte-macrophage colony-stimulating factor and interleukin-5.[242]

SUMMARY

Although they have lung or airway eosinophilia or both as a common denominator, the eosinophilic lung diseases correspond to a wide and heterogeneous spectrum of disorders. Eosinophilic lung disease may manifest clinically by a pulmonary disease of varying severity, ranging from chronic or transient infiltrates with mild symptoms to the acute severe eosinophilic pneumonia resembling ALI or acute respiratory distress syndrome and necessitating mechanical ventilation.

The etiologic diagnosis of eosinophilic lung diseases is crucial, and the workup will be directed by the clinical syndrome. Blood eosinophilia greater than 1×10^9 eosinophils/L (and preferably greater than 1.5×10^9/L) is of considerable help in narrowing the diagnosis. However, blood eosinophilia may be absent in the early phase of IAEP, or when patients are already taking corticosteroids. On BAL differential cell count, high eosinophilia (greater than 25%, and preferably over 40%) may be considered diagnostic of eosinophilic pneumonia in a compatible setting. There is currently little, if any, indication for pulmonary biopsy in the diagnosis of the eosinophilic lung diseases.

Inquiry as to drug intake must be meticulous, and any suspected drug should be withdrawn. Travel history or residence in areas endemic for parasitic infection must be recorded, and laboratory investigations for parasitic causes must take into account the specific epidemiology of parasites throughout the world. The appropriate diagnostic laboratory tests for parasites must be done according to the instructions of a specialist. The other known causes of eosinophilic lung disease must also be investigated (with the help of a checklist if possible). If no cause is found, the eosinophilic lung disease is considered idiopathic. When present, extrathoracic manifestations raise the suspicion of a systemic eosinophilic disease such as CSS or HES, thus necessitating specific diagnostic investigations.

If a determined cause has been found, its treatment may provide improvement (e.g., drug withdrawal in drug-induced disease). Corticosteroids remain the cornerstone of symptomatic treatment for eosinophilic disorders, and these are necessary in the idiopathic eosinophilic pneumonias, ABPA flares, and CSS (with adjunct immunosuppressants in patients with poor prognostic factors). The response to corticosteroids is usually dramatic in ICEP and in most cases of CSS, but relapses often occur when tapering the doses or after stopping treatment. Imatinib, a tyrosine kinase inhibitor, has recently proven very effective in the treatment of the myeloproliferative variant of HES, a disorder heretofore often resistant to treatment.

ACKNOWLEDGMENT

This work was supported by grant HCL-PRNC 93.97-005 from Ministère de la Santé et de l'Action Humanitaire, France.

REFERENCES

1. Marone G (ed): Human Eosinophils: Biological and Clinical Aspects. Basel: Karger, 2000.
2. Rothenberg ME: Eosinophilia. N Engl J Med 338:1592–1600, 1998.
3. Reeder WH, Goodrich BE: Pulmonary infiltration with eosinophilia (PIE syndrome). Ann Intern Med 36:1217–1240, 1952.
4. Crofton JW, Livingstone JL, Oswald NC, et al: Pulmonary eosinophilia. Thorax 7:1–35, 1952.
5. McCarthy DS, Pepys J: Cryptogenic pulmonary eosinophilias. Clin Allergy 3:339–351, 1973.
6. Carrington C, Addington W, Goff A, et al: Chronic eosinophilic pneumonia. N Engl J Med 280:787–798, 1969.
7. Liebow AA, Carrington CB: The eosinophilic pneumonias. Medicine (Baltimore) 48:251–285, 1969.
8. Jederlinic PJ, Sicilian L, Gaensler EA: Chronic eosinophilic pneumonia: A report of 19 cases and a review of the literature. Medicine (Baltimore) 67:154–162, 1988.
9. Olopade CO, Crotty TB, Douglas WW, et al: Chronic eosinophilic pneumonia and idiopathic bronchiolitis obliterans organizing pneumonia: Comparison of eosinophil number and degranulation by immunofluorescence staining for eosinophil-derived major basic protein. Mayo Clin Proc 70:137–142, 1995.
10. Tazelaar HD, Linz LJ, Colby TV, et al: Acute eosinophilic pneumonia: Histopathologic findings in nine patients. Am J Respir Crit Care Med 155:296–302, 1997.
11. The BAL Cooperative Group Steering Committee: Bronchoalveolar lavage constituents in healthy individuals, idiopathic pulmonary fibrosis, and selected comparison groups. Am Rev Respir Dis 141:S169–S202, 1990.
12. Velay B, Pages J, Cordier JF, et al: Hyperéosinophilie du lavage broncho-alvéolaire: Valeur diagnostique et corrélations avec l'éosinophilie sanguine. Rev Mal Respir 4:257–260, 1987.

13. Marchand E, Etienne-Mastroianni B, Chanez P, et al: Idiopathic chronic eosinophilic pneumonia and asthma: How do they influence each other? Eur Respir J 22:8–13, 2003.

14. Marchand E, Reynaud-Gaubert M, Lauque D, et al: Idiopathic chronic eosinophilic pneumonia: A clinical and follow-up study of 62 cases. Medicine (Baltimore) 77:299–312, 1998.

15. Pope-Harman AL, Davis WB, Allen ED, et al: Acute eosinophilic pneumonia: A summary of 15 cases and a review of the literature. Medicine (Baltimore) 75:334–342, 1996.

16. Pearson DJ, Rosenow EC: Chronic eosinophilic pneumonia (Carrington's): A follow-up study. Mayo Clin Proc 53:73–78, 1978.

17. Naughton M, Fahy J, FitzGerald MX: Chronic eosinophilic pneumonia: A long-term follow-up of 12 patients. Chest 103:162–165, 1993.

18. Hayakawa H, Sato A, Toyoshima M, et al: A clinical study of idiopathic eosinophilic pneumonia. Chest 105:1462–1466, 1994.

19. Wubbel C, Fulmer D, Sherman J: Chronic eosinophilic pneumonia: A case report and national survey. Chest 123:1763–1766, 2003.

20. Libby DM, Murphy TF, Edwards A, et al: Chronic eosinophilic pneumonia: An unusual cause of acute respiratory failure. Am Rev Respir Dis 122:497–500, 1980.

21. Mayo J, Müller N, Road J, et al: Chronic eosinophilic pneumonia: CT findings in six cases. AJR Am J Roentgenol 153:727–730, 1989.

22. Ebara H, Ikezoe J, Johkoh T, et al: Chronic eosinophilic pneumonia: Evolution of chest radiograms and CT features. J Comput Assist Tomogr 18:737–744, 1994.

23. Gaensler EA, Carrington CB: Peripheral opacities in chronic eosinophilic pneumonia: The photographic negative of pulmonary edema. AJR Am J Roentgenol 128:1–13, 1977.

24. Johkoh T, Muller NL, Akira M, et al: Eosinophilic lung diseases: Diagnostic accuracy of thin-section CT in 111 patients. Radiology 216:773–780, 2000.

25. Arakawa H, Kurihara Y, Niimi H, et al: Bronchiolitis obliterans with organizing pneumonia versus chronic eosinophilic pneumonia: High-resolution CT findings in 81 patients. AJR Am J Roentgenol 176:1053–1058, 2001.

26. Cottin V, Deviller P, Tardy F, et al: Urinary eosinophil-derived neurotoxin/protein X: A simple method for assessing eosinophil degranulation in vivo. J Allergy Clin Immunol 101:116–123, 1998.

27. Pesci A, Bertorelli G, Manganelli P, et al: Bronchoalveolar lavage in chronic eosinophilic pneumonia: Analysis of six cases in comparison with other interstitial lung diseases. Respiration 54(Suppl 1):16–22, 1988.

28. Takahashi H, Arakawa Y, Oki K, et al: Analysis of bronchoalveolar lavage cells in chronic eosinophilic pneumonia before and during corticosteroid therapy. Int Arch Allergy Immunol 108(Suppl 1):2–5, 1995.

29. Janin A, Torpier G, Courtin P, et al: Segregation of eosinophil proteins in alveolar macrophage compartments in chronic eosinophilic pneumonia. Thorax 48:57–62, 1993.

30. Jorens PG, Van Overveld FJ, Van Meerbeeck JP, et al: Evidence for marked eosinophil degranulation in a case of eosinophilic pneumonia. Respir Med 90:505–509, 1996.

31. Beninati W, Derdak S, Dixon PF, et al: Pulmonary eosinophils express HLA-DR in chronic eosinophilic pneumonia. J Allergy Clin Immunol 92:442–449, 1993.

32. Mukae H, Kadota JI, Kohno S, et al: Increase of activated T-cells in BAL fluid of Japanese patients with bronchiolitis obliterans organizing pneumonia and chronic eosinophilic pneumonia. Chest 108:123–128, 1995.

33. Weynants P, Riou R, Vergnon JM, et al: Pneumopathies chroniques idiopathiques à éosinophiles: Étude de 16 cas. Rev Mal Respir 2:63–68, 1985.

34. Steinfeld S, Golstein M, De Vuyst P: Chronic eosinophilic pneumonia (CEP) as a presenting feature of Churg-Strauss syndrome (CSS). Eur Respir J 7:2098, 1994.

35. Hueto-Perez-de-Heredia JJ, Dominguez-del-Valle FJ, Garcia E, et al: Chronic eosinophilic pneumonia as a presenting feature of Churg-Strauss syndrome. Eur Respir J 7:1006–1008, 1994.

36. Durieu J, Wallaert B, Tonnel AB: Long term follow-up of pulmonary function in chronic eosinophilic pneumonia. Eur Respir J 10:286–291, 1997.

37. Allen JN, Pacht ER, Gadek JE, et al: Acute eosinophilic pneumonia as a reversible cause of noninfectious respiratory failure. N Engl J Med 321:569–574, 1989.

38. Cheon JE, Lee KS, Jung GS, et al: Acute eosinophilic pneumonia: Radiographic and CT findings in six patients. AJR Am J Roentgenol 167:1195–1199, 1996.

39. King MA, Pope-Harman AL, Allen JN, et al: Acute eosinophilic pneumonia: Radiologic and clinical features. Radiology 203:715–719, 1997.

40. Philit F, Etienne-Mastroianni B, Parrot A, et al: Idiopathic acute eosinophilic pneumonia: A study of 22 patients. Am J Respir Crit Care Med 166:1235–1239, 2002.

41. Rom WN, Weiden M, Garcia R, et al: Acute eosinophilic pneumonia in a New York City firefighter exposed to World Trade Center dust. Am J Respir Crit Care Med 166:797–800, 2002.

42. Nakajima M, Manabe T, Niki Y, et al: Cigarette smoke-induced acute eosinophilic pneumonia. Radiology 207:829–831, 1998.

43. Shintani H, Fujimura M, Yasui M, et al: Acute eosinophilic pneumonia caused by cigarette smoking. Intern Med 39:66–68, 2000.

44. Shintani H, Fujimura M, Ishiura Y, et al: A case of cigarette smoking-induced acute eosinophilic pneumonia showing tolerance. Chest 117:277–279, 2000.

45. Nakajima M, Manabe T, Niki Y, et al: A case of cigarette smoking-induced acute eosinophilic pneumonia showing tolerance. Chest 118:1517–1518, 2000.

46. Kawayama T, Fujiki R, Honda J, et al: High concentration of (1 → 3)-beta-D-glucan in BAL fluid in patients with acute eosinophilic pneumonia. Chest 123:1302–1307, 2003.

47. Shorr AF, Scoville SL, Cersovsky SB, et al: Acute eosinophilic pneumonia among US military personnel deployed in or near Iraq. JAMA 292:2997–3005, 2004.

48. Taniguchi H, Kadota J, Fujii T, et al: Activation of lymphocytes and increased interleukin-5 levels in bronchoalveolar lavage fluid in acute eosinophilic pneumonia. Eur Respir J 13:217–220, 1999.

49. Ogawa H, Fujimura M, Matsuda T, et al: Transient wheeze: Eosinophilic bronchobronchiolitis in acute eosinophilic pneumonia. Chest 104:493–496, 1993.

50. Kawayama T, Fujiki R, Morimitsu Y, et al: Fatal idiopathic acute eosinophilic pneumonia with acute lung injury. Respirology 7:373–375, 2002.

51. Buddharaju VL, Saraceno JL, Rosen JM, et al: Acute eosinophilic pneumonia associated with shock. Crit Care Med 27:2014–2016, 1999.

52. Buchheit J, Eid N, Rodgers G, et al: Acute eosinophilic pneumonia with respiratory failure: A new syndrome? Am Rev Respir Dis 145:716–718, 1992.

53. Chiappini J, Arbib F, Heyraud JD, et al: Pneumopathie éosinophilique subaiguë idiopathique d'évolution favorable sans corticothérapie. Rev Mal Respir 12:25–28, 1995.

54. Churg J, Strauss L: Allergic granulomatosis, allergic angiitis, and periarteritis nodosa. Am J Pathol 27:277–301, 1951.

55. Jennette JC, Falk RJ, Andrassy K, et al: Nomenclature of systemic vasculitides: Proposal of an international consensus conference. Arthritis Rheum 37:187–192, 1994.

56. Katzenstein AL: Diagnostic features and differential diagnosis of Churg-Strauss syndrome in the lung: A review. Am J Clin Pathol 114:767–772, 2000.

57. Churg A: Recent advances in the diagnosis of Churg-Strauss syndrome. Mod Pathol 14:1284–1293, 2001.

58. Guillevin L, Cohen P, Gayraud M, et al: Churg-Strauss syndrome: Clinical study and long-term follow-up of 96 patients. Medicine (Baltimore) 78:26–37, 1999.

59. Della Rossa A, Baldini C, Tavoni A, et al: Churg-Strauss syndrome: Clinical and serological features of 19 patients from a single Italian centre. Rheumatology (Oxf) 41:1286–1294, 2002.

60. Solans R, Bosch JA, Perez-Bocanegra C, et al: Churg-Strauss syndrome: Outcome and long-term follow-up of 32 patients. Rheumatology (Oxf) 40:763–771, 2001.

61. Churg A, Brallas M, Cronin SR, et al: Formes frustes of Churg-Strauss syndrome. Chest 108:320–323, 1995.

62. Lanham JG, Elkon K, Pusey C, et al: Systemic vasculitis with asthma and eosinophilia: A clinical approach to the Churg-Strauss syndrome. Medicine (Baltimore) 63:65–81, 1984.

63. Reid AJC, Harrison BDW, Watts RA, et al: Churg-Strauss syndrome in a district hospital. QJM 91:219–229, 1998.

64. Mouthon L, le Toumelin P, Andre MH, et al: Polyarteritis nodosa and Churg-Strauss angiitis: Characteristics and outcome in 38 patients over 65 years. Medicine (Baltimore) 81:27–40, 2002.

65. Keogh KA, Specks U: Churg-Strauss syndrome: Clinical presentation, antineutrophil cytoplasmic antibodies, and leukotriene receptor antagonists. Am J Med 115:284–290, 2003.

66. Chumbley LC, Harrison EG, De Remee RA: Allergic granulomatosis and angiitis (Churg-Strauss syndrome): Report and analysis of 30 cases. Mayo Clin Proc 52:477–484, 1977.

67. Degesys GE, Mintzer RA, Vrla RF: Allergic granulomatosis: Churg-Strauss syndrome. AJR Am J Roentgenol 135:1281–1282, 1980.

68. Choi YH, Im JG, Han BK, et al: Thoracic manifestation of Churg-Strauss syndrome: Radiologic and clinical findings. Chest 117:117–124, 2000.

69. Worthy SA, Muller NL, Hansell DM, et al: Churg-Strauss syndrome: The spectrum of pulmonary CT findings in 17 patients. AJR Am J Roentgenol 170:297–300, 1998.

70. Olsen KD, Neel HB 3d, De Remee RA, et al: Nasal manifestations of allergic granulomatosis and angiitis (Churg Strauss syndrome). Otolaryngol Head Neck Surg 88:85–89, 1995.

71. Wallaert B, Gosset P, Prin L, et al: Bronchoalveolar lavage in allergic granulomatosis and angiitis. Eur Respir J 6:413–417, 1993.

72. Erzurum SC, Underwood GA, Hamilos DL, et al: Pleural effusion in Churg-Strauss syndrome. Chest 95:1357–1359, 1989.

73. Cottin V, Tardy F, Gindre D, et al: Urinary eosinophil-derived neurotoxin in Churg-Strauss syndrome. J Allergy Clin Immunol 96:261–264, 1995.

74. Mouthon L, Khaled M, Cohen P, et al: Antigen inhalation as a triggering factor in systemic small-sized-vessel vasculitis: Four cases. Ann Med Interne (Paris) 152:152–156, 2001.

75. Guillevin L, Guittard T, Bletry O, et al: Systemic necrotizing angiitis with asthma: Causes and precipitating factors in 43 cases. Lung 165:165–172, 1987.

76. Rich MW, Thomas RA: A case of eosinophilic pneumonia and vasculitis induced by diflunisal. Chest 111:1767–1769, 1997.

77. Hubner C, Dietz A, Stremmel W, et al: Macrolide-induced Churg-Strauss syndrome in a patient with atopy. Lancet 350:563, 1997.

78. Yermakov VM, Hitti IF, Sutton AL: Necrotizing vasculitis associated with diphenylhydantoin: Two fatal cases. Hum Pathol 13:182–184, 1983.

79. Lilly CM, Churg A, Lazarovich M, et al: Asthma therapies and Churg-Strauss syndrome. J Allergy Clin Immunol 109:S1–S19, 2002.

80. Masi AT, Hunder GG, Lie JT, et al: The American College of Rheumatology 1990 criteria for the classification of Churg-Strauss syndrome (allergic granulomatosis and angiitis). Arthritis Rheum 33:1094–1100, 1990.

81. Yousem SA, Lombard CM: The eosinophilic variant of Wegener's granulomatosis. Hum Pathol 19:682–688, 1988.

82. Vidal E, Liozon F, Rogues AM, et al: Concurrent temporal arteritis and Churg-Strauss syndrome. J Rheumatol 19:1312–1314, 1992.

83. Lie JT: Limited forms of Churg-Strauss syndrome. Pathol Annu 28:199–220, 1993.

84. Guillevin L, Lhote F, Gayraud M, et al: Prognostic factors in polyarteritis nodosa and Churg-Strauss syndrome: A prospective study in 342 patients. Medicine (Baltimore) 75:17–28, 1996.

85. Abu-Shakra M, Smythe H, Lewtas J, et al: Outcome of polyarteritis nodosa and Churg-Strauss syndrome. Arthritis Rheum 37:1798–1803, 1994.

86. Langford CA: Treatment of polyarteritis nodosa, microscopic polyangiitis, and Churg-Strauss syndrome: Where do we stand? Arthritis Rheum 44:508–512, 2001.

87. Chow CC, Mac-Moune Lai F: Allergic granulomatosis and angiitis (Churg-Strauss syndrome): Response to "pulse" intravenous cyclophosphamide. Ann Rheum Dis 48:605–608, 1989.

88. Guillevin L, Lhote F, Jarrousse B, et al: Treatment of polyarteritis nodosa and Churg-Strauss syndrome: A meta-analysis of 3 prospective controlled trials including 182 patients over 12 years. Ann Med Interne (Paris) 143:405–416, 1992.

89. Gayraud M, Guillevin L, le Toumelin P, et al: Long-term followup of polyarteritis nodosa, microscopic polyangiitis, and Churg-Strauss syndrome: Analysis of four prospective trials including 278 patients. Arthritis Rheum 44:666–675, 2001.

90. Cohen P, Pagnoux C, Mahr A, et al: Treatment of Churg-Strauss syndrome (CSS) without poor prognostic factor at baseline with corticosteroids (CS) alone: Preliminary results of a prospective multicenter trial. Arthritis Rheum 48:S209, 2003.

91. Tatsis E, Schnabel A, Gross WL: Interferon-alpha treatment of four patients with the Churg-Strauss syndrome. Ann Intern Med 129:370–4, 1998.

92. Chusid MJ, Dale DC, West BC, et al: The hypereosinophilic syndrome: Analysis of fourteen cases with review of the literature. Medicine (Baltimore) 54:1–27, 1975.

93. Bain BJ: Eosinophilic leukaemias and the idiopathic hypereosinophilic syndrome. Br J Haematol 95:2–9, 1996.

94. Brito-Babapulle F: Clonal eosinophilic disorders and the hypereosinophilic syndrome. Blood Rev 11:129–145, 1997.

95. Oliver JW, Deol I, Morgan DL, et al: Chronic eosinophilic leukemia and hypereosinophilic syndromes: Proposal for classification, literature review, and report of a case with a unique chromosomal abnormality. Cancer Genet Cytogenet 107:111–117, 1998.

96. Schoffski P, Ganser A, Pascheberg U, et al: Complete haematological and cytogenetic response to interferon alpha-2a of a myeloproliferative disorder with eosinophilia associated with a unique t(4;7) aberration. Ann Hematol 79:95–98, 2000.

97. Chang HW, Leong KH, Koh DR, et al: Clonality of isolated eosinophils in the hypereosinophilic syndrome. Blood 93:1651–1657, 1999.

98. Bigoni R, Cuneo A, Roberti MG, et al: Cytogenetic and molecular cytogenetic characterization of 6 new cases of idiopathic hypereosinophilic syndrome. Haematologica 85:486–491, 2000.

99. Roufosse F, Cogan E, Goldman M: The hypereosinophilic syndrome revisited. Annu Rev Med 54:169–184, 2003.

100. Simon HU, Plotz SG, Dummer R, et al: Abnormal clones of T cells producing interleukin-5 in idiopathic eosinophilia. N Engl J Med 341:1112–1120, 1999.

101. Roufosse F, Schandene L, Sibille C, et al: Clonal Th2 lymphocytes in patients with the idiopathic hypereosinophilic syndrome. Br J Haematol 109:540–548, 2000.

102. Cogan E, Schandené L, Crusiaux A, et al: Clonal proliferation of type 2 helper T cells in a man with the hypereosinophilic syndrome. N Engl J Med 330:535–538, 1994.

103. Cools J, DeAngelo DJ, Gotlib J, et al: A tyrosine kinase created by fusion of the PDGFRA and FIP1L1 genes as a therapeutic target of imatinib in idiopathic hypereosinophilic syndrome. N Engl J Med 348:1201–1214, 2003.

104. Griffin JH, Leung J, Bruner RJ, et al: Discovery of a fusion kinase in EOL-1 cells and idiopathic hypereosinophilic syndrome. Proc Natl Acad Sci U S A 100:7830–7835, 2003.

105. Hirshberg B, Kramer MR, Lotem M, et al: Chronic eosinophilic pneumonia associated with cutaneous T-cell lymphoma. Am J Hematol 60:143–147, 1999.

106. Weller PF, Bubley GJ: The idiopathic hypereosinophilic syndrome. Blood 83:2759–2779, 1994.

107. Fauci AS, Harley JB, Roberts WC, et al: The idiopathic hypereosinophilic syndrome: Clinical, pathophysiologic and therapeutic considerations. Ann Intern Med 97:78–92, 1982.

108. Spry CJF, Davies J, Tai PC, et al: Clinical features of fifteen patients with the hypereosinophilic syndrome. Q J Med 205:1–22, 1983.

109. Roberts WC, Ferrans VJ: Pathologic anatomy of the cardiomyopathies: Idiopathic dilated and hypertrophic types, infiltrative types, and endomyocardial disease with and without eosinophilia. Hum Pathol 6:287–342, 1975.

110. Lefebvre C, Bletry O, Degoulet P, et al: Facteurs pronostiques du syndrome hyperéosinophilique: Étude de 40 observations. Ann Med Interne (Paris) 140:253–257, 1989.

111. Ommen SR, Seward JB, Tajik AJ: Clinical and echocardiographic features of hypereosinophilic syndromes. Am J Cardiol 86:110–113, 2001.

112. Kazmierowski JA, Chusid MJ, Parrillo JE, et al: Dermatologic manifestations of the hypereosinophilic syndrome. Arch Dermatol 114:531–535, 1978.

113. Kang EY, Shim JJ, Kim JS, et al: Pulmonary involvement of idiopathic hypereosinophilic syndrome: CT findings in five patients. J Comput Assist Tomogr 21:612–615, 1997.

114. Cordier JF, Faure M, Hermier C, et al: Pleural effusions in an overlap syndrome of idiopathic hypereosinophilic syndrome and erythema elevatum diutinum. Eur Respir J 3:115–118, 1990.

115. Dussopt C, Schandené L, Perrin-Fayolle M, et al: Augmentation du taux d'interleukine 5 sérique au cours d'un syndrome hyperéosinophilique. Presse Med 26:166, 1997.

116. Parrillo JE, Borer JS, Henry WL, et al: The cardiovascular manifestations of the hypereosinophilic syndrome: Prospective study of 26 patients, with review of the literature. Am J Med 67:572–582, 1979.

117. Butterfield JH, Gleich GJ: Interferon-α treatment of six patients with the idiopathic hypereosinophilic syndrome. Ann Intern Med 121:648–653, 1994.

118. Butterfield JH, Gleich GJ: Response of six patients with idiopathic hypereosinophilic syndrome to interferon alfa. J Allergy Clin Immunol 94:1318–1326, 1994.

119. Ceretelli S, Capochiani E, Petrini M: Interferon-α in the idiopathic hypereosinophilic syndrome: Consideration of five cases. Ann Hematol 77:161–164, 1998.

120. Yoon TY, Ahn GB, Chang SH: Complete remission of hypereosinophilic syndrome after interferon-alpha therapy: Report of a case and literature review. J Dermatol 27:110–115, 2000.

121. Coutant G, Bletry O, Prin L, et al: Traitement des syndromes hyperéosinophiliques à expression myéloproliférative par l'association hydroxyurée-interféron alpha: À propos de 7 observations. Ann Med Interne (Paris) 144:243–250, 1993.

122. Demiroglu H, Dundar S: Combination of interferon-alpha and hydroxyurea in the treatment of idiopathic hypereosinophilic syndrome. Br J Haematol 97:928–930, 1997.

123. Weingarten RJ: Tropical eosinophilia. Lancet 1:103–105, 1943.

124. Malavige GN: Chronic cough ... and tropical pulmonary eosinophilia. BMJ 326:1036–1037, 2003.

125. Ottesen EA, Neva FA, Paranjape RS, et al: Specific allergic sensitisation to filarial antigens in tropical eosinophilia syndrome. Lancet 2:1158–1161, 1979.

126. Kazura JW: The filariases. In Mahmoud AAF (ed): Parasitic Lung Diseases. New York: Marcel Dekker, 1997, pp 109–124.

127. Ong RK, Doyle RL: Tropical pulmonary eosinophilia. Chest 113:1673–1679, 1998.

128. Chitkara RK, Sarinas PS: Dirofilaria, visceral larva migrans, and tropical pulmonary eosinophilia. Semin Respir Infect 12:138–148, 1997.

129. Bartoloni A, Dini F, Farese A, et al: Tropical pulmonary eosinophilia: Report of a case. Ann Med Interne (Paris) 148:321–322, 1997.

130. Jiva TM, Israel RH, Poe RH: Tropical pulmonary eosinophilia masquerading as acute bronchial asthma. Respiration 63:55–58, 1996.

131. Rom WN, Vijayan VK, Cornelius MJ, et al: Persistent lower respiratory tract inflammation associated with interstitial lung disease in patients with tropical pulmonary eosinophilia following conventional treatment with diethylcarbamazine. Am Rev Respir Dis 142:1088–1092, 1990.

132. Sandhu M, Mukhopadhyay S, Sharma SK: Tropical pulmonary eosinophilia: A comparative evaluation of plain chest radiography and computed tomography. Australas Radiol 40:32–37, 1996.

133. Rohatgi PK, Smirniotopoulos TT: Tropical eosinophilia. Semin Respir Med 12:98–106, 1991.

134. Ray D, Saha K: Serum immunoglobulin and complement levels in tropical pulmonary eosinophilia, and their

correlation with primary and relapsing stages of the illness. Am J Trop Med Hyg 27:503–507, 1978.

135. Pinkston P, Vijayan VK, Nutman TB, et al: Acute tropical pulmonary eosinophilia: Characterization of the lower respiratory tract inflammation and its response to therapy. J Clin Invest 80:216–225, 1987.

136. O'Bryan L, Pinkston P, Kumaraswami V, et al: Localized eosinophil degranulation mediates disease in tropical pulmonary eosinophilia. Infect Immun 71:1337–1342, 2003.

137. Vijayan VK, Kuppu Rao KV, Sankaran K, et al: Tropical eosinophilia: Clinical and physiological response to diethylcarbamazine. Respir Med 85:17–20, 1991.

138. Vijayan VK, Sankaran K, Venkatesan P, et al: Effect of diethylcarbamazine on the alveolitis of tropical eosinophilia. Respiration 58:255–259, 1991.

139. Udwadia FE: Tropical eosinophilia—a correlation of clinical, histopathologic, and lung function studies. Dis Chest 52:531–538, 1967.

140. Poh SC: The course of lung function in treated tropical pulmonary eosinophilia. Thorax 29:710–712, 1974.

141. Neva FA, Ottesen EA: Tropical (filarial) eosinophilia. N Engl J Med 298:1129–1131, 1978.

142. Cooray JH, Ismail MM: Re-examination of the diagnostic criteria of tropical pulmonary eosinophilia. Respir Med 93:655–659, 1999.

143. Salata RA: Intestinal nematodes. In Mahmoud AAF (ed): Parasitic Lung Diseases. New York: Marcel Dekker, 1997, pp 89–108.

144. Gelpi AP, Mustafa A: Ascaris pneumonia. Am J Med 44:377–389, 1968.

145. Sarinas PS, Chitkara RK: Ascariasis and hookworm. Semin Respir Infect 12:130–137, 1997.

146. Khuroo MS: Ascariasis. Gastroenterol Clin North Am 25:553–577, 1996.

147. Beaver PC, Snyder CH, Carrera GM, et al: Chronic eosinophilia due to visceral larva migrans: Report of three cases. Pediatrics 9:7–19, 1952.

148. Schantz PM, Glickman LT: Current concepts in parasitology: Toxocaral visceral larva migrans. N Engl J Med 298:436–439, 1978.

149. Beshear JR, Hendley JO: Severe pulmonary involvement in visceral larva migrans. Am J Dis Child 125:599–600, 1973.

150. Roig J, Romeu J, Riera C, et al: Acute eosinophilic pneumonia due to toxocariasis with bronchoalveolar lavage findings. Chest 102:294–296, 1992.

151. Bartelink AK, Kortbeek LM, Huidekoper HJ, et al: Acute respiratory failure due to toxocara infection. Lancet 342:1234, 1993.

152. Feldman GJ, Parker HW: Visceral larva migrans associated with the hypereosinophilic syndrome and the onset of severe asthma. Ann Intern Med 116:838–840, 1992.

153. Igra-Siegman Y, Kapila R, Sen P, et al: Syndrome of hyperinfection with strongyloides stercoralis. Rev Infect Dis 3:397–407, 1981.

154. Davidson RA: Infection due to Strongyloides stercoralis in patients with pulmonary disease. South Med J 85:28–31, 1992.

155. Jamil SA, Hilton E: The strongyloides hyperinfection syndrome. N Y State J Med 92:67–68, 1992.

156. Williams J, Nunley D, Dralle W, et al: Diagnosis of pulmonary strongyloidiasis by bronchoalveolar lavage. Chest 94:643–644, 1988.

157. Harris RA, Musher DM, Fainstein V, et al: Disseminated strongyloidiasis: Diagnosis made by sputum examination. JAMA 244:65–66, 1980.

158. Salata RA: Approach to diagnosis and management. In Mahmoud AAF (ed): Parasitic Lung Diseases. New York: Marcel Dekker, 1997, pp 191–210.

159. Ambrus JL, Klein E: Löffler syndrome and Ancylostomiasis brasiliensis. N Y State J Med 88:498–499, 1988.

160. King CL: Schistosomiasis. In Mahmoud AAF (ed): Parasitic Lung Diseases. New York: Marcel Dekker, 1997, pp 135–155.

161. Barrett-Connor E: Parasitic pulmonary disease. Am Rev Respir Dis 126:558–563, 1982.

162. Schwartz E, Rozenman J, Perelman M: Pulmonary manifestations of early schistosome infection among nonimmune travelers. Am J Med 109:718–722, 2000.

163. Davidson BL, El-Kassimi F, Uz-Zaman A, et al: The "lung shift" in treated schistosomiasis: Bronchoalveolar lavage evidence of eosinophilic pneumonia. Chest 89:455–457, 1986.

164. Gershwin LJ, Gershwin ME, Kritzman J: Human pulmonary dirofilariasis. Chest 66:92–96, 1974.

165. Feldman GJ, Worth Parker H: Visceral larva migrans associated with the hypereosinophilic syndrome and the onset of severe asthma. Ann Intern Med 116:838–840, 1992.

166. Fleury-Feith J, Van Nhieu J, Picard C, et al: Bronchoalveolar lavage eosinophilia associated with Pneumocystis carinii pneumonitis in AIDS patients. Chest 95:1198–1201, 1989.

167. Addis B: Pulmonary mycotic disease. In Hasleton PS (ed): Spencer's Pathology of the Lung (5th ed). New York: McGraw-Hill, 1996, pp 257–304.

168. Chandler FW, Watts JC: Fungal infections. In Dail DH, Hammar SP (eds): Pulmonary Pathology (2nd ed). New York: Springer-Verlag, 1994, pp 351–427.

169. Corrin B: Fungal diseases. In Corrin B (ed): The Lungs. London: Churchill Livingstone, 1990, pp 125–145.

170. Marty AM, Neafie RC: Fungal diseases. In Saldana MJ (ed): Pathology of Pulmonary Disease. Philadelphia: JB Lippincott, 1994, pp 477–487.

171. Sobonya RE: Fungal diseases, including allergic bronchopulmonary aspergillosis. In Thurlbeck WM, Churg AM (eds): Pathology of the Lung (2nd ed). New York: Thieme Medical, 1995, pp 303–331.

172. Geller DE, Kaplowitz H, Light MJ, et al: Allergic bronchopulmonary aspergillosis in cystic fibrosis: Reported prevalence, regional distribution, and patient characteristics. Chest 116:639–646, 1999.

173. Mastella G, Rainisio M, Harms HK, et al: Allergic bronchopulmonary aspergillosis in cystic fibrosis: A European epidemiological study. Eur Respir J 16:464–471, 2000.

174. Shah A, Khan ZU, Chaturvedi S, et al: Concomitant allergic Aspergillus sinusitis and allergic bronchopulmonary aspergillosis associated with familial occurrence of allergic bronchopulmonary aspergillosis. Ann Allergy 64:507–512, 1990.

175. Shah A, Bhagat R, Panchal N, et al: Allergic bronchopulmonary aspergillosis with middle lobe syndrome and allergic Aspergillus sinusitis. Eur Respir J 6:917–918, 1993.

176. Ponikau JU, Sherris DA, Kern EB, et al: The diagnosis and incidence of allergic fungal sinusitis. Mayo Clin Proc 74:877–884, 1999.

177. Torres C, Ro JY, el-Naggar AK, et al: Allergic fungal sinusitis: A clinicopathologic study of 16 cases. Hum Pathol 27:793–799, 1996.

178. Schubert MS, Goetz DW: Evaluation and treatment of allergic fungal sinusitis. I. Demographics and diagnosis. J Allergy Clin Immunol 102:387–394, 1998.

179. Venarske DL, deShazo RD: Sinobronchial allergic mycosis: The SAM syndrome. Chest 121:1670–1676, 2002.

180. Leonard CT, Berry GJ, Ruoss SJ: Nasal-pulmonary relations in allergic fungal sinusitis and allergic bronchopulmonary aspergillosis. Clin Rev Allergy Immunol 21:5–15, 2001.

181. Mehta SK, Sandhu RS: Immunological significance of *Aspergillus fumigatus* in cane-sugar mills. Arch Environ Health 38:41–46, 1983.

182. Marchand E, Verellen-Dumoulin C, Mairesse M, et al: Frequency of cystic fibrosis transmembrane conductance regulator gene mutations and 5T allele in patients with allergic bronchopulmonary aspergillosis. Chest 119:762–767, 2001.

183. Kauffman HF, Tomee JF, van der Werf TS, et al: Review of fungus-induced asthmatic reactions. Am J Respir Crit Care Med 151:2109–2116, 1995.

184. Patterson R, Grammer LC: Immunopathogenesis of allergic bronchopulmonary aspergillosis. *In* Patterson R, Greenberger PA, Roberts ML (eds): Allergic Bronchopulmonary Aspergillosis. Providence, RI: OceanSide Publications, 1995, pp 35–38.

184a. Wark P: Pathogenesis of allergic bronchopulmonary aspergillosis and an evidence-based review of azoles in treatment. Respir Med 98:915–923, 2004.

185. Rosenberg M, Patterson R, Mintzer R, et al: Clinical and immunologic criteria for the diagnosis of allergic bronchopulmonary aspergillosis. Ann Intern Med 86:405–414, 1977.

186. Patterson R, Greenberger PA, Roberts M: The diagnosis of allergic bronchopulmonary aspergillosis. *In* Patterson R, Greenberger PA, Roberts ML (eds): Allergic Bronchopulmonary Aspergillosis. Providence, RI: OceanSide Publications, 1995, pp 1–3.

187. Greenberger PA: Allergic bronchopulmonary aspergillosis. J Allergy Clin Immunol 110:685–692, 2002.

188. Patterson R, Roberts M: Classification and staging of allergic bronchopulmonary aspergillosis. *In* Patterson R, Greenberger PA, Roberts ML (eds): Allergic Bronchopulmonary Aspergillosis. Providence, RI: OceanSide Publications, 1995, pp 5–10.

189. Bosken C, Myers J, Greenberger P, et al: Pathologic features of allergic bronchopulmonary aspergillosis. Am J Surg Pathol 12:216–222, 1988.

190. Panchal N, Bhagat R, Pant C, et al: Allergic bronchopulmonary aspergillosis: The spectrum of computed tomography appearances. Respir Med 91:213–219, 1997.

191. Angus RM, Davies ML, Cowan MD, et al: Computed tomographic scanning of the lung in patients with allergic bronchopulmonary aspergillosis and in asthmatic patients with a positive skin test to *Aspergillus fumigatus*. Thorax 49:586–589, 1994.

192. Ward S, Heyneman L, Lee MJ, et al: Accuracy of CT in the diagnosis of allergic bronchopulmonary aspergillosis in asthmatic patients. AJR Am J Roentgenol 173:937–942, 1999.

193. McCarthy DS, Simon G, Hargreave FE: The radiological appearances in allergic broncho-pulmonary aspergillosis. Clin Radiol 21:366–375, 1970.

194. Sulavik S: Bronchocentric granulomatosis and allergic bronchopulmonary aspergillosis. Clin Chest Med 9:609–621, 1988.

195. Mintzer RA, Rogers LF, Kruglik GD, et al: The spectrum of radiologic findings in ABPA. Radiology 127:301–307, 1978.

196. Wardlaw A, Geddes DM: Allergic bronchopulmonary aspergillosis: A review. J R Soc Med 85:747–751, 1992.

197. Greenberger PA: Allergic fungal sinusitis. *In* Patterson R, Greenberger PA, Roberts ML (eds): Allergic Bronchopulmonary Aspergillosis. Providence, RI: OceanSide Publications, 1995, pp 53–59.

198. Patterson R, Greenberger PA, Lee TM, et al: Prolonged evaluation of patients with corticosteroid-dependent asthma stage of allergic bronchopulmonary aspergillosis. J Allergy Clin Immunol 80:663–668, 1987.

199. Wark PA, Gibson PG: Allergic bronchopulmonary aspergillosis: New concepts of pathogenesis and treatment. Respirology 6:1–7, 2001.

200. Salez F, Brichet A, Desurmont S, et al: Effects of itraconazole therapy in allergic bronchopulmonary aspergillosis. Chest 116:1665–1668, 1999.

201. Stevens DA, Schwartz HJ, Lee JY, et al: A randomized trial of itraconazole in allergic bronchopulmonary aspergillosis. N Engl J Med 342:756–762, 2000.

202. Wark PA, Hensley MJ, Saltos N, et al: Anti-inflammatory effect of itraconazole in stable allergic bronchopulmonary aspergillosis: A randomized controlled trial. J Allergy Clin Immunol 111:952–957, 2003.

203. Parmar JS, Howell T, Kelly J, et al: Profound adrenal suppression secondary to treatment with low dose inhaled steroids and itraconazole in allergic bronchopulmonary aspergillosis in cystic fibrosis. Thorax 57:749–750, 2002.

204. Skov M, Main KM, Sillesen IB, et al: Iatrogenic adrenal insufficiency as a side-effect of combined treatment of itraconazole and budesonide. Eur Respir J 20:127–133, 2002.

205. Liebow AA: Pulmonary angiitis and granulomatosis. Am Rev Respir Dis 108:1–18, 1973.

206. Katzenstein AL, Askin FB: Katzenstein and Askin's Surgical Pathology of Non-neoplastic Lung Disease. Philadelphia: WB Saunders, 1997.

207. Katzenstein AL, Liebow AA, Friedmann PJ: Bronchocentric granulomatosis, mucoid impaction and hypersensitivity reaction to fungi. Am Rev Respir Dis 111:497–537, 1975.

208. Robinson RG, Wehnut WD, Tsou E, et al: Bronchocentric granulomatosis: Roentgenographic manifestations. Am Rev Respir Dis 125:751–756, 1982.

209. Ward S, Heyneman LE, Flint JD, et al: Bronchocentric granulomatosis: Computed tomographic findings in five patients. Clin Radiol 55:296–300, 2000.

210. Rich AR: The role of hypersensitivity in periarteritis nodosa as indicated by seven cases developing during serum sickness and sulfonamide therapy. Bull Johns Hopkins Hosp 71:123–141, 1942.

211. Hertzman PA, Clauw DJ, Kaufman LD, et al: The eosinophilia-myalgia syndrome: Status of 205 patients and results of treatment 2 years after onset. Ann Intern Med 122:851–855, 1995.

212. Strumpf IJ, Drucker RD, Anders KH, et al: Acute eosinophilic pulmonary disease associated with the ingestion of L-tryptophan containing products. Chest 99:8–13, 1991.

213. Tazelaar HD, Myers JL, Drage CW, et al: Pulmonary disease associated with L-tryptophan-induced eosinophilic myalgia syndrome: Clinical and pathologic features. Chest 97:1032–1036, 1990.

214. Alonso-Ruiz A, Calabozo M, Perez-Ruiz F, et al: Toxic oil syndrome: A long-term follow-up of a cohort of 332 patients. Medicine (Baltimore) 72:285–295, 1993.

215. Cottin V, Frognier R, Monnot H, et al: Chronic eosinophilic pneumonia after radiation therapy for breast cancer. Eur Respir J 23:9–13, 2004.

216. Crestani B, Valeyre D, Roden S, et al: Bronchiolitis obliterans organizing pneumonia syndrome primed by

radiation therapy to the breast. Am J Respir Crit Care Med 158:1929–1935, 1998.

217. Cordier JF: Cryptogenic organizing pneumonitis: Bronchiolitis obliterans organizing pneumonia. Clin Chest Med 14:677–692, 1993.

218. Bousquet J, Chanez P, Vignola AM, et al: Eosinophil inflammation in asthma. Am J Respir Crit Care Med 150:S33–S38, 1994.

219. Bousquet J, Chanez P, Lacoste JY, et al: Eosinophilic inflammation in asthma. N Engl J Med 323:1033–1039, 1990.

220. Van Vyve T, Chanez P, Lacoste JY, et al: Comparison between bronchial and alveolar samples of bronchoalveolar lavage fluid in asthma. Chest 102:356–361, 1992.

221. Gibson PG, Fujimura M, Niimi A: Eosinophilic bronchitis: Clinical manifestations and implications for treatment. Thorax 57:178–182, 2002.

222. Niimi A, Amitani R, Suzuki K, et al: Eosinophilic inflammation in cough variant asthma. Eur Respir J 11:1064–1069, 1998.

223. Brightling CE, Woltmann G, Wardlaw AJ, et al: Development of irreversible airflow obstruction in a patient with eosinophilic bronchitis without asthma. Eur Respir J 14:1228–1230, 1999.

223a. Park SW, Lee YM, Jang AS, et al: Development of chronic airway obstruction in patients with eosinophilic bronchitis. A prospective follow-up study. Chest 125:1998–2004, 2004.

224. Quirce S, Fernandez-Nieto M, de Miguel J, et al: Chronic cough due to latex-induced eosinophilic bronchitis. J Allergy Clin Immunol 108:143, 2001.

225. Turner-Warwick ME, Haslam PL: The value of serial bronchoalveolar lavages in assessing the clinical progress of patients with cryptogenic fibrosing alveolitis. Am Rev Respir Dis 135:26–34, 1987.

226. Haslam PL, Turton CWG, Lukoszek A, et al: Bronchoalveolar lavage fluid cell counts in cryptogenic fibrosing alveolitis and their relation to therapy. Thorax 35:328–339, 1980.

227. Rudd RM, Haslam PL, Turner-Warwick M: Cryptogenic fibrosing alveolitis: Relationships of pulmonary physiology and bronchoalveolar lavage to response to treatment and prognosis. Am Rev Respir Dis 124:1–8, 1981.

228. Yousem SA: Eosinophilic pneumonia-like areas in idiopathic usual interstitial pneumonia. Mod Pathol 13:1280–1284, 2000.

229. Travis WD, Matsui K, Moss J, et al: Idiopathic nonspecific interstitial pneumonia: Prognostic significance of cellular and fibrosing patterns. Survival comparison with usual interstitial pneumonia and desquamative interstitial pneumonia. Am J Surg Pathol 24:19–33, 2000.

230. Basset F, Corrin B, Spencer H, et al: Pulmonary histiocytosis X. Am Rev Respir Dis 118:811–820, 1978.

231. Powers MA, Askin FB, Cresson DH: Pulmonary eosinophilic granuloma: 25-year follow-up. Am Rev Respir Dis 129:503–507, 1984.

232. Lieberman PH, Jones CR, Steinman RM, et al: Langerhans cell (eosinophilic) granulomatosis: A clinicopathologic study encompassing 50 years. Am J Surg Pathol 20:519–552, 1996.

233. Friedman PJ, Liebow AA, Sokoloff J: Eosinophilic granuloma of the lung: Clinical aspects of primary pulmonary histiocytosis in the adult. Medicine (Baltimore) 60:385–396, 1981.

234. Travis WD, Borok Z, Roum JH, et al: Pulmonary Langerhans cell granulomatosis (histiocytosis X): A clinicopathologic study of 48 cases. Am J Surg Pathol 17:971–986, 1993.

235. Bewig B, Stewart S, Bottcher H, et al: Eosinophilic alveolitis in BAL after lung transplantation. Transpl Int 12:266–272, 1999.

236. Mogayzel PJ Jr, Yang SC, Wise BV, et al: Eosinophilic infiltrates in a pulmonary allograft: A case and review of the literature. J Heart Lung Transplant 20:692–695, 2001.

237. Yousem SA: Graft eosinophilia in lung transplantation. Hum Pathol 23:1172–1177, 1992.

238. Gerhardt SG, Tuder RM, Girgis RE, et al: Pulmonary eosinophilia following lung transplantation for sarcoidosis in two patients. Chest 123:629–632, 2003.

239. Anonymous: Asthma and eosinophilia in a 66-year-old woman. Am J Med 87:439–444, 1989.

240. Shijubo N, Fujishima T, Morita S, et al: Idiopathic chronic eosinophilic pneumonia associated with noncaseating epithelioid granulomas. Eur Respir J 8:327–330, 1995.

241. Renston JP, Goldman ES, Hsu RM, et al: Peripheral blood eosinophilia in association with sarcoidosis. Mayo Clin Proc 75:586–590, 2000.

242. Horie S, Okubo Y, Suzuki J, et al: An emaciated man with eosinophilic pneumonia. Lancet 348:166, 1996.

243. Parry SD, Barbatzas C, Peel ET, et al: Sulphasalazine and lung toxicity. Eur Respir J 19:756–764, 2002.

244. Terzano C, Petroianni A: Clarithromycin and pulmonary infiltration with eosinophilia. BMJ 326:1377–1378, 2003.

245. Trojan A, Meier R, Licht A, et al: Eosinophilic pneumonia after administration of fludarabine for the treatment of non-Hodgkin's lymphoma. Ann Hematol 81:535–537, 2002.

246. Gagnadoux F, Roiron C, Carrie E, et al: Eosinophilic lung disease under chemotherapy with oxaliplatin for colorectal cancer. Am J Clin Oncol 25:388–390, 2002.

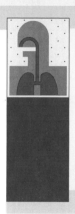

58 Lymphangioleiomyomatosis

Francis X. McCormack, M.D., Eugene J. Sullivan, M.D.

INTRODUCTION

Lymphangioleiomyomatosis (LAM) is a rare lung disease characterized by a strong association with the neurocutaneous syndrome known as tuberous sclerosis complex (TSC), marked female gender predominance, cystic destruction of the lung, progressive dyspnea on exertion, recurrent pneumothorax, and chylous fluid accumulation in the chest and abdomen.[1] LAM first appeared in the literature in 1918,[2] and not again until 1937.[3] In the 1950s through the late 1960s, there were solitary case reports or small case series with a varied and confusing pathologic nomenclature. Cornog and Enterline,[4] for example, described six cases of "lymphangiomyoma" and reviewed 14 cases in the literature with similar pathology that had been labeled "lymphangioma," "lymphangiomyoma," "lymphangiopericytoma," "leiomyomatosis," "lymphangiomatosis malformation," and "intrathoracic angiomatous hyperplasia." However, over the last 3 decades, larger case studies have better defined the natural history, pathologic classification, and clinical presentation of LAM.[5–12] Most significantly, recent synergistic interactions between pulmonary investigators, tuberous sclerosis geneticists, *Drosophila* biologists, and patient advocacy groups have resulted in truly significant progress in our understanding of the molecular and cellular basis of LAM.

EPIDEMIOLOGY

LAM almost exclusively affects young women, primarily in their reproductive years. It occurs in the setting of tuberous sclerosis complex (TSC-LAM), and also in a sporadic form in women who do not have TSC (S-LAM) (Table 58.1).[1] TSC-LAM is accompanied by the multiple system involvement and varied clinical presentations that characterize TSC. TSC is an autosomal dominant genetic disorder associated with development of hamartomas and dysplastic lesions in several organs, including cortical tubers, giant cell astrocytomas, and subependymal nodules in the central nervous system; angiofibromas, shagreen patches and ash-leaf macules of the skin; and angiomyolipomas and cysts of the kidney.[13] In S-LAM, by contrast, disease manifestations that accompany the thoracic changes include only angiomyolipomas and cysts in the kidney, and smooth muscle infiltration of the lymphatic system. Clinical presentations consistent with LAM have also been described in a few men with TSC,[14] including two biopsy-documented cases,[15,16] but never in men without TSC. Most of the LAM patients in the literature are from the United States, England, France, Japan, and Korea.[8–12] Although the geographic and racial distribution of LAM appears skewed, it is likely that all races are affected and that countries and populations with the greatest access to health care resources are overrepresented in these analyses.

The prevalence of LAM can be roughly estimated from TSC population data and LAM registries in England,[17] France,[12] and the United States.[18] The incidence of TSC is about 1 in 6000 births, and occurs equally in both genders.[19] The estimated worldwide prevalence of TSC is approximately 1.2 to 1.5 million people. Cystic pulmonary changes are found in 26% to 40% of women with TSC,[20–22] suggesting a TSC-LAM prevalence of approximately 150,000 to 250,000. In contrast, the global prevalence of S-LAM is roughly estimated to be 1 to 5 per million women, representing up to 25,000 to 50,000 patients. All together, therefore, there may be 300,000 or more LAM

The views expressed in this chapter do not necessarily represent those of the Food and Drug Administration.

Table 58.1 Comparison of the Two Forms of Lymphangioleiomyomatosis

	TSC-LAM	S-LAM
Estimated no. patients worldwide	250,000	30,000–50,000
Reported in males	+	−
Reported in children	+	+
Ascertainment	Mostly by screening	Dyspnea and pneumothorax
Germline *TSC* mutations	+	−
Both hits are somatic mutations	−	+
Inheritable	+	−
TSC1/TSC2 mutations reported	33%/66%	0%/100%
Angiomyolipomas	70–80% Often multiple/bilateral	40–50% Often single/unilateral
MMPH	+	Very rare, if ever
CNS/skin/eye/cardiac lesions	+	−
Retroperitoneal, thoracic adenopathy	+	+
Dyspnea	Less common	More common
Chylothorax	Less common	33%
Pneumothorax	Less common	66%
Respiratory failure	Less common	More common

CNS, central nervous system; MMPH, multifocal micronodular pneumocyte hyperplasia; S-LAM, sporadic form of lymphangioleiomyomatosis; TSC-LAM, tuberous sclerosis complex-lymphangioleiomyomatosis.

patients worldwide. The disparate population estimates for S-LAM and TSC-LAM highlight a curious paradox in the epidemiology of LAM: Although TSC-LAM appears to be much more common than S-LAM, most patients who seek medical attention for LAM-related pulmonary complaints have S-LAM. This observation suggests that either TSC-LAM is a milder disease than S-LAM, or that other TSC comorbidities overshadow the pulmonary manifestations of TSC-LAM. The National Heart, Lung and Blood Institute has established a National LAM Registry based at the Cleveland Clinic, which is currently collecting data on over 250 LAM patients, including over 30 with TSC.

INHERITANCE

Due to the severe clinical consequences of TSC, large TSC families are rare.[23] Approximately two thirds of new TSC cases arise from de novo mutations, which occur during embryogenesis. There have been several reports of familial TSC-LAM,[20,24] but mother-daughter transmission of S-LAM has never been reported.

ETIOLOGY

Our understanding of the genetic and molecular basis of TSC and LAM has increased substantially in the past 5 years. The most significant findings have included that LAM is quite common in women with TSC; that *TSC* mutations occur in the lungs, kidneys, and lymph nodes of patients

with S-LAM[25,26]; and that dysregulation of the Akt signaling pathway plays a central role in TSC and LAM cell growth, motility, and survival.[27,28,28a]

CONTROL OF CELL GROWTH BY TUMOR SUPPRESSOR PROTEINS

Clinicians have long recognized that the lung disease that occurs in women with TSC is pathologically indistinguishable from that which occurs in women with S-LAM.[4,29] However, the demonstration that S-LAM and TSC-LAM are genetically linked was reported only recently.[30] The lag period in our understanding was due, in part, to the failure to appreciate that a nonfamilial disease could share a common genetic basis with an inheritable disease. There are actually several precedents for this phenomenon among the class of diseases known as tumor suppressor syndromes (including neurofibromatosis and von Hippel-Lindau disease), of which TSC is a member. Tumor suppressor proteins regulate orderly cell growth and differentiation by sensing the surrounding environment, transmitting signals to the nucleus, and directly affecting transcription, translation, survival, or cell division. In the classic "two hit" paradigm,[31] a mutant copy of a tumor suppressor gene is inherited, but a tumor or dysplastic lesion develops only when the second "good" copy of the tumor suppressor gene is inactivated through a random, somatic mutation. The first (inherited) hit, often a point mutation or a small insertion or deletion, results in heterozygosity for the wild-type allele. The second mutational event is usually a large deletion, resulting in the loss of a chromosomal segment. A polymerase chain reaction technique can be used to detect the loss of heterozygosity for the wild-type allele caused by the deletion. When both copies of a tumor suppressor gene contain critical mutations, the protein produced by the gene is defective or deficient, protein function is lost, and cell growth, survival, and synthetic function become dysregulated.

REGULATION OF SIGNALING THROUGH AKT PATHWAY BY HAMARTIN AND TUBERIN

TSC is due to inactivating mutations in either of the two known *TSC* loci, *TSC1* on chromosome 9q34[32] and *TSC2* on chromosome 16p13.[33] The proteins encoded by *TSC1* and *TSC2* are hamartin and tuberin, respectively. Hamartin has no informative homologies with other proteins in the National Center for Biotechnology Information database, whereas tuberin has a domain with GTPase activating protein (GAP) homology.[34] Until recently, very little was known about the function of TSC proteins other than that they modulated cell growth. In 1999, Ito and Rubin[35] first reported that the enlarged eye cells characteristic of the mutant fruit fly, *Gigas*, could be induced by genetic inactivation of the fly homologue for tuberin. The loss of tuberin resulted in a defect in cell cycle control, which caused the cells to repeat S phase without entering M phase. Several laboratories subsequently reported that tuberin and hamartin regulate signaling through the PI3K/PKB(Akt)/S6K pathway, which controls cellular size and proliferation.[36–38] Delineation of the function and positioning of the TSC proteins in the Akt/S6K pathway has been a rapidly evolving process, and the available data to date are modeled in Figure 58.1. Tuberin and hamartin associate into a complex that functions as a master regulator for the kinase mTOR, or mammalian target of rapamycin (otherwise known as sirolimus), through an intermediate G protein called Rheb.[39,40,40a] The intact tuberin-hamartin complex acts as a GAP for Rheb, and maintains Rheb in an inactivated, nonphosphorylated state (Rheb-GDP). Phosphorylation of tuberin by Akt inactivates the GAP activity of the tuberin-hamartin complex, increases the abundance of Rheb-GTP, and permits phosphorylation and activation of downstream targets through mTOR to S6 and the initiation factor 4E binding protein (4E-BP1).

Thus, genetic mutations that result in the absence or dysfunction of tuberin or hamartin, as occur in patients with TSC and LAM, cause constitutive activation of S6K and 4E-BP1, two proteins that are intimately involved in the regulation of protein translation. The end result is the inappropriate stimulation of protein synthesis, cell motility, and cell growth.[28] Multiple mTOR effectors and mTOR itself were found to be highly phosphorylated in renal tumors of rats,[41] mice,[42] and humans[43] with mutations in *TSC* genes. Sirolimus, a microbial product that binds the intracellular receptor FKBP12 (an FK-506 binding protein) to inhibit mTOR activity, extinguished phospho-S6 expression and caused widespread apoptosis in the rat renal tumors.[41]

TSC MUTATIONS IN LUNG AND KIDNEY LESIONS OF PATIENTS WITH S-LAM

TSC patients have germline mutations in *TSC* genes, but S-LAM patients do not.[44] Smolarek and colleagues[45] first

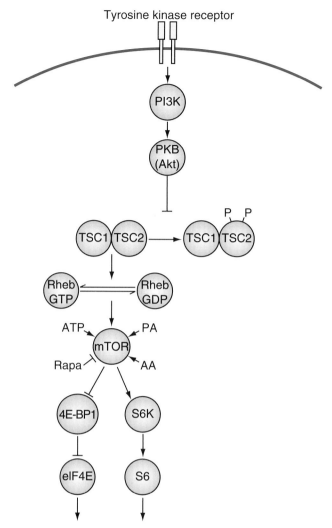

Figure 58.1 Tuberous sclerosis proteins regulate signaling through the Akt growth and protein translation pathway. The binding of a ligand to a growth factor receptor activates PI3K, followed by Akt. Activated pAkt phosphorylates TSC2, which blocks its GTPase activating protein (GAP) activity. When not phosphorylated, TSC2 complexed with TSC1 functions as a GAP for Rheb, maintaining Rheb in an inactivated Rheb-GDP state. Activated Rheb (Rheb-GTP) is therefore abundant when TSC1 or TSC2 is missing or when TSC2 is phosphorylated. Rheb-GTP activates mTOR in a manner that is potentiated by the availability of amino acids (AA), phosphatidic acid (PA), and ATP, and is blocked by the absence of these substrates or the presence of sirolimus (rapa). Activated mTOR phosphorylates downstream targets S6K and 4E binding protein (4E-BP1). pS6K phosphorylates S6 and 4E-BP1 releases elF4E, which together activate the cellular translational machinery and promote cell growth. (Adapted from Kwiatkowski DJ: Rhebbing up mTOR: New insights on TSC1 and TSC2, and the pathogenesis of tuberous sclerosis. Cancer Biol Ther 2:471–476, 2003.)

implicated *TSC* genes in the pathogenesis of S-LAM by finding that loss of heterozygosity for *TSC2* was present in fat- and smooth muscle–containing kidney tumors called angiomyolipomas and in lymph nodes from S-LAM patients. Proof that that loss of tuberin function was responsible for lung disease in LAM was provided by Carsillo and associates,[30] who demonstrated the presence of missense and protein-truncating TSC2 mutations associated with loss of heterozygosity in the abnormal lung and kidney tissue of patients with S-LAM. Samples taken from the normal regions of lung and kidney in those patients did not exhibit TSC mutations.[44] These findings were subsequently confirmed by Sato and colleagues,[46] and all S-LAM mutations described to date have been TSC2 mutations.[30,46,47] These data indicate that S-LAM is caused by mutations in the TSC2 gene that cause defects or deficiency in tuberin, and that both mutations likely occur after conception. TSC1 mutations have been described in TSC-LAM,[48] and future studies may reveal them to be causative in S-LAM as well.

GENETIC EVIDENCE THAT S-LAM MAY BE METASTATIC

Carsillo and coworkers[30] found that the mutations present in the kidney and lung of individual S-LAM patients were identical, suggesting that they had a common origin. A model for LAM was proposed in which the lung infiltration is a consequence of benign metastasis of LAM cells from the kidney tumor, axial lymph nodes, or other source. Reports of recurrence of LAM in the donor lung of LAM patients who had undergone lung transplant are also consistent with this metastatic theory[49-52a]; in two cases, lung metastases of recipient origin were proven by genetic and molecular techniques.[52,53] These data contradicted earlier reports that the recurrent lesions were derived from donor cells[49,50]; the techniques employed in those studies relied on antibody staining of lung sections, and were dependent on a degree of spatial resolution that is difficult to accomplish by immunohistochemistry. Other rare diseases that result from metastases of benign smooth muscle cells in women include leiomyomatosis peritonealis disseminata,[54] intravenous leiomyomatosis,[55] and benign metastasizing leiomyomatosis.[56] The metastatic theory of LAM suggests new avenues for treatment based on early intervention.[26]

The demonstration that S-LAM is also due to TSC mutations proves that TSC-LAM and S-LAM share a common genetic mechanism, and has focused attention on the Akt pathway that has proven to be central to TSC pathogenesis. Goncharova and colleagues[57] reported abundant S6 phosphorylation and unregulated cell proliferation in LAM cells isolated from explanted LAM lungs (harvested at lung transplant). They further demonstrated that sirolimus blocked the hyperphosphorylation of S6 and restored orderly cell growth. These and other studies form the basis for the trial of sirolimus in patients with TSC and LAM, currently underway in the United States and Europe. Recent evidence that tuberin regulates vascular endothelial growth factor in a sirolimus-reversible manner suggests additional and equally exciting therapeutic strategies based on inhibition of angiogenesis.[58,59] The development of adequate cell and animal models for LAM to test novel therapies remains a high priority for the field.

FUTURE DIRECTIONS IN RESEARCH

There are many unresolved questions regarding LAM. Although all current therapies are based on inhibition of estrogen activity, the role of estrogen in LAM pathogenesis remains unclear. Estrogen regulates the transcription of many genes, and there is some evidence that estrogen can modulate signaling through the Akt pathway.[60,61] Estrogen may play a role in LAM cell migration, infiltration, proliferation, or secretion of destructive proteases.[28,61] The mechanism of cyst formation is also the subject of debate. Although previous investigators had postulated that airflow obstruction due to smooth muscle cell infiltration was responsible for air space dilation, few investigators currently subscribe to this theory. Similar cystic changes occur in patients with metastatic endometrial stromal sarcoma, benign metastasizing leiomyoma, and mesenchymal cystic hamartoma of the lung, implicating an inherent capability of ectopic smooth muscle cells to effect cystic remodeling in the lungs. LAM lesions have been shown to be associated with protease imbalances, including up-regulation of matrix metalloproteinases 2 and 9,[62,63] and down-regulation of tissue inhibitor of metalloproteinase-3.[64] Several metalloproteinase inhibitors being tested for the other diseases may become candidate therapies for LAM as the role of matrix metalloproteinases in lung destruction becomes better defined.

CLINICAL FEATURES

The clinical onset of LAM usually occurs during the reproductive years. In most series, the mean age at the onset of symptoms of the disease has been the early to middle 30s.[7,8,12,65] Although new diagnoses of LAM have been reported in patients ranging in age from 12 to 75 years,[66,67] documented cases of the disease prior to menarche are rare. A number of reports in the literature describe women in whom the diagnosis was made after menopause.[7,8,12,65,68-71] In some of these cases, even the symptoms of LAM appeared after menopause.[8,12] The disease does not appear to be smoking-related, as the majority of patients in the largest case series were nonsmokers.[8,11,12]

Because LAM is rare and the symptoms are often nonspecific, the diagnosis is often delayed. Initial incorrect diagnoses have included asthma, chronic obstructive pulmonary disease, and idiopathic pulmonary fibrosis. In larger series, the mean interval between the onset of symptoms and diagnosis has averaged 3 to 4 years.[7,10,12]

The most common presenting symptoms of LAM are dyspnea and pneumothorax. In the series reported by Urban and colleagues,[12] exertional dyspnea and spontaneous pneumothorax were the initial symptoms in 49% and 46% of patients, respectively. During the course of the illness, dyspnea developed in 87% of patients, pneumothorax developed in 68% of patients, and chylothorax developed in 33% of patients. The first pneumothorax precedes the diagnosis of LAM in 82% of patients; in fact, most patients have two pneumothoraces before the diagnosis is made. Pneumothorax is often recurrent.[6,10,12] In LAM patients who have a pneumothorax, the likelihood of an ipsilateral recurrence is greater than 70%, and the likelihood of a contralateral pneumothorax is greater than 70%. Pneumothorax likely results from the rupture of subpleural blebs, but whether the event is triggered by progressive degradation of connective tissue matrix or airflow obstruction and overdistention of distal air spaces, or both, is unclear.

Other signs and symptoms of LAM, which may be present at the onset or may develop during the course of the disease, include cough, hemoptysis, chest pain, and symptoms related to reflux of chylous fluid into extrapleural locations, such as the peritoneum (chylous ascites) or pericardium (chylopericardium), airways (chyloptysis), and genitourinary tract (chyluria and chylous metrorrhea). It is likely that the chylous complications of LAM result from obstruction of lymphatic channels due to infiltration by smooth muscle cells.

Angiomyolipomas, unusual hamartomas composed of fat, smooth muscle, and abnormal blood vessels, may occur in virtually any location in the chest and abdomen, but are most common in the kidney. About 50% of S-LAM patients have renal angiomyolipomas, compared to 70% to 80% of TSC or TSC-LAM patients.[20] Angiomyolipomas are more commonly unilateral and solitary in S-LAM patients, and more commonly bilateral and multiple in TSC-LAM patients. Blood vessels in angiomyolipomas are often tortuous and aneurysmal, and are composed of cells with normal genotype and cells with *TSC* mutations,[72] which may partially explain their propensity to bleed. Spontaneous hemorrhage into angiomyolipomas may produce severe flank or abdominal pain, acute hypotension, and/or anemia, occasionally in association with circulatory collapse. Rarely, LAM presents as adenopathy or retroperitoneal masses that mimic lymphoma, ovarian or renal cancer, or other malignancy.[73,74]

There have been case reports of exacerbation of LAM associated with birth control pill use[75] or during pregnancy.[76-80] In a group of 69 patients with sporadic LAM, the onset of pulmonary symptoms occurred during pregnancy in 9 of the 46 patients (20%) with a history of pregnancy before or at the time of diagnosis.[12] In this same group, a marked exacerbation of previously diagnosed pulmonary LAM was observed in 2 (14%) patients during pregnancy. The effect of pregnancy or exogenous estrogen use on LAM has not been systematically studied, however.

PHYSICAL EXAMINATION

The physical examination in LAM is often nonspecific. Lung auscultation is usually uninformative but may reveal crackles in 15% to 20% of patients, and rhonchi or wheezing in less than 15%.[8,10,12] Clubbing is apparently uncommon, being reported in 3% and 5% of patients in two larger case series.[8,10] Physical examination may also reveal evidence of pleural effusion, ascites, or pneumothorax, if present. Careful dermatologic, ocular, and dental surveys should be performed for evidence of TSC, including facial angiofibromas, subungual fibromas, palpable dysplastic cutaneous lesions called shagreen patches, hypomelanotic macules (including those with ash-leaf or confetti configurations), and dental pitting.[13]

IMAGING STUDIES

The chest radiographic findings in LAM are nonspecific. Early in the disease, the chest radiograph may appear normal or may suggest hyperinflation only. As the disease progresses, the chest radiograph demonstrates diffuse, bilateral and symmetrical reticulonodular infiltrates, which can progress to cysts, bullae, or a "honeycomb" appearance in the later stages[8,12] (Fig. 58.2).

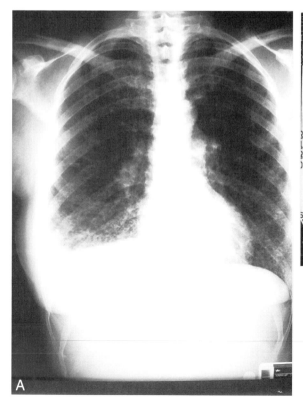

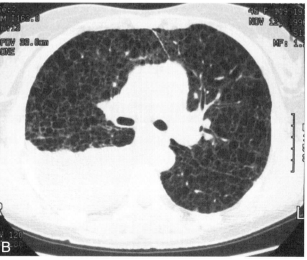

Figure 58.2 Chest radiograph **(A)** and high-resolution computed tomography scan **(B)** of the chest from a patient with lymphangioleiomyomatosis. Diffuse cystic changes and a right-sided chylothorax are present.

One characteristic radiographic feature of LAM is the preservation of lung volumes despite the presence of increased interstitial markings. This finding distinguishes LAM from most other interstitial lung diseases, in which alveolar septal and interstitial expansion tends to increase the lung's elastic recoil properties and decrease lung volumes. The chest radiograph may also reveal one of the common complications of LAM, pneumothorax or chylous pleural effusion. The presence of a pneumothorax may allow visualization of cystic changes in the deflated lung, which are not visible in the fully inflated lung.[81]

The high-resolution computed tomography (CT) scan of the chest is much more sensitive than the chest radiograph in detecting the cystic parenchymal disease, and is usually abnormal at the time of diagnosis, even when the chest radiograph and pulmonary function assessments are normal.[8,10,12,82] The CT shows diffuse, bilateral, thin-walled cysts of varying sizes ranging from 1 to 45 mm in diameter (see Fig. 58.2).[10,12] Blinded expert radiologists can correctly identify LAM among a pool of CTs consisting of a variety of other cystic lung diseases about 72% of the time.[83] Other CT features include linear densities (29%), ground-glass opacities (12%),[8] nodular densities (11%), hilar or mediastinal lymphadenopathy (9%), pleural effusion, pneumothorax, lymphangiomyomata, and dilated thoracic duct.[10,12]

In patients with TSC, nodular densities on high-resolution CT may represent multifocal micronodular pneumocyte hyperplasia (MMPH), clusters of hyperplastic type II pneumocytes.[20,84,85] MMPH may be present in men or women with TSC, and is very rare in patients with S-LAM.[86] MMPH has no known physiologic or prognostic consequences.

Chu and colleagues[10] reported that ventilation-perfusion scans were abnormal in 34 of 35 women with LAM. The most common abnormality was nonspecific, diffuse heterogeneity, usually grossly matched. These authors also described an unusual "speckling pattern" on the ventilation images in 74% of patients, consisting of "small, often peripheral collections of radioisotope."[10]

Abnormalities on abdominal imaging, such as renal angiomyolipoma and enlarged lymphatic structures, are also common in LAM (Fig. 58.3). Fat density within a renal mass is pathognomonic of angiomyolipomata. Angiomyolipomas are more common and more frequently bilateral and large in TSC-LAM than in S-LAM. In one report, angiomyolipoma size was found to correlate with the prevalence of pulmonary cysts in patients with TSC.[20] Chu and colleagues[10] reported the results of abdominal CT and ultrasound imaging in 35 patients with LAM. Twenty-two (63%) of these patients were found to have solid renal masses. In nine patients the solid masses were multiple, and in six they were bilateral. Renal abnormalities with features suggesting angiomyolipoma were seen in 18 patients (51%), consistent with prior studies.[87] These lesions were multiple in six patients and bilateral in four. Axial lymphadenopathy was also commonly seen in this series, including the presence of retroperitoneal nodes in 66% of patients. Less common findings were ascites (four patients), and renal cysts (three patients). Avila and associates[88] reported that abdominal lymphangioleiomyomas, often containing both cystic and solid components, were seen in 27 of 128 LAM patients.

Central nervous system abnormalities, such as cortical or subependymal tubers and astrocytomas, are common in patients with TSC, including those with TSC-LAM, but are not found in women with S-LAM. Moss and coworkers[89] reported that women with S-LAM and TSC-LAM may have an increased incidence of meningioma, but the significance of that finding has been questioned.[90]

PULMONARY FUNCTION TESTING

Pulmonary function testing in patients with LAM may be normal, or may reveal obstructive, restrictive, or mixed patterns, with obstructive physiology being the most common abnormality. For instance, initial pulmonary function testing in 69 patients with LAM revealed normal spirometry in 28 (42%), obstructive physiology in 23 (35%), restrictive physiology in 9 (14%), and combined obstructive and restrictive findings in 6 (9%).[12] Approximately 25% of patients with obstructive physiology may demonstrate bronchodilator responsiveness.[11] An increase in the residual volume–to–total lung capacity ratio, indicative of thoracic gas trapping, is common. The obstructive physiologic defect in LAM is attributable primarily to airflow obstruction, and to a lesser degree to a modest increase in lung compliance.[91] The most common finding on initial pulmonary function testing in various case series was abnormal gas transfer, as assessed by the diffusion coefficient for carbon monoxide (DL_{CO}), described in 82% to 97% of patients.[7,8,10,12] This led Urban and colleagues[12] to conclude that the diffusion coefficient "is the most sensitive functional abnormality in LAM and precedes any ventilatory defect in the natural history of the disease." Disease progression is characterized by a progressive obstructive ventilatory defect, and declines in FEV_1 and FEV_1/FVC ratio are most commonly used to monitor disease progression.

Crausman and coworkers[92] studied the mechanism of exercise limitation in 16 patients with LAM. They concluded that poor exercise performance was primarily due to airflow obstruction and increased dead space ventilation, caused by

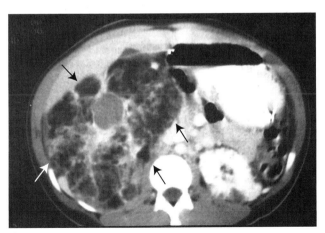

Figure 58.3 Abdominal computed tomography scan of an angiomyolipoma in a patient with lymphangioleiomyomatosis. Note tumor containing extensive fat density (bounded by *arrows*) that replaces the right kidney.

pulmonary vascular disease or extensive cystic change. Cardiopulmonary exercise testing in a much larger cohort of patients with LAM revealed a reduced maximum oxygen uptake and anaerobic threshold in 217 patients.[93] Exercise-induced hypoxemia occurred even in patients who did not have resting abnormalities in FEV_1 and DL_{CO}. In most patients, exercise was believed to be ventilation limited, due to airflow obstruction and increased dead space ventilation.

Taveira-DaSilva and colleagues[11] correlated lung function testing with lung histology in 74 patients and reported that a positive bronchodilator response was associated with a predominantly solid pattern of lung lesions (as opposed to cystic pattern), but not with airway inflammation (bronchiolitis), which was identified in 61% of lung biopsies. They also found that the DL_{CO} correlated with the lung maximum oxygen uptake and the lung histology score, a quantification of the extent of involvement with cystic lesions and LAM cells. However, FEV_1 and DL_{CO} were the best predictors of maximum oxygen uptake.

PATHOLOGY

Grossly, LAM lungs are enlarged and diffusely cystic, with dilated air spaces as large as 2.0 cm in diameter[6,94] (Fig. 58.4). Microscopic examination of the lung reveals foci of smooth muscle cell infiltration of the lung parenchyma, airways, lymphatics, and blood vessels, associated with areas of thin-walled cystic change (Fig. 58.5). There are two major cell morphologies that comprise LAM foci: small spindle-shaped cells and cuboidal epithelioid cells.[95] All such LAM cells stain positively for smooth muscle actin, vimentin, and desmin. The cuboidal cells within LAM lesions also react with a monoclonal antibody called HMB-45, developed against the premelanosomal protein gp 100, an enzyme in the melanogenesis pathway.[95,95a] This immunohistochemical study is very useful diagnostically, because other smooth muscle–predominant lesions in the lung do not react with the antibody.[96] The spindle-shaped cells of the LAM lesion are more frequently proliferating cell nuclear antigen positive than the cuboidal cells, consistent with a proliferative phenotype.[95] Compared to cigar-shaped normal smooth muscle cells, spindle-shaped LAM cells contain less abundant cytoplasm, and are less

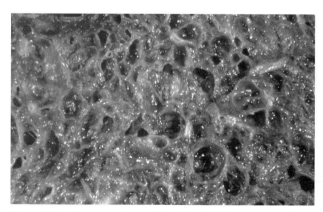

Figure 58.4 Gross specimen of lymphangioleiomyomatosis lung tissue. Extensive cystic changes are evident. *See Color Plate*

eosinophilic. Estrogen and progesterone receptors may also be present in LAM lesions,[97,98] but not in normal lung tissue.[99] The smooth muscle–like cells of angiomyolipomas are morphologically and immunohistochemically similar to LAM cells, including reactivity with antibodies directed against actin, desmin, vimentin, and HMB-45, as well as estrogen and progesterone receptors.[100,101] Unlike the dilated air spaces in emphysema, the cystic spaces are uniformly lined with hyperplastic type II cells.[102] Diffuse nodular proliferation of type II cells indicative of MMPH may occur in patients with TSC, in the presence or absence of LAM (Fig. 58.6).[86]

DIAGNOSIS

The diagnosis of LAM is often delayed, with many patients being treated for several years for alternative diagnoses. This unfortunate circumstance arises because the disease is rare, the symptoms are often nonspecific, and the radiographic manifestations can be protean. Many young women presenting with mild dyspnea are treated for asthma without extensive evaluation. Indeed, the findings of airflow limitation on spirometry found in LAM patients are consistent with asthma. Unless full pulmonary function testing is ordered, "red flags" such as reduced DL_{CO} will not be appreciated. Sadly, it is unusual for young dyspneic women with LAM to receive the correct diagnosis until a pneumothorax or chylothorax develops, or interstitial lung disease or an angiomyolipoma is discovered.

The differential diagnosis of the thin-walled cystic change that is characteristic of LAM also includes emphysema, Langerhans cell histiocytosis, lymphocytic interstitial pneumonitis, Birt-Hogg-Dubé syndrome,[103] and Sjögren's syndrome. Rare syndromes of benign or malignant smooth muscle metastasis may also produce cystic change and closely mimic LAM, including benign metastasizing leiomyoma,[56] endometrial stromal sarcoma,[104] and low-grade leiomyosarcomas. Other diseases that are confused with LAM include lymphangiomatosis, lymphangiectasis, and lymphatic dysplasia.[105]

In the proper clinical context, a diagnosis of LAM may be reasonably established based on radiographic findings if the differential diagnosis specific to each clinical setting is considered. For instance, classic LAM findings on high-resolution CT of the lung along with CT evidence of renal masses consistent with angiomyolipomata establish the diagnosis. Another disorder that presents with renal masses and lung cysts is Birt-Hogg-Dubé syndrome,[103] but skin nodules are also usually present and the renal lesions have a characteristic "chromophobe" histology. Pulmonary cystic change in a nonsmoking woman with TSC is consistent with LAM and does not usually require biopsy. In smoking patients, the diagnoses of emphysema and Langerhans cell histiocytosis[106] must be seriously entertained. Chylothorax in patients with pulmonary cysts is suggestive of LAM, but can be consistent with lymphangiomatosis,[107–109] a presumably unrelated lymphatic disorder associated with an equal gender distribution, bony disease, and no known hormonal responsiveness.

The diagnosis of LAM is most definitively established by lung biopsy. HMB-45 staining is quite specific for LAM and

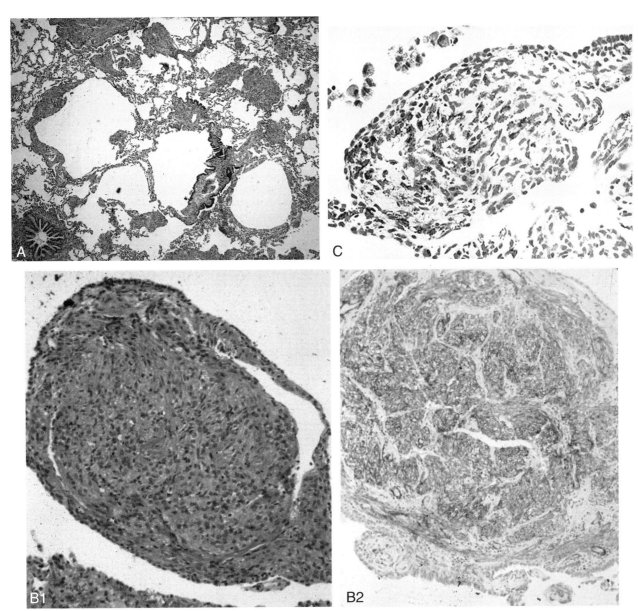

Figure 58.5 Histopathology of lymphangioleiomyomatosis (LAM). **A,** Smooth muscle cell infiltration, cystic change, and distorted pulmonary architecture characteristic of LAM. **B,** LAM nodule stained with hematoxylin and eosin (*B1*) or smooth muscle α-actin (*B2*). **C,** HMB-45 staining of LAM lung tissue. *See Color Plate*

can be used to differentiate LAM from other causes of smooth muscle proliferation in the lung, including idiopathic pulmonary fibrosis, benign metastasizing leiomyoma, and leiomyosarcoma. Successful bronchoscopic diagnoses, using transbronchial biopsies with appropriate immunohistochemical staining, are the exception, and surgical lung biopsy should generally be performed if there is any doubt about the diagnosis.

TREATMENT

There are no well-designed studies on which to base therapeutic decisions in LAM, and there is no consensus on optimal treatment of the disease. The three largest recent series, from Japan, England, and France,[8,12,110] reviewed ret-

rospective experiences with multiple therapies that can only be described as inconclusive. The definitions of evaluable treatments and response to therapy in these studies varied greatly. Each study reported a few responses, often in the chylous manifestations, but most patients remained stable or progressed. The few apparent pulmonary responses were often based on soft end points, such as a 15% increase in FEV_1, and none of the studies was statistically powered to address the question of therapeutic efficacy.

In the face of such uncertainty, decisions to treat are best made jointly by the patient and physician after thorough discussions of the risks and limited available data (Table 58.2). Therapies that are currently offered to patients who suffer progressive decline in lung function include progestins[110a] (both oral or intramuscular) and gonadotropin-releasing hormone agonists. For patients interested in therapy, oral

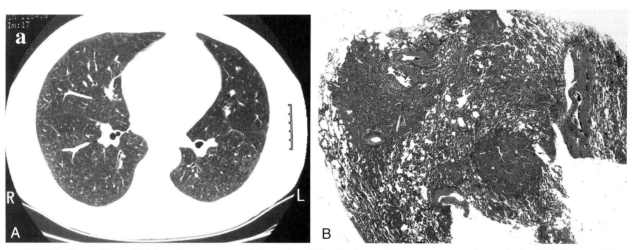

Figure 58.6 Radiographic and histopathologic presentation of multifocal micronodular pneumocyte hyperplasia (MMPH). **A,** High-resolution computed tomography scan of the chest of a patient with MMPH reveals miliary nodules throughout both lungs. **B,** Low-power view of the lung biopsy from a patient with MMPH reveals diffuse nodular proliferation of alveolar type II cells. *See Color Plate*

Table 58.2 Recommended Interventions, Studies, and Immunizations in Patients with Lymphangioleiomyomatosis

Interventions/Recommendations
Stop smoking
Stop all estrogen-containing medications
Counsel regarding pregnancy
Inform patient of symptoms of pneumothorax, chylothorax
Refer large angiomyolipomas (>4 cm diameter) for possible embolization
Refer for transplantation evaluation for FEV_1 <30%

Studies
High-resolution CT of the chest (follow every 1–2 yr)
Pulmonary function testing (follow every 6–12 mo)
Alpha$_1$-antitrypsin level
Abdominal CT or ultrasound for angiomyolipoma (follow every yr)
Rule out TSC with head CT or MRI, dermatologic, and ophthalmologic exams
Oximetry with rest, sleep, exercise
Bone densitometry

Indications for Lung Biopsy
Cystic pulmonary change without corroborating features of known TSC or angiomyolipomata
In smokers, lung biopsy may be required to distinguish LAM from emphysema and Langerhans cell histiocytosis

Immunizations
Yearly flu shot and Pneumovax

CT, computed tomography; FEV_1, forced expiratory volume in 1 second; LAM, lymphangioleiomyomatosis; MRI, magnetic resonance imaging; TSC, tuberous sclerosis complex.

progestins at doses that are sufficient to suppress serum estrogen production (e.g., norethindrone acetate [Aygestin], 10 mg PO daily or twice a day) are preferred over the suprapharmacologic intramuscular progesterone doses that have been promulgated in the literature (e.g., medroxy-progesterone acetate [Depo-Provera], 400 mg IM each month). Progestins at such high doses can cause fluid retention, depression, and mood swings. Gonadotropin-releasing hormone agonists (e.g., leuprolide [Lupron]) have been used in patients with LAM, but benefits are unproven and induction of early menopause is distressing and morbid in young women. There is no proven role for corticosteroids, immunomodulatory cytotoxic agents, or ovarian irradiation in the treatment of LAM. Ovariectomy is no longer widely recommended because the benefits are unknown and the risk of bone and heart disease is increased.[7,8,12]

Estrogen-containing medications may have adverse effects[75] and should be discontinued. Patients should be advised that pregnancy has been reported to result in exacerbations of LAM in some cases.[76–80] However, the risk of pregnancy in LAM has not been rigorously studied, and decisions regarding the advisability of pregnancy should be made on an individual basis.

A trial of bronchodilators should be considered in patients with LAM.[10] Extrapolating from chronic obstructive pulmonary disease populations, it is reasonable to speculate that oxygen use prolongs life in hypoxic patients. Oxygen should be administered to maintain oxyhemoglobin saturations of greater than 90% with rest, exercise, and sleep. Bone densitometry should be considered in all patients who are immobilized or on antiestrogen therapies, and appropriate therapy instituted for osteoporotic patients. Proper attention should be paid to cardiovascular health in patients who are rendered menopausal by therapy. Pulmonary rehabilitation seems to be particularly rewarding in this young, motivated population with obstructive lung disease, but studies to assess improvements in exercise tolerance, conditioning, and quality of life have not been done.

LAM patients may be at increased risk of pneumothorax during air travel due to the effects of changes in cabin pressure on noncommunicating cystic spaces in the lung. Of 395 patients who responded to the LAM Foundation enrollment questionnaire, 8 reported an episode of pneumothorax during air travel. In four cases, symptoms consistent with pneumothorax were present at the time the patient boarded the plane, such as preexisting chest pain or shortness of breath.[1] Although the denominator of the number of hours flown for the 395 patients is not known, four pneumothoraces in the group probably represents elevated risk compared to the risk of staying on the ground. In advising LAM patients about air travel, it is reasonable to consider several factors, including a history of prior pneumothorax (unless treated with a definitive surgical procedure), extensive cystic disease on high-resolution CT, and the overall extent of cardiopulmonary impairment. Patients with poor cardiopulmonary reserve may tolerate even small pneumothoraces poorly. It is prudent for LAM patients to obtain a medical evaluation, including a chest radiograph, prior to boarding a plane if pleuritic chest pain or unexplained persistent shortness of breath is present. Hypoxemia during flight presents independent risks. Patients should consult with their physicians regarding recommendations for on-board oxygen use.

Pleural disease should be aggressively managed. Over 65% of patients with LAM develop pneumothorax during the course of their illness, and the average number of pneumothoraces per LAM patient is 3.5. We advocate the use of a pleural symphysis procedure on the first pneumothorax, given the greater than 70% chance of recurrence. Contralateral pneumothoraces are equally likely, and bilateral pleurodesis is a reasonable therapeutic alternative at the time of the initial pneumothorax. Chemical sclerosis (preferably with talc), mechanical abrasion, talc poudrage, and pleurectomy have all been effective in patients with LAM. Although prior pleural procedures can increase perioperative bleeding in transplant patients, they do not appear to affect candidacy or survival.[111] Chyle does not generally cause pleural inflammation or fibrosis, and small chylous effusions most often require no intervention once the diagnosis of LAM is made. However, shortness of breath may mandate drainage—in some cases repeatedly. Pleural symphysis may be required to prevent nutritional and lymphocyte deficiencies that can result from repeated taps or persistent drainage. Chemical pleurodesis is generally an effective therapy for chylothorax, as is mechanical abrasion and talc poudrage.[112]

Urban and colleagues[12] reported the outcome of transplantation in 13 patients (associated with renal transplantation in 1 case). The mean interval between time of onset of LAM and transplantation was 7.8 ± 5.2 years (range 2.1 to 16.8 years). Mean FEV$_1$ before transplantation was 0.57 ± 0.15 L. Boehler and associates[113] conducted a retrospective questionnaire-based study on 34 LAM patients who had undergone lung transplantation. The actuarial survival after 2 years was 58%, which is similar to rates in other lung disease categories. The incidence of perioperative bleeding appeared to be higher, especially in patients with extensive pleural adhesions related to prior pleural procedures.

As with other obstructive lung diseases, referral for lung transplantation should be considered as the FEV$_1$ approaches 30% of the predicted value. Some patients who fail to meet this criterion qualify based on other factors that profoundly affect quality of life, such as disabling dyspnea or problems maintaining oxygen saturation. The question of bilateral versus unilateral transplantation has not been directly studied in LAM. Although bilateral lung transplantation produces better functional outcomes in some types of obstructive lung disease,[114] it is not always feasible due to the limited availability of organs and the urgency of the procedure in some patients.

Renal angiomyolipomas may require embolization or cauterization if bleeding occurs, which is thought to be more common when the diameter of the tumor exceeds 4 cm.[115] Others believe that the extent of aneurysmal change determines bleeding risk. Nephron-sparing partial resections may be required for very large tumors.[116]

PROGNOSIS

The clinical course of patients with LAM is quite variable. In general, the disease is believed to be slowly progressive.[116a] Estimates of the average rate of decline in lung function (FEV$_1$) range from 60 to 118 mL/yr.[11,117] A positive bronchodilator response, which was associated with a lower FEV$_1$, was found to be a predictor of a more rapid rate of decline in FEV$_1$ over time.[11] The data from the larger case series indicate that 38% to 78% of patients are alive 8.5 years from the time of disease onset.[7,8] Urban and colleagues[12] reported a 91% probability of survival at 8.5 years, 79% at 10 years, and 71% at 15 years. Matsui and colleagues[118] found that the actuarial survival, based on time from lung biopsy to death or transplantation, was 85% and 71% after 5 and 10 years, respectively. These investigators also developed a lung histology scoring system based on semiquantitative analyses of smooth muscle cell infiltration and cystic change, which correlated with survival. Using the Kaplan-Meier method, they found that patients with lung histology scores of 1, 2, and 3 had 5- and 10-year survival rates of 100% and 100%, 81% and 74%, and 63% and 52%, respectively. Other negative prognostic indicators that have been reported include a reduced FEV$_1$/FVC ratio, increased total lung capacity, and a predominantly cystic, rather than smooth muscle hyperplastic, histology.[8] No prognostic data are available for TSC-LAM, but the survival of patients identified through screening is almost certainly more favorable than that of patients who present with dyspnea.[20,22]

SUMMARY

LAM is an uncommon, progressive cystic lung disease that is almost exclusively restricted to women. Pulmonary parenchymal changes consistent with LAM are found in about one third of women with the autosomal dominant tumor suppressor syndrome TSC, but only a small fraction of these patients (probably <10%) develop significant pulmonary limitation. LAM also occurs in a sporadic form (S-LAM) that is associated with somatic (i.e., not germline) mutations in TSC genes, which commonly results in respiratory impairment. Conceptually, S-LAM can be considered as TSC isolated to the lung, kidney, and lymphatic system. Dysfunction or deficiency of the tuberous sclerosis proteins tuberin and hamartin causes TSC-LAM and S-LAM. LAM may be a metastatic illness, based on recent evidence that recurrent LAM after lung transplantation results from seeding of the graft from a recipient source.

The most common presentation of LAM is progressive dyspnea on exertion, often in association with a history of pneumothorax or chylothorax. The histopathologic hallmark of the disease is dilated distal air spaces and diffuse infiltration of the pulmonary interstitium with atypical smooth muscle cells, including spaces surrounding airways, vessels, and lymphatics. Renal angiomyolipomas, unusual hamartomas containing fat, smooth muscle, and blood vessels, are present in about 70% to 80% of patients with TSC-LAM and 50% of patients with S-LAM. Angiomyolipoma cells share numerous morphologic, histologic, immunohistochemical, and genetic similarities with LAM cells. Hemorrhage into an angiomyolipoma can produce a range of symptoms from chronic intermittent flank pain to acute abdomen with hypovolemic shock. When a history of chylothorax, angiomyolipomata, or known TSC is present, lung biopsy is usually not required for the diagnosis of LAM in nonsmoking females with typical thoracic radiographic changes on high-resolution CT. In the absence of these corroborating features, pathologic confirmation is usually prudent.

Patients with LAM should avoid exposure to tobacco smoke, discontinue estrogen-containing supplements, and become informed regarding the potential risks of pregnancy. Current therapies for LAM are targeted at antagonizing the action of estrogen, especially with progesterone or gonadotropin-releasing hormone agonists, but there is no convincing evidence that these empirical strategies are effective. Pneumothorax should be managed aggressively with pleural symphysis procedures, because the likelihood of recurrence is greater than 70%. Large angiomyolipomas (>4 cm) should be evaluated for angiographic embolization. Lung transplantation is an important option for patients with end-stage LAM, and outcomes are similar to those for patients with other diseases, but the perioperative complication rate appears to be somewhat higher. Support organizations available for LAM patients include the LAM Foundation (http://lam.uc.edu/), the Tuberous Sclerosis Alliance (http://www.tsalliance.org/), and LAM organizations in Japan (http://www7.plala.or.jp/lam_japan/public/), France (http://www.orpha.net/nestasso/FLAM/), England (http://www.lamaction.org/), Italy (http://www.ailam.it/), Germany (http://lam-info.de/), Australia (http://www.LAM.org.au/), and New Zealand (http://www.lam.org.nz/).

REFERENCES

1. Sullivan EJ: Lymphangioleiomyomatosis: A review. Chest 114:1689–1703, 1998.
2. Lautenbacher R: Dysembryomes metotipiques des reins, carcinose submiliere aigü poumon avec amphyseme généralise et double pneumothorax. Ann Med Interne (Paris) 5:435–450, 1918.
3. von Stossel E: Uber muskulare Cirrhose der Lunge (Muscular cirrhosis of the lung). Beitr Klin Tuberk 90:432–442, 1937.
4. Cornog JL Jr, Enterline HT: Lymphangiomyoma, a benign lesion of chyliferous lymphatics synonymous with lymphangiopericytoma. Cancer 19:1909–1930, 1966.
5. Silverstein EF, Ellis K, Wolff M, et al: Pulmonary lymphangiomyomatosis. Am J Roentgenol Radium Ther Nucl Med 120:832–850, 1974.
6. Corrin B, Leibow AA, Friedman PJ: Pulmonary lymphangiomyomatosis: A review. Am J Pathol 79:348–382, 1975.
7. Taylor JR, Ryu J, Colby TV, et al: Lymphangioleiomyomatosis: Clinical course in 32 patients. N Engl J Med 323:1254–1260, 1990.
8. Kitaichi M, Nishimura K, Itoh H, et al: Pulmonary lymphangioleiomyomatosis: A report of 46 patients including a clinicopathologic study of prognostic factors. Am J Respir Crit Care Med 151:527–533, 1995.
9. Oh YM, Mo EK, Jang SH, et al: Pulmonary lymphangioleiomyomatosis in Korea. Thorax 54:618–621, 1999.
10. Chu SC, Horiba K, Usuki J, et al: Comprehensive evaluation of 35 patients with lymphangioleiomyomatosis. Chest 115:1041–1052, 1999.
11. Taveira-DaSilva AM, Hedin C, Stylianou MP, et al: Reversible airflow obstruction, proliferation of abnormal smooth muscle cells, and impairment of gas exchange as predictors of outcome in lymphangioleiomyomatosis. Am J Respir Crit Care Med 164:1072–1076, 2001.
12. Urban T, Lazor R, Lacronique J, et al: Pulmonary lymphangioleiomyomatosis: A study of 69 patients. Groupe d'Etudes et de Recherche sur les Maladies "Orphelines" Pulmonaires (GERM"O"P). Medicine (Baltimore) 78:321–337, 1999.
13. Gomez M, Sampson J, Whittemore V: The Tuberous Sclerosis Complex (3rd ed). Oxford: Oxford University Press, 1999.
14. Dwyer JM, Hickie JB, Garvan J: Pulmonary tuberous sclerosis: Report of three patients and a review of the literature. Q J Med 40:115–125, 1971.
15. Aubry MC, Myers JL, Ryu JH, et al: Pulmonary lymphangioleiomyomatosis in a man. Am J Respir Crit Care Med 162:749–752, 2000.
16. Kim NR, Chung MP, Park CK, et al: Pulmonary lymphangioleiomyomatosis and multiple hepatic angiomyolipomas in a man. Pathol Int 53:231–235, 2003.
17. Johnson S: Rare diseases. 1. Lymphangioleiomyomatosis: Clinical features, management and basic mechanisms. Thorax 54:254–264, 1999.
18. Sullivan EJ, Beck GJ, Peavy HH, et al: Lymphangioleiomyomatosis Registry. Chest 115:301, 1999.
19. Sampson JR, Scahill SJ, Stephenson JB, et al: Genetic aspects of tuberous sclerosis in the west of Scotland. J Med Genet 26:28–31, 1989.
20. Franz DN, Brody A, Meyer C, et al: Mutational and radiographic analysis of pulmonary disease consistent with lymphangioleiomyomatosis and micronodular pneumocyte hyperplasia in women with tuberous sclerosis. Am J Respir Crit Care Med 164:661–668, 2001.
21. Costello LC, Hartman TE, Ryu JH: High frequency of pulmonary lymphangioleiomyomatosis in women with tuberous sclerosis complex. Mayo Clin Proc 75:591–594, 2000.
22. Moss J, Avila NA, Barnes PM, et al: Prevalence and clinical characteristics of lymphangioleiomyomatosis (LAM) in patients with tuberous sclerosis complex. Am J Respir Crit Care Med 164:669–671, 2001.
23. Dabora SL, Jozwiak S, Franz DN, et al: Mutational analysis in a cohort of 224 tuberous sclerosis patients indicates increased severity of TSC2, compared with TSC1, disease in multiple organs. Am J Hum Genet 68:64–80, 2001.
24. Slingerland JM, Grossman RF, Chamberlain D, et al: Pulmonary manifestations of tuberous sclerosis in first degree relatives. Thorax 44:212–214, 1989.
25. McCormack FX, Smolarek T, Menon A: Lymphangioleiomyomatosis and leiomyoma: Possibility of shared origins. In Moss J (ed): Lymphangioleiomyomatosis and Other Disorders of Smooth Muscle Proliferation. New York: Marcel Dekker, 1998, pp 373–406.
26. Henske EP: Metastasis of benign tumor cells in tuberous sclerosis complex. Genes Chromosomes Cancer 38:376–381, 2003.

27. Kwiatkowski DJ: Rhebbing up mTOR: New insights on TSC1 and TSC2, and the pathogenesis of tuberous sclerosis. Cancer Biol Ther 2:471–476, 2003.

28. Astrinidis A, Cash TP, Hunter DS, et al: Tuberin, the tuberous sclerosis complex 2 tumor suppressor gene product, regulates Rho activation, cell adhesion and migration. Oncogene 21:8470–8476, 2002.

28a. Goncharova E, Goncharov D, Noonan D, Krymskaya VP: TSC2 modulates actin cytoskeleton and focal adhesion through TSC1-binding domain and the Rac1 GTPase. J Cell Biol 167:1171–1182, 2004.

29. Stovin PG, Lum LC, Flower CD, et al: The lungs in lymphangiomyomatosis and in tuberous sclerosis. Thorax 30:497–509, 1975.

30. Carsillo T, Astrinidis A, Henske EP: Mutations in the tuberous sclerosis complex gene TSC2 are a cause of sporadic pulmonary lymphangioleiomyomatosis. Proc Natl Acad Sci U S A 97:6085–6090, 2000.

31. Knudson AG: Two genetic hits (more or less) to cancer. Nat Rev Cancer 1:157–162, 2001.

32. van Slegtenhorst M, de Hoogt R, Hermans C, et al: Identification of the tuberous sclerosis gene TSC1 on chromosome 9q34. Science 277:805–808, 1997.

33. Identification and characterization of the tuberous sclerosis gene on chromosome 16. The European Chromosome 16 Tuberous Sclerosis Consortium. Cell 75:1305–1315, 1993.

34. Wienecke R, Konig A, DeClue JE: Identification of tuberin, the tuberous sclerosis-2 product: Tuberin possesses specific Rap1GAP activity. J Biol Chem 270:16409–16414, 1995.

35. Ito N, Rubin GM: Gigas, a Drosophila homolog of tuberous sclerosis gene product-2, regulates the cell cycle. Cell 96:529–539, 1999.

36. Potter CJ, Huang H, Xu T: Drosophila Tsc1 functions with Tsc2 to antagonize insulin signaling in regulating cell growth, cell proliferation, and organ size. Cell 105:357–368, 2001.

37. Tapon N, Ito N, Dickson BJ, et al: The Drosophila tuberous sclerosis complex gene homologs restrict cell growth and cell proliferation. Cell 105:345–355, 2001.

38. Gao X, Pan D: TSC1 and TSC2 tumor suppressors antagonize insulin signaling in cell growth. Genes Dev 15:1383–1392, 2001.

39. Stocker H, Radimerski T, Schindelholz B, et al: Rheb is an essential regulator of S6K in controlling cell growth in Drosophila. Nat Cell Biol 5:559–565, 2003.

40. Zhang Y, Gao X, Saucedo LJ, et al: Rheb is a direct target of the tuberous sclerosis tumour suppressor proteins. Nat Cell Biol 5:578–581, 2003.

40a. Karbowniczek M, Cash T, Cheung M, et al: Regulation of B-Raf kinase activity by tuberin and Rheb is mammalian target of rapamycin (mTOR)-independent. J Biol Chem 279:29930–29937, 2004.

41. Kenerson HL, Aicher LD, True LD, et al: Activated mammalian target of rapamycin pathway in the pathogenesis of tuberous sclerosis complex renal tumors. Cancer Res 62:5645–5650, 2002.

42. Kwiatkowski DJ, Zhang H, Bandura JL, et al: A mouse model of TSC1 reveals sex-dependent lethality from liver hemangiomas, and up-regulation of p70S6 kinase activity in Tsc1 null cells. Hum Mol Genet 11:525–534, 2002.

43. El-Hashemite N, Zhang H, Henske EP, et al: Mutation in TSC2 and activation of mammalian target of rapamycin signalling pathway in renal angiomyolipoma. Lancet 361:1348–1349, 2003.

44. Astrinidis A, Khare L, Carsillo T, et al: Mutational analysis of the tuberous sclerosis gene TSC2 in patients with pulmonary lymphangioleiomyomatosis. J Med Genet 37:55–57, 2000.

45. Smolarek TA, Wessner LL, McCormack FX, et al: Evidence that lymphangiomyomatosis is caused by TSC2 mutations: Chromosome 16p13 loss of heterozygosity in angiomyolipomas and lymph nodes from women with lymphangiomyomatosis. Am J Hum Genet 62:810–815, 1998.

46. Sato T, Seyama K, Fujii H, et al: Mutation analysis of the TSC1 and TSC2 genes in Japanese patients with pulmonary lymphangioleiomyomatosis. J Hum Genet 47:20–28, 2002.

47. Yu J, Astrinidis A, Henske EP: Chromosome 16 loss of heterozygosity in tuberous sclerosis and sporadic lymphangiomyomatosis. Am J Respir Crit Care Med 164:1537–1540, 2001.

48. Jones AC, Shyamsundar MM, Thomas MW, et al: Comprehensive mutation analysis of TSC1 and TSC2 and phenotypic correlations in 150 families with tuberous sclerosis. Am J Hum Genet 64:1305–1315, 1999.

49. Bittmann I, Dose TB, Muller C, et al: Lymphangioleiomyomatosis: Recurrence after single lung transplantations. Hum Pathol 26:1420–1423, 1997.

50. Nine JS, Yousem SA, Paradis IL, et al: Lymphangioleiomyomatosis: Recurrence after lung transplantation. J Heart Lung Trans 13:714–719, 1994.

51. O'Brien JD, Lium JH, Parosa JF, et al: Lymphangioleiomyomatosis recurrence in the allograft after single-lung transplantation. Am J Respir Crit Care Med 151:2033–2036, 1995.

52. Bittmann I, Rolf B, Amann G, et al: Recurrence of lymphangioleiomyomatosis after single lung transplantation: New insights into pathogenesis. Hum Pathol 34:95–98, 2003.

52a. Crooks DM, Pacheco-Rodriguez G, Decastro RM, et al: Molecular and genetic analysis of disseminated neoplastic cells in lymphangioleiomyomatosis. Proc Natl Acad Sci U S A 101:17462–17467, 2004.

53. Karbowniczek M, Astrinidis A, Balsara BR, et al: Recurrent lymphangiomyomatosis after transplantation: Genetic analyses reveal a metastatic mechanism. Am J Respir Crit Care Med 167:967–982, 2002.

54. Buckshee K, Verma A, Karak AK: Leiomyomatosis peritonealis disseminata. Int J Gynaecol Obstet 61:191–192, 1998.

55. Dal Cin P, Quade BJ, Neskey DM, et al: Intravenous leiomyomatosis is characterized by a der(14)t(12;14)(q15;q24). Genes Chromosomes Cancer 36:205–206, 2003.

56. Shin MS, Fulmer JD, Ho KJ: Unusual computed tomographic manifestations of benign metastasizing leiomyomas as cavitary nodular lesions or interstitial lung disease. Clin Imaging 20:45–49, 1996.

57. Goncharova EA, Goncharov DA, Eszterhas A, et al: Tuberin regulates p70 S6 kinase activation and ribosomal protein S6 phosphorylation: A role for the TSC2 tumor suppressor gene in pulmonary lymphangioleiomyomatosis (LAM). J Biol Chem 277:30958–30967, 2002.

58. El-Hashemite N, Walker V, Zhang H, et al: Loss of Tsc1 or Tsc2 induces vascular endothelial growth factor production through mammalian target of rapamycin. Cancer Res 63:5173–5177, 2003.

59. Arbiser JL, Brat D, Hunter S, et al: Tuberous sclerosis-associated lesions of the kidney, brain, and skin are angiogenic neoplasms. J Am Acad Dermatol 46:376–380, 2002.

60. Pedram A, Razandi M, Aitkenhead M, et al: Integration of the non-genomic and genomic actions of estrogen:

Membrane-initiated signaling by steroid to transcription and cell biology. J Biol Chem 277:50768–50775, 2002.

61. Razandi M, Pedram A, Park ST, et al: Proximal events in signaling by plasma membrane estrogen receptors. J Biol Chem 278:2701–2712, 2003.

62. Hayashi T, Fleming MV, Stetler-Stevenson WG, et al: Immunohistochemical study of matrix metalloproteinases (MMPs) and their tissue inhibitors (TIMPs) in pulmonary lymphangioleiomyomatosis. Hum Pathol 28:1071–1078, 1997.

63. Hayashi T, Stetler-Stevenson WG, Fleming MV, et al: Immunohistochemical study of metalloproteinases and their inhibitors in the lungs of patients with diffuse alveolar damage and idiopathic pulmonary fibrosis. Am J Pathol 149:1241–1256, 1996.

64. Zhe X, Yang Y, Jakkaraju S, et al: Tissue inhibitor of metalloproteinase-3 downregulation in lymphangioleiomyomatosis: Potential consequence of abnormal serum response factor expression. Am J Respir Cell Mol Biol 28:504–511, 2003.

65. Sieker HO, McCarty KS Jr: Lymphangiomyomatosis: A respiratory illness with an endocrinologic therapy. Trans Am Clin Climatol Assoc 99:57–67, 1987.

66. Awai K, Fujikawa K, Sato T, et al: Pulmonary lymphangiomyomatosis. Radiat Med 8:132–135, 1990.

67. Hancock E, Tomkins S, Sampson J, et al: Lymphangioleiomyomatosis and tuberous sclerosis. Respir Med 96:7–13, 2002.

68. Joliat G, Stalder H, Kapanci Y: Lymphangiomyomatosis: A clinico-anatomical entity. Cancer 31:455–461, 1973.

69. Sinclair W, Wright JL, Churg A: Lymphangioleiomyomatosis presenting in a postmenopausal woman. Thorax 40:475–476, 1985.

70. Baldi S, Papotti M, Valente ML, et al: Pulmonary lymphangioleiomyomatosis in postmenopausal women: Report of two cases and review of the literature. Eur Respir J 7:1013–1016, 1994.

71. Zanella A, Toppan P, Nitti D, et al: Pulmonary lymphangioleiomyomatosis: A case report in postmenopausal woman treated with pleurodesis and progesterone (medroxyprogesterone acetate). Tumori 82:96–98, 1996.

72. Karbowniczek M, Yu J, Henske EP: Renal angiomyolipomas from patients with sporadic lymphangiomyomatosis contain both neoplastic and non-neoplastic vascular structures. Am J Pathol 162:491–500, 2003.

73. Matsui K, Tatsuguchi A, Valencia J, et al: Extrapulmonary lymphangioleiomyomatosis (LAM): Clinicopathologic features in 22 cases. Hum Pathol 31:1242–1248, 2000.

74. Avila NA, Kelly JA, Chu SC, et al: Lymphangioleiomyomatosis: Abdominopelvic CT and US findings. Radiology 216:147–153, 2000.

75. Shen A, Iseman MD, Waldron JA, et al: Exacerbation of pulmonary lymphangioleiomyomatosis by exogenous estrogens. Chest 91:782–785, 1987.

76. Hughes E, Hodder RV: Pulmonary lymphangiomyomatosis complicating pregnancy: A case report. J Reprod Med 32:553–557, 1987.

77. Yockey CC, Riepe RE, Ryan K: Pulmonary lymphangioleiomyomatosis complicated by pregnancy. Kans Med 87:277–278, 293, 1986.

78. Sleiman C, Mal H, Jebrak G, et al: Pulmonary lymphangiomyomatosis treated by single lung transplantation. Am Rev Respir Dis 145:964–966, 1992.

79. Kerr LA, Blute ML, Ryu JH, et al: Renal angiomyolipoma in association with pulmonary lymphangioleiomyomatosis: Forme fruste of tuberous sclerosis? Urology 41:440–444, 1993.

80. Johnson SR, Tattersfield AE: Pregnancy in lymphangioleiomyomatosis. Am J Respir Crit Care Med 157:A807, 1998.

81. Case Records of the Massachusetts General Hospital. Weekly Clinicopathological Exercises. Case 24–1988: A 32-year-old woman with recurrent pneumothorax. N Engl J Med 318:1601–1610, 1988.

82. Muller NL, Chiles C, Kullnig P: Pulmonary lymphangiomyomatosis: Correlation of CT with radiographic and functional findings. Radiology 175:335–339, 1990.

83. Koyama M, Johkoh T, Honda O, et al: Chronic cystic lung disease: Diagnostic accuracy of high-resolution CT in 92 patients. AJR Am J Roentgenol 180:827–835, 2003.

84. Popper HH, Juettner-Smolle FM, Pongratz MG: Micronodular hyperplasia of type II pneumocytes—a new lung lesion associated with tuberous sclerosis. Histopathology 18:347–354, 1991.

85. Lantuejoul S, Ferretti G, Negoescu A, et al: Multifocal alveolar hyperplasia associated with lymphangioleiomyomatosis in tuberous sclerosis. Histopathology 30:570–575, 1997.

86. Muir TE, Leslie KO, Popper H, et al: Micronodular pneumocyte hyperplasia. Am J Surg Pathol 22:465–472, 1998.

87. Bernstein SM, Newell JD Jr, Adamczyk D, et al: How common are renal angiomyolipomas in patients with pulmonary lymphangiomyomatosis? Am J Respir Crit Care Med 152:2138–2143, 1995.

88. Avila NA, Bechtle J, Dwyer AJ, et al: Lymphangioleiomyomatosis: CT of diurnal variation of lymphangioleiomyomas. Radiology 221:415–421, 2001.

89. Moss J, DeCastro R, Patronas NJ, et al: Meningiomas in lymphangioleiomyomatosis. JAMA 286:1879–1881, 2001.

90. Franz DN: Meningiomas in women with lymphangioleiomyomatosis. JAMA 287:1397–1398, 2002.

91. Burger CD, Hyatt RE, Staats BA: Pulmonary mechanics in lymphangioleiomyomatosis. Am Rev Respir Dis 143:1030–1033, 1991.

92. Crausman RS, Jennings CA, Mortenson RL, et al: Lymphangioleiomyomatosis: The pathophysiology of diminished exercise capacity. Am J Respir Crit Care Med 153:1368–1376, 1996.

93. Taveira-DaSilva AM, Stylianou MP, Hedin CJ, et al: Maximal oxygen uptake and severity of disease in lymphangioleiomyomatosis. Am J Respir Crit Care Med 168:1427–1431, 2003.

94. Carrington CB, Cugell DW, Gaensler EA, et al: Lymphangioleiomyomatosis: Physiologic-pathologic-radiologic correlations. Am Rev Respir Dis 116:977–995, 1977.

95. Matsumoto Y, Horiba K, Usuki J, et al: Markers of cell proliferation and expression of melanosomal antigen in lymphangioleiomyomatosis. Am J Respir Cell Mol Biol 21:327–336, 1999.

95a. Zhe X, Schuger L: Combined smooth muscle and melanocytic differentiation in lymphangioleiomyomatosis. J Histochem Cytochem 52:1537–1542, 2004.

96. Hoon V, Thung SN, Kaneko M, et al: HMB-45 reactivity in renal angiomyolipoma and lymphangioleiomyomatosis. Arch Pathol Lab Med 118:732–734, 1994.

97. McCarty KS Jr, Mossler JA, McLelland R, et al: Pulmonary lymphangiomyomatosis responsive to progesterone. N Engl J Med 303:1461–1465, 1980.

98. Colley MH, Geppert E, Franklin WA: Immunohistochemical detection of steroid receptors in a case of pulmonary lymphangioleiomyomatosis. Am J Surg Pathol 13:803–807, 1989.

99. Berger U, Khaghani A, Pomerance A, et al: Pulmonary lymphangioleiomyomatosis and steroid receptors: An immunocytochemical study. Am J Clin Pathol 93:609–614, 1990.

100. Logginidou H, Ao X, Russo I, et al: Frequent estrogen and progesterone receptor immunoreactivity in renal angiomyolipomas from women with pulmonary lymphangioleiomyomatosis. Chest 117:25–30, 2000.

101. Henske EP, Ao X, Short MP, et al: Frequent progesterone receptor immunoreactivity in tuberous sclerosis-associated renal angiomyolipomas. Mod Pathol 11:665–668, 1998.

102. Matsui K, K Riemenschneider W, Hilbert SL, et al: Hyperplasia of type II pneumocytes in pulmonary lymphangioleiomyomatosis. Arch Pathol Lab Med 124:1642–1648, 2000.

103. Nickerson ML, Warren MB, Toro JR, et al: Mutations in a novel gene lead to kidney tumors, lung wall defects, and benign tumors of the hair follicle in patients with the Birt-Hogg-Dube syndrome. Cancer Cell 2:157–164, 2002.

104. Aubry MC, Myers JL, Colby TV, et al: Endometrial stromal sarcoma metastatic to the lung: A detailed analysis of 16 patients. Am J Surg Pathol 26:440–449, 2002.

105. Faul JL, Berry GJ, Colby TV, et al: Thoracic lymphangiomas, lymphangiectasis, lymphangiomatosis, and lymphatic dysplasia syndrome. Am J Respir Crit Care Med 161:1037–1046, 2000.

106. Vassallo R, Ryu JH, Schroeder DR, et al: Clinical outcomes of pulmonary Langerhans'-cell histiocytosis in adults. N Engl J Med 346:484–490, 2002.

107. Tazelaar HD, Kerr D, Yousem SA, et al: Diffuse pulmonary lymphangiomatosis. Hum Pathol 24:1313–1322, 1993.

108. Swensen SJ, Hartman TE, Mayo JR, et al: Diffuse pulmonary lymphangiomatosis: CT findings. J Comput Assist Tomogr 19:348–352, 1995.

109. Swank DW, Hepper NG, Folkert KE, et al: Intrathoracic lymphangiomatosis mimicking lymphangioleiomyomatosis in a young woman. Mayo Clin Proc 64:1264–1268, 1989.

110. Johnson SR, Tattersfield AE: Treatment and outcome of lymphangioleiomyomatosis in the UK. Am J Respir Crit Care Med 155:A327, 1997.

110a. Taveira-Dasilva AM, Stylianou MP, Hedin CJ, et al: Decline in lung function in patients with lymphangioleiomyomatosis treated with or without progesterone. Chest 126:1867–1874, 2004.

111. Boehler A, Speich R, Russi EW, et al: Lung transplantation for lymphangioleiomyomatosis. N Engl J Med 335:1275–1280, 1996.

112. Ryu JH, Doerr CH, Fisher SD, et al: Chylothorax in lymphangioleiomyomatosis. Chest 123:623–627, 2003.

113. Boehler A, Speich R, Russi EW, et al: Lung transplantation for lymphangioleiomyomatosis. N Engl J Med 335:1275–1280, 1996.

114. Bando K, Paradis IL, Keenan RJ, et al: Comparison of outcomes after single and bilateral lung transplantation for obstructive lung disease. J Heart Lung Transplant 14:692–698, 1995.

115. De Luca S, Terrone C, Rossetti SR: Management of renal angiomyolipoma: A report of 53 cases. BJU Int 83:215–218, 1999.

116. Bissler JJ, Kingswood JC: Renal angiomyolipomata. Kidney Int 66:924–934, 2004.

116a. Johnson SR, Whale CI, Hubbard RB, et al: Survival and disease progression in UK patients with lymphangioleiomyomatosis. Thorax 59:800–803, 2004.

117. Johnson SR, Tattersfield AE: Decline in lung function in lymphangioleiomyomatosis: Relation to menopause and progesterone treatment. Am J Respir Crit Care Med 160:628–633, 1999.

118. Matsui K, Beasley MB, Nelson WK, et al: Prognostic significance of pulmonary lymphangioleiomyomatosis histologic score. Am J Surg Pathol 25:479–484, 2001.

59 Pulmonary Alveolar Proteinosis

**Mani S. Kavuru, M.D., Tracey L. Bonfield, Ph.D.,
Mary Jane Thomassen, Ph.D.**

INTRODUCTION

Pulmonary alveolar proteinosis (PAP) is a rare idiopathic lung disease characterized by the accumulation of lipoproteinaceous material within the alveoli of the lungs. Since this disease was first described in 1958, fewer than 500 cases have been reported in the medical literature.[1,2] Although the pathogenesis of PAP has remained unknown, most investigators have postulated a decreased clearance of lipids and surfactant proteins from the air spaces by the alveolar macrophages and type II epithelial cells. Historically, there has been no effective pharmacotherapy for PAP, and sequential whole-lung lavage (WLL) under general anesthesia has become the mainstay of treatment. In fact, WLL is the only therapy that has emerged to improve symptoms and oxygenation in patients with PAP.

Over the past 10 years, important advances have been made in the understanding of alveolar proteinosis and surfactant homeostasis, offering new directions for research as well as patient management.[3–5] First, genetically altered mice that are homozygous for a disrupted granulocyte-macrophage colony-stimulating factor (GM-CSF) gene develop a lung lesion with histologic resemblance to the lung disease in PAP patients, but with normal steady-state hematopoiesis. The biochemical properties of the material filling the air

spaces in these mutant mice are similar to those of patients with PAP. Surfactant is thought to be cleared or catabolized by predominantly alveolar macrophages, a process apparently dependent on GM-CSF. These studies for the first time have indicated that the growth factor GM-CSF plays a pivotal role in normal surfactant homeostasis and suggests a role for GM-CSF deficiency in the pathogenesis of PAP. Second, all patients with idiopathic PAP, but not healthy controls, have neutralizing anti–GM-CSF autoantibodies both in the circulation and in the lung. These observations raised the previously unsuspected notion that human alveolar proteinosis may be an autoimmune disease, and that the GM-CSF antibody has potential utility as a diagnostic test. Adult idiopathic PAP has emerged as an autoimmune disease with localized deficiency in biologically active GM-CSF due to circulating autoantibodies. Additional data from several small case series suggests that exogenous therapy with GM-CSF may improve the lung disease in a subset of patients with PAP. Intervention directed at treating this relative GM-CSF deficiency or lowering the circulating antibody level may have promise in the therapy of this disease.

Alveolar proteinosis may be the first human disease wherein a circulating antibody against a specific growth factor is linked to disease pathogenesis. Over a relatively short time, studies from genetically altered murine models have been translated to human studies for new approaches to both diagnostics and therapeutics. Several exhaustive and recent reviews on PAP are available for additional information.[2,6–9b]

CLASSIFICATION

The cardinal feature of PAP is the filling of lung alveoli with periodic acid–Schiff–positive, lipid-rich material with preservation of normal lung architecture and paucity of inflammation or fibrosis. PAP may be viewed as a syndrome consisting of a heterogeneous group of diseases resulting from failure to clear surfactant. Excess accumulation of alveolar surfactant can occur by various mechanisms (Fig. 59.1): relative GM-CSF deficiency, abnormal or dysfunctional surfactant, or overwhelming of clearance mechanisms. There are several potential ways to classify this syndrome clinically:

1. PAP occurring in the presence of circulating anti–GM-CSF
2. Neonatal or congenital presentation of PAP
3. PAP in the setting of a systemic inflammatory disease or malignancy (most often hematologic)
4. PAP in association with specific exogenous or occupational exposures

ADULT IDIOPATHIC PULMONARY ALVEOLAR PROTEINOSIS

Most of the published reports of the PAP syndrome involve its occurrence in adults, usually as an isolated idiopathic lung disease without an underlying malignancy, immunologic abnormality, exogenous occupational exposure, or infection. This sporadic rare disorder may be referred to as "primary" or "idiopathic." Since the initial report of neutralizing anti–GM-CSF antibodies in the circulation of PAP patients by Kitamura and colleagues,[5] all of the published cases of idiopathic PAP in adults have been associated with the presence of this antibody.[10–12]

NEONATAL/CONGENITAL PULMONARY ALVEOLAR PROTEINOSIS

Congenital PAP was first described in 1981 in a consanguineous family with four affected siblings.[13] In the spectrum of neonatal or congenital respiratory distress syndrome, congenital PAP may account for 1% of all infant deaths within 6 months of life.[14] There are two well-characterized but very rare gene mutations that result in congenital alveolar proteinosis due to surfactant protein (SP) B deficiency[15–18] and GM-CSF receptor β chain abnormality.[18a] Since the initial description by Nogee and colleagues, there have been about 50 cases of this inherited autosomal recessive SP-B deficiency that presents in full-term infants with respiratory distress.[13,17] A clinical clue to the diagnosis is a term baby with respiratory distress not responsive to surfactant replacement or corticosteroids. This disorder is uniformly fatal within the first few months of life, and the only hope for survival is lung transplantation. The gene abnormality results in the markedly reduced or absent active SP-B. The diagnosis can be established by polymerase chain reaction assay for the known mutations of SP-B deficiency. Interestingly, the heterozygote for SP-B mutation is clinically asymptomatic and lives into

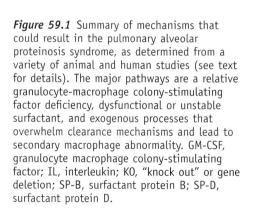

Figure 59.1 Summary of mechanisms that could result in the pulmonary alveolar proteinosis syndrome, as determined from a variety of animal and human studies (see text for details). The major pathways are a relative granulocyte-macrophage colony-stimulating factor deficiency, dysfunctional or unstable surfactant, and exogenous processes that overwhelm clearance mechanisms and lead to secondary macrophage abnormality. GM-CSF, granulocyte macrophage colony-stimulating factor; IL, interleukin; KO, "knock out" or gene deletion; SP-B, surfactant protein B; SP-D, surfactant protein D.

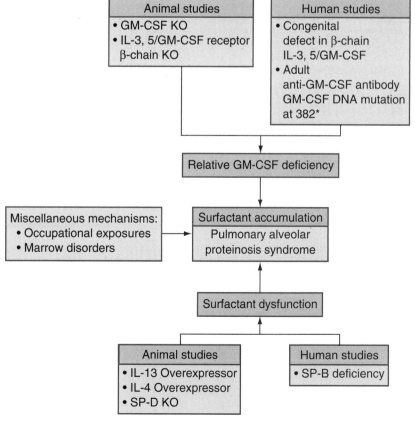

adulthood with normal lung function.[19] In addition, there are also isolated reports of a congenital alveolar proteinosis disorder due to a genetic mutation in the GM-CSF receptor gene β chain, radiographically and histologically indistinguishable from SP-B deficiency.[20] These infants present a bit later at several months of age and may have associated hematologic disorders.[21,21a]

SECONDARY PULMONARY ALVEOLAR PROTEINOSIS

There are many reports in the literature of alveolar proteinosis–like lung disease in the setting of other systemic disorders (Table 59.1). When PAP develops in association with another medical condition, it is often referred to as "secondary PAP." Chronic myelogenous leukemia and myelodysplastic syndrome are the most frequently noted underlying marrow disorders, but several others have also been reported.[22-24] Cordonnier and colleagues[24] recently reported that PAP accompanied 5.3% of all hematologic malignancies at their institution, which rose to 8.8% among neutropenic patients. Among their 10 patients with PAP, 5 had acute myeloid leukemia, 4 had chronic myelogenous leukemia, and 1 had acute lymphocytic leukemia. Three patients had undergone bone marrow transplantation. Nine of their 10 patients were neutropenic when they developed PAP, and most patients recovered spontaneously at the time of bone marrow restoration. A recent report of acute lymphoid leukemia with secondary PAP during the neutropenic

phase resolved with granulocyte-colony stimulating factor.[25] Several possible mechanisms have been advanced for this form of secondary PAP, including the malignant clone affecting the monocyte-alveolar macrophage lineage (i.e., leukemic cells lacking expression of the β$_c$ chain of the GM-CSF receptor), the effects of chemotherapy and radiation on macrophage number and function, and possibly the use of corticosteroid in this setting causing increased production of phospholipids.[21,26,27] Isolated case reports of systemic disease with effects on cell-mediated immunity have also been described in association with secondary PAP, including thymic alymphoplasia,[28] immunoglobulin A deficiency,[29] solid organ transplantation,[30] and acquired immunodeficiency syndrome.[31]

EXOGENOUS/OCCUPATIONAL EXPOSURE

PAP has been linked to several occupational exposures since it was first described (Table 59.2). Davidson and Macleod[32] found that approximately half of the first 138 patients had significant exposures to dust and fumes. Silica has been the most commonly reported exposure, with 10 of the 139 patients having heavy exposure to silica. With modern occupational precautions, this form of "acute silico-proteinosis" is quite rare.[33,34] Five patients in the original report of PAP by Rosen and colleagues[1] had been exposed to wood dust. Since these initial reports, multiple case reports of additional associations with occupational exposures have appeared in the literature, including exposures to aluminum dust,[35] cellulose fibers, cement dust (maybe related to silica), titanium dioxide,[36,37] and nitrogen dioxide. Unfortunately, it is difficult to implicate causality in these cases, and most of these associations remain unproven (see Table 59.2). However,

Table 59.1 Underlying Systemic Disorders Associated with Isolated Reports of Pulmonary Alveolar Proteinosis

Marrow Disorders
Acute lymphocytic leukemia
Acute myeloid leukemia
Aplastic anemia
Chronic lymphocytic leukemia
Chronic myelogenous leukemia
Myelodysplastic syndromes
Multiple myeloma
Non-Hodgkin's lymphoma
Waldenström's macroglobulinemia

Other Malignancies
Adenocarcinoma
Glioblastoma
Melanoma

Immune Deficiency Syndromes/Chronic Inflammation
Acquired immunodeficiency syndrome
Amyloidosis
Congenital lymphoplasia
Fanconi's syndrome
Hypogammaglobulinemia
Idiopathic thrombocytopenic purpura
Juvenile dermatomyositis
Renal tubular acidosis
Subacute combined immunodeficiency disease

Chronic Infections
Cytomegalovirus
Mycobacterium tuberculosis
Nocardia
Pneumocystis jirovecii (formerly *carinii*)

Table 59.2 Occupational Exposures Associated with Pulmonary Alveolar Proteinosis

| Agricultural dust |
| Aluminum dust |
| Bakery flour dust |
| Cement dust |
| Chlorine |
| Cleaning products |
| Fertilizer dust |
| Gasoline fumes |
| Nitrogen dioxide |
| Paint |
| Petroleum |
| Sawdust |
| Silica |
| Synthetic plastic fumes |
| Titanium |
| Varnish |

instillation of quartz (silica dioxide) in rodents produces alveolar proteinosis pathology and is a common way of increasing the amount of surfactant for isolating the surfactant proteins.[38]

EPIDEMIOLOGY

By all available data, PAP should be considered a rare or "orphan" lung disease. As mentioned earlier, there are only 500 reported cases in the literature to date.[1,2,7,9,39] Although the exact incidence and prevalence of PAP are unknown, it is likely that the published literature underestimates the disease prevalence.

A recent analysis of 410 published cases of PAP indicates that the median age at diagnosis was 39 years, the median duration of symptoms before diagnosis was 7 months, the majority of the patients were men (male-to-female ratio of 2.65:1.0), and 72% were smokers in the series that specified a smoking history.[2] There was no male predominance among nonsmokers, indicating that smoking may be a more important cofactor than gender, although this remains unknown.

CLINICAL CHARACTERISTICS

CLINICAL PRESENTATION

The clinical presentation of adult idiopathic PAP is variable and nonspecific. Patients typically present with subacute symptoms of cough and dyspnea, and a minority present with more acute symptoms, including fever, occasional hemoptysis, and constitutional symptoms. This nonspecific presentation may lead to months or years of misdiagnosis as "chronic bronchitis." The symptoms are frequently milder than expected from the radiographic findings. The physical examination is likewise nonspecific. The lung examination is frequently normal despite grossly abnormal chest radiographs, although crackles, clubbing, and cyanosis have been reported.

IMAGING STUDIES

Many patterns of chest radiographic abnormalities have been described in PAP. Typically a bilateral, symmetrical alveolar filling pattern is seen. Infiltrates classically are perihilar, extending to the periphery (lower more than upper) and sparing the costophrenic angles, yielding a "butterfly" distribution. This pattern is similar to that of pulmonary edema or *Pneumocystis jirovecii* (formerly *carinii*) pneumonia. Interstitial, mixed alveolar and interstitial, nodular, asymmetrical, and focal patterns have all been described. Although the absence of pleural effusions, adenopathy, and cardiomegaly helps to narrow the differential diagnosis of the chest radiographic pattern, the plain film appearance is generally nonspecific.

Computed tomography (CT) more clearly defines the extent, distribution, and nature of the infiltrates.[40–42] This is particularly true when thin sections are used. The infiltrates have been described as patchy or diffuse, and central or peripheral. Reticulonodular, ground-glass, and patchy or confluent air space patterns can be seen, often in the same

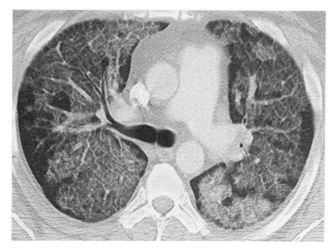

Figure 59.2 Computed tomography of the chest at the level of the tracheal bifurcation showing bilateral ground-glass air space disease with areas of "crazy paving" and "geographic distribution," typical of pulmonary alveolar proteinosis.

patient. The infiltrates are often delineated with sharp margins surrounded by normal lung (unexplained by normal anatomic landmarks). These areas have been referred to as "geographical" in appearance. The term *ground glass* has been used to describe a background homogeneous haze with preservation of the normal branching of vessels and airways. A branching pattern of white linear areas forming geometric shapes of around 10 mm in diameter is seen overlying consolidated or ground-glass areas.[43] This pattern, described as "crazy paving" (Fig. 59.2), has been seen in other diseases, including bronchoalveolar carcinoma.[44,45] Air bronchograms are variably reported, and the visibility of the pulmonary vessels is often preserved. Pleural effusions and adenopathy are usually absent. The CT appearance is quite characteristic of PAP, if not pathognomonic for the disease. Chest radiographic and high-resolution CT appearances have been shown to correlate with the presence of a restrictive ventilatory defect, reduced diffusing capacity, and hypoxemia.[41] An important current limitation of all radiographic techniques is the lack of a validated quantitative algorithm to assess lung disease burden.

PHYSIOLOGIC TESTING

In general, the most common pulmonary function abnormality is restriction.[2,9,40] The forced vital capacity and total lung capacity are mildly reduced in most series, with a disproportionate reduction in diffusing capacity. Patients tend to be mildly hypoxemic, with an elevated alveolar-arterial PO_2 difference along with a compensated respiratory alkalosis. The shunt fraction has been shown to be elevated as compared to patients with other diffuse lung diseases.[46]

LABORATORY EVALUATION

Routine laboratory studies are usually normal in PAP. Serum lactate dehydrogenase (LDH) is frequently elevated, although it is nonspecific.[46,47] In 36 PAP patients for whom the serum LDH level and the normal range were given, the level was 168% ± 66% of the upper limit of the normal range.[2] A recent report indicates that a normal LDH level may be predictive of a favorable response to GM-CSF therapy. However, the correlation between LDH level and arterial PO_2 is poor ($r^2 = 0.372$).[11] Surfactant proteins SP-A, SP-B, and SP-D have been reported to be elevated in the sera of patients with PAP.[11,48–50a] However, increased serum levels of these surfactant proteins is a nonspecific finding and has been noted in other lung diseases, including acute lung injury and idiopathic pulmonary fibrosis.[50,51] Krebs von den Lungen (KL-6), a mucin-like protein secreted by type II epithelial cells, is also elevated in serum and bronchoalveolar lavage (BAL) fluid in patients with PAP and is higher than in other interstitial diseases.[52] However, none of these serologic markers is particularly useful in the initial diagnosis of PAP. Their role in assessing disease severity or in monitoring disease activity is presently unclear.

DIAGNOSTIC EVALUATION

Although history, physical examination, radiographic studies, and physiologic testing may suggest PAP, further evaluation is usually needed to confirm the diagnosis. The most promising diagnostic test is determination of anti–GM-CSF serum titer (see section on discovery of anti–GM-CSF antibody later for a detailed discussion of current experience with this assay). BAL fluid from patients with PAP has fairly dramatic and characteristic features. This is true whether the fluid is obtained from a diagnostic bronchoscopy (i.e., 100 to 300 mL) or a therapeutic lung lavage. Most often, a transbronchial biopsy from an initial bronchoscopy or open-lung biopsy is performed to obtain tissue to confirm a diagnosis of idiopathic PAP and exclude other secondary etiologies for the pulmonary infiltrates. The more recent case series have used bronchoscopy with transbronchial biopsy as a diagnostic end point for PAP.[7,39] Our experience indicates that a characteristic CT scan and bronchoscopic findings are usually adequate.

BRONCHOALVEOLAR LAVAGE

BAL fluid from patients with PAP is grossly "milky" and opaque. When the lavage fluid is allowed to settle in a container, the effluent layers into a thick sediment and a more translucent supernatant (Fig. 59.3). A cytospin examination of the milky effluent contains large amounts of granular, acellular eosinophilic lipoproteinaceous material.[53,54] Papanicolaou-stained smears of the BAL fluid sediment reveal fat globules. The most striking observation from a cytospin preparation or cell blocks of the BAL sediment is the gross appearance of the alveolar macrophage. These cells are enlarged and engorged with lipid material with a foamy, vacuolated appearance under light microscopy (Fig. 59.4). Electron microscopy studies show the granular debris to be composed of tubular myelin, lamellar bodies, and fused membrane structures resembling surfactant. The presence of concentrically laminated structures called lamellar bodies can confirm that the acellular material is surfactant and further support a diagnosis of PAP.[9]

It is difficult to get an accurate cellular count from the lavage fluid because the large amounts of extracellular debris trap the cells with the centrifugation techniques. BAL

Figure 59.3 Gross appearance of the first liter of bronchoalveolar lavage fluid obtained at therapeutic whole-lung lavage, demonstrating "milky appearance" and a dense lipoproteinaceous sediment.

cellular differential counts from 36 unique PAP patients from the Cleveland Clinic have shown predominantly alveolar macrophages with lymphocytes, neutrophils, and eosinophils (Fig. 59.5). The majority of patients have a relatively normal differential cell count. In contrast, Milleron and colleagues,[55] in a group of seven all-male smokers with idiopathic PAP, noted a lower percentage of macrophages (39%) and increased lymphocytes (57%). Evaluation of the lymphocytes in these patients showed an increase in both CD4 and CD8 cells. Some reasons for the differences in the two studies include the fact that the latter study used a lower volume for BAL and different processing techniques.

Analysis of BAL fluid has revealed increased concentrations of lipids and proteins, particularly those associated with surfactant. The classes and distribution of surfactant phospholipids do not substantially differ from normal. Doyle and coworkers[51] reported that lavage fluid cholesterol from patients with idiopathic PAP is sevenfold greater than normal, making it the most abundant nonphospholipid component. Surfactant protein levels vary considerably from patient to patient, though they are consistently elevated. Both SP-A and SP-B have been reported to increase, and the SP-A–to-phospholipid and SP-B–to-phospholipid ratios are increased, with a normal SP-B:SP-A ratio. A dimeric form of surfactant protein C is present in increased quantities. SP-D has also been identified to be elevated in patients, though to a smaller degree than other surfactant proteins. This accumulated PAP material has been shown to have normal surface activity after processing.

PATHOLOGY

Macroscopically, both biopsy and necropsy specimens reveal multiple, up to 2 to 3 cm, yellow-gray nodular areas of consolidation. These areas are firm and exude a fatty substance when cut. On light microscopy, the alveoli are filled with a granular and floccular acidophilic acellular material that is

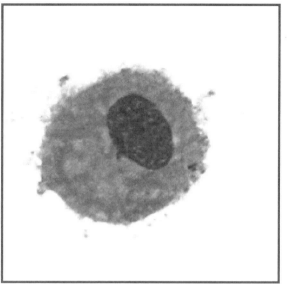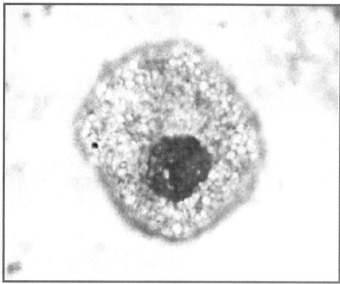

Figure 59.4 *Left,* Alveolar macrophage from a normal lung contains a single central nucleus with ample cytoplasm and long microvilli visible on the cell surface. (Original magnification ×400; hematoxylin stain.) *Right,* Alveolar macrophage from the lung of a patient with pulmonary alveolar proteinosis contains foamy cytoplasm, a result of phagocytosis of the surfactant phospholipids. (Original magnification ×400; hematoxylin stain.)

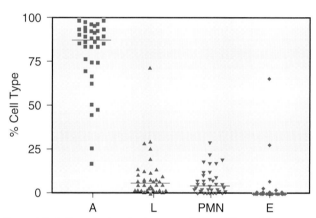

Figure 59.5 Bronchoalveolar lavage cellular differential counts in pulmonary alveolar proteinosis patients ($N = 36$), with median number of alveolar macrophages (A) = 88%, lymphocytes (L) = 6%, and polymorphonuclear leukocytes (PMN) = 5%. E, eosinophils.

amorphous and stains pink on hematoxylin and eosin (Fig. 59.6). This material stains intensely positive with periodic acid-Schiff after diastase digestion. This substance extends to the small bronchioles at times. Staining these specimens with SP-A antibody reveals uniform localization in the air spaces in primary PAP and patchy distribution in secondary PAP. Alveolar and interstitial architecture are typically preserved, though infiltration of bronchial walls with lymphocytes and thickening or fibrosis may be seen. The vasculature appears normal. Rare cases of pulmonary fibrosis have been described with long-standing PAP (see later discussion under Natural History and Prognosis).[56–59] Electron microscopy reveals characteristic multilamellated structures visible in the alveolar material as well as inclusions in the cytoplasm of macrophages.

PATHOGENESIS

SURFACTANT COMPOSITION AND HOMEOSTASIS

Surfactant is a complex mixture of phospholipids and proteins that is uniquely present in the normal lung at the interface of alveolar gas and the epithelial surface. Surfactant is reviewed in detail in Chapter 11.

Although the pathogenesis of PAP is unknown, most investigators postulate a decreased clearance of surfactant from air spaces rather than increased production.[60] Investigations of alveolar macrophages and PAP have suggested that macrophage surfactant uptake is normal but catabolism of surfactant is decreased. This leads to an accumulation of surfactant with subsequent inhibition of macrophage function (phagocytosis, migration, phagolysosome fusion, and subsequent killing).[61] These defects do not appear to be caused by an intrinsic cellular defect.

MURINE MODELS OF GM-CSF GENE OR RECEPTOR DELETION

An unexpected clue to the pathogenesis of PAP recently came to light when scientists working with genetically altered mice discovered that mice that are homozygous for a disrupted GM-CSF gene developed a lung lesion by 8 weeks of age with histologic resemblance to PAP.[3,4] Based upon quantification of surfactant protein messenger ribonucleic acid and immunohistochemical staining of wild-type and mutant murine lungs, the PAP that develops in these animals is believed to be the result of impaired surfactant clearance.[62] Further insight into the role of GM-CSF and surfactant metabolism was provided by Huffman and associates,[63] who demonstrated that local pulmonary epithelial cell–specific expression of GM-CSF using the promoter from the human SP-C gene corrects the alveolar proteinosis in the GM-CSF–deficient mice. Bone marrow transplantation and hematopoietic reconstitution of GM-CSF–deficient mice have also been shown to reverse the lung disease.[63] Additional studies demonstrated that exogenous administration of aerosolized GM-CSF corrects the lung lesion in the GM-CSF knockout mice.[64] Taken together, these studies strongly indicate that GM-CSF regulates the clearance of surfactant proteins and lipids.

Mice having a targeted deletion of the common β chain of the GM-CSF/interleukin-3/interleukin-5 receptor also develop PAP, which can be reversed by bone marrow transplantation and hematopoietic reconstitution by 8 to 12 weeks after transplant.[20,65,66] These observations indicate that the alveolar macrophage (which is marrow derived) is the cell that is restored in this model and is the likely target

of GM-CSF. Dirksen and colleagues[20] described four children who had defects in the β chain on peripheral blood monocytes; three were confirmed to have PAP. In contrast to the studies with knockout mice, which have suggested that PAP may be due to low or absent GM-CSF or to a defect in the GM-CSF receptor, no mutations in the receptor have been described in adult PAP patients. There is one report of a mutation in the GM-CSF coding sequence at position 382.[67] Studies at the Cleveland Clinic have demonstrated that circulating monocytes and alveolar macrophages from adult PAP patients are able to produce GM-CSF (in response to a proinflammatory stimulus such as lipopolysaccharide), suggesting an intact GM-CSF gene. In addition, the PAP cells were capable of responding to GM-CSF, indicating a functional receptor and downstream

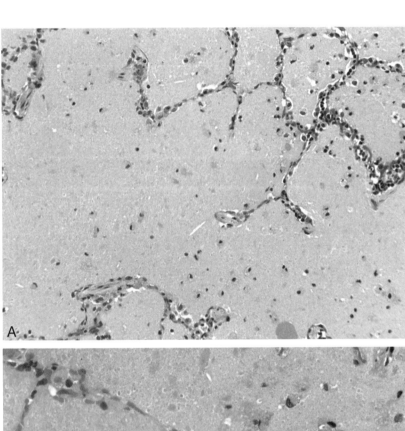

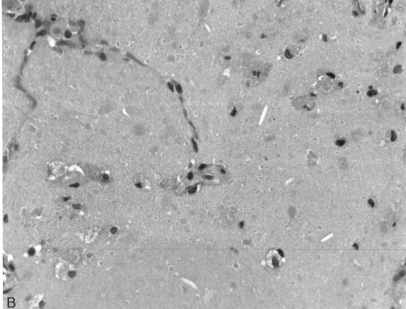

Figure 59.6 Lung histopathology section obtained by open-lung biopsy from a patient with idiopathic pulmonary alveolar proteinosis. **A,** Amorphous, extracellular pinkish eosinophilic material within the alveolar space with scattered alveolar macrophages and lymphocytes. The alveolar architecture is well preserved and the walls are essentially unremarkable. (Original magnification ×100; hematoxylin and eosin [H&E] stain.) **B,** High-power view of H&E-stained section showing eosinophilic material that completely fills the alveolar spaces. There are a few "cholesterol clefts" and scattered resident alveolar macrophages that are enlarged and vacuolated. (Original magnification ×400.)

Figure continued on opposite page

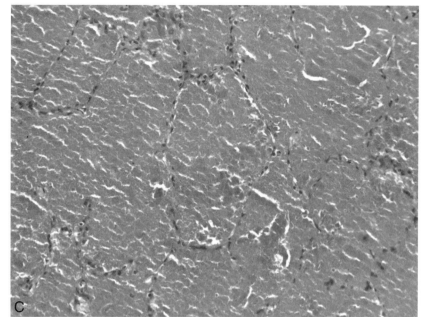

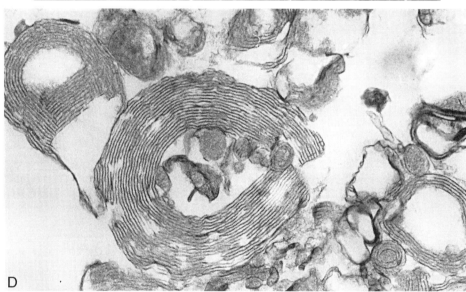

Figure 59.6 cont'd C, Medium-power view showing eosinophilic material present within the alveolar spaces that stains strongly positive with periodic acid–Schiff after diastase digestion. (Original magnification ×200.) **D,** Electron micrograph of alveolar debris. The structure of the material is lamellated, resembling surfactant. (Original magnification ×30,000.) (**A–C** Courtesy of Dr. Carol Farver, Cleveland Clinic; D from Wasserman K, Mason GR: Pulmonary alveolar proteinosis. *In* Murray JF, Nadel JA, Mason RJ, Boushey HA [eds]: Textbook of Respiratory Medicine [3rd ed]. Philadelphia: WB Saunders, 2000, pp 1789–1801.)

signaling pathway.[68] Similarly, Carraway and coworkers[69] have also demonstrated that PAP alveolar macrophages are able to produce GM-CSF, which is detectable both in BAL fluid and in the circulation. In summary, available data suggests that, in contrast to the murine GM-CSF knockout model, an inability to produce GM-CSF protein is not etiologic in PAP patients, and that the GM-CSF receptor is functional in the adult idiopathic PAP.

Additional murine studies indicate that a pulmonary lipidosis can result from several other pathways, including interleukin-4 overexpression in Clara cells,[70] interleukin-13 overexpression,[71] and SP-D gene deletion.[72,73] Interleukin-4 overexpression in Clara cells increases surfactant lipid synthesis and clearance, establishing a new equilibrium with an elevated surfactant pool and an alveolar proteinosis with a selective increase in SP-D.[70] Table 59.3 presents a list of known mechanisms producing the PAP syndrome.

DISCOVERY OF ANTI–GM-CSF AUTOANTIBODY IN PATIENTS WITH PULMONARY ALVEOLAR PROTEINOSIS

Kitamura and colleagues[5] were first to recognize the presence of circulating anti–GM-CSF autoantibodies that neutralize GM-CSF biologic activity in adult PAP. This group reported neutralizing immunoglobulin G (IgG) antibodies against GM-CSF in BAL fluid and sera from 11 and 24 patients with idiopathic PAP, respectively. Antibody was not detected in patients with secondary PAP ($n = 2$), in healthy controls ($n = 53$), or in patients with other lung disease ($n = 14$). These investigators further characterized the autoantibody as neutralizing and polyclonal, and composed of IgG1 and IgG2 subclasses. None of these patients had previously been treated with exogenous GM-CSF.

Several recent reports describe spontaneously occurring autoantibodies to a variety of cytokines and growth factors,

Table 59.3 Known Mechanisms Producing Pulmonary Alveolar Proteinosis Syndrome

Congenital/Neonatal
SP-B genetic defect
GM-CSF, IL-3, IL-5 receptor β chain genetic defect

Adult
Anti–GM-CSF antibody
GM-CSF cDNA mutation at 382 (single report)
Occupational exposures, "overload"
Miscellaneous (i.e., macrophage dysfunction)

Animal Models
GM-CSF gene deletion
GM-CSF receptor β chain deletion
Silica overload
IL-13 overexpressor
IL-4 overexpressor
SP-D knockout

cDNA, complementary deoxyribonucleic acid; GM-CSF, granulocyte-macrophage colony-stimulating factor; IL, interleukin; SP, surfactant protein.

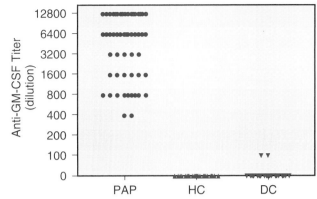

Figure 59.7 Serum anti–granulocyte-macrophage colony-stimulating factor antibody titers from adult idiopathic pulmonary alveolar proteinosis patients (PAP; $n = 72$), healthy controls (HC; $n = 49$), and disease controls (DC; $n = 44$).

including GM-CSF.[74] One study noted the presence of low to moderate levels of autoantibodies binding the GM-CSF in serum in 41 of 425 patients with various autoimmune diseases.[75] Myasthenia gravis was most prevalent; however, only three of the patients had neutralizing GM-CSF antibody. In addition, a very low prevalence of anti–GM-CSF autoantibodies has been described in healthy individuals (4 of 1258, or 0.3%), although these individuals were not tested for neutralizing activity.[76]

Studies at the Cleveland Clinic indicate that, in 72 patients with biopsy-proven adult idiopathic PAP, all have high titers of neutralizing anti–GM-CSF antibodies in their circulation, whereas none of the healthy ($n = 49$) or disease ($n = 44$) controls have elevated levels of the antibody ($P < 0.0001$) (Fig. 59.7). The lowest end titer for the PAP subjects was 1:400 ($n = 2$), and the highest end titers were 1:12,800 or higher.[10] The sensitivity of the serum anti–GM-CSF assay is 100% for a diagnosis of idiopathic PAP, and the specificity is greater than 91%; using a titer of 1:400 or higher, the specificity of the assay improves to 100%. These antibodies were shown to be neutralizing in the PAP patients by an inhibitory activity of the patient's serum on a myeloid cell line (TF-1) that is dependent on GM-CSF for growth.

Several recent studies have investigated the relationship between the anti–GM-CSF antibody level and disease activity in PAP. Bonfield and colleagues[12] noted that, in 11 adult patients with idiopathic PAP, the anti–GM-CSF titer was higher in patients with active disease and lower in patients in remission. The anti–GM-CSF titer at baseline was lower in a group of patients who were responders to exogenous GM-CSF therapy. This therapy did not induce or further increase the anti–GM-CSF titer. There was no leukocytosis with GM-CSF administration in any of the PAP patients. The data from this study indicate that the anti–GM-CSF titer correlates with PAP disease activity as well as the likelihood of response to GM-CSF therapy. Seymour and coworkers[11] measured blood levels of anti–GM-CSF antibodies by enzyme-linked immunosorbent assay as well as levels of SP-A, SP-B, LDH, and alveolar-arterial oxygen gradient in a cohort of 12 patients with PAP. The anti–GM-CSF antibody titer fell in all patients during treatment with GM-CSF (5 µg/kg/day), but the change in antibody concentration did not differ significantly between responders and nonresponders to GM-CSF therapy. There are several possible explanations for the disparate results between the Bonfield and Seymour studies regarding the predictive value of anti–GM-CSF antibody: (1) the two studies differ as to the duration of therapy (12 vs. 3 months); (2) the two assays may be measuring different epitopes of the anti–GM-CSF antibody, because neither assay directly measures the binding capacity for GM-CSF or biologic potency in neutralizing GM-CSF; and (3) the kinetics of the compartmentalization between the antibody in circulation and local lung antibody concentration is not known.

Uchida and associates[77] noted that the BAL fluid from patients with idiopathic PAP had anti–GM-CSF autoantibodies that were in very high concentration with a neutralizing capacity that far exceeds the concentration of GM-CSF in BAL fluid from normal lungs. These antibodies bind with very high affinity to GM-CSF such that adding excess GM-CSF can overcome effects of the antibody so the neutralizing capacity is "saturable." Although there was epitope heterogeneity, all patients had antibody epitopes in the region of amino acids 78 to 74, which is an important functional domain of GM-CSF.

In summary, available data suggest that an inability to produce GM-CSF protein is not etiologic in PAP patients and the GM-CSF receptor is functional in PAP. However, neutralizing anti–GM-CSF antibody, which is found in all idiopathic PAP patients tested, results in decreased functional GM-CSF. Thus, the common pathway between human PAP and the GM-CSF knockout mouse appears to be a deficiency of biologically active GM-CSF.

CONSEQUENCE OF GM-CSF DEFICIENCY FOR SURFACTANT METABOLISM

The exact mechanism by which GM-CSF is related to lung homeostasis and surfactant catabolism is unknown. Inefficient surfactant catabolism by alveolar macrophages has been shown to be related to GM-CSF deficiency (Fig. 59.8). Additionally, the lack of maturation and/or

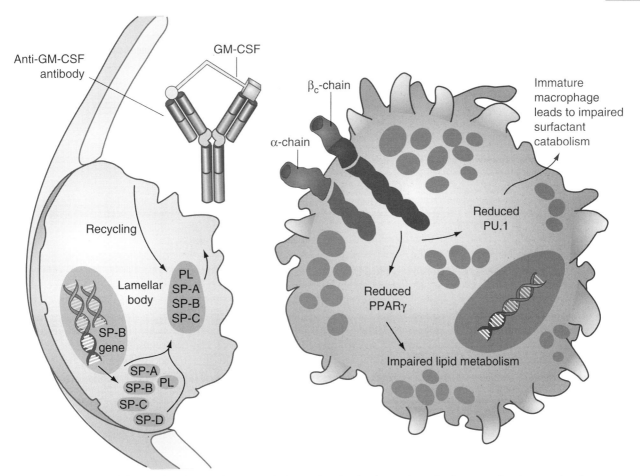

Figure 59.8 Schematic of abnormal surfactant homeostasis in an alveolus in the setting of pulmonary alveolar proteinosis. Anti–granulocyte-macrophage colony-stimulating factor (GM-CSF) antibody binds available GM-CSF to prevent triggering of the receptor on alveolar macrophages. In the absence of receptor binding, downstream signaling pathways that include peroxisome proliferator–activated receptor-γ and PU.1 are reduced, which leads to impaired lipid metabolism as well as lack of differentiation of the macrophage. PL, phospholipid; SP, surfactant protein.

differentiation of the monocyte/macrophage lineage has also been implicated in PAP. Data by Shibata and colleagues[78] indicate that the GM-CSF–deficient state in the GM-CSF knockout mouse is associated with decreased expression of the nuclear transcription factor PU.1. In these studies, the absence of PU.1 protein expression in the alveolar macrophage correlated with decreased maturation, differentiation, and surfactant catabolism. Correction of the GM-CSF defect in vitro resulted in increased expression of PU.1 and up-regulation of PU.1-dependent markers CD32, mannose receptor, and macrophage colony-stimulating factor receptor (M-CSFR).[79] This resulted in improved surfactant catabolism, adherence, and maturation.

Bonfield and coworkers[80] extended these murine observations and demonstrated that PU.1 messenger ribonucleic acid expression in PAP BAL cells is deficient compared with healthy controls. In vitro studies demonstrated that exogenous GM-CSF treatment up-regulated PU.1 and M-CSFR gene expression in the human PAP alveolar macrophages. Finally, in vivo studies showed that PAP patients treated with GM-CSF have higher levels of PU.1 and M-CSFR expression in alveolar macrophages compared with healthy controls or PAP patients before GM-CSF therapy. These observations suggest that differentiation as measured by the expression of PU.1 is critical in human alveolar macrophage surfactant catabolism.

Another direction for research in this area involves nuclear transcription factors that regulate intracellular lipid metabolism.[81] Peroxisome proliferator–activated receptor-γ (PPAR-γ) is a ligand-activated, nuclear transcription factor that regulates genes involved in lipid and glucose metabolism, inflammation, and other pathways. Bonfield and coworkers[82] demonstrated that PPAR-γ messenger ribonucleic acid and protein are highly expressed in alveolar macrophages of healthy control subjects but severely deficient in PAP alveolar macrophages. In addition, PPAR-γ–regulated lipid scavenger receptor CD36 is also deficient in PAP alveolar macrophages. Using both in vitro and in vivo data from patients with PAP, GM-CSF treatment restores PPAR-γ to control levels. These data suggest that GM-CSF regulates lung homeostasis and surfactant metabolism through PPAR-γ–dependent pathways in alveolar macrophages.

MURINE MODELS VERSUS HUMAN DISEASE

The murine models of PAP and the human disease have in common the lack of available functional GM-CSF. In the murine models, GM-CSF or its receptor is completely

Table 59.4 Comparison of Mouse/Human Pulmonary Alveolar Proteinosis (PAP) Lungs

		GM-CSF Knockout	Human PAP
Cytokine dysregulation	GM-CSF bioactivity	—	↓[5,68]
	MCP-1	↑[84]	↑[10,83]
	M-CSF	↑[78]	↑[10]
	IL-10	?	↑
Alveolar macrophage dysfunction	Phagocytosis/killing	↓[79]	±[61,124]
	TRL/mannose	↓[78]	↓
	PU.1	↓[78,79]	↓
	PPAR-γ	?	↓[82]
	LPS response	↓[78]	≥[68]

deficient.[3,4] In congenital PAP, gene deletions create abnormal surfactant proteins or GM-CSF receptor.[17,20] In idiopathic PAP, GM-CSF and its receptor are present and function in a normal fashion[68,69]; however, GM-CSF is ineffective due to its neutralization by anti–GM-CSF antibodies. The total absence of GM-CSF versus its neutralization by antibody may account for some of the differences observed between the murine models and human disease (Table 59.4). With this in mind, it is noteworthy that there are more similarities than differences between the PAP syndromes.

A common denominator between the GM-CSF knockout mouse and human idiopathic PAP was the observation of elevated BAL levels of monocyte chemotactic protein-1 (MCP-1) and macrophage colony-stimulating factor (M-CSF).[10,78,83] The presence of increased levels of M-CSF has been described as a compensatory mechanism for the loss of GM-CSF in both forms of PAP.[10,78,78a] Even with the high compensatory levels of M-CSF detected in the lungs of both the GM-CSF knockout mouse and human idiopathic PAP, the system may not work effectively due to the lack of appropriate terminal alveolar macrophage differentiation as measured by M-CSFR (c-fms) expression. The M-CSFR expression is enhanced with differentiation of myeloid cells. Thus, the decreased expression of M-CSFR in PAP may result in the inefficient response to the compensatory M-CSF in both murine and human PAP.

The elevated concentrations of MCP-1 in BAL fluid are thought to contribute to the increased pulmonary lymphocytosis in the murine model and in idiopathic PAP. Some studies suggest that the differential cell counts obtained from BAL samples from PAP patients have elevated levels of lymphocytes.[55] Other studies suggest that the term *lymphocytosis* is relative. In these studies, it is suggested that the increased number of lymphocytes sometimes observed in these patients is relatively modest given extremely high levels of MCP-1.[83] The alveolar macrophage appears to be the main source of MCP-1 in the murine model and in human PAP.[84] Carraway and colleagues[85] also showed elevated levels of MCP-1 in BAL cells from PAP patients using gene array analysis.

TREATMENT

Many therapies have been utilized through the years. The original report by Rosen and colleagues described unsuc-

cessful treatment with antibiotics, corticosteroids, and postural drainage.[1,86] Other novel therapies reported to be successful in isolated cases include intermittent positive-pressure breathing with aerosolized acetylcysteine, heparin, and saline; aerosolized ambroxol, a mucolytic agent; and aerosolized trypsin.[87–91] Despite these anecdotal reports, whole-lung lavage (WLL) emerged early on as a standard of care.[92,93]

THERAPEUTIC WHOLE-LUNG LAVAGE

In 1964, Ramirez and associates[94] performed a trial of WLL using up to 3 L of saline with addition of heparin or acetylcysteine initially under local anesthesia. They applied "repeated segmental flooding" as a means of physically removing the accumulated alveolar lipoproteinaceous material. Such segmental flooding provided proof that physical removal of adequate amounts of the material provided improvement in both symptoms and pulmonary function studies. Subsequently, this WLL procedure has seen refinement in the form of routine use of general anesthesia, increased lavage volumes, saline use alone, addition of chest percussion, and the successful completion of bilateral sequential WLL in the same session of anesthesia.[59,95,96] Therapeutic WLL is performed in a variety of referral settings around the world. However, there are no systematic surveys of the precise technique utilized in clinical practice or the numbers of WLL procedures performed. Also, there are no controlled studies of effectiveness of lung lavage or durability of response compared to observation alone.

At the Cleveland Clinic, therapeutic WLL is performed in the operating room under general anesthesia by a team that consists of two anesthesiologists, a pulmonologist, and a nurse anesthetist. All WLLs are performed as bilateral lung lavage (i.e., both lungs lavaged sequentially during one anesthesia session). We use total intravenous anesthesia consisting of a sedative (propofol) with narcotic (fentanyl), and a muscle relaxant (atracurium or rocuronium) instead of inhalation anesthetics. We use standard noninvasive monitoring, including a pulse oximeter, noninvasive blood pressure monitoring, and continuous electrocardiogram during the procedure. We do not routinely use arterial lines for blood pressure or pulmonary artery pressure monitoring. The patient is kept in the supine position throughout the procedure. We use a left-sided double-lumen endotracheal tube (Mallinckrodt Medical Inc., St. Louis, MO) of size 37 French in women and 39 French in men. A critical step after the double-lumen endotracheal tube placement is the verification of proper cuff position. We accomplish this meticulously by the use of a pediatric fiberoptic bronchoscope. The patient is kept ventilated using the pressure control mode with a fraction of inspired oxygen of 1.0 and positive end-expiratory pressure of 10 to 12 cm H_2O. Single-lung ventilation is instituted for the nonlavage lung. A disposable 3 L normal saline bag with a "Y" connector that leads to a drip chamber is placed 10 cm above the level of the patient's head. The nonventilated lung is lavaged with normal saline warmed to 37° C in 500 mL to 1 L aliquots. It is essential to use normal saline (0.9% sodium) for WLL. There have been serious complications, including hemolysis, renal failure, and death, after WLL with dextrose 5% in water. After each aliquot, the chest is allowed to drain by gravity

Table 59.5 Prelavage and Postlavage Pulmonary Parameters for Patients with Acquired PAP

Parameter	n	Mean change (SD)	95% CI of the Mean	P Value*
Arterial P_{O_2} (mm Hg)	41	20.1 (14.3)	15.6 to 24.6	<0.0001
$(A-a)P_{O_2}$ (mm Hg)	21	−30.6 (18.0)	−38.8 to −22.4	<0.0001
FEV_1 (L)	33	0.26 (0.47)	0.09 to 0.42	0.0034
Vital capacity (L)	40	0.50 (0.54)	0.33 to 0.67	<0.0001
DL_{CO} (mL/mm Hg per min)	25	4.4 (4.5)	2.6 to 6.3	<0.0001

$(A-a)P_{O_2}$, alveolar-arterial oxygen gradient; CI, confidence interval; DL_{CO}, diffusing capacity for carbon monoxide; PAP, pulmonary alveolar proteinosis.
* Value is for the comparison of prelavage versus postlavage data for individual patients for each parameter for only those patients with available data using a two-sample *t* test.
From Seymour JF, Presneill JJ: Pulmonary alveolar proteinosis: Progress in the first 44 years. Am J Respir Crit Care Med 166:215–235, 2002.

with intermittent chest percussion facilitating the drainage of the lavage fluid. Hammon and colleagues[97] noted that manual chest percussion is superior to mechanical percussion or no percussion based on optical density of the effluent. However, we use intermittent chest percussion provided by the Vest Airway Clearance System (Advanced Respiratory, St. Paul, MN). The procedure is repeated until the return fluid is clear. The patient receives a dose of intravenous furosemide 40 mg IV after the first lung is lavaged. After a 10-minute stabilization period, the contralateral lung is lavaged in a similar fashion. After the procedure, patients are sent to the postanesthesia recovery unit, where they are continued on pressure control ventilation with fraction of inspired oxygen of 1.0 and on F_{IO_2} 1.0 and positive end-expiratory pressure of 10 cm H_2O. Extubation typically occurs 3 hours after completion of the procedure. We do not usually image the chest either during or after the procedure unless we suspect complications.

Since its introduction into practice, therapeutic WLL has largely remained anecdotal as an art rather than science. However, practitioners of this procedure widely believe that patients with PAP improve symptomatically as well as by gas-exchange criteria with WLL.[92,98] A retrospective review of all published reports by Seymour and Presneill[2] indicates that the overall survival at 5 years from the time of diagnosis is higher for patients who underwent therapeutic lung lavage during the course of their disease ($94 \pm 2\%$ compared to $85 \pm 5\%$, for those not lavaged, $P = 0.04$; Fig. 59.9). This was based on 146 patients who were lavaged and 85 patients who were not. This review also indicated that the median total number of lavages performed was two and that about 70% of the patients were lavaged within 5 years of diagnosis. In 55 instances of reported response to lavage in a review of PAP literature, the median duration of clinical benefit from lavage was 15 months, with less than 20% of those patients followed beyond 3 years remaining free of recurrent PAP. This review also reported on 41 patients with paired gas-exchange data before and after lavage, and noted that the arterial P_{O_2} improved by 20.1 mm Hg (SD ± 14.3) (Table 59.5). The improvement in other pulmonary function parameters or diffusing capacity is less impressive.

There are no clearcut guidelines for the timing or indications for WLL or the end point for the lavage procedure

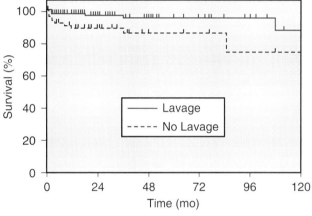

Figure 59.9 Overall survival from the time of diagnosis of acquired pulmonary alveolar proteinosis was significantly improved ($P = 0.044$) if patients had received therapeutic lung lavage at anytime during their disease course (lavage, $n = 146$; no lavage, $n = 85$). (From Seymour JF, Presneill JJ: Pulmonary alveolar proteinosis: Progress in the first 44 years. Am J Respir Crit Care Med 166:215–235, 2002.)

in the operating room. In practice, the patient's dyspnea, his or her feeling of activity intolerance, and the impact on daily life are perhaps the most important factors in performing lung lavage. The primary reason for performing lung lavage is to improve patient symptoms and relieve the patient of the need for supplemental oxygen therapy. Currently, there are no data or specific indications to perform this procedure to effect the natural history of the disease or prevent long-term complications. Various recommendations for WLL include

1. Dyspnea limiting patient's daily activities
2. Partial pressure of oxygen less than 60 mm Hg while breathing room air
3. Shunt fraction more than 10% to 12%

As lung lavage is a nonspecific physical removal of the accumulated material from the alveoli, and because we are investigating other specific treatments at the Cleveland Clinic (such as GM-CSF, as discussed later), we reserve lung lavage for the most symptomatic patients requiring supplemental oxygen of 4 L or more by nasal cannula. The only end point that is clinically used for terminating lung lavage in the operating room is the visual clarity of the lavage effluent. There is a subset of patients who do not respond despite aggressive lung lavage, for reasons that are unclear.

Physical removal of the lipoproteinaceous material through repeated dilution with saline solution is believed to be the mechanism for the beneficial effects of WLL. Additional benefits may include the bulk removal of anti–GM-CSF antibody as well as immunologic effects of WLL on the effector cells, such as the alveolar macrophage or the epithelial cell. Complications of WLL include hypoxemia, pneumonia, sepsis, hydropneumothorax, and adult respiratory distress syndrome. It is critical not to perform WLL when a patient has active bacterial pneumonia, because this can result in generalized sepsis and shock.

There have been isolated case reports about the use of flexible bronchoscopy for performing therapeutic bronchopulmonary lavage in PAP. Recently, Cheng and coworkers[99] suggested that bronchoscopic lobar lavage is simple and safe, and may find application in patients in whom WLL with general anesthesia may be hazardous due to severe and refractory hypoxemia. In patients who are too hypoxemic to tolerate lung lavage under general anesthesia as described, alternative approaches have been reported, including performing the lavage in a hyperbaric chamber,[100] use of complete cardiopulmonary bypass,[100–103] and liquid ventilation.[104]

GM-CSF THERAPY

International experience with GM-CSF therapy for PAP is summarized in Table 59.6.[105–110a] The first clinical trial was initiated by Seymour and associates in Australia in 1995, and a preliminary case report was published in 1996 of a single adult patient with idiopathic PAP, in whom gas exchange improved significantly with administration of GM-CSF.[111] This patient subsequently worsened with discontinuation of the drug, and improved again with readministration of GM-CSF.

The largest published series of GM-CSF therapy involved 14 adult patients with moderate disease (room air arterial PO_2 63 mm Hg; range, 49 to 83 mm Hg). Of the 14 patients, 12 of 12 tested were positive for circulating anti–GM-CSF.[105] The initial therapy included 5 µg/kg/day of GM-CSF subcutaneously for 6 to 12 weeks. Four of 14 patients responded at this dose of 5 µg, and 1 of these 4 patients underwent dose escalation with a single response at 20 µg/kg/day. The overall response rate was 5 of 14 (43%) (mean improvement in alveolar-arterial oxygen gradient = 23.2 mm Hg). The patients tolerated this therapy, and, interestingly, there was no leukocytosis with GM-CSF therapy, which is seen in normal volunteers. The protocol at the Cleveland Clinic involves a rapid dose escalation to 18 µg/kg/day maintained for a 6- to 12-month duration. Fourteen of 25 patients, or 60%, had a clinical response as defined by a 10 mm Hg or greater improvement in room

Table 59.6 Granulocyte-Macrophage Colony-Stimulating Factor (GM-CSF) Therapy for Pulmonary Alveolar Proteinosis: Summary of Published Reports

Study (year)	N	Dose (µg/kg/day)	Duration of Therapy	Duration of Response	Anti-GM-CSF-Ab?	$(A - a)PO_2$ Base–Final	Response Rate	Peak WBC Count	Comment
Seymour et al.[105] (2001)	14	5–20	1–3 mo	39 wk	12/12	45–22 (mean)	5/14 (43%)	7.2–8.4	Eosinophilia was a predictor of response
Barraclough and Gillies[106] (2001)	1	5	3 mo	NS	NS	Baseline PaO_2 ~76	1/1	29K	39% eosinophilia with therapy; CXR, PaO_2, PFTs normalized
Schoch et al.[107] (2002)	1	8		NS	1/1	55–9	1/1	NS	
De Vega et al.[108] (2002)	1	6	5 mo	>18 mo	NS	61–20	1/1	NS	
Acosta et al.[109] (2002)	1	5	2 mo	NS	NS	Dyspnea & cough PaO_2 from 71 to 82	1/1	Not increased	Improved PFTs, CT
Khanjari et al.[110] (2003)	1	5	3 mo	>1 yr	Negative	PaO_2 from 55 to 65	1/1	NS	Idiopathic marrow aplasia HRCT score improved from 18 to 14
Kavuru (2004)	25	Dose escalation to 18	3–12 mo		25/25	39–28	14/25 (60%)	<10 K	

$(A - a)PO_2$, alveolar-arterial PO_2 difference; Ab, antibody; CT, computed tomography; HRCT, high-resolution computed tomograph; PaO_2, arterial PO_2; PFTs, pulmonary function tests; WBC, white blood cell.

air arterial PO_2. There are several overall conclusions from published GM-CSF trials:

1. About 50% of the patients obtained an objective clinical improvement.
2. There is a lag time of greater than 8 weeks from start of therapy to observed clinical response.
3. There is variability in both required dose and duration of therapy.
4. There is a uniform lack of (or blunted) hematopoietic response to GM-CSF.
5. There is a reduction in anti–GM-CSF titer in both serum and BAL fluid with GM-CSF therapy.[12,107]
6. GM-CSF therapy is not curative, and some patients relapse after discontinuing therapy.

GM-CSF is a naturally occurring molecule that displays hematopoietic effects on multiple cell lines, including granulocytes, macrophages, megakaryocytes, erythroid colonies, and B and T lymphocytes.[112] Recombinant human GM-CSF is a glycoprotein that is commercially available.

Reed and colleagues[64] noted that aerosolized GM-CSF corrected the lung lesion in the GM-CSF knockout mouse. The improvement was dependent on both dose and duration of therapy. Interestingly, mice treated with intraperitoneal recombinant murine GM-CSF did not have resolution of lung disease. However, there was no other evidence to indicate systemic GM-CSF effect—neither hematopoietic studies nor drug levels were measured. The GM-CSF administered was not pegylated and therefore was unstable, with a short half-life. This study did not fully address whether systemic administration of GM-CSF produces a local biologic effect in the lungs. There have been isolated case reports in three patients with aerosolized GM-CSF producing a beneficial effect in alveolar proteinosis.[113,114,114a]

OTHER TREATMENT APPROACHES

Available human studies indicate that primary PAP is an autoimmune disease characterized by circulating, neutralizing anti–GM-CSF autoantibodies. These antibodies produce a state of relative GM-CSF deficiency in the lung microenvironment, leading to alveolar macrophage dysfunction and impaired surfactant catabolism. Therefore, approaches to reduce or deplete the antibody by targeted removal with plasmapheresis or targeted B-lymphocyte–depleting therapies may be rational in the treatment of this disease. There are currently no reports of the use of these agents in idiopathic PAP, but this appears to be a reasonable approach.

NATURAL HISTORY AND PROGNOSIS

Because PAP is an extraordinarily rare disease, the published series are small, retrospective, and from different institutions. There are no prospective studies with long-term follow-up or an international registry. The most recent review, by Seymour and Presneill,[2] indicates that actuarial survival rates on 343 patients reported with acquired PAP are 78% ± 8% at 2 years, 75 ± 8% at 5 years, and 68 ± 9% at 10 years. More than 80% of the deaths attributable to PAP during a 5-year observation period occurred during the first 12 months after diagnosis. Seymour and Presneill noted

that, of the 69 reported deaths, the cause of death was directly due to respiratory failure from PAP in 47 patients (72%), to uncontrolled infection in 13 (20%), and to unrelated causes in 5 cases (8%).

SPONTANEOUS RESOLUTION

The notion of spontaneous improvement or remission of PAP was noted in the initial report by Rosen and colleagues[1] and has been reinforced in several case series without very good documentation. The best objective analysis of all individual patient reports indicates that only 24 of 303 patients (7.9%) demonstrated significant objective spontaneous improvement (Table 59.7). In general, most of the reports of spontaneous remission are from literature prior to 1965 and usually involved a short duration of follow-up. We have not seen spontaneous resolution of this disease.

INFECTIONS

Although some older reports suggest that idiopathic PAP patients have increased susceptibility to infection,[115] this is certainly not a prominent finding in most of these patients. Routine lavage fluid cultures from patients undergoing WLL are usually sterile. Occasionally cultures are positive for a nonbacterial pathogen such as nontuberculous mycobacteria, which are usually colonizers because they do not persist on repeat lavage despite the absence of specific therapy. Seymour and Presneill's review noted that 13% of the lung washings from acquired PAP patients (representing 62 discrete cases) grew an organism.[2] Most of these reports are from prior to 1980. In the earlier series, some of the included patients had received immunosuppressive therapy or had underlying marrow or systemic diseases predisposing them to infection. One notable report by Witty and associates[116] gave impetus to the association of infection with PAP by reporting that 42% of the lavages between 1984 and 1992 grew nontuberculous mycobacteria, although in final analysis none of these patients was thought to have clinically significant infection (i.e., these organisms were likely colonizers or contaminants, possibly from laboratory processing). *Nocardia* was reported in 34 instances in Seymour and Presneill's review, with some patients having extrapulmonary infection as well.[2] The original reports are not clear about other coexisting conditions such as alcoholism. *Nocardia* is known to have tropism for the brain and often occurs in the absence of an underlying systemic disease (in one review of 1050 cases of nocardiosis, 36% did not have underlying immune dysfunction).[117] Therefore, *Nocardia* central nervous system disease does not necessarily indicate a predisposition for systemic infection in PAP. In summary, despite diffuse filling of alveoli with lipoproteinaceous material on a chronic basis, clinically important lung infection is quite rare. This phenomenon suggests that, despite alterations in alveolar macrophage function due to insufficient levels of biologically active GM-CSF, other defense mechanisms may be sufficient to protect against infections.

PULMONARY FIBROSIS

A PAP-like disease with areas of pulmonary fibrosis has been described in an experimental rat model exposed to inhaled

Table 59.7 Features of Patients with Acquired PAP Who Claimed to Have Manifested "Spontaneous Resolution"

Characteristic	Median			Median			P Value[2]
	n	%	(I.Q. range)[1]	n	%	(I.Q. range)[1]	
Age at diagnosis	24		38 (25–45)	278		38 (30–45)	0.6
Gender (% male)	24	71		273	73		0.8
Publication date (% pre-1965)	24	33		279	20		0.1
Duration of symptoms	20		4 (3–14)	178		8 (3–24)	0.1
Smoker (%)[3]	17	88		105	73		0.2
Serum LDH (% elevated)[4]	5	60		56	80		0.3
Arterial Pao$_2$ (mm Hg)	12		62 (52–69)	123		60 (48–70)	0.9
(A – a)Do$_2$ (mm Hg)[5]	11		47 (33–57)	102		47 (33–57)	0.8
Duration of follow-up (mo)	24		33 (12–76)	218		22 (10–48)	0.1

[1] Interquartile range is the range from the 25th to 75th centiles of the distribution.
[2] Values shown are calculated using the Mann-Whitney U-test or Kruskall-Wallis test for numerical data and the χ^2 test for categorical data, as appropriate.
[3] At the time of onset of symptoms, patients 10 years of age of less at diagnosis were assumed to be nonsmokers.
[4] Serum level of lactate dehydrogenase above upper limit of cited reference range.
[5] Alveolar-arterial oxygen gradient; where the actual figure is not provided, this has been calculated assuming BTPS conditions.
BTPS, body temperature, ambient pressure, and saturated with water vapor; I.Q., interquartile; LDH, lactate dehydrogenase; PAP, pulmonary alveolar proteinosis.
From Seymour JF, Presneill JJ: Pulmonary alveolar proteinosis: Progress in the first 44 years. Am J Respir Crit Care Med 166:215–235, 2002.

fine quartz or silica dust.[38] Isolated reports of interstitial fibrosis following alveolar proteinosis have been reported in three patients.[56,57,118] In the few reports of lung fibrosis, it is difficult to be certain whether this is due to the underlying PAP or is a complication of treatment used for PAP. Specifically, repeated WLL as well as exposure to a high fraction of inspired oxygen that is typical during these procedures may potentially produce lung fibrosis. My experience is that "end-stage lung disease" or irreversible scarring of the lung is a rare phenomenon.

ORGAN TRANSPLANTATION

With regard to the role of transplantation in PAP, there are three distinct scenarios to consider: (1) lung transplantation as therapy for underlying end-stage PAP; (2) PAP occurring incidentally in patients who have received a lung transplant; and (3) bone marrow transplantation as therapy for PAP.

A recent report on lung transplantation in children indicates that 12 of 190 transplants were performed for a diagnosis of PAP.[119] The details of these patients have not been published, but they are presumed to have had neonatal PAP (i.e., SP-B deficiency or ABC-A3 deficiency). Data on the number of adults receiving a transplant for a diagnosis of PAP in the United States are not available. Parker and Novotny[120] described the case of a 41-year-old woman with a 15-year history of disease who was thought to have end-stage idiopathic PAP despite repeated lung lavages. She underwent double-lung transplantation. Three years after transplantation, she developed pulmonary infiltrates with subsequent bronchoscopic evaluation indicating recurrent PAP, with all cultures being negative for infection. The level of chronic immunosuppression and the anti–GM-CSF antibody status were not specified. The mechanism for recurrent PAP in this patient remains unknown. Although the risk of recurrence of PAP in the lung allograft needs to be considered in the overall transplant decision, it may not be an absolute contraindication in those rare patients with idiopathic adult PAP and end-stage lung disease.

Bone marrow transplantation has been advanced as an option for some patients with PAP.[121] In the GM-CSF receptor knockout mouse, bone marrow transplantation led to resolution of the lung disease. The mechanism for benefit probably involves the donor stem cells, which would differentiate into alveolar macrophages with an intact GM-CSF receptor. There are no reports of a similar experiment wherein bone marrow transplantation was performed for neonatal PAP with the GM-CSF receptor defect. Whether this approach will be of benefit in adult autoimmune PAP by replacing the stem cells and therefore B lymphocytes is unknown. Patients with malignant marrow disorders with secondary PAP have resolved their lung disease after bone marrow transplantation to cure the underlying marrow disorder.[122]

GAPS IN CURRENT UNDERSTANDING: UNRESOLVED ISSUES, FUTURE DIRECTIONS

MECHANISMS

Table 59.3 summarizes the known mechanisms producing the PAP syndrome, as derived both from animal models and from neonatal and adult data. Studies to date strongly support an autoimmune basis for human PAP. There is no autoimmune animal model for PAP, and it is difficult to be certain whether the antibody observed in patients is causally related to the disease or is an epiphenomenon. The available murine studies suggest that GM-CSF is essential for surfactant homeostasis, and human studies indicate that circulating neutralizing antibodies to GM-CSF (along with lung-specific reduction in GM-CSF bioactivity) is a ubiquitous finding in all idiopathic PAP patients. These data strongly suggest a pathogenic role for anti–GM-CSF antibodies. In addition, response to GM-CSF therapy is inversely correlated with circulating anti–GM-CSF antibody titer. Patients with lower titers respond more favorably to therapy; conversely, patients with higher titers do not respond to GM-CSF therapy. Observations in a single PAP patient treated with plasmapheresis also showed that the reduction of antibody titer results in marked improvement of the lung disease.[123] Therefore, the development of an autoimmune animal model of PAP, which mimics the presumed mechanism in the human disease, would accelerate improvement in therapy for human PAP.

The initial trigger for the anti–GM-CSF antibody production remains unknown. In the most common form of this acquired disorder, in contrast to the congenital/neonatal disease, it may be speculated that an exogenous agent such as an infection or an environmental trigger not yet identified results in anti–GM-CSF production. Further progress is needed in elucidating the autoimmune cascade that leads to a particular subtype of B lymphocyte that produces the specific antibody. Also, the relative role of the T lymphocyte needs to be defined, as well as the reasons for organ-specific autoimmunity (i.e., clinical manifestation in patients being limited to the lungs). The circulating anti–GM-CSF antibody produces a GM-CSF–deficient state in the lungs that may lead to relative reduction in activation of the GM-CSF receptor on the alveolar macrophages. Subsequent downstream signaling pathways may specifically affect surfactant catabolism. This may provide new targets for further therapy.

CLINICAL MANAGEMENT

Many issues remain regarding the optimal therapy of patients with PAP. From a therapeutic lung lavage standpoint, the optimal timing and indications for lung lavage need to be prospectively defined. More objective markers of disease activity or disease burden are necessary to evaluate the effectiveness of conventional WLL or experimental therapies in the future. These objective markers may include quantitative CT scan with algorithms to measure disease burden, or perhaps new biomarkers. Augmentation of GM-CSF in the lung is a promising approach. However, the optimal route of delivery (inhaled vs. parenteral) as well as the dose and duration of therapy remain to be defined. If the anti–GM-CSF antibody is central to the pathogenesis of this disease, as the current evidence suggests, then therapies specifically targeting the antibody need to be pursued. These include physical removal of the antibody by approaches such as apheresis, perhaps combined with other modalities, such as targeted immunosuppression of the B lymphocyte to reduce antibody production. Finally, it may be possible to completely cure this disease by removing "memory" of anti–GM-CSF antibody production from the immune system.

SUMMARY

Pulmonary alveolar proteinosis is a syndrome consisting of a heterogeneous group of diseases that result in deposition of extracellular granular material in the lung. It is a rare yet chronic pulmonary disease with a variable natural history. Recent scientific data from both transgenic murine models and human studies have strongly linked GM-CSF to the normal homeostasis and clearance of surfactant from air spaces. These studies suggest that a relative deficiency in GM-CSF is important in the pathogenesis of PAP. This has transformed our approach to initial diagnosis of PAP by the use of a serologic test for anti–GM-CSF and has introduced the concept of GM-CSF replacement therapy. Determination of GM-CSF autoantibody in the sera will likely serve as a useful and simple noninvasive diagnostic test for this disease as well as possibly a test forecasting the clinical course. It is becoming clear that manipulating the relative GM-CSF availability in the lung will be important in the future treatment of patients with PAP. Further studies are required to determine the optimal approach in this regard.

REFERENCES

1. Rosen SH, Castleman B, Liebow AA: Pulmonary alveolar proteinosis. N Engl J Med 258:1123–1142, 1958.
2. Seymour JF, Presneill JJ: Pulmonary alveolar proteinosis: Progress in the first 44 years. Am J Respir Crit Care Med 166:215–235, 2002.
3. Dranoff G, Crawford AD, Sadelain M, et al: Involvement of granulocyte-macrophage colony-stimulating factor in pulmonary homeostasis. Science 264:713–716, 1994.
4. Stanley E, Lieschke GJ, Grail D, et al: Granulocyte/macrophage colony-stimulating factor-deficient mice show no major perturbation of hematopoiesis but develop a characteristic pulmonary pathology. Proc Natl Acad Sci U S A 91:5592–5596, 1994.
5. Kitamura T, Tanaka N, Watanabe J, et al: Idiopathic pulmonary alveolar proteinosis as an autoimmune disease with neutralizing antibody against granulocyte/macrophage colony-stimulating factor. J Exp Med 190:875–880, 1999.
6. Trapnell BC, Whitsett JA, Nakata K: Pulmonary alveolar proteinosis. N Engl J Med 349:2527–2539, 2003.
7. Goldstein LS, Kavuru MS, Curtis-McCarthy P, et al: Pulmonary alveolar proteinosis: Clinical features and outcomes. Chest 114:1357–1362, 1998.
8. Shah PL, Hansell D, Lawson PR, et al: Pulmonary alveolar proteinosis: Clinical aspects and current concepts on pathogenesis. Thorax 55:67–77, 2000.
9. Prakash UB, Barham SS, Carpenter HA, et al: Pulmonary alveolar phospholipoproteinosis: Experience with 34 cases and a review. Mayo Clin Proc 62:499–518, 1987.
9a. Venkateshiah SB, Thomassen MJ, Kavuru MS: Pulmonary alveolar proteinosis. Clinical manifestations and optimal treatment strategies. Treat Respir Med 3:217–227, 2004.
9b. Akin MR, Nguyen GK: Pulmonary alveolar proteinosis. Pathol Res Pract 200:693–698, 2004.
10. Bonfield TL, Russell D, Burgess S, et al: Autoantibodies against granulocyte macrophage colony-stimulating factor are diagnostic for pulmonary alveolar proteinosis. Am J Respir Cell Mol Biol 27:481–486, 2002.
11. Seymour JF, Doyle IR, Nakata K, et al: Relationship of anti-GM-CSF antibody concentration, surfactant protein A and B levels, and serum LDH to pulmonary parameters

and response to GM-CSF therapy in patients with idiopathic alveolar proteinosis. Thorax 58:252–257, 2003.

12. Bonfield TL, Kavuru MS, Thomassen MJ: Anti-GM-CSF titer predicts response to GM-CSF therapy in pulmonary alveolar proteinosis. Clin Immunol 105:342–350, 2002.

13. Teja K, Cooper PH, Squires JE, Schnatterly PT: Pulmonary alveolar proteinosis in four siblings. N Engl J Med 305:1390–1392, 1981.

14. DeMello DE, Nogee LM, Heyman S, et al: Molecular and phenotypic variability in the congenital alveolar proteinosis syndrome associated with inherited surfactant protein B deficiency. J Pediatr 125:43–50, 1994.

15. Nogee LM, DeMello DE, Dehner LP, Colten HR: Deficiency of pulmonary surfactant protein B in congenital alveolar proteinosis. N Engl J Med 328:406–410, 1999.

16. Nogee LM, Garnier G, Dietz HC, et al: A mutation in the surfactant protein B gene responsible for fatal neonatal respiratory disease in multiple kindreds. J Clin Invest 93:1860–1863, 1994.

17. Nogee LM, DeMello DE, Dehner LP, Colten HR: Brief report: Deficiency of pulmonary surfactant protein B in congenital alveolar proteinosis. N Engl J Med 328:406–410, 1993.

18. Mahut B, Delacourt C, Scheinmann P, et al: Pulmonary alveolar proteinosis: Experience with eight pediatric cases and a review. Pediatrics 97:117–122, 1996.

18a. Latzin P, Tredano M, Wust Y, et al: Anti-GM-CSF antibodies in paediatric pulmonary alveolar proteinosis. Thorax 60:39–44, 2005.

19. Yusen RD, Cohen AH, Hamvas A: Normal lung function in subjects heterozygous for surfactant protein-B deficiency. Am J Respir Crit Care Med 159:411–414, 1999.

20. Dirksen U, Nishinakamura R, Groneck P, et al: Human pulmonary alveolar proteinosis associated with a defect in GM-CSF/IL-3/IL-5 receptor common β chain expression. J Clin Invest 100:2211–2217, 1997.

21. Dirksen U, Hattenhorst U, Schneider P, et al: Defective expression of granulocyte-macrophage colony-stimulating factor/interleukin-3/interleukin-5 receptor common beta chain in children with acute myeloid leukemia associated with respiratory failure. Blood 92:1097–1103, 1998.

21a. de Blic J: Pulmonary alveolar proteinosis in children. Paediatr Respir Rev 5:316–322, 2004.

22. Carnovale R, Zornoza J, Goldman AM, Luna M: Pulmonary alveolar proteinosis: Its association with hematologic malignancy and lymphoma. Radiology 122:303–306, 1977.

23. Shoji N, Ito Y, Kimura Y, et al: Pulmonary alveolar proteinosis as a terminal complication in myelodysplastic syndromes: A report of four cases detected on autopsy. Leuk Res 26:591–595, 2002.

24. Cordonnier C, Fleury-Feith J, Escudier E, et al: Secondary alveolar proteinosis is a reversible cause of respiratory failure in leukemic patients. Am J Respir Crit Care Med 149:788–794, 1994.

25. Pamuk GE, Turgut B, Vural O, et al: Pulmonary alveolar proteinosis in a patient with acute lymphoid leukemia regression after G-CSF therapy. Leuk Lymphoma 44:871–874, 2003.

26. Winston DJ, Territo MC, Ho WG, et al: Alveolar macrophage dysfunction in human bone marrow transplant recipients. Am J Med 73:859–866, 1982.

27. Springmeyer SC, Altman LC, Kopecky KJ, et al: Alveolar macrophage kinetics and function after interruption of canine marrow function. Am Rev Respir Dis 125:347–351, 1982.

28. Haworth JC, Hoogstraten J, Taylor H: Thymic alymphoplasia. Arch Dis Child 42:40–54, 1967.

29. Webster JR Jr, Battifora H, Furey C, et al: Pulmonary alveolar proteinosis in two siblings with decreased immunoglobulin A. Am J Med 69:786–789, 1980.

30. Yousem SA, Burke CM, Billingham M: Pathologic pulmonary alterations in long-term human heart-lung transplantation. Hum Pathol 16:911–923, 1985.

31. Israel RH, Magnussen CR: Are AIDS patients at risk for pulmonary alveolar proteinosis? Chest 96:641–642, 1989.

32. Davidson JM, Macleod WM: Pulmonary alveolar proteinosis. Br J Dis Chest 63:13–28, 1969.

33. Xipell JM, Ham KN, Price CG, Thomas DP: Acute silicoproteinosis. Thorax 32:104–111, 1977.

34. Ziskind M, Jones RN, Weill H: Silicosis. Am Rev Respir Dis 113:643–665, 1976.

35. Miller RR, Churg AM, Hutcheon M, Lom S: Pulmonary alveolar proteinosis and aluminum dust exposure. Am Rev Respir Dis 130:312–315, 1984.

36. Keller CA, Frost A, Cagle PT, Abraham JL: Pulmonary alveolar proteinosis in a painter with elevated pulmonary concentrations of titanium. Chest 108:277–280, 1995.

37. Humble S, Allan TJ, Boudreaux C, et al: Titanium particles identified by energy-dispersive x-ray microanalysis within the lungs of a painter at autopsy. Ultrastruct Pathol 27:127–129, 2003.

38. Heppleston AG, Wright NA, Stewart JA: Experimental alveolar lipo-proteinosis following the inhalation of silica. J Pathol 101:293–307, 1970.

39. Asamoto H, Kitaichi M, Nishimura K, et al: Primary pulmonary alveolar proteinosis—clinical observation of 68 patients in Japan (in Japanese). Nihon Kyobu Shikkan Gakkai Zasshi 33:835–845, 1995.

40. Godwin JD, Muller NL, Takasugi JE: Pulmonary alveolar proteinosis: CT findings. Radiology 169:609–613, 1988.

41. Lee KN, Levin DL, Webb WR, et al: Pulmonary alveolar proteinosis: High-resolution CT, chest radiographic, and functional correlations. Chest 111:989–995, 1997.

42. Holbert JM, Costello P, Li W, et al: CT features of pulmonary alveolar proteinosis. AJR Am J Roentgenol 176:1287–1294, 2001.

43. Rossi SE, Erasmus JJ, Volpacchio M, et al: "Crazy-paving" pattern at thin-section CT of the lungs: Radiologic-pathologic overview. Radiographics 23:1509–1519, 2003.

44. Johkoh T, Itoh H, Muller NL, et al: Crazy-paving appearance at thin-section CT: Spectrum of disease and pathologic findings. Radiology 211:155–160, 1999.

45. Tan RT, Kuzo RS: High-resolution CT findings of mucinous bronchioloalveolar carcinoma: A case of pseudopulmonary alveolar proteinosis. AJR Am J Roentgenol 168:99–100, 1997.

46. Martin RJ, Rogers RM, Myers NM: Pulmonary alveolar proteinosis: Shunt fraction and lactic acid dehydrogenase concentration as aids to diagnosis. Am Rev Respir Dis 117:1059–1062, 1978.

47. Hoffman RM, Rogers RM: Serum and lavage lactate dehydrogenase isoenzymes in pulmonary alveolar proteinosis. Am Rev Respir Dis 143:42–46, 1991.

48. Honda Y, Takahashi H, Shijubo N, et al: Surfactant protein-A concentration in bronchoalveolar lavage fluids of patients with pulmonary alveolar proteinosis. Chest 103:496–499, 1993.

49. Honda Y, Kuroki Y, Matsuura E, et al: Pulmonary surfactant protein D in sera and bronchoalveolar lavage fluids. Am J Respir Crit Care Med 152:1860–1866, 1995.

50. Kuroki Y, Tsutahara S, Shijubo N, et al: Elevated levels of lung surfactant protein A in sera from patients with idiopathic pulmonary fibrosis and pulmonary alveolar proteinosis. Am Rev Respir Dis 147:723–729, 1993.

50a. Brasch F, Birzele J, Ochs M, et al: Surfactant proteins in pulmonary alveolar proteinosis in adults. Eur Respir J 24:426–435, 2004.

51. Doyle IR, Davidson KG, Barr HA, et al: Quantity and structure of surfactant proteins vary among patients with alveolar proteinosis. Am J Respir Crit Care Med 157:658–664, 1998.

52. Takahashi T, Munakata M, Suzuki I, Kawakami Y: Serum and bronchoalveolar fluid KL-6 levels in patients with pulmonary alveolar proteinosis. Am J Respir Crit Care Med 158:1294–1298, 1998.

53. Maygarden SJ, Iacocca MV, Funkhouser WK, Novotny DB: Pulmonary alveolar proteinosis: A spectrum of cytologic, histochemical, and ultrastructural findings in bronchoalveolar lavage fluid. Diagn Cytopathol 24:389–395, 2001.

54. Burkhalter A, Silverman JF, Hopkins MB III, Geisinger KR: Bronchoalveolar lavage cytology in pulmonary alveolar proteinosis. Am J Clin Pathol 106:504–510, 1996.

55. Milleron BJ, Costabel U, Teschler H, et al: Bronchoalveolar lavage cell data in alveolar proteinosis. Am Rev Respir Dis 144:1330–1332, 1991.

56. Clague HW, Wallace AC, Morgan WK: Pulmonary interstitial fibrosis associated with alveolar proteinosis. Thorax 38:865–866, 1983.

57. Hudson AR, Halprin GM, Miller JA, Kilburn KH: Pulmonary interstitial fibrosis following alveolar proteinosis. Chest 65:700–702, 1974.

58. Kaplan AI, Sabin S: Case report: Interstitial fibrosis after uncomplicated pulmonary alveolar proteinosis. Postgrad Med 61:263, 265, 1977.

59. Wasserman K, Blank N, Fletcher G: Lung lavage (alveolar washing) in alveolar proteinosis. Am J Med 44:611–617, 1968.

60. Ramirez J, Harlan WR Jr: Pulmonary alveolar proteinosis: Nature and origin of alveolar lipid. Am J Med 45:502–512, 1968.

61. Harris JO: Pulmonary alveolar proteinosis: Abnormal in vitro function of alveolar macrophages. Chest 76:156–159, 1979.

62. Ikegami M, Ueda T, Hull W, et al: Surfactant metabolism in transgenic mice after granulocyte macrophage-colony stimulating factor ablation. Am J Physiol 270:L650–L658, 1996.

63. Huffman JA, Hull WM, Dranoff G, et al: Pulmonary epithelial cell expression of GM-CSF corrects the alveolar proteinosis in GM-CSF-deficient mice. J Clin Invest 97:649–655, 1996.

64. Reed JA, Ikegami M, Cianciolo ER, et al: Aerosolized GM-CSF ameliorates pulmonary alveolar proteinosis in GM-CSF-deficient mice. Am J Physiol 276:L556–L563, 1999.

65. Cooke KR, Nishinakamura R, Martin TR, et al: Persistence of pulmonary pathology and abnormal lung function in IL-3/GM-CSF/IL-5 βc receptor-deficient mice despite correction of alveolar proteinosis after BMT. Bone Marrow Transplant 20:657–662, 1997.

66. Nishinakamura R, Wiler R, Dirksen U, et al: The pulmonary alveolar proteinosis in granulocyte macrophage colony-stimulating factor/interleukins 3/5 βc receptor-deficient mice is reversed by bone marrow transplantation. J Exp Med 183:2657–2662, 1996.

67. Bewig B, Wang XD, Kirsten D, et al: GM-CSF and GM-CSF βc receptor in adult patients with pulmonary alveolar proteinosis. Eur Respir J 15:350–357, 2000.

68. Thomassen MJ, Yi T, Raychaudhuri B, et al: Pulmonary alveolar proteinosis is a disease of decreased availability of GM-CSF rather than an intrinsic cellular defect. Clin Immunol 95:85–92, 2000.

69. Carraway MS, Ghio AJ, Carter JD, Piantadosi CA: Detection of granulocyte-macrophage colony-stimulating factor in patients with pulmonary alveolar proteinosis. Am J Respir Crit Care Med 161:1294–1299, 2000.

70. Ikegami M, Whitsett JA, Chroneos C, et al: IL-4 increases surfactant and regulates metabolism in vivo. Am J Physiol Lung Cell Mol Physiol 278:L75–L80, 2000.

71. Homer RJ, Zheng T, Chupp G, et al: Elias. Pulmonary type II cell hypertrophy and pulmonary lipoproteinosis are features of chronic IL-13 exposure. Am J Physiol Lung Cell Mol Physiol 283:L52–L59, 2002.

72. Korfhagen TR, Sheftelyevich V, Burhans MS, et al: Surfactant protein-D regulates surfactant phospholipid homeostasis in vivo. J Biol Chem 273:28438–28443, 1998.

73. Fisher JH, Sheftelyevich V, Ho YS, et al: Pulmonary-specific expression of SP-D corrects pulmonary lipid accumulation in SP-D gene-targeted mice. Am J Physiol Lung Cell Mol Physiol 278:L365–L373, 2000.

74. Wadhwa M, Meager A, Dilger P, et al: Neutralizing antibodies to granulocyte-macrophage colony-stimulating factor, interleukin-1α but not other cytokines in human immunoglobulin preparations. Immunology 99:113–123, 2000.

75. Meager A, Wadhwa M, Bird C, et al: Spontaneously occurring neutralizing antibodies against granulocyte-macrophage colony-stimulating factor in patients with autoimmune disease. Immunology 97:526–532, 1999.

76. Svenson M, Hansen MB, Ross C, et al: Antibody to granulocyte-macrophage colony-stimulating factor is a dominant anti-cytokine activity in human IgG preparations. Blood 91:2054–2061, 1998.

77. Uchida K, Nakata K, Trapnell BC, et al: High affinity autoantibodies specifically eliminate granulocyte-macrophage colony stimulating factor activity in the lung of patients with idiopathic pulmonary alveolar proteinosis. Blood 103:1089–1098, 2004.

78. Shibata Y, Berclaz YP, Chroneos ZC, et al: GM-CSF regulates alveolar macrophage differentiation and innate immunity in the lung through PU.1. Immunity 15:557–567, 2001.

78a. Bonfield TL, John N, Malur A, et al: Elevated monocyte chemotactic proteins 1, 2, and 3 in pulmonary alveolar proteinosis are associated with chemokine receptor suppression. Clin Immunol 114:79–85, 2005.

79. Berclaz P-Y, Shibata Y, Whitsett JA, Trapnell BC: GM-CSF, via PU.1, regulates alveolar macrophage FcgR-mediated phagocytosis and the IL-18/IFN-γ-mediated molecular connection between innate and adaptive immunity in the lung. Blood 100:4193–4200, 2002.

80. Bonfield TL, Raychaudhuri B, Malur A, et al: PU.1 regulation of human alveolar macrophage differentiation requires granulocyte-macrophage colony-stimulating factor. Am J Physiol Lung Cell Mol Physiol 285:L1132–L1136, 2003.

81. Chawla A, Repa JJ, Evans RM, Mangelsdorf DJ: Nuclear receptors and lipid physiology: Opening the X-files. Science 294:1866–1870, 2001.

82. Bonfield TL, Farver CF, Barna BP, et al: PPARγ is deficient in alveolar macrophages from patients with alveolar proteinosis. Am J Respir Cell Mol Biol 29:677–682, 2003.

83. Iyonaga K, Suga M, Yamamoto T, et al: Elevated bronchoalveolar concentrations of MCP-1 in patients with pulmonary alveolar proteinosis. Eur Respir J 14:383–389, 1999.

84. Paine R, Morris SB, Jin H, et al: Impaired functional activity of alveolar macrophages from GM-CSF-deficient mice. Am J Physiol Lung Cell Mol Physiol 281:L1210–L1218, 2001.

85. Carraway MS, Stonehuerner J, Ghio AJ, Piantadosi CA: DNA microarray analysis in patients with pulmonary alveolar proteinosis. Am J Respir Crit Care Med 167:A952, 2003.

86. Gumpert BC, Nowacki MR, Amundson DE: Pulmonary alveolar lipoproteinosis: Remission after antibiotic treatment. West J Med 161:66–68, 1994.

87. Arora PL, Rogers RM, Mayock RL: Alveolar proteinosis: Experience with trypsin therapy. Am J Med 44:889–899, 1968.

88. Farca A, Maher G, Miller A: Pulmonary alveolar proteinosis: Home treatment with intermittent positive pressure breathing. JAMA 224:1283–1285, 1973.

89. Sunderland WA, Klein RL: Heparin absorption during heparin-saline lung lavage in a patient with pulmonary alveolar proteinosis. Chest 63:1033–1034, 1973.

90. Diaz JP, Manresa PF, Benasco C, et al: Response to surfactant activator (ambroxol) in alveolar proteinosis. Lancet 1:1023, 1984.

91. Hashizume T: Pulmonary alveolar proteinosis successfully treated with ambroxol. Intern Med 41:1175–1178, 2002.

92. Rogers RM, Levin DC, Gray BA, Moseley LW Jr: Physiologic effects of bronchopulmonary lavage in alveolar proteinosis. Am Rev Respir Dis 118:255–264, 1978.

93. Martin RJ, Coalson JJ, Rogers RM, et al: Pulmonary alveolar proteinosis: The diagnosis by segmental lavage. Am Rev Respir Dis 121:819–825, 1980.

94. Ramirez J, Kieffer RF Jr, Ball WC Jr: Bronchopulmonary lavage in man. Ann Intern Med 63:819–828, 1965.

95. Kao D, Wasserman K, Costley D, Benfield JR: Advances in the treatment of pulmonary alveolar proteinosis. Am Rev Respir Dis 111:361–363, 1975.

96. Ben Abraham R, Greenfeld A, Rozenman J, Ben Dov I: Pulmonary alveolar proteinosis: Step-by-step perioperative care of whole lung lavage procedure. Heart Lung 31:43–49, 2002.

97. Hammon WE, McCaffree DR, Cucchiara AJ: A comparison of manual to mechanical chest percussion for clearance of alveolar material in patients with pulmonary alveolar proteinosis (phospholipidosis). Chest 103:1409–1412, 1993.

98. Selecky PA, Wasserman K, Benfield JR, Lippmann M: The clinical and physiological effect of whole-lung lavage in pulmonary alveolar proteinosis: A ten-year experience. Ann Thorac Surg 24:451–461, 1977.

99. Cheng SL, Chang HT, Lau HP, et al: Pulmonary alveolar proteinosis: Treatment by bronchofiberscopic lobar lavage. Chest 122:1480–1485, 2002.

100. van der Kleij AJ, Peper JA, Biervliet JD, et al: Whole lung lavage under hyperbaric conditions: 2. Monitoring tissue oxygenation. Adv Exp Med Biol 317:121–124, 1992.

101. Cooper JD, Duffin J, Glynn MF, et al: Combination of membrane oxygenator support and pulmonary lavage for acute respiratory failure. J Thorac Cardiovasc Surg 71:304–308, 1976.

102. Zapol WM, Wilson R, Hales C, et al: Venovenous bypass with a membrane lung to support bilateral lung lavage. JAMA 251:3269–3271, 1984.

103. Cohen ES, Elpern E, Silver MR: Pulmonary alveolar proteinosis causing severe hypoxemic respiratory failure treated with sequential whole-lung lavage utilizing venovenous extracorporeal membrane oxygenation: A case report and review. Chest 120:1024–1026, 2001.

104. Tsai WC, Lewis D, Nasr SZ, Hirschl RB: Liquid ventilation in an infant with pulmonary alveolar proteinosis. Pediatr Pulmonol 26:283–286, 1998.

105. Seymour JF, Presneill JJ, Schoch OD, et al: Therapeutic efficacy of granulocyte-macrophage colony-stimulating

106. Barraclough RM, Gillies AJ: Pulmonary alveolar proteinosis: A complete response to GM-CSF therapy. Thorax 56:664–665, 2001.

107. Schoch OD, Schanz U, Koller M, et al: BAL findings in a patient with pulmonary alveolar proteinosis successfully treated with GM-CSF. Thorax 57:277–280, 2002.

108. de Vega MG, Sanchez-Palencia A, Ramirez A, et al: GM-CSF therapy in pulmonary alveolar proteinosis. Thorax 57:837–838, 2002.

109. Acosta O, Maranes I, Perez A, et al: Therapeutic efficacy of GM-CSF in pulmonary alveolar proteinosis (in Spanish). Arch Bronconeumol 38:191–193, 2002.

110. Khanjari F, Watier H, Domenech J, et al: GM-CSF and proteinosis. Thorax 58:645, 2003.

110a. Seymour JF, Presneill JJ: Pulmonary alveolar proteinosis. What is the role of GM-CSF in disease pathogenesis and treatment? Treat Respir Med 3:229–234, 2004.

111. Seymour JF, Dunn AR, Vincent JM, et al: Efficacy of granulocyte-macrophage colony-stimulating factor in acquired alveolar proteinosis (letter). N Engl J Med 335:1924–1925, 1996.

112. Lieschke GJ, Burgess AW: Granulocyte colony-stimulating factor and granulocyte-macrophage colony-stimulating factor (1). N Engl J Med 327:28–35, 1992.

113. Wylam ME, Katzmann JA: Aerosolized GM-CSF improves pulmonary function in idiopathic pulmonary alveolar proteinosis. Am J Respir Crit Care Med 161:A889, 2000.

114. Tazawa R, Ishimoto O, Suzuki T, et al: Granulocyte-macrophage colony stimulating factor inhalation therapy as a treatment for pulmonary alveolar proteinosis. Eur Respir J 22:377s–378s, 2003.

114a. Arai T, Hamano E, Inoue Y, et al: Serum neutralizing capacity of GM-CSF reflects disease severity in a patient with pulmonary alveolar proteinosis successfully treated with inhaled GM-CSF. Respir Med 98:1227–1230, 2004.

115. Bedrossian CW, Luna MA, Conklin RH, Miller WC: Alveolar proteinosis as a consequence of immunosuppression: A hypothesis based on clinical and pathologic observations. Hum Pathol 11:527–535, 1980.

116. Witty LA, Tapson VF, Piantadosi CA: Isolation of mycobacteria in patients with pulmonary alveolar proteinosis. Medicine (Baltimore) 73:103–109, 1994.

117. Beaman BL, Burnside J, Edwards B, Causey W: Nocardial infections in the United States, 1972–1974. J Infect Dis 134:286–289, 1976.

118. Arbiser ZK, Guidot DM, Pine JR, et al: Pulmonary alveolar proteinosis mimicking idiopathic pulmonary fibrosis. Ann Diagn Pathol 7:82–86, 2003.

119. Huddleston CB, Bloch JB, Sweet SC, et al: Lung transplantation in children. Ann Surg 236:270–276, 2002.

120. Parker LA, Novotny DB: Recurrent alveolar proteinosis following double lung transplantation. Chest 111:1457–1458, 1997.

121. Gaine SP, O'Marcaigh AS: Pulmonary alveolar proteinosis: Lung transplant or bone marrow transplant? Chest 113:563–564, 1998.

122. Rodriguez-Luaces M, Lafuente A, Martin MP, et al: Haematopoietic transplantation in pulmonary alveolar proteinosis associated with chronic myelogenous leukaemia. Bone Marrow Transplant 20:507–510, 1997.

123. Kavuru MS, Bonfield TL, Thomassen MJ: Plasmapheresis, GM-CSF, and alveolar proteinosis. Am J Respir Crit Care Med 167:1036, 2003.

124. Golde DW, Territo M, Finley TN, Cline MJ: Defective lung macrophages in pulmonary alveolar proteinosis. Ann Intern Med 85:304–309, 1976.

ENVIRONMENTAL AND OCCUPATIONAL DISORDERS

60

Occupational Asthma

John R. Balmes, M.D.

INTRODUCTION

Work-related asthma is the most common form of occupational lung disease in the developed world at the present time, and the contribution of occupational exposures to the overall disease burden of asthma is considerable. Workplace exposure is an important cause of both new-onset asthma and exacerbations of preexisting disease. Although the term *occupational asthma* usually refers to new-onset asthma caused by exposure at the workplace, exacerbations of preexisting asthma are a potentially more important cause of morbidity at the workplace because there are more workers with work-aggravated asthma than work-caused asthma.

In this chapter, the epidemiology, pathogenesis/mechanisms, and clinical presentations of new-onset occupational asthma (both sensitizer-and irritant-induced) are discussed. A diagnostic approach is presented, including history and exposure assessment, physical examination, and objective tests used to confirm both the diagnosis of asthma and its relation to work. Management of the worker with occupational asthma is also addressed, including work modifications, prognosis, and impairment/disability assessment. Finally, the prevention of occupational asthma and future research needs are highlighted.

DEFINITION/CLASSIFICATION

Workplace exposure is an important cause of both new-onset asthma and exacerbations of preexisting disease. The term *occupational asthma* usually refers to new-onset asthma caused by exposure at the workplace; however, exacerbations of preexisting asthma are a potentially more important cause of morbidity at the workplace because there are more workers with *work-aggravated asthma* than work-caused asthma.

EXACERBATIONS OF PREEXISTING ASTHMA (WORK-AGGRAVATED ASTHMA)

Asthma is a common disease in the general population (affecting approximately 5%).[1] Because many people with asthma have mild disease and can function normally under most circumstances, every common occupation involves a significant number of workers with asthma. Extreme sensitivity of the airways to chemical, physical, and pharmacologic stimuli is a characteristic feature of asthma. Thus, many agents encountered in the workplace that have little or no effect on nonasthmatic workers can cause pronounced symptomatic airflow limitation in workers with asthma.

Irritants

Although numerous agents that irritate mucous membranes are commonly encountered in industry, little is known about their effects on airway function in people with asthma. Because regulatory standards for exposure at the workplace, unlike air pollution standards, are generally not designed to protect the most susceptible persons, allowable concentrations of irritants in the workplace may be orders of magnitude higher than the concentrations needed to cause exacerbations of asthma. An example is sulfur dioxide (SO_2), a highly water-soluble gas encountered in significant concentrations in many work sites. On the basis of data showing little effect of SO_2 in concentrations under 5 parts per million (ppm) in people with no pulmonary abnormalities, the current U.S. Occupational Safety and Health Administration (OSHA) threshold limit value for SO_2 allows exposure to an average concentration of 5 ppm over an 8-hour work shift. However, controlled human exposure studies have shown that, in persons with mild asthma, pronounced symptomatic airflow limitation can develop after 5 minutes of breathing concentrations of SO_2 of 0.5 ppm or less.[2,3]

The cellular and biochemical mechanisms by which SO_2 causes bronchoconstriction have not been determined. The bronchoconstrictor response does not seem directly related to the irritant properties of the gas, because 0.5 ppm is near the sensory detection threshold for SO_2. In contrast, exposure to a concentration of formaldehyde that causes marked eye and throat irritation does not cause bronchoconstriction in subjects with asthma.[4] Thus, it is not possible to predict the likely bronchoconstrictor response of workers with asthma to a given irritant without directly studying the effects of that material on asthmatic subjects.

Allergens

Inhalation of specific allergens is a well-recognized cause of exacerbations of asthma. Allergen inhalation not only causes immediate and late-phase airflow limitation but can also cause an increase in nonspecific airway hyperresponsiveness[5] and may thus increase the overall clinical severity of asthma. Specific allergens are an important cause of new-onset asthma related to occupation and are discussed later, but they are also an important cause of work-associated exacerbations of preexisting asthma. Animal proteins, encountered by laboratory workers, veterinarians, and farmers, are examples of allergens that have been implicated both in exacerbating existing asthma and in causing new-onset asthma.[6,7]

Other Stimuli

Many of the other stimuli known to cause bronchoconstriction in patients with asthma may contribute to work-induced exacerbations of asthma. These include environmental tobacco smoke; exercise, particularly in cold or dry environments; and viral upper respiratory infections, a well-recognized occupational risk among teachers and child care workers. Emotional stress is also an important feature of many jobs that may contribute to exacerbations of asthma.

NEW-ONSET ASTHMA CAUSED AT WORK (OCCUPATIONAL ASTHMA)

How the various types of occupational asthma are defined often depends on the setting (e.g., epidemiologic research, disease surveillance, or workers' compensation). An accepted operational definition of occupational asthma for clinical purposes is variable airflow limitation or airway hyperresponsiveness, or both, due to exposure to a specific agent or conditions in a particular work environment and not to stimuli encountered outside the workplace.[8] This definition includes no reference to the mechanism of asthma induction, and therefore work-related variable airway obstruction caused by antigen-induced hypersensitivity reactions, pharmacologic effects, nonspecific inflammatory processes, and direct airway irritation can qualify as occupational asthma (Table 60.1). In the past, the term *occupational asthma* often was used only to refer to patients with reversible airflow limitation due to sensitization to a substance encountered at work (i.e., *sensitizer-induced asthma*) that involves a latent period. With such an approach, workers who develop persistent symptoms of asthma and nonspecific airway hyperresponsiveness promptly after short-term, high-intensity inhalational exposure to irritant materials would not be considered to have occupational asthma. The term *reactive airways dysfunction syndrome* (RADS) has been coined to refer to this latter condition.[9]

Recently, a consensus appears to be developing around the concept that there is a type of occupational asthma without latency that may occur after single or multiple exposures to nonspecific irritant chemicals at concentrations high enough to induce airway injury and inflammation.[8,10] Because RADS refers only to asthma occurring after a single high-intensity exposure, the term *irritant-induced asthma* is used in this chapter in referring to the single or multiple exposure type. Recurrent exposure to an irritant before the

Table 60.1 Possible Causes of Occupational Asthma

Mechanisms	Examples
Without "Sensitization"	
Endotoxin effects	Cotton dust
Anticholinesterase effect	Organophosphate pesticides
Inflammatory response	Ammonia, chlorine
Irritant response	Dusts, fumes, vapors, cold
With "Sensitization"	
High-Molecular-Weight Compounds	
IgE-mediated (complete allergens)	Animal, plant, bacterial proteins
Low-Molecular-Weight Compounds	
IgE-mediated (haptens)	Platinum, antibiotics
? Mechanism	Isocyanates, amines, acid anhydrides, plicatic acid

IgE, immunoglobulin E.

onset of asthmatic symptoms may lead to blurring of the distinction based on latency.

Another type of disorder characterized by work-related variable airway limitation is associated with occupational exposure to organic dusts such as cotton, flax, hemp, jute, sisal, and various grains. Many but not all occupational lung disease experts consider organic dust–induced airway disease to be an asthma-like disorder rather than "true" asthma.[8] Reasons for this distinction include lack of airway eosinophilia, less frequent airway hyperresponsiveness, and a tendency to develop chronic bronchitis (by clinical definition) and chronic airflow limitation with chronic exposure.

Occupational asthma may need to be approached differently for epidemiologic and disease surveillance purposes than for medical-legal purposes. An inclusive approach is appropriate for use in a surveillance system in which identification triggers an investigation or intervention. If prevention of work-related asthma disability and loss of productivity is the goal, then variable airflow limitation and/or airway hyperresponsiveness caused *or* aggravated by exposures at the workplace must be considered.

EPIDEMIOLOGY

Reports from several surveillance programs have suggested that occupational asthma is probably the most common type of occupational lung disease in industrialized countries. Occupational asthma accounted for 26% of all work-related respiratory diseases reported to the Surveillance of Work and Occupational Respiratory Disease (SWORD) program in the United Kingdom[11] and 52% of such cases in British Columbia, where there is a particularly high prevalence due to the use of western red cedar.[12] However, the overall prevalence of occupational asthma in the general population is not clearly known. In the United States, analysis of 1978 Social Security Disability data indicated that approximately 15% of individuals disabled from asthma attributed it to workplace exposures.[13]

A number of studies have attempted to address the issue of attributable risk of asthma or wheezing in the general population due to occupation (i.e., what fraction of all asthma is due to occupational exposures?). This issue is complicated by the acknowledged lack of a standardized definition of asthma. A recent review of the existing literature on the population attributable risk of asthma due to occupational exposures provided a range from 8% to 21%, depending on the definition of exposure.[14]

The prevalence of occupational asthma in various occupational cohort studies depends on the agent(s) to which the workers are exposed, the levels of exposure, and host susceptibility factors such as atopy and cigarette smoking. The highest prevalences of occupational asthma have been reported with exposures to platinum salts and proteolytic enzymes used in the detergent industry (up to 50%).[15,16] In general, however, the prevalence of occupational asthma in most cohorts of workers exposed to a known sensitizing agent is less than 10%.[17] There are convincing data to indicate that the level of exposure is an important risk factor for sensitizer-induced occupational asthma.[18]

Atopy appears to be an important risk factor for occupational asthma due to immunoglobulin E (IgE)–dependent

mechanisms. Psyllium workers,[19] bakers,[20] and laboratory animal handlers who are atopic have been shown to be at increased risk of developing occupational asthma as compared to their nonatopic coworkers.[7] Cigarette smoking also appears to increase the risk of IgE-mediated occupational asthma. Workers exposed to platinum salts, acid anhydrides, snow crab, green coffee beans, and ispaghula who smoke have been shown to have greater risk of developing occupational asthma than their nonsmoking coworkers.[21] In contrast, for most sensitizing agents that cause asthma through mechanisms not involving specific IgE antibodies, such as diisocyanates and western red cedar, atopy and smoking do not appear to be risk factors.[22,23]

Little is known about the epidemiology of irritant-induced asthma, but it is likely to be a relatively rare outcome of irritant exposure. SWORD data suggest that less than 10% of reported inhalational injuries are followed by persistent asthma.[24] Irritant exposures may deserve greater attention as an important preventable cause of occupational asthma. Recent data from the Sentinel Health Notification System for Occupational Risk (SENSOR) program in the United States indicate that exposures to irritants are reported as frequently as exposures to sensitizers as causes of new-onset asthma.[25] Level of exposure is likely to be a risk factor for irritant-induced asthma. In a study of hospital laboratory workers exposed to a spill of glacial acetic acid, the risk of irritant-induced asthma increased with level of exposure as assessed by distance from the spill.[26] Several studies have also suggested that atopy and smoking are risk factors for irritant-induced asthma.[27,28]

Although exposure at the workplace has been recognized for more than 250 years as a cause of asthma, the incidence and prevalence of work-induced asthma remain unknown in most jurisdictions, principally because of the lack of an appropriate reporting system. Because asthma is a common disease that often presents de novo in adulthood, the association between onset of asthma and exposure to a specific material in the workplace is often missed.[28a] With the introduction of thousands of new chemicals into workplaces each year, the list of responsible agents is likely to continue to grow.

PATHOGENESIS/MECHANISMS

The mechanisms by which previously healthy adults develop asthma are poorly understood. Because many who develop asthma in adulthood do not report a family history of asthma or atopic disease, environmental factors are thought to be at least as important as genetic factors in causing adult-onset asthma. In most patients, these presumed "environmental factors" cannot be identified. Patients with work-induced asthma are a notable exception, and work-induced asthma provides a unique opportunity to study the mechanisms underlying the development of adult-onset asthma in general. For further discussion of the pathogenesis of asthma, see Chapter 37.

IMMUNOLOGIC OR SENSITIZER-INDUCED OCCUPATIONAL ASTHMA

Over 250 agents have been adequately documented to cause immunologic occupational asthma.[29] Table 60.2 lists

Table 60.2 Suspected Causes of Occupational Asthma

Material	Industry or Occupation at Risk	Material	Industry or Occupation at Risk
Low-Molecular-Weight Chemicals		Fish (glue)	Bookbinders, postal workers
Isocyanates		Silkworms	Silk sericulturers
Toluene diisocyanate	Polyurethane, insulators, laminators, roofers	Grain mites, weevils	Grain mill and storage workers, bakers
Diphenylmethane diisocyanate	Laminators, polyurethane foam	Prawns	Processors
Hexamethylene diisocyanate	Painters, plastics	Crabs	Processors
Naphthalene diisocyanate	Chemists, rubber workers	*Plants*	
Anhydrides		Wheat	Farmers, grain handlers
Trimellitic anhydride	Chemical workers	Buckwheat	Bakers
Phthalic anhydride	Paint, plastics	Grain dust	Farmers, grain handlers, bakers
Hexahydrophthalic anhydride	Epoxy resins	Rye flour	Bakers
Tetrachlorophthalic anhydride	Epoxy resins	Hops	Brewers
Metals		Tamarind seeds	Millers, spice processors
Chromium	Chrome platers, welders	Castor beans	Farmers, castor bean workers
Platinum	Platinum refiners	Coffee beans	Farmers, coffee bean workers
Nickel	Nickel platers, welders	Wool	Textile workers
Cobalt	Tool grinders, diamond polishers	Tobacco dust	Cigarette manufacturers
Aluminum?	Aluminum pot-room workers	Tea	Food processors
Drugs		Cotton, flax, hemp	Textile workers
Benzyl penicillin	Pharmaceuticals	Latex from natural rubber	Health care workers, food processors
Ampicillin	Pharmaceuticals	*Vegetable Gums*	
Sulfathiazole	Pharmaceuticals	Acacia	Printing
Tetracycline	Pharmaceuticals	Tragacanth	Printing, food processing
Psyllium	Pharmaceuticals	Karaya	Food processing
Methyldopa	Pharmaceuticals	Arabic	Printing
Salbutamol	Pharmaceuticals	*Wood Dusts*	
Piperazine dihydrochloride	Pharmaceuticals	Western red cedar	Woodworkers
Chloramine T	Pharmaceuticals, laboratory workers	Cedar of Lebanon	Woodworkers
Organophosphates	Farm workers, pesticide formulators, fumigators	Mahogany	Woodworkers
Miscellaneous Chemicals		California redwood	Woodworkers
Formaldehyde	Laboratory workers, embalmers, insulators, textile workers	Oak	Woodworkers
		Iroko	Woodworkers
Glutaraldehyde	Hospital staff (disinfection)	Boxwood	Woodworkers
Dimethylethanolamine	Paint sprayers	Cocabolla	Woodworkers
Ethylenediamine	Rubber workers, photographic processors	Zebrawood	Woodworkers
		Mansonia	Woodworkers
Persulfate salts	Chemical workers, beauticians	Mulberry	Woodworkers
Ethylene oxide	Medical sterilizers	*Dyes*	
Pyrethrin	Fumigators	Anthraquinone	Fabric dyeing
Ammonium thioglycolate	Beauticians	Carmine	Cosmetics, dyes
Monoethanolamine	Beauticians	Paraphenyl diamine	Fur dyeing
Hexamethylenamine	Beauticians	Hexafix brilliant yellow	Dye manufacturers
Polyvinyl chloride vapor	Meat wrappers	Drimaren brilliant blue	Dye manufacturers
Aminoethylethanolamine	Aluminum soldering	Cibachrome brilliant scarlet	Dye manufacturers
High-Molecular-Weight Organic Materials		Henna extract	Beauticians
Animals		*Fluxes*	
Domestic animals	Farmers, veterinarians, meat processors	Colophony (soft-core solder)	Solderers, electronics workers
		Enzymes	
Birds	Poultry breeders, bird fanciers	Pancreatic extracts	Pharmaceutical workers
Bats, mice, guinea pigs	Laboratory workers	*Bacillus subtilis*	Detergent manufacturers
Sea squirt	Oyster farmers	Papain	Food processors
		Trypsin	Plastics and rubber workers
		Flaviastase	Pharmaceutical workers
		Bromelain	Food processors
		Pectinase	Food processors

some of the more common agents and workers at risk. The mechanisms of sensitization by which these agents induce asthma can be somewhat arbitrarily divided based on molecular weight of the agents. High-molecular-weight (HMW) compounds ($\geq$5000 D) and some low-molecular-weight (LMW) compounds (<5000 D), such as platinum salts and acid anhydrides, induce asthma by specific IgE antibody-dependent reactions. However, the use of the term *immunologic* does not necessarily imply an IgE-mediated response; cell-mediated responses may be involved. IgE antibodies specific for the sensitizing agent in the workplace frequently cannot be demonstrated in cases of occupational asthma caused by LMW compounds, such as diisocyanates and plicatic acid (the agent responsible for causing asthma in workers exposed to western red cedar).

Whereas HMW compounds act as complete antigens, LMW compounds need to react with proteins (autologous or heterologous) to produce a complete antigen. In IgE-mediated occupational asthma, inhaled sensitizers bind to specific IgE on the surface of mast cells, basophils, and probably macrophages, eosinophils, and platelets. The specific reaction between allergen and IgE causes a cascade of events that produces the activation of inflammatory cells. Mast cell activation leads to early bronchoconstriction as a result of preformed mediator release (e.g., histamine, leukotrienes C_4, D_4, and E_4, and prostaglandin D_2). IgE-dependent activation of mast cells also leads to release of multiple cytokines/chemokines and increased expression of various adhesion molecules that are involved in modulating the late inflammatory reaction after allergen exposure.

As noted above, for a number of LMW compounds, specific IgE compounds either have not been found or have been found in only a subset of affected workers. A study using basophils from patients with western red cedar showed that plicatic acid did not induce histamine release from basophils by a tyrosine kinase–mediated mechanism as would be expected in an IgE-dependent response.[30] However, in a companion study, it was shown that T lymphocytes from such patients did specifically respond to a conjugate of plicatic acid and human serum albumin, suggesting an underlying immunologic mechanism.[31] A recent study using a murine model confirmed that transfer of toluene diisocyanate-induced asthma-related responses could be accomplished by transfusion of lymphocytes from sensitized to naive mice.[31a]

Whether immunologic occupational asthma is induced by HMW or LMW sensitizers, T cells appear to play an important role in the orchestration of the inflammatory process, and eosinophils, mast cells, epithelial cells, and neutrophils are the main effector cells that produce the characteristic features of asthma (i.e., smooth muscle contraction, mucus hypersecretion, airway inflammation, and epithelial injury). It has been hypothesized that allergic asthma is driven and maintained by the persistence of a specialized subset of chronically activated T memory cells sensitized against aeroallergenic, occupational, or viral antigens. Studies showing proliferation of peripheral blood lymphocytes after stimulation with cobalt and nickel[32] or diisocyanates[33] in sensitized subjects support this hypothesis. In nonoccupational allergic asthma, the majority of T-cell clones derived from the bronchial mucosa are CD4+, whereas in diiso-

cyanate-induced asthma, the majority may be CD8^{+34} or even CD4$^-$/CD8$^-\delta$/γ T cells.[33] Interestingly, an increased percentage of CD8+ T cells and increased production of interleukin-5 have been found in bronchoalveolar lavage fluid from nonatopic asthmatics.[35] One component of the signaling pathway involved in T-cell induction of diiso-cyanate asthma appears to be enhanced production of monocyte chemoattractant protein-1.[36]

Recent investigations into the genetic determinants of risk for sensitizer-induced occupational asthma have suggested that polymorphisms in genes encoding major histocompatibility complex class II proteins may be important determinants of the specificity of response to sensitizing agents. In workers with exposure to diisocyanates, human leukocyte antigen (HLA)-DQB1*0503 and DQB1*0201/0301 alleles are associated with asthma, whereas HLA-DQB1*0501 and DQA1*0101-DQB1*0501-DR1 alleles appear to be protective.[37] The alleles HLA-DQB1*0503 and HLA-DQB1*0501 differ at residue 57 for a single amino acid, aspartic acid in DQB1*0503 and valine in DQB1*0501, suggesting that residue 57 is potentially a critical location in the development of asthma.[38] Associations with major histocompatibility complex proteins have also been described in acid anhydride–induced asthma,[39] in platinum salts–induced asthma,[40] and in red cedar–induced asthma.[41] The DRB1*13 marker was associated with the risk of soybean epidemic asthma in Barcelona,[42] and the phenotype frequencies of DR1 and DR4 are slightly increased in subjects sensitized to latex.[43] Another set of genetic risk factors appears to be polymorphisms in genes coding for glutathione S-transferase enzymes. An association between increased risk of asthma related to occupational exposure to diisocyanates and the *GSTM1* null genotype has been reported.[44] In a different study of diisocyanate-exposed workers, homozygosity for *GSTP1* Val105 was correlated with a decreased risk of both diisocyanate-induced asthma and airway hyperresponsiveness.[45]

NONIMMUNOLOGIC OR IRRITANT-INDUCED OCCUPATIONAL ASTHMA

The mechanisms of irritant-induced asthma are largely unknown, but a localized airway inflammatory response is probably involved. It is important to note that most patients who have sustained a toxic inhalational injury to their airways (chemical bronchitis) will recover without developing asthma. There are bronchial biopsy data from patients who developed clinically evident asthma after exposure to high concentrations of irritants (RADS) that suggest that the histopathologic changes are similar to those of typical asthma (i.e., subepithelial fibrosis and infiltration of the mucosa/submucosa by eosinophils and T cells). However, the fibrosis tends to be greater and the T-cell infiltration/activation tends to be less.[9,46,47]

It has been hypothesized that irritant-induced epithelial damage is followed by direct activation of nonadrenergic, noncholinergic pathways via axon reflexes and the onset of neurogenic inflammation.[48] Nonspecific macrophage activation and mast cell degranulation may also occur. Recruitment of other inflammatory cells likely enhances the inflammatory response. The damaged bronchial epithelium may contribute to the persistence of the inflammatory response by release of proinflammatory mediators, but also may exhibit impaired function (i.e., reduced neutral endopeptidase activity, decreased generation of epithelial-derived relaxing factor). Irritant-induced airway inflammation may alter epithelial permeability such that subepithelial irritant receptors are more likely to be exposed to nonspecific stimuli such as cold air, exercise, cigarette smoke, and other inhaled irritants. Stimulation of these receptors may further increase the likelihood of persistence of airway inflammation and nonspecific airway hyperresponsiveness. Recovery from irritant-induced asthma appears to occur over time in many cases. However, the greater the initial injury, the more unlikely complete recovery will occur. With severe injury, whether after a single high-concentration inhalation or multiple lower concentration exposures, there may be sufficient airway remodeling (i.e., deposition of type III collagen under the basement membrane) that complete recovery cannot occur.

Although much insight into the pathogenesis of sensitizer-induced asthma has been gained over the past several decades, little of this information has clinical applicability at this point due to important data gaps. A better understanding of the mechanism(s) underlying asthma due to exposure to LMW sensitizing agents, such as the diisocyanates, is needed. This caveat is especially relevant to the issue of testing of workers for genetic susceptibility. Such testing cannot be recommended because there is insufficient understanding of interactions among genetic and environmental determinants of risk of occupational asthma. Of even greater need is a data-based framework for understanding the pathogenesis of irritant-induced asthma. Development of appropriate animal models would be a major advance. Although considerable progress has been made with regard to models of HMW sensitizer–induced asthma, models of LMW sensitizer–induced asthma[49] and irritant-induced asthma following a single, high-concentration exposure are still in a relatively early stage of development.[50] To date, there is no model of irritant-induced asthma due to multiple lower concentration exposures.

DIAGNOSIS

The diagnosis of occupational asthma is made by confirming the diagnosis of asthma and by establishing a relationship between asthma and work.[51,52] Occupational asthma should be considered in every case of adult-onset asthma or asthma that worsens in adult life.[15,52] Making a diagnosis of asthma requires the presence of both intermittent respiratory symptoms (e.g., cough, wheezing, chest tightness, dyspnea) *and* physiologic evidence of reversible/variable airway obstruction or hyperresponsiveness. After the diagnosis of asthma is confirmed, the next step is to assess the relationship with work, preferably by means of objective tests. In general, the patient's history alone is not sufficient for the diagnosis of occupational asthma and is more likely to exclude than confirm the diagnosis of occupational asthma.[51,53] Objective confirmation of the diagnosis is necessary for both appropriate medical care and compensation purposes. It is important to recognize that no single test can be used to confirm the diagnosis in all cases.

CLINICAL FEATURES

A large number of new causes of occupational asthma have been described over the past 25 years, and new chemicals are continually being introduced into the workplace. It is therefore reasonable to assume that many of the agents responsible for occupational asthma have not yet been identified. Furthermore, in many industries workers are exposed to multiple chemicals that can cause asthma, making it difficult to identify the specific chemical responsible for causing asthma in an individual worker. Consequently, the diagnosis of occupational asthma often must be entertained primarily from recognition of the clinical features, particularly the pattern of presentation.[54]

In general, occupational asthma presents clinically in the same way as asthma of nonoccupational origin. Signs and symptoms include wheezing, cough, chest tightness, shortness of breath, and dyspnea on exertion. Some patients with occupational asthma develop work-related "bronchitis," characterized by recurrent episodes of cough and sputum production. Others may experience nocturnal awakening as an early manifestation of occupational asthma.

Rhinoconjunctivitis, which is manifested by ocular and nasal discharge and pruritus, and sneezing, may accompany respiratory symptoms.[54a] In a study comparing the occurrence of rhinoconjunctivitis symptoms in workers exposed to HMW versus LMW substances, rhinoconjunctivitis occurred prior to the onset of occupational asthma in workers exposed to HMW substances; those exposed to LMW substances developed symptoms concurrently with their respiratory symptoms.[55] It was postulated that HMW substances are more likely to invoke IgE-mediated immune responses, resulting in this temporal symptom pattern.

In sensitizer-induced occupational asthma, symptoms typically develop months or years after the onset of exposure. Substances that cause sensitizer-induced asthma may induce early, late, or dual airway responses (Fig. 60.1). An early asthmatic reaction occurs within a few minutes of inhalation, with maximal bronchoconstriction occurring within 30 minutes. Late asthmatic reactions occur within 4 to 8 hours of inhalation. Dual, or biphasic, asthmatic reactions are characterized by both early and late bronchoconstriction. IgE-dependent agents, such as HMW substances, may induce both early and biphasic reactions.[15,56] IgE-independent agents are more likely to induce late or biphasic reactions.[15,56] For example, such reactions occur in up to 80% of workers with asthma caused by dust of the western red cedar.[57] Occasionally, a single exposure to the offending agent can cause repeated asthmatic reactions over several days.[58] The temporal patterns of airway responses discussed here are most clearly demonstrated in controlled exposure settings, rather than in typical workplace settings, which are more likely to involve exposures that vary over the course of the day and workweek.

Nonimmunologic or irritant-induced asthma is caused by exposure to gases, fumes, mists, smoke, or dusts that are directly irritating to the airways. Chemical bronchitis often precedes the development of irritant-induced asthma. In RADS, asthmatic symptoms occur relatively promptly and persistently after a single, high-concentration inhalational exposure. In irritant-induced asthma involving multiple lower concentration exposures, although recurrent symp-

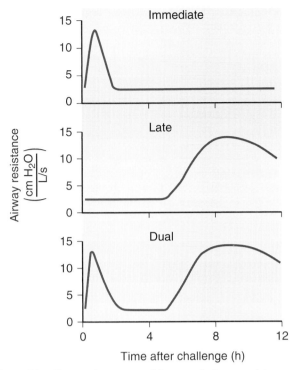

Figure 60.1 Temporal patterns of increased airway resistance after exposure to agents that cause occupational asthma.

toms of mucosal irritation are often experienced earlier, symptoms of asthma may be more gradual in onset.

HISTORY AND EXPOSURE ASSESSMENT

As in the evaluation of any patient with a possible work-related injury or illness, the evaluation of occupational asthma includes a detailed medical and occupational history. In the history of the present illness, the temporal relationship between recent exposures and respiratory symptoms must be investigated. A relationship between asthmatic symptoms and workplace exposures is suggested if any of the following patterns is present: (1) symptoms that occur only at work; (2) symptoms that improve on weekends or vacations; (3) symptoms that occur regularly after the work shift; (4) symptoms that progressively increase over the course of the workweek; and (5) symptoms that improve after a change in the work environment.[59]

Potential exposures to all "asthmagens" in the workplace as well as the home environment should be assessed. Workers also must be queried regarding moonlighting positions and hobbies, which might expose them to other asthmagens. Specific occupational history questions include not only the job title of the worker, but also specific job duties performed. In the event of accidents or spills, information regarding the role the worker played, proximity to the point source, size of the room, ventilation, duration of exposure, and type and efficacy of respiratory protection (i.e., personal protective equipment) should be evaluated. Evaluation also includes assessing the intensity or magnitude of exposure, including review of available industrial hygiene records; types of industrial processes used, such as those involving chemicals with high vapor pressure or heating; job charac-

teristics, such as spray painting; and geographic and climatic factors. In addition, other workers who have developed episodic respiratory symptoms must be identified, and their complete chronologic occupational histories obtained.

The past medical history should focus on any history of asthma, including current and past medications, the frequency of use of as-needed medications, the pattern of use of medications in relation to work, a history of hospitalizations or emergency room evaluations, and intubations. Other pertinent history includes childhood asthma, allergic rhinitis, atopic dermatitis, and other respiratory conditions such as chronic obstructive pulmonary disease. The cardiac history, including angina, and gastrointestinal history, including gastroesophageal reflux, which may present with dyspnea, must also be evaluated. A history of allergies, previous allergy testing, and cigarette smoking should be assessed, as should a history of airway hyperresponsiveness to nonallergenic stimuli such as exercise, cold air, or irritants.

PHYSICAL EXAMINATION

The physical examination in a patient with asthma is frequently completely normal. Physical examination should be focused on the upper and lower respiratory tract, including visualizing nasal and oropharyngeal mucous membranes, palpating the sinuses, and inspecting for nasal polyps. The chest should be auscultated during quiet breathing and forced exhalation, noting wheezes, rhonchi, or crackles. Cardiac examination should be performed to exclude a cardiac etiology for respiratory distress. The skin should be inspected for eczematous dermatitis and the extremities inspected for clubbing, cyanosis, and edema.

OBJECTIVE TESTS

Most asthmatic patients have normal chest radiographs because asthma involves the airways rather than the lung parenchyma. During exacerbations, hyperinflation and flattening of the diaphragms may be visualized due to air trapping. Bronchial wall thickening, reflecting chronic inflammation, and mucus plugging, manifested by fleeting infiltrates, may be seen.

Because there are no physical examination findings specific for asthma and because work-related wheezing is difficult to detect, repeated pulmonary function testing (both at and away from work) is usually required to make the diagnosis of occupational asthma. Spirometry, both before and after use of a bronchodilator, is the most reliable method of determining the presence of airflow limitation. It can be used to measure the response to a bronchodilator, which generally confirms the diagnosis of asthma. The American Thoracic Society defines a 12% improvement in the FEV_1 or an absolute value increase of at least 200 mL after bronchodilator administration as evidence of reversibility of airflow limitation.[60] A decrease of 10% in the FEV_1 across a work shift is objective evidence for work-related bronchoconstriction.[61]

Peak expiratory flow (PEF), which is measured in liters per minute via a hand-held peak flowmeter, is a simple and inexpensive method to assess airflow limitation and can be performed by the patient outside of medical or work settings. The patient is instructed to exhale as forcefully as possible into this device, and to use it to determine PEF preferably at least four times per day: prior to work, during various times in the work shift, after work, and prior to bedtime. The patient is then asked to maintain a symptom diary, recording the time of day, the PEF reading, and any respiratory symptoms for evaluation by the physician on medical follow-up. At least 2 weeks of serial PEF recordings are needed to assess whether occupational asthma is likely. A 20% or greater diurnal variability in PEF has been used to diagnose workers with occupational asthma, and a computerized system of analysis is under development, but visual inspection of whether there is a work-related pattern of increased diurnal variability is probably the best approach to the analysis of serial peak flow recordings at the present time.[51,62]

There is current debate as to whether PEF readings are accurate, because they are dependent on patient effort and reliability. In a study of 17 subjects instructed in the use of a portable computerized peak flowmeter who were unaware that their readings were being stored by the flowmeter, it was found that only 55% of the records were completely accurate in terms of the recorded value and timing of the measurements.[63] Worker training may improve the accuracy of measurements,[64] and portable computerized peak flowmeters are becoming increasingly affordable. Despite concerns about accuracy of patient-recorded PEF data, some investigators have found such data to have reasonable sensitivity and specificity for the diagnosis of occupational asthma.[62]

In a worker who is suspected of having occupational asthma but who has normal spirometry, inhalation challenge testing with methacholine or histamine can demonstrate the presence of nonspecific airway hyperresponsiveness. Progressive doses of histamine or methacholine are administered to the patient and serial FEV_1 measurements are obtained to generate a dose-response curve. Testing continues until the PC_{20}, the provocative concentration of histamine or methacholine that induces a 20% drop in FEV_1, is reached, after which the test is terminated. This test can be performed on an outpatient basis, and several published protocols are available.[65] On occasion, workers with occupational asthma will not show clear evidence of work-related lung function changes until after a prolonged period of removal from the causative exposure. In other words, it may take several weeks away from the patient's usual work before a clear improvement in spirometry, PEF, or methacholine responsiveness is noted.

Specific inhalation challenge tests, also called specific bronchial provocation studies, are performed rarely in the United States. When performed, the purpose of a specific challenge is often to determine the precise etiology in a complex exposure scenario or to investigate an unreported sensitizer. Historically, a specific inhalation challenge test has been considered a potentially dangerous procedure because the specific agent that is thought to induce occupational asthma is administered to the subject. These tests should be administered in a very controlled situation with careful monitoring in a hospital setting. However, recent studies in Quebec indicate that, if stringent exposure and safety protocols are followed, specific inhalation challenge tests can be performed with minimal risk to the subjects.[66]

Atopy, which is a risk factor for HMW sensitizer–induced asthma, can be established by administering skin prick tests with common aeroallergens. Extracts are available for confirming immediate hypersensitivity to some occupational sensitizers such as flour, animal proteins, and coffee. Patients can also be tested for the presence of specific IgE antibodies against HMW sensitizers and some LMW sensitizers (diisocyanates, acid anhydrides).[67,68]

DIAGNOSTIC CRITERIA

As noted earlier, the diagnosis of occupational asthma involves confirming the diagnosis of asthma and establishing its relatedness to work. The American College of Chest Physicians established the following criteria in 1995: (1) a history compatible with occupational asthma; (2) the presence of airflow limitation and its reversibility; (3) in the absence of airflow limitation, the presence of nonspecific airway hyperresponsiveness; and (4) the demonstration of work-relatedness of asthma by objective means.[51] The Canadian Thoracic Society has suggested a similar approach in making the diagnosis of occupational asthma, by demonstrating the presence of asthma with pulmonary function tests and then assessing the relationship between asthma and work.[52]

The National Institute for Occupational Safety and Health has recently updated its surveillance case definition and surveillance classification criteria for its state-based SENSOR programs for work-related asthma, which currently exist in California, Massachusetts, Michigan, and New Jersey.[25] Sentinel health events, which include cases of work-related asthma, indicate the need for preventive measures. Surveillance of work-related asthma may be accomplished by requiring health care professionals to report all diagnosed or suspected cases to state health departments. In analysis of these cases, the relative frequencies of classes of work-related asthma can be determined, as can gender frequencies; specific asthma-inducing agents, whether previously known or newly discovered; and the most common industries in which workers develop work-related asthma.

The SENSOR surveillance case definition for state health departments for work-related asthma includes (1) a health care professional's diagnosis consistent with asthma; and (2) an association between symptoms of asthma and work. The SENSOR programs classify work-related asthma into three broad categories by using surveillance case classification criteria (Table 60.3): (1) occupational asthma, or work-induced asthma that is new in onset; (2) work-aggravated asthma, which occurs in workers with preexisting asthma that has been treated within the past 2 years; and (3) RADS, or irritant-induced asthma. Cases of occupational asthma are subclassified on the basis of exposure to known asthma inducers. Although the SENSOR surveillance case definition and classification criteria were designed for epidemiologic purposes, they provide a reasonable approach for the clinical evaluation of patients.

MANAGEMENT

The mainstay of treatment of occupational asthma is prompt diagnosis and removal of the worker from further exposure to the inciting agent if substitution with a less hazardous substance is not possible.[15,51,52,56] This is crucial in cases of

Table 60.3 SENSOR Surveillance Case Classification Criteria for Work-Related Asthma

1. Preexisting asthma that was symptomatic and/or treated with asthma medication within the 2 years prior to entering the occupational setting associated with the patient's asthma symptoms = work-aggravated asthma.

2. New asthma symptoms that develop within 24 hours after a one-time high-level inhalation exposure (at work) to an irritant gas, fume, smoke, or vapor and that persist for at least 3 months = reactive airways dysfunction syndrome (RADS).

3. Workplace exposure to an agent previously associated with occupational asthma.*

4. Work-related changes in serially measured FEV$_1$ or peak expiratory flow.*

5. Work-related changes in bronchial responsiveness as measured by serial nonspecific inhalation challenge testing.*

6. Positive response to specific inhalation challenge testing with an agent to which the patient has been exposed at work.*

* Criteria 3 through 6 are used to define "classic" or work-induced asthma.

sensitizer-induced occupational asthma because very low exposures may trigger asthmatic reactions, including status asthmaticus. Substances such as toluene diisocyanate have been reported to induce asthma in sensitized workers in the parts per billion range. Workers with irritant-induced or work-aggravated asthma may continue to work in their usual jobs if their exposure to the inciting agent is diminished via proper engineering controls or by using respiratory protective equipment if engineering controls are not feasible.

TREATMENT

Patients diagnosed with occupational asthma should receive medical management following published guidelines.[1] Because asthma is characterized by airway inflammation, inhaled corticosteroids have become a mainstay of treatment. Malo and colleagues[69] have demonstrated that inhaled corticosteroids induce a small but significant overall improvement in patients with sensitizer-induced occupational asthma due to both HMW and LMW agents after withdrawal from exposure. In their double-blind crossover study, it was found that inhaled steroids were more beneficial if administered earlier rather than later after the diagnosis of occupational asthma was made. Better data on the long-term course of irritant-induced asthma, especially regarding the efficacy of inhaled steroids in improving outcome, would be of great value in managing patients with this condition.

PROGNOSIS

Occupational asthma can become a very disabling disease, resulting in long-term illness and a high rate of unemploy-

ment.[70] Subjects with occupational asthma have been found to suffer increased hospitalization rates for all causes, including cardiac and respiratory disease, compared to patients without asthma, but lower hospitalization rates than among patients with nonoccupational asthma at a tertiary care center.[71] Quality-of-life questionnaires have been administered to subjects with occupational asthma, and compared to those of patients with nonoccupational asthma. Subjects with occupational asthma have been found to have statistically significant impairments in quality of life. They demonstrate increased asthma symptoms, increased limitation of activities, and increased emotional dysfunction. These clinical and functional variables may be diminished due to the severity of asthma, loss of usual job, need for job retraining, or need for early retirement.[72]

Multiple studies have confirmed that the majority of workers with sensitizer-induced occupational asthma do not completely recover even after cessation of exposure to the causative agent.[73,74] Persistent nonspecific airway hyperresponsiveness is frequent and is associated with chronic airway inflammation. Risk factors for persistent asthmatic symptoms and airway hyperresponsiveness are duration of exposure, duration of symptoms before removal from exposure, and severity of asthma at time of diagnosis.[57,73] Early removal from exposure to a sensitizer increases the likelihood of recovery, and continued exposure in sensitized workers is associated with a worsening of asthma.[75]

With cessation of exposure, spirometry and airway responsiveness tend to improve over time. In general, spirometric measures plateau in 1 year, and bronchial responsiveness plateaus in 2 years.[76,76a] Lemiere and colleagues[77] found that a majority of subjects (60%) demonstrated decreased but persistent specific airway responsiveness after removal from exposure to the offending agent. Cessation of exposure to toluene diisocyanate in sensitized workers with occupational asthma is associated with a decrease in both the number of inflammatory cells in the airway mucosa and the amount of subepithelial fibrosis observed with serial bronchial biopsies.[78]

Follow-up data on workers with irritant-induced asthma are sparse, but in one study a majority of pulp mill workers who developed symptoms of asthma after acute "gassing" episodes continued to have nonspecific airway hyperresponsiveness up to 2 years following their last exposures.[79]

IMPAIRMENT/DISABILITY ASSESSMENT

Because the majority of workers with occupational asthma continue to have some degree of respiratory impairment even several years after cessation of exposure, disability (i.e., decreased ability to work in one's usual and customary job or, if severe, in any job) is a common outcome. Rates of job loss or job change are high.[80–84] Disease severity plays a major role, but working conditions are a potent factor in determining who experiences disability and who does not.[85–87] As a consequence of this high rate of disability, occupational asthma often has a substantial socioeconomic impact, with approximately 50% of affected workers suffering a reduction in income 3 years after the diagnosis was made in one study.[83] Physicians are often asked to assist their patients with occupational asthma in obtaining workers' compensation for any disability caused by the disease.

Evaluation of level of impairment due to occupational asthma should be carried out as soon as the condition has been optimally treated and stabilized. Guidelines for impairment evaluation have been developed by the American Thoracic Society and endorsed by the American Medical Association.[88,89] These guidelines use a scoring system that involves the following categories: (1) postbronchodilator FEV_1; (2) reversibility of FEV_1 *or* degree of nonspecific airway hyperresponsiveness; and (3) minimum asthma medication need for optimal control of the disease. Ideally, follow-up evaluation should again be carried out when there is a change in clinical status. Data-based validation of these expert panel–generated guidelines would be an important contribution.

PREVENTION

Prevention must be the primary tool for decreasing the incidence of, and morbidity and disability from, occupational asthma, which can become a chronic disabling disease. Prevention must involve the expertise of occupational health personnel, industrial hygienists, engineers, chemists, and allergists.[90] It must also involve cooperation between employers, workers and their representatives, regulators, and medical personnel.[91]

The goal of primary prevention is to prevent occupational exposure. Primary prevention methods include eliminating the sensitizing agent altogether by substitution with less hazardous substances, changing industrial processes, or reducing exposures. Despite some important efforts with regard to HMW sensitizers,[92,93] more exposure-response data on LMW sensitizers and irritants are critical to developing effective primary prevention programs. Secondary prevention detects asthma early so its duration and severity can be minimized. The early detection of asthma in workers in high-risk industries such as the spray painting industry, in which there is high exposure to diisocyanates, is an example of secondary prevention. Tertiary prevention applies to individuals who have already been diagnosed with occupational asthma. It includes institution of appropriate health care and an effort to prevent permanent asthma by early removal from exposure.[91] Unfortunately, although withdrawal of workers from the asthma-inducing agent may lead to symptomatic improvement, it may not prevent persistent asthma.

Engineering controls may be instituted in order to lower the risk of exposure to irritants and sensitizers, when substitutes cannot be found. Such controls include necessary local exhaust ventilation, process enclosure, containment/isolation of hazardous exposures, and maintenance programs. Personal protective equipment, such as respirators, should only be considered measures of last resort. As in any industry with potential work-related hazards, proper worker education and training in work processes, safety equipment and procedures, and the use of material safety data sheets are of utmost importance.

WORKPLACE SURVEILLANCE

Another essential component in the prevention of occupational asthma is surveillance for occupational asthma in the workplace. Surveillance programs are a type of secondary prevention, in that their principal goal is the early detection of asthma. In making an earlier diagnosis, morbidity and disability can be prevented via timely intervention. Any diagnosis of occupational asthma must be considered a sentinel event; other exposed workers are at risk and need to be identified promptly.[25,52,59]

A general approach to surveillance programs includes medical screening of coworkers as well as exposure monitoring.[52,59,91] The former falls under the jurisdiction of a medical department, whereas the latter is performed by industrial hygiene professionals. Ideally, the medical and industrial hygiene components should be performed in tandem. Performing surveillance in high-risk industries such as those using diisocyanates is a prime example. In medical surveillance, brief symptoms questionnaires can be administered annually that include questions such as improvement in respiratory symptoms on weekends and holidays.[52,59,91] In addition, periodic spirometry can be performed on an annual basis and compared to baseline spirometric testing at the time of hire. Review of PEF records over several weeks can also detect workers at risk for developing occupational asthma. Industrial hygienists can perform air sampling to ensure that appropriate engineering controls are in place to protect worker safety. Reviewing and updating lists of agents used in a given industry should be performed on a periodic basis, to identify possible asthma-inducing agents.

Development of medical surveillance protocols and interventions with documented efficacy in reducing new cases of occupational asthma in high-risk settings should be a key research priority. In Ontario, diisocyanate exposures were the most common cause of occupational asthma in workers' compensation claims in the recent past. Medical and industrial surveillance programs have resulted in the earlier removal of diisocyanate-exposed workers, thus shortening the duration of their asthmatic symptoms.[94]

Medical screening can also include skin prick testing in high-risk industries. Skin testing is available for some HMW antigens, such as flours, proteolytic enzymes, and laboratory animal proteins. Questionnaires can be administered that address allergic symptoms, skin sensitization, and respiratory symptoms. Cross-shift spirometry can detect workers with acute work-related decrements in FEV_1, but is insensitive for detecting late responses that may occur after work hours and requires on-site medical personnel to conduct the tests. Annual methacholine challenge testing has some theoretical appeal, but is impractical to apply to a large number of exposed workers.

SUMMARY

Occupational asthma is currently the most common form of occupational lung disease in the developed world. The prevalence of this disease is likely to remain high for many years, because about 250 industrial agents are known to cause the disease and new chemicals are continuously being introduced into the workplace. The diagnosis is generally established on the basis of a suggestive history of a temporal association between exposure and the onset of symptoms, and objective evidence that these symptoms are related to airflow limitation. Current evidence suggests that early diagnosis, elimination of exposure to the responsible agent, and early use of inhaled steroids may play important roles in the prevention of long-term persistence of asthma.

Persistent occupational asthma is often associated with substantial disability and consequent impacts on income and quality of life. Prevention of new cases is the best approach to reducing the burden of asthma attributable to occupational exposures. Despite considerable advances in our understanding of occupational asthma, more research on pathogenesis, risk factors, exposure-response, long-term outcome, and effective preventive strategies is needed.

REFERENCES

1. National Asthma Education and Prevention Program Expert Panel Report 2: Guidelines for the Diagnosis and Management of Asthma (NHLBI Publication No. 97-4051). Bethesda, Md: U.S. Department of Health and Human Services, 1997, p xiii.
2. Horstman DH, Seal E, Folinsbee LJ, et al: The relationship between exposure duration and sulfur dioxide–induced bronchoconstriction in asthmatic subjects. Am Ind Hyg Assoc J 49:38–47, 1988.
3. Balmes JR, Fine JM, Sheppard D: Symptomatic bronchoconstriction after short-term inhalation of sulfur dioxide. Am Rev Respir Dis 136:1117–1121, 1987.
4. Sheppard D, Eschenbacher WL, Epstein J: Lack of bronchomotor response to up to 3 ppm formaldehyde in subjects with asthma. Environ Res 35:133–139, 1984.
5. Cockcroft DW, Ruffin RE, Dolovich J, et al: Allergen-induced increase in non-allergic bronchial reactivity. Clin Allergy 7:503–513, 1977.
6. Nguyen B, Ghezzo H, Malo JL, et al: Time course of onset of sensitization to common and occupational inhalants in apprentices. J Allergy Clin Immunol 111:807–812, 2003.
7. Gautrin D, Infante-Rivard C, Ghezzo H, Malo J-L: Incidence and host determinants of probable occupational asthma in apprentices exposed to laboratory animals. Am J Respir Crit Care Med 163:899–904, 2001.
8. Bernstein IL, Chan-Yeung M, Malo J-L, et al: Definition and classification of asthma. In Bernstein IL, Chan-Yeung M, Malo J-L, Bernstein DI (eds): Asthma in the Workplace. New York: Marcel Dekker, 1999, pp 1–3.
9. Brooks SM, Weiss MA, Bernstein IL: Reactive airways dysfunction syndrome (RADS): Persistent asthma syndrome after high level irritant exposure. Chest 88:376–384, 1985.
10. Alberts WM, do Pico GA: Reactive airways dysfunction syndrome. Chest 109:1618–1626, 1996.
11. Meredith SK, Taylor VM, McDonald JC: Occupational respiratory disease in the United Kingdom in 1989: A report to the British Thoracic Society and the Society of Occupational Medicine by the SWORD project group. Br J Ind Med 48:292–298, 1991.
12. Contreras G, Rousseau R, Chan-Yeung M: Short report: Occupational respiratory diseases in British Columbia. Occup Environ Med 51:710–712, 1994.
13. Blanc P: Occupational asthma in a national disability survey. Chest 92:613–617, 1987.
14. Balmes J, Becklake M, Blanc P, et al: Occupational contribution to the burden of airway disease (an official statement of the American Thoracic Society). Am J Respir Crit Care Med 167:787–797, 2003.
15. Venables KM, Dally MB, Nunn AJ, et al: Smoking and occupational allergy in workers in a platinum refinery. Br J Ind Med 299:939–942, 1989.
16. Mitchell CA, Gandevia B: Respiratory symptoms and skin reactivity in workers exposed to proteolytic enzymes in the detergent industry. Am Rev Respir Dis 104:1–12, 1971.
17. Becklake MR, Malo J-L, Chan-Yeung M: Epidemiological approaches in occupational asthma. In Bernstein IL, Chan-Yeung M, Malo J-L, Bernstein DI (eds): Asthma in the Workplace. New York: Marcel Dekker, 1999, pp 27–65.
18. Nieuwenhuijsen MJ, Putcha V, Gordon S, et al: Exposure-response relations among laboratory animal workers exposed to rats. Occup Environ Med 60:104–108, 2003.
19. Malo J-L, Cartier A, L'Archeveque J, et al: Prevalence of occupational asthma and immunologic sensitization to psyllium among health care personnel in chronic care hospitals. Am Rev Respir Dis 142:1359–1366, 1990.
20. Droste J, Myny K, Van Sprundel M, et al: Allergic sensitization, symptoms, and lung function among bakery workers as compared with a nonexposed work population. J Occup Environ Med 45:648–655, 2003.
21. Zetterstrom O, Osterman K, Machado L, et al: Another smoking hazard: Raised serum IgE concentration and risk of occupational allergy. Br Med J (Clin Res Ed) 283:1215–1217, 1981.
22. Venables KM, Chan-Yeung M: Occupational asthma. Lancet 349:1465–1469, 1997.
23. Siracusa A, Kennedy SM, DyBuncio A, et al: Prevalence and predictors of asthma in working groups in British Columbia. Am J Ind Med 28:411–423, 1995.
24. Sallie B, McDonald JC: Inhalation accidents reported to the SWORD surveillance project 1990–1993. Ann Occup Hyg 40:211–221, 1996.
25. Jajosky RA, Harrison R, Flattery J, et al: Surveillance of work-related asthma in selected U.S. States—California, Massachusetts, Michigan, and New Jersey, 1993–1995. MMWR Morb Mortal Wkly Rep 48(SS-3):1–20, 1999.
26. Kern DG: Outbreak of the reactive airways dysfunction syndrome after a spill of glacial acetic acid. Am Rev Respir Dis 144:1058–1064, 1991.
27. Blanc P, Galbo M, Hiatt P, et al: Morbidity following acute irritant inhalation in a population-based study. JAMA 266:664–669, 1991.
28. Brooks SM, Hammad Y, Richards I, et al: The spectrum of irritant-induced asthma: Sudden and not-so-sudden and the role of allergy. Chest 113:42–49, 1998.
28a. Sama SR, Hunt PR, Cirillo CI, et al: A longitudinal study of adult-onset asthma incidence among HMO members. Environ Health 2:10, 2003.
29. Chan-Yeung M, Malo J-L: Etiologic agents in occupational asthma. Eur Respir J 7:346–371, 1994.
30. Frew A, Chan H, Salari H, et al: Is tyrosine kinase activation involved in basophil histamine release in asthma due to western red cedar? Allergy 53:139–143, 1998.
31. Frew A, Chang JH, Chan H, et al: T-lymphocyte responses to plicatic acid-human serum albumin conjugate in occupational asthma caused by western red cedar. J Allergy Clin Immunol 101:841–847, 1998.
31a. Matheson JM, Johnson VJ, Vallyathan V, Luster MI: Exposure and immunological determinants in a murine model for toluene diisocyanate (TDI) asthma. Toxicol Sci 2005, in press.
32. Kusaka Y, Nakano Y, Shirakawa T, et al: Lymphocyte transformation with cobalt in hard metal asthma. Ind Health 27:155–163, 1989.
33. Wisnewski AV, Herrick CA, Liu Q, et al: Human gamma/delta T-cell proliferation and IFN-gamma production induced by hexamethylene diisocyanate. J Allergy Clin Immunol 112:538–546, 2003.
34. Maestrelli P, Del Prete GF, De Carli M, et al: CD-8 T-cells producing interleukin-5 and interferon-gamma in bronchial

mucosa of patients with asthma induced by toluene diisocyanate. Scand J Work Environ Health 20:376–381, 1994.

35. Walker C, Bode E, Boer I, et al: Allergic and nonallergic asthmatics have distinct patterns of T cell activation and cytokine production in peripheral blood and bronchoalveolar lavage. Am Rev Respir Dis 146:109–115, 1992.

36. Bernstein DI, Cartier A, Côté J, et al: Diisocyanate antigen-stimulated monocyte chemoattractant protein-1 synthesis has greater test efficiency than specific antibodies for identification of diisocyanate asthma. Am J Respir Crit Care Med 166:445–450, 2002.

37. Bignon JS, Aron L, Ju LY, et al: HLA class II alleles in isocyanate-induced asthma. Am J Respir Crit Care Med 149:71–75, 1994.

38. Balboni A, Baricordi OR, Fabbri LM, et al: Association between toluene diisocyanate induced asthma and DQB1 markers: A possible role for aspartic acid at position 57. Eur Respir J 9:207–210, 1996.

39. Jones MG, Nielsen J, Welch J, et al: Association of HLA-DQ5 and HLA-DR1 with sensitization to organic acid anhydrides. Clin Exp Allergy 34:812–816, 2004.

40. Newman-Taylor A, Cullinan P, Lympany PA, et al: Interaction of HLA phenotype and exposure intensity in sensitisation to complex platinum salts. Am J Respir Crit Care Med 160:435–438, 1999.

41. Horne C, Quintana PJ, Keown PA, et al: Distribution of DRB1 and DQB1 HLA class II alleles in occupational asthma due to western red cedar. Eur Respir J 15:911–914, 2000.

42. Soriano JB, Ercilla G, Sunyer J, et al: HLA class II genes in soybean epidemic asthma patients. Am J Respir Crit Care Med 156:1394–1398, 1997.

43. Raulf-Heimsoth M, Chen Z, Rihs HP, et al: Analysis of T-cell reactive regions and HLA-DR4 binding motifs on the latex allergen Hev b 1 (rubber elongation factor). Clin Exp Allergy 28:339–348, 1998.

44. Piirila P, Wikman H, Luukkonen R, et al: Glutathione S-transferase genotypes and allergic responses to diisocyanate exposure. Pharmacogenetics 11:437–445, 2001.

45. Mapp CE, Fryer AA, De Marzo N, et al: Glutathione S-transferase GSTP1 is a susceptibility gene for occupational asthma induced by isocyanates. J Allergy Clin Immunol 109:867–872, 2002.

46. Gautrin D, Boulet L-P, Boutet M, et al: Is reactive airways dysfunction syndrome (RADS) a variant of occupational asthma? J Allergy Clin Immunol 93:12–22, 1994.

47. Chan-Yeung M, Lam S, Kennedy S, et al: Persistent asthma after repeated exposure to high concentrations of gases in pulpmills. Am J Respir Crit Care Med 149:1676–1680, 1994.

48. Gautrin D, Bernstein IL, Brooks S: Reactive airways dysfunction syndrome, or irritant-induced asthma. In Bernstein IL, Chan-Yeung M, Malo J-L, Bernstein DI (eds): Asthma in the Workplace. New York: Marcel Dekker, 1999, pp 565–593.

49. Ebino K, Kramarik J, Lemus R, et al: A mouse model for the study of localized toluene diisocyanate (TDI) adducts following intrabronchial administration of the chemical: Inflammation and antibody production. Inhal Toxicol 10:503–529, 1998.

50. Demnati R, Fraser R, Ghezzo H, et al: Time-course of functional and pathological changes after a single high acute inhalation of chlorine in rats. Eur Respir J 11:922–928, 1998.

51. Chan-Yeung M, Brooks S, Alberts WM, et al: ACCP Consensus Statement: Assessment of asthma in the workplace. Chest 108:1084–1117, 1995.

52. Tarlo SM, Boulet L-P, Cartier A, et al: Canadian Thoracic Society guidelines for occupational asthma. Can Respir J 5:289–300, 1998.

53. Mapp CE, Saetta M, Maestrelli P, Fabbri L: Occupational asthma. In Mapp CE (ed): European Respiratory Monographs, Vol 4: Occupational Lung Disorders (Monograph 11). Sheffield, UK: European Respiratory Society, 1999, pp 255–285.

54. Malo J-L, Ghezzo H, L'Archeveque J, et al: Is the clinical history a satisfactory means of diagnosing occupational asthma? Am Rev Respir Dis 143:528–532, 1991.

54a. Barnard CG, McBride DI, Firth HM, Herbison GP: Assessing individual employee risk factors for occupational asthma in primary aluminum smelting. Occup Environ Med 61:604–608, 2004.

55. Malo J-L, Lemiere C, Desjardins A, et al: Prevalence and intensity of rhinoconjunctivitis in subjects with occupational asthma. Eur Respir J 10:1513–1515, 1997.

56. Chan-Yeung M, Malo J-L: Occupational asthma. N Engl J Med 333:107–112, 1995.

57. Chan-Yeung M, Lam S, Koener S: Clinical features and natural history of occupational asthma due to western red cedar (Thuja plicata). Am J Med 72:411–415, 1982.

58. Zammit-Tabona M, Sherkin M, Kijek K, et al: Asthma caused by dimethyl methane diisocyanate in foundry workers: Clinical bronchoprovocation and immunologic studies. Am Rev Respir Dis 128:226–230, 1983.

59. Balmes JR: Surveillance for occupational asthma. Occup Med 6:101–110, 1991.

60. American Thoracic Society: Lung function testing: Selection of reference values and interpretation strategies. Am Rev Respir Dis 144:1202–1208, 1991.

61. Bright P, Burge PS: The diagnosis of occupational asthma from serial measurements of lung function at and away from work. Thorax 51:857–863, 1996.

62. Quirce S, Contreras G, Dybuncio A, et al: Peak expiratory flow monitoring is not a reliable method for establishing the diagnosis of occupational asthma. Am J Respir Crit Care Med 152:1100–1102, 1995.

63. Gannon PF, Belcher J, Pantin CF, et al: The effect of patient technique and training on the accuracy of self-recorded peak expiratory flow. Eur Respir J 14:28–31, 1999.

64. Gannon PF, Dickinson SA, Hitchings DJ, et al: The quality of self recorded peak expiratory flow (PEF). Eur Respir J 6:492s, 1993.

65. American Thoracic Society: Guidelines for methacholine and exercise challenge testing—1999. Am J Respir Crit Care Med 161:309–329, 2000.

66. Vandenplas O, Malo J-M: Inhalation challenges with agents causing occupational asthma. Eur Respir J 10:2612–2629, 1997.

67. Grammar LC, Shaughnessy MA, Henderson J, et al: A clinical and immunologic study of workers with trimellitic-anhydride-induced immunologic lung disease after transfer to low exposure jobs. Am Rev Respir Dis 148:54–57, 1993.

68. Karol MH, Tollerud DJ, Campbell TP, et al: Predictive value of airways hyperresponsiveness and circulating IgE for identifying types of responses to toluene diisocyanate challenge. Am J Respir Crit Care Med 149:611–615, 1994.

69. Malo J-L, Cartier A, Cote J, et al: Influence of inhaled steroids on recovery from occupational asthma after cessation of exposure: An 18-month double-blind crossover study. Am J Respir Crit Care Med 153:953–960, 1996.

70. Gassert TH, Hu H, Kelsey KT: Long-term health and employment outcomes of occupational asthma and their determinants. J Occup Environ Med 40:481–491, 1998.

71. Liss GM, Tarlo SM, MacFarlane Y, et al: Hospitalization among subjects compensated for occupational asthma. Am J Respir Crit Care Med 162:112–118, 2000.

72. Malo J-L, Boulet L-P, Dewitte J-D, et al: Quality of life of subjects with occupational asthma. J Allergy Clin Immunol 91:1121–1127, 1993.

73. Paggiaro PL, Vagaggini B, Bacci E, et al: Prognosis of occupational asthma. Eur Respir J 7:761–767, 1994.

74. Chan-Yeung M, Malo J-L: Natural history of occupational asthma. *In* Bernstein IL, Chan-Yeung M, Malo J-L, Bernstein DI (eds): Asthma in the Workplace. New York: Marcel Dekker, 1999, pp 129–143.

75. Cote J, Kennedy S, Chan-Yeung M: Outcome of patients with cedar asthma with continuous exposure. Am Rev Respir Dis 141:373–376, 1990.

76. Malo J-L, Cartier A, Ghezzo H, et al: Patterns of improvement in spirometry, bronchial hyperresponsiveness, and specific IgE antibody levels after cessation of exposure in occupational asthma caused by snow-crab processing. Am Rev Respir Dis 138:807–812, 1988.

76a. Malo JL, Ghezzo H: Recovery of methacholine responsiveness after end of exposure in occupational asthma. Am J Respir Crit Care Med 169:1304–1307, 2004.

77. Lemiere C, Cartier A, Dolovich J, et al: Outcome of specific bronchial responsiveness to occupational agents after removal from exposure. Am J Respir Crit Care Med 154:329–333, 1996.

78. Saetta M, Maestrelli P, Turato G, et al: Airway wall remodeling after cessation of exposure to isocyanates in sensitized asthmatic subjects. Am J Respir Crit Care Med 151:489–494, 1995.

79. Bherer L, Cushman R, Courteau JP, et al: Survey of construction workers repeatedly exposed to chlorine over a three to six month period in a pulp mill: II. Follow-up of affected workers by questionnaire, spirometry, and assessment of bronchial responsiveness 18 to 24 months after exposure ended. Occup Environ Med 51:225–228, 1994.

80. Cannon J, Cullinan P, Taylor AN: Consequences of occupational asthma. BMJ 311:602–603, 1995.

81. Axon EJ, Beach JR, Burge PS: A comparison of some of the characteristics of patients with occupational and non-occupational asthma. Occup Environ Med 45:109–111, 1995.

82. Mrabani A, Dimich-Ward H, Kwan SYL: Clinical and socioeconomic features of subjects with red cedar asthma: A follow-up study. Chest 104:821–824, 1993.

83. Ameille J, Pairon JC, Bayeux MC, et al: Consequences of occupational asthma on employment and financial status: A follow-up study. Eur Respir J 10:55–58, 1997.

84. Gannon PFG, Weir DC, Robertson AS, et al: Health, employment, and financial outcomes in workers with occupational asthma. BMJ 50:491–496, 1993.

85. Blanc PD, Jones M, Besson C, et al: Work disability among adults with asthma. Chest 104:1371–1377, 1993.

86. Blanc PD, Cisternas M, Smith S, et al: Asthma, employment status, and disability among adults treated by pulmonary and allergy specialists. Chest 109:688–696, 1996.

87. Yelin E, Henke J, Katz PP, et al: The work dynamics of adults with asthma. Am J Ind Med 35:472–480, 1999.

88. American Thoracic Society: Guidelines for the evaluation of impairment/disability in patients with asthma. Am Rev Respir Dis 147:1056–1061, 1993.

89. American Medical Association: Respiratory system. *In* Cocchiarella L, Andersson GBJ (eds): Guides to the Evaluation of Permanent Impairment (5th ed). Chicago: American Medical Association, 2001, pp 87–115.

90. Nordman H: Occupational asthma—time for prevention. Scand J Work Environ Health 20:108–115, 1994.

91. Venables KM: Prevention of occupational asthma. Eur Respir J 7:768–778, 1994.

92. Cullinan P, Lowson D, Nieuwenshuijsen MJ, et al: Work related symptoms, sensitisation, and estimated exposure in workers not previously exposed to flour. Occup Environ Med 51:579–583, 1994.

93. Cullinan P, Lowson D, Nieuwenshuijsen MJ, et al: Work related symptoms, sensitisation, and estimated exposure in workers not previously exposed to laboratory rats. Occup Environ Med 51:589–592, 1994.

94. Tarlo SM, Liss GM, Yeung KS: Changes in rates and severity of compensation claims for asthma due to diisocyanates: A possible effect of medical surveillance measures. Occup Environ Med 59:58–62, 2002.

61

Pneumocconioses

Robert L. Cowie, M.D., Jill Murray, M.B.B.Ch., F.F.Path.(SA),
Margaret R. Becklake, M.D.

INTRODUCTION

DEFINITIONS

The term *pneumoconiosis* derives from the Greek (*pneuma* = air and *konis* = dust) and was introduced in the 19th century to describe lung diseases consequent to the inhalation of mineral dusts. It has been adapted to indicate the nature of the putative dust, for example, silicosis (silica), asbestosis (asbestos), or siderosis (iron); or to indicate the occupation at risk, for example, coal workers' pneumoconiosis. The *Encyclopedia of Occupational Health and Safety* of the International Labour Organization (ILO)[1] defines pneumoconiosis as "the accumulation of dust in the lungs and the tissue reactions to its presence." The main reaction to mineral dust in the lungs is fibrosis. Not included in the definition of pneumoconiosis are conditions such as asthma, chronic obstructive pulmonary disease (COPD), and

hypersensitivity pneumonitis, in which there is no requirement for dust to accumulate in the lungs in the long term.

ACCUMULATION OF DUST IN THE LUNG AND TISSUE REACTIONS

The deposition of dust in the lungs depends on the size and the geometric and aerodynamic properties of the particles. Particle clearance is determined by the mucociliary escalator and cellular mechanisms, in particular, the macrophage (see Chapter 14). Dust accumulation in the lungs is determined by deposition and clearance. The biologic response depends upon the amount and duration of the accumulation and the nature of the dust. Tissue responses to inorganic dusts depend on particle size and on the biologic activity of the dust, which in turn depends on its surface chemical and physical properties.[1] Some dusts, such as coal, appear relatively inert and may accumulate in considerable amounts with minimal tissue response; others, in particular silica and asbestos, have potent biologic effects.[2] Parenchymal responses include nodular fibrosis (the classic example is the silicotic islet), diffuse fibrosis (the classic example is asbestosis), and macule formation with focal emphysema (the classic example is the coal dust macule).[3] Irregular and mixed fibrotic patterns also have been described as a consequence of mixed exposures involving other mineral dusts or fibers in addition to silica dust exposure. For any given dust exposure, the severity of the tissue reaction appears to be related to the cumulative lung dust burden.

EXPOSURE-RESPONSE RELATIONSHIPS

In epidemiologic studies, the dust burden in the lung can be assessed only indirectly. However, at an individual level, exposure can be estimated more directly from the job history, from the engineering history of the plant, including the efficiency of dust control, and from environmental measurements. Based on these estimates, convincing exposure-response relationships for pneumoconiosis can invariably be demonstrated in work force studies (Fig. 61.1; see also Fig. 61.9). At the public health level, the demonstration of exposure-response relationships is supportive evidence that the abnormality, dysfunction, or disease in question is causally related to the exposure.

The demonstration of exposure-response relationships also has implications for clinical practice. For instance, a clinical diagnosis of pneumoconiosis is strengthened greatly when there has been exposure to dust levels known to be associated with an increased risk of disease. Although exposure-response relationships generally describe the events in a work force, there may be heavily exposed individuals who remain unaffected and lightly exposed individuals with disease. Thus, environmental standards such as threshold limit values set by the American Conference of Government and Industrial Hygienists are levels that, if maintained throughout an individual's working life, are unlikely to be associated with disease. However, dust sampling may be problematic, and even in a workplace where average dust concentrations are below the threshold limit value, nearly half the samples exceed this value.[4] Thus, a clinician never should reject the diagnosis of a pneumoconiosis solely on the grounds that exposure was too remote, too short, or in a workplace where the threshold limit value was maintained. The patient in question may be unusually susceptible, may have had an unusual exposure profile, or may retain more dust than others similarly exposed.

CHEST IMAGING

The use of the ILO standard films for the descriptive interpretation of the radiologic appearance of diffuse parenchymal lung disease is well described in detail elsewhere.[5,6] The system, originally developed for epidemiologic studies of occupational lung disease, also may assist clinical interpretation. Apart from improving consistency in the reading of parenchymal disease, which is notoriously subject to reader variability, the system enables the clinician to set an individual case in the context of the available epidemiologic information. An important feature of the system is that the reader, after noting the quality of the film, is asked to classify "all appearances consistent with those defined and represented in the standard radiographs and guidelines for use of the ILO International Classification of Radiographs of Pneumoconiosis."[5] Small opacities in the parenchyma are classified by shape and size: p, q, or r for rounded opacities (of <1.5 mm, 1.5 to 3 mm, or >3 mm diameter, respectively) and s, t, or u for irregular opacities (of <1.5 mm, 1.5 to 3 mm, or >3 mm width, respectively). Profusion category (or concentration) is next read on a 12-point scale (0/−, 0/0, 0/1 up to 3/2, 3/3, and 3/+) in comparison with the standard radiographs. Large opacities are classified as category A (for one or more such opacities with a diameter of 1 cm but not exceeding a combined diameter of 5 cm), category B (one or more opacities larger than 10 cm in diameter and whose combined area does not exceed one upper zone), and category C (larger than B). Provision is made to grade pleural thickening for width ($a \leq 5$ mm, $b >$ 5 mm but <10 mm, and $c \geq 10$ mm) and extent ($1 =$ up to one quarter, $2 =$ one quarter to one half, and $3 =$ over one half of the lateral chest wall). The extent of pleural calcification also is graded, and there are provisions for comment on other features.

In the United States, the National Institute of Occupational Safety and Health (NIOSH) administers the National Coal Workers' Health Surveillance Program, which provides coal miners with the opportunity of a periodic medical examination. The program incorporates quality control in terms of radiographic technique and reading procedures

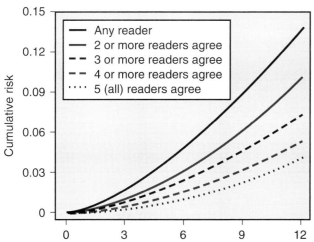

Figure 61.1 The cumulative risk of developing silicosis in relation to cumulative exposure to respirable silica (mg/m^3 × years), lagged by 5 years, among hard rock miners. The cohort consisted of all miners on the Ontario Workmen's Compensation Board's master file of miners who started work between 1941 and 1959 and were followed by chest radiography until their dust exposure ended or until 1982, whichever came first. The figure shows fitted Weibull models for one to five levels of reader consensus. The criterion for silicosis was a chest radiograph reading of small rounded opacities of profusion 1/1 or greater, using the ILO standard reference films, on the miner's most recent film. The films of 32 of 2109 miners were considered by one or more readers to have silicosis and were retained for the purposes of this analysis. (From Muir DCF, Shannon HS, Julian JA, et al: Silica exposure and silicosis among Ontario hardrock miners: III. Analysis and risk estimates. Am J Ind Med 16:29–43, 1989.)

using the ILO classification and reader training. This involves training seminars for physicians who may qualify as "A" readers (i.e., attended the seminars) or "B" readers, who passed a comprehensive examination on the basis of 120 radiographs read into the ILO classification. Many U.S. clinics and hospitals now conform to these standards.

Chest radiographs are the cornerstone of surveillance for pneumoconiosis in the workplace.[6] The common practice in some countries of using miniature films has been shown to be valid and even superior to standard radiographs in the detection of silicosis.[7] Computed tomography (CT) and high-resolution computed tomography (HRCT) have revolutionized clinical case evaluation. CT and HRCT are able to characterize lung and pleural lesions, as to their extent and confluence, with remarkable precision and are considerably more sensitive than the conventional chest radiograph.[6,8]

CLINICAL ISSUES, LUNG FUNCTION, AND PRINCIPLES OF MANAGEMENT

The clinician is faced with two main tasks when evaluating a case of suspected pneumoconiosis. First is the meticulous assessment of the nature of the disease process, including its site (airways or pulmonary parenchyma or pleura?), its extent, and whether it has decreased the individual's performance, in particular for his or her current job (is there evidence of impairment or disability?).[9] Assessment of impairment is based on symptoms and measurements of pulmonary function at rest and during exercise where indicated[9] (see Chapter 24). Pneumoconiosis may be associated with apparently normal lung function, or with a predominantly obstructive, restrictive, or mixed pattern of dysfunction. In the individual case, interpretation of results in terms of lung function profiles is usually done by the use of reference or predicted values.[10] However, these may be misleading given that those who undertake dusty occupations on average have higher initial spirometric lung volumes than the general population, on whom most predicted values are based.[11] Thus, it is not appropriate to minimize the functional significance of pneumoconiosis on the grounds of apparently normal lung function. Assessment of disability is made in the wider context of whether the patient is fit for his or her job, and thus requires expert knowledge of the job content; it usually is made by qualified professionals from the fields of law and economics, as well as other health sciences.[9]

Second is the need to determine whether there has been environmental or occupational exposure of duration, intensity, and character sufficient to account in full or in part for the patient's present condition. For this task, the key tool is the occupational history, which can be completed with the addition of the often extensive knowledge the worker can provide concerning his or her occupations, the materials handled, and the processes involved. Because pneumoconiosis is a reaction to retained dust, it may appear and progress after exposure has ceased,[12] hence the importance of a complete exposure history, including student summer jobs, military service, and short-term jobs. In addition, in industrialized countries, between 25% and 60% of men and up to 30% of women report exposure to dust or fumes at work,[13] further testimony to the fact that an occupational

history is as essential as the smoking history in the practice of respiratory medicine. On occasion, it may be necessary to establish occupational exposure on the basis of analysis of biologic material (sputum, bronchoalveolar lavage [BAL], transbronchial or open-lung biopsy specimen) for the putative dust or its breakdown products. This is particularly so in cases in which the exposure is remote and the exposure history incomplete or unreliable. Figure 61.2 presents examples of cases in which the putative dust was demonstrated in the pathologic specimens. The case record presented later in Figure 61.11 is an example of the use of lung dust burden measurements in establishing attributability.

Tuberculosis was a common complication of pneumoconiosis in the early part of the 20th century, when infection levels were high in parent populations from which work forces were drawn and drug therapy was not yet available. Although now relatively rare in industrialized countries, tuberculosis remains an important issue in industrializing countries and has increased dramatically, especially in South Africa, in response to the human immunodeficiency virus epidemic.[14]

Pneumoconiosis does not regress and may appear and progress only after work exposure ceases.[15] Medical management is limited to symptomatic treatment. Thus, the main issue for the patient, whether to quit the present job, depends on a knowledge of current dust levels in the patient's workplace. This information is not usually available to the treating physician, who nevertheless must ensure that the patient is advised appropriately. Relevant, too, are the patient's age, socioeconomic circumstances, proximity to retirement, and compensation status, all of which need to be taken into account in making this difficult decision.

The physician should be aware that, each time the diagnosis of pneumoconiosis is substantiated, it carries with it several important public health implications. In many jurisdictions, the physician has the legal responsibility to report all cases of pneumoconiosis.[16] The diagnosis of pneumoconiosis reflects a failure of environmental controls in the workplace that may require intervention by an appropriate authority. There are differences in disease notification practice and compensation legislation among states and among countries, and physicians should be aware of the appropriate procedure in the location of their practice.

EPIDEMIOLOGY AND IMPLICATIONS FOR CLINICAL PRACTICE

Information on the distribution of these diseases within and between work forces and the factors that influence distribution (the essence of epidemiology) provides the scientific base that the physician uses to reach a diagnosis, set prognosis, and plan management. Thus, knowledge of pneumoconiosis rates in the industries located in the local area assists the physician in diagnosis. Likewise, determining prognosis depends on work force–based information, on knowing which factors influence disease progression favorably and unfavorably, and the likely effect of further exposure even at low levels.

In the discussion that follows, the various types of pneumoconioses are considered separately with respect to occupations at risk, pathophysiology, and epidemiology, as well

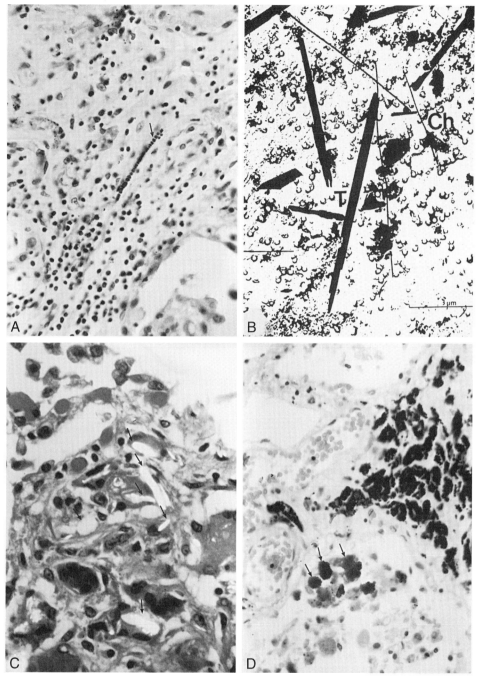

Figure 61.2 The putative agent in the lung tissue in four cases of pneumoconiosis is demonstrated. **A,** Typical asbestos body (*arrow*) in the lung of a 65-year-old long-term chrysotile asbestos miner with asbestosis, from the Thetford area. (Original magnification × 250, light microscopy.) **B,** Lung digest from the case of a 67-year-old long-term chrysotile miner with asbestosis from the Thetford area, photographed on a filter of pore diameter 0.2 mm (pores are evident as small punched-out areas in the photograph). The thin fibers labeled Ch were identified as chrysotile using morphologic criteria and energy-dispensive x-ray spectrometry (EDS). The thick fibers labeled T were identified as tremolite by EDS. In this mining area, there is a small amount of tremolite in the mined ore that accumulates preferentially in the lung tissue.[175] Amphiboles such as crocidolite, amosite, and tremolite most frequently form the core of asbestos bodies. For each asbestos body found in lung tissue, the number of uncoated fibers is at least several orders of magnitude greater. (Original magnification × 10,000, transmission electron microscopy.) **C,** Lung section from a 45-year-old man who died of pulmonary fibrosis due to talc. The talc particles, some examples of which are identified (*arrows*), appear as birefringent (*bright white*) elongated particles. (Original magnification × 250, light microscopy using polarizers.) **D,** Lung section from a 65-year-old welder showing amorphous carbon particles (*upper right*) and a cluster of rounded iron-coated particles (*arrows*). Particle clusters like this frequently are seen in the lung sections of welders and of foundry workers who have had exposure to iron dusts and fumes. (Original magnification × 250, light microscopy.) (Courtesy of Drs. Bruce Case and R. S. Fraser, Department of Pathology, and Dr. Patrick Sébastien, formerly of the School of Occupational Health, McGill University, Montreal.)

Table 61.1 Industries and Occupations at Risk for Silicosis

Industries, with Examples	Occupations Implicated
Mining, tunneling, and excavating *Underground:* gold, copper, iron, tin, uranium, civil engineering projects *Surface:* coal, iron, excavation of foundations	Miner, driller, tunneler, developer, stoper Mobile rig drill operator
Quarrying Granite, sandstone, slate, sand, chinastone/clay	Driller, hammerer, digger
Stonework Granite sheds, monumental masonry	Cutter, dresser, driller, polisher, grinder, mason
Foundries Ferrous and nonferrous metals	Molder, knockout man, fettler, coremaker, caster
Abrasives *Production:* silica flour, metal polish, and sandpapers; fillers in paint, rubber, and plastics *Sandblasting:* oil rigs, tombstones	Crusher, pulverizer, and mixer; workers in the manufacture of abrasives Operators of high-speed jets
Ceramics Manufacture of pottery, stoneware, refractory bricks for ovens and kilns	Workers at any stage of process if products are dry
Others Glass making, boiler scaling, traditional crafts, stone grinders, gemstone workers, dental technicians, concrete reconstruction	

as the clinical issues of diagnosis, prognosis, and management. On all continents and in many countries, a substantial proportion of individuals are exposed to dust at work and therefore potentially at risk for pneumoconiosis.[13] Lists of occupations and jobs at risk are never exhaustive (Table 61.1) but are a guide for use in general office practice, where it may be more important to raise the suspicion of a diagnosis of pneumoconiosis than to be knowledgeable about the particular exposures a given job title implies. Indeed, the latter often falls into the expertise of the industrial hygienist. For those in occupational health or occupational medicine practice, reference should be made to one of the more specialized texts that describe the occupations at risk in greater detail.[1,17,18]

SILICOSIS

DEFINITION

Silicosis is a fibrotic lung disease attributable to the inhalation of crystalline silica, usually in the form of quartz and, less commonly, as cristobalite and tridymite. Amorphous silica is relatively nontoxic[1,19]; silicates such as asbestos, mica, and talc evoke a different type of pulmonary response and are considered separately.

INDUSTRIES AND OCCUPATIONS STILL AT RISK

Silicosis, an ancient disease, continues to be a major disease worldwide in men and women exposed to silica dust in a variety of occupations.[1,20,21,21a,21b] Table 61.1 provides some common examples of industries in which workers are at risk for silica exposure. Construction, and surface and underground rock drilling have all been subjects of recent alert documents from the NIOSH. Foundries are also a main

source of silica dust.[1,16,22,23] A recent report has shown a silicosis risk for workers involved with the repair, rehabilitation, or demolition of concrete structures.[24]

Many of the current cases of silicosis come from industries using relatively new technology that, if unaccompanied by modern controls, may result in exposures to finer dust particles than in traditional industries and jobs.[24a] New types of pneumoconiosis often turn out to be silicosis in an industry not previously thought to be at risk or a mixed-dust pneumoconiosis in which silica is implicated with other dusts.[25,26] Silicosis is often the result of exposure in the remote past and not in the current workplace. The risks for silicosis depend upon the level of exposure and, although this can be controlled, there is evidence that dust levels are monitored appropriately in less than 10% of these workplaces.[23]

Outbreaks of silicosis and death from the disease continue to be reported worldwide,[16,23,27] even in countries with developed legislative systems and environmental surveillance programs, such as the United States,[28] Canada,[29] Europe,[30] and South Africa.[31,31a] In the United States, NIOSH has estimated that at least 1.7 million workers are exposed to silica, of whom between 1500 and 2360 will develop silicosis each year.[23] Estimates made in the 1980s of workers at risk in mines and quarries are as follows: 839,000 in 14 countries in Europe (excluding Poland and former U.S.S.R. countries); 189,000 in 8 countries in Australasia (excluding China); and 394,000 in 6 countries in Africa.[13] More recently, there have been reports of silicosis and of silica exposure in the general environment[32–34] and in agriculture.[35]

PATHOLOGY

Three clinicopathologic types of silicosis have been described: *chronic silicosis,* which typically follows exposure, measured in decades rather than years, to respirable dust usually containing less than 30% quartz; *accelerated silicosis,* which follows shorter, heavier exposure; and *acute silicosis* (silicoproteinosis), which follows intense exposure to fine dust of high silica content, such as that found in sandblasting industries, for periods measured in months rather than years.[19,36]

Chronic silicosis is the most common form of the disease. The hallmark of chronic silicosis is the silicotic nodule, one of the few agent-specific lesions in pathology[37] (Fig. 61.3A and B). The mature lesion is characterized by a central area of whorled hyalinized collagen fibers, with a more peripheral zone of dust-laden macrophages. Birefringent particles can be seen in the nodule with light microscopy.[38] Early in the course of the disease, dust-filled macrophages may be the most prominent finding. Silicotic nodules develop first in the hilar lymph nodes[39] and may be confined to this area; they may become encased in calcification and impinge on or erode into airways. The disease process next involves the lung parenchyma, where the nodules are discrete (3 to 5 mm in diameter), palpable, and grayish black in color. They are usually bilateral, involving the upper zones. Similar nodules can be found in the visceral pleura

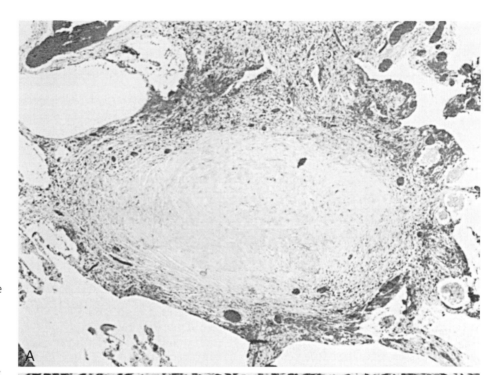

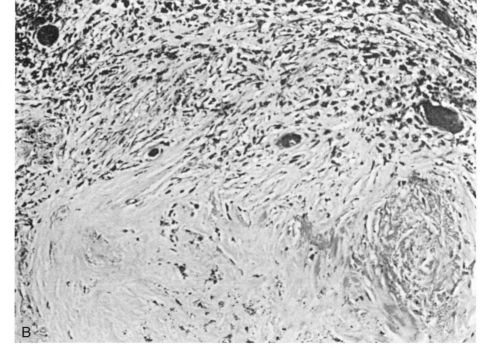

Figure 61.3 Pathologic lesions of chronic silicosis. **A,** Silicotic nodule characterized by a central zone of a cellular hyalinized collagen with a whorled appearance, and a peripheral zone of macrophages in which abundant foreign material is situated (original magnification × 40, light microscopy). **B,** Silicotic nodule at higher magnification to show these characteristics to better advantage (original magnification × 150, light microscopy).

Figure continued on following page

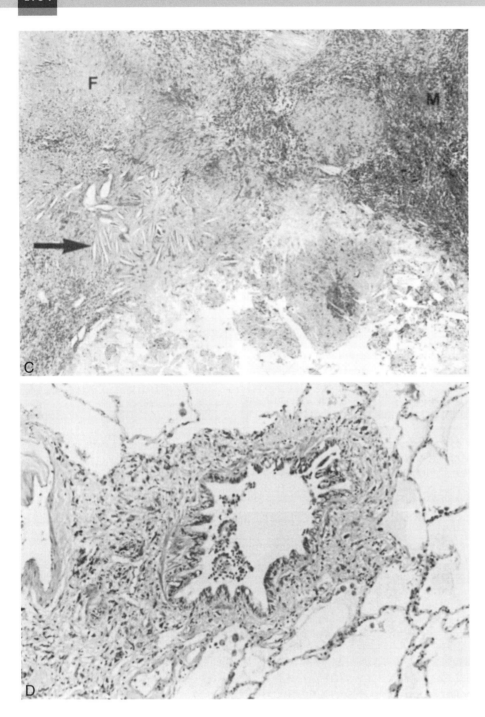

Figure 61.3 cont'd C, Progressive massive fibrosis from a case of silicosis showing fibrosis (F), aggregates of pigment-laden macrophages (M), and multiple cholesterol clefts (*arrow*). The tissue in the lower half is necrotic and has undergone liquefaction. (Original magnification × 25, light microscopy.) **D,** Mineral dust small airway disease, characterized by peribronchiolar fibrous tissue containing a moderate amount of foreign particulate material; occasional silicotic nodules were present elsewhere in the lung parenchyma (original magnification × 150, light microscopy). (**A** through **C** from Fraser RG, Paré JAP, Fraser RS, Genereux GP: Diagnosis of Diseases of the Chest [3rd ed]. Philadelphia: WB Saunders, 1990, pp 2288–2289. **D** courtesy of Dr. R. S. Fraser, McGill University, Montreal.)

and often develop in the lymphatic drainage channels of the lung, particularly in the perivascular sheath.

In accelerated silicosis, the changes are similar to those seen in chronic silicosis. However, the nodules develop sooner (after 3 to 10 years of exposure), and are more cellular than fibrotic in nature. A more diffuse interstitial pulmonary fibrosis may also develop.[40]

With disease progression in both chronic and accelerated silicosis, the nodules become confluent, leading to the development of *progressive massive fibrosis* (PMF) (Fig. 61.3C), also known as *complicated silicosis*. These lesions, which are at least 1 cm in diameter (and often larger), usually involve the upper lobes. They tend to obliterate lung structure and may cavitate, which may be an indication of tuberculosis.[36] *Rheumatoid nodules* may also occur in the setting of silicosis and may be seen in patients with rheumatoid arthritis or high levels of circulating rheumatoid factor, or both.[41] These nodules may be larger than the usual silicotic lesion (up to 5 cm in diameter) and have light gray necrotic centers surrounded by palisading histiocytes, fibroblasts, collagen, and neutrophils.[36] There may be few silicotic nodules in the background. Rheumatoid nodules are less frequently associated with silica than with coal dust exposure (see subsequent discussion in this chapter).

Acute silicosis shows all the features of pulmonary alveolar proteinosis (see Chapter 59). Silica particles and various

Table 61.2 Diseases Associated with Exposure to Silica Dust

Silicosis
Chronic silicosis
Accelerated silicosis
Acute silicosis (silicoproteinosis)
Progressive massive fibrosis

Chronic Obstructive Pulmonary Disease
Emphysema
Chronic bronchitis
Mineral dust–induced small airway disease

Lung Cancer

Mycobacterial Infection
Mycobacterium tuberculosis
Nontuberculous *Mycobacteria*

Immune-Related Diseases
Progressive systemic sclerosis
Rheumatoid arthritis
Chronic renal disease
Systemic lupus erythematosus

biomarkers of tissue reaction can be identified in the proteinaceous material from the alveolar spaces as well as in lavage material.[42]

The lungs of exposed individuals, whether or not they show silicosis, also may demonstrate the features of other diseases associated with occupational dust exposure (Table 61.2), such as chronic bronchitis and emphysema. The pathologic features are similar whether associated with occupational exposure to dusts and fumes encountered in the workplace or with exposure to cigarette smoke. Abnormalities of the small airways, including fibrosis and pigmentation of respiratory bronchioles (Fig. 61.3D), are seen in association with exposures to a variety of mineral dusts, including those responsible for silicosis.[43]

Silicotic nodules may also develop in the cervical and abdominal lymph nodes, and occasionally in the liver, spleen, and bone marrow.[16,44]

PATHOGENESIS

The pathogenicity pathogen of silica dust is dependent on the physical/mechanical and chemical properties of the particles. An excellent review of this topic summarizes the processes whereby silica produces inflammation and fibrogenesis in the lung.[45] Silica-induced inflammation and fibrosis result from complex interactions between the particles and lung macrophages, alveolar epithelial cells, fibroblasts, neutrophils, lymphocytes, and complex networks, stimulating the production of oxidants, chemokines, and cytokines. However, the cellular mechanisms that initiate and drive the process of inflammation and fibrosis are not fully understood. The surface characteristics of the silica particles determine their redox potential and ability to react with hydrogen, oxygen, and nitrogen. There is agreement that freshly fractured silica, such as that generated during sandblasting, is more toxic to the alveolar macrophages than is "aged" silica,[46] presumably because of its increased redox potential. Other minerals, particularly clay components, may adhere to the surfaces of silica particles, pro-

ducing "coated" silica, which is less toxic than uncoated silica dust. This may explain the relatively nonfibrogenic response to silica in coal and hematite miners and the observation that the incidence of silicosis is decreased by concomitant exposure to other dusts.[47] Silica particles of less than 5 μm reach the lower respiratory tract, and small particles may enter the alveoli. There is some debate as to whether the fibrogenicity of the particles is dependent on their actual size. The intensity of the exposure determines the nature of the lung injury. Low-intensity exposure generally produces aggregates of fibrosis with relative sparing of the lung architecture, whereas high-intensity exposure causes widespread pulmonary inflammation and collagen deposition.[40]

Tumor necrosis factor-α and interleukin-1 play an important role in the initiation of silicosis, and experimental inhibition of these cytokines has been shown to prevent silicosis.[45] Growth factors, including transforming growth factor-β, are important in fibrogenesis (and also have been implicated in carcinogenesis) in association with silica.[48,49] Although the major determinant of silicosis is the level of exposure to silica-containing dust, individual susceptibility to the disease may play a role.[50,51]

EPIDEMIOLOGY: SECULAR TRENDS AND THEIR IMPLICATIONS FOR THE CLINICIAN

Over the course of the 20th century, silicosis changed from a rapidly fatal disease to an indolent and disabling disorder. Reasons include improved environmental controls, falling rates of tuberculosis, and the advent of drug therapy for tuberculosis. Nevertheless, there is still well-warranted concern that this avoidable disease remains a significant cause of morbidity[16,52,52a] and mortality in the 21st century.[53-55]

The prevalence of silicosis is difficult to estimate, given the large number of industries at risk (see Table 61.1), the transient labor force in industrializing as well as in industrialized countries, and the frequent appearance of disease after the worker has left the work force.[20,56] Silicosis has been reported in workers from a variety of industries in Michigan who commenced work after 1970, and the reported cases have been estimated to represent only one third of the total cases of silicosis.[21] The prevalence of silicosis in South Africa has been rising.[31] The risk of developing disease is determined by the lung dust burden, which in turn is related primarily to the intensity, nature, and duration of exposure. The disease may progress even after exposure has ceased.[52,56,57] In calculating an individual's risk for silicosis, duration and intensity of exposure are of primary interest but peak exposure also may be important.[58] The physician should never dismiss the diagnosis of silicosis when that diagnosis is suggested by clinical and radiologic features, even when exposure appears to have been insignificant or in an occupation not known to be associated with silicosis.

Tuberculosis

The association between silicosis and tuberculosis has long been recognized. Rates for active tuberculosis in silicotic patients range from 2- to 30-fold more than those in the same workforce without silicosis.[59] Factors that influence the development of tuberculosis in the patient with silicosis include the severity and type of disease (the risk is considerably higher in patients with acute and accelerated silicosis),[19] the prevalence of tuberculosis in the population from which the work force was drawn, and the age, general health, and human immunodeficiency status of the work force population.[59-61] Exposure to silica, without silicosis, may also predispose individuals to tuberculosis[57,59] (see Table 61.2).

Tuberculosis is characterized by necrotizing epithelioid granulomas. These are never seen with silicosis alone. Although *Mycobacterium tuberculosis* is the usual organism, nontuberculous mycobacteria (NTM) account for a large proportion of the mycobacterial disease in some populations.[16,62,63] The proportion of tuberculosis and of disease caused by NTM in silica-exposed individuals probably reflects the profile of infection in the population from which the particular work force is drawn.

Airflow Obstruction and Chronic Bronchitis

COPD and chronic bronchitis are common manifestations of long-term occupational exposure to environments contaminated by silica dust, and can develop in silica-exposed individuals with or without silicosis.[16,52,64-70] Abnormalities of the small airways, including fibrosis and pigmentation of respiratory bronchioles (see Fig 61.3D), are also seen in association with exposures to a variety of mineral dusts, including those responsible for silicosis.[43] Smoking can potentiate the effect of silica dust on airflow obstruction.[69,70]

Connective Tissue Diseases and Renal Disease

Associations have been reported between exposure to silica and certain connective tissue diseases, including progressive systemic sclerosis, systemic lupus erythematosus, and, as previously mentioned, rheumatoid arthritis.[16,71] Epidemiologic evidence indicates that the prevalence of rheumatoid arthritis is increased in individuals with exposure to silica as well as in those with silicosis.[72] It has also been suggested that rheumatoid arthritis may initiate or aggravate silicosis.[73] Systemic sclerosis has been shown to be associated with silicosis,[72] but may also be associated with silica dust exposure without silicosis.[74,75] The evidence for an association between lupus erythematosus and silicosis is strongest for acute or accelerated silicosis but is inconclusive for chronic silicosis.[16,72]

Renal disease has also been reported in silica-exposed workers. Some studies have implicated an immune complex glomerulitis or a direct toxic effect of silica.[16,18,72]

Lung Cancer

In 1996, the International Agency for Research in Cancer (IARC) classified silica dust as "carcinogenic to humans."[76] The association between silicosis and lung cancer has been difficult to establish because of the high prevalence of smoking in silica-exposed workers and because of frequent concomitant radon exposure.[16,77] Studies of non–radon-exposed, nonsmoking workers with silicosis suggest a clear relationship between silicosis and lung cancer, but there remains some doubt as to whether silica exposure, in the absence of silicosis, carries an increased risk for lung cancer.[16,72,78,79,79a]

CLINICAL FEATURES

The symptoms and signs of chronic silicosis, a disease characterized by focal pulmonary fibrosis, are no different from those of focal pulmonary fibrosis caused by other agents; their evolution and time course are related to the type and severity of the disease process. The main symptom is breathlessness, first noted during exertion and later at rest as the large working reserve of the lung is diminished. In chronic silicosis, in the absence of other respiratory disease, even this symptom may be absent. It is not unusual for a patient with chronic silicosis to present without symptoms for assessment of an abnormal chest radiograph. The appearance of breathlessness may mark the development of a complication such as progressive massive fibrosis or tuberculosis, or may reflect associated airway disease. Cough and sputum production are common symptoms and usually relate to chronic bronchitis, but may reflect the development of tuberculosis or lung cancer. Chest pain is not a feature of silicosis, nor are systemic symptoms such as fever and weight loss, which should be attributed to tuberculosis or lung cancer until proven otherwise. Clubbing is also not a feature of silicosis and should raise concern about lung cancer.

In accelerated and acute silicosis, the time scale of symptom evolution is in years or months rather than decades. In acute silicosis, breathlessness may become disabling within months, followed by impaired gas exchange and respiratory failure.

RADIOGRAPHIC FEATURES

Uncomplicated silicosis is characterized by the presence of small rounded opacities on the chest radiograph,[1,8,19] as graded in the ILO classification (as described previously).[5] However, occasionally even advanced silicosis, determined by histology, may not be apparent on a chest radiograph.[80]

Silicotic nodules are usually, although not invariably, symmetrically distributed and tend to occur first in the upper zones (Fig. 61.4); later, although not invariably, other zones are involved. Occasionally the nodules are calcified, resembling microlithiasis. Enlargement of the hilar nodes may precede the development of the parenchymal lesions.[8] "Eggshell" calcification, when present, is strongly suggestive although not pathognomonic, of silicosis (Fig. 61.5; see also Fig. 61.4). Pleural plaques may occur but are not a common feature.

Progressive massive fibrosis is characterized by the coalescence of small rounded opacities to form larger lesions (see Fig. 61.5); they are graded on the ILO scale according to size and extent (categories A to C). CT assessment is superior to the chest radiograph not only in assessing the presence and extent of silicotic nodulation, but also in revealing early conglomeration.[81] With time, the mass lesions tend to contract, usually to the upper lobes, leaving hypertranslucent zones at their margins and often at the lung bases. In this process, small rounded opacities, previously evident, may disappear, resulting in a picture that needs to be distinguished from tuberculosis. The rapid development of several large lesions suggests rheumatoid

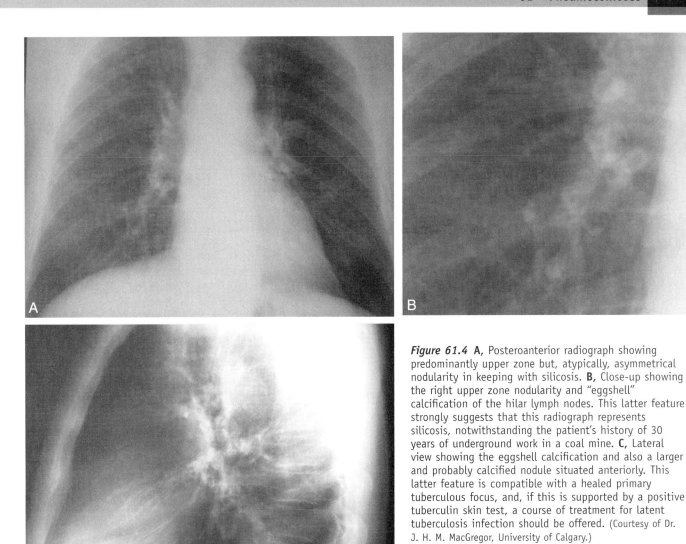

Figure 61.4 **A,** Posteroanterior radiograph showing predominantly upper zone but, atypically, asymmetrical nodularity in keeping with silicosis. **B,** Close-up showing the right upper zone nodularity and "eggshell" calcification of the hilar lymph nodes. This latter feature strongly suggests that this radiograph represents silicosis, notwithstanding the patient's history of 30 years of underground work in a coal mine. **C,** Lateral view showing the eggshell calcification and also a larger and probably calcified nodule situated anteriorly. This latter feature is compatible with a healed primary tuberculous focus, and, if this is supported by a positive tuberculin skin test, a course of treatment for latent tuberculosis infection should be offered. (Courtesy of Dr. J. H. M. MacGregor, University of Calgary.)

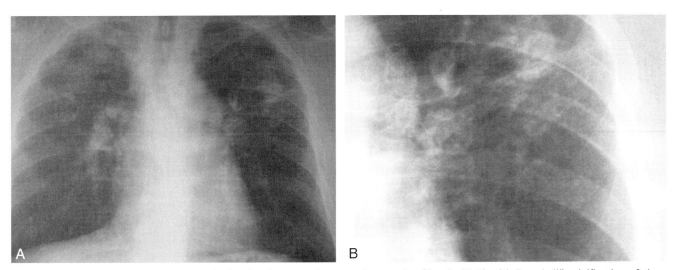

Figure 61.5 **A,** Posteroanterior radiograph showing features of progressive massive fibrosis (PMF) with "eggshell" calcification of the hilar nodes, in keeping with complicated silicosis, in a man who had shoveled sand in a glass factory. **B,** Close-up view showing the PMF with a background of smaller nodules and the eggshell calcification. (Courtesy of Dr. J. H. M. MacGregor, University of Calgary.)

silicosis, but new lesions, especially if cavitated, should be regarded as evidence of mycobacterial disease. Acute silicosis is characterized radiologically by diffuse changes that usually display an air space and interstitial pattern rather than the usual nodularity.[1,82]

LUNG FUNCTION

The lung function profile is determined by the extent of silicosis as well as associated or concomitant airway and vascular changes. In chronic silicosis, spirometric tests (FEV_1, FEV_1/FVC, and maximal midexpiratory flow[43]) usually reflect airflow limitation.[16,56,65,83] Reduction in diffusing capacity is generally apparent in more advanced chronic silicosis and probably reflects associated emphysema.[68,84] It is possible that most of the lung function changes associated with chronic silicosis can be attributed to the associated emphysema.[68,84]

In the accelerated and acute forms, functional changes are more marked and progression is more rapid. In acute silicosis, lung function shows a restrictive defect and impairment of gas exchange, which leads to respiratory failure and eventually to death from intractable hypoxemia. Interpretation of pulmonary function tests is discussed in Chapter 24.

DIAGNOSIS AND COMPLICATIONS

Silicosis is diagnosed on the basis of a history of exposure and the characteristic radiographic changes.[19] Problems arise when the history of exposure is remote, forgotten, or missed or has occurred outside of one of the recognized occupations (hence the importance of a careful and comprehensive occupational history). Occasionally the radiologic features are unusual; examples include the presence of hilar lymphadenopathy or of large lung opacities in the absence of typical small nodular opacification. Detection of silica in BAL material may suggest the diagnosis. Lung biopsy (transbronchial, transthoracic, or open) may be necessary to distinguish PMF or other atypical features from lung cancer, tuberculosis, and other diagnoses. Biopsy material should be submitted for microanalysis for dust, including silica.

Less common complications include cor pulmonale, spontaneous pneumothorax, broncholithiasis, and tracheobronchial obstruction in the neighborhood of enlarged calcified hilar nodes.[19] Diagnosis of active tuberculosis in the silicotic patient may be more difficult than in the nonsilicotic patient, but in general a good sample of sputum or sputum induced by nebulized hypertonic saline, sent for mycobacterial culture, provides the diagnosis. The presence of cough, hemoptysis, weight loss, fever, or any new radiologic feature should be pursued with culture of sputum or BAL fluid or with culture and histologic examination of tissue. In many instances, it is the chest radiograph rather than clinical features that gives the first indication of tuberculosis in the presence of silicosis, but it should be noted that patients with silicosis are also at risk for extrapulmonary tuberculosis.[59]

MANAGEMENT AND CONTROL

Once established, the fibrotic process of chronic silicosis is thought to be irreversible. Management of the individual case is thus directed toward preventing progression and the development of complicated disease. A change in occupation to an environment free of silica-containing dust should be advised unless this would adversely affect a person who is close to retirement and pension. The disease will generally progress even without further exposure,[56] but the rate of deterioration is probably reduced.

Interventions to interrupt the inflammatory process that leads to chronic silicosis including the inhalation of aluminum or polyvinylpynidine-N-oxide and oral tetrandine have not been shown to be successful. There is currently interest in the use of lung lavage to remove silica from the lung, but a favorable impact on progression of acute or chronic silicosis has not been demonstrated. Treatment of all forms of silicosis should be directed toward control of mycobacterial disease. This is especially true for acute and accelerated silicosis and silicosis in workers with human immunodeficiency virus infection.[19,55,61] All patients with silicosis should have a tuberculin skin test and, if it is positive, be offered treatment for latent tuberculosis infection.[55,85]

The interaction between silica exposure and smoking in the development of COPD[69,70] makes it particularly important to implement smoking cessation programs in the workplace.

Because acute and accelerated silicosis carry such a poor prognosis and tend to occur in younger persons,[53] consideration should be given to lung transplantation in such cases (see Chapter 89).

The most important aspect of the management of silicosis relates to its prevention. To achieve this, a sustained effort must be made to increase awareness of silicosis. Recent deaths from silicosis in younger individuals in the United States have occurred after exposure in the construction and manufacturing sectors, with none from mining.[53] This suggests a lack of awareness of the hazards of silica outside the traditional occupations associated with silicosis.

COAL WORKERS' PNEUMOCONIOSIS

DEFINITION AND OCCUPATIONS AT RISK

Coal workers' pneumoconiosis (CWP) is a distinct pathologic entity resulting from the deposition of coal dust in the lungs.[1,4,41] The tissue reactions to deposits of dust include the *coal macule* and the *coal nodule* (simple CWP), and PMF (complicated CWP) (Fig. 61.6).[41]

The main occupation at risk for CWP is coal mining, an industry that in the 1970s, despite modern mechanization, still employed approximately 250,000 people in the United Kingdom, and a comparable number in Western Europe.[13] Approximately 175,000 coal miners were employed in the United States in 1986; there has since been a steady decrease in the numbers to approximately 80,000 in 1999.[28] Coal is also mined in Eastern Europe, India, and China and on the African, Australian, and South American continents. With mechanization, output and potential for dust exposure has increased. Thus, although the industry employs fewer workers, former as well as current coal workers are likely to be seen with CWP for several decades to come.

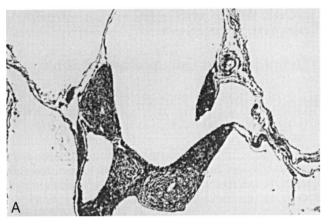

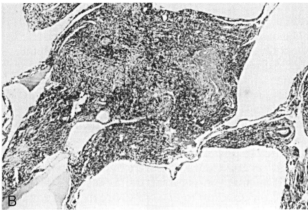

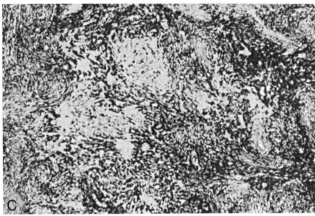

Figure 61.6 Pathologic lesions of coal workers' pneumoconiosis: examples from South African coal miners. **A,** Dust and dust-laden phagocytes in the wall of a distal airway in which reticulin and collagen fibers were demonstrated. Focal emphysema is associated with the lesion. **B,** Coal macule consisting of dust and dust-laden phagocytes, reticulin, and dense, irregular depositions of collagen. This lesion would be palpable. There also was associated focal emphysema. **C,** Progressive massive fibrosis with coalescence of macules and dense collagen deposition. (Original magnification × 100.) (Courtesy of Dr. B. Goldstein, National Center for Occupational Health, Johannesburg.)

Coal mine dust contains a variable amount of quartz depending on the nature of the ore-bearing rock, the size of the coal seam, and the processes used to mine the seam (including the degree of mechanization). Coal miners may also develop silicotic nodules when the coal seams that they mine are in hard rock. Silicosis is more common in mines with a high grade of coal and in workers such as roof bolters who work outside of the coal seams.[4,41] Current evidence shows that coal mining, even in the absence of CWP, is associated with chronic (industrial) bronchitis,[86] chronic airflow limitation,[4,87,88] and emphysema.[4,41]

Other occupations at risk for exposure to coal or carbon dust include coal trimming (which involves loading and stowing coal in stores or ships' holds), the mining and milling of graphite in carbon plants and in the manufacture of carbon electrodes, and the manufacture and use of carbon black.

PATHOLOGY

The primary lesion in CWP is the *coal macule,* which can be seen (although not palpated) on macroscopic examination as a small (up to 4-mm) pigmented lesion, distributed initially in the upper lobes, although the lower lobes may subsequently become involved.[41] On microscopic examination, the coal macule consists of a stellate aggregation of dust and dust-laden macrophages, around respiratory bronchioles, with reticulin fibers and a variable amount of collagen (see Fig. 61.6).[41] *Focal emphysema,* a form of centriacinar emphysema, occurs within and around the coal macule, and together they form the characteristic lesion of CWP.[41] The *coal nodule* is a palpable lesion that, in addition to dust-laden macrophages and reticulin, contains a substantial number of haphazardly arranged collagen fibers.[41] Coal nodules, which result from exposure to coal dust admixed with silica, usually occur on a background of coal macules.[1] Classic silicotic lesions are seen in approximately 12% of U.S. coal miners[41] and form when lung dust residue contains 18% or more quartz. Other features include subpleural dust deposits, enlargement of the hilar and mediastinal nodes, and, on occasion, tattooing of the parietal pleural lymphatic channels by coal dust.

PMF (complicated CWP) is defined as a fibrotic pneumoconiotic lesion 1 cm or greater in diameter. These bulky, often irregular, well-defined, heavily pigmented rubbery black tissue masses usually occur in a background of severe simple CWP. PMF usually develops in the posterior segment of the upper lobes or apical segments of the lower lobes and is typically bilateral (Figs. 61.7 and 61.8). Microscopically, the lesions contain the same elements as the coal nodule (see Fig. 61.6C). They may impinge on and obliterate airways and vessels and cross interlobar fissures. Cavitation is not uncommon, probably as a consequence of ischemic necrosis.

Rheumatoid pneumoconiosis,[41] one variant of which is called Caplan's syndrome, is a form of CWP associated with rheumatoid arthritis or a rheumatoid diathesis. It is characterized by necrobiotic nodules that are larger than coal nodules (up to 5 cm in diameter) and have smoother borders. Pigmentation is arranged in concentric laminations

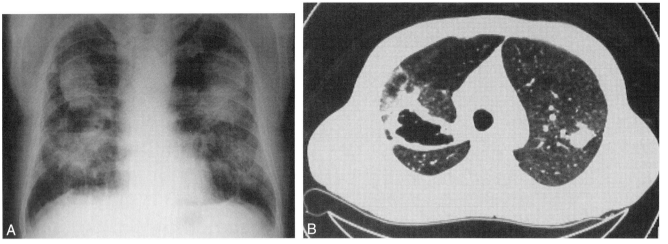

Figure 61.7 **A,** Chest radiograph showing progressive massive fibrosis (PMF) with evidence of cavitation in the right lower zone. The film represents complicated coal worker's pneumoconiosis. **B,** Computed tomography scan showing the background nodularity and the lesions of PMF with cavitation on the right. (Courtesy of Dr. J. H. M. MacGregor, University of Calgary.)

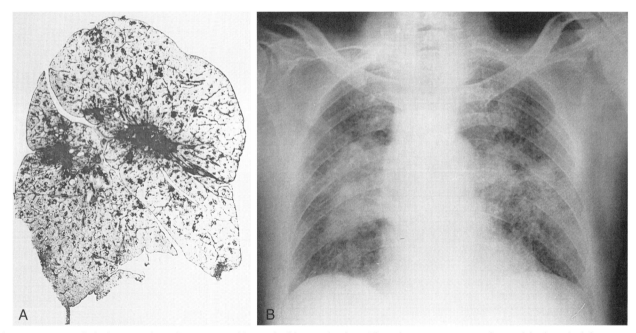

Figure 61.8 **A,** Whole-lung section of a 71-year-old Appalachian coal miner. The miner was a nonsmoker and had worked for 28 years underground, primarily at face work. The midsagittal section of the left lung shows massive lesions in the apical portion of the lower lobe and in the central area of the upper lobe. Progressive massive fibrosis (PMF) is seen against a background of simple nodular and macular coal workers' pneumoconiosis. In several areas, there is evidence of coalescence of nodules. There is mild focal emphysema associated with the coal dust macules. **B,** Chest radiograph showing features of PMF against a background of nodularity. The mass lesion on the right shows the propensity of PMF to move toward the hilum. The opacities are somewhat atypical for their predominantly lower zone situation. (Case from the NIOSH W. Laqueur collection, courtesy of Drs. V. Vallyathan and F. H. Y. Green.)

and, relative to PMF lesions, these nodules contain little dust. These lesions may cavitate or calcify. The microscopic features are similar to those described for the rheumatoid silicotic lesion (see under the discussion of the pathology of silicosis). Active areas in the nodules contain dust-laden macrophages, lymphocytes, polymorphonuclear leukocytes, and plasma cells. When activity ceases, they may collapse or calcify. Vasculitis is seen in vessels within and surrounding these lesions. Rheumatoid pneumoconiosis lesions were originally described in Welsh coal miners and are reported in Belgian coal miners, but are uncommon in North American coal miners.[89]

Diffuse interstitial fibrosis has also been reported in coal miners[90]; the fibrosis may contain black carbon pigment but is otherwise pathologically indistinguishable from usual interstitial fibrosis. However, it has a relatively benign clinical course compared with that of the same condition in the general population.[41]

PATHOGENESIS

The risk for CWP increases with the intensity and duration of exposure to coal dust. The effect of coal on the lung is also related to its rank, which is based on its carbon content. Anthracite ranks highest (93% carbon), followed by bituminous, sub-bituminous, and the lowest ranked lignite, with the lowest carbon content.[4,41] In epidemiologic studies, CWP is more common in mines of high-rank coal than in those of low-rank coal. This may relate to the greater relative surface area of the coal dust particles, higher surface free radicals, and silica in the high- rather than the low-rank coal.[91] The coal dust macule and nodule are ascribed to the accumulation of large amounts of relatively inert dust in the lung. As the lung burden of dust increases, alveolar macrophages are activated and reactive oxygen species are released. These in turn trigger the release of cytokines, including interleukins and tumor necrosis factor, which set in motion the processes of inflammation and fibrogenesis that are responsible for the development of pneumoconiosis, and the release of proteases which contribute to the associated emphysema. However, the fibrosis is considerably less intense and extensive than that evoked by the more bioactive dusts, such as silica and asbestos.[92]

Although the exact pathogenic mechanisms underlying the development of PMF remain in doubt, these lesions are thought to relate to the amount of coal dust accumulated in the lung, the proportion of inhaled silica in the dust and its surface bioactivity, individual immunologic factors, and whether tuberculosis is present.[41,91] Of these factors, the total dust burden appears to be the most important. In addition, there are striking differences in rates of simple pneumoconiosis and PMF between different coal pits, mining areas, and countries,[41,93] suggesting that other characteristics of the dust particles, including their shape, size, composition, bioactivity, and durability in lung tissue, also make a contribution to the risk of developing CWP.

EPIDEMIOLOGY AND NATURAL HISTORY

Early studies of coal miners suggested that the occupation and even the presence of CWP were not associated with higher mortality rates. These studies probably did not take the healthy worker effect into account, but, overall, the life expectancy of coal miners is comparable with that of the general population. However, coal workers with PMF do have reduced survival rates and increased morbidity associated with impaired pulmonary function. The prevalence of CWP has been falling consistently in the United States during the last 30 years: Rates in miners who have worked more than 24 years have fallen from 35% in 1973 to less than 5% in 1999 among the miners included in the NIOSH Coal Workers' X-ray Surveillance Program.[28,93a] Similar trends have been noted in Europe.[1] The presence of PMF is associated with more severe adverse effects on the health and life expectancy of coal miners than those of simple CWP. Risk factors for PMF include the presence and stage of CWP, the intensity of dust exposure, and the age of the patient.[94] The role of silica in the development of PMF is controversial but is generally believed to be important.[4,41]

Rheumatoid Pneumoconiosis

Rheumatoid pneumoconiosis (Caplan's syndrome) was originally described as a variant of PMF in coal workers on the basis of its distinctive radiologic features. Active arthritis or circulating rheumatoid factor was commonly associated with rheumatoid pneumoconiosis.[1] At present, most evidence suggests that the presence of rheumatoid arthritis, a rheumatoid diathesis, or both, is a host factor that modifies the response of an individual to coal mine dust exposure. Conversely, dust exposure does not appear to be a risk factor for rheumatoid arthritis.[1] CWP does not appear to have an association with other connective tissue disorders apart from a single report of an association with systemic sclerosis.

Role of Silica

Although it is recognized that silica does not play a primary role in the causation of CWP, coal miners, especially those mining anthracite, may develop the lesions of silicosis (see Fig. 61.4). When present, silicosis is usually associated with CWP.[41] Although combined exposure to silica and coal dust may produce less silicosis than would a similar pure exposure to silica, silica exposure is nevertheless thought to contribute to the risk of developing PMF.[4]

Airflow Obstruction and Chronic Bronchitis

With the generally decreasing rates for CWP in most countries, the focus of interest has shifted to an examination of the relationship of coal mining exposure with chronic bronchitis and emphysema.[64,87] Earlier studies demonstrated an association between occupational exposure and airflow limitation, but the confounding effects of smoking were not uniformly taken into account. In the early 1980s, the evidence for causality was strengthened greatly by the publication of two longitudinal studies,[95,96] involving approximately 1600 and 1000 men, respectively. Both studies showed that mine dust exposure resulted in an FEV_1 loss during the follow-up period that was approximately one third as severe as the effects of smoking. This effect increased to be comparable to that of smoking with higher dust exposure levels. A recent study of 909 young coal miners followed over 10 years demonstrated loss of forced vital capacity (FVC), FEV_1, and lung diffusing capacity that was apparent without CWP and persisted after controlling for smoking.[97] Studies based on autopsy material have implicated coal mining exposure in the production of emphysema, which was shown to be related to the amount of dust accumulated in the lung but not to the presence of CWP. In their comprehensive 1998 review, Coggan and Taylor concluded that (1) the balance of evidence points overwhelmingly to coal mine dust being a cause of impaired lung function; (2) this can be disabling; and (3) the best estimate of the loss of FEV_1 in relation to exposure of coal miners is 0.76 mL/gram hours/m³.[88] The issue of attributability, and thus compensation, in miners who had smoked and who had COPD remained controversial. This was clarified by Mr. Justice Turner in his judgment in a 1998 personal injury case. He concluded that exposure to coal dust, at a level that might be associated with a risk for pneumoconiosis, should be considered year for year to be equivalent to smoking as a cause of COPD.[98]

Mucus hypersecretion (chronic bronchitis) is common in coal workers but does not appear to play a direct role in their development of COPD. Mucus hypersecretion generally resolves after withdrawal from dust exposure, as it does after smoking cessation. However, bronchial hyperresponsiveness does appear to predispose coal workers to develop COPD. In U.S. coal miners, acute cross-shift changes in ventilatory capacity, suggesting bronchial hyperresponsiveness to the working environment, have been documented.[99] Longitudinal studies have shown that patients with persistent airway hyperresponsiveness to methacholine over a 5-year period show a greater FEV_1 decline compared with those whose airway hyperresponsiveness reverses over the same time period.[100] This raises the possibility that acute airway reactions to coal mine dust are a determinant of annual FEV_1 decline.[64]

Tuberculosis and Cancer

Mycobacterial infection, either by *M. tuberculosis* or NTM, has not been demonstrated to be more common in association with CWP in the absence of silicosis. Most evidence suggests that the occupation of coal mining is associated with a decreased risk of lung cancer but an increased risk of stomach cancer.[4,41,101]

CLINICAL FEATURES

Simple CWP is regarded as a disease state without symptoms or physical signs. The diagnosis is based on the radiologic features. The symptoms of cough and sputum reported by most coal miners are likely to be the consequence of dust-induced chronic bronchitis.[86] Breathlessness during exertion is usually caused by associated chronic airflow limitation or by the development of PMF.[4] Respiratory impairment and disability develop as PMF progresses, although patients with category A PMF (lesions 1 to 5 cm in diameter) may be symptom free. Lesions of PMF that impinge on airways may cause abnormal breath sounds. Large or bilateral PMF lesions may be associated with the signs and symptoms of pulmonary heart disease. The presence of new lung lesions with rheumatoid arthritis, subcutaneous rheumatoid nodules, or positive rheumatoid factor raises the possibility of rheumatoid pneumoconiosis. The lung lesions may or may not develop concomitantly with joint disease.

CHEST RADIOGRAPHY

The hallmark of simple CWP on the posteroanterior chest radiograph is the presence of small rounded opacities in the lung parenchyma.[1,8] (See the discussion of chest radiographs in the introduction to this chapter.) Coal macules are usually associated with small (<1.5 mm) *p* nodules on the chest radiograph, but the radiograph may show no nodularity with mild to moderate grades of CWP. The highest levels of coal dust are found in association with small, rounded *p* nodules. When the larger *q* and *r* nodules are visible radiologically, this usually reflects the presence of coal nodules and a higher proportion of quartz in the lungs.[102,103]

Because the chest radiograph has been shown to be insensitive to the presence of macules and nodules,[103] in individual cases CT may be useful. Small rounded opacities are usually seen first in the upper zones and involve the other zones at a later stage; all lung zones are unlikely to be involved unless profusion category 3 is present.[1,8] The nodule profusion is closely related to the lung dust content at autopsy. Small irregular opacities also occur in a profusion up to 1/0 in association with increasing age and smoking and, in coal workers, may relate to coexisting fibrosis and emphysema.[104] Small rounded opacities probably never regress, but the presence of emphysema appears to reduce the reading of profusion on the chest radiograph. Some enlargement of hilar nodes is usual, but eggshell calcification is unusual.

PMF is diagnosed radiologically when the parenchymal opacities exceed 1 cm in diameter, a cutoff point that is arbitrary in what is obviously a continuous process, as shown by the pathologic demonstration of PMF without associated radiologic features.[103] Conversely, approximately one third of cases diagnosed as PMF on the radiograph have been shown at autopsy to represent other lesions, including tumors, rheumatoid nodules, and tuberculosis scars.[103] PMF lesions are more common in the upper lobes, situated posteriorly, and are usually well demarcated from the adjacent lung. As PMF becomes more advanced, the lesions are nearly always bilateral (see Figs. 61.7 and 61.8). They may take on bizarre shapes, cavitate, or calcify. As the lesions shrink toward the hilum or to the apex, bullous lesions may be seen in the surrounding lung.

Lesions seen on the chest radiograph in rheumatoid pneumoconiosis are similar to those of PMF but are usually multiple and peripherally located. The lesions, which range in diameter from 0.5 to 5.0 cm, may appear within weeks. These lesions generally appear in the presence of lesser degrees of nodule profusion than are usual for PMF. They may cavitate, contain fluid levels, and show some calcification surrounding the cavity. In some cases, the lesions disappear, often completely, but may be followed at a later date by a fresh crop of lesions. The ILO classification of radiographs provides a special notation for lesions thought to be rheumatoid pneumoconiosis.[5]

LUNG FUNCTION

The controversy regarding the association between simple CWP and abnormal lung function has persisted largely because coal dust has been shown to cause both obstructive lung disease[97] and pneumoconiosis.[88] In general, it is probably true that simple CWP is a condition with little demonstrable effect on lung function. In part, this may be due to the health selection effect into a dusty job.[105,106] Small irregular opacities and PMF have each been shown to be associated with abnormal lung function.[4,107] Lung function deficits in complicated CWP include reduction in FVC and FEV_1, increased total lung capacity and residual volume, and decreased carbon monoxide diffusing capacity (particularly in the presence of mixed rounded and irregular opacities). Similar changes have also been noted in nonsmoking coal miners without CWP.[4,88,97] Pulmonary hypertension may develop in proportion to the reduction of the vascular bed associated with advanced PMF.

DIAGNOSIS, COMPLICATIONS, AND MANAGEMENT

A history of occupational exposure to coal and a chest radiograph are the fundamental elements in the diagnosis of CWP. A CT scan of the chest may be used to demonstrate evidence of CWP when the features on the radiograph are inconclusive.

There are no data to suggest that CWP alone carries an increased risk for mycobacterial infection, either by *M. tuberculosis*[107a] or NTM, but treatment of latent tuberculosis infection should be considered for coal workers who are thought to have had significant silica dust exposure or who have evidence of silicosis[85] (see section on silicosis). Other complications include rheumatoid nodules, which are associated more commonly with coal mining than with gold mining exposure, and scleroderma, in which the opposite is true. Most evidence suggests that the occupation of coal mining is associated with a decreased risk of lung cancer but an increased risk of stomach cancer.[101,108]

The principles of management are those summarized in the introduction to this chapter and elaborated in the section on silicosis. Younger patients with radiologic disease of profusion category 1 or greater should be advised to change their occupation to one in which they are no longer exposed to dust because of their risk of developing PMF. Management of other dust-related, smoking-related, or dust- and smoking-related diseases, such as chronic bronchitis and emphysema, is less straightforward. Smoking cessation counseling should be given on general principles. Although there are no data to show any interaction between smoking and CWP, both coal mining and smoking have the capacity to cause COPD.

ASBESTOS-RELATED FIBROSIS OF THE LUNGS (ASBESTOSIS) AND PLEURA

ASBESTOS MINERALS

History and Uses

Asbestos is an ancient mineral exploited by humans from prehistoric times because of its durability and heat resistance and its fibrous nature, which enabled it to be spun.[1,109] It was used by the Finns in the fashioning of pottery as early as 2500 BC; the Vestal Virgins in Rome used it for the wicks of their oil lamps; and Marco Polo marveled at the fire-resistant cloth made with asbestos by the Chinese he encountered in his Asian travels. Commercial use of asbestos, which started in the 19th century with open pit mining, grew as mechanization replaced hand cobbing,[1] and growth was exponential between the two world wars. Annual production peaked at over 5 million tons in 1976 and stabilized at approximately 4 million tons in the early 1980s. Production began to fall in Europe and North America only in the late 1980s, when the ill health effects of exposure became a matter of increasing public concern.[1] The use of substitutes has increased proportionately as the use of asbestos has been restricted or banned (as of 1999, 25 countries had banned or severely restricted the use of asbestos). On the African, Asian, and South American continents, asbestos continues to be in demand as a cheap, durable material for use in water reticulation and in housing projects for rapidly urbanizing populations.[109a]

The word *asbestos* (meaning "unquenchable" in Greek) is used currently as a collective term for naturally occurring mineral silicates of the serpentine and amphibole groups. Despite different origins and physical and chemical properties, these silicates have in common a fibrous habit, that is, they occur naturally in bundles from which fibers can be easily separated.

What is meant by the term *fiber* is of more than academic importance, because the dimensions of a fiber are determinants of its biologic potency. Thus, the mineralogist defines a fiber as a particle whose length-to-diameter (called aspect) ratio is equal to or greater than 10:1, whereas the definition used by the Occupational Safety and Health Administration as a basis for standard setting is a particle more than 5 μm in length with an aspect ratio equal to or greater than 3:1. This covers the many needle-like fragments found in the air, where asbestos is being mined, milled, fabricated, or installed.[110]

Table 61.3 lists some of the mineral silicates found in human lung tissue and gives a general (but not exhaustive) indication of their commercial uses. From the point of view of health effects, the most important are asbestos fibers and man-made mineral fibers. By contrast, annual world production of the nonasbestos mineral silicates is almost eightfold greater (approximately 30 million tons) than that of the asbestos mineral silicates.[110,111] Biologic potency (and disease-producing potential) depends in general on dose delivered to the target organ, fiber dimensions, and durability in the lung tissue. The role of each of these parameters may not be the same for all fibers and all disease entities.[110] Nonfibrous particles greater than 10 μm seldom reach the lung parenchyma, whereas fibers up to 200 μm can be found in the lungs if their diameter is less than 3 μm.[111,112]

Sources of Human Exposure

Given its many uses, the potential sources for human exposure to asbestos are legion.[1,111,113,114] The list given in Table 61.3 should be regarded as a short guide for clinical use. The discussion that follows deals mainly with exposure to asbestos fibers; however, the principles apply equally to exposure to other fibers.

In industrialized countries, and increasingly in industrializing countries, human exposure is most likely to be *occupational* and may occur in mining, milling, transporting, manufacturing, and applying or using raw fiber for manufactured products.[114,114a] In World War II, a major source of exposure was in the naval shipbuilding, repair, or refitting industries; in the post–World War II period, major sources of exposure were in the construction and transport industries, although exposures in shipbuilding, repair, or refitting continued to pose risks.[115] Asbestos-containing materials in post–World War II buildings include boards, panels, surfacing, insulation, tile and floor covering, roofing, and caulking. Exposure also occurs in maintenance operations or demolition of plants and buildings in which asbestos-containing materials have been used. Other sources of human exposure are the removal of asbestos lagging or insulation from ships or buildings and the disposal of industrial waste, such as the dumps of defunct asbestos plants. In most industrialized countries, these sources of exposure have diminished in response to heightened public awareness and control regulations.[1,114,115]

Table 61.3 Mineral Silicates That Have Been Found in Human Lung Tissue*

Mineral: Group and Form	Location of Major Deposits, Commercial or Other	Main Commercial Uses and/or Other Sources of Human Exposure
Asbestos Minerals		
Serpentine		
Chrysotile† (white asbestos)	Canada (Quebec, British Columbia, Yukon, Newfoundland‡), Russia, China (Szechwan), Brazil, Mediterranean countries (Cyprus, Corsica, Greece, Italy), southern Africa (South Africa, Zimbabwe, Swaziland)	Brake lining, ship building and repair, polishing of precious stones, stone cutting, whetstone cutting, foundry operations (mainly for insulation) Asbestos cement products (pipes, gutters, tiles, roofing); insulation, fireproofing, reinforced plastics (fan blades, electric switchgear); textiles; friction materials; paper products; filters; spray-on products
Amphibole		
Crocidolite (blue asbestos)	South Africa (Northwest Cape‡), western Australia‡	Used in combination, mostly in cement but also in some of the products listed above
Amosite (brown asbestos)	South Africa (Northern Province, former Transvaal)	
Anthophyllite	Finland‡	Filler in rubber and plastics
Tremolite	Contaminates ore in certain asbestos, talc, iron, and vermiculite mines; also found in some agricultural soils	May or may not be removed in processing; has rural domestic uses (e.g., stucco)
Cummington-grunerite	Contaminates ore in certain iron mines (often not fibrous)	No commercial use
Nonasbestos Mineral Silicates		
Clay minerals (usually fine-grained, powder-like) such as kaolin and montmorillanite (bentonite)	40 countries, including China, US (Georgia, North Carolina), UK (Cornwall), Czechoslovakia, Germany, Egypt, Japan	Functional filler in paper, plastic, bricks and cement, rubber, paint, etc.; fireclays, refractories, ceramics, lubricants
Attapulgite and sepiolite	US (Georgia, Florida), Spain, Australia, South Africa	Oil absorbants; pesticide carriers; pet litter
Talcs (usually platelike but can roll into scrolls)	US (Vermont, Montana, New York, California); Italy, Spain, Norway, China, Japan, Korea, Canada	Ceramics; paper making; cosmetics; pharmaceuticals; animal feed; fertilizer; anticaking; paints; varnishes; plastic reinforcer
Micas (usually flaky) Muscovite	US (North Carolina, Georgia, and other states); France, Spain, China, India, Italy	Filler in plastics, drill sites, special paints; refractories; semiconductors; insulation; anticorrosion materials; welding rods
Vermiculite (expands when heated)	South Africa, US (Montana, Virginia), Australia, Kenya	Absorbants (horticulture); plasters; boards; insulation; fire resistance
Wollastonite (occurs as needles or fibers in limestones)	US (California, New York), Japan, former USSR, Finland, Mexico, Australia	Filler/flux in ceramic industry; used in latex and oil-based paint; in welding fluxes; asbestos substitute in hardboard, insulation, and brake linings
Zeolite (fibrous) (e.g., erionite)	Turkey (Cappadocia and Anatolia regions): noncommercial deposits	Houses constructed in erionite rock; soil containing fibers mixed with tremolite; sepiolite used in stucco and plaster
Other (mainly nonfibrous)	Worldwide (in filling of lava cavities); mined in 16 countries, including several in Europe, in the US, and in Japan	Pollutant and radioactive waste control; also used in catalysts, adsorbants, conditioners
Man-Made Mineral Fibers		
Glasswool and filament, rock wool, slagwool, ceramic fiber	Production in factories around the world	Many uses previously reserved for asbestos: glass filament used in mats, lamination, yarns; glass-, rock-, and slagwool used as insulation in buildings and in car and naval construction; ceramic fiber used in reinforced cloth, discs, brakes, gaskets, board, and paper; high-performance ceramic fiber used in jet engines, spacecraft

* The list is not exhaustive, and the reader should consult other sources for further information.[1,3,111,113-115] Asbestos minerals invariably exhibit the fibrous habit; nonasbestos mineral silicates also may do so. Most silicate deposits are mineralogically heterogeneous, as are most of the commercial forms of the minerals.[111]

† Accounts for more than 90% of the world's commercial production; other fibers still used in combination with chrysotile.

‡ Mining no longer in operation.

§ In one of three epidemics of mesothelioma in Turkish villages, erionite was implicated; in the other two, tremolite and/or chrysotile were implicated.[121] As of 2003, 23 countries have prohibited the use of asbestos or severely restricted its use, but in all countries exemptions are allowed for certain uses. A prohibition decree was also adopted and will be enforced in the European Union in 2005. Currently, the Jeffrey Mine in Canada suspends its mining operations intermittently depending on demand.

Indirect occupational exposure, also called *bystander exposure,* describes the exposure of persons whose trades require them to work in the vicinity of others who were working directly with asbestos or asbestos-containing materials. Examples are carpenters and welders, who may work in close contact with insulators and laggers who mix asbestos on site, often in closed spaces. These exposures often occurred in the shipbuilding, repair, and refitting industries, and in the construction industries.

Domestic exposure occurs primarily as a consequence of fiber-laden work clothes being brought home. The dust they shed settles in the furnishings, carpets, upholstered sofas, and drapes and is repeatedly resuspended in the air by human activity, in particular house cleaning. Domestic exposure still accounts for a small proportion of cases of asbestos-related disease, mainly pleural, and is reported to have accounted for up to 15% of malignant mesothelioma in one U.K. study.[116] Given the long incubation period of this tumor (from 20 to 40 years), domestic exposure is likely to be the source of cases presenting well into the 21st century.[1,117]

Environmental and residential exposure occurs as a consequence of living in the neighborhood of asbestos mines, mills, or plants.[118] This source of exposure was first dramatically brought to medical attention in 1960 in a report of a cluster of 31 cases of malignant mesothelioma among residents and crocidolite asbestos miners of the Northwest Cape, South Africa.[119] Cases continued to be reported from this area at least until 1989.[120] Environmental exposures from nonindustrial sources have been documented among residents of rural areas in Eastern Europe where the soil is contaminated with various fibers.[121,121a] In addition, epidemics of asbestos-related pleural disease, nonmalignant as well as malignant, have occurred among residents of Turkish villages whose homes were constructed in erionite tuff rock or who used erionite and tremolite in stucco and plaster.[121] By contrast, a cohort study comparing the mortality experience of more than 4500 women living in the vicinity of the Quebec chrysotile mines with that of 1.375 million women from 60 reference areas in the province revealed no excess of lung or digestive system cancer, but seven deaths from mesothelioma occurred in women living in the asbestos mining area.[118]

A major concern since the 1980s has been the potential risk of exposure to occupants of public (including schools), commercial, and residential buildings constructed during the post–World War II period, when asbestos-containing materials were widely used in construction. A health review mandated by the U.S. Congress concluded that exposure in buildings was less by an order of magnitude than that encountered in the workplace except for custodians and others responsible for building maintenance.[122,123] The report also provided estimates of lifetime cancer risk (see Asbestosis, Asbestos Exposure, Lung Cancer, and Mesothelioma section later).

The Fate of Inhaled Fibers

Accumulation of fibers in the lung is the outcome of exposure, deposition, clearance, and retention, all processes that depend on fiber dimensions and the level, intensity, and profile of exposure.[124,125] Clearance of fibers from the lung

is greater for short and for chrysotile fibers than for long and for amphibole fibers.[126] Retention of fibers is inhomogeneous, with more fibers being found in the lung regions with shorter pathways and greater accumulations of longer fibers with asbestosis than in lungs in which only airway lesions have developed.[126] Fibers of 3 μm or less are phagocytosed by activated macrophages, then translocated to lymphatic channels, and eventually drained to the pleural space. Longer fibers are incompletely phagocytosed, often by more than one macrophage, and become the core of what were originally called *asbestos bodies* because of their association with asbestos exposure. Although most coated fibers in human lungs have been shown to contain asbestos (usually amphibole) when subjected to radiographic diffraction analysis,[109,112] the term *ferruginous bodies* has been suggested to underline the fact that other mineral fibers may undergo coating in human lungs. The mechanism by which fibers transmigrate to the parietal pleura to produce pleural plaques remains uncertain.[127]

In the lungs of exposed individuals, the number of uncoated, or bare, fibers (only visible on electron microscopy) exceeds the number of coated fibers (*asbestos* or *ferruginous bodies*), visible by light microscopy, by 5000- to 10,000-fold.[110,128] For many years, the coated asbestos fiber (*asbestos body*) has been considered the hallmark of exposure, past or current, no doubt because of its distinctive structure and because it was readily visible under the light microscope. The presence of more than one coated fiber has been cited (and challenged) as a necessary criterion for the pathologic diagnosis of asbestosis even in a patient with an appropriate exposure history.[128] Asbestos bodies may be found in sputum or in BAL fluid when lung tissue levels are very high. Asbestos bodies found in sputum or BAL fluid have been shown to reflect lung dust burden. They are also more commonly found when exposure has been recent and to amphibole rather than chrysotile fibers.[112,129,130] BAL fluid may also show characteristic cellular, biochemical, and mineralogic features in workers exposed to asbestos and in those with asbestosis.[131]

Exposure versus Dose-Response Relationships

Epidemiologic studies have consistently demonstrated exposure-response relationships for asbestos-related parenchymal lung fibrosis (Fig. 61.9).[132] There are differences in the slopes of the exposure-response relationships between industrial sectors, which probably reflects the fiber size (smaller fibers causing more disease) and the nature of the fibers, as well as their retention and biopersistence in lung tissue (amphiboles causing more disease than chrysotile). For asbestos-related pleural disease, exposure-response relationships can also usually be demonstrated, but the residence time of the dust in the lungs is more important than cumulative exposure.[125,127] Mineralogic analysis has also shown that fibrosis grade correlates with fiber concentration, both in chrysotile- and amosite-exposed workers. The toxicity of mineral fibers is determined by their physical and aerodynamic properties, which determine deposition and retention. Also relevant in fibrogenesis and probably in carcinogenesis is the solubility of the fibers (which determines their survival in lung tissue), and their surface properties and electrical charge (which may affect their toxicity for cell membranes and the formation of free radicals).[45,117]

ASBESTOSIS (PULMONARY PARENCHYMAL FIBROSIS)

Pathology and Pathogenesis

Asbestosis tends to be prominent in the lower lobes and in the subpleural areas. When disease is advanced, the lungs are small, streaks of fibrosis outline lobar and interlobar

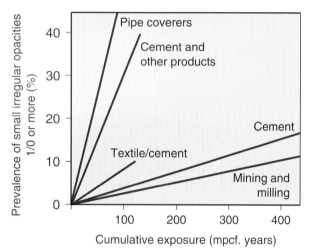

Figure 61.9 The figure shows the prevalence (%) of small irregular radiographic opacities (1/0 or more) in relation to cumulative exposure in millions of particles per cubic foot × years (mpcf. years) in different work forces exposed to asbestos. Idealized exposure-response relationships are shown for various sectors of the asbestos industry, including mining and milling, cement, and textile production (studies carried out in Quebec), and cement and other products and pipe covering (studies carried out in the United States). Further details are given elsewhere.[169] (From Becklake MR: Occupational lung disease: Past record and future trend using the asbestos case as an example. Clin Invest Med 6:305–317, 1983.)

septa, and the visceral pleura is invariably thickened. "Honeycombing" may be prominent subpleurally and in the lower lobes. Unlike silicosis, the tracheobronchial lymph nodes do not show characteristic changes, and PMF is unusual.[128] Advanced asbestos-related fibrosis is distinguishable from advanced fibrosis due to any other cause only by the presence of asbestos bodies or uncoated asbestos fibers (Fig. 61.10B).[112] At the other end of the disease spectrum, the lesions of mild asbestosis tend to occur at scattered sites, and usually consist of foci of peribronchiolar fibrosis[133] with local chronic interstitial inflammation, accumulation of macrophages in the air spaces, and proliferation of type II pneumocytes.[134] Second- and third-order bronchioles and alveolar ducts tend to be involved as the disease progresses and the fibrosis spreads to involve the alveolar interstitium (Fig. 61.10A).

In general, the grade of pulmonary fibrosis relates to the fiber burden carried by the lungs.[112] On the basis of animal and human data,[45,123,135] the sequence of events leading to asbestosis is thought to commence with an alveolitis that may resolve if the fiber burden is low and the fibers are cleared. If the fiber load is low but retained, a nonprogressive distal airway lesion (mineral dust–induced peripheral airway disease) may develop.[45,123,126,133,135] If the dust load retained is high, and phagocytosis of fibers by alveolar and interstitial macrophages is incomplete, fibronectin is released together with other proinflammatory and cytotoxic agents such as oxygen free radicals. These interact with and recruit fibroblasts to the site of the injury, where they proliferate and lay down collagen. If sustained, this process leads to irreversible damage, loss of alveolar spaces, and the development of chronic interstitial lung fibrosis—in other words, asbestosis.[126]

Epidemiology and Natural History

Clinical asbestosis, like clinical silicosis, is becoming less frequent and less severe as exposure levels in workplaces around the world are increasingly meeting currently

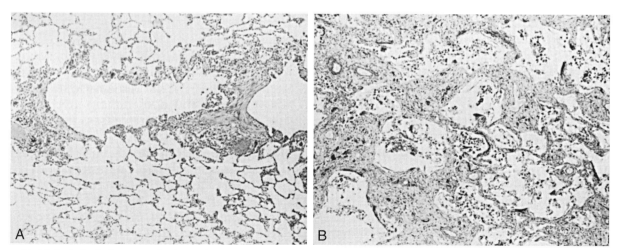

Figure 61.10 Pathologic features of asbestosis: examples from South African asbestos workers. **A,** Dust-laden phagocytes in the lumen and wall of a terminal bronchiole with commencing fibrosis. Giant cells, fibers, and asbestos bodies also are seen in the lesion. The architecture of the surrounding lung parenchyma is preserved. **B,** Diffuse interstitial fibrosis with destruction of the lung architecture and honeycombing; dust-laden phagocytes, fibers, and asbestos bodies are seen in the air spaces and interstitial tissue. (Original magnification × 100, light microscopy.) (Courtesy of Dr. B. Goldstein, National Center for Occupational Health, Johannesburg.)

recommended control levels.[20,125] In the United States, crude mortality rates and hospital discharges for asbestosis are still rising,[135a] but adjusted mortality rates are stable,[28] and in the United Kingdom and Canada, rates of certification of death or disability from asbestosis are falling.[136,137] With low-level exposure to asbestos, the interval between exposure and disease increases.[125] The pattern of exposure also determines the nature of the disease. In occupations in which exposure is intermittent but of high intensity, the ratio of pleural to parenchymal radiologic abnormality may exceed 20:1, whereas a 2:1 pleural-to-parenchymal ratio is more usual in occupations in which workers are more consistently exposed.[12,125] Exposure at a young age is an independent determinant of both attack and progression rates of parenchymal and pleural radiologic abnormalities, suggesting that residence time of dust in the lung is important in their pathogenesis.[12,125,138] Other determinants of progression are level and duration of exposure, cumulative exposure, and fiber type (more frequent after exposure to the amphiboles, crocidolite and amosite, or mixtures of amphibole and chrysotile than to chrysotile alone) (see Fig. 61.9).[125] Once established, radiologic asbestosis may remain static or it may progress; rarely has regression been recorded.[12] Radiologic asbestosis may appear and progress long after exposure ceases; in a study of chrysotile miners and millers in Quebec, appearance and progression rates of 31% and 9%, respectively, were recorded for pleuroparenchymal disease over an average follow-up period of 17 years since last exposure.[12,125] Progression in the absence of further exposure relates to cumulative exposure up to the time of quitting.[125,138] There is no evidence that human leukocyte antigen (HLA) phenotype influences risk[125]; however, there is currently research interest in other gene-environment interactions, including occupational exposures.[139]

Smoking deserves comment because of its role as a universal risk factor for respiratory disease, both malignant and nonmalignant. Thus, the long-term inhalation of cigarette smoke in individuals with no asbestos exposure is associated with bronchiolitis and peribronchiolar fibrosis, and there is some evidence that the milder grades of radiologic small irregular opacities in the ILO classification may be caused by smoking.[140] Pathologic studies do not show evidence of an association between asbestosis grade and smoking,[141] although there is evidence to suggest that smoking enhances the retention of fibers in the lungs.[117,141]

Clinical Features

Asbestosis has been called a monosymptomatic disease because the earliest, most consistently reported, and most distressing symptom is dyspnea. It occurs first during heavy effort, then at progressively diminishing levels of effort as the disease progresses. Dyspnea often precedes other evidence of disease and therefore may be underrated by the physician because of its subjective nature. However, the consistency of its relationship to exposure levels[125] suggests that it is related to early parenchymal asbestosis. Persistent cough is reported commonly, almost as frequently as dyspnea in some series.[127,142] The cough is usually dry, often occurs with distressing spasms, and has been attributed to the stimulation of lung receptors. A productive cough is usually associated with smoking. Chest tightness or pain, or both, are not uncommon and may be caused by acute asbestos-associated pleural reactions.

Basal crackles, an early and distinctive feature of asbestosis, are fine crisp sounds, often heard first over axillary and basal regions, and then more generally as the disease advances. Features of note are their persistence (they usually are unaffected by coughing), their timing (at first, at mid to late inspiration, and eventually during most of inspiration), and their high-pitched quality.[143] Other sounds, including coarse crackles and rhonchi, reflect airway disease that may be related to cigarette smoking or to dust in the occupational environment.[64] Clubbing of the fingers and occasionally the toes develops in some patients. Late manifestations include respiratory and circulatory failure, and these, with cancer, are common causes of death.

Radiographic Features

The posteroanterior chest radiograph remains a key tool in the initial clinical diagnosis of asbestosis, and in the health surveillance of exposed workers.[6] The ILO classification[5] uses the term *small irregular opacities* to describe the irregular linear shadows that develop in the lung parenchyma and obscure the normal bronchovascular arborization pattern seen in disease-free lungs. The parenchymal opacities are usually seen first in the lower lateral zones between the rib shadows. As their profusion increases, the borders of the heart are obscured. Small rounded opacities are unusual when the exposure has been primarily to fibers but are more likely to be seen in workers who also have had silica exposure (e.g., asbestos cement workers).[1,24]

Early fibrotic changes are better visualized by HRCT with supplementary prone images,[6] particularly for subpleural parenchymal changes that may be obscured by overlying pleural fibrosis on the chest radiograph.[144] Visceral pleural thickening of the interlobar fissures is common.[127] Changes in the parietal pleura (see later) are also common, and the presence of pleural plaques (particularly if they are bilateral) or of pleural thickening provides additional evidence that the parenchymal disease is asbestos related. Hilar node enlargement is not a feature of asbestosis, and PMF lesions, including rheumatoid pneumoconiosis, are less common than in workers exposed to coal or silica. The radiologic features of well-developed disease seldom present a diagnostic problem; interpretation of the less marked changes is much more subjective, and hence the use of ILO films and of HRCT are proportionately more valuable.[6,144,145] The CT scan is also useful in characterizing localized pleuropulmonary lesions, including rounded atelectasis, which must be distinguished from lung cancer because it presents as a solid localized lesion. HRCT can also identify coexisting lung disease such as emphysema and distinguish subpleural fat from pleural thickening and plaques.[6]

Lung Function

Established asbestosis is often but certainly not always associated with a restrictive lung function profile (see Chapter 24).[125] With less advanced radiologic disease, FVC and diffusing capacity are reduced, and reduction in flow at low lung volumes (maximal midexpiratory flow) is a common finding in keeping with small airway abnormality.[43,127] In studies of exposed populations, a substantial proportion of patients (up to half in some series)[12] exhibit a mixed or obstructive function profile in keeping with the parallel development of airway and parenchymal effects of working in dusty occupations contaminated by mineral dusts.[87] When repeated lung function tests are used to assess evolution of disease, simple volume measurements such as FVC appear to be the most useful.[12,109,146]

Diagnosis and Complications

Criteria for diagnosis depend on the purpose for which a diagnosis is required. Clinical diagnosis depends on establishing the presence, extent, and nature of pulmonary fibrosis (see earlier) and that the exposure has been of a duration and intensity sufficient to put the individual at risk for developing asbestosis.[147,147a] The fewer the features, the less certain the diagnosis; the more trivial the exposure, the less likely that it is causal. When radiologic or lung function changes are marginal, other imaging, including CT or HRCT, often reveals the presence of parenchymal abnormality and associated pleural thickening or plaques. In the absence of what appears to be an adequate exposure history, it may be appropriate to perform a biopsy of the lung to establish the nature of the disease and the presence and burden of asbestos in the lung (see previous discussion of fibers in the section on asbestos minerals). BAL may also be useful because the presence of asbestos bodies in BAL fluid is a reflection of lung dust burden.[131,148,148a] Diagnosis of asbestosis for the purpose of legal attributability calls for greater certainty and the use of criteria that vary according to the legal administrative system involved. Most published criteria consider histopathology as the best means of establishing the diagnosis.[123,126] In its absence, the following criteria are proposed: (1) a reliable history of asbestos exposure; (2) an appropriate lag time between exposure and detection; (3) evidence of lung fibrosis on the chest radiograph or HRCT scan; (4) a restrictive pattern of lung function; (5) bilateral fixed inspiratory crackles; and (6) clubbing of the fingers or toes, or both. Of these, history of exposure and imaging evidence (radiographic or HRCT) are considered essential and the others confirmatory.[126]

The individual with asbestosis is at increased risk for cancer of the lung[149,150] and, by virtue of asbestos exposure, is also at risk for mesothelioma. Working in a dusty occupation (as is the case for most workplaces contaminated by asbestos dust) also puts the worker at risk for developing COPD.[87] Tuberculosis and rheumatoid pneumoconiosis are uncommon complications of asbestosis.[151]

Asbestosis, Asbestos Exposure, Lung Cancer, and Mesothelioma

The observation reported in 1951 that lung cancer occurred more frequently in association with asbestosis than with several other types of pneumoconiosis was responsible for first directing attention to the potential of asbestos exposure for carcinogenesis.[152] At first, cancers seen in association with asbestosis were assumed to be scar cancers, analogous to those seen in diffuse interstitial fibrosis from other causes. Consistent with this theory were their

location (more common in the lower lobes, where asbestos-related fibrosis tends to be more severe), their often multicentric origin, and possibly their cell type (a preponderance of adenocarcinoma).[128] Subsequently, mortality studies of exposed work forces confirmed the excess lung cancer risk and showed it to be related to the intensity and duration of exposure[117,153] and to decrease after exposure ceases, thus providing evidence for causality. Autopsy analyses of lung fiber burden in those dying from asbestosis versus lung cancer were 30 million versus 13 million fibers per gram of dry lung tissue.[141] In a 2002 Italian study, over 1000 asbestos bodies per gram of dried lung tissue established lung burdens consistent with occupational exposure to asbestos in 56 out of 924 unselected surgical cases of lung cancer with no occupational exposure in their clinical records.[154]

In 1977, the IARC classified asbestos as a human carcinogen, the target sites being the lung, larynx, and pleura.[150] The report stated that there is "no scientific documentation indicating that these entities (asbestosis and lung cancer) are interrelated in any way other than (by their being) associated causally with exposure to asbestos. . . ." Since that date, a considerable body of evidence has accumulated in support of this view that lung cancer is associated with asbestos exposure with or without asbestosis,[155–158] although there are still dissenting views.[117] Experimental studies (cellular and molecular) support this view and suggest that asbestos may have multiple roles in the pathogenesis of malignancy, a question that touches on the whole issue of the interrelationship of inflammation, fibrogenesis, and carcinogenesis; for instance, profibrotic mediators also may lead to carcinogenicity.[45] The lung cancer risk is enhanced by cigarette smoking (although the previously held multiplicative model has recently been challenged[159]) but is also demonstrable in nonsmokers.[122,158,160] A 1999 analysis estimated the attributable proportion due to synergy to be as high as one third.[161] Other factors influencing the risk of lung cancer in exposed work forces include industry (risk greater in the textile vs. the asbestos cement industry), fiber type (risk greater when exposure is to amphibole-crocidolite, amosite or tremolite, or mixed amphibole-chrysotile than when it is only to chrysotile), and fiber dimensions (longer fibers are more carcinogenic than shorter fibers).[126,162]

The emergence of cancer as an important cause of death in asbestos-exposed individuals can be attributed in part to workplace controls, introduced in the 1970s and implemented over the latter half of the 20th century, resulting in a decrease in the competing risk from asbestosis, and greater chance of survival into the cancer age group. Lung dust burden studies in workers coming to autopsy with different asbestos-related diseases have confirmed that the dust burden associated with asbestosis is on average severalfold greater than that associated with asbestos-related lung cancer.[163] For instance, in chrysotile miners in Quebec, the fiber concentrations in those dying of asbestosis versus those dying of lung cancer versus nonexposed miners were 30 versus 13 versus 2 million chrysotile fibers per gram of dry lung tissue, respectively; for those engaged in trades with asbestos exposure in the Pacific Northwest, where amosite was the dominant fiber, the equivalent figures were 10.0 versus 1.0 versus 0.7 million fibers per gram of dry lung tissue.[141] All histologic cell types of lung cancer have been shown to be associated with asbestos exposure, which further supports the direct role of asbestos, independently from asbestosis, as a carcinogen.[158] In addition to its biologic importance, the issue is also of practical interest in terms of legal attributability, and this varies between jurisdictions. There is obviously a much stronger case for attributing lung cancer in a particular individual to asbestos exposure in the presence of asbestosis and in the absence of a smoking history than in the absence of asbestosis and in the presence of a smoking history. Despite the methodologic variation in asbestos fiber and body counting, all available information about exposure, including any measures of asbestos fiber in BAL or biopsy material, should be assembled in such evaluations; in other words, the presence of asbestosis should not be used as the only indicator of important occupational exposure.

Of great concern to the public is the risk of cancer from attending school or working in a building constructed with asbestos-containing materials. The lifetime risk for premature cancer death from exposure at school from age 5 to 18 years has been estimated at 6 per million exposed, and for working in an office building with asbestos-containing material, at 4 per million exposed, compared with a risk of 2000 per million for 20 years' employment in a workplace conforming to the 0.1 fiber/mL limit, that is, in compliance with the current permissible exposure limit proposed by the Occupational Safety and Health Administration.[122] Malignant mesothelioma has been reported in 16 teachers from different parts of the United States, 12 of whom had no identified exposure outside of school employment, but other population studies have failed to show an increase in the incidence of mesothelioma in relation to the use of asbestos in buildings.[122] However, residential environmental exposure has been implicated in mesothelioma production.[118]

PLEURAL PLAQUES

Pathology and Pathogenesis

Pleural plaques are distinctive, smooth, white, raised, irregular lesions usually found on the parietal and rarely on the visceral pleura. They may vary from small to extensive (up to 50 cm^2) and are usually nonadherent. Common sites are the posterolateral mid-lung zones, where they may follow the rib contour, and on the diaphragm. They are less commonly found on the pleura adjacent to the mediastinum and pericardium, and rarely in the apices and costophrenic sulci.[127] On microscopic section, pleural plaques consist of avascular, acellular, laminated collagen fibers arranged parallel to the surface or in whorls, with hyaline changes and occasional fibroblasts. Macroscopic calcification is common, and microscopic calcification extremely common, especially in the parietal lesions. The lesions are usually covered by mesothelium. Fine asbestos fibers are seen on electron microscopy.[127] The lungs of patients from the general population who have plaques have been shown to contain a 50- to 250-fold excess of long, thin, mainly amphibole fibers.[112] In asbestos miners and millers in Quebec, and in those engaged in the Pacific Northwest trades that involve exposure to asbestos, the lung burden is similar to that seen in

association with lung cancer (see earlier).[141] Pleural plaques are thought to develop from the release of fibers into the pleural space by mechanisms open to conjecture.[112] Release or escape probably occurs from subpleural accumulations of usually short, fine fibers that are able to penetrate the deeper lung spaces and are cleared via subpleural lymphatic channels.[112] Within the pleural space, macrophage and cellular interactions may determine fiber localization and plaque formation. In the absence of macrophages, the pleural reaction tends to be disorganized and diffuse.[164] The parietal location may be due to the fact that, for fibers, as for macrophages, the only exit from the pleural space is via stomas that communicate directly with the parietal pleural lymphatic channels. Pleural fibrosis and pleural plaques may have the same pathogenesis.[112]

Clinical Features

Pleural plaques, in the absence of parenchymal disease, often do not cause signs and symptoms and may be detected as an incidental finding on a routine chest radiograph. Their visualization depends on their thickness and the orientation of the x-ray beam. Only a modest proportion of those seen at autopsy are detected on posteroanterior chest radiographs; oblique views increase the yield. CT and HRCT scans can identify plaques at an earlier, less well-developed stage and can differentiate plaques from extrapleural fat pads. In the past, pleural plaques have been labeled as "visiting cards" for asbestos exposure, implying that they had no impact on lung function at rest or on effort. In fact, in epidemiologic studies, lung volumes (mainly vital capacity and FVC) are on average modestly but consistently reduced. The diffusion constant (the ratio of carbon monoxide diffusing capacity to total lung capacity) may be paradoxically increased by the presence of pleural plaques, after associated parenchymal fibrosis has been taken into account,[12,127,146] a change attributed to the decreased vital capacity while pulmonary capillary blood flow remains unaltered. Increasingly, too, it is recognized that in some individuals pleural plaques may be associated with disability[165]; the underlying mechanism may be inhibition of inspiratory capacity during exercise resulting in an increase in the work of breathing.

Epidemiology

Pleural plaques continue to be the most frequent and often the only manifestation of asbestos exposure,[127,137,166] and asbestos exposure is the most common cause of pleural plaques. For instance, for the period 1996–1998, pleural plaques constituted 28% of 4393 incident cases of occupational respiratory disease reported to the Surveillance System of Work-Related and Occupational Respiratory Disease (SWORD), which has been operating in the United Kingdom since 1989.[166] Bilateral pleural plaques are more likely to be associated with occupational exposure than unilateral plaques, for which other causes should be considered. Age and residence time of dust in the lungs are determinants of these distinctive pleural lesions[127]; smoking is considered to be a determinant by some[1] but not in general.[127] Domestic and residential exposures have been implicated in the production of pleural plaques (see earlier discussion of human exposure in the section on asbestos minerals), with remarkably high rates for pleural calcification (up to 30%) being described in some rural communities in the eastern Mediterranean countries of Corsica, Greece, Cyprus, and Turkey.[121] Of greater concern to the patient and the clinician is the prognostic significance of plaques: In one study, they were associated with alveolitis, as reflected in bronchoalveolar cell counts,[164] and by implication with an increased likelihood of developing parenchymal disease. The results of a Swedish cohort mortality study involving 1596 men were interpreted as showing that pleural plaques on the chest radiograph indicated significant exposure to asbestos, as well an increased risk of mesothelioma and possibly also lung cancer.[167]

PLEURAL FIBROSIS AND VISCEROPARIETAL REACTIONS

Pathology

Like pleural plaques, pleural fibrosis and visceroparietal pleural reactions may be localized or diffuse, and may vary in thickness from a milky discoloration of the lung surface to a thick, white peel encasing much of one or both lungs. The interlobar fissures are commonly involved.[6] Even severe visceral pleural disease may occur in the presence of minimal parenchymal reaction.[127,128] Occasionally, a localized pleural reaction may fold on itself and the surfaces synthesize, trapping the underlying lung and leading to a well-defined pleuroparenchymal lesion or pseudo-tumor, also called *rounded atelectasis*[127] (Fig. 61.11). Asbestos bodies and fibers are usually found in the visceral pleura, the underlying parenchyma, or both,[127] and the lung dust burden usually reflects the occupational exposure, but with electron microscopy fiber counts considerably less than those seen in asbestosis.[168]

Epidemiology

Like pleural plaques, pleural fibrosis and visceroparietal reactions may occur in the absence of radiologic parenchymal fibrosis, and are increasing in frequency.[127] The exposures implicated (see Table 61.3) are often short, heavy, remote, and related to amphiboles. Latency is usually long (>20 years), reflected in the fact that these reactions relate to time since first exposure (a proxy for residence time of dust in the lung) and not to cumulative exposure dose.[12,127] In the United States, radiographic pleural abnormality has been reported in approximately 1% of men without known exposure.[127] Pleural fibrosis has been reported in association with environmental exposures from mining operations (see previous discussion under sources of human exposure) in Finland and South Africa, and from nonmining (agricultural) operations in Bulgaria, Czechoslovakia, Poland, Greece, and Turkey. Epidemiologic studies are also consistent in showing that the presence of pleural fibrosis is associated with reduction in lung function, after any associated parenchymal fibrosis has been taken into account.[12,127,146]

Diagnosis

Pleural fibrosis is less specific for asbestos exposure than are pleural plaques, and other causes need to be considered in the differential diagnosis. Diagnosis of asbestos-related pleural thickening is usually based initially on the chest radiograph. Clinical presentation, like that of pleural plaques, is often as an incidental abnormality detected on a routine chest radiograph. After careful inquiry, a remote history of exposure, often quite brief but usually heavy, can be obtained from the patient. Rounded atelectasis may present as a radiologic abnormality in an asymptomatic patient, usually with a clear history of exposure, past or current. Conversely, some patients present with breathlessness[127] or chest pain, or both, with or without a history of acute episodes, attributed to benign pleural effusions (see later). Pleural fibrosis restricts the movement of the lungs; in the absence of associated parenchymal disease, clinical signs may be minimal, even though functional impairment is detectable. Impairment may be modest even in the presence of severe pleural disease.[12,127,169] In one study, any pleural abnormality was associated with an average deficit of 0.22 L and 0.40 L for FEV_1 and FVC, respectively,[165] but pleural fibrosis occasionally becomes severe enough to precipitate respiratory and cardiac failure and to require pleurectomy.[127,170]

The radiologic and CT features of pleural fibrosis are discussed in the section on pleural plaques. Given a history of exposure, obliteration of the costophrenic angle is likely to represent the residuum of asbestos pleural effusion.[127] In rounded atelectasis, the CT scan is particularly useful in delineating the relationship of the rounded lesion to other pleural changes.[144] Nevertheless, the differential diagnosis of rounded atelectasis includes lung cancer, and in some cases the diagnosis can only be established by surgery.

BENIGN ASBESTOS-RELATED PLEURAL EFFUSIONS

Benign asbestos-related pleural effusions may occur in lungs free of other stigmata of asbestos exposure or may mark an increase in the extent or severity of an already present pleural reaction. The term *benign* does not imply a lack of clinical significance, but rather that the effusion is not associated with mesothelioma.[127] Benign asbestos-related pleural effusions usually occur within 15 years of the first exposure and may occur after exposure has ceased.[127] They are more common in the age range 20 to 30 years and may be the most common manifestation of asbestos pleural disease in that age group. The episodes are usually transient and may be silent, but may be associated with chest tightness and, occasionally, pleural pain, fever, and dyspnea.[127] A pleural rub may be heard. The effusion is usually small, exudative, and blood stained[112] and contains leukocytes. Asbestos bodies are rarely found in the fluid, but they may be seen in the underlying parenchyma on biopsy.[171] The sedimentation rate often is raised.[171] Diagnosis is by exclusion, and suggested criteria include (1) an exposure history; (2) the absence of other causes; and (3) absence of tumor on a 3-year follow-up.[126] Because cytologic examination of the pleural fluid is rarely conclusive, a thoracoscopic biopsy is usually required to exclude other causes; to establish the presence of fibers in the pleural fluid (rarely demonstrable), the pleura (sometimes demonstrable), or the underlying lung parenchyma (not infrequently demonstrable); and to rule out malignancy, in particular malignant pleural mesothelioma. The usual pathologic findings in benign asbestos-related pleural effusion are those of chronic fibrous pleurisy with minimal cellularity.

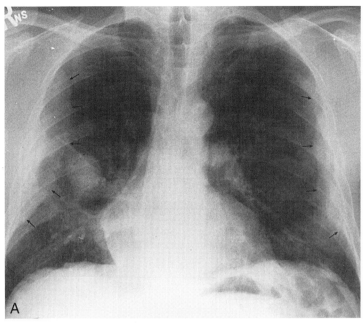

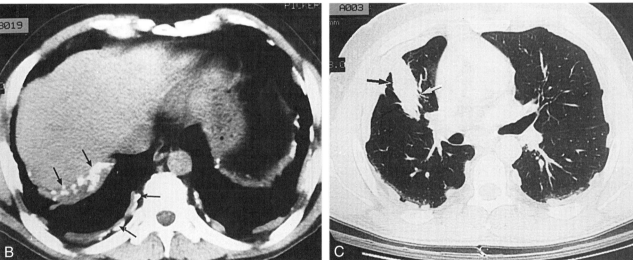

Figure 61.11 Asbestos-related pulmonary parenchymal and pleural disease (bilateral pleural fibrosis and rounded atelectasis) in a 50-year-old man. The patient had worked as an electrician since the age of 17 years, first in construction for 10 years (with known exposure to asbestos), then briefly on naval ships during World War II, and in a chemical plant (with known exposure to talc) for the past 20 years. His exercise tolerance was excellent and his only complaint was a dry cough. Chest radiographic abnormalities had been noted 4 years previously. **A,** Posteroanterior chest radiograph showing bilateral diaphragmatic plaques, extensive bilateral pleural thickening (category c3 using the ILO reference radiographs), and a circumscribed lesion in the right mid-lung zone that had increased in size over the past year. **B,** On the computed tomography scan, the pleural plaques were shown to be much more extensive than appeared from the posteroanterior chest radiograph. Many plaques (*arrows*) were calcified. In addition, high-resolution computed tomography at multiple levels revealed bands of subpleural fibrosis related to the pleural plaques or thickening, or both. Lung volumes and carbon monoxide diffusing capacity were greater than 100% and 98% of predicted values, respectively. Because the circumscribed lesion (**C,** *arrows*) had enlarged over the past year, it was removed surgically. The lesion, which was nonmalignant and pleural based, consisted of pleural, subpleural, and interstitial fibrosis. Analysis of lung digest revealed the following: 36,000 asbestos bodies per gram of dry lung tissue, and 7570 fibers per milligram of dry lung tissue, more than half of which were asbestos fibers and less than 1% of which were talc. These findings implicated his earlier rather than his more recent occupational exposures as the cause of his pleural disease. (Dr. J. Kosiuk, Department of Radiology, Royal Victoria Hospital, Montreal, carried out the radiographic studies. Dr. A. Dufresne, School of Occupational Health, McGill University, carried out the lung dust analyses.)

The prognosis of benign asbestos-related pleural effusions is generally good; most clear spontaneously, whether it is the first episode or a recurrence. Recurrence may be on the opposite side. Although effusion is a common form of presentation for malignant mesothelioma (see Chapter 70), there is no evidence that a benign effusion signals a future pleural malignancy. It appears rather to represent a stage in the evolution of asbestos-related pleural fibrosis, and carries the same risk (in one series, approximately 10%) of developing parenchymal fibrosis (asbestosis) as chronic pleural fibrosis. The pathogenesis is unknown.[112] Both mechanical irritation by fibers permeating the pleura and a direct cytotoxic effect on the surface mesothelial layer have been invoked.[127]

MANAGEMENT, PREVENTION, AND HEALTH MONITORING

The principles guiding clinical management of all these asbestos-related lung and pleural conditions are no different from those guiding this management when there is no history of asbestos exposure. These are discussed in Chapters 53 and 68. The specific issues involved in the management of work-related or potentially work-related disease are discussed in the introduction to this chapter under Epidemiology and Implications for Clinical Practice. The physician is reminded of the importance of making the appropriate notification of any case of asbestos-related disease. Notification, together with any procedures related to compensation, depends on the local jurisdiction in the area of the physician's practice. The physician must advise or refer the affected individual for advice concerning future employment (assuming employment is not out of the question for reasons of disability). Advice should be guided by our knowledge of the impact of further exposure on the natural history of the disease processes,[12,127,128] and by the risks for developing additional asbestos-related disease. In particular, it is important to emphasize that, even in the absence of any further exposure, progression of all nonmalignant asbestos-related diseases discussed here may occur on the basis of dust load already in the lungs. Current evidence suggests that, once there is definite parenchymal radiologic abnormality, the prudent option is to avoid all further exposure. Furthermore, continued exposure is likely to be associated with persistent industrial bronchitis, if present, and an increasing risk of chronic airflow limitation.[64] The possible role of smoking in the initiation and progression of fibrotic parenchymal disease and its established role in multiplying the risk of lung cancer are strong indications for antismoking advice to be given to the individual and for instituting smoking cessation programs in workplaces contaminated by asbestos dust.

No active treatment measures have been shown to influence the course of asbestosis. Corticosteroids and other anti-inflammatory and cytotoxic agents advocated for other interstitial lung diseases are less effective in asbestosis, possibly because the responsible agent remains in situ in the lungs. Patients with end-stage asbestosis have been the recipients of lung and heart-lung transplants, but technical difficulties may arise because of the associated pleural disease (see the previous discussion on the management of acute silicosis). Lung transplantation is discussed in Chapter 89.

For the nonmalignant asbestos-related pleural disorders, the evidence is now reasonably clear that patients with pleural fibrosis (and effusion seems to be a phase in the natural history of pleural fibrosis) are at greater risk for parenchymal fibrosis in the future.[125] It is appropriate to advise against further exposure (even in a workplace adherent to modern fiber limits) once pleural fibrosis becomes manifest and probably also (although this is less certain) once a pleural effusion has occurred. The presence of pleural

fibrosis or pleural plaques does not increase the individual's risk of malignant pleural mesothelioma beyond that associated with the dust load already carried by the lungs.

Control and prevention of asbestos-related lung diseases are public health issues, well discussed elsewhere.[1] An international ban on asbestos has been advocated as a public health measure for its control.[172] However, issues associated with an international ban, imposed by the industrialized world, include the lack of inexpensive alternatives for asbestos, especially important in the industrializing world (which currently accounts for much of the asbestos use), and the lack of studies comparable with those conducted on asbestos to examine the safety and effectiveness of substitutes, including man-made fibers.[173] Concern still exists about the potential ill health effects of the man-made substitutes,[173,174] even though the most recent data do not suggest that persons exposed occupationally have an increased risk of lung cancer or mesothelioma.[175–177]

Successful public control requires control of the work force environment, setting and enforcing of standards, and preemployment or in-service health examinations for exposed workers as part of a health-monitoring program. Implicit in the latter examination, which has the elements of a screening examination, is the hope that early detection might avoid later damaging disease, a hypothesis still to be tested. Nor is the interpretation of small changes between examinations (in physical signs and in radiologic, lung function, and cytologic examinations) an easy task. Such examinations are best regarded as biologic monitoring (for the purpose of detecting average trends within a work force) rather than as a method of case identification. Nevertheless, some individuals seek this type of health examination from their personal physician or clinic, and the clinician must make a judgment on the basis of available information. There is also some encouraging information for the individual with past exposure. First, only a minority of those exposed are likely to develop radiologic changes, and only a minority of those with radiologic changes develop clinical manifestations and any degree of disablement.[178] Furthermore, the additional chance of developing a carcinoma of the lung in the face of frank asbestosis is likely to be considerably lower than the 10% to 30% quoted on the basis of case data from patients exposed before the 1960s, when exposure levels were higher and asbestosis was, as far as can be judged, a more severe disease.[142] Quitting cigarette smoking should benefit the asbestos-exposed individual even more than the nonexposed individual because of the multiplicative interaction of these two agents.[161,179] According to one expert view,[143] for the current worker whose exposure has occurred only since the present control levels (0.1 fiber/mL for a 50-year working life) have been in place, ill-health effects are unlikely to be demonstrable by any practicable method of study. The mesothelioma risk, perhaps more disquieting for those with past occupational exposure, may also be expected to decline with time. Although in the United Kingdom it had been estimated that this would occur only by the second decade of the 21st century,[180] a 2003 report from a British naval dockyard indicates that rates had already peaked in 1991 and have since fallen.[181] Similar trends have been observed in Sweden, where the rate in men peaked in 1995 and has subsequently fallen,[182] and in Holland.[183] This improvement is attributed, at least in part, to the introduction of asbestos safety guidelines in the 1970s in these countries.

NONASBESTOS MINERAL SILICATES (FIBROUS OR NONFIBROUS) AND LUNG DISEASE

Exposure to some of the nonasbestos mineral silicates listed in Table 61.3 has been associated with lung disease. Silicate dust particles are found in the lungs of most urban dwellers,[109,134] and in general they appear to have low biologic activity.[111] Disease may develop after long, heavy exposure; initially it is characterized by accumulation of dust-laden macrophages around respiratory bronchioles, and later by fiber deposits with little mature collagen; the disease appears to progress in relation to lung dust overload.[111,113,121,134] Silicates are used widely as filling materials (kaolin, talc, and chlorite), as insulation (mica, vermiculite), and as absorbents (attapulgite, sepiolite), among other uses.[111] The clay minerals, talcs and mica (also called phyllosilicates because of their sheet structure),[111] constitute an important group. World production and use (estimated in 1991 as 5.3 million tons for talc alone) considerably exceed that of the asbestos minerals, which peaked at 5 million tons in the late 1970s. Before a 1989 North Atlantic Treaty Organization workshop, their toxicity as a group for humans had been studied little,[111] although three (talc, attapulgite, and sepiolite) had been evaluated for carcinogenic risk for humans by the IARC.[111] The information in this section is derived from the report of this workshop[111] and other sources.[115,123,184,185]

Talc and, more often, mica particles may form the core of ferruginous bodies. In general, the nonfibrous silicates have pulmonary effects similar to those caused by coal, unless they contain fibrous forms of these minerals or are contaminated by asbestos fibers, in which case their effects are closer to those produced by asbestos. The biologic effects of silica (quartz) may be modulated by the presence of silicates.[134]

KAOLIN PNEUMOCONIOSIS

The lesions of kaolin pneumoconiosis tend to be cellular and dust packed.[111] In its simple form, this pneumoconiosis is not usually associated with clinical or lung function changes, but rarely interstitial fibrosis or progressive massive fibrosis may occur and be associated with impairment.[184] In 10 surveys of kaolin-exposed work forces, the radiologic prevalence of simple pneumoconiosis (mostly small round opacities) ranged from less than 1% to 26.3%, whereas complicated pneumoconiosis and pleural change were unusual.[185] In general, prevalence was related to level and duration of dust exposure and probably contamination by other materials, including silica. Although lung cancers have been mentioned in relation to kaolin exposure,[186] no cohort mortality studies have been reported.

TALC PNEUMOCONIOSIS

The lesions of talc pneumoconiosis include peribronchial and perivascular interstitial accumulations of dust-filled macrophages, ill-defined nodular lesions in which birefringent talc crystals can be seen,[123] and foreign body granulomas.[111,184] In general, the disease evolves slowly, and PMF occurs infrequently; tuberculosis may complicate the condition but might reflect concomitant silica exposure. Interstitial fibrosis also may occur. A granulomatous arteritis caused by talc embolism is described in drug addicts who use an intravenous route for talc-containing drug tablets. Pleural changes, including plaques, are common; they are usually associated with mining exposures and may be due to contamination of mine dust by fiber (tremolite or anthophyllite).[111,184] Reactions to talc can be difficult to distinguish from those caused by silica or by asbestos, which often contaminate or even predominate in industrial grade talc.[184] In six surveys of talc-exposed work forces, prevalence of small opacities ranged from less than 1% to 37.2%; the latter were found in long-time workers and the lower rates were noted in some studies in which exposure was to pure talc.[185,187,187a] In three of seven cohort mortality studies in talc-exposed workers, excess deaths were recorded from nonmalignant respiratory disease, including pneumoconiosis. In addition, an excess of respiratory cancer mortality was found in five of the seven cohorts, but these findings must be interpreted with caution, because they were based on only 13 or fewer deaths in each cohort. In four of these, coexposure to other carcinogenic agents (mineral fibers, radon, silica) could have been implicated.[185] Several cases of mesothelioma were reported, but all in cohorts exposed to fiber-contaminated dusts.[185]

MICA PNEUMOCONIOSIS

The lesions of mica pneumoconiosis comprise dust particles surrounded by reticulin but usually with relatively little cellular reaction, although there are case reports of interstitial fibrosis[188] in which granulomas also have been described.[185] In three surveys of mica-exposed work forces, the prevalence of radiologic pneumoconiosis ranged from 1% to 44%, the latter work force being exposed to quartz-contaminated mica.[185] No mortality studies have been reported, but there has been one case report of a peritoneal mesothelioma in a mica-exposed worker.[185] Vermiculite, also a mica, does not appear to be toxic to the lungs of animals. However, in four surveys of vermiculite-exposed mine workers, the prevalence of radiologic pneumoconiosis ranged from less than 1% to 18%, and of pleural changes from 3% to 28%; in a processing plant, rates were higher and were related to cumulative exposure.[111,185] In one study, lung function was not affected,[189] although health selection may have operated to minimize an exposure effect. Pleural effusions and pleural thickening have been reported in mica-exposed work forces, in one of which mortality from malignant and nonmalignant respiratory disease was elevated. However, the role of mica was unclear as the cancer deaths were more common in patients with less exposure and there was amphibole contamination of the vermiculite.[190,190a]

The authors of a 1990 review[185] concluded that (1) there is little evidence that occupational exposure to pure kaolin, talc, mica, or vermiculite carries any important risk for health; (2) long and heavy exposure to kaolin and mica may result in low-grade radiographic changes, but clinically important pneumoconioses in work forces exposed to these phyllosilicates are likely to be the result of contamination by silica or asbestos fiber; (3) pleural lesions are common in talc-exposed workers but are probably caused by fiber contaminants; and (4) the increased rates of lung cancer or mesothelioma recorded in several exposed work forces probably result from exposure to fiber or silica contaminants of the ore or milled products.

MAN-MADE VITREOUS FIBERS

The production of man-made vitreous fibers (MMVFs) (including glass fibers and mineral wool, and refractory ceramic fibers as well as man-made mineral fibers such as carbon graphite, Kevlar Aramid, silicon carbide, and aluminum oxide), has increased markedly since the restriction or banning of asbestos in several countries. As with asbestos fibers, determinants of MMVF toxicity are (1) their dimensions (greatest risk with fine, long fibers less than 0.25 µm in diameter and longer than 8 µm); (2) their biopersistence, which can be altered in the production process according to the end use; and (3) dose to the target organ. MMVFs differ from asbestos fibers in being more soluble, less durable, and less biopersistent along a gradient of glass > rock > ceramic fibers.[191] Fibers are also coarser along a gradient of continuous glass filament > insulation wool > ceramic fibers > special purpose fibers.[191] Airborne levels in plants manufacturing MMVFs are commonly lower than 1 fiber/mL and lower in most applications except the application of insulation in confined spaces.[191] Airborne fiber diameters, with the exception of ceramic fiber, are generally large (1 mm) and thus nonrespirable. Despite their intensely irritating effects on skin and mucous membranes, there is no firm evidence that these fibers produce lung fibrosis, pleural lesions, or nonspecific respiratory disease in humans. However, refractory ceramic fibers may enhance the effects of smoking in producing airway disease.[191,192] Although the increased standardized mortality ratio for lung cancer in several cohorts exposed to MMVFs has been attributed to smoking,[175,177] several agencies have recommended exposures of 0.5 to 1 fiber/mL based on persisting concern about an excess working lifetime risk for lung cancer.[193,193a] There is no current evidence of an increased mesothelioma risk for MMVF workers.[176]

OTHER PNEUMOCONIOSES, OLD AND NEW

The pneumoconioses already discussed account for the majority of cases in most countries of the world. They exemplify a range of pulmonary reactions, from minimal reaction to a large lung particulate dust load, as in CWP, to a very specific fibrotic reaction to a comparatively small lung dust particulate load, as in silicosis. In the case of mineral fibers, the pulmonary reaction appears to be determined by lung fiber load of a particular size range (the long, fine fiber), as well as by fiber durability.

Several long-recognized, well-catalogued but less common pneumoconioses, which fall into the group in which the dust load is heavy but pulmonary reaction minimal, have not yet been mentioned. They include the pneumoconioses resulting from inhalation of iron in welding fumes or in iron or hematite mine dust (siderosis),

those that result from the inhalation of barytes by barium miners or workers (baritosis), and those that result from exposure to tin dust (stannosis). Other dusts that fall into this category include bismuth, manganese, Fuller's earth, and titanium. A more comprehensive list can be found elsewhere.[194] At the other end of the scale, lung disorders originally described as unusual or new forms of pneumoconiosis often turn out to be silicosis, which escaped recognition because exposure levels to quartz were higher than originally appreciated or the features of the pulmonary response were modified by the presence of other dusts. Examples include "Labrador lung" (named after exposure of iron miners to ore dust containing silica and some anthophyllite fibers)[25] and disease in bentonite workers that also turned out to be silicosis.[195] The pneumoconiosis of foundrymen is also an example of a response to mixed dust, in which the proportion of quartz is a key determinant of the character of the response. Careful case reports by observant clinicians continue to identify interstitial lung disease associated with various exposures and thus provide the information to stimulate the epidemiologic studies necessary to place them in proper context.

BERYLLIUM LUNG DISEASE

BERYLLIUM: USES, HUMAN TOXICITY, AND EXPOSURES

Beryllium is a rare metal that has many applications in modern industry because of its light weight, tensile strength, high melting point (1500°C), excellent alloying properties (beryllium-copper the most widely used), good thermal and electrical conductivity, resistance to corrosion, and ability to reduce the speed of nuclear fission.[1] Major sources are Argentina, Brazil, India, Zimbabwe, South Africa, and the United States. Its toxicity for humans was first recognized in Europe in the 1930s. In the United States, an epidemic of chronic beryllium disease occurred as a result of exposure in the fluorescent light industry during the 1940s, leading to discontinuation of its use in that industry and the institution of engineering controls in other industries handling beryllium.[1] However, the number of cases continued to increase and in 1987 reached 904 in a U.S. case registry.[196] Initially a large number of cases of acute berylliosis, an acute, toxic pneumonitis, were documented, but acute cases are now uncommon. Chronic berylliosis, a disease with features similar to sarcoidosis, continues to be reported. Cases arise from beryllium exposure in a wide variety of industries, including the manufacture of alloys, ceramics, radiographic equipment, and vacuum tubes, and in the extraction and smelting of beryllium. The number of individuals potentially exposed in the United States in 1987 was estimated at between 30,000 and 800,000 in the following industries: aerospace, electronics, ceramics, metal (including refining of scrap metal), nuclear (reactors, weapons), telecommunications, tool and die, and welding.[196] A survey of 646 workers in a beryllium metal alloy and oxide production plant showed that 9.4% were sensitized to beryllium on the basis of their positive beryllium lymphocyte proliferation test (BeLPT), and 4.6% had evidence of disease.[197] A British registry of deaths from beryllium exposure found that most cases had been exposed as machinists or in the manufacture of fluorescent lamps.[198] Survival rates ranged from 1 to 29 years.[198] Cases of berylliosis have also been reported in residents living near a beryllium refinery[199] and in a wife who laundered her exposed husband's clothing.[200] Beryllium contamination inside the personal vehicles of workers has also been documented.[201]

PATHOLOGY AND IMMUNE PATHOGENESIS

Acute beryllium disease in humans has been attributed to toxic, dose-related lung injury characterized by acute inflammatory reactions in the upper airways, bronchiolitis, pulmonary edema, and chemical pneumonitis. Recovery is usual, but 17% of cases progress to chronic beryllium disease.[196] Chronic beryllium disease is a multisystem disorder characterized by noncaseating granulomas that occur throughout the body, although their primary manifestation is in the lung.[17,196] On pathologic examination, chronic beryllium disease is characterized by the presence of a lymphocytic (helper/inducer T cell) alveolitis, as well as noncaseating epithelioid granulomas indistinguishable from those of sarcoidosis. There is a variable amount of fibroblastic activity that progresses to interstitial fibrosis as the lesions mature. Granulomatous lesions may occasionally be found in other sites, including thoracic and abdominal lymph nodes, spleen, liver, kidneys, and adrenal glands.

Beryllium enters the body by inhalation, and occasionally via the skin, where it acts as a specific antigen (alone or as a hapten through an interleukin-2 receptor pathway), leading to a proliferation of specific CD4 lymphocytes, release of lymphokines, and granuloma formation.[1] Because the agent persists in the lung, its slow release over time explains the appearance and progression of disease, even without further exposure.[1,17] There is also some evidence for an underlying genetic basis for susceptibility to beryllium disease, linked to a major histocompatibility complex class II marker (HLA-DPβ-1 Glu69) carrier status, which adds to the effect of the process (exposure) risk factor.[202] Evidence for delayed hypersensitivity in beryllium disease includes positive reactions to skin testing and in vitro responses of the lymphocytes to stimulation by beryllium (the BeLPT).[203] Skin testing, which may activate the pulmonary lesions, has been replaced by the BeLPT. Although these reactions are thought to indicate exposure and sensitization, not disease, in one series, six of eight sensitized individuals had granulomas on transbronchial biopsy.[204]

Beryllium is now considered to be a human carcinogen, especially in the presence of beryllium lung disease; in 1993 the IARC classified beryllium as a class 1 human carcinogen.[205]

CLINICAL FEATURES

The clinical features of acute beryllium disease include cough, chest pain, blood-tinged sputum, crackles, and patchy air space disease on the chest radiograph. The disorder is associated with high, and usually accidental, exposure and may present with an acute syndrome with features of acute respiratory distress syndrome or in a subacute form with features of pneumonitis. High levels of exposure to beryllium may also cause irritation and inflammation of the upper respiratory tract and conjunctivitis.[196] Although resolution generally occurs within a year, historically, the acute form was associated with death in 10% of cases and 17% progressed to chronic berylliosis.[196] No new case has been reported to the U.S. Beryllium Case Registry since 1987. Chronic beryllium disease may follow an acute beryllium pneumonitis, but more usually develops without antecedent events. The clinical features of chronic beryllium disease are similar to those of pulmonary sarcoidosis. There may be no associated symptoms,[203] but symptoms often include dyspnea, cough, chest pain, weight loss, fatigue, and arthralgias. Physical signs may include crackles, but signs of lung disease are often absent. Radiographic changes may precede the development of symptoms. The usual finding is ill-defined nodular or irregular opacities; hilar adenopathy is seen in approximately 40% of cases but is usually mild.[196] In the later stages of the disease, patchy fibrosis occurs with adjacent hyperinflation or distortion and extensive honeycombing. In chronic beryllium disease, pulmonary function usually shows a restrictive defect in advanced disease, but features including obstruction or isolated reduction in carbon monoxide diffusing capacity may occur with mild or moderate disease. Hypersensitivity to beryllium can be demonstrated by the BeLPT, which is increasingly used to determine whether exposed individuals have become sensitized. The diagnosis of chronic berylliosis depends upon the finding of lung disease, which is often indistinguishable from sarcoidosis, in the setting of current or past exposure to beryllium, and a positive BeLPT. Because the disease may occur following nonoccupational exposure, clinicians should give consideration to performing a BeLPT in cases of sarcoidosis in which the possibility of beryllium exposure exists.[206] The clinical course of chronic beryllium disease is variable. Some cases remain stable, some relapse and remit, and some progress inexorably.[196]

DIAGNOSIS AND MANAGEMENT

The diagnosis of chronic beryllium disease has been defined by criteria that include documented exposure to beryllium, evidence of lung disease compatible with the diagnosis, and a positive BeLPT performed on blood or BAL fluid.[207] The introduction of the BeLPT allowed for the introduction of three categories of beryllium-associated disorders: beryllium sensitization (positive blood or BAL fluid BeLPT but negative biopsy), subclinical beryllium disease (positive BeLPT and biopsy but no clinical or radiologic features of the disease), and chronic berylliosis (positive BeLPT and biopsy with clinical and radiologic features of disease).[207]

Most patients with chronic beryllium disease present in a fashion indistinguishable from pulmonary sarcoidosis, although extrapulmonary manifestations of disease (splenomegaly, hilar and mediastinal adenopathy), not unusual in sarcoidosis, are less common in chronic beryllium disease.[196,208] Evidence of sensitization to beryllium can be obtained in most instances by performing BeLPT on blood or BAL fluid (the yield from blood is lower than from BAL fluid). During the "epidemic" of beryllium disease during the 1940s and 1950s, chronic beryllium disease was very likely to have been considered in the differential diagnosis of sarcoidosis. Given the potentially long latency time for chronic beryllium disease, and despite the generally lower exposures that have occurred since the 1950s and its decreasing frequency, chronic beryllium disease still should remain in the differential diagnosis of sarcoidosis.[208a] Clusters of sarcoidosis occurring in a workplace should alert the clinician to the possibility that these represent examples of chronic berylliosis. In this context, note should be made of the very wide range of occupations associated with potential exposure to beryllium.

The most important step in case management is complete cessation of further exposure to beryllium. Corticosteroid therapy has been recommended in chronic beryllium disease, and long-term steroid therapy is believed to alter the course of the disease favorably, although there are no reports of permanent cure.

Chronic beryllium disease is controlled through the maintenance of the environmental levels in conformity with recommended control levels in all workplaces in which beryllium is used (the Atomic Energy Commission's environmental standards are 2 $\mu g/m^3$ averaged over an 8-hour day, not exceeding a peak of 25 $\mu g/m^3$ for 30 minutes).[1] The engineering controls that were introduced in the United States in the 1950s have been generally successful, but cases continue to be recognized, and the resultant review of exposure has shown industries in which the environmental standards were far exceeded.[206] Peak exposures, usually related to equipment failure or repair, may be more likely to induce sensitization, although this also has occurred in plants with median levels below 2 $\mu g/m^3$, especially where high-temperature operations produce beryllium fumes.[206]

Medical surveillance of exposed work forces, both by biologic monitoring for sensitization using blood BeLPT[204] and by case detection, plays a role in allowing this versatile mineral to be used safely. In case detection, a combination of the traditional clinical tools and criteria just referred to is used, as well as bronchoscopy for the harvesting of BAL lymphocytes for the BeLPT and for transbronchial biopsy with tissue analysis. Management of the sensitized individual should include advice to avoid further exposure. This advice is based on the likelihood that sensitized individuals usually have granulomas on transbronchial biopsy, even when chest radiograph and lung function tests are normal.

HARD-METAL DISEASE

Hard-metal disease, first described in Germany in the 1940s, has now been reported from many countries. Hard metal is manufactured by a sintering process that involves pressurization plus heating to 1500°C a mixture of tungsten carbide powder (often with tantalum carbide or titanium carbide added) and 10% cobalt.[1] Because of their diamond-like hardness, extreme strength, and heat resistance, "hard-metal" products have wide application in industry as drill tips (from dental to engineering drilling and diamond polishing), cutting and tunneling tools, grinding wheels, molds, jet engines, and ferromagnets. Human exposure occurs in the manufacturing of hard-metal products and in their maintenance and use. The grinding of sintered pieces generates high dust and cobalt concentrations.

Work-related illness in hard-metal workers may be acute (rhinitis and asthma), subacute (fibrosing alveolitis), or chronic (diffuse and progressive interstitial fibrosis).[209] The interstitial fibrosis is characterized by unusual multinu-

cleated giant cells comprising alveolar type II cells and macrophages that can be recovered from BAL fluid. The interstitial lung disease is thought to be a hypersensitivity pneumonitis to cobalt, which reacts with metallic carbides to produce active oxygen species.[210] A genetic association with some HLA-DP alleles may also be implicated.[211] This affords a plausible explanation of why only a small proportion of those exposed develop disease. A 1998 industry-wide cohort study in 10 facilities in France documented an increased mortality from lung cancer associated with simultaneous exposure to cobalt and tungsten carbide.[212] A review of workplace surveys indicates that interstitial disease is quite rare, whereas airway disease, including bronchitis and asthma, are both more frequent.[209,213] Both interstitial and airway disease may, of course, occur in the same individual. Diagnosis is based on an exposure history, a compatible clinical presentation, and pathologic and mineralogic features on biopsy: Tungsten carbide can usually be identified, but cobalt is generally not identified because, it is believed, of its solubility.[209] Cobalt exposure can be confirmed by skin patch test, or in urine, blood, or hair samples. Lymphocyte (blood or BAL fluid) transformation or leukocyte inhibition factor in response to cobalt may be useful.[209,214] Prompt diagnosis and removal from exposure may reverse acute disease, including asthma, and prevent the development of chronic disease. There have been several reports of response to withdrawal from exposure and treatment with corticosteroid.[17] Prevention requires control of exposure; for monitoring work force exposure, urinary cobalt may be useful.

SILICON CARBIDE (CARBORUNDUM) PNEUMOCONIOSIS

Carborundum pneumoconiosis is associated with exposure in the manufacture of carborundum, which is used as an abrasive because of its hardness. Under current exposure levels, this is generally a mild and nonprogressive disorder.[215] However, there is some evidence that workers exposed to this material, which has a silica and a fibrous component, are at risk for pneumoconiosis associated with lung dysfunction,[216,217] and possibly for lung cancer.[218]

FLOCK WORKER'S LUNG

A specific interstitial lung disorder characterized by lymphocytic bronchiolitis and peribronchiolitis with lymphoid hyperplasia[219] has been described in workers involved with the manufacture of nylon flock.[220-222] The disorder appears to be related to a specific form of cutting machine. The workers are exposed to a wide range of aerosolized material, including bioaerosols, nylon fiber, tannic acid, potato starch, carbon black, and zeolite, but respirable nylon fibers are currently thought to be the causative agent.

SUMMARY

This chapter has dealt with the classic pneumoconioses (silicosis, CWP, asbestosis, and asbestos-related pleural disease) as well as with some of the interstitial lung diseases that do not correspond to the ILO definition of pneumoconiosis, in which the agent is not necessarily a dust and does not necessarily remain in the lung (e.g., beryllium and hard-metal lung disease). The emphasis has been on providing information pertinent to the clinical encounter with a patient at risk for, or with, pneumoconiosis or other work-related lung disease. Occupational exposures need to be considered in the full range of respiratory disorders, including asthma, COPD, interstitial lung disease, pleural disease, lung infections, and mass lesions. The range of the intensity and nature of the exposure as well as the "latent period" between exposure and disease detection is sufficiently broad that a work-related cause should be considered in any adult patient with a respiratory disorder. Lack of knowledge of workplaces should not deter the physician from recording a complete occupational history. The current tools for diagnosis are complex and comprehensive and even allow for the identification of the agent in biologic material, but the occupational history remains the most important method for the detection of work-related diseases.[223]

REFERENCES

1. International Labour Office: Encyclopedia of Occupational Health and Safety (4th ed). Geneva: International Labour Office, 1997.
2. Nagelschmidt G: The relation between lung dust and lung pathology in pneumoconiosis. Br J Ind Med 17:247–259, 1960.
3. Churg A, Green FHY: Pathology of Occupational Lung Disease (2nd ed). Baltimore: Williams & Wilkins, 1998.
4. National Institute for Occupational Safety and Health: Occupational Exposure to Respirable Coal Mine Dust. Cincinnati, Ohio: National Institute for Occupational Safety and Health, 1995.
5. International Labour Office: Guidelines for the Use of the ILO International Classification of Radiographs of Pneumoconioses (rev ed). Geneva: International Labour Office, 2000.
6. Copley S, Hansell DM: Imaging. In Hendrick DJ, Burge PS, Beckett WS, et al (eds): Occupational Disorders of the Lung. London: WB Saunders, 2002, pp 483–501.
7. Corbett EL, Murray J, Churchyard GJ, et al: Use of miniradiographs to detect silicosis: Comparison of radiological with autopsy findings. Am J Respir Crit Care Med 160:2012–2017, 1999.
8. Fraser RS, Colman N, Muller NL, et al: Fraser and Pare's Diagnosis of Diseases of the Chest (4th ed). Philadelphia: WB Saunders, 1999.
9. American Thoracic Society: Evaluation of impairment/disability secondary to respiratory disorders. Am Rev Respir Dis 133:1205–1209, 1986.
10. American Thoracic Society: Lung function testing: Selection of reference values and interpretative strategies. Am Rev Respir Dis 134:363–368, 1991.
11. Becklake MR, White N: Sources of variation in spirometric measurements: Identifying the signal and dealing with noise. Occup Med 8:241–264, 1993.
12. Becklake MR: Asbestos and other fiber-related diseases of the lungs and pleura: Distribution and determinants in exposed populations. Chest 100:248–254, 1991.
13. Becklake MR: Occupational pollution. Chest 96:372S–378S, 1989.
14. Corbett EL, Churchyard GJ, Clayton TC, et al: HIV infection and silicosis: The impact of two potent risk factors on the incidence of mycobacterial disease in South African miners. AIDS 14:2759–2768, 2000.
15. Westerholm P: Silicosis: Observations on a case register. Scand J Work Environ Health 6:1–86, 1980.
16. American Thoracic Society: Adverse effects of crystalline silica exposure. Am J Respir Crit Care Med 155:761–768, 1997.
17. Churg A, Colby TV: Diseases caused by metals and related compounds. In Churg A, Green FH (eds): Pathology of Occupational Lung Disease (2nd ed). Baltimore: Williams & Wilkins, 1998, pp 77–128.
18. National Institute for Occupational Safety and Health: NIOSH Hazard Review: Health Effects of Occupational Exposure to Respirable Crystalline Silica. Cincinnati, Ohio: National Institute for Occupational Safety and Health, 2002.
19. Ziskind M, Jones RN, Weill H: Silicosis. Am Rev Respir Dis 113:643–665, 1976.
20. Becklake MR: The mineral dust diseases. Tuberc Lung Dis 73:13–20, 1992.
21. Rosenman KD, Reilly MJ, Kalinowski DJ, et al: Silicosis in the 1990s. Chest 111:779–786, 1997.
21a. Rosenman KD, Reilly MJ, Henneberger PK: Estimating the total number of newly-recognized silicosis cases in the United States. Am J Ind Med 44:141–147, 2003.
21b. Tjoe Nij E, Burdorf A, Parker J, et al: Radiographic abnormalities among construction workers exposed to quartz containing dust. Occup Environ Med 60:410–417, 2003.
22. Ehrlich RI, Rees D, Zwi AB: Silicosis in non-mining industry on the Witwatersrand. S Afr Med J 73:704–708, 1988.
23. Valiante DJ, Rosenman KD: Does silicosis still occur? JAMA 262:3003–3007, 1989.
24. Linch KD: Respirable concrete dust—silicosis hazard in the construction industry. Appl Occup Environ Hyg 17:209–221, 2002.
24a. Antao VC, Pinheiro GA, Kavakama J, Terra-Filho M: High prevalence of silicosis among stone carvers in Brazil. Am J Ind Med 45:194–201, 2004.
25. Edstrom HW, Rice DM: "Labrador lung": An unusual mixed dust pneumoconiosis. Can Med Assoc J 126:27–30, 1982.
26. Wagner JC, Pooley FD, Gibbs A, et al: Inhalation of china stone and china clay dusts: Relationship between the mineralogy of dust retained in the lungs and pathological changes. Thorax 41:190–196, 1986.
27. White NW, Chetty R, Bateman ED: Silicosis among gemstone workers in South Africa: Tiger's-eye pneumoconiosis (see comment). Am J Ind Med 19:205–213, 1991.
28. National Institute for Occupational Safety and Health: Work Related Lung Disease Surveillance Report, 2002. Cincinnati, Ohio: National Institute of Occupational Safety and Health, 2003.
29. Finkelstein MM: Silicosis surveillance in Ontario from 1979 to 1992. Scand J Work Environ Health 21:55–57, 1995.
30. Cavariani F, Di Pietro A, Miceli M, et al: Incidence of silicosis among ceramic workers in central Italy. Scand J Work Environ Health 21:58–62, 1995.
31. Murray J, Kielkowski D, Reid P: Occupational disease trends in black South African gold miners: An autopsy-based study. Am J Respir Crit Care Med 153:706–710, 1996.
31a. Churchyard GJ, Ehrlich R, teWaterNaude JM, et al: Silicosis prevalence and exposure-response relations in South African goldminers. Occup Environ Med 61:811–816, 2004.

32. Patial RK: Mountain desert silicosis. J Assoc Physicians India 47:503–504, 1999.

33. Norboo T, Angchuk PT, Yahya M, et al: Silicosis in a Himalayan village population: Role of environmental dust. Thorax 46:341–343, 1991.

34. Searl A, Nicholl A, Baxter PJ: Assessment of the exposure of islanders to ash from the Soufriere Hills volcano, Montserrat, British West Indies. Occup Environ Med 59:523–531, 2002.

35. Archer JD, Cooper GS, Reist PC, et al: Exposure to respirable crystalline silica in eastern North Carolina farm workers. AIHA J (Fairfax, Va) 63:750–755, 2002.

36. Gibbs AR, Wagner JC: Diseases due to silica. In Churg A, Green FHY (eds): Pathology of Occupational Lung Disease (2nd ed). Baltimore: Williams & Wilkins, 1998, pp 209–233.

37. Anonymous: Diseases associated with exposure to silica and nonfibrous silicate minerals. Silicosis and Silicate Disease Committee. Arch Pathol Lab Med 112:673–720, 1988.

38. McDonald JW, Roggli VL: Detection of silica particles in lung tissue by polarizing light microscopy. Arch Pathol Lab Med 119:242–246, 1995.

39. Murray J, Webster I, Reid G, et al: The relation between fibrosis of hilar lymph glands and the development of parenchymal silicosis. Br J Ind Med 48:267–269, 1991.

40. Velan GM, Kumar RK, Cohen DD: Pulmonary inflammation and fibrosis following subacute inhalational exposure to silica: Determinants of progression. Pathology 25:282–290, 1993.

41. Green F, Vallyathan V: Coal workers' pneumoconiosis and pneumoconiosis due to other carbonaceous dusts. In Churg A, Green FHY (eds): Pathology of Occupational Lung Disease (2nd ed). Baltimore: Williams & Wilkins, 1998, pp 129–207.

42. Castranova V, Porter D, Millecchia L, et al: Effect of inhaled crystalline silica in a rat model: Time course of pulmonary reactions. Mol Cell Biochem 234–235:177–184, 2002.

43. Churg A, Wright JL, Wiggs B, et al: Small airways disease and mineral dust exposure: Prevalence, structure, and function. Am Rev Respir Dis 131:139–143, 1985.

44. Slavin RE, Swedo JL, Brandes D, et al: Extrapulmonary silicosis: A clinical, morphologic, and ultrastructural study. Hum Pathol 16:393–412, 1985.

45. Mossman BT, Churg A: Mechanisms in the pathogenesis of asbestosis and silicosis. Am J Respir Crit Care Med 157:1666–1680, 1998.

46. Vallyathan V, Castranova V, Pack D, et al: Freshly fractured quartz inhalation leads to enhanced lung injury and inflammation: Potential role of free radicals. Am J Respir Crit Care Med 152:1003–1009, 1995.

47. Wallace WE, Keane MJ, Harrison JC: Surface properties of silica in mixed dusts. In Castranova V, Vallyathan V, Wallace WE (eds): Silica and Silica-Induced Disease: Boca Raton, Fla: CRC Press, 1995, pp 107–117.

48. Vanhee D, Gosset P, Boitelle A, et al: Cytokines and cytokine network in silicosis and coal workers' pneumoconiosis. Eur Respir J 8:834–842, 1995.

49. Williams AO, Knapton AD, Saffiotti U: Growth factors and gene expression in silica-induced fibrogenesis and carcinogenesis. Appl Occup Environ Hyg 10:1089–1098, 1995.

50. Koskinen H, Tiilikainen A, Nordman H: Increased prevalence of HLA-Aw19 and of the phenogroup Aw19,B18 in advanced silicosis. Chest 83:848–852, 1983.

51. Kreiss K, Danilovs JA, Newman LS: Histocompatibility antigens in a population based silicosis series. Br J Ind Med 46:364–369, 1989.

52. Cowie RL: The influence of silicosis on deteriorating lung function in gold miners. Chest 113:340–343, 1998.

52a. Goodwin SS, Stanbury M, Wang ML, et al: Previously undetected silicosis in New Jersey decedents. Am J Ind Med 44:304–311, 2003.

53. Anonymous: Silicosis deaths among young adults—United States, 1968–1994. MMWR Morb Mortal Wkly Rep 47:331–335, 1998.

54. Park R, Rice F, Stayner L, et al: Exposure to crystalline silica, silicosis, and lung disease other than cancer in diatomaceous earth industry workers: A quantitative risk assessment. Occup Environ Med 59:36–43, 2002.

55. Churchyard GJ, Kleinschmidt I, Corbett EL, et al: Factors associated with an increased case-fatality rate in HIV-infected and non-infected South African gold miners with pulmonary tuberculosis. Int J Tuberc Lung Dis 4:705–712, 2000.

56. Ng TP, Chan SL, Lam KP: Radiological progression and lung function in silicosis: A ten year follow up study. Br Med J (Clin Res Ed) 295:164–168, 1987.

57. Hnizdo E, Murray J: Risk of pulmonary tuberculosis relative to silicosis and exposure to silica dust in South African gold miners. Occup Environ Med 55:496–502, 1998.

58. Buchanan D, Miller BG, Soutar CA: Quantitative relations between exposure to respirable quartz and risk of silicosis. Occup Environ Med 60:159–164, 2003.

59. Cowie RL: The epidemiology of tuberculosis in gold miners with silicosis. Am J Respir Crit Care Med 150:1460–1462, 1994.

60. Sherson D, Lander F: Morbidity of pulmonary tuberculosis among silicotic and nonsilicotic foundry workers in Denmark. J Occup Med 32:110–113, 1990.

61. Churchyard GJ, Kleinschmidt I, Corbett EL, et al: Mycobacterial disease in South African gold miners in the era of HIV infection. Int J Tuberc Lung Dis 3:791–798, 1999.

62. Corbett EL, Churchyard GJ, Hay M, et al: The impact of HIV infection on Mycobacterium kansasii disease in South African gold miners. Am J Respir Crit Care Med 160:10–14, 1999.

63. Sonnenberg P, Murray J, Glynn JR, et al: Risk factors for pulmonary disease due to culture-positive M. tuberculosis or nontuberculous mycobacteria in South African gold miners. Eur Respir J 15:291–296, 2000.

64. Becklake MR: Occupational exposures: Evidence for a causal association with chronic obstructive pulmonary disease. Am Rev Respir Dis 140:S85–S91, 1989.

65. Cowie RL, Mabena SK: Silicosis, chronic airflow limitation, and chronic bronchitis in South African gold miners. Am Rev Respir Dis 143:80–84, 1991.

66. Oxman AD, Muir DC, Shannon HS, et al: Occupational dust exposure and chronic obstructive pulmonary disease: A systematic overview of the evidence. Am Rev Respir Dis 148:38–48, 1993.

67. Becklake MR, Irwig L, Kielkowski D, et al: The predictors of emphysema in South African gold miners. Am Rev Respir Dis 135:1234–1241, 1987.

68. Cowie RL, Hay M, Thomas RG: Association of silicosis, lung dysfunction, and emphysema in gold miners. Thorax 48:746–749, 1993.

69. Hnizdo E, Baskind E, Sluis-Cremer GK: Combined effect of silica dust exposure and tobacco smoking on the prevalence of respiratory impairments among gold miners. Scand J Work Environ Health 16:411–422, 1990.

70. Hnizdo E, Vallyathan V: Chronic obstructive pulmonary disease due to occupational exposure to silica dust: A review of epidemiological and pathological evidence. Occup Environ Med 60:237–243, 2003.

71. Koeger AC, Lang T, Alcaix D, et al: Silica-associated connective tissue disease: A study of 24 cases. Medicine (Baltimore) 74:221–237, 1995.

72. Calvert GM, Rice FL, Boiano JM, et al: Occupational silica exposure and risk of various diseases: An analysis using death certificates from 27 states of the United States. Occup Environ Med 60:122–129, 2003.

73. Sluis-Cremer GK, Hessel PA, Hnizdo E, et al: Relationship between silicosis and rheumatoid arthritis. Thorax 41:596–601, 1986.

74. Cowie RL: Silica-dust-exposed mine workers with scleroderma (systemic sclerosis). Chest 92:260–262, 1987.

75. Sluis-Cremer GK, Hessel PA, Nizdo EH, et al: Silica, silicosis, and progressive systemic sclerosis. Br J Ind Med 42:838–843, 1985.

76. International Agency for Research in Cancer: Silica, Some Silicates, Coal Dust and *Para*-aramid Fibrils (Scientific Publication No. 68). Lyon, France: International Agency for Research in Cancer, 1996.

77. Checkoway H, Hughes JM, Weill H, et al: Crystalline silica exposure, radiological silicosis, and lung cancer mortality in diatomaceous earth industry workers. Thorax 54:56–59, 1999.

78. McDonald AD, McDonald JC, Rando RJ, et al: Cohort mortality study of North American industrial sand workers. I. Mortality from lung cancer, silicosis and other causes. Ann Occup Hyg 45:193–199, 2001.

79. Wong O: The epidemiology of silica, silicosis and lung cancer: Some recent findings and future challenges. Ann Epidemiol 12:285–287, 2002.

79a. Attfield MD, Costello J: Quantitative exposure-response for silica dust and lung cancer in Vermont granite workers. Am J Ind Med 45:129–138, 2004.

80. Hnizdo E, Murray J, Sluis-Cremer GK, et al: Correlation between radiological and pathological diagnosis of silicosis: An autopsy population based study. Am J Ind Med 24:427–445, 1993.

81. Begin R, Ostiguy G, Fillion R, et al: Computed tomography scan in the early detection of silicosis. Am Rev Respir Dis 144:697–705, 1991.

82. Marchiori E, Ferreira A, Muller NL: Silicoproteinosis: High-resolution CT and histologic findings. J Thorac Imaging 16:127–129, 2001.

83. Begin R, Ostiguy G, Cantin A, et al: Lung function in silica-exposed workers: A relationship to disease severity assessed by CT scan. Chest 94:539–545, 1988.

84. Bergin CJ, Muller NL, Vedal S, et al: CT in silicosis: Correlation with plain films and pulmonary function tests. AJR Am J Roentgenol 146:477–483, 1986.

85. American Thoracic Society: Targeted tuberculin testing and treatment of latent tuberculosis infection. Am J Respir Crit Care Med 161:S221–S247, 2000.

86. Morgan WK: Industrial bronchitis. Br J Ind Med 35:285–291, 1978.

87. Becklake MR: Chronic airflow limitation: its relationship to work in dusty occupations. Chest 88:608–617, 1985.

88. Coggon D, Newman Taylor A: Coal mining and chronic obstructive pulmonary disease: A review of the evidence. Thorax 53:398–407, 1998.

89. Benedek TG: Rheumatoid pneumoconiosis: Documentation of onset and pathogenic considerations. Am J Med 55:515–524, 1973.

90. McConnochie K, Green FHY, Vallyathan V, et al: Interstitial fibrosis in coal workers—experience in Wales and West Virginia. Ann Occup Hyg 32(Suppl 1):553–560, 1988.

91. Attfield MD, Seixas NS: Prevalence of pneumoconiosis and its relationship to dust exposure in a cohort of U.S. bituminous coal miners and ex-miners. Am J Ind Med 27:137–151, 1995.

92. Begin R, Cantin A, Masse S: Recent advances in the pathogenesis and clinical assessment of mineral dust pneumoconioses: Asbestosis, silicosis and coal pneumoconiosis. Eur Respir J 2:988–1001, 1989.

93. Hurley JF, Burns J, Copland L, et al: Coalworkers' simple pneumoconiosis and exposure to dust at 10 British coalmines. Br J Ind Med 39:120–127, 1982.

93a. Anonymous: Pneumoconiosis prevalence among working coal miners examined in federal chest radiograph surveillance programs—United States, 1996–2002. MMWR Morb Mortal Wkly Rep 52:336–340, 2003.

94. Hurley JF, Alexander WP, Hazledine DJ, et al: Exposure to respirable coalmine dust and incidence of progressive massive fibrosis. Br J Ind Med 44:661–672, 1987.

95. Love RG, Miller BG: Longitudinal study of lung function in coal-miners. Thorax 37:193–197, 1982.

96. Attfield MD: Longitudinal decline in FEV_1 in United States coalminers. Thorax 40:132–137, 1985.

97. Carta P, Aru G, Barbieri MT, et al: Dust exposure, respiratory symptoms, and longitudinal decline of lung function in young coal miners. Occup Environ Med 53:312–319, 1996.

98. Rudd R: Coal miners' respiratory disease litigation. Thorax 53:337–340, 1998.

99. Lapp NL, Hankinson JL, Burgess DB, et al: Changes in ventilatory function in coal miners after a work shift. Arch Environ Health 24:204–208, 1972.

100. Hodgins P, Henneberger PK, Wang ML, et al: Bronchial responsiveness and five-year FEV_1 decline: A study in miners and nonminers. Am J Respir Crit Care Med 157:1390–1396, 1998.

101. Swaen GM, Meijers JM, Slangen JJ: Risk of gastric cancer in pneumoconiotic coal miners and the effect of respiratory impairment. Occup Environ Med 52:606–610, 1995.

102. Ruckley VA, Fernie JM, Chapman JS, et al: Comparison of radiographic appearances with associated pathology and lung dust content in a group of coalworkers. Br J Ind Med 41:459–467, 1984.

103. Vallyathan V, Brower PS, Green FH, et al: Radiographic and pathologic correlation of coal workers' pneumoconiosis. Am J Respir Crit Care Med 154:741–748, 1996.

104. Seaton A: Coalmining, emphysema, and compensation. Br J Ind Med 47:433–435, 1990.

105. Becklake MR, Lalloo U: The 'healthy smoker': A phenomenon of health selection? Respiration 57:137–144, 1990.

106. Becklake MR: The work relatedness of airway dysfunction. *In* Proceedings of the 9th International Conference in Epidemiology in Occupational Health. Washington, DC: National Institute for Occupational Safety and Health, 1994, pp 1–28.

107. Collins HP, Dick JA, Bennett JG, et al: Irregularly shaped small shadows on chest radiographs, dust exposure, and lung function in coalworkers' pneumoconiosis. Br J Ind Med 45:43–55, 1988.

107a. Isidro Montes I, Rego Fernandez G, Reguero J, et al: Respiratory disease in a cohort of 2,579 coal miners followed up over a 20-year period. Chest 126:622–629, 2004.

108. Meijers JM, Swaen GM, Slangen JJ, et al: Long-term mortality in miners with coal workers' pneumoconiosis in the Netherlands: A pilot study. Am J Ind Med 19:43–50, 1991.

109. Becklake MR: Asbestos-related diseases of the lung and other organs: Their epidemiology and implications for clinical practice. Am Rev Respir Dis 114:187–227, 1976.

109a. McCulloch J: Asbestos Blues. Labor, Capital, Physicians and the State in South Africa. Bloomington: Indiana University Press, 2002.

110. Walton WH: Airborne dusts. *In* Liddell D, Miller K (eds): Mineral Fibers and Health. Boca Raton, Fla: CRC Press, 1991, pp 55–78.

111. Bignon J: Health-Related Effects of Phyllosilicates. Berlin: Springer-Verlag, 1990.

112. Churg A: Nonneoplastic asbestos-induced disease. *In* Churg A, Green FHY (eds): Pathology of Occupational Lung Disease (2nd ed). Baltimore: Williams & Wilkins, 1998, pp 277–338.

113. Liddell D, Miller K: Mineral Fibers and Health. Boca Raton, Fla: CRC Press, 1991.

114. Selikoff I, Lee DHK: Asbestos and Disease. New York: Academic Press, 1978.

114a. Takahashi K, Karjalainen A: A cross-country comparative overview of the asbestos situation in ten Asian countries. Int J Occup Environ Health 9:244–248, 2003.

115. Rom WN: Environmental and Occupational Medicine (3rd ed). Philadelphia: Lippincott–Raven, 1998.

116. McDonald JC, McDonald AD: Epidemiology of mesothelioma. *In* Liddell D, Miller K (eds): Mineral Fibers and Health. Boca Raton, Fla: CRC Press, 1991, pp 147–168.

117. Churg A: Neoplastic asbestos-induced disease. *In* Churg A, Green FHY (eds): Pathology of Occupational Lung Disease (2nd ed). Baltimore: Williams & Wilkins, 1998, pp 339–391.

118. Camus M, Siemiatycki J, Meek B: Nonoccupational exposure to chrysotile asbestos and the risk of lung cancer. N Engl J Med 338:1565–1571, 1998.

119. Wagner JC, Sleggs CA, Marchand P: Diffuse pleural mesothelioma and asbestos exposure in the North Western Cape Province. Br J Ind Med 17:260–271, 1960.

120. Zwi AB, Reid G, Landau SP, et al: Mesothelioma in South Africa, 1976–84: Incidence and case characteristics. Int J Epidemiol 18:320–329, 1989.

121. Bignon J, Peto J, Souracci R, et al: Non-occupational Exposure to Mineral Fibers (Scientific Publication No. 90). Lyon, France: International Agency for Research in Cancer, 1989.

121a. Hasanoglu HC, Gokirmak M, Baysal T, et al: Environmental exposure to asbestos in eastern Turkey. Arch Environ Health 58:144–150, 2003.

122. Health Effects Institute, Asbestos Research: Asbestos in Public and Commercial Buildings. Cambridge, Mass: Health Effects Institute, Asbestos Research, 1991.

123. Harber P, Schenker MB, Balmes JR: Occupational and Environmental Respiratory Disease. St. Louis: Mosby, 1995.

124. Copes R, Thomas D, Becklake MR: Temporal patterns of exposure and nonmalignant pulmonary abnormality in Quebec chrysotile workers. Arch Environ Health 40:80–87, 1985.

125. Becklake M: Asbestosis. *In* Liddell D, Miller K (eds): Mineral Fibers and Health. Boca Raton, Fla: CRC Press, 1991, pp 103–119.

126. Begin R, Samet JM, Shaikh RA: Asbestos. *In* Harber, P, Schenker MB, Balmes JR (eds): Occupational and Environmental Respiratory Disease. St. Louis: Mosby, 1995, pp 293–329.

127. Ernst P, Zejda J: Pleural and airway disease associated with mineral fibers. *In* Liddell D, Miller K (eds): Mineral Fibers and Health. Boca Raton, Fla: CRC Press, 1991, pp 121–134.

128. Craighead JE, Abraham JL, Churg A, et al: The pathology of asbestos-associated diseases of the lungs and pleural cavities: Diagnostic criteria and proposed grading schema. Arch Pathol Lab Med 106:544–596, 1982.

129. Case BW, Sebastien P: Environmental and occupational exposures to chrysotile asbestos: A comparative microanalytic study. Arch Environ Health 42:185–191, 1987.

130. Dumortier P, Coplu L, de Maertelaer V, et al: Assessment of environmental asbestos exposure in Turkey by bronchoalveolar lavage. Am J Respir Crit Care Med 158:1815–1824, 1998.

131. De Vuyst P, Gevenois PA: Asbestosis. *In* Hendrick DJ, Burge PS, Beckett WS, et al. (eds): Occupational Disorders of the Lung. London: WB Saunders, 2002, pp 143–162.

132. Becklake MR: Occupational lung disease—past record and future trend using the asbestos case as an example. Clin Invest Med 6:305–317, 1983.

133. Wright JL, Cagle P, Churg A, et al: Diseases of the small airways. Am Rev Respir Dis 146:240–262, 1992.

134. Craighead JE: Diseases associated with exposure to silica and nonfibrous silicate minerals. Arch Pathol Lab Med 112:673–720, 1988.

135. Green FH, Harley R, Vallyathan V, et al: Exposure and mineralogical correlates of pulmonary fibrosis in chrysotile asbestos workers. Occup Environ Med 54:549–559, 1997.

135a. Anonymous: Changing patterns of pneumoconiosis mortality—United States, 1968–2000. MMWR Morb Mortal Wkly Rep 53:627–632, 2004.

136. Meredith SK, Taylor VM, McDonald JC: Occupational respiratory disease in the United Kingdom 1989: A report to the British Thoracic Society and the Society of Occupational Medicine by the SWORD project group. Br J Ind Med 48:292–298, 1991.

137. Provencher S, Labreche FP, De Guire L: Physician based surveillance system for occupational respiratory diseases: The experience of PROPULSE, Quebec, Canada. Occup Environ Med 54:272–276, 1997.

138. Becklake MR, Liddell FD, Manfreda J, et al: Radiological changes after withdrawal from asbestos exposure. Br J Ind Med 36:23–28, 1979.

139. Putnam EA, Schwanke C, Groves A, et al: Investigations of genetic susceptibility to asbestos-related disease. Am J Respir Crit Care Med 167:A580, 2003.

140. Blanc PD, Gamsu G: Cigarette smoking and pneumoconiosis: Structuring the debate. Am J Ind Med 16:1–4, 1989.

141. Becklake MR, Case BW: Fiber burden and asbestos-related lung disease: Determinants of dose-response relationships. Am J Respir Crit Care Med 150:1488–1492, 1994.

142. Huuskonen MS: Clinical features, mortality and survival of patients with asbestosis. Scand J Work Environ Health 4:265–274, 1978.

143. American Thoracic Society: The diagnosis of non-malignant diseases related to asbestos exposure. Am Rev Respir Dis 134:363–368, 1986.

144. Gamsu G, Aberle DR, Lynch D: Computed tomography in the diagnosis of asbestos-related thoracic disease. J Thorac Imaging 4:61–67, 1989.

145. Muller NL, Miller RR: Computed tomography of chronic diffuse infiltrative lung disease. Part 2. Am Rev Respir Dis 142:1440–1448, 1990.

146. Miller A, Lilis R, Godbold J, et al: Relationship of pulmonary function to radiographic interstitial fibrosis in 2,611 long-term asbestos insulators: An assessment of the International Labour Office profusion score. Am Rev Respir Dis 145:263–270, 1992.

147. Jones RN: The diagnosis of asbestosis. Am Rev Respir Dis 144:477–478, 1991.

147a. American Thoracic Society: Diagnosis and initial management of nonmalignant diseases related to asbestos. Am J Respir Crit Care Med 170:691–715, 2004.

148. De Vuyst P, Dumortier P, Moulin E, et al: Diagnostic value of asbestos bodies in bronchoalveolar lavage fluid. Am Rev Respir Dis 136:1219–1224, 1987.

148a. Dumortier P, Thimpont J, de Maertelaer V, De Vuyst P: Trends in asbestos body counts in bronchoalveolar lavage fluid over two decades. Eur Respir J 22:519–524, 2003.

149. Hughes JM: Epidemiology of lung cancer in relation to asbestos exposure. *In* Liddell D, Miller K (eds): Mineral Fibers and Health. Boca Raton, Fla: CRC Press, 1991, pp 136–145.

150. International Agency for Research in Cancer: Monographs on the Evaluation of Carcinogenic Risk of Chemicals to Man: Asbestos. Lyon, France: International Agency for Research in Cancer, 1977.

151. Segarra-Obiol F, Lopez-Ibanez P, Perez Nicolas J: Asbestosis and tuberculosis. Am J Ind Med 4:755–757, 1983.

152. Gloyne SR: Pneumoconiosis: A histological survey of necropsy material in 1205 cases. Lancet 1:820–817, 1951.

153. Becklake MR: Asbestos-related diseases of the lungs and pleura: Current clinical issues. Am Rev Respir Dis 126:187–194, 1982.

154. Mollo F, Magnani C, Bo P, et al: The attribution of lung cancers to asbestos exposure: A pathologic study of 924 unselected cases. Am J Clin Pathol 117:90–95, 2002.

155. Finkelstein MM: Radiographic asbestosis is not a prerequisite for asbestos-associated lung cancer in Ontario asbestos-cement workers. Am J Ind Med 32:341–348, 1997.

156. Nelson HH, Christiani DC, Wiencke JK, et al: k-Ras mutation and occupational asbestos exposure in lung adenocarcinoma: Asbestos-related cancer without asbestosis. Cancer Res 59:4570–4573, 1999.

157. Egilman D, Reinert A: Lung cancer and asbestos exposure: Asbestosis is not necessary. Am J Ind Med 30:398–406, 1996.

158. Gong NM, Christiani D: Lung cancer. *In* Hendrick DJ, Burge PS, Beckett WS, et al (eds): Occupational Disorders of the Lung. London: WB Saunders, 2002, pp 305–326.

159. Liddell FD, Armstrong BG: The combination of effects on lung cancer of cigarette smoking and exposure in Quebec chrysotile miners and millers. Ann Occup Hyg 46:5–13, 2002.

160. International Agency for Research in Cancer: Mechanisms of Fiber Carcinogenesis (Scientific Publication No. 140). Lyon, France: International Agency for Research in Cancer, 1996.

161. Erren TC, Jacobsen M, Piekarski C: Synergy between asbestos and smoking on lung cancer risks. Epidemiology 10:405–411, 1999.

162. McDonald JC, McDonald AD: Chrysotile, tremolite and carcinogenicity. Ann Occup Hyg 41:699–705, 1997.

163. Kayser K, Becker C, Seeberg N, et al: Quantitation of asbestos and asbestos-like fibers in human lung tissue by hot and wet ashing, and the significance of their presence for survival of lung carcinoma and mesothelioma patients. Lung Cancer 24:89–98, 1999.

164. Constantopoulos SH, Dalavanga YA, Sakellariou K, et al: Lymphocytic alveolitis and pleural calcifications in nonoccupational asbestos exposure: Protection against neoplasia? Am Rev Respir Dis 146:1565–1570, 1992.

165. Bourbeau J, Ernst P, Chrome J, et al: The relationship between respiratory impairment and asbestos-related pleural abnormality in an active work force. Am Rev Respir Dis 142:837–842, 1990.

166. Meyer JD, Holt DL, Chen Y, et al: SWORD '99: Surveillance of work-related and occupational respiratory disease in the UK. Occup Med (Lond) 51:204–208, 2001.

167. Hillerdal G: Pleural plaques and risk for bronchial carcinoma and mesothelioma: A prospective study. Chest 105:144–150, 1994.

168. Stephens M, Gibbs AR, Pooley FD, et al: Asbestos induced diffuse pleural fibrosis: Pathology and mineralogy. Thorax 42:583–588, 1987.

169. Kilburn KH, Warshaw R: Pulmonary functional impairment associated with pleural asbestos disease: Circumscribed and diffuse thickening. Chest 98:965–972, 1990.

170. Miller A, Teirstein AS, Selikoff IJ: Ventilatory failure due to asbestos pleurisy. Am J Med 75:911–919, 1983.

171. Hillerdal G, Ozesmi M: Benign asbestos pleural effusion: 73 exudates in 60 patients. Eur J Respir Dis 71:113–121, 1987.

172. LaDou J, Landrigan P, Bailar JC 3rd, et al: A call for an international ban on asbestos. Public Health Rev 29:241–246, 2001.

173. Siemiatycki J: Should Canadian health care professionals support the call for a worldwide ban on asbestos? CMAJ 164:495–497, 2001.

174. Camus M: A ban on asbestos must be based on a comparative risk assessment. CMAJ 164:491–494, 2001.

175. Marsh GM, Buchanich JM, Youk AO: Historical cohort study of US man-made vitreous fiber production workers: VI. Respiratory system cancer standardized mortality ratios adjusted for the confounding effect of cigarette smoking. J Occup Environ Med 43:803–808, 2001.

176. Marsh GM, Gula MJ, Youk AO, et al: Historical cohort study of US man-made vitreous fiber production workers: II. Mortality from mesothelioma. J Occup Environ Med 43:757–766, 2001.

177. Boffetta P, Andersen A, Hansen J, et al: Cancer incidence among European man-made vitreous fiber production workers. Scand J Work Environ Health 25:222–226, 1999.

178. Becklake MR, Thomas D, Liddell F, et al: Follow-up respiratory measurements in Quebec chrysotile asbestos miners and millers. Scand J Work Environ Health 8:105–110, 1982.

179. Walker AM: Declining relative risks for lung cancer after cessation of asbestos exposure. J Occup Med 26:422–426, 1984.

180. Peto J, Hodgson JT, Matthews FE, et al: Continuing increase in mesothelioma mortality in Britain. Lancet 345:535–539, 1995.

181. Hilliard AK, Lovett JK, McGavin CR: The rise and fall in incidence of malignant mesothelioma from a British Naval Dockyard, 1979–1999. Occup Med (Lond) 53:209–212, 2003.

182. Hemminki K, Li X: Mesothelioma incidence seems to have leveled off in Sweden. Int J Cancer 103:145–146, 2003.

183. Segura O, Burdorf A, Looman C: Update of predictions of mortality from pleural mesothelioma in the Netherlands. Occup Environ Med 60:50–55, 2003.

184. Green F, Churg A: Diseases due to nonasbestos silicates. *In* Churg A, Green FHY (eds): Pathology of Occupational Lung Disease (2nd ed). Baltimore: Williams & Wilkins, 1998, pp 235–276.

185. Cullinan P, McDonald JC: Respiratory disease from occupational exposure to nonfibrous mineral silicates. *In* Bignon J (ed): The Health-Related Effects of Phyllosilicates. Berlin: Springer-Verlag, 1990, pp 161–178.

186. Szadkowska-Stanczyk I, Szymczak W: Nested case-control study of lung cancer among pulp and paper workers in

relation to exposure to dusts. Am J Ind Med 39:547–556, 2001.

187. Wegman DH, Peters JM, Boundy MG, et al: Evaluation of respiratory effects in miners and millers exposed to talc free of asbestos and silica. Br J Ind Med 39:233–238, 1982.

187a. Coggiola M, Bosio D, Pira E, et al: An update of a mortality study of talc miners and millers in Italy. Am J Ind Med 44:63–69, 2003.

188. Landas SK, Schwartz DA:. Mica-associated pulmonary interstitial fibrosis. Am Rev Respir Dis 144:718–721, 1991.

189. Hessel PA, Sluis-Cremer GK: X-ray findings, lung function, and respiratory symptoms in black South African vermiculite workers. Am J Ind Med 15:21–29, 1989.

190. McDonald JC, McDonald AD, Sebastien P, et al: Health of vermiculite miners exposed to trace amounts of fibrous tremolite. Br J Ind Med 45:630–634, 1988.

190a. Howard TP: Pneumoconiosis in a vermiculite end-product user. Am J Ind Med 44:214–217, 2003.

191. De Vuyst P, Dumortier P, Swaen GM, et al: Respiratory health effects of man-made vitreous (mineral) fibres. Eur Respir J 8:2149–2173, 1995.

192. Trethowan WN, Burge PS, Rossiter CE, et al: Study of the respiratory health of employees in seven European plants that manufacture ceramic fibres. Occup Environ Med 52:97–104, 1995.

193. Utell MJ, Lockey JE: Disorders due to manmade vitreous fibers. In Hendrick DJ, Burge PS, Beckett WS, et al. (eds): Occupational Disorders of the Lung. London: WB Saunders, 2002, pp 191–199.

193a. Stone RA, Youk AO, Marsh GM, et al: Historical cohort study of U.S. man-made vitreous fiber production workers IX: summary of 1992 mortality follow up and analysis of respiratory system cancer among female workers. J Occup Environ Med 46:55–67, 2004.

194. Mapel D, Coultas D: Disorders due to minerals other than silica, coal, and asbestos, and to metals. In Hendrick DJ, Burge PS, Beckett WS, et al. (eds): Occupational Disorders of the Lung. London: WB Saunders, 2002, pp 163–190.

195. Phibbs BP, Sundin RE, Mitchell RS: Silicosis in Wyoming bentonite workers. Am Rev Respir Dis 103:1–17, 1971.

196. Kriebel D, Brain JD, Sprince NL, et al: The pulmonary toxicity of beryllium. Am Rev Respir Dis 137:464–473, 1988.

197. Kreiss K, Mroz MM, Zhen B, et al: Risks of beryllium disease related to work processes at a metal, alloy, and oxide production plant. Occup Environ Med 54:605–612, 1997.

198. Williams WJ: United Kingdom Beryllium Registry: Mortality and autopsy study. Environ Health Perspect 104S:949–951, 1996.

199. Hardy HL: Beryllium disease: A clinical perspective. Environ Res 21:1–9, 1980.

200. Newman LS, Kreiss K: Nonoccupational beryllium disease masquerading as sarcoidosis: Identification by blood lymphocyte proliferative response to beryllium. Am Rev Respir Dis 145:1212–1214, 1992.

201. Sanderson WT, Henneberger PK, Martyny J, et al: Beryllium contamination inside vehicles of machine shop workers. Am J Ind Med Sep(Suppl 1):72–74, 1999.

202. Richeldi L, Kreiss K, Mroz MM, et al: Interaction of genetic and exposure factors in the prevalence of berylliosis. Am J Ind Med 32:337–340, 1997.

203. Kreiss K, Newman LS, Mroz MM, et al: Screening blood test identifies subclinical beryllium disease. J Occup Med 31:603–608, 1989.

204. Kreiss K, Mroz MM, Newman LS, et al: Machining risk of beryllium disease and sensitization with median exposures below 2 micrograms/m³. Am J Ind Med 30:16–25, 1996.

205. Anonymous: Meeting of the IARC working group on beryllium, cadmium, mercury and exposures in the glass manufacturing industry. Scand J Work Environ Health 19:360–363, 1993.

206. Cullen MR, Kominsky JR, Rossman MD, et al: Chronic beryllium disease in a precious metal refinery: Clinical epidemiologic and immunologic evidence for continuing risk from exposure to low level beryllium fume. Am Rev Respir Dis 135:201–208, 1987.

207. Newman LS, Kreiss K, King TE Jr, et al: Pathologic and immunologic alterations in early stages of beryllium disease: Re-examination of disease definition and natural history. Am Rev Respir Dis 139:1479–1486, 1989.

208. Freiman DG, Hardy HL: Beryllium disease: The relation of pulmonary pathology to clinical course and prognosis based on a study of 130 cases from the U.S. beryllium case registry. Hum Pathol 1:25–44, 1970.

208a. Fireman E, Haimsky E, Noiderfer M, et al: Misdiagnosis of sarcoidosis in patients with chronic beryllium disease. Sarcoidosis Vasc Diffuse Lung Dis 20:144–148, 2003.

209. Balmes JR: Respiratory effects of hard-metal dust exposure. Occup Med 2:327–344, 1987.

210. Lison D, Lauwerys R, Demedts M, et al: Experimental research into the pathogenesis of cobalt/hard metal lung disease. Eur Respir J 9:1024–1028, 1996.

211. Potolicchio I, Mosconi G, Forni A, et al: Susceptibility to hard metal lung disease is strongly associated with the presence of glutamate 69 in HLA-DP beta chain. Eur J Immunol 27:2741–2743, 1997.

212. Moulin JJ, Wild P, Romazini S, et al: Lung cancer risk in hard-metal workers. Am J Epidemiol 148:241–248, 1998.

213. Auchincloss JH, Abraham JL, Gilbert R, et al: Health hazard of poorly regulated exposure during manufacture of cemented tungsten carbides and cobalt. Br J Ind Med 49:832–836, 1992.

214. Della Torre F, Cassani M, Segale M, et al: Trace metal lung diseases: A new fatal case of hard metal pneumoconiosis. Respiration 57:248–253, 1990.

215. Durand P, Begin R, Samson L, et al: Silicon carbide pneumoconiosis: A radiographic assessment. Am J Ind Med 20:37–47, 1991.

216. Begin R, Dufresne A, Cantin A, et al: Carborundum pneumoconiosis: Fibers in the mineral activate macrophages to produce fibroblast growth factors and sustain the chronic inflammatory disease. Chest 95:842–849, 1989.

217. Marcer G, Bernardi G, Bartolucci GB, et al: Pulmonary impairment in workers exposed to silicon carbide. Br J Ind Med 49:489–493, 1992.

218. Masse S, Begin R, Cantin A: Pathology of silicon carbide pneumoconiosis. Mod Pathol 1:104–108, 1988.

219. Boag AH, Colby TV, Fraire AE, et al: The pathology of interstitial lung disease in nylon flock workers. Am J Surg Pathol 23:1539–1545, 1999.

220. Eschenbacher WL, Kreiss K, Lougheed MD, et al: Nylon flock-associated interstitial lung disease. Am J Respir Crit Care Med 159:2003–2008, 1999.

221. Kern DG, Crausman RS, Durand KT, et al: Flock worker's lung: Chronic interstitial lung disease in the nylon flocking industry. Ann Intern Med 129:261–272, 1998.

222. Anonymous: Chronic interstitial lung disease in nylon flocking industry workers—Rhode Island, 1992–1996. MMWR Morb Mortal Wkly Rep 46:897–901, 1997.

223. Ramazzini B, Wright WC: De morbis artificium diatriba (Diseases of Workers: The Latin Text of 1733) (rev; WC Wright, transl). Chicago: University of Chicago Press, 1940.

62 Hypersensitivity Pneumonitis

Cecile S. Rose, M.D., M.P.H.

INTRODUCTION

Hypersensitivity pneumonitis (HP), also known as extrinsic allergic alveolitis, constitutes a spectrum of granulomatous, interstitial, bronchiolar, and alveolar-filling lung diseases resulting from repeated inhalation of and sensitization to a wide variety of organic aerosols and low-molecular-weight chemical antigens. HP was considered a rare disease, but increasing recognition of the ubiquity of environmental antigens, more sensitive diagnostic tools, and recent epidemiologic analyses using national disease registries have shown that HP is the most frequently occurring interstitial lung disease after sarcoidosis and idiopathic pulmonary fibrosis.[1]

The nature of the inhaled antigen, the circumstances of exposure, and the immunologic reactivity of the host all contribute to the risk for HP. Disease is characterized by a lymphocytic alveolitis and granulomatous pneumonitis, usually with improvement or complete recovery if antigen exposure ceases. Continued antigen exposure commonly leads to progressive interstitial fibrosis. No single historical or clinical feature is pathognomonic for HP. Rather, diagnosis relies on a strong index of suspicion and a constellation of clinical findings. When the diagnosis is suspected, the clinician must undertake appropriate clinical assessment and exposure control to prevent progressive, irreversible lung damage.

ETIOLOGY

The list of specific agents that cause HP is lengthy, and new exposure circumstances and disease entities continue to be described. The three major categories of antigens causing HP are microbial agents (bacteria, fungi and their components), animal proteins, and low-molecular-weight chemicals (Table 62.1). Recent investigations suggest that some exposures causing HP are complex mixtures and that disease is not always attributable to a single antigen.[2] A case of HP following anthrax vaccination has been described, though such occurrences appear to be rare.[3] Increasing numbers of pharmacologic agents have been shown to cause hypersensitivity reactions in the lung, but these are beyond the scope of this chapter and are covered under the subject of drug-induced lung diseases (see Chapter 67).

MICROBIAL AGENTS

Microbial organisms, including bacteria and fungi, are the most commonly recognized causes of HP. Microbial contaminants are common in indoor environments and probably cause many more cases of HP than are recognized clinically. Warm, moist environments often provide ideal circumstances for the amplification and proliferation of microbial antigens that, if disseminated and inhaled, can cause sensitizing lung disease.

Bacteria

Bacteria are unicellular prokaryotic organisms with cell membranes but no organized nuclei or membrane-bound organelles. Most bacteria take the form of rods (bacilli), spheres (cocci), or branched filaments (actinomycetes), and are generally 1 to 5 μm in diameter. Bacteria have adapted to a wide variety of ecologic habitats and segregate under

Table 62.1 Etiologic Categories of Hypersensitivity Pneumonitis, with Examples

Etiologic Category	Examples
Microbial Agents	
Bacteria	Thermophilic actinomyces, *Bacillus subtilis, Klebsiella, Epicoccum nigrum,* nontuberculous mycobacteria
Fungi	*Aspergillus, Penicillium, Cladosporium, Trichosporon, Alternaria, Aureobasidium, Cephalosporium* species
Animal Proteins	Avian, fish meal, rat urine, mollusk shell, wheat weevil, silkworm larvae
Chemical Sensitizers	Isocyanates, acid anhydrides, pyrethrum, Pauli's reagent (sodium diazobenzene sulfate)

different physical and chemical conditions in indoor and outdoor environments.

Thermophilic actinomycetes, including *Saccharopolyspora rectivirgula* (formerly *Micropolyspora faeni*) and the *Thermoactinomyces* species *vulgaris, sacchari, viridis,* and *candidus,* are associated causally with the prototypical example of HP, farmer's lung disease (FLD), first described by Campbell in 1932.[4] These bacteria thrive at 50° C to 55° C and in moist conditions, and secrete enzymes that cause decay of vegetable matter such as hay (FLD), sugar cane (bagassosis), and mushroom compost ("mushroom worker's lung").[5,6] They may be found contaminating ventilation and humidification systems ("humidifier lung") where temperatures reach 60° C and stagnant water is present.[7]

Indoor bacteria that prefer lower temperatures also can cause HP. An outbreak of *Bacillus subtilis* alveolitis occurred in six family members exposed during renovation to contaminated wood dust from bathroom flooring.[8,9] HP due to contamination of humidifiers has been associated with several gram-negative bacteria, including *Klebsiella* species and *Cytophaga* endotoxin.[10] Two children developed HP after exposure to an unventilated basement shower contaminated with the bacterium *Epicoccum nigrum.*[11] In addition to gram-negative bacteria themselves, endotoxins contained in their cell walls stimulate the cytokines tumor necrosis factor-α and interleukin-1 and may act as adjuvants, enhancing the inflammatory events leading to alveolitis and granuloma formation.[12]

A spectrum of occupational respiratory diseases including HP occurs with exposure to metalworking fluids. Risk for illness exists where water-based fluids are used and unusual microbial contaminants (probably nontuberculous mycobacteria or fungi) predominate.[13] Recreational as well as occupational exposures to bacterially contaminated water aerosols can cause HP. Nontuberculous mycobacteria contaminating hot tubs cause a granulomatous lung disease with features of HP that may resolve simply with removal from exposure.[14,15] Bacteria contained in water aerosols were associated with an outbreak of granulomatous pneumonitis called "lifeguard lung" affecting 33 lifeguards at an indoor swimming pool, with increased levels of airborne endotoxin in comparison with unaffected indoor pools.[16]

Fungi

Fungi are nonmotile, eukaryotic organisms that have rigid cell walls, lack chlorophyll, and reproduce by means of spores, most of which are designed for airborne transport (disseminators). Fungal spores germinate to produce morphologically diverse forms, including molds and yeasts. Molds are branching hyphal filaments; yeasts are round, oval, or elongated single cells that reproduce mostly by budding and form moist or mucoid colonies. The cell walls of fungi contain polysaccharides (including glucan and chitin) and glycoproteins. Many components of fungi are capable of becoming airborne and acting as antigen sources, including fungal spores, mycelial fragments, metabolites and partially degraded substrates, and fungal toxins.[17]

Fungal spore content in air comes mainly from species adapted to using wind energy for dispersal. The particular species and concentration in air at any given time depend on prevailing winds, temperature, seasonal climatologic factors, circadian patterns of sunlight and darkness, degree of precipitation, availability of substrates, and extent of substrate and atmospheric moisture content. The indoor pattern of fungal spores reflects both the outdoor spore composition and indoor fungal flora dominated by the Deuteromycetes, including *Penicillium, Aspergillus, Rhizopus, Mucor,* and yeasts. Among the interior sites for mold growth are garbage containers, food storage areas, wallpaper, upholstery, areas of increased moisture such as shower curtains, window moldings, window air conditioners, damp basements, and emissions from cool mist vaporizers.[18–23] Saunas, hot tubs, and even tap water also may become contaminated with microorganisms capable of causing hypersensitivity lung disease.[24–26]

Many fungal species have been associated causally with hypersensitivity lung diseases in a wide variety of occupational and environmental circumstances. The respirable conidia of *Aspergillus* species are ubiquitous in nature and commonly found in water, soil, and organic debris. A variety of *Aspergillus* species have been associated with HP in persons with diverse occupations, including soy sauce brewers, bird breeders, farmers, and compost, sawmill, mushroom, greenhouse, tobacco, cane mill, grain, and brewery workers,[27–31] and in those exposed to contaminated esparto grass used in the production of ropes, canvas, sandals, mats, baskets, and paper paste.[32] Similarly, a number of *Penicillium* species have been associated with HP, producing illness in cork workers (*P. frequentans*), cheese workers (*P. casei, P. roqueforti*), laboratory workers, farmers, and tree cutters.[33–37] *Penicillium citreonigrum* and *Monocillium* species contaminating peat moss were associated with cases of HP among workers in a peat moss processing plant.[38] Fatal HP in three Canadian farmers was traced to *P. brevicompactum* and *P. olivicolor* contaminating agricultural dusts.[39] *Alternaria, Cladosporium, Aureobasidium,* and many other fungal species can cause HP. For example, mixed fungal contaminants in wood dust, bark, and chips have caused HP in sawmill workers, tree cutters, and other wood handlers.[40–42]

Fungal antigens often are implicated in HP cases associated with microbial contamination in homes. Summer-type hypersensitivity pneumonitis, the most prevalent form of HP in Japan, is caused by seasonal mold contamination (mainly *Trichosporon asahii*, formerly *T. cutaneum* serotype II) in the home environment.[43] Domestic fungal exposure associated with decaying wood and damp walls in inner city dwellings is the most common cause of HP in Australia.[27] Multiple fungal species were identified in the homes of individuals with disease, including *Serpula lacrymans*, *Geotrichum candidum*, *Penicillium* species, *Alternaria tenuis*, *Fusarium solani*, and *Aspergillus* species. Similarly, *Rhodotorula* species, along with *Aspergillus* and *Candida* species, were implicated in a case of HP from a contaminated home ultrasonic humidifier.[44] These and other investigations suggest that sensitizing microbial exposures may be complex mixtures and that HP may not always be attributable to a single, well-defined antigen.

ANIMAL PROTEINS

Particulates from a variety of animal sources can cause HP, with exposure to birds the most clinically important and well-recognized form. HP from exposure to avian antigens, referred to as bird breeder's or bird fancier's lung, was first described by Plessner in 1960.[45] Avian antigens have been demonstrated in the feathers, droppings, and serum of turkeys, chickens, geese, ducks, parakeets, parrots, budgerigars, pigeons, doves, love birds, canaries, and even native birds and are highly immunogenic.[46,47] Highest exposures are associated with cleaning out bird lofts, cages, and coops. Bird breeder's lung is the more common form of HP in Great Britain, where approximately 12% of the general population keep budgerigars as pets.[48]

Animal handlers, such as laboratory workers, are at risk for HP from exposure to inhaled animal proteins (including rats and gerbils) in pelts, serum, and excreta.[49,50] Inhalation of grain infested with the wheat weevil *Sitophilus granarius* can cause a form of HP known as "miller's lung."[51] Sericulturists engaged in silk production can develop HP from exposure to larval secretions and cocoon particulates.[52] The dust from mollusk shells cut and polished to make buttons may cause HP in production workers.[53]

CHEMICAL SENSITIZERS

The chemical-induced forms of HP are probably less common than are microbial- and animal protein–induced cases, although some of the inorganic antigens that can cause disease are common in industry.

Isocyanates are used widely for large-scale production of polyurethane polymers in the manufacture of flexible and rigid foams, elastomers, adhesives, and surface coatings. Isocyanates, including toluene diisocyanate (TDI), diphenylmethane diisocyanate (MDI), hexamethylene diisocyanate (HDI), and 1,5-naphthalene diisocyanate (NDI), can cause HP (occasionally accompanied by pulmonary hemorrhage) in addition to the more common occupational asthma associated with their exposure.[54–56] Exposure to isocyanate prepolymers (having lower vapor pressures and thus believed to pose a lower risk of sensitization than the diisocyanates) was shown to induce an acute HP-like reaction among workers in automobile parts manufacturing.[57] Specific immunoglobulin (Ig) G antibodies to isocyanates have been detected in the serum and bronchoalveolar lavage (BAL) fluid of affected workers,[58,59] with a CD8+-predominant T-lymphocyte alveolitis.

Trimellitic anhydride, used in plastics, paints, and resins, has been associated with an HP-like syndrome often accompanied by anemia.[60] Trimellitic anhydride appears to act as a hapten, combining with endogenous proteins to create new antigenic determinants capable of eliciting IgE or IgG responses. Phthalic anhydride emitted from heated epoxy resin or contained in epoxy paints can cause HP.[61] Rare case reports of HP have been described from exposure to the pesticide pyrethrum; from Pauli's reagent (sodium diazobenzene sulfate), used in chromatography; and from copper sulfate, used in Bordeaux mixture to spray vineyards.[62–64]

EPIDEMIOLOGY

The worldwide prevalence of HP is unknown. Most of the population-based studies of HP focus on the prevalence of illness among agricultural workers. Using a questionnaire survey, Grant and coworkers[65] found the prevalence of FLD in three agricultural areas in Scotland to range from 2.3% to 8.6%. A questionnaire survey of western Wyoming dairy and cattle ranchers elicited a history typical of acute FLD in 3% of those surveyed.[66] A study of Wisconsin farmers described a disease prevalence of 9% to 12% in men exposed to moldy hay.[67] A cross-sectional respiratory morbidity survey of mushroom farm workers found that 20% of the heavily exposed workers reported symptoms consistent with mushroom worker's lung.[30] In Finland, data on clinically confirmed FLD showed a mean annual incidence rate of 44 per 100,000 persons in farming,[68] similar to the rate reported in Sweden of 23 per 100,000. Not surprisingly, HP symptom prevalence rates among agricultural workers are substantially higher than disease prevalence rates based on clinically confirmed cases, which reflects the challenges of HP diagnosis. Similarly, reports of disease outbreaks in microbially contaminated office buildings have described widely varying but usually low attack rates, although in some reports up to 70% of exposed individuals are affected.[69]

The prevalence of HP among bird hobbyists is estimated to range between 0.5% and 21% and probably varies depending on exposure circumstances.[70] A cross-sectional study of nacre button workers found a 23% prevalence of mollusk shell HP.[71] Prevalence data for HP associated with exposure to animal proteins is less variable than for the microbially induced hypersensitivity pneumonitides, probably because the measurement of serum precipitins is more reliable in these settings for case confirmation.

Fewer data exist on the prevalence of HP in workers exposed to chemical antigens. Using specific inhalation challenge, Vandenplas and coworkers[72] detected MDI-induced HP in 8 (4.7%) of 167 workers employed in a wood chipboard manufacturing plant. Interestingly, only one of the eight workers worked continuously near the source of MDI, indicating that intermittent exposures can lead to illness. Affected subjects were identified through workers' compensation claims, undoubtedly underestimating the actual prevalence of HP in the plant.

Reported disease prevalence and attack rates vary widely and depend on the populations studied, the nature and intensity of antigen exposure, the case definition chosen, and host factors that are poorly understood. However, epidemiologic studies of agricultural workers and bird fanciers suggest that HP may be quite common in some high-risk occupational settings.

OCCUPATIONAL AND ENVIRONMENTAL EXPOSURES

Although acute symptoms often are attributed to intense, intermittent antigen exposure and chronic forms of HP are thought to result from lower level, more prolonged exposure, the paucity of environmental exposure data provides little insight into dose-response relationships. Understanding of these relationships is further complicated by the fact that the latency period between initial exposure to an environmental antigen and onset of HP symptoms may vary from a few weeks to years.

Environmental risk factors, including antigen concentration, duration of exposure before onset of symptoms, frequency and intermittency of exposure, particle size, antigen solubility, use of respiratory protection, and variability in work practices, may influence disease prevalence, latency, and severity. FLD is most common in late winter, when stored hay is used to feed cattle, and in regions with heavy rainfall and harsh winter conditions, where feed is likely to become damp and therefore an ideal substrate for microbial proliferation. Summer-type HP in Japan,[73] and more recently described in Korea,[74] is characterized by recurrent seasonal symptoms, familial occurrence of cases, and symptom provocation on occupancy of homes containing *Trichosporon*-contaminated damp and decayed wood and woven straw tatami mats. Bird breeder's lung often occurs in late summer, associated with the sporting season, or in autumn when pigeons moult, shedding feather dust (bloom).[75] Thus, the most common forms of HP show both seasonal and geographic variation in incidence.

Indirect and apparently trivial antigen exposures can be important in the risk for avian antigen–induced HP. The illness developed in two spouses of pigeon hobbyists, one exposed to her husband's dusty coveralls and the other to a room adjacent to the pigeons.[76] A duvet containing goose feathers was a source of avian antigen–induced HP, and down comforters and pillows can create similar exposure risks.[77] Feathers used for making fishing lures and those contained in decorative wreaths have been associated with cases of HP.[78,79] These findings suggest that avian antigens are extremely potent inducers of immunologic lung disease, and a careful search for their presence must be included in the history taking of patients with suspected HP.

HOST FACTORS

Although many people are exposed to environmental antigens associated with HP, and some develop serum antibodies or BAL lymphocytosis, or both, fewer manifest

disease. This suggests that unique host susceptibility or resistance influences individual responses to inhaled antigen. Early studies of human leukocyte antigen haplotypes in patients with either FLD or bird fancier's HP showed no clear association of disease with a specific histocompatibility locus.[80,81] More recent investigations suggest that polymorphisms in tumor necrosis factor-α are associated with a genetic predisposition for FLD and bird breeder's lung.[82,83]

A number of studies have shown that HP occurs more frequently in nonsmokers than in smokers; the mechanisms for this effect are not known.[84,85] Pigeon fanciers who smoked had a lower incidence of precipitating antibodies to pigeon antigens and lower serum IgG and IgA antibodies to pigeon proteins in enzyme-linked immunosorbent assay in comparison with nonsmoking and ex-smoking pigeon fanciers, which suggests that cigarette smoking depresses both T-cell–independent and T-cell–dependent responses to inhaled antigens.[85] Smokers with FLD had more frequent illness recurrence, were more likely to have insidious than acute symptoms, had lower percent predicted vital capacities, and had poorer 10-year survival in comparison with nonsmokers with FLD.[86] Thus, although HP appears to occur more commonly in nonsmokers, prognosis is poorer in those who smoke, which underlines the importance of smoking cessation or avoidance in those with disease.

HP can occur in infants and children, most commonly from exposure to birds and also from inhalation of microbial aerosols. In a study of five children with bird breeder's lung, Stiehm and coworkers[87] found that children are more likely to present with the subacute or chronic forms of HP than with acute illness. Microbial antigen exposures are described in several case reports of childhood HP.[88,89] HP should be considered in the differential diagnosis of children with recurrent febrile respiratory illnesses and in those with unexplained interstitial lung disease, and parents should be questioned carefully regarding potential antigen exposures in the home and school.

Pregnancy and delivery appear to trigger symptoms and overt illness in women with bird breeder's lung, but the associated hormonal and immunologic changes are not understood.[90]

IMMUNOPATHOGENESIS

Despite a rich scientific literature, the complex immunopathogenesis of HP remains incompletely defined. Requirements for disease development include (1) repeated antigen exposure; (2) immunologic sensitization of the host to the antigen; and (3) immune-mediated damage to the lung. The immune inflammation resulting in lymphocytic alveolitis, granulomatous pneumonitis, and, in some cases, fibrosis appears to involve a combination of immune complex–mediated, humoral, and, most importantly, cell-mediated or delayed (type IV) immune reactions to inhaled antigen.[90a]

A cascade of cellular and humoral events characterize HP in its acute, subacute, and chronic forms. After inhalation, soluble antigens bind IgG antibody, immune complexes initiate the complement cascade, and macrophage activation occurs.[91] These macrophages secrete chemokines (including interleukin-8, regulated on activation normal T cell expressed and secreted [RANTES], and macrophage inflammatory protein-1α) and cytokines (including interleukin-1 and tumor necrosis factor-α) that first attract neutrophils and later attract and activate circulating T lymphocytes and monocytes. Studies using BAL show that, within the first 48 hours after exposure of a sensitized host to the antigen, there is an immediate influx of neutrophils,[92] probably stimulated by formation of intra-airway immune complexes, activation of the alternative complement pathway, or endotoxin effects of the inhaled antigen.[93,94] Several days later, the local immune response shifts to a T-lymphocyte–predominant alveolitis, often with 60% to 70% lymphocytes.[95] Cellular redistribution from peripheral blood to lung, in situ lymphocyte proliferation, and decreased apoptosis of lung lymphocytes contribute to the increased number of lung T cells.[96] Natural killer cells also are increased in BAL fluid from patients with HP in comparison with nonsmokers and with those with sarcoidosis.[97] Mast cell numbers are increased in BAL fluid after antigen exposure, returning to the normal range within 1 to 3 months after removal from exposure. Mast cells in HP are predominantly of the connective tissue type, and may play a role in the fibrosis seen in advanced or chronic HP.[98] A mild BAL neutrophilia (8% to 10%) may persist, and there appears to be an increase in lung tissue neutrophils in patients with subacute or chronic HP at risk for fibrosis.[99,100]

Examination of BAL lymphocyte subsets in patients with symptomatic HP reveals activated T lymphocytes, often with a predominance of CD8+ cells having suppressor/cytotoxic functions. CD4+/CD8+ ratios are usually less than 1.[101] However, a number of investigators have shown that these ratios vary widely in patients with HP, with some having normal or increased numbers of CD4+ cells.[102–104] Reasons for this variability are unclear, but data suggest that the forms of HP (acute vs. chronic) and the timing of last antigen exposure in relation to BAL may affect cellular phenotypes. A CD4+-predominant BAL lymphocytosis has been described in patients with the fibrotic stage of HP.[105] Smoking also affects the cellular phenotypes seen.

Animal models support the importance of cell-mediated immunity in HP. Cultured lymphocytes passively transferred from sensitized animals, including guinea pigs, rats,[106] rabbits,[107] and inbred mice,[108] to unexposed, nonsensitized animals results in disease similar to human HP when the naive animals subsequently are challenged with inhaled or infused intrapulmonary antigens. Similar results occur using passively transferred T lymphocytes that have been activated in vitro with either mitogen or antigen. Interferon-γ was found to be essential for the expression of HP in studies using "knockout" mice incapable of expressing the gene coding for interferon-γ, and other experimental studies support the type 1 T helper cell subset of lymphocytes as important in HP pathogenesis. Enhancement of HP has been shown in mice undergoing repeated intranasal instillation of S. rectivirgula and infected concurrently with Sendai virus,[109] suggesting that viral illness may affect host susceptibility to HP.

HISTOPATHOLOGY

The histopathology of HP is distinctive, but it is not pathognomonic, and histologic features vary depending on

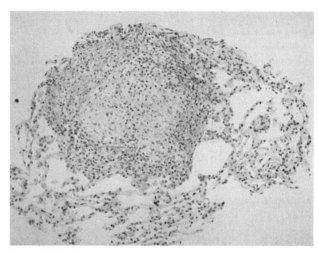

Figure 62.1 Photomicrograph of a hematoxylin and eosin–stained transbronchial lung biopsy from a patient with hypersensitivity pneumonitis (original magnification ×40). A small, discrete, non-necrotizing interstitial granuloma.

the stage of illness at the time of biopsy. The typical histologic triad of HP includes (1) cellular bronchiolitis (airway-centered inflammation), (2) interstitial mononuclear cell infiltrate, and (3) scattered, small, non-necrotizing granulomas,[110] but an appreciable number of HP cases do not show these classic features. HP represents an important fraction of histologically confirmed cases of nonspecific interstitial pneumonitis, and the finding of nonspecific interstitial pneumonitis on biopsy should prompt careful history taking for relevant environmental antigen exposures.[111]

In the acute and subacute forms of HP, there is a patchy infiltrate of the alveolar walls with mononuclear cells (predominantly lymphocytes and plasma cells) in a bronchiolocentric distribution, usually with accompanying epithelioid granulomas or giant cells (Fig. 62.1). Neutrophils and eosinophils are uncommon, although luminal neutrophils can be seen after acute exposure. Air space foam cells (foamy macrophages) are a distinctive part of the airway inflammatory process. In a 1982 case series of 60 patients with acute FLD, Reyes and coworkers[112] found interstitial inflammatory infiltrates in 100%, granulomas in 70%, unresolved (organizing) pneumonia in 65%, interstitial fibrosis in 65%, foam cells in 65%, foreign body material (demonstrable by polarized light) in 60%, solitary giant cells in 53%, and bronchiolitis obliterans in 50%. In a study of 475 Japanese patients with summer-type HP, interstitial inflammation was found in 95%, granulomas in 65%, and bronchiolitis obliterans with organizing pneumonia ("Masson bodies") in approximately 30%.

Interstitial fibrosis with honeycombing is found late in disease, usually accompanying chronic HP, by which time the granulomatous phase may have resolved. The interstitial fibrosis may show airway centering or may be indistinguishable from a usual interstitial pneumonia pattern.[113,114] Because the histopathologic findings of HP vary and overlap with other diseases, additional clinical data must be considered in confirming the diagnosis.

CLINICAL FEATURES

SIGNS AND SYMPTOMS

Detailed history taking is the mainstay of HP diagnosis and is essential for planning exposure intervention (Table 62.2). A clinical history suggesting a temporal relationship between symptoms and certain activities is often the first clue to the diagnosis of HP, although such a pattern may not occur in subacute or chronic forms of disease. The work history should include a chronology of current and previous occupations, with a description of specific work processes and exposures. Antigen exposures capable of causing HP can occur in almost any indoor environment under appropriate circumstances, and a simple job title cannot be used to exclude potential risk. For example, a schoolteacher developed chronic HP associated with indoor air quality problems in the school environment; the disease went unrecognized for years.[115]

The environmental history should explore exposure to pets and other domestic animals, particularly birds; hobbies such as gardening and lawn care, which may involve exposures to sensitizing chemicals such as pyrethrins; recreational activities such as use of hot tubs and indoor swimming pools, from which microbial bioaerosols can be generated; use of humidifiers, cool mist vaporizers, and humidified air conditioners, which can be sources of microbial bioaerosols; moisture indicators such as leaking, flooding, or previous water damage to carpets and furnishings;

Table 62.2 Components of an Occupational and Environmental History for Patients with Suspected Hypersensitivity Pneumonitis

Occupational History

Chronology of current and previous occupations

Description of job processes and specific work practices

List of specific chemicals, dusts, and other aerosol exposures (e.g., grain dust; animal handling; food and plant processing; cooling towers, fountains, and other water sprays; metalworking fluids)

Review of material safety data sheets (MSDSs) to identify known chemical sensitizers

Reports of industrial hygiene evaluations or environmental testing at the workplace

Symptom improvement away from work or symptom worsening with specific workplace exposures

Presence of persistent respiratory or constitutional symptoms in exposed coworkers

Use of respiratory protection at work

Environmental and Residential History

Pets and other domestic animals (especially birds)

Hobbies and recreational activities (especially those involving chemicals, feathers or fur, plant materials, and organic dusts)

Presence of humidifiers, dehumidifiers, swamp coolers, clothes dryers vented indoors, and other humidity sources

Use of hot tubs or saunas

Leaking or flooding indoors

Water damage to carpets or furnishings

Visible fungal growth

Feather pillows, comforters, or bedding

Similar symptoms in other family members or home occupants

---

and visible mold or mildew contamination in occupied spaces. Use of medications (both prescription and nonprescription) should be elicited to assess for possible drug-induced hypersensitivity lung disease.

The classification of illness into distinct acute, subacute, and chronic forms can be misleading because clinical manifestations frequently overlap. Nevertheless, the varying presentations are associated with variable clinical findings. Acute illness typically begins 4 to 12 hours after exposure, with onset of respiratory and constitutional symptoms of cough, dyspnea, chest tightness, fevers, chills, malaise, and myalgias. Symptoms may be accompanied by physical findings of fever, tachypnea, tachycardia, and lung inspiratory crackles. Peripheral blood leukocytosis with neutrophilia and lymphopenia may be present. Eosinophilia is unusual. Acute symptoms of HP are nonspecific and probably frequently are mistaken for infectious respiratory illnesses. Recurrent acute symptom episodes should prompt consideration of hypersensitivity lung disease and a careful historical search for relevant exposures.

The subacute and chronic presentations of illness also require a high degree of clinical suspicion to confirm the diagnosis and initiate appropriate management. Exertional dyspnea and cough are the predominant symptoms, and patients frequently report sputum production, fatigue, malaise, anorexia, and weight loss. Physical examination findings may be normal or may reveal basilar crackles. Wheezing occurs in some patients, probably reflecting antigen-mediated inflammatory effects on the airways. Cyanosis and right-sided heart failure may be evident with severe fibrotic disease. Clubbing occurred in approximately half the patients in a case series of bird breeder's lung and is associated with a poorer prognostic outcome[116]; however, this is an uncommon finding in other forms of HP.

PRECIPITATING ANTIBODIES

Although positive precipitating antibodies once were thought to be the hallmark of HP, they are unfortunately neither sensitive nor specific. The finding of specific IgG precipitating antibodies in the serum of a patient with suspected HP indicates exposure sufficient to generate a humoral immunologic response and may be a helpful diagnostic clue. However, serum precipitins are found in 3% to 30% of asymptomatic farmers and in up to 50% of asymptomatic pigeon breeders.[117,117a] The prevalence of positive tests in asymptomatic individuals fluctuates over time, with subjects testing variably positive or negative at different times, perhaps reflecting variable exposures.[118]

Specific precipitating antibodies frequently are not demonstrable in patients with HP.[118a] In one study, 30% to 40% of patients with FLD had no detectable precipitins to commonly tested antigens (*S. rectivirgula*, *Aspergillus* species, and *T. vulgaris*).[119] False-negative results may occur because of poorly standardized antigens, improper quality controls, insensitive techniques, the wrong choice of antigen, or underconcentrated sera.[120] The antibody response in some patients may be too meager to give a precipitin reaction using the traditional Ouchterlony double immunodiffusion technique. More sensitive assays such as enzyme-linked immunosorbent assay for specific IgG antibodies may lead to confusion because of decreased specificity. Serum precipitins may disappear over variable periods of time after exposure ceases, which adds to the difficulty of antigen-specific diagnosis.[121] In some cases, particularly those associated with complex microbial bioaerosol exposures, disease may not be a reaction to one organism alone but rather a cumulative reaction to a number of airborne antigens, which may not be reflected in available laboratory antigen panels.

OTHER LABORATORY STUDIES

Mild elevations in erythrocyte sedimentation rate, C-reactive protein, and immunoglobulins of IgG, IgM, or IgA isotypes are occasionally evident, reflecting acute or chronic inflammation. Serum angiotensin-converting enzyme concentrations rarely may be increased in patients with recurrent acute symptoms.[122] Antinuclear antibodies and other autoantibodies rarely are detected. Skin tests for both immediate and delayed-type hypersensitivity reactions are unhelpful in diagnosis.

PHYSIOLOGY

Complete pulmonary function tests (PFTs), including lung volumes, spirometry, and diffusing capacity, should be obtained when feasible in all patients with suspected HP. Lung function abnormalities in acute HP are classically restrictive, with a decrease in forced vital capacity, total lung capacity, and diffusion capacity. Hypoxemia is often present, and an exercise-induced decrease in PO_2 is an early sign of functional impairment.[123] Four to 6 weeks may be required for complete resolution of these acute abnormalities.[124] PFT results may be normal if performed after resolution of an acute episode but before onset of chronic interstitial fibrosis.

PFT results also may fall within normal limits in subacute forms of HP and may be particularly misleading if no premorbid PFT values are available for comparison. Both restrictive and obstructive defects in pulmonary function occur in subacute and chronic HP, and a combined restrictive and obstructive pattern is common. In 1965, Pepys and Jenkins[125] reported that 10% of 205 patients with FLD showed obstruction alone rather than restriction. Decreased diffusion capacity also is commonly observed. Gas-exchange abnormalities, particularly with exercise, may be marked. Nonspecific bronchial hyperreactivity measured by methacholine challenge has been described in 22% to 60% of patients with HP.[126] Thus, HP should be considered in the differential diagnosis of nonsmokers presenting with physiologic findings of emphysema and in patients with airflow limitation and nonspecific bronchial hyperreactivity.

Although both rest and exercise PFTs are important components in the diagnostic evaluation of patients with HP, findings are neither sensitive nor specific. Normal spirometry should not be used to exclude the diagnosis. Once diagnostic confirmation of HP is obtained, serial PFTs should be measured to assess response to therapy and to guide treatment decisions until recovery or stability, or both, of lung function is maintained.

RADIOGRAPHY

The chest radiograph in acute HP typically reveals a fine micronodular pattern or diffuse, patchy, ground-glass opacity (Fig. 62.2A).[127] Hilar or mediastinal adenopathy rarely is seen on the plain radiograph. The chest film may be normal, particularly in early disease stages, and is a poor screening tool in populations at risk for HP.[128] In one study, 4% of acute cases of FLD had normal films and another 40% to 45% had minimal changes that might easily be overlooked; the extent of radiographic abnormality correlated poorly with the severity of symptoms or functional impairment.[129] Radiographic abnormalities in acute illness regress or resolve over 4 to 6 weeks if further exposure is avoided. In subacute disease, small nodules and fine linear opacities are evident. In chronic HP, fibrosis may be manifested by linear reticular opacity, volume loss, and "honeycombing."

Computed tomography (CT) scanning is more sensitive than chest radiography in the diagnosis of HP. The most typical CT finding in HP is profuse, diffuse, poorly defined, centrilobular micronodules, probably reflecting a cellular bronchiolitis (Fig. 62.2B).[130–132] Diffuse ground-glass attenuation may be the predominant or only CT abnormality in some cases. The CT appearance of HP may be normal if disease is diagnosed early.[130] In chronic HP, findings of lung fibrosis may include reticular opacities, lobar volume loss, or honeycombing (Fig. 62.2C). In one case series, diffuse ground-glass attenuation was observed in most subacute and chronic forms of bird breeder's HP[133]; honeycombing was seen in only 50% of the chronic cases, a number of whom also had concurrent micronodules or ground-glass attenuation, or both. Emphysematous changes, predominantly in the lower lung zones, have been observed in subacute and chronic HP cases, most of whom were nonsmokers, perhaps related to bronchiolar inflammation and obstruction.[132–134] Focal areas of hyperlucency (mosaic pattern), perhaps due to bronchiolocentric inflammation with associated air trapping, may be a prominent feature.[135] In a retrospective study of 182 patients with subacute HP, high-resolution CT showed small (<15-mm diameter), thin-walled cysts in 13%.[136] Mild reactive mediastinal lymphadenopathy is a common CT finding,[137] typically involving only a few nodes with a maximal short-axis diameter less than 15 mm.

INHALATION CHALLENGE

The use of laboratory inhalation challenge in the diagnosis of HP is limited by the lack of standardized antigens and techniques. Inhalation of an aerosolized antigen suspected to be causative is most helpful when acute symptoms and clinical abnormalities are part of the disease presentation and likely to occur within hours after exposure.[138] In experienced laboratories, provocative testing may be useful in discriminating chronic HP induced by avian antigens from other interstitial lung diseases.[139] In some patients with acute symptoms, exposure to the suspect environment with post-exposure monitoring of symptoms, temperature, leukocyte count, spirometry, diffusing capacity, and chest radiograph may be preferable to laboratory challenge. Interpretation of results is often difficult, and routine inhalation challenge is not recommended in most patients with suspected HP.[140]

BRONCHOALVEOLAR LAVAGE

BAL provides a sensitive tool confirming the presence of alveolitis in patients with HP.[141] Typically, a marked lavage

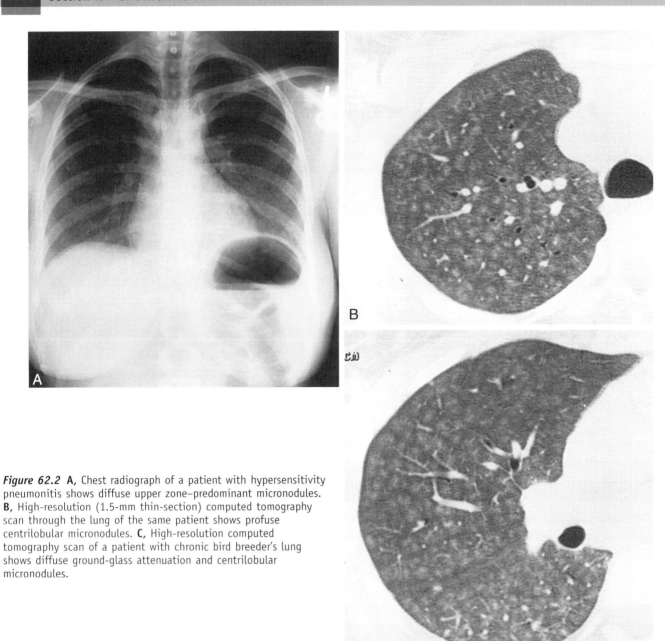

Figure 62.2 **A,** Chest radiograph of a patient with hypersensitivity pneumonitis shows diffuse upper zone–predominant micronodules. **B,** High-resolution (1.5-mm thin-section) computed tomography scan through the lung of the same patient shows profuse centrilobular micronodules. **C,** High-resolution computed tomography scan of a patient with chronic bird breeder's lung shows diffuse ground-glass attenuation and centrilobular micronodules.

lymphocytosis (30% to 70%) without eosinophilia or neutrophilia is found, often but not always with a CD8+ lymphocyte predominance. Total white blood cell numbers are increased, often up to fivefold normal. The absolute number of macrophages is similar to that in controls, although their percentage in lavage is reduced because of the high number of lymphocytes. Increased numbers of mast cells have been reported in symptomatic patients with HP.[142] Concentrations of IgG, IgM, and IgA antibodies typically are increased in BAL in subjects with HP (although smoking may mitigate this effect), as are total protein and albumin.[143]

The lavage cellular profile may vary considerably depending on the stage of illness and the time interval between BAL and last antigen exposure.[144] The BAL lymphocytosis of HP may persist for years after apparent removal from antigen exposure and despite improvement in other clinical parameters, limiting its utility as a tool to follow the course and progression of disease or to assess adequacy of antigen removal.[102] Individuals exposed to HP antigens but without reported symptoms or other clinical abnormalities may develop a lymphocytic alveolitis,[145] further limiting the diagnostic specificity of BAL. There appears to be little correlation between BAL findings and other clinical abnormalities, including radiographic changes, pulmonary function, and the presence of precipitating antibody.

LUNG BIOPSY

Lung biopsy is usually recommended in patients without sufficient clinical criteria for definitive diagnosis or to rule out other diseases that necessitate different treatment. Transbronchial biopsies are often sufficient, especially if directed by CT findings, and diagnostic yield increases when 6 to 10 samples are obtained.[146] Interstitial lymphocytic inflammation, granulomas, and bronchiolar inflammation can be seen on transbronchial biopsy; however, appreciation of the airway-centered inflammatory reaction of HP usually requires a surgical lung biopsy. Special stains and cultures are important to distinguish HP from infectious granulomatous conditions, including fungal and mycobacterial diseases. HP differs from sarcoidosis in the finding of inflammatory infiltrates at interstitial sites distant from granulomas, whereas in sarcoidosis such infiltrates generally are found in and around the granulomas.[140,147] Given the substantial overlap in the histologic appearance of these granulomatous processes, pathology without clinical correlation usually is not sufficient for diagnosis.

DIAGNOSTIC APPROACH

Because the diagnosis of HP carries such import for prevention of further antigen exposure, I typically perform the following diagnostic studies on all patients with suspected HP (Table 62.3): (1) detailed clinical history; (2) physical examination; (3) chest high-resolution CT (unless the plain film is clearly abnormal); (4) complete PFTs, including lung volumes, pre- and postbronchodilator spirometry, and carbon monoxide diffusing capacity; and (5) fiberoptic bronchoscopy, usually with BAL and transbronchial biopsies, including special stains and cultures for infectious agents. In patients with exertional dyspnea and normal or minimally abnormal PFTs, exercise physiology is often helpful in defining impairment and important in guiding treatment decisions, including the need for supplemental oxygen. Methacholine challenge does not distinguish asthma from HP and is generally not necessary. Serum precipitins are helpful when positive in confirming the diagnosis in bird breeder's lung and in other circumstances in which the putative antigen has been identified. However,

Table 62.3 Diagnostic Approach to the Patient with Possible Hypersensitivity Pneumonitis (HP)

Obtain detailed occupational and environmental exposure histories, along with regular clinical history
Physical examination
Pulmonary function, including spirometry, lung volumes, DL_{CO}
Chest radiographs, PA and lateral
HRCT if chest film is negative or nonspecific
Assess exercise ventilatory and gas-exchange parameters if exertional dyspnea is prominent
Consider serum precipitin analysis; negative results do not rule out HP, but a positive precipitin result helps confirm relevant antigenic exposures
FOB with bronchoalveolar lavage if diagnosis is in doubt; surgical lung biopsy may be indicated if FOB is nondiagnostic

DL_{CO}, carbon monoxide diffusing capacity; FOB, fiberoptic bronchoscopy; HRCT, high-resolution computed tomography; PA, posteroanterior.

negative precipitins should not be used to exclude the diagnosis.

DIAGNOSTIC CRITERIA

A number of diagnostic criteria for HP have been proposed, though none has been validated.[148] Recent guidelines[149] consider the diagnosis of HP confirmed if the patient fulfills four major and at least two minor criteria and if other diseases with similar findings have been excluded. The major criteria are (1) history of compatible symptoms that appear or worsen within hours after antigen exposure; (2) exposure confirmation based on history, environmental investigation, serum precipitin testing, and/or BAL antibody; (3) compatible abnormalities on chest radiograph or high-resolution CT; (4) BAL lymphocytosis; (5) compatible histologic changes on biopsy; and (6) positive "natural challenge" (reproduction of symptoms and laboratory abnormalities after exposure to the suspected environment) or by controlled inhalation challenge. Minor criteria include (1) basilar crackles on lung examination; (2) decreased diffusion capacity; and (3) arterial hypoxemia, at rest or with exercise. Following an outbreak of HP among metalworkers, a promising diagnostic index for HP was developed using a number of noninvasive tests, including a high alveolar-arterial PO_2 difference and/or decreased carbon monoxide diffusing capacity, elevated erythrocyte sedimentation rate, and dry crackles on examination in a patient with appropriate work-related symptoms.[150]

Stringent diagnostic criteria may underestimate milder cases of HP in which the chest radiograph is normal or when symptoms are subtle or insidious. Meta-analysis showed a decline in the sensitivity of the chest radiograph for diagnosis of HP over the years 1950 to 1980.[128] Because a positive exposure history is part of the case definition for disease, absent or inadequate occupational and environmental history taking probably results in underrecognition of disease. The likelihood that unrecognized HP occurs also is based on several other factors: (1) the signs and symptoms of illness and clinical diagnostic findings are nonspecific and mimic many other diseases, such as asthma, influenza, viral pneumonia, sarcoidosis, and idiopathic pulmonary fibrosis (Table 62.4); (2) early disease may be accompanied by a normal auscultatory lung examination and resting pulmonary function as well as a normal chest radiograph; (3) many of the microbial antigens that cause HP proliferate in common environmental niches, and relevant exposures may be difficult to elicit historically; and (4) precipitating antibodies are often negative and may disappear after exposure ceases, so that a patient with fibrotic lung disease from previous episodes of HP may not be recognized as such.[151]

NATURAL HISTORY AND PROGNOSIS

The clinical course of HP is variable, but, if illness is recognized early, the prognosis for recovery is usually quite good.[152]

In acute HP, symptoms of fever, chills, and cough usually disappear within days after exposure ceases. Malaise, fatigue,

Table 62.4 Differential Diagnosis of Hypersensitivity Pneumonitis*

	Clinical Presentation	BAL Lymphocytosis	Histopathology
Asthma	++	+	−
Sarcoidosis	++	++	+
Inhalation fever (e.g., ODTS)	++	−	−
Viral/mycoplasma pneumonias	++	+	−
Mycobacterial infections	++	++	+
Fungal infections	+	+	+
Other ILD (collagen vascular, IPF)	+	+	+
Chronic beryllium disease	+	++	+
Lymphoma/leukemia	+	+	+
Toxic fume inhalation	+	−	−

* Designations reflect other illnesses compared with hypersensitivity pneumonitis (acute, subacute, or chronic presentation).
++, very similar; +, similar; −, dissimilar.
BAL, bronchoalveolar lavage; ILD, interstitial lung disease; IPF, idiopathic pulmonary fibrosis; ODTS, organic dust toxic syndrome.

and dyspnea may persist for several weeks. There is usually rapid improvement in lung vital capacity and diffusion capacity in the first 2 weeks after an acute attack, but mild abnormalities in pulmonary function often persist for several months. In general, single acute episodes are self-limited. Occasionally, disease may progress despite removal from exposure. Continued symptoms and progressive lung impairment have been reported after recurrent acute attacks and even after a single severe attack.[153,154]

The subacute or chronic forms of HP, with insidious symptoms and more subtle clinical abnormalities, are often recognized later in the course of illness and consequently often have a poorer prognosis than acute disease.[154a] Symptomatic pigeon breeders monitored for 18 years showed a fourfold average rate of decline in pulmonary function in comparison with the expected rate.[155] Four children and five adults with chronic avian HP were monitored from 6 months to 10 years after treatment with corticosteroids and reduction or elimination of exposure.[156] Only five of the nine were completely asymptomatic, all had persistent positive serum precipitins, several had lung function abnormalities, and one ultimately died of HP after unsuccessful lung transplantation. Fatal diffuse alveolar damage has been described as a complication of chronic bird breeder's lung.[157] Overall, long-term mortality rates for patients with chronic HP range from 1% to 10%.[158,159]

Both emphysema (more common in late-stage FLD) and fibrosis (more common as an outcome of bird breeder's lung) are potential sequelae of HP. In a case-control study of 88 farmers with FLD, emphysema was found significantly more often (23%) in those with FLD in comparison with matched control farmers (7%), occurring in 18% of non-smoking and 44% of smoking FLD patients.[160] Recurrent attacks of FLD were associated in this study with risk for emphysema. In comparison with matched control farmers, those with FLD monitored for 14 years had significant reductions in diffusing capacity and more marked airflow limitation.[161] In another follow-up study of farmers with a history of FLD,[162] obstructive abnormalities from emphysema were the most common findings in those whose disease did not completely resolve; only 50% had no residual disease. In a study of Finnish farmers meeting strict diagnostic criteria for FLD, the risk for asthma necessitating medication was found to increase within the first 3 years after a diagnosis of FLD, with significantly higher asthma prevalence rates in the population with FLD at 5-year follow-up in comparison with the reference population.[163] Patients with HP from avian antigens appear to have a higher risk of developing fibrotic restrictive lung disease in comparison with those with FLD,[164] with a poor 5-year survival similar to that of patients with idiopathic pulmonary fibrosis. Thus, although some patients with HP recover completely, permanent sequelae of the disease include asthma, emphysema, and (sometimes progressive) interstitial fibrosis.

Continued antigen exposure may not lead to clinical deterioration in some cases.[165] Bourke and colleagues[166] found that 18 of 21 individuals with acute bird breeder's lung had continued regular exposure to pigeons 10 years after diagnosis, although many used improved ventilation and respiratory protection; only 6 reported continued respiratory symptoms. This phenomenon may be reflected in some animal models of disease, in which repeated antigen inhalation in sensitized animals results in resolution rather than progression of the pulmonary inflammatory response.[167] This modulation of the inflammatory response is not well understood, and there is as yet no role for immunotherapy in disease management.

No functional or biochemical marker exists to predict resolution or progression of disease. The BAL lymphocytosis associated with HP may persist for years after removal from exposure and despite clinical recovery. Age at diagnosis, duration of antigen exposure after onset of symptoms, and total years of exposure before diagnosis seem to have predictive value in the likelihood of recovery from bird breeder's lung.[168] Pigeon breeders with HP were more likely to improve or recover completely if they had been in contact with birds for less than 2 years. Neither the form of clinical presentation (acute vs. chronic) nor the degree of lung function abnormality at the time of diagnosis was related to recovery in another study of bird breeder's lung.[169] Rather, younger age at diagnosis and exposure to antigen for less than 6 months after symptom onset were associated with complete recovery.

TREATMENT

An accelerated decline in lung function with continued antigen exposure has been demonstrated for most forms of HP. Thus, early diagnosis and avoidance of antigen exposure are the mainstays of treatment, with pharmacologic therapy an important adjunct in some cases. Identification of the causative antigen is often challenging.

ANTIGEN AVOIDANCE

Elimination of a causative antigen from the patient's environment not only is the first step in treatment but also prevents occurrence of hypersensitivity diseases in others who are exposed. For example, maple bark disease and bagassosis are now quite rare in the United States after changes in the handling of material, which resulted in diminished opportunity for microbial growth. Removal of damaged and colonized areas, disinfection, and elimination of conditions leading to seasonal mold contamination are effective in preventing recurrence of summer-type HP in Japan.[170] An outbreak of HP traced to fungal contamination of an open water-spray ventilation system was controlled by extensive cleaning of the system and corresponding work areas and replacement of the system with a dry (closed-coil) ventilation system.[171] In another large outbreak caused by microbial contamination of a chilled water air-conditioning system, a variety of cleaning and water treatment measures were used to reduce antigen concentration. A solid-phase radioimmunoassay method using antiserum from affected workers was used thereafter to assess levels of airborne antigen and monitor the efficacy of control measures.[172] In an outbreak of HP associated with exposure to metalworking fluids, 51% (18) of the affected employees were able to return to work following implementation of several exposure control recommendations.[173] Recommended interventions included improving metalworking fluid management practices, enclosing selected metalworking fluid machining operations, eliminating mist cooling, ventilation improvements, and worker training. In cases of humidifier lung and "hot tub lung," removal of the contaminated sources is usually straightforward.

On-site investigation of the work and home environments by an experienced industrial hygienist may be helpful in cases in which the exposure history is uncertain, particularly when disease is progressive. For fungal contaminants, both area and personal spore sampling and indirect immunofluorescence testing for spore-specific IgG have been used to assess indoor air quality and individual mold sensitization.[174] However, quantitative bioaerosol sampling for indoor microbial antigens is time consuming, expensive, and not readily available to most clinicians, and requires an experienced industrial hygienist and analytical laboratory. Even when properly performed, results are often difficult to interpret.[175] Negative results should not be used to disprove disease or exposure. Settle plates are unreliable in assessing indoor microbial contaminants.

Avoidance of exposure by eliminating the offending antigen from the environment may be difficult in some circumstances. In five homes monitored serially after bird removal, antigen levels measured by inhibition enzyme-linked immunosorbent assay declined gradually despite extensive environmental control measures, with high levels still detectable at 18 months in one home.[176] Avian antigens can be found in homes without birds if wild bird excrement is deposited heavily outside the house and tracked in on shoes. Tannic acid application, used effectively in decreasing indoor cat and mite allergen levels, is not effective in decreasing bird antigen levels in patients with bird breeder's lung.[177]

When elimination of the antigen is not feasible or the etiologic agent is not identified specifically, exposure avoidance usually is accomplished by removing the affected individual from the likely antigen-containing environment. This approach may be simple and adequate for recovery. However, the social consequences and economic disruption to the affected individual may preclude strict abstinence from exposure. A 6-year follow-up study of affected farmers revealed that 50% to 60% remained on the farm[121]; by 15 years, as many as 70% had returned to farming.[159] Especially when antigen exposure avoidance is likely to be inadequate, regular follow-up of pulmonary function, radiography, and symptoms is essential to assess response to treatment, to detect clinical deterioration, and to direct efforts to mitigate ongoing antigen exposure.

PHARMACOLOGIC THERAPY

There are anecdotal reports of the beneficial effects of systemic steroids in acute attacks of HP, but controlled clinical trials are lacking. In cases in which pulmonary function abnormalities are minor and spontaneous recovery is likely with removal from exposure, steroids are probably unnecessary. More severe attacks may necessitate treatment with prednisone, typically beginning at 60 mg/day, plus bed rest, supplemental oxygen for hypoxemia, and other appropriate supportive measures. Pulmonary function should be monitored within the first 4 weeks after initiation of treatment. If there is objective improvement, a gradual taper to minimum sustaining corticosteroid doses should follow; otherwise, steroids should be tapered and discontinued. Monkare[178] showed that 12 weeks of steroid treatment did not produce better results than 4 weeks of treatment in patients with FLD. Repeated courses of intravenous methylprednisolone pulse therapy (15 mg/kg on 3 consecutive days) was efficacious in a child with HP.[179] Given the paucity of treatment studies and the known side effects of systemic corticosteroids, clinical judgment and careful medical follow-up must guide individual patient management.

The effect of corticosteroids on the long-term course of various forms of HP has received limited attention. In one study, 36 patients, most having suffered only one acute attack of FLD, were assigned randomly to receive prednisolone or placebo for 2 months.[180] The steroid-treated group showed more rapid improvement in physiologic abnormalities (particularly diffusion capacity) at 1-month follow-up, but no differences were found between the treated and untreated groups 5 years later. Interestingly, the group treated with steroids suffered more frequent recurrences of symptomatic FLD during the 5-year follow-up period, although this finding did not reach statistical significance. In a study of pigeon breeders with HP, there were no significant clinical outcome differences between cases who were treated with steroids and those who were not; the mean time for improvement or normalization of pulmonary function after treatment and removal from exposure was 3.4 months.[169]

Inhaled steroids and β-agonists may be helpful in patients with HP manifested by symptoms of chest tightness and cough and with airflow limitation on PFT.[181] There are as yet no data from controlled clinical trials on the efficacy of inhaled steroids in the treatment of HP.

Cytotoxic agents such as cyclophosphamide, cyclosporine,[182] and azathioprine have been used in patients with refractory progressive HP, but their efficacy is largely unexplored. Lung transplantation may be a last resort in such patients unresponsive to medical therapy.

PREVENTION

Recognition of an index case of HP is often a sentinel health event, indicating the need for further investigation and intervention in the implicated environment where others may be at risk and where opportunities for prevention may be identified. For example, indoor microbial contamination often is related to problems with control of moisture. Source, dilution, and administrative controls should be used when appropriate to reduce these indoor contaminants. Source control includes preventing leaking and flooding, removing stagnant water sources, eliminating aerosol humidifiers, hot tubs, and vaporizers, and maintaining indoor relative humidity below 70%. If humidifiers are used, frequent cleaning and water changes minimize the risk of microbial growth. Dilution of contaminants can be affected by increasing the amount of outdoor air in a building, and high-efficiency filters can be added to the ventilation system to clean recirculated air.[175] Complete elimination of indoor allergens is probably impossible, and it is often necessary to relocate immunologically sensitized individuals once hypersensitivity lung disease has occurred.

Work practices recommended to reduce the prevalence of FLD include efficient drying of hay and cereals before storage, use of mechanical feeding systems, and better ventilation of farm buildings.[65,183] In a study of French farmers, the presence of serum precipitins and the risk for FLD were associated with handling of barn-stored cattle fodder.[184] Efforts to diminish disease prevalence were not affected significantly by changing from traditional drying methods to artificial barn fodder drying in this occupational setting.[185] Education of individuals in at-risk occupations in antigen avoidance and early symptom recognition may be helpful.

The efficacy of various types of respirators in preventing antigen sensitization and disease progression once sensitization has occurred is unknown. Helmet-type powered air-purifying respirators have been used to prevent episodic exposure in individuals with previous acute episodes of FLD.[186] Respiratory protection has been examined in bird breeders with HP, many of whom are reluctant to abandon their high-risk hobby. Serial measurements of pigeon-specific IgG antibodies were obtained in 22 pigeon fanciers with HP who had ongoing exposure, 13 of whom wore a powered air-purifying respirator and 9 of whom refused respiratory protection.[187] Serum antibody levels declined by 65% over 14 months in those wearing respirators in comparison with no decline in antibody levels in those without respirators; no data were reported on changes in symptoms or pulmonary function in the two groups. Prolonged wearing of respiratory protection is limited by the fact that most respirators are hot and cumbersome. Dust respirators offer substantial, but in some cases incomplete, protection against organic dusts[188] and are not recommended as preventive measures once sensitization has occurred.

SUMMARY

Increasing recognition of the ubiquity of environmental antigen exposures and improved diagnostic tools have led to increasing recognition of cases and outbreaks of HP in a wide variety of occupational and nonoccupational settings. HP remains a diagnostic challenge because of the spectrum of clinical findings and the lack of a simple "gold standard" for diagnosis. Rather, the diagnosis depends on a strong clinical index of suspicion, a careful exposure history, and the integration of a constellation of radiographic, physiologic, and histopathologic findings that, by themselves, are nonspecific and mimic a variety of other chest illnesses. HP is both treatable (and even curable if detected early) and preventable (if exposure is recognized and antigen abatement is effective). Unrecognized or untreated, the illness may lead to permanent sequelae, including asthma, emphysema, and interstitial fibrosis.[189] Confirmation of the diagnosis often generates broader public health implications regarding the potential risks from ongoing antigen exposure to others sharing the environment. The diagnosis of even one case of HP should prompt a search for additional cases in the shared environment as well as initiation of measures to eliminate further exposure.

REFERENCES

1. Demedts M, Wells AU, Anto JM, et al: Interstitial lung diseases: An epidemiological overview. Eur Respir J Suppl 32:2s–16s, 2001.
2. Morell F, Roger A, Cruz MJ, et al: Suberosis: Clinical study and new etiologic agents in a series of eight patients. Chest 124:1145–1152, 2003.
3. Timmer SJ, Amundson DE, Malone JD: Hypersensitivity pneumonitis following anthrax vaccination. Chest 122:741–745, 2002.
4. Campbell J: Acute symptoms following work with hay. Br Med J 2:1143–1144, 1932.
5. Dickie HA, Rankin J: Farmer's lung: An acute granulomatous interstitial pneumonitis occurring in agricultural workers. J Am Med Assoc 167:1069–1076, 1958.
6. Buechner H, Prevatt A, Thompson J, et al: Bagassosis: Review with further historical data, studies of pulmonary function, and results of adrenal steroid therapy. Am J Med 25:234–237, 1958.

7. Banaszak EF, Thiede WH, Fink JN: Hypersensitivity pneumonitis due to contamination of an air conditioner. N Engl J Med 283:271–276, 1970.

8. Johnson CL, Bernstein IL, Gallagher JS, et al: Familial hypersensitivity pneumonitis induced by Bacillus subtilis. Am Rev Respir Dis 122:339–348, 1980.

9. Kane GC, Marx JJ, Prince DS: Hypersensitivity pneumonitis secondary to Klebsiella oxytoca: A new cause of humidifier lung. Chest 104:627–629, 1993.

10. Nordness ME, Zacharisen MC, Schlueter DP, et al: Occupational lung disease related to Cytophaga endotoxin exposure in a nylon plant. J Occup Environ Med 45:385–392, 2003.

11. Hogan MB, Patterson R, Pore RS, et al: Basement shower hypersensitivity pneumonitis secondary to Epicoccum nigrum. Chest 110:854–856, 1996.

12. Brade H, Brade L, Shchade U: Structure, endotoxicity, immunogenicity and antigenicity of bacterial lipopolysaccharides (endotoxins, O-antigens). In Levin J (ed): Bacterial Endotoxins: Pathophysiological Effects, Clinical Significance, and Pharmacological Control. New York: Alan R. Liss, 1993, pp 17–45.

13. Kreiss K, Cox-Ganser J: Metalworking fluid-associated hypersensitivity pneumonitis: A workshop summary. Am J Ind Med 32:423–432, 1997.

14. Embil J, Warren P, Yakrus M, et al: Pulmonary illness associated with exposure to Mycobacterium-avium complex in hot tub water: Hypersensitivity pneumonitis or infection? Chest 111:813–816, 1997.

15. Kahana LM, Kay JM, Yakrus MA, et al: Mycobacterium avium complex infection in an immunocompetent young adult related to hot tub exposure. Chest 111:242–245, 1997.

16. Rose CS, Martyny JW, Newman LS, et al: "Lifeguard lung": Endemic granulomatous pneumonitis in an indoor swimming pool. Am J Public Health 88:1795–1800, 1998.

17. Burge HA: Airborne allergenic fungi: Classification, nomenclature, and distribution. Immunol Allergy Clin North Am 92:307–319, 1989.

18. Reynolds S, Streifel A, McJilton C: Elevated airborne concentrations of fungi in residential and office environments. Am Ind Hyg Assoc J 51:601–604, 1990.

19. Siersted HC, Gravesen S: Extrinsic allergic alveolitis after exposure to the yeast Rhodotorula rubra. Allergy 48:298–299, 1993.

20. Hodges G, Fink J, Schlueter D: Hypersensitivity pneumonitis caused by a contaminated cool-mist vaporizer. Ann Intern Med 80:501–504, 1974.

21. Burke GW, Carrington CB, Strauss R, et al: Allergic alveolitis caused by home humidifiers: Unusual clinical features and electron microscopic findings. JAMA 238:2705–2708, 1977.

22. Baur X, Richter G, Pethran A, et al: Increased prevalence of IgG-induced sensitization and hypersensitivity pneumonitis (humidifier lung) in nonsmokers exposed to aerosols of a contaminated air conditioner. Respiration 59:211–214, 1992.

23. Fink JN, Banaszak EF, Barboriak JJ, et al: Interstitial lung disease due to contamination of forced air systems. Ann Intern Med 84:406–413, 1976.

24. Metzger WJ, Patterson R, Fink J, et al: Sauna-takers disease: Hypersensitivity pneumonitis due to contaminated water in a home sauna. JAMA 236:2209–2211, 1976.

25. Jacobs RL, Thorner RE, Holcomb JR, et al: Hypersensitivity pneumonitis caused by Cladosporium in an enclosed hot-tub area. Ann Intern Med 105:204–206, 1986.

26. Muittari A, Kuusisto P, Virtanen P, et al: An epidemic of extrinsic allergic alveolitis caused by tap water. Clin Allergy 10:77–90, 1980.

27. Bryant DH, Rogers P: Allergic alveolitis due to wood-rot fungi. Allergy Proc 12:89–94, 1991.

28. Meeker DP, Gephardt GN, Cordasco EM Jr, et al: Hypersensitivity pneumonitis versus invasive pulmonary aspergillosis: Two cases with unusual pathologic findings and review of the literature. Am Rev Respir Dis 143:431–436, 1991.

29. Tsuchiya Y, Shimokata K, Ohara H, et al: Hypersensitivity pneumonitis in a soy sauce brewer caused by Aspergillus oryzae. J Allergy Clin Immunol 91:688–689, 1993.

30. Sanderson W, Kullman G, Sastre J, et al: Outbreak of hypersensitivity pneumonitis among mushroom farm workers. Am J Ind Med 22:859–872, 1992.

31. Yoshida K, Ueda A, Yamasaki H, et al: Hypersensitivity pneumonitis resulting from Aspergillus fumigatus in a greenhouse. Arch Environ Health 48:260–262, 1993.

32. Quirce S, Hinojosa M, Blanco R, et al: Aspergillus fumigatus is the causative agent of hypersensitivity pneumonitis caused by esparto dust. J Allergy Clin Immunol 102:147–148, 1998.

33. Schlueter DP: "Cheesewasher's disease": A new occupational hazard? Ann Intern Med 78:606–613, 1973.

34. Avila R, Lacey J: The role of Penicillium frequentans in suberosis (respiratory disease in workers in the cork industry). Clin Allergy 4:109–117, 1974.

35. Fergusson RJ, Milne LJ, Crompton GK: Penicillium allergic alveolitis: Faulty installation of central heating. Thorax 39:294–298, 1984.

36. van Assendelft AH, Raitio M, Turkia V: Fuel chip-induced hypersensitivity pneumonitis caused by Penicillium species. Chest 87:394–396, 1985.

37. Dykewicz MS, Laufer P, Patterson R, et al: Woodman's disease: Hypersensitivity pneumonitis from cutting live trees. J Allergy Clin Immunol 81:455–460, 1988.

38. Cormier Y, Israel-Assayag E, Bedard G, et al: Hypersensitivity pneumonitis in peat moss processing plant workers. Am J Respir Crit Care Med 158:412–417, 1998.

39. Nakagawa-Yoshida K, Ando M, Etches RI, et al: Fatal cases of farmer's lung in a Canadian family: Probable new antigens, Penicillium brevicompactum and P. olivicolor. Chest 111:245–248, 1997.

40. Emanuel DA, Wenzel FJ, Lawton BR: Pneumonitis due to Cryptostroma corticale (maple-bark disease). N Engl J Med 274:1413–1418, 1966.

41. Belin L: Clinical and immunological data on "wood trimmer's disease" in Sweden. Eur J Respir Dis Suppl 107:169–176, 1980.

42. Enarson DA, Chan-Yeung M: Characterization of health effects of wood dust exposures. Am J Ind Med 17:33–38, 1990.

43. Ando M, Suga M, Nishiura Y, et al: Summer-type hypersensitivity pneumonitis. Intern Med 34:707–712, 1995.

44. Alvarez-Fernandez JA, Quirce S, Calleja JL, et al: Hypersensitivity pneumonitis due to an ultrasonic humidifier. Allergy 53:210–212, 1998.

45. Plessner MM: Une maladie des trieurs de plumes: La fievre du canard. Arch Mal Prof 21:67–69, 1960.

46. Moore VL, Fink JN, Barboriak JJ, et al: Immunologic events in pigeon breeders' disease. J Allergy Clin Immunol 53:319–328, 1974.

47. Kokkarinen J, Tukiainen H, Seppa A, et al: Hypersensitivity pneumonitis due to native birds in a bird ringer. Chest 106:1269–1271, 1994.

48. Boyd G, McSharry CP, Banham SW, et al: A current view of pigeon fancier's lung: A model for pulmonary extrinsic allergic alveolitis. Clin Allergy 12:53–59, 1982.

49. Carroll KB, Pepys J, Longbottom JL, et al: Extrinsic allergic alveolitis due to rat serum proteins. Clin Allergy 5:443–456, 1975.

50. Pimental J: Furrier's lung. Thorax 25:387–398, 1970.

51. Lunn JA, Hughes DT: Pulmonary hypersensitivity to the grain weevil. Br J Ind Med 24:158–161, 1967.

52. Nakazawa T, Umegae Y: Sericulturist's lung disease: Hypersensitivity pneumonitis related to silk production. Thorax 45:233–234, 1990.

53. Orriols R, Manresa JM, Aliaga JL, et al: Mollusk shell hypersensitivity pneumonitis. Ann Intern Med 113:80–81, 1990.

54. Vandenplas O, Malo JL, Saetta M, et al: Occupational asthma and extrinsic alveolitis due to isocyanates: Current status and perspectives. Br J Ind Med 50:213–228, 1993.

55. Yoshizawa Y, Ohtsuka M, Noguchi K, et al: Hypersensitivity pneumonitis induced by toluene diisocyanate: Sequelae of continuous exposure. Ann Intern Med 110:31–34, 1989.

56. Baur X, Chen Z, Marczynski B: Respiratory diseases caused by occupational exposure to 1,5-naphthalene-diisocyanate (NDI): Results of workplace-related challenge tests and antibody analyses. Am J Ind Med 39:369–372, 2001.

57. Simpson C, Garabrant D, Torrey S, et al: Hypersensitivity pneumonitis-like reaction and occupational asthma associated with 1,3-bis(isocyanatomethyl)cyclohexane pre-polymer. Am J Ind Med 30:48–55, 1996.

58. Selden AI, Belin L, Wass U: Isocyanate exposure and hypersensitivity pneumonitis—report of a probable case and prevalence of specific immunoglobulin G antibodies among exposed individuals. Scand J Work Environ Health 15:234–237, 1989.

59. Walker CL, Grammer LC, Shaughnessy MA, et al: Diphenylmethane diisocyanate hypersensitivity pneumonitis: A serologic evaluation. J Occup Med 31:315–319, 1989.

60. Patterson R, Zeiss CR, Pruzansky JJ: Immunology and immunopathology of trimellitic anhydride pulmonary reactions. J Allergy Clin Immunol 70:19–23, 1982.

61. Piirila P, Keskinen H, Anttila S, et al: Allergic alveolitis following exposure to epoxy polyester powder paint containing low amounts (<1%) of acid anhydrides. Eur Respir J 10:948–951, 1997.

62. Carlson JE, Villaveces JW: Hypersensitivity pneumonitis due to pyrethrum: Report of a case. JAMA 237:1718–1719, 1977.

63. Evans WV, Seaton A: Hypersensitivity pneumonitis in a technician using Pauli's reagent. Thorax 34:767–770, 1979.

64. Pimental J, Marques S: Vineyard sprayer's lung: A new occupational disease. Thorax 24:678–683, 1969.

65. Grant IW, Blyth W, Wardrop VE, et al: Prevalence of farmer's lung in Scotland: A pilot survey. Br Med J 1:530–534, 1972.

66. Madsen D, Klock LE, Wenzel FJ, et al: The prevalence of farmer's lung in an agricultural population. Am Rev Respir Dis 113:171–174, 1976.

67. Marx JJ, Guernsey J, Emanuel DA, et al: Cohort studies of immunologic lung disease among Wisconsin dairy farmers. Am J Ind Med 18:263–268, 1990.

68. Terho I, Heinonen OP, Lammi S: Incidence of clinically confirmed farmer's lung disease in Finland. Am J Ind Med 10:330, 1986.

69. Hodgson M, Morey P, Simon J: An outbreak of recurrent acute and chronic hypersensitivity pneumonitis in office workers. Am J Epidemiol 125:631–638, 1987.

70. Christensen LT, Schmidt CD, Robbins L: Pigeon breeders' disease—a prevalence study and review. Clin Allergy 5:417–430, 1975.

71. Orriols R, Aliaga JL, Anto JM, et al: High prevalence of mollusc shell hypersensitivity pneumonitis in nacre factory workers. Eur Respir J 10:780–786, 1997.

72. Vandenplas O, Malo JL, Dugas M, et al: Hypersensitivity pneumonitis-like reaction among workers exposed to diphenylmethane [correction to piphenylmethane] diisocyanate (MDI). Am Rev Respir Dis 147:338–346, 1993.

73. Ando M, Arima K, Yoneda R, et al: Japanese summer-type hypersensitivity pneumonitis: Geographic distribution, home environment, and clinical characteristics of 621 cases. Am Rev Respir Dis 144:765–769, 1991.

74. Yoo CG, Kim YW, Han SK, et al: Summer-type hypersensitivity pneumonitis outside Japan: A case report and the state of the art. Respirology 2:75–77, 1997.

75. McSharry C, Lynch PP, Banham SW, et al: Seasonal variation of antibody levels among pigeon fanciers. Clin Allergy 13:293–299, 1983.

76. Riley DJ, Saldana M: Pigeon breeder's lung: Subacute course and the importance of indirect exposure. Am Rev Respir Dis 107:456–460, 1973.

77. Haitjema T, van Velzen-Blad H, van den Bosch JM: Extrinsic allergic alveolitis caused by goose feathers in a duvet. Thorax 47:990–991, 1992.

78. Kim KT, Dalton JW, Klaustermeyer WB: Subacute hypersensitivity pneumonitis to feathers presenting with weight loss and dyspnea. Ann Allergy 71:19–23, 1993.

79. Meyer FJ, Bauer PC, Costabel U: Feather wreath lung: Chasing a dead bird. Eur Respir J 9:1323–1324, 1996.

80. Flaherty DK, Braun SR, Marx JJ, et al: Serologically detectable HLA-A, B, and C loci antigens in farmer's lung disease. Am Rev Respir Dis 122:437–443, 1980.

81. Rodey GE, Fink J, Koethe S, et al: A study of HLA-A, B, C, and DR specificities in pigeon breeder's disease. Am Rev Respir Dis 119:755–759, 1979.

82. Camarena A, Juarez A, Mejia M, et al: Major histocompatibility complex and tumor necrosis factor-alpha polymorphisms in pigeon breeder's disease. Am J Respir Crit Care Med 163:1528–1533, 2001.

83. Schaaf BM, Seitzer U, Pravica V, et al: Tumor necrosis factor-alpha -308 promoter gene polymorphism and increased tumor necrosis factor serum bioactivity in farmer's lung patients. Am J Respir Crit Care Med 163:379–382, 2001.

84. Warren CP: Extrinsic allergic alveolitis: A disease commoner in non-smokers. Thorax 32:567–569, 1977.

85. Baldwin CI, Todd A, Bourke S, et al: Pigeon fanciers' lung: Effects of smoking on serum and salivary antibody responses to pigeon antigens. Clin Exp Immunol 113:166–172, 1998.

86. Munakata M, Tanimura K, Ukuta H: Smoking promotes insidious and chronic farmer's lung disease, and deteriorates the clinical outcome. Intern Med 34:966–971, 1995.

87. Stiehm ER, Reed CE, Tooley WH: Pigeon breeder's lung in children. Pediatrics 39:904–915, 1967.

88. Fan LL: Hypersensitivity pneumonitis in children. Curr Opin Pediatr 14:323–326, 2002.

89. Eisenberg JD, Montanero A, Lee RG: Hypersensitivity pneumonitis in an infant. Pediatr Pulmonol 12:186–190, 1992.

90. Lama M, Chapela R, Salas J: Hypersensitivity pneumonitis: Clinical approach and an integral concept about its pathogenesis. A Mexican point of view. In Lama MS, Barrios R (eds): Interstitial Pulmonary Diseases: Selected Topics. Boca Raton, Fla: CRC Press, 1991, pp 171–195.

90a. Facco M, Trentin L, Nicolardi L, et al: T cells in the lung of patients with hypersensitivity pneumonitis accumulate in a clonal manner. J Leukoc Biol 75:798–804, 2004.

91. Patel AM, Ryu JH, Reed CE: Hypersensitivity pneumonitis: Current concepts and future questions (see comment). J Allergy Clin Immunol 108:661–670, 2001.

92. Fournier E, Tonnel AB, Gosset P, et al: Early neutrophil alveolitis after antigen inhalation in hypersensitivity pneumonitis. Chest 88:563–566, 1985.

93. Yoshizawa Y, Nomura A, Ohdama S, et al: The significance of complement activation in the pathogenesis of hypersensitivity pneumonitis: sequential changes of complement components and chemotactic activities in bronchoalveolar lavage fluids. Int Arch Allergy Appl Immunol 87:417–423, 1988.

94. Yoshizawa Y, Ohdama S, Tanoue M, et al: Analysis of bronchoalveolar lavage cells and fluids in patients with hypersensitivity pneumonitis: Possible role of chemotactic factors in the pathogenesis of disease. Int Arch Allergy Appl Immunol 80:376–382, 1986.

95. Mornex JF, Cordier G, Pages J, et al: Activated lung lymphocytes in hypersensitivity pneumonitis. J Allergy Clin Immunol 74:719–727, 1984.

96. Laflamme C, Israel-Assayag E, Cormier Y: Apoptosis of bronchoalveolar lavage lymphocytes in hypersensitivity pneumonitis. Eur Respir J 21:225–231, 2003.

97. Denis M, Bedard M, Laviolette M, et al: A study of monokine release and natural killer activity in the bronchoalveolar lavage of subjects with farmer's lung. Am Rev Respir Dis 147:934–939, 1993.

98. Walls A, Roberts J, Godfrey R, et al: Histochemical heterogeneity of human mast cells: Disease-related differences in mast cell subsets recovered by bronchoalveolar lavage. Int Arch Allergy Appl Immunol 92:233–241, 1990.

99. Pardo A, Barrios R, Gaxiola M, et al: Increase of lung neutrophils in hypersensitivity pneumonitis is associated with lung fibrosis. Am J Respir Crit Care Med 161:1698–1704, 2000.

100. Haslam PL, Dewar A, Butchers P, et al: Mast cells, atypical lymphocytes, and neutrophils in bronchoalveolar lavage in extrinsic allergic alveolitis: Comparison with other interstitial lung diseases. Am Rev Respir Dis 135:35–47, 1987.

101. Semenzato G, Agostini C, Zambello R, et al: Lung T cells in hypersensitivity pneumonitis: Phenotypic and functional analyses. J Immunol 137:1164–1172, 1986.

102. Cormier Y, Belanger J, Laviolette M: Prognostic significance of bronchoalveolar lymphocytosis in farmer's lung. Am Rev Respir Dis 135:692–695, 1987.

103. Brummund W, Kurup VP, Resnick A, et al: Immunologic response to *Faenia rectivirgula* (*Micropolyspora faeni*) in a dairy farm family. J Allergy Clin Immunol 82:190–195, 1988.

104. Ratjen F, Costabel U, Griese M, et al: Bronchoalveolar lavage fluid findings in children with hypersensitivity pneumonitis. Eur Respir J 21:144–148, 2003.

105. Murayama J, Yoshizawa Y, Ohtsuka M, et al: Lung fibrosis in hypersensitivity pneumonitis: Association with CD4+ but not CD8+ cell dominant alveolitis and insidious onset. Chest 104:38–43, 1993.

106. Richerson HB, Coon JD, Lubaroff D: Adoptive transfer of experimental hypersensitivity pneumonitis in the LEW rat. Am J Respir Crit Care Med 151:1205–1210, 1995.

107. Bice DE, Salvaggio J, Hoffman E: Passive transfer of experimental hypersensitivity pneumonitis with lymphoid cells in the rabbit. J Allergy Clin Immunol 58:250–262, 1976.

108. Schuyler M, Gott K, Cherne A, et al: Th1 CD4+ cells adoptively transfer experimental hypersensitivity pneumonitis. Cell Immunol 177:169–175, 1997.

109. Cormier Y, Samson N, Israel-Assayag E: Viral infection enhances the response to *Saccharopolyspora rectivirgula* in mice prechallenged with this farmer's lung antigen. Lung 174:399–407, 1996.

110. Coleman A, Colby TV: Histologic diagnosis of extrinsic allergic alveolitis. Am J Surg Pathol 12:514–518, 1988.

111. Vourlekis JS, Schwarz MI, Cool CD, et al: Nonspecific interstitial pneumonitis as the sole histologic expression of hypersensitivity pneumonitis. Am J Med 112:490–493, 2002.

112. Reyes CN, Wenzel FJ, Lawton BR, et al: The pulmonary pathology of farmer's lung disease. Chest 81:142–146, 1982.

113. Yoshizawa Y, Ohtani Y, Hayakawa H, et al: Chronic hypersensitivity pneumonitis in Japan: a nationwide epidemiologic survey. J Allergy Clin Immunol 103:315–320, 1999.

114. Hayakawa H, Shirai M, Sato A, et al: Clinicopathological features of chronic hypersensitivity pneumonitis. Respirology 7:359–364, 2002.

115. Thorn A, Lewne M, Belin L: Allergic alveolitis in a school environment. Scand J Work Environ Health 22:311–314, 1996.

116. Sansores R, Salas J, Chapela R, et al: Clubbing in hypersensitivity pneumonitis: Its prevalence and possible prognostic role. Arch Intern Med 150:1849–1851, 1990.

117. Roberts RC, Wenzel FJ, Emanuel DA: Precipitating antibodies in a midwest dairy farming population toward the antigens associated with farmer's lung disease. J Allergy Clin Immunol 57:518–524, 1976.

117a. Cormier Y, Letourneau L, Racine G: Significance of precipitins and asymptomatic lymphocytic alveolitis: a 20-yr follow-up. Eur Respir J 23:523–525, 2004.

118. Cormier Y, Belanger J: The fluctuant nature of precipitating antibodies in dairy farmers. Thorax 44:469–473, 1989.

118a. Trout DB, Seltzer JM, Page EH, et al: Clinical use of immunoassays in assessing exposure to fungi and potential health effects related to fungal exposure. Ann Allergy Asthma Immunol 92:483–491, 2004.

119. Cormier Y, Belanger J, LeBlanc P, et al: Bronchoalveolar lavage in farmers' lung disease: Diagnostic and physiological significance. Br J Ind Med 43:401–405, 1986.

120. Krasnick J, Meuwissen HJ, Nakao MA, et al: Hypersensitivity pneumonitis: Problems in diagnosis. J Allergy Clin Immunol 97:1027–1030, 1996.

121. Barbee RA, Callies Q, Dickie HA, et al: The long-term prognosis in farmer's lung. Am Rev Respir Dis 97:223–231, 1968.

122. Huls G, Lindemann H, Velcovsky HG: Angiotensin converting enzyme (ACE) in the follow-up control of children and adolescents with allergic alveolitis (in German). Monatsschr Kinderheilkd 137:158–161, 1989.

123. Schwaiblmair M, Beinert T, Vogelmeier C, et al: Cardiopulmonary exercise testing following hay exposure challenge in farmer's lung. Eur Respir J 10:2360–2365, 1997.

124. Cormier Y, Belanger J: Long-term physiologic outcome after acute farmer's lung. Chest 87:796–800, 1985.

125. Pepys J, Jenkins PA: Precipitin (FLH) test in farmer's lung. Thorax 20:21–35, 1965.

126. Freedman PM, Ault B: Bronchial hyperreactivity to methacholine in farmers' lung disease. J Allergy Clin Immunol 67:59–63, 1981.

127. Akira M, Kita N, Higashihara T, et al: Summer-type hypersensitivity pneumonitis: Comparison of high-resolution CT and plain radiographic findings. AJR Am J Roentgenol 158:1223–1228, 1992.

128. Hodgson MJ, Parkinson DK, Karpf M: Chest x-rays in hypersensitivity pneumonitis: A metaanalysis of secular trend. Am J Ind Med 16:45–53, 1989.

129. Monkare S, Ikonen M, Haahtela T: Radiologic findings in farmer's lung: Prognosis and correlation to lung function. Chest 84:460–466, 1985.

130. Lynch DA, Rose CS, Way D, et al: Hypersensitivity pneumonitis: Sensitivity of high-resolution CT in a population-based study. AJR Am J Roentgenol 159:469–472, 1992.

131. Buschman DL, Gamsu G, Waldron JA Jr, et al: Chronic hypersensitivity pneumonitis: Use of CT in diagnosis. AJR Am J Roentgenol 159:957–960, 1992.

132. Adler BD, Padley SP, Muller NL, et al: Chronic hypersensitivity pneumonitis: High-resolution CT and radiographic features in 16 patients. Radiology 185:91–95, 1992.

133. Remy-Jardin M, Remy J, Wallaert B, et al: Subacute and chronic bird breeder hypersensitivity pneumonitis: Sequential evaluation with CT and correlation with lung function tests and bronchoalveolar lavage. Radiology 189:111–118, 1993.

134. Malinen A, Erkinjuntti-Pekkanen R, Partanen P, et al: Long-term sequelae of farmer's lung disease in HRCT: A 14-year follow-up study of 88 patients and 83 matched control farmers. Chest 13:2212–2221, 2003.

135. Hansell DM, Wells AU, Padley SP, et al: Hypersensitivity pneumonitis: Correlation of individual CT patterns with functional abnormalities. Radiology 199:123–128, 1996.

136. Franquet T, Hansell DM, Senbanjo T, et al: Lung cysts in subacute hypersensitivity pneumonitis. J Comput Assist Tomogr 27:475–478, 2003.

137. Niimi H, Kang EY, Kwong JS, et al: CT of chronic infiltrative lung disease: Prevalence of mediastinal lymphadenopathy. J Comput Assist Tomogr 20:305–308, 1996.

138. Hendrick DJ, Marshall R, Faux JA, et al: Positive "alveolar" responses to antigen inhalation provocation tests: Their validity and recognition. Thorax 35:415–427, 1980.

139. Ramirez-Venegas A, Sansores RH, Perez-Padilla R, et al: Utility of a provocation test for diagnosis of chronic pigeon breeder's disease. Am J Respir Crit Care Med 158:862–869, 1998.

140. Richerson HB, Bernstein IL, Fink JN, et al: Guidelines for the clinical evaluation of hypersensitivity pneumonitis: Report of the Subcommittee on Hypersensitivity Pneumonitis. J Allergy Clin Immunol 84:839–844, 1989.

141. Drent M, Mulder PG, Wagenaar SS, et al: Differences in BAL fluid variables in interstitial lung diseases evaluated by discriminant analysis. Eur Respir J 6:803–810, 1993.

142. Laviolette M, Cormier Y, Loiseau A, et al: Bronchoalveolar mast cells in normal farmers and subjects with farmer's lung: Diagnostic, prognostic, and physiologic significance. Am Rev Respir Dis 144:855–860, 1991.

143. Calvanico NJ, Ambegaonkar SP, Schlueter DP, et al: Immunoglobulin levels in bronchoalveolar lavage fluid from pigeon breeders. J Lab Clin Med 96:129–140, 1980.

144. Trentin L, Marcer G, Chilosi M, et al: Longitudinal study of alveolitis in hypersensitivity pneumonitis patients: An immunologic evaluation. J Allergy Clin Immunol 82:577–585, 1988.

145. Cormier Y, Belanger J, Laviolette M: Persistent bronchoalveolar lymphocytosis in asymptomatic farmers. Am Rev Respir Dis 133:843–847, 1986.

146. Descombes E, Gardiol D, Leuenberger P: Transbronchial lung biopsy: An analysis of 530 cases with reference to the number of samples. Monaldi Arch Chest Dis 52:324–329, 1997.

147. Colby TV, Coleman A: The histologic diagnosis of extrinsic allergic alveolitis and its differential diagnosis. Prog Surg Pathol 10:11–26, 1989.

148. Terho EO: Diagnostic criteria for farmer's lung disease. Am J Ind Med 10:329, 1986.

149. Lacasse Y, Selman M, Costabel U, et al: Clinical diagnosis of hypersensitivity pneumonitis. Am J Respir Crit Care Med 168:952, 2003.

150. Dangman KH, Cole SR, Hodgson MJ, et al: The hypersensitivity pneumonitis diagnostic index: Use of non-invasive testing to diagnose hypersensitivity pneumonitis in metalworkers. Am J Ind Med 42:150–162, 2002.

151. Rose C, King TE Jr: Controversies in hypersensitivity pneumonitis (editorial). Am Rev Respir Dis 145:1–2, 1992.

152. Monkare S, Haahtela T: Farmer's lung—a 5-year follow-up of eighty-six patients. Clin Allergy 17:143–151, 1987.

153. Chasse M, Blanchette G, Malo J, et al: Farmer's lung presenting as respiratory failure and homogeneous consolidation. Chest 90:783–784, 1986.

154. Greenberger PA, Pien LC, Patterson R, et al: End-stage lung and ultimately fatal disease in a bird fancier. Am J Med 86:119–122, 1989.

154a. Vourlekis JS, Schwarz MI, Cherniack RM, et al: The effect of pulmonary fibrosis on survival in patients with hypersensitivity pneumonitis. Am J Med 116:662–668, 2004.

155. Schmidt CD, Jensen RL, Christensen LT, et al: Longitudinal pulmonary function changes in pigeon breeders. Chest 93:359–363, 1988.

156. Grammer LC, Roberts M, Lerner C, et al: Clinical and serologic follow-up of four children and five adults with bird-fancier's lung. J Allergy Clin Immunol 85:655–660, 1990.

157. Tasaka S, Kanazawa M, Kawai D: Fatal diffuse alveolar damage from bird fanciers' lung. Respiration 64:307–309, 1997.

158. Kokkarinen J, Tukiainen H, Terho EO: Mortality due to farmer's lung in Finland. Chest 106:509–512, 1994.

159. Braun SR, doPico GA, Tsiatis A, et al: Farmer's lung disease: Long-term clinical and physiologic outcome. Am Rev Respir Dis 119:185–191, 1979.

160. Erkinjuntti-Pekkanen R, Rytkonen H, Kokkarinen JI, et al: Long-term risk of emphysema in patients with farmer's lung and matched control farmers. Am J Respir Crit Care Med 158:662–665, 1998.

161. Erkinjuntti-Pekkanen R, Kokkarinen JI, Tukiainen HO, et al: Long-term outcome of pulmonary function in farmer's lung: A 14 year follow-up with matched controls. Eur Respir J 10:2046–2050, 1997.

162. Lalancette M, Carrier G, Laviolette M, et al: Farmer's lung: Long-term outcome and lack of predictive value of bronchoalveolar lavage fibrosing factors. Am Rev Respir Dis 148:216–221, 1993.

163. Kokkarinen JI, Tukiainen HO, Terho EO: Asthma in patients with farmer's lung during a five-year follow-up. Scand J Work Environ Health 23:149–151, 1997.

164. Perez-Padilla R, Salas J, Chapela R, et al: Mortality in Mexican patients with chronic pigeon breeder's lung compared with those with usual interstitial pneumonia. Am Rev Respir Dis 148:49–53, 1993.

165. Cuthbert OD, Gordon MF: Ten year follow up of farmers with farmer's lung. Br J Ind Med 40:173–176, 1983.

166. Bourke SJ, Banham SW, Carter R, et al: Longitudinal course of extrinsic allergic alveolitis in pigeon breeders. Thorax 44:415–418, 1989.

167. Richerson HB, Richards DW, Swanson PA, et al: Antigen-specific desensitization in a rabbit model of acute hypersensitivity pneumonitis. J Allergy Clin Immunol 68:226–234, 1981.

168. Allen DH, Williams GV, Woolcock AJ: Bird breeder's hypersensitivity pneumonitis: Progress studies of lung function after cessation of exposure to the provoking antigen. Am Rev Respir Dis 114:555–566, 1976.

169. de Gracia J, Morell F, Bofill JM, et al: Time of exposure as a prognostic factor in avian hypersensitivity pneumonitis. Respir Med 83:139–143, 1989.

170. Yoshida K, Ando M, Sakata T, et al: Prevention of summer-type hypersensitivity pneumonitis: Effect of elimination of *Trichosporon cutaneum* from the patients' homes. Arch Environ Health 44:317–322, 1989.

171. Woodard ED, Friedlander B, Lesher RJ, et al: Outbreak of hypersensitivity pneumonitis in an industrial setting. JAMA 259:1965–1969, 1988.

172. Reed CE, Swanson MC, Lopez M, et al: Measurement of IgG antibody and airborne antigen to control an industrial outbreak of hypersensitivity pneumonitis. J Occup Med 25:207–210, 1983.

173. Bracker A, Storey E, Yang C, et al: An outbreak of hypersensitivity pneumonitis at a metalworking plant: A longitudinal assessment of intervention effectiveness. Appl Occup Environ Hyg 18:96–108, 2003.

174. Zwick H, Popp W, Braun O, et al: Personal spore sampling and indirect immunofluorescent test for exploration of hypersensitivity pneumonitis due to mould spores. Allergy 46:277–283, 1991.

175. American Conference of Governmental Industrial Hygienists: Developing an Investigation Strategy. *In* Macher JM (ed): Bioaerosols Assessment and Control. Cincinnati, Ohio: American Conference of Governmental Industrial Hygienists, 1999.

176. Craig TJ, Hershey J, Engler RJ, et al: Bird antigen persistence in the home environment after removal of the bird. Ann Allergy 69:510–512, 1992.

177. Craig TJ, Hershey J, Engler RJ, et al: Tannic acid's effect on bird antigen. Ann Allergy Asthma Immunol 75:348–350, 1995.

178. Monkare S: Influence of corticosteroid treatment on the course of farmer's lung. Eur J Respir Dis 64:283–293, 1983.

179. Chen C, Kleinau I, Niggemann B, et al: Treatment of allergic alveolitis with methylprednisolone pulse therapy. Pediatr Allergy Immunol 14:66–70, 2003.

180. Kokkarinen JI, Tukiainen HO, Terho EO: Effect of corticosteroid treatment on the recovery of pulmonary function in farmer's lung. Am Rev Respir Dis 145:3–5, 1992.

181. Carlsen KH, Leegaard J, Lund OD, et al: Allergic alveolitis in a 12-year-old boy: Treatment with budesonide nebulizing solution. Pediatr Pulmonol 12:257–259, 1992.

182. Losa Garcia JE, Mateos Rodriguez F, Jimenez Lopez A, et al: Effect of cyclosporin A on inflammatory cytokine production by human alveolar macrophages. Respir Med 92:722–728, 1998.

183. Zejda JE, McDuffie HH, Dosman JA: Epidemiology of health and safety risks in agriculture and related industries: Practical applications for rural physicians. West J Med 158:56–63, 1993.

184. Dalphin JC, Toson B, Monnet E, et al: Farmer's lung precipitins in Doubs (a department of France): Prevalence and diagnostic value. Allergy 49:744–750, 1994.

185. Mauny F, Polio JC, Monnet E, et al: Longitudinal study of respiratory health in dairy farmers: Influence of artificial barn fodder drying. Eur Respir J 10:2522–2528, 1997.

186. Nuutinen J, Terho EO, Husman K, et al: Protective value of powered dust respirator helmet for farmers with farmer's lung. Eur J Respir Dis Suppl 152:212–220, 1987.

187. Anderson K, Walker A, Boyd G: The long-term effect of a positive pressure respirator on the specific antibody response in pigeon breeders. Clin Exp Allergy 19:45–49, 1989.

188. Hendrick DJ, Marshall R, Faux JA, et al: Protective value of dust respirators in extrinsic allergic alveolitis: Clinical assessment using inhalation provocation tests. Thorax 36:917–921, 1981.

189. Yoshizawa Y, Ohtani Y, Hayakawa H, et al: Chronic hypersensitivity pneumonitis in Japan: A nationwide epidemiologic survey. J Allergy Clin Immunol 103:315–320, 1999.

63

Air Pollution

John R. Balmes, M.D., Ira B. Tager, M.D., M.P.H., Mark D. Eisner, M.D., M.P.H.

INTRODUCTION

Appreciation of a general relationship between disease and breathing air contaminated by the products of human activity is ancient. Steps were taken to regulate the use of coal in England during the reign of Richard II (1377–1399).[1] It later became apparent that the danger was not confined to workers exposed to the highest concentrations of pollutants at sites of production; those living in the areas immediately surrounding certain industries were also at risk. That whole communities were at risk was most forcefully brought home by a series of air pollution episodes: in the Meuse Valley of Belgium in 1930; in Donora, Pennsylvania, in 1948; and in London, England, in 1952.[2] In these episodes, several days of air stagnation resulted in greatly increased concentrations of atmospheric pollutants, especially of sulfur dioxide and particulates, followed by a striking increase in mortality. In the worst of these episodes, in London, the death rate reached a level that had been exceeded in the 20th century only in the influenza pandemic of 1917–1918.[3] Although all age groups shared to some extent in the increase in mortality, most deaths occurred in the very young, the elderly, and persons already suffering from heart or lung disease. The excess mortality was largely due to bronchitis, pneumonia, and other respiratory and cardiac diseases. Individuals seemed also to differ in their sensitivity to the nonlethal consequences of these crises. In Donora, for example, there was one report of exacerbations in 88% of patients with asthma surveyed.[4]

Stimulated by the respiratory health effects of these episodes of extreme ambient air pollution, a large number of investigations have been carried out to define more clearly the impact of ambient air pollution on the respiratory tract and human health. Since 1975, these investigations have identified a variety of respiratory health effects at pollutant concentrations that are just above or within the levels set by the U.S. Environmental Protection Agency (EPA) (Table 63.1).[5]

A comprehensive review of the published research would be encyclopedic, because the effects of air pollution include not just impairment of human health but also what are collectively referred to as "welfare" effects, such as reductions in visibility and damage to buildings and structures, to agriculture, and to whole ecosystems. Similarly, the number of pollutants is legion, reflecting the ever-increasing complexity of the production, storage, and destruction of industrial products. Thus, this chapter discusses mainly the so-called criteria air pollutants (see Table 63.1), except for lead and carbon monoxide, and reviews what has been learned about the adverse effects of these pollutants on the lungs and airways. Criteria pollutants are those for which the EPA has determined there is an adequate scientific database on health effects to justify the regulation of air quality. The regulation of ambient concentration of each specific criteria pollutant is known as the National Ambient Air Quality Standard (NAAQS) for the particular pollutant. The circumscribed nature of this review should be kept in mind, for materials dispersed in the air are not absorbed uniquely through the respiratory tract. Particles settle, for example, on crops and waters destined for ingestion. And even if pollutants are absorbed through the respiratory tract, their adverse effects need not be confined to the lungs and airways, for materials are absorbed through mucosal surfaces into the circulation, and some have been implicated in impairing function of the central nervous system, bone marrow, and other organs.

POLLUTANTS

The definition of the term *pollutant* is elusive. Some experts consider an air pollutant to be any gas or particle that is increased in concentration to levels above those generally accepted as normal. At some sites, however, gases normally present in the atmosphere, as in caves, may be lethal for humans. Others consider a material to be a pollutant only if it is detectable as an unpleasant or hazardous material. The problem with this definition is apparent, for the definition of a pollutant must now start with the identification of an effect. This is, in fact, the approach that has been taken toward considering products of industrial activity that contaminate the atmosphere, and the definition of what constitutes an "adverse health effect" has been the subject of debate[6] that remains under periodic review. For the purposes of this review, any effect that impairs function or that indicates the initiation of a sequence of events known to result in the impairment of function is considered an "adverse health effect."

Three major types of air pollutants are recognized: the sulfur dioxide and particulate complex, photochemical oxidants, and a miscellaneous category of pollutants arising from industrial and mobile sources (so-called toxic air contaminants). Only the first two of these types of pollution are discussed in this chapter because the primary adverse health effects associated with toxic air contaminants are non-

respiratory cancers and reproductive dysfunction. However, several recent reports have also implicated volatile organic compounds as triggers of asthma exacerbations.[7,8] This conventional method of grouping pollutants is based on the conditions that lead to their production and not necessarily on common biologic effects. For example, atmospheric acids can be generated by by-products of sulfur dioxide (e.g., sulfuric acid) and of oxides of nitrogen (nitric acid). Epidemiologic evidence has implicated atmospheric acidity as a possible contributing factor in the development of adverse respiratory health effects. However, the biologic effects of these acids are quite different from those of the parent compounds from which they are derived. Some of the commonly encountered pollutants associated with adverse pulmonary effects are listed in Table 63.2.

Indoor air quality has assumed increasing importance. As levels of outdoor ambient air pollution have decreased in many areas throughout the United States, the relative impact of indoor air pollution has increased. North American residents spend the majority of their time indoors, increasing the importance of indoor exposures.[9] In particular, most children and adults spend the greatest proportion of their average day inside the home. At the same time, changes in home and office building construction have resulted in lower air exchange rates, increasing personal exposure to pollutants emitted indoors.[3] To adequately characterize personal exposure to air pollution, indoor air quality must be taken into account (Fig. 63.1).

GENERAL PROPERTIES, SOURCES, AND DISTRIBUTION

Sulfur oxides, particulate matter, ozone, and nitrogen dioxide (NO_2) are the most widely encountered pollutants that have been shown to cause adverse pulmonary effects. Sulfur dioxide is produced by the combustion of sulfur contained in fossil fuels such as coal and crude oil, and the major sources of environmental pollution with sulfur dioxide are power plants, oil refineries, smelters, and paper pulp mills. In the United States, sulfur dioxide levels are generally higher in the northeastern and midwestern states, primarily because of the use of high–sulfur-content coal in

Table 63.1 National Primary Air Quality Standards in the United States (Criteria Pollutants)

Pollutant	Standard	Averaging Period
Carbon monoxide	9 ppm (10 mg/m^3) 35 ppm (40 mg/m^3)	8 hr 1 hr
Nitrogen dioxide	0.053 ppm (100 µg/m^3)	1 yr
Ozone	0.12 ppm (235 µg/m^3) 0.08 ppm (157 µg/m^3)	1 hr 8 hr
Particulate <10 µm (PM$_{10}$)	50 µg/m^3 150 µg/m^3	1 yr 24 hr
Particulate <2.5 µm (PM$_{2.5}$)	15 µg/m^3 65 µg/m^3	1 yr 24 hr
Sulfur dioxide	0.03 ppm (80 µg/m^3) 0.14 ppm (365 µg/m^3)	1 yr 24 hr
Lead	1.5 µg/m^3	3 mo

Table 63.2 Major Pollutants Associated with Adverse Pulmonary Effects

Pollutant	Outdoor Sources	Indoor Sources	Adverse Effects
Sulfur oxides	Power plants, oil refineries, smelters	Kerosene space heaters	Bronchoconstriction
Oxides of nitrogen	Motor vehicle exhaust, power plants, oil refineries	Gas stoves and furnaces, kerosene space heaters	Airway injury (respiratory bronchiolitis), impaired lung defenses, enhanced response to allergen
Ozone	Motor vehicle exhaust	Aircraft cabins, welding, copiers, ozone generators	Airway injury (respiratory bronchiolitis), decreased lung function, exacerbations of asthma, enhanced response to allergen
Particulate matter	Motor vehicle exhaust, power plants	Tobacco and wood smoke	Exacerbations of asthma and chronic obstructive pulmonary disease, increased cardiopulmonary mortality
Radon		Residential basements	Lung cancer
Polycyclic hydrocarbons	Diesel exhaust	Tobacco smoke	Lung cancer

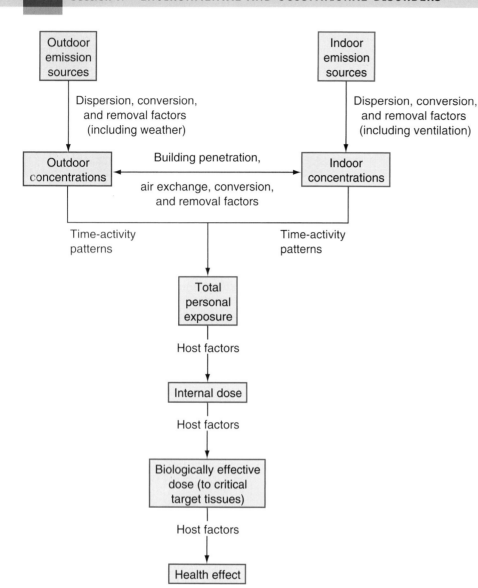

Figure 63.1 Relationship among outdoor pollution, indoor pollution, and health effects.

power plants. Sulfur dioxide itself is a clear, highly water-soluble gas, so it is effectively absorbed by the mucosal surfaces of the upper airways. A very small proportion of inhaled sulfur dioxide reaches the distal regions of the lungs.[10] However, the sulfur dioxide released into the atmosphere does not remain uniquely in the form of a gas; rather, it undergoes chemical reactions with water, trace metals, and other pollutants to form a variety of particulate aerosols. The nature of particles generated from sulfur-containing fuels varies from place to place, but sulfuric acid and various metallic, acidic, and ammonium sulfates are commonly present. Other nonsulfur products of fossil fuel combustion (soot; fly ash; oxides of iron, zinc, and copper; silicates; nitrates) contribute to the type of pollution present in urban areas where coal is burned in many residences and industrial emissions are not well controlled (e.g., London in the 1950s). This mixture of sulfur oxides and small particles may be blown great distances from its site of production, undergoing continuous transformation from gas to particle phase and ultimately becoming "acid rain" capable of profoundly affecting flora and fauna.[11]

In the western United States and many other areas of the world, particulate pollution is not driven by the combustion of sulfur-containing fuels. Atmospheric particulate air pollution arises from a variety of sources, both natural (e.g., sea spray, windblown dust) and synthetic sources (e.g., power plants, motor vehicles).[1,12,13] Particulate material that enters the atmosphere can be primary (particles emitted directly) and secondary (particles that form by chemical reactions that involve gas-phase precursors, such as sulfur dioxide and oxides of nitrogen).[4] Particles span a wide range of diameters from 0.003 μm (e.g., from automobiles, power generation) to as large as 1 μm (particles produced in the atmosphere). Photochemical processes produce particles in the range of 0.003 to 2 μm in diameter. Windblown dust, pollens, and cement dust are generally larger than 2 μm.[14] To date, most studies of the health effects of particles have focused on particle mass. Environmental monitoring before 1987 evaluated particles up to approximately 50 μm in aerodynamic diameter; however, since the 1970s, the focus has been on particle sizes that can be deposited in the human respiratory tract (generally <10 μm in diameter).[15]

Particles classified as "fine" (<2.5 μm) can travel for long distances and remain in the atmosphere for days to weeks; "coarse" particles (>2.5 μm) travel for rather short distances and have atmospheric half-lives of minutes to hours.[15] "Ultrafine" particles (<0.1 μm) are typically generated from combustion processes and have short atmospheric half-lives.[16] For example, the concentration of ultrafine particles emitted from motor vehicles on a major roadway has a rapid falloff with distance from the roadway, so by 300 m the concentration is back to the background level.[17] The distribution of the number of particles is inversely rated to particle size.[18] "Fine" mode particles are composed mainly of varying amounts of water and six major components (sulfates, acids, nitrates, elemental carbon, organic carbon, and trace metals), several of which can be further subdivided on the basis of chemical constituents and sources.[15] They are formed from gases by nucleation, condensation, or liquid-phase reactions. "Coarse" mode particles are composed primarily of crustal (rock, soil), biologic (pollen, spores), and industrial components; they are formed primarily by mechanical processes that produce small particles from larger particles.

Ozone and nitrogen oxides are primarily products of the action of sunlight on emissions of internal combustion engines.[19] The most important of these products are unburned hydrocarbons and NO_2, an oxidation product of nitrogen oxide, which is in turn a product of the fixation of atmospheric nitrogen with oxygen under conditions of high-temperature combustion. Ultraviolet irradiation of this mixture in the atmosphere results in a complex series of chemical reactions, producing ozone, alkyl nitrates, peroxyacyl nitrates, alcohols, ethers, acids, peroxyacids, and other organic and inorganic compounds that exist in both gas and particulate aerosol phases.[19] This mixture of pollutants typifies the "smog" of areas with large numbers of automobiles and abundant sunlight, such as the Los Angeles basin. Because ozone and NO_2 are the gases present in highest concentration and because they clearly cause toxic effects in animals and humans excessively exposed to them, they have been the oxidant pollutants most extensively studied. Both gases are relatively insoluble and poorly absorbed by the upper airways. A high proportion of the dose inhaled thus reaches the peripheral portion of the lungs and can cause injury at any site from the upper airways to the alveoli.[20]

Outdoor urban air contains a number of known carcinogens, including polycyclic hydrocarbons, n-nitroso compounds, and asbestos. However, the concentrations of these carcinogens in ambient air are quite low. Epidemiologic studies of exposure to diesel exhaust have provided consistent evidence of an excess risk of lung cancer in workers exposed to diesel exhaust,[21] and diesel exhaust is considered a probable carcinogen in humans by several agencies on the basis of experimental and epidemiologic data.[22] Several large population-based epidemiologic studies also have indicated an increased risk of lung cancer in relation to long-term exposure to ambient concentrations of particulate air pollutants, sulfur dioxide, and ozone.[23-25a]

INDOOR AIR POLLUTION

Whereas most attention has been given to pollutants present in outdoor air, it is now apparent that elevated concentra-

Table 63.3 Indoor Air Pollutants
Secondhand smoke exposure
Gas stove exposure
Wood smoke exposure
Kerosene heaters

Building materials that emit volatile compounds
    Plywood
    Particleboard
    Carpeting
    Paints

Cleaning materials

tions of airborne contaminants are common inside homes, public buildings, and other indoor microenvironments (Table 63.3).[26] Because urban residents typically spend 90% of their time indoors and because some contaminants are present in higher concentrations in indoor air, public health officials have become aware that measurement of outdoor air quality does not adequately characterize the risks of personal exposure.[26] Among the pollutants of indoor air of greatest concern are the by-products of cigarette smoking ("passive smoking" or second-hand smoke [SHS]), which appear to increase the risk of lower respiratory tract infection and asthma in children and the risk of cardiovascular disease and lung cancer among adults.[27] NO_2, a product of natural gas and kerosene combustion, may be present in indoor air in concentrations many times higher than those in outdoor air.[28] This has been suspected to increase the prevalence of respiratory illnesses in small children in the age range of 5 to 12 years raised in homes with natural gas, rather than electricity, as an energy source for cooking and heating,[29,30] but not in infants in the first 18 months of life.[31] Sulfur dioxide concentrations can reach levels 20 times higher than the present U.S. primary air quality standard of 0.14 part per million (ppm) in rooms heated by commercially available kerosene-burning space heaters[32]; ozone levels three times or more greater than the permitted level in outdoor air may be encountered in the cabins of high-altitude commercial aircraft[33]; and formaldehyde is released into the air of buildings insulated with urea-formaldehyde foam insulation and in mobile homes in which there is extensive use of plywood.[34]

A pollutant of indoor air that has caused particular concern is radon, a naturally occurring radioactive gas in the decay series of uranium (^{238}U) present in building materials made from rocks and soils. Epidemiologic studies of underground miners have provided strong and consistent evidence that radon causes lung cancer,[22] and surveys conducted by the EPA have documented high levels of radon in some homes in many regions of the United States, especially in the northeastern states.[35] The lung cancer risk from radon exposure in household air has so far proved difficult to define precisely.[22,36] The EPA has nonetheless estimated that about 15,000 to 20,000 lung cancer deaths annually are attributable to indoor radon.[35] In the meantime, some experts have suggested that the most cost-efficient way to reduce the incidence of radon-induced lung cancer is through smoking cessation and education of occupants of radon-contaminated homes to take such simple steps as improving the ventilation system, avoiding the use of basements as living areas, and discouraging the display of actinide-containing mineral collections in living areas.[37]

Ironically, the importance of pollution of indoor air became apparent as a result of steps taken to reduce the need for heat production from the combustion of fossil fuels. With more efficient insulation of buildings, the turnover of indoor air is reduced, permitting the accumulation of greater quantities of contaminants.

Sources of Indoor Pollutants

The concentrations of indoor air pollutants depend on both indoor and outdoor emission sources (see Fig. 63.1). Outdoor emission sources determine outdoor pollution concentrations, which, in turn, can affect indoor air quality. In addition to outdoor air pollution concentrations, the degree of penetration of outdoor pollution into the indoor environment depends largely on the rate of air infiltration from outdoors to indoors.[38] The rate of air infiltration is a complex function of the "tightness" of building construction and insulation, building location and orientation, number of exterior walls and windows, surrounding terrain and barriers, wind speed and direction, indoor-outdoor temperature gradient, and ventilation system type and efficiency.[38-41]

Time-activity patterns will influence personal exposure. The relative time spent indoors versus outdoors will affect the contribution of indoor pollutants to total personal exposure. Time spent in specific locations within the home will affect exposure to particular pollutants, as the distribution of indoor pollutant concentrations will vary among different zones of a building, especially for pollutants generated indoors.[38,42] In addition, activity level will affect metabolic rate and ventilatory rate, which will also influence personal exposure to indoor pollutants.[43]

Indoor Combustion: the Major Source of Indoor Air Pollution. The major source of indoor pollution is from combustion, particularly SHS exposure, gas stove use, and wood burning in stoves and fireplaces. Kerosene space heaters are also an important source of indoor air pollution. Table 63.2 shows the major indoor pollutants that are released from these sources and are associated with adverse pulmonary effects.

Second-hand Smoke Exposure and Airway Disease. SHS exposure is perhaps the best known and studied indoor pollutant. Strong evidence implicates it as a cause of lung cancer.[44,45] In addition to these carcinogenic effects, SHS contains respiratory irritants, such as sulfur dioxide, ammonia, and formaldehyde.[46] Passive smoking has also been linked with allergic phenomena, such as elevated serum immunoglobulin E levels.[47,48] As a consequence, SHS has the potential to induce new cases of asthma through irritant or sensitizing mechanisms. Among persons with established asthma, SHS exposure may adversely affect asthma control.

Numerous studies have evaluated the impact of SHS exposure on childhood asthma induction.[49] The 1997 California Environmental Protection Agency (Cal EPA) report included a meta-analysis of 37 studies conducted between 1975 and 1995 that evaluated SHS exposure as a risk factor for induction of childhood asthma. The pooled relative risk for asthma was 1.44 (95% confidence interval, 1.27 to 1.64). These data supported a causal association between SHS and new onset of childhood asthma cases.[46] Since the Cal EPA report, nearly 40 additional studies strongly support the original conclusion that SHS exposure is causally associated with new-onset asthma among children.[50-86]

Although it has received less study, SHS exposure also appears to be associated with new-onset asthma in adulthood. Cross-sectional, case-control, and cohort studies have suggested a link between SHS exposure and adult-onset asthma.[87-99] Workplace SHS exposure, in particular, appears to be related to adult asthma induction.[90,91,94,95]

SHS exposure may also cause other respiratory symptoms, such as wheezing, and impaired lung function.[97,98,100-108] A study of the impact of a legislative ban on smoking in bars and taverns on the respiratory health of bartenders showed a marked reduction in respiratory symptoms and a significant improvement in spirometric parameters of lung function.[109] The consistency of findings linking SHS exposure with different related respiratory health outcomes, including new-onset asthma and wheezing, supports a deleterious causal effect of SHS exposure on adult asthma.

Beyond asthma induction, SHS exposure is a probable cause of asthma exacerbation in both children and adults. A review by the EPA in 1992 concluded that: "There is now sufficient evidence to conclude that passive smoking is causally associated with additional episodes and increased severity of asthma in children who already have the disease."[46] Numerous subsequent studies indicate that SHS exposure, which is mostly due to parental smoking, causes increased symptoms, poorer pulmonary function, and other indicators of worsened asthma control among children with established asthma.[110-121] Similarly, SHS exposure, both at home and at work, appears to cause asthma exacerbation among adults.[106,122-130] Moreover, the negative impact of SHS exposure on pulmonary function appears to be greater among adults with asthma than in the general population.[103]

Gas Stove Exposure and Asthma Exacerbation. Domestic gas stove use releases NO_2, a potential respiratory irritant, into the indoor environment.[39,131] Most epidemiologic studies examining the impact of gas stove use have focused on healthy members of the general population. In both children[24,39,132-136] and adults,[39,98,137-142] the impact of gas stove exposure on respiratory symptoms and pulmonary function has been inconclusive. In the few prospective studies of healthy adults, gas stove use was associated with an increased risk of respiratory symptoms in one study,[138] whereas other investigators demonstrated no association with either respiratory symptoms[143] or pulmonary function.[144,145]

Because they have chronic airway inflammation, persons with asthma may be more susceptible to the effects of NO_2 and other combustion products released by gas stoves. Cross-sectional epidemiologic studies demonstrate an increased risk of prevalent childhood asthma cases in gas stove homes compared with electric stove homes,[52,54,74,146] although this has not been observed in adults.[98] In adults with established asthma, a prospective panel study found an association between gas stove use and increased risk of respiratory symptoms, restricted activity, and emergency department visits.[147] Another time-series analysis found a negative impact of gas stove use on daily peak expiratory flow and respiratory symptoms.[148] In contrast, a longitudinal U.K. cohort study found no effect of gas stove exposure on persistence of adult asthma or on respiratory symptoms among asthmatics.[149] In a prospective cohort study of adults with asthma, we found no impact of gas stove exposure on asthma severity or other aspects of asthma status.[130] Moreover, there was no association between gas stove exposure and pulmonary function impairment in a population-based sample of U.S. adults.[150] Overall, the evidence has not been sufficient to implicate gas stove use as an exacerbating factor in preexisting adult asthma.

One limitation of most epidemiologic studies is the difficulty in examining the timing and intensity of exposure. In a prospective study of 16 nonsmoking asthmatic women, investigators found that acute peak NO_2 exposure during gas cooking was associated with diminished peak expiratory flow, whereas mean NO_2 exposure over a 2-week period had no impact on peak flow.[151] The deleterious consequences of acute peak NO_2 exposure on adults with asthma are supported by epidemiologic studies that assessed gas stove use on a daily basis[147,148] and controlled human exposure studies of acute NO_2 exposure.[152–155] Average daily gas stove exposure, as assessed by most epidemiologic studies, appears to have no clinically meaningful impact on adults with asthma.

Wood Smoke Exposure: Respiratory Effects.
Wood smoke, which is produced from domestic fireplace or wood stove use, contains potent respiratory irritants such as formaldehyde, acrolein, nitrogen oxides, and sulfur dioxide.[156] It is also a major source of particulate air pollution.[157] In previous studies, exposure to extremely high wood smoke levels has been linked with respiratory problems. After a work shift, forest firefighters experienced an acute decrement in pulmonary function.[158] Similarly, Florida wildfires were associated with increased emergency department visits for asthma and acute bronchitis.[159] In developing countries, where prolonged wood stove use in poorly ventilated homes occurs, often in conjunction with other biomass fuels, wood smoke exposure has been associated with chronic respiratory symptoms and airway obstruction.[39,160–162] However, these exposure levels are much higher than those encountered in modern buildings.

The respiratory health effects of residential wood smoke exposure in developed countries, which occurs at lower levels, have not been clearly characterized. In a small study from Michigan, children living in homes heated by wood-burning stoves had a greater prevalence of cough and wheeze than those without domestic wood smoke exposure.[163] Similarly, children with asthma residing in a region of Seattle with high wood smoke exposure had lower FEV_1 than those living in less polluted areas.[164] Infants who live in homes with wood stoves had a greater risk of cough during the first year of life, although there was no effect of fireplace use.[135,136] However, other studies have found no effect of domestic wood smoke exposure on respiratory symptoms in children[54,165,166] or adults.[167]

Previous evidence evaluating the effects of wood smoke exposure on adult asthma is limited. A prospective cohort study of adults with asthma found that wood stove or fireplace use was related to greater respiratory symptoms.[147] In contrast, we found no evidence that wood smoke exposure adversely influenced adult asthma status during an 18-month longitudinal follow-up period.[130]

Kerosene Heater Use: Respiratory Effects.
Although kerosene heaters are less commonly used than other indoor heaters in developed countries, they can substantially increase indoor levels of fine particulate matter ($PM_{2.5}$), sulfate aerosol (SO_4^{2-}), and acidic aerosol (H^+), which have been linked with respiratory symptoms.[168] Kerosene heater use has been associated with cough, but not wheeze, among infants during the first year of life.[135] In an urban area of Ethiopia where biomass fuels are universally used, kerosene use was related to a greater risk of allergic sensitization and wheeze; these results may not generalize to more developed countries.[169] Other studies have shown no association between kerosene heater use and the risk of asthma, wheeze, or bronchial hyperreactivity.[54,76,170,171]

Other Indoor Pollutants.
Besides indoor combustion, there are many other sources of indoor pollutants. Building materials, such as plywood or particleboard, and carpeting can emit formaldehyde; furniture may release formaldehyde and volatile organic compounds; paints, cleaning compounds, and photocopiers may release volatile organic compounds.[39,40] Review of the respiratory health risks associated with these compounds is outside the scope of this chapter.

DEFENSE AGAINST INHALED POLLUTANTS

Given that the lung is a delicate structure with a large surface area and encounters about 9000 L of air daily, with each liter containing millions of particles, it is not surprising that an effective system has evolved for removing impurities from the air inhaled and for clearing and destroying particles or microorganisms that gain entry into the respiratory tract. The various mechanisms of defense are interrelated and work in a coordinated manner. A perturbation in any mechanism, whether because of congenital deficiency, disease, or the effect of an inhaled pollutant, may result in the breakdown of the coordinated defense system and in the development of disease. Definition of the mechanisms of defense normally present thus permits the inferential identification of subgroups of the population that may be at particularly high risk for adverse effects from inhaling polluted air.

Air pollutants exist as either gases or suspended particles. As gases, their site of deposition in the respiratory tract is largely a function of their solubility, the duration of exposure, and the airflow pattern of breathing. For highly soluble gases, the nose serves an important defensive function, because the air inhaled transnasally is passed over the large, irregular surface of the turbinates. The promotion of turbulent flow prolongs contact with the mucosal surface, increasing adsorption. Under conditions of quiet breathing, when most air is inspired transnasally, this is an efficient system. For example, the concentration of sulfur dioxide that reaches the glottis is less than 2% of the concentration inspired at the nose.[10] Under other circumstances, the importance of the nose diminishes. The more rapid the inspiratory flow, the smaller the proportion of sulfur dioxide removed.[10] Furthermore, the mouth is substantially less efficient at absorbing gases than is the nose, and the proportion of air inhaled through the mouth increases with the increased ventilatory demands of exercise. Thus the dose of a soluble pollutant delivered to the lower airways is increased by exercise for three reasons: the inspiratory flow is higher, the proportion inhaled through the mouth is increased, and the total quantity inhaled over time is greater (quantity = concentration × volume). The importance of the level of ventilation (in turn a function of the level of exercise) and of the oral-nasal distribution of breathing has perhaps best been shown in studies of the bronchoconstrictor response to sulfur dioxide.[172] Therefore, people with obstructive nasal disease also appear to be at greater risk for adverse respiratory effects of soluble pollutant gases.

For inhaled particles, the duration of retention in the lung, and therefore the likelihood of an adverse effect, is in large part a function of the site of deposition, which is largely determined by the size of the particles themselves.[173] Large particles (diameter > 10 μm) are efficiently removed by simple filtration through nasal cilia. Those that are not removed by filtration tend to become deposited by impaction; because of their great inertia, they cannot easily change direction to follow the abrupt changes in the direction of airflow in the nose, pharynx, and tracheobronchial tree; therefore, they impact on the mucosa of the upper respiratory tract and large airways, especially at points of bifurcation. The mechanisms of filtration and impaction are so efficient that few particles more than 10 μm in diameter are deposited in the lower respiratory tract.

The sites of deposition of smaller particles are determined much more by sedimentation and diffusion. Sedimentation, the tendency to fall at a constant rate under the influence of gravity, is influenced by the density and diameter of the particle and by the viscosity of the surrounding gas. Sedimentation probably accounts for the predominant deposition of particles of intermediate size (diameter, 0.5 to 3.0 μm) in the small airways and alveoli. For the smallest particles, diffusion is the mechanism by which deposition occurs. Many of these particles are not deposited at all but remain in suspension in the exhaled air; those that are deposited tend to settle in the terminal bronchioles and alveoli.

To some extent, deposition of particles can be influenced by the pattern of breathing. At the same minute ventilation, small, rapid breaths promote deposition in central airways, whereas slow, deep breaths increase the time for diffusion and sedimentation and favor deposition in the distal airways and alveoli.[174] Because there is intersubject variability in the pattern of breathing adopted to achieve the same increase in ventilation with exercise, it is possible that the sites of deposition, and therefore the effects of particles, differ among people performing similar tasks in the same atmosphere.

For the particles deposited in the tracheobronchial tree, cough and mucociliary clearance are the most important mechanisms of defense. Cough is especially effective in clearing particles deposited in large central airways; it is provoked by stimulation of afferent nerves ("cough receptors"), which are found in greatest density in the mucosa of the larynx and at branch points in the tracheobronchial tree,[175] the sites where particles are most likely to be deposited. (Cough is discussed further in Chapter 29.) The mucociliary system operates over the length of the conducting airways, from the proximal trachea to the terminal bronchioles. The mucus blanket is the product of secretion by goblet and serous cells of the epithelium and by the mucous and serous cells of the submucosal glands (see Chapter 13). The mucus blanket is discontinuous and is propelled mouthward by the cilia of the epithelial cells. The effective removal of particles by the mucociliary system thus requires secretion of glycoproteins by specialized secretory cells, maintenance of liquefaction by the transport of water and solute by airway epithelial cells (discussed in Chapter 13), and coordinated function of airway cilia. Impairment of any of these functions, whether by congenital or acquired diseases affecting mucus or water secretion (e.g., cystic fibrosis, chronic bronchitis) or ciliary function (e.g., dysmotile cilia syndrome), leads to prolongation of the retention time of particles, increasing the likelihood of adverse effects due to the particles themselves or to the materials (e.g., heavy metals) entrained on their surface. Such an impairment of function probably accounts for the finding that exposure to low levels of ozone enhanced pulmonary retention of asbestos fibers in rats.[176]

The clearance of particles deposited beyond the mucociliary blanket, in the distal, gas-exchanging part of the lung, involves primarily the alveolar macrophage. This cell scavenges particles deposited in the alveoli and either digests them or migrates with them to the respiratory bronchiole, where it ascends the mucociliary escalator. A small number of macrophages ingest particles and migrate to peribronchial or perivascular connective tissue. Clearance by this route is slow, and particle-laden macrophages may still be found in lung connective tissue many weeks after exposure.[177]

Although the macrophage usually functions to protect the lungs, it is possible that in some circumstances it contributes to lung injury. It is now hypothesized, for example, that the lung fibrosis caused by silica and asbestos particles is due to the continued attempt by macrophages to ingest and destroy the inhaled dusts. This activity results in the continuous release of connective tissue proteases from the macrophages themselves and in the continuous release of other mediators that secondarily activate lung fibroblasts and attract and activate polymorphonuclear leukocytes.[178]

Appreciation of the macrophage's role as the cell that makes initial contact with inhaled particles and that then communicates with other cells, amplifying the response to challenge, has led to its being regarded as the pivotal cell in lung defense. However, research during the 1990s has led to increased appreciation of the role of airway epithelial cells in mediating lung injury and repair after pollutant exposure.[179]

The role of noncellular mechanisms of lung defense in the mediation of adverse respiratory effects related to air pollutants has become increasingly apparent. To minimize oxidant damage to biologic molecules, the human lung has an integrated antioxidant system of enzymatic and expendable soluble antioxidants. This system includes several antioxidant defense mechanisms that detoxify reactive products or convert them to products that are quenched by other antioxidants. If the oxidant burden is sufficiently great, the reactive species may overwhelm or inactivate the antioxidant system. An imbalance between the production of reactive oxygen species and reactive nitrogen species and antioxidant capacity leads to a state of "oxidative stress" that contributes to the pathogenesis of a number of respiratory diseases. The resulting excess oxygen species can damage major cellular components, including membrane lipids, protein, carbohydrates, and deoxyribonucleic acid. Pathophysiologic consequences of this injury are inflammation and tissue damage. One mechanism by which oxidative stress induces inflammation is through activation of the nuclear transcription factors, nuclear factor-κB and activator protein-1, which play critical roles in turning on both allergic and nonspecific inflammatory responses by inducing increased expression of multiple cytokine genes (e.g., interleukin-8, granulocyte-macrophage colony-stimulating factor, and regulated on activation normal T cell expressed and secreted [RANTES]).[179a] Oxidant pollutants (e.g., ozone and diesel exhaust) cause a striking increase in polymorphonuclear cells in the lungs and airways.[180,181] Studies in humans and animals indicate that antioxidant defenses are likely to be important in the expression of air pollutant–induced injury of the respiratory tract.[182–184]

METHODS OF STUDYING ADVERSE EFFECTS OF AIR POLLUTION

What has been learned about the complex, integrated systems responsible for defending the lungs permits a rational prediction of potential harm from various pollutants and allows inferences about subgroups of the population that might be at greatest risk from harmful effects of different pollutants. However, even sound, scientifically based conjecture is far from an adequate basis for initiating the major industrial and social changes needed to reduce atmospheric pollution. The scientific basis for the actions needed must rest on the demonstration of a high likelihood of harmful effects, as shown by studies of disease in populations exposed to polluted air, acute effects in human subjects after short-term exposure to controlled levels of pollutants in a laboratory, effects on lung structure and function in animals, and in vitro studies of mechanisms of toxicity. Each of these forms of study presents various advantages and disadvantages, and none provides irrefutable proof of harmful effects from a particular pollutant under natural conditions of exposure. Standards are based, therefore, on the coherence of evidence provided by epidemiologic, clinical, animal, and in vitro research and are set to provide a margin of safety, with the recognition that harmful effects may occur in sensitive subgroups of the population even with exposure to levels below those that have been shown to cause effects in published studies.

EPIDEMIOLOGIC STUDIES

Of the four sources of evidence that relate to air pollution health effects, only epidemiologic studies permit the investigation of large numbers of people who are exposed to the ambient air quality conditions that are of interest. The demonstration by such studies of adverse health effects in relation to specific ambient conditions can provide strong support for regulatory intervention. However, by their nature, epidemiologic studies are complex, and to provide valid data, they must overcome certain inherent difficulties.

Many factors other than air pollutants can give rise to acute and chronic respiratory symptoms and functional changes. Modern epidemiologic studies of air pollution health effects do account for the influence of factors such as age, cigarette and other tobacco use, occupational exposures, socioeconomic influences, and underlying medical illnesses. However, it is not possible to be entirely sure that residual effects of such factors have not affected the results of these studies. Since 1990, the use of daily time-series studies has increased, inasmuch as these studies provide for control of important confounders that do not change over relatively short periods of time.[185] These studies have led to important advances in the delineation of the potential respiratory health effects of ambient air pollution.

A major difficulty for large-scale epidemiologic studies stems from the fact that many, if not most, ambient environments are complex mixtures of pollutants with potential health effects from a single agent or from the interaction of several agents, or both. A number of studies have nonetheless been designed to provide the detail necessary to separate out the individual and interactive effects of various pollutants.[186,187] Such studies, for example, have been able to identify the subcomponent of the particulate component of ambient air pollution that is most strongly associated with the occurrence of chronic respiratory symptoms in children[186] and to distinguish effects of individual pollutants within the complex mixture of ambient pollutants.[188–190]

The assignment of individual exposures and doses also poses a challenge for epidemiologic studies. Factors such as the time spent indoors versus outdoors and activity patterns are important determinants of exposure and dose. Although still heavily dependent on area-wide monitoring, epidemiologic studies are increasingly capable of providing multiple metrics of exposure (e.g., hourly peaks, hourly averages, 24-hour averages) for a wide variety of pollutants[191] and of evaluating their relationship to the health outcomes of interest. Technologic advances have led to the development of devices that permit personal monitoring of individuals in their breathing zones[192] and offer the prospect of even more refined exposure/dose assignment. Creative epidemiologic designs have led to the study of groups of individuals functioning under well-measured conditions of activity in ambient environments that are dominated by single species of pollutants and that are well characterized in terms of other relevant pollutants,[193–195] temperature, and humidity. Finally, advances in statistical analytic techniques[185,196] have permitted more realistic modeling of the complex interplay of the components of the environment in relation to health outcomes of interest.

CLINICAL HUMAN RESEARCH

Experimental studies of human subjects exposed to carefully controlled conditions can demonstrate the occurrence of acute responses to various doses of a single pollutant or pollutant mixture. Such studies can detect the minimal concentrations that induce measurable effects on tests of function and can assess responses in segments of the population predicted to have increased susceptibility to adverse effects under a range of exposure conditions (e.g., rest, vigorous exercise, oral breathing, nasal breathing). These studies are powerful tools for analyzing the effects of a pollutant on an important acute event, such as the precipitation of myocardial ischemia by carbon monoxide in a patient with coronary artery disease[197] or of bronchospasm by sulfur dioxide in a patient with asthma.[198] The limitation of these studies in analyzing the effects of chronic exposure is obvious, and at present the relationship between the effects of low or short-term exposure and the development of disease with long-term exposure is unknown. The finding that a brief exposure to ozone causes acute decrements in lung function does not, for example, necessarily indicate that prolonged or repeated exposure will lead to the development of chronic obstructive lung disease. For even a reasoned guess at the relationship, much more needs to be known about the pathogenesis of chronic obstructive lung disease, about the mechanisms of injury from ozone, and about the mechanisms responsible for tolerance of or adaptation to repeated exposures. With this information, it might be possible to determine whether acute exposure to the pollutant produces an effect known to be a marker indicating the initiation of the pathogenetic sequence responsible for disease.

ANIMAL RESEARCH

Study of animals offers the best opportunity to determine the pathogenetic mechanisms and nature of the changes in lung structure and function that result from chronic exposure to specific pollutants. In addition, animal studies permit assessment of the effects of a range of concentrations, so that a dose-response curve can be constructed: from the dose producing the first measurable change in structure or function to the dose producing a fatal outcome. Studies of animals uniquely offer a means of identifying possible "markers" of events that will lead to disease with chronic exposure, because only in animals is it feasible to relate the changes in measurements of physiologic or biochemical function produced by short-term exposures to the changes in structure and function produced by long-term exposure.

The major limitation of animal studies is that large interspecies variations in the response to pollutants make prediction of human dose-response relationships hazardous. Dogs, for example, can tolerate up to 200 ppm of sulfur dioxide without developing significant bronchoconstriction, whereas guinea pigs appear to be especially sensitive to the bronchomotor effects of the gas,[199] and rodents are relatively insensitive to ozone.[200] Another limitation is that some relatively common human diseases, such as asthma and cystic fibrosis, do not occur in animals, and so the response of people with these diseases cannot be estimated from animal studies.

IN VITRO RESEARCH

The use of cultured cells that can be directly exposed to various pollutants has helped to elucidate potential mechanisms by which these pollutants cause lung injury, inflammation, and adverse respiratory health effects. For example, multiple studies involving the treatment of either monocyte or epithelial cell lines as well as primary bronchial epithelial cells with diesel exhaust particles have documented that these particles induce oxidative stress; that the organic fraction of the extractable material from the particles is responsible for this pro-oxidant effect; that the oxidative stress induces the up-regulation of nuclear transcription factors nuclear factor-κB and activator protein-1, which promote increased expression of inflammatory cytokines; that the oxidative stress is also associated with mitochondrial injury and the induction of apoptosis; and that blocking the oxidative stress with antioxidant agents can prevent the downstream effects.[201] Another example of the value of in vitro studies is in determining the components of fine particles that are most toxic. Transition metals (e.g., zinc, copper, vanadium) have been shown to be the toxic factors on combustion-source particles.[201a]

ADVERSE EFFECTS OF SPECIFIC POLLUTANTS

SULFUR DIOXIDE AND PARTICULATE MATTER

A large body of accumulated data indicate that many of the health effects that have been attributed to sulfur dioxide in the past may in fact have been due to effects of particulate pollution that includes acid derivatives of sulfur dioxide as well as components that are not related to sulfur dioxide. Nonetheless, these two pollutant categories are discussed together, because many early studies cannot distinguish between their effects.

As mentioned previously, the strongest piece of evidence linking air pollution with adverse health effects is the observation of dramatic increases in mortality during severe episodes of air pollution in the Meuse Valley, Belgium (1930); in Donora, Pennsylvania (1948); and in London, England (1952).[2,3] During each of these episodes, the concentrations of sulfur dioxide and particulate matter are thought to have been extremely high. Several reanalyses of the London episode have provided evidence that the particulate component and not sulfur dioxide was primarily responsible for the excess deaths that were observed.[202,203]

Since these episodes, many *epidemiologic studies* have been performed in urban areas around the world to examine the relationship between mortality and fluctuations in the ambient concentrations of sulfur dioxides and particulate matter.[204] Overall, these studies show a consistent pattern of association between increased sulfur oxide and particulate concentrations and mortality.[2,202–207] Of particular importance is the observation that effects on daily mortality have been observed over ranges of particulate concentrations that are below the current NAAQS.[203–209a] Because a high correlation exists between particulate air pollution and components of sulfur pollution (SO_2, H_2SO_4, $[H^+]$), studies have been undertaken to distinguish the mortality effects of each of these components.[203,204,206,207,209] The preponderance of evidence suggests that particulate matter has a greater effect on daily mortality than do various measures of sulfur species.[203,204,206,209–212] Some studies have found H_2SO_4 to have the largest effect,[207] and studies from European countries[206,207,213] and Canada[214] have identified independent effects for sulfur dioxide. Mortality effects have been observed to occur largely in people 65 years of age or older and in those with underlying cardiopulmonary disease.[215] The mechanisms underlying this excess mortality are not well understood. Inflammatory mediator release into the systemic circulation as a result of the deposition in the lung of fine and ultrafine particles capable of inducing oxidative stress has been suggested as one possible mechanism by which particulate matter could lead to cardiovascular mortality by triggering endothelial dysfunction, atherosclerosis, and thrombosis.[216-218] Other possible mechanisms include (1) effects on the autonomic nervous system; (2) alterations of ion channel function in myocardial cells; and (3) ischemic responses in the myocardium. Particle exposure–related increases in plasma viscosity, C-reactive protein, fibrinogen, and arrhythmias as well as decreased heart rate variability have been observed in epidemiologic studies.[219-222] Two cohort studies have provided data to suggest that there are increasing all-cause, cardiopulmonary, and lung cancer mortality rates that are associated with environments that have increasing levels of fine particle air pollution ($PM_{2.5}$).[24,25] Support for a particulate matter–lung cancer association is also provided by an additional cohort study.[25a] Numerous epidemiologic studies have repeatedly found an association between (1) the presence of acute respiratory symptoms and short-term reductions in pulmonary function and (2) higher concentrations of particulate matter.[186,223-225] Results have been less consistent for studies of acid sulfates, although some studies clearly have shown increases in respiratory hospital admissions that are related to sulfur dioxide–derived acid species,[226] and there are data suggesting that acid species derived from sulfur dioxide (e.g., H_2SO_4, NH_4HSO_4, $[H^+]$) are important contributors to the respiratory health effects associated with particulate pollution.[186] A detailed panel study of over 200 asthmatics from Denver, Colorado, demonstrated a consistent effect of $[H^+]$ on the occurrence of increased symptoms and worsening asthma.[195] This study controlled for such variables as daily activity, time spent indoors versus outdoors, and meteorologic factors. Respiratory hospital admissions in 22 acute care hospitals in eastern Canada were found to be associated with increased acid aerosols ($[H^+] > SO_4^- > PM_{2.5} > PM_{10}$) during summertime haze, and these effects were independent of those related to ambient ozone concentrations.[226]

A large study of the respiratory health effects of acid aerosols in children in 24 North American cities has provided evidence that acids derived from sulfur dioxide have effects on chronic respiratory symptoms and lung function. Levels of sulfate particles were associated with increased prevalence of bronchitis in the previous year, and the sulfate particle effect was identical in magnitude to that for total particle acidity (which includes acids derived from NO_2), and greater than that for inhalable particles and total acid.[227] The same study reported small reductions in a variety of lung function measures derived from forced expiratory maneuvers that were related to sulfate particles, but in this analysis the effects related to sulfates were somewhat weaker than those for total particle strong acidity ($[H^+]$).[228] During the Donora, Pennsylvania, air pollution episode in 1948, one study reported respiratory symptoms in 88% of patients with asthma.[4] This observation suggested that patients with asthma are especially sensitive to the adverse effects of sulfur oxide and particulate pollution. Data from the Harvard Six Cities Study and the Children's Health Study in southern California have also suggested that asthmatic persons are more likely to have increased respiratory symptoms in relation to particulate matter than are nonasthmatic persons.[186,229] A Canadian study with 18 months of follow-up and a nonasthmatic control group found that children with asthma and exercise-induced decreases in peak expiratory flow rate were more likely than nonasthmatic children to have decreases in peak expiratory flow rate with daily increases in PM_{10}.[230] Coughing was increased only in asthmatics. Virtually all daily levels in this study were below the 24-hour PM_{10} NAAQS.[230] Increased use of medications by asthmatic children has been reported to be associated with 5-day mean sulfate levels, and this increased medication use did not alter the reductions in peak expiratory flow rate that were associated with increased sulfates.[231] A study in southern California found that asthma severity and medication use in teenage asthmatics influenced the response to ambient particulate air pollution.[232] Subjects with more severe asthma were more sensitive to the changes in ambient particle concentrations than were those with less severe asthma. Asthmatic children not taking anti-inflammatory medications (inhaled steroids, cromolyn) had the strongest response to particle air pollution.

The acute bronchoconstrictor effects of sulfur dioxide have been well established since the mid-1970s.[233,234] Inhalation of high concentrations of sulfur dioxide has been repeatedly shown to increase airway resistance in healthy human volunteers.[198,233,234] In general, this effect of sulfur dioxide has been observed only after inhalation of concentrations in excess of 5 ppm, well above the concentration found even in the most polluted ambient air. However, multiple studies in humans have shown that subjects with asthma are exquisitely sensitive to the bronchoconstrictor effects of sulfur dioxide.[172,198,235] Because sulfur dioxide is highly soluble in water, nearly all of the inspired gas is removed from the upper airways under normal resting conditions. By increasing the delivery of sulfur dioxide to the intrathoracic airways, exercise greatly potentiates sulfur dioxide–induced bronchoconstriction.[172] Concentrations of sulfur dioxide as low as 0.25 ppm can cause symptomatic bronchoconstriction when inhaled during exercise by subjects with asthma.[172,235,236] Such concentrations sometimes occur in polluted urban air, especially in the vicinity of point sources such as power plants and smelters. This bronchoconstrictor effect occurs after exposures as brief as 1 minute in duration.[237] Thus, sulfur dioxide–induced bronchoconstriction is not necessarily prevented by the current EPA standard of 0.14 ppm as a 24-hour maximal average, because this standard does not set limits for maximal concentrations over periods shorter than 24 hours. The 24-hour maximum of 0.14 ppm is far more likely to be exceeded in developing countries than in highly developed countries, because of the use of high–sulfur-content coal and oil in domestic heating, industry, and power plants. Moreover, because the nose is an efficient filter for sulfur dioxide, ambient concentration greatly overestimates the amount of gas that penetrates below the nose.

Some of the most important findings regarding pollutant effects on respiratory health have come from the large Children's Health Study conducted in Southern California that has followed thousands of schoolchildren over a period of years. In this study, both fine particulate matter and acid vapor (primarily nitric acid in Southern California) have been associated with a reduced rate of growth of lung function.[238,239] The magnitude of effect of air pollution on lung function has been compared to that of active smoking.[240]

Another important component of particulate pollution is diesel exhaust particulate. Because of a number of desirable properties of diesel combustion engines (e.g., lower emission of carbon dioxide than gasoline engines), there is intense interest in diesel technology. Diesel exhaust from heavy-duty trucks and diesel-engine cars is a major contributor to particulate air pollution in many parts of the world. Diesel exhaust particles have become the subject of intensive research interest because of reported associations with lung cancer and suggestive data of a role as an "adjuvant" in immunoglobulin E–mediated immune responses.

Diesel exhaust is a complex mixture of very small particles (90% < 1 μg by mass). The particles have hundreds of chemicals adsorbed onto their surfaces, which include known mutagens and carcinogens.[241,242] A large number of epidemiologic studies have provided estimates of the risk of lung cancer associated with exposure to diesel exhaust in occupational settings.[243] A meta-analysis of 35 studies of occupational exposure to diesel exhaust reported an overall relative risk for lung cancer of 1.33 (95% confidence interval, 1.24 to 1.44) with diesel exhaust exposure. Results were similar for various study designs and in studies that did and did not control for cigarette smoking. Railroad workers and truck drivers were at highest risk.[244] Human epidemiologic data are supported by toxicologic data for rats (but not hamsters and mice) that demonstrate the carcinogenic potential of diesel exhaust, the carbon black component having been identified as an important contributor.[245]

Several studies in mice have shown that repeated intratracheal instillation of diesel exhaust particulate can induce nonspecific airway hyperresponsiveness and enhance the inflammatory response to allergen challenge in previously sensitized animals.[246,247] There are also data from intranasal instillation studies in both mice and humans indicating that diesel exhaust particles can enhance local type 2 T helper cell cytokine and immunoglobulin E antibody production in already sensitized individuals as well as sensitization to a new antigen.[248-251] The mechanism of these effects appears to be related to the ability of the organic chemicals on diesel exhaust particles to induce oxidative stress.[201,252] Recent data using the human model of nasal instillation of diesel exhaust particles to enhance local responses to allergen have shown that polymorphisms of two genes for the antioxidant enzyme glutathione-S-transferase (*GSTM1* and *GSTP1*) confer susceptibility to the adjuvant effects of these particles.[253] As a result of these findings, the potential of diesel exhaust exposures to induce exacerbations of asthma is of increasing research interest.[254]

Relatively few controlled studies of human exposure to particulate matter have been conducted, but the results of several such studies indicate that both concentrated ambient particles and diesel exhaust particles are capable of inducing airway inflammation.[180,255] The levels of exposure used in these studies greatly exceed those typically found in ambient air.

PHOTOCHEMICAL OXIDANTS: OZONE AND NITROGEN DIOXIDE

The findings of numerous studies suggesting that air pollution by the sulfur dioxide–particulate complex correlates with mortality and morbidity from lung disease raise the concern that a similar correlation may exist for the photochemical oxidant group of pollutants. This concern is heightened by the broad distribution of photochemical pollution. In 1991, the then NAAQS for ozone, 0.12 ppm over 1 hour, was exceeded in 94 of 231 U.S. metropolitan areas, which represent a substantial fraction of the nation's population.[256] The highest levels were recorded in the Los Angeles basin, but the "summer haze" that extends over most of the Northeast of the continent, from northern Florida to southern Ontario, contains high levels of ozone as well as aerosol sulfuric and nitric acids, ammonium sulfate, and nitrates.[257] Although there have been fewer studies that have shown associations between oxidant pollution and mortality than is the case for particulate pollution, the available data are such that potential effects of photochemical oxidants on daily mortality cannot be ignored.[258,259,259a]

In terms of morbidity, several epidemiologic studies provided suggestive but far from definitive evidence that photochemical oxidants increase the incidence of chronic obstructive pulmonary disease (COPD).[260-262] An indirect association can be inferred from the findings that lower respiratory tract illness is more common in children raised in homes with natural gas heating and cooking[29,30] and that lower respiratory tract illness in childhood is more often recalled by patients with COPD than by healthy controls.[263] Direct study of the question has shown that long-term residence in areas with high levels of photochemical oxidants is associated with a greater prevalence of symptoms of respiratory disease, with slight but significant abnormalities in tests of airway function or greater rate of decline in ventilatory function, or both.[264-268] Results of two recent studies of college freshmen suggest that lifetime exposure to ozone in southern California can lead to slight but measurable differences in lung function.[269,270] A study from Austria also showed reduced growth of lung function in children living in areas with higher ozone levels.[271] Whether these abnormalities in pulmonary function tests indicate higher risk for developing the clinical syndromes of chronic obstructive bronchitis and emphysema is not yet known. Because individual susceptibility to developing COPD appears to be so variable, and because cigarette smoking has such a dominant role in causing the disease, considerably more data than are currently available will be needed to implicate or exclude photochemical oxidants definitively as important risk factors for the development of COPD.

Provocative data have been presented from an autopsy study of young people in Los Angeles County who died suddenly without evidence of overt disease. These data suggest the possibility that respiratory bronchiolitis with extension of inflammation into adjacent alveoli in the centriacinar region of the lung may result from residence in a metropolitan area characterized by photochemical oxidant pollution.[272] Another provocative report presented suggestive evidence that chronic exposure to high ambient ozone levels in Mexico City led to nasal mucosal dysplasia.[273] That levels of ozone at or below the old NAAQS for ozone, 0.12 ppm, can cause decrements in lung function in human subjects under "real-world" conditions has been shown in multiple studies.[193,194,274,275] The decrements in lung function found in children at summer camps are greater than those found in children exposed to comparable concentrations of ozone in chambers for 1 or 2 hours. Two explanations are possible: the cumulative dose of ozone was greater in the summer camp setting, or the response to ozone was potentiated by other pollutants in the ambient air.[193,274] In addition to the camp study results, exercising adults have also been shown to have decrements in lung function in response to ambient ozone.[194,275]

The epidemiologic case for photochemical oxidants as a cause of exacerbation of preexisting respiratory disease is stronger for asthma than for COPD. Several panel studies of asthmatics, in southern California, Houston, and Tucson, have shown that the risk of asthmatic exacerbation was enhanced by an increase in ozone.[276–279] Additional evidence comes from at least four other North American studies that have shown that the number of emergency room visits for asthma exacerbations in Montreal, New Brunswick, Atlanta, and New Jersey was correlated with ozone levels.[280–283] The most provocative data in support of ozone as a cause of asthma are again from the Children's Health Study.[284] Children who spend a lot of time exercising outside (i.e., those who play in three or more outdoor sports per year) in a community with high ozone levels had a threefold increased risk of developing new-onset asthma compared to similar children living in a low-ozone community.

The effect of photochemical oxidants on exacerbations of COPD has been less studied. In general, epidemiologic studies have shown that exacerbations of COPD are more strongly associated with levels of sulfur dioxide and particulate mass than with levels of ozone or NO_2,[285] and acute exposure studies have not shown patients with COPD to be more responsive to ozone.[286,287] In fact, smokers tend to be less responsive to ozone than are nonsmokers in terms of acute decrements in lung function.[288] Perhaps the most persuasive evidence that ambient ozone exposure can lead to exacerbations of COPD comes from studies in southern Ontario that found that the number of hospital admissions for all respiratory diseases, including exacerbations of chronic bronchitis and emphysema, correlated with ozone concentrations during summer months.[289,290] Unfortunately, there is also exposure to other pollutants with "summer haze" in Ontario, so that the effect of ozone cannot be entirely disentangled from that of other pollutants, especially acid sulfate particulate.

Other, less severe consequences have been more firmly linked to atmospheric oxidant levels. Performance in running events decreases in Los Angeles track meets when oxidant concentrations exceed 0.25 ppm, and this has been confirmed in a chamber study of competitive cyclists.[291,292] Headache, eye irritation, cough, and chest discomfort have all been found more commonly when oxidant levels rise above 0.15 ppm.[293]

NO_2 is another of the criteria pollutants named by the EPA and, in ambient air, is often found in association with ozone or other pollutants. Although it is less potent as an oxidant, high concentrations found in silos can cause the acute and sometimes lethal pulmonary edema of "silo-filler's disease."[294] Until recently, the low levels of NO_2 in outdoor air had not been definitively linked to adverse health effects in epidemiologic studies. However, the results of several studies have provoked renewed interest in this pollutant.[295,296] In the late 1970s, it became apparent that indoor concentrations often exceeded outdoor concentrations, particularly in homes equipped with gas stoves, and may be extremely high in inner city homes heated by ovens.[28] Because indoor air is relatively free of the other pollutants normally associated with NO_2 in outdoor air, this discovery enabled epidemiologic study of this potentially important pollutant. Research interest focused on the possibility that exposure to NO_2 in indoor air might increase the occurrence of respiratory infections, in part because of animal studies showing that NO_2 exposure reduces the clearance of infecting organisms. Unfortunately, epidemiologic studies of this question have not been definitive.[29–31] In addition, the Children's Health Study referred to earlier with regard to fine particulate matter and acid vapor also provided evidence of a negative effect of NO_2, but interestingly not of ozone, on growth of lung function.[238,239] Most recently, multiple studies have linked asthma exacerbations to urban exposures to NO_2.[295,296] In these studies, the question remains whether NO_2 is the pollutant primarily responsible for the observed effect on asthmatic patients or merely a marker of the traffic pollution mix.

The results of studies of the acute effects of exposure of human volunteers to ozone correspond well, but not perfectly, with the results of epidemiologic studies. At first, these studies focused almost exclusively on symptoms and changes in lung mechanics produced by short (1- to 2-hour) exposure to ozone and NO_2. For ozone, the effects most consistently observed are cough, substernal discomfort, decreases in the FEV_1 and forced vital capacity, a rise in airway resistance, and a fall in lung compliance. These effects were first noted in healthy subjects exposed to 0.30 ppm or more while performing light exercise,[297] but they have also been observed with exposure to concentrations at and below the former NAAQS of 0.12 ppm when the duration of exposure was prolonged to 6.5 hours and moderate, intermittent exercise was performed.[298–300] With this longer exposure, the functional decrements became progressively greater after each hour of exposure[298] but returned to baseline by the following day. A wide variability in responsiveness to ozone is found between healthy subjects: FEV_1 falls sharply in 20% to 25% of the subjects and not at all in others exposed under identical conditions.[298] The basis for the greater responsiveness of some individuals is unknown, but because responses are highly reproducible within individuals,[301] there is clearly a subgroup in the healthy population with heightened sensitivity to ozone. One of the genetic polymorphisms associated with increased susceptibility to the adjuvant effects of diesel exhaust particles (GSTM1 null) may also be linked to susceptibility to the acute effects of ozone.[289,302] With repeated daily exposures to ozone, both the symptoms and the changes in lung mechanics diminish.[303,304] Without further exposure, this tolerance lasts for 7 to 10 days.

Studies of the effects of NO_2 on healthy subjects have yielded qualitatively similar results, with the important exception that the concentration needed to produce unequivocal respiratory dysfunction (2.5 ppm) is well above the levels measured in ambient air during pollution episodes.[305] The effect of concentrations attainable in severe episodes (0.5 to 1.0 ppm) has been studied in subjects performing moderate exercise; the changes in symptoms and in lung mechanics were modest in comparison with those produced by the levels of ozone likely to be present in the same atmosphere.[305,306]

In addition to the changes in lung mechanics, increases in nonspecific airway responsiveness also occur with oxidant exposure. For ozone, it is firmly established that concentrations commonly reached in urban air can increase airway responsiveness, both in healthy subjects and in those with preexisting airway hyperresponsiveness.[154,300,301,307] In some studies, exposure of exercising asthmatic subjects to 0.30 ppm of NO_2 caused an increase in airway responsiveness, but in others, no such effects were found, even when conducted by the same investigators who had previously found an effect.[308] In view of the results of epidemiologic studies demonstrating an association between increased levels of ozone and increased risk of exacerbations of asthma,[276-283] the possibility that ozone may directly narrow the airways in people with asthma has been examined. Because airway hyperresponsiveness is characteristic of asthma, and because ozone causes increased airway responsiveness in healthy people, it was expected that ozone would cause bronchoconstriction in subjects with asthma. However, most studies of asthmatic subjects have shown no increased lung function responses to ozone in comparison to healthy subjects,[309,310] although at least two studies did show modestly greater changes in expiratory flow rates.[311,312] This is not really surprising because the acute decrements in lung function in response to ozone are restrictive in nature as a result of neural reflex inhibition of deep inspiration.[313]

The failure of clinical exposure studies to demonstrate a markedly heightened responsiveness of asthmatics to the acute effects of ozone on lung function is not necessarily inconsistent with the epidemiologic findings, for ozone could act by heightening responsiveness to another stimulus. Indeed, prior exposure to ozone has been shown to potentiate the early bronchoconstrictor response of allergic asthmatics to subsequent exposure to antigen.[314,315] There is also evidence that prior exposure to NO_2 can enhance both the early and late responses to inhaled antigen in allergic asthmatic subjects.[152,316] The mechanisms of the effects of ozone on the lungs and airways have been examined by analyzing ozone-induced changes in the cellular and chemical composition of bronchoalveolar lavage (BAL) fluid. In subjects exposed to 0.4 or 0.6 ppm of ozone for 2 hours, the proportion of polymorphonuclear leukocytes in lavage fluid obtained 2 hours later increased strikingly, especially in the subjects in whom airway responsiveness increased most.[317] BAL fluid obtained 18 hours after exposure to 0.4 ppm for 2 hours contains an increased proportion of polymorphonuclear leukocytes and increased concentrations of total protein, albumin, interleukin-6, fibronectin, and several other proteins, which suggests the presence of airway epithelial injury and inflammation.[180] Generically similar changes have been found in BAL fluid obtained 18 hours after 4 hours of exposure to 0.2 ppm or after 6.6 hours of exposure of healthy subjects to 0.12 and 0.08 ppm of ozone, as well as in nasal lavage fluid from subjects exposed to 0.5 ppm of ozone.[181,318,319] It is thus clear that

ozone can initiate inflammatory changes in the airways and is capable of producing tissue damage at real-world levels.[320] However, the clinical and public health significance of these findings cannot be defined without careful study of basic mechanisms in animals and without correlation with the results of long-term studies of effects in chronically exposed populations. In contrast to their lack of heightened response to the acute effects of ozone on lung function, asthmatic subjects do appear to have enhanced ozone-induced airway inflammation in comparison with healthy subjects.[310,321]

The inflammatory effect of NO_2, like that of ozone, has been studied by examining BAL fluid. Even multihour exposures to a high concentration, such as 2.0 ppm over 4 days, cause only mild airway inflammation.[322] In view of the hypothesized relationship between NO_2 exposure and increased risk of respiratory infection, the finding that alveolar macrophages obtained from NO_2-exposed subjects are less effective at inactivating influenza virus is particularly interesting.[323]

Numerous studies of the acute effects of ozone and NO_2 have been undertaken in animals. Death from pulmonary edema results from exposure to high concentrations of both pollutants, as has been reported for humans accidentally exposed to lethal levels. Ozone causes similar types of alterations in lung morphology in all animal species studied.[324] The most affected cells are the ciliated epithelial cells of the airways and type I cells in the gas-exchange region. Within the nasal cavity, anterior portions of the respiratory and transitional epithelium are affected.[325] Cilia are lost or damaged; some ciliated cells become necrotic, are lost, and are replaced with nonciliated cells. Mucus-secreting cells are affected as well.

The primary site of injury after brief (<24-hour) exposure to ozone is the centriacinar region of the lung in animals; injury is also evident to a lesser extent in the trachea and proximal bronchi; at equivalent exposures, nonhuman primates appear to be more sensitive than rats.[200] The cellular characteristics of the injury consist of a sloughing of alveolar type I cells, proliferation of alveolar type II cells, and a loss of ciliated cells. Inflammatory cells, mostly macrophages and polymorphonuclear leukocytes, appear in the lumina of the bronchioles and alveolar ducts.[326] With increased duration of exposure, alveolar septa in the centriacinar region thicken as a result of increased matrix, basement membrane, collagen, and fibroblasts and a thickened alveolar epithelium.

In rats and monkeys, ciliated and type I cells become necrotic and are sloughed from the epithelium as early as 2 to 4 hours after exposure to 0.5 ppm.[327] Repair, as shown by increased deoxyribonucleic acid synthesis, begins by about 18 to 24 hours of exposure, although cell damage continues.[328-330] The lesion is fully developed by 3 days of exposure, after which the rate of repair exceeds the rate of damage. There is an increase in antioxidant activity in damaged alveoli, presumably because of proliferation of type II cells, which are rich in these enzymes.[329] The up-regulation of antioxidant enzymes is site specific (i.e., different between proximal airways and distal lung).[331] Chronic exposures to ozone can lead to distal airway remodeling.[324] So-called bronchiolarization of centriacinar alveoli means that bronchial epithelium has replaced type I and II cells typical of alveolar ducts (i.e., increased respiratory bronchioles). Bronchiolarization has been observed at exposures as low as 0.25 ppm (8 hr/day for 18 months) in monkeys and can persist for months after exposure ceases.[332] Exposure regimens that have attempted to model ozone "episodes" or "seasons" with intermittent clean-air periods have affected experimental outcomes.[332–334] Although a simple pattern of responses has not emerged from intermittent-exposure studies, it is clear that the basic toxicologic principle of dose (i.e., concentration × time) is not sufficient to understand the complexity of the ozone dose-response relationship. Recent results of a study using rhesus monkeys showed that neonatal exposure (i.e., during a time when lung development was still occurring) to ozone actually caused abnormally reduced branching of airways.[335]

Studies of animals exposed to NO_2 provide generally similar results, except that morphologic abnormalities are produced by short-term exposure only if the concentrations used are well above those found even in severely polluted outdoor air. Short-term exposures to 5.0 ppm generally produce minimal or no morphologic effects in the rat.[336] Long-term exposures to levels greater than 2.0 ppm NO_2 are necessary to produce persistent changes in the lungs, such as bronchiolitis and collagen deposition.[336,337]

Multiple studies have shown that NO_2 enhances susceptibility to bacterial and viral infection, probably mediated at least in part through effects on alveolar macrophages.[336,338] Infectivity model experiments involving exposure to NO_2 followed by challenge with viable bacteria or viruses have demonstrated that NO_2 enhances microbe-induced mortality after short-term exposure to 2.0 ppm or more or after long-term exposure to 0.5 ppm.[336,339–341] Only cautious extrapolations to human responses can be drawn from these studies of animals. The finding that NO_2 is less directly toxic than ozone is probably applicable to humans, because it fits with what has been learned from controlled human exposure studies. It is uncertain whether the levels of NO_2 currently found in outdoor urban air pose a hazard by themselves; however, there are grounds for concern that the high levels of NO_2 sometimes found in indoor air lead to increased risk of respiratory tract infection. It seems likely that acute exposure to near ambient concentrations of ozone causes damage in the centriacinar region of the human lung, because this is the site of greatest damage in all the animal species that have been studied. This likelihood may be a cause for concern over the possible interaction of ozone with cigarette smoking in the pathogenesis of COPD, because the changes of chronic bronchitis and emphysema are thought to occur in this region first.

SUMMARY

The potential of air pollution as a hazard to human health became unmistakable between 1930 and 1952, when a series of air pollution crises caused striking increases in mortality. The properties, sources, and distribution of pollutants have since been defined. Their effects on the lungs and airways have been determined by short-term controlled exposures of human volunteers, by acute and chronic exposures of laboratory animals, and by epidemiologic studies of exposed populations. For major, widespread classes of pollutants, such as the photochemical oxidants, sulfur dioxide,

and particulate matter, the effects of high concentrations on healthy subjects have been described, and measures to reduce the production of pollutants at mobile and stationary sources have improved air quality, so large, acute increases in mortality associated with air pollution crises no longer occur in developed countries. However, epidemiologic data collected over the past 2 decades from multiple urban areas indicate that fluctuations in daily mortality are correlated with current levels of particulate pollution in these countries. Given the increased morbidity from asthma seen in the developed world, concern has also been raised about the potential of both oxidant gaseous pollutants and particulate matter (especially diesel-exhaust particles) to induce exacerbations of asthma, either through direct effects or through enhancement of allergic responses. The interactive effects of pollutants with other inhaled agents, such as antigens, cigarette smoke, and respiratory viruses, are not yet adequately defined.

REFERENCES

1. Ayres SM, Evans RG, Buehler ME: Air pollution: A major public health problem. CRC Crit Rev Clin Lab Sci 3:1–40, 1972.
2. Shy CM, Goldsmith JR, Hackney JD, et al: Health Effects of Air Pollution. New York: American Lung Association, 1978.
3. Logan WPD: Mortality in the London fog incident. Lancet 1:336–339, 1953.
4. Schrenk HH, Heiman H, Clayton GD, et al: Air Pollution in Donora, Pennsylvania: Epidemiology of the Unusual Smog Episode of October 1948. Washington, DC: U.S. Department of Public Health, 1949, p 306.
5. American Thoracic Society: State of the art: Health effects of outdoor air pollution. Am J Respir Crit Care Med 153:3–50, 477–498, 1996.
6. American Thoracic Society: What constitutes an adverse health effect of air pollution? Official statement of the American Thoracic Society. Am J Respir Crit Care Med 161:665–673, 2000.
7. Delfino RJ: Epidemiological evidence for asthma and exposure to air toxics: Linkages between occupational, indoor, and community air pollution research. Environ Health Perspect 110(Suppl 4):573–589, 2002.
8. Delfino RJ, Gong H Jr, Linn WS, et al: Asthma symptoms in Hispanic children and daily ambient exposures to toxic and criteria air pollutants. Environ Health Perspect 111:647–656, 2003.
9. Leech JA, Nelson WC, Burnett RT, et al: It's about time: A comparison of Canadian and American time-activity patterns. J Expo Anal Environ Epidemiol 12:427–432, 2002.
10. Frank NR, Yoder RE, Brain JD, et al: SO_2 (^{35}S-labeled) absorption by the nose and mouth under conditions of varying concentration and flow. Arch Environ Health 18:315–322, 1969.
11. Gorman E, Martin FB, Litzau JT: Acid rain: Ionic correlations in the eastern United States, 1980–1981. Science 225:407–409, 1984.
12. Environmental Protection Agency: Sources and emissions of atmospheric particles. In Air Quality Criteria for Particulate Matter (Vol 1). Washington, DC: National Center for Environmental Assessment Office of Research and Development, 1996, pp 5–1 to 5–34.
13. Wark K, Warner CF: Air Pollution: Its Origin and Control. New York: Harper-Collins, 1981, pp 143–151.

14. Environmental Protection Agency: Physics and chemistry of particulate matter. *In* Air Quality Criteria for Particulate Matter (Vol 1). Washington, DC: National Center for Environmental Assessment Office of Research and Development, 1996, pp 3–1 to 3–11.

15. Environmental Protection Agency: Integrative synthesis of key points: PM exposure, dosimetry, and health effects. *In* Air Quality Criteria for Particulate Matter (Vol 3). Washington, DC: National Center for Environmental Assessment Office of Research and Development, 1996, pp 13–1 to 13–28.

16. Renwick LC, Brown D, Clouter A, et al: Increased inflammation and altered macrophage chemotactic responses caused by two ultrafine particle types. Occup Environ Med 61:442–447, 2004.

17. Zhu Y, Hinds WC, Kim S, et al: Concentration and size distribution of ultrafine particles near a major highway. J Air Waste Manag Assoc 52:1032–1042, 2002.

18. Peters A, Wichmann HE, Tuch T, et al: Respiratory health effects are associated with the number of ultrafine particles. Am J Respir Crit Care Med 155:1376–1383, 1997.

19. Environmental Protection Agency: Tropospheric ozone chemistry. *In* Air Quality Criteria for Ozone and Related Photochemical Oxidants (Vol 1). Washington, DC: National Center for Environmental Assessment Office of Research and Development, 1996, pp 3–16 to 3–37.

20. Miller FJ: Similarity between man and laboratory animals in regional pulmonary deposition of ozone. Environ Res 17:84–101, 1978.

21. Cohen AJ, Higgins MWP: Health effects of diesel exhaust: Epidemiology. *In* Diesel Exhaust: A Critical Analysis of Emissions, Exposure, and Health Effects—A Special Report of the Institute's Diesel Working Group (No. 293). Cambridge, Mass: Health Effects Institute, 1995, pp 253–288.

22. Samet JM, Cohen AJ: Air pollution and lung cancer. *In* Swift DL, Foster WM (eds): Air Pollutants and the Respiratory Tract. New York: Marcel Dekker, 1999, pp 181–217.

23. Beeson WL, Abbey DE, Knutsen SF: Long-term concentrations of ambient air pollutants and incident lung cancer in California adults: Results from the ASHMOG Study. Environ Health Perspect 106:813–823, 1998.

24. Dockery DW, Pope CA, Xu X, et al: An association between air pollution and mortality in six U.S. cities (see comments). N Engl J Med 329:1753–1759, 1993.

25. Pope CA, Thun MJ, Namboodiri MM, et al: Particulate air pollution as a predictor of mortality in a prospective study of U.S. adults. Am J Respir Crit Care Med 151:669–674, 1995.

25a. Pope CA, Burnett RT, Thun MJ, et al: Lung cancer, cardiopulmonary mortality, and long-term exposure to fine particulate air pollution. JAMA 287:1132–1141, 2002.

26. Lambert WE, Samet JM: Indoor air pollution. *In* Harber P, Schenker M, Balmes J (eds): Occupational and Environmental Respiratory Disease. St. Louis: Mosby–Year Book, 1996, pp 784–807.

27. Hanrahan JP, Weiss ST: Environmental tobacco smoke. *In* Harber P, Schenker M, Balmes J (eds): Occupational and Environmental Respiratory Disease. St. Louis: Mosby–Year Book, 1996, pp 767–783.

28. Spengler JD, Duffy C, Letz R, et al: Nitrogen dioxide inside and outside 137 homes and implications for ambient air quality standards and health effects research. Environ Sci Technol 17:164–168, 1983.

29. Neas LM, Dockery DW, Ware JH, et al: Association of indoor nitrogen dioxide with respiratory symptoms and pulmonary function in children. Am J Epidemiol 134:204–219, 1991.

30. Hasselbad V, Kotchmar JJ, Eddy DM: Synthesis of environmental evidence: Nitrogen dioxide epidemiology studies. J Air Waste Manag Assoc 42:662–671, 1992.

31. Samet JM, Lambert WE, Skipper BJ, et al: A study of respiratory illnesses in infants and nitrogen dioxide exposure. Arch Environ Health 47:57–63, 1992.

32. Leaderer BP: Air pollutant emissions from kerosene space heaters. Science 218:1113–1115, 1982.

33. Bennett G: Ozone contamination of high altitude aircraft cabins. Aerospace Med 33:969–973, 1962.

34. Marbury MC, Krieger RA: Formaldehyde. *In* Samet JM, Spengler JD (eds): Indoor Air Pollution. Baltimore: Johns Hopkins University Press, 1991, pp 223–251.

35. Puskin JS, Nelson CB: EPA's perspective on risks from residential radon exposure. J Air Pollut Control Assoc 39:915–920, 1989.

36. Lubin JH, Boice JD: Lung cancer risk from residential radon: Meta-analysis of eight epidemiologic studies. J Natl Cancer Inst 89:49–57, 1997.

37. Stigum H, Strand T, Magnus P: Should radon be reduced in homes? A cost-effect analysis. Health Phys 84:227–235, 2003.

38. National Research Council CoIP: Indoor Pollutants. Washington, DC: National Academy Press, 1981.

39. Samet JM, Marbury MC, Spengler JD: Health effects and sources of indoor air pollution. Part I. Am Rev Respir Dis 136:1486–1508, 1987.

40. Samet JM, Marbury MC, Spengler JD: Health effects and sources of indoor air pollution. Part II. Am Rev Respir Dis 137:221–242, 1988.

41. Seppanen O, Fisk WJ: Association of ventilation type with SBS symptoms in office workers. Indoor Air 12:273–277, 2002.

42. Fortmann R, Kariher P, Clayton R: Indoor Air Quality: Residential Cooking Exposures (Final Report, ARB Contract No. 97-330). Sacramento: California Air Resources Board, 2001.

43. Jaakkola MS, Jaakkola JJ: Assessment of exposure to environmental tobacco smoke. Eur Respir J 10:2384–2397, 1997.

44. Boffetta P: Involuntary smoking and lung cancer. Scand J Work Environ Health 28(Suppl 2):30–40, 2002.

45. Hackshaw AK, Law MR, Wald NJ: The accumulated evidence on lung cancer and environmental tobacco smoke (see comments). BMJ 315:980–988, 1997.

46. California Environmental Protection Agency: Health effects of exposure to environmental tobacco smoke. Sacramento, CA: Office of Environmental Health Hazard Assessment, 1997.

47. Oryszczyn MP, Annesi-Maesano I, Charpin D, et al: Relationships of active and passive smoking to total IgE in adults of the Epidemiological Study of the Genetics and Environment of Asthma, Bronchial Hyperresponsiveness, and Atopy (EGEA). Am J Respir Crit Care Med 161:1241–1246, 2000.

48. Lindfors A, van Hage-Hamsten M, Rietz H, et al: Influence of interaction of environmental risk factors and sensitization in young asthmatic children. J Allergy Clin Immunol 104:755–762, 1999.

49. Chilmonczyk BA, Salmun LM, Megathlin KN, et al: Association between exposure to environmental tobacco smoke and exacerbations of asthma in children (see comments). N Engl J Med 328:1665–1669, 1993.

50. Cunningham J, O'Connor GT, Dockery DW, Speizer FE: Environmental tobacco smoke, wheezing, and asthma in children in 24 communities. Am J Respir Crit Care Med 153:218–224, 1996.

51. Mannino DM, Moorman JE, Kingsley B, et al: Health effects related to environmental tobacco smoke exposure in children in the United States: Data from the Third National Health and Nutrition Examination Survey. Arch Pediatr Adolesc Med 155:36–41, 2001.

52. Lanphear BP, Aligne CA, Auinger P, et al: Residential exposures associated with asthma in US children. Pediatrics 107:505–511, 2001.

53. Gergen PJ, Fowler JA, Maurer KR, et al: The burden of environmental tobacco smoke exposure on the respiratory health of children 2 months through 5 years of age in the United States: Third National Health and Nutrition Examination Survey, 1988 to 1994. Pediatrics 101:E8, 1998.

54. Maier WC, Arrighi HM, Morray B, et al: Indoor risk factors for asthma and wheezing among Seattle school children. Environ Health Perspect 105:208–214, 1997.

55. Kivity S, Sade K, Abu-Arisha F, Lerman Y: Epidemiology of bronchial asthma and chronic rhinitis in schoolchildren of different ethnic origins from two neighboring towns in Israel. Pediatr Pulmonol 32:217–221, 2001.

56. Wang TN, Ko YC, Chao YY, et al: Association between indoor and outdoor air pollution and adolescent asthma from 1995 to 1996 in Taiwan. Environ Res 81:239–247, 1999.

57. Agabiti N, Mallone S, Forastiere F, et al: The impact of parental smoking on asthma and wheezing. SIDRIA Collaborative Group. Studi Italiani sui Disturbi Respiratori nell'Infanzia e l'Ambiente. Epidemiology 10:692–698, 1999.

58. Hu FB, Persky V, Flay BR, et al: Prevalence of asthma and wheezing in public schoolchildren: Association with maternal smoking during pregnancy. Ann Allergy Asthma Immunol 79:80–84, 1997.

59. Ronmark E, Jonsson E, Platts-Mills T, Lundback B: Different pattern of risk factors for atopic and nonatopic asthma among children—report from the Obstructive Lung Disease in Northern Sweden Study. Allergy 54:926–935, 1999.

60. Gilliland FD, Li YF, Peters JM: Effects of maternal smoking during pregnancy and environmental tobacco smoke on asthma and wheezing in children. Am J Respir Crit Care Med 163:429–436, 2001.

61. Lister SM, Jorm LR: Parental smoking and respiratory illnesses in Australian children aged 0–4 years: ABS 1989–90 National Health Survey results. Aust N Z J Public Health 22:781–786, 1998.

62. Al-Dawood K: Parental smoking and the risk of respiratory symptoms among schoolboys in Al-Khobar City, Saudi Arabia. J Asthma 38:149–154, 2001.

63. Stoddard JJ, Miller T: Impact of parental smoking on the prevalence of wheezing respiratory illness in children. Am J Epidemiol 141:96–102, 1995.

64. Chen Y, Rennie DC, Dosman JA: Influence of environmental tobacco smoke on asthma in nonallergic and allergic children. Epidemiology 7:536–539, 1996.

65. Farber HJ, Wattigney W, Berenson G: Trends in asthma prevalence: The Bogalusa Heart Study. Ann Allergy Asthma Immunol 78:265–269, 1997.

66. Peters J, Hedley AJ, Wong CM, et al: Effects of an ambient air pollution intervention and environmental tobacco smoke on children's respiratory health in Hong Kong. Int J Epidemiol 25:821–828, 1996.

67. Beckett WS, Belanger K, Gent JF, et al: Asthma among Puerto Rican Hispanics: A multi-ethnic comparison study of risk factors. Am J Respir Crit Care Med 154:894–899, 1996.

68. Lam TH, Chung SF, Betson CL, et al: Respiratory symptoms due to active and passive smoking in junior secondary school students in Hong Kong. Int J Epidemiol 27:41–48, 1998.

69. Lam TH, Hedley AJ, Chung SF, Macfarlane DJ: Passive smoking and respiratory symptoms in primary school children in Hong Kong. Child Health and Activity Research Group (CHARG). Hum Exp Toxicol 18:218–223, 1999.

70. Shamssain MH, Shamsian N: Prevalence and severity of asthma, rhinitis, and atopic eczema: The north east study. Arch Dis Child 81:313–317, 1999.

71. Selcuk ZT, Caglar T, Enunlu T, Topal T: The prevalence of allergic diseases in primary school children in Edirne, Turkey. Clin Exp Allergy 27:262–269, 1997.

72. Kendirli GS, Altintas DU, Alparslan N, et al: Prevalence of childhood allergic diseases in Adana, Southern Turkey. Eur J Epidemiol 14:347–350, 1998.

73. Hajnal BL, Braun-Fahrlander C, Grize L, et al: Effect of environmental tobacco smoke exposure on respiratory symptoms in children. SCARPOL Team. Swiss Study on Childhood Allergy and Respiratory Symptoms with Respect to Air Pollution, Climate and Pollen. Schweiz Med Wochenschr 129:723–730, 1999.

74. Strachan DP, Carey IM: Home environment and severe asthma in adolescence: A population based case-control study. BMJ 311:1053–1056, 1995.

75. Lindfors A, Wickman M, Hedlin G, et al: Indoor environmental risk factors in young asthmatics: A case-control study. Arch Dis Child 73:408–412, 1995.

76. Azizi BH, Zulkifli HI, Kasim S: Indoor air pollution and asthma in hospitalized children in a tropical environment. J Asthma 32:413–418, 1995.

77. Jones RC, Hughes CR, Wright D, Baumer JH: Early house moves, indoor air, heating methods and asthma. Respir Med 93:919–922, 1999.

78. Infante-Rivard C, Gautrin D, Malo JL, Suissa S: Maternal smoking and childhood asthma. Am J Epidemiol 150:528–531, 1999.

79. Infante-Rivard C: Childhood asthma and indoor environmental risk factors. Am J Epidemiol 137:834–844, 1993.

80. Yang CY, Lin MC, Hwang KC: Childhood asthma and the indoor environment in a subtropical area. Chest 114:393–397, 1998.

81. Ponsonby AL, Couper D, Dwyer T, et al: The relation between infant indoor environment and subsequent asthma. Epidemiology 11:128–135, 2000.

82. Tariq SM, Hakim EA, Matthews SM, Arshad SH: Influence of smoking on asthmatic symptoms and allergen sensitisation in early childhood. Postgrad Med J 76:694–699, 2000.

83. Tariq SM, Matthews SM, Hakim EA, et al: The prevalence of and risk factors for atopy in early childhood: A whole population birth cohort study. J Allergy Clin Immunol 101:587–593, 1998.

84. Wennergren G, Amark M, Amark K, et al: Wheezing bronchitis reinvestigated at the age of 10 years. Acta Paediatr 86:351–355, 1997.

85. Jaakkola JJ, Nafstad P, Magnus P: Environmental tobacco smoke, parental atopy, and childhood asthma. Environ Health Perspect 109:579–582, 2001.

86. Oddy WH, Holt PG, Sly PD, et al: Association between breast feeding and asthma in 6 year old children: Findings of a prospective birth cohort study. BMJ 319:815–819, 1999.

87. Kronqvist M, Johansson E, Pershagen G, et al: Risk factors associated with asthma and rhinoconjunctivitis among Swedish farmers. Allergy 54:1142–1149, 1999.

88. Iribarren C, Friedman GD, Klatsky AL, Eisner MD: Exposure to environmental tobacco smoke: Association

with personal characteristics and self reported health conditions. J Epidemiol Community Health 55:721–728, 2001.

89. Larson ML, Frisk M, Hallstrom J, et al: Environmental tobacco smoke exposure during childhood is associated with increased prevalence of asthma in adults. Chest 120:711–717, 2001.

90. Janson C, Chinn S, Jarvis D, et al: Effect of passive smoking on respiratory symptoms, bronchial responsiveness, lung function, and total serum IgE in the European Community Respiratory Health Survey: A cross-sectional study. Lancet 358:2103–2109, 2001.

91. Flodin U, Jeonsson P, Ziegler J, Axelson O: An epidemiologic study of bronchial asthma and smoking. Epidemiology 6:503–505, 1995.

92. Thorn J, Brisman J, Toren K: Adult-onset asthma is associated with self-reported mold or environmental tobacco smoke exposures in the home. Allergy 56:287–292, 2001.

93. Hu FB, Persky V, Flay BR, Richardson J: An epidemiological study of asthma prevalence and related factors among young adults. J Asthma 34:67–76, 1997.

94. Greer JR, Abbey DE, Burchette RJ: Asthma related to occupational and ambient air pollutants in nonsmokers. J Occup Med 35:909–915, 1993.

95. McDonnell WF, Abbey DE, Nishino N, Lebowitz MD: Long-term ambient ozone concentration and the incidence of asthma in nonsmoking adults: The AHSMOG Study. Environ Res 80:110–121, 1999.

96. Dayal HH, Khuder S, Sharrar R, Trieff N: Passive smoking in obstructive respiratory disease in an industrialized urban population. Environ Res 65:161–171, 1994.

97. Leuenberger P, Schwartz J, Ackermann-Liebrich U, et al: Passive smoking exposure in adults and chronic respiratory symptoms (SAPALDIA Study). Swiss Study on Air Pollution and Lung Diseases in Adults, SAPALDIA Team (see comments). Am J Respir Crit Care Med 150:1222–1228, 1994.

98. Ng TP, Hui KP, Tan WC: Respiratory symptoms and lung function effects of domestic exposure to tobacco smoke and cooking by gas in non-smoking women in Singapore. J Epidemiol Commun Health 47:454–458, 1993.

99. Robbins AS, Abbey DE, Lebowitz MD: Passive smoking and chronic respiratory disease symptoms in non-smoking adults. Int J Epidemiol 22:809–817, 1993.

100. Kauffmann F, Dockery DW, Speizer FE, Ferris BG Jr: Respiratory symptoms and lung function in relation to passive smoking: A comparative study of American and French women. Int J Epidemiol 18:334–344, 1989.

101. Comstock GW, Meyer MB, Helsing KJ, Tockman MS: Respiratory effects on household exposures to tobacco smoke and gas cooking. Am Rev Respir Dis 124:143–148, 1981.

102. Jaakkola MS, Jaakkola JJ, Becklake MR, Ernst P: Effect of passive smoking on the development of respiratory symptoms in young adults: An 8-year longitudinal study. J Clin Epidemiol 49:581–586, 1996.

103. Eisner MD: Environmental tobacco smoke exposure and pulmonary function among adults in NHANES III: Impact on the general population and adults with current asthma. Environ Health Perspect 110:765–770, 2002.

104. Jaakkola MS, Jaakkola JJ, Becklake MR, Ernst P: Passive smoking and evolution of lung function in young adults: An 8-year longitudinal study. J Clin Epidemiol 48:317–327, 1995.

105. Carey IM, Cook DG, Strachan DP: The effects of environmental tobacco smoke exposure on lung function in a longitudinal study of British adults. Epidemiology 10:319–326, 1999.

106. Kunzli N, Schwartz J, Stutz EZ, et al: Association of environmental tobacco smoke at work and forced expiratory lung function among never smoking asthmatics and non-asthmatics. The SAPALDIA-Team. Swiss Study on Air Pollution and Lung Disease in Adults. Soz Praventivmed 45:208–217, 2000.

107. Withers NJ, Low L, Holgate ST, Clough JB: The natural history of respiratory symptoms in a cohort of adolescents (see comments). Am J Respir Crit Care Med 158:352–357, 1998.

108. Strachan DP, Butland BK, Anderson HR: Incidence and prognosis of asthma and wheezing illness from early childhood to age 33 in a national British cohort (see comments). BMJ 312:1195–1199, 1996.

109. Eisner MD, Smith AK, Blanc PD: Bartenders' respiratory health after establishment of smoke-free bars and taverns (see comments). JAMA 280:1909–1914, 1998.

110. Crombie IK, Wright A, Irvine L, et al: Does passive smoking increase the frequency of health service contacts in children with asthma? Thorax 56:9–12, 2001.

111. Ehrlich R, Jordaan E, Du Toit D, et al: Household smoking and bronchial hyperresponsiveness in children with asthma. J Asthma 38:239–251, 2001.

112. Dubus JC, Oddoze C, Badier M, et al: Possible interaction between exposure to environmental tobacco smoke and therapy in children with asthma. Clin Sci (Lond) 95:143–149, 1998.

113. Oddoze C, Dubus JC, Badier M, et al: Urinary cotinine and exposure to parental smoking in a population of children with asthma. Clin Chem 45:505–509, 1999.

114. Willers S, Axmon A, Feyerabend C, et al: Assessment of environmental tobacco smoke exposure in children with asthmatic symptoms by questionnaire and cotinine concentrations in plasma, saliva, and urine. J Clin Epidemiol 53:715–721, 2000.

115. Li YF, Gilliland FD, Berhane K, et al: Effects of in utero and environmental tobacco smoke exposure on lung function in boys and girls with and without asthma. Am J Respir Crit Care Med 162:2097–2104, 2000.

116. Venners SA, Wang X, Chen C, et al: Exposure-response relationship between paternal smoking and children's pulmonary function. Am J Respir Crit Care Med 164:973–976, 2001.

117. Mannino DM, Homa DM, Redd SC: Involuntary smoking and asthma severity in children: Data from the Third National Health and Nutrition Examination Survey. Chest 122:409–415, 2002.

118. Abulhosn RS, Morray BH, Llewellyn CE, Redding GJ: Passive smoke exposure impairs recovery after hospitalization for acute asthma. Arch Pediatr Adolesc Med 151:135–139, 1997.

119. Melen E, Wickman M, Nordvall SL, et al: Influence of early and current environmental exposure factors on sensitization and outcome of asthma in pre-school children. Allergy 56:646–652, 2001.

120. Schwartz J, Timonen KL, Pekkanen J: Respiratory effects of environmental tobacco smoke in a panel study of asthmatic and symptomatic children. Am J Respir Crit Care Med 161:802–806, 2000.

121. Meijer GG, Postma DS, van der Heide S, et al: Exogenous stimuli and circadian peak expiratory flow variation in allergic asthmatic children. Am J Respir Crit Care Med 153:237–242, 1996.

122. Dales RE, Kerr PE, Schweitzer I, et al: Asthma management preceding an emergency department visit. Arch Intern Med 152:2041–2044, 1992.

123. Abramson MJ, Kutin JJ, Rosier MJ, Bowes G: Morbidity, medication and trigger factors in a community sample of adults with asthma. Med J Aust 162:78–81, 1995.

124. Blanc PD, Ellbjar S, Janson C, et al: Asthma-related work disability in Sweden. Am J Respir Crit Care Med 160:2028–2033, 1999.

125. Mannino DM, Siegel M, Rose D, et al: Environmental tobacco smoke exposure in the home and worksite and health effects in adults: Results from the 1991 National Health Interview Survey. Tob Control 6:296–305, 1997.

126. Jindal SK, Jha LK, Gupta D: Bronchial hyper-responsiveness of women with asthma exposed to environmental tobacco smoke. Indian J Chest Dis Allied Sci 41:75–82, 1999.

127. Sippel JM, Pedula KL, Vollmer WM, et al: Associations of smoking with hospital-based care and quality of life in patients with obstructive airway disease. Chest 115:691–696, 1999.

128. Eisner MD, Katz PP, Yelin EH, et al: Measurement of environmental tobacco smoke exposure among adults with asthma. Environ Health Perspect 109:809–814, 2001.

129. Tarlo SM, Broder I, Corey P, et al: A case-control study of the role of cold symptoms and other historical triggering factors in asthma exacerbations. Can Respir J 7:42–48, 2000.

130. Eisner MD, Yelin EH, Katz PP, et al: Exposure to indoor combustion and adult asthma outcomes: Environmental tobacco smoke, gas stoves, and woodsmoke. Thorax 57:973–978, 2002.

131. Samet JM, Lambert WE, Skipper BJ, et al: Nitrogen dioxide and respiratory illness in children. Part I: Health outcomes. Res Rep Health Eff Inst 58:1–32, 1993 [discussion appears in Res Rep Health Eff Inst 51–80, 1993].

132. Pershagen G, Rylander E, Norberg S, et al: Air pollution involving nitrogen dioxide exposure and wheezing bronchitis in children. Int J Epidemiol 24:1147–1153, 1995.

133. Garrett MH, Hooper MA, Hooper BM, Abramson MJ: Respiratory symptoms in children and indoor exposure to nitrogen dioxide and gas stoves. Am J Respir Crit Care Med 158:891–895, 1998.

134. Volkmer RE, Ruffin RE, Wigg NR, Davies N: The prevalence of respiratory symptoms in South Australian preschool children. II. Factors associated with indoor air quality. J Paediatr Child Health 31:116–120, 1995.

135. Triche EW, Belanger K, Beckett W, et al: Infant respiratory symptoms associated with indoor heating sources. Am J Respir Crit Care Med 166:1105–1111, 2002.

136. Belanger K, Beckett W, Triche E, et al: Symptoms of wheeze and persistent cough in the first year of life: Associations with indoor allergens, air contaminants, and maternal history of asthma. Am J Epidemiol 158:195–202, 2003.

137. Jarvis D, Chinn S, Luczynska C, Burney P: Association of respiratory symptoms and lung function in young adults with use of domestic gas appliances (see comments). Lancet 347:426–431, 1996.

138. Ostro BD, Lipsett MJ, Mann JK, et al: Air pollution and respiratory morbidity among adults in southern California. Am J Epidemiol 137:691–700, 1993.

139. Jarvis D, Chinn S, Sterne J, et al: The association of respiratory symptoms and lung function with the use of gas for cooking. European Community Respiratory Health Survey. Eur Respir J 11:651–658, 1998.

140. Viegi G, Paoletti P, Carrozzi L, et al: Effects of home environment on respiratory symptoms and lung function in a general population sample in north Italy. Eur Respir J 4:580–586, 1991.

141. Viegi G, Carrozzi L, Paoletti P, et al: Effects of the home environment on respiratory symptoms of a general population sample in middle Italy. Arch Environ Health 47:64–70, 1992.

142. Dow L, Phelps L, Fowler L, et al: Respiratory symptoms in older people and use of domestic gas appliances. Thorax 54:1104–1106, 1999.

143. Keller MD, Lanese RR, Mitchell RI, Cote RW: Respiratory illness in households using gas and electricity for cooking. II. Symptoms and objective findings. Environ Res 19:504–515, 1979.

144. Fischer P, Remijn B, Brunekreef B, et al: Indoor air pollution and its effect on pulmonary function of adult non-smoking women: II. Associations between nitrogen dioxide and pulmonary function. Int J Epidemiol 14:221–226, 1985.

145. Keller MD, Lanese RR, Mitchell RI, Cote RW: Respiratory illness in households using gas and electricity for cooking. I. Survey of incidence. Environ Res 19:495–503, 1979.

146. Dekker C, Dales R, Bartlett S, et al: Childhood asthma and the indoor environment. Chest 100:922–926, 1991.

147. Ostro BD, Lipsett MJ, Mann JK, et al: Indoor air pollution and asthma: Results from a panel study (see comments). Am J Respir Crit Care Med 149:1400–1406, 1994.

148. Lebowitz MD, Collins L, Holberg CJ: Time series analyses of respiratory responses to indoor and outdoor environmental phenomena. Environ Res 43:332–341, 1987.

149. Moran SE, Strachan DP, Johnston ID, Anderson HR: Effects of exposure to gas cooking in childhood and adulthood on respiratory symptoms, allergic sensitization and lung function in young British adults. Clin Exp Allergy 29:1033–1041, 1999.

150. Eisner MD, Blanc PD: Gas stove use and respiratory health among adults with asthma in NHANES III. Occup Environ Med 60:759–764, 2003.

151. Ng TP, Seet CS, Tan WC, Foo SC: Nitrogen dioxide exposure from domestic gas cooking and airway response in asthmatic women. Thorax 56:596–601, 2001.

152. Tunnicliffe WS, Burge PS, Ayres JG: Effect of domestic concentrations of nitrogen dioxide on airway responses to inhaled allergen in asthmatic patients. Lancet 344:1733–1736, 1994.

153. Salome CM, Brown NJ, Marks GB, et al: Effect of nitrogen dioxide and other combustion products on asthmatic subjects in a home-like environment. Eur Respir J 9:910–918, 1996.

154. Orehek J, Massari JP, Gayrard P, et al: Effect of short-term, low-level nitrogen dioxide exposure on bronchial sensitivity of asthmatic patients. J Clin Invest 57:301–307, 1976.

155. Jenkins HS, Devalia JL, Mister RL, et al: The effect of exposure to ozone and nitrogen dioxide on the airway response of atopic asthmatics to inhaled allergen: Dose- and time-dependent effects. Am J Respir Crit Care Med 160:33–39, 1999.

156. Larson TV, Koenig JQ: Wood smoke: Emissions and noncancer respiratory effects. Annu Rev Public Health 15:133–156, 1994.

157. Boman BC, Forsberg AB, Jarvholm BG: Adverse health effects from ambient air pollution in relation to residential wood combustion in modern society. Scand J Work Environ Health 29:251–260, 2003.

158. Betchley C, Koenig JQ, van Belle G, et al: Pulmonary function and respiratory symptoms in forest firefighters. Am J Ind Med 31:503–509, 1997.

159. Surveillance of morbidity during wildfires—Central Florida, 1998. MMWR Morb Mortal Wkly Rep 48:78–79, 1999.

160. Mishra V: Indoor air pollution from biomass combustion and acute respiratory illness in preschool age children in Zimbabwe. Int J Epidemiol 32:847–853, 2003.

161. Ozbay B, Uzun K, Arslan H, Zehir I: Functional and radiological impairment in women highly exposed to indoor biomass fuels. Respirology 6:255–258, 2001.

162. Perez-Padilla R, Regalado J, Vedal S, et al: Exposure to biomass smoke and chronic airway disease in Mexican women: A case-control study. Am J Respir Crit Care Med 154:701–706, 1996.

163. Honicky RE, Osborne JS, Akpom CA: Symptoms of respiratory illness in young children and the use of wood-burning stoves for indoor heating. Pediatrics 75:587–593, 1985.

164. Koenig J, Hanley A, Rebolledo V, et al: The effects of wood smoke air pollution on spirometric lung function values in young asthmatic children. J Allergy Clin Immunol 85:178, 1990.

165. Tuthill RW: Woodstoves, formaldehyde, and respiratory disease. Am J Epidemiol 120:952–955, 1984.

166. von Mutius E, Illi S, Nicolai T, Martinez FD: Relation of indoor heating with asthma, allergic sensitisation, and bronchial responsiveness: Survey of children in south Bavaria. BMJ 312:1448–1450, 1996.

167. Levesqu B, Allaire S, Gauvin D, et al: Wood-burning appliances and indoor air quality. Sci Total Environ 281:47–62, 2001.

168. Leaderer BP, Naeher L, Jankun T, et al: Indoor, outdoor, and regional summer and winter concentrations of PM_{10}, $PM_{2.5}$, SO_4^{2-}, H^+, NH_4^+, NO_3^-, NH_3, and nitrous acid in homes with and without kerosene space heaters. Environ Health Perspect 107:223–231, 1999.

169. Venn AJ, Yemaneberhan H, Bekele Z, et al: Increased risk of allergy associated with the use of kerosene fuel in the home. Am J Respir Crit Care Med 164:1660–1664, 2001.

170. Azizi BH, Henry RL: The effects of indoor environmental factors on respiratory illness in primary school children in Kuala Lumpur. Int J Epidemiol 20:144–150, 1991.

171. Ng'ang'a LW, Odhiambo JA, Mungai MW, et al: Prevalence of exercise induced bronchospasm in Kenyan school children: An urban-rural comparison. Thorax 53:919–926, 1998.

172. Bethel RA, Erle DJ, Epstein J, et al: Effect of exercise rate and route of inhalation on sulfur dioxide–induced bronchoconstriction in asthmatic subjects. Am Rev Respir Dis 128:592–596, 1983.

173. Lippman M, Yeates DB, Albert RE: Deposition, retention, and clearance of inhaled particles. Br J Ind Med 37:337–362, 1980.

174. Martin D, Jacobi W: Diffusion of small-sized particles in the bronchial tree. Health Phys 23:23–29, 1972.

175. Fillenz M, Woods RI: Sensory innervation of the airways. *In* Porter R (ed): Ciba Foundation Symposium. Breathing: Herring-Breuer Centenary Symposium. London: Churchill, 1970, pp 101–107.

176. Pinkerton KE, Brody AR, Miller FJ, et al: Exposure to low levels of ozone results in enhanced pulmonary retention of inhaled asbestos fibers. Am Rev Respir Dis 140:1075–1081, 1989.

177. Sorokin SP, Brain JD: Pathways of clearance in mouse lungs exposed to iron oxide aerosols. Anat Rec 181:581–588, 1975.

178. Mossman BT, Churg A: Mechanisms in the pathogenesis of asbestosis and silicosis. Am J Respir Crit Care Med 157:1666–1680, 1998.

179. Devlin RB, McKinnon TL, Noah TL, et al: Cytokine and fibronectin production by human alveolar macrophages and airway epithelial cells exposed to ozone in vitro. Am J Physiol 266:1612–1619, 1994.

179a. Bernstein JA, Alexis N, Barnes C, et al: Health effects of air pollution. J Allergy Clin Immunol 114:1116–1123, 2004.

180. Salvi S, Blomberg A, Rudell B, et al: Acute inflammatory responses in the airways and peripheral blood after short-term exposure to diesel exhaust in healthy human volunteers. Am J Respir Crit Care Med 159:702–709, 1999.

181. Aris RM, Christian D, Hearne PQ, et al: Ozone-induced airway inflammation in human subjects as determined by airway lavage and biopsy. Am Rev Respir Dis 148:1363–1372, 1993.

182. Romieu I, Sienra-Monge JJ, Ramirez-Aguilar M, et al: Genetic polymorphism of GSTM1 and antioxidant supplementation influence lung function in relation to ozone exposure in asthmatic children in Mexico City. Thorax 59:8–10, 2004.

183. Plopper CG, Hatch GE, Wong V, et al: Relationship of inhaled ozone concentration to acute tracheobronchial epithelial injury, site-specific ozone dose, and glutathione depletion in rhesus monkeys. Am J Respir Cell Mol Biol 19:387–399, 1998.

184. Li N, Hao M, Phalen RF, et al: Particulate air pollutants and asthma: A paradigm for the role of oxidative stress in PM-induced adverse health effects. Clin Immunol 109:250–265, 2003.

185. Schwartz J, Spix C, Touloumi G, et al: Methodologic issues in studies of air pollution and daily counts of deaths or hospital admissions. J Epidemiol Commun Health 50(Suppl 1):S3–S11, 1996.

186. Dockery DW, Speizer FE, Stram DO, et al: Effects of inhalable particles on respiratory health of children. Am Rev Respir Dis 139:587–594, 1989.

187. Detels R, Tashkin DP, Sayre JW, et al: The UCLA population study of COPD: X. A cohort study of changes in respiratory disease associated with chronic exposure to SO_x, NO_x, and hydrocarbons. Am J Public Health 81:350–359, 1991.

188. Spix C, Anderson HR, Schwartz J, et al: Short-term effects of air pollution on hospital admissions of respiratory diseases in Europe: A quantitative summary of APHEA study results. Arch Environ Health 53:54–64, 1998.

189. Abbey DE, Burchette RJ, Knutsen SF, et al: Long-term particulate and other air pollutants and lung function in nonsmokers. Am J Respir Crit Care Med 158:289–298, 1998.

190. Burnett RT, Cakmak S, Brook JR, et al: The role of particulate size and chemistry in the association between summertime ambient air pollution and hospitalization for cardiorespiratory diseases. Environ Health Perspect 105:614–620, 1997.

191. Higgins ITT, D'Arcy JB, Gibbons DI, et al: Effect of exposure to ambient ozone on ventilatory lung function in children. Am Rev Respir Dis 141:1336–1346, 1990.

192. Liu L-JS, Koutrakis P, Olson MP, et al: Evaluation of the Harvard ozone passive sampler on human subjects indoors. Environ Sci Technol 28:915–923, 1994.

193. Spektor DM, Lippmann M, Thurston GD, et al: Effects of ambient ozone on respiratory function in active normal children. Am Rev Respir Dis 137:313–330, 1988.

194. Spektor DM, Lippmann M, Thurston GD, et al: Effects of ambient ozone on respiratory function in healthy adults exercising outdoors. Am Rev Respir Dis 138:821–828, 1988.

195. Ostro BD, Lipsett MJ, Wiener MB, et al: Asthmatic responses to airborne acid aerosols. Am J Public Health 81:694–702, 1991.

196. Zeger SL, Dominici F, Samet JM: Harvesting-resistant estimates of air pollution effects on mortality. Ann Epidemiol 10:171–175, 1999.

197. Aronow WS, Isbell MW: Carbon monoxide effect on exercise induced angina pectoris. Ann Intern Med 79:392–395, 1973.

198. Sheppard D, Wong SC, Uehara CF, et al: Lower threshold and greater bronchomotor responsiveness of asthmatic subjects to sulfur dioxide. Am Rev Respir Dis 122:873–878, 1980.

199. Amdur MO, Underhill DW: The effect of various aerosols on the response of guinea pigs to sulfur dioxide. Arch Environ Health 16:460–468, 1968.

200. Environmental Protection Agency: Respiratory tract effects of ozone. *In* Air Quality Criteria for Ozone and Related Photochemical Oxidants (Vol 3). Washington, DC: National Center for Environmental Assessment Office of Research and Development, 1996, pp 6–80 to 6–81.

201. Li N, Wang M, Oberley TD, et al: Comparison of the pro-oxidative and proinflammatory effects of organic diesel exhaust particle chemicals in bronchial epithelial cells and macrophages. J Immunol 169:4531–4541, 2002.

201a. Ghio AJ: Biological effects of Utah Valley ambient particles in humans: a review. J Aerosol Med 17:157–164, 2004.

202. Thurston GD, Ito K, Lippmann M, et al: Reexamination of London, England, mortality in relation to exposure to acidic aerosols during 1963–1972 winters. Environ Health Perspect 79:73–82, 1989.

203. Schwartz J, Marcus A: Mortality and air pollution in London: A time series analysis. Am J Epidemiol 131:185–194, 1990.

204. Vedal S: Ambient particles and health: Lines that divide. J Air Waste Manag Assoc 47:551–581, 1997.

205. Schwartz J: Air pollution and daily mortality: A review and meta-analysis. Environ Res 64:36–52, 1994.

206. Venners SA, Wang B, Xu Z, et al: Particulate matter, sulfur dioxide, and daily mortality in Chongqing, China. Environ Health Perspect 111:562–567, 2003.

207. Ballester F, Saez M, Perez-Hoyos S, et al: The EMECAM project: A multicentre study on air pollution and mortality in Spain. Combined results for particulates and for sulfur dioxide. Occup Environ Med 59:300–308, 2002.

208. Fairley D: The relationship of daily mortality to suspended particulates in Santa Clara County, 1980–1986. Environ Health Perspect 89:159–168, 1990.

209. Dockery DW, Schwartz J, Spengler JD: Air pollution and daily mortality: Associations with particulates and acid aerosols. Environ Res 59:362–373, 1992.

209a. Samoli E, Analitis A, Touloumi G, et al: Estimating the exposure-response relationships between particulate matter and mortality within the APHEA Multicity Project. Environ Health Perspect 113:88–95, 2005.

210. Borja-Aburto VH, Loomis DP, Bangdiwals SI, et al: Ozone, suspended particulates and daily mortality in Mexico City. Am J Epidemiol 145:258–268, 1997.

211. Samet JM, Dominici F, Curriero FC, et al: Fine particulate air pollution and mortality in 20 U.S. cities, 1987–1994. N Engl J Med 343:1742–1749, 2000.

212. Schwartz J, Dockery DW, Neas LM: Is daily mortality associated specifically with fine particles? J Air Waste Manag Assoc 46:927–939, 1996.

213. Zmirou D, Schwartz J, Saez M, et al: Time-series analysis of air pollution and cause-specific mortality. Epidemiology 9:495–503, 1998.

214. Brunett RT, Cakmak S, Brook JR: The effect of the urban ambient air pollution mix on daily mortality rates in 11 Canadian cities. Can J Public Health 89:152–156, 1998.

215. Brook RD, Franklin B, Cascio W, et al: Air pollution and cardiovascular disease: A statement for healthcare professionals from the Expert Panel on Population and Prevention Science of the American Heart Association. Circulation 109:2655–2671, 2004.

216. Seaton A, MacNee W, Donaldson K, et al: Particulate air pollution and acute health effects. Lancet 345:176–178, 1995.

217. Donaldson K, Stone V, Seaton A, et al: Ambient particle inhalation and the cardiovascular system: Potential mechanisms. Environ Health Perspect 109(Suppl 4):523–527, 2001.

218. van Eeden SF, Hogg JC: Systemic inflammatory response induced by particulate matter air pollution: The importance of bone-marrow stimulation. J Toxicol Environ Health A 65:1597–1613, 2002.

219. Peters A, Doring A, Wichmann H-E, Koenig W: Increased plasma viscosity during an air pollution episode: A link to mortality. Lancet 349:1582–1587, 1997.

220. Pope CA, Dockery DW, Kanner RE, et al: Oxygen saturation, pulse rate associated with particulate air pollution. Am J Respir Crit Care Med 159:365–372, 1999.

221. Peters A, Frohlich M, Doring A, et al: Particulate air pollution is associated with an acute phase response in men: Results from the MONICA-Augsburg Study. Eur Heart J 22:1198–1204, 2001.

222. Peters A, Liu E, Verrier RL, et al: Air pollution and incidence of cardiac arrhythmia. Epidemiology 11:11–17, 2000.

223. Pope CA, Dockery DW: Epidemiology of particle effects. *In* Holgate ST, Samet JM, Koren HS, Maynard RL (eds): Air Pollution and Health. New York: Academic Press, 1999, pp 673–705.

224. Dockery DW, Pope CA: Acute respiratory effects of particulate air pollution. Annu Rev Public Health 15:107–132, 1994.

225. Schwartz J: Air pollution and hospital admissions for respiratory disease. Epidemiology 7:20–28, 1995.

226. Thurston GD, Ito K, Hayes CG, et al: Respiratory hospital admissions and summertime haze air pollution in Toronto, Ontario: Consideration of the role of acid aerosols. Environ Res 65:271–290, 1994.

227. Dockery DW, Cunningham J, Damokosh AI, et al: Health effects of acid aerosols on North American children: Respiratory symptoms. Environ Health Perspect 104:500–505, 1996.

228. Raizenne M, Neas LM, Damokosh AI, et al: Health effects of acid aerosols on North American children: Pulmonary function. Environ Health Perspect 104:506–514, 1996.

229. McConnell R, Berhane K, Gilliland F, et al: Prospective study of air pollution and bronchitic symptoms in children with asthma. Am J Respir Crit Care Med 168:790–797, 2003.

230. Vedal S, Petkau J, White R, et al: Acute effect of ambient inhalable particles in asthmatic and non-asthmatic children. Am J Respir Crit Care Med 157:1034–1043, 1998.

231. Peters A, Dockery DW, Heinrich J, et al: Medication use modifies the health effects of particulate sulfate air pollution in children with asthma. Environ Health Perspect 105:430–435, 1997.

232. Delfino RJ, Zeiger RS, Seltzer JM, et al: Symptoms in pediatric asthmatics and air pollution: Differences in effects by symptom severity, anti-inflammatory medication use and particulate averaging time. Environ Health Perspect 106:751–761, 1998.

233. Frank NR, Amdur MO, Worcester J, et al: Effects of acute controlled exposure to SO_2 on respiratory mechanics in healthy male adults. J Appl Physiol 17:252–258, 1962.

234. Nadel JA, Salem H, Tamplin B, et al: Mechanism of bronchoconstriction during inhalation of sulfur dioxide. J Appl Physiol 20:164–167, 1965.

235. Linn WS, Venet TG, Shamoo DA, et al: Respiratory effects of sulfur dioxide in heavily exercising asthmatics: A dose-response study. Am Rev Respir Dis 127:278–283, 1983.

236. Horstman D, Roger LJ, Kehrl H, et al: Airway sensitivity of asthmatics to ozone. Toxicol Ind Health 2:289–298, 1986.

237. Balmes JR, Fine JM, Sheppard D: Symptomatic bronchoconstriction after short-term inhalation of sulfur dioxide. Am Rev Respir Dis 136:1117–1121, 1987.

238. Gauderman WJ, McConnell R, Gilliland F, et al: Association between air pollution and lung function growth in southern California children. Am J Respir Crit Care Med 162:1383–1390, 2000.

239. Gauderman WJ, Gilliland GF, Vora H, et al: Association between air pollution and lung function growth in southern California children: Results from a second cohort. Am J Respir Crit Care Med 166:76–84, 2002.

240. Avol EL, Gauderman WJ, Tan SM, et al: Respiratory effects of relocating to areas of differing air pollution levels. Am J Respir Crit Care Med 164:2067–2072, 2001.

241. Johnson JH: Automotive emissions. *In* Watson AY, Bates RR, Kennedy D (eds): Air Pollution, the Automobile, and Public Health. Cambridge, Mass: Health Effects Institute, 1988, pp 65–68.

242. Nauss KM: Critical issues in assessing the carcinogenesis of diesel exhaust: A synthesis of current knowledge. *In* Diesel Exhaust: A Critical Analysis of Emissions, Exposure, and Health Effects. Cambridge, Mass: Health Effects Institute, 1995, p 14.

243. Cohen AJ, Nikula K: The health effects of diesel exhaust: Laboratory and epidemiologic Studies. *In* Holgate ST, Samet JM, Koren HS, Maynard RL (eds): Air Pollution and Health. New York: Academic Press, 1999, pp 707–745.

244. Bhatia R, Lopipero P, Smith AH: Diesel exhaust exposure and lung cancer. Epidemiology 9:84–91, 1997.

245. Busby WF, Newberne PM: Diesel emissions and other substances associated with animal carcinogenicity. *In* Diesel Exhaust: A Critical Analysis of Emissions, Exposure, and Health Effects. Cambridge, Mass: Health Effects Institute, 1995, pp 187–220.

246. Takano H, Yoshikawa T, Ichinose T, et al: Diesel exhaust particles enhance antigen-induced airway inflammation and local cytokine expression in mice. Am J Respir Crit Care Med 156:36–42, 1997.

247. Nel AE, Diaz-Sanchez D, Ng D, et al: Enhancement of allergic inflammation by the interaction between diesel exhaust particles and the immune system. J Allergy Clin Immunol 102:539–557, 1998.

248. Takafuji S, Suzuki S, Koizumi K, et al: Diesel exhaust particulates inoculated by the intranasal route have an adjuvant activity for IgE production in mice. J Allergy Clin Immunol 79:639–645, 1987.

249. Diaz-Sanchez D, Dotson AR, Takenaka H, et al: Diesel exhaust particles induce local IgE production in vivo and alter the pattern of IgE messenger RNA isoforms. J Clin Invest 94:1417–1425, 1994.

250. Takenaka H, Zhang K, Diaz-Sanchez D, et al: Enhanced human IgE production results from exposure to the aromatic hydrocarbons from diesel exhaust: Direct effects on B-cell IgE production. J Allergy Clin Immunol 95:103–115, 1995.

251. Diaz-Sanchez D, Garcia MP, Wang M, et al: Nasal challenge with diesel exhaust particles can induce sensitization to a neoallergen in the human mucosa. J Allergy Clin Immunol 104:1183–1188, 1999.

252. Whitekus MJ, Li N, Zhang M, et al: Thiol antioxidants inhibit the adjuvant effects of aerosolized diesel exhaust particles in a murine model for ovalbumin sensitization. J Immunol 168:2560–2567, 2002.

253. Gilliland FD, Li YF, Saxon A, et al: Effect of glutathione-S-transferase M1 and P1 genotypes on xenobiotic enhancement of allergic responses: Randomised, placebo-controlled crossover study. Lancet 363:119–125, 2004.

254. Pandya RJ, Solomon G, Kinner A, et al: Diesel exhaust and asthma: Hypotheses and molecular mechanisms of action. Environ Health Perspect 110(Suppl 1):103–112, 2002.

255. Ghio AJ, Kim C, Devlin RB: Concentrated ambient air particles induce mild pulmonary inflammation in healthy human volunteers. Am J Respir Crit Care Med 162:981–988, 2000.

256. Environmental Protection Agency: Environmental concentrations, patterns, and exposure estimates. *In* Air Quality Criteria for Ozone and Related Photochemical Oxidants (Vol 1). Washington, DC: National Center for Environmental Assessment Office of Research and Development, 1996, pp 4–15 to 4–19.

257. Bates DV: Ozone: Myth and reality. Environ Res 50:230–237, 1989.

258. Saez M, Ballester F, Barcelo MA, et al: A combined analysis of the short-term effects of photochemical air pollutants on mortality within the EMECAM project. Environ Health Perspect 110:221–228, 2002.

259. Vedal S, Brauer M, White R, et al: Air pollution and daily mortality in a city with low levels of pollution. Environ Health Perspect 111:45–52, 2003.

259a. Bell ML, McDermott A, Zeger SL, et al: Ozone and short-term mortality in 95 US urban communities, 1987–2000. JAMA 292:2372–2378, 2004.

260. Hodgkin JE, Abbey DE, Euler GL, et al: COPD prevalence in nonsmokers in high and low photochemical air pollution areas. Chest 86:830–838, 1984.

261. Abbey DE, Mills PK, Petersen FF, et al: Long-term ambient concentrations of total suspended particulates and oxidants as related to incidence of chronic disease in California Seventh-Day Adventists. Environ Health Perspect 94:43–50, 1991.

262. Euler GL, Abbey DE, Hodgkin JE, et al: Chronic obstructive pulmonary disease symptom effects of long-term cumulative exposure to ambient levels of total oxidants and nitrogen dioxide in California Seventh-Day Adventist residents. Arch Environ Health 43:279–285, 1988.

263. Burrows B, Knudson RJ, Lebowitz MD: The relationship of childhood respiratory illness to adult obstructive airway disease. Am Rev Respir Dis 115:751–760, 1977.

264. Detels R, Sayre JW, Coulson AH, et al: The UCLA population studies of chronic obstructive respiratory disease: IV. Respiratory effects of long-term exposure to photochemical oxidants, nitrogen dioxide, and sulfates on current and never-smokers. Am Rev Respir Dis 124:673–680, 1981.

265. Stern B, Jones L, Raizenne M, et al: Respiratory health effects associated with ambient sulfates and ozone in two rural Canadian communities. Environ Res 49:20–39, 1985.

266. Kilburn KH, Warshaw R, Thornton JC: Pulmonary function impairment and symptoms in women in the Los Angeles Harbor area. Am J Med 79:23–28, 1985.

267. Detels R, Tashkin DP, Sayre JW, et al: The UCLA population studies of chronic obstructive respiratory disease: 9. Lung function changes associated with chronic

exposure to photochemical oxidants: A cohort study among never smokers. Chest 92:594–603, 1987.

268. Schwartz J: Lung function and chronic exposure to air pollution: A cross-sectional analysis of NHANES II. Environ Res 50:309–321, 1989.

269. Kunzli N, Lurmann F, Segal M, et al: Association between lifetime ambient ozone exposure and pulmonary function in college freshman—results of a pilot study. Environ Res 72:8–23, 1997.

270. Galizia A, Kinney PL: Long-term residence in areas of high ozone: Associations with respiratory health in a nationwide sample of nonsmoking young adults. Environ Health Perspect 107:675–679, 1999.

271. Frischer T, Studnicka M, Gartner C, et al: Lung function growth and ambient ozone: A three-year population study in school children. Am J Respir Crit Care Med 160:390–396, 1999.

272. Sherwin RP: Air pollution: The pathobiologic issues. J Toxicol Clin Toxicol 29:385–400, 1991.

273. Calderon-Garciduenas L, Osorno-Velasquez A, Bravo-Alvarez H, et al: Histopathologic changes of the nasal mucosa in southwest metropolitan Mexico City inhabitants. Am J Pathol 140:225–232, 1992.

274. Kinney PL, Thurston GD, Raizenne M: The effects of ambient ozone on lung function in children: A reanalysis of six summer camp studies. Environ Health Perspect 104:170–174, 1996.

275. Korrick SA, Neas LM, Dockery DW, et al: Effects of ozone and other pollutants on the pulmonary function of adult hikers. Environ Health Perspect 106:93–99, 1998.

276. Whittemore AS, Korn EL: Asthma and air pollution in the Los Angeles area. Am J Public Health 70:687–696, 1980.

277. Holguin AH, Buffler PA, Contant CF: The effects of ozone on asthmatics in the Houston area. *In* Lee SD (ed): Evaluation of the Scientific Basis for Ozone/Oxidants Standards (APCA International Specialty Conference Transactions TR-4). Pittsburgh: Air Pollution Control Association, 1982, pp 262–280.

278. Krzyzanowski M, Quackenboss JJ, Lebowitz MD: Relation of peak expiratory flow rates and symptoms to ambient ozone. Arch Environ Health 47:107–115, 1992.

279. Delfino RJ, Coate BD, Zeiger RS, et al: Daily asthma severity in relation to personal ozone exposure and outdoor fungal spores. Am J Respir Crit Care Med 154:633–641, 1996.

280. Steib DM, Burnett RT, Beveridge RC, et al: Association between ozone and asthma emergency department visits in St. John, New Brunswick, Canada. Environ Health Perspect 104:1354–1360, 1996.

281. White MC, Etzel RA, Wilcox WD, et al: Exacerbations of childhood asthma and ozone pollution in Atlanta. Environ Res 65:56–68, 1994.

282. Cody RP, Weisel CP, Birnbaum G, et al: The effect of ozone associated with summertime photochemical smog on the frequency of asthma visits to hospital emergency departments. Environ Res 58:184–194, 1992.

283. Delfino RJ, Murphy-Moulton AM, Burnett RT, et al: Effects of air pollution on emergency room visits for respiratory illnesses in Montreal, Quebec. Am J Respir Crit Care Med 155:568–576, 1997.

284. McConnell R, Berhane K, Gilliland F, et al: Asthma in exercising children exposed to ozone: A cohort study. Lancet 359:386–391, 2002. [published erratum appears in Lancet 359:896, 2002].

285. Sunyer J, Anto JM, Murillo C, et al: Effects of urban air pollution on emergency room admissions for chronic obstructive pulmonary disease. Am J Epidemiol 134:277–286, 1991.

286. Linn WS, Shamoo DA, Venet TG, et al: Response to ozone in volunteers with chronic obstructive pulmonary disease. Arch Environ Health 38:278–283, 1983.

287. Gong H, Shamoo DA, Anderson KR, et al: Responses of older men with and without chronic obstructive pulmonary disease to prolonged ozone exposure. Arch Environ Health 52:18–25, 1997.

288. Frampton MW, Morrow PE, Torres A, et al: Ozone responsiveness in smokers and nonsmokers. Am J Respir Crit Care Med 155:116–121, 1997.

289. Bates DV, Sitzo R: Air pollution and hospital admissions in southern Ontario: The acid summer haze effect. Environ Res 43:317–331, 1987.

290. Burnett RT, Dales RE, Raizenne M, et al: Effects of low ambient levels of ozone and sulfates on the frequency of respiratory admissions to Ontario hospitals. Environ Res 65:172–194, 1994.

291. Pierson WE: Impact of air pollutants on athletic performance. Allergy Proc 10:209–214, 1989.

292. Gong H, Bradley PW, Simmons MS, et al: Impaired exercise performance and pulmonary function in elite cyclists during low-level ozone exposure in a hot environment. Am Rev Respir Dis 134:726–733, 1986.

293. Hammer DI, Hasselblad R, Portnoy B, et al: Los Angeles student nurse study: Daily symptom reporting and photochemical oxidants. Arch Environ Health 28:255–260, 1974.

294. Douglas WW, Hepper NG, Colby TV: Silo-filler's disease. Mayo Clin Proc 64:291–304, 1989.

295. Lee JT, Kim H, Song H, et al: Air pollution and asthma among children in Seoul, Korea. Epidemiology 13:481–484, 2002.

296. Lin M, Chen Y, Villeneuve PJ, et al: Gaseous air pollutants and asthma hospitalization of children with low household income in Vancouver, British Columbia, Canada. Am J Epidemiol 159:294–303, 2004.

297. Bates DV, Bell GM, Burnham CD, et al: Short-term effects of ozone on the lung. J Appl Physiol 32:176–181, 1977.

298. McDonnell WF, Horstman DH: Pulmonary effects of ozone exposure during exercise: Dose-response characteristics. J Appl Physiol 54:1345–1352, 1983.

299. Horstman DH, Folinsbee LF, Ives PJ, et al: Ozone concentration and pulmonary response relationships for 6.6-hour exposures with five hours of moderate exercise to 0.08, 0.10, and 0.12 ppm. Am Rev Respir Dis 142:1158–1163, 1990.

300. McDonnell WF, Kehrl HR, Abdul-Salaam S, et al: Respiratory response of humans exposed to low levels of ozone for 6.6 hours. Arch Environ Health 46:145–150, 1991.

301. McDonnell WF, Horstmann DH, Abdul-Salaam S, et al: Reproducibility of individual responses to ozone exposure. Am Rev Respir Dis 131:36–40, 1985.

302. Bergamaschi E, De Palma G, Mozzoni P, et al: Polymorphism of quinone-metabolizing enzymes and susceptibility to ozone-induced acute effects. Am J Respir Crit Care Med 163:1426–1431, 2001.

303. Hackney JD, Linn WS, Mohler JG, et al: Adaptation to short-term respiratory effects of ozone in men exposed repeatedly. J Appl Physiol 43:82–85, 1977.

304. Christian DL, Chen LL, Scannell CH, et al: Ozone-induced inflammation is attenuated with multiday exposure. Am J Respir Crit Care Med 158:532–537, 1998.

305. Hackney JD, Triede FC, Linn WS, et al: Experimental studies on human health effects of air pollutants: IV. Short-term physiological and clinical effects of nitrogen dioxide exposure. Arch Environ Health 33:176–181, 1978.

306. Folinsbee LJ, Horvath SM, Bedi JF, et al: Effects of 0.62 ppm NO_2 on cardiopulmonary function in young male non-smokers. Environ Res 15:199–205, 1978.

307. Bauer MA, Utell MJ, Morrow PE, et al: 0.30 ppm nitrogen dioxide potentiates exercise-induced bronchospasm in asthmatics. Am Rev Respir Dis 134:1203–1208, 1986.

308. Samet JM, Utell MJ: The risk of nitrogen dioxide: What have we learned from epidemiological and clinical studies? Toxicol Ind Health 6:247–262, 1990.

309. Balmes JR: The role of ozone exposure in the epidemiology of asthma. Environ Health Perspect 101:219–224, 1993.

310. Scannell C, Chen L, Aris RM, et al: Greater ozone-induced inflammatory responses in subjects with asthma. Am J Respir Crit Care Med 154:24–29, 1996.

311. Kreit JW, Gross KB, Moore TB, et al: Ozone-induced changes in pulmonary function and bronchial responsiveness in asthmatics. J Appl Physiol 66:217–222, 1989.

312. Horstman DH, Ball BA, Brown J, et al: Comparison of pulmonary responses of asthmatic and nonasthmatic subjects performing light exercise while exposed to a low level of ozone. Toxicol Ind Health 11:369–385, 1995.

313. Hazucha MJ, Bates DV, Bromberg PA: Mechanisms of action of ozone on the human lung. J Appl Physiol 67:1535–1541, 1989.

314. Molfino NA, Wright SC, Satz I, et al: Effect of low concentrations of ozone on inhaled allergen responses in asthmatic subjects. Lancet 338:199–203, 1991.

315. Jorres R, Nowak D, Magnussen H: The effect of ozone exposure on allergen responsiveness in subjects with asthma or rhinitis. Am J Respir Crit Care Med 153:56–64, 1996.

316. Strand V, Rak S, Svartengren M, et al: Nitrogen dioxide exposure enhances asthmatic reactions to inhaled allergen in subjects with asthma. Am J Respir Crit Care Med 155:881–887, 1997.

317. Seltzer J, Bigby BG, Stulbarg MS, et al: Ozone-induced change in bronchial reactivity and airway inflammation in human subjects. J Appl Physiol 60:1321–1326, 1986.

318. Devlin RB, McDonnell WF, Mann R, et al: Exposure of humans to ambient levels for 6.6 hours causes cellular and biochemical changes in the lung. Am J Respir Cell Mol Biol 4:72–81, 1991.

319. Graham D, Henderson F, House D: Neutrophil influx measured in nasal lavages of humans exposed to ozone. Arch Environ Health 43:228–233, 1988.

320. Kinney, PL, Nilsen DM, Lippmann M, et al: Biomarkers of lung inflammation in recreational joggers exposed to ozone. Am J Respir Crit Care Med 154:1430–1435, 1996.

321. Basha MA, Gross KB, Gwizdala CJ, et al: Bronchoalveolar lavage neutrophilia in asthmatic and healthy volunteers after controlled exposure to ozone and filtered air. Chest 106:1757–1765, 1994.

322. Blomberg A, Krishna MT, Helleday R, et al: Persistent airway inflammation but accommodated antioxidant and lung function responses after repeated daily exposure to nitrogen dioxide. Am J Respir Crit Care Med 159:536–543, 1999.

323. Frampton MW, Smeglin M, Roberts NJ, et al: Nitrogen dioxide exposure in vivo and human alveolar macrophage inactivation of influenza virus in vitro. Environ Res 48:179–192, 1989.

324. Environmental Protection Agency: Respiratory tract effects of ozone. *In* Air Quality Criteria for Ozone and Related Photochemical Oxidants (Vol 3). Washington, DC: National Center for Environmental Assessment Office of Research and Development, 1996, pp 6–54 to 6–76.

325. Harkema JR, Plopper CG, Hyde DM, et al: Response of the macaque nasal epithelium to ambient levels of ozone: A morphometric study of the transitional and respiratory epithelium. Am J Pathol 128:29–44, 1987.

326. Dungworth DL: Noncarcinogenic responses of the respiratory tract to inhaled toxicants. *In* McClellan RO, Henderson RF (eds): Concepts in Inhalation Toxicology. New York: Hemisphere Publishing, 1989, pp 273–298.

327. Stephens RJ, Sloan MF, Evans MJ, et al: Early response of lung to low levels of ozone. Am J Pathol 74:31–58, 1974.

328. Evans MJ, Johnson LV, Stephens RJ, et al: Cell renewal in the lungs of rats exposed to low levels of ozone. Exp Mol Pathol 24:70–83, 1976.

329. Castleman WL, Dungworth DL, Schwartz LW, et al: Acute respiratory bronchiolitis: An ultrastructural and autoradiographic study of epithelial cell injury and renewal in rhesus monkeys exposed to ozone. Am J Pathol 98:811–840, 1980.

330. Bassett DJP, Bowen-Kelly E, Elbon CL, et al: Rat lung recovery from 3 days of continuous exposure to 0.75 ppm ozone. J Toxicol Environ Health 25:329–347, 1988.

331. Weller BL, Crapo JD, Slot J, et al: Site- and cell-specific alteration of lung copper/zinc and manganese superoxide dismutases by chronic ozone exposure. Am J Respir Cell Mol Biol 17:552–560, 1997.

332. Tyler WS, Tyler NK, Last JA, et al: Comparison of daily and seasonal exposures of young monkeys to ozone. Toxicology 50:131–144, 1988.

333. Chang L-Y, Huang Y, Stockstill BL, et al: Epithelial injury and interstitial fibrosis in the proximal alveolar regions of rats chronically exposed to a simulated pattern of urban ambient ozone. Toxicol Appl Pharmacol 109:219–234, 1992.

334. Barr BC, Hyde DM, Plopper CG, et al: A comparison of terminal airway remodeling in chronic daily versus episodic ozone exposure. Toxicol Appl Pharmacol 106:384–407, 1990.

335. Schelegle ES, Miller LA, Gershwin LJ, et al: Repeated episodes of ozone inhalation amplifies the effects of allergen sensitization and inhalation on airway immune and structural development in Rhesus monkeys. Toxicol Appl Pharmacol 191:74–85, 2003.

336. Environmental Protection Agency: Studies of the effects of nitrogen compounds on animals. *In* Air Quality Criteria for Oxides of Nitrogen (Vol 3). Washington, DC: National Center for Environmental Assessment Office of Research and Development, 1993, pp 13–202 to 13–205.

337. Chang Y-L, Mercer RR, Stockstill BL, et al: Effects of low levels of NO_2 on terminal bronchiolar cells and its relative toxicity compared to O_3. Toxicol Appl Pharmacol 96:451–464, 1988.

338. Schlesinger RB: Intermittent inhalation of nitrogen dioxide: Effects on rabbit alveolar macrophages. J Toxicol Environ Health 21:127–139, 1987.

339. Ehrlich R, Findlay JC, Fenters JD, et al: Health effects of short-term inhalation of nitrogen dioxide and ozone mixtures. Environ Res 10:217–233, 1977.

340. Ehrlich R, Henry MC: Chronic toxicity of nitrogen dioxide: I. Effect on resistance to bacterial pneumonia. Arch Environ Health 17:860–865, 1968.

341. Rose RM, Fuglestad JM, Skornik WA, et al: The pathophysiology of enhanced susceptibility to murine cytomegalovirus respiratory infection during short-term exposure to nitrogen dioxide. Am Rev Respir Dis 137:912–917, 1988.

64 Acute Pulmonary Responses to Toxic Exposures

Paul D. Blanc, M.D., M.S.P.H.

INTRODUCTION

This chapter focuses on the acute effects on the lung after exposure to toxic substances. As used in this chapter, "acute" subsumes short-term exposures (minutes to hours), with the initial onset of pulmonary responses within a similarly rapid time period. As a general rule, the relevant exposures are of high intensity, far in excess of recommended safety limits for the workplace or the environment. Moreover, this chapter does not address brief exposures inducing acute responses mediated by amnestic (e.g., allergic) mechanisms. These responses require prior exposures that already have led to sensitization, such as occupational asthma (Chapter 60) or hypersensitivity pneumonitis (Chapter 62). The lung is the target organ for toxicity in the acute pulmonary responses addressed in this chapter. *Target organ* does not equate with *route of exposure*. For many acute exposures the route of delivery for toxins may be by inhalation, yet the primary toxic insult is not to the lung (e.g., solvent inhalation that causes central nervous system depression). Inhalation exposures such as these are not addressed here. In contrast, paraquat and hydrocarbon aspiration, two examples of ingested toxins with severe acute target organ effects on the lung, are included in this chapter.

PATHOGENESIS OF IRRITANT LUNG INJURY

Acute lung toxicity results from a variety of exposures but is manifest by a fairly narrow repertoire of injury. Irritant gases and aerosols represent a group of heterogeneous agents that are capable of causing extensive cell injury throughout the respiratory tract. The primary location of lung injury and the onset of clinical symptoms are partly dependent on the solubility of the gas or aerosol involved. However, overwhelming exposures to any irritant inhalant can cause extensive damage throughout the respiratory tract. Ammonia[1] and sulfur dioxide[2] are examples of substances that are highly soluble in water. Such highly soluble substances cause immediate irritation of the conjunctival mucosa and upper airways. In contrast, oxides of nitrogen,[3] ozone,[4] and phosgene[5] have relatively low water solubility. For this reason, exposure to one of these agents may *not* be characterized by immediate mucous membrane symptoms. This may lead to more prolonged exposures and delays in seeking medical attention. Both more and less soluble irritant exposures can lead to distal lung injury, but in the case of highly soluble materials, a history of severe upper respiratory symptoms should precede the presentation of distal airway and alveolar damage. In addition to solubility and the amount of gas or aerosol inhaled, other physical properties that may be pertinent to the pathogenesis of acute irritant injury include pH, chemical reactivity, and, in the case of fumes or aerosols, particle or droplet physical characteristics. On the cellular level, respiratory tract injury may be mediated through the deposition or formation of an acid, alkali, or free radical. In most cases, the precise cellular mechanisms of injury from irritant inhalants have not been well delineated. This is true even for relatively common irritants such as chlorine, an agent for which a great deal of human and experimental animal data exist.[6]

Irritants reaching the lower respiratory tract, either because of their inherent physical characteristics or because of exposures that overwhelm the absorptive capacity of the upper airway, can injure both the lung epithelium and endothelium. Pathophysiologically, irritant injury at this level leads to a nonspecific pattern of diffuse alveolar damage similar to that seen from a variety of different causes (see Chapter 51). Thus, the outstanding research agenda needed to address the mechanisms of action for irritant inhalants parallels that of acute lung injury generally.[7] The pathologic changes in fatal cases of irritant lung injury include focal and confluent areas of edema with protein-rich fluid in the alveolar spaces, hyaline membrane formation, and denudation of the alveolar epithelium.[8,9] In addition, mucous membranes of the bronchial and bronchiolar walls may be destroyed or denuded. A component of pulmonary hemorrhage may occur in irritant lung injury but typically is not a major clinical manifestation. Its presence should raise suspicion of other syndromes.[10]

OTHER PATHOGENIC PROCESSES

Acute irritant injury is the predominant, but not the only, pathophysiologic mechanism underlying acute toxic lung syndromes. Some of the diverse agents causing these syndromes are detailed subsequently in this chapter. After exposure to other toxins, unlike with irritant chemical–related injury, it is difficult to delineate a descending, hierarchical pattern from upper airway to lower lung injury. Nonetheless, many of these exposures lead to adult respiratory distress syndrome in their most severe manifestations. These exposures produce syndromes including heavy metal pneumonitis,[11] hydrocarbon aspiration,[12] and paraquat lung injury.[13] The inhalation fever syndromes mark the principal exception to this general phenomenon.[14] The pathophysiology of these self-limited acute lung syndromes appears to be cytokine mediated, without obvious lung injury.

ACUTE MANAGEMENT

Diffuse alveolar damage after severe acute toxic lung injury is nonspecific. Therefore, the treatment of acute toxin-related lung injury should be consistent with the basic management of acute lung injury with diffuse alveolar damage (acute respiratory distress syndrome) due to other causes (see Chapters 51 and 85). A beneficial role for corticosteroids in the acute phase of irritant and other chemical toxin injury to the lungs has not been established by controlled trials. Experimental animal models of smoke inhalation injury, which can be generalized to other irritants, have not supported the use of corticosteroids.[15–17] However, concomitant airway injury with acute bronchospasm often warrants the empirical use of corticosteroids (along with bronchodilators) on the basis of airway obstruction. Animal exposure data for steroid treatment following chlorine inhalation support a beneficial effect measured by airway resistance and nonspecific responsiveness to methacholine, while being equivocal in terms of lung injury.[18,19] In smoke inhalation models, other therapies such as N-acetylcysteine and heparin have also demonstrated poor or equivocal outcomes.[17,20,21] Prophylactic antibiotic drugs have not proven to be efficacious in toxic lung injury; antibiotics should be reserved for those patients with clinical evidence of infection. In the management of acute respiratory distress syndrome, oxygen toxicity is a particular issue after paraquat exposure, because of its specific mechanism of action.[13] In the case of certain metal toxins, chelation may have a therapeutic role, as is addressed later in relation to the specific exposures involved. Inhalation fever is self-limited, so the principal clinical management issue is to exclude other exposures with less benign outcomes.[14,22]

CHRONIC PATHOLOGIC SEQUELAE AND RESIDUAL EFFECTS

Among persons surviving symptomatic exposure to acute irritants, persistent structural and functional effects may occur. Long-term follow-up evaluation after recovery from acute respiratory distress syndrome due to heterogeneous causes (predominantly associated with sepsis) suggests that residual deficits in lung volumes, airflow, and gas exchange may persist long after recovery.[23] Follow-up studies of more homogeneous populations evaluated after inhalation injury (with only a minority experiencing severe injury) suggest that airflow obstruction and nonspecific airway hyperresponsiveness are the most common persistent abnormalities after irritant injury. Even so, epidemiologic data suggest that these outcomes only occur in a minority of those exposed.[24–26]

The term *reactive airway dysfunction syndrome* has been applied to the persistence of airway reactivity after acute exposure to respiratory irritants.[27–29] The more general term *irritant-induced asthma* has also been used to describe this condition.[30,31] Insofar as this syndrome represents a form of work-related asthma, it is addressed in Chapter 60. Other outcomes of inhalation injury are uncommon. Bronchiolitis obliterans (BO),[32–39] bronchiectasis,[1,38,40–43] and bronchiolitis obliterans with organizing pneumonia[44] (BOOP) may occur, but are rare. Irritants have long been known to cause BO.[45] Nitrogen dioxide is the single agent (excluding fire smoke by-products) best documented to do so. Yet even with nitrogen dioxide, BO is an infrequent event; for example, only one case was found in a series of 20 moderate to severe exposures.[33] Pathologically, irritant-induced BO usually is characterized by intrabronchial granulation tissue (to which the term *proliferative bronchiolitis obliterans* is applied), as opposed to constrictive (obliterative) BO.[8,9] There are nosologic distinctions between proliferative BO and BOOP; importantly, both tend to be steroid responsive.[46]

In addition to residual obstructive ventilatory deficits, restrictive deficits may also occur following severe irritant inhalation injury.[40,47] There is also some indication that an isolated reduction in residual volume may be noted in the follow-up of such cases.[48,49] In addition to syndromes such as BO and BOOP, respiratory complaints after irritant inhalation can be a manifestation of a psychological disorder, rather than representing a primary pulmonary process.[50,51]

SPECIFIC EXPOSURES

CHLORINE, CHLORAMINES, HYDROCHLORIC ACID, AND RELATED CHEMICALS

Among the toxic agents causing pulmonary responses (Table 64.1), chlorine is one of the most common and potent irritant inhalants known.[6,52,53] Common forms of exposure include industrial leaks,[54] environmental releases occurring primarily in transport,[55] water purification,[56] swimming pool–related events,[57] and household-cleaning product misadventures.[58] In the form of a yellow-green acrid gas, industrial and environmental releases typically present clear-cut exposure histories. Because the gas is

Table 64.1 Selected Toxic Agents Causing Pulmonary Responses

Agent	Common Exposure Scenarios	References
Acid aerosols	Plating; microelectronics; other manufacturing	77, 88–91
Acrolein	Structural or wildland fires; other combustion	76, 186, 190
Ammonia	Industrial refrigeration leaks; fertilizers	1, 212–214
Brevetoxin	Aerosolization of "red tide" toxin	203, 204
Bromine	Water treatment; chemical manufacturing	39, 217, 219
Cadmium fume	Flame cutting of soldered or sheet metal materials	115–117
Chloramines and nitrogen trichloride	Bleach + ammonia mix; chlorination + ammonia	61, 62
Chlorine gas	Gas leak; water treatment; bleach + acid mix	4, 6, 53, 54
Chlorine dioxide	Pulp paper bleaching	63, 82
Crowd control agents	Military and police training and operations	108–110
Dimethyl sulfate	Industrial chemical yielding sulfuric acid	87
Fluorocarbons	Overheating polymers, spray applications	93, 134, 135
Hydrocarbons	Aspiration of low-viscosity materials	12, 170
Hydrogen sulfide	Sewers and manure pits; fossil fuel extraction	223, 226
Mercury vapor	Gold amalgam volatilization	118, 119, 121
Methyl bromide	Pesticide fumigant	220, 221
Methyl isocyanate	Pesticide manufacturing	227, 229
Methyl isothiocyanate	Breakdown product of metam sodium fumigant	230
Mustard gas	Chemical warfare agent	40, 96
Nickel carbonyl	Nickel processing	123, 124
Nitrogen dioxide	Silage; combustion; welding; nitric acid mixes	3, 33
Organic dusts/aerosols	Contaminated dust or bioaerosol generation	152, 153
Organophosphates	Pesticide application; chemical warfare	102, 103
Ozone	Bleaching; water treatment; plasma welding	78, 82
Paraquat	Herbicide skin contamination or ingestion	176, 183
Phosgene	Chlorinated solvent breakdown by-product	5, 99
Phosphine	Fumigation with aluminum or zinc phosphide	232, 233
Sulfur dioxide	Refrigeration; cement manufacture; mining	2, 83–85
Tributyltin (bis[tributyltin] oxide)	Paint additive for mold inhibition	133
Vanadium	Ore processing; fossil fuel by-product, catalyst use	129, 130
Zinc chloride	Smoke bombs	112–114
Zinc oxide fume	Welding galvanized steel; brass casting	137, 159, 168

heavier than air, higher contamination can be expected in low-lying areas (hence its use in trench warfare in World War I).[59] However, other environmental conditions may supervene. Examples include one well-documented case of the gas rising along the heated outside wall of a factory where rooftop workers were exposed.[54] In another case, chlorine initially collected in a basement, but then it was sucked up into the central heating system of a dormitory.[60]

The history of exposure to chlorine may be less straightforward when inhalation occurs after de novo generation of gas from chlorine-containing liquids or powders. The most common *liquid* formulation associated with chlorine gas release is hypochlorite bleach, whereas the active chlorine component of dry *powdered* bleaching cleansers is typically a chlorinated phosphate. In either liquid or powdered bleaches, the liberation of chlorine gas is pH dependent, occurring on contact with acids in common household products containing muriatic (hydrochloric), phosphoric, or hydrofluoric acid.[58] In contrast, mixing chlorine-containing products with ammonia leads to release of chloramines (monochloramine [NH_2Cl] and dichloramine [$NHCl_2$]) and related chemicals, especially nitrogen trichloride (NCl_3), chemicals whose irritant effects are attributed to in situ pulmonary reactions releasing chlorine, hypochlorous acid, and ammonia.[58,61,62] In chlorinated swimming pools, inadvertent mixing with nitrogen donors also occurs, with potential irritant effects attributed to nitrogen trichloride in particular.[62]

Irritant effects after inhalation of hypochlorite aerosols in confined spaces without a history of combining products (not an uncommon scenario when cleaning bathrooms) also can be associated with irritant effects. Similarly, in certain industrial operations, hydrochloric (hydrogen chloride in water) or hypochlorous acid aerosols are also respiratory irritants. Other sources of chlorine exposure occur in specific industrial processes that use a large number of inorganic chlorine derivatives. Worthy of particular mention are chlorine dioxide (used in pulp paper processing),[63] chlorinated silanes (gases used in microelectronics),[64] reactive metal halides (e.g., titanium or antimony chlorides),[11] and thionyl chloride (which breaks down to yield hydrogen chloride and sulfur dioxide).[35,65]

For chlorine and related chemicals, the acute respiratory response corresponds to the effective dose delivered to the lungs. All of these compounds appear to share final common toxic pathways. As noted in the general discussion of acute toxic inhalations, water solubility is an important determinant of the dose reaching the lower airways. For chlorine, chlorine dioxide, chloramines, and nitrogen trichloride, lower solubility favors deeper penetration with a more effective delivered dose compared with an equivalent inhalation of acid aerosols. However, exposure to any of these compounds is associated with some degree of immediate mucous membrane and upper airway irritation. In fact, the absence of acute irritant effects is not clinically consistent with chlorine gas or related exposures.

Chlorine inhalation may manifest any of the full spectrum of respiratory tract irritant effects, from minor mucosal responses to upper airway responses to diffuse alveolar damage.[54–59,66] Persistent airway hyperresponsiveness after irritant exposure has been associated particularly with chlorine gas and chlorine-containing products, although this may reflect the frequency of such exposures, rather than a propensity for chlorine to have this effect.[6,30,31] There is also limited evidence that persons with underlying airway hyperreactivity may be more responsive to chlorine.[67] Use of inhaled bronchodilators and steroids may be indicated for both acute and residual bronchospasm following chlorine inhalation. Although several case reports and series have touted the potential benefits of nebulized sodium bicarbonate inhalation in the acute treatment of chlorine inhalation, the efficacy of this intervention has never been assessed in a controlled trial.[62,68–71]

OXIDES OF NITROGEN, OZONE, SULFUR DIOXIDE, AND ACID AEROSOLS

These inhalants are major air pollutants; the effects of low-level exposure are discussed in detail in Chapter 63. When they are inhaled in high concentrations, these irritants also cause acute lung injury. Because of lower solubility, longer exposure with a greater predilection for lung injury may occur with ozone[4] and, even more commonly, nitrogen dioxide.[72] Nonetheless, with sulfur dioxide and acid aerosols, sufficient intensity of exposure leads to diffuse alveolar damage.

High-intensity exposure to oxides of nitrogen occurs through decomposition of organic matter. Examples include nitrogen dioxide–induced lung injury among farmers (also known as silo filler's disease),[33,73] use of internal combustion engines in enclosed spaces (with large outbreaks associated with ice resurfacing equipment used in indoor skating rinks),[3,74,75] thermal degradation of polymers (e.g., in structural fires),[76] explosives or industrial mishaps,[32,77] and welding by-products, particularly when "gas-shielded" techniques are employed (manual inert gas welding or tungsten inert welding).[78] Historically, the detonation of explosives has been one of the most important sources of exposure to nitrogen oxides.[79] Nitric oxide, an inhalant used therapeutically, breaks down to nitrogen dioxide in the presence of oxygen, and thus must be monitored with appropriate delivery devices.[80,81] High-intensity occupational ozone exposure is unusual, but it can occur with welding conditions similar to those associated with oxides of nitrogen.[78] More recently, ozone in water treatment and in pulp paper bleaching also has emerged as a health issue.[82]

Important sources of high-level sulfur dioxide exposure include mining and ore refining,[2] Portland cement manufacturing,[83] sulfur treatment of fruit,[84] and industrial releases.[85] Historically, sulfur dioxide has also been important in pulp paper processing[82] and as a refrigerant.[86] In ambient air pollution, the acid aerosols of primary concern are sulfuric and nitric acids, but they can also be encountered occupationally. Sulfuric acid exposure occurs both through direct use and through the breakdown of a highly toxic industrial chemical, dimethyl sulfate.[87] Nitric acid also has many industrial uses.[77] When nitric acid reacts with organic materials such as wood, substantial amounts of nitrogen dioxide can be rapidly released. A number of other inorganic and organic acid vapors and aerosols are also important potential causes of acute lung injury, including chromic,[88] acetic,[89] formic,[90] and hydrofluoric[91] acids.

Hydrofluoric acid (hydrogen fluoride), in addition to nonspecific irritant effects, can induce clinically significant hypocalcemia.[92] Exposures occur in manufacturing of both microelectronics and phosphate fertilizers, in household use of hydrofluoric acid rust removal agents (the mixture of which with hypochlorite bleach can evolve both chlorine and hydrogen fluoride), and in pyrolysis of fluorinated polymers.[93] Hydrogen fluoride is a chronic exposure problem in the aluminum smelting industry. Hydrogen fluoride is also released as a breakdown product of sulfur hexafluoride, an electrical insulating liquid chemical used in equipment.[94]

MILITARY AND CROWD CONTROL AGENTS

Unfortunately, these exposures are not of mere historical interest.[59,95,95a] Of the major World War I chemical weapons, only sulfur mustard (mustard gas) has been used "militarily" since World War II. Classified as a vesicant because of blistering induced by skin contact, mustard gas inhalation causes severe respiratory injury. Survivors exhibit residual tracheobronchitis and bronchiectasis.[40,96,97] Phosgene, another World War I toxic gas, is currently encountered as a thermal breakdown product or ultraviolet photoreactant of chlorinated solvents (e.g., methylene chloride).[5,98] A common cause of exposure is inadvertent phosgene production from welding metals "degreased" with solvents.[78] Phosgene is the prototypic deeply penetrating inhalant exhibiting a delayed onset of symptoms (12 to 24 hours after exposure).[99] Chloropicrin, another World War I gas, is a low-threshold irritant currently encountered in chemical manufacturing and as a component of fumigants.[100,101,101a] The modern chemical warfare armamentarium is dominated by systemic toxins developed from organophosphate pesticides.[102,103] These highly lethal neurotoxins have important respiratory effects, including manifestations of both muscarinic receptor stimulation (bronchorrhea and bronchospasm) and nicotinic receptor depolarization blockade (respiratory muscle paralysis).

Crowd control agents ("tear gases"), as opposed to the war gases, are intended to incapacitate persons via immediate mucous membrane irritation.[104] The agents in greatest use worldwide are chloroacetophenone ("mace"), and orthochlorobenzamalonitrile.[105,106] In addition to their mucous membrane effects, case reports have implicated these agents in lower respiratory injury and even persistent effects following high-intensity exposures (e.g., in enclosed buildings).[107-110] Unlike tear gas, the primary component of "smoke bombs," zinc chloride, is a potent lower respiratory tract irritant.[111] Military, police, and other exposures (including training exercises) have resulted in severe pulmonary edema.[112-114]

CADMIUM, MERCURY, AND OTHER TOXIC METALS

Inhalation of certain metal fumes or vapors causes acute pneumonitis.[11] The two metals most important clinically are cadmium and mercury. In both instances, the most important factor in pulmonary insult is acute inhalation at a heavy level of exposure. With cadmium, exposure typically occurs through welding, brazing (high-temperature soldering), or flame cutting metal under conditions of poor ventilation.[115-117] The usual source of cadmium is the welding rod, brazing solder, or a metal coating, rather than the base metal itself.[78] For mercury, high levels of the relatively volatile metal can be generated effectively from many nonenclosed operations, most notably through heated metal reclamation processes (e.g., home refining of mercury-gold amalgams).[118-120] Exposure has also occurred through burning mercury sulfide (Chinese red cinnabar) and mercuric oxide for medicinal purposes.[121,122] Other metals, including antimony, manganese, and beryllium, are sometimes cited as causes of acute metal pneumonitis, but there are few reports in the last 50 years providing documentation of such disorders.[11] Nickel carbonyl is an organic metal derivative and potent pulmonary toxin, with exposure primarily limited to nickel refining.[123,124] Inorganic nickel, although a sensitizing substance, is not associated with pneumonitis.

Dangerous exposures to cadmium, mercury, and nickel carbonyl occur in part because these agents are not immediately irritating, analogous to the delayed symptoms after phosgene gas inhalation. Patients typically present in respiratory distress 12 to 24 hours after exposure.[115-122] The exposure history often remains occult unless aggressively pursued. Metal pneumonitis from these materials also can include fever as a clinical manifestation of the toxic syndrome. However, the term *metal fume fever* should not be used in this context.[125]

The toxic mechanism in heavy metal pneumonitis is presumed to be inhibition of enzymatic and other critical cellular functions. Chelation treatment has not been shown to be effective in heavy metal pneumonitis due to cadmium or mercury, although chelation is often initiated in the case of mercury injury.[121,122] The agent dithiocarb (diethyldithiocarbamate) has been used as a chelating antidote for nickel carbonyl pneumonitis, based on supportive animal data.[126,127] Disulfiram has been suggested as a potential alternative treatment, although experimental data to support this practice are weak.[127,128]

Two other metal compounds are well-documented bronchial irritants in humans. Vanadium, which is encountered in metal processing and, in lower concentrations, as a fossil fuel by-product, causes acute bronchitis.[129] Among boilermakers, vanadium-rich fuel oil ash is suspected to be a key exposure related to acute respiratory symptoms.[130] In a single case report, high-intensity exposure to ash from an oil-burning furnace was associated with diffuse alveolar damage; although vanadium was detectable in the residue, the toxic mechanism in this case was unclear.[131] In another case report, vanadium was linked to pneumonitis.[132] Tributyltin (bis[tributyltin] oxide), an organotin compound employed as a mildew and mold retardant in paint, is also an airway irritant.[133]

METAL FUME FEVER, POLYMER FUME FEVER, AND ORGANIC DUST TOXIC SYNDROME

There are a number of febrile flulike pulmonary syndromes reflecting similar clinical responses to a diverse group of acute inhalational exposures.[14,134] Their hallmark is chills, fever, malaise, and myalgia with onset 4 to 8 hours after intense inhalation of fumes or dust.[14,22,125,135] Common respiratory complaints include cough or mild dyspnea, but findings of chest radiographic infiltrates or hypoxemia are inconsistent with this disorder. Peripheral leukocytosis usually accompanies the syndrome; bronchoalveolar lavage shows a marked influx of neutrophils.[136-138] These syndromes all are self-limited, resolving clinically within 12 to 48 hours. Signs or symptoms of pneumonitis should suggest alternative, less benign diagnoses, such as cadmium pneumonitis,[116,117] hypersensitivity pneumonitis (Chapter 62), or inhalation of more toxic temperature-dependent fluoropolymer pyrolysis by-products (which include hydrogen fluoride and carbonyl fluoride).[93,139,140] Toxic pneumonitis, which should be distinguished from fume fever, has been associated with exposure to fluoropolymer-containing protective sprays for leather products that did not involve thermal breakdown by-products.[141-143]

Metal fume fever and organic dust toxic syndrome share a common feature of tachyphylaxis, with a blunted response to daily repeated inhalation (and hence the name "Monday morning fever") among both brass founders and cotton mill workers.[14,144,145] Metal fume fever is associated with zinc oxide inhalation from welding galvanized metal or brass working.[146] There is only limited clinical evidence that other metals (magnesium and copper) cause a similar response,[125,147] and experimental data further discount magnesium as a potential cause of fume fever.[148] Organic dust toxic syndrome is associated with inhalation of materials contaminated with thermophilic bacteria and fungal spores, including wood chips,[149] straw,[150] silage,[151] and textile raw materials.[145] The increasing industrialization of agricultural processes, especially the use of animal confinement techniques, is an additional source of exposure leading to organic dust toxic syndrome, although these same settings can produce irritant gases such as hydrogen sulfide and ammonia.[152,153] The syndrome includes variously named conditions including pulmonary mycotoxicosis,[154] silo unloader's syndrome,[151] and mill fever.[155] One of the best documented historical outbreaks of organic dust toxic syndrome occurred among individuals who work with stained (contaminated) cotton mattresses.[145] Inhalation of aerosols from contaminated water sources produces a similar febrile syndrome, some of which is attributable to *Legionella* species (Pontiac fever) as well as to other organisms.[14] Polymer fume fever is associated with thermal breakdown products of fluoropolymers (e.g., Teflon and related materials).[135,156-158] The pathophysiologic mechanisms underlying all these syndromes have not been established, but research suggests that pulmonary cytokines may play a key role.[159-168]

HYDROCARBON PNEUMONITIS AND BABY POWDER ASPIRATION

Hydrocarbon pneumonitis occurs with oral ingestion of hydrocarbons. This is a prominent issue in the pediatric age group, accounting for many hospital admissions each year. The common hydrocarbons involved are mineral spirits, mineral seal oil (common in furniture polish), lamp oil, kerosene (paraffin), turpentine (pine oil), gasoline, and lighter fluid.[12,169-172] Even though these substances have systemic toxic effects such as central nervous system depression, life-threatening complications of ingestion are predominantly the result of concomitant hydrocarbon aspiration and subsequent pulmonary compromise, making the lung the target organ of concern in hydrocarbon ingestion. In contradistinction to aspiration hydrocarbon pneumonitis, the toxicity of hydrocarbon (solvent) inhalation manifests primarily in either central nervous system or cardiac effects. Major pulmonary target organ damage associated with acute hydrocarbon exposure by inhalation is unusual but has been reported.[173]

Hydrocarbon aspiration can occur at the time of initial ingestion or subsequently with vomiting. Low viscosity of an ingested hydrocarbon is considered a major factor promoting aspiration (presumably for mechanical reasons), for example, with mineral seal oil.[12,170] Although theoretical consideration has been given to potential effects on surfactant as being mediators of hydrocarbon aspiration toxicity, the chemical pneumonitis of the syndrome appears to be nonspecific.

Another acute inhalational pediatric syndrome is caused by baby (talcum) powder aspiration.[174,175] Within hours, the inhaled powder can cause a severe and potentially fatal pneumonitis. The pathophysiology of baby powder pneumonitis may not be specific to talc per se and is distinct from talcosis, a chronic granulomatous lung disease. There is no proposed specific mechanism of the acute syndrome. Pediatricians emphasize prevention through discontinuing the use of such powders in infants, but exposures still occur.

PARAQUAT

Paraquat is a widely used herbicide and a potent toxin. Ingestion rather than inhalation is the typical route of exposure associated with human toxicity. Contamination through skin absorption can also occur. The theoretical risk of smoking contaminated materials has never been established clinically. Most paraquat deaths result from suicidal intent.[13,176,177] Paraquat ingestion is a relatively uncommon method of suicide in the United States, but its incidence is greater in a number of other countries, perhaps related to patterns of crop utilization and ease of access.[176,178] Although paraquat ingestion leads to acute gastrointestinal tract necrosis and multiorgan failure, the lung is the target organ for toxicity among those surviving the immediate postingestion period. Diquat, a related dipyridyl herbicide, does not cause the syndrome of lung toxicity associated with paraquat.[179]

The pulmonary toxicity of paraquat, in contrast to its gastrointestinal effects, does not reflect caustic irritant injury. Rather, paraquat is notable in its ability to induce an accelerated, chemically induced pulmonary fibrosis. After stabilization following acute multiorgan paraquat toxic effects, disease progression is marked by rapidly worsening respiratory distress, hypoxemia, and a restrictive ventilatory defect, with decreased lung compliance and diffusing capacity, ending in death from ventilatory failure within days to weeks.[13,176] Survivors may demonstrate modest and slow improvement in lung function.[180] Diagnosis of paraquat exposure is usually clear on the basis of the patient's history, but confirmatory blood or urine levels are available through the manufacturer of the chemical.

The mechanism of paraquat toxicity is attributed to the generation of superoxide radicals that may be partly iron dependent.[181] Consistent with an oxidant mechanism, supplemental oxygen and radiation therapy may worsen the outcome.[14,176,182] There are no known antidotes for paraquat poisoning, and enhanced elimination (hemoperfusion) has not demonstrated a clear benefit.[13,176] Data from a single prospective clinical trial suggest that brief high-dose methylprednisolone (Solu-Medrol) therapy combined with cyclophosphamide may be associated with increased survival following moderate to severe paraquat ingestion.[183]

SMOKE INHALATION

The generic term *smoke inhalation* includes potential exposure to a wide array of substances because of the complex chemistry of heat decomposition and pyrolysis. Although cytotoxic anoxia from carbon monoxide, cyanide, and oxidants represents a major manifestation of toxic insult from acute smoke inhalation, this *nonpulmonary target organ* effect is not covered here.[76,184-186] However, there are a number of chemical irritants produced as pyrolysis by-products that do have significant potential target organ pulmonary toxicity. In contrast to thermal injury to the respiratory tract, which is typically limited to upper airways, with laryngeal edema the major potential medical management problem,[187,188] smoke inhalation from fires can affect the entire respiratory tract through irritant injury.

In certain cases, irritant chemicals from fires result from liberation of preformed substances, but, most commonly, the toxins of concern are formed de novo. These irritants are produced by the thermal degradation of both naturally occurring and synthetic polymers. The predominant by-products of heat breakdown are determined by the nature of the polymers consumed, but the precise mixture of agents released in any specific event may be difficult to predict, varying in particular according to temperature and oxygen availability.[76,189]

As a general rule, the chemical monomer precursor is not a significant polymer breakdown product, although residual monomers can be evolved under certain circumstances. For example, hydrogen chloride rather than vinyl chloride is released when polyvinyl chloride is burned.[76] Many of the specific chemical irritants that can be released as common thermal breakdown by-products are addressed elsewhere in this chapter. These include the following: hydrochloric acid (hydrogen chloride), hydrofluoric acid (hydrogen fluoride), and other acids; ammonia; phosgene; and oxides of nitrogen. The zinc chloride "smoke" of smoke bombs (in contrast to the heterogeneous character of "natural smoke") is also discussed separately.

Aldehydes merit specific attention, however, because smoke from fires may represent the most common source of high-intensity irritant inhalant injury caused by this group of chemicals. These chemicals include formaldehyde, acetaldehyde, and acrolein. Of these aldehydes, acrolein (CH_2=CHCHO), although the most severe irritant, is least familiar to most health-care providers. Acrolein, a highly reactive chemical, is formed as an important pyrolysis product of both synthetic (e.g., acrylic) and natural polymers.[190]

The general considerations concerning irritant exposure discussed previously, including air concentration and water solubility, come into play in smoke inhalation. These factors are further complicated by the potential interactive effects of multiple simultaneous exposures, as well as the modifying impact of physical cofactors such as airborne respirable particulates (e.g., soot) that may serve as adsorbent carriers facilitating deep lung penetration. In practice, detailed exposure data delineating the irritant contents of a specific smoke exposure are rarely available. Information that may help to elucidate exposure conditions include identity of the products involved (e.g., specific synthetic polymers, if known), history of inhalation within an enclosed or confined space, evidence of thermal injury, and carboxyhemoglobin and methemoglobin levels as markers of inhalation severity based on other concomitant exposures (carbon monoxide and oxidants).[184-186]

Firefighters (both urban and wildland) and non–occupationally exposed victims of irritant smoke inhalation have proved important groups in which to study acute inhalational syndromes. Large-scale conflagrations (e.g., urban "wildland" fires) can expose substantial numbers of people to irritant combustion by-products, as can smoke drift from intentional burning of agricultural residue. Studies of such populations have demonstrated acute and persistent airflow obstruction and increased nonspecific airway hyperresponsiveness after smoke inhalation.[191-198] Bronchiectasis and BO have both been associated with combustion by-product exposure.[35,38] The acute respiratory effects of exposure to the plume generated by the destruction of the World Trade Center appear to relate to alkaline (high-pH) dust from concrete, gypsum, and glass fibers, rather than to smoke particulate.[199,200]

PHARMACOLOGIC SYNDROMES

Certain natural and synthetic chemical exposures exert acute target organ lung effects mediated by specific mechanisms consistent with known pharmacologic actions. These chemicals are site specific for key cellular functions leading to adverse respiratory effects. As noted previously, the most potent chemical warfare agents act through acetylcholinesterase inhibition, with profound impacts on respiratory function.[102,103] Similar, albeit less potent, agents have widespread use as agricultural chemicals. Both organophosphate and carbamate pesticides lead to respiratory compromise as a principal toxic effect. For example, in one case series, a considerable number of poisonings from these pesticides led to respiratory failure, accompanied by a high case-fatality rate; in contrast, all the patients without concomitant respiratory failure survived.[201]

Inhaled capsaicin, of interest as a research tool to study substance P–mediated effects, is associated with cough in occupational settings (e.g., in chili pepper processing).[202] Another naturally occurring toxin with a primary respiratory effect is brevetoxin. This toxin, produced by dinoflagellates, is associated with "red tides." Environmental inhalation exposure from airborne aerosols of red tide (due to wind and surf action) causes cough, sneeze, and wheeze.[203-205] The toxin appears to act by stimulating sodium channels in the lung. Respiratory irritation is also a manifestation of Pfiesteria dinoflagellate toxin inhalation[206,207] and also has been reported in association with another marine organism, Lyngbya majuscula.[208]

OTHER INHALANT EXPOSURES

Ammonia

Anhydrous ammonia is a gas at room temperature and ambient pressure, although ammonia more commonly is encountered in aqueous form (e.g., in cleaning solutions). In addition to incidents in the chemical industry and in hazardous transportation, commercial refrigeration systems and farming represent important sources of potential exposure to ammonia gas.[1,209-214] Anhydrous ammonia release has also occurred from illicit methamphetamine laboratory operations.[215] Ammonia has prominent irritant warning properties (such as burning eyes). It is linked with lung injury chiefly in settings of overwhelming exposure or where immediate escape has been possible. Bronchiectasis has been documented after ammonia exposure.[1] Acute ammonia exposure has also been reported to have residual upper airway effects, including decreased olfactory acuity.[216]

Bromine and Methyl Bromide

Bromine is an irritant halogen. It usually is handled as a liquid rather than as a gas, but it vaporizes readily. Sources of bromine exposure other than environmental releases include chemical synthesis and water purification.[39,217–219] Methyl bromide is a major industrial fumigant with far greater potential for public exposure. Methyl bromide is also a potent respiratory irritant, but central nervous system effects may account for more important target organ toxicity in typical exposures.[220,221]

Ethylene Oxide

Ethylene oxide is a common sterilizing agent used in medical centers.[222] The gas has poor odor-threshold warning properties. Health concerns over nonpulmonary chronic low-level exposure effects have spurred strict exposure controls and detection alarm systems. Nonetheless, ethylene oxide's widespread use provides ample opportunity for nonintentional release. At exposures near its odor threshold, pulmonary injury may occur.[222]

Hydrogen Sulfide

Hydrogen sulfide is a common by-product of petroleum extraction and refining as well as a potential hazard from the breakdown of organic materials (hence its common name, "sewer gas").[223] Hydrogen sulfide is a respiratory irritant, but it is an even more potent cytotoxic asphyxiant, impairing cytochrome oxidase and cellular respiration. Therefore, in cases of severe hydrogen sulfide exposure, rapid cardiovascular collapse and death overshadow any pulmonary organ effects, with irritant symptoms of importance only in lower intensity exposures.[223–226]

Methyl Isocyanate and Methyl Isothiocyanate

Methyl isocyanate (MIC) use is restricted to a narrow industrial application in the synthesis of pesticides. The mass fatalities at Bhopal, India, make MIC an important toxin for historical reasons. The toxicity of MIC was the result of its severe irritant properties leading to pulmonary edema.[227–229] No cyanide-mediated mechanism was involved. Methyl isothiocyanate, a breakdown product of the soil fumigant metam sodium, is an irritant chemically related to MIC that was also involved in a mass exposure episode, although less severe than the MIC release at Bhopal.[230] Methyl isothiocyanate also has been detected as a low-level contaminant in cigarettes, but its link to potential symptoms is unclear.[231] Urethane exposures do not involve MIC; the isocyanates associated with urethane, such as toluene diisocyanate (TDI), diphenylmethane diisocyanate (MDI), and hexamethylene diisocyanate (HDI), are pulmonary irritants as well as sensitizers (see Chapter 60) but do not have toxicity similar to MIC.

Phosphine

Phosphine is another important commercial fumigant gas with pulmonary and systemic toxicity. Phosphine is generated on site from aluminum or zinc phosphide in agricultural fumigation applications, in particular grain storage facilities. Phosphine also has industrial applications, particularly in the production of microelectronics.[232,233]

Miscellaneous Exposures

A number of other occupational and environmental agents result in acute pulmonary syndromes. Examples of such exposures include *diethylaminoethanol* and *cyclohexylamine* (both anticorrosive boiler additives),[234,235] *amitrole* and *glyphosphate* (both common herbicides),[236,237] *sodium azide* (used in a variety of chemical applications but important as a potential inhalant through automobile airbag deployment),[238] *diborane* (an irritant gas used in manufacturing microelectronic equipment),[239,240] *barium* (inhalation can cause bronchospasm and respiratory muscle weakness, in addition to life-threatening hypokalemia),[241] and *hydrogen selenide* (an irritant gas used in several industrial processes as well as being a potential metal processing by-product).[242,243] *Acetic anhydride* (used in making epoxy and other resins) has also been associated with acute lung injury.[244] A distinctly different pattern of injury is associated with a related epoxy chemical, *trimellitic anhydride,* which causes severe pulmonary hemorrhage after subacute exposure.[10]

Another outbreak of unusual subacute toxicity occurring after weeks or months of exposure has been linked to *Acramin* textile dyes. Labeled the "Ardystil" syndrome, its principal pulmonary manifestation is rapidly progressive BOOP.[44,245–247] Two other recently documented syndromes, an interstitial process labeled "flock worker's lung" and a bronchiolitis-like syndrome linked to a popcorn flavoring, also appear to follow subacute or chronic inhalation exposures without an acute irritant phase.[248–251a]

In addition to these synthetic substances, naturally occurring exposures are also associated with acute and subacute lung responses, although these syndromes are poorly characterized. Epidemiologically, *Stachybotrys chartarum* (*atra*) mold growth indoors in water-damaged residential structures was initially linked to a cluster of cases of pulmonary hemorrhage in infants, although the association was later retracted in a follow-up review by the U.S. Centers for Disease Control and Prevention.[252,253] The potential link between *Stachybotrys* and other human diseases is even more questionable.[254] Other case reports have occasionally linked other molds or mold by-products with lung injury (as opposed to self-limited organic dust toxic syndrome, discussed previously).[255] Lycoperdonosis is a potentially severe, acute pulmonary syndrome following intentional inhalation of puffball mushroom (*Lycoperdon*) spores.[256] The pathophysiology of the syndrome is not understood, but its high attack rate with heavy exposure suggests a toxic rather than allergic or infective mechanism.

SUMMARY

Short-term inhalation exposures to toxic substances may have important effects on the lung as the target organ for damage. A number of substances cause acute respiratory tract toxicity, but the repertoire of pulmonary pathologic responses to such injury is limited. Although modified by the solubility and other physical properties of the toxic agent, injury in large part depends on the intensity and duration of exposure. Extensive injury can lead to acute pulmonary edema and diffuse alveolar damage. Specific exposures of importance include chlorine, oxides of nitrogen, sulfur dioxide, acid aerosols, toxic metal fumes, and pyrolysis by-products. Aside from acute irritant or toxic lung insult leading to airway injury and diffuse alveolar damage, other patterns of acute responses include the inhalation fevers (which are self-limited and appear to be cytokine mediated) and certain target-specific effects, such as those elicited by cholinesterase inhibition. In addition, exposure by ingestion of some substances (e.g., hydrocarbons and paraquat) can cause important acute pulmonary target organ toxicity.

REFERENCES

1. Leduc D, Gris G, Lheureux P, et al: Acute and long term respiratory damage following inhalation of ammonia. Thorax 47:755–757, 1992.
2. Rabonowitz S, Greyson ND, Weiser W, et al: Case report: Clinical and laboratory features of acute sulfur dioxide inhalation poisoning: Two year follow-up. Am Rev Respir Dis 139:556–558, 1989.
3. Karlson-Stiber C, Hojer J, Sjoholm A, et al: Nitrogen dioxide pneumonitis in ice hockey players. J Intern Med 239:451–456, 1996.
4. Menzel DB: Ozone: An overview of its toxicity in man and animals. J Toxicol Environ Health 13:183–204, 1984.
5. Snyder RW, Mishel HS, Christensen GC: Pulmonary toxicity following exposure to methylene chloride and its combustion product, phosgene. Chest 101:860–861, 1992.
6. Das R, Blanc PD: Chlorine gas exposure and the lung. Toxicol Ind Health 9:439–455, 1993.
7. Matthay MA, Zimmerman GA, Esmon C, et al: Future research directions in acute lung injury. Am J Respir Crit Care 167:1027–1035, 2003.
8. Katzenstein A-LA, Askin FB: Surgical Pathology of Non-neoplastic Lung Disease (2nd ed). Philadelphia: WB Saunders, 1990, pp 9–57.
9. Wright JL, Churg A: Diseases caused by gases and fumes. In Churg A, Green FHY (eds): Pathology of Occupational Lung Disease (2nd ed). Baltimore: Williams & Wilkins, 1998, pp 57–76.
10. Blanc PD, Golden JA: Unusual occupationally related disorders of the lung: Case reports and a literature review. Occup Med 7:403–422, 1992.
11. Nemery B: Metal toxicity and the respiratory tract. Eur Respir J 3:202–219, 1990.
12. Truemper E, Reyes De La Rocha S, Atkinson SD: Clinical characteristics, pathophysiology and management of hydrocarbon ingestion: Case report and review of the literature. Pediatr Emerg Care 3:187–193, 1987.
13. Pond SM: Manifestations and management of paraquat poisoning. Med J Aust 152:256–259, 1990.
14. Rose CS, Blanc PD: Inhalation fever. In Rom WN (ed): Environmental and Occupational Medicine (3rd ed). Boston: Little, Brown, 1998, pp 467–480.
15. Sheridan R: Specific therapies for inhalation injury. Crit Care Med 30:718–719, 2002.
16. Nieman GF, Clark WR, Hakim T: Methylprednisolone does not protect the lung from inhalation injury. Burns 17:384–390, 1991.
17. Critchley JAJH, Beeley JM, Clark RJ, et al: Evaluation of N-acetylcysteine and methylprednisolone as therapies for oxygen and acrolein-induced lung damage. Environ Health Perspect 85:89–94, 1990.
18. Demnati R, Fraser R, Martin JG, et al: Effects of dexamethasone on functional and pathological changes in rat bronchi caused by high acute exposure to chlorine. Toxicol Sci 45:242–246, 1998.
19. Gunnarsson M, Walther SM, Seidal T, Lennquist S: Effects of inhalation of corticosteroids immediately after experimental chlorine gas injury. J Trauma 48:101–107, 2000.
20. Tasaki O, Mozingo DW, Dubick MA, et al: Effects of heparin and lisofylline on pulmonary function after smoke inhalation injury in an ovine model. Crit Care Med 30:637–643, 2003.
21. Murakami K, Enkhbaatar P, Shimoda K, et al: High-dose heparin fails to improve acute lung injury following smoke inhalation in sheep. Clin Sci 104:349–356, 2003.
22. Von Essen S, Robbins RA, Thompson AB, et al: Organic dust toxic syndrome: An acute febrile reaction distinct from hypersensitivity pneumonitis. Clin Toxicol 28:389–420, 1990.
23. Suchyta MR, Elliot CG, Jensen RL, et al: Predicting the presence of pulmonary impairment in adult respiratory distress syndrome survivors. Respiration 60:103–106, 1993.
24. Blanc PD, Galbo M, Hiatt P, et al: Morbidity following acute irritant inhalation in a population-based study. JAMA 266:664–669, 1991.
25. Blanc PD, Galbo M, Hiatt P, et al: Symptoms, lung function and airway responsiveness following irritant inhalation. Chest 103:1699–1705, 1993.
26. Blanc PD: Chemical inhalation injury and its sequelae. West J Med 160:2–3, 1994.
27. Brooks SM, Weiss MA, Bernstein IL: Reactive airways dysfunction syndrome (RADS). Chest 88:376–384, 1985.
28. Alberts WM, Do Pico GA: Reactive airways dysfunction syndrome. Chest 109:1618–1626, 1996.
29. Blanc PD: RADS—a special entity? The role of irritant exposure in asthma. Proceedings of the first Jack Pepys Occupational Asthma Symposium. Am J Respir Crit Care Med 167:450–471, 2003.
30. Tarlo S, Broder I: Irritant-induced occupational asthma. Chest 96:297–300, 1989.
31. Boulet LP: Increases in airway responsiveness following acute exposure to respiratory irritants: Reactive airway dysfunction syndrome or occupational asthma? Chest 94:476–481, 1988.
32. Yockey CC, Eden BM, Byrd RB: The McConnell missile accident: Clinical spectrum of nitrogen dioxide exposure. JAMA 244:1221–1223, 1980.
33. Zwemer FL, Pratt DS, May JJ: Silo filler's disease in New York State. Am Rev Respir Dis 146:650–653, 1992.
34. Lenci G, Wacker G, Schulz V, et al: Bronchiolitis obliterans nach Stickstoffdiozyd (NO$_2$)–Inhalation: Klinisch-roentgenologisch-histologische beobachung [Bronchiolitis obliterans after inhalation of nitrogen dioxide (NO$_2$): Clinical, radiological, histological observations]. Pneumonologie 44:32–36, 1990.
35. Konichezsky S, Schatter A, Ezri T, et al: Thionyl-chloride-induced lung injury and bronchiolitis obliterans. Chest 104:971–973, 1993.
36. Janigan DT, Kiolp T, Michael R, et al: Bronchiolitis obliterans in a man who used his wood-burning stove to burn synthetic construction materials. CMAJ 156:1171–1173, 1997.
37. Segev JS, Mason UG, Worthen S, et al: Bronchiolitis obliterans: Report of three cases with detailed physiologic studies. Chest 83:169–174, 1983.

38. Tasaka S, Kanazawa M, Mori M, et al: Long-term course of bronchiectasis and bronchiolitis obliterans as late complication of smoke inhalation. Respiration 62:40–42, 1995.

39. Kraut A, Lilis R: Chemical pneumonitis due to exposure to bromine compounds. Chest 94:208–210, 1988.

40. Emad A, Rezaian GR: The diversity of the effects of sulfur mustard gas inhalation on respiratory system 10 years after a single, heavy exposure: Analysis of 197 cases. Chest 112:734–738, 1997.

41. Kass I, Zamel N, Dobry CA, et al: Bronchiectasis following ammonia burns of the respiratory tract. Chest 62:282–285, 1972.

42. Breton D, Jouvet P, de Blic J, et al: Toxicite des fumees d'incendie: A propos de deux observations pediatriques [Smoke inhalation injury: Two pediatric cases]. Arch Fr Pediatr 50:43–45, 1993.

43. Mahut B, Delacourt C, de Blic J, et al: Bronchiectasis in a child after acrolein inhalation. Chest 104:1286–1287, 1993.

44. Moya C, Anto JM, Newman Taylor AJ: Outbreak of organizing pneumonia in textile printing sprayers. Lancet 344:498–502, 1994.

45. Wagner JH: Bronchiolitis obliterans following the inhalation of acrid fumes. Am J Med Sci 154:511–522, 1917.

46. Myers JL, Colby TV: Pathologic manifestations of bronchiolitis, constrictive bronchiolitis, cryptogenic organizing pneumonia, and diffuse panbronchiolitis. Clin Chest Med 14:611–622, 1993.

47. Piirla PL, Nordman H, Korhonen OS, et al: A thirteen-year follow-up of respiratory effect of acute exposure to sulfur dioxide. Scand J Work Environ Health 22:191–196, 1996.

48. Owens MW: Clinical significance of an isolated reduction in residual volume. Am Rev Respir Dis 136:1377–1380, 1987.

49. Buick JB, Lowry RC, Magee TRA: Is a reduction in residual volume a sub-clinical manifestation of hydrogen sulfide intoxication? Am J Ind Med 37:296–299, 2000.

50. Bowler RM, Mergler D, Huel G, et al: Psychological, psychosocial, and psychophysiological sequelae in a community affected by a railroad chemical disaster. J Trauma Stress 7:601–624, 1994.

51. Shusterman D: Upper and lower airway sequelae of irritant inhalations. Clin Pulm Med 6:18–31, 1999.

52. Blanc PD, Galbo MS, Balmes JR, et al: Occupational factors in work-related inhalations: Inferences for prevention strategy. Am J Ind Med 25:783–791, 1994.

53. Winder C: The toxicology of chlorine. Environ Res A 85:105–114, 2001.

54. Schwartz DA, Smith DD, Lakshminarayan S: The pulmonary sequelae associated with accidental inhalation of chlorine gas. Chest 97:820–825, 1990.

55. Jones RN, Hughes JM, Glindmeyer H, et al: Lung function after acute chlorine exposure. Am Rev Respir Dis 134:1190–1195, 1986.

56. Fleta J, Calvo C, Zuniga J, et al: Intoxication of 76 children by chlorine gas. Hum Toxicol 5:99–100, 1986.

57. Wood BR, Colombo JL, Benson BE: Chlorine inhalation toxicity from vapors generated by swimming pool chlorinator tablets. Pediatrics 79:427–430, 1987.

58. Centers for Disease Control: Chlorine gas toxicity from mixture of bleach with other cleaning products—California. MMWR Morb Mortal Wkly Rep 40:619–621, 627–629, 1991.

59. Eckert WG: Mass deaths by gas or chemical poisoning. Am J Forensic Med Pathol 12:119–125, 1991.

60. Hasan FM, Geshan A, Fuleihan FJD: Resolution of pulmonary dysfunction following acute chlorine exposure. Arch Environ Health 38:76–80, 1983.

61. Bernard A, Carbonelle S, Michel O, et al: Lung hyperpermeability and asthma prevalence in school children: Unexpected associations with the attendance at indoor chlorinated swimming pools. Occup Environ Med 60:385–394, 2003.

62. Pascuzzi TA: Mass casualties from acute inhalation of chloramine gas. Mil Med 163:102–104, 1998.

63. Salisbury DA, Enarson DA, Chan-Yeung M, et al: First-aid reports of acute chlorine gassing among pulpmill workers as predictors of lung health consequences. Am J Ind Med 20:71–81, 1991.

64. Promisloff RA, Phan A, Lenchner GS, et al: Reactive airway dysfunction syndrome in three police officers following a roadside chemical spill. Chest 98:928–929, 1990.

65. Dunkel R, Wermke R, Felgenhauer N, et al: Short term thionylchloride exposure causing delayed airway obstruction (abstract). J Toxicol Clin Toxicol 37:417, 1999.

66. Shusterman D, Balmes J, Avila PC, et al: Chlorine inhalation produces nasal congestion in allergic rhinitics without mast cell degranulation. Eur Respir J 21:652–657, 2003.

67. D'Alessandro A, Kuschner W, Wong H, et al: Exaggerated responses to chlorine inhalation among persons with non-specific airway hyperreactivity. Chest 109:331–337, 1996.

68. Vinsel PJ: Treatment of acute chlorine gas inhalation with nebulized sodium bicarbonate. J Emerg Med 8:327–329, 1990.

69. Bosse GM: Nebulized sodium bicarbonate in the treatment of chlorine gas inhalation. Clin Toxicol 232:233–241, 1994.

70. Douidar SM: Nebulized sodium bicarbonate in acute chlorine inhalation. Ped Emerg Care 13:406–407, 1997.

71. Guloglu C, Kara IH, Erten PG: Acute accidental exposure to chlorine gas in the southeast of Turkey: A study of 108 cases. Environ Res A 88:29–33, 2002.

72. Ainslie G: Inhalational injuries produced by smoke and nitrogen dioxide. Respir Med 87:169–174, 1993.

73. Douglas WW, Hepper NG, Colby TV: Silo-filler's disease. Mayo Clin Proc 64:291–304, 1989.

74. Hedberg K, Hedberg CW, Iber C, et al: An outbreak of nitrogen dioxide induced respiratory illness among ice hockey players. JAMA 262:3014–3017, 1989.

75. Centers for Disease Control: Nitrogen dioxide and carbon monoxide intoxication in an indoor ice arena—Wisconsin, 1992. MMWR Morb Mortal Wkly Rep 41:383–385, 1992.

76. Prien T, Traber DL: Toxic smoke compounds and inhalation injury—a review. Burns 14:451–460, 1988.

77. Hajela R, Janigan DT, Landrigan PL, et al: Fatal pulmonary edema due to nitric acid inhalation in three pulp-mill workers. Chest 97:487–489, 1990.

78. National Institute for Occupational Safety and Health: Criteria for a Recommended Standard: Welding, Brazing and Thermal Cutting (Publication No. 88-110). Cincinnati, Ohio: U.S. Department of Health and Human Services, 1988.

79. Ellis FP: The hazards of toxic gases in warships excluding agents of chemical warfare. In Cope VZ (ed): History of the Second World War: Medicine and Pathology. London: Her Majesty's Stationary Office, 1952, pp 304–318.

80. Weinberger B, Laskin DL, Heck DE, et al: The toxicology of inhaled nitric oxide. Toxicol Sci 59:5–16, 2001.

81. Quereshi MA, Shah NJ, Hemmen CW, et al: Exposure of intensive care nurses to nitric oxide and nitrogen dioxide

during therapeutic use of inhaled nitric oxide in adults with acute respiratory distress syndrome. Am J Crit Care 11:147–153, 2002.

82. Toren K, Blanc PD: The history of pulp and paper bleaching with special emphasis on its respiratory health effects. Lancet 349:1316–1318, 1997.

83. Centers for Disease Control: Sulfur dioxide exposure in Portland cement plants. MMWR Morb Mortal Wkly Rep 33:195–196, 1984.

84. Koksal N, Hasanoglu HC, Gokirmak M, et al: Apricot sulfurization: An occupation that induces an asthma-like syndrome in agricultural environments. Am J Ind Med 43:447–453, 2003.

85. Centers for Disease Control: Acute occupational exposure to sulfur dioxide—Missouri. MMWR Morb Mortal Wkly Rep 32:541–542, 1983.

86. Galea M: Fatal sulfur dioxide inhalation. Can Med Assoc J 91:345–347, 1964.

87. Ip M, Wong K-L, Wong K-F, et al: Lung injury in dimethyl sulfate poisoning. J Occup Med 31:141–143, 1989.

88. National Institute for Occupational Safety and Health: Criteria for a Recommended Standard: Chromic Acid (Publication No. 73-11021). Cincinnati, Ohio: U.S. Department of Health, Education and Welfare, 1973.

89. Kern DG: Outbreak of the reactive airways dysfunction syndrome after a spill of glacial acetic acid. Am Rev Respir Dis 144:1058–1064, 1991.

90. Yelon JA, Simpson RL, Gudjonsson O: Formic acid inhalation injury: A case report. J Burn Care Rehabil 17:241–242, 1996.

91. Wing J, Sanderson LM, Bender JD, et al: Acute health effects in a community after a release of hydrofluoric acid. Arch Environ Health 46:155–160, 1991.

92. Upfal M, Doyle C: Medical management of hydrofluoric acid exposure. J Occup Med 32:726–731, 1990.

93. Zanen AL, Rietveld AP: Inhalation trauma due to overheating in a microwave oven. Thorax 48:300–302, 1993.

94. Kraut A, Lillis R: Pulmonary effects of acute exposure to degradation products of sulphur hexafluoride during electrical cable repair work. Br J Ind Med 47:829–832, 1990.

95. Institute of Medicine, Pechura CM, Rall DP (eds): Veterans at Risk: The Health Effects of Mustard Gas and Lewisite. Washington, DC: National Academy Press, 1993.

95a. Kales SN, Christiani DC: Acute chemical emergencies. N Engl J Med 350:800–808, 2004.

96. Freitag L, Firusian N, Stamatis G, et al: The role of bronchoscopy in pulmonary complications due to mustard gas inhalation. Chest 100:1436–1441, 1991.

97. Blanc PD: The legacy of war gas (editorial). Am J Med 106:689–690, 1999.

98. English JM: A case of probable phosgene poisoning. Br Med J 1:38, 1964.

99. Borak J, Diller WF: Phosgene exposure: Mechanisms of injury and treatment strategies. J Occup Environ Med 43:110–119, 2000.

100. TeSlaa G, Kaiser M, Biederman L, et al: Chloropicrin toxicity involving animal and human exposure. Vet Hum Toxicol 28:323–324, 1986.

101. Gonmori K, Muto H, Yamamoto T, et al: A case of homicidal intoxication by chloropicrin. Am J Forensic Med Pathol 8:135–138, 1987.

101a. Centers for Disease Control and Prevention: Illness associated with drift of Chloropicrin soil fumigant into a residential area—Kern County, California, 2003. MMWR Morb Motal Wkly Rep 53:740–742, 2004.

102. Dunn MA, Sidell FR: Progress in medical defense against nerve agents. JAMA 262:649–652, 1989.

103. Danon YL, Shemer J (eds): Chemical Warfare Medicine: Aspects and Perspectives of the Persian Gulf War. Jerusalem: Gefen Publishing, 1994.

104. Reider MJ: Lacrimators. Clin Toxicol Rev 9:1–4, 1987.

105. Jones GRN: CS and its chemical relatives. Nature 235:257–261, 1972.

106. Beswick FW: Chemical agents used in riot control and warfare. Hum Toxicol 2:247–256, 1983.

107. Spark S, Giammona ST: Toxic effect of tear gas on an infant following prolonged exposure. Am J Dis Child 123:245–246, 1972.

108. Hu H, Fine JM, Epstein P, et al: Tear gas—harassing agent or toxic chemical weapon? JAMA 262:660–663, 1989.

109. Roth VS, Franzblau A: RADS after exposure to a riot-control agent: A case report (letter). J Occup Environ Med 38:863–865, 1996.

110. Hill AR, Silverberg NB, Mayorga D, et al: Medical hazards of the tear gas CS. Medicine 79:234–240, 2000.

111. Brown RFR, Marrs TC, Rice P, et al: The histopathology of rat lung following exposure to zinc oxide/hexachlorethane smoke or instillation of zinc chloride followed by treatment with 70% oxygen. Environ Health Perspect 85:81–87, 1990.

112. Evans EH: Casualties following exposure to zinc chloride smoke. Lancet 2:368–369, 1945.

113. Schenker MR, Speizer FE, Taylor JO: Acute upper respiratory symptoms resulting from exposure to zinc chloride aerosol. Environ Res 25:317–324, 1981.

114. Pettila V, Takkunen O, Tukiainen P: Zinc chloride smoke inhalation: A rare case of severe acute respiratory distress syndrome. Intensive Care Med 26:215–217, 2000.

115. Anthony JS, Zamel N, Aberman A: Abnormalities in pulmonary function after brief exposure to toxic metal fumes. J Can Med Assoc 119:586–588, 1978.

116. Barnhart S, Rosenstock L: Cadmium chemical pneumonitis. Chest 86:789–791, 1984.

117. Fuortes L, Leo A, Ellerbeck PG, et al: Acute respiratory fatality associated with exposure to sheet metal and cadmium fumes. Clin Toxicol 29:279–283, 1991.

118. Levin M, Jacobs J, Polos PG: Acute mercury poisoning and mercurial pneumonitis from gold ore purification. Chest 94:551–556, 1988.

119. Rowens B, Guerrero-Bentacourt D, Gottlieb CA, et al: Respiratory failure and death following acute inhalation of mercury vapor. Chest 99:185–190, 1991.

120. Moromisato DY, Anas N, Goodman G: Mercury inhalation poisoning and acute lung injury in a child: Use of high-frequency oscillatory ventilation. Chest 105:613–615, 1994.

121. Ho BSJ, Lin J-L, Huang C-C, et al: Mercury vapor inhalation from Chinese red (cinnabar). J Toxicol Clin Toxicol 41:75–78, 2003.

122. Mohan S, Tamilarasan A, Buhl A: Inhalational mercury poisoning masquerading as toxic shock syndrome. Anaesth Intensive Care 22:305–306, 1994.

123. Vuopala V, Huhti E, Takkunen J, et al: Nickel carbonyl poisoning: Report of 25 cases. Ann Clin Res 2:214–222, 1970.

124. Zicheng S: Acute nickel carbonyl poisoning: A report of 179 cases. Br J Ind Med 43:422–424, 1986.

125. Blanc P, Boushey HA: The lung in metal fume fever. Semin Respir Med 14:212–225, 1993.

126. Kurta DL, Dean BS, Krenzelok EP: Acute nickel carbonyl poisoning. Am J Emerg Med 11:64–66, 1993.

127. Bradberry SM, Vale JA: Therapeutic review: Do diethyldithiocarbamate and disulfiram have a role in acute nickel carbonyl poisoning? Clin Toxicol 37:259–264, 1999.

128. Scott LK, Grier LR, Arnold TC, et al: Respiratory failure from inhalational nickel carbonyl exposure treated with continuous high-volume hemofiltration and disulfiram. Inhal Toxicol 14:1103–1109, 2002.

129. Irsigler GB, Visser PJ, Spangenberg PAL: Asthma and chemical bronchitis in vanadium plant workers. Am J Ind Med 35:366–374, 1999.

130. Woodin MA, Liu Y, Neuberg D, et al: Acute respiratory symptoms in workers exposed to vanadium-rich fuel-oil ash. Am J Respir Crit Care Med 37:353–363, 2000.

131. Ghio AJ, Gilbey JG, Roggli VL, et al: Diffuse alveolar damage after exposure to an oil fly ash. Am J Respir Crit Care Med 164:1514–1518, 2001.

132. Vandenplas O, Binard-van Cangh F, Gregoire J, et al: Fever and neutrophilic alveolitis caused by a vanadium based catalyst. Occup Environ Health 59:785–787, 2002.

133. Wax PM, Dockstader L: Tributyltin use in interior paints: A continuing health hazard. Clin Toxicol 33:239–241, 1995.

134. Rask-Andersen A, Pratt DS: Inhalation fever: A proposed unifying term for febrile reactions to inhalation of noxious substances. Br J Ind Med 49:40, 1992.

135. Centers for Disease Control: Polymer-fume fever associated with cigarette smoking and the use of tetrafluoroethylene— Mississippi. MMWR Morb Mortal Wkly Rep 36:515–516, 521–522, 1987.

136. Volgelmeier C, Konig G, Bencze K, et al: Pulmonary involvement in zinc fume fever. Chest 92:946–948, 1987.

137. Blanc P, Wong H, Bernstein MS, et al: An experimental model of metal fume fever. Ann Intern Med 114:930–936, 1991.

138. Lecours R, Laviolette M, Cormier Y: Bronchoalveolar lavage in pulmonary mycotoxicosis (organic dust toxic syndrome). Thorax 41:924–926, 1986.

139. Robbins JJ, Ware RL: Pulmonary edema from Teflon fumes. N Engl J Med 271:360–361, 1964.

140. Evans EA: Pulmonary edema after inhalation of fumes from polytetra-fluoroethylene (PTFE). J Occup Med 15:599–601, 1973.

141. Centers for Disease Control and Prevention: Severe acute respiratory illness linked to use of shoe sprays—Colorado, November 1993. MMWR Morb Mortal Wkly Rep 42:885–887, 1993.

142. Laliberte M, Sanfacon G, Blais R: Acute pulmonary toxicity linked to use of a leather protector. Ann Emerg Med 25:841–844, 1995.

143. Carson MF, White CM: Pneumonitis following inhalation of a commercially available water repellant. Clin Toxicol 39:179–180, 2001.

144. Drinker P, Thomson RM, Finn JL: Metal fume fever: II. Resistance acquired by inhalation of zinc oxide on two successive days. J Ind Hyg 9:98–105, 1927.

145. Neal PA, Schneiter R, Camanita BH: Report on acute illness among rural mattress makers using low grade, stained cotton. JAMA 119:1074–1082, 1942.

146. National Institute for Occupational Safety and Health: Occupational Exposure to Zinc (Publication No. 76-104). Washington, DC: U.S. Department of Health, Education and Welfare, 1976.

147. Borak J, Cohen H, Hethman TA: Copper exposure and metal fume fever: Lack of evidence for a causal relationship. Am Ind Hyg Assoc J 61:832–836, 2000.

148. Kuschner WG, Wong H, D'Alessandro A, et al: Human pulmonary responses to experimental inhalation of high concentration fine and ultrafine magnesium oxide particles. Environ Health Perspect 105:1234–1237, 1997.

149. Centers for Disease Control: Acute respiratory illness following occupational exposure to wood chips—Ohio.

MMWR Morb Mortal Wkly Rep 35:483–484, 489–490, 1986.

150. Brinton WT, Vastbinder EE, Greene JW, et al: An outbreak of organic dust toxic syndrome in a college fraternity. JAMA 258:1210–1212, 1987.

151. May JJ, Stallones L, Darrow D, et al: Organic dust toxicity (pulmonary mycotoxicosis) associated with silo unloading. Thorax 41:919–923, 1986.

152. Schenker MB, Christiani D, Cormier Y, et al: Respiratory health hazards in agriculture. Am J Respir Crit Care Med 158:S1–S76, 1998.

153. Seifert SA, Von Essen S, Jacobitz K, et al: Organic dust toxic syndrome: A review. J Toxicol Clin Toxicol 41:185–193, 2003.

154. Emanuel DA, Wenzel FJ, Lawton BR: Pulmonary mycotoxicosis. Chest 67:293–297, 1975.

155. Taylor G: Acute systemic effects of inhaled occupational agents. In Merchant JA (ed): Occupational Respiratory Diseases. Washington, DC: U.S. Department of Health and Human Services, 1986, pp 607–625.

156. Cavagna G, Finulli M, Vigliani EC: Studio sperimentale sulla patagenesi della febbre da inaliazaione di fumi di Teflon (politetrafluoroetilene) [Experimental study on the pathogenesis of Teflon fume fever]. Med Lav 52:251–261, 1961.

157. Lewis CE, Kerby GR: An epidemic of polymer fume fever. JAMA 191:375–378, 1965.

158. Wegman D, Peters JM: Polymer fume fever and cigarette smoking. Ann Intern Med 81:55–57, 1974.

159. Blanc PD, Boushey HA, Wong H, et al: Cytokines in metal fume fever. Am Rev Respir Dis 147:134–138, 1993.

160. Kuschner WG, D'Alessandro A, Wintermeyer SF, et al: Pulmonary responses to purified zinc oxide fume. J Investig Med 43:371–378, 1995.

161. Kuschner WG, D'Allesandro A, Wong H, et al: Early pulmonary cytokine responses to zinc oxide fume inhalation. Environ Res 75:7–11, 1997.

162. Wintermeyer SF, Kuschner WG, Wong H, et al: Pulmonary responses following wood chip mulch exposure. J Occup Environ Med 39:308–314, 1997.

163. Wang Z, Malmberg P, Larsson P, et al: Time course of interleukin-6 and tumor necrosis factor-alpha increase in serum following inhalation of swine dust. Am J Respir Crit Care Med 143:147–152, 1996.

164. Cormier Y, Duchaine C, Israel-Assayag E, et al: Effects of repeated swine building exposures on normal naive subjects. Eur Respir J 10:1516–1522, 1997.

165. Deetz DC, Jagielo PJ, Quinn TJ, et al: The kinetics of grain dust-induced inflammation of the lower respiratory tract. Am J Crit Care Med 115:254–259, 1997.

166. Borm PJA, Schins ROF, Derhaag TJJM, et al: Cross-shift changes in blood inflammatory markers occur in the absence of airway obstruction in workers exposed to grain dust. Chest 109:1078–1085, 1996.

167. Wohlford-Lenane CL, Deetz DC, Schwartz DA: Cytokine gene expression after inhalation of corn dust. Am J Physiol 27:L737–L743, 1999.

168. Fine JM, Gordon T, Chen LC, et al: Characterization of tolerance to inhaled zinc oxide in naive subjects and sheet metal workers. J Occup Environ Med 42:1085–1091, 2000.

169. Beamon RF, Siegel CJ, Landers G, et al: Hydrocarbon ingestion in children: A six year retrospective study. J Am Coll Emerg Physicians 5:771–775, 1976.

170. Klein BL, Simon JE: Hydrocarbon poisonings. Pediatr Clin North Am 33:411–419, 1986.

171. Dice WH, Ward G, Kelly J, et al: Pulmonary toxicity following gastrointestinal ingestion of kerosene. Ann Emerg Med 11:138–142, 1982.

172. Brook MP, McCarron MM, Mueller JA: Pine oil cleaner ingestion. Ann Emerg Med 18:391–395, 1989.

173. Nirenberg DW, Horowitz MB, Harris KM, et al: Mineral spirits inhalation associated with hemolysis, pulmonary edema, and ventricular fibrillation. Arch Intern Med 151:1437–1440, 1991.

174. Gould SR, Bernardo DE: Respiratory distress after talc inhalation. Br J Dis Chest 66:230–233, 1972.

175. Motomatsu K, Adachi H, Uno T: Two infant deaths after inhaling baby powder. Chest 75:448–450, 1979.

176. Bismuth C, Garnier R, Baud FJ, et al: Paraquat poisoning: An overview of the current status. Drug Safety 5:243–251, 1990.

177. Smith JC: Paraquat poisoning by skin absorption: A review. Hum Toxicol 7:15–19, 1988.

178. Im JQ, Lee KS, Han MC, et al: Paraquat poisoning: Findings on chest radiography and CT in 42 patients. AJR Am J Roentgenol 157:697–701, 1991.

179. Smith EA, Oehme FW: A review of selected herbicides and their toxicities. Vet Hum Toxicol 33:596–608, 1991.

180. Lin J-L, Liu L, Leu M-L: Recovery of respiratory function in survivors of paraquat intoxication. Arch Environ Health 50:432–439, 1995.

181. Van Der Wal NAA, Smith LL, Van Oirschot JFLM, et al: Effect of iron chelators on paraquat toxicity in rats and alveolar type II cells. Am Rev Respir Dis 145:180–186, 1992.

182. Saenghirunvattana S, Sermswan A, Piratchvej V, et al: Effect of lung irradiation on mice following paraquat intoxication. Chest 101:833–835, 1992.

183. Lin J-L, Leu M-L, Liu Y-C, et al: A prospective clinical trial of pulse therapy with glucocorticoid and cyclophosphamide in moderate to severe paraquat-poisoned patients. Am J Respir Crit Care Med 159:357–360, 1999.

184. Summer W, Haponik E: Inhalation of irritant gases. Clin Chest Med 2:273–287, 1981.

185. Schwartz DA: Acute inhalational injury. Occup Med 2:297–318, 1987.

186. Miller K, Chang A: Acute inhalation injury. Emerg Med Clin North Am 21:533–557, 2003.

187. Haponik EF, Meyers DA, Munster AM, et al: Acute upper airway injury in burn patients: Serial changes of flow volume curves and nasopharyngoscopy. Am Rev Respir Dis 135:360–366, 1987.

188. Kuo DC, Jerrard DA: Environmental insults: Smoke inhalation, submersion, diving, and high altitude. Emerg Med Clin North Am 21:475–497, 2003.

189. Alarie Y: Toxicity of fire smoke. Crit Rev Toxicol 32:259–289, 2002.

190. Hale CA, Barkin PW, Jung W, et al: Synthetic smoke with acrolein but not HCl produces pulmonary edema. J Appl Physiol 64:1121–1133, 1988.

191. Sheppard D, Distefano S, Morse L, et al: Acute effects of routine firefighting on lung function. Am J Ind Med 9:333–340, 1986.

192. Stenton SC, Kelly CA, Waiters EH, et al: Induction of bronchial hyperresponsiveness following smoke inhalation injury. Br J Dis Chest 82:436–438, 1988.

193. Chia KS, Jeyaratnam J, Chan TB, et al: Airway responsiveness of firefighters after smoke exposure. Br J Ind Med 47:524–527, 1990.

194. Kinsella J, Carter R, Reid WH, et al: Increased airways reactivity after smoke inhalation. Lancet 337:595–597, 1991.

195. Liu D, Tager IB, Balmes JR, et al: The effect of smoke inhalation on lung function and airway responsiveness in wildland fire fighters. Am Rev Respir Dis 146:1469–1473, 1992.

196. Shusterman D, Kaplan JZ, Canabarro C: Immediate health effects of an urban wildfire. West J Med 158:133–138, 1993.

197. Long A, Tate RB, Neuman M, et al: Respiratory symptoms in a susceptible population due to burning of agricultural residue. Chest 113:351–357, 1998.

198. Park GY, Park JW, Jeong DH, et al: Prolonged airway and systemic inflammatory reactions after smoke inhalation. Chest 123:475–480, 2003.

199. McGee JK, Chen LC, Cohen MD, et al: Chemical analysis of World Trade Center fine particulate matter for use in toxicologic assessment. Environ Health Perspect 111:972–980, 2003.

200. Beckett WS: A New York City firefighter. Am J Respir Crit Care Med 166:785–786, 2002.

201. Tsao TC-Y, Juang Y-C, Lan R-S, et al: Respiratory failure of acute organophosphate and carbamate poisoning. Chest 98:631–636, 1990.

202. Blanc P, Liu D, Juarez C, Boushey HA: Cough in hot pepper workers. Chest 99:27–32, 1991.

203. Asai S, Krzanowski JJ, Anderson WH, et al: Effects of the toxin of red tide, *Ptychodiscus brevis*, on canine tracheal smooth muscle: A possible new asthma-triggering mechanism. J Allergy Clin Immunol 69:418–428, 1982.

204. Pierce RH: Red tide (*Ptychodiscus brevis*) toxin aerosols: A review. Toxicon 24:955–965, 1986.

205. Krzanowski JJ: Natural products and bronchial asthma. J Fla Med Assoc 1:357–358, 1994.

206. Matuszak DL, Sanders M, Taylor JL, et al: Toxic *Pfiesteria* and human health. Md Med J 46:515–520, 1997.

207. Haselow DT, Brown E, Tracy JK, et al: Gastrointestinal and respiratory tract symptoms following brief environmental exposure to aerosols during a *Pfiesteria*-related fish kill. J Toxicol Environ Health A 63:553–564, 2001.

208. Osborne NJ, Webb PM, Shaw GR: The toxins of *Lyngbya majuscula* and their human and ecological health effects. Environ Int 27:381–392, 2001.

209. Walton M: Industrial ammonia gassing. Br J Ind Med 30:78–86, 1973.

210. Sobanya R: Fatal anhydrous ammonia inhalation. Hum Pathol 8:293–299, 1977.

211. Montague TJ, Macneil AR: Mass ammonia inhalation. Chest 77:496–498, 1980.

212. Flury KE, Dines DE, Rodarte JR, et al: Airway obstruction due to inhalation of ammonia. Mayo Clin Proc 64:291–304, 1989.

213. De La Hoz RE, Schlueter DP, Rom WN: Chronic lung disease secondary to ammonia inhalation injury: A report on three cases. Am J Ind Med 29:209–214, 1996.

214. Weisskopf MG, Drew JM, Hanrahan LP, et al: Hazardous ammonia releases: Public health consequences and risk factors for evacuation and injury, United States, 1993–1998. J Occup Environ Med 45:197–204, 2003.

215. Centers for Disease Control and Prevention: Public health consequences among first responders to emergency events associated with illicit methamphetamine laboratories—selected states, 1996–1999. MMWR Morb Mortal Wkly Rep 49:1021–1023, 2000.

216. Prudhomme JC, Shusterman DJ, Blanc PD: Acute-onset persistent olfactory deficit resulting from multiple over-exposures to ammonia vapor at work. J Am Board Fam Pract 11:66–69, 1998.

217. Morabia A, Selleger C, Landry JC, et al: Accidental bromine exposure in an urban population: An acute epidemiological assessment. Int J Epidemiol 17:148–152, 1988.

218. Lossos IS, Abolnik I: Pneumomediastinum: A complication of exposure to bromine. Br J Ind Med 47:784, 1990.

219. Burns MJ, Linden CH: Another hot tub hazard: Toxicity secondary to bromine and hydrobromic acid exposure. Chest 111:816–819, 1997.

220. Hertzman J, Cullen MR: Methyl bromide intoxication in four field workers during removal of soil fumigation sheets. Am J Ind Med 17:321–326, 1990.

221. Centers for Disease Control: Unintentional methyl bromide gas release. MMWR Morb Mortal Wkly Rep 38:880–882, 1990.

222. National Institute for Occupational Safety and Heath: Ethylene Oxide, Current Intelligence Bulletin 35 (Publication No. 81–130). Cincinnati, Ohio: U.S. Department of Health and Human Services, 1981.

223. Centers for Disease Control: Occupational fatality following exposure to hydrogen sulfide—Nebraska. MMWR Morb Mortal Wkly Rep 35:533–535, 1986.

224. Jappinen P, Vilkka V, Marttila O, et al: Exposure to hydrogen sulphide and respiratory function. Br J Ind Med 47:824–828, 1990.

225. Parra O, Monso E, Gallego M, et al: Inhalation of hydrogen sulphide: A case of subacute manifestations and long term sequelae. Br J Ind Med 48:286–287, 1991.

226. Guidotti TL: Hydrogen sulphide. Occup Med 46:367–371, 1996.

227. Mehta PS, Mehta AS, Mehta SJ, et al: Bhopal tragedy's health effects: A review of methyl isocyanate. JAMA 264:2781–2787, 1990.

228. Dhra VR, Kriebel D: The Bhopal disaster: It's not too late for sound epidemiology (editorial). Arch Environ Health 48:436–438, 1993.

229. Cullinan P, Acquilla S, Ramana Dhara V: Respiratory morbidity 10 years after the Union Carbide gas leak at Bhopal: A cross sectional survey. BMJ 314:338–343, 1997.

230. Cone JE, Wugofski L, Balmes JR, et al: Persistent respiratory health effects after a metam sodium pesticide spill. Chest 106:500–508, 1994.

231. Centers for Disease Control and Prevention: Recall of Philip Morris cigarettes, May 1995–March 1996. MMWR Morb Mortal Wkly Rep 45:251–254, 1996.

232. Garry VF, Good PF, Manivel JC, et al: Investigation of a fatality from non-occupational aluminum phosphide exposure: Measurement of aluminum in tissue and body fluids as a marker of exposure. J Lab Clin Med 122:739–747, 1993.

233. Feldstein A, Heumann M, Barnett M: Fumigant intoxication during transport of grain by railroad. J Occup Med 33:64–65, 1991.

234. Centers for Disease Control: Workplace exposures to corrosion-inhibiting chemicals from a steam humidification system—Ohio, 1988. MMWR Morb Mortal Wkly Rep 39:863–865, 1990.

235. Gadon ME, Melius JM, McDonald GJ, et al: New-onset asthma after exposure to the steam system additive 2-diethylaminoethanol. J Occup Med 36:623–626, 1994.

236. Balkisson R, Murray D, Hoffstein V: Alveolar damage due to inhalation of amitrole-containing herbicide. Chest 101:1174–1175, 1992.

237. Pushnoy LA, Avnon LS, Carel RS: Herbicide (Roundup) pneumonitis. Chest 114:1769–1770, 1998.

238. Gross KB, Haidar AH, Basha MA, et al: Acute pulmonary response of asthmatics to aerosols and gases generated by airbag deployment. Am J Respir Crit Care Med 150:408–414, 1994.

239. Lowe HJ, Freeman G: Boron hydride (Borane) intoxication in man. Arch Ind Health 16:523–533, 1957.

240. Wald PH, Becker CE: Toxic gases used in the micro-electronics industry. Occup Med 1:105–117, 1986.

241. Jacobs IA, Taddeo J, Kelly K, et al: Poisoning as a result of barium styphnate explosion. Am J Ind Med 41:285–288, 2002.

242. Schecter A, Shanske W, Stenzler A, et al: Acute hydrogen selenide inhalation. Chest 77:554–555, 1980.

243. Banerjee BD, Dwivedi S, Singh S: Acute hydrogen selenide gas poisoning admissions in one of the hospitals in Delhi, India: A case report. Hum Exp Toxicol 16:276–278, 1997.

244. Sinclair JS, McManus DT, Ohara MD, et al: Fatal inhalation injury following an industrial accident involving acetic anhydride. Burns 20:469–470, 1994.

245. Ould Kadi F, Mohammed-Brahim B, Fyad A, et al: Outbreak of pulmonary disease in textile sprayers in Algeria (letter). Lancet 344:962–963, 1994.

246. Cordero P, Solé A: Bronchiolitis obliterans organizing pneumonia (Ardystil syndrome) and chronic demyelinating disease of the central nervous system. Arch Bronconeumol 31:89–92, 1995.

247. Camus P, Nemery B: A novel cause for bronchiolitis obliterans organizing pneumonia: Exposure to paint aerosols in textile workshops. Eur Respir J 11:259–262, 1998.

248. Kern DG, Crausman RS, Durand KTH: Flock worker's lung: Chronic interstitial lung disease in the nylon flocking industry. Ann Intern Med 129:261–272, 1998.

249. Eschenbacher WL, Kreiss K, Lougheed MD, et al: Nylon flock-associated interstitial lung disease. Am J Respir Crit Care Med 159:2002–2008, 1999.

250. Kuschner W: What exactly is flock worker's lung? Chest 117:10–13, 2000.

251. Kreiss K, Gomma A, Kullman G, et al: Clinical bronchiolitis obliterans in workers at a microwave-popcorn plant. N Engl J Med 347:330–338, 2002.

251a. Akpinar-Elci M, Travis WD, Lynch DA, Kreiss K: Bronchiolitis obliterans syndrome in popcorn production plant workers. Eur Respir J 24:298–302, 2004.

252. Centers for Disease Control and Prevention: Update: Pulmonary hemorrhage/hemosiderosis among infants—Cleveland, Ohio, 1993–1996. MMWR Morb Mortal Wkly Rep 46:33–35, 1997.

253. Centers for Disease Control and Prevention: Update: Pulmonary hemorrhage/hemosiderosis among infants—Cleveland, Ohio, 1993–1996. MMWR Morb Mortal Wkly Rep 49:180–184, 2000.

254. Terr AI: *Stachybotrys*: Relevance to human disease. Ann Allergy Asthma Immunol 87:57–63, 2001.

255. Yoshida K, Masayki A, Araki S: Acute pulmonary edema in a storehouse of moldy oranges: A severe case of the organic dust toxic syndrome. Arch Environ Health 44:382–384, 1989.

256. Centers for Disease Control and Prevention: Respiratory illness associated with inhalation of mushroom spores—Wisconsin, 1994. MMWR Morb Mortal Wkly Rep 43:525–526, 1994.

65

High Altitude

Robert B. Schoene, M.D., Erik R. Swenson, M.D.

INTRODUCTION

The survival of a species depends on its ability to adapt to acute and chronic stress. High altitude represents a natural stress wherein barometric pressure is lower than at sea level and, consequently, a lower PO_2 is present. Adaptation to this hypoxia will determine whether a species can thrive and reproduce in such an environment.

Nearly 30 million people live at altitudes greater than 2500 m, primarily in the Rocky Mountains of North America, the Andes Mountains of South America, the Ethiopian Highlands of East Africa, and the Himalaya Mountains of South-Central Asia. Although climatic conditions above 5000 m can be habitable, experience suggests that human populations fail to thrive and reproduce above this altitude. Brief forays above 5000 m are possible, but prolonged survival is not.

Increasing numbers of lowlanders are venturing to high altitudes for recreation and adventure. Modern methods of transportation allow access to remote areas and ascension to high altitude very rapidly. Consequently, the frequency with which illnesses either caused or exacerbated by high altitude occur is also increasing. With growing awareness of the risks, persons are seeking advice on traveling to these regions, including older persons with cardiovascular, pulmonary, or other illnesses and women who are pregnant.

The first purpose of this chapter is to review the compensatory mechanisms that take place in the transport of oxygen from the air to the tissues when barometric pressure is lower—normal adaptation. We discuss both acute and chronic adaptation and explore factors determining the limits of adaptation and performance at high altitude. Our second goal is to review the consequences of maladaptation—the acute and chronic illnesses of high altitude.

HISTORICAL PERSPECTIVE

For most of its approximately 4.6 billion years, the Earth's atmosphere contained essentially no oxygen. About a half billion years ago photosynthetic activity increased, such that about 100 million years ago the oxygen level became sufficient to permit life of multicellular organisms. Subsequently, the amount of oxygen in the atmosphere up to 110,000 m (69 miles) increased and for some time has remained at about 20.9%. The PO_2 in the air we breathe, therefore, is simply $0.2093 \times$ barometric pressure (Table 65.1).

Our awareness of the existence of this life-giving gas and of the consequences of its lack is more recent. In 1590, a Jesuit priest, Father Joseph de Acosta, described both the adaptation and the maladaptation occurring on ascent to Pariacaca, a 4500-m Andean pass in South America. He speculated that it was the "thin air" that was responsible for the sensations of headache, dyspnea, and light-headedness that often occur on acute ascent. During the 17th century, a phenomenal growth occurred in our understanding of the atmosphere. Air was discovered to have weight. In 1641, Berti and Maignan designed the first water barometer, which they placed against the side of a house. On September 18, 1648, the French scientist Perier carried a barometer to the summit of Puy-de-Dome (1067 m), where he found the pressure to be 78 mm Hg less than at the base of the mountain. A French physiologist, Paul Bert, is credited with being the father of high-altitude research. His steel bell chambers allowed simulated ascent by decompression. In 1875, he helped design the experiments for the flight of the hot-air balloon Zenith, in which two of the three scientists ascending to over 8000 m died. Haldane[1] and Kellogg[2] give a perspective on the prodigious work that was being done early in the 20th century. West[3] published an excellent treatise of the history of humans' encounters at

Table 65.1 U.S. Standard Atmosphere: Altitude, Barometric Pressure, and Inspired Partial Pressure of Oxygen*

Altitude (m)	Altitude (feet)	Barometric Pressure (mm Hg)	Inspired P_{O_2} (mm Hg)
0	0	760.0	159.1
1,000	3,280	674.4	141.2
2,000	6,560	596.3	124.9
3,000	9,840	525.8	110.1
4,000	13,120	462.8	96.9
5,000	16,400	405.0	84.8
6,000	19,680	354.0	79.1
8,000	26,240	267.8	56.1
8,848	29,028	253.0	43.1

* Values except 8,848 m, are taken for mid latitude (45° N). There is greater variation at higher altitudes.
Modified with permission from Altman PL, Dittmer DS (eds): Respiration and Circulation. Bethesda, Md: Federation of American Societies for Experimental Biology, 1971, pp 12–13.

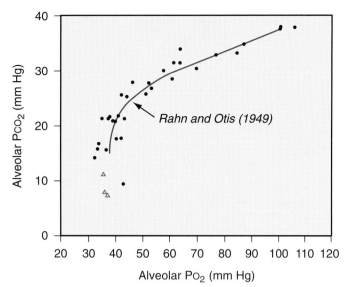

Figure 65.1 Oxygen–carbon dioxide diagram of Rahn and Otis with values of alveolar gas composition in acclimatized subjects at high altitude. At extreme altitudes, marked hyperventilation maintains alveolar P_{O_2} at approximately 35 mm Hg. (From West JB, Hackett PH, Maret KH, et al: Pulmonary gas exchange on the summit of Mt. Everest. J Appl Physiol 55:678–687, 1983.)

high altitude. We emphasize the research that has built upon the work of these pioneers and others, which has been extensively documented.[4]

ADAPTATION

The P_{O_2} diminishes as the oxygen molecules move from air to blood and then to the tissues that require a constant supply of this vital gas. Ventilation, matching of ventilation with blood flow, diffusion of oxygen from the gas to the blood, circulation, diffusion to and into tissue, and metabolism in the cell are all links in the chain of oxygen transport. A number of compensatory mechanisms improve oxygen delivery, when its inspired concentration is reduced.

VENTILATION: ACUTE AND CHRONIC ADAPTATION

Control of Ventilation

Mechanisms regulating breathing are reviewed in Chapter 4. The ventilatory response to high altitude is the most immediate and noticeable physiologic event to occur on acute ascent. The oxygen and carbon dioxide concentrations in alveolar air are a direct reflection of barometric pressure and alveolar ventilation. Measurement of the partial pressures of alveolar gases by Rahn and Otis[5] in 1946 clearly demonstrated that, as barometric pressure decreases, ventilation increases to minimize the drop in alveolar P_{O_2} (Fig. 65.1). These studies attempted to predict the pressure of alveolar gases at the summit of Mt. Everest (8848 m, barometric pressure about 253 mm Hg), which were measured on the 1981 American Medical Research Expedition to Mt. Everest (see Fig. 65.1). In a single individual, increased breathing resulted in an alveolar P_{CO_2} of 7.5 mm Hg and

an alveolar P_{O_2} of 34 mm Hg (inspired P_{O_2} = 43 mm Hg). Data collected in a simulated, 40-day ascent of Mt. Everest in a hypobaric chamber showed slightly higher levels of alveolar P_{CO_2} (11.2 ± 1.7 mm Hg) in six subjects, which also reflects an extraordinary degree of hyperventilation to preserve a viable level of oxygenation.

The ventilatory response to a relatively constant hypoxic stimulus varies over time (Fig. 65.2): the initial increase on ascent, the subsequent course over hours and weeks, and the deacclimatization on descent. In addition, high-altitude inhabitants exhibit a different long-term response, which results in lower ventilation at any given altitude than sojourners would demonstrate at similar altitudes.[6]

Acute Response. With acute hypoxia, ventilation increases immediately, followed 10 to 15 minutes later by a lower level of hyperventilation in spite of sustained carotid chemoreceptor output. This response is called the hypoxic ventilatory response (HVR). As the arterial P_{O_2} decreases from that at sea level to about 60 mm Hg, the increase in ventilation is slight; but as the arterial P_{O_2} drops lower, both carotid chemoreceptor activity and ventilation increase substantially, but with individual variability. This individual variability plays an important role in human adaptation, maladaptation, and performance at high altitude, as well as low altitude. Recent work in mice has identified a locus on chromosome 9 that influences the variation in HVR.[7] This work may lead to insight into the variability of human ventilatory responses, which have long been known to have an inherited component.

The role of the carotid body in the ventilatory response to hypoxia has been based on extensive direct and indirect evidence.[8] Neural discharge from the whole carotid sinus nerve is related hyperbolically to decreasing P_{O_2} in arterial blood, such as the ventilatory response to hypoxia. Surgical

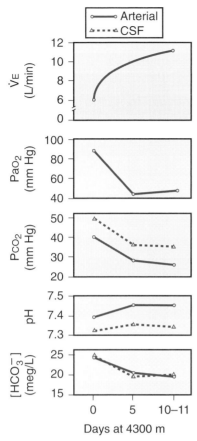

Figure 65.2 Ventilatory acclimatization during 10- to 11-day sojourn to 4300 m. Ventilation continues to increase as cerebrospinal fluid (CSF) acid-base alterations parallel plasma changes. HCO_3^-, bicarbonate; Pa_{O_2}, arterial oxygen tension; Pco_2, carbon dioxide tension; $\dot{V}_E$, minute volume of ventilation. (From Forster HV, Dempsey JA, Chosy LW: Incomplete compensation of CSF [H⁺] in man during acclimatization to high altitude [4300 m]. J Appl Physiol 38:1067–1072, 1975.)

ablation of carotid body input in animals results in loss of the ventilatory response to acute hypoxia.

The acute increase in ventilation is inhibited by the resulting respiratory alkalosis and drop in Pco_2 at the medullary and peripheral chemosensors.[9] In addition, beginning a few minutes after hypoxic exposure and lasting for perhaps half an hour, a decrease in breathing not explained by hypocapnia is observed; the mechanism causing this transient, hypoxia-related decrease in breathing, referred to as hypoxia ventilatory decline or "roll off," is the subject of current investigation but is not thought to be secondary to hypocapnia.[10] Subsequently, over days, ventilation increases. Although the mechanism is not fully understood, the classic explanation of the progressive increase in ventilation after several days was that renal compensation for the resulting respiratory alkalosis permitted full realization of the hypoxic stimulus to ventilation. However, measurement of blood pH revealed that alkalosis persists as ventilation increases, whereas the cerebrospinal fluid (CSF) pH affecting the medullary chemosensors might return to normal by virtue of H^+/HCO_3^- regulation across the blood-brain barrier. The sustained hyperventilation on sudden hyperoxia and in the presence of continued alkalinity of blood was thought to be secondary to a relative CSF acidosis.

Subsequent investigators could not confirm these findings, and found that not only blood but also lumbar CSF of humans remained alkaline during high-altitude (3100 m) sojourns of up to 3 weeks. During deacclimatization, when arterial Pco_2, ventilation, and blood and CSF pH have returned toward normal, a sustained hyperventilation persists for days.[11]

The inability to account for the ventilatory response at high altitude based on traditional stimuli led some investigators to explore the environment in which the central chemoreceptors exist, namely, the brain interstitial fluid and intracellular fluid, which were found to be acidotic in spite of alkalinity of the CSF. Using nuclear magnetic resonance spectroscopy in humans, Goldberg and colleagues[12] looked at brain tissue pH after 7 days at 4300 m in a hypobaric chamber. At the end of the altitude exposure, brain tissue pH was unchanged from before exposure. These results suggest that some mediator(s), other than H⁺, sustain the hyperventilation during a stay at high altitude.

Subsequent Ventilatory Adaptation. Over subsequent hours to weeks at high altitude, ventilation continues to increase. Data from extreme altitude show that ventilatory change may be ongoing for months.[13] A number of factors, such as regulation of brain pH, metabolic rate, and turnover of neurotransmitters, might contribute to this hyperventilation.

One important factor in the progressive hyperventilation may be an increase in the sensitivity over time of the carotid body to hypoxia,[14,15] which is supported by the observation that carotid body–denervated animals do not undergo ventilatory acclimatization. This resetting of the hypoxic sensitivity is not understood but may be secondary to a change in neurotransmitters in the carotid body. There also appears to be a role for carbon dioxide sensitivity that is mediated in the brain stem. An increase in the ventilatory response to carbon dioxide occurs during and after exposure to high altitude, which suggests that the set point for carbon dioxide chemosensitivity changes.

Intermittent Hypoxic Exposure. Patients with sleep disorders or heart and lung disease and travelers to high altitude undergo bouts of hypoxia, which has led to interest in the physiology, chemistry, and gene signaling of the chemosensor response when exposed to intermittent hypoxia.[7,16,17] Studies have focused on the "dose" and frequency of the hypoxic stimulus necessary to induce a physiologic response. Ren and colleagues[18] used 8 hours of exposure in humans to comparable levels of hypoxia, hemodilution, and carboxyhemoglobinemia to reconfirm that it is the P_{O_2} in the blood that stimulates HVR. Eight hours of exposure to isocapnic and poikilocapnic hypoxia (end-tidal P_{O_2} ($P_{ET}O_2$ = 55 mm Hg) substantially augmented the chemosensitivity to carbon dioxide in humans compared to controls. Fatemian and associates[19] documented an increase in HVR after 8 hours in the modest simulated environment of a pressurized aircraft (inspired P_{O_2} = 127 mm Hg). Katayama coworkers[20] exposed six subjects for 1 hr/day for 7 days to a simulated 4500-m altitude and found increased HVR, ventilatory equivalent ($\dot{V}_E/\dot{V}_{O_2}$), and arterial oxygen saturation (S_{O_2}) during hypoxic exercise after the exposure. As little as 20 min/day of hypoxic exposure ($P_{ET}O_2$ = 51 to

55 mm Hg) resulted in an augmented HVR, but only after 2 weeks of exposure.[21] Athletes who trained by spending 20 consecutive nights alternating between sleeping 5 nights at 2650 m and 2 nights at low altitude had normal resting ventilation but markedly increased HVR.[22]

Using briefer, more frequent bouts of hypoxia (5 minutes of 11% to 12% oxygen alternating with 5 minutes of air for 12 hr/night, for 7 nights) in awake rats, investigators induced long-term facilitation of ventilatory drives without an increase in resting ventilation or metabolic rates. This effect lasted at least 3 days after the exposure and was completely gone by 7 days.[23] Reeves and colleagues[24] exposed rats to sustained hypoxia (10% oxygen), intermittent hypoxia (90 seconds of air, 90 seconds of 10% oxygen), or air for 30 days and found that both sustained and intermittent hypoxia stimulated resting minute ventilation and the HVR. Further implications of intermittent hypoxia are discussed in subsequent sections on the hemodynamic, erythropoietic, and exercise training–related responses to hypoxia.

Ventilation on Descent. Individuals who have acclimatized to high altitude and who return to low altitude continue to hyperventilate and have increased ventilatory responses to hypoxia and carbon dioxide for several days. Because the subjects are no longer hypoxemic, this continued ventilatory stimulation cannot be attributed to hypoxemia. The persistent hyperventilation on descent could be secondary to a rise in carbon dioxide that results from the loss of hypoxic stimulus to ventilation,[12,14] but this complex interaction of events on descent or cessation of exposure to hypoxia is not well understood.

Chronic Ventilatory Adaptation. With residence at high altitude, ventilation diminishes, and resting arterial P_{CO_2}, although generally below that at sea level, is higher than that observed in acclimatized lowlanders at high altitude. Most noteworthy is the diminished ventilatory response to an acute hypoxic challenge seen in many high-altitude residents. This diminution of hypoxic chemosensitivity, found in highlanders,[25–27] is an acquired phenomenon associated with prolonged residence. The mechanism for this blunting of hypoxic ventilatory response with chronic hypoxia is not known, but blunting occurs in conjunction with hypertrophy of the carotid bodies and may be an adaptive phenomenon in which the disadvantage of the lower arterial P_{O_2} is offset by the lower energy expenditure of the lower ventilation.

High-altitude natives from the Himalayan Mountains in Tibet and Nepal, populations in which chronic mountain sickness is rare, do not exhibit hypoventilation or blunted hypoxic chemosensitivity to the same extent as South American high-altitude dwellers. Huang and coworkers[28] compared Tibetan highlanders, well-acclimatized sojourners, and sojourners who had developed polycythemia. Highlanders and well-acclimatized sojourners had higher resting minute ventilations, lower arterial P_{CO_2}, higher pH values, higher arterial S_{O_2}, and higher diffusing capacities for carbon monoxide than sojourners with polycythemia. Hackett and colleagues[29] noted similar responses in Sherpas, highland natives living in the Himalayan Mountains who are descendants of inhabitants of the Tibetan plateau. These results are in contrast to the many studies in South America

that have found that high-altitude natives hypoventilate as compared with lowlanders.[25–27] The study by Hackett and colleagues[29] also showed that hypoxic chemosensitivity in the Sherpa population, when corrected for their smaller body size, had a normal distribution with a mean and standard deviation comparable to sojourners. The potential difference between Himalayan and Andean highlanders suggests an intriguing possibility that these two populations may have adapted differently. The seemingly more successful adaptation of the Tibetans may be a result of their longer exposure (~60,000 to 75,000 years) as a population to high altitude than the Andeans (~14,000 years or so).

Pulmonary Function and Mechanics at Altitude

On ascent, the lung undergoes a number of changes that may alter its function. This topic was recently reviewed by Milic-Emili and coworkers.[30] Vital capacity decreases in the first 24 hours.[31,32] Coates and colleagues[31] noted an increase in residual volume and in the slope of the alveolar plateau of the single-breath nitrogen test. These changes are all compatible with an increased interstitial fluid volume, resulting in airway narrowing, gas trapping, and delayed emptying of some lung units. Using transthoracic electrical impedance, Jaeger and associates[32] and Hoon and coworkers[33] reported increased lung water on acute ascent to altitude. In the study by Hoon and coworkers, the increased lung water cleared uneventfully within 24 hours in those subjects who remained asymptomatic but continued to increase in those in whom symptoms of high-altitude pulmonary edema developed. These data also suggest that an initial transient increase in intravascular or extravascular lung water may account for the decrease in vital capacity and other mechanical changes. Although hypoxia and hypocapnia may cause airway narrowing, thus increasing airway resistance, Gautier and associates[34] found a decrease in resistance at high altitude, presumably secondary to decreased air density.

Chronic exposure causes other changes in the high-altitude dweller. Hurtado[35] reported larger vital capacities in high-altitude natives (2720 mL/m² in natives; 2610 mL/m² in non-native high-altitude residents, and 2460 mL/m² in sea-level whites). Similarly, Brody and associates[36] described larger vital capacities in Peruvian highlanders than in lowlanders (5.11 ± 0.64 vs. 3.73 ± 0.32 L). Frisancho[37] later discovered that the increase in vital capacity was dependent on the age at which the subjects began living at high altitude. Young, growing subjects develop larger vital capacities than those who move to high altitude later in life.

Gas Exchange

Ventilation and Perfusion. The ascent of Mt. Everest (8848 m) without supplemental oxygen by Messner and Habeler in 1978 and the subsequent measurements of the barometric pressure and alveolar gas composition on the summit of Mt. Everest by Pizzo[38] have stimulated interest in pulmonary gas exchange during severe hypoxia, but one need not go to such extremes to observe the remarkable adaptations to hypobaric conditions. Excellent updates on the subject are available.[39,40]

The initial increase in ventilation during acute hypoxia is matched by an increase in cardiac output and pulmonary perfusion.[41] Additionally, hypoxia causes pulmonary arterial constriction and pulmonary hypertension. At rest at altitude or with regional hypoxia in the lung, this adaptive response is advantageous by improving ventilation-perfusion ($\dot{V}A/\dot{Q}$) matching.[41] The increased pulmonary vascular resistance causes redistribution of blood flow to areas of the lung that are usually poorly perfused at sea level. Gale and coworkers,[41] using the multiple inert gas elimination technique in an altitude chamber, found that $\dot{V}A/\dot{Q}$ matching was optimized at rest up to 4550 m. These studies, using two different techniques, indicate that a normal pulmonary vascular response to hypoxia results in improved gas exchange at rest by optimizing $\dot{V}A/\dot{Q}$ matching.

Diffusion. At high altitude, diffusion of oxygen from alveolus to blood appears to be a major rate-limiting step in oxygen transport. In fact, the higher one goes, the greater the portion of the alveolar-arterial PO_2 difference (($A - a$)PO_2) is due to diffusion limitation, especially during exercise.[42] An additional factor at extreme altitudes may be the worsening of the $\dot{V}A/\dot{Q}$ relationship.[42] Oxygen flux is dependent on the pressure gradient for oxygen from the alveolus to capillary blood, gas permeability of the alveolar-capillary membrane (DM), capillary blood volume, and the surface area for gas exchange (discussed in Chapters 4 and 24). Several factors serve to limit oxygen transfer. First is the decreasing PO_2 as one ascends. Equilibration is time dependent, requiring approximately 0.25 second at sea level. At altitude, even the estimated pulmonary transit time at rest of 0.75 second may not be adequate for end-capillary equilibrium of oxygen to occur, and diffusion limitation is exacerbated during exercise as a consequence of the shortened transit time of blood across the pulmonary capillary and the fall in mixed venous PO_2. Because the low arterial PO_2 lies on the steep portion of the oxygen-hemoglobin dissociation curve, a small decrease in PO_2 will result in a proportionately greater drop in pulmonary capillary oxygen content than occurs at sea level. All of these factors may result in an increased ($A - a$)PO_2 at extreme altitude, which will be accentuated by exercise.

West and Wagner[43] modeled these factors as they pertain to the summit of Mt. Everest, where the barometric pressure was assumed to be about 250 mm Hg. Using assumed reasonable values for hemoglobin concentration, oxygen consumption, diffusion (DM), acid-base status, and capillary transit time, they predicted that at this altitude equilibration of oxygen tension between the alveolus and end-capillary blood is far from complete (Fig. 65.3). Alterations in any single variable, especially DM, could drastically reduce the end-capillary PO_2.

With long-term or lifelong residence at high altitude, diffusing capacity of the lung increases. Whether this increase in diffusing capacity results from an increased DM and/or capillary blood volume is not clear. Attempts to document either an increased alveolar surface area or increased capillary blood volume have not been successful. The ($A - a$)PO_2 was found to be lower or the diffusing capacity was found to be higher in high-altitude residents in a number of other studies.[44-47] Dempsey and associates[44] and Schoene and coworkers[47] have obtained data on sojourners and high-landers at rest and during exercise that provide a convincing argument for more efficient oxygen transfer across the lung in long-term dwellers at high altitude. In spite of a modestly lower level of minute ventilation during exercise in high-altitude natives than in sojourners at high altitude, the high-altitude inhabitants exhibited a higher arterial PO_2 both at rest and during exercise, suggesting a more efficient oxygen transfer from alveolus to blood.

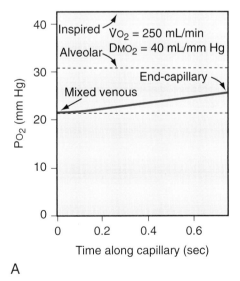

A

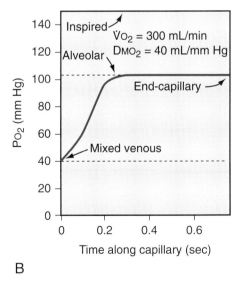

B

Figure 65.3 Comparison of the calculated time course of oxygen tension (PO_2) in the pulmonary capillary of a climber at rest on the summit of Mt. Everest (**A;** barometric pressure = 250 m, inspired PO_2 = 43 mm Hg) to sea-level values (**B;** barometric pressure = 760 mm Hg, inspired PO_2 = 150 mm Hg). At sea level, there is adequate time for equilibration of alveolar and end-capillary oxygen, whereas at extreme altitude, even at rest, when transit time for the red blood cell is presumably similar to that at sea level, full equilibration is not realized, resulting in end-capillary blood that is not fully saturated. $\dot{V}O_2$, oxygen consumption; DMO_2, diffusion capacity of the alveolar capillary membrane. (From West JB, Wagner PD: Predicted gas exchange on the summit of Mt. Everest. Respir Physiol 42:1–16, 1980.)

CARDIOVASCULAR ADAPTATION

The cardiovascular adaptations to high altitude are numerous and involve changes in cardiac output, the pulmonary and systemic vasculatures, and the microcirculation and have been summarized by Wolfel and Levine.[48]

Cardiac Response

In response to acute hypoxia, an increased cardiac output helps sustain oxygen delivery in spite of the decreased arterial oxygen content. The increase in cardiac output is a result of an increased heart rate with little change in stroke volume. The initial increase in cardiac output during hypoxia is mediated by an increase in release of and sensitivity to catecholamines that overrides the augmented parasympathetic tone. Over a few days at high altitude, cardiac output decreases, primarily as a result of a decrease in stroke volume, thought to be secondary to a diminished preload from a shrinkage in plasma volume. An increase in sympathetic tone overrides the vasodilatory effects of epinephrine[49] and endothelium-derived adenosine.[50]

Peak exercise heart rates decrease from sea-level values. Norepinephrine levels rise, but down-regulation of β-receptors in the myocardium contributes to the lower exercise heart rate.[51] Autonomic function, especially parasympathetic tone, plays a role in the decreased heart rate, but the lower heart rate is not a limiting factor in oxygen delivery.[52] In Tibetan high-altitude natives, adolescents retain a more accentuated parasympathetic tone and heart rate variability even after 3 years at low altitude.[53] In sojourners, as acclimatization proceeds further, hemoglobin concentration and blood volume increase and oxygen transport is improved by an increase in stroke volume and arterial oxygen content. Steady-state exercise after acclimatization does not decrease as blood flow to the muscle decreases and vascular resistance increases.[54] After prolonged exposure to high altitude, stroke volume, cardiac output, and muscle blood flow are reduced at any given exercise level, whereas systemic vascular resistance is increased.[55]

Wolfel and colleagues[54] used β-adrenergic blockade in subjects acclimatized to 4300 m over 21 days and found that oxygen delivery was decreased secondary to slower heart rates that was not compensated for by an increase in stroke volume. Total body oxygen consumption was maintained by increased oxygen extraction across the tissue beds, as reflected in mixed venous PO_2 values that were as low as documented in studies at simulated 8000 m. This study demonstrates the impressive compensatory mechanisms the body can employ to maintain energy output.

Hemodynamic changes seen in sojourners at high altitude are not found in healthy people living at high altitude. In fact, a lower systemic blood pressure is generally found in the high-altitude natives in South America, which may be acquired in as little as a year after moving to high altitude. This lower systemic pressure is thought in this population to be secondary to a primary vasodilatory effect of hypoxia on the musculature of the systemic arterial wall.

Hemodynamic Response

On ascent to high altitude, hypoxic pulmonary vasoconstriction causes pulmonary hypertension.[40] On acute

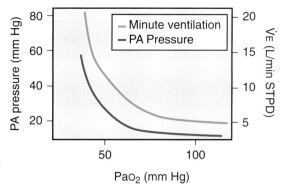

Figure 65.4 Relationship of arterial oxygen tension (PaO_2) to minute ventilation ($\dot{V}E$) and pulmonary arterial (PA) pressure. Although there is variability among individuals, both the ventilatory and the pulmonary vascular response do not increase until PaO_2 falls below 70 mm Hg. (From Reeves JT, Wagner WW Jr, McMurtry F, et al: Physiological effects of high altitude on the pulmonary circulation. *In* Robertshaw D [ed]: International Review of Physiology: Environmental Physiology III. Baltimore: University Park Press, 1979, pp 289–310.)

exposure to hypoxia, pulmonary artery pressure increases little until the alveolar PO_2 drops below 70 mm Hg, then increases markedly (Fig. 65.4). Chronic exposure to high altitude results in an even greater increase in pulmonary vascular resistance and pulmonary hypertension, which in some individuals can be severe, secondary both to pulmonary vasoconstriction and the increase in pulmonary vascular resistance from the extreme polycythemia.

There is both individual and interspecies variation of the hypoxic pulmonary vascular response. For instance, some cattle suffer severe pulmonary hypertension, whereas the Tibetan yak, an animal that has adapted well to high altitude, has no evidence of muscular hypertrophy of the pulmonary arterioles or right ventricular hypertrophy.[56] Months at high altitude (about 3000 m) are required for lowlanders to develop pulmonary hypertension comparable to that of highlanders. Once this level of pulmonary hypertension is reached, these lowlanders exhibit a more reactive hypoxic pulmonary vascular response than do the high-altitude natives. As counterpoint, a study by Groves and coworkers[57] reported normal, sea-level values for pulmonary artery pressure in a small sample of native Tibetan highlanders. In spite of the resting values of pulmonary artery pressures, high-altitude dwellers in both Bolivia and Tibet show high levels of pulmonary capillary nitric oxide (NO), a potent pulmonary vasodilator.[58] These authors speculated that this response may limit the degree to which nature will allow pressures to rise.

Anatomically, pulmonary arterioles are thought to be the site of the constriction that precedes smooth muscle hypertrophy and persistent pulmonary hypertension. Heath and colleagues[59] confirmed these findings in autopsies of humans born and raised at 3800 m and found distal extension of vascular smooth muscle into pulmonary arterioles as small as 20 μm in diameter. Depending on the severity of changes, particularly intimal fibrosis, the pulmonary hypertension may or may not be reversible, but a return to normal pressures requires months or years at low altitude. In contrast, a study of autopsies on high-altitude natives of the Himalaya Mountains showed no hypertrophy of pulmonary arteriolar smooth muscle.[60] This finding, along with that of Groves and coworkers,[57] suggests that Himalayan natives, who have lived longer at high altitude than have the Andeans, have undergone a different pattern of microvascular adaptation in the lung. Thus, there appear to be important ethnic differences in the pulmonary vascular response to sustained hypoxia.

HEMATOLOGIC ADAPTATION

With sustained hypoxia, blood undergoes changes that improve oxygen transport to tissues. The two basic adaptations are (1) an increased oxygen-carrying capacity from an increase in the number of erythrocytes and (2) an altered affinity of hemoglobin for the oxygen molecule. There is also a decrease in plasma volume over time that is secondary to a water diuresis. Recent reviews are available.[61]

Erythropoietic Response

Hemoglobin concentration increases within 1 or 2 days of ascent and continues to rise for a number of weeks. The initial rise is due to hemoconcentration resulting from the diuresis that occurs on initial ascent. The continued increase results from increased red blood cell production; this adaptation helps sustain oxygen delivery in the presence of a decreased arterial SO_2.

Erythropoietin stimulates red blood cell production; hypoxia per se is the primary stimulus for erythropoietin release. Serum erythropoietin levels increase rapidly within 24 to 48 hours of ascent to high altitude, and then start to decline within 3 weeks as acclimatization progresses.[62] Both red blood cell volume and total blood volume increase, along with a decrease in plasma volume, and these changes increase oxygen content and presumably oxygen delivery at high altitude. The erythropoietic response quickly ceases on descent. A return to sea-level hemoglobin values occurs in approximately 3 weeks.

Although hematocrit values generally increase with altitude, a marked variability in erythropoiesis exists between individuals, both sojourners[63] and highlanders,[64] and between different highland populations. The difference in erythropoiesis between Andean and Himalayan natives is noteworthy, with Andean natives · having substantially higher values. Recent data from Jefferson and colleagues[65] described extraordinary degrees of polycythemia in high-altitude natives of Cerro de Pasco, Peru, at over 4300 m. The group with the highest hematocrits (>75%) had high erythropoietin concentrations as well as high serum cobalt levels. Cobalt is known to be an erythropoietic stimulant and may be a contaminant from the mining industry. Whether the excessive erythropoiesis in Andean high-altitude dwellers is secondary to an up-regulation of the erythropoietic response or to the renal sensing of hypoxia is not clear. Hochachka and Rupert[66] found no abnormalities in the genes encoding for the erythropoietic response and suggested that the renal sensing of hypoxia is the genesis of the extraordinary polycythemia.

Whereas the increase in hemoglobin concentration augments arterial oxygen content, a number of changes detrimental to oxygen delivery may also occur. At sea level, a small increase in hemoglobin concentration (1.2 g/dL) improves aerobic performance in trained, elite runners. As hematocrit approaches 60%, viscosity increases and first cardiac output and then oxygen delivery may actually decrease. This decrease in oxygen delivery is thought to be due to an impairment of perfusion of the microcirculation in the exercising muscles as a consequence of increased blood viscosity.

Excessive polycythemia may be deleterious, and phlebotomy may, therefore, be beneficial. In a study on Mt. Everest, four climbers with hematocrits of 60% or greater underwent both psychometric and exercise testing before and after isovolumic hemodilution to produce hematocrits lowered to about 50%.[67] Psychometric test performance improved, whereas maximum exercise performance did not change. These results imply that cerebral oxygen delivery may have been improved, whereas delivery to exercising muscles was unchanged. The optimal hematocrit remains elusive, but, clearly, high-altitude survival and performance are impaired by an excessive polycythemic response (see Maladaptation later).

Oxygen-Hemoglobin Affinity

The transport of oxygen by blood is also influenced by the ease with which it is taken up by hemoglobin in the pulmonary capillaries and released from hemoglobin in tissue capillaries. A number of variables affect the process, one of which is the affinity of hemoglobin for oxygen, as defined by the shape and position of the oxygen-hemoglobin dissociation curve. An important feature of the oxygen-hemoglobin relationship is that, over a large range of physiologic oxygen partial pressure values (arterial PO_2 of 60 to 100 mm Hg), hemoglobin is more than 90% saturated with oxygen. Thus, a change in arterial PO_2 within that range has only a modest effect on arterial oxygen content. At arterial PO_2 values less than 60 mm Hg, oxygen content of hemoglobin drops precipitously with only small decreases in PO_2. At high altitude, certain adaptations of oxygen-hemoglobin affinity occur that may help facilitate oxygen transfer.

The concentrations of three substances in blood—hydrogen ion, carbon dioxide, and 2,3-diphosphoglycerate (2,3-DPG)—influence the position of the oxygen-hemoglobin dissociation curve: Increases in one or more of these cause a right shift, allowing unloading of oxygen from hemoglobin to the tissues at a higher mean capillary PO_2. Although a rightward shift of the oxygen-hemoglobin dissociation curve was initially thought to be advantageous at high altitude, not all studies support these results. More precise measurements of the curve have allowed better documentation of human hemoglobin physiology at altitude. Investigators found that humans at altitude in South America have a modestly left-shifted curve. Part of the difficulty in the interpretation of these data resides in the finding of increased 2,3-DPG levels in high-altitude natives. Winslow and colleagues[68] in Peru and Samaja and coworkers[69] in Nepal found increased 2,3-DPG concentrations, which should result in a right shift, but they also found that persistent respiratory alkalosis more than counterbalanced the 2,3-DPG effect, shifting the curve back to normal or slightly to the left.

At very high altitude, a rightward shift of the oxygen-hemoglobin dissociation curve could be a disadvantage to oxygen transport: The benefit to unloading oxygen from hemoglobin with decreased oxygen affinity at the tissues may be offset by a decrease in loading of oxygen at the lung. A left-shifted curve at extreme altitude would theoretically result in enhanced oxygen loading in the lungs and a higher arterial oxygen content. Marked respiratory alkalosis and hemoglobin with a high affinity for oxygen both yield a leftward shift of the oxygen-hemoglobin dissociation curve and are two characteristics found in migrating birds, especially bar-headed geese, which can withstand relatively acute exposure to extreme altitude (>8000 m) while in full flight.[70]

Winslow and associates[71] observed that, after 2 months at 6300 m, the polycythemic response (mean hematocrit = 54.4 ± 4.0%) in climbers was less than had been anticipated. Although the level of 2,3-DPG increased, the persistent, uncompensated respiratory alkalosis resulted in a much lower P_{50} (PO_2 at which 50% of the binding sites on hemoglobin are saturated) (Fig. 65.5). As discussed earlier, this leftward shift may convey an important advantage to climbers to extreme altitude.

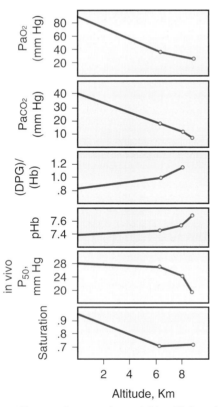

Figure 65.5 Effectors of oxygen-hemoglobin affinity. The net result at extreme altitude is a protected arterial oxygen saturation. DPG, diphosphoglycerate; P_{50}, PO_2 at which 50% of the binding sites on hemoglobin are saturated; PaO_2, arterial oxygen tension; $PaCO_2$, arterial carbon dioxide tension; pHb, blood pH. For explanation, see text. (From Winslow RM, Samaja M, West JB: Red cell function at extreme altitude on Mount Everest. J Appl Physiol 56:109–116, 1984.)

TISSUE ADAPTATION

The final stages in the journey of oxygen molecules from ambient air to the mitochondria involve the transfer of oxygen from blood to tissues. Within this critical portion of the oxygen cascade are several steps in the movement of oxygen from within the capillary blood, across the vascular endothelium, through the cytoplasm to the mitochondria, where oxidative phosphorylation occurs. This process depends largely on diffusion and distance. A driving pressure of only 1 to 2 mm Hg is necessary to cause oxygen to diffuse from the cytoplasm to the mitochondria, whereas as much as 10 mm Hg may be needed for sufficient flux from the capillary plasma to the cytoplasm. A PO_2 in the capillary blood exists below which the final steps of the oxygen cascade may become impaired.

Certain adaptive changes take place to optimize oxygen transfer from blood to tissue during extreme hypoxia: (1) anatomic changes that minimize the distance for radial diffusion of oxygen from the blood vessel to the mitochondria and (2) biochemical changes that improve the metabolic readiness in the mitochondria. The process of tissue adaptation has been recently reviewed.[72]

Morphologic Adaptation

A decrease in diffusion distance can be achieved by increasing the concentration of blood vessels in the tissues or increasing the surface area for gas exchange by increasing capillary tortuosity around the muscle cell.[73,74] Krogh[75] calculated the decreasing maximum distances over which oxygen could diffuse at increasing altitudes to sustain oxidative metabolism. Banchero[76] documented an increase in capillary density and a decrease in the skeletal muscle cell size in dogs after a 3-week exposure to simulated altitude (barometric pressure = 435 mm Hg). Both alterations presumably decrease diffusion distance of oxygen to the mitochondria. However, these findings have been challenged.[77]

The mechanism of angiogenesis results from increased messenger RNA levels of HIF-1 and subsequent induction of vascular endothelial growth factor (VEGF), which has been found in animal models during hypoxia[78] but not in humans.[79] VEGF messenger RNA decreases after chronic exposure to high-altitude training in animals while capillary density appears to have increased.[80] Some level of exercise is necessary to induce angiogenesis with or without hypoxia, and it appears that hypoxia without exercise is not adequate to stimulate capillarization. In fact, chronic hypoxia alone may suppress angiogenesis.

Another confounding factor is that, during sojourns at altitudes above 5000 m, a decrease in muscle cell size[81] results in a decreased distance for oxygen to diffuse to the mitochondria; it is not clear whether this shrinkage is secondary to decreased physical activity or to a breakdown of muscle protein for fuel induced by severe hypoxia. The functional outcome may be a decrease in muscle strength and aerobic capacity, which may not be totally recoupable when the hypoxic exposure is terminated.

The mitochondria are the subcellular structures in which oxidative metabolism takes place. Oxygen consumption depends on mitochondrial numbers and function. The results of morphologic observations vary. Ou and Tenney[82] compared two groups of cattle, one raised at high altitude (4250 m) and the other at sea level, and found mitochondrial density in myocardial cells to be increased by 40% in the high-altitude animals. Using different species and techniques for quantifying mitochondria, other investigators have not noted increases. Human studies in the chamber study Operation Everest II[81] described a decrease in mitochondrial volume; at lower altitudes, a decrease has not been observed.[77]

Biochemical Alterations

Diffusion of oxygen from the blood to the mitochondria of muscle is facilitated by myoglobin, an intracellular protein that binds with oxygen at a very low tissue PO_2. This molecule may therefore facilitate diffusion of oxygen to muscle mitochondria. Myoglobin concentration correlates quantitatively with the aerobic capacity of the muscle cell, and is increased with training and is elevated in animals native to and exposed to high altitude. The role of myoglobin in intracellular oxygen flux was thrown into doubt by the observation that mice genetically engineered to have no myoglobin still had normal oxygen consumption at various levels of energy expenditure.[83]

Investigations of oxidative enzyme alterations during hypoxia have also yielded varied results, depending on the species, the tissue, and the stress.[84] The data in humans, particularly at very high altitudes, suggest that the glycolytic capacity, which is responsible for high levels of oxygen consumption, is decreased, whereas fatty acid metabolism, which contributes to endurance exercise, is conserved.

CENTRAL NERVOUS SYSTEM RESPONSE

The organ most crucially affected by a decrease in oxygenation is the brain.[85] A number of mechanisms exist that optimize oxygen delivery to the brain in spite of profound degrees of hypoxemia, but even these have limits.

Cerebral Blood Flow

On initial exposure to high altitude, the hypoxia-induced increase in cerebral blood flow is in part offset by hypocapnic cerebral vasoconstriction[86]; the net result is a modest increase in cerebral blood flow. Severinghaus and colleagues[87] found that cerebral blood flow in humans increased 33% after 12 hours at 3800 m in spite of a fall in arterial PCO_2 from 40 to 35 mm Hg. After 4 to 5 days, cerebral blood flow decreased but was still 13% greater than the sea level value. Thus, oxygen delivery is ensured initially by an increase in cerebral blood flow when arterial oxygen content is lowest, and then as ventilation and blood oxygen increase and other cellular mechanisms of acclimatization ensue, cerebral blood flow drops toward low-altitude ranges with the priority of oxygen delivery superseding the hypocapnic cerebral vasoconstriction.

Cerebral Function

The flight of the hot-air balloon Zenith in 1875, during which two of the three scientists died after ascending to above 8000 m, is a grim reminder of the potentially catastrophic effect of acute, severe hypoxia. Many other anecdotal accounts of impaired mental function after rapid ascent to high altitude can be cited. As one ascends, motor, sensory, and complex cognitive abilities are progressively impaired. New tasks are learned with difficulty at 3048 m, and simulated altitudes of 6100 m result in a decrement in sensory, perceptual, and motor performance. Even acute, modest decreases in arterial SO_2 to 85% impair mental concentration and fine motor coordination; a further decrease to 75% results in poor judgment, irritability, and decreased muscle function.

Several studies have addressed the question of whether the psychometric, behavioral, or cognitive dysfunction occurs and, if so, persists after return to low altitude. Clark and colleagues[88] did not find residual abnormalities in climbers who had been above 5100 m on Himalayan expeditions. However, subjects who had been at high altitude for 10 months had dysfunction of both motor coordination and speed that resolved over 1 and 2 years, respectively.[89] Symptoms compatible with organic brain syndrome were present in half of the climbers, whereas 11 of the 30 had abnormal electroencephalograms on descent. Psychological tests were mildly to severely abnormal in all of them. Impairment of short-term memory and concentration was documented by Regard and associates[90] in climbers ascending without supplemental oxygen to 8500 m or higher.

From measurements made on climbers before and after an expedition to Mt. Everest and in subjects of Operation Everest II, Hornbein and coworkers[91] found transient deterioration in learning, memory, and expression of verbal material after descent, which returned to baseline 1 year later; however, a symmetrical reduction in motor speed, quantified by a finger-tapping test, remained abnormal 1 year later. Of particular interest was that, contrary to expectations, individuals with high HVRs and consequently higher arterial SO_2 and who performed better physically had more pronounced neuropsychometric dysfunction. One explanation for these findings is that those with a more brisk HVR might have greater hypocapnic cerebral vasoconstriction and, consequently, a lower cerebral oxygen delivery. The bulk of evidence suggests that exposure to very high altitude results not only in acute but also in some residual alterations in neuropsychological function in certain individuals, as well as possible cortical atrophy after extreme altitude exposure.

Respiration and Sleep at High Altitude

Regulation of breathing during sleep is reviewed in Chapter 74. Periodic breathing is common in sojourners to high altitude. At moderate altitudes, this periodic breathing diminishes over several days as ventilatory acclimatization proceeds. Variability in incidence is thought to be due to differences in individual hypoxic and hypercapnic chemosensitivity.

Respiration during sleep at high altitude has been recently reviewed.[92,93] The consensus is that sleep eliminates most cortical influence on respiration, leaving hypoxemia via carotid chemoreceptors as a more prominent drive. The effect of hypoxically induced changes in PCO_2 on hypoxic drive may set up oscillations of ventilation in a poorly damped system (Fig. 65.6).

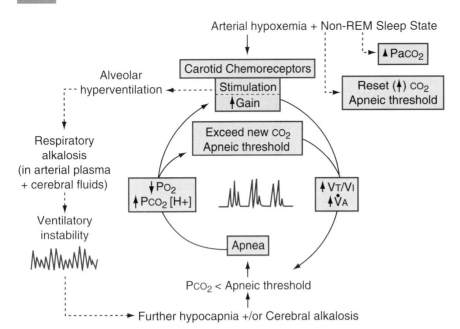

Figure 65.6 Schema of possible mechanism for pathogenesis of hypoxia-induced periodic breathing during non–rapid eye movement (non-REM) sleep. Increased peripheral chemoreceptor activity lowers P_{CO_2} and $[H^+]$ in arterial plasma and cerebral fluids to near apnea threshold. Subsequent ventilatory oscillations occur with the inherent instability arising from phase delays of the chemical stimuli to the respiratory centers. (From Berssenbrugge A, Dempsey J, Skatrud J: Hypoxic versus hypocapnic effects on periodic breathing during sleep. *In* West JB, Lahiri S [eds]: High Altitude and Man. Bethesda, Md: American Physiological Society, 1984, pp 115–128.)

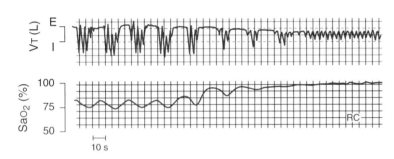

Figure 65.7 Periodic breathing in lowlander at 5400 m during sleep while breathing ambient air (*left half of tracings*) and oxygen (*right half of tracings*). Upper panel is tidal volume (V_T, inspiration downward), and lower panel is arterial oxygen saturation (Sa_{O_2}, %). (From Lahiri S, Maret K, Sherpa MG: Dependence of high-altitude sleep apnea on ventilatory sensitivity to hypoxia. Respir Physiol 52:281–301, 1983.)

Lahiri and associates,[94] studying both sojourners and high-altitude natives at 5400 m, observed a correlation between hypoxic chemosensitivity and presence of periodic breathing (Fig. 65.7). High-altitude natives, who have lower HVRs, had virtually no periodic breathing. Sojourners' periodic breathing was ablated by administration of oxygen. These findings suggested that those individuals with higher HVRs had greater instability of the peripheral-central oxygen–carbon dioxide interaction, resulting in more pronounced periodicity. On this same expedition, the climbers who were studied at 6300 m continued to have periodic breathing 6 weeks later, suggesting that the extreme hypoxia at this altitude causes continued instability of the control of ventilation that was not diminished by acclimatization.[95] At moderate altitude, periodic breathing tends to diminish with acclimatization.

Although the mechanism of periodic breathing during sleep at high altitude is not fully understood, it is clear that the most severe hypoxemia experienced by both sojourners and natives occurs during sleep. Marked drops in S_{O_2} during periodic breathing have been noted primarily in sojourners and have been corrected in part by respiratory stimulants such as acetazolamide,[96,97] medroxyprogesterone acetate,[97] and almitrine,[98] each of which may be acting by a different mechanism. The continual wake-sleep cycle may contribute to loss of sleep and inordinate fatigue. Anecdotal evidence suggests that some patients with obstructive sleep apnea may have obliteration of the apnea, presumably secondary to the respiratory stimulation of hypoxia.

FLUID HOMEOSTASIS

High altitude may induce a dysfunction of osmoregulation, with a difference in fluid homeostasis between healthy persons who ascend to high altitude and those who get altitude illness. The normal response is a diuresis that persists during the stay at high altitude. In the healthy individual, there does not appear to be an alteration in antidiuretic hormone or aldosterone in resting subjects. Exercise over a number of days, on the other hand, activates the renin-angiotensin system. Fluid shifts result in an increase in interstitial and plasma volume and a decrease in intracellular volume. In humans, the overall diuresis may be promoted by a rise in atrial natriuretic peptide. The potential role of fluid balance in the etiology of acute altitude illness is discussed later.

EXERCISE

Maximal Work

Both acute and prolonged exposures to hypoxia result in a decrease in maximal oxygen consumption ($\dot{V}_{O_2}max$) and work performance.[41,99–102] Exercise capacity undergoes a progressive decline with increasing altitude, such that $\dot{V}O_2max$ decreases about 10% per 1000 m of altitude gain. At approximately 0.5 atm, $\dot{V}O_2max$ is about half of its sea level value, and at 0.33 atm (as at the summit of Mt. Everest), $\dot{V}O_2max$ is about 23% of that at sea level (Fig. 65.8). A number of factors contribute to this decline in exercise capacity as a function of increasing hypoxia.

Ventilation

The usual ventilatory response to exercise is further stimulated by hypoxia. This response is proportional to altitude.[99,103] For instance, the amount of ventilation for a given metabolic rate (the ventilatory equivalent, $\dot{V}E/\dot{V}O_2$) in sojourners to 6300 m is almost four times as great as at

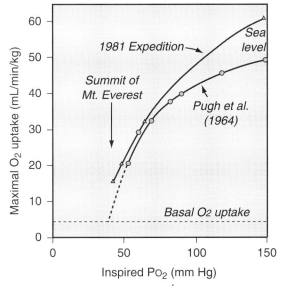

Figure 65.8 Maximal oxygen uptake ($\dot{V}O_2max$) versus inspired PO_2. There is a predictable decrease in $\dot{V}O_2max$ at higher altitudes. The more recent data demonstrate that a small amount of work is possible on the summit of Mt. Everest. (From West JB, Boyer SJ, Graber DJ, et al: Maximal exercise at extreme altitudes on Mount Everest. J Appl Physiol 55:688–702, 1983.)

sea level (Fig. 65.9). The costs of these extraordinary levels of breathing are both metabolic and subjective. The oxygen cost of exercise hyperpnea at extreme altitude may be as high as 40% of the overall metabolic rate at high levels of exercise; the aversion to extreme dyspnea may limit both intensity and duration of exercise and result in allocation of a proportion of cardiac output to the muscles of respiration that otherwise could be dedicated to the muscles of locomotion.

The degree of hyperpnea at moderate levels of exercise is determined both by the magnitude of the hypoxic stimulus and by the individual's hypoxic ventilatory response. In a group of climbers on Mt. Everest, Schoene and associates[103] found that exercise hyperpnea at sea level and at 6300 m correlated with values for HVR obtained at rest at both sea level and after adaptation to 5400 m. These data also demonstrated that those with higher HVRs had less arterial oxygen desaturation during exercise and were able to climb higher. Additional studies also indicate that most successful climbers to extreme altitude exhibit higher values for HVR at sea level than normal subjects.[104,105]

On the other hand, chronic or lifelong exposure to high altitude results in a lower ventilatory response to exercise.[47,106] Dempsey and associates[44] studied sojourners and high-altitude inhabitants in Colorado and found relative hypoventilation (increased PCO_2, decreased minute ventilation) during work by the residents. Even so, arterial oxygen saturation was preserved in the high-altitude resident by virtue of a lower $(A-a)PO_2$ that did not increase significantly from rest to exercise. Similar results were described in the Quechua Indians of northern Chile.[47] These findings suggest improved gas exchange in the high-altitude resident, reflected by an increased diffusing capacity at rest and during exercise. This increased diffusing capacity likely results from an increased surface area for gas exchange, diminishing the $(A-a)PO_2$ and enabling a decreased ventilatory work requirement.

Gas Exchange

In contrast to exercise in most healthy people at sea level, exercise at extreme altitude results in a decrease in maximal

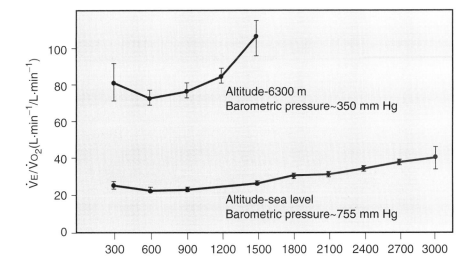

Figure 65.9 The ventilatory equivalent ($\dot{V}E/\dot{V}O_2$) for given workloads in a group of climbers at sea level *(lower line)* and at 6300 m *(upper line)*. The data demonstrate that the stimulation for ventilation from hypoxia results in a $\dot{V}E/\dot{V}O_2$ that is nearly four times greater than that at sea level. (From Schoene RB: Hypoxic ventilatory response and exercise ventilation at sea level and high altitude. *In* West JB, Lahiri S [eds]: High Altitude and Man. Bethesda, Md: American Physiological Society, 1984, pp 19–30.)

ventilation and heart rate (Fig. 65.10).[99,100] Arterial oxygen saturation decreases both acutely[41] (Fig. 65.11) and after prolonged stay at high altitude.[99] A review of gas exchange at high altitude is available.[39]

Although $(A - a)PO_2$ increases during hypoxic exercise in sojourners at high altitude,[42,100] this increase does not appear to occur in high-altitude natives.[44,47] Using the multiple inert gas elimination technique, Torre-Bueno and coworkers[107] noted a substantial role for diffusion limitation

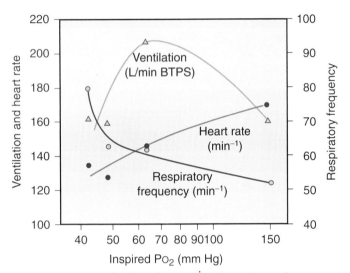

Figure 65.10 Maximal ventilation ($\dot{V}E_{max}$), respiratory frequency, and heart rate versus inspired PO_2. At 6300 m, $\dot{V}E_{max}$ is increased because of the stimulation to ventilation from hypoxia as well as a decreased density of the inspired air, whereas at over 8000 m, $\dot{V}E_{max}$ is decreased, probably as a result of a diminished metabolic demand from low work rates. Frequency continues to increase. Maximum heart rate decreases with increasing altitude. (From West JB, Boyer SJ, Graber DJ, et al: Maximal exercise at extreme altitudes on Mount Everest. J Appl Physiol 55:688–702, 1983.)

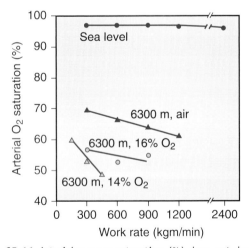

Figure 65.11 Arterial oxygen saturation (%) does not decrease with exercise at sea level but drops progressively with higher workloads at greater altitudes. There is a diffusion limitation of oxygen transfer across the alveolar-hemoglobin interface. (From West JB, Boyer SJ, Graber DJ, et al: Maximal exercise at extreme altitudes on Mount Everest. J Appl Physiol 55:688–702, 1983.)

as a factor in the widened $(A - a)PO_2$ during exercise at simulated 3030 and 4550 m altitude. Gale and associates[41] also found an increasing contribution of $\dot{V}A/\dot{Q}$ mismatch at these same altitudes and exercise levels, which they believed to be secondary to a nonuniform hypoxic pulmonary vascular response, and which may possibly lead to some interstitial pulmonary edema and thus some $\dot{V}A/\dot{Q}$ heterogeneity and impairment of gas exchange.

These studies, therefore, quantified the contribution of a number of factors to arterial oxygen desaturation during exercise at high altitude. Increasing diffusion limitation is probably secondary to a number of factors, primarily a decreased driving pressure for oxygen from the air to the blood due to alveolar hypoxia, coupled with a decreased transit time for blood across the pulmonary capillary due to an increased cardiac output with exercise (see Fig. 65.4).

Cardiovascular Response

With acute exposure to hypoxia, cardiac output and heart rate increase above sea-level values at equivalent submaximal workloads. With prolonged exposure, cardiac output at submaximal workloads is comparable to sea-level values. However, maximum cardiac output is decreased. Maximal heart rate and stroke volume are decreased with prolonged exposure.[108] The reason for the decrease in maximum heart rate is not understood, but heart rate and cardiac output remain appropriate to the oxygen consumption even up to altitudes of 8000 m. Additionally, during Operation Everest II, echocardiographic studies demonstrated that cardiac contractility was preserved.[108] The decrease in maximum heart rate during exercise is more pronounced in sojourners than it is in high-altitude dwellers. This lower maximum heart rate in sojourners may be secondary to increased vagal tone, but more likely it represents the normal response for a given metabolic demand, which is limited by other factors at high altitude. Maximal cardiac output is decreased at high altitude, probably secondary both to a maximal heart rate that is lower than at sea level and to the decrease in stroke volume.[109] There are some data suggesting a down-regulation of β-receptors that are partly responsible for the lower maximum heart rate at high altitude.

Pulmonary artery pressures reach high levels during exercise at high altitudes.[110] These pressures did not return to normal when subjects were given oxygen, which suggests some structural changes in the pulmonary vasculature. With the maintenance of a cardiac output appropriate for the level of work rates, the increase in pulmonary vascular resistance in healthy sojourners to high altitude does not seem to limit exercise.

Using data from Operation Everest II, Roca and colleagues[111] speculated that a diffusion limitation for oxygen from the blood to the muscle might limit its extraction in the peripheral tissues. This hypothesis was tested in an isolated muscle preparation exercised by electrical stimulation by Hogan and associates.[112] Blood flow was held constant, and oxygen delivery was varied at several levels of hypoxia. $\dot{V}O_2max$ was related to effluent PO_2, oxygen delivery, and calculated capillary PO_2, which supports the contention that aerobic function at high altitude may be limited at least in part by limitation of driving pressure or diffusion of oxygen from the blood to the peripheral tissues. However, the delivery of oxygen from the blood to the mitochondria is a complex interaction of blood flow in the capillary network, the content of oxygen on the hemoglobin, the P_{50} of the blood, and the cell membrane/cytosol/mitochondrial interphase. Hypoxia results in an increase of blood flow, which appears to compensate for the decreased oxygen content.

The importance of the distribution of flow in the capillary network cannot be overlooked. Both athletic training and hypoxic stress result in similar proliferation of capillaries, which would optimize delivery of oxygen.[113,114] The increased angiogenesis may be secondary to an increase in VEGF.

The diffusion of oxygen from the blood to the tissue is the final hurdle in the oxygen transport chain. Wagner[115] has discussed the theoretical reasons why extraction might be limited during hypoxic exercise. Using mixed venous blood as a reflection of the limits of extraction can be misleading because there are obviously tissue beds that are metabolically much more active during exercise and thus must have a lower oxygen content in the effluent blood than would be reflected in mixed venous blood. Hogan and coworkers[116] exercised canine gastrocnemius muscle under different levels of hypoxia and found the effluent PO_2 to be as low as 11 mm Hg; by keeping flow constant, they found that further extraction was possible. Richardson and colleagues[117] looked at blood flow during maximal human leg exercise with normoxia and hypoxia and found similar blood flow yet a lower work rate during hypoxic conditions. They concluded that there was diffusion limitation during hypoxia. Using nuclear magnetic resonance spectroscopy during leg extension exercise in humans to determine myoglobin saturation as a reflection of tissue oxygenation, they also found that during hypoxia myoglobin saturation was about 50% with a PO_2 of about 3 mm Hg.[118] Thus they believed that diffusion of oxygen from the cytosol to the mitochondria encountered less resistance than at the 1- to 5-μm barrier from the red cell sarcolemma.

Tissue Alterations

The decrease in $\dot{V}O_2$max that remains even after prolonged exposure to high altitude may also be a reflection of factors at the tissue level.[72] Several of the animal studies dealing with morphologic and biochemical changes with hypoxia were discussed earlier. Human data are sparse, but Cerretelli and di Prampero[119] studied climbers returning from 2 months at extremely high altitude. After performing muscle biopsies, they found (1) an unchanged ratio of capillaries to muscle fiber; (2) a 10% to 15% decrease in muscle mass, which was secondary to a reduction in fiber diameter; (3) a consequent 20% increase in mitochondria-to-fiber volume ratio; and (4) a 45% decrease in succinic dehydrogenase activity. Although the radial diffusion distance for oxygen was less, the overall effect was a decrease in oxidative capacity of the muscle after a prolonged sojourn at high altitude. Similar observations were made during Operation Everest II by Green and associates.[120]

Further metabolic changes occur at the muscle cell level that are not understood. On acute exposure to high altitude, blood lactate levels are higher at any given workload than at sea level.[56,121] This increase in lactate is probably secondary to increased glycogenolysis from the hormonal stresses of tissue hypoxia. However, acclimatization results in increased endurance and a lower level of muscle and blood lactate than is seen at comparable levels of exercise at sea level.[119,120] The mechanism of the "lactate paradox" (lower blood lactate concentrations than expected if the tissue during exercise is oxygen supply limited) is not well understood. It may be a consequence of an inhibition of glycogenolysis during acclimatization, an increased dependence on free fatty acid oxidation for energy, an increased liver and muscle uptake of lactate, or an optimization of the cell-to-cell lactate shuttle.

Exercise Performance at High Altitude

Maximal oxygen consumption decreases about 3.5% for every 300 m altitude above 1500 m. At moderate altitudes, where many athletic competitions take place, the initial decrease in athletic performance on acute exposure can be partly regained after several weeks of habitation. Performance for running events of less than 2 minutes' duration at less than 3000 m altitude is not impaired and may even be slightly improved because of decreased air density. Performances in events of longer duration are predictably diminished and cannot be restored to sea-level capacity with prolonged stay or training at high altitude.

Submaximal exercise may be more pertinent to daily life or prolonged athletic events than is rapid and intense exercise to exhaustion. Improved endurance testing after 2 weeks at 4300 m is associated with lower blood lactate concentrations.

Training at High Altitude

Much controversy existed concerning the benefit of training at high altitude, much of it generated during the 1968 Olympics in Mexico City; subsequently, a number of elite endurance runners have lived and trained at moderate altitude (2000 to 2500 m). More recently the debate has been further fueled by the interest in intermittent hypoxia.[122] Earlier the hope was that the beneficial changes bestowed by this exposure would improve performance at low altitude, but beneficial effects on performance after return to sea level were generally not found. The intensity of training at high altitude necessarily was less, provoking the idea that detraining actually took place in sea-level–trained athletes. Beidleman and coworkers[123] found that intermittent exposure to 4300 m for 3 weeks improved both ergometrics and strength in trained cyclists. They concluded that intermittent hypoxia (4 hr/day, 5 days per week for 3 weeks) is a valid alternative to more prolonged exposures. In their landmark study, Levine and colleagues[124] studied four groups of athletes: (1) those who lived low and trained low (1350 m), (2) those who lived low and trained high (3000 m), (3) those who lived high and trained high, and (4) those who lived high and trained low. Although there were no great differences in the groups, those who lived high and trained low seemed to have gained the benefit of hypoxic conditioning while not losing the intensity of training sessions. This advantage was conveyed presumably by the modestly elevated hemoglobin from the altitude exposure. Of interest was that there was individual variability in the erythropoietic response in that some athletes did not get a rise in hemoglobin and thus got no benefit in performance.[125] This observation is not much different from findings in patients with hypoxic lung disease, who have a spectrum of responses with equivalent degrees of hypoxemia that suggests that the stimulus is more subtle and complex than can be discerned from blood partial pressures of oxygen. In summary, it appears that most of the data support an "adequate" dose of hypoxic exposure, either at altitude or artificially induced, for rest or sleep while continuing to maintain an intensity of training at low altitude. The benefit is presumably conveyed by a modest erythropoietic response and thus oxygen-carrying capacity, but even in this regard there is individual variability in erythropoiesis.

MALADAPTATION

Sudden ascent from sea level to the summit of Mt. Everest (8848 m or 29,028 ft) would lead to unconsciousness within minutes and death soon thereafter. Yet mountain climbing over a period of weeks to this altitude is usually without obvious adverse effects. However, rapid ascent to much lower altitudes (2500 to 4000 m) can also lead to problems in some individuals. These acute disorders of high altitude include acute mountain sickness (AMS), high-altitude pulmonary edema (HAPE), and high-altitude cerebral edema (HACE) (Table 65.2). The incidence and severity of illness depend on several factors, including the speed of ascent and amount of altitude gained, the length of stay, and individual susceptibility[126] (Table 65.3). A trip to and from high altitude on the same day is much less stressful than an overnight stay because hypoxia is accentuated during sleep and because of more prolonged exposure.

PROBLEMS OF LOWLANDERS ON ASCENT TO HIGH ALTITUDE

Susceptibility to altitude illness is highly variable, but for a single individual the symptoms are often reproducible given the same rate of ascent and other circumstances. Men and women are equally susceptible to AMS.[127,128] Younger adults may be slightly more vulnerable to AMS,[127] and preverbal children recently were found to have the same prevalence as adults.[129]

In addition to individual differences in susceptibility, any factors aggravating hypoxemia, such as alcohol or other respiratory depressants, carbon monoxide poisoning, or respiratory infection, may enhance vulnerability to altitude illness. Although essentially no information exists on how prior or coexisting illnesses might contribute to susceptibility to altitude sickness, one may assume that any condition

Table 65.2 Disorders Associated with High Altitude

Disorder		Problems Potentially Aggravated (Partial List)
In the Unacclimatized	*In High-Altitude Residents*	
Acute mountain sickness	Chronic mountain sickness	Hypertension
Cerebral edema	Reentry pulmonary edema	Arteriosclerotic heart disease
Pulmonary edema	Problems of pregnancy	Congestive heart failure
Peripheral edema		Chronic lung disease
Retinopathy		Arteriosclerotic cerebrovascular disease
Thromboembolic problems		Pulmonary hypertension
Sleep periodic breathing		Disorders of pregnancy and childbirth

Table 65.3 Incidence of Altitude Illness in Various Groups

Study Group	Sleeping Altitude	Maximum Altitude Reached (m)	Average Rate of Ascent*	AMS (%)	HAPE and/or HACE	Deaths	Reference
Colorado skiers	2400–3000	3500	1–2	15–40	0.1–0.01	?	127
Mt. Everest trekkers	3000–5200	5500	1–2 (fly in)	47	1.6	1:2,500	127, 268
			10–13 (walk in)	23	0.05		
Mt. McKinley climbers	3000–5000	6195	3–7	50	2–3	1:625	127
Mt. Rainier climbers	3000	4392	1–2	67	0.1	1:10,000	269
Indian soldiers	3000–5000	5500	1–2	1.9	2.3–15.5	?	132

* Days to sleeping altitude from sea level.
? = data not supplied.
AMS, acute mountain sickness; HACE, high-altitude cerebral edema; HAPE, high-altitude pulmonary edema.

that causes hypoventilation, hypoxemia, pulmonary hypertension, increased intracranial pressure, or fluid retention will induce or exacerbate altitude illnesses.

Acute Mountain Sickness

Clinical Presentation. Headache is the most common and prominent symptom of AMS. Typically, the headache, often frontal, occurs within a few hours after ascent to high altitude or is present on awakening the next morning. Associated symptoms and signs in approximate order of frequency are lassitude, insomnia, anorexia, nausea, dizziness, breathlessness, reduced urination, and vomiting, which are accompanied by evidence of fluid retention.[130] The early symptoms of AMS are remarkably similar to those of an alcohol hangover. It is a curious fact that the symptoms of AMS do not usually evince themselves at once. The majority of newcomers have expressed themselves as being quite well on arrival. As a rule, toward the evening the patient begins to feel rather slack and disinclined for exertion. He or she goes to bed, but has a restless and troubled night, and wakes next morning with a severe headache. There may be vomiting, and frequently there is a sense of oppression in the chest, but there is rarely any respiratory distress or alteration in the normal rate of breathing so long as the patient is at rest. The patient may feel slightly giddy on rising from bed, and any attempt at exertion increases the headache.

On examination the face may be slightly cyanosed; the eyes look dull and heavy. The pulse is nearly always high, being generally in the neighborhood of 100 beats/min, but may be as high as 150 beats/min. The temperature is normal,[131] but the patient feels cold and shivery, possibly as a result of hypoxic vasodilation, which may account for heat loss and drop in body temperature. Periodic breathing during sleep is normal at altitude, not indicative of AMS, and is therefore not a diagnostic sign.

The headache increases toward evening, as does the pulse rate; all appetite is lost, and the patient wishes to be left alone—to sleep if possible. Generally, during the second night he or she is able to do so, and as a rule wakes the next morning feeling better. As the day draws on, the patient probably feels worse again, the symptoms all tending to reappear on any exertion; however, if the patient keeps to his or her bed, by the fourth day after arrival he or she is probably very much better and at the end of the week is quite fit again.

Although most studies report tachycardia, Singh and associates[132] found a relative bradycardia (mean heart rate 66 beats/min) in two thirds of soldiers with severe AMS and possible incipient HACE. There are no characteristic changes in blood pressure. Localized crackles can present in 25% to 35% of the cases.[132] Decreased urine output in spite of adequate hydration is an especially helpful sign if present.[127] Differential diagnosis includes dehydration, hypothermia, exhaustion, alcohol hangover, carbon monoxide poisoning, and respiratory or cerebral infectious diseases.

Singh and associates[132] described the natural course of the illness in soldiers who were airlifted to between 3300 and 5500 m. Incapacitating illness in 840 soldiers lasted 2 to 5 days. However, full recovery took much longer: 38%

recovered fully within 3 days, 40% were still ill after 1 week, and 13% had symptoms after 1 month. Three individuals died of pulmonary and cerebral edema. Ski resort tourists sleeping at a more modest altitude of 2700 m exhibited symptoms lasting an average of 15 hours (range: 6 to 94 hours).[133] Most individuals tolerate or treat their own symptoms as the illness resolves over 1 to 3 days while acclimatization occurs, but some persons with AMS seek medical help or are forced to descend. A small percentage of those with AMS (2% to 8%) go on to develop cerebral edema or pulmonary edema, especially if ascent is continued in spite of illness (see Table 65.3). The hallmarks of progression to HACE are truncal ataxia and altered mental status, with or without respiratory distress.

Pathophysiology. Current concepts of pathophysiology emphasize the cerebral etiology of AMS. Elevated intracranial pressure has been demonstrated in severe illness, and cerebral edema has been noted with various imaging techniques[134,135] and with brain biopsy.[132] The edema observed in these advanced cases of AMS appears to be due to passage of fluid from the intravascular to the extravascular space; initially the edema is confined to the white matter.[135] Using magnetic resonance imaging, Hackett and colleagues[135] found swelling in the white matter and none in the gray matter in patients with HACE, which suggested to them that the extravascular leak was of a vasogenic origin. However, whether increased intracranial pressure or brain swelling actually causes the milder symptoms of AMS is not established. There is only one study in subjects with early AMS, and it found no increase in CSF pressure.[136] Despite this, patients with AMS appear to have slightly higher increases in brain volume by magnetic resonance imaging (0.8% vs. 0.4%) than those without symptoms[137] and decreases in intracerebral CSF volume.[137,138] It has been suggested that development of AMS may depend to some extent on the ability to shift CSF out of the cranium, and those individuals with smaller total CSF volumes may be at a disadvantage, such as younger persons versus older persons, in whom age-related increases in volume of the sulci may provide a greater compliance to mitigate mild brain swelling.[136] A very recent study reported no changes in various magnetic resonance imaging–derived indices of cerebral edema in patients with moderate to severe AMS.[138] The classic explanation that the headache and other symptoms of AMS are due to cerebral vasodilation alone seems unlikely,[139,140] because attempts to link AMS symptom severity with middle cerebral artery blood flow velocity have shown no correlation.[141,142]

The progression of AMS to HACE makes attractive the view that AMS symptoms represent the effect of early cerebral edema with increased intracranial pressure. Although elevated intracranial pressure has been demonstrated in severe illness and cerebral edema has been demonstrated with brain imaging techniques,[134,135] a study in patients with early AMS found no increase in CSF pressure.[136] Headache, even severe headache, can be an early symptom of AMS, at a time when edema and significant increases in intracranial pressure are unlikely explanations for its origin. Noting that most headaches are generally thought to be due to stimulation of pain fibers in meninges or larger cerebral vessels, the possibility that at least some of the early symptoms of

AMS are of a different cause than brain swelling, such as migraine-type headache, must be considered.[143] Lastly, given the failure to date of all imaging and quantitation of brain and CSF volumes, brain blood volume, blood flow, and edema to demonstrate sufficient changes in magnitude and consistency with symptoms, another possibility must be considered—that of changes in the blood-brain barrier with hypoxia that alter its permeability to plasma compounds with potential neurotoxicity or irritation, independent of any changes in volumes or pressures in any compartment of the brain. Studies in animals and cell culture have established hypoxic-mediated increased permeability of the blood-brain barrier to large molecules, but no direct measurements have been made in humans. What actually might alter the blood-brain barrier with hypoxia is presently uncertain, but oxygen free radical species, NO production, and possibly VEGF, which all increase in response to hypoxia, have been suggested.[138,144,145] Although Maloney and colleagues[146] found that changes or levels in VEGF did not correlate with AMS or arterial SO_2 percent, a more recent study reported that VEGF levels were higher in subjects with AMS.[146a]

Studies of patients suffering from AMS have consistently found arterial hypoxemia, widened $(A - a)PO_2$ differences that point to some degree of $\dot{V}A/\dot{Q}$ mismatching. Whatever the mechanism, this further component to arterial hypoxemia only adds to the central nervous system stress of high altitude. In fact, Roach and associates[147] found that lower arterial SO_2 measured at 4200 m on Mt. McKinley in asymptomatic climbers was predictive of later development of AMS as the subjects went higher to the summit. The impairment of gas exchange has been attributed to radiologically occult lung edema,[148] causing a small reduction in vital capacity, increases in closing volume, and reductions of diffusing capacity in AMS.[149-151] Increased lung water, consistent with changes in thoracic impedance,[150] may lead to small airway bronchoconstriction or extrinsic compression by increased lymph flow through bronchovascular bundles. Whether the efficiency of normal $\dot{V}A/\dot{Q}$ matching mechanisms is altered is unknown, but animal work suggests a range of enhanced $\dot{V}A/\dot{Q}$ matching with mild inspired hypoxia to impaired $\dot{V}A/\dot{Q}$ matching with more severe hypoxia.[152] At what level of hypoxia this crossover point might occur in any individual is unknown, and it is unlikely to be the same for different individuals, given the heterogeneity in the strength of hypoxic responses such as HVR, hypoxic pulmonary vasoconstriction (HPV), diuresis, and sympathetic activation, which may differ by an order of magnitude in healthy individuals.[153-155]

The findings in severe AMS of possible cerebral edema, peripheral edema, and proteinuria all point to a general defect in salt and water homeostasis, and possibly to increased capillary permeability. Persons susceptible to AMS have elevated aldosterone and antidiuretic hormone levels when compared with controls.[156] In contrast, persons acclimatizing well exhibit diuresis, net water loss, and low antidiuretic hormone values.[156] Although it would seem plausible that a generalized increase in systemic capillary permeability and endothelial cell dysfunction might exist, this was not so in a study that found no differences in the transvascular escape of labeled protein in subjects with and without AMS.[157]

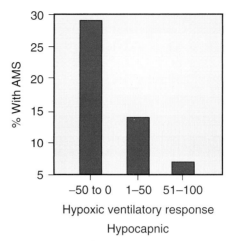

Figure 65.12 Percentage of subjects who developed acute mountain sickness (AMS), grouped into preascent low, medium, and high hypoxic ventilatory responses. Tests were done without holding carbon dioxide constant. Those with lower hypoxic drives had a higher incidence of illness. (From Hackett PH, Reeves JT, Grover RF, Weil JV: Ventilation in human populations native to high altitude. *In* West JB, Lahiri S [eds]: High Altitude and Man. Bethesda, Md: American Physiological Society, 1984, pp 179–191.)

Hypoventilation has long been considered a strong contributor to development of AMS. A brisk increase in ventilation on ascent to altitude is associated with a lower incidence of AMS, and those with AMS tend to have a lower HVR when tested at sea level (Fig. 65.12).[158] If this were the case, then hypoventilation would aggravate the hypoxemia, diminish the alkalosis, and be responsible for the fluid retention and weight gain associated with AMS (Fig. 65.13). However compelling this scenario, others have not found a correlation of sea-level HVR with AMS.[159,160] Yet, Bartsch and colleagues[160] found that, as subjects developed AMS, they did hypoventilate, suggesting a blunting of HVR that developed with illness, not vice versa. To what extent hypoventilation initially may be principally responsible for the greater degree of hypoxemia in subjects with AMS is not entirely certain, because inspired hypoxia and hypoxemia also cause changes in lung function and $\dot{V}A/\dot{Q}$ matching, as discussed previously. That acetazolamide and theophylline, a respiratory stimulant and a diuretic, respectively, are effective agents for prevention and treatment reinforces the importance of ventilation, arterial oxygenation, and diuresis (see Fig. 65.13)[161] in the pathophysiology of AMS.

Prevention. A number of measures are effective in preventing or ameliorating AMS. Gradual ascent, with pauses for acclimatization, is the method of choice. The Himalayan Rescue Association recommends an acclimatization day (2 nights at the same altitude) for every 600-m gain in sleeping altitude above 3000 m. In one study, a diet high in carbohydrates (>80%) improved oxygenation and reduced symptoms of AMS in soldiers taken to 4200 m.[162] The presumed mechanism of benefit is that carbohydrates increase the respiratory quotient, resulting in a higher alveolar PO_2.[163] However, a subsequent study showed no difference in symptom scores or cytokine expression in subjects on a reasonably tolerable high (68%) carbohydrate and nutritionally complete diet.[164]

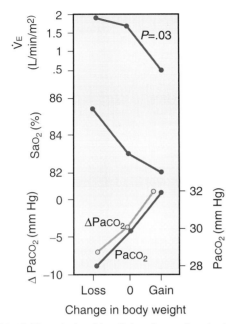

Figure 65.13 The relationship of the change in minute ventilation from low to high altitude ($\Delta\dot{V}_E$), arterial oxygen saturation by ear oximeter (S_{aO_2}%), the change in arterial carbon dioxide tension from low to high altitude (ΔP_{aCO_2}), and arterial carbon dioxide tension (P_{aCO_2}) to change in body weight (>2%) on ascent to altitude in trekkers in Nepal. Weight gain was associated with acute mountain sickness. (From Hackett PH, Rennie D, Hofmeister SE, et al: Fluid retention and relative hypoventilation in acute mountain sickness. Respiration 43:321–329, 1982.)

Acetazolamide is a well-established prophylactic agent[127,165–167] at doses between 250 and 500 mg twice daily. Its principal action is renal carbonic anhydrase inhibition, which causes a bicarbonate diuresis and a metabolic acidosis. These stimulate ventilation, increase alveolar P_{O_2} and arterial oxygen saturation, and enhance tissue capillary oxygen off-loading by an acidosis-mediated right shift of the oxygen-hemoglobin dissociation curve. In effect, the drug speeds the process of natural acclimatization by accelerating the pace of ventilatory adaptation from several days to one. Other actions of acetazolamide and related carbonic anhydrase inhibitors on carbonic anhydrase elsewhere in the body that may contribute to their preventative and therapeutic (see discussion later) action include reduction in CSF formation and slight carbon dioxide retention in the peripheral and central chemoreceptors by inhibition of carbonic anhydrase in the capillary endothelium of these sites.[166] The drug is well tolerated, although paresthesias are common. Nausea and drowsiness occasionally occur, and carbonated beverages taste flat, probably secondary to the inhibition of hydration of carbon dioxide on the palette. Acetazolamide has a sulfonamide (-SO_2NH_2) group and shares the cautions common to all sulfa drugs. A dosage of 125 mg twice daily for the first 2 to 3 days at altitude appears to be adequate for most individuals climbing or trekking.[168] This may represent the lowest possible dose, because it was not effective in sedentary tourists at 3800 m when compared to 250 mg twice daily.[169]

Dexamethasone also provides effective prevention when used in a dosage of 4 mg every 6 to 12 hours, starting at least 6 hours before ascent.[170] Studies comparing dexamethasone and acetazolamide have revealed approximately equal effectiveness of the two drugs in preventing AMS.[171,172] Experts generally consider acetazolamide the drug of choice for prophylaxis because of its greater safety and because it enhances acclimatization; dexamethasone does not speed the acclimatization process and may be associated with reappearance of symptoms when discontinued. Dexamethasone should be available, especially in remote areas where rapid treatment of evolving symptoms may keep the victim ambulatory and thus able to ambulate and help him/herself down. The patient is, therefore, much less of a burden to rescuers.

Pharmacologic prophylaxis should probably be reserved for those who are known to be susceptible to AMS or for those who must ascend to altitude quickly (e.g., rescue or military teams) without the benefit of staged ascent. In other circumstances, it is reasonable to delay use of acetazolamide until the symptoms of AMS first develop, at which time acetazolamide can be taken in the usual dosage until symptoms improve.

Treatment. The key to successful treatment is early diagnosis. Persons with mild illness may resolve their symptoms by resting and staying under observation at the same altitude and may respond well to a descent of as little as 300 m, whereas more severe illness requires further descent.[130] Descent should continue until the individual improves and, in severe cases, should not be delayed to wait for a doctor, a rescue team, or a helicopter. At times, field conditions may be such that descent is impractical or impossible, or the illness may be mild enough not to warrant the inconvenience of descending.

With the use of a portable hyperbaric chamber, "low altitude" can be brought to the patient. Although chambers have been used for decades in fixed locations, a new lightweight nylon chamber (6 kg) is now being taken on expeditions and treks to high-altitude regions. Pressurization to 2 psi (110 mm Hg) is equivalent to a descent of approximately 1500 m. By means of a foot pump, sufficient gas flow is maintained to keep the carbon dioxide concentration low and the oxygen concentration close to 21%.[173] Supplemental oxygen can also be added to the bag. Studies have documented the chamber to be as effective as administering 26% to 30% oxygen; the critical factor for resolution of illness is the P_{O_2}. These devices are particularly useful when oxygen is not readily available. In ski resorts and other areas with medical facilities, persons suffering from AMS or HAPE prefer oxygen breathing to being treated in a chamber. As with oxygen therapy, relief of symptoms is generally immediate, but treatment is necessary for a number of hours for continued clinical improvement after removal from the chamber. The duration of therapy depends on the severity of illness.[173,174]

Only a few medications have been evaluated for treatment of AMS. Singh and colleagues[132] found aspirin helpful for headache and promoting sleep, whereas ammonium chloride and potassium chloride were of no value. Ibuprofen,[175] acetaminophen,[175] and sumatriptan[176] also treat the headache of AMS. Prochlorperazine is useful for treating nausea and vomiting and, unlike some other antiemetics, does not depress ventilation but, rather, may actually increase HVR.[177] Sedative hypnotics, alcohol, opiates, and other ventilatory depressants should be avoided in persons with AMS, although in a recent report, low-dose temazepam (10 mg at bedtime) reduced periodic breathing and improved nocturnal oxygen saturation and perceived sleep quality without causing AMS.[178]

High-Altitude Cerebral Edema

HACE is defined as the presence of a change in mental status or ataxia, or both, in a person with AMS, or the presence of both central nervous system abnormalities in a person without AMS who has recently ascended to altitude.

The initial symptoms of HACE are usually those of severe AMS plus neurologic abnormalities. Headache may be incapacitating, nausea and vomiting persistent, and lassitude debilitating. Ataxic gait, usually present and associated with altered mental status, is a reliable diagnostic sign. Among the protean neurologic signs accompanying the illness are papilledema, visual changes, cranial nerve palsies, bladder dysfunction, abnormal reflexes, paresthesias, pareses, aphasia, clonus, hallucinations, seizures, and behavioral changes, terminating in coma and death.[127,142,179]

The incidence of HACE is difficult to assess because the boundary of progression from AMS may be hard to define and the symptoms and signs may be similar to those of cerebral hypoxia secondary to *severe* hypoxemia from pulmonary edema. At higher altitudes, HACE may affect 5% to 10% of those experiencing AMS and is more common in those with HAPE.[127,132,180] Differential diagnosis includes all other causes of encephalopathy, such as carbon monoxide poisoning, hypertensive crisis, severe cerebral hypoxia secondary to HAPE, cerebral ischemia secondary to thrombosis or hemorrhage, meningitis, and migrainous encephalopathy. Magnetic resonance imaging reveals a pattern of reversible increased T2-weighted signal in the corpus callosum, especially in the splenium, which may help differentiate HACE from other conditions.[135]

Pathology reports revealed gross cerebral edema in seven of eight persons who had died of altitude illness; five also had pulmonary edema.[179,181] Findings included swelling and flattening of the cerebral gyri, compression of the sulci, herniation of cerebellar tonsils and unci, small petechial hemorrhages, and venous and sinus thromboses.

The definitive treatment of HACE is descent. However, recovery is not as rapid as in AMS and HAPE, and a descent in altitude of more than 1000 m may be necessary. Oxygen or hyperbaric therapy may be a lifesaving temporizing measure. In the only study of therapy, severe neurologic symptoms and signs responded to furosemide and betamethasone; the drugs were not studied separately.[132] Dexamethasone is now routinely used in hopes of reducing brain swelling but may be less effective if given after onset of coma. Mannitol and glycerol have been suggested for treatment but are difficult to use safely in the field and should only be used in a hospital or clinic setting.

High-Altitude Pulmonary Edema

HAPE is the most common cause of death from high-altitude illness (see Table 65.3). Although it was probably a problem even when Hannibal's troops crossed the Alps in 217 BC, until recently the condition was misdiagnosed as pneumonia, bronchitis, or congestive heart failure. Not until reports by Hultgren[182] and Houston,[183] and subsequent studies by Hultgren and coworkers,[184] was HAPE shown to be a noncardiogenic form of pulmonary edema. Like other causes of noncardiac pulmonary edema, the exact pathophysiology is under active investigation.

Clinical Presentation. Victims are often young, physically fit men and women who ascend rapidly from sea level and have not had HAPE before in spite of repeated altitude exposures. HAPE occurs within the first 2 to 4 days of ascent to higher altitudes (>2500 m), most commonly on the second night.[185] The earliest indications are decreased exercise performance and slow recovery from exercise. The victim usually notices fatigue, weakness, and dyspnea on exertion, often ascribing these nonspecific symptoms to various other causes. Signs of AMS such as headache, anorexia, and lassitude are frequently present as well. A persistent dry cough develops. Nail beds become cyanotic. The condition typically worsens at night, and tachycardia and tachypnea develop at rest. Dyspnea at rest and audible congestion in the chest finally signal the presence of a serious pulmonary problem. Orthopnea is common. Pink frothy sputum is a late finding. The severe hypoxemia with or without concomitant cerebral edema may produce mental changes, ataxia, and a decreased level of consciousness. Descents of even 600 m can be lifesaving, but recovery is faster with further descent.

On admission to the hospital, the patient does not generally appear as ill as one would expect based on blood gases and radiographic findings. A temperature of up to 38.5° C is common. Tachycardia is present and correlates with an increased respiratory rate and severity of illness. Crackles appear in the right mid-lung fields first. Concomitant respiratory infection is sometimes present. Radiographs and computed tomography scans show a patchy, fluffy-type exudate, which may be limited to one area (the right lung field predominating initially) or generalized, depending on the severity of the illness (Fig. 65.14). Pulmonary artery pressure is high, but pulmonary wedge pressure is normal and heart size is not increased.[184,185]

Pathologic Findings. A total of 22 autopsies have been reported in persons dying of HAPE.[132,181] A proteinaceous exudate with hyaline membranes is characteristic. All had some areas of pneumonitis, with neutrophil accumulation, although none was noted to contain bacteria. Pulmonary veins were not dilated. Most reports mention capillary and arteriolar thrombi and deposits of fibrin, as well as hemorrhage and infarcts. The autopsy findings thus suggest a protein-rich edema and the possibility that clotting abnormalities may play a role in the illness.

Analyses of alveolar fluid in persons with non-lethal HAPE provide additional insight into the mechanism of HAPE. Schoene and associates[186] obtained the first bronchoalveolar lavage samples in climbers with AMS and HAPE, as well as in healthy subjects. The lavage fluid confirmed that HAPE is a high-protein fluid, higher than in patients with acute respiratory distress syndrome (ARDS), and that the fluid was highly cellular (Fig. 65.15). However, unlike ARDS lavage fluid, which has primarily neutrophils, HAPE fluid contained a higher percentage of alveolar

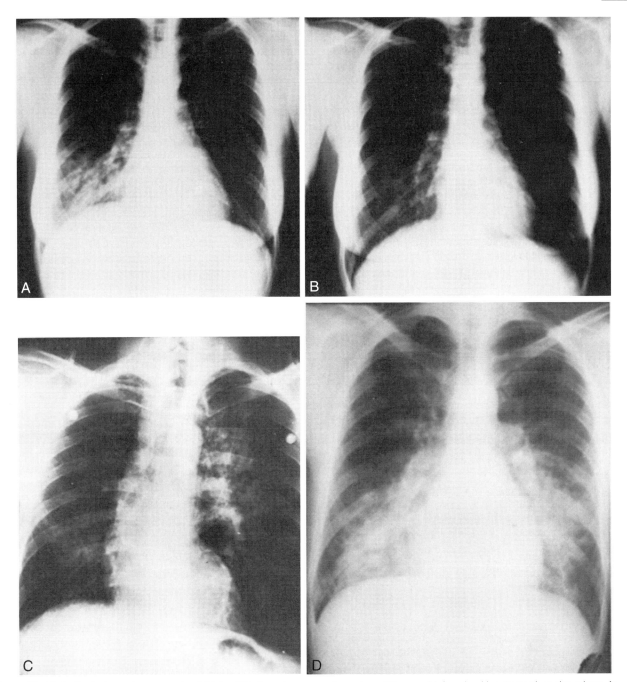

Figure 65.14 **A,** Typical roentgenograph of high-altitude pulmonary edema in a 29-year-old female skier. Note that the edema is unilateral, right sided, and predominantly in the right middle lobe. **B,** Roentgenograph of the same patient 1 day later, after descent and oxygen. Note the rapid clearing. **C,** Severe unilateral pulmonary edema in a 21-year-old male with no history of any previous illness. **D,** Severe pulmonary edema of altitude. Note normal heart size.

macrophages, but in some cases elevated neutrophils. Additionally, chemotactic (leukotriene B$_4$) and vasoactive (thromboxane B$_2$) mediators were present. The climbers with AMS who had some degree of arterial oxygen desaturation had alveolar fluid that was similar to that of the control subjects. Similar lavage findings emerged from the Japanese Alps in patients with HAPE discovered at moderate altitude and brought down to a hospital, with lavages performed after several days of rest and treatment. In these cases, there was neutrophilia and numerous cytokines (interleukin [IL]-1, IL-6, IL-8, and tumor necrosis

factor-α) were found to be elevated compared with controls, whereas IL-1α, IL-10, and P-selectin were not.[187] The inflammatory milieu in the lavages was quite surprising, given the well-established findings of very elevated pulmonary artery pressures and strong HPV in subjects with HAPE and the absence of alveolar space inflammation in other forms of severe pulmonary artery hypertension.

Resolution of this conundrum came with lavages obtained in the first 24 hours of HAPE onset at 4559 m (Monte Rosa, Italy) performed in conjunction with echocardiographic measurement of systolic pulmonary

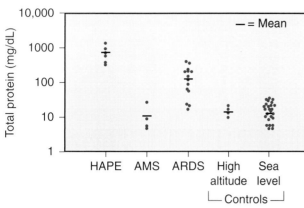

Figure 65.15 Protein concentration in bronchoalveolar lavage fluid (on the vertical axis) in high-altitude pulmonary edema (HAPE), acute mountain sickness (AMS), acute respiratory distress syndrome (ARDS), and high-altitude and sea-level controls. (From Schoene RB, Swenson ER, Pizzo CJ, et al: The lung at high altitude: Bronchoalveolar lavage in acute mountain sickness and pulmonary edema. J Appl Physiol 64:2605–2613, 1988.)

artery pressures.[188] This study confirmed the high protein content and in some cases alveolar hemorrhage in those with the highest pulmonary artery pressures (systolic >80 mm Hg). Despite the high-permeability leak characteristics of the lavage fluid, there was no evidence of cytokine expression or neutrophil recruitment in the earliest phase of the disease. These studies taken together establish definitively that HAPE is a noninflammatory injury of the lung with secondary inflammation.

Possible Mechanisms. Three basic mechanisms for pulmonary edema in HAPE have been hypothesized: increased microvascular pressure, increased microvascular permeability, or a combination of the two. Because we know HAPE to be due to increased permeability, it is grouped with the pulmonary edemas of noncardiogenic origin: near drowning, narcotic overdose, neurogenic pulmonary edema, and perhaps ARDS (see Chapters 51 and 85).

However, in contrast to ARDS, rapid clearing of the edema without fibrosis or long-term sequelae is usual in HAPE as observed at autopsy. Although the HAPE data are limited, the available evidence suggests that, although there are markers of some inflammation in HAPE, it is not the same inflammatory-mediated driven process as ARDS.[186,188] It is most likely that high intravascular pressures (see discussion later) initiate a sequence of events that induces a modest post facto inflammatory response that is far less severe than what is seen in ARDS.

The search for what triggers the leak continues. In 1967, Hultgren[189] suggested that edema resulted from uneven hypoxic vasoconstriction, resulting in overperfusion of the microvasculature in areas of the lung where arteriolar vasoconstriction failed to protect downstream vessels. Further support for this concept came from Hackett and colleagues,[190] who found a susceptibility to HAPE of persons born without a right pulmonary artery. Uneven perfusion is suggested clinically by the typical patchy roentgenographic appearance (see Fig. 65.13) and by nuclear lung scan and magnetic resonance studies in persons breathing hypoxic gas mixtures,[191,191a] which showed considerable

differences in regional perfusion in HAPE-susceptible subjects. Thus, overperfusion of some areas of the pulmonary vasculature in the setting of a generally constricted vascular bed (greater perfusing pressure) may be a factor involved in the pathogenesis of HAPE. The mechanism of leak in overperfusion edema may be due to high pressure and high flow, subjecting precapillary arterioles and capillaries to injury or biomechanical stress from high shear forces. This concept has been termed *capillary stress failure* by West and colleagues.[192-195]

The mechanism(s) by which high pressures and shear stress lead to a high permeability–type leak may involve a continuum of pressure-related phenomena by which pericellular (between cell) and transcellular (across cell) movement of plasma (and even red cells) occurs into the lung interstitium and thence into the alveolar space. At lower levels of pressure elevation, stretch on collagen and other supporting extracellular matrix elements may induce dynamic and quickly reversible changes in barrier permeability[196,197] that, with greater duration and further pressure elevation, may lead to capillary rupture and alveolar hemorrhage, which is seen in the most severe cases of HAPE.[186,188] The anatomic correlates of stress failure in experimental models of hypoxia-mediated pulmonary artery hypertension have included demonstration of a variety of capillary endothelial and alveolar epithelial breaks with platelet and erythrocyte movement through these sites of discontinuity in the alveolar-capillary barrier.[198] The fact that only a poor correlation between histologic discontinuities in the alveolar capillary barrier and leak as assessed by lung water measurements can be found suggests that stress failure is more than just traumatic breaks, also involving noninjurious pressure-induced alterations in permeability that can quickly regress with reduction in pressure.[198,199]

Markedly elevated pulmonary artery pressure is a consistent finding in HAPE. Persons susceptible to HAPE have an abnormally high pulmonary artery pressure response during hypoxic breathing, as well as on ascent to high altitude,[200,201] before onset of edema. The cause of exaggerated hypoxic pulmonary vasoconstrictor response (HPV) in HAPE susceptible subjects is not known. In addition to a possibly increased hypoxic pulmonary vasoconstrictor response, lower HVR[202-205] and slightly lower lung volumes[203,206,207] may contribute to increased pulmonary artery pressure by causing greater alveolar hypoxia[208] and reducing the number of recruitable vessels. Increased sympathetic tone may also contribute to stronger pulmonary vasoconstriction, because skeletal muscle micro-neurography in HAPE subjects demonstrates increased muscle sympathetic activity during hypoxia at low altitude and prior to HAPE at high altitude.[209] In accordance with these findings, increased plasma or urinary levels of norepinephrine compared to controls were found to precede[210] and accompany[210,211] HAPE. It is conceivable that increased sympathetic activity contributes to the brisk hypoxic pulmonary vasoconstrictor response and that HAPE may have some resemblance to neurogenic pulmonary edema.[212]

Other evidence suggests that susceptibility to HAPE may be associated with alterations in vasoactive mediator production by endothelial cells in the pulmonary circulation that lead to a phenotype of strong hypoxic vasoconstriction which may be genetically determined.[212a] Increased endothelin concentrations are found in the plasma.[213,214] Furthermore, there is indirect evidence that NO production is reduced in HAPE-susceptible individuals, because they have lower exhaled NO during acute[215] and prolonged[216] exposure to hypoxia and lower concentrations of nitrate and nitrite in bronchoalveolar lavage fluid[188] than control subjects. The observation that inhaled NO did not normalize pulmonary artery pressure in HAPE-susceptible individuals, but did so in those resistant to HAPE,[217] indicates that impaired NO synthesis cannot fully account for the excessive pulmonary vascular reactivity in HAPE-prone subjects. It is likely that additional factors mentioned previously, such as sympathetic activity and other vasoconstrictors such as prostanoid metabolites, contribute to the increased pulmonary artery pressures in HAPE-susceptible subjects.

Although the data largely establish a hydrostatic basis to HAPE, one cannot overlook the potential role of inflammation in some individuals that may predispose or contribute at some point to make the microvascular endothelium vulnerable to a subsequent increase in pressure. The published lavage studies taken together provide rough sequential data that establish the fact that inflammatory mediators are not present in nascent HAPE, but that they may be expressed later in reaction possibly to alveolar-capillary trauma of stress failure.[186-188] Any process altering the permeability of the alveolar-capillary barrier will lower the pressure required for edema formation. Indeed, increased fluid accumulation during hypoxic exposure after priming by endotoxin or virus in animals[218] and the association of preceding respiratory viral infections with HAPE in children[219] support this concept. Under conditions of increased permeability, HAPE may also occur in individuals with normal hypoxic pulmonary vascular responses. Thus, upper respiratory tract infections shortly before a sojourn in the mountains and vigorous exercise at altitudes between 2000 and 3000 m may explain in some cases why HAPE can develop at a surprisingly low altitude.[220] Other causes to be considered include left ventricular diastolic dysfunction in those patients with systemic hypertension and diabetes, and undiagnosed pathology causing or amplifying HPV, such as silent pulmonary embolism, possibly triggered by preceding long bus, car, or airline travel.[221]

Another theory of HAPE pathogenesis is that HAPE is a form fruste of neurogenic pulmonary edema. It is probably more appropriate to consider that they share features of a common final pathway to pulmonary edema. The presence of red blood cells, the spectrum of serum proteins in HAPE lavage fluid, and the absence of architectural damage are all similar to neurogenic pulmonary edema.[222] One component of neurogenic pulmonary edema is thought to be increased microvascular pressure secondary to sympathetically mediated pulmonary venous constriction.[223] Recent work has suggested that α-adrenergic blockade may be of value in the treatment of HAPE[224]; the authors speculated that relief of pulmonary venous constriction could play a role because they also found accentuated sympathetic activity in HAPE-susceptible individuals.[209] Also, studies have demonstrated simultaneous cerebral edema in some individuals with HAPE,[135,225] as well as elevated plasma and urine catecholamines.[156,226] Despite the similarities of neurogenic pulmonary edema with HAPE, it must be realized that most subjects with HAPE have little or no evidence of any central

nervous system abnormalities, in contrast to the profound central nervous system alterations in neurogenic pulmonary edema. Further investigation may help clarify the role of the central and sympathetic nervous systems in HAPE.

Unlike the equivocal link of hypoventilation with AMS (see earlier), control of ventilation plays a key role in the pathophysiology of HAPE.[227] Persons with a low HVR have an increased risk of pulmonary edema, whereas a brisk response may be protective. This has been well established in subjects who are susceptible to HAPE when compared to people who do not develop HAPE. In addition, dangerous hypoxic depression of ventilation may develop in those who have a low hypoxic drive and who become extremely hypoxic from HAPE.[227] Persons who hypoventilate are more hypoxemic and have greater pulmonary hypertension, and this may be particularly important during sleep. Supporting this concept is the frequency with which the onset of HAPE occurs during sleep, and indeed sleeping medications may provoke HAPE. Interestingly, the association of low HVR and strong HPV in HAPE-susceptible subjects may be linked at the peripheral chemoreceptors. Animal studies of carotid body and lung denervation have shown that hypoxic stimulation of the peripheral chemoreceptors reduces the magnitude of HPV.[228] Thus, those who are driven to breathe more in hypoxia not only maintain a higher alveolar PO_2 and a reduced stimulus to HPV, but the strength of HPV itself is blunted.

A further mechanism that may be central in the pathophysiology of HAPE is the little-appreciated capacity of the lung to reabsorb fluid by active transport. Investigations in cell culture and animal models suggest that impairment of active alveolar fluid clearance by hypoxia may be involved, because water and sodium transport by type I and II alveolar epithelial cells is important in normal lung fluid balance, particularly at the moment of birth when the formerly fluid-filled lung must be quickly aerated. Hypoxia decreases alveolar transepithelial sodium transport[229] and accounts for decreased fluid clearance from the alveoli of hypoxic rats at fraction of inspired oxygen of 8%.[230] Mice partially deficient in the apical (alveolar-facing) epithelial sodium channel accumulate more lung water in hypoxia[231] and develop more pulmonary edema with other forms of acute lung injury.[231a] Transalveolar sodium transport can be increased by β2-receptor stimulation, and a recent field study reported successful prevention of HAPE with inhalation of salmeterol, a long-acting β2-agonist.[232] However, it should be noted that doses 2.5 times higher than recommended for treatment of obstructive lung disease were used, and, owing multiple actions of this drug, such as pulmonary artery vasodilation, increased ventilatory response to hypoxia, and tightening of cell-to-cell contacts, the contribution of enhanced alveolar fluid clearance to the positive outcome of the study remains uncertain.[233] We need more selective and specific drugs to better evaluate the role of alveolar fluid clearance in the pathophysiology of HAPE.

In an effort to determine the importance of active transport in HAPE and whether differences exist in this capacity in the susceptibility to HAPE, Sartori and colleagues[232] found lower transepithelial nasal potentials in normoxia in HAPE-susceptible individuals versus nonsusceptible controls. The easily measured potential difference across the nasal mucosa is considered to be a good, but not perfect, surrogate for the alveolar epithelium. The reduced nasal potential difference in HAPE-susceptible individuals can be attributed to lower sodium transport by the epithelial sodium channel. These findings may point to a constitutional, possibly genetically determined reduction of sodium transport across the respiratory epithelium. Although a recent investigation confirmed the difference in nasal potential between HAPE-susceptible individuals and controls in normoxia, this difference could not be attributed to differences in epithelial sodium channel activity.[234] Furthermore, this study showed that the nasal epithelium may not adequately reflect ion transport across the alveolar epithelium due to differences in chloride transport between the two epithelia. Therefore, the significance and predictive power of a lower nasal potential difference in HAPE-susceptible individuals is not clear at present.

Treatment. Proper treatment of HAPE depends on the severity of the illness and the nature of the environment. The sooner the diagnosis is made, the easier the illness can be reversed. In the wilderness, where oxygen and medical expertise may not be available, most persons with HAPE should be evacuated to a lower altitude as soon as possible, keeping in mind the desirability of minimal exertion by the victim. If HAPE is diagnosed early, recovery is rapid with a descent of only 500 to 1000 m, and the victim may be able to reascend cautiously 2 or 3 days later. A portable hyperbaric chamber,[235] or supplemental oxygen, if available, will immediately increase arterial SO_2 and reduce pulmonary artery pressure, heart rate, respiratory rate, and symptoms. In situations in which descent is difficult, these treatments can be lifesaving. Rescue groups should make delivery of oxygen to the victim the highest priority if descent may be delayed.

Keeping the patient warm may be important, because cold stress elevates pulmonary artery pressure.[236] The use of an expiratory positive airway pressure mask was shown to improve oxygenation in HAPE and may be useful as a temporizing measure, although its efficacy has not been well evaluated.[237] In high-altitude locations with clinics or hospitals, bed rest alone can be adequate treatment for mild cases, and bed rest with supplemental oxygen generally suffices for moderate and severe illness. Complete resolution of the edema may require 24 to 72 hours of oxygen therapy if treated near the altitude of onset, whereas removing the patient to a lower altitude results in prompter clearing of edema. Curiously, even higher concentrations of oxygen do not seem to be more useful as long as arterial SO_2 is maintained above 90%.[235] Apparently, when a threshold PO_2 is reached, the pulmonary artery pressure drops and the edema starts to clear, and higher PO_2 values do not further accelerate this process. Occasionally, life-threatening HAPE being treated at a medical facility will require descent to a lower altitude as well as a high inspired oxygen concentration if arterial saturation cannot be maintained or if severe encephalopathy develops. Intubation may then be required, as well as therapy directed to the cerebral edema. Pulmonary embolism, pneumothorax, myocardial infarction, and congestive heart failure should also be suspected in patients not responding rapidly to oxygen therapy.

Drugs are not as effective for treatment of HAPE as descent and/or oxygen. Although Singh and colleagues[132] reported good results with furosemide, concerns about hypovolemia and hypotension have constrained its use in North America and by the Himalayan Rescue Association in Nepal. Morphine sulfate, used cautiously and when central nervous system function is intact, can relieve dyspnea, improve oxygenation and comfort, and reduce heart and respiratory rates, much as it does in cardiogenic pulmonary edema.[238] Digitalis, isoproterenol, and corticosteroids have had no demonstrated benefit. Other measures that reduce pulmonary hydrostatic pressure by decreasing venous return may be of value. Vasodilators have recently been shown to lower pulmonary artery pressure and pulmonary vascular resistance, as well as to improve oxygenation.[239] Nifedipine can be given in an initial dose of 10 mg orally, followed by 10-mg doses every 4 hours, or preferably followed by the extended-release preparation, 30 mg two to three times a day.[239] Experience with hydralazine and phentolamine is limited, and currently calcium channel blockers, such as nifedipine and amlodipine, are the drug therapy of choice. Acetazolamide may be useful, primarily in the early stage of illness, given its therapeutic potential in AMS, and recent animal studies that show it reduces HPV.[240] Beyond the well-proven calcium channel blockers, there has been a significant interest in phosphodiesterase-5 inhibitors, such as sildenafil. Several ongoing studies should soon determine their efficacy. Despite progress in evaluating drug therapy, the best management of this uncommon illness in the back country is early recognition and descent.

Prevention. The preventive measures previously described for AMS also apply to HAPE. A fast rate of ascent is an important contributing factor, and graded ascent with adequate time for acclimatization will reduce the risk of HAPE. Because unrecognizable subclinical pulmonary edema might be converted to clinical edema by exercise, avoidance of overexertion, especially when fatigued, may help prevent HAPE. Persons on acetazolamide have occasionally developed HAPE during extremely rapid ascents, but clinical experience suggests that this drug may prevent HAPE in persons with a history of recurrent episodes in the presence of a reasonable rate of ascent. Nifedipine was recently found effective in preventing HAPE in subjects with a past history of the illness[241]; the dose used was 20 mg (slow release) every 8 hours. Because the incidence of HAPE is low, prophylactic nifedipine should be reserved for those known to be susceptible. A single study has established that high-dose inhaled salmeterol may be considered for prophylaxis.[232] A recent investigation to test whether inhibition of HPV by phosphodiesterase-5 inhibitors and stimulation of active alveolar salt and water transport by dexamethasone show strong promise.[241a]

Thrombosis: Coagulation and Platelet Changes

The higher than expected incidence of venous thrombosis, pulmonary embolism, and stroke in mountaineers, as well as autopsy findings of widespread thrombi in the brain and lungs, have led to investigations of the clotting mechanism at high altitude. Changes in platelets and in coagulation have been observed in rabbits, mice, rats, calves, and humans on ascent to altitude and have been extensively reviewed.[242] Coagulation studies on individuals with HAPE are limited. Singh and colleagues[243] reported that HAPE patients had increased fibrinogen levels and prolonged clot lysis times, which they attributed to a breakdown of fibrinolysis. Singh[244] also reported thrombotic, occlusive hypertensive pulmonary vascular disease in soldiers who had recently arrived at altitude. Dickinson and associates[181] concluded that hypercoagulability of the blood and sequestration of platelets in the pulmonary vascular bed provoke pulmonary thrombosis and may contribute to the pathogenesis of HAPE. Bartsch and associates,[245,246] on the other hand, with careful longitudinal studies done while subjects were developing HAPE, concluded that platelet and coagulation changes were epiphenomena and not causative.

Taken together, the work done to date does not confirm a causative role for abnormal coagulation in the pathophysiology of altitude illnesses. Peripheral thrombotic events in mountaineers and, therefore, some embolic events may be explained on the basis of dehydration, polycythemia, cold, constrictive clothing, and venous stasis from prolonged periods of weather-imposed inactivity.

Subacute Mountain Sickness

Recently, two syndromes of pulmonary hypertension and right-sided heart failure have been described in lowlanders who move to high altitude. These may be the human counterparts to brisket disease in cattle, a problem affecting susceptible bovine strains after months of exposure to altitude. Subacute infantile mountain sickness was described in Han Chinese infants who were born at low altitude and then moved to Lhasa, Tibet (3600 m).[247] The adult syndrome was reported by Anand and associates[248] in Indian soldiers posted for over 3 months at altitudes over 5800 m. In both syndromes, congestive heart failure and severe pulmonary hypertension inevitably led to death unless the victim was removed to a lower altitude. Polycythemia is not a feature of the disease in children but was present in the adults. In addition to the pulmonary hypertension, pathogenic features in adults include myocardial dysfunction, fluid and salt retention, and impaired renal function.[249] To date, the syndrome has not been noted in other populations.

PROBLEMS OF HIGH-ALTITUDE RESIDENTS

Chronic Mountain Sickness

Chronic mountain sickness (CMS) occurs in persons born and living at high altitude as well as in lowlanders who move to high altitudes and stay for prolonged periods of time. The entity was first described in Andean dwellers by Monge[250] in 1928 and is often referred to as Monge's disease. Excessive erythrocytosis, that is, a hematocrit above 60% to 70% or more than 2 standard deviations above the average value for healthy residents at a given high altitude, is an essential characteristic of the syndrome; the illness therefore is also referred to as chronic mountain polycythemia, but the term *chronic mountain sickness* is most commonly used. CMS has been reported in North America, China, and the republics of the former Soviet Union, as well as in South America.

The incidence in women before menopause is low but increases appreciably after approximately 45 years of age.[251]

There are geographic and ethnic differences in the prevalence of CMS. It is rarely found in natives of the Tibetan plateau but is frequently encountered in the Andes, in the North American Rockies, and in other mountainous regions where lowlanders have moved.[252,253] The reason for this difference is only speculative, but it is thought possibly to be secondary to more advantageous adaptations that the Tibetans have undergone because of the much greater duration of their existence on the Tibetan plateau (~250,000 years) compared with that of the Andeans (~13,000 to 15,000 years). Especially important may be the findings that Tibetans have a much lower pulmonary vasoconstrictive response to hypoxia, lower hematocrits, and lower sea-level birth weights of their children as compared with other high-altitude populations.

Clinical Presentation. Symptoms of CMS are similar to those found in persons suffering polycythemia at low altitude: headache, dizziness, lethargy, impaired memory and mentation, and poor sleep. Consistent findings are cyanosis, plethoric appearance, and elevated hematocrit and hemoglobin. The diagnosis can only be established by eliminating all other causes of polycythemia. Indeed, much confusion in the literature regarding incidence and other aspects of CMS may be due to inadequate validation of the diagnosis. Monge,[250] for example, noted a high frequency of bronchial complications in patients with CMS, whereas Kryger and associates[253] found evidence of lung disease in 50% of those with CMS in Leadville, Colorado. Indeed, when viewed as a syndrome, it is possible that many cases represent an interaction between some underlying chronic lung disease, high altitude, and heavy metal toxicity (see later). The incidence of cases of pure, or so-called primary, CMS has not been determined.

Pathophysiology. Physiologic studies of CMS show a tendency toward excessive hypoxemia in many but not all cases, a blunted HVR, relative hypoventilation, a widened $(A-a)PO_2$, frequent pulmonary hypertension that can lead to right-sided heart failure, an increase in red blood cell mass without an increase in plasma volume, and excessive arterial oxygen desaturation during sleep.[253–256] How all these factors interact in a cause-and-effect role is not clear.

The excessive polycythemia of CMS may be due to greater hypoxemia, but the actual hematocrit values obtained are often higher than expected for the measured arterial SO_2.[255] Thus, an excessive hematopoietic response to a given hypoxic stimulus may be a factor.[256] Hypoventilation appears to be a significant contributor to the greater hypoxemia. Hypoxia itself may ultimately contribute to the ventilatory depression, as evidenced by an increase in ventilation in some natives with CMS when given oxygen to breathe. Severe nocturnal desaturation may also occur (Fig. 65.16).[257] In fact, the Denver investigators thought that the greater hypoxemia during sleep might be adequate to explain the higher hematocrits. These observations also point out that disorders causing mild hypoxemia at sea level, such as sleep apnea or chronic lung disease, can have more serious consequences when superimposed on the hypoxia of high altitude.

Most recently, Jefferson and associates[258] found that a majority of subjects with CMS and excessive erythrocytosis (as high as 91% hematocrit) in an Andean mining commu-

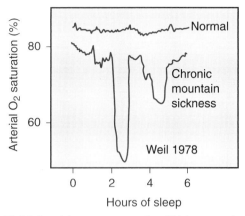

LEADVILLE COLORADO 3100m

Figure 65.16 Arterial oxygen saturation (%) by ear oximeter during sleep in a normal resident of Leadville, Colorado, and in a patient with chronic mountain sickness. Severe and prolonged desaturation occurred in the individual with chronic mountain sickness. (From Weil JV, Kryger MH, Scoggin CH: Sleep and breathing at high altitude. *In* Guilleminault C, Dement WC [eds]: Sleep Apnea Syndromes. New York: Alan R Liss, 1978, pp 119–136.)

nity had detectable serum concentrations of cobalt, a heavy metal known to independently stimulate renal erythropoietin production.

Treatment. Patients with CMS are treated by reducing red blood cell mass. Improving oxygenation and thereby reducing the hypoxic stimulus for red blood cell production is the most physiologic approach to therapy. Therefore, the definitive treatment for CMS is relocation to a lower altitude. Because a move is not always compatible with the patient's lifestyle, other treatments are often invoked. Phlebotomy has long been used, not only for CMS but also for any cause of excessive polycythemia. Despite the common clinical practice and prompt subjective improvement, long-term benefits have not been well documented. Low-flow oxygen during sleep is probably effective, especially for those with marked sleep desaturation. Respiratory stimulants, by increasing alveolar PO_2, have also been found to be effective in treating CMS. Medroxyprogesterone acetate, given in dosages of 20 to 60 mg/day for 10 weeks, increased tidal volume and minute ventilation, lowered arterial PCO_2, and improved oxygenation both awake and asleep.[259] Hematocrit values declined from a mean of 60% to 52%, which is in the normal range for 3100 m. Acetazolamide was also beneficial. The response to respiratory stimulants underscores the contribution of hypoventilation to the pathogenesis of CMS. Theophylline and acetazolamide (respiratory stimulants as well) and angiotensin-converting enzyme inhibitors directly suppress renal erythropoietin synthesis and release. Recently it was shown that the need for repeated phlebotomies could be eliminated in patients with CMS by daily treatment with an angiotensin-converting enzyme inhibitor.[260]

Reentry Pulmonary Edema

Some persons living for years at high altitude, who then descend to lower altitudes, develop HAPE on reascent.

Authors have suggested that the incidence of HAPE on reascent may be higher than during initial ascent by sojourners,[261,262] but data on true incidence are lacking. Children and adolescents are more susceptible than adults. Hultgren and Marticorena[261] found in Peruvian natives an incidence of reentry HAPE of 6.4 per 100 exposures in the 1- to 20-year-old age group and 0.4 per 100 exposures in those older than 21. The phenomenon has been most often observed in Peru, where high-altitude residents can return from sea level to high altitude quite rapidly. Cases have also been reported in Leadville, Colorado,[262] but reports are conspicuously absent from Nepal and Tibet, possibly because rapid return to high altitude is not so readily available. It has been postulated that the increased muscularization of pulmonary arterioles that develops with chronic high-altitude exposure generates an inordinately high pulmonary artery pressure on reascent, causing the edema. Mountaineers have learned that adequate acclimatization to a given altitude will not necessarily protect against HAPE on rapid ascent to a yet higher altitude.

ILLNESSES INFLUENCED BY HIGH ALTITUDE

Millions of lowlanders of all ages travel to high altitude for work and recreation. Because of increasing ease of travel to these places, this phenomenon has increased a great deal over the past couple of decades. Thus, many low-altitude dwellers with preexisting diseases compound their maladies with the added stress of hypoxia. Ironically, very few studies have been done to understand what happens to people with respiratory diseases when they visit high-altitude destinations, and even fewer data are available about how to treat them before and after their exposure.

Lung Disease

The effects of acute or transient altitude exposure on persons with preexisting lung disease are minimally explored despite the large numbers of such patients at risk. Any person hypoxemic from chronic obstructive pulmonary disease at sea level will be more hypoxemic at altitude and therefore likely to be more symptomatic. However, Graham and Houston[263] found that persons with moderate chronic obstructive pulmonary disease (but without cor pulmonale or carbon dioxide retention) tolerated 2000 m well, complaining only of mild fatigue. Arterial PO_2 fell from 66 to 51 mm Hg at rest and from 63 to 46 mm Hg with exercise. Persons with blunted carotid body function from lung disease may not exhibit the normal increase in ventilation on ascent or the usual increased breathlessness associated with more severe hypoxemia. Many patients with chronic airflow obstruction who venture to high altitude report reduced exercise ability at high altitude, and many initiate supplemental oxygen or increase their usual rate of oxygen administration. The effect of altitude on lung disorders is an important area for future research.

Symptomatic pulmonary hypertension, whether primary or secondary, is a contraindication to ascent to high altitude because pulmonary artery pressure will increase further, exacerbating illness and possibly predisposing to HAPE.

Guidelines are available on how to evaluate and treat patients with hypoxemia who are going to travel by air.[264–266]

The methods to predict air-flight hypoxemia (altitude in cabin approximately 2000 to 2500 m) are tedious and generally not available in most clinical laboratories. It is probably reasonable to prescribe 2 L/min oxygen by nasal prongs for patients with low-altitude oxygen saturations of 88% to 92%, while merely increasing the flow by approximately 2 L/min in patients already on oxygen.

Sleep Apnea

For patients with sleep apnea, the degree of nocturnal desaturation and hypoxemia will be greater at high altitude, which could lead to increased arrhythmias, greater pulmonary hypertension, poorer quality of sleep, and daytime fatigue. Supplemental oxygen, in addition to the patient's standard therapy such as nasal continuous positive airway pressure, may be necessary to maintain adequate oxygenation. On the other hand, recent data suggest that obstructive sleep apnea improves with a night of simulated altitude ascent[267] but at the cost of increased central apneas. The net effect of these changes in control of breathing and their mechanisms during sleep at altitude in patients with sleep apnea remains undefined.

SUMMARY

We have reviewed the normal processes that the body undergoes in adapting to the low-oxygen environment of high altitude. These steps optimize the delivery of oxygen from the air to the cells. Additionally, we have discussed the clinical situations in which adaptation is not successful, leading to a spectrum of altitude illnesses, from the milder form (AMS) to the more severe manifestations of pulmonary and cerebral edemas. The pathophysiology of acute altitude illnesses is not completely understood, but it is associated with leakage of fluid from the intravascular to the extravascular spaces, primarily in the brain and lungs.

REFERENCES

1. Haldane JS: Acclimatization to high altitude. Physiol Rev 7:363–384, 1927.
2. Kellogg RH: Altitude acclimatization: An historical introduction emphasizing the regulation of breathing. Physiologist 11:37–57, 1968.
3. West JB: Highlife: A History of High Altitude Physiology and Medicine. Oxford: Oxford University Press, 1998.
4. Hornbein TF, Schoene RB (eds): High Altitude: An Exploration of Human Adaptation (Lung Biology in Health and Disease, Vol 161). New York: Marcel Dekker, 2001.
5. Rahn H, Otis AB: Man's respiratory response during and after acclimatization to high altitude. Am J Physiol 157:445–559, 1946.
6. Winslow RM, Monge C: Hypoxia, Polycythemia, and Chronic Mountain Sickness. Baltimore: Johns Hopkins University Press, 1987, pp 98–117.
7. Tankersley CG: Selected contribution: Variation in acute hypoxic ventilatory response is linked to mouse chromosome 9. J Appl Physiol 90:1615–1622, 2001.
8. Smith CA, Dempsey JA, Hornbein TF: Control of breathing at high altitude. In Hornbein TF, Schoene RB (eds): High Altitude: An Exploration of Human Adaptation (Lung Biology in Health and Disease, Vol 161). New York: Marcel Dekker, 2001, pp 139–174.
9. Daristotle L, Berssenbrugge AD, Engwall MJ, et al: The effects of carotid body hypocapnia on ventilation in goats. Respir Physiol 79:123–135, 1990.
10. Smith CA, Saupe KW, Henderson KS, Dempsey JA: Ventilatory effects of specific carotid body hypocapnia in dogs during wakefulness and sleep. J Appl Physiol 79:689–699, 1995.
11. Dempsey JA, Forster HV, Bisgard GE, et al: Role of cerebrospinal fluid in ventilatory deacclimatization from chronic hypoxia. J Clin Invest 64:199–205, 1979.
12. Goldberg S, Schoene RB, Haynor D, et al: Brain tissue pH and ventilatory acclimatization to high altitude. J Appl Physiol 72:58–63, 1991.
13. West JB: Rate of ventilatory acclimatization to extreme altitude. Respir Physiol 74:323–333, 1988.
14. Schoene RB, Roach RC, Hackett PH, et al: Operation Everest II: Ventilatory adaptation during gradual decompression to extreme altitude. Med Sci Sports Exerc 22:804–810, 1990.
15. Vizek M, Pickett CK, Weil JV: Increased carotid body hypoxic sensitivity during acclimatization to hypobaric hypoxia. J Appl Physiol 63:2403–2410, 1987.
16. Neubauer JA: Invited review: Physiological and pathophysiological responses to intermittent hypoxia. J Appl Physiol 90:1593–1599, 2001.
17. Prabhakar NR: Oxygen sensing during intermittent hypoxia: Cellular and molecular mechanisms. J Appl Physiol 90:1986–1994, 2001.
18. Ren X, Dorrington KL, Robbins PA: Respiratory control in humans after 8 h of lowered arterial PO_2, hemodilution, or carboxyhemoglobinemia. J Appl Physiol 90:1189–1195, 2001.
19. Fatemian M, Kim DY, Poulin MJ, Robbins PA: Very mild exposure to hypoxia for 8 h can induce ventilatory acclimatization in humans. Pflugers Arch 441:840–843, 2001.
20. Katayama K, Sato Y, Morotomi Y, et al: Intermittent hypoxia increases ventilation and Sa_{O_2} during hypoxic exercise and hypoxic chemosensitivity. J Appl Physiol 90:1431–1440, 2001.
21. Mahamed S, Duffin J: Repeated hypoxic exposures change respiratory chemoreflex control in humans. J Physiol (Lond) 534:595–603, 2001.
22. Townsend NE, Gore CJ, Hahn AG, et al: Living high–training low increases hypoxic ventilatory response of well-trained endurance athletes. J Appl Physiol 93:1498–1505, 2002.
23. McGuire M, Zhang Y, White DP, Ling L: Chronic intermittent hypoxia enhances ventilatory long-term facilitation in awake rats. J Appl Physiol 95:1499–1508, 2003.
24. Reeves SR, Gozal E, Guo SZ, et al: Effect of long-term intermittent and sustained hypoxia on hypoxic ventilatory and metabolic responses in the adult rat. J Appl Physiol 95:1767–1774, 2003.
25. Weil JV, Byrne-Quinn E, Sodal I, et al: Acquired attenuation of chemoreceptor function in chemically hypoxic man at high altitude. J Clin Invest 50:186–195, 1971.
26. Sorensen SC, Severinghaus JW: Irreversible respiratory insensitivity to acute hypoxia in men born at high altitude. J Appl Physiol 25:217–220, 1968.
27. Lahiri S, DeLaney RB, Brody JS, et al: Relative role of environmental and genetic factors in respiratory adaptation to high altitude. Nature 261:133–135, 1976.

28. Huang, SY, Ning XH, Zhou ZN, et al: Ventilatory function in adaptation to high altitude: Studies in Tibet. *In* West JB, Lahiri S (eds): High Altitude and Man. Bethesda, Md: American Physiological Society, 1984, pp 173–177.

29. Hackett PH, Reeves JT, Reeves CD, et al: Control of breathing in Sherpas at low and high altitude. J Appl Physiol 49:374–379, 1980.

30. Milic-Emili J, Kayser B, Gautier H: Mechanics of breathing. *In* Hornbein TF, Schoene RB (eds): High Altitude: An Exploration of Human Adaptation (Lung Biology in Health and Disease, Vol 161). New York: Marcel Dekker, 2001, pp175–198.

31. Coates G, Gray G, Mansell A, et al: Changes in lung volume, lung density, and distribution of ventilation during hypobaric decompression. J Appl Physiol 46:752–755, 1979.

32. Jaeger JJ, Sylvester JT, Cymerman A, et al: Evidence for increased intrathoracic fluid volume in man at high altitude. J Appl Physiol 47:670–676, 1979.

33. Hoon RS, Balasubramanio V, Tiwari BC, et al: Changes in transthoracic electrical impedance at high altitude. Br Heart J 39:61–66, 1977.

34. Gautier H, Peslin R, Grassine A, et al: Mechanical properties of the lungs during acclimatization to altitude. J Appl Physiol 52:1407–1415, 1982.

35. Hurtado A: Respiratory adaptations in the Indian natives of the Peruvian Andes. Am J Phys Anthropol 17:137–161, 1932.

36. Brody JS, Lahiri S, Simpsen M, et al: Lung elasticity and airway dynamics in Peruvian natives to high altitude. J Appl Physiol 42:245–251, 1977.

37. Frisancho AR: Functional adaptation to high altitude hypoxia. Science 187:313–319, 1975.

38. West JB, Hackett PH, Maret KH, et al: Pulmonary gas exchange on the summit of Mt. Everest. J Appl Physiol 55:678–687, 1983.

39. Wagner PD: Gas exchange. *In* Hornbein TF, Schoene RB (eds): High Altitude: An Exploration of Human Adaptation (Lung Biology in Health and Disease, Vol 161). New York: Marcel Dekker, 2001, pp 199–234.

40. Reeves JT, Stenmark KR: The pulmonary circulation at high altitude. *In* Hornbein TF, Schoene RB (eds): High Altitude: An Exploration of Human Adaptation (Lung Biology in Health and Disease, Vol 161). New York: Marcel Dekker, 2001, pp 293–342.

41. Gale GE, Torre-Bueno JR, Moon RE, et al: Ventilation-perfusion inequality in normal humans during exercise at sea level and simulated altitude. J Appl Physiol 58:978–988, 1985.

42. Wagner PD, Sutton JR, Reeves JT, et al: Operation Everest II: Pulmonary gas exchange during simulated ascent of Mt. Everest. J Appl Physiol 63:2348–2359, 1987.

43. West, JB, Wagner PD: Predicted gas exchange on the summit of Mt. Everest. Respir Physiol 42:1–16, 1980.

44. Dempsey JA, Reddan WG, Birnbaum ML, et al: Effects of acute through life-long hypoxic exposure in exercise pulmonary gas exchange. Respir Physiol 13:62–89, 1971.

45. Cerny FC, Dempsey JA, Reddan WG: Pulmonary gas exchange in non-native residents of high altitude. J Clin Invest 52:2993–2999, 1973.

46. Guleria JS, Pande JN, Sethi PK, et al: Pulmonary diffusing capacity at high altitude. J Appl Physiol 31:536–543, 1971.

47. Schoene RB, Roach RC, Lahiri S, et al: Increased diffusion capacity maintains arterial saturations during exercise in the Quechua Indians of the Chilean Altiplano. Am J Hum Biol 2:663–668, 1990.

48. Wolfel EE, Levine BD: The cardiovascular system at high altitude: Heart and systemic circulation. *In* Hornbein TF,

Schoene RB (eds): High Altitude: An Exploration of Human Adaptation (Lung Biology in Health and Disease, Vol 161). New York: Marcel Dekker, 2001, pp 235–292.

49. Halliwill JR, Minson CT: Effect of hypoxia on arterial baroreflex control of heart rate and muscle sympathetic nerve activity in humans. J Appl Physiol 93:857–864, 2002.

50. MacLean M, Sinoway LI, Leuenberger U: Systemic hypoxia elevates skeletal muscle interstitial adenosine levels in humans. Circulation 98:1990–1992, 1998.

51. Antezana AM, Kacimi R, Le Trong JL, et al: Adrenergic status of humans during prolonged exposure to the altitude of 6,542 m. J Appl Physiol 76:1055–1059, 1994.

52. Bogaard HJ, Hopkins SR, Yamaya Y, et al: Role of the autonomic nervous system in the reduced maximal cardiac output at altitude. J Appl Physiol 93:271–279, 2002.

53. Zhaung J, Zhu H, Zhou Z: Reserved higher vagal tone under acute hypoxia in Tibetan adolescents long-term migration to sea level. Jpn J Physiol 52:51–56, 2002.

54. Wolfel EE, Groves BM, Brooks GA, et al: Oxygen transport during steady-state submaximal exercise in chronic hypoxia. J Appl Physiol 70:1129–1136, 1991.

55. Bender PR, Groves BM, McCullough RE, et al: Oxygen transport to exercising leg in chronic hypoxia. J Appl Physiol 65:2592–2597, 1988.

56. Heath D, Williams D, Dickinson J: The pulmonary arteries of the yak. Cardiovasc Res 18:133–139, 1984.

57. Groves BM, Droma T, Sutton JR, et al: Minimal hypoxic pulmonary hypertension in normal Tibetans at 3658 m. J App Physiol 74:312–318, 1993.

58. Beall CM, Laskowski D, Strohl KP, et al: Pulmonary nitric oxide in mountain dwellers. Nature 414:411–412, 2001.

59. Heath D, Smith P, Rios Dalenz J, et al: Small pulmonary arteries in some natives of La Paz, Bolivia. Thorax 36:599–604, 1981.

60. Gupta ML, Rao KS, Anand IS, et al: Lack of smooth muscle in the small pulmonary arteries of the native Ludakhi: Is the Himalayan highlander adapted? Am Rev Respir Dis 145:1201–1204, 1992.

61. Grover RF, Bärtsch P: Blood. *In* Hornbein TF, Schoene RB (eds): High Altitude: An Exploration of Human Adaptation (Lung Biology in Health and Disease, Vol 161). New York: Marcel Dekker, 2001, pp 493–523.

62. Knaupp W, Khilnani S, Sherwood J, et al: Erythropoietin response to acute normobaric hypoxia in humans. J Appl Physiol 73:837–840, 1992.

63. Ge R, Witkowski S, Zhang Y, et al: Determinants of erythropoietin release in response to short-term hypobaric hypoxia. J Appl Physiol 92:2361–2367, 2002.

64. Schmidt W, Spielvogel H, Eckhardt KU, et al: Effects of chronic hypoxia and exercise on plasma erythropoietin in high-altitude residents. J Appl Physiol 74:1874–1878, 1993.

65. Jefferson JA, Escudero E, Hurtado ME, et al: Excessive erythrocytosis, chronic mountain sickness, and serum cobalt levels. Lancet 359:407–408, 2002.

66. Hochachka PW, Rupert JL: Fine tuning the HIF-1 "global" O_2 sensor for hypobaric hypoxia in Andean high-altitude natives. Bioessays 25:515–519, 2003.

67. Sarnquist FH, Schoene RB, Hackett PH: Exercise tolerance and cerebral function after acute hemodilution of polycythemic mountain climbers. Aviat Space Environ Med 57:313–317, 1986.

68. Winslow RM, Monge CC, Statham NJ, et al: Variability of oxygen affinity of blood: Human subjects native to high altitude. J Appl Physiol 51:1411–1416, 1981.

69. Samaja M, Veicsteinas A, Cerritelli P: Oxygen affinity of blood in altitude Sherpas. J Appl Physiol 47:337–341, 1979.

70. Faraci FM, Kilgore DL Jr, Feddle MR: Oxygen delivery to the heart and brain during hypoxia: Peking duck vs. bar-headed goose. Am J Physiol 247:R69–R75, 1984.

71. Winslow RM, Samaja M, West JB: Red cell function at extreme altitude on Mount Everest. J Appl Physiol 56:109–116, 1984.

72. Green HJ, Sutton JR: The effects of altitude on skeletal muscle. *In* Hornbein TF, Schoene RB (eds): High Altitude: An Exploration of Human Adaptation (Lung Biology in Health and Disease, Vol 161). New York: Marcel Dekker, 2001, pp 443–492.

73. Mathieu-Costello O: Muscle adaptation to altitude: Tissue capillarity and capacity for aerobic metabolism. High Alt Med Biol 2:413–25, 2001.

74. Mathiew-Costello O: Capillary tortuosity and degree of contraction or extension of skeletal muscle. Microvasc Res 33:98–117, 1987.

75. Krogh A: Number and distribution of capillaries in muscles with calculations of the oxygen pressure head necessary to supply the tissue. J Physiol (Lond) 52:409–415, 1919.

76. Banchero N: Capillary density of skeletal muscle in dogs exposed to simulated altitude. Proc Soc Exp Biol Med 148:435–439, 1975.

77. Green HJ, Sutton JR, Wolfel EE, et al: Altitude acclimatization and energy metabolic adaptations in skeletal muscle during exercise. J Appl Physiol 73:2701–2708, 1992.

78. Breen EC, Johnson EC, Wagner H, et al: Angiogenic growth factor mRNA responses in muscle to a single bout of exercise. J Appl Physiol 81:355–361, 1996.

79. Richardson RS, Wagner H, Mudaliar SR, et al: Human VEGF gene expression in skeletal muscle: Effect of acute normoxic and hypoxic exercise. Am J Physiol 277:H2247-H2252, 1999.

80. Olfert IM, Breen EC, Mathieu-Costello O, Wagner PD: Chronic hypoxia attenuates resting and exercise-induced VEGF, flt-1, and flk-1 mRNA levels in skeletal muscle. J Appl Physiol 90:1532–1538, 2001.

81. MacDougall JD, Green HJ, Sutton JR, et al: Operation Everest II: Structural adaptations in skeletal muscle in response to extreme simulated altitude. Acta Physiol Scand 142:421–427, 1991.

82. Ou LC, Tenney SM: Properties of mitochondria from hearts of cattle acclimatized to high altitude. Respir Physiol 8:151–159, 1970.

83. Garry DJ, Ordway GA, Lorrenz JN, et al: Mice without myoglobin. Nature 395:905–908, 1998.

84. Hochachka PW, Stanley C, Merkt J, et al: Metabolic meaning of elevated levels of oxidative enzymes in high altitude adapted animals: An interpretive hypothesis. Respir Physiol 52:303–313, 1982.

85. Raichle ME, Hornbein TF: The high-altitude brain. *In* Hornbein TF, Schoene RB (eds): High Altitude: An Exploration of Human Adaptation (Lung Biology in Health and Disease, Vol 161). New York: Marcel Dekker, 2001, pp 377–423.

86. Severinghaus JW: Cerebral circulation at high altitude. *In* Hornbein TF, Schoene RB (eds): High Altitude: An Exploration of Human Adaptation (Lung Biology in Health and Disease, Vol 161). New York: Marcel Dekker, 2001, pp 343–375.

87. Severinghaus JW, Chiodi H, Eger EL II, et al: Cerebral blood flow in man at high altitude: Role of cerebrospinal fluid pH in normalization of flow in chronic hypocapnia. Circ Res 19:274–282, 1966.

88. Clark CF, Heaton RK, Wiens AN: Neuropsychological functioning after prolonged high altitude exposure in mountaineering. Aviat Space Environ Med 54:202–207, 1983.

89. Sharma VM, Malhotra MS: Ethnic variations in psychological performance under altitude stress. Aviat Space Environ Med 47:248–251, 1976.

90. Regard M, Oelz O, Brugger P, et al: Persistent cognitive impairment in climbers after repeated exposure to high altitude. Neurology 39:210–213, 1989.

91. Hornbein TF, Townes B, Houston CS: The cost to the central nervous system of climbing to extremely high altitude. N Engl J Med 321:1714–1719, 1989.

92. Lahiri S, Maret KH, Sherpa MG, et al: Sleep and periodic breathing at high altitude: Sherpa natives versus sojourners. *In* West JB, Lahiri S (eds): High Altitude and Man. Bethesda, Md: American Physiological Society, 1984, pp 73–90.

93. Berssenbrugge A, Dempsey J, Skatrud J: Hypoxic versus hypocapnic effects on periodic breathing during sleep. *In* West JB, Lahiri S (eds): High Altitude and Man. Bethesda, Md: American Physiological Society, 1984, pp 115–128.

94. Lahiri S, Maret K, Sherpa MG: Dependence of high-altitude sleep apnea on ventilatory sensitivity to hypoxia. Respir Physiol 52:281–301, 1983.

95. West JB, Peters RM Jr, Aksnes G, et al: Nocturnal periodic breathing at altitudes of 6300 and 8050 meters. J Appl Physiol 61:280–287, 1987.

96. Sutton JR, Houston CS, Mansele AL, et al: Effect of acetazolamide on hypoxia during sleep at high altitude. N Engl J Med 301:1329–1331, 1979.

97. Kryger M, McCullough RE, Collins D, et al: Treatment of chronic mountain polycythemia with respiratory stimulation. Am Rev Respir Dis 117:455–464, 1978.

98. Hackett PH, Roach RC, Harrison G, et al: Respiratory stimulants and sleep periodic breathing at high altitude: Almitrine versus acetazolamide. Am Rev Respir Dis 135:896–898, 1987.

99. West JB, Boyer SJ, Graber DJ, et al: Maximal exercise at extreme altitudes on Mount Everest. J Appl Physiol 55:688–702, 1983.

100. Sutton JR, Reeves JT, Wagner PD, et al: Operation Everest II: Oxygen transport during exercise at extreme simulated altitude. J Appl Physiol 64:1309–1321, 1988.

101. Wagner PD, Gale GE, Moon RE, et al: Pulmonary gas exchange in humans exercising at sea level and simulated altitude. J Appl Physiol 61:280–287, 1986.

102. Roach R, Kayser B: Exercise and hypoxia: Performance, limits, and training. *In* Hornbein TF, Schoene RB (eds): High Altitude: An Exploration of Human Adaptation (Lung Biology in Health and Disease, Vol 161). New York: Marcel Dekker, 2001, pp 663–705.

103. Schoene RB, Lahiri S, Hackett PH, et al: Relationship of hypoxic ventilatory response to exercise performance on Mount Everest. J Appl Physiol 56:1478–1483, 1984.

104. Schoene RB: The control of ventilation in climbers to extreme altitude. J Appl Physiol 53:886–890, 1982.

105. Masuyama S, Kimura H, Sugita T, et al: Control of ventilation in extreme-altitude climbers. J Appl Physiol 61:500–506, 1986.

106. Lahiri S, Kao FF, Velasquez T, et al: Respiration of man during exercise at high altitude: Highlanders vs. lowlanders. Respir Physiol 8:361–375, 1970.

107. Torre-Bueno JR, Wagner PD, Saltzman HA, et al: Diffusion limitation in normal humans during exercise at sea level and simulated altitude. J Appl Physiol 58:989–995, 1985.

108. Reeves, JT, Groves BM, Sutton JR, et al: Operation Everest II: Preservation of cardiac function at extreme altitude. J Appl Physiol 63:531–539, 1987.

109. Grover RF, Reeves JT, Grover EB, et al: Muscular exercise in young men native to 3100 m altitude. J Appl Physiol 22:555–564, 1967.

110. Groves BM, Reeves JT, Sutton JR, et al: Operation Everest II: Elevated high altitude pulmonary resistance unresponsive to oxygen. J Appl Physiol 63:521–530, 1987.

111. Roca J, Hogan MC, Story D: Evidence for peripheral tissue diffusion limitation of maximum O_2 uptake. J Appl Physiol 67:291–299, 1989.

112. Hogan MC, Roca J, Wagner PD, et al: Limitation of maximal O_2 uptake and performance by acute hypoxia in dog muscle in situ. J Appl Physiol 65:815–821, 1988.

113. Crenshaw AG, Fryden J, Thornell L, et al: Extreme endurance training: Evidence of capillary and mitochondrial compartmentalization in human skeletal muscle. Eur J Appl Physiol 63:173–178, 1991.

114. Roca J, Agusti AG, Alonso A, et al: Effects of training on muscle O_2 transport at VO2max. J Appl Physiol 73:1067–1076, 1992.

115. Wagner PD: Determinants of maximal oxygen transport and utilization. Annu Rev Physiol 58:21–50, 1996.

116. Hogan MC, Bebout DE, Wagner PD, et al: Maximal oxygen uptake of in situ dog muscle during acute hypoxemia with constant perfusion. J Appl Physiol 69:570–576, 1990.

117. Richardson RS, Knight DR, Poole DC, et al: Determinants of maximal exercise VO2 during single leg knee-extensor exercise in humans. Am J Physiol 268:H1453–H1461, 1995.

118. Richardson RS, Noyszewski EA, Kendrick KF, et al: Myoglobin O_2 desaturation during exercise: Evidence of a limited O_2 transport. J Clin Invest 96:1916–1926, 1995.

119. Cerretelli P, di Prampero PE: Aerobic and anaerobic metabolism during exercise at altitude. Med Sport Sci 19:1–19, 1985.

120. Green HJ, Sutton JR, Young P, et al: Operation Everest II: Muscle energetics during maximal exhaustive exercise. J Appl Physiol 66:142–150, 1989.

121. Van Hall G, Calbet JA, Sondergaard H, Saltin B: Similar carbohydrate but enhanced lactate utilization during exercise after 9 wk of acclimatization to 5,620 m. Am J Physiol Endocrinol Metab 283:E1203–E1213, 2002.

122. Levine BD: Intermittent hypoxic training: Fact and fancy. High Alt Med Biol 3:177–193, 2002.

123. Beidleman BA, Muza SR, Fulco CS, et al: Intermittent altitude exposures improve muscular performance at 4,300 m. J Appl Physiol 95:1824–1832, 2003.

124. Levine BD, Stray-Gundersen J: "Living high-training low": Effect of moderate altitude acclimatization with low-altitude training on performance. J Appl Physiol 83:102–112, 1997.

125. Chapman RF, Stray-Gundersen J, Levine BD: Individual variation in response to altitude training. J Appl Physiol 85:1448–1456, 1998.

126. Bärtsch P, Grunig E, Hohenhaus E, Dehnert C: Assessment of high altitude tolerance in healthy individuals. High Alt Med Biol 2:287–296, 2001.

127. Hackett PH, Rennie D, Levine HD: The incidence, importance, and prophylaxis of acute mountain sickness. Lancet 2:1149–1154, 1976.

128. Honigman B, Theis MK, Koziol-McClain J, et al: Acute mountain sickness in a general tourist population at moderate altitudes. Ann Intern Med 118:587–592, 1993.

129. Pollard AJ, Niermeyer S, Barry P, et al: Children at high altitude: An international consensus statement by an ad hoc committee of the International Society for Mountain Medicine. High Alt Med Biol 2:389–403, 2001.

130. Bärtsch P, Roach RC: Acute mountain sickness and high-altitude pulmonary edema. In Hornbein TF, Schoene RB (eds): High Altitude: An Exploration of Human Adaptation. New York: Marcel Dekker, 2001, pp 731–776.

131. Roach RC, Icenogle MV, Maes D, et al: Body temperature, autonomic responses, and acute mountain sickness. High Alt Med Biol 4:367–373, 2003.

132. Singh I, Khanna PK, Srivastava MC, et al: Acute mountain sickness. N Engl J Med 280:175–184, 1969.

133. Montgomery AB, Mills J, Luce JM: Incidence of acute mountain sickness at intermediate altitude. JAMA 261:732–734, 1989.

134. Levine BD, Yoshimura K, Kobayashi T, et al: Dexamethasone in the treatment of acute mountain sickness. N Engl J Med 321:1707–1713, 1989.

135. Hackett PH, Yarnell PR, Hill R, et al: High altitude cerebral edema evaluated with magnetic resonance imaging: Clinical correlation and pathophysiology. JAMA 280:1920–1925, 1998.

136. Roach RC, Hackett PH: Frontiers of hypoxia research: Acute mountain sickness. J Exp Biol 204:3161–3170, 2001.

137. Hackett PH, Roach RC: High-altitude illness. N Engl J Med 345:107–114, 2001.

138. Fischer R, Vollmar C, Thiere M et al: No evidence of cerebral oedema in severe acute mountain sickness. Cephalalgia 24:66–71, 2004.

139. Jensen JB, Wright AD, Lassen NA, et al: Cerebral blood flow in acute mountain sickness. J Appl Physiol 69:430–433, 1990.

140. Jansen GF, Krins A, Basnyat B: Cerebral vasomotor reactivity at high altitude in humans. J Appl Physiol 86:681–686, 1999.

141. Baumgartner RW, Spyridopoulos I, Bärtsch P, et al: Acute mountain sickness is not related to cerebral blood flow: A decompression chamber study. J Appl Physiol 86:1578–1582, 1999.

142. Lysakowski C, Von Elm E, Dumont L, et al: The effect of magnesium, high altitude, and acute mountain sickness on blood flow velocity in the middle cerebral artery. Clin Sci (Lond) 106:279–285, 2004.

143. Buzzi MG, Bonamini M, Moskowitz MA: Neurogenic model of migraine. Cephalalgia 15:277–280, 1995.

144. Bailey DM, Kelger GR, Holzgraefe M, et al: Pathophysiological significance of peroxidative stress, neuronal damage and membrane permeability in acute mountain sickness. J Appl Physiol 96:1459–1463, 2004.

145. Mark KS, Burroughs AR, Brown RC, et al: Nitric oxide mediates hypoxia-induced changes in paracellular permeability of cerebral microvasculature. Am J Physiol Heart Circ Physiol 286:H174–H180, 2004.

146. Maloney J, Wang D, Duncan T, et al: Plasma vascular endothelial growth factor in acute mountain sickness. Chest 118:47–52, 2000.

146a. Tissot van Patot MC, Leadbetter G, Keyes LE, et al: Greater free plasma VEGF and lower soluble VEGF receptor-1 in acute mountain sickness. J Appl Physiol 2005, in press.

147. Roach RC, Greene ER, Schoene RB, Hackett PH: Arterial oxygen saturation for prediction of acute mountain sickness. Aviat Space Environ Med 69:1182–1185, 1998.

148. Grissom CK, Roach RC, Sarnquist FH, et al: Acetazolamide in the treatment of acute mountain sickness: Clinical efficacy and effect on gas exchange. Ann Intern Med 116:461–465, 1992.

149. Cremona G, Asnaghi R, Baderna P, et al: Pulmonary extravascular fluid accumulation in recreational climbers: A prospective study. Lancet 359:303–309, 2002.

150. Mason NP, Petersen M, Melot C, et al: Serial changes in nasal potential difference and lung electrical impedance tomography at high altitude. J Appl Physiol 94:2043–2050, 2003.

151. Ge RL, Matsuzawa Y, Takeoka M, et al: Low pulmonary diffusing capacity in subjects with acute mountain sickness. Chest 111:58–64, 1997.

152. Hlastala MP, Lamm WJ, Karp A, et al: Spatial distribution of hypoxic pulmonary vasoconstriction in the supine pig. J Appl Physiol 96:1589–1599, 2004.

153. Swenson ER, Duncan TB, Goldberg SV, et al: Diuretic effect of acute hypoxia in humans: Relationship to hypoxic ventilatory responsiveness and renal hormones. J Appl Physiol 78:377–383, 1995.

154. Maggiorini M, Melot C, Pierre S, et al: High-altitude pulmonary edema is initially caused by an increase in capillary pressure. Circulation 103:2078–2083, 2001.

155. Duplain H, Vollenweider L, Delabays A, et al: Augmented sympathetic activation during short-term hypoxia and high-altitude exposure in subjects susceptible to high-altitude pulmonary edema. Circulation 99:1713–1718, 1999.

156. Grissom CK, Roach RC, Sarnquist FH, et al: Acetazolamide in the treatment of acute mountain sickness: Clinical efficacy and effect on gas exchange. Ann Intern Med 116:461–465, 1992.

157. Kleger GR, Bärtsch P, Vock P, et al: Evidence against an increase in capillary permeability in subjects exposed to high altitude. J Appl Physiol 81:1917–1923, 1996.

158. Moore LG, Harrison GL, McCullough RE, et al: Low acute hypoxic ventilatory response and hypoxic depression in acute altitude sickness. J Appl Physiol 60:1407–1412, 1986.

159. Milledge JS, Thomas PS, Beeley JM, English JS: Hypoxic ventilatory response and acute mountain sickness. Eur Respir J 1:948–951, 1998.

160. Bärtsch P, Swenson ER, Paul A, et al: Hypoxic ventilatory response, ventilation, gas exchange, and fluid balance in acute mountain sickness. High Alt Med Biol 3:361–376, 2003.

161. Fischer R, Lang SM, Leitl M, et al: Theophylline and acetazolamide reduce sleep-disordered breathing at high altitude. Eur Respir J 23:47–52, 2004.

162. Hansen JE, Hartley LH, Hogan RP: Arterial oxygen increase by high carbohydrate diet at altitude. J Appl Physiol 33:441–445, 1972.

163. Consolazio CF, Matoush LO, Johnson HL, et al: Effects of a high carbohydrate diet on performance and clinical symptomatology after rapid ascent to high altitude. Fed Proc 28:937–943, 1969.

164. Swenson ER, MacDonald A, Vathever M, et al: Acute mountain sickness is not altered by a high carbohydrate diet nor associated with elevated circulating cytokines. Aviat Space Environ Med 68:499–503, 1997.

165. Birmingham Medical Research Expeditionary Society Mountain Sickness Study Group: Acetazolamide in control of acute mountain sickness. Lancet 1:180–183, 1981.

166. Swenson ER: Carbonic anhydrase inhibitors and ventilation: A complex interplay of stimulation and suppression. Eur Respir J 12:1242–1247, 1998.

167. Greene MK, Kerr AM, McIntosh IB, et al: Acetazolamide in prevention of acute mountain sickness: A double blind controlled cross-over study. BMJ 283:811–813, 1981.

168. Basnyat B, Gertsch JH, Johnson EW, et al: Efficacy of low-dose acetazolamide (125 mg BID) for the prophylaxis of acute mountain sickness: A prospective, double-blind, randomized, placebo-controlled trial. High Alt Med Biol 4:45–52, 2003.

169. Carlsten C, Swenson ER, Ruoss S: A dose response trial of acetazolamide for acute mountain sickness prevention in visitors to 13,000 feet. High Alt Med Biol 5:33–39, 2004.

170. Johnson TS, Rock PB, Fulco CS, et al: Prevention of acute mountain sickness by dexamethasone. N Engl J Med 310:683–686, 1984.

171. Ellsworth AJ, Meyer EF, Larson EB: Acetazolamide and dexamethasone use versus placebo to prevent acute mountain sickness on Mount Rainier. West J Med 154:289–293, 1991.

172. Zell SC, Goodman PH: Acetazolamide and dexamethasone in the prevention of acute mountain sickness. West J Med 148:541–545, 1988.

173. Taber RL: Protocols for the use of a portable hyperbaric chamber for the treatment of high altitude disorders. J Wilderness Med 1:181–192, 1990.

174. Kasic JF, Yaron M, Nicholas RA, et al: Treatment of acute mountain sickness: Hyperbaric versus oxygen therapy. Ann Emerg Med 20:1109–1112, 1991.

175. Harris NS, Wenzel RP, Thomas SH: High altitude headache: Efficacy of acetaminophen vs. ibuprofen in a randomized, controlled trial. J Emerg Med 24:383–387, 2003.

176. Utiger D, Eichenberger U, Bernasch D, et al: Transient minor improvement of high altitude headache by sumatriptan. High Alt Med Biol 3:387–393, 2002.

177. Olson LG, Hensley MJ, Saunders NA: Augmentation of ventilatory response to asphyxia by prochlorperazine in humans. J Appl Physiol 53:637–643, 1982.

178. Dubowitz G: Effect of temazepam on oxygen saturation and sleep quality at high altitude: Randomised placebo controlled crossover trial. BMJ 316:587–589, 1998.

179. Houston CS, Dickinson JD: Cerebral form of high altitude illness. Lancet 2:758–761, 1975.

180. Yarnell PR, Heit J, Hackett PH: High-altitude cerebral edema (HACE): The Denver/Front Range experience. Semin Neurol 20:209–217, 2000.

181. Dickinson JD, Heath D, Gosney J, et al: Altitude-related deaths in seven trekkers in the Himalayas. Thorax 38:646–656, 1983.

182. Hultgren H, Spickard W: Medical experiences in Peru. Stanford Med Bull 18:76–95, 1960.

183. Houston CS: Acute pulmonary edema of high altitude. N Engl J Med 263:478–480, 1960.

184. Hultgren HN, Lopez CE, Lundberg E, et al: Physiologic studies of pulmonary edema at high altitude. Circulation 29:393–408, 1964.

185. Schoene RB, Hultgren HN, Swenson ER: High-altitude pulmonary edema. *In* Hornbein TF, Schoene RB (eds): High Altitude: An Exploration of Human Adaptation (Lung Biology in Health and Disease, Vol 161). New York: Marcel Dekker, 2001, pp 778–814.

186. Schoene RB, Swenson ER, Pizzo CJ, et al: The lung at high altitude: Bronchoalveolar lavage in acute mountain sickness and pulmonary edema. J Appl Physiol 64:2605–2613, 1988.

187. Kubo K, Hanaoka M, Yamaguchi S, et al: Cytokines in bronchoalveolar lavage fluid in patients with high altitude pulmonary oedema at moderate altitude in Japan. Thorax 51:739–742, 1996.

188. Swenson ER, Maggiorini M, Mongovin S, et al: Pathogenesis of high-altitude pulmonary edema: Inflammation is not an etiologic factor. JAMA 287:2228–2235, 2002.

189. Hultgren HN: High altitude pulmonary edema. *In* Hegnauer A (ed): Biomedical Problems of High Terrestrial Altitudes. Springfield, Va: Federal Scientific and Technical Information, 1967, pp 131–141.

190. Hackett PH, Creagh CE, Grover RF, et al: High altitude pulmonary edema in persons without the right pulmonary artery. N Engl J Med 302:1070–1073, 1980.

191. Viswanathan R, Subramanian S, Radha TG: Effect of hypoxia on regional lung perfusion, by scanning. Respiration 37:142–147, 1979.

191a. Hopkins SR, Garg J, Bolar DS, et al: Pulmonary blood flow heterogeneity during hypoxia and high-altitude pulmonary edema. Am J Respir Crit Care Med 171:83–87, 2005.

192. West JBV, Mathieu-Costello O: Structure, strength, failure, and remodeling of the pulmonary blood-gas barrier. Annu Rev Physiol 61:543–572, 1999.

193. Tsukimoto K, Yoshimura N, Ichioka M, et al: Protein, cell, and leukotriene B$_4$ concentrations of lung edema fluid produced by high capillary pressures in rabbit. J Appl Physiol 76:321–327, 1994.

194. West JB, Mathieu-Costello O: Strength of the pulmonary blood-gas barrier. Respir Physiol 88:141–148, 1992.

195. West JB, Tsukimoto K, Mathieu-Costello O, et al: Stress failure in pulmonary capillaries. J Appl Physiol 70:1731–1742, 1991.

196. Parker JC, Ivey CL, Tucker JA: Gadolinium prevents high airway pressure-induced permeability increases in isolated rat lungs. J Appl Physiol 84:1113–1118, 1998.

197. Parker JC, Ivey CL: Isoproterenol attenuates high vascular pressure-induced permeability increases in isolated rat lungs. J Appl Physiol 83:1962–1967, 1997.

198. West JB: Thoughts on the pulmonary blood-gas barrier. Am J Physiol Lung Cell Mol Physiol 285:L501–L513, 2003.

199. Maron MB, Fu Z, Mathieu-Costello O, West JB: Effect of high transcapillary pressures on capillary ultrastructure and permeability coefficients in dog lung. J Appl Physiol 90:638–648, 2001.

200. Yagi H, Yamada H, Kobayashi T, et al: Doppler assessment of pulmonary hypertension induced by hypoxic breathing in subjects susceptible to high altitude pulmonary edema. Am Rev Respir Dis 142:796–801, 1990.

201. Hultgren HN, Grover RF, Hartley LH: Abnormal circulatory responses to high altitude in subjects with a previous history of high altitude pulmonary edema. Circulation 44:759–770, 1971.

202. Hackett PH, Roach RC, Schoene RB, et al: Abnormal control of ventilation in high-altitude pulmonary edema. J Appl Physiol 64:1268–1272, 1988.

203. Matsuzawa Y, Fujimoto K, Kobayashi T, et al: Blunted hypoxic ventilatory drive in subjects susceptible to high-altitude pulmonary edema. J Appl Physiol 66:1152–1157, 1989.

204. Hohenhaus E, Paul A, McCullough RE, et al: Ventilatory and pulmonary vascular response to hypoxia and susceptibility to high altitude pulmonary oedema. Eur Respir J 8:1825–1833, 1995.

205. Selland MA, Stelzner TJ, Stevens T, et al: Pulmonary function and hypoxic ventilatory response in subjects susceptible to high-altitude pulmonary edema. Chest 103:111–116, 1993.

206. Podolsky A, Eldridge MW, Richardson RS, et al: Exercise-induced VA/Q inequality in subjects with prior high-altitude pulmonary edema. J Appl Physiol 81:922–932, 1996.

207. Steinacker J, Tobias P, Menold E, et al: Lung diffusing capacity and exercise in subjects with previous high altitude pulmonary edema. Eur Respir J 11:643–650, 1998.

208. Bärtsch P: High altitude pulmonary edema. Respiration 64:435–444, 1997.

209. Duplain H, Vollenweider L, Delabays A, et al: Augmented sympathetic activation during short-term hypoxia and high-altitude exposure in subjects susceptible to high-altitude pulmonary edema. Circulation 99:1713–1718, 1999.

210. Bärtsch P, Shaw S, Franciolli M, et al: Atrial natriuretic peptide in acute mountain sickness. J Appl Physiol 65:1929–1937, 1988.

211. Koyama S, Kobayashi T, Kubo K, et al: The increased sympathoadrenal activity in patients with high altitude pulmonary edema is centrally mediated. Jpn J Med 27:10–16, 1988.

212. Lear GH: Neurogenic pulmonary oedema. Acta Paediatr Scand 79:1131–1133, 1990.

212a. Mortimer H, Patel S, Peacock AJ: The genetic basis of high-altitude pulmonary oedema. Pharmacol Ther 101:183–192, 2004.

213. Sartori C, Vollenweider L, Löffler B-M, et al: Exaggerated endothelin release in high-altitude pulmonary edema. Circulation 99:2665–2668, 1999.

214. Droma Y, Hayano T, Takabayashi Y, et al: Endothelin-1 and interleukin-8 in high altitude pulmonary oedema. Eur Respir J 9:1947–1949, 1996.

215. Busch T, Bärtsch P, Pappert D, et al: Hypoxia decreases exhaled nitric oxide in mountaineers susceptible to high altitude pulmonary edema. Am J Respir Crit Care Med 163:368–373, 2001.

216. Duplain H, Sartori C, Lepori M, et al: Exhaled nitric oxide in high-altitude pulmonary edema: Role in the regulation of pulmonary vascular tone and evidence for a role against inflammation. Am J Resp Crit Care Med 162:221–224, 2000.

217. Bärtsch P, Swenson ER, Maggiorini M: Update: High altitude pulmonary edema. Adv Exp Med Biol 502:89–106, 2001.

218. Stelzner TJ, O'Brien RF, Sato K, Weil JV: Hypoxia-induced increases in pulmonary trans-vascular protein escape in rats: Modulation by glucocorticoids. J Clin Invest 82:1840–1847, 1988.

219. Durmowicz AG, Noordeweir E, Nicholas R, Reeves JT: Inflammatory processes may predispose children to high-altitude pulmonary edema. J Pediatr 130:838–840, 1997.

220. Gabry AL, Ledoux X, Mozziconacci M, Martin C: High-altitude pulmonary edema at moderate altitude (<2,400 m; 7,870 feet): A series of 52 patients. Chest 123:49–53, 2003.

221. Ferrari E, Chevallier T, Chapelier A, Baudouy M: Travel as a risk factor for venous thromboembolic disease: A case-control study. Chest 115:440–444, 1999.

222. Maron MB: Analysis of airway fluid protein concentration in neurogenic pulmonary edema. J Appl Physiol 62:470–476, 1987.

223. Malik AB: Pulmonary vascular response to increase in intracranial pressure: Role of sympathetic mechanisms. J Appl Physiol 42:335–343, 1977.

224. Hackett PH, Roach RC, Hartig GS, et al: The effect of vasodilators on pulmonary hemodynamics in high altitude pulmonary edema: a comparison. Int J Sports Med 13(Suppl 1)S68–S71, 1992.

225. Kobayashi T, Koyama S, Kubo K, et al: Clinical features of patients with high altitude pulmonary edema in Japan. Chest 92:814–821, 1987.

226. Koyama S, Kobayashi T, Kubo K, et al: The increased sympathoadrenal activity in patients with high altitude pulmonary edema is centrally mediated. Jpn J Med 27:10–16, 1988.

227. Hackett PH, Roach RC, Schoene RB, et al: Abnormal control of ventilation in high-altitude pulmonary edema. J Appl Physiol 64:1268–1272, 1988.

228. Wilson MB, Levitzky MG: Chemoreflex blunting of hypoxic pulmonary vasoconstriction is vagally mediated. J Appl Physiol 66:782–791, 1989.

229. Wodopia R, Ko HS, Billian J, et al: Hypoxia decreases proteins involved in epithelial electrolyte transport in A549 cells and rat lung. Am J Physiol Lung Cell Mol Physiol 279:L1110–L1119, 2000.

230. Vivona ML, Matthay M, Chabaud MB, et al: Hypoxia reduces alveolar epithelial sodium and fluid transport in rats: Reversal by beta-adrenergic agonist treatment. Am J Respir Cell Mol Biol 25:554–561, 2001.

231. Egli M, Cook L, Hugli O, et al: Delayed resolution of pulmonary edema in mice with deficient Na-transport dependent alveolar fluid clearance. FASEB J 15:860, 2001.

231a. Egli M, Duplain H, Lepori M, et al: Defective respiratory amiloride-sensitive sodium transport predisposes to pulmonary oedema and delays its resolution in mice. J Physiol 560:857–865, 2004.

232. Sartori C, Allemann Y, Duplain H, et al: Salmeterol for the prevention of high-altitude pulmonary edema. N Engl J Med 346:1631–1636, 2002.

233. Bärtsch P, Mairbaurl M: Salmeterol for prevention of high altitude pulmonary edema. N Engl J Med 347:1282–1285, 2002.

234. Mairbaurl H, Weymann J, Mohrlein A, et al: Nasal epithelium potential difference at high altitude (4,559 m): Evidence for secretion. Am J Respir Crit Care Med 167:862–872, 2003.

235. Hackett PH, Roach RC, Goldberg S, et al: A portable, fabric hyperbaric chamber for treatment of high altitude pulmonary edema (abstract). In Sutton JR, Coates G, Remmers JE (eds): Hypoxia: The Adaptations. Philadelphia: BC Decker, 1990, p 291.

236. Chauca D, Bligh J: An additive effect of cold exposure and hypoxia on pulmonary artery pressure in sheep. Res Vet Sci 21:123–124, 1976.

237. Schoene RB, Roach RC, Hackett PH, et al: High altitude pulmonary edema and exercise at 4400 meters on Mount McKinley: Effect of expiratory positive airway pressure. Chest 87:330–333, 1985.

238. Menon ND: High altitude pulmonary edema. N Engl J Med 273:66–72, 1965.

239. Oelz O, Maggiorini M, Ritter M, et al: Nifedipine for high altitude pulmonary edema. Lancet 2:1241–1244, 1989.

240. Deem S, Hedges RG, Kerr ME, Swenson ER: Acetazolamide reduces hypoxic pulmonary vasoconstriction in isolated perfused rabbit lungs. Respir Physiol 123:109–119, 2000.

241. Bärtsch P, Maggiorini M, Ritter M, et al: Prevention of high-altitude pulmonary edema by nifedipine. N Engl J Med 325:1284–1289, 1991.

241a. Maggiorini M, Brunner-La Rocca HP, Bärtsch P, et al: Dexamethasone and tadalafil prophylaxis prevent both excessive pulmonary constriction and high altitude pulmonary edema in susceptible subjects. Eur Respir J 24:110s, 2004.

242. Heath D, Williams DR: Man at High Altitude (2nd ed). Edinburgh, Churchill Livingstone, 1981.

243. Singh I, Chohan IS, Mathew NT: Fibrinolytic activity in high altitude pulmonary edema. Indian J Med Res 57:210–217, 1969.

244. Singh I: Pulmonary Hypertension in New Arrivals at High Altitude: Proceedings of World Health Organization Meeting on Primary Pulmonary Hypertension, October 1973. Geneva, World Health Organization, 1974.

245. Bärtsch P, Haeberli A, Franciolli M, et al: PW: Coagulation and fibrinolysis in acute mountain sickness and beginning pulmonary edema. J Appl Physiol 66:2136–2144, 1989.

246. Bärtsch P: Hypobaric hypoxia. Lancet 357:955–956, 2001.

247. Sui GJ, Liu YH, Cheng XS, et al: Subacute infantile mountain sickness. J Pathol 155:161–170, 1988.

248. Anand IS, Malhotra RM, Chandrashekhar Y, et al: Adult subacute mountain sickness: A syndrome of congestive heart failure in man at very high altitude. Lancet 335:561–565, 1990.

249. Anand IS, Phil D, Chandrashekhar Y: Subacute mountain sickness syndromes: Role of pulmonary hypertension. In Sutton JR, Coates G, Houston CS (eds): Hypoxia and Mountain Medicine. Burlington, Vt: Queen City Printers, 1992, pp 241–251.

250. Monge MC: La enfermedad de los Andes: Sindromes eritremicos. Ann Fac Med Univ San Marcos (Lima) 11:1–316, 1928.

251. Leon-Velarde F, Ramos MA, Hernandez JA, et al: The role of menopause in the development of chronic mountain sickness. Am J Physiol 272(1 Pt 2):R90–R94, 1997.

252. Xie C-F, Pei S-X: Some physiological data on sojourners and native highlanders at three different altitudes in Xizang. In Shang LD (ed): Proceedings of Symposium on Tibet Plateau. New York, Gordon and Breach Science Publishers, 1981, pp 1449–1452.

253. Kryger M, McCullough R, Doekel R, et al: Excessive polycythemia of high altitude: Role of ventilatory drive and lung disease. Am Rev Respir Dis 118:659–666, 1978.

254. Kryger MH, Grover RF: Chronic mountain sickness. Semin Respir Med 5:164–168, 1983.

255. Monge CC: Natural Acclimatization to High Altitudes: Clinical Conditions in Life at High Altitudes (Scientific Publication No. 140). Washington, DC, Pan American Health Organization, 1996, pp 46–52.

256. Winslow RM: Relationship between erythropoiesis and ventilation in high altitude natives. In Lahiri S, Cherniack NS, Fitzerland RS (eds): Response and Adaptation to Hypoxia: Organ to Organelle. New York, Oxford University Press, 1991, pp 143–156.

257. Weil JV, Kryger MH, Scoggin CH: Sleep and breathing at high altitude. In Guilleminault C, Dement WC (eds): Sleep Apnea Syndromes. New York, Alan R Liss, 1978, pp 119–136.

258. Jefferson JA, Escudero E, Hurtado ME, et al: Excessive erythrocytosis, chronic mountain sickness, and serum cobalt levels. Lancet 359:407–408, 2002.

259. Kryger M, McCullough RE, Collins D, et al: Treatment of excessive polycythemia of high altitude with respiratory stimulant drugs. Am Rev Respir Dis 117:455–464, 1978.

260. Plata R, Cornejo A, Arratia C, et al: Angiotensin-converting-enzyme inhibition therapy in altitude polycythaemia: A prospective randomised trial. Lancet 359:663–666, 2002.

261. Hultgren HN, Marticorena EA: High altitude pulmonary edema: Epidemiologic observations in Peru. Chest 74:372–376, 1978.

262. Scoggin CH, Hyers TM, Reeves JT, et al: High altitude pulmonary edema in the children and young adults of Leadville, Colorado. N Engl J Med 297:1269–1273, 1977.

263. Graham WG, Houston CS: Short-term adaptation to moderate altitude: Patients with chronic obstructive pulmonary disease. JAMA 240:1491–1494, 1978.

264. Dillard T, Rosenberg A, Berg B, et al: Hypoxemia during altitude exposure: A meta-analysis of chronic obstructive pulmonary disease. Chest 103:422–425, 1993.

265. Gong H Jr, Tashkin DP, Lee EY, et al: Hypoxia-altitude simulation test: Evaluation of patients with chronic airway obstruction. Am Rev Respir Dis 130:980–986, 1984.

266. Gong H Jr: Air travel and oxygen therapy in cardiopulmonary patients. Chest 101:1104–1113, 1992.

267. Burgess KR, Johnson PL, Edwards N: Central and obstructive sleep apnoea during ascent to high altitude. Respirology 9:222–229, 2004.

268. Hackett PH, Rennie D: Avoiding mountain sickness. Lancet 2:938, 1978.

269. Larson EB, Roach RC, Schoene RB, Hornbein TF: Acute mountain sickness and acetazoleamide: Clinical efficacy and effect on ventilation. JAMA 2248:328–332, 1982.

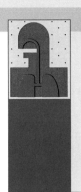

66

Diving Medicine

Alfred A. Bove, M.D., Ph.D., **Tom S. Neuman,** M.D.

INTRODUCTION

INCREASED PRESSURE

Humans are exposed to increased pressure when submerged underwater and when subjected to elevated pressures in closed pressure vessels. Underwater exposure is experienced by divers, who are subject to increasing pressure directly proportional to depth (Table 66.1). Pressure vessels include hyperbaric chambers used for treatment of medical and diving-related diseases, pressurized tunnels and caissons used for underwater construction, and underwater habitats. As depth and pressure increase, the diver breathes gas of increased density using breathing equipment that provides oxygen and allows for elimination of carbon dioxide.

RELATION TO ALTITUDE

Excursions to high altitude expose blood and tissues to the risk of free gas formation (see discussion later). Divers with increased inert gas in tissues from diving can develop free gas in tissues when going to altitude after diving even though they follow established protocols for ascent from depth to the surface. Flying after diving is a common occurrence among sport divers, who may fly in commercial aircraft (about 8000 feet equivalent altitude) shortly after diving. The excursion above sea level produces inert gas supersaturation, which may cause free gas to form in tissues and blood.

Aviators ascending to altitudes above 18,000 feet (0.5 atmosphere absolute [ATA]) are also subject to free gas formation due to supersaturation of tissue inert gases dissolved at atmospheric pressure.[1]

WATER IMMERSION

Increases in intrathoracic blood volume occur with water immersion.[2] Intrathoracic pressure at end-expiration increases from −5 cm H_2O while standing in air to −2 cm H_2O during immersion,[3,4] and abdominal pressure increases from −6 cm H_2O in air to +12 cm H_2O during immersion.[3,5] The hydrostatic pressure prevents blood from pooling in the peripheral veins. The increase in transdiaphragmatic pressure and the absence of venous blood pooling increase venous return during immersion. (In this respect, immersion in water is analogous to a gravity-free state.) The magnitude of the increase in the intrathoracic blood volume during head-out immersion has been estimated to be about 700 mL.[2,6] The central blood shifts result in an increase in cardiac output[7] and an increase in central venous pressure. The increase in intrathoracic blood volume causes a diuresis due to release of natriuretic hormones.

Although immersion effects are found in all divers, breath-hold divers also exhibit effects from diving while apneic.[8] Breath-hold divers can develop sudden unconsciousness during ascent from long apneic dives.[9] This phenomenon is called *shallow water blackout* and is due to a progressive reduction in arterial PO_2 as the breath-hold

Table 66.1 Pressure Equivalents for Altitude and Depth

	Feet	ATM	mm Hg	psi
Altitude above sea level	12,000	0.636	483	9.3
	8,000	0.742	564	10.9
	4,000	0.863	656	12.7
Sea level	0	1	760	14.7
Depth in sea water	33	2	1,520	29.4
	66	3	2,280	44.1
	99	4	3,040	58.8
	132	5	3,800	73.5

ATM, atmospheres absolute; psi, pounds/square inch.

diver ascends with arterial Po_2 already reduced due to metabolic needs.

THERMAL EXPOSURE

Most diving is done in water with temperature below the skin temperature (30° C), and the diver loses heat throughout the dive. Therefore, hypothermia is a constant hazard in diving and will occur rapidly in the absence of protective garments even in relatively warm water (e.g., 22° to 23° C). Heat loss is inhibited in divers doing moderate work in water above 30° C, and hyperthermia can develop. A diver must be in 33° C water to be thermoneutral at rest.

As in other forms of hypothermia, initial sensations of cold give way to shivering as a means of heat production. Below 23° C, an unprotected diver will become hypothermic after a short exposure. When body core temperature falls below 35° C, severe shivering is present; muscles of the forearm and hand are stiff, and fine motor function of the hands is impaired.[10] Inability to use the hands may become a safety hazard in cold water diving. Thermal protection for diving generally can be classified as "wet" or "dry." Wet suits are foam neoprene and contain an insulating layer of water situated between the skin and the garment. Dry suits are designed to keep the diver free from water contact. A thin outer garment is an impenetrable barrier. The insulation is derived from undergarments, which utilize trapped air as an insulating medium. The trapped water layer and the nitrogen gas contained in the foam neoprene account for the resistance to heat transfer characteristic of wet suits. Compression of neoprene occurs with increasing depth, and reduces the effectiveness of the insulation. The undergarments of a dry suit tend to be compressed less because compressed air is added to the dry suit to maintain a constant suit volume as depth increases. Wearing a wet suit in relatively warm water (25° C) increases the risk of hyperthermia during physical exertion. Divers wearing no thermal protection in 15° to 18° C water maintain a normal core temperature during continuous exercise at an oxygen consumption ($\dot{V}o_2$) level of 1.5 to 1.8 L/min. On the other hand, intermittent exercise at an equivalent intensity results in a decrease in core temperature in 25° C water.[11] Likewise, brief periods of exercise at a $\dot{V}o_2$ of 2.4 L/min are insufficient to prevent a decline in rectal temperature in thermally protected divers in 5° C water. Combinations of higher water temperatures, greater or longer exercise inten-

sities, and thermal protection may actually produce an increase in core temperature. Divers face heat loss even in tropical waters, which have temperatures ranging from 29° to 31° C.

Diving dress for thermal protection has been developed for different levels of cold exposure. For exposures exceeding 1 to 2 hours with minimal work in 22° C water, a wet suit will provide adequate thermal protection.[12] When water temperature reaches 17° C, a dry suit with an air layer between the diver and the water is required for moderate working exposures; a wet suit can be used for short exposures. When temperature reaches 4° C, a heated wet suit is used to maintain a stable body temperature. At depths exceeding 330 feet, breathing gas must be heated to prevent respiratory heat loss. Cold stress also evokes adaptive thermogenic responses, reflected by changes in $\dot{V}o_2$. The increase in $\dot{V}o_2$ relative to thermoneutral conditions may be immediate upon submersion and persist throughout continuous exercise. A rise in $\dot{V}o_2$ upon exposure to cold water represents an adaptive response that generates additional body heat in order to minimize a change in core temperature. A slower rise in $\dot{V}o_2$ can occur in divers wearing thermal protection. Slow heat loss is often unrecognized until severe hypothermia is present.

Peripheral vasoconstriction occurs in response to the stress of cold water diving. The magnitude of the vasoconstriction is dependent on body core temperature, which, in turn, is affected by the amount of thermal protection and the water temperature. Cold-induced vasoconstriction can persist throughout light to moderate exercise. The same adaptive response can contribute to nonfreezing cold injury when finger or toe temperatures remain below 8° to 10° C for more than 30 minutes.

ENERGY NEEDS FOR DIVING

A scuba diver swimming underwater at a speed of 1.0 knot (about 100 feet/min) consumes about 25 mL of oxygen/kg per minute (Fig. 66.1). This is a high workload and is uncommon in sport scuba diving. Because swimming energy is proportional to the square of velocity, only extremely fit divers tolerate workloads for higher swimming speeds. A diver with a maximum $\dot{V}o_2$ of 40 mL/kg per minute would be able to tolerate swimming at 1.3 knots for a few minutes but would become extremely tachypneic to compensate for lactate production. Swimming at 60% of maximum $\dot{V}o_2$ (about 8 metabolic equivalents), a work level that is at or slightly below the anaerobic threshold,[13] can be sustained for long periods of time. For a diver with a maximum $\dot{V}o_2$ of 40 mL/kg per minute, sustainable swimming speed, working at 60% to 65% of maximum capacity, would be about 100 feet/min, whereas the diver with a maximum $\dot{V}o_2$ of 25 mL/kg per minute would be able to sustain a swimming speed of about 70 feet/min. Safety considerations suggest that the sport diver should be able to tolerate a peak workload of about 40 mL/kg per minute and a sustained workload of about 24 mL/kg per minute (60% of maximum). Scuba divers who maintain this level of physical conditioning can be expected to respond appropriately to most diving workloads. Divers who do not achieve this conditioning level may have difficulty with adverse conditions related to diving. As a result, severe dyspnea may

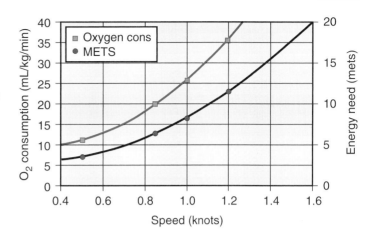

Figure 66.1 Oxygen consumption and metabolic equivalents (METS) are shown for underwater swimming. (Data from Navy Department: U.S. Navy Diving Manual. Vol 1, Rev 3: Air Diving [Publication No. NAVSEA 0994-LP-001–9110]. Washington, DC: U.S. Navy Department, 1996.)

Figure 66.2 The schematics show two types of self-contained diving systems. The open-circuit scuba is the system commonly used for recreational diving. Air is exhaled into the surrounding water. Rebreather systems allow exhaled breathing gas to be recycled through a carbon dioxide scrubber, mixed with additional breathing gas, and returned to the diver through a breathing bag. Breathing gas is replenished via a demand valve. This system can be used with 100% oxygen or oxygen-enriched air mixtures. Other forms of rebreather systems contain separate oxygen and inert gas supplies, and mixing is controlled with a small computer to maintain a constant oxygen partial pressure.

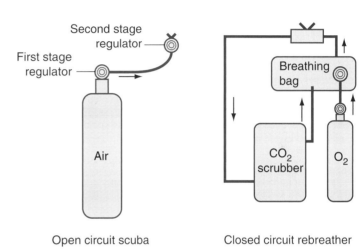

accompany workloads above 65% of maximum aerobic capacity, a physical stress that often leads to panic and increases the risk for drowning.

EQUIPMENT

OPEN-CIRCUIT SCUBA

The most commonly used breathing support system in diving is the open-circuit scuba (self-contained underwater breathing apparatus). This equipment (Fig. 66.2) consists of a pressurized metal cylinder containing compressed air connected to a pressure regulator that lowers pressure first to about 150 psi over ambient pressure and then to ambient pressure in a demand-type regulator with a mouthpiece in the diver's mouth. This device delivers ambient-pressure air only when inhalation is initiated and allows flow that matches the minute volume of the diver. The device may not deliver adequate flow at extremes of exercise, or at depths where gas density is significantly increased, but such high flow rates and depth exposures are uncommon. Its reliability and ease of use have allowed millions of amateur divers to partake in diving as a recreation. Use of open-circuit scuba is limited by the amount of compressed air available in the cylinder carried by the diver. A typical scuba cylinder can supply approximately 2100 L of air at the surface (1 ATA).

This volume is reduced in direct proportion to ambient pressure. For example, at a depth of 66 feet of seawater (fsw) or 3 ATA pressure, the effective volume of air is decreased to 700 L. With a minute ventilation of 20 L/min, this air supply would last 35 minutes. Open-circuit scuba is usually limited to depths above 200 feet because of limited air supply, nitrogen narcosis, and concern for oxygen toxicity.

CLOSED-CIRCUIT SCUBA

To increase diving exposure time, self-contained equipment has advanced to a form that uses a carbon dioxide absorbent to remove exhaled carbon dioxide and replenishes only the oxygen used per minute. Inert gas is conserved by recycling the exhaled gas through the carbon dioxide absorbent and then adding oxygen before the gas is rebreathed in the closed system (see Fig. 66.2). This equipment has several advantages: little gas is released into the surrounding water, oxygen can be carried in volumes adequate for several hours of exposure, and gas consumption is independent of depth. With a mixture of oxygen and inert gas, some of these units can be used to depths exceeding 300 feet.[14] With 100% oxygen, depth is limited to 25 feet because of oxygen toxicity. Although use of closed-circuit scuba in the past was confined to commercial and military divers, simplified rebreather systems are becoming popular among recreational divers.

SURFACE-SUPPLIED EQUIPMENT

Commercial diving developed when compressed air pumps were perfected and an appropriate diving helmet was developed. The diver breathes compressed air pumped from the surface to the helmet, while the excess air flows out through the bottom of the helmet. The modern diving helmet is attached at the collar to a diving suit so that air flows from the helmet into the suit to maintain an air layer for thermal protection. Excess air leaves the closed suit-helmet system via an exhaust valve.

NOMENCLATURE OF THE DISORDERS RELATED TO DIVING

Golding and coworkers[15] described a scheme for categorizing decompression-related disorders that has become the standard nomenclature for describing pressure-related disorders. They described disorders related to supersaturation of inert gases in tissues with subsequent bubble formation as *decompression sickness* (DCS). They described a systemic form of DCS that involves the central nervous system, the lungs, and the circulation ("serious," type II) and a non-systemic (peripheral) form that involves the skin, bones, and joints ("minor," type I). *Barotrauma* and *arterial gas embolism* have been named separately based on different pathophysiologic mechanisms.

Francis and Smith[16] suggest that the two illnesses (DCS and arterial gas embolism) are difficult to separate from one another clinically, and both require the same therapy. *Decompression illness* is proposed to encompass both DCS and arterial gas embolism in a single term. In this chapter, we use a pathophysiologic classification of the pressure disorders whenever possible.

PRESSURE EFFECTS: BOYLE'S LAW

RELATION OF GAS VOLUME TO DEPTH

Boyle's law states that, if the temperature of a fixed mass of an ideal gas is kept constant, the relationship between the volume and pressure will vary in such a way that the product of the pressure and volume will remain constant.[17] This relationship is described by the equation PV = K, where P is absolute pressure, V is volume, and K is a constant. Thus, at a constant temperature and mass, the volume of a gas is inversely proportional to the pressure exerted on that gas. Consequently, when the pressure is doubled, the volume is reduced to one half of the original volume. This relationship is graphically illustrated in Figure 66.3. Two different states of a gas at the same temperature may be denoted by subscripts 1 and 2. With this type of notation, Boyle's law may also be written as

$$P_1 V_1 = P_2 V_2$$

Because the gas volume is proportional to the absolute pressure, the volume change from 33 to 66 fsw (from 2 to 3 ATA) is less than the change from the surface to 33 fsw (from 1 to 2 ATA). Changes of depth in shallow water cause

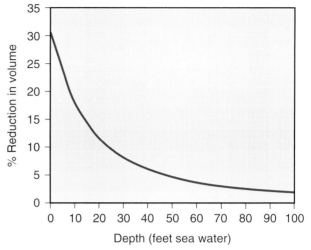

Figure 66.3 The relation of volume changes to depth underwater. Volume changes are greater per foot of depth change near the surface than in deeper depths.

greater volume changes than equivalent changes of depth in deeper water. Rapid volume expansion resulting from depth changes in shallow water can cause tissue injury.

BAROTRAUMA

Because of Boyle's law, volume in the lungs, middle ear, paranasal sinuses, and gastrointestinal tract all are reduced as pressure increases. Displacement of tissues into the diminishing volume of these spaces causes a phenomenon called *squeeze*, which damages tissues and may cause dysfunction of the organ involved. Barotrauma can affect a paranasal sinus with a blocked orifice (sinus squeeze), a small residual air pocket left between a tooth filling and the base of the tooth (tooth squeeze), or the air space within a diving mask (mask squeeze) or between the skin and a fold in a dry diving suit (suit squeeze). All can produce tissue injury due to displacement of tissues into the diminishing air space. Although lung squeeze is theoretically possible by breath-hold diving to a depth that reduces the lung volume below the residual volume,[6] in practice this has not been observed because of the increased intrapulmonary blood volume and compression of the thorax. Middle ear barotrauma is the most common diving-related disorder encountered in divers.[18]

Pulmonary Barotrauma and Arterial Gas Embolism

Injury to the lungs is a potentially lethal complication most often due to poor diving practices. When a diver subjected to increasing pressure breathes from an air supply at depth, the breathing gas is pressurized to the ambient pressure so that pressure gradients from breathing supply to the airways are not altered as the diver descends. Divers in swimming pools at depths greater than 4 feet are susceptible to pulmonary barotrauma. In the 1930s, a number of deaths were observed during submarine escape training in the U.S. Navy. Studies by Behnke[19] and by Polak and Adams[20] reported the features of lung barotrauma as separate from those of DCS (see later). Subsequently, fatalities were identified in which no evidence of prior pulmonary disease was present but pulmonary barotrauma occurred, resulting in air embolism. In some cases, obstruction of a single bronchus was thought to cause overexpansion of a lung segment. Based on those observations, diving and submarine training was prohibited for subjects with a history of any disease that causes airway obstruction. Later studies[21,22] provided further insight into mechanisms and prevention of pulmonary barotrauma. Asymptomatic anatomic abnormalities of the lung[20] and asthma were thought to contribute to the risk of barotrauma. Recent data suggest that asthma is not an absolute contraindication (see later).

Pathophysiology. Under experimental conditions, it has been demonstrated that transpulmonary pressures (i.e., the difference between intratracheal and intrapleural pressures) of 95 to 110 cm H_2O are sufficient to disrupt pulmonary parenchyma and allow gases into the interstitium.[21] Extra-alveolar gas can migrate through the perivascular sheaths of the pulmonary vasculature to cause mediastinal emphysema and pneumothorax.[21] Gas can also dissect into the retroperitoneum and into the subcutaneous tissues of the neck. When intrathoracic pressure drops at the time of the first breath on the surface after the pulmonary barotrauma, extra-alveolar gas can pass into ruptured blood vessels, travel to the left side of the heart, and enter the arterial circulation as gaseous emboli.[22] Pulmonary barotraumas and arterial gas embolism can also occur before reaching the surface. The dissemination of gas bubbles throughout the arterial circulation causes injury to other organ systems and to skeletal muscle, which is evident by a rise in serum creatine kinase level.[23]

Pulmonary barotrauma can occur in divers who would not be considered at risk for lung overpressure. Wilmshurst and coworkers[24] found that occult lung disease and probably smoking increase the risk of pulmonary barotrauma and cerebral air embolism. Tetzlaff and colleagues[25] suggested that prospective pulmonary function testing could be used as a means of separating individuals with a history of asthma who can dive safely from those who might be at risk for pulmonary barotrauma. They identified changes in the flow-volume curve, specifically reduced midexpiratory flow at 25% of vital capacity, in pulmonary barotrauma patients compared with patients who had DCS but not pulmonary barotrauma. FEV_1 was similar in both groups. The authors also performed computed tomography of the chest and found 13 lung abnormalities among the 15 patients with pulmonary barotrauma. Although only four cases in the control group had computed tomography of the chest, none had an abnormal finding. Both studies suggest that occult lung disease and asthma may contribute to unexplained cerebral air embolism. However, other authors have disagreed with these interpretations.[26]

Epidemiologic studies have not demonstrated a significant relationship between asthma and an increased risk for pulmonary barotrauma (see later in the section on Medical Qualifications for Diving). In a retrospective study of submarine candidates undergoing submarine escape training, Benton and associates[27] identified a small forced vital capacity as a risk factor for pulmonary barotrauma.

Clinical Manifestations of Arterial Air Embolism. The most commonly involved organ is the brain, where strokelike symptoms occur within minutes after the diver surfaces. The most frequently observed signs are loss of consciousness, hemiplegia, and stupor and confusion. Also frequently seen are seizures, vertigo, visual disturbances, sensory changes, headache, and circulatory collapse.[28] In a study of pulmonary barotrauma resulting from submarine escape training, Elliott and associates[28] found that most individuals fully recovered if they were promptly recompressed. However, one fourth to one third of victims in this group had recurrence of symptoms during decompression from the initial hyperbaric treatment and required a second recompression treatment. The signs and symptoms of this secondary process are similar to the initial presentation but are more gradual in onset and may include headache, progressive stupor, visual disturbances, and convulsions.

Victims of arterial gas embolism frequently suffer near drowning episodes, when they lose consciousness in the water. Chest radiographs (Fig. 66.4) may show a diffuse lung edema pattern. About 5% of patients immediately develop apnea, unconsciousness, and cardiac arrest. This catastrophic course results from filling of the heart and great vessels with air. Many of these individuals are unresponsive to cardiopulmonary resuscitation and advanced life support measures.[29] Harker and coworkers[30] reported the pulmonary findings of 31 patients with cerebral air embolism from diving: 25% demonstrated pneumomediastinum; 10%, subcutaneous emphysema; 6%, pneumocardium; 3%, pneumoperitoneum; and 3%, pneumothorax. Fifty-two percent had pulmonary infiltrates indicating associated near drowning.

Extra-alveolar gas can enter the mediastinum and the subcutaneous spaces of the neck and can enter the pleural space. Mediastinal emphysema is generally associated with mild substernal pain or no symptoms. The pain is described as either a dull ache or tightness and may be exacerbated by

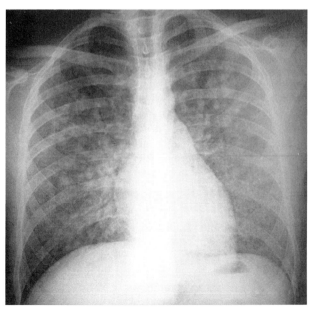

Figure 66.4 Chest radiograph from a diver showing pulmonary barotrauma and near drowning. The diffuse pulmonary edema pattern is suggestive of water aspiration.

inspiration, coughing, or swallowing. The pain may radiate to any portion of the upper torso. Unless massive, this condition is not usually associated with respiratory symptoms. On physical examination, a crunching sound synchronous with cardiac action may be auscultated (Hamman's sign). The chest radiograph confirms the diagnosis. No treatment is usually necessary.

Air dissecting cephalad from the mediastinum causes subcutaneous emphysema in the neck. Swelling and crepitus in the root of the neck and supraclavicular fossa, sore throat, hoarseness, and dysphagia may result. Radiographs may be helpful in detecting subtle cases. When extra-alveolar gas ruptures into the pleural space (either from the mediastinum through the parietal pleura or from the perivascular tissues through the visceral pleura), a pneumothorax results. Laboratory evaluation may show an elevated hematocrit level and elevation of several serum enzyme levels.[31] Treatment for arterial gas embolism requires recompression in a hyperbaric chamber (see later).

Middle Ear Barotrauma

Middle ear barotrauma ("ear squeeze") occurs when the eustachian tube is blocked during descent and the middle ear space cannot equilibrate with the increasing ambient pressure.[32] The tympanic membrane is displaced inward and may ultimately rupture. The middle ear may fill with blood from engorged mucous membranes. Infection and hearing loss are complications. Symptoms occur during descent and include pain in the affected ear that increases with depth. Relief of pain without proper ventilation of the middle ear usually indicates that the tympanic membrane has ruptured. Cold water entering the middle ear when the tympanic membrane ruptures may cause vertigo due to unilateral vestibular stimulation. Late complications include acute otitis media, serous otitis media, and chronic tympanic membrane perforation.[18] In rare cases of middle ear barotrauma, the facial nerve is injured by the increased pressure and a temporary facial paralysis results.[33]

Prevention is achieved by ensuring that the eustachian tube is patent and that the ears can be equilibrated at surface pressure before descending. A modified Valsalva maneuver is commonly used to accomplish this goal. Several grading schemes for middle ear barotrauma have been proposed. The grading by Teed[34] is commonly used for descriptive purposes. Because middle ear barotrauma causes edema and hemorrhage into the middle ear, equalization is usually impossible to achieve until healing is complete. The presence of middle ear barotrauma usually prohibits diving until it is resolved.

Alternobaric Vertigo.
Alternobaric vertigo occurs on ascent when the reduction of middle ear pressure is not uniform in both ears. The pressure imbalance causes differential stimulation of the labyrinths, resulting in vertigo. The sensation of vertigo occurs on ascent, usually within 30 to 40 feet of the surface, and may persist for 1 to 2 hours after diving. Vertigo is self-limiting and gradually disappears without therapy. Symptoms are similar to labyrinthitis and can include nausea, vomiting, and generalized malaise. Onset of vertigo underwater may be dangerous due to disorientation, particularly in novice divers.

The disorder must be differentiated from vestibular DCS, which is usually associated with deeper, prolonged diving or saturation diving.[35] Some subjects may be particularly susceptible to alternobaric vertigo if they have had previous injury or infection of the labyrinths. No therapy is required in most cases because the disorder is self-limiting. In susceptible individuals, use of moderate doses of antihistamines or decongestants may prevent symptoms.

Inner Ear Barotrauma

Inner ear barotrauma occurs on descent in divers who perform a forceful Valsalva maneuver to equalize middle ear pressure. If the eustachian tube is blocked, middle ear pressure becomes progressively more negative relative to ambient pressure.[18,36] When a Valsalva maneuver is performed, intrathoracic pressure, central venous pressure, spinal fluid pressure, and inner ear pressure rise above ambient pressure, thereby increasing the gradient between the inner ear perilymph and the middle ear. If the middle ear pressure is already below ambient pressure, the differential pressure from inner ear to middle ear may become large enough to rupture the round or oval window. When one of these structures ruptures, perilymph flows from the inner ear to the middle ear, and auditory and vestibular dysfunction follows. Symptoms include sudden onset of vertigo, nausea, vomiting, tinnitus, and loss of hearing on the affected side.[37] Severity may vary, and some divers will complain of hearing loss, tinnitus, or vertigo only after diving.

Prevention is by training and attention to eustachian tube function. Treatment varies from conservative therapy to surgical repair of the round or oval window. Vertigo and nausea can be treated with benzodiazepine medications. Tinnitus and reduced hearing may become chronic, particularly if no treatment is provided.

In some divers who exhibit clinical evidence of inner ear barotrauma, the round and oval windows are found to be intact upon surgical exploration. These divers are thought to have a pressure injury to the organ of Corti and the vestibular system.[38]

Sinus Barotrauma

When a sinus orifice is blocked, pressure within the sinus becomes negative with respect to ambient pressure, and mucosal blood vessels become engorged and eventually rupture.[39] The resulting mucosal hemorrhage fills the sinus with blood. Symptoms are usually reported as pain over the affected sinus during descent and epistaxis on ascent when the expanding residual air in the sinus discharges the blood. Headache following a dive may indicate sphenoid sinus barotrauma. The disorder usually is self-limiting; treatment is decongestants to reestablish orifice patency and maneuvers to drain the affected sinus. Persistence of blood in the sinus may result in acute bacterial sinusitis. Prevention is accomplished by avoiding diving with congestion of the nasopharynx and prudent use of decongestants. If a maxillary sinus orifice is occluded, the maxillary branch of the trigeminal nerve may be compressed during ascent and result in infraorbital paresthesias that usually resolve in 2 to 3 hours.

Facial Barotrauma

Facial barotrauma has been called "mask squeeze" because it occurs in the distribution of the diving mask. Diving masks cover the mouth and nose, and, like other air-containing spaces, require continuous pressure equilibration by exhaling through the nose into the mask. If pressure within the mask is not equilibrated with ambient pressure during descent, blood vessels in the face and conjunctiva become engorged and eventually rupture.[40] Facial edema, ecchymoses, and conjunctival hemorrhages are noted after diving, usually in novice divers. Retro-orbital hematoma has been described as a complication.[41] The disorder is self-limiting; no treatment is needed. Proper training prevents the disorder.

Skin Barotrauma

An infrequent injury to the skin occurs in divers using air-containing diving suits (dry suits). Folds in the suit may become compressed against the skin and allow prolapse of skin into the fold. The result is linear ecchymoses on the trunk or extremities. No therapy is required. The injury is uncommon in newer design neoprene dry suits.

Tooth Barotrauma

Barodontalgia occurs on descent when air pockets under fillings or in areas of decay become compressed. Severe toothache results, which is relieved by ascending. Rarely, an air pocket under a filling expands on ascent and ejects the filling from the tooth. Careful dental work prevents this disorder.[42]

Gastrointestinal Barotrauma

Air may enter the stomach and intestines during diving due to faulty breathing apparatus or by air swallowing. On ascent, the air will expand and distend the stomach or intestine. Gastric distention can occlude the esophageal-gastric junction and prevent eructation. Distention of the stomach may occasionally cause stomach rupture and pneumoperitoneum.[43] The diver experiences abdominal pain, which increases during ascent. Treatment may require surgical repair of the ruptured viscus. Divers with previous gastric surgery may be prone to gastric air trapping.[44] The disorder is prevented by attention to equipment maintenance and avoidance of air swallowing.

DISSOLVED INERT GAS EFFECTS

GAS SOLUBILITY AND HENRY'S LAW

Pressure determines the amount of gas that is dissolved in tissues and fluids of the body. A person subjected to increased ambient pressure takes up gases into the tissues of the body according to an exponential kinetics process. At equilibrium, the partial pressure of the gas and the solubility of the gas in the specific tissue (Table 66.2) determine dissolved gas content of tissues. Of the gases involved in diving, oxygen is not a problem with regard to DCS due to its low partial pressure at the cellular level[45]; carbon dioxide also does not cause concern for DCS because of its high

Table 66.2 Characteristics of Inert Gases*

Gas	Molecular Weight	Lipid Solubility[†]	Water Solubility[†]	Narcotic Potential[‡]
Helium	4	0.015	0.009	0.23
Neon	20	0.019	0.009	0.28
Hydrogen	2	0.036	0.018	0.55
Nitrogen	28	0.067	0.013	1.00
Argon	40	0.140	0.026	2.32

* Solubility of the various gases in lipid is related to their narcotic potential. Helium is the least, and argon the most, narcotic gas in the list.
[†] Expressed as gas volume/solute volume at 1 bar.
[‡] Values relative to nitrogen.
Adapted from Bennett PB: Inert gas narcosis and HPNS. *In* Bove AA (ed): Bove and Davis' Diving Medicine (4th ed). Philadelphia: WB Saunders, 2004, pp 225–240.

solubility and low partial pressure. However, inert gases (nitrogen, helium) are limiting factors in diving because, as the diver ascends with increased dissolved gas in the tissues, these gases are able to supersaturate quickly and form a gas phase.

INERT GAS KINETICS

Gases dissolve in tissues, fats, and water according to Henry's law:

$$V = K \cdot P$$

where K, a solubility coefficient, and P, the partial pressure of the gas, determine the quantity (V) of dissolved inert gas. Solubility coefficients for water and lipid are provided in Table 66.2. Although Henry's law determines the amount of gas in the tissue, there is a finite time required for equilibrium to be achieved. Gases entering tissues approximate a first-order relationship, wherein rate of gas flow into tissue is proportional to the pressure difference between blood and tissue. Factors that affect the rate of entry include blood flow to the tissue and the rate of diffusion of gases into the tissue.[46] The concentration of gas in tissues follows the kinetics equation

$$dC/dt = K \cdot \Delta C$$

where the change in concentration over time (dC/dt) is proportional to a constant (K) times the difference in concentration between blood and tissues (ΔC). Solution of the equation describes an asymptotic curve in which the tissue gas concentration approaches the maximum concentration for the given pressure after time has elapsed. There is a family of curves for different values of K. These curves represent different tissues that have different gas exchange characteristics.[47] Similar kinetics control the washout of inert gas from tissues when ambient pressure is reduced.

The majority of diving is of short duration (i.e., minutes to hours) and shallow exposure (i.e., in depths shallower that 200 feet). Such diving exposures allow only a few tissues to reach equilibrium based on Henry's law, while most are not fully saturated. Divers can return to the surface from these short-duration dives by following a schedule of ascent based on depth and time.[47] Tables describing decompression protocols are available throughout the world and are usually developed for military or commercial diving needs.[12] Decompression tables have been incorporated into submersible wrist-mounted computers, which provide instantaneous information on decompression during diving.

When diving exposure is long enough, all tissues reach equilibrium at the new ambient pressure and are fully saturated with inert gas. Bond[48] demonstrated that divers could spend prolonged periods (weeks) under pressure, with all tissues saturated at the increased pressure, without serious physiologic changes. Working dives conducted with Bond's techniques have been performed at depths over 1000 feet in open sea for periods up to 3 to 4 weeks. Breathing gases for these saturation dives are mixed with extreme care because dives of 1000 feet with normoxic mixtures (0.3 to 0.5 bar oxygen) require that oxygen concentrations be held to tolerances of 0.01% to avoid hypoxia or oxygen toxicity.

GAS SUPERSATURATION IN TISSUES

When the diver ascends, pressure is reduced rapidly, and tissues become supersaturated with gas. When the degree of supersaturation becomes excessive, dissolved gas will leave the solution and form bubbles. Boycott and colleagues[49] first demonstrated that a diver could prevent bubble formation by keeping the degree of supersaturation below a certain level. They suggested that a 2:1 ratio of initial to final tissue partial pressure after ascent would prevent bubble formation. Their concept of a critical pressure ratio for bubble formation is the basis for most decompression tables used to prevent decompression sickness.

Boycott and colleagues[49] assumed that the body could be considered as a set of "tissues" with different rates of gas diffusion. Although these tissues do not represent discrete anatomic structures, they provide a convenient means to understand the kinetics of inert gas exchange. Examples of tissues with rapid gas exchange are blood and lung alveolar cells; those with slow gas exchange are ligaments, tendons, and the vitreous humor of the eye. In most decompression tables, stops during ascent are selected to avoid excess supersaturation in tissues with specific gas-exchange rates (Fig. 66.5). Operations involving exposure to increased partial pressure of inert gas must always consider the decompression procedures as well as the diving procedures. For long or deep exposures, the technique of saturation diving is used (see earlier). Decompression procedures are well defined for air and other mixtures of nitrogen and oxygen; helium and oxygen; nitrogen, helium, and oxygen (trimix); hydrogen and oxygen; and a few rare earth gases such as argon and neon used in experimental exposures.

DECOMPRESSION SICKNESS

Excess supersaturation causes dissolved gases to change phase to the gaseous form, and bubbles form in blood and tissues.[50] Expansion of gases in blood and tissues on ascent results in damage and dysfunction of tissues and organs and venous gas embolism to the lungs. Sudden decompression

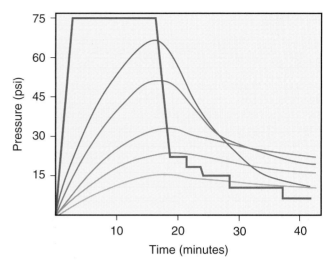

Figure 66.5 Theoretical nitrogen gas concentrations are expressed in units of pressure for an exposure of 75 psi (5.1 ATA) following the depth-time profile indicated by the *heavy line*. Curves are shown for five theoretical tissue compartments with different rates of gas exchange. Tissue gas concentration increases during exposure to pressure. When pressure is reduced, gas concentration in tissues begins to fall. Stops during return to baseline allow tissue concentration to fall to a safe level of supersaturation before reducing pressure further. (Data from Boycott AE, Damant GCC, Haldane J: The prevention of compressed air illness. J Hyg [Cambridge] 8:342–443, 1908.)

following a long, deep dive can be fatal. DCS is the disorder caused by damage to organs and tissues as a result of bubble production and growth.

In the 19th century, Bert[51] described the pathophysiology of DCS. Several investigators in the early 20th century concluded from autopsies on divers and caisson workers that DCS is caused by inert gas bubbles in the blood and tissues.[52] Based on bubble volume and location, they were able to explain the variety and severity of the symptoms. Paralysis resulted from bubbles in the spinal cord, cerebral dysfunction was thought to result from bubbles in the brain, and dyspnea was associated with bubbles in the pulmonary circulation. Muscle and joint pain may be due to bubbles in ligaments, fascia, periosteum, marrow, or nerve sheaths.

Hallenbeck and colleagues[53] described effects of bubbles in blood and tissues that were not caused by mechanical obstruction. Subsequent studies identified clotting and platelet activation by bubbles, intravascular coagulation, plasma leakage from the intravascular space, hemoconcentration, and hypovolemia[54] as manifestations of bubble surface effects. Hematologic abnormalities are infrequent in mild cases.[55]

Bubbles and tissue injury result in activation of acute inflammation.[56] The inflammatory response alters vascular permeability, causing fluid to leak into the interstitial tissues of the systemic and pulmonary vascular beds.[57] In severe cases, pulmonary edema can occur; hypovolemia with significant plasma loss and hemoconcentration result.

Factors Affecting Risk of Decompression Sickness

The use of Doppler ultrasound for intravascular bubble detection has provided insight into the presence of bubbles following diving.[58] Many divers demonstrate venous gas emboli but no manifestations of DCS. The concept of a threshold or dose-response effect has been postulated, wherein a clinical disorder requires a certain volume of free gas; lesser amounts are asymptomatic.[59] However, the presence of bubbles in asymptomatic divers and aviators is associated with increased risk of developing symptoms of DCS after diving or altitude exposure.[60,61]

Patent Foramen Ovale. Moon and coworkers[62] reported 30 patients with a history of DCS who were studied with bubble contrast echocardiography for identification of a patent foramen ovale (PFO). Sixty-one percent of 18 patients with serious DCS had shunting, whereas a 25% prevalence was seen in normal volunteers. Wilmshurst and associates[63] identified a single patient with paradoxical gas embolism through an atrial septal defect and suggested that the atrial septal defect augmented symptoms of DCS in this patient. Moon and coworkers[64] evaluated 90 divers with previous DCS who were studied using bubble contrast echocardiography and color flow Doppler to detect right-to-left shunting through a PFO. Fifty-nine of 90 had experienced serious decompression symptoms, whereas 31 had experienced pain only or mild symptoms. Forty-nine percent of the serious DCS subjects had evidence of a right-to-left shunt either during Valsalva maneuver or at rest compared with 19.8% of controls. With musculoskeletal DCS, there was no difference in PFO prevalence between the diving subjects and the controls. Prevalence of PFO in a normal population ranges from 25% to 34% depending on age.

Wilmshurst and colleagues[65] found no difference in PFO prevalence when comparing control subjects to divers with onset of neurologic symptoms later than 30 minutes after surfacing or with joint pain. In divers who had neurologic symptoms within 30 minutes of surfacing, the prevalence of shunt was significantly higher than in controls. The authors pointed out that cerebral dysfunction is usually thought to be due to cerebral gas embolism. However, in the presence of a PFO, cerebral gas embolism caused by venous bubbles transiting a PFO may blur the distinction between neurologic DCS and air embolism. Wilmshurst and coworkers[65] found variability in the severity of shunting among different tests and times. They suggest that this variability may occur during diving and would explain the fact that divers with PFO may dive for many years without developing symptoms. Germonpré and associates[66] found that divers with cerebral DCS have a high incidence of large PFO compared to control subjects and divers with spinal DCS. De novo formation of bubbles in spinal cord and other tissue remains a well-documented pathogenesis in DCS; however, the presence of a PFO is associated with an increase in the risk of DCS of about twofold.[66a] The high prevalence of PFO in the population and the very low incidence of DCS suggest that a PFO can only play a minor role in the pathophysiology of DCS. There is no current need to close a PFO as a prophylactic measure.[66b]

Age. Attempts to determine the impact of age on susceptibility to DCS have aroused much debate. A 10-year study by the U.S. Air Force on flight exposures ranging from 1500 to 30,000 feet show a threefold increase in susceptibility when comparing aviators 18 to 21 years of age with aviators 42 years of age and older.[67] The study suggests a trend toward increased DCS susceptibility in individuals over age 42. Carturan and colleagues[68] examined the effects of age and physical condition on venous bubble formation in sport divers. They found a correlation between bubble formation, increased age, and decreased physical condition.

Clinical Manifestations

Based on the nomenclature proposed by Golding and coworkers,[15] DCS has been divided into a systemic form (type II) and a nonsystemic, musculoskeletal form (type I). Divers can suffer DCS even after a "safe profile" indicated by either diving tables or wrist-mounted computers.

Sport and military divers have similar rates of type I and type II DCS (Table 66.3). Commercial divers have the highest incidence of DCS. In this population, the incidence of musculoskeletal DCS is high. In the late 1990s, the incidence of DCS was about 2 in 10,000 dives for the sport diver compared with about 1 in 100,000 for those who participated in diving for scientific or academic purposes.[69]

There is a spectrum of signs and symptoms in DCS that can mimic a variety of other disorders (Table 66.4). The disease develops after an ascent from depth when a diver does not follow the established procedures for returning to the surface that are designed to prevent effervescence of dissolved inert gas (nitrogen). Free gas entering the vascular system from the peripheral tissues will transit the veins and cause varying degrees of pulmonary vascular obstruction.

Table 66.3 Frequency and Incidence of Decompression Sickness (DCS) in Sport, Military, and Commercial Air Diving Populations

Source	Military	Sport	Commercial	All
Total dives*	648,488	2,577,680	43,063	3,269,231
Frequency				
Total DCS*	172	878	152	1,202
Type II DCS*	86	649	9	744
Incidence DCS[†]	2.65	3.41	35.3	3.68
Incidence DCS II[†]	1.33	2.52	2.09	2.28

* Values are number of events. Type II DCS is systemic, serious DCS.
[†] Incidence per 10,000 dives; DCS II, DCS type II.
From Bove AA: Risk of decompression sickness with patent foramen ovale. Undersea Biomed Res 25:175–178, 1998.

Table 66.4 Frequency of Decompression Sickness (DCS) Symptoms in 100 Cases

Symptom	Percentage of All DCS Symptoms
Skin itch	4
Headache	11
Fatigue/malaise	13
Bone/joint pain	54
Spinal/back pain	11
Spinal/neurologic	22
Respiratory	21

Adapted from Navy Department: U.S. Navy Diving Manual. Vol 1, Rev 3: Air Diving (Publication No. NAVSEA 0994-LP-001-9110). Washington, DC: U.S. Navy Department, 1996.

When pulmonary obstruction occurs, a classic syndrome ("chokes") is described.[70] This syndrome is manifested by chest pain, dyspnea, and cough.[71]

DCS is often associated with free gas in the blood and with mechanical tissue injury from expanding gas. Bubbles and tissue injury result in activation of acute inflammation,[56] damage to vascular endothelium,[71] microvascular occlusion, and focal regions of tissue ischemia. A common manifestation of DCS in divers is evidence of spinal cord dysfunction usually at levels below the diaphragm.[72,73] Symptoms include paresthesias, muscle weakness, paralysis of the lower extremities, bowel or bladder incontinence, urinary retention, and sexual impotence. In cases of sudden ascent from deep depth ("blowup"), usually found in commercial diving exposures, a massive DCS syndrome will occur with both cerebral and spinal neurologic symptoms, unconsciousness, hypovolemic shock, pulmonary edema, and a high mortality rate.[71] A rare but important symptom of systemic (type II) decompression sickness is sudden acute neurologic hearing loss and vestibular dysfunction. DCS of this type usually occurs from deep, prolonged commercial diving exposures and, if untreated, can result in permanent deafness.[74] Presence of cerebral involvement in DCS has been suggested, but the overlap in cerebral involvement with arterial gas embolism makes unclear the exact etiology of cerebral injury. Presence of a PFO (see earlier) can contribute to cerebral gas embolism in DCS.

The musculoskeletal form of DCS is manifested by pains in the extremities and joints.[75] Symptoms of local joint pain are often confused with pain from injuries, and the diagnosis of DCS may be missed. In some populations, a high incidence of aseptic bone necrosis is found in divers who have experienced DCS of the joints in the distant past or who have experienced deep, prolonged dives in caisson work[75] and in commercial operations.[76] An erythematous or purpuric skin rash may also be a manifestation of DCS. Leffler and White[77] described their experience with a large diving operation (5000 dives) to salvage a crashed airliner. They treated 19 divers for decompression-related illness, 18 of whom recovered fully.

Treatment

The clinical manifestations of arterial air embolism and DCS can overlap, and treatment goals for both disorders include recompression and other adjunctive measures. Bubble-induced injury can result in local hemorrhages in the spinal cord, brain, and other organs and direct tissue injury due to distortion as bubbles expand.

The initial treatment of DCS and arterial gas embolism should always be a return to pressure by recompression in a hyperbaric chamber and administration of oxygen at increased ambient pressure (hyperbaric oxygen). Fluid replacement and antiplatelet agents are also a part of the initial treatment. Once stabilized with pressure and oxygen, the patient must be decompressed slowly to permit the inert gas to be carried away from tissues by the circulatory system and then to be exhaled by the lungs. With early treatment, DCS and air embolism generally have an excellent prognosis for recovery. When delay occurs, or when the injury is severe, permanent injury to the brain or spinal cord may occur.

Hyperbaric Therapy. Treatment of DCS and arterial gas embolism should be instituted with recompression as soon as possible after the injury. A history and physical evaluation, including a neurologic examination and cognitive assessment, should be obtained before treatment when possible. Therapy is provided in a hyperbaric chamber by a trained medical team. Return to depth underwater is not a satisfactory method of recompression for DCS or air embolism. However, this treatment has been used in remote areas with a support team properly equipped and trained in open water treatment of these disorders. Hyperbaric therapy should be postponed for further diagnostic studies only if the findings from such studies could influence the choice of therapy.

The usual practice is to follow the standard protocols for pressure treatment outlined in the *U.S. Navy Diving Manual*.[12] Treatment for minor or type I DCS, manifested by symptoms of joint or bone pain, is a pressure exposure equivalent to a 60-foot depth in seawater (60 fsw) using intermittent oxygen therapy. Itching and erythema of the skin may also be signs of type I DCS, but skin findings alone usually do not require recompression therapy. Recompression therapy for cutis marmorata resulting from DCS has been recommended by some, but most cases, when not associated with other evidence of DCS, resolve spontaneously.

Two protocols established by the U.S. Navy have been recommended: U.S. Navy Treatment Table 5, a 135-minute exposure, and U.S. Navy Treatment Table 6, a 285-minute exposure with 100% oxygen at 60 fsw with air breaks to avoid pulmonary oxygen toxicity. The designation of these treatment protocols as Treatment Table 5 and Treatment Table 6 is arbitrary and is based on their position in the list of treatment tables published in the *U.S. Navy Diving Manual*.[12] Most practitioners use Treatment Table 6 for treatment of type 1 DCS to account for the possibility of accompanying serious signs or symptoms that might be missed on examination. For serious or type II DCS, Treatment Table 6 is recommended.

When a diver ascends from extreme depths with significant missed decompression, the medical officer may choose to use recompression tables that pressurize the diver to a "depth of relief," to use alternate gas mixtures (i.e., helium and oxygen), or to hold the diver for over 24 hours at a single depth to stabilize the medical status (saturation treatment).[78] For surface-supplied air and scuba divers, the principal treatment gases are oxygen and air. For treatment depths greater than 60 fsw (18 meters of seawater), enriched nitrogen-oxygen (nitrox) or helium-oxygen (heliox) may also be used. Helium-oxygen mixtures are used for treatments deeper than 200 to 220 fsw (60 to 67 meters of seawater).

Repeated hyperbaric oxygen treatments can be given, although end points for repetitive therapy are not well defined. Treatments can be administered until no further change of symptoms is found or for a fixed number of exposures (e.g., five). However, controlled trials to determine efficacy of repetitive treatments are not available, and neurologic injuries may return to normal without further hyperbaric treatment. Treatment of arterial gas embolism follows similar protocols. Recompression to 60 fsw and oxygen therapy are usually successful.[79] Recompression to 165 fsw depth equivalent (5 ATA) is recommended if symptoms persist after recompression to 60 fsw.[12]

Supplemental Oxygen and Fluids. Early administration of supplemental oxygen on the surface is thought to be beneficial for treating both DCS and arterial gas embolism; optimal inspired concentration of oxygen is 100%. Although oxygen first aid has been widely recommended, available data do not demonstrate a dramatic difference in long-term outcome in persons treated with oxygen prior to recompression compared with those who do not get such treatment. Intravenous fluid administration also may be a useful initial treatment. Central nervous system injury may be exacerbated by hyperglycemia, and glucose-containing intravenous solutions should be administered cautiously. Measurement of hematocrit and urine-specific gravity is useful to guide fluid replacement therapy.

Diagnostic Testing

Chest radiography can be used to diagnose pneumothorax, pneumomediastinum associated with pulmonary overpressure accidents, and the pulmonary abnormalities associated with aspiration or capillary leakage associated with chokes. In most cases, it is not necessary to postpone recompression treatment in order to obtain radiographic studies. If pneumothorax is suspected, a chest radiograph can be helpful in making the decision to insert a chest tube. Neurologic and psychological testing may be useful in determining response to treatment when brain injury is present. Electronystagmography and audiography may be useful in distinguishing inner ear DCS from inner ear barotraumas. Inner ear DCS requires recompression, whereas inner ear barotrauma is managed with bed rest, avoidance of straining, and possibly surgical intervention. The circumstances causing the two syndromes are distinct (see earlier) and are helpful in the differential diagnosis; however, in the event the distinction cannot be made, recompression therapy may be of benefit. Central nervous system injury is best diagnosed by magnetic resonance imaging (MRI). Areas of cerebral and spinal cord ischemia or infarction can be identified by MRI and correlate with clinical findings.[80,81] MRI images

of the brain in divers with no history of decompression-related disorders are also found to be abnormal in some studies[82]; the significance of MRI findings in these individuals is unclear.

Emergency Treatment

Because divers may be injured in areas remote from medical care, treatment measures should be instituted during transit to a hyperbaric chamber facility. Emergency treatment before transfer of an injured diver should include 100% oxygen by mask, aspirin 325 to 975 mg by mouth, and Ringer's lactate intravenously. One study of oxygen, aspirin, intravenous fluids, and hydrocortisone 1 to 2 g intravenously during transit to a hyperbaric chamber found that two thirds of the cases had a favorable outcome[83]; however, it remains unproven whether such emergency treatment alters long-term outcome. A favorable response to urgent care should not prolong transfer to the closest chamber facility capable of providing recompression therapy.

INERT GAS NARCOSIS

Inert gas narcosis (nitrogen narcosis) results from breathing air at depths greater than 100 fsw.[84,85] Symptoms include loss of fine motor control and high-order mental skills, bizarre and inappropriate behavior, improper response to emotional stress, hostility, and unconsciousness. Symptoms increase with depth from 100 feet. At 300 to 400 feet, unconsciousness may occur owing to the anesthetic effect of nitrogen at this pressure. In diving deeper than 200 feet, helium replaces nitrogen as the inert gas to prevent narcosis. Fatigue, heavy work, and cold water can augment the narcotic effect of nitrogen. Symptoms disappear immediately on ascending to a shallow depth. Often there is amnesia for the events that occurred below.[84] Nitrogen effects on nervous function are thought to have the same mechanism of action as anesthetic gases. Gas effects on cell membrane function result in reduced cellular activity and, ultimately, general anesthesia. Narcotic potential varies among the inert gases (see Table 66.2).

OXYGEN TOXICITY

Acute toxicity to the brain occurs when oxygen partial pressure exceeds 1.4 ATA. Higher partial pressures can be tolerated for brief periods. The toxic diver usually suffers a grand mal seizure. When underwater, a seizure often leads to drowning. Use of enriched oxygen mixtures by sport divers has increased the incidence of acute oxygen toxicity in this population. A detailed discussion of oxygen toxicity can be found in standard textbooks on diving.[86]

MEDICAL QUALIFICATIONS FOR DIVING

The type of diving dictates the medical requirements. Military divers have the most stringent requirements, whereas recreational divers have the most relaxed requirements. Commercial divers, caisson and tunnel workers, and hyperbaric chamber workers all have unique standards. Disorders that limit cardiovascular or pulmonary function during exercise, physical deconditioning, metabolic disorders that limit exercise capacity, and certain physical handicaps can compromise diving safety.

EXERCISE REQUIREMENTS

Workloads in diving vary based on the type of diving. A diver swimming underwater at a speed of 1.0 knot consumes about 25 mL of oxygen per kilogram per minute.[87] Safety considerations suggest that divers should tolerate a peak workload of about 40 mL/kg per minute and a sustained workload of about 24 mL/kg per minute to ensure safety under adverse diving conditions. Divers who do not achieve this level of fitness should avoid exposures that may require high levels of physical exertion.

DISORDERS CAUSING SUDDEN UNCONSCIOUSNESS

Disorders that may cause sudden unconsciousness underwater are considered to be contraindications to diving. Seizure disorders are considered to be a contraindication to diving because increased oxygen partial pressure, hyperventilation, and increased catecholamines during stress all can lower seizure threshold. A diver sustaining an underwater seizure is at risk for drowning and may compromise the safety of others who attempt a rescue. A diving candidate with a history of a seizure disorder should be seizure free without antiseizure medications for 4 years before being considered for diving.[88] Insulin-dependent diabetes mellitus is considered a contraindication to commercial and military diving due to the risk of hypoglycemia; however, special training for diabetic recreational divers has allowed safe diving for some insulin-dependent sport divers.

PULMONARY DISORDERS

Asthma has been a subject of controversy in diving because of possible air trapping and pulmonary overinflation during ascent. However, an increased risk for pulmonary barotrauma has not been supported by clinical observation. Neuman and coworkers[89] suggested that blanket prohibition is not justified by published data. Criteria for safe diving by patients with a history of asthma include evidence that expiratory airflow at 50% of peak (mid-expiratory flow) is not reduced after exercise by greater than 50%.[90] A more detailed discussion of issues related to asthma and diving has been published.[90] Clinical and operational experience suggests that patients with a history of spontaneous pneumothorax may be at risk for lung collapse and development of a progressively worsening tension pneumothorax during diving. Treatment requires immediate decompression of the pleural space through an intercostal needle or chest tube and may be difficult in remote diving sites.

CARDIAC DISORDERS

Patients with coronary disease may develop manifestations (angina pectoris, myocardial infarction, sudden death) while diving. Caruso[91] found that the highest incidence of diving related death from cardiovascular disease occurs in the age range from 60 to 70 years (Fig. 66.6). Mebane and colleagues[92] reported the mortality experience from the Diving Alert Network. Of 33 cases of sudden death while diving, 31 were attributed to coronary disease, one was related to a cerebral vascular accident, and one was related to aortic stenosis. Screening of diving candidates for coronary disease is particularly important in the sport diving community, in which candidates at increased risk for coronary disease due to age and chronic illness may present for training.

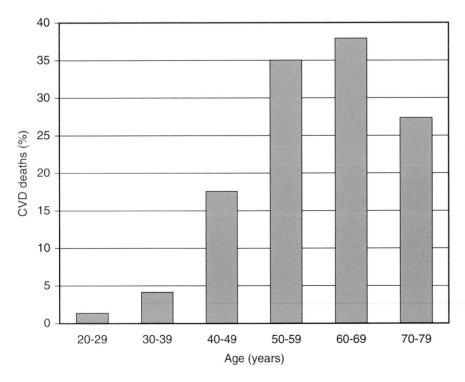

Figure 66.6 Incidence of cardiovascular related diving deaths as a percentage of all deaths in different age groups of recreational divers. (Data from Caruso JL, Bove AA, Uguccioni DM, et al: Recreational diving deaths associated with cardiovascular disease [abstract]. Undersea Hyperb Med 28:76, 2001.)

Diving candidates with atrial septal defects risk paradoxical embolism of gas bubbles that form in the venous circulation during decompression.[87] The presence of an atrial septal defect is considered to be a contraindication to diving. PFO effects on diving are discussed in an earlier section. A ventricular septal defect does not appear to produce a risk for paradoxical embolization of bubbles. In patients with minimal or no symptoms who have either atrial or ventricular septal defects with normal pressures in the central circulation, the shunt will be directed from left to right and no arterial desaturation occurs. Patients with a right-to-left shunt and arterial hypoxemia will normally have severely limited exercise capacity and should not dive. A detailed treatment of this topic can be found elsewhere.[87]

Diving-Induced Arrhythmias

Reflex bradycardia from diving has been described by a number of investigators.[93,94] This arrhythmia is thought to be related to facial immersion and cooling, and is found in diving mammals[95] as well as humans. The autonomic adjustments to apneic diving in marine mammals appear to be an oxygen-conserving reflex, but this effect does not appear to be significant in humans in spite of a well-developed reflex in many free divers. Ackerman and colleagues[96] described a series of drowning and near drowning cases that demonstrated a familial inherited long QT syndrome. The syndrome was confirmed by genetic testing. Although their cases were related to drowning, the same risk is likely to occur in divers with the long QT syndrome. It is unclear whether drug-induced long QT syndrome when combined with diving would increase risk for sudden death.

NEAR DROWNING

Drowning is reported as the leading cause of death in the approximately 100 to 150 scuba fatalities in the United States each year.[97] Arterial gas embolism may be the precipitating factor or even the cause of death in many of these accidents.[98] In the United States, drowning of males is approximately five times more common than of females.[99] As with fatal automobile accidents, the single most important factor in drowning incidents involving adults is alcohol. Multiple studies done in widely different geographical areas, such as the United States,[99] New Zealand,[100] South Africa,[101] and Australia,[102] reveal that, in well over half of the adults who drown, alcohol is a significant contributing factor. With scuba-related drowning or near drowning incidents, the most common factor is entanglement or the diver running out of air at depth or in a cave.

There is strong evidence that intentional hyperventilation before breath-hold diving is associated with both drowning and near drowning episodes.[9] Hyperventilation reduces the arterial P_{CO_2}, so the breath-hold break point is prolonged sufficiently for hypoxemia to occur before the individual is forced to breathe.[103] The hypoxemia in turn causes the individual to lose consciousness, and the submersion incident then occurs.

Hypothermia leading to drowning and near drowning incidents has been reported frequently; however, in diving fatalities this is an unusual occurrence due to the almost universal use of either wet suits or dry suits by divers for thermal protection. Hypothermia reduces a person's ability to function until the point of unconsciousness or helplessness is reached. At that time, the victim's head falls into the water, resulting in drowning or near drowning. Maximum breath-hold times of normally clothed individuals drop dramatically in cold water, further compromising their ability to survive in rough water where they may be intermittently submerged. However, in rare circumstances, hypothermia can have a protective effect on the near drowning victim (see later).

Hypothermia is one of many conditions that can precipitate drowning by causing unconsciousness. In the case of scuba diving incidents, contamination of the diver's air supply with carbon monoxide produces rapid unconsciousness, and oxygen-induced seizures (see earlier) have been implicated as the cause of death in divers using oxygen-enriched air as a breathing mixture.

PATHOPHYSIOLOGY

Approximately 10% to 15% of near drowning victims appear not to aspirate fluid during immersion.[104,105] To account for the lack of aspiration in these individuals, it has been hypothesized that reflex laryngospasm occurs and persists until reflex ventilatory activity ceases. However, experimental data to support this hypothesis are lacking. In near drowning victims who do not aspirate, the period of hypoxemia generally is as long as the immersion incident itself. If ventilation can be reestablished before the development of injury secondary to hypoxemia, recovery typically is rapid and uneventful. Until recently it was largely reported that there was a percentage of drowning victims who also did not aspirate. Ultimately these reports were based on the work of Cot,[105] published in French. Review of that work and a more recent translation[106] do not support this hypothesis. It is much more likely that so-called dry drownings do not occur and that they actually represent arrhythmic deaths.

Unlike the victim without aspiration, the individual who aspirates remains hypoxemic, even after being removed from the fluid medium and even after ventilation is reestablished. As a result, in the latter group the period of hypoxemia is longer, and secondary damage due to the hypoxemia is more likely to occur. The continuing hypoxemia is most frequently due to direct lung injury from the aspirated fluid, which causes areas of low ventilation-perfusion ratio to develop.

The mechanism by which hypoxemia develops has not been completely elucidated. With saltwater aspiration, it is believed that hyperosmotic fluid causes transudation of fluid into alveoli, and the aspiration of debris (sand, diatoms, algae, etc.) causes a reactive exudate. As a result, alveoli become filled and are not ventilated. In freshwater aspiration, it is believed surfactant is washed out of the lungs, causing areas of focal alveolar collapse, leading to areas of shunt and low ventilation-perfusion ratio, again resulting in hypoxemia. These abnormalities persist until the lung damage resolves or until surfactant can be regenerated.

Victims often swallow large amounts of fluid during the near drowning episode, so further decreases in ventilatory function may occur as a result of elevation of the diaphragm from gastric distention. Vomiting and aspiration of gastric contents may further complicate the near drowning episode. Hypoxemia and decreased alveolar ventilation produce a number of consequences. Elevations of arterial PCO_2 and decreases in pH occur quickly. Metabolic acidosis can be extremely severe because the victim often struggles during the near drowning episode. Finally, cardiovascular collapse may occur, resulting in cardiac arrest. If hypoxemia and decreased cardiac output persist long enough, anoxic cerebral damage can ensue.[107-109] Although electrolyte disturbances are usually not a significant problem in near drowning, the exception to this situation appears to be drowning victims in the Dead Sea, where electrolyte concentrations are greater than those in usual seawater. Victims of near drowning in that unique environment have major electrolyte abnormalities, and it is believed that these disturbances are responsible for fatal arrhythmias in that group.[110] The remaining specific consequence of aspiration is pneumonia, which can occur in near drowning victims. The pathogens and the clinical picture of pneumonia associated with near drowning have recently been reviewed extensively.[111]

Because cardiac arrest is secondary to hypoxemia in near drowning, it presumably takes a significant amount of time to occur. If the water in which the victim is immersed is cold enough during this time, if the surface area–to-mass ratio of the victim is large enough, and if the victim swallows enough water, core temperature may decrease sufficiently that oxygen demands are markedly decreased. However, it is unclear whether this mechanism is adequate to explain the degree of cooling and the amount of cerebral protection that appears to occur in some incidents.[112]

CLINICAL PRESENTATION

The clinical presentation of drowning or near drowning victims is highly variable. The patient who is unconscious and apparently without vital signs at the site of the accident may be hemodynamically stable and neurologically intact in the emergency room, whereas the victim initially hemodynamically stable at the scene might deteriorate significantly before arrival at the hospital.

Cardiovascular System

Victims of significant near drowning often suffer cardiac arrest, but frequently respond to resuscitative measures. However, it is not uncommon for a victim to be brought to the emergency room still requiring cardiopulmonary resuscitation. If the patient responds to cardiopulmonary resuscitation with a stable rhythm or if the patient never suffers a cardiac arrest, supraventricular tachycardias are commonly seen. If the patient presents with a viable rhythm, it will most likely be supraventricular tachycardia secondary to hypoxemia and acidosis.[107,108] Usually, however, the patient is hemodynamically intact (i.e., adequate blood pressure and pulse with a presumably adequate cardiac output). Some patients may have a primary cardiac arrest that may mimic a drowning episode. This is known to occur in patients with coronary ischemia and in patients with the long QT syndrome (see earlier). Pathologic diagnoses may be further complicated by terminal aspiration secondary to agonal breathing after cardiac arrest.

Table 66.5 Average Blood Gas Measurements in Hospitalized Near-Drowning Victims Breathing Room Air upon Admission

	pH	Paco$_2$ (mm Hg)	Pao$_2$ (mm Hg)	Base Excess (mEq)
Fresh water	7.26	38	66	−9
Sea water	7.37	36	56	−5
All	7.30	37	62	−7

Adapted from Modell JH, Davis JH, Giammona ST, et al: Blood gas and electrolyte changes in human near-drowning victims. JAMA 203:337–343, 1968.

Pulmonary System

Patients with water aspiration may present with few or no respiratory complaints or with severe pulmonary edema.[113] The latter is probably due to direct lung injury and is not usually cardiac in origin. Patients who have aspirated any significant quantity of water frequently have a widened alveolar-arterial oxygen gradient and anything from mild to severe hypoxemia. Arterial PCO_2 can be low or elevated depending on alveolar ventilation (Table 66.5). Chest radiographs can show patchy infiltrates, which are most common in the periphery or in the medial basal regions, or frank pulmonary edema (see Fig. 66.4).[114] The pulmonary edema is a form of the acute respiratory distress syndrome.[114] The clinical course cannot be predicted with certainty by the radiographic picture of lung injury.[115] Victims with clear-cut pulmonary difficulties may show minimal radiographic abnormalities, and those with minimal clinical injury may have severely abnormal radiographic pictures.

An interesting form of pulmonary edema found in divers was described by Wilmshurst[116] and by Hampson and Dunford.[117] This is manifest as severe dyspnea while diving, associated with arterial hypoxemia, lung congestion, and a normal cardiovascular system. The syndrome may be related to negative-pressure pulmonary edema, a phenomenon well described in the anesthesia literature.[118]

Neurologic Status

The neurologic status of patients can also be quite varied. To compare results among different groups, a classification scheme has been suggested to describe these patients.[119,120] In this classification system, patients are placed into category A, B, or C based on their initial neurologic status. Category A patients are awake; category B patients are blunted; and category C patients are comatose. Within category C, patients are further classified as C1, C2, or C3, depending on their best motor response. The C1 comatose patient has a decorticate response, the C2 patient has a decerebrate response, and the C3 patient has no motor response at all.

TREATMENT

Restoration of normal neurologic function, although unusual, has been described even after prolonged drowning-induced cardiac arrest.[121-123] As cardiac arrest in this setting is invariably due to hypoxemia and acidosis, the first goal must be to establish a reliable airway and to supply as high an inspired oxygen concentration as possible. Until the results of arterial blood gas determinations are available, 100% oxygen should be provided. Endotracheal intubation is the preferred method for establishing an airway. This approach needs to take into account the possibility of a concomitant unstable neck injury if there is associated trauma,[124,125] and the risk of aspiration. At present there are insufficient data to warrant the routine use of the Heimlich maneuver in near drowning victims.[126]

Patients with cardiac arrest due to near drowning can have a profound metabolic acidosis. The doses of bicarbonate required to reverse such acidosis may be far larger than the doses recommended for patients suffering cardiac arrest from primary heart disease.[127] Arterial blood gas determinations are necessary to guide precise bicarbonate dosing. Concurrently, a nasogastric tube should be inserted to decompress the stomach, and body temperature readings should be obtained to rule out hypothermia. In the presence of a significantly lowered body temperature, aggressive rewarming measures should be instituted.

Once an adequate airway has been obtained and spontaneous cardiac activity achieved, adequate oxygen delivery to the tissues needs to be ensured, which requires an adequate arterial PO_2. Generally, in the near drowning victim, hemodynamic stability is relatively easy to achieve. Occasional patients will have marked decreases in blood pressure and cardiac output. The initial therapy for hypotension of most etiologies is a trial of fluids, but for a near drowning victim with pulmonary edema, this may not be appropriate. As a result, this group of patients may require invasive hemodynamic monitoring. With knowledge of pulmonary artery wedge pressure and cardiac output, more rational decisions concerning the need for fluids or pressors can then be made.[113] Isolated measurement of the central venous pressure is generally not an accurate method of judging intravascular volume status in the presence of noncardiac pulmonary edema. In addition, changes in central venous pressure do not necessarily correspond to changes in left ventricular filling pressures. In the case of immersion pulmonary edema in a diver, the cause of hypoxemia is not water aspiration, and therapy should include diuretics to reduce lung congestion.[117]

Positive end-expiratory pressure is extremely effective in reversing the abnormal ventilation-perfusion relationships leading to hypoxemia. Usually only modest amounts of pressure are necessary to achieve adequate oxygenation, and the improvement in pulmonary function can be quite dramatic. Positive end-expiratory pressure apparently does not alter the course of the underlying pulmonary injury but rather allows for adequate oxygenation while the lung is recovering. It also allows this recovery to take place at a level of inspired oxygen that is not in itself toxic to the lung.[128] Usually the pulmonary injury resolves over a period of 48 to 72 hours, and ventilatory support in most circumstances is relatively brief, unless infection develops. Consequently, in patients who are able to tolerate it, nasal continuous or bilevel positive airway pressure may be a reasonable method for short-term ventilatory support. However, the risk of aspiration is not inconsequential with this treatment.[100,129,130] At present there are insufficient data to warrant the use of inverse-ratio ventilation in cases of

near drowning.[131] It may be prudent to manage some near drowning victims with modern high-flow oxygen delivery systems for relatively brief periods before resorting to more invasive methods of providing adequate oxygenation.

The use of antibiotics in the near drowning victim who aspirates ocean water or swimming pool water is generally necessary only for those individuals who become febrile, develop new pulmonary infiltrates, or develop purulent secretions.[132] Prophylactic antibiotics do not improve mortality or decrease morbidity.[107] Because most pulmonary infections in the near drowning victim appear to be hospital acquired, prophylactic antibiotics seem to select for more resistant organisms.[133] In addition to clinical experience, experimental evidence also suggests that the use of prophylactic antibiotics is not indicated. If the victim aspirates heavily contaminated water with a known or suspected organism, the use of prophylactic antibiotics may be appropriate. A rare complication of near drowning is the aspiration of sand or gravel.[134] Although bronchoscopy for the routine management of the near drowning victim is probably not warranted, consideration for this procedure should be made when unexpected difficulties with mechanical ventilation occur.

Routine use of adrenocorticosteroids to treat the lung injury associated with near drowning is unwarranted. Experimental evidence with this form of aspiration as well as others strongly suggests that steroids do not improve the long-term outcome or short-term morbidity.[135,136] However, there is one uncontrolled series of four cases that suggests high-dose steroids may be beneficial to near drowning victims who present with pulmonary edema.[137] Artificial surfactant[138] and extracorporeal membrane oxygenation[139] have also been used to treat the pulmonary injury associated with near drowning. Any victim who has more than minimal respiratory symptoms, an abnormal chest radiograph, or abnormal arterial blood gas measurements should be admitted to the hospital, because pulmonary damage may not be clinically manifest for several hours after the incident.[140] Nearly all patients who will demonstrate significant problems of gas exchange will do so by 4 to 8 hours after the incident; therefore, consideration for discharge from the emergency department may be appropriate in people who can be observed in this fashion.[141] In the setting of a diving accident, an unconscious victim may have sustained an air embolism as well. Whenever doubt exists, both conditions should be treated simultaneously.

PROGNOSIS

The prognosis for the near drowning victim depends mainly on the duration of immersion, the length of the anoxic period, and the degree of damage secondary to the anoxic episode. Patients who arrive at the hospital neurologically intact have an excellent prognosis and should survive neurologically unimpaired. Additionally, the occurrence of an apparent "cardiac arrest" does not in itself suggest a poor outcome. Cardiac arrest that persists through the period of initial first aid and transport to the hospital is a poor prognostic sign, but the presence of spontaneous respirations on presentation to the emergency department following cardiac arrest in the field is a good prognostic sign.[142] The duration of immersion correlates with the degree of damage secondary to the anoxic episode and therefore with the outcome. No prognostic test has proven to be a reliable basis for treatment decisions, and predictions concerning outcome cannot be made in the presence of severe hypothermia.

SUMMARY

Diving and work in compressed air have produced occupational exposure to hazardous environments for over 100 years. In the past 50 years, diving has become a recreation participated in by millions of individuals throughout the world. Besides the medical support for commercial diving and the unique training needed by physicians who support military diving, any physician may encounter a recreational diver seeking consultation about an illness related to a diving exposure, or medical clearance for diving. Therefore, knowledge of the basic physiology and pathophysiology is important in understanding the patient's illness or evaluation requirements. Occasionally a physician may be confronted with treatment for an acute medical emergency related to diving exposure, such as DCS, arterial gas embolism, or near drowning. This chapter provides a basic introduction and a basis for initiating treatment, seeking consultation, or furthering education in this interesting area of environmental medicine.

REFERENCES

1. Ryles MT, Pilmanis AA: The initial signs and symptoms of altitude decompression sickness. Aviat Space Environ Med 67:983–989, 1996.
2. Hong SK, Cerretelli P, Cruz JC, et al: Mechanics of respiration during submersion in water. J Appl Physiol 27:537–538, 1969.
3. Agostoni E, Gurtner G, Torri G, et al: Respiratory mechanics during submersion and negative pressure breathing. J Appl Physiol 21:251–258, 1966.
4. Johnson LF, Lin YC, Hong SK: Gastroesophageal dynamics during immersion in water to the neck. J Appl Physiol 38:449–454, 1975.
5. Hong SK, Ting EY, Rahn H: Lung volumes at different depths of submersion. J Appl Physiol 23:18–22, 1967.
6. Craig AB Jr, Ware DE: Effect of immersion in water on vital capacity and residual volume of the lungs. J Appl Physiol 23:423–425, 1967.
7. Arborelius M, Balldin UI, Lidja B, et al: Hemodynamic changes in man during immersion with the head above water. Aerosp Med 43:592–598, 1972.
8. Hong SK, Rahn H, Kang DH, et al: Diving pattern, lung volumes, and alveolar gas in the Korean diving women (Ama). J Appl Physiol 18:457–465, 1963.
9. Craig AB Jr: Causes of loss of consciousness during underwater swimming. J Appl Physiol 16:583–586, 1961.
10. Tipton M, Mekjavic I, Golden F: Hypothermia. In Bove AA (ed): Bove and Davis' Diving Medicine (4th ed): Philadelphia: WB Saunders, 2004, pp 261–274.
11. Pendergast DR, Tedesco M, Nawrocki DM, et al: Energetics of underwater swimming with SCUBA. Med Sci Sports Exerc 28:573–580, 1996.
12. Navy Department: U.S. Navy Diving Manual. Vol 1, Rev 3: Air Diving (Publication No. NAVSEA 0994-LP-001-9110). Washington, DC: U.S. Navy Department, 1996.
13. Wasserman K, Whipp BJ, Koyal SN, et al: Anaerobic threshold and respiratory gas exchange during exercise. J Appl Physiol 35:236–247, 1973.
14. Navy Department: U.S. Navy Diving Manual. Vol 2: Mixed Gas Diving (Publication No. NAVSEA 0994 LP-001-9120). Washington, DC: U.S. Navy Department, 1996, pp 12–1 to 12–44.
15. Golding FC, Griffiths P, Hempleman HV, et al: Decompression sickness during construction of the Dartford Tunnel. Br J Ind Med 17:167–180, 1960.
16. Francis TJR, Smith DH: Describing Decompression Illness (42nd UHMS Workshop). Kensington, Md: Undersea and Hyperbaric Medical Society, 1991.
17. Boyle R: New pneumatic experiments about respiration. Philos Trans R Soc Lond 5:2011–2031, 1670.
18. Hunter SE, Farmer JC: Ear and sinus problems in diving. In Bove AA (ed): Bove and Davis' Diving Medicine (4th ed): Philadelphia: WB Saunders, 2004, pp 431–460.
19. Behnke AR: Analysis of accidents occurring in training with the submarine "lung." US Naval Med Bull 30:177–184, 1932.
20. Polak B, Adams H: Traumatic air embolism in submarine escape training. US Naval Med Bull 30:165–177, 1932.
21. Schaefer KE, Nulty WP, Carey C, et al: Mechanisms in development of interstitial emphysema and air embolism on decompression from depth. J Appl Physiol 13:15–29, 1958.
22. Malhotra MC, Wright CAM: Arterial air embolism during decompression and its prevention. Proc R Soc Med B 154:418–427, 1960.
23. Smith R, Neuman T: Elevation of serum creatine kinase in divers with arterial gas embolism. N Engl J Med 330:19–24, 1994.
24. Wilmshurst P, Davidson C, O'Connell G, et al: Role of cardio-respiratory abnormalities, smoking and dive characteristics in the manifestations of neurological decompression illness. Clin Sci 86:297–303, 1994.
25. Tetzlaff K, Reuter M, Leplow B, et al: Risk factors for pulmonary barotrauma in divers. Chest 112:654–659, 1997.
26. Neuman TS, Clausen JL: Recommend caution in defining risk factors for barotrauma. Chest 114:1791–1792, 1998.
27. Benton PJ, Francis TJR, Pethybridge RJ: Spirometric indices and the risk of pulmonary barotrauma in submarine escape training. Undersea Hyperb Med 26:213–218, 1999.
28. Elliott DH, Harrison JAB, Barnard EEP: Clinical and radiographic features of 88 cases of decompression barotrauma. In Shilling CW, Beckett MW (eds): Proceedings of the Sixth Symposium on Underwater Physiology. Bethesda, Md: Federation of American Societies for Experimental Biology, 1978, pp 527–535.
29. Neuman TS, Jacoby I, Bove AA: Fatal pulmonary barotrauma due to obstruction of the central circulation with air. J Emerg Med 16:413–417, 1998.
30. Harker CP, Neuman TS, Olson LK, et al: The roentgenographic findings associated with air embolism in sport scuba divers. J Emerg Med 11:443–449, 1993.
31. Smith RM, Van Hoesen KB, Neuman TS: Arterial gas embolism and hemoconcentration. J Emerg Med 12:147–153, 1994.
32. Vail HH: Traumatic conditions of the ear in workers in an atmosphere of compressed air. Arch Otolaryngol 10:113–126, 1929.
33. Whelan TR: Facial nerve palsy associated with underwater barotrauma. Postgrad Med J 66:465–466, 1990.
34. Teed RW: Factors producing obstruction of the auditory tube in submarine personnel. US Naval Med Bull 44:293–306, 1944.

35. Lundgren C, Tjernstrom O, Ornhagen H: Alternobaric vertigo and hearing disturbances in connection with diving: An epidemiologic study. Undersea Biomed Res 1:251–258, 1974.

36. Freeman P, Edmonds C: Inner ear barotrauma. Arch Otolaryngol 95:556–563, 1972.

37. Pullen FW: Perilymphatic fistula induced by barotrauma. Am J Otol 13:270–272, 1992.

38. Sheridan MF, Hetherington HH, Hull JJ: Inner ear barotrauma from scuba diving. Ear Nose Throat J 78:181, 184, 186–187, 1999.

39. Fagan P, McKenzie B, Edmonds E: Sinus barotrauma in divers. Ann Otol Rhinol Laryngol 85:61–64, 1976.

40. Butler FK: Diving and hyperbaric ophthalmology. Surv Ophthalmol 39:347–366, 1995.

41. Butler F: Orbital hemorrhage following facemask barotrauma. Undersea Hyperb Med 28:31–34, 2001.

42. Kieser J, Holborow D: The prevention and management of oral barotrauma. N Z Dent J 93:114–116, 1997.

43. Cramer FS, Heimbach RD: Stomach rupture as a result of gastrointestinal barotrauma in a SCUBA diver. J Trauma 22:238–240, 1982.

44. Hayden JD, Davies JB, Martin IG: Diaphragmatic rupture resulting from gastrointestinal barotrauma in a scuba diver. Br J Sports Med 32:75–76, 1998.

45. Lambertsen CJ: Therapeutic gases: Oxygen, carbon dioxide and helium. *In* DiPalma JR (ed): Drill's Pharmacology in Medicine (4th ed). New York: McGraw-Hill, 1971, pp 1145–1179.

46. Kety S: The theory and applications of the exchange of inert gas at the lungs and tissues. Pharmacol Rev 3:1–41, 1951.

47. Vann RD: Mechanisms and risk of decompression sickness. *In* Bove AA (ed): Bove and Davis' Diving Medicine (4th ed): Philadelphia: WB Saunders, 2004, pp 127–164.

48. Bond G: New developments in high pressure living. Arch Environ Health 9:310–314, 1964.

49. Boycott AE, Damant GCC, Haldane J: The prevention of compressed air illness. J Hyg (Cambridge) 8:342–443, 1908.

50. Harvey EN, Barnes DK, McElroy WD, et al: Bubble formation in animals. I. Physical factors. J Cell Comp Physiol 24:1–22, 1944.

51. Bert P: Barometric Pressure: Researches in Experimental Physiology (Hitchcock MA, Hitchcock FA, transl). Columbus Book Co, 1943. Reprinted by the Undersea Medical Society, Bethesda, Md, 1878.

52. Erdman S: Aeropathy of compressed air illness among tunnel workers. JAMA 49:1665–1670, 1907.

53. Hallenbeck JM, Bove AA, Moquin R, et al: Accelerated coagulation of whole blood and cell free plasma by bubbling in vitro. Aerosp Med 44:712–714, 1973.

54. Bove AA, Hallenbeck JM: Changes in blood and plasma volumes in dogs during decompression sickness. Aerosp Med 45:49–55, 1974.

55. Boussuges A, Sainty JM, Juhan-Vague I, et al: Activation of coagulation in decompression illness. Aviat Space Environ Med 69:129–132, 1998.

56. Bove AA: Basis for drug therapy in decompression sickness. Undersea Biomed Res 9:91–112, 1982.

57. Levin LL, Stewart GJ, Lynch PR, et al: Blood and blood vessel wall changes induced by decompression sickness in dogs. J Appl Physiol 50:944–949, 1981.

58. Spencer MP: Decompression limits for compressed air determined by ultrasonically detected blood bubbles. J Appl Physiol 40:227–235, 1976.

59. Butler BD, Robinson R, Fife C, et al: Doppler detection of decompression bubbles with computer assisted digitization of ultrasonic signals. Aviat Space Environ Med 62:997–1004, 1991.

60. Conkin J, Waligora JM, Foster PP, et al: Information about venous gas emboli improves prediction of hypobaric decompression sickness. Aviat Space Environ Med 69:8–16, 1998.

61. Kumar VK, Waligora JM, Billica RD: Utility of Doppler-detectable microbubbles in the diagnosis and treatment of decompression sickness. Aviat Space Environ Med 68:151–158, 1997.

62. Moon RE, Camporesi EM, Kisslo JA: Patent foramen ovale and decompression sickness in divers. Lancet 1:513–514, 1989.

63. Wilmshurst PT, Byrne JC, Webb-Peploe MM: Relation between intraatrial shunts and decompression sickness in divers. Lancet 2:1302–1305, 1989.

64. Moon RE, Kisslo JA, Massey EW, et al: Patent foramen ovale (PFO) and decompression illness. Undersea Biomed Res 13(Suppl):15, 1991.

65. Wilmshurst PT, Treacher DF, Crowther A, et al: Effects of a patent foramen ovale on arterial saturation during exercise and on cardiovascular responses to deep breathing, Valsalva manoeuvre, and passive tilt: Relation to history of decompression illness in divers. Br Heart J 71:229–231, 1994.

66. Germonpré P, Dendale P, Unger P, Balestra C: Patent foramen ovale and decompression sickness in sports divers. J Appl Physiol 84:1622–1626, 1998.

66a. Torti SR, Billinger M, Schwerzmann M, et al: Risk of decompression illness among 230 divers in relation to the presence and size of patent foramen ovale. Eur Heart J 25:1014–1020, 2004.

66b. Moon RE, Bove AA: Transcatheter occlusion of patent foramen ovale: A prevention for decompression illness? Undersea Hyperb Med 31:271–274, 2004.

67. Sulaiman ZM, Pilmanis AA, O'Conner RB: Relationship between age and susceptibility to altitude decompression sickness. Aviat Space Environ Med 68:695–698, 1997.

68. Carturan D, Boussuges A, Vanuxem P, et al: Ascent rate, age, maximal oxygen uptake, adiposity, and circulating venous bubbles after diving. J Appl Physiol 93:1349–1356, 2002.

69. Hart AJ, White SAS, Conboy PJ, et al: Open water scuba diving accidents in Leicester: Five years' experience. J Accid Emerg Med 16:198–200, 1999.

70. Neuman TS, Spragg RG, Wagner PD, et al: Cardiopulmonary consequences of decompression sickness. Respir Physiol 41:143–155, 1980.

71. Norman JN, Childs CM, Jones C, et al: Management of a complex diving accident. Undersea Biomed Res 6:209–216, 1979.

72. Hallenbeck JM, Bove AA, Elliott DH: Mechanisms underlying spinal cord damage in decompression sickness. Neurology 25:308–316, 1975.

73. Nix WA, Hopf HC: Central nervous system damage after decompression accidents. Deutsch Med Wochenschr 105:302–306, 1980.

74. Farmer JC, Thomas WG, Youngblood DG, et al: Inner ear decompression sickness. Laryngoscope 86:1315–1326, 1976.

75. McCallum RI, Walder DN: Bone lesions in compressed air workers. J Bone Joint Surg 48:207–235, 1966.

76. Elliott DH: Decompression inadequacy in aseptic bone necrosis. Proc R Soc Med 64:1278–1280, 1971.

77. Leffler CT, White JC: Recompression treatments during the recovery of TWA Flight 800. Undersea Hyperb Med 24:301–308, 1997.

78. Moon RE: Treatment of decompression illness. *In* Bove AA (ed): Bove and Davis' Diving Medicine (4th ed): Philadelphia: WB Saunders, 2004, pp 195–224.

79. Bove AA, Clark JM, Simon AJ, et al: Successful therapy of cerebral air embolism with hyperbaric oxygen at 2.8 ATA. Undersea Biomed Res 9:76–80, 1982.

80. Reuter M, Tetzlaff K, Hutzelmann A, et al: MR imaging of the central nervous system in diving-related decompression illness. Acta Radiol 38:940–944, 1997.

81. Sparacia G, Banco A, Sparacia B, et al: Magnetic resonance findings in scuba diving-related spinal cord decompression sickness. MAGMA 5:111–115, 1997.

82. Reul J, Weis J, Jung A, et al: Central nervous system lesions and cervical disc herniations in amateur divers. Lancet 345:1403–1405, 1995.

83. Saumarez RC, Bolt JF, Gregory RJ: Neurologic decompression sickness treated without recompression. Br Med J 1:151–152, 1973.

84. Bennett PB: Inert gas narcosis and HPNS. *In* Bove AA (ed): Bove and Davis' Diving Medicine (4th ed): Philadelphia: WB Saunders, 2004, pp 225–240.

85. Behnke AR, Thompson RM, Motley EP: The psychologic effects from breathing air at 4 atmospheres pressure. Am J Physiol 112:554–558, 1935.

86. Clark JM, Thom SR: Toxicity of oxygen, carbon dioxide, and carbon monoxide. *In* Bove AA (ed): Bove and Davis' Diving Medicine (4th ed): Philadelphia: WB Saunders, 2004, pp 241–260.

87. Bove AA: Cardiovascular disorders and diving. *In* Bove AA (ed): Bove and Davis' Diving Medicine (4th ed): Philadelphia: WB Saunders, 2004, pp 485–506.

88. Massey EW, Greer HD: Neurologic consequences of diving. *In* Bove AA (ed): Bove and Davis' Diving Medicine (4th ed): Philadelphia: WB Saunders, 2004, pp 461–474.

89. Neuman TS, Bove AA, O'Connor RD, et al: Asthma and diving. Ann Allergy 73:344–350, 1994.

90. Elliott DE: Are Asthmatics Fit To Dive? Kensington, Md: Undersea and Hyperbaric Medical Society, 1996.

91. Caruso JL, Bove AA, Uguccioni DM, et al: Recreational diving deaths associated with cardiovascular disease (abstract). Undersea Hyperb Med 28:76, 2001.

92. Mebane GY, Low N, Dovenbarger J: A review of autopsies on recreational scuba divers: 1989–1992. Undersea Hyperb Med 20(Suppl):70, 1993.

93. Arborelius M Jr, Balldin UI, Lilja B, Lundgren CEG: Hemodynamic changes in man during immersion with the head above water. Aerospace Med 43:592–598, 1972.

94. Irving L: Bradycardia in human divers. J Appl Physiol 18:489–491, 1963.

95. Irving L, Solandt OM, Solandt DY, Fischer KC: The respiratory metabolism of the seal and its adjustment to diving. J Cell Comp Physiol 7:137–151, 1935.

96. Ackerman MJ, Tester DJ, Porter CJ: Swimming, a gene-specific arrhythmogenic trigger for inherited long QT syndrome. Mayo Clin Proc 74:1088–1094, 1999.

97. McAniff JJ: United States Underwater Fatality Statistics, 1970–82, Including a Preliminary Assessment of 1983 Fatalities (Report No. URI-SSR-84–17). Providence: National Underwater Accident Data Center, University of Rhode Island, 1984.

98. Powers AT, Bass B, Stewart J, et al: A six year review of SCUBA diving fatalities in San Diego County. Undersea Biomed Res 19(Suppl):20, 1992.

99. Dietz PE, Baker SP: Drowning: Epidemiology and prevention. Am J Public Health 64:303–312, 1974.

100. Cairns FJ, Koelmeyer TD, Smeeton WM: Deaths from drowning. N Z Med J 97:65–67, 1984.

101. Davis S, Smith LS: Alcohol and drowning in Cape Town. S Afr Med J 62:931–933, 1999.

102. Plueckhahn VD: The aetiology of 134 deaths due to "drowning" in Geelong during the years 1957–1971. Med J Aust 2:1183–1187, 1972.

103. Lanphier EH, Rahn H: Alveolar gas exchange during breath holding with air. J Appl Physiol 18:478–482, 1963.

104. Modell JH, Davis JH, Giammona ST, et al: Blood gas and electrolyte changes in human near-drowning victims. JAMA 203:337–343, 1968.

105. Cot C: Asphyxia from drowning: Treatment based on experimental findings. Bull Acad Nat Med (Paris) 105:758, 1931.

106. Modell JH, Bellefleur M, Davis JH: Drowning without aspiration: Is this an appropriate diagnosis? J Forensic Sci 44:1119–1123, 1999.

107. Modell JH, Moya F, Newby EJ, et al: The effects of fluid volume in sea water drowning. Ann Intern Med 67:68–80, 1967.

108. Modell JH, Moya F: Effects of volume of aspirated fluid during chlorinated fresh-water drowning. Anesthesiology 27:662–672, 1966.

109. Giammona ST, Modell JH: Drowning by total immersion: Effects on pulmonary surfactant of distilled water, isotonic saline and sea water. Am J Dis Child 114:612–616, 1967.

110. Yagil Y, Stalnikowicz R, Michaeli J, et al: Near drowning in the Dead Sea: Electrolyte imbalances and therapeutic implications. Arch Intern Med 145:50–53, 1985.

111. Szpilman D: Near-drowning and drowning classification: A proposal to stratify mortality based on the analysis of 1,831 cases. Chest 112:660–665, 1997.

112. Xu X, Tikuissis P, Giesbrecht G: A mathematical model for brain cooling during cold water near drowning. J Appl Physiol 86:265–272, 1999.

113. Lheureux P, Vincent JL, Brimioulle S: Fulminant pulmonary edema after near drowning: Remarkably high colloid osmotic pressure in tracheal fluid. Intensive Care Med 10:205–207, 1984.

114. Fine NL, Myerson DA, Myerson PJ, et al: Near drowning presenting as the adult respiratory distress syndrome. Chest 65:347–349, 1974.

115. Rosenbaum HT, Thompson WL, Fuller RH: Radiographic pulmonary changes in near drowning. Radiology 83:306–312, 1964.

116. Wilmshurst PT, Nuri M, Crowther A, Webb-Peploe MM: Cold-induced pulmonary oedema in scuba divers and swimmers and subsequent development of hypertension. Lancet 1:62–65, 1989.

117. Hampson NB, Dunford RG: Pulmonary edema of scuba divers. Undersea Hyperb Med 24:29–33, 1997.

118. Deepika K, Kenaan CA, Barrocas AM, et al: Negative pressure pulmonary edema after acute upper airway obstruction. J Clin Anesth 9:403–408, 1997.

119. Conn AW, Montes JE, Barker GA, et al: Cerebral salvage in near drowning following neurological classification by triage. Can Anaesth Soc J 27:201–210, 1980.

120. Modell JH, Graves SA, Kuck EJ: Near drowning: Correlation of level of consciousness and survival. Can Anaesth Soc J 27:211–215, 1980.

121. Sekar TS, McDonnell KF, Namsirikul P, et al: Survival after prolonged immersion in cold water without neurologic sequelae. Arch Intern Med 140:775–779, 1980.

122. Wolford JP: Cold water near-drowning response. J Emerg Med Services 3:5–8, 1984.

123. Young RSK, Zaineraitis ED, Dooling EO: Neurologic outcome in cold-water drowning. JAMA 244:1233–1235, 1980.

124. Hwang V, Shofer FS, Durbin DR, Baren JM: Prevalence of traumatic injuries in drowning and near drowning in

children and adolescents. Arch Pediatr Adolesc Med 175:50–53, 2003.
125. Watson RS, Cummings P, Quan L, et al: Cervical spine injuries among submersion victims. J Trauma 51:658–662, 2001.
126. Rosen P, Soto M, Harley J: The use of the Heimlich maneuver in near drowning. J Emerg Med 13:397–405, 1995.
127. Guidelines for cardiopulmonary resuscitation (CPR) and emergency cardiac care (ECC). JAMA 268:2171–2302, 1992.
128. Rutledge RR, Flor RJ: The use of mechanical ventilation with positive end expiratory pressure in the treatment of near drowning. Anesthesiology 38:194–196, 1973.
129. Meyer TJ, Hill NS: Noninvasive positive pressure ventilation to treat respiratory failure. Ann Intern Med 120:760–770, 1994.
130. Lapinsky SE, Mount DB, Mackey D, et al: Management of acute respiratory failure due to pulmonary edema with nasal positive pressure support. Chest 105:229–231, 1994.
131. Shanholtz C, Brower R: Should inverse ratio ventilation be used in the adult respiratory distress syndrome? Am Rev Respir Dis 149:1354–1358, 1994.
132. Kizer KW: Resuscitation of submersion casualties. Emerg Med Clin North Am 1:643–652, 1983.
133. Hughes JA: Drowning—an overview. J Am Coll Emerg Physicians 6:172, 1977.

134. Dunagan DP, Cox JE, Chang MC, et al: Sand aspiration with near drowning: Radiographic and bronchoscopic findings. Am J Respir Crit Care Med 156:292–295, 1997.
135. Calderwood HW, Modell JH, Ruiz BC: The ineffectiveness of steroid therapy for treatment of fresh-water near drowning. Anesthesiology 43:642–650, 1975.
136. Downs JB, Chapman RL, Modell JH, et al: An evaluation of steroid therapy in aspiration pneumonitis. Anesthesiology 40:129–135, 1974.
137. Sladen A, Zauder HL: Methyl prednisolone therapy for pulmonary edema following near drowning. JAMA 215:1793–1795, 1971.
138. McBrian M, Katumba JJ, Mukhtar AI: Artificial surfactant in the treatment of near drowning. Lancet 342:1485–1486, 1993.
139. Thalmann M, Trampitsch E, Haberfellner N, et al: Resuscitation in near drowning with extracorporeal membrane oxygenation. Ann Thorac Surg 72:607–608, 2001.
140. Putman CE: Drowning: Another plunge. Am J Roentgenol Radium Ther Nucl Med 125:543–549, 1975.
141. Causey AL, Tilelli JA, Swanson ME: Predicting discharge in uncomplicated near-drowning. Am J Emerg Med 18:9–11, 2000.
142. Jacobsen WK, Mason LJ, Briggs BA, et al: Correlation of spontaneous respiration and neurologic damage in near drowning. Crit Care Med 11:487–489, 1983.

67 Drug-Induced Pulmonary Disease

Andrew H. Limper, M.D.

INTRODUCTION

It is estimated that 2% to 5% of hospitalized patients experience an adverse drug reaction. Approximately 0.3% of hospital deaths are drug related, which results in tens of thousands of deaths in the United States each year.[1] Adverse drug reactions, which are for the most part preventable, account for considerable morbidity, mortality, and expense. Table 67.1 lists the classification of drug reactions.

We know little about the pharmacokinetic properties of drugs in individual patients. Some metabolites last only a fraction of a second and are not measurable. Many drug-related injuries are not reproducible in animals and therefore cannot be studied in depth. Moreover, if a drug administered in the therapeutic dose range caused an adverse reaction in most of the patients who received it, the drug would not be usable. Thus, the very success of many drugs and the fact that only a small percentage of the population reacts adversely to drugs have also limited understanding of pulmonary toxicities. Even though we know the mechanism of injury for some agents, we do not know why the injury only occurs in a few people. Nor do we understand why a patient can be rechallenged months and years later with the same drug and not develop a similar reaction. These deficiencies in our knowledge will eventually need to be corrected. Nevertheless, drug-induced pulmonary disease can be a significant problem. Analysis of a case series of open-lung biopsies in immunocompromised hosts with diffuse pulmonary disease disclosed that 21% of patients had disease that was likely to have been caused by a chemotherapeutic drug. Finally, our knowledge is limited because there is no requirement to report adverse drug reactions. It is estimated that less than 5% of all adverse drug-induced pulmonary diseases are formally reported.

There are in excess of 300 drugs known to affect the lungs adversely; many are listed in Table 67.2. To minimize mortality and significant morbidity, it is incumbent upon the clinician to keep in mind at least the more common drugs that may induce pulmonary disease.[2-6]

Table 67.1 Classification of Drug Reactions

| Allergic or hypersensitivity reactions |
| Overdosage |
| Intolerance |
| Idiosyncratic reaction |
| Side effects |
| Secondary effects |

MECHANISMS OF DRUG-INDUCED PULMONARY INJURY

Four mechanisms of drug injury to the lungs are recognized: (1) oxidant injury, such as during chronic nitrofurantoin ingestion; (2) direct cytotoxic effects on alveolar capillary endothelial cells by cytotoxic drugs (and these effects may be aggravated by oxidant injuries); (3) deposition of phospholipids within cells, such as produced by cationic amphophilic drugs such as amiodarone; and (4) immune-mediated injury through drug-induced systemic lupus erythematosus (SLE).[4,7-11] Although extensive investigation has been undertaken to look for other forms of immune system–mediated injury, only the SLE induced by drugs has been proven.

In addition to their respiratory functions, the lungs are actively involved in the regulation of several important vasoactive endogenous substances, including prostaglandins, angiotensin, serotonin, and bradykinin. However, except for angiotensin conversion, there has been no proof that inhibition of this metabolic function produces systemic

Table 67.2 Classification of Drug-Induced and Related Pulmonary Diseases by Type of Medication

Chemotherapeutic
Cytotoxic
  Azathioprine
  *Bleomycin
  Busulfan
  Chlorambucil
  Cyclophosphamide
  Etoposide
  Interleukin-2
  Melphalan
  *Mitomycin C
  Nitrosoamines
  Procarbazine
  Tumor necrosis factor
  Vinblastine
  Zinostatin
Noncytotoxic
  *Bleomycin
  *Cytosine arabinoside
  *Gemcitabine
  *Methotrexate
  *Procarbazine

Antibiotic
*Amphotericin B
Nitrofurantoin
  *Acute
  Chronic
Sulfasalazine

Anti-inflammatory
*Acetylsalicylic acid
Gold
Interferons
Leukotriene antagonists
Methotrexate
Nonsteroidal anti-inflammatory agents
*Penicillamine

Analgesic
*Heroin
*Methadone
*Naloxone
*Placidyl
*Propoxyphene
*Salicylates

Cardiovascular
*Amiodarone
Angiotensin-converting enzyme inhibitors
Anticoagulants
*β-Blockers
Dipyridamole
Flecainide
*Protamine
Tocainide

Inhalant
Aspirated oil
*Oxygen

Intravenous
*Blood products
*Ethanolamide maolate (sodium morrhuate)
Ethiodized oil (lymphangiogram)
Talc

Miscellaneous
Appetite suppressants
Bromocriptine
Dantrolene
*Hydrochlorothiazide
Methysergide
*Tocolytic agents
*Tricyclics
L-Tryptophan
Radiation
Systemic lupus erythematosus (drug-induced)
*Complement-mediated leukostasis

* Typically present as acute or subacute respiratory insufficiency.

effects; no other specific function of an extrapulmonary organ has been reported to be directly regulated by the lung. Although the lung is rich in cytochrome P-450 enzymes and known to metabolize some xenobiotics, very little is known about the metabolic handling of most drugs by the lungs.

Oxidant-mediated injury is believed to play a significant role in several of the drug-induced pulmonary diseases, namely, the chronic fibrosis related to nitrofurantoin, and possibly many of the chemotherapeutic drug–induced pulmonary injuries.[5] In vitro, nitrofurantoin is capable of generating toxic oxygen-derived substances such as hydrogen peroxide, hydroxyl radical, superoxide, and singlet oxygen. These oxygen radicals generate singlet electron transfers that disrupt critical cell functions. Nitrofurantoin may produce pulmonary fibrosis by accelerating the generation of oxygen radicals within lung cells and by overwhelming the normal antioxidant protective mechanisms. This in turn incites inflammatory and fibrotic reactions.

It is postulated that chemotherapeutic drug injury represents a direct toxic reaction. Considerable research has been done on bleomycin-induced lung injury. Bleomycin does not have a major effect on the bone marrow or on immunocompetency. The exact mechanism of bleomycin lung injury is unknown. However, epithelial cells in the lung and skin contain lower levels of a specific inactivating enzyme against bleomycin than do epithelial cells in other organs. Thus, the drug is allowed to accumulate within the cell and induce deoxyribonucleic acid (DNA) fragmentation.[8] Because bleomycin toxicity appears to be related to dosage and age, the toxicity probably is related to the levels of inactivating enzyme in certain individuals. Bleomycin apparently overwhelms this enzyme with a large total dose. It is also likely that there is a relative deficiency of the enzyme in individuals over 70 years of age. Some individuals of any age may be relatively deficient in this enzyme and hence especially sensitive to bleomycin lung toxicity.

The first cells to be affected by bleomycin are the type I epithelial cells. Repair of injured type I cells is accomplished by type II cells, which proliferate and differentiate into type I cells to restore the normal air-blood barrier. The vulnerability of the type II cell to bleomycin depends on the state of its cell cycle. If it is in the resting G_0 phase, the cell appears resistant to bleomycin injury, whereas if the cell is proliferating or differentiating, atypical exaggerated metaplasia occurs. Consequently, with net loss of type I alveolar epithelial cells, a fibroblastic reparative process is initiated. Bleomycin can also stimulate fibroblasts directly to increase collagen synthesis. Type I cells are particularly vulnerable to injury by bleomycin, but in the steady state the type II cell is generally considered to be injury resistant. By dosing bleomycin repeatedly, the likelihood increases that type II cells will be exposed during their vulnerable proliferative or differentiating periods.

Additional information indicates that bleomycin injures lung cells through the generation of reactive oxidants.[12] Antioxidant defenses may be of value in the amelioration of bleomycin-induced lung toxicity.[13] Accordingly, breathing supplementary oxygen potentiates bleomycin-induced oxidant injury. However, not all of the reactions to chemotherapeutic drugs are as dose- and age-related as bleomycin, nor does oxygen potentiate the toxicity of most drugs.

Amiodarone has brought to light another potential mechanism of drug-induced lung injury. Amiodarone has been demonstrated to produce phospholipidosis in alveolar macrophages and type II cells. In amiodarone pulmonary toxicity, there is a marked accumulation of abnormal alveolar macrophages containing lamellar inclusions, which in turn contain a variety of phospholipids.[7] It is not known whether this phospholipidosis is directly related to the accompanying interstitial pneumonitis. There are more than two dozen cationic amphophilic drugs known to induce a phospholipid storage disorder in cells, particularly in the lungs. It is believed that these drugs impair phospholipid catabolism. The process is reversible with discontinuation of the agent.

Drug-induced SLE is another established mechanisms of drug-induced pulmonary disease.[10] There are two groups of drugs associated with drug-induced SLE. The first group commonly elicits antinuclear antibody formation in a large percentage of the persons taking the drug, but only a small percentage of these develop clinical symptoms of SLE. The second group is made up of numerous drugs that have been reported to induce antinuclear antibodies only rarely, but virtually all persons afflicted develop SLE.

In drug-induced SLE, the antibodies are primarily directed against histones. In contrast, during idiopathic SLE, the antinuclear antibodies are heterogeneous and consist of antibodies recognizing native DNA, histones, and nonhistone ribonuclear proteins, as well as antibodies formed against extranuclear host components such as clotting factors.[10] Exactly how drugs incite antibodies to nuclear protein is not clear, because these agents are in themselves nonimmunogenic. A current hypothesis proposes that the drug acts as an adjuvant or immunostimulant to augment responses to "self" antigens. Autoimmunity then develops from the clonal expansion of cell-reacting lymphocytes, which are ordinarily held in check by a balance of helper and suppressor influences.

CHEMOTHERAPEUTIC AGENTS

Chemotherapeutic agent are extensively used in solid and hematologic malignancies, but also are increasingly employed for their immunosuppressive properties in the management of various inflammatory disorders. Pulmonary reactions to these agents can prove quite severe and rapidly fatal. In addition, the presentations of drug-induced pulmonary disease must be rapidly differentiated from other etiologies, including pulmonary infection, whose clinical presentations, including fever and diffuse radiographic abnormalities, may be extremely similar to chemotherapy-induced pulmonary reactions. Chemotherapy-associated pulmonary reactions have become a major problem, particularly in relation to therapeutic regimens containing bleomycin, methotrexate, cyclophosphamide, and a host of newer agents (Table 67.3). Virtually all patients taking these drugs are immune suppressed, both from their underlying disease and from the chemotherapy agents themselves, enhancing their susceptibility to a variety of usual and atypical infections. In addition, recurrence of their underlying disease needs to be excluded, which makes a specific diagnosis difficult in these complicated clinical situations.

Table 67.3 Pharmacologic Action of Selected Chemotherapeutic Agents with Associated Pulmonary Toxicities

Antibiotic-Derived Agents
Bleomycin
Mitomycin C

Alkylating Agents
Busulfan
Cyclophosphamide
Chlorambucil
Melphalan

Antimetabolites
Methotrexate
6-Mercaptopurine
Azathioprine
Cytosine arabinoside
Gemcitabine
Fludarabine

Nitrosoamines
Bischloroethyl nitrosourea (BCNU)
Chloroethyl cyclohexyl nitrosourea (CCNU)
Methyl-CCNU

Podophyllotoxins
Etoposide
Paclitaxel
Docetaxel

Novel Antitumor Agents
All-*trans* retinoic acid (ATRA)
Gefitinib
Imatinib mesylate
Irinotecan

Immune Modulatory Agents Used in Malignancy
Interferons
Interleukin-2
Tumor necrosis factor-α

Other Miscellaneous Chemotherapy Agents
Procarbazine
Zinostatin
Vinblastine

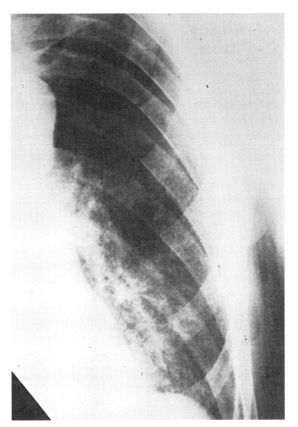

Figure 67.1 A close-up chest roentgenogram showing an alveolar interstitial pattern that is characteristic but not diagnostic of cytotoxic lung disease.

Hence, the differential diagnosis in these settings commonly includes infection, recurrence of the underlying disease, and other causes of interstitial lung disease, as well as drug toxicity.

The diagnosis of cytotoxic lung damage rests upon an appropriate history of drug exposure, histologic evidence of lung injury, and, most importantly, the exclusion of other causes of the lung damage. Unfortunately, there is no single diagnostic test or tissue biopsy that can definitively confirm the diagnosis of chemotherapy-associated lung disease. Thus, a careful and thorough evaluation to eliminate the possibilities of other conditions producing these effects, particularly infection, is warranted. Clinicians caring for these patients must be aware of myriad chemotherapeutic agents that can injure the lungs. Overall, less than 10% of the patients receiving chemotherapeutic agents will develop pulmonary toxicities.[2,14] Thus, the clinician must maintain a high index of suspicion, and be aware of other competing causes of pulmonary injury that may affect these immune-compromised patients.[2–20]

The clinical presentation of many chemotherapy drug effects is quite similar, with the exception that some present more acutely, whereas others tend to be more insidious in their onset. In general, nonproductive cough, dyspnea, and often fever begin weeks to years after the agent is first administered. Fever is common with most chemotherapeutic drug–induced pulmonary injury, but it may not be consistently present. Chills are usually absent and weight loss is often present. The chest radiograph in cases of chemotherapy-induced lung disease may be unremarkable for days or weeks before showing typical changes of a diffuse interstitial infiltrative pattern. Alternatively, there may be a diffuse mixed alveolar-interstitial pattern, which may occasionally be useful in recognizing early drug effects (Fig. 67.1).[21,22] However, these patterns are not fully diagnostic. There is no characteristic radiographic pattern specific for any particular chemotherapy agent, with the possible exception of hilar lymphadenopathy associated with "methotrexate lung."[23,24] Auscultation of the lungs will frequently reveal crackles, which are also nonspecific. In some instances, small pleural effusions may be present during adverse drug reactions, but these are not consistently present. Clubbing has not been reported in any chemotherapeutic pulmonary toxicity.

The results of lung function studies are abnormal in almost all patients with cytotoxic drug–induced lung disease when compared with pretreatment testing. The carbon monoxide diffusing capacity may decrease before reduced volumes are detected. In addition, this decrease in carbon monoxide diffusing capacity may precede the onset of symptoms and radiographic changes by days or weeks.[2] In several prospective investigations, diffusing capacity has been used to detect early onset of pulmonary reactions, at which time the agents are discontinued to minimize progression into overt clinical disease.[25] Gallium (^{67}Ga) uptake has, in the past, also been shown to be increased in the lungs of most patients with chemotherapeutic drug reactions, even before the chest radiograph appears abnormal. However, in recent years the use of gallium scanning has significantly decreased. Bronchoalveolar lavage may be another means of assessing early lung damage from these drugs; however, the results are often variable. In general, the greatest utility of bronchoalveolar lavage is to exclude infection.

Some reactions related to chemotherapeutic agents have been associated with cytologic atypia in affected pulmonary tissues. The histologic finding of markedly atypical type II pneumocytes, with relative fewer type I cells, has been reported. These type II pneumocytes may appear "bizarre"; however, the nuclear-to-cytoplasmic ratio remains normal, and there is no increase in mitotic activity in these cells.[4] Therefore, these changes should not be interpreted as a harbinger of malignancy. The simple presence of cytologic atypia cannot by itself definitely establish chemotherapy-associated lung injury. For instance, cytologic atypia may be present in occasional busulfan-treated patients without radiographic, clinical, or pathologic evidence of lung injury. In addition, cellular atypia can also be observed in the setting of a severe viral infection. Therefore, although cytologic atypia may suggest significant drug exposure, its presence cannot be viewed as diagnostic of toxicity.[26] In addition, tissue examination in chemotherapy-associated lung injury may demonstrate an inflammatory cell infiltrate in the interstitium as well as deposition of collagen in the septal walls. Lung remodeling can progress to severe fibrosis, resulting in respiratory insufficiency.

ANTIBIOTIC-DERIVED AGENTS

Bleomycin

Bleomycin pulmonary toxicity is the most prevalent and best understood chemotherapeutic-induced pulmonary disease.[25] Surveillance pulmonary function testing and chest radiographs reveal that as many as 20% of patients treated with bleomycin develop overt pulmonary disease, and as many as 1% die from pulmonary consequences of bleomycin therapy.[2] The incidence of bleomycin-related pulmonary disease is significantly greater in those who have received a cumulative dose of over 450 U, with a 10% death rate in those having received a total dose greater than 550 U of bleomycin. Pulmonary toxicity is also increased in patients over 70 years of age and in those with preexisting lung disease. In these investigations, frequent monitoring of the carbon monoxide diffusing capacity has been shown to predict subsequent clinical deterioration. Therefore, progressive fall in the carbon monoxide diffusing capacity should prompt withdrawal of further bleomycin administration.[27] In addition, the enhanced sensitivity of computed tomography scanning may also be useful in establishing an early diagnosis of bleomycin pneumonitis.[28,29] In one series of 100 patients receiving bleomycin, thoracic computed

tomography scan was abnormal in 38%, whereas the chest radiographs were abnormal in only 15%.[28]

Several other agents predispose patients toward developing bleomycin pneumonitis synergistically. Prior or concomitant thoracic radiation therapy is associated with a markedly increased incidence of severe bleomycin pulmonary toxicity. Furthermore, there is strong evidence of synergistic toxicity between prior bleomycin exposure and subsequent exposure to high inspired oxygen concentrations. This is often a problem during anesthesia and in the postoperative recovery period.[30,31] The length of time after bleomycin exposure during which breathing high inspired concentrations of oxygen predisposes to bleomycin toxicity is not known. Bleomycin exposures within the previous 6 months should be considered risky, though the hazard may extend for month or years beyond this interval. High concentrations of oxygen should be avoided whenever possible. In addition, there also appears to be synergistic toxicity between bleomycin and concomitant administration of cyclophosphamide.

One study demonstrated that, if the patient survives the acute injury from bleomycin, pulmonary findings may improve substantially over time.[32] However, if significant fibrosis is present, the process may progress insidiously despite the administration of corticosteroids. Histologically, end-stage bleomycin pneumonitis may be indistinguishable from idiopathic usual interstitial pneumonitis.

A less frequent form of bleomycin pneumonitis has also been described, namely, a hypersensitivity type of bleomycin reaction associated with acute onset, fever, and peripheral blood or bronchoalveolar lavage eosinophilia.[2,25] Discontinuation of bleomycin and initiating corticosteroids usually brings about rapid reversal of this hypersensitivity variant of bleomycin pneumonitis.

An additional rare, but clinically important, presentation of bleomycin pneumonitis can occur: the clinical presentation of nodular pulmonary lesions mimicking tumor metastasis (Fig. 67.2).[33,34] These reactions to bleomycin have been described in the setting of lymphoma or seminoma,

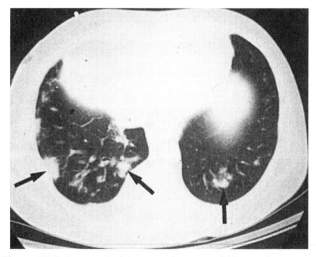

Figure 67.2 A computed tomography scan of bleomycin pneumonitis showing a nodular pattern. The histologic features of this form of bleomycin-induced lung injury are typical of bronchiolitis obliterans with organizing pneumonitis.

requiring surgical biopsy to differentiate bleomycin-associated lung injury from recurrence of the primary malignancy. These nodular lesions from bleomycin often exhibit the histologic pattern of bronchiolitis obliterans with organizing pneumonitis.[4] Similar reactions have been described in association with other chemotherapeutic agents, including methotrexate, cyclophosphamide, chlorambucil, mitomycin, and interferon, and also with nonchemotherapeutic agents such as amiodarone, gold, and nitrofurantoin.[4]

Mitomycin C

Mitomycin C has been employed in the management of bladder tumors, lung cancer, anal canal cancer, metastatic breast carcinoma, metastatic liver tumors, and esophageal malignancies. One series estimated the incidence of mitomycin-induced pneumonitis to be approximately 8%, with two additional series suggesting the incidence to range from 12% to as high as 39%.[35,36] The symptomatology, radiographic abnormalities, and histologic findings of mitomycin-induced pneumonitis are similar to those of other alkylating drug toxicities. However, it has been suggested that the carbon monoxide diffusing capacity may not fall prior the onset of clinical symptoms.[35] In addition, a favorable response to corticosteroid therapy has also been quite dramatic in many of these patients, possibly greater than in other forms of chemotherapy-associated lung injury.

In addition to mitomycin-induced pneumonitis, there are reports of an unusual reaction to mitomycin C consisting of microangiopathic hemolytic anemia with associated noncardiogenic pulmonary edema and renal failure.[37] Most of these patients developed side effects between 6 and 12 months after beginning mitomycin C chemotherapy. Up to one half of these patients evolve into the acute respiratory distress syndrome, with mortality as high as 95% in some series. The mortality in patients with mitomycin C–associated hemolytic uremic syndrome who do not develop acute respiratory distress syndrome is still in the range of 50%. In some instances, this unusual drug reaction appears to be precipitated by blood transfusions. Microangiopathic changes are present in the lungs and kidneys with intimal hyperplasia of the arterioles, along with prominent nuclear atypia of the capillary cells and capillary fibrin thrombi.

ALKYLATING AGENTS

Busulfan

Busulfan has been used for the management of chronic myeloproliferative disorders. The average duration from the initiation of therapy to the onset of respiratory symptoms is roughly 3.5 years, ranging between 8 months and as late as 10 years. However, busulfan pulmonary toxicity can occur as soon as 6 weeks following initiation of therapy. The incidence of busulfan pulmonary toxicity is estimated to be 6%, with a reported range of 2.5% to 43%.[38] Dyspnea, fever, and cough begin in a more insidious fashion with busulfan than with many other chemotherapy lung toxicities. Such symptoms have even been reported to begin months after busulfan therapy has been discontinued. Withdrawal of the agent and administration of corticosteroids results in variable responses. Although a few patients improve, the majority

experience progressive respiratory impairment and death. It is further not clear whether busulfan-related lung injury is a dose-related toxicity. Concomitant radiation therapy may potentiate the effect of busulfan. The chest radiograph in busulfan toxicity reveals a combined alveolar and interstitial process to a greater degree than in other chemotherapy reactions. This is likely due to a high degree of desquamation of injured epithelial cells into the alveolar spaces. This alveolar debris may be so extensive as to suggest alveolar proteinosis in some patients receiving busulfan. This form of alveolar proteinosis is more refractory to therapeutic lavage than is idiopathic alveolar proteinosis.[39–41]

Cyclophosphamide

Cyclophosphamide is widely included in combination chemotherapy for hematologic malignancies and solid tumors, including breast cancer. Accumulating evidence suggests that the incidence of cyclophosphamide-induced pneumonitis may be largely underestimated.[42,42a] A clinical review identified six patients in whom cyclophosphamide was the only factor contributing toward pulmonary injury.[43] Clinical features of cyclophosphamide-associated pulmonary toxicity include fever, dyspnea, cough, gas-exchange abnormalities, parenchymal infiltrates, and pleural thickening. Two patterns of cyclophosphamide-induced lung toxicity have been described. First, an early-onset pneumonitis can occur within the first 1 to 6 months after institution of therapy. This form generally responds to withdrawal of cyclophosphamide. In contrast, a late-onset pneumonitis may develop after months or even years of therapy, and result in progressive lung fibrosis and bilateral pleural thickening. This late-onset variety unfortunately has minimal response to withdrawal of cyclophosphamide or to corticosteroid therapy.[43] The dose of cyclophosphamide and development of lung disease are not clearly related. There have also been very rare reports of negative rechallenge with cyclophosphamide without subsequent recurrence of the pulmonary toxicity. However, this is not recommended.

Chlorambucil

This agent has been prescribed primarily for chronic lymphocytic disorders. The clinical presentation, chest radiographic abnormalities, and histologic features of chlorambucil-associated pneumonitis are remarkably similar to those described in other alkylating agent–induced pulmonary toxicities.[14] The presentation is usually insidious, occurring 6 months to a year or more after the start of therapy. Surveillance of lung function, particularly diffusing capacity, may be of benefit in anticipating which patients will deteriorate and require discontinuation of the agent. Few data are available on the efficacy of corticosteroid therapy in chlorambucil-related lung toxicity.

Melphalan

Melphalan has been enlisted in the treatment of multiple myeloma. There have been relatively few well-documented cases of pulmonary toxicity associated with melphalan, although the overall incidence may be underestimated.[21] The course of melphalan-associated pulmonary injury varies from acute to more subacute in tempo. Patients present with insidious to abrupt onset of dyspnea, cough, and frequently fever. There are no particular clues for predicting which patients will develop side effects. The incidence of pulmonary side effects from melphalan must be generally low, in view of the fact that this agent has been widely employed in the long-term management of myeloma.

ANTIMETABOLITES

Methotrexate

Methotrexate is present in many combination regimens for malignancies, and also is in used extensively for nonmalignant conditions, including psoriasis and rheumatoid arthritis. Several hundred cases of adverse pulmonary reactions related to methotrexate have been described. Methotrexate pneumonitis is unique and fortunately has been associated with only a few fatalities. Dyspnea, nonproductive cough, and fever usually commence a few days to several weeks after initiation of therapy. However, in rare cases, symptoms may be observed a few months or years after onset of therapy.[44] Methotrexate-associated pneumonitis is almost always reversible with or without the addition of corticosteroids. Eosinophilia is seen in at least half of the cases, and the disease is therefore believed to represent a hypersensitivity reaction.[2] The intriguing feature of this reaction is that the drug may be reinstituted following resolution of methotrexate pneumonitis without necessarily triggering a subsequent recurrence of symptoms or findings. In about one third of the patients, weakly formed granulomas are identified in lung biopsy, which is very unusual in other forms of chemotherapy-associated lung disease.[4] There is no cellular atypia, such as is seen in many other cytotoxic drug toxicities.

The chest radiograph tends to reveal a homogeneous infiltrate throughout all lung fields. Hilar adenopathy or pleural effusion occurs in at least 10% to 15% of patients with methotrexate lung toxicity. In distinct contrast to most of the other chemotherapy pulmonary toxicities, prospective investigations of patients receiving methotrexate have not demonstrated a diminished diffusing capacity that might predate subclinical toxicity. In addition, pulmonary toxicity in response to methotrexate does not appear to be dose related. There have been a few reports of fatal reactions occurring either from intrathecal methotrexate or from oral ingestion after previous intrathecal injections. Exclusion of opportunistic infections in the setting of methotrexate use is particularly important. *Pneumocystis* pneumonia has been reported in patients receiving methotrexate, either alone or in combination with corticosteroids.[45] The clinical presentation, chest radiography, and other clinical features can be quite similar to methotrexate lung.[45]

Azathioprine

There are over two dozen case reports of azathioprine-associated pneumonitis. However, the net overall incidence must be quite low, considering the widespread use of this agent for neoplastic as well as non-neoplastic conditions.[21] Nevertheless, the possibility of an azathioprine pneumonitis must be considered in any individual receiving this agent. Azathioprine is metabolized to 6-mercaptopurine, and there

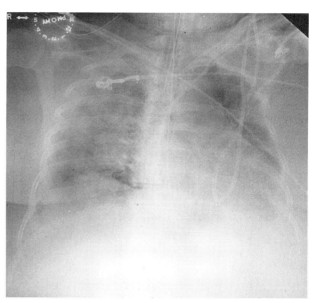

Figure 67.3 A chest radiograph of a 44-year-old woman showing acute noncardiac pulmonary edema that resulted from cytosine arabinoside–induced pulmonary disease. Histologic examination typically demonstrates intense intra-alveolar proteinaceous material forming hyaline membranes, but little other reaction.

have been a handful of reports detailing cytotoxic interstitial pneumonitis in association with this metabolite.[6] However, most of these patients have also received other agents that potentially could be implicated in the lung injury described.

Cytosine Arabinoside

Cytosine arabinoside (ara-C) is a cytotoxic agent used to induce remission in acute leukemia and other hematologic malignancies prior to bone marrow transplantation. Intensive ara-C treatment regimens have been associated with rapidly fatal noncardiac pulmonary edema (Fig. 67.3).[6] Histologic examination of lung tissue during ara-C pulmonary toxicity reveals substantial accumulation of intra-alveolar proteinaceous material without the cellular atypia and mononuclear infiltration described with other cytotoxic drugs. In two large series, 13% to 28% of the patients with toxicity developed respiratory distress during the administration of the drug, and nearly one half developed symptoms within a month of completing drug adminstration.[46,47] The mechanism underlying this reaction is unknown, and the associated mortality is high. Treatment for ara-C pulmonary toxicity is largely supportive, with mechanical ventilation, careful management of fluid status, and surveillance for superimposed infectious complications.

Gemcitabine

Gemcitabine is a pyrimidine analogue, with structure and activities similar to cytarabine (ara-C). It is highly active against non–small cell lung cancer, as well as breast, pancreatic, and ovarian cancers. It is usually well tolerated, with the most prevalent toxicity being bone marrow suppression, as well as nausea, rash, transaminase elevation, and edema in some cases. The evidence of pulmonary toxicity in association with gemcitabine has only recently emerged, and the incidence has probably been underestimated.[48] Dyspnea has been reported in 10% of treated patients, with severe dyspnea reported in up to 5%.[49–51] There are three major patterns of respiratory involvement in gemcitabine-related pulmonary toxicity. The first pattern is a nonspecific, self-limiting dyspnea occurring within hours to days of treatment. A second, relatively uncommon, pattern is that of an acute hypersensitivity reaction with bronchospasm. Lastly, a third pattern of severe respiratory involvement is occasionally seen. This is a severe idiosyncratic reaction with profound dyspnea and pulmonary infiltrates that may progress to life-threatening respiratory insufficiency. Most cases of gemcitabine-related pulmonary toxicity resolve with discontinuation of this drug. In cases of severe symptoms, discontinuation of the agent along with institution of corticosteroids, careful fluid management, and diuretic therapy may be warranted.[50]

Fludarabine

Fludarabine, another nucleoside analogue, is widely employed in the management of chronic lymphoproliferative disorders. The incidence of pulmonary toxicity related to fludarabine has been estimated to be approximately 8.6%.[52,52a,52b] Affected individuals experience dyspnea as early as 3 days after the first round of chemotherapy, though later onset of pulmonary symptoms has also been reported. The chest radiograph reveals either interstitial or mixed alveolar-interstitial infiltrates. Most patients respond to discontinuation of this drug, and receive symptomatic and objective benefits from additional corticosteroid therapy.

NITROSOAMINES

Nitrosourea compounds have a role in the treatment of gliomas and other central nervous system tumors, as well as in conditioning protocols preceding autologous bone marrow stem cell transplantation. Pulmonary toxicity related to nitrosoureas is well recognized and represents one of the most common side effects of these agents.[53] In particular, bischloroethyl nitrosourea (BCNU, carmustine) has been described to induce both acute-onset pulmonary injury and delayed-onset pulmonary fibrosis, with a predilection for the upper lobes.[53] The incidence of pulmonary toxicity associated with the administration of BCNU varies from 1.5% to 20% and is dose related, with up to a 50% incidence of lung disease in those receiving a total dose of over 1500 mg/m^2.[54] However, there have also been reports of pulmonary effects occurring with much lower doses.[54] The duration of therapy before the onset of pulmonary toxicity for the acute variant of nitrosourea lung injury has generally ranged from 6 months to 3 years. There appears to be a synergistic effect with cyclophosphamide, with radiation therapy, and possibly with other chemotherapeutic agents. The outcome may be unpredictable and sometimes fatal. There have been fewer case reports of pulmonary toxicity with methyl-chloroethyl cyclohexyl nitrosourea and chloroethyl cyclohexyl nitrosourea. Apparently, fever is less commonly associated with this form of

pulmonary toxicity than with many other chemotherapeutic drugs. Therapy usually consists of withholding the offending agent, and institution of corticosteroids, which has variable and often only transient beneficial effects.[55]

A long-term complication of BCNU toxicity is upper lobe fibrosis that may appear many years after the completion of chemotherapy. O'Driscoll and colleagues followed 17 patients for up to 17 years, and 12 of the 17 (71%) developed delayed upper lobe fibrosis.[56] The fibrosis is insidious in onset and, once discovered, appears to be intractably progressive. Corticosteroid therapy has not proven to be effective in delayed BCNU upper lobe fibrosis. Another unusual reported complication that is almost exclusively associated with nitrosourea compounds is pneumothorax.[57] This may be related to the upper lobe fibrobullous changes present in patients with BCNU lung toxicity.

NOVEL AND EMERGING AGENTS

All-*Trans* Retinoic Acid

All-*trans* retinoic acid (ATRA) has been employed in acute promyelocytic leukemia, in which it promotes differentiation of myeloid precursors and stimulates the maturation of leukemic cells, thereby promoting remission. It has also been reported to reduce disseminated intravascular coagulation and hemorrhagic complications during promyelocytic leukemia. The drug is associated with a number of toxicites, including edema, pleuropericardial effusions, and fluid retention that may evolve into a generalized capillary leak syndrome. In addition, multiple hemorrhagic complications have also been described. In one study, 9 of 35 patients with promyelocytic leukemia receiving ATRA developed respiratory distress.[58] Respiratory symptoms occurred between 2 and 21 days of treatment. Intravenous corticosteroid therapy seemed to be of benefit to these patients. Based upon these observations, an additional study has suggested that the incidence of ATRA-associated pulmonary syndrome may be reduced to roughly 10% through the use of preventative treatment with oral corticosteroids.[59] Tissue examinations of lungs affected by ATRA have revealed interstitial infiltration with maturing myeloid cells. However, the overall spectrum of the ATRA-associated pulmonary syndrome is continuing to evolve and includes the presence of myeloid cells and blasts in bronchoalveolar lavage fluid, nodular pulmonary infiltrates, pulmonary leukostasis, noncardiogenic pulmonary edema, acute respiratory distress syndrome, Sweet's syndrome, and diffuse alveolar hemorrhage.[60]

Gefitinib and Imatinib

Gefitinib (Iressa, ZD1839) is a selective tyrosine kinase inhibitor active on the epidermal growth factor receptor. It is used in patients with advanced non–small cell lung cancer who have failed to respond to platinum-based chemotherapy. At least six cases of acute interstitial pneumonia have been associated with this drug, and the overall incidence of gefitinib-associated interstitial lung disease may be in the range of 1%.[61,61a] Diffuse ground-glass opacities have been reported on computed tomography scan, with tissue examination demonstrating diffuse alveolar damage. Although some patients respond to withdrawal of the agent and institution of corticosteroid therapy, others progress to fulminant respiratory insufficiency. Hence, the clinician needs to remain mindful of this pulmonary complication of gefitinib therapy, and discontinue the agent if symptoms and radiograpic abnormalities occur. Recently, a limited number of cases showing pulmonary infiltration have also been reported in association with imatinib mesylate (Gleevec, ST1571), a novel tyosine kinase inhibitor used in the treatment of chronic myelogenous leukemia and gastrointestinal stromal tumors.[62]

Irinotecan

Irinotecan, a semisynthetic camptothecin, has been employed for advanced colorectal cancer either alone or in combination with 5-fluorouracil, and in some lung cancer trials. Early studies of irinotecan in Japan documented a 1.8% incidence of pneumonitis.[63,64,64a] In those studies, clinical features included dyspnea, fever, and reticulonodular pulmonary infiltrates. Empirical corticosteroids were recommended, but some patients progressed to fatal respiratory failure. In subsequent U.S. trials, cough and dyspnea were described in roughly 20% of treated patients.[65] However, many of these patients had intrathoracic malignancies. The reported incidence of serious pulmonary toxicity related to irinotecan was much lower in these subsequent trials (approximately 0.4%).[65] Nonetheless, cases of serious irinotecan-associated interstitial pneumonitis have been reported in the United States. Patients with preexisting pulmonary disease may be at enhanced risk.

PODOPHYLLOTOXINS

Etoposide

Etoposide (VP-16) has been widely used in combination chemotherapy for non–small cell and small cell lung carcinoma. Despite its extensive use, only a few cases of etoposide-associated pulmonary toxicity have been reported.[66] Onset may occur shortly after the first round of chemotherapy. However, most of the associated cases present after prolonged treatment. Tissue examination reveals features of alveolar edema, diffuse alveolar damage, and atypical type II pneumocytes. Therapy consists of withdrawal of the agent and administration of corticosteroids, which provide variable improvement.

Paclitaxel

Paclitaxel (Taxol) is a highly potent chemotherapeutic agent used in the treatment of lung, breast, and ovarian carcinomas. A few case reports have associated this agent with respiratory symptoms, including cough, dyspnea, wheezing, and chest tightness.[67] Interstitial and reticulonodular infiltrates have been reported on chest radiographic studies.[68] Cases of transient pulmonary infiltrates and suspected interstitial pneumonitis have also been described. The true incidence of lung toxicity directly related to paclitaxel is not well understood. A prospective study of lung function in 33 patients receiving paclitaxel with carboplatin (an agent with little lung toxicity) in the setting of nonthoracic malignancy revealed an isolated decrease in diffusing capacity without

other clinical or radiographic evidence of pulmonary toxicity.[69] In other studies, conducted on patients with lung carcinoma, significant early and late pulmonary toxicity has been noted in 10% and 68% of patients, respectively.[70] Attributing the toxicity directly to paclitaxel is confounded by the underlying thoracic neoplasm, as well as other cytotoxic agents used in these patients.[71] Nonetheless, clinicians should be aware of the potential of paclitaxel impairing pulmonary function.

Docetaxel

Docetaxel (Taxotere) is a new taxane compound that has activity in the treatment of breast and non–small cell lung cancer. Occasional pulmonary toxicity based on a hypersensitivity reaction has been observed.[72] These patients have responded rapidly to corticosteroid therapy. Recently, a small case series has suggested that the combination of docetaxel and gemcitabine has a particular propensity to induce severe pulmonary toxicity.[73]

IMMUNOMODULATORY AGENTS

Interferons

Interferons have been used in a wide variety of malignant, infectious, and inflammatory disorders. Interferon-alfa and interferon beta have been employed in the treatment of hairy cell leukemia, myeloma, T-cell lymphoma, chronic myelogenous leukemia, malignant pleural effusions, melanoma, renal cell carcinoma, and Kaposi's sarcoma. Interferon gamma has been included in investigative trials for mesothelioma, non–small cell lung carcinoma, and idiopathic pulmonary fibrosis.

Administration of interferons has been associated with a variety of pulmonary reactions. For instance, interferon-alfa has been linked to severe exacerbation of bronchospasm in patients with preexisting asthma.[74] In addition, a granulomatous reaction indistinguishable from sarcoidosis has been described in relation to interferon therapy.[75] These toxicities usually respond to either reduction or withdrawal of the interferon treatment with or without the addition of corticosteroids. Noncaseating granulomas have been documented in the lung, lymph nodes, liver, and skin of affected patients.

Interferon-associated interstitial lung disease has also been reported.[76] Dyspnea and cough are observed and bilateral infiltrates are present on chest radiography. A CD8-predominant lymphocytic response is found in the bronchoalveolar lavage, and a cellular interstitial pattern is present on histology. In some cases, interferon therapy has also been associated with bronchiolitis obliterans with organizing pneumonia.[77] Most affected patients respond to discontinuation of the interferon and administration of corticosteroids. Recently, interferon gamma has been used in idiopathic pulmonary fibrosis. A series has been reported in which four patients with advanced idiopathic pulmonary fibrosis developed acute hypoxemic respiratory failure during interferon gamma treatment.[78] This was not reponsive to corticosteroids and was fatal in three cases. Interferon gamma is also associated with a high incidence of severe radiation pneumonitis, when it is used in multimodality therapy for non–small cell lung carcinoma.[79]

Interleukin-2

Interleukin-2 has been employed with or without lymphokine-activated killer cells as an investigational treatment of certain malignancies.[80–82] Over 50% of the patients treated with interleukin-2 have developed one or more pulmonary complications, including noncardiogenic pulmonary edema, acute respiratory distress syndrome, and bronchospasm, as well as cardiac dysfunction leading to cardiogenic pulmonary edema. In some individuals, a generalized capillary leak syndrome has been reported.

Tumor Necrosis Factor

Tumor necrosis factor-α promotes inflammation and induces necrosis of certain neoplasms. It has been employed as an investigational therapy for patients with advanced malignancies.[83,84] In one series of tumor necrosis factor-α–treated patients, pulmonary function tests showed a significant decline in carbon monoxide diffusing capacity in all patients, beginning roughly 2 weeks after initiation of therapy. The results of other tests of pulmonary function did not change significantly.[84] Associated respiratory impairment has been noted in some patients.

Granulocyte-Macrophage and Granulocyte Colony-Stimulating Factors

Granulocyte-macrophage colony-stimulating factor and granulocyte colony-stimulating factor are widely applied in the treatment of bone marrow suppression following chemotherapy, thereby enhancing the immune response of treated patients. A number of case reports and small series have proposed that these biologic factors may potentiate pulmonary toxicity of other chemotherapeutic agents.[85] It has also been suggested that granulocyte-macrophage colony-stimulating factor may induce a recall phenomenon of toxicity from other drugs.

OTHER CHEMOTHERAPEUTIC AGENTS

Procarbazine

Procarbazine has found use in Hodgkin's disease and other lymphoproliferative disorders. Adverse pulmonary reactions related to procarbazine are fairly rare, with only a few cases of probable procarbazine pneumonitis being described.[21] These lung reactions may be cytotoxic in nature. In other patients, toxicity has been related to a rapid-onset hypersensitivity reaction associated with eosinophilia that declines after the drug has been discontinued.

Zinostatin

Zinostatin has been associated with occasional reports of pulmonary toxicity, usually only occurring in patients who have received the drug for prolonged periods of time.[21] Interestingly, this agent has been associated with the unique drug reaction of hypertrophy of the pulmonary vasculature, which may be associated with pulmonary hypertension. This may be related to a direct cytotoxic effect of the drug on the pulmonary endothelium.

Vinblastine

Vinblastine, a vinca plant alkaloid, is one of the oldest chemotherapeutic agents still in use. Vinblastine continues to be included in a wide variety of chemotherapeutic regimens for hematologic and solid malignancies. Traditionally, vinblastine was thought to have little if any pulmonary toxicity. However, reports have associated vinblastine with pulmonary complications when it is combined with other agents, particularly mitomycin C. This combination has been complicated by bronchospasm, interstitial pneumonitis, and a noncardiac pulmonary edema.[86,87]

RADIATION

The acute effects of radiation can produce histologic changes mimicking cytotoxic lung responses and may occasionally involve areas of lung outside the port of radiation. The process is generally heralded by fever beginning 3 to 8 weeks after initiation of radiation therapy and may rapidly progress to a fatal outcome in spite of institution of corticosteroids. The disease may improve spontaneously but usually progresses to chronic radiation effects. Bronchoalveolar lavage predominantly demonstrates lymphocytes in the contralateral lung as well as in the involved lung.[88] The chronic effects of radiation are well known. They begin 3 to 6 months or later after radiation therapy, and their primary effect is vascular.[89] Recently, a form of radiation pneumonitis has been observed outside the treatment fields, usually in patients with breast cancer.[90] Tissue examination has revealed bronchiolitis obliterans with organizing pneumonitis in these cases.[90]

ANTIMICROBIAL AGENTS

NITROFURANTOIN

Acute Reaction

Acute nitrofurantoin pneumonitis may be one of the most common drug-induced pulmonary diseases.[91–93] The Swedish Adverse Drug Reaction Committee reported 921 patients with adverse reactions to this drug: 43% were acute pulmonary reactions, and another 5% were due to chronic interstitial pneumonitis.[91,92] They estimated that all of these reactions occurred in less than 1% of those taking the drug. Seventy-one percent of all reactions were severe enough to require hospitalization, but only 1% were fatal. The fatalities included 4 of 49 patients with chronic pulmonary fibrosis and 2 of 398 with acute pulmonary reactions.

Acute pulmonary reactions are probably underestimated.[93] The incidence has been estimated to be anywhere from 1 in 550 to 1 in 5400 individuals.[93] The mechanism of the acute nitrofurantoin reaction is unknown. There are only a few studies on the lung histology in individuals with acute nitrofurantoin pneumonitis, and these have shown a proliferation of fibroblasts and a lymphoplasmacytic infiltrate, occasionally with an intra-alveolar desquamation of cells. In spite of peripheral blood eosinophilia, eosinophils are not usually seen in the lung tissue.

The typical reaction begins a few hours to several days after initiation of therapy.[93] It appears to be much more common in women, but this is probably related to the increased use of this drug for urinary tract infections in women. Fever is present in the majority of cases, dyspnea is almost always present, and cough is present in about two thirds of cases. Other incidental findings include leukocytosis and eosinophilia in one third and an elevation in sedimentation rate in nearly one half of cases. The chest roentgenogram shows either an alveolar or an interstitial process or both. The reaction may be unilateral or asymmetrical. It is generally most prominent at the bases. Pleural effusion has been found in one third of patients, most commonly unilaterally. Bronchospasm has been reported in a number of cases, but its incidence is unknown. It may occur in the absence of pulmonary parenchymal or pleural disease.[93]

The onset of the acute symptoms does not appear to be dose related. Pleuritic chest pain occurs in about one third of patients, mimicking acute pulmonary embolism and, in some cases, pneumonitis and myocardial infarction. Crackles are present in most cases. There is no way of diagnosing acute nitrofurantoin pneumonitis other than suspecting that the drug is responsible for the patient's symptoms. The treatment consists of discontinuing the medication and providing supportive care. It is not known whether corticosteroids accelerate the resolution, and there is probably no indication for their use. There is also no role for rechallenge to confirm the diagnosis. Nitrofurantoin-induced SLE with pleuropulmonary disease and positive antinuclear antibody has also been reported. Little information is available on this form of lung disease.

Chronic Reaction

There is no clinical overlap between the acute and chronic pulmonary reaction to nitrofurantoin. Chronic reactions occur far less commonly than acute pulmonary reactions. In chronic reactions, fever and eosinophilia are much less common.[91,93,94] The onset of dyspnea and cough is usually insidious, beginning 6 months to many years after the chronic (either continuous or intermittent) use of nitrofurantoin. These reactions are more common in women.

The chest roentgenogram shows a diffuse interstitial process.[93,94] There is no associated bronchospasm or obstructive airway disease. Pulmonary function testing demonstrates a restrictive pattern. Bronchoalveolar lavage usually shows a lymphocytic reaction.[95] Histologic analysis of lung tissue shows inflammatory cells and fibrosis. Clinically, radiologically, and histologically, this condition often mimics other forms of interstitial lung disease, including usual interstitial pneumonia, with the single exception that these patients have ingested nitrofurantoin chronically.

The literature varies as to the utility of corticosteroids. Our experience is that they are almost always required before significant resolution occurs. Others imply that the infiltrates resolve spontaneously on discontinuation of the medication.[94] Our policy is to observe the patient for 2 to 4 months after discontinuing nitrofurantoin and then repeating the chest roentgenogram and pulmonary function studies. If there is no improvement, a trial of corticosteroids is given.

SULFASALAZINE

Sulfasalazine is an antimicrobial drug that has been used for many years for the treatment of inflammatory bowel disease.[96] There appear to be two separate types of adverse pulmonary reactions: one is a pulmonary infiltrate and eosinophilia, and the other a bronchiolitis obliterans with organizing pneumonitis. The onset of symptoms of cough, dyspnea, and, in about half of cases, fever begins 1 to 8 months after initiation of continuous therapy. The dosage ranges from 1.5 to 8 g/day. The chest roentgenogram shows a variable pattern of lung infiltrates, ranging from upper lobe alveolar infiltrates to a diffuse interstitial process. Over half of the patients had significant blood eosinophilia, but none had migratory pulmonary infiltrates. The majority of the resolution occurs within 1 week to 6 months after discontinuing the drug and, if necessary, adding corticosteroids. Sulfasalazine is metabolized to 5-aminosalicylic acid and sulfapyridine, both of which have been implicated in eosinophilic pneumonitis. In cases of suspected sulfasalazine-associated pulmonary disorders, it important to keep in mind that inflammatory bowel disease has been associated with a variety of pulmonary abnormalities independent of sulfasalazine use. Inflammatory bowel disease has been independently linked to airway inflammation, interstitial lung disease including bronchiolitis obliterans with organizing pneumonia, neutrophilic necrotic pulmonary nodules, and serositis.[96] Most of these disorders respond to corticosteroid therapy.

MISCELLANEOUS ANTIMICROBIAL DRUGS

There are many scattered reports of unusual reactions to various antimicrobial drugs.[97] In view of the wide use of these agents, the incidence is extremely small. Many of these reactions appear to be pulmonary infiltrates with eosinophilia. The polymyxin and aminoglycoside antibiotics are known to produce respiratory muscle weakness when they reach an excessive level in the blood.[98] Toxic levels in the blood occur in patients to whom these drugs are given by direct instillation into the peritoneal or pleural space, in persons with renal failure, or when the patient receiving them has been given a muscle-relaxing agent at the time of general anesthesia. These effects are reversible with physostigmine. The combined administration of granulocytes with amphotericin B may predispose some patients to transient deterioration in pulmonary function.[99]

ILLICIT DRUGS

HEROIN

Although nitrofurantoin appears to be the most commonly reported prescribed drug with adverse pulmonary effects, heroin pulmonary edema may be the most common drug-induced pulmonary disease worldwide. Hospitals in all major cities of the United States receive hundreds of patients with heroin pulmonary edema. Heroin is diacetylmorphine and, because of its increased lipid solubility, it crosses the blood-brain barrier much more readily than morphine.[100,101] There are several postulated mechanisms of heroin-induced noncardiac pulmonary edema. These include a direct toxic effect on the alveolar-capillary membrane, leading to an increased permeability and extravasation of fluid into the alveolar spaces; a neurogenic response to central nervous system injury; an allergic or hypersensitivity reaction; and an acute hypoxic effect on the alveolar-capillary membrane in association with secondary increased permeability. The hypoxemic theory is the one most commonly touted, but other causes of acute hypoxia, such as barbiturate overdosage with depression of the respiratory center, rarely result in noncardiac pulmonary edema.[66]

Heroin pulmonary edema can occur with the first intravenous use of the drug. It is believed that the effects of heroin are related to the dose. However, the exact dose is almost always unknown. Up to 40% of addicts hospitalized for acute drug overdose have acute pulmonary edema with severe hypoxemia and hypercapnia. The noncardiac pulmonary edema is indistinguishable at the outset from other forms of acute respiratory distress syndrome. The pulmonary capillary wedge pressure is usually within normal range. Typically, symptoms of dyspnea and somnolence begin within minutes of the intravenous "push," but reports of delayed onset of hours and even a few days have been published. The patient hypoventilates, producing hypoxemia and hypercapnia. The pupils are small. Auscultation of the lungs discloses crackles. The chest roentgenogram shows changes of noncardiac pulmonary edema. Acidosis can be metabolic as well as respiratory.

Up to one half of these patients vomit and aspirate, which leads to secondary bacterial infection. This should be suspected if the pulmonary infiltrates do not clear within 24 to 48 hours of treatment. Other pulmonary abnormalities include septic emboli from infected thrombophlebitis or tricuspid endocarditis. Treatment consists of assisted ventilation using positive end-expiratory pressure, oxygen, and intravenous naloxone to reverse the respiratory depression. This is usually sufficient treatment for the noncardiac pulmonary edema, which will reverse with time. Corticosteroids are unnecessary. Because up to half of these patients have aspirated and have bacterial infections, appropriate use of antimicrobial drugs is indicated.

Bronchiectasis and necrotizing bronchitis in chronic heroin abusers have been reported. These may be more sequelae of recurrent gastric aspiration than the effects of heroin, with or without pulmonary edema. Pulmonary function is abnormal in patients with pulmonary edema. Even after the roentgenographic clearance of the edema and the return of the lung volumes to normal, a reduction in the carbon monoxide diffusing capacity may persist. In chronic abusers of heroin and other illicit intravenous drugs, pulmonary function abnormalities are more likely to be related to talc granulomatosis than to sequelae of a single acute injury.

METHADONE AND PROPOXYPHENE

Pulmonary sequelae similar to those associated with heroin have been reported with methadone and propoxyphene and likely have similar mechanisms. Treatment is the same as for heroin-induced sequelae. Addicts in drug rehabilitation programs have free access to methadone. They accumulate the drug illegally, dissolve it, and inject it. Noncardiac pulmonary edema has been reported in cases of both oral and intravenous overdose of methadone. Propoxyphene is a rapidly absorbed drug, and, even after oral ingestion, death can occur within 30 minutes from respiratory depression

and arrest and noncardiac pulmonary edema. In some parts of the United States, propoxyphene is a commonly used drug in attempted suicide.

METHYLPHENIDATE

Methylphenidate may have more serious adverse side effects than either heroin or cocaine.[102,103] Methylphenidate can be abused either intravenously or orally. In one series of methylphenidate abuse, all 22 patients had chest pain and wheezing and most had abnormal pulmonary function tests and hemoptysis.[102] In another series, severe panlobular emphysema was found in seven patients who died as a result of the abnormalities.[103]

COCAINE

Cocaine use remains a major problem throughout the world, and there are increasing reports of adverse pulmonary effects from both intravenous and inhalation use of the drug. These are over and above the known cardiac effects of cocaine, which produces left ventricular failure with pulmonary congestion and edema. The principal long-term effects of cocaine are infection and aspiration, noncardiac pulmonary edema, particulate embolization, talcosis, diffuse alveolar damage, alveolar hemorrhage, intra-alveolar eosinophilic infiltration, lung mass with or without cavitation, and bronchiolitis obliterans with organizing pneumonia (Table 67.4).[104,105]

TALC GRANULOMATOSIS

Talc (magnesium silicate) is used as a filler in many medications intended for oral use. Addicts who abuse oral medications such as meperidine, methadone, propoxyphene, methylphenidate, amphetamines, and tripelennamine often crush the tablets, mix them with various solutions, and inject them intravenously. This results in the insidious onset of granulomatous interstitial fibrosis, granulomatous pulmonary arterial occlusion, or both.[101,104,106] This usually does not occur in heroin addicts, because heroin is mixed in soluble fillers such as quinine, lactose, or maltose. In large series of consecutive autopsies done on addicts, depending on the type of addiction, the incidence of talc granulomatosis ranges from 15% to 80%.

Table 67.4 Principal Effects of Cocaine
Infection and aspiration leading to noncardiac pulmonary edema
Particulate embolization
Talcosis
Diffuse alveolar damage
Alveolar hemorrhage
Intra-alveolar eosinophilic infiltration
Lung mass with or without cavitation
Bronchiolitis obliterans with organizing pneumonia

Dyspnea is the major symptom, cough occurs in some patients, and, in more advanced stages of pulmonary hypertension, symptoms of exercise-induced syncope, right-sided heart failure, and even sudden death occur. The chest roentgenogram may be normal in up to half of patients with proven talc granulomatosis. Thus, a normal chest roentgenogram does not eliminate the possibility of this condition. Pulmonary function studies characteristically show a low diffusing capacity before any other abnormalities are evident, because of occlusion of pulmonary blood vessels. This may remain the only abnormality. Chest roentgenograms in these patients show diffuse micronodular densities varying in size between 1 and 3 mm, which may mimic alveolar microlithiasis. Therapy with corticosteroids provides little consistent improvement.

Histologically, the pulmonary tissue demonstrates granulomatous changes, with multinucleated giant cells, mononuclear inflammatory cells, lymphocytes, and fibrosis.[106] Talc is detected by the presence of strongly birefringent crystals (using polarized light) within the granulomas. Bronchoalveolar lavage shows an increased lymphocytosis, and intracellular and free talc have been identified in the bronchoalveolar lavage fluid. Talc retinopathy occurs in over half the patients. Talc emboli presenting as small, whitish, glistening foci near the macula within a small vessel are fairly characteristic.

CARDIOVASCULAR DRUGS

ANGIOTENSIN-CONVERTING ENZYME INHIBITORS

Angiotensin-converting enzyme (ACE) inhibitors are widely used for control of hypertension and in the management of congestive heart failure. Soon after their introduction, these agents were associated with nonproductive cough and more rarely with angioneurotic edema.[107,108] Dry cough occurs in 5% to 20% of patients on ACE inhibitors, being reported with captopril, enalapril, lisinopril, and virtually all other ACE inhibitors. The mechanism of ACE inhibitor–induced cough likely involves accumulation of kinins and substance P, which are degraded by ACE and other endopeptidases. The cough generally is reported in the first few weeks after beginning therapy but may not be appreciated for a number of months. ACE cough is usually benign but can be quite annoying, and causes the discontinuation of these agents in half of the patients affected. Exacerbation of bronchospasm has been associated with ACE inhibitors only on very rare occasions. Fortunately, most patients can be switched to other classes of drugs. Rechallenge with a different ACE antagonist is not recommended as the cough will usually reoccur. Cough generally abates within 4 days of discontinuation of the agent, providing confirmation of the diagnosis. Of note, selective angiotensin receptor antagonists have much lower incidence of dry cough compared to ACE inhibitors and may represent a therapeutic option for many patients.[109]

ACE inhibitors cause angioneurotic edema much less frequently; this condition is reported in 0.1% to 0.2% of patients receiving ACE inhibitors. This complication usually occurs within hours to, at most, 1 week after initiating therapy. This reaction may be mediated by bradykinins but may also involve autoantibodies and complement system activation. Treatment involves airway protection, epinephrine, antihistamines, and corticosteroid administration. The ACE inhibitor must be discontinued and future use avoided in these patients.

AMIODARONE

Amiodarone has significant benefit for ventricular and supraventricular dysrhythmias in patients who do not respond to most other antiarrhythmic agents. This drug is associated with a number of side effects, which include corneal microdeposits (in nearly 100% of the patients); peripheral neuropathy; liver dysfunction; thyroid dysfunction, including hypo- and hyperthyroidism; and bluish pigmentation of the skin. However, the most serious side effect is an interstitial pneumonitis, which occurs in up to 6% of patients and may be fatal.[7,110]

The mechanism of amiodarone toxicity is unknown, but the toxicity is dose related and has distinctive histologic features. The histologic findings generally include foamy alveolar macrophages and type II pneumocytes containing lamellar inclusions. In one half of the patients on amiodarone who die of nonpulmonary causes, macrophages and type II pneumocytes contain a markedly increased amount of phospholipid.

The incidence of pulmonary toxicity from amiodarone varies widely but probably averages 4% to 6% of those patients on the drug.[7,111] The majority are men, but this may be related to increased use in men. Symptoms consist of insidious dyspnea, nonproductive cough, and occasionally a low-grade fever without chills, followed by subtle chest roentgenographic findings, which initially may be asymmetrical or even limited to the upper lobes. If the drug is continued, the process may diffusely involve the lungs with an interstitial or alveolar process (Fig. 67.4). Pleural effusion is uncommon. Pleuritic chest pain occurs in about 10% of patients. Clubbing has not been reported. Crackles may be heard, but it is difficult to be certain whether these are due to pulmonary edema, because congestive heart failure is common in these patients. In about 20% of patients with amiodarone pneumonitis, the presentation will be acute, mimicking pneumonia.

Laboratory studies disclose a normal to mildly elevated leukocyte count, generally no eosinophilia, and an elevated sedimentation rate, with little or no reactivity to antinuclear antibody. Pulmonary function studies disclose a decrease in the total lung capacity and carbon monoxide diffusing capacity as well as hypoxemia. However, a decrease in the lung volumes and carbon monoxide diffusing capacity can occur as a result of congestive heart failure, and thus a change in these parameters is not diagnostic of impending clinical amiodarone pneumonitis. There are reports of using ^{67}Ga radionuclide lung scanning that demonstrate its benefit in differentiating amiodarone pneumonitis from congestive heart failure.[112] There may be an increased predisposition to amiodarone pneumonitis if either pulmonary function or chest roentgenographic findings are abnormal before administration of the drug begins.

The majority of the patients who develop amiodarone pneumonitis have been taking the drug for at least a month, and some for a few years. Most are receiving at least

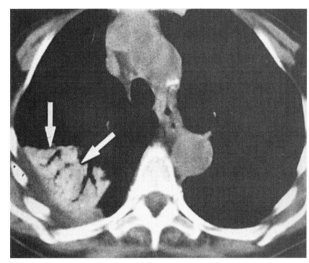

Figure 67.5 A chest computed tomography (CT) scan showing large pulmonary masses from amiodarone pneumonitis. Note that the masses are appreciably denser than the surrounding soft tissue in the chest wall in this CT scan obtained without contrast.

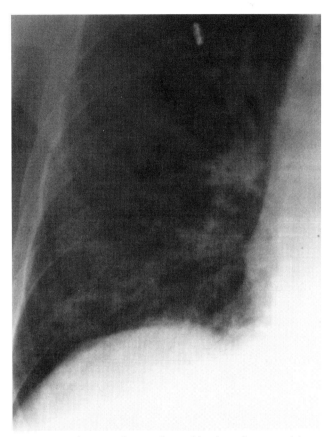

Figure 67.4 Close-up chest radiographic view of a man with amiodarone-induced lung disease. The pattern is predominantly interstitial and nonuniform.

400 mg/day. However, there have been a number of reports of amiodarone pneumonitis occurring with as little as 200 mg/day. There are also reports of patients receiving 200 mg/day for months or even years and not developing amiodarone pneumonitis until the dose is boosted for purposes of better control of the arrhythmia. Generally, the systemic side effects from amiodarone, such as peripheral neuropathy and liver dysfunction, correlate with the serum levels, but this is not necessarily the case with the pulmonary toxicity. Perhaps the greater phospholipid turnover in the lung explains the greater chance for lung toxicity from amiodarone. The diagnosis of amiodarone pneumonitis is one of exclusion.

Normally, amiodarone pneumonitis is thought to be primarily an interstitial or alveolar process (or both) sometimes mimicking eosinophilic pneumonitis with peripheral infiltrates, but there are a number of reports of confluent lesions occurring as a result of amiodarone pneumonitis. Many of these lesions are bronchiolitis obliterans.[113,114] Computed tomography of the lung can further define these processes because amiodarone, being an iodinated compound, is radiopaque, and on a computed tomography scan the amiodarone pneumonitis lesions are denser than the surrounding soft tissue in the chest wall (Fig. 67.5). This latter finding may confirm the diagnosis.[115]

Treatment consists of drug withdrawal and leads to a variety of responses. Some patients who were not treated with corticosteroids have died of pulmonary fibrosis and respiratory failure. Others have died in spite of being treated with corticosteroids. The majority respond to discontinuation of the drug and addition of corticosteroids, which are usually required for a period of at least 2 and perhaps 6 months or longer. There are many case reports of patients who continued on amiodarone because it was the only drug that controlled their ventricular dysrhythmia and who at the same time were given corticosteroids to suppress their pneumonic reaction.[116] For some patients, implantable automatic cardiac defibrillators provide a therapeutic option to chronic high-dose amiodarone therapy.

Initially, it was believed that tissue confirmation by biopsy was necessary to establish a diagnosis, although stopping the drug and adding corticosteroids may offer a presumptive diagnosis if the process clears. Bronchoalveolar lavage produces variable results.[7] The presence of foamy macrophages in lavage fluid or on biopsy only confirms exposure to the drug; their presence alone does not necessarily indicate amiodarone toxicity. Their absence does eliminate the diagnosis, however. Although not used frequently in recent years, a positive ^{67}Ga scan can be highly suggestive of an inflammatory pneumonitis rather than congestive heart failure. If the diagnosis has not been established, the clinician must decide whether to proceed with an open-lung biopsy to rule out other disease processes or to consider diminishing the dose or discontinuing the drug, or adding corticosteroids, or both. A lung biopsy usually reveals the foamy macrophages and epithelial cells, and variable inflammatory cell infiltration. In some cases, the tissue pattern of bronchiolitis obliterans with organizing pneumonia has been observed (Table 67.5). Reductions in sedimentation rate following discontinuation or reduction of amiodarone dosage may be of further value in establishing the diagnosis.

There are reports of postoperative acute respiratory distress syndrome in patients on amiodarone.[117,118] Several of these patients have died as a result of the acute respiratory distress syndrome, which begins 18 to 72 hours after

Table 67.5 Drugs or Treatment Associated with the Induction of Bronchiolitis Obliterans with Organizing Pneumonitis

Bleomycin
Amiodarone
Gold
Penicillamine
Sulfasalazine
Radiation
Interferons
Methotrexate
Mitomycin C
Cyclophosphamide
Cocaine

surgery. In one series, the acute respiratory distress syndrome occurred in 50% of the patients on or recently on amiodarone.[118] It has been postulated that the high fraction of inspired oxygen given during the operation and the postoperative period contributed to this complication.

PROTAMINE

Protamine sulfate is used to reverse the anticoagulant effects of heparin following cardiovascular surgical procedures. Systemic hypotension is not an uncommon sequela of administering this drug. However, there have been a number of cases of noncardiogenic pulmonary edema occurring within minutes to 1 or 2 hours after the administration of the drug.[119] It is frequently associated with an anaphylactic reaction and bronchospasm, an increase in pulmonary artery pressure with normal wedge pressure, and hypotension. In at least half of the patients there is a history of previous use of protamine, either in a similar situation or as protamine zinc insulin. Skin testing can confirm the sensitization. Therapy is supportive, including reintubation if the patient has been extubated, assisted ventilation with high inspired oxygen concentrations, administration of high-dose corticosteroids, and treatment of hypotension with an α-adrenergic agonist. In patients whose skin test is positive to protamine or who have a history of reaction to protamine, an alternative method of reversing the effects of heparin is to use intravenous hexadimethrine.[96]

β-ADRENERGIC ANTAGONISTS

β-Adrenergic antagonists are among the most commonly prescribed drugs. β-Adrenergic receptors can be divided into excitatory β_1-receptors, located in the heart, and inhibitory β_2-receptors, located in the bronchi. The β-adrenergic blockers, or β-blockers, are competitive antagonists.

Propranolol was the first β-adrenergic antagonist introduced. It was quickly recognized that it had adverse effects on individuals with known obstructive lung disease.[113]

Studies have also demonstrated increased airway resistance in normal persons and in asymptomatic asthmatic patients who use propranolol.[120] Thus, this agent should be avoided in all patients with known obstructive lung disease, even those who are asymptomatic. The following β-adrenergic antagonists, presented in decreasing order of bronchoprovocation potential, are available for clinical use in the United States: propranolol, timolol, nadolol, metoprolol, atenolol, pindolol, and labetalol.[121]

There are two features of β-adrenergic antagonists that predict their potential for bronchoprovocation. The first is their cardioselectivity, and the second is their intrinsic sympathomimetic activity. Generally, cardioselectivity is the more important of the two. If the drug is cardioselective, it has little effect on the inhibitory β-receptors located in the bronchial walls. Propranolol, timolol, and nadolol have essentially no cardioselectivity.[98] Metoprolol has some cardioselectivity, and atenolol has considerable cardioselectivity, making atenolol the drug of choice in an individual with obstructive airway disease who needs a β-adrenergic antagonist. The other mechanism important in β-adrenergic antagonists is intrinsic sympathomimetic activity, with pindolol having strong intrinsic sympathomimetic activity. Labetalol is unique in that it has combined α- and β-antagonist effects. It is not cardioselective, nor does it have intrinsic sympathomimetic activity; therefore, it is assumed that it is its α-adrenergic antagonist potential that causes it to be bronchoprotective.

Thus, among the seven drugs listed, atenolol and then metoprolol and probably labetalol are the three that can be used with relative safety in persons with obstructive lung disease, if absolutely necessary. However, these should always be given in conjunction with an aerosolized β_2-adrenergic agent. Calcium channel blockers may be a good alternative to β-blocking drugs, if indicated, because they also may have some bronchodilating capabilities.

The same findings have been shown to occur in asthmatic patients receiving timolol eye drops for glaucoma. There are many case reports of the adverse effects of topical ocular timolol, including a number of fatal cases of status asthmaticus.[122] Topically applied timolol is absorbed through the conjunctiva and bypasses the liver, resulting in a higher concentration than when given orally. A novel ocular β-adrenergic antagonist, betaxolol, has been shown to be safer in patients with known airway disease. There are scattered reports of β-blocker–associated interstitial pneumonitis.[123] Propafenone is an additional membrane-stabilizing antiarrhythmic agent that is structurally similar to propranolol and has the potential to aggravate bronchospasm.[124]

TOCAINIDE AND FLECAINIDE

Tocainide is used in the treatment of refractory ventricular arrhythmias. There are over 40 known cases of acute interstitial pneumonitis beginning 3 weeks to several months after initiation of therapy.[125] The response to discontinuing the drug is good; corticosteroids may be necessary in some cases. Flecainide, another antidysrhythmic agent, has been reported to be associated with the acute respiratory distress syndrome and an interstitial lymphocytic pneumonitis.[126,127]

ANTI-INFLAMMATORY AGENTS

ASPIRIN

Anti-inflammatory agents are among the most commonly used drugs, and many have pulmonary side effects.[128] Aspirin is the most commonly used drug in the world. In the United States, there are over 200 proprietary drugs that contain aspirin. It is estimated that up to 5% of asthmatics are sensitive to aspirin; ingestion may cause fatal aggravation of bronchospasm.[129] The exact cause of aspirin-sensitive asthma is unknown. One theory is that acetylsalicylic acid and similar compounds inhibit cyclooxygenase, and thus prevent the generation of cyclooxygenase products. If bronchodilator prostaglandins (such as prostaglandin E_2), are normally released by these subjects, their inhibition could cause bronchospasm.

The aspirin-asthma triad consists of asthma, rhinitis, and nasal polyposis. Almost always there are other associated side effects, such as cutaneous rashes and gastrointestinal symptoms. These adverse reactions are not dose related, because they can occur with very small doses. In addition, salicylate-induced noncardiac pulmonary edema can occur when the serum salicylate level is greater than 40 mg/dL. This can occur without an intentional overdosage in patients chronically ingesting salicylates.[130] It occurs more commonly in elderly persons who are smokers than in younger nonsmokers. The mechanism is unknown, although it may be a direct effect on the alveolar capillary wall as a result of an increase in the capillary permeability. It may be related to the effect of salicylates on platelets or prostaglandins or occur through a central nervous system effect. It does not occur in every individual with very high serum salicylate levels. Because of the respiratory center stimulation by salicylates, hyperventilation occurs, resulting in a low arterial PCO_2, frequently less than 20 mm Hg. In spite of hyperventilation, the arterial PO_2 may be paradoxically low because of the presence of pulmonary edema. In one review of the 177 consecutive patients admitted to an intensive care unit for salicylate intoxication, 47% had respiratory failure, 94% required mechanical ventilation, abnormal clotting studies were noted in 38%, and 36% were acidemic.[131] There was a 15% mortality. Treatment of salicylate-induced noncardiac pulmonary edema depends on the severity of the edema; some patients require intubation and even hemodialysis. Treatment with forced alkaline diuresis is often recommended, but this is dangerous in patients who already have pulmonary edema.

Leatherman and Schmitz have described a pseudosepsis syndrome associated with chronic salicylate ingestion.[132] Most patients had fever, leukocytosis, hypotension, and multiple organ failure, including acute respiratory distress syndrome. This condition is easily missed unless salicylate intoxication is suspected and the blood salicylate level is measured.

OTHER NONSTEROIDAL ANTI-INFLAMMATORY DRUGS

Most of the nonsteroidal anti-inflammatory agents can produce the same side effects as aspirin, including aggravation of asthma, noncardiac pulmonary edema, drug-induced SLE, and pulmonary infiltrates with eosinophilia.

Naproxen may be more commonly associated with an infiltrate and eosinophilia than are the other agents.[133] A few agents can cause hypervolemia and, in turn, pulmonary edema through the mechanism of increased sodium retention through the kidneys.

GOLD

Gold has been used since ancient times for treating various immunologic disorders, including rheumatoid arthritis.[128,134] There are now a number of reports of diffuse interstitial pneumonitis and fibrosis associated with gold that are believed to be separate from that of rheumatoid lung. Interstitial pneumonitis is more commonly observed in patients taking sodium aurothiomalate than in those taking aurothioglucose, but this may reflect the more common use of the former drug. Symptoms of dyspnea with or without fever begin insidiously several weeks to months after initiation of weekly intramuscular injections of gold. A few reports have demonstrated peripheral blood eosinophilia, but this is uncommon. Pleural effusion is not associated with this reaction.

In diffuse interstitial pneumonitis and fibrosis, the chest roentgenogram shows a predominantly interstitial process. Bronchoalveolar lavage usually demonstrates a high percentage of lymphocytes.[134] Histologically, the lung demonstrates fibrosis with an interstitial infiltrate of lymphocytes and plasma cells and focal hyperplasia of type II pneumocytes. Electron microscopy demonstrates electron-dense structures within lysosomes of endothelial cells of the alveolar capillaries and interstitial macrophages. Microanalysis with an electron probe shows that these electron-dense structures contain gold, suggesting that a direct toxic effect might be an important mechanism in the pathogenesis of gold-induced pulmonary reactions. However, there are no control studies of lungs in patients who are taking gold but do not develop gold pneumonitis.

Other associated complications of gold are often present, such as dermatitis, neuropathy, and proteinuria. Secondary infections have not been reported as a complication of gold pneumonitis, nor have there been deaths reported from irreversible lung fibrosis. The treatment may be as simple as withdrawing the drug and allowing the process to resolve spontaneously. However, a number of patients have required corticosteroids for reversal. Gold pneumonitis is not thought to be related to rheumatoid fibrosis, in that the parenchymal disease improves spontaneously with stopping gold or almost always regresses with use of corticosteroids.

PENICILLAMINE

There are three possible pulmonary complications with the use of penicillamine with no apparent overlap: penicillamine-induced SLE, bronchiolitis obliterans, and Goodpasture's syndrome. Some patients with penicillamine-associated pneumonitis or alveolitis have high titers of antinuclear antibodies. Penicillamine-induced disease appears to be one of the more common causes of drug-induced SLE.[135] This condition should always be considered in the patient receiving penicillamine, especially if a pleural effusion is present. A normal concentration of sugar in the effusion fluid virtually eliminates the possibility of a rheumatoid effusion.

Penicillamine-associated bronchiolitis obliterans is probably underestimated in its incidence and severity.[136] There is little information on pulmonary function in rheumatoid patients before initiation of penicillamine that compares patients who subsequently develop bronchiolitis obliterans with those who do not experience obstructive physiology. Perhaps there is a predisposing obstructive lung disease in the rheumatoid patient that is worsened by penicillamine in the form of a bronchiolitis obliterans. Corticosteroids have little benefit in treating this condition, which usually presents in an advanced state.

There have also been several case reports of penicillamine-associated Goodpasture's syndrome with diffuse alveolar hemorrhage.[137] If recognized early enough, appropriate therapy with hemodialysis, plasmapheresis, and immunosuppression may prevent a serious outcome.

LEUKOTRIENE ANTAGONISTS

Recent reports have associated zafirlukast and related leukotriene antagonists with manifestations of Churg-Strauss syndrome.[138,139] These potent agents have been employed in treating asthma. As zafirlukast is added to an asthmatic treatment regimen, corticosteroids are frequently tapered. A number of cases have been described with patients exhibiting pulmonary infiltrates, cardiomyopathy, and eosinophilia while receiving zafirlukast. It is currently unknown whether these medications actually trigger these reactions, or whether they are unmasking a preexistent infiltrative eosinophilic disorder as the corticosteroids are withdrawn. In either event, the pulmonary reaction responds to discontinuation of zafirlukast and reinstitution of corticosteroids.

CORTICOSTEROIDS

Corticosteroids given in immunosuppressive doses are well known for predisposing patients to the development of opportunistic infections. A most unusual adverse effect of corticosteroids is mediastinal lipomatosis, the deposition of mediastinal fat, which produces a widening of the mediastinum that mimics lymphadenopathy or other neoplasms (Fig. 67.6). Clinically, these patients have a cushingoid appearance, with rounded facies and a "buffalo hump." The same kind of fat that deposits in the buffalo hump occurs in the mediastinum. The chest roentgenogram does not show the lumpiness usually expected with adenopathy. Computed tomography can usually make this diagnosis by establishing radiographic fat density throughout the mediastinal mass (see Fig. 67.6).[140] Mediastinal lipomatosis does not necessitate tapering corticosteroids because the fat does not compromise vital structures.

DRUG-INDUCED SYSTEMIC LUPUS ERYTHEMATOSUS

There are over 50 drugs that have been reported to induce the SLE syndrome, but only 5 regularly induce antinuclear antibodies in patients taking them: hydralazine, procainamide, isoniazid, hydantoins, and penicillamine.[141,142] Only a small percentage of the patients on these drugs develop the clinical syndrome that involves the pleuropulmonary system in over half the cases (see the earlier discussion on mechanisms of drug-induced injury). It is thought that patients who develop antinuclear antibodies to these drugs are "slow acetylators." Symptoms almost always begin insidiously after the patient has been taking the drug for many months or even years. Systemic signs and symptoms of polyarthralgia, myalgia, fever, pleurisy, and cutaneous lesions are common. However, renal disease is very uncommon, possibly because complement is not as often involved in the drug-induced form of SLE compared to the spontaneous type.

The antinuclear antibody assay is positive in all patients with drug-induced SLE. However, the test for anti-native (anti–double-stranded) DNA is negative. The complement level may or may not be abnormal. A Coombs test is positive in about one third of patients. An elevated erythrocyte sedimentation rate and hypergammaglobulinemia are common nonspecific findings.

The chest roentgenographic findings of the drug-induced form of the disease are indistinguishable from spontaneous-onset SLE and include pleural effusions in one third of patients, basilar infiltrates, pneumonitis with atelectasis, and apparent cardiomegaly from pericardial effusion. Pleural fluid glucose is normal or at least correlates with the blood glucose levels.

The symptoms usually resolve once the drug is discontinued. However, occasionally it is necessary to add corticosteroids for more rapid resolution of disabling symptoms. If the offending drug cannot be discontinued for clinical reasons, the lowest dose should be used, along with the addition of corticosteroids.

INHALANTS

OIL

Aspirated oil can produce a variety of pulmonary diseases, ranging from an asymptomatic solitary nodule to diffuse disease with severe respiratory insufficiency.[143,144] Most commonly, however, the diseases present in an asymptomatic individual with an incidental finding of an abnormal chest roentgenogram that mimics a more serious process such as bronchogenic carcinoma. Because patients rarely consider oily nose drops, oily eye lubricants, or mineral oil as a medication, they rarely volunteer that they are taking oil-containing medications.

There are three types of oil: mineral oils, neutral oils, and animal fats. Mineral oils are the most commonly aspirated oils. Oily droplets are taken up by macrophages that eventually disintegrate and release the oil, which in turn inhibits ciliary activity.[143] Thus, the oil is not expectorated and the cycle is repeated again. Eventually, a fibrotic or granulomatous reaction occurs. Neutral or vegetable oils (e.g., olive or castor oil) do not elicit a local reaction and are removed by expectoration. Animal fats (e.g., milk, butter) are rapidly hydrolyzed, with the liberated fatty acids producing tissue necrosis and subsequent fibrosis. The diagnosis can be established with the demonstration of oil in the lung tissue. Computed tomography and magnetic resonance imaging have been used in diagnosing lipoid-induced infiltrates.[144] Treatment involves the discontinuation of the oil-containing medication. Once this occurs, progression is unlikely.

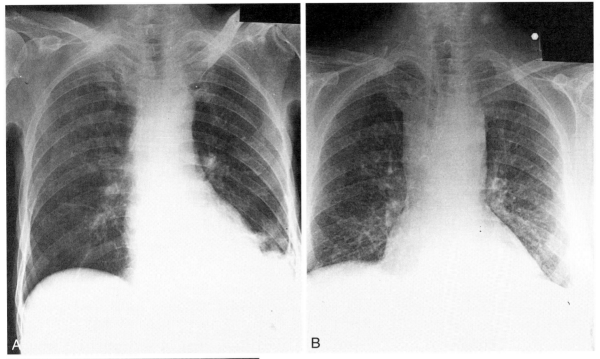

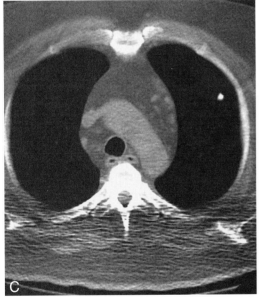

Figure 67.6 Mediastinal lipomatosis in response to corticosteroids. **A,** Chest roentgenogram prior to systemic corticosteroid administration. **B,** Chest roentgenogram after corticosteroid administration shows widened mediastinum. **C,** Computed tomography scan of the chest shows mediastinal lipomatosis, with radiographic fat density surrounding the great vessels and tracheal shadows.

OXYGEN

Exposure to high concentrations of oxygen may contribute to or aggravate the acute respiratory distress syndrome.[145–149] There are two theories as to the mechanism of oxygen-induced pulmonary disease. The first is that a high fraction of inspired oxygen induces formation and release of free oxidant radicals. These short-lived molecules damage DNA, destroy lipid membranes, and inactivate intracellular enzymes.[145] The other theory is that hyperoxia produces a direct injury to endothelial cells and type I epithelial cells, which results in alveolar-capillary leak.[146]

Studies in volunteers breathing 100% oxygen for 6 to 48 hours produced variable effects, but in some a tracheobronchitis occurred, with symptoms of substernal burning, chest tightness, and nonproductive cough.[149] It also produced a reduction in vital capacity and carbon monoxide diffusing capacity.[147] The development of tolerance to hyperoxia appears to be related to the ability of the individual to increase the production of antioxidants, a mechanism that may be determined genetically.[145]

The sequelae of oxygen toxicity are separable into two phases, the acute, or exudative, phase and the subacute proliferative phase; however, there is considerable overlap between the two phases, with the proliferative phase beginning after the fourth to seventh day. The exudative phase begins within 48 to 72 hours, depending on the fraction of inspired oxygen, and is associated with perivascular, interstitial, and alveolar edema with atelectasis, as well as alveolar hemorrhage. This phase appears to be reversible.

The proliferative phase is characterized by progressive resorption of exudates and hyperplasia of type II cells. This is followed by the deposition of collagen and elastin in the interstitium and hyaline membrane deposition. This is usually an irreversible phase. Clinically, hypoxemia and diminished compliance progress, requiring a greater fraction of inspired oxygen and assisted ventilation, further aggravating the problem. The chest roentgenogram shows an alveolar-interstitial pattern in an irregular distribution, with evidence of moderate loss of volume from patchy atelectasis.

There is no clinical way of diagnosing oxygen toxicity. A lung biopsy specimen may show changes consistent with oxygen toxicity, but the primary value of the biopsy is to exclude other causes of lung injury. Keeping the arterial PO_2 less than 80 mm Hg or the inspired fraction of oxygen below 0.40 to 0.50 minimizes the chance of oxygen toxicity developing. Barotrauma and ventilator-induced injury may accompany and be indistinguishable from oxygen toxicity.

TRANSFUSION-RELATED ACUTE ALVEOLAR DAMAGE

Acute alveolar damage as a result of transfusion reaction is probably one of the more rarely recognized adverse drug reactions, if one considers transfused blood or its products a form of drug. The damage is usually the result of donor antibodies against leukocyte antigens or donor leukocyte-specific immune cells reacting against the recipient's leukocytes.[150] In about 5% of the cases, the recipient's antileukocyte antibodies react against the donor leukocytes. The acute alveolar damage reaction is not a hemolytic transfusion reaction or an anaphylactic reaction.

The clinical presentation is that of onset of dyspnea, cough, fever, and hypotension within a few hours of receiving a transfusion. A urticarial rash occurs in about half of these patients. The onset of symptoms can occur in response to as little as 50 mL of transfused blood or blood products. The pulmonary artery wedge pressure is always normal. Any blood product containing plasma and plasma proteins can produce this form of reaction.

The source of the antibodies is almost always blood taken from multiparous women who have had three or more pregnancies. Approximately 7% of all multiparous women carry human leukocyte antigen antibodies in their blood.[150] It is recommended that donor blood of all multiparous women be screened for these antibodies and, if found, only the frozen or washed erythrocytes should be used.

The treatment of leukoagglutinin-mediated noncardiac pulmonary edema is supportive, including assisted ventilation if necessary and supplemental oxygen. It is unknown whether a short course of high-dose corticosteroids is beneficial, but it is certainly worth considering. The course of the noncardiac pulmonary edema is usually limited to 72 hours or less.

RADIOGRAPHIC CONTRAST MEDIUM–INDUCED LEUKOSTASIS

The symptoms and signs produced by complement-induced granulocyte aggregation associated with radiographic contrast media are frequently attributed to an allergic reaction and may cause noncardiac pulmonary edema.[151,152] Anaphylaxis as a cause can be eliminated by the absence of urticaria or other rash, and by the absence of significant laryngeal edema or bronchospasm. Histologic examination of the lungs demonstrates aggregates of granulocytes obstructing microscopic pulmonary arterioles and capillaries. These findings can be overlooked if not carefully sought or if the autopsy or examination of lung tissue is not done within a few hours of the reaction.

Clinically, the onset of symptoms of dyspnea and hypoxemia begins within a few minutes to an hour of the injection of the radiographic contrast medium. There is not necessarily a history of an allergic reaction to iodine. Treatment is supportive and includes a trial of high-dose corticosteroids, although this may be ineffective.

The activation of complement and, in turn, the generation of C5a stimulates granulocytes to aggregate and to adhere to endothelium, releasing proteases and toxic oxygen compounds. These, in turn, produce endothelial damage and capillary leakage. One study found high postmortem plasma histamine levels, which were thought to represent mast cell activation.[152]

MISCELLANEOUS DRUGS

TOCOLYTIC-INDUCED PULMONARY EDEMA

Tocolytics are agents that have been widely used in the treatment of premature labor. The most commonly used drugs are terbutaline, albuterol, ritodrine, and other β-mimetic drugs. There are many reports of these agents inducing pulmonary edema in otherwise healthy women.[153] The incidence varies from 0.5% to 5% of those receiving these drugs. Predisposing factors include the use of corticosteroids, twin gestation, fluid overload (particularly with saline), and anemia. The β-mimetic drugs typically stimulate $β_2$-adrenergic receptors, increase the maternal pulse rate and the cardiac output, and produce peripheral vasodilation. Hemodilution occurs and can be detected by a drop in the hemoglobin, hematocrit, and albumin. The blood pressure may drop as a result of the peripheral vasodilation and be a sign that too much tocolytic drug has been given.

A typical clinical scenario is as follows. In spite of the tocolytic agent, labor continues; the tocolytic agent is then stopped, and corticosteroids are added to accelerate fetal lung maturation. With the discontinuation of the tocolytic, the vasodilated vessels return to normal tone with a reduction of the intravascular volume. During delivery, further autotransfusion due to uterine contractions occurs, and pulmonary edema develops, usually in the postpartum period.

There are conflicting reports of the wedge pressure ranging from normal to elevated. In one study, patients with an elevated wedge pressure had normal left ventricular function by echocardiography. At this point, it is uncertain whether the pulmonary edema is truly cardiac or noncardiac in origin.

The treatment is oxygen and diuresis. In certain cases, consideration has been given to resuming the tocolytic agent merely to reproduce the peripheral vasodilation and allow an increase in the resumption of the intravascular volume that was present before the tocolytic agent was withdrawn. Corticosteroids aggravate the situation by their mineralocorticoid effect, which promotes fluid retention. The differential diagnosis includes aspiration of gastric contents, left-sided heart failure, amniotic fluid embolism, and overtransfusion.

HYDROCHLOROTHIAZIDE

There are over 40 reported cases of acute onset of diffuse pulmonary infiltrates associated with the ingestion of hydrochlorothiazide.[154] It may begin with the first dose or days later; 90% of cases occur in women who take the drug intermittently rather than daily, presumably for fluid retention. Symptoms consist of fairly rapid onset of dyspnea that clears within 48 to 72 hours of discontinuing the drug. A low-grade fever may be present. There is no eosinophilia and no positive antinuclear antibodies. The chest roentgenogram shows a diffuse bilateral alveolar-interstitial infiltrate. In the few cases studied, the pulmonary capillary wedge pressure was normal.

METHYSERGIDE, BROMOCRIPTINE, AND CABERGOLINE

Methysergide, bromocriptine, and cabergoline are structurally similar and produce similar pleuropulmonary reactions.[155,156] Methysergide is now rarely used to treat vascular headaches because there are better alternative drugs. Bromocriptine and cabergoline are used for the treatment of Parkinson's disease. The pleuropulmonary disease produced by both of these agents has an insidious onset. The predominant feature is pleural thickening and effusion, which is reversible by discontinuing the medication. Effusions are rarely large, are not commonly associated with pleuritic pain, and may show lymphocytosis.[155]

DEXTRAN

Hyskon is a low-molecular-weight dextran that is capable of producing a noncardiac pulmonary edema.[157] It is used principally in hysteroscopic surgery, most often for improving fertility, during which the endometrial cavity is distended with approximately 500 mL of low-molecular-weight dextran. The incidence of noncardiac pulmonary edema increases significantly if more than 500 mL is used, endometrial surfaces are excessively irritated, or the procedure lasts more than 45 minutes. In addition to noncardiac pulmonary edema, coagulopathy can also occur.

APPETITE SUPPRESSANTS

In the 1960s, excess cases of pulmonary hypertension were associated with the potent anorexigen aminorex fumarate. More recently, pulmonary hypertension has been associated with dexfenfluramine, fenfluramine, and phenteramine.[158] Valvular heart disease has also been associated with these agents.[159] A careful drug history must be taken to exclude this possibility in patients presenting with dyspnea, cardiovascular symptoms, or heart murmurs. Drug-associated pulmonary hypertension may be progressive and fatal despite discontinuation of the agents.[158]

ESOPHAGEAL VARICEAL SCLEROTHERAPY

Esophageal variceal sclerotherapy with either sodium morrhuate, sodium tetradecyl sulfate, or ethanolamine oleate can lead to multiple abnormalities.[160,161] Typically about 1 mL of one of these substances is injected into or around the varices, and up to 15 to 20 injections are made during a single procedure. Chest roentgenograms taken shortly after the procedure were abnormal in 85% of the cases at the Mayo Clinic, but this was rarely of clinical significance.[160] Pleural effusion occurred in about 25% of patients, mediastinal widening in 33%, atelectasis in 12%, and pulmonary infiltrates in 9%. Fever, chest pain, and difficulty in swallowing were common after the procedure but rarely amounted to a serious problem.

In the literature, pleural effusion occurred in anywhere from zero to 50% of the patients, and most of these patients were asymptomatic.[161] Effusions were more common when a large volume of fluid was injected and the volume per site was increased. Serious complications such as mediastinitis or frank esophageal rupture are rare, but should be suspected if the fever persists for more than 24 hours, the pleural effusion is large, or there is persistent chest pain. The acute respiratory distress syndrome can occur but happens in less than 1% of the patients in whom the procedure is carried out.

TRICYCLIC ANTIDEPRESSANT OVERDOSE

Tricyclic antidepressant overdose is one of the more common causes of drug emergencies seen in the emergency room setting. About one third of the pulmonary complications that these patients develop are either noncardiac pulmonary edema or aspiration. If hypotension results, cardiac pulmonary edema can occur.[162-164] Nearly 80% of the patients have an initially widened alveolar-arterial oxygen gradient. Mechanical ventilation may be required in up to three fourths of patients. The greater the drug level, the more likely the patient is to develop pulmonary complications. Nearly one half of the patients have an abnormal chest roentgenogram, and about 10% of the patients develop acute respiratory distress syndrome.

HYDANTOIN

There has been much confusion in the literature as to whether or not hydantoin produces parenchymal pulmonary disease and mediastinal adenopathy. Reports in the affirmative have been followed by a more detailed patient study refuting the possibility of pulmonary parenchymal disease.[165,166] The only two hydantoin-induced pulmonary diseases are drug-induced SLE and a few rare cases of hypersensitivity pneumonitis that show a predominance of lymphocytes found in the bronchoalveolar lavage fluid or biopsied tissue. The fact that hydantoin is one of the more commonly used drugs over extremely long periods of time and that it has not shown an obvious relationship for the induction of significant pulmonary disease makes it unlikely that there is a true relationship of any consequence.

DANTROLENE

Dantrolene is a long-acting skeletal muscle relaxant used in treating patients with spastic neurologic disorders.[167] There have been several case reports of chronic pleural effusion or pericarditis, or both, associated with this drug. Peripheral blood eosinophilia was seen in some patients who were taking dantrolene.

SUMMARY

Clinicians must maintain a high index of suspicion that unexplained pulmonary disease may be caused by medications. Most drug-induced pulmonary reactions are reversible if the drug is stopped in time. If necessary, additional measures such as judicious use of corticosteroids may be helpful. There are almost no diagnostic studies available that will confirm the presence of drug-induced lung disease. Rechallenging the patient with the suspected drug is dangerous and generally not indicated. If there is a question of whether or not a medication may be the cause of a particular pulmonary abnormality, one option is to call the medical director of the drug manufacturer, listed in the *Physicians' Desk Reference* (PDR). In addition, a timely website can be accessed at http://www.pneumotox.com.

REFERENCES

1. Classen DC, Pestotnik SL, Evans RS, et al: Computerized surveillance of adverse drug events in hospital patients. JAMA 266:2847–2851, 1991.
2. Limper AH: Drug induced lung disease: New developments. *In* Braunwald E (ed): Harrison's OnLine. New York: McGraw-Hill Health Professions Division, 2000.
3. Limper AH, Rosenow EC 3rd: Drug-induced interstitial lung disease. Curr Opin Pulm Med 2:396–404, 1996.
4. Myers JL: Pathology of drug-induced lung disease. *In* Katzenstein AL, Askin F (eds): Surgical Pathology of Non-neoplastic Lung Disease (2nd ed). Philadelphia: WB Saunders, 1990, pp 97–127.
5. Rosenow EC III, Myers JL, Swensen SJ, Pisani RJ: Drug-induced pulmonary disease: An update. Chest 102:239–250, 1992.
6. Cooper JAD Jr, White DA, Matthay RA: Drug-induced pulmonary disease. Part 1: Cytotoxic drugs; Part 2: Noncytotoxic drugs. Am Rev Respir Dis 133:321–340; 488–505, 1986.
7. Martin WJ II, Rosenow EC III: Amiodarone pulmonary toxicity: Recognition and pathogenesis (part 2). Chest 93:1242–1248, 1988.
8. Israel-Biet D, Labrune S, Huchon GJ: Drug-induced lung disease. Eur Respir J 4:465–478, 1991.
9. Beinert T, Binder D, Stuschke M, et al: Oxidant-induced lung injury in anticancer therapy. Eur J Med Res 4:43–53, 1999.
10. Schoen RT, Trentham DE: Drug-induced lupus: An adjuvant disease. Am J Med 71:5–8, 1981.
11. Wesselius LJ: Pulmonary complications of cancer therapy. Compr Ther 18:17–20, 1992.
12. Oury TD, Thakker K, Menache M, et al: Attenuation of bleomycin-induced pulmonary fibrosis by a catalytic antioxidant metalloporphyrin. Am J Respir Cell Mol Biol 25:164–169, 2001.
13. Tamagawa K, Taooka Y, Maeda A, et al: Inhibitory effects of a lecithinized superoxide dismutase on bleomycin-induced pulmonary fibrosis in mice. Am J Respir Crit Care Med 161:1279–1284, 2000.
14. Rosenow EC III, Limper AH: Drug induced pulmonary disease. Semin Respir Infect 10:86–95, 1995.
15. Aronchick JM, Gefter WB: Drug-induced pulmonary disease: An update. J Thorac Imaging 6:19–29, 1991.
16. Snyder LS, Hertz MI: Cytotoxic drug-induced lung injury. Semin Respir Infect 3:217–228, 1988.
17. Lehne G, Lote K: Pulmonary toxicity of cytotoxic and immunosuppressive agents. Acta Oncol 29:113–124, 1990.
18. Twohig KJ, Matthay RA: Pulmonary effects of cytotoxic agents other than bleomycin. Clin Chest Med 11:31–54, 1990.
19. Brooks BJ Jr, Seifter EJ, Walsh TE, et al: Pulmonary toxicity with combined modality therapy for limited stage small cell lung cancer. J Clin Oncol 4:200–209, 1986.
20. Ginsberg SJ, Comis RL: The pulmonary toxicity of antineoplastic agents. Semin Oncol 9:34–51, 1982.
21. Akoun GM, White JP: Treatment-induced respiratory disorders. *In* Dukes MNG (ed): Drug-Induced Disorders (Vol 3). Amsterdam: Elsevier, 1989, pp 1–377.
22. Klein DS, Wilds PR: Pulmonary toxicity of antineoplastic agents: Anaesthetic and postoperative implications. Can Anesth Soc J 30:399–405, 1983.
23. Carson CW, Cannon GW, Egger MJ, et al: Pulmonary disease during the treatment of rheumatoid arthritis with low dose pulse methotrexate. Semin Arthritis Rheum 16:186–195, 1987.
24. Gispen JG, Alarcaon GS, Johnson JJ, et al: Toxicity of methotrexate in rheumatoid arthritis. J Rheumatol 14:73–79, 1987.
25. Jules-Elysee K, White DA: Bleomycin-induced pulmonary toxicity. Clin Chest Med 11:1–20, 1990.
26. Heard B, Cooke R: Busulphan lung. Thorax 23:187–193, 1968.
27. Wolkowicz J, Sturgeon MB, Rawji M, et al: Bleomycin-induced pulmonary function abnormalities. Chest 101:97–101, 1992.
28. Bellamy EA, Husband JE, Blaquiere RM, et al: Bleomycin-related lung damage: CT evidence. Radiology 156:155–158, 1985.
29. Mills P, Husband J: Computed tomography of pulmonary bleomycin toxicity. Semin Ultrasound CT MR 11:417–422, 1990.
30. Ingrassia TS III, Ryu JH, Trastek VF, et al: Oxygen-exacerbated bleomycin pulmonary toxicity. Mayo Clin Proc 66:173–178, 1991.
31. Goldiner PL, Carlon GC, Cvitkovic E, et al: Factors influencing postoperative morbidity and mortality in patients treated with bleomycin. Br Med J 1:1664–1667, 1978.
32. Van Barneveld RWC, Sleijfer DT, VanDerMark TW, et al: Natural course of bleomycin-induced pneumonitis: A follow-up study. Am Rev Respir Dis 135:48–51, 1987.
33. Santrach PJ, Askin FB, Wells RJ, et al: Nodular form of bleomycin-related pulmonary injury in patients with osteogenic sarcoma. Cancer 64:806–811, 1989.
34. Cohen MB, Austin JH, Smith-Vaniz A, et al: Nodular bleomycin toxicity. Am J Clin Pathol 92:101–104, 1989.
35. Verweij J, van Zanten T, Souren T, et al: Prospective study on the dose relationship of mitomycin C-induced interstitial pneumonitis. Cancer 60:756–761, 1987.
36. Linette DC, McGee KH, McFarland JA: Mitomycin-induced pulmonary toxicity: Case report and review of the literature. Ann Pharmacother 26:481–484, 1992.
37. Sheldon R, Slaughter D: A syndrome of microangiopathic hemolytic anemia, renal impairment, and pulmonary edema in chemotherapy-treated patients with adenocarcinoma. Cancer 58:1428–1436, 1986.
38. Fernandez HF, Tran HT, Albrecht F, et al: Evaluation of safety and pharmacokinetics of administering intravenous

busulfan in a twice-daily or daily schedule to patients with advanced hematologic malignant disease undergoing stem cell transplantation. Biol. Blood Marrow Transplant 8:486–492, 2002.

39. Bedrossian CWM, Luna MA, Conklin RH, et al: Alveolar proteinosis as a consequence of immunosuppression. Hum Pathol 11:527–535, 1980.

40. Aymard JP, Gyger M, Lavallee R, et al: A case of pulmonary alveolar proteinosis complicating chronic myelogenous leukemia. Cancer 53:954–956, 1984.

41. Watanabe K, Sueishi K, Tanaka K, et al: Pulmonary alveolar proteinosis and disseminated atypical mycobacteriosis in a patient with busulfan lung. Acta Pathol Jpn 40:63–66, 1990.

42. Morgan M, Dodds A, Atkinson K, et al: The toxicity of busulphan and cyclophosphamide as the preparative regimen for bone marrow transplantation. Br J Haematol 77:529–534, 1991.

42a. Tanaka N, Newell JD, Brown KK, et al: Collagen vascular disease-related lung disease: high-resolution computed tomography findings based on the pathologic classification. J Comput Assist Tomogr 28:351–360, 2004.

43. Malik SW, Myers JL, DeRemee RA, Specks U: Lung toxicity with cyclophosphamide use: Two distinct patterns. Am J Respir Crit Care Med 154:1851–1856, 1996.

44. Hasan FM, Mark EJ: A 28-year-old man with increasing dyspnea, dry cough, and fever after chemotherapy for lymphoma. N Engl J Med 323:737–747, 1990.

45. Hilliquin P, Renoux M, Perrot S, et al: Occurrence of pulmonary complications during methotrexate therapy in rheumatoid arthritis. Br J Rheumatol 35:441–445, 1996.

46. Andersson BS, Luna MA, Yee C, et al: Fatal pulmonary failure complicating high-dose cytosine arabinoside therapy in acute leukemia. Cancer 65:1079–1084, 1990.

47. Jehn J, Göldel N, Rienmauller R, et al: Noncardiogenic pulmonary edema complicating intermediate and high-dose Ara C treatment for relapsed acute leukemia. Med Oncol Tumor Pharmacother 5:41–47, 1988.

48. Joerger M, Gunz A, Speich R, Pestalozzi BC: Gemcitabine-related pulmonary toxicity. Swiss Med Wkly 132:17–20, 2002.

49. Nelson R, Tarasoff P: Dyspnea with gemcitabine is commonly seen, often disease related, transient, and rarely severe. Eur J Cancer 31:197–198, 1995.

50. Gupta N, Ahmed I, Steinberg H, et al: Gemcitabine-induced pulmonary toxicity: Case report and review of the literature Am J Clin Oncol 25:96–100, 2002.

51. Rosado MF, Kett DH, Schein RM, et al: Severe pulmonary toxicity in a patient treated with gemcitabine. Am J Clin Oncol 25:31–33, 2002.

52. Helman DL Jr, Byrd JC, Ales NC, Shorr AF: Fludarabine-related pulmonary toxicity: A distinct clinical entity in chronic lymphoproliferative syndromes. Chest 122:785–790, 2002.

52a. Casper J, Knauf W, Blau I, et al: Treosulfan/fludarabine: a new conditioning regimen in allogeneic transplantation. Ann Hematol 83(Suppl 1):S70–S71, 2004.

52b. Nusair S, Breuer R, Shapira MY, et al: Low incidence of pulmonary complications following nonmyeloablative stem cell transplantation. Eur Respir J 23:440–445, 2004.

53. Massin F, Coudert B, Foucher P, et al: Nitrosourea-induced lung diseases (in French). Rev Mal Respir 9:575–582, 1992.

54. Parish JM, Muhm JR, Leslie KO: Upper lobe pulmonary fibrosis associated with high-dose chemotherapy containing BCNU for bone marrow transplantation. Mayo Clin Proc 78:630–634, 2003.

55. Weinstein AS, Diener-West M, Nelson DF, Pakuris E: Pulmonary toxicity of carmustine in patients treated for malignant glioma. Cancer Treat Rep 70:943–946, 1986.

56. O'Driscoll BR, Hasleton PS, Taylor PM, et al: Active lung fibrosis up to 17 years after chemotherapy with carmustine (BCNU) in childhood. N Engl J Med 323:378–382, 1990.

57. Durant JR, Norgard MJ, Murad TM, et al: Pulmonary toxicity associated with bischloroethyl nitrosourea (BCNU). Ann Intern Med 90:191–194, 1979.

58. Frankel SR, Eardley A, Lauwers G, et al: The "retinoic acid syndrome" in acute promyelocytic leukemia. Ann Intern Med 117:292–296, 1992.

59. Wiley JS, Firkin FC: Reduction of pulmonary toxicity by prednisolone prophylaxis during all-trans retinoic acid treatment of acute promyelocytic leukemia. Leukemia 9:774–778, 1995.

60. Nicolls MR, Terada LS, Tuder RM, et al: Diffuse alveolar hemorrhage with underlying pulmonary capillaritis in the retinoic acid syndrome. Am J Respir Crit Care Med 158:1302–1305, 1998.

61. Cohen MH, Williams GA, Sridhara R, et al: FDA drug approval summary: Gefitinib (ZD1839) (Iressa) tablets. Oncologist 8:303–306, 2003.

61a. Ieki R, Saitoh E, Shibuya M: Acute lung injury as a possible adverse drug reaction related to gefitinib. Eur Respir J 22:179–181, 2003.

62. Rosado MF, Donna E, Ahn YS: Challenging problems in advanced malignancy: Imatinib mesylate-induced interstitial pneumonitis. J Clin Oncol 21:3171–3173, 2003.

63. Fukuoka M, Niitani H, Suzuki A, et al: A Phase II study of CPT-11, a derivative of camptothecin, for previously untreated non small cell lung cancer. J Clin Oncol 10:16–20, 1992.

64. Masuda N, Fukuoka M, Kusunoki Y, et al: CPT-11: A new derivative of camptothecin for the treatment of refractory or relapsed small cell lung cancer. J Clin Oncol 10:1225–1229, 1992.

64a. Yamada M, Kudoh S, Fukuda H, et al: Dose-escalation study of weekly irinotecan and daily carboplatin with concurrent thoracic radiotherapy for unresectable stage III non-small cell lung cancer. Br J Cancer 87:258–263, 2002.

65. Madarnas Y, Webster P, Shorter AM, et al: Irinotecan-associated pulmonary toxicity. Anticancer Drugs 11:709–713, 2000.

66. Gurjal A, An T, Valdivieso M, Kalemkerian GP: Etoposide-induced pulmonary toxicity. Lung Cancer 26:109–112, 1999.

67. Shannon VR, Price KJ: Pulmonary complications of cancer therapy. Anesth Clin North Am 16:563–586, 1998.

68. Ramanathan RK, Reddy VV, Holbert JM, Belani CP: Pulmonary infiltrates following administration of paclitaxel. Chest 110:289–292, 1996.

69. Dimopoulou I, Galani G, Dafni U, et al: A prospective study of pulmonary function in patients treated with paclitaxel and carboplatin. Cancer 94:452–458, 2002.

70. Robert F, Spencer SA, Childs HA, et al: Concurrent chemo-radiation therapy with cisplatin and paclitaxel for locally advanced non-small cell lung cancer: Long-term follow-up of a Phase I trial. Lung Cancer 37:189–199, 2002.

71. Robert F, Childs HA, Spencer SA, et al: Phase I/IIa study of concurrent paclitaxel and cisplatin with radiation therapy in locally advanced non-small cell lung cancer: Analysis of early and late pulmonary morbidity. Semin Radiat Oncol 9:136–147, 1999.

72. Etienne B, Perol M, Nesme P, et al: Acute diffuse interstitial pneumopathy following docetaxel (Taxotere):

Apropos of 2 cases (in French). Rev Mal Respir 15:199–203, 1998.

73. Dunsford ML, Mead GM, Bateman AC, et al: Severe pulmonary toxicity in patients treated with a combination of docetaxel and gemcitabine for metastatic transitional cell carcinoma. Ann Oncol 18:943–947, 1999.

74. Bini EJ, Weinshel EH: Severe exacerbation of asthma: A new side effect of interferon-alpha in patients with asthma and chronic hepatitis C. Mayo Clin Proc 74:367–370, 1999.

75. Rubinowitz AN, Naidich DP, Alinsonorin C: Interferon-induced sarcoidosis. J Comput Assist Tomogr 27:279–283, 2003.

76. Kumar KS, Russo MW, Borczuk AC, et al: Significant pulmonary toxicity associated with interferon and ribavirin therapy for hepatitis C. Am J Gastroenterol 97:2432–2440, 2002.

77. Patel M, Ezzat W, Pauw KL, Lowsky R: Bronchiolitis obliterans organizing pneumonia in a patient with chronic myelogenous leukemia developing after initiation of interferon and cytosine arabinoside. Eur J Haematol 67:318–321, 2001.

78. Honore I, Nunes H, Groussard O, et al: Acute respiratory failure after interferon-gamma therapy of end-stage pulmonary fibrosis. Am J Respir Crit Care Med 167:953–957, 2003.

79. Shaw EG, Deming RL, Creagan ET, et al: Pilot study of human recombinant interferon gamma and accelerated hyperfractionated thoracic radiation therapy in patients with unresectable stage IIIA/B nonsmall cell lung cancer. Int J Radiat Oncol Biol Phys 31:827–831, 1995.

80. Lazarus DS, Kurnick JT, Kradin RL: Alterations in pulmonary function in cancer patients receiving adoptive immunotherapy with tumor-infiltrating lymphocytes and interleukin-2. Am Rev Respir Dis 141:193–198, 1990.

81. Saxon RR, Klein JS, Bar MH, et al: Pathogenesis of pulmonary edema during interleukin-2 therapy: Correlation of chest radiographic and clinical findings in 54 patients. AJR Am J Roentgenol 156:281–285, 1991.

82. Conant EF, Fox KR, Miller WT: Pulmonary edema as a complication of interleukin-2 therapy. AJR Am J Roentgenol 152:749–752, 1989.

83. Hocking DC, Phillips PG, Ferro TJ, et al: Mechanisms of pulmonary edema induced by tumor necrosis factor-alpha. Circ Res 67:68–77, 1990.

84. Kuei JH, Tashkin DP, Figlin RA: Pulmonary toxicity of recombinant human tumor necrosis factor. Chest 96:334–338, 1989.

85. Vial T, Descoates J: Clinical toxicity of cytokines used as hematopoietic growth factors. Drug Saf 13:371–406, 1995.

86. Rao SX, Ramaswamy G, Levin M, et al: Fatal acute respiratory failure after vinblastine-mitomycin therapy in lung carcinoma. Arch Intern Med 145:1905–1907, 1985.

87. Hoelzer KL, Harrison BR, Luedke SW, et al: Vinblastine-associated pulmonary toxicity in patients receiving combination therapy with mitomycin and cisplatin. Drug Intel Clin Pharm 20:287–289, 1986.

88. Roberts CM, Foulcher E, Zaunders JJ, et al: Radiation pneumonitis: A possible lymphocyte-mediated hypersensitivity reaction. Ann Intern Med 118:696–700, 1993.

89. Boyars MC: Clinical management of radiation-induced lung disease. J Respir Dis 11:167–183, 1990.

90. Arbetter KR, Prakash UB, Tazelaar HD, Douglas WW: Radiation-induced pneumonitis in the "nonirradiated" lung. Mayo Clinic Proc 74:27–36, 1999.

91. Holmberg L, Boman G, Bottiger IE, et al: Adverse reactions to nitrofurantoin: Analysis of 921 reports. Am J Med 69:733–738, 1980.

92. Holmberg L, Boman G: Pulmonary reactions to nitrofurantoin: 447 cases reported to the Swedish Adverse Drug Reaction Committee 1966–1976. Eur J Respir Dis 62:180–189, 1981.

93. Prakash UBS: Pulmonary reaction to nitrofurantoin. Semin Respir Dis 2:71–75, 1980.

94. Robinson BWS: Nitrofurantoin-induced interstitial pulmonary fibrosis. Med J Aust 1:72–76, 1983.

95. Akoun GM, Cadranel JL, Rosenow EC III, et al: Bronchoalveolar lavage cell data in drug-induced pneumonitis. Allergy Immunol 23:245–252, 1991.

96. Camus P, Piard F, Ashcroft T, et al: The lung in inflammatory bowel disease. Medicine 72:151–183, 1993.

97. Kohno S, Yamaguchi K, Yasuoka A, et al: Clinical evaluation of 12 cases of antimicrobial drug-induced pneumonitis. Jpn J Med 29:248–254, 1990.

98. Warner WA, Sanders E: Neuromuscular blockade associated with gentamicin therapy. JAMA 215:1153–1154, 1971.

99. Levine SJ, Walsh TJ, Martinez A, et al: Cardiopulmonary toxicity after liposomal amphotericin B infusion. Ann Intern Med 114:664–666, 1991.

100. Heffner JE, Harley RA, Schabel SI: Pulmonary reactions from illicit substance abuse. Clin Chest Med 11:151–162, 1990.

101. O'Donnell AE, Pappas LS: Pulmonary complications of intravenous drug abuse. Chest 94:251–253, 1988.

102. Parran TV Jr, Jasinski DR: Intravenous methylphenidate abuse. Arch Intern Med 151:781–783, 1991.

103. Schmidt RA, Glenny RW, Godwin JD, et al: Panlobular emphysema in young intravenous Ritalin abusers. Am Rev Respir Dis 143:649–656, 1991.

104. McCarroll KA, Roszler MH: Lung disorders due to drug abuse. J Thorac Imaging 6:30–35, 1991.

105. Forrester JM, Steele AW, Waldron JA, et al: Crack lung: An acute pulmonary syndrome with a spectrum of clinical and histopathologic findings. Am Rev Respir Dis 142:462–467, 1990.

106. Crouch E, Churg A: Progressive massive fibrosis of the lung secondary to intravenous injection of talc: A pathologic and mineralogic analysis. Am J Clin Pathol 80:520–526, 1983.

107. Israili ZH, Hall WD: Cough and angioneurotic edema associated with angiotensin-converting enzyme inhibitor therapy: A review of the literature and pathophysiology. Ann Intern Med 117:234–242, 1992.

108. Alderman CP: Adverse effects of the angiotensin converting enzyme inhibitors. Ann Pharmacother 30:55–61, 1996.

109. Elliott WJ: Double-blind comparison of eprosartan and enalapril on cough and blood pressure in unselected hypertensive patients. Eprosartan Study Group. J Hum Hypertens 13:413–417, 1999.

110. Kennedy JI Jr: Clinical aspects of amiodarone pulmonary toxicity. Clin Chest Med 11:119–129, 1990.

111. Dusman RE, Stanton MS, Miles WM, et al: Clinical features of amiodarone-induced pulmonary toxicity. Circulation 82:51–59, 1990.

112. Xaubet A, Roca J, Rodriguez-Roisin R, et al: Bronchoalveolar lavage cellular analysis and gallium lung scan in the assessment of patients with amiodarone-induced pneumonitis. Respiration 52:272–280, 1987.

113. Camus P, Lombard JN, Perrichon M, et al: Bronchiolitis obliterans organizing pneumonia in patients taking acebutolol or amiodarone. Thorax 44:711–715, 1989.

114. Piccione W Jr, Faber LP, Rosenberg MS: Amiodarone-induced pulmonary mass. Ann Thorac Surg 47:918–919, 1989.

115. Kuhlman JE, Teigen C, Ren H, et al: Amiodarone pulmonary toxicity: CT findings in symptomatic patients. Radiology 177:121–125, 1990.

116. Zaher C, Hamer A, Peter T, et al: Low-dose steroid therapy for prophylaxis of amiodarone-induced pulmonary infiltrates (letter). N Engl J Med 308:779, 1983.

117. Kay GN, Epstein AE, Kirklin JK, et al: Fatal postoperative amiodarone pulmonary toxicity. Am J Cardiol 62:490–493, 1988.

118. Greenspon AJ, Kidwell GA, Hurley W, et al: Amiodarone-induced postoperative adult respiratory distress syndrome. Circulation 84(Suppl III):III-407 to III-415, 1991.

119. Just-Viera JO, Fischer CR, Gago O, et al: Acute reaction to protamine: Its importance to surgeons. Am Surg 50:52–60, 1984.

120. Chester EH, Schwartz HJ, Fleming GM: Adverse effect of propranolol on airway function in nonasthmatic chronic obstructive lung disease. Chest 79:540–544, 1981.

121. Reynolds RJ, Burford JG, George RB: Using beta-blockers safely in asthma and COPD patients. J Respir Dis 3:95–113, 1982.

122. Everitt DE, Avorn J: Systemic effects of medications used to treat glaucoma. Ann Intern Med 112:120–125, 1990.

123. Gauthier-Rahman S, Akoun GM, Milleron BJ, et al: Leukocyte migration inhibition in propranolol-induced pneumonitis. Chest 97:238–241, 1990.

124. Ganau G, Lenzi T: Intravenous propafenone for converting recent onset atrial fibrillation in emergency departments: A randomized placebo-controlled multicenter trial. J Emerg Med 16:383–387, 1998.

125. Feinberg L, Travis WD, Ferrans V, et al: Pulmonary fibrosis associated with tocainide. Am Rev Respir Dis 141:505–508, 1990.

126. Hanston P, Evrard P, Mahieu P, et al: Flecainide-associated interstitial pneumonitis. Lancet 337:371–372, 1991.

127. Akoun GM, Cadranel JL, Israel-Biet D, et al: Flecainide-associated pneumonitis. Lancet 337:49, 1991.

128. Cannon GW: Pulmonary complications of antirheumatic drug therapy. Semin Arthritis Rheum 19:353–364, 1990.

129. Ameisen JC, Capron A: Aspirin-sensitive asthma. Clin Exp Allergy 20:127–129, 1990.

130. McGuigan MA: A two-year review of salicylate deaths in Ontario. Arch Intern Med 147:510–512, 1987.

131. Thisted B, Krantz T, Strom J, et al: Acute salicylate self-poisoning in 177 consecutive patients treated in ICU. Acta Anaesthesiol Scand 31:312–316, 1987.

132. Leatherman JW, Schmitz PG: Fever, hyperdynamic shock, and multiple-system organ failure: A pseudo-sepsis syndrome associated with chronic salicylate intoxication. Chest 100:1391–1396, 1991.

133. Londino AV Jr, Wolf GL, Calabro JJ, et al: Naproxen and pneumonitis (letter). JAMA 252:1853, 1984.

134. Evans RB, Ettensohn DB, Fawaz-Estrup F, et al: Gold lung: Recent developments in pathogenesis, diagnosis, and therapy. Semin Arthritis Rheum 16:196–205, 1987.

135. Chalmers A, Thompson D, Stein HB, et al: Systemic lupus erythematosus during penicillamine therapy for rheumatoid arthritis. Ann Intern Med 97:659–663, 1982.

136. Murphy KC, Atkins CJ, Offer RC, et al: Obliterative bronchiolitis in two rheumatoid arthritis patients treated with penicillamine. Arthritis Rheum 24:557–560, 1981.

137. Peces R, Riera JR, Arboleya LR, et al: Goodpasture's syndrome in a patient receiving penicillamine and carbimazole. Nephron 45:316–320, 1987.

138. Wechsler ME, Garpestad E, Flier SR, et al: Pulmonary infiltrates, eosinophilia, and cardiomyopathy following corticosteroid withdrawal in patients with asthma receiving zafirlukast. JAMA 279:455–457, 1998.

139. Knoell DL, Lucas J, Allen JN: Churg-Strauss syndrome associated with zafirlukast. Chest 114:332–334, 1998.

140. Bien ME, Mancuso AA, Mink JH, et al: Computed tomography in the evaluation of mediastinal lipomatosis. J Comput Assist Tomogr 2:379–383, 1978.

141. Totoritis MC, Rubin RL: Drug-induced lupus. Postgrad Med 78:149–161, 1985.

142. Hess EV, Mongey AB: Drug-related lupus. Bull Rheum Dis 40:1–8, 1991.

143. Lipinski JK, Weisbrod GL, Sanders DE: Exogenous lipoid pneumonitis. J Can Assoc Radiol 31:92–98, 1980.

144. Laurent F, Philippe JC, Vergier B, et al: Exogenous lipoid pneumonia: HRCT, MR, and pathologic findings. Eur Radiol 9:1190–1196, 1999.

145. Frank L, Massaro FL: Oxygen toxicity. Am J Med 69:117–126, 1980.

146. Davis WB, Rennard SI, Bitterman PB, et al: Pulmonary oxygen toxicity: Early reversible changes in human alveolar structures induced by hyperoxia. N Engl J Med 309:878–883, 1983.

147. Jackson RM: Pulmonary oxygen toxicity. Chest 88:900–905, 1985.

148. Fox RB, Hoidal JR, Brown DM, et al: Pulmonary inflammation caused by oxygen toxicity: Involvement of chemotactic factors and polymorphonuclear leukocytes. Am Rev Respir Dis 123:521–523, 1981.

149. Sackner MA, Landa J, Hirsch J, et al: Pulmonary effects of oxygen breathing: A 6–hour study in normal men. Ann Intern Med 82:40–43, 1975.

150. Popovsky MA, Abel MD, Moore SB: Transfusion-related acute lung injury associated with passive transfer of antileukocyte antibodies. Am Rev Respir Med 128:185–189, 1983.

151. Schneiderman H, Hammerschmidt DE, McCall AR, et al: Fatal complement-induced leukostasis after diatrizoate injection: Principles of clinicopathologic diagnosis. JAMA 250:2340–2342, 1983.

152. Vandenplas O, Hantson P, Dive A, et al: Fulminant pulmonary edema following intravenous administration of radiocontrast media. Acta Clin Belg 45:334–339, 1990.

153. Pisani RJ, Rosenow EC III: Pulmonary edema associated with tocolytic therapy. Ann Intern Med 110:714–718, 1989.

154. Biron P, Dessureault J, Napke E: Acute allergic interstitial pneumonitis induced by hydrochlorothiazide. Can Med Assoc J 145:28–34, 1991.

155. Kinnunen E, Viljanen A: Pleuropulmonary involvement during bromocriptine treatment. Chest 94:1034–1036, 1988.

156. Ling LL, Ahlskog JE, Munger TM, et al: Constrictive pericarditis and pleuropulmonary disease associated with cabergoline therapy for Parkinson's disease. Mayo Clin Proc 74:371–375, 1999.

157. McLucas B: Hyskon complications in hysteroscopic surgery. Obstet Gynecol Surv 46:196–200, 1991.

158. Mark EJ, Patalas ED, Chang HT, et al: Fatal pulmonary hypertension associated with the short-term use of fenfluramine and phentermine. N Engl J Med 337:602–606, 1997.

159. Connolly HM, Crary JL, McGoon MD, et al: Valvular heart disease associated with fenfluramine-phentermine. N Engl J Med 337:581–588, 1997.

160. Zeller FA, Cannon CR, Prakash UBS: Thoracic manifestations after esophageal variceal sclerotherapy. Mayo Clin Proc 66:727–732, 1991.

161. Edling JE, Bacon BR: Pleuropulmonary complications of endoscopic variceal sclerotherapy. Chest 99:1252–1257, 1991.

162. Roy TM, Ossorio MA, Cipolla LM, et al: Pulmonary complications after tricyclic antidepressant overdose. Chest 96:852–856, 1989.

163. Varnell RM, Godwin JD, Richardson ML, et al: Adult respiratory distress syndrome from overdose of tricyclic antidepressants. Radiology 170:667–670, 1989.

164. Shannon M, Lovejoy FH Jr: Pulmonary consequences of severe tricyclic antidepressant ingestion. J Toxicol Clin Toxicol 25:443–461, 1987.

165. Michael JR, Rudin ML: Acute pulmonary disease caused by phenytoin. Ann Intern Med 95:452–454, 1981.

166. Chamberlain DW, Hyland RH, Ross DJ: Diphenylhydantoin-induced lymphocytic interstitial pneumonia. Chest 90:458–460, 1986.

167. Miller DH, Haas LF: Pneumonitis, pleural effusion and pericarditis following treatment with dantrolene. J Neurol Neurosurg Psychiatry 47:553–554, 1984.

DISORDERS OF THE PLEURA

68

Pleural Effusion

V. Courtney Broaddus, M.D., Richard W. Light, M.D.

INTRODUCTION

The pleural space is bounded by two membranes, the visceral pleura covering the lung and the parietal pleura covering the chest wall and diaphragm. Into this space, normal liquid and protein enter from the systemic circulation and are removed by the parietal pleural lymphatics. Pleural pressure is subatmospheric and mediates inflation of the lung. Because the mesothelial boundaries are leaky, excess liquid can move across into this lower pressure, high-capacitance space and collect as a pleural effusion. Thus, pleural effusions are common and of highly diverse etiology. These effusions can form based on disease of the pleural membranes themselves or disease of thoracic or abdominal organs. Depending on the protein and lactate dehydrogenase (LDH) concentrations of the liquid and the cellular composition, these effusions can be primarily approached as to the likely underlying causes. Exudative pleural effusions meet at least one of the following criteria (Light's criteria), whereas transudative effusions meet none: pleural fluid protein–to–serum protein ratio of more than 0.5, pleural fluid LDH–serum LDH ratio of more than 0.6, and pleural fluid LDH more than two thirds of the upper normal limit for serum. In this chapter, we discuss both the physiology and pathophysiology of liquid movement in the pleural space.

THE PLEURA: FORM AND FUNCTION

The pleura consists of two membranes, the visceral pleura covering the lung, and the parietal pleura covering the chest wall and diaphragm. These two pleural membranes meet at the hilar root of the lung. In the sheep, an animal with a pleural anatomy similar to humans, the surface area of the visceral pleura of one lung, including that invaginating into the lung fissures, is similar to that of the parietal pleura of one hemithorax, approximately 1000 cm[2].[1] The normal pleural space is approximately 18 to 20 μm in width, although it widens at its most dependent areas.[1] Although at one time controversial, it is now clear that pleural membranes do not touch each other, and that the pleural space is a real, not a potential, space[1] (Fig. 68.1).

It is likely that the primary function of the pleural membranes is to allow extensive movement of the lung relative to the chest wall. If the lung adhered directly to the chest wall, its expansion and deflation would be more limited. Encased in its slippery coat, the lung, although still coupled mechanically to the chest wall, is able to expand across a breadth of several intercostal spaces. Nonetheless, in clinical and exper-imental studies, pleural symphysis has not been associated with large abnormalities in lung function.[2,3] The most common findings have been a decrease in volume of the affected lung[2] and, in one study, of the opposite lung as well.[4] If pleural thickening accompanies pleural symphysis, abnormalities of lung function may result more from fibrothorax than from obliteration of the pleural space alone.

The visceral pleura may also provide mechanical support for the lung: contributing to the shape of the lung,[5] providing a limit to expansion,[6] and contributing to the work of deflation.[7] Because the submesothelial connective tissue is continuous with the connective tissue of the lung parenchyma, the visceral pleura may help to distribute the forces produced by negative inflation pressures evenly over the lung. In this way, overdistention of alveoli at the pleural surface may be avoided, lessening the chance of rupture and pneumothorax.

One recently recognized function of the pleural space is to provide a route by which edema can escape the lung.[8] As has been shown in several experimental studies of either hydrostatic or increased-permeability lung edema,[9,10] the pleural space can function as an additional safety factor protecting against the development of alveolar edema. The formation of transudative effusions in patients with congestive heart failure apparently reflects the movement of edema from the lung to a space where its effects on lung function are relatively small.[11]

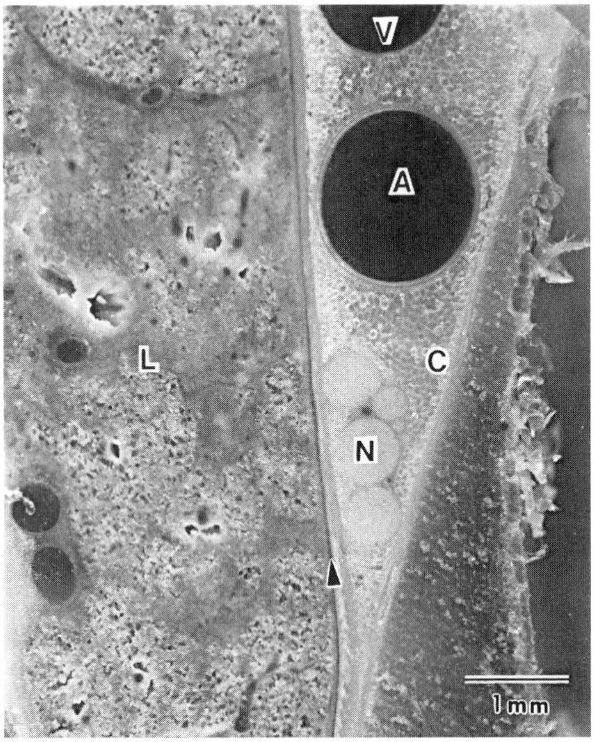

EMBRYOLOGY AND ANATOMY

By 3 weeks of gestational age, the pleural, pericardial, and peritoneal spaces begin to form from the mesoderm, and, by 9 weeks, the pleural cavity has become separated from both the pericardial and peritoneal spaces.[12] Various cysts, diverticula, and defects can result from incomplete partitioning of the three mesodermal spaces. As the lung develops, the lung buds invaginate into the visceral pleura, and henceforth retain a pleural covering.

The pleural membranes are smooth, glistening coverings for the constantly moving lung. Overlying each pleural membrane is a single cell layer of mesothelial cells. These cells can vary in shape from flat to cuboidal or columnar, perhaps based on the degree of stretching of the underlying submesothelial tissue. These cells, the most numerous cell type of the pleural space, may have a variety of functions important to pleural biology. Mesothelial cells can secrete the macromolecular components of the extracellular matrix and organize them into mature matrix,[13] phagocytose particles,[14] produce fibrinolytic and procoagulant factors,[15] and secrete neutrophil and monocyte chemotactic factors[16] that may be important for inflammatory cell recruitment into the pleural spaces.[17] The mesothelial cells also produce cytokines such as transforming growth factor-β, epidermal growth factor, and platelet-derived growth factor, which are important in pleural inflammation and fibrosis.[18]

On the surface of the mesothelial cells are microvilli, which are irregularly distributed over the pleural surfaces. Although microvilli presumably exist to increase surface area for metabolic activity, the function of these prominent features is unknown. Mesothelial cells produce hyaluronan but not mucin, express keratin microfilaments, stain negatively

Figure 68.1 The pleural space is depicted in a frozen sheep thorax by reflected-light microscopy. The pleural space is seen as a continuous dark band (*arrowhead*) between the lung (L) and the chest wall (C). Because the section was removed from beneath a rib, the intercostal vein (V), artery (A), and nerve (N) are seen. (From Albertine KH, Wiener-Kronish JP, Bastacky J, Staub NC: No evidence for mesothelial cell contact across the costal pleural space of sheep. J Appl Physiol 70:123–134, 1991.)

with epithelial-specific antibodies (Ber-EP4, B72.3, Leu.M1, and CEA), and stain positively for calretinin and mesothelin—all features that are important for histochemical and immunohistochemical identification of the cells in pleural effusions.[19,20]

The cells lie on a thin basement membrane overlying a varying region of connective tissue containing mostly collagen and elastin. Although the parietal pleural connective tissue layer is of a consistent thickness, the visceral connective tissue layer varies greatly. In a single individual, the visceral pleura varies from a thinner layer at the cranial region to a thicker layer at the caudal region.[21] Analysis of the constituents of the visceral pleura has shown that there is more collagen relative to elastin than is found in the lung parenchyma, a finding consistent with a mechanical role for the pleura.[22] This connective tissue layer contains blood vessels and lymphatics and joins with the connective tissue of the lung.

BLOOD SUPPLY

The parietal pleura is supplied by intercostal arteries[23] (Fig. 68.2A). The visceral pleura in humans, like that in sheep, is exclusively supplied by the bronchial circulation, which drains into pulmonary veins[21] (Fig. 68.2B). The drainage route via pulmonary veins may have contributed to earlier confusion about whether the visceral pleural blood supply was from a systemic (bronchial) or pulmonary circulation. Both pleurae in humans therefore have a systemic circulation, although the visceral pleural bronchial circulation may have a slightly lower perfusion pressure than the parietal pleural intercostal circulation because of its drainage into a lower pressure venous system.

LYMPHATICS

If one injects carbon particles into the pleural space as a visible marker of lymphatic drainage pathways, one later finds that the black carbon has been taken up into lymphatics on the parietal side, not the visceral side (Fig. 68.3). The visceral pleura has extensive lymphatics, but they do not connect to the pleural space.[21] Demonstrated in rabbits, sheep, and now in humans, the parietal pleural lymphatics connect to the pleural space via stomas, holes of 8 to 10 μm in diameter that are formed by discontinuities in the mesothelial layer where mesothelium joins to the underlying

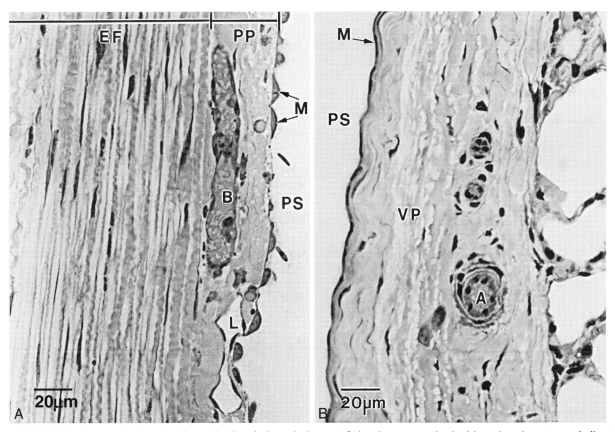

Figure 68.2 Light micrographs showing the parietal and visceral pleurae of the sheep, an animal with a pleural anatomy similar to that of humans. Both membranes are covered by a single layer of mesothelial cells (M). **A,** The parietal pleura (PP) is the layer of loose connective tissue between the pleural space (PS) and the dense connective tissue of the endothoracic fascia (EF). Within the loose connective tissue are blood microvessels (B) from the intercostal arteries, and lymphatic lacunae (L) that open into the pleural space via stomata. **B,** The visceral pleural (VP) lies between the pleural space (PS) and the alveoli. The blood supply to the visceral pleura is via the bronchial arteries (A), which drain into pulmonary veins. The pleura contains dense bands of elastin and collagen. (From Staub NC, Wiener-Kronish JP, Albertine KH: Transport through the pleura: Physiology of normal liquid and solute exchange in the pleural space. *In* Chrétien J, Bignon J, Hirsch A [eds]: The Pleura in Health and Disease [Lung Biology in Health and Disease, Vol 30]. New York: Marcel Dekker, 1985, pp 174–175.)

Figure 68.3 Macroscopic photograph of lymphatic lacunae in the parietal pleura over an intercostal space. Colloidal carbon was instilled into the pleural space to label the draining lymphatics. When one looks down upon the pleura, the lymphatic lacunae (L) appear as broad cisterns. B, blood vessel. (Original magnification ×39.) (From Albertine KH, Wiener-Kronish JP, Staub NC: The structure of the parietal pleura and its relationship to pleural liquid dynamics in sheep. Anat Rec 208:406, 1984.)

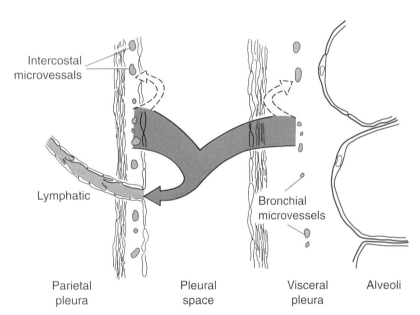

Figure 68.4 Schema showing normal pleural liquid turnover. The initial microvascular filtrate in the parietal and visceral pleura is partly reabsorbed (*dashed arrows*). The remaining low-protein interstitial liquid flows across the leaky pleural mesothelial layers into the pleural space. The pleural liquid exits the pleural space via the parietal pleural lymphatic stomata. (From Staub NC, Wiener-Kronish JP, Albertine KH: Transport through the pleura: Physiology of normal liquid and solute exchange in the pleural space. *In* Chrétien J, Bignon J, Hirsch A [eds]: The Pleura in Health and Disease [Lung Biology in Health and Disease, Vol 30]. New York: Marcel Dekker, 1985, p 182.)

lymphatic endothelium.[24–26] The stomas can accommodate particles as large as erythrocytes. In various experimental studies, these lymphatics have been shown to be the major route of exit of liquid from the pleural space.[27] From the stomas, liquid drains to lacunae, spider-like submesothelial collecting lymphatics, which then drain to infracostal lymphatics, to parasternal and periaortic nodes, to the thoracic duct, and into the systemic venous system. Lymphoid cells have been described lying within aggregates underneath morphologically different mesothelial cells, forming raised structures called *Kampmeier's foci* that may have an immune function.[28]

NERVE SUPPLY

Only the parietal pleura contains sensory nerve fibers, supplied by the intercostal and phrenic nerves. The costal and peripheral diaphragmatic regions are innervated by the intercostal nerves, and pain from these regions is referred to the adjacent chest wall. The central diaphragmatic region is innervated by the phrenic nerve, and pain from this region is referred to the ipsilateral shoulder. The visceral pleura does not contain sensory nerve fibers; therefore, pain, whether from inflammation, tumor, or catheters

advanced far out in the lung during bronchoscopy, indicates involvement of the adjacent parietal pleura.

PHYSIOLOGY OF THE PLEURAL SPACE

NORMAL PLEURAL LIQUID AND PROTEIN TURNOVER

In the last 10 to 15 years, a consensus has developed that normal pleural liquid arises from the systemic pleural vessels in both pleurae, flows across the leaky pleural membranes into the pleural space, and exits the pleural space via the parietal pleural lymphatics[29] (Fig. 68.4). In this way, the pleural space is analogous to other interstitial spaces of the body. There are several lines of evidence for this explanation:

1. Intrapleural pressure is lower than the interstitial pressure of either of the pleural tissues.[30] This pressure difference constitutes a gradient for liquid movement into but not out of the pleural space.
2. The pleural membranes are leaky to liquid and protein. Whether tested in vitro[31,32] or in situ,[33] the pleura offers little resistance to liquid or protein movement.
3. Mesothelial cells have not been shown to generate an electrical potential difference, as would be expected if

there were active transport across them.[31,32] Although normal pleural liquid has been reported to be alkaline with a higher bicarbonate than plasma,[34] there is no evidence yet for mesothelial participation in generating a bicarbonate gradient. If indeed the mesothelial layer is leaky, it is difficult to explain how mesothelial cells could maintain such a gradient.

4. The entry of pleural liquid is slow and compatible with known interstitial flow rates. By noninvasive studies of the equilibration of radiolabeled albumin, the entry rate of pleural liquid is approximately 0.01 mL/kg per hour in a sheep, or about 0.5 mL hourly in a grown man.[35] The half-time of pleural liquid turnover in sheep and rabbits is 6 to 8 hours.[35,36]

5. The protein concentration of normal pleural liquid is low in sheep[35] and probably in humans, which implies sieving of the protein across a high-pressure gradient. The protein concentration of sheep pleural liquid (10 g/L) and pleural-to-plasma protein concentration ratio (0.15) are similar to those of filtrates from high-pressure systemic vessels. By comparison, a filtrate from low-pressure pulmonary vessels has a higher protein concentration (45 g/L) and ratio (lymph-to-plasma protein concentration ratio 0.69).[37]

6. The majority of liquid exits the pleural space by bulk flow, not by diffusion or active transport. This is evident because the protein concentration of pleural effusions remains constant as the effusion is absorbed, as is expected with bulk flow. If liquid were absorbed by diffusion or active transport, then proteins would diffuse at a slower rate, and the protein concentration would progressively increase. In addition, erythrocytes instilled into the pleural space are absorbed intact,[38,39] and in almost the same proportion as the liquid and protein.[27] This indicates that the major route of exit is via holes large enough to accommodate sheep erythrocytes (6 to 8 μm diameter). The only possible exit is via the parietal pleural stomas (10 to 12 μm diameter) and the pleural lymphatics. Of note, these lymphatics have a large capacity for absorption. When artificial effusions were instilled into the pleural space of awake sheep, the exit rate (0.28 mL/kg per hour) was nearly 30 times the baseline exit rate (0.01 mL/kg per hour).[27]

PLEURAL PRESSURE

A controversy has existed over whether there are two pleural pressures, or one.[40] Two pressures had been proposed to explain a discrepancy between two ways of measuring pleural pressure. One pressure, a liquid pressure measured using catheters, varied at 1 cm H_2O/cm lung height as would a static column of liquid. The other pressure, a surface pressure measured using surface balloons and suction cups, varied by less than 1 cm H_2O/cm height and was equal and opposite to pulmonary recoil pressure. It appears now that the controversy arose because of the difficulty of measuring pleural pressure with catheters. The catheters were large relative to the narrow pleural space, distorted the space, and created a static column of liquid. With the use of relatively noninvasive micropipettes, it is clear that pleural pressure is the same in the liquid as on the pleural surface, and varies by approximately 0.5 cm/cm height.[40]

The existence of this vertical pressure gradient implies that pleural liquid does not form a static column, but slowly flows from the top to the bottom of the space.

The actual pleural pressure in humans is approximately −5 cm H_2O at midchest at functional residual capacity and −30 cm H_2O at total lung capacity.[41] If the lung were less compliant at these volumes, these pressures would be more negative. In one study of patients undergoing thoracentesis, those with more negative pleural pressures had a smaller improvement in lung volume than those with less negative pressures, presumably reflecting the presence of underlying diseased, noncompliant lung.[42]

Although the pleural space pressure is subatmospheric, gases do not accumulate there. The sum of all partial pressures of gases in capillary blood is approximately 700 mm Hg, or 60 mm Hg below atmospheric ($P_{H_2O} = 47$, $P_{CO_2} = 46$, $P_{N_2} = 570$, and $P_{O_2} = 40$ mm Hg). The subatmospheric pressure of dissolved gases in capillary blood helps to maintain the pleural space free of gas and facilitates absorption of any gas that does enter the pleural space. Of note, to increase the gradient favoring absorption of gas, one can lower the partial pressure of nitrogen in the blood by having a patient breathe increased concentrations of inspired oxygen. The oxygen displaces alveolar nitrogen, thereby lowering the partial pressure of nitrogen in capillary blood; because of the limited absorption of oxygen due to the plateau of the oxygen-hemoglobin dissociation curve, however, the increase in inspired oxygen does not add greatly to the partial pressure of oxygen in capillary blood.

PATHOPHYSIOLOGY OF THE PLEURAL SPACE

PLEURAL EFFUSIONS

For pleural liquid to accumulate, either the entry rate of liquid must increase to a sustained rate more than 30 times normal (to exceed the reserve lymphatic removal capacity), the exit rate of liquid must decrease, or both rates must change.[43] In the clinical setting, it is most likely that excess pleural liquid accumulates due to changes in both entry and exit rates. Although clinicians are more aware of the problem of an increased entry rate of liquid, many of the causes of pleural effusions probably also decrease the exit rate of pleural liquid by interfering with pleural lymphatic drainage. The lymphatic exit rate may be decreased by obstruction of the parietal pleural stomas, inhibition of lymphatic contractility, infiltration of draining parasternal lymph nodes, or elevation of the systemic venous pressure into which the lymph drains.[43] Decreases in lymphatic clearance have been confirmed in patients with tuberculous and malignant effusions,[44] and in those with the yellow nail syndrome, a disease of lymphatic function.[45]

To determine the origin of effusions, a classic and useful distinction is between transudates and exudates.[46] Transudates (protein ratio [pleural/plasma] <0.50 *and* LDH ratio [pleural/plasma] <0.60) form by leakage of liquid across an intact barrier, owing to increases in hydrostatic pressures or decreases in osmotic pressures across that barrier. Transudates generally indicate that the pleural membranes are not themselves diseased. Exudates (protein ratio >0.50 *or* LDH ratio >0.60) form from leakage of liquid and protein across an altered barrier with increased permeability. The protein ratio, the LDH ratio, and the absolute pleural LDH concentration constitute Light's criteria.

The circulatory barrier across which the liquid and protein leak is not always obvious. Most transudates are due to congestive heart failure. The pleural effusions form from leakage of edema from the pulmonary interstitium across the leaky visceral pleura into the pleural space.[9,11] Other transudates, those associated with the nephrotic syndrome or atelectasis, may form because of altered pressures (osmotic or hydrostatic) across the pleural capillaries. Some transudates may develop because of an isolated decrease in exit rate.[47] Finally, hepatic hydrothorax and effusions from peritoneal dialysis develop when liquid flows from the peritoneal space into the lower pressure pleural space across macroscopic holes in the diaphragm.

Exudates arise from injured capillary beds, either in the lung, the pleura, or adjacent tissues. Most exudates, such as those associated with pneumonia or pulmonary embolism, probably form following lung inflammation and injury when a high-protein lung edema leaks into the pleural space. Another large category of exudates arise from pleural injury due to inflammation, infection, or malignancy. Exudates can form when exudative liquid in the mediastinum (esophageal rupture or chylothorax), retroperitoneum (pancreatic pseudocyst), or peritoneum (ascites with spontaneous bacterial peritonitis or Meigs' syndrome) finds its way into the lower pressure pleural space.

For either transudates or exudates, lymphatic obstruction may contribute to the accumulation of the effusion.[43] Nonetheless, because lymphatic clearance does not alter the pleural fluid protein concentration, the protein concentration gives information about the formation of the fluid, not its removal.

EFFECTS OF PLEURAL EFFUSIONS ON LUNG FUNCTION

In the presence of a space-occupying liquid in the pleural space, the lung recoils inward, the chest wall recoils outward, and the diaphragm is depressed inferiorly. If the lung and chest wall have normal compliances, the decrease in lung volume accounts for approximately a third of the volume of the pleural effusion, and the increase in the size of the hemithorax accounts for the remaining two thirds. As a result, lung volumes are reduced by less than the pleural effusion volume. If the lung is otherwise normal, there is no evidence that an effusion causes significant hypoxemia, presumably because ventilation and perfusion decrease similarly. In fact, in one study, hypoxemia was noted only after liquid was removed by thoracentesis,[48] when perfusion presumably was restored while ventilation remained inadequate.

Common symptoms of patients with effusions are pleuritic chest pain, cough, and dyspnea. It appears that the three symptoms are due to different causes. Pleuritic chest pain derives from inflammation of the parietal pleura, the site of pleural pain fibers. Occasionally, this symptom is accompanied by an audible or palpable pleural rub, reflecting the movement of abnormal pleural tissues. Cough may be due to distortion of the lung, in the same way as cough follows lung collapse from a pneumothorax. Dyspnea is most likely caused by the mechanical inefficiency of the res-

piratory muscles that are stretched by the outward displacement of the chest wall and the downward displacement of the diaphragm. After the removal of large amounts of pleural liquid, dyspnea is generally relieved promptly, although the reduction in pleural liquid volume is associated with only small increases in lung volume and little improvement, or an actual decrease, in PO_2. In one study, nine patients underwent removal of over 1800 mL of pleural liquid, and, despite increases in vital capacity of only 300 mL, all patients experienced immediate relief of dyspnea.[49] Although the vital capacity changed little, patients could generate a more negative pleural pressure at the same lung volume after thoracentesis than before. This ability to generate a more negative pleural pressure was evidence of an improved efficiency of the respiratory muscles following the return of the chest wall to a more normal position after thoracentesis. This improved efficiency of respiration may explain the relief of dyspnea after removal of pleural liquid.

APPROACH TO PATIENTS WITH PLEURAL EFFUSION

The possibility of a pleural effusion should be considered whenever a patient with an abnormal chest radiograph is evaluated. Increased densities on the chest radiograph are frequently attributed to parenchymal infiltrates when they actually represent pleural fluid. Free pleural fluid gravitates to the most dependent part of the thoracic cavity, which is the posterior costophrenic sulcus when the patient is upright. Therefore, if the posterior costophrenic angle is blunted or if the posterior part of the diaphragm is not visible on the lateral chest radiograph, bilateral decubitus chest radiographs or an ultrasonic examination of the pleural space should be obtained to ascertain whether free pleural fluid is present. If the distance between the inside of the thoracic cavity and the outside of the lung is less than 10 mm, the pleural effusion is not likely to be clinically significant and, in any case, will be difficult to sample by thoracentesis. If the distance is greater than 10 mm, an effort should be made to determine the cause of the pleural effusion.

DIFFERENTIAL DIAGNOSIS OF PLEURAL EFFUSION

Many different diseases may have an accompanying pleural effusion (Table 68.1). The vigor with which various diagnoses are pursued should depend on the likelihood that the person has that particular disease. Table 68.2 shows rough estimates of the annual incidence of the most common causes of pleural effusions. Congestive heart failure and cirrhosis are responsible for almost all transudative pleural effusions. Pneumonia, malignant pleural disease, pulmonary embolism, and gastrointestinal disease account for at least 90% of all exudative pleural effusions.

SEPARATION OF EXUDATES FROM TRANSUDATES

A diagnostic thoracentesis should be performed on nearly every patient with free pleural fluid that measures more than 10 mm on the decubitus radiograph. If the patient has

Table 68.1 Differential Diagnoses of Pleural Effusions

Transudative Pleural Effusions
Congestive heart failure
Pericardial disease
Hepatic hydrothorax
Nephrotic syndrome
Peritoneal dialysis
Urinothorax
Myxedema
Fontan procedure
Central venous occlusion
Subarachnoid-pleural fistula
Veno-occlusive disease
Bone marrow transplantation
Iatrogenic

Exudative Pleural Effusions
Neoplastic diseases
　Metastatic disease
　Mesothelioma
　Primary effusion lymphoma
　Pyothorax-associated lymphoma
Infectious diseases
　Pyogenic bacterial infections
　Tuberculosis
　Actinomycosis and nocardiosis
　Fungal infections
　Viral infections
　Parasitic infections
Pulmonary embolism
Gastrointestinal disease
　Esophageal perforation
　Pancreatic disease
　Intra-abdominal abscesses
　Diaphragmatic hernia
　Post–abdominal surgery
Collagen vascular diseases
　Rheumatoid pleuritis
　Systemic lupus erythematosus
　Drug-induced lupus
　Immunoblastic lymphadenopathy
　Sjögren's syndrome
　Churg-Strauss syndrome
　Wegener's granulomatosis
Post–cardiac injury syndrome
Post–coronary artery bypass surgery
Asbestos exposure
Sarcoidosis
Uremia
Meigs' syndrome
Ovarian hyperstimulation syndrome
Yellow nail syndrome
Drug-induced pleural disease
　Nitrofurantoin
　Dantrolene
　Methysergide
　Bromocriptine
　Procarbazine
　Amiodarone
Trapped lung
Radiation therapy
Electrical burns
Iatrogenic injury
Hemothorax
Chylothorax

Table 68.2 Approximate Annual Incidence of Various Types of Pleural Effusions in the United States*

Type of Effusion	Incidence
Congestive heart failure	500,000
Pneumonia (bacterial)	300,000
Malignant disease	200,000
Lung	60,000
Breast	50,000
Lymphoma	40,000
Other	50,000
Pulmonary embolization	150,000
Viral disease	100,000
Post–coronary artery bypass surgery	60,000
Cirrhosis with ascites	50,000
Gastrointestinal disease	25,000
Collagen vascular disease	6,000
Tuberculosis	2,500
Asbestos exposure	2,000
Mesothelioma	1,500

* Adapted from Light RW: Pleural Diseases (4th ed). Philadelphia: Lippincott Williams & Wilkins, 2001, p 89.

obvious congestive heart failure, consideration can be given to postponing the thoracentesis until the heart failure is treated. However, if the patient is febrile or has pleuritic chest pain or if the effusions are not of comparable size on both sides, a thoracentesis should be performed without delay.

Thoracentesis is a safe procedure when performed by an experienced operator. Because of the small-bore needle required, it can be safely performed in patients with coagulopathies and thrombocytopenia, and in patients on positive mechanical ventilation.[50] Descriptions of technique emphasize proper positioning of the patient, identification of the area of decreased tactile fremitus that is a sensitive physical finding for the level of the effusion, and adequate local anesthesia of the parietal pleura as well as of the skin.[50] The needle should run over the top of the rib to avoid the neurovascular bundle that travels in each intercostal space. Of note, this bundle travels in the middle of the intercostal space from the spine for approximately 5 to 6 inches (13 cm) before taking its safer position beneath the upper rib.[50] Thus, one should avoid thoracentesis medial to the midclavicular line.

Complications from thoracentesis include pneumothorax and hemothorax. Estimates of each complication from prospective studies are low (4% to 5% for pneumothorax; 1% for hemothorax), with only half of the pneumothoraces requiring chest thoracostomy.[51,52] In such studies, pneumothorax was associated with procedural events such as aspiration of air, multiple needle passes, and development of new symptoms. The risk for pneumothorax appears to be higher in patients with prior radiotherapy to the chest or multiple prior thoracenteses. In an uncomplicated thoracentesis that is well tolerated by the patient, there appears to be no value to routine chest radiography.[51,52]

The first question that should be answered with the diagnostic thoracentesis is whether the patient has a transudative or an exudative pleural effusion (see Pleural Effusions earlier). The identification of transudates or exudates is made by analysis of the levels of protein and LDH in the pleural fluid and the serum. Exudative pleural effusions meet at least one of Light's criteria, whereas transudative pleural effusions meet none[46]: (1) protein ratio (pleural fluid/serum) greater than 0.50; (2) LDH ratio (pleural fluid/serum) greater than 0.60; and (3) pleural fluid LDH greater than two thirds of the upper normal limit for serum. If none of these criteria is met, the patient has a transudative pleural effusion, and the pleural surfaces can be ignored while the congestive heart failure, cirrhosis, or nephrosis is treated. In the rare cases in which malignancy has been associated with a transudate, extrapleural effects of the tumor or other causes such as concurrent congestive heart failure are the most likely cause, as evidenced by the rarity of a positive cytology in those effusions.[47,53]

The Light criteria may misidentify a transudative effusion as an exudative effusion in as many as 25% of cases. If a patient appears to have a transudative effusion clinically, but the pleural fluid meets exudative criteria, the difference between the serum and pleural fluid protein levels should be assessed. Romero-Candeira and coworkers[54] have shown that, if this difference exceeds 3.1 g/dL, the patient in all probability has a transudative effusion. Other tests such as the effusion cholesterol concentration and pleural fluid/serum bilirubin concentration have not proven to be superior to Light's criteria.[55,56]

Most studies dichotomize pleural effusions into transudates or exudates based on a single cutoff point. An alternative approach recommended by Heffner and coworkers[57,58] is to use likelihood ratios for identifying whether a pleural fluid is a transudate or an exudate. The idea behind this approach is that the higher a value (e.g., the pleural fluid LDH), the more likely the effusion is to be an exudate and the lower the value, the less likely the effusion is to be an exudate. Heffner and coworkers have derived multilevel[57] and continuous[58] likelihood ratios for the usual biochemical tests used to differentiate transudates and exudates. When these likelihood ratios are used in conjunction with pretest probabilities using Bayes' theorem, posttest probabilities can be derived.[58] The difficulty in using this approach is that the pretest probabilities vary significantly from physician to physician. Moreover, most physicians do not understand the mathematics involved. However, this approach does emphasize that it is important to take into consideration the absolute value of the measurements. Very high or very low measurements are almost always indicative of exudates and transudates, respectively, whereas values near the cutoff levels can be associated with either transudates or exudates.

When dealing with a patient who has a high likelihood of having a transudative pleural effusion, the most cost-effective use of the laboratory is to order only protein and LDH levels on the pleural fluid and obtain other laboratory tests only if the fluid turns out to be an exudate. In one study, of 320 pleural fluid specimens submitted for analysis, 83 were found to be transudative. For these 83 effusions, 725 additional laboratory tests had been ordered, increasing both cost and the incidence of false-positive tests (seven of nine).[59] If one suspects initially that the patient has an exudate or if the fluid turns out to be an exudate, specimens can then be sent for cytology, amylase, glucose, cell count and differential, and cultures.

DIFFERENTIATING EXUDATIVE PLEURAL EFFUSIONS

Once it has been determined that the patient has an exudative pleural effusion, one should attempt to determine which of the diseases listed in Table 68.1 is responsible for the effusion, remembering that pneumonia, malignancy, and pulmonary embolism account for the great majority of all exudative pleural effusions. In all patients with undiagnosed exudative pleural effusions, the appearance of the fluid should be noted, and the pleural fluid protein and LDH levels (if not already obtained), glucose level, differential cell count, and microbiologic and cytologic studies should be measured or carried out.[60] In selected patients, other tests on the pleural fluid, such as pH, amylase level, antinuclear antibody (ANA) level, rheumatoid factor level, adenosine deaminase (ADA) level, lipid analysis, and so forth, may be of value. However, it is certainly not cost-effective to obtain all these tests routinely on patients with undiagnosed exudative pleural effusions.

Appearance of Pleural Fluid

The gross appearance of the pleural fluid should always be described and its odor noted. If the pleural fluid smells putrid, the patient has a bacterial infection (probably anaerobic) of the pleural space. If the fluid smells like urine, the patient probably has a urinothorax. If the pleural fluid is bloody, a pleural fluid hematocrit should be obtained. If the pleural fluid hematocrit is greater than 50% that of the peripheral blood, the patient has a hemothorax and the physician should strongly consider inserting chest tubes. If the pleural fluid hematocrit is less than 1%, the blood in the pleural fluid has no clinical significance. If the pleural fluid hematocrit is between 1% and 50%, the patient most likely has malignant pleural disease, a pulmonary embolus, or a traumatically induced pleural effusion.[61]

The supernatant of the pleural fluid should be examined if the pleural fluid is turbid, milky, or bloody. If the pleural fluid is turbid when originally obtained, but the turbidity clears with centrifugation, the turbidity is due to cells or debris in the pleural fluid. If the turbidity persists after centrifugation, the patient probably has a chylothorax or a pseudochylothorax. These two entities can be differentiated by the patient's history, examination of the sediment for cholesterol crystals, and lipid analysis of the supernatant. With chylothorax, the disease process is acute, the pleural surfaces are not thickened, there are no cholesterol crystals present, and the pleural fluid triglyceride level is usually above 110 mg/dL (1.24 mmol/L).[62] With pseudochylothorax, the disease process is chronic, the pleural surfaces are thickened, there may be cholesterol crystals, and the pleural fluid triglyceride level is usually not elevated. (For further discussion of chylothorax, see Chapter 69).

Pleural Fluid Protein

The pleural fluid protein level tends to be elevated to a comparable degree with all exudative pleural effusions and is therefore not generally useful in the differential diagnosis of an exudative pleural effusion. However, if the protein level is above 5.0 g/dL, the likelihood of the diagnosis of tuberculous pleurisy is increased. If the pleural fluid protein level is very low (<0.5 g/dL), the patient probably has a urinothorax, an effusion secondary to peritoneal dialysis, a leak of cerebrospinal fluid into the pleural space, or an effusion secondary to the misplacement of a central intravascular line.

Pleural Fluid Lactate Dehydrogenase

Whereas pleural liquid protein and LDH arise from filtration from serum and thus serve as indicators of vascular permeability, LDH, as an intracellular enzyme, may also indicate the degree of cell turnover within the pleural space. The pleural fluid LDH level is increased to a comparable degree in patients with all categories of exudative pleural effusions and therefore is of no utility in the differential diagnosis of exudative pleural effusion.[46] Likewise, the pleural fluid LDH isoenzymes are of limited use in the differential diagnosis of exudative pleural effusions.[63] However, pleural fluid LDH concentration should be measured every time a diagnostic thoracentesis is performed, because the level of LDH in the pleural fluid reflects the degree of inflammation in the pleural space. If the pleural fluid LDH concentration increases with serial thoracenteses, the degree of inflammation in the pleural space is worsening and the physician should be more aggressive in pursuing the diagnosis. Alternatively, if the pleural fluid LDH level decreases with serial thoracenteses, the pleural disease is resolving and observation of the patient is indicated.[64]

Pleural Fluid Glucose

A low glucose concentration probably indicates the coexistence of two abnormalities: a thickened, infiltrated pleura leading to an impaired diffusion of glucose into the pleural space plus increased metabolic activity leading to increased glucose utilization within the pleural space. The glucose level should be measured in all undiagnosed exudative pleural effusions because the demonstration of a reduced pleural fluid glucose level (<60 mg/dL, or 3.33 mmol/L) narrows the diagnostic possibilities to seven: parapneumonic effusion, malignant effusion, tuberculous effusion, rheumatoid effusion, hemothorax, paragonimiasis, and Churg-Strauss syndrome.[64] If a patient with a parapneumonic effusion has a pleural fluid glucose level below 40 mg/dL (2.22 mmol/L), tube thoracostomy should be considered. Many patients with rheumatoid pleural effusions have a pleural fluid glucose level below 30 mg/dL (1.66 mmol/L).[65] In contrast, most patients with pleural effusion secondary to systemic lupus erythematosus will have a pleural fluid glucose level above 80 mg/dL (4.44 mmol/L).[66] Patients with malignant pleural disease and a low pleural fluid glucose level usually have a positive pleural fluid cytology, pleural biopsy, or both. In addition, their prognosis is poor, with a mean survival of less than 2 months.[67]

Pleural Fluid White Cell Count and Differential

Pleural liquid that is submitted for white cell count and differential should be sent in a tube with an anticoagulant to prevent the cells from clumping.[68] Of note, however, the absolute pleural fluid white blood cell count is of limited value. A pleural fluid white blood cell count of 1000/μL roughly separates transudative from exudative pleural effusion. Pleural fluid white blood cell counts above 10,000/μL are most common with empyemas and parapneumonic effusions, but are also seen with pancreatitis, pulmonary embolism, and collagen vascular diseases and, occasionally, with malignancy and tuberculosis.[61]

The differential cell count on the pleural fluid is much more useful than the white cell count itself. When the pleural fluid differential cell count is performed, the cells should be partitioned into the following categories: polymorphonuclear leukocytes, eosinophils, small lymphocytes, mesothelial cells, and other mononuclear cells. Pleural effusions due to an acute disease process such as pneumonia, pulmonary embolization, pancreatitis, intra-abdominal abscess, or early tuberculosis contain predominantly polymorphonuclear leukocytes. Pleural effusions due to a chronic disease process contain predominantly mononuclear cells.

Pleural fluid eosinophilia (10% or more eosinophils by differential count) is most commonly due to air or blood in the pleural space. Interleukin (IL)-5 appears to be an important factor because the number and percentage of eosinophils in the pleural space are closely correlated with the pleural liquid IL-5 levels.[69] Occasionally, no pleural fluid eosinophils are found in the initial thoracentesis, but many eosinophils are seen in a subsequent thoracentesis, most likely due to a small pneumothorax caused by the initial thoracentesis.[70] With traumatic hemothorax, pleural fluid eosinophilia does not occur until the second week. The eosinophilia appears to be due to production of IL-5 by CD4+ T-cells within the pleural space.[71] At times, the pleural fluid eosinophilia associated with a hemothorax can lead to eosinophilia in the peripheral blood.[72] The bloody pleural effusion complicating pulmonary embolism frequently contains many eosinophils.[73] With pneumothorax, pleural eosinophilia appears within 3 days of the pneumothorax and reaches a peak after 6 days.[74] Again, the degree of pleural fluid eosinophilia is correlated with the pleural fluid IL-5 level.[74]

After excluding air or blood as the underlying cause, the etiologies of 392 cases of eosinophilic pleural effusions have been reported as follows: idiopathic, 40%; malignancy, 17%; parapneumonic, 13%; tuberculosis, 6%; pulmonary embolism, 4%; transudates, 8%; and other, 13%.[75] If the etiology of the eosinophilia is not evident, several unusual diagnoses should be considered. Benign asbestos pleural effusions are frequently eosinophilic. In one series, 15 of 29 patients (52%) with benign asbestos pleural effusions had pleural fluid eosinophilia.[70] Patients with pleural effusions secondary to drug reactions (nitrofurantoin or dantrolene) typically have pleural fluid eosinophilia.[64] The pleural fluid of patients with pleural paragonimiasis is typically eosinophilic with low glucose, low pH, and high LDH levels.[76] Churg-Strauss syndrome is the only other disease that produces this constellation of pleural fluid findings.[77]

Mesothelial cells line the pleural cavities. It is unusual to find mesothelial cells in effusions due to tuberculosis; in one series of 65 patients with tuberculous pleuritis, only 1 patient had more than 1 mesothelial cell/1000 cells.[78] However, the absence of mesothelial cells is also common with other conditions in which the pleura becomes coated with fibrin, such as a complicated parapneumonic effusion.

The demonstration that more than 50% of the white blood cells in an exudative pleural effusion are small lymphocytes indicates that the patient probably has a malignant or a tuberculous pleural effusion. Ninety of 96 exudative pleural effusions (94%) in two series with more than 50% small lymphocytes were due to tuberculosis or malignant disease.[61,79] Because these two diseases can be diagnosed with needle biopsy of the pleura, the presence of pleural fluid lymphocytosis should alert the physician to consider needle biopsy of the pleura for diagnosis. In general, separation of pleural lymphocytes into T and B lymphocytes has not been useful diagnostically, because most lymphocytic effusions contain mostly T cells (CD4+) whether the diagnosis is malignancy or tuberculosis.[80,81] Such partitioning can be useful diagnostically, however, when a diagnosis of chronic lymphocytic leukemia or lymphoma is suspected. With these diseases, the pleural lymphocytes are usually of B-cell origin.[82,83]

Pleural Fluid Cytology

A pleural fluid specimen from every patient with an undiagnosed exudative pleural effusion should be sent for cytopathologic studies. The first pleural fluid cytologic study is positive for malignant cells in up to 60% of the effusions caused by pleural malignancy.[61] If three separate specimens are submitted, up to 90% with pleural malignancy have positive cytopathology. The percentage of cases in which cytologic study of the pleural fluid establishes the diagnosis of a malignant pleural effusion ranges from 40% to 87%.[61,84,85] The frequency of positive pleural fluid cytologic tests is dependent on the tumor type. For example, less than 25% of patients with Hodgkin's disease have positive cytology,[86] whereas most patients with adenocarcinomas have positive cytology.[85] The percentage of positive diagnoses is higher if both cell blocks and smears are prepared by standard protocols and examined by an experienced cytologist.[87] Each additional sample may increase diagnostic yield in part by providing a higher percentage of fresher cells, as older degenerated cells are largely removed by the earlier thoracenteses. During thoracoscopy, pleural lavage has been found to increase the diagnostic yield, perhaps by harvesting more fresh cells for analysis.[88] The percentage of positive diagnoses is obviously dependent on the skill of the cytologist.

Other Diagnostic Tests for Malignancy

Cytology may be nondiagnostic either because of a problem of specificity (e.g., the malignant cells cannot be differentiated from reactive mesothelial cells and "atypical" benign cells) or because of a problem of sensitivity (e.g., the malignant cells are rare). Several assays are being evaluated for their ability to increase the specificity of cytology for diagnosis of malignancy. Fluorescent in situ hybridization with chromosome-specific probes can confirm abnormal numbers of specific chromosomes (aneuploidy), thereby confirming that abnormal cells are indeed malignant.[89] Chromosomal analysis can be useful for the diagnosis of pleural leukemia or lymphoma.[90] With greater understanding of specific malignant molecular abnormalities, similar cytogenetic approaches may become increasingly useful for diagnosing solid tumors involving the pleura, such as by detection of loss of heterozygosity[91] or by comparative genomic hybridization.[92] Argyrophilic nucleolar organizing regions, areas of nuclear deoxyribonucleic acid (DNA) coding for ribosomal ribonucleic acid, are found in greater numbers and a larger size in malignant cells compared to benign reactive cells, although the degree of overlap limits the diagnostic value.[93] In addition, many assays have been tested in an attempt to increase sensitivity for the diagnosis of malignancy. Many of these tests, such as the detection of tumor markers in pleural liquid, are limited by their lack of specificity for malignant effusions. Future directions, such as detection by a polymerase chain reaction (PCR)–based assay of tumor-specific markers, such as those of telomerase, may hold promise,[94] although nonspecificity is always a concern.[95]

Immunohistochemical and Other Studies for Diagnosing Malignancy

Immunohistochemical stains of malignant cells are used to confirm a diagnosis and to specify tumor type, with many new markers recently available.[87,96] The most common application of immunocytochemistry is to distinguish adenocarcinoma from mesothelioma. In the recent past, a panel of antibodies was used that generally stained adenocarcinoma but not mesothelioma. Currently, several antibodies have been introduced that generally stain mesothelioma but not adenocarcinoma. Thus, adenocarcinoma can be identified and separated from mesothelioma or reactive mesothelial cells by its positive staining with a panel of antibodies to epithelial markers (B72.3, Ber-EP4, or Leu-M1); mesothelioma will stain with antibodies to calretinin (a calcium-binding protein), mesothelin (a glycoprotein identified on the surface of mesothelial cells), or specific cytokeratins (cytokeratin 5/6)[87,96] (see Chapter 70).

Culture and Bacteriologic Stains

Pleural fluid from patients with undiagnosed exudative pleural effusions should be cultured for bacteria (both aerobically and anaerobically), mycobacteria, and fungi. A Gram stain should also be obtained. In the case of a probable complicated parapneumonic effusion with an initial negative Gram stain, the sediment of the pleural fluid should be stained because the bacteria will be precipitated in the sediment along with the white blood cells and the debris.

One potentially useful adjunct is detection of bacterial antigens by countercurrent immunoelectrophoresis[97] or latex agglutination,[98] or of bacterial DNA by PCR.[99] The antigen-specific assays may be especially useful in children, whose common pathogens, *Staphylococcus aureus*, *Streptococcus pneumoniae*, and *Haemophilus influenzae*, have antigens available for identification. The antigens for anaerobic bacteria, the more common pathogen in adults, are not available.

OTHER DIAGNOSTIC TESTS FOR PLEURAL FLUID

Pleural Fluid pH and Pco₂

The pleural fluid pH can be reduced to less than 7.20 by 10 different conditions: complicated parapneumonic effusion, esophageal rupture, rheumatoid pleuritis, tuberculous pleuritis, malignant pleural disease, hemothorax, systemic acidosis, paragonimiasis, lupus pleuritis, and urinothorax.[64] The decreased pleural fluid pH appears to result from lactic acid and carbon dioxide accumulation in the pleural fluid.[100] The pleural fluid pH is most useful in determining whether chest tubes should be inserted in patients with parapneumonic effusions.[101] A fall in the pleural fluid pH appears to be a sensitive indicator that the patient has a highly inflammatory parapneumonic pleural effusion that will require drainage.

The routine measurement of pleural fluid pH is recommended only in patients with parapneumonic effusions. In general, pleural fluids with a low pH also have a low glucose and a high LDH level.[100] In many institutions, pleural fluid glucose is used as an alternative to the pH measurement. When the pleural fluid pH is used as a diagnostic test, it must be measured with the same care as arterial pH. The fluid should be collected anaerobically in a heparinized syringe and placed on ice. If the sample is left open to air, a spuriously high pH value can be obtained because of the rapid loss of carbon dioxide. The pH must be measured with a blood gas machine; a pH meter or indicator paper is not sufficiently accurate.[102]

Pleural Fluid Amylase

The pleural fluid amylase is elevated in patients with pleural effusions secondary to esophageal perforation, pancreatic disease, or malignant disease. However, because such a small percentage of effusions are due to esophageal perforation or pancreatic disease, the routine measurement of pleural fluid amylase is not indicated.[103] In the case of esophageal rupture, the origin of the amylase is the salivary glands.[104] In animal models of esophageal rupture, the pleural fluid amylase concentration is elevated within 2 hours of esophageal rupture.[105] In effusions due to pancreaticopleural fistulas, the amylase concentration is extremely high (>4000 IU/mL), reflective of the concentrations in pancreatic secretions.[106] In approximately 10% of malignant effusions, the pleural fluid amylase level is mildly elevated. The site of the primary tumor in such patients is usually not the pancreas.[107] Malignancy can be differentiated from pancreatic disease with amylase isoenzymes because the amylase with malignant effusions is primarily of the salivary type.[108]

Tests for Collagen Vascular Diseases

About 5% of patients with rheumatoid arthritis[109] and 50% of patients with systemic lupus erythematosus[110] have a pleural effusion sometime during the course of their disease. At times, the effusions may be the first manifestation of the disease; therefore, these diagnostic possibilities should be considered in patients with undiagnosed exudative pleural effusion.

Measurement of the ANA titer is the best screening test for lupus pleuritis, although it is now evident that a positive pleural fluid ANA is not specific for the diagnosis. Although all patients with lupus pleuritis have a positive pleural liquid ANA (>1:40), the finding of a positive ANA has been found in between 11% and 27% of all other effusions.[111] In one prospective study, neither the titer of ANA, the ratio of pleural to plasma ANA, or the pattern of staining increased the specificity for systemic lupus erythematosus.[112] In fact, a positive pleural fluid ANA in patients without systemic lupus erythematosus may be associated with malignancy.[112]

When a rheumatoid pleural effusion is suspected, the clinical picture usually establishes the diagnosis. If any question exists, the level of rheumatoid factor in the pleural fluid should be measured. Only patients with rheumatoid pleuritis have a pleural fluid rheumatoid factor titer equal to or greater than 1:320 and equal to or greater than the serum titer.[113]

Adenosine Deaminase

ADA, a product of activated lymphocytes, catalyzes the conversion of adenosine to inosine and is important for normal immune function. The pleural fluid ADA levels are elevated in almost all patients with tuberculous pleuritis, but not with other conditions even when associated with lymphocytic effusions.[114,115] Despite earlier concerns about false-negative values in human immunodeficiency virus (HIV)–positive patients, ADA appears to retain its usefulness in patients with HIV.[116] An occasional patient with empyema, lymphoma, or leukemia may have elevated pleural fluid ADA levels; however, these entities should be relatively easy to differentiate from tuberculosis clinically. Because it is a highly sensitive test, the ADA can be a useful test to exclude the diagnosis of tuberculosis when the ADA level is low (<40 U/L).[117]

Interferon-γ

Interferon-γ, a T-cell lymphokine, plays a critical role in the effective clinical response to *Mycobacterium tuberculosis*. Pleural liquid interferon-γ is elevated almost exclusively in tuberculous effusions.[118]

Molecular Techniques for Diagnosis of *Mycobacterium tuberculosis*

Four molecular techniques are now available for diagnosis of *M. tuberculosis*: PCR to detect specific mycobacterial DNA sequences in clinical specimens (pleural liquid or biopsy), nucleic acid probes to identify the organism in culture, restriction fragment length polymorphism to compare strains in epidemiologic studies, and gene-based susceptibility studies to screen for known genes associated with drug resistance.[119]

In theory, PCR tests have a great potential for providing a rapid, highly sensitive and specific diagnosis of mycobacterial infection. In practice, PCR amplification of clinical samples has been limited by a low sensitivity, often little better than culture itself.[120] The decreased sensitivity may be due to degradation of the target DNA by sample processing or by inhibitors of amplification in clinical fluids. Before wide application of PCR assays, considerations will also include its cost and its current inability to identify antibiotic resistance of the organism. In the future, molecular techniques for diagnosis of tuberculosis and other slow-growing microorganisms will likely prove increasingly important.

Other Enzymes and Proteins

Over the past several years, many articles have been written on the utility of measuring various enzymes and proteins in the pleural space, including hyaluronic acid, lysozyme or its components, mucoproteins, mucopolysaccharides, beta$_2$-microglobulin, alpha-fetoprotein, aldolase, glutamic oxaloacetic transaminase, glutamic pyruvic transaminase, and alkaline and acid phosphatases. None has proved of value in the differential diagnosis or management of patients with pleural effusions.[64]

USEFUL IMAGING STUDIES IN PATIENTS WITH SUSPECTED PLEURAL DISEASE

Radiographic Studies

The possibility of a pleural effusion should be considered whenever a patient with an abnormal chest radiograph is evaluated. Two main factors influence the distribution of free fluid in the pleural space. First, the fluid collects in the most dependent part of the thoracic cavity because the lung is less dense than the pleural fluid. Second, because of their elastic recoil, the lobes of the lung maintain their traditional shape at all stages of collapse.

When the patient is upright, the fluid first accumulates between the inferior surface of the lower lobe and the diaphragm. If there is less than 75 mL of fluid, it may occupy only this position without overflowing into the costophrenic sinuses. When more fluid accumulates, it spills over into the posterior costophrenic angle and obliterates the posterior part of the diaphragm on the lateral projection. The possibility of a pleural effusion should be suspected whenever the posterior part of one or both diaphragms is obscured. The presence of a clinically significant amount of free pleural fluid can be excluded if both posterior costophrenic angles are clear.

When there are larger amounts of pleural fluid, the lateral costophrenic angle on the posteroanterior radiograph becomes blunted. Collins and associates[121] demonstrated that at least 175 mL of pleural fluid had to be injected into the pleural space of cadavers before the lateral costophrenic angle was blunted. In some of their cases, more than 500 mL of pleural fluid could be present without blunting the lateral costophrenic angle. As more fluid accumulates, the entire outline of the diaphragm on the affected side is lost, and the fluid extends upward around the anterior, lateral, and posterior thoracic walls, producing opacification of the lung base and the typical meniscus shape of the fluid.

The changes just discussed are suggestive rather than diagnostic of the presence of pleural fluid. Lateral decubi-

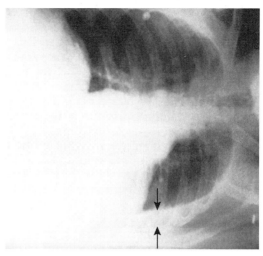

Figure 68.5 Left lateral decubitus chest radiograph demonstrating the presence of free pleural fluid. The amount of pleural fluid can be semiquantified by measuring the distance between the two *arrows*.

tus radiographs or ultrasonic examination should be obtained in most instances when free pleural fluid is suspected. If the entire hemithorax is opacified, decubitus radiographs are of no use, because there is no air-containing lung in the hemithorax. The basis for the use of the lateral decubitus view is that free fluid gravitates to the most dependent part of the pleural space. When a patient is placed in the lateral recumbent position, the free pleural fluid on the dependent side accumulates between the chest wall and the lung (Fig. 68.5). As little as 5 mL of pleural fluid can be demonstrated with properly exposed decubitus radiographs.[122] The amount of pleural fluid can be semiquantitated by measuring the distance between the inner border of the chest wall and the outer border of the lung (see Fig. 68.5). As already stated, when this distance is less than 10 mm, the amount of pleural fluid is small, and a diagnostic thoracentesis is usually not attempted.

Pleural fluid may become encapsulated by adhesions anywhere between the parietal and the visceral pleurae or in the interlobar fissures. Such loculation occurs most frequently in association with conditions that cause intense pleural inflammation, such as complicated parapneumonic effusion or tuberculous pleuritis. When the loculation is situated between the lung and the chest wall, there is a characteristic radiographic picture. The loculation is D-shaped, with the base of the "D" against the chest wall and the smooth convexity protruding inward toward the lung. The absence of air bronchograms helps differentiate a loculated pleural effusion from a parenchymal infiltrate. A definite diagnosis of loculated pleural effusion is best established by ultrasonography or computed tomography (CT).

Ultrasound

One way to document and locate loculated pleural fluid is with ultrasound. In the presence of pleural fluid, the proximal echoes from the skin, intercostal muscles, and parietal pleura are separated from the distal echoes arising from the visceral pleura and the lung by a central echo-free space. The advantages of ultrasound over CT are the ease and speed with which the examination can be performed, the lack of ionizing radiation, the relatively low cost, and the ability to provide continuous guidance for thoracentesis or pleural biopsy.[123,124]

The appropriate site for a thoracentesis can be identified using ultrasound, although its routine use is probably not cost-effective. If a patient has a moderate or large effusion, ultrasound is indicated only if no fluid is obtained after two or three attempts.[125] When ultrasound is used to identify the site for thoracentesis, it is important to perform the thoracentesis at the time of the ultrasonic examination. If the skin is marked and the patient returned to his or her room, thoracentesis is frequently unsuccessful, because the relationship between the skin and the pleural fluid may have changed. In addition, when the thoracentesis is performed at the time of the ultrasonic examination, there is immediate feedback that is valuable in improving the skill of the ultrasonographer.

Computed Tomography

CT is currently the best way to visualize the pleural space.[124,126] CT of the chest has its greatest utility in distinguishing parenchymal and pleural abnormalities. With current protocols involving the rapid injection of intravenous contrast medium, the unaerated perfused lung parenchyma will enhance, whereas the pleural abnormality will not.[127]

Chest CT is quite useful in distinguishing a parenchymal lung abscess located near the chest wall from an empyema with an air-fluid level. The most distinctive features are the margins of the abnormality. With empyema, the cavity walls are of uniform thickness both internally and externally, and the adjacent lung is usually compressed. The angle of contact with the chest wall may be obtuse. In addition, most empyemas have a lenticular shape and demonstrate the "split pleura" sign (Fig. 68.6A).[128] With lung abscess, the walls of the cavity are not of uniform thickness, and the adjacent lung is not compressed. The angle of contact with the chest wall may be acute (Fig. 68.6B).

In diffuse pleural disease, chest CT is useful in distinguishing malignant from benign causes. Features associated with malignancy include circumferential pleural thickening, pleural nodules, parietal thickening greater than 1 cm, and mediastinal pleural involvement.[129] The distinction of metastatic disease from mesothelioma can be difficult, although hilar adenopathy is more common with metastatic disease.[124] In patients with pleural abnormalities consistent with malignancy, CT-guided cutting-needle biopsies may supplant closed pleural biopsy for diagnosis.[130]

Magnetic Resonance Imaging

Pleural effusions generally have long T1 and T2 values on magnetic resonance imaging. The intensity of pleural effusions is therefore low to extremely low on T1-weighted images.[124] However, at the present time, magnetic resonance imaging of the chest is less satisfactory than ultrasound or CT in identifying the presence of pleural fluid. It is possible that, with improved magnetic resonance technology, the characteristics of pleural fluid can be determined noninvasively. At the present time, respiratory and cardiac

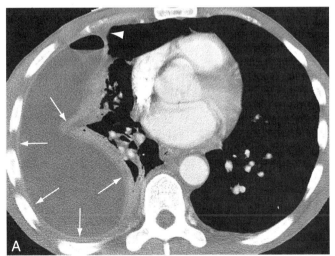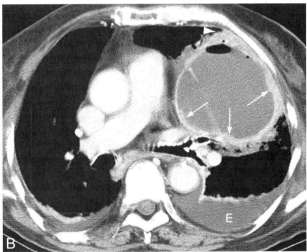

Figure 68.6 Typical CT features of a pleural empyema versus a lung abscess. **A,** Axial computed tomography (CT) scan through the lower thorax in a patient with fever and pleuritic chest pain shows features typical of empyema, including the formation of obtuse angles between the lesion and chest wall (*arrowhead*), a lenticular shape, a smooth internal surface (*arrows*), and mass effect on surrounding structures (note leftward shift of the heart and great vessels). Note enhancement of the parietal and visceral pleura, representing the "split pleura" sign (*arrows*) and the presence of an air-fluid level, indicating the presence of a bronchopleural fistula. **B,** Axial CT scan through the mid-thorax in a patient with fever and cough productive of foul-smelling sputum shows features typical of a pulmonary abscess, including the formation of acute angles between the lesion and the chest wall (*arrowhead*); a round shape; a thick, irregular internal surface (*arrows*); and relatively little mass effect on surrounding structures, despite the large size of the lesion. The latter occurs because pulmonary abscesses tend to destroy adjacent lung more than they displace it. Note the presence of an associated pleural effusion (E). (Courtesy of Michael B. Gotway, MD, Department of Radiology, University of California, San Francisco.)

motion are the major limitations in evaluating specific intensity patterns of fluid collections of various compositions.

Positron Emission Tomography

Positron emission tomography visualizes tissues that are metabolically active by their concentration of the radioisotope ^{18}F-fluorodeoxyglucose. Because most malignant cells have a higher metabolic rate than nonmalignant cells, positron emission tomography can help differentiate malignant from benign lesions, help stage patients with malignancy, and help identify recurrence.[124]

Other Imaging Studies

Pulmonary embolism (see Chapter 48) is one of the leading causes of pleural effusion. The evaluation of a patient with a pleural effusion for pulmonary embolism can begin with a Doppler ultrasound of the lower extremities. If the ultrasound identifies thrombus, the patient can then be treated for thromboembolic disease. If it is negative, the patient may still have a pulmonary embolism. The standard approach has been to proceed to lung ventilation-perfusion scanning. However, the interpretation of the perfusion lung scan is difficult in patients with pleural fluid because of shifting of the fluid when the patient moves from the supine position for the perfusion scan to the upright position for the ventilation scan.[131] Spiral CT angiography instead is highly sensitive and specific for pulmonary emboli in the proximal, segmental pulmonary arteries.[132,133] In contrast to lung scanning, spiral CT can establish alternate diagnoses as well.[133] Where spiral CT is not available, lung scanning can be used, perhaps after efforts to improve accuracy by withdrawing as much pleural liquid as possible. A diagnostic scan (normal or high probability) can then be used either to exclude the diagnosis or initiate anticoagulation. If nondiagnostic (e.g., of low or intermediate probability), the scan should be followed by pulmonary angiography.

INVASIVE TESTS IN PATIENTS WITH UNDIAGNOSED EXUDATIVE PLEURAL EFFUSIONS

In the patient with an undiagnosed exudative pleural effusion, there are several invasive tests that might be considered, including needle biopsy of the pleura, bronchoscopy, thoracoscopy, and open biopsy of the pleura. It is important to remember that no diagnosis is ever established for approximately 20% of all exudative pleural effusions and that many resolve spontaneously, leaving no residua.[117,134] In patients with undiagnosed exudative pleural effusions, three factors should influence the vigor with which one pursues the diagnosis with invasive tests:

1. The symptoms and the clinical course of the patient. If the symptoms of the patient are minimal or if the symptoms are improving with time, a less aggressive approach is indicated.
2. The trend of the pleural fluid LDH level with time. If the pleural fluid LDH increases with serial thoracenteses, a more aggressive approach is indicated.
3. The attitude of the patient. If the patient is anxious, and eager to know the cause of the pleural effusion, an aggressive approach should be taken.

Needle Biopsy of the Pleura

Small specimens of the parietal pleura can be obtained with needle biopsy. The needles most commonly used for this procedure are the Cope needle and the Abrams needle.[64,135] Because needle biopsy of the pleura is useful mainly to establish the diagnosis of malignant or tuberculous pleural effusions, this procedure should be considered when one of these diagnoses is suspected.

In malignant pleural disease, the needle biopsy of the pleura will be positive in 40% to 60% of patients.[134,136] Overall, the yield from pleural fluid cytology tends to be higher. In one series of 281 patients with malignant pleural effusions, the pleural biopsy was positive in 43%, whereas the pleural fluid cytology was positive in 58%.[134] In only 7% was the pleural biopsy positive and the pleural fluid cytology negative.[134] However, in a second series of 189 patients with malignant pleural effusions, the pleural biopsy was positive in 60%, whereas the cytology was positive in 52%. Both pleural fluid cytology and biopsy were positive in 33%, only the biopsy was positive in 27%, and only the cytology was positive in 19%.[136] A prudent approach to the patient with a suspected malignant pleural effusion is to obtain a pleural biopsy only if the cytology obtained at the time of the initial diagnostic thoracentesis is nondiagnostic.

Needle biopsy of the pleura has its greatest utility in diagnosing tuberculous pleuritis. The initial biopsy is positive for granulomas in 50% to 80% of patients.[137] The demonstration of granulomas on the pleural biopsy is virtually diagnostic of tuberculous pleuritis; caseous necrosis or acid-fast bacilli need not be demonstrated, although on rare occasions fungal diseases, sarcoidosis, or rheumatoid pleuritis can produce granulomatous pleuritis. When tuberculous pleuritis is suspected, a portion of the pleural biopsy specimen should be cultured for mycobacteria. In one series of 21 patients with tuberculous pleuritis, either the microscopic examination or the biopsy culture was positive in 20 of the 21 patients (95%).[138] If the initial biopsy is nondiagnostic and the patient has tuberculous pleuritis, a second biopsy will be diagnostic 10% to 40% of the time.[137,139]

The greatest value of needle biopsy for a patient with tuberculosis is obtaining material for culture of *M. tuberculosis* for the determination of drug susceptibility. Often, the presentation of a patient with a recent purified protein derivative conversion and an exudative pleural effusion with lymphocytosis is classic and unlikely to be due to any diagnosis other than tuberculous pleurisy. The diagnosis can be further supported by measurements, where available, of pleural fluid ADA or interferon-γ. In those cases, treatment for tuberculosis can be offered with confidence without needle biopsy confirmation. However, when the patient may have been exposed to drug-resistant organisms, needle biopsy will increase the likelihood of obtaining organisms for culture and is recommended. In cases of pleural tuberculosis, sputum induction can be useful for culturing the organism, even when the chest radiograph shows no pulmonary involvement; it was recently shown to have a yield similar to culture of the pleural biopsy (52% vs. 62%).[140]

The two major complications of needle biopsy of the pleura are pneumothorax and bleeding. Pneumothoraces large enough to require a chest tube occur in only about 1% of pleural biopsies.[134,141] It is likely that many pneumothoraces develop because of leakage of air through the biopsy needle and do not necessarily indicate puncture of the lung. A hemothorax can result if an intercostal artery or vein is inadvertently biopsied. In one series a fatal hemothorax occurred in 2 of 227 biopsy procedures.[141] The pleural biopsy needle can also be mistakenly inserted into the liver, spleen, or kidney, which can lead to hemorrhage in these organs. However, bleeding complications are rare.

If no diagnosis is obtained after routine laboratory tests, including cytology and one needle biopsy of the pleura, what can be said concerning the patient? Poe and coworkers[141] followed 143 such patients for 12 to 72 months, during which time 29 patients were diagnosed with malignant pleural disease and one patient with tuberculous pleuritis. In all 29 cases in which malignancy was eventually diagnosed, the diagnosis of malignant neoplasm was suggested by clinical criteria such as weight loss, constitutional symptoms, or a history of previous cancer. These authors concluded that most patients with undiagnosed exudative pleural effusions in whom the clinical picture does not suggest malignancy are best managed by observation. In those with symptoms suggestive of malignancy, thoracoscopy is probably the procedure of choice.

Bronchoscopy

Another procedure that should be considered in the patient with an undiagnosed pleural effusion is bronchoscopy (see Chapter 22). If the patient has an associated parenchymal lesion or hemoptysis, fiberoptic bronchoscopy will provide a diagnosis in nearly 75% of cases.[142] If the patient has neither a parenchymal abnormality nor hemoptysis, a diagnosis for the pleural effusion is established less than 10% of the time.[143] At the present time, CT scan of the chest should be performed in all patients with undiagnosed exudative pleural effusions. Bronchoscopy should then be performed only if the CT scan demonstrates parenchymal abnormalities or if the patient has hemoptysis. At the time of bronchoscopy, special attention is paid to those portions of the lung in which the parenchymal abnormalities were demonstrated.

Pleuroscopy or Video-Assisted Thoracoscopic Surgery

Pleuroscopy and video-assisted thoracoscopic surgery are discussed fully in Chapter 23. Pleuroscopy may be useful diagnostically in patients in whom the origin of a pleural effusion remains unclear after routine fluid analysis and needle biopsy of the pleura. In many cases, especially for the evaluation of malignancy, pleuroscopy may supplant needle biopsy because of a greater diagnostic yield and the added ability to provide pleural sclerosis. Pleuroscopy can be performed by pulmonologists using local anesthesia and conscious sedation for direct visualization of the pleural surfaces, tissue sampling, and pleurodesis; thoracoscopy performed by thoracic surgeons, generally referred to as video-assisted thoracoscopic surgery, utilizes general anesthesia and single-lung ventilation by double-lumen intubation and allows greater access to the pleura and lung for surgical procedures.[144]

Two separate studies, each with 102 patients, report diagnostic yields of 93%[145] and 80%.[146] However, when the studies are examined in detail, one finds that the only diagnosis that is definitely established with thoracoscopy is malignancy. Thoracoscopy is efficient at establishing the diagnosis of malignancy. In the two series,[145,146] the diagnosis was established in 99 of 117 patients (85%) with malignancy, including 51 of 56 (91%) of those with mesothelioma.

Which patients with undiagnosed pleural effusions should undergo thoracoscopy? A diagnosis can be established in over 80% of patients with malignancy, including those with mesothelioma. Moreover, talc can be insufflated at the time of the procedure, and this will control the effusion in the great majority of patients. Nonetheless, there are minor risks of the procedure, a need for postprocedure chest tube(s), and a procedure cost that should be considered. Pleuroscopy is therefore recommended for the patient with an undiagnosed pleural effusion after diagnostic thoracentesis and needle biopsy of the pleura in whom the diagnosis of malignancy is strongly suspected and in whom one wishes to establish this diagnosis.

Open Biopsy of the Pleura

Thoracotomy with direct biopsy of the pleura provides the best visualization of the pleura and the best biopsy specimens. Nowadays, the less invasive thoracoscopy techniques (pleuroscopy or VATS) can replace thoracotomy in most instances. The main indication for open pleural biopsy is progressive undiagnosed pleural disease that cannot be approached by or has failed to be diagnosed by thoracoscopy. In the past, for example, the diagnosis of malignant mesothelioma was usually made with open biopsy of the pleura, but now the diagnosis can be established in the majority of the cases with thoracoscopy.

It should be emphasized that open pleural biopsy does not always provide a diagnosis in patients with pleural effusions. Douglass and associates[147] reported that thoracotomy failed to provide a specific diagnosis for 7 of 21 patients with undiagnosed pleural effusion. Over the 11-year period from 1962 to 1972, 51 patients with pleural effusion seen at the Mayo Clinic had no diagnosis after an open pleural biopsy.[148] In 31 of these patients (61%), there was no recurrence of the pleural effusion, and no cause ever became apparent. However, 13 of the patients were eventually proved to have malignancy; 6 had lymphoma and 4 had malignant mesothelioma. Thus, observation of patients with undiagnosed pleural effusions is often warranted unless there is compelling reason to pursue the diagnosis of malignancy.

TRANSUDATIVE PLEURAL EFFUSIONS

Transudative pleural effusions frequently accompany many common clinical disorders. It is noteworthy that the primary abnormality in most cases of transudative pleural effusions originates in organs other than the pleura or lungs, especially the heart, liver, and kidneys. This association emphasizes the fact that, although patients may visit their physicians for respiratory complaints, these symptoms may be caused by extrapulmonary disorders. Further discussion of the pulmonary manifestations of primary diseases in extrapulmonary organ systems is found in Chapters 75 to 83.

CONGESTIVE HEART FAILURE

Congestive heart failure is the most common cause of pleural effusion.[64] The incidence of pleural effusion in patients with congestive heart failure is high. In one series of 60 patients with an exacerbation of stable congestive heart failure, chest CT scans demonstrated that 50 patients (83%) had a right-sided pleural effusion and 46 patients had a left-sided effusion. Approximately one third of the effusions had a volume that exceeded 700 mL.[149] In an older autopsy series of 402 patients with congestive heart failure at the Mayo Clinic, 290 of the patients (72%) had pleural effusions with volumes greater than 250 mL.[150]

Pathophysiology

It appears that the pleural fluid that accumulates with congestive heart failure is related to the clearance of pulmonary interstitial fluid across a leaky mesothelium into the pleural space.[8] In studies in which sheep lungs were isolated in situ, volume loading led to an increased transudation across the lung into the pleural space.[9] The pleural fluid had the same protein concentration as that of the lung lymph and the interstitial edema liquid in the lung. The volume of pleural fluid constituted about 25% of all edema formed in the lung.[9] In the clinical situation, patients with congestive heart failure are much more likely to have a pleural effusion if there is radiologically apparent pulmonary edema; the presence of pleural effusions correlates more closely with

the pulmonary venous pressure than with either systemic venous pressure or pulmonary artery pressure.[151]

Clinical Manifestations

Patients with pleural effusion resulting from congestive heart failure usually have symptoms and signs of heart failure, such as dyspnea on exertion, orthopnea, nocturia, peripheral edema, distended neck veins, crackles, and a cardiac gallop. The chest radiograph almost always reveals cardiomegaly in addition to the pleural effusion.

The pleural effusions that occur with congestive heart failure tend to be bilateral, with larger effusions on the right (Fig. 68.7A). On CT imaging, interstitial and alveolar edema can often be detected by the presence of thickened septa and patchy infiltrates (Fig. 68.7B). In an autopsy study of 250 patients with congestive heart failure and pleural effusion, 88% of the patients had bilateral pleural effusions, with the mean volume of pleural fluid in the right pleural space (1084 mL) slightly greater than the mean volume of fluid in the left pleural space (913 mL).[150] Moreover, of the 35 patients who did have unilateral pleural effusions, 46% had either pulmonary embolism or pneumonia.[150] Weiss and Spodick[152] reported that 73% of 51 patients with congestive heart failure had bilateral effusions, 19% had unilateral right-sided effusions, and 9% had unilateral left-sided effusions. In a study of patients with congestive heart failure in which CT was used to estimate pleural liquid volume, 30% of effusions on the right were moderate to large, compared to 17% on the left.[149]

The reason that effusions are generally larger on the right side may lie in the fact that they originate from the larger lung on the right side.[47] In volume-overloaded sheep, the

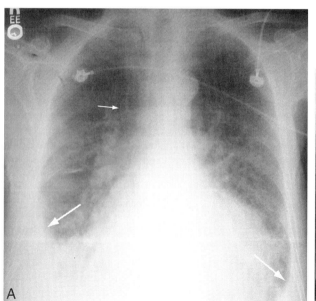

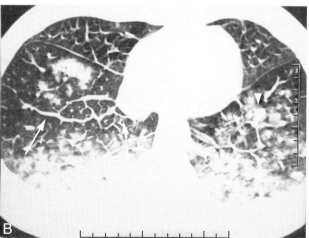

Figure 68.7 Effusion from congestive heart failure. **A,** Frontal chest radiograph in a patient with pulmonary edema shows cardiomegaly, bilateral pleural effusions (*larger arrows*), and central interstitial thickening, including Kerley's A lines (*small arrow*). Note that the right effusion is slightly larger than the left effusion. **B,** High-resolution computed tomography scan in a patient with pulmonary edema shows interstitial edema with bilateral, basilar centrilobular ground-glass opacity nodules (*arrowhead*) and smooth interlobular septal thickening (*arrows*). Bilateral pleural effusions are also present. (Courtesy of Michael B. Gotway, MD, Department of Radiology, University of California, San Francisco.)

rate of liquid leakage from the right lung was higher than from the left, likely due to the larger volume and surface area of the right lung.[9] In another study in awake sheep, there was no difference in the rate of absorption of effusions from the right and left pleural spaces,[27] suggesting that differences in size result from the difference in formation.[27,47]

Although congestive heart failure is by far the most common cause of bilateral pleural effusions, an alternate explanation should be sought if there is no cardiomegaly. In one series of 78 patients with bilateral effusions but a normal-sized heart, only 4% of the effusions were caused by congestive heart failure.[153]

Diagnosis and Management

The diagnosis is usually suggested by the clinical picture of congestive heart failure. The initial decision to be made is whether or not to perform a diagnostic thoracentesis. In a patient with congestive heart failure and a pleural effusion, a diagnostic thoracentesis should be performed if the pleural effusion is unilateral, if bilateral effusions are not comparable in size, if the patient is febrile, if the patient has pleuritic chest pain, or if the patient does not have cardiomegaly.[64] If none of these conditions is met, one can treat the congestive heart failure and perform a diagnostic thoracentesis only if the effusion does not resolve. However, the biochemical characteristics of the pleural fluid may change with diuresis. In one study of 15 patients with congestive heart failure who underwent thoracentesis every 48 hours, the mean pleural fluid protein level increased from 2.3 to 3.5 g/dL and the mean pleural fluid LDH level increased from 176 to 262 U/L.[54]

The pleural fluid from a patient with congestive heart failure is usually a transudate, as defined previously by Light's criteria.[46] However, if the patient has been on diuretics, the pleural fluid protein and LDH ratios may be increased sufficiently that the pleural fluid meets Light's exudative criteria. A similar phenomenon has been described in the ascites literature.[154] The LDH ratio can also increase if intrapleural LDH increases due to injury from repeated taps and if serum LDH falls when diuresis reduces liver congestion.[154] Generally, if the effusion protein and LDH values meet Light's criteria for an exudate, it is only by a small amount.[58] The transudative nature of the pleural fluids can be established in such patients if the serum minus the pleural fluid protein level is greater than 3.1 g/dL.[54] If congestive heart failure is suspected, the most cost-effective approach to diagnosis is to order only protein and LDH levels initially. Other tests are ordered only if the fluid turns out to be an exudate.[59]

Patients with congestive heart failure and pleural effusion should be treated with afterload reduction, diuretics, and inotropes, as needed. When the heart failure is successfully managed, the pleural effusion usually resolves. If the patient is markedly dyspneic when first evaluated, a therapeutic thoracentesis to relieve the dyspnea should be considered. Rarely, despite intensive therapy of the congestive heart failure, a patient has persistent large effusions. If such patients are dyspneic and if their dyspnea is relieved by a therapeutic thoracentesis, consideration can be given to controlling the effusions with a pleurodesis using a sclerosing agent, such as doxycycline or talc slurry[155]; further details about pleurodesis are provided in Chapter 70.

PERICARDIAL DISEASE

There is a high incidence of pleural effusion in patients with pericardial disease. In one series of 35 patients with constrictive pericarditis, 60% of the patients had radiologically demonstrable pleural effusions.[156] Weiss and Spodick[157] reviewed 124 patients with pericardial disease and found that 35 (28%) had a pleural effusion. In this series the pleural effusions tended to be left sided. Of the 35 patients, 21 had only a left-sided pleural effusion, 2 had only a right-sided pleural effusion, and the remaining 12 were bilateral. However, in another series of 21 patients with constrictive pericarditis and pleural effusion, the pleural effusion was right sided only in 9 (43%) and was bilateral in the remaining 12 (57%).[156]

The mechanism responsible for the pleural effusion associated with pericardial disease is not clear. In constrictive pericarditis, one explanation for the effusions is that the pulmonary and systemic capillary pressures are elevated secondary to the pericardial disease, resulting in a transudative pleural effusion. However, one would expect these effusions to be bilateral. In inflammatory pericardial disease, however, the pleural effusion tends to be left sided and, although the characteristics of the fluid have not been well described, it is probable that the effusion forms from extension of the pericardial inflammation to the adjacent pleura.[157]

HEPATIC HYDROTHORAX

Patients with cirrhosis of the liver may develop a pleural effusion. In two large series, approximately 6% of patients with cirrhosis had pleural effusions.[158,159] The incidence appears to be much higher if ascites is present; however, in some patients with hepatic hydrothorax, no ascites can be detected, presumably because all ascitic fluid moves to the pleural space because of prevailing pressure gradients and low-resistance diaphragmatic defects.[47,160]

Pathophysiology

The predominant mechanism leading to a pleural effusion in a patient with cirrhosis and ascites appears to be the movement of the ascitic fluid from the peritoneal cavity through defects in the diaphragm into the pleural space.[161] The decreased plasma oncotic pressure is only a secondary factor.

The diaphragmatic defects have been demonstrated in many ways. Lieberman and coworkers[158] introduced 500 to 1000 mL of air into the peritoneal cavity of five patients with cirrhosis, ascites, and pleural effusions and found that a pneumothorax developed in all patients within 48 hours. In addition, they were able to demonstrate air bubbles coming through an otherwise undetectable diaphragmatic defect at thoracoscopy in one of their patients. In two of their patients, diaphragmatic defects were demonstrated at postmortem examination.[158] Mouroux and coworkers[162] performed thoracoscopy on eight patients and were able to identify diaphragmatic defects in six. There are no direct lymphatic connections between the peritoneal and the pleural spaces. Thus, the connections between the spaces either are preexisting developmental defects or are defects caused by trauma or stretching.

Clinical Manifestations

The clinical situation in patients with pleural effusions from cirrhosis and ascites is usually dominated by the cirrhosis and ascites. At times, however, the presence of a large pleural effusion may produce severe dyspnea. The pleural effusion associated with cirrhosis and ascites is frequently large and can occupy the entire hemithorax. The large effusions occur because the diaphragmatic defect permits fluid to flow from the peritoneal cavity into the pleural cavity until the pleural pressure approaches the peritoneal pressure. The pleural pressures in patients with pleural effusions secondary to ascites are higher than those in patients with other transudative pleural effusions.[163] The pleural effusions are usually right sided (80%) but occasionally are left sided (17%) or bilateral (3%).[161]

Diagnosis and Treatment

It is usually easy to establish the diagnosis of hepatic hydrothorax from the clinical picture. If doubt exists, the diagnosis can be confirmed by scanning the chest after technetium-99m–labeled sulfur colloid is injected into the peritoneal cavity.[164] Both a paracentesis and a thoracentesis should be performed to confirm that the ascites and the pleural fluid are both transudates. Xiol and associates[165] performed thoracentesis on 60 patients with cirrhosis and ascites. The pleural fluid analysis yielded a diagnosis other than hepatic hydrothorax in 18 (30%), including 9 cases of spontaneous bacterial pleuritis, 2 cases of tuberculosis, 2 adenocarcinomas, 2 parapneumonic effusions, and 3 undiagnosed exudates.[165] The protein level with hepatic hydrothorax in the pleural fluid is usually higher than that in the ascitic fluid but is still below 3.0 g/dL.[158] If the polymorphonuclear cell count is greater than 500 cells/μL, the diagnosis of spontaneous bacterial pleuritis in conjunction with spontaneous bacterial peritonitis should be considered.[166]

The initial management of the pleural effusion associated with cirrhosis and ascites should be directed toward treatment of the ascites. The patient should be given a low-salt diet and treated with diuretics. If diet and diuretics do not control the effusion, the treatment of choice is liver transplantation, but rarely is transplantation immediately available.[160] Chest tube insertion should be avoided because the ascitic fluid will also drain through the chest tube, which can lead to massive protein depletion and even fatal cardiovascular collapse.[160] The next best approach is probably implantation of a transjugular intrahepatic portosystemic shunt (TIPS).[166a] TIPS is usually effective in the management of hepatic hydrothorax. Kinasewitz and Keddissi[160] summarized the literature on 115 patients who received TIPS for refractory hepatic hydrothorax and reported that the procedure controlled the hydrothorax in 80%, but 12% of the patients developed encephalopathy.

If neither TIPS nor liver transplantation is feasible, the best alternative treatment is probably videothoracoscopy with closure of the diaphragmatic defects and pleurodesis.

De Campos and associates[167] performed 21 thoracoscopies in 18 patients with hepatic hydrothorax with an overall success rate of 48%. The procedure prevented recurrence in four of five patients who had defects identified and sutured.[167] In this series, the median hospital stay was 15 days and the mortality in the 3 months following surgery was 39%.[167] In another thoracoscopic study, even though diaphragmatic defects were identified in only 2 of 9 patients, efforts to seal the diaphragm completely were highly successful in resolving the hepatic hydrothorax. Nonetheless, as might be expected in this high risk population, mortality in the following 2 years remained high (8 of 9).[167a]

Spontaneous Bacterial Pleuritis

Spontaneous bacterial pleuritis is, by definition, infection of a preexisting hepatic hydrothorax in which a parapneumonic infection has been excluded. Originally termed *spontaneous bacterial empyema*, we prefer the term *pleuritis* to emphasize its similarity to spontaneous bacterial peritonitis, and to indicate that its treatment does not require tube thoracostomy. In one series in Spain, 16 of 120 patients (13%) admitted with a diagnosis of hepatic hydrothorax had a spontaneous bacterial pleuritis.[166] The diagnosis is made if the pleural fluid culture is positive, the pleural fluid neutrophil count is greater than 250 cells/μL, and a pneumonic process has been excluded. If the pleural fluid neutrophil count is greater than 500 cells/μL and the pleural fluid cultures are negative, culture-negative spontaneous bacterial pleuritis is diagnosed.[166] In the series from Spain, 10 of 24 episodes (43%) of spontaneous bacterial empyema were not associated with bacterial peritonitis.[166] Appropriate treatment of spontaneous bacterial pleuritis requires systemic antibiotics, but tube thoracostomy does not appear to be necessary. It remains to be seen whether spontaneous bacterial pleuritis is a common occurrence in the United States.

NEPHROTIC SYNDROME

There is a high incidence of pleural effusion in patients with the nephrotic syndrome. In one study of 52 patients, 21% had pleural effusions.[168] The mechanism responsible for the transudative pleural effusion associated with the nephrotic syndrome is probably the combination of decreased plasma oncotic pressure and increased hydrostatic pressure. The increased hydrostatic pressure is due to salt retention, which produces hypervolemia. The pleural effusions in patients with a nephrotic syndrome are usually bilateral and are frequently infrapulmonary in location.[168]

A diagnostic thoracentesis should be performed in all patients with the nephrotic syndrome and a pleural effusion to prove that the pleural fluid is a transudate. Nonetheless, the possibility of pulmonary embolism should always be considered in patients with the nephrotic syndrome and a pleural effusion. In one series of 36 patients with the nephrotic syndrome, 22% had pulmonary emboli.[169] If the pleural fluid is an exudate, a scintigraphic lung scan or a spiral CT scan should be obtained.

The treatment of the pleural effusion associated with the nephrotic syndrome should be aimed at increasing the level of protein in the serum by decreasing the protein loss in urine. If this is unsuccessful, pleurodesis with a sclerosing agent should be considered in selected patients who are symptomatic from the pleural effusion.[170]

PERITONEAL DIALYSIS

Peritoneal dialysis is occasionally complicated by the development of an acute hydrothorax. In a review of 3195 patients receiving continuous ambulatory peritoneal dialysis in Japan, 1.6% developed a pleural effusion as a result of the movement of the dialysate from the peritoneal cavity into the pleural cavity.[171] The effusion developed within 30 days of initiation of the dialysis in 50% of the patients, but 18% had been receiving dialysis for more than a year before the effusion developed.[171] The effusions are right sided in about 90%.[171,172]

The pleural fluid in these patients is characterized by a glucose level intermediate between that of the dialysate and the serum, a protein level below 1.0 g/dL, and a low LDH level. The LDH level is higher and the glucose level is lower in the pleural fluid than in the ascitic fluid.[172] Although the communication closes spontaneously in some patients, a surgical approach is usually required if continuous ambulatory peritoneal dialysis is to be continued. The treatment of choice is probably thoracoscopy with closure of the diaphragmatic defects, followed by pleurodesis.[173] Alternative treatments are pleurodesis alone or thoracotomy with repair of the diaphragmatic defects.

URINARY TRACT OBSTRUCTION (URINOTHORAX)

Obstruction of the urinary tract resulting in a retroperitoneal urine collection (urinoma) can lead to a pleural effusion.[174] The mechanism by which the pleural fluid accumulates is unknown, but it is thought that this retroperitoneal fluid drains along pressure gradients into the pleural space. The collection of fluid actually represents urine, and the pleural fluid smells like urine. The diagnosis can be established with simultaneous measurement of the creatinine levels in the pleural fluid and serum. Only patients with urinary tract obstruction have pleural fluid creatinine levels higher than those in serum.[174] In 12 reported cases, the average pleural to serum creatinine ratio was 9.1 (1.1–19.8).[174a] When the urinary tract obstruction is relieved, the pleural effusion rapidly disappears.

MYXEDEMA

A pleural effusion sometimes occurs as a complication of myxedema.[175] Most patients with myxedema and pleural effusion have a concomitant pericardial effusion. In one series of 25 patients with pericardial effusions secondary to myxedema, 13 of the patients (52%) had concomitant pleural effusion.[176] When the pleural effusion occurs simultaneously with a pericardial effusion, the pleural fluid is usually a transudate.[176] The isolated pleural effusion seen in conjunction with myxedema is generally borderline between a transudate and an exudate.[175] Although the mechanism of formation of the effusion is unknown, a decrease in lymphatic function due to low thyroid levels may contribute.[47] Thyroid replacement is the obvious treatment for pleural effusions associated with myxedema.

FONTAN PROCEDURE

With the Fontan procedure, an anastomosis is created between the superior vena cava, the right atrium, or the inferior vena cava and the pulmonary artery to bypass the right ventricle, usually because of tricuspid atresia or a univentricular heart. Pleural effusion occurs in many patients after surgery and contributes significantly to postoperative morbidity. Pleural effusions are more likely to occur in patients who have significant aortopulmonary collateral vessels before surgery; thus, Spicer and colleagues[177] recommended that these vessels be embolized during preoperative angiography. The amount of pleural drainage postoperatively is decreased by about 50% if the Fontan circuit is fenestrated to allow shunt of deoxygenated blood to the systemic circulation.[178] The treatment of choice for these effusions is usually insertion of a pleuroperitoneal shunt.[179] Alternative treatments are creation of a late fenestration to create a right-to-left shunt or chemical pleurodesis.

OTHER CAUSES OF TRANSUDATIVE PLEURAL EFFUSIONS

On rare occasions a subarachnoid pleural fistula can develop, which results in the accumulation of cerebrospinal fluid in the pleural space. The pleural fluid looks like cerebrospinal fluid, with very low protein and LDH levels.[180] Subarachnoid pleural fistula can occur following ventriculopleural shunting and with penetrating injuries, fractures, or surgery of the thoracic spine.[64] The fistula rarely closes without surgical intervention.[181]

Large, persistent transudative effusions can result from central venous obstruction, perhaps due to increases in venous pressure leading to increased formation of liquid and to decreases in lymphatic clearance. Such cases have been reported from occlusions of the hemiazygous vein,[182] brachiocephalic vein,[183] and superior vena cava.[184] Relief of the obstruction can lead to resolution of the effusion.[183]

Patients with pulmonary veno-occlusive disease frequently have small pleural effusions.[185] The characteristics of the pleural fluid have not been described, but it is probably a transudate because the effusions are likely related to the increased interstitial fluid.[185] This is the only condition associated with pulmonary hypertension, with the exception of pulmonary embolism, that is frequently associated with a pleural effusion.

Pulmonary embolism has been reported to be associated with a transudative pleural effusion. However, in recent paper on the pleural fluid findings with pulmonary embolism, all 60 pleural fluids were exudates.[73] Pleural amyloidosis is associated with transudative effusions, probably due to a combination of heart failure and pleural infiltration with amyloid.[186]

Bone marrow transplantation has also been associated with transudative effusions. In one review, 7 (0.4%) of 1905 patients who had received a bone marrow transplant developed at least two significant effusions for which there was no clear-cut explanation involving the pleural, peritoneal, or pericardial cavities.[187] This complication was seen only in children and only in recipients of allogeneic transplants. The effusions are large, require chest tubes, and are transudates.

It appears that the effusions are due to either acute or chronic graft-versus-host disease.[187]

EXUDATIVE PLEURAL EFFUSIONS

Exudative pleural effusions, defined according to Light's criteria (see discussion earlier), are common clinical problems. These effusions may develop as a result of inflammation, injury, or malignancy, which can involve the pleural surfaces, the adjacent lung, or more distant tissues, such as mediastinal and abdominal organs. Further discussion of effusions secondary to pleural tumors is presented in Chapter 70, and special types of effusions (chylothorax and hemothorax) are discussed in Chapter 69.

PARAPNEUMONIC EFFUSIONS AND EMPYEMA

A parapneumonic effusion is any pleural effusion associated with bacterial pneumonia, lung abscess, or bronchiectasis. Parapneumonic effusions are probably the most common exudative pleural effusion in the United States. The annual incidence of bacterial pneumonia in the United States is estimated to be 4 million.[188] Approximately 20% to 40% of patients hospitalized with bacterial pneumonia have an accompanying pleural effusion.[101,189] The morbidity and mortality in patients with pneumonia and pleural effusion are higher than in patients with pneumonia alone. In one study of patients with community-acquired pneumonia, the relative risk of mortality was 7.0 times higher for patients with bilateral pleural effusions and 3.4 times higher for patients with unilateral pleural effusions of moderate or greater size than that in other patients with community-acquired pneumonia.[190] Although it is possible that comorbidity from diseases such as congestive heart failure might cause both the effusions and the excess mortality, at least some of the increase in morbidity and mortality may be due to improper management of the pleural effusion.

When one is managing a patient with a parapneumonic effusion, the main decision to make is whether or not chest tubes should be inserted. The term *complicated parapneumonic effusion* is used to refer to those effusions that require tube thoracostomy for their resolution. An empyema is, by definition, pus in the pleural space. Approximately 60% of empyemas are complicated parapneumonic effusions, whereas 20% occur after thoracic surgical procedures, and the remaining 20% occur as complications of various conditions, such as thoracic trauma, esophageal perforation, thoracentesis, and subdiaphragmatic infection.[64]

Pathophysiology

The evolution of a parapneumonic pleural effusion can be divided into three stages, which are not sharply defined but rather represent a continuous spectrum. In the first stage, the exudative stage, a focus of parenchymal infection leads to increased pulmonary interstitial fluid, some of which traverses the visceral pleura and causes the accumulation of a small sterile pleural effusion. The pleural fluid in this stage is an exudate with primarily polymorphonuclear leukocytes, a normal glucose level, and a normal pH. With institution of appropriate antibiotic therapy during this stage, both the pneumonic process and the pleural effusion resolve.

The next stage is the fibropurulent stage, characterized by infection of the previously sterile pleural fluid with the offending bacteria. In this stage, more pleural fluid accumulates and contains many polymorphonuclear leukocytes, bacteria, and cellular debris. In addition, fibrin is deposited as continuous sheets that cover both the visceral and the parietal pleura in the involved area. As this stage progresses, there is a tendency for the fibrin membranes to partition the involved pleural space into multiple locules. This loculation hinders extension of the empyema but makes complete drainage of the pleural space with chest tubes increasingly difficult. The pleural fluid pH and glucose level decrease, and the LDH level increases progressively as this stage evolves.

In the last stage, the organization stage, fibroblasts grow into the exudate from both the visceral and the parietal pleural surfaces to produce an inelastic membrane. This membrane, sometimes called a *pleural peel*, can encase the lung and hinder the reexpansion of the underlying lung when the pleural fluid is evacuated. If the underlying lung cannot reexpand, consideration should be given to decortication, because it is virtually impossible to eradicate the infection if the space persists after the fluid is evacuated. However, if the infection is already controlled, the peel frequently resolves spontaneously over the ensuing 3 to 6 months.

Classification

An expert panel from the American College of Chest Physicians has developed a new categorization of patients with parapneumonic effusions.[191] This new categorization is modeled somewhat on the tumor-metastasis-node (TMN) classification of tumors and is based upon the anatomy of the effusion, the bacteriology of the pleural fluid, and the chemistry of the pleural fluid (Table 68.3).

The *category 1* effusion is a small (<10 mm thickness on decubitus radiograph, CT, or ultrasound studies), free-flowing effusion. Because the effusion is small, no thoracentesis is performed and the bacteriology and chemistry of the fluid are unknown. The risk of a poor outcome with a category 1 effusion is very low.

The *category 2* effusion is small to moderate in size (>10 mm thickness and < one half the hemithorax) and is free flowing. The Gram stain and culture of the pleural fluid are negative and the pleural fluid pH is more than 7.20 or the glucose more than 60 mg/dL. The risk of a poor outcome with a category 2 effusion is low.

The *category 3* effusion meets at least one of the following criteria: (a) the effusion occupies more than one half the hemithorax, is loculated, or is associated with a thickened parietal pleura; (b) the Gram stain or culture is positive; or (c) the pleural fluid pH is less than 7.20 or the pleural fluid glucose is less than 60 mg/dL. The risk of a poor outcome with a category 3 effusion is moderate.

The *category 4* effusion is characterized by pleural fluid that is pus. The risk of a poor outcome with a category 4 effusion is high.

Table 68.3 Categorizing Risk for Poor Outcome in Patients with Parapneumonic Effusion

Pleural Space Anatomy		Pleural Fluid Bacteriology		Pleural Fluid Chemistry	Category	Risk of Poor Outcome	Drainage
A_0: Minimal, free-flowing effusion (<10 mm on lateral decubitus)	*and*	B_x: Culture and Gram stain results unknown	*and*	C_x: pH, glucose unknown	1	Very low	No
A_1: Small to moderate free-flowing effusion (>10 mm and $<^1/_2$ hemithorax)	*and*	B_0: Negative culture and Gram stain	*and*	C_0: pH $\geq$ 7.20, glucose > 60 mg/dL	2	Low	No
A_2: Large, free-flowing effusion ($\geq^1/_2$ hemithorax), loculated effusion, or effusion with thickened parietal pleura	*or*	B_1: Positive culture and Gram stain	*or*	C_1: pH < 7.20, glucose < 60 mg/dL	3	Moderate	Yes
		B_2: Pus			4	High	Yes

From Colice GL, Curtis A, Deslauriers J, et al: Medical and surgical treatment of parapneumonic effusions: An evidence-based guideline. Chest 118:1158–1171, 2000.

Bacteriology

Before the antibiotic era, *Streptococcus pneumoniae* or hemolytic streptococci were responsible for most empyemas.[192] Then, between 1955 and 1965, *Staphylococcus aureus* was the bacterium most commonly isolated from pleural fluid.[192] In the 1970s, in a study with meticulous methods of isolation, anaerobic organisms were most commonly isolated.[193] However, it appears that aerobic organisms are now responsible for most empyemas.[64,194]

In a patient with a bacterial pneumonia, the incidence of associated pleural effusion and the frequency with which the pleural fluid becomes infected depend on the infecting organism.[64] For example, approximately 35% of patients with anaerobic pneumonia have a culture-positive pleural effusion,[193] whereas fewer than 5% of patients with pneumococcal pneumonia have culture-positive pleural effusions.[101]

Clinical Manifestations

Aerobic Bacterial Infections. Patients with aerobic bacterial pneumonia and pleural effusion initially have an acute febrile illness consisting of chest pain, sputum production, and leukocytosis. The incidence of pleuritic chest pain and the degree of leukocytosis are comparable whether or not there is an accompanying pleural effusion.[101]

Anaerobic Bacterial Infections. Patients with anaerobic bacterial infections involving the pleural space usually present with a subacute illness. In one series, the duration of symptoms before presentation averaged 10 days, with 70% of the patients having symptoms for more than 7 days.[195] Most patients with anaerobic pleuropulmonary infections have significant weight loss (mean: 13.2 kg in one series) as well as leukocytosis and mild anemia.[195] In addition, most patients have risk factors for aspiration of an anaerobic inoculum; these risk factors include alcoholism, an episode of unconsciousness, and infected gums.

Because of the nonspecificity of the symptoms associated with empyema, the diagnosis may not be considered and thus may be delayed. In one series of 119 patients from England in the late 1980s, empyema was considered the most likely diagnosis by the admitting doctor in only 35 patients (29%).[196] In this same series, the diagnosis was delayed for more than 1 week in 28 patients and for more than 1 month after admission in 5 patients.[196] In this series, the most common symptom was malaise (73%), and only 56% of the patients were febrile. In a more recent series from Canada, the mean delay from admission to the time of correct diagnosis was 44 days.[197]

Diagnosis

Parapneumonic effusion and empyema should be included in the differential diagnosis of all undiagnosed exudative effusions. The possibility of a parapneumonic effusion should be considered whenever a patient with a bacterial pneumonia is initially evaluated. If costophrenic angles show blunting or if the diaphragm is not visible throughout its length, bilateral decubitus chest radiographs or ultrasound should be obtained to evaluate the possibility of a pleural effusion.

With the involved side dependent, the amount of free pleural fluid can be semiquantitated by measuring the distance between the inside of the chest wall and the outside of the lung. If this distance is less than 10 mm, the effusion is not clinically significant, and thoracentesis is not indicated.[101,191] If the thickness of the fluid exceeds 10 mm, then a thoracentesis should be performed immediately.[191,194] Only by examining the pleural fluid can one distinguish a complicated from an uncomplicated parapneumonic effusion. The pleural fluid should be examined grossly for color, turbidity, and odor. Aliquots are sent for determination of the pleural fluid glucose, LDH, and protein concentrations, the pH (with a blood gas machine),[102] a differential and total leukocyte count, a Gram stain, and aerobic and anaerobic bacterial cultures. In most instances, the pleural fluid should also be submitted for mycobacterial and fungal smears and cultures.

Not all patients with an acute illness, parenchymal infiltrates, and pleural effusion have an acute bacterial pneumonia. This clinical picture may also be seen with pulmonary embolization, acute pancreatitis, tuberculosis, Dressler's syndrome, and other diseases. The diagnostic workup of each patient should be individualized based on the clinical situation.

Patients with parapneumonic effusions may have mediastinal lymphadenopathy secondary to the pneumonia.[198,199] Kearney and associates[199] obtained chest CT scans in 50 patients with parapneumonic effusion and reported that 18 (36%) had at least one lymph node greater than 1 cm in its short axis. None of the patients developed evidence of malignant disease during the 1-year follow-up, and lymphadenopathy tended to decrease in size in those who had repeated studies.[199]

Treatment

When a patient with pneumonia and a pleural effusion is initially evaluated, an appropriate antibiotic must be selected, and the decision whether to initiate invasive therapy for the pleural effusion must be made. Bacterial cultures of the sputum, blood, and pleural fluid should be obtained before antibiotic therapy is instituted. Antibiotic therapy for bacterial pneumonia is discussed in Chapter 32.

Prognostic Factors. Findings in the pleural fluid that suggest that a more aggressive approach will be necessary for a parapneumonic effusion are listed in Table 68.4. The more purulent the pleural fluid, the lower the glucose level, and the lower the pH, the more likely the patient is to require increasingly invasive procedures for complete drainage. Other pleural fluid measurements that have been reported to be useful as markers for identifying complicated parapneumonic effusions include the pleural fluid myeloperoxidase level,[200] the complement activation product SC5b-9,[201] and the polymorphonuclear elastase level.[202] Additional studies are necessary to assess the utility of these measurements.

Overall Treatment Plan. The treatment options for patients with parapneumonic effusions and empyema, in order of increasing invasiveness, are diagnostic thoracentesis, therapeutic thoracentesis, tube thoracostomy, tube thoracostomy with thrombolytics, thoracoscopy, and thoracotomy with decortication. If the patient has any of the poor prognostic factors, it is likely that one of these treatments will be necessary. It is important not to continue any one treatment that is not working for more than a day or so.[203,204]

Table 68.4 Pleural Fluid Factors Suggesting a More Invasive Approach for the Resolution of a Parapneumonic Effusion*

1. Pus is present in the pleural space
2. Positive pleural fluid Gram stain
3. Pleural fluid glucose below 60 mg/dL
4. Pleural fluid pH below 7.20
5. Positive pleural fluid culture
6. Pleural fluid LDH more than 3 times upper normal limit for serum
7. Loculated pleural fluid

* Listed in order of decreasing seriousness.
LDH, lactate dehydrogenase.

The effectiveness of a given treatment is evaluated by the clinical status of the patient together with the amount and the characteristics of the pleural fluid. If the patient appears to be responding, if the amount of pleural fluid is not large, and if the characteristics of the fluid are improving, the treatment should be considered successful. More invasive procedures are not indicated for pleural thickening alone. Chest CT scans are very useful in evaluating the adequacy of drainage of the pleural space.[205]

Patients with effusions that measure more than 10 mm in thickness on the decubitus radiograph, or that are loculated, should have a thoracentesis within hours of admission. If poor prognostic factors are present, one should attempt to remove all the fluid with a therapeutic thoracentesis or tube thoracostomy on the day of admission. If these maneuvers are unsuccessful, thrombolytics or thoracoscopy should be tried within 48 hours. If the drainage is still unsuccessful, surgical consultation concerning decortication with open drainage and débridement should be obtained.

Diagnostic Versus Therapeutic Thoracentesis. To determine whether the patient has any of the prognostic factors listed in Table 68.4, a thoracentesis must be performed. Should a therapeutic thoracentesis or a diagnostic thoracentesis initially be performed? Because the risks of a diagnostic thoracentesis and a therapeutic thoracentesis are comparable, and a therapeutic thoracentesis might obviate the necessity for further procedures, a therapeutic thoracentesis is recommended.[203] If the pleural fluid never recurs, one need not worry about the pleural fluid. If the pleural fluid recurs after a therapeutic thoracentesis, poor prognostic findings in the pleural fluid indicate the need for more drainage—either an additional therapeutic thoracentesis or a tube thoracostomy. The absence of poor prognostic findings in a patient who is improving clinically indicates that additional drainage is not necessary. No more than three therapeutic thoracenteses are recommended.[203] If the pleural fluid cannot be completely removed because it is loculated, tube thoracostomy should be performed if any of the other poor prognostic factors listed in Table 68.4 are present.

Therapeutic Thoracentesis. Although therapeutic thoracentesis is not commonly used in the treatment of parapneumonic effusions, a few studies suggest that it may have a role. Sasse and coworkers[206] reported that therapeutic thoracentesis was at least as good as chest tube placement in the treatment of early pleural infections in a rabbit model of empyema. In a clinical retrospective study, Storm and associates[207] reported that 48 of 51 patients (94%) with empyema (purulent pleural fluid or positive microbiologic studies on the pleural fluid) were managed successfully with daily thoracentesis combined with a saline lavage. There have been no controlled studies comparing therapeutic thoracentesis with small-tube thoracostomy in the treatment of patients with complicated parapneumonic effusions. Obviously, therapeutic thoracentesis will not be adequate if the pleural fluid is loculated or if the fibrinous coating over the visceral pleura prevents the underlying lung from expanding.

Chest Tubes. Once it is decided that tube thoracostomy is necessary, there should be no delay in its performance, because a complicated parapneumonic effusion can progress

from free-flowing pleural fluid to loculated pleural fl[...]
within hours. In one older series of 47 anaerobic emp[...]
mas, five patients died, and all deaths were attributed t[...]
delay in obtaining adequate pleural drainage.[195] In a subs[...]
quent series, a delay in instituting chest tube draina[...]
resulted in a mortality increase from 3.4% to 16%.[208] Th[...]
chest tube should be positioned in the most dependent pa[...]
of the effusion.

There is no consensus on the optimal size of the chest tub[...]
for drainage.[194] In the past, relatively large (26- to 36[...]
French) chest tubes were recommended because of th[...]
belief that smaller tubes would become obstructed by th[...]
thick fluid. However, it appears that many patients can be
managed with much smaller tubes. In one recent study, 103
patients with empyema were treated with 8- to 12-French
pigtail or 10- to 14-French Malecot catheters inserted with
the Seldinger technique under either ultrasound or CT
scan.[209] In this study, these small catheters served as the
definitive treatment in 80 of the 103 patients (78%).[209]
These results are as good as those reported in some series in
which larger tubes were utilized.[208,210] The small chest tubes
in the aforementioned series were inserted percutaneously
by interventional radiologists. It is likely that the excellent
results are related to accurate image-guided placement of the
catheter. If small tubes are used, regular flushing and suction
are recommended to avoid catheter blockage.[194] If the
pleural fluid is frank pus, it is still preferable to insert a large
chest tube.[211] The chest tube should be left in place until the
volume of the pleural drainage per 24 hours is less than
50 mL and until the draining fluid becomes clear yellow.

Successful closed-tube drainage of a complicated parapneumonic effusion is associated with improvement in the
clinical and radiologic status of the patient within 24 to 48
hours. If there is no significant improvement after this
period, either the pleural drainage is unsatisfactory or the
patient is receiving the wrong antibiotic. In such situations,
the culture results should be reviewed and the adequacy of
the pleural drainage should be assessed by chest radiographs, CT scans, or ultrasound examination. If the pleural
space is inadequately drained, another chest tube should be
inserted, a fibrinolytic agent should be injected intrapleurally, or a more extensive surgical procedure should be
performed. Inadequate drainage can be caused by poor
positioning of the tube, obstruction of the chest tube,
loculated pleural fluid, or inadequate expansion of the
underlying lung caused by coating of the visceral pleura.

Intrapleural Thrombolytic Agents. These agents have been
recommended in the treatment of loculated parapneumonic
effusions because they may facilitate drainage as a result of
their fibrinolytic action. In the past several years, there have
been several uncontrolled studies that purported to show
the utility of streptokinase or urokinase in the treatment of
multiloculated pleural infections. The usual dose of streptokinase is 250,000 IU, in 30 to 60 mL of normal saline
given intrapleurally via the chest tube. The usual dose of
urokinase is 100,000 IU diluted in the same manner. At the
present time urokinase but not streptokinase is available in
the United States. An alternative fibrinolytic agent is tissue
plasminogen activator.[212,213] The chest tube is clamped for
1 to 2 hours after instillation. The administration of these
agents intrapleurally has not been shown to have an effect

tube bottles.[223] After the procedure, the cavity sh[...]
irrigated daily with a mild antiseptic solution[...]
drainage from the tubes can be collected in a[...]
placed over the tubes. Open drainage is pr[...]
tication only in those patients who are[...]
ill to tolerate the more extensive proc[...]
by open drainage can expect to h[...]
for a prolonged period. In on[...]
treated by an open-drainage[...]
healing the drainage site[...]

Bronchopleural Fi[...]

When an e[...]
bronchopl[...]
The pl[...]
tub[...]

...rmation about
[...] the extent of the empyema cavity. The finding
of a thickened visceral pleural peel without septations suggests that the empyema may be chronic and probably will
not be amenable to thoracoscopic débridement alone.
Most patients who undergo thoracoscopy need no additional therapy. When four recent studies with a total of 232
patients are combined, thoracoscopy was the definitive procedure in 77% of the patients.[218-221] After thoracoscopy,
the median hospital stay ranged from 5.3 to 12.3 days, the
median time for postprocedure chest tube drainage ranged
from 3.3 to 7.1 days, and the overall mortality was 3%.[218-221]

Decortication. This procedure should be considered in
patients who require additional drainage after tube thoracostomy and thoracoscopy.[222] With this procedure, a full
thoracotomy is performed to remove all fibrous tissue and
pus from the pleural space. The primary advantage that
thoracotomy has over thoracoscopy is that decortication is
easier to perform with thoracotomy. Decortication eliminates the pleural sepsis and allows the underlying lung to
expand. Decortication is major thoracic surgery and should
not be performed on patients who are markedly debilitated.
It should not be performed just to remove thickened pleura,
because such thickening usually resolves spontaneously over
several months. After 6 months, however, if the pleural
thickening persists and the pulmonary function is sufficiently reduced to limit the patient's activities, decortication
should be considered.

Open Drainage (Eloesser Flap). With this relatively minor
surgical procedure, which can be performed under local
anesthesia, a U-shaped incision is made to provide a skin
flap overlying the lower part of the empyema collection; the
exposed rib segments and underlying parietal pleura are
excised to open the empyema cavity; then, the skin flap is
sutured inside the cavity to create a semipermanent opening
into which one or more large-bore short tubes are inserted.
The open-drainage procedure allows more complete
drainage and frees the patient from attachment to chest-

of an intrathoracic muscle transposition[227] or a pedicled omental flap are usually required.[226]

TUBERCULOUS PLEURITIS

In many parts of the world, the most common cause of an exudative pleural effusion is tuberculosis. However, in the United States, the annual incidence of tuberculous pleural effusion is only 1000 patients. In Tennessee, a low-incidence state, 1 in every 30 cases of tuberculosis is tuberculous pleuritis,[228] whereas, in some African countries, the percentage of patients with tuberculosis who have a pleural effusion exceeds 30%.[229] The effect of HIV on the incidence of tuberculous pleurisy is still uncertain; in some studies, HIV appears to increase the incidence[230] and in others it does not.[229] The confusion may in part be due to the state of immunocompromise: The prevalence of tuberculous pleurisy is also higher in patients with CD4 counts above 200 cells/μL than in those with CD4 counts below 200 cells/μL,[231] in keeping with the understanding of the role of delayed hypersensitivity in the development of the effusion.

A pleural effusion as a manifestation of tuberculosis has been likened to a primary chancre as a manifestation of syphilis. Both are self-limited and of little immediate concern, but both may lead to serious disease many years later. A recent molecular epidemiologic study has confirmed that tuberculous pleurisy is an early manifestation of tuberculosis infection.[231a] Most instances of pleural effusion secondary to tuberculosis resolve spontaneously; however, if patients are not treated with antituberculous therapy, they have about a 50% likelihood of developing active tuberculosis in the subsequent 5 years.[232]

Pathogenesis

A tuberculous pleural effusion can either be a sequel to a primary infection acquired 3 to 6 months previously or represent reactivation tuberculosis.[233] As discussed in Chapter 33, two different pathogenetic mechanisms can lead to tuberculous pleural effusions. By far, the more common is the entry of only a few *M. tuberculosis* into the pleural space; in the presence of specific cell-mediated immunity, tubercle bacilli provoke an intense hypersensitivity reaction and outpouring of fluid.[234] Chest radiographs may or may not reveal associated parenchymal involvement. In the second variety, a subpleural caseous focus or cavity ruptures into the pleural space and results in a pleural effusion. In this case, chest radiographs nearly always show parenchymal abnormalities.

As just mentioned, delayed hypersensitivity appears to play a large role in the pathogenesis of tuberculous pleuritis. In animal models, the intrapleural injection of tuberculous protein in sensitized animals results in the rapid appearance of an exudative pleural effusion.[234] When the animals are given antilymphocyte serum, the development of the effusion is suppressed. It is probable that delayed hypersensitivity also plays a large role in the development of tuberculous pleural effusions in humans. The mycobacterial burden in the pleural space is low because the pleural fluid cultures from only about 35% of patients with tuberculous pleuritis are positive.[235] T lymphocytes specifically sensitized to tuberculous protein are present in the pleural fluid.[234]

ould be , and the olostomy bag ferred to decor- thought to be too edure. Patients treated ave an open chest wound recent series of 53 patients procedure, the median time for was over 120 days.[224]

stula Complicating Empyema

pyema is complicated by the presence of a eural fistula, adequate pleural drainage is crucial. eural fluid that is not drained exteriorly with chest s is likely to drain interiorly throughout the tracheo- ronchial tree, producing a severe diffuse pneumonia. A bronchopleural fistula should be suspected whenever the chest radiograph reveals an air-fluid level or when the patient expectorates copious quantities of sputum while lying on one side (as the empyema drains into the bronchial tree) and not while lying on the other side.

At times, it is difficult to determine whether an air-fluid level is in the lung or in the pleural space. It is important to make this differentiation because a lung abscess should be treated with antibiotics alone, whereas it is imperative to drain the pleural space if a bronchopleural fistula exists. Chest CT is quite valuable in making this differentiation, as described earlier (see Fig. 68.6A).

Postpneumonectomy Empyema

The incidence of empyema after pneumonectomy is about 7.5%.[225] This diagnosis should be suspected in any patient who undergoes pneumonectomy and becomes febrile, starts expectorating large amounts of sputum, has purulent drainage from the thoracotomy wound, or has a mediastinum that is midline or shifted to the contralateral side. The diagnosis is established with a diagnostic thoracentesis that reveals organisms on Gram stain or culture.

A postpneumonectomy empyema is an extremely serious complication because it is impossible to eliminate the space containing the infection and, consequently, it is difficult to sterilize the pleural space. Approximately 60% to 80% of patients with postpneumonectomy empyema have a bronchopleural or an esophagopleural fistula.[225,226] Therefore, all patients with this complication should undergo a chest CT scan and a bronchoscopy.

The treatment of a postpneumonectomy empyema involves two different aspects, draining the infected pleural fluid and closing the bronchopleural fistula. The pleural fluid is best drained by tube thoracostomy if the empyema occurs in the first few days after pneumonectomy. Subsequently, most patients require open drainage. If the patient does not have a bronchopleural fistula, operative irrigation and filling of the residual space with an antibiotic-containing solution[226] or thoracoscopic debridement[226a] may be curative.

If a bronchopleural fistula is present, it must be treated. Attempts can be made to close the fistula bronchoscopically, but a thoracotomy and surgical closing of the fistula by use

Although delayed hypersensitivity to tuberculous protein is believed to be primarily responsible for tuberculous pleuritis, approximately one third of patients with tuberculous pleuritis have a negative tuberculin skin test result when first evaluated.[235] Occasionally, the immunosuppression may result from a relative depletion of the circulating purified protein derivative–reactive lymphocytes as they sequester in the pleural space. More commonly, immunosuppression is thought to be due to suppressor cells, either adherent monocytes or Fc-bearing lymphocytes that are found in the blood but not in the pleural space.[234]

Clinical Manifestations

Tuberculous pleuritis occurs as an acute illness in about two thirds of cases and as a chronic illness in the remaining one third. The acute illness is marked by cough and chest pain in about 75% of patients and often mimics a bacterial pneumonia with parapneumonic effusion. The chronic form is characterized by low-grade fever, weakness, and weight loss.[236]

Effusions secondary to tuberculous pleuritis are almost always unilateral (Fig. 68.8) and are usually small to moderate in size, although they may occupy the entire hemithorax.[237] About 50% of patients have smooth pleural thickening of greater than 1 cm on CT scan. About one third of patients have coexisting parenchymal disease.[237] In such patients, the pleural effusion is almost always on the side of the parenchymal infiltrate and invariably indicates active parenchymal disease[236] (see Fig. 68.8). It is likely that, even in cases with no radiographic evidence of parenchymal involvement, the effusion is associated with a subpleural focus of infection. Evidence to support this contention is provided by a recent study in which the yield of sputum induction for *M. tuberculosis* was as high in patients with no

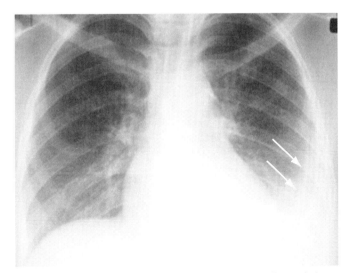

Figure 68.8 Tuberculous effusion. Frontal chest radiograph in an immunocompromised patient with *Mycobacterium tuberculosis* infection shows left lower lobe consolidation (note retrocardiac density and absence of left hemidiaphragm contour) and left pleural effusion (*arrows*). Smears and cultures of sputum were positive for *M. tuberculosis*. (Courtesy of Michael B. Gotway, MD, Department of Radiology, University of California, San Francisco.)

radiographic evidence of parenchymal involvement (55%) as in those with evidence of parenchymal disease (45%).[140]

Pleural Fluid

The pleural fluid from patients with tuberculous pleuritis is an exudate that usually contains predominantly small lymphocytes. If symptoms have been present only a few days, neutrophils may be predominant. The pleural fluid glucose level is usually similar to that of serum, but at times, it is reduced. A pleural fluid protein level above 5.0 g/dL is suggestive of tuberculous pleuritis.

Diagnosis

The possibility of tuberculous pleuritis should be considered in every patient with an undiagnosed exudative pleural effusion, even though only a small percentage of such effusions are due to tuberculosis in the United States.[64] For the past 40 years, the most common way to establish the diagnosis of tuberculous pleuritis has been through needle biopsy of the pleura. However, in recent years, three tests that can be performed on pleural fluid have been developed that may be useful in establishing or excluding the diagnosis of tuberculous pleuritis[238]: (1) the level of ADA in the pleural fluid, (2) the level of interferon-γ in the pleural fluid, and (3) PCR for mycobacterial DNA. These studies are described in detail earlier in this chapter; as mentioned, one disadvantage of these tests is that they do not provide bacterial cultures for antibiotic sensitivity testing.

All patients with an undiagnosed exudative pleural effusion should undergo mycobacterial cultures of their pleural fluid and should have one of the aforementioned three tests performed on their pleural fluid. An induced sputum sample should also be sent for smear and culture, because it will be positive in approximately 50%.[140] If the culture of the fluid or sputum is positive, treatment for tuberculosis should be initiated. If one of the other tests is positive for tuberculosis, the patient should also be treated for tuberculosis unless the patient has a disease that is known to be associated with a positive result or if there is no pleural fluid lymphocytosis. In areas with a high likelihood of resistant tuberculosis, one may also want to obtain pleural tissue for cultures via needle biopsy of the pleura or thoracoscopy. If the patient does not respond to therapy, then further investigations are warranted. Needle biopsy of the pleura can be performed in questionable cases, but, unless the likelihood of tuberculosis is high, the invasive diagnostic test of choice is usually thoracoscopy.

Treatment

Patients with tuberculous pleuritis should be treated with antituberculous medications in the same treatment regimens that are administered to patients with pulmonary tuberculosis; these are fully discussed in Chapter 33. With treatment, patients generally become afebrile within about 2 weeks, and the pleural effusion resolves within 6 weeks. On occasion, the pleural effusion worsens after antituberculous therapy is initiated[239] or a pleural effusion develops while patients are being treated for tuberculosis.[240] In these situations, the possibility of a wrong diagnosis must be considered, but the paradoxical worsening can occur with the correct diagnosis and appropriate antituberculous medications.[239,240] Mild degrees of pleural fibrosis are present a year after therapy is begun in about 50% of patients. The presence of fibrosis is not related to the initial pleural fluid findings and is of limited clinical significance.[241]

The role of systemic corticosteroids in the treatment of tuberculous pleuritis remains controversial. There were no benefits with the use of systemic corticosteroids in two controlled studies in which therapeutic thoracentesis was also performed,[241,242] but the duration of fever and the time required for fluid resorption were decreased in a third study in which no therapeutic thoracentesis was performed.[243] Use of corticosteroids may be considered for those who are markedly symptomatic, but only after the institution of appropriate antituberculosis therapy. Therapeutic thoracentesis is indicated if the patient has a moderate-sized or larger pleural effusion producing symptoms. Otherwise, complete drainage of the pleural space has no significant effects on the long-term outcome.[244]

ACTINOMYCOSIS

More than 50% of patients with thoracic actinomycosis have pleural involvement.[245] In one series of 15 patients, 6 had pleural effusion, and an additional 6 had marked pleural thickening.[245] The characteristic chest radiographic finding is a localized lung lesion extending to the chest wall with pleural thickening or effusion. The pleural fluid with actinomycosis may be either frank pus with predominantly polymorphonuclear leukocytes or serous fluid with predominantly lymphocytes.

The diagnosis of actinomycosis should be considered when a chronic infiltrative pulmonary lesion extends to adjacent lobes through intralobar fissures. The presence of chest wall abscesses or draining sinus tracts suggests the diagnosis, as do bone changes consisting of periosteal proliferation or bone destruction. The definitive diagnosis is established with the demonstration of *Actinomyces israelii* by anaerobic cultures. Patients with pleural actinomycosis should be treated with high doses of penicillin or another suitable antimicrobial (see Chapter 32) for prolonged periods. The management of the pleural effusion is similar to that for patients with any other bacterial pneumonia.

NOCARDIOSIS

Pleural effusions develop in approximately 50% of patients with pulmonary nocardiosis.[246] Patients with pleural effusion secondary to nocardiosis almost always have an associated parenchymal infiltrate. The pleural fluid can range from serous fluid to frank pus, and pleural fluid cultures may or may not be positive. Because most patients who develop nocardiosis are immunosuppressed,[246] this diagnosis should be considered in the immunosuppressed patient with a parenchymal infiltrate and a pleural effusion. The diagnosis is established with aerobic cultures, which should be observed for at least 2 weeks, because *Nocardia asteroides* is a slow-growing organism. Patients with pleural nocardiosis should be treated with sulfonamides or suitable alternative antimicrobials (see Chapter 32), and the pleural effusion should be managed as any pleural effusion complicating a pneumonia.

FUNGAL INFECTIONS

Fungal infections of the lungs are discussed in Chapter 34. This section considers the pleural complications of aspergillosis, blastomycosis, coccidioidomycosis, cryptococcosis, and histoplasmosis. In addition, *Pneumocystis jirovecii* (formerly *carinii*) has been included.

Aspergillosis

The pleural space occasionally becomes infected with *Aspergillus*, usually *Aspergillus fumigatus*.[247] Pleural aspergillosis usually occurs in one of two settings. Most commonly, it occurs in patients who were treated in the past with artificial pneumothorax therapy for tuberculosis. Pleural aspergillosis may also complicate lobectomy or pneumonectomy, in which situation a bronchopleural fistula is almost always present.[248]

The diagnosis of pleural aspergillosis should be suspected in any patient with a history of artificial pneumothorax therapy for tuberculosis who has signs and symptoms of a chronic infection, such as weight loss, malaise, low-grade fever, and chronic cough. The chest radiograph reveals increasing degrees of pleural thickening and usually an air-fluid level in the pleural space, indicating the presence of a bronchopleural fistula.[247] In some patients, fungus balls or mycetoma may be evident in either the lungs or the pleural space. The diagnosis is confirmed by the demonstration of *Aspergillus* on fungal cultures of the pleural fluid. Patients with pleural aspergillosis almost always have positive precipitin blood test results for antibodies against *Aspergillus*.

The optimal treatment for pleural aspergillosis is surgical removal of the involved pleura and resection of the involved lobe or the entire ipsilateral lung, if necessary.[247] Lung resection is usually necessary because the infection tends to invade and destroy the underlying lung. Surgery should be performed as early as possible to avoid progressive destruction of the lung. Itraconazole or amphotericin B should be administered systemically before and after the surgery to prevent postoperative pleural infection with *Aspergillus*. Some patients with pleural aspergillosis are too debilitated to undergo a major surgical procedure. Such patients should undergo open drainage (Eloesser flap) with daily insertion of gauze impregnated with amphotericin B.[249]

The clinical picture of postoperative *Aspergillus* pleural infection is similar to that of other postpneumonectomy infections. Once the diagnosis is established, a chest tube should be inserted, and the pleural space should be irrigated daily with 25 mg of amphotericin B or 75,000 U of nystatin.[250] Over an extended period, most patients are cured with this treatment.

Blastomycosis

Infection with *Blastomyces dermatitidis* produces a pleural effusion in about 10% of patients, and an additional 40% or more have pleural thickening.[251] Patients with pleural blastomycosis have signs and symptoms similar to those of tuberculous pleuritis. The pleural fluid is usually an exudate with predominantly small lymphocytes, although polymorphonuclear leukocytes may predominate.[252] Because pleural biopsy may reveal noncaseating granulomas, one should consider the diagnosis of blastomycosis in patients with a clinical picture compatible with tuberculous pleuritis and granulomas on pleural biopsy. The diagnosis is established by demonstrating the organism in secretions, pleural fluid, or histologic sections. Patients with pleural blastomycosis should be treated with itraconazole or amphotericin B, as described in Chapter 34.

Coccidioidomycosis

Two types of pleural disease occur in association with coccidioidomycosis. The first is associated with a primary benign infection and may or may not have concomitant parenchymal involvement. The second occurs when a coccidioidal cavity ruptures to produce a hydropneumothorax.

Primary Coccidioidomycosis. The incidence of pleural effusion with symptomatic primary coccidioidomycosis is about 7%.[253] Most patients are febrile and have pleuritic chest pain, and nearly 50% have either erythema nodosum or erythema multiforme. The pleural effusion is almost always unilateral, often occupying more than 50% of the hemithorax.[253] There is a coexisting parenchymal infiltrate in about 50%. The pleural fluid is an exudate containing predominantly small lymphocytes and has a glucose level above 60 mg/dL (3.33 mmol/L).[253] Pleural fluid cultures are positive for *Coccidioides immitis* in about 20%, whereas cultures of pleural biopsy specimens are almost always positive.

Most patients with primary coccidioidomycosis and pleural effusion require no systemic antifungal therapy. Only patients with a negative skin test result or other evidence of dissemination should be treated. The complement fixation titers are usually high in patients with coccidioidal pleural effusion, and a high titer alone should not be used as an indication for treatment.

Rupture of Coccidioidal Cavity. Hydropneumothoraces develop in 1% to 5% of patients with chronic cavitary coccidioidomycosis. The rupture of the cavity into the pleural space is usually heralded by the development of an acute illness with systemic signs of toxicity. These patients should undergo tube thoracostomy immediately to drain the air and fluid from the pleural space. Most patients require a thoracotomy with a partial or total lobectomy, and most require some degree of decortication.[254]

Cryptococcosis

Pleural involvement with cryptococcosis appears to result from extension of a primary subpleural cryptococcal nodule into the pleural space. About 50% of patients with pleural cryptococcosis have disseminated disease, and most have an accompanying parenchymal abnormality.[255] Most patients who have a cryptococcal pleural effusion are immunosuppressed, and many of the patients have acquired immunodeficiency syndrome (AIDS).[256,257] The pleural fluid is an exudate, usually with a predominance of small lymphocytes.

Not all patients with pleural cryptococcosis require treatment with systemic antifungal therapy.[258] Treatment should be initiated in patients with cryptococcal antigen in their blood or cerebrospinal fluid; in immunosuppressed patients,

including those with AIDS; and in those with enlarging effusions, especially if pleural cell counts and LDH concentrations are increasing.[256]

Histoplasmosis

Pleural effusion is rare with histoplasmosis. In one review of 259 patients with pulmonary histoplasmosis, only one had a pleural effusion.[259] Patients with pleural effusions secondary to histoplasmosis usually have a subacute illness characterized by low-grade fever and pleuritic chest pain. The chest radiograph usually reveals an infiltrate or a subpleural nodule in addition to the pleural effusion.[260] The pleural fluid is an exudate in which lymphocytes predominate, and the pleural biopsy usually reveals noncaseating granulomas. No systemic treatment is usually necessary for a pleural effusion secondary to histoplasmosis because the effusion normally resolves spontaneously over several weeks. Systemic therapy should be administered if the effusion persists over 3 to 4 weeks or if the patient is immunosuppressed (see Chapter 34).

Pneumocystis jirovecii

Pleural effusions are rare in patients with *P. jirovecii* pneumonia (see Chapter 75), but they have been reported. The pleural effusion appears to be an extension of the pulmonary process, and concurrent pneumothoraces are common.[261] The pleural fluid is an exudate with a relatively low protein level but an LDH level above the upper normal limit for serum. At times, organisms can be visualized in the pleural fluid.[261]

VIRAL INFECTIONS

Viral infections probably account for a sizable percentage of undiagnosed exudative pleural effusions. However, the diagnosis is rarely established because it usually depends on the isolation of the virus or the demonstration of a significant increase in antibody titers to the virus. These studies are not routinely obtained on patients with undiagnosed pleural effusions.

Primary Atypical Pneumonia

The incidence of pleural effusions with so-called primary atypical pneumonia (usually caused by *Mycoplasma* or viruses) is as high as 20%.[262] The effusions associated with atypical pneumonia are usually small, are exudative, and contain predominantly neutrophils. Thoracentesis should be performed in such patients to exclude a complicated parapneumonic effusion.

Other Viruses

Viral infection is probably responsible for a much higher percentage of pleural effusion without parenchymal infiltrates than is generally recognized. In one epidemic, 559 soldiers in Turkey had an acute febrile illness characterized by pleuritic chest pain and a mononuclear cell–predominant pleural effusion without parenchymal infiltrates. No pathogens were demonstrated, and it was assumed that this self-limited disease was due to a virus, although serologic studies were not performed.[263]

A pleural effusion can occur with infectious hepatitis. In one prospective study of 156 hepatitis patients, 70% had at least a small pleural effusion. In this situation the pleural fluid is an exudate with predominantly mononuclear cells.[264] One must be careful in handling pleural fluid when infectious hepatitis is suspected because the infectious hepatitis B antigen has been demonstrated in pleural fluid.[265]

Almost all patients with the hantavirus pulmonary syndrome (see Chapter 31) have a pleural effusion. Initially, the fluid is a transudate, probably resulting from cardiac dysfunction, but subsequently, the fluid becomes exudative.[266] Almost all patients with severe cases of dengue hemorrhagic fever also have pleural effusions, which are either right sided or bilateral.[267] Pleural effusions have also been reported to result from infection with infectious mononucleosis, respiratory syncytial virus, influenza viruses, measles after the administration of inactivated virus vaccine, cytomegalovirus, herpes simplex virus, and Lassa fever virus. Interestingly, none of 136 patients with severe acute respiratory syndrome (SARS) had a pleural effusion in one series.[268]

Acquired Immunodeficiency Syndrome

As discussed in Chapter 75, pleural effusions occur in patients with AIDS but are less common than are parenchymal infiltrates. In a recent series of 1225 consecutive hospital admissions of patients with AIDS in Jacksonville, Florida, the incidence of pleural effusion was 15%.[269] The distribution of the diseases responsible for pleural effusions in patients with AIDS varies widely from series to series.[270] In series from industrialized countries that included predominantly intravenous drug users, the most common cause is parapneumonic effusions; in contrast, in series with predominantly homosexuals, the most common cause is Kaposi's sarcoma. In series from Africa, tuberculosis is the most common cause.[270] Other causes of pleural effusions in patients with AIDS include body-cavity lymphoma, *Pneumocystis jiroveci* (formerly *carinii*), opportunistic infections, renal failure, and congestive heart failure.[271]

Patients with AIDS and parapneumonic effusions should be managed as would any patient with a parapneumonic effusion, but the incidence of complicated parapneumonic effusion is higher in patients with AIDS.[272] The incidence of pleural effusion with pulmonary Kaposi's sarcoma is approximately 50%.[270] Most patients with a pleural effusion due to Kaposi's sarcoma have bilateral parenchymal infiltrates. The diagnosis of pleural involvement is difficult and often depends on the demonstration of pulmonary Kaposi's sarcoma, either by bronchoscopic examination, high-resolution CT, or thoracoscopy. The pleural fluid is an exudate that is usually serosanguineous or hemorrhagic. Pleural fluid cytologic examinations are invariably negative with pleural Kaposi's sarcoma; pleural biopsy results are also usually negative because the parietal pleura is not involved.[270]

Patients with AIDS with an exudative pleural effusion should have a diagnostic thoracentesis that includes bacterial, mycobacterial, and fungal cultures and measurement of the pleural fluid ADA or interferon-γ level. If this does not establish a diagnosis, consideration should be given to performing thoracoscopy, at which time a pleurodesis may be considered in symptomatic patients.

PARASITIC DISEASES

Parasitic infections of the lungs are discussed in Chapter 35. Those that may also involve the pleura—amebiasis, echinococcosis, and paragonimiasis—are also considered in this section.

Amebiasis

Pleural effusions arise by two different mechanisms in conjunction with amebic liver abscess. First, an amebic liver abscess may irritate the diaphragm and produce a sympathetic pleural effusion in a manner analogous to that of pyogenic liver abscess. Second, a pleural effusion develops when an amebic liver abscess ruptures into the pleural space through the diaphragm.[273]

The sympathetic effusion in amebic liver abscess is more common than rupture of an abscess through the diaphragm.[273] Patients with sympathetic effusions frequently have pleuritic chest pain referred to the tip of the scapula or the shoulder. The chest radiograph reveals a small to moderate-sized pleural effusion and often elevation of the hemidiaphragm with platelike atelectasis.[274] The pleural fluid has not been well characterized. The diagnosis can be established by positive gel diffusion, indirect hemagglutination, or enzyme-linked immunosorbent assay tests, the results of which are positive in more than 98% of patients with extraintestinal invasive amebiasis.[273] Patients with amebic abscess and a sympathetic pleural effusion should be treated with antiamebic drugs, as described in Chapter 35.

The transdiaphragmatic rupture of an amebic liver abscess is usually heralded by an abrupt exacerbation of pain in the right upper quadrant and may be accompanied by a tearing sensation.[274] Shortly thereafter, progressive respiratory distress, sepsis, and occasionally shock develop. The pleural effusion is frequently massive, with opacification of the entire hemithorax and shift of the mediastinum to the contralateral side.[274] The diagnosis of amebic abscess with transdiaphragmatic rupture is suggested by the discovery of "anchovy paste"—or "chocolate sauce"—like pleural fluid on diagnostic thoracentesis.

Patients with transdiaphragmatic rupture should undergo tube thoracostomy. Large-bore tubes should be used because the pleural fluid can be quite viscid.[274] The patients should also be treated with the same antiamebic drugs recommended for patients with amebic sympathetic effusions. Most patients are cured with the drugs together with pleural drainage.[275] Because bacterial infection of the pleural space complicates the process in about one third of patients,[276] bacterial cultures of the pleural fluid should be obtained routinely. If bacterial infection is present, appropriate antibiotic therapy should be initiated.

Echinococcosis

Pleural involvement with hydatid disease can develop in one of three situations: (1) a pulmonary hydatid cyst may rupture into the pleural space; (2) a hepatic hydatid cyst or, on rare occasions, a splenic cyst may rupture through the diaphragm into the pleural space; or (3) the pleura maybe be primarily involved by the slowly enlarging cyst.[277] When a cyst ruptures into the pleural space, either an empyema or a pneumothorax can result.[277] In a recent series of 474 patients with pulmonary hydatid disease, 6% had pleural thickening or effusion.[277a]

When a hydatid cyst ruptures into the pleural space, the patient develops acute symptoms, with sudden tearing chest pain, dyspnea, and shock from the antigenic challenge to the body.[278] The cyst frequently also ruptures into the tracheobronchial tree, producing a bronchopleural fistula with a hydropneumothorax that may become secondarily infected.[277]

The diagnosis of pleural echinococcosis is established by the demonstration of echinococcal scolices with hooklets in the pleural fluid or the pleural biopsy specimen. Eosinophils are frequently present in the pleural fluid unless it is secondarily infected.[279] Patients with pleural echinococcosis should be immediately subjected to thoracotomy to remove the parasite, to excise the original cyst, and to close the bronchopleural fistula.[277] Patients with hydatid cysts should be treated with antiprotozoal therapy if all the cysts cannot be removed, or when rupture of a cyst has occurred.

Paragonimiasis

Pleural disease is common with paragonimiasis. In one series of 71 patients, 43 (61%) had pleural disease, including 20 with unilateral pleural effusions, 6 with bilateral pleural effusions, 6 each with unilateral and bilateral hydropneumothorax, and 5 with pleural thickening.[280] In a review of 25 Indochinese refugees with paragonimiasis, 48% had pleural effusions, which were massive in 6 patients and the sole manifestation in 5.[76] Paragonimiasis can occur in natives of the United States who have never left the country.[281]

Patients with pleural paragonimiasis present with a chronic illness. There is also a parenchymal infiltrate in approximately 50% of patients. The pleural fluid in patients with pleural paragonimiasis is characteristic. It is an exudate with a glucose level of less than 10 mg/dL (0.56 mmol/L), an LDH level of more than three times the upper limit of normal for serum, a pH below 7.10, and a differential revealing a high percentage of eosinophils.[76] In addition, cholesterol crystals are frequently present.[76] Pleural paragonimiasis is one of only two conditions in which the pleural fluid is characterized by a low pH, a low glucose level, and many eosinophils; the other is Churg-Strauss syndrome. Usually, there are no ova in the pleural fluid.

The diagnosis of pleural paragonimiasis is strongly suggested by the unique pleural fluid findings of low glucose level, low pH, and pleural fluid eosinophilia. The diagnosis is established definitively by demonstrating the typical operculated eggs in sputum, stool, or pleural fluid. A complement fixation titer above 1:8 for *Paragonimus westermani* is strongly suggestive of the diagnosis.[76]

The treatment of choice for paragonimiasis is praziquantel, 25 mg/kg body weight three times a day for 3 days.[282] If the pleural disease has been present for such a prolonged period that the pleural surfaces are abnormally thickened, penetration of antiparasitic agents into the pleural space may be insufficient to eradicate the infection, and thoracotomy with decortication may be necessary.[283]

PULMONARY EMBOLISM

The diagnosis most commonly overlooked in the differential diagnosis of a patient with an undiagnosed pleural effusion is pulmonary embolism. It has been estimated that at least 500,000 persons develop venous thromboembolism annually in the United States. Because at least 30% of patients with pulmonary emboli have an associated pleural effusion,[284] over 150,000 pleural effusions secondary to pulmonary emboli should occur annually. Therefore, one should expect to see more cases of pleural effusion secondary to pulmonary embolization than to bronchogenic carcinoma. Nevertheless, in most large series, pulmonary embolization accounts for fewer than 5% of pleural effusions. This discrepancy probably occurs because the diagnosis is frequently not considered in patients with undiagnosed pleural effusions. The diagnosis and treatment of pulmonary embolism are discussed in Chapter 48.

Pathophysiology

The mechanism by which pulmonary embolization produces pleural effusions is unknown. The pleural fluid in association with a pulmonary embolus is almost always exudative.[73] Exudative effusions result from an increase in the permeability of the capillaries either in the lung or in the pleura as a result of ischemia or inflammation. Any excess lung liquid can then move to the pleural space in a fashion similar to that shown for pulmonary edema.[9] Soluble factors, such as vascular endothelial growth factor, may play a role in at least some patients because the pleural fluid vascular endothelial growth factor level was very high in one patient with pulmonary embolism.[285] Transudative effusions, if they occur, may result from increased central venous pressure and decreased intrapleural pressure.

Clinical Manifestations

Patients with pulmonary embolism can be divided into three categories, depending on their presenting symptoms: (1) pleuritic pain or hemoptysis, (2) isolated dyspnea, and (3) circulatory collapse. In the Prospective Investigation of Pulmonary Embolism Diagnosis (PIOPED) study, 56% of the patients with pleuritic pain or hemoptysis had pleural effusion, and 26% of those with isolated dyspnea had pleural effusion, but none of the patients with circulatory collapse had pleural effusion.[284]

Approximately 50% of patients with paraembolic effusions have parenchymal infiltrates seen on chest radiographs.[286] The infiltrates are usually in the lower lobes, are pleura based, and are convex toward the hilum. Paraembolic effusions are usually small; in one series, 48 of 56 patients (86%) had only blunting of the costophrenic angle, and no patient had an effusion that occupied more than one third of a hemithorax.[284] Patients with parenchymal infiltrates tend to have larger effusions. The pleural effusions may be unilateral or bilateral. In one study of 57 patients with pulmonary emboli and pleural effusion, the effusions were bilateral in 20 (35%).[287] Interestingly, in more recent studies using spiral CT angiography in patients suspected of having pulmonary embolism, those patients found to have pulmonary embolism were no more likely to have pleural effusions than those without embolism (50% vs. 58%[288]; 57% vs. 56%[289]). Patients suspected of having pulmonary embolism likely have other underlying conditions that predispose them to pleural effusions, such as congestive heart failure or pneumonia.

Pleural fluid analysis is of limited value in establishing the diagnosis of paraembolic effusion because there is nothing characteristic about the fluid. The pleural fluid is almost always an exudate.[73] The pleural fluid red blood cell count exceeds 100,000/μL in fewer than 20% and is below 10,000/μL in at least 30%. The pleural fluid white blood cell count can vary from under 100 to over 50,000/μL. The differential white blood cell count may reveal predominantly polymorphonuclear leukocytes or mononuclear cells.

Diagnosis

The possibility of pulmonary embolization should be considered in every patient with a pleural effusion, even if the patient has obvious congestive heart failure. In an autopsy series of 290 patients with congestive heart failure and pleural effusion, 60 (21%) had pulmonary emboli.[150] When a paraembolic effusion is strongly suspected, the patient should be started on heparin treatment and a test for pulmonary embolism should be performed before a thoracentesis is attempted.[185]

The best screening test for pulmonary emboli appears to be measurement of the D-dimers in the peripheral blood (see Chapter 48). Although the D-dimer test is very sensitive, it is not particularly specific.[185] Therefore, if the D-dimer test is positive, an additional test is necessary to confirm the diagnosis. The spiral CT scan appears to be the preferred test if it is available, because it is more accurate than lung scans and also provides addition information about the status of the lung parenchyma and the mediastinum.[290] Another reason to obtain the spiral CT scan rather than a perfusion scan in patients with pleural effusions suspected of having pulmonary emboli is that the presence of the effusion makes the lung scan more difficult to interpret.[290] An alternative approach is to study the legs to see if there is any evidence of deep venous thrombosis with duplex ultrasonography with venous compression. This test has a sensitivity that exceeds 90% and a specificity that exceeds 95%.[291] If deep venous thrombosis is not demonstrated, then additional studies are necessary to delineate the etiology of the pleural effusion.

Treatment

The treatment of the patient with a paraembolic effusion is the same as for any patient with pulmonary emboli (see Chapter 48). The presence of bloody pleural fluid is not a contraindication to the administration of heparin or, if indicated, thrombolytic therapy. Bynum and Wilson[286] treated three patients who had pleural fluid red blood cell counts above 100,000/μL with intravenous heparin and observed no increase in the size of the effusion.

Paraembolic effusions usually reach their maximum size within the first 3 days.[292] If the effusion increases in size after this time, the patient probably has recurrent emboli or another complication. Bynum and Wilson[286] reported two patients in whom an enlarging ipsilateral effusion developed; one had recurrent pulmonary emboli, whereas the other had a pleural infection. Of two additional patients in whom contralateral pleural effusions developed, both had recurrent emboli. A diagnostic thoracentesis is therefore indicated in patients in whom the effusion enlarges after therapy is instituted. If bloody pleural fluid is discovered, a pleural fluid hematocrit value should be obtained. If the pleural fluid hematocrit value is greater than 50% of the peripheral hematocrit, a hemothorax is present that cannot be attributed to pulmonary embolism. If this is the case, anticoagulation should be discontinued, and tube thoracostomy should be performed.[293]

With treatment, paraembolic effusions gradually resolve. The resolution is much more rapid in patients without parenchymal infiltrates; in most of these patients, complete resolution occurs within 7 days. In contrast, resolution is rarely complete within 7 days in those with parenchymal infiltrates.

ABDOMINAL DISEASES

As discussed in Chapter 78, many abdominal diseases can cause pulmonary signs and symptoms. This section describes the most important of these disorders that cause pleural effusion. The pleural effusions occurring in patients with chronic liver disease and ascites and in those with infectious hepatitis have already been discussed.

Esophageal Perforation

The diagnosis of esophageal rupture should always be considered in the differential diagnosis of exudative pleural effusions because, if this condition is not rapidly treated, the mortality increases, with current estimates ranging between 30% and 60%.[294] Approximately 60% of patients with esophageal perforation have a pleural effusion, whereas about 25% have a pneumothorax.[295] The pleural effusion is usually left sided (Fig. 68.9), but it may be right sided or bilateral.

Esophageal perforation most commonly occurs as a complication of esophagoscopy and is more likely to occur when there is an attempt to remove a foreign body or to dilate an esophageal stricture.[296] Overall, the incidence of esophageal perforation with esophagoscopic examination is 0.15% to 0.70%.[295] The insertion of a Blakemore-Sengstaken tube for esophageal varices is sometimes complicated by esophageal rupture. Frequently, the diagnosis is missed in these patients because of the severity of their illness and the multiple coexisting problems.[295] Esophageal perforation may also result from transesophageal echocardiography, foreign bodies, esophageal carcinoma, gastric intubation, chest trauma, chest surgery, or vomiting (Boerhaave's syndrome).

Clinical Manifestations. The symptoms associated with esophageal perforation result from the acute mediastinitis produced by contamination of the mediastinum by the oropharyngeal contents. Most of the morbidity from esophageal perforation is caused by infection of the mediastinum and the pleural space by the oropharyngeal bacterial flora.[105]

A patient with an esophageal perforation is usually acutely ill. With a spontaneous rupture, there is frequently a sensation of tearing or bursting in the lower part of the chest or the

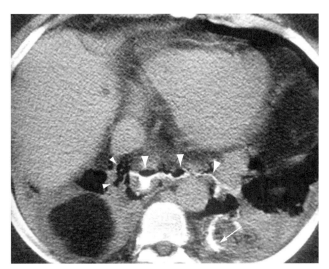

Figure 68.9 Effusion due to esophageal perforation. Axial computed tomography scan through the lower thorax in a patient with chest pain shows pneumomediastinum (*small arrowheads*) and leakage of water-soluble oral contrast from the ruptured esophagus (*large arrowheads*) through the mediastinum into the left pleural space (*arrow*). (From Fadoo F, Ruiz DE, Dawn SK, et al: Helical CT esophagography for the evaluation of suspected esophageal perforation or rupture. AJR Am J Roentgenol 182:1177–1179, 2004.)

ferred contrast medium has been in question, because barium, although it has better radiographic density and lower cost, may lead to granulomatous inflammation or fibrosis after leakage into the mediastinum or pleura. Therefore, instead of barium, aqueous iodinated contrast media are used primarily to detect leaks, due to their safety and rapid absorption[301]; one such medium, Hexabrix (ioxaglate meglumine and ioxaglate sodium), has been suggested as a contrast agent of choice because it does not elicit much of an inflammatory reaction in the pleura.[302] With fluoroscopic studies, water-soluble contrast agents may fail to reveal small leaks because of their lower radiographic density compared to barium; therefore, it has been recommended that negative studies with water-soluble contrast be followed by confirmatory studies with barium.[301] Currently, for reasons of speed and thoroughness, CT studies may supplant fluoroscopic studies for evaluation of possible esophageal tears. Given the higher resolution of CT scans, water-soluble contrast dyes appear to be sufficient to visualize leaks[303] (see Fig. 68.9).

Treatment. The treatment of mediastinitis from esophageal perforation and other causes is discussed in detail in Chapter 78. Prompt surgical exploration of the mediastinum with primary repair of the esophageal tear and drainage of the pleural space and the mediastinum should be carried out.[296] Parenteral antibiotics should be given to treat the mediastinitis and pleural infection. If exploration of the mediastinum is delayed for more than 48 hours after rupture, primary repair is usually not possible because of the damaged tissue. Such patients are probably best managed with T-tube intubation of the esophageal defect.[296]

Pancreatic Disease

Three different types of nonmalignant pancreatic disease can have an accompanying pleural effusion: acute pancreatitis, chronic pancreatitis with pseudocyst, and pancreatic ascites.

Acute Pancreatitis. In a study of 133 patients with their first attack of acute pancreatitis, 50% of the patients had a pleural effusion on chest CT scan.[304] Of those with effusions, the effusion was bilateral in 51 (77%), unilateral left sided in 10 (15%), and unilateral right sided in 5 (8%). Patients with acute pancreatitis and a pleural effusion had more severe disease and a higher mortality rate than did those without effusions.[304] The exudative pleural effusion accompanying acute pancreatitis results from the diaphragmatic inflammation and transdiaphragmatic transfer of the exudative fluid arising from acute pancreatic inflammation.

The clinical picture is usually dominated by abdominal symptoms, including pain, nausea, and vomiting. However, at times, respiratory symptoms consisting of pleuritic chest pain and dyspnea may dominate the clinical picture. In addition to the small to moderate-sized pleural effusion, the chest radiograph may reveal an elevated diaphragm and basilar infiltrates.[305] Demonstration of an elevated pleural fluid amylase level is highly suggestive of the diagnosis, but the diagnosis of esophageal rupture must be excluded. The pleural fluid is an exudate with predominantly polymorphonuclear leukocytes and a normal glucose level.

epigastrium. The chest pain is characteristically excruciating and is often unrelieved by opiates. Dyspnea is frequently a prominent symptom. More than 50% of patients have small amounts of hematemesis. The presence of subcutaneous emphysema in the suprasternal notch is suggestive of the diagnosis. However, less than 10% of patients have subcutaneous emphysema within the first 4 hours of rupture.[297] When the esophagus is perforated during esophagoscopy, the endoscopist generally does not realize it; however, the patients usually develop persistent chest or epigastric pain within a few hours after completion of the procedure.

Diagnosis. The diagnosis of esophageal rupture should be considered in all acutely ill patients with an exudative pleural effusion. The best screening test for esophageal rupture appears to be the level of amylase in the pleural fluid.[297] In the experimental model, the pleural fluid amylase level is elevated within 2 hours of rupture.[105] Only one patient has been reported in the literature with a perforated esophagus without an elevated pleural fluid amylase level. This patient was unable to produce saliva because of Sjögren's syndrome with keratoconjunctivitis sicca.[298] The pleural fluid amylase level is elevated owing to saliva, with its high amylase content, entering the pleural space.[104]

The pleural fluid pH is usually decreased below 7.00 in patients with pleural effusion secondary to esophageal perforation.[299] The mechanism for the low pleural fluid pH appears to be the intense inflammatory response resulting from the mediastinitis and not the regurgitation of gastric juice into the pleural space.[299] The demonstration of either squamous epithelial cells or food particles in the pleural fluid is highly suggestive of the diagnosis.[300]

The diagnosis is established when esophageal perforation is confirmed by contrast studies of the esophagus. The pre-

Patients with pancreatitis and a pleural effusion should be treated for their pancreatitis in the usual manner (see Chapter 78). If the pleural effusion does not resolve within 2 weeks of the initiation of treatment, the possibility of a pancreatic abscess or a pancreatic pseudocyst must be considered.

Chronic Pancreatic Pleural Effusion. Patients with chronic pancreatic disease sometimes have a large chronic pleural effusion. Most of these patients have a pancreatic pseudocyst. When the pancreatic ductal system is disrupted, a pseudocyst may form in the pancreas. A sinus tract may extend from the pseudocyst through the aortic or esophageal hiatus into the mediastinum. Once the sinus tract reaches the mediastinum, the process may be contained to form a mediastinal pseudocyst or it may rupture into one or both pleural spaces, resulting in a large chronic pleural effusion[106] (Fig. 68.10).

The clinical picture of patients with chronic pancreatic disease and pleural effusion is usually dominated by chest symptoms, such as dyspnea, cough, and chest pain. Most patients do not have abdominal symptoms because the pancreaticopleural fistula decompresses the pseudocyst. The pleural effusion is usually massive and recurs rapidly after thoracentesis.[106] The effusion is usually left sided but may be right sided or bilateral.

The key to the diagnosis is a markedly elevated pleural fluid amylase level, generally greater than 1000 U/L, while the serum level of amylase may be only mildly elevated. Patients with chronic pancreatic pleural disease are generally easily differentiated from those with malignant pleural effusion, who also may have an elevated pleural fluid amylase level, because the amylase level is much higher with the pseudocyst. In rare cases in which the differentiation is not obvious, the diagnosis can be made by measuring amylase isoenzymes because the amylase associated with malignancy is of the salivary, not the pancreatic, type.[108] Both ultrasound and CT are useful in establishing the diagnosis of pancreatic pseudocyst. Endoscopic retrograde

cholangiopancreatography usually documents the fistulous tract or other pancreatic pathology.

Patients with chronic pancreatic pleural effusions should be given a trial of conservative therapy for 2 to 3 weeks that consists of nasogastric suction, no oral intake, suppression of pancreatic secretion with atropine, and repeated therapeutic thoracenteses.[106] The administration of a continuous infusion of somatostatin may decrease the secretions through the fistula and facilitate closure.[306] Conservative treatment is successful within 4 weeks in about 40% of patients. If conservative treatment fails, a laparotomy should be performed. The anatomy of the pancreatic ductal system should be assessed before surgery with endoscopic retrograde cholangiopancreatography or at the time of operation with operative pancreatography. If a sinus tract is found, it should be ligated or excised. The pancreas should be partially resected, drained with a Roux-en-Y loop, or both, depending on the pancreatographic findings.[106] An alternative approach is to attempt percutaneous abdominal pseudocyst drainage by use of CT guidance.[307] Decortication of the pleura may be necessary for some patients in order to remove the thick pleural peel created by the intense inflammation caused by the presence of pancreatic enzymes.

Pancreatic Ascites. Some patients with pancreatic disease develop ascites characterized by high amylase and protein levels. If such patients should happen to have or develop a defect in their diaphragm, they develop a large pleural effusion as a result of the flow of fluid from the peritoneal cavity to the pleural cavity. The treatment for pancreatic ascites is the same as for pancreatic pleural effusion, except serial paracenteses rather than serial thoracenteses are performed.[308]

Intra-Abdominal Abscesses

Pleural effusions frequently occur with intra-abdominal abscesses. The possibility of an intra-abdominal abscess should be considered strongly in any patient with an undiagnosed exudative pleural effusion containing predominantly polymorphonuclear leukocytes, particularly when there are no pulmonary parenchymal infiltrates. The mechanism responsible for the development of the exudative pleural effusion is probably diaphragmatic irritation.

Subphrenic abscess is the intra-abdominal abscess most commonly associated with a pleural effusion; pleural effusions occur in approximately 80% of patients with subphrenic abscess.[309] The approximate incidence of effusions with other intra-abdominal abscesses is 40% in pancreatic abscesses,[310] 30% in splenic abscess,[311] and 20% in intrahepatic abscesses.[312] With pancreatic abscess, the pleural fluid has a high amylase level.

Clinical Manifestations. Subphrenic abscess most commonly develops as a postoperative complication 1 to 3 weeks after intra-abdominal surgery.[309] Splenectomy and gastrectomy are particularly likely to be complicated by left subphrenic abscess. There is no antecedent abdominal surgery in approximately 10% of patients with subphrenic abscess.[309] The abscess may result from perforation of the stomach, duodenum, appendix, colon, or a diverticulum, or from diverticulitis, cholecystitis, pancreatitis, or trauma.

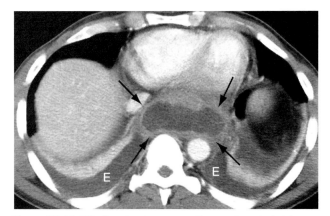

Figure 68.10 Effusion due to pancreatic pseudocyst. Axial computed tomography scan through the lower thorax in a patient with chronic pancreatitis shows bilateral pleural effusions (E) and a cystic mass in the middle mediastinum (*arrows*) representing a pseudocyst. (Courtesy of Michael B. Gotway, MD, Department of Radiology, University of California, San Francisco.)

Most patients have fever, leukocytosis, and abdominal pain, but, frequently, there are no localizing signs or symptoms.

Most patients with pyogenic intrahepatic abscesses have fever and anorexia. Abdominal pain is common, but, frequently, it is not localized to the right upper quadrant. On physical examination, an enlarged, tender liver can be demonstrated. Laboratory tests reveal leukocytosis, anemia, elevated alkaline phosphatase levels, and hyperbilirubinemia.[313]

Pancreatic abscess usually follows an episode of acute pancreatitis. This diagnosis should be suspected if the patient does not respond to the initial therapy or if fever, abdominal pain, and leukocytosis develop within 3 weeks of the episode of acute pancreatitis.[310] Splenic abscess is uncommon and usually occurs in patients with systemic infection. Bacterial endocarditis is the most common underlying infection.[311]

The pleural fluid that accumulates in patients with intra-abdominal abscesses is an exudate with predominantly polymorphonuclear leukocytes. The pleural fluid white blood cell count may exceed 50,000/µL, but the pleural fluid pH and glucose concentration usually remain above 7.20 and 60 mg/dL (3.33 mmol/L), respectively. Only rarely does the pleural fluid become infected.

Diagnosis and Treatment. The diagnosis of intra-abdominal abscess is best established with an abdominal CT scan,[314] which should be obtained in every patient with an undiagnosed exudative pleural effusion characterized by predominantly polymorphonuclear leukocytes if there are no parenchymal infiltrates. The appropriate treatment for a patient with an intra-abdominal abscess and a pleural effusion is drainage of the abscess combined with parenteral antibiotics.[315]

Diaphragmatic Hernia

Hernias through the diaphragm are important in two ways in the differential diagnosis of patients with suspected pleural disease. First, they may mimic a pleural effusion, and second, a pleural effusion is usually present with a strangulated diaphragmatic hernia. The possibility of a diaphragmatic hernia should be considered whenever an apparent pleural effusion has an atypical shape or location. If air is present in the herniated intestine, the diagnosis is easily established. If no air is present, an upper gastrointestinal series and a small bowel follow-through, a barium enema, or both, may be required to establish the diagnosis.

Most patients with a strangulated diaphragmatic hernia have a pleural effusion; in fact, the development of an effusion may indicate that chronic hernias have strangulated.[316] Usually, diaphragmatic hernias are traumatic in origin, but the strangulation may not occur for months to years after the original injury, which usually is an automobile accident.[316] More than 90% of strangulated diaphragmatic hernias are on the left side, perhaps because the liver protects the right hemidiaphragm. Strangulation usually occurs suddenly and progresses rapidly, and the patient presents with signs of intestinal obstruction. Left shoulder pain is typically present owing to diaphragmatic irritation. The diagnosis is suggested by the presence of air-fluid levels in the strangulated viscera within the left pleural space. The pleural fluid is a serosanguineous exudate with predominantly polymorphonuclear leukocytes. The proper treatment is immediate surgery to prevent gangrene of the strangulated viscera.[316]

Abdominal Surgery

Approximately 50% of patients undergoing abdominal surgery develop a pleural effusion in the first few days after surgery.[317,318] The incidence of postoperative pleural effusion is greater in patients undergoing upper abdominal surgery, in patients with postoperative atelectasis, and in patients with free abdominal fluid at surgery.[317,318] The accumulation of pleural fluid within the first 72 hours after abdominal surgery is probably related to either diaphragmatic irritation or transdiaphragmatic movement of intra-abdominal fluid. A postoperative patient with a significant amount of pleural fluid, particularly when associated with fever, should have a diagnostic thoracentesis to rule out pleural infection as a cause of the effusion. In addition, the possibility of pulmonary embolization should be considered. If the effusion develops more than 72 hours after surgery, it is probably not related to the surgical procedure itself, and alternative explanations must be sought, such as pulmonary embolization, intra-abdominal abscess, and hypervolemia.

Liver Transplantation

Most patients who undergo an orthotopic liver transplantation develop a pleural effusion after surgery. In one study, 68% of 300 patients undergoing liver transplantation developed a pleural effusion, and the effusion occupied more than 25% of the hemithorax in 21 patients (7%).[319] The effusion was unilateral right sided in 153 and bilateral in 53. The effusions are large enough to require therapeutic thoracentesis or tube thoracostomy in approximately 10%.[319] The natural history of these effusions is that they increase in size over the first 3 postoperative days and then gradually resolve over several weeks to several months.[320] The pathogenesis of these effusions is probably related to injury or irritation of the right hemidiaphragm caused by the extensive right upper quadrant dissection. These pleural effusions can be largely prevented if a fibrin sealant is sprayed on the undersurface of the diaphragm around the insertion of the liver ligaments at the time of the transplantation.[321]

Bilious Pleural Effusion

Bilious pleural effusions are due to a fistula from the biliary tree to the pleural space.[322] The fistula may be secondary to trauma, suppurative complications of biliary tract infections, or surgery, particularly when biliary obstruction is present. The diagnosis should be suspected in any patient with an obstructed biliary tract. The pleural fluid usually appears bilious, but, at times, the diagnosis may depend on the demonstration that the ratio of pleural fluid to serum bilirubin is greater than 1.0. Appropriate treatment consists of reestablishment of biliary drainage. The incidence of empyema with bilious pleural effusion is approximately 50%. Most patients who have a bilious pleural effusion require decortication and diaphragmatic repair.[322]

MISCELLANEOUS DISEASES

Rheumatoid Pleuritis

The pleura is occasionally involved in the course of rheumatoid arthritis. Approximately 5% of patients with rheumatoid arthritis have a pleural effusion, and approximately 20% experience pleuritic chest pain.[109,323] Rheumatoid pleurisy has a striking male predominance, despite the higher prevalence of rheumatoid disease in women; more than 10% of men, but less than 2% of women, with rheumatoid disease have a pleural effusion.[109,323] Additional information about rheumatoid pleuritis and other pulmonary manifestations of rheumatoid arthritis is found in Chapter 54.

The pathogenesis of the pleuritis or the pleural effusion associated with rheumatoid arthritis is not definitely known but probably involves cellular immune reactions. Evidence for this immune mechanism includes elevated pleural fluid levels of soluble IL-2 receptor, T lymphocytes, and ADA.[324] Autopsy examination usually reveals only thickened pleura, with nonspecific chronic inflammation. The thickened visceral pleural surfaces are frequently studded with small nodules with the histologic features of rheumatoid nodules.

Clinical Manifestations. Rheumatoid pleural effusions classically occur in the older male patient with rheumatoid arthritis and subcutaneous nodules. Almost all patients with rheumatoid pleural effusions are older than 35 years; moreover, approximately 80% are men and approximately 80% have subcutaneous nodules. The pleural effusion usually develops only after the arthritis has been present for several years,[109] but on rare occasions a patient may present with a pleural effusion.[325]

Patients with rheumatoid pleuritis may be asymptomatic or symptomatic with pleuritic chest pain, fever, or both,[109,113] and some patients experience dyspnea secondary to the presence of pleural fluid. In most patients, the chest radiograph reveals a small or moderate-sized pleural effusion. In approximately 25% of patients, the effusion is bilateral.[109] With time, the effusion may alternate from one side to the other or may come and go on the same side. Other intrathoracic manifestations of rheumatoid disease are present in up to one third of patients.[109]

Diagnosis. The diagnosis is suggested by the clinical picture of rheumatoid arthritis and the presence of a pleural effusion. The pleural fluid with rheumatoid pleuritis is distinctive, characterized by a glucose level less than 30 mg/dL (1.67 mmol/L), a high LDH level (>700 IU/L), a low pH (<7.20), and a high rheumatoid factor titer (>1:320).[113] Occasionally, the pleural fluid glucose is not reduced when the patient is first seen, but serial pleural fluid glucose determinations reveal progressively lower pleural fluid glucose levels. Another interesting characteristic of rheumatoid pleural effusions is their tendency to contain cholesterol crystals or high levels of cholesterol.[326] A unique cytologic appearance of elongated comet-shaped or "tadpole" cells is also considered specific for the diagnosis.[325,327]

With the characteristic pleural fluid findings, the primary alternative diagnosis to exclude is complicated parapneumonic effusion. The incidence of complicated parapneumonic effusion is high in patients with rheumatoid pleuritis,[328] so this differentiation is important. It is particularly important to examine the Gram stain of the pleural fluid and to culture the fluid both aerobically and anaerobically.

Prognosis and Treatment. The natural history of rheumatoid pleuritis varies. Most patients experience a spontaneous resolution within 3 months, but the effusion is persistent in an occasional patient, and massive pleural thickening sometimes develops. There are no studies that demonstrate that anti-inflammatory therapy has any influence on the course of rheumatoid pleuritis. The results after intrapleural corticosteroids have been mixed.[329] Decortication should be considered in patients with thickened pleura, who are symptomatic with dyspnea. This procedure is particularly difficult in patients with rheumatoid pleuritis because it is not easy to develop a plane of dissection between the lung and the fibrous peel.[330]

Lupus Pleuritis

Approximately 40% of patients with systemic lupus erythematosus or drug-induced lupus have a pleural effusion during the course of their disease.[110]

Clinical Manifestations. Most patients with lupus pleuritis have arthritis or arthralgias before the development of a pleural effusion. Almost all patients with lupus pleuritis have pleuritic chest pain, and most are also febrile. Lupus pleuritis frequently develops in association with an exacerbation of the underlying disease. The pleural effusions secondary to lupus are usually small and are bilateral in about 50% of patients.[331]

Many medications have been incriminated for producing drug-induced lupus erythematosus (see Chapter 67).[64] Hydralazine, procainamide, isoniazid, phenytoin, and chlorpromazine are the ones most commonly associated with drug-induced lupus, but there are more that 70 other drugs that possibly induce lupus.[332] The presenting signs, symptoms, and radiographic abnormalities are similar, whether the pleuritis is due to spontaneous or to drug-induced lupus. The symptoms associated with drug-induced lupus characteristically abate within days of discontinuing the offending drug.

Diagnosis. The possibility of lupus pleuritis should be considered in any patient with an exudative pleural effusion of unknown cause. The pleural fluid can contain a predominance of either polymorphonuclear or mononuclear cells, depending on the timing of the thoracentesis in relation to the development of the symptoms.[66] Although it was believed in the past that elevated ANA titers in the pleural fluid were diagnostic of lupus pleuritis, it appears that such elevated titers are neither specific nor sensitive for diagnosing lupus pleuritis.[111,333] Likewise, because the presence of lupus erythematosus cells in pleural fluid is not specific for lupus pleuritis, this test should not be ordered.[334] The diagnosis is based primarily on the clinical picture and the serologic findings for lupus.

Treatment. In contrast to rheumatoid pleuritis, the pleuritis with systemic lupus responds to corticosteroid administration. It is recommended that patients with lupus pleuritis be treated with oral prednisone, 80 mg every other day, with rapid tapering once the symptoms are controlled. At times, the effusion is large, is symptomatic, and does not respond to corticosteroid therapy. In such a situation, consideration should be given to chemical pleurodesis.[335] Of course, if the patient has drug-induced lupus, the offending drug should be withdrawn.[64]

Post–Cardiac Injury Syndrome (PCIS)

This syndrome, which is also known as the postpericardiectomy or the post–myocardial infarction (Dressler's) syndrome, is characterized by combinations of pericarditis, pleuritis, and pneumonitis that develop after injury to the myocardium or pericardium.[336] In a recent paper, noncomplicated PCIS was defined as the presence of temperature greater than 100.5° F, patient irritability, pericardial friction rub, and a small pericardial effusion with or without pleural effusion following cardiac trauma.[337] A complicated PCIS is defined as a noncomplicated PCIS plus the need for hospital readmission with or without the need for pericardiocentesis or thoracentesis.[337] PCIS has occurred after myocardial infarction, cardiac surgery, blunt chest trauma, percutaneous left ventricle puncture, and implantation of a pacemaker.[336] The incidence of PCIS is approximately 1% after myocardial infarction and is somewhat higher after cardiac surgery.[64] The exact pathogenesis of this syndrome is unknown, but it appears to have an immunologic basis. Engle and colleagues[338] reported that there was a close relationship between the development of the syndrome and the presence of anti-heart antibodies, but it is unclear whether the anti-heart antibodies instigate or result from the syndrome.

Clinical Manifestations. The syndrome typically develops about 3 weeks after the injury, but it can occur any time between 3 days and 1 year later. The two cardinal symptoms are fever and chest pain. The chest pain often precedes the onset of fever and can vary from an agonizing crush to a dull ache. At times, it may have a pleuritic component. Most patients have a pericardial friction rub, and echocardiography can demonstrate pleural fluid in more than 50% of the patients.[339] Pulmonary infiltrates are present in about 50% of patients, and laboratory evaluation reveals leukocytosis with an elevated erythrocyte sedimentation rate.[339–341]

A pleural effusion occurs in about two thirds of patients with PCIS.[341] The pleural effusions are bilateral and small in most patients.[339,341] The pleural fluid is an exudate that is frequently serosanguineous or bloody.[339] The pleural fluid glucose level exceeds 60 mg/dL (3.33 mmol/L), and the pH is usually above 7.40. The pleural fluid differential may reveal either predominantly polymorphonuclear leukocytes or mononuclear cells, depending on the acuteness of the process.[339]

Diagnosis. The diagnosis of PCIS should be considered in any patient who develops a pleural effusion after injury to the heart. The diagnosis of the syndrome is established by the clinical picture and by excluding congestive heart failure, pulmonary embolism, and pneumonia. A spiral CT scan or a perfusion lung scan should be obtained to exclude the diagnosis of pulmonary embolization. An advantage of spiral CT is that it can also document pericardial and parenchymal involvement or an alternative diagnosis.

Treatment. PCIS usually responds to treatment with anti-inflammatory agents, such as aspirin and indomethacin.

Corticosteroids may be necessary in more severe cases, and may be indicated to prevent coronary bypass graft occlusion, a potential complication of PCIS following coronary artery bypass graft (CABG) surgery.[340]

Post–Coronary Artery Bypass Surgery

More than 600,000 patients undergo CABG surgery in the United States each year. Because approximately 10% of patients who undergo CABG surgery will develop a pleural effusion that occupies more than 25% of their hemithorax in the subsequent month,[342] CABG surgery is one of the more common causes of pleural effusions in the United States. The prevalence of small pleural effusions is high following CABG surgery. In one study, the prevalence of pleural effusions in 47 patients as detected by ultrasound was 89% at 7 days, 77% at 14 days, and 57% at 30 days.[343] In a recent study of 349 patients post-CABG, the prevalence of pleural effusion on chest radiograph 30 days postoperatively was 62%; 40 of the 349 patients (11%) had an effusion that occupied more than 25% of the hemithorax.[342] The pleural effusions after CABG surgery tend to be left sided or bilateral and, if bilateral, the effusion is usually larger on the left.[342]

The primary symptom of a patient with a large pleural effusion post-CABG is dyspnea.[342] The presence of either chest pain or fever should alert the physician to an alternative diagnosis. When all patients with large pleural effusions after CABG surgery are considered, the effusions can be divided into those that are bloody and those that are serous. The bloody effusions are probably secondary to bleeding into the pleural space. They reach their maximal size within 30 days of surgery, are frequently associated with pleural fluid or peripheral eosinophilia or both, have a high pleural fluid LDH level,[344] and respond to one or two therapeutic thoracenteses.[344] In contrast, the cause of the serous pleural effusions is unknown. They tend to reach their maximal size more than 30 days after surgery, have more than 50% small lymphocytes, and have a relatively low pleural fluid LDH level.[344] Most of these late effusions can also be managed with one or two therapeutic thoracenteses,[342] but some are very refractory. It is unknown whether anti-inflammatory agents or diuretics are beneficial in the treatment of these effusions. An occasional patient will require thoracoscopy with decortication because of a lung trapped by a thin fibrous membrane.[345]

Other Collagen Vascular Diseases

Pleural effusions occasionally occur in the course of Churg-Strauss syndrome, Wegener's granulomatosis, Sjögren's syndrome, and angioimmunoblastic lymphadenopathy, which are described in detail in other chapters. The pleural disease that occurs with these diseases constitutes a relatively minor portion of the clinical picture.

Lung Transplantation

With lung transplantation, the lymphatics that normally drain the lung are severed. Accordingly, the fluid that normally leaves the lung via these lymphatics drains through the pleural space. The presence of chest tubes in the first few days after lung transplantation prevents the accumulation of pleural fluid. Pleural complications such as hemothorax, empyema, and persistent air leak contribute substantially to the postoperative morbidity and mortality. The incidence of pleural effusions at 3 months posttransplant is about 30% to 60%.[346,347] The incidence of effusion at 12 months is less than 10%.[347] The effusions are characteristically a lymphocyte-predominant exudate with a benign course.[346] However, patients who develop complications after lung transplantation are likely to develop pleural effusions. In one study, pleural effusions occurred with 14 (74%) of 19 episodes of acute rejection, 7 (88%) of 8 instances of chronic rejection, 6 (55%) of 11 episodes of infection, and 3 (75%) of 4 instances of lymphoproliferative disease.[348] An occasional individual who donates a lobe of his or her lung for lung transplantation will also develop a pleural effusion.[349] (More details about lung transplantation are provided in Chapter 89.)

Asbestos Exposure

An otherwise unexplained pleural effusion may occur after exposure to asbestos, which may have been brief or intermittent, and in the immediate or distant past. Epler and coworkers[350] reviewed the medical histories of 1135 asbestos workers whom they had followed up for several years and found that 35 (3%) of the workers had pleural effusions for which there was no other ready explanation. The heavier the asbestos exposure, the more likely the patient is to develop a pleural effusion. The pleural effusion sometimes develops within 5 years of the initial exposure, but in one large series, the mean latency was 30 years.[351]

The pathogenesis of the pleural effusion occurring after asbestos exposure is unknown.[19] Asbestos fibers, both long and short, may move from the lung to the pleural space and lodge in the parietal pleura, where they appear to be concentrated in specific locations that correlate with the lymphatic drainage. Here, their presence leads to a continuous low-grade inflammation.[19] This chronic inflammation can either decrease the lymphatic clearance of the pleural space or increase the permeability of the capillaries in the parietal pleura, either of which could lead to the development of an exudative pleural effusion. An immune mechanism has been invoked to explain the fluctuations in the degree of pleuritis with time.[351]

Clinical Manifestations. Patients with pleural effusion secondary to asbestos exposure have surprisingly few symptoms. In the series of Epler and coworkers,[350] 66% had no symptoms. The chest radiograph usually reveals a small to moderate-sized effusion, which is bilateral in about 10%. The pleural fluid is an exudate, and the pleural fluid differential can reveal either predominantly polymorphonuclear leukocytes or mononuclear cells.[352] Interestingly, pleural fluid eosinophilia was present in 15 (52%) of the 29 patients with asbestos pleural effusions for whom pleural fluid differentials were reported.[70]

Diagnosis. The diagnosis of benign asbestos effusion is one of exclusion. It requires the following criteria: history of direct or indirect exposure to asbestos; exclusion of other causes, notably infection, pulmonary embolism, and malig-

nancy; and follow-up of at least 2 years to verify that the effusion is benign.[351]

Prognosis. The natural history of the patient with an asbestos pleural effusion is one of chronicity, with frequent recurrences and sometimes the development of extensive fibrosis of the parietal pleura.[350,352] On average, the pleural effusion persists for 3 months but eventually clears and leaves no residual pleural disease. Massive pleural fibrosis develops in about 20% of patients, and ipsilateral blunting of the costophrenic angle occurs in another 20%.[350,352] Rounded atelectasis also develops in about 10% of patients.[352] There is no known treatment for asbestos pleural effusion. Further information about asbestos-induced lung disease is provided in Chapter 61.

Sarcoidosis

A pleural effusion occasionally occurs in patients with sarcoidosis (see Chapter 55). The incidence of pleural effusion with sarcoidosis is probably less than 1%.[353] Patients with pleural effusion due to sarcoid usually have extensive parenchymal sarcoidosis and, frequently, extrathoracic sarcoidosis.[353] The symptoms of pleural involvement with sarcoidosis vary; many patients have no symptoms, although an equal number have pleuritic chest pain or dyspnea.[354]

The pleural effusions with sarcoidosis are usually small and are bilateral in approximately one third of cases. The pleural fluid is almost always an exudate, and its cell differential is characterized by predominantly small lymphocytes.[353]

The diagnosis of sarcoidosis depends initially on histologic demonstration of noncaseating granulomas in biopsy specimens from conventional sites, including pleural biopsy. In the patient with known sarcoidosis, one can attribute the presence of the pleural effusion to sarcoid only when other causes of exudative lymphocyte-predominant pleural effusions, such as tuberculosis, are excluded. The pleural effusion secondary to sarcoidosis may resolve spontaneously, or corticosteroid therapy may be required for its resolution.[355]

Uremia

Uremia may be complicated by a fibrinous pleuritis and pleural effusion.[356,357] The pathogenesis of the pleural effusion associated with uremia is unclear. It is probably somewhat analogous to that for uremic pericarditis because more than half of the patients with uremic pleuritis also have uremic pericarditis. The incidence of pleural effusions with uremia is approximately 3%.[357] A close relationship does not appear to exist between the degree of uremia and the occurrence of a pleural effusion. The incidence of pleural effusion in patients who are receiving chronic hemodialysis is approximately 50% on chest CT scan.[358] The etiologies of 100 effusions occurring in hospitalized patients with uremia were as follows: heart failure, 46; uremia, 16; parapneumonic, 15, atelectasis, 11; and miscellaneous, 12.[359]

The pleural effusion seen with uremia frequently occupies more than 50% of the hemithorax and is bilateral in about 20% of patients.[357] More than 50% of patients are symptomatic from the pleural disease, with fever (50%), chest pain (30%), cough (35%), and dyspnea (20%) being the most common symptoms. The pleural fluid is an exudate that is frequently serosanguineous or bloody. The glucose level is within normal limits, and the differential white blood cell count reveals predominantly lymphocytes.[357] Pleural biopsy specimens invariably reveal chronic fibrinous pleuritis.

The diagnosis of uremic pleuritis is one of exclusion in the patient with chronic renal failure. After beginning dialysis, the effusion gradually disappears within 4 to 6 weeks in about 75% of patients. In the remaining patients, the effusion persists, progresses, or recurs. An occasional patient develops marked pleural thickening that may require decortication.[360]

Meigs' Syndrome

Meigs and Cass[361] originally described a syndrome characterized by ascites and pleural effusion in association with solid benign ovarian tumors. Subsequently, it has become apparent that a similar syndrome can occur with benign cystic ovarian tumors, with benign tumors of the uterus (fibromyomas), and with low-grade ovarian malignant tumors without evidence of metastases.[64] The ascites appears to result from the secretion of large amounts of fluid by the tumors.[64] Vascular endothelial growth factor plays an important role in the pathogenesis of the ascites and pleural fluid, because vascular endothelial growth factor levels are high in both the ascites and pleural fluid.[362] It is thought that the pleural effusion results from the ascitic fluid passing through defects in the diaphragm into the pleural space.[363]

Patients with Meigs' syndrome usually have a chronic illness characterized by weight loss, pleural effusion, ascites, and a pelvic mass. It is important to realize that not all patients with this constellation of symptoms have a disseminated malignancy. Approximately 70% of the effusions are right sided, and 20% are bilateral. The pleural fluid is usually an exudate with a relatively low white blood cell count ($<1000/\mu L$) and occasionally is bloody. The level of CA-125 in the pleural fluid may be elevated, and this should not be taken as an indication of malignancy.[364]

The diagnosis of Meigs' syndrome should be considered in all women who have a pelvic mass, ascites, and a pleural effusion. If the cytology of the pleural fluid is negative in such patients, a diagnostic laparoscopy or an exploratory laparotomy should be performed to determine whether there are peritoneal metastases. The diagnosis is confirmed when the ascites and the pleural fluid resolve after the primary neoplasm is removed and do not recur. The pleural fluid disappears from the chest within the first 2 weeks after surgery.

Endometriosis

An occasional patient with severe endometriosis presents with massive ascites. In one review, 10 of 27 patients (37%) also had a pleural effusion.[365] The effusions are usually right sided but may be bilateral. The pleural fluid is a bloody or a chocolate-colored exudate. The serum carcinoembryonic antigen level may be elevated, suggesting ovarian carcinoma. Hormonal therapy, including gonadotropin-releasing hormone agonists, may be attempted, but frequently it is ineffective, and many patients require total abdominal hysterectomy plus bilateral salpingo-oophorectomy.[365]

Ovarian Hyperstimulation Syndrome

This syndrome is a serious complication of ovulation induction. The dramatic clinical picture is characterized by massive ovarian enlargement with multiple cysts, hemoconcentration, and the third-space accumulation of fluid.[366] The full-blown syndrome may be complicated by renal failure, hypovolemic shock, thromboembolic episodes, acute respiratory distress syndrome, and death. Although the pathophysiology of this syndrome is incompletely understood, it is likely that the increased capillary permeability is due to the up-regulation of vascular endothelial growth factor expression in the ovarian granulosa cells by the exogenous human chorionic gonadotropin.[367]

Patients with the syndrome present within 2 to 3 weeks of receiving the human chorionic gonadotropin. Patients typically present with abdominal pain and distention, nonproductive cough, and dyspnea caused by the ascites, pleural effusion, or both. The pleural effusion is usually bilateral, and the pleural fluid is an exudate with predominantly neutrophils and a relatively low LDH level. The treatment of severe cases requires restoration of intravascular volume, correction of electrolyte abnormalities, and venous thromboembolism prophylaxis.[364]

Extramedullary Hematopoiesis

Patients with severe chronic anemia may develop pleural effusions as a result of extramedullary hematopoiesis of the pleura.[368] Thoracentesis reveals a bloody pleural fluid with granulocytic and erythroid progenitors and megakaryocytes.[368] Management of the effusions is difficult, but low-dose radiotherapy to the pleura has been effective in controlling the pleural effusion.[368]

Yellow Nail Syndrome

This syndrome consists of the triad of deformed yellow nails, lymphedema, and pleural effusions. The three entities may become manifest at widely disparate times and therefore are not all concurrently present in every patient. One patient developed lymphedema in childhood, chronic nail changes at age 78 years, and a pleural effusion in her ninth decade.[369] The basic abnormality responsible for this syndrome appears to be hypoplasia of the lymphatic vessels,[370,371] although increased vascular permeability has been proposed to explain the high protein pleural effusions.[371a]

Typically, the nails are pale yellow to greenish in color and are excessively curved from side to side. They are also thickened and may show transverse ridging or onycholysis (separation of nail from bed). The pleural effusions are bilateral in about 50% of cases and can be massive. Once a pleural effusion has developed with this syndrome, it tends to persist and to recur rapidly after thoracentesis.[370] The pleural fluid is usually a clear exudate with predominantly lymphocytes.[370] The pleural fluid LDH tends to be relatively low relative to the pleural fluid protein level.[64]

The diagnosis is usually established by the presence of the triad of pleural effusion, lymphedema, and yellow nails. The diagnosis may be difficult to establish if the pleural effusion is the first manifestation of the syndrome. There is no specific treatment for the syndrome, but if the effusion is large and is producing symptoms, the effusion can be treated with pleurodesis, parietal pleurectomy, or a pleuroperitoneal shunt.[64]

Drug Reactions Producing Pleural Effusions

Lupus-like syndromes occur in conjunction with the administration of many different medications and have been discussed earlier in this chapter and in Chapter 67. Although there are case reports of pleural disease associated with administration of many drugs,[332] the following drugs are known to induce pleural disease.

Nitrofurantoin. Pleuropulmonary reactions occasionally result from the administration of nitrofurantoin. Such reactions can have an acute or a chronic presentation.[372] The acute presentation occurs within 1 month of initiation of therapy and is manifested by dyspnea, nonproductive cough, and fever. About 20% of patients have an infiltrate and an effusion, and about 3% have only an effusion. Most patients have both peripheral eosinophilia (>350/µL) and lymphopenia (<1000/µL).[373] Pleural fluid analysis revealed 17% eosinophils in the one patient for whom pleural fluid analysis was reported.[373]

The chronic syndrome occurs when the patient has been taking nitrofurantoin for 2 months to 5 years and is much less common than the acute syndrome. Pleural effusion occurs in less than 10% of patients, and no patient with the chronic syndrome has had a pleural effusion without an infiltrate.[372]

The diagnosis of nitrofurantoin pleuropulmonary reaction should be suspected in all patients with a pleural effusion who are taking nitrofurantoin. If the drug is discontinued, the patient usually improves clinically within 1 to 4 days, and the chest radiograph becomes normal within a week with the acute syndrome, whereas the time course is much longer for the chronic syndrome.[372]

Dantrolene. Dantrolene sodium is a long-acting skeletal muscle relaxant with a chemical structure similar to that of nitrofurantoin. Its administration can lead to the development of pleural or pericardial disease.[374] The pleural effusion is unilateral and develops 2 months to 12 years after the initial administration of dantrolene. Patients may be febrile and may have pleuritic chest pain. The pleural fluid is an eosinophilic exudate with a normal glucose level.[374] When dantrolene is discontinued, the patient improves symptomatically within days, but it may take several months for the pleural effusion to resolve completely.

Methysergide. The administration of methysergide can lead to a pleuropulmonary disease similar to that seen with nitrofurantoin.[375] Symptoms consisting of chest pain, dyspnea, and fever develop 1 month to 3 years after methysergide therapy is initiated. The chest radiograph commonly shows bilateral loculated pleural effusions and pleural thickening.[375] When methysergide is discontinued, the symptoms of the patients improve. However, in one series of 13 patients, severe pleural fibrosis persisted in the 2 patients who had continued to take the drug for the longest period (18 and 36 months) after the onset of the pleurisy.[375]

Ergot Alkaloids. The long-term administration of ergot alkaloid drugs such as bromocriptine, ergotamine, dihy-droergotamine, nicergoline, pergolide, and dopergine in the long-term treatment of Parkinson's disease can lead to pleuropulmonary changes.[332] As of 1988, a total of 23 patients had been reported. All the patients were men, and the drug had been taken for 6 months to 4 years before symptoms developed. Two to 5% of patients receiving long-term ergot alkaloid therapy develop pleuropulmonary disease. The incidence of pleural disease is higher if the patient has previous exposure to asbestos.[376] The chest radiograph reveals unilateral or bilateral pleural thickening or effusion in most patients. Analysis of the pleural fluid reveals an exudate with predominantly lymphocytes and frequently eosinophilia.[377] The natural history of pleuropulmonary disease during ergot alkaloid therapy is unclear. The disease progresses only in some of the patients who continue taking the drug.[377]

Procarbazine. There have been two detailed case reports in which pleuropulmonary reactions consisting of chills, cough, dyspnea, and bilateral pulmonary infiltrates with pleural effusion occurred after treatment with procarbazine.[378,379] In both cases, symptoms developed within hours after procarbazine therapy; in both instances, rechallenge with procarbazine again produced the infiltrates and pleural effusions. With discontinuation of the drug, the symptoms and radiographic changes resolved within several days.

Amiodarone. Amiodarone is an antiarrhythmic that may produce severe pulmonary toxicity (see Chapter 67). Pleural effusions occur as a manifestation of amiodarone toxicity, but they are uncommon. Most cases have concomitant parenchymal involvement, but cases have been reported in which there is none.[332] The pleural fluid is an exudate and may have predominantly lymphocytes, macrophages, or polymorphonuclear leukocytes.[332]

Interleukin-2. Recombinant IL-2 is sometimes used in the treatment of malignancies, especially melanoma or renal cell carcinoma. One of the primary side effects of IL-2 administration is the development of pulmonary infiltrates and pleural effusion that are probably related to a generalized capillary leak syndrome.[64] The incidence of pleural effusion after IL-2 administration is approximately 50%.[332] The characteristics of the pleural fluid have not been described. After the IL-2 therapy is stopped, the effusions tend to disappear. However, in one study 17% of patient still had a pleural effusion 4 weeks after therapy cessation.[380]

Trapped Lung

As a result of inflammation, a fibrous peel may form over the visceral pleura. This peel can prevent the underlying lung from expanding fully, thereby "trapping" the underlying lung. The resulting negative pleural pressure leads to the development of a chronic pleural effusion.[64,163]

A patient with a chronic pleural effusion secondary to trapped lung may experience shortness of breath or may be asymptomatic. Symptoms of acute pleural inflammation, such as pleuritic chest pain and fever, are distinctly uncommon, but the patient often gives a history of such events in the past. One characteristic of the pleural effusion secondary to trapped lung is that the amount of fluid is remarkably constant from one study to another. With trapped lung, the pleural fluid is a borderline exudate; the ratio of pleural fluid to serum protein is about 0.5, and the ratio of pleural fluid LDH to serum LDH is about 0.6.[64]

The diagnosis of pleural effusion secondary to trapped lung should be suspected in any patient with a stable, chronic pleural effusion, particularly if the patient has a history of pneumonia, pneumothorax, hemothorax, or thoracic operation. The thickened visceral pleura can be demonstrated if 200 to 400 mL of air is injected into the pleural space at the time of a thoracentesis. Alternatively, the thickened visceral pleura can be demonstrated by CT of the chest. Measurement of the pleural pressure as fluid is withdrawn during therapeutic thoracentesis is useful diagnostically. With trapped lung compared with normal lung, the pleural pressure is low initially and decreases rapidly as fluid is removed.[163]

The definitive therapy for trapped lung is thoracotomy with decortication. However, this major surgery is indicated only in patients who are symptomatic from the disease. If the patient is asymptomatic or minimally symptomatic, the patient can be observed if the clinical picture, pleural fluid findings, and pleural pressure measurements are all compatible with the diagnosis.

Therapeutic Radiation Exposure

Radiotherapy to the chest can cause the development of a pleural effusion. Bachman and Macken[381] followed 200 patients treated with 4000 to 6000 rads to the hemithorax for breast carcinoma and reported that 11 patients (6%) developed a pleural effusion. The pleural effusion developed within 6 months of the completion of the radiotherapy, and every patient had concomitant radiation pneumonitis. The pleural effusion tends to be small and to resolve gradually over many months.[381] The pleural fluid is an exudate with many mesothelial cells.[382] It is important to recognize that this entity exists, and that the development of a pleural effusion in a patient after radiotherapy does not necessarily indicate that the patient has a recurrence of the malignancy.

Iatrogenic Pleural Effusions

The iatrogenic pleural effusions that are secondary to various pharmacologic agents, radiotherapy, endoscopic esophageal sclerotherapy, coronary artery bypass surgery, abdominal surgery, and fluid overload are discussed earlier in this chapter. However, pleural effusions can result from misplacement of a percutaneously inserted catheter or a nasogastric catheter, both of which are discussed here.

Both internal jugular and subclavian vein catheterization can be complicated by misplacement of the catheter tip into the mediastinum or pleural space that results in a large unilateral or bilateral pleural effusion. The pleural fluid may have the characteristics of the intravenous fluid, or it may be bloody from laceration of the blood vessels.[383] If the patient is receiving lipids through a central line, the fluid may look chylous.[384] The diagnosis of a misplaced central venous catheter should be considered in all patients with such lines who rapidly develop pleural effusions, and the patients should be evaluated by diagnostic thoracentesis.

Small pleural effusions may also develop after translumbar aortographic examination and after percutaneous transhepatic coronary vein occlusion. The effusions in these circumstances are usually small and resolve spontaneously.

In the past several years, the development of soft, flexible, small-bore polyurethane feeding tubes has made nasogastric and nasoenteric feeding more practical and comfortable for patients. However, misplacement of these tubes can lead to serious pleural complications. Pneumothorax is the most common complication,[385] but infusion of the enteral formula into the pleural space, or the development of an empyema, or both, also occur relatively frequently.[385] These small flexible tubes are inserted with a stylet in place that enables easier advancement of the device. However, with the stylet in place, the tubing becomes stiff enough that it can perforate structures relatively easily. The risk is much greater if the patient has an endotracheal tube in place or is obtunded.[385] To prevent these complications, these tubes should be inserted only by experienced persons, and the tube should be immediately removed if the patient starts coughing. The tube should not be advanced if resistance is felt, and, before feeding is initiated, the position of the tip of the tube should be confirmed radiographically.[386] If enteral solutions enter the pleural space, tube thoracostomy should be performed to remove the solution. In addition, the patient should be carefully observed for the development of an empyema.[385]

SUMMARY

Pleural effusion is a common clinical finding in patients with underlying disease of the neighboring lung or of the pleura itself. Pleural effusion is also a common manifestation of extrapulmonary disorders, particularly diseases of the heart (congestive heart failure) or abdominal organs; unilateral or bilateral effusion is found in certain connective tissue diseases, especially rheumatoid arthritis and lupus erythematosus, and may complicate the administration of many different drugs. The evaluation of a patient with clinically significant pleural effusion of unknown cause begins with a diagnostic thoracentesis and measurement of the protein and LDH levels to differentiate a transudate from an exudate. This distinction helps guide subsequent workup, if necessary, with the goal of defining the underlying disorder that led to the accumulation of the fluid. Treatment varies considerably and depends on the specific cause. Cure is possible in many instances, and symptomatic relief can be provided for nearly all patients with pleural effusion.

REFERENCES

1. Albertine KH, Wiener-Kronish JP, Bastacky J, et al: No evidence for mesothelial cell contact across the costal pleural space of sheep. J Appl Physiol 70:123–134, 1991.
2. Deschamps C, Rodarte JR: Effects of unilateral pleural symphysis on respiratory system mechanics and gas exchange in anesthetized dogs. Am Rev Respir Dis 137:1385–1389, 1988.
3. Ukale V, Bone D, Hillerdal G, et al: The impact of pleurodesis in malignant effusion on respiratory function. Respir Med 93:898–902, 1999.
4. Davidson FF, Glazier JB: Unilateral pleuritis and regional lung function. Ann Intern Med 77:37–42, 1972.

5. Stamenovic D: Mechanical properties of pleural membrane. J Appl Physiol 57:1189–1194, 1984.
6. Humphrey JD: A possible role of the pleura in lung mechanics. J Biomech 20:773–777, 1987.
7. Hajji MA, Wilson TA, Lai-Fook SJ: Improved measurements of shear modulus and pleural membrane tension of the lung. J Appl Physiol 47:175–181, 1979.
8. Broaddus VC, Light RW: What is the origin of transudates and exudates? Chest 102:658–659, 1992.
9. Broaddus VC, Wiener-Kronish JP, Staub NC: Clearance of lung edema into the pleural space of volume-loaded, anesthetized sheep. J Appl Physiol 68:2623–2630, 1990.
10. Wiener-Kronish JP, Broaddus VC, Albertine KH, et al: Relationship of pleural effusions to increased permeability pulmonary edema in anesthetized sheep. J Clin Invest 82:1422–1429, 1988.
11. Wiener-Kronish JP, Broaddus VC: Interrelationship of pleural and pulmonary interstitial liquid. Annu Rev Physiol 55:209–226, 1993.
12. Gray SW, Skandalakis JE: Development of the pleura. In Chrétien J, Bignon J, Hirsch A (eds): The Pleura in Health and Disease (Lung Biology in Health and Disease, Vol 30). New York: Marcel Dekker, 1985, pp 3–19.
13. Rennard SI, Jaurand M-C, Bignon J, et al: Role of pleural mesothelial cells in the production of the submesothelial connective tissue matrix of lung. Am Rev Respir Dis 130:267–274, 1984.
14. Boylan AM, Sanan DA, Sheppard D, et al: Vitronectin enhances internalization of crocidolite asbestos by rabbit pleural mesothelial cells via the integrin $\alpha v \beta 5$. J Clin Invest 96:1987–2001, 1995.
15. Idell S, Zwieb C, Kuman A, et al: Pathways of fibrin turnover of human pleural mesothelial cells in vitro. Am J Respir Cell Mol Biol 7:414–426, 1992.
16. Antony VB, Hott JW, Kunkel SL, et al: Pleural mesothelial cell expression of C-C (monocyte chemotactic peptide) and C-X-C (interleukin-8) chemokines. Am J Respir Cell Mol Biol 12:581–588, 1995.
17. Boylan AM, Rüegg C, Kim KJ, et al: Evidence of a role for mesothelial cell-derived interleukin-8 in the pathogenesis of asbestos-induced pleurisy in rabbits. J Clin Invest 89:1257–1267, 1992.
18. Lee YCG, Lane KB: Cytokines in pleural diseases. In Light RW, Lee YCG (eds): Textbook of Pleural Diseases. London: Arnold Publishing, 2003, pp 63–77.
19. Nishimura SL, Broaddus VC: Asbestos-induced pleural disease. Clin Chest Med 19:311–329, 1998.
20. Ordonez NG: Immunohistochemical diagnosis of epithelioid mesotheliomas: A critical review of old markers, new markers. Hum Pathol 33:953–967, 2002.
21. Albertine KH, Wiener-Kronish JP, Roos PJ, et al: Structure, blood supply, and lymphatic vessels of the sheep's visceral pleura. Am J Anat 165:277–294, 1982.
22. Oldmixon EH, Hoppin FGJ: Comparison of amounts of collagen and elastin in pleura and parenchyma of dog lung. J Appl Physiol 56:1383–1388, 1956.
23. Albertine KH, Wiener-Kronish JP, Staub NC: The structure of the parietal pleura and its relationship to pleural liquid dynamics in sheep. Anat Rec 208:401–409, 1984.
24. Wang N-S: The preformed stomas connecting the pleural cavity and the lymphatics in the parietal pleura. Am Rev Respir Dis 111:12–20, 1975.
25. Li J: Ultrastructural study on the pleural stomata in human. Funct Dev Morphol 3:277–280, 1993.
26. Li Y-Y, Li J-C: Ultrastructure and three-dimensional study of the lymphatic stomata in the costal pleura of the rabbit. Microsc Res Tech 62:240–246, 2003.
27. Broaddus VC, Wiener-Kronish JP, Berthiaume Y, et al: Removal of pleural liquid and protein by lymphatics in awake sheep. J Appl Physiol 64:384–390, 1988.
28. Pereira ADD, Aguas AP, Oliveira MJ, et al: Experimental modulation of the reactivity of pleural milky spots (Kampmeier's foci) by Freund's adjuvants, betamethasone and mycobacterial infection. J Anat 185:471–479, 1994.
29. Staub NC, Wiener-Kronish JP, Albertine KH: Transport through the pleura: Physiology of normal liquid and solute exchange in the pleural space. In Chrétien J, Bignon J, Hirsch A (eds): The Pleura in Health and Disease (Lung Biology in Health and Disease, Vol 30). New York: Marcel Dekker, 1985, pp 169–193.
30. Bhattacharya J, Gropper MA, Staub NC: Interstitial fluid pressure gradient measured by micropuncture in excised dog lung. J Appl Physiol 56:271–277, 1984.
31. Payne DK, Kinasewitz GT, Gonzalez E: Comparative permeability of canine visceral and parietal pleura. J Appl Physiol 65:2558–2564, 1988.
32. Kim KJ, Critz AM, Crandall ED: Transport of water and solutes across sheep visceral pleura. Am Rev Respir Dis 120:883–892, 1979.
33. Negrini D, Townsley MI, Taylor AE: Hydraulic conductivity of the canine parietal pleura in vivo. J Appl Physiol 69:438–442, 1990.
34. Rolf LL, Travis DM: Pleural fluid-plasma bicarbonate gradients in oxygen-toxic and normal rats. Am J Physiol 224:857–861, 1973.
35. Wiener-Kronish JP, Albertine KH, Licko V, et al: Protein egress and entry rates in pleural fluid and plasma in sheep. J Appl Physiol 56:459–463, 1984.
36. Broaddus VC, Araya M: Liquid and protein dynamics using a new, minimally invasive pleural catheter in rabbits. J Appl Physiol 72:851–857, 1992.
37. Erdmann AJ, Vaughan TR, Brigham KL, et al: Effect of increased vascular pressure on lung fluid balance in unanesthetized sheep. Circ Res 37:271–284, 1975.
38. Wilson JL, Herrod CM, Searle GL, et al: The absorption of blood from the pleural space. Surgery 48:766–774, 1960.
39. Courtice FC, Morris B: The effect of diaphragmatic movement on the absorption of protein and of red cells from the pleural cavity. Aust J Exp Biol 31:227–238, 1953.
40. Lai-Fook SJ, Rodarte JR: Pleural pressure distribution and its relationship to lung volume and interstitial pressure. J Appl Physiol 70:967–978, 1991.
41. Murray JF: The Normal Lung (2nd ed). Philadelphia: WB Saunders, 1986.
42. Light RW, Stansbury DW, Brown SE: The relationship between pleural pressures and changes in pulmonary function after therapeutic thoracentesis. Am Rev Respir Dis 133:658–661, 1986.
43. Nahid P, Broaddus VC: Liquid and protein exchange. In Light RW, Lee GYC (eds): Textbook of Pleural Diseases. London: Arnold, 2003, pp 35–44.
44. Leckie WJH, Tothill P: Albumin turnover in pleural effusions. Clin Sci 29:339–352, 1965.
45. Runyon BA, Forker EL, Sopko JA: Pleural-fluid kinetics in a patient with primary lymphedema, pleural effusions, and yellow nails. Am Rev Respir Dis 119:821–825, 1979.
46. Light RW, MacGregor MI, Luchsinger PC, et al: Pleural effusions: The diagnostic separation of transudates and exudates. Ann Intern Med 77:507–513, 1972.
47. Broaddus VC: Transudative pleural effusions. In Loddenkemper R, Antony VB (eds): Pleural Diseases (European Respiratory Monograph, Vol 7, Monograph 22). Sheffield, UK: European Respiratory Society Journals, 2002, pp 157–176.

48. Brandstetter RD, Cohen RP: Hypoxemia after thoracentesis: A predictable and treatable condition. JAMA 242:1060–1061, 1979.

49. Estenne M, Yernault J-C, de Troyer A: Mechanism of relief of dyspnea after thoracocentesis in patients with large pleural effusions. Am J Med 74:813–819, 1983.

50. Colt H: Drainage and biopsy techniques. In Light RW, Lee GYC (eds): Textbook of Pleural Diseases. London: Arnold, 2003, pp 481–497.

51. Doyle JJ, Hnatiuk OW, Torrington KG, et al: Necessity of routine chest roentgenography after thoracentesis. Ann Intern Med 124:816–820, 1996.

52. Aleman C, Alegre J, Armadans L, et al: The value of chest roentgenography in the diagnosis of pneumothorax after thoracentesis. Am J Med 107:340–343, 1999.

53. Ashchi M, Golish J, Eng P, et al: Transudative malignant pleural effusions: Prevalence and mechanisms. South Med J 91:23–26, 1998.

54. Romero-Candeira S, Fernandez C, Martin C, et al: Influence of diuretics on the concentration of proteins and other components of pleural transudates in patients with heart failure. Am J Med 110:681–686, 2001.

55. Burgess LJ, Maritz FJ, Taljaard JJF: Comparative analysis of the biochemical parameters used to distinguish between pleural transudates and exudates. Chest 107:1604–1609, 1995.

56. Heffner JE, Brown LK, Barbieri CA, et al: Diagnostic value of tests that discriminate between exudative and transudative pleural effusions. Chest 111:970–980, 1997.

57. Heffner JE, Sahn SA, Brown LK: Multilevel likelihood ratios for identifying exudative pleural effusions. Chest 121:1916–1920, 2003.

58. Heffner JE, Highland K, Brown LK: A meta-analysis derivation of continuous likelihood ratios for diagnosing pleural fluid exudates. Am J Respir Crit Care Med 15:1591–1599, 2003.

59. Peterman TA, Speicher CE: Evaluating pleural effusions: A two-stage approach. JAMA 252:1051–1053, 1984.

60. Light RW: Pleural effusion. N Engl J Med 346:1971–1977, 2002.

61. Light RW, Erozan YS, Ball WC: Cells in pleural fluid: Their value in differential diagnosis. Arch Intern Med 132:854–860, 1973.

62. Staats BA, Ellefson RD, Budahn LL, et al: The lipoprotein profile of chylous and nonchylous pleural effusions. Mayo Clin Proc 55:700–704, 1980.

63. Light RW, Ball WC: Lactate dehydrogenase isoenzymes in pleural effusions. Am Rev Respir Dis 108:660–664, 1973.

64. Light RW: Pleural Diseases (4th ed). Baltimore: Lippincott, Williams & Wilkins, 2001.

65. Lillington GA, Carr DT, Mayne JG: Rheumatoid pleurisy with effusion. Arch Intern Med 128:764–768, 1971.

66. Good JTJ, King TE, Antony VB, et al: Lupus pleuritis: Clinical features and pleural fluid characteristics with special reference to pleural fluid antinuclear antibodies. Chest 84:714–718, 1983.

67. Sahn SA, Good JTJ: Pleural fluid pH in malignant effusions: Diagnostic, prognostic, and therapeutic implications. Ann Intern Med 108:345–349, 1988.

68. Conner BD, Lee YCG, Branca P, et al: Variations in pleural fluid WBC count and differential counts with different sample containers and different methods. Chest 123:1181–1187, 2003.

69. Mohamed KH, Abdelhamid AI, Lee YCG, et al: Pleural fluid levels of interleukin-5 and eosinophils are closely correlated. Chest 122:567–580, 2002.

70. Adelman M, Albelda SM, Gottlieb J, et al: Diagnostic utility of pleural fluid eosinophilia. Am J Med 77:915–920, 1984.

71. Schandene L, Namias B, Crusiaux A, et al: IL-5 in post-traumatic eosinophilic pleural effusion. Clin Exp Immunol 93:115–119, 1993.

72. Maltais F, Laberge F, Cormier Y: Blood hypereosinophilia in the course of posttraumatic pleural effusion. Chest 98:348–351, 1990.

73. Romero-Candeira S, Hernandez Blasco L, Soler MJ, et al: Biochemical and cytologic characteristics of pleural effusions secondary to pulmonary embolism. Chest 121:465–469, 2002.

74. Smit HJ, van den Heuvel MM, Barbierato SB, et al: Analysis of pleural fluid in idiopathic spontaneous pneumothorax: Correlation of eosinophil percentage with the duration of air in the pleural space. Respir Med 93:262–267, 1999.

75. Kalomenidis I, Light RW: Eosinophilic pleural effusions. Curr Opin Pulm Med 9:254–260, 2003.

76. Johnson RJ, Johnson JR: Paragonimiasis in Indochinese refugees. Am Rev Respir Dis 128:534–538, 1983.

77. Erzurum SE, Underwood GA, Hamilos DL, et al: Pleural effusion in Churg-Strauss syndrome. Chest 95:1357–1359, 1989.

78. Spriggs AI, Boddington MM: The Cytology of Effusions (2nd ed). New York: Grune & Stratton, 1968, pp 5–11.

79. Yam LT: Diagnostic significance of lymphocytes in pleural effusions. Ann Intern Med 66:972–982, 1967.

80. Lucivero G, Pierucci G, Bonomo L: Lymphocytes subsets in peripheral blood and pleural fluid. Eur Respir J 1:337–340, 1988.

81. Elis A, Mulchanov I, Radnay J, et al: The diagnostic significance of polyclonal lymphocytosis in pleural effusions. N Z Med J 113:56–58, 2000.

82. Domagala W, Emerson EE, Kos LG: T and B lymphocytes enumeration in the diagnosis of lymphocyte-rich pleural fluids. Acta Cytol 25:471–477, 1981.

83. Katz RL, Raval P, Manning JT, et al: A morphologic, immunologic, and cytometric approach to the classification of non-Hodgkin's lymphoma in effusions. Diagn Cytopathol 3:91–101, 1987.

84. Jarvi OH, Kunnas RJ, Laitio MT, et al: The accuracy and significance of cytologic cancer diagnosis of pleural effusions. Acta Cytol 16:152–157, 1972.

85. Dekker A, Bupp PA: Cytology of serous effusions: An investigation into the usefulness of cell blocks versus smears. Am J Clin Pathol 70:855–860, 1978.

86. Melamed MR: The cytological presentation of malignant lymphomas and related diseases in effusions. Cancer 16:413–431, 1963.

87. Fetsch PA, Abati A: Immunocytochemistry in effusion cytology: A contemporary review. Cancer 93:293–308, 2001.

88. Mohamed KH, Mobasher AA, Yousef AI, et al: Pleural lavage: A novel diagnostic approach for diagnosing exudative pleural effusion. Lung 178:371–379, 2000.

89. Fiegl M, Kaufmann H, Zojer N, et al: Malignant cell detection by fluorescence in situ hybridization (FISH) in effusions from patients with carcinoma. Hum Pathol 31:448–455, 2000.

90. Dewald G, Dines DE, Weiland LH, et al: Usefulness of chromosome examination in the diagnosis of malignant pleural effusions. N Engl J Med 295:1494–1500, 1976.

91. de Matos Granja N, Soares R, Rocha S, et al: Evaluation of breast cancer metastases in pleural effusion by molecular biology techniques. Diagn Cytopathol 27:210–213, 2002.

92. Nagel H, Schulten HJ, Gunawan B, et al: The potential value of comparative genomic hybridization analysis in effusion and fine needle aspiration cytology. Mod Pathol 15:818–825, 2002.

93. Bethwaite PB, Delahunt B, Holloway LJ, et al: Comparison of silver-staining nucleolar organizer region (AgNOR) counts and proliferating cell nuclear antigen (PCNA) expression in reactive mesothelial hyperplasia and malignant mesothelioma. Pathology 27:1–4, 1995.

94. Yang C-T, Lee M-H, Lan R-S, et al: Telomerase activity in pleural effusions: Diagnostic significance. J Clin Oncol 16:567–573, 1998.

95. Braunschweig R, Guilleret I, Delacretaz F, et al: Pitfalls in TRAP assay in routine detection of malignancy in effusions. Diagn Cytopathol 25:225–230, 2001.

96. Ordonez NG: The immunohistochemical diagnosis of mesothelioma: A comparative study of epithelioid and lung adenocarcinoma. Am J Surg Pathol 27:1031–1051, 2003.

97. Coonrod JD, Wilson HD: Etiologic diagnosis of intrapleural empyema by counterimmunoelectrophoresis. Am Rev Respir Dis 113:637–641, 1976.

98. Boersma WG, Lowenberg A, Holloway Y, et al: Rapid detection of pneumococcal antigen in pleural fluid of patients with community acquired pneumonia. Thorax 48:160–162, 1993.

99. Falguera M, Lopez A, Nogues A, et al: Evaluation of the polymerase chain reaction method for detection of *Streptococcus pneumoniae* DNA in pleural fluid samples. Chest 122:2212–2216, 2002.

100. Potts DE, Willcox MA, Good JTJ, et al: The acidosis of low-glucose pleural effusions. Am Rev Respir Dis 117:665–671, 1978.

101. Light RW, Girard WM, Jenkinson SG, et al: Parapneumonic effusions. Am J Med 69:507–512, 1980.

102. Cheng D-S, Rodriguez RM, Rogers J, et al: Comparison of pleural fluid pH values obtained using blood gas machine, pH meter and pH indicator strip. Chest 114:1368–1372, 1998.

103. Branca P, Rodriguez RM, Rogers JT, et al: Routine measurement of pleural fluid amylase is not indicated. Arch Intern Med 161:228–232, 2001.

104. Sherr HP, Light RW, Merson MH, et al: Origin of pleural fluid amylase in esophageal rupture. Ann Intern Med 76:985–986, 1972.

105. Maulitz RM, Good JTJ, Kaplan RL, et al: The pleuropulmonary consequences of esophageal rupture: An experimental model. Am Rev Respir Dis 120:363–367, 1979.

106. Rockey DC, Cello JP: Pancreaticopleural fistula: Report of 7 patients and review of the literature. Medicine 69:332–344, 1990.

107. Light RW, Ball WC: Glucose and amylase in pleural effusions. JAMA 225:257–260, 1973.

108. Kramer MR, Saldana MJ, Cepero RJ, et al: High amylase in neoplasm-related pleural effusion. Ann Intern Med 110:567–569, 1989.

109. Walker WC, Wright V: Rheumatoid pleuritis. Ann Rheum Dis 26:467–474, 1967.

110. Winslow WA, Ploss LN, Loitman B: Pleuritis in systemic lupus erythematosus: Its importance as an early manifestation in diagnosis. Ann Intern Med 49:70–88, 1958.

111. Khare V, Baethge B, Lang S, et al: Antinuclear antibodies in pleural fluid. Chest 106:866–871, 1994.

112. Wang DY, Yang PC, Yu WL, et al: Comparison of different diagnostic methods for lupus pleuritis and pericarditis: A prospective three-year study. J Formos Med Assoc 99:375–380, 2000.

113. Halla JT, Schrohenloher RE, Volanakis JE: Immune complexes and other laboratory features of pleural effusions. Ann Intern Med 92:748–752, 1980.

114. Jimenez Castro D, Diaz Nuevo G, Perez-Rodriguez E, et al: Diagnostic value of adenosine deaminase in nontuberculous lymphocytic pleural effusions. Eur Respir J 21:220–224, 2003.

115. Lee YCG, Rogers JT, Rodriguez RM, et al: Adenosine deaminase levels in nontuberculous lymphocytic pleural effusions. Chest 120:356–361, 2001.

116. Riantawan P, Chaowalit P, Wongsangiem M, et al: Diagnostic value of pleural fluid adenosine deaminase in tuberculous pleuritis with reference to HIV coinfection and a Bayesian analysis. Chest 116:97–103, 1999.

117. Ferrer JS, Muñoz XG, Orriols RM, et al: Evolution of idiopathic pleural effusion: A prospective, long-term follow-up study. Chest 109:1508–1513, 1996.

118. Villena V, Lopez-Encuentra A, Pozo F, et al: Interferon gamma levels in pleural fluid for the diagnosis of tuberculosis. Am J Med 115:365–370, 2003.

119. Su WJ: Recent advances in the molecular diagnosis of tuberculosis. J Microbiol Immunol Infect 35:209–214, 2002.

120. Forbes BA: Critical assessment of gene amplification approaches on the diagnosis of tuberculosis. Immunol Invest 26:105–116, 1997.

121. Collins JD, Burwell D, Furmanski S, et al: Minimal detectable pleural effusions. Radiology 105:51–53, 1972.

122. Moskowitz H, Platt RT, Schachar R, et al: Roentgen visualization of minute pleural effusion. Radiology 109:33–35, 1973.

123. Tsai T-H, Yang P-C: Ultrasound in the diagnosis and management of pleural disease. Curr Opin Pulm Med 9:282–290, 2003.

124. Davies CL, Gleeson FV: Diagnostic radiology. *In* Light RW, Lee GYC (eds): Textbook of Pleural Diseases. London: Arnold, 2003, pp 210–237.

125. Kohan JM, Poe RH, Israel RH, et al: Value of chest ultrasonography versus decubitus roentgenography for thoracentesis. Am Rev Respir Dis 133:1124–1126, 1986.

126. McLoud TC: CT and MR in pleural disease. Clin Chest Med 19:261–276, 1998.

127. Bressler EL, Francis IR, Glazer GM, et al: Bolus contrast medium enhancement for distinguishing pleural from parenchymal lung disease: CT features. J Comput Assist Tomogr 11:436–440, 1987.

128. Stark DD, Federle MP, Goodman PC, et al: Differentiating lung abscess and empyema: radiography and computed tomography. AJR Am J Roentgenol 141:163–167, 1983.

129. Leung AN, Muller NL, Miller RR: CT in differential diagnosis of diffuse pleural disease. AJR Am J Roentgenol 154:487–492, 1990.

130. Maskell NA, Gleeson FV, Davies RJ: Standard pleural biopsy versus CT-guided cutting-needle biopsy for diagnosis of malignant disease in pleural effusions: A randomised controlled trial. Lancet 361:1326–1330, 2003.

131. Goddard P, Henson J, Davies ER: Pleural effusion causing unmatched ventilation defects in ventilation and perfusion scanning. Clin Radiol 37:285–286, 1986.

132. Remy-Jardin M, Remy J, Deschildre F, et al: Diagnosis of pulmonary embolism with spiral CT: Comparison with pulmonary angiography and scintigraphy. Radiology 200:699–706, 1996.

133. MacDonald SL, Mayo JR: Computed tomography of acute pulmonary embolism. Semin Ultrasound CT MR 24:217–231, 2003.

134. Prakash UBS, Relman HM: Comparison of needle biopsy with cytologic analysis for the evaluation of pleural effusion: Analysis of 414 cases. Mayo Clin Proc 60:158–164, 1985.

135. Kirsch CM, Kroe M, Jensen WA, et al: A modified Abrams needle biopsy technique. Chest 108:982–986, 1995.

136. Bueno CE, Clemente G, Castro BC, et al: Cytologic and bacteriologic analysis of fluid and pleural biopsy specimens with Cope's needle. Arch Intern Med 150:1190–1194, 1990.

137. Scerbo J, Keltz H, Stone DJ: A prospective study of closed pleural biopsies. JAMA 218:377–380, 1971.

138. Levine H, Metzger W, Lacera D, et al: Diagnosis of tuberculous pleurisy by culture of pleural biopsy specimens. Arch Intern Med 126:269–271, 1970.

139. Von Hoff DD, LiVolsi V: Diagnostic reliability of needle biopsy of the parietal pleura. Am J Clin Pathol 64:200–203, 1975.

140. Conde MB, Loivos AC, Rezende VM, et al: Yield of sputum induction in the diagnosis of pleural tuberculosis. Am J Respir Crit Care Med 167:723–725, 2003.

141. Poe RH, Israel RH, Utell MJ, et al: Sensitivity, specificity, and predictive values of closed pleural biopsy. Arch Intern Med 144:325–328, 1984.

142. Chang SC, Perng RP: The role of fiberoptic bronchoscopy in evaluating the causes of pleural effusions. Arch Intern Med 149:855–857, 1989.

143. Feinsilver SH, Barrows AA, Braman SS: Fiberoptic bronchoscopy and pleural effusion of unknown origin. Chest 90:516–519, 1986.

144. Hartman DL, Antony VB: Thoracoscopy: The pulmonologist's role. Semin Respir Crit Care Med 16:354–360, 1995.

145. Menzies R, Charbonneau M: Thoracoscopy for the diagnosis of pleural disease. Ann Intern Med 114:271–276, 1991.

146. Hucker J, Bhatnagar ND, al-Jailaihawi AN, et al: Thoracoscopy in the diagnosis and management of recurrent pleural effusions. Ann Thorac Surg 52:1145–1147, 1991.

147. Douglass BE, Carr DT, Bernatz PE: Diagnostic thoracotomy in the study of 'idiopathic' pleural effusion. Am Rev Tuberc 74:954–957, 1956.

148. Ryan CJ, Rodgers RF, Unni KK, et al: The outcome of patients with pleural effusion of indeterminate cause at thoracotomy. Mayo Clin Proc 56:145–149, 1981.

149. Kataoka H, Takada S: The role of thoracic ultrasonography for evaluation of patients with decompensated chronic heart failure. J Am Coll Cardiol 35:1638–1646, 2000.

150. Race GA, Scheifley CH, Edwards JE: Hydrothorax in congestive heart failure. Am J Med 22:83–89, 1957.

151. Wiener-Kronish JP, Matthay MA, Callen PW, et al: Relationship of pleural effusions to pulmonary hemodynamics in patients with heart failure. Am Rev Respir Dis 132:1253–1256, 1985.

152. Weiss JM, Spodick DH: Laterality of pleural effusions in chronic congestive heart failure. Am J Cardiol 53:951, 1984.

153. Rabin CB, Blackman NS: Bilateral pleural effusions: Its significance in association with a heart of normal size. J Mt Sinai Hosp N Y 24:45–63, 1957.

154. Broaddus VC: Diuresis and transudative effusions—changing the rules of the game. Am J Med 110:732–735, 2002.

155. Glazer M, Berkman N, Lafair JS, et al: Successful talc slurry pleurodesis in patients with nonmalignant pleural effusion. Chest 117:1404–1409, 2000.

156. Plum GE, Bruwer AJ, Clagett OT: Chronic constrictive pericarditis: Roentgenologic findings in 35 surgically proved cases. Mayo Clin Proc 32:555–566, 1957.

157. Weiss JM, Spodick DH: Association of left pleural effusions with pericardial disease. N Engl J Med 308:696–697, 1983.

158. Lieberman FL, Hidemura R, Peters RL, et al: Pathogenesis and treatment of hydrothorax complicating cirrhosis with ascites. Ann Intern Med 64:341–351, 1966.

159. Johnston RF, Loo RV: Studies to determine the source of the fluid and report of thirteen cases. Ann Intern Med 61:385–401, 1964.

160. Kinasewitz GT, Keddissi JI: Hepatic hydrothorax. Curr Opin Pulm Med 9:261–265, 2003.

161. Xiol X: Hepatic hydrothorax. In Light RW, Lee GYC (eds): Textbook of Pleural Diseases, London: Arnold, 2003, pp 402–409.

162. Mouroux J, Perrin C, Venissac N, et al: Management of pleural effusion of cirrhotic origin. Chest 109:1093–1096, 1996.

163. Light RW, Jenkinson SG, Minh V, et al: Observations on pleural pressures as fluid is withdrawn during thoracentesis. Am Rev Respir Dis 121:799–804, 1980.

164. Bhattacharya A, Mittal BR, Biswas T, et al: Radioisotope scintigraphy in the diagnosis of hepatic hydrothorax. J Gastroenterol Hepatol 16:317–321, 2001.

165. Xiol X, Castellote J, Cortes-Beut R, et al: Usefulness and complications of thoracentesis in cirrhotic patients. Am J Med 111:67–69, 2001.

166. Xiol X, Castellvi JM, Guardiola J, et al: Spontaneous bacterial empyema in cirrhotic patients: A prospective study. Hepatology 23:719–723, 1996.

166a. Hassoun Z, Pomier-Layrargues G: The transjugular intrahepatic portosystemic shunt in the treatment of portal hypertension. Eur J Gastroenterol Hepatol 16:1–4, 2004.

167. de Campos JRM, Filho LOA, Werebe EC, et al: Thoracoscopy and talc poudrage in the management of hepatic hydrothorax. Chest 118:13–17, 2000.

167a. Takayama T, Kurokawa Y, Daiwa Y, et al: A new technique of thoracoscopic pleurodesis for refractory hepatic hydrothorax. Surg Endosc 18:140–143, 2004.

168. Cavina G, Vichi G: Radiological aspects of pleural effusions in medical nephropathy in children. Ann Radiol Diagn 31:163–202, 1958.

169. Llach F, Arieff AI, Massry SG: Renal vein thrombosis and nephrotic syndrome: A prospective study of 36 adult patients. Ann Intern Med 83:8–14, 1975.

170. Jenkins PG, Shelp WD: Recurrent pleural transudate in the nephrotic syndrome: A new approach to treatment. JAMA 230:587–588, 1974.

171. Nomoto Y, Suga T, Nakajima K, et al: Acute hydrothorax in continuous ambulatory peritoneal dialysis: A collaborative study of 161 centers. Am J Nephrol 9:363–367, 1989.

172. Tang S, Chui WH, Tang AW, et al: Video-assisted thoracoscopic talc pleurodesis is effective for maintenance of peritoneal dialysis in acute hydrothorax complicating peritoneal dialysis. Nephrol Dial Transplant 18:804–808, 2003.

173. Di Bisceglie M, Paladini P, Voltolini L, et al: Videothoracoscopic obliteration of pleuroperitoneal fistula in continuous peritoneal dialysis. Ann Thorac Surg 62:1509–1510, 1996.

174. Baron RL, Stark DD, McClennan BL: Intrathoracic extension of retroperitoneal urine collections. AJR Am J Roentgenol 137:37–41, 1981.

174a. Garcia-Pachon E, Padilla-Navas I: Urinothorax: case report and review of the literature with emphasis on biochemical diagnosis. Respiration 71:533–536, 2004.

175. Gottehrer A, Roa J, Stanford GG, et al: Hypothyroidism and pleural effusions. Chest 98:1130–1132, 1990.

176. Marks PA, Roof BS: Pericardial effusions associated with myxedema. Ann Intern Med 39:230–240, 1953.

177. Spicer RL, Uzark KC, Moore JW, et al: Aortopulmonary collateral vessels and prolonged pleural effusions after modified Fontan procedures. Am Heart J 131:1164–1168, 1996.

178. Lemler MS, Scott WA, Leonard SR, et al: Fenestration improves clinical outcome of the Fontan procedure: A prospective, randomized study. Circulation 105:207–212, 2002.

179. Sade RM, Wiles HB: Pleuroperitoneal shunt for persistent pleural drainage after Fontan procedure. J Thorac Cardiovasc Surg 100:621–623, 1990.

180. D'Souza R, Doshi A, Bhojraj S, et al: Massive pleural effusion as the presenting feature of a subarachnoid-pleural fistula. Respiration 69:96–99, 2002.

181. Lloyd C, Sahn SA: Subarachnoid pleural fistula due to penetrating trauma: Case report and review of the literature. Chest 122:2252–2256, 2002.

182. Moulopoulos SD, Kelekis D, Diamantopoulos EJ, et al: Hemiazygous vein thrombosis as a cause of unexplained left-sided pleural effusion. Angiology 37:352–357, 1986.

183. Muthuswamy P, Alausa M, Reilly J: The effusion that would not go away. N Engl J Med 345:756–759, 2001.

184. Good JTJ, Moore JB, Fowler AA, et al: Superior vena cava syndrome as a cause of pleural effusion. Am Rev Respir Dis 125:246–247, 1982.

185. Light RW: Effusions from vascular causes. In Light RW, Lee GYC (eds): Textbook of Pleural Diseases. London: Arnold, 2003, pp 289–296.

186. Berk JL, Keane J, Seldin DC, et al: Persistent pleural effusions in primary systemic amyloidosis: Etiology and prognosis. Chest 124:969–977, 2003.

187. Seber A, Khan SP, Kersey JH: Unexplained effusions: Association with allogeneic bone marrow transplantation and acute or chronic graft-versus-host disease. Bone Marrow Transplant 17:207–211, 1996.

188. Neiderman MS, Bass JB, Campbell GD: Guidelines for the initial management of adults with community-acquired pneumonia: Diagnosis, assessment of severity, and initial antimicrobial therapy. Am Rev Respir Dis 148:1418–1426, 1993.

189. Musher DM, Alexandraki I, Graviss EA, et al: Bacteremic and nonbacteremic pneumococcal pneumonia: A prospective study. Medicine 79:210–221, 2000.

190. Hasley PB, Albaum MN, Li Y-H, et al: Do pulmonary radiographic findings at presentation predict mortality in patients with community-acquired pneumonia? Arch Intern Med 156:2206–2212, 1996.

191. Colice GL, Curtis A, Deslauriers J, et al: Medical and surgical treatment of parapneumonic effusions: An evidence-based guideline. Chest 118:1158–1171, 2000.

192. Finland M, Barnes MW: Changing ecology of acute bacterial empyema: Occurrence and mortality at Boston City Hospital during 12 selected years from 1935 to 1972. J Infect Dis 127:274–291, 1978.

193. Bartlett JG, Gorbach SL, Thadepalli H: Bacteriology of empyema. Lancet 1:338–340, 1974.

194. Davies CL, Gleeson FV, Davies RJ: BTS guidelines for the management of pleural infection. Thorax 58(Suppl II):II18–II28, 2003.

195. Bartlett JG, Finegold SM: Anaerobic infections in the lung and pleural space. Am Rev Respir Dis 110:56–77, 1974.

196. Ferguson AD, Prescott RJ, Selkon JB: The clinical course and management of thoracic empyema. QJM 89:285–289, 1996.

197. Chu MW, Dewar LR, Burgess JJ, et al: Empyema thoracis: Lack of awareness results in a prolonged clinical course. Can J Surg 44:284–288, 2001.

198. Haramati LB, Alterman DD, White CS, et al: Intrathoracic lymphadenopathy in patients with empyema. J Comput Assist Tomogr 21:608–611, 1997.

199. Kearney SE, Davies CW, Tattersall DJ, et al: The characteristics and significance of thoracic lymphadenopathy in parapneumonic effusion and empyema. Br J Radiol 73:583–587, 2000.

200. Alegre J, Jufresa J, Aleman C, et al: Pleural fluid myeloperoxidase as a marker of infectious pleural effusions. Eur J Intern Med 12:357–362, 2001.

201. Vives M, Porcel JM, Gazquez I, et al: SC5b-9: A test for identifying complicated parapneumonic effusions. Respiration 67:433–438, 2000.

202. Aleman C, Alegre J, Segura R, et al: Polymorphonuclear elastase in the early diagnosis of complicated pyogenic pleural effusions. Respiration 70:462–467, 2003.

203. Light RW, Rodriguez RM: Management of parapneumonic effusions. Clin Chest Med 19:373–382, 1998.

204. Lim TK, Chin NK: Empirical treatment with fibrinolysis and early surgery reduces the duration of hospitalization in pleural sepsis. Eur Respir J 13:514–518, 1999.

205. Kearney SE, Davies CW, Davies RJ, et al: Computed tomography and ultrasound in parapneumonic effusions and empyema. Clin Radiol 55:542–547, 2000.

206. Sasse SA, Nguyen TK, Teixera LR, et al: Utility of daily therapeutic thoracentesis for the treatment of empyema. Chest 116:1703–1708, 1999.

207. Storm HKR, Krasnik M, Bang K, et al: Treatment of pleural empyema secondary to pneumonia: Thoracocentesis regimen versus tube drainage. Thorax 47:821–824, 1992.

208. Ashbaugh DG: Empyema thoracis: Factors influencing morbidity and mortality. Chest 99:1162–1165, 1991.

209. Shankar S, Gulati M, Kang M, et al: Image-guided percutaneous drainage of thoracic empyema: Can sonography predict the outcome? Eur Radiol 10:495–499, 2000.

210. Ali I, Unruh H: Management of empyema thoracis. Ann Thorac Surg 50:355–359, 1990.

211. Light RW: Management of parapneumonic effusions. Chest 100:892–893, 1991.

212. Walker CA, Shirk MB, Tschampel MM, et al: Intrapleural alteplase in a patient with complicated pleural effusion. Ann Pharmacother 37:376–379, 2003.

213. Bishop NB, Pon S, Ushay HM, et al: Alteplase in the treatment of complicated parapneumonic effusion: A case report. Pediatrics 111:E188–E190, 2003.

214. Davies RJ, Traill ZC, Gleeson FV: Randomised controlled trial of intrapleural streptokinase in community acquired pleural infection. Thorax 52:416–421, 1997.

215. Bouros D, Schiza S, Tzanakis N, et al: Intrapleural urokinase vs normal saline in the treatment of complicated parapneumonic effusions and empyema: A randomized, double-blind study. Am J Respir Crit Care Med 159:37–42, 1999.

216. Maskell NA, Davies CWH, Nunn AJ, et al. U.K. controlled trial of intrapleural streptokinase for pleural infection. N Engl J Med 352:865–874, 2005.

217. Waller DA: Thoracoscopy in management of postpneumonic pleural infections. Curr Opin Pulm Med 8:323–326, 2002.

218. Landreneau RJ, Keenan RJ, Hazelrigg SR, et al: Thoracoscopy for empyema and hemothorax. Chest 109:18–24, 1995.

219. Cassina PC, Hauser M, Hillejan L, et al: Video-assisted thoracoscopy in the treatment of pleural empyema: Stage-based management and outcome. J Thorac Cardiovasc Surg 117:234–238, 1999.

220. Lawrence DR, Ohri SK, Moxon RE, et al: Thoracoscopic debridement of empyema thoracis. Ann Thorac Surg 64:1448–1450, 1997.
221. Striffeler H, Gugger M, Im Hof V, et al: Video-assisted thoracoscopic surgery for fibrinopurulent pleural empyema in 67 patients. Ann Thorac Surg 65:319–323, 1998.
222. Thurer RJ: Decortication in thoracic empyema: Indications and surgical technique. Chest Surg Clin N Am 6:461–490, 1996.
223. Deslauriers J, Jacques LF, Gregoire J: Role of Eloesser flap and thoracoplasty in the third millennium. Chest Surg Clin N Am 12:605–623, 2002.
224. Maruyama R, Ondo K, Mikami K, et al: Clinical course and management of patients undergoing open window thoracotomy for thoracic empyema. Respiration 68:606–610, 2001.
225. Pairolero PC: Empyema and bronchopleural fistula after pneumonectomy: Factors affecting incidence. Ann Thorac Surg 72:243–247, 2001.
226. Wain JC: Management of late postpneumonectomy empyema and bronchopleural fistula. Chest Surg Clin N Am 6:529–541, 1996.
226a. Gossot D, Stern JB, Galetta D, et al: Thoracoscopic management of postpneumonectomy empyema. Ann Thorac Surg 78:273–276, 2004.
227. Deschamps C, Pairolero PC, Allen MS, et al: Management of postpneumonectomy empyema and bronchopleural fistula. Chest Surg Clin N Am 6:519–527, 1996.
228. Mehta JB, Dutt A, Harvill L: Epidemiology of extrapulmonary tuberculosis. Chest 99:1134–1138, 1991.
229. Mlika-Cabanne N, Brauner M, Kamanfu G, et al: Radiographic abnormalities in tuberculosis and risk of coexisting human immunodeficiency virus infection. Am J Respir Crit Care Med 152:794–799, 1995.
230. Lawn SD, Evans AJ, Sedgwick PM, et al: Pulmonary tuberculosis: Radiological features in west Africans coinfected with HIV. Br J Radiol 72:339–344, 1999.
231. Jones BE, Young SMM, Antoniskis D, et al: Relationship of the manifestations of tuberculosis to CD4 cell counts in patients with human immunodeficiency virus infection. Am Rev Respir Dis 148:1292–1297, 1993.
231a. Ong A, Creasman J, Hopewell PC, et al: A molecular epidemiological assessment of extrapulmonary tuberculosis in San Francisco. Clin Infect Dis 38:25–31, 2004.
232. Roper WH, Waring JJ: Primary serofibrinous pleural effusion in military personnel. Am Rev Respir Dis 71:616–634, 1955.
233. Moudgil H, Sridhar G, Leitch AG: Reactivation disease: The commonest form of tuberculous pleural effusion in Edinburgh, 1980–1991. Respir Med 88:301–304, 1994.
234. Ellner JJ, Barnes PF, Wallis RS, et al: The immunology of tuberculous pleurisy. Semin Respir Infect 3:335–342, 1988.
235. Valdes L, Alvarez D, San Jose E, et al: Tuberculous pleurisy: A study of 254 patients. Arch Intern Med 158:2017–2021, 1998.
236. Berger HW, Mejia E: Tuberculous pleurisy. Chest 63:88–92, 1973.
237. Yilmaz MU, Kumcuoglu Z, Utkaner G, et al: Computed tomography findings of tuberculous pleurisy. Int J Tuberc Lung Dis 2:164–167, 1998.
238. Light RW: Useful tests on the pleural fluid in the management of patients with pleural effusions. Curr Opin Pulm Med 5:245–249, 1999.
239. Al-Majed SA: Study of paradoxical response to chemotherapy in tuberculous pleural effusion. Respir Med 90:211–214, 1996.
240. Gupta RC, Dixit R, Purohit SD, et al: Development of pleural effusion in patients during anti-tuberculosis chemotherapy. Indian J Chest Dis Allied Sci 42:161–168, 2000.
241. Barbas CSV, Cukier A, de Varvalho CRR, et al: The relationship between pleural fluid findings and the development of pleural thickening in patients with pleural tuberculosis. Chest 100:1264–1267, 1991.
242. Galarza I, Cañete C, Granados A, et al: Randomised trial of corticosteroids in the treatment of tuberculous pleurisy. Thorax 50:1305–1307, 1995.
243. Lee CH, Wang WJ, Lan RS, et al: Corticosteroids in the treatment of tuberculous pleurisy: A double-blind, placebo-controlled, randomized study. Chest 94:1256–1259, 1988.
244. Lai YF, Chao TY, Wang YH, et al: Pigtail drainage in the treatment of tuberculous pleural effusions: A randomised study. Thorax 58:149–151, 2003.
245. Flynn MW, Felson B: The roentgen manifestations of thoracic actinomycosis. Am J Roentgenol Radium Ther Nucl Med 110:707–716, 1970.
246. Feigin DS: Nocardiosis of the lung: Chest radiographic findings in 21 cases. Radiology 159:9–14, 1986.
247. Hillerdal G: Pulmonary aspergillus infection invading the pleura. Thorax 36:745–751, 1981.
248. Wex P, Utta E, Drozdz W: Surgical treatment of pulmonary and pleuropulmonary *Aspergillus* disease. Thorac Cardiovasc Surg 41:64–70, 1993.
249. Shirakusa T, Ueda H, Saito T, et al: Surgical treatment of pulmonary aspergilloma and *Aspergillus* empyema. Ann Thorac Surg 48:779–782, 1989.
250. Colp CR, Cook WA: Successful treatment of pleural aspergillosis and bronchopleural fistula. Chest 68:96–98, 1975.
251. Kinasewitz GT, Penn RL, George RB: The spectrum and significance of pleural disease in blastomycosis. Chest 86:580–584, 1985.
252. Failla PJ, Cerise FP, Karam GH, et al: Blastomycosis: Pulmonary and pleural manifestations. South Med J 88:405–410, 1995.
253. Lonky SA, Catanzaro A, Moser KM, et al: Acute coccidioidal pleural effusion. Am Rev Respir Dis 114:681–688, 1976.
254. Cunningham RT, Einstein H: Coccidioidal pulmonary cavities with rupture. J Thorac Cardiovasc Surg 84:172–177, 1982.
255. Young EJ, Hirsh DD, Fainstein V, et al: Pleural effusions due to *Cryptococcus neoformans*. Am Rev Respir Dis 121:743–747, 1980.
256. Wasser L, Talavera W: Pulmonary cryptococcosis in AIDS. Chest 92:692–695, 1987.
257. Conces DRJ, Vix VA, Tarver RD: Pleural cryptococcosis. J Thorac Imaging 5:84–86, 1990.
258. Duperval R, Hermans PE, Brewer NS, et al: Cryptococcosis, with emphasis on the significance of isolation of *Cryptococcus neoformans* from the respiratory tract. Chest 72:13–19, 1977.
259. Connell JVJ, Mumh JR: Radiographic manifestations of pulmonary histoplasmosis: A 10-yr review. Radiology 121:281–285, 1976.
260. Weissbluth M: Pleural effusion in histoplasmosis. J Pediatr 88:894–895, 1976.
261. Horowitz ML, Schiff M, Samuels J, et al: *Pneumocystis carinii* pleural effusion: Pathogenesis and pleural fluid analysis. Am Rev Respir Dis 148:232–234, 1993.
262. Fine NL, Smith LR, Sheedy PF: Frequency of pleural effusions in mycoplasma and viral pneumonias. N Engl J Med 283:790–793, 1970.
263. Alptekin F: An epidemic of pleurisy with effusion in Bitlis, Turkey: Study of 559 cases. US Armed Forces Med J 9:1–11, 1958.

264. Gross PA, Gerding DN: Pleural effusion associated with viral hepatitis. Gastroenterology 60:898–902, 1971.

265. Tabor E, Russell RP, Gerety RJ, et al: Hepatitis B surface antigen and e antigen in pleural effusion: A case report. Gastroenterology 73:1157–1159, 1977.

266. Bustamante EA, Levy H, Simpson SQ: Pleural fluid characteristics in hantavirus pulmonary syndrome. Chest 112:1133–1136, 1997.

267. Setiawan MW, Samsi TK, Wulur H, et al: Dengue haemorrhagic fever: Ultrasound as an aid to predict the severity of the disease. Pediatr Radiol 16:1–4, 1998.

268. Wong KT, Antonio GE, Hui DS, et al: Severe acute respiratory syndrome: Radiographic appearances and pattern of progression in 138 patients. Radiology 228:401–406, 2003.

269. Afessa B: Pleural effusion and pneumothorax in hospitalized patients with HIV infection. Chest 117:1031–1037, 2000.

270. Light RW, Hamm H: Pleural disease and the acquired immune deficiency syndrome. Eur Respir J 10:2638–2643, 1997.

271. Hamm H: Effusions in immunocompromised hosts. *In* Light RW, Lee GYC (eds): Textbook of Pleural Diseases. London: Arnold, 2003, pp 357–361.

272. Gil Suay V, Cordero PJ, Martinez E, et al: Parapneumonic effusions secondary to community-acquired bacterial pneumonia in human immunodeficiency virus-infected patients. Eur Respir J 8:1934–1939, 1995.

273. Lyche KD, Jensen WA: Pleuropulmonary amebiasis. Semin Respir Infect 12:106–112, 1997.

274. Ibarra-Perez C: Thoracic complications of amebic abscess of the liver. Chest 79:672–676, 1981.

275. Baijal SS, Agarwal DK, Roy S, et al: Complex ruptured amebic liver abscesses: The role of percutaneous catheter drainage. Eur J Radiol 20:65–67, 1995.

276. Cameron EWJ: The treatment of pleuropulmonary amebiasis with metronidazole. Chest 73:647–650, 1978.

277. Aribas OK, Kanat F, Gormus N, et al: Pleural complications of hydatid disease. J Thorac Cardiovasc Surg 123:492–497, 2002.

277a. Ozvaran MK, Ersoy Y, Uskul B, et al: Pleural complications of pulmonary hydatid disease. Respirology 9:115–119, 2004.

278. Xanthakis DS, Katsaras E, Efthimiadis M, et al: Hydatid cysts of the liver with intrathoracic rupture. Thorax 36:497–501, 1981.

279. Teixeira LR, Vargas FS: Effusions from atypical infections. *In* Light RW, Lee GYC (eds): Textbook of Pleural Diseases. London: Arnold, 2003, pp 345–356.

280. Im JG, Whang HY, Kim WS, et al: Pleuropulmonary paragonimiasis: Radiologic findings in 71 patients. AJR Am J Roentgenol 159:39–43, 1992.

281. Pachucki CT, Levandowski RA, Brown VA, et al: American paragonimiasis treated with praziquantel. N Engl J Med 311:582–583, 1984.

282. Drugs for parasitic infections. Med Lett Drugs Ther 40:1–7, 1998.

283. DeFrain M, Hooker R: North American paragonimiasis: Case report of a severe clinical infection. Chest 121:1368–1372, 2002.

284. Stein PD, Henry JW: Clinical characteristics of patients with acute pulmonary embolism stratified according to their presenting syndromes. Chest 112:974–979, 1997.

285. Cheng D, Rodriguez RM, Perkett EA, et al: Vascular endothelial growth factor in pleural fluid. Chest 116:760–765, 1999.

286. Bynum LJ, Wilson JEI: Radiographic features of pleural effusions in pulmonary embolism. Am Rev Respir Dis 117:829–834, 1978.

287. Goldberg SN, Richardson DD, Palmer EL, et al: Pleural effusion and ventilation/perfusion scan interpretation for acute pulmonary embolus. J Nucl Med 37:1310–1313, 1996.

288. Coche EE, Muller NL, Kim KI, et al: Acute pulmonary embolism: Ancillary findings at spiral CT. Radiology 207:753–758, 1998.

289. Shah AA, Davis SD, Gamsu G, et al: Parenchymal and pleural findings in patients with and patients without acute pulmonary embolism detected at spiral CT. Radiology 211:147–153, 1999.

290. Coche E, Verschuren F, Keyeux A, et al: Diagnosis of acute pulmonary embolism in outpatients: Comparison of thin-collimation multi-detector row spiral CT and planar ventilation-perfusion scintigraphy. Radiology 229:757–765, 2003.

291. Tapson VF, Carroll BA, Davidson BL, et al: The diagnostic approach to acute venous thromboembolism: Clinical practice guideline. Am J Respir Crit Care Med 160:1043–1066, 1999.

292. Bynum LJ, Wilson JEI: Characteristics of pleural effusions associated with pulmonary embolism. Arch Intern Med 136:159–162, 1976.

293. Rostand RA, Feldman RL, Block ER: Massive hemothorax complicating heparin anticoagulation for pulmonary embolus. South Med J 70:1128–1130, 1977.

294. Reeder LB, DeFilippi VJ, Ferguson MK: Current results of therapy for esophageal perforation. Am J Surg 169:615–617, 1995.

295. Michel L, Grillo HC, Malt RA: Operative and nonoperative management of esophageal perforations. Ann Surg 194:57–63, 1981.

296. Bufkin BL, Miller JIJ, Mansour KA: Esophageal perforation: Emphasis on management. Ann Thorac Surg 61:1447–1451, 1996.

297. Abbott OA, Mansour KA, Logan WD, et al: Atraumatic so-called 'spontaneous' rupture of the esophagus. J Thorac Cardiovasc Surg 59:67–83, 1970.

298. Rudin JS, Ellrodt AG, Phillips EH: Low pleural fluid amylase associated with spontaneous rupture of the esophagus. Arch Intern Med 143:1034–1035, 1983.

299. Good JT, Antony VB, Reller LB, et al: The pathogenesis of the low pleural fluid pH in esophageal rupture. Am Rev Respir Dis 127:702–704, 1983.

300. Eriksen KR: Oesophageopleural fistula diagnosed by microscopic examination of pleural fluid. Acta Chir Scand 128:771–777, 1964.

301. Tanomkiat W, Galassi W: Barium sulfate as contrast medium for evaluation of postoperative anastomotic leaks. Acta Radiol 41:482–485, 2000.

302. Ginai AZ: Experimental evaluation of various available contrast agents for use in the gastrointestinal tract in case of suspected leakage. Effects on pleura. Br J Radiol 59:887–894, 1986.

303. Fadoo F, Ruiz DE, Dawn SK, et al: Helical CT esophagography for the evaluation of suspected esophageal perforation or rupture. AJR Am J Roentgenol 182:1177–1179, 2004.

304. Lankisch PG, Droge M, Becher R: Pleural effusions: A new negative prognostic parameter for acute pancreatitis. Am J Gastroenterol 89:1849–1851, 1994.

305. Roseman DM, Kowlessar OD, Sleisenger MH: Pulmonary manifestations of pancreatitis. N Engl J Med 263:294–296, 1960.

306. Pederzoli P, Bassi C, Falconi M, et al: Conservative treatment of external pancreatic fistulas with parenteral nutrition alone or in combination with continuous

68 • Pleural Effusion   1959

intravenous infusion of somatostatin, glucagon or calcitonin. Surg Gynecol Obstet 163:428–432, 1986.

307. Lang EK, Paolini RM, Pottmeyer A: The efficacy of palliative and definitive percutaneous versus surgical drainage of pancreatic abscesses and pseudocysts. South Med J 84:55–64, 1991.

308. Lipsett PA, Cameron JL: Internal pancreatic fistula. Am J Surg 163:216–220, 1992.

309. van der Sluis RF: Subphrenic abscess. Surg Gynecol Obstet 158:427–430, 1984.

310. Miller TA, Lindenauer SM, Frey CF, et al: Pancreatic abscess. Arch Surg 108:545–551, 1974.

311. Johnson JD, Raff MJ, Barnwell PA, et al: Splenic abscess complicating infectious endocarditis. Arch Intern Med 143:906–912, 1983.

312. Rubin RH, Swartz MN, Malt R: Hepatic abscess: Changes in clinical, bacteriologic and therapeutic aspects. Am J Med 57:601–610, 1974.

313. Chu K-M, Fan S-T, Lai ECS, et al: Pyogenic liver abscess. Arch Surg 131:148–153, 1996.

314. Haaga JR, Weinstein AJ: CT-guided percutaneous aspiration and drainage of abscesses. AJR Am J Roentgenol 135:1187–1194, 1980.

315. Men S, Akhan O, Koroglu M: Percutaneous drainage of abdominal abscess. Eur J Radiol 43:204–218, 2002.

316. Aronchick JM, Epstein DM, Gefter WB, et al: Chronic traumatic diaphragmatic hernia: The significance of pleural effusion. Radiology 168:675–678, 1988.

317. Light RW, George RB: Incidence and significance of pleural effusion after abdominal surgery. Chest 69:621–626, 1976.

318. Nielsen PH, Jepsen SB, Olsen AD: Postoperative pleural effusion following upper abdominal surgery. Chest 96:1133–1135, 1989.

319. Golfieri R, Giampalma E, Morselli Labate AM, et al: Pulmonary complications of liver transplantation: Radiological appearance and statistical evaluation of risk factors in 300 cases. Eur Radiol 10:1169–1183, 2000.

320. Afessa B, Gay P, Plevak DJ, et al: Pulmonary complications of orthotopic liver transplantation. Mayo Clin Proc 68:427–434, 1993.

321. Uetsuji S, Komada Y, Kwon AH, et al: Prevention of pleural effusion after hepatectomy using fibrin sealant. Int Surg 79:135–137, 1994.

322. Delco F, Domenighetti G, Kauzlaric D, et al: Spontaneous biliothorax following cholecystopleural fistula presenting as an acute respiratory insufficiency: Successful removal of gallstones from the pleural space. Chest 106:961–963, 1994.

323. Horler AR, Thompson M: The pleural and pulmonary complications of rheumatoid arthritis. Ann Intern Med 51:1179–1203, 1959.

324. Pettersson T, Soderblom T, Nyberg P, et al: Pleural fluid soluble interleukin 2 receptor in rheumatoid arthritis and systemic lupus erythematosus. J Rheumatol 21:1820–1824, 1994.

325. Chou CW, Chang SC: Pleuritis as a presenting manifestation of rheumatoid arthritis: Diagnostic clues in pleural fluid cytology. Am J Med Sci 323:158–161, 2002.

326. Ferguson GC: Cholesterol pleural effusion in rheumatoid lung disease. Thorax 21:577–582, 1966.

327. Naylor B: The pathognomonic cytologic picture of rheumatoid pleuritis. Acta Cytol 34:465–473, 1990.

328. Jones FL, Blodgett RC: Empyema in rheumatoid pleuropulmonary disease. Ann Intern Med 74:665–671, 1971.

329. Chapman PT, O'Donnell JL, Moller PW: Rheumatoid pleural effusion: Response to intrapleural corticosteroid. Rheumatology 19:478–480, 1992.

330. Yarbrough JW, Sealy WC, Miller JA: Thoracic surgical problems associated with rheumatoid arthritis. J Thorac Cardiovasc Surg 68:347–354, 1975.

331. Wang DY: Diagnosis and management of lupus pleuritis. Ann Intern Med 49:70–88, 2002.

332. Kalomenidis IT: Effusions due to drugs. *In* Light RW, Lee YCG (eds): Textbook of Pleural Diseases. London: Arnold, 2003, pp 382–393.

333. Wang DY, Yang P-C, Yu WL, et al: Serial antinuclear antibodies titre in pleural and pericardial fluid. Eur Respir J 15:1106–1110, 2000.

334. Chao TY, Huang SH, Chu CC: Lupus erythematosus cells in pleural effusions: Diagnostic of systemic lupus erythematosus? Acta Cytol 41:1231–1233, 1997.

335. Vargas FS, Milanez JR, Filomeno LT, et al: Intrapleural talc for the prevention of recurrence in benign or undiagnosed pleural effusions. Chest 106:1771–1775, 1994.

336. Light RW: Pleural effusions following cardiac injury and coronary artery bypass graft surgery. Semin Respir Crit Care Med 22:657–664, 2001.

337. Mott AR, Fraser CDJ, Kusnoor AV, et al: The effect of short-term prophylactic methylprednisolone on the incidence and severity of postpericardiotomy syndrome in children undergoing cardiac surgery with cardiopulmonary bypass. J Am Coll Cardiol 37:1700–1706, 2001.

338. Engle MA, Gay WAJ, Kaminsky ME, et al: The postpericardiotomy syndrome then and now. Curr Probl Cardiol 3:1–40, 1978.

339. Stelzner TJ, King TEJ, Antony V, et al: The pleuropulmonary manifestations of the postcardiac injury syndrome. Chest 84:383–387, 1983.

340. Urschel HCJ, Razzuk MA, Gardner M: Coronary artery bypass occlusion second to postcardiotomy syndrome. Ann Thorac Surg 22:528–531, 1976.

341. Dressler W: The post-myocardial infarction syndrome. Arch Intern Med 103:28–42, 1959.

342. Light RW, Rogers JT, Moyers JP, et al: Prevalence and clinical course of pleural effusions at 30 days after coronary artery and cardiac surgery. Am J Respir Crit Care Med 166:1563–1566, 2002.

343. Vargas FS, Cukier A, Hueb W, et al: Relationship between pleural effusion and pericardial involvement after myocardial revascularization. Chest 105:1748–1752, 1994.

344. Sadikot RT, Rogers JT, Cheng DS, et al: Pleural fluid characteristics of patients with symptomatic pleural effusion after coronary artery bypass graft surgery. Arch Intern Med 160:2665–2668, 2000.

345. Lee YCG, Vaz MA, Ely KA, et al: Symptomatic persistent post-coronary artery bypass graft pleural effusions requiring operative treatment: Clinical and histologic features. Chest 119:795–800, 2001.

346. Shitrit D, Izbicki G, Fink G, et al: Late postoperative pleural effusion following lung transplantation: Characteristics and clinical implications. Eur J Cardiothorac Surg 23:494–496, 2003.

347. Ferrer JS, Roldan J, Roman A, et al: Acute and chronic pleural complications in lung transplantation. J Heart Lung Transplant 22:1217–1225, 2003.

348. Medina LS, Siegel MJ, Bejarano PA, et al: Pediatric lung transplantation: Radiographic-histopathologic correlation. Radiology 187:807–810, 1993.

349. Battafarano RJ, Anderson RC, Meyers BF, et al: Perioperative complications after living donor lobectomy. J Thorac Cardiovasc Surg 120:909–915, 2000.

350. Epler GR, McCloud CT, Gaensler EA: Prevalence and incidence of benign asbestos pleural effusion: Diagnosis and cause. JAMA 267:617–622, 1982.

351. Hillerdal G: Nonmalignant pleural disease related to asbestos exposure. Clin Chest Med 6:141–152, 1985.

352. Hillerdal G, Ozesmi M: Benign asbestos pleural effusion: 73 exudates in 60 patients. Eur J Respir Dis 71:113–121, 1987.

353. Soskel NT, Sharma OP: Pleural involvement in sarcoidosis. Curr Opin Pulm Med 6:455–468, 2000.

354. Chusid EL, Siltzbach LE: Sarcoidosis of the pleura. Ann Intern Med 81:1990–1994, 1974.

355. Nicholls AJ, Friend JA, Legge JS: Sarcoid pleural effusion: Three cases and review of the literature. Thorax 35:277–281, 1980.

356. Nidus BD, Matalon R, Cantacuzino D, et al: Uremic pleuritis—a clinicopathological entity. N Engl J Med 281:255–256, 1969.

357. Berger HW, Rammohan G, Neff MS, et al: Uremic pleural effusion: A study in 14 patients on chronic dialysis. Ann Intern Med 82:362–364, 1975.

358. Coskun M, Boyvat F, Bozkurt B, et al: Thoracic CT findings in long-term hemodialysis patients. Acta Radiol 40:181–186, 1998.

359. Jarratt MJ, Sahn SA: Pleural effusions in hospitalized patients receiving long-term hemodialysis. Chest 108:470–474, 1995.

360. Rodelas R, Rakowski TA, Argy WP, et al: Fibrosing uremic pleuritis during hemodialysis. JAMA 243:2424–2425, 1980.

361. Meigs JV, Cass JW: Fibroma of the ovary with ascites and hydrothorax. Am J Obstet Gynecol 33:249–267, 1937.

362. Ishiko O, Yoshida H, Sumi T, et al: Vascular endothelial growth factor levels in pleural and peritoneal fluid in Meigs' syndrome. Eur J Obstet Gynaecol Reprod Biol 98:129–130, 2001.

363. Kirschner PA: Porous diaphragm syndromes. Chest Surg Clin N Am 8:449–472, 1998.

364. Light RW: Pleural effusions due to obstetric and gynecological conditions. In Light RW, Lee YCG (eds): Textbook of Pleural Diseases. London: Arnold, 2003, pp 419–427.

365. Bhojawala J, Heller DS, Cracchiolo B, et al: Endometriosis presenting as bloody pleural effusion and ascites—report of a case and review of the literature. Arch Gynecol Obstet 264:39–41, 2000.

366. Abramov Y, Eichalal U, Schenker JG: Pulmonary manifestations of severe ovarian hyperstimulation syndrome: A multicenter study. Fertil Steril 71:645–651, 1999.

367. Wang TH, Horng SG, Chang CL, et al: Human chorionic gonadotropin-induced ovarian hyperstimulation syndrome is associated with upregulation of vascular endothelial growth factor. J Clin Endocrinol Metab 87:3300–3308, 2002.

368. Oren I, Goldman A, Hadda N, et al: Ascites and pleural effusion secondary to extramedullary hematopoiesis. Am J Med Sci 318:286–288, 1999.

369. Eastwood HD, Williams TJ: Pleural effusions and yellow nails of late onset. Postgrad Med J 49:364–365, 1973.

370. Beer DJ, Pereira WJ, Snider GL: Pleural effusion associated with primary lymphedema: A perspective on the yellow nail syndrome. Am Rev Respir Dis 117:595–599, 1978.

371. Lewis M, Kallenbach JA, Zaltzman M, et al: Pleurectomy in the management of massive pleural effusion associated with primary lymphoedema: Demonstration of abnormal pleural lymphatics. Thorax 38:637–639, 1983.

371a. D'Alessandro A, Muzi G, Monaco A, et al: Yellow nail syndrome: does protein leakage play a role? Eur Respir J 17:149–152, 2001.

372. Holmberg L, Boman G: Pulmonary reactions to nitrofurantoin: 447 cases reported to the Swedish Adverse Drug Reaction Committee, 1966–1976. Eur J Respir Dis 62:180–189, 1981.

373. Geller M, Flaherty DK, Dickie HA, et al: Lymphopenia in acute nitrofurantoin pleuropulmonary reactions. J Allergy Clin Immunol 59:445–448, 1977.

374. Petusevsky ML, Faling LJ, Rocklin RE, et al: Pleuropericardial reaction to treatment with dantrolene. JAMA 242:2772–2774, 1979.

375. Kok-Jensen A, Lindeneg O: Pleurisy and fibrosis of the pleura during methysergide treatment of hemicrania. Scand J Respir Dis 51:218–222, 1970.

376. Hillerdal G, Lee J, Blomkvist A, et al: Pleural disease during treatment with bromocriptine in patients previously exposed to asbestos. Eur Respir J 10:2711–2715, 1997.

377. McElvaney NG, Wilcox PG, Churg A, et al: Pleuropulmonary disease during bromocriptine treatment of Parkinson's disease. Arch Intern Med 148:2231–2236, 1988.

378. Jones SE, Moore M, Blank N, et al: Hypersensitivity to procarbazine (Matulane) manifested by fever and pleuropulmonary reaction. Cancer 29:498–500, 1972.

379. Ecker MD, Jay B, Keohane MF: Procarbazine lung. AJR Am J Roentgenol 131:527–528, 1978.

380. Vogelzang PJ, Bloom SM, Mier JW, et al: Chest roentgenographic abnormalities in IL-2 recipients: Incidence and correlation with clinical parameters. Chest 101:746–752, 1992.

381. Bachman AL, Macken K: Pleural effusions following supervoltage radiation for breast carcinoma. Radiology 72:699–709, 1959.

382. Fantanes de Torres E, Guevara E: Pleuritis by radiation: Report of two cases. Acta Cytol 25:427–429, 1981.

383. Duntley P, Siever J, Korwes ML, et al: Vascular erosion by central venous catheter. Clinical features and outcome. Chest 101:1633–1638, 1992.

384. Wothuis A, Landewe RB, Theunissen PH, et al: Chylothorax or leakage of total parenteral nutrition? Eur Respir J 12:1233–1235, 1998.

385. Roubenoff R, Ravich WJ: Pneumothorax due to nasogastric feeding tubes: Report of four cases, review of the literature, and recommendations for prevention. Arch Intern Med 149:184–188, 1989.

386. Miller KS, Tomlinson JR, Sahn SA: Pleuropulmonary complications of enteral tube feedings. Chest 88:231–233, 1985.

69 Pneumothorax, Chylothorax, Hemothorax, and Fibrothorax

Richard W. Light, M.D., Y. C. Gary Lee, M.B.Ch.B., Ph.D., F.R.A.C.P.

INTRODUCTION

By definition, a pneumothorax is present when there is air in the pleural space. Pneumothoraces are classified as *spontaneous pneumothoraces,* which occur without preceding trauma or other obvious cause, and *traumatic pneumothoraces,* which occur as a result of direct or indirect trauma to the chest, sometimes as a result of a diagnostic or therapeutic maneuver *(iatrogenic pneumothorax).* Spontaneous pneumothoraces are subclassified as *primary* or *secondary spontaneous pneumothoraces.* A primary spontaneous pneumothorax occurs in an otherwise healthy person without underlying lung disease. A secondary spontaneous pneumothorax complicates an underlying lung disease, most commonly chronic obstructive pulmonary disease (COPD).

Most pleural effusions prove to be either an exudate or a transudate according to the criteria provided in Chapter 68. Occasionally, the liquid contents turn out to be chyle, pseudochyle, or blood. This chapter describes the pathogenesis and clinical manifestations of chylothorax, pseudochylothorax, and hemothorax. In addition, the sequela of chronic organizing pleural disease of any origin—fibrothorax—is also considered.

PATHOPHYSIOLOGY OF PNEUMOTHORAX

In normal people, the pressure in the pleural space is negative with respect to the alveolar pressure during the entire respiratory cycle. The pressure gradient between the alveoli and the pleural space, the transpulmonary pressure, is the result of the inherent elastic recoil of the lung. During spontaneous breathing, the pleural pressure is also negative with respect to the atmospheric pressure. The functional residual capacity, or resting end-expiratory volume of the lung, is the volume at which the inherent outward pull of the chest wall is equal to, but opposite in direction to, the inward pull (recoil) of the lung.[1]

When a communication develops between an alveolus or other intrapulmonary air space and the pleural space, air will flow from the alveolus into the pleural space until there is no longer a pressure difference or until the communication is sealed. Similarly, when a communication develops through the chest wall between the atmosphere and the pleural space, air will enter the pleural space until the pressure gradient is eliminated or the communication is closed. The influence of a pneumothorax on the volume of the hemithorax and the lung is illustrated in Figure 69.1. When sufficient air enters the pleural space to increase the pleural pressure from -5 to -2.5 cm H_2O, the transpulmonary or recoil pressure decreases from 5 to 2.5 cm H_2O. The amount of air necessary to effect this change in the pleural pressure is equal to 33% of the patient's vital capacity. The largest portion of this pleural air (25% of the vital capacity) displaces air from the lung. The increase in pleural pressure also changes the recoil pressure acting across the chest wall, which allows the thoracic cavity to expand along its pres-

sure-volume curve (by 8% of the vital capacity). The increase in the pleural pressure also causes a shift of the mediastinum to the contralateral side, an enlarged hemithorax, and a depressed hemidiaphragm. These findings do not necessarily indicate that a tension pneumothorax is present.[1]

The main physiologic consequences of a pneumothorax are a decrease in the vital capacity (as illustrated in Fig. 69.1) and a decrease in the arterial PO₂. In patients with primary spontaneous pneumothorax, the decrease in the vital capacity is usually well tolerated. If the lung function of the patient is abnormal before the development of the pneumothorax, however, the decrease in vital capacity may lead to respiratory insufficiency with alveolar hypoventilation and respiratory acidosis.

Most patients with a pneumothorax have a reduced arterial PO₂ and an increase in the alveolar-arterial oxygen tension difference. In a series of 12 patients with spontaneous pneumothorax, the arterial PO₂ was below 80 mm Hg in 9 (75%) and was below 55 mm Hg in two patients, both of whom had secondary spontaneous pneumothorax.[2]

The reduction in arterial PO₂ appears to be caused by areas with low ventilation-perfusion ratios, anatomic shunts, and, occasionally, alveolar hypoventilation. Norris and coworkers[2] reported that the average right-to-left shunt in their 12 patients with spontaneous pneumothorax was more than 10%. Larger pneumothoraces were associated with greater shunts. When the pneumothorax occupied less than 25% of the hemithorax, the shunt was not increased.[2]

After air is evacuated from the pleural space, the arterial PO₂ usually improves, but the improvement may take several hours. Norris and colleagues[2] evacuated the pleural air from three patients with a pneumothorax and an initial anatomic shunt above 20%; within 90 minutes, the shunt had decreased below 10%, but it still remained above 5% in all patients. The delay in improvement may be related to the duration of the pneumothorax.

PRIMARY SPONTANEOUS PNEUMOTHORAX

INCIDENCE

The incidence of primary spontaneous pneumothorax in the residents of Olmsted County, Minnesota, between 1959 and 1978 was 7.4 per 100,000 per year for men and 1.2 per 100,000 per year for women.[3] In a more recent study from the United Kingdom, the incidence of spontaneous pneumothorax was 24.0 per 100,000 per year for men and 9.8 per 100,000 per year for women,[4] and about one half of the pneumothoraces were primary spontaneous pneumothoraces. If the incidence is assumed to be 10.0 per 100,000 per year for men and 5.0 per 100,000 per year for women, the annual incidence in the United States would be about 22,500.

ETIOLOGIC FACTORS

Primary spontaneous pneumothorax is believed to result from rupture of a subpleural emphysematous bleb, which is usually located in the apex of the lung.[5] Blebs can be found in more than 75% of patients undergoing thoracoscopy for treatment of primary spontaneous pneumothorax.[5] The pathogenesis of these subpleural blebs is unclear. Such blebs have been attributed to congenital abnormalities, inflam-

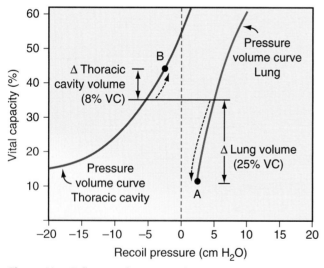

Figure 69.1 Influence of a pneumothorax on the volumes of the lung and hemithorax. In this illustration, the pneumothorax has caused the intrapleural pressure to rise from -5 to -2.5 cm H_2O. The lung and thoracic cavity move on their respective pressure volume curves (*dashed lines*) to new volumes for the lung (A) and thoracic cavity (B). Note that the volume of the hemithorax becomes larger as the volume of the lung becomes smaller. The changes in volumes of the hemithorax and lung are unequal because of the differences in the slopes of two pressure-volume curves. VC, vital capacity. (From Light RW: Pleural Diseases [3rd ed]. Philadelphia: Lea & Febiger, 1995, p 244.)

mation of the bronchioles, and disturbances of the collateral ventilation.[5] There is a strong association between smoking and the development of a primary spontaneous pneumothorax. When four separate series of patients with primary spontaneous pneumothorax are combined, 461 of 505 patients (91%) with primary spontaneous pneumothorax were smokers or ex-smokers.[1] The occurrence of a spontaneous pneumothorax is related to the level of cigarette smoking. In men the relative risk of a pneumothorax is 7 times higher in light smokers (1 to 12 cigarettes/day), 21 times higher in moderate smokers (13 to 22 cigarettes/day), and 102 times higher in heavy smokers (>22 cigarettes/day) than in nonsmokers.[6] It is probable that smoking-induced disease of small airways contributes to the development of the subpleural blebs.

Patients with primary spontaneous pneumothorax tend to be taller and thinner than control persons. In one study of military recruits with primary spontaneous pneumothorax, persons with a pneumothorax were on average 2 inches taller and 25 pounds lighter than the typical military recruit.[1] An increased length of the chest may contribute to the formation of the subpleural blebs. Because pleural pressure falls about 0.20 cm H_2O per centimeter of vertical height, pleural pressure will be more negative at the apex of the lung in tall than in short people; accordingly, the alveoli at their lung apex are subjected to a greater mean distending pressure. Over an extended period, this could lead to the formation of subpleural blebs in those tall people who are genetically predisposed to bleb formation.

A tendency for the development of a primary spontaneous pneumothorax can be inherited. Some cases are due to an autosomal dominant gene with incomplete penetrance, the penetrance being lower in women (21%) than in men (50%). There also appears to be an inheritance due to an X-linked recessive gene.[7] Recently a syndrome called the Birt-Hogg-Dubé syndrome has been described in which there is an increased incidence of spontaneous pneumothorax, benign skin tumors, and renal tumors.[8] This is an autosomal dominant cancer syndrome in which the gene has been mapped to chromosome 17p11.2.[8] In one study of 111 patients with this syndrome, pneumothorax occurred in 25 (22.5%).[9] Pneumothorax also occurs with increased frequencies with the Marfan syndrome and homocystinuria.

CLINICAL MANIFESTATIONS

The peak age for the occurrence of a primary spontaneous pneumothorax is in the early 20s, and it rarely occurs after age 40. Primary spontaneous pneumothorax usually develops while the patient is at rest, and only rarely do the initial symptoms arise during heavy exercise.[10] Surprisingly, many patients with spontaneous pneumothorax do not seek medical attention immediately after the development of symptoms. In one series, 18% of patients waited more than 1 week after development of symptoms before obtaining medical help.[11]

Chest pain and dyspnea are the two main symptoms associated with the development of primary spontaneous pneumothorax. In one series of 39 patients with primary spontaneous pneumothorax, every patient had chest pain or dyspnea, and both symptoms were present in 25 of 39 patients (64%).[12] The chest pain usually has an acute onset

and is localized to the side of the pneumothorax. A rare complication of spontaneous pneumothorax is Horner's syndrome, which is thought to result from traction on the sympathetic ganglion produced by a shift of the mediastinum.

On physical examination, the vital signs are usually normal, with the exception of a moderate tachycardia. A tension pneumothorax should be suspected if the pulse rate exceeds 140 beats/min or if hypotension, cyanosis, or electromechanical dissociation is present. On examination of the chest, the side with pneumothorax is larger than the contralateral side and moves less during the respiratory cycle. Tactile fremitus is absent, the percussion note is hyperresonant, and the breath sounds are absent or reduced on the affected side. The lower edge of the liver may be shifted inferiorly with a right-sided pneumothorax. With a large pneumothorax, the trachea may be shifted toward the contralateral side.

The presence of a pneumothorax may elicit electrocardiographic changes. With left pneumothorax, all of the following changes have been noted: rightward shift of the frontal QRS axis, diminution of precordial R voltage, decrease in QRS amplitude, and precordial T-wave inversion. With right pneumothorax, the following changes have been noted: diminution of precordial QRS voltage, right-axis deviation, and a prominent R wave in lead V_2 with associated loss of S-wave voltage mimicking posterior myocardial infarction.[13] All these changes are thought to be due to mechanical effects and should not be mistaken for cardiac ischemia or infarction.

DIAGNOSIS

The diagnosis is usually suggested by the clinical history and the physical examination. The diagnosis is established by demonstrating a pleural line on the chest radiograph (Fig. 69.2). In doubtful cases, lateral decubitus films may facilitate the diagnosis. Expiratory films are no more sensitive than inspiratory films in detecting pneumothoraces and are

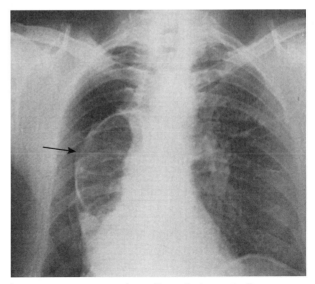

Figure 69.2 Posteroanterior radiograph demonstrating a pneumothorax on the right side. Note the obvious pleural line (*arrow*) that separates the lung from the air in the pleural space. (From Light RW: Pleural Diseases [2nd ed]. Philadelphia: Lea & Febiger, 1990, p 36.)

not recommended.[5] A small pleural effusion is associated with a primary spontaneous pneumothorax in approximately 15% of cases and is manifested radiographically as an air-fluid level.[11,12] When the pleural fluid is analyzed, it frequently contains a large percentage of eosinophils.[14] On rare occasions, spontaneous pneumothorax is complicated by brisk bleeding into the pleural space, producing a hemopneumothorax.[15] If the patient's vital signs are unstable in this situation, emergency surgery is indicated.[15]

The amount of lung collapse should be estimated when one is managing a patient with a pneumothorax. Because the volumes of the lung and the hemithorax are roughly proportional to the cube of their diameters, one can estimate the degree of collapse (PNX %) by measuring average diameters of the lung and the hemithorax, cubing these diameters, and using the following equation, known as the Light index[1]:

$$PNX\% = 100\left[1 - \frac{lung^3}{hemithorax^3}\right]$$

It has recently been shown that there is an excellent correlation ($r = 0.84$) between the Light index and the amount of air that can be aspirated from a pneumothorax.[16]

RECURRENCE RATES

Following a primary spontaneous pneumothorax, a patient is at risk of recurrence particularly in the months immediately after the first episode. Sadikot and associates[17] followed 153 patients with primary spontaneous pneumothorax for a mean of 54 months and reported that 39% had a recurrent ipsilateral pneumothorax, most within the first year. Once a patient has a primary spontaneous pneumothorax, there is also an increased risk of having a pneumothorax on the contralateral side. In the report of Sadikot and coworkers,[17] 15% of the 153 patients developed a pneumothorax on the contralateral side.

There have been several attempts to predict who will develop recurrent pneumothorax. Patients who are tall and those who continue to smoke are more likely to have a recurrence.[17] Yet, there is no relationship between the number of blebs or the size of the blebs on computed tomography (CT),[18] or the appearance of the lung at thoracotomy,[19] and the risk of recurrence. Once a patient has had one recurrence, the risk of another recurrence increases to more than 50%.[20]

TREATMENT

There are two goals to managing a patient with a primary spontaneous pneumothorax: to rid the pleural space of its air and to decrease the likelihood of a recurrence. There are several different approaches to the treatment of patients with primary spontaneous pneumothorax. These include observation, supplemental oxygen, simple aspiration of the pneumothorax, simple tube thoracostomy, tube thoracostomy with instillation of a pleurodesing agent, thoracoscopy with oversewing of the blebs and pleurodesis, and open thoracotomy. When the treatment for any given patient is selected, it should be remembered that primary spontaneous pneumothorax is mainly a nuisance and rarely life-threatening to the patient. Recently, the American College of Chest Physicians[21] and the British Thoracic Society[22] have published guidelines on the treatment of spontaneous pneumothorax. The former guideline emphasized how few controlled studies exist on the treatment of pneumothorax.[21]

Observation

Once the communication between the alveoli and the pleural space is eliminated, the air in the pleural space will be gradually reabsorbed. The rate of spontaneous reabsorption is slow. Kircher and Swartzel[23] estimated that 1.25% of the volume of the hemithorax is absorbed each 24 hours. Therefore, if a patient has a 20% pneumothorax, it will take 16 days for pleural air to be absorbed spontaneously. For this reason, it is recommended that only asymptomatic patients with pneumothoraces occupying less than 15% of the hemithorax be considered for this type of treatment. If the patient is hospitalized, supplemental oxygen should be administered to increase the rate of pleural air absorption.

Supplemental Oxygen

In pneumothorax, gases move in and out of the pleural space from the capillaries in the visceral and parietal pleura. The movement of each gas depends on the gradient between its partial pressure in the capillaries and in the pleural space, the blood flow per unit surface area available for gas exchange, and the solubility of each gas in the surrounding tissues. Normally, the sum of all the partial pressures in the capillary blood with a patient breathing room air is about 706 mm Hg ($P_{H_2O} = 47$, $P_{CO_2} = 46$, $P_{N_2} = 573$, and $P_{O_2} = 40$ mm Hg). If it is assumed that the pleural pressure is approximately 0 when there is a pneumothorax, then the net gradient for gas absorption is only 54 mm Hg (760 − 706). If the patient is placed on 100% oxygen, however, the sum of all the partial pressures in the capillary blood will probably fall below 200 mm Hg (the P_{N_2} will approach 0, whereas the P_{O_2} will remain under 100 mm Hg). Accordingly, the net gradient for gas absorption will exceed 550 mm Hg or be 10 times greater than it was with the patient breathing room air.[1]

Indeed, the administration of supplemental oxygen accelerates the rate of pleural air absorption in clinical and experimental situations. Chernick and Avery[24] demonstrated that the administration of humidified 100% oxygen to rabbits with experimentally induced pneumothoraces increased the rate of absorption by about sixfold. Subsequent studies in patients with a spontaneous pneumothorax have demonstrated that pleural air is absorbed about four times faster when the patients are given high concentrations of supplemental oxygen to breathe.[25] It is recommended that hospitalized patients with any type of pneumothorax who are not subjected to aspiration or tube thoracostomy be treated with supplemental oxygen at high concentrations.

Simple Aspiration

The initial treatment for most patients with primary spontaneous pneumothoraces greater than 15% of the volume of the hemithorax should be simple aspiration.[26–28] This procedure is successful in approximately 60% of patients with spontaneous pneumothorax.[29] The advantages of this procedure are that, if successful, hospitalization is not required and there is less pain from the smaller tube. The recurrence rates appear to be similar after simple aspiration and after tube thoracostomy.[26-28]

With this procedure, a relatively small needle (~16 gauge) with an internal polyethylene catheter is inserted into the second anterior intercostal space at the mid-clavicular line after local anesthesia. An alternative site is selected if the pneumothorax is loculated or if adhesions are present. After the needle is inserted, it is extracted, leaving the catheter tip in the pleural space. A three-way stopcock and a 60-mL syringe are attached to the catheter. Air is manually withdrawn until no more can be aspirated. The catheter is then occluded for several hours. If the chest radiograph confirms that there has been no recurrence, the catheter is removed and the patient is discharged. Alternatively, the patient can be observed in the hospital overnight or can be discharged with a Heimlich one-way valve attached to the catheter. If the total volume of air aspirated exceeds 4 L and no resistance has been felt, it is assumed that there has been no expansion, and alternative procedures are initiated.

It is recommended that most patients with their first primary spontaneous pneumothorax be managed initially with simple aspiration on an outpatient basis. For patients who reside more than 15 minutes from the hospital, consideration can be given to observing them overnight in the hospital. Patients should return in 24 to 72 hours for a follow-up chest radiograph. If aspiration is unsuccessful, then either thoracoscopy or tube thoracostomy should be undertaken. Because a patient with a first primary spontaneous pneumothorax has less than a 50% likelihood of developing a recurrent ipsilateral spontaneous pneumothorax and because a pneumothorax is primarily a nuisance rather than life-threatening, there is little reason to go to great lengths to prevent a recurrence. Simple aspiration is not recommended for patients with secondary spontaneous pneumothoraces or with recurrent primary spontaneous pneumothoraces.

Tube Thoracostomy

For the past several decades, most patients with primary spontaneous pneumothorax have been managed initially with tube thoracostomy. This procedure is recommended if simple aspiration proves ineffective and thoracoscopy is not readily available; it rapidly results in the reexpansion of the underlying lung and does not require prolonged hospitalization. In one series of 81 patients treated with tube thoracostomy, the average duration of hospitalization was only 4 days, with a range of 3 to 6 days. Only three patients (4%) had persistent air leaks after several days of chest tube drainage.[11]

When a spontaneous pneumothorax is managed with tube thoracostomy, relatively small tubes (12 to 16 French)[22,30] or pigtail catheters (8 to 10 French)[31] appear to be as effective as larger tubes. Because the risk of reexpansion pulmonary edema is greater when the lung is reexpanded rapidly, it is probably better to use water seal and to avoid suction for the first 24 hours of tube thoracostomy.

After the lung has reexpanded and the air leak has ceased for 24 hours, the chest tube can be removed. Air leaks are present when there is bubbling through the water seal chamber of the drainage system. If there is no bubbling on quiet respiration, the patient should be asked to cough. The absence of bubbling indicates there is no air leak. There is probably no reason to clamp the tube before its removal.[21,22] If the lung remains unexpanded or if there is a persistent air leak 72 hours after tube thoracostomy, consideration should be given to performing thoracoscopy or thoracotomy. There is no evidence that the intrapleural injection of a pleurodesing agent facilitates closure of a bronchopleural fistula.[32]

Tube Thoracostomy with Instillation of a Pleurodesing Agent

Because many patients with an initial primary spontaneous pneumothorax will have a recurrence, efforts have been made to diminish the recurrence rates by injecting pleurodesing agents into the pleural space at the time of initial episode. The two agents most commonly used are doxycycline and talc slurry. The administration of one of these agents will reduce the recurrence rates from approximately 40% to 25% (Fig. 69.3).[32] However, because thoracoscopy with stapling of blebs and pleural abrasion reduces the recurrence rate to less than 5%,[1,33] the thoracoscopic procedure is preferred if it is readily available. Because the

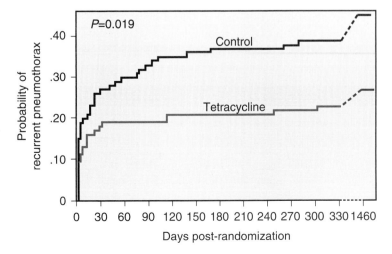

Figure 69.3 Probability of recurrent pneumothorax after assignment to the tetracycline or the control group in the Veterans Administration cooperative study on spontaneous pneumothorax. (From Light RW, O'Hara VS, Moritz TE, et al: Intrapleural tetracycline for the prevention of recurrent spontaneous pneumothorax. JAMA 264:2224–2230, 1990.)

administration of talc intrapleurally may be associated with the development of acute respiratory distress syndrome,[34,35] a tetracycline derivative (e.g., doxycycline 500 mg) is probably the agent of choice. Bleomycin is not recommended for pneumothoraces because it does not produce a pleurodesis in animals with a normal pleura,[36] and has not been studied with pneumothorax in humans.

The procedure for the intrapleural instillation of doxycycline is outlined in Chapter 70 in the discussion of malignant pleural effusions. Because the injection of a tetracycline derivative can be very painful, particularly in a patient with a pneumothorax and a relatively normal pleura, heavy sedation should be given before sclerosis is attempted.

Thoracoscopy

As video-assisted thoracoscopic surgery (VATS) becomes more widely available, patients with spontaneous pneumothorax are increasingly being managed with VATS (see also Chapter 23). It is the procedure of choice if aspiration fails or if the patient has a recurrent pneumothorax. During VATS, attempts are made to eliminate the blebs responsible for the pneumothorax and to create a pleurodesis. There is no reason to obtain a CT scan before the thoracoscopy. The primary means by which the blebs are treated is with endo-stapling. The disadvantage of endo-stapling is that it is expensive, with the consumables costing more than $400 per procedure.[37] When this is a concern, the apical blebs and bullae can be managed by thoracoscopic suturing.[37] Pleurodesis is probably best induced by pleural abrasion.[38,39]

VATS is effective management for primary spontaneous pneumothorax. When four series with a total of 551 patients are combined, only 19 (3.4%) of the patients had a recurrence with a follow-up period of more than 1 year.[38,40-42] The median duration of hospitalization for patients treated with thoracoscopy is about 3 days. The most common complication of VATS for the treatment of primary spontaneous pneumothorax is a persistent air leak, which occurs in less than 5% of cases.[40] VATS is preferred to thoracotomy because the hospitalization times are shorter and there is less morbidity.[43]

Some have proposed that medical thoracoscopy or pleuroscopy with the insufflation of talc is the preferred way to manage primary spontaneous pneumothorax.[44,45] With pleuroscopy the anesthesia is local and no treatment is provided for the blebs. Controlled studies are needed to determine whether this method is as effective as VATS with stapling of the blebs and pleural abrasion. In one study of 59 patients, pleuroscopy with the insufflation of talc had a recurrence rate of 5% during a follow-up period of 5 years.[45]

Open Thoracotomy

When VATS is not available, open thoracotomy with oversewing of the blebs and pleural abrasion is a reasonable alternative. If a thoracotomy is performed for pneumothorax, a transaxillary mini-thoracotomy should be performed to minimize the trauma and the length of the scar.[46] Thoracotomy is effective in preventing recurrences.[47] In one large series of 362 patients undergoing parietal pleurectomy combined with excision of blebs, there were only two documented ipsilateral recurrences during an average follow-up

period of 4.5 years in 310 patients.[47] There was a single death attributable to the operative procedure, and the average postoperative period of hospitalization was only 6 days.[47] Various methods have been used for scarification of the pleural surfaces, ranging from visceral and parietal pleurectomy to abrasion of the pleura with dry sponges. Because all appear to be equally effective, pleural abrasion with dry gauze is recommended because it is less traumatic than pleurectomy and does not affect a subsequent thoracotomy.

Summary of Treatment

Most patients with their first primary spontaneous pneumothorax should be managed initially with simple aspiration of the pleural air with a plastic catheter. If this is ineffective, VATS should be performed promptly, with endo-stapling of blebs and pleural abrasion to create a pleurodesis. When thoracoscopy is unavailable, patients who fail aspiration should be managed with tube thoracostomy with an attempt at pleurodesis with either doxycycline or talc. If, after 3 days of thoracostomy drainage, there is a persistent air leak or the lungs have not reexpanded, thoracoscopy should be considered. Patients with recurrent primary spontaneous pneumothorax should undergo VATS or thoracotomy.

SECONDARY SPONTANEOUS PNEUMOTHORAX

A secondary spontaneous pneumothorax is more serious than a primary spontaneous pneumothorax because it further decreases the pulmonary function of a patient whose reserve is already diminished. In addition, the presence of the underlying lung disease makes management of the pneumothorax more difficult.

INCIDENCE

The incidence of secondary spontaneous pneumothorax is similar to that of primary spontaneous pneumothorax.[3] An estimated 15,000 new cases of secondary spontaneous pneumothorax occur annually in the United States. Men over the age of 75 have the highest per capita rate of pneumothorax, 60 per 100,000 per year.[4]

ETIOLOGIC FACTORS

COPD is the most common underlying disease in patients with secondary spontaneous pneumothorax, although almost every lung disease has been associated with secondary spontaneous pneumothorax. In one recent series of 505 patients with secondary spontaneous pneumothorax, 348 patients had COPD, 93 had tumors, 26 had sarcoidosis, 9 had tuberculosis, 16 had other pulmonary infections, and 13 had miscellaneous diseases.[48] Among patients with COPD, the incidence of secondary spontaneous pneumothorax increases with progressive severity of the COPD. In the Veterans Administration cooperative study[32] on pneumothorax, 27% of the 229 participants had an FEV_1/FVC ratio below 0.40. One of the most common causes of secondary spontaneous pneumothorax is

Pneumocystis jirovecii (formerly *carinii*) infection in the patient with acquired immunodeficiency syndrome (AIDS).[49] There is also a high incidence of spontaneous pneumothorax in patients with cystic fibrosis. In a series of 144 patients older than 10 years with cystic fibrosis, 12.5% had experienced a secondary spontaneous pneumothorax.[50] Patients with lymphangioleiomyomatosis (see Fig. 69.6 and Chapter 58) and histiocytosis X[50a] (Langerhans cell granulomatosis; see Chapter 57) also have a high incidence of spontaneous pneumothorax.

CLINICAL MANIFESTATIONS

In general, the clinical symptoms associated with secondary spontaneous pneumothorax are more severe than those associated with primary spontaneous pneumothorax. In the series of 57 patients with COPD and pneumothorax reported by Dines and coworkers,[51] all patients complained of shortness of breath, 74% had chest pain on the side of the pneumothorax, 9% were cyanotic, and 7% were hypotensive. Although earlier studies reported a mortality rate that exceeded 10% with pneumothorax secondary to COPD,[51,52] in the large Veterans Administration cooperative study, the mortality rate from pneumothorax was only 1%.[32]

DIAGNOSIS

The possibility of a pneumothorax should be considered in every patient with COPD who suddenly has increasing shortness of breath, particularly if there is associated chest pain. The physical examination of a patient with a secondary spontaneous pneumothorax is less helpful in establishing the diagnosis than it is in a patient with a primary spontaneous pneumothorax. Patients with underlying disease may already have hyperexpanded lungs, decreased tactile fremitus, a hyperresonant percussion note, and distant breath sounds over both lung fields. Accordingly, when a pneumothorax develops, side-to-side differences in the physical examination may not be apparent.

The diagnosis of secondary spontaneous pneumothorax is established by the demonstration of a pleural line on the chest radiograph. It is sometimes difficult to see this line in radiographs of patients with COPD because the hyperlucent emphysematous lung shows little difference in radiodensity from the pneumothorax. Frequently, the presence of the pneumothorax is overlooked on the initial chest radiograph, particularly when the film is overexposed. In patients with lung disease, the radiographic appearance of the pneumothorax can be altered by the underlying abnormalities. Areas of normal lung collapse more evenly and completely than do diseased areas with large bullae or severe emphysema, which have a decreased elastic recoil and may trap gas.

It is important to distinguish a spontaneous pneumothorax from a large, thin-walled, air-containing bulla in patients with COPD. The apparent pleural line with a large bulla is usually concave toward the lateral chest wall because it represents the medial border of the bulla, whereas the pleural line with a pneumothorax is usually oriented convexly toward the lateral chest wall. At times, CT examination of the chest is necessary to make this differentiation.[53]

RECURRENCE RATES

It appears that the recurrence rates for secondary spontaneous pneumothoraces are somewhat higher than those for primary spontaneous pneumothoraces if the patients are not treated with pleurodesing agents or thoracotomy. In two series of patients with both primary and secondary spontaneous pneumothoraces, the recurrence rates were somewhat higher in the patients with secondary spontaneous pneumothorax (~45%) than they were in patients with primary spontaneous pneumothorax (~30%) over a 3- to 5-year observation period.[32,54]

TREATMENT

Urgent evaluation is indicated for any patient suspected of having a secondary spontaneous pneumothorax. Patients with secondary spontaneous pneumothoraces occasionally die before a chest tube can be inserted. Such deaths were reported in 3 of 57 patients (5%) with pneumothorax secondary to COPD[51] and in 3 of 15 patients (20%) with cystic fibrosis.[55] The high immediate mortality rate emphasizes that an important secondary treatment goal for these patients is reducing the likelihood of a recurrence.

The initial treatment for nearly every patient with a secondary spontaneous pneumothorax should be tube thoracostomy. Simple aspiration should not be performed because it frequently is ineffective and, in addition, does not decrease the likelihood of a recurrence. The evacuation of even a small pneumothorax can lead to a rapid improvement in symptoms. If respiratory failure occurs, necessitating mechanical ventilation, a chest tube should be placed immediately because the pneumothorax is likely to enlarge during mechanical ventilation.

It is more difficult to expand the lung and air leaks persist longer in patients with secondary spontaneous than in patients with primary spontaneous pneumothorax who are treated with tube thoracostomy. In secondary spontaneous pneumothorax caused by COPD, the median time for lung expansion is 5 days compared with 1 day for primary spontaneous pneumothorax,[51] and more patients require prolonged chest tube drainage.[56] In one series, 35% of patients with cystic fibrosis required multiple chest tubes[55]; similarly, in another series, 29% of patients with COPD required more than one chest tube. After 7 days of tube thoracostomy drainage, the lung remains unexpanded or the air leak persists in about 20% of patients with secondary spontaneous pneumothorax.[51,55]

Following thoracostomy, a case can be made for subjecting most patients with secondary spontaneous pneumothorax to thoracoscopy. Thoracoscopy should certainly be performed in patients with a persistent air leak or an unexpanded lung after 72 hours of tube thoracostomy. If the lung expands and the air leak ceases within the first 72 hours, an attempt should be made to prevent a recurrence. For preventing recurrences, thoracoscopy is superior to chemical pleurodesis as the recurrence rates after thoracoscopy are less than 5%, whereas those after chemical pleurodesis are approximately 20%.[32] If thoracoscopy is not available, it is recommended that doxycycline (500 mg) be instilled into the pleural space in an attempt to prevent a recurrent pneumothorax. If thoracoscopy is unavailable and there is a persistent air leak or an unexpanded lung after 5 days, consideration should be given to thoracotomy.

One consideration for patients with secondary spontaneous pneumothorax is the effect that a pleurodesing agent might have on a future lung transplant. In the past, if attempts at pleurodesis had been made on the side of the proposed transplant, patients were excluded from lung transplantation due to the risk of excess bleeding. In 1998, however, a consensus conference statement on lung transplantation in cystic fibrosis stated that pleurodesis is not a contraindication to lung transplantation.[57] Although not a contraindication to lung transplantation, pleurodesis, especially with talc, would be expected to make future lung transplantation more difficult and should be avoided if possible. It would be advisable to consult local transplant surgeons when contemplating pleurodesis for candidates for future lung transplant.

PNEUMOTHORAX SECONDARY TO *PNEUMOCYSTIS* IN PATIENTS WITH ACQUIRED IMMUNODEFICIENCY SYNDROME

Patients with AIDS and *P. jirovecii* infection have a relatively high incidence of spontaneous pneumothorax. Approximately 5% of patients with AIDS who receive prophylactic pentamidine will have a spontaneous pneumothorax.[1] Most patients with AIDS who have a spontaneous pneumothorax have a history of *P. jirovecii* infection, many are taking prophylactic pentamidine, and most have a recurrence of their *P. jirovecii* infection.[1,49] The explanation for the high incidence of spontaneous pneumothorax in these patients appears to be the presence of multiple subpleural lung cavities, which are associated with subpleural necrosis.[58] Once such a patient has a pneumothorax, he or she is likely to experience a contralateral pneumothorax. It should be noted that iatrogenic pneumothoraces, particularly those related to mechanical ventilation or pulmonary procedures, are also common in patients with AIDS.[49]

Perhaps due to the necrotic lung surrounding the ruptured cavity, the spontaneous pneumothorax associated with AIDS and *P. jirovecii* infection is notoriously difficult to treat. In one report of 20 patients, the median duration of tube thoracostomy was 20 days; 11 patients underwent pleurodesis, whereas 5 patients had thoracotomy.[59]

Patients with AIDS and a spontaneous pneumothorax should be treated with tube thoracostomy. If the air leak persists for more than a few days, there are two options: a Heimlich valve or VATS. The intrapleural injection of a pleurodesing agent has not been shown to be effective in expediting closure of the leak. In general, the Heimlich valve is preferred because the patient can be managed as an outpatient. Vricella and Trachiotis[60] discharged 10 patients with Heimlich valves and reported that there were no instances of morbidity or mortality related to the valve, and the valves were removed from all patients as outpatients at a mean of 17 days after discharge.

If the patient cannot be managed with a Heimlich valve because the airflow through the bronchopleural fistula is too high, VATS can be performed. Wait[61] reported that 30 of 32 patients (94%) with AIDS and spontaneous pneumothorax were managed successfully with talc insufflation without endo-stapling. If operative intervention is planned, it should be carried out early to avoid prolonged air leak, hospitalization, and morbidity.

PNEUMOTHORAX SECONDARY TO TUBERCULOSIS

Between 1% and 3% of patients hospitalized for pulmonary tuberculosis will have a pneumothorax.[62] All such patients should be treated initially with tube thoracostomy. In one series of 28 patients, of 11 treated by observation or repeated pleural aspiration, 7 (64%) died,[62] whereas of 17 patients treated with tube thoracostomy, only 1 (6%) died. Obviously, antituberculous chemotherapy should be given concomitantly with the tube thoracostomy. Open thoracotomy should not be considered until the patient has received antituberculous therapy for at least 6 weeks.

IATROGENIC PNEUMOTHORAX

Iatrogenic pneumothoraces are probably more common than primary and secondary spontaneous pneumothoraces combined. The relative incidence of iatrogenic pneumothorax has increased over the past few decades because of the increased use of invasive procedures such as transbronchial biopsy, percutaneous lung aspiration, central vein catheterization, and ventilation with high levels of positive end-expiratory pressure, all of which are associated with a high incidence of pneumothorax. Indeed, in the period between November 1, 1983, and January 1, 1989, at the Veterans Administration Hospital in Long Beach, California, there were 108 instances of iatrogenic pneumothorax compared with 90 instances of spontaneous pneumothorax. The causes of the 108 cases of iatrogenic pneumothorax at that facility were as follows: transthoracic needle aspiration in 35, thoracentesis in 31, insertion of subclavicular intravenous line in 23, positive-pressure ventilation in 6, transbronchial biopsy in 3, and miscellaneous in 10.[63]

Currently, the leading cause of iatrogenic pneumothorax is transthoracic needle aspiration. The incidence of iatrogenic pneumothorax with this procedure is about 25%, and 10% of the patients with pneumothorax receive tube thoracostomy.[64,65] This procedure is more likely to result in a pneumothorax if the patient has COPD, if the lesion is deep within the lung, or if the angle of the needle route is wide.[65,66] Various maneuvers such as positioning the patient with the biopsied side down[67] or using the blood patch technique have not proved useful in diminishing the incidence of pneumothorax.

Another common cause of iatrogenic pneumothorax is mechanical ventilation. In one early series of 553 patients undergoing mechanical ventilation, 4% developed a pneumothorax.[68] The frequency of the pneumothorax was increased if the patient had aspiration pneumonia (37%), was treated with positive end-expiratory pressure (15%), had intubation of the right main-stem bronchus (13%), or had COPD (8%).[68] In a more recent study, the incidence of pneumothorax in 725 patients with acute respiratory distress syndrome was 6.9%.[69] In patients with acute respiratory distress syndrome, the incidence of barotrauma is higher if the ventilator plateau pressure exceeds 35 cm H_2O or if the lung compliance is below 30 mL/cm H_2O.[70]

Other common causes of iatrogenic pneumothorax (with approximate incidences) are thoracentesis (2.5%),[71] pleural biopsy (8%),[72] and transbronchial lung biopsy (6%).[73] Iatrogenic pneumothorax also frequently complicates cardiopulmonary resuscitation. Other procedures associated with the development of an iatrogenic pneumothorax include subclavian or internal jugular vein catheterization, tracheostomy, intercostal nerve block, mediastinoscopy, liver biopsy, and the insertion of small nasogastric tubes.[1]

DIAGNOSIS

The diagnosis of iatrogenic pneumothorax should be suspected in any patient treated by mechanical ventilation whose clinical condition suddenly deteriorates. A sensitive indicator of the development of a pneumothorax in such patients is increased peak and plateau pressures if the patient is on a volume-cycled ventilator or a decreased tidal volume if the patient is on a pressure-cycled ventilator. The diagnosis should also be suspected in any patient who becomes more dyspneic after a medical or surgical procedure that is known to be associated with the development of a pneumothorax. It should be emphasized that the pneumothorax may not be evident immediately after thoracic procedures, and symptoms may not develop for 24 hours or longer.[74,74a] The diagnosis is readily confirmed by a chest radiograph. In patients with extensive pulmonary infiltrates, there may be little evidence of lung collapse, but the air in the pleural space may instead be indicated by the "deep sulcus" sign (Fig. 69.4).

TREATMENT

The treatment of iatrogenic pneumothorax differs from that of spontaneous pneumothorax in that one does not have to worry about preventing a recurrent pneumothorax. The symptoms can vary from none to severe respiratory distress when an iatrogenic pneumothorax develops after a procedure. If the patient has at most minimal symptoms and the pneumothorax occupies less than 15% of the volume of the hemithorax, the patient can be observed. The administration of supplemental oxygen increases the rate at which the pneumothorax is absorbed for the reasons described in the previous section. If the patient has more than minimal symptoms or if the pneumothorax occupies more than 15% of the hemithorax, the procedure of choice is simple aspiration with a plastic catheter,[75] as described for primary spontaneous pneumothorax. If simple aspiration does not control the pneumothorax, then tube thoracostomy should be performed. Small-bore chest tubes (gauge 7 to 9 French) with Heimlich valves are quite effective in this situation.[76]

The management of patients with an iatrogenic pneumothorax secondary to positive-pressure mechanical ventilation should include tube thoracostomy to prevent the development of a tension pneumothorax. Tension pneumothorax can easily develop because the positive pressure during inspiration forces air into the pleural space under high pressure until it soon exceeds atmospheric pressure. If the patient continues to receive mechanical ventilation, the chest tube should be left in place for at least 48 hours after the air leak stops. At times, a bronchopleural fistula is so large that a high percentage of the total inspired volume exits through the chest tube. The air exiting through the chest tube still provides effective ventilation, however, because it contains levels of carbon dioxide similar to those of exhaled gas.[77] Although the use of high-frequency ventilators has been recommended in this situation, two studies in adults[78,79] have demonstrated that high-frequency ventilation does not consistently improve gas exchange or decrease the flow through the fistula.

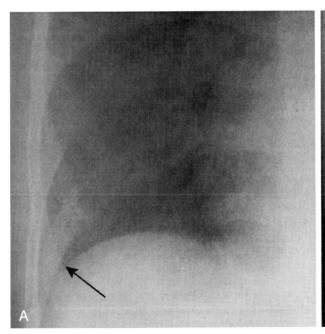 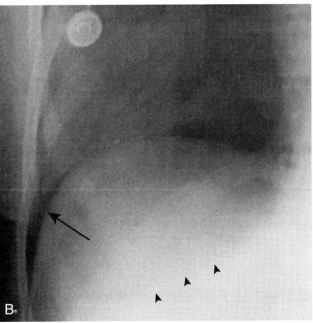

Figure 69.4 Detailed views of right costophrenic angle from successive supine chest radiographs taken before **(A)** and after **(B)** the development of a pneumothorax. Both illustrations show diffuse infiltrations in the right lower lung field. Note change in costophrenic angles (*arrows*) caused by air in the pleural space between the diaphragm and chest wall: the "deep sulcus" sign. Air in the anterior pleural space can also be recognized by an air-tissue interface (*arrowheads*).

TRAUMATIC (NONIATROGENIC) PNEUMOTHORAX

The incidence of pneumothorax after blunt trauma depends on the severity of the trauma. The incidence of pneumothorax has exceeded 35% in some series.[80]

MECHANISM

A traumatic pneumothorax can result from either penetrating or nonpenetrating chest trauma. With penetrating chest trauma, the mechanism of the pneumothorax is easily understood because the wound allows air to enter the pleural space via the chest wall or via the visceral pleura from the tracheobronchial tree.

With nonpenetrating trauma, a pneumothorax may develop if the visceral pleura is lacerated secondary to a rib fracture or dislocation. In the majority of patients with pneumothorax secondary to nonpenetrating trauma, however, there are no associated rib fractures. In this instance, it is thought that the sudden chest compression abruptly increases the alveolar pressure, which may cause alveolar rupture. Once the alveolus is ruptured, air enters the interstitial space and dissects toward either the visceral pleura or the mediastinum. A pneumothorax develops when either the visceral or the mediastinal pleura ruptures, allowing air to enter the pleural space.

DIAGNOSIS AND TREATMENT

The diagnosis of pneumothorax is made by the chest radiograph or the chest CT. A pneumothorax that is apparent on the chest CT, but not on the chest radiograph, is called an *occult* pneumothorax.[81] About 40% of traumatic pneumothoraces are occult.[82] In recent years ultrasonography performed by emergency room physicians or surgeons has been used increasingly to determine whether a pneumothorax is present.[83,84] Ultrasound is more sensitive that supine chest radiographs in identifying pneumothoraces.[84]

Most traumatic pneumothoraces should be treated initially with tube thoracostomy. If the patient has an occult pneumothorax or if the distance between the lung and chest wall does not exceed 1.5 cm, however, tube thoracostomy is probably not indicated unless the patient is receiving mechanical ventilation.[82,85] In one series, 333 patients with pneumothoraces less than 1.5 cm were initially managed without chest tubes, and only 33 (10%) subsequently required tube thoracostomy.[85] When traumatic pneumothoraces are treated with tube thoracostomy, the lung usually expands and the air leak ceases within 24 hours.[85] If the leak persists for more than a few days, consideration should be given to performing thoracoscopy. Carrillo and associates[86] performed thoracoscopy in 11 such patients and were able to identify and repair the site of the air leak in 10 of the 11 patients. In the eleventh patient, a chemical pleurodesis was performed. There were no further air leaks in any of the patients, and all chest tubes were removed within 24 hours.[86]

Two uncommon diagnoses, both of which are indications for immediate thoracotomy, should be considered for any patient with a traumatic pneumothorax. The first diagnosis, fracture of the trachea or a major bronchus, usually occurs in the presence of an anterior or lateral fracture of one or more of the first three ribs. Most patients will have at least some hemoptysis.[87] Therefore, in patients with a traumatic pneumothorax, the presence of a large pneumothorax with continued leakage of air into the pleural space after tube thoracostomy, a fracture of one or more of the first three ribs, or hemoptysis should serve as an indication for fiberoptic bronchoscopy to assess the possibility of a bronchial tear.[87] Primary surgical repair of the tear usually results in full restoration of function of the distal lung.[87]

The second diagnosis that should be considered is traumatic rupture of the esophagus; a hydropneumothorax almost always accompanies this condition. A reliable screening test for esophageal rupture is measurement of the pleural fluid amylase concentration.[1] If this level is elevated, contrast radiographic studies of the esophagus should be performed. It is important to establish the diagnosis of esophageal rupture expeditiously because the mortality approaches 100% if surgical treatment is not carried out promptly.

AIR TRAVEL AND PNEUMOTHORAX

If a patient has suffered a pneumothorax, how long should they wait before they travel by air? The Aerospace Medical Association has suggested that patients should be able to fly 2 to 3 weeks after radiologic resolution of the pneumothorax.[88] One study of 12 patients with traumatic pneumothorax reported that the 10 patients who waited at least 14 days before travel were all asymptomatic in-flight, whereas 1 of 2 patients who flew earlier than 14 days developed respiratory distress in-flight with symptoms suggesting a recurrent pneumothorax.[89]

NEONATAL PNEUMOTHORAX

A spontaneous pneumothorax is present shortly after birth in 1% to 2% of all infants, and the pneumothorax is symptomatic in approximately half of these.[24,90] The incidence of spontaneous neonatal pneumothorax is twice as high in male as in female infants. Affected infants are usually full term or post-term.[24] Usually, the infant has a history of fetal distress requiring resuscitation or a difficult delivery with evidence of aspiration of meconium, blood, or mucus.[24]

There is a high incidence of pneumothorax in infants with neonatal respiratory distress syndrome. In one series of 295 newborn infants with the syndrome, 19% had a pneumothorax.[91] Pneumothorax developed in 29% of those requiring intermittent positive-pressure ventilation with positive end-expiratory pressure, in 11% of those requiring continuous positive airway pressure, and in only 4% of those not requiring respiratory assistance.[91] In a recent series of 26,007 babies with birth weights between 401 and 1500 g born in 1999, the incidence of pneumothorax was 6.3%, but, in babies weighing less than 750 g, the incidence was 15%.[92]

PATHOGENESIS

The development of a spontaneous neonatal pneumothorax is related to the mechanical problems of expanding the lung for the first time. During the first few breaths of life, the transpulmonary pressures average 40 cm H_2O, with occasional pressures as high as 100 cm H_2O.[93] At birth, the alveoli usually open in rapid sequence, but, if bronchial obstruction is present from the aspiration of blood, meconium, or mucus, high transpulmonary pressures may lead to rupture of the lung. A transpulmonary pressure of 60 cm H_2O ruptures an adult lung,[24] whereas a transpulmonary pressure of 45 cm H_2O ruptures a neonatal rabbit lung.[94]

CLINICAL MANIFESTATIONS

With neonatal spontaneous pneumothorax, the signs vary from none to severe acute respiratory distress, depending on the size of the pneumothorax. With a small pneumothorax, there may be mild apneic spells with some irritability or restlessness. With a large pneumothorax, there may be severe respiratory distress with marked tachypnea, grunting, retractions, and cyanosis.[24] In newborn babies, the detection of pneumothorax by physical examination is often difficult. Because breath sounds are widely transmitted in the small neonatal thorax, diminished breath sounds on the affected side may be difficult to appreciate. The most reliable sign is a shift of the apical heart impulse away from the side of the pneumothorax.[24] The diagnosis of neonatal spontaneous pneumothorax is confirmed by a high-quality chest radiograph.

The development of a pneumothorax in a patient with neonatal respiratory distress syndrome is usually heralded by a change in the vital signs. In one series of 49 patients, cardiac arrest marked the development of the pneumothorax in 12 patients (24%); most of the other patients had a decrease in the blood pressure, pulse, or respiratory rate.[91] In another series, however, the earliest signs were an increase in the blood pressure, heart rate, or pulse pressure.[95] The occurrence of a pneumothorax in an infant with the neonatal respiratory distress syndrome is associated with mortalities exceeding 60% in some studies.[96]

TREATMENT

An infant with a spontaneous pneumothorax who is asymptomatic or mildly symptomatic can be observed closely because the pneumothorax will resolve within a few days in the majority. It is necessary to observe the patient closely because of the possibility that the pneumothorax will enlarge or that a tension pneumothorax will develop.[24] Supplemental oxygen can hasten the resolution of the pneumothorax, but it should be administered with care because of the dangers of retrolental fibroplasia.[24] Tube thoracostomy should be performed on any neonate who is more than mildly symptomatic. One recent study demonstrated that 18-gauge venous catheters were comparable to 12-French chest tubes in managing pneumothorax in neonates.[97] Tube thoracostomy should be performed in virtually all infants with the neonatal respiratory distress syndrome and pneumothorax, because the pneumothorax further compromises the ventilatory status of the patient and tends to increase in size.

CATAMENIAL PNEUMOTHORAX

A catamenial pneumothorax is a pneumothorax that occurs in conjunction with menstruation (Fig. 69.5).[97a] This is an

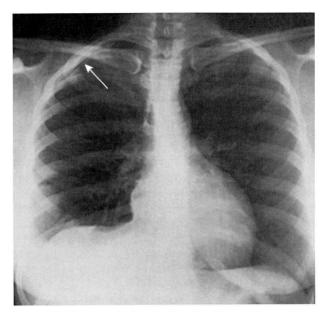

Figure 69.5 Posteroanterior chest roentgenogram from a 32-year-old woman showing a small right-sided pneumothorax (*arrow*). This was the fourth episode with onset during menses. (Courtesy of Dr. Louis S. Lehman, San Francisco.)

uncommon entity; only 80 cases had been reported by 1996.[98] However, catamenial pneumothorax is probably underdiagnosed and underreported. In one recent study from Italy, eight cases of catamenial pneumothorax were seen over an 18-month period.[99] With catamenial pneumothorax, respiratory symptoms usually develop within 24 to 48 hours of the onset of the menstrual flow.[98] Most pneumothoraces are right sided, but left-sided and even bilateral pneumothoraces have been reported.[98] Catamenial pneumothoraces tend to be recurrent unless there is a therapeutic intervention. On the average, patients have about five pneumothoraces before the diagnosis is recognized.

PATHOGENESIS

The pathogenesis of catamenial pneumothorax is not definitely established. When the syndrome was initially described by Maurer and colleagues,[100] it was hypothesized that air gained access to the peritoneal cavity during menstruation and then entered the pleural cavity through a diaphragmatic defect. In a subsequent review of 18 patients who had undergone thoracotomy, however, diaphragmatic defects were demonstrable in only three, whereas six had pleural or diaphragmatic endometriosis.[101] However, in a recent series of eight cases in which a careful thoracoscopic examination was performed, diaphragmatic abnormalities were detected in all; four patients had both diaphragmatic defects and endometriosis, three patients had only diaphragmatic endometriosis, and one patient had only a diaphragmatic defect.[99] It has been suggested that, with diaphragmatic endometriosis, the endometrial tissue on the diaphragm undergoes cyclical necrosis leading to a diaphragmatic defect.[102] These authors concluded that diaphragmatic abnormalities play a fundamental role in the pathogenesis of catamenial pneumothorax.[102]

DIAGNOSIS AND TREATMENT

Any woman who has a spontaneous pneumothorax within the first 48 hours of her menstrual period should be suspected of having a catamenial pneumothorax. The treatment of catamenial pneumothorax is aimed at treating endometriosis, known or suspected, by suppressing the ectopic endometrium. This can be attempted by suppression of ovulation with oral contraceptives or by suppression of gonadotropins with danazol or gonadotropin-releasing hormone to produce a medical oophorectomy.[98] However, these measures are effective in less than 50% of patients.[98] Alternative treatments include thoracoscopy with stapling of blebs, closure of diaphragmatic defects and parietal abrasion or pleurectomy, or chemical pleurodesis.[98] A recent paper suggested that the best treatment includes lining the diaphragm with a polyglactin mesh to treat occult diaphragmatic defects.[102]

TENSION PNEUMOTHORAX

A tension pneumothorax is said to be present when the intrapleural pressure exceeds the atmospheric pressure throughout expiration and often during inspiration as well.[1] Most patients who develop a tension pneumothorax are receiving positive pressure to their airways, either during mechanical ventilation or during resuscitation.[103] For a tension pneumothorax to develop in a spontaneously breathing person, some type of one-way valve mechanism must be present so more air enters the pleural space on inspiration than leaves the pleural space on expiration, so air accumulates in the pleural space under positive pressure.[1]

PATHOPHYSIOLOGY

The development of a tension pneumothorax is usually heralded by a sudden deterioration in the cardiopulmonary status of the patient. The explanation for this sudden deterioration is probably related to the combination of a decreased cardiac output due to impaired venous return and profound hypoxia due to ventilation-perfusion mismatches. Carvalho and associates[104] induced tension pneumothorax with a mean pleural pressure of +25 cm H_2O in 10 adult mechanically ventilated sheep. They found that the mean cardiac output decreased from 3.5 to 1.1 L/min. In their preparation, the arterial PO_2 fell from a baseline value of 159 to 59 mm Hg. Barton and associates[105] induced tension pneumothoraces in pigs and found that, at a pleural pressure of +10 cm H_2O, there was profound hypoxemia (arterial oxygen saturation fell from 97% to 55%) and a moderate decrease in the cardiac output (2.8 to 1.8 L/min). Daly and associates[106] reported that, in intubated and ventilated dogs, the cardiac output decreased when the mean intrathoracic pressure exceeded 3 mm Hg (4.1 cm H_2O) and the arterial oxygen saturation fell bellow 90% when the pressure exceeded 10 mm Hg (13.6 cm H_2O). In patients on mechanical ventilation who develop tension pneumothorax, there is a large drop in the cardiac output.[107]

CLINICAL MANIFESTATIONS

Patients most commonly have a tension pneumothorax while they are receiving positive-pressure mechanical ventilation or

during cardiopulmonary resuscitation.[103] Tension pneumothorax has also been reported to occur as a complication of hyperbaric oxygen therapy.[108] Occasionally, a tension pneumothorax will evolve during the course of a spontaneous pneumothorax. Cases have been reported in which the tension pneumothorax developed due to improper connection of one-way flutter valves with small-caliber chest tubes.[109]

The clinical picture associated with the development of a tension pneumothorax is striking. The patient appears distressed, with rapid labored respirations, cyanosis, marked tachycardia, and profuse diaphoresis. The physical findings are those of a very large pneumothorax. Arterial blood gases reveal marked hypoxemia and sometimes respiratory acidosis.

Tension pneumothorax should be suspected in patients receiving mechanical ventilation who suddenly deteriorate. In this situation, the peak pressures on the ventilator usually increase markedly if the patient is on volume-type ventilation, whereas the tidal volumes decrease markedly if the patient is on pressure-support ventilation.[1] Tension pneumothorax should also be suspected in any patient undergoing cardiopulmonary resuscitation in whom ventilation is difficult. In one series of 3500 autopsies, an unsuspected tension pneumothorax was found in 12 cadavers; 10 of these had received mechanical ventilation, and 9 had undergone cardiopulmonary resuscitation.[110] Tension pneumothorax should also be suspected in any patient with a known pneumothorax who deteriorates suddenly or in any patient who has undergone a procedure known to cause a pneumothorax.

DIAGNOSIS AND TREATMENT

A tension pneumothorax is a medical emergency. One should not waste time trying to establish the diagnosis of tension pneumothorax radiologically because the clinical situation and the physical findings usually strongly suggest the diagnosis.[1] When the diagnosis is suspected, the patient should immediately be given a high concentration of supplemental oxygen to alleviate the hypoxia. A large-bore (14- to 16-gauge) catheter with needle should be immediately inserted into the pleural space through the second anterior intercostal space.[1] After the catheter and needle are inserted into the chest, the needle is removed and a large syringe containing a few milliliters of sterile saline is attached to the indwelling catheter. The plunger is then pulled out of the syringe. If air bubbles through the saline after the plunger is withdrawn, the diagnosis of tension pneumothorax is established. If the fluid enters the pleural space from the syringe, the patient does not have a tension pneumothorax and the catheter should be removed.

If the procedure just described confirms the diagnosis of a tension pneumothorax, the catheter should be left in place and in communication with the atmosphere until air ceases to exit through the syringe. Additional air can be withdrawn from the pleural space with the syringe and the three-way stopcock. The patient should be prepared for immediate tube thoracostomy.

REEXPANSION PULMONARY EDEMA

Unilateral pulmonary edema (*reexpansion pulmonary edema*) may develop in certain patients whose lung has been rapidly reinflated after a period of collapse secondary to a pneumothorax or a pleural effusion. Patients with reexpansion pulmonary edema have various degrees of hypoxia and hypotension. On occasion, the pulmonary edema becomes bilateral, and the patient requires intubation and mechanical ventilation. On rare occasions, the syndrome is fatal; the seriousness of the syndrome is emphasized by the fact that it has been fatal in otherwise healthy, young persons.[111,112] Although the incidence of reexpansion pulmonary edema is not known, it is probably relatively low because there were no instances of reexpansion pulmonary edema in the Veterans Administration cooperative study of more than 200 patients with spontaneous pneumothorax.[32] In a retrospective study of 320 episodes of pneumothorax, reexpansion pulmonary edema occurred in 3 patients (1.0%).[113] In 1988, Mahfood and associates[114] reviewed the literature on reexpansion pulmonary edema and were able to find only 53 cases; however, the syndrome was fatal in 11 (21%). It is probable that the mortality rate is much less than 20% because nonfatal cases are less likely to be reported and some patients are essentially asymptomatic.[115]

PATHOPHYSIOLOGY

Reexpansion pulmonary edema appears to be due to increased permeability of the pulmonary vasculature. In both experimental animals[116] and humans,[117] the edema fluid has a high protein content, suggesting that edema forms due to increased leakiness of the capillaries rather than increased hydrostatic pressure. It has been hypothesized that the mechanical stresses applied to the lung during reexpansion damage the capillaries and lead to pulmonary edema.[116] Reperfusion injury due to reactive oxygen species (ROS) is another possibility. Three separate studies in animals[118-120] demonstrated that the administration of ROS-scavenging compounds such as dimethylthiourea, catalase, or superoxide dismutase all partially inhibit the neutrophilic infiltration associated with the development of reexpansion pulmonary edema, but do not impressively decrease the amount of edema in the experimental situation. Moreover, neutrophil depletion does not affect the amount of edema.

In experimental animals, reexpansion pulmonary edema occurs only if the lung has been collapsed for several days and only if negative pressure is applied to the pleural space. In humans, most cases of reexpansion pulmonary edema develop when the pneumothorax or pleural effusion has been present for at least 3 days[114] and when negative pressure has been applied to the pleural space.[111]

CLINICAL MANIFESTATIONS

Patients with reexpansion pulmonary edema typically have pernicious coughing or chest tightness during or immediately after tube thoracostomy or thoracentesis. The symptoms usually progress for 12 to 24 hours, and serial chest radiographs reveal progressive ipsilateral pulmonary edema, which may progress to involve the contralateral lung. If the patient does not die within the first 48 hours, recovery is usually complete. Treatment is primarily supportive, with the administration of supplemental oxygen and diuretics, and intubation and mechanical ventilation when necessary. One report suggested that the syndrome could be aborted

if the patient is treated with continuous positive airway pressure within the first hour of the development of the syndrome.[121] Chest tubes should be placed to underwater-seal drainage if the syndrome develops.

PREVENTION

Because reexpansion pulmonary edema can be fatal, it is important to prevent it when possible. The possibility of its development should be considered in any patient with a large pneumothorax or pleural effusion subjected to tube thoracostomy or thoracentesis. When tube thoracostomy is performed for spontaneous pneumothorax, the tubes should initially be connected to an underwater-seal drainage apparatus rather than to negative pleural pressure. If underwater-seal drainage does not cause reexpansion of the underlying lung within 24 to 48 hours, then negative pressure can be applied to the pleural space.[1]

When a thoracentesis is performed, the procedure should be terminated if the patient develops tightness of the chest or experiences coughing. At our hospital, no limit is put on the amount of air or fluid withdrawn, but the procedure is stopped if symptoms develop.[71] Over a 3-year period, 941 thoracenteses were performed, including 119 procedures in which more than 1500 mL was removed. Infiltrates consistent with reexpansion pulmonary edema were noted on the post-thoracentesis radiograph in two patients (0.2%) from whom 1000 and 1200 mL of pleural fluid had been removed.[71] Neither patient was symptomatic or required treatment.[71]

CHYLOTHORAX

Pleural fluid is occasionally found to be milky or at least turbid. When this cloudiness persists after centrifugation, it is almost always due to a high lipid content in the pleural fluid. Two different situations bring about the accumulation of high levels of lipid in pleural liquid. In one, chyle enters the pleural space as a result of disruption of the thoracic duct, producing a chylothorax or a chylous pleural effusion. In the second, large amounts of cholesterol or lecithin-globulin complexes accumulate in a long-standing pleural effusion to produce a pseudochylothorax or a chyliform pleural effusion.[1] It is not only important to recognize but also to differentiate these two conditions because their etiology and management are completely different.

PATHOPHYSIOLOGY

A chylothorax forms when the thoracic duct, which carries dietary fat in the form of chylomicrons, becomes disrupted. Chylomicrons are formed in the intestine, after which they enter the intestinal lacteal vessels and are then transported to the cisterna chyli. The thoracic duct leaves the cisterna chyli and passes through the aortic hiatus of the diaphragm on the anterior surface of the vertebral body between the aorta and the azygos vein into the posterior mediastinum. The thoracic duct then ascends extrapleurally in the posterior mediastinum along the right side of the anterior surface of the vertebral column. Between the level of the fourth and sixth thoracic vertebrae, the duct crosses to the left side of the vertebral column and continues cephalad to enter the superior mediastinum between the aortic arch and the subclavian artery and the left side of the esophagus. Rupture of the thoracic duct before it crosses over the midline tends to produce right-sided chylothoraces, and interruptions of the duct while it ascends on the left of the vertebral column tend to result in left-sided chylothoraces.[122]

Once the thoracic duct passes the thoracic inlet, it arches above the clavicle and passes anterior to the left subclavian artery, vertebral artery, and thyrocervical trunk to terminate in the region of the left jugular and subclavian veins. Although this route is the typical one, there are wide anatomic variations throughout the course of the duct. Also, many collateral vessels and lymphaticovenous anastomoses are known to exist. Presumably these channels transport the chyle to the blood following therapeutic ligation of the thoracic duct.

Chyle, the drainage from the thoracic duct, is a milky, opalescent fluid that usually separates into three layers on standing: a creamy uppermost layer containing chylomicrons, a milky intermediate layer, and a dependent layer containing cellular elements. Chyle is bacteriostatic[123] and resists becoming infected even if it stands at room temperature for several weeks. In addition, chyle is not irritating and usually does not induce thickening of the pleural membrane.

The thoracic duct normally conveys between 1500 and 2500 mL of chyle daily.[122] The flow varies considerably, depending on the diet of the person. The ingestion of fat can increase the flow of lymph in the thoracic duct by a factor of 2 to 10 for several hours. The ingestion of liquid, but not protein or carbohydrate, also increases the flow. The electrolyte composition of chyle is similar to that of serum, and the protein content is usually above 3 g/dL (30 g/L).[1] The primary cellular component of chyle is the T lymphocyte.[1] Prolonged loss of chyle results in severe nutritional depletion, water and electrolyte loss, hypolipemia, and depletion of T lymphocytes with resulting immunodeficiency.[123]

ETIOLOGY

The factors responsible for chylothorax in five separate series totaling 143 patients are shown in Table 69.1. More than 50% of chylothoraces are caused by tumors and, of those due to tumors, lymphoma is found in approximately 75%. In recent years, chylothorax has been reported in patients with AIDS and Kaposi's sarcoma.

Trauma, most often due to a cardiovascular or thoracic surgical procedure, is the second leading cause of chylothorax. Surgery or trauma involving the posterior mediastinum is associated with higher risks of chylothorax. Esophagectomy, for example, is complicated by chylothorax in 1% to 4% of cases.[124] Overall, the incidence of chylothorax after cardiothoracic operations is generally low (about 0.5% to 2.5%[125–127]), but in view of the large number of such procedures being performed each year, chylothorax remains an important consideration. Surgical procedures that involve mobilization of the left subclavian artery are particularly likely to be complicated by chylothorax.[128] Transplantation of the lung and heart (or both) can sever the lymphatic drainage and has been associated with

Table 69.1 Causes of Chylothorax from Five Separate Series

Cause	Number	%
Tumor	76	54
Lymphoma	57	
Other	19	
Trauma	36	25
Surgical	31	
Other	5	
Idiopathic	22	15
Congenital	8	
Other	14	
Miscellaneous	9	6

Adapted from Light RW: Pleural Diseases (3rd ed). Baltimore: Williams & Wilkins, 1995, p 285.

chylothoraces.[129] Chylothorax has been reported as a complication of a wide range of other operations, including esophagoscopy, stellate ganglion blockade, thoracic sympathectomy, high translumbar aortography, lung resections,[125,126] and spinal surgery.[1] Of note, bilateral chylothoraces can develop following bilateral neck dissection.[130] In the pediatric setting, chylothorax is particularly common after surgical repair of congenital diaphragmatic hernia (up to 10% of cases) and is usually left sided.[131]

As the course of the thoracic duct is variable, and is often difficult to identify during surgery, oral administration of cream before high-risk operations (e.g., esophagectomy) has been advocated. Ingestion of fat increases the flow (and size) of the thoracic duct and may therefore allow easy identification of the duct during surgery.[132]

Nonsurgical trauma can also lead to chylothorax. The thoracic duct may be disrupted with penetrating injuries involving the neck or thorax. Nonpenetrating trauma in which the spine is hyperextended or a vertebra is fractured can lead to chylothorax, particularly if the injury occurs shortly after the ingestion of a fatty meal. Less impressive traumas such as weight lifting, straining, severe bouts of coughing or vomiting, childbirth, and vigorous stretching while yawning have been reported to cause chylothorax.[122] Chylothoraces secondary to closed trauma are usually on the right side, with the site of rupture being in the region of the 9th or 10th thoracic vertebra.

Chylothoraces can also arise from chylous ascites that moves across the diaphragm into the pleural space. Causes of chylous ascites include many of the causes of chylothorax. In addition, cirrhosis may be a cause of chylous ascites and associated chylothorax. Romero and colleagues[133] described five cirrhotic patients in whom chylothorax was associated with chylous ascites; when a radioisotope was injected into the peritoneal cavity of these patients, it rapidly appeared in the pleural cavity. Interestingly, these chylothoraces were transudative, suggesting that the chyle was diluted by low-protein cirrhotic ascitic fluid.

There are many other causes of chylothorax, but, even when all are grouped together, they account for only a small percentage of all chylothoraces. Pulmonary lymphangioleiomyomatosis is the most common other cause of chylothorax[134] and is discussed later in this chapter (see also Chapter 58). Other disease entities associated with chylothorax are abnormalities of the lymphatic vessels,[1] such as intestinal lymphangiectasis or reticular hyperplasia, yellow nail syndrome, superior vena caval or subclavian vein thrombosis/obstruction, filariasis, lymph node enlargement, mediastinal fibrosis, lymphangitis of the thoracic duct, tuberous sclerosis, amyloidosis, and Gorham's syndrome (disappearing bone disease; massive osteolysis).

If no cause can be found for the chylothorax, it is labeled *idiopathic*. Before attaching this label, however, lymphoma should be excluded. In one series, the diagnosis of lymphoma was not established in four patients until at least 6 months after they presented with a chylothorax.[135]

Fetal and Neonatal Chylothorax

Fetal chylothorax is increasingly recognized as an uncommon but important condition that requires monitoring and management to avoid serious complications, including spontaneous abortion or death after birth.[136] Fetal chylothoraces are often termed *primary* fetal pleural effusions, as no obvious causes can be identified in most cases.[136] Congenital lymphangiectasis is a rare condition that can produce fetal chylothorax.[137] The integrin $\alpha_9\beta_1$ is widely expressed in smooth muscles and is a receptor for extracellular matrix proteins (e.g., osteopontin and tenascin C) and vascular cell adhesion molecule-1. Recent animal studies suggested that the α_9 subunit of the integrin $\alpha_9\beta_1$ is required for the normal development of the lymphatic system, including the thoracic duct, and mice with homozygous null mutation of the α_9 subunit develop large bilateral congenital chylothoraces.[138]

Chylothorax is the most common type of neonatal pleural effusion.[136] It may be a result of persistent fetal chylothorax,[136] but can also be due to rupture of the thoracic duct from trauma during delivery or to developmental abnormalities of the thoracic duct.[139] Increased venous pressure, especially from congenital heart diseases or from thrombosis of central venous catheters, is another recognized mechanism of neonatal chylothorax.[136] In many cases, the chylothorax is idiopathic. Before milk feeding, the pleural fluid is clear in appearance; once the infant begins milk feeding, the pleural fluid takes on the milky appearance of chyle.[136]

CLINICAL MANIFESTATIONS

The symptoms, physical findings, and radiographic features of chylothorax are the same as those encountered in patients with comparably sized pleural effusions of any cause. Pleuritic chest pain and fever are rare, however, because chyle is not irritating to the pleural surface. With nontraumatic chylothorax, the onset of symptoms is usually gradual, with the patient complaining of dyspnea on exertion, and discomfort on the affected side.

With traumatic chylothorax, there is usually a latent period of 2 to 10 days between the trauma and the clinical presentation of the pleural effusion.[140] During this latent period, chyle may accumulate in the posterior mediastinum to form a chyloma, which may be visible on the chest radiograph as a posterior mediastinal mass.[1] The mass disappears when the mediastinal pleura ruptures and the chylothorax is formed.

Neonatal chylothorax may present with respiratory distress in the first few days of life. Fifty percent of the infants have symptoms within the first 24 hours, whereas 75% have symptoms by the end of the first week. Most neonatal chylothoraces are either right sided or bilateral; only rarely are they left sided.[139] There is a high frequency of neonatal chylothoraces in infants with hydramnios.[139] Fetal chylothorax is often diagnosed only on ultrasonography.

The main threat to life with chylothorax is inanition from malnutrition if the chyle is drained externally. The daily loss of 1500 to 2500 mL of fluid containing substantial amounts of protein, fats, electrolytes, and lymphocytes will rapidly make any patient malnourished and immunocompromised.

DIAGNOSIS

It is usually easy to establish the diagnosis of chylothorax because chyle has a distinctive white, odorless, milky appearance. Chylous pleural fluid must be differentiated from empyema fluid and chyliform pleural fluid in pseudochylothorax. In empyema, the milky appearance is caused by suspended white blood cells and debris, which will sediment upon centrifugation, leaving a clear supernatant. In chylous and chyliform pleural effusions, the milky appearance is caused by high lipid levels and the supernatant will remain cloudy after centrifugation. The lipids in chyliform effusion are cholesterol or lecithin-globulin complexes rather than chylomicrons (as in chylothoraces).

It should be emphasized that the pleural fluid with chylothorax does not always look like typical chyle. In a series of 24 patients,[133] 14 pleural fluid samples were milky, 5 were bloody, 3 were turbid yellow, and 2 were clear yellow. The possibility of a chylothorax should be considered whenever a turbid, serosanguineous, or bloody pleural fluid sample is obtained during a diagnostic thoracentesis. Such fluids should be centrifuged. If turbidity persists in the supernatant, the possibility of a chylothorax should be explored.

Usually it is relatively easy to differentiate chylous from chyliform pleural fluid by the clinical picture. In contrast to a chylothorax, a pseudochylothorax usually has been long-standing (often 5 years or more). The patient with a pseudochylothorax has markedly thickened pleura on CT scan, whereas the pleura with chylothorax is normal. Examination of the pleural liquid may reveal cholesterol crystals that are present in some patients with pseudochylothorax.[1]

When doubt exists as to whether a patient has a chylothorax, pleural fluid and serum triglyceride and cholesterol levels should be measured. Patients who have a chylothorax usually have a pleural fluid triglyceride level above 110 mg/dL (1.24 mmol/L), a ratio of the pleural fluid to the serum triglyceride of greater than 1.0, and a ratio of the pleural fluid to the serum cholesterol of less than 1.0.[133] However, it should be remembered that fasting may significantly reduce the triglyceride level in the pleural fluid and produce false-negative results. If doubt persists after the lipid measurements, one approach is to feed the patient a high-fat meal before sampling the pleural fluid. Alternatively, the demonstration of chylomicrons in lipoprotein analysis of the pleural fluid confirms the diagnosis of chylothorax.[141]

Once it is established that a patient has a chylothorax, it is important to determine a cause. Because lymphoma is the most common (and treatable) cause of nontraumatic chylothorax, every effort should be made to establish or exclude this diagnosis. CT studies of the mediastinum and abdomen should be obtained in all patients with a nontraumatic chylothorax to look for lymphadenopathy. Another possibility to consider in women with chylothorax and parenchymal infiltrates is pulmonary lymphangioleiomyomatosis.

Another useful diagnostic procedure in the patient with nontraumatic chylothorax is bipedal lymphangiography.[142] Not only may a lymphangiogram point toward a site of chyle leak along the thoracic duct, it can at times help point toward a specific diagnosis.[143] Lymphoscintigraphy (e.g., with technetium-99m–labeled human serum albumin) has been used as an alternative to lymphangiography.[144]

It should be emphasized that, unlike the situation with most other types of pleural effusions, examination of the pleura is unlikely to provide insight to the etiology of the chylothorax. Hence, pleural biopsy or thoracoscopy is not usually indicated in the workup of patients with a chylothorax.

TREATMENT

General Approaches

Management strategies of chylothoraces should be directed toward (1) maintaining nutrition and reducing the flow of chyle, (2) relieving dyspnea by removing the chyle, and (3) closure of the defect (Table 69.2).

Maintaining Nutrition and Reducing the Flow of Chyle. With chylothorax, the main dangers to the patient are malnutrition and a compromised immunologic status caused by the removal of large amounts of protein, fat, electrolytes, and lymphocytes from repeated thoracenteses or chest tube drainage. Therefore, when managing a patient with a chylothorax, it is important to treat the chylothorax definitively before the patient becomes too cachectic to tolerate the treatment. Early involvement of an experienced dietitian is recommended.

Table 69.2 Management of a Chylothorax

Maintaining nutrition and reducing the volume of chyle circulation
    Dietary: medium-chain triglyceride diet or total parental nutrition
    Octreotide

Relieving dyspnea by stopping reaccumulation of chyle in the pleural cavity
    Thoracentesis
    Pleuroperitoneal shunting
    Tube thoracostomy
    Pleurodesis

Treatment of the underlying defect
    Thoracic duct embolization
    Ligation of the thoracic duct (VATS or thoracotomy)
    Clipping or fibrin glue to the thoracic duct leak
    Radiotherapy for mediastinal lymphoma

VATS, video-assisted thoracoscopic surgery.

Regardless of the cause, closure of the thoracic duct leak may be facilitated by efforts to minimize the flow of chyle. Chyle flow can be minimized by using parenteral hyperalimentation to provide nutrition. Alternatively, a low-fat diet with most fats in the form of medium-chain triglycerides can also reduce chyle flow because the medium-chain triglycerides are absorbed directly into the blood.[123]

Octreotide, a somatostatin analogue, has been reported in case series (in both adult and pediatric patients[145–147]) to be effective in hastening the closure of thoracic duct leak,[148] although large prospective studies are lacking. The mechanism of its action is not clear but is believed to be related to a reduction of intestinal fat (especially triglyceride) absorption and an increase in fecal fat excretion.[145]

Relieving Dyspnea by Removing Chyle. There are several methods to remove the chylous effusion. Repeated thoracentesis or tube thoracostomy may be used initially, but every attempt should be made to minimize the duration of tube drainage because persistent chyle loss rapidly leads to malnutrition or immunosuppression. Hence, dietary measures to minimize the flow of chyle in patients with tube drainage are of paramount importance.

Pleuroperitoneal shunts are advisable if the chylothorax fails to resolve quickly.[149] Indeed, some authors recommend it as the first line of management as soon as the diagnosis is established. To date, most series on pleuroperitoneal shunts are based in pediatric populations. In one series, 14 of the 17 pediatric chylothoraces were treated successfully with a pleuroperitoneal shunt.[150] The advantage of the pleuroperitoneal shunt is that the lymph is not removed from the body, and thus one can avoid malnourishment or immunodeficiency in the patient. Following the same principle, autoinfusion of the chyle back into systemic circulation has been performed successfully in a patient undergoing chronic hemodialysis.[151] Pleuroperitoneal shunts should not be inserted if ascites is present. Also, pleuroperitoneal shunting is less likely to be successful in patients whose chylothoraces result from central venous thrombosis.[149]

Closure of the Defect. With traumatic chylothorax, the defect in the thoracic duct frequently closes spontaneously. If the pleuroperitoneal shunt is ineffective in draining the pleural space, or if the patient has a chest tube and the drainage of chyle continues unabated beyond 7 days, a more aggressive treatment plan should be considered. In a series of 27 patients with chylothorax following lung resection, those with large-volume drainage (>500 mL per 24 hours) despite total parenteral nutrition were more likely to require reoperation.[125] In another series of patients with post–lung resection chylothorax, 13 of the 15 patients with lower initial drainage volume (mean 300 mL/day) responded to conservative treatment, whereas only 6 of 11 patients with larger drainage volume responded to conservative treatment.[152]

Several options exist to control the chyle leak. A simple but effective method is the creation of a chemical pleurodesis via the intrapleural injection of a pleurodesing agent. Thoracoscopic talc pleurodesis resulted in obliteration of the pleural space and control of the chylothorax in all 19 patients in one series.[153]

Recently, lymphatic embolization and blockade has been shown in a large series of 42 patients to be safe with a complete or partial response rate of 74%.[154] The thoracic duct is punctured via a peritoneal cannula and the duct is embolized with various devices (e.g., microcoils). In patients whose thoracic duct cannot be cannulated, disruption of the duct with needles may also reduce or stop the chyle leak.[154] If available, lymphatic embolization should be attempted before more invasive procedures (e.g., surgery) are performed.

Most chylothoraces can be successfully managed with VATS, during which one should attempt to find the actual site of leakage from the duct. In some cases, VATS has to be converted to an exploratory thoracotomy. The duct is ligated on both sides of the leak or ligated at the lowest point in the chest.[155] Preoperatively, the site of the leak may be identified by a lymphangiogram. The identification of the thoracic duct can also be facilitated with preoperative oral administration of cream.[156] If for technical reason the thoracic duct cannot be successfully ligated during VATS, a pleurodesis (e.g., partial pleurectomy or talc insufflation) should be performed to obliterate the pleural space at the same operation. Recently, laparoscopic ligation of the thoracic duct has also been attempted with success.[157]

Special Considerations

Nontraumatic Chylothorax. If the patient is known to have either lymphoma or metastatic carcinoma, the chylothorax often responds to mediastinal radiation. In one series, mediastinal radiation adequately controlled the chylothorax for the remainder of the patient's life in 68% of those with lymphoma and in 50% of those with metastatic carcinoma.[135] If radiation therapy fails, consideration should be given to embolization, pleurodesis, or pleuroperitoneal shunting.[158]

If the cause of a nontraumatic chylothorax is unknown, the initial management is similar to that for a patient with a traumatic chylothorax, as discussed previously. A pleuroperitoneal shunt should be inserted to allow time for a thorough evaluation. Both a chest CT and a lymphangiogram should be obtained. If both are normal, the chylothorax can be assumed to be due to minor trauma, and spontaneous closure can be expected within weeks. If there is mediastinal lymphadenopathy, a diagnosis should be pursued.

Fetal and Congenital Chylothorax. Congenital chylothorax, diagnosed either in utero or after birth, can cause developmental abnormalities or at times be fatal.[136] If diagnosed in utero, maternal dietary restriction should be initiated.[159] Thoracentesis can be performed under ultrasound guidance to evacuate the chylothorax,[160] as large effusions can cause pulmonary hypoplasia and respiratory distress at birth.[136] If the chylothorax reaccumulates, pleuro-amniotic shunting should be considered.[161] In a small number of reported cases, ultrasound-guided intrapleural administration of OK-432,[162] a penicillin-treated streptococcal preparation, or maternal blood[163] has offered effective control of the chylothorax, presumably via creating a pleurodesis.

If the congenital chylothorax is diagnosed after birth, the baby should be treated conservatively with repeated thoracenteses for respiratory compromise while nutrition is maintained by the parenteral route or with medium-chain triglycerides.[164] Octreotide should be tried. If the chylothorax recurs after the third pleural aspiration, however, a pleuroperitoneal shunt should be placed. If the shunt is

unsuccessful, consideration should be given to thoracic duct ligation.[136]

PULMONARY LYMPHANGIOLEIOMYOMATOSIS

Pulmonary lymphangioleiomyomatosis (LAM) is a rare condition, affecting mostly women of reproductive age, and is characterized by progressive dyspnea, recurrent pneumothoraces, and chylous effusions. It is further discussed in Chapter 58. The reported incidence of chylothorax in patients with LAM ranges from 10%[134] to 30%.[165] It can occur in both the sporadic and the tuberous sclerosis complex–associated types of LAM.[134] Whereas the mean age of presentation of LAM is in the early 30s,[166] the mean age of presentation of chylothorax is in the early 40s.[134] The chylothorax is usually unilateral but can be bilateral[134] or associated with chyloascites. The chylothorax is thought to be the result of the combination of perilymphatic proliferation of smooth muscle leading to lymphatic obstruction and of infiltration of the lymph nodes in the mediastinum and retroperitoneal space by immature smooth muscle cells.[167] CT scan is usually diagnostic for LAM (Fig. 69.6).

The general principles for the management of a chylothorax secondary to LAM are similar to those for any nontraumatic chylothorax. The course of these chylothoraces is highly variable.[134] In some cases, simple thoracentesis for symptomatic relief is adequate.[134] However, in two recent series combined, 12 of the 19 LAM patients with chylothoraces required either pleurodesis or thoracic duct ligation to control the reaccumulation of chyle.[134,168]

It should be emphasized that lung transplantation is a treatment option for a proportion (19% in one series[169]) of patients with LAM. The morbidity and mortality of transplantation is increased in these patients, especially from intraoperative bleeding,[170] which is attributed to pleural adhesions from recurrent pneumothoraces. Although pleurodesis is not an absolute contraindication for future transplantation, a transplant surgeon should be consulted before

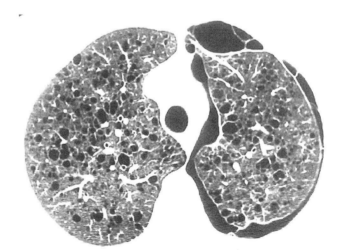

Figure 69.6 Chest computed tomography scan of a patient with lymphangioleiomyomatosis. Note the numerous thin-walled cysts, rounded and relatively uniform in shape, and a pneumothorax. (Courtesy of Dr. Lisete Teixeira, University of Sao Paulo, Brazil.)

subjecting LAM patients with a chylothorax to pleurodesis or thoracotomy (to ligate the thoracic duct).

CHYLIFORM PLEURAL EFFUSIONS AND PSEUDOCHYLOTHORAX

A pseudochylothorax with its attendant chyliform pleural effusion may also be the cause of milky turbid pleural fluid. In this instance the turbidity is related to high levels of cholesterol or lecithin-globulin complexes in the fluid. Pseudochylothoraces are rare, with fewer than 200 reported cases in the literature[171]—much less common than chylothoraces.

PATHOGENESIS

Although chyliform pleural effusion was first reported over a century ago, its precise pathogenesis remains unknown. Most patients with a pseudochylothorax have pleural surfaces that are markedly thickened and sometimes calcified, and most have had a pleural effusion for at least 5 years. It appears that, if an exudative effusion persists for a lengthy period—months to years—in a fibrotic area of grossly thickened pleura, it has a high tendency to become enriched with cholesterol.[123]

Most of the cholesterol in chyliform pleural effusions is associated with high-density lipoproteins, in contrast to the cholesterol in acute exudates, which is mostly bound to low-density lipoproteins.[172] It has been hypothesized that, during acute inflammation, there is increased filtration of cholesterol into the pleural fluid.[172] In addition, the cholesterol can originate from degeneration of the red and white blood cells that enter the pleural space as part of the underlying disease process.[173] The cholesterol becomes "trapped" in the pleural space and undergoes a change in lipoprotein-binding characteristics. The thickened pleura inhibits the exit of cholesterol out of the pleural space.[172] Serum cholesterol levels and systemic cholesterol metabolism appear to be normal in patients with pseudochylothorax.

The most common situations in which chyliform pleural effusions occur are after tuberculous pleurisy (54%), and chronic rheumatoid pleurisy (9%).[171] Pseudochylothorax can also develop in patients who have been treated with artificial pneumothorax for pulmonary tuberculosis and who have chronic pleural effusions secondary to the atelectatic lung.[173] However, successful treatment of an acute tuberculous pleurisy does not preclude the development of long-term complications such as pseudochylothorax.[171] Pleural paragonimiasis may also be associated with chyliform pleural effusion, as may any disease state that is associated with thickened pleura and chronic pleural effusion. Rare cases of pseudochylothorax have also been associated with trauma or surgery.[174]

CLINICAL MANIFESTATIONS

Pseudochylothorax develops in patients with long-standing pleural effusions. The mean duration of the effusion is 5 years before it turns chyliform, but an occasional pleural effusion has become chyliform within 1 year of onset.[175] Many patients with chyliform pleural effusions are asymptomatic or at least no more symptomatic than when they initially developed the pleural effusion. When symptoms do occur, they are usually related to the underlying disease process or to the impairment of pulmonary function produced by the effusion and the thickened pleura. In some cases, the effusion gradually enlarges with time, with resultant progressive dyspnea.[123]

DIAGNOSIS

The diagnosis of chyliform pleural effusion is usually not difficult. The pleural effusion is long-standing, and the pleura is thickened or calcified. In such patients, the two other diagnostic possibilities are chylothorax and empyema. The pleural surfaces are usually normal, however, if the patient has a chylothorax. If the patient has an empyema, centrifugation of the pleural fluid will produce a clear supernatant. If the supernatant remains turbid, the sediment should be examined for cholesterol crystals because their presence is diagnostic of pseudochylothorax. The cholesterol crystals give a distinct satin-like sheen to the pleural fluid. Microscopically, these crystals have a typical rhomboid appearance.[1] Not all patients with chyliform pleural effusion have cholesterol crystals in their pleural fluid; however, most have an elevated pleural fluid cholesterol level (>250mg/dL, or 6.45 mmol/L).[1] CT chest scan can reveal a layering of fat in nondependent sites, as shown in a series of pseudochylothorax patients.[176]

TREATMENT

The possibility of tuberculosis should always be considered when a patient is found to have a chyliform pleural effusion. However, tuberculous pseudochylothorax is usually culture negative.[171] We advise draining only the symptomatic cases and treating with antituberculous chemotherapy those patients with positive Ziehl-Neelsen stain or Löwenstein culture and those with enlarging effusions of suspected tuberculous origin (see Chapter 33).

When the patient's exercise capacity is limited by shortness of breath, a therapeutic thoracentesis should be performed. Hillerdal[173] reported that the removal of several hundred milliliters of pleural fluid from patients with pseudochylothorax resulted in a markedly improved exercise tolerance. Thoracentesis can be difficult in a pseudochylothorax because of the very thickened pleura and the negative pressure inside the cavity.[123] Although a few successful cases have been reported,[177] decortication should only be considered if the patient is symptomatic and the underlying lung is believed to be functional.

HEMOTHORAX

Hemothorax is the presence of blood in the pleural space, specifically when the hematocrit of the pleural fluid is at least 50% that of the peripheral blood.[1] When bloody pleural fluid is obtained with a diagnostic thoracentesis, the hematocrit should always be measured. Frequently, even though the pleural fluid appears to be pure blood, the hematocrit of the fluid will be less than 5%.[1]

TRAUMATIC HEMOTHORAX

Blood may enter the pleural space from injury to the chest wall, diaphragm, lung, blood vessels, or mediastinum. On entering the pleural space, the blood coagulates rapidly, but, presumably as a result of the physical agitation produced by movement of the heart and lungs, the clot may be defibrinated. Loculation occurs early in the course of hemothorax.

Diagnosis

The diagnosis of traumatic hemothorax should be suspected in any patient with penetrating or nonpenetrating trauma of the chest (Fig. 69.7). It should be emphasized that the hemothorax may not be apparent on the initial chest radiograph. In one series of 130 patients with hemothorax secondary to nonpenetrating trauma, the hemothorax was not appreciated on the initial chest radiograph in 24% of the patients.[178] Although the hemothorax was missed in some of the patients because the initial radiograph was obtained with the patient supine, other patients had no evidence of a hemothorax on the upright radiograph.[178]

The CT scan is more sensitive than the chest radiograph in detecting hemothoraces. In a study of 103 patients with blunt trauma, Trupka and colleagues[80] demonstrated that thoracic CT detected a hemothorax in 21 patients (20%) in whom the routine chest radiograph showed no pleural fluid. When patients experience severe thoracic trauma, a CT scan of the chest is indicated not only for its ability to identify hemothorax but also to identify pneumothoraces, lung contusion, and bone fractures.[80] The diagnosis is established if the pleural fluid hematocrit is greater than 50% of that of the peripheral blood.

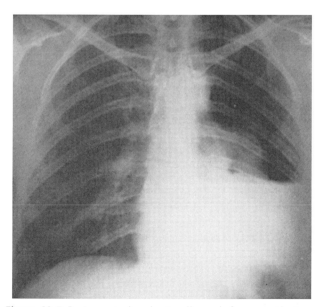

Figure 69.7 Posteroanterior chest radiograph from a patient who suffered multiple injuries in an automobile accident. The patient had a hemopneumothorax. With the prompt institution of tube thoracostomy, the air and blood were evacuated from the pleural space and the chest radiograph was normal 1 week later.

Ultrasound is now available in many emergency rooms, and has been applied for the detection of traumatic hemothoraces. In one study of 240 patients, ultrasonography was comparable to initial chest radiograph in detecting hemothoraces, with a specificity and sensitivity of 100% and 96%, respectively.[179] Ultrasonography is therefore valuable in expediting the diagnosis in patients with severe trauma.

It should also be noted that a delayed hemithorax is not uncommon. In one series of 36 blunt trauma cases, the hemithorax presented late (18 hours to 6 days after the initial injury) in one third of the patients. Most of these patients had multiple or displaced rib fractures.[180]

Treatment

A patient with a traumatic hemothorax should undergo immediate tube thoracostomy for the following reasons: it permits nearly complete evacuation of the blood from the pleural space; it can stop the bleeding, if the bleeding is from pleural lacerations, by bringing the two pleural surfaces into apposition; it enables quantification of the degree of continued bleeding; and it may decrease the incidence of subsequent empyema.[181] The blood drained from the pleural space may be autotransfused.[182] The rapid evacuation of the blood from the pleural space may decrease the incidence of a subsequent fibrothorax.[183]

It is recommended that the chest tube be inserted relatively high (fourth or fifth intercostal space) in the midaxillary line because the ipsilateral hemidiaphragm may be elevated secondary to the trauma.[181] Alternatively, it should be inserted under image guidance. Large-bore chest tubes should be used because the blood frequently clots. Chest tubes should be removed as soon as they stop draining or cease to function, because they can serve as conduits for pleural infection.

Approximately 20% of patients with hemothorax require surgical intervention for suspected cardiac tamponade, vascular injury, pleural contamination, débridement of devitalized tissue, chest wounds, major bronchial air leaks,[184] or continued pleural hemorrhage. Posttraumatic hemithorax was traditionally managed exclusively by thoracotomy, but advances in VATS have made it the procedure of choice in many centers,[185] with thoracotomy reserved only for massive acute hemorrhages. Before surgery is performed for this reason, it is important to ascertain that the bleeding is not from a misplaced central venous catheter. This diagnosis is readily established by examining the appearance of the pleural drainage when the character of the infusion fluid is changed. There are no precise criteria for the amount of pleural bleeding that should serve as an indication for thoracoscopy or thoracotomy, and each case must be individualized; however, if the bleeding is more than 200 mL/hr and shows no signs of slowing, surgical intervention should be seriously considered.[186]

Complications

The four main pleural complications of traumatic hemothorax are the retention of clotted blood in the pleural space, pleural infection, pleural effusion, and fibrothorax. In one retrospective series, 24 (1.4%) of 1728 chest trauma patients had a residual hemithorax.[187] Most patients with small to moderate amounts of clotted blood remaining in their pleural space have no residual pleural abnormalities even if no intervention is undertaken.[184] If more than 30% of the hemithorax is occupied by clotted blood, the hemithorax should be evacuated. Decisions regarding thoracoscopic evacuation should not be made from the plain chest radiograph alone and require CT studies.[188] VATS is the mainstay of management, and conversion to thoracostomy is seldom required.[185,187] The clotted blood should be evacuated within 7 days because after this time it begins to become organized and is much more difficult to remove.[185] In a prospective, randomized trial, VATS was more effective than thoracostomy tube drainage for removing retained hemothoraces. In this study, both the length of hospital stay (7 vs. 3.6 days) and the duration of tube drainage (4.5 vs. 2.5 days) were shorter in the group receiving VATS.[189] In another series, thoracoscopic evacuation performed within 3 days of admission was associated with a lower operative difficulty score (and shorter operation time) and shorter inpatient stay, compared with patients operated at later time points.[187]

Intrapleural administration of fibrinolytic agents (e.g., streptokinase or urokinase) may be safe in patients with hemithorax and retained clots, according to several descriptive studies.[190,191] However, there have been no comparative studies to confirm the efficacy of fibrinolysis versus conservative management or surgical evacuation.

Empyema occurs in 1% to 4% of patients with traumatic hemothoraces.[181,184] Empyema is more frequent in patients who are admitted in shock, have gross contamination of their pleural space, have associated abdominal injuries, or undergo prolonged pleural drainage.[184] The administration of prophylactic antibiotics (e.g., cefazolin 500 mg every 6 hours until tube removal) results in a significant decrease in the incidence of pleural infection.[192] The treatment of empyema complicating hemothorax is similar to that of any bacterial infection of the pleural space (see Chapters 32 and 68).

In more than 10% of patients with a traumatic hemothorax, a pleural effusion will develop after the chest tubes are removed.[184] Most such pleural effusions resolve spontaneously, leaving no residual pleural abnormalities. It is important to perform a diagnostic thoracentesis in such patients, however, to verify that no pleural infection is present.

Fibrothorax develops in less than 1% of patients with hemothorax. Fibrothorax appears to develop more frequently when a hemopneumothorax is present or when a hemothorax becomes infected. The definitive treatment for fibrothorax is decortication. Decortication for fibrothorax should be delayed for several months after the injury, however, to allow time for spontaneous resolution of the pleural thickening, which is often considerable.

IATROGENIC HEMOTHORAX

Whenever a hemothorax is discovered, the possibility of an iatrogenic origin should be considered. The most common cause of iatrogenic hemothorax is thoracic surgery,[193] but perforation of a central vein or artery by a percutaneously inserted catheter[194] or leaking from the aorta after translumbar aortographic study are also common. Iatrogenic hemothorax can also follow thoracentesis, pleural biopsy, chest tube insertion,[195] percutaneous lung aspiration or biopsy, transbronchial biopsy, endoscopic esophageal variceal therapy,[196] and cardiopulmonary resuscitation.[197] Patients with iatrogenic hemothoraces should be managed, as are patients with traumatic hemothoraces, with chest tubes and thoracoscopy or thoracotomy as needed.

NONTRAUMATIC HEMOTHORAX

Nontraumatic hemothoraces are distinctly uncommon. The most common cause is malignant pleural disease,[198] and the second most common cause is a complication of anticoagulation therapy for pulmonary embolization.[199] The cause of the hemothorax in some patients remains unknown despite exploratory thoracotomy.[200]

A spontaneous hemothorax may result from rupture of an abnormal intrathoracic blood vessel, such as subpleural arteriovenous malformations,[201] aneurysm of the aorta[202] or pulmonary artery, patent ductus arteriosus, or coarctation of the aorta.[1] Other causes of a spontaneous hemothorax include a complication of bleeding disorders (such as hemophilia or thrombocytopenia), a complication of spontaneous pneumothoraces, bronchopulmonary sequestration, thoracic endometriosis,[98] chickenpox pneumonia,[203] or intrathoracic extramedullary hematopoiesis.[204] Spontaneous hemithorax is a rare but potentially life-threatening complication of neurofibromatosis, either from aneurysmal changes in large arteries (e.g., aorta) or from dysplastic changes in small vessels.[205]

Mediastinal tumors can also produce a spontaneous large hemothorax, which can be bilateral.[206] Blood can also accumulate in the pleural space due to pathologies of abdominal organs, such as rupture of a splenic artery aneurysm through the diaphragm, pancreatic pseudocysts,[207] and rupture of hepatocellular carcinomas.[208]

Hemothoraces complicating anticoagulant therapy (warfarin[209] or heparin—low molecular weight[210] or unfractionated[199]) or intrapleural fibrinolytics[209] have been reported. The hemothorax usually becomes apparent 4 to 7 days after anticoagulation therapy is initiated, but it may occur much later. When the hemothorax develops, the coagulation studies are usually within the acceptable therapeutic range.[199]

Chest tubes should be inserted into patients with spontaneous hemothorax to remove the blood from the pleural space and to quantify the degree of continued bleeding. An attempt should be made to determine the cause of the hemothorax. If brisk (>100 mL/hr) bleeding persists, emergency thoracotomy should be performed.[211]

FIBROTHORAX

A dense layer of fibrous tissue may be deposited over the pleural surface for a variety of underlying reasons. Pleural fibrosis usually follows intense inflammation of the pleura; however, the mechanisms following the inflammatory process leading up to fibrosis are unclear. Recent evidence suggests that profibrotic cytokines,[209] especially transforming growth factor-β, probably play a significant role.[212]

A fibrothorax most commonly develops as a complication of an empyema or a hemothorax. Fibrothorax has also developed as a complication of tuberculosis, collagen vascular disease, uremia, paragonimiasis, and drug reactions. Pleural fibrosis can be idiopathic, and isolated familial cases have been reported.[213] Whereas tuberculous pleuritis is common, fibrothorax is a rare complication.[214] In one study, restrictive functional sequelae were found in 10% of 81 patients with tuberculous pleuritis, but were mostly mild.[215] Neither the early drainage of the pleural effusion[216] nor the use of systemic corticosteroids[217] has significant impact on subsequent development of pleural thickening or restrictive lung function in patients with tuberculous pleuritis. Pleural fluid inflammatory markers are, at best, weak predictors of eventual pleural thickening.[215]

Asbestos exposure may also lead to a fibrothorax (also called diffuse pleural thickening), which is usually bilateral.[218] In these cases, extensive fibrosis of the visceral pleura develops, together with areas of adhesion with the parietal surfaces, thus obliterating the pleural space.[218] Diffuse pleural thickening is known to follow benign asbestos pleural effusions, and it has been suggested that this is a necessary precursor of fibrothorax.[219] In one series of 44 patients with diffuse pleural thickening, half had a history of benign asbestos effusion; conversely, 54% of those who had a benign asbestos effusion had residual pleural thickening.[219] Diffuse pleural thickening is usually,[218] but not inevitably, associated with heavy asbestos exposure, and its incidence increases with increasing time since first exposure.[219] The pleural fibrosis is often progressive, resulting in restrictive lung defects, especially if the costophrenic angle is obliterated.[220]

Pleural (with or without concurrent pulmonary) fibrosis can also occur with the use of ergot alkaloids (e.g., bromocriptine, pergolide, and methysergide).[1,209,221] It has been suggested that subjects with asbestos exposure may be more susceptible to bromocriptine-induced pleural fibrosis.[222] Onset of dyspnea from ergot-induced pleural fibrosis is usually insidious and in the majority of cases presents at least 6 months after starting the medication.[209] The pleural thickening is usually bilateral but can be unilateral, and may be associated with pleuritic pain. Constitutional symptoms and elevated serologic inflammatory markers have also been reported.[221] In the case of bromocriptine, the fibrothorax will stop progressing on cessation of the drug use, and may even regress.[209] However, complete resolution of the pleural thickening is rare. Corticosteroids are often administered, but their effectiveness has never been established.[209]

Although pleural fibrosis is usually an undesirable event, it is commonly used therapeutically in the form of pleurodesis to control pleural effusions and pneumothoraces. Pleurodesis is the iatrogenic induction of pleural fibrosis, leading to symphysis of the visceral and parietal pleurae to obliterate the pleural space to prevent fluid or air reaccumulation.[223] Interestingly, neither chemical nor surgical pleurodesis appears to produce significant disturbance in pulmonary function, even after decades. A retrospective review of young patients treated 22 to 35 years ago for spontaneous pneumothoraces showed that those who received talc pleurodesis ($n = 80$) had a higher incidence of pleural thickening on radiographs, as expected. Despite that, there were minimal restrictive changes in their lung function when compared with those treated by simple drainage ($n = 34$) only.[224] Several small human and animal studies also revealed no significant impairment in lung

volumes and gas exchange at rest or during exercise following pleurodesis.[225–227] Such observations imply that, for a fibrothorax to be clinically significant, it must involve either very extensive pleural fibrosis (in excess of therapeutic pleurodesis) or concomitant parenchymal fibrosis.

DIAGNOSIS

In typical cases, the diagnosis of fibrothorax can easily be made from the roentgenographic findings plus a history of a predisposing cause (e.g., an old injury or infection). Radiologically, a peel of uniform thickness surrounds the lung. Calcification occurs frequently on the inner aspect of the peel (Fig. 69.8) and provides an indicator by which the thickness of the peel may be accurately measured. Apparent pleural thickening can occur, especially in obese subjects (body mass index > 30), presumably the result of extrapleural fat deposition.[228] A CT scan can easily discriminate between fat and thickening.

Recently, a new CT scoring system that quantifies the thickness of the pleura and the fractional circumference of the hemithorax involved (as well as other pleural changes, such as rounded atelectasis and pleural plaques) has been shown to correlate with impairment in pulmonary function measures (especially total lung capacity and carbon monoxide diffusing capacity).[220]

Routine pulmonary function testing usually reveals mild to severe restrictive ventilatory dysfunction.[219] In the case of asbestos-induced diffuse pleural thickening, the restriction is due to inflammatory involvement of the costal surfaces of the diaphragm and lower costal pleura, thus producing a pleurodesis that limits the movement of the diaphragm and rib cage during inspiration.[229] Reduction in rib cage expansion is the main cause of restriction, because the reduction in volume contributed by the diaphragm movement is partly compensated by the flattening of its dome.[229] In one study, 95% of patients with asbestos-induced diffuse pleural thickening complained of exertional dyspnea.[230] Objective reduction of exercise work capacity had also been shown.[231]

Pulmonary function may be severely compromised in patients with an extensive fibrothorax. As a result of the marked pleural thickening, the hemithorax becomes contracted, and its mobility is reduced.[232] As the fibrothorax progresses, the intercostal spaces may narrow, the size of the involved hemithorax may diminish, and the mediastinum may be displaced ipsilaterally. In patients with bilateral fibrothorax resulting from asbestos exposure, hypercapnic respiratory failure may develop and may be amenable to home noninvasive ventilation.[233]

TREATMENT

It should be emphasized that patients with a recent hemothorax, empyema, or tuberculous pleuritis frequently show marked spontaneous improvement in their symptoms and the degree of pleural thickening in the 3 to 6 months after the acute episode.[234] Patients with a fibrothorax should avoid drugs that can induce pleural fibrosis.

Decortication, surgical removal of the fibrous peel from the pleural surface, has been attempted to treat fibrothorax. However, the degree of improvement after decortication

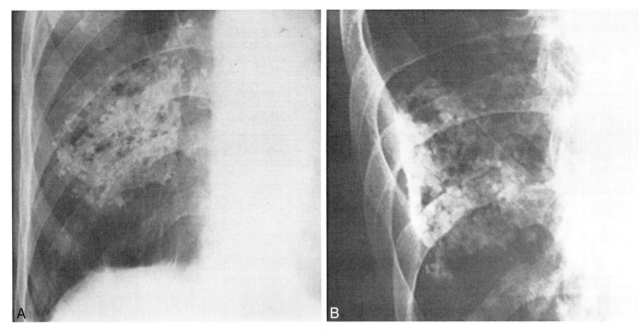

Figure 69.8 Detailed views from posteroanterior **(A)** and oblique **(B)** chest roentgenograms of a 62-year-old man showing a localized fibrothorax with calcified plaque on the right. Patient had had right-sided empyema 32 years before. (From Hinshaw HC, Murray JF: Diseases of the Chest. Philadelphia: WB Saunders, 1980, p 912.)

varies, with many series showing disappointing results.[235,236] Success in part depends on the condition of the underlying lung. The vital capacity may improve more than 50% after decortication if the underlying lung is normal, but it may even decrease after decortication in patients with extensive parenchymal disease. The duration of the fibrothorax does not seem helpful in predicting the outcome. Therefore, decortication should be considered only if the pleural thickening has been present for several months and if the lifestyle of the patient is compromised by exertional dyspnea. If CT scans of the chest reveal significant parenchymal disease, decortication is not advisable. The results of decortication in patients with bilateral fibrothoraces secondary to asbestos exposure have been disappointing; this is probably because of the presence of concomitant pulmonary fibrosis.[235] Finally, decortication is a major surgical procedure and should not be performed on patients debilitated by other diseases.

SUMMARY

Pneumothorax is increasing in frequency mainly because of the large number of diagnostic or therapeutic maneuvers that enable air to enter the pleural space. Spontaneous pneumothorax in otherwise healthy persons and traumatic (noniatrogenic) pneumothorax continue to be common and sometimes serious clinical problems. Tension pneumothorax is life-threatening and requires immediate relief. A less common, but also serious, complication is reexpansion pulmonary edema. These and other aspects of pneumothorax are described in detail in this chapter.

Chylothorax is not a common disorder, but it is important to recognize it when it occurs. Most cases are caused either by tumors, especially lymphoma, or by trauma. Chylothorax can usually be differentiated from pseudochy-lothorax by differences in the clinical picture. With chylothorax, symptoms are acute and the pleural surfaces are normal, whereas with pseudochylothorax symptoms are chronic and the pleural surfaces are thickened. A hemothorax is defined as a bloody pleural fluid with a hematocrit more than 50% of that in peripheral blood, and is usually caused by trauma, either accidental or iatrogenic. A few cases are spontaneous in origin or are related to anticoagulant therapy. Fibrothorax most commonly develops as a complication of empyema or hemothorax, which organizes into a thick fibrous layer on one or both pleural surfaces.

REFERENCES

1. Light RW: Pleural Diseases (4th ed). Baltimore: Lippincott, Williams & Wilkins, 2001.
2. Norris RM, Jones JG, Bishop JM: Respiratory gas exchange in patients with spontaneous pneumothorax. Thorax 23:427–433, 1968.
3. Melton LJ, Hepper NG, Offord KP: Incidence of spontaneous pneumothorax in Olmsted County, Minnesota: 1950 to 1974. Am Rev Respir Dis 120:1379–1382, 1979.
4. Gupta D, Hansell A, Nichols T, et al: Epidemiology of pneumothorax in England. Thorax 55:666–671, 2000.
5. Schramel FM, Postmus PE, Vanderschueren RG: Current aspects of spontaneous pneumothorax. Eur Respir J 10:1372–1379, 1997.
6. Bense L, Eklung G, Wiman LG: Smoking and the increased risk of contracting spontaneous pneumothorax. Chest 92:1009–1012, 1987.
7. Abolnik IZ, Lossos IS, Zlotogora J, et al: On the inheritance of primary spontaneous pneumothorax. Am J Med Genet 40:155–158, 1991.
8. Khoo SK, Giraud S, Kahnoski K, et al: Clinical and genetic studies of Birt-Hogg-Dube syndrome. J Med Genet 39:906–912, 2002.

9. Zbar B, Alvord WG, Glenn G, et al: Risk of renal and colonic neoplasms and spontaneous pneumothorax in the Birt-Hogg-Dube syndrome. Cancer Epidemiol Biomarkers Prev 11:393–400, 2002.

10. Bense L, Wiman LG, Hedenstierna G: Onset of symptoms in spontaneous pneumothorax: Correlations to physical activity. Eur J Respir Dis 71:181–186, 1987.

11. Seremetis MG: The management of spontaneous pneumothorax. Chest 57:65–68, 1970.

12. Vail WJ, Alway AE, England NJ: Spontaneous pneumothorax. Chest 38:512–515, 1960.

13. Alikhan M, Biddison JH: Electrocardiographic changes with right-sided pneumothorax. South Med J 91:677–680, 1998.

14. Smit HJ, van den Heuvel MM, Barbierato SB, et al: Analysis of pleural fluid in idiopathic spontaneous pneumothorax: Correlation of eosinophil percentage with the duration of air in the pleural space. Respir Med 93:262–267, 1999.

15. Wu YC, Lu MS, Yeh CH, et al: Justifying video-assisted thoracic surgery for spontaneous hemopneumothorax. Chest 122:1844–1847, 2002.

16. Noppen M, Alexander P, Driesen P, et al: Quantification of the size of primary spontaneous pneumothorax: Accuracy of the Light index. Respiration 68:396–399, 2001.

17. Sadikot RT, Greene T, Meadows K, et al: Recurrence of primary spontaneous pneumothorax. Thorax 52:805–809, 1997.

18. Smit HJ, Wienk MA, Schreurs AJ, et al: Do bullae indicate a predisposition to recurrent pneumothorax? Br J Radiol 73:356–359, 2000.

19. Janssen JP, Schramel FM, Sutedja TG, et al: Videothoracoscopic appearance of first and recurrent pneumothorax. Chest 108:330–334, 1995.

20. Gobbel WG Jr, Rhea WG Jr, Nelson IA, et al: Spontaneous pneumothorax. J Thorac Cardiovasc Surg 46:331–345, 1963.

21. Baumann MH, Strange C, Heffner JE, et al: Management of spontaneous pneumothorax: An American College of Chest Physicians Delphi Consensus Statement. Chest 119:590–602, 2001.

22. Henry M, Arnold T, Harvey J: BTS guidelines for the management of spontaneous pneumothorax. Thorax 58(Suppl II):II39–II52, 2003.

23. Kircher LT Jr, Swartzel RL: Spontaneous pneumothorax and its treatment. J Am Med Assoc 155:24–29, 1954.

24. Chernick V, Avery ME: Spontaneous alveolar rupture at birth. Pediatrics 32:816–824, 1963.

25. Northfield TC: Oxygen therapy for spontaneous pneumothorax. Br Med J 4:86–88, 1971.

26. Harvey J, Prescott RJ: Simple aspiration versus intercostal tube drainage for spontaneous pneumothorax in patients with normal lungs. British Thoracic Society Research Committee. BMJ 309:1338–1339, 1994.

27. Andrivet P, Djedaini K, Teboul J-L, et al: Spontaneous pneumothorax: Comparison of thoracic drainage vs immediate or delayed needle aspiration. Chest 108:335–340, 1995.

28. Noppen M, Alexander P, Driesen P, et al: Manual aspiration versus chest tube drainage in first episodes of primary spontaneous pneumothorax: A multicenter, prospective, randomized pilot study. Am J Respir Crit Care Med 165:1240–1244, 2002.

29. Light RW: Manual aspiration: The preferred method for managing primary spontaneous pneumothorax? Am J Respir Crit Care Med 165:1202–1203, 2002.

30. Ponn RB, Silverman HJ, Federico JA: Outpatient chest tube management. Ann Thorac Surg 64:1437–1440, 1997.

31. Liu CM, Hang LW, Chen WK, et al: Pigtail tube drainage in the treatment of spontaneous pneumothorax. Am J Emerg Med 21:241–244, 2003.

32. Light RW, O'Hara VS, Moritz TE, et al: Intrapleural tetracycline for the prevention of recurrent spontaneous pneumothorax: Results of a Department of Veterans Affairs cooperative study. JAMA 264:2224–2230, 1990.

33. Almind M, Lange P, Viskum K: Spontaneous pneumothorax: Comparison of simple drainage, talc pleurodesis, and tetracycline pleurodesis. Thorax 44:627–630, 1989.

34. Campos JR, Werebe EC, Vargas FS, et al: Respiratory failure due to insufflated talc. Lancet 349:251–252, 1997.

35. Light RW: Talc should not be used for pleurodesis. Am J Respir Crit Care Med 162:2024–2026, 2000.

36. Vargas FS, Wang NS, Lee HM, et al: Effectiveness of bleomycin in comparison to tetracycline as pleural sclerosing agent in rabbits. Chest 104:1582–1584, 1993.

37. Yim AP: Video-assisted thoracoscopic suturing of apical bullae: An alternative to staple resection in the management of primary spontaneous pneumothorax. Surg Endosc 9:1013–1016, 1995.

38. Bertrand PC, Regnard JF, Spaggiari L, et al: Immediate and long-term results after surgical treatment of primary spontaneous pneumothorax by VATS. Ann Thorac Surg 61:1641–1645, 1996.

39. Casadio C, Rena O, Giobbe R, et al: Stapler blebectomy and pleural abrasion by video-assisted thoracoscopy for spontaneous pneumothorax. J Cardiovasc Surg (Torino) 43:259–262, 2002.

40. Yim AP, Liu HP: Video assisted thoracoscopic management of primary spontaneous pneumothorax. Surg Laparosc Endosc 7:236–240, 1997.

41. Naunheim KS, Mack MJ, Hazelrigg SR, et al: Safety and efficacy of video-assisted thoracic surgical techniques for the treatment of spontaneous pneumothorax. J Thorac Cardiovasc Surg 109:1198–1203, 1995.

42. Lang-Lazdunski L, Chapuis O, Bonnet PM, et al: Videothoracoscopic bleb excision and pleural abrasion for the treatment of primary spontaneous pneumothorax: Long-term results. Ann Thorac Surg 75:960–965, 2003.

43. Crisci R, Coloni GF: Video-assisted thoracoscopic surgery versus thoracotomy for recurrent spontaneous pneumothorax: A comparison of results and costs. Eur J Cardiothorac Surg 10:556–560, 1996.

44. Tschopp JM, Boutin C, Astoul P, et al: Talcage by medical thoracoscopy for primary spontaneous pneumothorax is more cost-effective than drainage: A randomised study. Eur Respir J 20:1003–1009, 2002.

45. Noppen M: Management of primary spontaneous pneumothorax. Curr Opin Pulm Med 9:272–275, 2003.

46. Yim AP, Ng CS: Thoracoscopy in the management of pneumothorax. Curr Opin Pulm Med 7:210–214, 2001.

47. Nkere UU, Griffin SC, Fountain SW: Pleural abrasion: A new method of pleurodesis. Thorax 46:596–598, 1991.

48. Weissberg D, Refaely Y: Pneumothorax. Chest 117:1279–1285, 2000.

49. Afessa B: Pleural effusion and pneumothorax in hospitalized patients with HIV infection: The Pulmonary Complications, ICU Support, and Prognostic Factors of Hospitalized Patients with HIV (PIP) Study. Chest 117:1031–1037, 2000.

50. Luck SR, Raffensperger JG, Sullivan HJ, et al: Management of pneumothorax in children with chronic pulmonary disease. J Thorac Cardiovasc Surg 74:834–839, 1977.

50a. Mendez JL, Nadrous HF, Vassallo R, et al: Pneumothorax in pulmonary Langerhans cell histiocytosis. Chest 125:1028–1032, 2004.

51. Dines DE, Clagett OT, Payne WS: Spontaneous pneumothorax in emphysema. Mayo Clin Proc 45:481–487, 1970.

52. George RB, Herbert SJ, Shames JM, et al: Pneumothorax complicating pulmonary emphysema. JAMA 234:389–393, 1975.

53. Phillips GD, Trotman-Dickenson B, Hodson ME, et al: Role of CT in the management of pneumothorax in patients with complex cystic lung disease. Chest 112:275–278, 1997.

54. Lippert HL, Lund O, Blegvad S, et al: Independent risk factors for cumulative recurrence rate after first spontaneous pneumothorax. Eur Respir J 4:324–331, 1991.

55. Boat TF, Di Sant' Agnese PA, Warwick WJ, et al: Pneumothorax in cystic fibrosis. JAMA 209:1498–1504, 1969.

56. Videm V, Pillgram-Larsen J, Ellingsen O, et al: Spontaneous pneumothorax in chronic obstructive pulmonary disease: Complications, treatment and recurrences. Eur J Respir Dis 71:365–371, 1987.

57. Yankaskas MR, Mallory GBJ, and the Consensus Committee: Lung transplantation in cystic fibrosis. Chest 113:217–226, 1998.

58. Light RW, Hamm H: Pleural disease and the acquired immune deficiency syndrome. Eur Respir J 10:2638–2643, 1997.

59. Sepkowitz KA, Telzak EE, Gold JW, et al: Pneumothorax in AIDS. Ann Intern Med 114:455–459, 1991.

60. Vricella LA, Trachiotis GD: Heimlich valve in the management of pneumothorax in patients with advanced AIDS. Chest 120:15–18, 2001.

61. Wait MA: AIDS-related pneumothorax. Ann Thorac Surg 64:290–291, 1997.

62. Wilder RJ, Beacham EG, Ravitch MM: Spontaneous pneumothorax complicating cavitary tuberculosis. J Thorac Cardiovasc Surg 43:561–573, 1962.

63. Despars JA, Sassoon CSH, Light RW: Significance of iatrogenic pneumothoraces. Chest 105:1147–1150, 1994.

64. Li H, Boiselle PM, Shepard JO, et al: Diagnostic accuracy and safety of CT-guided percutaneous needle aspiration biopsy of the lung: Comparison of small and large pulmonary nodules. AJR Am J Roentgenol 167:105–109, 1996.

65. Vitulo P, Dore R, Cerveri I, et al: The role of functional respiratory tests in predicting pneumothorax during lung needle biopsy. Chest 109:612–615, 1995.

66. Saji H, Nakamura H, Tsuchida T, et al: The incidence and the risk of pneumothorax and chest tube placement after percutaneous CT-guided lung biopsy: The angle of the needle trajectory is a novel predictor. Chest 121:1521–1526, 2002.

67. Tanisaro K: Patient positioning after fine needle lung biopsy—effect on pneumothorax rate. Acta Radiol 44:52–55, 2003.

68. de Latorre FJ, Tomasa A, Klamburg J, et al: Incidence of pneumothorax and pneumomediastinum in patients with aspiration pneumonia requiring ventilatory support. Chest 72:141–144, 1977.

69. Weg JG, Anzueto A, Balk RA, et al: The relation of pneumothorax and other air leaks to mortality in the acute respiratory distress syndrome. N Engl J Med 338:341–346, 1998.

70. Boussarsar M, Thierry G, Jaber S, et al: Relationship between ventilatory settings and barotrauma in the acute respiratory distress syndrome. Intensive Care Med 28:406–413, 2002.

71. Jones PW, Moyers JP, Rogers JT, et al: Ultrasound-guided thoracentesis: Is it a safer method? Chest 123:418–423, 2003.

72. Poe RH, Israel RH, Utell MJ, et al: Sensitivity, specificity, and predictive values of closed pleural biopsy. Arch Intern Med 144:325–328, 1984.

73. Herf SM, Suratt PM, Arora NS: Deaths and complications associated with transbronchial lung biopsy. Am Rev Respir Dis 115:708–711, 1977.

74. Levy H, Kallenbach JM, Feldman C, et al: Delayed pneumothorax after transbronchial lung biopsy. Thorax 41:647–648, 1986.

74a. Choi CM, Um SW, Yoo CG, et al: Incidence and risk factors of delayed pneumothorax after transthoracic needle biopsy of the lung. Chest 126:1516–1521, 2004.

75. Yamagami T, Nakamura T, Iida S, et al: Management of pneumothorax after percutaneous CT-guided lung biopsy. Chest 121:1159–1164, 2002.

76. Conces DJJ, Tarver RD, Gray WC, et al: Treatment of pneumothoraces utilizing small caliber chest tubes. Chest 94:55–57, 1988.

77. Bishop MJ, Benson MS, Pierson DJ: Carbon dioxide excretion via bronchopleural fistulas in adult respiratory distress syndrome. Chest 91:400–402, 1987.

78. Bishop MJ, Benson MS, Sato P, et al: Comparison of high frequency jet ventilation with conventional mechanical ventilation for bronchopleural fistula. Anesth Analg 66:833–838, 1987.

79. Albelda SM, Hansen-Flaschen JH, Taylor E, et al: Evaluation of high-frequency jet ventilation in patients with bronchopleural fistulas by quantitation of the airleak. Anesthesiology 63:551–554, 1985.

80. Trupka A, Waydhas C, Hallfeldt KK, et al: Value of thoracic computed tomography in the first assessment of severely injured patients with blunt chest trauma: Results of a prospective study. J Trauma 43:405–411, 1997.

81. Bridges KG, Welch G, Silver M, et al: CT detection of occult pneumothorax in multiple trauma patients. J Emerg Med 11:179–186, 1993.

82. Wolfman NT, Myers WS, Glauser SJ, et al: Validity of CT classification in management of occult pneumothorax: A prospective study. AJR Am J Roentgenol 171:1317–1320, 1998.

83. Dulchavsky SA, Schwarz KL, Kirkpatrick AW, et al: Prospective evaluation of thoracic ultrasound in the detection of pneumothorax. J Trauma 50:201–205, 2001.

84. Rowan KR, Kirkpatrick AW, Liu D, et al: Traumatic pneumothorax detection with thoracic US: Correlation with chest radiography and CT—initial experience. Radiology 225:210–214, 2002.

85. Knottenbelt JD, van der Spuy JW: Traumatic pneumothorax: A scheme for rapid patient turnover. Br J Accident Surg 21:77–80, 1990.

86. Carrillo EH, Schmacht DC, Gable DR, et al: Thoracoscopy in the management of posttraumatic persistent pneumothorax. J Am Coll Surg 186:636–639, 1998.

87. Kunisch-Hoppe M, Hoppe M, Rauber K, et al: Tracheal rupture caused by blunt chest trauma: Radiological and clinical features. Eur Radiol 10:480–483, 2000.

88. Medical guidelines for air travel. Aerospace Medical Association, Air Transport Medicine Committee, Alexandria, Va. Aviat Space Environ Med 67(10 Suppl):B1–B16, 1996.

89. Cheatham ML, Safcsak K: Air travel following traumatic pneumothorax: When is it safe? Am Surg 65:1160–1164, 1999.

90. Steele RW, Metz JR, Bass JW, et al: Pneumothorax and pneumomediastinum in the newborn. Radiology 98:629–632, 1971.

91. Ogata ES, Gregory GA, Kitterman JA, et al: Pneumothorax in the respiratory distress syndrome:

Incidence and effect on vital signs, blood gases, and pH. Pediatrics 58:177–183, 1976.

92. Horbar JD, Badger GJ, Carpenter JH, et al: Trends in mortality and morbidity for very low birth weight infants, 1991–1999. Pediatrics 110:143–151, 2002.

93. Karlberg P, Cherry RB, Escardo F, et al: Respiratory studies on newborns. II. Pulmonary ventilation and mechanics of breathing in the first minutes of life including the onset of respiration. Acta Pediatr 51:121–136, 1962.

94. Adler SM, Wyszogrodski I: Pneumothorax as a function of gestational age: Clinical and experimental studies. J Pediatr 87:771–775, 1975.

95. Goldberg RN: Sustained arterial blood pressure elevation associated with pneumothoraces: Early detection via continuous monitoring. Pediatrics 68:775–777, 1981.

96. Walker MW, Shoemaker M, Riddle K, et al: Clinical process improvement: Reduction of pneumothorax and mortality in high-risk preterm infants. J Perinatol 22:641–645, 2002.

97. Arda IS, Gurakan B, Aliefendioglu D, et al: Treatment of pneumothorax in newborns: Use of venous catheter versus chest tube. Pediatr Int 44:78–82, 2002.

97a. Korom S, Canyurt H, Missbach A, et al: Catamenial pneumothorax revisited: clinical approach and systematic review of the literature. J Thorac Cardiovasc Surg 128:502–508, 2004.

98. Joseph J, Sahn SA: Thoracic endometriosis syndrome: New observations from an analysis of 110 cases. Am J Med 100:164–170, 1996.

99. Alifano M, Roth T, Broet SC, et al: Catamenial pneumothorax: A prospective study. Chest 124:1004–1008, 2003.

100. Maurer ER, Schaal JA, Mendez FL: Chronic recurrent spontaneous pneumothorax due to endometriosis of the diaphragm. J Am Med Assoc 168:2013–2014, 1958.

101. Lillington GA, Mitchell SP, Wood GA: Catamenial pneumothorax. JAMA 219:1328–1332, 1972.

102. Bagan P, Le Pimpec Barthes F, Assouad J, et al: Catamenial pneumothorax: Retrospective study of surgical treatment. Ann Thorac Surg 75:378–381, 2003.

103. Baumann MH: Non-spontaneous pneumothorax. In Light RW, Lee YCG (eds): Textbook of Pleural Diseases. London: Arnold, 2003, pp 464–474.

104. Carvalho P, Hilderbrandt J, Charan NB: Changes in bronchial and pulmonary arterial blood flow with progressive tension pneumothorax. J Appl Physiol 81:1664–1669, 1996.

105. Barton ED, Rhee P, Hutton KC, et al: The pathophysiology of tension pneumothorax in ventilated swine. J Emerg Med 15:147–153, 1997.

106. Daly CM, Swalec-Tobias K, Tobias AH, et al: Cardiopulmonary effects of intrathoracic insufflation in dogs. J Am Anim Hosp Assoc 38:515–520, 2002.

107. Beards SC, Lipman J: Decreased cardiac index as an indicator of tension pneumothorax in the ventilated patient. Anesthesiology 49:137–141, 1994.

108. Murphy DG, Sloan EP, Hart RG, et al: Tension pneumothorax associated with hyperbaric oxygen therapy. Am J Emerg Med 9:176–179, 1991.

109. Mainini SE, Johnson FE: Tension pneumothorax complicating small-caliber chest tube insertion. Chest 97:759–760, 1990.

110. Ludwig J, Kienzle GD: Pneumothorax in a large autopsy population. Am J Clin Pathol 70:24–26, 1978.

111. Trapnell DH, Thurston JGB: Unilateral pulmonary edema after pleural aspiration. Lancet 1:1367–1369, 1970.

112. Peatfield RC, Edwards RR, Johnson NM: Two unexpected deaths from pneumothorax. Lancet 1:356–358, 1979.

113. Rozenman J, Yellin A, Simansky DA, et al: Re-expansion pulmonary oedema following spontaneous pneumothorax. Respir Med 90:235–238, 1996.

114. Mahfood S, Hix WR, Aaron BL, et al: Reexpansion pulmonary edema. Ann Thorac Surg 45:340–345, 1988.

115. Gowrinath K, Varma DM, Kavitha VP, et al: Re-expansion pulmonary oedema: Revisited. Indian J Chest Dis Allied Sci 44:267–270, 2002.

116. Pavlin DJ, Nessly ML, Cheney FW: Increased pulmonary vascular permeability as a cause of re-expansion edema in rabbits. Am Rev Respir Dis 124:422–427, 1981.

117. Sprung CL, Loewenherz JW, Baier H, et al: Evidence for increased permeability in re-expansion pulmonary edema. Am J Med 71:497–500, 1981.

118. Jackson RM, Veal CF, Beckman JS, et al: Polyethylene glycol-conjugated superoxide dismutase in unilateral lung injury due to re-expansion (re-oxygenation). Am J Med Sci 300:22–28, 1990.

119. Jackson RM, Veal CF, Alexander CB, et al: Re-expansion pulmonary edema: A potential role for free radicals in its pathogenesis. Am Rev Respir Dis 137:1165–1171, 1988.

120. Doerschuk CM, Allard MF, Oyarzun MJ: Evaluation of reexpansion pulmonary edema following unilateral pneumothorax in rabbits and the effect of superoxide dismutase. Exp Lung Res 16:355–367, 1990.

121. Smolle-Juettner FM, Prause G, Ratzenhofer B, et al: The importance of early detection and therapy of reexpansion pulmonary edema. Thorac Cardiovasc Surg 39:162–166, 1991.

122. Hillerdal G: Chylothorax and pseudochylothorax. Eur Respir J 10:1157–1162, 1997.

123. Hillerdal G: Effusions from lymphatic disruptions. In Light RW, Lee YCG (eds): Textbook of Pleural Diseases. London: Arnold, 2003, pp 362–369.

124. Alexiou C, Watson M, Beggs D, et al: Chylothorax following oesophagogastrectomy for malignant disease. Eur J Cardiothorac Surg 14:460–466, 1998.

125. Shimizu K, Yoshida J, Nishimura M, et al: Treatment strategy for chylothorax after pulmonary resection and lymph node dissection for lung cancer. J Thorac Cardiovasc Surg 124:499–502, 2002.

126. Merigliano S, Molena D, Ruol A, et al: Chylothorax complicating esophagectomy for cancer: A plea for early thoracic duct ligation. J Thorac Cardiovasc Surg 119:453–457, 2000.

127. Shimizu J, Hayashi Y, Oda M, et al: Treatment of postoperative chylothorax by pleurodesis with the streptococcal preparation OK-432. Thorac Cardiovasc Surg 42:233–236, 1994.

128. Strausser JL, Flye MW: Management of nontraumatic chylothorax. Ann Thorac Surg 31:520–526, 1981.

129. Shitrit D, Izbicki G, Starobin D, et al: Late-onset chylothorax after heart-lung transplantation. Ann Thorac Surg 75:285–286, 2003.

130. Kamasaki N, Ikeda H, Wang ZL, et al: Bilateral chylothorax following radical neck dissection. Int J Oral Maxillofac Surg 32:91–93, 2003.

131. Hanekamp MN, Tjin A Djie GCM, van Hoek-Ottenkamp WG, et al: Does V-A ECMO increase the likelihood of chylothorax after congenital diaphragmatic hernia repair? J Pediatr Surg 38:971–974, 2003.

132. Shackcloth MJ, Poullis M, Lu J, et al: Preventing of chylothorax after oesophagectomy by routine pre-operative administration of oral cream. Eur J Cardiothorac Surg 20:1035–1036, 2001.

133. Romero S, Martin C, Hernandez L, et al: Chylothorax in cirrhosis of the liver: Analysis of its frequency and clinical characteristics. Chest 114:154–159, 1998.

134. Ryu JH, Doerr CH, Fisher SD, et al: Chylothorax in lymphangioleiomyomatosis. Chest 123:623–627, 2003.

135. Roy PH, Carr DT, Payne WS: The problem of chylothorax. Mayo Clin Proc 42:457–467, 1967.

136. Perkett EA: Pediatric pleural diseases. *In* Light RW, Lee YCG (eds): Textbook of Pleural Diseases. London: Arnold, 2003, pp 475–480.

137. Jacquemont S, Barbarot S, Boceno M, et al: Familial congenital pulmonary lymphangiectasia, non-immune hydrops fetalis, facial and lower limb lymphedema: Confirmation of Njolstad's report. Am J Med Genet 93:264–268, 2000.

138. Huang XZ, Wu JF, Ferrando R, et al: Fatal bilateral chylothorax in mice lacking the integrin $\alpha 9\beta 1$. Mol Cell Biol 20:5208–5215, 2000.

139. Van Aerde J, Campbell AN, Smyth JA, et al: Spontaneous chylothorax in newborns. Am J Dis Child 138:961–964, 1984.

140. Miller JIJ: Diagnosis and management of chylothorax. Chest Surg Clin N Am 6:139–148, 1996.

141. Staats BA, Ellefson RD, Budahn LL, et al: The lipoprotein profile of chylous and nonchylous pleural effusions. Mayo Clin Proc 55:700–704, 1980.

142. Sachs PB, Zelch MG, Rice TW, et al: Diagnosis and localization of laceration of the thoracic duct: Usefulness of lymphangiography and CT. AJR Am J Roentgenol 157:703–705, 1991.

143. Browse NL, Allen DR, Wilson NM: Management of chylothorax. Br J Surg 84:1711–1716, 1997.

144. Stavngaard T, Mortensen J, Brenoe J, et al: Lymphoscintigraphy using technetium-99m human serum albumin in chylothorax. Thorac Cardiovasc Surg 50:250–252, 2002.

145. Al-Zubairy SA, Al-Jazairi AS: Octreotide as a therapeutic option for management of chylothorax. Ann Pharmacother 37:679–682, 2003.

146. Buettiker V, Hug MI, Burger R, et al: Somatostatin: A new therapeutic option for the treatment of chylothorax. Intensive Care Med 27:1083–1086, 2001.

147. Evans J, Clark MF, Mincher L, et al: Chylous effusions complicating lymphoma: A serious event with octreotide as a treatment option. Hematol Oncol 21:77–81, 2003.

148. Rosti L, Bini RM, Chessa M, et al: The effectiveness of octreotide in the treatment of post-operative chylothorax. Eur J Pediatr 161:149–150, 2002.

149. Murphy MC, Newman BM, Roadgers BM: Pleuroperitoneal shunts in the management of persistent chylothorax. Ann Thorac Surg 48:195–200, 1989.

150. Wolff AB, Silen ML, Kokoska ER, et al: Treatment of refractory chylothorax with externalized pleuroperitoneal shunts in children. Ann Thorac Surg 68:1053–1057, 1999.

151. Urizar RE, Kolnacki K, Kaslovsky R, et al: Chylothorax fluid autoinfusion in a chronic hemodialysis patient. Pediatr Nephrol 18:403–406, 2003.

152. Le Pimpec-Barthes F, D'Attellis N, Dujon A, et al: Chylothorax complicating pulmonary resection. Ann Thorac Surg 73:1714–1719, 2002.

153. Mares DC, Mathur PN: Medical thoracoscopic talc pleurodesis for chylothorax due to lymphoma: A case series. Chest 114:731–735, 1998.

154. Cope C, Kaiser LR: Management of unremitting chylothorax by percutaneous embolization and blockage of retroperitoneal lymphatic vessels in 42 patients. J Vasc Interv Radiol 13:1139–1148, 2002.

155. Robinson CLN: The management of chylothorax. Ann Thorac Surg 39:90–95, 1985.

156. Janssen JP, Joosten HJ, Postmus PE: Thoracoscopic treatment of postoperative chylothorax after coronary bypass surgery. Thorax 49:1273, 1994.

157. Vassallo BC, Cavadas D, Beveraggi E, et al: Treatment of postoperative chylothorax through laparoscopic thoracic duct ligation. Eur J Cardiothorac Surg 21:556–557, 2002.

158. Romero S: Nontraumatic chylothorax. Curr Opin Pulm Med 6:287–291, 2000.

159. Bartha JL, Comino-Delgado R: Fetal chylothorax response to maternal dietary treatment. Obstet Gynecol 97:820–823, 2001.

160. Tanemura M, Nishikawa N, Kojima K, et al: A case of successful fetal therapy for congenital chylothorax by intrapleural injection of OK-432. Ultrasound Obstet Gynecol 18:371–375, 2001.

161. Brito T, Oliveira C, Sousa L, et al: Congenital chylothorax: A case report. Ultrasound Obstet Gynecol 21:70–71, 2003.

162. Jorgensen C, Brocks V, Bang J, et al: Treatment of fetal chylothorax associated with pronounced hydrops with intrapleural injection of OK-432. Ultrasound Obstet Gynecol 21:66–69, 2003.

163. Parra J, Amenedo M, Muniz-Diaz E, et al: A new successful therapy for fetal chylothorax by intrapleural injection of maternal blood. Ultrasound Obstet Gynecol 22:290–294, 2003.

164. Beghetti M, La Scala G, Belli D, et al: Etiology and management of pediatric chylothorax. J Pediatr 136:653–658, 2000.

165. Taylor JR, Ryu J, Colby TV, et al: Lymphangioleiomyomatosis: Clinical course in 32 patients. N Engl J Med 323:1254–1260, 1990.

166. Sullivan EJ: Lymphangioleiomyomatosis: A review. Chest 114:1689–1703, 1998.

167. Kalassian KG, Doyle R, Kao P, et al: Lymphangioleiomyomatosis: New insights. Am J Respir Crit Care Med 155:1183–1186, 1997.

168. Johnson SR, Tattersfield AE: Clinical experience of lymphangioleiomyomatosis in the UK. Thorax 55:1052–1057, 2000.

169. Urban T, Lazor R, Lacronique J, et al: Pulmonary lymphangioleiomyomatosis: A study of 69 patients. Medicine 78:321–337, 1999.

170. Boehler A, Speich R, Russi EW, et al: Lung transplantation for lymphangioleiomyomatosis. N Engl J Med 335:1275–1280, 1996.

171. Garcia-Zamalloa A, Ruiz-Irastorza G, Aguayo FJ, et al: Pseudochylothorax: Report of 2 cases and review of the literature. Medicine 78:200–207, 1999.

172. Hamm H, Pfalzer B, Fabel H: Lipoprotein analysis in a chyliform pleural effusion: Implications for pathogenesis and diagnosis. Respiration 58:294–300, 1991.

173. Hillerdal G: Chyliform (cholesterol) pleural effusion—eleven new cases. Chest 86:426–428, 1985.

174. Garcia-Pachon E, Fernandez LC, Lopez-Azorin F, et al: Pseudochylothorax in pleural effusion due to coronary artery bypass surgery. Eur Respir J 13:1487–1488, 1999.

175. Nogueras C, Monteagudo M, Vila M, et al: Recent-onset tuberculous pleurisy presenting as pseudochylothorax. Am J Med 113:166–168, 2002.

176. Song JW, Im JG, Goo JM, et al: Pseudochylous pleural effusion with fat-fluid levels: Report of six cases. Radiology 216:478–480, 2000.

177. Goldman A, Burford TH: Cholesterol pleural effusion: A report of three cases with a cure by decortication. Dis Chest 18:586–594, 1950.

178. Drummond DS, Craig RH: Traumatic hemothorax: Complications and management. Am Surg 33:403–408, 1967.

179. Ma OJ, Mateer JR: Trauma ultrasound examination versus chest radiography in the detection of hemothorax. Ann Emerg Med 29:312–315, 1997.
180. Simon BJ, Chu Q, Emhoff TA, et al: Delayed hemothorax after blunt thoracic trauma: An uncommon entity with significant morbidity. J Trauma 45:673–676, 1998.
181. Beall ACJ, Crawford HW, DeBakey ME: Considerations in the management of acute traumatic hemothorax. J Thorac Cardiovasc Surg 52:351–360, 1966.
182. Anderson CB: Autotransfusion in traumatic hemothorax. Mo Med 72:541–544, 1975.
183. Griffith GL, Todd EP, McMillin RD, et al: Acute traumatic hemothorax. Ann Thorac Surg 26:204–207, 1978.
184. Wilson JM, Boren CHJ, Peterson SR, et al: Traumatic hemothorax: Is decortication necessary? J Thorac Cardiovasc Surg 77:489–495, 1979.
185. Carrillo EH, Richardson JD: Thoracoscopy in the management of hemothorax and retained blood after trauma. Curr Opin Pulm Med 4:243–246, 1998.
186. Liu DW, Liu HP, Lin PJ, et al: Video-assisted thoracic surgery in treatment of chest trauma. J Trauma 42:670–674, 1997.
187. Vassiliu P, Velmahos GC, Toutouzas KG: Timing, safety, and efficacy of thoracoscopic evacuation of undrained post-traumatic hemothorax. Am Surg 67:1165–1169, 2001.
188. Velmahos GC, Demetriades D, Chan L, et al: Predicting the need for thoracoscopic evacuation of residual traumatic hemothorax: Chest radiograph is insufficient. J Trauma 46:65–70, 1999.
189. Meyer DM, Jessen ME, Wait MA, et al: Early evacuation of traumatic retained hemothoraces using thoracoscopy: A prospective, randomized trial. Ann Thorac Surg 64:1396–1400, 1997.
190. Inci I, Ozcelik C, Ulku R, et al: Intrapleural fibrinolytic treatment of traumatic clotted hemothorax. Chest 114:160–165, 1998.
191. Jerjes-Sanchez C, Ramirez-Rivera A, Elizalde JJ, et al: Intrapleural fibrinolysis with streptokinase as an adjunctive treatment in hemothorax and empyema: A multicenter trial. Chest 109:1514–1519, 1996.
192. Brunner RG, Vinsant GO, Alexander RH, et al: The role of antibiotic therapy in the prevention of empyema in patients with an isolated chest injury (ISS 9–10): A prospective study. J Trauma 30:1148–1153, 1990.
193. Waller DA, Edwards JG, Martin-Ucar AE: Surgery of the pleural cavity. In Light RW, Lee YCG (eds): Textbook of Pleural Diseases. London: Arnold, 2003, pp 513–525.
194. Krauss D, Schmidt GA: Cardiac tamponade and contralateral hemothorax after subclavian vein catheterization. Chest 99:517–518, 1991.
195. Rashid MA, Wikstrom T, Ortenwall P: Mediastinal perforation and contralateral hemothorax by a chest tube. Thorac Cardiovasc Surg 46:375–376, 1998.
196. Hussain A, Raja AJ: Occurrence of hemothorax (unilateral) after sclerotherapy. Am J Gastroenterol 86:1553–1554, 1991.
197. Wagner RB: Massive hemothorax secondary to foreign body and CPR. Ann Thorac Surg 59:1241–1242, 1995.
198. Berliner K: Hemorrhagic pleural effusion. Ann Intern Med 14:2266–2284, 1941.
199. Rostand RA, Feldman RL, Block ER: Massive hemothorax complicating heparin anticoagulation for pulmonary embolus. South Med J 70:1128–1130, 1977.
200. Yung CM, Bessen SC, Hingorani V, et al: Idiopathic hemothorax. Chest 103:638–639, 1993.
201. Edinburgh KJ, Chung MH, Webb WR: CT of spontaneous hemothorax from intrapleural rupture of a pulmonary arteriovenous malformation. AJR Am J Roentgenol 170:1399–1400, 1998.
202. Ootaki Y, Okada M, Yamashita C, et al: Tension hemothorax caused by a ruptured aneurysm of the descending thoracic aorta: Report of a case. Surg Today 30:558–560, 2000.
203. Rodriguez E, Martinez MJ, Javaloyas M, et al: Haemothorax in the course of chickenpox. Thorax 41:491, 1986.
204. Xiros N, Economopoulos T, Papageorgiou E, et al: Massive hemothorax due to intrathoracic extramedullary hematopoiesis in a patient with hereditary spherocytosis. Ann Hematol 80:38–40, 2001.
205. Pezzetta E, Paroz A, Ris HB, et al: Spontaneous hemothorax associated with von Recklinghausen's disease. Eur J Cardiothorac Surg 23:1062–1064, 2003.
206. Santelmo N, Hirschi S, Sadoun D, et al: Bilateral hemothorax revealing mediastinal parathyroid adenoma. Respiration 66:176–178, 1999.
207. Tanaka A, Takeda R, Utsunomiya H, et al: Severe complications of mediastinal pancreatic pseudocyst: Report of esophagobronchial fistula and hemothorax. J Hepatobiliary Pancreat Surg 7:86–91, 2000.
208. Sohara N, Takagi H, Yamada T, et al: Hepatocellular carcinoma complicated by hemothorax. J Gastroenterol 35:240–244, 2000.
209. Kalomenidis IT: Effusions due to drugs. In Light RW, Lee YCG (eds): Textbook of Pleural Diseases. London: Arnold, 2003, pp 383–393.
210. Mrug M, Mishra PV, Lusane HC, et al: Hemothorax and retroperitoneal hematoma after anticoagulation with enoxaparin. South Med J 95:936–938, 2002.
211. Light RW: Effusions from vascular causes. In Light RW, Lee YCG (eds): Textbook of Pleural Diseases. London: Arnold, 2003, pp 289–296.
212. Lee YCG, Lane KB: The many faces of transforming growth factor beta in pleural diseases. Curr Opin Pulm Med 7:173–179, 2001.
213. Azoulay E, Paugam B, Heymann MF, et al: Familial extensive idiopathic bilateral pleural fibrosis. Eur Respir J 14:971–973, 1999.
214. Chan CH, Arnold M, Chan CY, et al: Clinical and pathological features of tuberculous pleural effusion and its long-term consequences. Respiration 58:171–175, 1991.
215. Candela A, Andujar J, Hernandez L, et al: Functional sequelae of tuberculous pleurisy in patients correctly treated. Chest 123:1996–2000, 2003.
216. Lai YF, Chao TY, Wang YH, et al: Pigtail drainage in the treatment of tuberculous pleural effusions: A randomised study. Thorax 58:149–151, 2003.
217. Matchaba PT, Volmink J: Steroids for treating tuberculous pleurisy. Cochrane Database Syst Rev 2:CD001876, 2000.
218. Chapman SJ, Cookson WO, Musk AW, et al: Benign asbestos pleural disease. Curr Opin Pulm Med 9:266–271, 2003.
219. Musk AW, De Klerk NH: Benign asbestos pleural diseases. In Light RW, Lee YCG (eds): Textbook of Pleural Diseases. London: Arnold, 2003, pp 428–434.
220. Copley SJ, Wells AU, Rubens MB, et al: Functional consequences of pleural disease evaluated with chest radiography and CT. Radiology 220:237–243, 2001.
221. Pfitzenmeyer P, Foucher P, Dennewald G, et al: Pleuropulmonary changes induced by ergoline drugs. Eur Respir J 9:1013–1019, 1996.
222. Hillerdal G, Lee J, Blomkvist A, et al: Pleural disease during treatment with bromocriptine fib in patients previously exposed to asbestos. Eur Respir J 10:2711–2715, 1997.

223. Lee YCG, Rodriguez RM, Lane KB, et al: Pleurodesis for recurrent pleural effusions in the new millennium. Recent Adv Res Updates 2:81–89, 2001.

224. Lange P, Mortensen J, Groth S: Lung function 22–35 years after treatment of idiopathic spontaneous pneumothorax with talc poudrage or simple drainage. Thorax 43:559–561, 1988.

225. Ukale V, Bone D, Hillerdal G, et al: The impact of pleurodesis in malignant effusion on respiratory function. Respir Med 93:898–902, 1999.

226. Fleetham JA, Forkert L, Clarke H, et al: Regional lung function in the presence of pleural symphysis. Am Rev Respir Dis 122:33–38, 1980.

227. McGahren ED, Teague WG, Flanagan TJ, et al: The effects of talc pleurodesis on growing swine. J Pediatr Surg 25:1147–1151, 1990.

228. Lee YCG, Runnion CK, Pang SC, et al: Increased body mass index is related to apparent circumscribed pleural thickening on plain chest radiographs. Am J Ind Med 39:112–116, 2001.

229. Singh B, Eastwood PR, Finucane KE, et al: Effect of asbestos-related pleural fibrosis on excursion of the lower chest wall and diaphragm. Am J Respir Crit Care Med 160:1507–1515, 1999.

230. Yates DH, Browne K, Stidolph PN, et al: Asbestos-related bilateral diffuse pleural thickening: natural history of radiographic and lung function abnormalities. Am J Respir Crit Care Med 153:301–306, 1996.

231. Picado C, Laporta D, Grassino A, et al: Mechanisms affecting exercise performance in subjects with asbestos-related pleural fibrosis. Lung 165:45–57, 1987.

232. Gaensler EA: Lung displacement: Abdominal enlargement, pleural space disorder, deformities of the thoracic cage. *In* Fenn WO, Rahn H (eds): Handbook of Physiology. Section 3: Respiration (Vol II). Washington, DC: American Physiological Society, 1965, pp 1623–1661.

233. Munoz X, Roger A, Pallisa E, et al: Ventilatory insufficiency due to asbestos-related diffuse pleural fibrosis successfully treated with noninvasive home mechanical ventilation. Respiration 68:533–536, 2001.

234. Neff CC, vanSonnenberg E, Lawson DW, et al: CT follow-up of empyemas: Pleural peels resolve after percutaneous catheter drainage. Radiology 176:195–197, 1990.

235. Hillerdal G: Non-malignant asbestos pleural disease. Thorax 36:669–675, 1981.

236. Fielding DI, McKeon JL, Oliver WA, et al: Pleurectomy for persistent pain in benign asbestos-related pleural disease. Thorax 50:181–183, 1995.

70

Tumors of the Pleura

Alice M. Boylan, M.D., V. Courtney Broaddus, M.D.

INTRODUCTION

Tumors of the pleural space can be primary or secondary. The secondary tumor due to metastatic spread of malignancy, usually from lung or breast cancer, is the most common and is discussed first. Pleural metastatic disease is estimated to affect 200,000 persons per year in the United States, and serves as the most common cause of exudative pleural effusion after infection.[1] Unfortunately, because it represents metastatic spread, treatment goals are generally those of palliation, not cure. Survival is poor, with an average of 4 months. Primary tumors of the pleural space are more uncommon. The most common primary tumor, malignant mesothelioma, affects approximately 2300 persons per year in the United States, although the incidence is growing worldwide.[1] Interestingly, despite its grim reputation, mesothelioma offers better survival than does metastatic pleural disease, with mean survival of 9 to 12 months. Although curative treatments are not yet available, progress is being made. Other rare but interesting tumors, such as solitary fibrous tumor of the pleura, primary effusion lymphoma, and pyothorax-associated lymphoma, are also discussed.

METASTATIC PLEURAL DISEASE

TYPES OF TUMOR

Certain tumors appear to have a predilection for metastasis to the pleura, particularly lung cancer, breast cancer, and lymphomas, and less commonly gastrointestinal and genitourinary malignancies (Table 70.1). In approximately half the cases of metastatic pleural disease, the patient will have an associated pleural effusion, most often exudative.[2] However, in up to 10% of the malignant pleural effusions, the tumor of origin is not identified.[3] After infectious disease, malignant pleural effusions are the leading cause of exudative effusions.

The pattern of metastatic spread can provide some clues to the identity of the primary tumor. Whereas malignant mesotheliomas generally originate on the parietal pleura and then spread to the visceral pleura, metastases due to bronchogenic carcinoma usually are first found on the visceral pleura and then spread to the parietal pleura, and are rarely found exclusively on the parietal pleura.[2] In addition, the side of a malignant effusion is usually the same as the tumor of origin in most cases of bronchogenic carcinoma, with 17 of 24 cases ipsilateral in one autopsy series.[4] In patients with pleural metastasis due to other cancers, evidence from two autopsy series suggests that the malignancy initially involves the visceral pleura and moves to the pleural space from there.[2,4]

CLINICAL FEATURES

The most common symptom associated with a malignant pleural disease is dyspnea, most often from the presence of a pleural effusion. Cough is also a symptom that may be due to the presence of a pleural effusion. If the effusion is the cause of these symptoms, both dyspnea and cough can be relieved promptly by thoracentesis. When a thoracentesis fails to relieve these symptoms, tumor infiltration of lung or pleura or another medical condition should be suspected. Chest pain can often be described as a dull ache; this may indicate involvement of the chest wall and sensory neurons of the parietal pleura and chest wall. In one series, 34% of patients with malignant pleural effusion described a dull chest ache and 24% described a pleuritic chest pain.[5] This differed from those patients with benign causes of their effusions, who were more likely to describe pleuritic chest pain.[5] Systemic symptoms may include malaise and anorexia.

MALIGNANT PLEURAL EFFUSIONS

As mentioned, pleural effusion is not present in all cases of malignant pleural disease. In autopsy studies of patients with malignancy, malignant pleural disease was associated with an effusion in 55%[2] to 60%[4] of cases. It is increasingly recognized that malignant cells can reach the pleural space without effusion because cytology of pleural lavage can be positive in patients undergoing resection for lung cancer who have no effusion. In one study, 4.5% of patients at

thoracotomy for lung cancer without effusion had positive pleural lavage cytology.[6] The development of an effusion may depend on characteristics of the tumor cells; in an experimental study of lung cancer cell lines, the production of pleural effusion was associated with the invasiveness of the cell lines and with their production of vascular endothelial growth factor.[7]

Lung cancer is the most common cause of malignant pleural effusions[8] (see Table 70.1). Lung cancer and breast cancer together account for more than half of all malignant pleural effusions. Of the histologic types of bronchogenic cancers, adenocarcinomas are most frequently associated with malignant pleural effusions, but effusions may be seen with all types.[9]

Breast cancer is the second most common cause of malignant pleural effusions.[8,10] The time course of development of the effusion from the time of initial diagnosis of breast cancer is usually 2 years, but can be up to 20 years. The effusion usually is ipsilateral to the site of the original tumor (50%), but can also be contralateral (40%) and less commonly bilateral (10%).[11]

Lymphoma is the third most common cause in most series,[8] but is possibly the most common cause in young adults.[10] Pleural effusions are common both in non-Hodgkin's and in Hodgkin's lymphoma.[12] In patients with non-Hodgkin's lymphoma, approximately 16% will develop malignant effusions and most will have the effusion at the time of initial diagnosis in association with evidence of disease elsewhere.[13] The high yield of pleural fluid cytology[14] suggests frequent invasion of the pleural space. Chylothorax may also develop in some patients with non-Hodgkin's disease. In Hodgkin's lymphoma, effusions may be caused by hilar or mediastinal lymph node involvement as well as pleural involvement.[12]

Malignancies probably produce pleural effusions both by decreasing the normal exit of liquid and by increasing the production of liquid (Table 70.2) (see Chapter 68). The entry of liquid can be increased in several ways: (1)

Table 70.1 Primary Tumors Responsible for Malignant Pleural Effusion*

Primary Tumor Site	Total (%)
Lung	37.5
Breast	16.8
Lymphoma	11.5
Gastrointestinal	6.9
Genitourinary	9.4
Other	7.3
Unknown	10.7

* A compilation of data from five different reports with a total of 2040 patients. The "other" category includes ovarian carcinoma, sarcomas, uterine and cervical carcinomas, and other carcinomas. From Antunes G, Neville E, Duffy J, et al: BTS guidelines for the management of malignant pleural effusions. Thorax 58:II29–II38, 2003.

Table 70.2 Physiologic Mechanisms (Neoplastic and Paraneoplastic) by which Malignancy May Cause Pleural Effusions*

Means of Increasing Liquid	Mechanism	Site/Source	Examples
Increased entry	Increased vascular permeability	Pleural vessels	Invasion by tumor Cytokines (e.g., VEGF) Injury (e.g., radiation)
		Pulmonary vessels	Infection (e.g., postobstructive pneumonitis) Cytokines/injury
	Increased vascular hydrostatic gradient	Pleural vessels	Decreased pleural pressure (e.g., atelectasis) Increased venous pressure (e.g., SVC syndrome) Decreased plasma osmotic pressure (e.g., hypoproteinemia)
	Nonvascular entry	Thoracic duct	Chylothorax
Decreased exit	Increased resistance to lymphatic flow	Pleural lymphatics Lymph nodes	Infiltration of parietal pleura Infiltration of mediastinal lymph nodes
	Increased gradient opposing lymphatic flow		Decreased pleural pressure (e.g., atelectasis) Increased venous pressure (e.g., SVC syndrome)

* Most likely, both an increase in entry and a decrease in exit are required to produce a stable pleural effusion. "Paraneoplastic" refers to mechanisms taking place outside the pleural space.
SVC, superior vena cava; VEGF, vascular endothelial growth factor.
Adapted from Nahid P, Broaddus VC: Liquid and protein exchange. *In* Light RW, Lee GYC (eds): Textbook of Pleural Diseases. London: Arnold, 2003, pp 35–44.

increased permeability of the pleural vessels by direct invasion of tumor cells, inflammatory and vasoactive cytokines (e.g. vascular endothelial growth factor), or injury (e.g., radiation-induced), (2) increased permeability of *pulmonary* vessels by infection, pulmonary embolism, or pulmonary infarct with movement of liquid from lung to pleural space, (3) increased hydrostatic forces due to venous obstruction or hypoproteinemia, and (4) entry of other sources of liquid, such as chyle from a disrupted thoracic duct. The exit of liquid from the pleural space can be decreased by infiltration of parietal pleural lymphatics or mediastinal lymph nodes. Further changes that can decrease lymphatic removal from the pleural space include decreased pleural pressure, as from atelectasis with bronchial obstruction, or elevation of the downstream central venous pressure, as from a superior vena cava syndrome. We suspect that several factors combine to form a pleural effusion in association with malignancy.[15] Abnormalities due to malignancy itself may be sufficient to tip the balance between the entry and exit of liquid toward accumulation of excess pleural liquid. Alternatively, the malignancy may alter the balance gradually without the development of an overt effusion; the advent of another nonmalignant condition, such as heart failure or pneumonia, may then tip the balance and precipitate the appearance of a symptomatic pleural effusion. In these cases, malignancy may contribute to but not be the sole cause of the effusion.[15] Such processes may explain how malignancy can be associated with transudative effusions.[16]

PLEURAL FLUID ANALYSIS

The pleural fluid is almost always an exudate. The effusion may meet exudative criteria by the lactate dehydrogenase (LDH) ratio or absolute level only and not by the protein ratio.[17] Such an observation may indicate that an increased cell turnover and cell lysis is the source of the elevated LDH, but the increased vascular permeability needed to produce pleural fluid with increased protein concentration is not present. In some studies, perhaps 5% of malignant effusions are found to be transudates.[18] In most of these cases, the primary cause of these "malignant" transudative effusions appears to be congestive heart failure or other known causes of a transudate (e.g., superior vena cava syndrome, volume overload), and the malignancy may contribute to the effusion formation.[18] Malignancy could be a sole cause of a transudate if, for example, the malignancy primarily interfered with lymphatic absorption of pleural liquid.[16] In such cases, one could imagine that the accumulation of normal pleural liquid would produce a transudative effusion. In one interesting case report, a patient with metastatic colon cancer but without other comorbid conditions presented with transudative pleural effusions and negative cytology; within 1 month, the effusions were exudative with positive cytology.[19] Biopsy showed parietal pleural lymphatic infiltration, suggesting that the cause of the initial transudative effusion was primarily blockage of pleural liquid lymphatic clearance, followed by invasion of the pleural space and development of an exudate.

The effusion may be grossly bloody; indeed, malignant disease is the most common cause of bloody effusions.[20] However, about half of malignant effusions are not bloody in appearance and have pleural fluid red blood cell counts under 10,000/μL.[20] On cell differential, a predominance of lymphocytes is usual, but a mononuclear or eosinophilic predominance does not exclude the diagnosis. The presence of pleural fluid eosinophilia (>10% eosinophils) has been thought to be unusual in malignant effusion and to argue against the diagnosis.[21] However, in a more recent study of 476 effusions, 20% of the eosinophilic effusions were found to be malignant; this was the same as the percentage of noneosinophilic effusions that was found to be malignant (20%),[22] showing not only that eosinophilic effusions could be malignant but also that the presence of eosinophilia did not alter the likelihood of malignancy. Eosinophilia in many of these situations may be caused by other factors, such as the prior entry of air or blood into the pleural space. In another study in which care was taken to study only initial thoracenteses to avoid the entry of air or blood, eosinophilia was present in 12.6% of all effusions tapped, and the presence of eosinophilia did not differentiate malignant from benign etiologies.[23]

The pleural glucose concentration is lower than 60 mg/dL in approximately 20% of malignant pleural effusions.[24] Effusions with a low glucose level also tend to have a low pleural pH and a larger tumor burden in the pleural space. It would therefore be expected that those patients with a low pleural glucose or pH would have a shorter survival. Indeed, some groups have found that a pleural fluid pH less than 7.30 is associated with a median survival of 1 to 2 months.[25,26] However, a recent study assessing different methods for deriving likelihood ratios from pleural fluid pH raises doubts about using the pleural fluid pH as a predictor. After evaluating studies that included information for 850 patients, the authors concluded that pleural fluid pH (≤7.20) is useful for predicting failure of pleurodesis, but has marginal value for predicting death within 3 months.[27]

Pleural fluid amylase concentration is elevated in 10% of patients with malignant pleural effusions.[28,29] However, the origin of the amylase is not the pancreas, as shown by its identification as salivary rather than pancreatic amylase.[30] In one series of consecutive effusions, a very high amylase in malignant pleural fluid (>600 IU/L) was a poor prognostic factor.[29]

RADIOGRAPHIC EVALUATION

The size of malignant effusions may vary greatly. Some may be small, amounting to a few milliliters and only causing blunting of the costophrenic angle, whereas others are large enough to obscure the hemithorax. In fact, malignancy is the most common cause of effusions that are either large, opacifying more than two thirds of the hemithorax, or massive, opacifying the entire hemithorax. In one retrospective series of 766 patients, malignancy was found as the cause of 55% of large and massive effusions[31]; the other causes were pleural empyema and tuberculous effusions. Of these large malignant effusions, most were caused by lung or breast cancer. Interestingly, cytologic examination was no more likely to be positive in these large/massive effusions than in smaller ones (63%, large; 53%, small).

If the effusion is large, it is important to note the position of the mediastinum. It is expected that, in an uncomplicated situation, the mediastinum will be shifted away from a large effusion. If the mediastinum is midline, one can suspect one of two things: (1) the pleural pressures are equal on the two sides, implying that significant lung collapse is present offsetting the increase in pressure expected from the presence of the effusion; or (2) the mediastinum is fixed in position and cannot shift in response to a pressure differential. If the mediastinum is shifted toward the side of the effusion, the pressure is demonstrably lower on the side of the effusion than on the other side. The lung must be collapsed and unable to expand in response to this abnormally low pressure. Because the lung is trapped, either collapsed due to main-stem bronchial obstruction or infiltrated by tumor, it is unlikely to reinflate with chest tube thoracostomy. In situations in which the mediastinum is shifted toward a massive effusion, placement of chest tubes is not recommended.

Computed tomography (CT) has the advantage of providing detailed information about the pleural surfaces, as well as information about the lung parenchyma, chest wall, and mediastinum. Thus, one obtains clues about the presence of malignancy and the identity of the tumor of origin as well as staging information. The typical features found in malignant pleural disease are pleural thickening (>1 cm), irregularity, and nodules (Fig. 70.1). In CT studies of patients with diffuse pleural thickening with or without effusions, such features were reported to be useful in differentiating malignant from benign disease.[32] In a prospective CT study of 40 patients with suspected malignant effusions, these pleural characteristics discriminated well between malignant and benign disease, with a sensitivity for malignancy of 84% and a specificity of 100%.[33] In a larger CT study of 211 consecutive patients with effusions, the most specific findings for malignancy were pleural nodules and nodular thickening.[34] Pleural thickening alone was not as specific and was seen in malignancy and empyema.

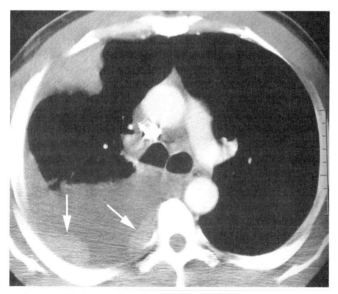

Figure 70.1 Metastatic adenocarcinoma. Axial contrast-enhanced thoracic computed tomography scan shows right pleural effusion associated with enhancing nodular masses (*arrows*) emanating from the parietal pleura, later shown to be metastatic adenocarcinoma.

Although the presence of pleural nodules was highly specific, it was not sensitive; pleural nodules were found in only 17% of malignant effusions. Interestingly, half of the patients with malignant effusions had no pleural abnormalities on the CT. Other CT findings such as the presence of a pulmonary mass, chest wall involvement, large mediastinal nodes, and hepatic metastases, suggested malignancy.[34]

Although magnetic resonance imaging (MRI) is not advocated for routine evaluation of malignant effusions, its excellent soft-tissue contrast may be useful for detailed evaluation of tumor invasion.[35] It may be particularly useful in evaluating the chest wall and pleura in the apices of the hemithoraces. In one study, MRI characteristics of pleural effusions including heterogeneity, loculation, and size of effusions were not useful for determining the etiology of effusions.[36]

Positron emission tomography (PET) with ^{18}F-fluorodeoxyglucose radiolabeling can be very useful for differentiating benign pleural fibrosis from malignancy and provides useful information for staging in cases of documented malignancy. However, it may not always be able to differentiate pleural malignancy from benign pleural inflammation, such as that due to talc pleurodesis.[37]

DIAGNOSIS

Cytology is reportedly diagnostic in approximately 60% of patients,[38] but the diagnostic yield varies with the type of tumor, the extent of tumor involvement of the pleural space, and the skill of the cytologist. Cytology is more likely to be positive in adenocarcinoma than in squamous cell lung cancer, for example, perhaps because of the increased tendency of adenocarcinoma to involve the pleural space.[20] Cytology may be positive more often in effusions with a low pH, indicating a greater tumor burden.[24,26] Interestingly, cytologic yield does not vary greatly with the size of the effusion; in one study, cytology was positive as often in large or massive effusions (63%) as in small or moderate-sized effusions (53%).[31]

In the past, closed pleural biopsy was performed as a next step in cases in which cytology was negative. However, this procedure can no longer be advocated with the advent of advanced imaging techniques and pleuroscopy. The patchy involvement of the parietal pleura by malignancy appears to make closed pleural biopsy a "hit or miss" technique, and, not surprisingly, image-directed biopsies have now been shown to be more accurate. In one randomized study comparing CT-guided biopsy with closed pleural biopsy using an Abrams needle, CT-guided biopsy was significantly more sensitive (87% vs. 47%) with a better negative predictive value (80% vs. 44%).[39]

Pleural biopsy via pleuroscopy is a well-tolerated procedure that permits excellent visualization of the entire pleural surface (see also Chapter 23). Directed biopsies of suspicious areas lead to a correct identification of metastatic pleural disease in nearly 100% of cases.[40] This technique has additional advantages, including the ability to obtain large biopsies for immunohistochemical analysis or electron microscopy, to provide information about the gross appearance of tumor, to provide information for staging, to lyse adhesions, and to drain the pleural space completely for talc pleurodesis.

Biologic markers for malignancy may be discovered as the molecular biology of cancer is better understood, and would potentially assist the cytologic diagnosis. One potential marker is telomerase, a ribonucleoprotein enzyme that maintains chromosomal telomere length and is associated with cell immortality and malignant transformation. In a study of 109 consecutive patients with a histologically confirmed diagnosis of benign or malignant effusion, telomerase activity was determined in cells from pleural effusions using a polymerase chain reaction–based technique. The sensitivity of telomerase activity for malignancy was 83% and specificity was 80%. When telomerase activity was combined with cytologic analysis, the sensitivity of the tests combined rose to 92% compared to cytologic examination alone (54%).[41] In a similar study, telomerase activity was measured in cells from pleural fluid in 144 consecutive patients. Excluding patients with equivocal histopathology, positive telomerase activity had a sensitivity of 91% and a specificity of 94%. Of note, all nonmalignant, telomerase-positive pleural effusion samples were obtained from patients with tuberculosis.[42] Like many tests, this particular test has limitations due to false positives and false negatives, although it suggests that, in the future, such molecular tests may improve diagnostic yield either alone or together with cytology.[43]

Other biomarkers have the potential to identify a particular tumor type. For example, surfactant protein A, a specific marker for alveolar type II cells and Clara cells, has increased expression in the majority of primary lung adenocarcinomas, but not in other types of lung cancer or other malignancies. In a study evaluating cells from pleural effusions due to a variety of malignancies and benign processes using reverse transcriptase–polymerase chain reaction to detect surfactant protein A messenger ribonucleic acid, the sensitivity for detection of primary lung adenocarcinomas was 83%. Although there were some false negatives, none of the samples from patients with other diagnoses were positive.[44] Others have used an enzyme-linked immunosorbent assay to measure levels of surfactant protein A in pleural effusions. They found that 40% of pleural effusions from lung adenocarcinomas (27 of 67) had levels greater than 500 ng/mL, whereas effusions from other histologic types of lung cancers, adenocarcinomas of different primary sites, and tuberculosis had low levels.[45] Future diagnostic assays in pleural effusions hold promise for increased accuracy of diagnosis of malignancy in general and also of the specific malignancy.

THERAPY AND PALLIATION

The therapeutic and palliative approach to malignant pleural effusions is guided by several factors (Table 70.3). The options are several and of increasing invasiveness. First of all, the clinician should determine that the effusion is symptomatic, causing either dyspnea, cough, or chest pain. Symptomatic effusions require an effort to control the effusion, usually by obliterating the pleural space and the ability of effusions to form or by draining the effusion, either internally or externally. Important issues that help the clinician decide on the approach are the ability of the lung to reinflate fully, the clinical status of the patient, and the availability of approaches such as pleuroscopy. Obviously the overall goal is to provide the greatest relief of symptoms using the least invasive, least morbid, and least expensive therapy. Management issues mainly focusing on palliation have been addressed in guidelines from the European Respiratory Society/American Thoracic Society[46] and the British Thoracic Society.[8]

The possibility of definitive therapy is dictated by the primary malignancy and usually entails chemotherapy for control of metastatic, systemic disease. Malignant pleural effusions that may respond to chemotherapy include those due to breast cancer, small cell lung cancer, and lymphoma.[11,47,48] Radiation therapy may be useful for treatment of the primary tumor or to treat local areas of chest wall invasion, but is limited by the radiosensitive organs adjacent to the pleura, such as the lung and heart. As stated previously, the most common and most debilitating symptom caused by malignant effusions is dyspnea, leading to control of dyspnea as the primary focus of palliative therapy in most cases.

Repeated thoracentesis to remove a symptomatic effusion may be preferred in those unusual circumstances when the fluid reaccumulates slowly and patient preference dictates. Nonetheless, most malignant effusions recur rapidly and would need frequent drainage, making this approach useful only in a few cases, such as in a patient with a very short life expectancy.

Chemical pleurodesis can be considered when the lung can reinflate so it comes in contact with the parietal pleura. Even if contact can be achieved over a large but not total pleural surface area, pleurodesis may still be effective at preventing the recurrence of large symptomatic effusions.[49] Pleurodesis with talc is effective in most cases with a success

Table 70.3 Options for Control of Symptomatic Malignant Effusions

Option	Patient Eligibility and Considerations
Chemotherapy	Chemoresponsive tumor
Thoracentesis	Slowly recurring effusion Used for patients with very short life expectancy

Pleurodesis
  Via chest tube
  Via pleuroscopy
	Lung able to reinflate
	Can free up lung tacked down by adhesions
	Pleuroscopy must be available
	When pleuroscopy already needed for biopsies

Indwelling catheter	Good outpatient situation Good for trapped lung
Pleuroperitoneal shunt	Patient can operate pump Good for trapped lung Excellent for chylothorax
Pleurectomy Via pleuroscopy or thoracotomy	When other less invasive options have failed Good patient status and life expectancy

rate of >90% at preventing recurrence at 30 days, and is more effective than pleurodesis with other agents, including tetracycline and bleomycin.[49a] Talc pleurodesis can be painful and, in a small percentage of patients, can lead to pulmonary edema and acute respiratory failure.[1] In one retrospective study of 120 patients who underwent pleurodesis with talc, 7% developed arterial desaturation within 1 day of the procedure.[50] However, it remains uncertain whether the respiratory complications are directly related to talc or to other factors such as reexpansion pulmonary edema, comorbid disease, or premedication. Some evidence suggests that a smaller size of talc particle allows systemic distribution from the pleural space; in a recent randomized study, pleurodesis with graded talc (with most particles less than 10 μm removed) was associated with fewer systemic complications than a mixed talc.[51] Alternative sclerosing agents have been investigated, but currently talc is the preferred agent as it consistently produces the highest success rates, followed by the tetracyclines and bleomycin.[52] Other agents studied include iodopovidone, quinacrine, and *Corynebacterium parvum*.[53,53a,54]

The mode of administration of talc has inspired some controversy. Prospective trials have shown no benefit of standard large-bore tubes over small-bore tubes (12 French) for pleurodesis, although talc was used in a minority of these patients,[55] and no benefit from rotation of patients as determined by instillation of radiolabeled talc and by outcome.[49] For most patients, a chest tube can be inserted and pleurodesis performed within 24 hours.[56] Talc can be administered via slurry through chest tubes or by poudrage (insufflation) via pleuroscopy or video-assisted thoracoscopic surgery. In a retrospective study of 34 patients, poudrage was associated with shorter hospital stay and chest tube duration than slurry[57]; however, in an earlier prospective randomized study of 57 patients, talc poudrage and talc slurry had similar outcomes.[58] Pleuroscopy or video-assisted thoracoscopic surgery clearly has the ability to drain the pleural space completely at the time of talc instillation and to lyse adhesions, which may allow more success in selected patients. In reported studies of a total of nearly 1000 patients, pleuroscopic insufflation of talc for pleurodesis has an excellent success rate (93%) and low operative mortality (<0.8%).[40,59] In 393 patients with malignant pleural effusions and talc insufflation, complications included empyema (3%), pulmonary edema (2%), and respiratory failure (2%).[59]

Chronic indwelling catheters to drain the pleural effusion have been shown to be effective alternatives to chemical pleurodesis. They not only control effusion-related symptoms in 80% to 90% of patients, but also lead to pleurodesis in 44%.[60] Effusions in patients with trapped lungs and large locules can still be treated in this way. Complications are usually minor.[60]

Pleuroperitoneal shunting is another alternative for palliation when the lung cannot reexpand or pleurodesis is unsuccessful, but it is reserved primarily for patients with chylous effusions. Although it is a more invasive procedure, the pleuroperitoneal shunt allows the drainage of chyle into the abdomen and thus minimizes protein loss. In most series, operative and in-house mortality are very low,[61,62] and not significantly different from that following tube thoracotomy with talc pleurodesis.[62] The mean duration of

patency has been reported at 26 months, with fewer than 25% of the shunts clotting before the death of the patient.[63] Rarely malignant seeding along the chest wall can develop at the site of shunt insertion. Importantly, improvement in dyspnea is achieved in most patients (95%).[61,62] Of note, the external pump chamber must be manually compressed several times each day to move the pleural fluid into the peritoneal space.

Pleurectomy via thoracotomy can achieve a pleural symphysis when other treatment fails, but should be reserved for patients with an expected survival of greater than 6 months. This technique is reportedly very effective, but the operative mortality is relatively high (12.5%).[64] Pleurectomy via video-assisted thoracoscopic surgery has a lower operative mortality and morbidity. However, in a prospective study of 19 patients, the hospital stay was a median of 5 days and 2 patients developed recurrent effusions,[65] making chronic indwelling catheter placement or pleuro-peritoneal shunting more appealing for many of these patients who fail pleurodesis.

PROGNOSIS

The overall prognosis is poor for most patients with malignant pleural effusions. In an analysis of several studies with a total of over 400 patients, the median survival was 4.0 months.[66] The survival varied by tumor of origin; patients with malignant effusions from lung cancer had lower median survivals of 3.0 months, whereas those with pleural effusions from cancer of the breast had 5.0 months; from mesothelioma, 6.0 months; and from lymphoma, 9.0 months. When used to predict survival for any individual patient, pleural fluid pH or glucose is not sufficiently robust.[66] One of the strongest predictors appears to be the Karnovsky Performance Scale score; in a prospective trial of 85 consecutive patients with malignant pleural effusions referred for pleuroscopic pleurodesis, those with a Karnovsky score above 70 had a median survival of 13.2 months, whereas those with a score below 30 had a median survival of 1.1 months.[67] Interestingly, in this study, when compared to other measures such as pleural fluid pH, glucose, or extent of carcinomatous involvement of the pleural surface, performance scoring was the only significant predictor of survival.

MESOTHELIOMA

INCIDENCE AND ETIOLOGY

Malignant pleural mesothelioma is an uncommon cancer, but can no longer be considered rare with more than 2000 cases per year diagnosed in the United States alone. The number of cases is anticipated to continue to increase in the United States and Western Europe until at least 2020[68] due to the increase in occupational exposures to asbestos and asbestos-containing products that occurred after World War II. During the heyday of excitement about asbestos, asbestos was viewed as a modern innovation and was used widely, even in such products as toothpaste[69] and cigarette filters![70]

After 2020, the number of cases is anticipated to plateau and then decline in these countries due to the reduction in occupational exposures caused by restrictions on asbestos use, worker protection, and asbestos abatement efforts that were instituted from the mid-1970s to the 1990s. Unfortunately, asbestos is a naturally occurring substance that continues to be mined, and whose use is actually increasing in many developing countries[71] such as India, Brazil, Korea, and South Africa. Of Asian countries, only Japan and Singapore have adopted a ban on asbestos.[72] As a consequence of continued asbestos use, the incidence of malignant mesothelioma in many developing countries is expected to reach high levels in the future.

Groups in the United States with significant asbestos exposure and increased rates of mesotheliomas include workers in the asbestos industry, insulators, pipe fitters, shipyard workers, brake mechanics, railroad workers, construction workers, carpenters, plumbers, electricians, painters, non-asbestos miners, welders, machinists, manufacturers of mineral products, bricklayers, and workers who perform maintenance and repair in buildings with asbestos insulation.[73,74] In addition, it is not uncommon to see women with asbestos-induced mesothelioma whose only clear asbestos exposure was from exposure to their spouses' contaminated clothing. Incidence may rise due to recent population exposures such as from the dust that settled after the collapse of the World Trade Center.[75]

Other causes of mesothelioma have been postulated. Recently, there has been a great deal of controversy as to whether simian virus 40 (SV40), which contaminated the polio vaccine administered from 1955 through 1963, may be contributing to the development of mesotheliomas in the United States and other countries. SV40 is an intriguing candidate because it can immortalize cells by binding and inactivating both the retinoblastoma (Rb) protein and p53, key control steps for proliferation and apoptosis, respectively. SV40 sequences have been found in approximately 50% of mesotheliomas.[76] However, a causal relationship has not been established, and epidemiologic studies to date have not shown an increase in the incidence of mesotheliomas in populations exposed to this virus.[77,78] Further complicating the analysis is the recognition that the presence of SV40 deoxyribonucleic acid (DNA) sequences alone does not prove the role of SV40 in tumor development. Viral proteins must be expressed and impair the function of cell proteins necessary for normal cell function. One group of investigators found no evidence of SV40 large T antigen protein expression in mesothelioma cell lines, and showed that some antibody preparations are contaminated by a protein of a size (90 kd) similar to SV40 large T antigen leading to false-positive signals.[79] At this time, SV40 is still a subject of intense discussion, more as a possible co-carcinogen with asbestos than as a primary cause of mesothelioma. See recent arguments addressing the evidence for[79a] and against[79b] SV40 as a cause of mesothelioma.

Cigarette smoking is not associated with an increased incidence of mesotheliomas.[80] Talc or man-made vitreous fibers (rock wool/slagwool and fiberglass) have not been found to be associated with occupational mesotheliomas.[81,82] Excess cases of mesotheliomas have been identified in oil refinery workers. This was once thought to be due to exposure to petroleum oil and its products, but is now attributed to occupational asbestos exposure.[83] Therapeutic radiation may cause or contribute to the development of mesothelioma. Multiple cases of patients who developed mesothelioma in the area of prior radiation have been reported.[84] However, a contribution of asbestos exposure cannot be excluded because analysis of tissues for asbestos bodies was not performed in most cases, and the demographics of the patients is similar to those with known asbestos-induced tumors.[85] Nonetheless, although a causal relationship cannot be proved, the data suggest that radiotherapy causes a small increase in the risk of developing mesothelioma.[85]

Environmental asbestos exposures have been associated with the development of mesothelioma in Australia and South Africa. Studies of household contacts of asbestos workers who develop mesothelioma have shown that these patients often have pulmonary asbestos concentrations similar to occupationally exposed individuals.[86] Exposure of occupants in buildings with asbestos-containing materials is generally not associated with increased asbestos fiber burden in the lung or an increase in mesothelioma incidence. However, there is one case report of mesothelioma in a teacher's aide whose only known exposure was working in a building that contained asbestos. Lung fiber burden was shown to be increased in this case.[86] In Turkey, an extraordinarily high incidence of mesothelioma is found in certain villages in central Turkey with exposure to erionite dust, a nonasbestos crystalline fibrous form of the mineral zeolite.[87] Finally, chronic inflammation of the pleura, as in familial Mediterranean fever, has been postulated to cause mesothelioma. At least four cases of mesothelioma have been reported in patients with this disease, presumedly due to recurrent serositis.[88] Asbestos may still be an underlying cause or contributing factor in patients without a clear occupational exposure given that fiber burden studies suggest that most urban dwellers have some asbestos fibers in their lungs.[89,90]

Although millions of workers have been exposed to significant amounts of asbestos, only a few develop mesothelioma, making it likely that there are genetic factors that increase susceptibility. Supporting the notion of genetic susceptibility is the identification of multiple clusters of this disease in families,[91] although clusters may also be explained by common environmental exposure to asbestos. Nonetheless, in the Cappadocian region of Turkey, where exposure to erionite is widespread, the susceptibility to mesothelioma appears to be inherited in an autosomal dominant pattern.[91a]

GENETIC CHARACTERISTICS

Mesothelioma is characterized by a high degree of aneuploidy, but there is no one oncogene or tumor suppressor gene that has yet been found to underlie the tumor. The gene for p53, a tumor suppressor gene mutated in most lung cancers and other solid tumors, is not frequently mutated in mesothelioma.[92] (For discussion of genetic abnormalities in lung cancer, see Chapter 42). Nonetheless, abnormalities in the p53 pathway may still be present. K-ras, a proto-oncogene frequently activated in lung cancer, is also not found to be abnormal in mesothelioma.[93] Cytogenetic and loss of heterozygosity studies show consistent losses of chromosomal regions, suggesting that these regions may contain genes for key tumor suppressors. Losses are consistently found in regions 1p, 3p, 6q, 9p, 13q,

15q, and 22q. Tumor suppressors located in those regions and found to be associated with mesothelioma include the neurofibromatosis type 2 (NF2) gene (22q12) and p16INIC4A-p14ARF (9p21).[94] In addition, chromosomal gains or activating mutations may be anticipated to lead to activation of proto-oncogenes. Oncogenes suspected to play a role in mesothelioma include those coding for c-*myc* and for growth factors or growth factor receptors (e.g., platelet-derived growth factor, epidermal growth factor receptor). Gene expression profiling may provide additional insights into genetic abnormalities critical for mesothelioma and, in so doing, may also provide prognostic information, guide therapy, and suggest future therapeutic approaches.[95,96]

The long latency period between exposure to asbestos and development of mesothelioma suggests that multiple genetic abnormalities are required. Unlike the situation for bronchogenic carcinoma where the natural history can be studied by repeatedly accessing the bronchial epithelium, the pleural space is not easily sampled, making the natural history of mesothelioma more opaque. From cell and animal studies, it appears that asbestos can injure the chromosomes both by generating reactive oxygen species that damage DNA and by mechanical breakage of chromosomes.[97] Asbestos fibers translocate from the lung to the pleural space and accumulate at the parietal pleura, where they can interact with mesothelial cells over decades. During this time, ongoing DNA and chromosomal damage in asbestos-exposed mesothelial cells may lead ultimately to malignant change. In the process, the cells develop unregulated proliferation and an increased resistance to apoptosis.[98] Losses of key genetic areas containing tumor suppressors may be critical steps in generating mesothelioma. If SV40 contributes to this process, it may be by binding and inactivating key regulators of cell growth and survival, Rb and p53 proteins.

CLINICAL FEATURES

The mean age at presentation is 60 years because of the long latency (usually 30 to 40 years) from the time of first exposure to asbestos to the development of clinically evident disease.[68] The incidence is higher in men, presumably because more men have worked in asbestos-related trades.

Symptoms and physical findings are generally not specific for the disease. Most patients present with nonpleuritic chest pain or dyspnea.[99] Compared to that of metastatic pleural diseases, the pain from mesothelioma can be severe, aching, and often very difficult to control. Less common complaints are cough, fevers, chills, sweats, and fatigue. Physical examination is usually only remarkable for signs related to the presence of a pleural effusion or mass. Later in the course of disease, one can often appreciate volume loss and decreased mobility of the chest wall on the side of the primary tumor. Occasionally, the tumor may extend directly into the chest wall, and be detected as a tender or nontender chest wall mass.

Laboratory findings are also nonspecific, and include anemia and thrombocytosis. Thrombocytosis (platelets >400,000/μL) can be seen in 40% of patients, may be due to production of interleukin-6 by the tumor, and augurs a poor prognosis.[100,101] Measurement of mesothelin-family

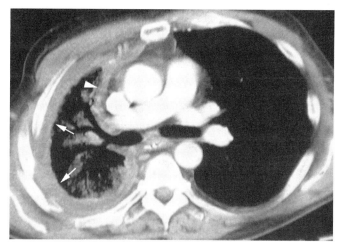

Figure 70.2 Mesothelioma. Axial thoracic computed tomography scan shows diffuse right pleural thickening (*arrows*) associated with marked volume loss in the right thorax. Note the presence of mediastinal pleural involvement (*arrowhead*).

proteins in serum shows future promise for the diagnosis of mesothelioma and for monitoring of disease progression.[102]

RADIOGRAPHIC EVALUATION

The most common findings on chest radiograph are a moderate to large unilateral pleural effusion or unilateral pleural thickening (nodular or smooth)[99] (Fig. 70.2). In a study of 99 patients with malignant mesothelioma, the most common finding on CT was a rindlike extension of tumor on the pleural surfaces (70%).[103] Other findings included circumferential lung encasement by multiple nodules (28%), pleural thickening with an irregular margin between the lung and pleura (26%), and pleural thickening with pleural-based nodules (20%). Invasion of soft tissues and the chest wall with rib destruction may also be seen. As the disease progresses and the lung becomes more encased with tumor, there is often volume loss with a shift of the mediastinum toward the side of the primary tumor (see Fig. 70.2). Signs of lymphatic metastasis may be seen, but are more commonly evident late in the course of disease. Further tumor progression may lead to invasion through the mediastinum into the contralateral chest. It is important to note that pleural plaques are often not visible; only 28% of patients have radiographically apparent plaques.[104] Large mediastinal lymph nodes are more consistent with metastatic disease than with mesothelioma. Mediastinal adenopathy as the initial presentation of mesothelioma has been reported, but is exceedingly rare.[105] Radiographic features that favor the diagnosis of malignant mesothelioma over metastatic pleural disease were found by multivariate analysis to include rindlike pleural involvement, mediastinal pleural involvement, and pleural thickness more than 1 cm.[103]

Some clinicians prefer MRI over CT for staging and preoperative evaluation because, as reported in one study, MRI may demonstrate extent of disease and chest wall and diaphragmatic invasion better than CT (Fig. 70.3).[106] However, this has not yet been shown to confer an important clinical advantage. In an earlier study, Heelan and coworkers[107] also found MRI superior in detection of tissue

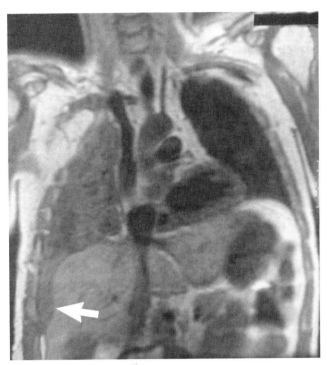

Figure 70.3 Mesothelioma. Magnetic resonance image of the same patient as in Figure 70.2 with malignant mesothelioma showing invasion across the diaphragm by tumor (*arrow*).

invasion in these areas; nonetheless, they found no improvement in staging and no alteration in therapy due to its use.

[18]F-Fluorodeoxyglucose PET imaging shows promise as a tool to differentiate benign from malignant disease and as an adjunctive tool for staging (Fig. 70.4). In one study, it was found to be superior to CT for detecting lymph node involvement.[108] However, in another study of 63 patients with malignant mesothelioma, the sensitivity for identification of local extent of tumor was only 19%, and for determination of nodal status was 11%.[109] The rare distant metastasis was identified with this technique. Interestingly, these authors also found that a high standard uptake value in the primary tumor correlated with N2 disease.

In patients being considered for an extensive debulking procedure such as extrapleural pneumonectomy, we believe every effort should be made to define the extent of disease. A combination of the imaging techniques may be necessary for determining the best approach to the patient.[110] In addition to CT, we therefore routinely perform MRI and PET imaging of patients being evaluated for surgery as well as endoscopic ultrasound with biopsy of suspicious nodes.

DIAGNOSIS

Effusions in these patients are usually exudative in nature and are bloody in more than half of the cases. Pleural fluid cytology is often the first diagnostic test performed but is diagnostic in less than 30% of cases.[111] Pleural biopsy by a closed technique is only marginally better,[99,111] but may be improved using CT guidance.[112] In one study in which patients were randomly assigned to closed pleural biopsy or CT-guided biopsy, mesothelioma was diagnosed by closed pleural biopsy with a sensitivity of 55% (6/11) and by CT-guided biopsy with a sensitivity of 88% (8/9); although the difference was not significant because of small numbers, a similar diagnostic advantage of CT-guided biopsy was found for other pleural malignancies.[39] However, even with current immunohistochemical stains, mesothelioma may be difficult to differentiate from metastatic adenocarcinoma or benign pleural inflammation. In those cases, surgical biopsy is required to establish a definitive diagnosis. A surgical biopsy not only provides larger specimens for immunohistochemistry and electron microscopy,[113] but also provides critical information about the biologic behavior of the tumor. The behavior of mesothelioma is unique in that it usually starts on the parietal pleural surface with multiple colonies of cells that coalesce and spread to the visceral pleura. Distant metastases are generally a very late finding. In contrast, metastatic adenocarcinoma is usually more prominent on the visceral pleural surface and often associated with distant metastasis. Benign inflammation lacks the surface irregularity usually (but not always) seen with malignant disease.

The preferred approach for surgical biopsy is via pleuroscopy (see Chapter 23). Not only does pleuroscopy have the advantage of obtaining large samples, but also it permits the drainage of effusions and the freeing up of a trapped lung.[114,115] In addition, if the lung is not trapped, talc can be insufflated at the end of the procedure to achieve a pleurodesis. Intraoperative talc insufflation has been reported to have a greater than 95% success rate of preventing recurrent pleural effusion in this setting[58] and does not interfere with later attempts at tumor debulking. The insertion site of the pleuroscope is an important consideration if tumor debulking is attempted in the future because of the tendency of mesotheliomas to seed biopsy and chest tube sites.[111] Misdiagnosis with pleuroscopy has rarely been reported and in those cases was thought to be due to adhesions preventing access to the primary tumor.[114] If pleuroscopy cannot be performed due to the absence of at least a small pleural effusion, an incisional biopsy has an equally high diagnostic yield.

PATHOLOGIC FEATURES

The dilemma for the pathologist is in differentiating mesothelioma from metastatic adenocarcinoma or reactive mesothelium. Because of the difficulties in establishing the diagnosis in some cases, an expert panel of pathologists from the United States and Canada was formed.[116] In their statement, they stressed the need for the pathologist to have information about the biologic behavior of the tumor from the radiographic and intraoperative observations. In addition, they stressed the need to obtain larger specimens to permit multiple immunohistochemical stains and electron microscopy. Ultrastructural features seen by electron microscopy that are typical of mesothelioma include cytoplasmic tonofilaments and long, sinuous, branching microvilli.[117] In contrast, the microvilli of adenocarcinomas are relatively short, wide, and straight. For electron microscopy, some biopsy material must be preserved in glutaraldehyde, whereas formalin-fixed specimens can be analyzed by immunohistochemistry. Although a variety of immunohistochemical stains have been used to differentiate

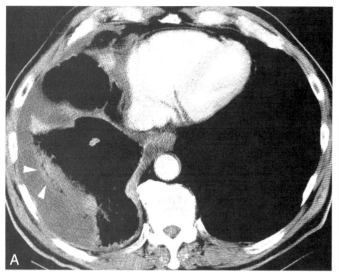

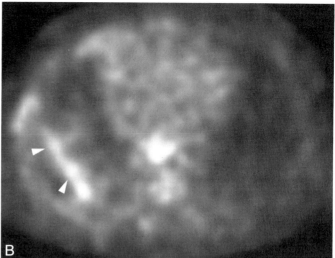

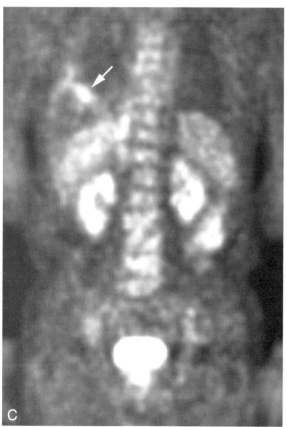

Figure 70.4 Mesothelioma. **A,** Axial computed tomography scan showing mesothelioma of the right chest with effusion and thickened visceral pleura with underlying pulmonary atelectasis (*arrowheads*). **B,** Axial positron emission tomography (PET) scan indicates high activity in the area of thickened pleura, indicating likely involvement by tumor, suggesting at least a T2 lesion by International Mesothelioma Interest Group staging (*arrowheads*). The bright central uptake appears to indicate malignant involvement, either of a mediastinal lymph node or mediastinal pleura. **C,** Coronal view of PET scan also showing high activity of visceral pleura in fissure (*arrow*). (Courtesy of Michael B. Gotway, MD, Department of Radiology, University of California, San Francisco.)

adenocarcinoma of the lung and mesothelioma, none is specific, especially with less well-differentiated tumors. Use of a panel of immunohistochemical stains is recommended.[116] In a study analyzing a variety of cancers, including 60 epithelioid mesotheliomas and 50 lung adenocarcinomas, it was concluded that the best combination of markers for discrimination of these tumors based on sensitivity and specificity are calretinin and cytokeratin 5/6 (or WT1) (favoring mesothelioma) and CEA and MOC-31 (or B72.3, Ber-EP4, or BG-8) (favoring adenocarcinoma).[118] Another marker, mesothelin, has been found to be a highly sensitive positive marker for epithelioid mesotheliomas; however, as with many markers previously studied, it has low specificity.[119] Of note, most of these studies do not include analysis of the less common cell types of mesothelioma, biphasic and sarcomatous.

PROGNOSIS AND STAGING

The median survival for patients with malignant mesothelioma is between 4 and 12 months from the time of diagnosis.[120] Regardless of therapy, patients with the epithelial cell type do best and those with the sarcomatous cell type the worst, with mixed or biphasic falling between the two

Table 70.4 International Mesothelioma Interest Group (IMIG) Staging System for Malignant Pleural Mesothelioma

T1	Tumor involving ipsilateral parietal pleura
	T1a No involvement of visceral pleura
	T1b Some scattered foci involving visceral pleura
T2	Tumor involving entire ipsilateral pleura, both visceral and parietal
	Plus, invasion of diaphragmatic muscle
	Or, confluent involvement of visceral pleura, including the fissures
	Or, invasion from visceral pleura into pulmonary parenchyma
T3	Tumor locally advanced but potentially resectable
T4	Tumor locally advanced but technically unresectable
NX	Regional nodes cannot be assessed
N0	No lymph node metastasis
N1	Metastasis to ipsilateral bronchopulmonary or hilar lymph nodes
N2	Metastasis to subcarinal or ipsilateral mediastinal nodes
N3	Metastasis to contralateral mediastinal or internal mammary nodes, or to any supraclavicular node
MX	Distant metastasis cannot be assessed
M0	No distant metastasis
M1	Distant metastasis present

Stage:	Description:
Stage I	
Ia	T1aN0M0
Ib	T1bN0M0
Stage II	T2N0M0
Stage III	Any T3M0
	Any N1M0
	Any N2M0
Stage IV	Any T4
	Any N3
	Any M1

From Rusch VW for the International Mesothelioma Interest Group: A proposed new international TNM staging system for malignant pleural mesothelioma. Chest 108:1122–1128, 1995.

Table 70.5 The Brigham Staging System for Malignant Pleural Mesothelioma

Stage	Description
I	Completely resectable
II	Positive surgical margins and/or intrapleural adenopathy*
III	Local extension and extrapleural disease
IV	Distant metastasis

* Intrapleural adenopathy is any node present in the resected pleural envelope.
From Sugarbaker DJ, Norberto JJ, Swanson SJ: Surgical staging and work-up of patients with diffuse malignant pleural mesothelioma. Semin Thorac Cardiovasc Surg 9:356–360, 1997.

other types.[120] By univariate analysis, age 75 years or greater, male gender, smoking history, advanced stages above stage I disease, Karnofsky Performance Scale score less than 70, white blood cell count greater than or equal to 8450/μL, and LDH level greater than or equal to 500 IU/L have all been associated with a worse prognosis.[121] In addition, pathologic findings of microvessel density and of tumor necrosis, which was found to correlate with vessel density, are poor prognostic factors.[122,123]

Staging continues to be controversial. Prior to the proposal of a tumor-node-metastasis (TNM)-based staging system by the International Mesothelioma Interest Group,[124] there had been at least six other systems proposed for staging of mesotheliomas. None of the six was clearly shown to predict survival, including the most widely used Butchart staging system.[125] The TNM-based staging system is organized in a manner similar to the system currently in use for non–small cell carcinoma of the lung (Table 70.4). Further surgical studies at the Memorial Sloan Kettering Cancer Center supported the prognostic value of this system.[126,127] For example, patients with stage I disease had

a median survival of 30 months and those with stage IV had a median survival of 8 months.[127] However, the Brigham group found it less useful for determination of surgical resectability, and have proposed yet another staging system that is also widely used[128] (Table 70.5). It should be noted that this staging system requires resection to determine the involvement of surgical margins, limiting its applicability mostly to postsurgical staging.

Staging systems may be supplemented by prognostic scoring systems that do not require surgical staging. Prognostic scoring systems proposed by the European Organisation for Research and Treatment of Cancer (EORTC) and by the Cancer and Leukemia Group B (CALGB) incorporate performance status, histopathology, and other laboratory studies.[101]

THERAPY AND PALLIATION

Surgical Therapy

The two goals of surgical therapy at the current time are palliation of symptoms and debulking of tumor with therapeutic intent. Many believe that therapy should follow the paradigm of treatment developed for ovarian cancer because of the similarities in biologic behavior of the cancer and the similar embryologic origin of the cells of the primary tumor.[129] In both diseases, surgical resection alone does not prevent disease recurrence. However, the approach of surgical debulking followed by systemic chemotherapy has shown significant success for the treatment of ovarian cancer. For surgical debulking of mesotheliomas, two surgical approaches are commonly employed, pleurectomy with decortication or extrapleural pneumonectomy (EPP). Pleurectomy with decortication removes all gross disease from all pleural surfaces and preserves the underlying lung. EPP entails en bloc removal of the lung along with surrounding parietal pleura, pericardium, and diaphragm. The pericardium and diaphragm are then replaced by synthetic grafts. These are both technically challenging procedures and should be performed only by surgeons with extensive experience. EPP is especially difficult, and was originally associated with an unacceptably high morbidity of 30%. However, with advances in surgical, anesthetic, and critical care techniques, and more exacting patient selection, experienced centers now report mortality rates of 4%, comparable to standard pneumonectomy.[130] Both pleurectomy with decortication and EPP are accomplished through an extended posterolateral thoracotomy, and, as mentioned earlier, previous talc pleurodesis is not a contraindication to either procedure and may occasionally facilitate the separation of the pleura from the chest wall.

Preoperative evaluation of patients considered for surgery includes a thorough assessment of tumor stage, cardiac function, and pulmonary function. Most surgery is confined to those patients with the epithelial cell morphology. If debulking surgery is to be of benefit, it is essential that the tumor is early stage and confined to one hemithorax. Chest CT or MRI is the usual first step in staging. MRI is preferred by some centers for assessment of transdiaphragmatic extension of tumor (see Fig. 70.3), and many now request fluorodeoxyglucose PET as well (see Fig. 70.4). Recognition that mediastinal lymph node involvement is a poor prognostic sign has prompted centers to require either cervical mediastinoscopy or endoscopic ultrasound with biopsy of suspicious nodes prior to EPP. In addition, some groups perform laparoscopy prior to opening the chest because mesothelioma often spreads through the diaphragm and seeds the peritoneum.[131]

For patients who successfully complete such extensive screening, a few large series suggest that surgical debulking procedures may provide a survival advantage. In the first studies in which both surgeries were performed, it appeared as if pleurectomy was superior, with better survival than EPP.[126,132] However, in a follow-up report, the same investigators found that there was no difference in median survival between the two surgical debulking procedures.[127] Both series showed that failure after pleurectomy is more often local, whereas failure after EPP is more often extrathoracic. These results underscore the difficulty in eradicating mesothelioma with surgery alone.

Based on such studies showing that surgery alone is insufficient to cure mesothelioma, Sugarbaker and colleagues[130] at the Brigham and Women's Hospital have developed a strategy of tumor debulking using EPP followed by chemotherapy and high-dose radiation therapy to destroy residual tumor cells. This multimodality strategy was reported to yield a median survival of 19 months and a 5-year survival of 15%. However, patients with all three positive variables (an epithelial cell type, clean margins after resection, and negative extrapleural lymph nodes) had a median survival of 51 months and a 5-year survival of 46%. Of note, patients with sarcomatous cell type did poorly. Although these results are exciting, they have been criticized for selection bias. For example, only 23% of patients had involvement of mediastinal lymph nodes. In contrast, Rusch and Venkatraman[127] found nodal involvement in 57% and Pass and colleagues[133] found nodal involvement in 79% of their patients. Given the lack of prospective randomized studies comparing surgery with or without adjuvant therapy to medical management or supportive care, the therapeutic or even palliative benefit of surgical debulking followed by chemotherapy and radiation therapy remains unknown. Some critics point out that there are some long-term survivors without treatment and that surgery may actually harm patients without improving survival.[134] For example, in one unrandomized prospective study, 52 patients receiving surgery and other treatments (chemotherapy or radiotherapy) were compared to 64 patients without treatment. Although the treatments were believed to provide palliation, there was no significant difference in survival between treated and untreated patients.[135] In the untreated group, median survival was 18 months, and 7 of the 64 patients lived for 4 years (11% 4-year survival). Until randomized studies are performed, the best treatment plan for patients with mesothelioma will remain unknown.

Surgical debulking has been combined with a variety of other approaches to kill residual tumor cells on the surface of the thoracic cavity, including hyperthermia and photodynamic therapy, without convincing success. Strategies employing hyperthermia usually involve heating of chemotherapeutic agents to 40° to 42° C followed by instillation into the thoracic or peritoneal cavity after surgical debulking. This may be associated with significant morbidity such as has been reported with instillation of cisplatin and doxorubicin after debulking.[136] Complications include the development of bronchopleural fistula, diaphragmatic rupture, wound dehiscence, persistent air leakage, and chylous effusion. Others have tried whole-body hyperthermia combined with chemotherapy (the patient heated to 41.8° C plus ifosfamide, carboplatin, and etoposide, every 4 weeks).[137] Although most of the treatment toxicities were manageable and included severe neutropenia, one patient died due to sepsis and the 2-year overall survival was only 20%.

Photodynamic therapy requires preoperative administration of a drug that sensitizes cells to a particular wavelength of light. The patient is then taken to the operating room, as much of the tumor is removed as possible, and a light source is placed in the chest. Serious complications include myocardial perforation and systemic capillary leak syndrome. In a Phase III trial conducted by Pass and colleagues,[133] patients were randomized to pleurectomy and decortication with or without intraoperative photodynamic therapy. The authors found no difference in median survival or time to progression between the two groups. More recently, a newer photosensitizing agent (Foscan) has been studied in a dose-escalation Phase I trial. Foscan was injected 6 days before surgery. Fourteen patients were treated at the maximal tolerated dose without significant complications.[138] Phase II studies were believed to be warranted.

At this time the value of surgical debulking and adjunctive measures such as hyperthermia, photodynamic therapy, chemotherapy, and radiation therapy are not known. It may be that an approach of debulking followed by some modality to eradicate residual tumor will improve outcome. However, until randomized trials are undertaken and a consensus is reached on staging, this will not be known with confidence.

Chemotherapy

Most patients with mesothelioma are not candidates for surgical or radiotherapy treatment, and chemotherapy is their only option. Choosing the best agents based on trials is difficult because the number of patients in such trials is usually small and because staging systems are not uniform. In two extensive reviews of chemotherapy trials,[139,140] antimetabolites were found to have the highest antitumor activity, with platinum compounds and plant alkaloids showing the least.

Combination chemotherapies were not superior to single-agent chemotherapy.[139] Until recently, the best combinations appeared to be cisplatin with gemcitabine[141] or cisplatin with irinotecan.[142] With both combinations, in initial trials a significant number of patients had improvement in symptoms such as chest pain and dyspnea, but there was no significant improvement in survival. A follow-up multicenter trial of cisplatin and gemcitabine showed similar results, with nearly half of the patients noting symptom improvement, 33% a partial response, and 60% stable disease; again, there was no survival benefit compared to historical controls.[143] Similarly, treatment with the combination of gemcitabine and oxaliplatin has been reported improve symptoms, but not significantly improve survival (median survival of 13 months).[144]

There is now considerable excitement about a new antifolate, pemetrexed, when used together with cisplatin. The use of this combination has been compared to cisplatin alone in a large Phase III study of 456 patients.[145] Response rates were significantly better in the pemetrexed/cisplatin arm than in the cisplatin-alone arm (41.3% vs. 16.7%), and survival was significantly better as well (median survival 12.1 months versus 9.3 months). Importantly, the addition of folic acid and vitamin B_{12} significantly reduced toxicity without altering survival benefit.[145]

Newer Agents under Study. Studies of the molecular biology of mesothelioma and the cellular mechanisms leading to a malignant phenotype have led to the identification of several possible therapeutic targets for treatment of this disease. Some of these are already under investigation in clinical trials. For example, several receptor tyrosine kinases are aberrantly expressed in these tumors, including the epidermal growth factor receptor.[146] Inhibitors of these proteins are now available in oral form and are being evaluated in patients with mesothelioma. Other novel agents targeting growth factors found to be overexpressed in mesothelioma are under investigation. In addition to epidermal growth factor, these targets include vascular endothelial growth factor and its receptor and platelet-derived growth factor receptor.[139]

Radiation Therapy

Although in vitro studies suggest that mesothelioma is sensitive to radiation,[147] the clinical experience reported by radiation oncologists suggests that it is an especially radio-resistant tumor. In addition, radiation of the involved chest is limited by the presence of radiosensitive organs. As a consequence, its use appears limited to adjunctive therapy for patients who have undergone EPP, and to palliative treatment of painful chest wall lesions. In patients with malignant pleural mesothelioma, radiotherapy can be useful in the palliation of symptoms of chest pain and painful masses. In addition, prophylactic chest wall irradiation has been shown in a randomized trial to reduce the incidence of chest wall recurrences at incision sites.[148] An area of active ongoing research is the role of high-dose hemithorax irradiation after EPP for early-stage disease. This approach has resulted in a marked reduction in local tumor recurrences. Nonetheless, almost half of patients subsequently developed distant metastases.[149]

Immunotherapy

It is known that the immune response plays an important role in the control of malignant tumor growth and elimination of malignant cells. This knowledge has prompted a number of investigators to study the intrapleural instillation of cytokines to stimulate an antitumor immune response. Cytokine treatment is limited by the short half-life of most cytokines, necessitating repeated injections or continuous infusion via a pleural catheter. In a prospective multicenter study using intrapleural interferon-γ twice weekly for 2 months, Boutin and associates[150] reported a response rate of 45% in stage I disease. With intrapleural infusions of interleukin-2, Goey and colleagues[151] found a partial response in 4 of 21 patients and an overall survival of 16 months. In both cases, side effects were minimal and consisted primarily of fever and constitutional symptoms. Studies in animals suggest that interferons have an antiproliferative effect on mesothelioma cells and enhance the cytotoxic effect of cisplatin. The results from these studies led to the development of a Phase II trial of cisplatin-doxorubicin and interferon alfa-2b in advanced malignant mesothelioma.[152] The overall response rate was 29% and the median survival was 9.3 months, with a 1-year survival of 45% and 2-year survival of 34%. However, at least one episode of severe myelosuppression was seen in 76% of patients, limiting the application of this treatment.[152]

Gene Therapy

Gene therapy strategies that have been investigated for the treatment of mesothelioma include genetic immunopotentiation, mutation compensation, and molecular chemotherapy. Genetic immunopotentiation employs the genetic induction of an inflammatory antitumor response. For example, vaccinia virus carrying the gene for interleukin-2 has been studied in patients to determine toxicity.[153] Not only was intratumoral injection well tolerated, but 50% of tumors were found to have T-cell infiltration. Mutation compensation attempts to block or replace abnormally expressed genes. The best example of this in mesothelioma is compensation for the absence of p16 gene expression, a consistent abnormality in mesothelioma.[94] Reexpression of p16INK4A using an adenoviral vector improved survival in a murine model of mesothelioma.[154] Molecular chemotherapy is a technique of genetically modifying cells to make them susceptible to a drug. Investigators at the University of Pennsylvania are instilling an adenoviral vector containing the herpes simplex thymidine kinase *(HSVtk)* gene into the pleural space of patients.[155] This virus is taken up by mesothelial cells and the *HSVtk* gene product makes the cells metabolize ganciclovir to a toxic by-product. In humans, the viral uptake is patchy, and repeated dosing is limited by the development of immunity to the virus. However, work using a murine model suggests that repeated dosing may actually improve survival despite the presence of preexisting immunity to the virus.[156] Investigators at Louisiana State University are using a similar strategy, but instead instill terminally irradiated ovarian cancer cells transfected with the *HSVtk* gene into the pleural space of patients.[157] In clinical trials, these cells have been shown to adhere preferentially to mesothelioma cells, where they may then be able to exert an antitumor effect.[158] Animal studies suggest this strategy exerts an antitumor effect through a direct toxic effect on tumor cells, and also perhaps through an immune-mediated antitumor effect.[159]

Palliative Therapy

Pain, dyspnea, and cough are common and often disabling. The pain can be so severe that the doses of narcotics required for control may suppress respiration or lead to aspiration. If a specific site of chest wall invasion can be identified, radiation to that site may effectively control pain. However, the pain is often diffuse or multifocal. In these cases, the placement of a chronic epidural catheter with instillation of a narcotic can provide dramatic relief without the clouded sensorium associated with narcotics.

Dyspnea and cough are often due to large pleural effusions. The approach to palliation has been described for malignant pleural effusions earlier in this chapter, and some of these options are applicable to the effusions due to mesothelioma as well (see Table 70.3). Effusions due to mesothelioma can usually be controlled with pleurodesis or placement of an indwelling catheter (Pleurx; Denver Biomedical, Golden, Colorado). Pleurodesis with talc is an effective and relatively inexpensive agent for this task. As described earlier, it can be administered as a slurry through a chest tube or as an aerosol during thoracoscopy with equal effect. Regardless, with either technique, the affected lung must be capable of expanding so that the visceral and parietal pleura are in contact. Placement of a Pleurx pleural catheter for chronic pleural drainage is another option for these patients. With this system, an indwelling pleural catheter is placed during an outpatient procedure. Patients access the catheter at home at regular intervals to drain accumulated pleural fluid. This provides symptomatic relief without the need for hospitalization in most cases, and over a period of weeks to months may produce pleural symphysis.[60,160]

CHEMOPREVENTION

The existence of populations with known exposure to asbestos suggests that an effective chemoprevention strategy could reduce the incidence of mesothelioma. In one such study, former workers of the Wittenoom asbestos mines of Australia were assigned randomly to daily use of vitamin A (retinol) or β-carotene, without a placebo group.[161] Interestingly, in each group of approximately 250 persons, 9 cases of mesothelioma would have been expected. In the group taking retinol, there were only 3 mesotheliomas, whereas in the group taking β-carotene, there were 12. In the groups who were not in the study, the incidence of mesothelioma was similar to the expected incidence. Studies of retinol are continuing. Such studies have the potential of preventing a disease for which curative therapies do not yet exist.

Additional information on clinical and basic research concerning mesothelioma can be found in reports of biannual meetings of the International Mesothelioma Interest Group.[161a] Web sites that provide additional information include the following: the International Mesothelioma Interest Group (http://www.imig.org); the National Cancer Institute (http://www.nci.nih.gov); and Oncolink (Abramson Cancer Center, University of Pennsylvania) (http://www.oncolink.com).

SOLITARY FIBROUS TUMOR OF THE PLEURA

The term *solitary fibrous tumor* is now used in preference to earlier terms such as "benign mesothelioma" or "localized mesothelioma" for several reasons: to distinguish it clearly from malignant mesothelioma, to acknowledge that it may contain malignancy within it, and also to recognize that its cellular origin is more likely from pleuripotential fibroblasts than from mesothelial cells.[1,162] These localized tumors of the pleura are more rare than malignant mesotheliomas, accounting for 8% of all benign pathologies of the chest and 10% of all primary pleural neoplasms.[163] The majority of solitary fibrous tumors act in a benign fashion (80–90%) whereas the remainder act as malignant tumors.[162] More than 50% cause no symptoms and are identified as an incidental finding on radiographic examination.[164] When symptoms do occur, they are usually chronic and related to the mechanical effects of the tumor. Most commonly noted are cough, dyspnea, and chest pain.[162,165]

Paraneoplastic syndromes are associated with this tumor. Hypertrophic osteoarthropathy has been described in 14%[165] to 19%[162] of cases and usually resolves over a few months following resection of the tumor.[162,166] Hypoglycemia has been described in between 4%[162] and 14%[165] of patients with solitary fibrous tumors, although the percentage may be elevated because the hypoglycemia may bring the patient to medical attention. The hypoglycemia arises from the production by the tumor of insulin-like growth factor-II, which has insulin activity peripherally and at the liver.[167] As for other non–islet cell tumors associated with hypoglycemia, the hypoglycemia can be treated best by full resection of the tumor.[168] If this is not possible or while awaiting surgical resection, patients have been treated successfully with corticosteroids, which can suppress insulin-like growth factor-II production.[168]

Most solitary fibrous tumors arise from the visceral pleura, but some arise from the parietal.[162,165] In cases in which they appear within the lung parenchyma, the tumor border may be attached to the pleura via a pedicle or stalk. They are usually round and firm with clear borders, and can grow to be several centimeters in diameter. On cut section, the tumor has a fibrous whorled appearance with occasional calcification, hemorrhage, and central necrosis. Cells are elongated and spindle shaped on histologic examination.[166] By immunohistochemistry, the solitary fibrous tumor can be distinguished from malignant mesothelioma by its staining for vimentin and CD34 (a hematopoietic progenitor cell antigen) and its lack of staining for keratin.[165,169]

Radiographic evaluation usually reveals a solitary circumscribed and homogeneous lesion (Fig. 70.5). It rarely may occupy the entire hemothorax, but the average size is about 6 cm.[166] In one study, most of the masses appeared to have an atypical appearance for pleural-based tumors in that they appeared to form an acute angle with the chest wall on radiographic examinations.[170] This may be due to the size of the lesions and the tendency for them to hang from a pedicle into the lung.[170] In some cases the mass may be mobile due to the

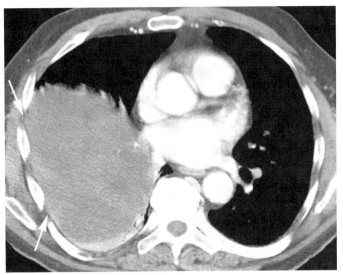

Figure 70.5 Solitary fibrous tumor of the pleura. Axial computed tomography scan shows a large, somewhat heterogeneous mass in the right lower chest with extensive chest wall contact (*arrows*). (Courtesy of Michael B. Gotway, MD, Department of Radiology, University of California, San Francisco.)

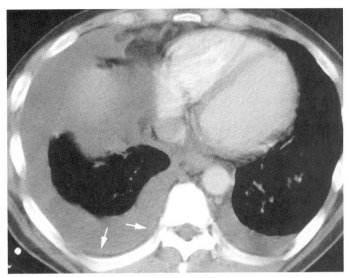

Figure 70.6 Primary effusion lymphoma. On axial computed tomography scan, the malignancy is manifest by bilateral effusions. *Arrows* indicate a minimally thickened parietal pleura, without nodularity. (Courtesy of Michael B. Gotway, MD, Department of Radiology, University of California, San Francisco.)

pedicle, and occasionally movement can be documented using decubitus views. CT scans may reveal heterogeneous areas of enhancement in some larger tumors that correlate pathologically with vascularity, and areas of low attenuation that correlate with cystic necrosis and hemorrhage.[171] All have contours that are smooth and lobulated without evidence of invasion into underlying tissues. Occasionally dense calcification is seen.[171] MRI findings are consistent with a fibrous tumor, with low signal on T1- and T2-weighted images.[172,173] There is little information about the use of PET to differentiate solitary fibrous tumors from malignant mesothelioma. However, the few cases in the literature support the finding of low or absent uptake of fluorodeoxyglucose on PET imaging of the solitary fibrous tumor.[174]

The diagnosis is strongly suggested by the chest radiograph and CT scan. If a paraneoplastic syndrome is present together with a large tumor of the pleural space, the diagnosis of solitary fibrous tumor is likely. Needle biopsy may be unhelpful and, even if malignancy is present within a portion of the tumor, may miss the areas of concern. Surgery is advised in most cases both for diagnosis by excision and for definitive treatment.

Surgical resection will be curative in most cases. When the tumor arises from the visceral pleura, surgical resection may involve wedge resection or lobectomy. Recurrences do occur,[164,175] and have been documented up to 17 years after resection, sometimes with malignant transformation.[162,166] Yearly chest radiographs are recommended to follow these patients after resection. Sometimes, return of a paraneoplastic syndrome can accompany a recurrence of the solitary fibrous tumor.[165]

PRIMARY EFFUSION LYMPHOMA

Primary effusion lymphoma (PEL) is a type of high-grade B-cell lymphoma that grows within the serous body cavi-

ties (pleural, peritoneal, and pericardial) without a detectable tumor mass (Fig. 70.6). Because of its tropism for serosal spaces, it is considered one of the entities within the group of body cavity lymphomas.[176] PEL is a body cavity lymphoma caused by the human herpes virus 8 (HHV8),[176] the same virus that is the etiologic cause of Kaposi's sarcoma. Most cases of PEL are found in homosexual men with advanced human immunodeficiency virus (HIV) disease. In a few cases, PEL has also been described in HIV-negative patients, usually elderly persons of Eastern European/Mediterranean descent, in an epidemiologic pattern similar to that of HIV-negative, classic Kaposi's sarcoma.[176] Many PELs in HIV-positive patients are coinfected by Epstein-Barr virus (EBV),[176] suggesting a cooperative etiologic role between HHV8 and EBV. Nonetheless, the HHV8 is thought to be the primary etiologic factor and the identification of HHV8 is required for the diagnosis of PEL.[176]

PEL tends to occur as a late manifestation of HIV infection. Therefore, it should be considered in patients with advanced HIV disease with large exudative lymphocytic effusions. CT scan will show a small degree of pleural thickening, without any tumor mass or mediastinal adenopathy[177] (see Fig. 70.6). Pleural fluid may have a very elevated LDH level.[1] Cytologic examination will show pleomorphic large lymphocytes and suggest the diagnosis. The lymphocytes stain negatively for B- and T-cell antigens. Identification of HHV8 can be performed by extracting DNA from involved tissues followed by Southern blot analysis, by in situ hybridization of slides from paraffin-embedded samples, and by in situ reverse transcriptase–polymerase chain reaction of cytologic smears or cell blocks.[178]

Treatment is usually attempted with chemotherapy. In one study of HIV-positive patients with PEL, a CHOP-like regimen (cyclophosphamide, doxorubicin, vincristine, and prednisone) achieved a complete remission in 42% of patients, with a median survival of 6 months; this outcome was similar to that for immunoblastic lymphoma but worse than that for centroblastic B-cell lymphoma.[179] Other treatment options include highly active antiretroviral therapy, although this has no effect on HHV8 replication.[176] Also, broad-spectrum antiviral agents are now under consideration in patients with PEL.[180]

PYOTHORAX-ASSOCIATED LYMPHOMA

Pyothorax-associated lymphoma is an HHV8-negative body cavity lymphoma, associated with EBV.[176] It is a high-grade non-Hodgkin's lymphoma occurring as a mass in the pleural space of patients with long-standing chronic pleural inflammation usually following artificial pneumothorax for pleuropulmonary tuberculosis.[181] This entity is mainly seen in Japan but has also been reported in western countries.[181,182] The few series available report a strong association with EBV, with 70% of tumors having evidence of EBV in one study.[183] The cell type is usually B cell, with frequent plasmacytoid features, but occasionally an aberrant dual B/T phenotype may be seen.[182] As opposed to PEL, which is associated with systemic immunodeficiency as from HIV infection or old age, pyothorax-associated lymphoma is associated with a local pleural immunosuppression and antigenic stimulation.[176]

A relatively large review of 106 patients with pyothorax-associated lymphoma in Japan showed the median age at the time of diagnosis to be 64 years (range, 46 to 82 years).[183] In these patients, there was at least a 20-year history of pyothorax (mean 37 years, maximum 64 years), and patients were predominately male (12:1). All had a history of chronic inflammation of the pleura, either due to artificial pneumothorax for treatment of pulmonary tuberculosis (80%) or tuberculous pleuritis (17%). Fever and back pain were the common symptoms on presentation, and chest radiograph or CT scan showed a localized pleural mass in an area of chronic pleural disease. There are no large series evaluating specific treatments for this disease. In some reports, it appears that patients may do better with radiotherapy than with chemotherapy.[184,185] In a review of 106 patient records, patients underwent a variety of treatments, including surgical resection, chemotherapy with a CHOP-like regimen, and radiotherapy.[183] Patients appeared to respond initially to chemotherapy, but clinical outcome was poor, with a 5-year survival of 22%.[183] In one patient undergoing treatment, the serum EBV load measured by a quantitative real-time polymerase chain reaction correlated well with tumor size, suggesting that monitoring of the serum EBV load might be helpful in the management of EBV-positive patients with this disease.[185]

SUMMARY

Metastatic, secondary tumors of the pleura are a common clinical problem for the pulmonologist. Diagnosis is now often made from core needle specimens obtained using CT or ultrasound guidance or from biopsies obtained under direct visualization during pleuroscopy. When treatment of the primary tumor fails, talc pleurodesis or placement of an indwelling catheter often provides effective palliation. Conversely, primary tumors of the pleura remain uncommon and, when malignant, are difficult to diagnose and treat. Diagnosis is aided by intraoperative and radiographic observations that provide information as to the biologic behavior of the tumor and by staining pathologic specimens with a panel of immunohistochemical stains. Staging remains controversial, and treatment is often frustratingly ineffective. However, new understanding of the molecular biology of these tumors provides hope for major advances in both diagnosis and treatment in the near future.

REFERENCES

1. Light RW: Pleural Diseases (4th ed). Philadelphia: Lippincott Williams & Wilkins, 2001.
2. Rodriguez-Panadero F, Borderas Naranjo F, Lopez Mejias J: Pleural metastatic tumours and effusions: Frequency and pathogenic mechanisms in a post-mortem series. Eur Respir J 2:366–369, 1989.
3. Johnston WW: The malignant pleural effusion: A review of cytopathologic diagnoses of 584 specimens from 472 consecutive patients. Cancer 56:905–909, 1985.
4. Meyer PC: Metastatic carcinoma of the pleura. Thorax 21:437–443, 1966.
5. Marel M, Stastny B, Melinova L, et al: Diagnosis of pleural effusions: Experience with clinical studies, 1986 to 1990. Chest 107:1598–1603, 1995.
6. Lim E, Ali A, Theodorou P, et al: Intraoperative pleural lavage cytology is an independent prognostic indicator for staging non-small cell lung cancer. J Thorac Cardiovasc Surg 127:1113–1118, 2004.
7. Yano S, Shinohara H, Herbst RS, et al: Production of experimental malignant pleural effusions is dependent on invasion of the pleura and expression of vascular endothelial growth factor/vascular permeability factor by human lung cancer cells. Am J Pathol 157:1893–1903, 2000.
8. Antunes G, Neville E, Duffy J, et al: BTS guidelines for the management of malignant pleural effusions. Thorax 58:II29–II38, 2003.
9. Chernow B, Sahn SA: Carcinomatous involvement of the pleura: An analysis of 96 patients. Am J Med 63:695–702, 1977.
10. Hsu C: Cytologic detection of malignancy in pleural effusion: A review of 5255 samples from 3811 patients. Diagn Cytopathol 3:8–12, 1987.
11. Fentiman IS, Millis R, Sexton S, et al: Pleural effusion in breast cancer: A review of 105 cases. Cancer 47:2087–2092, 1981.
12. Alexandrakis MG, Passam FH, Kyriakou DS, et al: Pleural effusions in hematologic malignancies. Chest 125:1546–1555, 2004.
13. Berkman N, Breuer R, Kramer MR, et al: Pulmonary involvement in lymphoma. Leuk Lymphoma 20:229–237, 1996.
14. Das DK, Gupta SK, Ayyagari S, et al: Pleural effusions in non-Hodgkin's lymphoma: A cytomorphologic, cytochemical and immunologic study. Acta Cytol 31:119–124, 1987.
15. Nahid P, Broaddus VC: Liquid and protein exchange. In Light RW, Lee GYC (eds): Textbook of Pleural Diseases. London: Arnold, 2003, pp 35–44.
16. Broaddus VC: Transudative pleural effusions. In Loddenkemper R, Antony VB (eds): Pleural Diseases (European Respiratory Monograph, Vol 7, Monograph 22). Sheffield, UK: European Respiratory Society Journals, 2002, pp 157–176.

17. Light RW, MacGregor MI, Luchsinger PC, et al: Pleural effusions: The diagnostic separation of transudates and exudates. Ann Intern Med 77:507–513, 1972.

18. Ashchi M, Golish J, Eng P, et al: Transudative malignant pleural effusions: Prevalence and mechanisms. South Med J 91:23–26, 1998.

19. Fernandez C, Martin C, Aranda I, et al: Malignant transient pleural transudate: A sign of early lymphatic tumoral obstruction. Respiration 67:333–336, 2000.

20. Light RW, Erozan YS, Ball WC: Cells in pleural fluid: Their value in differential diagnosis. Arch Intern Med 132:854–860, 1973.

21. Adelman M, Albelda SM, Gottlieb J, et al: Diagnostic utility of pleural fluid eosinophilia. Am J Med 77:915–920, 1984.

22. Rubins JB, Rubins HB: Etiology and prognostic significance of eosinophilic pleural effusions: A prospective study. Chest 110:1271–1274, 1996.

23. Martinez-Garcia MA, Cases-Viedma E, Cordero-Rodriguez PJ, et al: Diagnostic utility of eosinophils in the pleural fluid. Eur Respir J 15:166–169, 2000.

24. Rodriguez-Panadero F, Lopez Mejias J: Low glucose and pH levels in malignant pleural effusions. Am Rev Respir Dis 139:663–667, 1989.

25. Rodriguez-Panadero F, Lopez-Mejias J: Survival time of patients with pleural metastatic carcinoma predicted by glucose and pH studies. Chest 95:320–324, 1989.

26. Sahn SA, Good JT Jr: Pleural fluid pH in malignant effusions. Ann Intern Med 108:345–349, 1988.

27. Heffner JE, Heffner JN, Brown LK: Multilevel and continuous pleural fluid pH likelihood ratios for evaluating malignant pleural effusions. Chest 123:1887–1894, 2003.

28. Light RW, Ball WC: Glucose and amylase in pleural effusions. JAMA 225:257–260, 1973.

29. Villena V, Perez V, Pozo F, et al: Amylase levels in pleural effusions: A consecutive unselected series of 841 patients. Chest 121:470–474, 2002.

30. Kramer MR, Saldana MJ, Cepero RJ, et al: High amylase levels in neoplasm-related pleural effusion. Ann Intern Med 110:567–569, 1989.

31. Porcel JM, Vives M: Etiology and pleural fluid characteristics of large and massive effusions. Chest 124:978–983, 2003.

32. Leung A, Muller N, Miller R: CT in differential diagnosis of diffuse pleural disease. AJR Am J Roentgenol 154:487–492, 1990.

33. Traill ZC, Davies RJ, Gleeson FV: Thoracic computed tomography in patients with suspected malignant pleural effusions. Clin Radiol 56:193–196, 2001.

34. Arenas-Jimenez J, Alonso-Charterina S, Sanchez-Paya J, et al: Evaluation of CT findings for diagnosis of pleural effusions. Eur Radiol 10:681–690, 2000.

35. Knisely BL, Broderick LS, Kuhlman JE: MR imaging of the pleura and chest wall. Magn Reson Imaging Clin N Am 8:125–141, 2000.

36. Davis SD, Henschke CI, Yankelevitz DF, et al: MR imaging of pleural effusions. J Comput Assist Tomogr 14:192–198, 1990.

37. Kwek BH, Aquino SL, Fischman AJ: Fluorodeoxyglucose positron-emission tomography and CT after talc pleurodesis. Chest 125:2356–2360, 2004.

38. Prakash UB, Reiman HM: Comparison of needle biopsy with cytologic analysis for the evaluation of pleural effusions: Analysis of cytologic analysis in 414 cases. Mayo Clin Proc 60:158–164, 1985.

39. Maskell NA, Gleeson FV, Davies RJ: Standard pleural biopsy versus CT-guided cutting-needle biopsy for diagnosis of malignant disease in pleural effusions: A randomised controlled trial. Lancet 361:1326–1330, 2003.

40. Cardillo G, Facciolo F, Carbone L, et al: Long-term follow-up of video-assisted talc pleurodesis in malignant recurrent pleural effusions. Eur J Cardiothorac Surg 21:302–305, 2002 (discussion appears in Eur J Cardiothorac Surg 21:305–306, 2002).

41. Dikmen G, Dikmen E, Kara M, et al: Diagnostic implications of telomerase activity in pleural effusions. Eur Respir J 22:422–426, 2003.

42. Yang CT, Lee MH, Lan RS, et al: Telomerase activity in pleural effusions: Diagnostic significance. J Clin Oncol 16:567–573, 1998.

43. Braunschweig R, Guilleret I, Delacretaz F, et al: Pitfalls in TRAP assay in routine detection of malignancy in effusions. Diagn Cytopathol 25:225–230, 2001.

44. Takezawa C, Takahashi H, Fujishima T, et al: Assessment of differentiation in adenocarcinoma cells from pleural effusion by peripheral airway cell markers and their diagnostic values. Lung Cancer 38:273–281, 2002.

45. Shijubo N, Tsutahara S, Hirasawa M, et al: Pulmonary surfactant protein A in pleural effusions. Cancer 69:2905–2909, 1992.

46. Antony VB, Loddenkemper R, Astoul P, et al: Management of malignant pleural effusions. Eur Respir J 18:402–419, 2001.

47. Livingston RB, McCracken JD, Trauth CJ, et al: Isolated pleural effusion in small cell lung carcinoma: Favorable prognosis. Chest 81:208–211, 1982.

48. Elis A, Blickstein D, Mulchanov I, et al: Pleural effusion in patients with non-Hodgkin's lymphoma: A case-controlled study. Cancer 83:1607–1611, 1998.

49. Mager HJ, Maesen B, Verzijlbergen F, et al: Distribution of talc suspension during treatment of malignant pleural effusion with talc pleurodesis. Lung Cancer 36:77–81, 2002.

49a. West SD, Davies RJ, Lee YC: Pleurodesis for malignant pleural effusions: current controversies and variations in practices. Curr Opin Pulm Med 10:305–310, 2004.

50. Bondoc AY, Bach PB, Sklarin NT, et al: Arterial desaturation syndrome following pleurodesis with talc slurry: Incidence, clinical features, and outcome. Cancer Invest 21:848–854, 2003.

51. Maskell NA, Lee YC, Gleeson FV, et al: Randomized trials describing lung inflammation after pleurodesis with talc of varying particle size. Am J Respir Crit Care Med 170:377–382, 2004.

52. Sahn SA: Management of malignant pleural effusions. Monaldi Arch Chest Dis 56:394–399, 2001.

53. Olivares-Torres CA, Laniado-Laborin R, Chavez-Garcia C, et al: Iodopovidone pleurodesis for recurrent pleural effusions. Chest 122:581–583, 2002.

53a. Ukale V, Agrenius V, Hillerdal G, et al: Pleurodesis in recurrent pleural effusions: a randomized comparison of a classical and a currently popular drug. Lung Cancer 43:323–328, 2004.

54. Senyigit A, Bayram H, Babayigit C, et al: Comparison of the effectiveness of some pleural sclerosing agents used for control of effusions in malignant pleural mesothelioma: A review of 117 cases. Respiration 67: 623–629, 2000.

55. Parulekar W, Di Primio G, Matzinger F, et al: Use of small-bore vs large-bore chest tubes for treatment of malignant pleural effusions. Chest 120:19–25, 2001.

56. Spiegler PA, Hurewitz AN, Groth ML: Rapid pleurodesis for malignant pleural effusions. Chest 123:1895–1898, 2003.

57. Erickson KV, Yost M, Bynoe R, et al: Primary treatment of malignant pleural effusions: Video-assisted thoracoscopic surgery poudrage versus tube thoracostomy. Am Surg

68:955–959, 2002 (discussion appears in Am Surg 68:959–960, 2002).

58. Yim AP, Chan AT, Lee TW, et al: Thoracoscopic talc insufflation versus talc slurry for symptomatic malignant pleural effusion. Ann Thorac Surg 62:1655–1658, 1996.

59. de Campos JR, Vargas FS, de Campos Werebe E, et al: Thoracoscopy talc poudrage: A 15-year experience. Chest 119:801–806, 2001.

60. Pollak JS: Malignant pleural effusions: Treatment with tunneled long-term drainage catheters. Curr Opin Pulm Med 8:302–307, 2002.

61. Genc O, Petrou M, Ladas G, et al: The long-term morbidity of pleuroperitoneal shunts in the management of recurrent malignant effusions. Eur J Cardiothorac Surg 18:143–146, 2000.

62. Petrou M, Kaplan D, Goldstraw P: Management of recurrent malignant pleural effusions: The complementary role talc pleurodesis and pleuroperitoneal shunting. Cancer 75:801–805, 1995.

63. Lee KA, Harvey JC, Reich H, et al: Management of malignant pleural effusions with pleuroperitoneal shunting. J Am Coll Surg 178:586–588, 1994.

64. Fry WA, Khandekar JD: Parietal pleurectomy for malignant pleural effusion. Ann Surg Oncol 2:160–164, 1995.

65. Waller DA, Morritt GN, Forty J: Video-assisted thoracoscopic pleurectomy in the management of malignant pleural effusion. Chest 107:1454–1456, 1995.

66. Heffner JE, Nietert PJ, Barbieri C: Pleural fluid pH as a predictor of survival for patients with malignant pleural effusions. Chest 117:79–86, 2000.

67. Burrows CM, Mathews C, Colt HG: Predicting survival in patients with recurrent symptomatic malignant pleural effusions. Chest 117:73–78, 2000.

68. Britton M: The epidemiology of mesothelioma. Semin Oncol 29:18–25, 2002.

69. Alleman JE, Mossman BT: Asbestos revisited. Sci Am 277:70–75, 1997.

70. Talcott JA, Thurber WA, Kantor AF, et al: Asbestos-associated diseases in a cohort of cigarette-filter workers. N Engl J Med 321:1220–1223, 1989.

71. Harris LV, Kahwa IA: Asbestos: Old foe in 21st century developing countries. Sci Total Environ 307:1–9, 2003.

72. Takahashi K, Karjalainen A: A cross-country comparative overview of the asbestos situation in ten Asian countries. Int J Occup Environ Health 9:244–248, 2003.

73. Yeung P, Rogers A: An occupation-industry matrix analysis of mesothelioma cases in Australia 1980–1985. Appl Occup Environ Hyg 16:40–44, 2001.

74. Teschke K, Morgan MS, Checkoway H, et al: Mesothelioma surveillance to locate sources of exposure to asbestos. Can J Public Health 88:163–168, 1997.

75. Landrigan PJ, Lioy PJ, Thurston G, et al: Health and environmental consequences of the World Trade Center disaster. Environ Health Perspect 112:731–739, 2004.

76. Gazdar AF, Butel JS, Carbone M: SV40 and human tumours: myth, association or causality? Nat Rev Cancer 2:957–964, 2002.

77. Engels EA, Katki HA, Nielsen NM, et al: Cancer incidence in Denmark following exposure to poliovirus vaccine contaminated with simian virus 40. J Natl Cancer Inst 95:532–539, 2003.

78. Strickler HD, Goedert JJ, Devesa SS, et al: Trends in U.S. pleural mesothelioma incidence rates following simian virus 40 contamination of early poliovirus vaccines. J Natl Cancer Inst 95:38–45, 2003.

79. Pilatte Y, Vivo C, Renier A, et al: Absence of SV40 large T-antigen expression in human mesothelioma cell lines. Am J Respir Cell Mol Biol 23:788–793, 2000.

79a. Pass HI, Bocchetta M, Carbone M: Evidence of an important role for SV40 in mesothelioma. Thorac Surg Clin 14:489–495, 2004.

79b. Shah KV: Causality of mesothelioma: SV40 question. Thorac Surg Clin 14:497–504, 2004.

80. Muscat J, Wydner E: Cigarette smoking, asbestos exposure and malignant mesothelioma. Cancer Res 51:2263–2267, 1991.

81. Coggiola M, Bosio D, Pira E, et al: An update of a mortality study of talc miners and millers in Italy. Am J Ind Med 44:63–69, 2003.

82. Marsh GM, Gula MJ, Youk AO, et al: Historical cohort study of US man-made vitreous fiber production workers: II. Mortality from mesothelioma. J Occup Environ Med 43:757–766, 2001.

83. Gennaro V, Finkelstein MM, Ceppi M, et al: Mesothelioma and lung tumors attributable to asbestos among petroleum workers. Am J Ind Med 37:275–282, 2000.

84. Weissmann LB, Corson JM, Neugut AI, et al: Malignant mesothelioma following treatment for Hodgkin's disease. J Clin Oncol 14:2098–2100, 1996.

85. Cavazza A, Travis LB, Travis WD, et al: Post-irradiation malignant mesothelioma. Cancer 77:1379–1385, 1996.

86. Roggli V: Mineral fiber content of lung tissue in patients with malignant mesothelioma. *In* Henderson D, et al (eds): Malignant Mesothelioma. New York: Hemisphere Publishing, 1992, pp 201–222.

87. Emri S, Demir AU: Malignant pleural mesothelioma in Turkey, 2000–2002. Lung Cancer 45:S17–S20, 2004.

88. Lidar M, Pras M, Langevitz P, et al: Thoracic and lung involvement in familial Mediterranean fever (FMF). Clin Chest Med 23:505–511, 2002.

89. Mollo F, Andrion A, Bellis D, et al: Optical determination of coated and uncoated mineral fibers in lungs of subjects without professional exposure. Appl Pathol 1:276–282, 1983.

90. Kobayashi H, Watanabe H, Zhang WM, et al: A quantitative and histological study on pulmonary effects of asbestos exposure in general autopsied lungs. Acta Pathol Jpn 36:1781–1791, 1986.

91. Huncharek M: Non-asbestos related diffuse malignant mesothelioma. Tumori 88:1–9, 2002.

91a. Roushdy-Hammady I, Siegel J, Emri S, et al: Genetic-susceptibility factor and malignant mesothelioma in the Cappadocian region of Turkey. Lancet 357:444–445, 2001.

92. Mor O, Yaron P, Huszar M, et al: Absence of p53 mutations in malignant mesothelioma. Am J Respir Cell Mol Biol 16:9–13, 1997.

93. Ni Z, Liu Y, Keshava N, et al: Analysis of K-ras and p53 mutations in mesotheliomas from humans and rats exposed to asbestos. Mutat Res 468:87–92, 2000.

94. Murthy SS, Testa JR: Asbestos, chromosomal deletions, and tumor suppressor gene alterations in human malignant mesothelioma. J Cell Physiol 180:150–157, 1999.

95. Singhal S, Wiewrodt R, Malden LD, et al: Gene expression profiling of malignant mesothelioma. Clin Cancer Res 9:3080–3097, 2003.

96. Pass HI, Liu Z, Wali A, et al: Gene expression profiles predict survival and progression of pleural mesothelioma. Clin Cancer Res 10:849–859, 2004.

97. Broaddus VC, Jaurand M-C: Asbestos fibers and their interaction with mesothelial cells in vitro and in vivo. *In* Chahinian AP, Robinson BWS (eds): Mesothelioma. London: Martin Dunitz, 2002, pp 267–287.

98. Leard L, Broaddus VC: Mesothelial cell proliferation and apoptosis. Respirology 9:292–299, 2004.

99. Ruffie P, Minkin F, Cormier Y, et al: Diffuse malignant mesothelioma of the pleura in Ontario and Quebec: A

retrospective study of 332 patients. J Clin Oncol 7:1157–1168, 1989.

100. Nakano T, Chahinian AP, Shinjo M, et al: Interleukin 6 and its relationship to clinical parameters in patients with malignant pleural mesothelioma. Br J Cancer 77:907–912, 1998.

101. Edwards JG, Abrams KR, Leverment JN, et al: Prognostic factors for malignant mesothelioma in 142 patients: Validation of CALGB and EORTC prognostic scoring systems. Thorax 55:731–735, 2000.

102. Robinson BW, Creaney J, Lake R, et al: Mesothelin-family proteins and diagnosis of mesothelioma. Lancet 362:1612–1616, 2003.

103. Metintas M, Ucgun I, Elbek O, et al: Computed tomography features in malignant pleural mesothelioma and other commonly seen pleural diseases. Eur J Radiol 41:1–9, 2002.

104. Huncharek M: Changing risk groups for malignant mesothelioma. Cancer 69:2704–2711, 1992.

105. Sussman J, Rosai J: Lymph node metastasis as the initial manifestation of malignant mesothelioma: Report of six cases. Am J Surg Pathol 14:819–828, 1990.

106. Knuuttila A, Kivisaari L, Kivisaari A, et al: Evaluation of pleural disease using MR and CT: With special reference to malignant pleural mesothelioma. Acta Radiol 42:502–507, 2001.

107. Heelan RT, Rusch VW, Begg CB, et al: Staging of malignant pleural mesothelioma: Comparison of CT and MR imaging. AJR Am J Roentgenol 172:1039–1047, 1999.

108. Benard F, Sterman D, Smith R, et al: Metabolic imaging of malignant pleural mesothelioma with fluorodeoxyglucose positron emission tomography. Chest 111:106–109, 1998.

109. Flores RM, Akhurst T, Gonen M, et al: Positron emission tomography defines metastatic disease but not locoregional disease in patients with malignant pleural mesothelioma. J Thorac Cardiovasc Surg 126:11–16, 2003.

110. Wang ZJ, Reddy GP, Gotway MB, et al: Malignant pleural mesothelioma: Evaluation with CT, MR imaging, and PET. Radiographics 24:105–119, 2004.

111. Boutin C, Rey F: Thoracoscopy in pleural malignant mesothelioma: A prospective study of 188 patients. Cancer 72:389–393, 1993.

112. Adams RF, Gray W, Davies RJ, et al: Percutaneous image-guided cutting needle biopsy of the pleura in the diagnosis of malignant mesothelioma. Chest 120:1798–1802, 2001.

113. Johansson L, Linden D-J: Aspects of histopathologic subtype as a prognostic factor in 85 pleural mesotheliomas. Chest 109:109–114, 1996.

114. Blanc FX, Atassi K, Bignon J, et al: Diagnostic value of medical thoracoscopy in pleural disease: A 6-year retrospective study. Chest 121:1677–1683, 2002.

115. Grossebner MW, Arifi AA, Goddard M, et al: Mesothelioma—VATS biopsy and lung mobilization improves diagnosis and palliation. Eur J Cardiothorac Surg 16:619–623, 1999.

116. McCaughey W, Colby T, Battifora H, et al: Diagnosis of diffuse malignant mesothelioma: Experience of a US/Canadian Mesothelioma Panel. Mod Pathol 4:342–353, 1991.

117. Yang GC: Long microvilli of mesothelioma are conspicuous in pleural effusions processed by Ultrafast Papanicolaou stain. Cancer 99:17–22, 2003.

118. Ordonez NG: The immunohistochemical diagnosis of mesothelioma: A comparative study of epithelioid mesothelioma and lung adenocarcinoma. Am J Surg Pathol 27:1031–1051, 2003.

119. Ordonez NG: Value of mesothelin immunostaining in the diagnosis of mesothelioma. Mod Pathol 16:192–197, 2003.

120. Zellos LS, Sugarbaker DJ: Diffuse malignant mesothelioma of the pleural space and its management. Oncology (Huntingt) 16:907–913, 2002.

121. Metintas M, Metintas S, Ucgun I, et al: Prognostic factors in diffuse malignant pleural mesothelioma: Effects of pretreatment clinical and laboratory characteristics. Respir Med 95:829–835, 2001.

122. Edwards JG, Cox G, Andi A, et al: Angiogenesis is an independent prognostic factor in malignant mesothelioma. Br J Cancer 85:863–868, 2001.

123. Edwards JG, Swinson DE, Jones JL, et al: Tumor necrosis correlates with angiogenesis and is a predictor of poor prognosis in malignant mesothelioma. Chest 124:1916–1923, 2003.

124. Rusch VW for the International Mesothelioma Interest Group: A proposed new international TNM staging system for malignant pleural mesothelioma. Chest 108:1122–1128, 1995.

125. Butchart E, Ashcroft T, Barnsley W, et al: Pleuropneumonectomy in the management of diffuse malignant mesothelioma of the pleura: Experience in 29 patients. Thorax 31:15–24, 1976.

126. Rusch VW, Venkatraman E: The importance of surgical staging in the treatment of malignant pleural mesothelioma. J Thorac Cardiovasc Surg 111:815–826, 1996.

127. Rusch VW, Venkatraman ES: Important prognostic factors in patients with malignant pleural mesothelioma, managed surgically. Ann Thorac Surg 68:1799–1804, 1999.

128. Sugarbaker DJ, Norberto JJ, Swanson SJ: Surgical staging and work-up of patients with diffuse malignant pleural mesothelioma. Semin Thorac Cardiovasc Surg 9:356–360, 1997.

129. Piquette GN, Timms BG: Isolation and characterization of rabbit ovarian surface epithelium, granulosa cells, and peritoneal mesothelium in primary culture. In Vitro Cell Dev Biol 26:471–481, 1990.

130. Sugarbaker DJ, Flores RM, Jaklitsch MT, et al: Resection margins, extrapleural nodal status, and cell type determine postoperative long-term survival in trimodality therapy of malignant pleural mesothelioma: Results in 183 patients. J Thorac Cardiovasc Surg 117:54–63, 1999.

131. Conlon KC, Rusch VW, Gillern S: Laparoscopy: An important tool in the staging of malignant pleural mesothelioma. Ann Surg Oncol 3:489–494, 1996.

132. Pass HI, Kranda K, Temeck BK, et al: Surgically debulked malignant pleural mesothelioma: Results and prognostic factors. Ann Surg Oncol 4:215–222, 1997.

133. Pass H, Temeck B, Kranda K, et al: Phase III randomized trial of surgery with or without intraoperative photodynamic therapy and postoperative immunochemotherapy for malignant pleural mesothelioma. Ann Surg Oncol 4:628–633, 1997.

134. Lee YCG, Light RW, Musk AW: Management of malignant pleural mesothelioma: A critical review. Curr Opin Pulm Med 6:267–274, 2000.

135. Law MR, Gregor A, Hodson ME, et al: Malignant mesothelioma of the pleura: A study of 52 treated and 64 untreated patients. Thorax 39:255–259, 1984.

136. van Ruth S, Baas P, Haas RL, et al: Cytoreductive surgery combined with intraoperative hyperthermic intrathoracic chemotherapy for stage I malignant pleural mesothelioma. Ann Surg Oncol 10:176–182, 2003.

137. Bakhshandeh A, Bruns I, Traynor A, et al: Ifosfamide, carboplatin and etoposide combined with 41.8 degrees C whole body hyperthermia for malignant pleural mesothelioma. Lung Cancer 39:339–345, 2003.

138. Friedberg JS, Mick R, Stevenson J, et al: A Phase I study of Foscan-mediated photodynamic therapy and surgery in patients with mesothelioma. Ann Thorac Surg 75:952–959, 2003.

139. Vogelzang NJ: Emerging insights into the biology and therapy of malignant mesothelioma. Semin Oncol 29:35–42, 2002.

140. Ryan C, Herndon J, Vogelzang N: A review of chemotherapy trials for malignant mesothelioma. Chest 113:66S–73S, 1998.

141. Byrne MJ, Davidson JA, Musk AW, et al: Cisplatin and gemcitabine treatment for malignant mesothelioma: A Phase II study. J Clin Oncol 17:25–30, 1999.

142. Nakano T, Chahinian AP, Shinjo M, et al: Cisplatin in combination with irinotecan in the treatment of patients with malignant pleural mesothelioma. Cancer 85:2375–2384, 1999.

143. Nowak AK, Byrne MJ, Williamson R, et al: A multicentre Phase II study of cisplatin and gemcitabine for malignant mesothelioma. Br J Cancer 87:491–496, 2002.

144. Schutte W, Blankenburg T, Lauerwald K, et al: A multicenter Phase II study of gemcitabine and oxaliplatin for malignant pleural mesothelioma. Clin Lung Cancer 4:294–297, 2003.

145. Vogelzang NJ, Rusthoven JJ, Symanowski J, et al: Phase III study of pemetrexed in combination with cisplatin versus cisplatin alone in patients with malignant pleural mesothelioma. J Clin Oncol 21:2636–2644, 2003.

146. Janne PA, Taffaro ML, Salgia R, et al: Inhibition of epidermal growth factor receptor signaling in malignant pleural mesothelioma. Cancer Res 62:5242–5247, 2002.

147. Carmichael J, Degraff WG, Gamson J, et al: Radiation sensitivity of human lung cancer cell lines. Eur J Cancer Clin Oncol 25:527–534, 1989.

148. Boutin C, Rey F, Viallat JR: Prevention of malignant seeding after invasive diagnostic procedures in patients with pleural mesothelioma: A randomized trial of local radiotherapy. Chest 108:754–758, 1995.

149. Senan S: Indications and limitations of radiotherapy in malignant pleural mesothelioma. Curr Opin Oncol 15:144–147, 2003.

150. Boutin C, Nussbaum E, Monnet I, et al: Intrapleural treatment with recombinant gamma-interferon in early stage malignant pleural mesothelioma. Cancer 74:2460–2467, 1994.

151. Goey S, Eggermont A, Punt C, et al: Intrapleural administration of interleukin 2 in pleural mesothelioma: A Phase I-II study. Br J Cancer 72:1283–1288, 1995.

152. Parra HS, Tixi L, Latteri F, et al: Combined regimen of cisplatin, doxorubicin, and alpha-2b interferon in the treatment of advanced malignant pleural mesothelioma: A Phase II multicenter trial of the Italian Group on Rare Tumors (GITR) and the Italian Lung Cancer Task Force (FONICAP). Cancer 92:650–656, 2001.

153. Mukherjee S, Haenel T, Himbeck R, et al: Replication-restricted vaccinia as a cytokine gene therapy vector in cancer: Persistent transgene expression despite antibody generation. Cancer Gene Ther 7:663–670, 2000.

154. Frizelle SP, Rubins JB, Zhou JX, et al: Gene therapy of established mesothelioma xenografts with recombinant p16INK4a adenovirus. Cancer Gene Ther 7:1421–1425, 2000.

155. Sterman DH, Kaiser LR, Albelda SM: Gene therapy for malignant pleural mesothelioma. Hematol Oncol Clin North Am 12:553–568, 1998.

156. Lambright ES, Force SD, Lanuti ME, et al: Efficacy of repeated adenoviral suicide gene therapy in a localized murine tumor model. Ann Thorac Surg 70:1865–1870, 2000 (discussion appears in Ann Thorac Surg 70:1870–1861, 2000).

157. Schwarzenberger P, Harrison L, Weinacker A, et al: The treatment of malignant mesothelioma with a gene modified cancer cell line: A Phase I study. Hum Gene Ther 9:2641–2649, 1998.

158. Harrison LH Jr, Schwarzenberger PO, Byrne PS, et al: Gene-modified PA1-STK cells home to tumor sites in patients with malignant pleural mesothelioma. Ann Thorac Surg 70:407–411, 2000.

159. Schwarzenberger P, Lei D, Freeman SM, et al: Antitumor activity with the HSV-tk-gene-modified cell line PA-1-STK in malignant mesothelioma. Am J Respir Cell Mol Biol 19:333–337, 1998.

160. Putnam JB Jr, Walsh GL, Swisher SG, et al: Outpatient management of malignant pleural effusion by a chronic indwelling pleural catheter. Ann Thorac Surg 69:369–375, 2000.

161. de Klerk NH, Musk AW, Ambrosini GL, et al: Vitamin A and cancer prevention II: Comparison of the effects of retinol and beta-carotene. Int J Cancer 75:362–367, 1998.

161a. Mutti L, Broaddus VC: Malignant mesothelioma as both a challenge and an opportunity. Oncogene 23:9155–9161, 2004.

162. Briselli M, Mark EJ, Dickersin GR: Solitary fibrous tumors of the pleura: Eight new cases and review of 360 cases in the literature. Cancer 47:2678–2689, 1981.

163. Mezzetti M, Panigalli T, Giudice FL, et al: Surgical experience of 15 solitary benign fibrous tumor of the pleura. Crit Rev Oncol Hematol 47:29–33, 2003.

164. Robinson LA, Reilly RB: Localized pleural mesothelioma: The clinical spectrum. Chest 106:1611–1615, 1994.

165. Rena O, Filosso PL, Papalia E, et al: Solitary fibrous tumour of the pleura: Surgical treatment. Eur J Cardiothorac Surg 19:185–189, 2001.

166. Okike N, Bernatz PE, Woolner LB: Localized mesothelioma of the pleura: Benign and malignant variants. J Thorac Cardiovasc Surg 75:363–372, 1978.

167. Le Roith D: Tumor-induced hypoglycemia. N Engl J Med 341:757–758, 1999.

168. Teale JD, Wark G: The effectiveness of different treatment options for non-islet cell tumour hypoglycaemia. Clin Endocrinol 60:457–460, 2004.

169. Chang YL, Lee YC, Wu CT: Thoracic solitary fibrous tumor: Clinical and pathological diversity. Lung Cancer 23:53–60, 1999.

170. Mendelson DS, Meary E, Buy JN, et al: Localized fibrous pleural mesothelioma: CT findings. Clin Imaging 15:105–108, 1991.

171. Lee KS, Im JG, Choe KO, et al: CT findings in benign fibrous mesothelioma of the pleura: Pathologic correlation in nine patients. AJR Am J Roentgenol 158:983–986, 1992.

172. Harris GN, Rozenshtein A, Schiff MJ: Benign fibrous mesothelioma of the pleura: MR imaging findings. AJR Am J Roentgenol 165:1143–1144, 1995.

173. Padovani B, Mouroux J, Raffaelli C, et al: Benign fibrous mesothelioma of the pleura: MR study and pathologic correlation. Eur Radiol 6:425–428, 1996.

174. Cortes J, Rodriguez J, Garcia-Velloso MJ, et al: [^{18}F]-FDG PET and localized fibrous mesothelioma. Lung 181:49–54, 2003.

175. Suter M, Gebhard S, Boumghar M, et al: Localized fibrous tumours of the pleura: 15 new cases and review of the literature. Eur J Cardiothorac Surg 14:453–459, 1998.

176. Ascoli V, Lo-Coco F: Body cavity lymphoma. Curr Opin Pulm Med 8:317–322, 2002.

177. Morassut S, Vaccher E, Balestreri L, et al: HIV-associated human herpesvirus 8-positive primary lymphomatous

effusions: Radiologic findings in six patients. Radiology 205:459–463, 1997.

178. Wakely PE Jr, Menezes G, Nuovo GJ: Primary effusion lymphoma: Cytopathologic diagnosis using in situ molecular genetic analysis for human herpesvirus 8. Mod Pathol 15:944–950, 2002.

179. Simonelli C, Spina M, Cinelli R, et al: Clinical features and outcome of primary effusion lymphoma in HIV-infected patients: A single-institution study. J Clin Oncol 21:3948–3954, 2003.

180. Hocqueloux L, Agbalika F, Oksenhendler E, et al: Long-term remission of an AIDS-related primary effusion lymphoma with antiviral therapy. AIDS 15:280–282, 2001.

181. Androulaki A, Drakos E, Hatzianastassiou D, et al: Pyothorax-associated lymphoma (PAL): A western case with marked angiocentricity and review of the literature. Histopathology 44:69–76, 2004.

182. Petitjean B, Jardin F, Joly B, et al: Pyothorax-associated lymphoma: A peculiar clinicopathologic entity derived from B cells at late stage of differentiation and with occasional aberrant dual B- and T-cell phenotype. Am J Surg Pathol 26:724–732, 2002.

183. Nakatsuka S, Yao M, Hoshida Y, et al: Pyothorax-associated lymphoma: A review of 106 cases. J Clin Oncol 20:4255–4260, 2002.

184. Aruga T, Itami J, Nakajima K, et al: Treatment for pyothorax-associated lymphoma. Radiother Oncol 56:59–63, 2000.

185. Shide K, Henzan H, Nagafuji K, et al: Dynamics of Epstein-Barr virus load in pyothorax-associated lymphoma. J Med Virol 70:137–140, 2003.

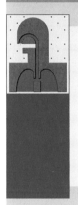

71

Tumors and Cysts of the Mediastinum

David R. Park, M.D., Eric Vallières, M.D.

INTRODUCTION

The mediastinum is the region in the chest between the pleural cavities that contains the heart and other thoracic viscera except for the lungs. It is bounded laterally by the parietal pleurae, anteriorly by the sternum, posteriorly by the vertebral column and paravertebral gutters, superiorly by the thoracic inlet, and inferiorly by the diaphragm. Interest in the mediastinum as a separate body region stems from the diversity and vital importance of the structures it contains, and the multiplicity of disease processes by which it can be affected. The nonspecific nature of the clinical manifestations of most of these disorders and the mediastinum's relative inaccessibility for diagnostic examination result in a considerable challenge to the clinician evaluating mediastinal disease.

This chapter begins by describing the normal anatomy and contents of the mediastinum, the clinical manifestations produced by disease in this region, and the means available for diagnostic investigation, including techniques for imaging the mediastinal contents and methods for obtaining tissue for cytologic or histologic examination. It then describes the features of specific tumors and cysts that occur in the mediastinum. The last part of this chapter outlines an overall clinical approach to the evaluation of mediastinal disease.

THE NORMAL MEDIASTINUM

The anatomy of the mediastinum can be described in several ways, depending on whether it is being considered from the

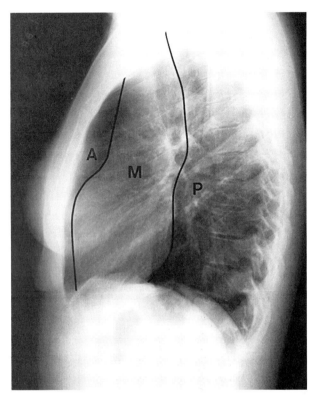

Figure 71.1 By convention the mediastinum is divided into anterior (A), middle (M), and posterior (P) compartments, according to its appearance on lateral chest radiograph. Although other more complex subdivisions exist, this one is most helpful to the clinician.

Table 71.1 Normal Mediastinal Contents
Anterior Compartment Thymus gland Substernal extensions of thyroid and parathyroid glands Lymphatic vessels and lymph nodes Connective tissue
Middle Compartment Heart Pericardium Aortic arch and great vessels Innominate veins and superior vena cava Trachea and main bronchi Hila Lymph nodes Phrenic and upper vagus nerves Connective tissue
Posterior Compartment Esophagus Descending aorta Azygos and hemiazygos veins Thoracic duct Lymph nodes Vagus nerves (lower portions) Sympathetic chains Connective tissue

point of view of the radiologist[1,2] or that of the operating surgeon.[3] Most clinicians simply divide the mediastinum into anterior, middle, and posterior compartments, as seen on the lateral chest radiograph (Fig. 71.1).[4]

The anterior compartment consists of everything lying forward of and superior to the heart shadow; its boundaries are the sternum, the first rib, and an imaginary curved line following the anterior heart border and brachiocephalic vessels from the diaphragm to the thoracic inlet. Within the anterior compartment lie the thymus gland, any substernal extensions of the thyroid and parathyroid glands, and lymphatic tissue (Table 71.1).

The middle compartment, dorsal to the anterior mediastinum, extends from the lower edge of the sternum along the diaphragm and then cephalad along the posterior heart border and posterior wall of the trachea. It contains the heart, the pericardium, the aortic arch and its major branches, the innominate veins and superior vena cava, the pulmonary arteries and hila, the trachea, and several groups of lymph nodes. In addition, the phrenic and upper vagus nerves course through the middle mediastinal compartment.

The posterior mediastinum occupies the space between the back of the heart and trachea and the front of the posterior ribs and paravertebral gutters. It extends from the diaphragm cephalad to the first rib. In it are the esophagus, descending aorta, azygous and hemiazygous veins, paravertebral lymph nodes, and thoracic duct. The lower portions of the vagus nerve and sympathetic chains also lie within the posterior mediastinum.

This three-compartment model is consistent with embryonic development of the region and also with the characteristic distribution of individual disorders encountered clinically. However, other classifications exist. Some authors include the most superior portion of the anterior mediastinum as a separate, fourth compartment. Others subdivide the mediastinum into seven distinct regions: thoracic inlet, anterior mediastinum, supra-aortic area, infra-aortic area, supra-azygos area, infra-azygos area, and hila.[1] This classification has been praised for enabling radiologists to localize lesions more accurately and for permitting more precise differential diagnosis, but it seems unnecessarily complicated for the clinician. A similar categorization, based on surgical landmarks, is used for the mapping of lymph node locations during mediastinal staging of bronchogenic carcinoma.[5]

Separation of mediastinal structures into anterior, middle, and posterior compartments follows logically from the appearance of the chest on conventional radiography. And, because evaluation of a mediastinal abnormality nearly always starts with a conventional chest radiograph, these compartments will likely remain the fundamental anatomic units of the mediastinum. However, the anatomic relationships of the mediastinal viscera and tissue planes are best appreciated on axial images such as produced by computed tomography (CT) scans (see Fig. 72.1).[6] The anatomy of the tissues planes in the mediastinum, and their continuity with spaces in the neck and abdomen, are discussed further in Chapter 72.

CLINICAL SETTINGS AND PRESENTATIONS OF MEDIASTINAL DISEASE

ASYMPTOMATIC MASS

The incidental discovery of a mediastinal mass that has produced no symptoms is the most common setting in which the clinician encounters primary mediastinal disease. At least half of all mediastinal masses are asymptomatic and detected by chest radiography performed for unrelated reasons. About 80% of such asymptomatic masses are benign, whereas more than half are malignant if they have produced symptoms.[3,7–10]

EFFECTS OF COMPRESSION OR INVASION OF ADJACENT TISSUES

Symptoms in patients with mediastinal mass lesions are usually due to compression by mass effect, or invasion of adjacent intrathoracic structures. Masses in the mediastinum can produce a wide variety of symptoms.[7,8] Chest pain, from traction on mediastinal tissues, tissue invasion, or bone erosion, is common. Cough also occurs frequently because of extrinsic compression of the trachea or bronchi, or erosion into the airway itself. Either of these processes predisposes to postobstructive pneumonia. Hemoptysis, hoarseness, or stridor also may be part of the clinical presentation. Invasion or irritation of the pleural surface may produce a pleural effusion, and can cause pain and dyspnea. Compression or direct invasion of the esophagus may lead to dysphagia. Rarely, anterior mediastinal tumors can cause pericarditis or pericardial tamponade,[11,12] and masses in the middle mediastinum can produce right ventricular outflow obstruction and cor pulmonale.[11,13]

The superior vena cava is especially vulnerable to extrinsic compression and obstruction because it is thin walled, its intravascular pressure is low, and it is relatively confined by lymph nodes and other more rigid structures. A distinct "superior vena cava syndrome" results from the resulting increased venous pressure in the upper thorax, head, and neck,[3,14,15] and is characterized by dilation of collateral veins in the upper portion of the thorax and neck; edema and plethora of the face, neck, and upper torso; suffusion and edema of the conjunctiva; and cerebral symptoms, such as headache, disturbance of consciousness, and visual distortion.[16] Tinnitus and epistaxis also may occur, and all symptoms are exacerbated in the supine position. Tuberculous mediastinitis and syphilitic aneurysms were once the most common causes of superior vena cava obstruction. Numerous benign causes of superior vena cava syndrome are described,[17] but bronchogenic carcinoma and lymphoma are now the most common etiologies,[3,18,19] and fewer than 20% of cases are due to nonmalignant disease.[18,19] Bronchogenic carcinoma and the superior vena cava syndrome are discussed further in Chapter 44.

Mediastinal masses can produce a variety of symptoms by invading or compressing nerves. These include hoarseness from recurrent laryngeal nerve involvement, Horner's syndrome from involvement of sympathetic ganglia, dyspnea from phrenic nerve involvement causing diaphragmatic paralysis, tachycardia secondary to vagus nerve involvement, and clinical manifestations of spinal cord compression.

SYSTEMIC SYMPTOMS AND SYNDROMES

Fever, anorexia, weight loss, and other systemic symptoms are nonspecific features of malignancy and granulomatous inflammation that occur frequently in patients with mediastinal disease. In addition, primary mediastinal tumors are associated with a wide array of distinctive systemic syndromes (Table 71.2).[7,8,20–22] Some typically have endocrine function, such as thyrotoxicosis, rarely seen with intrathoracic goiter; Cushing's syndrome, associated with thymomas and carcinoid tumors; gynecomastia, seen in patients with human chorionic gonadotropin–secreting germ cell tumors; hypertension, typical in patients with pheochromocytoma but also reported in patients with ganglioneuroma; hypercalcemia, observed in patients with parathyroid adenoma and lymphoma; and diarrhea, often present in children with neuroblastoma and ganglioneuroma. Hypoglycemia in patients with certain pleural tumors, teratomas, fibrosarcomas, and neurosarcomas is also believed to be the result of tumor products with endocrine function.

Thymomas are associated with numerous systemic syndromes, most of which appear to be autoimmune in origin.[7,8,21,23] The most familiar of these is myasthenia gravis; others include pure red blood cell aplasia, myocarditis, and hypogammaglobulinemia. Patients with thymoma also have an increased incidence of collagen vascular disease, Whipple's disease, and malignancy elsewhere in the body.

Table 71.2 Systemic Syndromes Associated with Mediastinal Masses

Syndrome	Associated Conditions
Endocrine Effects	
Hypothyroidism or hyperthyroidism	Mediastinal goiter
Hypercalcemia	Parathyroid adenoma, lymphoma
Hypertension	Pheochromocytoma, ganglioneuroma, chemodectoma
Cushing's syndrome	Carcinoid, thymoma
Hypoglycemia	Mesenchymal tumor
Gynecomastia	Germ cell tumor
Diarrhea	Ganglioneuroma, neuroblastoma
Autoimmune Effects	
Opsomyoclonus	Neuroblastoma
Myasthenia gravis	Thymoma
Red cell aplasia	Thymoma
Myocarditis	Thymoma
Hypogammaglobulinemia	Thymoma
Congenital Syndromes	
Neurofibromatosis	Neurofibroma
Multiple endocrine neoplasia	Parathyroid adenoma, pheochromocytoma
Unknown Causes	
Alcohol-induced pain	Hodgkin's disease
Fever and night sweats	Lymphoma

Other mediastinal tumors associated with systemic syndromes or diseases include carcinoid and parathyroid adenoma (multiple endocrine neoplasia), neurofibromas (neurofibromatosis), and lymphomas (fever of unknown origin and alcohol-induced pain). Osteoarthropathy is a known feature of primary pleural tumors, neurofibroma, and neurilemoma. Finally, neuroblastoma may be associated with opsomyoclonus, a condition characterized by ataxia and rapid, random eye movements, thought to be caused by an autoantibody against cerebellar tissues.[24]

INVESTIGATION OF THE MEDIASTINUM IN PATIENTS WITH MALIGNANCY

The most common clinical circumstance under which the clinician's attention is focused on the mediastinum is in the staging of patients with lung cancer. Bronchogenic carcinoma is the leading cause of cancer deaths in the United States, with 170,000 new cases and nearly 160,000 deaths per year.[25] Crucial to the management of patients with non–small cell carcinoma, affecting both initial therapy and ultimate survival, is whether and to what extent the mediastinum is involved.[26,27] Controversy has surrounded the question of whether ipsilateral lymph node metastasis should preclude surgical resection for cure. Although metastatic involvement of the mediastinum has traditionally been considered a contraindication to such surgery, increasing attention is being focused on multimodality treatment approaches for these patients, and treatment options are rapidly evolving (see Chapter 44 for additional information). Regardless of the latest treatment options, careful preoperative evaluation of the mediastinum is crucial to the decision-making process.[28]

Nonthoracic malignancies also may metastasize to the mediastinum. This is particularly common with tumors originating in the head and neck, the esophagus, the genitourinary tract, the breasts, and the skin (malignant melanoma).[2]

PNEUMOMEDIASTINUM AND MEDIASTINITIS

Air in the mediastinum (pneumomediastinum) is a common complication of mechanical ventilation and may also be encountered in spontaneously breathing patients under a wide variety of circumstances. Pain is the most common symptom[6] and presumably results from stretching of mediastinal tissues. It is characteristically substernal and aggravated by breathing and changes in position. Other manifestations of air in the mediastinum include dyspnea, dysphagia, dysphonia, and subcutaneous crepitation. Acute inflammation within the confined space of the mediastinum (mediastinitis) causes a dramatic clinical picture dominated by substernal chest pain, chills, high fever, and prostration. Chronic forms of mediastinitis typically result in symptoms due to compression or constriction of the mediastinal viscera. Pneumomediastinum and mediastinitis are discussed further in Chapter 72.

TECHNIQUES FOR VISUALIZING THE MEDIASTINUM AND ITS CONTENTS

The diagnostic approach to disorders of the mediastinum may be divided into two phases: noninvasive imaging and invasive procedures for obtaining tissue samples. The mediastinum is relatively inaccessible for examination or exploration. Accordingly, imaging studies play an important role in the initial evaluation of mediastinal disease. These include conventional radiographic studies, CT, magnetic resonance imaging (MRI), transthoracic and endoscopic ultrasonography (discussed in Chapter 20), and various radionuclide studies (discussed in Chapter 21).

CONVENTIONAL RADIOGRAPHIC TECHNIQUES

Standard posteroanterior and lateral chest radiographs are the means by which most mediastinal abnormalities are first detected, and certain mediastinal mass lesions have characteristic findings (Table 71.3). For example, teratomas are usually anterior and may contain areas of calcium (sometimes teeth or bone), fat, and soft tissue. Neural tumors are usually far posterior, with sharply delineated margins. Pericardial cysts usually lie against the pericardium, on the diaphragm, or against the anterior chest wall. Foregut duplications of the type commonly called bronchogenic cysts tend to lie against the trachea, carina, or main bronchus. These findings give clues to the possible origin of a mediastinal mass, but further imaging evaluation is usually required.

Special conventional radiographic views, fluoroscopy, and tomography have largely been replaced by CT and MRI. In the appropriate clinical settings, contrast studies remain important diagnostic tools in mediastinal disease. Barium esophagrams can demonstrate extrinsic compression, esophageal diverticulum, tumor invasion, or fistula formation.[7] Angiography may be helpful in identifying vascular compression or invasion, can define the vascular supply of tumors, and can sample blood for hormonal localization of certain tumors. Myelography may help to delineate intraspinal extension of posterior mediastinal tumors and to differentiate neurogenic neoplasms from meningoceles, but it has largely been supplanted by CT and MRI.

Air contrast studies are seldom used intentionally in the United States today, but can be helpful even when inadvertent.[29] These include diagnostic pneumothorax, to show whether a mass is adherent to the mediastinum or chest wall[30,31]; diagnostic pneumoperitoneum, which can demonstrate diaphragmatic herniation through the foramina of Morgagni (anterior) and Bochdalek (posterior); and diagnostic pneumomediastinum, which can outline mediastinal structures.[7]

COMPUTED TOMOGRAPHY

Evaluation of mediastinal disease has changed dramatically since the advent of CT imaging. The transaxial plane of CT is well suited for assessment of mediastinal structures, most of which are oriented perpendicularly to this plane. Certain patterns and densities on CT images are virtually pathognomonic. These include the high density of calcified tissue and contrast-enhanced blood vessels, and fat, whose characteristic low density enables it to be identified with certainty (Fig. 71.2).[32,33] Normal anatomic variations and fluid-filled cysts can be distinguished confidently from other processes, and the site of origin of mediastinal masses

Table 71.3 Some Characteristic Imaging Findings in Mediastinal Disease

Feature	Likely Etiology
Huge mass on initial presentation	Neurogenic tumor Meningocele Mesenchymal tumor
Teardrop-shaped mass within interlobar fissure	Pericardial or bronchogenic cyst
Fat density on computed tomography scan	Mediastinal lipomatosis or lipoma

Calcification in mass	In rim of mass
	  Cystic thymoma or thyroid adenoma
	  Aneurysm
	  Silicosis ("eggshell" calcification)
	In center of mass
	  Thyroid adenoma
	  Teratoma

Teeth or bone	Teratoma
Phleboliths	Hemangioma
Air-fluid level in mass	Esophageal disease Diaphragmatic hernia Developmental cyst Cystic teratoma Abscess
Mass with associated parenchymal infiltrate	Granulomatous infection Metastatic bronchogenic carcinoma Lymphoma with direct extension into lung Esophageal abnormality with aspiration pneumonitis Bronchial compression by primary mediastinal mass
Mass with associated pleural effusion	Metastatic malignancy with pleural involvement Granulomatous inflammation of lymph nodes

Superior vena cava obstruction	Recent onset
	  Bronchogenic carcinoma
	  Lymphoma
	  Catheter-associated thrombosis
	Long-standing
	  Mediastinal fibrosis

Erosion or destruction of bone	Arterial aneurysm Tumors of peripheral nerves or sympathetic ganglia Meningocele
Spine or rib deformity	Enteric cyst

can be better identified.[2,32] Characteristic CT findings in a variety of mediastinal disorders have now been described (see Table 71.3). A recent report described 100% specificity for the CT appearance of teratomas, thymolipomas, and omental fat herniation, but the overall accuracy for predicting the diagnosis of all mediastinal masses was only 48%.[33]

CT has several other limitations for mediastinal imaging. Although vertically oriented structures (e.g., those in the paratracheal area), are well seen on cross-sectional CT images, horizontally oriented structures and boundaries are much more difficult to evaluate.[34] Abnormalities in the aortopulmonary window area and the subcarinal region are examples. Certain distinctions cannot be made reliably by CT, such as between the proximity of a mass and its invasion of central structures, between tumor invasion of the lung parenchyma and associated atelectasis or consolidation,[34] and between benign and malignant causes of mediastinal lymph node enlargement.

Lymph nodes are readily identifiable on CT scan and can be categorized as normal in size and shape, enlarged, coalescent, or grossly replaced by tumor mass.[2] For practical purposes, most authors consider mediastinal lymph nodes greater than 1.0 cm in diameter along the short axis as abnormal. However, in numerous studies of CT in mediastinal staging of lung cancer, the sensitivity of the 1.0-cm cutoff for detecting cancerous nodes by CT has ranged from 18% to 94% (reviewed by Gould and colleagues[35]). The specificity of the 1.0-cm cutoff in these studies ranged from 43% to 100%, although in most it was well under 90%. Mediastinal lymph nodes greater than 2.0 cm in diameter are virtually always abnormal,[36,37] and most nodes greater than 2.0 cm in diameter in patients with lung cancer contain metastatic disease.[37] However, even in series of patients with proven bronchogenic carcinoma, benign findings were present in 10% of lymph nodes either larger than 2.0 cm in diameter or with evidence of central necrosis.[38] In another study, no cancer was found in 37% of lymph nodes sized 2 to 4 cm in diameter.[39] Thus, normal appearing nodes often contain metastatic cancer, whereas even markedly enlarged nodes with abnormal appearance may not.

Nevertheless, CT has become the initial imaging procedure of choice for the evaluation of the mediastinum in patients with a primary mediastinal mass[20-22] or with suspected lung cancer.[40-42] In the majority of patients, CT cannot establish a diagnosis with certainty, prove unresectability, or confidently exclude the possibility of mediastinal lymph node metastases. However, CT can be helpful by precisely defining the mediastinal anatomy and guiding subsequent invasive diagnostic and staging procedures, or by confirming a clinical suspicion of extensive mediastinal involvement or visceral organ invasion that precludes curative resection.

MAGNETIC RESONANCE IMAGING

MRI assesses tissues by measuring radiofrequency-induced nuclear resonance emissions instead of measuring the attenuation of transmitted ionizing radiation as detected by conventional radiography and CT (see additional discussion in Chapter 20). This facilitates the construction of magnetic resonance images not only in axial cross section but also in coronal and sagittal planes better suited to evaluating vertically oriented structures and tissue boundaries[34,43,44] (Figs. 71.3 and 71.4). Magnetic resonance images of blood vessels are identifiable without the need for contrast enhancement (Fig. 71.5).[34,45] Metallic objects that cause artifact on CT scans do not interfere with MRI, although some metallic devices may be subjected to magnetic forces.[46]

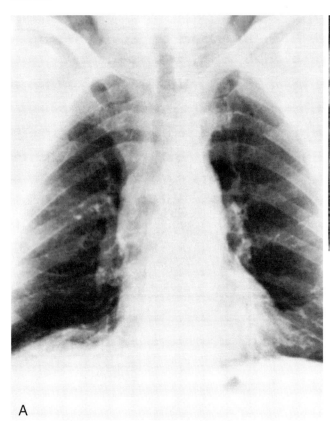

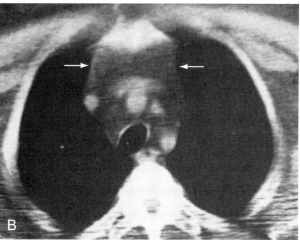

Figure 71.2 Computed tomography (CT) scan **(B)** showing the superior aspect of the mediastinum in a patient with mediastinal lipomatosis, appearing on standard chest radiograph **(A)** as diffuse mediastinal widening. The low radiographic density of fat evident on the CT scan is pathognomonic (*arrows*). (From Shepard JG: Computed tomography of the mediastinum. Clin Chest Med 5:291–305, 1984.)

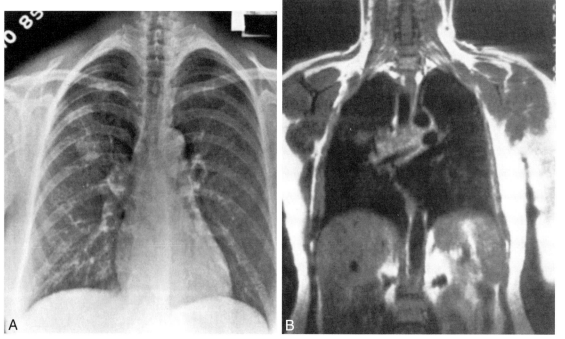

Figure 71.3 Chest radiograph **(A)** and coronal magnetic resonance image **(B)** of a patient with adenocarcinoma of the right upper lung field, showing metastases to the right hilum and mediastinum. (From Martini N, Heelan R, Westcott J, et al: Comparative merits of conventional, computed tomographic, and magnetic resonance imaging in assessing mediastinal involvement in surgically confirmed lung carcinoma. J Thorac Cardiovasc Surg 90:639–648, 1985.)

MRI is finding increasing use in evaluation of the mediastinum, both in general applications in chest disease,[2,43,44,47] and in more specific circumstances such as bronchogenic carcinoma,[41,42,48] and in various benign conditions. Whether current MRI techniques are superior to CT for staging the mediastinum in lung cancer remains unclear. A large multicenter study comparing the two techniques found similar accuracy for the detection of mediastinal node involvement, although MRI was superior for detecting direct mediastinal tumor invasion.[49] Based on this experience and numerous smaller studies, most authorities now recommend CT for routine staging purposes, and MRI for defining anatomy in special circumstances such as prior to surgical resection of superior sulcus tumors or those invading the mediastinum, chest wall, or diaphragm.[28,41,42]

Like CT, MRI has limitations. Both imaging techniques distinguish poorly between hilar masses and adjacent collapsed or consolidated lung. Both can also show displacement or compression of the esophagus or trachea by tumor, but often are unable to indicate whether there is also invasion of these structures. Most importantly, neither technique reliably distinguishes between benign and malignant causes for lymph node enlargement.

ULTRASONOGRAPHY

Ultrasonography may be useful in confirming the cystic nature of mediastinal masses. Successful diagnosis of pericardial and other developmental cysts has been accomplished using this technique, although it cannot readily distinguish between benign and malignant cystic lesions. Both transthoracic and endoscopic ultrasound probes may be useful in the evaluation of mediastinal disease.[50,51] Ultrasound may be most useful in guiding endoscopic biopsy techniques, as discussed later in this chapter.[52,53]

RADIONUCLIDE IMAGING

Radionuclide imaging studies rely on the localization of markers based on specific metabolic or immunologic properties of the target tissue (discussed further in Chapter 21). Compared with CT or MRI, the spatial resolution of radionuclide scans is relatively poor, but the overall diagnostic accuracy may be greatly improved over that of anatomic/morphologic images if a sufficiently specific probe is available. An additional appeal is the potential ability to diagnose and stage a malignancy, and identify distant metastases with a single scan of the entire body.

Planar imaging with gallium-67 (^{67}Ga) has been used in preoperative mediastinal assessment in patients with bronchogenic carcinoma, but early enthusiasm was eventually replaced by disenchantment with this technique. In their comparison of ^{67}Ga scans with standard chest radiographs and CT, Dooms and Hricak[54] determined that the radionuclide test was the least accurate. ^{67}Ga scans produced too many false positives because of nonspecific uptake by benign inflammatory nodes, and missed small neoplastic nodes.[54] In general, results using planar imaging of thallium-201 (^{201}Tl) tracer have been similarly disappointing.

Radionuclide imaging techniques occasionally have applicability in evaluation of the mediastinum under other circumstances. For instance, ^{67}Ga scans have been used in the

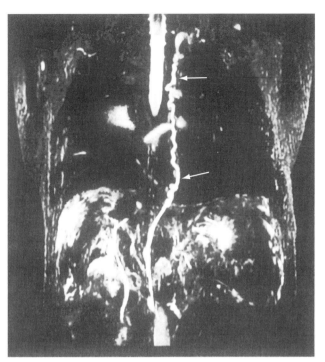

Figure 71.4 Magnetic resonance lymphogram of the thoracic duct. The normal course of the thoracic duct can be seen diagonally crossing the lower mediastinum from the patient's right to left and then ascending along the left mediastinum to reach the subclavian vein (*arrows*). In this case, the duct is somewhat more dilated and tortuous than normal due to the presence of hepatic cirrhosis. (From Takahashi H, Kuboyama S, Abe H, et al: Clinical feasibility of noncontrast-enhanced magnetic resonance lymphography of the thoracic duct. Chest 124:2136–2142, 2003.)

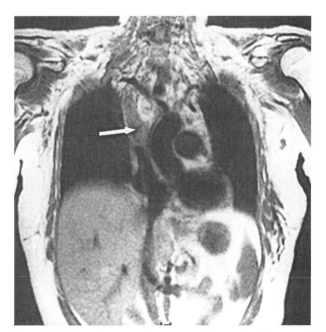

Figure 71.5 Coronal magnetic resonance image of a 52-year-old woman with multiple myeloma, experiencing symptoms of superior vena cava obstruction following placement of an indwelling central venous catheter in preparation for bone marrow transplantation. Vertically oriented structures are clearly discernible, and a black "flow void" is present within the heart and great vessels. The SVC is completely obstructed by thrombus (*arrow*).

evaluation of patients with sarcoidosis. Characteristic "lambda" and "panda" signs result from uptake in the lacrimal and salivary glands and the mediastinal lymph nodes.[55] However, the lack of specificity has relegated the use of ^{67}Ga scans to selected cases with high pretest probability, or to detect subclinical extrathoracic sites of involvement.[56] Radioiodine scanning may detect ectopic thyroid tissue, a positive result of which is pathognomonic for that condition.[7] Various radionuclide studies that may be used to characterize specific primary mediastinal masses are discussed later in this chapter.

Immunolocalization is a theoretically appealing means of targeting a probe to tumor tissues. However, experience with technetium-labeled antibodies has been disappointing due to a high rate of false-positive signals in the mediastinum.[57,58]

Single-photon emission computed tomography (SPECT) permits imaging of standard gamma-emitting probes in a cross-sectional fashion similar to conventional CT. This results in improved sensitivity, resolution, and anatomic information relative to planar images. The accuracy of ^{201}Tl-SPECT for determining mediastinal node involvement by lung cancer compares favorably with CT, but is not sensitive or specific enough to supplant surgical staging.[59,60]

Positron emission tomography (PET) is perhaps the most promising imaging technique available for use in the evaluation of lung cancer.[35,61] PET technology relies on high-energy photon–emitting probes such as (^{18}F)fluo-rodeoxyglucose (FDG), which are metabolically trapped within tumor cells. The result is a high signal-to-background ratio, excellent spatial resolution, and high accuracy (Fig. 71.6). Unfortunately, PET technology is costly and not universally available, and efforts to use modified SPECT equipment have failed to match the performance of dedicated PET scanners.[62] Continuous technological advances will undoubtedly improve both the performance and the cost of this technique. Already, improved specificity has been achieved by analyzing the differential uptake of FDG versus ^{11}C-labeled choline probes in malignant verus inflammatory lymph nodes.[63] Also, dedicated machines that generate coregistered CT and PET fusion images,[64] and artificial neural network algorithms for image interpretation,[65] have improved the accuracy of PET.

The precise role of PET in the mediastinal staging of lung cancer remains to be determined. Some authorities consider a negative FDG-PET scan sufficiently reassuring to proceed directly to thoracotomy.[66] However, in a series from our institution, FDG-PET scans failed to detect mediastinal metastases in 8 of 118 patients with surgically established nodal stage.[67] Seven of these eight cases had positive lymph nodes discovered during mediastinoscopy, and thus avoided an unnecessary up-front thoracotomy. Additional advantages of FDG-PET in our series included the identification of unsuspected sites of distant metastasis in 17% of patients, and the ability to focus invasive staging procedures on lymph node stations that are most likely to be involved with cancer.[67]

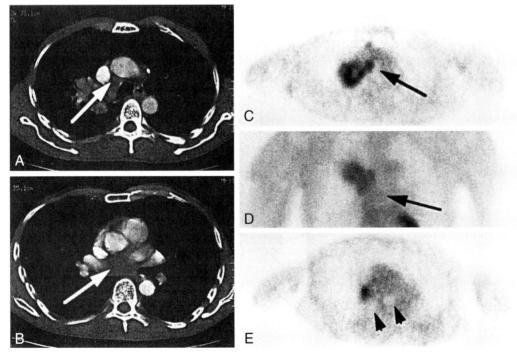

Figure 71.6 Computed tomography (CT) and positron emission tomography (PET) scans of a patient with right upper lobe squamous cell carcinoma. The primary tumor and right paratracheal adenopathy **(A)** and subcarinal adenopathy **(B)** are evident on the standard CT images (*arrows*). PET images reveal uptake in the primary tumor and right paratracheal nodes on axial **(C)** (*arrow*) and coronal **(D)** views, but not in the subcarinal node on coronal **(D)** (*arrow*) and axial **(E)** views. The *arrowheads* in **E** point to the main bronchi. At mediastinoscopy, the right paratracheal nodes were found to be malignant, and the subcarinal nodes were enlarged but benign. (From Vansteenkiste JF, Stroobants SG, De Leyn PR, et al: Mediastinal lymph node staging with FDG-PET scan in patients with potentially operable non-small cell lung cancer: A prospective analysis of 50 cases. Leuven Lung Cancer Group. Chest 112:1480–1486, 1997.)

Most published series describing the use of PET in staging lung cancer have been single institution series, usually from highly specialized units. In a review of 39 such studies comparing CT and FDG-PET in the staging of lung cancer, PET detected mediastinal metastases with sensitivity and specificity ranging from 50% to 100% and from 63% to 100%, respectively.[35] Recently, the American College of Surgeons Oncology Group reported the results of the only prospective multicenter evaluation of PET in staging resectable non–small cell lung cancer.[68] In this more realistic setting, the sensitivity of PET in determining mediastinal nodal involvement was 61%, its specificity was 84%, the negative predictive value was 87%, and the positive predictive value was only 56%. Based on this experience, it seems prudent to confirm both positive and negative FDG-PET findings if the findings of mediastinal involvement would alter the subsequent surgical approach.[68]

TECHNIQUES FOR OBTAINING MEDIASTINAL TISSUE

Definitive diagnosis of most mediastinal masses requires the evaluation of a tissue sample. Available approaches for biopsy of mediastinal lesions include needle aspiration and biopsy via transbronchial, percutaneous, or transesophageal approaches; and surgical biopsies obtained by more invasive procedures, including mediastinoscopy, mediastinotomy, and thoracoscopy.

NEEDLE ASPIRATION AND BIOPSY

Transbronchial Needle Aspiration

Transbronchial needle aspiration (TBNA) via the fiberoptic bronchoscope is an appealing technique, because it can yield definitive proof of the presence of malignancy in the mediastinum using a procedure less hazardous and costly than mediastinoscopy (see additional discussion in Chapter 22).[69] The procedure was initially carried out via the rigid bronchoscope, then adapted for use through the flexible fiberoptic bronchoscope.[70,71] Subsequently, larger needles were developed that can yield tissue fragments suitable for histologic evaluation.[72-74] Despite the proximity of major vessels and lung parenchyma to the areas routinely biopsied, TBNA appears to be a safe procedure; few significant complications (pneumothorax and hemomediastinum) have been reported in over 1500 reported procedures. Although experience with TBNA in patients receiving mechanical ventilation is limited, no complications were reported in a recent series of eight patients.[75]

In the setting of bronchogenic carcinoma, TBNA focuses on the subcarinal lymph nodes and the right paratracheal nodes, both of which are common metastatic sites. Experience with TBNA in this setting has been reported mostly in terms of the "yield" of positive results, without definitive surgical confirmation of both positive and negative TBNA results.[76-80] A careful prospective study found that only 15% of patients with the established diagnosis of lung cancer had a positive result from TBNA, but in 69% of these the TBNA specimen was the only preoperative evidence for mediastinal metastases.[77] The true sensitivity and specificity of TBNA appear to range from 14% to 50% and from 96% to 100%, respectively.[81,82] Thus, negative results require definitive operative confirmation, but the risk of false-positive TBNA results appears to be quite low. Of four false-positive results reported in the literature, two were believed to have resulted from aspiration of the primary tumor adjacent to a major airway, and two were attributed to tumor cells picked up from tracheobronchial secretions.[81,83,84] Accordingly, it is sensibly recommended that TBNA be performed prior to bronchial exploration or biopsy of any endobronchial lesions.[76,77]

To achieve comparable results in clinical practice, training and experience with TBNA are necessary,[85,86] along with appropriate selection of patients. The yield is improved in patients with visible endobronchial lesions, or with widening or erythema of the carina,[76,77,87] and mediastinal adenopathy on plain radiographs and subcarinal adenopathy on CT also are associated with improved yield.[88] The yield of TBNA can be improved by guidance of the biopsy needle placement using CT[89] or endoscopic ultrasound,[90-93a] and improves incrementally as up to five to seven needle passes are made without guidance.[94,95] Notably, the first aspirate may be diagnostic in 42% to 58% of cases, suggesting that rapid on-site cytopathologic examination could spare many patients repeated biopsy attempts.[94,95]

Finally, TBNA may have utility in other clinical situations, such as the diagnosis of a variety of primary mediastinal masses and cysts, metastases from extrathoracic malignancies, miscellaneous benign conditions,[69,79,96,97] and the evaluation of mediastinal adenopathy associated with human immunodeficiency virus (HIV) infection.[98]

Percutaneous Needle Aspiration and Biopsy

Percutaneous needle aspiration and biopsy of mediastinal masses, used sporadically for several decades, has experienced renewed utilization using ultrasound[99-102] or, more often, CT guidance[103,104] (Fig. 71.7). When performed by experienced clinicians, percutaneous needle aspiration of the mediastinum has acceptable morbidity and yields comparable to those from percutaneous biopsy of pulmonary lesions. As with TBNA, serious bleeding is seldom encountered,[103,104] and accurate diagnosis of a wide variety of lesions has been reported.[105,106] Accuracy undoubtedly varies with the skill and persistence of the operator and is enhanced when immediate cytopathologic examination is used to determine whether or not an adequate sample has been obtained.[104]

Endoscopic Ultrasound-Guided Needle Aspiration and Biopsy

Endoscopic ultrasonography-guided needle aspiration and biopsy relies on the availability of endoscopic ultrasound probes to guide the placement of biopsy needles, which are passed through the working channel of a gastroscope.[93,107] The proximity of the esophagus to areas of the mediastinum relatively inaccessible to mediastinoscopy, such as the posterior subcarinal lymph nodes, makes this approach particularly appealing. Preliminary studies suggest that it is highly accurate and well tolerated.[52,53,108,109] Endoscopic ultrasonography-guided biopsy has similar sensitivity compared

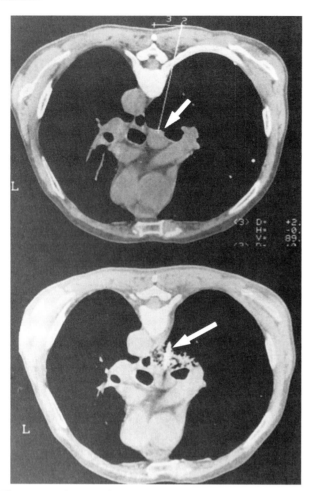

Figure 71.7 Computed tomography–guided needle aspiration of a mediastinal mass. The upper image shows the planned course of the biopsy needle, entering the left paraspinal area to reach a subcarinal lymph node (*arrow*). The lower image shows the tip of the needle extending into the mass (*arrow*). (From Akamatsu H, Terashima M, Koike T, et al: Staging of primary lung cancer by computed tomography-guided percutaneous needle cytology of mediastinal lymph nodes. Ann Thorac Surg 62:352–355, 1996.)

to PET, and superior specificity (100%).[110] In selected cases it can confirm the presence of mediastinal metastases and obviate the need for surgical staging procedures.[111]

MEDIASTINOSCOPY, ANTERIOR MEDIASTINOTOMY, AND THORACOSCOPY

Mediastinoscopy is a procedure that allows direct inspection and biopsy of lymph nodes or other masses in the superior portion of the anterior mediastinum.[3,112,113] In its present form, it was introduced by Carlens in 1959.[114] Although more invasive than any of the techniques discussed previously in this chapter, mediastinoscopy can provide large specimens for histologic examination, including entire lymph nodes, rather than the cellular aspirates or small tissue fragments produced by needle biopsy techniques.

Mediastinal anatomy from the mediastinoscopist's perspective is different from that based on the lateral chest radiograph as described earlier: Structures are considered according to whether they lie anterior, posterior, or imme-diately to the right or left of the trachea.[5,115] Not all of the mediastinal lymph nodes can be reached by the medi-astinoscope. Those readily accessible include the right para-tracheal nodes to the level of the tracheal bifurcation, the left paratracheal nodes as far as the aortic arch, and the anterior subcarinal nodes.[2] Posterior subcarinal nodes and nodes in aortic and para-aortic locations cannot be reached via the standard cervical approach, but are accessible using extended cervical mediastinoscopy[116] or anterior medi-astinotomy through an incision in the left second intercostal space (the Chamberlain procedure).[2,117–119] Mediastinoscopy and anterior mediastinotomy usually require general anes-thesia, but may be performed as outpatient procedures when subsequent thoracotomy is not planned immediately.[120]

Mediastinoscopy has utility in evaluating mediastinal adenopathy or mass lesions in a variety of settings, includ-ing the evaluation of complications of HIV infection.[121] However, its most frequent application is in the staging of bronchogenic carcinoma.[122] Surgeons debate whether to perform this procedure at the time of thoracotomy or to schedule thoracotomy at a later time, after final pathology results are available. The former approach has the disad-vantages of extending anesthesia time and relying on pre-liminary results in the determination of resectability, whereas the latter approach requires two separate episodes of anesthesia and postoperative recuperation. Recent evi-dence suggests that either frozen section or imprint cytol-ogy methods can provide rapid, accurate results and facilitate immediate decisions about the feasibility of cura-tive resection.[123,124]

In addition to limitations in the accessibility of certain nodal groups,[82,125,126] and the necessity for general anesthe-sia, mediastinoscopy has potential but rare complications. A recent retrospective 10-year review of 2137 consecutive mediastinoscopies in one center reported only one death attributable to the procedure (0.05%) and 12 complications (0.6%).[112] Potential complications include pneumothorax, hemorrhage, recurrent laryngeal nerve paralysis, elevation of one hemidiaphragm, injury to the trachea, esophageal perforation, thoracic duct laceration, air embolism, and mediastinitis. Morbidity and mortality from anterior medias-tinotomy in 62 patients were 16.1% and 1.6%, respectively.[127]

Precise indications for mediastinoscopy in non–small cell lung cancer are controversial. The presence of enlarged nodes is an important indication for mediastinoscopy, so that patients with resectable tumors are not incorrectly assumed to have inoperable mediastinal spread (Fig. 71.8). Some advocate the routine use of mediastinoscopy in the evaluation of all cases of potentially resectable disease because neither CT, MRI, nor even PET imaging reliably excludes metastatic lymph node involvement.[112,128] In an attempt to reduce the incidence of unnecessary medi-astinoscopy, some authors use mediastinoscopy more selec-tively and omit the procedure if all nodes are less than 1.0 cm or 1.5 cm in short axis diameter by CT scan,[2,129] or if the primary tumor is small, peripheral, or located in either of the lower lobes.[125,130] Despite these guidelines, the deci-sion about whom to subject to mediastinoscopy or anterior mediastinotomy for lung cancer staging remains a variable one that depends on local resources, personal experience, institutional biases, and treatment preferences for patients with minimal mediastinal nodal involvement.

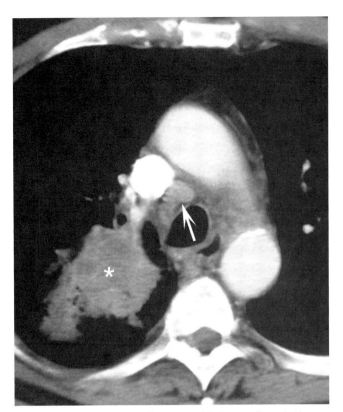

Figure 71.8 Axial computed tomographic image through the lower trachea shows a squamous cell carcinoma in the posterior right upper lobe (*) and right paratracheal lymphadenopathy (*arrow*). The right paratracheal lymph node, which was more than 2.0 cm in short axis diameter, did not show abnormal tracer accumulation on PET. It was surgically sampled and proven to be free of tumor. (Courtesy of Michael B. Gotway, MD, Department of Radiology, University of California, San Francisco.)

Video-assisted thoracoscopic surgery, usually considered a tool for the evaluation of pleural and lung abnormalities, also can be helpful in the management of mediastinal diseases (see also Chapter 23). After dissection through the parietal mediastinal pleura, mediastinal lymph nodes can be sampled to aid in the staging of malignancies such as esophageal carcinoma[131] and for the diagnosis and resection of primary mediastinal tumors and cysts.[132-137] Video-assisted thoracoscopy can approach lesions in any mediastinal compartment, but appears to be particularly well suited to evaluating lesions in the middle and posterior compartments.[138]

THE MEDIASTINAL MASS

DEFINITION

Specific lesions that present as a mass in the mediastinum may be discovered incidentally or identified during evaluation of thoracic or systemic symptoms. Although they meet this definition, mediastinal metastases or tumors invading the mediastinum from other intrathoracic sites are customarily omitted. Likewise, primary lesions of the trachea, heart, or esophagus are not discussed, even though they lie within the mediastinum. Several of the masses mentioned, such as thyroid and fat, are not tumors or even disease

processes per se, but are instead aberrantly located or overabundant normal tissues. Justification for their inclusion comes from the similarity of their presentation to that of mediastinal tumors and the fact that, in most instances, they require the same evaluation as any other mediastinal mass. The clinical problem is a "mediastinal mass," and this discussion focuses on the main disease processes that are the cause of this presentation.

Diseases that are relatively unique to the mediastinum, such as thymic neoplasms and developmental cysts, are discussed in some detail. Other conditions that commonly occur elsewhere in the body, such as lymphoma, are considered mainly in terms of the features of their presentation in the mediastinum; for a comprehensive discussion of these topics, the reader is referred elsewhere.

CLASSIFICATION AND INCIDENCE

The most practical classification of mediastinal masses from the clinical standpoint is by location, grouping together lesions that are characteristically found in the anterior, middle, and posterior mediastinal compartments. Table 71.4 lists the disorders that present as a mediastinal mass and the compartments in which they characteristically arise. This simple scheme is followed in this chapter, recognizing that such a classification ignores embryologic or histologic similarities between some lesions,[3] and the fact that mediastinal masses often present in mediastinal compartments other than their most typical location (Fig. 71.9).

Primary mediastinal masses are not uncommon, although their real incidence is difficult to ascertain reliably. An overall incidence of 1 case per 100,000 population per year may be a reasonable estimation.[139] The tumors and cysts that account for this incidence are individually much less frequent. Table 71.5 estimates the relative frequencies of the most common mediastinal tumors and cysts, based on the collection by Silverman and Sabiston[7] of nearly 2400 cases from the literature. More recent series suggest a similar pattern,[9,10,140,141] although Cohen and associates[10] have observed a rising incidence of mediastinal masses in general and an increasing proportion of lymphoma and malignant neurogenic tumors over the course of their 45-year survey. The precise frequencies of individual disorders vary in different series, probably because of differences in referral sources and patient populations, but neurogenic tumors, thymomas, and developmental cysts account for around 60% of all mediastinal masses. Lymphomas and germ cell tumors such as teratoma and seminoma account for about one fourth, and a large number of other lesions, both benign and malignant, constitute the remaining 15%.

There are some differences in the incidence of mediastinal masses between adults and children: Thymoma and thyroid masses rarely occur in infants and children, whereas neurogenic tumors are less common in adults. The likelihood of malignancy is higher in infants and children than in adults: In adults, about one fourth of all mediastinal mass lesions are malignant, whereas in children, the percentage is 40% to 45%.[7] In addition, HIV infection substantially alters the spectrum of mediastinal disease. In the HIV-positive population, mediastinal masses are most often due to granulomatous inflammation from mycobacterial and other infections, lymphoma, and other opportunistic processes, and multiple

Table 71.4 Disorders Presenting as a Mass in the Mediastinum

Anterior Mediastinum
Thymic neoplasms
Germ cell tumors
  Teratoma
  Seminoma
  Nonseminomatous germ cell tumors
    Embryonal cell carcinoma
    Choriocarcinoma
Lymphoma
  Hodgkin's disease
  Non-Hodgkin's lymphoma
Thyroid neoplasms
Parathyroid neoplasms
Mesenchymal tumors
  Lipoma
  Fibroma
  Lymphangioma
  Hemangioma
  Mesothelioma
  Others
Diaphragmatic hernia (Morgagni)
Primary carcinoma

Middle Mediastinum
Lymphadenopathy
  Reactive and granulomatous inflammation
  Metastasis
  Angiofollicular lymphoid hyperplasia (Castleman's disease)
Lymphoma
Developmental cysts
  Pericardial cyst
  Foregut duplication cysts
    Bronchogenic cyst
    Enteric cyst
  Others
Vascular enlargements
Diaphragmatic hernia (hiatal)

Posterior Mediastinum
Neurogenic tumors
  Arising from peripheral nerves
  Arising from sympathetic ganglia
  Arising from paraganglionic tissue
Meningocele
Esophageal lesions
  Carcinoma
  Diverticula
Diaphragmatic hernia (Bochdalek)
Miscellaneous

diseases may be present simultaneously,[121,142] including bronchogenic carcinoma.[143] Finally, surgical case series are likely to underrepresent causes of mediastinal masses, such as goiter, that do not routinely lead to surgical intervention.

SPECIFIC MEDIASTINAL TUMORS AND CYSTS

LESIONS TYPICALLY IN THE ANTERIOR MEDIASTINUM

Thymic Neoplasms

Thymoma is the most common neoplasm occurring in the anterior mediastinum,[2,7–9,23,144–147] and has been recognized

more often recently because of increased aggressiveness in evaluating patients with myasthenia gravis.[7,9] Histologically, thymoma is composed of lymphocytes and epithelial cells and is described according to predominating cell type.[148] However, a thymoma's histologic appearance correlates poorly with its biologic behavior, and clinically these tumors are categorized according to their local invasiveness rather than their appearance under the microscope.[8,149] Thus biologically aggressive thymomas are termed "invasive" rather than "malignant" thymoma.

The peak incidence of thymomas is between the ages of 40 and 60 years, with equal gender predilection. These neoplasms are rare in children. Two thirds of patients are asymptomatic at the time of diagnosis; an anterior mediastinal mass is discovered incidentally on the chest roentgenogram. The rest of the patients typically have nonspecific chest pain, cough, or dyspnea.[150] However, from 40% to 70% have at least laboratory evidence of one or more of the two dozen systemic "parathymic" syndromes that have been recognized.[7,146] Myasthenia gravis is most frequent among these, reported in 10% to 50% of patients with thymoma.[7] How thymoma produces myasthenia gravis is unknown, but autoantibodies to the postsynaptic acetylcholine receptor appear to explain the dysfunction of the neuromuscular junction[151] and are found in the majority of patients with myasthenia.[152]

Radiographically, thymomas are usually detected near the junction of the heart and great vessels; typically, they are round or oval and their margins smooth or lobulated (Fig. 71.10). Compared with thymic hyperplasia, which is typically symmetrical, thymoma usually distorts the gland's normal shape and extends to one side.[144,153] As with virtually all solid mass lesions of the mediastinum, thymoma is diagnosed with certainty only by examination of tissue.[148] However, CT can reveal gross invasion and MRI can demonstrate the continuity of a mediastinal mass with the thymus,[154] and discern invasion of vascular structures.[155] Preliminary experience with somatostatin receptor scintigraphy[156] and FDG-PET[157] appears promising for discerning thymoma and other thymic tumors from benign thymic hyperplasia.

Thymomas are neoplastic, but most have relatively benign biologic behavior. Patients whose tumors are fully encapsulated can expect survival equal to that of the general population. Invasive tumors have a poorer prognosis, with 50% to 77% 5-year and 30% to 55% 10-year survival.[158,159] Recurrence after resection occurs in nearly a third of patients.[159] The presence of a thymoma-associated systemic syndrome has traditionally been regarded as a poor prognostic sign.[7,8] However, with improvements in perioperative management of patients with myasthenia gravis, the adverse effect of parathymic manifestations on the prognosis of patients with thymoma appears to be offset by the earlier diagnosis of thymoma discovered because of myasthenic symptoms.[144,147,158]

Thymomas may respond to hormonal therapy[159a] but are usually managed by resection via a median sternotomy approach,[7,145,147] or via video-assisted thoracoscopic surgery.[136] Most authors favor removal of as much tumor mass as possible, even when it invades surrounding tissues. Adjunctive treatment with postoperative radiotherapy is provided,[8,147,160] and the addition of preoperative or adjuvant chemotherapy appears promising.[146,161–163] Thymectomy may also improve symptoms in some patients with myasthenia

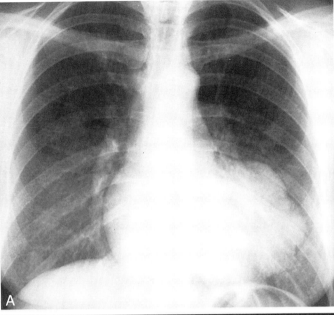

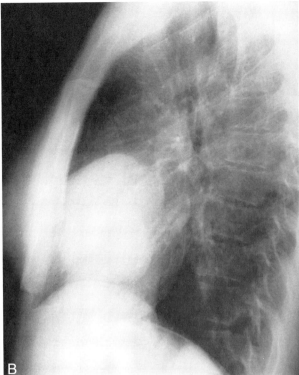

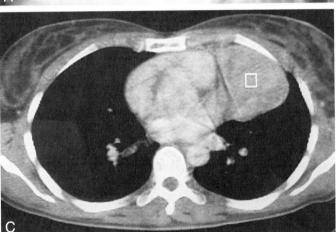

Figure 71.9 Typical findings on chest radiographs (**A,** posteroanterior view; **B,** lateral view) and thoracic computed tomogram (**C**) showing a mass presenting in the middle mediastinum. At surgery, this mass proved to be a benign thymoma, originating in the anterior mediastinum and extending by a slender stalk into the middle radiographic compartment. (Courtesy of Dr. Robert Stevens, Wenatchee, WA.)

gravis,[164] although survival appears to be improved primarily in those without an actual thymoma found at thymectomy.[165]

Other thymic mass lesions include benign conditions such as thymic hyperplasia, thymic cysts,[148] and lipothymoma.[166] Thymic carcinoma is a histologically malignant process that invades locally and frequently metastasizes.[167] The prognosis depends on the histologic grade and the anatomic stage and is generally poor. Resection and combined chemotherapy and radiation therapy are advocated.[168] Carcinoid tumors occasionally occur in the thymus.[169,170] They may cause Cushing's syndrome[171] and be associated with multiple endocrine adenomatosis. Locally invasive carcinoids may be difficult to resect completely, but characteristically have a prolonged clinical course.[7] Interestingly, the thymus is also a common site for mediastinal Hodgkin's lymphoma, and normal thymic tissue may enlarge following chemotherapy for lymphoma (a process termed *thymic rebound*), mimicking recurrence of the primary disease.[172]

Germ Cell Tumors

Approximately 10% to 12% of primary mediastinal masses are derived from germinal tissues, both in adults and in children.[3,7,8,173,174] These neoplasms are classified into four main groups: teratoma and teratocarcinoma, seminoma, embryonal cell carcinoma, and choriocarcinoma.[175] They are believed to arise from remnant multipotent germ cells that have migrated abnormally during embryonic development.[176] Next to the sacrococcygeal area in children and the gonads in adults, the mediastinum is the most common site for these tumors.[7,174]

Teratomas are the most common germ cell tumors. By definition, they are made up of tissues foreign to the area in which they occur. Ectodermal derivatives predominate, but structures originating in all three primary germ cell layers may be found. When only the epidermis and its derivatives are present, the term *dermoid cyst* is appropriate. Teratomas occur most often in young adults, but have been reported in all age groups, and men and women are affected with equal frequency. Most (80%) are benign, but teratocarcinoma, the malignant counterpart, is an aggressive, rapidly spreading neoplasm with a poor prognosis.

Most patients with teratomas have symptoms caused by the tumor; only about a third are asymptomatic.[7,177] Usual symptoms are pain, cough, and dyspnea. If the tumor erodes into a bronchus, hemoptysis or even the expectoration of

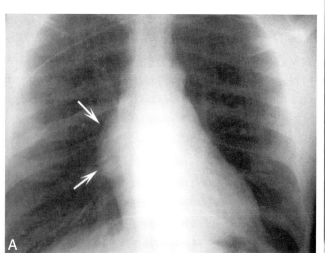
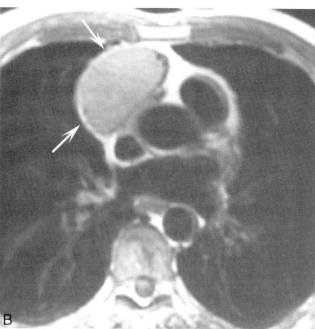

Figure 71.10 A, Frontal chest radiograph shows a smoothly marginated mass along the right side of the mediastinum (*arrows*). The obscuration of a portion of the right atrial border indicates that the mass lies within the anterior mediastinum. **B,** Axial magnetic resonance T1-weighted image through the base of the heart shows that the mass (*arrows*) is slightly hyperintense compared to skeletal muscle and resides within the anterior mediastinum. Note the smooth, well defined margins of the mass, consistent with encapsulated thymoma. (Courtesy of Michael B. Gotway, MD, Department of Radiology, University of California, San Francisco.)

Table 71.5 Relative Frequencies of Mediastinal Masses in Adults and Children

Lesion	Adults (%)	Children (%)
Thymoma	19	—
Developmental cysts	21	18
Bronchogenic	7	8
Pericardial	7	<1
Enteric	3	8
Other cysts	4	2
Neurogenic tumors	21	40
Lymphoma	13	18
Germ cell tumors	11	11
Endocrine (thyroid, parathyroid, carcinoid)	6	—
Mesenchymal tumors	7	9
Primary carcinoma	—	—
Other malignancies	3	4

Data from Silverman NA, Sabiston DC: Mediastinal masses. Surg Clin North Am 60:757–777, 1980, and based on their review of reported mediastinal masses in 1950 adults and 437 children.

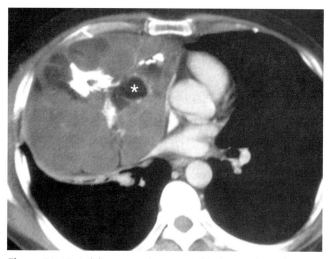

Figure 71.11 Axial computed tomographic image through the base of the heart shows a large right-sided anterior mediastinal mass with heterogeneous attenuation. Elements of calcium, soft tissue, and fat (*) are present. The presence of fat within an anterior mediastinal mass is characteristic of teratoma. (Courtesy of Michael B. Gotway, MD, Department of Radiology, University of California, San Francisco.)

differentiated tissue such as hair (trichoptysis) or sebaceous material may occur.[177] Teratomas may also rupture into the pleural space and produce acute respiratory distress or enter the pericardium, causing pericardial tamponade.

On chest radiographs, teratomas are generally smooth, rounded, and well circumscribed if they are cystic and more lobulated and asymmetrical if they are solid. Soft tissue, fat, and calcification (occasionally, fully formed teeth and bone) can be identified on CT images, rendering this one of few mediastinal tumors that can be diagnosed confidently before operation (Fig. 71.11).[33] All teratomas should be resected because of the uncertainty as to whether they are benign and the possibility of further enlargement with impingement on adjacent structures. In malignant teratoma, adjuvant combination chemotherapy may result in improved survival.[178]

Seminoma (dysgerminoma) differs from teratoma in numerous respects.[8,148,179] It occurs almost exclusively in men, usually in the third decade of life. Most patients seek medical attention because of chest pain, dyspnea, cough, hoarseness, or dysphagia. Superior vena cava obstruction can occur.[7] Seminomas are aggressive malignant tumors that extend locally and metastasize distantly, usually to skeletal bones. They may secrete human chorionic gonadotropin, but not alpha-fetoprotein. Factors associated with a poorer prognosis include age over 35 years; superior vena cava obstruction; supraclavicular, cervical, or hilar adenopathy; and presentation with fever.[180,181] Seminomas are extremely radiosensitive and may respond dramatically to chemotherapy even in cases with dissemination.[176,182] With aggressive cisplatin-based regimens, long-term survival with all mediastinal seminomas is approximately 80%.[176,183]

Nonseminomatous mediastinal germ cell tumors have been classified variously,[8] but may be grouped into embryonal cell carcinoma and choriocarcinoma.[7,180] A nonseminomatous malignancy usually grouped with embryonal cell carcinoma is called endodermal sinus or yolk sac tumor. These highly malignant aggressive tumors often secrete human chorionic gonadotropin, alpha-fetoprotein, or carcinoembryonic antigen, which may also produce clinical manifestations, such as gynecomastia, in 50% of patients.[8] Associations have been noted with Klinefelter's syndrome[184,185] and with hematologic malignancy.[186,187] Like seminoma, these tumors occur mainly in men in the third and fourth decades and are usually symptomatic. Although most patients present with disseminated disease and the prognosis has been less favorable than in seminoma,[8] cisplatin-based treatment regimens have markedly improved the outcome, with over 50% of patients achieving long-term survival.[176,187] Even disseminated and refractory malignant germ cell tumors may respond to aggressive chemotherapy[188] and salvage regimens involving bone marrow transplantation.[189,190]

Lymphoma

Lymphoma is a common cause of a mediastinal mass in both adults and children and represents between 10% and 20% of cases in most series.[3,7–10,141] Hodgkin's disease occurs bimodally in adolescents and young adults and in those over 50, whereas non-Hodgkin's lymphomas occur most commonly in older adults. Although 50% to 60% of patients with Hodgkin's disease have mediastinal lymph node involvement at the time of diagnosis,[191] and non-Hodgkin's lymphomas involve the mediastinum in only 20% of cases,[192] Hodgkin's disease accounts for only a third of all cases of mediastinal lymphoma because of the greater overall incidence of non-Hodgkin's lymphomas.[7] Approximately 5% of patients with either type of lymphoma have disease confined to the mediastinum.[191,193] Lymphoma is especially common as a thoracic complication in HIV-infected patients.[194–196] HIV-associated lymphomas are usually immunoblastic,[194] although Hodgkin's disease also is more common in patients with HIV infection than in the general population.[195,197]

Incidental discovery of a mass on a chest radiograph is a common presentation of lymphoma, although many patients have systemic symptoms or more localized complaints such as cough and chest pain. Tracheal compromise and superior vena cava obstruction are common, as are pericardial and pleural involvement,[193,198] and Hodgkin's disease often involves the hilar nodes and lung parenchyma.[198] Resection is not a necessary part of therapy, but anterior thoracotomy or mediastinoscopy is usually required to confirm the diagnosis if adenopathy is not evident outside the mediastinum. The prognosis of Hodgkin's and other lymphomas has improved strikingly in the last 2 decades as more effective and less toxic combinations of radiotherapy and chemotherapy have evolved, and effective salvage regimens, including bone marrow transplantation, have been developed to treat relapsed disease. More detailed discussions of Hodgkin's disease and non-Hodgkin's lymphomas in pediatric and adult populations are available in several excellent reviews.[199–204]

Thyroid Lesions

Ectopic thyroid glands account for fewer than 10% of mediastinal masses in surgical series, but are probably more common in clinical practice. Thyroid tissue within the mediastinum is of two distinct origins. Most commonly, a cervical goiter extends substernally into the anterior mediastinum.[205] Primary intrathoracic goiter, presumably originating from a rest of heterotopic thyroid tissue, is rare. Most such goiters are in the anterior mediastinum, but they may occur in the middle or posterior mediastinum as well.[7,8] Intrathoracic goiter occurs predominantly in women of middle age or older; it is usually asymptomatic, although hoarseness, cough, or swelling of the face and arms may occur. Intrathoracic thyroid tissue is easily recognized by radioactive iodine scanning,[206] and may be suspected on the basis of high radiodensity on CT scans, particularly after iodinated contrast injection.[207,208] Most mediastinal goiters, being of cervical origin, can be resected by a transcervical approach, without need for sternotomy.[209]

Parathyroid Lesions

Mediastinal parathyroid tissue accounts for as many as 10% of cases of hyperparathyroidism,[210] and the mediastinum is the most common site for ectopic parathyroid adenomas in surgically resistant hyperparathyroidism.[211,212] Half of ectopic parathyroid adenomas lie in the anterior mediastinum, usually near the thymus.[213] Parathyroid cysts may enlarge sufficiently to appear as a mass on the chest radiograph and to produce symptoms.[214–217] Otherwise, location of aberrant functioning parathyroid tissue can be a difficult clinical problem that may be aided preoperatively by CT, ultrasound, or MRI.[218–220] Selective arteriography and venous sampling for parathormone levels have largely been supplanted by radionuclide scans, unless therapeutic embolization is anticipated.[219]

Technetium-99m sestamibi scans are highly accurate in the detection of aberrant parathyroid tissue,[220,221] and their routine use has been proposed as cost-effective because it may lessen the chance of protracted and/or failed cervical explorations in cases of primary hyperparathyroidism.[222] However, another study found no differences in meaningful perioperative or ultimate outcomes of patients who did and did not undergo preoperative localization studies.[223] Localization studies may be better justified in patients who have failed a prior attempt at resection, in whom an aberrantly located adenoma would be more likely.[220,224,225] Parathyroid adenomas are cured by complete resection, and resection via video-assisted thoracoscopic surgery is increasingly advocated.[132,133,226]

Parathyroid carcinoma, like parathyroid adenoma, is often functional, resulting in varying degrees of hyperparathyroidism, but is also locally invasive and may metastasize.[227] Cure is possible with aggressive surgical management.[228]

Mesenchymal Tumors

Included in this group of unusual mediastinal masses are lipomas, fibromas, mesotheliomas, and lymphangiomas, plus several other rare tumors (see Table 71.4).[7] They arise from connective tissue, fat, smooth muscle, striated muscle, blood vessels, or lymphatic channels and can occur in any region of the mediastinum. Histologically and clinically, they are not substantially different from their counterparts elsewhere in the body. Unless the lesion is very large, the presence of symptoms usually means that the lesion is malignant.[2,7]

Lipoma is the most common mesenchymal tumor of the mediastinum and is most often anterior. It may be encapsulated or unencapsulated, but in either case it is smooth and rounded with sharply defined margins. The characteristic low density of lipomas on CT images (Fig. 71.12) permits a confident diagnosis unless there is associated inhomogeneity, invasion of surrounding tissues, or poor demarcation of the mass's perimeter, in which case malignancy (liposarcoma or lipoblastoma) or teratoma must be excluded.[2,229]

Considerably more common than lipoma is mediastinal lipomatosis, or generalized overabundance of histologically normal unencapsulated fat.[230] The presence of some fat in the anterior mediastinum is normal, usually in and around the thymus. Accumulation of excess fat is associated with generalized obesity[231] or Cushing's syndrome, or with the use of exogenous corticosteroids and other drugs,[232,233] and in some cases occurs without explanation.[230] Mediastinal lipomatosis appears on the conventional radiograph as a smooth widening or bulging of normal mediastinal contours, and its low homogeneous CT density confirms the diagnosis (see Fig. 71.2).[2] Compression or displacement of other mediastinal structures does not occur.[231,232]

Multiple symmetrical lipomatosis is a rare disorder, distinct from those just described, that can cause tracheal compression.[234] However, this disorder generally does not affect the anterior mediastinum, cardiophrenic angles, or paraspinal areas.

Sarcomas involving the mediastinum are rare. Nerve sheath sarcoma, spindle cell sarcoma, leiomyosarcoma, and liposarcoma are the four most common types.[235] Prior radiation therapy appears to be a predisposing factor in some cases.[236,237]

LESIONS TYPICALLY IN THE MIDDLE MEDIASTINUM

Enlargement of Lymph Nodes

Enlargement of lymph nodes represents one of the most common causes of mediastinal abnormality on chest radi-

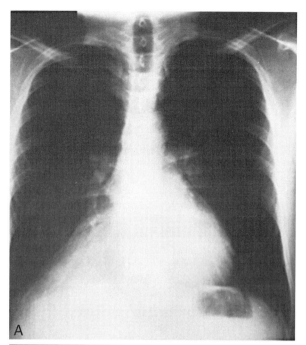

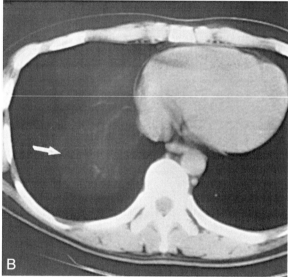

Figure 71.12 A, The chest radiograph of a 31-year-old man showing an abnormality at the right cardiophrenic angle noted as an incidental finding. **B,** Computed tomogram demonstrates a well-circumscribed homogenous fat-density mass characteristic of mediastinal lipoma extending into the right hemithorax (*arrow*).

ographs. Numerous classifications exist for the mediastinal lymph nodes, a comprehensive example of which is the 11-region scheme of the American Thoracic Society.[5] Figure 71.13 presents a simplified grouping of the main mediastinal nodes that corresponds to findings on conventional radiography and CT scans.[238] Nodes in the subcarinal, paratracheal, and hilar areas tend to be larger than those elsewhere,[2,239,240] but most authors consider a short axis diameter of 1.0 cm to be the upper limit of normal size.

Mediastinal lymph node enlargement is most often due to three general categories of disease process: lymphoma,[241,242] metastatic cancer,[238] and granulomatous

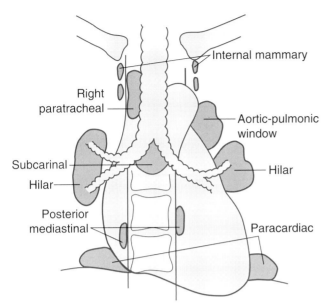

Figure 71.13 Simplified schematic diagram depicting mediastinal lymph node groups. (From McLoud TC, Meyer JE: Mediastinal metastases. Radiol Clin North Am 20:453–468, 1982.)

inflammation (granulomatous mediastinitis is discussed in Chapter 72). Numerous less common causes are described, including Castleman's disease or angiofollicular lymphoid hyperplasia. Mediastinal adenopathy is common in HIV-infected patients and is usually infection related, although lymphoma, Kaposi's sarcoma, and other processes may be responsible.[142] As discussed previously, lymph node enlargement can be detected accurately by CT and MRI, but imaging studies cannot reliably distinguish between benign and malignant causes of node enlargement (see Fig. 71.8).

Developmental Cysts

Developmental cysts of various sorts comprise 10% to 20% of all mediastinal masses in both adults and children.[7,243–245] Although some are histologically unclassifiable, most can be identified as pericardial, bronchogenic, or enteric on the basis of their lining tissues.[7,246] Bronchogenic and enteric cysts are often referred to as *foregut duplication cysts* because of their origin from aberrant portions of the ventral and dorsal foregut, respectively.

Pericardial cysts account for about one third of cystic masses in adults, but are much less common in children (see Table 71.5). They typically lie against the pericardium, diaphragm, or anterior chest wall in the right cardiophrenic angle. Rarely, pericardial cysts may communicate with the pericardium. Although typically harmless, pericardial cysts may enlarge to cause right ventricular outflow obstruction,[247] or rupture and hemorrhage to cause pericardial tamponade,[248] or sudden cardiac death.[249]

Bronchogenic cysts are typically found near the large airways, often just posterior to the carina, although they may be attached to the esophagus or even inside the pericardium.[7] The cyst wall often contains cartilage and respiratory epithelium. Most are discovered incidentally and cause no symptoms; however, they may communicate with the tracheobronchial tree and become infected[250]; enlarge

to cause airway obstruction (especially in infants),[251] pulmonary artery compression,[252] or hemodynamic collapse[253]; or rupture with disastrous consequences.[254] Spillage of cyst contents into the airway during anesthesia also has been reported.[255]

Enteric or enterogenous cysts are similar in location and appearance to bronchogenic cysts, but have digestive tract epithelium. They are relatively uncommon in adults, but are the most common cysts found in infants and children, in whom they may be associated with spinal extension and malformations of the vertebral column (called "neurenteric" cysts). Enteric cysts can occasionally be multiple and associated with duplications of other portions of the gastrointestinal tract.

Developmental cysts can usually be identified by CT or ultrasonography, and the diagnosis may be confirmed by aspiration cytology. MRI is valuable in cases of suspected spinal extension. In the appropriate clinical setting, benign cysts need not be resected unless they cause symptoms.[256] However, most authorities favor resection because of diagnostic uncertainties and the potential for development of complications.[243,244,250,254,257] Alternatives to thoracotomy include therapeutic aspiration,[258,259] and thoracoscopic or mediastinoscopic excision.[134,260,261] Resection is usually curative, but cases of recurrence are described.[262,263]

Vascular Masses and Enlargements

Although not technically masses, a variety of vascular lesions must be considered in the differential diagnosis of mediastinal enlargement seen on the chest radiograph.[8,264,265] These include poststenotic aortic dilation, aneurysms or tortuosity of the aorta and great vessels, aortic coarctation, innominate vein and superior vena cava aneurysms, persistent left vena cava, azygous and hemiazygos vein enlargement, anomalous pulmonary venous return, pulmonary venous varix, and cardiophrenic angle varices associated with portal hypertension.[266] Idiopathic dilation of the pulmonary trunk and pulmonary arterial hypertension of any cause may appear as a mediastinal mass, and traumatic aortic transection and more subtle vascular injuries may result in mediastinal hematoma.

Angiography has been the traditional means of diagnosing mediastinal masses of vascular origin, but CT imaging with intravenous contrast injection permits more convenient detection in most cases today.[267,268] MRI shows great promise in enabling definitive diagnosis without radiation or contrast exposure.[269–271] However, both CT and MRI can be misleading if the vascular lumen is obscured.[272]

Diaphragmatic Hernia

The protrusion of omental fat or other abdominal contents through the diaphragm may occur via several potential routes, and mediastinal mass lesions in any compartment can be the result.[2] A hernia through the foramen of Morgagni produces a cardiophrenic angle mass, usually on the right side. Bochdalek's hernia, in the posterior mediastinum, generally appears on the left side, presumably because the liver prevents herniation on the right. Herniation of fat around the esophagus is believed to precede hiatal hernia formation, and either may appear as a mediastinal mass. In the latter instance, an air-fluid level is intermittently seen on horizontal beam films. Fine linear densities are often demonstrable in diaphragmatic fat herniations on CT imaging. These are thought to represent omental vessels within the hernia, and they may help differentiate a hernia from a lipoma.[2] Although diaphragmatic herniations are usually incidental radiographic findings, traumatic central diaphragmatic hernias may protrude into the mediastinum and result in cardiac compromise.[273,274]

LESIONS TYPICALLY IN THE POSTERIOR MEDIASTINUM

Neurogenic Tumors

Neoplasms arising from neural tissues constitute the largest single group of mediastinal masses,[7,8,275-277] accounting for about 20% of adult cases and twice that proportion in children (see Table 71.5). They are classified according to specific tissue of origin into those arising from peripheral nerves, from sympathetic ganglia, and from paraganglionic (chemoreceptor) tissue (Table 71.6).[276] As a group, neurogenic tumors usually appear radiographically as a unilateral paravertebral mass.[7] Most are benign and asymptomatic in adults, but in children more than half are malignant and symptomatic.[277] Clinical manifestations include chest pain from nerve or bone erosion, dyspnea secondary to tracheal compression, and neurologic deficits resulting from spinal cord compression by intraspinal tumor extension. In addition, many neurogenic tumors are hormonally active.

Tumors arising from peripheral nerves include neurofibromas, neurilemomas or schwannomas, and neurosarcomas.[229] Neurofibromas contain both nerve sheath cells and nerve elements and are the most common tumor of this group. They are incompletely encapsulated and may grow quite large, producing symptoms by nerve compression or space occupation. Mediastinal neurofibroma may be one manifestation of von Recklinghausen's disease (neurofibromatosis). As with these tumors elsewhere, malignant degeneration into neurosarcoma eventually occurs in 10% to 15% of patients with Von Recklinghausen's disease.[8] Although patients with von Recklinghausen's neurofibromatosis do develop mediastinal neurofibromas, a meningocele is said to be a more likely cause of a posterior mediastinal mass in such persons.[7]

Table 71.6 Neurogenic Tumors of the Mediastinum

Neoplasms Arising from Peripheral Nerves
Neurofibroma
Neurilemoma (Schwannoma)
Neurosarcoma

Neoplasms Arising from Sympathetic Ganglia
Ganglioneuroma
Ganglioneuroblastoma
Neuroblastoma
Sympathicoblastoma

Neoplasms Arising from Paraganglionic Tissue
Pheochromocytoma
Paraganglioma (Chemodectoma)

Neurilemoma, or schwannoma, is another common neurogenic tumor that arises from the neural sheath. Most often seen in the third to fifth decade of life, neurilemoma usually causes no symptoms and appears as a well-circumscribed, homogeneous density on chest radiograph (Fig. 71.14A).[7,8,229] It is always completely encapsulated and does not invade surrounding tissues, although neurilemomas may extend into intervertebral foramina (Fig. 71.14B and C). They occasionally calcify, and cyst formation may occur, with subsequent mucoid degeneration or hemorrhage. Treatment of both neurilemoma and solitary neurofibroma is resection.

Malignant tumors of nerve sheath origin are also known as malignant neurofibroma, malignant schwannoma, or neurogenic fibrosarcoma. These tumors behave aggressively, with both local invasion and distant metastasis. Half occur in patients with neurofibromatosis.[22,278] Treatment requires wide excision and usually adjuvant radiation.[22]

Tumors arising from nerve cells in sympathetic ganglia display a spectrum of neoplastic behavior ranging from ganglioneuroma, a benign tumor occurring mainly in children, to the malignant tumors ganglioneuroblastoma and neuroblastoma. Ganglioneuromas cause symptoms merely by mass effect, and are usually cured by surgical excision. Ganglioneuroblastomas have intermediate behavior and can invade locally but are less likely to metastasize.[8] Neuroblastoma rapidly displaces and invades adjacent structures and may be widely metastatic at the time of presentation.[279,280] Neuroblastoma accounts for 13% to 23% of childhood mediastinal masses and is the second or third most common cause behind the lymphomas.[281,282] One series of older patients found that 13% of primary tumors were found in the mediastinum,[283] and some authors report that neuroblastoma arising in the mediastinum has a somewhat more favorable prognosis than the same malignancy elsewhere in the body.[284,285] These tumors often elaborate endocrine peptides and catecholamines, and are associated with diarrhea, fever, anorexia, and weight loss.[7] The propensity to produce catecholamines is used to advantage by imaging tumor uptake of the catecholamine precursor iodine-123–labeled metaiodobenzylguanidine for purposes of diagnosis and identification of distant tumor metastases.[286] Treatment of neuroblastoma involves surgical resection of stage I disease, and combination chemotherapy and radiation for advanced stages.[287] Radical excision of mediastinal neuroblastoma appears to offer no advantages over standard therapy.[284]

Neoplasms arising from paraganglionic or chemoreceptor tissue include pheochromocytomas, which are rare in the mediastinum and indistinguishable clinically or histologically from their counterparts in the abdomen, and paragangliomas (chemodectomas).[115,169,288] Paragangliomas may secrete catecholamines just as do pheochromocytomas. They appear benign under the microscope and seldom metastasize, but spread locally in an aggressive fashion and thus have high morbidity and mortality rates.[7,115]

MISCELLANEOUS MEDIASTINAL MASSES

Numerous rare causes of mass lesions in the mediastinum have been described.[8,289] These include malignancies known

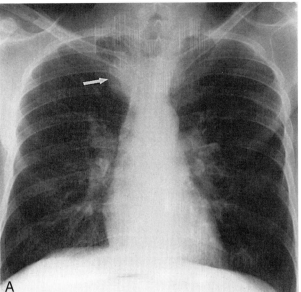
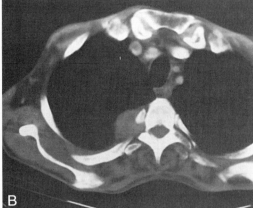
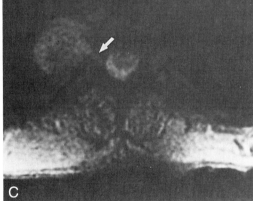

Figure 71.14 Series of imaging studies of a 64-year-old asymptomatic man with a surgically proved neurilemoma, or schwannoma. **A,** Posteroanterior chest radiograph showing an incidental finding of a discrete mass behind the right clavicular head (*arrow*). **B,** Computed tomogram showing homogeneous, well-circumscribed appearance and posterior location adjacent to the vertebral column. **C,** Magnetic resonance image showing extension of the tumor into the neural foramen (*arrow*).

as primary carcinoma and sarcoma of the mediastinum.[7,290] Primary carcinoma usually occurs in the anterior or middle mediastinum and is believed to be distinct from bronchogenic carcinoma and from other primary mediastinal neoplasms. It occurs primarily in adults, usually in men, and has an aggressive, rapidly fatal course with little response to therapy. Primary mediastinal sarcoma is a rare lesion of children, which otherwise clinically resembles primary carcinoma. Poorly differentiated carcinoma of the mediastinum ("Adkins tumor"[291]) is a rare neoplasm whose histology does not permit identification of a likely tissue or site of origin.[290]

Miscellaneous benign causes of a mediastinal mass have been described. Pancreatic pseudocysts may extend into the mediastinum, usually through the aortic or esophageal hiatus.[8,289,292] They have been reported in all three mediastinal compartments. Hydatid cysts also rarely occur in the mediastinum.[8,289] The posterior mediastinum is occasionally the site of a thoracic duct cyst.[7,141] Also, extramedullary hematopoiesis in patients with chronic hemolytic anemia may appear as a mediastinal mass, often in a posterior location. Meningoceles, outgrowths of spinal meninges that protrude along the course of a spinal nerve, produce posterior mediastinal masses.

Finally, it must be remembered that masses found within any of the mediastinal compartments may be lesions more commonly found in another mediastinal compartment or may occasionally have extended from another area in the mediastinum (see Fig. 71.9).

GENERAL APPROACH TO DIAGNOSTIC INVESTIGATION

EVALUATION OF A PRIMARY MEDIASTINAL MASS

Occasionally, mass lesions in the mediastinum can be diagnosed based on clinical information and noninvasive test results alone, without need for a biopsy. Only a few masses fall into this category. These include mediastinal thyroid tissue, which can be identified by radioactive iodine scans; certain granulomatous lesions that are densely calcified and have remained unchanged on serial radiographs; and mediastinal lipomatosis with typical CT findings. Determining that a mass is cystic does not unequivocally establish it as benign: Solid tumors may become cystic (especially thymomas and degenerating nerve sheath tumors), and teratomas may be solid, cystic, or a combination of these. In addition, some cystic lesions become so densely packed with secreted material and detritus that they appear solid on CT.[243,244,250] Lymphoma or other malignancy diagnosed by biopsy of tissues outside the thorax does not require separate demonstration that it is also the cause of a mediastinal mass. Confirmed active pulmonary tuberculosis or sarcoidosis usually warrants a trial of therapy and period of observation before invasive approaches are used to evaluate coexistent mediastinal abnormalities. However, for the large majority of mediastinal masses, thorough diagnostic evaluation must lead to examination of tissue obtained from the lesion (Table 71.7).

Table 71.7 Diagnostic Approach to the Primary Mediastinal Mass

History
Symptoms of local effects or complications
Systemic syndromes as clues to diagnosis (see Table 71.2)

Physical Examination
Physiologic compromise
Extrathoracic manifestations as clues to diagnosis
  (see Table 71.2)
Potential extrathoracic biopsy sites
General condition and candidacy for surgery

Chest Radiography and Computed Tomography
Anatomic location (see Table 71.4)
Appearance (size, shape, density, invasion)
Characteristic features (see Table 71.3)

Special Imaging Studies
Thyroid scan (suspected goiter, abnormal thyroid function tests)
Gallium-67 scan (suspected sarcoidosis)
Somatostatin receptor scintigraphy (suspected thymoma)
Technetium-99m scan (suspected parathyroid adenoma)
Positron emission tomography (suspected lung cancer)

Laboratory Studies
Complete blood count
Routine chemistries (hypercalcemia, hypoglycemia)
Thyroid function tests (suspected goiter)
Anti–acetylcholine receptor antibody (myasthenic symptoms or
  mass contiguous with thymus)
Alpha-fetoprotein and β-human chorionic gonadotropin
  (suspected germ cell tumor)
Catecholamine levels (suspected neurogenic tumor)

Tissue Biopsy
Transbronchial needle biopsy (especially if bronchoscopy is
  already indicated)
Transthoracic or transesophageal needle biopsy (for accessible
  lesions when primary resection is not feasible)
Mediastinoscopy or mediastinotomy (for accessible lesions, if
  less invasive approaches are unsuccessful)

Primary Surgical Resection
Appropriate diagnostic approach when ultimate goal is
  resection and no evidence precludes therapeutic resection

Primary mediastinal tumors usually require biopsy in order to determine the cause. However, as most primary mediastinal masses should be removed regardless of the diagnosis, consideration should be given to surgical resection as the initial invasive diagnostic approach in the appropriate settings. In general, even lesions discovered to be benign should be removed.[3,7,8] Resection of benign neoplasms is advisable because they may subsequently enlarge, compress vital mediastinal structures, hemorrhage, rupture, become infected, or, with varying degrees of likelihood, undergo malignant degeneration. Bizarre complications of benign lesions, such as a case of fatal air embolism resulting from the rupture of an air-containing bronchogenic cyst during ascent in an aircraft, highlight the potential hazards of unresected benign mediastinal lesions.[254]

In light of these factors, the basic focus of the diagnostic evaluation of a mediastinal mass is an orderly preparation for obtaining a tissue diagnosis. The goals of diagnostic evaluation should be to assess the patient's general health and suitability for curative operation, clinical syndromes, and laboratory clues suggesting a specific diagnosis. For instance, elevated thyroid hormone levels suggest goiter—one of the few circumstances in which tissue examination may not be required if functioning mediastinal thyroid tissue is identified on radionuclide scanning. Elevated human chorionic gonadotropin or alpha-fetoprotein levels can suggest the presence of a malignant germ cell tumor, and anti–acetylcholine receptor antibodies can identify even asymptomatic patients with myasthenia gravis due to thymoma. These distinctions may be important because, as in the case of lymphoma, a biopsy confirming a malignant germ cell tumor should prompt combined radiation and chemotherapy rather than radical surgical resection. Awareness of the possibility of thymoma and myasthenia gravis can help the surgeon and anesthesiologist avoid or recognize perioperative complications of neuromuscular weakness.

Conventional chest radiographs are the first diagnostic tool in all cases, and certain mediastinal mass lesions have characteristic appearances (see Table 71.3). A stable appearance, in comparison to older films, can obviate the need for further investigation in selected patients. Imaging by CT or MRI will more completely depict the mass's size, location, density, homogeneity, and gross involvement of surrounding tissues than standard chest radiographs and will also help guide the surgeon. The need for specialized studies such as a thyroid scan will be dictated by the clinical setting and by suspicion of a specific diagnosis. Sometimes a more accessible site for biopsy is discovered on general evaluation of the patient, as in cases of lymphoma with extrathoracic lymphadenopathy. However, in most cases, tissue from the mediastinal mass must be obtained, and the optimal management of mediastinal tumors and cysts usually includes complete resection of the mass. Therefore, if the patient is a candidate for potentially curative surgical resection, surgery should be the next step in most cases.

MEDIASTINAL EVALUATION TO STAGE BRONCHOGENIC CARCINOMA

Mediastinal tissue sampling is central to the management of bronchogenic carcinoma because noninvasive assessment of the mediastinum usually cannot definitively confirm or exclude the presence of metastases, and because findings of mediastinal metastases may drastically alter the surgical and other therapeutic options. Thus, in patients who appear to be candidates for surgical resection, staging should consist of a deliberate search for metastases in the mediastinal lymph nodes.[66,293,294] Ideally, the presence or absence of nodal metastases would be determined without subjecting patients to invasive procedures. Unfortunately, the clinician's ability to achieve such an ideal is hampered by the failure of noninvasive techniques to confirm or exclude that a given node contains malignant cells. To refuse surgery for a patient with curable disease is a greater loss than to perform mediastinoscopy or even thoracotomy on another who is unresectable. It thus seems logical to progress through the staging process from diagnosis to imaging of the mediastinum, to examination of nodal tissue, to surgical exploration, stopping the sequence on the confident discovery of metastatic disease but otherwise proceeding to resection.

Which imaging procedures to employ, how to obtain diagnostic tissue, and what constitutes the confident identification of metastases that contraindicate surgery are decisions that must be made but have no absolute answers. Most clinicians would currently favor delineating the extent of the primary tumor and the location and size of mediastinal lymph nodes using CT. The choice of subsequent steps is increasingly being guided by the mediastinal anatomy and the estimated likelihood of metastasis.[66,294] Thus, for a patient with extensive mediastinal invasion evident on CT, the best approach to confirm mediastinal involvement may be transbronchial, transthoracic, or transesophageal needle aspiration because of the low morbidity and good yield of these procedures in this setting. A patient with a normal mediastinal appearance on CT (but possibly false negative) might be referred next for PET scanning to help guide invasive mediastinal evaluation and to identify unsuspected distant metastases. A patient with enlarged discrete lymph nodes on CT (but possibly false positive) might be referred directly for mediastinoscopy in order to exclude mediastinal involvement with the greatest confidence, assuming that the nodes are in accessible areas. For posterior subcarinal nodes or aortopulmonary window nodes, ultrasound-guided biopsy or anterior mediastinotomy might be considered. In addition, the local availability of CT or PET, and clinical experience with transbronchial, transthoracic, and transesophageal needle aspiration, mediastinoscopy, thoracoscopy, or other procedures, will all influence the individual clinician's approach.

Finally, the general condition and wishes of the patient with lung cancer must enter into the clinical staging process. A systematic extrathoracic assessment may indicate that curative resection is not an option,[293] either because the patient has obvious signs of distant metastases or because severe chronic pulmonary, cardiac, or other systemic disease precludes aggressive, curative therapy.

SUMMARY

The mediastinum contains numerous vital structures in a confined and poorly accessible space, and may be involved by a variety of different diseases. This chapter reviews the anatomic compartments of the mediastinum and their normal contents, the clinical settings and clinical manifestations of common diseases that affect the mediastinum, and the available imaging and biopsy techniques that are helpful in evaluating patients with mediastinal disorders. At least half the patients with mediastinal masses are asymptomatic and the lesions are detected as an incidental finding on a chest radiograph obtained for other purposes. Asymptomatic lesions tend to be benign; symptoms are usually caused by compression or invasion of neighboring structures. Occasionally, mediastinal tumors are associated with paraneoplastic manifestations, which are typically endocrine in origin. Specific mediastinal tumors and cysts are most conveniently characterized by their location within the mediastinum: anterior, middle, or posterior. The evaluation involves special imaging, usually CT, but definitive diagnosis nearly always requires examination of tissue. Most mediastinal masses, whether benign or malignant, should be treated by surgical resection. A variety of approaches may be used to evaluate the mediastinum in patients with lung cancer. The optimal approach depends on the individual anatomy, the likelihood of mediastinal metastases, and the clinical guidance sought from the results.

ACKNOWLEDGMENTS

The authors wish to acknowledge the contributions of David J. Pierson, MD, who wrote this chapter for the first and second editions, and coauthored this chapter with DRP for the third edition.

REFERENCES

1. Heitzman ER: The Mediastinum: Radiologic Correlations with Anatomy and Pathology (2nd ed). New York: Springer-Verlag, 1988.
2. Naidich DP, Zerhouni EA, Siegelman SS: Computed Tomography and Magnetic Resonance of the Thorax (2nd ed). New York: Raven Press, 1991.
3. Beszniak I, Szende B, Lapis K: Mediastinal Tumors and Pseudotumors. Basel: Karger, 1984.
4. Fraser RG, Paré JAP: The normal chest. In Synopsis of Diseases of the Chest (2nd ed). Philadelphia: WB Saunders, 1994, pp 1–116.
5. American Thoracic Society. Medical section of the American Lung Association. Clinical staging of primary lung cancer. Am Rev Respir Dis 127:659–669, 1983.
6. Maunder RJ, Pierson DJ, Hudson LD: Subcutaneous and mediastinal emphysema: Pathophysiology, diagnosis, and management. Arch Intern Med 144:1447–1453, 1984.
7. Silverman NA, Sabiston DC Jr: Mediastinal masses. Surg Clin North Am 60:757–777, 1980.
8. LeRoux BT, Kallichurum S, Shama DM: Mediastinal cysts and tumors. Curr Probl Surg 21:1–76, 1984.
9. Davis RD Jr, Oldham HN Jr, Sabiston DC Jr: Primary cysts and neoplasms of the mediastinum: Recent changes in clinical presentation, methods of diagnosis, management, and results. Ann Thorac Surg 44:229–237, 1987.
10. Cohen AJ, Thompson L, Edwards FH, Bellamy RF: Primary cysts and tumors of the mediastinum. Ann Thorac Surg 51:378–384, 1991.
11. Oldham HN Jr, Sabiston DC Jr: Primary tumors and cysts of the mediastinum: Lesions presenting as cardiovascular abnormalities. Arch Surg 96:71–75, 1968.
12. Weinberg BA, Conces DJ Jr, Waller BF: Cardiac manifestations of noncardiac tumors. Part I: Direct effects. Clin Cardiol 12:289–296, 1989.
13. Weinberg BA, Conces DJ Jr, Waller BF: Cardiac manifestations of noncardiac tumors. Part II: Direct effects. Clin Cardiol 12:347–354, 1989.
14. Markman M: Diagnosis and management of superior vena cava syndrome. Cleve Clin J Med 66:59–61, 1999.
15. Wudel LJ Jr, Nesbitt JC: Superior vena cava syndrome. Curr Treat Options Oncol 2:77–91, 2001.
16. Bell DR, Woods RL, Levi JA: Superior vena caval obstruction: A 10-year experience. Med J Aust 145:566–568, 1986.
17. Mahajan V, Strimlan V, van Ordstrand HS, Loop FD: Benign superior vena cava syndrome. Chest 68:32–35, 1975.
18. Yellin A, Rosen A, Reichert N, et al: Superior vena cava syndrome: The myth—the facts. Am Rev Respir Dis 141:1114–1118, 1990.

19. Chen JC, Bongard F, Klein SR: A contemporary perspective on superior vena cava syndrome. Am J Surg 160:207–211, 1990.

20. Hoffman OA, Gillespie DJ, Aughenbaugh GL, Brown LR: Primary mediastinal neoplasms (other than thymoma). Mayo Clin Proc 68:880–891, 1993.

21. Strollo DC, Rosado de Christenson ML, Jett JR: Primary mediastinal tumors. Part I: Tumors of the anterior mediastinum. Chest 112:511–522, 1997.

22. Strollo DC, Rosado de Christenson ML, Jett JR: Primary mediastinal tumors. Part II: Tumors of the middle and posterior mediastinum. Chest 112:1344–1357, 1997.

23. Shields TW: Thymic tumors. In Shields TW (ed): Mediastinal Surgery. Philadelphia: Lea & Febiger, 1991, pp 153–173.

24. Connolly AM, Pestronk A, Mehta S, et al: Serum autoantibodies in childhood opsoclonus-myoclonus syndrome: An analysis of antigenic targets in neural tissues. J Pediatr 130:878–884, 1997.

25. Jemal A, Murray T, Samuels A, et al: Cancer statistics, 2003. CA Cancer J Clin 53:5–26, 2003.

26. Mountain CF: Revisions in the International System for Staging Lung Cancer (see comments). Chest 111:1710–1717, 1997.

27. Naruke T, Tsuchiya R, Kondo H, et al: Implications of staging in lung cancer. Chest 112:242S–248S, 1997.

28. Pretreatment evaluation of non-small-cell lung cancer. The American Thoracic Society and The European Respiratory Society. Am J Respir Crit Care Med 156:320–332, 1997.

29. Takasugi JE: Diagnostic use of inadvertent pneumothorax after CT-guided percutaneous lung biopsy. J Thorac Imaging 9:138–140, 1994.

30. Watanabe A, Shimokata K, Saka H, et al: Chest CT combined with artificial pneumothorax: Value in determining origin and extent of tumor. AJR Am J Roentgenol 156:707–710, 1991.

31. Yokoi K, Mori K, Miyazawa N, et al: Tumor invasion of the chest wall and mediastinum in lung cancer: Evaluation with pneumothorax CT. Radiology 181:147–152, 1991.

32. Brown K, Aberle D, Batra P, et al: Current use of imaging in the evaluation of primary mediastinal masses. Chest 98:466–473, 1990.

33. Ahn JM, Lee KS, Goo JM, et al: Predicting the histology of anterior mediastinal masses: Comparison of chest radiography and CT. J Thorac Imaging 11:265–271, 1996.

34. Martini N, Heelan R, Westcott J, et al: Comparative merits of conventional, computed tomographic, and magnetic resonance imaging in assessing mediastinal involvement in surgically confirmed lung carcinoma. J Thorac Cardiovasc Surg 90:639–648, 1985.

35. Gould MK, Kuschner WG, Rydzak CE, et al: Test performance of positron emission tomography and computed tomography for mediastinal staging in patients with non-small-cell lung cancer: A meta-analysis. Ann Intern Med 139:879–892, 2003.

36. Schnyder PA, Gamsu G: CT of the pretracheal retrocaval space. AJR Am J Roentgenol 136:303–308, 1981.

37. Baron RL, Levitt RG, Sagel SS, et al: Computed tomography in the preoperative evaluation of bronchogenic carcinoma. Radiology 145:727–732, 1982.

38. Ratto GB, Frola C, Cantoni S, Motta G: Improving clinical efficacy of computed tomographic scan in the preoperative assessment of patients with non-small cell lung cancer. J Thorac Cardiovasc Surg 99:416–425, 1990.

39. McLoud TC, Bourgouin PM, Greenberg RW, et al: Bronchogenic carcinoma: Analysis of staging in the mediastinum with CT by correlative lymph node mapping and sampling (see comments). Radiology 182:319–323, 1992.

40. Colice GL: Chest CT for known or suspected lung cancer. Chest 106:1538–1550, 1994.

41. Quint LE, Francis IR, Wahl RL, et al: Preoperative staging of non-small-cell carcinoma of the lung: Imaging methods. AJR Am J Roentgenol 164:1349–1359, 1995.

42. Bonomo L, Ciccotosto C, Guidotti A, Storto ML: Lung cancer staging: The role of computed tomography and magnetic resonance imaging. Eur J Radiol 23:35–45, 1996.

43. Gamsu G, Sostman D: Magnetic resonance imaging of the thorax. Am Rev Respir Dis 139:254–274, 1989.

44. Link KM, Samuels LJ, Reed JC, et al: Magnetic resonance imaging of the mediastinum and its contents. J Thorac Imaging 8:34–53, 1993.

45. Hansen ME, Spritzer CE, Sostman HD: Assessing the patency of mediastinal and thoracic inlet veins: Value of MR imaging. AJR Am J Roentgenol 155:1177–1182, 1990.

46. Dujovny M, Alp MS, Dujovny N, et al: Aneurysm clips: Magnetic quantification and magnetic resonance imaging safety. Technical note. J Neurosurg 87:788–794, 1997.

47. Weinreb JC, Naidich DP: Thoracic magnetic resonance imaging. Clin Chest Med 12:33–54, 1991.

48. Kono M, Adachi S, Kusumoto M, Sakai E: Clinical utility of Gd-DTPA-enhanced magnetic resonance imaging in lung cancer. J Thorac Imaging 8:18–26, 1993.

49. Webb WR, Gatsonis C, Zerhouni EA, et al: CT and MR imaging in staging non-small cell bronchogenic carcinoma: Report of the Radiologic Diagnostic Oncology Group. Radiology 178:705–713, 1991.

50. Wernecke K, Diederich S: Sonographic features of mediastinal tumors. AJR Am J Roentgenol 163:1357–1364, 1994.

51. Herth F, Becker HD: Endobronchial ultrasound of the airways and the mediastinum. Monaldi Arch Chest Dis 55:36–44, 2000.

52. Wiersema MJ, Kochman ML, Cramer HM, Wiersema LM: Preoperative staging of non-small cell lung cancer: Transesophageal US-guided fine-needle aspiration biopsy of mediastinal lymph nodes. Radiology 190:239–242, 1994.

53. Pedersen BH, Vilmann P, Folke K, et al: Endoscopic ultrasonography and real-time guided fine-needle aspiration biopsy of solid lesions of the mediastinum suspected of malignancy. Chest 110:539–544, 1996.

54. Dooms GC, Hricak H: Radiologic imaging modalities, including magnetic resonance, for evaluating lymph nodes. West J Med 144:49–57, 1986.

55. Sulavik SB, Spencer RP, Weed DA, et al: Recognition of distinctive patterns of gallium-67 distribution in sarcoidosis. J Nucl Med 31:1909–1914, 1990.

56. Maná J: Nuclear imaging: [67]Gallium, [201]thallium, ^{18}F-labeled fluoro-2-deoxy-D-glucose positron emission tomography. Clin Chest Med 18:799–811, 1997.

57. Vansant JP, Johnson DH, O'Donnell DM, et al: Staging lung carcinoma with a Tc-99m labeled monoclonal antibody. Clin Nucl Med 17:431–438, 1992.

58. Rusch V, Macapinlac H, Heelan R, et al: NR-LU-10 monoclonal antibody scanning: A helpful new adjunct to computed tomography in evaluating non-small-cell lung cancer. J Thorac Cardiovasc Surg 106:200–204, 1993.

59. Matsuno S, Tanabe M, Kawasaki Y, et al: Effectiveness of planar image and single photon emission tomography of thallium-201 compared with gallium-67 in patients with primary lung cancer. Eur J Nucl Med 19:86–95, 1992.

60. Yokoi K, Okuyama A, Mori K, et al: Mediastinal lymph node metastasis from lung cancer: Evaluation with Tl-201 SPECT—comparison with CT. Radiology 192:813–817, 1994.

61. Lowe VJ, Naunheim KS: Positron emission tomography in lung cancer. Ann Thorac Surg 65:1821–1829, 1998.

62. Shreve PD, Steventon RS, Deters EC, et al: Oncologic diagnosis with 2-[fluorine-18]fluoro-2-deoxy-D-glucose imaging: Dual-head coincidence gamma camera versus positron emission tomographic scanner. Radiology 207:431–437, 1998.

63. Hara T, Kosaka N, Suzuki T, et al: Uptake rates of ^{18}F-fluorodeoxyglucose and ^{11}C-choline in lung cancer and pulmonary tuberculosis: A positron emission tomography study. Chest 124:893–901, 2003.

64. Lardinois D, Weder W, Hany TF, et al: Staging of non-small-cell lung cancer with integrated positron-emission tomography and computed tomography. N Engl J Med 348:2500–2507, 2003.

65. Vesselle H, Turcotte E, Wiens L, Haynor D: Application of a neural network to improve nodal staging accuracy with ^{18}F-FDG PET in non-small cell lung cancer. J Nucl Med 44:1918–1926, 2003.

66. Kramer H, Groen HJ: Current concepts in the mediastinal lymph node staging of nonsmall cell lung cancer. Ann Surg 238:180–188, 2003.

67. Vesselle H, Pugsley JM, Vallières E, Wood DE: The impact of fluorodeoxyglucose F 18 positron-emission tomography on the surgical staging of non-small cell lung cancer. J Thorac Cardiovasc Surg 124:511–519, 2002.

68. Reed CE, Harpole DH, Posther KE, et al: Results of the American College of Surgeons Oncology Group Z0050 trial: The utility of positron emission tomography in staging potentially operable non-small cell lung cancer. J Thorac Cardiovasc Surg 126:1943–1951, 2003.

69. Shure D: Transbronchial needle aspiration—current status. Mayo Clin Proc 64:251–254, 1989.

70. Oho K, Kato H, Ogawa I, et al: A new needle for transfiberoptic bronchoscopic use. Chest 76:492, 1979.

71. Wang KP, Terry PB: Transbronchial needle aspiration in the diagnosis and staging of bronchogenic carcinoma. Am Rev Respir Dis 127:344–347, 1983.

72. Wang KP: Flexible transbronchial needle aspiration biopsy for histologic specimens. Chest 88:860–863, 1985.

73. Mehta AC, Kavuru MS, Meeker DP, et al: Transbronchial needle aspiration for histology specimens. Chest 96:1228–1232, 1989.

74. Schenk DA, Strollo PJ, Pickard JS, et al: Utility of the Wang 18-gauge transbronchial histology needle in the staging of bronchogenic carcinoma. Chest 96:272–274, 1989.

75. Ghamande S, Rafanan A, Dweik R, et al: Role of transbronchial needle aspiration in patients receiving mechanical ventilation. Chest 122:985–989, 2002.

76. Wang KP, Brower R, Haponik EF, Siegelman S: Flexible transbronchial needle aspiration for staging of bronchogenic carcinoma. Chest 84:571–576, 1983.

77. Shure D, Fedullo PF: The role of transcarinal needle aspiration in the staging of bronchogenic carcinoma. Chest 86:693–696, 1984.

78. Harrow EM, Oldenburg FA Jr, Lingenfelter MS, Smith AM Jr: Transbronchial needle aspiration in clinical practice: A five-year experience. Chest 96:1268–1272, 1989.

79. Gay PC, Brutinel WM: Transbronchial needle aspiration in the practice of bronchoscopy. Mayo Clin Proc 64:158–162, 1989.

80. Utz JP, Patel AM, Edell ES: The role of transcarinal needle aspiration in the staging of bronchogenic carcinoma. Chest 104:1012–1016, 1993.

81. Schenk DA, Bower JH, Bryan CL, et al: Transbronchial needle aspiration staging of bronchogenic carcinoma. Am Rev Respir Dis 134:146–148, 1986.

82. Ratto GB, Mereu C, Motta G: The prognostic significance of preoperative assessment of mediastinal lymph nodes in patients with lung cancer. Chest 93:807–813, 1988.

83. Cropp AJ, DiMarco AF, Lankerani M: False-positive transbronchial needle aspiration in bronchogenic carcinoma. Chest 85:696–697, 1984.

84. Carlin BW, Harrell JH, Fedullo PF: False-positive transcarinal needle aspirate in the evaluation of bronchogenic carcinoma. Am Rev Respir Dis 140:1800–1802, 1989.

85. Haponik EF, Cappellari JO, Chin R, et al: Education and experience improve transbronchial needle aspiration performance. Am J Respir Crit Care Med 151:1998–2002, 1995.

86. Rodríguez de Castro F, Díaz Lopez F, Serda GJ, et al: Relevance of training in transbronchial fine-needle aspiration technique. Chest 111:103–105, 1997.

87. Shields GW, Coggeshall JW, Witt WS, et al: Transbronchoscopic needle aspiration in the diagnosis and staging of lung cancer. South Med J 79:694–695, 1986.

88. Harrow E, Halber M, Hardy S, Halteman W: Bronchoscopic and roentgenographic correlates of a positive transbronchial needle aspiration in the staging of lung cancer. Chest 100:1592–1596, 1991.

89. Rong F, Cui B: CT scan directed transbronchial needle aspiration biopsy for mediastinal nodes (see comments). Chest 114:36–39, 1998.

90. Herth FJ, Becker HD, Ernst A: Ultrasound-guided transbronchial needle aspiration: An experience in 242 patients. Chest 123:604–607, 2003.

91. Herth F, Becker HD, Ernst A: Conventional vs endobronchial ultrasound-guided transbronchial needle aspiration: A randomized trial. Chest 125:322–325, 2004.

92. Krasnik M, Vilmann P, Larsen SS, Jacobsen GK: Preliminary experience with a new method of endoscopic transbronchial real time ultrasound guided biopsy for diagnosis of mediastinal and hilar lesions. Thorax 58:1083–1086, 2003.

93. Falcone F, Fois F, Grosso D: Endobronchial ultrasound. Respiration 70:179–194, 2003.

93a. Rintoul RC, Skwarski KM, Murchison JT, et al: Endoscopic and endobronchial ultrasound real-time fine-needle aspiration for staging of the mediastinum in lung cancer. Chest 126:2020–2022, 2004.

94. Xie HB, Cornwell R, Grossman JE, et al: Bronchoscopy-guided transtracheal and transbronchial fine-needle aspiration biopsy: A 5-year institutional review of 111 cases. Diagn Cytopathol 27:276–281, 2004.

95. Chin R Jr, McCain TW, Lucia MA, et al: Transbronchial needle aspiration in diagnosing and staging lung cancer: How many aspirates are needed? Am J Respir Crit Care Med 166:377–381, 2002.

96. Trisolini R, Agli LL, Cancellieri A, et al: The value of flexible transbronchial needle aspiration in the diagnosis of stage I sarcoidosis. Chest 124:2126–2130, 2003.

97. Cetinkaya E, Yildiz P, Kadakal F, et al: Transbronchial needle aspiration in the diagnosis of intrathoracic lymphadenopathy. Respiration 69:335–338, 2002.

98. Harkin TJ, Ciotoli C, Addrizzo-Harris DJ, et al: Transbronchial needle aspiration (TBNA) in patients infected with HIV. Am J Respir Crit Care Med 157:1913–1918, 1998.

99. Wernecke K, Vassallo P, Peters PE, von Bassewitz DB: Mediastinal tumors: Biopsy under US guidance. Radiology 172:473–476, 1989.

100. Sheppard MN: Percutaneous biopsy of mediastinal tumours under sonographic guidance. Thorax 46:740, 1991.

101. Morrissey B, Adams H, Gibbs AR, Crane MD: Percutaneous needle biopsy of the mediastinum: Review of 94 procedures. Thorax 48:632–637, 1993.

102. Otani Y, Yoshida I, Ishikawa S, et al: Use of ultrasound-guided percutaneous needle biopsy in the diagnosis of mediastinal tumors. Surg Today 26:990–992, 1996.

103. Akamatsu H, Terashima M, Koike T, et al: Staging of primary lung cancer by computed tomography-guided percutaneous needle cytology of mediastinal lymph nodes. Ann Thorac Surg 62:352–355, 1996.

104. Belfiore G, Camera L, Moggio G, et al: Middle mediastinum lesions: Preliminary experience with CT-guided fine-needle aspiration biopsy with a suprasternal approach. Radiology 202:870–873, 1997.

105. Westcott JL: Transthoracic biopsy and drainage procedures. *In* Freundlich I, Bragg D (eds): A Radiologic Approach to Diseases of the Chest. Baltimore: Williams & Wilkins, 1992, pp 374–386.

106. Rosenberger A, Adler OB: Mediastinal biopsy. *In* Dondelinger R, Rossi P, Kurdziel J, et al (eds): Interventional Radiology. New York: Thieme, 1990, pp 18–26.

107. Krasnik M: Endoscopic transesophageal and endoscopic transbronchial real-time ultrasound-guided biopsy. Respiration 70:293–298, 2003.

108. Silvestri GA, Hoffman BJ, Bhutani MS, et al: Endoscopic ultrasound with fine-needle aspiration in the diagnosis and staging of lung cancer. Ann Thorac Surg 61:1441–1445, 1996.

109. Fritscher-Ravens A, Soehendra N, Schirrow L, et al: Role of transesophageal endosonography-guided fine-needle aspiration in the diagnosis of lung cancer. Chest 117:339–345, 2000.

110. Fritscher-Ravens A, Davidson BL, Hauber HP, et al: Endoscopic ultrasound, positron emission tomography, and computerized tomography for lung cancer. Am J Respir Crit Care Med 168:1293–1297, 2003.

111. Gress FG, Savides TJ, Sandler A, et al: Endoscopic ultrasonography, fine-needle aspiration biopsy guided by endoscopic ultrasonography, and computed tomography in the preoperative staging of non-small-cell lung cancer: A comparison study. Ann Intern Med 127:604–612, 1997.

112. Hammoud ZT, Anderson RC, Meyers BF, et al: The current role of mediastinoscopy in the evaluation of thoracic disease. J Thorac Cardiovasc Surg 118:894–899, 1999.

113. Kelemen JJ 3rd, Naunheim KS: Minimally invasive approaches to mediastinal neoplasms. Semin Thorac Cardiovasc Surg 12:301–306, 2000.

114. Carlens E: Mediastinoscopy: A method for inspection and tissue biopsy in the superior mediastinum. Dis Chest 36:343–352, 1959.

115. Marchevsky AM, Kaneko M: Surgical Pathology of the Mediastinum. New York: Raven Press, 1984, pp 1–3.

116. Ginsberg RJ, Rice TW, Goldberg M, et al: Extended cervical mediastinoscopy: A single staging procedure for bronchogenic carcinoma of the left upper lobe. J Thorac Cardiovasc Surg 94:673–678, 1987.

117. McNeill TM, Chamberlain JM: Diagnostic anterior mediastinotomy. Ann Thorac Surg 2:532–539, 1966.

118. Olak J: Parasternal mediastinotomy (Chamberlain procedure). Chest Surg Clin N Am 6:31–40, 1996.

119. Adegboye VO, Obajimi MO, Ogunsehinde OO, et al: Anterior mediastinotomy—a diagnostic tool. Afr J Med Med Sci 30:341–344, 2001.

120. Vallières E, Pagé A, Verdant A: Ambulatory mediastinoscopy and anterior mediastinotomy. Ann Thorac Surg 52:1122–1126, 1991.

121. Mouroux J, Riquet M, Padovani B, et al: Surgical management of thoracic manifestations in human immunodeficiency virus-positive patients: Indications and results. Br J Surg 82:39–43, 1995.

122. Ginsberg RJ: Evaluation of the mediastinum by invasive techniques. Surg Clin North Am 67:1025–1035, 1987.

123. Clarke MR, Landreneau RJ, Borochovitz D: Intraoperative imprint cytology for evaluation of mediastinal lymphadenopathy. Ann Thorac Surg 57:1206–1210, 1994.

124. de Montpréville VT, Dulmet EM, Nashashibi N: Frozen section diagnosis and surgical biopsy of lymph nodes, tumors and pseudotumors of the mediastinum. Eur J Cardiothorac Surg 13:190–195, 1998.

125. Dillemans B, Deneffe G, Verschakelen J, Decramer M: Value of computed tomography and mediastinoscopy in preoperative evaluation of mediastinal nodes in non-small cell lung cancer: A study of 569 patients. Eur J Cardiothorac Surg 8:37–42, 1994.

126. Funatsu T, Matsubara Y, Ikeda S, et al: Preoperative mediastinoscopic assessment of N factors and the need for mediastinal lymph node dissection in T1 lung cancer. J Thorac Cardiovasc Surg 108:321–328, 1994.

127. Best LA, Munichor M, Ben-Shakhar M, et al: The contribution of anterior mediastinotomy in the diseases of the mediastinum and lung. Ann Thorac Surg 43:78–81, 1987.

128. Boyle EM, Vallières E: Mediastinoscopy in the staging of lung cancer. Curr Surg 58:47–54, 2001.

129. Daly BD, Mueller JD, Faling LJ, et al: N2 lung cancer: Outcome in patients with false-negative computed tomographic scans of the chest. J Thorac Cardiovasc Surg 105:904–910, 1993.

130. Mentzer SJ, Swanson SJ, DeCamp MM, et al: Mediastinoscopy, thoracoscopy, and video-assisted thoracic surgery in the diagnosis and staging of lung cancer. Chest 112:239S–241S, 1997.

131. Krasna MJ: Advances in staging of esophageal carcinoma. Chest 113:107S–111S, 1998.

132. Prinz RA, Lonchyna V, Carnaille B, et al: Thoracoscopic excision of enlarged mediastinal parathyroid glands. Surgery 116:999–1004, 1994.

133. Knight R, Ratzer ER, Fenoglio ME, Moore JT: Thoracoscopic excision of mediastinal parathyroid adenomas: A report of two cases and review of the literature. J Am Coll Surg 185:481–485, 1997.

134. Hazelrigg SR, Landreneau RJ, Mack MJ, Acuff TE: Thoracoscopic resection of mediastinal cysts. Ann Thorac Surg 56:659–660, 1993.

135. Naunheim KS: Video thoracoscopy for masses of the posterior mediastinum. Ann Thorac Surg 56:657–658, 1993.

136. Sugarbaker DJ: Thoracoscopy in the management of anterior mediastinal masses. Ann Thorac Surg 56:653–656, 1993.

137. Roviaro G, Rebuffat C, Varoli F, et al: Videothoracoscopic excision of mediastinal masses: Indications and technique. Ann Thorac Surg 58:1679–1683, 1994.

138. Demmy TL, Krasna MJ, Detterbeck FC, et al: Multicenter VATS experience with mediastinal tumors. Ann Thorac Surg 66:187–192, 1998.

139. LeRoux BT: Cysts and tumors of the mediastinum. Surg Gynecol Obstet 115:695–703, 1962.

140. Blegvad S, Lippert H, Simper LB, Dybdahl H: Mediastinal tumours: A report of 129 cases. Scand J Thorac Cardiovasc Surg 24:39–42, 1990.

141. Adegboye VO, Brimmo AI, Adebo OA, et al: The place of clinical features and standard chest radiography in

evaluation of mediastinal masses. West Afr J Med 22:156–160, 2003.

142. Haramati LB, Choi Y, Widrow CA, Austin JH: Isolated lymphadenopathy on chest radiographs of HIV-infected patients. Clin Radiol 51:345–349, 1996.

143. Fishman JE, Schwartz DS, Sais GJ, et al: Bronchogenic carcinoma in HIV-positive patients: Findings on chest radiographs and CT scans. AJR Am J Roentgenol 164:57–61, 1995.

144. Verstandig AG, Epstein DM, Miller WT Jr, et al: Thymoma—report of 71 cases and a review. Crit Rev Diagn Imaging 33:201–230, 1992.

145. Cooper JD: Current therapy for thymoma. Chest 103:334S–336S, 1993.

146. Debono DJ, Loehrer PJ: Thymic neoplasms. Curr Opin Oncol 8:112–119, 1996.

147. Kohman LJ: Controversies in the management of malignant thymoma. Chest 112:296S–300S, 1997.

148. Tao L-C: Guides to Clinical Aspiration Biopsy: Lung, Pleura, and Mediastinum. New York: Igaku-Shoin, 1988, pp 273–328.

149. LeGolvan DP, Abell MR: Thymomas. Cancer 39:2142–2157, 1977.

150. Morgenthaler TI, Brown LR, Colby TV, et al: Thymoma. Mayo Clin Proc 68:1110–1123, 1993.

151. Lennon VA, Lambert EH: Myasthenia gravis induced by monoclonal antibodies to acetylcholine receptors. Nature 285:238–240, 1980.

152. Beekman R, Kuks JB, Oosterhuis HJ: Myasthenia gravis: Diagnosis and follow-up of 100 consecutive patients. J Neurol 244:112–118, 1997.

153. Rosado de Christenson ML, Galobardes J, Moran CA: Thymoma: Radiologic-pathologic correlation. Radiographics 12:151–168, 1992.

154. Kiyosue H, Miyake H, Komatsu E, Mori H: MRI of cervical masses of thymic origin. J Comput Assist Tomogr 18:206–208, 1994.

155. Sakai F, Sone S, Kiyono K, et al: MR imaging of thymoma: Radiologic-pathologic correlation. AJR Am J Roentgenol 158:751–756, 1992.

156. Lastoria S, Vergara E, Palmieri G, et al: In vivo detection of malignant thymic masses by indium-111-DTPA-D-Phe1-octreotide scintigraphy. J Nucl Med 39:634–639, 1998.

157. Liu RS, Yeh SH, Huang MH, et al: Use of fluorine-18 fluorodeoxyglucose positron emission tomography in the detection of thymoma: A preliminary report. Eur J Nucl Med 22:1402–1407, 1995.

158. Lewis JE, Wick MR, Scheithauer BW, et al: Thymoma: A clinicopathologic review. Cancer 60:2727–2743, 1987.

159. Blumberg D, Port JL, Weksler B, et al: Thymoma: A multivariate analysis of factors predicting survival. Ann Thorac Surg 60:908–913, 1995.

159a. Kurup A, Loehrer PJ Sr: Thymoma and thymic carcinoma: therapeutic approaches. Clin Lung Cancer 6:28–32, 2004.

160. Curran WJ Jr, Kornstein MJ, Brooks JJ, Turrisi AT 3rd: Invasive thymoma: The role of mediastinal irradiation following complete or incomplete surgical resection. J Clin Oncol 6:1722–1727, 1988.

161. Loehrer PJ Sr, Kim K, Aisner SC, et al: Cisplatin plus doxorubicin plus cyclophosphamide in metastatic or recurrent thymoma: Final results of an intergroup trial. The Eastern Cooperative Oncology Group, Southwest Oncology Group, and Southeastern Cancer Study Group. J Clin Oncol 12:1164–1168, 1994.

162. Loehrer PJ Sr, Chen M, Kim K, et al: Cisplatin, doxorubicin, and cyclophosphamide plus thoracic radiation therapy for limited-stage unresectable thymoma: An intergroup trial. J Clin Oncol 15:3093–3099, 1997.

163. Venuta F, Rendina EA, Longo F, et al: Long-term outcome after multimodality treatment for stage III thymic tumors. Ann Thorac Surg 76:1866–1872, 2003 [discussion appears in Ann Thorac Surg 76:1872, 2003].

164. Busch C, Machens A, Pichlmeier U, et al: Long-term outcome and quality of life after thymectomy for myasthenia gravis. Ann Surg 224:225–232, 1996.

165. Cosi V, Romani A, Lombardi M, et al: Prognosis of myasthenia gravis: A retrospective study of 380 patients. J Neurol 244:548–555, 1997.

166. Rosado de Christenson ML, Pugatch RD, Moran CA, Galobardes J: Thymolipoma: Analysis of 27 cases. Radiology 193:121–126, 1994.

167. Hsu CP, Chen CY, Chen CL, et al: Thymic carcinoma: Ten years' experience in twenty patients. J Thorac Cardiovasc Surg 107:615–620, 1994.

168. Weide LG, Ulbright TM, Loehrer PJ Sr, Williams SD: Thymic carcinoma: A distinct clinical entity responsive to chemotherapy. Cancer 71:1219–1223, 1993.

169. Wick MR, Rosai J: Neuroendocrine neoplasms of the mediastinum. Semin Diagn Pathol 8:35–51, 1991.

170. Economopoulos GC, Lewis JW Jr, Lee MW, Silverman NA: Carcinoid tumors of the thymus. Ann Thorac Surg 50:58–61, 1990.

171. Wick MR, Carney JA, Bernatz PE, Brown LR: Primary mediastinal carcinoid tumors. Am J Surg Pathol 6:195–205, 1982.

172. Burns DE, Schiffman FJ: Beguiled by the gallium: Thymic rebound in an adult after chemotherapy for Hodgkin's disease. Chest 104:1916–1919, 1993.

173. Trastek VF, Pairolero PC: Benign germ cell tumors of the mediastinum. In Shields TW (ed): Mediastinal Surgery. Philadelphia: Lea & Febiger, 1991, pp 205–210.

174. Dehner LP: Germ cell tumors of the mediastinum. Semin Diagn Pathol 7:266–284, 1990.

175. Nichols CR, Fox EP: Extragonadal and pediatric germ cell tumors. Hematol Oncol Clin North Am 5:1189–1209, 1991.

176. Nichols CR: Mediastinal germ cell tumors. Semin Thorac Cardiovasc Surg 4:45–50, 1992.

177. Lewis BD, Hurt RD, Payne WS, et al: Benign teratomas of the mediastinum. J Thorac Cardiovasc Surg 86:727–731, 1983.

178. Dulmet EM, Macchiarini P, Suc B, Verley JM: Germ cell tumors of the mediastinum: A 30-year experience. Cancer 72:1894–1901, 1993.

179. Hainsworth JD, Greco FA: Clinical features of malignant germ cell tumors and primary seminomas of the mediastinum. In Shields TW (ed): Mediastinal Surgery. Philadelphia: Lea & Febiger, 1991, pp 211–218.

180. Knapp RH, Hurt RD, Payne WS, et al: Malignant germ cell tumors of the mediastinum. J Thorac Cardiovasc Surg 89:82–89, 1985.

181. Hurt RD, Bruckman JE, Farrow GM, et al: Primary anterior mediastinal seminoma. Cancer 49:1658–1663, 1982.

182. Bukowski RM, Wolf M, Kulander BG, et al: Alternating combination chemotherapy in patients with extragonadal germ cell tumors. A Southwest Oncology Group study. Cancer 71:2631–2638, 1993.

183. Bukowski RM: Management of advanced and extragonadal germ-cell tumors. Urol Clin North Am 20:153–160, 1993.

184. Dexeus FH, Logothetis CJ, Chong C, et al: Genetic abnormalities in men with germ cell tumors. J Urol 140:80–84, 1988.

185. Nichols CR, Heerema NA, Palmer C, et al: Klinefelter's syndrome associated with mediastinal germ cell neoplasms. J Clin Oncol 5:1290–1294, 1987.

186. Nichols CR, Hoffman R, Einhorn LH, et al: Hematologic malignancies associated with primary mediastinal germ-cell tumors. Ann Intern Med 102:603–609, 1985.

187. Nichols CR, Roth BJ, Heerema N, et al: Hematologic neoplasia associated with primary mediastinal germ-cell tumors. N Engl J Med 322:1425–1429, 1990.

188. Nichols CR, Catalano PJ, Crawford ED, et al: Randomized comparison of cisplatin and etoposide and either bleomycin or ifosfamide in treatment of advanced disseminated germ cell tumors: An Eastern Cooperative Oncology Group, Southwest Oncology Group, and Cancer and Leukemia Group B Study. J Clin Oncol 16:1287–1293, 1998.

189. Nichols CR, Andersen J, Lazarus HM, et al: High-dose carboplatin and etoposide with autologous bone marrow transplantation in refractory germ cell cancer: An Eastern Cooperative Oncology Group protocol. J Clin Oncol 10:558–563, 1992.

190. Nichols CR, Saxman S: Primary salvage treatment of recurrent germ cell tumors: Experience at Indiana University. Semin Oncol 25:210–214, 1998.

191. Vaeth JM, Moskowitz SA, Green JP: Mediastinal Hodgkin's disease. Am J Roentgenol 126:123–126, 1976.

192. Jones SE, Fuks Z, Bull M, et al: Non-Hodgkin's lymphomas. IV. Clinicopathologic correlation in 405 cases. Cancer 31:806–823, 1973.

193. Levitt LJ, Aisenberg AC, Harris NL, et al: Primary non-Hodgkin's lymphoma of the mediastinum. Cancer 50:2486–2492, 1982.

194. Wang CY, Snow JL, Su WP: Lymphoma associated with human immunodeficiency virus infection. Mayo Clin Proc 70:665–672, 1995.

195. Straus DJ: Human immunodeficiency virus-associated lymphomas. Med Clin North Am 81:495–510, 1997.

196. Klencke B, Kaplan L: Advances and future challenges in non-Hodgkin's lymphoma. Curr Opin Oncol 10:422–427, 1998.

197. L'Evy R, Colonna P, Tourani JM, et al: Human immunodeficiency virus associated Hodgkin's disease: Report of 45 cases from the French Registry of HIV-Associated Tumors. Leuk Lymphoma 16:451–456, 1995.

198. Strickler JG, Kurtin PJ: Mediastinal lymphoma. Semin Diagn Pathol 8:2–13, 1991.

199. Jacobs P: Hodgkin's disease and the malignant lymphomas. Dis Mon 39:213–297, 1993.

200. DeVita VT Jr, Hubbard SM: Hodgkin's disease. N Engl J Med 328:560–565, 1993.

201. Armitage JO: Treatment of non-Hodgkin's lymphoma. N Engl J Med 328:1023–1030, 1993.

202. Sandlund JT, Downing JR, Crist WM: Non-Hodgkin's lymphoma in childhood. N Engl J Med 334:1238–1248, 1996.

203. Hudson MM, Donaldson SS: Hodgkin's disease. Pediatr Clin North Am 44:891–906, 1997.

204. Shad A, Magrath I: Non-Hodgkin's lymphoma. Pediatr Clin North Am 44:863–8690, 1997.

205. Chin SC, Rice H, Som PM: Spread of goiters outside the thyroid bed: A review of 190 cases and an analysis of the incidence of the various extensions. Arch Otolaryngol Head Neck Surg 129:1198–1202, 2003.

206. Park HM, Tarver RD, Siddiqui AR, et al: Efficacy of thyroid scintigraphy in the diagnosis of intrathoracic goiter. AJR Am J Roentgenol 148:527–529, 1987.

207. Glazer HS, Molina PL, Siegel MJ, Sagel SS: High-attenuation mediastinal masses on unenhanced CT. AJR Am J Roentgenol 156:45–50, 1991.

208. Jennings A: Evaluation of substernal goiters using computed tomography and MR imaging. Endocrinol Metab Clin North Am 30:401–414, ix, 2001.

209. Katlic MR, Grillo HC, Wang CA: Substernal goiter: Analysis of 80 patients from Massachusetts General Hospital. Am J Surg 149:283–287, 1985.

210. Yousem DM, Scheff AM: Thyroid and parathyroid gland pathology: Role of imaging. Otolaryngol Clin North Am 28:621–649, 1995.

211. Jaskowiak N, Norton JA, Alexander HR, et al: A prospective trial evaluating a standard approach to reoperation for missed parathyroid adenoma. Ann Surg 224:308–320, 1996.

212. Shen W, Duren M, Morita E, et al: Reoperation for persistent or recurrent primary hyperparathyroidism. Arch Surg 131:861–867, 1996.

213. Stark DD, Gooding GA, Moss AA, et al: Parathyroid imaging: Comparison of high-resolution CT and high-resolution sonography. AJR Am J Roentgenol 141:633–638, 1983.

214. Rangnekar N, Bailer WJ, Ghani A, et al: Parathyroid cysts: Report of four cases and review of the literature. Int Surg 81:412–414, 1996.

215. Gurbuz AT, Peetz ME: Giant mediastinal parathyroid cyst: An unusual cause of hypercalcemic crisis—case report and review of the literature. Surgery 120:795–800, 1996.

216. Hauet EJ, Paul MA, Salu MK: Compression of the trachea by a mediastinal parathyroid cyst. Ann Thorac Surg 64:851–852, 1997.

217. Landau O, Chamberlain DW, Kennedy RS, et al: Mediastinal parathyroid cysts. Ann Thorac Surg 63:951–953, 1997.

218. Hopkins CR, Reading CC: Thyroid and parathyroid imaging. Semin Ultrasound CT MR 16:279–295, 1995.

219. Moinuddin M, Whynott C: Ectopic parathyroid adenomas: Multi-imaging modalities and its management. Clin Nucl Med 21:27–32, 1996.

220. Fayet P, Hoeffel C, Fulla Y, et al: Technetium-99m sestamibi scintigraphy, magnetic resonance imaging and venous blood sampling in persistent and recurrent hyperparathyroidism. Br J Radiol 70:459–464, 1997.

221. Caixas A, Berna L, Hernández A, et al: Efficacy of preoperative diagnostic imaging localization of technetium 99m-sestamibi scintigraphy in hyperparathyroidism. Surgery 121:535–541, 1997.

222. Sofferman RA, Nathan MH: The ectopic parathyroid adenoma: A cost justification for routine preoperative localization with technetium Tc 99m sestamibi scan. Arch Otolaryngol Head Neck Surg 124:649–654, 1998.

223. Roe SM, Brown PW, Pate LM, et al: Initial cervical exploration for parathyroidectomy is not benefited by preoperative localization studies. Am Surg 64:503–507, 1998.

224. Blanco I, Carril JM, Banzo I, et al: Double-phase Tc-99m sestamibi scintigraphy in the preoperative location of lesions causing hyperparathyroidism. Clin Nucl Med 23:291–297, 1998.

225. Sarfati E, Billotey C, Halimi B, et al: Early localization and reoperation for persistent primary hyperparathyroidism. Br J Surg 84:98–100, 1997.

226. Smythe WR, Bavaria JE, Hall RA, et al: Thoracoscopic removal of mediastinal parathyroid adenoma. Ann Thorac Surg 59:236–238, 1995.

227. Cordeiro AC, Montenegro FL, Kulcsar MA, et al: Parathyroid carcinoma. Am J Surg 175:52–55, 1998.

228. Vázquez Quintana E: Parathyroid carcinoma: Diagnosis and management. Am Surg 63:954–957, 1997.

229. Swanson PE: Soft tissue neoplasms of the mediastinum. Semin Diagn Pathol 8:14–34, 1991.

230. Homer JM, Wechsler RJ, Carter BL: Mediastinal lipomatosis. Radiology 128:657–661, 1978.

231. Lee WJ, Fattal G: Mediastinal lipomatosis in simple obesity. Chest 70:308–309, 1976.

232. Koerner HF, Sun DIC: Mediastinal lipomatosis secondary to steroid therapy. Am J Roentgenol Radium Ther Nucl Med 98:461–464, 1966.

233. Miller WT Jr: Drug-related pleural and mediastinal disorders. J Thorac Imaging 6:36–51, 1991.

234. Enzi G, Biondetti PR, Fiore D, Mazzoleni F: Computed tomography of deep fat masses in multiple symmetrical lipomatosis. Radiology 144:122–124, 1982.

235. Burt M, Ihde JK, Hajdu SI, et al: Primary sarcomas of the mediastinum: Results of therapy. J Thorac Cardiovasc Surg 115:671–680, 1998.

236. Killion MJ, Brodovsky HS, Schwarting R: Pericardial angiosarcoma after mediastinal irradiation for seminoma: A case report and a review of the literature. Cancer 78:912–917, 1996.

237. Ducatman BS, Scheithauer BW: Postirradiation neurofibrosarcoma. Cancer 51:1028–1033, 1983.

238. McLoud TC, Meyer JE: Mediastinal metastases. Radiol Clin North Am 20:453–468, 1982.

239. Genereux GP, Howie JL: Normal mediastinal lymph node size and number: CT and anatomic study. AJR Am J Roentgenol 142:1095–1100, 1984.

240. Glazer GM, Gross BH, Quint LE, et al: Normal mediastinal lymph nodes: Number and size according to American Thoracic Society mapping. AJR Am J Roentgenol 144:261–265, 1985.

241. Filly R, Blank M, Castellino RA: Radiographic distribution of intrathoracic disease in previously untreated patients with Hodgkin's disease and non-Hodgkin's lymphoma. Radiology 120:277–281, 1976.

242. Burgener FA, Hamlin D: Intrathoracic histiocytic lymphoma. AJR Am J Roentgenol 136:499–504, 1981.

243. St Georges R, Deslauriers J, Duranceau A, et al: Clinical spectrum of bronchogenic cysts of the mediastinum and lung in the adult. Ann Thorac Surg 52:6–13, 1991.

244. Patel SR, Meeker DP, Biscotti CV, et al: Presentation and management of bronchogenic cysts in the adult. Chest 106:79–85, 1994.

245. Cioffi U, Bonavina L, De Simone M, et al: Presentation and surgical management of bronchogenic and esophageal duplication cysts in adults. Chest 113:1492–1496, 1998.

246. Salyer DC, Salyer WR, Eggleston JC: Benign developmental cysts of the mediastinum. Arch Pathol Lab Med 101:136–139, 1977.

247. Ng AF, Olak J: Pericardial cyst causing right ventricular outflow tract obstruction. Ann Thorac Surg 63:1147–1148, 1997.

248. Borges AC, Gellert K, Dietel M, et al: Acute right-sided heart failure due to hemorrhage into a pericardial cyst. Ann Thorac Surg 63:845–847, 1997.

249. Fredman CS, Parsons SR, Aquino TI, Hamilton WP: Sudden death after a stress test in a patient with a large pericardial cyst. Am Heart J 127:946–950, 1994.

250. Ribet ME, Copin MC, Gosselin B: Bronchogenic cysts of the mediastinum. J Thorac Cardiovasc Surg 109:1003–1010, 1995.

251. Lippmann M, Solit R, Goldberg SK, Najjar D: Mediastinal bronchogenic cyst: A cause of upper airway obstruction. Chest 102:1901–1903, 1992.

252. Worsnop CJ, Teichtahl H, Clarke CP: Bronchogenic cyst: A cause of pulmonary artery obstruction and breathlessness. Ann Thorac Surg 55:1254–1255, 1993.

253. Fratellone PM, Coplan N, Friedman M, Stelzer P: Hemodynamic compromise secondary to a mediastinal bronchogenic cyst. Chest 106:610–612, 1994.

254. Zaugg M, Kaplan V, Widmer U, et al: Fatal air embolism in an airplane passenger with a giant intrapulmonary bronchogenic cyst. Am J Respir Crit Care Med 157:1686–1689, 1998.

255. Politis GD, Baumann R, Hubbard AM: Spillage of cystic pulmonary masses into the airway during anesthesia. Anesthesiology 87:693–696, 1997.

256. Bolton JW, Shahian DM: Asymptomatic bronchogenic cysts: What is the best management? (see comments). Ann Thorac Surg 53:1134–1137, 1992.

257. Kirwan WO, Walbaum PR, McCormack RJ: Cystic intrathoracic derivatives of the foregut and their complications. Thorax 28:424–428, 1973.

258. Schwartz AR, Fishman EK, Wang KP: Diagnosis and treatment of a bronchogenic cyst using transbronchial needle aspiration. Thorax 41:326–327, 1986.

259. Tobert DG, Midthun DE: Bronchogenic cyst. J Bronch 3:295–299, 1996.

260. Urschel JD, Horan TA: Mediastinoscopic treatment of mediastinal cysts. Ann Thorac Surg 58:1698–1700, 1994.

261. Smythe WR, Bavaria JE, Kaiser LR: Mediastinoscopic subtotal removal of mediastinal cysts. Chest 114:614–617, 1998.

262. Read CA, Moront M, Carangelo R, et al: Recurrent bronchogenic cyst: An argument for complete surgical excision. Arch Surg 126:1306–1308, 1991.

263. Gharagozloo F, Dausmann MJ, McReynolds SD, et al: Recurrent bronchogenic pseudocyst 24 years after incomplete excision: Report of a case. Chest 108:880–883, 1995.

264. Kelley MJ, Mannes EJ, Ravin CE: Mediastinal masses of vascular origin: A review. J Thorac Cardiovasc Surg 76:559–572, 1978.

265. Backer CL: Vascular masses of the mediastinum. In Shields TW (ed): Mediastinal Surgery. Philadelphia: Lea & Febiger, 1991, pp 138–149.

266. Wachsberg RH, Yaghmai V, Javors BR, et al: Cardiophrenic varices in portal hypertension: Evaluation with CT. Radiology 195:553–556, 1995.

267. Marotta R, Franchetto AA: The CT appearance of aortic transection. AJR Am J Roentgenol 166:647–651, 1996.

268. Gavant ML, Menke PG, Fabian T, et al: Blunt traumatic aortic rupture: Detection with helical CT of the chest (see comments). Radiology 197:125–133, 1995.

269. Berlin SC: Magnetic resonance imaging of the cardiovascular system and airway. Pediatr Clin North Am 44:659–679, 1997.

270. Burkill GJ, Burn PR, Padley SP: Aneurysm of the left brachiocephalic vein: An unusual cause of mediastinal widening. Br J Radiol 70:837–839, 1997.

271. Soler R, Rodríguez E, Requejo I, et al: Magnetic resonance imaging of congenital abnormalities of the thoracic aorta. Eur Radiol 8:540–546, 1998.

272. Podbielski FJ, Sam AD 2nd, Halldorsson AO, et al: Giant azygos vein varix. Ann Thorac Surg 63:1167–1169, 1997.

273. D'Cruz IA, Sugathan P: Compression of right atrium by traumatic diaphragmatic hernia. Am Heart J 133:380–383, 1997.

274. Colliver C, Oller DW, Rose G, Brewer D: Traumatic intrapericardial diaphragmatic hernia diagnosed by echocardiography. J Trauma 42:115–117, 1997.

275. Gale AW, Jelihovsky T, Grant AF, et al: Neurogenic tumors of the mediastinum. Ann Thorac Surg 17:434–443, 1974.

276. Reed JC, Hallet KK, Feigin DS: Neural tumors of the thorax: Subject review from the AFIP. Radiology 126:9–17, 1978.

277. Saenz NC, Schnitzer JJ, Eraklis AE, et al: Posterior mediastinal masses. J Pediatr Surg 28:172–176, 1993.

278. Matsui I, Tanimura M, Kobayashi N, et al: Neurofibromatosis type 1 and childhood cancer. Cancer 72:2746–2754, 1993.

279. Shields TW, Reynolds M: Neurogenic tumors of the thorax. Surg Clin North Am 68:645–668, 1988.

280. Matthay KK: Neuroblastoma: A clinical challenge and biologic puzzle. CA Cancer J Clin 45:179–192, 1995.

281. Simpson I, Campbell PE: Mediastinal masses in childhood: A review from a paediatric pathologist's point of view. Prog Pediatr Surg 27:92–126, 1991.

282. Grosfeld JL, Skinner MA, Rescorla FJ, et al: Mediastinal tumors in children: Experience with 196 cases. Ann Surg Oncol 1:121–127, 1994.

283. Franks LM, Bollen A, Seeger RC, et al: Neuroblastoma in adults and adolescents: An indolent course with poor survival. Cancer 79:2028–2035, 1997.

284. Adams GA, Shochat SJ, Smith EI, et al: Thoracic neuroblastoma: A Pediatric Oncology Group study. J Pediatr Surg 28:372–377, 1993.

285. Morris JA, Shochat SJ, Smith EI, et al: Biological variables in thoracic neuroblastoma: A Pediatric Oncology Group study. J Pediatr Surg 30:296–302, 1995.

286. Rufini V, Fisher GA, Shulkin BL, et al: Iodine-123-MIBG imaging of neuroblastoma: Utility of SPECT and delayed imaging. J Nucl Med 37:1464–1468, 1996.

287. Katzenstein HM, Cohn SL: Advances in the diagnosis and treatment of neuroblastoma. Curr Opin Oncol 10:43–51, 1998.

288. Shapiro B, Orringer MB, Gross MD: Mediastinal paragangliomas and pheochromocytomas. *In* Shields TW (ed): Mediastinal Surgery. Philadelphia: Lea & Febiger, 1991, pp 254–271.

289. Pantoja E, Kattan KR, Thomas HA: Some uncommon lower mediastinal densities. Radiol Clin North Am 22:633–646, 1984.

290. Hainsworth JD, Greco FA: Poorly differentiated carcinoma of the mediastinum. *In* Shields TW (ed): Mediastinal Surgery. Philadelphia: Lea & Febiger, 1991, pp 225–227.

291. Adkins RB Jr, Maples MD, Hainsworth JD: Primary malignant mediastinal tumors. Ann Thorac Surg 38:648–653, 1984.

292. Jaffe BM, Ferguson TB, Holtz S: Mediastinal pancreatic pseudocysts. Am J Surg 124:600–606, 1972.

293. Spiro SG, Goldstraw P: The staging of lung cancer. Thorax 39:401–407, 1984.

294. Detterbeck FC, DeCamp MM Jr, Kohman LJ, Silvestri GA: Lung cancer: Invasive staging: the guidelines. Chest 123:167S–175S, 2003.

72

Pneumomediastinum and Mediastinitis

David R. Park, M.D., Eric Vallières, M.D.

Introduction
General Anatomic Considerations
Pneumomediastinum
    Pathophysiology
    Clinical Settings and Syndromes
    Clinical Manifestations and Diagnosis

Approach to Management
Sequelae
Mediastinitis
    Acute Mediastinitis
    Granulomatous Mediastinitis and Mediastinal Fibrosis
Summary

INTRODUCTION

Pneumomediastinum (air in the mediastinum) and mediastinitis (infection or inflammation in the mediastinum) are disorders that predominantly involve the potential spaces and interstitial and lymphatic tissues of the mediastinum rather than the visceral organs. Although both may occur together, as following esophageal rupture, the term *pneumomediastinum* usually refers to the presence of aberrant air in the mediastinum without accompanying infection. *Mediastinitis* is the appropriate term when infection or inflammation is the primary disease process regardless of the variable presence of air. These conditions are each seen in a variety of unique clinical circumstances. However, both tend to result from breaches in the integrity of mediastinal structures, or from the continuity of mediastinal tissue planes with sites of involvement elsewhere in the body. Thus, anatomic considerations are similar for the two processes and are considered together at the beginning of this chapter. The pathophysiology, clinical settings, management approaches, and impact on patient well-being of pneumomediastinum and mediastinitis are quite different and are discussed separately.

GENERAL ANATOMIC CONSIDERATIONS

The mediastinum is traversed by air-filled structures (trachea and esophagus) that also may contain colonizing microorganisms. In addition, mediastinal lymph nodes drain the airways and lung parenchyma where inhaled organisms, antigens, and dusts are encountered. Consequently, entry of air or inflammatory and infectious materials into the mediastinum is readily accomplished by breaches in the integrity of these mediastinal structures, or when materials deposited in the airways or distal lung enter the lymphatic system.

How air reaches the mediastinum from ruptured alveoli or from outside the chest, and its physiologic and clinical effects once it is there, can be understood by referring to the soft-tissue compartments of the neck, thorax, and abdomen, as illustrated in Figure 72.1. The visceral space surrounding the trachea, esophagus, and great vessels of the neck continues into the chest to envelop the mediastinal structures and passes through the diaphragm with the esophagus to communicate with the retroperitoneal space. A continuum thus connects the viscera-containing portions of the neck, chest, and retroperitoneal space.[1] A similar continuum exists between the endothoracic fascia of the outer chest wall and the abdominal transversalis fascia. Furthermore, within the mediastinum, the vessels and airways of the pulmonary hilum are surrounded by the visceral space, which extends distally into the lung and eventually merges with the distal bronchovascular sheaths (see Fig. 72.1).[1] The same anatomic relationships that permit air to dissect freely throughout the mediastinum also predispose to the spread of infection and inflammation.[1,2]

Thus, it is possible for air that originates within any of the structures mentioned, or inflammation originating at any site in the mediastinum, to dissect around or spread to involve any of these structures. Although air in the mediastinum does not usually cause serious clinical consequences unless it is under tension, the proximity of the mediastinal tissue planes to many vital organs makes the mediastinum uniquely vulnerable to inflammatory injury. Consequently, mediastinal inflammation can give rise to widely varying manifestations that are related more to the functions of the affected structures than to symptoms or signs of the inflammation itself. In the remainder of this chapter, pneumomediastinum and the various forms of mediastinitis are discussed in turn.

PNEUMOMEDIASTINUM

Pneumomediastinum consists of air or other gas in the mediastinum. Also known as mediastinal emphysema, it is one of several forms of aberrant extra-alveolar air, or air outside the confines of the respiratory and gastrointestinal tracts; the others include subcutaneous emphysema, pulmonary interstitial emphysema, pneumopericardium,

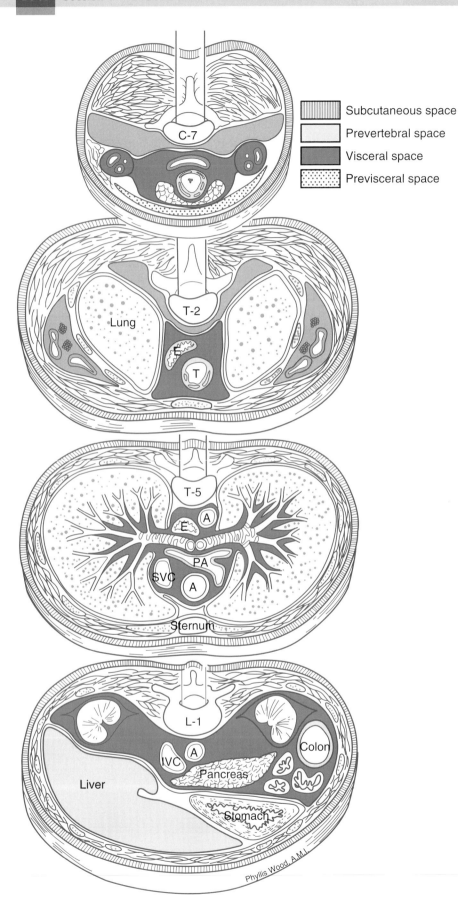

Figure 72.1 Soft-tissue compartments of the mediastinum (levels of T2 and T5) in relation to those of the neck (level of C7) and the upper abdomen (level of L1), demonstrating continuity of the visceral space. A, aorta; E, esophagus; IVC, inferior vena cava; PA, pulmonary artery; SVC, superior vena cava; T, trachea. (From Maunder RJ, Pierson DJ, Hudson LD: Subcutaneous and mediastinal emphysema: Pathophysiology, diagnosis, and management. Arch Intern Med 144:1447–1453, 1984.)

pneumoperitoneum, pneumoretroperitoneum, pneumo-cephalus, and pneumorrhachis (air in the spinal canal). Pneumothorax, the most common life-threatening form of extra-alveolar air, is discussed elsewhere (Chapter 69) and mentioned only briefly here.

Extra-alveolar air in the form of pneumomediastinum and subcutaneous emphysema occurs in a wide variety of clinical settings, the earliest of which to be recognized was during childbirth. In her "Observations" of 1617 (as cited by Gordon[3]), Louise Bourgeois, midwife to the queen of France, wrote, "I saw that she tried to stop crying out, and I implored her not to stop, for fear that her throat might swell." According to Faust,[4] the first formal medical documentation of pneumomediastinum and subcutaneous emphysema following Valsalva's maneuver during labor was by Simmons in 1784, and this association was reported in over 130 patients by 1927.[3] Within 2 decades thereafter, Hamman[5,6] had thoroughly established the clinical features of spontaneous pneumomediastinum and Macklin and Macklin[7] had elegantly elucidated its pathophysiology. Little has been added to the pioneering descriptions of these investigators, but pneumomediastinum and other forms of extra-alveolar air are encountered today in a greater variety of clinical circumstances. These include mechanical ventilation and other aspects of critical care, decompression in diving and other settings, chest trauma, asthma, and numerous other situations in addition to childbirth.[1]

PATHOPHYSIOLOGY

The pathophysiology of pneumomediastinum depends on the clinical circumstances in which it is encountered. Pneumomediastinum most commonly results from microscopic alveolar rupture but can also result from air escaping from the upper respiratory tract, intrathoracic airways, or gastrointestinal tract. Gas can be generated by bacteria causing infection of the visceral space, and outside air can reach the mediastinum after trauma or surgery. These potential sources for mediastinal emphysema are summarized in Table 72.1 and discussed in the following sections.

Air Originating in the Upper Respiratory Tract

Mediastinal air dissecting downward from the head and neck can originate in several ways. Retropharyngeal abscess is a long-established cause of gas in the neck,[8] but other infections, including dental abscess, cervical adenitis, salivary gland infection, tonsillitis, and osteomyelitis of the facial bones, can also produce this finding.[1,2,9,10] Odontogenic infections are said to be the most common of these.[11]

Dental extractions or drilling, especially in the lower molar teeth and if an air-turbine drill is used, can be followed by pneumomediastinum.[12] Although drilling has been considered necessary for this to occur, pneumomediastinum can be massive and associated with complications even after simple dental extraction.[13] Passage of air into the soft tissues from the socket of an extracted tooth can be increased dramatically if positive pressure is applied at the mouth—as illustrated by the case of a soldier whose neck swelled on resumption of his duties as a bugler immediately after a tooth extraction.[14]

Table 72.1 Possible Origins of Air in the Mediastinum

Upper Respiratory Tract
Head and neck infection (odontogenic, salivary glands, cervical adenitis, tonsillitis, peritonsillar abscess, osteomyelitis of facial bones)
Fractures (involving paranasal sinuses, orbit, mandibles, other facial bones)
Other mucosal disruption (trauma, surgery, attempted endotracheal intubation)
Dental procedures (extractions, air-turbine drilling)

Intrathoracic Airways
Blunt or penetrating chest trauma
Foreign body
Iatrogenic (bronchoscopy, bronchial brushing, transbronchial biopsy, needle aspiration)
Neoplasm

Lung Parenchyma
Direct disruption of alveoli (penetrating trauma, surgery, transbronchial biopsy, needle aspiration)
"Spontaneous" alveolar rupture (between alveolus and adjacent bronchovascular sheath)*

Gastrointestinal Tract
Esophageal perforation
Via pneumoperitoneum or pneumoretroperitoneum (gastric or intestinal perforation, diverticulitis, pneumatosis cystoides intestinalis, endoscopy, biopsy, infection)
Infection with gas-producing organisms
Acute bacterial mediastinitis
Head and neck infections

Air from Outside the Body
Penetrating trauma to neck or chest
Surgical procedures (tracheotomy, mediastinoscopy, sternotomy)
Via subcutaneous emphysema in association with chest tube insertion
Artificial pneumothorax
Artificial pneumoperitoneum

* See Table 72.2 for clinical settings.

Injury to the paranasal sinuses, orbit, mandible, and other facial bones adjacent to the upper airways can provide access of air to the fascial planes of the neck,[15,16] especially following nose blowing.[9] Surgical procedures involving the upper respiratory tract may produce air in the neck, via breaches either in the oropharyngeal mucosa[17] or in the trachea and skin.[18] Pneumomediastinum and subcutaneous emphysema are common following tracheotomy: These findings were noted in 13% of cases in one prospective series in adults.[19,20]

Pneumomediastinum can also occur following attempts at endotracheal intubation or after overinflation of the endotracheal tube cuff when the hypopharyngeal mucosa or membranous trachea is injured.[21] Tracheal injury and esophageal rupture leading to pneumomediastinum can happen also when air is forced into the open mouth.[22–24]

Air Originating in the Intrathoracic Airways

Blunt thoracic trauma, particularly deceleration injury as sustained in motor vehicle accidents, may lacerate or fracture the trachea or main bronchi and allow air to enter the mediastinum.[25] Although this may occur in the proximal trachea,[26] the majority of such injuries are within 3 cm of the carina, probably owing to the relative fixation of the airway at the carina and the development of a shearing force when the more mobile parts are displaced by the sudden impact.[25,27]

Other potential sources of mediastinal air from the major intrathoracic airways include perforation by an aspirated foreign body and erosion by bronchogenic or esophageal neoplasm.[28,28a] Visceral perforation is much less frequently associated with bronchoscopy than with esophagoscopy. However, increasing use of bronchoscopic biopsy techniques and endobronchial therapies for bronchial obstruction render this source for mediastinal air increasingly likely.

Air Originating in the Lung Parenchyma

Most instances of pneumomediastinum are the result of alveolar disruption. This may occur after direct injury to the lung parenchyma, which allows air to escape from torn alveoli and terminal bronchioles after penetrating thoracic trauma, or from cut surfaces during surgery. The lung may be nicked in the course of tracheotomy or central venous access procedures, and this mechanism may also be the source of extra-alveolar air following percutaneous or trans-bronchial lung biopsy. However, the majority of cases of pneumomediastinum follow "spontaneous" microscopic alveolar rupture.

Mechanism of Alveolar Rupture. Disruption of alveolar walls and entry of air into the bronchovascular sheath can result when a sudden increase in alveolar pressure, or a fall in perivascular interstitial pressure, establishes a gradient of sufficient magnitude to disrupt the alveolar walls at their bases and introduce air into the pulmonary interstitium, as depicted in Figure 72.2.[1,7,29,30] In both circumstances, alveolar rupture occurs by the same mechanism: a transient gradient between the alveolus and bronchovascular sheath. Although it has been speculated that a sufficient increase in intrapulmonic pressure was capable of producing alveolar rupture,[31] animal experiments have demonstrated that an increase in alveolar volume, due to increased transpulmonary pressure, is a more important determinant of disruption of the alveolar walls.[32] This finding may explain the rarity of alveolar rupture following coughing and sneezing, acts that buttress the chest and abdominal walls to counter the transient high intrapulmonic pressures.[33]

High alveolar volumes undoubtedly contribute to alveolar rupture after sudden decompression due to decreases in external pressure.[33,34] The mechanism of alveolar rupture presumably relates to overdistention due to the expansion of gas trapped in the lungs during ascent. Accordingly, alveolar rupture is especially prevalent after sudden ascent from shallow depths, as the proportional volume expansion of intrathoracic gas is greater: Ascent from 99 to 66 feet beneath the surface increases gas volume by 33%, whereas rising from 33 feet to the surface doubles it.[35,36]

Pneumomediastinum and other forms of ventilator-related barotrauma are almost always associated with parenchymal abnormalities in the affected lung,[33,37] and this is also the case in the majority of instances occurring during spontaneous ventilation.[1,7]

Spread of Air after Alveolar Rupture. Entry of air into the bronchovascular sheath, as depicted schematically in Figure 72.2, produces pulmonary interstitial emphysema. This is the initial consequence of alveolar rupture and may be the only overt manifestation of extra-alveolar air, especially in neonates with infant respiratory distress syndrome.[38-40] According to Munsell,[41] Laennec called this condition "interlobular emphysema." The clinical description of pulmonary interstitial emphysema, which is rarely observed in adults,[33] is attributed to Hamman.[42]

Because the mean pressure in the mediastinum, like that in the pleural space, is always somewhat negative with respect to the pressure in the pulmonary parenchyma, the pressure difference causes air to move centripetally, perhaps facilitated by the pumping action of breathing.[27,43] This is illustrated in Figure 72.3, and convincingly described in the 1944 paper by Macklin and Macklin,[7] which first confirmed the sequence in experimental animals:

> [T]he first step . . . was air passing through numerous minute ruptures in the strained bases of the alveoli of the overinflated region into the underlying vascular sheaths. The air bubbles, at the very first minute, moved along the vascular sheaths, coalescing and gaining in size. This streaming of air through the pulmonic interstitium reminded one of the flow of a river that ever increases in size by addition of new tributaries as it proceeds on its course. Reaching the root of the lung, the train of air bubbles passed into and distended the mediastinum. With continued insufflation an actual overflow into the retroperitoneum, anterior mediastinum and subcutaneous tissues of the root of the neck and axillae occurred. In extreme cases the mediastinal wall ruptured, producing a pneumothorax.

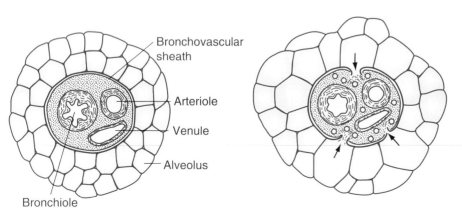

Figure 72.2 Schematic diagram showing mechanism of alveolar rupture into the bronchovascular sheath resulting from a momentary pressure gradient between them. (From Maunder RJ, Pierson DJ, Hudson LD: Subcutaneous and mediastinal emphysema: Pathophysiology, diagnosis, and management. Arch Intern Med 144:1447–1453, 1984.)

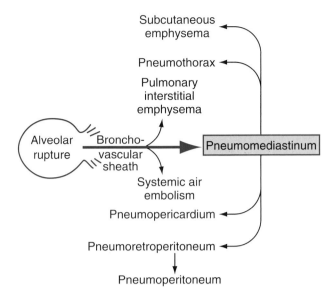

Subcutaneous
emphysema

Pneumothorax

Pulmonary
interstitial
emphysema

Alveolar
rupture   Broncho-
           vascular
           sheath   Pneumomediastinum

Systemic air
embolism

Pneumopericardium

Pneumoretroperitoneum

Pneumoperitoneum

Figure 72.3 One likely mechanism to explain the different forms of extra-alveolar air resulting from alveolar rupture.

These classic observations have since been confirmed in other studies, but little has been added conceptually.

Entry of Air into the Pleural Space. Pneumothorax following alveolar rupture occurs most commonly through the sequence depicted in Figure 72.3. Once in the mediastinum, air follows the path of least resistance and may rupture through the delicate mediastinal fascia and overlying pleura into the pleural space. The observations that, in animal experiments, lower sustained inflation-hold pressures are required to produce pulmonary interstitial emphysema than to create a pneumomediastinum or pneumothorax,[38] and that pneumomediastinum preceded pneumothorax in the majority of mechanically ventilated patients with the acute respiratory distress syndrome (ARDS) in one series, lend substantial support to this model.[44] Another mechanism for pneumothorax following alveolar rupture has been proposed,[45] in which air dissects toward the periphery of the lung rather than toward the mediastinum and ruptures via subpleural blebs through the visceral surface of the lung. Which of these mechanisms most often accounts for "spontaneous" pneumothorax is uncertain.

Entry of Air into the Abdomen. Extra-alveolar air having its origin from disrupted alveoli may appear below the diaphragm, in the form of either *pneumoperitoneum* or *pneumoretroperitoneum*.[46–49] To reach the retroperitoneal space, and thence into the peritoneal cavity, air from the mediastinum usually extends via the loosely packed paraesophageal connective tissue to pass through and beneath the diaphragm. An alternative route directly through the diaphragm has also been suggested. In a review of 28 cases of pneumoperitoneum occurring during mechanical ventilation, Hillman[50] noted subcutaneous emphysema in 19, pneumothorax in 18, and pneumomediastinum in only 13. Pneumoperitoneum has also occurred without evidence of pneumomediastinum after emergency ascent during scuba diving.[51]

Entry of Air into the Vasculature. Extra-alveolar air also may enter pulmonary blood vessels, with resultant *arterial air embolism*.[34,52] This complication is particularly common in the setting of decompression illness,[52,53] yet is relatively rare as a complication of mechanical ventilation, despite a high incidence of alveolar rupture and other forms of aberrant air.[54,55]

Why is air embolism recognized commonly in decompression illness and rarely during mechanical ventilation, despite the rupture of alveoli in both circumstances? Perhaps the more common recognition in decompression illness relates to a larger volume of air entering the circulation, to a greater injury to the pulmonary venules and veins where aberrant air would enter the systemic circulation, to the relative ease in recognizing subtle forms of air embolism in otherwise healthy patients, or to the upright posture of ascending divers favoring clinically overt cerebral embolization of any air entering the systemic circulation. Also, bubbles may form directly within systemic circulation during decompression, leading to arterial air embolism in the absence of pulmonary barotrauma. Diving medicine is discussed further in Chapter 66.

Although commonly believed to require septal defects or pulmonary arteriovenous shunts,[56] systemic air embolism can follow introduction of air into the venous system without the obvious presence of such right-to-left shunts.[57–59]

Air Originating in the Gastrointestinal Tract

Mediastinal air can be of gastrointestinal origin, from either above or below the diaphragm, although this is probably less common than the spread of mediastinal air into the abdomen as discussed earlier. In *Boerhaave's syndrome,* rupture of the esophagus allows air and other material to enter the mediastinum.[60] In this circumstance, pneumomediastinum is accompanied by acute mediastinitis, as described later in this chapter. Pneumomediastinum can also be a consequence of esophageal perforation during upper gastrointestinal endoscopy,[61] or following the ingestion of a caustic such as paraquat[62] or lye (sodium hydroxide).

Air or other gas originating in the retroperitoneal space also can spread to the mediastinum,[1] although this is rare. Possible causes of pneumomediastinum from such a sequence include perforation of a duodenal ulcer, ulcerative colitis, sigmoid diverticulitis, pneumatosis cystoides intestinalis, "rectal barotrauma,"[63] and procedures such as sigmoidoscopy, colonoscopy, and barium enema.[64]

Air Originating from External and Miscellaneous Sources

Pneumomediastinum can arise from air entering the body from external sources, particularly if positive pressure is applied to the subcutaneous tissue planes. Air can enter the cervical soft tissues during tracheotomy[19,20] or the chest wall during arthroscopic shoulder surgery,[65,66] and subsequently reach the mediastinum. Pneumothorax can be the source of mediastinal air by an unusual mechanism when treated with tube thoracostomy,[67] as first described by Sauerbruch.[68] Once a connection is established from the pleural space to the skin by means of a chest tube, air can enter the subcutaneous tissues, dissect to the neck, and then penetrate down into the mediastinum. Air introduced into the pleural space under tension, as in the era of deliberate pneumothorax as treatment for tuberculosis, could conceivably enter the mediastinum directly across the parietal pleura.[69]

Pneumomediastinum has also been observed following the deliberate insufflation of air into the peritoneal cavity, both in tuberculosis treatment[70] and during the course of modern-era laparoscopy.[71] Presumably, air introduced into the peritoneal cavity by any mechanism could migrate, by the reverse of the sequence shown in Figure 72.3, to the mediastinum. This would include air entering the peritoneal cavity via the female genital tract during pelvic examination,[72] douche,[73] postpartum exercise,[74] or blowing into the vagina,[75,76] especially during pregnancy.[77-79]

Gas can form in the mediastinum during acute bacterial mediastinitis caused by gas-producing organisms. More commonly, pneumomediastinum associated with mediastinitis is due to communication with the gastrointestinal tract (as in Boerhaave's syndrome), respiratory tract (as in necrotizing pneumonia or head-neck soft-tissue infection), or outside air (as in traumatic or post-sternotomy mediastinitis). These conditions are described in more detail in the second part of this chapter.

CLINICAL SETTINGS AND SYNDROMES

Pneumomediastinum following alveolar rupture is encountered clinically in two general settings: "spontaneous" mediastinal emphysema and "barotrauma," or pneumomediastinum occurring during positive-pressure ventilation or associated with other externally applied distending pressures (Table 72.2). Two dramatic clinical syndromes deserve separate discussion: pneumopericardium, in which the mediastinal air is confined to the pericardium, sometimes with profound physiologic effects; and systemic air embolism, in which morbid microvascular complications are common.

Spontaneous Pneumomediastinum

Voluntary Alterations in Breathing Pattern. Alveolar rupture can sometimes be induced by voluntarily manipulating the breathing pattern such that lung volume is increased or sudden pressure changes occur. A typical example is pneumomediastinum reported after marijuana smoking.[80,81] Vigorous straining against a closed glottis after inhaling to total lung capacity, the Valsalva maneuver, is the presumed mechanism. The same complication has occurred after inhaling free-base cocaine,[82-84] during which users sometimes add additional external airway pressure by having an accomplice blow vigorously into their mouths through a cardboard tube.[85] Pneumomediastinum has also been reported in two college fraternity brothers following the recreational inhalation of nitrous oxide from disposable canisters.[86]

Mediastinal and subcutaneous emphysema occurred in a medical student after pulmonary function testing,[87] and these findings have also been observed in other healthy young individuals after dancing,[88] and strenuous shouting, yelling, and singing during the course of basic training for the U.S. Marines.[89] Other circumstances in which healthy persons have developed pneumomediastinum include playing the trumpet,[90] inflating a balloon,[90,91] and moun-

Table 72.2 Alveolar Rupture: Reported Clinical Settings
Spontaneous
Deliberate alteration in breathing pattern
Marijuana smoking and cocaine inhalation
Pulmonary function testing
Mountain climbing
Wind instrument playing
Yelling, shouting, and singing
Straining and other involuntary alterations in breathing pattern
Childbirth
Vomiting
Seizures; status epilepticus
Violent coughing; sneezing; hiccupping
Heavy lifting; athletic competition
Straining at stool
Associated lung diseases
"Idiopathic" (Hamman's Syndrome)
Due to External Pressure Changes (Barotrauma)
Decompression; gas expansion
Scuba diving
Air travel
Positive intrathoracic pressure of external origin
Mechanical ventilation
Continuous positive airway pressure
Manual ventilation during resuscitation, anesthesia, or transport
Equipment malfunction or misconnection in anesthesia or oxygen therapy
Heimlich maneuver
Deceleration injury

tain climbing.[92] In mountaineers, alveolar rupture may be related to "voluntary pressure breathing," a practice originally proposed for fliers during World War II that consists of slow, deep inhalations followed by forced exhalation through tightly pursed lips. This maneuver has been advocated by some climbers as a means of getting more oxygen into the blood, but it could well lead to alveolar rupture. The cases reported by Vosk and Houston[92] were members of the same climbing party, and both had practiced "voluntary pressure breathing" during ascent.

Inadvertent Manipulation of Breathing Pattern. Much more common than the voluntary maneuvers just discussed is the inadvertent manipulation of the breathing pattern in the course of straining or exertion. As mentioned earlier, the first recorded pneumomediastinum occurred during childbirth,[3] and this complication of labor has been cited many times since.[4,93] It has also been noted after vomiting in association with bulimia,[94] hyperemesis gravidarum,[95] diabetic ketoacidosis,[96-98] and other settings. Prolonged straining during convulsive seizures can be followed by mediastinal emphysema,[99] as can athletic competition[100,101] and violent coughing.[102] It is reasonable to expect that any activity producing large momentary swings in intrathoracic pressure could result in alveolar rupture and pneumomediastinum; other authors have listed sneezing, hiccupping, and straining at stool among such predispositions.[1,7]

Associated Lung Diseases. Localized airway obstruction can overdistend lung tissue, disrupt alveoli, and lead to all the reported forms of extra-alveolar air. This is easiest to visualize in the case of an obstructing foreign body,[103] blood clot,[104] or tumor,[105] but it may also explain the observation of extra-alveolar air in diffuse obstructive and parenchymal lung diseases. Pneumomediastinum is well described as a complication of acute asthma.[106–111] Although chest radiographs are not routinely obtained during attacks of asthma, pneumomediastinum is not infrequent, having been noted in 5.4% of 479 radiographs of children admitted with asthma attacks.[112]

Parenchymal lung diseases associated with pneumomediastinum include atelectasis,[7] bronchiolitis,[113,114] pneumonia,[115,116] influenza,[7,41] measles,[117] hematogenous tumor metastases,[118] and miliary tuberculosis.[118a]

Idiopathic. Although a history of a potential predisposing event or disease process is elicited in most patients with "spontaneous" pneumomediastinum or other forms of extra-alveolar air, cases without such associations do occur and are known as *Hamman's syndrome*.[42] Hamman's original patient was a 51-year-old physician in whom no predisposing factor could be identified.[42] Hamman later reported several additional cases of truly "idiopathic" pneumomediastinum, and modern series confirm that this may occur even in patients with normal lung parenchyma as determined by chest computed tomography (CT).[5,119,119a]

Barotrauma or Pneumomediastinum Associated with Pressure Changes

Decreases in external pressure, such as during decompression events, may lead to alveolar overdistention and rupture. As mentioned earlier, alveolar rupture is a relatively common complication of sudden decompression.[34,52,120] Extra-alveolar air may develop following scuba diving,[51,121] during decompression in a hyperbaric chamber,[122] or with sudden atmospheric pressure changes during air travel.

Externally applied positive airway pressure is another general category of clinical settings associated with extra-alveolar air. Most familiar within this category is "barotrauma" during mechanical ventilation; however, this term is in part a misnomer because alveolar overinflation, rather than high airway pressures per se, may play the major role.[33,123]

Whether abetted by positive-pressure ventilation or occurring as a result of severe lung dysfunction, extra-alveolar air is common in mechanically ventilated patients.[54,124] Alveolar rupture during positive-pressure ventilation is thought to result from overdistention in an area with abnormal airways or lung parenchyma. Delivered tidal volumes in excess of 15 mL/kg, particularly when combined with high levels of positive end-expiratory pressure, predispose to barotrauma, although the disease processes traditionally managed in this fashion are themselves associated with alveolar rupture.[33] In fact, Gammon and associates found that ARDS was the lung disease most commonly associated with barotrauma,[44] and was the only independently associated risk factor for barotrauma among all ventilated patients.[37] These authors attributed previously reported univariate associations between airway pressures and barotrauma to the fact that airway pressures serve as a marker of the severity of lung injury (or dysfunction) rather than a causative risk factor for pulmonary barotrauma.[37] Further supporting this hypothesis, recent studies have found that

the generally modest airway pressures and delivered volumes used were not different among those ARDS patients who developed and did not develop barotrauma.[125–127] In fact, it is likely that both the severity of underlying lung dysfunction and particular styles of ventilator management that result in higher pressures and regional overdistention are responsible.[128]

Several distinct modes of mechanical ventilation have been introduced with the main purpose of decreasing the incidence of overt barotrauma. These include pressure-limited modes of mechanical ventilation (e.g., inspiratory pressure support; pressure-control ventilation; airway pressure-release ventilation), and high-frequency ventilation.[128] The hope that barotrauma would be lessened by these modes is based on rational theory,[129] but no controlled clinical trials comparing the incidence of barotrauma with pressure-limited versus volume-limited ventilation have been reported.[123] Anecdotal reports have suggested that high-frequency jet ventilation may reduce the incidence of barotrauma, but two recent large randomized trials comparing high-frequency oscillation with conventional volume ventilation showed no differences in barotrauma among patients with acute respiratory failure with either risk factors for[130] or established[131] ARDS.

An alternative approach is the use of conventional volume-limited ventilatory modes with parameters selected to avoid overdistention (and also the repetitive opening and collapse of lung units). Such "protective" ventilatory strategies, designed to reduce microscopic ventilator-induced lung injury, might also reduce the incidence of barotrauma. Several randomized trials have compared this approach with more traditional ventilatory management, but found no differences in the incidence of barotrauma.[132–135] These findings may be the result of a long-term trend toward the use of less injurious ventilatory parameters; even the control arms in these studies used relatively modest tidal volumes and distending pressures compared with historical practice, resulting in a lower incidence of barotrauma overall.[127]

Theoretic analysis[136] and studies on experimental animals[137] suggest that a gradual inhalation, followed by a pause at peak inflation, produces optimum intrapulmonary gas distribution and oxygenation. However, in clinical practice, this is of dubious value and may be hazardous. Prolonged inspiratory times reduce the time available for lung emptying, so that air trapping and occult positive end-expiratory pressure or "auto-PEEP" ensue, especially when airflow obstruction or high minute ventilation needs are present.[138,139] This "dynamic air trapping" results in overinflation and can lead to alveolar rupture and overt barotrauma. Clinical observations suggest that, in the setting of severe asthma, any attempt to increase total minute volume (regardless of the specific ventilatory pattern) is associated with increased auto-PEEP and barotrauma,[140] leading to strategies using intentional hypoventilation (see Chapter 86). In patients with ARDS, auto-PEEP is associated with greater overall minute ventilation rates, but a rapid and shallow breathing pattern appears to increase auto-PEEP more than a slower, deeper pattern.[141]

Noninvasive forms of positive-pressure ventilation are less often associated with barotrauma than conventional mechanical ventilation. This is probably because of the lower airway pressures used, and the less severe lung diseases being treated. For instance, continuous positive airway pressure applied by mask was associated with pneumomediastinum in only 1 of 331 applications of this therapy cited in one review.[142]

Barotrauma is especially likely when excessive manual ventilation or insufflation of air or oxygen under high pressure occurs. Barotrauma is a well-documented complication of manual ventilation during cardiopulmonary resuscitation,[143,144] not only from lung puncture during attempted line placement but also from excessive lung distention. Improperly connected oxygen tubing for in-hospital transport of intubated patients, such that exhalation is prevented, has resulted in life-threatening barotrauma,[145] as have similar errors following anesthesia and surgery.[146] A variety of other anesthesia-related causes of alveolar rupture have been attributed to inadvertent overinflation or mechanical obstruction to exhalation.[45]

Deceleration injury commonly results in extra-alveolar air, even when there is no open chest wound or displaced rib fracture. Although motor vehicle accidents are currently the most common setting for such injuries, they can also follow blows to the chest or falls into water with the glottis closed.[29,30] Pneumomediastinum has also occurred after resuscitation from choking by use of the Heimlich maneuver.[147]

Pneumopericardium

Alveolar rupture can be followed by dissection of air into the pericardium, and pneumopericardium may be the only evidence of extra-alveolar air detected on chest radiograph. This occurs less frequently in adults[148,149] than in infants, in whom it is recognized as a potentially lethal complication of ventilatory management for the infant respiratory distress syndrome.[38,40] Hemodynamically significant pneumopericardium in adult patients undergoing mechanical ventilation has been considered less likely, because the adult pericardium communicates less readily with the rest of the mediastinum than is the case with neonates. However, one thorough literature review documented the occurrence of pericardial tamponade resulting from pneumopericardium in adults as well as in infants.[149] In 252 cases reported in 81 cited articles, pericardial air was hemodynamically significant in 37%.[149] The majority of the patients were either neonates or adults with severe thoracic trauma, but the rest presented in a variety of clinical settings. In several instances, immediate pericardial decompression was lifesaving.[148,149] One adult patient experienced life-threatening pneumopericardium during continuous positive airway pressure therapy following cardiac surgery, which undoubtedly had altered the tissue planes between the mediastinum and pericardium. In this case, spontaneous resolution followed discontinuation of continuous positive airway pressure.[150]

Another complication of mechanical ventilation in infants, having a clinical presentation similar to pericardial tamponade, is when pulmonary interstitial emphysema becomes hemodynamically significant in the form of "air block."[151] In this entity, extra-alveolar air accumulates sufficiently within the lung to compress the airways, resulting in distal air trapping, interference with pulmonary blood flow, and acute cor pulmonale.[151]

Arterial Air Embolism

Entry of aberrant air into the pulmonary vessels results in systemic or arterial air embolism. This is particularly common in the setting of decompression illness (detectable in 3% of submarine escape trainees[53]), and is often accompanied by pneumomediastinum.[52] When a predisposing condition such as asthma is present, even ascents from the bottom of a swimming pool can cause air embolism.[152] The clinical manifestations depend on the amount and the distribution of the bubbles, but cerebral air embolism is often fatal.[32,34,52,121,152]

As discussed previously, arterial air embolism is relatively rare as a complication of mechanical ventilation. In this setting, it is reported more frequently in infants[153,154] than in adults,[55] except after thoracotomy for penetrating lung injury.[155–157] Fatal air embolism has also been reported after recreational inhalation of helium from a pressurized cylinder.[158]

Systemic air embolism may occur in circumstances other than alveolar rupture. These include direct air entry into ruptured blood vessels in pulmonary cavities, after artificial pneumothorax for treatment of tuberculosis, and in a variety of iatrogenic settings.[34,159] Included in this last group are cardiac bypass, intracranial or cervical vascular procedures in the semiupright position, and hemodialysis. Dramatic cases of air embolism have followed the rupture of an air-filled bronchogenic cyst during ascent in an aircraft,[160] and the establishment of a bronchial–left atrial fistula due to a mediastinal abscess complicating lung transplantation.[161]

CLINICAL MANIFESTATIONS AND DIAGNOSIS

Symptoms, Physical Signs, and Laboratory Findings

Pain is the most common symptom reported by patients with pneumomediastinum[1,41,119,162–165] and probably results from stretching of mediastinal tissues by dissecting air. It occurs in 80% to 90% of patients with "spontaneous" mediastinal emphysema and may account for some cases of unexplained acute chest pain in otherwise healthy young people.[119,162] The pain is characteristically substernal in location and aggravated by movement, breathing, and position changes[41,164,166]; it often radiates to the back, shoulder, or arm. Discomfort may extend into the neck, and retropharyngeal or perilaryngeal air dissection may give rise to dysphagia[41,167] or dysphonia, with the characteristic muffled, "hot potato" voice as if talking with a mouthful of hot potato. Dyspnea is present in about half of the cases,[119] and extension of air into retroperitoneal or peritoneal areas may give rise to abdominal discomfort,[41] although this is less frequent.

Physical examination reveals palpable crepitation in the neck and supraclavicular area in perhaps 50% of cases.[162] Percussion of the border of cardiac dullness may be difficult because of interposed air, and cyanosis and neck vein distention have been observed.[41] The most characteristic physical finding in pneumomediastinum is *Hamman's sign*,[5,41] a crunching or clicking sound synchronous with the heartbeat, heard over the precordium, and increased in intensity during inspiration and in the left lateral decubitus position.[1,41,164] *Hamman's crunch* has been described as similar to the noise produced by rubbing two rubber balloons together.[41] Although considered by Hamman to be pathognomonic for mediastinal air, it can occasionally be heard in other circumstances, such as pneumothorax without radiographic evidence for pneumomediastinum.[1] A second characteristic auscultatory finding, described in cases of pneumopericardium, is the *bruit de moulin* ("mill-wheel murmur"),[168] described as a metallic splashing sound generated when the pericardium contains both air and fluid, and present in 57 of 159 cases of pneumopericardium in one series.[149]

Low-grade fever is frequently noted in patients with pneumomediastinum without associated infection or other illness.[41,169] Fever, along with mild to moderate leukocytosis,[1,41,170] likely results from reactive inflammation associated with air dissection in the mediastinum. Leukocyte counts of over 10,000/μL in 16 patients and over 20,000/μL in 5 patients were noted in one series of 23 patients, but returned to normal without treatment within 1 to 2 days.[41]

Electrocardiographic changes occur in some cases of pneumomediastinum without evidence of other cardiac abnormalities.[41] These may consist of diffusely low voltage, nonspecific axis shifts, ST-T wave changes, and ST segment elevation in the lateral precordial leads.[41] These changes are also observed in association with pneumothorax and may be in part related to physical displacement of mediastinal structures.

Radiographic Features

Pneumomediastinum is most often detected by standard chest radiography. In cases without obvious subcutaneous emphysema, the finding of pneumomediastinum is often the first manifestation of extra-alveolar air. The diagnosis is usually made by demonstrating a thin line of radiolucency, best seen along the left heart border (Fig. 72.4).[1] Other

common signs are highlighting of the aortic knob, which is surrounded by increased radiolucency, and the "continuous diaphragm" sign,[171] an unbroken radiolucent line extending from one hemidiaphragm to the other beneath the heart (Fig. 72.5). Mediastinal air may be easier to see on films taken in lateral projection, which may demonstrate retrosternal air or vertical lucent streaks outlining the aorta, pulmonary artery, or other mediastinal structures.[1] A variety of more subtle findings may be present.[172] Distinguishing between mediastinal emphysema and a small pneumothorax may be difficult. A film taken in the lateral decubitus position may show air rising to the most elevated portion of the thorax if it is free to move in the pleural space, whereas mediastinal air moves little with changes in position.[172] A radiograph obtained at end-expiration may accentuate both forms of extra-alveolar air.[172]

Detection of pneumomediastinum (and pneumothorax) may be rendered more difficult by confusion with visual phenomena known as Mach bands.[173] These are apparent areas of radiolucency (negative Mach bands) or radiodensity (positive Mach bands) that are perceived at the borders of object density contours.[174] Mach bands are optical illusions caused by lateral inhibition in the retina and are not actually present on the radiographic film; they disappear if the adjacent object contour is covered so that the viewer no longer perceives a sharp contrast. In some instances, detection of mediastinal air may be made easier because of the Mach effect that can accentuate differences in radiodensity between the mediastinal border and adjacent air.[175]

The sensitivity of standard chest radiographs for detecting pneumomediastinum is largely unknown because most published case series include only patients with positive find-

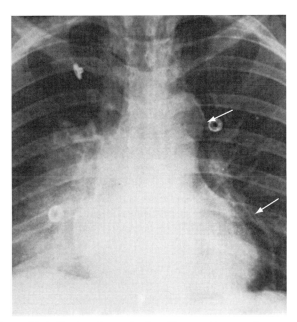

Figure 72.4 Chest radiograph of a 47-year-old man who developed mediastinal emphysema while hospitalized for treatment of right lower lobe pneumonia showing displacement of the mediastinal pleura by air (*arrows*).

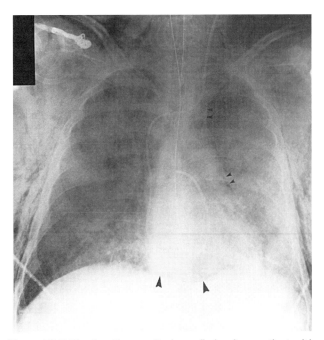

Figure 72.5 The "continuous diaphragm" sign in a patient with pneumomediastinum that developed during mechanical ventilation for severe acute respiratory distress syndrome. An unbroken radiolucent line (*arrowheads*) is visible from one hemidiaphragm to the other, rendering the inferior heart border clearly visible. Air is also present in the mediastinum (*small arrowheads*) and the soft tissues of both shoulders and neck.

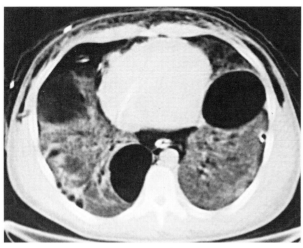

Figure 72.6 Computed tomogram of the chest showing pneumomediastinum associated with extensive subcutaneous emphysema in a patient undergoing mechanical ventilation for severe acute respiratory distress syndrome. Mediastinal air is seen in both the middle and posterior mediastinal compartments.

ings.[119] As many as half of all radiographically detectable instances of pneumomediastinum may be undetected if only a posteroanterior exposure is made.[100] Careful examination of routine posteroanterior and lateral films may yield adequate information in most cases, but CT is probably more accurate than plain radiography for detecting aberrant air in all its forms and should be considered when important management decisions rest on a given distinction.[172]

Air in the lung interstitium (pulmonary interstitial emphysema) is rarely identified in adults.[176] Characteristic findings are subpleural blebs or cysts[176] and perivascular air. The latter is especially difficult to identify with certainty, particularly on bedside films taken in critically ill patients. In a series of 12 cases of pulmonary interstitial emphysema confirmed at autopsy, only 3 had convincing evidence on films taken prior to death.[176] Chest CT is much more sensitive for detecting interstitial emphysema,[177,178] identifying this finding in 39% of high-risk blunt trauma patients in one series.[178]

Subcutaneous emphysema is readily detected as streaks or pockets of air outlining the visceral planes in the neck or within subcutaneous tissues. It often outlines the tissue compartments of the chest wall, clearly identifying the pectoral muscles (Fig. 72.6; see also Fig. 72.5). Both subcutaneous emphysema and pneumomediastinum are common findings in patients on mechanical ventilators,[179,180] being present in 7% of cases in one early series.[179] These signs of alveolar rupture during positive-pressure ventilation are important clinical danger signals, as half or more will go on to pneumothorax.[44,180]

APPROACH TO MANAGEMENT

Natural History of Pneumomediastinum

In most cases of pneumomediastinum, the air tends to spread throughout the mediastinum and to vent out of the thorax into the subcutaneous tissue planes.[1,181] Subcutaneous emphysema can become massive and prove distressing to both patient and physician, but it is seldom dangerous in itself. Subcutaneous air collections will resolve spontaneously without surgical decompression once the primary air leak has sealed. Depending upon the circumstances, other forms of aberrant air may require intervention, virtually always for the relief of mechanical effects that compromise organ function.

Management of Spontaneous Pneumomediastinum

Most cases of spontaneous pneumomediastinum can be linked to one or more predisposing factors such as bronchospasm, infection, or foreign body, and treatment or removal of these is followed by gradual resolution of the aberrant air. Pain and other symptoms should be alleviated, and supplemental oxygen may hasten reabsorption, but specific therapy for pneumomediastinum is rarely needed. Treatment in a hyperbaric chamber has been carried out in cases related to submarine training,[182] but pneumomediastinum is not one of the currently accepted indications for hyperbaric therapy.[35,36] Most cases resolve with conservative management alone.

Although pneumomediastinum rarely becomes physiologically significant, in rare instances it can produce life-threatening cardiovascular collapse.[3,7,183] An early, well-documented incident was described by Laennec more than 150 years ago, as related by Munsell.[41] The great French clinician was called to see a small boy who had been run over by a dung cart. Laennec describes how his 4-year-old patient was placed in a tent; with a candle for light, Laennec inserted sharp sticks into the boy's neck, supraclavicular areas, and anterior portion of the chest. A subsequent, rapid, large outpouring of air extinguished the candle, and the boy, previously in extremis, recovered. Modern medicine can add little more to this emergency decompression regimen except for the substitution of needles for sticks.

Other equally convincing if less eloquently described instances of life-threatening pneumomediastinum and its immediate surgical relief have been recorded.[183] Although surgical treatment of massive or symptomatic subcutaneous emphysema has been advocated, a careful examination of the literature reveals very few instances in which this has actually been carried out. Techniques that have been used include aspiration of the mediastinum with needles,[6,184,185] cervical mediastinotomy,[102,108,181,183,186,187] infraclavicular incisions,[188] placement of subcutaneous drains,[189,190] and even splitting or completely excising the sternum.[191] Tracheotomy has also been advocated by some, both to permit mediastinal air to vent outward and to prevent glottis closure and positive intrathoracic pressure generation during coughing.[191,192] Others feel that tracheotomy is contraindicated.[108] Most experienced clinicians reserve invasive therapy for cases of increasing airway impingement or cardiovascular compromise. In these instances, which must be exceedingly rare, small infraclavicular incisions or placement of drains into the mediastinal fascia seem to be the most prudent initial approach.

Management of Pneumomediastinum during Positive-Pressure Ventilation

The appearance of mediastinal or subcutaneous air in a patient receiving positive-pressure ventilation is always a cause for concern. Although not usually physiologically significant without associated pneumothorax, pneumomediastinum may progress rapidly to the latter.[44] Pneumothorax in a mechanically ventilated patient requires prompt tube thoracostomy, and some clinicians favor "prophylactic" chest tube placement when extra-alveolar air first appears. This practice is probably not justified because of the hazards and complications of chest tube drainage in such patients, but a tube thoracostomy tray should be kept at the bedside for prompt use if the clinical picture of tension pneumothorax should develop.

Discontinuation of positive-pressure ventilation, if feasible, would seem advantageous for patients with ventilator-related extra-alveolar air in any form. Short of this, several adjustments should theoretically diminish the tendency of air to enter the mediastinum, although no clinical studies support these recommendations. Delivered tidal volumes and distending pressures should be reduced if possible. Positive end-expiratory pressure should be reduced or discontinued, and mean intrathoracic pressure should be minimized through adjustment of inspiratory flow and timing. Patient-triggered pressure-limited ventilation (e.g., inspiratory pressure support) or low-rate intermittent mandatory ventilation would probably be preferable to mandatory volume-limited ventilation if clinically feasible.[129] Cough suppression, increased sedation, or use of airway pressure-release ventilation to minimize positive pressure due to coughing can be considered.

Occult positive end-expiratory pressure, or "auto-PEEP," can augment air leakage, and steps to minimize this complication should be taken when it occurs[139]; these would include reducing minute ventilation and minimizing inspiratory time by increasing inspiratory flow rate and using ventilatory circuitry of low compressible volume. Finally, bronchospasm and other potentially reversible contributors to air trapping during mechanical ventilation should be treated vigorously.

Tracheobronchial disruption causing extra-alveolar air requires prompt diagnosis and surgical repair.[25,27,193] This condition should be considered in a patient with blunt thoracic trauma in the presence of extensive soft-tissue emphysema, airway bleeding, or nonresolving pneumothorax,[1,29,193,194] especially if on chest radiography the collapsed lung tissue appears to have fallen away from the hilum.[195] When these findings are present, emergent bronchoscopy should be carried out to establish the diagnosis.[1,29,193,196]

Pneumopericardium in the neonate during mechanical ventilation is considered a medical emergency that should be treated with prompt drainage.[197] Most authors recommend drainage with a pericardial tube.[197,198] Although much less common, tension pneumopericardium in the adult may be adequately relieved by pericardiocentesis, followed by close observation.[149]

SEQUELAE

Pneumomediastinum subsides uneventfully in the vast majority of instances once the precipitating event or process has resolved. Recurrence of spontaneous mediastinal emphysema is unusual, although it has been described in both children[112] and adults.[92,119,162]

Air in the pleural space can induce a localized eosinophilic inflammation called reactive eosinophilic pleuritis, and a presumed mediastinal analogue to this phenomenon has also been described.[199] Diagnostic pneumomediastinum was performed 1 week prior to thymectomy in 63 patients with myasthenia gravis and, at surgery, the thymuses of 29 of them contained "histioeosinophilic" granulomas.[199] This interesting observation suggests that pneumomediastinum in other clinical settings could be followed by similar changes, although whether they persist or could have clinical significance is unknown.

MEDIASTINITIS

The term *mediastinitis* encompasses a number of loosely related processes that involve inflammation of mediastinal structures and its sequelae. Most forms of mediastinitis are infectious in etiology, and variations in their clinical presentation depend largely on the chronicity of the underlying process rather than the specific microbial cause. Thus, it seems logical to classify this family of disorders according to "acute" and "chronic" forms rather than into more specific etiologic categories. For largely anatomic reasons, acute mediastinitis is a distinct, usually catastrophic, disorder. The chronic forms of mediastinal inflammation comprise a spectrum of disease, defined usually by radiographic or histologic features, that ranges from active granulomatous inflammation to "burned-out" mediastinal fibrosis. In the remainder of this chapter, the various forms of acute mediastinitis are discussed, then chronic mediastinitis is dealt with as a continuum from chronic inflammation to fibrosis rather than as separate disease processes.

ACUTE MEDIASTINITIS

Acute mediastinitis was once a rare and dramatic condition of a fulminating and usually fatal course seen after rupture of the esophagus from forceful vomiting or in conjunction with penetrating trauma. However, beginning in the 1950s and 1960s, with the proliferation of endoscopic procedures, and since the 1970s with the rise of cardiac surgery via median sternotomy, acute mediastinitis has become somewhat more common and more varied in its clinical presentation. Because of this clinical variation, which may include relatively indolent infections, the term *suppurative mediastinitis* has been proposed as more accurate than "acute." In either case, a distinction is drawn between these disorders and chronic "granulomatous" and "fibrosing" mediastinitis.

Typical Clinical Features of Acute Mediastinitis

The classic clinical description of acute mediastinitis is as follows. Onset is sudden and dramatic, with chills, high fever, and prostration. Patients are restless and irritable, with a sense of impending doom. Tachycardia, tachypnea, and signs of systemic toxicity are prominent. Most patients complain of severe substernal chest pain, worsened by breathing or coughing, and unrelieved by opiates. The pain may be referred into the neck and ear if the process involves the superior mediastinum, whereas posterior or inferior mediastinal involvement may cause radicular pain radiating around the chest and pain between the scapulae. Examination may reveal supraclavicular fullness and tenderness over the sternum or sternoclavicular joints, and crepitus and other signs of mediastinal and subcutaneous emphysema may be prominent. Hamman's sign (a crunching sound synchronous with cardiac systole, heard over the anterior thorax) is characteristic but not always present. Later, tracheal deviation, jugular venous distention, and other signs of compression of mediastinal structures may appear. These features are typical after spontaneous esophageal rupture as seen in Boerhaave's syndrome, but the presentation varies considerably in other settings.[200]

Clinical Classification of Acute Mediastinitis

Involvement of different mediastinal regions tends to have typical causes: infection in the superior mediastinum is most often the result of direct extension from neck infection; anterior mediastinal infection is typical after surgery or penetrating wounds to the anterior thorax; and posterior mediastinal abscesses are characteristic for tuberculous or pyogenic spinal infections.[201] However, because the clinical picture of acute mediastinitis is influenced most strongly by the route and circumstances of infection, classification according to these factors seems most reasonable. The following discussion characterizes the clinical picture and management of acute mediastinitis in different settings classified according to the mechanism of mediastinal entry (Table 72.3).

Mediastinitis Resulting from Visceral Perforation

Boerhaave's syndrome refers to esophageal rupture associated with forceful vomiting, classically after overeating or excessive drinking. It is the most familiar example of acute mediastinitis,[202,203] although no longer the most common. In addition to the clinical manifestations described previously, hematemesis may be present before the actual rupture, and tends to diminish or stop after rupture occurs.[204] Unilateral or bilateral hydropneumothorax is common and quickly progresses to empyema (Fig. 72.7). Spontaneous esophageal rupture can be difficult to diagnose, especially in the patient with altered sensorium who may delay seeking medical attention and who may not be able to relate a clear history. Adding to the clinician's confusion is the fact that lower esophageal rupture may be mistaken for an abdominal catastrophe.[204]

The mechanism of esophageal rupture, as elucidated by Rogers and associates,[194] involves hydrostatic forces that overcome the tensile strength of the normal esophageal wall. A momentary rise in intragastric pressure, as in vomiting, trauma, seizure, or other straining, accompanied by relaxation of the lower esophageal sphincter, permits gastric contents to enter and distend the lower esophagus. If the upper sphincter does not open so that regurgitation of esophageal contents can occur, hydrostatic pressure in the esophagus may rise to the point that its wall gives way at its weakest point. This is usually in the lower left posterolateral wall, where the muscle bundles in the longitudinal layer of the esophagus separate, allowing a bubble of mucosa to protrude through into the mediastinum and burst. This mechanism may be similar to that in pneumatic esophageal

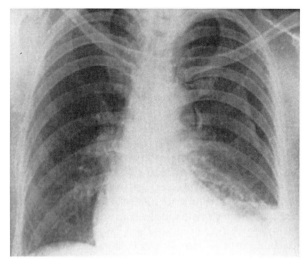

Figure 72.7 Chest roentgenogram of a 64-year-old woman taken 16 hours after traumatic perforation of the esophagus. The classic features of pneumomediastinum and left-sided hydropneumothorax are evident.

Table 72.3 Acute Mediastinitis: Etiologies and Clinical Settings

Perforation of a thoracic viscus
  Esophagus
    "Spontaneous": forceful vomiting (Boerhaave's syndrome); pneumatic trauma
    Direct penetrating trauma
    Impacted foreign body
    Instrumentation: esophagoscopy; sclerotherapy; esophageal obturator airway
    Erosion: carcinoma; necrotizing infection
  Trachea or main bronchi
    Direct penetrating trauma
    Instrumentation: bronchoscopy; intubation
    Foreign body
    Erosion of carcinoma

Direct extension of infection from elsewhere
  Intrathoracic: lung; pleura; pericardium; lymph node; paraspinous abscess
  Extrathoracic
    From above: retropharyngeal space; odontogenic
    From below: pancreatitis

Mediastinitis following sternotomy for cardiothoracic surgery

"Primary" mediastinal infection: inhalational anthrax

rupture, a bizarre occurrence related to biting and puncturing an automobile tire inner tube, or closing the mouth around the leaking valve of an automobile tire.[205]

In the present era, the most common cause of acute mediastinitis is esophageal perforation during diagnostic or therapeutic endoscopic procedures.[201,206] A review of 30 years of experience with esophageal perforation before the widespread use of flexible fiberoptic endoscopy instruments found 77% of cases to be due to endoscopy.[207] Actual passage of the instrument may be less traumatic today, but perforation of the diseased esophagus is still a recognized complication.

In a review by Wesdorp and associates,[208] of 54 esophageal perforations related to endoscopy or instrumentation, 35 instances were in patients with inoperable esophageal malignancy and 19 were in patients with benign disease. Most occurred after stent placement or dilation procedures. The diagnosis was made within 2 hours in 94% of these patients. Fourteen of the 19 patients with benign disease were treated conservatively, and 5 with surgery; there were no deaths among these patients, probably reflecting the influences of an empty gut lumen, prompt recognition of the complication, and immediate treatment.

Endoscopic injection sclerotherapy is associated with mediastinal complications in a significant number of patients receiving this therapy, particularly with repeated treatments.[206,209] Frank perforation, associated with necrosis of the esophageal wall and usually occurring 2 to 14 days after the procedure, has been reported in approximately 6% of patients.[209,210] More common is pleural effusion, presumably associated with subclinical chemical mediastinitis without actual perforation, which has been noted in up to 14% of patients.[206,211] In most instances this complication is benign and self-limited, responding to conservative therapy in this chronically ill patient population.[211]

Other reported causes of traumatic esophageal perforation include the esophageal obturator airway, and swallowed foreign bodies, particularly if the swallowed object is chosen with self-inflicted injury as the intent. One series describes six prison inmates who swallowed hypodermic needles fashioned in the shape of "stars" to win temporary reprieves from incarceration.[212] Unfortunately, all required surgical management and one patient experienced a lengthy and complicated hospital course. Accidental or intentional ingestion of caustic solutions such as paraquat or lye also can lead to esophageal perforation.[62]

The diagnosis of esophageal perforation depends on an appropriate degree of clinical suspicion. On the chest roentgenogram, the hallmarks are diffuse mediastinal widening, and the presence of air in the mediastinum and elsewhere in soft tissues. Mediastinal air-fluid levels may be seen, and pneumothorax or hydropneumothorax may be present. CT can delineate these abnormalities more clearly. Passage of ingested contrast material into the periesophageal space or pleura may be observed (see Fig. 68.9).[213,214] The diagnosis is usually established by contrast studies, endoscopic examination, or at operation, although percutaneous mediastinal aspiration, using a subxiphoid approach, is advocated by some as a means of earlier diagnosis.[215]

Successful management of frank, uncontained esophageal perforation requires early surgical repair, drainage of the mediastinum and often the pleural space, and administration of appropriate antibiotics.[216–218] Percutaneous catheter aspiration of mediastinal abscesses, under CT guidance, has been used when the infection is localized and the clinical setting is less urgent.[219]

Complications of acute mediastinitis after esophageal rupture may include localized abscess formation, extensive pleural empyema, and persistent esophagocutaneous fistulas. A prolonged stormy course is usual, and reexploration may be necessary to assure adequate drainage.

Mortality reported due to acute mediastinitis after esophageal rupture has ranged from 10% to 20%[207,220] to as high as 40% to 50%[204,220]; variations are attributed to differences in patient selection and management approaches. Timing of surgical drainage has been of prime importance in determining the clinical outcome; in one series of 39 cases, mostly after esophagoscopy, survival was 70% when surgery was performed within 24 hours of injury, and 20% when done after 24 hours.[220] Modern series reporting the use of consistently aggressive surgical management cite 89% to 90% survival after spontaneous esophageal rupture.[221,222]

Other potential iatrogenic causes of mediastinitis include bronchoscopic perforation and migration of indwelling central venous catheters. Bronchoscopy is a much less frequently reported cause of mediastinitis than esophagoscopy. However, increasing use of laser and mechanical endobronchial procedures, often performed in the setting of malignancy with chronic airway colonization or postobstructive pneumonia, add to the likelihood of potential mediastinal complications. Intravascular catheters may be another source of acute mediastinitis when the catheter tip erodes through the vessel wall into the mediastinum. Instillation of hyperosmotic,[223] vesicant, or vasoactive substances via these catheters may induce a chemical, rather than an infectious, inflammation (Fig. 72.8).

Direct Extension of Infection from Other Sites

Direct extension of infection into the mediastinum from elsewhere has become rare in the antibiotic era.[224] Earlier, however, it was more frequent, and a series of 100 patients with suppurative mediastinitis reported in 1938 included 21 patients in whom it was secondary to oropharyngeal infection.[8] Infection originating in periodontal tissues, in the tonsillar region, or after pharyngeal perforation may extend via the prevertebral, visceral, or pretracheal spaces or in the carotid sheaths,[2,225] although the usual route is via the retropharyngeal space to the posterior mediastinum (Fig. 72.9).[11,226,227] Mediastinal infection occurring in this fashion, which has been given the name *descending necrotizing mediastinitis,* is perhaps the most clinically devastating form of the disorder.[11,226–228]

Odontogenic infection is consistently the most common source of descending necrotizing mediastinitis.[11,224,229] Most are mixed infections with both aerobic and anaerobic organisms on culture,[11,230] and purulent pleural and pericardial involvement is common.[11,224]

In addition to the clinical signs described previously for acute mediastinitis after esophageal perforation, patients with this form of the disease may have widening of the retropharyngeal space, with or without associated air-fluid levels, anterior displacement of the tracheal air column, and loss of the normal cervical spine lordosis on lateral films of the neck.[11] CT scans of the neck and chest are usually definitive (Fig. 72.10).[226,231]

Treatment of descending necrotizing mediastinitis requires aggressive surgical drainage, usually via a cervical approach.[11,224] Whether or not to explore the mediastinum via a thoracic approach depends on the imaging findings. Some authors have suggested that thoracic exploration be reserved for cases in which the infection extends below the level of the fourth vertebral body or the tracheal bifurcation.[11] Others have argued that any evidence of mediastinal involvement should prompt transthoracic exploration and

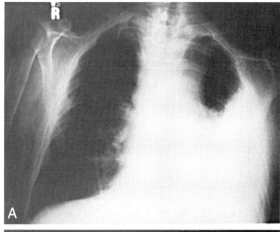

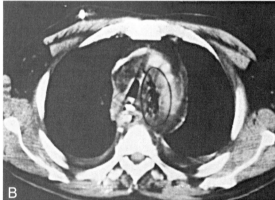

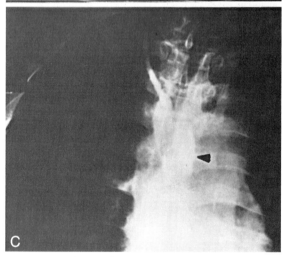

Figure 72.8 Imaging studies of a 74-year-old man with mediastinitis due to erosion of an indwelling central venous catheter tip into the mediastinum. **A,** The chest radiograph shows mediastinal widening, radiolucency in the left upper mediastinum, left pleural effusion, and medial deviation of the catheter tip. **B,** The chest computed tomogram shows a gas-containing mediastinal abscess between the trachea and contrast-enhanced great vessels (an indelible elliptical line was drawn around the area on the original film). **C,** Although blood could be aspirated from the catheter, contrast material injected through the catheter passed directly into the mediastinum (*arrowhead*).

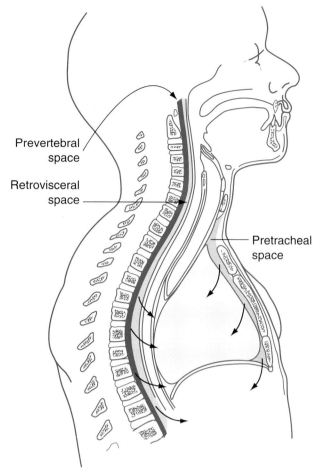

Figure 72.9 The three deep spaces of the neck and their communication with the mediastinum. (From Freeman RK, Vallières E, Verrier ED, et al: Descending necrotizing mediastinitis: An analysis of the effects of serial surgical debridement on patient mortality. J Thorac Cardiovasc Surg 119:260–267, 2000.)

drainage.[224,229,231] In fact, this more aggressive approach may be warranted. In a retrospective case series and extensive literature review, Corsten and coworkers[226] found that the mortality rate of patients treated with cervical drainage alone was 47% compared with 19% when thoracic mediastinal drainage was added. Routine serial postoperative cervicothoracic CT imaging and aggressive reexploration and drainage guided by these imaging findings appear to reduce the mortality of this condition even further.[227] Although thoracoscopic and other percutaneous drainage procedures have been described and may be appropriate in selected patients, thorough open drainage and irrigation remain the standard approach.

Direct extension of infection from elsewhere in the chest is a rare cause of acute mediastinitis, but can occur with eroding neoplasms. Extension from anterior chest wall and neck infections has been described in injection drug users,[224,232] and acute purulent mediastinitis has also been reported after closed-chest cardiopulmonary resuscitation,[233] although the pathogenesis in such a case is unclear. A less acute form, occurring as a complication of vertebral or costal tuberculous infection,[11] also is rare today in developed countries.

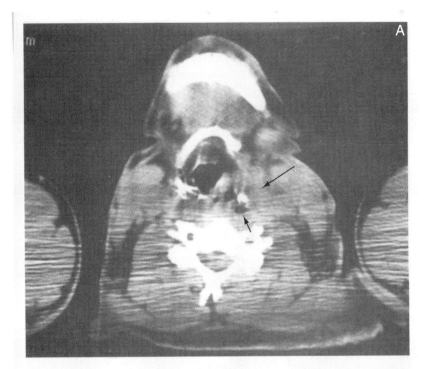

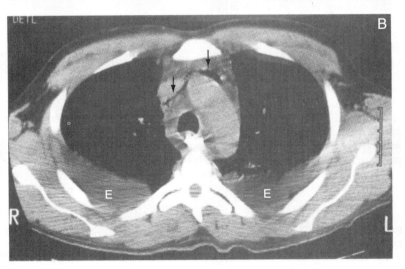

Figure 72.10 Computed tomography scans of a 35-year-old man with descending necrotizing mediastinitis. **A,** At the level of the hyoid bone in the neck, there is gas in the retropharyngeal soft tissues (*short arrow*) and inflammatory changes in the parapharyngeal space (*long arrow*). **B,** At the level of the aortic arch in the chest, gas is seen outlining the great vessels (*arrows*). There are inflammatory changes in the paratracheal tissues and bilateral pleural effusions (empyema, E). (From Corsten MJ, Shamji FM, Odell PF, et al: Optimal treatment of descending necrotizing mediastinitis. Thorax 52:702–708, 1997.)

Penetrating chest injuries may result in acute mediastinitis, especially if the wound causes visceral perforation or is grossly contaminated, and if there has been a delay in reaching medical attention. In such instances the diagnosis of acute mediastinitis may not be apparent if the patient has other serious injuries.

Pancreatitis has been reported to extend into the mediastinum, presenting as mediastinal widening with the clinical picture of acute mediastinitis.[234] Spread in such a circumstance would presumably be via the aortic and esophageal hiatuses and could also explain the reported occurrence of pancreatic pseudocysts in the mediastinum.[201] Both gastric and esophageal ulcers have been reported as causes of mediastinitis, sometimes eroding directly into the pericardium.

Mediastinitis after Cardiac Surgery

Whereas some other forms of acute mediastinitis have been decreasing in frequency, bacterial mediastinitis after median sternotomy for coronary artery bypass, valve replacement, or correction of congenital heart disease has become an increasingly important entity,[216,235–237] and several cases of acute bacterial mediastinitis have occurred after heart and heart-lung transplantation.[238–240] Along with the occurrence of mediastinitis as a complication of endoscopy, this form illustrates the predominately iatrogenic character of acute mediastinitis in the present era.

The incidence of mediastinal infection after cardiac surgery has been variously reported at 0.4% to 5.0%, but recent series report rates of less than 1%.[241] Post-sternotomy mediastinitis has become a substantial clinical problem not because of a high case incidence, but because cardiac surgery via median sternotomy has become such a widely used procedure.

Risk factors that appear to predispose to development of mediastinitis after cardiac surgery have been reported in a myriad of case series, as comprehensively reviewed by Ulicny and Hiratzka[242] and El Oakley and Wright.[241] Preoperative risk factors include advanced age and male gender, diabetes mellitus, obesity, the need for immunosuppressive therapy, smoking, obstructive lung disease, a history of previous sternotomy or mediastinal irradiation, and poorer preoperative cardiac dysfunction and New York Heart Association functional class. Perioperative risk factors include shaving rather than clipping for hair removal, the use of bilateral internal mammary artery grafts, a longer duration of the surgical procedure and of perfusion time, greater use of cautery or bone wax, a low cardiac output state in the early postoperative period, and greater amounts of postoperative bleeding. The incidence of postoperative mediastinitis appears to be increased further if reoperation is required to control bleeding, when multiple valve replacement accompanies coronary artery bypass, or if the patient requires more than 48 hours of mechanical ventilation postoperatively. Preoperative use of β-adrenergic drugs was associated with mediastinitis in one study, most likely because of its association with obstructive lung diseases where increased stress can be placed on sternal wounds in the presence of airflow obstruction and cough.[243]

The pathogenesis of mediastinitis following sternotomy is debated, although most cases appear to result from direct contamination of the mediastinum at the time of operation. Three possible routes of infection are postulated. Some authorities suspect that primary sternal instability leads to failure of the skin closure and subsequent penetration of bacteria through the wound.[244] Others suspect that a focus of sternal osteomyelitis is the initial site of infection, leading to secondary sternal instability and deeper penetration of the infection.[245,246] A third postulated mechanism is bacterial seeding of an undrained mediastinal fluid collection.[241] In the acute stages, the mediastinal structures are involved with pliable fibrinous exudates, and osteomyelitis, if present, is confined to the wound margins. Subacute infections are characterized by increasingly dense adhesions entrapping the visceral organs, sinus tract formation, and more extensive sternal bone involvement.[241]

The epidemiology of cases within an institution suggests that sound general infection control and careful asepsis in the operating room remain the most effective means of prevention.[235,241] Although definitive proof of their efficacy is still lacking, prophylactic antibiotics are widely used in the perioperative management of cardiac surgery patients.[241] The prophylactic intranasal application of mupirocin ointment has been shown to reduce by 50% the rate of *Staphylococcus aureus* nosocomial infections in carriers who undergo major surgery[247] and there is a suggestion that its general use in cardiac surgery may significantly decrease the rates of post-sternotomy wound infections and osteomyelitis,[248] but confirmatory randomized controlled trials are awaited.

Mediastinitis may occur as early as 3 days or as long as 6 months after surgery,[236] although most cases occur within 2 weeks.[235] Because the clinical features, microbiology, management, and prognosis of post-sternotomy mediastinitis all vary with the "incubation time" between surgery and presentation with mediastinitis, classification of mediastinitis cases on this basis has been advocated to permit more uniform comparisons between reports.[241]

The bacteriology of postoperative mediastinitis varies and parallels that of early prosthetic valve endocarditis. *Staphylococcus epidermidis* and *S. aureus* have been the most frequent organisms in several series,[235,236,245,246,249] and as many as 40% of cases have mixed infections.[235] Anaerobes and gram-negative bacilli are rare,[235,250] and *Candida* species[235,251] and atypical mycobacteria (especially *Mycobacterium chelonae* and *Mycobacterium fortuitum*)[216] are infrequently reported. Infection with the last two groups tends to be more indolent and is more likely to involve the sternum or costochondral tissues. Presentation within the first postoperative week is more often associated with gram-negative infection and also more likely to be accompanied by bacteremia, whereas presentation after the second week increases the likelihood that *Staphylococcus* is the infecting agent.[236]

Acute mediastinitis occurring after cardiac surgery tends to be less devastating than that seen in the settings described previously, perhaps because it remains relatively localized longer and tends to be recognized earlier. Only 4 of the 21 patients in the series of Bor and coworkers[236] developed the classic signs of mediastinitis. Typically, the clinical course consists of fever and systemic signs, followed by bacteremia and local signs of wound infection.[236] Drainage from the sternotomy incision and other localizing findings are present in the great majority of patients.[235,236,245]

The diagnosis is usually made at the time of reexploration of the sternotomy wound and rests on a heightened clinical suspicion in the appropriate setting. Distinguishing between superficial and deep wound infections may be difficult, especially if the clinical signs of infection are modest. A variety of diagnostic tests have been used in reported series, including gallium scanning, CT, and ultrasonography. CT is particularly helpful in identifying and discerning soft-tissue swelling, fluid collections, and sternal erosion or dehiscence.[252] However, these first two findings are common in the early postoperative period, and their significance is much more clear when they persist or develop after 14 days.[252,253] Some authors use subxiphoid[215] or transsternotomy[246] needle aspiration in suspected cases, although, as with the other tests mentioned, the potential exists to delay diagnosis in a condition that can progress rapidly. Patients with fever, positive blood cultures, and wound abnormalities in the post-sternotomy period should probably be explored.

As in other settings, therapy for post-sternotomy mediastinitis consists of early surgical exploration, débridement and drainage, irrigation, and prolonged administration of systemic antibiotics.[235,241,254,255] There has been disagreement in the past as to whether the incision should be left open or closed around drains for irrigation. Most authors now advocate early closure, even though reexploration may be necessary. This approach avoids the respiratory and cardiovascular compromise from the open chest wound, and patients managed with their wounds left open stay substantially longer in the hospital.[235,241,255,256] A variety of surgical

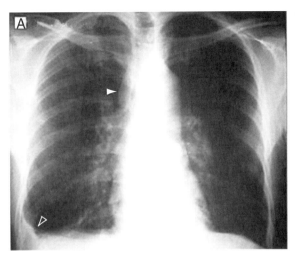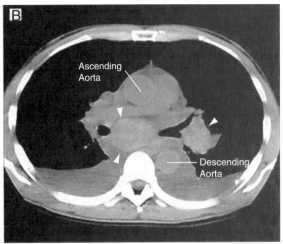

Figure 72.11 Imaging studies from a 56-year-old man with inhalational anthrax. **A,** The chest radiograph shows a widened mediastinum (*white arrowhead*), perihilar infiltrates, and right pleural effusion (*dark arrowhead*). **B,** The non-contrast chest computed tomogram confirms mediastinal edema, mediastinal and hilar adenopathy, and bilateral pleural effusions. Note large hyperdense lymph nodes (*arrowheads*) in subcarinal space and left hilum. (From Mayer TA, Bersoff-Matcha S, Murphy C, et al: Clinical presentation of inhalational anthrax following bioterrorism exposure. JAMA 286:2549–2553, 2001.)

options exist for the débridement, establishment of irrigation, and buttressing and closure of sternal wounds.[255]

Reported mortality from mediastinitis after cardiac surgery varies considerably,[235,257] partly because of varying incidence of coexisting disease, different treatment regimens, use of prophylactic antibiotics, and when the patients were seen—some series extend back to the 1950s. Currently, most patients should survive, with mortality rates of 20% to 40%.[236,241] Hospitalization of survivors is usually prolonged by this complication.[258]

Spread of infection to contiguous prosthetic material or valves is a devastating complication that usually portends a fatal outcome.[236] Infection may occasionally spread to adjacent pericardium, lung, or chest wall. Significant sternal osteomyelitis and costochondritis, once seen in as many as one third of cases,[259] have become less common complications with earlier aggressive management.

The possibility of progressive mediastinal fibrosis and other disabling long-term sequelae in survivors was addressed in a series of patients evaluated at a mean of 50 months after surgery.[260] Five of the 11 patients had pleural thickening on the chest roentgenogram, but there were no significant clinical or physiologic sequelae.

"Primary Mediastinitis": Inhalational Anthrax

Anthrax, caused by infection with *Bacillus anthracis,* is primarily a disease of cattle, sheep, and goats and is most prevalent in the Middle East, although it is now recognized as an important disease of bioterrorism (see later). Most cases of anthrax are the cutaneous form of the disease, which is contracted by direct inoculation, usually from handling hides or hair from infected animals. Traditionally the less common form, inhalational anthrax, or *woolsorter's disease,* is contracted by inhaling *B. anthracis* spores from animal sources. Inhalation of anthrax spores into the distal air spaces is followed by ingestion by alveolar macrophages and transport to the mediastinal lymph nodes. A hemorrhagic

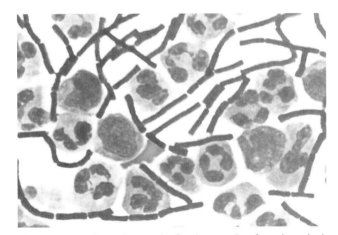

Figure 72.12 Photomicrograph of a Gram stain of cerebrospinal fluid from a 63-year-old man with inhalational anthrax. The field is packed with leukocytes and boxcar-shaped gram-positive rods typical of *Bacillus anthracis*. (From Jernigan JA, Stephens DS, Ashford DA, et al: Bioterrorism-related inhalational anthrax: The first 10 cases reported in the United States. Emerg Infect Dis 7:933–944, 2001.)

mediastinitis rapidly evolves, followed by bacteremia, overwhelming sepsis, and usually death.[261–263]

Clinically, patients typically experience a biphasic illness with an initial insidious flulike illness lasting 2 to 4 days and characterized by fever, malaise, myalgias, and nonproductive cough. This is followed by a fulminant phase of acute mediastinitis, with respiratory distress, chest pain, cyanosis, and prostration.[262–265] The chest radiograph and CT scan typically show mediastinal widening and pleural effusions (Fig. 72.11).[266] The diagnosis is established by demonstration of gram-positive, boxcar-shaped bacilli in tissue or body fluid specimens or in the blood buffy coat (Fig. 72.12). A direct fluorescent antibody test, polymerase chain reaction, and serologic tests are available for confirmation.

Sporadic anthrax is fortunately rare, with one report documenting only two confirmed cases in this country in 25 years.[267] However, anthrax has remained a very real concern because of its devastating clinical effects and its ominous potential as an agent of biologic warfare and bioterrorism.[262,263,268,269] In the fall of 2001, this potential was realized when *B. anthracis* spores were intentionally dispersed through the U.S. postal system. An outbreak followed, with many cases of cutaneous anthrax and at least 10 cases of inhalational anthrax identified by astute local physicians, local public health officers, and an investigative team headed by the Centers for Disease Control and Prevention.[264,265] All patients became ill within 4 to 6 days of presumed exposure, presented within 2 to 5 days of symptom onset, and had abnormal chest radiographs. Most had evidence of bacteremia.[264,265]

Inhalational anthrax has historically been a devastating disease even with appropriate treatment: 12 of 13 well-documented sporadic cases in the United States had fatal outcomes.[261] However, in the bioterrorism outbreak, prompt diagnosis and initiation of antibiotic therapy plus aggressive drainage of mediastinal and pleural collections resulted in survival of 6 of the 10 patients.[264] High-dose intravenous penicillin has traditionally been the treatment of choice,[261] although penicillin-resistant strains have been reported.[270] Cephalosporin resistance is typical, and most patients in the bioterrorism outbreak were treated with multiple agents, including a fluoroquinolone.[264]

GRANULOMATOUS MEDIASTINITIS AND MEDIASTINAL FIBROSIS

Mediastinal disease that is chronic in nature may be considered in the broad categories of granulomatous mediastinitis and mediastinal fibrosis. These conditions are not so much separate disease processes, however, as they are two ends of a spectrum of chronic inflammation and fibrosis. This pathophysiologic continuum is not evident in most of the literature, which mainly reports groups of cases at one or another end of the spectrum. Among the larger series, some cases have been based on pathologic material, selected according to the presence of granulomas[271] or fibrosis[272,273]; others have reported only cases of proved etiology,[274,275] with mediastinal widening or mass on the chest radiograph,[276] or who presented with superior vena cava (SVC) obstruction.[277–279] Attempts to garner large numbers of cases from the literature[280,281] have necessarily been hampered by this lack of uniformity in selection. Further, because nearly all published series are retrospective, the clinical descriptions of chronic mediastinitis are incomplete and biased toward especially prominent or commonly recorded features.

Disorders falling along the continuum from active granulomatous mediastinitis to pure mediastinal fibrosis have been designated by the following terms, among others: mediastinal adenitis, mediastinal granulomatosis, sclerosing mediastinitis, mediastinal collagenosis, and fibrosing mediastinitis. Most recently, the term *idiopathic fibroinflammatory lesion of the mediastinum* has been proposed in order to reflect the usually unknown cause and the heterogeneous histopathologic features of these disorders.[282] Conceptually, all these processes may be thought of as variations of a common process that differ in the nature of the host response and in the point in their natural history at which they are examined (Fig. 72.13).

Pathophysiology and Etiologies

The genesis of granulomatous mediastinitis and mediastinal fibrosis, and of their varying manifestations, is most easily understood using histoplasmosis or tuberculosis as an example. Infection begins as a primary focus in the lung, which drains to mediastinal lymph nodes, and leads to mediastinal adenitis. This is accompanied by some degree of periadenitis and, eventually, a cluster of caseating lymph nodes, which breaks down into an irregular mass and which heals by fibrous encapsulation. In some cases, dense calcification may occur within this mass. In most instances, the medi-

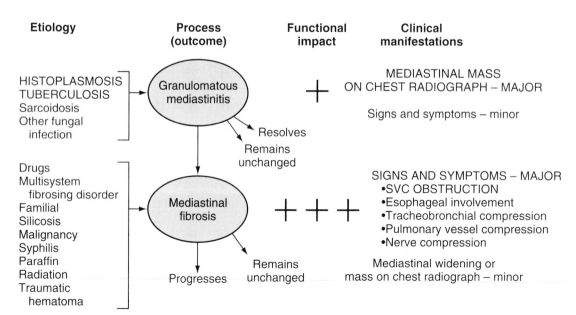

Figure 72.13 Pathophysiologic relationships between granulomatous mediastinitis and mediastinal fibrosis. Predominant etiologies and clinical manifestations for each process are shown in capital letters. SVC, superior vena cava.

astinal mass is 4 to 6 cm in diameter, although it may be as large as 10 cm.[216] The thickness of the fibrotic capsule is the main determinant of the clinical picture: In most cases it is 2 to 5 mm in thickness and has little clinical impact, but in some cases the capsule reaches 6 to 9 mm and invades or engulfs adjacent tissues.[216,274] This benign localized process produces physiologically important effects because of the compact nature of the mediastinum and the importance and vulnerability of the structures it contains (Fig. 72.14).

Symptoms and physiologic effects of this process are determined by which lymph nodes are involved.[283] Most commonly, they are in the right perihilar region, perhaps accounting in part for the high prevalence of SVC obstruction observed in this condition. Later, in instances in which the process progresses to generalized fibrosis, the entire upper portion of the mediastinum may be involved.

Why inflammation and fibrosis progress in some patients and not in others has been the subject of considerable debate. Goodwin and associates[274] postulated that prolonged gradual seepage of some soluble antigen or other substance from the involved lymph nodes, at least in patients with histoplasmosis, causes fibrosis. This theory is supported by the finding of stronger histoplasmin skin test reactivity in patients with mediastinal fibrosis than in others with chronic histoplasmosis,[274] and the observation that coccidioidomycosis, which also produces an exuberant granulomatous mediastinal lymphadenitis, is virtually never associated with mediastinal fibrosis.[283] Other authors reject this theory in favor of an abnormality in collagen organization, which, when provoked by various stimuli, leads to mediastinal fibrosis.[272] Whether either of these concepts or some other mechanism is responsible, it is evident that the nature and vigor of the host's response is vitally important.

The development of both mediastinal and retroperitoneal fibrosis in the same patients,[273,284,285] and of idiopathic isolated mediastinal fibrosis in others,[286] has led some investigators to postulate an autoimmune mechanism.[287] The finding of mediastinal and retroperitoneal fibrosis, along with other forms of fibrosis in members of the same family, has led to the term *familial multifocal fibrosclerosis.*[288] Fibrosing processes elsewhere in the body that could be related, in at least some cases, to mediastinal fibrosis, include retroperitoneal fibrosis, Riedel's thyroiditis, sclerosing cholangitis, orbital pseudotumor, sclerosing cervicitis, ligneous perityphlitis of the cecum, and keloids.[272,288] Others have pointed out dissimilarities between mediastinal and retroperitoneal fibrosis and disagree with this unitary concept.[274]

Most cases of granulomatous mediastinitis are caused by histoplasmosis (especially in North America) or tuberculosis.[216,271,272,274,280,284] However, as the disease progresses from active caseous inflammation to largely acellular fibrosis, it becomes more and more difficult to establish the cause with certainty. In 180 cases reviewed by Schowengerdt and colleagues,[280] a definite diagnosis could be established in 33 of 103 examples of "granulomatous mediastinitis," but in only 3 of 77 categorized as "mediastinal fibrosis." Histoplasmosis and tuberculosis together accounted for 83% of the confirmed diagnoses.[280]

Other reported infectious causes of mediastinal fibrosis include actinomycosis,[289] syphilis,[289,290] nematode infection with *Wuchereria bancrofti,*[291] and "pyogenic" causes,[290] although it appears that the last of these (acute mediastinitis) seldom results in chronic sequelae.[260]

Granulomatous infection is the usual cause of mediastinal fibrosis as diagrammed in Figure 72.13. However, the same histologic and clinical picture can be the ultimate

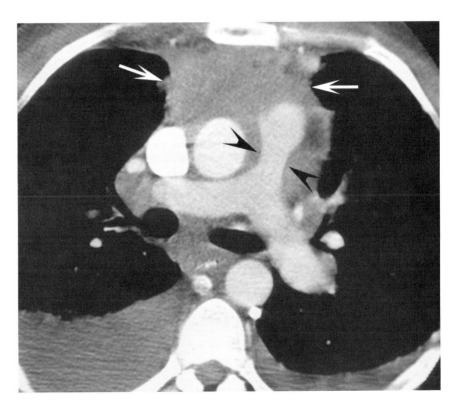

Figure 72.14 Axial computed tomographic image through the main pulmonary artery shows abnormal soft tissue infiltrating the mediastinum (*arrows*), compressing the main pulmonary artery (*arrowheads*). The presence of mass effect on vessels and bronchi is characteristic of mediastinal fibrosis. (Courtesy of Michael B. Gotway, MD, Department of Radiology, University of California, San Francisco.)

result of other disease processes. Fibrosis associated with use of methysergide (Sansert), a drug used in the control of severe vascular headache, is perhaps the best known of these. Graham and associates[292] reported 27 patients treated with methysergide in whom retroperitoneal fibrosis developed; three of these patients also had pulmonary and mediastinal involvement. Perhaps because the offending agent can be completely removed from the body, the symptoms and signs of methysergide-induced fibrosis regress or remit completely in most patients when the drug is stopped.[292]

In addition to accounting for 11% of the cases of granulomatous mediastinitis of known cause in the review by Schowengerdt and colleagues,[280] sarcoidosis has been reported as a cause of SVC obstruction owing to mediastinal fibrosis.[293] Other reported noninfectious causes of mediastinal fibrosis include silicosis,[294] paraffin (as a late complication of plombage for tuberculosis), and traumatic mediastinal hematoma.[216,273] Nodular sclerosing Hodgkin's disease also may masquerade as mediastinal fibrosis,[295] emphasizing the importance of careful review of adequately representative biopsy samples when evaluating a mediastinal mass. Although there are reports of SVC and bronchial obstruction thought to be caused by mediastinal irradiation,[296,297] radiotherapy as a cause of mediastinal fibrosis must be distinctly unusual in view of its widespread use and the rare documentation of this complication.

Clinical Manifestations

On the continuum from active granulomatous mediastinitis to "burned-out" mediastinal fibrosis, the former tends to be asymptomatic and to be discovered incidentally by chest radiography and the latter tends to cause clinical manifestations.[298,299] In the largest collection of cases to date, 74% of the patients with granulomatous mediastinitis were asymptomatic, whereas all but 17% with fibrosis presented with symptoms or signs.[280] In 52 patients with mediastinal fibrosis and evidence of histoplasmosis reviewed by Loyd and coworkers,[281] initial symptoms included cough in 41%, dyspnea in 32%, hemoptysis in 31%, and chest pain in 23%. Clinical manifestations develop either because the fibrotic process invades or compresses mediastinal structures, or because a calcified mass erodes into adjacent structures. These manifestations can be grouped into those related to involvement of the airways, the SVC, the esophagus, the major pulmonary vessels, and mediastinal nerves. In some cases, findings are present in more than one of these categories.

Airway Involvement. Clinical manifestations due to involvement of the trachea or major bronchi are common in patients with granulomatous mediastinitis or mediastinal fibrosis. Airway complications, including dyspnea, cough, and hemoptysis, were the most common clinical manifestations in several series[281,282,298,300,301] and constituted the most common indication for surgical intervention.[298] Any of the main airways may be compromised, but involvement of the right middle lobe is reported as most frequent and is often accompanied by features of the *right middle lobe syndrome*.[216] Bronchoesophageal fistula is rare but has been observed,[280] and may be heralded by simultaneous hemop-

tysis and hematemesis.[302] Symptomatic mediastinal adenitis can present, especially in children, with a characteristic "brassy" cough resulting from tracheal or bronchial compression; this syndrome is self-limited and lasts for several weeks to a few months.[216]

Superior Vena Cava Obstruction. SVC obstruction has been the most frequent complication of granulomatous mediastinitis and mediastinal fibrosis in some series.[280,303] Although most patients with SVC obstruction have malignancy, depending on the case selection criteria used, benign causes comprise about 3% to 6% of large published series,[277,304] of which most are due to granulomatous mediastinitis or mediastinal fibrosis.[284] SVC obstruction can occur at any stage of granulomatous or fibrotic involvement[216,280]; this complication was present in 77% of symptomatic patients designated as having granulomatous mediastinitis and in 52% of those with symptoms in the setting of mediastinal fibrosis in Schowengerdt's series.[280]

The typical presentation is *superior vena cava syndrome* (also described in Chapter 44).[305] Because obstruction develops gradually, collateral channels tend to divert much of the venous flow (Fig. 72.15). Therefore, symptoms may be less prominent than might be expected and may improve with time.[271,283,284] However, even chronic SVC obstruction can cause serious complications such as hemorrhage from esophageal varices, recurrent upper extremity thrombophlebitis, and postphlebitic syndrome.[283,306] Less commonly, the inferior vena cava can be involved,[280] as can the azygos vein.[216] Thoracic duct obstruction is rare[280] but can produce chylothorax[283] and its associated clinical manifestations.

Esophageal Involvement. Esophageal involvement can consist of extrinsic compression, traction diverticula, disturbances of esophageal motility, or bleeding.[216] Symptoms of dysphagia, chest pain, and eructation are experienced by perhaps one third of patients who have any complaints from their disease.[271,280]

Pulmonary Vascular Involvement. Mediastinal fibrosis can involve major vessels on either side of the heart.[272,274,280] When this occurs, the prognosis is not as benign as in the other clinical presentations discussed.[283] Progressive obstruction of one or both main pulmonary arteries can result in pulmonary hypertension, cor pulmonale, and refractory right-sided heart failure (Fig. 72.16).[283,307] Patients with pulmonary hypertension from fibrosing mediastinitis may have clinical and radiographic features in common with chronic thrombotic obstruction of major pulmonary arteries.[308] Stenosis of proximal pulmonary veins can cause a clinical picture similar to severe valvular mitral stenosis, with pulmonary venous hypertension and recurrent episodes of hemoptysis.[283] Pulmonary venous hypertension can be unilateral when the veins from only one lung are involved, and thus may result in unilateral pulmonary fibrosis.[216]

Mediastinal Nerve Involvement. Additional manifestations may result from the involvement of mediastinal nerves. Entrapment or compression of the recurrent laryngeal nerve can produce hoarseness.[272,280] Other possible manifestations include diaphragmatic paralysis owing to involvement of

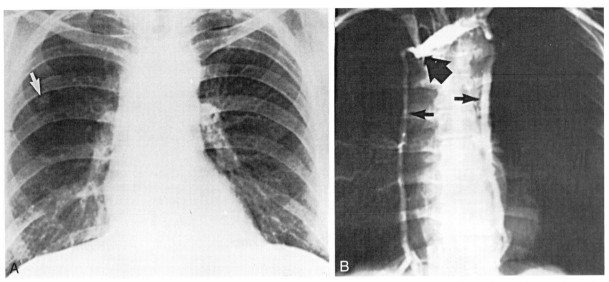

Figure 72.15 Mediastinal fibrosis (in this instance from histoplasmosis) with superior vena cava obstruction and extensive collateral circulation. **A,** The standard frontal radiograph shows smooth widening of the superior mediastinum with a peripheral granuloma in the right lung (*arrow*). **B,** Another film taken just after rapid injection of contrast material into an antecubital vein shows complete obstruction of the superior vena cava (*thick arrow*), with filling of the internal mammary veins bilaterally (*thin arrows*). (From Fraser RG, Paré JAP, Paré PD, et al: Diagnosis of Diseases of the Chest [3rd ed, Vol II]. Philadelphia: WB Saunders, 1989, p 955.)

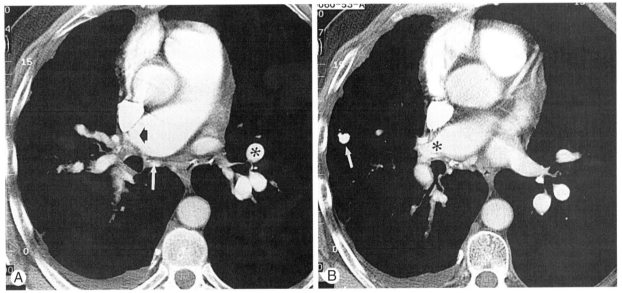

Figure 72.16 Computed tomography scan of a 45-year-old man with pulmonary hypertension caused by fibrosing mediastinitis due to histoplasmosis. **A,** At the level of the main pulmonary artery, findings include calcification within the middle mediastinum (*white arrow*), pleural thickening and calcification, smooth tapering stenosis of the right pulmonary artery (*black arrow*), and post-stenotic dilation of the left lower lobe pulmonary artery branches (*asterisk*). Stenosis of the left pulmonary artery was also present but not clearly demonstrated on a single image. **B,** At a lower level, a calcified pulmonary granuloma (*arrow*) and stenosis of the superior pulmonary veins (*asterisk*) are evident.

one or both phrenic nerves, Horner's syndrome from impingement on autonomic ganglions or nerves, and persistent tachycardia from damage to the vagus nerve.

Diagnosis and Management

In most instances, surgical exploration is necessary to distinguish between benign and malignant causes for SVC syndrome, localized mediastinal mass, or other manifestation that brings the patient with chronic mediastinitis to the physician's attention. In occasional cases, radiographs from previous years documenting an unchanged appearance, or dense calcification within the mass, will permit a confident diagnosis without operation.

Chest radiographs are abnormal in most patients. Granulomatous mediastinitis more often presents a localized mass, usually in the right paratracheal area, and the later fibrotic state more frequently produces generalized widening of the superior portion of the mediastinum, but these characteristics vary.[271,272,284,299] Mass lesions tend to be smooth and lobulated[284] and contrast studies in cases of SVC obstruction typically show the affected area to be smooth and tapered,[272] in contrast to the more ragged appearances usually seen with cancer. In some cases, the mediastinum is normal in appearance on standard chest films, and venography or CT is necessary to demonstrate the anatomic basis of a clinically evident obstruction.[284]

The role of specific medical therapy for granulomatous mediastinitis or mediastinal fibrosis is unclear.[298] Some evidence suggests that selected cases with active inflammation associated with histoplasmosis may benefit from antifungal therapy,[303,309,310] but specific indications, if any, for antifungal therapy remain unknown. A similarly conservative approach should be taken to tuberculosis-related mediastinal complications, unless sputum or tissue samples are positive for mycobacteria, or convincing clinical evidence of active tuberculosis is present.

The clinical manifestations of this disease appear to be the result of host factors as much as the infection itself. Accordingly, therapy directed at the host inflammatory response has also been attempted. Anecdotal reports of treatment of mediastinal and retroperitoneal fibrosis with corticosteroids have reached opposite conclusions.[311,312] It appears that diffuse forms of fibrosis may be more likely to respond.[301] As in the case of antimicrobial therapy, the appropriate role for anti-inflammatory therapy for granulomatous mediastinitis and mediastinal fibrosis is presently unknown.[313]

At the time of exploration for diagnosis, some surgeons advise removal of as much of the inflammatory or fibrous mass as possible, in order to reduce its bulk and perhaps diminish its later impact on adjacent tissues.[271,313] Despite the difficulties presented by fibrotic and granulomatous encasement, bronchoplastic procedures may be quite successful in these patients.[298] Surgery to bypass an obstructed vena cava is technically difficult and not always effective,[271] although this may still be considered if bleeding esophageal varices or recurrent upper extremity thrombophlebitis occurs.[283] Endovascular caval stent placement is another option.[314] Obstruction of major pulmonary vessels is a poor prognostic sign. Therapeutic options are limited, but angiographic dilation and stent placement may be successful in selected cases (Fig. 72.17).[315]

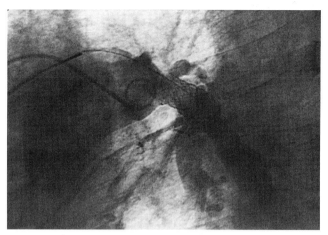

Figure 72.17 Digital subtraction angiogram (same patient as in Fig. 72.16) of the left pulmonary artery immediately following insertion of an expandable wire mesh stent that eliminated the pressure gradient between the main pulmonary artery and left lobar pulmonary arteries. The stent and guidewire lie across the area of previous stenosis, and a pigtail catheter is in the prestenotic pulmonary artery.

the underlying disease process, although, rarely, direct intervention is indicated to decompress air in the mediastinum or pericardium.

Acute mediastinitis is usually a sudden and severe disease that is now most commonly caused by perforation of the esophagus during endoscopic procedures. "Spontaneous" rupture of the esophagus during vomiting and descending infections originating in the neck remain important causes of acute mediastinitis, and infectious complications after surgical procedures that incorporate sternotomy incisions are being encountered with increasing frequency. All forms of acute mediastinitis are life-threatening and require prompt diagnosis, surgical drainage, and antimicrobial treatment.

Chronic mediastinitis is less common than the acute variety and generally is related to granulomatous involvement of the mediastinum and its fibrotic sequelae. Complications include bronchial obstruction, SVC syndrome, esophageal disorders, and pulmonary vessel obstruction. Management is aimed at relief of these mechanical complications. The role of anti-inflammatory and antimicrobial therapy is presently unclear.

SUMMARY

Pneumomediastinum, the presence of air or other gas in the mediastinum, is not a common clinical disorder, even though it may occur in a wide variety of different circumstances. The gas that causes pneumomediastinum usually originates from the lungs, but may arise from the upper respiratory tract or the gastrointestinal tract (especially the esophagus). Less often, pneumomediastinum follows penetrating injuries or complicates infection by gas-forming bacteria. Substernal chest pain signals the onset of pneumomediastinum, and the diagnosis is usually established by detecting the presence of aberrant air radiographically. Treatment depends primarily on successful management of

ACKNOWLEDGMENTS

The authors wish to acknowledge the contributions of David J. Pierson, MD, who wrote this chapter for the first and second editions, and coauthored this chapter with DRP for the third edition.

REFERENCES

1. Maunder RJ, Pierson DJ, Hudson LD: Subcutaneous and mediastinal emphysema: Pathophysiology, diagnosis, and management. Arch Intern Med 144:1447–1453, 1984.
2. Moncada R, Warpeha R, Pickleman J, et al: Mediastinitis from odontogenic and deep cervical infection: Anatomic pathways of propagation. Chest 73:497–500, 1978.

3. Gordon CA: Respiratory emphysema in labor: With two new cases and a review of 130 cases in the literature. Am J Obstet Gynecol 14:633–646, 1927.

4. Faust RC: Subcutaneous emphysema during labor. Northwest Med 39:24–26, 1940.

5. Hamman L: Spontaneous mediastinal emphysema. Bull Johns Hopkins Hosp 64:1–21, 1939.

6. Hamman L: Mediastinal emphysema. J Am Med Assoc 128:1–6, 1945.

7. Macklin MT, Macklin CC: Malignant interstitial emphysema of the lungs and mediastinum as an important occult complication in many respiratory diseases and other conditions: An interpretation of the clinical literature in the light of laboratory experiment. Medicine 23:281–352, 1944.

8. Pearse HE Jr: Mediastinitis following cervical suppuration. Ann Surg 108:588–604, 1938.

9. Thawley SE: Air in the neck. Laryngoscope 9:1445–1453, 1974.

10. Schweitzer V: Osteolytic sinusitis and pneumomediastinum: Deceptive otolaryngologic complications of cocaine abuse. Laryngoscope 96:206–210, 1986.

11. Estrera AS, Landay MJ, Grisham JM, et al: Descending necrotizing mediastinitis. Surg Gynecol Obstet 157:545–552, 1983.

12. Shackelford D, Casani JA: Diffuse subcutaneous emphysema, pneumomediastinum, and pneumothorax after dental extraction. Ann Emerg Med 22:248–250, 1993.

13. Sandler CM, Libshitz HI, Marks G: Pneumoperitoneum, pneumomediastinum, and pneumopericardium following dental extraction. Radiology 115:539–540, 1975.

14. Turnbull A: A remarkable coincidence in dental surgery. Br Med J 1:1131, 1900.

15. Flood TR: Mediastinal emphysema complicating a zygomatic fracture: A case report and review of the literature. Br J Oral Maxillofac Surg 26:141–148, 1988.

16. Henry CH, Hills EC: Traumatic emphysema of the head, neck, and mediastinum associated with maxillofacial trauma: Case report and review. J Oral Maxillofac Surg 47:876–882, 1989.

17. Gudlaugsson O, Geirsson AJ, Benediktsdottir K: Pneumoparotitis: A new diagnostic technique and a case report. Ann Otol Rhinol Laryngol 107:356–358, 1998.

18. Padovan IF, Dawson CA, Henschel EO, Lehman RH: Pathogenesis of mediastinal emphysema and pneumothorax following tracheotomy. Chest 66:553–556, 1974.

19. Stauffer JL, Olson DE, Petty TL: Complications and consequences of endotracheal intubation and tracheotomy: A prospective study of 150 critically ill patients. Am J Med 70:65–76, 1981.

20. Stauffer JL, Silvestri RC: Complications of endotracheal intubation, tracheostomy, and artificial airways. Respir Care 27:417–434, 1982.

21. Marty Ané CH, Picard E, Jonquet O, Mary H: Membranous tracheal rupture after endotracheal intubation. Ann Thorac Surg 60:1367–1371, 1995.

22. Frascone RJ, Cicero JJ, Sturm JT: Pneumopericardium occurring during a high-speed motorcycle ride. J Trauma 23:163–164, 1983.

23. Buntain WL, Lynn HB: Traumatic pneumatic disruption of the esophagus. J Thorac Cardiovasc Surg 63:553–560, 1972.

24. Curci MR, Dibbins AW, Grimes CK: Compressed air injury to the esophagus: Case report. J Trauma 29:1713–1715, 1989.

25. Wiot JF: Tracheobronchial trauma. Semin Roentgenol 18:15–22, 1983.

26. Chitre VV, Prinsley PR, Hashmi SM: Pneumopericardium: An unusual manifestation of blunt tracheal trauma. J Laryngol Otol 111:387–388, 1997.

27. Bertelson S, Howitz P: Injuries of the trachea and bronchi. Thorax 27:188–194, 1972.

28. Sridhar KS, Hussein AM, Patten JE: Spontaneous pneumomediastinum in esophageal carcinoma. Am J Clin Oncol 13:527–531, 1990.

28a. Libeer C, Verbeken E, De Wever W, et al: Mediastinal emphysema and small cell lung cancer (SCLC): a case-report. Lung Cancer 47:139–142, 2005.

29. Robertson HT, Lakshminarayan S, Hudson LD: Lung injury following a 50-metre fall into water. Thorax 33:175–180, 1978.

30. Alveolar rupture (editorial). Lancet 2:137–138, 1978.

31. Joannides M, Tsoulsos GD: The etiology of interstitial and mediastinal emphysema. Arch Surg 21:333–339, 1930.

32. Schaefer KE, McNulty WP Jr, Carey C, Liebow AA: Mechanisms in development of interstitial emphysema and air embolism on decompression from depth. J Appl Physiol 13:15–29, 1958.

33. Pierson DJ: Alveolar rupture during mechanical ventilation: Role of PEEP, peak airway pressure, and distending volume. Respir Care 33:472–483, 1988.

34. Peirce ECI: Cerebral gas embolism (arterial) with special reference to iatrogenic accidents. Hyperb Oxygen Rev 1:161–184, 1980.

35. Melamed Y, Shupak A, Bitterman H: Medical problems associated with underwater diving. N Engl J Med 326:30–35, 1992.

36. Grim PS, Gottlieb LJ, Boddie A, et al: Hyperbaric oxygen therapy. JAMA 263:2216–2220, 1990.

37. Gammon RB, Shin MS, Groves RH Jr, et al: Clinical risk factors for pulmonary barotrauma: A multivariate analysis. Am J Respir Crit Care Med 152:1235–1240, 1995.

38. Crosfield JL, Boger D, Clatworthy HW: Hemodynamic and manometric observations in experimental air-block syndrome. J Pediatr Surg 6:339–344, 1971.

39. Madansky DL, Lawson EE, Chernick V, Taeusch HW Jr: Pneumothorax and other forms of pulmonary air leak in newborns. Am Rev Respir Dis 120:729–737, 1979.

40. Taylor J, Dibbins A, Sobel DB: Neonatal pneumomediastinum: Indications for, and complications of, treatment. Crit Care Med 21:296–298, 1993.

41. Munsell WP: Pneumomediastinum. JAMA 202:689–693, 1967.

42. Hamman L: Spontaneous interstitial emphysema of the lungs. Trans Assoc Am Physicians 52:311–319, 1937.

43. Macklin CC: Transport of air along sheaths of blood vessels from alveoli to mediastinum: Clinical implications. Arch Intern Med 64:913–926, 1939.

44. Gammon RB, Shin MS, Buchalter SE: Pulmonary barotrauma in mechanical ventilation: Patterns and risk factors. Chest 102:568–572, 1992.

45. Newton NI, Adams AP: Excessive airway pressure during anesthesia: Hazards, effects, and prevention. Anaesthesia 33:689–699, 1978.

46. Powner DJ, Snyder JV, Morris CW, Grenvik A: Retroperitoneal air dissection associated with mechanical ventilation. Chest 69:739–742, 1976.

47. Turner W, Fry WJ: Pneumoperitoneum complicating mechanical ventilation therapy. Arch Surg 112:723–726, 1977.

48. Gutkin Z, Iellin A, Meged S, et al: Spontaneous pneumoperitoneum without peritonitis. Int Surg 77:219–223, 1992.

49. Mularski RA, Sippel JM, Osborne ML: Pneumoperitoneum: A review of nonsurgical causes. Crit Care Med 28:2638–2644, 2000.

50. Hillman KM: Pneumoperitoneum—a review. Crit Care Med 10:476–481, 1982.

51. Rose DM, Jarczyk PA: Spontaneous pneumoperitoneum after scuba diving. JAMA 239:223, 1978.

52. Strauss RH: Diving medicine. Am Rev Respir Dis 119:1001–1023, 1979.

53. Ingvar DH, Adolfson J, Lindemark C: Cerebral air embolism during training of submarine personnel in free escape: An encephalographic study. Aerosp Med 44:628–635, 1973.

54. Zwillich CW, Pierson DJ, Creagh CE, et al: Complications of assisted ventilation: A prospective study of 354 consecutive episodes. Am J Med 57:161–174, 1974.

55. Marini JJ, Culver BH: Systemic gas embolism complicating mechanical ventilation of adult respiratory distress syndrome. Ann Intern Med 110:699–707, 1989.

56. Foster PP, Boriek AM, Butler BD, et al: Patent foramen ovale and paradoxical systemic embolism: A bibliographic review. Aviat Space Environ Med 74:B1–B64, 2003.

57. Spencer MP, Oyama Y: Pulmonary capacity for dissipation of venous gas emboli. Aerosp Med 42:822–827, 1971.

58. Gottdiener JS, Papademetriou V, Notargiacomo A, et al: Incidence and cardiac effects of systemic venous air embolism: Echocardiographic evidence of arterial embolization via noncardiac shunt. Arch Intern Med 148:795–800, 1988.

59. Black M, Calvin J, Chan KL, Walley VM: Paradoxic air embolism in the absence of an intracardiac defect. Chest 99:754–755, 1991.

60. Jaworski A, Fischer R, Lippmann M: Boerhaave's syndrome. Arch Intern Med 148:223–224, 1988.

61. Minocha A, Richards R: Pneumomediastinum as a complication of upper gastrointestinal endoscopy. J Emerg Med 9:325–329, 1991.

62. Chen KW, Wu MH, Huang JJ, Yu CY: Bilateral spontaneous pneumothoraces, pneumopericardium, pneumomediastinum, and subcutaneous emphysema: A rare presentation of paraquat intoxication. Ann Emerg Med 23:1132–1134, 1994.

63. Mirzayan R, Cepkinian V, Asensio JA: Subcutaneous emphysema, pneumomediastinum, pneumothorax, pneumopericardium, and pneumoperitoneum from rectal barotrauma. J Trauma 41:1073–1075, 1996.

64. Bakker J, van Kersen F, Bellaar-Spruyt J: Pneumopericardium and pneumomediastinum after polypectomy. Endoscopy 23:46–47, 1991.

65. Lee HC, Dewan N, Crosby L: Subcutaneous emphysema, pneumomediastinum, and potentially life-threatening tension pneumothorax: Pulmonary complications from arthroscopic shoulder decompression. Chest 101:1265–1267, 1992.

66. Lau KY: Pneumomediastinum caused by subcutaneous emphysema in the shoulder: A rare complication of arthroscopy. Chest 103:1606–1607, 1993.

67. Liebig S, Siemoneit KD: Mediastinalemphysem und Begleitpneumothorax: Entstehung und Behandlung. Prax Pneumol 28:1133–1138, 1974.

68. Sauerbruch F: Die Bedeutung des Mediastinalemphysems in der Pathologie des Spannungspneumothorax. Beitr Klin Chir 60:450–478, 1908.

69. Banyai A: Direct and indirect pneumoperitoneum incidental to artificial pneumothorax. Am J Med Sci 186:513–518, 1933.

70. Simmonds F: Air embolism and pneumomediastinum in artificial pneumoperitoneum. Lancet 1:530–533, 1946.

71. Chui PT, Gin T, Chung SC: Subcutaneous emphysema, pneumomediastinum and pneumothorax complicating laparoscopic vagotomy. Report of two cases. Anaesthesia 48:978–981, 1993.

72. Cass LJ, Dow EC, Brooks JR: Pneumoperitoneum following pelvic examination. Am J Gastroenterol 45:209–211, 1966.

73. Walker MA: Pneumoperitoneum following a douche. J Kans Med Soc 43:55, 1942.

74. Lozman H, Newman AJ: Spontaneous pneumoperitoneum occurring during postpartum exercises in the knee-chest position. Am J Obstet Gynecol 72:903–905, 1956.

75. Ashai S, Lipton D, Colon A, Niebyl JR: Pneumoperitoneum secondary to cunnilingus. N Engl J Med 295:117, 1976.

76. Varon J, Laufer MD, Sternback GL: Recurrent pneumoperitoneum following vaginal insufflation. Am J Emerg Med 9:447–448, 1991.

77. Aronson ME, Nelson PK: Fatal air embolism in pregnancy resulting from an unusual sex act. Obstet Gynecol 30:127–130, 1967.

78. Fyke FEI, Kazmier FJ, Harms RW: Venous air embolism: Life-threatening complication of orogenital sex during pregnancy. Am J Med 78:333–336, 1985.

79. Collins KA, Davis GJ, Lantz PE: An unusual case of maternal-fetal death due to vaginal insufflation of cocaine. Am J Forensic Med Pathol 15:335–339, 1994.

80. Miller WE, Spiekerman RE, Hepper NG: Pneumomediastinum resulting from performing Valsalva maneuvers during marijuana smoking. Chest 62:233–234, 1972.

81. Hazouard E, Koninck JC, Attucci S, et al: Pneumorachis and pneumomediastinum caused by repeated Muller's maneuvers: Complications of marijuana smoking. Ann Emerg Med 38:694–697, 2001.

82. Shesser R, Davis C, Edelstein S: Pneumomediastinum and pneumothorax after inhaling alkaloidal cocaine. Ann Emerg Med 10:213–215, 1981.

83. Seaman ME: Barotrauma related to inhalational drug abuse. J Emerg Med 8:141–149, 1990.

84. Sullivan TP, Pierson DJ: Pneumomediastinum after freebase cocaine use. AJR Am J Roentgenol 168:84, 1997.

85. Adrouny A, Magnusson P: Pneumopericardium from cocaine inhalation. N Engl J Med 313:48–49, 1985.

86. LiPuma JP, Wellman J, Stern H: Nitrous oxide abuse: A new cause for pneumomediastinum. Radiology 145:602, 1982.

87. Varkey B, Kory RC: Mediastinal and subcutaneous emphysema following pulmonary function tests. Am Rev Respir Dis 108:1393–1396, 1973.

88. Jabourian Z, McKenna EL, Feldman M: Spontaneous pneumomediastinum and subcutaneous emphysema. J Otolaryngol 17:50–53, 1988.

89. McMahon DJ: Spontaneous pneumomediastinum. Am J Surg 131:550–551, 1976.

90. Lorge HJ: The etiology of idiopathic pneumothorax. Am J Med Sci 199:635–641, 1940.

91. Mumford AD, Ashkan K, Elborn S: Clinically significant pulmonary barotrauma after inflation of party balloons. BMJ 313:1619, 1996.

92. Vosk A, Houston CS: Mediastinal emphysema in mountain climbers: Report of two cases and review. Heart Lung 6:799–805, 1977.

93. Seidl JJ, Brotzman GL: Pneumomediastinum and subcutaneous emphysema following vaginal delivery: Case report and review of the literature. J Fam Pract 39:178–180, 1994.

94. Mitchell JE, Seim HC, Colon E, et al: Medical complications and medical management of bulimia. Ann Intern Med 107:71–77, 1987.

95. Schwartz M, Rossoff L: Pneumomediastinum and bilateral pneumothoraces in a patient with hyperemesis gravidarum. Chest 106:1904–1906, 1994.

96. Beigelman PM, Miller LV, Martin HE: Mediastinal and subcutaneous emphysema in diabetic coma with vomiting. JAMA 208:2315–2318, 1969.

97. Girard DE, Carlson V, Natelson EA, Fred HL: Pneumomediastinum in diabetic ketoacidosis: Comments on mechanism, incidence, and management. Chest 60:455–459, 1971.

98. Watson JP, Barnett AH: Pneumomediastinum in diabetic ketoacidosis. Diabet Med 6:173–174, 1989.

99. Kistner RW: Acute mediastinal emphysema complicating eclampsia. N Engl J Med 244:873–875, 1951.

100. Millard CE: Pneumomediastinum. Chest 56:297–300, 1969.

101. Morgan EJ, Henderson DA: Pneumomediastinum as a complication of athletic competition. Thorax 36:155–156, 1981.

102. Kobak AJ, Abrams RH: Pregnancy complicated by massive subcutaneous emphysema of mediastinal origin (Hamman's syndrome). Am J Obstet Gynecol 57:789–792, 1949.

103. Gay BB: Radiologic evaluation of the nontraumatized child with respiratory distress. Radiol Clin North Am 16:91–112, 1978.

104. Popovich J, Babcock R: Intraluminal blood cast causing obstructive emphysema and recurrent pneumothorax. Crit Care Med 10:482–483, 1982.

105. Janetos GP, Ochsner SF: Bilateral pneumothorax in metastatic osteogenic sarcoma. Am Rev Respir Dis 88:73–76, 1963.

106. Cooley JC, Gillespie JB: Mediastinal emphysema: Pathogenesis and management. Chest 49:104–108, 1966.

107. Kirsch MM, Orvald TO: Mediastinal and subcutaneous emphysema complicating acute bronchial asthma. Chest 57:580–581, 1970.

108. Steffey WR, Cohn AM: Spontaneous subcutaneous emphysema of the head, neck, and mediastinum. Arch Otolaryngol 100:32–35, 1974.

109. Karetsky MS: Asthma mortality: An analysis of one year's experience, review of the literature, and assessment of current modes of therapy. Medicine 54:471–484, 1975.

110. Dattwyler RJ, Goldman MA, Bloch KJ: Pneumomediastinum as a complication of asthma in teenage and young adult patients. J Allergy Clin Immunol 63:412–416, 1979.

111. Zegel HG, Miller WT: Subcutaneous emphysema in a young man. JAMA 241:1273–1274, 1979.

112. Eggleston PA, Ward BH, Pierson WE, Bierman CW: Radiographic abnormalities in acute asthma in children. Pediatrics 54:442–449, 1974.

113. Wohl MEB, Chernick V: Bronchiolitis. Am Rev Respir Dis 118:759–781, 1978.

114. Gapany-Gapanavicius M, Yellin A, Almog S, Tirosh M: Pneumomediastinum: A complication of chlorine exposure from mixing household cleaning agents. JAMA 248:349–350, 1982.

115. Ozonoff MB: Pneumomediastinum associated with asthma and pneumonia in children. Am J Roentgenol Radium Ther Nucl Med 95:112–117, 1965.

116. Greenberg LF, Benham Kahn S: *Klebsiella* pneumonia with pneumothorax, pneumomediastinum, and pneumoperitoneum. Dis Chest 43:546–550, 1963.

117. Odita JC, Akamaguna AI: Mediastinal and subcutaneous emphysema associated with childhood measles. Eur J Pediatr 142:33–36, 1984.

118. Sharma S, Rajani M, Aggarwal S, et al: Spontaneous pneumothorax and pneumothorax in metastatic lung disease. Indian J Chest Dis Allied Sci 30:125–132, 1988.

118a. Das M, Chandra U, Natchu M, et al: Pneumomediastinum and subcutaneous emphysema in acute miliary tuberculosis. Indian J Pediatr 71:553–554, 2004.

119. Gerazounis M, Athanassiadi K, Kalantzi N, Moustardas M: Spontaneous pneumomediastinum: A rare benign entity. J Thorac Cardiovasc Surg 126:774–776, 2003.

119a. Weissberg D, Weissberg D: Spontaneous mediastinal emphysema. Eur J Cardiothorac Surg 26:885–888, 2004.

120. Elliott DH, Harrison JAB, Barnard EEP: Clinical and radiological features of 88 cases of decompression barotrauma. *In* Shilling CW, Beckett MW (eds): Underwater Physiology VI. Bethesda, Md: Federation of American Societies for Experimental Biology, 1978, pp 1011–1013.

121. Boettger ML: Scuba diving emergencies: Pulmonary overpressure accidents and decompression sickness. Ann Emerg Med 12:563–567, 1983.

122. Unsworth IP: Pulmonary barotrauma in hyperbaric chamber. Anaesthesia 28:675–678, 1973.

123. Pierson DJ: Barotrauma and bronchopleural fistula. *In* Tobin M (ed): Principles and Practice of Mechanical Ventilation. New York: McGraw-Hill, 1994, pp 813–836.

124. Peterson GW, Baier H: Incidence of pulmonary barotrauma in a medical ICU. Crit Care Med 11:67–69, 1983.

125. Schnapp LM, Chin DP, Szaflarski N, Matthay MA: Frequency and importance of barotrauma in 100 patients with acute lung injury. Crit Care Med 23:272–278, 1995.

126. Weg JG, Anzueto A, Balk RA, et al: The relation of pneumothorax and other air leaks to mortality in the acute respiratory distress syndrome. N Engl J Med 338:341–346, 1998.

127. Boussarsar M, Thierry G, Jaber S, et al: Relationship between ventilatory settings and barotrauma in the acute respiratory distress syndrome. Intensive Care Med 28:406–413, 2002.

128. Kacmarek RM: Methods of providing mechanical ventilatory support. *In* Pierson D, Kacmarek R (eds): Foundations of Respiratory Care. New York: Churchill Livingstone, 1992, pp 953–972.

129. Kacmarek RM: Management of the patient-ventilator system. *In* Pierson D, Kacmarek R (eds): Foundations of Respiratory Care. New York: Churchill Livingstone, 1992, pp 973–998.

130. Hurst JM, Branson RD, Davis K Jr, et al: Comparison of conventional mechanical ventilation and high-frequency ventilation: A prospective, randomized trial in patients with respiratory failure. Ann Surg 211:486–491, 1990.

131. Derdak S, Mehta S, Stewart TE, et al: High-frequency oscillatory ventilation for acute respiratory distress syndrome in adults: A randomized, controlled trial. Am J Respir Crit Care Med 166:801–808, 2002.

132. Amato MB, Barbas CS, Medeiros DM, et al: Effect of a protective-ventilation strategy on mortality in the acute respiratory distress syndrome. N Engl J Med 338:347–354, 1998.

133. Stewart TE, Meade MO, Cook DJ, et al: Evaluation of a ventilation strategy to prevent barotrauma in patients at high risk for acute respiratory distress syndrome. Pressure- and Volume-Limited Ventilation Strategy Group. N Engl J Med 338:355–361, 1998.

134. Brower RG, Shanholtz CB, Fessler HE, et al: Prospective, randomized, controlled clinical trial comparing traditional versus reduced tidal volume ventilation in acute respiratory distress syndrome patients. Crit Care Med 27:1492–1498, 1999.

135. Ventilation with lower tidal volumes as compared with traditional tidal volumes for acute lung injury and the acute respiratory distress syndrome. The Acute Respiratory Distress Syndrome Network. N Engl J Med 342:1301–1308, 2000.

136. Jansson L, Johson B: A theoretical study on flow patterns of ventilators. Scand J Respir Dis 53:237–246, 1972.

137. Modell HI, Cheney FW: Effects of inspiratory flow pattern on gas exchange in normal and abnormal lungs. J Appl Physiol Respir Environ Exercise Physiol 46:1103–1107, 1979.

138. Pepe PE, Marini JJ: Occult positive and end-expiratory pressure in mechanically ventilated patients with airflow obstruction. Am Rev Respir Dis 114:166–169, 1982.

139. Benson MS, Pierson DJ: Auto-PEEP during mechanical ventilation of adults. Respir Care 33:557–565, 1988.

140. Williams TJ, Tuxen DV, Scheinkestel CD, et al: Risk factors for morbidity in mechanically ventilated patients with acute severe asthma. Am Rev Respir Dis 146:607–615, 1992.

141. de Durante G, del Turco M, Rustichini L, et al: ARDSNet lower tidal volume ventilatory strategy may generate intrinsic positive end-expiratory pressure in patients with acute respiratory distress syndrome. Am J Respir Crit Care Med 165:1271–1274, 2002.

142. Branson RD, Hurst JM, DeHaven CBJ: Mask CPAP: State of the art. Respir Care 30:846–857, 1985.

143. McClure JN, Skardasos GM, Brown JM: Cardiac arrest in the operating area. Am Surg 38:241–242, 1972.

144. Atcheson SG, Peterson GV, Fred HL: Ill effects of cardiac resuscitation: Report of two unusual cases. Chest 67:615–616, 1975.

145. Vestal BK, Vestal RE: Iatrogenic pneumothorax: An unusual cause. JAMA 235:1879–1880, 1976.

146. Chiles DG, Mannheimer WN, Miller FE: Pneumothorax, pneumomediastinum, and massive subcutaneous emphysema after general anesthetic: Report of a case. J Oral Surg 28:845–847, 1970.

147. Agia G, Hurst E: Pneumomediastinum following the Heimlich maneuver. Ann Emerg Med 8:473–475, 1979.

148. Hurd TE, Novak R, Gallagher TJ: Tension pneumopericardium: A complication of mechanical ventilation. Crit Care Med 12:200–201, 1984.

149. Cummings RG, Wesly RLR, Adams DH, Lowe JE: Pneumopericardium resulting in cardiac tamponade. Ann Thorac Surg 37:511–517, 1984.

150. McEachern RC, Patel RG: Pneumopericardium associated with face-mask continuous positive airway pressure. Chest 112:1441–1443, 1997.

151. Crosfield JL, Clatworthy HW, Frye TR: Surgical therapy in neonatal air-block syndrome. J Thorac Cardiovasc Surg 60:392–401, 1970.

152. Weiss LD, Van Meter KW: Cerebral air embolism in asthmatic scuba divers in a swimming pool. Chest 107:1653–1654, 1995.

153. Bowen F, Chandra R, Avery G: Pulmonary interstitial emphysema with gas embolization in hyaline membrane disease. Am J Dis Child 126:117–118, 1973.

154. Banagle R: Massive intracranial air embolism: A complication of mechanical ventilation. Am J Dis Child 134:799–800, 1980.

155. Graham JM, Beall ACJ, Mattox KL, Vaughan GD: Systemic air embolism following penetrating trauma to the lung. Chest 72:449–454, 1977.

156. Thomas AN, Stephens BG: Air embolism: A cause of morbidity and death after penetrating chest trauma. J Trauma 14:633–637, 1974.

157. Donato AT, Arciniegas E, Lam CR: Fatal air embolism during thoracotomy for gunshot injury to the lung. J Thorac Cardiovasc Surg 69:296–298, 1975.

158. Pao BS, Hayden SR: Cerebral gas embolism resulting from inhalation of pressurized helium. Ann Emerg Med 28:363–366, 1996.

159. O'Quin RJ, Lakshminarayan S: Venous air embolism. Arch Intern Med 142:2173–2176, 1982.

160. Zaugg M, Kaplan V, Widmer U, et al: Fatal air embolism in an airplane passenger with a giant intrapulmonary bronchogenic cyst. Am J Respir Crit Care Med 157:1686–1689, 1998.

161. Karmy-Jones R, Vallières E, Culver B, et al: Bronchial-atrial fistula after lung transplant resulting in fatal air embolism. Ann Thorac Surg 67:550–551, 1999.

162. Yellin A, Gapany-Gapanavicius M, Lieberman Y: Spontaneous pneumomediastinum: Is it a rare cause of chest pain? Thorax 38:383–385, 1983.

163. Versteegh FG, Broeders IA: Spontaneous pneumomediastinum in children. Eur J Pediatr 150:304–307, 1991.

164. Holmes KD, McGuirt WF: Spontaneous pneumomediastinum: Evaluation and treatment. J Fam Pract 31:422, 425–426, 1990.

165. Smith BA, Ferguson DB: Disposition of spontaneous pneumomediastinum. Am J Emerg Med 9:256–259, 1991.

166. Karns JR, Daue EO Jr: Mediastinotomy in spontaneous mediastinal emphysema. J Am Med Assoc 136:622–623, 1948.

167. Shuster MJ: Pneumomediastinum as a cause of dysphagia and pseudodysphagia. Ann Emerg Med 10:648–651, 1981.

168. Tucker WS Jr: Symptoms and signs of syndromes associated with mill wheel murmurs. N C Med J 49:569–572, 1988.

169. Draper AJ: Spontaneous mediastinal emphysema and pneumothorax. Am J Med 5:59–68, 1948.

170. Aisner M, Franco JE: Mediastinal emphysema. N Engl J Med 241:818–825, 1949.

171. Levin B: The continuous diaphragm sign. Radiology 24:337–338, 1973.

172. Bejvan SM, Godwin JD: Pneumomediastinum: Old signs and new signs. AJR Am J Roentgenol 166:1041–1048, 1996.

173. Whitley MA, Pierson DJ: Does this patient have a pneumomediastinum? Respir Care 31:1151–1153, 1986.

174. Lane EJ, Proto AV, Phillips TW: Mach bands and density perception. Radiology 121:9–17, 1976.

175. Friedman AC, Lautin EM, Rothenberg L: Mach bands and pneumomediastinum. J Can Assoc Radiol 32:232–235, 1981.

176. Westcott JC, Cole SR: Interstitial pulmonary emphysema in children and adults: Roentgenographic features. Radiology 111:367–378, 1974.

177. Kemper AC, Steinberg KP, Stern EJ: Pulmonary interstitial emphysema: CT findings. AJR Am J Roentgenol 172:1642, 1999.

178. Wintermark M, Schnyder P: The Macklin effect: A frequent etiology for pneumomediastinum in severe blunt chest trauma. Chest 120:543–547, 2001.

179. Rohlfing BM, Webb WR, Schlobohm RM: Ventilator-related extra-alveolar air in adults. Radiology 121:25–31, 1976.

180. Zimmerman JE, Dunbar BS, Klingenmaier CH: Management of subcutaneous emphysema, pneumomediastinum, and pneumothorax during respirator therapy. Crit Care Med 3:69–73, 1975.
181. Van Stiegmann G, Brantigan CO, Hopeman AR: Tension pneumomediastinum. Arch Surg 112:1212–1215, 1977.
182. Norman J, Rizzolo P: Subcutaneous, mediastinal, and probable subpericardial emphysema treated with recompression. N Engl J Med 261:269–272, 1959.
183. Beg MH, Reyazuddin N, Ansari MM: Traumatic tension pneumomediastinum mimicking cardiac tamponade. Thorax 43:576–577, 1988.
184. Brandfass RT, Martinez DM: Mediastinal and subcutaneous emphysema in labor. South Med J 69:1554–1555, 1976.
185. Jewett TC, Adler RH, Taheri SA: Tension pneumomediastinum in the newborn. J Thorac Cardiovasc Surg 43:540–547, 1962.
186. Webb WR, Johnston JH, Geisler JW: Pneumomediastinum: Physiologic observations. J Thorac Cardiovasc Surg 35:309–315, 1958.
187. Rydell JR: Emergency cervical mediastinotomy for massive mediastinal emphysema. Arch Surg 70:647–653, 1955.
188. Herlan DB, Landreneau RJ, Ferson PF: Massive spontaneous subcutaneous emphysema: Acute management with infraclavicular "blow holes." Chest 102:503–505, 1992.
189. Kelly MC, McGuigan JA, Allen RW: Relief of tension subcutaneous emphysema using a large bore subcutaneous drain. Anaesthesia 50:1077–1079, 1995.
190. Beck PL, Heitman SJ, Mody CH: Simple construction of a subcutaneous catheter for treatment of severe subcutaneous emphysema. Chest 121:647–649, 2002.
191. Zukerman H, Sadovsky E, Frankel M, Brzezinski A: Subcutaneous and mediastinal emphysema during labor. Gynaecologia 153:12–18, 1962.
192. Pecora DV, Yegian D, Hochwald A: Tracheotomy in the treatment of severe mediastinal emphysema. J Am Med Assoc 166:354–356, 1958.
193. Kirsch MM, Orringer MB, Behrendt DM, Sloan H: Management of tracheobronchial disruption secondary to nonpenetrating trauma. Ann Thorac Surg 22:93–101, 1976.
194. Rogers LF, Puig AW, Dooley BN, Cuello L: Diagnostic considerations in mediastinal emphysema: A pathophysiologic-roentgenologic approach to Boerhaave's syndrome and spontaneous pneumomediastinum. Am J Roentgenol Radium Ther Nucl Med 115:495–511, 1972.
195. Oh KS, Fleischner FG, Wyman SM: Characteristic pulmonary finding in traumatic complete transection of a main-stem bronchus. Radiology 92:371–372, 1969.
196. Grover FL, Ellestad C, Arom KV, et al: Diagnosis and management of major tracheobronchial injuries. Ann Thorac Surg 28:384–391, 1979.
197. Emery RW, Landes RG, Lindsay WG, et al: Surgical treatment of pneumopericardium in the neonate. World J Surg 2:631–637, 1978.
198. Cohen DJ, Baumgart S, Stephenson LW: Pneumopericardium in neonates: Is it PEEP or is it PIP? Ann Thorac Surg 35:179–183, 1983.
199. Halicek F, Rosai J: Histioeosinophilic granulomas in the thymuses of 29 myasthenic patients: A complication of pneumomediastinum. Hum Pathol 15:1137–1144, 1984.
200. Henderson JAM, Peloquin AJM: Boerhaave revisited: Spontaneous esophageal perforation as a diagnostic masquerader. Am J Med 86:559–567, 1989.
201. Forrest JV, Shackelford GD, Bramson RT, Anderson LS: Acute mediastinal widening. Am J Roentgenol Radium Ther Nucl Med 117:881–885, 1973.
202. Bjerke HS: Boerhaave's syndrome and barogenic injuries of the esophagus. Chest Surg Clin N Am 4:819–825, 1994.
203. Brauer RB, Liebermann Meffert D, Stein HJ, et al: Boerhaave's syndrome: Analysis of the literature and report of 18 new cases. Dis Esophagus 10:64–68, 1997.
204. Marston EL, Valk HL: Spontaneous perforation of the esophagus: Review of the literature and report of a case. Ann Intern Med 51:590–607, 1959.
205. Bar-Maor J, Hayari L: Pneumatic perforation of the esophagus in children. J Pediatr Surg 27:1532–1533, 1992.
206. Edling JE, Bacon BR: Pleuropulmonary complications of endoscopic variceal sclerotherapy. Chest 99:1252–1257, 1991.
207. Berry BE, Ochsner JL: Perforation of the esophagus: A 30-year review. J Thorac Cardiovasc Surg 65:1–7, 1973.
208. Wesdorp ICE, Bartelsman JFWM, Huibregtse K, et al: Treatment of instrumental esophageal perforation. Gut 25:398–404, 1984.
209. Schuman BM, Beckman JW, Tedesco FJ, et al: Complications of endoscopic injection sclerotherapy: A review. Am J Gastroenterol 82:823–830, 1987.
210. Perino LE, Gholson CF, Goff JS: Esophageal perforation after fiberoptic variceal sclerotherapy. J Clin Gastroenterol 9:286–289, 1987.
211. Baydur A, Korula J: Cardiorespiratory effects of endoscopic esophageal variceal sclerotherapy. Am J Med 89:477–482, 1990.
212. Vassilev BN, Kazandziev PK, Losanoff JE, et al: Esophageal "stars": A sinister foreign body ingestion. South Med J 90:211–214, 1997.
213. Fraser RG, Paré JAP: Diagnosis of Diseases of the Chest (2nd ed, Vol III). Philadelphia: WB Saunders, 1979.
214. Gollub MJ, Bains MS: Barium sulfate: A new (old) contrast agent for diagnosis of postoperative esophageal leaks. Radiology 202:360–362, 1997.
215. Sarr MG, Watkins LJ, Stewart JR: Mediastinal tap as a useful method for the early diagnosis of mediastinal infection. Surg Gynecol Obstet 159:79–81, 1984.
216. Goodwin RA Jr: Disorders of the mediastinum. In Fishman AP (ed): Pulmonary Diseases and Disorders. New York: McGraw-Hill, 1980, pp 1479–1486.
217. Loop FD, Groves LK: Esophageal perforations. Ann Thorac Surg 10:571–587, 1971.
218. Krizek TJ, Lease JG: Surgical management of suppurative mediastinitis. In Sabiston DJ (ed): Textbook of Surgery (14th ed). Philadelphia: WB Saunders, 1991, pp 1796–1800.
219. Gobien RP, Stanley JH, Gobien BS, et al: Percutaneous catheter aspiration and drainage of suspected mediastinal abscess. Radiology 151:69–71, 1984.
220. Craddock DR, Logan A, Mayell M: Traumatic rupture of the esophagus and stomach. Thorax 23:657–662, 1968.
221. Ohri SK, Liakakos TA, Pathi V, et al: Primary repair of iatrogenic thoracic esophageal perforation and Boerhaave's syndrome. Ann Thorac Surg 55:603–606, 1993.
222. Sakamoto Y, Tanaka N, Furuya T, et al: Surgical management of late esophageal perforation. Thorac Cardiovasc Surg 45:269–272, 1997.
223. Keung YK, Gendreau J, Barber A, Cobos E: Acute mediastinitis secondary to leakage of parenteral nutrition from a migrated central venous catheter in a patient undergoing autologous bone marrow transplant. Bone Marrow Transplant 17:871–872, 1996.
224. Kiernan PD, Hernandez A, Byrne WD, et al: Descending cervical mediastinitis. Ann Thorac Surg 65:1483–1488, 1998.

225. Garatea-Crelgo J, Gay-Escoda C: Mediastinitis from odontogenic infection: Report of three cases and review of the literature. Int J Oral Maxillofac Surg 20:65–68, 1991.

226. Corsten MJ, Shamji FM, Odell PF, et al: Optimal treatment of descending necrotising mediastinitis. Thorax 52:702–708, 1997.

227. Freeman RK, Vallières E, Verrier ED, et al: Descending necrotizing mediastinitis: An analysis of the effects of serial surgical debridement on patient mortality. J Thorac Cardiovasc Surg 119:260–267, 2000.

228. Wheatley MJ, Stirling MC, Kirsh MM, et al: Descending necrotizing mediastinitis: Transcervical drainage is not enough. Ann Thorac Surg 49:780–784, 1990.

229. Marty-Ane CH, Berthet JP, Alric P, et al: Management of descending necrotizing mediastinitis: An aggressive treatment for an aggressive disease. Ann Thorac Surg 68:212–217, 1999.

230. Brook I, Frazier EH: Microbiology of acute purulent pericarditis: A 12-year experience in a military hospital. Arch Intern Med 156:1857–1860, 1996.

231. Sancho LM, Minamoto H, Fernandez A, et al: Descending necrotizing mediastinitis: A retrospective surgical experience. Eur J Cardiothorac Surg 16:200–205, 1999.

232. Dreyfuss D, Djedaini K, Bidault Lapomme C, Coste F: Nontraumatic acute anterior mediastinitis in two HIV-positive heroin addicts. Chest 101:583–585, 1992.

233. Mensah GA, Gold JP, Schreiber T, et al: Acute purulent mediastinitis and sternal osteomyelitis after closed-chest cardiopulmonary resuscitation: A case report and review of the literature. Ann Thorac Surg 46:353–355, 1988.

234. Poppel MH: Some migratory aspects of inflammatory collections of pancreatic origin. Radiology 72:323–329, 1959.

235. Sarr MG, Gott VL, Townsend TR: Mediastinal infection after cardiac surgery. Ann Thorac Surg 38:415–423, 1984.

236. Bor DH, Rose RM, Modlin JF, et al: Mediastinitis after cardiovascular surgery. Rev Infect Dis 5:885–897, 1983.

237. Newman LS, Szczukowski LC, Bain RP, et al: Suppurative mediastinitis after open heart surgery. Chest 94:546–553, 1988.

238. Karwande S, Renlund D, Olsen S, et al: Mediastinitis in heart transplantation. Ann Thorac Surg 54:1039–1045, 1992.

239. Baldwin R, Radovancevic B, Sweeney M, Frazier O: Bacterial mediastinitis after heart transplantation. J Heart Lung Transplant 11:545–549, 1992.

240. Bassiri AG, Girgis RE, Theodore J: *Actinomyces odontolyticus* thoracopulmonary infections: Two cases in lung and heart-lung transplant recipients and a review of the literature. Chest 109:1109–1111, 1996.

241. El Oakley RM, Wright JE: Postoperative mediastinitis: Classification and management. Ann Thorac Surg 61:1030–1036, 1996.

242. Ulicny KS Jr, Hiratzka LF: The risk factors of median sternotomy infection: A current review. J Card Surg 6:338–351, 1991.

243. Bitkover CY, Gardlund B: Mediastinitis after cardiovascular operations: A case-control study of risk factors. Ann Thorac Surg 65:36–40, 1998.

244. Stoney WS, Alford WC Jr, Burrus GR, et al: Median sternotomy dehiscence. Ann Thorac Surg 26:421–426, 1978.

245. Grossi EA, Culliford AT, Krieger KH, et al: A survey of 77 major infectious complications of median sternotomy: A review of 7,949 consecutive operative procedures. Ann Thorac Surg 40:214–223, 1985.

246. Culliford AT, Cunningham JJ, Zeff RH, et al: Sternal and costochondral infections following open-heart surgery: A review of 2594 cases. J Thorac Cardiovasc Surg 72:714–725, 1976.

247. Perl TM, Cullen JJ, Wenzel RP, et al: Intranasal mupirocin to prevent postoperative *Staphylococcus aureus* infections. N Engl J Med 346:1871–1877, 2002.

248. Kluytmans JA, Mouton JW, VandenBergh MF, et al: Reduction of surgical-site infections in cardiothoracic surgery by elimination of nasal carriage of *Staphylococcus aureus*. Infect Control Hosp Epidemiol 17:780–785, 1996.

249. Demmy TL, Park SB, Liebler GA, et al: Recent experience with major sternal wound complications. Ann Thorac Surg 49:458–462, 1990.

250. Kohman LJ, Coleman MJ, Parker FB Jr: Bacteremia and sternal infection after coronary artery bypass grafting. Ann Thorac Surg 49:454–457, 1990.

251. Glower DD, Douglas JM Jr, Gaynor JW, et al: *Candida* mediastinitis after a cardiac operation. Ann Thorac Surg 49:157–163, 1990.

252. Misawa Y, Fuse K, Hasegawa T: Infectious mediastinitis after cardiac operations: Computed tomographic findings. Ann Thorac Surg 65:622–624, 1998.

253. Jolles H, Henry DA, Roberson JP, et al: Mediastinitis following median sternotomy: CT findings. Radiology 201:463–466, 1996.

254. Craver JM, Rand RP, Bostwick JI, et al: Management of postcardiotomy mediastinitis. *In* Waldhausen J, Orringer M (eds): Complications in Thoracic Surgery. St Louis: Mosby–Year Book, 1991, pp 125–131.

255. Robicsek F: Postoperative sterno-mediastinitis. Am Surg 66:184–192, 2000.

256. El Gamel A, Yonan NA, Hassan R, et al: Treatment of mediastinitis: Early modified Robicsek closure and pectoralis major advancement flaps. Ann Thorac Surg 65:41–46, 1998.

257. Milano CA, Kesler K, Archibald N, et al: Mediastinitis after coronary artery bypass graft surgery: Risk factors and long-term survival. Circulation 92:2245–2251, 1995.

258. Lazar HL, Fitzgerald C, Gross S, et al: Determinants of length of stay after coronary artery bypass graft surgery. Circulation 92(Suppl II):II-20–II-24, 1995.

259. Englemam RM, Williams CD, Gouge TH, et al: Mediastinitis following open-heart surgery: Review of two years experience. Arch Surg 107:772–778, 1973.

260. Grigas D, Bor DH, Kosinski E, et al: Cardiopulmonary function following post-cardiac surgical mediastinitis. Chest 85:729–732, 1984.

261. LaForce FM: Anthrax. Clin Infect Dis 19:1009–1013, 1994.

262. Shafazand S, Doyle R, Ruoss S, et al: Inhalational anthrax: Epidemiology, diagnosis, and management. Chest 116:1369–1376, 1999.

263. Shafazand S: When bioterrorism strikes: Diagnosis and management of inhalational anthrax. Semin Respir Infect 18:134–145, 2003.

264. Jernigan JA, Stephens DS, Ashford DA, et al: Bioterrorism-related inhalational anthrax: The first 10 cases reported in the United States. Emerg Infect Dis 7:933–944, 2001.

265. Jernigan DB, Raghunathan PL, Bell BP, et al: Investigation of bioterrorism-related anthrax, United States, 2001: Epidemiologic findings. Emerg Infect Dis 8:1019–1028, 2002.

266. Mayer TA, Bersoff-Matcha S, Murphy C, et al: Clinical presentation of inhalational anthrax following bioterrorism exposure: Report of 2 surviving patients. JAMA 286:2549–2553, 2001.

267. Brachman PS: Inhalation anthrax. Ann N Y Acad Sci 353:83–93, 1980.

268. Abramova FA, Grinberg LM, Yampolskaya OV, Walker DH: Pathology of inhalational anthrax in 42 cases from the Sverdlovsk outbreak of 1979. Proc Natl Acad Sci U S A 90:2291–2294, 1993.

269. Pile JC, Malone JD, Eitzen EM, Friedlander AM: Anthrax as a potential biological warfare agent. Arch Intern Med 158:429–434, 1998.

270. Lalitha MK, Thomas MK: Penicillin resistance in *Bacillus anthracis*. Lancet 349:1522, 1997.

271. Strimlan CV, Dines DE, Payne WS: Mediastinal granuloma. Mayo Clin Proc 50:702–705, 1975.

272. Feigin DS, Eggleston JC, Siegelman SS: The multiple roentgen manifestations of sclerosing mediastinitis. Johns Hopkins Med J 144:1–8, 1979.

273. Light AM: Idiopathic fibrosis of the mediastinum: A discussion of three cases and review of the literature. J Clin Pathol 31:78–88, 1978.

274. Goodwin RA, Nickell JA, DesPrez RM: Mediastinal fibrosis complicating healed primary histoplasmosis and tuberculosis. Medicine 51:227–246, 1972.

275. Bloomberg TJ, Dow CJ: Contemporary mediastinal tuberculosis. Thorax 35:392–396, 1980.

276. Rabinowitz JG, Prater W, Silver J, et al: Mediastinal histoplasmosis. Mt Sinai J Med 47:356–363, 1980.

277. Lokich JJ, Goodman R: Superior vena cava syndrome: Clinical management. JAMA 231:58–61, 1975.

278. Schechter MM: The superior vena cava syndrome. Am J Med Sci 227:46–56, 1954.

279. Mahajan V, Strimlan V, van Ordstrand HS, Loop FD: Benign superior vena cava syndrome. Chest 68:32–35, 1975.

280. Schowengerdt CG, Suyemoto R, Main FB: Granulomatous and fibrous mediastinitis: A review and analysis of 180 cases. J Thorac Cardiovasc Surg 57:365–379, 1969.

281. Loyd JE, Tillman BF, Atkinson JB, et al: Mediastinal fibrosis complicating histoplasmosis. Medicine 67:295–310, 1988.

282. Flieder DB, Suster S, Moran CA: Idiopathic fibroinflammatory (fibrosing/sclerosing) lesions of the mediastinum: A study of 30 cases with emphasis on morphologic heterogeneity. Mod Pathol 12:257–264, 1999.

283. Rohwedder JJ: Neoplastic disease and mediastinal disorders. *In* Guenter CA, Welch MH (eds): Pulmonary Medicine, 2nd ed. Philadelphia: JB Lippincott, 1982, pp 880–883.

284. Fraser RG, Paré JAP, Paré PD, et al: Diagnosis of Diseases of the Chest (3rd ed, Vol IV). Philadelphia: WB Saunders, 1991.

285. Cameron DD, Ing ST, Boyle M, Mathews WH: Idiopathic mediastinal and retroperitoneal fibrosis. Can Med Assoc J 85:227–232, 1961.

286. Cunningham T, Farrell J, Veale D, Fitzgerald O: Anterior mediastinal fibrosis with superior vena caval obstruction complicating the synovitis-acne-pustulosis-hyperostosis-osteomyelitis syndrome. Br J Rheumatol 32:408–410, 1993.

287. Kalweit G, Huwer H, Straub U, Gams E: Mediastinal compression syndromes due to idiopathic fibrosing mediastinitis—report of three cases and review of the literature. Thorac Cardiovasc Surg 44:105–109, 1996.

288. Comings DE Skubi K-B, Eyes JV, Motulsky AG: Familial multifocal fibrosclerosis. Ann Intern Med 66:884–892, 1967.

289. McIntire FT, Sykes EM Jr: Obstruction of the superior vena cava: A review of the literature and report of two personal cases. Ann Intern Med 30:925–960, 1949.

290. Ochsner A, Dixon JL: Superior vena cava thrombosis: Review of the literature and report of cases of traumatic and infectious origin. J Thorac Surg 5:641–672, 1936.

291. Gilbert HM, Hartman BJ: Short report: A case of fibrosing mediastinitis caused by *Wuchereria bancrofti*. Am J Trop Med Hyg 54:596–599, 1996.

292. Graham JR, Suby HI, LeCompte PR, Sadowsky NL: Fibrotic disorders associated with methysergide therapy for headache. N Engl J Med 274:359–368, 1966.

293. Gordonson J, Trachtenberg S, Sargent EN: Superior vena cava obstruction due to sarcoidosis. Chest 63:292–293, 1973.

294. Ray RL, Truscott DE: Silicosis as a cause of superior vena cava obstruction. Br J Dis Chest 57:210–212, 1963.

295. Flannery MT, Espino M, Altus P, et al: Hodgkin's disease masquerading as sclerosing mediastinitis. South Med J 87:921–923, 1994.

296. Smith AR, Richards V: Superior vena cava obstruction. Am J Surg 96:353–359, 1958.

297. Dechambre S, Dorzee J, Fastrez J, et al: Bronchial stenosis and sclerosing mediastinitis: An uncommon complication of external thoracic radiotherapy. Eur Respir J 11:1188–1190, 1998.

298. Mathisen DJ, Grillo HC: Clinical manifestation of mediastinal fibrosis and histoplasmosis. Ann Thorac Surg 54:1053–1057, 1992.

299. Rossi SE, McAdams HP, Rosado-de-Christenson ML, et al: Fibrosing mediastinitis. Radiographics 21:737–757, 2001.

300. Mole TM, Glover J, Sheppard MN: Sclerosing mediastinitis: A report on 18 cases. Thorax 50:280–283, 1995.

301. Sherrick AD, Brown LR, Harms GF, Myers JL: The radiographic findings of fibrosing mediastinitis. Chest 106:484–489, 1994.

302. Kefri M, Dyke S, Copeland S, et al: Hemoptysis and hematemesis due to a broncholith: Granulomatous mediastinitis. South Med J 89:243–245, 1996.

303. Urschel HC Jr, Razzuk MA, Netto GJ, et al: Sclerosing mediastinitis: Improved management with histoplasmosis titer and ketoconazole. Ann Thorac Surg 50:215–221, 1990.

304. Wychulis AR, Payne WS, Clagett OT, Woolner LB: Surgical treatment of mediastinal tumors: A 40-year experience. J Thorac Cardiovasc Surg 62:379–391, 1971.

305. Yellin A, Rosen A, Reichert N, et al: Superior vena cava syndrome: The myth—the facts. Am Rev Respir Dis 141:1114–1118, 1990.

306. Basaranoglu M, Ozdemir S, Celik AF, et al: A case of fibrosing mediastinitis with obstruction of superior vena cava and downhill esophageal varices: A rare cause of upper gastrointestinal hemorrhage. J Clin Gastroenterol 28:268–270, 1999.

307. Espinosa RE, Edwards WD, Rosenow EC 3rd, Schaff HV: Idiopathic pulmonary hilar fibrosis: An unusual cause of pulmonary hypertension. Mayo Clin Proc 68:778–782, 1993.

308. Berry DF, Buccigrossi D, Peabody J, et al: Pulmonary vascular occlusion and fibrosing mediastinitis. Chest 89:296–301, 1986.

309. Maholtz MS, Dauber JH, Yousem SA: Case report: Fluconazole therapy in histoplasma mediastinal granuloma. Am J Med Sci 307:274–277, 1994.

310. Mocherla S, Wheat LJ: Treatment of histoplasmosis. Semin Respir Infect 16:141–148, 2001.

311. Field C, Arnold W, Gloster ES, et al: Steroid therapy as treatment for idiopathic fibrosis of the retroperitoneum and mediastinum. Pediatrics 78:936–938, 1986.

312. Gran JT: Chronic idiopathic mediastinal fibrosis presenting with malaise, pleuritis and thoracic back pain. Br J Rheumatol 32:757–759, 1993.

313. Dunn EJ, Ulicny KS Jr, Wright CB, Gottesman L: Surgical implications of sclerosing mediastinitis: A report of six cases and review of the literature. Chest 97:338–346, 1990.

314. Dodds GA 3rd, Harrison JK, O'Laughlin MP, et al: Relief of superior vena cava syndrome due to fibrosing mediastinitis using the Palmaz stent. Chest 106:315–318, 1994.

315. Guerrero A, Hoffer EK, Hudson L, et al: Treatment of pulmonary artery compression due to fibrous mediastinitis with endovascular stent placement. Chest 119:966–968, 2001.

DISORDERS IN THE CONTROL OF BREATHING

73

Hypoventilation and Hyperventilation Syndromes

Eliot A. Phillipson, M.D., James Duffin, Ph.D.

INTRODUCTION

Breathing is regulated by two anatomically distinct but functionally integrated elements referred to as the metabolic (or automatic) and the behavioral (or voluntary) respiratory control systems. The metabolic system is concerned primarily with acid-base balance and blood gas homeostasis. Appropriate to this function, it receives afferent input from peripheral and central chemoreceptors that are sensitive to pH, PCO_2, and PO_2 and from bronchopulmonary mechanoreceptors that are sensitive to the degree of lung stretch and rate of airflow. In contrast, the behavioral control system utilizes the ventilatory apparatus for functions whose primary purpose is not gas exchange, the most notable examples being speaking and singing.

Disorders in the control of breathing can arise because of disturbances in either of these two control systems. In broad terms, defects in the behavioral system result in dysphasia, dyspraxia, or alveolar *hyper*ventilation syndromes but do not produce clinically important *hypo*ventilation syndromes.[1,2] Rather, hypoventilation disorders arise because of either defects in the metabolic control system or defects in the respiratory neuromuscular apparatus, chest wall, lungs, or airways. Such disorders can be acute or chronic.

Acute hypoventilation disturbances, which represent life-threatening emergencies, are considered in Chapter 85. This chapter deals with disturbances in respiratory control that result in chronic hypoventilation or chronic hyperventilation syndromes.

CONTROL OF BREATHING

BASIC PRINCIPLES

Breathing is responsible for providing sufficient oxygen for metabolism and for eliminating the carbon dioxide produced by metabolism. The respiratory control system accomplishes this goal by sensing the tissue partial pressures of oxygen (PO_2) and carbon dioxide (PCO_2), and adjusting pulmonary ventilation so that oxygen uptake at the lungs equals oxygen consumption by the tissues, and carbon dioxide elimination at the lungs equals carbon dioxide production by the tissues (Fig. 73.1). Under these conditions, pulmonary gas exchange matches metabolism, and PO_2 and PCO_2 remain constant.

In the case of PO_2 the requirement is relatively simple; it must be kept at a level sufficient to saturate arterial hemoglobin and to provide a pressure gradient that supplies tissue

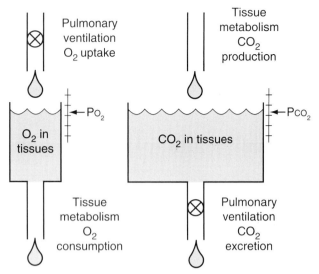

Figure 73.1 A conceptual model showing the balance between metabolic requirements and pulmonary gas exchange of oxygen and carbon dioxide. Note the difference in size of the tissue storage compartments of the two gases, as a result of which changes in P_{O_2} are fast and changes in P_{CO_2} are slow.

metabolic requirements for oxygen. Because hemoglobin saturation can be achieved over a wide range of P_{O_2} levels, P_{O_2} need not be closely regulated, as long as tissue hypoxia is avoided. In contrast, the requirement for carbon dioxide elimination is less dependent on a pressure gradient because carbon dioxide diffuses much more readily through an aqueous environment than does oxygen. However, P_{CO_2} must be controlled at a level that ensures that hydrogen ion concentration ($[H^+]$) remains within the narrow limits necessary for optimal protein function (normally 40 nM/L). This requirement can be considered as the second goal of the respiratory control system, although renal regulation of ionic concentrations is also involved.

Under resting conditions, P_{CO_2} is maintained within a narrow range by a negative feedback regulator involving two chemoreceptors that sense $[H^+]$, one in the brain (central chemoreceptors) and one in the carotid bodies (peripheral chemoreceptors). When these chemoreceptors sense an increase in $[H^+]$, breathing is stimulated. This *chemoreflex control system* also protects against asphyxia by increasing the sensitivity of the peripheral chemoreceptors to $[H^+]$ under conditions of hypoxia. During exercise, however, rapid increases in metabolism must be accompanied by rapid changes in ventilation if pulmonary gas exchange is to match metabolism. In this situation, fast neural response mechanisms are activated, including afferent feedback from the exercising muscles and a parallel activation of ventilation with activation of the exercising muscles, termed *central command*. If the level of ventilation produced as a result of these fast *exercise control system* mechanisms does not match the increased level of metabolism induced by exercise, the slower chemical feedback control system produces the necessary corrections.

The two elements involved in matching pulmonary gas exchange to metabolic requirements, the chemoreflex and exercise control systems, collectively constitute the *metabolic* or *automatic control system*. However, other

physiologic functions also utilize the ventilatory apparatus, notably speaking, singing, and voluntary breath-holding.[3] These activities impact on the respiratory muscles through the *behavioral control system*.[4-7] Breath-holding exemplifies the competition that may exist between the behavioral and metabolic control systems for use of the respiratory muscles. At the initiation of a breath-hold, voluntary control dominates and breathing is halted; but as the chemoreflex drive to breathe increases progressively, the metabolic control system overrides behavioral control and the breath-hold is terminated. In the process of this competition, the discrepancy between the chemoreflex drives to breathe, on the one hand, and the lack of ventilation, on the other, results in a sensation of dyspnea.[8,9]

Subsidiary to the metabolic and behavioral systems are other control systems, including those responsible for choice of efficient patterns of breathing in terms of tidal volume and respiratory rate, and for protection of the airways by pulmonary reflexes, such as cough. This hierarchical system of controllers can be put into perspective by examination of the organization of the central respiratory control system.

ORGANIZATON OF THE RESPIRATORY CONTROL SYSTEM

General Organization

Taken together, the demands of the various respiratory control systems vary from moment to moment, and may place conflicting demands on the respiratory muscles, depending upon a set of conflicting priorities. The site of much of this competition is the spinal respiratory motoneuron, where the various drives to breathing arrive via separate pathways (Fig. 73.2). Thus, behavioral or voluntary control from the motor cortex is mediated by the corticospinal tracts in the dorsolateral spinal cord; metabolic or automatic control from the central controller in the medulla is mediated by ventrolateral spinal cord pathways, as are the inputs from hypothalamic, limbic, and reticular formation systems that mediate such behaviors as anxiety hyperventilation, the sudden gasp of a startle, the changes in breathing during sleep, and the response to sensory afferents such as pain. The separation of the spinal pathways for behavioral and metabolic control in humans has been deduced from observations of spinal cord injuries that involve only one pathway. For example, some patients are able breathe on command but lack the automatic chemoreflex response to carbon dioxide, whereas others have a response to carbon dioxide but cannot voluntarily influence breathing.[5]

The metabolic respiratory control system can be viewed as a complex hierarchical control system with multiple feedback loops (Fig. 73.3). The system is centered in the brain stem (medulla), where respiratory rhythm and drives are sent to the respiratory motoneurons in the spinal cord, based on feedback from various afferents. Details of this system are provided in a number of reviews.[10,11] The afferent inputs to the system include those from the central chemoreceptors within the medulla, the peripheral chemoreceptors in the carotid bodies, and airway and lung receptors. Although these signals also reach higher areas of the central nervous system, where they may contribute to respiratory sensations such as dyspnea, little is known about

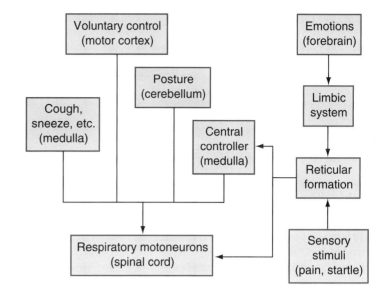

Figure 73.2 A general scheme showing various elements controlling the spinal respiratory motoneurons.

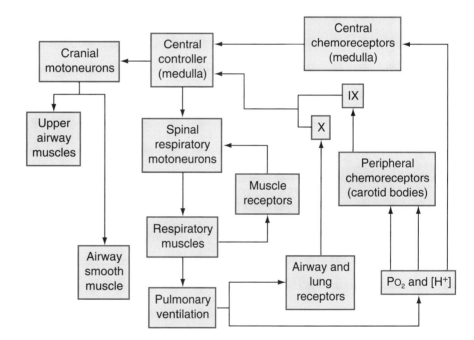

Figure 73.3 A schematic diagram of some of the feedback loops involved in the automatic control of breathing. IX, glossopharyngeal nerve; X, vagus nerve.

the pathways involved. In addition to the medullary feedback loops, there are also local control loops to spinal motoneurons from respiratory muscle receptors, particularly in the intercostal muscles.

Spinal Organization

The spinal organization of respiratory motoneuron control is complex and not fully understood. Four groups of respiratory neurons have been identified in the spinal cord: upper cervical inspiratory neurons in C1–3; phrenic motoneurons and interneurons in C3–5; intercostal motoneurons and interneurons in T1–12; and abdominal motoneurons and interneurons in T6–L3. The interneurons within the motoneuron segments and those more remote in the upper cervical cord probably mediate the segmental and suprasegmental reflex control of the motoneurons.

The upper cervical inspiratory neurons are located bilaterally in longitudinal columns extending caudally from the medulla to mid-C3.[12] These neurons receive a direct drive from the medullary inspiratory neurons, as well as inputs from intercostal afferents. Their axons descend the spinal cord ipsilaterally as far as the upper lumbar segments, and arborize within the phrenic, intercostal, and abdominal motoneuron segments of the spinal cord. As yet, the functional connections of these neurons are undetermined because they do not appear to connect synaptically with spinal respiratory neurons.[13,14]

The respiratory motoneurons, including the phrenic motoneurons driving the diaphragm, the intercostal motoneurons driving the intercostal muscles, and the abdominal motoneurons driving the abdominal muscles,[15–17] receive a rhythmic respiratory drive from two sources: the nearby respiratory interneurons in the spinal cord,[18] and the respiratory neurons located in the medulla. These motoneurons produce a ramp of inspiratory nerve activity by an increasing firing frequency and by the recruitment of additional motoneurons. Because the medullary respiratory neurons are also the source of the rhythmic drive to the spinal respiratory interneurons, the medullary neurons are often referred to as the respiratory premotor neurons.

Central Organization

The network that generates and transmits respiratory rhythm to the spinal respiratory motoneurons via bulbospinal projections, and to various respiratory muscles of the airway via cranial nerves, lies within the medulla and pons.[19,20] The medullary respiratory neurons are located in two main groups, longitudinally distributed on either side of the neuraxis, referred to as the ventral respiratory group (VRG) and the dorsal respiratory group (DRG), because of their relative anatomic positions. The groups are located near the obex, the point where the central canal widens into the fourth ventricle (Fig. 73.4). The DRG includes the respiratory afferent relay neurons of the nucleus tractus solitarius,[21] and the VRG includes cranial motoneurons of the nucleus ambiguus.[22] Pontine respiratory groups include the Kolliker fuse and parabrachial nuclei.[23,24] The Bötzinger complex, rostral to the VRG, and the pre-Bötzinger complex, located between it and the VRG, are thought to be the site of respiratory rhythm generation.[25]

The medullary respiratory neurons can be classified according to several overlapping criteria: the nucleus in which they are located, pattern of activity, destination of axon projections, and synaptic function (inhibitory or excitatory). The patterns of activity are of two main types, inspiratory (I) and expiratory (E), corresponding to the phases of respiration in which they are active. Within these phases, the pattern of firing frequency may be augmenting, constant, or decrementing. The expiratory phase can be subdivided into early and late portions, sometimes also called E1 (or postinspiratory) and E2, corresponding to the declining and quiescent periods, respectively, of phrenic nerve activity.

The axon destinations also help to classify these neurons. For example, the axons of neurons in the nucleus ambiguus (which may have any of the patterns of activity described previously) leave the medulla ipsilaterally in the vagus or glossopharyngeal nerves, and innervate several different muscles of the airways.[26,27] The hypoglossal motoneurons that innervate the tongue are similar. These various cranial motoneurons are respiratory in the sense that a component of their activity is related to the respiratory cycle, but they are also involved in other functions, such as speech and swallowing. Because this dual function dictates the requirement for looser respiratory control than the respiratory pump muscles, the cranial motoneurons are not driven by the same premotor neurons as the pump muscles.[28]

The premotor neurons for the respiratory pump muscles are found in the VRG and DRG, from where most of their axons course contralaterally within the medulla before descending the cord to the respiratory motoneurons and interneurons. These premotor neurons are termed *bulbospinal neurons*, in contrast to respiratory neurons whose axons do not leave the medulla (propriobulbar neurons). The latter neurons are found primarily in the VRG and in the Bötzinger and pre-Bötzinger complexes; and because they have constant, augmenting, or decrementing firing patterns, they are considered to be elements of the neural network involved in generation of respiratory rhythm.

Although the function of the inspiratory, bulbospinal premotor neurons in driving the inspiratory motoneurons of the diaphragm and external intercostal muscles is obvious, that of the expiratory, bulbospinal premotor neurons is not, given that expiration is passive under most conditions. It is thought that these neurons may serve to prevent activation of the inspiratory muscles during expiration, by exciting inhibitory spinal interneurons that synapse with the

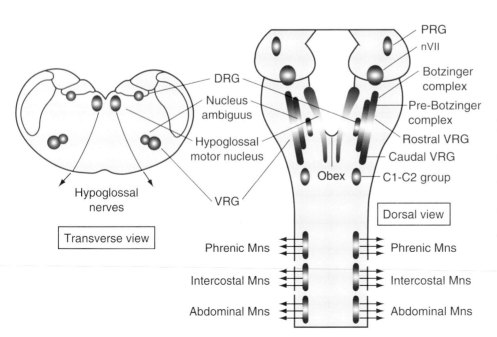

Figure 73.4 A schematic diagram of the medulla showing the main groups of respiratory neurons. The dorsal view has the cerebellum removed, and the transverse view is at the level of the obex. C1-C2, cervical cord levels 1 and 2; DRG, dorsal respiratory group; PRG, pontine respiratory group; VRG, ventral respiratory group.

inspiratory motoneurons. In addition, the expiratory bul-bospinal neurons provide excitation to the spinal expiratory motoneurons when needed under conditions of increased ventilation. Some of the neurons are well characterized. The Bötzinger complex expiratory neurons, for example, are unique in that they provide an inhibitory input to all of the medullary inspiratory neurons, and to the phrenic motoneurons. The functions of the other neurons are less well understood and the subject of continuing research.

The Respiratory Rhythm Generator

There are two main theories regarding the generation of respiratory rhythm: the pacemaker hypothesis, and the network hypothesis.[20,29,29a] The former suggests that respiratory rhythm is an intrinsic property of some cells in the pre-Bötzinger complex, and that these cells drive the others.[30,31] In contrast, the network hypothesis suggests that respiratory rhythm results from the pattern of synaptic interconnections among neurons in a distributed network in the rostral VRG, pre-Bötzinger complex, and Bötzinger complex.[32,33] Definitive proof for these hypotheses is difficult to establish. Rather, the hypotheses have emerged largely from studies based on different experimental preparations (the network hypothesis from adult in vivo preparations, and the pacemaker hypothesis from neonatal in vitro preparations). These differences may account for the different findings. Indeed, it has been suggested that the pacemaker behavior is one of "gasping" induced by hypoxia, an alternative to the "eupneic" breathing pattern produced by the network.[34] This conflict between hypotheses may be resolved using a new perfused preparation that can be applied to both neonates and adults, the working heart–brain stem preparation.[35,36] Experiments using this preparation have already demonstrated the importance of synaptic inhibition in normal respiratory rhythm generation.[37]

A number of specific models for each hypothesis have been proposed. All of the network models have two basic principles in common. First, mutual inhibition must exist between at least two major groups of neurons of opposite respiratory phase (inspiratory and expiratory). Second, at least one of the neuron types must be self-limiting through an accommodative mechanism whereby the responsiveness of the neuron is decreased by its own activity. Figure 73.5 shows a connection diagram for such a model. The model proposes mutual inhibition between expiratory decrementing and inspiratory decrementing neurons, with both types of neurons considered to be accommodating (the process that produces their declining pattern of activity). Thus, the alternating phases of activity result from mutual inhibition (a bistable oscillator), and accommodation of the neurons ensures that the model does not stick in one phase or the other. It is apparent that the slow time course of the accommodation process largely determines the inherent respiratory rhythm timing.

CONTROL OF THE BREATHING PATTERN

Two main types of receptors from the lungs and airways provide feedback information to the medullary controller that determines the pattern of breathing; specifically, rapidly adapting irritant receptors and slowly adapting stretch

Figure 73.5 A simple model of respiratory rhythm generation based upon mutual inhibition (*filled circles*) between propriobulbar inspiratory and expiratory neurons of the ventral respiratory group with a decrementing pattern of activity (E-DEC and I-DEC). Both neurons are accommodating and control the output of the inspiratory and expiratory augmenting neurons (I-AUG and E-AUG). The network requires a tonic excitation (*open circles*) from the chemoreceptors to oscillate. I-AUG, E-AUG, inspiratory and expiratory augmenting neurons, respectively; I-DEC, E-DEC, inspiratory and expiratory decrementing neurons, respectively.

receptors.[38–41] The rapidly adapting receptors are found throughout the airway from the nose to the alveoli, and are stimulated by irritants in the inspired air, and by rapid and excessive lung inflation or deflation. These receptors are classified as rapidly adapting because, following stimulation, their activation declines rapidly even if the stimulus persists. Some irritant receptors produce stereotyped patterns of breathing, such as coughing, and all share the property of stimulating inspiration and inducing bronchoconstriction. Stimulation of these receptors during an asthmatic attack exacerbates airway narrowing by producing bronchoconstriction in addition to that produced by the local release of chemical mediators. The pattern of breathing induced by irritant receptor stimulation depends upon their location in the airway: nasal receptors (trigeminal nerves) result in sneezing; epipharyngeal receptors (glossopharyngeal nerves) result in the aspiration or sniff reflex; laryngeal and tracheal receptors (vagus nerves) result in coughing; tracheal, bronchial, and bronchiolar receptors (vagus nerves) result in Head's paradoxical reflex and the deflation reflex; and juxtapulmonary capillary or J receptors (vagus nerves) result in rapid, shallow breathing.

The stretch receptors, which are located in the main airways of the bronchial tree, respond to lung inflation and produce afferent feedback to the medullary controller through the vagus nerves that is proportional to lung volume. These receptors are responsible for the Hering-Breuer inflation reflex, whereby lung inflation switches respiratory phase from inspiration to expiration. This reflex is very apparent in animals, even at normal lung volumes, so that blockade or section of the vagi results in slow, deep breathing because inspiration continues to larger tidal volumes and longer inspiration times. In humans, however, the inflation reflex is weak, and difficult to demonstrate except at high lung volumes. It is thought that the stretch receptors provide information to the central respiratory controller that enables a judgment to be made of the effectiveness of respiratory muscle activity. Such information may be used for adjustment of the breathing pattern in response to altered loading the respiratory muscles.[42]

Although the level of ventilation required for metabolic gas exchange can be achieved by several different combinations of tidal volume and respiratory rate, there is a particular combination that will result in minimum work.[43] Stretch receptor information may help to determine this combination. In addition, stretch receptor information may also be sensed consciously, providing information with regard to lung volume and pulmonary ventilation. Discrepancies between the level of ventilation demanded by the central controller (which can also be sensed) and the actual pulmonary ventilation achieved is thought to produce the sensation of dyspnea.[5]

CHEMOREFLEX CONTROL OF BREATHING

The chemical control of breathing is based on a negative feedback loop and chemoreflex (Fig. 73.6). Thus, when the central and peripheral chemoreceptors sense an increase in [H+], breathing is stimulated by a chemoreflex that includes the central nervous system, respiratory muscles, and changes in alveolar ventilation, resulting in correction of the [H+], hence the negative feedback designation of the system. However, in addition to chemical stimuli, non-chemical drives to breathe also contribute to the level of ventilation, independently of the chemoreflexes. These drives include the central nervous system "state" of the subject, which is referred to as the "waking neural drive," because it is withdrawn during sleep.[5,44–46]

The relationship between the feedback and feed-forward elements of the chemoreflex control of breathing can be described using graphic models of ventilation and PCO_2. The feed-forward part of the loop (see Fig. 73.6) relates the dependence of [H+], PCO_2, and PO_2 on ventilation. The regulation of PCO_2 by ventilation controls [H+], whereas (as described later) PO_2 acts only by changing the sensitivity of the peripheral chemoreflex to carbon dioxide. Therefore, the feed-forward part of the loop can be characterized by the relationship between ventilation and PCO_2, as dictated by the requirements for elimination of carbon dioxide by the lungs. The product of ventilation and alveolar PCO_2 is proportional to the amount of carbon dioxide eliminated; hence, in any steady metabolic state, PCO_2 depends on the rate of carbon dioxide elimination divided by the rate of ventilation. This relationship results in a rectangular hyperbola, referred to as the *metabolic hyperbola* (Fig. 73.7, dashed line).

The two chemoreflexes, central and peripheral, are defined by the location of their sensors. The central chemoreceptors are located somewhere in the medulla (probably near the ventrolateral surface and scattered within the brain tissue) and respond to the [H+] of their local environment.[47,48] They are considered to be carbon dioxide receptors because central [H+] is directly dependent on the PCO_2 of chemoreceptor tissue. Two factors complicate the physiology of the central chemoreceptors. First, the blood-brain barrier to polar solutes prevents changes in arterial [H+] from reaching the central environment, whereas carbon dioxide passes freely across the barrier. As a result, central [H+] may differ from arterial [H+]. The central chemoreceptors are therefore somewhat isolated from arterial acid-base disturbances, except as they involve changes in arterial PCO_2. Second, because the central chemoreceptors are in brain tissue, they are relatively slow in responding even to changes in PCO_2 in arterial blood. For example, the time constant for the central chemoreceptor response

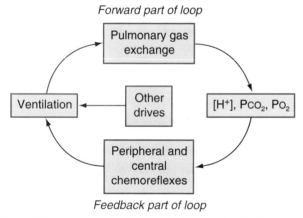

Figure 73.6 A schematic diagram of the negative feedback chemoreflex control of breathing.

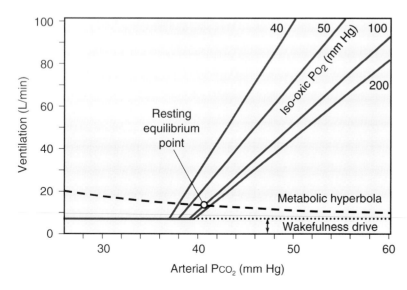

Figure 73.7 A graphic solution for the negative feedback chemoreflex control of breathing. The peripheral chemoreflex contribution to ventilatory drive, which varies with PO_2, is added to the central chemoreflex contribution, but only increases ventilation once a threshold is exceeded. The chemoreflex control of ventilation, dependent on both PCO_2 and PO_2, is therefore shown as a series of isoxic lines. Below the threshold, ventilation is driven by the waking neural drive (*dotted line*). The intersection of the control lines with the metabolic hyperbola (*long-dashed line*) defines the equilibrium point of the feedback and feed-forward components of the control system, and the resting ventilation and PCO_2.

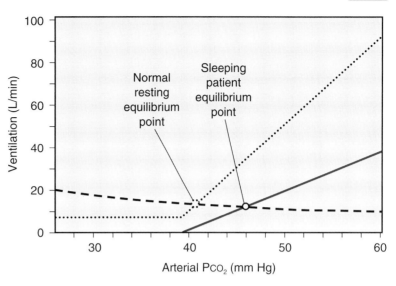

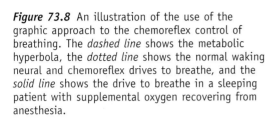

Figure 73.8 An illustration of the use of the graphic approach to the chemoreflex control of breathing. The *dashed line* shows the metabolic hyperbola, the *dotted line* shows the normal waking neural and chemoreflex drives to breathe, and the *solid line* shows the drive to breathe in a sleeping patient with supplemental oxygen recovering from anesthesia.

to a change in alveolar P_{CO_2} is about 100 seconds; hence, it takes 5 minutes (three time constants) for the system to respond fully to changes in inspired carbon dioxide.

The increase in pulmonary ventilation in response to stimulation of the central chemoreceptors by hydrogen ions is referred to as the *central chemoreflex*. The drive to breathe from the central chemoreceptors increases linearly with [H+] (or P_{CO_2}) above a chemoreceptor threshold ($\approx$28 mm Hg arterial P_{CO_2}), and the slope of this response is its sensitivity. The central chemoreflex response to any particular P_{CO_2} is therefore determined by both its sensitivity and threshold.

The peripheral chemoreceptors, located in the carotid bodies at the bifurcation of the carotid arteries, are able to "taste" the blood approaching the brain. Signals from the receptors are sent to the respiratory control center in the medulla via the carotid sinus nerve (a branch of the glossopharyngeal or IXth cranial nerve).[48a] The peripheral chemoreceptors respond to both the [H+] and the P_{O_2} of arterial blood, such that, in response to hypoxia, the sensitivity of the chemoreceptor response to [H+] or P_{CO_2} is increased (see Fig. 73.7). Thus, the receptors are maximally stimulated by a simultaneous increase in [H+] and decrease in P_{O_2}—in other words, by asphyxia.[49]

Like the central chemoreflex, the drive to breathe from peripheral chemoreceptors increases linearly with [H+] (or P_{CO_2}) above a chemoreceptor threshold ($\approx$34 mm Hg arterial P_{CO_2}), with the slope of the response representing its sensitivity. Thus, the peripheral chemoreflex response to any particular P_{CO_2} is determined by both its sensitivity and threshold. However, for the peripheral chemoreceptors, the sensitivity of the response also depends on the P_{O_2}, such that hypoxia increases the P_{CO_2} sensitivity markedly, and hyperoxia decreases it almost to zero.

The central and peripheral chemoreceptor drives to breathe summate to provide the chemoreflex drive to breathe, but do not affect pulmonary ventilation until the total ventilatory drive exceeds a drive threshold. Thus, an increase in P_{CO_2} does not increase ventilation until a threshold P_{CO_2} has been exceeded, referred to as the *ventilatory recruitment threshold* P_{CO_2}. Above the threshold, the ventilatory chemoreflex response is linear with a slope (sensitivity) varying with P_{O_2} (see Fig. 73.7). When P_{O_2} is high,

the ventilatory to response carbon dioxide is due almost entirely to the central chemoreflex. When P_{CO_2} is below the ventilatory recruitment threshold, ventilation is maintained above zero by the waking neural drive. However, when this drive is lost during sleep, a P_{CO_2} below the ventilatory recruitment threshold results in apnea (see Chapter 74).

The peripheral chemoreceptors have traditionally been considered to be primarily hypoxia sensors. Although correct in one sense, this notion is somewhat misleading as it implies an independent drive to breathe associated with hypoxia. Although the peripheral chemoreceptors do sense hypoxia, the only effect of hypoxia acutely (as noted previously) is to increase the sensitivity of the chemoreceptors to [H+] (or P_{CO_2}). This feature of the peripheral chemoreflex has two important clinical implications: if the P_{O_2} is high, there is little (if any) peripheral chemoreflex response to P_{CO_2}; and if the P_{CO_2} is low (and therefore below the ventilatory recruitment P_{CO_2} threshold), there is little (if any) peripheral chemoreflex response to hypoxia.[50] However, in the presence of prolonged continuous or intermittent hypoxia, the chemoreflex may undergo modifications.[51]

The graphic representation of the chemoreflex control of breathing is useful for predicting ventilation and P_{CO_2} under a variety of conditions. Figure 73.8 shows one example, that of a sleeping patient recovering from anesthesia and breathing supplemental oxygen. In this case the waking neural drive is absent, the peripheral chemoreflex drive is minimal because the P_{O_2} is high, and the central chemoreflex sensitivity is depressed by the anesthesia. As a result, the patient is operating on the flat portion of the metabolic hyperbola, and, under these conditions, a small decrease in ventilation results in a large increase in P_{CO_2}.

HYPOVENTILATION SYNDROMES

GENERAL PRINCIPLES AND DIAGNOSTIC APPROACH

Pathogenesis

Alveolar hypoventilation exists when arterial P_{CO_2} increases above the normal range of 37 to 43 mm Hg. In clinically important hypoventilation syndromes, arterial P_{CO_2} is

45 mm Hg or higher and typically ranges from 50 to 70 mm Hg.[52-55] Numerous disease entities can result in chronic alveolar hypoventilation (Table 73.1), but in all cases the underlying mechanism involves a defect in either the sensors or the integrating neurons of the metabolic (automatic) respiratory control system or in the effector organs of breathing (i.e., the neuromuscular system or the ventilatory apparatus) (Table 73.2).

Defects in the metabolic control system result in hypoventilation because abnormalities in blood gases and cerebral acid-base status are not sensed or, if sensed, do not produce an appropriate change in motor output of the medullary respiratory neurons. Patients with such defects fail to breathe normally in response to metabolic respiratory stimuli, but because the behavioral control system, respiratory motor pathways, and ventilatory apparatus are intact, they are capable of voluntarily driving respiration. As a result, patients with defects in the metabolic control system typically demonstrate normal ventilatory mechanics, but they have impaired responses to metabolic respiratory stimuli and often hypoventilate severely during sleep, when ventilation is critically dependent on the metabolic control system.[52,56-62] As a result of chronic hypoventilation, these patients have a primary respiratory acidosis leading

to a secondary increase in extracellular bicarbonate ion concentration.[63,64] In contrast, patients with a primary metabolic alkalosis may develop secondary hypoventilation as a compensatory response. This type of hypoventilation represents not a defect in respiratory control but rather an appropriate response of the metabolic control system to a disturbance in acid-base status. It can be said that patients with metabolic alkalosis "shouldn't" breathe, in contrast to those with control defects, who "won't" breathe, and those with mechanical defects, who "can't" breathe. However, the degree of hypoventilation that develops in response to metabolic alkalosis depends on several factors, including associated electrolyte disturbances and the sensitivity of the peripheral chemoreceptors to the accompanying hypoxia.[65,66] Thus, patients with weak hypoxic responsiveness tend to hypoventilate more than do patients with brisk hypoxic responsiveness.

Chronic hypoventilation resulting from defects in effector elements of the respiratory system (see Table 73.2) represents disturbances of ventilatory motor and mechanical function, and these defects do not in themselves mean that the metabolic control system is defective. Because the same effector elements also serve the behavioral control system, these patients are usually unable to breathe normally even when consciously attempting to do so. Hence, such defects are characterized either by reductions in the maximum respiratory pressures that can be generated voluntarily or by impairment of lung volumes and flow rates.[67] In the presence of such neural or mechanical defects, coexisting disturbances in respiratory control are often difficult to identify, because the neuromuscular or mechanical defect may preclude normal responses to chemical respiratory stimuli even when the control system is intact.

Physiologic and Clinical Consequences

Regardless of the underlying cause, the fundamental disturbance in all hypoventilation syndromes is a global reduction in the level of alveolar ventilation, resulting in an

---

Table 73.1 Classification of Disorders Associated with Chronic Alveolar Hypoventilation

Disorders of Chemosensitivity
Carotid body dysfunction, trauma[137]
Prolonged hypoxia[138,139]
Metabolic alkalosis[65]

Disorders of Brain-Stem–Integrating and Rhythm-Generating Networks and Brain-Stem Motor Neurons
Bulbar poliomyelitis, encephalitis[94,105]
Infarction[95,108]
Neoplasms[140]
Sarcoidosis[106]
Demyelinating disorders[107]
Chronic drug administration[141]
Primary alveolar hypoventilation syndrome[57,58,142]

Disorders of Spinal Cord, Peripheral Nerves, and Respiratory Muscles
Poliomyelitis[54,61,73]
Motor neuron disease[67,74,110,111]
Peripheral neuropathy[143]
Myasthenia gravis[54,754]
Muscular dystrophy[54,75,116,117,130]
Chronic myopathy[54,75,116,117]

Disorders of Chest Wall Structure
Obesity-hypoventilation syndrome[53,84,86,92]
Kyphoscoliosis[144]
Fibrothorax[144]
Post-thoracoplasty[144]
Ankylosing spondylitis[144]

Disorders of Lungs and Airways
Chronic obstructive pulmonary disease (Chapter 36)
Cystic fibrosis (Chapter 38)
Laryngeal and tracheal stenosis[145,146]
Obstructive sleep apnea syndrome (Chapter 74)

Table 73.2 Mechanisms Underlying Chronic Alveolar Hypoventilation

Mechanisms Involved	Site or Type of Defect	Major Distinguishing Features
Sensors	Metabolic alkalosis Peripheral chemoreceptors Central chemoreceptors	Alkaline pH Impaired response to hypoxia Impaired response to hyperoxic hypercapnia
Controller	Brain-stem respiratory neurons or networks	Impaired chemoresponses Sleep-induced hypoventilation Normal ventilatory mechanics
Effectors	Neuromuscular apparatus Ventilatory apparatus	Reduced maximal respiratory pressures Impaired ventilatory mechanics

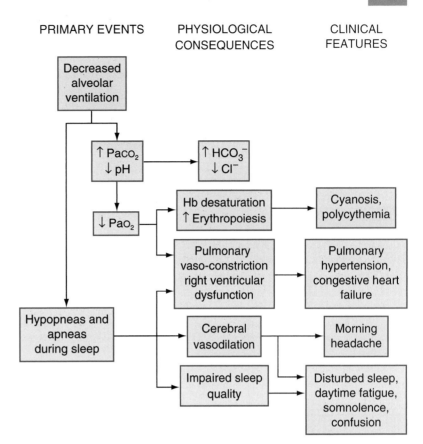

PRIMARY EVENTS   PHYSIOLOGICAL CONSEQUENCES   CLINICAL FEATURES

Figure 73.9 Schema showing the primary events, physiologic responses, and clinical features resulting from alveolar hypoventilation. $Paco_2$, arterial Pco_2; Pao_2, arterial Po_2.

increase in alveolar Pco_2 and therefore in arterial Pco_2. Because of the inverse relationship between alveolar Pco_2 and Po_2 defined by the alveolar air equation, the rise in alveolar Pco_2 produces an obligatory decrease in alveolar Po_2, resulting in hypoxemia (Fig. 73.9). These disturbances are typically magnified during sleep because of further reductions in alveolar ventilation secondary to a reduction in overall respiratory drive (see Chapter 74).

The primary disturbances produced by alveolar hypoventilation lead to a series of secondary physiologic responses that in turn produce the clinical features of chronic hypoventilation (see Fig. 73.9). These features consist predominantly of hematologic, cardiovascular, and neurologic manifestations. There is considerable debate as to whether the cardiovascular and neurologic features of hypoventilation result from the chronic hypercapnia or from the chronic hypoxemia, but it appears likely that both disturbances play a role. For example, alleviation of hypoxemia alone by the administration of supplemental oxygen reverses the polycythemia and may attenuate the severity of pulmonary hypertension, but supplemental oxygen can also aggravate the degree of hypercapnia and the severity of neurologic complaints.[55,68,69]

Laboratory Assessment

The investigation of the patient with chronic alveolar hypoventilation involves the use of a series of laboratory tests that examine one or more components of the respiratory system (Fig. 73.10). Analysis of the pattern of test results usually enables localization of the site of the underlying defect to the metabolic control system, the respiratory neuromuscular system, or the ventilatory apparatus.

Defects in Metabolic Control. The patient with a defect in the chemoreceptors or medullary integrating and premotor neurons that constitute the metabolic control system typically demonstrates impaired ventilatory responses to hypercapnia, hypoxia, asphyxia, and often exercise.[52,56–59,68–70] Because central drive is impaired, occlusion pressure responses and diaphragm electromyographic (EMG) responses to chemical stimuli are also diminished, although few systematic measurements have been reported in these patients. Furthermore, during sleep these patients tend to hypoventilate even more than while awake, as a result of the loss of the stimulatory effect of wakefulness on breathing, and central apneas during sleep may be frequent.[55,59,69–72] In contrast, in the absence of intrinsic bronchopulmonary or chest wall disease, tests of respiratory system resistance and compliance give normal results and the alveolar-arterial Po_2 difference $((A - a)Po_2)$ is not widened. Because the behavioral control system and neuromuscular apparatus are intact, these patients can usually hyperventilate voluntarily and can generate normal lung volumes and flow rates.[56,58,59,64] Similarly, tests of respiratory muscle activation and strength yield normal results, including normal maximum inspiratory and expiratory mouth pressures generated against an occluded airway, normal transdiaphragmatic pressure, and normal diaphragmatic EMG responses.

Neuromuscular Defects. Patients with defects in the spinal cord, respiratory nerves, or respiratory muscles resemble

SITE OF DEFECT   TEST RESULTS

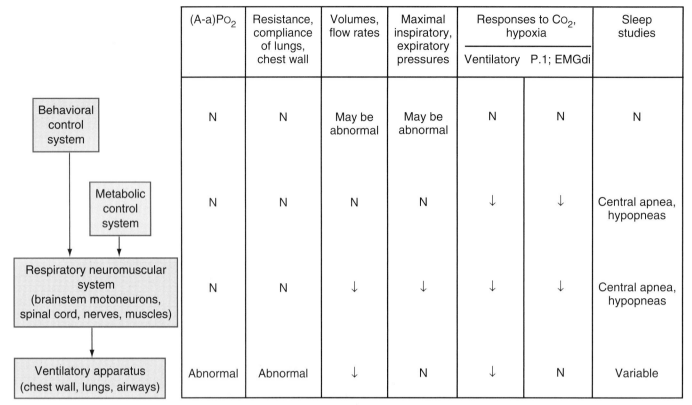

	(A-a)PO$_2$	Resistance, compliance of lungs, chest wall	Volumes, flow rates	Maximal inspiratory, expiratory pressures	Responses to CO$_2$, hypoxia — Ventilatory	Responses to CO$_2$, hypoxia — P.1; EMGdi	Sleep studies
Behavioral control system	N	N	May be abnormal	May be abnormal	N	N	N
Metabolic control system	N	N	N	N	↓	↓	Central apnea, hypopneas
Respiratory neuromuscular system (brainstem motoneurons, spinal cord, nerves, muscles)	N	N	↓	↓	↓	↓	Central apnea, hypopneas
Ventilatory apparatus (chest wall, lungs, airways)	Abnormal	Abnormal	↓	N	↓	N	Variable

Figure 73.10 Pattern of laboratory test results in alveolar hypoventilation syndromes, based on the site of defect. (A − a)PO$_2$, alveolar-arterial PO$_2$ difference; EMGdi, diaphragmatic electromyogram; N, normal; P.1, pressure generated in first 1/10 second after airway occlusion.

patients with disturbances in the control system, in that the former also have impaired ventilatory, occlusion pressure, and EMG responses to chemical respiratory stimuli.[54,67,73–76] In addition, however, patients with neuromuscular disease are unable to generate normal lung volumes (particularly total lung capacity), flow rates (particularly peak flow and maximum voluntary ventilation), and static respiratory pressures.[67]

Ventilatory Apparatus Defects. Patients with intrinsic disease of the lungs, airways, or chest wall demonstrate abnormalities in the values of respiratory resistance or compliance. Because of these abnormalities, values of lung volumes and flow rates are typically abnormal, and ventilatory responses to chemical respiratory stimuli are impaired. In contrast, because the respiratory neuromuscular system is intact in these patients, static tests of respiratory muscle strength and activity, which are not influenced by the resistance or compliance of the respiratory system, usually yield normal results.[77,78] Thus, maximum inspiratory and expiratory pressures, transdiaphragmatic pressure, and occlusion pressure and diaphragm EMG responses to hypercapnia or hypoxia may be quite normal.[79–81]

PRIMARY ALVEOLAR HYPOVENTILATION

Primary alveolar hypoventilation is a disorder of unknown origin characterized by chronic hypercapnia and hypoxemia

in the absence of identifiable neurologic disease, respiratory muscle weakness, or mechanical ventilatory defects. The disorder is considered to occur from a failure in the metabolic (or automatic) respiratory control system, which results in a diminished central respiratory drive. In most patients, hypoventilation is more severe during sleep, and apneic periods are common. In contrast, because the behavioral respiratory control system is intact, patients with primary alveolar hypoventilation are able to hyperventilate voluntarily and to reduce arterial PCO$_2$ to normal levels.

The clinical syndrome of primary alveolar hypoventilation in its isolated form is a relatively rare disease. However, an element of primary alveolar hypoventilation may play a role in several clinical disorders of the respiratory neuromuscular and ventilatory systems in which the degree of alveolar hypoventilation is out of keeping with the magnitude of underlying neuromuscular or mechanical defect. Such disorders include diseases of the respiratory muscles,[82] the obesity-hypoventilation syndrome,[53,82–86] and the "blue bloater" chronic obstructive pulmonary disease syndrome.[80,81] In these disorders, the impairment of the respiratory muscles or the increased mechanical impedance to breathing may unmask a weakness in central respiratory drive,[87] analogous to the weakness that can be uncovered in some otherwise healthy subjects by the imposition of mechanical ventilatory loads.[88] However, whether the underlying cause of decreased respiratory drive in these patients is the same as in patients with isolated primary alveolar hypoventilation is not known.

Pathogenesis

Primary alveolar hypoventilation is thought to result from a failure of the chemoreceptors or of the medullary neuronal networks that make up the metabolic respiratory control system. As such, it represents a pure disease of the respiratory controller rather than of the respiratory muscles or mechanical ventilatory apparatus. In the majority of patients, this interpretation is based on the clinical and laboratory features of the illness and not on the demonstration of specific lesions in any component of the metabolic control system. In fact, autopsy studies have reported neuropathologic findings in extremely few patients and have found either no abnormalities or only nonspecific lesions in the area of the medullary respiratory neurons.[2] However, studies in both animals and humans indicate an important role for genetic and metabolic factors in the pathogenesis of hypoventilation syndromes.[62,89–93] In contrast to primary alveolar hypoventilation, lesions involving the medullary reticular formation have been demonstrated in several patients with central alveolar hypoventilation secondary to known neurologic disease.[2,94–97] In some infants who died of sudden infant death syndrome, which may represent a primary alveolar hypoventilation disorder, structural abnormalities of the carotid body chemoreceptors have been demonstrated.[98] Removal of the carotid bodies in experimental animals results in a chronic hypoventilation syndrome that closely resembles the human disorder.[99] However, no studies of carotid body structure have been reported in patients with primary alveolar hypoventilation.

Clinical Features

Primary alveolar hypoventilation occurs in all age groups, including infancy and childhood,[62,91,100] but the majority of reported cases in adults have been in men 20 to 50 years of age.[56–59,71] Rare familial cases have been described.[101] In most patients, the development of symptoms is insidious, and the disease is often overlooked because the patient is typically free of respiratory complaints. In particular, dyspnea is uncommon in this condition, in contrast to other hypoventilation disorders, and the arterial PCO_2 may be relatively normal when measured during wakefulness. Often, the diagnosis is first suspected only when the patient develops severe respiratory depression after conventional doses of anesthesia or sedation.

The common presenting complaints of patients with primary alveolar hypoventilation are lethargy, fatigue, daytime somnolence, disturbed sleep, and morning headache (see Fig. 73.9). Cyanosis and secondary polycythemia are also frequent. As the severity of chronic hypoventilation and hypoxemia increases, patients develop clinical evidence of pulmonary hypertension, right ventricular hypertrophy, and, eventually, congestive cardiac failure. The congestive heart failure is due to right ventricular dysfunction and is manifested by elevation of the jugular venous pressure, hepatomegaly, and peripheral edema.

Diagnosis

The key diagnostic findings in primary alveolar hypoventilation are hypercapnia, hypoxemia, and chronic respiratory acidosis in the absence of respiratory muscle weakness or mechanical ventilatory defects (see Fig. 73.10). The degree of blood gas abnormality is often surprising, in that arterial PCO_2 levels of 50 to 70 mm Hg and arterial PO_2 levels of 40 to 50 mm Hg may be associated with relatively mild symptoms. Typically, patients can voluntarily hyperventilate and reduce the arterial PCO_2 to normal or even to hypocapnic levels. As a result, hypercapnia may not be detected in a single arterial blood sample, but the presence of an elevated serum bicarbonate should draw attention to the underlying chronic disturbance. The $(A - a)PO_2$ is usually normal but may be elevated, presumably because of areas of low ventilation-perfusion matching or microatelectasis, although the mechanism has not been clearly defined.

In addition to normal lung volumes and airflow rates, patients with primary alveolar hypoventilation typically maintain a normal maximum voluntary ventilation and normal maximum inspiratory and expiratory airway pressures (see Fig. 73.10). In contrast, the ventilatory and occlusion pressure responses to hypercapnia are reduced or absent, and the responses to hypoxia are often diminished.[52,56–59,70] In most patients, some hypoxic chemosensitivity persists, in that inhalation of high oxygen concentrations further reduces the level of ventilation.[52,69] Paradoxically, in a few patients, supplemental oxygen produces an increase in ventilation, which suggests that chronic hypoxia may have contributed to central respiratory depression.[57,59] In the typical patient, the ventilatory response to exercise is also abnormal, with further increases in arterial PCO_2 and decreases in arterial PO_2, in keeping with a failure of metabolic respiratory control. Breath-holding time may be markedly prolonged, without any accompanying sensation of dyspnea.[56]

Patients with primary alveolar hypoventilation are generally able to maintain rhythmic breathing during wakefulness, although at a lower than normal level of ventilation, because of the stimulatory effect of brain-stem reticular activation on the respiratory neurons.[62,102,103] During sleep, however, breathing is critically dependent on the metabolic respiratory control system.[102] Hence, these patients are apt to cease rhythmic breathing during sleep. Sleep studies in patients with alveolar hypoventilation usually demonstrate a further deterioration in ventilation, with frequent episodes of central hypopnea or outright apnea followed by arousal or awakening. These sleep-related events presumably account for the clinical complaints of disturbed sleep and morning headache; they contribute to daytime fatigue, lethargy, and somnolence; and they play a role in the development of polycythemia and pulmonary hypertension. Support for this concept is derived from the fact that the daytime symptoms of primary alveolar hypoventilation, as well as the polycythemia and pulmonary hypertension, can be alleviated by improving nocturnal ventilation alone.[56,59]

Differential Diagnosis

Primary alveolar hypoventilation, in which there is no other identifiable neurologic disease, must be distinguished from central alveolar hypoventilation secondary to underlying neurologic disease (see Table 73.1), although the clinical and laboratory features of the two disorders are often very similar. This distinction requires a careful neurologic history and examination for evidence of other brain-stem or autonomic disturbances. The classic example of chronic alveolar hypoventilation secondary to brain-stem disease is that which follows bulbar poliomyelitis or encephalitis.[61,94,104,105] The disorder has also been reported in association with brain-stem vascular insufficiency or stroke, infections, neoplasms, sarcoidosis, multiple sclerosis, and autonomic insufficiency syndromes.[2,95,97,106–108] These secondary causes of central alveolar hypoventilation are usually signified by the other features of the underlying disease process and by the fact that the patient may not be able to increase the level of ventilation voluntarily. A form of subacute central alveolar hypoventilation that follows cervical cordotomy for pain and other forms of spinal surgery has also been described.[109]

Primary alveolar hypoventilation can be confused with chronic disorders of the respiratory neuromuscular system (see Chapter 82) that are often unrecognized clinically (see Table 73.1). Increasingly common in this group of disorders is the postpolio syndrome, a form of chronic respiratory insufficiency that typically develops 20 to 30 years after recovery from poliomyelitis.[61,73] In addition to the history of polio many years earlier, these patients demonstrate weakness of the respiratory muscles (see Fig. 73.10), and many have developed kyphoscoliosis. Motoneuron disease, an idiopathic degeneration of motoneurons from anterior horn cells to cortex, can manifest as chronic respiratory failure, particularly when the phrenic motoneurons are involved.[67,74,110,111] The disease typically occurs in men 50 to 70 years old and is distinguished from primary alveolar hypoventilation by the presence of muscle weakness and atrophy, often with fasciculation and spasticity. Laboratory investigation reveals a pattern of test results typical of respiratory neuromuscular disease (see Fig. 73.10). Furthermore, the abnormalities are progressive, as is the clinical course of the disease; death, from respiratory complications, usually occurs 2 to 5 years after onset of the disease.

Unilateral diaphragmatic paralysis can result from phrenic nerve trauma, inflammation, or neoplastic infiltration, but in most cases the cause is unknown.[112–115] Patients with unilateral diaphragmatic paralysis are often asymptomatic and do not usually hypoventilate. Bilateral diaphragm weakness or paralysis can result from phrenic neuropathy or from intrinsic diaphragmatic disease, including muscular dystrophies, polymyositis, and acid maltase deficiency.[54,75,76,116–118] Bilateral diaphragmatic disease may lead to severe chronic alveolar hypoventilation. Distinguishing features include the presence of orthopnea, paradoxical movement of the abdomen in the supine posture, deterioration in lung volumes and in arterial blood gas values in the supine posture, rapid deterioration in ventilation during a maximum voluntary ventilation maneuver, and reduction of the maximum inspiratory pressures that can be generated against an occluded airway. Transdiaphragmatic pressures, calculated from simultaneous measurement of esophageal and gastric pressures, are reduced or absent, and the EMG response of the diaphragm, recorded by an esophageal electrode, reveals a reduction in diaphragm discharge in response to transcutaneous phrenic nerve stimulation in the neck.[54,118–120]

Management

Patients with primary alveolar hypoventilation must be cautioned against the use of sedative medications, which may

Table 73.3 Management of Primary Alveolar Hypoventilation

Pharmacologic techniques	Respiratory stimulant drugs (progesterone, acetazolamide) Supplemental oxygen
Mechanical techniques	Rocking bed Negative-pressure ventilator Positive-pressure ventilator Phrenic nerve stimulation

readily induce acute respiratory failure. Respiratory stimulants may be useful in some patients. Several pharmacologic agents, including methylxanthines and analeptics, have been used to treat patients with primary alveolar hypoventilation (Table 73.3), with variable but generally disappointing results. Long-term administration of progesterone has been beneficial in some patients, particularly those with mechanical ventilatory defects and an element of reduced respiratory drive, such as the obesity-hypoventilation syndrome and hypercapnic obstructive lung disease.[121–123] Acetazolamide is effective in increasing respiratory drive in patients with primary metabolic alkalosis superimposed on chronic carbon dioxide retention,[124] but is not indicated in pure respiratory acidosis. A few patients with primary alveolar hypoventilation have responded favorably to long-term nocturnal oxygen administration, which suggests that cerebral hypoxia during sleep was aggravating the hypoventilation disorder.[59,69] However, in the majority of patients, supplemental oxygen aggravates the degree of nocturnal hypoventilation and further increases arterial carbon dioxide levels by removing hypoxic ventilatory drive.

In most patients with primary alveolar hypoventilation, neuromuscular disease, or the obesity-hypoventilation syndrome, mechanical ventilatory assistance is required for effective management (see Table 73.3). Noninvasive positive-pressure ventilation, delivered through a nasal mask, is currently the preferred method of treatment,[55,125–133] but diaphragmatic pacing by electrophrenic stimulation can also be very effective.[56,134–136] The administration of this treatment only during sleep generally produces dramatic clinical improvement, with alleviation of daytime symptoms, reversal of polycythemia and pulmonary hypertension, and lowering of daytime arterial PCO_2 values.

HYPERVENTILATION SYNDROMES

Hyperventilation refers to an increase in the rate of alveolar ventilation that is excessive for the rate of metabolic carbon dioxide production, resulting in a decrease in arterial PCO_2 to below the normal range of 37 to 43 mm Hg. Hyperventilation should be distinguished from *tachypnea*, an increase in respiratory frequency, and from *hyperpnea*, an increase in minute volume of ventilation. Neither of these conditions derives from nor implies a change in arterial PCO_2. Hyperventilation is often associated with dyspnea, but not all patients with hyperventilation complain of shortness of breath; conversely, patients with dyspnea need not be hyperventilating.

INPUTS   CONTROL SYSTEMS

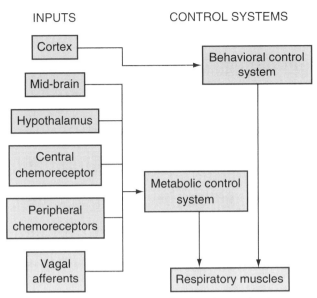

Figure 73.11 Schematic diagram showing the mechanisms involved in alveolar hyperventilation.

Table 73.4 Hyperventilation Syndromes
Hypoxemia High altitude Pulmonary disease Cardiac shunts
Pulmonary Disorders Pneumonia Interstitial pneumonitis, fibrosis, edema Pulmonary embolic or vascular disease Bronchial asthma Pneumothorax Chest wall disorders
Cardiovascular Disorders Congestive heart failure Hypotension
Metabolic Disorders Acidosis (diabetic, renal, lactic) Hyperthyroidism Hepatic failure
Neurologic and Psychogenic Disorders Psychogenic or anxiety hyperventilation Central nervous system infection, tumors, infarction
Drug-Induced Salicylates Methylxanthine derivatives β-Adrenergic agonists Progesterone
Miscellaneous Fever, sepsis Pain Pregnancy

From Phillipson EA: Disorders of ventilation. *In* Fauci AS, Braunwald E, Isselbacher KJ, et al (eds): Harrison's Principles of Internal Medicine (14th ed). New York: McGraw-Hill, 1998, pp 1476–1480.

PATHOGENESIS

Alveolar hyperventilation arises from excessive ventilatory drive that is mediated through either the behavioral or the metabolic control system (Fig. 73.11). Many pathophysiologic conditions and diseases can result in an increase in respiratory drive (Table 73.4). In some cases, the mechanism involved is well understood (e.g., hypoxemic sensitization of the peripheral chemoreceptors); in other cases, several potential mechanisms have been postulated but as yet have not been clearly established (e.g., hyperventilation associated with hepatic failure). Therefore, hyperventilation syndromes are best considered through the use of a clinical rather than mechanistic approach (see Table 73.4).

Hypoxemia

In most clinical settings, hypoxemia is a potent ventilatory stimulus and results in hyperventilation by virtue of its action on the peripheral chemoreceptors (i.e., the carotid bodies). The response of minute volume of ventilation (or alveolar ventilation) to decreases in arterial PO_2 is not linear: it is substantially greater when arterial PO_2 falls below 60 mm Hg.[147] In contrast, although the oxygen content per se of arterial blood is not the primary hypoxic stimulus of the carotid bodies, the ventilatory response to hypoxemia is relatively linear with regard to decreases in arterial oxygen saturation.[147,148] However, the magnitude of response is attenuated by reduced levels of arterial PCO_2 and increased levels of arterial pH (see "Control of Breathing" section earlier). The hyperventilation associated with hypoxia can be dramatic, particularly in persons with normal ventilatory mechanics. For example, at the summit of Mount Everest, where arterial PO_2 was estimated to be 27 mm Hg, alveolar PCO_2 was reduced to 7.5 mm Hg.[149] Clinically, however, impaired mechanical properties of the chest wall or lungs often attenuate the degree of alveolar hyperventilation induced by hypoxia. Conversely, in many pulmonary disor-

ders that produce hypoxemia, the associated hypocapnia may not be due to the hypoxia and persists even when the hypoxia is alleviated with supplemental oxygen.[150]

The degree of alveolar hyperventilation induced by hypoxia is highly variable; the variation is determined, at least in part, by genetic factors.[151] In addition, there also appears to be a temporal influence that may, in part, reflect the effects of hypoxia on cerebral blood flow, metabolism, and release of excitatory and inhibitory neuromodulators, all of which secondarily affect breathing.[152–154] Typically, the ventilatory response to acute hypoxia is initially brisk but then decreases after several minutes,[155,156] only to increase again after 12 to 24 hours as the longer term process of respiratory acclimatization comes into play. However, sustained hypoxemia of many years' duration, as occurs in long-time residents at high altitudes and in patients with cyanotic congenital heart disease, is associated with considerable attenuation of hypoxic ventilatory drive.[157,158]

Pulmonary Disorders

One of the most common causes of hyperventilation in patients with pulmonary disease is stimulation of bronchopulmonary receptors that reflexly increase ventilatory drive and, directly or indirectly, contribute to the sensation of dyspnea (see Chapter 28). These receptors, which are sensitive to a variety of mechanical and chemical stimuli, send impulses to the central nervous system through the afferent vagus nerves, resulting in cough, bronchoconstriction, and hyperventilation (see "Control of Breathing" section earlier). Direct evidence implicating these receptors in the alveolar hyperventilation of lung disease is derived largely from animal studies,[159,160] but there are also supportive studies in a few patients who have undergone vagal blockade.[161] Indirect support for this notion is derived from the fact that administration of supplemental oxygen to patients with hypoxemic interstitial or pulmonary vascular disease does not necessarily abolish the hyperventilation.[150,162-164]

Stimulation of chest wall receptors may contribute to the hyperventilation that accompanies asthma, pulmonary fibrosis, and restrictive chest wall disorders.[159,165] The mechanisms involved have not been clearly established but are thought to include stimulation of respiratory muscle spindles and other chest wall receptors. The same mechanisms may also play a role in the pathogenesis of dyspnea in these disorders.

Cardiovascular Disorders

Patients with congestive heart failure and states of low cardiac output typically hyperventilate at rest, during exercise, and even during sleep.[166-170] The mechanisms involved probably include stimulation of pulmonary vascular and interstitial receptors as a result of pulmonary congestion.[171] In addition, low cardiac output states and hypotension stimulate breathing through the arterial baroreceptors[172] and may also stimulate breathing secondary to "stagnant hypoxia" of the carotid body chemoreceptor cells.

Metabolic Disorders

Alveolar hyperventilation is a well-described compensatory response to metabolic acidosis. Although respiratory compensation is generally effective, physiologic compensation for metabolic acidosis is not complete. For example, in a severe metabolic acidosis that reduces serum bicarbonate levels to 8 mEq/L, the uncompensated arterial pH would be 6.92; with hyperventilation to 20 mm Hg (a typical response), pH increases to 7.22. The degree of compensation varies among patients, depending on differences in chemosensitivity and ventilatory mechanics, but in general a decrease in bicarbonate level of 1 mEq/L results in a compensatory decrease in arterial PCO_2 of about 1 mm Hg.[173,174] The specific mechanisms involved in the hyperventilation of metabolic acidosis are controversial, but probably include stimulation of both the peripheral and central chemoreceptors.[175-178] Metabolic acidosis also increases the sensitivity of the peripheral chemoreceptors to hypoxia.

Hyperthyroidism is frequently associated with hyperventilation and increased ventilatory chemoreflexes, both of which return to normal after treatment.[179] Hyperventilation is also a common feature in patients with severe liver disease.[180,1181] Several possible mechanisms have been proposed, including increased blood levels of progesterone, ammonia, and vasoactive intestinal peptide, and increased brain levels of ammonia and glutamine, all of which may stimulate respiration.[154,180,181] In addition, patients with severe hepatocellular dysfunction or portal hypertension may develop small pulmonary arteriovenous anastomoses ("spider nevi" of the lungs) or portal-pulmonary venous shunts, resulting in hypoxemia and hyperventilation due to stimulation of the peripheral chemoreceptors.

Neurologic and Psychogenic Disorders

Psychogenic hyperventilation[182-185] is thought to arise from anxiety or stress, both of which act on the behavioral respiratory control system (see Fig. 73.11). In support of this mechanism is the fact that this type of hyperventilation usually abates during sleep, when the behavioral control system is quiescent and breathing is driven by the metabolic system.[102,184] Apart from psychogenic causes, central neurogenic hyperventilation is relatively rare.[2] Indeed, in most patients with intracranial disturbances who are hyperventilating, the immediate cause is either pulmonary edema or hypoxemia.[186,187] In rare cases, however, disorders of the midbrain and hypothalamus induce hyperventilation.[2] In addition, patients with head trauma or intracranial hemorrhage may hyperventilate as a secondary reaction to red blood cell glycolysis and acidosis in the cerebrospinal fluid, and patients with brain-stem infiltration by tumor may hyperventilate as a result of lactic acidosis produced by the malignant cells.[186-190] In other rare cases, severe cerebrovascular insufficiency or infarction is associated with hyperventilation, possibly by interference with the inhibitory influence normally exerted by cortical structures on the brain-stem respiratory neurons.[191-193]

Drug-Induced Hyperventilation

Several drugs cause hyperventilation[194] by stimulating the peripheral or central chemoreceptors or by direct action on the brain-stem respiratory neurons (see Table 73.4). The acid-base disturbance resulting from salicylate overdose is biphasic, consisting of an initial primary respiratory alkalosis followed by a metabolic acidosis that induces secondary hyperventilation.[195,196]

Miscellaneous Causes

Fever and sepsis, even in the absence of hypotension, are commonly associated with hyperventilation, over and above any associated increase in metabolic rate.[197-199] The mechanisms involved are not clear, but they could include either carotid body or hypothalamic stimulation by increased temperature. Pain is also frequently accompanied by hyperventilation.[200] The mechanisms involved may include adrenergic stimulation of the peripheral and central chemoreceptors.[201,202] In addition, painful stimuli may act through the behavioral control system. From a practical clinical standpoint, there is often concern that a painful arterial puncture required for blood gas assessment could result in a spuriously low arterial PCO_2 and inappropriate diagnosis of hyperventilation. However, there is little difference in arterial PCO_2 between samples obtained with and without the use of local anesthetic.[203] Chronic hyperventilation is a normal feature of pregnancy and of the luteal phase of the menstrual cycle and may result from the effects of progesterone (and perhaps other hormones) acting directly on the medullary respiratory neurons.[204–206]

PHYSIOLOGIC AND CLINICAL FEATURES

Respiratory

Because hyperventilation involves an increase in respiratory drive, respiratory muscle effort, and minute volume of ventilation, the most frequent symptom associated with hyperventilation is dyspnea. However, there is considerable discrepancy between the degree of hyperventilation, as assessed by arterial PCO_2, and the degree of dyspnea.

From a physiologic standpoint, hyperventilation is clearly beneficial in patients who are hypoxemic because the alveolar hypocapnia is associated with an increase in alveolar PO_2 and with a varied increase in arterial PO_2 (dependent on pulmonary ventilation-perfusion inhomogeneities). The relationship among these variables is governed by the alveolar air equation (see Chapter 4). This physiologic consequence of hyperventilation is clinically important in patients with hypoxemic pulmonary disease and in healthy persons at high altitude. Indeed, the successful ascent of Mount Everest without the use of supplemental oxygen was critically dependent on the increase in alveolar and arterial PO_2 generated by profound alveolar hyperventilation.[149]

Conversely, alveolar hyperventilation can also have detrimental respiratory effects, including a decrease in or loss of respiratory drive immediately after cessation of the hyperventilation, secondary to the low arterial and cerebral PCO_2. Under these conditions, hypoxemia can develop quickly without an associated return of respiratory drive or a sensation of dyspnea, because of the persisting hypocapnia that reverses at a considerably slower rate. This sequence of events has been implicated in the deaths of healthy underwater divers who, in advance of diving, voluntarily hyperventilate to decrease alveolar PCO_2 and increase alveolar oxygen stores, and thereby prolong underwater breath-holding time. A less dramatic but more common clinical problem resulting from hyperventilation during wakefulness is periodic breathing during sleep, with or without associated central sleep apnea. This sequence of events gives rise to the most common type of central sleep apnea syndrome (see Chapter 74).

Blood

Respiratory alkalosis produces a leftward shift in the oxygen-hemoglobin dissociation curve (the Bohr effect), which increases loading of oxygen onto hemoglobin in the lungs but decreases release of oxygen at the tissue level. This change can be beneficial or detrimental, depending on the specific conditions. In general, the detrimental effects of impaired oxygen release at the tissues outweigh the beneficial effects of increased oxygen loading in the lungs, because even under conditions of moderate hypoxemia, hemoglobin is well saturated with oxygen without a leftward shift of the dissociation curve (e.g., at an arterial PO_2 of 60 mm Hg, hemoglobin is 90% saturated). However, under conditions of severe hypoxia, as at very high altitudes or in utero, the loading of oxygen onto hemoglobin becomes critical to survival, and therefore a respiratory alkalosis and the resulting leftward shift of the dissociation curve can be beneficial.

Respiratory alkalosis also results in several electrolyte shifts that are clinically important, including hypokalemia, hypophosphatemia, and decreased ionizable calcium.[207–210] These shifts contribute to many of the clinical features of hyperventilation, including dizziness, peripheral paresthesias, carpopedal spasm, tetany, and muscle weakness.

Cardiovascular and Cerebrovascular

The most important clinical consequences of alveolar hyperventilation are those related to vasoconstriction, that is secondary to alkalemia.[211–214] Severe alkalemia can induce cardiac arrhythmias (possibly related to electrolyte disturbances) and cardiac ischemia, which probably results from both acute coronary vasoconstriction and the increased oxygen affinity of hemoglobin.[212–216] Alkalemia also induces intense cerebrovascular constriction that can result in dizziness, visual impairment, syncope, and seizures.[152,183,217] Acutely, every 1 mm Hg decrease in arterial PCO_2 reduces cerebral blood flow by 2%,[218] resulting in cerebral hypoxia, as assessed by metabolic, electroencephalographic, and corneoretinal indices and by direct measurements of cerebral PO_2.[219–222] In patients with sickle cell disease, the degree of cerebral hypoxia may be sufficient to induce red blood cell sickling and cerebral infarction.[223] In general, the severity of cerebral vasoconstriction induced by hyperventilation decreases within hours, as the degree of cerebral alkalosis is attenuated.[183,224]

DIAGNOSIS

Although hyperventilation may be suspected clinically in the presence of tachypnea or noticeable hyperpnea, the diagnosis can be confirmed only by analysis of arterial blood gases and pH. The key measurements are the arterial PCO_2, a decrease in which indicates the presence of hyperventilation, and the pH, which determines whether the disorder is classified as a primary respiratory alkalosis (increased pH) or a primary metabolic acidosis (decreased pH).[173,174] However, in mixed acid-base disorders, arterial pH may not be alkalemic despite primary alveolar hyperventilation. Measurement of arterial PO_2 and calculation of $(A - a)PO_2$ is also helpful, because a widened $(A - a)PO_2$ suggests a pulmonary disorder as the underlying cause of the hyperventilation. The finding of a decreased serum bicarbonate concentration establishes the chronic nature of the disorder and points to an organic cause, as opposed to psychogenic hyperventilation. In patients with suspected psychogenic hyperventilation, measurements of minute volume of ventilation and of arterial or transcutaneous PCO_2 during sleep can be useful because the hyperventilation does not usually persist during sleep.

Once the presence of alveolar hyperventilation has been established, the underlying cause can generally be identified on the basis of history, physical examination, and knowledge of coexisting medical disorders (see Table 73.4). Two disorders may not be readily apparent clinically and frequently give rise to "unexplained hyperventilation": pulmonary vascular disease (particularly chronic or recurrent thromboembolism) and psychogenic or anxiety hyperventilation.[183,185] However, the two disorders can usually be identified and distinguished on the basis of clinical and laboratory features. Hyperventilation secondary to pulmonary vascular disease is invariably accompanied by exertional dyspnea and often by exertional presyncope and clinical signs of pulmonary arterial hypertension. In addition, these patients usually have a widened $(A - a)P_{O_2}$, often have a reduced pulmonary diffusing capacity for carbon monoxide, and usually maintain their hyperventilation during exercise. In contrast, patients with psychogenic hyperventilation typically complain of the need to sigh frequently and of dyspnea at rest and not necessarily during exercise.[184,225] Symptoms of acute hyperventilation, including paresthesias, carpopedal spasm, and tetany, are frequent, and anxiety is often prominent.[225] Half the patients present with cardiovascular symptoms, including palpitation, tachycardia, and chest pain, and about 25% present with neurologic complaints, including lightheadedness, headache, or memory impairment.[183,225] In contrast to pulmonary vascular disease, in psychogenic hyperventilation the $(A - a) P_{O_2}$ and pulmonary function tests yield normal results, and during mild to moderate exercise, the hyperventilation tends to disappear. However, during exercise, heart rate and cardiac output may be high in relation to metabolic rate.

MANAGEMENT

Alveolar hyperventilation can usually be managed by appropriate treatment of the underlying cause (see Table 73.4). However, in the few patients in whom alkalemia is thought to be inducing acute cerebral vasoconstriction, cardiac arrhythmias or ischemia, or paresthesias and tetany, inhalation of a low concentration of carbon dioxide can provide relief.

The long-term management of patients with disabling psychogenic hyperventilation can be problematic. Careful explanation of the basis of the symptoms is helpful and reassures the patient that no serious cardiac or cerebral disorder is present. Such reassurance is often sufficient to allay the patient's anxiety. If not, more intense psychotherapy or medications that relieve anxiety maybe required.[187,226,227] Some patients have responded well to β-adrenergic antagonists or to an exercise program.[202,228]

SUMMARY

Alveolar hypoventilation can result from numerous disease entities but is ultimately attributable to defects in the metabolic respiratory control system, the respiratory neuromuscular system, or the ventilatory apparatus. Detailed clinical and laboratory investigations can generally distinguish among these underlying mechanisms and locate the site of the defect. In most patients, alveolar hypoventilation is secondary to obstructive airway disease, mechanical chest wall disturbances, neurologic disease affecting the brain stem or spinal cord, or respiratory muscle weakness. In a small percentage of cases, no underlying cause can be found, and these patients are said to have primary alveolar hypoventilation, which is considered to represent a failure of the metabolic respiratory control system. Patients with primary alveolar hypoventilation are able to hyperventilate volun-

tarily, but during sleep, hypoventilation becomes more severe and central apneas are common. Management of patients with primary alveolar hypoventilation, as well as those with respiratory neuromuscular disorders, usually involves mechanical ventilatory assistance. Administration of such treatment only during sleep often produces dramatic clinical improvement and alleviates daytime symptoms.

Hyperventilation can result from several diseases that produce an increase in respiratory drive, including disorders associated with hypoxemia, pulmonary vascular and interstitial disease, congestive heart failure, metabolic acidosis, intracranial disorders, anxiety, and drugs. Patients who are hyperventilating may complain of dyspnea, but there is often a considerable discrepancy between the degree of hyperventilation, as assessed by arterial P_{CO_2}, and the degree of dyspnea. Hyperventilation may produce important secondary effects on respiratory drive, on the unloading of oxygen from hemoglobin at the tissue level, and on cardiac and cerebral function. The underlying cause of hyperventilation can often be identified by the associated clinical features and measurements of arterial blood gases, pH, bicarbonate, and the $(A - a)$ P_{O_2}. The two disorders that most frequently give rise to "unexplained hyperventilation" are pulmonary vascular disease and anxiety, or psychogenic hyperventilation. Treatment of hyperventilation is generally directed at the underlying disorder.

REFERENCES

1. Plum F: Neurological integration of behavioral and metabolic control of breathing. *In* Porter R (ed): Breathing: Hering-Breuer Centenary Symposium. London: Churchill, 1970, pp 159–181.
2. Plum F, Leigh RJ: Abnormalities of central mechanisms. *In* Hornbein TF (ed): Lung Biology in Health and Disease. Vol 17: Regulation of Breathing (Part 2). New York: Marcel Dekker, 1981, pp 989–1067.
3. Phillipson EA, McClean PA, Sullivan CE, et al: Interaction of metabolic and behavioral respiratory control during hypercapnia and speech. Am Rev Respir Dis 117:903–909, 1978.
4. Orem J, Trotter RH: Behavioral control of breathing. News Physiol Sci 9:228–232, 1994.
5. Shea SA: Behavioural and arousal-related influences on breathing in humans. Exp Physiol 81:1–26, 1996.
6. Murphy K, Corfield DR, Guz A, et al: Cerebral areas associated with motor control of speech in humans. J Appl Physiol 83:1438–1447, 1997.
7. Horn EM, Waldrop TG: Suprapontine control of respiration. Respir Physiol 114:201–211, 1998.
8. Killian KJ: Sense of effort and dyspnoea. Monaldi Arch Chest Dis 53:654–660, 1998.
9. Manning HL, Mahler DA: Pathophysiology of dyspnea. Monaldi Arch Chest Dis 56:325–330, 2001.
10. Bianchi AL, Denavit-Saubié M, Champagnat J: Central control of breathing in mammals: Neuronal circuitry, membrane properties, and neurotransmitters. Physiol Rev 75:1–45, 1995.
11. Feldman JL, McCrimmon DR: Neural control of breathing. *In* Zigmond MJ, Bloom FE, Landis SC, et al (eds): Fundamental Neuroscience. New York: Academic Press, 1999, pp 1063–1090.
12. Lipski J, Duffin J: An electrophysiological investigation of propriospinal inspiratory neurons in the upper cervical cord of the cat. Exp Brain Res 61:625–637, 1986.

13. Lipski J, Duffin J, Kruszewska B, et al: Upper cervical inspiratory neurons in the rat: An electrophysiological and morphological study. Exp Brain Res 95:477–487, 1993.

14. Tian GF, Duffin J: Connections from upper cervical inspiratory neurons to phrenic and intercostal motoneurons studied with cross-correlation in the decerebrate rat. Exp Brain Res 110:196–204, 1996.

15. Berger AJ: Phrenic motoneurons in the cat: Subpopulations and nature of respiratory drive potentials. J Neurophysiol 42:76–90, 1979.

16. Kirkwood PA, Munson JB, Westgaard RH, et al: The organization of the respiratory input to intercostal motoneurones: The contribution from interneurones. In Sieck GC, Gandevia SC, Cameron WE (eds): Respiratory Muscles and Their Neuromotor Control. New York: Alan R Liss, 1987, pp 157–166.

17. Iscoe S: Control of abdominal muscles. Prog Neurobiol 56:433–506, 1998.

18. Kirkwood PA, Schmid K, Sears TA: Functional identities of thoracic respiratory interneurones in the cat. J Physiol (Lond) 461:667–687, 1993.

19. Ezure K: Synaptic connections between medullary respiratory neurons and considerations on the genesis of respiratory rhythm. Prog Neurobiol 35:429–450, 1990.

20. Richter DW, Spyer KM: Studying rhythmogenesis of breathing: Comparison of in vivo and in vitro models. Trends Neurosci 24:464–472, 2001.

21. Ezure K, Tanaka I, Saito Y, et al: Axonal projections of pulmonary slowly adapting receptor relay neurons in the rat. J Comp Neurol 446:81–94, 2002.

22. Nunez-Abades PA, Pasaro R, Bianchi AL: Study of the topographical distribution of different populations of motoneurons within rat's nucleus ambiguus, by means of four different fluorochromes. Neurosci Lett 135:103–107, 1992.

23. Dick TE, Bellingham MC, Richter DW: Pontine respiratory neurons in anesthetized cats. Brain Res 636:259–269, 1994.

24. St-John WM: Neurogenesis of patterns of automatic ventilatory activity. Prog Neurobiol 56:97–117, 1998.

25. Smith JC, Ellenberger HH, Ballanyi K, et al: Pre-Bötzinger complex: A brainstem region that may generate respiratory rhythm in mammals. Science 254:726–729, 1991.

26. Canning BJ, Fischer A: Neural regulation of airway smooth muscle tone. Respir Physiol 125:113–127, 2001.

27. Jordan D: Central nervous pathways and control of the airways. Respir Physiol 125:67–81, 2001.

28. Peever JH, Shen L, Duffin J: Respiratory pre-motor control of hypoglossal motoneurons in the rat. Neuroscience 110:711–722, 2002.

29. Ramirez JM, Zuperku EJ, Alheid GF, et al: Respiratory rhythm generation: Converging concepts from in vitro and in vivo approaches? Respir Physiol Neurobiol 131:43–56, 2002.

29a. Duffin J: Functional organization of respiratory neurons: a brief review of current questions and speculations. Exp Physiol 89:517–529, 2004.

30. Rekling JC, Feldman JL: PreBotzinger complex and pacemaker neurons: Hypothesized site and kernel for respiratory rhythm generation. Ann Rev Physiol 60:385–405, 1998.

31. Feldman JL, Gray PA: Sighs and gasps in a dish. Nat Neurosci 3:531–532, 2000.

32. Richter DW, Ballanyi K, Schwarzacher S: Mechanisms of respiratory rhythm generation. Curr Opin Neurobiol 2:788–793, 1992.

33. Duffin J, Ezure K, Lipski J: Breathing rhythm generation: Focus on the rostral ventrolateral medulla. News Physiol Sci 10:133–140, 1995.

34. St. John WM, Paton JF: Characterizations of eupnea, apneusis and gasping in a perfused rat preparation. Respir Physiol 123:201–213, 2000.

35. Paton JF: The ventral medullary respiratory network of the mature mouse studied in a working heart-brainstem preparation. J Physiol (Lond) 493:819–831, 1996.

36. Paton JF: A working heart-brainstem preparation of the mouse. J Neurosci Methods 65:63–68, 1996.

37. Busselberg D, Bischoff AM, Paton JF, et al: Reorganisation of respiratory network activity after loss of glycinergic inhibition. Pflugers Arch 441:444–449, 2001.

38. Lee LY, Pisarri TE: Afferent properties and reflex functions of bronchopulmonary C-fibers. Respir Physiol 125:47–65, 2001.

39. Sant'Ambrogio G, Widdicombe J: Reflexes from airway rapidly adapting receptors. Respir Physiol 125:33–45, 2001.

40. Schelegle ES, Green JF: An overview of the anatomy and physiology of slowly adapting pulmonary stretch receptors. Respir Physiol 125:17–31, 2001.

41. Widdicombe J: Airway receptors. Respir Physiol 125:3–15, 2001.

42. Benchetrit G: Breathing pattern in humans: Diversity and individuality. Respir Physiol 122:123–129, 2000.

43. McIlroy M, Eldridge F, Thomas JP, et al: The effect of added elastic and non-elastic resistances on the pattern of breathing in normal subjects. Clin Sci 15:337–344, 1956.

44. Fink BR: Influence of cerebral activity in wakefulness on regulation of breathing. J Appl Physiol 16:15–20, 1961.

45. Orem J: The nature of the wakefulness stimulus for breathing. Prog Clin Biol Res 345:23–30, 1990.

46. Orem J, Lovering AT, Dunin-Barkowski W, et al: Tonic activity in the respiratory system in wakefulness, NREM and REM sleep. Sleep 25:488–496, 2002.

47. Nattie EE: Central chemosensitivity, sleep, and wakefulness. Respir Physiol 129:257–268, 2001.

48. Morrell MJ, Heywood P, Moosavi SH, et al: Central chemosensitivity and breathing asleep in unilateral medullary lesion patients: Comparisons to animal data. Respir Physiol 129:269–277, 2001.

48a. Iturriaga R, Alcayaga J: Neurotransmission in the carotid body: transmitters and modulators between glomus cells and petrosal ganglion nerve terminals. Brain Res Rev 47:46–53, 2004.

49. Torrance RW: Prolegomena: Chemoreception upstream of transmitters. Adv Exp Med Biol 410:13–38, 1996.

50. Jounieaux V, Parreira VF, Aubert G, et al: Effects of hypocapnic hyperventilation on the response to hypoxia in normal subjects receiving intermittent positive-pressure ventilation. Chest 121:1141–1148, 2002.

51. Duffin J, Mahamed S: Adaptation in the respiratory control system. Can J Physiol Pharmacol 81:765–773, 2003.

52. Mellins RB, Balfour HH Jr, Turino GM, et al: Failure of automatic control of ventilation (Ondine's curse). Medicine 49:487–504, 1970.

53. Rochester DF, Enson Y: Current concepts in the pathogenesis of the obesity-hypoventilation syndrome. Am J Med 57:402–420, 1974.

54. Newsom Davis J, Goldman M, Loh L, et al: Diaphragm function and alveolar hypoventilation. Q J Med 45:87–100, 1976.

55. Goldstein RS: Hypoventilation: Neuromuscular and chest wall disorders. Clin Chest Med 13:507–521, 1992.

56. Hyland RH, Jones NL, Powles ACP, et al: Primary alveolar hypoventilation treated with nocturnal electrophrenic respiration. Am Rev Respir Dis 117:165–172, 1978.

57. Rodman T, Close HP: The primary hypoventilation syndrome. Am J Med 26:808–817, 1959.

58. Rhoads GG, Brody JS: Idiopathic alveolar hypoventilation: Clinical spectrum. Ann Intern Med 71:271–278, 1969.

59. McNicholas WT, Carter JL, Rutherford R, et al: Beneficial effect of oxygen in primary alveolar hypoventilation with central sleep apnea. Am Rev Respir Dis 125:773–775, 1982.

60. Gozal D, Marcus CL, Shoseyof D, et al: Peripheral chemoreceptor function in children with the congenital hypoventilation syndrome. J Appl Physiol 74:379–387, 1993.

61. Hsu AA, Staats BA: "Postpolio" sequelae and sleep-related disordered breathing. Mayo Clin Proc 73:216–224, 1998.

62. Spengler CM, Gozal D, Shea SA: Chemoreceptive mechanisms elucidated by studies of congenital central hypoventilation syndrome. Respir Physiol 129:247–255, 2001.

63. Schwartz WB, Brackett NC Jr, Cohen JJ: The response of extracellular hydrogen ion concentration to graded degrees of chronic hypercapnia: The physiologic limits of the defense of pH. J Clin Invest 44:291–301, 1965.

64. Goldring RM, Turino GM, Heinemann HO: Respiratory-renal adjustments in chronic hypercapnia in man. Am J Med 51:772–784, 1971.

65. Goldring RM, Cannon PJ, Heinemann HO, et al: Respiratory adjustment to chronic metabolic alkalosis in man. J Clin Invest 47:188–202, 1968.

66. Heinemann HO, Goldring RM: Bicarbonate and the regulation of ventilation. Am J Med 57:361–370, 1974.

67. Jackson CE, Rosenfeld J, Moore DH, et al: A preliminary evaluation of a prospective study of pulmonary function studies and symptoms of hypoventilation in ALS/MND patients. J Neurol Sci 191:75–78, 2001.

68. Barlow PB, Bartlett D Jr, Hauri P, et al: Idiopathic hypoventilation syndrome: Importance of preventing nocturnal hypoxemia and hypercapnia. Am Rev Respir Dis 121:141–145, 1980.

69. Bubis MJ, Anthonisen NR: Primary alveolar hypoventilation treated by nocturnal administration of O_2. Am Rev Respir Dis 118:947–953, 1978.

70. Farmer WC, Glenn WWL, Gee JBL: Alveolar hypoventilation syndrome: Studies of ventilatory control in patients selected for diaphragm pacing. Am J Med 64:39–49, 1978.

71. Bradley TD, Phillipson EA: Central sleep apnea. Clin Chest Med 13:493–505, 1992.

72. McNicholas WT, Phillipson EA: Central hypoventilation syndromes and hypercapnic central sleep apnea. *In* McNicholas WT, Phillipson EA (eds): Breathing Disorders in Sleep. London: WB Saunders, 2002, pp 239–245.

73. Lane DJ, Hazleman B, Nicholas PJR: Late onset respiratory failure in patients with previous poliomyelitis. Q J Med 43:551–568, 1974.

74. Gupta RG: Respiratory dysfunction in motor neuron disease. *In* Weiner WJ (ed): Respiratory Dysfunction in Neurologic Disease. Mount Kisco, NY: Futura, 1980, pp 71–81.

75. Gibson GJ, Pride NB, Newsom Davis J, et al: Pulmonary mechanics in patients with respiratory muscle weakness. Am Rev Respir Dis 115:389–395, 1977.

76. Rosenow EC III, Engel AG: Acid maltase deficiency in adults presenting as respiratory failure. Am J Med 64:485–491, 1978.

77. Black LF, Hyatt RE: Maximal respiratory pressures: Normal values, and relationship to age and sex. Am Rev Respir Dis 99:696–701, 1969.

78. Whitelaw WA, Derenne JP, Milic-Emili J: Occlusion pressure as a measure of respiratory center output in conscious man. Respir Physiol 23:181–199, 1975.

79. Altose MD, McCauley WC, Kelsen SG, et al: Effects of hypercapnia and inspiratory flow-resistive loading on respiratory activity in chronic airways obstruction. J Clin Invest 59:500–507, 1977.

80. Gelb AF, Klein E, Schiffman P, et al: Ventilatory response and drive in acute and chronic obstructive pulmonary disease. Am Rev Respir Dis 116:9–16, 1977.

81. Lourenco RV, Miranda JM: Drive and performance of the ventilatory apparatus in chronic obstructive lung disease. N Engl J Med 279:53–59, 1968.

82. Riley DJ, Santiago TV, Daniele RP, et al: Blunted respiratory drive in congenital myopathy. Am J Med 63:459–466, 1977.

83. Bradley TD, Rutherford R, Lue F, et al: Role of diffuse airway obstruction in the hypercapnia of obstructive sleep apnea. Am Rev Respir Dis 134:920–924, 1986.

84. Lopata M, Onal E: Mass loading, sleep apnea, and the pathogenesis of obesity hypoventilation. Am Rev Respir Dis 126:640–645, 1982.

85. Rapoport DM, Garay SM, Epstein H, et al: Hypercapnia in the obstructive sleep apnea syndrome: A reevaluation of the "Pickwickian syndrome." Chest 89:627–635, 1986.

86. Berger KI, Ayappa I, Chatr-Amontri B, et al: Obesity hypoventilation syndrome as a spectrum of respiratory disturbances during sleep. Chest 120:1231–1238, 2001.

87. Mountain R, Zwillich C, Weil J: Hypoventilation in obstructive lung disease: The role of familial factors. N Engl J Med 298:521–525, 1978.

88. Schiffman PL, Westlake RE, Santiago TV, et al: Ventilatory control in parents of victims of sudden-infant-death syndrome. N Engl J Med 302:486–491, 1980.

89. Tankersley CG, Fitzgerald RS, Levitt RC, et al: Genetic control of differential baseline breathing pattern. J Appl Physiol 82:874–881, 1997.

90. O'Donnell CP, Schaub CD, Haines AS, et al: Leptin prevents respiratory depression in obesity. Am J Respir Crit Care Med 159:1477–1484, 1999.

91. Weese-Mayer DE, Silvestri JM, Huffman AD, et al: Case/control family study of autonomic nervous system dysfunction in idiopathic central hypoventilation syndrome. Am J Med Gen 100:237–245, 2001.

92. Phipps PR, Starritt E, Caterson I, et al: Association of serum leptin with hypoventilation in human obesity. Thorax 57:75–76, 2002.

93. Weil JV: Variation in human ventilatory control-genetic influence on the hypoxic ventilatory response. Respir Physiol Neurobiol 135:239–246, 2003.

94. Plum F, Swanson AG: Abnormalities in central regulation of respiration in acute and chronic convalescent poliomyelitis. Arch Neurol Psychiatry 80:267–285, 1958.

95. Devereaux MW, Keane JR, Davis RL: Automatic respiratory failure associated with infarction of the medulla. Arch Neurol 29:46–52, 1973.

96. Baker AB, Matzke HA, Brown JR: Poliomyelitis: III. Bulbar poliomyelitis: A study of medullary function. Arch Neurol Psychiatry 63:257–281, 1950.

97. Levin BE, Margolis G: Acute failure of automatic respirations secondary to a unilateral brainstem infarct. Ann Neurol 1:583–586, 1977.

98. Cole S, Lindenberg LB, Galioto FM Jr, et al: Ultrastructural abnormalities of the carotid body in sudden infant death syndrome. Pediatrics 63:13–17, 1979.

99. Bowes G, Andrey S, Kozar L, et al: Effect of chronic carotid body denervation on respiratory drive and stability in sleeping dogs. Am Rev Respir Dis 129(Suppl):A244, 1984.

100. Gaultier C: Abnormalities of the chemical control of breathing: Clinical correlates in infants and children. Ped Pulmonol Suppl 23:114–117, 2001.

101. Moore GC, Zwillich CW, Battaglia JD, et al: Respiratory failure associated with familial depression of ventilatory response to hypoxia and hypercapnia. N Engl J Med 295:861–865, 1976.

102. Phillipson EA, Bowes G: Control of breathing during sleep. In Cherniack NS, Widdicombe JG (eds): Handbook of Physiology. Section 3: The Respiratory System. Vol II: Control of Breathing (Part 2). Bethesda, Md: American Physiological Society, 1986, pp 649–689.

103. Shea SA: Life without ventilatory chemosensitivity. Respir Physiol 110:199–210, 1997.

104. Cohn JE, Kuida H: Primary alveolar hypoventilation associated with western equine encephalitis. Ann Intern Med 56:633–644, 1962.

105. Solliday NH, Gaensler EA, Schwaber JR, et al: Impaired central chemoreceptor function and chronic hypoventilation many years following poliomyelitis. Respiration 31:177–192, 1974.

106. Daum JJ, Canter HG, Katz S: Central nervous system sarcoidosis with alveolar hypoventilation. Am J Med 38:893–898, 1965.

107. Bloor JW, Johnson RJ, Canales L, et al: Reversible paralysis of automatic respiration in multiple sclerosis. Arch Neurol 34:686–689, 1977.

108. Smyth A, Riley M: Chronic respiratory failure: An unusual cause and treatment. Thorax 57:835–836, 2002.

109. Krieger AJ, Rosomoff HL: Sleep-induced apnea: I. A respiratory and autonomic dysfunction syndrome following bilateral percutaneous cervical cordotomy. J Neurosurg 39:168–180, 1974.

110. Sivak ED, Streib EW: Management of hypoventilation in motor neuron disease presenting with respiratory insufficiency. Ann Neurol 7:188–191, 1980.

111. Thorpy MJ, Schmidt-Nowara WW, Pollak CP, et al: Sleep-induced nonobstructive hypoventilation associated with diaphragmatic paralysis. Ann Neurol 12:308–311, 1982.

112. Arborelius M Jr, Lilja B, Senyk J: Regional and total lung function studies in patients with hemidiaphragmatic paralysis. Respiration 32:253–264, 1975.

113. Ridyard JB, Stewart RM: Regional lung function in unilateral diaphragmatic paralysis. Thorax 31:438–442, 1976.

114. Easton PA, Fleetham JA, De La Rocha A, et al: Respiratory function after paralysis of the right hemidiaphragm. Am Rev Respir Dis 127:125–128, 1983.

115. Riley EA: Idiopathic diaphragmatic paralysis. Am J Med 32:404–416, 1962.

116. Inkley SR, Oldenburg FC, Vignos PJ Jr: Pulmonary function in Duchenne muscular dystrophy related to stage of disease. Am J Med 56:297–306, 1974.

117. Coccagna G, Mantovani M, Parchi C, et al: Alveolar hypoventilation and hypersomnia in myotonic dystrophy. J Neurol Neurosurg Psychiatry 38:977–984, 1975.

118. Derenne JP, Macklem PT, Roussos C: The respiratory muscles: Mechanics, control, and pathophysiology, Part III. Am Rev Respir Dis 118:581–601, 1978.

119. Newsom Davis J: Phrenic nerve conduction in man. J Neurol Neurosurg Psychiatry 30:420–426, 1967.

120. Loh L, Goldman M, Newsom Davis J: The assessment of diaphragm function. Medicine 56:165–169, 1977.

121. Lyons HA, Hwang CT: Therapeutic use of progesterone in alveolar hypoventilation associated with obesity. Am J Med 44:881–888, 1968.

122. Sutton FD Jr, Zwillich CW, Creagh CE, et al: Progesterone for outpatient treatment of Pickwickian syndrome. Ann Intern Med 83:476–479, 1975.

123. Skatrud JB, Dempsey JA, Bhansali P, et al: Determinants of chronic carbon dioxide retention and its correction in humans. J Clin Invest 65:813–821, 1980.

124. Bear R, Goldstein M, Phillipson E, et al: Effect of metabolic alkalosis on respiratory function in patients with chronic obstructive lung disease. Can Med Assoc J 117:900–903, 1977.

125. Garay SM, Turino GM, Goldring RM: Sustained reversal of chronic hypercapnia in patients with alveolar hypoventilation syndromes: Long term maintenance with noninvasive nocturnal mechanical ventilation. Am J Med 70:269–274, 1981.

126. Ellis ER, Bye PTP, Bruderer JW, et al: Treatment of respiratory failure during sleep in patients with neuromuscular disease: Positive pressure ventilation through a nose mask. Am Rev Respir Dis 135:148–152, 1987.

127. Kerby GR, Mayer LS, Pingleton SK: Nocturnal positive pressure ventilation via nasal mask. Am Rev Respir Dis 135:738–740, 1987.

128. Bach JR, Alber AS: Management of chronic alveolar hypoventilation by nasal ventilation. Chest 97:52–57, 1990.

129. Goldstein RS, De Rosie JA, Avendano MA, et al: Influence of non-invasive positive pressure ventilation on inspiratory muscles. Chest 99:408–415, 1991.

130. Hukins CA, Hillman DR: Daytime predictors of sleep hypoventilation in Duchenne muscular dystrophy. Am J Respir Crit Care Med 161:166–170, 2000.

131. Masa JF, Celli BR, Riesco JA, et al: The obesity hypoventilation syndrome can be treated with noninvasive mechanical ventilation. Chest 119:1102–1107, 2001.

132. Hida W, Okabe S, Tatsumi K, et al: Nasal continuous positive airway pressure improves quality of life in obesity hypoventilation syndrome. Sleep Breath 7:3–12, 2003.

133. Annane D, Chevrolet JC, Chevret S, et al: Nocturnal mechanical ventilation for chronic hypoventilation in patients with neuromuscular and chest wall disorders. Cochrane Database Syst Rev 2:CD001941, 2000.

134. Glenn WWL, Holcomb WG, Gee JB, et al: Central hypoventilation: Long term ventilatory assistance by radiofrequency electrophrenic respiration. Ann Surg 172:755–773, 1970.

135. Langou RA, Cohen LS, Sheps D, et al: Ondine's curse: Hemodynamic response to diaphragm pacing (electrophrenic respiration). Am Heart J 95:295–300, 1978.

136. Weese-Mayer DE, Silvestri JM, Kenny AS, et al: Diaphragm pacing with a quadripolar phrenic nerve electrode: An international study. Pacing Clin Electrophysiol 19:1311–1319, 1996.

137. Wade JG, Larson CP Jr, Hickey RF, et al: Effect of carotid endarterectomy on carotid chemoreceptor and baroreceptor function in man. N Engl J Med 282:823–829, 1970.

138. Severinghaus JW, Bainton CR, Carcelen A: Respiratory insensitivity to hypoxia in chronically hypoxic man. Respir Physiol 1:308–334, 1966.

139. Weil JV, Byrne-Quinn E, Sodal IE, et al: Acquired attenuation of chemoreceptor function in chronically hypoxic man at high altitude. J Clin Invest 50:186–195, 1971.

140. Hughes JMB: Central respiratory failure reversed by treatment. Brain 90:675–680, 1967.

141. Marks CE Jr, Goldring RM: Chronic hypercapnia during methadone maintenance. Am Rev Respir Dis 108:1088–1093, 1973.

142. Fishman AP, Turino GM, Bergofsky EH: The syndrome of alveolar hypoventilation. Am J Med 23:333–339, 1957.

143. Goldstein RL, Hyde RW, Lapham LW, et al: Peripheral neuropathy presenting with respiratory insufficiency as the primary complaint. Am J Med 56:443–449, 1974.

144. Bergofsky EH: Respiratory failure in disorders of the thoracic cage. Am Rev Respir Dis 119:643–669, 1979.

145. Shim C, Corro P, Park SS, et al: Pulmonary function studies in patients with upper airway obstruction. Am Rev Respir Dis 106:233–238, 1972.

146. Proctor DF: The upper airways: II. The larynx and trachea. Am Rev Respir Dis 115:315–342, 1977.

147. Weil JV, Byrne-Quinn E, Sodal ID, et al: Hypoxic ventilatory drive in normal man. J Clin Invest 49:1061–1072, 1970.

148. Rebuck AS, Campbell EJM: A clinical method for assessing the ventilatory response to hypoxia. Am Rev Respir Dis 109:345–350, 1974.

149. West JB, Hackett PH, Maret KH, et al: Pulmonary gas exchange on the summit of Mount Everest. J Appl Physiol 55:678–687, 1983.

150. Anthonisen NR, Cherniack RM: Ventilatory control in lung disease. *In* Hornbein TF (ed): Regulation of Breathing (Part II). New York: Marcel Dekker, 1981, pp 965–987.

151. Kawakami Y, Yamamoto H, Yoshikawa T, et al: Chemical and behavioral control of breathing in adult twins. Am Rev Respir Dis 129:703–707, 1984.

152. Kety SS, Schmidt CF: The effects of active and passive hyperventilation on cerebral blood flow, cerebral oxygen consumption, cardiac output, and blood pressure in normal young men. J Clin Invest 25:107–119, 1946.

153. Lee LY, Milhorn HT: Central ventilatory response to O_2 and CO_2 at three levels of carotid chemoreceptor stimulation. Respir Physiol 25:319–333, 1975.

154. Neubauer JA, Melton JE, Edelman NH: Modulation of respiration during hypoxia. J Appl Physiol 68:441–451, 1990.

155. Easton PA, Slykerman LJ, Anthonisen NR: Ventilatory response to sustained hypoxia in normal adults. J Appl Physiol 61:906–911, 1986.

156. Easton PA, Slykerman LJ, Anthonisen NR: Recovery of the ventilatory response to hypoxia in normal adults. J Appl Physiol 64:521–528, 1988.

157. Edelman NH, Lahiri S, Broudo L, et al: The blunted ventilatory response to hypoxia in cyanotic congenital heart disease. N Engl J Med 282:405–411, 1970.

158. Weil JV: Ventilatory control at high altitude. *In* Cherniack NS, Widdicombe JG (eds): Handbook of Physiology. Section 3: The Respiratory System. Vol II: Control of Breathing (Part 2). Bethesda, Md: American Physiological Society, 1986, pp 703–728.

159. Phillipson E, Murphy E, Kozar LF, et al: Role of vagal stimuli in exercise ventilation in dogs with experimental pneumonitis. J Appl Physiol 39:76–85, 1975.

160. Cotton DJ, Bleecker ER, Fisher SP, et al: Rapid shallow breathing after *Ascaris suum* antigen inhalation: Role of vagus nerves. J Appl Physiol 42:101–106, 1977.

161. Guz A, Noble MI, Eisele JH, et al: Experimental results of vagal blockade in cardiopulmonary disease. *In* Porter R (ed): Breathing: Hering-Breuer Centenary Symposium. London: Churchill, 1970, pp 315–329.

162. Lourenco RV, Turino GM, Davidson LAG, et al: The regulation of ventilation in diffuse pulmonary fibrosis. Am J Med 38:199–216, 1965.

163. Jones NL, Rebuck AS: Tidal volume during exercise in patients with diffuse fibrosing alveolitis. Bull Eur Physiopathol Respir 15:321–328, 1979.

164. DiMarco AF, Kelsen SG, Cherniack NS, et al: Occlusion pressure and breathing pattern in patients with interstitial lung disease. Am Rev Respir Dis 127:425–430, 1983.

165. von Euler C: On the role of proprioceptors in perception and execution of motor acts with special reference to breathing. *In* Pengelly LD, Rebuck AS, Campbell EJM (eds): Loaded Breathing. Edinburgh: Churchill-Livingstone, 1974, pp 139–149.

166. Takasaki Y, Orr D, Popkin J, et al: Effect of nasal continuous positive airway pressure on sleep apnea in congestive heart failure. Am Rev Respir Dis 140:1578–1584, 1989.

167. Dowdell WT, Javaheri S, McGinnis W: Cheyne-Stokes respiration presenting as sleep apnea syndrome. Am Rev Respir Dis 141:871–879, 1990.

168. Bradley TD: Right and left ventricular functional impairment and sleep apnea. Clin Chest Med 13:459–479, 1992.

169. Naughton M, Benard D, Tam A, et al: Role of hyperventilation in the pathogenesis of central sleep apneas in patients with congestive heart failure. Am Rev Respir Dis 148:330–338, 1993.

170. Lorenzi-Filho G, Rankin F, Bies I, et al: Effects of inhaled carbon dioxide and oxygen on Cheyne-Stokes respiration in patients with heart failure. Am J Respir Crit Care Med 159:1490–1498, 1999.

171. Tkacova R, Hall MJ, Liu PP, et al: Left ventricular volume in patients with heart failure and Cheyne-Stokes respiration during sleep. Am J Respir Crit Care Med 156:1549–1555, 1997.

172. De Burgh Daly M: Interactions between respiration and circulation. *In* Cherniack NS, Widdicombe JG (eds): Handbook of Physiology. Section 3: The Respiratory System. Vol II: Control of Breathing (Part 2). Bethesda, Md: American Physiological Society, 1986, pp 529–594.

173. Arbus GS, Hebert LA, Levesque RR, et al: Characterization and clinical application of the "significance band" for acute respiratory alkalosis. N Engl J Med 280:117–123, 1969.

174. Gennari FJ, Goldstein MB, Schwartz WB: The nature of the renal adaptation to chronic hypocapnia. J Clin Invest 51:1722–1730, 1972.

175. Hamilton RW, Epstein PE, Henderson LW, et al: Control of breathing in uremia: Ventilatory response to CO_2 after hemodialysis. J Appl Physiol 41:216–222, 1976.

176. Kaehny WD, Jackson JT: Respiratory response to HCl acidosis in dogs after carotid body denervation. J Appl Physiol 46:1138–1142, 1979.

177. Forster HV, Dempsey JA: Ventilatory adaptations. *In* Hornbein TF (ed): Regulation of Breathing. New York: Marcel Dekker, 1981, pp 845–904.

178. Teppema LJ, Barts PW, Folgering HT, Evers JA: Effects of respiratory and (isocapnic) metabolic arterial acid base disturbances on medullary extracellular fluid pH and ventilation in cats. Respir Physiol 53:379–395, 1983.

179. Pino-Garcia JM, Garcia-Rio F, Diez JJ, et al: Regulation of breathing in hyperthyroidism: Relationship to hormonal and metabolic changes. Eur Respir J 12:400–407, 1998.

180. Stanley NN, Salisbury BG, McHenry LC Jr, et al: Effect of liver failure on the response of ventilation and cerebral circulation to carbon dioxide in man and in the goat. Clin Sci Mol Med 49:157–169, 1975.

181. Karetzky MS, Mithoefer JC: The cause of hyperventilation and arterial hypoxia in patients with cirrhosis of the liver. Am J Med Sci 254:797–804, 1967.

182. Lum LC: The syndrome of habitual chronic hyperventilation. *In* Hill O (ed): Modern Trends in Psychosomatic Medicine. London: Butterworths, 1976, pp 196–230.

183. Margarian GJ: Hyperventilation syndromes: Infrequently recognized common expressions of anxiety and stress. Medicine 61:219–236, 1982.

184. Brashear RE: Hyperventilation syndrome. Lung 161:257–273, 1983.

185. Jack S, Rossiter HB, Warburton CS, et al: Behavioral influences and physiological indices of ventilatory control in subjects with idiopathic hyperventilation. Behav Modif 27:637–652, 2003.

186. Plum F, Posner JB: The Diagnosis of Stupor and Coma. Philadelphia: FA Davis, 1966.

187. Plum F, Swanson AG: Central neurogenic hyperventilation in man. Arch Neurol Psychiatry 81:535–544, 1959.

188. Froman C, Crampton-Smith A: Hyperventilation associated with low pH of cerebrospinal fluid after intracranial hemorrhage. Lancet 1:780–782, 1966.

189. North JB, Jennett S: Abnormal breathing patterns associated with acute brain damage. Arch Neurol 31:338–344, 1974.

190. Leigh RF, Shaw DA: Rapid respiration in unconscious patients. Arch Neurol 33:356–361, 1976.

191. Fink BR, Katz R, Reinhold H, et al: Suprapontine mechanisms in regulation of respiration. Am J Physiol 202:217–220, 1962.

192. Tenney SM, Ou LC: Ventilatory response of decorticate and decerebrate cats to hypoxia and CO_2. Respir Physiol 29:81–92, 1976.

193. Johnston SC, Singy V, Ralston HJ 3rd, et al: Chronic dyspnea and hyperventilation in an awake patient with small subcortical infarcts. Neurology 57:2131–2133, 2001.

194. Hickey RF, Severinghaus JW: Regulation of breathing: Drug effects. *In* Hornbein TF (ed): Regulation of Breathing (Part II). New York: Marcel Dekker, 1981, pp 1251–1312.

195. Tenney SM, Miller RM: Respiratory and circulatory actions of salicylate. Am J Med 19:498–508, 1955.

196. Millhorn DE, Eldridge FL, Waldrop TG: Effects of salicylate and 2,4-dinitrophenol on respiration and metabolism. J Appl Physiol 53:925–929, 1982.

197. Cunningham DJC, Oriordan JLH: The effect of a rise in temperature on the respiratory response to carbon dioxide. Q J Exp Physiol 42:329–345, 1957.

198. Simmons DH, Nicoloff J, Guze LB: Hyperventilation and respiratory alkalosis as signs of gram-negative bacteremia. JAMA 174:2196–2199, 1960.

199. Gaudio R Jr, Abramson N: Heat-induced hyperventilation. J Appl Physiol 25:742–746, 1968.

200. Aronson PR: Hyperventilation from organic disease. Ann Intern Med 50:554–559, 1959.

201. Joels N, White H: The contribution of the arterial chemoreceptors to the stimulation of respiration by adrenaline and noradrenaline in the cat. J Physiol (Lond) 197:1–23, 1968.

202. Heistad DD, Wheeler RC, Mark AL, et al: Effects of adrenergic stimulation on ventilation in man. J Clin Invest 51:1469–1475, 1972.

203. Morgan EJ, Baidwan B, Petty TL, et al: The effects of unanesthetized arterial puncture on PCO_2 and pH. Am Rev Respir Dis 120:795–798, 1979.

204. Lyons HA: Respiratory effects of gonadal hormones. *In* Salhanick HA, Kipnis DM, Van de Wiele RL (eds):

Metabolic Effects of Gonadal Hormones and Contraceptive Steroids. New York: Plenum, 1969, pp 394–402.

205. Skatrud JB, Dempsey JA, Kaiser DG: Ventilatory response to medroxyprogesterone acetate in normal subjects: Time course and mechanism. J Appl Physiol 44:939–944, 1978.

206. Bayliss DA, Millhorn DE: Central neural mechanisms of progesterone action: Application to the respiratory system. J Appl Physiol 73:393–404, 1992.

207. Brown EB: Physiological effects of hyperventilation. Physiol Rev 33:445–471, 1953.

208. Mostellar ME, Tuttle EP Jr: Effects of alkalosis on plasma concentration and urinary excretion of inorganic phosphate in man. J Clin Invest 43:138–149, 1964.

209. Fitzgerald F: Clinical hypophosphatemia. Annu Rev Med 29:177–189, 1978.

210. Brautbar N, Leibovici H, Finlander P, et al: Mechanism of hypophosphatemia during acute hyperventilation (abstract). Clin Res 28:387A, 1980.

211. Richardson DW, Kontos HA, Raper AJ, et al: Systemic circulatory responses to hypocapnia in man. Am J Physiol 223:1308–1312, 1972.

212. Neill WA, Hattenhauer M: Impairment of myocardial O_2 supply due to hyperventilation. Circulation 52:854–858, 1975.

213. Yasue H, Nagao M, Omote S, et al: Coronary arterial spasm and Prinzmetal's variant form of angina induced by hyperventilation and Tris-buffer infusion. Circulation 58:56–62, 1978.

214. Laffey JG, Kavanagh BP: Hypocapnia. N Engl J Med 347:43–53, 2002.

215. Chen CC, Chen SA, Tai CT, et al: Hyperventilation facilitates induction of supraventricular tachycardia: A novel method and the possible mechanism. J Cardiovasc Electrophysiol 12:1242–1246, 2001.

216. Yasue H, Omote S, Takizawa A, et al: Alkalosis-induced coronary vasoconstriction: Effects of calcium, diltiazem, nitroglycerin and propranolol. Am Heart J 102:206–210, 1981.

217. Hauge A, Thoresen M, Walloe L: Changes in cerebral blood flow during hyperventilation and CO_2 breathing measured transcutaneously in humans by a bidirectional, pulsed, ultrasound Doppler blood velocity meter. Acta Physiol Scand 110:167–173, 1980.

218. Raichle ME, Posner JB, Plum F: Cerebral blood flow during and after hyperventilation. Arch Neurol 23:394–403, 1970.

219. Reivich MP, Cohen PJ, Greenbaum L: Alterations in the electroencephalogram of awake man produced by hyperventilation effects of 100% oxygen at 3 atmospheres pressure. Neurology 16:304, 1966.

220. Kogure K, Busto R, Matsumoto A, et al: Effect of hyperventilation on dynamics of cerebral energy metabolism. Am J Physiol 228:1862–1867, 1975.

221. Rebuck AS, Davis C, Longmire D, et al: Arterial oxygenation and carbon dioxide tensions in the production of hypoxic electroencephalographic changes in man. Clin Sci Mol Med 50:301–306, 1976.

222. Kennealy JA, McLennan JE, Loudon RG, et al: Hyperventilation-induced cerebral hypoxia. Am Rev Respir Dis 122:407–412, 1980.

223. Arnow PM, Panwalker A, Garvin JS, et al: Aspirin, hyperventilation, and cerebellar infarction in sickle-cell disease. Arch Intern Med 138:148–149, 1978.

224. Severinghaus JW: The role of cerebrospinal fluid pH in normalization of cerebral blood flow in chronic hypocapnia. Acta Neurol Scand 14(Suppl):116–120, 1965.

225. Lewis BI: Hyperventilation syndrome: A clinical and physiological evaluation. Calif Med 21:259–271, 1959.
226. Rosenbaum JF: Current concepts in psychiatry. The drug treatment of anxiety. N Engl J Med 306:401–404, 1982.
227. Van Doorn P, Folgering H, Colla P: Control of end-tidal PCO_2 in the hyperventilation syndrome: Effects of biofeedback and breathing instructions compared. Bull Eur Physiopathol Respir 18:829–836, 1982.
228. Folgering H, Rutlen H, Roumen Y: Beta-blockade in the hyperventilation syndrome: A retrospective assessment of symptoms and complaints. Respiration 44:19–25, 1983.

74

Sleep Disorders

T. Douglas Bradley, M.D., Eliot A. Phillipson, M.D.

INTRODUCTION

Since 1990, respiratory disturbances during sleep have come to be recognized as extremely common disorders with important clinical consequences. In addition to affecting the quality of sleep, there is a growing realization that respiratory-related sleep disturbances can interact closely with, and even contribute to, several common cardiovascular and metabolic disorders. Thus, the field of sleep medicine has now firmly entered the mainstream of clinical practice.

IMPACT OF SLEEP ON BREATHING

Sleep is not a homogeneous phenomenon but rather consists of two distinct states, referred to as non–rapid eye movement (non-REM) or quiet sleep and rapid eye movement (REM) or active sleep.[1-4] The two states are distinguished by a combination of behavioral and electrographic criteria. Non-REM sleep consists of four stages that are thought to represent progressively deeper sleep, with the deepest stages (3 and 4) being referred to as slow-wave sleep. REM sleep, during which dreaming occurs, is characterized by intense cerebral metabolic activity and central nervous system excitation, despite which incoming sensory information and outgoing motor activity are actively inhibited. In the normal adult, non-REM sleep and REM sleep alternate cyclically, with periods of REM sleep lasting 10 to 20 minutes and occurring every 90 to 120 minutes.

Non-REM sleep and REM sleep have several important physiologic influences on breathing, particularly on respiratory drive, stability, and ventilatory mechanics.[5,6] Overall respiratory drive is decreased during non-REM sleep, owing to loss of the stimulatory effect of wakefulness on breathing and to a reduction in chemosensitivity. As a result, during stages 1 and 2 of non-REM sleep, as the central nervous system state fluctuates between awake and asleep, there is a fluctuation in respiratory drive that predisposes to periodic breathing. Once slow-wave sleep is fully established, nonchemical respiratory inputs are minimized, and breathing is regulated by the metabolic respiratory control system. Under these conditions, overall respiratory drive is usually stable but less than during wakefulness. As a result, minute volume of ventilation is reduced by 1 to 2 L/min compared with wakefulness, arterial P_{CO_2} is increased by 2 to 8 mm Hg, and arterial P_{O_2} is decreased by 5 to 10 mm Hg.

During REM sleep, respiratory drive is often irregular, ventilatory responses to chemical and mechanical respiratory stimuli may be transiently reduced or abolished, and short periods of central apnea lasting 10 to 20 seconds are relatively common. In addition, intercostal and accessory muscle activity is reduced coincident with the generalized inhibition of skeletal muscle tone characteristic of this state. As a result, thoracoabdominal coupling may be diminished, resulting in further decreases in ventilation, and functional residual capacity may be reduced. The influences of non-REM and REM sleep on respiratory drive and muscle activity are exerted on the muscles of the upper airway in addition to those of the chest wall.[7] Therefore, upper airway resistance is increased during non-REM sleep compared with wakefulness, and increased even more during REM sleep.

The physiologic impact of sleep on breathing is of little consequence in healthy persons. In patients with disturbances of respiratory structure or function, however, the imposition of these sleep-related changes on the underlying disturbance may have important clinical consequences. For example, in patients with defects in metabolic respiratory drive, such as occur in the primary alveolar hypoventilation syndrome, withdrawal of the stimulatory effect of wakefulness on breathing may result in marked hypoventilation or apnea. In patients with diaphragmatic weakness or paralysis, inhibition of intercostal and accessory respiratory muscle activity during REM sleep may result in profound hypoventilation. In persons with a structurally small oropharyngeal cavity, reduced activation of the upper airway muscles during non-REM sleep and further inhibition in REM sleep may predispose to upper airway collapse.

IMPACT OF SLEEP ON CARDIOVASCULAR FUNCTION

The shift of central nervous system state from wakefulness to non-REM sleep is normally accompanied by progressive reductions in metabolic rate, sympathetic nervous system activity, heart rate, stroke volume, cardiac output, and systemic blood pressure, and by a progressive increase in vagal tone.[8-11] An important consequence of these physiologic changes is a reduction in myocardial workload. Compared to wakefulness, non-REM sleep is a time of relative autonomic and circulatory stability. This stability is disrupted from time to time by brief microarousals from sleep that provoke sudden transient increases in sympathetic nervous activity, heart rate, and blood pressure.[11,12]

The effects of REM sleep on cardiovascular activity are more complex than those of non-REM sleep. In animals, renal sympathetic nerve activity decreases during REM sleep, but in humans sympathetic outflow to skeletal muscle vasculature increases and blood pressure rises to levels comparable to those of wakefulness.[9,11] Whether these differences are species related or are caused by nonuniform activation of various branches of the sympathetic nervous system remains to be determined. Despite these changes, because adults spend approximately 80% to 85% of their total sleep time in non-REM sleep, the overall effect of sleep is to rest the cardiovascular system. Disruptions of sleep, as occur in such disorders as sleep apnea, interfere with this state of cardiovascular quiescence and, in so doing, stress the heart and circulation.

AROUSAL RESPONSES

The ability to awaken from sleep or to arouse to a lighter stage of sleep is an important element of several sleep-related respiratory disturbances. The arousal response, which requires reticular and cortical activation, results in a number of physiologic responses that are of potential benefit.[13] These include immediate increases in respiratory drive and level of ventilation, which serve to correct any preceding hypoventilation; activation of the upper airway dilator and abductor muscles, which serves to terminate obstructive apneas; activation of the cough reflex, which serves to protect the lower airways and lungs from aspiration; and initiation of behavioral responses that may protect life, such as escape from a smoke-filled room. However, the role of the arousal response in the pathogenesis of respiratory disturbances related to sleep is complex. For example, arousal in response to an episode of apnea terminates the respiratory event and limits the degree of asphyxic exposure, but arousal also interferes with the continuity of sleep and over time may expose the individual to the complications of sleep fragmentation or deprivation. Similarly, arousal from sleep may result in transient surges in blood pressure that represent an added burden on the cardiovascular system. Therefore, although the arousal response may be of immediate protective value, it can be maladaptive in the long term and may contribute to the pathophysiology of sleep-related respiratory disturbances.

PHYSIOLOGIC AND CLINICAL CONSEQUENCES

Disorders of ventilation during sleep can result in several physiologic and clinical disturbances (Table 74.1). In broad terms, these complications are thought to arise either because of interference with the quality, quantity, or structure of sleep or because of recurrent nocturnal hypoxemia or asphyxia. The disturbances in sleep structure result in neuropsychological and behavioral manifestations rather than respiratory complaints, whereas the complications of nocturnal hypoxemia or asphyxia are predominantly cardiovascular and respiratory in nature.

LABORATORY ASSESSMENT

Because the clinical consequences of sleep-related respiratory disturbances are thought to arise either from disruptions in sleep quality and architecture or from derangements in blood gases, the laboratory assessment of such disorders is designed to focus on sleep structure and respiratory function. The simplest type of laboratory investigation is the continuous monitoring of arterial oxygen saturation using an ear or finger oximeter. The response time of such instruments is sufficiently rapid to detect transient falls in saturation, such as might occur during an apnea episode lasting 10 to 20 seconds. The pattern of saturation recorded during overnight oximetry can be highly characteristic of specific respiratory disturbances (Fig. 74.1),[14] but the diagnostic accuracy of oximetry as a screening test for any specific disease is relatively low. The addition of transcutaneous

Table 74.1 Consequences of Respiratory Disturbances during Sleep

Physiologic Disturbance	Clinical Consequences
Fragmentation of sleep by frequent arousals; loss of slow-wave sleep	Recurrent awakenings Restless sleep Unrefreshing sleep Morning headache Daytime sleepiness Cognitive impairment Personality changes
Recurrent nocturnal hypoxemia or asphyxia; increased cardiac afterload	Nocturnal cardiac arrhythmias Paroxysmal nocturnal dyspnea Nocturnal angina Pulmonary hypertension Systemic hypertension Left ventricular dysfunction Chronic respiratory failure

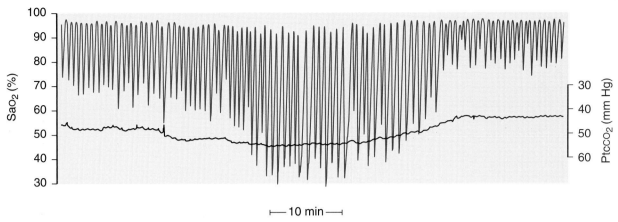

Figure 74.1 Recorder tracings of arterial oxygen saturation (SaO_2) measured by ear oximetry and of transcutaneous PCO_2 ($PtcCO_2$) in a patient with obstructive sleep apnea show recurrent episodes of desaturation typical of this disorder. (From Stradling JR, Phillipson EA: Breathing disorders during sleep. Q J Med 58:3–18, 1986.)

PCO_2 monitoring to an overnight screening test provides information regarding changes in the mean level of arterial PCO_2 over a period of several minutes but cannot detect fluctuations in arterial PCO_2 on a breath-by-breath basis or during the course of a single apnea episode. Nevertheless, such information can be helpful in assessing overall trends in alveolar ventilation during sleep (see Fig. 74.1). Overnight Holter monitoring of heart rate and rhythm can also be a useful screening procedure,[15] but abnormalities of cardiac rhythm are neither sufficiently sensitive nor specific enough to stand alone as a screening test for any particular respiratory disturbance during sleep.

Full overnight sleep studies, referred to as polysomnography, involve the recording of several electrographic variables, including the electroencephalogram, electrooculogram, and submental electromyogram, which allow sleep to be staged and quantitated and brief arousals or awakenings from sleep to be identified.[4] The tibialis electromyogram is also usually recorded to determine the presence of periodic leg movements during sleep (nocturnal myoclonus).[16] Standard respiratory measurements include arterial oxygen saturation by ear or finger oximetry, often transcutaneous PCO_2, and recordings of breathing movements that permit the identification of apneas or hypopneas and their classification as obstructive or nonobstructive (Fig. 74.2).[17] The latter distinction can usually be made with appropriate surface transducers such as the respiratory inductive plethysmograph.[18] In some cases, more sensitive techniques may be required, such as measurement of intrapleural pressure swings (with an esophageal catheter) or diaphragm electromyographic response.[19,20]

OBSTRUCTIVE SLEEP APNEA

The clinical importance of sleep apnea arises from the fact that it is one of the leading causes of excessive daytime sleepiness and may contribute to the development of several cardiorespiratory and metabolic disturbances.[21–24] During the past 15 years, it has come to be recognized as a common disorder, affecting at least 2% of middle-aged women and 4% of middle-aged men.[25] Prevalence rates are

higher in postmenopausal than in premenopausal women, and higher in the elderly than in the middle-aged.[26,27] Despite increasing awareness of the disorder, most cases remain undiagnosed.[28]

Sleep apnea is defined as cessation of airflow at the nose and mouth during sleep. In obstructive sleep apnea, airflow ceases because of complete occlusion of the upper airway at the oropharyngeal level, despite continued activation of the inspiratory muscles.[29,30] In contrast, in central sleep apnea, airflow ceases because drive to all the respiratory muscles is transiently abolished. Isolated central apneas may occur in healthy subjects, particularly during REM sleep.[5] Obstructive apneas are generally considered to be pathologic. In patients with clinically important obstructive sleep apnea, there are usually at least 15 obstructive apnea and hypopnea episodes per hour of sleep. However, evidence has emerged that a high upper airway resistance during sleep (manifested by snoring) that is accompanied by recurrent arousals from sleep, even in the absence of outright apneas and hypopneas, can also result in a clinically important "sleep apnea" syndrome.[31,32] Therefore, the absence of apneas and hypopneas in a symptomatic patient does not unequivocally exclude a sleep-related respiratory disorder.

PATHOGENESIS

The definitive event in obstructive sleep apnea is posterior movement of the tongue and palate into apposition with the posterior pharyngeal wall, resulting in occlusion of the nasopharynx and oropharynx.[29,30] The resulting airway obstruction initiates a primary sequence of events (Fig. 74.3) that may repeat itself hundreds of times each night. With the onset of sleep, the upper airway occludes, resulting in cessation of airflow despite continuing respiratory efforts. As a result of apnea, progressive asphyxia develops, until there is a brief arousal from sleep, restoration of upper airway patency, and resumption of airflow. With the relief of asphyxia, the patient quickly returns to sleep, only to have the sequence of events repeated over and over again.[33]

Several underlying mechanisms contribute to the onset and termination of upper airway occlusion during sleep.[34] In general terms, upper airway collapse occurs when the

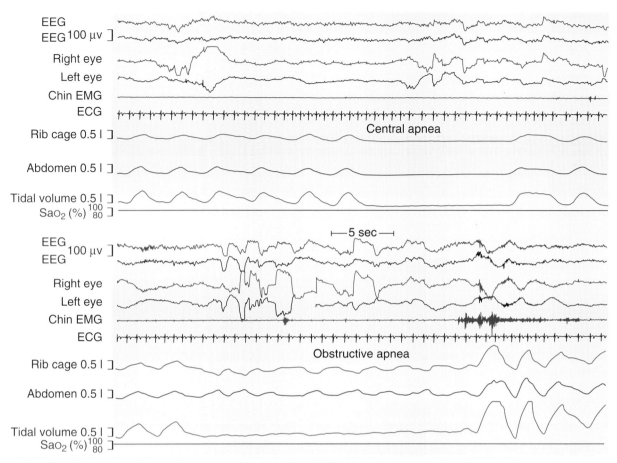

Figure 74.2 Recorder tracings during polysomnographic study show distinction between central and obstructive apneas, using a respiratory inductive plethysmograph. Upper and lower panels form a continuous record in rapid eye movement sleep. Channels from the top down show the following: electroencephalogram (EEG), right and left eye movements, submental electromyogram (EMG), electrocardiogram (ECG), movements of rib cage and abdomen, tidal volume, and arterial oxygen saturation (Sao_2). Note that during central apnea the absence of tidal volume excursion was accompanied by absence of rib cage and abdominal movements; during obstructive apnea, paradoxical rib cage and abdominal movements were present. (From Phillipson EA, Bowes G: Sleep disorders. *In* Fishman AP [ed]: Update of Pulmonary Diseases and Disorders. New York: McGraw-Hill, 1982, pp 256–273.)

subatmospheric pharyngeal pressure generated during inspiration exceeds by some critical amount the stabilizing forces generated by the dilator and abductor muscles of the upper airway.[7,34–37] Both structural and functional factors contribute to the development of a critical airway-collapsing pressure.[34] A minority of patients have obvious anatomic narrowing of the upper airway, as a result of micrognathia and retrognathia, adenotonsillar hypertrophy, macroglossia, or acromegaly.[38–40] However, in the majority of patients who are free of such disorders, the structural defect is subtle but can be demonstrated during wakefulness by a variety of imaging techniques, including computed tomography scanning of the upper airway, acoustic reflection measurements of the pharyngeal area, cephalometric roentgenography, magnetic resonance imaging, and videoendoscopy.[7,29,41–46] Obesity frequently contributes to the upper airway narrowing.[41,45,47] In addition to a reduction in oropharyngeal size, the compliance of the upper airway may be increased, resulting in a tendency for the airway to be floppy and to collapse when subjected to a negative pressure.[36,37,48–50]

Because the apneas occur only during sleep, it is obvious that the state of the central nervous system plays an important role in pathogenesis of the disorder. During wakeful-

ness, upper airway muscle activity is greater than normal in patients with obstructive sleep apnea, presumably to compensate for airway narrowing and a high airway resistance.[34,51,52] The normal decrease in upper airway muscle activity that occurs at onset of sleep[7,53,54] may be sufficient to allow the development of a critical airway-collapsing pressure during inspiration in susceptible individuals.[7,34] In addition, the fluctuation of central nervous system state that normally occurs at the onset of sleep results in a transient instability in respiratory drive (characterized by periodic breathing) that is also exerted on the muscles of the upper airway.[55,56] As a result, the transient reductions in upper airway muscle activity may be excessive in relation to the reductions in diaphragmatic activity.[57–60] Under these conditions, the negative airway pressure generated during inspiration can become sufficient to collapse the pharynx. Therefore, sleep can be considered to exert a permissive influence on upper airway function that predisposes to upper airway collapse in persons who are susceptible because of a small airway lumen.

Physiologic reductions in upper airway muscle activity are particularly marked during REM sleep, which probably accounts for the tendency for obstructive sleep apnea to first

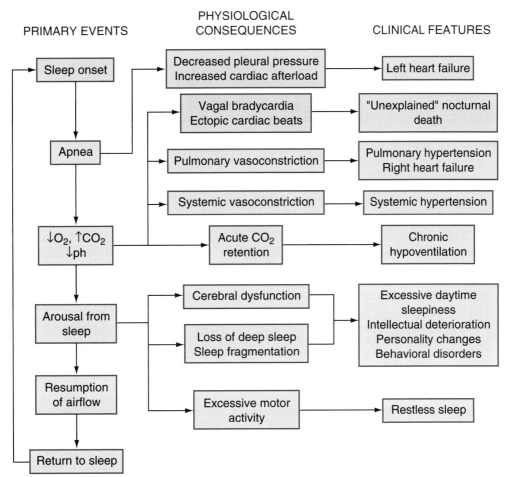

PRIMARY EVENTS   PHYSIOLOGICAL CONSEQUENCES   CLINICAL FEATURES

Figure 74.3 Schema shows the primary sequence of events, physiologic responses, and clinical features of obstructive sleep apnea. (Modified from Phillipson EA: Sleep apnea. Med Clin North Am 23:2314–2323, 1982.)

develop in this stage of sleep.[4,48] Alcohol and other sedatives that selectively depress upper airway muscle activity may also promote upper airway collapse in susceptible individuals.[61-64] In many of these patients, varying degrees of nasal obstruction are also present. The resulting high upstream resistance predisposes to upper airway collapse by increasing the degree of subatmospheric pressure generated in the pharynx during inspiration, because the strength of diaphragmatic contraction is increased to overcome airflow resistance in the nose.

Termination of obstructive apnea depends on a brief arousal to a lighter stage of sleep, which is accompanied by activation of the upper airway dilator and abductor muscles and restoration of airway patency.[7,35,65] In some cases there may be an outright awakening from sleep. The specific factors involved in the arousal response probably involve chemical stimuli related to asphyxia and mechanical stimuli related to breathing against an occluded airway.[13,66,67] Carotid body defects markedly prolong obstructive apneas in experimental animals[68] and are thought to play a similar role in hypercapnic patients with this condition.[69] Arousal can also be delayed by factors that interfere with reticular activation, such as REM sleep, which probably accounts for the fact that apneas are typically longer and associated with more severe degrees of asphyxia in this stage of sleep.[13,69] Alcohol, sedative medications, and chronic sleep deprivation also impair central nervous system arousability and prolong obstructive apneas.[61,63,70,71]

CLINICAL FEATURES

The primary sequence of nocturnal events that characterizes obstructive sleep apnea elicits a series of secondary physiologic responses, which in turn give rise to the clinical features and complications of the syndrome (see Fig. 74.3). In broad terms, the clinical manifestations segregate into two groups. One group is predominantly neuropsychological and behavioral and is thought to arise ultimately from the recurrent arousals that terminate each apnea, although recurrent cerebral hypoxia also plays a role. The second group, predominantly cardiorespiratory, is related largely but not exclusively to the recurrent episodes of nocturnal asphyxia.

The most common manifestations of obstructive sleep apnea are neuropsychological and behavioral, with excessive daytime sleepiness, decreased energy, and fatigue being the most common complaints.[72] Initially, daytime sleepiness develops under passive conditions such as watching television and reading, but as the disorder progresses, sleepiness encroaches progressively into all daily activities and can become severely disabling and dangerous. Tests of driving ability reveal significant impairment in patients with obstructive sleep apnea, and rates of motor vehicle accidents among these patients are considerably increased compared with those among control subjects.[73-76] Frequently associated with excessive daytime sleepiness are signs of intellectual impairment, memory loss, poor judgment, and personality changes.[72,77-79] Although these manifestations of obstructive sleep apnea are probably related to nocturnal sleep fragmentation and loss of the deeper stages of sleep, patients with apparently similar nocturnal disturbances may demonstrate widely varying degrees of daytime impairment. Furthermore, the patient is frequently unaware of excessive daytime sleepiness or intellectual deterioration; therefore, questioning of family members is an important aspect of history taking.

The most common nocturnal symptom is loud snoring, indicative of upper airway narrowing. Typically, snoring has been present for many years before other symptoms develop, at which time the snoring takes on a temporal character, being interrupted periodically by episodes of silence corresponding to the occlusive events. The termination of each apnea episode is usually heralded by a very loud snoring gasp, accompanied by body movement and flailing of the limbs. The patient may be unaware of these events but often complains of a disturbed or restless sleep, as does the bed partner. Occasionally, the patient awakens fully and may complain of choking, air hunger, or insomnia. Most patients complain of an unrefreshing sleep, mental fogginess and disorientation, and, occasionally, a headache on arising in the morning.[72]

CARDIOVASCULAR COMPLICATIONS

Mounting epidemiologic evidence points to an association between obstructive sleep apnea and several cardiovascular disorders, although a causal relationship has yet to be firmly established.[80,81] The strongest evidence is that between obstructive sleep apnea and systemic hypertension, with large cross-sectional and prospective cohort studies demonstrating significantly increased odds of prevalent and new hypertension in subjects with obstructive sleep apnea.[82-84] Conversely, among unselected patients with hypertension, up to 35% have obstructive sleep apnea,[85-87] and in those with drug-resistant hypertension, the prevalence of obstructive sleep apnea has been reported to be as high as 85%.[88] Cross-sectional data from the Sleep Heart Health Study also indicate an association between obstructive sleep apnea and ischemic heart disease, stroke, and congestive heart failure, independent of other known risk factors.[89]

Several physiologic mechanisms may contribute to the cardiovascular disorders associated with obstructive sleep apnea. For example, systemic blood pressure usually rises transiently during obstructive apneas or at apnea termination as a result of sympathetic activation and reflex vasoconstriction secondary to asphyxia, arousal from sleep, and changes in intrathoracic pressure[90-93] (Fig. 74.4). Blood pressure then falls toward baseline on resumption of breathing, but unlike healthy subjects, patients with obstructive sleep apnea fail to lower their overall blood pressure during sleep.[90,94] More than 50% of patients with obstructive sleep apnea have systemic hypertension, possibly related to chronically excessive sympathetic nervous system activity and elevated plasma norepinephrine concentrations,[91,93,95-98] and to impaired endothelial-mediated vasodilatory responsiveness.[99-102] Experimental studies in an animal model of the disorder directly demonstrate that obstructive sleep apnea can lead to sustained increases in waking blood pressure.[103]

In addition to systemic hypertension, there is mounting clinical and experimental evidence that obstructive sleep

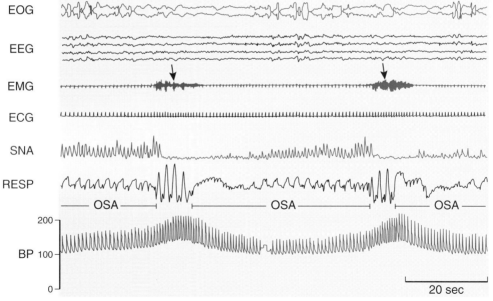

Figure 74.4 Recordings of sympathetic activity (from the peroneal nerve) and of arterial blood pressure in a patient with obstructive sleep apnea (OSA). Muscle sympathetic nerve activity (SNA) is suppressed at the beginning of the apnea but increases as arterial oxygen saturation (not shown) decreases, reaching a peak at termination of the apnea, after which it is abruptly inhibited by lung inflation. Surges in blood pressure (BP) peak shortly after peak muscle SNA and arousal from sleep (*arrows*). Other channels show the electroencephalogram (EEG), electrocardiogram (ECG), electromyogram (EMG), electro-oculogram (EOG), and respirations (RESP). (From Somers VK, Dyken ME, Clary MP, et al: Sympathetic neural mechanisms in obstructive sleep apnea. J Clin Invest 96:1897–1904, 1995.) *See Color Plate*

apnea may adversely affect left ventricular function both acutely and chronically. Acutely, the exaggerated negative intrathoracic pressure generated during obstructive apneas reduces stroke volume and cardiac output by increasing left ventricular afterload and reducing left ventricular preload.[104,105] Negative intrathoracic pressure, which can reach as much as −90 cm H_2O (−65 mm Hg), increases left ventricular transmural pressure, an important determinant of left ventricular afterload, and reduces left ventricular preload through its effect on ventricular interactions.[104,106–111] These adverse effects of exaggerated negative intrathoracic pressure on stroke volume are more pronounced in patients with underlying left ventricular dysfunction than in healthy subjects.[107,112] The acute hemodynamic disturbances induced by obstructive apneas could play a role in the development of nocturnal angina and pulmonary edema that have been reported in patients with obstructive sleep apnea.[113–116]

Intermittent hypoxia during obstructive apneas can also adversely affect left ventricular performance through its effects on preload, afterload, and contractility. Elevations in pulmonary artery pressure due to apnea-related hypoxia impede right ventricular emptying and reduce the rate of relaxation of both ventricles.[117] These effects, along with those related to negative intrathoracic pressure, can compromise left ventricular filling.[110,118,119] Hypoxia can also contribute to acute elevations in systemic blood pressure through stimulation of the sympathetic nervous system,[120] an effect that is exaggerated in patients with congestive heart failure.[121] As a result of these elevations in left ventricular afterload and in sympathetic cardiac stimulation, the oxygen demands of the myocardium are likely to be increased, which could precipitate myocardial ischemia, nocturnal angina, and cardiac arrhythmias in patients with underlying coronary artery disease.[93,113,115,116,121–123] Given these associations, the notion has developed that obstructive sleep apnea can result in sudden death during sleep,[115,124] but rigorous data in support of this notion are lacking.

Emerging data also point to an association between obstructive sleep apnea and chronic left ventricular dysfunction, although it has not been established that obstructive sleep apnea can result in overt left ventricular failure in the absence of chronic hypertension, coronary artery disease, or underlying myocardial dysfunction.[125–127] Nevertheless, alleviation of obstructive sleep apnea in some patients with congestive heart failure has produced a remarkable improvement in left ventricular ejection fraction and a decrease in exertional dyspnea.[106,128,129] Furthermore, studies in a canine model of obstructive sleep apnea have demonstrated a decrease in left ventricular ejection fraction after 1 to 3 months of exposure to recurrent upper airway occlusion during sleep.[108] Muscle sympathetic nerve activity and plasma norepinephrine concentrations are chronically increased in patients with obstructive sleep apnea.[91,93,97,98] It is known that survival of patients with congestive heart failure is inversely proportional to cardiac sympathetic nerve activity and plasma norepinephrine concentration,[130,131] providing a possible explanation for the deleterious effects of obstructive sleep apnea in patients with congestive heart failure.

Obstructive sleep apnea may also impact on the cardiovascular system by causing increases in platelet aggregability, blood coagulability, inflammatory mediators, and reactive oxygen species, all of which have been implicated in atherogenesis and arterial thrombus formation.[132–137] Furthermore, treatment of obstructive sleep apnea lowers production of reactive oxygen species, adhesion molecule expression, leukocyte adherence to endothelial cells, and vascular endothelial growth factor.[137,138] Emerging data also suggest that obstructive sleep apnea may be an independent risk factor for the metabolic syndrome, increased insulin resistance, and glucose intolerance, and that treatment of the disorder improves insulin sensitivity, independent of weight loss.[139–142]

Ten percent to 15% of patients with obstructive sleep apnea develop sustained pulmonary hypertension leading to right-sided heart failure.[143] Acute pulmonary vasoconstriction has been well documented during obstructive apneas, but pulmonary arterial pressure during wakefulness is typically normal.[15,90] The development of sustained pulmonary hypertension may require the presence of daytime hypoxemia and hypercapnia in addition to severe nocturnal desaturation.[143–144] The daytime blood gas disturbances can generally be attributed to the combined effects of obesity, diffuse airway obstruction, and reduced respiratory drive. In contrast, it is not clear that severe nocturnal hypoxemia alone is associated with the development of right-sided heart failure. Ten percent to 15% of patients with obstructive sleep apnea also develop chronic hypercapnia.[145] When combined with right-sided heart failure, obesity, and daytime sleepiness, such patients are said to have the *pickwickian* or obesity-hypoventilation syndrome. The development of chronic carbon dioxide retention appears to require the presence of obesity, mild to moderate diffuse airway obstruction, and reductions in ventilatory chemosensitivity and respiratory drive.[145–147] Together, these disturbances attenuate the normal hyperpnea that typically develops between nocturnal obstructive events, thereby preventing correction of the blood gas disturbances that develop during the apnea episodes.[146]

DIAGNOSIS

The typical patient with obstructive sleep apnea is a middle-aged or elderly man or woman, mildly to moderately overweight and hypertensive, who presents with a history of snoring, restless and unrefreshing sleep, nocturnal choking or dyspnea, and excessive daytime sleepiness or fatigue.[72] In women, particularly postmenopausal women, the complaint of snoring is less frequent than in men, and daytime fatigue may be more frequent than outright sleepiness. The disease is less common in premenopausal women, children, young men, and nonobese individuals. Because the symptoms of obstructive sleep apnea may resemble those of congestive heart failure, sleep apnea is frequently overlooked in patients with underlying cardiac disease, an important oversight that should be avoided, given the increased rate of mortality that sleep apnea confers on such patients.[148,149] In the patient with a typical clinical picture and a high pretest probability of obstructive sleep apnea, the diagnosis can often be confirmed by overnight screening tests (see "Laboratory Assessment" section earlier), particularly the finding of recurrent episodes of arterial oxygen desaturation (see Fig. 74.1). In contrast, negative screening test results do not exclude the diagnosis.[150–152] There is considerable interest in the role of unattended home sleep-monitoring in the investigation of obstructive sleep apnea, and some evidence of its usefulness, but the role of such studies in routine practice has yet to be established.[152,153] Thus, laboratory polysomnography (see "Laboratory Assessment" section earlier) remains the definitive approach to diagnosis, by the demonstration of recurrent episodes of airflow cessation accompanied by continuing respiratory effort (see Fig. 74.2).

A common clinical dilemma in the investigation of possible obstructive sleep apnea is the patient with a history of mild snoring who is otherwise completely asymptomatic and in good health and in whom no apnea episodes have been witnessed by the bed partner. Although some of these patients may well have a mild degree of sleep apnea, it has not been clearly established that snoring per se or even mild sleep apnea is associated with long-term health complications.[154] Hence, there is no firm indication for sleep studies in such patients, because management, which consists of counseling regarding the need for reduction of weight and of alcohol consumption (where appropriate), cessation of smoking, and avoidance of sleeping in the supine posture,[155,156] is unlikely to be changed by the demonstration of a few obstructive events during sleep.

MANAGEMENT

The indications for treatment of patients with obstructive sleep apnea have not been firmly established, but useful guidelines have been developed.[156] In establishing a treatment strategy, it is essential that the severity of the disorder be defined, based on the clinical symptoms and the objective level of nocturnal respiratory and sleep disturbance.[152,157] There is general agreement that patients with neuropsychological or cardiorespiratory complications of the disorder warrant treatment. In contrast, there is uncertainty regarding the approach to treatment in patients who snore but are completely asymptomatic, most of whom will be found to have an increased upper airway resistance during sleep but fewer than 10 apneas and hypopneas and arousals per hour of sleep. This uncertainty relates to the fact that the natural history of untreated snoring or very mild obstructive sleep apnea has not been defined. However, even in the absence of such definitive knowledge, because snoring can be highly disruptive to the sleep of the bed partner, at minimum asymptomatic snorers should receive preventive counseling that is designed to alleviate snoring and to delay its progression to outright sleep apnea. This counseling includes measures that are similar to those prescribed for patients with mild to moderate symptoms, including weight reduction (where appropriate), avoidance of alcohol and sedatives, and avoidance of sleeping in the supine posture (to the extent possible).[155,158]

More invasive approaches to asymptomatic snoring include oral appliances that are designed to keep the tongue forward or to advance the entire mandible. The efficacy of such devices in abolishing snoring has been reported to be 55% to 100%.[158–161] Nasal continuous positive airway pressure (nasal CPAP, to be described later) is highly effective in relieving snoring but is generally not well accepted by asymptomatic snorers.[162] Apart from the conservative measures already noted, currently the most popular invasive

treatment for simple snoring is pharyngeal surgery, including both traditional uvulopalatopharyngoplasty and laser-assisted uvulopalatoplasty.[163,164] Relief of snoring has been reported in up to 80% of patients.

Several different treatments are currently prescribed for patients with symptomatic obstructive sleep apnea, including intraoral appliances, surgery, and nasal CPAP during sleep. Intraoral appliances are designed to keep the mandible and tongue forward and thereby increase the size of the upper airway lumen. Several devices have been demonstrated to be of benefit in selected cases.[159–161,165,166] Surgical approaches include uvulopalatopharyngoplasty, which is designed to increase the size of the oropharyngeal lumen by removing redundant soft tissue.[163] The rate of overall long-term cure is less than 50%,[167] but higher rates of success can be achieved by more discriminating selection of appropriate patients.[167–169] Other surgical approaches, including mandibular advancement, hyoid osteotomy, and similar procedures, have a more limited application but higher rates of success in selected patients.[167]

At present, the most effective and widespread treatment for obstructive sleep apnea is nasal CPAP,[156] which provides a pneumatic splint to the airway and prevents development of a critical subatmospheric collapsing pressure.[170] Nasal CPAP is highly effective in the sleep laboratory and is well tolerated by most patients (60% to 85%), even over a period of years.[171–173] Furthermore, nasal CPAP has been demonstrated to improve sleep quality, reduce daytime sleepiness and driving accidents, and decrease nocturnal hypertension.[173] In some centers, nasal CPAP treatment is initiated during the diagnostic study night once the diagnosis has been established, but proper patient training and education on a subsequent day are critically important to ensure long-term compliance. Patients who are unable to tolerate conventional nasal CPAP despite an adequate trial may respond well to second- and third-generation devices that provide more flexible algorithms in titrating the airway pressure.[156,173]

The only treatment for obstructive sleep apnea that has been tested specifically in patients with cardiovascular disease is nasal CPAP. In patients with obstructive sleep apnea and hypertension, CPAP at optimal therapeutic pressures reduces both nocturnal and daytime blood pressure.[174] Preliminary studies have demonstrated similar benefits even in patients with obstructive sleep apnea and refractory hypertension.[175] In patients with ischemic heart disease and nocturnal angina who are receiving appropriate pharmacologic therapy for angina, treatment of obstructive sleep apnea with CPAP can markedly reduce the frequency of nocturnal cardiac ischemic events.[116] Similarly, in patients with obstructive sleep apnea and congestive heart failure, CPAP has immediate beneficial effects, including improvements in nocturnal oxygenation, reductions in the frequency of arousals, consolidation of sleep, and augmentation of cardiac output.[106] In addition, long-term treatment with nocturnal nasal CPAP results in marked improvements in left ventricular ejection fraction during the daytime and in reductions in exertional dyspnea.[106,128,129] Because the beneficial effects of unloading the heart at night lead to improvements in left ventricular function and cardiac functional status that are sustained throughout the day, CPAP should be considered the treatment of choice for obstructive sleep apnea in patients with ischemic heart disease or congestive heart failure.

In patients with severe obstructive sleep apnea in whom all other treatment approaches are ineffective or not tolerated, tracheostomy is indicated and provides immediate relief by bypassing the site of oropharyngeal obstruction during sleep.[176,177] In such cases, the tracheostomy needs to be opened only at night and can be plugged during waking hours. However, tracheostomy is now performed very rarely in most centers, having been replaced by other treatment modalities, notably nasal CPAP during sleep.

PERIODIC BREATHING AND CENTRAL SLEEP APNEA

Central sleep apnea is defined as a cessation of breathing during sleep that results from transient abolition of drive to the respiratory muscles. *Periodic breathing* refers to a regular waxing and waning of ventilation as a result of fluctuations in central respiratory drive. In some persons, the waning phase of periodic breathing may include a short period of outright apnea that is typically central in type. In such cases, central sleep apnea can be considered a manifestation and exaggeration of periodic breathing. Because this form of central sleep apnea is the type most frequently encountered in clinical practice and shares common underlying mechanisms with periodic breathing,[57,178] these two sleep-related breathing disturbances are best considered together.

PATHOGENESIS

Central sleep apnea is not a single disease entity but rather includes several disorders in which the definitive event is the withdrawal of effective central drive to the respiratory muscles.[178,179] The resulting decrease in ventilation initiates a primary sequence of events similar to those that occur in the obstructive sleep apnea syndrome (see Fig. 74.3). On the basis of theoretical, experimental, and clinical considerations, two distinct underlying mechanisms have been invoked to account for cessation of central respiratory output during sleep. First are outright defects in the respiratory control system or in the respiratory neuromuscular apparatus. Such defects generally result in a chronic alveolar hypoventilation syndrome, manifested by some degree of daytime hypercapnia (see Chapter 73). However, the full impact of such defects usually becomes apparent only during sleep, when the stimulatory influence of behavioral, cortical, and reticular inputs to the brain-stem respiratory neurons (referred to as the waking neural drive to breathing[180]) is minimized and breathing becomes critically dependent on the defective metabolic respiratory control system.[5,181]

In contrast to central sleep apnea that results from underlying defects in the respiratory controller or neuromuscular systems are central apneic disorders that arise from transient fluctuations or instabilities in an otherwise intact respiratory control system. These instabilities, manifested by periodic breathing, typically occur only during drowsiness and light sleep, and because there is no defect in respiratory control or drive, arterial P_{CO_2} levels during steady-state wakefulness or slow-wave sleep are normal or even low.[178,179,182] Several

theoretical and experimental models have been developed to account for such transient fluctuations in central respiratory drive.[183–187] Common to all these models is a P_{CO_2} level during sleep that falls transiently below the critical threshold value required for maintenance of respiratory rhythm.

Such transient discrepancies in P_{CO_2} levels arise in a number of conditions, the most common of which is the transition from wakefulness to sleep. Because of the waking neural drive to breathing, ventilation is higher and P_{CO_2} levels are lower during wakefulness than during established sleep.[5] Withdrawal of this drive at the transition from wakefulness to sleep results in a P_{CO_2} level that (although appropriate for wakefulness) is below the steady-state value appropriate for sleep (Fig. 74.5). If this P_{CO_2} level of wakefulness is below the threshold value for rhythm generation during sleep, an outright apnea will ensue at onset of sleep until P_{CO_2} rises to the critical threshold value. If sleep becomes firmly established at this point, regular breathing follows without further apneas or hypopneas. However, the transition from waking to sleep is often characterized by repeated fluctuations in central nervous system state between "awake" and "asleep." With each momentary arousal from sleep toward wakefulness, the P_{CO_2} levels that were present during sleep represent a hypercapnic stimulus during wakefulness, and ventilation therefore increases in accordance with the awake response to carbon dioxide, resulting in the

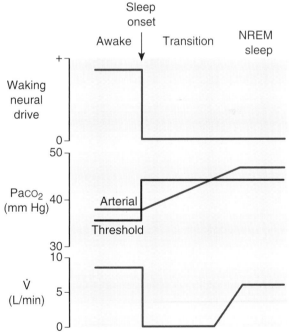

Figure 74.5 Schematic diagram showing a proposed mechanism underlying central sleep apnea at sleep onset. With the loss of the waking neural drive to breathing at sleep onset, there is an increase in the arterial threshold P_{CO_2} required to maintain respiratory rhythm. As a result, the arterial P_{CO_2} (Pa_{CO_2}) that was present during wakefulness may be below the threshold P_{CO_2} for rhythm generation in sleep; hence, ventilation ($\dot{V}$) falls to zero and apnea ensues until arterial P_{CO_2} rises above the threshold level for rhythm generation in sleep, whereupon rhythmic breathing resumes. NREM, non–rapid eye movement. (From Bradley TD, Phillipson EA: Central sleep apnea. Clin Chest Med 13:493–505, 1992.)

hyperpneic phase of periodic breathing. The changes in ventilation from the sleeping to the waking phase are a mirror image of those that occur in the waking-to-sleeping phase. This cycle of hypopnea (or apnea) alternating with hyperpnea is repeated until sleep becomes established.

In this scheme, the magnitude of fluctuation in ventilation with changes in central nervous system state depends on the difference between the awake and sleeping values of PCO_2 and the steepness of the ventilatory response to carbon dioxide during wakefulness.[187a] Any factor that magnifies these variables enhances the tendency to periodic breathing and central sleep apnea. For example, at high altitude, the alveolar hyperventilation that results from hypoxia drives arterial and cerebral PCO_2 levels well below the critical threshold value required for maintenance of respiratory rhythm during sleep.[188,189] Hypoxia may also increase the steepness of the ventilatory response to carbon dioxide. As a result, periodic breathing, characterized by brief central apneas alternating with vigorous hyperpneas, is typical among sojourners at high altitude.[190] Similarly, any cardiac or pulmonary disorder that results in hypoxia and alveolar hyperventilation during wakefulness is likely to be associated with periodic breathing and central apnea during light sleep.

CENTRAL SLEEP APNEA IN PATIENTS WITH LEFT VENTRICULAR HEART DISEASE

Periodic breathing with central sleep apnea is frequently observed in patients with congestive heart failure, in whom the periodic breathing is characterized by a prolonged classic crescendo-decrescendo pattern of tidal volume (Cheyne-Stokes respiration).[191,192] In contrast to obstructive sleep apnea, Cheyne-Stokes respiration appears to result from, rather than cause, congestive heart failure, but can have secondary pathologic consequences for patients with heart failure.

The key factor in the pathogenesis of central sleep apnea in congestive heart failure is similar to that described previously and involves oscillations in arterial PCO_2 below and above the threshold for apnea.[193,194] Reductions in arterial PCO_2 below the threshold transiently shut off the central respiratory drive and trigger central apnea, the length of which is proportional to the preceding degree of hyperventilation and the magnitude of reduction of arterial PCO_2 below the apnea threshold.[186,195] For the same degree of left ventricular systolic dysfunction, patients with Cheyne-Stokes respiration hyperventilate more and have a lower arterial PCO_2 both awake and asleep than do patients without Cheyne-Stokes respiration.[193,196] The higher ventilation and lower arterial PCO_2 are associated with higher left ventricular end-diastolic volumes and filling pressures, as well as increased peripheral and central chemoreceptor sensitivity.[197–199] Therefore, the chronic hyperventilation is probably caused mainly by stimulation of pulmonary vagal receptors by pulmonary congestion, and by augmented ventilatory responses to chemical stimuli.[199,200] As a result of the chronic hyperventilation, the arterial PCO_2 levels in patients with central sleep apnea are very close to the apneic threshold. Under these conditions, abrupt increases in ventilation, frequently triggered by arousals from sleep, drive arterial PCO_2 below the threshold, precipitating central apneas.[193,195]

The critical role of reductions in arterial PCO_2 in precipitating central apneas is demonstrated by the observation that raising the PCO_2 by just 1 to 3 mm Hg (e.g., by inhalation of a carbon dioxide–enriched gas mixture) abolishes central sleep apnea in patients with and without congestive heart failure[194,201] (Fig. 74.6).

As in patients with obstructive sleep apnea, sleep fragmentation due to arousals at the termination of apneas is probably an important cause of excessive daytime sleepiness and fatigue in patients with congestive heart failure and central sleep apnea.[202] Hypoxia and arousals from sleep are also associated with stimulation of the sympathetic nervous system.[11,91,93,203] Nocturnal and daytime norepinephrine concentrations are markedly higher in congestive heart failure patients with Cheyne-Stokes respiration and central sleep apnea than in those without sleep apnea and are directly proportional to the frequency of arousals from sleep and the degree of apnea-related hypoxia, but not to left ventricular ejection fraction.[204] Therefore, it appears that central sleep apnea can trigger sympathetic activation in patients with congestive heart failure and thereby exert a secondary deleterious effect on the underlying disorder.

CLINICAL FEATURES

In some persons, recurrent central apneas during sleep are not associated with any clinical manifestations or physiologic disturbances and are therefore of little clinical importance. In others, the primary sequence of nocturnal events that characterize central apnea may give rise to a series of clinical features and complications that are similar to those resulting from obstructive sleep apnea (see Fig. 74.3). Because several different mechanisms can produce central apnea, the associated clinical manifestations are variable.

In patients whose central apnea is a manifestation of an underlying defect in respiratory control or in neuromuscular function, the clinical picture is usually dominated by recurrent episodes of respiratory failure and features of a chronic alveolar hypoventilation syndrome, including carbon dioxide retention, hypoxemia, pulmonary hypertension, right-sided heart failure, and polycythemia.[178,179] Restless sleep, morning headache, chronic fatigue, and daytime sleepiness are also common in these patients, presumably as a consequence of nocturnal aggravation of hypoxemia and hypercapnia and disruption of normal sleep patterns. In contrast, patients whose central apnea is caused by transient fluctuations in respiratory drive during sleep do not have daytime hypercapnia and do not develop the cardiopulmonary complications of sleep apnea.[178,179] Rather, they typically present with features of disturbed sleep, including recurrent nocturnal awakenings, morning fatigue, and daytime sleepiness.[178,179] Because many of these patients also have a history of nasal obstruction and snoring, they are often initially thought to have obstructive sleep apnea. Patients with this type of central sleep apnea may present without any other associated clinical disorder (idiopathic central sleep apnea), but in many the central sleep apnea is secondary to the presence of congestive heart failure.[178,205] Some of the fatigue that characterizes the heart failure syndrome may be a result of sleep apnea rather than heart failure per se. Patients with heart failure and central sleep apnea may also complain of insomnia and paroxysmal nocturnal dyspnea.[191,206–208]

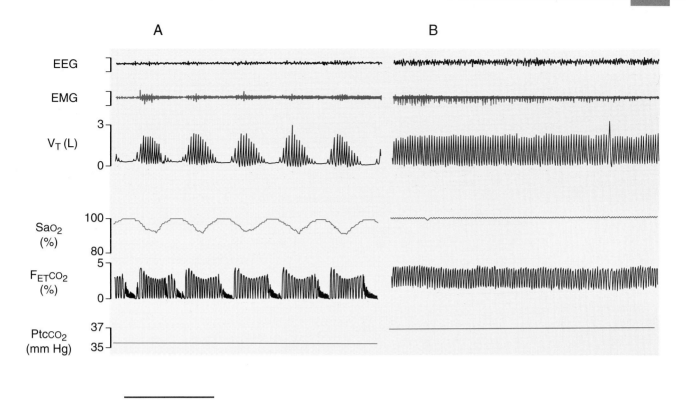

Figure 74.6 Polysomnographic recordings are shown from a patient during stage 2 sleep while breathing air **(A)** and 1% carbon dioxide in air **(B)**. Note abolition of central apneas on the tidal volume (V_T) trace and of recurrent decreases in arterial oxygen saturation (SaO_2) during carbon dioxide inhalation, in association with an increase in transcutaneous PCO_2 ($PtcCO_2$) of 1.6 mm Hg. EEG, electroencephalogram; EMG, submental electromyogram; $F_{ET}CO_2$, end-tidal carbon dioxide concentration. (From Lorenzi-Filho G, Rankin F, Bies I, et al: Effects of inhaled carbon dioxide and oxygen on Cheyne-Stokes respiration in patients with heart failure. Am J Respir Crit Care Med 159:1490–1498, 1999.)

The increased nocturnal and daytime sympathetic nervous activity associated with central sleep apnea in patients with congestive heart failure can aggravate myocardial dysfunction and contribute to disease progression.[123,204] For example, congestive heart failure patients with central sleep apnea have a higher rate of ventricular tachycardia than do patients without sleep apnea, and the timing of ventricular ectopic beats is linked to the central sleep apnea ventilatory cycle and its associated dips in arterial oxygen saturation.[209] The underlying cause of this relationship is unknown, but it could be a result of the apnea-related hypoxia, greater sympathetic nervous activity, recurrent surges in systemic blood pressure, or larger left ventricular volume in patients with central sleep apnea.[123,197,204] Because one third of patients with congestive heart failure die suddenly, presumably as a result of cardiac arrhythmias,[210] these relationships deserve further investigation. One or more of these factors may contribute to the increased mortality reported in congestive heart failure patients who have sleep apnea, compared with those who do not.[211]

DIAGNOSIS

The definitive diagnosis of a central sleep apnea disorder requires a polysomnographic study to demonstrate recurrent episodes of apnea accompanied by an absence of ventilatory effort. The latter criterion can best be confirmed by recording of pleural pressure swings with an esophageal catheter[19] (Fig. 74.7). In most patients, however, the cessation of respiratory drive can be reliably inferred from the coincident absence of rib cage and abdominal movements and of electromyographic activity of the diaphragm (recorded with surface electrodes).

In addition to confirming the presence of central sleep apnea, the polysomnographic findings usually provide an indication of whether the disorder is secondary to defects or to instabilities in the respiratory control system. In patients with defective metabolic respiratory control or neuromuscular disorders, there is a gradual reduction in ventilation to the point of apnea as the waking neural drive to breathing is withdrawn. The hypopneas and apneas are generally distributed across all stages of sleep but are more prolonged in REM sleep.[179] Furthermore, the reductions in ventilation are usually accompanied by marked decreases in arterial oxygen saturation and by increases (often of 10 to 20 mm Hg) in PCO_2 that can be measured continuously with a transcutaneous sensor. In contrast to these findings, in patients whose central sleep apnea is secondary to transient instabilities in respiratory drive, the apneas and hypopneas are typically associated with the transition from wakefulness to sleep and alternate with recurrent episodes of hyperpnea associated with arousals from sleep. Once

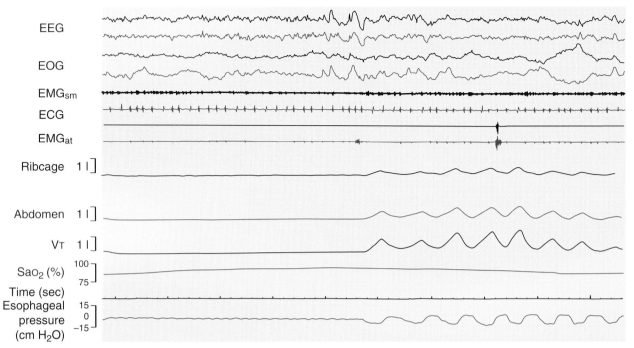

Figure 74.7 Polysomnographic recording of a central sleep apnea in a patient with congestive heart failure. Note the absence of rib cage and abdominal motion and of esophageal pressure excursions when there is no tidal volume (VT) excursion, indicating an absence of central respiratory drive. Other channels show the electroencephalogram (EEG), electrocardiogram (ECG), anterior tibialis and submental electromyogram (EMGat and EMGsm), and electro-oculogram (EOG). (From Takasaki Y, Orr D, Popkin J, et al: Effect of nasal continuous positive airway pressure on sleep apnea in congestive heart failure. Am Rev Respir Dis 140:1578–1584, 1989.)

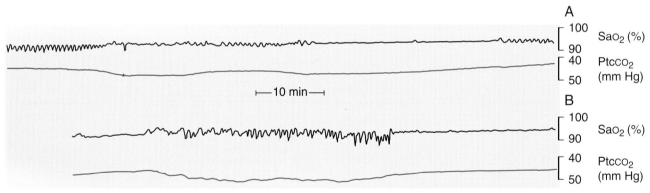

Figure 74.8 Compressed records of nocturnal arterial oxygen saturation (SaO_2) and transcutaneous PCO_2 ($PtcCO_2$) in a patient with idiopathic central sleep apnea **(A)**, and in a patient with obstructive sleep apnea **(B)**. Record reads from right to left. Note that in patient **A** the segments containing recurrent apneas (indicated by oscillations in SaO_2) are preceded by a small decrease in $PtcCO_2$. In contrast, in patient **B** the segment containing recurrent apneas is accompanied by a small increase in $PtcCO_2$. (From Bradley TD, Phillipson EA: Central sleep apnea. Clin Chest Med 13:493–505, 1992.)

sleep is established, breathing usually becomes regular, so during slow-wave and REM sleep, apneas and hypopneas are distinctly unusual. In most patients with this type of central sleep apnea, the apneic events are associated with only mild degrees of arterial oxygen desaturation and usually a small decrease in PCO_2 (Fig. 74.8). The *decrease* in PCO_2 related to state transitions plays a critical role in *generating* central apneas during sleep (see "Pathogenesis" section earlier), whereas in patients with defective respiratory control or muscle function, the *increase* in PCO_2 that occurs during sleep is the *result* of the central apneas.

MANAGEMENT

The management of central sleep apnea syndrome depends on the presence or absence of an underlying defect in respiratory drive or neuromuscular function. In patients with such defects, the management is usually the same as for a chronic alveolar hypoventilation syndrome (see Chapter 73). It is important that the patient be cautioned against the use of sedative medications that can aggravate the central sleep apnea and induce acute respiratory failure. Patients are occasionally improved by respiratory stimulant drugs, particularly medroxyprogesterone.[212] Supplemental nocturnal oxygen is of benefit in attenuating nocturnal hypoxemia but may result in more severe hypoventilation and prolongation of apnea episodes.[213,214] Despite such measures, the majority of patients with severe nocturnal hypoventilation and central apnea require some type of ventilatory assistance. For those with central alveolar hypoventilation syndromes, electrophrenic pacing of the diaphragm during sleep can be extremely effective.[215] When phrenic stimulation is not available or is inappropriate (as in neuromuscular disorders), mechanical ventilation is usually required, by means of either a positive-pressure ventilator applied through a tracheostomy or nose mask or a negative-pressure ventilator applied to the chest wall.[216–218] The administration of such treatment only during sleep often produces dramatic clinical improvement, with alleviation of daytime symptoms, lowering of daytime arterial PCO_2, and reversal of cardiovascular complications.[219,220]

The management of nonhypercapnic central sleep apnea disorders has not been clearly defined.[182] As would be expected from knowledge of the underlying mechanisms (see "Pathogenesis" section earlier), patients who are hypoxemic generally respond well to supplemental oxygen,[221] and others have benefited, at least in the short term, from acidification with acetazolamide.[222] More recently, this condition has been effectively managed with nasal CPAP, as for obstructive sleep apnea.[223,224] The mechanisms whereby nasal CPAP abolishes idiopathic central sleep apnea are not entirely clear but may involve an increase in PCO_2 above the apneic threshold as a result of the increase in expiratory mechanical load. Nasal CPAP is particularly effective in patients with central sleep apnea associated with congestive heart failure and results in improvements in daytime exercise tolerance and cardiac function, as well as sleep quality.[202,225] Randomized clinical trials of 1 to 3 months' duration have shown that nasal CPAP has a beneficial effect on several surrogate markers of mortality in patients with congestive heart failure, including increases in left ventricular ejection fraction, reductions in functional mitral regurgitation, and decreases in atrial natriuretic peptide and norepinephrine concentrations.[202,204,226,227] These findings suggest the potential for nasal CPAP to improve survival in patients with congestive heart failure and central sleep apnea, as has been demonstrated in small, randomized trials.[228]

SUMMARY

Breathing disorders during sleep can result in a broad range of clinical manifestations, the most prevalent of which are unrefreshing sleep, daytime sleepiness and fatigue, and cognitive impairment. There is also mounting evidence that respiratory-related sleep disturbances can contribute to several common cardiovascular and metabolic disorders, including systemic hypertension, cardiac dysfunction, and insulin resistance. The most common breathing disorder during sleep is obstructive sleep apnea, for which the most frequently prescribed treatment is the application of nasal CPAP during sleep. Central sleep apnea can occur as an isolated disturbance or in conjunction with central hypoventilation disorders, but is more commonly associated with

periodic breathing (Cheyne-Stokes respiration) in the setting of congestive heart failure, where it is thought to aggravate myocardial dysfunction and to contribute to disease progression. Nasal CPAP can be an effective treatment for central sleep apnea, and may have a beneficial effect on cardiac function in patients with Cheyne-Stokes respiration.

REFERENCES

1. Aserinsky E, Kleitman N: Regularly occurring periods of eye motility, and concomitant phenomena, during sleep. Science 118:273–274, 1953.
2. Dement WC, Kleitman N: Cyclic variations in EEG during sleep and their relation to eye movements, body motility, and dreaming. Electroencephalogr Clin Neurophysiol 9:673–690, 1957.
3. Jouvet M: Neurophysiology of the sleep states. Physiol Rev 47:117–177, 1967.
4. Rechtschaffen A, Kales A: A Manual of Standardized Terminology: Techniques and Scoring System for Sleep Stages of Human Subjects (Publication No. 204). Washington, DC: National Institutes of Health, 1968.
5. Phillipson EA, Bowes G: Control of breathing during sleep. In Cherniack NS, Widdicombe JG (eds): Handbook of Physiology. Section 3: The Respiratory System. Vol II: Control of Breathing (Part 2). Bethesda, Md: American Physiological Society, 1986, pp 649–689.
6. Morrell MJ, Dempsey JA: Impact of sleep on ventilation. In McNicholas WT, Phillipson EA (eds): Breathing Disorders in Sleep. London: WB Saunders, 2002, pp 3–17.
7. Horner RL: Motor control of the pharyngeal musculature and implications for the pathogenesis of obstructive sleep apnea. Sleep 19:827–853, 1996.
8. White DP, Weil JV, Zwillich CW: Metabolic rate and breathing during sleep. J Appl Physiol 59:384–391, 1985.
9. Somers VK, Dyken ME, Mark AL, et al: Sympathetic-nerve activity during sleep in normal subjects. N Engl J Med 328:303–307, 1993.
10. Shepard JW Jr: Gas exchange and hemodynamics during sleep. Med Clin North Am 69:1243–1264, 1985.
11. Hornyak M, Cejnar M, Elam M, et al: Sympathetic muscle nerve activity during sleep in man. Brain 114:1281–1295, 1991.
12. Davies RJ, Belt PJ, Roberts SJ, et al: Arterial blood pressure responses to graded transient arousal from sleep in normal humans. J Appl Physiol 74:1123–1130, 1993.
13. Bowes G, Phillipson EA: Arousal responses to respiratory stimuli during sleep. In Saunders NA, Sullivan CE (eds): Lung Biology in Health and Disease. Vol 21: Sleep and Breathing. New York: Marcel Dekker, 1984, pp 137–161.
14. Stradling JR, Phillipson EA: Breathing disorders during sleep. Q J Med 58:3–18, 1986.
15. Motta J, Guilleminault C, Schroeder JS, et al: Tracheostomy and hemodynamic changes in sleep-induced apnea. Ann Intern Med 89:454–458, 1978.
16. Coleman RM: Periodic movements in sleep (nocturnal myoclonus) and restless legs syndrome. In Guilleminault C (ed): Sleep and Waking Disorders: Indications and Techniques. Menlo Park, Calif: Addison-Wesley, 1982, pp 265–295.
17. Phillipson EA, Bowes G: Sleep disorders. In Fishman AP (ed): Update of Pulmonary Diseases and Disorders. New York: McGraw-Hill, 1982, pp 256–273.
18. Stradling JR, Chadwick GA, Quirk C, et al: Respiratory inductance plethysmography: Calibration techniques, their

validation and the effects of posture. Bull Eur Physiopathol Respir 21:317–324, 1985.

19. Staats BA, Bonekat HW, Harris CD, et al: Chest wall motion in sleep apnea. Am Rev Respir Dis 130:59–63, 1984.

20. Onal E, Lopata M, Ginzburg AS, et al: Diaphragmatic EMG and transdiaphragmatic pressure measurements with a single catheter. Am Rev Respir Dis 124:563–565, 1981.

21. Kreiger A: Assessment of the sleepy patient. In McNicholas WT, Phillipson EA (eds): Breathing Disorders in Sleep. London: WB Saunders, 2002, pp 3–17.

22. Bradley TD, Floras JS (eds): Lung Biology in Health and Disease. Vol 146: Sleep Apnea: Implications in Cardiovascular and Cerebrovascular Disease. New York: Marcel Dekker, 2000.

23. Grunstein RR: Hormonal and metabolic disturbances in sleep apnea. In McNicholas WT, Phillipson EA (eds): Breathing Disorders in Sleep. London: WB Saunders, 2002, pp 209–221.

24. Young T, Peppard PE, Gottlieb DJ: Epidemiology of obstructive sleep apnea. Am J Respir Crit Care Med 165:1217–1239, 2002.

25. Young T, Palta M, Dempsey J, et al: The occurrence of sleep-disordered breathing among middle-aged adults. N Engl J Med 328:1230–1235, 1993.

26. Young T, Finn L, Austin D, Peterson A: Menopausal status and sleep-disordered breathing in the Wisconsin Sleep Cohort Study. Am J Respir Crit Care Med 167:1181–1185, 2003.

27. Ancoli-Israel S, Kripke DF, Klauber MR, et al: Sleep disordered breathing in community-dwelling elderly. Sleep 14:486–495, 1991.

28. Young TB, Peppard P: Epidemiology of obstructive sleep apnea. In McNicholas WT, Phillipson EA (eds): Breathing Disorders in Sleep. London: WB Saunders, 2002, pp 31–43.

29. Suratt PM, Dee P, Atkinson RL, et al: Fluoroscopic and computed tomographic features of the pharyngeal airway in obstructive sleep apnea. Am Rev Respir Dis 127:487–492, 1983.

30. Hudgel DW: Variable site of airway narrowing among obstructive sleep apnea patients. J Appl Physiol 61:1403–1409, 1986.

31. Guilleminault C, Stoohs R, Clerk A, et al: Cause of excessive daytime sleepiness: The upper airway resistance syndrome. Chest 104:781–787, 1993.

32. Guilleminault C, Beck J, Carillo O: EEG arousal and upper airway resistance syndrome. Electroencephalogr Clin Neurophysiol 103:501, 1999.

33. Bradley TD, Phillipson EA: Pathogenesis and pathophysiology of the obstructive sleep apnea syndrome. Med Clin North Am 69:1169–1185, 1985.

34. Malhotra A, White DP: Pathogenesis of obstructive sleep apnea syndrome. In McNicholas WT, Phillipson EA (eds): Breathing Disorders in Sleep. London: WB Saunders, 2002, pp 441–463.

35. Remmers JE, de Groot WJ, Sauerland EK, et al: Pathogenesis of upper airway occlusion during sleep. J Appl Physiol 44:931–938, 1978.

36. Smith PL, Wise RA, Gold AR, et al: Upper airway pressure-flow relationships in obstructive sleep apnea. J Appl Physiol 64:789–795, 1988.

37. Schwartz AR, Smith PL, Wise RA, et al: Effect of positive nasal pressure on upper airway pressure-flow relationships. J Appl Physiol 66:1626–1634, 1989.

38. Bear SE, Priest JH: Sleep apnea syndrome: Correction with surgical advancement of the mandible. J Oral Maxillofac Surg 35:543–549, 1980.

39. Mezon BJ, West P, Maclean JP, et al: Sleep apnea in acromegaly. Am J Med 69:615–618, 1980.

40. Orr WC, Martin RJ: Obstructive sleep apnea associated with tonsillar hypertrophy in adults. Arch Intern Med 141:990–992, 1981.

41. Haponik EF, Smith PL, Bohlman ME, et al: Computerized tomography in obstructive sleep apnea. Am Rev Respir Dis 127:221–226, 1983.

42. Riley R, Guilleminault C, Herran J, et al: Cephalometric analyses and flow-volume loops in obstructive sleep apnea patients. Sleep 6:303–311, 1983.

43. Rivlin J, Hoffstein V, Kalbfleisch J, et al: Upper airway morphology in patients with idiopathic obstructive sleep apnea. Am Rev Respir Dis 129:355–360, 1984.

44. Lowe AA, Gionhaker N, Takeuchi K, et al: Three dimensional CT reconstructions of tongue and airway in adult subjects with obstructive sleep apnea. Am J Orthod Dentofacial Orthop 90:364–374, 1986.

45. Horner RL, Mohiaddin RH, Lowell DG, et al: Sites and sizes of fat deposits around the pharynx in obese patients with obstructive sleep apnoea and weight matched controls. Eur Respir J 2:613–622, 1989.

46. Schwab RJ, Pasirstein M, Pierson R, et al: Identification of upper airway anatomic risk factors for obstructive sleep apnea with volumetric magnetic resonance imaging. Am J Respir Crit Care Med 168:522–530, 2003.

47. Davies RJO, Stradling JR: The relationship between neck circumference, radiographic pharyngeal anatomy, and the obstructive sleep apnea syndrome. Eur Respir J 3:509–514, 1990.

48. Issa FG, Sullivan CE: Upper airway closing pressures in obstructive sleep apnea. J Appl Physiol 57:520–527, 1984.

49. Brown IG, Bradley TD, Phillipson EA, et al: Pharyngeal compliance in snoring subjects with and without obstructive sleep apnea. Am Rev Respir Dis 132:211–215, 1985.

50. Bradley TD, Brown IG, Grossman RF, et al: Pharyngeal size in snorers, non-snorers, and patients with obstructive sleep apnea. N Engl J Med 315:1327–1331, 1986.

51. Mezzanotte WS, Tangel DJ, White DP: Waking genioglossal electromyogram in sleep apnea patients versus normal controls (a neuromuscular compensatory mechanism). J Clin Invest 89:1571–1579, 1992.

52. Hendricks JC, Petrof BL, Panckeri K, et al: Compensatory hyperactivity of an upper airway dilator in bulldogs. Am Rev Respir Dis 148:185–194, 1993.

53. Sauerland EK, Harper RM: The human tongue during sleep: Electromyographic activity of the genioglossus muscle. Exp Neurol 51:160–170, 1976.

54. Wheatley JR, Mezzanote WS, Tangel DJ, et al: Influence of sleep on genioglossus muscle activation by negative pressure in normal men. Am Rev Respir Dis 148:597–605, 1993.

55. Onal E, Lopata M, O'Connor T: Pathogenesis of apneas in hypersomnia-sleep apnea syndrome. Am Rev Respir Dis 125:167–174, 1982.

56. Onal E, Lopata M: Periodic breathing and the pathogenesis of occlusive sleep apneas. Am Rev Respir Dis 126:676–680, 1982.

57. Cherniack NS: Sleep apnea and its causes. J Clin Invest 73:150–156, 1984.

58. Hudgel DW, Chapman KR, Faulks C, et al: Changes in inspiratory muscle electrical activity and upper airway resistance during periodic breathing induced by hypoxia during sleep. Am Rev Respir Dis 135:899–906, 1987.

59. Parisi RA, Neubauer JA, Frank MM, et al: Correlation between genioglossal and diaphragmatic responses to

hypercapnia during sleep. Am Rev Respir Dis 135:378–382, 1987.

60. Hudgel DW, Harasick T: Fluctuations in timing of upper airway and chest wall inspiratory muscle activity in obstructive sleep apnea. J Appl Physiol 69:443–450, 1990.

61. Taasan VC, Block AJ, Boysen PG, et al: Alcohol increases sleep apnea and oxygen desaturation in asymptomatic men. Am J Med 71:240–245, 1981.

62. Dolly FR, Block AJ: Effect of flurazepam on sleep-disordered breathing and nocturnal oxygen desaturation in asymptomatic subjects. Am J Med 73:239–243, 1982.

63. Issa FG, Sullivan CE: Alcohol, snoring and sleep apnea. J Neurol Neurosurg Psychiatry 45:353–359, 1982.

64. Krol RC, Knuth SL, Bartlett D Jr: Selective reduction of genio-glossal muscle activity by alcohol in normal human subjects. Am Rev Respir Dis 129:247–250, 1984.

65. Martin RJ, Pennock BE, Orr WC, et al: Respiratory mechanics and timing during sleep in occlusive sleep apnea. J Appl Physiol 48:432–437, 1980.

66. Vincken W, Guilleminault C, Silvestri L, et al: Inspiratory muscle activity as a trigger causing the airways to open in obstructive sleep apnea. Am Rev Respir Dis 135:372–377, 1987.

67. Yasuma F, Kozar LF, Kimoff RJ, et al: Interaction of chemical and mechanical respiratory stimuli in the arousal response to hypoxia in sleeping dogs. Am Rev Respir Dis 143:1274–1277, 1991.

68. Bowes G, Townsend ER, Bromley SM, et al: Role of the carotid body and of afferent vagal stimuli in the arousal response to airway occlusion in sleeping dogs. Am Rev Respir Dis 123:644–647, 1981.

69. Sullivan CE, Issa FG, Berthon-Jones M, et al: Pathophysiology of sleep apnea. In Saunders NA, Sullivan CE (eds): Lung Biology in Health and Disease. Vol 21: Sleep and Breathing. New York: Marcel Dekker, 1984, pp 299–363.

70. Bowes G, Woolf GM, Sullivan CE, et al: Effect of sleep fragmentation on ventilatory and arousal responses of sleeping dogs to respiratory stimuli. Am Rev Respir Dis 122:899–908, 1980.

71. Guilleminault C, Rosekind M: The arousal threshold: Sleep deprivation, sleep fragmentation, and obstructive sleep apnea syndrome. Bull Eur Physiopathol Respir 17:341–349, 1981.

72. Flemons WW, Whitelaw WA: Clinical features of obstructive sleep apnea syndrome. In McNicholas WT, Phillipson EA (eds): Breathing Disorders in Sleep. London: WB Saunders, 2002, pp 64–85.

73. George CF, Nickerson PW, Hanly PJ, et al: Sleep apnoea patients have more automobile accidents. Lancet 2:447, 1987.

74. Findley L, Fabrizio M, Thommi G, et al: Severity of sleep apnea and automobile crashes. N Engl J Med 320:868–869, 1989.

75. Barbe F, Pericas J, Munoz A, et al: Automobile accidents in patients with sleep apnea syndrome. Am J Respir Crit Care Med 158:18–22, 1998.

76. Teran-Santos J, Jiminez-Gomez A, Cordero-Guevara J: The association between sleep apnea and the risk of traffic accidents. N Engl J Med 340:847–851, 1999.

77. Telakivi T, Kajaste S, Partinen M, et al: Cognitive function in middle-aged snorers and controls: Role of excessive daytime somnolence and sleep related hypoxic events. Sleep 11:454–462, 1988.

78. Bedard MA, Montplaisir J, Richer F, et al: Obstructive sleep apnea syndrome: Pathogenesis of neuropsychological deficits. Clin Exp Neuropsychol 13:950–964, 1991.

79. Naegele B, Thouvard V, Pepin JL, et al: Deficits of cognitive executive functions in patients with sleep apnea syndrome. Sleep 18:43–52, 1995.

80. Lavie P: Pro: Sleep apnea causes cardiovascular disease. Am J Respir Crit Care Med 169:147–148, 2004.

81. Stradling J: Con: Sleep apnea does not cause cardiovascular disease. Am J Respir Crit Care Med 169:148–149, 2004.

82. Young T, Peppard P, Palta M, et al: Population-based study of sleep-disordered breathing as a risk factor for hypertension. Arch Intern Med 157:1746–1752, 1997.

83. Nieto FJ, Young TB, Lind BK, et al: Association of sleep-disordered breathing, sleep apnea, and hypertension in a large community-based study. Sleep Heart Health Study. JAMA 283:1829–1836, 2000.

84. Pepparad PE, Young T, Palta M, et al: Prospective study of the association between sleep-disordered breathing and hypertension. N Engl J Med 342:1378–1384, 2000.

85. Kales A, Cadieux RJ, Shaw LC III, et al: Sleep apnoea in a hypertensive population. Lancet 2:1005–1008, 1984.

86. Fletcher ED, DeBehnke RD, Lovoi MS, et al: Undiagnosed sleep apnea in patients with essential hypertension. Ann Intern Med 103:190–195, 1985.

87. Worsnop CJ, Naughton MT, Barter CE, et al: The prevalence of sleep apnea in hypertensives. Am J Respir Crit Care Med 157:111–115, 1998.

88. Logan AG, Perlikowski SM, Mente A, et al: High prevalence of obstructive sleep apnea in drug resistant hypertension. J Hypertens 19:2271–2277, 2001.

89. Shahar E, Whitney CW, Redline S, et al: Sleep-disordered breathing and cardiovascular disease: Cross-sectional results of the Sleep Heart Health Study. Am J Respir Crit Care Med 163:19–25, 2001.

90. Coccagna G, Mantovani M, Brignani F, et al: Continuous recording of the pulmonary and systemic arterial pressure during sleep in syndromes of hypersomnia with periodic breathing. Bull Eur Physiopathol Respir 8:1159–1172, 1972.

91. Hedner J, Ejnell H, Sellgren J, et al: Is high and fluctuating muscle nerve sympathetic activity in the sleep apnoea syndrome of pathogenetic importance for the development of hypertension? J Hypertens 6(Suppl 4):S529–S531, 1988.

92. Morgan BJ, Denahan T, Ebert TJ: Neurocirculatory consequences of negative intrathoracic pressure vs. asphyxia during voluntary apnea. J Appl Physiol 74:2969–2975, 1993.

93. Somers VK, Dyken ME, Clary MP, et al: Sympathetic neural mechanisms in obstructive sleep apnea. J Clin Invest 96:1897–1904, 1995.

94. Mateika JH, Mateika S, Slutsky AS, et al: The effect of snoring on mean arterial blood pressure during non-REM sleep. Am Rev Respir Dis 145:141–146, 1992.

95. Millman RP, Redline S, Carlisle CC, et al: Daytime hypertension in obstructive sleep apnea: Prevalence and contributing risk factors. Chest 99:861–866, 1991.

96. Fletcher EC, Miller J, Schaaf JW, et al: Urinary catecholamines before and after tracheostomy in patients with obstructive sleep apnea and hypertension. Sleep 10:35–44, 1987.

97. Carlson JT, Hedner J, Elam M, et al: Augmented resting sympathetic nerve activity in awake patients with obstructive sleep apnea. Chest 103:1763–1768, 1993.

98. Narkiewicz K, van de Borne PJ, Cooley RL, et al: Sympathetic activity in obese subjects with and without obstructive sleep apnea. Circulation 98:772–776, 1998.

99. Ip MS, Lam B, Chan LY, et al: Circulating nitric oxide is suppressed in obstructive sleep apnea and is reversed by

nasal continuous positive airway pressure. Am J Respir Crit Care Med 162:2166–2171, 2000.

100. Imadojemu VA, Gleeson K, Quraishi SA, et al: Impaired vasodilator responses in obstructive sleep apnea are improved with continuous positive airway pressure therapy. Am J Respir Crit Care Med 165:950–953, 2002.

101. Ip MSM, Tse HF, Lam B, et al: Endothelial function in obstructive sleep apnea and response to treatment. Am J Respir Crit Care Med 169:348–353, 2004.

102. Nieto FJ, Herrington DM, Redline S, et al: Sleep apnea and markers of vascular endothelial function in a large community sample of older adults. Am J Respir Crit Care Med 169:354–360, 2004.

103. Brooks D, Horner RL, Kozar LF, et al: Obstructive sleep apnea as a cause of systemic hypertension: Evidence from a canine model. J Clin Invest 99:106–109, 1997.

104. Buda AJ, Pinsky MR, Ingels NBJ, et al: Effect of intrathoracic pressure on left ventricular performance. N Engl J Med 301:453–459, 1979.

105. Bradley TD, Holloway RM, McLaughlin PR, et al: Cardiac output response to continuous positive airway pressure in congestive heart failure. Am Rev Respir Dis 145:377–382, 1992.

106. Malone S, Liu PP, Holloway R, et al: Obstructive sleep apnoea in patients with dilated cardiomyopathy: Effects of continuous positive airway pressure. Lancet 338:1480–1484, 1991.

107. Scharf SM, Bianco JA, Tow DE, et al: The effects of large negative intrathoracic pressure on left ventricular function in patients with coronary artery disease. Circulation 63:871–875, 1981.

108. Parker JD, Brooks D, Kozar LF, et al: Acute and chronic effects of airway obstruction on canine left ventricular performance. Am J Respir Crit Care Med 160:1888–1896, 1999.

109. Buda AJ, Schroeder JS, Guilleminault C: Abnormalities of pulmonary artery wedge pressures in sleep-induced apnea. Int J Cardiol 1:67–74, 1981.

110. Peters J, Fraser C, Stuart RS, et al: Negative intrathoracic pressure decreases independently left ventricular filling and emptying. Am J Physiol 257:H120–H131, 1989.

111. Virolainen J, Ventila M, Turto H, et al: Effect of negative intrathoracic pressure on left ventricular pressure dynamics and relaxation. J Appl Physiol 79:455–460, 1995.

112. Hall MJ, Ando SI, Floras JS, et al: Magnitude and time course of hemodynamic responses to Mueller maneuvers in patients with congestive heart failure. J Appl Physiol 85:1476–1484, 1998.

113. Hanly P, Sasson Z, Zuberi N, et al: ST-segment depression during sleep in obstructive sleep apnea. Am J Cardiol 71:1341–1345, 1993.

114. Chaudhary BA, Ferguson DS, Speir WA: Pulmonary edema as a presenting feature of sleep apnea syndrome. Chest 82:122–124, 1982.

115. Chan HS, Chiu HF, Tse LK, et al: Obstructive sleep apnea presenting with nocturnal angina, heart failure, and near-miss sudden death. Chest 99:1023–1025, 1991.

116. Franklin KA, Nilsson JB, Sahlin C: Sleep apnoea and nocturnal angina. Lancet 345:1085–1087, 1995.

117. Cargill RI, Kiely DG, Lipworth BJ: Adverse effects of hypoxaemia on diastolic filling in humans. Clin Sci 89:165–169, 1995.

118. Tolle FA, Judy WV, Yu PL, et al: Reduced stroke volume related to pleural pressure in obstructive sleep apnea. J Appl Physiol 55:1718–1724, 1983.

119. Stoohs R, Guilleminault C: Cardiovascular changes associated with obstructive sleep apnea syndrome. J Appl Physiol 72:583–589, 1992.

120. Somers VK, Mark AL, Zavala DC, et al: Contrasting effects of hypoxia and hypercapnia on ventilation and sympathetic activity in humans. J Appl Physiol 67:2101–2106, 1989.

121. Galatius-Jensen S, Hansen J, Rasmussen V, et al: Nocturnal hypoxaemia after myocardial infarction: Association with nocturnal myocardial ischaemia and arrhythmias. Br Heart J 72:23–30, 1994.

122. Shepard JW Jr, Garrison MW, Guther DA, et al: Relationship of ventricular ectopy to nocturnal O_2 desaturation in patients with obstructive sleep apnea. Chest 88:325–340, 1985.

123. Daly PA, Sole MJ: Myocardial catecholamines and the pathophysiology of heart failure. Circulation 82(Suppl I):I-35–I-43, 1990.

124. Seppala T, Partinen M, Penttila A, et al: Sudden death and sleeping history among Finnish men. J Intern Med 229:23–28, 1991.

125. Hender J, Ejnell H, Caidahl K: Left ventricular hypertrophy independent of hypertension in patients with obstructive sleep apnea. J Hypertens 8:941–946, 1990.

126. Hanly P, Sasson Z, Zuberi N, et al: Ventricular function in snorers and patients with obstructive sleep apnea. Chest 102:100–105, 1992.

127. Amin R, Kimball T, Bean J, et al: Left ventricular hypertrophy and abnormal ventricular geometry in children and adolescents with obstructive sleep apnea. Am J Respir Crit Care Med 165:1395–1399, 2002.

128. Kaneko Y, Floras JS, Usui K, et al: Cardiovascular effects of continuous positive airway pressure in patients with heart failure and obstructive sleep apnea. N Engl J Med 348:1233–1241, 2003.

129. Mansfield DR, Gollogly NC, Kaye DM, et al: Controlled trial of continuous positive airway pressure in obstructive sleep apnea and heart failure. Am J Respir Crit Care Med 169:361–366, 2004.

130. Kaye DM, Lambert GM, Lefkovits J, et al: Neurochemical evidence of cardiac sympathetic activation and increased central nervous system norepinephrine turnover in severe congestive heart failure. J Am Coll Cardiol 23:570–578, 1994.

131. Cohn JN, Levine TB, Olivary MT, et al: Plasma norepinephrine as a guide to prognosis in patients with congestive heart failure. N Engl J Med 311:819–823, 1984.

132. Sanner BM, Konermann M, Tepel M, et al: Platelet function in patients with obstructive sleep apnoea syndrome. Eur Respir J 16:648–652, 2000.

133. Bokinsky G, Miller M, Ault K, et al: Spontaneous platelet activation and aggregation during obstructive sleep apnea and its response to therapy with nasal continuous positive airway pressure: A preliminary investigation. Chest 108:625–630, 1995.

134. Nobili L, Schiavi G, Bozano E, et al: Morning increase in whole blood viscosity in obstructive sleep apnea syndrome. Clin Hemorheol Microcirc 22:21–27, 2000.

135. Shamsuzzaman AS, Winnicki M, Lanfranchi P, et al: Elevated C-reactive protein in patients with obstructive sleep apnea. Circulation 105:2462–2464, 2002.

136. Schulz R, Mahmoudi S, Hattar K, et al: Enhanced release of superoxide from polymorphonuclear neutrophils in obstructive sleep apnea: Impact of continuous positive airway pressure therapy. Am J Respir Crit Care Med 162:566–570, 2000.

137. Dyugovskaya L, Lavie P, Lavie L: Increased adhesion molecule expression and production of reactive oxygen species in leukocytes of sleep apnea patients. Am J Respir Crit Care Med 165:934–939, 2002.

138. Lavie L, Kraiczi H, Hefetz A, et al: Plasma vascular endothelial growth factor in sleep apnea syndrome: Effects of nasal continuous positive air pressure treatment. Am J Respir Crit Care Med 165:1624–1628, 2002.

139. Ip MS, Lam B, Ng MMT, et al: Obstructive sleep apnea is independently associated with insulin resistance. Am J Respir Crit Care Med 165:670–676, 2002.

140. Punjabi NM, Sorkin JD, Karzel LI, et al: Sleep-disordered breathing and insulin resistance in middle-aged and overweight men. Am J Respir Crit Care Med 165:677–682, 2002.

141. Chin K, Shimizu K, Nakamura T, et al: Changes in intra-abdominal visceral fat and serum leptin levels in patients with obstructive sleep apnea syndrome following nasal continuous positive airway pressure therapy. Circulation 100:706–712, 1999.

142. Harsch IA, Schahin SP, Radespiel-Troger M, et al: Continuous positive airway pressure treatment rapidly improves insulin sensitivity in patients with obstructive sleep apnea syndrome. Am J Respir Crit Care Med 169:156–162, 2004.

143. Bradley TD, Rutherford R, Grossman RF, et al: Role of daytime hypoxemia in the pathogenesis of right heart failure in the obstructive sleep apnea syndrome. Am Rev Respir Dis 131:835–839, 1985.

144. Weitzenblum E, Krieger J, Apprill M, et al: Daytime pulmonary hypertension in patients with obstructive sleep apnea syndrome. Am Rev Respir Dis 138:345–349, 1988.

145. Bradley TD, Rutherford R, Lue F, et al: Role of diffuse airway obstruction in the hypercapnia of obstructive sleep apnea. Am Rev Respir Dis 134:920–924, 1986.

146. Garay SM, Rapoport D, Sorkin B, et al: Regulation of ventilation in the obstructive sleep apnea syndrome. Am Rev Respir Dis 124:451–457, 1981.

147. Lopata M, Onal E: Mass loading, sleep apnea, and the pathogenesis of obesity hypoventilation. Am Rev Respir Dis 126:640–645, 1982.

148. Lavie P, Herer P, Peled R, et al: Mortality in sleep apnea patients: A multivariate analysis of risk factors. Sleep 18:149–157, 1995.

149. Ancoli-Israel S, Kripke DF, Klauber MR, et al: Morbidity, mortality and sleep disordered breathing in community dwelling elderly. Sleep 19:277–282, 1996.

150. Gyulay S, Olson LG, Hensley MR, et al: A comparison of clinical assessment and home oximetry in the diagnosis of obstructive sleep apnea. Am Rev Respir Dis 147:50–53, 1993.

151. Series F, Marc I, Cormier Y, et al: Utility of nocturnal home oximetry for case finding in patients with suspected sleep apnea syndrome. Ann Intern Med 119:449–453, 1993.

152. Loube DI, Strohl KP: Obstructive sleep apnea syndrome: Screening and diagnosis. In McNicholas WT, Phillipson EA (eds): Breathing Disorders in Sleep. London: WB Saunders, 2002, pp 86–102.

153. Whittle AT, Finch SP, Mortimore IL, et al: Use of home sleep studies for diagnosis of the sleep apnoea/hypopnoea syndrome. Thorax 52:1068–1073, 1997.

154. Hoffstein V: Is snoring dangerous to your health? Sleep 19:506–516, 1996.

155. Braver HM, Block AJ, Perri MG: Treatment for snoring: Combined weight loss, sleeping on the side, and nasal spray. Chest 107:1283–1288, 1995.

156. American Thoracic Society: Indications and standards for use of nasal continuous positive airway pressure (CPAP) in sleep apnea syndromes. Am J Respir Crit Care Med 150:1738–1745, 1994.

157. Lévy P, Pépin JL: Management options in obstructive sleep apnea syndrome. In McNicholas WT, Phillipson EA (eds): Breathing Disorders in Sleep. London: WB Saunders, 2002, pp 105–115.

158. Hoffstein V: Clinical significance and management of snoring without obstructive sleep apnea syndrome. In McNicholas WT, Phillipson EA (eds): Breathing Disorders in Sleep. London: WB Saunders, 2002, pp 164–178.

159. O'Sullivan RA, Hillman DR, Mateljan R, et al: Mandibular advancement splint: An appliance to treat snoring and obstructive sleep apnea. Am J Respir Crit Care Med 151:194–198, 1995.

160. Ferguson KA, Ono T, Lowe A, et al: A randomized cross-over trial of an oral appliance vs. nasal continuous positive airway pressure in the treatment of mild-moderate obstructive sleep apnea. Chest 109:1269–1275, 1996.

161. Stradling JR, Negus TW, Smith D, et al: Mandibular advancement devices for the control of snoring. Eur Respir J 11:447–450, 1998.

162. Engleman HE, Kingshott RN, Wraith PK, et al: Randomized placebo-controlled crossover trial of continuous positive airway pressure for mild sleep apnea/hypopnea syndrome. Am J Respir Crit Care Med 159:461–467, 1999.

163. Fujita S, Conway W, Zorick F, et al: Surgical correction of anatomic abnormalities in obstructive sleep apnea syndrome: Uvulopalatopharyngoplasty. Otolaryngol Head Neck Surg 89:923–934, 1981.

164. Kamami YV: Laser CO_2 for snoring: Preliminary results. Acta Otorhinolaryngol Belg 44:451–456, 1990.

165. Schmidt-Nowara WW, Meade TE, Hays MB: Treatment of snoring and obstructive sleep apnea with a dental orthosis. Chest 99:1378–1385, 1991.

166. Ng AT, Gotsopoulos H, Qian J, Cistulli PA: Effect of oral appliance therapy on upper airway collapsibility in obstructive sleep apnea. Am J Respir Crit Care Med 168:238–241, 2003.

167. Sher AE, Schechtman KB, Piccirillo JF: The efficacy of surgical modifications of the upper airway in adults with obstructive sleep apnea syndrome. Sleep 19:156–177, 1996.

168. Ryan CF, Lowe AA, Li D, et al: Three dimensional upper airway computed tomography in obstructive sleep apnea: A prospective study in patients treated by uvulopalatopharyngoplasty. Am Rev Respir Dis 144:428–432, 1991.

169. Launois SH, Feroah TR, Campbell WN, et al: Site of pharyngeal narrowing predicts outcome of surgery for obstructive sleep apnea. Am Rev Respir Dis 147:182–189, 1993.

170. Sullivan CE, Issa FG, Berthon-Jones M, et al: Reversal of obstructive sleep apnea by continuous positive airway pressure applied through the nares. Lancet 1:862–865, 1981.

171. Sullivan CE, Issa FG, Berthon-Jones M, et al: Home treatment of obstructive sleep apnea with continuous positive airway pressure applied through a nose-mask. Bull Eur Physiopathol Respir 20:49–54, 1984.

172. Hoffstein V, Viner S, Mateika S, et al: Treatment of obstructive sleep apnea with nasal continuous positive airway pressure: Patient compliance, perception of benefits, and side effects. Am Rev Respir Dis 145:841–845, 1992.

173. McNicholas WT: Nasal continuous positive airway pressure therapy for obstructive sleep apnea syndrome. In McNicholas WT, Phillipson EA (eds): Breathing Disorders in Sleep. London: WB Saunders, 2002, pp 116–133.

174. Becker HF, Jerrentrup A, Ploch T, et al: Effect of nasal continuous positive airway pressure treatment on blood

pressure in patients with obstructive sleep apnea. Circulation 107:68–73, 2003.

175. Logan AG, Tkacova R, Perlikowski SM, et al: Refractory hypertension and sleep apnea: Effect of CPAP on blood pressure and baroreflex. Eur Respir J 21:241–247, 2003.

176. Weitzman ED, Kahn E, Pollack CP: Quantitative analysis of sleep and sleep apnea before and after tracheostomy in patients with the hypersomnia-sleep apnea syndrome. Sleep 3:407–423, 1980.

177. Guilleminault C, Simmons FB, Motta J, et al: Obstructive sleep apnea syndrome and tracheostomy: Long-term followup experience. Arch Intern Med 141:985–988, 1981.

178. Bradley TD, Phillipson EA: Central sleep apnea. Clin Chest Med 13:493–505, 1992.

179. Bradley TD, McNicholas WT, Rutherford R, et al: Clinical and physiologic heterogeneity of the central sleep apnea syndrome. Am Rev Respir Dis 134:217–221, 1986.

180. Orem J: The nature of the wakefulness stimulus to breathing. Prog Clin Biol Res 345:23–31, 1990.

181. McNicholas WT, Phillipson EA: Central hypoventilation syndromes and hypercapnic central sleep apnea. *In* McNicholas WT, Phillipson EA (eds): Breathing Disorders in Sleep. London: WB Saunders, 2002, pp 239–245.

182. Bradley TD: Nonhypercapnic central sleep apnea. *In* McNicholas WT, Phillipson EA (eds): Breathing Disorders in Sleep. London: WB Saunders, 2002, pp 246–264.

183. Phillipson EA: Control of breathing during sleep. Am Rev Respir Dis 118:909–939, 1978.

184. Khoo MCK, Kronauer RE, Strohl KP, et al: Factors inducing periodic breathing in humans: A general model. J Appl Physiol 53:644–659, 1982.

185. Skatrud JB, Dempsey JA: Interaction of sleep state and chemical stimuli in sustaining rhythmic ventilation. J Appl Physiol 55:813–822, 1983.

186. Datta AK, Shea SA, Horner RL, et al: The influence of induced hypocapnia and sleep on the endogenous respiratory rhythm in humans. J Physiol (Lond) 440:17–33, 1991.

187. Khoo MCK, Gottschalk A, Pack AI: Sleep-induced periodic breathing and apnea: A theoretical study. J Appl Physiol 70:2014–2024, 1991.

187a. Dempsey JA, Smith CA, Przybylowski T, et al: The ventilatory responsiveness to CO_2 below eupnoea as a determinant of ventilatory stability in sleep. J Physiol (Lond) 560:1–11, 2004.

188. Berssenbrugge A, Dempsey J, Iber C, et al: Mechanisms of hypoxia-induced periodic breathing during sleep in humans. J Physiol (Lond) 343:507–524, 1983.

189. Lahiri S, Maret K, Sherpa MG: Dependence of high altitude sleep apnea on ventilatory sensitivity to hypoxia. Respir Physiol 52:281–301, 1983.

190. Weil JV: Sleep at high altitude. Clin Chest Med 6:615–621, 1985.

191. Javaheri S, Parker TJ, Liming JD, et al: Sleep apnea in 81 ambulatory male patients with stable heart failure. Circulation 97:2154–2159, 1998.

192. Sin DD, Fitzgerald F, Parker JD, et al: Risk factors for central and obstructive sleep apnea in 450 men and women with congestive heart failure. Am J Respir Crit Care Med 160:1101–1106, 1999.

193. Naughton M, Benard D, Tam A, et al: Role of hyperventilation in the pathogenesis of central sleep apneas in patients with congestive heart failure. Am Rev Respir Dis 148:330–338, 1993.

194. Lorenzi-Filho G, Rankin F, Bies I, et al: Effects of inhaled carbon dioxide and oxygen on Cheyne-Stokes respiration in patients with heart failure. Am J Respir Crit Care Med 159:1490–1498, 1999.

195. Xie A, Wong B, Phillipson EA, et al: Interaction of hyperventilation and arousal in the pathogenesis of idiopathic central sleep apnea. Am J Respir Crit Care Med 150:489–495, 1994.

196. Javaheri S: A mechanism of central sleep apnea in patients with heart failure. N Engl J Med 341:949–954, 1999.

197. Tkacova R, Hall MJ, Liu PP, et al: Left ventricular volume in patients with heart failure and Cheyne-Stokes respiration during sleep. Am J Respir Crit Care Med 156:1549–1555, 1997.

198. Solin P, Bergin P, Richardson M, et al: Influence of pulmonary capillary wedge pressure on central apnea in heart failure. Circulation 99:1574–1579, 1999.

199. Solin P, Roebuck T, Johns DP, et al: Peripheral and central ventilatory responses in central sleep apnea with and without congestive heart failure. Am J Respir Crit Care Med 162:2194–2200, 2000.

200. Churchill ED, Cope O: The rapid shallow breathing resulting from pulmonary congestion and edema. J Exp Med 49:531–537, 1929.

201. Xie A, Rankin F, Rutherford R, et al: Effects of inhaled CO_2 and added dead space on idiopathic central sleep apnea. J Appl Physiol 82:918–926, 1997.

202. Naughton MT, Liu PP, Bernard DC, et al: Treatment of congestive heart failure and Cheyne-Stokes respiration during sleep by continuous positive airway pressure. Am J Respir Crit Care Med 151:92–97, 1995.

203. van de Borne P, Oren R, Abouassaly C, et al: Effect of Cheyne-Stokes respiration on muscle sympathetic nerve activity in severe congestive heart failure secondary to ischemic or idiopathic dilated cardiomyopathy. Am J Cardiol 81:432–436, 1998.

204. Naughton MT, Benard DC, Liu PP, et al: Effects of nasal CPAP on sympathetic activity in patients with heart failure and central sleep apnea. Am J Respir Crit Care Med 152:473–479, 1995.

205. Bradley TD: Right and left ventricular functional impairment and sleep apnea. Clin Chest Med 13:459–479, 1992.

206. Harrison TR, King CE, Calhoun JA, et al: Cheyne-Stokes respiration as the cause of paroxysmal dyspnea at the onset of sleep. Arch Intern Med 53:891–910, 1934.

207. Hanly PJ, Millar TW, Steljes DG, et al: Respiration and abnormal sleep in patients with congestive heart failure. Chest 96:480–488, 1989.

208. Dowdell WT, Javaheri S, McGinnis W: Cheyne-Stokes respiration presenting as sleep apnea syndrome: Clinical and polysomnographic features. Am Rev Respir Dis 141:871–879, 1990.

209. Javaheri S, Corbett WS: Association of low $PaCO_2$ with central sleep apnea and ventricular arrhythmias in ambulatory patients with stable heart failure. Ann Intern Med 128:204–207, 1998.

210. Goldman S, Johnson G, Cohn JN, et al: Mechanism of death in heart failure: The vasodilator-heart failure trials. Circulation 87(Suppl VI):VI-24–VI-31, 1993.

211. Hanly PJ, Zuberi-Khokhar NS: Increased mortality associated with Cheyne-Stokes respiration in patients with congestive heart failure. Am J Respir Crit Care Med 153:272–276, 1996.

212. Sutton FD Jr, Zwillich CW, Creagh CE, et al: Progesterone for outpatient treatment of Pickwickian syndrome. Ann Intern Med 83:476–479, 1975.

213. Bubis MJ, Anthonisen NR: Primary alveolar hypoventilation treated by nocturnal administration of O_2. Am Rev Respir Dis 118:947–953, 1978.

214. Barlow PB, Bartlett D Jr, Hauri P, et al: Idiopathic hypoventilation syndrome: Importance of preventing nocturnal hypoxemia and hypercapnia. Am Rev Respir Dis 121:141–145, 1980.

215. Farmer WC, Glenn WWL, Gee JBL: Alveolar hypoventilation syndrome: Studies of ventilatory control in patients selected for diaphragm pacing. Am J Med 64:39–49, 1978.

216. Garay SM, Turino GM, Goldring RM: Sustained reversal of chronic hypercapnia in patients with alveolar hypoventilation syndromes. Am J Med 70:269–274, 1981.

217. Goldstein RS, Molotiu N, Skrastins R, et al: Reversal of sleep-induced hypoventilation and chronic respiratory failure by nocturnal negative pressure ventilation in patients with restrictive ventilatory impairment. Am Rev Respir Dis 135:1049–1055, 1987.

218. Ellis ER, Bye PTP, Bruderer JW, et al: Treatment of respiratory failure during sleep in patients with neuromuscular disease: Positive pressure ventilation through a nose mask. Am Rev Respir Dis 135:148–152, 1987.

219. Bach JR, Alber AS: Management of chronic alveolar hypoventilation by nasal ventilation. Chest 97:52–57, 1990.

220. Goldstein RS, Avendano MA, DeRosie JA, et al: Influence of non-invasive positive pressure ventilation on inspiratory muscles. Chest 99:408–415, 1991.

221. Martin RJ, Sanders MH, Gray BA, et al: Acute and long-term ventilatory effects of hypoxia in the adult sleep apnea syndrome. Am Rev Respir Dis 125:175–180, 1982.

222. White DP, Zwillich CW, Pickett CK, et al: Central sleep apnea: Improvement with acetazolamide therapy. Arch Intern Med 142:1816–1819, 1982.

223. Issa FG, Sullivan CE: Reversal of central sleep apnea using nasal CPAP. Chest 90:165–171, 1986.

224. Hoffstein V, Slutsky AS: Central sleep apnea reversed by continuous positive airway pressure. Am Rev Respir Dis 135:1210–1212, 1987.

225. Bradley TD, Holloway R, McLaughlin P, et al: Cardiac output response to continuous positive airway pressure in congestive heart failure. Am Rev Respir Dis 145:377–382, 1992.

226. Tkacova R, Liu PP, Naughton MT, et al: Effect of continuous positive airway pressure on mitral regurgitant fraction and atrial natriuretic peptide in patients with heart failure. J Am Coll Cardiol 30:739–745, 1997.

227. Naughton MT, Bradley TD: Sleep apnea in congestive heart failure. Clin Chest Med 19:99–113, 1998.

228. Sin DD, Logan AG, Fitzgerald FS, et al: Effects of continuous positive airway pressure on cardiovascular outcomes in heart failure patients with and without Cheyne-Stokes respiration. Circulation 102:61–66, 2000.

RESPIRATORY MANIFESTATIONS OF EXTRAPULMONARY DISORDERS

75
Pulmonary Complications of Human Immunodeficiency Virus Infection

Laurence Huang, M.D., **John D. Stansell**, M.D.

INTRODUCTION

Published observations in 1981 of opportunistic infection and Kaposi's sarcoma in previously healthy homosexual men and injection drug users brought into public and scientific awareness the complications of a then unknown viral infection, which eventually would be identified as the acquired immunodeficiency syndrome (AIDS).[1,2] A few years later, scientists at the Pasteur Institute and National Institutes of Health discovered the first of the causative viruses, human immunodeficiency virus type-1 (HIV-1), and developed an accurate test to detect its presence in humans.[3,4] Since then, wide genetic variation in HIV-1 has been appreciated[5] and a second virus (HIV-2) has been discovered.[6,7] In the 24 years since the recognition of these first cases of AIDS, our understanding of HIV and its myriad infectious and noninfectious complications has increased enormously. A quick search of PubMed for journal articles referencing HIV yields over 130,000 citations. Furthermore, during this period, the prognosis for those persons infected by HIV has undergone dramatic change in industrialized countries. The use of quantitative measures of immune function and HIV viral burden, antiretroviral drug combinations that suppress HIV viral replication below the limit of quantitation, and

therapies that can treat and prevent HIV-associated complications have become widely available in North America and Western Europe. These therapeutic advances have resulted in a dramatic decline in the incidence of new AIDS cases and in the number of AIDS-associated deaths in those countries where these methods are available.[8] Unfortunately, access to medications is far from universal, a cure for HIV is likely unattainable, and an HIV vaccine of proven effectiveness remains elusive. Therefore, efforts to prevent the spread of new HIV infection and to identify and treat those persons who are already HIV infected continue to be worldwide priorities.

The lungs are one of the chief target organs of HIV disease and, accordingly, a major source of morbidity and mortality. The spectrum of pulmonary manifestations is broad, and many infectious and noninfectious complications have been recognized (Table 75.1).[9-11] These complications include diseases that are AIDS defining or HIV associated, as well as disorders whose association with HIV is inconclusive or purely coincidental. This chapter provides a brief review of the epidemiology of HIV infection and its immunologic abnormalities. Then, a diagnostic approach to the evaluation of HIV infection and HIV-associated pulmonary disease is detailed, followed by a discussion of the

Table 75.1 Spectrum of Pulmonary Complications

Infections
Bacteria*
  Streptococcus pneumoniae
  Haemophilus species
  Pseudomonas aeruginosa
  Other bacteria
Mycobacteria
  Mycobacterium tuberculosis[†]
  Mycobacterium avium complex[‡]
  Mycobacterium kansasii[‡]
  Other mycobacteria[‡]
Fungi
  Pneumocystis jirovecii (formerly P. carinii)[§]
  Cryptococcus neoformans[‡]
  Histoplasma capsulatum[‡]
  Coccidioides immitis[‡]
  Aspergillus species
  Blastomyces dermatitidis
  Penicillium marneffei
Viruses
  Cytomegalovirus[§]
  Other viruses
Parasites
  Toxoplasma gondii[||]
  Other parasites

Malignancies
Kaposi's sarcoma[§]
Non-Hodgkin's lymphoma[§]
Bronchogenic carcinoma

Interstitial Pneumonitides
Lymphocytic interstitial pneumonitis[¶]
Nonspecific interstitial pneumonitis

Other
Chronic obstructive pulmonary disease
Pulmonary hypertension
Alveolar proteinosis
Diffuse alveolar damage
Bronchiolitis obliterans with organizing pneumonia
Sarcoidosis
Hypersensitivity pneumonitis
Immune reconstitution syndromes

* Acquired immunodeficiency syndrome (AIDS)–defining diagnosis in adults and adolescents (>13 years) if recurrent (≥2 episodes in 12 months). Not applicable as AIDS-defining diagnosis in children.
[†] AIDS-defining diagnosis in adults and adolescents. AIDS-defining diagnosis in children if extrapulmonary or disseminated.
[‡] AIDS-defining diagnosis if extrapulmonary or disseminated.
[§] AIDS-defining diagnosis.
[||] AIDS-defining diagnosis if central nervous system is involved.
[¶] AIDS-defining diagnosis in children. Not applicable as AIDS-defining diagnosis in adults or adolescents.
Modified from Murray JF, Mills J: Pulmonary infectious complications of human immunodeficiency virus infection. Am Rev Respir Dis 141:1356–1372, 1582–1598, 1990.

major HIV-associated pulmonary diseases, with emphasis on clinical features, diagnosis, treatment, and prevention.

EPIDEMIOLOGY

The AIDS epidemic has had a major impact in the United States and throughout the world. From the dawn of the epidemic through 2002, the Centers for Disease Control and Prevention (CDC) reported that nearly 1 million AIDS cases and nearly 500,000 deaths from AIDS have occurred in the United States and its territories alone.[12] However, this number pales in comparison to the estimated 30 million deaths from AIDS worldwide. In the United States, the annual incidence of AIDS-defining opportunistic illnesses increased each year until 1996, when it decreased for the first time, declining 6.5%.[13] In 1996, the number of AIDS deaths also decreased for the first time, declining by a staggering 25%.[13] Because the decline in AIDS deaths has far exceeded the decline in new AIDS cases, more people are living with AIDS in the United States than ever before.[12] Although the national incidence and prevalence of HIV can only be estimated because of incomplete reporting, the CDC now estimates that there are at least 1 million people living with HIV in the United States.[12]

Men who have sex with men (MSM) and injection drug users are the main risk categories for acquiring HIV infection in the United States and account for more than 85% of the cumulative AIDS cases in adults and adolescents.[12] A much lower percentage of cases are attributable to heterosexual contact. Transfusion of contaminated blood, blood components, or tissue now accounts for less than 2% of cumulative cases, and the blood and blood products in the United States and Europe are generally considered safe from HIV contamination. Intrauterine or perinatal transmission from mother to fetus or child is responsible for most of the pediatric cases, although these cases have plummeted since the routine application of improved HIV perinatal techniques and antiretroviral prophylaxis.[14] The gender and racial/ethnic demographics of HIV/AIDS in the United States have dramatically changed. Women comprise an increasing percentage of adult AIDS cases (currently 34% of adult cases), as do African Americans and Hispanics (currently 60% of adult cases).[12] The percentage of cases in MSM is declining relative to that in injection drug users and those with heterosexual contact. In addition, the epidemic has shifted from its initial predominance in large urban cities along the East and West coasts to increasingly include smaller cities and towns throughout the United States, in the South, and in the Midwest.

Although the U.S. statistics and estimates, among the most accurate available, paint an improving picture, the global picture is worsening at a staggering rate. As of 2004, the Joint United Nations Programme on HIV/AIDS estimated that there were 40 million people living with HIV/AIDS throughout the world, that 5 million acquired HIV in 2003, and that 3 million died due to HIV in 2003. An estimated 14,000 persons per day became infected with HIV in 2003.[15] If the current trends continue, the Global AIDS Policy Coalition projects that 60 to 70 million adults will have been infected with HIV by the end of the year 2010.

In contrast to the situation in the United States, heterosexual contact is the predominant mode of HIV transmission worldwide.[15] Women comprise 64% of the existing adult AIDS cases and two thirds of newly infected cases in developing countries, where 95% of all worldwide AIDS cases reside. AIDS is orphaning an increasing number of children. Sadly, it is estimated that one in every three children orphaned by this disease is under the age of 5 years, and an estimated 10.4 million children have been orphaned by AIDS since the epidemic began. An estimated 2.3 million children under the age of 15 were orphaned in 2002 alone.

More than 95% of all the HIV-infected people in the world live in developing countries.[15] Most of these people are unaware that they are infected with HIV, a fact that promotes the continued spread of the disease. Sub-Saharan Africa is the hardest hit region, with an estimated 25 to 28 million people living with HIV/AIDS, but substantial increases are occurring in Asia, India, Latin America, and Eastern Europe. Accompanying the regional differences in AIDS prevalence are differences in the prevalences of HIV-associated pulmonary diseases. For example, *Pneumocystis* pneumonia (PCP), the most common AIDS-defining opportunistic infection and one of the most common HIV-associated pulmonary infections in the United States, is relatively uncommon in sub-Saharan Africa. Conversely, tuberculosis, the sovereign HIV-associated infection in Africa, has a considerably smaller impact in the United States. *Penicillium marneffei*, the third most common HIV-associated opportunistic infection in northern Thailand, is practically unheard of outside of Southeast Asia.

IMMUNOLOGIC ABNORMALITIES

After infection with HIV and without effective antiretroviral therapy, HIV-infected persons experience a gradual but inexorable loss of host immunity that has been characterized as a syndrome of immune dysregulation, dysfunction, and deficiency, involving many components of the immune system.[16] Prominent among these deficits and most important clinically are a depletion of CD4$^+$ T lymphocytes, suppression of host responses to T-cell–dependent antigens, and abnormal activation of B cells.

HIV infection yields deletion of CD4$^+$ memory cells and suppresses the host response to T-cell–dependent antigens.[17,18] After encountering a pathogen, T cells normally undergo clonal expansion, which amplifies their response. In HIV-infected patients, however, this proliferation is attenuated in response to both recall mitogens and viruses to which patients have serologic evidence of prior exposure.

Similar dysregulation is seen in the abnormal activation of B cells. Although generally held to be "polyclonal," evidence indicates that HIV infection induces both virus-specific and broadly nonspecific B-cell activation.[19]

DIAGNOSTIC APPROACH

When a patient seeks medical attention for new respiratory complaints, the differential diagnosis may include HIV infection and one of its complications. In these cases, the physician faces two problems: first, to determine whether the patient is infected with HIV and, second, to elucidate the nature of the respiratory complaints that prompted the visit. Each of these two responsibilities is briefly considered.

EVALUATION OF HUMAN IMMUNODEFICIENCY VIRUS INFECTION

The diagnosis of HIV infection itself is made by detection of specific antibodies to the virus with a screening enzyme-linked immunosorbent assay (ELISA) test followed by a confirmatory test such as the Western blot. After acute HIV infection, however, there is a delay of several weeks until the development of detectable antibodies. In these patients, measurement of the plasma HIV ribonucleic acid (RNA, viral load) may indicate acute HIV infection that should be confirmed by repeated HIV antibody testing. Confirmation is necessary because the plasma HIV RNA may be falsely positive at low titers; thus, this test should never be used to establish the diagnosis of HIV infection. However, HIV viral loads in excess of 5000 copies/mL are rarely false positives.[20,21]

Several laboratory tests have been used to document the stage of HIV disease and to predict the development of AIDS. Currently, the most widely used tests are the determination of the absolute number or percentage of circulating CD4$^+$ T lymphocytes and the measurement of plasma HIV RNA. The CD4$^+$ T lymphocyte count has proved to be especially useful in the evaluation of HIV-associated complications (including pulmonary disease), as it predicts the development of these diseases.[22] The plasma HIV RNA level has proved to be useful in guiding the management of HIV infection. In addition, evidence suggests that the plasma HIV RNA level is a predictor for the development of AIDS and death due to infection independent of the CD4$^+$ lymphocyte count in the untreated HIV-infected subject.[23-27]

EVALUATION OF HUMAN IMMUNODEFICIENCY VIRUS–ASSOCIATED PULMONARY DISEASE

The evaluation of an HIV-infected patient with pulmonary disease is aimed at making a specific diagnosis. In general, definitive diagnosis is preferred to empirical therapy for a number of reasons. Although each of the HIV-associated pulmonary diseases has characteristic clinical and radiographic features, these features overlap. Occasionally, the presenting features are atypical, or more than one pulmonary disease is present. Without appropriate therapy, HIV-infected patients with pneumonia can progress rapidly to respiratory failure and death. Therapies used to treat HIV-associated pulmonary diseases have important toxicities and interactions with other medications that a patient may be receiving for prophylaxis, for a comorbid condition, or as part of highly active antiretroviral therapy (HAART). Thus, empirical therapy without an attempted diagnostic evaluation is seldom justified.

The evaluation should begin with the history and physical examination. Laboratory testing should be performed and a chest radiograph obtained from patients with suspected pulmonary disease. Frequently, the results of this evaluation suggest a specific differential diagnosis and management plan. Occasionally, additional studies, including pulmonary function testing, chest computed tomography

(CT), high-resolution computed tomography (HRCT), and gallium-67 (^{67}Ga) scanning, are needed to narrow the differential diagnosis and to refine the management plan.

Once the differential diagnosis is established, empirical therapy for the suspected diagnosis should be initiated while awaiting the results of diagnostic studies. The diagnostic studies chosen depend on a number of factors, including the specific diagnosis being considered, the sensitivity and specificity of the diagnostic tests, and the availability (including cost) of the tests. In most cases, sputum and blood cultures should be performed. Depending on the suspected diagnosis, bronchoscopy should be performed if sputum results are nondiagnostic. The decision to perform bronchoalveolar lavage (BAL) with or without transbronchial biopsy (TBBX) depends on the suspected diagnosis and the sensitivities of these procedures for that diagnosis. Thoracentesis (and possibly pleural biopsy) should be considered for patients presenting with pleural effusion. At institutions with expertise, CT-guided transthoracic needle aspiration or surgical procedures such as thoracoscopy or mediastinoscopy can be used. Occasionally, video-assisted or open-lung biopsy is required. The choice of specific diagnostic tests relies on an accurate differential diagnosis derived from a number of factors.

Prevalence of Pulmonary Diseases

The prevalence of each of the HIV-associated pulmonary diseases depends on a number of factors, especially the clinical setting in which the patient is evaluated, the patient's CD4$^+$ lymphocyte count, the patient's use of HAART, and the use of specific prophylaxis against opportunistic infection.[28-31]

Clinical Setting. The clinical setting in which the patient is seen influences the prevalence of pulmonary diseases observed. The Pulmonary Complications of HIV Infection Study (PCHIS) was a prospective, observational cohort study that followed more than 1150 HIV-infected subjects for approximately 5 years (1988–1993) at six sites across the United States.[32] The investigators found that ambulatory HIV-infected subjects presenting to a clinic with respiratory complaints had upper respiratory tract infections (URIs) and acute bronchitis more often than pneumonia due to bacteria, mycobacteria, Pneumocystis, fungi, viruses, and parasites combined.[33] Wallace and colleagues[33] of the PCHIS reported an annual incidence of upper respiratory tract infection ranging from 35 to 52 episodes per 100 person-years, totaling 1810 episodes during the study period. This exceeded the annual incidence and total number of episodes of bacterial pneumonia (3.9 to 7.3 cases per 100 person-years, 232 total cases), PCP (2.8 to 9.5 cases per 100 person-years, 220 total cases), and pneumonias due to other opportunistic infections (69 total cases) combined. However, patients with upper respiratory tract infection or acute bronchitis are usually treated as outpatients, whereas patients with opportunistic pneumonia often require hospitalization.

Over the course of the AIDS epidemic, the frequencies of specific pulmonary diseases among HIV-infected patients have changed. Early in the epidemic, PCP accounted for the majority of pneumonias seen.[10,11] More recently, bacterial pneumonia has become the leading pneumonia observed. At San Francisco General Hospital, bacterial pneumonia is currently the most common pulmonary disease seen in hospitalized HIV-infected patients. In contrast to 1992, when 25 cases of PCP were diagnosed per month at San Francisco General Hospital, the current caseload has declined to four to six per month. Most of these cases are in individuals with previously undiagnosed HIV or those who were nonadherent to PCP prophylaxis (L. Huang and J. Stansell, unpublished data). Tuberculosis, cryptococcal pneumonia, and pulmonary Kaposi's sarcoma are now rarely encountered. In published series of critically ill HIV-infected patients, PCP remains the most common pulmonary disease seen in some but not all series.[34,35,35a,35b]

CD4$^+$ Lymphocyte Count. The CD4$^+$ lymphocyte count is an excellent indicator of an HIV-infected patient's risk of developing a specific opportunistic infection or neoplasm, and it is therefore an essential element of the evaluation of pulmonary disease. Many of the HIV-associated pulmonary diseases usually present at or below a characteristic CD4$^+$ lymphocyte count and seldom occur above that count.[22] The exceptions are diseases that can present in persons with or without HIV infection, such as bacterial pneumonia, tuberculosis, and non-Hodgkin's lymphoma. In HIV-infected persons, these diseases can present at any CD4$^+$ lymphocyte count, although their incidence increases and their characteristic presentation changes as the CD4$^+$ count declines (see subsequent disease discussion).

At CD4$^+$ lymphocyte counts less than 200 cells/μL, bacterial pneumonia is often accompanied by bacteremia, and Mycobacterium tuberculosis disease is often extrapulmonary or disseminated. Moreover, below this CD4$^+$ count, Pneumocystis and Cryptococcus neoformans pneumonia become important considerations, whereas neither typically occurs in a patient with a count significantly higher than 200 cells/μL. At CD4$^+$ lymphocyte counts below 100 cells/μL, and, especially at CD4$^+$ lymphocyte counts below 50 cells/μL, endemic fungi, certain viruses (cytomegalovirus), nontuberculous mycobacteria (Mycobacterium avium complex [MAC]) and Kaposi's sarcoma become important considerations. At this degree of immunosuppression, many of these diseases present with extrapulmonary or disseminated manifestations that may dominate the clinical presentation.

Antiretroviral drug combinations can effectively suppress HIV replication and reverse the previously inexorable decline in a patient's CD4$^+$ lymphocyte count. In many cases, patients experience a dramatic increase in their CD4$^+$ count, an increase that may be sustained for as long as the patient adheres to treatment and the antiretroviral combination is effective at suppressing HIV. This result raised a number of important questions about whether a patient's risk for specific opportunistic infection was lessened by the increase in CD4$^+$ lymphocyte count and, if so, whether specific prophylaxis could be discontinued. As clinical research and clinical experience accumulates, it appears that the risk of opportunistic infections is best reflected by the current CD4$^+$ lymphocyte count.[36] Multiple studies indicate that primary and secondary Pneumocystis prophylaxis can be safely discontinued in patients whose CD4$^+$ lymphocyte counts increase above 200 cells/μL for at least 3 months.[37-49a] Similar evidence has emerged that indicates that it is safe to discontinue primary and secondary prophylaxis against MAC,[44,50-56] *Cryptococcus neoformans*,[54,57-60] and *Toxoplasma gondii*[40,42-44,54,61,62] when CD4+ lymphocyte counts have been restored to greater than 100 (MAC) to 200 cells/μL (*C. neoformans*) for at least 3 (primary prophylaxis) to 6 (secondary prophylaxis) months.[36] Although an invaluable tool in assessing disease-specific risk in the HIV-immunocompromised patient, the CD4+ lymphocyte count cannot replace the history and physical examination, laboratory tests, and chest radiograph in the diagnostic evaluation.

History and Physical Examination

Many aspects of the history and physical examination can provide important diagnostic clues to the cause of HIV-associated pulmonary disease.

Symptoms. Respiratory symptoms are common in HIV-infected persons, are more frequent in HIV-infected persons than HIV-negative controls, and are more frequent in HIV-infected smokers than in HIV-infected nonsmokers.[63] In general, respiratory symptoms are nonspecific; all of the HIV-associated pulmonary diseases can present with cough, dyspnea, and, less commonly, pleuritic chest pain. However, a productive cough with purulent sputum suggests a bacterial process, whereas a nonproductive cough and dyspnea are more characteristic of PCP or other fungal infection. The duration of symptoms can also be useful in distinguishing bacterial pneumonia (usually 3 to 5 days of symptoms) from PCP (usually 2 to 4 weeks of symptoms).

Constitutional symptoms such as fever, night sweats, anorexia, and weight loss, although nonspecific, often suggest the presence of a systemic or disseminated infection or represent "B" symptoms of non-Hodgkin's lymphoma.

The presence of extrapulmonary symptoms may suggest a disease that has both pulmonary and extrapulmonary manifestations. For example, cryptococcal disease causing both pneumonia and meningitis should be strongly considered in an HIV-infected patient whose CD4+ lymphocyte count is below 200 cells/μL and who presents with cough, dyspnea, and headache.

Past Medical History. Many aspects of the past medical history can provide important diagnostic clues to the current cause of HIV-associated pulmonary disease.

HIV Risk Category and Habits. MSM have a significantly higher incidence of Kaposi's sarcoma than do patients without this risk factor, and approximately 95% of HIV-associated Kaposi's sarcoma occurs in MSM. Injection drug users have a higher incidence of bacterial pneumonia and tuberculosis than do persons without a history of injection drug use.[64,65] In addition, injection and other illicit drug use can cause important non–HIV-associated pulmonary illnesses such as aspiration pneumonia secondary to altered sensorium, endocarditis-related septic pulmonary emboli, pulmonary vascular disease, and drug-induced pulmonary edema.[66]

As in the general population, HIV-infected patients who are cigarette smokers are at an increased risk for a variety of pulmonary illnesses. Cigarette smokers have a higher incidence of both bacterial bronchitis and bronchopneumonia than do nonsmokers or former smokers, especially if their CD4+ lymphocyte counts are below 200 cells/μL.[64] Although it is currently debated whether HIV infection itself is associated with an increased risk of bronchogenic carcinoma, HIV-infected cigarette smokers are more likely than nonsmokers to develop this disease. In addition, patients with a long history of cigarette smoking may present with manifestations of chronic obstructive pulmonary disease as the cause of their respiratory symptoms.[67]

Residence and Travel. A history of residence in or travel to a geographic region that is endemic for fungi such as *H. capsulatum*, *C. immitis*, *Blastomyces dermatitidis*, or *P. marneffei* is a strong determinant of the risk of disease. Patients without such a history are unlikely to develop these diseases. Tuberculosis is more common in certain geographic areas and in certain populations.[68] Patients who were born in or have traveled to a country with a high prevalence of *M. tuberculosis* and patients who are homeless, unstably housed, or previously incarcerated are at high risk of *M. tuberculosis* infection. Geography has also been associated with the risk of PCP.[69,70]

Prior Pulmonary Diseases and Prophylaxis Use. As is discussed later in this chapter, many of the HIV-associated opportunistic infections recur, especially in the absence of secondary prophylaxis or immune reconstitution. Thus, knowledge of a patient's prior pulmonary history may suggest the etiology of the current illness. Patients who fail to receive or to adhere to recommended prophylaxis have an increased risk for HIV-associated opportunistic infections such as PCP.

Signs. As with symptoms, vital signs are nonspecific. Patients with pneumonia may be febrile, tachycardic, and tachypneic. Evidence of systemic hypotension suggests a fulminant disease process (e.g., bacterial septicemia or disseminated histoplasmosis) and is cause for concern. Pulse oximetry often reveals a decrease in the oxygen saturation and provides an estimate of disease severity.

Physical examination of the chest may provide important diagnostic clues. Focal lung findings are detected more often in patients with bacterial pneumonia than in those with PCP, many of whom have a normal examination. However, common physical findings in patients with PCP are tachypnea and low tidal volumes. Occasionally, chest findings are the result of nonpulmonary disease. For example, crackles in association with an S_3 cardiac gallop and an elevated jugular venous pressure suggest a cardiac etiology.

The remainder of the physical examination is often suggestive of a specific pulmonary disease. Headache or altered mental status suggests *C. neoformans*, whereas focal neurologic abnormalities usually implicate *T. gondii* or central nervous system lymphoma. Concurrent visual and respiratory complaints may indicate cytomegalovirus. New cutaneous lesions may be a manifestation of disseminated fungal, bacterial, or mycobacterial disease, and mucocutaneous Kaposi's sarcoma lesions are seen in most patients with pulmonary Kaposi's sarcoma. However, the absence of mucocutaneous Kaposi's sarcoma lesions does not preclude the presence of pulmonary disease.[71] Hepatosplenomegaly or peripheral lymphadenopathy may be signs of disseminated mycobacterial or fungal disease or non-Hodgkin's lymphoma.

Laboratory Tests

Laboratory tests may provide important diagnostic clues. However, HIV-infected patients often have a host of laboratory abnormalities that are nonspecific or are due to conditions that are unrelated to the pulmonary disease. Laboratory tests that may be useful include the white blood cell (WBC) count and differential and serum lactate dehydrogenase (LDH) and arterial blood gas measurements. The last two tests are better as prognostic markers and as baseline values for subsequent measurements than as diagnostic tests. Serial measurements are useful whenever a patient fails to exhibit a clinical response or deteriorates despite appropriate therapy.

White Blood Cell Count. When a CD4$^+$ lymphocyte count is unavailable, the WBC and differential (percentage of lymphocytes) can be used to estimate the stage of HIV disease and the risk of specific diseases. The WBC is frequently elevated (or, if normal, elevated relative to the patient's baseline value) in patients with bacterial pneumonia. These patients often have an associated "left shift." Neutropenia is a risk factor for bacterial and certain fungal infections such as *Aspergillus*. Pancytopenia may suggest the presence of mycobacterial or fungal disease or non-Hodgkin's lymphoma involving the bone marrow. With other types of pulmonary diseases, the WBC more often reflects the stage of the HIV disease or the use of bone marrow–suppressive medications than the presence of a specific disease.

Serum Lactate Dehydrogenase. The serum LDH level is often elevated in patients with PCP.[67,72] It is also elevated in many other pulmonary and nonpulmonary conditions, however, limiting its diagnostic use. In patients with PCP, the degree of LDH elevation correlates with prognosis and response to therapy. Those patients with an initial LDH level that is markedly elevated have a worse prognosis than do patients whose LDH is normal or mildly elevated. With successful therapy, the LDH level declines; an increasing LDH level in a patient who is receiving PCP treatment is often a sign of therapeutic failure.

Arterial Blood Gas. Values of arterial blood gas analysis are frequently abnormal in patients with pulmonary disease. Although nonspecific, the arterial blood gas results can be an important factor in the decision whether to hospitalize a patient and are used to determine whether adjunctive corticosteroids are indicated for patients with PCP.

Chest Radiograph

In the absence of respiratory symptoms, chest radiographic screening for pulmonary disease is rarely useful.[73,74] Patients who have new-onset symptoms or signs that are suggestive of pulmonary disease should have a posteroanterior and lateral chest radiograph. The most common chest radiographic features of each of the pulmonary diseases are discussed separately. In general, the distribution (unilateral or bilateral, focal, multifocal, diffuse, specific lung zone[s]) and pattern (interstitial/reticular, granular, alveolar/consolidation, nodular) of any parenchymal abnormalities and the presence or absence of associated findings such as nodules, masses, cysts, cavities, pleural effusions, or intrathoracic adenopathy provide important diagnostic clues and help to direct subsequent evaluation. However, no constellation of radiographic abnormalities is specific for a particular pulmonary disease; the patterns seen only suggest a differential diagnosis.

Pulmonary Function Tests

Many of the indications for pulmonary function testing are the same for HIV-infected persons as for any person and are discussed in Chapter 24. In HIV-infected patients, pulmonary function testing, specifically measurement of the diffusing capacity for carbon monoxide (DL_{CO}), can be useful in the evaluation of suspected PCP.[75] The DL_{CO} is a sensitive but nonspecific test for PCP in patients with clinically suspected PCP who have a normal or unchanged chest radiograph. Patients whose DL_{CO} is greater than 75% of predicted value are unlikely to have PCP; for these patients, neither diagnostic procedures to detect *Pneumocystis* nor empirical PCP therapy is indicated, and clinical observation or evaluation for another pulmonary process is recommended. Patients whose DL_{CO} is 75% or below of predicted value require a diagnostic procedure for PCP, usually sputum induction or bronchoscopy.

Although the DL_{CO} has clinical utility in the evaluation of suspected PCP, it should only be obtained when there is a reasonable suspicion for this disease, and it has no role as a screening test to detect early PCP in asymptomatic persons. In a PCHIS study of 64 HIV-infected patients who had a decline of 20% or more in their DL_{CO} value from a baseline value—in the absence of new respiratory symptoms or new chest radiographic findings—none of the patients had PCP (or another opportunistic infection) diagnosed on sputum induction, bronchoscopy, or clinical follow-up.[76]

Unfortunately, utilization of the DL_{CO} in the diagnosis of infectious pulmonary disease in HIV-infected persons has largely fallen into disuse. The reasons for this neglect are several, including the nonspecific nature of reduced measures of diffusing capacity, the fear of transmission of communicable organisms to pulmonary laboratory personnel and other immunocompromised patients, and reliance upon radiographic technology, specifically chest CT. Given the easy availability, low cost, and excellent negative predictive value of a normal DL_{CO}, the authors believe this switch to a new diagnostic algorithm is unwarranted in many cases.

Chest Computed Tomography or High-Resolution Chest Tomography

Many of the indications for chest CT or HRCT scans are the same for HIV-infected patients as for any patient and are discussed in Chapter 20. Clearly, a chest CT is more sensitive than a chest radiograph for detecting the presence and describing the characteristics and extent of pulmonary disease. In HIV-infected patients, the clinical and chest radiographic presentations usually are sufficient to suggest a specific diagnosis. Occasionally, however, the presentation is confusing. In these cases, chest CT or HRCT scans can be extremely useful because each of the HIV-associated pulmonary diseases has a characteristic CT/HRCT appearance that often allows radiologists to provide a confident diagnosis.[77-81] However, the choice of performing a chest CT or HRCT must be weighed against the cost of the procedure and should never delay the pursuit of a definitive diagnostic procedure and empirical therapy, if warranted.

In the experience of Naidich and McGuinness,[77] CT can be especially useful in the identification of occult pulmonary disease and the characterization of diffuse parenchymal disease such as PCP or pulmonary Kaposi's sarcoma. In our experience at San Francisco General Hospital, chest CT can also be useful in the evaluation of multiple pulmonary nodules or hilar/mediastinal adenopathy.[79–81] Finally, a normal CT scan makes pulmonary opportunistic infection or neoplasm unlikely.[78]

Radionuclide Imaging

Three radionuclides have been used to study the lungs in HIV-infected persons: gallium citrate (^{67}Ga-citrate), technetium-99m diethylenetriamine pentaacetate (^{99m}Tc-DTPA), and thallium-201 (^{201}Tl). Similar to pulmonary function testing, ^{67}Ga-citrate was used extensively during the early years of the AIDS epidemic as a guide to further diagnostic studies. Specifically, these tests were recommended in cases of clinically suspected pulmonary disease, most often PCP, where the chest radiograph was normal. Currently, these tests are rarely used. A chest CT scan or definitive diagnostic procedure is probably preferred over a ^{67}Ga scan in most instances because they have a higher sensitivity and specificity than [67]Ga.[82–84]

Sputum

Studies of sputum, either expectorated or induced, can establish the diagnosis of many of the HIV-associated pulmonary diseases. Most patients with pyogenic pneumonia complain of a cough that is productive of purulent sputum. In these cases, an expectorated sputum specimen can be useful in focusing the diagnostic evaluation and selecting the initial antimicrobial therapy.[85]

Most patients with PCP report a nonproductive cough. In these cases, examination of induced sputum, obtained by inhalation of a hypertonic saline aerosol generated by an ultrasonic handheld nebulizer, is a sensitive technique for diagnosing PCP and decreases the need for invasive diagnostic procedures.[86] The sensitivity of induced sputum examination for *Pneumocystis* varies by institution; at San Francisco General Hospital, the sensitivity has remained consistent throughout the AIDS epidemic in the range of 74% to 83%.[86,87] However, this range of sensitivities implies that a significant percentage of patients (17% to 26%) will have a false-negative induced sputum examination for *Pneumocystis* and that further diagnostic studies are indicated in these cases.

Sputum examination and culture are the foundations for the diagnosis of tuberculosis.[88,89] Several studies report that the sensitivity of sputum acid-fast bacilli (AFB) smear and culture in HIV-infected patients is similar to the sensitivity in the overall population.[90–94] However, other studies report a lower sensitivity of sputum smear or culture in HIV-infected patients.[95–98] Typically, the probability of a particular patient with tuberculosis having a positive sputum AFB smear is related to the specific radiographic features and the extent of radiographic disease. Patients with cavitary disease on radiograph are more likely to have a positive AFB smear

than patients with a normal or minimally abnormal radiograph. Most patients with tuberculosis can produce expectorated specimens suitable for examination and culture; in those patients who are unable to provide an adequate expectorated specimen, induced sputum can be used.

Although the experience and published literature about the value of sputum studies in other infections are limited compared with those for PCP and tuberculosis, sputum examination and culture can establish the diagnosis of a number of HIV-associated pulmonary infections, including those due to nontuberculous mycobacteria (e.g., *Mycobacterium kansasii*), fungi (e.g., *C. neoformans*, *H. capsulatum*, *C. immitis*, and *P. marneffei* but not *Aspergillus*), and parasites (e.g., *T. gondii*), but not cytomegalovirus.

Bronchoscopy

Fiberoptic bronchoscopy is a cornerstone in the evaluation of HIV-associated pulmonary disease. In general, bronchoscopy should be considered for any known or suspected HIV-infected patient with pulmonary disease whose severity warrants a prompt and accurate diagnosis, for patients with suspected pulmonary Kaposi's sarcoma, for patients with suspected non-Hodgkin's lymphoma (if other diagnostic procedures are thought to be more hazardous or less likely to provide the diagnosis), for patients whose diagnosis remains unknown despite less invasive diagnostic studies (e.g., induced sputum), and for patients whose empirical therapy is failing.

The decision to perform BAL with or without TBBX depends on the suspected diagnosis and on the sensitivities of these procedures for that diagnosis. At the beginning of the AIDS epidemic, both BAL and TBBX were usually performed during the initial bronchoscopy. Studies demonstrated that the yield from these two procedures was complementary in identifying pathogens: The sensitivity of BAL was 86% and that of TBBX 87%; when the two procedures were combined, the sensitivity was 98% for all pathogens and 100% for *Pneumocystis*.[83] Currently, at San Francisco General Hospital, in cases in which PCP is the suspected pathogen, we perform only BAL during the initial bronchoscopy.[84,87] Our experience is that the sensitivity of BAL fluid examination for *Pneumocystis* is 97% or higher, and, therefore, a negative BAL fluid examination for *Pneumocystis* rules out the diagnosis of PCP in all but the rarest of cases. To estimate the sensitivity of BAL for PCP, Huang and colleagues[87] reviewed the medical records of 100 randomly selected HIV-infected patients who had both a negative induced sputum test and a negative BAL fluid examination for *Pneumocystis* and had no other diagnosis established. The authors found that two patients were diagnosed with PCP in the 60 days after their negative BAL, one 46 days and the other 51 days after the negative bronchoscopy. Furthermore, TBBX rarely provided the sole diagnosis of PCP. In this consecutive series of 992 cases of PCP over a 4-year period, TBBX was the sole diagnostic procedure in only two cases (0.2%).

In contrast to PCP, TBBX improves the sensitivity of bronchoscopy for diagnosing a number of other important pathogens, including tuberculosis and endemic fungal pneumonias. Furthermore, tissue confirmation from TBBX or another biopsy specimen is mandatory to establish the diagnosis of invasive aspergillosis, cytomegalovirus pneumonia, and pulmonary non-Hodgkin's lymphoma. Therefore, when the clinical and radiographic features suggest one of these pulmonary diseases, both BAL and TBBX are warranted during the initial bronchoscopy.

Other Procedures

Several other procedures have been used in the diagnostic evaluation of patients with HIV-associated pulmonary disease. Diagnostic thoracentesis should be considered for any HIV-infected patient with pleural effusion in whom other studies are nondiagnostic or in whom there is a concern about empyema. Although the addition of pleural biopsy increases the sensitivity of this procedure for tuberculosis, pleural fluid culture alone is often sufficient to establish the diagnosis of bacterial and fungal infections, and pleural fluid cytology can establish the diagnosis of non-Hodgkin's lymphoma. Transthoracic needle aspiration of the lungs can be used to diagnose focal mass lesions and mediastinal adenopathy.[99-101] Video-assisted thoracoscopy has made a number of important contributions. As a result, open-lung biopsy is only occasionally indicated in the evaluation of HIV-associated pulmonary disease. However, when used, open-lung biopsy can establish a diagnosis in most cases.[102-104]

INFECTIOUS COMPLICATIONS

The lungs are the principal targets of the many infections that lead to a diagnosis of AIDS and are often involved in earlier stages of HIV disease as well. In this section, the major pulmonary infectious complications of HIV disease are reviewed according to the category of infectious microorganism that causes them (see Table 75.1).

BACTERIA

Early in the AIDS epidemic, bacterial pneumonia accounted for only a small proportion of pulmonary diseases reported. In 1984, the National Heart, Lung, and Blood Institute conducted a workshop on AIDS-associated pulmonary complications, the purpose of which was to report on the shared experiences of six institutions that had considerable experience with AIDS.[105] Although PCP, either alone or with coexisting infection, accounted for 373 (85%) of the 441 serious pulmonary diseases reported, bacterial pneumonia was seen in only 11 cases (2.5%). Subsequently, bacterial pneumonia became recognized as a frequent complication of HIV infection and one that often preceded other opportunistic infections. The recognition that the incidence of bacterial pneumonia is increased in HIV-infected persons and is frequently recurrent led to the inclusion of recurrent bacterial pneumonia (defined as two or more episodes within 12 months) as an AIDS-defining illness in the 1993 CDC Expanded Surveillance Case Definition for AIDS.[106]

Prior to the HAART era, Hirschtick and coworkers[64] of the PCHIS confirmed the increased incidence of bacterial pneumonia in HIV-infected persons and provided important new insights into the relationship between bacterial pneumonia and HIV infection. The PCHIS, which ended in 1994, remains the only prospective multicenter cohort study specifically designed to study pulmonary disease in HIV-infected persons and, therefore, was an important source of information. In this study, there were 5.5 episodes of bacterial pneumonia per 100 person-years in the HIV-infected cohort compared with 0.9 episodes per 100 person-years in the HIV-seronegative control cohort ($P < 0.001$). Bacterial pneumonia was more common in HIV-infected patients than in the HIV-seronegative controls, even in the subset of HIV-infected patients with CD4+ lymphocyte counts above 500 cells/μL ($P = 0.004$). Furthermore, the rate of bacterial pneumonia increased as the CD4+ lymphocyte count declined. The authors also found that the incidence of bacterial pneumonia was greater in injection drug users (11.1 episodes per 100 person-years) than in either MSM (4.1 episodes per 100 person-years, $P < 0.001$) or female partners (3.8 episodes per 100 person-years, $P < 0.003$). Cigarette smoking was also associated with an increased incidence of bacterial pneumonia, especially in HIV-infected subjects with a CD4+ lymphocyte count below 200 cells/μL. Osmond and colleagues[107] of the PCHIS found that patients who developed bacterial or PCP had a significantly shorter median duration of survival compared with CD4+ count–matched control subjects without one of these pneumonias. Finally, Morris and associates[108] of the PCHIS found that the occurrence of bacterial or PCP was associated with permanent decreases in FEV$_1$, FEV$_1$/FVC, forced vital capacity, and DL$_{CO}$.

During the HAART era (1996 to present), the incidence of bacterial pneumonia among HIV-infected persons has declined. Data from large prospective cohorts document this decline. The CDC-sponsored Adult/Adolescent Spectrum of HIV Disease project is a prospective medical record review of HIV-infected persons of age 13 years or older that is conducted in 11 U.S. cities. In this study, Jones and colleagues[109] found that the incidence of recurrent pneumonia declined from 22.0 per 1000 person-years in 1992 to 10.7 per 1000 person-years in 1997. Data from single institutions have reported similar results. In a study from 1995 to 1998, Afessa and Green[110] reported that bacterial pneumonia accounted for 9% of the 1225 consecutive hospital admissions for HIV-infected adults. Sullivan and associates[111] reported that the incidence of bacterial pneumonia decreased from 22.7 episodes per 100 person-years in 1993 to 9.1 episodes per 100 person-years in 1997. In this study, the use of protease inhibitor (PI)–containing antiretroviral regimens was associated with a decreased risk of bacterial pneumonia. The use of trimethoprim-sulfamethoxazole (TMP-SMX) has also been found to decrease the risk of bacterial pneumonia.[112,113]

Overall, *Streptococcus pneumoniae* and *Haemophilus* species are the most frequently identified bacteria causing community-acquired pneumonia in HIV-infected persons. *Pseudomonas aeruginosa* is an important consideration as a community-acquired pathogen in persons with advanced AIDS and CD4+ lymphocyte counts below 50 cells/μL. Other bacteria are occasionally identified as causes of pneumonia in HIV-infected persons, including *Legionella* species, *Rhodococcus equi,* and *Nocardia* species.

Streptococcus pneumoniae and *Haemophilus* Species

Similar to published series of community-acquired bacterial pneumonia in other populations, *S. pneumoniae* and *Haemophilus* species are the most frequently identified pathogens in HIV-infected persons. Burack and coworkers[114] found that *S. pneumoniae* and *Haemophilus influenzae* were the two most common bacteria seen in their series of 216 cases. Streptococci, usually *S. pneumoniae,* were responsible for 81 cases (37.5%) of bacterial pneumonia, and *Haemophilus* species accounted for an additional 46 cases (21%). Mundy and colleagues[115] also reported that *S. pneumoniae* and *H. influenzae* were the most common bacteria seen in their series of 180 hospitalized HIV-infected patients with pneumonia. Finally, Hirschtick and colleagues[64] of the PCHIS noted that these two bacteria comprised 54% of the bacteria identified in their study of 237 cases of bacterial pneumonia. In the period immediately preceding the HAART era, Rimland and associates[116] reported that PCP, followed by *S. pneumoniae* and *H. influenzae,* were the most common causes of community-acquired pneumonia in their series of 230 cases. In the HAART era, Afessa and Green[110] found that *S. pneumoniae* and *P. aeruginosa* were the two most common bacteria seen in their series of 111 cases. The authors postulated that the use of empirical antibiotics prior to collection of respiratory specimens might have contributed to an underdiagnosis of *S. pneumoniae.*

Clinical Features. In HIV-infected persons, the clinical and radiographic features of bacterial pneumonia are similar to those in immunocompetent persons with a few important exceptions, which are detailed.[67,67a]

CD4⁺ Lymphocyte Count, Symptoms, and Signs. Bacterial pneumonia can occur throughout the course of HIV infection and at any CD4⁺ lymphocyte count. As the CD4⁺ count declines, however, the incidence of bacterial pneumonia and the frequency of bacteremia increase. Hirschtick and colleagues[64] of the PCHIS found that the rate of bacterial pneumonia increased from 2.3 episodes per 100 person-years in HIV-infected subjects with a CD4⁺ count above 500 cells/μL to 10.8 episodes per 100 person-years in subjects with a CD4⁺ count below 200 cells/μL. The rate of pneumococcal bacteremia in HIV-infected patients has been estimated to be almost 100 times greater than that in age-matched non–HIV-infected persons.[117] Bacterial pneumonia characteristically presents with fever (in 90% to 100%), cough (in 90% to 100%) that is often productive (60% to 100%), dyspnea (in 45% to 75%), and pleuritic chest pain (in 50% to 70%).[118] The onset of symptoms is usually acute (3 to 5 days). Physical examination of the chest frequently reveals signs of focal lung consolidation or pleural effusion. The WBC count is typically elevated or, if normal, is elevated relative to the patient's baseline value, and there is often an accompanying "left shift."

Chest Radiograph. The chest radiograph characteristically reveals focal consolidation that tends to involve segments or lobes; a single focus is usually seen, but multifocal disease appears to be more common than in non–HIV-infected persons (Fig. 75.1).[119] Studies suggest that this "classic" presentation may be seen more frequently in pneumonias

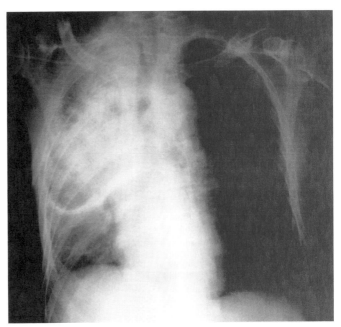

Figure 75.1 Posteroanterior chest radiograph of an HIV-seropositive patient showing focal right lung consolidation. Culture of blood and sputum revealed *Streptococcus pneumoniae.* In HIV-infected persons, *S. pneumoniae* is the most frequently identified bacterial pathogen and is often accompanied by bacteremia, especially when the CD4⁺ lymphocyte count is below 200 cells/μL. (Reproduced with permission from L. Huang.)

due to *S. pneumoniae* and, to a lesser extent, *Haemophilus* species than in those due to community-acquired *P. aeruginosa.* Several of the published series on HIV-associated bacterial pneumonia presented radiographic findings without regard to specific bacteria. One such study reported that 40% of 55 HIV-infected patients with bacterial pneumonia presented with focal, segmental or lobar, alveolar infiltrates, 38% had diffuse reticulonodular infiltrates, 16% had focal reticulonodular infiltrates, and 5% had nodular or cavitary infiltrates on chest radiograph.[120] Another study found that 54% of 99 HIV-infected patients with bacterial pneumonia had a lobar infiltrate, 17% had an interstitial infiltrate, 10% had a nodular infiltrate, and only 1% had a cavitary infiltrate on their radiograph.[65] In this study, multivariate analysis demonstrated that the presence of a lobar infiltrate on chest radiograph was an independent predictor of bacterial pneumonia (odds ratio = 5.8, 95% confidence interval = 2.1 to 16.1, $P < 0.001$). However, it is important to point out that these studies considered all bacterial pathogens together. Numerous reports as well as clinical experience demonstrate that the frequency of certain radiographic findings depends on the specific causative bacteria.

S. pneumoniae and *H. influenzae* pneumonia usually present with focal consolidation on chest radiograph, although *H. influenzae* may also present with bilateral interstitial or mixed interstitial-alveolar infiltrates similar to PCP. A review of all English-language published articles and abstracts from 1981 to 1990 about *S. pneumoniae* disease in HIV-infected persons found that three fourths of bacterial pneumonias due to *S. pneumoniae* presented with segmental, lobar, or multilobar consolidation on chest radiograph.[121] Garcia-Leoni and associates[122] reported a focal alveolar pattern in 67% and a diffuse alveolar pattern in 10% of the radiographs from 21 HIV-infected patients with *S. pneumoniae* pneumonia. Schlamm and Yancovitz[123] found similar proportions in 34 HIV-infected patients with *H. influenzae* pneumonia, in whom focal or diffuse lobar infiltrates were noted in 74% of the radiographs. However, another series of 12 HIV-infected patients with *H. influenzae* pneumonia discovered that the presentation was clinically and radiographically indistinguishable from that of PCP.[124] Patients complained of nonproductive cough and dyspnea with a median symptom duration of 4 weeks. All presented with bilateral interstitial or bilateral mixed interstitial-alveolar infiltrates similar to those in PCP.

Diagnosis. The diagnostic approach to bacterial pneumonia is the same for HIV-infected as for non–HIV-infected persons (see Chapter 32); most hospitalized patients should have sputum Gram stain and culture.[125,126] Blood cultures provide specific information and should be obtained.[125,126] Studies have documented a significantly higher rate of bacteremia, especially pneumococcal, among HIV-infected persons. In HIV-infected patients, 25% to 80% of those with pneumococcal pneumonia presented with bacteremia, and 5% to 25% of those with *H. influenzae* pneumonia presented with bacteremia. The presence of shock is an independent predictor associated with an increased morality.[127] Given these findings, blood cultures should be performed in most, if not all, cases. Finally, thoracentesis should be considered for patients with pleural effusion, especially if the effusion is large or if there is concern about possible empyema. In communities where drug-resistant bacteria are prevalent, attempts to culture the causative bacteria to enable drug susceptibility testing are especially important.

Treatment. The principles of the treatment of patients with community-acquired pneumonia are the same for HIV-infected as for non–HIV-infected persons.[125,126,128] The choice of antimicrobial agent should be based on a number of factors, such as the results of a sputum Gram stain, the presence of comorbid conditions (e.g., chronic obstructive pulmonary disease, congestive heart failure, alcohol use), the clinical and radiographic presentation, and the severity of the pneumonia. As for non-HIV-infected persons, treatment should be initiated promptly.[129] Initial empirical therapy should include coverage against frequently identified organisms (e.g., *S. pneumoniae* and *Haemophilus* species). Prevailing drug resistance patterns must be considered when the antibiotic is selected. For patients with CD4+ lymphocyte counts less than 100 cells/µL, especially if associated with recent hospitalization, neutropenia, and broad-spectrum antimicrobial use, consideration should be given to including coverage against *P. aeruginosa*. The duration of therapy is similar for HIV-infected and non–HIV-infected persons, and the response rates appear to be comparable. A large multicenter Italian study, the Pneumonia Outcome Predictors in HIV-Infected Patients (POP-HIV) study, reported that HIV-infected patients admitted to the hospital with community-acquired pneumonia reached what was a conservative definition of clinical stability after a median of 6 days (interquartile range, 3 to 10 days).[130]

Prevention. The U.S. Public Health Service and the Infectious Diseases Society of America (USPHS/IDSA)

recommend that the 23-valent polysaccharide pneumococcal vaccine be given to all HIV-infected patients with CD4+ lymphocyte counts above 200 cells/µL and be considered for patients with CD4+ lymphocyte counts below 200 cells/µL.[36] The efficacy of vaccination is greatest when the patient's CD4+ lymphocyte count is above 500 cells/µL.[131] Revaccination can be considered for patients who were initially immunized when their CD4+ lymphocyte count was below 200 cells/µL if their count has increased above 200 cells/µL in response to HAART. The duration of the protective effect of primary pneumococcal vaccination in HIV-infected persons is unknown; revaccination 5 years after the initial vaccination may be appropriate. Studies of HIV-infected patients with invasive pneumococcal disease demonstrate that greater than 80% of episodes and greater than 90% of recurrent episodes are caused by *S. pneumoniae* serotypes that are covered by the 23-valent vaccine.[132,133] Given the low incidence of *H. influenzae* type B infection among adults, the *H. influenzae* type B vaccine is not generally recommended for HIV-infected adults.[36] Patients who are cigarette smokers or who use injection drugs should be encouraged to quit. Patients who are receiving TMP-SMX for *Pneumocystis* or *T. gondii* prophylaxis or clarithromycin or azithromycin for disseminated MAC prophylaxis will receive added benefit in that these antimicrobial agents also offer protection against many bacterial infections.[133a] Because neutropenia is a strong risk factor for bacterial pneumonia, the discontinuation of myelosuppressive medications or the use of granulocyte colony-stimulating factor in HIV-infected patients with an absolute neutrophil count below 500 cells/µL has been suggested.[36] Patients who experience recurrent episodes of bacterial pneumonia can be considered for chronic antibiotic prophylaxis; however, this decision must balance the potential benefits against the risks of drug-resistant bacteria and potential adverse effects and toxicity.

Pseudomonas aeruginosa

In addition to being a cause of nosocomial disease, *P. aeruginosa* is well recognized as a cause of community-acquired bacterial pneumonia in HIV-infected persons. In contrast to non–HIV-infected persons, the classic risk factors for *P. aeruginosa* infection are often absent in HIV-infected patients, and the disease is often recurrent.[134]

P. aeruginosa infection produces a wide spectrum of disease in HIV-infected persons. The two most common presentations are pneumonia and bacteremia. Unlike pneumonia due to *S. pneumoniae* and *Haemophilus* species, however, pneumonia due to *P. aeruginosa* usually occurs at more profound degrees of immunosuppression, and the chest radiograph often reveals cavitary infiltrates.

CD4+ Lymphocyte Count, Symptoms, and Signs. Most cases of *P. aeruginosa* pneumonia occur in patients with a CD4+ lymphocyte count less than 100 cells/µL, usually less than 50 cells/µL. In one series of 16 HIV-infected patients with *P. aeruginosa* bronchopulmonary infection, the mean CD4+ count was 25 cells/µL, and only one patient had a CD4+ count above 50 cells/µL (56 cells/µL).[135] Another series of 15 HIV-infected patients with community-acquired *P. aeruginosa* pneumonia reported a mean CD4+ count of

27 cells/µL and noted that 80% had a CD4$^+$ count less than 50 cells/µL.[136] The usual symptoms include fever and cough that is productive, with dyspnea and chest pain seen less frequently.[136]

Chest Radiograph. Although the chest radiograph may resemble that seen in pneumococcal or *Haemophilus* pneumonias with focal consolidation, a significant proportion of radiographs demonstrate cavitary infiltrates. Schuster and Norris[136] reported that half of 16 HIV-infected patients with *Pseudomonas* pneumonia had cavitary infiltrates on their admission chest radiograph, and another 3 patients (19%) had cavities on subsequent radiographs. Less striking results were noted in a study of 58 HIV-infected patients with *P. aeruginosa infection* in which 24% of the 25 patients who had pneumonia had cavitary infiltrates on chest radiograph.[137]

Other Bacteria

Legionella species were originally thought to be an important cause of community-acquired bacterial pneumonia in HIV-infected patients. In the National Heart, Lung, and Blood Institute workshop, *Legionella* species either alone or with coexisting PCP accounted for 19 (4.3%) of the 441 serious pulmonary diseases seen.[105] In an update a few years later, it was noted that *Legionella* pneumonia was seldom seen.[138] Only a few series of *Legionella* pneumonia in HIV-infected patients have been reported. One series reported eight cases of *Legionella pneumophila* pneumonia occurring in seven HIV-infected patients (1.7% of the patients with Walter Reed stage 5 or 6 in their cohort).[139] Five of the cases were nosocomial. The median CD4$^+$ lymphocyte count was 83 cells/µL (range, 38 to 155 cells/µL). Another series reported 15 cases of *L. pneumophila* pneumonia that spanned the HAART era.[140] Ten of the 15 cases occurred in persons who were receiving HAART, and the mean CD4$^+$ lymphocyte count was 348 cells/µL (5 of the 10 also had an undetectable HIV RNA level). Fever (13 of 13), cough (12 of 13; productive in 8 of 13), and dyspnea (10 of 13) were the most common symptoms. Extrapulmonary manifestations (gastrointestinal, $n = 3$; neurologic, $n = 4$) were also seen. The chest radiograph revealed alveolar infiltrates in all 15 cases, with 8 of the 15 having bilateral involvement. Of note, 12 (80%) of the 15 persons developed respiratory failure and 3 died. Although *L. pneumophila* is the most common species identified, other *Legionella* species have also been reported.

There have been a number of reports of *R. equi* pulmonary disease occurring in HIV-infected persons. A review of over 100 reported cases found that approximately two thirds occurred in HIV-infected persons, with pulmonary disease present in the majority.[141] This review noted that HIV-infected persons were more likely to have *R. equi* bacteremia or extrapulmonary manifestations, or both, than persons without HIV infection. Most cases present when the CD4$^+$ lymphocyte count is less than 200 cells/µL and usually below 100 cells/µL.[141] In one multicenter series of 67 HIV-infected patients with *R. equi* infection, the mean CD4$^+$ count was 35 cells/µL (range, 1 to 183 cells/µL).[142] Fever (91%), cough (88%; productive in 85%), chest pain (45%), hemoptysis (31%), and dyspnea (30%) were the most

common presenting symptoms. The chest radiograph often reveals cavitary lesions that may mimic tuberculosis or nocardiosis, or focal consolidation that may mimic bacterial pneumonia. Donisi and associates[143] reported cavitary lesions in 5 (42%) of 12 radiographs and lobar consolidation in 4 (33%). Torres-Tortosa and coworkers[142] found cavitary lesions in 67% of cases (45 of 67), with upper lobe involvement common. Sputum, blood, bronchoscopy, and pleural fluid specimens can establish the diagnosis of *R. equi* pneumonia.[142,143] The optimum treatment regimen and duration have yet to be defined.[141] Combination antibiotic therapy is generally recommended, and potential choices include vancomycin, imipenem, rifampin, erythromycin, fluoroquinolones, and aminoglycosides. Treatment for 6 months is often required. Relapses are common, so chronic suppressive therapy is probably indicated. HIV-infected patients should avoid exposure to aerosolized soil containing farm animal manure.

There have been a handful of reports of *Nocardia* species infection in HIV-infected patients. *Nocardia asteroides* is the most common species identified, and the lung is the most commonly affected site. Most cases present when the CD4$^+$ lymphocyte count is below 200 cells/µL. In one series of 30 HIV-infected patients with nocardiosis, the mean CD4$^+$ count was 109 cells/µL (median = 92 cells/µL; range, 12 to 266 cells/µL).[144] The presenting symptoms often mimicked tuberculosis. Fever (30 of 30 cases), productive cough (22 of 30), and weight loss (21 of 30) were most common.[144] The chest radiograph usually reveals cavitary lesions or lobar or multilobar infiltrates, especially in the upper lung zones. In one series of 21 HIV-infected patients, cavitary lesions were seen in 62%, lobar or multilobar consolidation in 52%, reticulonodular infiltrates in 33%, solitary masses in 24%, and pleural effusions in 33% of radiographs.[145] Upper lobe involvement was seen in 71%. Uttamchandani and colleagues[144] reported alveolar infiltrates in 64%, reticulonodular infiltrates in 9%, and mixed reticulonodular-alveolar infiltrates in 27% of radiographs. Upper lobe involvement was seen in 64%, associated cavitation was noted in 18%, pleural effusions in 14%, and intrathoracic adenopathy in 9% of radiographs. Sputum or bronchoscopy can establish the diagnosis of pulmonary nocardiosis. A modified AFB stain may provide an early presumptive diagnosis in the proper clinical setting. Long-term TMP-SMX is the treatment of choice.

MYCOBACTERIA

Early in the AIDS epidemic, mycobacteria were recognized as major sources of HIV-associated morbidity and mortality. Initially, HIV-infected patients were noted to develop disseminated MAC. Subsequently, the relationship between HIV and *M. tuberculosis* and nontuberculous mycobacteria such as *M. kansasii* became clearer. Other nontuberculous mycobacteria are also occasionally identified as causes of pneumonia in HIV-infected persons.

Mycobacterium tuberculosis

Tuberculosis is the major opportunistic infection complicating the HIV epidemic worldwide. Although other pathogens may predominate in individual areas, no other pathogen poses as great a global threat to persons immunocompromised by HIV infection as *M. tuberculosis.* Moreover, unlike most of the HIV-associated opportunistic infections, *M. tuberculosis* is transmissible from person to person; it is also curable and preventable.

The AIDS epidemic has contributed to a veritable explosion of tuberculosis throughout the world, but especially in sub-Saharan Africa and Southeast Asia. The World Health Organization (WHO) Global Surveillance and Monitoring Project[146,147] estimated that approximately 10 to 11 million people are coinfected with HIV and *M. tuberculosis,* with the overwhelming majority (>90%) of these persons residing in the WHO African and Southeast Asian Regions. There were an estimated 8.3 million new tuberculosis cases in 2000; 9% of all new tuberculosis cases in adults (ages 15 to 49 years) were attributable to HIV infection, with the proportion being much greater in the WHO African Region (31%) and some developed countries, including the United States (26%).[147] There were an estimated 1.8 million deaths from tuberculosis, 12% of which were attributable to HIV. Overall, tuberculosis was the cause of death in 11% of all adult AIDS deaths.

The AIDS epidemic has also affected tuberculosis in the United States. Before 1985, the incidence of tuberculosis in the United States declined by 5% to 6% per year. From 1985 through 1992, tuberculosis cases increased by 20%, which resulted in 51,700 additional cases of tuberculosis being reported in excess of that predicted by the annual decline previously noted.[148] However, since 1992, tuberculosis cases have decreased steadily. In 2002, tuberculosis cases declined 43.5% from the 1992 peak, and the number of tuberculosis cases reported was the lowest recorded in the United States since reporting began in 1953.[149] Defining the precise proportion of tuberculosis cases occurring in HIV-infected persons in the United States is limited by incomplete HIV reporting. Nevertheless, the proportion of tuberculosis cases who were also HIV-positive declined from 15% in 1993 to 8% in 2001, including a decline from 29% in 1993 to 15% in 2001 among adults ages 25 to 44 years.[150]

It remains unclear whether HIV-infected persons are more likely to acquire tuberculous infection after exposure to *M. tuberculosis* than HIV-negative persons. Once an individual is infected, however, it is clear that HIV infection significantly increases the risk of developing primary tuberculosis as well as progressing from latent tuberculosis infection (LTBI) to active tuberculous disease. Studies have reported an annual rate of tuberculosis among untreated, tuberculin skin test–positive, HIV-infected persons in the United States of 4.5 to 10.4 cases per 100 person-years.[68,151] Instead of a 5% lifetime risk of "reactivation" disease, the antiretroviral-untreated HIV-infected person with latent, untreated *M. tuberculosis* infection risks almost certain active tuberculosis as immune competence wanes. The risk of "reactivation" disease among HIV-infected persons has been estimated to be as high as 10% per year.

Multidrug-resistant tuberculosis poses a particularly grim prospect for the HIV-infected person.[152] The risk of drug-resistant tuberculosis has been reported to be greater among HIV-infected patients than among others. In a multivariate analysis, HIV infection was found to be an independent risk factor for at least isoniazid resistance, for both

isoniazid and rifampin resistance, and especially for rifampin monoresistance.[153] The factors that lead to acquired drug resistance include an inadequate initial treatment regimen, patient nonadherence with the prescribed regimen, and the addition of a single drug to a failing regimen. Studies with restriction fragment length polymorphism analysis have shown that multidrug-resistant tuberculosis can occur as a result of both failure to adhere to tuberculous therapy and exogenous reinfection from a multidrug-resistant source.[154] This latter sequence is probably an expression of the increased risk of developing active new-onset tuberculosis among HIV-infected patients in these instances after exposure to a patient with multidrug-resistant organisms. Transmission of multidrug-resistant tuberculosis to health care workers and prison guards has been documented; several of these workers, many of whom were HIV seropositive, have developed multidrug-resistant tuberculosis and some have died.[155,156]

Clinical Features. Worldwide, tuberculosis is often the initial manifestation of underlying HIV infection. As in immunocompetent persons, the clinical and radiographic features of tuberculosis in HIV-infected persons vary.[88,89] Patients usually present with some combination of constitutional (fever, night sweats, weight loss), and respiratory (cough, dyspnea) symptoms. HIV infection is an independent risk factor associated with an increased risk for extrapulmonary tuberculosis.[157]

CD4⁺ Lymphocyte Count, Symptoms, and Signs. Tuberculosis can occur throughout the course of HIV infection and at any CD4⁺ lymphocyte count. In an early study, Theuer and associates[90] reported a median CD4⁺ lymphocyte count of 326 cells/µL (range, 23 to 742 cells/µL) among 11 HIV-infected persons with tuberculosis. Jones and colleagues[158] found a median CD4⁺ count of 97 cells/µL among 85 consecutive HIV-infected patients with tuberculosis; 63 patients had a CD4⁺ count equal to or less than 200 cells/µL, and 22 had a CD4⁺ count above 200 cells/µL. In a study of 111 South African HIV-infected persons with tuberculosis, the median CD4⁺ lymphocyte count was 169 cells/µL (range, 6 to 1125 cells/µL).[159] The clinical expression of tuberculosis in HIV-infected persons is largely dependent on the degree of host immunosuppression (Table 75.2).[88,160] HIV-infected persons with relatively early HIV disease typically present with a picture suggestive of reactivation tuberculosis. In these patients,

Table 75.2 Manifestations of AIDS-Related Tuberculosis in "Early" and "Late" HIV Infection

Feature	Early Infection	Late Infection
Tuberculin skin test	Positive	Negative
Extrapulmonary	10–15%	More than 50%
Radiographic distribution	Upper lung zones	Lower and middle lung zones
Cavitation	Common	Uncommon
Adenopathy	Uncommon	Common

Adapted from Murray JF: Cursed duet: HIV infection and tuberculosis. Respiration 57:210–220, 1990.

tuberculosis classically presents with fevers, cough that is usually productive, night sweats, and weight loss. Disease is usually limited to the lung, and signs of extrapulmonary disease are typically absent. In contrast, HIV-infected persons with more advanced HIV disease typically present with a picture reminiscent of primary pulmonary tuberculosis or disseminated tuberculosis. In these patients, symptoms and signs of extrapulmonary disease are often present. In a series of 97 HIV-infected patients with tuberculosis, Jones and colleagues[158] reported that extrapulmonary tuberculosis was seen in 30 (70%) of 43 patients with a CD4+ count of 100 cells/μL or less, 10 (50%) of 20 patients with a count between 101 and 200 cells/μL, 7 (44%) of 16 patients with a count between 201 and 300 cells/μL, and only 5 (28%) of 18 patients with a count above 300 cells/μL. Virtually any extrapulmonary site may be involved; common sites include lymph nodes (usually cervical, supraclavicular, and axillary), bone marrow, genitourinary tract, central nervous system, and liver.[161] Tuberculous meningitis is more frequent in HIV-infected persons.[162] Although nonspecific, routine laboratory tests such as the complete blood cell count and liver transaminases, when abnormal, are often indicative of tuberculous involvement.[161]

Chest Radiograph. The prevalences of specific chest radiograph features of tuberculosis also depend on the degree of host immunosuppression. Disease occurring early in the course of HIV infection mirrors that encountered in immunocompetent persons: upper lung zone infiltrates, often with cavitation, on chest radiograph. However, tuberculosis occurring later in the course of HIV infection often presents with middle and lower lung zone infiltrates (see Fig. 75.2); with diffuse infiltrates, including a miliary pattern; or with a normal chest radiograph. Greenberg and coworkers[91] noted a normal radiograph in 19 (14%) of 133 HIV-infected patients with tuberculosis. As the CD4+ lymphocyte count declines, cavitation becomes less common, and intrathoracic adenopathy (Fig. 75.3) becomes more common, on chest radiograph. Jones and colleagues[158] reported that adenopathy was seen on the radiographs of 20 (34%) of 58 HIV-infected patients with a CD4+ count of 200 cells/μL or less compared with 4 (14%) of 29 patients with a CD4+ count above 200 cells/μL (P = 0.04). Abouya and associates[163] found significant differences in the proportion of chest radiographs that showed cavitary infiltrates and those with intrathoracic adenopathy as the CD4+ count declined. In 111 patients coinfected with HIV and *M. tuberculosis,* the proportion of radiographs with cavitary infiltrates decreased from 63% to 44% to 29% as the CD4+ cell count declined from 400 cells/μL and above to 200 to 399 cells/μL and then to below 200 cells/μL (P < 0.05); in contrast, the proportion of radiographs with noncavitary infiltrates (33%, 44%, and 58%, respectively) and with intrathoracic adenopathy (0%, 14%, and 20%, respectively) increased as the CD4+ cell count declined (both P < 0.05). In settings in which HIV-infected persons may be receiving HAART, the proportion of patients with tuberculosis who present with a post-primary pattern on chest radiograph is increased. In one study of 209 patients, 82% of the patients receiving HAART presented with a post-primary pattern of tuberculosis compared to 44% of the patients not receiving HAART (P < 0.001).[164] During the course of the study, the proportion of patients with tuberculosis who present with a post-primary pattern on chest radiograph increased from 36% (1987–1991) to 44% (1992–1996) and then to 58% (1997–2001) (P = 0.02).

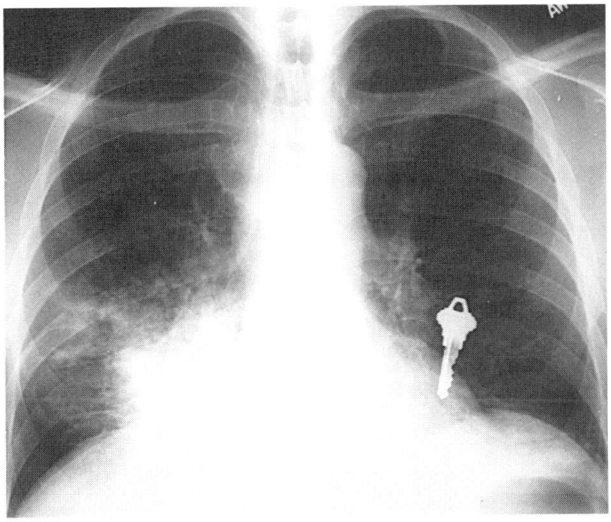

Figure 75.2 Posteroanterior chest radiograph of an HIV-seropositive patient showing focal right lung consolidation with air bronchograms. Culture of sputum revealed *Mycobacterium tuberculosis* that was mono-rifampin resistant. Knowledge of the patient's CD4+ lymphocyte count (<50 cells/μL) and understanding that tuberculosis can present with middle to lower lung zone consolidation during "late" HIV infection were instrumental in making the diagnosis of tuberculosis. The key was in the patient's pocket. (Reproduced with permission from L. Huang.)

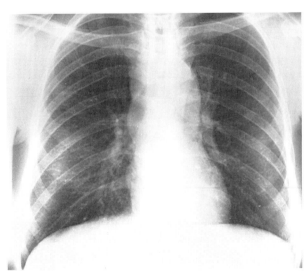

Figure 75.3 Posteroanterior chest radiograph of an HIV-seropositive patient showing mediastinal adenopathy. Culture of biopsy material revealed *Mycobacterium tuberculosis.* Among HIV-infected persons, the proportion of cases that present with intrathoracic adenopathy on chest radiograph increases as the CD4+ lymphocyte count decreases. (From Murray JF, Mills J: Pulmonary complications of HIV infection. Am Rev Respir Dis 141:1356–1372, 1582–1598, 1990.)

Slow recognition of late "atypical" HIV-associated tuberculosis delays institution of specific chemotherapy and increases the likelihood of transmission. A high index of suspicion should always be maintained when evaluating HIV-infected populations at high risk for tuberculosis, as the clinical and radiographic presentations vary. The key to the diagnosis is knowledge of the person's CD4+ lymphocyte count and understanding the role that host immunosuppression has in the presentation.

Diagnosis. The diagnostic approach to tuberculosis is the same for HIV-infected as for non–HIV-infected persons. Sputum AFB smears are the initial diagnostic tests. Three sputum specimens should be obtained for 3 consecutive days, examined for AFB, and cultured for mycobacteria. In patients with nonproductive cough or scant secretions, sputum induction should be performed. As described previously, several studies reported that the sensitivity of sputum AFB smear and culture in HIV-infected patients is similar to the sensitivity in the overall population. In addition, the sensitivity of sputum AFB culture for HIV-infected patients with pleural effusions due to tuberculosis has been reported to be as high as 77%.[165] The detection of AFB on smear, regardless of the source, is an indication for empirical antituberculosis treatment but cannot be considered diagnostic of tuberculosis. Several nontuberculous mycobacteria may present in HIV-infected persons and may be the cause of a smear-positive specimen. Molecular techniques, including the Roche Amplicor *Mycobacterium tuberculosis* Test and the Gen-Probe Amplified *Mycobacterium tuberculosis* Direct Test, are approved for use in the identification of *M. tuberculosis* in respiratory specimens. These tests are more sensitive than either AFB staining or auramine-rhodamine fluorescence for detecting *M. tuberculosis*. Sputum AFB smears are negative in a significant percentage (about 50%) of cases of tuberculosis. Even three negative AFB smears cannot exclude the diagnosis of tuberculosis. Therefore, patients with clinically suspected tuberculosis should remain on antituberculosis therapy while awaiting the results of culture or further diagnostic testing, or both. For patients in whom the clinical suspicion for tuberculosis remains high despite having negative sputum AFB smears, bronchoscopy with BAL and TBBX can be considered.

The "gold standard" diagnostic test for tuberculosis remains isolation and identification of *M. tuberculosis* by culture. Virtually any specimen can be examined for AFB, cultured for mycobacteria, and studied by polymerase chain reaction (PCR), including sputum, BAL fluid, TBBX specimen, Wang needle aspirate, pleural fluid or biopsy specimen, fine-needle aspirate of lymph node or other lesion, bone marrow aspirate or biopsy specimen, and urine, cerebrospinal fluid, and biopsy specimens of other suspicious sites (e.g., liver). Blood cultures are specific and should be obtained, especially from those persons with a CD4+ lymphocyte count below 200 cells/μL. The results of drug susceptibility studies are useful in tailoring definitive treatment and are essential in cases of drug resistance.

Treatment. Because tuberculosis is transmissible, persons with suspected tuberculosis should be started on empirical antituberculosis treatment promptly to reduce the risk of transmission. The detection of AFB on smear or in culture, regardless of the source, is an indication for empirical anti-

tuberculosis treatment while final identification is awaited. The American Thoracic Society, CDC, and IDSA Treatment of Tuberculosis guidelines recommend a 6-month treatment regimen for HIV-infected patients with drug-susceptible tuberculosis.[166] However, 6 months is the minimum duration of treatment for HIV-infected adults. Patients whose sputum cultures are still positive after 2 months of therapy should be considered candidates for a 9-month regimen.[166] The American Academy of Pediatrics recommends a 9-month treatment regimen for HIV-infected children with drug-susceptible tuberculosis.[166,167] Directly observed therapy and other adherence-promoting strategies should be used. Clearly, HIV-infected patients with drug-resistant tuberculosis require a longer duration of therapy, and expert consultation should be sought in these cases.

HIV-infected persons with suspected tuberculosis should be started on four antituberculous drugs: isoniazid, rifampin, pyrazinamide, and ethambutol.[166] These drugs should be given daily (56 doses) or 5 days a week (40 doses) for 8 weeks. If the cultures reveal drug-susceptible tuberculosis, patients should be continued on isoniazid and rifampin daily (or thrice weekly) for an additional 18 weeks. Although it is a potential continuation-phase option in immunocompetent patients, once-weekly isoniazid-rifapentine should never be given to HIV-infected patients as studies have reported increased rates of tuberculosis recurrence and development of acquired rifampin monoresistance.[166] If a strong clinical suspicion exists for MAC, multidrug therapy that is active against both *M. tuberculosis* and MAC can be initiated simultaneously (e.g., by adding a macrolide, either clarithromycin or azithromycin, to the previously noted four-drug regimen). The standard four-drug antituberculosis regimen is also effective therapy against *M. kansasii*, although the duration of treatment differs.[168]

All cultures positive for *M. tuberculosis* should be submitted for susceptibility testing. When results of susceptibility testing are available, drug therapy can be tailored. As in the treatment of all patients with tuberculosis, compliance is essential to a successful result. The response to therapy and the time to convert sputum cultures from positive to negative appear to be similar in HIV-infected and non–HIV-infected patients.[166] Among published studies, the tuberculosis recurrence rate has varied; however, most studies report rates of 5% or less when the standard four-drug regimen is prescribed and taken.[166]

HIV-infected patients with tuberculosis are more likely to experience toxicity from antituberculous drugs than are non–HIV-infected persons. However, HIV-infected patients are often receiving a number of additional medications, and it is often difficult to distinguish an adverse drug effect to antituberculous drugs from adverse effects from these other medications. As a result, the first-line antituberculous drugs (especially isoniazid and rifampin) should only be discontinued permanently if there is strong evidence that these medications were the cause.[166] HIV-infected patients with tuberculosis who begin dual therapy for *M. tuberculosis* and HIV infection may develop paradoxical reactions, a temporary exacerbation of clinical and radiographic features that appears to be related to decreases in plasma HIV RNA and increases in the CD4+ lymphocyte count.[169–171a] The diagnosis of paradoxical reaction is one of exclusion. Patients with paradoxical reactions only rarely require change or discontinuation of antituberculous or antiretroviral therapies, and symptomatic therapy is recommended.[166]

HIV-infected patients who are receiving or who are initiating antiretroviral therapy at the time that tuberculosis is diagnosed pose a special problem for the treatment of tuberculosis.[172] Current guidelines for the treatment of HIV infection recommend the use of combinations of antiretroviral therapies for symptomatic HIV-infected persons (AIDS or severe HIV-associated symptoms) and for asymptomatic HIV-infected persons with a CD4+ lymphocyte count below 200 cells/µL.[173] Antiretroviral therapy can also be considered for persons with less severe immunosuppression (manifested by a CD4+ lymphocyte count between 200 and 350 cells/µL); the level of plasma HIV RNA should also be taken into account. The recommended combinations include either a non-nucleoside reverse transcriptase inhibitor (NNRTI)–based regimen consisting of efavirenz (an NNRTI) plus lamivudine (a nucleoside reverse transcriptase inhibitor [NRTI]) plus a third drug (zidovudine, stavudine, or tenofovir DF, all NRTIs), or a protease inhibitor (PI)-based regimen consisting of lopinavir or ritonavir (a PI) plus lamivudine plus a third drug (zidovudine or stavudine). Once begun, it is crucial that antiretroviral therapy be continued without interruption for optimum, durable results. However, the optimal timing for initiating antiretroviral therapy in an HIV-infected patient who is being treated for tuberculosis remains to be defined.[173a] Moreover, the dual treatment of HIV and M. tuberculosis poses additional challenges.

Both PIs and NNRTIs have significant interactions with the rifamycins, principally related to the induction or inhibition (or both) of the hepatic cytochrome P-450 (CYP450) enzyme system.[166,173] In addition, the rifamycins are inducers of the CYP450 enzyme system. Of the rifamycins, rifampin is the most potent CYP450 inducer, followed by rifapentine and then rifabutin. In general, induction of the CYP450 system results in decreased drug levels, whereas inhibition results in increased levels. Decreased drug levels are associated with the development of resistance in both HIV and M. tuberculosis, whereas increased drug levels are correlated with toxicity. Previously, the use of rifampin to treat tuberculosis in a patient receiving or initiating PI therapy, NNRTI therapy, or both was contraindicated.[174] The current guidelines indicate that rifampin can be used with certain PIs and NNRTIs. Information on the interactions between specific antiretroviral drugs and different rifamycins is constantly being updated. Clinicians caring for HIV-infected patients with tuberculosis should consult experts in their management prior to initiating tuberculosis or HIV therapy. Another source of information, which is updated regularly, is the CDC website (http://www.cdc.gov/nchstp/tb/).

Prevention. HIV-infected persons are at the greatest risk for progressing from LTBI to active tuberculosis. Therefore, HIV-infected persons should be tested for LTBI when HIV infection is first identified.[36,175] Repeat testing each year should be considered for persons who have a negative tuberculin skin test and who are at risk for exposure to M. tuberculosis. In addition, strong consideration should be given to retesting persons who initially had a negative test but subsequently experienced an increase in their CD4+ lymphocyte count due to antiretroviral therapy.

The tuberculin skin test remains the best screening tool to document M. tuberculosis exposure. HIV-infected persons with CD4+ lymphocyte counts above 400 cells/µL are likely to have a positive response to purified protein derivative (PPD) skin testing in the presence of M. tuberculosis infection. However, the magnitude of the delayed hypersensitivity response is likely to be less than that seen in HIV-seronegative persons. Accordingly, 5-mm induration (rather than the conventional 10 mm) is recommended as the cutoff point for LTBI in HIV-infected persons. Despite this modification, there is a higher incidence of false-negative tests as the CD4+ count declines. Markowitz and colleagues[68] of the PCHIS found the sensitivity of delayed hypersensitivity/anergy testing to fall off after the CD4+ lymphocyte count declined below 400 cells/µL. Routine anergy testing is not generally recommended for HIV-infected patients.

HIV-infected persons with a positive response to PPD or a history of a positive response to PPD who have not received prior treatment for LTBI should receive isoniazid for 9 months.[36,175] This is a change from previous recommendations, which called for 12 months of therapy. An alternative treatment for LTBI is rifampin for 4 months; if the patient is also receiving antiretroviral therapy with a PI or with delavirdine, an NNRTI, expert consultation should be sought. The two-drug regimen of rifampin plus pyrazinamide for 2 months is no longer recommended due to an increased incidence of severe hepatotoxicity and death.[176] At present, the routine use of preventive therapy in anergic or PPD-negative, HIV-infected persons is not generally recommended.[36,175] However, some authorities recommend primary preventive therapy for anergic or PPD-negative, HIV-infected residents of locations where there is an ongoing significant risk for exposure to M. tuberculosis (e.g., prisons, jails, homeless shelters).[36,175] In addition, HIV-infected persons, including HIV-infected health care workers, who have experienced a significant tuberculosis exposure (sufficient to cause PPD conversions in immunocompetent persons) should be offered appropriate prophylaxis. Several studies document that the risk of reactivation tuberculosis is virtually eliminated if an HIV-infected person who has been infected with a drug-susceptible organism takes adequate prophylaxis.[36,175] HIV-seropositive persons who have converted their PPD test after exposure to multidrug-resistant tuberculosis or anergic HIV-seropositive persons who have experienced a significant contact with multidrug-resistant tuberculosis should be offered prophylaxis based on the susceptibilities of the multidrug-resistant tuberculosis to which they were exposed. Paramount in the management of such patients is the active involvement of an expert in the treatment of multidrug-resistant tuberculosis.

Although concern has been raised about the safety and efficacy of vaccination with bacille Calmette-Guérin (BCG), a live vaccine, data suggest that the incidence of local complications (ulceration and lymphadenitis) did not differ among HIV-infected babies who received bacille Calmette-Guérin compared with non–HIV-infected infants.[177]

Moreover, the WHO and the International Union Against Tuberculosis and Lung Diseases (IUATLD) continue to recommend using bacille Calmette-Guérin in developing countries where there is a high prevalence of HIV infection, but state that the vaccine should not be given to symptomatic HIV-infected children or adults.

Mycobacterium avium Complex

MAC consists of several related *Mycobacterium* species, including *M. avium* and *M. intracellulare*. Until 1980, only 24 cases of disseminated MAC had been reported.[178] After the onset of the AIDS epidemic, the number of cases rose dramatically. With the increased use of combinations of antiretroviral therapy, however, our experience at San Francisco General Hospital, and at many other institutions, is that the incidence of disseminated MAC has declined since 1996.[8,179,180]

The pathogenesis of disseminated MAC is incompletely understood, but it is believed to result from primary acquisition of the microorganism, which is ubiquitous in the environment, rather than reactivation of latent infection.[181,182] These mycobacteria probably enter the body chiefly through the gastrointestinal tract and occasionally through the lungs.[183,184] Person-to-person transmission is believed to be unlikely. Nearly all cases of disseminated MAC are caused by *M. avium* serotypes, which suggests that there are important differences in exposure to or virulence of these particular strains.

Clinical Features. Although the lungs are an important potential portal of entry for MAC into the bloodstream, isolated MAC pulmonary disease is rare.[185–188] The most common clinical presentation of disseminated MAC disease is a febrile, wasting syndrome consisting of fever, night sweats, fatigue, anorexia, and weight loss; other manifestations include abdominal pain and chronic diarrhea, hepatosplenomegaly, lymphadenopathy, progressive anemia, and, rarely, extrabiliary obstructive jaundice.[189,190]

CD4+ Lymphocyte Count, Symptoms, and Signs. More than 95% of cases of disseminated MAC occur in HIV-infected patients whose CD4+ count is 50 cells/μL or less.[190,191] Patients with disseminated MAC characteristically have nonspecific symptoms, signs, and laboratory abnormalities. Constitutional features dominate the clinical presentation, and respiratory symptoms are usually absent. In addition to these symptoms, patients with pulmonary MAC infection often present with cough, dyspnea, and occasionally hemoptysis.[188] Physical examination usually reveals evidence of weight loss; hepatosplenomegaly and lymphadenopathy may also be found. Laboratory abnormalities include anemia, often severe, and an elevated alkaline phosphatase level. The chest radiograph is typically normal, even when the organism is cultured from respiratory tract secretions.[183] Focal pneumonia has been reported but is extremely rare.[185–188] More frequently seen—but still uncommon—are endobronchial lesions without pneumonia.[192,193] These endobronchial lesions appear to be submucosal "pearls" that on biopsy are teeming with AFB. Accompanying the increased use of combinations of antiretroviral therapy has come an appreciation for the immune reconstitution syndrome. The immune reconstitution syndrome often presents with paradoxical worsening of an opportunistic infection that develops when patients are treated concurrently (or in close temporal proximity) for both the opportunistic infection and the underlying HIV infection. Alternatively, immune reconstitution syndrome results in atypical presentations of a previously undiagnosed opportunistic infection. Many of the reported cases of isolated pulmonary MAC occurred in patients who received antiretroviral therapy, thus raising the possibility that isolated pulmonary MAC is an example of immune reconstitution syndrome. Clinicians should be aware of this possibility when starting patients on antiretroviral therapy.

Diagnosis. MAC can be cultured from numerous sites, but the most productive sources are blood, bone marrow, liver, or lymph nodes.[190] Blood cultures for MAC are a sensitive method for establishing the diagnosis of disseminated disease. The sensitivity of blood cultures for disseminated MAC has ranged from 86% to 98% of cases in which disseminated disease was confirmed by autopsy. The diagnosis of disseminated MAC can also be established by cultures from any normally sterile body site. Often, MAC is cultured from respiratory specimens such as sputum or BAL fluid, but this finding cannot be considered indicative of either pulmonary or disseminated disease.[183,194] The pathologic findings of MAC infection are characteristic but not definitive. AFB are remarkably abundant and are often packed within foamy macrophages or histiocytes; granulomas are usually absent or poorly formed.

Treatment. Although there are several efficacious treatment regimens, the optimal one for treating disseminated MAC is still debated.[168] The key to any regimen is the inclusion of a macrolide, either clarithromycin (500 mg twice daily) or azithromycin (500 mg daily).[195] One of these should be combined with ethambutol (15 mg/kg/day). Some experts favor the addition of rifabutin (300 mg daily) to this combination, although the principal benefit appears to be in decreasing the risk of macrolide resistance among those patients who responded to therapy.[196] As with tuberculosis, the use of rifabutin must be carefully scrutinized with concurrent administration of an NNRTI or a PI. In the past, disseminated MAC treatment was considered lifelong. In the setting of combination antiretroviral therapy with increases in the CD4+ lymphocyte count to above 100 cells/μL, however, most patients have been able to discontinue therapy (after a minimum of 12 months of a macrolide-based MAC treatment regimen) without relapse.[54–56]

Prevention. Although MAC can be found in environmental sources such as food and water, there are no specific recommendations regarding exposure avoidance as a prevention strategy. Similarly, although the presence of MAC in a stool or respiratory specimen is predictive of disseminated disease, routine screening of either is not recommended. The USPHS/IDSA guidelines recommend that MAC prophylaxis be administered to HIV-infected patients with a CD4+ lymphocyte count less than 50 cells/μL and no clinical evidence of disseminated MAC.[36] There are a number of different MAC prophylaxis regimens available. Choices include azithromycin (1200 mg weekly), clarithromycin (500 mg twice daily), rifabutin

(300 mg daily), or the combination of azithromycin plus rifabutin; one of the first two regimens is the preferred prophylaxis.[36] Prophylaxis with one of the macrolides has the additional benefit of reducing the incidence of bacterial infections.[197] Primary MAC prophylaxis should be discontinued in persons who have experienced a significant response to HAART with an increase in their CD4$^+$ lymphocyte count to greater than 100 cells/µL for at least 3 months.[36,51-53]

Mycobacterium kansasii

Mycobacterium kansasii has a particular geographic distribution, predominantly in the southern and central United States.[168] Prior to the AIDS epidemic, infection and disease due to *M. kansasii* were uncommon. In 1980, the incidence of *M. kansasii* infection was estimated to be 0.52 cases per 100,000 persons.[198] Subsequent estimates documented a dramatic increase in the incidence of *M. kansasii* associated with HIV infection. Prior to the HAART era, we saw an increase in the number of cases in San Francisco, a nonendemic area. Bloch and associates[199] found a cumulative incidence of *M. kansasii* infection of 2.4 cases per 100,000 HIV-infected adults, a rate that is almost five times higher than the national rate. Although *M. kansasii* pulmonary disease can be clinically indistinguishable from tuberculosis,[200] no person-to-person transmission has been documented, and infection is thought to occur from environmental sources.

Clinical Features. *M. kansasii* is the second most common cause of nontuberculous mycobacterial pulmonary disease in the United States.[168] During the second decade of the AIDS epidemic, *M. kansasii* infection was increasingly described in HIV-infected patients. As mentioned, some of these cases have occurred outside of the endemic area. In the HAART era, cases of *M. kansasii* appear to have declined.

CD4$^+$ Lymphocyte Count, Symptoms, and Signs. Similar to tuberculosis in HIV-infected persons, *M. kansasii* pneumonia can occur at any CD4$^+$ lymphocyte count. Most HIV-infected patients with *M. kansasii*, however, have evidence of severe immunosuppression.[200] Witzig and coworkers[201] found a mean CD4$^+$ count of 62 cells/µL (median CD4$^+$ count, 24 cells/µL) among 49 HIV-infected patients with *M. kansasii* disease, and only four (8%) patients had a CD4$^+$ count above 200 cells/µL. In a study by Bloch and associates[199] that included 187 HIV-infected patients, the median CD4$^+$ lymphocyte count was 20 cells/µL (range, 0 to 541 cells/µL), and 94% had an AIDS diagnosis. In a study from the HAART era, Canueto-Quintero and colleagues[200] reported a mean CD4$^+$ count of 20 cells/µL among 25 HIV-infected patients with *M. kansasii*. *Mycobacterium kansasii* disease usually manifests itself with pulmonary involvement; accompanying disseminated disease or only extrapulmonary involvement is seen at the lowest CD4$^+$ lymphocyte counts.[190] Witzig and coworkers[201] found that 32 (65%) of 49 HIV-infected patients with *M. kansasii* had isolated pulmonary disease (mean CD4$^+$ count, 75 cells/µL), whereas the remainder had disseminated disease (mean CD4$^+$ count, 28 cells/µL). The characteristic symptoms of *M. kansasii* include fever, cough that is often productive, dyspnea, and constitutional symptoms such as weight loss, fatigue, and night sweats. Chest pain and hemoptysis are seen in a minority of cases. Physical examination of the chest may be normal; sometimes findings such as crackles and wheezes can be appreciated. Peripheral lymphadenopathy, hepatosplenomegaly, and new cutaneous lesions are extrapulmonary signs of disease.

Chest Radiograph. The chest radiographic findings of *M. kansasii* are varied. The most common radiographic findings include alveolar infiltrates, diffuse infiltrates, and cavities; masses, intrathoracic adenopathy, and pleural effusions have also been reported. In a series of 49 HIV-infected patients with *M. kansasii*, alveolar infiltrates were noted in 55%, interstitial infiltrates in 22%, cavitation in 22%, and mass lesions in 8%.[201] In 8%, the radiograph was normal, and these patients had disseminated disease. The radiographic findings were unilateral in 49% and bilateral in 43%, and the distribution was apical in 35%, mid-lung in 18%, and lower lung in 12%.

Diagnosis. The diagnosis of *M. kansasii* rests on its isolation and subsequent identification by culture. Pulmonary disease can be diagnosed by all of the techniques used for the diagnosis of tuberculosis. Unlike tuberculosis, however, in which identification of *M. tuberculosis* is diagnostic of disease, the identification of *M. kansasii* can occasionally represent colonization rather than disease.[201a] To assist clinicians, the American Thoracic Society outlined criteria for the diagnosis of nontuberculous mycobacterial pulmonary disease.[168] These criteria apply to HIV-infected and non–HIV-infected persons and presume that the patient is symptomatic and has either chest radiographic or HRCT evidence of parenchymal disease. The criteria for diagnosis are (1) if three sputum/bronchial wash results are available during the previous 12 months: three positive cultures or two positive cultures and one positive AFB smear; (2) if only one bronchial wash is available: positive culture with a strongly positive AFB smear or heavy growth on solid media (≥2+ for each); (3) if sputum/bronchial wash results are nondiagnostic or another concurrent disease cannot be excluded: transbronchial or lung biopsy specimen revealing *M. kansasii* or biopsy specimen demonstrating mycobacterial histopathologic features and at least one sputum or bronchial wash that is positive (even 1+). More recently, the use of subtyping defined by PCR-restriction enzyme analysis of the *hsp65* gene may help distinguish pathogenic from nonpathogenic isolates.[202]

Treatment. The American Thoracic Society recommends that a regimen consisting of isoniazid (300 mg daily), rifampin (600 mg daily), and ethambutol (25 mg/kg daily for the first 2 months, then 15 mg/kg daily) be used for treatment of *M. kansasii* pulmonary disease.[168,203] Of these, rifampin and ethambutol are the most crucial. Patients who are taking PI (or NNRTI) therapy for HIV infection should receive rifabutin or clarithromycin in place of rifampin. Pyrazinamide is unacceptable as an alternative drug because all *M. kansasii* isolates are resistant. Patients should receive treatment for 18 months or a minimum of 12 months after their cultures are converted to negative.

Prevention. There are no recommended prevention strategies for *M. kansasii*.

Other Mycobacteria

MAC and *M. kansasii* account for the majority of non-tuberculous mycobacterial infections complicating HIV disease. Other mycobacteria, however, including *M. xenopi, M. genavense, M. malmoense, M. gordonae, M. fortuitum, M. chelonae, M. terrae, M. celatum, M. conspicuum,* and *M. triplex,* have been occasionally identified.[184,190,204] The reason or reasons for this striking disparity are unknown. Increased frequency of exposure or the presence of specific defects in host defenses might account for the predominance of MAC and to a lesser extent *M. kansasii* in AIDS patients. The American Thoracic Society has summarized the diagnosis and treatment of nontuberculous mycobacterial disease and is in the process of updating and revising their recommendations.[168] Readers are referred to this summary as well as to Chapter 33 for details.

FUNGI

Early in the AIDS epidemic, fungi were recognized as major sources of morbidity and mortality. Despite the overall decline in HIV-associated opportunistic infections in the United States, fungi remain frequent causes of disease. Several fungi can cause pulmonary disease in HIV-infected persons. *Pneumocystis carinii,* now officially designated *P. jirovecii,* previously classified as a protozoan but currently considered a fungus, remains the most common AIDS-defining opportunistic infection in the United States and Western Europe and is a common cause of HIV-associated pneumonia. *Cryptococcus neoformans,* the most common cause of meningitis in HIV-infected persons, often presents with an associated pneumonia. The endemic fungi *H. capsulatum, C. immitis, P. marneffei,* and, to a lesser extent, *B. dermatitidis* are among the chief causes of HIV-associated disease seen in their particular geographic regions, and all have important pulmonary presentations. Finally, invasive aspergillosis is often a devastating pulmonary disease seen in HIV-infected persons with severe immunosuppression. Further information about fungal pulmonary diseases is provided in Chapter 34.

Pneumocystis jirovecii (Formerly *Pneumocystis carinii*)

PCP remains the most common AIDS-defining opportunistic infection in the United States, among children and adults/adolescents. However, its overall incidence is declining.[8] Early in the AIDS epidemic, PCP accounted for nearly two thirds of AIDS-defining diagnoses, and an additional 15% to 20% of patients developed PCP at some time during their HIV disease. Two factors, the use of combination antiretroviral therapy (HAART) and *Pneumocystis* prophylaxis, have combined to dramatically reduce the overall number of cases. At San Francisco General Hospital, we diagnosed between 200 and 290 cases of PCP annually from 1990 to 1994 (Fig. 75.4). In 1995 and 1996, the number of cases was below 200; since 1997, the number has been below 100 cases of PCP annually, and is currently below 50. This decline coincided with the use of dual NRTIs, first with PIs and subsequently with other antiretrovirals. Nevertheless, PCP continues to occur, chiefly among persons who are unaware of their HIV infection, those who fail to seek medical care, and those who fail to adhere to or are intolerant of antiretroviral therapy or *Pneumocystis* prophylaxis.[205–207]

History and Epidemiology. First identified early in the 20th century by Chagas, *Pneumocystis* was initially recognized as a human pathogen in the 1950s. Despite over a half-century of experience and an explosion of PCP cases since 1981, several gaps in our understanding of this omnipresent organism remain.[207a] In fact, it was only in 1988 that initial homology studies indicated that *Pneumocystis* was a fungus rather than a protozoan, as previously classified.[208,209] One major obstacle that has impeded further advances has been the inability to reliably culture human *Pneumocystis* in vitro, forcing researchers to rely on animal models for growth and

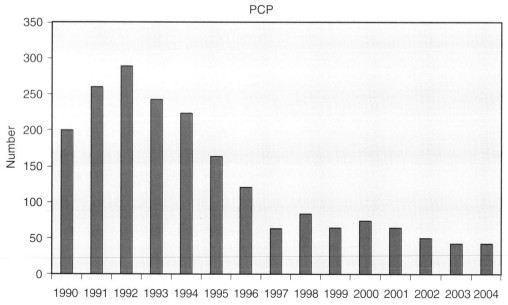

Figure 75.4 Annual cases of *Pneumocystis* pneumonia diagnosed at San Francisco General Hospital (1990–2004).

testing. Although mammals are the only known hosts of *Pneumocystis* and a number of mammals are susceptible to infection, *Pneumocystis* has been demonstrated to be species specific.[210,211] Although *Pneumocystis* can be easily transmitted between mammals of the same species, studies that have attempted to transmit *Pneumocystis* from one species to another have been unsuccessful.[212] In recognition of the host-species specificity of *Pneumocystis*, the *Pneumocystis* that causes *Pneumocystis* pneumonia in humans is now referred to as *P. jirovecii*, in honor of Otto Jirovec, the parasitologist who is credited with first identifying *Pneumocystis* as the cause of pulmonary disease in humans.[213]

The precise ecologic niche for *P. jirovecii* and its mode of transmission are unknown.[214,215] The inability to maintain human *Pneumocystis* in culture suggests that *P. jirovecii* may be unable to grow outside of its human host. Given its species specificity, it is doubtful that other mammals are the reservoir for *P. jirovecii*. This host-species specificity also implies coevolution of human and *P. jirovecii* that, in turn, implies long-term carriage in its human host. It has been shown that infection with *P. jirovecii* is almost ubiquitous. Up to 85% to 100% of the U.S. population have specific antibodies directed against *P. jirovecii* by the age of 3 years.[216–218] Clearly, most of these individuals never develop PCP. In the setting of severe immunosuppression, such as occurs in HIV infection, however, PCP can affect significant proportions of people. These studies and others suggest that reactivation of latent infection is a cause of *P. jirovecii* disease among immunocompromised hosts. However, reports of newly acquired infection after de novo exposure to persons with PCP have been documented; these outbreaks occurred among immunocompromised persons in pediatric wards, cancer clinics or wards, transplant units, and other confined spaces and suggest possible person-to-person transmission of *P. jirovecii* and the rapid development of disease. More recent studies that have used molecular tools to detect *Pneumocystis* are consistent with transmission of *P. jirovecii* from patients with PCP to their household and hospital contacts.[219,220] Transmission of *P. jirovecii* probably occurs via inhalation of a *Pneumocystis*-containing aerosol. Hughes and colleagues[221,222] demonstrated that immunocompromised axenic rats maintained in germ-free isolators did not develop PCP despite 3 months of immunosuppression with dexamethasone. In a selective manner, these rats were then exposed to potential sources of *P. carinii*, including air, food, and water. Rats who were exposed to filtered (sterile) air and to regular (unsterile) food and water did not develop PCP. However, rats exposed to room (unsterile) air but maintained on sterile food and water did develop PCP, implying that *P. carinii* is acquired as an airborne disease from de novo infection in the setting of immunocompromise. The duration of exposure necessary for transmission may be short. Soulez and associates[223] housed *Pneumocystis*-free severe combined immunodeficiency (SCID) mice near corticosteroid-treated non-SCID mice and found that a 1-day exposure was sufficient for transmission of *Pneumocystis* to the SCID mice. Transmission of *P. carinii* from PCP-infected SCID mice to other SCID mice via immunocompetent BALB/c mice that were colonized with *P. carinii* has been demonstrated.[224,225] Taken together, these studies offer a compelling extrapolation that humans are the reservoir for *P. jirovecii*, that

person-to-person transmission occurs, and that PCP can result from a recent exposure both to humans with PCP and to humans who are colonized with *P. jirovecii*. If correct, these studies have profound implications as to our current management of persons with PCP.

Clinical Features. Setting aside the question of whether person-to-person transmission of *P. jirovecii* is an important problem, the risk factors for the development of PCP among HIV-infected persons are clear. These risk factors for adults include a CD4$^+$ lymphocyte count less than 200 cells/μL (see next section for information on infants and children), a history of PCP, and 2 or more weeks of unexplained fever, or the presence of oropharyngeal candidiasis.[226,227]

CD4$^+$ Lymphocyte Count, Symptoms, and Signs. Approximately 95% of adolescent and adult cases of PCP occur in HIV-infected patients whose CD4$^+$ lymphocyte count is below 200 cells/μL.[227] The Multicenter AIDS Cohort Study found a markedly increased risk for PCP among HIV-infected subjects with a CD4$^+$ lymphocyte count of 200 cells/μL or less at study entry.[226] These subjects had a nearly fivefold greater risk of developing PCP than did subjects who had a CD4$^+$ lymphocyte count higher than 200 cells/μL at study entry (odds ratio = 4.9, 95% confidence interval = 3.1 to 8.0, $P < 0.001$). This study also demonstrated that the presence of fever for 2 weeks or more and the development of thrush were independent predictors for PCP. Stansell and colleagues[227] found that the incidence of PCP increased as the CD4$^+$ lymphocyte count declined. Subjects with a CD4$^+$ count between 101 and 200 cells/μL had an incidence of 5.95 cases of PCP per 100 person-years, whereas those with a CD4$^+$ count of 100 cells/μL or less had 11.13 cases per 100 person-years.

Concerning infants and children, a significant percentage of cases of PCP in HIV-infected infants 6 months of age or younger occur when the CD4$^+$ lymphocyte count is above 1500 cells/μL.[228] Furthermore, in these infants, the CD4$^+$ lymphocyte count can decline rapidly (700 to 1200 cells/μL) in the 3 months preceding PCP.[228] Accordingly, the guidelines for *Pneumocystis* prophylaxis differ for infants, children, and adults/adolescents (see subsequent section on prevention).[36]

HIV-infected adults, unlike other immunocompromised persons, usually have a prolonged prodromal illness associated with PCP. Kovacs and coworkers[229] found nearly 1 month of symptoms before presentation in most HIV-infected patients with PCP. In this study, the median duration of symptoms in 40 HIV-infected patients was 28 days, which was significantly longer than the median duration of 5 days seen in the 37 patients with other immunosuppressive diseases ($P < 0.0002$). Kales and colleagues[230] reported a median duration of symptoms of 3 weeks in 143 HIV-infected patients with PCP and found that 72 patients (50%) had a duration of symptoms of 2 weeks or longer. This duration of symptoms can often be used to distinguish PCP from pyogenic pneumonia, which typically presents with 3 to 5 days of symptoms.

Classically, PCP presents with fever, a nonproductive cough, and dyspnea on exertion. In one series of 145 HIV-infected patients with PCP, fever was noted in 86%, cough in 91%, and dyspnea in 95% of patients.[230] High fevers, rigors, purulent sputum, and pleuritic chest pain are uncommon and can be used to distinguish PCP from pyogenic pneumonia. In a multivariate analysis, Selwyn and associates[65] found that the presence of purulent sputum (odds ratio = 2.46, 95% confidence interval = 1.1 to 5.4, P = 0.03) or pleuritic chest pain (odds ratio = 2.99, 95% confidence interval = 1.4 to 6.6, P = 0.01) was an independent predictor of bacterial pneumonia rather than of PCP or tuberculosis.

Physical examination of the chest may be normal. In the series reported by Kales and colleagues,[230] 78 patients (54%) with PCP had a normal lung examination. When abnormal, the most frequent findings on lung auscultation are inspiratory crackles; the presence of crackles has been reported to be associated with a greater disease severity and an increased mortality.[230]

Numerous studies have shown that the serum LDH level is increased in patients with PCP. However, an elevated serum LDH level does not establish the diagnosis of PCP, nor does a normal serum LDH value rule out the diagnosis.[67]

Chest Radiograph. Classically, PCP presents with bilateral, symmetrical reticular or granular opacities (Fig. 75.5).[231] These opacities typically begin in the perihilar region and extend outward as the disease severity increases. Occasionally, the opacities will be unilateral or asymmetrical. Our experience has taught us that the pattern seen (reticular, granular) is more important in suggesting the diagnosis of PCP than the distribution (bilateral versus unilateral, symmetrical versus asymmetrical, diffuse versus focal). Thin-walled cysts, or pneumatoceles, are seen in 10% to 20% of cases (see Fig. 75.5).[232,233] Pneumatoceles may be present at the time of diagnosis or may develop during PCP therapy. Pneumatoceles may be single or multiple in number, and small or large in size, and predispose patients to pneumothorax, which is another radiographic presentation of PCP. Usually, pneumatoceles resolve but occasionally they persist despite successful therapy.

Virtually every possible radiographic finding, including focal, lobar, or segmental consolidation, nodules with or without cavitation, and a miliary pattern, can be seen occasionally.[233] Apical or upper lung zone disease that mimics tuberculosis is typically associated with aerosolized pentamidine prophylaxis, although this presentation can be seen as well in patients taking oral prophylaxis or no preventive therapy (Fig. 75.6). Intrathoracic adenopathy and pleural effusions are rarely due to PCP. These radiographic findings should prompt a search for an alternate or at least a coexisting process such as bacterial pneumonia, tuberculosis, fungal pneumonia, or pulmonary Kaposi's sarcoma.

PCP may present with a normal chest radiograph. Published studies report the incidence of a normal radiograph to range from 0% to 39%.[231,233,234] In our experience, PCP presents with a normal chest radiograph in less than 5% of cases.

Diagnosis. At San Francisco General Hospital, patients with a clinical presentation suggestive of PCP and a compatible chest radiograph undergo sputum induction.[67] If sputum induction examination is negative for *P. jirovecii* and other organisms, patients then undergo bronchoscopy with BAL. In our experience, a negative BAL rules out the diagnosis of PCP in all but the rarest of cases. Thus, we recommend

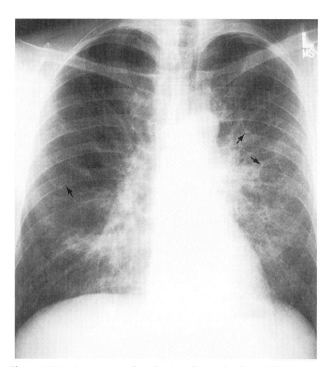

Figure 75.5 Posteroanterior chest radiograph of an HIV-seropositive patient with *Pneumocystis* pneumonia showing bilateral, predominantly perihilar, granular opacities and three pneumatoceles (*arrows*). Pneumatoceles may be single or multiple in number, and small or large in size, and may predispose patients to pneumothorax. (Reproduced with permission from L. Huang.)

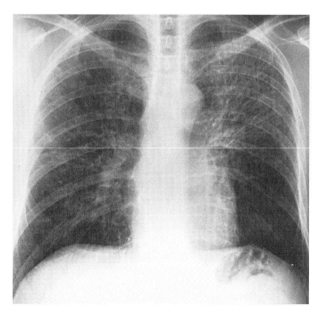

Figure 75.6 Posteroanterior chest radiograph of an HIV-seropositive patient who had been receiving aerosolized pentamidine showing reticular infiltration, predominantly of the upper lung zones, secondary to relapsed *Pneumocystis* pneumonia (PCP). This radiographic presentation, however, may also be seen in patients on no PCP prophylaxis. (From Murray JF, Mills J: Pulmonary complications of HIV infection. Am Rev Respir Dis 141:1356–1372, 1582–1598, 1990.)

that PCP treatment be discontinued in these patients and an alternative diagnosis and treatment be pursued, if warranted. However, the sensitivity of bronchoscopy with BAL differs at each institution; at some institutions, the sensitivity of bronchoscopy is improved with the addition of TBBX.

Patients with a suggestive clinical presentation but a normal or unchanged radiograph undergo either pulmonary function testing or chest HRCT to determine who warrants diagnostic testing (e.g., sputum induction). On pulmonary function testing, patients with PCP often display a restrictive ventilatory defect with decreased lung volumes and increased expiratory airflow. A more sensitive indicator of PCP, however, is a decrease in the DL_{CO}, which is caused by alveolar-capillary block.[235] The DL_{CO} is a sensitive indicator of PCP. Huang and colleagues[75] of the PCHIS demonstrated that a decreased DL_{CO} (defined as $\leq 75\%$ of the predicted value, corrected for hemoglobin) detected 90% of the cases of PCP in patients whose chest radiograph was normal or unchanged. Moreover, the combination of a normal or unchanged radiograph and a DL_{CO} of more than 75% of predicted value virtually rules out the possibility of PCP. Thus, these patients should probably be clinically observed without further evaluation or treatment for PCP, or they should be evaluated and treated for another process. One drawback to the DL_{CO} is its lack of specificity. The same study that reported a DL_{CO} sensitivity of 90% also found a specificity of 53%.[75] Therefore, a decreased DL_{CO} is not diagnostic of PCP, and patients with clinically suspected PCP who have a decreased DL_{CO} undergo sputum induction in our institution.

An alternate test to the DL_{CO} is chest HRCT. PCP has a characteristic appearance on HRCT: patchy areas of ground-glass opacity through which vessels are seen and a background of interlobular septal thickening. We found that HRCT was a sensitive test for persons with clinically suspected PCP but who had a normal, unchanged, or equivocal chest radiograph.[236] In this study of 51 HIV-infected patients with clinically suspected PCP but a normal, unchanged, or equivocal chest radiograph, all patients with PCP diagnosed by either sputum induction or BAL had an HRCT with ground-glass opacities (sensitivity was 100%). In addition, none of the 40 patients whose HRCT was without ground-glass opacities was found to have PCP on sputum induction, BAL, and clinical follow-up. Thus, an HRCT without these lesions rules out the diagnosis of PCP, and these patients should probably be clinically observed without further evaluation or treatment for PCP, or they should be evaluated and treated for another process. Although HRCT has a better specificity than does DL_{CO} (89% versus 53%), patients with suspected PCP and an HRCT with typical ground-glass densities still must undergo sputum induction in our institution.

The diagnosis of PCP rests on the microscopic visualization of the characteristic *P. jirovecii* cysts or trophic forms (or both) on stained respiratory specimens. *Pneumocystis jirovecii* can be detected in expectorated[237] or induced sputum; in pulmonary secretions obtained by nasotracheal suction, BAL, or percutaneous aspiration of the lung parenchyma; and in pulmonary tissue obtained by transbronchial, thoracoscopic, or open-lung biopsy. Of these, sputum induction and BAL are the most widely used. The standard method for detection of *P. jirovecii* has been with

cyst wall stains such as methenamine silver and toluidine blue-O or with Giemsa and Diff-Quik, which stain the intracystic sporozoites and the trophic forms.[238] Monoclonal antibodies to *P. jirovecii*, which react with both cysts and trophic forms, are also used.[238] PCR-based techniques have also been employed and have been reported to be more sensitive but also less specific than either of the other methods.[238,239] However, the increased sensitivity of PCR-based assays has allowed for their pairing with noninvasive, rapid (60-second) procedures such as oropharyngeal washing (i.e., gargling) for the diagnosis of PCP. Several studies have reported sensitivities and specificities for PCP of PCR-based assay using oropharyngeal washing that may permit its use in resource-limited settings where sputum induction and BAL are unavailable or too costly.[240-243]

A number of studies have examined the impact of PCP prophylaxis on the sensitivity of induced sputum and BAL examination for detecting the organisms.[244-251] Some authors reported a lower sensitivity of diagnostic studies for PCP among patients who were receiving aerosolized pentamidine compared with those having no prophylaxis, whereas others found no difference between the two groups. In patients undergoing bronchoscopy, the yield for *P. jirovecii* may be improved by performing upper lobe lavage or multiple lobe lavage with or without a more sensitive staining technique (e.g., monoclonal antibodies).[249-251] Our practice is to perform BAL in the most affected lobe visualized on chest radiograph. For patients with diffuse radiographic disease, we usually perform a single lavage in the right middle lobe. For patients with, for example, an upper lung zone predominance on radiograph, however, we often lavage both an upper lobe and the right middle lobe. Despite the widespread use of TMP-SMX and dapsone for PCP prophylaxis, no studies have evaluated whether the yield of diagnostic studies is changed in persons receiving one of these medications. Our clinical experience suggests that, although the severity of chest radiograph abnormalities may be milder in patients receiving prophylaxis than in those receiving no prophylaxis, the yields from sputum induction and BAL remain the same.

Treatment. The standard duration of PCP therapy is 21 days. The choice of specific treatment depends in part on the severity of disease (Table 75.3). TMP-SMX remains the treatment of choice for patients with mild, moderate, and severe PCP and is the regimen against which all others are measured. TMP and SMX act in concert to inhibit two different steps in folate metabolism. TMP inhibits dihydrofolate reductase, preventing the synthesis of tetrahydrofolate from dihydrofolate, and SMX inhibits dihydropteroate synthase, preventing the conversion of *para*-aminobenzoate to dihydrofolate. TMP-SMX possesses many benefits, including availability in both an intravenous and an oral form, availability as a single-drug combination, excellent oral bioavailability, and activity against many community-acquired bacteria that may cause concomitant pyogenic infection. The usual dose of TMP is 15 (range, 15 to 20) mg/kg/day and that of SMX is 75 (range, 75 to 100) mg/kg/day, divided into three or four daily doses. Dosing may be intravenous (recommended for patients with moderate or severe PCP) or oral. In general, we avoid a TMP dose exceeding 320 mg every 8 hours, instead increasing

Table 75.3 Treatment Regimens for *Pneumocystis* Pneumonia (PCP)*

Treatment Regimen	Dose(s), Frequency	Toxicities
Mild PCP[†] (Pao$_2$ >70 mm Hg *and* Alveolar-Arterial O$_2$ Difference <35 mm Hg)		
Trimethoprim (TMP)–sulfamethoxazole	15–20 mg/kg (TMP component) daily (q6–8h)	Fever, dermatologic, gastrointestinal, hematologic
Trimethoprim plus dapsone	15–20 mg/kg daily (q6–8h); 100 mg once daily	Dermatologic, gastrointestinal, hematologic
Clindamycin plus primaquine	1800 mg daily (q6–8h); 30 mg (base) once daily	Dermatologic, gastrointestinal, hematologic
Atovaquone	750 mg thrice daily	Dermatologic, gastrointestinal
Moderate–Severe PCP[‡] (Pao$_2$ ≤70 mm Hg *or* Alveolar-Arterial O$_2$ Difference ≥35 mm Hg)		
Trimethoprim (TMP)–sulfamethoxazole	15–20 mg/kg (TMP component) daily (q6–8h)	Fever, dermatologic, gastrointestinal, hematologic
Pentamidine	3–4 mg/kg once daily	Renal, pancreatic
Clindamycin plus primaquine	1800–2400 mg (q6–8h); 30 mg (base) PO once daily	Dermatologic, gastrointestinal, hematologic
Trimetrexate plus leucovorin[§] ± dapsone	45 mg/m^2 once daily; 20 mg/m^2 q6h ± 100 mg PO once daily	Hematologic, dermatologic, fever

* Recommended duration of therapy = 21 days.
[†] Oral route is preferred for patients with mild PCP who are treated as outpatients.
[‡] Intravenous route is preferred (at least until clinical improvement) for patients with moderate to severe PCP. Adjunctive corticosteroids (prednisone 40 mg PO twice daily for 5 days, then 40 mg PO once daily for 5 days, then 20 mg PO once daily for 11 days; or potency-equivalent Solu-Medrol IV) should also be administered.
[§] Leucovorin (folinic acid) must be given concomitantly and for 2 to 3 days after stopping Trimetrexate.

the frequency to every 6 hours. Unfortunately, adverse effects from TMP-SMX are frequent and include rash, fever, gastrointestinal complaints (nausea, vomiting), elevated liver transaminases, hyperkalemia, and bone marrow suppression, especially anemia and neutropenia. Often these effects develop during the second week of therapy. In a significant proportion of HIV-infected patients, the side effects are ultimately treatment limiting. Rare adverse reactions include Stevens-Johnson syndrome, toxic epidermal necrolysis, and a clinical syndrome resembling septic shock with hypotension, fever, pulmonary infiltrates, and renal and hepatic dysfunction.

For patients with an allergy to or intolerance of TMP-SMX, alternative treatment regimens include intravenous pentamidine, clindamycin plus primaquine, trimethoprim plus dapsone, trimetrexate (with or without dapsone), and atovaquone (see Table 75.3). Similar to tuberculosis, HIV-infected patients with PCP who begin dual therapy for *Pneumocystis* and HIV infection may develop paradoxical reactions, a temporary exacerbation of clinical and radiographic features.[252,253] The diagnosis of paradoxical reaction is one of exclusion. Patients with paradoxical reactions only rarely require change or discontinuation of antipneumocystis or antiretroviral therapies, and symptomatic therapy is recommended.

Corticosteroid Therapy. In 1990, the National Institutes of Health–University of California Expert Panel for Corticosteroids as Adjunctive Therapy for Pneumocystis Pneumonia[254] concluded that adjunctive corticosteroid therapy "can clearly reduce the likelihood of death, respiratory failure, or deterioration of oxygenation in patients with moderate-to-severe pneumocystis pneumonia." The panel recommended that adjunctive corticosteroids be given to adults or adolescents with documented or suspected PCP if they have an

arterial PO$_2$ level less than 70 mm Hg or an alveolar-arterial PO$_2$ difference greater than 35 mm Hg. Adjunctive corticosteroids, either oral prednisone or intravenous methylprednisolone, should be started when specific antipneumocystis treatment is begun.

Early in the AIDS epidemic, it was realized that acute respiratory failure secondary to PCP, if severe enough to warrant mechanical ventilation, had a mortality rate of 86% or greater.[254] Subsequent reports from individual hospitals confirmed this gloomy prognosis; 39 of 45 patients who were intubated and ventilated for PCP at San Francisco General Hospital from 1981 to 1985 died, a mortality rate of 87%.[255] Accordingly, many institutions, including our own, actively discouraged aggressive treatment of PCP-associated acute respiratory failure. Although the mortality associated with acute respiratory failure secondary to PCP remains significant (>50%), some encouraging progress has been made.[256-260]

Prevention. The natural reservoir for human *Pneumocystis* remains unknown. Both an environmental and a human reservoir have been suggested.[214,215] Whether PCP results solely from reactivation of latent infection or also from a recent infection is debated. Numerous reports have suggested that *Pneumocystis* may be transmitted from person to person and that PCP may result from a recent exposure to an individual with PCP. Reports of cluster outbreaks of PCP among different immunocompromised populations support the theory that PCP can result from person-to-person transmission and a recent exposure in the setting of immunosuppression. Thus, some authorities have argued that HIV-infected and other immunocompromised persons who are at risk for PCP should avoid close contact with any individuals who have PCP. Nevertheless, the current USPHS/IDSA Guidelines for Preventing Opportunistic

Infections state that "although certain authorities might recommend that HIV-infected persons who are at risk for PCP avoid sharing a hospital room with a patient who has PCP, data are insufficient to support this recommendation as standard practice."[36]

HIV-infected adults or adolescents (including those on HAART) who have a CD4+ lymphocyte count less than 200 cells/μL or a history of oropharyngeal candidiasis should receive primary *Pneumocystis* prophylaxis, and persons with prior PCP should receive secondary prophylaxis.[36] Infants born to HIV-infected mothers should receive *Pneumocystis* prophylaxis starting at 4 to 6 weeks of age, until the infant's HIV serostatus can be conclusively determined. Subsequently, infants who are HIV-negative can discontinue *Pneumocystis* prophylaxis, whereas HIV-infected infants should continue prophylaxis for at least their first year of life. After the first year, the need for subsequent *Pneumocystis* prophylaxis is based on age-specific CD4+ lymphocyte count thresholds: for children 1 to 5 years of age, CD4+ lymphocyte count less than 500 cells/μL or CD4 lymphocyte percentage less than 15%; and for children 6 years of age or older, CD4+ lymphocyte count less than 200 cells/μL (as for adults and adolescents) or CD4 lymphocyte percentage less than 15%. Once started, HIV-infected persons should remain on prophylaxis for life, unless their CD4+ lymphocyte counts increase from less than 200 cells/μL to greater than 200 cells/μL for at least 3 months as a result of HAART. Several studies have demonstrated that primary and secondary PCP prophylaxis can be safely discontinued in the vast majority of these persons.[37–49] In rare cases, however, PCP has recurred after the discontinuation of secondary PCP prophylaxis, despite an apparent HAART-associated immune reconstitution.[261]

TMP-SMX, dapsone, atovaquone suspension, and aerosolized pentamidine are the standard options for PCP prophylaxis (Table 75.4). TMP-SMX is the first-line prophylaxis choice, both primary and secondary, against *Pneumocystis*. For those patients intolerant of TMP-SMX, dapsone and atovaquone are both oral drugs that can be used. Many authorities would add pyrimethamine to these drugs for patients with a history of PCP or a CD4+ lymphocyte count less than 100 cells/μL, or both. For patients who are *T. gondii* immunoglobulin G antibody positive, pyrimethamine must be added. Aerosolized pentamidine remains an effective and well-tolerated prophylaxis option.

However, caution must be exercised when using this drug for secondary prophylaxis or for a patient with a CD4+ lymphocyte count below 100 cells/μL.

Cryptococcus neoformans

Cryptococcosis is a disease caused by the budding encapsulated yeast *C. neoformans*. It is the only encapsulated fungus that infects humans, and India ink or mucicarmine staining can identify its polysaccharide capsule.[262,263] Serotyping based on antigenic differences in the polysaccharide capsule demonstrate that serotypes A and D are the most common cause of infection and disease. *Cryptococcus neoformans* infection occurs after inhalation of a yeast-containing aerosol. The yeast is global in distribution and is most commonly isolated from bird excrement, decaying fruit, and soil. Unlike the situation with *H. capsulatum* and *C. immitis*, however, no clear-cut exposure-disease association exists. In addition, no human-to-human or animal-to-human transmission has been documented.

Early in the AIDS epidemic, approximately 5% to 8% of HIV-infected patients developed cryptococcal disease. Cryptococcosis occurred in 7% of the first 2087 AIDS patients seen at San Francisco General Hospital.[264] However, our experience and that of many other institutions is that the incidence of cryptococcosis has dramatically declined since 1996.[179,265,266] In one population-based surveillance study,[265] the annual incidence of cryptococcosis in HIV-infected persons decreased from 66 per 1000 persons with AIDS in 1992 to 7 per 1000 persons in 2000 in the Atlanta area, and from 24 per 1000 persons with AIDS in 1993 to 2 per 1000 persons in 2000 in the Houston area. Using national surveillance data, a study from France found a 46% decrease in the incidence of cryptococcosis in HIV-infected patients from the pre-HAART period (1985–1996) to the post-HAART period (1997–2001).[266] The annual percentage of cases of cryptococcosis among new cases of AIDS remained stable over time (3.5%). However, cryptococcosis was the AIDS-defining illness and the HIV-identifying diagnosis in significantly greater proportions of persons in the post-HAART period compared to the pre-HAART period.

Clinical Features. Although the portal of entry is the lung, cryptococcal pulmonary infection is often asymptomatic or

Table 75.4 Prevention of *Pneumocystis* Pneumonia

Prevention Regimens	Alternative Dosing	Comments
Trimethoprim-sulfamethoxazole 1 double-strength (DS) tablet daily Dapsone 100 mg daily	1 single strength tablet daily; 1 DS tablet thrice weekly	Also effective prophylaxis against *Toxoplasma gondii* and many bacterial pathogens Combine with pyrimethamine and leucovorin in persons who are *T. gondii* immunoglobulin G antibody positive. Consider combining with pyrimethamine and leucovorin when used for secondary prophylaxis.
Atovaquone suspension 1500 mg daily, divided into 1–2 doses		Improved bioavailability compared to tablets
Aerosolized pentamidine 300 mg monthly via Respirgard II nebulizer		May be associated with increased risk of extrapulmonary disease

minimally symptomatic, and the most commonly encountered manifestation of cryptococcal disease is meningitis.[264–267] In a large series of 106 HIV-infected patients with cryptococcal disease, 89 patients (84%) had meningitis, and only four patients (4%) had isolated pneumonia.[264] In a population-based surveillance study that included 1322 HIV-infected patients with cryptococcal disease, only 45 patients (3%) had pulmonary disease in the absence of both fungemia and meningitis.[265] Finally, in a national surveillance study that reported on 1644 HIV-infected patients, 74% had cryptococcal meningitis.[266]

CD4+ Lymphocyte Count, Symptoms, and Signs. Most cases of cryptococcosis occur in patients with a CD4+ lymphocyte count less than 200 cells/μL, usually below 100 cells/μL. One review of 76 patients with cryptococcal disease found a mean CD4+ count of 46 cells/μL (range, 2 to 220 cells/μL) in the 65 patients with meningitis.[268] A recent study of 1644 patients reported a median CD4+ count of 24 cells/μL with a range of 0 to 480 cells/μL.[266] The clinical presentation of cryptococcal disease is often subtle and nonspecific. The most common symptoms are fever, malaise, and headaches. Chuck and Sande[264] reported fever in 65%, malaise in 76%, and headache in 73% of 89 patients with meningitis. Classic symptoms of meningitis, such as nausea or vomiting (42%), altered mental status (28%), stiff neck (22%), and photophobia (18%), were present in only a minority. A study from Uganda reported fever (84%), headache (46%), stiff neck (18%), and an altered mental status (6%) in 69 patients with cryptococcal disease.[269] Thus, clinicians caring for HIV-infected persons must be alert to these protean manifestations and should entertain the possibility of cryptococcosis.

Pulmonary cryptococcosis is often clinically silent. Most cases of pulmonary involvement are discovered serendipitously on routine chest radiograph rather than as a result of specific symptoms or signs. Chuck and Sande[264] reported respiratory complaints (cough or dyspnea) in 31% of their 89 patients with cryptococcal meningitis. When present, the most frequent respiratory complaints are cough and dyspnea. French and colleagues[269] noted cough in 33% of their 69 patients with cryptococcal disease. Numerous studies have focused on HIV-infected patients with cryptococcal pneumonia.[268,270–279] In these series, cough and dyspnea were the most common respiratory symptoms, but pleuritic chest pain and productive cough were also reported, perhaps distinguishing pulmonary cryptococcosis from PCP. Batungwanayo and coworkers[276] noted cough in 94%, dyspnea in 46%, and pleuritic pain in 30% of 37 HIV-infected patients with cryptococcal pneumonia.

Similar to the symptoms, the signs of cryptococcal infection are often nonspecific. Chuck and Sande[264] reported that 56% of 89 patients with meningitis were febrile on examination, 27% had nuchal rigidity, and less than 20% had altered mentation or focal neurologic deficits. Papilledema is rare in patients with normal sensorium. In patients with pneumonia, tachypnea and fine crackles may be encountered.[275] Occasionally, cutaneous lesions mimicking molluscum contagiosum or Kaposi's sarcoma may be seen.

Chest Radiograph. Cryptococcal pneumonia most commonly presents with diffuse bilateral interstitial infiltrates.[280] In a series of 37 HIV-infected patients with cryptococcal

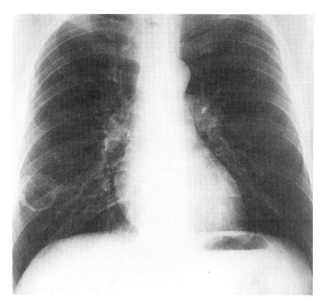

Figure 75.7 Posteroanterior chest radiograph of an HIV-seropositive patient showing a solitary cavitary lesion in the right lower lung field. Culture of bronchoalveolar lavage fluid revealed *Cryptococcus neoformans*. In HIV-infected patients, cryptococcal disease can present with a wide range of chest radiographic findings, including a normal chest radiograph. (From Stansell JD: Fungal disease in HIV-infected persons: Cryptococcosis, histoplasmosis, and coccidioidomycosis. J Thorac Imaging 6:28–35, 1991.)

pneumonia, diffuse interstitial or interstitial-alveolar infiltrates were seen in 76%.[276] Meyohas and associates[277] reported the radiographic findings of cryptococcal pneumonia in 17 patients and reviewed the findings in another seven studies that included a total of 75 cases; interstitial infiltrates were seen in 60 of the 92 radiographs (65%). In addition to bilateral and unilateral interstitial infiltrates, focal consolidation (13%), nodular opacities (11%), cavitation (11%) (Fig. 75.7), pleural effusion (14%), and hilar adenopathy (27%) were all noted in their review. Case reports also document the occurrence of a miliary pattern,[281] solitary pulmonary nodules,[282] pulmonary masses,[283] isolated pleural effusion,[271] and pneumothorax[284] due to *C. neoformans*. Finally, cryptococcal pneumonia may also present with a normal radiograph. In the review by Meyohas and associates,[277] a normal chest radiograph was seen in 11% of the 92 cases.

Diagnosis. The diagnosis of cryptococcal infection begins with the cryptococcal antigen (CRAG) test. The test can be performed on serum, cerebrospinal fluid, urine, BAL fluid,[285] or pleural fluid. The serum CRAG test is sensitive and specific for cryptococcemia. A negative serum CRAG test virtually rules out the diagnosis of cryptococcal meningitis but can be seen in cases of isolated pulmonary cryptococcosis. A positive serum CRAG test should prompt an evaluation for disseminated disease, especially meningitis, but can be seen in the presence of rheumatoid factor or infection with *Trichosporon beigelii*. Blood fungal cultures are specific and should be obtained as part of the diagnostic evaluation. New cutaneous lesions may be signs of dissemination, and their sudden appearance should prompt consideration for biopsy.

The diagnosis of pulmonary cryptococcosis is usually established by culture of sputum or BAL fluid and occasionally of pleural fluid. Biopsy specimens from TBBX and pleural biopsy can also be diagnostic. Batungwanayo and coworkers[276] found that BAL diagnosed 27 of 33 cases (sensitivity was 82%) of cryptococcal pneumonia compared with TBBX, which diagnosed 10 of 21 cases (sensitivity was 48%). In some cases cultures are negative, but BAL or pleural fluid CRAG test can establish the diagnosis.[277] Alternatively, because the treatment is identical, the diagnosis of pneumonia may be inferred in the presence of disseminated cryptococcal disease (e.g., meningitis) and a compatible radiographic presentation. However, caution must be exercised with this approach, because other opportunistic infections such as PCP may be present concurrently and can demonstrate identical radiographic findings.

Treatment. In contrast to cryptococcal meningitis, there are no randomized controlled trials for HIV-infected patients presenting with isolated cryptococcal pneumonia or with concurrent cryptococcal pneumonia and meningitis.[286] Therefore, the optimum treatment for these patients remains undefined. Some authorities would treat isolated cryptococcal pneumonia that is mild in severity with fluconazole alone (200 to 400 mg daily).[286] However, patients with clinically significant cryptococcal pneumonia should be considered at high risk for early deterioration and should be offered the best available therapy (Table 75.5). Ampho-tericin B plus 5-fluorocytosine is the treatment of choice for HIV-infected patients with cryptococcal meningitis.[286] In patients with isolated moderate to severe pneumonia or those with concurrent meningitis, this regimen should be used. Treatment should be continued until the patient is clinically improved, at which point the patient can be switched to fluconazole (400 mg daily) to complete a 10- to 12-week course. The patient should then be maintained on fluconazole (200 mg daily) for life unless he or she experiences an immune reconstitution due to HAART. Patients who have a CD4+ lymphocyte count greater than 100 to 200 cells/μL for at least 6 months due to HAART and who have completed their initial 10- to 12-week course for cryptococcosis and remain asymptomatic can be considered candidates for discontinuation of maintenance therapy.[36] Several studies have demonstrated that maintenance therapy can be safely discontinued in the vast majority of these persons.[54,58-60] Similar to tuberculosis and PCP, HIV-infected patients with cryptococcosis who begin dual therapy for *C. neoformans* and HIV infection may develop paradoxical reactions, a temporary exacerbation of clinical features.[287] Patients who had cryptococcal meningitis may present with aseptic meningitis and have elevated intracranial pressure. In addition, patients with cryptococcal pneumonia and nodules on chest radiograph may develop cavitation of their nodules or new intrathoracic adenopathy.[287,288] The diagnosis of paradoxical reaction is one of exclusion. Patients with paradoxical reactions only rarely require change or discontinuation of antifungal

Table 75.5 Treatment of Fungal Disease

Fungus	Moderate–Severe Disease	Mild Disease	Maintenance/Suppression
Cryptococcus neoformans	Amphotericin B (0.7–0.8 mg/kg/day) plus 5-fluorocytosine (100 mg/kg/day, four divided doses), until clinical improvement (minimum 2 wk), followed by fluconazole (400 mg daily) for total 10–12 wk	Fluconazole (800–1200 mg daily) plus 5-fluorocytosine (100 mg/kg/day, four divided doses), for 4 wk, followed by fluconazole (400 mg daily) for total 10–12 wk	Fluconazole (200 mg daily). Amphotericin B (0.7–0.8 mg/kg twice–thrice weekly)
Histoplasma capsulatum	Amphotericin B (0.8–1.0 mg/kg/day) until clinical improvement	Itraconazole (300 mg twice daily × 3 days, then 200 mg twice daily)	Itraconazole (200 mg twice daily).* Amphotericin B (0.8–1.0 mg/kg twice–thrice weekly).
Coccidioides immitis	Amphotericin B (1.0–1.2 mg/kg/day) until clinical improvement	Fluconazole (400–1200 mg daily)	Fluconazole (400 mg daily). Amphotericin B (1.0–1.2 mg/kg twice–thrice weekly).
Aspergillus species (usually *A. fumigatus*)	Amphotericin B (0.8–1.0 mg/kg/day) until clinical improvement	Itraconazole (300 mg twice daily × 3 days, then 200 mg twice daily)	Itraconazole (200 mg twice daily).* Amphotericin B (0.8–1.0 mg/kg twice–thrice weekly).
Blastomyces dermatitidis	Amphotericin B (0.8–1.0 mg/kg/day) until clinical improvement	Itraconazole (300 mg twice daily × 3 days, then 200 mg twice daily)	Itraconazole (200 mg twice daily)*
Penicillium marneffei	Amphotericin B (0.6 mg/kg/day for 2 weeks), followed by itraconazole (200 mg twice daily) for additional 10 wk	Itraconazole (300 mg twice daily × 3 days, then 200 mg twice daily)	Itraconazole (200 mg daily)

* Dose modification may be necessary to maintain adequate itraconazole serum levels (>2).

or antiretroviral therapies, and symptomatic therapy is recommended.

Primary Prevention. There are no specific recommendations regarding exposure avoidance as a prevention strategy for *C. neoformans*.[36] In addition, routine screening of asymptomatic persons with serum CRAG testing is not recommended. Fluconazole is effective primary prophylaxis against cryptococcosis.[289] However, long-term fluconazole administration raises a number of concerns, including the development of drug-resistant fungi. This, combined with clinical studies that failed to show a survival benefit resulting from a reduction in cryptococcal disease,[289] lessens the utility of fluconazole as primary prophylaxis for most patients. Thus, the current USPHS/IDSA guidelines do not recommend fluconazole for primary *C. neoformans* prophylaxis.[36]

Histoplasma capsulatum

Histoplasmosis is a disease caused by the dimorphic, soil-dwelling fungus *H. capsulatum*. The fungus is found on all continents except Antarctica, but it is most endemic to North America and the Caribbean basin.[262,290] The heaviest concentration is found in the Mississippi, Ohio, and St. Lawrence River valleys. The precise reasons for the endemicity of *H. capsulatum* are unknown but may relate to climate (moderate), humidity, and specific soil characteristics.[290] In these areas, the fungus exists in microfoci related to the enrichment of the soil with bird or bat excrement, which helps to promote sporulation. In soil, the fungus exists in a mycelial form with characteristic tuberculate macroconidia. The hyphae also have microconidia that are easily aerosolized when disturbed. Inhalation of these microconidia leads to primary pulmonary infection that is usually clinically silent.

Once deposited in the alveoli, *H. capsulatum* transforms into its yeast (or parasitic) form, and an area of pneumonitis develops. During this period before cell-mediated immunity develops, the organism spreads to regional lymph nodes and to reticuloendothelial organs. Two to 3 weeks after exposure, about 40% of immunocompetent individuals develop a flulike syndrome with fever, chills, myalgias, a nonproductive cough, and chest pain. Ninety-nine percent of these cases spontaneously resolve with the development of specific cell-mediated immunity. In contrast, progressive disseminated histoplasmosis develops in HIV-infected persons lacking cell-mediated immunity. Although most cases of HIV-associated histoplasmosis appear to result from de novo exposure, reactivation disease does occur. These cases account for the histoplasmosis seen in nonendemic areas such as San Francisco or New York.[291]

Clinical Features. Although the portal of entry is the lung, disseminated histoplasmosis most often presents as a febrile wasting illness in HIV-infected persons. In a large series of 72 HIV-infected patients with disseminated histoplasmosis, 69 patients (96%) presented with fever and weight loss.[292]

CD4⁺ Lymphocyte Count, Symptoms, and Signs. Most cases of disseminated histoplasmosis occur in patients with a $CD4^+$ lymphocyte count less than 100 cells/μL and often below 50 cells/μL. The clinical presentation of histoplas-

mosis is frequently subtle and nonspecific. The most common symptoms are fever and weight loss. Occasionally, the presentation is dramatic with a sepsis-like syndrome associated with hypotension, respiratory failure, liver and renal failure, and coagulopathy. Wheat and colleagues[292] reported a sepsis-like syndrome in 12.5% of 72 patients with disseminated histoplasmosis and noted its presence in 10% of 51 other cases reviewed.

The most frequent respiratory complaints are cough and dyspnea. These symptoms are usually found in patients with chest radiographic abnormalities and are often absent in patients with normal radiographs. A review of 51 cases of HIV-associated progressive disseminated histoplasmosis found that 16% presented with respiratory complaints. Subsequent series of 72 cases and 64 cases found that 53% and 38%, respectively, had respiratory complaints at presentation.[292,293]

Similar to symptoms, the signs of histoplasmosis are often nonspecific and most often reveal fever and wasting. Examination of the chest may reveal crackles. Hepatomegaly (26% to 29%), splenomegaly (12% to 35%), peripheral lymphadenopathy (17% to 37%), central nervous system findings (14% to 18%), and cutaneous lesions (1% to 18%) may also be seen.[292] One study found that cutaneous lesions were significantly more frequent in HIV-infected persons residing in Brazil than in their counterparts residing in the United States.[294] As described, a sepsis-like syndrome is present in 10% to 12.5% of cases and portends a poor outcome.[292] Frequent laboratory findings include anemia, leukopenia, thrombocytopenia, and liver function test elevations. Serum LDH and serum ferritin elevations, often pronounced, have also been reported.[290]

Chest Radiograph. Disseminated histoplasmosis will present with a normal chest radiograph in a significant proportion of cases.[280,292,293,295] Wheat and colleagues[292] reported normal radiographs in 43% of 72 HIV-infected patients and in 36% of the patients in the literature reviewed. In a series of 50 HIV-infected patients with disseminated histoplasmosis, Conces and coworkers[295] found that 54% had a normal radiograph. The most common radiographic findings are diffuse, often coarse reticular or reticulonodular (Fig. 75.8), occasionally alveolar infiltrates.[280] Wheat and colleagues[292] found diffuse infiltrates in 44% of their 72 patients, whereas Conces and coworkers[295] found diffuse nodular opacities or diffuse linear opacities in 13 of 50 patients (26% overall, but 57% of the patients with an abnormal radiograph). Focal opacities are less common but are found in 7% to 11% of cases.[292] Hilar and mediastinal adenopathy and calcified granulomata are each found in less than 5% of patients, attesting to the low incidence of reactivation disease.[292]

Diagnosis. The diagnosis of histoplasma infection begins with the histoplasma polysaccharide antigen (HPA) test. The test can be performed on urine, serum, cerebrospinal fluid, or BAL fluid. The sensitivity of the HPA test is greater in urine than in serum. Although the urine HPA is sensitive in disseminated histoplasmosis, it is often negative in isolated pulmonary disease. With successful therapy HPA values fall, and during relapses HPA values rise (usually by ≥2 HPA units), which are useful features for assessing response to therapy and for evaluating possible relapse.[296]

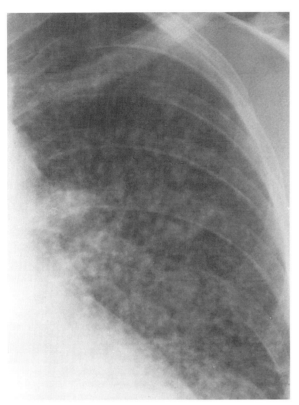

Figure 75.8 Posteroanterior chest radiographic close-up of the left mid-lung of an HIV-seropositive patient showing a medium to coarse reticulonodular pattern characteristic of disseminated fungal disease. (From Stansell JD: Fungal disease in HIV-infected persons: Cryptococcosis, histoplasmosis, and coccidioidomycosis. J Thorac Imaging 6:28–35, 1991.)

A false-positive HPA test can occur in patients with other disseminated fungal diseases (blastomycosis, paracoccidioidomycosis, and penicilliosis) but it has never been reported in patients with cryptococcosis, coccidioidomycosis, aspergillosis, or candidiasis. A persistently positive HPA test indicates continued disease and warrants continued therapy. Definitive diagnosis requires isolation and identification of the fungus by culture. Blood fungal cultures are specific and should be obtained as part of the diagnostic evaluation. Wheat and colleagues[292] reported that fungal blood cultures were positive in 65 of their 72 cases (90%). Occasionally, the peripheral blood smear reveals intracellular yeast. Other potential diagnostic sources include bone marrow, lymph node, and skin.

The diagnosis of pulmonary histoplasmosis can be established by direct examination and culture of sputum, BAL fluid,[297] or TBBX.

Treatment. Amphotericin B is the treatment of choice for HIV-infected patients with moderate to severe disseminated histoplasmosis, whereas itraconazole is an alternative for patients with mild disease (see Table 75.5).[298] Treatment with amphotericin B should be continued until the patient is clinically improved, at which point the patient can be switched to itraconazole to complete a 12-week course. The patient should then be maintained on lifelong suppressive therapy with itraconazole, which is superior to fluconazole.[299]

Primary Prevention. In those areas endemic for *H. capsulatum*, patients should avoid activities that will potentially increase their exposure, such as cleaning chicken coops; disturbing native soil beneath bird-roosting sites; cleaning, remodeling, or demolishing old buildings; and exploring caves.[36] Routine skin and serologic testing, even in histoplasmosis-endemic areas, is not recommended. Itraconazole is effective primary prophylaxis against histoplasmosis for persons who reside in endemic areas.[300] However, the results of clinical studies that failed to show a survival benefit resulting from a reduction in histoplasmosis[300] lessen the utility of itraconazole as primary prophylaxis for most patients. Thus, the current USPHS/IDSA guidelines do not recommend itraconazole for primary *H. capsulatum* prophylaxis.[36] Itraconazole, however, can be considered for primary prophylaxis for HIV-infected persons whose CD4+ lymphocyte count is less than 100 cells/μL and who reside in hyperendemic areas, if they participate in high-risk activities that involve frequent exposure to soil.[301]

Coccidioides immitis

Coccidioidomycosis is a disease caused by the dimorphic, soil-dwelling fungus *C. immitis*, which causes an uncommon, but devastating, disseminated disease that is often fatal in HIV-infected persons. The fungus is endemic to the semiarid regions of North America, notably the southwestern United States (central California, southern Arizona, southern New Mexico, and west Texas) and also northern Mexico.[262,302,303] California's southern San Joaquin Valley and southern Arizona are hyperendemic areas.[303] *Coccidioides immitis* is also found in South America, especially central Argentina. In soil, the fungus exists in a mycelial form with characteristic arthrospores.[303] These arthrospores are easily aerosolized when disrupted. After inhalation and deposition in the distal airways and alveoli, the arthrospores transform into spherules that may develop several hundred endospores. Rupture of the spherules allows widespread dissemination of the endospores, which then form additional spherules, replicating the cycle. Although most cases of HIV-associated coccidioidomycosis appear to result from de novo exposure, reactivation disease does occur.

Clinical Features. Although the portal of entry is the lung, coccidioidomycosis often presents with disseminated disease and meningitis. Other frequent sites include the skin and skeletal system. In one study, 42% of HIV-infected patients with coccidioidomycosis presented with disseminated disease; overall, 25% of the patients in this series died.[304] Cases of endotracheal or endobronchial involvement have been reported.[305] Bronchoscopic findings vary and may show mucosal involvement or intrinsic obstruction.

CD4+ Lymphocyte Count, Symptoms, and Signs. Most cases of disseminated coccidioidomycosis occur in patients with a CD4+ lymphocyte count below 100 cells/μL and often less than 50 cells/μL. One review of 91 patients with coccidioidal disease found a mean CD4+ count of 55 cells/μL among patients with diffuse pulmonary disease.[306] Another study of 153 patients with coccidioidomycosis found a median CD4+ count of 54 cells/μL.[304] The clinical presentation is often nonspecific. Fever, chills, night sweats, and weight loss are common. Singh and associates[306] reported fever and chills in 68%, weight loss in 50%, and night sweats in 36% of 91 patients with coccidioidomycosis. The most frequent respiratory complaint in these patients was cough, which was noted in 64%; dyspnea was less common, only 10%.

Similar to symptoms, the signs of coccidioidomycosis are often nonspecific. Fever and wasting are often present. Examination of the chest may reveal crackles. Lymphadenopathy (24%) and splenomegaly (<10%) may also be seen.[306]

Chest Radiograph. Coccidioidal pneumonia most commonly presents with diffuse reticulonodular infiltrates.[280] In a series of 91 HIV-infected patients with coccidioidomycosis, diffuse reticulonodular infiltrates were seen in 65%.[306] Focal opacities were less common but occurred in 14% of cases and consisted of focal infiltrates, single or multiple nodules, and cavities.[306] Pleural effusion and hilar adenopathy were also reported. Coccidioidomycosis also presents with a normal chest radiograph.

Diagnosis. Unlike cryptococcosis and histoplasmosis, there is no specific antigen test available for diagnosing coccidioidomycosis. Thus, definitive diagnosis requires the isolation and identification of the fungus by culture or identification of pathognomonic giant spherules in cytologic or histologic preparations. In cases of suspected coccidioidomycosis, it is critical to alert the microbiology laboratory so that proper laboratory precautions can be implemented. Serologic tests can be extremely useful in the evaluation of suspected coccidioidomycosis. Several studies have found an 80% to 90% sensitivity of complement fixation and tube precipitin tests.[307,308] False-negative titers most often occurred in the most severely immunocompromised patients with diffuse pulmonary disease. In those with positive tests, the titer appeared to reflect the disease activity and was useful for monitoring response to therapy.[308]

Direct examination and culture of sputum, BAL fluid, or transbronchial biopsy can establish the diagnosis of pulmonary coccidioidomycosis. Singh and associates[306] found that sputum culture (13 of 19, or 68%) and cytology (8 of 11, or 73%) were often diagnostic. BAL fluid culture diagnosed 29 of 42 cases (69%), and BAL fluid cytology diagnosed 32 of 48 cases (67%); in addition, TBBX culture diagnosed 8 of 10 cases (80%), and biopsy histology diagnosed all 14 cases (100%).

Treatment. Amphotericin B is the treatment of choice for HIV-infected patients with pulmonary or disseminated coccidioidomycosis (see Table 75.5).[302] Patients who have responded can be switched to fluconazole. The patient should then be maintained on lifelong suppressive therapy with fluconazole. Twice- to thrice-weekly amphotericin B is another alternative. The prognosis for pulmonary disease is related to its severity. Fish and coworkers[307] found that the 31 patients with diffuse pulmonary disease had a significantly higher mortality rate than the 20 with focal disease in one series. Singh and associates[306] reported similar results. Fluconazole is the treatment of choice for patients with meningitis.[302] Thus, fluconazole (400 to 800 mg daily) can be considered for patients with mild pulmonary disease and a concurrent meningitis.

Primary Prevention. In those areas endemic for *C. immitis*, patients should avoid activities that will potentially increase their exposure, such as visits to construction projects or sites where the soil is disturbed. Routine skin and serologic testing, even in endemic areas, is not recommended. Primary prophylaxis for persons living in or traveling to an endemic area is generally not recommended.[36]

Aspergillus Species

Aspergillus species are found worldwide, and exposure is universal. However, disease is infrequent unless phagocyte number or function is reduced.[309] Presently, greater than 180 species within the *Aspergillus* genus have been identified. *Aspergillus fumigatus*, however, is the most common disease-causing species, and it accounts for approximately 90% of cases of invasive aspergillosis. Although invasive aspergillosis is a well-documented complication of various immunosuppressive disorders, particularly in patients with hematologic malignancy or organ transplantation, it is an uncommon problem in patients with HIV disease. In 13 patients reported by Denning and colleagues,[310] pulmonary aspergillosis followed the diagnosis of AIDS by a median of 25 months; in these patients, risk factors for the development of aspergillosis besides HIV-induced immunosuppression included use of corticosteroids, neutropenia, marijuana, and broad-spectrum antimicrobial drugs. In the HAART era, the incidence of invasive aspergillosis has further declined. Holding and coworkers[311] reported an aspergillosis incidence of 3.5 cases per 1000 person-years among HIV-infected subjects enrolled in the CDC-led Adult and Adolescent Spectrum of HIV Disease study.

Clinical Features. The entire spectrum of *Aspergillus*-related lung disease has been observed in HIV-infected persons, from colonization of the respiratory tract[312] or a preexisting cavity,[313,314] to tracheobronchitis or obstructing bronchial aspergillosis,[315] to invasive aspergillosis.[310,312,316–321] We have also seen a case of allergic bronchopulmonary aspergillosis in an HIV-infected asthmatic patient, a case of an *Aspergillus* empyema, and an *Aspergillus* lung mass. We concentrate here on the most severe manifestation of *Aspergillus* pulmonary disease, invasive aspergillosis. Although most patients with invasive aspergillosis have a CD4+ lymphocyte count lower than 50 cells/μL, the classic risk factors for the disease relate more to phagocyte number and function (as determined by neutropenia and use of corticosteroids or broad-spectrum antibiotics) than to absolute CD4+ counts. Patients with aspergillosis typically present with fever, cough, dyspnea, and occasionally pleuritic chest pain. Hemoptysis is another presenting feature. The chest radiographic abnormalities are variable and include unilateral or bilateral infiltrates, cavitary lesions, nodular and pleural-based densities, and pleural effusions.[322]

Diagnosis. The definitive diagnosis of aspergillosis requires both demonstration of tissue invasion and isolation of the organism by culture. Neither sputum nor BAL is sufficient. Microscopy alone cannot distinguish *Aspergillus* species from *Fusarium* or *Pseudallescheria* species. The results of TBBX are usually negative, but specimens from sputum, BAL fluid, or percutaneous aspirates are often positive on culture. The absence of histologic proof of tissue invasion is always somewhat disquieting, especially in attempting to distinguish invasive disease from possible colonization of damaged airways. Repeated isolation of the fungus in large numbers with a compatible clinical setting makes the diagnosis more tenable.

Treatment. Compared with the fungi previously discussed, there is relatively little experience treating HIV-infected patients with aspergillosis.[309] Usually, amphotericin B or itraconazole has been administered with variable results (see Table 75.5).[323] We have also used liposomal amphotericin B for a few patients with similar outcomes. More recently, voriconazole has been touted as superior to amphotericin B for the treatment of invasive aspergillosis. Even with the prompt institution of therapy, the prognosis is poor, undoubtedly in large part because aspergillosis, when it occurs, is nearly always a late complication of advanced HIV disease.

Prevention. Given the ubiquitous nature of *Aspergillus* species, it is impossible to prevent exposure to the organism. However, patients with advanced HIV disease should avoid activities that will potentially increase their exposure, including being near decaying vegetation (e.g., compost) and soil.

Blastomyces dermatitidis

Blastomycosis is a disease caused by the endemic, dimorphic fungus *B. dermatitidis*. Blastomycosis is coendemic with histoplasmosis throughout much of the central United States. It is much less common than histoplasmosis, however, and reports of HIV-associated blastomycosis are uncommon.[324,325]

Clinical Features. The largest case series reported 15 cases of HIV-associated blastomycosis.[324] All but one had a CD4+ lymphocyte count less than 200 cells/μL. The authors noted two distinct patterns of disease. Although 12 of 15 patients (80%) had evidence of pulmonary involvement, one group of patients had disease that was clinically limited to the respiratory system. The other group had disseminated blastomycosis, commonly involving multiple organ systems, including the lungs. Eleven of 15 patients (73%) had abnormal chest radiographs, with diffuse interstitial or miliary disease (55%) being the most common radiographic finding. Definitive diagnosis requires the growth of *B. dermatitidis*, although visualization of the characteristic budding yeast form is strongly suggestive and warrants antifungal therapy while awaiting culture.

Treatment. Amphotericin B is the treatment of choice for HIV-infected patients with severe disease (see Table 75.5).[324, 326] Treatment with amphotericin B should be continued to a cumulative induction dose of 1.5 to 2.5 g. Patients who have improved can then be switched to itraconazole maintenance therapy for life, whereas those without significant improvement should continue taking amphotericin B. With prompt institution of therapy, most patients with disease limited to the lungs responded well; in contrast, patients with disseminated disease did poorly (40% mortality in 30 days).[324]

Penicillium marneffei

Penicilliosis is a disease caused by *P. marneffei*, a dimorphic, soil-dwelling fungus. With expansion of the HIV epidemic into southeastern Asia has come a dramatic increase in cases of penicilliosis.[327-333] *Penicillium marneffei* is endemic in southeastern Asian countries,[331] and, in Northern Thailand, it is the third most common opportunistic infection (after tuberculosis and cryptococcosis) in HIV-infected patients with AIDS, accounting for 15% to 20% of all AIDS-related illnesses. Disease is related to soil exposure, especially during the rainy season (May to October), but not to the consumption of bamboo rats, the only known nonhuman hosts of *P. marneffei*.[334,335] Infection is probably acquired via inhalation.

Clinical Features. Most cases of penicilliosis occur in patients with a CD4+ lymphocyte count less than 100 cells/μL. The clinical presentation is often mistaken for tuberculosis, cryptococcosis, or histoplasmosis. The most common symptoms include fever, weight loss, cough, and generalized papular skin lesions, usually with central umbilication. Symptoms are often present for weeks. In one series of 92 patients with *P. marneffei* infection, fever was present in 92%, weight loss in 76%, and skin lesions in 71%.[329] In addition to the cutaneous findings, physical examination often reveals peripheral lymphadenopathy and hepatomegaly. Anemia is a prominent laboratory finding.

Diagnosis. *Penicillium marneffei* is most commonly a disseminated disease in HIV-infected patients, and the diagnosis is usually made by blood fungal cultures. Other sites of diagnosis include the skin, lymph nodes, bone marrow, and respiratory specimens. In contrast to other *Penicillium* species that cause disease in humans, *P. marneffei* converts to a yeast form in its host, and yeast-laden macrophages can often be seen in peripheral blood, bone marrow aspirates, and touch preparations from tissue biopsies.

Treatment. Amphotericin B, followed by itraconazole, is the standard treatment for *P. marneffei* infection (see Table 75.5).[336] The duration of amphotericin B treatment is 2 weeks, followed by an additional 10 weeks of itraconazole. This regimen is reported to have a greater than 97% response rate for disseminated *P. marneffei* infection.[336] Without secondary prophylaxis, however, most patients will suffer a relapse within 6 to 12 months.

Prevention. In Thailand, a prospective, double-blind, placebo-controlled trial found that itraconazole (200 mg daily) is an effective primary prophylaxis against *P. marneffei*.[337] In this study, subjects randomized to itraconazole were significantly less likely to develop *P. marneffei* infection than were subjects randomized to placebo. A prospective double-blind, placebo-controlled trial determined that itraconazole (200 mg daily) is an effective secondary prophylaxis against *P. marneffei*.[338] In this study, none of the 36 patients randomized to itraconazole had a relapse of *P. marneffei* within 1 year compared with 20 of the 35 patients (57%) assigned to placebo. Given the strong association with soil exposure, especially during the rainy season, HIV-infected patients living in or traveling to endemic areas should avoid activities that will potentially increase their exposure.

Candida Species

Despite the high frequency of mucocutaneous candidiasis in HIV-infected patients, pulmonary candidiasis is distinctly uncommon and is rarely diagnosed during life.[339] Because of the small number of documented cases of pulmonary candidiasis, neither the clinical features nor the treatment is well established. However, it is clear that tissue invasion must be demonstrated by biopsy for a convincing diagnosis; the mere identification of the fungus in respiratory secretions by culture alone is insufficient.

VIRUSES

Many viruses are known to cause pulmonary disease in immunosuppressed persons, including members of the herpesvirus family (cytomegalovirus [CMV], herpes simplex virus, varicella-zoster virus, and Epstein-Barr virus), influenza virus, parainfluenza virus, respiratory syncytial virus, measles virus, adenovirus, rhinovirus, and human metapneumovirus. All of these viruses have been identified in HIV-infected patients; however, only CMV is regarded as an important agent of pulmonary disease. Although clearly the source of significant pathologic conditions in the retina, gastrointestinal tract, and nervous system, the role of CMV in producing pulmonary disease in HIV-infected persons is open to question. Many consider this ubiquitous virus a "passenger" rather than a pathogen in most instances. However, there are also instances in which documented pulmonary disease results from CMV.

Cytomegalovirus

Cytomegalovirus is a beta-herpesvirus. The risk of exposure to CMV increases with age, and evidence of CMV infection is extremely common in healthy persons. The results of serologic studies indicate that more than 50% to 70% of all adults and virtually 100% of male homosexuals are infected with the virus.[340] Cytomegalovirus is excreted in saliva, respiratory secretions, urine, and semen. In HIV-infected patients, CMV disease is believed to result chiefly from reactivation of latent infection. However, disease has been documented from de novo infection in recipients of solid organs, bone marrow, and blood, which raises the possibility that new infection or superinfection from exogenous sources may also occur in HIV-infected persons.

Clinical Features. Retinitis and gastrointestinal disease are the two most common forms of HIV-associated CMV disease. Cytomegalovirus is a frequent isolate from the BAL fluid of patients with advanced immunosuppression who undergo evaluation for opportunistic infections, notably *Pneumocystis*. Because CMV may be shed in respiratory secretions, its mere presence in BAL fluid cannot be construed as being diagnostic of CMV pulmonary disease. When dual pulmonary infection is discovered, treatment directed against the coexisting disease and not against CMV usually results in clinical resolution.[341,342] However, there are clearly instances when CMV causes pulmonary disease, and the challenge clinicians face is to recognize when these occur.[343–345]

CD4+ Lymphocyte Count, Symptoms, and Signs. Most cases of CMV disease occur in patients with a CD4+ lymphocyte count less than 50 cells/μL. In one study of 18 patients with biopsy-proven CMV pneumonia, the median CD4+ count was 4 cells/μL.[345]

The most common symptoms of CMV pneumonia are cough, dyspnea, and fever. In the study by Salomon and associates,[345] these symptoms were seen in 94%, 94%, and 89%, respectively, of the 18 patients reported. Respiratory symptoms were present for up to 2 weeks in 50% and between 2 and 4 weeks in an additional 44%. Physical examination of the chest may be normal or may reveal crackles or evidence of pleural effusion. The serum LDH has been reported to be elevated in CMV pneumonia.[345]

Chest Radiograph. The chest radiograph findings of CMV pneumonia vary and include reticular or ground-glass opacities, alveolar infiltrates, and nodules or nodular opacities.[345] Pleural effusions may be seen as well.

Diagnosis. When suspected CMV pulmonary disease occurs in conjunction with other end-organ disease (e.g., retinitis), CMV therapy must be initiated immediately. Treatment of one end-organ CMV disease in fact treats all, although the length of therapy can differ by organ system. The therapeutic dilemma is much greater when only the lungs appear to be afflicted. Patients suspected of having CMV pneumonitis should undergo a careful dilated retinal examination performed by an experienced ophthalmologist, even if there are no ocular complaints. CMV is usually a disseminated disease and commonly involves multiple organ systems in a single host. The only precise criterion for diagnosis of CMV pulmonary disease is the demonstration of widespread specific cytopathic changes in the lungs. Neither culture of BAL fluid [346,347] nor cytopathic inclusions on TBBX specimens are sufficient to make the diagnosis of CMV pneumonitis.

Treatment. Ganciclovir (dihydropropylguanosine), foscarnet (trisodium phosphonoformate, Foscavir), and cidofovir are the principal treatment options for CMV disease. With these drugs, an initial course of induction therapy is used. Unlike retinal and gastrointestinal disease, however, the length of induction therapy for CMV pneumonia is undetermined. Certainly, induction therapy should be continued until clinical improvement occurs, as with gastrointestinal disease. Some authorities have recommended a 21-day course for isolated CMV pneumonitis. In HIV-infected patients with CMV retinitis, ganciclovir is administered intravenously at 5 mg/kg twice a day for induction therapy followed by 5 mg/kg once a day for lifelong maintenance therapy. The usefulness of this maintenance therapy in preventing relapse of CMV pneumonitis is unclear. The principal toxicity of ganciclovir is myelosuppression (neutropenia in 20% to 40% and thrombocytopenia in 5%). Patients receiving ganciclovir must have their complete blood counts monitored closely. For patients who develop significant neutropenia, the addition of granulocyte colony-stimulating factor may permit continuation of ganciclovir. Those with persistent neutropenia despite granulocyte colony-stimulating factor should be switched to an alternate therapy such as foscarnet.

In HIV-infected patients with CMV retinitis, foscarnet is also administered intravenously at 90 mg/kg twice a day (or 60 mg/kg three times a day) for induction therapy and 90 to 120 mg/kg once a day for maintenance therapy. Because it can bind with calcium and significantly lower ionized calcium levels, foscarnet is usually administered by infusion pump over at least 1 hour. Too rapid an infusion may cause seizures and death. The principal toxicity of foscarnet is nephrotoxicity and electrolyte disturbance. Patients receiving foscarnet must have their renal function and electrolytes monitored closely.

Cidofovir is another alternative. One benefit of cidofovir is that it does not require phosphorylation by virus-induced enzyme and is therefore active against most ganciclovir-resistant viruses that have resistance mutations in the phosphorylating gene. Cidofovir has an extremely long half-life. The principal toxicity of cidofovir is nephrotoxicity that can be diminished by aggressive prehydration and concurrent probenecid therapy. Patients receiving cidofovir must have their renal function monitored closely.

Finally, valganciclovir may be used. Valganciclovir is an oral prodrug of ganciclovir and is rapidly hydrolyzed to ganciclovir when administered orally. The dose of valganciclovir is 900 mg twice daily. This dose achieves blood levels comparable to a 5-mg/kg intravenous dose of ganciclovir. In a randomized study, oral valganciclovir was as effective as intravenous ganciclovir in treatment of HIV-infected subjects with CMV retinitis.[348]

Prevention. HIV-infected persons belonging to groups of individuals with low rates of seropositivity for CMV should be tested for CMV antibodies.[36] HIV-infected patients who are CMV immunoglobulin G negative should be given CMV-negative blood in the event that a transfusion is necessary. Oral ganciclovir can be used for the prevention of CMV disease in HIV-infected patients who are CMV immunoglobulin G positive. However, this regimen is associated with conflicting data on its efficacy, a high pill burden, high cost, and significant toxicities. In addition, the specter of the development of ganciclovir resistance has combined to limit the general use of this prophylaxis regimen.[36]

Other Viruses

Symptomatic pulmonary viral infection other than CMV is uncommon.[349] Herpes simplex virus, while frequently cultured from BAL fluid, is usually a contaminant from upper airway carriage. Lower respiratory tract involvement is rare in HIV-infected persons (0.2% to 4% of autopsy cases) and appears to be more frequent in other immunosuppressed hosts. Herpes simplex virus pulmonary disease causes a focal pneumonia or a diffuse interstitial pneumonitis.[350] The focal pneumonias appear to result from contiguous spread of herpes simplex virus to the lung parenchyma and are often associated with necrotizing tracheobronchitis, whereas the diffuse interstitial pneumonias appear to be a manifestation of hematogenous herpes simplex virus dissemination.

Varicella-zoster virus is a rare cause of pneumonia in HIV-infected adult patients.[351,352] Epstein-Barr virus DNA has been identified in lung biopsy specimens of infants and children with lymphocytic interstitial pneumonitis (LIP), but the precise role of the virus in this disease is uncertain.[353] Influenza has been isolated from HIV-infected patients.[354] In this small series, neither the clinical presentation of influenza nor the rate of secondary complications appeared to be different from that in healthy persons. Nevertheless, it is generally recommended that all HIV-infected persons

be vaccinated annually.[36] A randomized, double-blind, placebo-controlled study of 102 HIV-infected persons found that influenza vaccine resulted in significant decreases in laboratory-confirmed influenza and respiratory symptoms and no substantial changes in CD4+ lymphocyte count or HIV RNA.[355] However, some HIV-infected patients, those with CD4+ lymphocyte counts below 100 cells/μL or HIV RNA levels above 100,000 copies/mL (or both), are unable to mount a protective antibody response.[356] HIV-infected children with measles appear to have a similar clinical presentation and outcome compared to HIV-uninfected children.[357] Human metapneumovirus has been described in HIV-infected infants.[358] HIV itself is present in the lungs of HIV-infected patients during all stages of disease. However, its pathogenic role in HIV-associated pulmonary disease is presently unclear.

PARASITES

Several unicellular and multicellular parasites cause pulmonary disease in HIV-infected hosts. Of these, *T. gondii* is the most frequent.

Toxoplasma gondii

Toxoplasma gondii is an intracellular protozoan. Toxoplasmosis is a zoonosis with domestic cats as its definitive host but with an infectious reservoir that encompasses all animals. Transmission to humans occurs when raw or undercooked meat that contains *T. gondii* is eaten. Domestic cat feces in litter boxes are an additional source of potential *T. gondii* infection. Vertical transmission can occur from mother to fetus. In HIV-infected patients, the overwhelming majority of cases of toxoplasmosis result from reactivation of chronic, latent infection. Thus, the keys to preventing toxoplasmosis are prevention of exposure for those not yet infected and prophylaxis for those already seropositive. The seroprevalence of *Toxoplasma* antibodies varies. In the United States, the seroprevalence is 10% to 50%, whereas in Western Europe, the seroprevalence may be as high as 90%.

Clinical Features. *Toxoplasma gondii* encephalitis is a well-recognized complication of advanced HIV disease and is an AIDS-defining condition. Although toxoplasmosis is the most common cause of focal brain abscesses in HIV-infected patients, pulmonary involvement is uncommon. Pulmonary disease may occur in patients with central nervous system or disseminated disease or with isolated pulmonary involvement.[359–362]

CD4+ Lymphocyte Count, Symptoms, and Signs. Toxoplasmosis presents at the lower range of CD4+ lymphocyte counts. In a large study of 64 patients with pulmonary toxoplasmosis conducted in France, the mean (±SD) CD4+ count was 40 (±75) cells/μL.[362] Pulmonary toxoplasmosis characteristically presents with cough, usually nonproductive, dyspnea, and fever. Physical examination of the chest may be normal or may reveal crackles. Focal neurologic findings are common. Hepatosplenomegaly can be seen.

Chest Radiograph. The chest radiograph usually reveals bilateral infiltrates, either fine reticulonodular infiltrates indistinguishable from PCP or a coarser nodular pattern similar to that seen with tuberculosis or fungal pneumonias.[363] Pleural effusions can be seen, and a variety of other radiographic findings have also been described.[361]

Diagnosis. The diagnosis of pulmonary toxoplasmosis is usually established by bronchoscopy with BAL fluid study. In one review, BAL fluid study was diagnostic in 16 of 17 immunocompromised patients with pulmonary disease.[361]

Treatment. The treatment for pulmonary toxoplasmosis is identical to that for central nervous system toxoplasmosis. Traditionally, treatment is with either pyrimethamine and sulfadiazine or pyrimethamine and clindamycin. Leucovorin (folinic acid) should be coadministered. A study of 77 patients with central nervous system toxoplasmosis compared TMP-SMX with pyrimethamine and sulfadiazine and found no significant difference in their efficacy.[364] In addition, atovaquone and pyrimethamine plus azithromycin have been used with reasonable success as salvage therapy for patients failing or intolerant of the standard treatment options.[365,366]

Prevention. HIV-infected persons should be tested for *T. gondii* antibodies.[36] Persons who are *Toxoplasma* antibody negative should be instructed to avoid potential sources of infection. HIV-infected patients who have cats should either have someone else change the litter box or, if unable to find someone, clean the litter box daily and wash their hands thoroughly afterward.[36] In addition, cats should be kept indoors, should not be allowed to hunt, and should not be fed raw or undercooked meat. Patients themselves should similarly avoid eating raw or undercooked meat. Approximately 30% to 40% of HIV-infected patients who are *Toxoplasma* antibody positive will develop toxoplasmosis unless they are provided prophylaxis. Accordingly, these persons should receive primary prophylaxis once their CD4$^+$ lymphocyte count falls below 100 cells/μL.[36] As a practical matter, this is often accomplished when the CD4$^+$ count reaches 200 cells/μL or less because the prophylaxis of choice (TMP-SMX) is also the prophylaxis of choice for *Pneumocystis*. For patients who are intolerant of TMP-SMX, dapsone plus pyrimethamine (and leucovorin) can be used. Because relapses are common, patients who recover from toxoplasmosis should receive secondary prophylaxis with either pyrimethamine, sulfadiazine, and leucovorin or pyrimethamine, clindamycin, and leucovorin.[36] Atovaquone (with or without pyrimethamine) is another option. Several studies have demonstrated that primary and secondary *T. gondii* prophylaxis can be safely discontinued in the vast majority of HIV-infected persons who have experienced an increase in their CD4$^+$ lymphocyte count to greater than 200 cells/μL for at least 3 months.[40,42-44,54,61]

Other Parasites

In general, helminth infections are reported infrequently in HIV-infected persons.[367,368] Several cases of both pulmonary cryptosporidiosis and pulmonary microsporidiosis in HIV-infected patients with concurrent intestinal disease have been reported.[369-379] In these cases, aspiration from the gastrointestinal tract appears to be the most probable route of pulmonary infection. Occasionally, patients have presented

with disseminated disease, raising the distinct possibility of hematogenous spread. The most common respiratory symptoms are cough, dyspnea, and pleuritic chest pain. One review found that these symptoms were present in 77%, 58%, and 33%, respectively, of patients with cryptosporidial pulmonary disease.[379] The diagnosis of pulmonary disease can be made by either sputum study or bronchoscopy.

The hyperinfection syndrome with *Strongyloides stercoralis* has been reported in HIV-infected patients.[380-390] However, *Strongyloides* hyperinfection does not appear to be an important HIV-associated complication, even in countries where the parasite is endemic.[391,391a] We have encountered several cases of pulmonary strongyloidiasis as part of a disseminated disease. All patients were from regions with a high incidence of helminthic infection. Fever with concurrent gastrointestinal and respiratory symptoms was typical. The diagnosis was made by sputum or BAL fluid study. The patients were treated successfully with either albendazole or ivermectin; however, relapses were quite common, and retreatment was often necessary.

NONINFECTIOUS DISORDERS

The evaluation of respiratory complications usually focuses on the diagnosis of HIV-associated opportunistic infections because of their frequency, the need for prompt therapy, and, in the case of tuberculosis, the concern for transmission to other persons, both HIV infected and non-HIV infected. However, HIV-infected patients are also susceptible to a number of noninfectious pulmonary complications, which are briefly reviewed here.

MALIGNANCIES

Two different HIV-associated malignancies, Kaposi's sarcoma and non-Hodgkin's lymphoma, may involve the lungs, involving the parenchyma, airways, pleura, or hilar or mediastinal lymph nodes. Intrathoracic disease from either neoplasm is usually a manifestation of disease already recognized elsewhere, but occasionally both Kaposi's sarcoma and non-Hodgkin's lymphoma may present with isolated pulmonary disease.

Kaposi's Sarcoma

The most common HIV-associated malignancy is Kaposi's sarcoma. One of the truly striking features of the AIDS epidemic in the early 1980s was the explosion of cases of this previously rare disease. Although the incidence of Kaposi's sarcoma has decreased dramatically since then, significant advances have been made in our understanding of its pathogenesis, including its association with a novel human herpesvirus, HHV8.[392]

The incidence of HIV-associated Kaposi's sarcoma has always been significantly higher in male homosexuals than in other HIV risk groups. Approximately 90% to 95% of cases occur in male homosexuals. It has been estimated that there is a 20,000- to 73,000-fold increased incidence of Kaposi's sarcoma in HIV-infected homosexual men than in the overall population.[393] These observations suggested the presence of a possible sexually transmitted cofactor. In

1994, Chang and colleagues[394] identified DNA fragments present in HIV-associated Kaposi's sarcoma specimens but absent in most non-Kaposi's specimens. The nucleotide sequence of these fragments demonstrated homology to two known gamma- (lymphotropic) herpesviruses, suggesting that the fragments derived from a novel herpesvirus, subsequently named human herpesvirus 8 (HHV8) or Kaposi's sarcoma–associated herpesvirus.[395] Subsequently, HHV8 has also been found in specimens from non–HIV-infected persons with classic, endemic (African), and transplant-associated Kaposi's sarcoma. These and other findings argue for a central role of HHV8 in the pathogenesis of Kaposi's sarcoma and provide new avenues for possible treatment of this disease.

Clinical Features. Pulmonary Kaposi's sarcoma is detected clinically in approximately one third of patients with known Kaposi's sarcoma, with the proportion detected at autopsy approaching 50% to 75%.

CD4+ Lymphocyte Count, Symptoms, and Signs. Pulmonary Kaposi's sarcoma presents at the lower range of CD4+ lymphocyte counts. In one study of 168 patients with pulmonary Kaposi's sarcoma, the median CD4+ count was 19 cells/μL; 68% had a CD4+ lymphocyte count below 50 cells/μL, and only 4% had a CD4+ count higher than 200 cells/μL.[71] Most but not all patients with clinically diagnosed pulmonary Kaposi's sarcoma have concomitant mucocutaneous disease. Huang and coworkers[71] found that 85% of 168 consecutive patients diagnosed with pulmonary Kaposi's sarcoma by bronchoscopy had evidence of mucocutaneous involvement at the time of bronchoscopy. The 15% without mucocutaneous involvement had pulmonary disease that ranged from isolated tracheal lesions to diffuse endobronchial involvement that was ultimately fatal. A significant proportion of patients with pulmonary Kaposi's sarcoma also have concurrent opportunistic infection. For example, Huang and coworkers[71] found that 45 (27%) of the 168 patients with pulmonary Kaposi's sarcoma had accompanying opportunistic infection, most frequently PCP. These observations underscore the need to evaluate each patient with Kaposi's sarcoma who presents with respiratory symptoms not only for pulmonary Kaposi's sarcoma but also for opportunistic infection. Patients with pulmonary Kaposi's sarcoma who develop opportunistic infection may also experience a rapid progression of their Kaposi's sarcoma that mimics an infectious process.

Pulmonary Kaposi's sarcoma characteristically presents with nonproductive cough, dyspnea, and fever. Chest pain and hemoptysis are less frequently noted and, in our experience, presage a precipitous clinical decline. Symptoms will usually be present for a few weeks but may also progress rapidly in a manner indistinguishable from opportunistic infection. Physical examination of the chest is often normal, but crackles, generalized or localized wheezes, and signs of pleural effusion can be observed.

Chest Radiograph. Pulmonary Kaposi's sarcoma characteristically presents with bilateral opacities in a central or perihilar distribution (Fig. 75.9). Typical findings include linear densities, nodules or nodular opacities of varying size, pleural effusions, and intrathoracic adenopathy. Gruden and associates[396] reviewed the chest radiographic presentation of

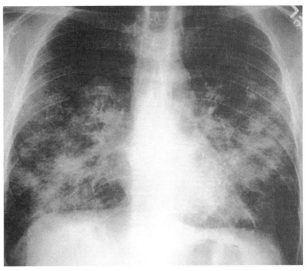

Figure 75.9 Posteroanterior chest radiograph of an HIV-seropositive patient with pulmonary Kaposi's sarcoma diagnosed by bronchoscopy showing the characteristic bilateral, perihilar distribution of abnormalities consisting of nodules and nodular opacities. Although most HIV-infected patients with pulmonary Kaposi's sarcoma will have concomitant mucocutaneous Kaposi's sarcoma, approximately 15% will have no evidence of cutaneous or oral involvement. (Reproduced with permission from L. Huang.)

76 consecutive patients with pulmonary Kaposi's sarcoma diagnosed by bronchoscopy whose BAL was negative for infectious organisms. In this study, 95% of the radiographs had peribronchial cuffing and "tram track" opacities, with or without more extensive perihilar coalescent opacities. Small nodules or nodular opacities were seen in 78%, Kerley's B lines in 71%, and pleural effusions in 53% of the radiographs. Of note, no chest radiograph had either Kerley's B lines or pleural effusions without concurrent parenchymal findings. Sixteen percent of the radiographs had hilar or mediastinal lymph node enlargement. Although this constellation of radiographic findings strongly suggests the diagnosis of pulmonary Kaposi's sarcoma in an HIV-infected male homosexual, no radiograph is diagnostic for Kaposi's sarcoma. Therefore, patients with suspected pulmonary Kaposi's sarcoma should have their diagnosis confirmed.

Diagnosis. The diagnosis of pulmonary Kaposi's sarcoma is usually established by bronchoscopy. The observation of characteristic endobronchial, red or violaceous, flat or slightly raised lesions is sufficient to diagnose pulmonary disease (Fig. 75.10). However, the presence of these lesions does not preclude a concurrent infection, nor does their absence in the observable airway preclude more distal disease or parenchymal, pleural, or nodal involvement. Although endobronchial or transbronchial biopsy of the airway or parenchymal abnormalities, respectively, is usually unnecessary, we have occasionally established the diagnosis by TBBX in patients in whom there was a strong clinical suspicion for pulmonary Kaposi's sarcoma but who had no endobronchial lesions detected. Patients with cutaneous Kaposi's sarcoma who develop new respiratory complaints should undergo evaluation according to the algorithm (sputum induction, followed by bronchoscopy) previously described. However, patients in whom there is a strong

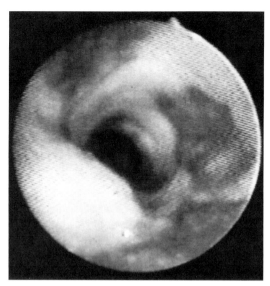

Figure 75.10 Characteristic Kaposi's sarcoma lesions in the trachea of an HIV-seropositive patient seen via bronchoscopy. (Reproduced with permission from L. Huang.)

clinical suspicion for pulmonary Kaposi's sarcoma should undergo bronchoscopy as the initial procedure.

Patients with pleural effusion may be considered candidates for thoracentesis, primarily to exclude the presence of a pyogenic, mycobacterial, or fungal infection, but also to provide symptomatic relief if the effusion is large. Although most Kaposi's sarcoma effusions are exudative, the effusions may be transudate or exudate, and serous, serosanguineous, or even frankly bloody. We have even seen chylous effusions due to lymphatic obstruction from intrathoracic Kaposi's sarcoma.

Kaposi's sarcoma is ^{67}Ga scan negative. In contrast, opportunistic infections and non-Hodgkin's lymphoma are ^{67}Ga avid. Among HIV-associated pulmonary disease, this unique feature of Kaposi's sarcoma has created a niche for the use of ^{67}Ga scans. In the absence of either a bronchoscopic or tissue diagnosis of pulmonary Kaposi's sarcoma, its presence may be inferred by the finding of significant chest radiographic abnormalities and a negative ^{67}Ga scan.

Treatment. Treatment of pulmonary Kaposi's sarcoma has seen tremendous advancement. Earlier in the AIDS epidemic, treatment was controversial. Many patients found to have pulmonary Kaposi's sarcoma also had a concurrent opportunistic infection. In many of these patients, treatment of the infection resulted in resolution of the respiratory symptoms. Given the significant toxicities of Kaposi's sarcoma chemotherapy regimens, oncologists often reserved treatment for pulmonary Kaposi's sarcoma to those moderately to severely symptomatic patients without concurrent opportunistic infection.

With advances in treatment for Kaposi's sarcoma and for HIV infection itself, several possibilities currently exist for treating pulmonary disease. One option is to use a liposomal anthracycline, either doxorubicin or daunorubicin. These new agents, used singly, have surpassed the old regimen of combined doxorubicin, bleomycin, and vincristine (ABV) as first-line therapy. Paclitaxel (Taxol) has been used as second-line therapy for those patients with

refractory disease. Another option is to aggressively treat the HIV disease with combination antiretroviral therapy (HAART). We have seen a number of cases in which this approach has resulted in dramatic improvement or resolution of pulmonary symptoms and chest radiographic abnormalities. For selected patients, a stepwise approach of aggressive antiretroviral therapy, followed by chemotherapy against Kaposi's sarcoma if the patient fails to respond to antiretroviral therapy, may be reasonable.

Primary Prevention. The association between HHV8 and Kaposi's sarcoma suggests that prevention of HHV8 infection is critical in the prevention of Kaposi's sarcoma. Although debated, the three main routes of HHV8 transmission are believed to be oral, semen, and through blood by sharing infected needles.[36] Proper precautions to avoid or minimize HHV8 exposure through these routes should be recommended.

Non-Hodgkin's Lymphoma

Almost all HIV-associated non-Hodgkin's lymphomas are of B-cell origin. Most are classified as diffuse large cell (19% to 34%); small, noncleaved Burkitt's (20% to 40%); or immunoblastic (25% to 46%).[397-399] At the time of diagnosis, 58% to 82% of patients are classified as stage III or IV. The etiology of non-Hodgkin's lymphoma is unknown. Although Epstein-Barr virus has been implicated in the pathogenesis of the primary central nervous system lymphomas and is often present in the body cavity lymphomas, it is found in only a minority of HIV-associated non-Hodgkin's lymphomas.

Clinical Features. Most HIV-infected patients with non-Hodgkin's lymphoma present with widely disseminated disease and extranodal involvement.[400] Frequent extranodal sites include the liver, spleen, bone marrow, meninges, gastrointestinal tract, and pericardium. Intrathoracic involvement is seen in a smaller proportion. The reported incidence of intrathoracic disease varies from 0% to 31% of patients at the time of clinical diagnosis and is usually higher at the time of autopsy. Occasionally, the lung is the only site involved.

CD4+ Lymphocyte Count, Symptoms, and Signs. Non-Hodgkin's lymphoma can present at a wide range of CD4+ lymphocyte counts. The median CD4+ T-lymphocyte count is approximately 100 cells/μL, and 75% of patients have a CD4+ T-lymphocyte count above 50 cells/μL. In one study of 38 patients with non-Hodgkin's lymphoma, the mean (±SD) CD4+ count was 67 (±65) cells/μL.[401]

When the lungs are involved, the most common symptoms are cough and dyspnea, with chest pain and hemoptysis occurring in a minority. Eisner and colleagues[401] found that these respiratory symptoms were present in 71%, 63%, 26%, and 11%, respectively, of the 38 patients reported. Systemic symptoms such as fever, sweats, and weight loss are common. Physical examination of the chest may reveal a variety of findings, including crackles, rhonchi, wheezes, dullness to percussion, decreased breath sounds, and occasionally egophony.

Chest Radiograph. The most common chest radiograph parenchymal findings include single (Fig. 75.11) or

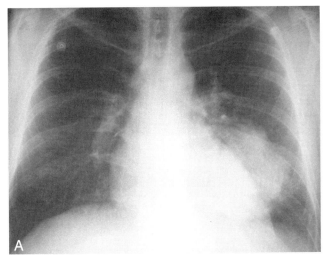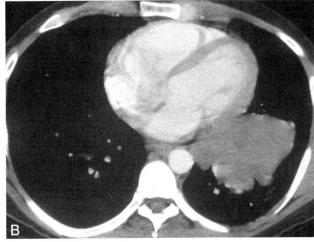

Figure 75.11 **A,** Frontal chest radiograph from an AIDS patient with non-Hodgkin's lymphoma showing a large left lower lobe mass. **B,** Axial computed tomogram shows a mass in the left lower lobe without an air bronchogram, suggestive of a neoplasm. (Courtesy of Michael B. Gotway, MD, Department of Radiology, University of California, San Francisco.)

multiple nodules, nodular opacities or masses, lobar infiltrates, and diffuse interstitial infiltrates.[401,402] More rarely, cases of endobronchial lesions have been reported.[403,404] Pleural effusions are the most common radiographic abnormality, occurring in 40% to 70% of cases.[401–405] Bilateral hilar and mediastinal adenopathy can be found in up to 60% of patients. However, it must be noted that isolated intrathoracic adenopathy without identifiable extrathoracic nodal involvement is a rare presentation for HIV-associated non-Hodgkin's lymphomas.[399]

Diagnosis. The diagnosis of non-Hodgkin's lymphoma requires demonstration of malignant lymphocytes on cytology or biopsy specimens. Most often the diagnosis is made by needle aspiration or biopsy of an extrathoracic site. Persons who present with isolated intrathoracic involvement should undergo bronchoscopy with Wang needle biopsy, if abnormal nodes are within reach through the bronchoscope, and with TBBX.[401] For lesions outside the sampling distance of the bronchoscope, fluoroscopic or CT-guided fine-needle aspiration should be considered. Other options include mediastinoscopy and open-lung biopsy. In all cases, the presence of a pathologist in the procedure room to immediately evaluate the adequacy of samples seems to improve the diagnostic yield. For patients with pleural effusions, pleural fluid cytology, biopsy, or both are often diagnostic.[375,377,398,401,405]

Treatment. Standard chemotherapy is usually CHOP or mBACOD, often with adjunctive colony-stimulating factors (granulocyte or granulocyte-macrophage).[406] Treatment of non-Hodgkin's lymphoma is frequently complicated by the development of opportunistic infections and by the presence of decreased bone marrow reserve, which results in a decreased chemotherapy dose intensity. Because of the frequency of death from opportunistic infection, specifically PCP, *Pneumocystis* prophylaxis is warranted in all cases, regardless of CD4+ T-lymphocyte count. In the HAART era, HIV-infected patients with non-Hodgkin's lymphoma have been treated with concurrent HAART with promising results.[407,408]

Primary Pleural Effusion Lymphoma. Primary pleural effusion lymphoma is a distinct subtype of non-Hodgkin's lymphoma that presents with isolated effusions in body cavities, including the pleura, pericardium, and peritoneum.[409] These lymphomatous effusions occur in the absence of a discrete nodal or extranodal mass. HIV-infected patients with primary pleural effusion lymphoma typically present with symptoms related to the space-occupying nature of the effusion (i.e., dyspnea). Diagnosis is established by pleural fluid histology. This entity is unique among HIV-associated lymphomas in that the malignant cells have no cell surface markers for B (or T) cells. Instead, common leukocyte antigen (CD45) alone is present. Interestingly, HHV8 has been found in all cases. Typically, chemotherapy regimens used for non-Hodgkin's lymphoma are used with variable results.

Bronchogenic Carcinoma

There is significant debate about whether other malignancies that involve the lung, namely, Hodgkin's disease[398,410,411] and especially bronchogenic carcinoma,[412–423] are also associated with HIV disease.

Epidemiology. In contrast to Kaposi's sarcoma and non-Hodgkin's lymphoma, there is no unequivocal increase in bronchogenic carcinoma in persons with non–HIV-associated immunosuppressive disorders. Nevertheless, there are a number of reports that suggest that bronchogenic carcinoma is increased in frequency, occurs at a younger age, and has a more aggressive course in HIV-infected patients. One study that cross-matched the HIV/AIDS and cancer registries in Texas found a 6.5-fold increased incidence of bronchogenic carcinoma in HIV/AIDS patients compared with the overall U.S. population.[419] The PCHIS found an observed rate of bronchogenic carcinoma of approximately 180 cases per 100,000 person-years in its HIV-infected cohort.[420] Other studies found no significant increase.[416] However, these studies were conducted in the pre-HAART era, and there is some concern that the incidence of bronchogenic cancer will increase as the population of HIV-infected patients lives longer (and continues to smoke).[422]

Clinical Features. Most HIV-infected patients who develop bronchogenic carcinoma are cigarette smokers. Although all pathologic types are seen, adenocarcinoma has been the most frequent type reported, similar to that seen in non–HIV-infected patients younger than 40 years of age who develop bronchogenic carcinoma. Bronchogenic carcinoma can develop at a wide range of CD4+ lymphocyte counts. In the PCHIS study, the range of CD4+ counts among the patients who developed lung cancer was 127 to 1026 cells/µL.[420] The characteristic presentation of bronchogenic carcinoma is familiar and includes respiratory symptoms such as cough, occasionally with hemoptysis, dyspnea, and chest pain. Constitutional symptoms such as fatigue and weight loss may also be present. The chest radiographic presentation appears to include parenchymal nodules or masses, pleural effusion, and central parenchymal or hilar masses and mediastinal adenopathy.[424–427] Chest CT scans provide additional important details.

Diagnosis and Treatment. The diagnosis and treatment of bronchogenic carcinoma in an HIV-infected patient is similar to that in a non–HIV-infected individual. HIV infection should be considered an important concurrent underlying medical problem, much the same as one would consider underlying cardiopulmonary disease. Surgical resection should be considered for any patient whose staging and medical condition support such an approach.[428] However, the prognosis is poor. The median survival in the reported cases has ranged from 1 to 6 months.

INTERSTITIAL PNEUMONITIDES

Although opportunistic infection and neoplasia dominate the clinical spectrum of HIV-associated pulmonary disease, a small number of patients present with signs and symptoms that are attributable to one of the interstitial pneumonitides, LIP or nonspecific interstitial pneumonitis (NSIP).

Lymphocytic Interstitial Pneumonitis

Although described by Carrington and Liebow over 30 years ago, it remains speculative whether LIP is a pathogenically distinct entity or whether it is a disorder of multiple causes that all produce a similar pathologic reaction. The facts that LIP occurs with increased frequency in HIV-infected persons (albeit rarely in adults) and is diagnostic of AIDS when it occurs in an HIV-infected child younger than 13 years of age favor the diverse-origin theory. Histologic abnormalities of LIP consist mainly of diffuse infiltration of the alveolar septa and peribronchiolar and perivascular interstitium by lymphocytes. Plasma cells and macrophages can also be seen.[429] An apparently related disorder, pulmonary lymphoid hyperplasia, has similar features, but the aggregates of lymphoid cells, with or without germinal centers, are more conspicuous and are located in peribronchovascular regions.[430]

Clinical Features. The most striking feature of HIV-associated LIP is the effect of age on its incidence. Earlier in the AIDS epidemic, one third to one half of AIDS-defining diagnoses in HIV-infected children were due to LIP. In contrast, LIP is rare in adults. We have encountered a handful of biopsy-proven LIP adult cases in our experience with several thousand AIDS patients at San Francisco General Hospital, and there are scattered case reports throughout the literature.[431–438]

The symptoms of LIP include slowly progressive dyspnea, nonproductive cough, and fever. Lung examination may be normal or may reveal inspiratory crackles. These clinical features are indistinguishable from those of opportunistic infection (e.g., PCP). In children, additional physical examination findings include clubbing, salivary gland enlargement, hepatosplenomegaly, and lymphadenopathy.

Chest Radiograph. The chest radiograph presentation of LIP is nonspecific and characteristically shows bilateral reticulonodular "interstitial" infiltrates with a middle to lower lung zone predominance (Fig. 75.12).[439] Areas of alveolar opacity believed to result from bronchial compression caused by more severe lymphocytic infiltration have been reported rarely.[440] Hilar or mediastinal adenopathy is occasionally seen. Pulmonary function tests often reveal a restrictive ventilatory defect and a decreased diffusing capacity. Chest CT scans may reveal small (2- to 4-mm) nodules, often in a peribronchovascular distribution, or diffuse areas of ground-glass opacity.[441,442] Gallium scintigraphy may detect diffuse pulmonary uptake, indistinguishable from PCP, although all patterns have been described.[440]

Diagnosis. The diagnosis of LIP requires histologic confirmation by biopsy.[443,444]

Treatment. There are so few cases of LIP among HIV-infected adults that neither definitive therapy nor benefit of therapy has been determined. The clinical course of LIP in adults ranges from mild disease with spontaneous resolution to progressive disease and respiratory failure. A few case

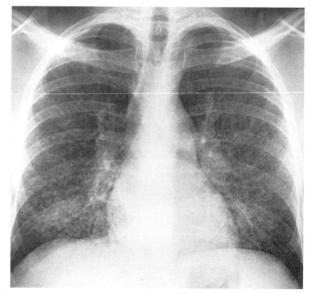

Figure 75.12 Posteroanterior chest radiograph of an HIV-seropositive patient showing diffuse reticulonodular infiltration. Biopsy specimen revealed lymphocytic interstitial pneumonitis, a rare disorder in HIV-infected adults that is more frequently seen in HIV-infected children.

reports of LIP that responded to antiretroviral therapy alone have been reported.[435,436,438]

Nonspecific Interstitial Pneumonitis

NSIP is a pulmonary disorder characterized histologically by the infiltration of mononuclear cells, predominantly lymphocytes and plasma cells, into the peribronchiolar and perivascular interstitium. In contrast to LIP, the alveolar septa are less frequently involved.[429] NSIP has been reported with various frequencies in HIV-infected patients. Because it is a histologic diagnosis, its incidence depends on the frequency with which biopsy is performed during the diagnostic evaluation.

Clinical Features. The symptoms of NSIP include dyspnea, nonproductive cough, and fever.[445-448] Lung examination may be normal. These clinical features are indistinguishable from those of PCP. However, NSIP may present at $CD4^+$ lymphocyte counts above 200 cells/μL, whereas PCP rarely (≤5%) does.[447,448] In one large series of 67 HIV-infected patients with NSIP, the mean $CD4^+$ lymphocyte count in the patients with NSIP was 492 cells/μL compared with 57 cells/μL for the matched control subjects with PCP.[448]

Chest Radiograph. The chest radiographic presentation of NSIP is nonspecific and usually indistinguishable from that of PCP. As with PCP, NSIP can present with a normal radiograph. One study of patients with NSIP found that 16 of 36 (44%) had a normal radiograph.[449] The most common radiographic abnormality seen was a diffuse interstitial pattern. Other abnormalities include pleural effusions, alveolar infiltrates, and nodules.[440,449] Pulmonary function tests often reveal a mildly decreased diffusing capacity.[446]

Diagnosis. The diagnosis of NSIP requires both histologic confirmation and the exclusion of other etiologies.[450]

Treatment. The natural history of HIV-associated NSIP is poorly understood, but it usually resolves or stabilizes without therapy.[447,448] Observation is all that is required, with the proviso that, if the patient becomes severely ill, repeat bronchoscopy and biopsy are indicated to look for a different, usually infectious, disorder.

OTHER DISORDERS

A variety of other noninfectious and nonmalignant lung diseases have been associated with HIV infection. In many instances, though, the linkage is uncertain.

Obstructive Lung Disease

Obstructive lung disease occurs frequently in HIV-infected patients, and a variety of pulmonary function test abnormalities can be seen. The PCHIS researchers performed serial pulmonary function tests in their more than 1100 HIV-infected subjects and demonstrated that advanced HIV infection, characterized by a $CD4^+$ lymphocyte count less than 200 cells/μL or HIV-associated symptoms, as well as race, cigarette smoking, and injection drug use, are all associated with reductions in diffusing capacity.[451] A PCHIS multivariate analysis found that both PCP and bacterial pneumonia were independently associated with an accelerated decline in the forced vital capacity, FEV_1, FEV_1/FVC, and DL_{CO}.[108] Studies have found that significant proportions of HIV-infected subjects self-report wheezing within the past 12 months[452] and have evidence of airflow obstruction.[453] In this later study, 33 of 99 persons with AIDS had decreased forced expiratory flow rates; 20 of the 33 (61%) experienced a significant response to inhaled bronchodilators.

HIV-infected patients may have asthma that precedes their HIV infection.[67] In one clinic-based study, a history of asthma was reported in 21% and current asthma in 17% of 136 patients attending a primary care clinic for HIV infection.[454] On questioning, 61% of the current asthmatic patients reported subjective worsening of their asthma after becoming HIV infected. Whether this worsening was secondary to an increase in upper respiratory tract illnesses, or acute bronchitis resulting from HIV infection or HIV itself played an etiologic role is unclear. HIV-infected patients are more likely than non–HIV-infected patients to have bronchial hyperresponsiveness to methacholine. In one study, a significantly greater proportion of HIV-infected smokers had a 20% or greater decrease in their FEV_1 at a cumulative dose of methacholine of 2 mg or less compared to non–HIV-infected control subjects.[452]

Obstructive airway disease, chronic bronchitis, and bronchiectasis are all well-recognized sequelae of opportunistic infection.[455-458] Evidence is emerging that suggests that HIV infection is associated with an increase in emphysema. Diaz and coworkers[459] reported four patients without antecedent pneumonia or opportunistic infection who presented with progressive dyspnea. Chest radiographs showed no infiltrations, and pulmonary function tests revealed increased functional residual capacity and residual volumes and decreased diffusing capacity suggestive of emphysema. However, only minimal airflow obstruction was noted. Chest HRCT scans revealed emphysema-like bullous changes even though known causes of emphysema were absent in these patients. Subsequently, Diaz and coworkers[460] examined HIV-infected persons with unexplained decreases in diffusing capacity by chest HRCT and by separation of the diffusing capacity into its membrane and capillary blood vessel components. The authors found HRCT evidence of early emphysema that correlated well with values of both diffusing capacity and its capillary blood vessel subdivision. In another study, HIV-infected subjects were compared to non-HIV infected control subjects matched for age and smoking history.[461] The authors found that the incidence of emphysema was significantly higher in the HIV-seropositive subjects (15%) compared to the HIV-seronegative subjects (2%, $P = 0.025$). The incidence of emphysema in subjects who had a smoking history of 12 pack-years or greater was also significantly higher in the HIV-seropositive group (37%) compared to the HIV-seronegative group (0%, $P = 0.011$). The percentage of cytotoxic lymphocytes in BAL fluid was much higher in HIV-seropositive smokers with emphysema. Increased oxidant stress may contribute to emphysema in HIV-infected patients.[461a]

Pulmonary Hypertension

Numerous reports of primary pulmonary hypertension (PPH) in HIV-infected patients are scattered in the literature.[462,462a,462b] One series compared 20 HIV-infected patients with PPH to 93 non–HIV-infected patients with PPH.[463] At PPH diagnosis, the HIV-infected patients were significantly younger and the proportion with New York Heart Association functional class III or IV was significantly lower (50% vs. 75%, $P < 0.01$). Pulmonary hypertension was thought to be the cause of death in 8 of the 10 HIV-infected patients who died within 1 year after the diagnosis of PPH. Pathologic findings resembled those of plexogenic pulmonary arteriopathy. In a review of the 131 cases of pulmonary hypertension in HIV-infected patients reported up to that time, 82% were thought to be due to HIV infection alone.[462] Presenting symptoms included progressive dyspnea (85%), pedal edema (30%), nonproductive cough (19%), fatigue (13%), syncope or near syncope (12%), and chest pain (7%). Chest radiographs demonstrated cardiomegaly (72%) and prominence of the pulmonary arteries (71%). Pulmonary function tests revealed mild restrictive patterns with a decreased DL_{CO}. Electrocardiograms frequently demonstrated right ventricular hypertrophy (67%), and echocardiograms invariably revealed dilation of the right heart chambers (98%). Plexogenic pulmonary arteriopathy was the most common histopathologic abnormality (78%). In a series from the HAART era, 82 HIV-infected patients with pulmonary hypertension were reported.[464] Subjects in New York Heart Association functional class III or IV at the time of diagnosis had a 1-, 2-, and 3-year survival of 60%, 45%, and 28%, respectively. In univariate analysis, CD4+ lymphocyte count, the use of HAART, and the use of epoprostenol infusion were associated with an improved survival.

Pulmonary Alveolar Hemorrhage

Pulmonary alveolar hemorrhage is a frequent finding on bronchoscopy.[465] In one study of 243 consecutive HIV-infected patients undergoing a total of 273 bronchoscopies, alveolar hemorrhage (assessed using the Golde score) was seen in 32%. Only one patient reported hemoptysis, supporting the conclusion that alveolar hemorrhage is usually mild and clinically silent. As expected, patients with alveolar hemorrhage were more likely to have platelet counts below 60,000 cells/μL, an activated partial thromboplastin time greater than 1.5, and renal dysfunction. Importantly, alveolar hemorrhage was observed in subjects with invasive aspergillosis (2 of 2, or 100%), CMV pneumonia (5 of 6, or 83%), and pulmonary Kaposi's sarcoma (15 of 20, or 75%).

Pulmonary Alveolar Proteinosis

Two cases of "secondary pulmonary alveolar proteinosis" have been reported.[466] Both patients had HIV-associated opportunistic infections. When they failed to improve, histologic examination revealed extensive intra-alveolar deposits of a lipoproteinaceous material that stained strongly with periodic acid–Schiff. The authors speculated that the alveolar proteinosis was secondary to opportunistic infection, as has been reported in non–HIV-infected persons. Another report demonstrated that both light and ultrastructural examinations of BAL fluid from 9 of 26 patients with PCP showed lipoproteinaceous material highly suggestive of that described in pulmonary alveolar proteinosis.[467] In comparison, none of the BAL fluid samples from 11 patients without PCP had these findings.

Diffuse Alveolar Damage and Interstitial Fibrosis

Diffuse alveolar damage is a nonspecific pattern of response resulting from acute injury to the alveolar epithelium and endothelium; in contrast, interstitial fibrosis may result from chronic injury. Given the potential severity of HIV-associated opportunistic infections (e.g., PCP) and their tendency to recur, pathologic findings of diffuse alveolar damage and interstitial fibrosis can be expected.[443,468,469]

Bronchiolitis Obliterans with Organizing Pneumonia

Bronchiolitis obliterans with organizing pneumonia has been reported in a handful of HIV-infected patients.[470-473] The clinical and radiographic presentation, diagnosis, and clinical course with corticosteroid therapy were similar to those of bronchiolitis obliterans with organizing pneumonia in non–HIV-infected persons.

Sarcoidosis

Sarcoidosis is one of the last disorders that one might expect to find among the pulmonary complications of HIV infection. In many respects, the coexistence of these two diseases is seemingly incompatible: Sarcoidosis is characterized by granuloma formation, which HIV infection inhibits; moreover, sarcoid-induced alveolitis consists predominantly of CD4+ lymphocytes, whereas HIV-associated lymphocytic alveolitis consists chiefly of CD8+ lymphocytes.[474] Nevertheless, several cases of sarcoidosis in HIV-infected patients have been reported.[475-478] Many of these cases have been reported during the HAART era and have correlated the use of HAART with the development of sarcoidosis.[479-484] In these cases, clinical improvement was noted with corticosteroid therapy.

Antiretroviral Therapy–Associated Pulmonary Disease

As more HIV-infected persons are treated with potent combinations of antiretroviral therapies with resultant improvement in immune function, it is quite possible that more cases of pulmonary disease will occur in which the invigorated immune system plays an important pathogenetic role.[484a] Several cases of a sarcoid-like pulmonary disorder have been reported in persons treated with antiretroviral therapy in whom BAL analysis revealed an intense CD4+ alveolitis and histopathology demonstrated noncaseating granulomas.[485] In addition, we have seen a striking case of acute hypersensitivity pneumonitis (to avian antigen) in a patient who only developed symptoms after she experienced a dramatic increase in her CD4+ lymphocyte count as a result of potent antiretroviral therapy.[486] In this case, removal of the birds resulted in resolution of her symptoms and radiographic abnormalities.

SUMMARY

The lungs are one of the chief target organs of HIV disease. This chapter reviews the current epidemiology of HIV/AIDS both in the United States and worldwide, contrasting the two. An overview of the immunologic abnormalities seen in HIV disease as well as an approach to the evaluation of HIV infection and HIV-associated pulmonary disease is provided. Finally, the chapter discusses the major infectious and noninfectious pulmonary complications of HIV infection, with an emphasis on their clinical features, diagnosis, treatment, and prevention.

REFERENCES

1. Gottlieb MS, Schroff R, Schanker HM, et al: *Pneumocystis carinii* pneumonia and mucosal candidiasis in previously healthy homosexual men: Evidence of a new acquired cellular immunodeficiency. N Engl J Med 305:1425–1431, 1981.
2. Masur H, Michelis MA, Greene JB, et al: An outbreak of community-acquired *Pneumocystis carinii* pneumonia: Initial manifestation of cellular immune dysfunction. N Engl J Med 305:1431–1438, 1981.
3. Barre-Sinoussi F, Chermann JC, Rey F, et al: Isolation of a T-lymphotropic retrovirus from a patient at risk for acquired immune deficiency syndrome (AIDS). Science 220:868–871, 1983.
4. Popovic M, Sarngadharan MG, Read E, et al: Detection, isolation, and continuous production of cytopathic retroviruses (HTLV-III) from patients with AIDS and pre-AIDS. Science 224:497–500, 1984.
5. Gurgo C, Guo HG, Franchini G, et al: Envelope sequences of two new United States HIV-1 isolates. Virology 164:531–536, 1988.
6. Barin F, M'Boup S, Denis F, et al: Serological evidence for virus related to simian T-lymphotropic retrovirus III in residents of West Africa. Lancet 2:1387–1389, 1985.
7. Barin F, Denis F, Baillou A, et al: A STLV-III related human retrovirus, HTLV-IV: Analysis of cross-reactivity with the human immunodeficiency virus (HIV). J Virol Methods 17:55–61, 1987.
8. Palella FJ Jr, Delaney KM, Moorman AC, et al: Declining morbidity and mortality among patients with advanced human immunodeficiency virus infection. HIV Outpatient Study Investigators. N Engl J Med 338:853–860, 1998.
9. White DA, Matthay RA: Noninfectious pulmonary complications of infection with the human immunodeficiency virus. Am Rev Respir Dis 140:1763–1787, 1989.
10. Murray JF, Mills J: Pulmonary infectious complications of human immunodeficiency virus infection. Part I. Am Rev Respir Dis 141:1356–1372, 1990.
11. Murray JF, Mills J: Pulmonary infectious complications of human immunodeficiency virus infection. Part II. Am Rev Respir Dis 141:1582–1598, 1990.
12. Centers for Disease Control and Prevention: Cases of HIV infection and AIDS in the United States, 2002. HIV/AIDS Surveill Rep 14:1–48, 2002.
13. Centers for Disease Control and Prevention: HIV/AIDS Surveillance Report 8:1–39, 1996.
14. Connor EM, Mofenson LM: Zidovudine for the reduction of perinatal human immunodeficiency virus transmission: Pediatric AIDS Clinical Trials Group Protocol 076—results and treatment recommendations. Pediatr Infect Dis J 14:536–541, 1995.
15. UNAIDS and World Health Organization: Report on the Global HIV/AIDS Epidemic. Geneva: World Health Organization, 2003.
16. Edelman AS, Zolla-Pazner S: AIDS: A syndrome of immune dysregulation, dysfunction, and deficiency. FASEB J 3:22–30, 1989.
17. Beck JM, Shellito J: Effects of human immunodeficiency virus on pulmonary host defenses. Semin Respir Infect 4:75–84, 1989.
18. Agostini C, Semenzato G: Immunologic effects of HIV in the lung. Clin Chest Med 17:633–645, 1996.
19. Shirai A, Cosentino M, Leitman-Klinman SF, et al: Human immunodeficiency virus infection induces both polyclonal and virus-specific B cell activation. J Clin Invest 89:561–566, 1992.
20. Rich JD, Merriman NA, Mylonakis E, et al: Misdiagnosis of HIV infection by HIV-1 plasma viral load testing: A case series. Ann Intern Med 130:37–39, 1999.
21. Havlichek DH Jr, Hage-Korban E: False-positive HIV diagnosis by HIV-1 plasma viral load testing. Ann Intern Med 131:794, 1999.
22. Hanson DL, Chu SY, Farizo KM, et al: Distribution of CD4$^+$ T lymphocytes at diagnosis of acquired immunodeficiency syndrome-defining and other human immunodeficiency virus-related illnesses. The Adult and Adolescent Spectrum of HIV Disease Project Group. Arch Intern Med 155:1537–1542, 1995.
23. O'Brien WA, Hartigan PM, Martin D, et al: Changes in plasma HIV-1 RNA and CD4$^+$ lymphocyte counts and the risk of progression to AIDS. Veterans Affairs Cooperative Study Group on AIDS. N Engl J Med 334:426–431, 1996.
24. Mellors JW, Munoz A, Giorgi JV, et al: Plasma viral load and CD4$^+$ lymphocytes as prognostic markers of HIV-1 infection. Ann Intern Med 126:946–954, 1997.
25. Vlahov D, Graham N, Hoover D, et al: Prognostic indicators for AIDS and infectious disease death in HIV-infected injection drug users: Plasma viral load and CD4$^+$ cell count. JAMA 279:35–40, 1998.
26. Kaplan JE, Hanson DL, Jones JL, et al: Viral load as an independent risk factor for opportunistic infections in HIV-infected adults and adolescents. AIDS 15:1831–1836, 2001.
27. Swindells S, Evans S, Zackin R, et al: Predictive value of HIV-1 viral load on risk for opportunistic infection. J Acquir Immune Defic Syndr 30:154–158, 2002.
28. Sepkowitz KA: Opportunistic infections in patients with and patients without acquired immunodeficiency syndrome. Clin Infect Dis 34:1098–1107, 2002.
29. Kaplan JE, Hanson D, Dworkin MS, et al: Epidemiology of human immunodeficiency virus-associated opportunistic infections in the United States in the era of highly active antiretroviral therapy. Clin Infect Dis 30(Suppl 1):S5–S14, 2000.
30. Mocroft A, Katlama C, Johnson AM, et al: AIDS across Europe, 1994–98: The EuroSIDA study. Lancet 356:291–296, 2000.
31. Serraino D, Puro V, Boumis E, et al: Epidemiological aspects of major opportunistic infections of the respiratory tract in persons with AIDS: Europe, 1993–2000. AIDS 17:2109–2116, 2003.
32. The Pulmonary Complications of HIV Study Group: Design of a prospective study of the pulmonary complications of human immunodeficiency virus infection. J Clin Epidemiol 46:497–507, 1993.
33. Wallace JM, Hansen NI, Lavange L, et al: Respiratory disease trends in the Pulmonary Complications of HIV Infection Study cohort. Pulmonary Complications of HIV Infection Study Group. Am J Respir Crit Care Med 155:72–80, 1997.
34. Rosen MJ, Clayton K, Schneider RF, et al: Intensive care of patients with HIV infection: Utilization, critical illnesses, and outcomes. Pulmonary Complications of HIV Infection Study Group. Am J Respir Crit Care Med 155:67–71, 1997.

35. Morris A, Creasman J, Turner J, et al: Intensive care of human immunodeficiency virus-infected patients during the era of highly active antiretroviral therapy. Am J Respir Crit Care Med 166:262–267, 2002.

35a. Morris A, Huang L: Intensive care of patients with HIV infection: HAART warming improvement but beware of future HAART (and heart) attacks. Chest 125:1602–1604, 2004.

35b. Narasimhan M, Posner AJ, DePalo VA, et al: Intensive care in patients with HIV infection in the era of highly active antiretroviral therapy. Chest 125:1800–1804, 2004.

36. Kaplan JE, Masur H, Holmes KK: Guidelines for preventing opportunistic infections among HIV-infected persons—2002: Recommendations of the U.S. Public Health Service and the Infectious Diseases Society of America. MMWR Recomm Rep 51(RR-8):1–52, 2002.

37. Furrer H, Egger M, Opravil M, et al: Discontinuation of primary prophylaxis against Pneumocystis carinii pneumonia in HIV-1-infected adults treated with combination antiretroviral therapy. Swiss HIV Cohort Study. N Engl J Med 340:1301–1306, 1999.

38. Schneider MM, Borleffs JC, Stolk RP, et al: Discontinuation of prophylaxis for Pneumocystis carinii pneumonia in HIV-1-infected patients treated with highly active antiretroviral therapy. Lancet 353:201–203, 1999.

39. Weverling GJ, Mocroft A, Ledergerber B, et al: Discontinuation of Pneumocystis carinii pneumonia prophylaxis after start of highly active antiretroviral therapy in HIV-1 infection. EuroSIDA Study Group. Lancet 353:1293–1298, 1999.

40. Kirk O, Lundgren JD, Pedersen C, et al: Can chemoprophylaxis against opportunistic infections be discontinued after an increase in CD4 cells induced by highly active antiretroviral therapy? AIDS 13:1647–1651, 1999.

41. Yangco BG, Von Bargen JC, Moorman AC, et al: Discontinuation of chemoprophylaxis against Pneumocystis carinii pneumonia in patients with HIV infection. HIV Outpatient Study (HOPS) Investigators. Ann Intern Med 132:201–205, 2000.

42. Mussini C, Pezzotti P, Govoni A, et al: Discontinuation of primary prophylaxis for Pneumocystis carinii pneumonia and toxoplasmic encephalitis in human immunodeficiency virus type I-infected patients: The Changes in Opportunistic Prophylaxis study. J Infect Dis 181:1635–1642, 2000.

43. Dworkin MS, Hanson DL, Kaplan JE, et al: Risk for preventable opportunistic infections in persons with AIDS after antiretroviral therapy increases CD4+ T lymphocyte counts above prophylaxis thresholds. J Infect Dis 182:611–615, 2000.

44. Soriano V, Dona C, Rodriguez-Rosado R, et al: Discontinuation of secondary prophylaxis for opportunistic infections in HIV-infected patients receiving highly active antiretroviral therapy. AIDS 14:383–386, 2000.

45. Lopez Bernaldo de Quiros JC, Miro JM, Pena JM, et al: A randomized trial of the discontinuation of primary and secondary prophylaxis against Pneumocystis carinii pneumonia after highly active antiretroviral therapy in patients with HIV infection. Grupo de Estudio del SIDA 04/98. N Engl J Med 344:159–167, 2001.

46. Ledergerber B, Mocroft A, Reiss P, et al: Discontinuation of secondary prophylaxis against Pneumocystis carinii pneumonia in patients with HIV infection who have a response to antiretroviral therapy. Eight European Study Groups. N Engl J Med 344:168–174, 2001.

47. Furrer H, Opravil M, Rossi M, et al: Discontinuation of primary prophylaxis in HIV-infected patients at high risk of Pneumocystis carinii pneumonia: Prospective multicentre study. AIDS 15:501–507, 2001.

48. Koletar SL, Heald AE, Finkelstein D, et al: A prospective study of discontinuing primary and secondary Pneumocystis carinii pneumonia prophylaxis after CD4 cell count increase to >200 × 106/L. AIDS 15:1509–1515, 2001.

49. Mussini C, Pezzotti P, Antinori A, et al: Discontinuation of secondary prophylaxis for Pneumocystis carinii pneumonia in human immunodeficiency virus-infected patients: A randomized trial by the CIOP Study Group. Clin Infect Dis 36:645–651, 2003.

49a. Zellweger C, Opravil M, Bernasconi E, et al: Long-term safety of discontinuation of secondary prophylaxis against Pneumocystis pneumonia: prospective multicentre study. AIDS 18:2047–2053, 2004.

50. Aberg JA, Yajko DM, Jacobson MA: Eradication of AIDS-related disseminated Mycobacterium avium complex infection after 12 months of antimycobacterial therapy combined with highly active antiretroviral therapy. J Infect Dis 178:1446–1449, 1998.

51. El-Sadr WM, Burman WJ, Grant LB, et al: Discontinuation of prophylaxis for Mycobacterium avium complex disease in HIV-infected patients who have a response to antiretroviral therapy. Terry Beirn Community Programs for Clinical Research on AIDS. N Engl J Med 342:1085–1092, 2000.

52. Currier JS, Williams PL, Koletar SL, et al: Discontinuation of Mycobacterium avium complex prophylaxis in patients with antiretroviral therapy-induced increases in CD4+ cell count: A randomized, double-blind, placebo-controlled trial. AIDS Clinical Trials Group 362 Study Team. Ann Intern Med 133:493–503, 2000.

53. Furrer H, Telenti A, Rossi M, et al: Discontinuing or withholding primary prophylaxis against Mycobacterium avium in patients on successful antiretroviral combination therapy. The Swiss HIV Cohort Study. AIDS 14:1409–1412, 2000.

54. Kirk O, Reiss P, Uberti-Foppa C, et al: Safe interruption of maintenance therapy against previous infection with four common HIV-associated opportunistic pathogens during potent antiretroviral therapy. Ann Intern Med 137:239–250, 2002.

55. Shafran SD, Mashinter LD, Phillips P, et al: Successful discontinuation of therapy for disseminated Mycobacterium avium complex infection after effective antiretroviral therapy. Ann Intern Med 137:734–737, 2002.

56. Aberg JA, Williams PL, Liu T, et al: A study of discontinuing maintenance therapy in human immunodeficiency virus-infected subjects with disseminated Mycobacterium avium complex. AIDS Clinical Trial Group 393 Study Team. J Infect Dis 187:1046–1052, 2003.

57. Martinez E, Garcia-Viejo MA, Marcos MA, et al: Discontinuation of secondary prophylaxis for cryptococcal meningitis in HIV-infected patients responding to highly active antiretroviral therapy. AIDS 14:2615–2617, 2000.

58. Aberg JA, Price RW, Heeren DM, et al: A pilot study of the discontinuation of antifungal therapy for disseminated cryptococcal disease in patients with acquired immunodeficiency syndrome, following immunologic response to antiretroviral therapy. J Infect Dis 185:1179–1182, 2002.

59. Vibhagool A, Sungkanuparph S, Mootsikapun P, et al: Discontinuation of secondary prophylaxis for cryptococcal meningitis in human immunodeficiency virus-infected patients treated with highly active antiretroviral therapy: A prospective, multicenter, randomized study. Clin Infect Dis 36:1329–1331, 2003.

60. Mussini C, Pezzotti P, Miro JM, et al: Discontinuation of maintenance therapy for cryptococcal meningitis in patients

with AIDS treated with highly active antiretroviral therapy: An international observational study. Clin Infect Dis 38:565–571, 2004.

61. Furrer H, Opravil M, Bernasconi E, et al: Stopping primary prophylaxis in HIV-1-infected patients at high risk of toxoplasma encephalitis. Swiss HIV Cohort Study. Lancet 355:2217–2218, 2000.

62. Guex AC, Radziwill AJ, Bucher HC: Discontinuation of secondary prophylaxis for toxoplasmic encephalitis in human immunodeficiency virus infection after immune restoration with highly active antiretroviral therapy. Clin Infect Dis 30:602–603, 2000.

63. Diaz PT, Wewers MD, Pacht E, et al: Respiratory symptoms among HIV-seropositive individuals. Chest 123:1977–1982, 2003.

64. Hirschtick RE, Glassroth J, Jordan MC, et al: Bacterial pneumonia in persons infected with the human immunodeficiency virus. Pulmonary Complications of HIV Infection Study Group. N Engl J Med 333:845–851, 1995.

65. Selwyn PA, Pumerantz AS, Durante A, et al: Clinical predictors of *Pneumocystis carinii* pneumonia, bacterial pneumonia and tuberculosis in HIV-infected patients. AIDS 12:885–893, 1998.

66. O'Donnell AE, Selig J, Aravamuthan M, et al: Pulmonary complications associated with illicit drug use. An update. Chest 108:460–463, 1995.

67. Huang L, Stansell JD: AIDS and the lung. Med Clin North Am 80:775–801, 1996.

67a. Jordano Q, Falco V, Almirante B, et al: Invasive pneumococcal disease in patients infected with HIV: still a threat in the era of highly active antiretroviral therapy. Clin Infect Dis 38:1623–1628, 2004.

68. Markowitz N, Hansen NI, Hopewell PC, et al: Incidence of tuberculosis in the United States among HIV-infected persons. The Pulmonary Complications of HIV Infection Study Group. Ann Intern Med 126:123–132, 1997.

69. Dohn MN, White ML, Vigdorth EM, et al: Geographic clustering of *Pneumocystis carinii* pneumonia in patients with HIV infection. Am J Respir Crit Care Med 162:1617–1621, 2000.

70. Morris AM, Swanson M, Ha H, et al: Geographic distribution of human immunodeficiency virus-associated *Pneumocystis carinii* pneumonia in San Francisco. Am J Respir Crit Care Med 162:1622–1626, 2000.

71. Huang L, Schnapp LM, Gruden JF, et al: Presentation of AIDS-related pulmonary Kaposi's sarcoma diagnosed by bronchoscopy. Am J Respir Crit Care Med 153:1385–1390, 1996.

72. Butt AA, Michaels S, Kissinger P: The association of serum lactate dehydrogenase level with selected opportunistic infections and HIV progression. Int J Infect Dis 6:178–181, 2002.

73. Schneider RF, Hansen NI, Rosen MJ, et al: Lack of usefulness of radiographic screening for pulmonary disease in asymptomatic HIV-infected adults. Pulmonary Complications of HIV Infection Study Group. Arch Intern Med 156:191–195, 1996.

74. Gold JA, Rom WN, Harkin TJ: Significance of abnormal chest radiograph findings in patients with HIV-1 infection without respiratory symptoms. Chest 121:1472–1477, 2002.

75. Huang L, Stansell J, Osmond D, et al: Performance of an algorithm to detect *Pneumocystis carinii* pneumonia in symptomatic HIV-infected persons. Pulmonary Complications of HIV Infection Study Group. Chest 115:1025–1032, 1999.

76. Kvale PA, Rosen MJ, Hopewell PC, et al: A decline in the pulmonary diffusing capacity does not indicate opportunistic lung disease in asymptomatic persons infected with the human immunodeficiency virus. Pulmonary Complications of HIV Infection Study Group. Am Rev Respir Dis 148:390–395, 1993.

77. Naidich DP, McGuinness G: Pulmonary manifestations of AIDS: CT and radiographic correlations. Radiol Clin North Am 29:999–1017, 1991.

78. Hartman TE, Primack SL, Muller NL, et al: Diagnosis of thoracic complications in AIDS: Accuracy of CT. AJR Am J Roentgenol 162:547–553, 1994.

79. Edinburgh KJ, Jasmer RM, Huang L, et al: Multiple pulmonary nodules in AIDS: Usefulness of CT in distinguishing among potential causes. Radiology 214:427–432, 2000.

80. Jasmer RM, Edinburgh KJ, Thompson A, et al: Clinical and radiographic predictors of the etiology of pulmonary nodules in HIV-infected patients. Chest 117:1023–1030, 2000.

81. Jasmer RM, Gotway MB, Creasman JM, et al: Clinical and radiographic predictors of the etiology of computed tomography-diagnosed intrathoracic lymphadenopathy in HIV-infected patients. J Acquir Immune Defic Syndr Hum Retrovirol 31:291–298, 2002.

82. Kirshenbaum KJ, Burke R, Fanapour F, et al: Pulmonary high-resolution computed tomography versus gallium scintigraphy: Diagnostic utility in the diagnosis of patients with AIDS who have chest symptoms and normal or equivocal chest radiographs. J Thorac Imaging 13:52–57, 1998.

83. Broaddus C, Dake MD, Stulbarg MS, et al: Bronchoalveolar lavage and transbronchial biopsy for the diagnosis of pulmonary infections in the acquired immunodeficiency syndrome. Ann Intern Med 102:747–752, 1985.

84. Golden JA, Hollander H, Stulbarg MS, et al: Bronchoalveolar lavage as the exclusive diagnostic modality for *Pneumocystis carinii* pneumonia: A prospective study among patients with acquired immunodeficiency syndrome. Chest 90:18–22, 1986.

85. Cordero E, Pachon J, Rivero A, et al: Usefulness of sputum culture for diagnosis of bacterial pneumonia in HIV-infected patients. Eur J Clin Microbiol Infect Dis 21:362–367, 2002.

86. Ng VL, Gartner I, Weymouth LA, et al: The use of mucolysed induced sputum for the identification of pulmonary pathogens associated with human immunodeficiency virus infection. Arch Pathol Lab Med 113:488–493, 1989.

87. Huang L, Hecht FM, Stansell JD, et al: Suspected *Pneumocystis carinii* pneumonia with a negative induced sputum examination: Is early bronchoscopy useful? Am J Respir Crit Care Med 151:1866–1871, 1995.

88. Havlir DV, Barnes PF: Tuberculosis in patients with human immunodeficiency virus infection. N Engl J Med 340:367–373, 1999.

89. Barnes PF, Lakey DL, Burman WJ: Tuberculosis in patients with HIV infection. Infect Dis Clin North Am 16:107–126, 2002.

90. Theuer CP, Hopewell PC, Elias D, et al: Human immunodeficiency virus infection in tuberculosis patients. J Infect Dis 162:8–12, 1990.

91. Greenberg SD, Frager D, Suster B, et al: Active pulmonary tuberculosis in patients with AIDS: Spectrum of radiographic findings (including a normal appearance). Radiology 193:115–119, 1994.

92. Smith RL, Yew K, Berkowitz KA, et al: Factors affecting the yield of acid-fast sputum smears in patients with HIV and tuberculosis. Chest 106:684–686, 1994.

93. Finch D, Beaty CD: The utility of a single sputum specimen in the diagnosis of tuberculosis: Comparison between HIV-infected and non-HIV-infected patients. Chest 111:1174–1179, 1997.

94. Conde MB, Soares SL, Mello FC, et al: Comparison of sputum induction with fiberoptic bronchoscopy in the diagnosis of tuberculosis: Experience at an acquired immune deficiency syndrome reference center in Rio de Janeiro, Brazil. Am J Respir Crit Care Med 162:2238–2240, 2000.

95. Pitchenik AE, Burr J, Suarez M, et al: Human T-cell lymphotropic virus-III (HTLV-III) seropositivity and related disease among 71 consecutive patients in whom tuberculosis was diagnosed: A prospective study. Am Rev Respir Dis 135:875–879, 1987.

96. Klein NC, Duncanson FP, Lenox TH 3rd, et al: Use of mycobacterial smears in the diagnosis of pulmonary tuberculosis in AIDS/ARC patients. Chest 95:1190–1192, 1989.

97. Bruchfeld J, Aderaye G, Palme IB, et al: Sputum concentration improves diagnosis of tuberculosis in a setting with a high prevalence of HIV. Trans R Soc Trop Med Hyg 94:677–680, 2000.

98. Bruchfeld J, Aderaye G, Palme IB, et al: Evaluation of outpatients with suspected pulmonary tuberculosis in a high HIV prevalence setting in Ethiopia: Clinical, diagnostic and epidemiological characteristics. Scand J Infect Dis 34:331–337, 2002.

99. Scott WW Jr, Kuhlman JE: Focal pulmonary lesions in patients with AIDS: Percutaneous transthoracic needle biopsy. Radiology 180:419–421, 1991.

100. Gruden JF, Klein JS, Webb WR: Percutaneous transthoracic needle biopsy in AIDS: Analysis in 32 patients. Radiology 189:567–571, 1993.

101. Falguera M, Nogues A, Ruiz-Gonzalez A, et al: Transthoracic needle aspiration in the study of pulmonary infections in patients with HIV. Chest 106:697–702, 1994.

102. Pass HI, Potter D, Shelhammer J, et al: Indications for and diagnostic efficacy of open-lung biopsy in the patient with acquired immunodeficiency syndrome (AIDS). Ann Thorac Surg 41:307–312, 1986.

103. Fitzgerald W, Bevelaqua FA, Garay SM, et al: The role of open lung biopsy in patients with the acquired immunodeficiency syndrome. Chest 91:659–661, 1987.

104. LoCicero J 3rd: Does every patient with enigmatic lung disease deserve a lung biopsy? The continuing dilemma. Chest 106:706–708, 1994.

105. Murray JF, Felton CP, Garay SM, et al: Pulmonary complications of the acquired immunodeficiency syndrome: Report of a National Heart, Lung, and Blood Institute workshop. N Engl J Med 310:1682–1688, 1984.

106. Centers for Disease Control and Prevention: 1993 revised classification system for HIV infection and expanded surveillance case definition for AIDS among adolescents and adults. JAMA 269:729–730, 1993.

107. Osmond DH, Chin DP, Glassroth J, et al: Impact of bacterial pneumonia and Pneumocystis carinii pneumonia on human immunodeficiency virus disease progression. Pulmonary Complications of HIV Study Group. Clin Infect Dis 29:536–543, 1999.

108. Morris AM, Huang L, Bacchetti P, et al: Permanent declines in pulmonary function following pneumonia in human immunodeficiency virus-infected persons. The Pulmonary Complications of HIV Infection Study Group. Am J Respir Crit Care Med 162:612–616, 2000.

109. Jones JL, Hanson DL, Dworkin MS, et al: Surveillance for AIDS-defining opportunistic illnesses, 1992–1997. Mor Mortal Wkly Rep CDC Surveill Summ 48:1–22, 1999.

110. Afessa B, Green B: Bacterial pneumonia in hospitalized patients with HIV infection: The Pulmonary Complications, ICU Support, and Prognostic Factors of Hospitalized Patients with HIV (PIP) Study. Chest 117:1017–1022, 2000.

111. Sullivan JH, Moore RD, Keruly JC, et al: Effect of antiretroviral therapy on the incidence of bacterial pneumonia in patients with advanced HIV infection. Am J Respir Crit Care Med 162:64–67, 2000.

112. Navin TR, Rimland D, Lennox JL, et al: Risk factors for community-acquired pneumonia among persons infected with human immunodeficiency virus. J Infect Dis 181:158–164, 2000.

113. Anglaret X, Messou E, Ouassa T, et al: Pattern of bacterial diseases in a cohort of HIV-1 infected adults receiving cotrimoxazole prophylaxis in Abidjan, Cote d'Ivoire. AIDS 17:575–584, 2003.

114. Burack JH, Hahn JA, Saint-Maurice D, et al: Microbiology of community-acquired bacterial pneumonia in persons with and at risk for human immunodeficiency virus type 1 infection: Implications for rational empiric antibiotic therapy. Arch Intern Med 154:2589–2596, 1994.

115. Mundy LM, Auwaerter PG, Oldach D, et al: Community-acquired pneumonia: Impact of immune status. Am J Respir Crit Care Med 152:1309–1315, 1995.

116. Rimland D, Navin TR, Lennox JL, et al: Prospective study of etiologic agents of community-acquired pneumonia in patients with HIV infection. AIDS 16:85–95, 2002.

117. Daley CL: Bacterial pneumonia in HIV-infected patients. Semin Respir Infect 8:104–115, 1993.

118. Noskin GA, Glassroth J: Bacterial pneumonia associated with HIV-1 infection. Clin Chest Med 17:713–723, 1996.

119. Feldman C, Glatthaar M, Morar R, et al: Bacteremic pneumococcal pneumonia in HIV-seropositive and HIV-seronegative adults. Chest 116:107–114, 1999.

120. Magnenat JL, Nicod LP, Auckenthaler R, et al: Mode of presentation and diagnosis of bacterial pneumonia in human immunodeficiency virus-infected patients. Am Rev Respir Dis 144:917–922, 1991.

121. Janoff EN, Breiman RF, Daley CL, et al: Pneumococcal disease during HIV infection: Epidemiologic, clinical, and immunologic perspectives. Ann Intern Med 117:314–324, 1992.

122. Garcia-Leoni ME, Moreno S, Rodeno P, et al: Pneumococcal pneumonia in adult hospitalized patients infected with the human immunodeficiency virus. Arch Intern Med 152:1808–1812, 1992.

123. Schlamm HT, Yancovitz SR: Haemophilus influenzae pneumonia in young adults with AIDS, ARC, or risk of AIDS. Am J Med 86:11–14, 1989.

124. Moreno S, Martinez R, Barros C, et al: Latent Haemophilus influenzae pneumonia in patients infected with HIV. AIDS 5:967–970, 1991.

125. Bartlett JG, Dowell SF, Mandell LA, et al: Practice guidelines for the management of community-acquired pneumonia in adults. Infectious Diseases Society of America. Clin Infect Dis 31:347–382, 2000.

126. Niederman MS, Mandell LA, Anzueto A, et al: Guidelines for the management of adults with community-acquired pneumonia: Diagnosis, assessment of severity, antimicrobial therapy, and prevention. Am J Respir Crit Care Med 163:1730–1754, 2001.

127. Cordero E, Pachon J, Rivero A, et al: Community-acquired bacterial pneumonia in human immunodeficiency virus-infected patients: Validation of severity criteria. The Grupo Andaluz para el Estudio de las Enfermedades Infecciosas. Am J Respir Crit Care Med 162:2063–2068, 2000.

128. Mandell LA, Bartlett JG, Dowell SF, et al: Update of practice guidelines for the management of community-acquired pneumonia in immunocompetent adults. Clin Infect Dis 37:1405–1433, 2003.

129. Uphold CR, Deloria-Knoll M, Palella FJ Jr, et al: US hospital care for patients with HIV infection and pneumonia: The role of public, private, and Veterans Affairs hospitals in the early highly active antiretroviral therapy era. Chest 125:548–556, 2004.

130. Viale P, Scudeller L, Petrosillo N, et al: Clinical stability in human immunodeficiency virus-infected patients with community-acquired pneumonia. Clin Infect Dis 38:271–279, 2004.

131. Dworkin MS, Ward JW, Hanson DL, et al: Pneumococcal disease among human immunodeficiency virus-infected persons: Incidence, risk factors, and impact of vaccination. Clin Infect Dis 32:794–800, 2001.

132. Nuorti JP, Butler JC, Gelling L, et al: Epidemiologic relation between HIV and invasive pneumococcal disease in San Francisco County, California. Ann Intern Med 132:182–190, 2000.

133. McEllistrem MC, Mendelsohn AB, Pass MA, et al: Recurrent invasive pneumococcal disease in individuals with human immunodeficiency virus infection. J Infect Dis 185:1364–1368, 2002.

133a. Hughes WT, Dankner WM, Yogev R, et al: Comparison of atovaquone and azithromycin with trimethoprim-sulfamethoxazole for the prevention of serious bacterial infections in children with HIV infection. Clin Infect Dis 40:136–145, 2005.

134. Manfredi R, Nanetti A, Ferri M, et al: *Pseudomonas* spp. complications in patients with HIV disease: An eight-year clinical and microbiological survey. Eur J Epidemiol 16:111–118, 2000.

135. Baron AD, Hollander H: *Pseudomonas aeruginosa* bronchopulmonary infection in late human immunodeficiency virus disease. Am Rev Respir Dis 148:992–996, 1993.

136. Schuster MG, Norris AH: Community-acquired *Pseudomonas aeruginosa* pneumonia in patients with HIV infection. AIDS 8:1437–1441, 1994.

137. Dropulic LK, Leslie JM, Eldred LJ, et al: Clinical manifestations and risk factors of *Pseudomonas aeruginosa* infection in patients with AIDS. J Infect Dis 171:930–937, 1995.

138. Murray JF, Garay SM, Hopewell PC, et al: NHLBI workshop summary. Pulmonary complications of the acquired immunodeficiency syndrome: An update. Report of the second National Heart, Lung and Blood Institute workshop. Am Rev Respir Dis 135:504–509, 1987.

139. Blatt SP, Dolan MJ, Hendrix CW, et al: Legionnaires' disease in human immunodeficiency virus-infected patients: Eight cases and review. Clin Infect Dis 18:227–232, 1994.

140. Pedro-Botet ML, Sabria M, Sopena N, et al: Legionnaires disease and HIV infection. Chest 124:543–547, 2003.

141. Weinstock DM, Brown AE: *Rhodococcus equi*: An emerging pathogen. Clin Infect Dis 34:1379–1385, 2002.

142. Torres-Tortosa M, Arrizabalaga J, Villanueva JL, et al: Prognosis and clinical evaluation of infection caused by *Rhodococcus equi* in HIV-infected patients: A multicenter study of 67 cases. Chest 123:1970–1976, 2003.

143. Donisi A, Suardi MG, Casari S, et al: *Rhodococcus equi* infection in HIV-infected patients. AIDS 10:359–362, 1996.

144. Uttamchandani RB, Daikos GL, Reyes RR, et al: Nocardiosis in 30 patients with advanced human immunodeficiency virus infection: Clinical features and outcome. Clin Infect Dis 18:348–353, 1994.

145. Kramer MR, Uttamchandani RB: The radiographic appearance of pulmonary nocardiosis associated with AIDS. Chest 98:382–385, 1990.

146. Dye C, Scheele S, Dolin P, et al: Consensus statement. Global burden of tuberculosis: Estimated incidence, prevalence, and mortality by country. WHO Global Surveillance and Monitoring Project. JAMA 282:677–686, 1999.

147. Corbett EL, Watt CJ, Walker N, et al: The growing burden of tuberculosis: Global trends and interactions with the HIV epidemic. Arch Intern Med 163:1009–1021, 2003.

148. Centers for Disease Control and Prevention: Tuberculosis morbidity—United States, 1992. MMWR Morb Mortal Wkly Rep 42:696–697, 703–704, 1993.

149. Centers for Disease Control and Prevention: Trends in tuberculosis morbidity—United States, 1992–2002. MMWR Morb Mortal Wkly Rep 52:217–220, 222, 2003.

150. Centers for Disease Control and Prevention: Reported Tuberculosis in the United States, 2002. Atlanta, Ga: Centers for Disease Control and Prevention, 2003.

151. Moreno S, Baraia-Etxaburu J, Bouza E, et al: Risk for developing tuberculosis among anergic patients infected with HIV. Ann Intern Med 119:194–198, 1993.

152. Bradford WZ, Daley CL: Multiple drug-resistant tuberculosis. Infect Dis Clin North Am 12:157–172, 1998.

153. Moore M, Onorato IM, McCray E, et al: Trends in drug-resistant tuberculosis in the United States, 1993–1996. JAMA 278:833–837, 1997.

154. Small PM, Shafer RW, Hopewell PC, et al: Exogenous reinfection with multidrug-resistant *Mycobacterium tuberculosis* in patients with advanced HIV infection. N Engl J Med 328:1137–1144, 1993.

155. Pearson ML, Jereb JA, Frieden TR, et al: Nosocomial transmission of multidrug-resistant *Mycobacterium tuberculosis*: A risk to patients and health care workers. Ann Intern Med 117:191–196, 1992.

156. Dooley SW, Jarvis WR, Martone WJ, et al: Multidrug-resistant tuberculosis. Ann Intern Med 117:257–259, 1992.

157. Ong A, Creasman J, Hopewell PC, et al: A molecular epidemiological assessment of extrapulmonary tuberculosis in San Francisco. Clin Infect Dis 38:25–31, 2004.

158. Jones BE, Young SM, Antoniskis D, et al: Relationship of the manifestations of tuberculosis to CD4 cell counts in patients with human immunodeficiency virus infection. Am Rev Respir Dis 148:1292–1297, 1993.

159. Morris L, Martin DJ, Bredell H, et al: Human immunodeficiency virus-1 RNA levels and CD4 lymphocyte counts, during treatment for active tuberculosis, in South African patients. J Infect Dis 187:1967–1971, 2003.

160. Hopewell PC: Impact of human immunodeficiency virus infection on the epidemiology, clinical features, management, and control of tuberculosis. Clin Infect Dis 15:540–547, 1992.

161. Shafer RW, Kim DS, Weiss JP, et al: Extrapulmonary tuberculosis in patients with human immunodeficiency virus infection. Medicine (Baltimore) 70:384–397, 1991.

162. Berenguer J, Moreno S, Laguna F, et al: Tuberculous meningitis in patients infected with the human immunodeficiency virus. N Engl J Med 326:668–672, 1992.

163. Abouya L, Coulibaly IM, Coulibaly D, et al: Radiologic manifestations of pulmonary tuberculosis in HIV-1 and HIV-2-infected patients in Abidjan, Cote d'Ivoire. Tuber Lung Dis 76:436–440, 1995.

164. Busi Rizzi E, Schinina V, Palmieri F, et al: Radiological patterns in HIV-associated pulmonary tuberculosis:

Comparison between HAART-treated and non-HAART-treated patients. Clin Radiol 58:469–473, 2003.

165. Conde MB, Loivos AC, Rezende VM, et al: Yield of sputum induction in the diagnosis of pleural tuberculosis. Am J Respir Crit Care Med 167:723–725, 2003.

166. Blumberg HM, Burman WJ, Chaisson RE, et al: American Thoracic Society/Centers for Disease Control and Prevention/Infectious Diseases Society of America: Treatment of tuberculosis. Am J Respir Crit Care Med 167:603–662, 2003.

167. American Academy of Pediatrics: Tuberculosis (25th ed). Elk Grove Village, Ill: American Academy of Pediatrics, 2000.

168. Diagnosis and treatment of disease caused by nontuberculous mycobacteria. American Thoracic Society. Medical section of the American Lung Association. Am J Respir Crit Care Med 156:S1–S25, 1997.

169. Narita M, Ashkin D, Hollender ES, et al: Paradoxical worsening of tuberculosis following antiretroviral therapy in patients with AIDS. Am J Respir Crit Care Med 158:157–161, 1998.

170. Fishman JE, Saraf-Lavi E, Narita M, et al: Pulmonary tuberculosis in AIDS patients: Transient chest radiographic worsening after initiation of antiretroviral therapy. AJR Am J Roentgenol 174:43–49, 2000.

171. Wendel KA, Alwood KS, Gachuhi R, et al: Paradoxical worsening of tuberculosis in HIV-infected persons. Chest 120:193–197, 2001.

171a. Breton G, Duval X, Estellat C, et al: Determinants of immune reconstitution inflammatory syndrome in HIV type 1-infected patients with tuberculosis after initiation of antiretroviral therapy. Clin Infect Dis 39:1709–1712, 2004.

172. Burman WJ, Jones BE: Treatment of HIV-related tuberculosis in the era of effective antiretroviral therapy. Am J Respir Crit Care Med 164:7–12, 2001.

173. Department of Health and Human Services: Guidelines for the use of antiretroviral agents in HIV-1-infected adults and adolescents. 2004. Available at http://AIDSinfo.nih.gov/.

173a. Dheda K, Lampe FC, Johnson MA, Lipman MC: Outcome of HIV-associated tuberculosis in the era of highly active antiretroviral therapy. J Infect Dis 190:1670–1676, 2004.

174. Centers for Disease Control and Prevention: Prevention and treatment of tuberculosis among patients infected with human immunodeficiency virus: Principles of therapy and revised recommendations. MMWR Recomm Rep 47(RR-20):1–58, 1998.

175. Targeted tuberculin testing and treatment of latent tuberculosis infection. Joint Statement of the American Thoracic Society/Centers for Disease Control and Prevention/Council of the Infectious Diseases Society of America. Am J Respir Crit Care Med 161:S221–S247, 2000.

176. Update: Adverse event data and revised American Thoracic Society/CDC recommendations against the use of rifampin and pyrazinamide for treatment of latent tuberculosis infection—United States, 2003. MMWR Morb Mortal Wkly Rep 52:735–739, 2003.

177. Lallemant-Le Coeur S, Lallemant M, Cheynier D, et al: Bacillus Calmette-Guerin immunization in infants born to HIV-1-seropositive mothers. AIDS 5:195–199, 1991.

178. Horsburgh CR Jr, Mason UG 3rd, Farhi DC, et al: Disseminated infection with Mycobacterium avium-intracellulare: A report of 13 cases and a review of the literature. Medicine (Baltimore) 64:36–48, 1985.

179. Holtzer CD, Jacobson MA, Hadley WK, et al: Decline in the rate of specific opportunistic infections at San Francisco General Hospital, 1994–1997. AIDS 12:1931–1933, 1998.

180. Kirk O, Gatell JM, Mocroft A, et al: Infections with Mycobacterium tuberculosis and Mycobacterium avium among HIV-infected patients after the introduction of highly active antiretroviral therapy. EuroSIDA Study Group JD. Am J Respir Crit Care Med 162:865–872, 2000.

181. Horsburgh CR Jr, Selik RM: The epidemiology of disseminated nontuberculous mycobacterial infection in the acquired immunodeficiency syndrome (AIDS). Am Rev Respir Dis 139:4–7, 1989.

182. Tobin-D'Angelo MJ, Blass MA, del Rio C, et al: Hospital water as a source of Mycobacterium avium complex isolates in respiratory specimens. J Infect Dis 189:98–104, 2004.

183. Horsburgh CR Jr, Metchock BG, McGowan JE Jr, et al: Clinical implications of recovery of Mycobacterium avium complex from the stool or respiratory tract of HIV-infected individuals. AIDS 6:512–514, 1992.

184. Falkinham JO 3rd: Nontuberculous mycobacteria in the environment. Clin Chest Med 23:529–551, 2002.

185. Rigsby MO, Curtis AM: Pulmonary disease from nontuberculous mycobacteria in patients with human immunodeficiency virus. Chest 106:913–919, 1994.

186. Kalayjian RC, Toossi Z, Tomashefski JF Jr, et al: Pulmonary disease due to infection by Mycobacterium avium complex in patients with AIDS. Clin Infect Dis 20:1186–1194, 1995.

187. Hocqueloux L, Lesprit P, Herrmann JL, et al: Pulmonary Mycobacterium avium complex disease without dissemination in HIV-infected patients. Chest 113:542–548, 1998.

188. Salama C, Policar M, Venkataraman M: Isolated pulmonary Mycobacterium avium complex infection in patients with human immunodeficiency virus infection: Case reports and literature review. Clin Infect Dis 37:e35–e40, 2003.

189. Horsburgh CR Jr: Mycobacterium avium complex infection in the acquired immunodeficiency syndrome. N Engl J Med 324:1332–1338, 1991.

190. Jones D, Havlir DV: Nontuberculous mycobacteria in the HIV infected patient. Clin Chest Med 23:665–674, 2002.

191. Chin DP, Reingold AL, Horsburgh CR Jr, et al: Predicting Mycobacterium avium complex bacteremia in patients infected with human immunodeficiency virus: A prospectively validated model. Clin Infect Dis 19:668–674, 1994.

192. Packer SJ, Cesario T, Williams JH Jr: Mycobacterium avium complex infection presenting as endobronchial lesions in immunosuppressed patients. Ann Intern Med 109:389–393, 1988.

193. Mehle ME, Adamo JP, Mehta AC, et al: Endobronchial Mycobacterium avium-intracellulare infection in a patient with AIDS. Chest 96:199–201, 1989.

194. Griffith DE, Brown-Elliott BA, Wallace RJ Jr: Diagnosing nontuberculous mycobacterial lung disease: A process in evolution. Infect Dis Clin North Am 16:235–249, 2002.

195. Dunne M, Fessel J, Kumar P, et al: A randomized, double-blind trial comparing azithromycin and clarithromycin in the treatment of disseminated Mycobacterium avium infection in patients with human immunodeficiency virus. Clin Infect Dis 31:1245–1252, 2000.

196. Gordin FM, Sullam PM, Shafran SD, et al: A randomized, placebo-controlled study of rifabutin added to a regimen of clarithromycin and ethambutol for treatment of disseminated infection with Mycobacterium avium complex. Clin Infect Dis 28:1080–1085, 1999.

197. Currier JS, Williams P, Feinberg J, et al: Impact of prophylaxis for Mycobacterium avium complex on bacterial infections in patients with advanced human immunodeficiency virus disease. Clin Infect Dis 32:1615–1622, 2001.

198. Good RC, Snider DE Jr: Isolation of nontuberculous mycobacteria in the United States, 1980. J Infect Dis 146:829–833, 1982.

199. Bloch KC, Zwerling L, Pletcher MJ, et al: Incidence and clinical implications of isolation of *Mycobacterium kansasii:* Results of a 5-year, population-based study. Ann Intern Med 129:698–704, 1998.

200. Canueto-Quintero J, Caballero-Granado FJ, Herrero-Romero M, et al: Epidemiological, clinical, and prognostic differences between the diseases caused by *Mycobacterium kansasii* and *Mycobacterium tuberculosis* in patients infected with human immunodeficiency virus: A multicenter study. Clin Infect Dis 37:584–590, 2003.

201. Witzig RS, Fazal BA, Mera RM, et al: Clinical manifestations and implications of coinfection with *Mycobacterium kansasii* and human immunodeficiency virus type 1. Clin Infect Dis 21:77–85, 1995.

201a. Marras TK, Morris A, Gonzalez LC, Daley CL: Mortality prediction in pulmonary *Mycobacterium kansasii* infection and human immunodeficiency virus. Am J Respir Crit Care Med 170:793–798, 2004.

202. Taillard C, Greub G, Weber R, et al: Clinical implications of *Mycobacterium kansasii* species heterogeneity: Swiss National Survey. J Clin Microbiol 41:1240–1244, 2003.

203. Griffith DE: Management of disease due to *Mycobacterium kansasii*. Clin Chest Med 23:613–621, 2002.

204. El-Solh AA, Nopper J, Abdul-Khoudoud MR, et al: Clinical and radiographic manifestations of uncommon pulmonary nontuberculous mycobacterial disease in AIDS patients. Chest 114:138–145, 1998.

205. Lundberg BE, Davidson AJ, Burman WJ: Epidemiology of *Pneumocystis carinii* pneumonia in an era of effective prophylaxis: The relative contribution of non-adherence and drug failure. AIDS 14:2559–2566, 2000.

206. Huang L, Hecht FM: Why does *Pneumocystis carinii* pneumonia still occur? AIDS 14:2611–2612, 2000.

207. Pulvirenti J, Herrera P, Venkataraman P, et al: *Pneumocystis carinii* pneumonia in HIV-infected patients in the HAART era. AIDS Patient Care STDS 17:261–265, 2003.

207a. Thomas CF Jr, Limper AH: *Pneumocystis* pneumonia. N Engl J Med 350:2487–2498, 2004.

208. Edman JC, Kovacs JA, Masur H, et al: Ribosomal RNA sequence shows *Pneumocystis carinii* to be a member of the fungi. Nature 334:519–522, 1988.

209. Stringer SL, Stringer JR, Blase MA, et al: *Pneumocystis carinii*: Sequence from ribosomal RNA implies a close relationship with fungi. Exp Parasitol 68:450–461, 1989.

210. Gigliotti F: Host species-specific antigenic variation of a mannosylated surface glycoprotein of *Pneumocystis carinii*. J Infect Dis 165:329–336, 1992.

211. Gigliotti F, Haidaris PJ, Haidaris CG, et al: Further evidence of host species-specific variation in antigens of *Pneumocystis carinii* using the polymerase chain reaction. J Infect Dis 168:191–194, 1993.

212. Gigliotti F, Harmsen AG, Haidaris CG, et al: *Pneumocystis carinii* is not universally transmissible between mammalian species. Infect Immun 61:2886–2890, 1993.

213. Stringer JR, Beard CB, Miller RF, et al: A new name (*Pneumocystis jiroveci*) for *Pneumocystis* from humans. Emerg Infect Dis 8:891–896, 2002.

214. Kovacs JA, Gill VJ, Meshnick S, et al: New insights into transmission, diagnosis, and drug treatment of *Pneumocystis carinii* pneumonia. JAMA 286:2450–2460, 2001.

215. Morris A, Beard CB, Huang L: Update on the epidemiology and transmission of *Pneumocystis carinii*. Microbes Infect 4:95–103, 2002.

216. Meuwissen JH, Tauber I, Leeuwenberg AD, et al: Parasitologic and serologic observations of infection with *Pneumocystis* in humans. J Infect Dis 136:43–49, 1977.

217. Pifer LL, Hughes WT, Stagno S, et al: *Pneumocystis carinii* infection: Evidence for high prevalence in normal and immunosuppressed children. Pediatrics 61:35–41, 1978.

218. Peglow SL, Smulian AG, Linke MJ, et al: Serologic responses to *Pneumocystis carinii* antigens in health and disease. J Infect Dis 161:296–306, 1990.

219. Vargas SL, Ponce CA, Gigliotti F, et al: Transmission of *Pneumocystis carinii* DNA from a patient with *P. carinii* pneumonia to immunocompetent contact health care workers. J Clin Microbiol 38:1536–1538, 2000.

220. Miller RF, Ambrose HE, Novelli V, et al: Probable mother-to-infant transmission of *Pneumocystis carinii* f. sp. *hominis* infection. J Clin Microbiol 40:1555–1557, 2002.

221. Hughes WT: Natural mode of acquisition for de novo infection with *Pneumocystis carinii*. J Infect Dis 145:842–848, 1982.

222. Hughes WT, Bartley DL, Smith BM: A natural source of infection due to *Pneumocystis carinii*. J Infect Dis 147:595, 1983.

223. Soulez B, Palluault F, Cesbron JY, et al: Introduction of *Pneumocystis carinii* in a colony of SCID mice. J Protozool 38:123S–125S, 1991.

224. Dumoulin A, Mazars E, Seguy N, et al: Transmission of *Pneumocystis carinii* disease from immunocompetent contacts of infected hosts to susceptible hosts. Eur J Clin Microbiol Infect Dis 19:671–678, 2000.

225. Gigliotti F, Harmsen AG, Wright TW: Characterization of transmission of *Pneumocystis carinii* f. sp. *muris* through immunocompetent BALB/c mice. Infect Immun 71:3852–3856, 2003.

226. Phair J, Munoz A, Detels R, et al: The risk of *Pneumocystis carinii* pneumonia among men infected with human immunodeficiency virus type 1. Multicenter AIDS Cohort Study Group. N Engl J Med 322:161–165, 1990.

227. Stansell JD, Osmond DH, Charlebois E, et al: Predictors of *Pneumocystis carinii* pneumonia in HIV-infected persons. Pulmonary Complications of HIV Infection Study Group. Am J Respir Crit Care Med 155:60–66, 1997.

228. Simonds RJ, Lindegren ML, Thomas P, et al: Prophylaxis against *Pneumocystis carinii* pneumonia among children with perinatally acquired human immunodeficiency virus infection in the United States. Pneumocystis carinii Pneumonia Prophylaxis Evaluation Working Group. N Engl J Med 332:786–790, 1995.

229. Kovacs JA, Hiemenz JW, Macher AM, et al: *Pneumocystis carinii* pneumonia: A comparison between patients with the acquired immunodeficiency syndrome and patients with other immunodeficiencies. Ann Intern Med 100:663–671, 1984.

230. Kales CP, Murren JR, Torres RA, et al: Early predictors of in-hospital mortality for *Pneumocystis carinii* pneumonia in the acquired immunodeficiency syndrome. Arch Intern Med 147:1413–1417, 1987.

231. DeLorenzo LJ, Huang CT, Maguire GP, et al: Roentgenographic patterns of *Pneumocystis carinii* pneumonia in 104 patients with AIDS. Chest 91:323–327, 1987.

232. Sandhu JS, Goodman PC: Pulmonary cysts associated with *Pneumocystis carinii* pneumonia in patients with AIDS. Radiology 173:33–35, 1989.

233. Kennedy CA, Goetz MB: Atypical roentgenographic manifestations of *Pneumocystis carinii* pneumonia. Arch Intern Med 152:1390–1398, 1992.

234. Opravil M, Marincek B, Fuchs WA, et al: Shortcomings of chest radiography in detecting *Pneumocystis carinii* pneumonia. J Acquir Immune Defic Syndr Hum Retrovirol 7:39–45, 1994.

235. Sankary RM, Turner J, Lipavsky A, et al: Alveolar-capillary block in patients with AIDS and *Pneumocystis carinii* pneumonia. Am Rev Respir Dis 137:443–449, 1988.

236. Gruden JF, Huang L, Turner J, et al: High-resolution CT in the evaluation of clinically suspected *Pneumocystis carinii* pneumonia in AIDS patients with normal, equivocal, or nonspecific radiographic findings. AJR Am J Roentgenol 169:967–975, 1997.

237. Metersky ML, Aslenzadeh J, Stelmach P: A comparison of induced and expectorated sputum for the diagnosis of *Pneumocystis carinii* pneumonia. Chest 113:1555–1559, 1998.

238. Shelhamer JH, Gill VJ, Quinn TC, et al: The laboratory evaluation of opportunistic pulmonary infections. Ann Intern Med 124:585–599, 1996.

239. Torres J, Goldman M, Wheat LJ, et al: Diagnosis of *Pneumocystis carinii* pneumonia in human immunodeficiency virus-infected patients with polymerase chain reaction: A blinded comparison to standard methods. Clin Infect Dis 30:141–145, 2000.

240. Helweg-Larsen J, Jensen JS, Benfield T, et al: Diagnostic use of PCR for detection of *Pneumocystis carinii* in oral wash samples. J Clin Microbiol 36:2068–2072, 1998.

241. Fischer S, Gill VJ, Kovacs J, et al: The use of oral washes to diagnose *Pneumocystis carinii* pneumonia: A blinded prospective study using a polymerase chain reaction-based detection system. J Infect Dis 184:1485–1488, 2001.

242. Larsen HH, Masur H, Kovacs JA, et al: Development and evaluation of a quantitative, touch-down, real-time PCR assay for diagnosing *Pneumocystis carinii* pneumonia. J Clin Microbiol 40:490–494, 2002.

243. Larsen HH, Huang L, Kovacs JA, et al: A prospective, blinded study of quantitative touch-down polymerase chain reaction using oral-wash samples for diagnosis of *Pneumocystis* pneumonia in HIV-infected patients. J Infect Dis 189:1679–1683, 2004.

244. Levine SJ, Masur H, Gill VJ, et al: Effect of aerosolized pentamidine prophylaxis on the diagnosis of *Pneumocystis carinii* pneumonia by induced sputum examination in patients infected with the human immunodeficiency virus. Am Rev Respir Dis 144:760–764, 1991.

245. Metersky ML, Catanzaro A: Diagnostic approach to *Pneumocystis carinii* pneumonia in the setting of prophylactic aerosolized pentamidine. Chest 100:1345–1349, 1991.

246. Fahy JV, Chin DP, Schnapp LM, et al: Effect of aerosolized pentamidine prophylaxis on the clinical severity and diagnosis of *Pneumocystis carinii* pneumonia. Am Rev Respir Dis 146:844–848, 1992.

247. Ng VL, Geaghan SM, Leoung G, et al: Lack of effect of prophylactic aerosolized pentamidine on the detection of *Pneumocystis carinii* in induced sputum or bronchoalveolar lavage specimens. Arch Pathol Lab Med 117:493–496, 1993.

248. Jules-Elysee KM, Stover DE, Zaman MB, et al: Aerosolized pentamidine: Effect on diagnosis and presentation of *Pneumocystis carinii* pneumonia. Ann Intern Med 112:750–757, 1990.

249. Levine SJ, Kennedy D, Shelhamer JH, et al: Diagnosis of *Pneumocystis carinii* pneumonia by multiple lobe, site-directed bronchoalveolar lavage with immunofluorescent monoclonal antibody staining in human immunodeficiency virus-infected patients receiving aerosolized pentamidine chemoprophylaxis. Am Rev Respir Dis 146:838–843, 1992.

250. Baughman RP, Dohn MN, Shipley R, et al: Increased *Pneumocystis carinii* recovery from the upper lobes in *Pneumocystis* pneumonia: The effect of aerosol pentamidine prophylaxis. Chest 103:426–432, 1993.

251. Read CA, Cerrone F, Busseniers AE, et al: Differential lobe lavage for diagnosis of acute *Pneumocystis carinii* pneumonia in patients receiving prophylactic aerosolized pentamidine therapy. Chest 103:1520–1523, 1993.

252. Wislez M, Bergot E, Antoine M, et al: Acute respiratory failure following HAART introduction in patients treated for *Pneumocystis carinii* pneumonia. Am J Respir Crit Care Med 164:847–851, 2001.

253. Koval CE, Gigliotti F, Nevins D, et al: Immune reconstitution syndrome after successful treatment of *Pneumocystis carinii* pneumonia in a man with human immunodeficiency virus type 1 infection. Clin Infect Dis 35:491–493, 2002.

254. Consensus statement on the use of corticosteroids as adjunctive therapy for *Pneumocystis* pneumonia in the acquired immunodeficiency syndrome. The National Institutes of Health-University of California Expert Panel for Corticosteroids as Adjunctive Therapy for Pneumocystis Pneumonia. N Engl J Med 323:1500–1504, 1990.

255. Wachter RM, Luce JM, Turner J, et al: Intensive care of patients with the acquired immunodeficiency syndrome: Outcome and changing patterns of utilization. Am Rev Respir Dis 134:891–896, 1986.

256. Wachter RM, Russi MB, Bloch DA, et al: *Pneumocystis carinii* pneumonia and respiratory failure in AIDS: Improved outcomes and increased use of intensive care units. Am Rev Respir Dis 143:251–256, 1991.

257. Wachter RM, Luce JM, Safrin S, et al: Cost and outcome of intensive care for patients with AIDS, *Pneumocystis carinii* pneumonia, and severe respiratory failure. JAMA 273:230–235, 1995.

258. Curtis JR, Yarnold PR, Schwartz DN, et al: Improvements in outcomes of acute respiratory failure for patients with human immunodeficiency virus-related *Pneumocystis carinii* pneumonia. Am J Respir Crit Care Med 162:393–398, 2000.

259. Nickas G, Wachter RM: Outcomes of intensive care for patients with human immunodeficiency virus infection. Arch Intern Med 160:541–547, 2000.

260. Morris A, Wachter RM, Luce J, et al: Improved survival with highly active antiretroviral therapy in HIV-infected patients with severe *Pneumocystis carinii* pneumonia. AIDS 17:73–80, 2003.

261. Crothers K, Huang L: Recurrence of *Pneumocystis carinii* pneumonia in an HIV-infected patient: Apparent selective immune reconstitution after initiation of antiretroviral therapy. HIV Med 4:346–349, 2003.

262. Stansell JD: Pulmonary fungal infections in HIV-infected persons. Semin Respir Infect 8:116–123, 1993.

263. Perfect JR, Casadevall A: Cryptococcosis. Infect Dis Clin North Am 16:837–874, 2002.

264. Chuck SL, Sande MA: Infections with *Cryptococcus neoformans* in the acquired immunodeficiency syndrome. N Engl J Med 321:794–799, 1989.

265. Mirza SA, Phelan M, Rimland D, et al: The changing epidemiology of cryptococcosis: An update from population-based active surveillance in 2 large metropolitan areas, 1992–2000. Clin Infect Dis 36:789–794, 2003.

266. Dromer F, Mathoulin-Pelissier S, Fontanet A, et al: Epidemiology of HIV-associated cryptococcosis in France (1985–2001): Comparison of the pre- and post-HAART eras. AIDS 18:555–562, 2004.

267. Zuger A, Louie E, Holzman RS, et al: Cryptococcal disease in patients with the acquired immunodeficiency syndrome: Diagnostic features and outcome of treatment. Ann Intern Med 104:234–240, 1986.

268. Darras-Joly C, Chevret S, Wolff M, et al: *Cryptococcus neoformans* infection in France: Epidemiologic features of

and early prognostic parameters for 76 patients who were infected with human immunodeficiency virus. Clin Infect Dis 23:369–376, 1996.

269. French N, Gray K, Watera C, et al: Cryptococcal infection in a cohort of HIV-1-infected Ugandan adults. AIDS 16:1031–1038, 2002.

270. Wasser L, Talavera W: Pulmonary cryptococcosis in AIDS. Chest 92:692–695, 1987.

271. Newman TG, Soni A, Acaron S, et al: Pleural cryptococcosis in the acquired immune deficiency syndrome. Chest 91:459–461, 1987.

272. Chechani V, Kamholz SL: Pulmonary manifestations of disseminated cryptococcosis in patients with AIDS. Chest 98:1060–1066, 1990.

273. Clark RA, Greer DL, Valainis GT, et al: *Cryptococcus neoformans* pulmonary infection in HIV-1-infected patients. J Acquir Immune Defic Syndr Hum Retrovirol 3:480–484, 1990.

274. Clark RA, Greer D, Atkinson W, et al: Spectrum of *Cryptococcus neoformans* infection in 68 patients infected with human immunodeficiency virus. Rev Infect Dis 12:768–777, 1990.

275. Cameron ML, Bartlett JA, Gallis HA, et al: Manifestations of pulmonary cryptococcosis in patients with acquired immunodeficiency syndrome. Rev Infect Dis 13:64–67, 1991.

276. Batungwanayo J, Taelman H, Bogaerts J, et al: Pulmonary cryptococcosis associated with HIV-1 infection in Rwanda: A retrospective study of 37 cases. AIDS 8:1271–1276, 1994.

277. Meyohas MC, Roux P, Bollens D, et al: Pulmonary cryptococcosis: Localized and disseminated infections in 27 patients with AIDS. Clin Infect Dis 21:628–633, 1995.

278. Driver JA, Saunders CA, Heinze-Lacey B, et al: Cryptococcal pneumonia in AIDS: Is cryptococcal meningitis preceded by clinically recognizable pneumonia? J Acquir Immune Defic Syndr Hum Retrovirol 9:168–171, 1995.

279. Friedman EP, Miller RF, Severn A, et al: Cryptococcal pneumonia in patients with the acquired immunodeficiency syndrome. Clin Radiol 50:756–760, 1995.

280. Stansell JD: Fungal disease in HIV-infected persons: Cryptococcosis, histoplasmosis, and coccidioidomycosis. J Thorac Imaging 6:28–35, 1991.

281. Douketis JD, Kesten S: Miliary pulmonary cryptococcosis in a patient with the acquired immunodeficiency syndrome. Thorax 48:402–403, 1993.

282. Miller KD, Mican JA, Davey RT: Asymptomatic solitary pulmonary nodules due to *Cryptococcus neoformans* in patients infected with human immunodeficiency virus. Clin Infect Dis 23:810–812, 1996.

283. Lacomis JM, Costello P, Vilchez R, et al: The radiology of pulmonary cryptococcosis in a tertiary medical center. J Thorac Imaging 16:139–148, 2001.

284. Torre D, Martegani R, Speranza F, et al: Pulmonary cryptococcosis presenting as pneumothorax in a patient with AIDS. Clin Infect Dis 21:1524–1525, 1995.

285. Baughman RP, Rhodes JC, Dohn MN, et al: Detection of cryptococcal antigen in bronchoalveolar lavage fluid: A prospective study of diagnostic utility. Am Rev Respir Dis 145:1226–1229, 1992.

286. Saag MS, Graybill RJ, Larsen RA, et al: Practice guidelines for the management of cryptococcal disease. Infectious Diseases Society of America. Clin Infect Dis 30:710–718, 2000.

287. Jenny-Avital ER, Abadi M: Immune reconstitution cryptococcosis after initiation of successful highly active antiretroviral therapy. Clin Infect Dis 35:e128–e133, 2002.

288. Lanzafame M, Trevenzoli M, Carretta G, et al: Mediastinal lymphadenitis due to cryptococcal infection in HIV-positive patients on highly active antiretroviral therapy. Chest 116:848–849, 1999.

289. Powderly WG, Finkelstein D, Feinberg J, et al: A randomized trial comparing fluconazole with clotrimazole troches for the prevention of fungal infections in patients with advanced human immunodeficiency virus infection. NIAID AIDS Clinical Trials Group. N Engl J Med 332:700–705, 1995.

290. Wheat LJ, Kauffman CA: Histoplasmosis. Infect Dis Clin North Am 17:1–19, 2003.

291. Huang CT, McGarry T, Cooper S, et al: Disseminated histoplasmosis in the acquired immunodeficiency syndrome: Report of five cases from a nonendemic area. Arch Intern Med 147:1181–1184, 1987.

292. Wheat LJ, Connolly-Stringfield PA, Baker RL, et al: Disseminated histoplasmosis in the acquired immune deficiency syndrome: Clinical findings, diagnosis and treatment, and review of the literature. Medicine (Baltimore) 69:361–374, 1990.

293. Sarosi GA, Johnson PC: Disseminated histoplasmosis in patients infected with human immunodeficiency virus. Clin Infect Dis 14(Suppl 1):S60–S67, 1992.

294. Karimi K, Wheat LJ, Connolly P, et al: Differences in histoplasmosis in patients with acquired immunodeficiency syndrome in the United States and Brazil. J Infect Dis 186:1655–1660, 2002.

295. Conces DJ Jr, Stockberger SM, Tarver RD, et al: Disseminated histoplasmosis in AIDS: Findings on chest radiographs. AJR Am J Roentgenol 160:15–19, 1993.

296. Wheat LJ, Connolly-Stringfield P, Kohler RB, et al: *Histoplasma capsulatum* polysaccharide antigen detection in diagnosis and management of disseminated histoplasmosis in patients with acquired immunodeficiency syndrome. Am J Med 87:396–400, 1989.

297. Wheat LJ, Connolly-Stringfield P, Williams B, et al: Diagnosis of histoplasmosis in patients with the acquired immunodeficiency syndrome by detection of *Histoplasma capsulatum* polysaccharide antigen in bronchoalveolar lavage fluid. Am Rev Respir Dis 145:1421–1424, 1992.

298. Wheat J, Sarosi G, McKinsey D, et al: Practice guidelines for the management of patients with histoplasmosis. Infectious Diseases Society of America. Clin Infect Dis 30:688–695, 2000.

299. Wheat J, MaWhinney S, Hafner R, et al: Treatment of histoplasmosis with fluconazole in patients with acquired immunodeficiency syndrome. National Institute of Allergy and Infectious Diseases Acquired Immunodeficiency Syndrome Clinical Trials Group and Mycoses Study Group. Am J Med 103:223–232, 1997.

300. McKinsey DS, Wheat LJ, Cloud GA, et al: Itraconazole prophylaxis for fungal infections in patients with advanced human immunodeficiency virus infection: Randomized, placebo-controlled, double-blind study. National Institute of Allergy and Infectious Diseases Mycoses Study Group. Clin Infect Dis 28:1049–1056, 1999.

301. Hajjeh RA, Pappas PG, Henderson H, et al: Multicenter case-control study of risk factors for histoplasmosis in human immunodeficiency virus-infected persons. Clin Infect Dis 32:1215–1220, 2001.

302. Galgiani JN, Ampel NM, Catanzaro A, et al: Practice guideline for the treatment of coccidioidomycosis. Infectious Diseases Society of America. Clin Infect Dis 30:658–661, 2000.

303. Chiller TM, Galgiani JN, Stevens DA: Coccidioidomycosis. Infect Dis Clin North Am 17:41–57, 2003.

304. Woods CW, McRill C, Plikaytis BD, et al: Coccidioidomycosis in human immunodeficiency virus-infected persons in Arizona, 1994–1997: Incidence, risk factors, and prevention. J Infect Dis 181:1428–1434, 2000.

305. Polesky A, Kirsch CM, Snyder LS, et al: Airway coccidioidomycosis—report of cases and review. Clin Infect Dis 28:1273–1280, 1999.

306. Singh VR, Smith DK, Lawerence J, et al: Coccidioidomycosis in patients infected with human immunodeficiency virus: Review of 91 cases at a single institution. Clin Infect Dis 23:563–568, 1996.

307. Fish DG, Ampel NM, Galgiani JN, et al: Coccidioidomycosis during human immunodeficiency virus infection: A review of 77 patients. Medicine (Baltimore) 69:384–391, 1990.

308. Galgiani JN, Ampel NM: Coccidioidomycosis in human immunodeficiency virus-infected patients. J Infect Dis 162:1165–1169, 1990.

309. Marr KA, Patterson T, Denning D: Aspergillosis: Pathogenesis, clinical manifestations, and therapy. Infect Dis Clin North Am 16:875–894, 2002.

310. Denning DW, Follansbee SE, Scolaro M, et al: Pulmonary aspergillosis in the acquired immunodeficiency syndrome. N Engl J Med 324:654–662, 1991.

311. Holding KJ, Dworkin MS, Wan PC, et al: Aspergillosis among people infected with human immunodeficiency virus: Incidence and survival. Adult and Adolescent Spectrum of HIV Disease Project. Clin Infect Dis 31:1253–1257, 2000.

312. Pursell KJ, Telzak EE, Armstrong D: *Aspergillus* species colonization and invasive disease in patients with AIDS. Clin Infect Dis 14:141–148, 1992.

313. Addrizzo-Harris DJ, Harkin TJ, McGuinness G, et al: Pulmonary aspergilloma and AIDS: A comparison of HIV-infected and HIV-negative individuals. Chest 111:612–618, 1997.

314. Greenberg AK, Knapp J, Rom WN, et al: Clinical presentation of pulmonary mycetoma in HIV-infected patients. Chest 122:886–892, 2002.

315. Kemper CA, Hostetler JS, Follansbee SE, et al: Ulcerative and plaque-like tracheobronchitis due to infection with *Aspergillus* in patients with AIDS. Clin Infect Dis 17:344–352, 1993.

316. Klapholz A, Salomon N, Perlman DC, et al: Aspergillosis in the acquired immunodeficiency syndrome. Chest 100:1614–1618, 1991.

317. Decker CF, Parenti DM: Invasive aspergillosis in patients with HIV infection: Report of two patients and a review of the literature. J Acquir Immune Defic Syndr 4:603–606, 1991.

318. Minamoto GY, Barlam TF, Vander Els NJ: Invasive aspergillosis in patients with AIDS. Clin Infect Dis 14:66–74, 1992.

319. Lortholary O, Meyohas MC, Dupont B, et al: Invasive aspergillosis in patients with acquired immunodeficiency syndrome: Report of 33 cases. French Cooperative Study Group on Aspergillosis in AIDS. Am J Med 95:177–187, 1993.

320. Miller WT Jr, Sais GJ, Frank I, et al: Pulmonary aspergillosis in patients with AIDS: Clinical and radiographic correlations. Chest 105:37–44, 1994.

321. Mylonakis E, Barlam TF, Flanigan T, et al: Pulmonary aspergillosis and invasive disease in AIDS: Review of 342 cases. Chest 114:251–262, 1998.

322. Staples CA, Kang EY, Wright JL, et al: Invasive pulmonary aspergillosis in AIDS: Radiographic, CT, and pathologic findings. Radiology 196:409–414, 1995.

323. Stevens DA, Kan VL, Judson MA, et al: Practice guidelines for diseases caused by *Aspergillus*. Infectious Diseases Society of America. Clin Infect Dis 30:696–709, 2000.

324. Pappas PG, Pottage JC, Powderly WG, et al: Blastomycosis in patients with the acquired immunodeficiency syndrome. Ann Intern Med 116:847–853, 1992.

325. Bradsher RW, Chapman SW, Pappas PG: Blastomycosis. Infect Dis Clin North Am 17:21–40, 2003.

326. Chapman SW, Bradsher RW Jr, Campbell GD Jr, et al: Practice guidelines for the management of patients with blastomycosis. Infectious Diseases Society of America. Clin Infect Dis 30:679–683, 2000.

327. Supparatpinyo K, Chiewchanvit S, Hirunsri P, et al: *Penicillium marneffei* infection in patients infected with human immunodeficiency virus. Clin Infect Dis 14:871–874, 1992.

328. Hilmarsdottir I, Meynard JL, Rogeaux O, et al: Disseminated *Penicillium marneffei* infection associated with human immunodeficiency virus: A report of two cases and a review of 35 published cases. J Acquir Immune Defic Syndr Hum Retrovirol 6:466–471, 1993.

329. Supparatpinyo K, Khamwan C, Baosoung V, et al: Disseminated *Penicillium marneffei* infection in southeast Asia. Lancet 344:110–113, 1994.

330. Heath TC, Patel A, Fisher D, et al: Disseminated *Penicillium marneffei*: Presenting illness of advanced HIV infection; a clinicopathological review, illustrated by a case report. Pathology 27:101–105, 1995.

331. Duong TA: Infection due to *Penicillium marneffei*, an emerging pathogen: Review of 155 reported cases. Clin Infect Dis 23:125–130, 1996.

332. Cooper CR Jr, McGinnis MR: Pathology of *Penicillium marneffei*: An emerging acquired immunodeficiency syndrome-related pathogen. Arch Pathol Lab Med 121:798–804, 1997.

333. Hung CC, Hsueh PR, Chen MY, et al: Invasive infection caused by *Penicillium marneffei*: An emerging pathogen in Taiwan. Clin Infect Dis 26:202–203, 1998.

334. Chariyalertsak S, Sirisanthana T, Supparatpinyo K, et al: Seasonal variation of disseminated *Penicillium marneffei* infections in northern Thailand: A clue to the reservoir? J Infect Dis 173:1490–1493, 1996.

335. Chariyalertsak S, Sirisanthana T, Supparatpinyo K, et al: Case-control study of risk factors for *Penicillium marneffei* infection in human immunodeficiency virus-infected patients in northern Thailand. Clin Infect Dis 24:1080–1086, 1997.

336. Sirisanthana T, Supparatpinyo K, Perriens J, et al: Amphotericin B and itraconazole for treatment of disseminated *Penicillium marneffei* infection in human immunodeficiency virus-infected patients. Clin Infect Dis 26:1107–1110, 1998.

337. Chariyalertsak S, Supparatpinyo K, Sirisanthana T, et al: A controlled trial of itraconazole as primary prophylaxis for systemic fungal infections in patients with advanced human immunodeficiency virus infection in Thailand. Clin Infect Dis 34:277–284, 2002.

338. Supparatpinyo K, Perriens J, Nelson KE, et al: A controlled trial of itraconazole to prevent relapse of *Penicillium marneffei* infection in patients infected with the human immunodeficiency virus. N Engl J Med 339:1739–1743, 1998.

339. Welch K, Finkbeiner W, Alpers CE, et al: Autopsy findings in the acquired immune deficiency syndrome. JAMA 252:1152–1159, 1984.

340. Mintz L, Drew WL, Miner RC, et al: Cytomegalovirus infections in homosexual men: An epidemiological study. Ann Intern Med 99:326–329, 1983.

341. Miles PR, Baughman RP, Linnemann CC Jr: Cytomegalovirus in the bronchoalveolar lavage fluid of patients with AIDS. Chest 97:1072–1076, 1990.

342. Jacobson MA, Mills J, Rush J, et al: Morbidity and mortality of patients with AIDS and first-episode *Pneumocystis carinii* pneumonia unaffected by concomitant pulmonary cytomegalovirus infection. Am Rev Respir Dis 144:6–9, 1991.

343. Rodriguez-Barradas MC, Stool E, Musher DM, et al: Diagnosing and treating cytomegalovirus pneumonia in patients with AIDS. Clin Infect Dis 23:76–81, 1996.

344. Waxman AB, Goldie SJ, Brett-Smith H, et al: Cytomegalovirus as a primary pulmonary pathogen in AIDS. Chest 111:128–134, 1997.

345. Salomon N, Gomez T, Perlman DC, et al: Clinical features and outcomes of HIV-related cytomegalovirus pneumonia. AIDS 11:319–324, 1997.

346. Mann M, Shelhamer JH, Masur H, et al: Lack of clinical utility of bronchoalveolar lavage cultures for cytomegalovirus in HIV infection. Am J Respir Crit Care Med 155:1723–1728, 1997.

347. Uberti-Foppa C, Lillo F, Terreni MR, et al: Cytomegalovirus pneumonia in AIDS patients: Value of cytomegalovirus culture from BAL fluid and correlation with lung disease. Chest 113:919–923, 1998.

348. Martin DF, Sierra-Madero J, Walmsley S, et al: A controlled trial of valganciclovir as induction therapy for cytomegalovirus retinitis. N Engl J Med 346:1119–1126, 2002.

349. Connolly MG Jr, Baughman RP, Dohn MN, et al: Recovery of viruses other than cytomegalovirus from bronchoalveolar lavage fluid. Chest 105:1775–1781, 1994.

350. Ramsey PG, Fife KH, Hackman RC, et al: Herpes simplex virus pneumonia: Clinical, virologic, and pathologic features in 20 patients. Ann Intern Med 97:813–820, 1982.

351. Fraisse P, Faller M, Rey D, et al: Recurrent varicella pneumonia complicating an endogenous reactivation of chickenpox in an HIV-infected adult patient. Eur Respir J 11:776–778, 1998.

352. Gnann JW Jr: Varicella-zoster virus: Atypical presentations and unusual complications. J Infect Dis 186(Suppl 1):S91–S98, 2002.

353. Andiman WA, Eastman R, Martin K, et al: Opportunistic lymphoproliferations associated with Epstein-Barr viral DNA in infants and children with AIDS. Lancet 2:1390–1393, 1985.

354. Safrin S, Rush JD, Mills J: Influenza in patients with human immunodeficiency virus infection. Chest 98:33–37, 1990.

355. Tasker SA, Treanor JJ, Paxton WB, et al: Efficacy of influenza vaccination in HIV-infected persons: A randomized, double-blind, placebo-controlled trial. Ann Intern Med 131:430–433, 1999.

356. Fuller JD, Craven DE, Steger KA, et al: Influenza vaccination of human immunodeficiency virus (HIV)-infected adults: Impact on plasma levels of HIV type 1 RNA and determinants of antibody response. Clin Infect Dis 28:541–547, 1999.

357. Moss WJ, Monze M, Ryon JJ, et al: Prospective study of measles in hospitalized, human immunodeficiency virus (HIV)-infected and HIV-uninfected children in Zambia. Clin Infect Dis 35:189–196, 2002.

358. Madhi SA, Ludewick H, Abed Y, et al: Human metapneumovirus-associated lower respiratory tract infections among hospitalized human immunodeficiency virus type 1 (HIV-1)-infected and HIV-1-uninfected African infants. Clin Infect Dis 37:1705–1710, 2003.

359. Oksenhendler E, Cadranel J, Sarfati C, et al: *Toxoplasma gondii* pneumonia in patients with the acquired immunodeficiency syndrome. Am J Med 88:18N–21N, 1990.

360. Schnapp LM, Geaghan SM, Campagna A, et al: *Toxoplasma gondii* pneumonitis in patients infected with the human immunodeficiency virus. Arch Intern Med 152:1073–1077, 1992.

361. Pomeroy C, Filice GA: Pulmonary toxoplasmosis: A review. Clin Infect Dis 14:863–870, 1992.

362. Rabaud C, May T, Lucet JC, et al: Pulmonary toxoplasmosis in patients infected with human immunodeficiency virus: A French National Survey. Clin Infect Dis 23:1249–1254, 1996.

363. Goodman PC, Schnapp LM: Pulmonary toxoplasmosis in AIDS. Radiology 184:791–793, 1992.

364. Torre D, Casari S, Speranza F, et al: Randomized trial of trimethoprim-sulfamethoxazole versus pyrimethamine-sulfadiazine for therapy of toxoplasmic encephalitis in patients with AIDS. Italian Collaborative Study Group. Antimicrob Agents Chemother 42:1346–1349, 1998.

365. Torres RA, Weinberg W, Stansell J, et al: Atovaquone for salvage treatment and suppression of toxoplasmic encephalitis in patients with AIDS. Atovaquone/Toxoplasmic Encephalitis Study Group. Clin Infect Dis 24:422–429, 1997.

366. Jacobson JM, Hafner R, Remington J, et al: Dose-escalation, Phase I/II study of azithromycin and pyrimethamine for the treatment of toxoplasmic encephalitis in AIDS. AIDS 15:583–589, 2001.

367. Karp CL, Neva FA: Tropical infectious diseases in human immunodeficiency virus-infected patients. Clin Infect Dis 28:947–963, 1999.

368. McCombs SB, Dworkin MS, Wan PC: Helminth infections in HIV-infected persons in the United States, 1990–1999. Clin Infect Dis 30:241–242, 2000.

369. Forgacs P, Tarshis A, Ma P, et al: Intestinal and bronchial cryptosporidiosis in an immunodeficient homosexual man. Ann Intern Med 99:793–794, 1983.

370. Ma P, Villanueva TG, Kaufman D, et al: Respiratory cryptosporidiosis in the acquired immune deficiency syndrome: Use of modified cold Kinyoun and Hemacolor stains for rapid diagnoses. JAMA 252:1298–1301, 1984.

371. Brady EM, Margolis ML, Korzeniowski OM: Pulmonary cryptosporidiosis in acquired immune deficiency syndrome. JAMA 252:89–90, 1984.

372. Weber R, Kuster H, Keller R, et al: Pulmonary and intestinal microsporidiosis in a patient with the acquired immunodeficiency syndrome. Am Rev Respir Dis 146:1603–1605, 1992.

373. Schwartz DA, Visvesvara GS, Leitch GJ, et al: Pathology of symptomatic microsporidial (*Encephalitozoon hellem*) bronchiolitis in the acquired immunodeficiency syndrome: A new respiratory pathogen diagnosed from lung biopsy, bronchoalveolar lavage, sputum, and tissue culture. Hum Pathol 24:937–943, 1993.

374. Weber R, Kuster H, Visvesvara GS, et al: Disseminated microsporidiosis due to *Encephalitozoon hellem*: Pulmonary colonization, microhematuria, and mild conjunctivitis in a patient with AIDS. Clin Infect Dis 17:415–419, 1993.

375. Remadi S, Dumais J, Wafa K, et al: Pulmonary microsporidiosis in a patient with the acquired immunodeficiency syndrome: A case report. Acta Cytol 39:1112–1116, 1995.

376. Gunnarsson G, Hurlbut D, DeGirolami PC, et al: Multiorgan microsporidiosis: Report of five cases and review. Clin Infect Dis 21:37–44, 1995.

377. Dore GJ, Marriott DJ, Hing MC, et al: Disseminated microsporidiosis due to *Septata intestinalis* in nine patients infected with the human immunodeficiency virus: Response to therapy with albendazole. Clin Infect Dis 21:70–76, 1995.

378. Meynard JL, Meyohas MC, Binet D, et al: Pulmonary cryptosporidiosis in the acquired immunodeficiency syndrome. Infection 24:328–331, 1996.

379. Clavel A, Arnal AC, Sanchez EC, et al: Respiratory cryptosporidiosis: Case series and review of the literature. Infection 24:341–346, 1996.

380. Maayan S, Wormser GP, Widerhorn J, et al: *Strongyloides stercoralis* hyperinfection in a patient with the acquired immune deficiency syndrome. Am J Med 83:945–948, 1987.

381. Schainberg L, Scheinberg MA: Recovery of *Strongyloides stercoralis* by bronchoalveolar lavage in a patient with acquired immunodeficiency syndrome. Am J Med 87:486, 1989.

382. Kramer MR, Gregg PA, Goldstein M, et al: Disseminated strongyloidiasis in AIDS and non-AIDS immunocompromised hosts: Diagnosis by sputum and bronchoalveolar lavage. South Med J 83:1226–1229, 1990.

383. Harcourt-Webster JN, Scaravilli F, Darwish AH: *Strongyloides stercoralis* hyperinfection in an HIV positive patient. J Clin Pathol 44:346–348, 1991.

384. Gompels MM, Todd J, Peters BS, et al: Disseminated strongyloidiasis in AIDS: Uncommon but important. AIDS 5:329–332, 1991.

385. Makris AN, Sher S, Bertoli C, et al: Pulmonary strongyloidiasis: An unusual opportunistic pneumonia in a patient with AIDS. AJR Am J Roentgenol 161:545–547, 1993.

386. Torres JR, Isturiz R, Murillo J, et al: Efficacy of ivermectin in the treatment of strongyloidiasis complicating AIDS. Clin Infect Dis 17:900–902, 1993.

387. Lessnau KD, Can S, Talavera W: Disseminated *Strongyloides stercoralis* in human immunodeficiency virus-infected patients: Treatment failure and a review of the literature. Chest 104:119–122, 1993.

388. Celedon JC, Mathur-Wagh U, Fox J, et al: Systemic strongyloidiasis in patients infected with the human immunodeficiency virus: A report of 3 cases and review of the literature. Medicine (Baltimore) 73:256–263, 1994.

389. Nomura J, Rekrut K: *Strongyloides stercoralis* hyperinfection syndrome in a patient with AIDS: Diagnosis by fluorescent microscopy. Clin Infect Dis 22:736, 1996.

390. Ferreira MS, Nishioka Sde A, Borges AS, et al: Strongyloidiasis and infection due to human immunodeficiency virus: 25 cases at a Brazilian teaching hospital, including seven cases of hyperinfection syndrome. Clin Infect Dis 28:154–155, 1999.

391. Lucas SB: Missing infections in AIDS. Trans R Soc Trop Med Hyg 84(Suppl 1):34–38, 1990.

391a. Viney ME, Brown M, Omoding NE, et al: Why does HIV infection not lead to disseminated strongyloidiasis? J Infect Dis 190:2175–2180, 2004.

392. Dukers NH, Rezza G: Human herpesvirus 8 epidemiology: What we do and do not know. AIDS 17:1717–1730, 2003.

393. Biggar RJ, Burnett W, Mikl J, et al: Cancer among New York men at risk of acquired immunodeficiency syndrome. Int J Cancer 43:979–985, 1989.

394. Chang Y, Cesarman E, Pessin MS, et al: Identification of herpesvirus-like DNA sequences in AIDS-associated Kaposi's sarcoma. Science 266:1865–1869, 1994.

395. Moore PS, Chang Y: Detection of herpesvirus-like DNA sequences in Kaposi's sarcoma in patients with and without HIV infection. N Engl J Med 332:1181–1185, 1995.

396. Gruden JF, Huang L, Webb WR, et al: AIDS-related Kaposi sarcoma of the lung: Radiographic findings and staging system with bronchoscopic correlation. Radiology 195:545–552, 1995.

397. Ziegler JL, Beckstead JA, Volberding PA, et al: Non-Hodgkin's lymphoma in 90 homosexual men: Relation to generalized lymphadenopathy and the acquired immunodeficiency syndrome. N Engl J Med 311:565–570, 1984.

398. Knowles DM, Chamulak GA, Subar M, et al: Lymphoid neoplasia associated with the acquired immunodeficiency syndrome (AIDS): The New York University Medical Center experience with 105 patients (1981–1986). Ann Intern Med 108:744–753, 1988.

399. Kaplan LD, Abrams DI, Feigal E, et al: AIDS-associated non-Hodgkin's lymphoma in San Francisco. JAMA 261:719–724, 1989.

400. Tirelli U, Spina M, Gaidano G, et al: Epidemiological, biological and clinical features of HIV-related lymphomas in the era of highly active antiretroviral therapy. AIDS 14:1675–1688, 2000.

401. Eisner MD, Kaplan LD, Herndier B, et al: The pulmonary manifestations of AIDS-related non-Hodgkin's lymphoma. Chest 110:729–736, 1996.

402. Goodman PC: Non-Hodgkin's lymphoma in the acquired immunodeficiency syndrome. J Thorac Imaging 6:49–52, 1991.

403. Judson MA, Sahn SA: Endobronchial lesions in HIV-infected individuals. Chest 105:1314–1323, 1994.

404. Keys TC, Judson MA, Reed CE, et al: Endobronchial HIV associated lymphoma. Thorax 49:525–526, 1994.

405. Sider L, Horton ES: Pleural effusion as a presentation of AIDS-related lymphoma. Invest Radiol 24:150–153, 1989.

406. Kaplan LD, Straus DJ, Testa MA, et al: Low-dose compared with standard-dose m-BACOD chemotherapy for non-Hodgkin's lymphoma associated with human immunodeficiency virus infection. National Institute of Allergy and Infectious Diseases AIDS Clinical Trials Group. N Engl J Med 336:1641–1648, 1997.

407. Antinori A, Cingolani A, Alba L, et al: Better response to chemotherapy and prolonged survival in AIDS-related lymphomas responding to highly active antiretroviral therapy. AIDS 15:1483–1491, 2001.

408. Vaccher E, Spina M, Talamini R, et al: Improvement of systemic human immunodeficiency virus-related non-Hodgkin lymphoma outcome in the era of highly active antiretroviral therapy. Clin Infect Dis 37:1556–1564, 2003.

409. Mbulaiteye SM, Biggar RJ, Goedert JJ, et al: Pleural and peritoneal lymphoma among people with AIDS in the United States. J Acquir Immune Defic Syndr 29:418–421, 2002.

410. Fajac I, Cadranel JL, Mariette X, et al: Pulmonary Hodgkin's disease in HIV-infected patient: Diagnosis by bronchoalveolar lavage. Chest 102:1913–1914, 1992.

411. Gerard L, Galicier L, Boulanger E, et al: Improved survival in HIV-related Hodgkin's lymphoma since the introduction of highly active antiretroviral therapy. AIDS 17:81–87, 2003.

412. Remick SC: Lung cancer: An HIV-related neoplasm or a coincidental finding? Chest 102:1643–1644, 1992.

413. Fraire AE, Awe RJ: Lung cancer in association with human immunodeficiency virus infection. Cancer 70:432–436, 1992.

414. Sridhar KS, Flores MR, Raub WA Jr, et al: Lung cancer in patients with human immunodeficiency virus infection compared with historic control subjects. Chest 102:1704–1708, 1992.

415. Karp J, Profeta G, Marantz PR, et al: Lung cancer in patients with immunodeficiency syndrome. Chest 103:410–413, 1993.
416. Chan TK, Aranda CP, Rom WN: Bronchogenic carcinoma in young patients at risk for acquired immunodeficiency syndrome. Chest 103:862–864, 1993.
417. Tenholder MF, Jackson HD: Bronchogenic carcinoma in patients seropositive for human immunodeficiency virus. Chest 104:1049–1053, 1993.
418. Aaron SD, Warner E, Edelson JD: Bronchogenic carcinoma in patients seropositive for human immunodeficiency virus. Chest 106:640–642, 1994.
419. Parker MS, Leveno DM, Campbell TJ, et al: AIDS-related bronchogenic carcinoma: Fact or fiction? Chest 113:154–161, 1998.
420. Johnson CC, Wilcosky T, Kvale P, et al: Cancer incidence among an HIV-infected cohort. Pulmonary Complications of HIV Infection Study Group. Am J Epidemiol 146:470–475, 1997.
421. Tirelli U, Spina M, Sandri S, et al: Lung carcinoma in 36 patients with human immunodeficiency virus infection. The Italian Cooperative Group on AIDS and Tumors. Cancer 88:563–569, 2000.
422. Bower M, Powles T, Nelson M, et al: HIV-related lung cancer in the era of highly active antiretroviral therapy. AIDS 17:371–375, 2003.
423. Dal Maso L, Polesel J, Serraino D, et al: Lung cancer in persons with AIDS in Italy, 1985–1998. AIDS 17:2117–2119, 2003.
424. Braun MA, Killam DA, Remick SC, et al: Lung cancer in patients seropositive for human immunodeficiency virus. Radiology 175:341–343, 1990.
425. White CS, Haramati LB, Elder KH, et al: Carcinoma of the lung in HIV-positive patients: Findings on chest radiographs and CT scans. AJR Am J Roentgenol 164:593–597, 1995.
426. Fishman JE, Schwartz DS, Sais GJ, et al: Bronchogenic carcinoma in HIV-positive patients: Findings on chest radiographs and CT scans. AJR Am J Roentgenol 164:57–61, 1995.
427. Gruden JF, Webb WR, Yao DC, et al: Bronchogenic carcinoma in 13 patients infected with the human immunodeficiency virus (HIV): Clinical and radiographic findings. J Thorac Imaging 10:99–105, 1995.
428. Thurer RJ, Jacobs JP, Holland FW 2nd, et al: Surgical treatment of lung cancer in patients with human immunodeficiency virus. Ann Thorac Surg 60:599–602, 1995.
429. Schneider RF: Lymphocytic interstitial pneumonitis and nonspecific interstitial pneumonitis. Clin Chest Med 17:763–766, 1996.
430. Joshi VV, Oleske JM, Minnefor AB, et al: Pathology of suspected acquired immune deficiency syndrome in children: A study of eight cases. Pediatr Pathol 2:71–87, 1984.
431. Grieco MH, Chinoy-Acharya P: Lymphocytic interstitial pneumonia associated with the acquired immune deficiency syndrome. Am Rev Respir Dis 131:952–955, 1985.
432. Solal-Celigny P, Couderc LJ, Herman D, et al: Lymphoid interstitial pneumonitis in acquired immunodeficiency syndrome-related complex. Am Rev Respir Dis 131:956–960, 1985.
433. Morris JC, Rosen MJ, Marchevsky A, et al: Lymphocytic interstitial pneumonia in patients at risk for the acquired immune deficiency syndrome. Chest 91:63–67, 1987.
434. Itescu S, Brancato LJ, Buxbaum J, et al: A diffuse infiltrative CD8 lymphocytosis syndrome in human immunodeficiency virus (HIV) infection: A host immune response associated with HLA-DR5. Ann Intern Med 112:3–10, 1990.
435. Scarborough M, Lishman S, Shaw P, et al: Lymphocytic interstitial pneumonitis in an HIV-infected adult: Response to antiretroviral therapy. Int J STD AIDS 11:119–122, 2000.
436. Dufour V, Wislez M, Bergot E, et al: Improvement of symptomatic human immunodeficiency virus-related lymphoid interstitial pneumonia in patients receiving highly active antiretroviral therapy. Clin Infect Dis 36:e127–e130, 2003.
437. Das S, Miller RF: Lymphocytic interstitial pneumonitis in HIV infected adults. Sex Transm Infect 79:88–93, 2003.
438. Innes AL, Huang L, Nishimura SL: Resolution of lymphocytic interstitial pneumonitis in an HIV infected adult after treatment with HAART. Sex Transm Infect 80:417–418, 2004.
439. Oldham SA, Castillo M, Jacobson FL, et al: HIV-associated lymphocytic interstitial pneumonia: Radiologic manifestations and pathologic correlation. Radiology 170:83–87, 1989.
440. Conces DJ Jr, Tarver RD: Noninfectious and nonmalignant pulmonary disease in AIDS. J Thorac Imaging 6:53–59, 1991.
441. Carignan S, Staples CA, Muller NL: Intrathoracic lymphoproliferative disorders in the immunocompromised patient: CT findings. Radiology 197:53–58, 1995.
442. McGuinness G, Scholes JV, Jagirdar JS, et al: Unusual lymphoproliferative disorders in nine adults with HIV or AIDS: CT and pathologic findings. Radiology 197:59–65, 1995.
443. Travis WD, Pittaluga S, Lipschik GY, et al: Atypical pathologic manifestations of *Pneumocystis carinii* pneumonia in the acquired immune deficiency syndrome: Review of 123 lung biopsies from 76 patients with emphasis on cysts, vascular invasion, vasculitis, and granulomas. Am J Surg Pathol 14:615–625, 1990.
444. Saldana MJ, Mones JM: Pulmonary pathology in AIDS: Atypical *Pneumocystis carinii* infection and lymphoid interstitial pneumonia. Thorax 49(Suppl):S46–S55, 1994.
445. Suffredini AF, Ognibene FP, Lack EE, et al: Nonspecific interstitial pneumonitis: A common cause of pulmonary disease in the acquired immunodeficiency syndrome. Ann Intern Med 107:7–13, 1987.
446. Ognibene FP, Masur H, Rogers P, et al: Nonspecific interstitial pneumonitis without evidence of *Pneumocystis carinii* in asymptomatic patients infected with human immunodeficiency virus (HIV). Ann Intern Med 109:874–879, 1988.
447. Griffiths MH, Miller RF, Semple SJ: Interstitial pneumonitis in patients infected with the human immunodeficiency virus. Thorax 50:1141–1146, 1995.
448. Sattler F, Nichols L, Hirano L, et al: Nonspecific interstitial pneumonitis mimicking *Pneumocystis carinii* pneumonia. Am J Respir Crit Care Med 156:912–917, 1997.
449. Simmons JT, Suffredini AF, Lack EE, et al: Nonspecific interstitial pneumonitis in patients with AIDS: Radiologic features. AJR Am J Roentgenol 149:265–268, 1987.
450. Travis WD, Fox CH, Devaney KO, et al: Lymphoid pneumonitis in 50 adult patients infected with the human immunodeficiency virus: Lymphocytic interstitial pneumonitis versus nonspecific interstitial pneumonitis. Hum Pathol 23:529–541, 1992.
451. Rosen MJ, Lou Y, Kvale PA, et al: Pulmonary function tests in HIV-infected patients without AIDS. Pulmonary Complications of HIV Infection Study Group. Am J Respir Crit Care Med 152:738–745, 1995.

452. Poirier CD, Inhaber N, Lalonde RG, et al: Prevalence of bronchial hyperresponsiveness among HIV-infected men. Am J Respir Crit Care Med 164:542–545, 2001.

453. O'Donnell CR, Bader MB, Zibrak JD, et al: Abnormal airway function in individuals with the acquired immunodeficiency syndrome. Chest 94:945–948, 1988.

454. Lin RY, Lazarus TS: Asthma and related atopic disorders in outpatients attending an urban HIV clinic. Ann Allergy Asthma Immunol 74:510–515, 1995.

455. Verghese A, al-Samman M, Nabhan D, et al: Bacterial bronchitis and bronchiectasis in human immunodeficiency virus infection. Arch Intern Med 154:2086–2091, 1994.

456. McGuinness G, Gruden JF, Bhalla M, et al: AIDS-related airway disease. AJR Am J Roentgenol 168:67–77, 1997.

457. King MA, Neal DE, St John R, et al: Bronchial dilatation in patients with HIV infection: CT assessment and correlation with pulmonary function tests and findings at bronchoalveolar lavage. AJR Am J Roentgenol 168:1535–1540, 1997.

458. Bard M, Couderc LJ, Saimot AG, et al: Accelerated obstructive pulmonary disease in HIV infected patients with bronchiectasis. Eur Respir J 11:771–775, 1998.

459. Diaz PT, Clanton TL, Pacht ER: Emphysema-like pulmonary disease associated with human immunodeficiency virus infection. Ann Intern Med 116:124–128, 1992.

460. Diaz PT, King MA, Pacht ER, et al: The pathophysiology of pulmonary diffusion impairment in human immunodeficiency virus infection. Am J Respir Crit Care Med 160:272–277, 1999.

461. Diaz PT, King MA, Pacht ER, et al: Increased susceptibility to pulmonary emphysema among HIV-seropositive smokers. Ann Intern Med 132:369–372, 2000.

461a. Diaz PT, Wewers MD, King M, et al: Regional differences in emphysema scores and BAL glutathione levels in HIV-infected individuals. Chest 126:1439–1442, 2004.

462. Mehta NJ, Khan IA, Mehta RN, et al: HIV-related pulmonary hypertension: Analytic review of 131 cases. Chest 118:1133–1141, 2000.

462a. Sitbon O, Gressin V, Speich R, et al: Bosentan for the treatment of human immunodeficiency virus-associated pulmonary arterial hypertension. Am J Respir Crit Care Med 170:1212–1217, 2004.

462b. Zuber JP, Calmy A, Evison JM, et al: Pulmonary arterial hypertension related to HIV infection: improved hemodynamics and survival associated with antiretroviral therapy. Clin Infect Dis 38:1178–1185, 2004.

463. Petitpretz P, Brenot F, Azarian R, et al: Pulmonary hypertension in patients with human immunodeficiency virus infection: Comparison with primary pulmonary hypertension. Circulation 89:2722–2727, 1994.

464. Nunes H, Humbert M, Sitbon O, et al: Prognostic factors for survival in human immunodeficiency virus-associated pulmonary arterial hypertension. Am J Respir Crit Care Med 167:1433–1439, 2003.

465. Vincent B, Flahault A, Antoine M, et al: AIDS-related alveolar hemorrhage: A prospective study of 273 BAL procedures. Chest 120:1078–1084, 2001.

466. Ruben FL, Talamo TS: Secondary pulmonary alveolar proteinosis occurring in two patients with acquired immune deficiency syndrome. Am J Med 80:1187–1190, 1986.

467. Tran Van Nhieu J, Vojtek AM, Bernaudin JF, et al: Pulmonary alveolar proteinosis associated with *Pneumocystis carinii*: Ultrastructural identification in bronchoalveolar lavage in AIDS and immunocompromised non-AIDS patients. Chest 98:801–805, 1990.

468. Askin FB, Katzenstein AL: Pneumocystis infection masquerading as diffuse alveolar damage: A potential source of diagnostic error. Chest 79:420–422, 1981.

469. Ramaswamy G, Jagadha V, Tchertkoff V: Diffuse alveolar damage and interstitial fibrosis in acquired immunodeficiency syndrome patients without concurrent pulmonary infection. Arch Pathol Lab Med 109:408–412, 1985.

470. Zahraa J, Herold B, Abrahams C, et al: Bronchiolitis obliterans organizing pneumonia in a child with acquired immunodeficiency syndrome. Pediatr Infect Dis J 15:448–451, 1996.

471. Allen JN, Wewers MD: HIV-associated bronchiolitis obliterans organizing pneumonia. Chest 96:197–198, 1989.

472. Leo YS, Pitchon HE, Messler G, et al: Bronchiolitis obliterans organizing pneumonia in a patient with AIDS. Clin Infect Dis 18:921–924, 1994.

473. Sanito NJ, Morley TF, Condoluci DV: Bronchiolitis obliterans organizing pneumonia in an AIDS patient. Eur Respir J 8:1021–1024, 1995.

474. Semenzato G: Immunology of interstitial lung diseases: Cellular events taking place in the lung of sarcoidosis, hypersensitivity pneumonitis and HIV infection. Eur Respir J 4:94–102, 1991.

475. Coots LE, Lazarus AA: Sarcoidosis diagnosed in a patient with known HIV infection. Chest 96:201–202, 1989.

476. Lowery WS, Whitlock WL, Dietrich RA, et al: Sarcoidosis complicated by HIV infection: Three case reports and a review of the literature. Am Rev Respir Dis 142:887–889, 1990.

477. Newman TG, Minkowitz S, Hanna A, et al: Coexistent sarcoidosis and HIV infection: A comparison of bronchoalveolar and peripheral blood lymphocytes. Chest 102:1899–1901, 1992.

478. Amin DN, Sperber K, Brown LK, et al: Positive Kveim test in patients with coexisting sarcoidosis and human immunodeficiency virus infection. Chest 101:1454–1456, 1992.

479. Gomez V, Smith PR, Burack J, et al: Sarcoidosis after antiretroviral therapy in a patient with acquired immunodeficiency syndrome. Clin Infect Dis 31:1278–1280, 2000.

480. Blanche P, Gombert B, Rollot F, et al: Sarcoidosis in a patient with acquired immunodeficiency syndrome treated with interleukin-2. Clin Infect Dis 31:1493–1494, 2000.

481. Haramati LB, Lee G, Singh A, et al: Newly diagnosed pulmonary sarcoidosis in HIV-infected patients. Radiology 218:242–246, 2001.

482. Lenner R, Bregman Z, Teirstein AS, et al: Recurrent pulmonary sarcoidosis in HIV-infected patients receiving highly active antiretroviral therapy. Chest 119:978–981, 2001.

483. Morris DG, Jasmer RM, Huang L, et al: Sarcoidosis following HIV infection: Evidence for CD4+ lymphocyte dependence. Chest 124:929–935, 2003.

484. Foulon G, Wislez M, Naccache JM, et al: Sarcoidosis in HIV-infected patients in the era of highly active antiretroviral therapy. Clin Infect Dis 38:418–425, 2004.

484a. Hirsch HH, Kaufmann G, Sendi P, Battegay M: Immune reconstitution in HIV-infected patients. Clin Infect Dis 38:1159–1166, 2004.

485. Naccache JM, Antoine M, Wislez M, et al: Sarcoid-like pulmonary disorder in human immunodeficiency virus-infected patients receiving antiretroviral therapy. Am J Respir Crit Care Med 159:2009–2013, 1999.

486. Morris AM, Nishimura S, Huang L: Subacute hypersensitivity pneumonitis in an HIV infected patient receiving antiretroviral therapy. Thorax 55:625–627, 2000.

76 Pulmonary Complications of Organ Transplantation and Primary Immunodeficiencies

Rodney J. Folz, M.D., Ph.D., John M. Routes, M.D.

INTRODUCTION

The human respiratory tract is well designed anatomically and incorporates a variety of defense mechanisms (see Chapters 11 through 15) to protect against both inhaled and aspirated microorganisms and toxic substances. Physical barriers and removal systems constitute the first line of defense, but the lungs are also protected by a complex series of integrated immunologic and cellular mechanisms. Hereditary or acquired deficiencies in any one of the components of this elaborate system are frequently announced by the development of recurrent infections, often of the lungs or upper respiratory tract.

The first part of this chapter briefly describes the many primary (heritable) immunodeficiency syndromes that arise from disorders of antibody production and function, cellular immune deficiencies, and phagocytic cell abnormalities. The chapter concludes with a discussion of bone marrow and stem-cell transplantation, an increasingly common cause of severe acquired immunodeficiency, with emphasis on the different types of infectious and noninfectious pulmonary complications as well as how to diagnosis and manage them.

PRIMARY IMMUNODEFICIENCIES

A diagnostic evaluation for primary immunodeficiency is a fundamental, but often overlooked issue in the evaluation of patients with pulmonary infections. This oversight may have significant, detrimental consequences for long-term survival and quality of life of the patient with a primary immunodeficiency. Several studies indicate the importance of the early diagnosis of primary immunodeficiencies in reducing the morbidity and mortality associated with recurrent infections. For example, early bone marrow transplantation (BMT) (<3 months of age) results in improved outcome in infants with severe combined immunodeficiency (SCID). Treatment with high-dose intravenous immunoglobulin (IVIG) can prevent many of the infectious sequelae in patients with primary antibody deficiency states.[1] Additionally, many routine childhood vaccines use attenuated organisms. The use of such vaccines may lead to disseminated infections in patients with antibody or cellular immunodeficiencies and are contraindicated.

Primary immunodeficiencies are disorders that increasingly affect adults. Of the estimated 20,000 patients in the United States receiving IVIG, 23% are 30 to 44 years of age and 34% are in the 45- to 65-year age group. Thus, the diagnosis or clinical manifestation of primary immunodeficiencies may be delayed into adulthood, and more patients who were diagnosed during infancy and childhood, with appropriate care, survive into the adult years.

The decision to evaluate patients with pulmonary infection for primary immunodeficiencies cannot be made in the context of the pulmonary infection alone. Several factors need to be considered (Table 76.1). Thus, a patient with first pneumonia, but with a history of intractable sinus disease or recurrent gastrointestinal infections, should be evaluated for a primary immunodeficiency. Elderly patients hospitalized for pneumonia are at high risk for recurrent pneumonia and early mortality. These patients should be evaluated for immunodeficiency and immunized against *Streptococcus pneumoniae*.[2] In addition, the prevalence of autoimmune disorders is increased in many primary immunodeficiencies. In general, an evaluation of the immune system is warranted in patients with two or more radiographically documented pneumonias.

There are several clues in the history and clinical presentation of patients with primary immunodeficiencies that suggest the type of immunologic defect present (Table 76.2). The onset of diseases associated with cellular immunodeficiencies usually begins soon after birth or in early infancy. Infections with opportunistic or unusual pathogens, mycobacteria, disseminated viral infections, and severe oral candidiasis may occur. Diarrhea and malabsorption are common,[3–5] and growth is delayed. In contrast, the onset of infections in patients with antibody deficiencies, such as

X-linked agammaglobulinemia (XLA), occurs after 6 months when maternal antibodies are no longer present. Recurrent and severe upper and lower respiratory tract infections are the usual mode of presentation. Complement deficiencies may present in a manner similar to antibody deficiencies or with recurrent *Neisseria* species infections. In contrast to patients with cellular immunodeficiencies, growth is usually unimpaired in patients with complement or antibody deficiencies.

One common misconception is that opportunistic pathogens are overwhelmingly the cause of most infections in patients with primary immunodeficiencies. In fact, many infections in immunodeficient patients occur with pathogens that are common in the community. However, these infections may be of unusual severity and respond poorly to therapy. Finally, although this section deals exclusively with primary immunodeficiency disorders, it is critically important to exclude secondary immunodeficiencies (e.g., lymphoproliferative disorders and malignancy, malnutrition, immunosuppressive drugs, protein-losing states) in patients who present with recurrent infection.

In summary, there are several criteria (see Table 76.1) that should prompt the clinician to evaluate a patient for immunodeficiency. An immunodeficiency evaluation should not be restricted to children, but is warranted in patients of any age. Recurrent infections, even infections that are common in the population in general, such as sinusitis, pneumonia, and gastrointestinal infections, should lead to a screening evaluation for immunodeficiency.

DIAGNOSTIC WORKUP

There are a number of readily available and fairly inexpensive screening tests that should be used in the evaluation of a patient for possible immunodeficiency (Table 76.3).[6] Abnormalities found in these screening tests indicate the need for more sophisticated studies in collaboration with a clinical immunologist. The goal in the evaluation of immunodeficient patients should be to define the specific genetic abnormality whenever possible.

Antibody Deficiencies

The quantitative measurement of immunoglobulin (Ig)G, IgA, and IgM is the single best test to screen for antibody

---

Table 76.1 General Criteria for Immunologic Evaluation

Chronic infection
Recurrent infection
Opportunistic or unusual pathogens
Unusual sites of infections
Incomplete clearing of infection
Poor response to antimicrobial therapy
Associated conditions (unusual facies, tetany, thrush, eczema, autoimmunity)

Table 76.2 Examples of Primary Immunodeficiencies

Type of Immunodeficiency	Example	Mode of Presentation
Antibody	XLA, CVID	Upper and lower respiratory tract infections (encapsulated and atypical bacteria), giardiasis
T cell	DiGeorge syndrome	Abnormal facies, lymphopenia, recurrent infections
Combined B cell and T cell	SCID (multiple causes)	Opportunistic infections, thrush, intractable diarrhea, failure to thrive
Cellular/complex	IFN-γ–IL-12 axis	Atypical mycobacterial and *Salmonella* infections
Phagocyte	CGD	Recurrent abscesses
Complement	C5–C9	Recurrent *Neisseria meningitidis* infections

CGD, chronic granulomatous disease; CVID, common variable immunodeficiency; IFN, interferon; IL, interleukin; SCID, severe combined immunodeficiency; XLA, X-linked agammaglobulinemia.

Table 76.3 Screening Tests for Immune Function

Immune Function	Enumeration/Flow Cytometry	Function
Cellular immunity	CBC with differential* CD3$^+$CD4$^+$ CD3$^+$CD8$^+$ CD16$^+$CD56$^+$	Cutaneous delayed hypersensitivity Enzyme assays (ADA, PNP) FISH for 22q11 and 10p11 deletion NK cell cytolysis assay
B cells	CD19$^+$ or CD20$^+$	IgG, IgA, IgM levels Antibody response to immunization
PMNs	CBC with differential LFA-1	Oxidase function (NBT, DHR, chemiluminescence) Enzyme assays (MPO, G6PD) Phagocyte function
Complement		AH$_{50}$ (alternative pathway) CH$_{50}$ (classic pathway) Complement split products Specific complement components

* Preferred initial screening tests are underlined.
ADA, adenosine deaminase; CBC, complete blood count; DHR, dihydrorhodamine; FISH, fluorescence in situ hybridization; G6PD, glucose-6-phosphate dehydrogenase; Ig, immunoglobulin; LFA-1, lymphocyte function antigen 1; MPO, myeloperoxidase; NK, natural killer; NPT, nitroblue tetrazolium; PMN, polymorphonuclear leukocytes; PNP, purine nucleoside phosphorylase.

Table 76.4 Typical Results of Screening Tests in Antibody Deficiencies

Disorder	B-Cell Numbers	IgG (mg/dL)	IgA (mg/dL)	IgM (mg/dL)	Response to Immunization
IgA deficiency	Normal	Normal	<10	Normal	Normal
XLA	Very low	<200	Extremely low	Extremely low	Absent
CVID	Usually normal	<400	Low	Low	Absent
Steroid induced	Normal or reduced	>400	Slightly reduced	Slightly reduced	May be reduced, not absent
Hyper-IgM syndrome	Normal	<400	Low	Normal/high	Small IgM response, no memory

CVID, common variable immunodeficiency; Ig, immunoglobulin; XLA, X-linked agammaglobulinemia.

deficiency states.[7] An abnormality in the level of one of the classes of immunoglobulins (IgG, IgA, and IgM) is present in the majority of patients with primary antibody deficiencies. The pattern of the levels of IgG, IgA, and IgM gives important insight into the likely etiology of the antibody deficiency (Table 76.4). For example, clinical immunologists are frequently consulted about the issue of whether a patient on corticosteroids has a primary antibody deficiency. In steroid-induced hypogammaglobulinemia, IgG levels are usually only moderately depressed (usually >400 mg/dL) and the magnitude of reduction reflects the dosage and duration of corticosteroid usage.[8] IgA and IgM levels tend to be preserved. In common variable immunodeficiency (CVID), IgG levels are usually more profoundly depressed (<400 mg/dL), IgA levels are reduced (<10 mg/dL) in 70% of patients, and IgM levels are reduced (<25 mg/dL) in over 80% of patients.[7] Finally, patients with CVID are unable to make specific antibody following immunization. In contrast, patients with steroid-induced hypogammaglobulinemia make specific antibodies, although the response may be blunted.[9]

The quantitation of B-cell numbers, typically measured by flow cytometry using the monoclonal antibodies directed against the CD19 or CD20 antigens, may also provide clues to the type of B-cell immunodeficiency present. XLA and autosomal recessive causes of antibody deficiency usually have severely reduced levels of B cells. In contrast, B-cell numbers in CVID are usually, but not always, normal.

In assessing response to immunization, it is important to immunize with both a protein and polysaccharide antigen and to assess the response 4 to 6 weeks postimmunization.[10] The immunologic requirements to make antibodies (e.g., T helper cell, cytokine requirements) in response to immunization with these antigens differ, a difference that may have important clinical implications. For example, some patients with normal quantitative immunoglobulins or selective IgA deficiency exhibit a selective inability to make antibody to polysaccharide, but not to protein antigens. This immunologic defect results in recurrent sinopulmonary infections.

Protein antigens commonly used to assess specific antibody responses include tetanus and diphtheria toxoids. The

Haemophilus influenzae type B vaccine in present use conjugates the capsular polysaccharide (polyribose phosphate) to a protein carrier. Thus, immunization with *H. influenzae* type B measures an antibody response to a protein, but not to a polysaccharide antigen. Many adults have not been immunized to *H. influenzae* type B, making this vaccine particularly useful in the evaluation of this group of patients.

There are two readily available vaccines that can be used to assess antibody responses to polysaccharide antigens, the pneumococcal polysaccharide and *Neisseria meningitidis* vaccines. Some pneumococcal vaccines are conjugated to a protein carrier and cannot be used to measure a response to the polysaccharide antigen. When using the pneumococcal vaccine, the measurement of antibody responses to several (12 or more) capsular antigens is indicated. There is considerable controversy about what constitutes a normal response to the pneumococcal vaccine. The authors believe that the only clearly abnormal response to a pneumococcal vaccine in adults is an absent response to all or nearly all capsular antigens. Finally, children less than 2 years of age frequently do not make antibody responses to polysaccharide antigens. Thus, the use of polysaccharide vaccines to diagnose antibody-deficient states in this age group is not indicated.

Cellular Immunodeficiencies

Most patients with impaired cellular immunity will have either reduced T-cell numbers or abnormal T-cell function, or both (see Table 76.3). Quantitation of T-cell numbers is easily screened by enumeration using flow cytometry. The CD3 antigen measures the total numbers of T cells, whereas CD4 and CD8 antigens are present on the T helper and T cytotoxic subsets, respectively. Cutaneous delayed hypersensitivity is an easily performed test for T-cell function. Because cutaneous delayed hypersensitivity responses are absent in normal infants, in vitro assays of T-cell function are indicated in this group of patients.[11] The measurement of natural killer (NK) cell numbers (CD16+/CD18+) and function is indicated in the evaluation of infants for possible SCID or patients with recurrent, severe herpesvirus infection. The pattern of abnormalities in the numbers of specific lymphocyte subpopulations (T cells, NK cells, B cells) is helpful in identifying the molecular abnormality in infants with SCID (Table 76.5).

Table 76.5 More Common Etiologies of Severe Combined Immunodeficiency (SCID)

Form of SCID	Prevalence	T/B/NK Cell Ratio	Inheritance
γc deficiency	45–50%	−/+/−	X-linked
ADA deficiency	15–20%	−/−/−	AR*
RAG1/RAG2	10%†	−/−/+	AR
JAK-3	5–10%	−/+/−	AR

* Autosomal recessive.

† Total prevalence of patients with mutations in either RAG1 or RAG2 gene.

Complement Deficiencies

The screening tests for complement deficiency states associated with increased infections are the CH_{50} and AH_{50}, which measure the integrity of the classic and alternative pathways of complement activation, respectively[12] (see Table 76.3). Abnormalities in the CH_{50} or AH_{50} could be due to deficiencies in individual components of the complement pathway or to inappropriate activation and consumption in the complement pathway. These possibilities are distinguished by the measurement of two or more individual components of the classic or alternative complement pathway and the measurement of complement split products. Complement consumption is indicated by the low levels of more than one component of complement and the elevation of complement split products. In contrast, complement deficiency states show depressed levels of individual members of the complement pathway with normal levels of complement split products.

Phagocyte Deficiencies

The initial screening test for phagocytic cell defects includes a complete blood count, with quantitation of leukocyte number and morphology (see Table 76.3). The nitroblue tetrazolium test and dihydrorhodamine test (DHR) are the assays most commonly used to detect defects in the generation of oxidase activation, such as seen in chronic granulomatous disease (CGD).[13] The DHR test is fast becoming the assay of choice due to the ease, rapidity, and reproducibility of the test, along with the capacity to readily detect CGD carrier states.[13,14] Both the nitroblue tetrazolium and DHR tests measure the products of oxidase metabolism. In the DHR test, phagocytes are loaded with a fluorescent dye (DHR) and activated with phorbol myristate acetate. The products of oxidase metabolism then interact with DHR, leading to a change in fluorescence that is quantitated by flow cytometry. Other functional assays for phagocytes include enzyme assays for myeloperoxidase and glucose-6-phosphate dehydrogenase, chemotactic assays, and phagocytic tests that may include measuring the capacity of phagocytes to both phagocytose and kill bacteria such as *Staphylococcus aureus*. Abnormalities in adhesion molecules such as leukocyte adhesion deficiency (LAD) types 1 and 2 are detected by flow cytometry.

ANTIBODY DEFICIENCIES

An increasing number of genetic abnormalities are known to cause primary antibody deficiencies.[15] However, despite tremendous progress in this area, the molecular basis underlying two common primary antibody deficiencies, IgA deficiency and CVID, remain unknown.

IVIG is the most commonly used form of antibody replacement for the treatment of profound antibody deficiencies such as XLA and CVID. Subcutaneous infusion of gamma globulin is an acceptable alternative form of therapy.[16] High-dose IVIG (500 to 600 mg/kg) is superior in preventing infections compared to conventional low-dose IVIG (100 to 150 mg/kg).[17] The bronchiectasis due to recurrent respiratory tract infections and sinusitis has also been shown to improve with high-dose IVIG.[18] Intercurrent sinopulmonary infections should be aggressively treated with appropriate antimicrobial therapy to include coverage of common encapsulated bacteria as well as atypical bacterial pathogens (including *Mycoplasma* species and *Ureaplasma*).[19]

A common mistake in managing patients with CVID is the inappropriate use of serologic assays in the diagnosis of infectious disorders. With the exception of IgA and IgG subclass deficiency, patients with antibody deficiency do not make specific antibodies in response to exogenous antigens. Therefore, the use of diagnostic studies to detect specific antibodies against pathogens is unreliable and, if positive, almost always simply reflect antibodies present in the IVIG used to treat such patients. Diagnostic studies that detect antigens or genome (polymerase chain reaction [PCR] assays) from the pathogen must be used in place of serologic assays.

IMMUNOGLOBULIN A DEFICIENCY

The prevalence of IgA deficiency varies among different ethnic groups, but the overall prevalence is approximately 1 per 700 live births.[15] There is considerable controversy on whether IgA deficiency alone predisposes people to infection.[15,20,21] Most patients with IgA deficiency do not have increased infection and are often discovered during evaluation unrelated to infection.[22,23] However, a significant minority of patients with IgA deficiency do have recurrent infections.[20]

Clinical manifestations of IgA deficiency are highly variable. Infectious complications of IgA deficiency include recurrent otitis media, sinusitis, and lower respiratory tract infections.[20] Gastrointestinal tract infections, in particular recurrent giardiasis, may be present. The prevalence of atopic (asthma, allergic rhinitis, eczema) and autoimmune (systemic lupus erythematosus, celiac disease, rheumatoid arthritis) diseases is increased in patients with IgA deficiency.[24] IgA deficiency may be discovered in the diagnostic evaluation of such patients.

The prevalence of atopy, the genetic predisposition to generate IgE antibodies in response to environmental antigens, is increased in patients with IgA deficiency. Multiparous women may develop IgE antibodies upon exposure to IgA from the infant during the birthing process. Many blood and blood products contain low amounts of IgA. IgA-deficient patients transfused with these blood products may produce IgE antibodies to the IgA commonly present in these preparations. Consequently, patients with IgA deficiency may be at risk to develop anaphylactic reactions following administration of blood or blood products. To prevent these anaphylactic reactions, patients with IgA deficiency should wear identification, such as a Medic Alert bracelet or necklace. Blood transfusions using products from IgA-deficient donors should be used whenever possible. Extensively washed, packed red blood cells may be used for transfusion in an emergency situation or when an IgA-deficient donor cannot be found.

Unlike in patients with more severe forms of antibody deficiency, such as CVID or XLA, replacement therapy with IVIG is not warranted in patients with isolated IgA deficiency. In patients with IgA deficiency and concomitant IgG

subclass deficiency who have recurrent and persistent respiratory tract infections, determination of the antibody response following vaccination should be used to ascertain if IVIG therapy is warranted.[22]

X-LINKED AGAMMAGLOBULINEMIA

Bruton's X-linked agammaglobulinemia is a primary antibody deficiency with an estimated prevalence of 1 per 50,000 live births.[25] Mutations in various locations of the cytoplasmic tyrosine kinase gene, Bruton's tyrosine kinase (*Btk*), are responsible for this immunodeficiency.[26] *Btk* function is required for B-cell receptor signaling, which is necessary for the survival and differentiation of immature B cells. Consequently, B-cell numbers and immunoglobulin levels are dramatically reduced in this disorder. *Btk* is not necessary for T-cell receptor signaling or T-cell survival. As a result, XLA is the prototypical pure B-cell immunodeficiency.[27] This contrasts with some other antibody deficiency disorders, such as CVID or hyper-IgM syndrome, where abnormalities in cellular immunity are frequently present. Several other, autosomal recessive, forms of antibody deficiency[15] have been characterized. The clinical manifestations of these disorders are similar to XLA.[28]

Small tonsils and absent lymph nodes are the only characteristic physical findings in XLA. The vast majority of patients with XLA have the onset of recurrent sinopulmonary infections, usually within the first 2 years of life. The most common pathogens are encapsulated bacteria such as *S. pneumoniae* and *H. influenzae*.[29,30] Infections with atypical bacteria such as *Mycoplasma pneumoniae* or *Ureaplasma urealyticum* are also frequently encountered. Although cellular immunity is the primary defense against pneumonias due to *Pneumocystis jirovecii* (formerly *carinii*), pneumonias due to this microorganism are well described, although uncommon.[31] Central nervous system infections with enteroviruses may occur and respond to antiviral therapy. Gastrointestinal tract infections with *Giardia lamblia*, in addition to common bacterial pathogens (*Salmonella, Shigella, Campylobacter*), frequently occur. Viral hepatitis B and C occur in a minority of patients and should be diagnosed using PCR-based assays to detect viral genome.

The pulmonary complications of XLA are a major cause of morbidity and mortality in XLA and include bronchiectasis, hypoxemia, and cor pulmonale. Complete pulmonary function tests (if possible) and high-resolution computed tomography (HRCT) scan of the chest are indicated in the initial evaluation of these patients and periodically thereafter. High-dose IVIG has been shown to decrease pulmonary infections in these patients, but may not totally prevent bronchiectasis. Bronchiectasis should be treated with daily pulmonary toilet, and vigorous antimicrobial therapy for intercurrent pulmonary infections is indicated. The efficacy of rotating antibiotics is unclear, so the practice should not be routinely used.

COMMON VARIABLE IMMUNODEFICIENCY

CVID, also known as acquired hypogammaglobulinemia, is a primary immunodeficiency affecting approximately 1 per 50,000 to 75,000 live births.[32] CVID is a clinical syndrome and represents a family of disorders that exhibit a common phenotype. Although variable, the mean onset of symptoms in patients with CVID is in the second decade of life. There remains a considerable delay between the onset of symptoms and the diagnosis of CVID (>5 years).[7] Unlike with XLA, T-cell abnormalities are common in patients with CVID and likely account for the more protean clinical manifestations of this disease.[7] The diagnosis of CVID should be considered in any person with recurrent respiratory tract infections (i.e., two or more confirmed pneumonias) who is more than 2 years of age.

The etiology of CVID is unknown. Recently, a European study reported that mutation in the inducible costimulator gene (*ICOS*) was present in 4 of 32 patients previously diagnosed with CVID.[33] These patients had reduced B-cell numbers and exhibited the typical infections associated with hypogammaglobulinemia. ICOS deficiency can be ascertained by flow cytometry that shows an absence of ICOS on T-cells following cellular activation. The prevalence of ICOS deficiency in a broader group of patients remains to be determined.

The laboratory evaluation of patients with CVID demonstrates the complex nature of the disease.[7] IgG levels are reduced by greater than 2 standard deviations from the mean in all patients. IgA levels are low in nearly all patients, whereas IgM levels are reduced in the majority of patients. B-cell numbers are usually normal in CVID, and, if reduced, may indicate a poorer prognosis. T-cell abnormalities occur in approximately 40% of patients and include anergy, T-cell lymphopenia, and poor proliferative responses to mitogens and antigens.

Nearly all patients present with recurrent upper and lower respiratory tract infections. Common pathogens include encapsulated (*H. influenzae, S. pneumoniae*) or atypical (*Mycoplasma* species) bacteria[7,19,34] and rarely *P. jirovecii*. Pulmonary infections with gram-negative rods should also be considered, in particular in patients with long-standing CVID or impaired cellular immunity. Patients with CVID appear to be particularly susceptible to infections with atypical bacteria. Apart from respiratory tract infections, joint and bone infections due to these organisms have also been reported. Gastrointestinal tract infections with pathogens similar to those found in XLA (*Campylobacter jejuni, G. lamblia*) are common.[7] The prevalence of hepatitis is increased in CVID, occurring in approximately 12% of patients. The etiology of the hepatitis in CVID is complex and includes viral infection (hepatitis B and C viruses), autoimmunity, and granulomatous hepatitis.

There are other conditions that further complicate the management of CVID. Although patients with CVID are unable to make antibodies to foreign antigens, they exhibit increased propensity to make autoantibodies. Consequently, the prevalence of autoimmune disorders such as autoimmune hemolytic anemia, idiopathic thrombocytopenic purpura, rheumatoid arthritis, juvenile rheumatoid arthritis, and systemic lupus erythematosus is increased.[7] Oral corticosteroids and the use of immunomodulatory dosages of IVIG (2 g/kg/month) are generally used to treat the autoimmune hemolytic anemia or idiopathic thrombocytopenic purpura.

Patients with CVID are at high risk to develop malignancy. In particular, the prevalence of non-Hodgkin's lymphomas and gastric carcinoma are dramatically increased in CVID and are a major cause of morbidity and mortality in this disorder.[35,36] Careful periodic examination of the lymph nodes and spleen is important, as patients with CVID also frequently have adenopathy and splenomegaly that is nonmalignant in nature. The use of periodic abdominal computed tomography (CT) scans to assess spleen size and the presence of intra-abdominal and retroperitoneal adenopathy, along with upper and lower endoscopic evaluation for gastrointestinal symptoms, is indicated.

The pulmonary disorders associated with CVID are also complex and a major cause of mortality. As might be expected, bronchiectasis is the most common pulmonary abnormality in CVID. Diffuse interstitial lung diseases (granulomatous lung disease, lymphocytic interstitial pneumonia, follicular bronchiolitis, and bronchiolitis obliterans with organizing pneumonia [BOOP]), disorders that are refractory to the use of IVIG, occur in approximately 25% of patients with CVID.[37,38]

There is considerable controversy regarding the nature and clinical course of granulomatous lung disease in CVID.[39,40] Some believe that the granulomatous disease in CVID represents a form of sarcoidosis. Common features shared with sarcoidosis include the systemic nature of the disease, frequent presence of mediastinal and hilar adenopathy, and noncaseating granulomas in the lung and other organs. In contrast, we and others believe this disorder represents a distinct disease entity. In the evaluation of patients with diffuse lung disease and CVID, we routinely perform open-lung biopsies. Unlike sarcoidosis, we have found that the granulomatous and lymphoproliferative histopathologic patterns (lymphocytic interstitial pneumonia, follicular bronchiolitis, and lymphoid hyperplasia) often appear together. Furthermore, the pulmonary disease does not remit spontaneously, responds poorly to corticosteroid therapy, and is associated with an increased risk to develop non-Hodgkin's lymphoma and early mortality.[40a] Limited anecdotal experience suggests that the granulomatous and lymphocytic lung disease responds to low-dose cyclosporine therapy.[41]

The combination of CVID in conjunction with thymoma is known as Good's syndrome.[42,43] Whether this disorder is unique from CVID or another manifestation of the disease is unclear. The thymoma is often not apparent on routine chest radiograph. Autoimmune disorders and opportunistic infections appear to be more common in this group of patients. Resection of the thymoma is recommended, although this will not result in resolution of the immunodeficiency or autoimmunity.[42,43]

Due to the complexity of the pulmonary disease, we recommend periodic chest radiographs, full pulmonary function tests, and HRCT scans of the chest in patients with CVID.[44] Patients with diffuse lung disease should undergo open-lung biopsy to characterize the nature of the lung disease and exclude lymphoma.

HYPER–IMMUNOGLOBULIN M SYNDROME

Hyper-IgM syndrome (HIM) is a descriptive term that reflects a laboratory abnormality (high IgM level with low IgA and IgG levels) common to several distinct types of immunodeficiencies (Table 76.6).[44a] Although all forms of HIM also have impaired humeral immunity, several types of HIM have abnormal cellular immunity.

Table 76.6 Etiologies of Hyper–Immunoglobulin M Syndrome

Mutation	Clinical Phenotype
CD40-L	X-linked, abnormal cellular immunity, neutropenia in 50%, early onset, recurrent sinopulmonary infections, fungal and opportunistic infections, intractable diarrhea
AICD or UNG AR	Normal cellular immunity, later age of onset, recurrent sinopulmonary infections, lymphadenopathy, no opportunistic infections, mutation in UNG with similar phenotype
CD40/AR NEMO (IKK-γ)	Similar presentation as CD40-L mutation Ectodermal dysplasia (most), impaired cellular immunity, hyper-IgM or hyper-IgA recurrent infections, mycobacterial infections

AICD, activation-induced cytidine deaminase; AR, autosomal recessive; Ig, immunoglobulin; UNG, uracil-N-glycosylase; see text for other abbreviations.

The classic, X-linked form of HIM, which accounts for approximately two thirds of the cases, is due to a mutation in the CD40 ligand (CD40-L) gene.[45-53] CD40-L is inducibly expressed on activated, CD4 T cells and interacts with CD40, which is expressed on the surface of B cells. The interaction of CD40 on B cells with CD40-L on activated T cells in conjunction with specific cytokines (interleukin [IL]-4) is required for immunoglobulin class switching. Consequently, mutations in CD40-L (or CD40 in HIM-3) results in a failure to class switch, leading to defective production of the later immunoglobulin isotypes (IgG, IgA, and IgE). High levels of IgM are an inconsistent finding, occurring in approximately 50% of patients.[45] Antibody responses to immunization show a weak IgM response, without development of IgG- or IgA-specific responses and the absence of immunologic memory. CD40 is also expressed on monocytes and dendritic cells. The lack of CD40-L T-cell interaction with CD40 on monocytes and dendritic cells leads to defective cellular immunity. Autosomal mutations within the CD40 gene cause a clinical phenotype similar to X-linked HIM. Patients with mutations in CD40 or CD40-L have recurrent infections, including infections with opportunistic pathogens, beginning early in life. Infections with *P. jirovecii* are particularly common, occurring in 30% to 40% of patients with HIM. High levels of IgM are inconsistently found in all forms of HIM.[45-47] Neutropenia is frequently found and may respond to treatment with granulocyte colony-stimulating factor (G-CSF).

Mutations within the nuclear factor-κB (NF-κB) essential modifier (NEMO) gene are another cause of HIM.[54-61] NEMO is involved in the activation and nuclear translocation of NF-κB. Ligation of CD40 on B cells activates the NF-κB pathway and appears to be important in immunoglobulin class switching. Therefore, an inability to activate the NF-κB pathway due to mutation in NEMO likely explains the plethora of immunologic abnormalities in this syndrome, including hypogammaglobulinemia, impaired production of inflammatory cytokines, and defec-tive cellular immunity, including abnormal NK cell function. Most, but not all, of these patients exhibit ectodermal dysplasia (abnormal teeth, decreased numbers of sweat glands, fine hair, and frontal bossing). Patients with NEMO have severe infections early in life, including infections with opportunistic organisms, mycobacteria, and herpesviruses.

Mutations in activation-induced cytidine deaminase (AICD),[62] or uracil-N-glycosylase (UNG)[63] are causes of autosomal recessive forms of HIM. The exact function of AICD or UNG in causing HIM is unclear at this point. Mutations in AICD or UNG appear to cause a similar clinical phenotype. Unlike other forms of HIM, the immunologic abnormalities in AICD or UNG mutations have impaired humoral immunity; cellular immunity is intact. Consequently, infections with opportunistic pathogens do not occur. BMT has been used to successfully treat X-linked HIM.[47,64-70] The efficacy of BMT in other forms of HIM is unclear.

SPECIFIC ANTIBODY DEFICIENCY

Specific antibody deficiency (SAD) is a primary antibody deficiency disorder that is characterized by normal levels of IgG, IgA, and IgM but an inability to make specific antibodies, most commonly in response to polysaccharide antigens such as those in the pneumococcal vaccine Pneumovax.[71-76] Patients with specific antibody deficiency present with recurrent sinopulmonary infections, similar to other forms of hypogammaglobulinemia. The diagnosis of SAD is made by measuring an absence of specific antibody responses following immunization with polysaccharide vaccines, most commonly the non-protein-conjugated pneumococcal vaccine. Cellular immunity is normal. As pointed out earlier in the chapter, considerable controversy exists in regard to what constitutes an "abnormal" response to the pneumococcal vaccine sufficient to make the diagnosis of SAD. Therefore, the prevalence of this disorder is unknown. It is the opinion of the authors that this disorder is frequently overdiagnosed based simply on poor antibody responses to some, but not all, pneumococcal capsular antigens following immunization with the pneumococcal vaccine. The initial treatment of SAD is similar to that of IgA deficiency. However, IVIG is indicated in patients with SAD who fail more conservative treatment.

IMMUNOGLOBULIN G SUBCLASS DEFICIENCY

There are four isotypes of IgG in humans, IgG1, IgG2, IgG3, and IgG4. The predominant subclass is IgG1, accounting for over 60% of the total IgG. In some patients evaluated for recurrent sinopulmonary infections, low levels of one of the IgG subclasses are found. However, the significance of IgG subclass abnormality is unclear.[77] Some believe that isolated IgG subclass deficiencies predispose patients to recurrent sinopulmonary infections. However, IgG subclass deficiencies, including genetic deletions of IgG subclass loci, are well documented in healthy individuals.[78,79] Because the clinical significance of isolated IgG subclass deficiencies is unclear, in most cases the measurement of IgG subclasses is not warranted in the evaluation of patients with recurrent sinopulmonary infections. In patients with an isolated IgG subclass deficiency and recurrent infections, the decision to use IVIG should be based on antibody responses following vaccination.

X-LINKED LYMPHOPROLIFERATIVE DISEASE

X-linked lymphoproliferative disease (XLP) is a rare primary immunodeficiency that is the result of mutations in the lymphocyte signaling-adaptor protein, in *SH2D1A* (also known as SAP, slam-associated protein, or DSHP).[80-82] The *SH2D1A* adaptor protein affects multiple intracellular signaling pathways in several different lymphocyte subpopulations, including T cells, B cells, and NK cells, a property that leads to the complex immunologic abnormalities seen in these patients. Patients with XLP have a unique predisposition to infection with Epstein-Barr virus (EBV), an infection that triggers the immunodeficiency in the vast majority of cases. Approximately 60% of patients with XLP present with overwhelming EBV infection. In 30% of patients, lymphomas develop after EBV infection, whereas 30% develop hypogammaglobulinemia.[83] Patients may have one or all of the manifestations of the syndrome at the same time. The onset of disease is variable, occurring as early as infancy or well into adulthood. Immunologic abnormalities apart from hypogammaglobulinemia include markedly reduced NK cell function and impaired T-cell responses. The only definitive therapy for XLP is BMT,[84-86] although IVIG is commonly used in an effort to prevent infections due to hypogammaglobulinemia.

CELLULAR DEFICIENCIES

DIGEORGE SYNDROME

DiGeorge syndrome (DGS) is one of the most common primary immunodeficiencies, occurring in approximately 1 per 4000 to 5000 live births. The vast majority of patients with DGS have deletions of varying degrees in chromosome 22q11.2. The molecular basis for many cases of DGS may be mutations within TBX1, a T-box transcription factor important in embryonic development.[87] Patients with DGS with 22q11.2 deletions exhibit a characteristic facies that includes hypertelorism, saddle nose, shortened philtrum, and low-set ears.[88] Other common features of DGS include hypoplasia of the thymus (leading to immunodeficiency) and parathyroid glands, abnormalities in the great vessels of the heart, and velopharyngeal insufficiency.

The immunodeficiency associated with DGS is highly variable and correlates with the degree of thymic hypoplasia. Patients with "complete DG," comprising approximately 2% of the overall numbers of DGS patients, have defects in T-cell function that require bone marrow or thymic transplantation.[89-91] In contrast, the majority of patients with DGS are referred to as having "partial DGS." Patients with partial DGS[92] generally have mild lymphopenia. T-cell defects in these patients are usually mild, and in vitro and in vivo (delayed-type hypersensitivity skin tests) assessment of T-cell function is normal. Humoral immunity is usually intact in DGS, except for the unusual patient with IgA deficiency. Intact thymic function is essential for deletion of autoreactive T cells. Consequently, patients with DGS have an increased prevalence of autoimmune disorders.

DEFECTS IN THE INTERFERON-γ/INTERLEUKIN-12 AXIS

CD4 T cells have been divided into at least two groups based on the cytokines they produce. Type 1 T helper (Th1) cells produce high levels of cytokines (IL-2, interferon-γ [IFN-γ], and tumor necrosis factor-α) that are essential in the generation of a robust cellular immune response. In contrast, type 2 T helper (Th2) cells produce cytokines (IL-4, IL-5) necessary for the elicitation of humoral immunity. IL-12, IL-18, and IFN-γ are critical cytokines involved in the differentiation of Th0 cells (T cells not committed to the Th1 or Th2 pathway) to the Th1 phenotype.

Primary immunodeficiencies leading to cellular immunodeficiency result from mutations in the genes coding for the IFN-γ receptors (IFN-γR1 or IFN-γR2),[93-99] IL-12 p40,[100] or the β1 chain of the IL-12 receptor,[101-106] or in the IFN-γ receptor signaling pathway (mutations of STAT1).[107] These various mutations may be partial or complete, which leads to differences in the clinical phenotypes. Screening tests of immune function, including serum IgG, IgA, and IgM levels, measurement of specific antibody responses, T-cell and B-cell enumeration, and lymphocyte proliferation assays, are generally normal.[108,109]

Deficiencies in the INF-γ–IL-12 axis lead to a predisposition to infections with low-virulence mycobacteria, *Salmonella*, and, less commonly, *Legionella*, *Listeria*, *Nocardia*, and viral infections (cytomegalovirus, herpes simplex virus, varicella-zoster virus, parainfluenza virus, and respiratory syncytial virus). Complete IFN-γ receptor deficiency leads to early-onset, severe mycobacterial infections, often following immunization with bacille Calmette-Guérin, and the deficiency is fatal unless treated with BMT. A complete deficiency of the IL-12 β1 receptor predisposes patients to infection with low-virulence *Salmonella*, weakly pathogenic types of mycobacteria, and tuberculosis. Patients with partial deficiencies of other components of the INF-γ–IL-12 axis exhibit a phenotype similar to that of deficiency of the IL-12 β1 receptor. In patients with mycobacterial infections and deficiency of IL-12 p40, IL-12 β1 receptor, or partial IFN-γ receptor deficiency, the addition of subcutaneous IFN-γ to standard antimicrobial therapy is useful.

AUTOIMMUNE POLYENDOCRINOPATHY–CANDIDIASIS–ECTODERMAL DYSTROPHY

Autoimmune polyendocrinopathy–candidiasis–ectodermal dystrophy (APECED) is an autosomal recessive disorder due to mutations within the autoimmune regulator gene (*AIRE*).[110] The clinical phenotype of APECED is highly variable and includes immune-mediated endocrinopathy (hypoparathyroidism, adrenal failure, and other endocrine disorders), mucocutaneous candidiasis, and ectodermal dysplasia (keratopathy, nail dystrophy).[111-113] The characteristic clinical features of endocrinopathy, ectodermal dystrophy, and candidiasis are not present in all patients. AIRE appears to function as a transcription factor that is necessary for presentation of specific autoantigens to developing T cells in the thymus.[114] Mutations of *AIRE* may lead to defective thymic deletion of autoreactive T cells (negative selection) due to the absence of these specific autoantigens in the thymus. The treatment of APECED may include immunosuppressive and antifungal therapy for the autoimmune and superficial *Candida* infections, respectively.[115]

IDIOPATHIC CD4 LYMPHOPENIA

Idiopathic CD4 lymphopenia is defined as a CD4 T-cell count of less than 300 cells/μL in the absence of other known causes of CD4 lymphopenia, such as infections with human immunodeficiency virus (HIV) type 1 or other retroviruses, iatrogenic immunosuppression, and lymphoreticular malignancies. The clinical presentation of idiopathic CD4 lymphopenia reflects the impairment in cellular immunity and includes infections with mycobacteria, fungi (histoplasmosis, *Cryptococcus neoformans*, mucocutaneous candidiasis), viruses (herpes zoster, human papillomaviruses), and opportunistic pathogens such as *P. jirovecii*.[116–125] Patients with idiopathic CD4 lymphopenia may benefit from antimicrobial prophylaxis against *P. jirovecii*. Therapy with IL-2 may also result in clinical and immunologic improvement.[126]

NATURAL KILLER CELL DEFICIENCY

Rare instances of primary NK cell deficiency have been described due to a mutation in the low-affinity IgG receptor (CD16).[127,128] Murine studies defining the role of NK cells indicate that they are important mediators of antiviral immunity, in particular against herpesviruses.[129] In agreement with murine models, patients with a primary NK cell deficiency are also prone to recurrent and severe infections with herpesviruses.

Secondary abnormalities of NK cell function are far more common than primary NK cell defects. NK cell dysfunction is present in several other primary immunodeficiencies, such as defects in the IFN-γ–IL-12 axis, XLP, some forms of SCID, hyper-IgM syndrome due to NEMO mutation (NF-κB essential modifier or IκB kinase γ chain), lymphocyte function antigen-1 (LFA-1) deficiency, and Chédiak-Higashi syndrome. HIV-1 infection also induces NK cell dysfunction,[130] a process reversed following treatment with highly active antiretroviral therapy. Interestingly, in patients with HIV-1—associated, human herpesvirus 8—induced Kaposi's sarcoma, the improvement of NK cell function following retroviral therapy temporally correlated with resolution of the Kaposi's sarcoma lesions,[131] further substantiating the role of NK cells in immunity against herpesviruses. The diagnosis of NK cell deficiency is made by the enumeration of CD16-positive NK cells by flow cytometry.

SEVERE COMBINED IMMUNODEFICIENCY

SCID is a syndrome that encompasses a variety of molecular defects that result in absent or severely impaired T-cell and B-cell function.[132] One commonly used method to classify SCID is based on whether the molecular defects decrease the numbers of T cells, T cells and B cells, or T cells, B cells, and NK cells (see Table 76.5).

The molecular defects that lead to the syndrome of SCID include mutations that lead to abnormalities in cytokine signaling (e.g., the common gamma chain [γc] of the IL-2 receptor; JAK-3) or T-cell receptor signaling (CD45, ZAP-70, CD3γ, CD3ε), defective T-cell and B-cell receptor gene recombination (RAG1, RAG2), a defective nucleotide salvage pathway (adenine deaminase [ADA] deficiency), and defects in the expression of major histocompatibility complex class I or class II molecules. X-linked SCID (γc mutation) is the most common form of SCID, accounting for approximately 50% of cases.[132] The γc of the IL-2 receptor is utilized by several other cytokine receptors, including the receptors for IL-4, IL-7, IL-11, IL-15, and IL-21. Consequently, the immunodeficiency due to mutation of the γc is due to the combined effects of loss of function in all these cytokine receptors. Milder or atypical forms of SCID due to gene defects usually associated with classic SCID may also occur.[133–135] There are additional gene defects that lead to SCID of variable severity, such as Wiskott-Aldrich syndrome (WAS), DGS, ataxia-telangiectasia (AT), XLP, and some forms of hyper-IgM syndrome. For purposes of this chapter, these latter diseases are discussed separately from SCID.

The clinical presentation of SCID is characterized by severe infections most commonly of the respiratory and gastrointestinal tract in early infancy. Infections are caused by common and opportunistic pathogens, and disseminated infections are frequent. The absence of a thymic shadow on chest radiograph in an infant with recurrent infections should prompt further studies to exclude the diagnosis of SCID. Other common manifestations of the syndrome include oral thrush, persistent diarrhea, interstitial pneumonitis, impaired growth, and the absence of lymph nodes. Engraftment of maternal T cells in an infant with SCID can lead to graft-versus-host disease (GVHD). The prompt treatment of infection, administration of IVIG, and prophylaxis against *P. jirovecii* are indicated until hematopoietic stem-cell transplantation (SCT) can take place. In the event blood transfusions are needed, only lymphocyte depleted, CMV negative blood should be used. No live vaccinations should be given to infants with known or suspected SCID.

Because early mortality due to disseminated infections is extremely common, it is essential to make a prompt diagnosis of SCID. Laboratory abnormalities in patients with SCID include panhypogammaglobulinemia and lymphopenia (<1000/μL) in the majority of cases. A defect in the capacity of T cells to proliferate in response to mitogens is the classic immunologic finding in SCID.[132,136,137]

With the exception of ADA deficiency, hematopoietic SCT is the preferred treatment for SCID.[138,139] Early BMT (<3 months of age) from a human lymphocyte antigen–identical donor improve the prognosis. The administration of polyethylene glycol–ADA is an alternative treatment for SCID due to ADA deficiency.

Recently, 10 patients with X-linked SCID have been immunologically reconstituted by gene therapy.[140–142] Replication-incompetent retroviruses encoding the γc of the IL-2 receptor were used to transduce autologous CD34+ stem cells, which were then infused into the infants. Immunologic evaluation of patients analyzed up to 2.5 years post–gene therapy revealed a return in T-cell and B-cell function in nearly all patients. Regrettably, retroviral insertion leading to activation of the proto-oncogene LMO-2 resulted in γδ T-cell leukemia in two patients.[141] Gene therapy using retroviral vectors has been suspended in the United States at the time of this writing.

WISKOTT-ALDRICH SYNDROME

WAS is an X-linked disorder characterized by recurrent infection, eczematous skin disease, and thrombocytopenia due to a mutation in the WAS protein (*WASP*) gene.[143] The function of WASP is complex, but through its interaction with a variety of adaptor molecules and kinases, WASP is involved in the integration of cytoplasmic signaling with the reorganization of the actin cytoskeleton. Consequently, WASP function is critical in the formation of the immunologic synapse, cellular motility, and cellular trafficking.[143,144]

The classic clinical expression of WAS includes recurrent infections, autoimmunity, eczematous dermatitis, and an increased prevalence of EBV-related lymphomas. Upper and lower respiratory infections are common in WAS.[145,146] Decreased platelet counts, platelet function, and platelet size are hallmarks of the disorder and lead to a marked bleeding diathesis. Infection and hemorrhage are common causes of death. Decreased levels of serum immunoglobulins and impaired antibody responses following immunization are common.[145-147] Abnormalities in T cell [145-147] and NK cell[148] function also frequently occur and likely contribute to the predisposition to infection.

The treatment of WAS includes the aggressive treatment of intercurrent infection and the administration of IVIG.[145] The thrombocytopenia usually responds to splenectomy.[146,149,150] BMT has been successfully employed in WAS.[151,152]

ATAXIA-TELANGIECTASIA

AT is an autosomal recessive disorder due to a mutation in the AT gene, which is involved in the repair of damaged DNA. The clinical manifestations of AT include neurologic dysfunction (cerebellar ataxia, oculomotor apraxia, delayed motor development), telangiectasias, and immunodeficiency. The mutation in the AT gene, with an attendant increased radiosensitivity, leads to the increased prevalence of malignancies (lymphomas, epithelial tumors) in this disorder. The manifestations of immunodeficiency typically begin in infancy or early childhood and resemble antibody deficiencies. Serum immunoglobulins are usually normal in AT, but hypogammaglobulinemia and defective responses to immunization with pneumococcal vaccine are not infrequent.[153,154] Elevated levels of carcinoembryonic antigen and alpha-fetoprotein are present in nearly all patients with AT.[155] There is no definitive treatment of AT. Patients with AT should be sent to tertiary referral centers with experience in these disorders to assist in their management.

PHAGOCYTIC CELL DISORDERS

Phagocytic defects can initially be separated by abnormalities intrinsic or extrinsic to the phagocyte. Examples of intrinsic phagocyte defects include defects in adhesion, chemotaxis, signaling, or killing (Table 76.7). Alternatively, there are examples of primary immunodeficiencies in which phagocytic cell function is normal, but auxiliary components necessary to optimal phagocytic function are absent. For example, immunoglobulins and complement are necessary for optimal phagocytic function.

It is often assumed that defects in phagocytic cell function must present early in life. However, an increasing number of adults are being diagnosed with phagocytic defects that include diverse molecular etiologies such as CGD and LAD-1. There are several indications for evaluation of patients for phagocytic abnormalities, including infections with unusual or opportunistic pathogens (e.g., fungi such as *Aspergillus* or *Nocardia*; bacteria such as *Serratia marcescens* or *Burkholderia cepacia*), unusual sites of infection (e.g., recurrent osteomyelitis; abscesses in the brain, lung, or liver), systemic bacterial infections, recurrent skin or upper or lower respiratory tract infections, and cold abscesses. Apart from infection, patients with phagocytic defects may have ongoing chronic inflammatory responses in the skin (e.g., eczematoid dermatitis) or mucous membranes (e.g., periodontitis, aphthous stomatitis) and disordered inflammatory responses leading to delayed or abnormal wound healing.

Table 76.7 Examples of Intrinsic Phagocytic Cell Defects

Defect	Disease	Abnormality/Clinical Presentation
Abnormal release from bone marrow	WHIM	Mutation in CXCR4; warts, hypo-Ig, decreased PMNs, URTI
Adhesion	LAD-1	Mutation in CD18; delayed umbilical cord separation, inability to form pus, infection
Chemotaxis	Hyper-IgE	Unknown; high levels of IgE, coarse facial features, recurrent pyogenic infections of skin and lung, skeletal and dental abnormalities
Signaling	IRAK-4	Recurrent pyogenic infections, septicemia, meningitis
Degranulation	Chédiak-Higashi syndrome	Mutation in *LYST*, silver-gray hair, dysmorphic granules (all cells), pyogenic infections
Oxidative killing	CGD	Mutations of subunits of NADPH oxidase; recurrent pyogenic infections of skin, bone, lungs

CGD, chronic granulomatous disease; Ig, immunoglobulin; IRAK-4, interleukin-1 receptor–associated kinase 4; LAD, leukocyte adhesion deficiency; NADPH, nicotinamide adenine dinucleotide phosphate; PMNs, polymorphonuclear leukocytes; URTI, upper respiratory tract infection; WHIM, warts, hypoglobulinemia, immunodeficiency, and myelokathexis.

ABNORMAL RELEASE OR PRODUCTION

Warts, Hypogammaglobulinemia, Immunodeficiency, and Myelokathexis Syndrome

Warts, hypogammaglobulinemia, immunodeficiency, and myelokathexis syndrome (WHIM) is a rare primary immunodeficiency that has recently been shown to be due to an activating mutation in CXCR4, which leads to inappropriate retention of mature neutrophils in the bone marrow (myelokathexis) and hypogammaglobulinemia.[156] Patients present with recurrent sinopulmonary infections and an unusual proclivity to infection with human papillomaviruses.[157] Apart from neutropenia, laboratory studies may demonstrate low levels of IgG or IgA, cutaneous anergy, and poor in vitro lymphocyte proliferation in response to mitogens and antigens. A reduction in bacterial infections is seen following treatment with IVIG,[158] and G-CSF or granulocyte-macrophage colony-stimulating factor has been used to treat the neutropenia.[157]

Cyclic Neutropenia and Congenital Agranulocytosis (Kostmann's Syndrome)

Cyclic neutropenia is an autosomal dominant disorder due to a mutation in the elastase-2 gene leading to regular, 21-day fluctuations in levels of neutrophils and other blood components (platelets, monocytes, reticulocytes). During the periods of neutropenia, patients are predisposed to bacterial infection with pyogenic bacteria and opportunistic pathogens. The diagnosis of cyclic neutropenia should be suspected in the context of cyclic hematopoiesis and neutropenia that coincides with recurrent infections. To document concurrent infection with neutropenia, serial complete blood counts (2 times per week) for at least 6 weeks should be performed.

Congenital agranulocytosis (Kostmann's syndrome) is a rare immunodeficiency due to a maturational arrest of neutrophil precursors in the bone marrow. The clinical manifestations of congenital agranulocytosis typically begin in early infancy with life-threatening infections (cellulitis, meningitis, perirectal abscesses, sepsis).[159] Patients with congenital agranulocytosis have severe neutropenia with an absolute neutrophil count of <200 cells/μL. The clinical manifestations of congenital agranulocytosis are more severe than those of cyclic neutropenia. The use of G-CSF is indicated in both cyclic neutropenia and congenital agranulocytosis; such treatment increases neutrophils counts and reduces infection in the vast majority of afflicted patients.[159] In patients with severe neutropenia unresponsive to G-CSF, BMT has been successfully performed.[160,161]

DECREASED ADHERENCE AND CHEMOTAXIS

The influx of leukocytes in general and neutrophils in particular to sites of infection is a complex process involving the production and release of neutrophils from the bone marrow, and the activation of neutrophils by chemotactic factors with subsequent adhesion of neutrophils to the endothelium, followed by transmigration of neutrophils through the endothelium of postcapillary venules. The first step in the egress of neutrophils from the circulation to sites of infection is mediated by the rolling (loose) adhesion of neutrophils to endothelium, mediated predominantly by CD15s (sialyl Lewis$_x$) on the neutrophil and its counterligands on the endothelium (E-selectin, P-selectin). The following step in adhesion, which is of higher affinity, is mediated predominantly by the interaction of the integrin LFA-1 (CD11a/CD18) on the leukocyte, with its counterligand intercellular adhesion molecule-1 on the endothelium. Integrins are composed of two subunits (α and β), which are noncovalently associated. The common α chain of CD18 associates with CD11a (LFA-1), CD11b (Mac-1 or CR3), and CD11c (gp150. 95), which are expressed on a variety of leukocytes. Therefore, mutations in the α chain of CD18 reduce the expression of CD11a, CD11b, and CD11c, resulting in defects in the endothelial adhesion of all leukocytes. Mutations in CD18 and CD15s lead to the primary immunodeficiencies LAD type 1 and LAD type 2, respectively.

Leukocyte Adhesion Deficiency Types 1 and 2

LAD-1 is divided into two broad categories based on whether the deficiency of LFA-1 is severe (<0.5% of normal levels) or moderate (5% to 10% of normal levels). Patients with a complete deficiency in LFA-1 expression often present in the neonatal period with delayed separation of the umbilical cord, omphalitis, and severe infections of the skin, gingiva, and gastrointestinal and upper and lower respiratory tracts. Moderate deficiencies of LFA-1 result in a milder phenotype, with the diagnosis delayed until adulthood in some instances.

Patients with LAD-1 exhibit neutrophilia, even in the absence of systemic infection, due to the inability of leukocytes to adhere to the endothelium. The definitive diagnosis of LAD-1 deficiency is made by the demonstration of extremely low levels of LFA-1 on unactivated and activated neutrophils by flow cytometry.[162,163] The treatment of LAD-1 deficiency includes the aggressive use of antimicrobials in the treatment of infection. BMT is the only definitive treatment for patients with severe deficiencies of LFA-1.[164] Moderate deficiencies of LFA-1 improve with recombinant IFN-γ therapy and chronic antimicrobial prophylaxis.

LAD-2 is an extremely rare disorder characterized by developmental delay, mental retardation, and recurrent infection similar to that in LAD-1. A mutation in the GDP-fucosyl transporter leads to the absence of CD15s on leukocytes[165] and the Bombay blood phenotype.[163] Interestingly, oral fucose administration can induce the expression of CD15s, leading to improvement of the central nervous system abnormalities and decreased infection.[166,167]

Hyper-IgE Syndrome

Hyper-IgE syndrome (HIES), also known as Job's syndrome, is an autosomal dominant disorder of unknown etiology. The clinical features of HIES include the onset of moderate to severe eczema (100%) and eosinophilic pustular folliculitis in early infancy, and skin and lower respiratory tract infections. Mucocutaneous candidiasis, pyogenic infections of the skin, and cold abscesses are common. Repeated pulmonary infections, most commonly caused by *S. aureus* and *H. influenzae,* lead to the formation of lung abscesses, pneumatoceles, and severe bronchiectasis. Secondary infection of the lung abscesses with *Pseudomonas* and *Aspergillus* is common.

Patients with HIES exhibit a characteristic facies that includes coarse facial features with a protuberant mandible and forehead, hypertelorism, and a broad, fleshy nasal tip. Skeletal abnormalities, hyperextensible joints, severe osteoporosis with skeletal fractures, and delayed resorption of the primary teeth are other common features of this disorder.[168] Lymphomas develop in approximately 5% of patients with HIES.

An elevated IgE (>2000 IV/mL), including high levels of IgE specific for *S. aureus*, and peripheral eosinophilia [169,170] are characteristic, but not pathognomonic, laboratory abnormalities. The same laboratory abnormalities may be present in patients with atopic dermatitis. Abnormal leukocyte chemotaxis and deficient production of IFN-γ by T cells may contribute to the pathogenesis of this disorder. The treatment of HIES is similar to that of other phagocytic disorders. IVIG or IFN-γ may benefit some patients.[171–173] HIES is not cured by BMT.[172]

DEFECT IN OXIDATIVE KILLING

Chronic Granulomatous Disease

CGD is a rare (1 per 1 million births) immunodeficiency due to mutation in one of the four subunits of the leukocyte nicotinamide adenine dinucleotide phosphate (NADPH) oxidase system. The function of NADPH oxidase is to transfer an electron to molecular oxygen (O_2), leading to the formation of superoxide. Approximately two thirds of cases of CGD are X-linked due to a mutation in the g91phox subunit of NADPH oxidase. Mutations of the other subunits of NADPH oxidase (p22, p47, p67) are inherited in an autosomal recessive pattern and account for the remainder of cases.

The previously widely accepted view explaining the underlying molecular basis for the increased infections seen in CGD has recently been challenged.[174,175] It was thought that the inability of neutrophils to kill catalase-positive organisms was due to the failure to generate superoxide, byproducts of superoxide metabolism such as hydrogen peroxide (H_2O_2), and the superoxide- and myeloperoxidase (MPO)-dependent formation of hypochlorous acid (HOCl). Many microorganisms produce H_2O_2, which may substitute for cellular H_2O_2 production. Therefore, it was reasoned that only catalase-positive microorganisms were pathogenic in CGD due to their capacity to degrade H_2O_2.

However, the following clinical and experimental observations challenged this hypothesis. Many microorganisms are catalase positive, but only a few are common pathogens in CGD. In murine models of CGD, catalase-negative and catalase-positive *S. aureus* are equally virulent.[176] Furthermore, primary MPO deficiency of neutrophils does not usually lead to an increased propensity to infection in humans. Rather than the simple generation of H_2O_2, superoxide production appears to be necessary for the activation and release of microbicidal enzymes, such as cathepsin G and elastase present in bound form in the matrix of primary granules of neutrophils.[174] These results explain why mice genetically deficient in neutrophil elastase and cathepsin G are highly susceptible to infection with catalase-positive

organisms, despite the normal NADPH function and generation of superoxide by neutrophils.[174,177]

The clinical manifestations of CGD usually begin early in life but may not present until adulthood. CGD is characterized by recurrent infections with catalase-positive organisms (*Aspergillus* species, *S. aureus, B. cepacia,* and others). Pneumonia, osteomyelitis, liver abscesses, lymphadenitis, skin and anorectal infections, and lymphadenitis occur frequently.[178] Invasive aspergillosis is the most common primary cause of death. As previously discussed, the diagnosis of CGD is readily made by the use of either the nitroblue tetrazolium or DHR tests.

Apart from infectious complications, disordered inflammation and wound healing are hallmark manifestations of the disease. Inflammatory granuloma formation may lead to urinary or gastrointestinal tract obstruction. Exuberant granulation tissue leads to disordered wound healing, including wound dehiscence following surgical procedures.

Recent studies provide insight into the molecular basis for the abnormal inflammatory responses that characterize CGD. Gene array experiments comparing global gene expression of normal and X-linked CGD neutrophils indicate that CGD neutrophils constitutively overproduce proinflammatory mediators and exhibit defective neutrophil apoptosis due to the overproduction of the antiapoptotic protein Bcl-xl.[179] Additionally, upon apoptosis, CGD neutrophils do not properly externalize phosphatidylserine. Phosphatidylserine is the ligand for the phosphatidylserine receptor, which is present on macrophages and mediates the efficient clearance of apoptotic cells.[180] Consequently, there is a delay in the removal of apoptotic CGD neutrophils by macrophages.[181] Thus, the increased production of proinflammatory mediators, reduced apoptosis, and delayed clearance of apoptotic neutrophils all likely lead to disordered inflammatory response in CGD.

The therapy of CGD includes aggressive treatment of infection, including surgical incision and drainage when indicated. The prophylactic administration of trimethoprim-sulfamethoxazole[182] markedly reduces infection, in particular infections caused by *S. aureus*.[182] Prophylactic itraconazole has also recently been shown to reduce serious fungal infections.[183] IFN-γ reduces infections and decreases mortality in both X-linked and autosomal recessive CGD.[184,185] Gastrointestinal and urinary tract obstruction due to granuloma formation are treated with systemic corticosteroids.

DISORDER IN LEUKOCYTE SIGNALING: IRAK-4 DEFICIENCY

Toll-like receptors (TLRs) are a family of pattern-recognition receptors that are activated following microbial infection and that, in turn, result in the activation of innate immune responses. TLRs recognize conserved motifs derived from a variety of pathogenic microorganisms, including bacteria, fungi, and viruses.[186] Members of the TLRs share a common intracytoplasmic domain, the Toll IL-1 receptor domain, which is responsible for the recruitment of the Toll IL-1 receptor—associated kinase (IRAK-4) following receptor ligation, which leads to subsequent downstream signaling and effector function. Recently, a primary immunodeficiency was described in children due to mutation in IRAK-4. Mutations in IRAK-4 lead to increased infections (cellulitis, arthritis, meningitis, osteomyelitis, sepsis) by pyogenic bacteria (*S. aureus* and *S. pneumoniae*).[187] Leukocytes isolated from patients with IRAK-4 deficiency fail to produce tumor necrosis factor-α following ligation of TLRs, IL-1, or IL-18. The proper management of patients with IRAK-4 mutations remains to be determined.

DISORDERS IN LEUKOCYTE GRANULE FORMATION AND DEGRANULATION

Chédiak-Higashi Syndrome

Chédiak-Higashi syndrome is a rare autosomal recessive disorder due to a mutation of the *LYST* gene. LYST is homologous to the yeast vacuolar sorting protein, which is involved in lysosomal sorting of proteins.[188,189] A mutation of the homologous gene is the cause of *beige* defect in mice. Patients with Chédiak-Higashi syndrome are predisposed to pyogenic infections (e.g., *S. aureus, Streptococcus pyogenes*), exhibit partial oculocutaneous albinism, and have a variety of neurologic defects.[190,191] All cells demonstrate oversized, dysmorphic lysosomes of storage granules. In neutrophils these lysosomes are visualized as large, azurophilic granules. Due to defects in degranulation, polymorphonuclear leukocyte and NK cell killing function is abnormal. Neutrophils also exhibit decreased chemotactic responses. Patients with Chédiak-Higashi syndrome may develop a lymphoma-like syndrome characterized by the abnormal proliferation of T cells, leading to hepatosplenomegaly, lymphadenopathy, and bone marrow failure. Without successful BMT,[192] this disorder is usually fatal.[191,192]

Myeloperoxidase Deficiency

MPO is present in the lysosomes of monocytes and azurophilic granules of polymorphonuclear leukocytes. MPO is responsible for the conversion of H_2O_2 to $HOCl$, leading to subsequent killing of a variety of microorganisms. Primary MPO deficiency is a fairly common immunodeficiency, occurring in approximately 1 per 4000 live births. Interestingly, patients with primary MPO deficiency do not appear to be predisposed to infection. However, in patients with diabetes mellitus, primary MPO deficiency predisposes to recurrent infection particularly with *Aspergillus* species and *Candida* species. The diagnosis of primary MPO deficiency is made by measurement of MPO activity in neutrophils.

Specific Granule Deficiency

Specific granule deficiency is a rare primary immunodeficiency due to a mutation in the transcription factor C/EBPε, leading to defective leukocyte maturation and the absence of secondary granules in neutrophils.[178,193] Neutrophils in patients with specific granule deficiency lack secondary granules and defensins and exhibit bilobed nuclei. Eosinophils are deficient in eosinophilic cationic protein, eosinophil-derived neurotoxin, and major basic protein. Patients with specific granule deficiency exhibit severe, frequent pyogenic infections. The prognosis of specific granule deficiency is poor without BMT.

COMPLEMENT DEFICIENCIES

Complement has many important functions that include the modulation of inflammatory responses (e.g., vasodilation, leukocytosis, and chemotaxis); clearance of immune complexes; modulation of the immune response (e.g., enhanced production of antibodies); and microbial elimination (e.g., opsonization, neutralization, and microbicidal activity). Complement may also be important in the efficient removal of apoptotic cells, preventing the presentation of self-antigens, and the induction of autoimmunity.[194] Deficiencies in components of the complement system are usually manifest by an increased propensity to infection or autoimmunity. There are several indications for the evaluation of the complement system, which include a strong family history of autoimmune diseases, recurrent infections caused by encapsulated bacteria, a family history of meningococcal disease, infection caused by unusual types of meningococcus (Y, W135), or age older than 9 years at the time of meningococcal disease and recurrent angioedema.

EARLY COMPONENTS

Defects in the early components of complement (C1q, C1s, C2, C4), which are inherited in an autosomal codominant manner, typically lead to an increased prevalence of autoimmune disease, such as systemic lupus erythematosus. Redundancies in the complement pathway, including the alternative and mannose-binding lectin pathways, likely explain the relative paucity of infections. Encapsulated bacteria (*S. pneumoniae, H. influenzae*) are the most common pathogens in people with recurrent infection due to deficiency in early complement components.[12] C2 deficiency is the most common early component deficiency, occurring in 1 per 10,000 to 28,000 live births.

MANNOSE-BINDING LECTIN

Mannose-binding lectin deficiency is inherited as an autosomal recessive trait. There is considerable debate whether mannose-binding lectin deficiency leads to an increased prevalence of infection. Many believe that this deficiency leads to an increased prevalence of infection in infants, but not in adults.[12]

C3 COMPONENT

The classic, alternative, and mannose-binding lectin pathway all converge at C3. For this reason, deficiencies in C3 result in more severe infection than deficiencies in other components of complement. Patients with C3 deficiency have an increased prevalence of autoimmune disease and present in a manner similar to those with antibody deficiency.

LATE COMPONENTS

Deficiencies in the terminal components of the complement pathway (C5 through C9) are inherited in an autosomal codominant manner. Patients with late component deficiencies are highly predisposed to infection with *Neisseria* species, usually types that are not commonly found in healthy individuals or patients with antibody deficiencies. The prevalence of autoimmune disease is also increased in these patients, but to a much lesser extent than deficiencies in the early components of complement. Patients with late component deficiencies usually have the onset of infection at an older age; many are without symptoms of infection well into adolescence.[12]

ALTERNATIVE PATHWAY

Deficiencies in components of the alternative pathway (factor D, or properdin) are extremely rare and present with increased bacterial infections, including infections with *Neisseria* species. Properdin deficiency is a X-linked inherited disorder, in contrast to the other complement deficiencies (with the exception of hereditary angioneurotic edema), which are inherited in an autosomal codominant manner.

THERAPY

Therapy for complement deficiencies is primarily supportive. Individuals should be vaccinated against common bacterial pathogens associated with complement deficiency (e.g., *S. pneumoniae, H. influenzae, N. meningitidis*). Prophylactic antibody may be helpful in selected situations.

BONE MARROW AND STEM-CELL TRANSPLANTATION

High-dose chemo/radiation therapy with hematopoietic SCT support has been evolving over the past 35 years[195] and is currently being used for the treatment of hematologic and solid organ malignancies, as well as other chronic nonmalignant conditions.[196–202] These dose-intensive chemo/immunotherapy regimens combined with localized or total-body irradiation, followed by autologous (same patient), allogeneic (genetically matched relative or nonrelative), or syngeneic (genetically identical sibling) hematopoietic SCT, are increasingly being used for both initial and salvage treatment of a large number of solid tissue and hematologic malignancies.[203–212] In the case of some hematologic cancers refractory to conventional-dose chemotherapy, including all forms of leukemia, several reports demonstrate allogeneic SCT as a treatment option that offers increased cure rates and increased long-term survival over conventional chemotherapy.[213–215] However, in many cases, and in particular with those regimens used for treating advanced-stage breast cancer,[216–219] the use of SCT is still being defined.[220] Most recently, nonmyeloablative regimens (so called minitransplants) are seeing increased popularity as oncologists attempt to apply the graft-versus-tumor effect while minimizing untoward side effects.[221] Thus, we are likely to see an increasing number of patients undergoing some form of SCT in the future.

PULMONARY COMPLICATIONS FOLLOWING SCT

Despite the excitement of this new and emerging combined-modality treatment, pulmonary side effects continue to thwart its success.[222,222a] In a large majority of cases, both

infectious and noninfectious forms of pulmonary toxicity continue to plague patients and inflict unwanted complications, resulting in increased morbidity and mortality.[223–230] The differential diagnoses for these infectious etiologies (Table 76.8) and noninfectious etiologies (Table 76.9) are described more fully below. The incidence of these

Table 76.8 Infectious Causes of Pulmonary Infiltrates following Stem-Cell Transplantation

Bacteria
Staphylococcus aureus
Streptococcus pneumoniae
Pseudomonas aeruginosa
Klebsiella
Legionella
Mycobacterium avium complex

Fungi
Aspergillus
Histoplasma capsulatum
Coccidioides immitis
Blastomyces
Trichosporon
Fusarium
Zygomycetes
Candida
Pneumocystis jirovecii

Viruses
Cytomegalovirus
Respiratory virus (respiratory syncytial virus, parainfluenza virus, influenza A and B, adenovirus)
Herpes simplex virus, varicella-zoster virus

Table 76.9 Noninfectious Causes of Pulmonary Infiltrates following Stem-Cell Transplantation (with Abbreviations)

Idiopathic pneumonia syndrome (IPS)
Diffuse alveolar hemorrhage (DAH) or pulmonary hemorrhage
Bronchiolitis obliterans (BO) or airflow obstruction
Delayed pulmonary toxicity syndrome (DPTS)
Bronchiolitis obliterans with organizing pneumonia (BOOP)
Diffuse alveolar damage (DAD) or drug toxicity
Engraftment syndrome (ES)
Cardiogenic or noncardiogenic pulmonary edema
Interstitial fibrosis
Hypersensitivity pneumonitis
Radiation pneumonitis
Pleural effusions
Hepatopulmonary syndrome
Vascular or malignant thromboemboli
Pulmonary cytolytic thrombi (PCT)
Posttransplant lymphoproliferative disorder (PTLD)
Transfusion-related acute lung injury

pulmonary toxicities following SCT has been estimated to be anywhere from 2% to 70%, varying with the specific patient population being analyzed, details of the individual therapeutic regimens, and the criteria used to define lung toxicity.[231] For example, idiopathic pneumonia syndrome, one of the most severe forms of SCT-related lung toxicity, represents a major iatrogenic cause of morbidity and mortality, and accounts for up to 40% of non–GVHD deaths in BMT recipients.[226,232]

The individual components of the conditioning regimen likely play a key role in the development of pulmonary toxicity. This may be particularly true for noninfectious etiologies. In the case of autologous SCT, for example, carmustine (BCNU), one of the chemotherapeutic agents used with auto-SCT, has been shown to cause pulmonary toxicity when used as a single agent or in combination with other agents.[233-238] In fact, a National Heart, Lung and Blood Institute workshop has suggested that more than 50% of breast cancer patients receiving regimens containing carmustine may develop clinically apparent lung injury.[239] By inhibiting antioxidant enzymes,[240,241] BCNU depletes epithelial lining fluid glutathione levels,[242-244] resulting in increased oxidative stress. Cyclophosphamide (also used with both autologous and allogeneic SCT regimens) has also been shown to cause lung injury, deplete glutathione stores,[245-247] increase the generation of reactive oxygen species by alveolar macrophages,[248] inhibit prostaglandin E$_2$ production by macrophages,[245] and modulate bronchoalve-

olar lavage (BAL) cell populations.[248] Acrolein, a cyclophosphamide metabolite, can also react directly with glutathione, forming irreversible conjugates.[249] Additionally, cisplatin has been shown to increase the production of superoxide anions[250] and to decrease the activity of lipid peroxide protecting enzymes, such as catalase, Cu,Zn-superoxide dismutase, glutathione peroxidase, and glutathione-S-transferase, in the liver and kidney of rats.[251] Animal models of lung toxicity following allogeneic SCT generally require the following three components: (1) infusion of alloreactive T cells, (2) total-body irradiation, and (3) cyclophosphamide.[252-257] The effects of other chemotherapeutic agents and radiation on lung pathophysiology are discussed in more depth elsewhere in this text.

Risk Factors and Prognostic Factors

Because pulmonary complications following hematopoietic SCT are associated with high morbidity and mortality, identification of pretransplant conditions that predispose to the development of these complications could guide specific therapeutic alternatives to lessen or minimize the impact pulmonary toxicities have in the post-SCT follow-up. Numerous risk factors have been identified that may predispose to the development of pulmonary complications following SCT (Table 76.10). This list is not intended to be all inclusive, as this would be difficult due to the large number of unique conditioning and consolidation regimens

---

Table 76.10 Predisposing Factors for the Development of Pulmonary Toxicity following Stem-Cell Transplantation (SCT)

Predisposing Factor	Study Findings
Autologous SCT	
Atopy	Multivariate logistic analysis showed a preexisting history of atopy to be highly predictive (odds ratio = 21, 95% confidence interval = 3.6–125, P = 0.0001) of noninfectious pulmonary complications in 34 pediatric patients with Hodgkin's disease.[209]
Anemia (hemoglobin <10 g/dL)	In one study, 94 patients with multiple myeloma underwent high-dose therapy with autologous SCT, with interstitial pneumonitis occurring in 29 of 94 patients (31%).[430] Mortality in patients who developed interstitial pneumonitis was high at 45%. Patients developing interstitial pneumonitis were more frequently anemic (P = 0.03) than those who did not have pulmonary complications prior to SCT.
Abnormal chest radiograph (CXR) pre-SCT	In the febrile post-SCT setting, patients with pretransplant CXR abnormalities were more likely to develop additional abnormalities than those who had a normal pre-SCT CXR.[270]
Severe nephrotoxicity	Severe nephrotoxicity, as defined by a doubling of the baseline creatinine or requiring dialysis, was associated with sepsis and liver and pulmonary dysfunction.[431]
Allogeneic SCT	
Pre-SCT FEV$_1$ ≤80%	A pretransplant FEV$_1$ ≤80% predicted is associated with an increased risk (risk ratio = 4.4; 95% confidence interval = 1.81–10.66) of developing severe pulmonary complications in adults.[266]
Type of graft-versus-host disease (GVHD) prophylaxis: CYA/MTX > TCD	GVHD prophylaxis using cyclosporin A + methotrexate (CYA/MTX) is associated with a > 4-fold increased incidence of severe pulmonary toxicity versus CD6+ T-cell depletion (TCD) (33% vs. 8%, P > 0.0001).[266] It had been shown previously that T-cell depletion reduced, but did not eliminate, interstitial pneumonitis–related mortality.[432]
Severe nephrotoxicity	Severe nephrotoxicity, as defined by a doubling of the baseline creatinine or requiring dialysis, was associated with significantly higher frequencies of lung toxicity, with mortality rates exceeding 80%.[433]
Auto- and Allo-SCT	
Thoracic radiation	
Older age and poor performance status pre-SCT	
Long interval between diagnosis and transplantation	
Synergistic reactions within conditioning regimens	
Underlying malignancy	
Conditioning chemotherapy (e.g., cyclophosphamide, carmustine [BCNU], bleomycin, busulfan, doxorubicin)	

being utilized at SCT centers around the world. Many of these risk factors are interrelated. For example, the development of chronic GVHD increases the risk for the subsequent development of bronchiolitis obliterans.[258] Additionally, multivariable analysis showed that age above 60 years, pretransplant FEV_1/FVC less than 80%, respiratory virus infection, and quiescent or progressive-onset chronic GVHD were all associated with the development of airflow obstruction.[259] Furthermore, the presence of airflow obstruction significantly and independently demonstrated an increased risk of 2.3 for mortality following SCT.[259]

Diffuse lung injury that follows hematopoietic SCT regimens can have different clinical courses depending on whether the transplant comes from allogeneic or autologous sources.[239] Reasons for this are not clearly defined but likely involve variable exposure to different agents or factors, each capable of causing lung injury. For example, following allogeneic BMT, the development of diffuse lung injury may be related to several factors, including the presence of severe GVHD, use of methotrexate to prevent GVHD, high doses of irradiation, older age, poorer performance ratings before transplantation, and infection with CMV.[260,261] However, many of these risk factors are not involved in the lung injury that follows autologous SCT because they are typically not used. More than likely, lung injury following autologous BMT is due to reagents associated with the conditioning regimens.[219,239,262-265] One recent study from the Dana-Farber Cancer Institute highlights important similarities and differences in severe pulmonary complications following autologous hematopoietic SCT versus allogeneic hematopoietic SCT protocols.[266] As shown in Figure 76.1, abnormal radiographs were seen in a higher percentage of allogeneic SCT (57%) than in autologous SCT (22%). Although each SCT group had a somewhat similar distribution of infectious and noninfectious etiologies, the allogeneic group had a markedly increased incidence of severe

pulmonary complications (48 of 199 patients, or 24%) when compared to the autologous SCT recipients (4 of 140 patients, or 2.8%). This report characterizes the often-quoted statement that pulmonary complications following allogeneic SCT occur more frequently and are of greater severity than those that follow autologous SCT.

Time Course

The relative time frame in which pulmonary complications occur following SCT can be very helpful in ranking the most likely diagnostic entities, both infectious and noninfectious.[267] This is primarily due to the effects of the conditioning and consolidation regimens and the varying states of immunosuppression over time. Specific diagnoses are discussed in more detail later.

Initially, there is the acute neutropenic phase before engraftment, which typically occurs within 30 days after SCT. We know that, following allogeneic SCT, the median time to neutrophil recovery is 9 to 18 days [268,269] and to platelet transfusion independence, 11 days.[269] It is highly likely that patients will develop fevers during the neutropenic phase following SCT; in the autologous SCT setting, the frequency of fever may be as high as 94%.[270] During this time period, common pathologic findings include drug toxicity, idiopathic pneumonia syndrome, pulmonary edema, and diffuse alveolar hemorrhage. Bacterial infections are common, as are fungal infections, primarily due to *Aspergillus*. However, surgical lung biopsy results in patients with radiographic infiltrates following SCT show the prevalence of infection to be low (19%) within the first 30 days after SCT among patients receiving broad-spectrum antibiotics.[271] Interestingly, in this early preengraftment phase of SCT, failure to demonstrate a specific etiology may lead to a worse outcome than in patients with proven infectious pneumonia after SCT.[272]

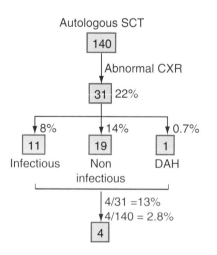

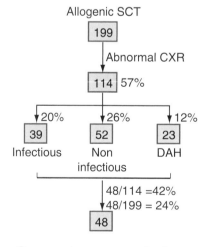

Figure 76.1 Pulmonary complications following stem-cell transplantation (SCT). CXR, chest radiograph; DAH, diffuse alveolar hemorrhage. (From Ho VT, Weller E, Lee SJ, et al: Prognostic factors for early severe pulmonary complications after hematopoietic stem cell transplantation. Biol Blood Marrow Transplant 7:223–229, 2001.)

In the early postengraftment phase, between 30 days and 100 days following SCT, the gradual return of polymorphonuclear leukocytes results in decreased susceptibility to bacterial and fungal infections, but the immunosuppression used for treatment of GVHD leads to deficits in cellular and humoral immunity. This is the period when we can see an engraftment syndrome that coincides with the return of neutrophils. Viral infections begin to come into play, and CMV now becomes much more readily detectable in pulmonary tissues, though CMV prophylaxis has successfully minimized the impact of CMV pneumonia in transplanted patients. *Pneumocystis* pneumonia (PCP) is rarely seen when trimethoprim-sulfamethoxazole prophylaxis is given. Additionally pulmonary cytolytic thrombi are seen during this interval.[273] Delayed pulmonary toxicity syndrome, in the autologous SCT setting, is seen beginning at 5 to 6 weeks. The prevalence of infections has been shown to increase to over 75%, at some centers, in patients who are more than 30 days post-SCT and who develop radiographic infiltrates despite broad-spectrum antibiotics.[271]

The late postengraftment phase begins at 100 days post-SCT. The immune system is now recovering, but this process can be significantly inhibited in allogeneic transplanted patients who require immunosuppressive therapy for acute or chronic GVHD. During this phase, noninfectious etiologies tend to dominate a clinical picture in which airflow obstruction, otherwise known as bronchiolitis obliterans, begins to emerge. Mixed restrictive-fibrotic lung disease, usually due to the repair and response of prior acute lung injury insults, becomes more prevalent. Bronchiolitis obliterans with organizing pneumonia (BOOP) may also be seen. Infectious agents may still play a role, primarily following allogeneic SCT, and include CMV and bacterial or fungal sinopulmonary disease. PCP may be seen in the chronically immunosuppressed transplanted patient not on appropriate prophylaxis.

INFECTIOUS PULMONARY COMPLICATIONS

Bacterial

The extent to which bacterial bronchopneumonia is present in patients after SCT is not known but has been estimated to be 2% by open-lung biopsy and greater than 25% when documented at autopsy.[274] Bacterial pathogens can account for over 50% of pulmonary infections and include *Pseudomonas aeruginosa, S. aureus, Mycobacterium tuberculosis,* atypical mycobacterial infection, *Escherichia coli, Xanthomonas maltophilia, Klebsiella pneumoniae, Serratia, Legionella* species, *Enterococcus faecium,* and *Mycoplasma* species.[275,276] In one series, staphylococcal species accounted for 24% and streptococcal species accounted for 13% of all pulmonary isolates.[277] Although the prevalence of *M. tuberculosis* infection following SCT has been estimated to be about 0.6%, delayed diagnoses due to slow growth of the bacterium can lead to delays in initiating therapy.[278] For this reason, a high index of suspicion should be maintained, particularly in endemic areas. The widespread use of empirical and prophylactic broad-spectrum antibiotics can make the diagnosis of bacterial pneumonia more challenging in this group of patients. Also, severe oral mucositis and concurrent use of narcotics likely increase aspiration

risks. *Nocardia asteroides* pneumonia is rare, but tends to occur at a median time of 210 days after SCT and is found almost universally in patients following allogeneic SCT.[279]

Viral

Cytomegalovirus Pneumonia. CMV pneumonia is a major cause of morbidity and mortality for patients undergoing SCT, with a mortality rate reported to be anywhere from 30% to 85%. In the 1980s, and before the routine use of preventive antiviral therapy, CMV pneumonia was found as the etiologic agent in 60% to 80% of diffuse pneumonias occurring in stem-cell transplant recipients.[280,281] Now, fortunately, the incidence of CMV pneumonia has been markedly reduced to approximately 4% when prophylactic ganciclovir is given to all CMV-seropositive patients or to patients who were considered at high risk for CMV disease on the basis of a positive surveillance culture (early treatment).[282] Additionally, CMV-seronegative recipients of hematopoietic stem cell transplants benefit greatly from the use of seronegative or leukocyte-filtered blood products, helping to maintain low CMV infection rates. The incidence of CMV infections is reported to be similar following both autologous and allogeneic SCT (40% to 50%), though the frequency of severe CMV disease is believed to be substantially lower in autologous recipients (0% to 1%) versus allograft recipients (16%).[226,283,284]

It is increasingly being recognized that CMV reactivation plays a significant role in post-SCT complications. However, although active CMV replication is typically accompanied by CMV antigenemia/DNAemia, local CMV (re)activation in the lung and colon, without detection of active CMV infection in the peripheral blood, is possible.[285] Hence, negative peripheral blood studies for CMV may not rule out active tissue CMV infection. Screening of patients scheduled for SCT by routine evaluation of blood, urine, or BAL samples can identify patients during CMV viral excretion, allowing for individualized treatment strategies, which have been shown to decrease CMV pneumonia and improve overall survival. Detection methods for CMV antigen and deoxyribonucleic acid are quite sensitive and specific ways of identifying patients at high risk for developing CMV pneumonia following SCT. For example, CMV screening using PCR is more sensitive than histologic examination and at least as sensitive as CMV viral culture.[286] In fact, PCR monitoring of CMV in plasma to guide both implementation and discontinuation of CMV therapy may help not only to reduce CMV disease, but also to attenuate the side effects of antiviral drugs.[287] It is controversial whether CMV antigenemia monitoring is superior to screening bronchoscopies for the detection of CMV pneumonia. In recipients of allogeneic stem-cell transplants, serum CMV antigenemia studies appear to be superior,[288] whereas in other studies BAL fluid analysis demonstrated an almost 50% greater sensitivity for identifying CMV when compared to peripheral blood sampling.[289]

CMV pneumonia more typically occurs within 30 days after SCT, though it can also occur more than 100 days afterward.[290] CMV pneumonia may also occur very late following SCT,[291,292] and this may be especially true in patients undergoing nonmyeloablative SCT.[293] Although the treatment of CMV pneumonia is discussed in detail in Chapter

31, several comments are worth making in the SCT setting. Preventive treatment of CMV has markedly reduced the incidence of severe CMV infections. However, the long-term use of ganciclovir in preventing CMV pneumonia should be weighed against factors limiting its overall effectiveness, principally drug-induced neutropenia. Treatment of patients for CMV pneumonia prior to the development of respiratory failure can result in a significantly higher survival rate than treatment after respiratory failure.[290] Other studies show that starting CMV treatment within 6 days of the onset of CMV antigenemia is associated with a positive response to therapy.[294] Thus, a favorable response depends on early diagnosis and treatment. Primary treatment for CMV pneumonia is composed of intravenous ganciclovir and high-dose IVIG.[295,296]

Other Viruses. Respiratory viral infections occurring in patients after SCT are a major cause of morbidity and mortality. The most commonly identified respiratory virus is *respiratory syncytial virus* (RSV), which accounts for 35% of respiratory viral isolates, followed by parainfluenza virus (30%), rhinovirus (25%), and influenza virus (11%).[297] Of these, pneumonia occurred in 49% of patients with RSV isolates, 22% of those with parainfluenza virus, less than 10% of those with influenza virus, and 3% of those with rhinovirus isolates.[297] Much is known about RSV in the post-SCT setting.

RSV pneumonia is frequently seen in stem-cell transplant recipients.[298] Over a 5-year period, McCarthy and colleagues[299] showed that 26 (6.3%) of 336 recipients of allo-SCT developed RSV pneumonia, which was correlated with lower respiratory tract infection and a poor overall outcome (19.2% mortality).

Primary treatment strategies for RSV pneumonia are to use the virus-static agent ribavirin either intravenously (25 mg/kg/day loading dose followed by 15 mg/kg/day in three divided doses) or given via nebulizer (6 g/day, over an 18-hour period), or by using pooled or RSV-specific immunoglobulin intravenously (0.2 to 0.4 g/kg given 2 or 3 times per week).[299] Furthermore, early diagnosis and treatment with ribavirin and RSV-specific immunoglobulin, while the RSV still remains in the upper airways, may prevent progression to RSV pneumonia.[299,300] However, it must be remembered that none of these agents has yet been proven effective in this patient population.[299] In fact, when no specific RSV treatment was given in a group of transplanted patients who developed RSV pneumonia, the overall outcome was favorable, but RSV infection in the preengraftment period was associated with delayed engraftment.[301] Newer agents, such as high-titer monoclonal antibody against RSV, show promise in experimental animals models of RSV pneumonia.[302] An infection control strategy involving (1) prompt identification, isolation, and cohorting of RSV-infected patients; (2) prompt therapy with aerosolized ribavirin; (3) screening visitors for respiratory symptoms; (4) restricting visitation by all children under 12 years of age and all family members and other visitors with upper respiratory tract infectious symptoms; and (5) restricting symptomatic hospital staff from working in the BMT unit can lead to a significant reduction in the frequency of nosocomial RSV infection in high-risk groups such as patients after SCT.[303] Simple glove and gown precautions can also substantially reduce nosocomial transmission of RSV,[304] as does the use of disposable eye-nose goggles.[305]

Parainfluenza virus has been isolated from the respiratory secretions of about 2.1% to 5% of adult stem-cell–transplanted patients, of whom about half (44%) go on to develop pneumonia with an associated mortality of 37% to 50%.[306–308] In children, the frequency of parainfluenza virus infection is 2.2%.[306] Both the frequency and mortality of parainfluenza pneumonia is higher in allogeneic versus autologous SCT. Types 3 and 1 parainfluenza virus are more commonly isolated from respiratory secretions of patients after SCT than is type 2.[297,308]

Influenza virus frequently causes community epidemics that can also affect stem-cell transplant recipients. In one SCT center, 29% of transplanted patients developed acute respiratory illness due to influenza virus type A.[309] The frequency of influenza infection was similar following both autologous and allogeneic SCT. Mortality was found to be 17%. Fortunately, annual vaccination for influenza and the prompt and early use of antiviral agents such as amantadine, rimantadine, zanamivir, or oseltamivir can be used to decrease morbidity and mortality from influenza pneumonia. Aerosolized ribavirin may also be effective for treating influenza A and B virus infection.[310–312]

Other herpes-group viruses, such as *herpes simplex virus* (HSV) and *varicella-zoster virus,* are less commonly seen in patients after SCT because of the prophylactic administration of acyclovir.[313] However, HSV may still cause a virus-associated interstitial pneumonia[314] and acyclovir-resistant HSV causing pneumonia has also been described.[315] When looked for, *rhinovirus* has been detected in 8% of BAL samples taken from patients with acute pulmonary infiltrates following SCT.[316] Although the isolation of rhinovirus is often associated with copathogens, it is not clear if the high mortality (83%) is due to rhinovirus or the copathogen. *Adenovirus* infection has been isolated in about 4.9% of patients undergoing SCT, and the source is thought to be endogenous viral reactivation.[317] The incidence of adenoviral pneumonia is less than 1%, but it has a mortality of up to 70%.

Fungal

Invasive fungal disease due to *Aspergillus, Zygomycetes,* and *Candida* species appears to be increasing in recipients of stem-cell transplants.[318] With improved prophylactic strategies to prevent CMV pneumonia, invasive fungal diseases have now become the leading cause of infectious mortality after SCT.[319] *Aspergillus* infection most often involves the lung and is seen in up to 10% to 25% of transplanted patients.[320,321] Airborne *Aspergillus* enter the body via the nasal passages and respiratory tract. The incidence of invasive *Aspergillus* in one large series of 2496 patients following SCT increased from 5.7% at the beginning of the study to 11.2% at the end of the study.[318] There was a bimodal distribution of *Aspergillus* that depended on the type of transplant. Following autologous SCT, aspergillosis occurred during the neutropenia phase and was rare after engraftment[318]; in contrast, *Aspergillus* infection was noted to occur almost exclusively after engraftment in patients following allogeneic SCT.[318] The mean diagnostic yield of bronchoscopy for histologically proven invasive pulmonary aspergillosis is low (43%).[322] Thus, a negative bronchoscopy does not rule out *Aspergillus* disease. A quantitative PCR method has been recently developed for the rapid diagnosis of invasive pulmonary aspergillosis in BAL fluid. To distinguish infection from airway contamination, lavage fluid from affected areas is compared to those from unaffected areas,[323] but it remains to be seen whether this will improve diagnostic yield.

Galactomannan, a component of the *Aspergillus* cell wall, is released into the serum following invasion of the fungus into tissue. Measuring serum levels of galactomannan antigen has shown promise in the early detection of invasive aspergillus fungal disease in patients undergoing SCT, preceding detection by conventional radiographic or computed tomography scans by a median of 8 days.[323a] However, false-positive results due to (1) cross-reactivity with other fungi, (2) the concomitant administration of piperacillin-tazobactam, or (3) translocation of galactomannan antigen present in milk and some cereals across the gut wall and/or intestines damaged by chemotherapies, and false-negatives results due to (1) the presence of anti-aspergillus antibodies, (2) localized or encapsulated infections, or (3) the use of antifungal therapy all may limit its usefulness as the sole diagnostic test for invasive fungal disease to that of an adjunct for the diagnosis of invasive aspergillus.[323b]

Radiographic-guided fine-needle aspiration can also be used to diagnose invasive pulmonary aspergillosis, but again with poor sensitivity (24%).[324] Radiographically, aspergillosis presents most commonly as a single or multiple nodular lesions, with about half showing evidence of cavitation.[325] Despite antifungal therapy, mortality associated with *Aspergillus* following SCT remains high, ranging from 75% to 90%.[326,327] The application of surgical lung resection in selected individuals with invasive pulmonary aspergillosis, combined with antifungal chemotherapy, may lead to higher rates of cure.[328] Invasive pulmonary aspergillosis treatment guidelines are discussed more fully in Chapter 34.

Although much less frequent than aspergillosis, fungal infections from endemic mycoses such as *Histoplasma capsulatum*, *Coccidioides immitis*, and *Blastomyces dermatitidis* should also be considered in this immunocompromised population. Invasive *Candida* infection is also prevalent in stem-cell transplant recipients, and autopsy data suggest that 50% of infected patients have pulmonary involvement.[274,328] Zygomycetes (which include *Mucor* and *Rhizopus*) appear to be emerging pathogens that have a particularly rapidly progressive course and are reported to occur in up to 1.2% of patients after SCT.[329,330] *Rhizopus* may also present as an endobronchial obstructing lesion following SCT.[331] The occurrence of *P. jirovecii*, which is always a threat, has been virtually eliminated by routine prophylaxis.[331a]

NONINFECTIOUS PULMONARY COMPLICATIONS

Idiopathic Pneumonia Syndrome

The National Heart, Lung and Blood Institute convened a workshop in 1991 to review clinical and pathologic features of lung toxicity following hematopoietic SCT, focusing primarily on idiopathic pneumonia syndrome (IPS), which is

Table 76.11 Diagnostic Criteria for Idiopathic Pneumonia Syndrome

1. Evidence of widespread alveolar injury as evidence by
   a. Multilobar infiltrates on routine chest radiographs or computed tomography scans
   b. Symptoms and signs of pneumonia (e.g., cough, dyspnea, crackles)
   c. Evidence of abnormal pulmonary physiology:
      1. Increased alveolar-arterial Po_2 gradient (compared with previous, if available)
      2. New or increased restrictive pulmonary function test abnormality

AND

2. Absence of active lower respiratory tract infection as evaluated by
   a. Bronchoalveolar lavage or transbronchial biopsy or open-lung biopsy negative for infectious pathogens (bacterial, cytomegalovirus, respiratory syncytial virus, parainfluenza virus, other respiratory viruses, fungi, *Pneumocystis jirovecii*, and other organisms)
   b. Ideally, a second confirmatory negative test is done 2–14 days after the initial negative bronchoscopy

From Clark JG, Hansen JA, Hertz MI, et al: NHLBI workshop summary: Idiopathic pneumonia syndrome after bone marrow transplantation. Am Rev Respir Dis 147:1601–1606, 1993.

the most severe form of stem-cell transplant–related lung toxicity, and is associated with widespread alveolar injury. In the absence of lower respiratory tract infection, IPS can lead to respiratory failure and death.[232,239] Early estimates reported a 35% incidence of IPS following SCT,[332] but in more recent studies, the overall incidence of IPS was about 10%.[226,332–334] Mortality can reach 65%.[262,263,335] Although steroids are often used to treat IPS,[228] the efficacy of such treatment is not proven.[334] The precise pathogenesis of IPS is under investigation and not yet understood. Clark and colleagues[336] showed that proinflammatory cytokine activation may play an important role in the development of lung injury. Analysis of BAL fluid in patient with IPS showed elevated levels of IL-1, IL-2, IL-6, and tumor necrosis factor-α, whereas transplanted patients without IPS showed levels of these inflammatory cytokines similar to those obtained from normal volunteers. The appearance of IPS is delayed by several weeks to months following SCT.[239]

Criteria for the diagnosis of IPS are listed in Table 76.11. Most patients with IPS have nonspecific radiographic abnormalities and abnormal pulmonary function. Infectious etiologies must be excluded by invasive diagnostic testing. There is a need for specific laboratory testing that could assist in the accurate diagnosis of IPS and perhaps help define prognosis. In this regard, KL-6, a mucinous high-molecular-weight glycoprotein expressed primarily on type 2 alveolar epithelial cells, has been shown to be elevated in the BAL and serum of patients with pulmonary complications following SCT, but KL-6 levels may turn out to be more useful for monitoring the severity of IPS after SCT.[337] Monitoring exhaled nitric oxide levels may also prove useful as a marker for IPS, as there was an inverse correlation between exhaled nitric oxide levels and diffusing capacity of carbon monoxide.[338]

Diffuse Alveolar Hemorrhage

Acute diffuse pulmonary hemorrhage has been described in patients receiving autologous and allogeneic marrow transplants and has been termed *diffuse alveolar hemorrhage* (DAH) to reflect the finding that sequential BAL samples become progressively bloodier as these later aliquots predominantly sample alveoli.[339–341] DAH is considered to be a syndrome with nonspecific radiologic and clinical presentations. Even though certain bacterial and fungal infections can lead to pulmonary hemorrhage,[342] the diagnosis of DAH is reserved for hemorrhage due to noninfectious etiologies.[343] The diagnostic criteria for DAH are listed in Table 76.12.

One report documented a higher incidence of DAH following allogeneic SCT (3% to 7%) compared to autologous SCT (1% to 5%),[344] though others have shown no difference in the incidence of DAH following autologous and allogeneic SCT (5% for both).[343] In patients admitted to the intensive care unit with respiratory failure following SCT, the prevalence of DAH may be as high as 40%.[345] Although most patients have low platelet counts at the time of DAH, there have been no statistically significant associations with the development of bleeding, nor have platelet transfusions been shown to improve DAH.[346] However, total-body irradiation, thoracic irradiation, old age, the pretransplant intensive chemotherapy, a second SCT, and pretransplant presence of bronchial neutrophils (>20%) and eosinophils (>0%) have all been associated with the development of DAH.[343,346–352] The pathogenesis of DAH is unclear but may involve proinflammatory cytokine release, vasculopathy, and elevated pulmonary artery pressures.

Clinically, DAH typically occurs early following SCT, usually within the first 4 weeks. Hemoptysis rarely occurs.[346] In patients who develop DAH, radiographic abnormalities typically develop on average 11 days after SCT and precede the clinical diagnosis by an average of 3 days.[353] The most common initial radiographic pattern is a bilateral interstitial process, with the second most common following an alveolar pattern. Radiographs typically progress rapidly over the course of several days into confluent alveolar patterns, which predominate over interstitial patterns.[353] DAH is associated with a 70% to 100% mortality.[345–347,353]

Although there are no randomized controlled trials evaluating the efficacy of high-dose corticosteroids for treatment of DAH, several studies suggest both an improvement in respiratory status and improved survival.[273] For example, treatment of DAH with high-dose corticosteroids currently remains the most promising therapeutic option, though not all studies demonstrate beneficial effects. The most commonly used treatment strategy was reported from the University of Nebraska, where methylprednisolone was used at a dose of 125 to 250 mg intravenously every 6 hours for 4 to 6 days and then tapered over 2 weeks.[354] In patients with DAH, treatment with this high-dose strategy showed improved total survival and survival to hospital discharge, and decreased development of respiratory failure when compared to DAH patients left untreated or treated with low-dose methylprednisolone (<30 mg/day). Others have also shown beneficial effects of high-dose methylprednisolone, at a dose of 1000 mg/day given for 3 days, then decreased by 50% every 3 days, though these studies only reported the effects on four patients with DAH following SCT.[355] Less beneficial effects were seen in 23 patients who developed DAH and treated with high-dose steroids. Although transient improvements in respiratory status were noted, 21 of these patients went on to develop respiratory failure and 17 (74%) ultimately died.[356] Treatment of DAH in pediatric patients following SCT using similar high-dose steroid regimens has not had much success.[357,358] High-dose steroids do not appear to increase the rate of infections.[354] Moreover, long-term survivors of DAH may demonstrate excellent recovery of pulmonary function 1 year later.[344]

Delayed Pulmonary Toxicity Syndrome

The term *delayed pulmonary toxicity syndrome* (DPTS) is used to describe lung injury following autologous SCT.[359,360] Clinically, DPTS manifests as an acute to subacute onset of progressive exertional dyspnea, shortness of breath, and dry cough, with or without fever and hypoxemia. Radiographic abnormalities may or may not be present.[360] Closely following the diffusing capacity of carbon monoxide is the best way to monitor the development of DPTS[361]; it reaches a nadir level in 15 to 18 weeks following high-dose chemotherapy and SCT.[361] When compared with IPS, DPTS has an overall higher incidence (72%) and lower mortality.[360] Lung specimens obtained either by open-lung biopsy, autopsy, or transbronchial biopsy in 10 patients who developed DPTS showed five major pathologic findings: (1) alveolar septal thickening with interstitial fibrosis; (2) atypical type II pneumocytes; (3) injury to the pulmonary arterial vasculature; (4) intra-alveolar edema; and (5) increased intra-alveolar macrophages.[264] DPTS is characterized by a loss of pulmonary function and a variable extent of peripheral ground-glass or consolidation opacities on chest CT, all occurring no sooner than 4 to 6 weeks (mean onset 11 weeks) following SCT.[360,362,363] A similar syndrome termed *pulmonary toxicity syndrome* also showed no survival differences in those who did and did not develop this lung toxicity.[364] There was an association in those who developed pulmonary toxicity syndrome with the development of a noncholestatic elevation of transaminases.[364] Overall, patients who develop DPTS or pulmonary toxicity syndrome appear to respond to corticosteroids, if started promptly; treatment is associated with improvements in radiographs, clinical physiology, and pulmonary function tests.[361,364,365]

Table 76.12 Diagnostic Criteria for Diffuse Alveolar Hemorrhage

1. Evidence for widespread/diffuse alveolar injury as manifest by
   a. Multilobar pulmonary infiltrates
   b. Abnormal pulmonary physiology with increased alveolar-arterial P_{O_2} difference
   c. Restrictive ventilatory defect

2. Absence of infectious etiologies compatible with the diagnosis

3. Bronchoalveolar lavage showing progressively bloodier return from three separate subsegmental bronchi or the presence of blood in at least 30% of the alveolar surfaces of lung tissue

Bronchiolitis Obliterans Syndrome or Airflow Obstruction

An increasingly common, noninfectious, posttransplant pulmonary complication primarily affecting the airways is best characterized by chronic progressive airflow obstruction, otherwise known as bronchiolitis obliterans (BO). BO occurring in patients after SCT was originally described in the mid 1980s and was seen exclusively following allogeneic transplantation; the condition was believed to be a manifestation of GVHD of the small airways.[366] Symptoms typically develop between 1.5 and 6 months post-SCT, starting with a cough and progressing to dyspnea and wheezing followed by severe airflow obstruction.[367] FEV_1 values were reported to fall to a mean of 35% of the predicted value, and the FEV_1/FVC ratio dropped below 60%.[367,368] Subsequent studies found that as many as 11% of long-term survivors of allogeneic SCT may develop airflow obstruction, but this number is dependent on the diagnostic criteria used.[369] These early studies defined airflow obstruction as a fall in FEV_1/FVC of less than 0.7 following transplantation.[369] However, using a new operational definition of chronic airflow obstruction, a decline in percent predicted FEV_1 of more than 5% per year (over at least a 5-year period) and the lowest documented posttransplant FEV_1/FVC ratio less than 0.8, the incidence of chronic airflow obstruction was found to be increased to 26%.[259] It is unlikely that the higher incidence reported actually reflects a true change in the incidence; rather, it probably represents the change in the definition.[370]

Fatality is high in cases with rapidly progressive or severe obstruction.[369] However, the overall case-fatality rates are quite variable, ranging from 14% to 100% with a mean value of 61%.[273] Using the definition of greater than 5% per year decline in percent predicted FEV_1, BO was associated with an attributable mortality rate of 9% at 3 years, 12% at 5 years, and 18% at 10 years; however, the subgroup of patients with chronic GVHD had an attributable mortality of 22% at 3 years, 27% at 5 years, and 40% at 10 years.[259] Risk factors for the development of BO include older age at the time of SCT, respiratory viral infection within the first 100 days, acute and chronic GVHD, total-body irradiation, hypogammaglobulinemia, GVHD prophylaxis with methotrexate, and respiratory viral infections.[259,371]

There are no specific radiographic findings diagnostic of BO in adults following SCT. In one study, HRCT of BO after SCT showed variable amounts of vascular attenuation, hypoattenuated areas, consolidation, and bronchial dilation[372]; another showed bronchial dilation to be the main imaging abnormality.[373] However, in children who develop severe airflow obstruction after SCT, HRCT may be a useful tool to assess for the development of BO. Of seven pediatric patients who developed BO after SCT, all had abnormal HRCT scans, with the most common findings being parenchymal hypoattenuation, expiratory "air trapping," and segmental or subsegmental bronchial dilation.[374]

Treatment options for BO are limited. No prospective trials have been conducted in this setting. Symptomatic relief may be obtained with bronchodilators. Because BO is thought to be a manifestation of GVHD, enhanced immunosuppression has been used for treatment. Prednisone 1 to 1.5 mg/kg/day, not to exceed 100 mg/day, is given for 4 to 6 weeks.[273,369] If this stabilizes the disease process, corticosteroids are slowly tapered and discontinued in 6 to 12 months. If no improvement is noted in 1 month, immunosuppression with cyclosporine or azathioprine is initiated. The dose of azathioprine is 2 to 3 mg/kg/day, not to exceed 200 mg daily.[273] Cyclosporine dosage is adjusted based on serum concentration measurements.

In selected patients with BO associated with extensive GVHD refractory to more conventional immunosuppresion, the successful use of lung transplantation has been reported.[374a,374b]

Bronchiolitis Obliterans with Organizing Pneumonia

BOOP has been reported to occur as a late pulmonary complication following SCT.[375,376] BOOP has been reported as the etiology of noninfectious pulmonary opacities in up to 26% of pediatric patients undergoing open-lung biopsy after SCT.[377] In adult patients who survive allogeneic SCT for more than 3 months, the incidence of BOOP is 1.3%.[378] The diagnosis of BOOP following SCT was associated with a long-term survival rate of 80%, presumably because BOOP can often be treated successfully with high-dose steroids.[377,378] Multiple single case reports of transplanted patients who developed BOOP also show a good response to corticosteroids.[379-383] Radiographic CT findings of BOOP in patients after SCT show patchy consolidation or ground-glass attenuation opacities, or both.[384] Thus, BOOP should be considered in the differential diagnosis of pulmonary opacities following SCT and appears to impart a good long-term prognosis. Initial therapy for BOOP is prednisone 0.75 to 1.5 mg/kg/day, up to 100 mg, for 1 to 3 months, and this is followed with lower doses for a total duration of 6 to 12 months.[273]

Vasculopathies, Pulmonary Artery Hypertension, and Pulmonary Veno-occlusive Disease

Although uncommon, vasculopathy has been described in a series of six pediatric patients following allogeneic SCT; the disorder occurred from 13 to 418 days after transplant and was characterized by an obliterative arteriopathy, which was hypothesized to be due to the effects of irradiation, chemotherapy, cyclosporine, and GVHD.[385] Somewhat similar findings were seen in a group of transplanted pediatric patients who presented with pulmonary nodular lesions ($n = 15$ patients), but the term *pulmonary cytolytic thrombi* (PCT) was used.[362] Distinct histopathologic features of PCT include occlusive vascular lesions and hemorrhagic infarcts.[362,386] The thrombi consist of intensive basophilic, amorphous material that occasionally extends into adjacent tissue through the damaged vascular wall. White blood cells are frequently seen entrapped in the thrombi. PCT appears to resolve without requiring specific therapy.

Severe pulmonary artery hypertension (PAH) as an etiology for acute dyspnea and hypoxia should also be considered, particularly in children undergoing allogeneic SCT for malignant infantile osteopetrosis; in this group, an incidence of PAH as high as 29% has been reported.[387] PAH occurring as a result of intimal fibrosis and veno-occlusion also occurs in adults.[388]

Pulmonary veno-occlusive disease of varying origin is a rare cause of PAH that can progress rapidly to death. Pulmonary veno-occlusive disease occurring as a pulmonary complication following SCT has been reported in both adults[389–391] and children.[392,393] In particular, infants with malignant infantile osteopetrosis treated with allogeneic SCT seem to have a particular high frequency of pulmonary veno-occlusive disease, reported to be 29% in one series.[387]

Lymphoproliferative Disorders

Posttransplant lymphoproliferative disorders (PTLDs) occur in 1.2% to 1.9% of patients following SCT[394,395] and can present as focal pulmonary opacities.[396,397] PTLDs occur almost exclusively after allogeneic SCT,[395] though a case report documents lymphomatoid granulomatosis following autologous SCT.[398] These EBV-associated lymphoproliferative disorders result from acquired immunodeficiency after SCT, with impaired T-cell immunity leading to a polyclonal expansion of B cells infected with EBV.[395,399] The major risk factors for the development of PTLDs after SCT are ex vivo T-cell depletion of the allograft and in vivo anti–T-cell therapy for GVHD.[394] PTLDs may respond to humanized anti-CD20 monoclonal antibody (Rituximab)[400] and interferon-alfa.[395]

Engraftment Syndrome

During reengraftment of neutrophils following SCT, the clinical constellation of noninfectious fever, erythrodermatous skin rash, and noncardiogenic pulmonary edema may be seen and is referred to as the engraftment syndrome (ES).[401,402] ES has been reported to occur in about 7% to 9% of patients undergoing SCT,[403,404] but the incidence may be as high as 59%,[402] depending on the criteria used for diagnosis.[405] Spitzer[401] has proposed a set of major and minor criteria for a uniform definition of ES (Table 76.13). Although the pathophysiology of ES is not entirely clear, it likely involves multiple pathways that include prominent interactions of T cells, monocytes, and proinflammatory

cytokine production and release.[401,403] The development of ES may also be associated with an early and steep recovery of neutrophils following SCT,[404] and thus is closely related to the use of either G-CSF[402,406,407] or granulocyte-macrophage colony-stimulating factor.[408] Although ES is more common after autologous SCT, it is also described following allogeneic SCT.[401] In children, ES has been reported to occur in 19.2% of patients who underwent SCT; of these, 66% developed hypoxia or pulmonary infiltrates or both.[407] Chest radiographs may be abnormal in 50% of individuals with engraftment syndrome, and the most common findings are pleural effusions and interstitial pulmonary edema.[409] Interestingly, the pulmonary edema aspect of ES can be eliminated in some cases by shielding the lung from radiation treatment.[410]

ES appears to have a prompt response to corticosteroid treatment,[403,404,410] though transplanted patients who develop ES may have significantly increased morbidity and mortality. This is particularly so for pediatric patients after SCT, in whom the difference in overall transplant-related mortality was 23% in those with ES versus 4.8% (P < 0.0001) in those without ES.[407] In some groups, such as breast cancer patients treated with SCT, ES may also be associated with poor long-term survival.[411]

MANAGEMENT ISSUES

Radiologic Studies

Chest Radiography. Chest radiographs (CXRs) are frequently obtained for routine follow-up of patients who have undergone SCT. The rationale for this practice is based, in part, on the identification of individuals who develop new pulmonary opacities but who do not have respiratory symptoms. In febrile neutropenic patients, but not necessarily those following SCT, the reported incidence of new pulmonary radiographic abnormalities without pulmonary signs or symptoms has been reported to be as low as 2% to 4%[412,413] or as high as 17% to 25%.[414] In a group of febrile patients after autologous SCT, 26% had new CXR abnormalities but were without pulmonary signs or symptoms.[270] However, the presence of pretransplant CXR abnormalities increased the risk almost threefold of developing additional abnormalities with fever. The specificity of the physical examination for new pulmonary infiltrates is low (30% to 40%) in the neutropenic febrile patient.[270,414] The clinical benefit of obtaining routine CXRs in febrile neutropenic patients has not been unequivocally determined, but reports so far suggest that routine CXRs in the initial management of the febrile neutropenic patient, whether from conventional chemotherapy or following auto-SCT, may not be necessary.[270,412,414] This likely results from the current practice of treating febrile neutropenic patients with high-dose, broad-spectrum antibiotics and antifungal agents. However, subsequent follow-up CXRs, in the setting of persistent fevers or new physical findings, would likely be beneficial to patients in localizing pulmonary infiltrates or suggesting new pulmonary disease processes.

A normal CXR in the setting of persistent fever in neutropenic patients after SCT does not necessarily rule out pneumonia. In a study from Germany, of 188 HRCTs performed prospectively in 112 neutropenic patients (54 of

---

Table 76.13 Diagnostic Criteria for Engraftment Syndrome (ES)*

Major Criteria

Temperature ≥38.3°C with no identifiable infectious etiology

Erythrodermatous rash involving more than 25% of body surface area and not attributable to a medication

Noncardiogenic pulmonary edema, manifested by diffuse pulmonary infiltrates consistent with this diagnosis, and hypoxia

Minor Criteria

Hepatic dysfunction with either total bilirubin ≥2 mg/dL or transaminase levels ≥2 times normal

Renal insufficiency (serum creatinine ≥2 times baseline)

Weight gain ≥2.5% of baseline body weight

Transient encephalopathy unexplainable by other causes

*A diagnosis of ES is established by the presence of all three major criteria or two major criteria and one or more minor criteria.[401] ES should occur within 96 hours of engraftment (polymorphonuclear leukocytes ≥500/µL for 2 consecutive days).
From Spitzer TR: Engraftment resyndrome following hematopoietic stem cell transplantation. Bone Marrow Transplant 27:893–898, 2001.

whom had a stem-cell transplant) who remained febrile for more than 48 hours despite empirical antibiotic treatment and who had a normal CXR, 112 (60%) were subsequently shown to have a pulmonary infiltrate by chest HRCT scan.[415] Of those with an abnormal HRCT scan, 54% were subsequently shown to have pneumonia.

Standard and High-Resolution Chest Computed Tomography.
The role of standard chest CT in the management of pulmonary disease following SCT is currently being defined. HRCT has been shown to have a sensitivity of 88% for identifying pneumonia in the febrile neutropenic patient after SCT if the patient remains febrile for over 48 hours.[415] The specificity was shown to be 67% but, more interestingly, the negative predictive value was 97%.[415] It was estimated that a time gain of up to 5 days can be achieved by the additional use of HRCT compared to the exclusive use of plain CXR. It has been recommended that all neutropenic patients with a fever of unknown origin and a normal CXR should undergo HRCT.[415,416] Patients who have a normal HRCT scan have a low likelihood of pneumonia during follow-up. Thus, in addition to identifying lung pathology otherwise missed by plain radiographs, chest CT will also help localize the area of abnormal lung, which should assist in directing subsequent invasive diagnostic procedures to the most involved segments of the lung.

Other Interventions

Where practical, sputum samples or induced sputum samples, or both, or nasal saline irrigation should be obtained. Although this relatively simple form of testing could provide useful information for infectious etiologies such as *Mycobacterium, P. jirovecii,* respiratory viruses, and *Aspergillus,* the majority of patients with pulmonary infiltrates after SCT are not capable of producing acceptable sputum samples, and more aggressive airway/parenchymal sampling techniques are needed.

Fiberoptic bronchoscopy (FB) has emerged as the intervention of choice for working up pulmonary infiltrates in patients following SCT, whereas fine-needle aspiration (FNA) (see later) and surgical lung biopsy (SLB) have taken a more limited role. However, in the appropriate clinical setting, both FNA and SLB may provide useful and timely information not otherwise obtainable via FB.

Fiberoptic Bronchoscopy.
Flexible FB is extremely useful in the workup of pulmonary opacities seen in patients after both autologous and allogeneic SCT. The diagnostic yield has been reported to be anywhere from 40% to as high as 89%, depending on the transplanted patient population and whether or not both BAL and transbronchial biopsy (TBBX) were performed.[417,417a] In a recent study, the diagnostic yield of FB was evaluated in 104 consecutive non–HIV-infected immunocompromised patients with lung infiltrates or pulmonary lesions, 20% of whom had undergone SCT.[275] From these patients, a total of 128 diagnoses were made either by FB (56.2%) or SLB (13.3%), or based on clinical criteria (30.5%). BAL was the most common procedure (performed in 95%), followed by TBBX (43%) and protected specimen brushing (29%).[275] The overall diagnostic yield from FB was 56%.[275] The diagnostic yield of BAL was 38%, TBBX 38%, and protected specimen brushing 13%. The combined diagnostic yield of BAL plus TBBX was 70%, whereas that of BAL plus TBBX plus protected specimen brushing reached 86%. FB was very good at diagnosing infectious etiologies (81% sensitivity) and DAH (90% sensitivity). TBBX provided an exclusionary diagnosis in 17 patients; 15 cases were due to noninfectious causes: radiation pneumonitis in 3, Wegener's granulomatosis in 2, diffuse alveolar damage in 4, BOOP in 2, and nonspecific pneumonitis, bronchopneumonia, sarcoidosis, and lymphoma in 1 each.[275] The overall complication rate of FB was 21.2%, with minor bleeding being the most common complication (13.5%, although one patient required a red blood cell transfusion), followed by worsening of hypoxemia (9.6%, with two patients requiring short-term ventilatory support). There were no deaths due to FB. However, not all patients in this study underwent TBBX, so the rate of complications due to this procedure may be underestimated.

FB has been evaluated in patients after autologous SCT. The utility of flexible FB in the workup of pulmonary infiltrates was evaluated in 23 advanced breast cancer patients (treated with high-dose chemotherapy and autologous SCT) who underwent 27 consecutive bronchoscopies.[417] These authors report that FB provided a diagnosis in 59% of these patients. All patients underwent BAL, and TBBX was performed in 14. TBBX provided a diagnosis in 10 of the 14 (71%), with pulmonary drug toxicity being the most common finding (8 of 10) followed by lymphangitic breast cancer (2 of 10).[417] BAL was diagnostic in six cases (22%): three cases of bacterial pneumonia, three of aspergillosis, and one each of *P. jirovecii* and influenza B infections.[417] Only one minor complication occurred, a small pneumothorax not requiring chest tube placement.[417]

FB has also been evaluated in the allogeneic adult stem-cell transplant setting and was found to have a diagnostic yield of 42%, of which infectious etiologies (CMV, *Mycobacterium avium* complex, and *Aspergillus* were most frequent), followed by DAH, were the most common.[276] Furthermore, the results of FB altered patient management in 32% of these patients; almost half of these changes included withdrawal of antimicrobial therapy.[276] However, no survival benefit was noted. The complication rate was 3.9%, which led to respiratory failure requiring mechanical ventilation in these cases.[276]

In a separate study that analyzed the diagnostic yield of BAL in patients being worked up for pulmonary infiltrates on CXR following both autologous and allogeneic SCT, BAL was diagnostic in 42 of 89 patients (47%).[418] The most common findings were DAH, bacterial pneumonia, RSV, aspergillosis, PCP, and CMV. BAL had a high false-negative rate when the pulmonary infiltrate was due to cardiogenic pulmonary edema, IPS, and BO.[418] Similar findings of yield and safety have been reported by others.[419,420] In contrast, some centers report FB to have substantially higher complication rates and lower diagnostic yields, and to have less frequently changed the patient treatment plan.[277,421] It is worth reemphasizing that FB has not clearly been shown to impact survival.

Transthoracic Fine-Needle Aspiration.
Transthoracic FNA can be useful in the diagnostic workup of focal peripheral radiographic abnormalities in patients with hematologic

malignancies and after SCT. Pulmonary nodules, masses, focal infiltrates, and cavitary lesions are all potentially approachable with FNA. In one recent study, 67 patients with underlying hematologic malignancies, or those who recently underwent SCT, were subjected to FNA for the workup of focal thoracic radiographic opacities.[422] Using a 22-gauge needle, a positive diagnosis was made in 72% of these patients.[422] The specific yield for malignancy was 77% (90% for lung cancer and 68% for lymphoma). A diagnosis of infection was correctly made in 67%. *Aspergillus fumigatus* was the organism most frequently diagnosed, whereas only one of three *C. neoformans* infections was identified by FNA. Several prior studies also reported similar diagnostic yields for FNA in the immunocompromised host. FNA correctly diagnosed fungal infections in 10 (67%) of 15 stem-cell–transplanted patients who presented with focal opacities not responsive to antibiotics.[423] A recent Finnish study retrospectively evaluated 30 FNAs in 21 allogeneic transplant recipients with focal pulmonary lesions.[324] They diagnosed invasive aspergillosis in 5 of 21 patients (24%), *Pseudomonas* in 2 of 21 (10%), and one case of *Nocardia* (5%) on the first FNA attempt. This method missed the diagnosis of invasive aspergillosis in 8 of 21 patients (38%), GVHD in 3 of 21 (14%), and BOOP in 1 of 21, and in 2 of 21 patients the underlying lung disease remained unknown.[324]

In 82 patients, primarily in the setting of heart and kidney transplant, FNA was reported to have a diagnostic yield of 73%, with a 26% pneumothorax rate (of which half required chest tube insertion) and 3% with limited hemoptysis.[424] Hwang and colleagues[425] recently reported a 79% diagnostic yield in 21 immunocompromised patients undergoing FNA, with *S. aureus* and *A. fumigatus* being the major bacterial and fungal agents identified.

Complications from FNA typically limit the effectiveness of this technique in the immunocompromised population. Pneumothorax is the most common complication, with rates that vary from 13% to 25%; next most common are hemothorax, hemoptysis, and chest tube placement.[324,422,423,425,426] Thus, in patients after SCT, the appropriate clinical setting for FNA is the workup of small peripheral focal pulmonary opacities; the diagnostic yield is particularly good for invasive pulmonary aspergillosis.

Surgical Lung Biopsy. The role for SLB in immunocompromised patients with persistent pulmonary infiltrates has not been clearly defined. SLB has the theoretical advantage of a high yield for a specific diagnosis, but is often associated with significant morbidity and mortality. In the 1980s, at a time before the routine use of antiviral, antibacterial, and antifungal prophylaxis, SLB performed in stem-cell–transplanted patients showed mixed findings depending on the patient population under study. For example, in 109 adult marrow transplant recipients, the use of SLB for diagnosis of diffuse pulmonary infiltrates showed a high incidence (63%) of patients with infectious etiologies.[271] Of these, CMV pneumonia was the major infectious etiologic agent found, comprising 90% of the total, whereas PCP was found in only 6%. Bacterial and yeast infections were found in 2% each, and simultaneous infection with two or more organisms was found in 4%. Somewhat surprisingly, autopsy examinations of 25 patients who died within 10 days of SLB revealed 4 patients with previously undetected fungal infec-

tions with *Aspergillus*.[271] In a separate study, 87 stem-cell–transplanted patients underwent 94 SLB procedures that led to a specific diagnosis in 60%.[427] Although there were no reported intraoperative complications, there was a 21% incidence of minor complications. Overall, 45% of the patients died within 30 days of their operation and 74% of patients died during the course of this study at a mean time of 43 days following SLB.[427] SLB may have less clinical utility in the pediatric transplant population. In 21 pediatric patients undergoing 22 SLBs, only 3 were shown to have CMV and 4 to have PCP[428]; a total of 14 of 21 showed no causative microorganisms. Thirteen of these patients eventually died after SLB, and only two patients had their management changed as a direct result of this procedure. These authors concluded that SLB is of limited value and that survival is dismal unless the patient has PCP.[428]

Recent studies support a limited role of SLB in today's patient with persistent pulmonary opacities following SCT. Most transplanted patients now receive routine antibacterial, antiviral, antifungal, and anti-*Pneumocystis* prophylaxis, and the resulting distribution of infectious etiologies of pulmonary infiltrates has changed. In one recent series of 12 stem-cell–transplanted patients undergoing SLB, 67% showed nonspecific findings consisting of organizing alveolitis, interstitial fibrosis, diffuse alveolar damage, and necrotizing granuloma.[429] Only 4 of 12 biopsies identified an infectious agent (1 each of invasive pulmonary aspergillosis, mycobacterial pneumonia, *Candida* pneumonia, and PCP), which led to a change in antimicrobial therapy in 3 of 12 patients.[429] Interestingly, no CMV pneumonia was found. In this small series, there were no reports of SLB-associated mortality or morbidity. However, overall mortality remained high, as 42% of the patients eventually died during their hospitalization. In this report, the authors argued that a nondiagnostic SLB has value because it excludes diagnoses that would require empirical hazardous therapies, such as amphotericin B.[429]

In Taiwan, 35 SCT patients with diffuse pulmonary infiltrates underwent SLB resulting in therapeutic changes in 22 (63%), of which clinical improvement was seen in 22 (63%).[429a] In this group of patients the leading diagnoses were interstitial pneumonitis (40%), cytomegalovirus pneumonitis (20%) and miliary tuberculosis (9%). Other diagnoses made were organizing pneumonia (14%) and 1 each of aspergillosis, alveolar hemorrhage, capillaritis, lymphoma relapse and post transplant lymphoproliferative disorder.

Complications from SLB may be increased in transplanted pediatric patients. Of 19 pediatric patients who underwent SLB for radiographic evidence of pulmonary infiltrates after SCT, 47% developed significant complications, including prolonged intubation (7 patients), pneumothorax (2 patients), and pleural effusion (1 patient).[377] Significant risk factors for SLB complications were allogeneic SCT, absolute neutrophil count below 500 cells/μL, multisystem organ failure, ventilator dependency, and concurrent high-dose steroid use. There was no mortality directly related to the procedure, though the overall 30-day mortality was 37%. A specific diagnosis was made in all patients who underwent SLB: 6 cases of infection (4 *Aspergillus*, 1 influenza, and 1 *Stenotrophomonas*), 5 cases of BOOP, 4 cases of interstitial pneumonitis, 1 case of gangliosidosis, and 1 of lymphocytic infiltrate.[377] This resulted in a change in therapy for 17 of 19 patients (90%), ultimately leading to an improved clinical condition in only 7 of these patients (41%). There are two scenarios in which SLB was considered to be beneficial. First, a histopathologic diagnosis of BOOP was likely to result in long-term survival benefit. Second, in patients with discrete solitary pulmonary nodules, surgical resection of lesions, which often showed *Aspergillus,* was likely to remove most of the disease burden, thus providing a significant advantage in postoperative recovery.[377]

SLB was performed in 33 pediatric and adult patients who developed pulmonary nodular lesions (7% incidence) after SCT and resulted in 33 specific diagnoses.[326] There was one death directly attributable to SLB. In this series, the most common pathologic finding was PCT, occurring in 15 patients, all of whom underwent allogeneic SCT. *Aspergillus* was the second most common finding, seen in eight patients, six of whom ultimately died from progressive fungal disease. Other specific findings were two cases of interstitial pneumonitis, two of intra-alveolar hemorrhage, two of organizing pneumonitis, and one each of thromboembolism, metastatic choriocarcinoma, hemorrhagic infarct, and foreign body embolus.[326]

SUMMARY

The diagnosis and management of patients with pulmonary diseases associated with underlying disorders of immune deficiency has become an increasingly common and, thereby, important part of the daily practice of medicine. HIV infection and its accompanying lethal partner—the acquired immunodeficiency syndrome (see Chapter 75)—contribute the majority of such patients, but more and more people are being seen with any one of a host of pulmonary complications related to BMT or SCT. As discussed in this chapter, these disorders not only are frequent, but can be life-threatening and involve a wide range of infectious and noninfectious etiologies. The pattern of infectious complications of transplantation has been greatly affected by the now routine use of prophylaxis against common viral, bacterial, and fungal agents, which has lowered the incidence of many previously familiar disorders but, in turn, has allowed other less common manifestations to supervene. The workup and treatment of these often deadly pulmonary conditions is described.

Although much less common, the primary (heritable) immunodeficiency syndromes that affect antibody production, cellular immune capacity, and phagocytic cell function are also discussed. Patients with these disorders are now surviving into adulthood or are being diagnosed as adults, so chest physicians need to know about these diseases as well as their particular pulmonary complications.

REFERENCES

1. Busse PJ, Razvi S, Cunningham-Rundles C: Efficacy of intravenous immunoglobulin in the prevention of pneumonia in patients with common variable immunodeficiency. J Allergy Clin Immunol 109:1001–1004, 2002.
2. Hedlund JU, Ortqvist AB, Kalin M, et al: Risk of pneumonia in patients previously treated in hospital for pneumonia. Lancet 340:396–397, 1992.
3. Paul ME, Shearer WT: Approach to the evaluation of the immunodeficient patient. *In* Rich RR, Fleisher TA, Shearer WT, et al (eds): Clinical Immunology: Principles and Practice. London: Mosby International, 2001, pp 33.1–33.11.
4. Paul ME, Shearer WT: The patient with too many infections. *In* Lieberman P, Anderson J (eds): Current Clinical Practice; Allergic Diseases: Diagnosis and Treatment. Totowa, NJ: Humana, 2000, pp 445–459.
5. Chapel HM, Webster DB: Assessment of the immune system. *In* Ochs HD, Smith CIE, Puck JM (eds): Primary Immunodeficiency Disease: A Molecular and Genetic Approach. New York: Oxford University Press, 1998, pp 419–431.
6. Folds JD, Schmitz JL: Clinical and laboratory assessment of immunity. J Allergy Clin Immunol 111:S702–S711, 2003.
7. Cunningham-Rundles C, Bodian C: Common variable immunodeficiency: Clinical and immunological features of 248 patients. Clin Immunol 92:34–48, 1999.
8. Nelson HS, Hamilos DL, Corsello PR, et al: A double-blind study of troleandomycin and methylprednisolone in asthmatic subjects who require daily corticosteroids. Am Rev Respir Dis 147:398–404, 1993.
9. Hamilos DL, Young RM, Peter JB, et al: Hypogammaglobulinemia in asthmatic patients. Ann Allergy 68:472–481, 1992.
10. Rodrigo MJ, Vendrell M, Cruz MJ, et al: Utility of the antibody response to a conjugated *Haemophilus influenzae* type B vaccine for diagnosis of primary humoral immunodeficiency. Am J Respir Crit Care Med 162:1462–1465, 2000.
11. Buckley RH: Primary cellular immunodeficiencies. J Allergy Clin Immunol 109:747–757, 2002.
12. Frank MM: Complement deficiencies. Pediatr Clin North Am 47:1339–1354, 2000.
13. Crockard AD, Thompson JM, Boyd NA, et al: Diagnosis and carrier detection of chronic granulomatous disease in five families by flow cytometry. Int Arch Allergy Immunol 114:144–152, 1997.
14. Vowells SJ, Sekhsaria S, Malech HL, et al: Flow cytometric analysis of the granulocyte respiratory burst: A comparison study of fluorescent probes. J Immunol Methods 178:89–97, 1995.
15. Ballow M: Primary immunodeficiency disorders: Antibody deficiency. J Allergy Clin Immunol 109:581–591, 2002.
16. Gardulf A, Andersen V, Bjorkander J, et al: Subcutaneous immunoglobulin replacement in patients with primary antibody deficiencies: Safety and costs. Lancet 345:365–369, 1995.
17. Eijkhout HW, van Der Meer JW, Kallenberg CG, et al: The effect of two different dosages of intravenous immunoglobulin on the incidence of recurrent infections in patients with primary hypogammaglobulinemia: A randomized, double-blind, multicenter crossover trial. Ann Intern Med 135:165–174, 2001.
18. Roifman CM, Lederman HM, Lavi S, et al: Benefit of intravenous IgG replacement in hypogammaglobulinemic patients with chronic sinopulmonary disease. Am J Med 79:171–174, 1985.
19. Gelfand EW: Unique susceptibility of patients with antibody deficiency to mycoplasma infection. Clin Infect Dis 17(Suppl 1):S250–S253, 1993.
20. Cunningham-Rundles C: Physiology of IgA and IgA deficiency. J Clin Immunol 21:303–309, 2001.
21. Lilic D, Sewell WA: IgA deficiency: What we should—or should not—be doing. J Clin Pathol 54:337–338, 2001.

22. Hammarstrom L, Vorechovsky I, Webster D: Selective IgA deficiency (SIgAD) and common variable immunodeficiency (CVID). Clin Exp Immunol 120:225–231, 2000.

23. Hanson LA, Bjorkander J, Carlsson B, et al: The heterogeneity of IgA deficiency. J Clin Immunol 8:159–162, 1988.

24. Alaswad B, Brosnan P: The association of celiac disease, diabetes mellitus type 1, hypothyroidism, chronic liver disease, and selective IgA deficiency. Clin Pediatr (Phila) 39:229–231, 2000.

25. Ochs HD, Smith CI: X-linked agammaglobulinemia: A clinical and molecular analysis. Medicine (Baltimore) 75:287–299, 1996.

26. Speletas M, Kanariou M, Kanakoudi-Tsakalidou F, et al: Analysis of Btk mutations in patients with X-linked agammaglobulinaemia (XLA) and determination of carrier status in normal female relatives: A nationwide study of Btk deficiency in Greece. Scand J Immunol 54:321–327, 2001.

27. Smith CIE, Bäckesjö C-M, Berglöf A, et al: X-linked agammaglobulinemia: Lack of mature B lineage cells caused by mutations in the Btk kinase. Springer Semin Immunopathol 19:369–381, 1998.

28. Minegishi Y, Rohrer J, Conley M: Recent progress in the diagnosis and treatment of patients with defects in early B-cell development. Curr Opin Pediatr 11:528–532, 1999.

29. Conley ME, Nortarangelo LD, Etzioni A: Diagnostic criteria for primary immunodeficiencies. Clin Immunol 93:190–197, 1999.

30. Conley M, Rohrer J, Minegishi Y: X-linked agammaglobulinemia. Clin Rev Allergy Immunol 19:183–204, 2000.

31. Alibrahim A, Lepore M, Lierl M, et al: *Pneumocystis carinii* pneumonia in an infant with X-linked agammaglobulinemia. J Allergy Clin Immunol 101:552–553, 1998.

32. Fasth A: Primary immunodeficiency disorders in Sweden: Cases among children, 1974–1979. J Clin Immunol 2:86–92, 1982.

33. Grimbacher B, Hutloff A, Schlesier M, et al: Homozygous loss of ICOS is associated with adult-onset common variable immunodeficiency. Nat Immunol 4:261–268, 2003.

34. Roifman CM, Rao CP, Lederman HM, et al: Increased susceptibility to mycoplasma infection in patients with hypogammaglobulinemia. Am J Med 80:590–594, 1986.

35. Mellemkjaer L, Hammarstrom L, Andersen V, et al: Cancer risk among patients with IgA deficiency or common variable immunodeficiency and their relatives: A combined Danish and Swedish study. Clin Exp Immunol 130:495–500, 2002.

36. Cunningham-Rundles C, Lieberman P, Hellman G, Chaganti RS: Non-Hodgkin lymphoma in common variable immunodeficiency. Am J Hematol 37:69–74, 1991.

37. Mechanic LJ, Dikman S, Cunningham-Rundles C: Granulomatous disease in common variable immunodeficiency. Ann Intern Med 127:613–617, 1997.

38. Popa V: Lymphocytic interstitial pneumonia of common variable immunodeficiency. Ann Allergy 60:203–206, 1988.

39. Kanathur N, Byrd RP Jr, Fields CL, Roy TM: Noncaseating granulomatous disease in common variable immunodeficiency. South Med J 93:631–633, 2000.

40. Fasano MB, Sullivan KE, Sarpong SB, et al: Sarcoidosis and common variable immunodeficiency: Report of 8 cases and review of the literature. Medicine (Baltimore) 75:251–261, 1996.

40a. Bates CA, Ellison MC, Lynch DA, et al: Granulomatous-lymphocytic lung disease shortens survival in common

41. Davies CW, Juniper MC, Gray W, et al: Lymphoid interstitial pneumonitis associated with common variable hypogammaglobulinaemia treated with cyclosporin A. Thorax 55:88–90, 2000.

42. Tarr PE, Sneller MC, Mechanic LJ, et al: Infections in patients with immunodeficiency with thymoma (Good syndrome): Report of 5 cases and review of the literature. Medicine (Baltimore) 80:123–133, 2001.

43. Good RA: Agammaglobulinemia—a provocative experiment of nature. Bull Univ Minn 26:1–19, 1954.

44. Kainulainen L, Varpula M, Liippo K, et al: Pulmonary abnormalities in patients with primary hypogammaglobulinemia. J Allergy Clin Immunol 104:1031–1036, 1999.

44a. Erdos M, Durandy A, Marodi L: Genetically acquired class-switch recombination defects: the multi-faced hyper-IgM syndrome. Immunol Lett 97:1–6, 2005.

45. Winkelstein JA, Marino MC, Ochs H, et al: The X-linked hyper-IgM syndrome: Clinical and immunologic features of 79 patients. Medicine (Baltimore) 82:373–384, 2003.

46. Bonilla FA, Geha RS: CD154 deficiency and related syndromes. Immunol Allergy Clin North Am 21:61–89, 2001.

47. Levy J, Espanol-Boren T, Thomas C, et al: Clinical spectrum of X-linked hyper-IgM syndrome. J Pediatr 131:47–54, 1997.

48. Ferrari S, Giliani S, Insalaco A, et al: Mutations of CD40 gene cause an autosomal recessive form of immunodeficiency with hyper IgM. Proc Natl Acad Sci U S A 98:12614–12619, 2001.

49. Aruffo A, Farrington M, Hollenbaugh D, et al: The CD40 ligand, gp39, is defective in activated T cells from patients with X-linked hyper-IgM syndrome. Cell 72:291–300, 1993.

50. DiSanto JP, Bonnefoy JY, Gauchat JF, et al: CD40 ligand mutations in X-linked immunodeficiency with hyper-IgM (see comments). Nature 361:541–543, 1993.

51. Fuleihan R, Ramesh N, Loh R, et al: Defective expression of the CD40 ligand in X chromosome-linked immunoglobulin deficiency with normal or elevated IgM. Proc Natl Acad Sci U S A 90:2170–2173, 1993.

52. Korthauer U, Graf D, Mages HW, et al: Defective expression of T-cell CD40 ligand causes X-linked immunodeficiency with hyper-IgM (see comments). Nature 361:539–541, 1993.

53. Allen RC, Armitage RJ, Conley ME, et al: CD40 ligand gene defects responsible for X-linked hyper-IgM syndrome (see comments). Science 259:990–993, 1993.

54. Orange JS, Brodeur SR, Jain A, et al: The spectrum of clinical phenotype and immunodeficiency due to NFκB essential modifier (NEMO) mutation. J Allergy Clin Immunol 111:S190, 2003.

55. Orange JS, Brodeur SR, Jain A, et al: Deficient natural killer cell cytotoxicity in patients with IKK-gamma/NEMO mutations. J Clin Invest 109:1501–1509, 2002.

56. Wisniewski SA, Kobielak A, Trzeciak WH, Kobielak K: Recent advances in understanding of the molecular basis of anhidrotic ectodermal dysplasia: Discovery of a ligand, ectodysplasin A and its two receptors. J Appl Genet 43:97–107, 2002.

57. Aradhya S, Courtois G, Rajkovic A, et al: Atypical forms of incontinentia pigmenti in male individuals result from mutations of a cytosine tract in exon 10 of NEMO (IKK-gamma). Am J Hum Genet 68:765–771, 2001.

58. Doffinger R, Smahi A, Bessia C, et al: X-linked anhidrotic ectodermal dysplasia with immunodeficiency is caused by

impaired NF-kappaB signaling. Nat Genet 27:277–285, 2001.

59. Jain A, Ma CA, Liu S, et al: Specific missense mutations in NEMO result in hyper-IgM syndrome with hypohidrotic ectodermal dysplasia. Nat Immunol 2:223–228, 2001.

60. Mansour S, Woffendin H, Mitton S, et al: Incontinentia pigmenti in a surviving male is accompanied by hypohidrotic ectodermal dysplasia and recurrent infection. Am J Med Genet 99:172–177, 2001.

61. Zonana J, Elder ME, Schneider LC, et al: A novel X-linked disorder of immune deficiency and hypohidrotic ectodermal dysplasia is allelic to incontinentia pigmenti and due to mutations in IKK-gamma (NEMO). Am J Hum Genet 67:1555–1562, 2000.

62. Revy P, Muto T, Levy Y, et al: Activation-induced cytidine deaminase (AID) deficiency causes the autosomal recessive form of the hyper-IgM syndrome (HIGM2). Cell 102:565–575, 2000.

63. Imai K, Slupphaug G, Lee WI, et al: Human uracil-DNA glycosylase deficiency associated with profoundly impaired immunoglobulin class-switch recombination. Nat Immunol 4:1023–1028, 2003.

64. Hadzic N, Pagliuca A, Rela M, et al: Correction of the hyper-IgM syndrome after liver and bone marrow transplantation. N Engl J Med 342:320–324, 2000.

65. Bordigoni P, Auburtin B, Carret AS, et al: Bone marrow transplantation as treatment for X-linked immunodeficiency with hyper-IgM. Bone Marrow Transplant 22:1111–1114, 1998.

66. Duplantier JE, Seyama K, Day NK, et al: Immunologic reconstitution following bone marrow transplantation for X- linked hyper IgM syndrome. Clin Immunol 98:313–318, 2001.

67. Kato T, Tsuge I, Inaba J, et al: Successful bone marrow transplantation in a child with X-linked hyper-IgM syndrome. Bone Marrow Transplant 23:1081–1083, 1999.

68. Kawai S, Sasahara Y, Minegishi M, et al: Immunological reconstitution by allogeneic bone marrow transplantation in a child with the X-linked hyper-IgM syndrome. Eur J Pediatr 158:394–397, 1999.

69. Scholl PR, O'Gorman MR, Pachman LM, et al: Correction of neutropenia and hypogammaglobulinemia in X-linked hyper-IgM syndrome by allogeneic bone marrow transplantation. Bone Marrow Transplant 22:1215–1218, 1998.

70. Thomas C, de Saint Basile G, Le Deist F, et al: Brief report: Correction of X-linked hyper-IgM syndrome by allogeneic bone marrow transplantation. N Engl J Med 333:426–429, 1995.

71. Ambrosino DM, Siber GR, Chilmonczyk BA, et al: An immunodeficiency characterized by impaired antibody responses to polysaccharides. N Engl J Med 316:790–793, 1987.

72. Ambrosino DM, Umetsu DT, Siber GR, et al: Selective defect in the antibody response to Haemophilus influenzae type b in children with recurrent infections and normal serum IgG subclass levels. J Allergy Clin Immunol 81:1175–1179, 1988.

73. French MAH, Harrison G: Systemic antibody deficiency in patients without serum immunoglobulin deficiency or with selective IgA deficiency. Clin Exp Immunol 56:18–22, 1984.

74. Saxon A, Kobayashi RH, Stevens RH, et al: In vitro analysis of humoral immunity in antibody deficiency with normal immunoglobulins. Clin Immunol Immunopathol 17:235–244, 1980.

75. Sorensen RU, Leiva LE, Giangrosso PA, et al: Response to a heptavalent conjugate Streptococcus pneumoniae vaccine in children with recurrent infections who are unresponsive to the polysaccharide vaccine. Pediatr Infect Dis J 17:685–691, 1998.

76. Sorensen RU, Leiva LE, Javier FC, et al: Influence of age on the response to Streptococcus pneumoniae vaccine in patients with recurrent infections and normal immunoglobulin concentrations. J Allergy Asthma Clin Immunol 102:215–221, 1998.

77. Maguire GA, Kumararatne DS, Joyce HJ: Are there any clinical indications for measuring IgG subclasses? Ann Clin Biochem 39:374–377, 2002.

78. Shackelford PG, Granoff DM, Madassery JV, et al: Clinical and immunologic characteristics of healthy children with subnormal serum concentrations of IgG2. Pediatr Res 27:16–21, 1990.

79. Lefranc MP, Lefranc G: Human immunoglobulin heavy-chain multigene deletions in healthy individuals. FEBS Lett 213:231–237, 1987.

80. Morra M, Silander O, Calpe S, et al: Alterations of the X-linked lymphoproliferative disease gene SH2D1A in common variable immunodeficiency syndrome. Blood 98:1321–1325, 2001.

81. Nistala K, Gilmour KC, Cranston T, et al: X-linked lymphoproliferative disease: Three atypical cases. Clin Exp Immunol 126:126–130, 2001.

82. Soresina A, Lougaris V, Giliani S, et al: Mutations of the X-linked lymphoproliferative disease gene SH2D1A mimicking common variable immunodeficiency. Eur J Pediatr 161:656–659, 2002.

83. Schuster V, Kreth HW: X-linked lymphoproliferative disease is caused by deficiency of a novel SH2 domain-containing signal transduction adaptor protein. Immunol Rev 178:21–28, 2000.

84. Gross TG, Filipovich AH, Conley ME, et al: Cure of X-linked lymphoproliferative disease (XLP) with allogeneic hematopoietic stem cell transplantation (HSCT): Report from the XLP Registry. Bone Marrow Transplant 17:741–744, 1996.

85. Hoffmann T, Heilmann C, Madsen HO, et al: Matched unrelated allogeneic bone marrow transplantation for recurrent malignant lymphoma in a patient with X-linked lymphoproliferative disease (XLP). Bone Marrow Transplant 22:603–604, 1998.

86. Pracher E, Panzer-Grumayer ER, Zoubek A, et al: Successful bone marrow transplantation in a boy with X-linked lymphoproliferative syndrome and acute severe infectious mononucleosis. Bone Marrow Transplant 13:655–658, 1994.

87. Yagi H, Furutani Y, Hamada H, et al: Role of TBX1 in human del22q11.2 syndrome. Lancet 362:1366–1373, 2003.

88. Bartsch O, Nemeckova M, Kocarek E, et al: DiGeorge/velocardiofacial syndrome: FISH studies of chromosomes 22q11 and 10p14, and clinical reports on the proximal 22q11 deletion. Am J Med Genet 117A:1–5, 2003.

89. Markert ML, Boeck A, Hale LP, et al: Transplantation of thymus tissue in complete DiGeorge syndrome. N Engl J Med 341:1180–1189, 1999.

90. Bowers DC, Lederman HM, Sicherer SH, et al: Immune constitution of complete DiGeorge anomaly by transplantation of unmobilised blood mononuclear cells. Lancet 352:1983–1984, 1998.

91. Bensoussan D, Le Deist F, Latger-Cannard V, et al: T-cell immune constitution after peripheral blood mononuclear cell transplantation in complete DiGeorge syndrome. Br J Haematol 117:899–906, 2002.

92. Chinen J, Rosenblatt HM, Smith EO, et al: Long-term assessment of T-cell populations in DiGeorge syndrome. J Allergy Clin Immunol 111:573–579, 2003.

93. Rosenzweig S, Dorman SE, Roesler J, et al: 561del4 defines a novel small deletion hotspot in the interferon-gamma receptor 1 chain. Clin Immunol 102:25–27, 2002.

94. Jouanguy E, Lamhamedi-Cherradi S, Lammas D, et al: A human IFNGR1 small deletion hotspot associated with dominant susceptibility to mycobacterial infection. Nat Genet 21:370–378, 1999.

95. Jouanguy E, Altare F, Lamhamedi S, et al: Interferon-gamma-receptor deficiency in an infant with fatal bacille Calmette-Guerin infection. N Engl J Med 335:1956–1961, 1996.

96. Jouanguy E, Lamhamedi-Cherradi S, Altare F, et al: Partial interferon-gamma receptor 1 deficiency in a child with tuberculoid bacillus Calmette-Guerin infection and a sibling with clinical tuberculosis. J Clin Invest 100:2658–2664, 1997.

97. Altare F, Jouanguy E, Lamhamedi-Cherradi S, et al: A causative relationship between mutant IFNgR1 alleles and impaired cellular response to IFNgamma in a compound heterozygous child. Am J Hum Genet 62:723–726, 1998.

98. Doffinger R, Jouanguy E, Dupuis S, et al: Partial interferon-gamma receptor signaling chain deficiency in a patient with bacille Calmette-Guerin and *Mycobacterium abscessus* infection. J Infect Dis 181:379–384, 2000.

99. Dorman SE, Holland SM: Mutation in the signal-transducing chain of the interferon-gamma receptor and susceptibility to mycobacterial infection. J Clin Invest 101:2364–2369, 1998.

100. Altare F, Lammas D, Revy P, et al: Inherited interleukin 12 deficiency in a child with bacille Calmette-Guerin and *Salmonella enteritidis* disseminated infection. J Clin Invest 102:2035–2040, 1998.

101. Altare F, Durandy A, Lammas D, et al: Impairment of mycobacterial immunity in human interleukin-12 receptor deficiency. Science 280:1432–1435, 1998.

102. Altare F, Ensser A, Breiman A, et al: Interleukin-12 receptor beta1 deficiency in a patient with abdominal tuberculosis. J Infect Dis 184:231–236, 2001.

103. de Jong R, Altare F, Haagen IA, et al: Severe mycobacterial and *Salmonella* infections in interleukin-12 receptor-deficient patients. Science 280:1435–1438, 1998.

104. Aksu G, Tirpan C, Cavusoglu C, et al: *Mycobacterium fortuitum-chelonae* complex infection in a child with complete interleukin-12 receptor beta 1 deficiency. Pediatr Infect Dis J 20:551–553, 2001.

105. Picard C, Fieschi C, Altare F, et al: Inherited interleukin-12 deficiency: IL12β genotype and clinical phenotype of 13 patients from six kindreds. Am J Hum Genet 70:336–348, 2002.

106. Sakai T, Matsuoka M, Aoki M, et al: Missense mutation of the interleukin-12 receptor beta1 chain-encoding gene is associated with impaired immunity against *Mycobacterium avium* complex infection. Blood 97:2688–2694, 2001.

107. Dupuis S, Dargemont C, Fieschi C, et al: Impairment of mycobacterial but not viral immunity by a germline human STAT1 mutation. Science 293:300–303, 2001.

108. Casanova JL, Abel L: Genetic dissection of immunity to mycobacteria: The human model. Annu Rev Immunol 20:581–620, 2002.

109. Lammas DA, Casanova JL, Kumararatne DS: Clinical consequences of defects in the IL-12-dependent interferon-gamma (IFN-gamma) pathway. Clin Exp Immunol 121:417–425, 2000.

110. An autoimmune disease, APECED, caused by mutations in a novel gene featuring two PHD-type zinc-finger domains. The Finnish-German APECED Consortium. Autoimmune Polyendocrinopathy-Candidiasis-Ectodermal Dystrophy. Nat Genet 17:399–403, 1997.

111. Heino M, Peterson P, Kudoh J, et al: APECED mutations in the autoimmune regulator (AIRE) gene. Hum Mutat 18:205–211, 2001.

112. Vogel A, Strassburg CP, Obermayer-Straub P, et al: The genetic background of autoimmune polyendocrinopathy-candidiasis-ectodermal dystrophy and its autoimmune disease components. J Mol Med 80:201–211, 2002.

113. Kumar PG, Laloraya M, She JX: Population genetics and functions of the autoimmune regulator (AIRE). Endocrinol Metab Clin North Am 31:321–338, vi, 2002.

114. Anderson MS, Venanzi ES, Klein L, et al: Projection of an immunological self shadow within the thymus by the AIRE protein. Science 298:1395–1401, 2002.

115. Ward L, Paquette J, Seidman E, et al: Severe autoimmune polyendocrinopathy-candidiasis-ectodermal dystrophy in an adolescent girl with a novel AIRE mutation: Response to immunosuppressive therapy. J Clin Endocrinol Metab 84:844–852, 1999.

116. Sinicco A, Maiello A, Raiteri R, et al: *Pneumocystis carinii* in a patient with pulmonary sarcoidosis and idiopathic CD4+ T lymphocytopenia. Thorax 51:446–447, 1996 [discussion appears in Thorax 51:448–449, 1996].

117. De Socio GV, Gerli R, Menichetti F: Disseminated tuberculosis and idiopathic CD4+ T-lymphocytopenia. Clin Microbiol Infect 5:653–654, 1999.

118. Gubinelli E, Posteraro P, Girolomoni G: Idiopathic CD4+ T lymphocytopenia associated with disseminated flat warts and alopecia areata. J Dermatol 29:653–656, 2002.

119. Kortsik C, Elmer A, Tamm I: Pleural effusion due to *Histoplasma capsulatum* and idiopathic CD4 lymphocytopenia. Respiration 70:118–122, 2003.

120. Menon BS, Shuaib IL, Zamari M, et al: Idiopathic CD4+ T-lymphocytopenia in a child with disseminated cryptococcosis. Ann Trop Paediatr 18:45–48, 1998.

121. Seddon M, Ellis-Pegler RB: Idiopathic CD4+ T-lymphocytopenia: Case report. N Z Med J 108:134, 1995.

122. Zanelli G, Sansoni A, Ricciardi B, et al: Muscular-skeletal cryptococcosis in a patient with idiopathic CD4+ lymphopenia. Mycopathologia 149:137–139, 2001.

123. Hirasaki S, Koide N, Ogawa H, Tsuji T: Active intestinal tuberculosis with esophageal candidiasis due to idiopathic CD4+ T-lymphocytopenia in an elderly woman. J Gastroenterol 35:47–51, 2000.

124. Manchado Lopez P, Ruiz de Morales JM, Ruiz Gonzalez I, Rodriguez Prieto MA: Cutaneous infections by papillomavirus, herpes zoster and *Candida albicans* as the only manifestation of idiopathic CD4+ T lymphocytopenia. Int J Dermatol 38:119–121, 1999.

125. Warnatz K, Draeger R, Schlesier M, Peter HH: Successful IL-2 therapy for relapsing herpes zoster infection in a patient with idiopathic CD4+ T lymphocytopenia. Immunobiology 202:204–211, 2000.

126. Cunningham-Rundles C, Murray HW, Smith JP: Treatment of idiopathic CD4 T lymphocytopenia with IL-2. Clin Exp Immunol 116:322–325, 1999.

127. Jawahar S, Moody C, Chan M, et al: Natural killer (NK) cell deficiency associated with an epitope-deficient Fc receptor type IIIA (CD16-II). Clin Exp Immunol 103:408–413, 1996.

128. de Vries E, Koene HR, Vossen JM, et al: Identification of an unusual Fcγ receptor IIIa (CD16) on natural killer cells in a patient with recurrent infections. Blood 88:3022–3027, 1996.

129. Lodoen M, Ogasawara K, Hamerman JA, et al: NKG2D-mediated natural killer cell protection against cytomegalovirus is impaired by viral gp40 modulation of retinoic acid early inducible 1 gene molecules. J Exp Med 197:1245–1253, 2003.

130. Mavilio D, Benjamin J, Daucher M, et al: Natural killer cells in HIV-1 infection: Dichotomous effects of viremia on inhibitory and activating receptors and their functional correlates. Proc Natl Acad Sci U S A 100:15011–15016, 2003.

131. Sirianni MC, Vincenzi L, Topino S, et al: NK cell activity controls human herpesvirus 8 latent infection and is restored upon highly active antiretroviral therapy in AIDS patients with regressing Kaposi's sarcoma. Eur J Immunol 32:2711–2720, 2002.

132. Buckley RH, Schiff RI, Schiff SE, et al: Human severe combined immunodeficiency: Genetic, phenotypic, and functional diversity in one hundred eight infants. J Pediatr 130:378–387, 1997.

133. Notarangelo LD, Mella P, Jones A, et al: Mutations in severe combined immune deficiency (SCID) due to JAK3 deficiency. Hum Mutat 18:255–263, 2001.

134. Frucht DM, Gadina M, Jagadeesh GJ, et al: Unexpected and variable phenotypes in a family with JAK3 deficiency. Genes Immun 2:422–432, 2001.

135. Moshous D, Pannetier C, Chasseval RR, et al: Partial T and B lymphocyte immunodeficiency and predisposition to lymphoma in patients with hypomorphic mutations in Artemis. J Clin Invest 111:381–387, 2003.

136. Stephan JL, Vlekova V, Le Deist F, et al: Severe combined immunodeficiency: A retrospective single-center study of clinical presentation and outcome in 117 patients. J Pediatr 123:564–572, 1993.

137. Rosen FS: Severe combined immunodeficiency: A pediatric emergency. J Pediatr 130:345–346, 1997.

138. Fischer A, Landais P, Friedrich W, et al: European experience of bone-marrow transplantation for severe combined immunodeficiency. Lancet 336:850–854, 1990.

139. Buckley RH, Schiff SE, Schiff RI, et al: Hematopoietic stem-cell transplantation for the treatment of severe combined immunodeficiency. N Engl J Med 340:508–516, 1999.

140. Cavazzana-Calvo M, Hacein-Bey S, de Saint Basile G, et al: Gene therapy of human severe combined immunodeficiency (SCID)-X1 disease. Science 288:669–672, 2000.

141. Hacein-Bey–Abina S, Le Deist F, Carlier F, et al: Sustained correction of X-linked severe combined immunodeficiency by ex vivo gene therapy. N Engl J Med 346:1185–1193, 2002.

142. Aiuti A, Slavin S, Aker M, et al: Correction of ADA-SCID by stem cell gene therapy combined with nonmyeloablative conditioning. Science 296:2410–2413, 2002.

143. Ochs HD: The Wiskott-Aldrich syndrome. Isr Med Assoc J 4:379–384, 2002.

144. Notarangelo LD, Ochs HD: Wiskott-Aldrich syndrome: A model for defective actin reorganization, cell trafficking and synapse formation. Curr Opin Immunol 15:585–591, 2003.

145. Ochs HD: The Wiskott-Aldrich syndrome. Clin Rev Allergy Immunol 20:61–86, 2001.

146. Sullivan KE, Mullen CA, Blaese RM, Winkelstein JA: A multiinstitutional survey of the Wiskott-Aldrich syndrome. J Pediatr 125:876–885, 1994.

147. Ochs HD, Slichter SJ, Harker LA, et al: The Wiskott-Aldrich syndrome: Studies of lymphocytes, granulocytes and platelets. Blood 55:243–252, 1980.

148. Orange JS, Ramesh N, Remold-O'Donnell E, et al: Wiskott-Aldrich syndrome protein is required for NK cell cytotoxicity and colocalizes with actin to NK cell-activating immunologic synapses. Proc Natl Acad Sci U S A 99:11351–11356, 2002.

149. Gaspoz JM, Waldvogel F, Cornu P, et al: Significant and persistent improvement of thrombocytopenia after splenectomy in an adult with the Wiskott-Aldrich syndrome and intra-cerebral bleeding. Am J Hematol 48:182–185, 1995.

150. Mullen CA, Anderson KD, Blaese RM: Splenectomy and/or bone marrow transplantation in the management of the Wiskott-Aldrich syndrome: Long-term follow-up of 62 cases. Blood 82:2961–2966, 1993.

151. Filipovich AH, Stone JV, Tomany SC, et al: Impact of donor type on outcome of bone marrow transplantation for Wiskott-Aldrich syndrome: Collaborative study of the International Bone Marrow Transplant Registry and the National Marrow Donor Program. Blood 97:1598–1603, 2001.

152. Ozsahin H, Le Deist F, Benkerrou M, et al: Bone marrow transplantation in 26 patients with Wiskott-Aldrich syndrome from a single center. J Pediatr 129:238–244, 1996.

153. Cabana MD, Crawford TO, Winkelstein JA, et al: Consequences of the delayed diagnosis of ataxia-telangiectasia. Pediatrics 102:98–100, 1998.

154. Sanal O, Ersoy F, Yel L, et al: Impaired IgG antibody production to pneumococcal polysaccharides in patients with ataxia-telangiectasia. J Clin Immunol 19:326–334, 1999.

155. Waldmann TA, McIntire KR: Serum-alpha-fetoprotein levels in patients with ataxia telangiectasia. Lancet 2:1112–1115, 1972.

156. Hernandez PA, Gorlin RJ, Lukens JN, et al: Mutations in the chemokine receptor gene CXCR4 are associated with WHIM syndrome, a combined immunodeficiency disease. Nat Genet 34:70–74, 2003.

157. Hord JD, Whitlock JA, Gay JC, Lukens JN: Clinical features of myelokathexis and treatment with hematopoietic cytokines: A case report of two patients and review of the literature. J Pediatr Hematol Oncol 19:443–448, 1997.

158. Wetzler M, Talpaz M, Kleinerman ES, et al: A new familial immunodeficiency disorder characterized by severe neutropenia, a defective marrow release mechanism, and hypogammaglobulinemia. Am J Med 89:663–672, 1990.

159. Zeidler C, Welte K: Kostmann syndrome and severe congenital neutropenia. Semin Hematol 39:82–88, 2002.

160. Zeidler C, Welte K, Barak Y, et al: Stem cell transplantation in patients with severe congenital neutropenia without evidence of leukemic transformation. Blood 95:1195–1198, 2000.

161. Toyoda H, Azuma E, Hori H, et al: Successful unrelated BMT in a patient with Kostmann syndrome complicated by pre-transplant pulmonary 'bacterial' abscesses. Bone Marrow Transplant 28:413–415, 2001.

162. Harris ES, Shigeoka AO, Li W, et al: A novel syndrome of variant leukocyte adhesion deficiency involving defects in adhesion mediated by beta1 and beta2 integrins. Blood 97:767–776, 2001.

163. Hogg N, Stewart MP, Scarth SL, et al: A novel leukocyte adhesion deficiency caused by expressed but nonfunctional beta2 integrins Mac-1 and LFA-1. J Clin Invest 103:97–106, 1999.

164. Farinha NJ, Duval M, Wagner E, et al: Unrelated bone marrow transplantation for leukocyte adhesion deficiency. Bone Marrow Transplant 30:979–981, 2002.

165. Lubke T, Marquardt T, Etzioni A, et al: Complementation cloning identifies CDG-IIc, a new type of congenital disorders of glycosylation, as a GDP-fucose transporter deficiency. Nat Genet 28:73–76, 2001.

166. Etzioni A, Tonetti M: Fucose supplementation in leukocyte adhesion deficiency type II. Blood 95:3641–3643, 2000.

167. Marquardt T, Luhn K, Srikrishna G, et al: Correction of leukocyte adhesion deficiency type II with oral fucose. Blood 94:3976–3985, 1999.

168. Grimbacher B, Holland SM, Gallin JI, et al: Hyper-IgE syndrome with recurrent infections—an autosomal dominant multisystem disorder. N Engl J Med 340:692–702, 1999.

169. Schopfer K, Baerlocher K, Price P, et al: Staphylococcal IgE antibodies, hyperimmunoglobulinemia E and *Staphylococcus aureus* infections. N Engl J Med 300:835–838, 1979.

170. Friedman SJ, Schroeter AL, Homburger HA: Whole organisms and purified cell walls compared as immunosorbents for the detection of IgE antibodies to *Staphylococcus aureus.* J Immunol Methods 66:369–375, 1984.

171. Wakim M, Alazard M, Yajima A, et al: High dose intravenous immunoglobulin in atopic dermatitis and hyper-IgE syndrome. Ann Allergy Asthma Immunol 81:153–158, 1998.

172. Kimata H: High-dose intravenous gamma-globulin treatment for hyperimmunoglobulinemia E syndrome. J Allergy Clin Immunol 95:771–774, 1995.

173. King CL, Gallin JI, Malech HL, et al: Regulation of immunoglobulin production in hyperimmunoglobulin E recurrent-infection syndrome by interferon gamma. Proc Natl Acad Sci U S A 86:10085–10089, 1989.

174. Reeves EP, Lu H, Jacobs HL, et al: Killing activity of neutrophils is mediated through activation of proteases by K+ flux. Nature 416:291–297, 2002.

175. Holland SM: Update on phagocytic defects. Pediatr Infect Dis J 22:87–88, 2003.

176. Messina CG, Reeves EP, Roes J, Segal AW: Catalase negative *Staphylococcus aureus* retain virulence in mouse model of chronic granulomatous disease. FEBS Lett 518:107–110, 2002.

177. Tkalcevic J, Novelli M, Phylactides M, et al: Impaired immunity and enhanced resistance to endotoxin in the absence of neutrophil elastase and cathepsin G. Immunity 12:201–210, 2000.

178. Segal BH, Holland SM: Primary phagocytic disorders of childhood. Pediatr Clin North Am 47:1311–1338, 2000.

179. Kobayashi SD, Voyich JM, Braughton KR, et al: Gene expression profiling provides insight into the pathophysiology of chronic granulomatous disease. J Immunol 172:636–643, 2004.

180. Fadok VA, Bratton DL, Rose DM, et al: A receptor for phosphatidylserine-specific clearance of apoptotic cells. Nature 405:85–90, 2000.

181. Hampton MB, Vissers MC, Keenan JI, Winterbourn CC: Oxidant-mediated phosphatidylserine exposure and macrophage uptake of activated neutrophils: Possible impairment in chronic granulomatous disease. J Leukoc Biol 71:775–781, 2002.

182. Mouy R, Fischer A, Vilmer E, et al: Incidence, severity, and prevention of infections in chronic granulomatous disease. J Pediatr 114:555–560, 1989.

183. Gallin JI, Alling DW, Malech HL, et al: Itraconazole to prevent fungal infections in chronic granulomatous disease. N Engl J Med 348:2416–2422, 2003.

184. Ahlin A, Larfars G, Elinder G, et al: Gamma interferon treatment of patients with chronic granulomatous disease is associated with augmented production of nitric oxide by polymorphonuclear neutrophils. Clin Diagn Lab Immunol 6:420–424, 1999.

185. Bemiller LS, Roberts DH, Starko KM, Curnutte JT: Safety and effectiveness of long-term interferon gamma therapy in patients with chronic granulomatous disease. Blood Cells Mol Dis 21:239–247, 1995.

186. Pasare C, Medzhitov R: Toll-like receptors and acquired immunity. Semin Immunol 16:23–26, 2004.

187. Picard C, Puel A, Bonnet M, et al: Pyogenic bacterial infections in humans with IRAK-4 deficiency. Science 299:2076–2079, 2003.

188. Barbosa MD, Nguyen QA, Tchernev VT, et al: Identification of the homologous beige and Chediak-Higashi syndrome genes. Nature 382:262–265, 1996.

189. Certain S, Barrat F, Pastural E, et al: Protein truncation test of LYST reveals heterogenous mutations in patients with Chediak-Higashi syndrome. Blood 95:979–983, 2000.

190. Introne W, Boissy RE, Gahl WA: Clinical, molecular, and cell biological aspects of Chediak-Higashi syndrome. Mol Genet Metab 68:283–303, 1999.

191. Carnide EM, Jacob CM, Pastorino AC, et al: Chediak-Higashi syndrome: Presentation of seven cases. Rev Paul Med 116:1873–1878, 1998.

192. Aslan Y, Erduran E, Gedik Y, et al: The role of high dose methylprednisolone and splenectomy in the accelerated phase of Chediak-Higashi syndrome. Acta Haematol 96:105–107, 1996.

193. Lekstrom-Himes JA, Dorman SE, Kopar P, et al: Neutrophil-specific granule deficiency results from a novel mutation with loss of function of the transcription factor CCAAT/enhancer binding protein epsilon. J Exp Med 189:1847–1852, 1999.

194. Boackle SA, Holers VM: Role of complement in the development of autoimmunity. Curr Dir Autoimmun 6:154–168, 2003.

195. Armitage JO: Bone marrow transplantation. N Engl J Med 330:827–838, 1994.

196. Walters MC, Patience M, Leisenring W, et al: Bone marrow transplantation for sickle cell disease. N Engl J Med 335:369–376, 1996.

197. Boulad F, Giardina P, Gillio A, et al: Bone marrow transplantation for homozygous beta-thalassemia: The Memorial Sloan-Kettering Cancer Center experience. Ann N Y Acad Sci 850:498–502, 1998.

198. Hernandez-Boluda JC, Marin P, Carreras E, et al: Bone marrow transplantation for severe aplastic anemia: The Barcelona Hospital Clinic experience. Haematologica 84:26–31, 1999.

199. Tyndall A, Fassas A, Passweg J, et al: Autologous haematopoietic stem cell transplants for autoimmune disease—feasibility and transplant-related mortality. Autoimmune Disease and Lymphoma Working Parties of the European Group for Blood and Marrow Transplantation, the European League Against Rheumatism and the International Stem Cell Project for Autoimmune Disease. Bone Marrow Transplant 24:729–734, 1999.

200. Brodsky RA, Smith BD: Bone marrow transplantation for autoimmune diseases. Curr Opin Oncol 11:83–86, 1999.

201. Wang B, Yamamoto Y, El-Badri NS, Good RA: Effective treatment of autoimmune disease and progressive renal disease by mixed bone-marrow transplantation that establishes a stable mixed chimerism in BXSB recipient mice. Proc Natl Acad Sci U S A 96:3012–3016, 1999.

202. Saba N, Sutton D, Ross H, et al: High treatment-related mortality in cardiac amyloid patients undergoing autologous stem cell transplant. Bone Marrow Transplant 24:853–855, 1999.

203. Armitage JO: Bone marrow transplantation. N Engl J Med 330:827–838, 1994.

204. Saba N, Abraham R, Keating A: Overview of autologous stem cell transplantation. Crit Rev Oncol Hematol 36:27–48, 2000.

205. Williams CD, Harrison CN, Lister TA, et al: High-dose therapy and autologous stem-cell support for chemosensitive transformed low-grade follicular non-Hodgkin's lymphoma: A case-matched study from the European Bone Marrow Transplant Registry. J Clin Oncol 19:727–735, 2001.

206. Seyfarth B, Kuse R, Sonnen R, et al: Autologous stem cell transplantation for follicular lymphoma: No benefit for early transplant? Ann Hematol 80:398–405, 2001.

207. Arranz R, Tomas JF, Gil-Fernandez JJ, et al: Autologous stem cell transplantation (ASCT) for poor prognostic Hodgkin's disease (HD): Comparative results with two CBV regimens and importance of disease status at transplant. Bone Marrow Transplant 21:779–786, 1998.

208. Fleming DR, Wolff SN, Fay JW, et al: Protracted results of dose-intensive therapy using cyclophosphamide, carmustine, and continuous infusion etoposide with autologous stem cell support in patients with relapse or refractory Hodgkin's disease: A Phase II study from the North American Marrow Transplant Group. Leuk Lymphoma 35:91–98, 1999.

209. Frankovich J, Donaldson SS, Lee Y, et al: High-dose therapy and autologous hematopoietic cell transplantation in children with primary refractory and relapsed Hodgkin's disease: Atopy predicts idiopathic diffuse lung injury syndromes. Biol Blood Marrow Transplant 7:49–57, 2001.

210. Alegre A, Diaz-Mediavilla J, San-Miguel J, et al: Autologous peripheral blood stem cell transplantation for multiple myeloma: A report of 259 cases from the Spanish Registry. Spanish Registry for Transplant in MM (Grupo Espanol de Trasplante Hematopoyetico-GETH) and PETHEMA. Bone Marrow Transplant 21:133–140, 1998.

211. Burdach S, van Kaick B, Laws HJ, et al: Allogeneic and autologous stem-cell transplantation in advanced Ewing tumors: An update after long-term follow-up from two centers of the European Intergroup study EICESS. Stem-Cell Transplant Programs at Dusseldorf University Medical Center, Germany and St. Anna Kinderspital, Vienna, Austria. Ann Oncol 11:1451–1462, 2000.

212. Stiff PJ, Veum-Stone J, Lazarus HM, et al: High-dose chemotherapy and autologous stem-cell transplantation for ovarian cancer: An autologous blood and marrow transplant registry report. Ann Intern Med 133:504–515, 2000.

213. Chao NJ, Forman SJ, Schmidt GM, et al: Allogeneic bone marrow transplantation for high-risk acute lymphoblastic leukemia during first complete remission. Blood 78:1923–1927, 1991.

214. Enright H, McGlave P: Bone marrow transplantation for chronic myelogenous leukemia. Curr Opin Oncol 10:100–107, 1998.

215. Flinn IW, Vogelsang G: Bone marrow transplantation for chronic lymphocytic leukemia. Semin Oncol 25:60–64, 1998.

216. Stadtmauer EA, O'Neill A, Goldstein LJ, et al: Conventional-dose chemotherapy compared with high-dose chemotherapy plus autologous hematopoietic stem-cell transplantation for metastatic breast cancer. Philadelphia Bone Marrow Transplant Group. N Engl J Med 342:1069–1076, 2000.

217. Vij R, DiPersio J, Brown R, et al: Outcomes of high-dose chemotherapy and autologous stem cell transplant in isolated locally recurrent breast cancer: A multicenter evaluation. Bone Marrow Transplant 26:947–953, 2000.

218. Pecora AL, Lazarus HM, Stadtmauer EA, et al: Effect of induction chemotherapy and tandem cycles of high-dose chemotherapy on outcomes in autologous stem cell transplant for metastatic breast cancer. Bone Marrow Transplant 27:1245–1253, 2001.

219. Peters WP, Ross M, Vredenburgh JJ, et al: High-dose chemotherapy and autologous bone marrow support as consolidation after standard-dose adjuvant therapy for high-risk primary breast cancer. J Clin Oncol 11:1132–1143, 1993.

220. Viens P, Maraninchi D: High-dose chemotherapy in advanced breast cancer. Crit Rev Oncol Hematol 41:141–149, 2002.

221. Spitzer TR: The expanding applications of non-myeloablative stem cell transplantation. Pediatr Transplant 7(Suppl 3):95–100, 2003.

222. Fisher VL: Long-term follow-up in hematopoietic stem-cell transplant patients. Pediatr Transplant 3(Suppl 1):122–129, 1999.

222a. Kotloff RM, Ahya VN, Crawford SW: Pulmonary complications of solid organ and hematopoietic stem cell transplantation. Am J Respir Crit Care Med 170:22–48, 2004.

223. Krowka MJ, Rosenow EC III, Hoagland HC: Pulmonary complications of bone marrow transplantation. Chest 87:237–246, 1985.

224. Breuer R, Lossos IS, Berkman N, Or R: Pulmonary complications of bone marrow transplantation. Respir Med 87:571–579, 1993.

225. Soubani AO, Miller KB, Hassoun PM: Pulmonary complications of bone marrow transplantation. Chest 109:1066–1077, 1996.

226. Wingard JR, Sostrin MB, Vriesendorp HM, et al: Interstitial pneumonitis following autologous bone marrow transplantation. Transplantation 46:61–65, 1988.

227. Gosselin MV, Adams RH: Pulmonary complications in bone marrow transplantation. J Thorac Imaging 17:132–144, 2002.

228. Griese M, Rampf U, Hofmann D, et al: Pulmonary complications after bone marrow transplantation in children: Twenty-four years of experience in a single pediatric center. Pediatr Pulmonol 30:393–401, 2000.

229. Fanfulla F, Pedrazzoli P, Da Prada GA, et al: Pulmonary function and complications following chemotherapy and stem cell support in breast cancer. Eur Respir J 15:56–61, 2000.

230. Ewig S, Torres A, Riquelme R, et al: Pulmonary complications in patients with haematological malignancies treated at a respiratory ICU. Eur Respir J 12:116–122, 1998.

231. Folz RJ: Mechanisms of lung injury following bone marrow transplantation. Am J Respir Cell Mol Biol 20:1097–1099, 1999.

232. Clark JG, Hansen JA, Hertz MI, et al: NHLBI workshop summary: Idiopathic pneumonia syndrome after bone marrow transplantation. Am Rev Respir Dis 147:1601–1606, 1993.

233. Durant JR, Norgard MJ, Murad TM, et al: Pulmonary toxicity associated with bischloroethylnitrosourea (BCNU). Ann Intern Med 90:191–194, 1979.

234. Lieberman A, Ruoff M, Estey E, et al: Irreversible pulmonary toxicity after single course of BCNU. Am J Med Sci 279:53–56, 1980.

235. Ryan BR, Walters TR: Pulmonary fibrosis: A complication of 1,3-bis(2-chloroethyl)-1- nitrosourea (BCNU) therapy. Cancer 48:909–911, 1981.

236. Litam JP, Dail DH, Spitzer G, et al: Early pulmonary toxicity after administration of high-dose BCNU. Cancer Treat Rep 65:39–44, 1981.

237. Weinstein AS, Diener-West M, Nelson DF, Pakuris E: Pulmonary toxicity of carmustine in patients treated for malignant glioma. Cancer Treat Rep 70:943–946, 1986.

238. Seiden MV, Elias A, Ayash L, et al: Pulmonary toxicity associated with high dose chemotherapy in the treatment of solid tumors with autologous marrow transplant: An analysis of four chemotherapy regimens. Bone Marrow Transplant 10:57–63, 1992.

239. Cherniack RM, Abrams J, Kalica AR: Pulmonary disease associated with breast cancer therapy. Am J Respir Crit Care Med 150:1169–1173, 1994.

240. Kehrer JP: The effect of BCNU (carmustine) on tissue glutathione reductase activity. Toxicol Lett 17:63–68, 1983.

241. Smith AC, Boyd MR: Preferential effects of 1,3-bis(2-chloroethyl)-1-nitrosurea (BCNU) on pulmonary glutathione reductase and glutathione/glutathione disulfide ratios: Possible implications for lung toxicity. J Pharmacol Exp Ther 229:658–663, 1984.

242. Baz MA, Tapson VF, Trigt PV, Piantadosi CA: Glutathione depletion in epithelial lining fluid of lung allografts. Am J Respir Crit Care Med 149:A744, 1994.

243. Cantin AM, Hubbard RC, Crystal RG: Glutathione deficiency in the epithelial lining fluid of the lower respiratory tract in idiopathic pulmonary fibrosis. Am Rev Respir Dis 139:370–372, 1989.

244. Pacht E, Timerman A, Lykens M, Merola A: Deficiency of alveolar fluid glutathione in patients with sepsis and adult respiratory distress syndrome. Chest 100:1397–1403, 1991.

245. Cooper JA Jr, Merrill WW: Modulation of endoperoxide product levels and cyclophosphamide-induced injury by glutathione repletion. J Appl Physiol 67:2316–2322, 1989.

246. Patel JM, Block ER: Cyclophosphamide-induced depression of the antioxidant defense mechanisms of the lung. Exp Lung Res 8:153–165, 1985.

247. Venkatesan N, Chandrakasan G: Cyclophosphamide induced early biochemical changes in lung lavage fluid and alterations in lavage cell function. Lung 172:147–158, 1994.

248. Cooper JA Jr, Merrill WW, Reynolds HY: Cyclophosphamide modulation of bronchoalveolar cellular populations and macrophage oxidative metabolism: Possible mechanisms of pulmonary pharmacotoxicity. Am Rev Respir Dis 134:108–114, 1986.

249. Grafstrom RC, Dypbukt JM, Willey JC, et al: Pathobiological effects of acrolein in cultured human bronchial epithelial cells. Cancer Res 48:1717–1721, 1988.

250. Masuda H, Tanaka T, Takahama U: Cisplatin generates superoxide anion by interaction with DNA in a cell-free system. Biochem Biophys Res Commun 203:1175–1180, 1994.

251. Sadzuka Y, Shoji T, Takino Y: Effect of cisplatin on the activities of enzymes which protect against lipid peroxidation. Biochem Pharmacol 43:1872–1875, 1992.

252. Cooke KR, Kobzik L, Martin TR, et al: An experimental model of idiopathic pneumonia syndrome after bone marrow transplantation: I. The roles of minor H antigens and endotoxin. Blood 88:3230–3239, 1996.

253. Cooke KR, Krenger W, Hill G, et al: Host reactive donor T cells are associated with lung injury after experimental allogeneic bone marrow transplantation. Blood 92:2571–2580, 1998.

254. Shankar G, Scott Bryson J, Darrell Jennings C, et al: Idiopathic pneumonia syndrome after allogeneic bone marrow transplantation in mice: Role of pretransplant radiation conditioning. Am J Respir Cell Mol Biol 20:1116–1124, 1999.

255. Shankar G, Bryson JS, Jennings CD, et al: Idiopathic pneumonia syndrome in mice after allogeneic bone marrow transplantation. Am J Respir Cell Mol Biol 18:235–242, 1998.

256. Panoskaltsis-Mortari A, Strieter RM, Hermanson JR, et al: Induction of monocyte- and T-cell-attracting chemokines in the lung during the generation of idiopathic pneumonia syndrome following allogeneic murine bone marrow transplantation. Blood 96:834–839, 2000.

257. Panoskaltsis-Mortari A, Taylor PA, Yaeger TM, et al: The critical early proinflammatory events associated with idiopathic pneumonia syndrome in irradiated murine allogeneic recipients are due to donor T cell infusion and potentiated by cyclophosphamide. J Clin Invest 100:1015–1027, 1997.

258. Socie G, Clift RA, Blaise D, et al: Busulfan plus cyclophosphamide compared with total-body irradiation plus cyclophosphamide before marrow transplantation for myeloid leukemia: Long-term follow-up of 4 randomized studies. Blood 98:3569–3574, 2001.

259. Chien JW, Martin PJ, Gooley TA, et al: Airflow obstruction after myeloablative allogeneic hematopoietic stem cell transplantation. Am J Respir Crit Care Med 168:208–214, 2003.

260. Weiner RS, Boymer MM, Gale RP, et al: Interstitial pneumonitis after bone marrow transplantation. Ann Intern Med 104:168–175, 1986.

261. Wingard JR, Mellits ED, Sostrin MB, et al: Interstitial pneumonitis after allogeneic bone marrow transplantation: Nine-year experience at a single institution. Medicine 67:175–186, 1988.

262. Weaver CH, Appelbaum FR, Peterson FB, et al: High-dose cyclophosphamide, carmustine, and etoposide followed by autologous bone marrow transplantation in patients with lymphoid malignancies who have received dose-limiting radiation therapy. J Clin Oncol 11:1329–1335, 1993.

263. Reece D, Barnett M, Shepherd J, et al: High-dose cyclophosphamide, carmustine (BCNU), and etoposide (VP16–213) with or without cisplatin (CBV ± P) and autologous transplantation for patients with Hodgkin's disease who fail to enter a complete remission after combination chemotherapy. Blood 86:451–456, 1995.

264. Todd NW, Peters WP, Ost AH, et al: Pulmonary drug toxicity in patients with primary breast cancer treated with high-dose combination chemotherapy and autologous bone marrow transplantation. Am Rev Respir Dis 147:1264–1270, 1993.

265. Jones RB, Matthes S, Shpall EJ, et al: Acute lung injury following treatment with high-dose cyclophosphamide, cisplatin, and carmustine: Pharmacodynamic evaluation of carmustine. J Natl Cancer Inst 85:640–647, 1993.

266. Ho VT, Weller E, Lee SJ, et al: Prognostic factors for early severe pulmonary complications after hematopoietic stem cell transplantation. Biol Blood Marrow Transplant 7:223–229, 2001.

267. Wah TM, Moss HA, Robertson RJ, Barnard DL: Pulmonary complications following bone marrow transplantation. Br J Radiol 76:373–379, 2003.

268. Schiller G, Lee M, Paquette R, et al: Transplantation of autologous peripheral blood progenitor cells procured after high-dose cytarabine-based consolidation chemotherapy for adults with secondary acute myelogenous leukemia in first remission. Leuk Lymphoma 33:475–484, 1999.

269. Klein JL, Hamm C, Dansey RD, et al: High-dose chemotherapy and CD34-selected peripheral blood progenitor cell transplantation for patients with breast cancer metastatic to bone and/or bone marrow. Bone Marrow Transplant 28:1023–1029, 2001.

270. Roy V, Ali LI, Selby GB: Routine chest radiography for the evaluation of febrile neutropenic patients after autologous stem cell transplantation. Am J Hematol 64:170–174, 2000.

271. Crawford SW, Hackman RC, Clark JG: Open lung biopsy diagnosis of diffuse pulmonary infiltrates after marrow transplantation. Chest 94:949–953, 1988.

272. Gruson D, Hilbert G, Portel L, et al: Severe respiratory failure requiring ICU admission in bone marrow transplant recipients. Eur Respir J 13:883–887, 1999.

273. Afessa B, Litzow MR, Tefferi A: Bronchiolitis obliterans and other late onset non-infectious pulmonary complications in hematopoietic stem cell transplantation. Bone Marrow Transplant 28:425–434, 2001.

274. Hackman R: Lower respiratory tract. *In* Sale G, Shulman H (eds): The Pathology of Bone Marrow Transplantation. New York: Masson, 1984, pp 156–170.

275. Jain P, Sandur S, Meli Y, et al: Role of flexible bronchoscopy in immunocompromised patients with lung infiltrates. Chest 125:712–722, 2004.

276. Feinstein MB, Mokhtari M, Ferreiro R, et al: Fiberoptic bronchoscopy in allogeneic bone marrow transplantation: Findings in the era of serum cytomegalovirus antigen surveillance. Chest 120:1094–1100, 2001.

277. Dunagan DP, Baker AM, Hurd DD, Haponik EF: Bronchoscopic evaluation of pulmonary infiltrates following bone marrow transplantation. Chest 111:135–141, 1997.

278. Aljurf M, Gyger M, Alrajhi A, et al: *Mycobacterium tuberculosis* infection in allogeneic bone marrow transplantation patients. Bone Marrow Transplant 24:551–554, 1999.

279. van Burik JA, Hackman RC, Nadeem SQ, et al: Nocardiosis after bone marrow transplantation: A retrospective study. Clin Infect Dis 24:1154–1160, 1997.

280. Meyers JD, Flournoy N, Thomas ED: Nonbacterial pneumonia after allogeneic marrow transplantation: A review of ten years' experience. Rev Infect Dis 4:1119–1132, 1982.

281. Crawford SW, Bowden RA, Hackman RC, et al: Rapid detection of cytomegalovirus pulmonary infection by bronchoalveolar lavage and centrifugation culture. Ann Intern Med 108:180–185, 1988.

282. Goodrich JM, Boeckh M, Bowden R: Strategies for the prevention of cytomegalovirus disease after marrow transplantation. Clin Infect Dis 19:287–298, 1994.

283. Wingard JR, Chen DY, Burns WH, et al: Cytomegalovirus infection after autologous bone marrow transplantation with comparison to infection after allogeneic bone marrow transplantation. Blood 71:1432–1437, 1988.

284. Mossad SB, Avery RK, Longworth DL, et al: Infectious complications within the first year after nonmyeloablative allogeneic peripheral blood stem cell transplantation. Bone Marrow Transplant 28:491–495, 2001.

285. Reinke P, Prosch S, Kern F, Volk HD: Mechanisms of human cytomegalovirus (HCMV) (re)activation and its impact on organ transplant patients. Transpl Infect Dis 1:157–164, 1999.

286. Burgart LJ, Heller MJ, Reznicek MJ, et al: Cytomegalovirus detection in bone marrow transplant patients with idiopathic pneumonitis: A clinicopathologic study of the clinical utility of the polymerase chain reaction on open lung biopsy specimen tissue. Am J Clin Pathol 96:572–576, 1991.

287. Leruez-Ville M, Ouachee M, Delarue R, et al: Monitoring cytomegalovirus infection in adult and pediatric bone marrow transplant recipients by a real-time PCR assay performed with blood plasma. J Clin Microbiol 41:2040–2046, 2003.

288. Humar A, Lipton J, Welsh S, et al: A randomised trial comparing cytomegalovirus antigenemia assay vs screening bronchoscopy for the early detection and prevention of disease in allogeneic bone marrow and peripheral blood stem cell transplant recipients. Bone Marrow Transplant 28:485–490, 2001.

289. Sakamaki H, Yuasa K, Goto H, et al: Comparison of cytomegalovirus (CMV) antigenemia and CMV in bronchoalveolar lavage fluid for diagnosis of CMV pulmonary infection after bone marrow transplantation. Bone Marrow Transplant 20:143–147, 1997.

290. Konoplev S, Champlin RE, Giralt S, et al: Cytomegalovirus pneumonia in adult autologous blood and marrow transplant recipients. Bone Marrow Transplant 27:877–881, 2001.

291. de Medeiros CR, Moreira VA, Pasquini R: Cytomegalovirus as a cause of very late interstitial pneumonia after bone marrow transplantation. Bone Marrow Transplant 26:443–444, 2000.

292. Machado CM, Menezes RX, Macedo MC, et al: Extended antigenemia surveillance and late cytomegalovirus infection after allogeneic BMT. Bone Marrow Transplant 28:1053–1059, 2001.

293. Junghanss C, Boeckh M, Carter RA, et al: Incidence and outcome of cytomegalovirus infections following nonmyeloablative compared with myeloablative allogeneic stem cell transplantation, a matched control study. Blood 99:1978–1985, 2002.

294. Machado CM, Dulley FL, Boas LS, et al: CMV pneumonia in allogeneic BMT recipients undergoing early treatment of pre-emptive ganciclovir therapy. Bone Marrow Transplant 26:413–417, 2000.

295. Emanuel D, Cunningham I, Jules-Elysee K, et al: Cytomegalovirus pneumonia after bone marrow transplantation successfully treated with the combination of ganciclovir and high-dose intravenous immune globulin. Ann Intern Med 109:777–782, 1988.

296. Reed EC, Bowden RA, Dandliker PS, et al: Treatment of cytomegalovirus pneumonia with ganciclovir and intravenous cytomegalovirus immunoglobulin in patients with bone marrow transplants. Ann Intern Med 109:783–788, 1988.

297. Bowden RA: Respiratory virus infections after marrow transplant: The Fred Hutchinson Cancer Research Center experience. Am J Med 102:27–30, 1997 [discussion appears in Am J Med 102:42–43, 1997].

298. Ghosh S, Champlin RE, Ueno NT, et al: Respiratory syncytial virus infections in autologous blood and marrow transplant recipients with breast cancer: Combination therapy with aerosolized ribavirin and parenteral immunoglobulins. Bone Marrow Transplant 28:271–275, 2001.

299. McCarthy AJ, Kingman HM, Kelly C, et al: The outcome of 26 patients with respiratory syncytial virus infection following allogeneic stem cell transplantation. Bone Marrow Transplant 24:1315–1322, 1999.

300. Ghosh S, Champlin RE, Englund J, et al: Respiratory syncytial virus upper respiratory tract illnesses in adult blood and marrow transplant recipients: Combination therapy with aerosolized ribavirin and intravenous immunoglobulin. Bone Marrow Transplant 25:751–755, 2000.

301. Abdallah A, Rowland KE, Schepetiuk SK, et al: An outbreak of respiratory syncytial virus infection in a bone marrow transplant unit: Effect on engraftment and outcome of pneumonia without specific antiviral treatment. Bone Marrow Transplant 32:195–203, 2003.

302. Ottolini MG, Curtis SR, Mathews A, et al: Palivizumab is highly effective in suppressing respiratory syncytial virus in an immunosuppressed animal model. Bone Marrow Transplant 29:117–120, 2002.

303. Garcia R, Raad I, Abi-Said D, et al: Nosocomial respiratory syncytial virus infections: Prevention and control in bone marrow transplant patients. Infect Control Hosp Epidemiol 18:412–416, 1997.

304. Leclair JM, Freeman J, Sullivan BF, et al: Prevention of nosocomial respiratory syncytial virus infections through compliance with glove and gown isolation precautions. N Engl J Med 317:329–334, 1987.

305. Gala CL, Hall CB, Schnabel KC, et al: The use of eye-nose goggles to control nosocomial respiratory syncytial virus infection. JAMA 256:2706–2708, 1986.

306. Wendt CH, Weisdorf DJ, Jordan MC, et al: Parainfluenza virus respiratory infection after bone marrow transplantation. N Engl J Med 326:921–926, 1992.

307. Lewis VA, Champlin R, Englund J, et al: Respiratory disease due to parainfluenza virus in adult bone marrow transplant recipients. Clin Infect Dis 23:1033–1037, 1996.

308. Whimbey E, Vartivarian SE, Champlin RE, et al: Parainfluenza virus infection in adult bone marrow transplant recipients. Eur J Clin Microbiol Infect Dis 12:699–701, 1993.

309. Whimbey E, Elting LS, Couch RB, et al: Influenza A virus infections among hospitalized adult bone marrow transplant recipients. Bone Marrow Transplant 13:437–440, 1994.

310. Knight V, McClung HW, Wilson SZ, et al: Ribavirin small-particle aerosol treatment of influenza. Lancet 2:945–949, 1981.

311. McClung HW, Knight V, Gilbert BE, et al: Ribavirin aerosol treatment of influenza B virus infection. JAMA 249:2671–2674, 1983.

312. Wilson SZ, Gilbert BE, Quarles JM, et al: Treatment of influenza A (H1N1) virus infection with ribavirin aerosol. Antimicrob Agents Chemother 26:200–203, 1984.

313. Winston DJ, Ho WG, Gale RP, Champlin RE: Prophylaxis of infection in bone marrow transplants. Eur J Cancer Clin Oncol 24(Suppl 1):S15–S23, 1988.

314. Kitabayashi A, Hirokawa M, Horiuchi T, et al: Late-onset herpes simplex virus-associated interstitial pneumonia after allogeneic bone marrow transplantation. Bone Marrow Transplant 25:225–226, 2000.

315. Ljungman P, Ellis MN, Hackman RC, et al: Acyclovir-resistant herpes simplex virus causing pneumonia after marrow transplantation. J Infect Dis 162:244–248, 1990.

316. Ison MG, Hayden FG, Kaiser L, et al: Rhinovirus infections in hematopoietic stem cell transplant recipients with pneumonia. Clin Infect Dis 36:1139–1143, 2003.

317. Shields AF, Hackman RC, Fife KH, et al: Adenovirus infections in patients undergoing bone-marrow transplantation. N Engl J Med 312:529–533, 1985.

318. Wald A, Leisenring W, van Burik JA, Bowden RA: Epidemiology of *Aspergillus* infections in a large cohort of patients undergoing bone marrow transplantation. J Infect Dis 175:1459–1466, 1997.

319. Wingard JR: Fungal infections after bone marrow transplant. Biol Blood Marrow Transplant 5:55–68, 1999.

320. Junghanss J, Marr K, Carter R: Incidence of bacterial and fungal infections after nonmyeloablative compared to myeloablative allogeneic stem cell transplantation (HSCT). Blood 98:479a, 2001.

321. McWhinney PH, Kibbler CC, Hamon MD, et al: Progress in the diagnosis and management of aspergillosis in bone marrow transplantation: 13 years' experience. Clin Infect Dis 17:397–404, 1993.

322. Reichenberger F, Habicht J, Kaim A, et al: Lung resection for invasive pulmonary aspergillosis in neutropenic patients with hematologic diseases. Am J Respir Crit Care Med 158:885–890, 1998.

323. Kawazu M, Kanda Y, Goyama S, et al: Rapid diagnosis of invasive pulmonary aspergillosis by quantitative polymerase chain reaction using bronchial lavage fluid. Am J Hematol 72:27–30, 2003.

323a. Maertens J, Van Eldere J, Verhaegen J, et al: Use of circulating galactomannan screening for early diagnosis of invasive aspergillosis in allogeneic stem cell transplant recipients. J Infect Dis 186:1297–1306, 2002.

323b. McLintock LA, Jones BL: Advances in the molecular and serological diagnosis of invasive fungal infection in haemato-oncology patients. Br J Haematol 126:289–297, 2004.

324. Jantunen E, Piilonen A, Volin L, et al: Radiologically guided fine needle lung biopsies in the evaluation of focal pulmonary lesions in allogeneic stem cell transplant recipients. Bone Marrow Transplant 29:353–356, 2002.

325. Jantunen E, Piilonen A, Volin L, et al: Diagnostic aspects of invasive *Aspergillus* infections in allogeneic BMT recipients. Bone Marrow Transplant 25:867–871, 2000.

326. Gulbahce HE, Pambuccian SE, Jessurun J, et al: Pulmonary nodular lesions in bone marrow transplant recipients: Impact of histologic diagnosis on patient management and prognosis. Am J Clin Pathol 121:205–210, 2004.

327. Jantunen E, Ruutu P, Piilonen A, et al: Treatment and outcome of invasive *Aspergillus* infections in allogeneic BMT recipients. Bone Marrow Transplant 26:759–762, 2000.

328. Goodrich JM, Reed EC, Mori M, et al: Clinical features and analysis of risk factors for invasive candidal infection after marrow transplantation. J Infect Dis 164:731–740, 1991.

329. Morrison VA, Haake RJ, Weisdorf DJ: Non-*Candida* fungal infections after bone marrow transplantation: Risk factors and outcome. Am J Med 96:497–503, 1994.

330. Penalver FJ, Romero R, Fores R, et al: Mucormycosis and hemopoietic transplants. Haematologica 83:950–951, 1998.

331. Maddox L, Long GD, Vredenburgh JJ, Folz RJ: *Rhizopus* presenting as an endobronchial obstruction following bone marrow transplant. Bone Marrow Transplant 28:634–636, 2001.

331a. Dummer JS: *Pneumocystis carinii* infections in transplant recipients. Semin Respir Infect 5:50–57, 1990.

332. Krowka MJ, Rosenow EC 3rd, Hoagland HC: Pulmonary complications of bone marrow transplantation. Chest 87:237–246, 1985.

333. Crawford SW, Longton G, Storb R: Acute graft-versus-host disease and the risks for idiopathic pneumonia after marrow transplantation for severe aplastic anemia. Bone Marrow Transplant 12:225–231, 1993.

334. Kantrow SP, Hackman RC, Boeckh M, et al: Idiopathic pneumonia syndrome: Changing spectrum of lung injury after marrow transplantation. Transplantation 63:1079–1086, 1997.

335. Demirer T, Weaver CH, Buckner CD, et al: High-dose cyclophosphamide, carmustine and etoposide followed by allogeneic bone marrow transplantation in patients with lymphoid malignancies who had received prior dose-limiting radiation therapy. J Clin Oncol 13:596–602, 1995.

336. Clark JG, Madtes DK, Martin TR, et al: Idiopathic pneumonia after bone marrow transplantation: Cytokine activation and lipopolysaccharide amplification in the bronchoalveolar compartment. Crit Care Med 27:1800–1806, 1999.

337. Ashida T, Higashishiba M, Sumimoto Y, et al: Serum KL-6 levels in patients with pulmonary complications after allogeneic bone marrow transplantation. Int J Hematol 74:464–468, 2001.

338. Qureshi MA, Girgis RE, Dandapantula HK, et al: Increased exhaled nitric oxide following autologous peripheral hematopoietic stem-cell transplantation: A potential marker of idiopathic pneumonia syndrome. Chest 125:281–287, 2004.

339. Robbins RA, Linder J, Stahl MG, et al: Diffuse alveolar hemorrhage in autologous bone marrow transplant recipients. Am J Med 87:511–518, 1989.

340. Agusti C, Ramirez J, Picado C, et al: Diffuse alveolar hemorrhage in allogeneic bone marrow transplantation. Am J Respir Crit Care Med 151:1006–1010, 1995.

341. Srivastava A, Gottlieb D, Bradstock KF: Diffuse alveolar haemorrhage associated with microangiopathy after allogeneic bone marrow transplantation. Bone Marrow Transplant 15:863–867, 1995.

342. Agusti C, Ramirez J, Picado C, et al: Diffuse alveolar hemorrhage in allogeneic bone marrow transplantation: A postmortem study. Am J Respir Crit Care Med 151:1006–1010, 1995.

343. Afessa B, Tefferi A, Litzow MR, et al: Diffuse alveolar hemorrhage in hematopoietic stem cell transplant recipients. Am J Respir Crit Care Med 166:641–645, 2002.

344. Weisdorf DJ: Diffuse alveolar hemorrhage: An evolving problem? Leukemia 17:1049–1050, 2003.

345. Huaringa AJ, Leyva FJ, Giralt SA, et al: Outcome of bone marrow transplantation patients requiring mechanical ventilation. Crit Care Med 28:1014–1017, 2000.

346. Robbins RA, Linder J, Stahl MG, et al: Diffuse alveolar hemorrhage in autologous bone marrow transplant recipients. Am J Med 87:511–518, 1989.

347. Jules-Elysee K, Stover DE, Yahalom J, et al: Pulmonary complications in lymphoma patients treated with high-dose therapy autologous bone marrow transplantation. Am Rev Respir Dis 146:485–491, 1992.

348. Crilley P, Topolsky D, Styler MJ, et al: Extramedullary toxicity of a conditioning regimen containing busulphan, cyclophosphamide and etoposide in 84 patients undergoing autologous and allogenic bone marrow transplantation. Bone Marrow Transplant 15:361–365, 1995.

349. Mulder PO, Meinesz AF, de Vries EG, Mulder NH: Diffuse alveolar hemorrhage in autologous bone marrow transplant recipients. Am J Med 90:278–281, 1991.

350. Raptis A, Mavroudis D, Suffredini A, et al: High-dose corticosteroid therapy for diffuse alveolar hemorrhage in allogeneic bone marrow stem cell transplant recipients. Bone Marrow Transplant 24:879–883, 1999.

351. Wojno KJ, Vogelsang GB, Beschorner WE, Santos GW: Pulmonary hemorrhage as a cause of death in allogeneic bone marrow recipients with severe acute graft-versus-host disease. Transplantation 57:88–92, 1994.

352. Sisson JH, Thompson AB, Anderson JR, et al: Airway inflammation predicts diffuse alveolar hemorrhage during bone marrow transplantation in patients with Hodgkin disease. Am Rev Respir Dis 146:439–443, 1992.

353. Witte RJ, Gurney JW, Robbins RA, et al: Diffuse pulmonary alveolar hemorrhage after bone marrow transplantation: Radiographic findings in 39 patients. AJR Am J Roentgenol 157:461–464, 1991.

354. Metcalf JP, Rennard SI, Reed EC, et al: Corticosteroids as adjunctive therapy for diffuse alveolar hemorrhage associated with bone marrow transplantation. University of Nebraska Medical Center Bone Marrow Transplant Group. Am J Med 96:327–334, 1994.

355. Chao NJ, Duncan SR, Long GD, et al: Corticosteroid therapy for diffuse alveolar hemorrhage in autologous bone marrow transplant recipients. Ann Intern Med 114:145–146, 1991.

356. Lewis ID, DeFor T, Weisdorf DJ: Increasing incidence of diffuse alveolar hemorrhage following allogeneic bone marrow transplantation: Cryptic etiology and uncertain therapy. Bone Marrow Transplant 26:539–543, 2000.

357. Ben-Abraham R, Paret G, Cohen R, et al: Diffuse alveolar hemorrhage following allogeneic bone marrow transplantation in children. Chest 124:660–664, 2003.

358. Haselton DJ, Klekamp JG, Christman BW, Barr FE: Use of high-dose corticosteroids and high-frequency oscillatory ventilation for treatment of a child with diffuse alveolar hemorrhage after bone marrow transplantation: Case report and review of the literature. Crit Care Med 28:245–248, 2000.

359. Wilczynski SW, Petros WP, Hussein AM, et al: Increased incidence of pulmonary toxicity in breast cancer patients undergoing high dose chemotherapy. Am J Respir Crit Care Med 153:A273, 1996.

360. Wilczynski SW, Erasmus JJ, Petros WP, et al: Delayed pulmonary toxicity syndrome following high-dose chemotherapy and bone marrow transplantation for breast cancer. Am J Respir Crit Care Med 157:565–573, 1998.

361. Wilczynski SW, Erasmus JJ, Petros WP, et al: Delayed pulmonary toxicity syndrome following high-dose chemotherapy and bone marrow transplantation for breast cancer. Am J Respir Crit Care Med 157:565–573, 1998.

362. Bhalla KS, Wilczynski SW, Abushamaa AM, et al: Pulmonary toxicity of induction chemotherapy prior to standard high-dose chemotherapy with autologous hematopoietic support. Am J Respir Crit Care Med 161:17–25, 2000.

363. Patz EF Jr, Peters WP, Goodman PC: Pulmonary drug toxicity following high-dose chemotherapy with autologous bone marrow transplantation: CT findings in 20 cases. J Thorac Imaging 9:129–134, 1994.

364. Cao TM, Negrin RS, Stockerl-Goldstein KE, et al: Pulmonary toxicity syndrome in breast cancer patients undergoing BCNU-containing high-dose chemotherapy and autologous hematopoietic cell transplantation. Biol Blood Marrow Transplant 6:387–394, 2000.

365. Bhalla KS, Wilczynski SW, Abushamaa AM, et al: Pulmonary toxicity of induction chemotherapy prior to standard or high-dose chemotherapy with autologous hematopoietic support. Am J Respir Crit Care Med 161:17–25, 2000.

366. Epler GR: Bronchiolitis obliterans and airways obstruction associated with graft-versus-host disease. Clin Chest Med 9:551–556, 1988.

367. Wyatt SE, Nunn P, Hows JM, et al: Airways obstruction associated with graft versus host disease after bone marrow transplantation. Thorax 39:887–894, 1984.

368. Ralph DD, Springmeyer SC, Sullivan KM, et al: Rapidly progressive air-flow obstruction in marrow transplant recipients: Possible association between obliterative bronchiolitis and chronic graft-versus-host disease. Am Rev Respir Dis 129:641–644, 1984.

369. Crawford SW, Clark JG: Bronchiolitis associated with bone marrow transplantation. Clin Chest Med 14:741–749, 1993.

370. Folz RJ: Allogeneic stem cell transplant, lung disease, and airflow obstruction. Am J Respir Crit Care Med 168:146–147, 2003.

371. Socie G, Curtis RE, Deeg HJ, et al: New malignant diseases after allogeneic marrow transplantation for childhood acute leukemia. J Clin Oncol 18:348–357, 2000.

372. Ooi GC, Peh WC, Ip M: High-resolution computed tomography of bronchiolitis obliterans syndrome after bone marrow transplantation. Respiration 65:187–191, 1998.

373. Philit F, Wiesendanger T, Archimbaud E, et al: Post-transplant obstructive lung disease ("bronchiolitis obliterans"): A clinical comparative study of bone marrow and lung transplant patients. Eur Respir J 8:551–558, 1995.

374. Sargent MA, Cairns RA, Murdoch MJ, et al: Obstructive lung disease in children after allogeneic bone marrow transplantation: Evaluation with high-resolution CT. AJR Am J Roentgenol 164:693–696, 1995.

374a. Rabitsch W, Deviatko E, Keil F, et al: Successful lung transplantation for bronchiolitis obliterans after allogeneic marrow transplantation. Transplantation 71:1341–1343, 2001.

374b. Pechet TV, de le Morena M, Mendeloff EN, et al: Lung transplantation in children following treatment for malignancy. J Heart Lung Transplant 22:154–160, 2003.

375. Mathew P, Bozeman P, Krance RA, et al: Bronchiolitis obliterans organizing pneumonia (BOOP) in children after allogeneic bone marrow transplantation. Bone Marrow Transplant 13:221–223, 1994.

376. Thirman MJ, Devine SM, O'Toole K, et al: Bronchiolitis obliterans organizing pneumonia as a complication of allogeneic bone marrow transplantation. Bone Marrow Transplant 10:307–311, 1992.

377. Hayes-Jordan A, Benaim E, Richardson S, et al: Open lung biopsy in pediatric bone marrow transplant patients. J Pediatr Surg 37:446–452, 2002.

378. Palmas A, Tefferi A, Myers JL, et al: Late-onset noninfectious pulmonary complications after allogeneic bone marrow transplantation. Br J Haematol 100:680–687, 1998.

379. Kanda Y, Takahashi T, Imai Y, et al: Bronchiolitis obliterans organizing pneumonia after syngeneic bone marrow transplantation for acute lymphoblastic leukemia. Bone Marrow Transplant 19:1251–1253, 1997.

380. Baron FA, Hermanne JP, Dowlati A, et al: Bronchiolitis obliterans organizing pneumonia and ulcerative colitis after allogeneic bone marrow transplantation. Bone Marrow Transplant 21:951–954, 1998.

381. Ishii T, Manabe A, Ebihara Y, et al: Improvement in bronchiolitis obliterans organizing pneumonia in a child after allogeneic bone marrow transplantation by a combination of oral prednisolone and low dose erythromycin. Bone Marrow Transplant 26:907–910, 2000.

382. Kanamori H, Mishima A, Tanaka M, et al: Bronchiolitis obliterans organizing pneumonia (BOOP) with suspected liver graft-versus-host disease after allogeneic bone marrow transplantation. Transpl Int 14:266–269, 2001.

383. Kleinau I, Perez-Canto A, Schmid HJ, et al: Bronchiolitis obliterans organizing pneumonia and chronic graft-versus-host disease in a child after allogeneic bone marrow transplantation. Bone Marrow Transplant 19:841–844, 1997.

384. Worthy SA, Flint JD, Muller NL: Pulmonary complications after bone marrow transplantation: High-resolution CT and pathologic findings. Radiographics 17:1359–1371, 1997.

385. Selby DM, Rudzki JR, Bayever ES, Chandra RS: Vasculopathy of small muscular arteries in pediatric patients after bone marrow transplantation. Hum Pathol 30:734–740, 1999.

386. Gulbahce HE, Manivel JC, Jessurun J: Pulmonary cytolytic thrombi: A previously unrecognized complication of bone marrow transplantation. Am J Surg Pathol 24:1147–1152, 2000.

387. Steward CG, Pellier I, Mahajan A, et al: Severe pulmonary hypertension: A frequent complication of stem cell transplantation for malignant infantile osteopetrosis. Br J Haematol 124:63–71, 2004.

388. Seguchi M, Hirabayashi N, Fujii Y, et al: Pulmonary hypertension associated with pulmonary occlusive vasculopathy after allogeneic bone marrow transplantation. Transplantation 69:177–179, 2000.

389. Williams LM, Fussell S, Veith RW, et al: Pulmonary veno-occlusive disease in an adult following bone marrow transplantation: Case report and review of the literature. Chest 109:1388–1391, 1996.

390. Salzman D, Adkins DR, Craig F, et al: Malignancy-associated pulmonary veno-occlusive disease: Report of a case following autologous bone marrow transplantation and review. Bone Marrow Transplant 18:755–760, 1996.

391. Kuga T, Kohda K, Hirayama Y, et al: Pulmonary veno-occlusive disease accompanied by microangiopathic hemolytic anemia 1 year after a second bone marrow transplantation for acute lymphoblastic leukemia. Int J Hematol 64:143–150, 1996.

392. Trobaugh-Lotrario AD, Greffe B, Deterding R, et al: Pulmonary veno-occlusive disease after autologous bone marrow transplant in a child with stage IV neuroblastoma: Case report and literature review. J Pediatr Hematol Oncol 25:405–409, 2003.

393. Hackman RC, Madtes DK, Petersen FB, Clark JG: Pulmonary venoocclusive disease following bone marrow transplantation. Transplantation 47:989–992, 1989.

394. Micallef IN, Chhanabhai M, Gascoyne RD, et al: Lymphoproliferative disorders following allogeneic bone marrow transplantation: The Vancouver experience. Bone Marrow Transplant 22:981–987, 1998.

395. Gross TG, Steinbuch M, DeFor T, et al: B cell lymphoproliferative disorders following hematopoietic stem cell transplantation: Risk factors, treatment and outcome. Bone Marrow Transplant 23:251–258, 1999.

396. Tolar J, Coad JE, Ramsay NK, et al: Lymphoproliferative disorder presenting as pulmonary nodules after bone marrow transplantation. Bone Marrow Transplant 28:808–810, 2001.

397. Shoji N, Ohyashiki JH, Suzuki A, et al: Multiple pulmonary nodules caused by B-cell post-transplant lymphoproliferative disorder after bone marrow transplantation: Monitoring Epstein-Barr virus viral load. Jpn J Clin Oncol 33:408–412, 2003.

398. Fassas A, Jagannath S, Desikan KR, et al: Lymphomatoid granulomatosis following autologous stem cell transplantation. Bone Marrow Transplant 23:79–81, 1999.

399. Cohen JI: Epstein-Barr virus infection. N Engl J Med 343:481–492, 2000.

400. Milpied N, Vasseur B, Parquet N, et al: Humanized anti-CD20 monoclonal antibody (Rituximab) in post transplant B-lymphoproliferative disorder: A retrospective analysis on 32 patients. Ann Oncol 11(Suppl 1):113–116, 2000.

401. Spitzer TR: Engraftment syndrome following hematopoietic stem cell transplantation. Bone Marrow Transplant 27:893–898, 2001.

402. Lee CK, Gingrich RD, Hohl RJ, Ajram KA: Engraftment syndrome in autologous bone marrow and peripheral stem cell transplantation. Bone Marrow Transplant 16:175–182, 1995.

403. Edenfield WJ, Moores LK, Goodwin G, Lee N: An engraftment syndrome in autologous stem cell transplantation related to mononuclear cell dose. Bone Marrow Transplant 25:405–409, 2000.

404. Ravoet C, Feremans W, Husson B, et al: Clinical evidence for an engraftment syndrome associated with early and steep neutrophil recovery after autologous blood stem cell

transplantation. Bone Marrow Transplant 18:943–947, 1996.

405. Maiolino A, Biasoli I, Lima J, et al: Engraftment syndrome following autologous hematopoietic stem cell transplantation: Definition of diagnostic criteria. Bone Marrow Transplant 31:393–397, 2003.

406. Kawano C, Muroi K, Kuribara R, et al: Engraftment syndrome after autologous peripheral blood stem cell transplantation with high numbers of peripheral blood stem cells followed by granulocyte colony-stimulating factor administration. Bone Marrow Transplant 25:228–229, 2000.

407. Madero L, Vicent MG, Sevilla J, et al: Engraftment syndrome in children undergoing autologous peripheral blood progenitor cell transplantation. Bone Marrow Transplant 30:355–358, 2002.

408. Akasheh M, Eastwood D, Vesole DH: Engraftment syndrome after autologous hematopoietic stem cell transplant supported by granulocyte-colony-stimulating factor (G-CSF) versus granulocyte-macrophage colony-stimulating factor (GM-CSF). Bone Marrow Transplant 31:113–116, 2003.

409. Ravenel JG, Scalzetti EM, Zamkoff KW: Chest radiographic features of engraftment syndrome. J Thorac Imaging 15:56–60, 2000.

410. Oyama Y, Cohen B, Traynor A, et al: Engraftment syndrome: A common cause for rash and fever following autologous hematopoietic stem cell transplantation for multiple sclerosis. Bone Marrow Transplant 29:81–85, 2002.

411. Khan SA, Gaa B, Pollock BH, et al: Engraftment syndrome in breast cancer patients after stem cell transplantation is associated with poor long-term survival. Biol Blood Marrow Transplant 7:433–438, 2001.

412. Jochelson MS, Altschuler J, Stomper PC: The yield of chest radiography in febrile and neutropenic patients. Ann Intern Med 105:708–709, 1986.

413. Feusner J, Cohen R, O'Leary M, Beach B: Use of routine chest radiography in the evaluation of fever in neutropenic pediatric oncology patients. J Clin Oncol 6:1699–1702, 1988.

414. Donowitz GR, Harman C, Pope T, Stewart FM: The role of the chest roentgenogram in febrile neutropenic patients. Arch Intern Med 151:701–704, 1991.

415. Heussel CP, Kauczor HU, Heussel GE, et al: Pneumonia in febrile neutropenic patients and in bone marrow and blood stem-cell transplant recipients: Use of high-resolution computed tomography. J Clin Oncol 17:796–805, 1999.

416. Heussel CP, Kauczor HU, Heussel G, et al: Early detection of pneumonia in febrile neutropenic patients: Use of thin-section CT. AJR Am J Roentgenol 169:1347–1353, 1997.

417. Soubani AO, Qureshi MA, Baynes RD: Flexible bronchoscopy in the diagnosis of pulmonary infiltrates following autologous peripheral stem cell transplantation for advanced breast cancer. Bone Marrow Transplant 28:981–985, 2001.

417a. Mulabecirovic A, Gaulhofer P, Auner HW, et al: Pulmonary infiltrates in patients with haematologic malignancies: transbronchial lung biopsy increases the diagnostic yield with respect to neoplastic infiltrates and toxic pneumonitis. Ann Hematol 83:420–422, 2004.

418. Huaringa AJ, Leyva FJ, Signes-Costa J, et al: Bronchoalveolar lavage in the diagnosis of pulmonary complications of bone marrow transplant patients. Bone Marrow Transplant 25:975–979, 2000.

419. Glazer M, Breuer R, Berkman N, et al: Use of fiberoptic bronchoscopy in bone marrow transplant recipients. Acta Haematol 99:22–26, 1998.

420. Lanino E, Sacco O, Kotitsa Z, et al: Fiberoptic bronchoscopy and bronchoalveolar lavage for the evaluation of pulmonary infiltrates after BMT in children. Bone Marrow Transplant 18(Suppl 2):117–120, 1996.

421. White P, Bonacum JT, Miller CB: Utility of fiberoptic bronchoscopy in bone marrow transplant patients. Bone Marrow Transplant 20:681–687, 1997.

422. Wong PW, Stefanec T, Brown K, White DA: Role of fine-needle aspirates of focal lung lesions in patients with hematologic malignancies. Chest 121:527–532, 2002.

423. Crawford SW, Hackman RC, Clark JG: Biopsy diagnosis and clinical outcome of persistent focal pulmonary lesions after marrow transplantation. Transplantation 48:266–271, 1989.

424. Castellino RA, Blank N: Etiologic diagnosis of focal pulmonary infection in immunocompromised patients by fluoroscopically guided percutaneous needle aspiration. Radiology 132:563–567, 1979.

425. Hwang SS, Kim HH, Park SH, et al: The value of CT-guided percutaneous needle aspiration in immunocompromised patients with suspected pulmonary infection. AJR Am J Roentgenol 175:235–238, 2000.

426. Poe RH, Kallay MC, Wicks CM, Odoroff CL: Predicting risk of pneumothorax in needle biopsy of the lung. Chest 85:232–235, 1984.

427. Snyder CL, Ramsay NK, McGlave PB, et al: Diagnostic open-lung biopsy after bone marrow transplantation. J Pediatr Surg 25:871–876, 1990 [discussion appears in J Pediatr Surg 25:876–877, 1990].

428. Shorter NA, Ross AJ 3rd, August C, et al: The usefulness of open-lung biopsy in the pediatric bone marrow transplant population. J Pediatr Surg 23:533–537, 1988.

429. Shaikh ZH, Torres HA, Walsh GL, et al: Open lung biopsy in bone marrow transplant recipients has a poor diagnostic yield for a specific diagnosis. Transpl Infect Dis 4:80–84, 2002.

429a. Wang JY, Chang YL, Lee LN, et al: Diffuse pulmonary infiltrates after bone marrow transplantation: the role of open lung biopsy. Ann Thorac Surg 78:267–272, 2004.

430. Chen CI, Abraham R, Tsang R, et al: Radiation-associated pneumonitis following autologous stem cell transplantation: Predictive factors, disease characteristics and treatment outcomes. Bone Marrow Transplant 27:177–182, 2001.

431. Merouani A, Shpall EJ, Jones RB, et al: Renal function in high dose chemotherapy and autologous hematopoietic cell support treatment for breast cancer. Kidney Int 50:1026–1031, 1996.

432. Breuer R, Or R, Lijovetzky G, et al: Interstitial pneumonitis in T cell-depleted bone marrow transplantation. Bone Marrow Transplant 3:625–630, 1988.

433. Parikh CR, McSweeney PA, Korular D, et al: Renal dysfunction in allogeneic hematopoietic cell transplantation. Kidney Int 62:566–573, 2002.

77 Pulmonary Complications of Heart Disease

J. Michael B. Hughes, D.M., F.R.C.P.

INTRODUCTION

The main way in which the heart influences the lungs is through the level of pulmonary venous pressure. Acute elevation of pulmonary venous pressure caused by mitral stenosis or inadequate left ventricular contraction leads to pulmonary edema once a mean pulmonary capillary pressure of 25 to 30 mm Hg has been exceeded. More common, nowadays, is the mild to moderate pulmonary venous hypertension of chronic treated heart failure, accompanied by profound dyspnea on exertion, a limited exercise capacity, and structural damage to the lungs. This chapter focuses on the pulmonary dysfunction caused by pulmonary hypertension associated with acute and chronic left-sided heart failure and discusses possible mechanisms for the breathlessness and exercise limitation that are the patients' main complaints. Other causes of pulmonary hypertension are described in Chapter 49; the effects of intracardiac shunts on lung function and how to measure them are discussed in Chapter 50.

CAUSES AND CONSEQUENCES OF RAISED PULMONARY VENOUS PRESSURE

INTERSTITIAL AND ALVEOLAR EDEMA

The causes of increased venous pressure are well known, the most common being congestive heart failure and mitral valve disease. Left ventricular dysfunction has many causes (e.g., ischemic heart disease, cardiomyopathy, myocarditis). Extracardiac causes are unusual, but include pericardial restriction, mediastinal fibrosis, and veno-occlusive disease.

The effects on the lungs are common to all, but they vary according to the severity of the pressure elevation and the chronicity of the condition. Further information about the pathogenesis of pulmonary edema is provided in Chapter 51.

As pulmonary venous pressure rises, so do pulmonary capillary and arterial pressures. Distention and recruitment of alveolar septal capillaries and recruitment of arteriolar domains occur.[1-3] An increasing proportion of the lung (in the gravity axis) is in West's zone 3,[4] in which pulmonary venous pressure exceeds alveolar pressure. (See Chapter 4 for more information about the effect of gravity on the lungs.) In accordance with Starling's principle, microvascular filtration and lymph flow increase when capillary pressure rises.[5] Before reaching the lymphatics, the filtrate accumulates in the interstitial spaces of the lung, first in the alveolar septa (where space is limited) and then in the loose peribronchial and perivascular tissue[6] and pleural space.[7] The latter two act as a sump or safety valve to prevent an excessive rise in interstitial pressure, which would flood the alveoli with edema fluid and impair gas exchange. In an experimental study of hydrostatic edema,[7] only one third of the microvascular filtrate was removed by the lymphatic vessels, the remainder being accommodated in the lungs (43%) and in the pleural space (23%). Pulmonary edema fluid is eventually cleared in the systemic venous system via the lymphatics; the elevation of systemic venous pressure in patients with congestive heart failure (CHF) slows lymph flow[8] even though lymphatic vessels have valves and contract actively, producing intralymphatic pressures up to 30 mm Hg. Pleural transudates are a reflection of the composition of pulmonary edema fluid, correlating better with increases in wedge pressure[9] than with rises in systemic venous pressure.[10]

HISTOPATHOLOGY OF CHRONIC PULMONARY VENOUS HYPERTENSION

Alveolar Damage

The earliest histologic changes arising from increases in pulmonary venous and capillary pressures occur in the alveolar-capillary wall,[11] which becomes edematous, particularly in the thicker, collagen-containing parts of the septum. The thinnest part of the alveolar barrier, consisting of the fused basement membranes of the epithelial and endothelial cells, is unaffected, leaving gas exchange unimpaired. The interstitial edema becomes organized and "hyaline" with the formation of a mucopolysaccharide ground substance. There is swelling of endothelial cells and proliferation of connective tissue (reticulin and elastin) in the interstitium and of epithelial type II cells, the last being a stereotyped response to injury.

The initial response to an elevation of capillary pressure is edema with a low protein content and distention of perivascular lymphatics. In experimental models (e.g., isolated perfused rabbit lungs), capillary hypertension leads to alveolar damage with endothelial and epithelial cell rupture (breaks or fractures), seen on transmission[12] and scanning[13] electron microscopy. The distribution of edema fluid and its protein content is very inhomogeneous.[14,15] Clearly, vascular barotrauma induced by elevated left atrial pressures can increase capillary permeability,[16] with leak of protein and erythrocytes into the interstitial and alveolar spaces. The extravascular red blood cells disintegrate, and their hemosiderin is ingested by tissue macrophages (see Fig. 16.11 in Chapter 16). Progressive fibrosis with collagen formation leads to obliteration of pulmonary capillaries.

The increased intraluminal pressure also leads to hypertrophy and fibrous change in the pulmonary arteries and veins. The main changes are medial hypertrophy of the muscular pulmonary arteries with intimal fibrosis and peripheral extension of the muscle coat into the smaller branches of the pulmonary arterial tree. The pulmonary veins show similar changes.[17] The basic pathophysiologic mechanism in acute heart failure is the same as in mitral stenosis, but progression to alveolar hyalinization and fibrosis and medial hypertrophy of vessels has not yet occurred, and a greater degree of functional reversibility can be expected.

Vascular Remodeling

The remodeling that occurs in pulmonary hypertension has been studied in detail in experimental models.[18,19] In response to a rise in pressure, pulmonary arteries and veins develop a thicker wall accompanied by a narrowing of the lumen. There is an increase in flow resistance and in stiffness of the wall. In vessel segments exposed to 50 mm Hg of mechanical stress, collagen messenger ribonucleic acid expression and synthesis are increased, provided the endothelium is present.[18] The crucial step appears to be induction of an endogenous vascular serine elastase,[20] which releases growth factors and glycoproteins (tenascin-C and fibronectin), stimulating smooth muscle growth and migration. The first step may be pressure-induced disruption of the endothelium allowing serum proteins into the vessel wall to activate endogenous vascular serine elastase and matrix metalloproteinases, which break up the elastic

lamina in the wall and stimulate smooth muscle growth and collagen and elastin synthesis. Elastase and matrix metalloproteinase inhibitors (not effective yet in vivo) can reverse the remodeling process, in part, by inducing apoptosis of smooth muscle cells and degradation of excess extravascular matrix.[21] In rats, pressure unloading, by transplanting hypertensive lungs into healthy rats, leads to regression of the remodeling changes.[22] Clinically, regression of pulmonary hypertension after reduction of pulmonary venous pressure by mitral valve surgery or cardiac transplantation is substantial but usually not complete.

Blood-Gas Barrier

In chronic pulmonary venous hypertension, marked thickening of the basement membranes of the capillary endothelial cells and alveolar epithelial cells occurs. West and Mathieu-Costello[23] reviewed the subject of *stress failure* of the pulmonary capillaries. The integrity of the blood-gas barrier on its thin (0.2 to 0.3 µm in width) gas-exchanging side depends on the lamina densa, the central core of the fused basement membranes of the alveolar epithelial and capillary endothelial cells. The lamina densa comprises a thin (50-nm) layer of type IV collagen. The thickness (and strength) of this layer of collagen varies according to the vascular stress imposed upon it. In the systemic circulation, there is a progression in capillary basement membrane thickness from the thigh to the calf, in keeping with the higher hydrostatic pressures in the lower leg,[24] and a similar thickening in pulmonary capillaries develops in patients with long-standing pulmonary venous hypertension,[11] as already mentioned. Changes in gene expression for extracellular matrix proteins (α_1 III and α_2 IV procollagen, fibronectin, fibroblast growth factor, and transforming growth factor-β) occur in response to the increase in capillary wall stress.[25] In addition to conditions associated with high pulmonary venous pressures, pulmonary capillary stress failure with breakdown of the alveolar-capillary membranes occurs consistently in several situations: in galloping thoroughbred racehorses, in intense exercise by elite human athletes, in neurogenic and high-altitude pulmonary edema, and in overinflation of the lung,[23] due not so much to the mean level of capillary pressure, but to the peak levels reached on exertion.

HEMODYNAMICS

Pressures at Rest and with Exercise

Butler and colleagues[26] documented pulmonary vascular pressures and pulmonary blood flows in 320 patients with heart failure at rest and at peak exercise during treadmill walking. Patients were divided into four groups according to the level of pulmonary vascular resistance (PVR) at rest. The data,[26-28] excluding those in the highest PVR category, are shown in Table 77.1, from which several points can be made:

1. PVR at rest in CHF is less than in mitral stenosis, in which it typically exceeds 6 Wood units (mm Hg/L per minute). Only 19% of patients in this series had a PVR greater than 3.5 Wood units.

2. A low left ventricular ejection fraction (LVEF) is an essential part of left ventricular dysfunction and

Table 77.1 Pulmonary Hemodynamics at Rest and on Maximal Exercise in Congestive Heart Failure Patients versus Age-Matched Controls

	Controls*	Congestive Heart Failure†		
Pulmonary hypertension	Nil	Nil	Mild	Moderate
Pulmonary vascular resistance (PVR) (mm Hg/L/min)	<1.5	<1.5	1.5–2.5	2.5–3.5
No. of subjects		90	115	54
LV ejection fraction (%)	65	24	23	24
Oxygen uptake (mL/min/kg)	35	13.9	13.7	11.8
Pulmonary artery pressure [mean] (mm Hg)				
Rest	12	20	24	33
Maximal exercise	30	34	38	44
Pulmonary wedge pressure (mm Hg)				
Rest	6	14	15	21
Maximal exercise	20	21	21	24
Cardiac output (L/min)				
Rest	6	5.2	4.6	4.2
Maximal exercise	18	10	9	7.4
PVR				
Rest	1.0	1.1	1.9	3.1
Maximal exercise	0.6	1.4	2.0	3.0

* Assumed values based on age-matched (age for CHF patients 52 ± 10 years) controls from data of Reeves JT, Grover RF, Dempsey JA: Pulmonary circulation during exercise. *In* Weir EK, Reeves JT (eds): Lung Biology in Health and Disease Series. Vol. 38: Pulmonary Vascular Physiology and Pathophysiology. New York: Marcel Dekker, 1988, pp 110–111; and Sullivan MJ, Higginbotham MB, Cobb FR: Increased exercise ventilation in patients with chronic heart failure: Intact ventilatory control despite hemodynamic and pulmonary abnormalities. Circulation 77:552–559, 1988.
† Data from Butler J, Chomsky DB, Wilson JR: Pulmonary hypertension and exercise intolerance in patients with heart failure. J Am Coll Cardiol 34:1802–1806, 1999.
LV, left ventricular; PVR, pulmonary vascular resistance.

"failure," but there is no relationship with the level of pulmonary hypertension (PHT) in this study or others.[29] LVEF in the group with PVR greater than 3.5 (not shown in Table 77.1) was 21%.

3. A severe reduction in maximal oxygen uptake ($\dot{V}O_2$max) accompanies CHF. $\dot{V}O_2$max is related to the severity of PHT ($P < 0.01$ for PVR < 1.5 vs. PVR 2.5 to 3.5) in this study, but not in another.[29]

4. Interestingly, the increase in pulmonary artery pressure (PPA) (mean) from rest to exercise diminishes as its resting level rises. This is related to an inability to increase cardiac output as PHT progresses.

5. Pulmonary wedge pressures at rest reflect both impaired left ventricular function and LVEF. On exercise, wedge pressures rise as left ventricular inflow and filling pressures rise. Left ventricular inflow in controls rises threefold from rest to exercise, but less than twofold in patients with CHF. The high wedge pressure on peak exercise in controls is a reflection of their high cardiac output.

6. Increasing PHT is accompanied by lower cardiac outputs at rest and on exercise ($P < 0.05$ for nil group vs. mild and moderate PHT).

7. Although the "nil PHT" group has a normal PVR at rest, the fall in PVR on exercise, a well-known feature in normal lungs (and seen in control subjects), does not occur. The fall in vascular resistance in the normal lung is caused by the rise in left ventricular filling pressure, which is transmitted back to all vascular pressures in the pulmonary circulation, causing distention of vessels and recruitment of capillaries in the microvascular bed.[2,30] This is shown most strikingly by an abrupt increase in apical blood flow distribution at the onset of exercise, from 5% of total pulmonary blood flow at rest to 9% with exercise,[31] despite rather modest increases in PPA with exercise in older compared to younger subjects.[32] This reserve of function is absent in patients with CHF, in whom no fall in PVR occurs with exercise (see Table 77.1).

From rest to exercise, the pressure-flow relationships of the normal pulmonary circulation (a very-low-pressure system) are under the control of the left ventricle, through rises in left ventricular filling and pulmonary venous pressures (change in pulmonary wedge pressure from rest to exercise, for controls, is 78% of ΔPPA; see Table 77.1). In pulmonary hypertension (from any cause), pressure-flow relationships are dominated by the vascular resistance of the pulmonary vessels themselves rather than by the left ventricle.

Wedge Pressure and Edema

High wedge pressures on exertion (or with a short burst of violent exercise) in patients with CHF may approach or exceed the colloid osmotic pressure of plasma proteins

(28 mm Hg) and may cause ultrastructural damage to the endothelium.[12-16] In normal subjects, there is no convincing evidence that a significant amount of pulmonary edema fluid accumulates during exercise, except in unacclimatized subjects at high altitude.[33] As discussed in detail in Chapters 6 and 51, and by Taylor and associates,[34] interstitial fluid and oncotic pressures and lymph flow, functioning as safety factors, act to limit edema formation in patients with CHF when their clinical state is stable. In addition, the basement membranes of the blood-gas barrier are considerably thickened.[11] It is generally believed that the parenchymal fibrosis caused by chronic pulmonary vascular congestion reduces the hydraulic conductivity of the pulmonary microcirculation. There is support for this view from a study of pacing-induced heart failure in dogs, in which the filtration coefficient for water and solutes was reduced by the increase in endothelial, interstitial, and epithelial thickness, leading to a calculated reduction in transvascular protein clearance of 50%.[35]

Ambulatory Pressures. Away from the laboratory and formalized exercise testing, pulmonary artery systolic and diastolic pressures have been monitored during everyday activities.[36] Climbing stairs caused pulmonary vascular pressures of patients with chronic heart failure to increase to values as high as 90% of the peak treadmill exercise pressure response. Walking on the level increased pressures to 73% of the peak. Eating and urination produced smaller effects, which were seen only in some patients. Pressures rose by 3 to 25 mm Hg on lying down, averaging 63% of peak exercise pressures. These episodes of brief pulmonary hypertension brought about by everyday activities are contributory factors to capillary stress failure and the microvascular damage in the heart failure lung.

Postoperative Hemodynamics

Treatment of the pulmonary complications of mitral valve disease or CHF is primarily by lowering pulmonary venous pressure, either by medical management or surgical intervention. The hemodynamic changes following surgical intervention[37-39] are shown in Table 77.2. In CHF, the LVEF increased from 16% to 56%.[40] Between the series, there is a wide range in mean PPA and PVR, but less so for the pulmonary wedge pressure. Patients with mitral stenosis have higher pressures but a longer history of pulmonary venous hypertension; consequently, structural changes in the vessels will have been more severe and less reversible. Note the higher postoperative PPA and PVR for patients with mitral stenosis than for the patients with CHF. The higher pulmonary wedge pressure (>19 mm Hg) of patients with mitral stenosis was due to late restenosis of the valve (pulmonary wedge pressure immediately after valvuloplasty was about 15 mm Hg).

In the CHF groups, pretransplant pulmonary vascular pressures in the series from Mettauer and associates[39] in the 1990s were significantly lower than those from Niset and colleagues,[38] whose patients were transplanted between 1984 and 1988. The mean age (48 to 49 years) was similar in both studies, but patients in the series of Niset and colleagues[38] were more likely to have been smokers. In fact, their FEV_1, vital capacity (VC), diffusing capacity of carbon monoxide (DL_{CO}), and DL/VA values were lower (see Table 77.7 later [A vs. C]). Although smoking is the most likely cause for the difference (Niset and colleagues,[38] but not Mettauer and associates,[39] found that their smokers had lower FEV_1/VC, DL_{CO}, and DL/VA values), there remains the possibility (see later section on diffusing capacity) that angiotensin-converting enzyme (ACE) inhibitor therapy in the 1990s "protected" the lung microvasculature from the effects of high pulmonary venous pressures.

Pathogenesis of Pulmonary Hypertension in Congestive Heart Failure

The primary cause of pulmonary hypertension in CHF is considered to be alveolar and microvascular injury (low DL_{CO}, low lung volumes) and vascular remodeling of the

---

Table 77.2 Pulmonary Hemodynamics before (Pre) and Changes after (Δ) Reduction of Pulmonary Venous Pressure by Surgery (Mitral Valvuloplasty or Cardiac Transplantation)

	Mitral Stenosis (Percutaneous Valvuloplasty)		Congestive Heart Failure (Cardiac Transplantation)			
	Levine et al. (1989)[37]		*Niset et al. (1993)*[38]		*Mettauer et al. (1999)*[39]	
No. of patients	14		47		21	
Parameter	Pre	Δ (post 7 mo)	Pre	Δ (post 12 mo)	Pre	Δ (post 33 mo)
Pulmonary artery pressure (mm Hg)	51.0	−16	36	−16	25	−5
Pulmonary wedge pressure (mm Hg)	26	−7	26	−14	19	−7
Cardiac output (L/min)	3.7	+0.6				
Cardiac index (L/min/m²)			2.23	+0.6	2.3	+0.5
Pulmonary vascular resistance (PVR) (mm Hg/L/min)	7.9	−4.2	3.0	−1.35	2.4	−1.0
PVR (post/pre %)	44.0		56.0		59	

pulmonary arteries and veins (see earlier sections). The rise in pulmonary venous pressure does not necessarily cause pulmonary hypertension. For example, there is a considerable rise of wedge pressure on exercise (see Table 77.1) without any rise of PVR in CHF patients, and a large fall in PVR in normal subjects because of the accompanying vascular distention and recruitment, mostly in the microvascular bed. In CHF, 80% to 90% of the structural change is reversible with heart transplantation (perhaps only 60% in mitral stenosis postsurgery), the "irreversible" element being in the microvasculature, because the $D_{L_{CO}}$ does not return to normal. Levine and coworkers[37] reported a significant fall in PVR (from 5.6 to 3.5 mm Hg/L per minute) between the immediate postoperative measurements and those found at follow-up 7 months later, suggesting that substantial resolution of the remodeling of the resistance vessels can take place over time. The vascular remodeling of the pulmonary arteries increases their smooth muscle mass, which may raise basal vascular tone (normally very low in the pulmonary circulation). Naeije and colleagues[41] found that an infusion of the vasodilator prostaglandin E_1 reduced PVR by 20% to 30% at rest and on exercise before and after transplantation in patients with CHF.

LUNG VOLUMES AND SPIROMETRY

Mitral Stenosis

Abnormalities of pulmonary function are related to the severity of the cardiac disease. In an early study in mitral stenosis, Frank and associates[42] documented an increasing fall in VC from New York Heart Association (NYHA) class I to class IV, accompanied by a fall in total lung capacity (TLC) and expiratory reserve volume and a rise in residual

volume (RV) (Fig. 77.1). Rhodes and coworkers,[43] in a study of 25 nonsmokers with mitral valve disease, showed a significant inverse correlation between VC and cardiac size or PVR. RV showed a positive correlation with pulmonary wedge pressure. Functional residual capacity (FRC) tends to remain normal,[44] although a fall has been described in class IV patients.[45]

Acute Heart Failure

In patients with acute on chronic failure, the reduction in lung volumes is broadly related to the extent of pulmonary edema.[46] Up to 30% improvement in all lung volumes can occur in the first 4 to 6 weeks after successful surgical[47] or medical[48] treatment. There are virtually no observations in patients with acute pulmonary edema, but serial measurements that were reported in a single case[45] showed a reduction in all volumes (including FRC) in proportion to the severity of the edema, with a 60% reduction shortly before death compared with an earlier remission.

Chronic Heart Failure

Compared to those with mitral stenosis, patients with CHF are older, but their disease duration may have been shorter. Pulmonary function, for a given NYHA class, tends to be better preserved in CHF than in mitral stenosis, but the predominant pattern of lung volume loss with subtle degrees of airflow obstruction is the same. TLC and FRC are reduced to about 80% to 90% of the predicted value, whereas RV may be normal[49] or slightly raised (110%)[50] (see Fig. 77.1).

But there are confounding factors: (1) cigarette smoking, currently or in the past; (2) previous sternotomy (e.g.,

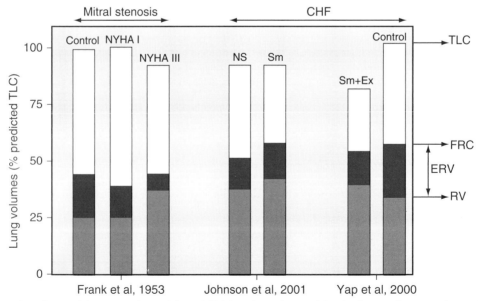

Figure 77.1 Mean values for total lung capacity and its subdivisions in patients with mitral stenosis grouped according to New York Heart Association classification (data from Frank NR, Cugell DW, Gaensler EA, et al: Ventilatory studies in mitral stenosis. Am J Med 15:60–70, 1953), and in patients with congestive heart failure (data from Johnson BD, Beck KC, Olson LJ, et al: Pulmonary function in patients with reduced left ventricular function. Chest 120:1869–1876, 2001; and Yap JCH, Moore D, Cleland JGF, et al: Effect of supine posture on respiratory mechanics in chronic left ventricular failure. Am J Respir Crit Care Med 162:1285–1291, 2000). ERV, expiratory reserve volume; Ex, ex-smokers; FRC, functional residual capacity; NS, never smokers; RV, residual volume; Sm, current smokers; TLC, total lung capacity.

coronary artery bypass grafting [CABG]); (3) intensive medical therapy with diuretics and ACE inhibition; and (4) obesity. Johnson and colleagues[49] subdivided their CHF population not according to NYHA class, but into four groups: (i) never smokers (NS), (ii) NS + previous sternotomy for CABG, (iii) smokers, and (iv) smokers + CABG; these groups were compared with a nonsmoking control group (NS with a history of coronary artery disease but no left ventricular failure). The results for smokers and NS with CHF are shown in Fig. 77.1. As expected, smokers had a lower VC, FEV_1, and FEV_1/VC, and a higher RV/TLC ratio than NS. Post-CABG patients (group ii) had a lower TLC than the other groups. If TLC is reduced, a high RV/TLC ratio does not by itself imply airflow obstruction. Although all groups had FEV_1/VC ratios of 75% or greater, maximum expiratory flow rates at a given fraction of the VC (50% [FEF_{50}] or 75% [FEF_{75}]) were reduced in all, especially in those with a smoking history. The inspiratory capacity (IC [= TLC − FRC]) has been promoted recently as an index of "dynamic hyperinflation" (reflecting the raised end-expiratory lung volume during tidal breathing). Nanas and associates[51] found that the decline in IC (79% of predicted) was greater than the fall in VC (89% of predicted), and, with pulmonary capillary wedge pressure (PCWP), was the best predictor of exercise capacity. Nevertheless, in absolute terms, the fall (if any) in RV in CHF is less than the fall in FRC, so the VC should remain the more sensitive index, and one that is easier to measure reproducibly than the IC.

Postural Change

In changing from the sitting to the supine position, patients with CHF behave rather differently from healthy persons[50] (Table 77.3). In contrast to normal subjects, those with CHF have no significant fall in FRC going from sitting to supine, although there is a decrease in VC caused by a rise in RV. Total *thoracic* volumes, as distinct from gas volumes, are significantly greater in patients with stable CHF in the supine posture. At FRC (sitting) the gas volumes in CHF are 0.4 L less than in controls (see Table 77.3), but the dilated cardiac chambers will contain an extra 300 to 500 mL of blood,[52] and the engorged pulmonary vessels and extra interstitial fluid contribute another 100 mL at least, making thoracic volume similar to that in normal subjects during resting tidal breathing. But, in the supine posture, because the gas volume in heart failure (at FRC) does not fall as it does in normal subjects, the total thoracic volume will be at least 400 to 600 mL greater. Unless there are compensatory increases in the compliances of the lung and chest wall, which is unlikely, the elastic work of breathing must increase and additional work must be done by the inspiratory muscles to maintain the thoracic volume at levels well above the relaxation volume of the system. In fact, the work of breathing, compared with that in normal subjects, is increased 2.5 times in the sitting position and threefold in the supine posture.[53]

DIFFUSING CAPACITY (TRANSFER FACTOR)

Background

The DL_{CO}—or its European equivalent, the transfer factor (TL_{CO})—when measured by the single-breath technique,[54] by far the most common method, is the multiple of two components: the transfer factor of carbon monoxide (KCO) and the volume of alveolar gas distribution (VA) ($DL_{CO} = KCO \times VA$). A low DL_{CO} can be caused by a low KCO (approximately the rate of alveolar uptake of inhaled CO, and equivalent, except in its units, to DL/VA) or by a low VA, or by both.[55] In the Roughton-Forster approach, DL_{CO} is measured first with an air and then with a hyperoxic carbon monoxide–helium mixture. The DL_{CO} (the overall alveolar-capillary conductance) can be partitioned into a

Table 77.3 Postural Effects on Pulmonary Mechanics in Normal Subjects and in Patients with Congestive Heart Failure (CHF)

Pulmonary variable	Patients with CHF (N = 10)		Normal Subjects (N = 10)	
	Sitting	Supine	Sitting	Supine
Visual analogue score of breathlessness	2.2	3.9*	0	0
Vital capacity (L)	2.6	2.4*	4.5	4.4
Functional residual capacity (L)	3.3	3.1	3.7	3.05†
FEV_1 (% predicted)	76	66†	103	97†
FEF_{50} (L/s)	2.2	1.6†	3.0	2.8
Total respiratory resistance (R_{RS}) (forced oscillation at 6 Hz; cm H_2O/L/s)	3.4	6.1‡	2.6	3.4†
Specific total respiratory resistance (SR_{RS}) (R_{RS} × midtidal lung volume)	12.1	21‡	10.2	11.8

*$P < 0.05$ (sitting versus supine).
†$P < 0.01$ (sitting versus supine).
‡$P < 0.001$ (sitting versus supine).
FEF_{50}, forced expiratory flow at 50% VC.
Data from Yap JCH, Moore D, Cleland JGF, et al: Effect of supine posture on respiratory mechanics in chronic left ventricular failure. Am J Respir Crit Care Med 162:1285–1291, 2000.

membrane diffusive conductance (DM) and a red cell conductance, which is proportional to pulmonary capillary volume (Vc); the KCO can be similarly subdivided into DM/VA and Vc/VA components.

Chronic Heart Failure

Guazzi,[56] in a review, tabulated 12 studies in the period 1990–1999 with 514 CHF patients in total, NYHA class III being the most common functional stage. The average DL_{CO} was 78% of predicted normal (range 63 to 90); the mean DL_{CO}/VA (from only six studies) was 89% of predicted (range 82 to 106). The large range of mean values between studies implies wide interindividual variation, wider than for spirometry or lung volumes. For example, Siegel and colleagues[57] found that, for the same level of VC, patients with audible crackles had lower DL_{CO} values than patients without crackles; measurements of DL_{CO} repeated after intensive treatment to eliminate the crackles would have been interesting. There is a correlation of DL_{CO} with NYHA class[58,59] and with exercise capacity (peak oxygen uptake [$\dot{V}O_2$])[29,59,60]; correlations with pulmonary hemodynamics (PCWP, 1/PVR) are weak but stronger with the components of DL_{CO}, DM, and Vc (see next section).

Partitioning DL_{CO} into Its Membrane and Capillary Volume Components

Puri and coworkers[58,59] showed that the reduction in DL_{CO} in CHF could be explained mostly by a reduction in the DM component. As it is relatively unusual in pulmonary function for DM to be "uncoupled" from Vc (both are usually affected), this finding generated much interest and some novel hypotheses about the pathogenesis of the reduction of DL_{CO} in CHF. DL_{CO} and DM have the units of conductance, so in terms of alveolar-capillary gas transfer, $1/DL_{CO}$ and $1/DM$ are the overall and membrane resistances, respectively. Puri and coworkers[58] showed that $1/DM$ accounted for 63% and 86% of the total resistance ($1/DL_{CO}$) in NYHA II and III patients, respectively, compared to 53% in control subjects. Table 77.4 summarizes the results from three studies for DL_{CO} and DL/VA and their components. Overall, the results are reasonably consistent. DL_{CO} and DM are reduced, especially in NYHA classes III and IV. A greater percentage of the total transfer resistance resides in the membrane component (DL_{CO}/DM %). DM was correlated inversely with PVR[59,61] and positively with peak $\dot{V}O_2$. DM (and DL_{CO}) correlate with the duration of heart failure, with a reduction in DL_{CO} to 75% of control occurring in 4.6 years.[39] In a more clinical sense, in 106 patients followed up for 17 months (17 died), impairment of DM and ACE inhibitor therapy were the only independent predictors of survival.[62] In contrast, Vc is relatively normal or increased (see Table 77.4). There is a suggestion that Vc may be reduced in the more severely affected patients. For example, Al-Rawas and colleagues[63] found an equal reduction of DM and Vc (80% of control values) in heart transplantation candidates with severely compromised left ventricular function (LVEF 6% to 26%). Vc is related to the level of PCWP.[60]

Like Vc, DL/VA is relatively well maintained in CHF, the reduced DM/VA being counterbalanced by an elevated Vc/VA (see Table 77.4). The DL_{CO}/VA is a more specific index of alveolar-capillary damage than the DL_{CO}, because DL_{CO} is also VA dependent (see "Background," above). In fact, a normal DL/VA coupled with a low VA (in CHF, VA is in the range of 70% to 80% of predicted) is still compatible with a degree of alveolar destruction/fibrosis, because with normal alveolar structure, a low VA is associated with a "compensatory" high DL/VA.[55]

Table 77.4 Measurements of Diffusing Capacity (DL_{CO}), and Its Subdivisions (Membrane Diffusing Capacity [DM] and Capillary Volume [Vc]), Membrane Resistance as % Total Gas Transfer Resistance (DL_{CO}/DM [$\approx 1/DM \div 1/DL$]), and DM, and Vc per Unit Alveolar Volume (VA), All as % of Value in Control Subjects for Each Study, in Patients with Congestive Heart Failure

	Puri et al. (1995)[59]		Assayeg et al. (1998)[61]		Mettauer et al. (1999)[39]
	NYHA II	*NYHA III*	*PVR Normal**	*PVR High†*	*NYHA III-IV*
n	40	10	30	17	21
DL_{CO} (% control)	80	72	93	78	71
DM (% control)	68	35	80	54	61
Vc (% control)	77	129	108	119	87
DL_{CO}/DM (%)	57	79‡			67§
DL/VA (% control)	95	85	91	90	98
DM/VA (% control)	75	47		92‖	84
Vc/VA (% control)	116	198		133‖	121

* Pulmonary vascular resistance (PVR) normal: mostly New York Heart Association (NYHA) class I-II.
† PVR raised: mostly NYHA class III-IV.
‡ Control group, 53%.
§ Control group, 58%.
‖ Both groups combined.

Table 77.5 Measurements of FEV$_1$, Diffusing Capacity (DL$_{CO}$), and Its Subdivisions (Membrane Diffusing Capacity [DM] and Capillary Volume [Vc]) in Patients with Congestive Heart Failure ($n = 9$; Mean Age, 62 Years; Mean Ejection Fraction, 37%) Receiving Successively Placebo, Isosorbide (40 mg tid), Washout (3 days), and Enalapril (10 mg bid)

	FEV$_1$ (L)	DL$_{CO}$ (mL/min/mm Hg)	DM (mL/min/mm Hg)	Vc (mL)
Placebo (1 wk)	2.8	22	29	130
Isosorbide (48 hr)	3.0	21	29	100*
Isosorbide (1 mo)	3.0*	20	27	110*
Enalapril (48 hr)	2.9*	21	29	105*
Enalapril (1 mo)	3.1*	24.5*†	33*†	100*†

* $P < 0.01$ versus placebo.

† $P < 0.01$ versus isosorbide (1 month).

Data from Guazzi M, Agostoni P: Angiotensin-converting enzyme inhibition restores the diffusing capacity for carbon monoxide in patients with chronic heart failure by improving the molecular diffusion across the alveolar capillary membrane. Clin Sci 96:17–22, 1999.

Saline Infusion and Ultrafiltration

The question arises whether the low DM value in CHF is "fixed" or there is also a variable component related to alveolar septal edema. Puri and coworkers[64] produced intravascular volume expansion with an infusion of about 800 mL saline, which reduced DM by 13%, a significant change (FEV$_1$ also changed, −10%). The reduction in DM had resolved 24 hours later. This finding was taken up by Guazzi and colleagues in an interesting series of papers.[56,65–71] First, Guazzi and associates[65] showed that a 150-mL infusion of saline produced the same changes in DM as 750 mL of saline, whereas a 750-mL infusion of isotonic glucose *increased* DM and DL$_{CO}$. None of these infusions changed right atrial pressure or pulmonary wedge pressure. Because no changes in DM were seen with saline infusions in normal subjects, Guazzi and associates[65] suggested that sodium transport from blood to interstitium must have been up-regulated specifically in the damaged lung of CHF patients. Sodium is absorbed from alveolar liquid via Na$^+$ channels on the apical surface of type II alveolar cells, and extruded into the interstitium from the basal surface of the cell via the Na$^+$,K$^+$-ATPase pump. This process can be up-regulated by β-adrenergic agonists and growth factors, including transforming growth factor-α.[72] Na$^+$ channel blockers (amiloride) and Na$^+$,K$^+$-ATPase pump inhibitors (ouabain) worsen pulmonary edema in an ischemia-reperfusion model.[73] However, amiodarone (400 mg/day) did not have any effects on DL$_{CO}$ in heart failure patients after 1 or 2 years' treatment (1% developed lung fibrosis).[74] The relevance of all this information to saline infusion in CHF patients is not clear at the moment.

The removal of fluid by ultrafiltration (with a loss of about 8 kg in body weight) lowered PPA and PCWP (from 25 to 15 mm Hg) but did not improve DL$_{CO}$ or DM (there was a small fall in Vc) in spite of improvements in FEV$_1$, VC, and VA. This shows that the variable component of DM cannot be induced by an improvement in hemodynamics.[75]

Enalapril and the Renin-Angiotensin System

Guazzi and associates[66] reasoned that ACE inhibitors might affect lung as well as cardiac function, because ACE is located on the pulmonary endothelium, where it converts angiotensin I and inactivates bradykinin. ACE inhibition reduces pulmonary microvascular levels of angiotensin II and enhances exposure to prostaglandins, especially prostacyclin (prostaglandin I$_2$), and nitric oxide, as a result of increases in local kinin concentrations.[76] After 2 weeks' treatment with enalapril (an ACE inhibitor), DL$_{CO}$ increased significantly from 84% to 96% of predicted[66]; in addition, peak V̇O$_2$ increased and exercise VD/VT fell. The beneficial effect of enalapril was opposed by aspirin given concurrently. Aspirin on its own had no deleterious effect.[67] Treatment with hydralazine and isosorbide was more effective than enalapril in reducing PCWP and improving exercise performance, but did not increase DL$_{CO}$. Treatment with enalapril for 1 year improved DL$_{CO}$ and DL/VA and functional indices of exercise performance (but not spirometry or lung volumes) in 20 patients with left ventricular dysfunction (cardiomyopathy), but not in a control group with hypertension and normal left ventricular function.[69] In a subsequent study, comparing placebo, isosorbide, and enalapril, the increase in DL$_{CO}$ with enalapril was clearly due to an increase in DM and accompanied by a fall in Vc (Table 77.5). A type 1 angiotensin blocker (losartan) had no effect on the DL$_{CO}$, which suggests that enalapril is acting via bradykinin potentiation and prostaglandin enhancement.[70] Losartan did improve peak V̇O$_2$ and exercise tolerance, an effect not opposed by aspirin.[68] The beneficial effects of ACE inhibition on DL$_{CO}$ starts within 48 hours and regresses within a week when aspirin is added, suggesting a role for prostaglandins[71] rather than structural changes.

Role of ACE Gene Polymorphisms

The ACE gene has a polymorphism that results in three genotypes (DD, ID, II). With or without ACE inhibitor therapy, ACE and angiotensin II levels in CHF patients were higher in those with the DD genotype than those with the II genotype,[77] and their functional status (lower DL$_{CO}$, FEV$_1$, and peak V̇O$_2$ and higher exercise V̇E/V̇CO$_2$ ratio) was worse[77] (Table 77.6). There was no difference in resting cardiac function between the DD and II types. The number of patients was small ($n = 57$) and such associations might become weaker when larger populations are investigated.[78]

Table 77.6 Serum Angiotensin-Converting Enzyme (ACE) and Angiotensin II (AII), FEV_1, Diffusing Capacity (DL_{CO}), Oxygen Uptake (peak $\dot{V}O_2$), and Ventilatory Equivalent for CO_2 ($\dot{V}E/\dot{V}CO_2$) on Exercise in Patients with Congestive Heart Failure Characterized According to ACE Genotype

	ACE Genotype		
	II	**ID**	**DD**
n	12	28	17
ACE (U/L)	3.4*	6.7	9.1
AII (pg/mL)	11	15	19.0
FEV_1 (% predicted)	92*†	83	77
DL_{CO} (% predicted)	97*†	90	83
Peak $\dot{V}O_2$ (mL/kg/min)‡	21*†	18	16
$\dot{V}E/\dot{V}CO_2$§	37*	34	32

* $P < 0.05$ II versus DD.
† $P < 0.05$ II versus ID
‡ Control values 32 to 34.
§ Control values 25 to 30.
Data from Abraham MR, Olson LJ, Joyner MJ, et al: Angiotensin genotype modulates pulmonary function and exercise capacity in treated patients with congestive heart failure. Circulation 106:1794–1799, 2002.

Pathogenesis of the Reduced DL_{CO}

Puri and coworkers[58,59] first suggested that there might be a link between capillary stress failure (see earlier section) and alveolar-capillary damage and its repair, leading to a reduction in DM. Since 1997, it has become clear that (1) the response to high capillary pressures in terms of lung function may be determined, in part, by the ACE genotype and its polymorphisms[77]; and (2) the DL_{CO} is not "fixed" but has a variable component.[56,65–71] The nature of the "plastic-ity" of DL_{CO} is not fully understood, but it may be related to Na^+ absorption from the alveolar-capillary cells and interstitium into the capillaries. The way in which ACE inhibition with enalapril up-regulates this process only in the lungs of patients with CHF remains to be determined. The beneficial effect of enalapril on the DL_{CO} is inhibited by aspirin; because losartan (type 1 angiotensin receptor blocker) has no effect on DL_{CO}, the enalapril effect is possibly mediated through vasodilator prostaglandins such as prostacyclin. Other factors, not fully understood, may (acutely) increase DL_{CO} in CHF patients, such as 8 weeks exercise training (+25%),[78a] a 10-unit insulin infusion in patients with type 2 diabetes (+21%),[79] or sildenafil (50 mg orally) – a phosphodiesterase-5 inhibitor (+11%).[79a]

PULMONARY FUNCTION AFTER LOWERING OF PULMONARY VENOUS PRESSURE

Thoracotomy and sternotomy themselves lead to a temporary (6-week) decrease in VC.[80] Ten weeks after mitral valve surgery, there are, overall, no significant changes in lung volumes or diffusing capacity. There is a small improvement in function over the next 3 months.[81] A fall in RV has been observed.[45] Irreversible structural changes (hyalinization of interstitial edema, collagen deposition, and fibrosis) are the reason why pulmonary function fails to improve.

On the other hand, lung volumes do improve after cardiac transplantation. Hosenpud[82] reported an average increase of 0.36 L in FEV_1 and 0.55 L in forced vital capacity in 17 patients studied 15 ± 10 months after transplantation. The change in forced vital capacity correlated with the decrease in cardiac volume ($r = 0.83$). Table 77.7 summarizes the lung function changes 12 to 33 months after transplantation for three series.[38,39,83] There is about a 1.0-L increase in TLC and a 0.9-L increase in VC. The FEV_1/VC ratio (not shown) averaged 73% to 77% (actual) before transplantation, and in two of the three series fell by 2% to 3% after transplant. Bussieres and colleagues[83] made serial

Table 77.7 Changes (Δ) in Pulmonary Function in Patients with Congestive Heart Failure before and after Heart Transplantation

Parameter	Before Transplantation			After Transplantation		
	A*	**B†**	**C‡**	**DA***	**DB†**	**DC‡**
No: of subjects/months post	47/12	14/12	21/33			
TLC (L)	5.2	5.4	5.2	+1.2	+1.1	+0.8
TLC (% predicted)	79	80	81	+19	+17	+14
FEV_1 (% predicted)	69	80	78	+14	+25	+6
VC (% predicted)	75	85	85	+19	+27	+13
DL_{CO} (% predicted)	64	61	71	+3	+7	−2
K_{CO} (DL/VA) (% predicted)	65	57	98	−7	−1	−12

* Data from (A) Niset G, Ninane V, Antoine M, et al: Respiratory dysfunction in congestive heart failure: Correction after heart transplantation. Eur Respir J 6:1197–1201, 1993.
† Data from (B) Bussieres LM, Pflugfelder PW, Ahmad D, et al: Evolution of resting lung function in the first year after cardiac transplantation. Eur Respir J 8:959–962, 1995.
‡ Data from (C) Mettauer B, Lampert E, Charloux A, et al: Lung membrane diffusing capacity, heart failure, and heart transplantation. Am J Cardiol 83:62–67, 1999.
DL_{CO}, diffusing capacity of carbon monoxide; K_{CO}, transfer factor of carbon monoxide; TLC, total lung capacity; VC, vital capacity.

measurements and noted that it was 3 months before FEV_1 improved (note the effect of sternotomy[80]) and that there was a further increase at 1 year. DL_{CO} improved only slightly (see Table 77.7), and the KCO (DL/VA) fell, both changes being consistent with alveolar reexpansion with the lung volume increase. Failure of the KCO to improve suggests irreversible microvascular damage.

LUNG COMPLIANCE

Effect of Acute Vascular Distention

The effects of an acute elevation of pulmonary venous pressure on lung compliance were investigated in normal subjects by rapid infusion of 2 L of saline, which is sufficient to raise pulmonary artery diastolic pressure (referred to the lung base) from 23 to 30 mm Hg.[84] There was no fall in lung compliance, nor did the subjects report chest discomfort or dyspnea. This contrasts with the findings of Pepine and Wiener,[85] who induced (by pacing) tachycardia and anginal symptoms in 16 patients with proved ischemic heart disease. Lung compliance did not fall with tachycardia alone, but only when anginal symptoms supervened and left ventricular end-diastolic pressure rose. The effect on lung compliance was reversed after sublingual administration of nitroglycerin. During the anginal episode, there was a fall in specific airway conductance, which was less impressive than the fall in compliance, and a minimal increase in resting lung volume. Pepine and Wiener[85] could not reproduce the fall in compliance in normal control subjects by inducing chest pain through electric stimulation. The rapidly reversible fall in lung compliance during angina must be linked with vascular distention rather than interstitial or alveolar edema; to date, their findings have not been reproduced. A similar instantaneous fall in compliance (also about 30%) occurs on changing from sitting to supine position.[53]

In excised lungs of rabbits and cats, acute vascular distention (without the induction of pulmonary edema) causes a subtle change in the pressure-volume curve, shifting it to the right above FRC and to the left below FRC.[86] The right shift at high lung volumes can be explained by air displacement due to vascular distention, whereas the left shift at low lung volumes (increase in volume for the same lung recoil pressure and reduction in compliance, $\Delta V/\Delta P$) is thought to be caused by the von Basch effect (the erectile nature of engorged capillaries, which was described in 1887). These effects have been reproduced in normal subjects with elevations of central venous pressure[87] and in patients with pulmonary plethora (atrial septal defect) or with mitral valve disease.[44] The shift to the right is more pronounced in mitral valve disease than in atrial septal defect, in which it is similar to the effects of vascular distention in animal lungs.

Chronic Changes

The reduction in static compliance in mitral stenosis correlates with the reduction in VC and TLC.[88] This may reflect the alveolar destruction and fibrosis produced by chronic elevation of pulmonary venous pressure. In contrast to pulmonary fibrotic disease, maximum lung recoil pressure is not increased. This is related to respiratory muscle weakness (see later discussion). In eight patients with acute pulmonary edema (on a background of CHF), lung compli-

ance was severely reduced, averaging 0.037 L/cm H_2O (normal, >0.2), rising to 0.09 cm H_2O after recovery.[89]

AIRFLOW OBSTRUCTION

Acute Heart Failure

In cases of acute left ventricular dysfunction (after myocardial infarction) reviewed by Hales and Kazemi,[46] airflow obstruction shown by a reduced FEV_1/FVC ratio was a frequent finding. Light and George[48] reported a ratio of 0.66 in 15 nonsmokers with acute congestive failure, which improved to 0.71 after treatment and recovery. Sharp and coworkers[89] studied seven patients with severe pulmonary edema and again after recovery; inspiratory resistance by the von Neergaard and Wirz method averaged 9.1 cm H_2O/L per second (330% of predicted), falling slightly to 8.7 after treatment. This rise in resistance is probably caused by a fall in FRC (geometric narrowing) and an increase in vagal tone (bronchoconstriction).[90] Peribronchial cuffs of edema fluid do not contribute to the airway narrowing.[91] More recently, Duguet and colleagues[92] looked for airflow limitation during tidal breathing in 12 patients with acute heart failure (mostly very elderly, 8 of 12 being $\geq$ 80 years old, and 5 subsequently died) admitted to an intensive care unit. Negative expiratory pressure (-3.5 cm H_2O) was applied at the mouth and flow limitation was assumed if expiratory flow did not increase during the maneuver. Flow limitation was seen in 4 of 12 patients in the sitting posture and 9 of 12 when supine. Control subjects did not show flow limitation. In four patients IC was measured; no change was seen with alteration of posture, and breathing pattern remained constant. Flow limitation diminished as the patients' condition improved; the authors believed that edema was the likely cause, but increases in vascular volume in recumbency may also have played a part.

Chronic Heart Failure

The overall pattern of pulmonary function is "restrictive" (low TLC) rather than "obstructive" (reduced FEV_1/VC), although a history of smoking will confound the issue.[49] The FEV_1/VC ratio (absolute) is typically around 80%.[49,50] Although FEF_{50} and FEF_{75} (flows related to the actual VC) are about 75% of control values,[49,50] maximal expiratory flows in relation to predicted TLC (i.e., on an absolute scale) are normal or supernormal.[93] The curvilinearity of the maximal expiratory flow volume (MEFV) curve hardly differs from that of controls.[49,93] Respiratory resistance, measured during tidal breathing using the forced oscillation technique, is greater (130%) than in control subjects,[50] but this is a relatively small increase in functional terms, and mostly explained by the lower FRC. Nevertheless, there is interest in the increase in resistance that occurs on changing from sitting to supine,[50] particularly in relation to orthopnea, and in whether exercise ventilation is constrained by maximal expiratory flow rates (see later sections on ventilatory constraints on exercise, and on orthopnea).

Postural Changes

Minor increases in respiratory resistance and maximal expiratory flows are amplified when patients with CHF assume the supine posture[50] (see Table 77.3). Respiratory resistance rose by 80% going from sitting to supine, as did specific resistance (not surprising because there was no change in FRC). FEF_{50} and FEF_{75} also decreased (35% and 54%, respectively) compared to sitting values (control subjects had a <7% fall in expiratory flows). Inhalation of the antimuscarinic agent ipratropium caused only a modest reduction in the elevated resistance in the supine posture. The changes were rapidly reversed on sitting up again, arguing against peribronchial edema as a cause. Resistance measurements with change of posture from sitting to prone would be of interest.

Pathogenesis

The rise in airway resistance in patients with mitral stenosis and heart failure, which is more marked in the recumbent posture, is not severe. The increase in resistance in the supine posture (see Table 77.3) awaits a good explanation. It is not related to a change in lung volume, nor to vagally induced bronchoconstriction, because there was no effect after inhaled ipratropium. Generalized mucosal swelling or airway wall edema with narrowing rather than closure of the bronchial lumen could lead to an increase in airway resistance without the regional inhomogeneity of ventilation that is characteristic of asthma and chronic obstructive pulmonary disease (but is absent in heart disease).

Bronchial Hyperreactivity

The issue of bronchial hyperreactivity has been reviewed by Snashall and Chung.[94] The studies of Cabanes and coworkers[95] and Rolla and associates[96,97] showed increased methacholine hyperresponsiveness in patients with CHF[96] and mitral stenosis,[97] in smokers and nonsmokers alike. Inhalation of a β-agonist reversed 50% of the fall in FEV_1 induced by methacholine. More interestingly, Cabanes and coworkers[95] inhibited the methacholine-induced bronchoconstriction almost completely by pretreatment with an α-adrenergic agonist and vasoconstrictor, methoxamine. Exercise duration increased (from 526 to 578 seconds) after inhalation of 10 mg of methoxamine.[98] They suggested that methacholine caused bronchial mucosal vessel dilation and edema, which were prevented by prior treatment with methoxamine.[95] The hypothesis is a provocative one. There have been reports (reviewed by Snashall and Chung[94]) that failed to find bronchial hyperresponsiveness in patients with heart failure; the incidence overall is about 30%, and the predisposing factors are still under investigation. However, no follow-up publications have appeared.

Conversely, the antimuscarinic drug ipratropium, when inhaled, causes more bronchodilatation (ΔFEV_1, 11%) in acute cardiac decompensation than after medical intensive treatment (ΔFEV_1, 4%), implying that airway edema increases cholinergic tone.[96]

RESPIRATORY MUSCLE FUNCTION

Measurement Techniques

The strength of the respiratory muscles is assessed traditionally from the mouth pressure generated by a maximal effort (from RV or FRC) against an obstructed mouthpiece, called maximal inspiratory pressure (MIP). The strength of the expiratory muscles (maximal expiratory pressure, MEP) is measured similarly but with an effort made from TLC. These are not natural maneuvers, and some patients find them hard to do. Sniffing (for inspiratory tests) and coughing (for expiratory tests) are easier tasks for patients to perform. The transmission of peak dynamic pressures in sniffing and coughing to the mouth may be delayed, so best practice is to measure peak (actually the minimum) esophageal pressure (Pes) during a sniff and the peak (maximum) gastric pressure[99] during a cough with balloons passed via the nose.

Chronic Heart Failure

Hughes and colleagues,[100] in a study of CHF patients, found that MIP was 70 cm H_2O (72% of control) but that sniff Pes was 95 cm H_2O (91% of control). Mouth pressures will no doubt continue as a standard test, useful for comparison with earlier work; a normal value, compared to age-matched in-house controls, excludes significant respiratory muscle weakness, but a subnormal value does not automatically prove that weakness is present. Table 77.8, in which the VC is used as a surrogate marker of the severity of CHF, shows that static respiratory muscle strength, at first unimpaired, diminishes as VC declines.[100-104] MIP tests principally the strength of the diaphragm; MEP is a measure of the strength of the truncal muscles involved in a Valsalva maneuver. Hughes and colleagues[100] looked for a correlation of MIP, MEP, and sniff Pes with VC but did not find one with their small numbers ($n = 10$). Meyer and coworkers,[105] in a larger study ($n = 145$), found that MIP correlated with $\dot{V}O_2max$ per kilogram, as well as with VD/VT (peak exercise) and VC. Meyer and coworkers[106] also showed that MIP was significantly lower (60% control) in nonsurvivors ($n = 57$) than in survivors (77%) ($n = 187$) in a 2-year follow-up study, and that the combination of MIP, $\dot{V}O_2max$, and LVEF was a sensitive predictor of 1-year survival. Another study,[107] but lacking MIP measurements, showed from gastrocnemius muscle biopsies that myosin heavy chain shifts (from slow aerobic to fast oxidative and glycolytic forms) correlated with $\dot{V}O_2max$.

Respiratory muscle endurance is reduced based on a reduction in the maximal sustainable ventilatory capacity on exercise.[108] In CHF patients walking on a treadmill until stopped by dyspnea, the maximum relaxation rate of a submaximal sniff was slowed during the first minute of recovery, compared to controls, suggesting excessive loading, and probably fatigue, of the inspiratory muscles.[109] A recent analysis using negative pressure threshold loading, rather than exercise, suggests that an abnormal breathing pattern (tachypnea with shortened expiratory time) may contribute importantly to a reduced endurance time.[109a] Twelve months after heart-lung transplantation (for Eisenmenger's syndrome or primary pulmonary hypertension), muscle pressures had improved but remained abnormal[110] (see Table 77.8); the persistence of muscle weakness may reflect, in part, the effects of immunosuppressive drugs, including corticosteroids, but deconditioning is probably the most important factor.

Table 77.8 Measurement of Skeletal Muscle Strength in Relation to Vital Capacity in Patients with Congestive Heart Failure

Parameter	McParland et al. (1995)[101]	Hughes et al. (1999)[100]	Mancini et al. (1992)[102]	Ambrosino et al. (1994)[103]	Hammond et al. (1990)[104]	Ambrosino et al. (1996)[110*]	
						Pre-HLT	Post-HLT
No. patients	15	20	10	45	16	11	11
Vital capacity (% predicted)	93	91	86	80	60	60	77
Max. expiratory pressure (MEP) (% controls)	100	80	80	78	49	40	50
Max. inspiratory pressure (MIP) (% controls)	81	72	76	76	40	50	88

* Pre-HLT, before heart-lung transplantation; post-HLT, 12 months after heart-lung transplantation.

Pathogenesis

In patients with CHF, there is abundant evidence of structural, biochemical, and functional abnormalities in skeletal (limb) muscle, including the respiratory muscles, in particular atrophy of the type I (slow twitch) fibers (see reviews by Stassijns and colleagues[111] and Piepoli and associates[112]). Recovery in skeletal muscle occurs after cardiac transplantation. There is also evidence that the diaphragm muscle fibers are "super-fit," because they have a shift in myosin isoforms and an increase in oxidative capacity similar to those seen in limb muscles after training.[113]

The precise reason for the muscle weakness in heart failure is still not clear. The morphologic and biochemical abnormalities are reversible, in part, after heart transplantation,[114] with an increase in fiber cross-sectional area (+40%), but without reaching normal values; there was no increase in capillary numbers, but improvements in muscle biochemistry were seen.[114] Piepoli and coworkers[112] suggested that left ventricular dysfunction and inactivity activate catabolic factors (tumor necrosis factor production, insulin resistance) and reduce anabolic ones, leading to a myopathic state that is only partially reversed by training programs. Nevertheless, deconditioning must play a major role in the *limb* muscle weakness, because highly strenuous training regimens can restore $\dot{V}O_2$max in heart transplant recipients to control values,[115] but whether that is "normal" for them is another matter. Deconditioning cannot be invoked for the weakness of the respiratory muscles, but this is relatively mild if Sn Pes is the yardstick.[100]

REGIONAL LUNG FUNCTION

Distribution of Ventilation

In patients with chronic heart failure, nitrogen washout tends to be normal, which is consistent with the normal FEV_1/FVC ratio and the mild increase in airway resistance. In one study, nitrogen washout was prolonged in 11 of 18 post–myocardial infarction patients,[116] but the smoking status of the group was not given.

Effect of Cardiomegaly

Most patients with CHF have cardiomegaly, and it is not uncommon to find a reduction in regional ventilation (in the sitting position). In a series of 180 patients, there was a significant relationship between heart size and reduced left lower lobe ventilation[117] (assessed with krypton-81m gas). Wiener and associates[118] used single-photon emission computed tomography to assess ventilation distribution in patients with CHF and cardiomegaly in recumbent postures; in all seven patients, but not in control subjects, there was a reduction in left lower lobe ventilation in the supine posture, which was reversed by turning the patient prone (Fig. 77.2). No effect was seen in the upper zones. During sleep, patients with CHF, especially those with large left ventricles, tend to avoid lying in the left lateral decubitus position, compared to controls.[119]

PULMONARY GAS EXCHANGE AT REST AND ON EXERCISE

Rest

There have been many studies of arterial PO_2 and PCO_2 in patients with acute hemodynamic pulmonary edema or after myocardial infarction.[120] Figure 77.3 shows the correlation between arterial PO_2 and clinical severity. Arterial PCO_2 remained normal (38 ± 6 mm Hg [mean $\pm$ SD]) in all classes and did not rise when 28% oxygen was inspired. Neither arterial PCO_2 nor pH correlated with severity. Arterial lactate rose progressively from 8 mg/dL in class I to 20 mg/dL in class IV,[120] consistent with the decline in cardiac output with increasing clinical severity.[121] Improvement in arterial PO_2 and measured right-to-left shunt fraction occurred after deep breathing or intermittent positive-pressure breathing,[122] but not after intravenous administration of diuretics.[116,122] This suggests that basal atelectasis, secondary to sedation and immobility, plays as important a role as pulmonary edema. In patients with mitral stenosis or chronic treated heart failure, the consensus is that arterial oxygenation is normal or nearly so.[121,123]

Exercise

The most recent data come from the multicenter study of Wasserman and colleagues.[124] The mean arterial PO_2 at peak exercise was 98 ± 15 mm Hg and the alveolar-arterial PO_2 difference ($(A - a)PO_2$) was 21 ± 14 mm Hg. Although

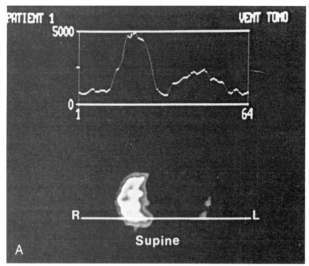

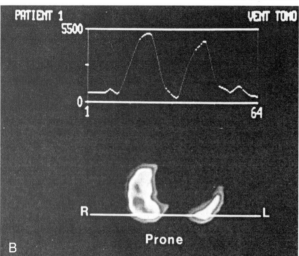

Figure 77.2 Tomographic reconstruction at midheart level (single-photon emission computed tomography) of regional ventilation during continuous inhalation of krypton-81m in a patient with congestive heart failure and cardiomegaly. Counts per pixel are plotted against distance along a horizontal axis through dorsal regions of both lungs. Note that the image of the prone patient **(B)** has been inverted. Reduced ventilation of the left lower lobe in supine patient **(A)** is restored when the patient is prone. (From Wiener C, Henderson B, McKenna WJ, et al: Left lower lobe ventilation is reduced in patients with cardiomegaly in the supine but not in the prone position. Am Rev Respir Dis 141:150–155, 1990.)

these mean values fall within the normal range and would be consistent with an increase in alveolar dead space (high $\dot{V}A/\dot{Q}$) rather than a physiologic shunt (low $\dot{V}A/\dot{Q}$) gas-exchange pattern, the dispersion was quite considerable. Aguilaniu and associates[125] commented that 30 of 85 patients in the Wasserman and colleagues study[124] had a (A – a)PO_2 greater than 30 mm Hg, suggesting a physiologic shunt from impaired distribution of ventilation. Unlike the situation in acute heart failure (see Fig. 77.3), low arterial PO_2 values on peak exercise were unrelated to clinical status, at least in terms of $\dot{V}O_2$max. Arterial PCO_2 was only slightly below resting values (35 mm Hg) and was similar to that in

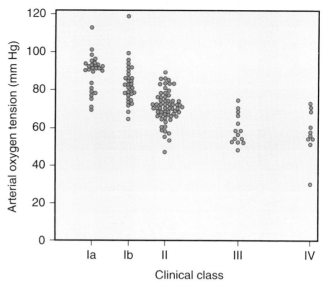

Figure 77.3 Arterial oxygen tension while breathing room air in patients with acute myocardial infarction. Class Ia, no heart failure; Ib, recovery from heart failure; II, moderate heart failure; III, pulmonary edema; and IV, cardiogenic shock. (From Fillmore SJ, Shapiro M, Killip T: Arterial oxygen tension in acute myocardial infarction: Serial analysis of clinical state and blood gas changes. Am Heart J 79:620–629, 1976.)

controls. At low metabolic rates, arterial pH is well controlled, even though the lactate rise is greater in patients with severe exercise impairment.[124]

Influence of Low Diffusing Capacity on Gas Exchange on Exercise

There is a correlation between the DL_{CO}[29,59,60] and $DL_{CO}/\dot{Q}$[126] and the pretransplant $\dot{V}O_2$max, and between DL_{CO}[63] and DL/VA[127] and the $\dot{V}O_2$max after transplant. These findings raise the possibility that a low DL_{CO} in CHF might lead to hypoxemia on exercise and limitation of $\dot{V}O_2$max. Support for this notion comes from Braith and coworkers,[128] who divided their posttransplant patients into those with DL_{CO} greater than 70% of predicted and those with DL_{CO} less than 70% of predicted (mean 60%). In the latter group, arterial PO_2 fell on exercise from 100 to 78 mm Hg (arterial oxygen saturation [SO_2] fell from 98% to 93%), and arterial PCO_2 fell more than the DL_{CO} greater than 70% of predicted group. Cardiac output was the same for both groups. On the other hand, Ville and colleagues[127] subdivided their patients similarly, but did not find oxygen desaturation in either group.

In idiopathic pulmonary fibrosis with DL_{CO} at rest less than 50% of predicted, substantial hypoxemia may arise on exercise (arterial SO_2, 71% to 92%; ΔSO_2 from rest, 3% to 15%).[129] This abnormality is recognized as being due to diffusion-limited gas exchange, the crucial parameter being a $DL_{CO}/\dot{Q}$ ratio less than 1.5. The trigger factors for diffusion-limited hypoxemia are (1) low alveolar PO_2 (e.g., altitude); (2) high $\dot{V}O_2$; (3) low DL_{CO} (which varies as DL_{O_2}); and (4) high $\dot{Q}$. Healthy subjects exercising at altitude and idiopathic pulmonary fibrosis patients with low DL_{CO} exercising in room air are the most susceptible. Smith and coworkers[126] measured $DL_{CO}/\dot{Q}$ ratios in CHF patients, at rest (3.6) and exercising (2.8) at 30 W (37% of max). DL_{CO} increased on mild exercise by 31%. It is difficult to predict their $DL_{CO}/\dot{Q}$ at the $\dot{V}O_2$max, but because these patients did not desaturate at peak exercise at 80 W (arterial SO_2 went from 98% to 96%), it is unlikely that the $DL_{CO}/\dot{Q}$ ratio fell from 2.8 at 30 W to less than 1.5 at 80 W. Agostoni and colleagues[60] exercised CHF patients (DL_{CO} at rest 70%) to maximum while breathing air or a hypoxic mixture (16% O_2); the hypoxic mixture should have "revealed" any diffusion limitation. In fact, the fall in arterial SO_2 was very modest (−3%) and ΔPO_2 and $\Delta(A - a)PO_2$ was no different from control subjects breathing 16% O_2.

Therefore, even with a DL_{CO} less than 75%, diffusion-limited hypoxemia is unlikely. The cause of exercise-induced hypoxemia in CHF patients (it occurs in 10%[124]) is physiologic shunting (low $\dot{V}A/\dot{Q}$ units), possibly secondary to smoking-related pathology.

EXERCISE RESPONSES

Ventilation

There have been many studies showing that patients with CHF hyperventilate on exercise in relation to their metabolic requirements, and that the ventilatory equivalents (the $\dot{V}E/\dot{V}CO_2$ and $\dot{V}E/\dot{V}O_2$ ratios) are high. Sullivan and colleagues[28] carried out a systematic study of $\dot{V}E/\dot{V}CO_2$ on exercise, and found a relationship at peak exercise with the physiologic dead space (VD/VT) (see discussion later) and, inversely, with cardiac output, but not with pulmonary artery or wedge pressures. Al-Rawas and associates[130] showed that $\dot{V}E/\dot{V}CO_2$ was also related (inversely) to $\dot{V}O_2$max. Marzo and coworkers[40] had found previously that the improvement in cardiac output following heart transplantation was associated with a reduction in exercise $\dot{V}E/\dot{V}CO_2$. Wasserman and colleagues,[124] in a multicenter study involving 132 CHF patients and 52 controls, showed that the equivalent ratio for oxygen ($\dot{V}E/\dot{V}O_2$) increased as the patient's $\dot{V}O_2$max declined. Discussion of possible causes for the increased ventilatory equivalents comes later.

Ventilatory Constraints on Exercise

The excess ventilation ($\dot{V}E$) in relation to metabolic demand has to be met in the light of a diminished ventilatory capacity (low maximal voluntary ventilation), a degree of airflow obstruction, and inspiratory muscle weakness (or a low threshold for fatigue). The maximal voluntary ventilation measured at rest may overestimate the minute ventilation that can be sustained on endurance exercise. In control subjects, the end-expiratory lung volume (EELV) on exercise decreases initially, but increases above the resting level at peak exercise.[93] A fall in EELV, produced by expiratory muscle effort, is beneficial for the subsequent inspiration because (1) lengthening the diaphragm muscle fibers increases their contractility (this is a small effect), (2) the outward recoil of the thoracic cage at volumes below FRC gives an additional "lift" to inspiration, and (3) peak end-inspiratory lung volume occurs at a lower thoracic volume, thus requiring less elastic work to be done. A rise in EELV on exercise is referred to as "dynamic hyper-inflation," the mechanism being that, as expiration becomes flow-limited (expiratory flows reaching the outer border of the exercise MEFV curve), so inspiration begins before expiration has been completed; thus, a new equilibrium is established at a higher EELV above the threshold for expiratory flow limitation. The downside is that there is more elastic work of breathing at the higher thoracic volumes.

At rest, the EELV in CHF patients is low (see Fig. 77.1) and the expiratory reserve volume is reduced. Because breathing is taking place close to RV, little reduction in EELV on exercise is possible in CHF (EELV falls in a few patients but never rises). According to Johnson and colleagues,[93] 50% of the expired tidal volume (VT) encroached on the exercise MEFV curve, and they calculated that, because of this flow limitation, CHF patients were operating at about 80% of their ventilatory capacity. The paradox is the failure of exercise EELV to rise in CHF patients as a compensatory mechanism, and this might indicate inspiratory muscle fatigue. Interestingly, $\dot{V}E$ at maximal exercise was not increased when 3% CO_2 was added to the inspired air, but $\dot{V}E$ did increase with 3% CO_2 at rest, and on exercise in control subjects; this might indicate mechanical constraints, or inspiratory muscle fatigue.

O'Donnell and coworkers[131] reached the same conclusion but from a different approach. They gave ventilatory assistance in the form of continuous positive airway pressure or inspiratory pressure support (both at +3.5 cm H_2O), which reduced the work of breathing, continuous positive airway pressure by 40% and inspiratory pressure support by 25%. Endurance time (at 60% $\dot{V}O_2$max) increased with pressure support by 2.8 minutes (43%). With or without pressure support, EELV increased (+0.3 L), but their CHF patients had more airflow obstruction (lower FEV_1/VC and more curvilinearity of the MEFV curve) than the patients of Johnson and colleagues.[93] Like Johnson and colleagues,[93] they found considerable flow limitation on exercise from analysis of a flow-volume curve.

Physiologic Dead Space

The physiologic dead space (VD/VT) is the sum of the anatomic dead space and the alveolar dead space (caused by high $\dot{V}A/\dot{Q}$ ratios in the alveolar regions). VD/VT is an expression of wasted ventilation; therefore, a high value implies an elevated $\dot{V}E/\dot{V}CO_2$ ratio.[28,130] Both indices are related to the cardiac index. Part of the physiologic dead space (VD) is due to the obligatory anatomic dead space of the upper respiratory tract. At an equivalent oxygen consumption, patients with heart failure breathe with a faster and shallower pattern, in keeping with their reduced VC. Wasserman and colleagues[124] found that VT on exercise declined in proportion to the fall in $\dot{V}O_2$max, being about 1.0 L (respiratory rate 50 breaths/min) at maximal exercise in the most disabled patients. For them, the anatomic dead space (about 200 mL on exercise) represents 20% of VT (but only 7% in normal subjects at peak exercise), which is a significant fraction, though not the major part of their total VD/VT (50% to 60%).[124] The bulk of the VD/VT excess in severe CHF, however, is caused by "alveolar" dead space (i.e., by gas-exchanging units with $\dot{V}A/\dot{Q}$ ratios higher than the ideal value of about 1.0). Because cardiac output tends to be low in patients with CHF for a given level of exercise or $\dot{V}O_2$, recruitment of blood flow at the lung apex that occurs normally on exercise[31] may not occur (or else the apical vessels are fully recruited at rest due to the pulmonary hypertension), accounting for the high VD/VT on exercise. Regional $\dot{V}A/\dot{Q}$ mismatch is another possibility, but it would have to be biased toward high and not low $\dot{V}A/\dot{Q}$ units, because the physiologic shunt is low in heart failure. Surprisingly, there have been no studies of $\dot{V}A/\dot{Q}$ distribution in chronic heart failure using the MIGET technique. A third possibility is that the high ratio of $\dot{V}E$ to cardiac output in patients with CHF during exercise is responsible by itself for the rise in physiologic dead space, because VD/VT increases as total ventilation ($\dot{V}E$) increases.[132]

Cardiac Transplantation and Exercise Performance

Only a few of the many studies on the effects of heart transplantation on exercise performance are mentioned here. There is considerable improvement in all peak exercise parameters (Table 77.9) resulting from an increase in the LVEF, resting cardiac index, and lung volumes, and a decrease in PVR (see Table 77.2), but none of the values becomes normal. Oxygen uptake, at best, reaches two thirds of the control values, having been 40% or less pretransplant. Patients achieve their maximum $\dot{V}O_2$ 1 year after transplant, with no improvement in subsequent years.[133,134] Minute ventilation and maximum VT increase following the improvement in ventilatory capacity (note FEV_1 and VC increases in Table 77.7). There is a decrease in the $\dot{V}E/\dot{V}CO_2$ and VD, indicating better $\dot{V}A/\dot{Q}$ matching (or just a global increase in $\dot{Q}$) and, perhaps, less $\dot{V}CO_2$ per unit of oxygen consumed (see Table 77.9). The reason for the low $\dot{V}O_2max$ (see review by Marconi and Marzorati[135]) is thought to be a low maximum heart rate (chronotropic incompetence) and suboptimal skeletal muscle function,[101] either cyclosporin induced or from deconditioning. Richard and coworkers,[115] however, have shown that prolonged and strenuous endurance exercise training can restore $\dot{V}O_2max$ (and heart rate max) to normal levels.

Oxygen Breathing

There is controversy about whether patients with CHF benefit from an increase in inspired oxygen concentration during exercise. Restrick and colleagues,[136] on the basis of ambulatory tests (6 minute or endurance walks), concluded that portable oxygen at 2 or 4 L/min had no effect on the distance walked or on symptoms of breathlessness in spite of an improvement in arterial SO_2 (from 90% to 93%). Moore and coworkers[137] (steady-state exercise at 40 W, cycle ergometer, breathing 50% O_2) and Chua and colleagues[138] (progressive work test, treadmill, breathing 100% O_2), both found an increase in exercise time (+14% and +15%) when oxygen was breathed. Russell and associates,[139] on the other hand (progressive work test, cycle ergometer, breathing 60% O_2), found no increase in exercise time, no reduction in blood lactate, and a reduction in blood flow and $\dot{V}O_2$ by the legs. All studies have found a small increase in arterial SO_2, but this may not be the limiting factor in submaximal exercise performance. In some patients, the benefits of oxygen breathing might stem from a lowering of PPA and PVR.

Causes of Exercise Hyperventilation

There are many suggestions and theories, but no consensus, concerning the mechanisms of exercise hyperventilation. Wasserman and associates[124] proposed a "metabolic" analysis on the basis of the alveolar air equation for carbon dioxide:

$$\dot{V}E = \dot{V}CO_2 \times \frac{863}{Pa_{CO_2} \times (1 - VD/VT)}$$

where $\dot{V}E$ and $\dot{V}CO_2$ are minute ventilation and metabolic carbon dioxide production (in liters or milliliters per minute), respectively; 863 is the correction factor from BTPS conditions (body temperature, ambient pressure, saturated with water) to STPD conditions (standard temperature and pressure, dry); and VD/VT is the physiologic dead space as a fraction of the tidal volume. In the study by Wasserman and associates,[124] a subset of 20 sub-

Table 77.9 Ventilatory Responses to Maximal Exercise in Patients with Congestive Heart Failure before and after Heart Transplantation

	Pretransplant*	Posttransplant*	Controls†
Oxygen consumption (peak) ($\dot{V}O_2$) (L/min/kg)	10–14	17–21	32–34
Oxygen consumption (% control)	30–42	52–64	
Minute ventilation ($\dot{V}E$) (L/min)	40–50	50–60	80–90
Tidal volume (VT) (L)	1.35	1.8	2.3
Ventilatory equivalent for CO_2 ($\dot{V}E/\dot{V}CO_2$)	40–50	35	25–30
Physiologic dead space (VD/VT) (%)	0.35	0.3	0.2

* Transplant data from Marzo KP, Wilson JR, Mancini DM: Effects of cardiac transplantation on ventilatory response to exercise. Am J Cardiol 69:547–553, 1992; and Al-Rawas OA, Carter R, Stevenson RD, et al: Exercise intolerance following heart transplantation: The role of pulmonary diffusing capacity impairment. Chest 118:1661–1670, 2000.
† Control data (combined) mainly from Sullivan MJ, Higginbotham MB, Cobb FR: Increased exercise ventilation in patients with chronic heart failure: Intact ventilatory control despite hemodynamic and pulmonary abnormalities. Circulation 77:552–559, 1988.

jects with moderate heart failure (peak $\dot{V}O_2$ <12 mL/min/kg) had mean peak $\dot{V}O_2$ of 0.77 L/min; $\dot{V}CO_2$, 1.093 L/min; $\dot{V}E$, 51.8 L/min; VD/VT, 0.48; and arterial PCO_2, 35 mm Hg. The increase in $\dot{V}E$ in the CHF group compared with normal subjects at the same $\dot{V}O_2$ (51.8 versus 22.5 L/min) can be apportioned roughly as follows: $\Delta\dot{V}CO_2$, 47%; $\Delta VD/VT$, 45%; and ΔPCO_2, 8%. Putting Wasserman and associates' arguments very simply, the high $\dot{V}E$ in patients with heart failure is a response to (1) excess carbon dioxide production due to the buffering of lactic acid with bicarbonate and carbon dioxide; (2) a high physiologic dead space (wasted ventilation in terms of gas exchange); and, less importantly, (3) a metabolic acidosis that, through chemoreceptor stimulation, lowers arterial PCO_2 and restores blood pH to normal (pH was maintained within 0.02 units of resting values).

Wasserman and associates' analysis,[124] and the earlier work of Sullivan and colleagues,[28] suggest that $\dot{V}E$ on exercise in CHF, although excessive for the metabolic load (high $\dot{V}E/\dot{V}CO_2$), is an appropriate response in the sense of maintaining normal arterial PO_2 and PCO_2 values. The mechanisms that "set" the level of ventilation during exercise are not fully understood, even in normal subjects. Patients with CHF have normal responses (increasing $\dot{V}E$ for a given metabolic load) to breathing hypoxic or hypercapnic gas mixtures during exercise (the chemoreceptor response).[93,138] There must be some hypoxic drive breathing air, because exercise ventilation in patients with CHF is reduced when 50%[137] or 100%[138] oxygen is breathed. Chua and colleagues[138] have shown that the hypoxic (single breath of N_2) and hypercapnic (rebreathing 7% CO_2) ventilatory responses at rest were increased in CHF, but the data are scattered, and only 30% of subjects were actually outside the range for normals.

Peripheral Factors and the Ergoreflex. Reflexes from exercising muscles, transmitted via small myelinated and unmyelinated fibers of groups III and IV,[140] also stimulate ventilation, although they may be more important at the onset of exercise than in the maintenance of the steady state. This so-called ergoreflex can be augmented by occluding an exercising limb immediately on cessation of exercise; this fixes the metabolic state of the muscle and prolongs the activation of the reflex.[112] This reflex promotes the sympathetic vasoconstrictor drive and stimulates ventilation. Compared with control subjects, patients with heart failure maintained their exercise (hand gripping) ventilation throughout the 3-minute period of postexercise limb occlusion at 86% of the exercise level, whereas only 55% of that level was maintained by normal subjects.[112] Among the many substances released into effluent blood by exercising muscle, such as H^+, HCO_3^-, K^+, lactate, phosphate, and bradykinin, only the increases in prostaglandins (E_2 and $F_{1\alpha}$) were predictors of the ergoreflex response[141]; blockade of cyclo-oxygenase with ketoprofen, reducing prostaglandin and bradykinin production, attenuated the ergoreflex in CHF.[141a] Infusions of sodium bicarbonate abolished the increased ergoreceptor activity in CHF by reducing serum (and presumably tissue) H^+ concentrations. The source of protons neutralized by bicarbonate is not known for certain, but it might be lactate production or the conversion of adenosine triphosphate to adenosine diphosphate and inorganic phosphate.[142]

Peripheral Muscle Function. Augmentation of the ergoreflex in CHF patients is related to structural[143,144] and functional[144,145] abnormalities in skeletal muscle, as revealed by muscle biopsies (see Stassijns and associates[111] for review). These changes, at least in their initial stages, are probably related to the deconditioning that takes place when the capacity and motivation to exercise is reduced. In support of this notion, training programs (both uncontrolled[146] and controlled[147,148]) increase overall performance on formal exercise testing, especially peripheral muscle function. Improvements were seen in exercise endurance time, $\dot{V}O_2$max, and $\dot{Q}$max[78a,146–148]; there were small reductions at submaximal work loads in $\dot{V}E$ (15%) and $\dot{V}E/\dot{V}CO_2$ slope (10%).[78a,147] There was no change with training in pulmonary hemodynamics on exercise, nor in LVEF, but significant improvements occurred in leg performance in terms of blood flow, oxygen delivery, arteriovenous oxygen content difference, and lactate production.[146] Mitochondrial density increased.[148] Training the forearm for 6 weeks damped down the ergoreflex.[112] As patients with heart failure deteriorate and with the onset of cachexia, muscle bulk declines and many catabolic processes are activated (e.g., raised tumor necrosis factor-α levels) and anabolic functions diminish (e.g., insulin and growth hormone resistance)[149] (see Coats[150] for a review). At this stage of progressive CHF, skeletal muscle impairment may be irreversible.

It is difficult to assess the contribution of the ergoreflex in setting ventilatory levels during exercise in CHF. In terms of arterial PCO_2, $\dot{V}E$ seems appropriate for the metabolic load and the high VD/VT. After training, with a decrease in the ergoreflex, $\dot{V}E$ at a given work load decreases by only 15%.[147] Perhaps mechanical constraints or incipient respiratory muscle fatigue limit the response to ergoreflex stimulation so that hypocapnia does not occur.

Prognostic Factors

There is a need for predictors of "event-free" survival for (1) assessing the need for transplantation, and (2) monitoring medical therapy. Ideally, prognostic factors should be simple, sensitive, and specific for CHF. Measurements of cardiopulmonary hemodynamics are not simple and are invasive. The performance of the heart under stress, such as at peak exercise, is likely to be a more sensitive index than an assessment under resting conditions. Above a certain exercise threshold, the arteriovenous oxygen content difference becomes relatively stable, so that $\dot{V}O_2$ reflects cardiac output. Traditionally, the peak $\dot{V}O_2$ has been used as a surrogate for "cardiac capacity," and there is a considerable literature devoted to finding even simpler indices to act as predictors of peak $\dot{V}O_2$ (i.e., measurements that are independent of patient motivation and effort). $\dot{V}O_2$max correlates with DL_{CO} at rest[29,59,60,63] more consistently than with other routine pulmonary function tests such as FEV_1, but the link between $\dot{V}O_2$max and lung function at rest is not a close one physiologically. Consequently, interest has shifted to submaximal exercise indices, particularly the $\dot{V}E/\dot{V}CO_2$ ratio, generally taken as the slope of $\dot{V}E$ plotted against $\dot{V}CO_2$ at different exercise levels. The most recent studies have found $\dot{V}E/\dot{V}CO_2$ alone[151] or the anaerobic threshold[152] a better predictor of event-free survival or death than

$\dot{V}O_2$max or other indices such as NYHA class or LVEF.[151] Of the components of the $\dot{V}E/\dot{V}CO_2$ ratio (VD/VT and $PaCO_2$), a low peak $PaCO_2$ has superior prognostic power.[152a] Robbins and coworkers[153] claimed that with nonparametric Kaplan-Meier plots, using $\dot{V}E/\dot{V}CO_2$ and peak $\dot{V}O_2$, low, intermediate, and high risk groups for death can be identified. Pardaens and associates,[154] on the other hand, found that peak $\dot{V}O_2$ had superior prognostic power.

SLEEP

Central Sleep Apnea

Periodic breathing (apnea or hypopnea, or both, alternating with hyperpnea) is frequently observed in patients with chronic heart failure. The CHF is usually severe and associated with a higher pulmonary wedge pressure *and poorer prognosis* than in other patients with CHF.[155,156] Another characteristic pattern of altered breathing is Cheyne-Stokes respiration, in which VT gradually increases and then decreases, with each cycle interrupted by a period of apnea (see Fig. 18.1 in Chapter 18). Cheyne-Stokes respiration occurs during sleep and is a form of sleep disorder known as central sleep apnea (CSA) (see Chapter 74). Both periodic breathing and Cheyne-Stokes respiration occur in healthy subjects, especially men and elderly persons, at high altitude. The pathogenesis of CSA is linked to a hyperactive ventilatory response to carbon dioxide during sleep.[157,158] In CHF patients with CSA, the end-tidal PCO_2 does not show the normal rise during non–rapid eye movement sleep (+2.5 mm Hg from wakefulness) and remains close to the carbon dioxide threshold for hypopnea (+1.7 mm Hg) and apnea (+2.8 mm Hg).[159] Inhaling carbon dioxide, either directly or via an external dead space attached to a face mask, is effective in stabilizing the breathing pattern and improving sleep quality.[160]

Obstructive Sleep Apnea

Another form of sleep-related apnea-hypopnea is the obstructive sleep apnea (OSA) syndrome (see Chapter 74), which occurs most often in obese men. Progressive collapse of the pharyngeal aperture, when complete, causes apnea (defined as cessation of airflow >10 seconds). Asynchronous chest and abdominal wall movements are seen during the apneic periods in OSA but are absent in CSA. Apneas are terminated by an arousal reflex, which may be explosive in OSA when the pharynx suddenly opens. At the end of apnea, severe arterial hypoxemia may occur. In both OSA and CSA, frequent arousal leads to sleep fragmentation with daytime sleepiness and poor concentration. Systemic blood pressure rises during arousal. There is also sympathetic nervous system activation with increased nocturnal urinary norepinephrine excretion.[161] OSA may be a risk factor in ischemic heart disease and probably worsens the prognosis of patients with CHF.

In one study using polysomnography of 81 patients with stable CHF, Javaheri and colleagues[162] found an incidence of CSA of 40% and of OSA of 11%, which is considerably greater than expected in this age group (2% to 4%). Patients with CSA and OSA were more likely to have atrial fibrillations, ventricular arrhythmias, and lower LVEFs. Their lowest nocturnal arterial SO_2 values were 76% ± 12% (SD) compared with 89% ± 4% in those without apneas. There was no difference in daytime oxygenation. The OSA patients were also more likely to be overweight and to snore than the CSA patients and, compared to CHF patients without OSA, to have systolic hypertension.[161] Treatment of OSA in the standard way with nasal continuous positive airway pressure improves left ventricular function.[162]

MECHANISMS OF DYSPNEA

ACUTE PULMONARY EDEMA

In patients with acute heart failure, breathlessness at rest is associated with an acute elevation of pulmonary venous pressure sufficient to cause interstitial and alveolar edema. The mechanism of the dyspnea, which is discussed in detail in Chapter 28, although clearly linked to these changes, is far from clear. Experimentally, an acute rise in pulmonary vascular pressures increases neural activity in unmyelinated C fibers, which were called by Paintal[163] juxtapulmonary capillary or J receptors, but a relationship with reflex tachypnea has not been established. Wead and associates[164] concluded from their own observations and a review of previous data that intrapulmonary vascular congestion failed to stimulate C fibers or other nerve endings (e.g., irritant or stretch receptors) sufficiently to change central inspiratory activity, nor was there experimental evidence in support of left atrial or pulmonary venous distention as a source. Of course, these experiments are carried out in anesthetized and often partially isolated animal preparations. In their review, Snashall and Chung[94] marshaled the evidence in favor of intrapulmonary interstitial pressure receptors, but the role of these receptors in pulmonary edema remains in doubt.

In humans, the induction of an attack of angina pectoris by atrial pacing,[85] which increased left atrial pressure and decreased lung compliance, caused "chest tightness, substernal discomfort, pressure, or constriction," but not dyspnea. Measurements of ventilation and ventilatory pattern were not made. It may be wrong to seek a single cause for the dramatic "air hunger" of patients with acute left ventricular failure, because factors such as arterial hypoxemia, low cardiac output, and tissue acidosis may combine with the rise of pulmonary interstitial pressure to produce the response. Another possibility is that the reflex tachypnea of acute pulmonary edema arises from expansion of the chest cage. In patients with acute left ventricular failure, the thorax may have to accommodate 500 mL or more of extra blood and new edema fluid. Unless FRC falls by a similar amount, the chest cage must expand. This increases the elastic work of breathing in a situation in which oxygen delivery to the respiratory muscles may already be compromised, and might contribute to the dyspnea and discomfort of the patient. A similar mechanism may contribute to the sensation of orthopnea (see next section).

ORTHOPNEA

Dyspnea, relieved in part by sitting upright, is a common symptom in patients with acute or chronic heart failure. Christie and Meakins,[165] who, using intrapleural catheters, were the first to show a decreased lung compliance in CHF, believed that pulmonary vascular congestion stimulated the Hering-Breuer reflex. Sitting up diminished the congestion and relieved the dyspnea. In chronic CHF, respiratory resistance rises (+80%) in the supine posture, and maximum expiratory flows fall (−40%), although FRC does not show the expected fall (see Table 77.3). Thus, patients with CHF must have a considerable degree of hyperinflation of the thorax when they lie flat, because although their air volumes (FRC) are similar to normal subjects, they need to accommodate at least an extra 500 mL in blood and tissue volume. Yap and associates[50] found that dyspnea scores in CHF increased from 2.2 (sitting) to 3.9 (supine) on a scale of 0 to 10. There was no score in controls in either posture. The higher the midtidal lung volume, the greater the elastic work of breathing.[53] Afferent signals from the inspiratory muscles, which are working at a shorter length and therefore at a mechanical disadvantage, may contribute to the sensation of orthopnea.

EXERCISE DYSPNEA

The symptoms experienced by patients with CHF, when they exercise, are dyspnea and fatigue. Figure 77.4 presents these symptoms at the end of chains of causation, starting

on the pulmonary side with a rise of pulmonary venous pressure, and on the systemic side with a decrease in cardiac reserve. Fatigue or dyspnea are equally common reasons for stopping exercise.[28,166] There is no difference in peak exercise variables (wedge or mean P_{PA}, $\dot{V}_E$, $\dot{V}_E/\dot{V}_{CO_2}$, V_D/V_T, and $\dot{V}_{O_2}$max) between patients limited by dyspnea and patients limited by fatigue.[28] At peak exercise, dyspnea scores were not related to any ventilatory parameters.[166] Thus the symptom of dyspnea on exercise cannot be easily related to ventilatory demand, or explained in simple terms as excess ventilation for the task at hand.

On the other hand, exertional dyspnea may relate to ventilatory difficulty in terms of an increase in the elastic or resistive work of breathing, which may have a peripheral component if there is respiratory muscle weakness or fatigue. Perceived dyspnea in heart failure correlates with respiratory muscle weakness (MIP and MEP), with the work of breathing (tension time index of the diaphragm), and with FEV_1.[102] Using near-infrared spectroscopy, patients with CHF showed significant accessory respiratory muscle (serratus anterior) deoxygenation compared to controls.[167] Lipkin and coworkers[168] found that exercise was terminated by fatigue in 23 of 25 patients with a "slow" exercise protocol, and by breathlessness in all 25 patients after a "fast" protocol. Minute ventilation and lactate and

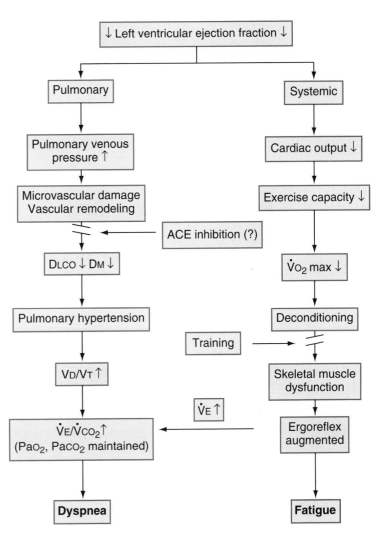

Figure 77.4 Flow chart showing a hypothetical sequence of events stemming from a reduction in left ventricular function for the lung and systemic tissues, particularly the skeletal muscles. The positive effect of training is generally accepted, but that of angiotensin-converting enzyme (ACE) inhibition on lung repair awaits further confirmation. The origin of the symptoms of dyspnea and fatigue is contentious.

H^+ ion concentrations were higher with the rapid protocol. One theory is that the location of a "critical" level of tissue hypoxia and acidosis (respiratory muscles versus the leg muscles) determines whether exercise is terminated by dyspnea or fatigue.

After cardiac transplantation, the demand for ventilation at a given $\dot{V}O_2$ declines[40] (note the fall in $\dot{V}E/\dot{V}CO_2$ in Table 77.9), and perceived dyspnea falls. The reduced sensation of dyspnea is not accompanied by any decrease in the work of breathing,[169] suggesting that the lungs remain stiff and noncompliant. The residual dyspnea in posttransplantation patients may relate to impaired lung mechanics and to skeletal muscle atrophy and deconditioning (see Table 77.8).

SUMMARY

In patients with heart disease, acute rises of pulmonary venous pressure increase the pulmonary blood volume, reduce lung compliance, and increase (moderately) airway resistance. Microvascular filtration and lymph flow increase. If the pressure increase is sufficient to exceed the rate of clearance of filtrate, interstitial and then alveolar edema ensues. Lung volumes decrease, and gas exchange is compromised (arterial PO_2 and DL_{CO} are reduced). Acutely (e.g., after acute myocardial infarction), these changes are reversible.

Chronic elevation of pulmonary venous pressure from whatever cause leads to alveolar and vascular damage with loss of lung volume, a reduction in the DL_{CO} (especially in DM), and pulmonary hypertension. DL_{CO} and DM improve by 15% to 20% after ACE inhibitor therapy, but not after ACE receptor blockade; the mechanism is thought to relate to Na^+ absorption from the alveolar septum. A rise in airway resistance is present but not severe. Respiratory muscle function is mildly impaired until the later stages of the disease.

The origin of the symptoms of dyspnea and orthopnea in patients with CHF is not well understood. Airway resistance rises in the supine posture, and the thoracic cage is relatively overexpanded. An intrapulmonary stimulus for orthopnea seems unlikely, and reflexes arising from overexpansion of the chest wall may play a role. Exercise capacity is limited, primarily because of a low cardiac output, high muscle vascular resistance, and deconditioning of the exercising muscles. Respiratory muscle fatigue may limit exercise capacity in some patients. Deconditioning is accompanied by structural and biochemical changes in muscle, but these changes and the poor muscle performance can be reversed by training programs.

Arterial PO_2 at rest and on exercise is usually within the normal range, but mixed venous PO_2 and pH are lower and lactate is higher than in healthy persons. Oxygen breathing may improve exercise capacity and duration. The cause of the hyperventilation with exercise is partly pulmonary, from an increase in VD ventilation, and partly peripheral, arising from excess lactate production and an augmented ergoreceptor reflex in exercising muscle. The origin of the symptom of dyspnea on exercise is poorly understood.

Reduction of pulmonary venous pressure by cardiac transplantation is accompanied by improvements in PVR, lung volumes (but not DL_{CO}), respiratory muscle function, and exercise capacity, and a reduction in exercise hyperventilation and in the sensation of dyspnea. Nevertheless, most indices remain at about two thirds of normal values, but a return to normal values can be achieved if a strenuous exercise program is undertaken.

REFERENCES

1. West JB: Respiratory physiology. *In* The Essentials (7th ed). Baltimore: Lippincott Williams & Wilkins, 2004, pp 1–186.
2. Glazier JB, Hughes JMB, Maloney JE, et al: Measurements of capillary dimensions and blood volume in rapidly frozen lungs. J Appl Physiol 26:65–76, 1969.
3. Warrell DA, Evans JW, Clarke RO, et al: Pattern of filling in the pulmonary capillary bed. J Appl Physiol 32:346–356, 1972.
4. West JB, Dollery CT, Naimark A: Distribution of blood flow in isolated lung: Relation to vascular and alveolar pressures. J Appl Physiol 19:713–724, 1964.
5. Erdmann J, Vaughan T, Brigham K, et al: Effect of increased vascular pressure on lung fluid balance in unanesthetized sheep. Circ Res 37:271–284, 1975.
6. Staub NC, Nagano H, Pearce ML: Pulmonary edema in dogs, especially the sequence of fluid accumulation in lungs. J Appl Physiol 22:227–240, 1967.
7. Broaddus VC, Wiener-Kronish JP, Staub NC: Clearance of lung edema into the pleural space of volume-loaded anesthetized sheep. J Appl Physiol 68:2623–2630, 1990.
8. Drake RE, Giesler M, Laine G, et al: Effect of outflow pressure on lung lymph flow in unanesthetized sheep. J Appl Physiol 58:70–76, 1985.
9. Wiener-Kronish JP, Matthay MA, Callen PW, et al: Relationship of pleural effusions to pulmonary hemodynamics in patients with congestive heart failure. Am Rev Respir Dis 132:1253–1256, 1985.
10. Wiener-Kronish JP, Goldstein R, Matthay MA, et al: Lack of association of pleural effusion with chronic pulmonary arterial and right atrial hypertension. Chest 92:967–970, 1987.
11. Haworth SG, Hall SM, Patel M: Peripheral pulmonary vascular and airway abnormalities in adolescents with rheumatic mitral stenosis. Int J Cardiol 18:405–416, 1988.
12. Tsukimoto K, Mathieu-Costello O, Prediletto R, et al: Ultrastructural appearances of pulmonary capillaries at high transmural pressures. J Appl Physiol 71:573–582, 1991.
13. Costello ML, Mathieu-Costello O, West JB: Stress failure of alveolar epithelial cells studied by scanning electron microscopy. Am Rev Respir Dis 145:1446–1455, 1992.
14. Bachofen H, Schürch S, Michel RP, et al: Experimental hydrostatic pulmonary edema in rabbit lungs: Morphology. Am Rev Respir Dis 147:989–996, 1993.
15. Bachofen H, Schürch S, Weibel ER: Experimental hydrostatic pulmonary edema in rabbit lungs: Barrier lesions. Am Rev Respir Dis 147:997–1004, 1993.
16. Crapo JD: New concepts in the formation of pulmonary edema (editorial). Am Rev Respir Dis 147:790–792, 1993.
17. Harris P, Heath D: The Human Pulmonary Circulation (3rd ed). New York: Churchill Livingstone, 1986.
18. Tozzi CA, Poiani GJ, Harangozo AM, et al: Pressure-induced connective tissue synthesis in pulmonary artery segments is dependent on intact endothelium. J Clin Invest 84:1005–1012, 1989.
19. Stenmark KR, Mecham RP: Cellular and molecular mechanisms of pulmonary vascular remodeling. Annu Rev Physiol 59:89–144, 1997.
20. Rabinovitch M: EVE and beyond, retro and prospective insights. Am J Physiol 277:L5–L12, 1999.

21. Cowan KN, Jones PL, Rabinovitch M: Elastase and matrix metalloproteinase inhibitors induce regression, and tenascin-C antisense prevents, progression of vascular disease. J Clin Invest 105:21–34, 2000.

22. O'Blenes SB, Fischer S, McIntyre B, et al: Hemodynamic unloading leads to regression of pulmonary vascular disease in rats. J Thorac Cardiovasc Surg 121:279–289, 2001.

23. West JB, Mathieu-Costello O: Structure, strength failure, and remodeling of the pulmonary blood-gas barrier. Annu Rev Physiol 61:543–572, 1999.

24. Williamson JR, Vogler NJ, Kilo C: Regional variations in the width of the basement membrane of muscle capillaries in man and the giraffe. Am J Pathol 63:359–370, 1971.

25. Berg JT, Fu Z, Breen EC, et al: High lung inflation increases mRNA levels of ECM components and growth factors in lung parenchyma. J Appl Physiol 83:120–128, 1997.

26. Butler J, Chomsky DB, Wilson JR: Pulmonary hypertension and exercise intolerance in patients with heart failure. J Am Coll Cardiol 34:1802–1806, 1999.

27. Reeves JT, Grover RF, Dempsey JA: Pulmonary circulation during exercise. In Weir EK, Reeves JT (eds): Lung Biology in Health and Disease. Vol 3: Pulmonary Vascular Physiology and Pathophysiology. New York: Marcel Dekker, 1988, pp 107–133.

28. Sullivan MJ, Higginbotham MB, Cobb FR: Increased exercise ventilation in patients with chronic heart failure: Intact ventilatory control despite hemodynamic and pulmonary abnormalities. Circulation 77:552–559, 1988.

29. Kraemer MD, Kubo SH, Rector TS, et al: Pulmonary and peripheral vascular factors are important determinants of peak exercise oxygen uptake in patients with heart failure. J Am Coll Cardiol 21:641–648, 1993.

30. Maseri A, Caldini P, Howard P, et al: Determinants of pulmonary vascular volume: Recruitment versus distensibility. Circ Res 31:218–228, 1972.

31. Harf A, Pratt T, Hughes JMB: Regional distribution of $\dot{V}A/\dot{Q}$ in man at rest and with exercise measured with krypton-81m. J Appl Physiol 44:115–123, 1978.

32. Granath A, Jonsson B, Strandell T: Circulation in healthy old men, studied by right heart catheterization at rest and during exercise in supine and sitting position. Acta Med Scand 176:425–446, 1964.

33. Hultgren H, Lopez C, Lundberg E, et al: Physiologic studies of pulmonary edema at high altitude. Circulation 29:393–408, 1964.

34. Taylor AE, Barnard JW, Barman SC, et al: Fluid balance. In Crystal RG, West JB, et al (eds): The Lung: Scientific Foundations (Vol 2). Philadelphia: Lippincott–Raven, 1997, pp 1558–1560.

35. Townsley MI, Fu Z, Mathieu-Costello O, et al: Pulmonary microvascular permeability: Responses to high vascular pressure after induction of pacing-induced heart failure in dogs. Circ Res 77:317–325, 1995.

36. Gibbs JSR, Keegan J, Wright C, et al: Pulmonary artery pressure changes during exercise and daily activities in chronic heart failure. J Am Coll Cardiol 15:52–61, 1990.

37. Levine MJ, Weinstein JS, Diver DJ, et al: Progressive improvement in pulmonary vascular resistance after percutaneous mitral valvuloplasty. Circulation 79:1061–1067, 1989.

38. Niset G, Ninane V, Antoine M, et al: Respiratory dysfunction in congestive heart failure: Correction after heart transplantation. Eur Respir J 6:1197–1201, 1993.

39. Mettauer B, Lampert E, Charloux A, et al: Lung membrane diffusing capacity, heart failure, and heart transplantation. Am J Cardiol 83:62–67, 1999.

40. Marzo KP, Wilson JR, Mancini DM: Effects of cardiac transplantation on ventilatory response to exercise. Am J Cardiol 69:547–553, 1992.

41. Naeije R, Lipski A, Abramowicz M, et al: Nature of pulmonary hypertension in congestive heart failure: Effects of cardiac transplantation. Am J Respir Crit Care Med 149:881–887, 1994.

42. Frank NR, Cugell DW, Gaensler EA, et al: Ventilatory studies in mitral stenosis. Am J Med 15:60–76, 1953.

43. Rhodes KM, Evemy K, Nariman S, et al: Relation between severity of mitral valve disease and routine lung function tests in non-smokers. Thorax 37:751–755, 1982.

44. Wood TE, McCleod P, Anthonisen NR, et al: Mechanics of breathing in mitral stenosis. Am Rev Respir Dis 104:52–60, 1971.

45. Richards DGB, Whitfield AGW, Arnott WM, et al: The lung volume in low output cardiac syndromes. Br Heart J 13:381–386, 1951.

46. Hales CA, Kazemi H: Pulmonary function after uncomplicated myocardial infarction. Chest 72:350–358, 1977.

47. Morris MJ, Smith MM, Clarke BG: Lung mechanics after cardiac valve replacement. Thorax 35:453–460, 1980.

48. Light RW, George RB: Serial pulmonary function in patients with acute heart failure. Arch Intern Med 143:429–433, 1983.

49. Johnson BD, Beck KC, Olson LJ, et al: Pulmonary function in patients with reduced left ventricular function. Chest 120:1869–1876, 2001.

50. Yap JCH, Moore D, Cleland JGF, et al: Effect of supine posture on respiratory mechanics in chronic left ventricular failure. Am J Respir Crit Care Med 162:1285–1291, 2000.

51. Nanas S, Nanas J, Papazachou O, et al: Resting lung function and hemodynamic parameters as predictors of exercise capacity in patients with chronic heart failure. Chest 123:1386–1393, 2003.

52. Hannan WJ, Vojacek J, Connell HM, et al: Radionuclide determined pulmonary blood volume in ischaemic heart disease. Thorax 36:922–927, 1981.

53. Cherniack RM, Cuddy TE, Armstrong JB: Significance of pulmonary elastic and viscous resistance in orthopnea. Circulation 15:859–864, 1957.

54. Ogilvie CM, Forster RE, Blakemore WS, et al: A standardized breath holding technique for the clinical measurement of the diffusing capacity of the lung for carbon monoxide. J Clin Invest 36:1–17, 1957.

55. Hughes JMB, Pride NB: In defence of the carbon monoxide transfer coefficient, KCO (TL/VA). Eur Respir J 17:1–7, 2001.

56. Guazzi M: Alveolar-capillary membrane dysfunction in chronic heart failure: Pathophysiology and therapeutic implications. Clin Sci 98:633–641, 2000.

57. Siegel JL, Miller A, Brown LK, et al: Pulmonary diffusing capacity in left ventricular dysfunction. Chest 98:550–553, 1990.

58. Puri S, Baker BL, Oakley CM, et al: Increased alveolar/capillary membrane resistance to gas transfer in patients with chronic heart failure. Br Heart J 72:140–144, 1994.

59. Puri SP, Baker BL, Dutka DP, et al: Reduced alveolar-capillary membrane diffusing capacity in chronic heart failure. Circulation 91:2769–2774, 1995.

60. Agostoni PG, Bussotti M, Palermo P, et al: Does lung diffusion impairment affect exercise capacity in patients with heart failure? Heart 88:453–459, 2002.

61. Assayeg P, Benamer H, Aubry P, et al: Alteration of the alveolar-capillary membrane diffusing capacity in chronic left heart disease. Am J Cardiol 82:459–464, 1998.

62. Guazzi M, Pontone G, Brambilla R, et al: Alveolar-capillary membrane gas conductance: A novel prognostic indicator in chronic heart failure. Eur Heart J 23:467–476, 2002.

63. Al-Rawas OA, Carter R, Stevenson RD, et al: The alveolar-capillary membrane diffusing capacity and the pulmonary capillary blood volume in heart transplantation candidates. Heart 83:156–160, 2000.

64. Puri S, Dutka DP, Baker BL, et al: Acute saline infusion reduces alveolar-capillary membrane conductance and increases airflow obstruction in patients with left ventricular dysfunction. Circulation 99:1190–1196, 1999.

65. Guazzi M, Agostoni P, Bussotti M, et al: Impeded alveolar-capillary gas transfer with saline infusion in heart failure. Hypertension 34:1202–1207, 1999.

66. Guazzi M, Marenzi G, Alimento M, et al: Improvement of alveolar-capillary membrane diffusing capacity with enalapril in chronic heart failure and counteracting effect of aspirin. Circulation 95:1930–1936, 1997.

67. Guazzi M, Pontone G, Agostoni P: Aspirin worsens exercise performance and pulmonary gas exchange in patients with heart failure who are taking angiotensin-converting enzyme inhibitors. Am Heart J 138:254–260, 1999.

68. Guazzi M, Melzi G, Agostoni P: Comparison of changes in respiratory function and exercise oxygen uptake with losartan versus enalapril in congestive heart failure secondary to ischemic or idiopathic dilated cardiomyopathy. Am J Cardiol 80:1572–1576, 1997.

69. Guazzi M, Melzi G, Marenzi GC, et al: Angiotensin-converting enzyme inhibition facilitates alveolar-capillary gas transfer and improves ventilation-perfusion coupling in patients with left ventricular dysfunction. Clin Pharmacol Ther 65:319–327, 1999.

70. Guazzi M, Agostoni P: Angiotensin-converting enzyme inhibition restores the diffusing capacity for carbon monoxide in patients with chronic heart failure by improving the molecular diffusion across the alveolar capillary membrane. Clin Sci 96:17–22, 1999.

71. Guazzi M, Agostoni P, Guazzi MD: Modulation of alveolar-capillary sodium handling as a mechanism of protection of gas transfer by enalapril, and not by losartan, in chronic heart failure. J Am Coll Cardiol 37:398–406, 2001.

72. Matthay MA, Folkesson HG, Verkman AS: Salt and water transport across alveolar and distal airway epithelia in the adult lung. Am J Physiol 270:L487–L503, 1996.

73. Taylor AE, Khimenko PL, Moore TM, et al: Fluid balance. In Crystal RG, West JB, et al (eds): The Lung: Scientific Foundations (Vol 2). Philadelphia: Lippincott–Raven, 1997, pp 1561–1562.

74. Singh SN, Fisher SG, Deedwania PC, et al: Pulmonary effect of amiodarone in patients with heart failure. The Congestive Heart Failure–Survival Trial of Antiarrhythmic Therapy (CHF-STAT) Investigators (Veterans Affairs Cooperative Study No. 320). J Am Coll Cardiol 30:514–517, 1997.

75. Agostoni PG, Guazzi M, Bussotti M, et al: Lack of improvement of lung diffusing capacity following fluid withdrawal by ultrafiltration in chronic heart failure. J Am Coll Cardiol 36:1600–1604, 2000.

76. Bhoola KD, Figueroa CD, Worthy K: Bioregulation of kinins: Kallikreins, kininogens and kininases. Pharmacol Rev 44:1–80, 1992.

77. Abraham MR, Olson LJ, Joyner MJ, et al: Angiotensin genotype modulates pulmonary function and exercise capacity in treated patients with congestive heart failure. Circulation 106:1794–1799, 2002.

78. Bonnici F, Keavney B, Collins R, et al: Angiotensin converting enzyme insertion or deletion polymorphism and coronary restenosis: Meta-analysis of 16 studies. BMJ 325:517–519, 2002.

78a. Guazzi M, Reina G, Tumminello G, et al: Improvement of alveolar–capillary membrane diffusing capacity with exercise training in chronic heart failure. J Appl Physiol 97:1866–1873, 2004.

79. Guazzi M, Brambilla R, De Vita S, et al: Diabetes worsens pulmonary diffusion in heart failure, and insulin counteracts this effect. Am J Respir Crit Care Med 166:978–982, 2002.

79a. Guazzi M, Tumminello G, Di Marco F, et al: The effects of phosphodiesterase-5 inhibition with sildenafil on pulmonary hemodynamics and diffusion capacity, exercise ventilatory efficiency, and oxygen uptake kinetics in chronic heart failure. J Am Coll Cardiol 44:2339–2348, 2004.

80. Estenne M, Yernault J-C, De Smet J-M, et al: Phrenic and diaphragm function after coronary artery bypass grafting. Thorax 40:293–299, 1985.

81. Mustafa KY, Nour MM, Shuhaiber H, et al: Pulmonary function before and sequentially after valve replacement surgery with correlation to preoperative haemodynamic data. Am Rev Respir Dis 130:400–406, 1984.

82. Hosenpud JD: Abnormal pulmonary function specifically related to congestive heart failure: Comparison of patients before and after cardiac transplantation. Am J Med 88:493–496, 1990.

83. Bussieres LM, Pflugfelder PW, Ahmad D, et al: Evolution of resting lung function in the first year after cardiac transplantation. Eur Respir J 8:959–962, 1995.

84. Muir AL, Flenley DC, Kirby BJ, et al: Cardiorespiratory effects of rapid saline infusion in normal man. J Appl Physiol 38:786–793, 1975.

85. Pepine CJ, Wiener J: Relationships of anginal symptoms to lung myocardial ischemia. Circulation 46:863–869, 1972.

86. Frank NR: Influence of acute pulmonary vascular congestion on recoiling force of excised cat's lung. J Appl Physiol 14:905–908, 1959.

87. Bondurant S, Mead J, Cook CD: A re-evaluation of effects of acute central congestion on pulmonary compliance in normal subjects. J Appl Physiol 15:875–877, 1960.

88. Frank NR, Lyons HA, Siebens AA, et al: Pulmonary compliance in patients with cardiac disease. Am J Med 22:516–523, 1957.

89. Sharp JT, Griffith GT, Bunnell IL, et al: Ventilatory mechanics in pulmonary edema in man. J Clin Invest 37:111–117, 1958.

90. Chung KF, Keyes SJ, Morgan BM, et al: Mechanisms of airway narrowing in acute pulmonary edema in dogs: Influence of the vagus and lung volume. Clin Sci 65:289–296, 1983.

91. Michel RP, Zocchi L, Rossi A, et al: Does interstitial lung edema compress airways and arteries? A morphometric study. J Appl Physiol 62:108–115, 1987.

92. Duguet A, Tantucci C, Lozinguez O, et al: Expiratory flow limitation as a determinant of orthopnea in acute left heart failure. J Am Coll Cardiol 35:690–700, 2000.

93. Johnson BD, Beck KC, Olson LJ, et al: Ventilatory constraints during exercise in patients with chronic heart failure. Chest 117:321–332, 2000.

94. Snashall PD, Chung KF: Airway obstruction and bronchial hyperresponsiveness in left ventricular failure and mitral stenosis. Am Rev Respir Dis 144:945–955, 1991.

95. Cabanes LR, Weber SN, Matran R, et al: Bronchial hyperresponsiveness to methacholine in patients with impaired left ventricular function. N Engl J Med 320:1317–1322, 1989.

96. Rolla G, Bucca C, Brussino L, et al: Bronchodilating effect of ipratropium bromide in heart failure. Eur Respir J 6:1492–1495, 1993.

97. Rolla G, Bucca C, Caria E, et al: Bronchial responsiveness in patients with mitral valve disease. Eur Respir J 3:127–131, 1990.

98. Cabanes L, Costes F, Weber S, et al: Improvement in exercise performance by inhalation of methoxamine in patients with impaired left ventricular function. N Engl J Med 326:1661–1665, 1992.

99. Mann WD-C, Kyroussis D, Fleming TA, et al: Cough gastric pressure and maximal expiratory mouth pressure in humans. Am J Respir Crit Care Med 168:714–717, 2003.

100. Hughes PD, Polkey MI, Hams ML, et al: Diaphragm strength in chronic heart failure. Am J Respir Crit Care Med 160:529–534, 1999.

101. McParland C, Resch EF, Krishnan B, et al: Inspiratory muscle weakness in chronic heart failure: Role of nutrition and electrolyte status and systemic myopathy. Am J Respir Crit Care Med 151:1101–1107, 1995.

102. Mancini D, Henson D, LaManca J, et al: Respiratory muscle function and dyspnea in patients with chronic congestive heart failure. Circulation 86:909–918, 1992.

103. Ambrosino N, Opasich C, Crotti P, et al: Breathing pattern, ventilatory drive and respiratory muscle strength in chronic heart failure. Eur Respir J 7:17–22, 1994.

104. Hammond MD, Bauer KA, Sharp JT, et al: Respiratory muscle strength in congestive heart failure. Chest 98:1091–1094, 1990.

105. Meyer FJ, Zugck C, Haass M, et al: Inefficient ventilation and reduced respiratory muscle capacity in congestive heart failure. Basic Res Cardiol 95:333–342, 2000.

106. Meyer FJ, Borst MM, Zugck C, et al: Respiratory muscle dysfunction in congestive heart failure: Clinical correlation and prognostic significance. Circulation 103:2153–2158, 2001.

107. Vescovo G, Serafini F, Dalla Libera L, et al: Skeletal muscle myosin heavy chains in heart failure: Correlation between magnitude of the isozyme shift, exercise capacity, and gas exchange measurements. Am Heart J 135:130–137, 1998.

108. Mancini DM, Henson D, LaManca J, et al: Evidence of reduced muscle endurance in patients with heart failure. J Am Coll Cardiol 24:972–981, 1994.

109. Hughes PD, Hart N, Hamnegård C-H, et al: Inspiratory muscle relaxation rate slows during exhaustive treadmill walking in patients with chronic heart failure. Am J Respir Crit Care Med 163:1400–1403, 2001.

109a. Hart N, Kearney MT, Pride NB, et al: Inspiratory muscle load and capacity in chronic heart failure. Thorax 59:477–482, 2004.

110. Ambrosino N, Bruschi C, Callegari G, et al: Time course of exercise capacity, skeletal and respiratory muscle performance after heart-lung transplantation. Eur Respir J 9:1508–1514, 1996.

111. Stassijns G, Lysens R, Decramer M: Peripheral and respiratory muscles in chronic heart failure. Eur Respir J 9:2161–2167, 1996.

112. Piepoli M, Clark AL, Volterrani M, et al: Contribution of muscle afferents to the hemodynamic, autonomic and ventilatory responses to exercise in patients with chronic heart failure. Circulation 93:940–952, 1996.

113. Tikunov B, Levine S, Mancini D: Chronic congestive heart failure elicits adaptations of endurance exercise in diaphragmatic muscle. Circulation 95:910–916, 1997.

114. Bussieres LM, Pflugfelder PW, Taylor AW, et al: Changes in skeletal muscle morphology and biochemistry after cardiac transplantation. Am J Cardiol 79:630–634, 1997.

115. Richard R, Verdier JC, Duvallet A, et al: Chronotropic competence in endurance trained heart transplant recipients: Heart rate is not a limiting factor for exercise capacity. J Am Coll Cardiol 33:192–197, 1999.

116. Pain MCF, Stannard M, Sloman G: Disturbances of pulmonary function after acute myocardial infarction. Br Med J 2:591–594, 1967.

117. Alexander MSM, Arnot RN, Lavender JP: Left lower lobe ventilation and its relation to cardiomegaly and posture. BMJ 229:94, 1989.

118. Wiener C, Henderson B, McKenna WJ, et al: Left lower lobe ventilation is reduced in patients with cardiomegaly in the supine but not the prone position. Am Rev Respir Dis 141:150–155, 1990.

119. Leung RS, Bowman ME, Parker JD, et al: Avoidance of the left lateral decubitus position during sleep in patients with heart failure: Relationship to cardiac size and function. J Am Coll Cardiol 41:227–230, 2003.

120. Fillmore SJ, Shapiro M, Killip T: Arterial oxygen tension in acute myocardial infarction: Serial analysis of clinical state and blood gas changes. Am Heart J 79:620–629, 1976.

121. Franciosa JA, Leddy CL, Wilen M, et al: Relation between hemodynamic and ventilatory responses in determining exercise capacity in severe congestive heart failure. Am J Cardiol 53:127–134, 1985.

122. Scheinman MM, Evans GT: Right to left shunt in patients with acute myocardial infarction. Am J Cardiol 29:757–766, 1972.

123. Rubin SA, Brown HA, Swan HJC: Arterial oxygenation and arterial oxygen transport in chronic myocardial failure at rest, during exercise and after hydralazine treatment. Circulation 66:143–148, 1982.

124. Wasserman K, Zhang YY, Gitt A, et al: Lung function and exercise gas exchange in chronic heart failure. Circulation 96:2221–2227, 1997.

125. Aguilaniu B, Page E, Peronnet F, et al: Lung function and exercise gas exchange in heart failure. Circulation 98:1043–1044, 1998.

126. Smith AA, Cowburn PJ, Parker ME, et al: Impaired pulmonary diffusion during exercise in patients with chronic heart failure. Circulation 100:1406–1410, 1999.

127. Ville N, Mercier J, Varray A, et al: Exercise tolerance in heart transplant patients with altered pulmonary diffusing capacity. Med Sci Sports Exerc 30:339–344, 1998.

128. Braith RW, Limacher MC, Mills RM Jr, et al: Exercise-induced hypoxemia in heart transplant recipients. J Am Coll Cardiol 22:768–776, 1993.

129. Hughes JMB, Lockwood DNA, Jones HA, et al: D/Q and diffusion limitation at rest and on exercise in patients with interstitial fibrosis. Respir Physiol 83:155–166, 1991.

130. Al-Rawas OA, Carter R, Richens D, et al: Ventilatory and gas exchange abnormalities on exercise in chronic heart failure. Eur Respir J 8:2022–2028, 1995.

131. O'Donnell DE, D'Arsigny C, Abdollah H, et al: Ventilatory assistance improves exercise endurance in stable congestive heart failure. Am J Respir Crit Care Med 160:1804–1811, 1999.

132. West JB: Ventilation-perfusion inequality and overall gas exchange in computer models of the lung. Respir Physiol 7:88–110, 1969.

133. Mandak JS, Aaronson KD, Mancini DM: Serial assessment of exercise capacity after heart transplantation. J Heart Lung Transplant 14:468–478, 1995.

134. Givertz MM, Hartley LH, Colucci WS: Long-term sequential changes in exercise capacity and chronotropic responsiveness after cardiac transplantation. Circulation 96:232–237, 1997.

135. Marconi C, Marzorati M: Exercise after heart transplantation. Eur J Appl Physiol 90:250–259, 2003.

136. Restrick LJ, Davies SW, Noone L, et al: Ambulatory oxygen in chronic heart failure. Lancet 340:1192–1193, 1992.

137. Moore DP, Weston AR, Hughes JMB, et al: Effects of increased inspired oxygen concentrations on exercise performance in chronic heart failure. Lancet 339:850–853, 1992.

138. Chua TP, Ponikowski PP, Harrington D, et al: Contribution of peripheral chemoreceptors to ventilation and the effects of their suppression on exercise tolerance in chronic heart failure. Heart 76:483–489, 1996.

139. Russell SD, Koshkarian GM, Medinger AE, et al: Lack of effect of increased inspired oxygen concentrations on maximal exercise capacity or ventilation in stable heart failure. Am J Cardiol 84:1412–1416, 1999.

140. McCloskey DI, Mitchell JH: Reflex cardiovascular and respiratory responses originating in exercising muscle. J Physiol (Lond) 224:173–186, 1972.

141. Scott AC, Wensel R, Davos CH, et al: Chemical mediators of the muscle ergoreflex in chronic heart failure: A putative role for prostaglandins in reflex ventilatory control. Circulation 106:214–220, 2002.

141a. Scott AC, Wensel R, Davos CH, et al: Putative contribution of prostaglandin and bradykinin to muscle reflex hyperactivity in patients on ACE–inhibitor therapy for chronic heart failure. Eur Heart J 25:1806–1813, 2004.

142. Scott AC, Wensel R, Davos CH, et al: Skeletal muscle reflex in heart failure patients: Role of hydrogen. Circulation 107:300–306, 2003.

143. Drexler H, Riede U, Munzel T, et al: Alterations of skeletal muscle in chronic heart failure. Circulation 85:1751–1759, 1992.

144. Sullivan MJ, Green HJ, Cobb FR: Skeletal muscle biochemistry and histology in ambulatory patients with long-term heart failure. Circulation 81:518–527, 1990.

145. Massie BM, Conway M, Rajagopalan B, et al: Skeletal muscle metabolism during exercise under ischemic conditions in congestive heart failure. Circulation 78:320–326, 1988.

146. Sullivan MJ, Higginbotham MB, Cobb FR: Exercise training in patients with severe left ventricular dysfunction. Circulation 78:506–515, 1988.

147. Coats AJS, Adamopoulos S, Radaelli A, et al: Controlled trial of physical training in chronic heart failure. Circulation 85:2119–2131, 1992.

148. Hambrecht R, Niebauer J, Fiehn E, et al: Physical training in patients with chronic stable heart failure: Effects on cardiorespiratory fitness and ultrastructural abnormalities of leg muscles. J Am Coll Cardiol 25:1239–1249, 1995.

149. Anker SD, Chua TP, Ponikowski P, et al: Hormonal changes and catabolic/anabolic imbalance in chronic heart failure and their importance for cardiac cachexia. Circulation 96:526–534, 1997.

150. Coats AJS: Heart failure: What causes the symptoms of heart failure? Heart 86:574–578, 2001.

151. Kleber FX, Vietzke G, Wernecke KD, et al: Impairment of ventilatory efficiency in heart failure: Prognostic impact. Circulation 101:2803–2809, 2000.

152. Gitt AK, Wasserman K, Kilkowski C, et al: Exercise anaerobic threshold and ventilatory efficiency identify heart failure patients for high risk of early death. Circulation 106:3079–3084, 2002.

152a. Guazzi M, Reina G, Tumminello G, et al: Exercise ventilation inefficiency and cardiovascular mortality in heart failure: the critical independent prognostic value of the arterial CO_2 partial pressure. Eur Heart J 2005, in press.

153. Robbins M, Francis G, Pashkow FJ, et al: Ventilatory and heart rate responses to exercise: Better predictors of heart failure mortality than peak oxygen consumption. Circulation 100:2411–2417, 1999.

154. Pardaens K, Van Cleemput J, Vanhaecke J, et al: Peak oxygen uptake better predicts outcome than submaximal data in heart transplant candidates. Circulation 101:1152–1157, 2000.

155. Solin P, Bergin P, Richardson M, et al: Influence of pulmonary capillary wedge pressure on central apnea in heart failure. Circulation 99:1574–1579, 1999.

156. Lanfranchi PA, Braghivoli A, Bosimini E, et al: Prognostic value of nocturnal Cheyne-Stokes respiration in chronic heart failure. Circulation 99:1435–1440, 1999.

157. Javaheri S: A mechanism of central sleep apnea in patients with heart failure. N Engl J Med 341:949–954, 1999.

158. Solin P, Roebuck T, Johns DP, et al: Peripheral and central ventilatory responses in central sleep apnea with and without congestive heart failure. Am J Respir Crit Care Med 162:2194–2200, 2000.

159. Xie A, Skatrud JB, Puleo DS, et al: Apnea-hypopnea threshold for CO_2 in patients with congestive heart failure. Am J Respir Crit Care Med 165:1245–1250, 2002.

160. Khayat RN, Xie A, Patel AK, et al: Cardiorespiratory effects of added dead space in patients with heart failure and central sleep apnea. Chest 123:1551–1560, 2003.

161. Naughton MT, Bradley TD: Sleep apnea in congestive heart failure. Clin Chest Med 19:99–113, 1998.

162. Javaheri S, Parker TJ, Liming JD: Sleep apnea in 81 ambulatory patients with stable heart failure. Circulation 97:2145–2159, 1998.

163. Paintal AS: Mechanism of stimulation of type J pulmonary receptors. J Physiol (Lond) 203:511–532, 1969.

164. Wead WB, Cassidy SS, Coast JR, et al: Reflex cardiorespiratory responses to pulmonary vascular congestion. J Appl Physiol 62:870–879, 1987.

165. Christie RV, Meakins JC: The intrapleural pressure in congestive heart failure and its clinical significance. J Clin Invest 13:323–345, 1934.

166. Russell SD, McNeer FR, Higginbotham MB: Exertional dyspnea in heart failure: A symptom unrelated to pulmonary function at rest or during exercise. Am Heart J 135:398–405, 1998.

167. Mancini DM, Ferraro N, Nazzaro D, et al: Respiratory muscle deoxygenation during exercise in patients with heart failure demonstrated with near-infra red spectroscopy. J Am Coll Cardiol 18:492–498, 1995.

168. Lipkin DP, Canepa-Anson R, Stephens MR, et al: Factors determining symptoms in heart failure: Comparison of fast and slow exercise tests. Br Heart J 55:439–445, 1986.

169. Mancini DM, LaManca J, Donchez L, et al: The sensation of dyspnea during exercise is not determined by the work of breathing in patients with heart failure. J Am Coll Cardiol 28:391–395, 1996.

78 Pulmonary Complications of Abdominal Disease

Robert Rodriguez-Roisin, M.D., Joan Albert Barberà, M.D.

INTRODUCTION

This chapter is devoted to the pulmonary complications of abdominal disease and begins with a discussion of the most relevant esophageal and bowel disorders. Then the lung-liver syndromes and the specific liver disorders associated with particular pulmonary complications are reviewed. Finally, the respiratory consequences of diseases of the pancreas and kidney are described. The objective in each section is the same: to update the most relevant clinical, pathophysiologic, pathogenetic, and therapeutic aspects of the principal abdominal disease states and thereby assist the clinician in diagnosing and managing their sometimes complex and challenging pulmonary complications.

GASTROESOPHAGEAL AND GASTROINTESTINAL DISORDERS

GASTROESOPHAGEAL REFLUX

Gastroesophageal reflux is defined as the retrograde movement of gastric contents into the esophagus. Gastroesophageal reflux is common, with more than one third of the population having intermittent complaints of this disorder.[1] Gastroesophageal reflux has long been associated with respiratory symptoms and diseases. These range from overt aspiration pneumonia to more chronic insidious respiratory disorders in which the relationship with gastroesophageal reflux is often difficult to establish. The latter subset includes some forms of bronchitis, bronchiectasis, pulmonary fibrosis, asthma, and chronic cough. The association of gastroesophageal reflux with asthma and chronic cough has been clearly documented, and the possible coexistence of gastroesophageal reflux must be considered especially in patients with refractory cough or wheezing.[2-4]

The prevalence of gastroesophageal reflux in patients with asthma is greater than in the general population. Approximately, 75% of asthmatics have reflux symptoms,[4] although the prevalence depends on the technique used to document gastroesophageal reflux. Using esophageal manometry and 24-hour ambulatory esophageal pH monitoring, Sontag and colleagues[5] observed that 82% of asthmatics had abnormal amounts of acid reflux. Furthermore, the use of 24-hour ambulatory esophageal pH monitoring revealed that gastroesophageal reflux may be the cause of chronic cough in up to 40% of patients with the symptom.[6,7] It is also important to note that patients with asthma or chronic cough can have significant reflux without describing classic reflux symptoms. Irwin and associates[8] reported that gastroesophageal reflux was clinically silent in 24% of patients with difficult-to-control asthma.

Pathogenesis

The pathogenesis of respiratory abnormalities associated with gastroesophageal reflux can be divided into three basic mechanisms. First, gross aspiration–linked pulmonary syndromes are usually the result of free esophageal reflux with large-volume retrograde flow. Frequently, there is reduced basal lower esophageal tone and impaired esophageal motility and clearance.[9] These patients may have recurrent pneumonia, bronchiectasis, or pulmonary infiltrates. The endoscopic examination usually reveals severe anatomic changes, such as grade 3 or 4 esophagitis or Barrett's epithelialization of the mucosa.

A second pathogenic mechanism is related to the microaspiration of gastric contents from the proximal (upper) esophagus. This results from small-volume aspirates that produce an exudative mucosal reaction in the larynx and in the tracheobronchial tree. Respiratory symptoms are less apparent and range from hoarseness or chronic cough to difficult-to-control asthma. Jack and coworkers,[10] using simultaneous tracheal and esophageal pH measurements in asthmatics with gastroesophageal reflux, showed that episodes of reflux that were followed by a fall in intratracheal pH resulted in a marked fall in peak expiratory flow rate (PEFR), which was several times greater than that observed when reflux was not followed by tracheal aspiration (Fig. 78.1). This indicates that microaspiration into the bronchial tree not only occurs but induces an important increase in airway resistance. Nevertheless, reflux episodes that do not reach the upper sphincter, and hence are without aspiration, may also induce changes in airway resistance.

The third pathogenic mechanism is produced by gastroesophageal reflux activation of a vagal reflex between the distal (lower) esophagus and the tracheobronchial tree. This reflex mechanism has been described both in patients with bronchial asthma and in those with persistent cough. It was first suggested by Mansfield and Stein,[11] who demonstrated in patients with asthma that the infusion of hydrochloric acid into the esophagus induced an increase in airflow resistance that was rapidly reversed by antacids. These changes occurred even with maximal bronchodilator therapy. In a later study in a canine model, a similar increase in airflow resistance that disappeared after bilateral interruption of the vagal nerves was reported,[12] indicating that it was a vagally mediated mechanism. Supporting the role of a vagal reflex in gastroesophageal reflux–induced bronchoconstriction are the results of Wright and colleagues,[13] who showed that the decrement in FEV_1 induced by acid infusion into the esophagus was abolished by pretreatment with intramuscular atropine.

However, not all asthmatic patients show significant changes in airflow resistance after esophageal acid infusion.[14] Mansfield and Stein[11] noted that the increase in airway resistance elicited by esophageal acid infusion was present only in those asthmatics with evidence of esophagitis, suggesting that prior esophageal mucosal injury is

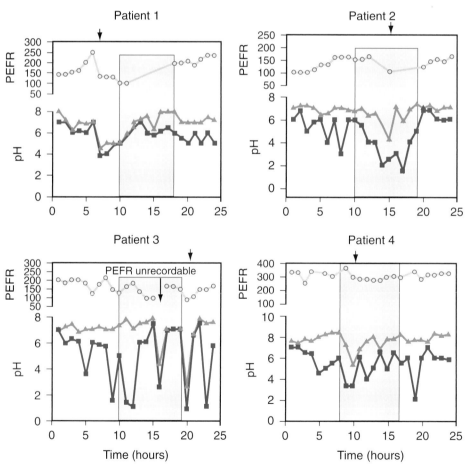

Figure 78.1 Graphs showing simultaneous esophageal (*solid squares*) and tracheal (*solid triangles*) pH measurements in four patients with both gastroesophageal reflux and asthma, along with recordings of peak expiratory flow rate (PEFR), over a 24-hour period. There were 37 significant falls in esophageal pH suggestive of gastroesophageal reflux. Five of these episodes were followed by a fall in tracheal pH and were associated with a significant decrease in PEFR (mean change −84 ± 16 L/min), whereas during the remaining 32 episodes of gastroesophageal reflux without tracheal aspiration the mean change in PEFR was minimal (−8 ± 4 L/min). *Arrows* show representative episodes. (From Jack CI, Calverley PMA, Donnelly RJ, et al: Simultaneous tracheal and oesophageal pH measurements in asthmatic patients with gastro-oesophageal reflux. Thorax 50:201–204, 1995.)

necessary to elicit acid-induced changes in airway resistance. Studies using dual-electrode esophageal pH testing seem to confirm this observation. In a study by Schan and co-workers,[15] PEFR decreased after esophageal acid infusion in control subjects, asthmatics with gastroesophageal reflux, asthmatics without gastroesophageal reflux, and subjects with gastroesophageal reflux alone; however, esophageal acid clearance improved PEFR in all groups except the asthmatics with gastroesophageal reflux, who had a further decrease in PEFR. The drop in PEFR did not depend on acid exposure of the upper esophagus, a prerequisite for microaspiration, and was partially reversed by vagolytic doses of intravenous atropine, implying the importance of a vagally mediated reflex.[3] The stimulation of acid-sensitive esophageal receptors may also enhance bronchial hyperre-activity, as shown by Hervé and colleagues,[16] who demonstrated a reduction in the dose of methacholine required to induce a fall in FEV_1 of 20% after esophageal acid infusion. Similarly, the vagus nerve may also play a role in the bronchoconstriction induced by microaspiration. In a cat model, Tuchman and coworkers[17] showed that the increase in lung resistance induced by intratracheal infusion of acid, which was several times greater than that induced by intraesophageal infusion, was abolished after bilateral vagotomy. The logical conclusions from these observations are that gastroesophageal reflux may induce bronchial changes via a vagally mediated reflex originating in the lower esophagus and that these effects are further amplified if reflux reaches the upper esophagus and microaspiration occurs.

The relationship between gastroesophageal reflux and respiratory disorders is further complicated by the fact that physiologic alterations associated with asthma or cough, or with bronchodilator therapy, may themselves promote gastroesophageal reflux. Episodes of bronchospasm and cough are accompanied by an increase in the negative pressure within the thorax, and hence in the esophagus, that may promote reflux. In addition, hyperinflation and "air trapping" may lead to flattening of the diaphragm, allowing the lower esophageal sphincter to be drawn up into the thorax, impairing the antireflux barrier. Bronchodilator therapy may also promote gastroesophageal reflux. Theophylline increases gastric acid secretion and decreases lower esophageal sphincter tone. Indeed, asthmatics with gastroesophageal reflux who receive theophylline show an increase in esophageal acid exposure and reflux symptoms.[18] Specific β-adrenergic agents relax smooth muscle tone throughout the body and thereby may promote gastroesophageal reflux. A decrease in lower esophageal sphincter pressure has been shown with β-adrenergic drugs administered orally or intravenously,[19] but not when these agents were given by inhalation.[20]

Diagnosis

The possibility of associated gastroesophageal reflux should be suspected in patients with refractory chronic cough or difficult-to-treat asthma.[4,21] Patients should be questioned about symptoms of gastroesophageal reflux, which include heartburn, regurgitation, or dysphagia. However, some patients may complain of atypical symptoms, including substernal chest pain, hoarseness, sore throat, otalgia, hiccups, teeth erosion, or a feeling of a "lump in the throat" (globus

sensation).[1] It is also important to record whether asthma or cough worsens with recumbency, after meals, or during alcohol ingestion. If the clinical history is typical of gastroesophageal reflux, no further diagnostic workup may be necessary and a trial of antireflux therapy will often confirm that the symptoms are due to acid reflux.

However, gastroesophageal reflux may be clinically silent in a number of patients. If dysphagia is present, a barium radiographic study should be performed in order to rule out esophageal obstruction or obvious motility abnormalities. In asymptomatic cases or when symptoms are atypical, ambulatory esophageal pH monitoring is the procedure of choice because of its high sensitivity and specificity to detect gastroesophageal reflux. However, demonstration of reflux by pH monitoring shows an association but not always a cause-and-effect relationship.[2,22,23] It has been proposed that, if respiratory symptoms and acid reflux episodes occur together more than 75% of the time, then the probability of a causal association is high.[23-25] If symptoms persist despite adequate treatment, an additional pH monitoring study with a dual intragastric and esophageal probe should be performed while the patient remains on therapy. If distal esophageal acid exposure continues, pharmacologic treatment should be increased.[1] On the contrary, if there is no esophageal acid exposure and the intragastric pH is greater than 4 more than 50% of the time, an alternative diagnosis for symptom persistence should be pursued. Endoscopy is indicated for those patients in whom complicated gastroesophageal reflux (e.g., esophagitis, Barrett's esophagus) is suspected.[3]

Treatment

Therapy for gastrointestinal reflux should be instituted by recommending several changes in lifestyle, such as raising the head of the bed, avoiding meals before bedtime, eating low-fat foods, reducing body weight, and eliminating caffeine and alcohol. Pharmacologic strategies for treating gastroesophageal reflux include antacids, which can be used for symptomatic relief; histamine receptor blockers (cimetidine, ranitidine, famotidine), which partially block gastric acid secretion; proton pump inhibitors (omeprazole, lansoprazole),[24] which directly inhibit gastric acid secretion; and prokinetic agents (cisapride, domperidone), which improve esophageal contractility, increase lower esophageal sphincter pressure, and increase gastric emptying. Surgical interventions include the Nissen-Toupet-Belsey fundoplication and the Hill gastropexy. Larrain and colleagues[25] evaluated the long-term effects of surgery or cimetidine compared with placebo; after 5 years, only the patients treated with surgery were free of symptoms, whereas those treated with cimetidine or placebo had persistent clinical abnormalities. Laparoscopic antireflux surgery has been developed and was shown to be effective in a series of 195 patients, all of whom had failed to respond to omeprazole.[26]

A recommended approach for treating patients with respiratory complications of gastroesophageal reflux would be to start with empirical therapy that includes both conservative antireflux measures and acid-suppressive therapy.[27] Administration of high doses of proton pump inhibitors (e.g., omeprazole, 20 mg twice a day; or lansoprazole, 30 mg twice a day) for 3 months is recommended, because some patients treated with lower doses or with histamine receptor blockers may not show adequate acid suppression.[3,28,29] If the patient's condition improves, then long-term therapy should be considered. Maintenance therapy can include a histamine receptor blocker or a proton pump inhibitor at the lowest dose necessary to control symptoms, a level that must be determined individually. A prokinetic agent can be added. In patients not responding to the initial trial and in those who report only partial improvement of their symptoms, ambulatory pH testing under acid-suppressive therapy is indicated. If symptoms persist and there is no evidence of esophageal reflux, the test is considered negative and respiratory symptoms are unlikely to be caused by gastroesophageal reflux. If the test confirms the persistence of reflux, then surgery should be considered.[20,30] Furthermore, the surgical option should be discussed with all patients who require a proton pump inhibitor to control gastroesophageal reflux, especially young patients, because there are still unanswered questions about the long-term safety of these drugs.[3,23]

INFLAMMATORY BOWEL DISEASE

Inflammatory bowel disease has been associated with a variety of extraintestinal manifestations, although pulmonary complications are considered to be infrequent. In an analysis of 1400 patients with inflammatory bowel disease, Rogers and colleagues[31] identified only 6 patients (0.4%) who had unexplained concurrent pulmonary disease. Nevertheless, the prevalence of pulmonary involvement in patients with inflammatory bowel disease may be higher than indicated by Rogers and colleagues, because pulmonary function abnormalities have been reported in a significant number of patients in the absence of respiratory symptoms.[32–36]

Most of the reported patients with pulmonary complications associated with inflammatory bowel disease had ulcerative colitis (88%),[37] and the remainder had Crohn's disease. Respiratory involvement can occur at any age and seems to be more prevalent in women than in men. Frequently, respiratory complications are associated with other extraintestinal manifestations, such as arthritis, skin changes, or pericarditis. In most cases, respiratory symptoms develop after the diagnosis of inflammatory bowel disease has been made, frequently several years afterward. Nonetheless, in some cases respiratory symptoms antedate or are concomitant with those of the bowel disease.[37]

Various patterns of respiratory impairment in inflammatory bowel disease have been described (Table 78.1).[36,37] The one most frequently observed is airway disease (51% of cases).[37] Unexplained purulent bronchitis, with or without bronchiectasis, in patients with inflammatory bowel disease was first reported by Kraft and associates[38] in 1976. Subsequent studies confirmed this association.[37,39,40] Unexplained productive cough is the predominant symptom; in some instances, it developed dramatically after proctocolectomy.[37] Involvement of the airways can occur at various levels of the tracheobronchial tree and can take the form of tracheal stenosis, chronic bronchitis, bronchiectasis, or bronchiolitis (see Table 78.1). Endoscopic examination shows marked erythema, swelling of the mucosa, and deformation of the airway lumen. Biopsy specimens have revealed mucosal

Table 78.1 Patterns of Respiratory Involvement in Inflammatory Bowel Disease

Disease Type	No. of Cases	%
Airway disease		
Subglottic stenosis	6	5.7
Chronic bronchitis	18	17.0
Chronic bronchial suppuration	7	6.6
Bronchiectasis	20	18.9
Chronic bronchiolitis	3	2.8
Interstitial lung disease		
BOOP	11	10.4
ILD–pulmonary sarcoidosis	16	15.1
Pulmonary infiltrates and eosinophilia	3	2.8
Necrotic nodules	5	4.7
Pleural disease		
Pleural effusion	4	3.8
Pleuropericarditis	13	12.3
TOTAL	106	100.1

BOOP, bronchiolitis obliterans with organizing pneumonia; ILD, interstitial lung disease.
From Camus P, Piard F, Ashcroft T, et al: The lung in inflammatory bowel disease. Medicine (Baltimore) 72:151–183, 1993.

ulceration, thickening of the basement membrane, and marked infiltration by neutrophils and plasma cells.[37,40] Some authors have found histologic similarities between the inflammatory infiltrate of the airways and that of the colon, suggesting that the bronchial disease may result from a common abnormality in immune regulation that affects both the bowel and the bronchial tree, organs with a common embryologic origin.[37–40] Pulmonary function testing in patients with airway involvement usually reveals an obstructive ventilatory defect.[40] One study demonstrated small airway dysfunction (obstruction) in patients with ulcerative colitis who had normal spirometric measurements, suggesting that subclinical abnormalities in the airways may be more prevalent than suspected in these patients.[35,36] In some cases, the inflammatory process in the subglottic area can take the form of pseudotumoral lesions, with the potential of producing life-threatening acute upper airway obstruction requiring aggressive airway management.[37,41]

Interstitial lung disease associated with inflammatory bowel disease has been less frequently observed (28% of cases).[37] Yet, such an association has occasionally been reported with other interstitial disorders, such as bronchiolitis obliterans with organizing pneumonia,[37] sarcoidosis, and desquamative interstitial pneumonitis, and in the form of the syndrome of pulmonary infiltrates and eosinophilia.[37,42] Because drugs used to treat ulcerative colitis and Crohn's disease (e.g., sulfasalazine, 5-aminosalicylic acid) may also induce interstitial pulmonary disease (e.g., bronchiolitis obliterans with organizing pneumonia, pulmonary infiltrates and eosinophilia),[37,42] it can be difficult to establish whether the pulmonary involvement is a result of the treatment or of the disease itself. Nonetheless, interstitial lung disorders have been reported in untreated patients, indicating that such an association may occur without exposure to drugs. A reduction in carbon monoxide diffusing capacity (DL_{CO}) during the active phases of the inflammatory bowel disease has been reported,[42] which also suggests that subclinical pulmonary parenchymal involvement may be more prevalent than previously suspected. Furthermore, bronchoalveolar lavage examination in patients with Crohn's disease revealed the presence of a lymphocytic alveolitis, chiefly owing to an increase of CD4-positive T lymphocytes, in patients who did not have clinical evidence of pulmonary involvement.[42]

Necrobiotic nodules, corresponding histologically to aggregates of neutrophils with areas of necrosis, have been reported in a few patients.[37] Serositis affecting the pleura or the pericardium, or both, has been reported in a small number of cases, especially during the periods of increased disease activity.[37]

Colobronchial fistulas have been reported in some cases of Crohn's disease, the majority of them presenting with left lower pneumonia.[36] Involvement of the esophagus is rare in Crohn's disease, but four cases of bronchoesophageal fistula associated with esophageal Crohn's disease have been reported.[36] Although conservative treatment can be attempted, the majority of cases with fistulas will require surgical treatment.

In the majority of patients with pulmonary disorders associated with inflammatory bowel disease, glucocorticosteroids given by inhalation or by mouth usually result in a rapid control of symptoms,[37,39,40] especially in those patients who do not have severe structural impairment (e.g., bronchiectasis). Lung transplantation has been performed in some cases of severe respiratory compromise.[37]

HEPATIC DISEASES

PLEURAL EFFUSION

Between 5% and 10% of patients with cirrhosis of the liver develop pleural effusion, traditionally referred to as *hepatic hydrothorax,* in the absence of a coexisting cardiopulmonary disease. (For further discussion of hepatic hydrothorax, see Chapter 68). This effusion is a transudate unless the pleural fluid is complicated by an infection. Although pleural effusions, which are most commonly located in the right hemithorax but which may also be left-sided or bilateral, are strongly associated with pronounced ascites, there are patients in whom ascites is almost undetectable. The effusion is usually mild to moderate in size and asymptomatic, but in some cases it can be massive and provoke shortness of breath.[43] The mechanism is basically related to the presence of communications (usually small diaphragmatic defects) and to the pressure gradient between the abdominal and pleural cavities that facilitates the movement of the liquid into the chest. The presence of pleural fluid disturbs lung mechanics, resulting in decreased lung volumes and pulmonary compliance. Accordingly, pulmonary gas exchange becomes abnormal and leads to moderate hypoxemia and an increased alveolar-arterial PO_2 gradient (($A - a)PO_2$), caused by both slight right-to-left intrapulmonary shunt and mild ventilation-perfusion imbalance. Either because of lasting effects of the effusion or because of coexistent hepatopulmonary syndrome (see later), these abnormalities do not easily reverse after thoracentesis.[44]

The clinical management of pleural effusion in the context of liver disease is often rather difficult. Repeated thoracenteses will have transitory effects only, and thoracic drainage may result in substantial protein loss. The use of transjugular intrahepatic portosystemic shunting to decrease portal hypertension, which in turn could reduce the size of the hydrothorax, seems to be more promising, at least in the short term.[45] If the patient is not a candidate for shunting, other approaches, including video-assisted thoracoscopic surgery to repair diaphragmatic defects and induce a pleurodesis, may also be considered (see Chapter 68).

PULMONARY FUNCTION DISTURBANCES

The most common lung function abnormality in patients with end-stage hepatic disease is a decreased DL_{CO}; likewise, both obstructive and restrictive ventilatory defects have been observed.[46] The coexistence of massive ascites can decrease lung compliance, increase pleural pressure, and reduce diaphragmatic motility. Together, these pathophysiologic alterations restrict ventilatory capacity and reduce the efficiency of gas exchange, causing increased ($A - a)PO_2$ values with or without associated hypoxemia.[47]

HEPATOPULMONARY SYNDROME

Mild to moderate arterial hypoxemia is relatively common in the setting of chronic liver diseases. Yet, unless intrinsic cardiopulmonary disease is present, severe hypoxemia (arterial $PO_2 < 60$ mm Hg) is not common.[48–50] Accordingly, the presence of severe hypoxemia in a patient with chronic hepatic disease without cardiopulmonary disease should strongly suggest hepatopulmonary syndrome (HPS). Because patients with advanced liver disorders characteristically hyperventilate and are hypocapnic, measurement of the ($A - a)PO_2$ becomes the most sensitive way to detect gas-exchange disturbances in HPS.

HPS is defined as a syndrome characterized by a clinical triad: advanced chronic liver disease; arterial oxygenation defect, which ultimately leads to severe arterial hypoxemia; and widespread intrapulmonary vascular dilations.[51,52] The pulmonary gas-exchange disturbance is characterized by arterial oxygen desaturation that may be mild, moderate, or severe. There is an increased ($A - a)PO_2$, commonly associated with hypocapnia and respiratory alkalosis.[52] At sea level, while breathing room air, resting ($A - a)PO_2$ values equal to or above 15 mm Hg can be considered abnormal, and, for patients older than 64 years, an ($A - a)PO_2$ equal to or above 20 mm Hg can be considered abnormal.[52] Although HPS is more prevalent in patients with all categories of hepatic cirrhosis, it also occurs in those with other common chronic liver diseases, such as chronic active hepatitis. In rare cases, HPS has been documented in other unusual liver disorders (noncirrhotic portal hypertension, alpha$_1$-antitrypsin deficiency, and Budd-Chiari syndrome).[53] Nevertheless, the term hepatopulmonary syndrome does not encompass all pleuropulmonary disorders that may coexist with liver disorders. At present, there is a special clinical interest in HPS because of its high prevalence (an estimated 20% in some series) among patients with end-stage hepatic disease, its

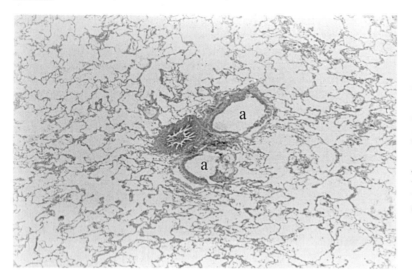

Figure 78.2 Photomicrograph of a lung biopsy from a patient with hepatopulmonary syndrome. Note the central presence of dilated pulmonary arteries (a) with a neighboring normal terminal bronchiole surrounded by an otherwise structurally intact pulmonary architecture. (Original magnification ×100.) (From Rodriguez-Roisin R, Roca J: Hepatopulmonary syndrome: The paradigm of liver-induced hypoxaemia. Ballieres Clin Gastroenterol 11:387–406, 1997.) (Courtesy of Dr. J. Ramírez, Hospital Clínic, Universitat de Barcelona, Barcelona.)

life-threatening nature, the lack of beneficial medical therapy, and its unique improvement or full resolution after liver transplantation in more than 80% of the reported cases.[50,52]

The most conspicuous pathologic finding is a pronounced vasodilation of all peripheral branches of the pulmonary vasculature, at both the precapillary and capillary levels of the lung (15 to 150 µm in diameter), near the gas-exchange area.[54] Widespread intrapulmonary vasodilation is present in an otherwise intact pulmonary parenchyma (Fig. 78.2).

Pathogenesis

Pathogenically, it can be hypothesized that chronic liver disease associated with portal hypertension and perhaps with portosystemic shunting may lead to hepatic failure, thereby inducing widespread vasodilation and a hyperkinetic state that results ultimately in HPS. Yet, the precise mechanism underlying HPS remains uncertain despite numerous investigations. Whether the mechanism of hemodynamic disturbances is related to failure of metabolism, to insufficient production of one or more circulating vasoactive substances by the injured liver, or to altered clearance of some of the vasodilator molecules produced by endothelial cells[55] remains concealed. Circulating humoral vasodilating substances such as glucagon and prostacyclin have been investigated and may contribute to the development of vascular abnormalities in patients with chronic hepatitis, including a blunted hypoxic pulmonary vasoconstrictor response. However, clear evidence of their involvement in HPS is not available.[56,57]

Nitric oxide (NO), a ubiquitous biologic agent considered to be a "fine-tuner" of vascular tone, has been presumed to be a pivotal signaling molecule of potential importance in the pathobiology of HPS.[58,59] Persistent induction of NO synthase (NOS) could account for the hyperkinetic circulatory hallmarks of HPS.[59] Both a constitutive isoform of NOS, expressed in endothelial cells (eNOS, or type III NOS),[60] and the inducible NOS (iNOS, or type II NOS), expressed in target tissues such as human bronchial epithelial cells after exposure to proinflammatory

cytokines,[61] have been implicated in experimental models in the pathogenesis of HPS. In keeping with this contention, increased levels of exhaled NO have been observed in patients with advanced hepatic cirrhosis and in those with HPS.[62,63] Moreover, there have been significant decrements in exhaled NO after interventions such as administration of methylene blue, which blocks the guanylate cyclase by which NO may mediate vasodilation,[64] or performance of liver transplantation.[65,66] More recently, it was shown in patients with liver cirrhosis that there are close correlations between exhaled NO concentration and Child-Pugh score, alkaline phosphatase, bilirubin, aspartate and alanine aminotransferases, and albumin, suggesting that NO formation in the lung may be triggered by stimulating factors normally inactivated by the liver.[64] Recent work suggests that endothelin-1 and tumor necrosis factor-α can both interact in the development of experimental HPS.[52,66a,66b]

Clinically, most of the patients with HPS are cyanotic, show conspicuous finger clubbing, may complain of shortness of breath and platypnea (increased dyspnea in the upright position relieved by recumbency), and have a hyperkinetic circulation. The majority of the patients exhibit the typical clinical and functional stigmata of advanced liver failure, including those of portal hypertension; in a few cases, severe pulmonary abnormalities may antedate those of hepatic dysfunction.[50,51] The presence of abundant cutaneous spider angiomata has been postulated as a clinical marker of the severity of both systemic and pulmonary circulatory and gas-exchange abnormalities observed in HPS.[67] The more severe the hepatic failure, the greater the severity of HPS, as suggested by a prospective study in cirrhotic patients in which the hypoxemic subpopulation exhibited more severe liver failure as well as higher Child-Pugh scores and hepatic venous pressure gradients.[68] Unlike the case in hereditary hemorrhagic telangiectasia and other pulmonary arteriovenous malformations (see Chapter 50), hemoptysis and paradoxic emboli are extremely uncommon clinical manifestations of HPS. A single case of brain abscess has been reported.[69] In approximately one third of HPS patients, the syndrome can coexist with other chronic respiratory comorbidities such as chronic obstructive (chronic obstructive pulmonary disease [COPD] or bronchial asthma) or restrictive (i.e., pulmonary fibrosis) respiratory disorders. Nevertheless, the prevailing clinical and functional pulmonary features in patients with such comorbidities are generally those of HPS.[70]

Diagnosis

The diagnostic criteria for HPS are as follows[51]: presence of chronic liver disease; normal or near-normal chest radiograph (e.g., basal medium-sized nodular or reticulonodular opacities); gas-exchange abnormalities, more specifically an increased $(A - a)PO_2$ (≥ 15 mm Hg), with or without concomitant arterial hypoxemia (arterial $PO_2 <$ 80 mm Hg); and a positive contrast-enhanced echocardiogram or an abnormal intravenous radiolabeled perfusion lung scan, or both. Other additional features that can be useful for further establishing the diagnosis of HPS include decreased DL_{CO}, dyspnea with or without platypnea and orthodeoxia (arterial hypoxemia that worsens when the patient is upright compared to recumbent), and a hyperkinetic circulatory state (high cardiac output and low systemic arterial pressures) with normal or low pulmonary artery pressure (PPA). Although thoracic computed tomography scan appears to be nonspecific, it may be useful to exclude coexistent respiratory comorbidities.[52]

Two-dimensional contrast-enhanced echocardiography appears to be the most sensitive and accurate noninvasive diagnostic procedure to identify right-to-left shunts of blood by finding microbubbles of air (or indocyanine green) in the left heart cavities within three to six beats of their visualization in the right-sided chambers[50,51] (Fig. 78.3). Normally, echogenicity in the left chambers is not detected because the intravenously injected microbubbles (60 to 90 µm in diameter) are trapped in the pulmonary capillaries. Contrast-enhanced echocardiography cannot distinguish among the different forms of pulmonary vascular deformities (i.e., precapillary, capillary, and pleural dilations versus direct arteriovenous communications), but it can clearly differentiate them from intracardiac malformations, such as a patent foramen ovale, in which the microbubbles would appear in the left heart almost simultaneously with their appearance in the right. Alternatively, the demonstration of technetium-99m–macroaggregated albumin activity over extrapulmonary organs (e.g., liver, spleen, kidneys, and brain) strongly suggests the presence of right-to-left intrapulmonary shunting, because under normal conditions the albumin macroaggregates (20 to 60 µm in diameter) are trapped in the pulmonary capillary bed. From a pulmonary function viewpoint, the spectrum of gas-exchange abnormalities is wide and includes severe hypoxemia at rest (conventionally measured while breathing room air and in the sitting position), low arterial PCO_2, increased $(A - a)PO_2$,[49] and decreased DL_{CO}. In general, expiratory flow rates and lung volumes are within normal limits.

To date, the exact prevalence of HPS remains unknown. Using contrast-enhanced echocardiography as the "gold standard" tool to identify intrapulmonary vascular dilations, the prevalence of a positive echocardiography test in patients with chronic liver disease is approximately 20%.[49,71] However, the relevance of a positive contrast-enhanced echocardiography result in patients without coexisting gas-exchange disturbances, some of whom may have a normal $(A - a)PO_2$, remains unsettled. These patients are considered to have a *forme fruste* of HPS whose natural history is unknown as yet.[71,72]

Systemic hypotension, a normal or low PPA with normal or low pulmonary vascular resistance (PVR) (<1.5 mm Hg/L per minute),[50] an inordinately high cardiac output, and a reduced pulmonary vascular reactivity are the hemodynamic hallmarks of HPS. When the constellation of hypoxemia, normal or low PPA, and finger clubbing are observed in a patient with advanced liver disease, the

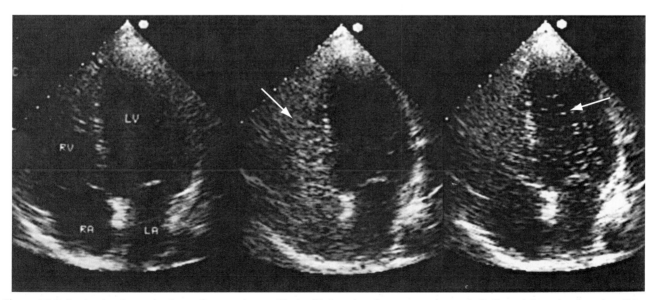

Figure 78.3 Contrast-enhanced echocardiograms in a patient with hepatopulmonary syndrome. *Left,* Normal four-chamber view (LA, left atrium; LV, left ventricle; RA, right atrium; RV, right ventricle). *Center,* Injected microbubbles appear in the RV (*arrow*). *Right,* Within 5 beats, microbubbles appear in the LV (*arrow*). The demonstration of microbubbles in the left cardiac chambers is highly suggestive of the presence of intrapulmonary vascular dilations, or, alternatively, of anatomic arteriovenous malformations. (Courtesy of Dr. C. Paré, Hospital Clínic, Universitat de Barcelona, Barcelona.)

diagnosis of HPS is strongly suggested. Although data describing the natural history of HPS are scant, it appears that HPS patients not undergoing liver transplantation worsen progressively and have an adverse outcome, with median survival of 41 months following diagnosis of HPS.[52] In a recent prospective study, HPS was an independent risk factor for poor prognosis in patients with cirrhosis; those with HPS had a significantly shorter median survival (approximately 11 months) than those without HPS (41 months) even after adjusting for differences in liver disease.[73]

Gas-Exchange Abnormalities

The multiple inert gas elimination technique has been used extensively to investigate the contribution of ventilation-perfusion mismatching to pulmonary gas-exchange abnormalities in patients with HPS, and also in patients with liver cirrhosis and varying degrees of hypoxemia.[67,74–78] When HPS is mild to moderate, the predominant mechanism of hypoxemia is ventilation-perfusion inequality, essentially due to the presence of areas in which ventilation is preserved but perfusion is profoundly increased. In contrast, when HPS is severe, increased intrapulmonary shunt is the primary abnormality. The response of arterial PO_2 to 100% oxygen breathing may be helpful to the clinician to estimate the principal intrapulmonary mechanism of hypoxemia in HPS. If arterial PO_2 remains basically unaltered (below 300 mm Hg) during hyperoxic breathing, the major mechanism of abnormal arterial oxygenation should be a marked right-to-left intrapulmonary shunt, most likely due to the predominance of arteriovenous communications.

Equally important, inert gas studies performed during hypoxic and normoxic conditions have confirmed the presence of reduced pulmonary vasopressor tone, as previously shown,[67,79,80] favoring the development of alveolar units with low ventilation-perfusion ratios. If the site of hypoxic pulmonary vasoconstriction is in small arteries, such as those smaller than 500 µm in diameter, then the vascular derangement observed in HPS must impair the ability of these pulmonary vessels to contract in response to vasoconstricting agents. Collectively, as the severity of the liver dysfunction advances, the greater the systemic and pulmonary vasodilation, the lower the hypoxic pulmonary vascular response, and the greater the degree of ventilation-perfusion inequalities, including increased intrapulmonary shunt.[67,74–78,80a] A "diffusion-perfusion defect" has also been postulated to explain an increased diffusion gradient for oxygen in dilated pulmonary capillaries.[81,82] The contention is that vasodilation causes inadequate diffusion of oxygen to the center of the enlarged capillary. Moreover, the coexistence of a hyperkinetic state and the resulting shorter transit time of red blood cells would exaggerate further this diffusion-induced gas-exchange disturbance.[52]

Treatment

Therapeutically, a vast armamentarium of pharmacologic agents has been tested in patients with HPS, with disappointing results overall. These agents include bismesylate almitrine, cyclophosphamide, garlic preparation, indomethacin, long-term oxygen therapy, methylene blue, propranolol, prostaglandin, and somatostatin.[50–52] In principle, all

these approaches held promise because of their efficacy in enhancing pulmonary vasoconstriction (e.g., bismesylate almitrine) or ablating vasodilation (e.g., propranolol). More aggressive palliative procedures, such as embolization of pulmonary fistulas, portal decompression after transjugular intrahepatic portosystemic shunting, and decompressive treatment of suprahepatic inferior vena cava obstruction in Budd-Chiari syndrome or plasma exchange, have not been successful or have at most shown modest effects that warrant further studies.[52,83] By contrast, orthotopic liver transplantation has proved to be a much more encouraging alternative approach for HPS.[52,84–87] In theory, replacement of the damaged organ should prevent all HPS-induced systemic and pulmonary effects, hence resolving or ameliorating gas-exchange abnormalities. Although a full comprehensive experience with liver transplantation in the setting of HPS is still unclear, it is currently estimated that approximately two thirds of both pediatric and adult patients with HPS show significant clinical and functional respiratory improvement after this radical surgical procedure.[88] Youth, a good arterial PO_2 response to 100% oxygen breathing, and lower presurgical hypoxemia are all factors that seem to predict a favorable response to liver transplantation.[87] Collectively, these elements may indicate a more reactive pulmonary vasculature and less profound intrapulmonary shunt. Recent work indicates that morbidity may be higher after liver transplantation in patients with advanced HPS with arterial PO_2 values below 50 mm Hg and abnormal (>20%) radionuclide extrapulmonary uptake.[89]

PORTOPULMONARY HYPERTENSION

Pulmonary hypertension (PH) associated with portal hypertension or portopulmonary hypertension (POPH) is another mysterious pulmonary vascular disorder that appears to be associated with chronic hepatic disease.[52,87] Because both the diagnosis and the outcome of POPH, particularly in relation to the therapeutic benefits of liver transplantation, appear to be substantially different from those of HPS, it is important to highlight the distinctions between the two disorders.[87,90] Currently, PH is defined as a mean PPA exceeding 25 mm Hg at rest or 30 mm Hg during exercise, in the presence of a mean pulmonary artery occlusion pressure below 15 mm Hg.[52,91,92]

Recent studies from liver transplant centers have indicated a 3.1% to 4.7% frequency of moderate POPH in patients with advanced liver disease.[52,88] Moreover, the interplay among PPA, PVR, and cardiac output in hepatic patients is especially complex. Increases in the pressures within the pulmonary circulation can be caused by three mechanisms, and it is clinically useful, therefore, to characterize the pulmonary hemodynamics that complicate liver disease into three subsets by measured hemodynamic variables.[52,93,94] First is the "hyperdynamic circulatory state" induced by a hyperkinetic circulation in which the increased minimal PPA is predominantly attributable to a high cardiac output due to passive distention of compliant arterial vessels and recruitment of upper lung blood vessels. This subset is most common in liver diseases, including HPS.[93] A second mechanism is manifested by volume increase reflecting excess volume or pressure increase (or both) due to limitation in pulmonary blood flow to the left atrium because of left ventricular dysfunction. This subgroup, called "increased pulmonary venous volume," occurs in alcoholic cirrhosis and combined liver-renal insufficiency. The third scenario, so-called vascular obstruction, represents true POPH, a condition with histologic features identical to those of plexogenic pulmonary arteriopathy (see Chapter 49), including medial hypertrophy, concentric intimal fibrosis, and plexiform lesions of the small arteries, with or without secondary thrombotic changes.[95] As PVR increases, right ventricular hypertrophy and failure ensue, characterized by falling cardiac output. According to a recent European Respiratory Society Task Force,[52] POPH should be suspected in patients with chronic liver disease who have an increased PPA (>25 mm Hg), an increased PVR (>3.0 mm Hg/L per minute or 240 dynes-sec/cm^5), and a normal pulmonary artery occlusion pressure.

In the classic retrospective postmortem studies, the prevalence of histopathologic evidence of PH in patients with liver cirrhosis or POPH (or both) ranged between 0.25% and 0.73%[95]; by contrast, PH was detected in only 0.13% of a noncirrhotic population. These data lend further support to the likelihood of a causal association between the two conditions. Subsequently, two prospective studies identified a higher incidence of PH, about 2%, in patients with chronic liver disease,[96,97] and more recently, two other groups of investigators observed a considerably higher figure, approximately 4%.[88,98] Furthermore, POPH has been classified as a category of secondary PH with hemodynamic criteria consistent with the definitions and classification proposed by the Third World Symposium on Pulmonary Artery Hypertension.[99] In a case-control study conducted by the International Primary Hypertension Study Group to investigate the incidence of primary PH, the condition was found in 7.3% of patients with cirrhosis, 3.1% of those with human immunodeficiency virus infection, 2.1% of those with a family history of primary PH, and none of the controls.[100]

From a histopathologic viewpoint, the vascular lesions are indistinguishable from those identified in primary PH, namely isolated medial hypertrophy, plexogenic pulmonary arteriopathy, and thrombotic pulmonary arteriopathy.[101] According to Hervé and colleagues,[92] vasoconstriction, remodeling of the walls of muscular pulmonary arteries, and in situ microthrombosis combine to increase the vascular resistance in POPH. It is postulated that the portosystemic shunting of vasoactive agents such as thromboxanes, serotonin, bradykinin, and neuropeptide Y, which are normally metabolized by the healthy liver, may result in pulmonary arterial vasoconstriction.[94] As in primary PH, an attractive alternative pathogenic hypothesis that cannot be ruled out is pulmonary endothelial dysfunction, with decreased production of the endogenous vasodilator NO.[94]

The most common symptom is shortness of breath on exertion; chest pain, syncope, and hemoptysis can also occur.[97,102] Radiographically, both an enlarged cardiac silhouette and pulmonary artery prominence are noted in approximately two thirds of patients with hemodynamic confirmation of POPH.[102] Overall, maximal airflow rates and lung volumes are within or near normal limits, whereas DL_{CO}, arterial PO_2, and $(A-a)PO_2$ are reduced, although not to the strikingly low levels observed in HPS.[88,103] Compared with patients with primary PH, the mean PPA is lower

in patients with POPH, and cardiac index and mixed venous oxygen saturation are higher.[92] Contrast-enhanced echocardiography does not show echogenicity in the left-sided cavities unless there is an abnormal communication at the atrial level.[103]

Transthoracic echocardiographic findings (increased tricuspid peak regurgitant jet velocity, pulmonic valve insufficiency, paradoxical septal motion, right ventricular hypertrophy-dilation, and an increased right ventricular systolic pressure estimate) in the setting of portal hypertension suggest, but do not prove, POPH.[50] Accordingly, pulmonary hemodynamics must be measured by right heart catheterization to confirm the diagnosis. Lung biopsy is not advised due to increased risk of bleeding. Because the presence of POPH increases the risk of transplantation, screening for POPH is extremely important when liver transplantation is considered. A retrospective analysis showed that a screening Doppler echocardiography with a right ventricular systolic pressure greater than 50 mm Hg identifies essentially all patients who should proceed to right heart catheterization.[52] Although data are scant, it is suggested that the pulmonary component of POPH is progressive.[97] Although it is generally assumed that patients with POPH have a shorter survival time, they actually lived longer than those with other categories of primary PH.[88]

Patients with a clinical suspicion of POPH, like all patients with primary PH, should have a pharmacologic vasodilator test to assess the degree of reversibility of the pulmonary vasculature in response to common drugs such as nifedipine, NO, and prostacyclin.[52] A 20% reduction in both PPA and PVR is considered to be a criterion of vascular responsiveness. The likelihood of response appears to be low in this population; in the series reported by Hervé and colleagues,[92] none of the patients with POPH showed a positive vasodilator response. Nonetheless, in those few with a positive response, oral vasodilator agents deserve a therapeutic trial. In addition, continuous infusion and inhaled preparations of the more powerful vasodilator epoprostenol (prostacyclin) have been shown to be beneficial in some patients with POPH.[52,92,94,104] Liver transplantation has been tried but with conflicting results; pediatric patients seem to show a better response than adults.[90] Of note, there is one case report of a successful outcome after orthotopic liver transplantation in an adult with POPH associated with a strikingly hyperdynamic circulatory state.[105] However, unlike the situation for HPS, POPH is not considered an indication for liver transplantation currently, because these patients are at extremely high risk from this elective surgical procedure.[88,92] Therefore, pulmonary vasodilators should be used to improve and optimize the underlying levels of PH prior to any consideration of surgery.[52]

PRIMARY BILIARY CIRRHOSIS

Primary biliary cirrhosis (PBC), considered to be an autoimmune disease, is characterized by a chronic, cholestatic, granulomatous and destructive process that involves the intrahepatic bile ducts.[106] When severe, these processes result in cholestasis, cirrhosis, and liver failure. The autoimmunologic basis is reflected in the presence of several immunologic alterations, such as depressed T-suppressor cell function, hypergammaglobulinemia, and the presence of antimitochondrial antibodies. Connective tissue diseases such as the sicca complex, Sjögren's syndrome, and scleroderma are frequently associated with PBC.[106,107] Several respiratory abnormalities have been associated with PBC: interstitial lung disorders, such as lymphocytic interstitial pneumonitis and fibrosing alveolitis; subclinical intrapulmonary granulomas that mimic sarcoidosis[108]; increased numbers of CD4$^+$ lymphocytes in the bronchoalveolar lavage fluid; and obstructive airway disease, such as bronchiectasis.[45] Occasionally, the pulmonary manifestations precede the liver involvement.[109] In addition, thoracic wall deformities secondary to osteopenic vertebral complications induced by abnormal vitamin D metabolism related to poor absorption of fat-soluble vitamins can be also observed.[45] A reduced DL_{CO}, with or without ventilatory defects, is one of the functional hallmarks of the disease, particularly when a connective tissue disorder coexists.[109–111] Furthermore, the clinical, radiographic, and functional respiratory abnormalities in patients with PBC are more likely to be associated with underlying connective tissue disorders than with PBC itself.[111] As with many chronic liver diseases, PBC can be complicated by HPS (discussed previously).

CHRONIC ACTIVE HEPATITIS

Chronic active hepatitis, an increasingly frequent liver disease that is characterized by diffuse parenchymal inflammation and hepatic cell necrosis, may be caused by viral hepatitis (most commonly hepatitis C virus), autoimmune disorders, and drug-related liver injury. Pulmonary fibrosis and lymphoid interstitial pneumonitis have been reported but are rare.[110,112] After years of smoldering inflammation, which is often asymptomatic, chronic active hepatitis can lead to cirrhosis and liver failure, which has been associated with HPS.[45] Patients with chronic hepatitis C virus infection and coexistent COPD may demonstrate an accelerated annual decline in FEV_1.[113]

SCLEROSING CHOLANGITIS

Sclerosing cholangitis is an unusual disease that results from chronic inflammation affecting both intrahepatic and extrahepatic bile ducts. It has been linked with inflammatory obstructive airway diseases such as bronchiectasis; however, the relationship remains unproven because ulcerative colitis, a frequent clinical accompaniment, has also been associated with the same respiratory complications.[114]

ALPHA$_1$-ANTITRYPSIN DEFICIENCY

The discovery that certain patients with COPD had low levels of circulating alpha$_1$-antitrypsin led to the current protease-antiprotease theory of the pathogenesis of pulmonary emphysema (see Chapter 36 for complete discussion). This hereditary disorder is nearly always associated with the homozygous PiZZ phenotype. Genetically predisposed infants often present with hepatomegaly or hepatosplenomegaly and evidence of cholestasis. Most children with alpha$_1$-antitrypsin–induced liver disease recover, but about 15% go on to develop cirrhosis, presumably from toxic effects of the mutant antitrypsin protein retained in the endoplasmic reticulum of hepatocytes[115]; HPS has been

reported as a complication of this form of cirrhosis.[116] By far the more common pulmonary complication, COPD is unrelated to the presence of liver disease, occurs in adults, and is characterized by panacinar emphysema and bronchial abnormalities, including bronchiectasis.[45]

PANCREATITIS

During episodes of acute pancreatitis, pulmonary complications are frequent and, when present, account for significant mortality. Intrathoracic complications have been implicated as important contributing factors to death from pancreatitis in 22% to 29% of fatal cases.[117] Furthermore, respiratory failure, as defined by an arterial PO_2 value lower than 60 mm Hg, is considered one of the major factors adversely affecting survival in acute pancreatitis.[118]

The two major respiratory complications associated with pancreatitis are respiratory failure and pleural effusion. A number of other intrathoracic complications have also been described, including pulmonary infiltrates, basilar atelectasis, unilateral elevation of the diaphragm, and pleural thickening.[119]

RESPIRATORY FAILURE

Gas-exchange disturbances, ranging from mild hypoxemia to acute respiratory distress syndrome (ARDS), may occur during episodes of acute pancreatitis. Arterial hypoxemia (arterial PO_2 < 80 mm Hg) with a normal chest radiograph is a frequent finding in the early stages of acute pancreatitis.[119] In one study of 116 patients, 69% showed an arterial PO_2 lower than 76 mm Hg during the first 48 hours of the episode.[120] Although arterial hypoxemia may be asymptomatic and mild during the initial hours of acute pancreatitis, it should not be dismissed, because these patients are at increased risk for respiratory failure.[121] Ranson and associates[120] reported that 67% of the patients who had an initial arterial PO_2 lower than 66 mm Hg developed clinical respiratory symptoms afterward, and 39% of them died. Accordingly, patients who present with hypoxemia during an episode of acute pancreatitis should be closely monitored for worsening respiratory failure.

The mechanisms of arterial hypoxemia with a normal chest radiograph during acute pancreatitis remain poorly understood. Murphy and associates[122] showed that hypoxemia in these patients was caused by an increase in the right-to-left shunt fraction, which improved after recovery in most cases. No changes in expiratory flow rates, lung volumes, or closing capacity were shown, compared with measurements performed after recovery. This suggests that the development of poorly ventilated alveolar units in dependent lung areas, due to pain-related breathing abnormalities, is unlikely to be the mechanism of the observed hypoxemia.[122] These authors suggested that hypoxemia in the absence of radiologic abnormalities may be related to changes in pulmonary vascular permeability, similar but milder than that described in ARDS.[122] In a similar group of patients, De Troyer and colleagues[123] measured a transient reduction of DL_{CO} during the episodes of pancreatitis. They suggested that factors released from the injured pancreas could have increased capillary permeability and impaired the $D_{L_{CO}}$.[123] In addition, Greenberg and coworkers[124] demonstrated a reduction in the oxygen affinity of hemoglobin in patients with acute pancreatitis, which was related to the increase in circulating fatty acids.

Because of the normal chest radiograph, arterial hypoxemia may be clinically undetected but profound; therefore, a high index of suspicion should be present for respiratory impairment in patients with acute pancreatitis, and arterial blood gases should be measured periodically during the initial 48 to 72 hours of hospitalization.[117] When hypoxemia occurs, the patient should receive supplemental oxygen to raise the arterial PO_2 to more than 70 mm Hg.[125]

Approximately 15% of patients with acute pancreatitis develop ARDS,[117] a complication associated with a mortality rate of approximately 75%.[120,126] The incidence of ARDS is higher in patients with hemorrhagic compared with nonhemorrhagic pancreatitis.[127,128] Respiratory symptoms appear 2 to 7 days after the onset of the acute episode. The chest radiograph usually shows signs of pulmonary vascular congestion that progress to bilateral, diffuse infiltrates. Studies of arterial blood gases confirm severe hypoxemia, usually associated with marked hypocapnia. Autopsy findings in these patients have revealed acute lung injury that is indistinguishable from that observed in ARDS attributable to other causes.[127]

The mechanisms of lung injury associated with acute pancreatitis are not completely understood. It is not clear whether the injury results from a direct toxic effect of pancreatic products or is secondary to the release of inflammatory mediators, or both. Several pancreatic products, production of which is markedly increased during acute pancreatitis, have the potential to induce lung injury. Phospholipase A_2 has been extensively studied as a putative mediator, because it binds to pulmonary capillaries and has the ability to induce the enzymatic degradation of the phospholipid components of surfactant, thereby promoting alveolar collapse and increased vascular permeability.[129,130] Free fatty acids, produced from triglyceride degradation by circulating lipase, may induce alveolar edema and hemorrhage.[131,132] Pancreatic enzymes also have the capability to induce lung injury and cause increased vascular permeability.[133,134] In addition to the direct effect of pancreatic products, the indirect effect of the intense inflammatory reaction associated with acute pancreatitis may lead to ARDS. Various inflammatory mediators that may be released during pancreatic injury, such as reactive oxygen species,[135] adhesion molecules, platelet-activating factor,[136,137] and cytokines (interleukin-8),[138] possess the potential to produce diffuse lung injury and increase pulmonary vascular permeability.

Treatment of pancreatitis-associated lung injury is essentially supportive and does not differ from that for other forms of ARDS (see Chapter 85). Additional measures include suppression of the secretory function of the pancreas by elimination of oral intake, use of nasogastric suction, and inhibition of gastric acid secretion with histamine$_2$ blockers. The benefit of inhibition of pancreatic enzyme secretion is controversial. In animal models, the protease inhibitor aprotinin (Trasylol) was shown to exert a protective effect[134]; however, in humans it did not reduce mortality rates.[139] Studies suggest that octreotide, a potent inhibitor of exocrine pancreatic secretion, may decrease mortality rates[140] and the incidence of ARDS among patients with severe acute pancreatitis.[140,141] Nevertheless, the effectiveness of octreotide in the treatment of pancreatitis-associated ARDS needs to be further evaluated in prospective, controlled, randomized trials.

PLEURAL EFFUSION

Pleural effusions may be associated with both acute and chronic pancreatitis (see also Chapter 68). In acute pancreatitis, pleural effusion is a relatively frequent finding, being present in about 20% of the patients.[142] In most cases these effusions are of small size and unilateral, usually affecting the left side.[143]

Various pathogenic mechanisms have been proposed to explain the presence of pleural effusions associated with acute pancreatitis[142]: (1) increased permeability of lymphatics and fluid leak caused by pancreatic enzymes that may diffuse from the peritoneal side to the thoracic side of the diaphragm; (2) impaired lymphatic drainage of pleural exudate caused by obstruction of lymphatic vessels by the high enzymatic content of the pleural fluid; and (3) increased permeability of diaphragmatic capillaries caused by the inflammatory process in the adjacent pancreas.

In patients with pleural effusion associated with acute pancreatitis, symptoms are primarily abdominal (abdominal pain, nausea and vomiting); occasionally, respiratory symptoms (pleuritic pain and dyspnea) may also be present. The diagnosis is established by demonstrating an elevated amylase concentration in the pleural fluid, which is usually greater than the concentration in plasma.[142] The pleural fluid usually is an exudate with a serosanguineous appearance and a high concentration of both protein and lactic acid dehydrogenase. The differential white blood cell count reveals a predominance of polymorphonuclear cells.

Pleural effusions associated with acute pancreatitis usually are self-limited and resolve when the pancreatic inflammation decreases without requiring therapeutic drainage. Therefore, if the pleural effusion does not resolve within 2 weeks after treatment for the pancreatic disease, the possibility of a pancreatic abscess or a pseudocyst should be considered.

Chronic pleural effusions are usually associated with chronic relapsing pancreatitis and pancreatic pseudocyst. In most cases a history of alcohol abuse is present.[144] Chronic effusions are large, may occupy the entire hemithorax, and reaccumulate rapidly after thoracentesis.

The typical mechanism of chronic effusion is a direct communication between the pancreas and the pleural space. In chronic pancreatitis, the pancreatic duct may rupture because of high internal pressure. Once it is disrupted, pancreatic secretions are able to flow into the retroperitoneum, from which they can enter the mediastinum through the esophageal or aortic hiatuses and then penetrate into the pleural space (Fig. 78.4). Occasionally, a direct communication exists between a pancreatic pseudocyst and the pleural cavity, through the diaphragmatic dome.[144]

Patients with chronic pancreatic effusions usually complain of respiratory symptoms such as chest pain and shortness of breath. Abdominal symptoms may be absent, probably because the pancreaticopleural communication decompresses the pseudocyst.[142] Therefore, the diagnosis of a chronic pancreatic pleural effusion should be suspected in

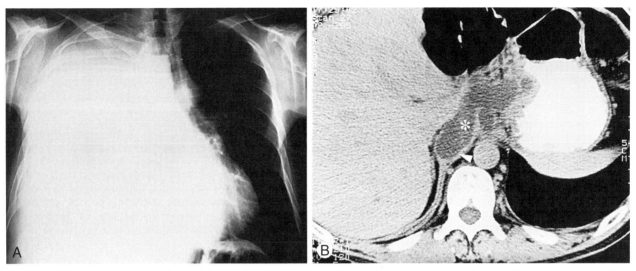

Figure 78.4 This massive pleural effusion is associated with a pancreatic pseudocyst. **A,** Chest radiograph demonstrates a massive pleural effusion in the right hemithorax. **B,** Computed tomography scan of the upper abdomen, performed after pleural drainage, shows the cephalad extension of the pseudocyst (*asterisk*) through the right crural insertion (*arrowhead*) and the esophageal hiatus. (Courtesy of Dr. S. Navarro, Hospital Clínic, Universitat de Barcelona, Barcelona.)

any patient with a large pleural effusion who appears to be chronically ill or has a history of pancreatic disease or alcohol abuse.[145] The diagnosis is established by the demonstration of a high concentration of amylase in the pleural fluid, which typically is several times higher than that in the serum. Ultrasonography and computed tomographic scanning of the chest and abdomen usually reveal the presence of a pseudocyst and occasionally may even show the pancreaticopleural fistula[146] (see Fig. 78.4). Endoscopic retrograde cholangiopancreatography provides additional information on ductal structures and may demonstrate passage of contrast material from the pancreatic duct or a pseudocyst into the peritoneal cavity, although visualization of the fistula may be difficult.[144,146] Endoscopic retrograde cholangiopancreatography and computed tomographic scanning together provide complementary information, which is useful especially if the patient has to undergo surgical intervention.

Patients with chronic pancreatic pleural effusions should be treated initially with nasogastric tube placement, no oral intake, parenteral nutrition, and repeated therapeutic thoracenteses. Inhibition of pancreatic secretion with octreotide has been shown to be useful in promoting the closure of pancreaticopleural fistulas in some cases.[147] Nonetheless, if, after 2 to 3 weeks of medical therapy, the pleural fluid continues to accumulate and the patient remains symptomatic, surgery to close the fistula should be considered.

CHRONIC RENAL FAILURE

Chronic renal diseases are associated with a variety of respiratory manifestations. Pulmonary edema, pleural disease, pulmonary calcification, and sleep apnea syndrome have been documented in patients with chronic renal failure. Furthermore, treatment with hemodialysis also produces transient changes in pulmonary gas exchange. These disorders are discussed in this section. Systemic necrotizing vasculitis and diseases associated with autoantibodies, which usually affect both the lung and the kidney, are considered in Chapters 49 and 54, respectively.

PULMONARY EDEMA

Pulmonary edema is common in patients with acute or chronic renal failure. A variety of conditions may favor edema formation: fluid overload, left ventricular failure, hypoalbuminemia, and increased pulmonary microvascular permeability. The relative importance of increased microvascular permeability versus left ventricular failure in the pathogenesis of pulmonary edema in renal failure has been largely a subject of controversy. Autopsy findings showing the presence of protein-rich edema fluid, hyaline membranes, and alveolar hemorrhage[148,149] all pointed to an increased vascular permeability to proteins as the likely mechanism of pulmonary edema formation. The demonstration of an increased protein content in edema fluid sampled directly by endotracheal aspiration reinforced this hypothesis.[150] Furthermore, pulmonary edema has been reported in the absence of volume overload and in the presence of normal intracardiac and pulmonary wedge pressures. However, studies using a double-isotope technique failed to show a significant accumulation of a radiolabeled plasma protein (transferrin) in patients with renal failure and pulmonary edema.[151] The rate of protein accumulation in patients with renal failure was similar to that in patients with cardiogenic pulmonary edema and in normal volunteers, and significantly lower than in patients with ARDS; these observations suggest that pulmonary edema associated with renal failure is probably not related to increased pulmonary vascular permeability to proteins.[151]

Conceivably, heart failure plays an important role in the development of pulmonary edema associated with renal failure. Cardiac disorders are common in end-stage renal disease, and a variety of factors, including hypertension, diabetes mellitus, anemia, surgical arteriovenous fistulas, and ischemic heart disease, may adversely affect cardiac function.[152,153] Left ventricular dysfunction may be reversible after dialysis or renal transplantation, which suggests that patients with chronic renal failure may have a specific "uremic cardiomyopathy."[152,154,155]

Subclinical lung congestion in patients with chronic renal failure may reduce lung volumes and maximal expiratory flow rates; these abnormalities usually reverse after hemodialysis.[156–158] In contrast to the findings in patients with left ventricular dysfunction,[159] subclinical pulmonary edema in renal failure is not associated with bronchial hyperresponsiveness; no changes in bronchial reactivity have been documented in these patients before and after hemodialysis.[160]

From a clinical standpoint, most instances of pulmonary edema associated with renal failure involve increased intravascular volume and abnormal left ventricular function. Accordingly, its treatment should essentially consist of removal of excess body fluid with dialysis.

PLEURAL DISEASE

Approximately 20% to 40% of patients who die from chronic renal failure have fibrinous pleuritis detected at autopsy.[148,161] This fibrinous pleuritis can be manifested as pleuritic chest pain with pleural rubs,[162] pleural effusion,[163] or fibrothorax.[164,165]

Pleural effusions are present in 3% of patients with chronic renal failure.[163] No relationship exists between the development of pleural effusion and the degree of uremia, the adequacy and duration of dialysis, or the interdialysis interval.[162,163] Patients may be asymptomatic, or they may present with fever, chest pain, cough, or dyspnea. The effusions usually are unilateral and in some cases may be large, occupying more than 50% of the hemithorax. The pleural fluid is an exudate with either a serosanguineous or a frankly hemorrhagic appearance.[166] The leukocyte count reveals predominance of lymphocytes, and the biopsy specimens usually demonstrate chronic fibrinous pleuritis.[142] The pathogenesis of pleural disease associated with renal failure is not known, but it is probably related to the effect of retained metabolic toxins.

The effusion usually disappears gradually after several weeks of dialysis. In about 25% of patients, it may persist, progress, or recur. If fibrothorax develops and produces a restrictive ventilatory impairment, surgical decortication should be considered.[164,165]

PULMONARY CALCIFICATION

Metastatic calcification is a complication of chronic renal failure that may affect many visceral organs[167] (see also Chapter 80). Pulmonary involvement is common, but it is usually undetectable by chest radiography and asymptomatic.[168] At times, the chest radiograph may show infiltrates composed of nodular opacities less than 2 mm in diameter that can be diffuse or localized. The infiltrates are relatively stable, in contrast to infectious processes. Pulmonary function tests may reveal a restrictive ventilatory defect or reduction in DL_{CO}.

The pathogenesis of pulmonary calcification in patients with chronic renal failure is not known. It has been sug-

gested that, especially in the setting of a highly elevated calcium-phosphorus product, undamaged soft tissues respond to a variety of chemical sensitizers with calcium deposition.[169] The patient's age, the type of underlying renal disease, and the duration of dialysis do not appear to be important in the development of this complication.[168]

The diagnosis of pulmonary calcification can be confirmed by pulmonary uptake during technetium-99m–diphosphonate scanning.[169] Treatment is generally unsatisfactory. Reduction of calcium intake or use of vitamin D analogues to reduce parathyroid hormone levels may be helpful.[169,170] In the rare patient with symptomatic respiratory compromise, renal transplantation has been suggested as a therapeutic alternative.[167]

SLEEP APNEA

Disturbed sleep has been recognized frequently in patients with end-stage renal disease. Other causes of sleep apnea are described in Chapter 74. Using polysomnography, Kimmel and Miller[171] found that sleep apnea was present in 16 (73%) of 22 patients with chronic renal failure whose history was suggestive of sleep apnea; these patients accounted for an overall prevalence of 7.2% of the hemodialysis population. Sleep disturbances consist of apneas and hypopneas, both central and obstructive types.[172]

Various mechanisms have been proposed to explain the high prevalence of sleep apnea in patients with chronic renal failure: narrowing of the upper airway by submucosal edema,[173] the effect of uremic toxins on the central nervous system,[173] an insufficient stimulus to breathe owing to the decreased arterial PCO_2 in patients with chronic metabolic acidosis,[174] or an abnormal ventilatory responsiveness due to a resetting of the threshold level of hydrogen ion concentration necessary for respiratory stimulation secondary to chronic acidosis.[175] Both hemodialysis[173] and renal transplantation[176] have been shown to improve sleep apnea. Nasal continuous positive airway pressure has also shown to be effective in improving daytime symptoms in some patients.[177]

HEMODIALYSIS-INDUCED HYPOXEMIA

During hemodialysis, the majority of patients develop a reduction in arterial PO_2. The arterial PO_2 falls within a few minutes of initiation of dialysis by 10 to 15 mm Hg, reaches a nadir after 30 to 60 minutes, and persists for the duration of the procedure.[178–180] The severity of hypoxemia varies according to the type of dialysis membrane and the chemical nature of the dialysate buffer.[181,182] Several mechanisms have been proposed to explain the decrease in arterial PO_2: (1) a shift in the oxyhemoglobin dissociation curve caused by the increase in pH during the procedure; (2) depression of central respiratory output due to alkalosis; (3) oxygen diffusion impairment; (4) ventilation-perfusion mismatching due to stasis of leukocytes in small pulmonary vessels; and (5) hypoventilation due to carbon dioxide excretion via the dialysate.

A once popular explanation, pulmonary vascular leukostasis, has been largely shown to be unrelated to the hypoxemia. Exposure of blood to dialysis membranes activates the alternative complement pathway, and within minutes C3a and C5a are generated. Complement activation may induce intrapulmonary sequestration of leukocytes and a fall in circulating leukocytes. Based on the temporal association between onset of hypoxemia and the transient leukopenia, it had been postulated that the decrease in arterial PO_2 results from ventilation-perfusion mismatching due to leukostasis in small pulmonary vessels.[183] However, studies performed specifically to measure ventilation-perfusion distributions during hemodialysis using the multiple inert gas elimination technique have ruled out ventilation-perfusion mismatching as the mechanism of hypoxemia.[184–186] On the contrary, Romaldini and colleagues[185] showed a tendency for ventilation-perfusion matching to improve during the dialysis procedure, which was most likely explained by a dialysis-induced decrease in extravascular lung water.[185] Furthermore, the fact that hypoxemia can be seen during dialysis with membranes that do not cause leukopenia,[187] and the fact that use of bicarbonate buffer or bubbling of carbon dioxide through the dialysate prevents the hypoxemia despite leukopenia, suggest that factors other than pulmonary leukocyte aggregation account for hemodialysis-associated hypoxemia.

Currently, the most accepted explanation for the decrease in arterial PO_2 during hemodialysis is the hypoventilation associated with the removal of carbon dioxide by the dialysate. During hemodialysis, carbon dioxide diffuses into the dialysis fluid and the amount of carbon dioxide output via the lung is reduced. The result of this nonrespiratory removal of carbon dioxide is a decrease in the minute ventilation[180,188]; in one study, minute ventilation dropped from an average of 7.2 L/min to 5.7 L/min within 15 minutes of the start of hemodialysis.[189] The $(A - a)PO_2$ value during hemodialysis actually remains stable despite a significant fall in arterial PO_2.[180,185] The amount of carbon dioxide "unloading" into the dialysate buffer depends on its composition; it is substantial with acetate buffer but appears to be minimal with bicarbonate buffer.[190] In addition, acetate buffer may further reduce respiratory carbon dioxide elimination due to carbon dioxide consumption during acetate metabolism.[191] An additional consequence of the nonrespiratory carbon dioxide "unloading" is to destabilize resting ventilation; the reduced overall ventilation is frequently accompanied by an irregular breathing pattern, with the development of periodicity and sometimes apneas.[192,193]

The decrease in arterial PO_2 during hemodialysis is unlikely to be important in patients with normal cardiopulmonary function, but it may be clinically relevant in those with preexisting lung disease.[194,195] Accordingly, the composition of the dialysis membrane and the chemical nature of the dialysate buffer should be considered when dialyzing patients who have cardiopulmonary disease. In these patients, cellulose or polyacrylonitrile filters and a bicarbonate bath are preferred. In addition, supplemental oxygen may be necessary during hemodialysis in some patients.

SUMMARY

The principal disorders highlighted in this review are the respiratory consequences of gastroesophageal reflux, the pulmonary vascular disease states associated with portal hypertension, and the pleural and lung parenchymal complications of acute pancreatitis. In addition, other pulmonary problems related to specific liver, gastrointestinal, and renal diseases are discussed. Over the last few years, the knowledge and understanding of some of these syndromes, particularly gastroesophageal reflux and HPS, has improved substantially and has offered promising therapeutic approaches.

REFERENCES

1. Katz PO, Castell DO: Diagnosis of gastroesophageal reflux disease. In Stein MR (ed): Gastroesophageal Reflux Disease and Airway Disease. New York: Marcel Dekker, 1999, pp 55–68.
2. Sontag SJ: Gastroesophageal reflux and asthma. Am J Med 103:84S–90S, 1997.
3. Harding SM, Richter JE: The role of gastroesophageal reflux in chronic cough and asthma. Chest 111:1389–1402, 1997.
4. Sontag SJ: The prevalence of GERD in asthma. In Stein MR (ed): Gastroesophageal Reflux Disease and Airway Disease. New York: Marcel Dekker, 1999, pp 115–138.
5. Sontag SJ, Schnell TG, Miller TQ, et al: Prevalence of oesophagitis in asthmatics. Gut 33:872–876, 1992.
6. Irwin RS, Curley FJ, French CL: Chronic cough: The spectrum and frequency of causes, key components of the diagnostic evaluation, and outcome of specific therapy. Am Rev Respir Dis 141:640–647, 1990.
7. Mello CJ, Irwin RS, Curley FJ: Predictive values of the character, timing, and complications of chronic cough in diagnosing its cause. Arch Intern Med 156:997–1003, 1996.
8. Irwin RS, Curley FJ, French CL: Difficult-to-control asthma: Contributing factors and outcome of a systematic management protocol. Chest 103:1662–1669, 1993.
9. DeMeester TR, Bonavina L, Iascone C, et al: Chronic respiratory symptoms and occult gastroesophageal reflux: A prospective clinical study and results of surgical therapy. Ann Surg 211:337–345, 1990.
10. Jack CI, Calverley PMA, Donnelly RJ, et al: Simultaneous tracheal and oesophageal pH measurements in asthmatic patients with gastro-oesophageal reflux. Thorax 50:201–204, 1995.
11. Mansfield LE, Stein MR: Gastroesophageal reflux and asthma: A possible reflex mechanism. Ann Allergy 41:224–226, 1978.
12. Mansfield LE, Hameister HH, Spaulding HS, et al: The role of the vagus nerve in airway narrowing caused by intraesophageal hydrochloric acid provocation and esophageal distention. Ann Allergy 47:431–434, 1981.
13. Wright RA, Miller SA, Corsello BF: Acid-induced esophagobronchial-cardiac reflexes in humans. Gastroenterology 99:71–73, 1990.
14. Tan WC, Martin RJ, Pandey R, et al: Effects of spontaneous and simulated gastroesophageal reflux on sleeping asthmatics. Am Rev Respir Dis 141:1394–1399, 1990.
15. Schan CA, Harding SM, Haile JM, et al: Gastroesophageal reflux-induced bronchoconstriction: An intraesophageal acid infusion study using state-of-the-art technology. Chest 106:731–737, 1994.
16. Hervé P, Denjean A, Jian R, et al: Intraesophageal perfusion of acid increases the bronchomotor response to methacholine and to isocapnic hyperventilation in asthmatic subjects. Am Rev Respir Dis 134:986–989, 1986.

17. Tuchman DN, Boyle JT, Pack AI, et al: Comparison of airway responses following tracheal or esophageal acidification in the cat. Gastroenterology 87:872–881, 1984.

18. Ekstrom T, Tibbling L: Influence of theophylline on gastro-oesophageal reflux and asthma. Eur J Clin Pharmacol 35:353–356, 1988.

19. DiMarino AJ, Cohen S: Effect of an oral beta-2 adrenergic agonist on lower esophageal sphincter pressure in normals and in patients with achalasia. Dig Dis Sci 27:1063–1066, 1982.

20. Schindlbeck NE, Heinrich C, Huber RM, et al: Effects of albuterol (salbutamol) on esophageal motility and gastroesophageal reflux in healthy volunteers. JAMA 260:3156–3158, 1988.

21. Irwin RS, Madison JM: The diagnosis and treatment of cough. N Engl J Med 343:1715–1721, 2000.

22. Pope CE: Acid-reflux disorders. N Engl J Med 331:656–660, 1994.

23. Wiener GJ, Richter JE, Cooper JB, et al: The symptom index: A clinically important parameter of ambulatory 24-hour esophageal pH monitoring. Am J Gastroenterol 83:358–361, 1988.

24. Harding SM, Richter JE: The role of gastroesophageal reflux in chronic cough and asthma. Chest 111:1389–1402, 1997.

25. Larrain A, Carrasco E, Galleguillos F, et al: Medical and surgical treatment of nonallergic asthma associated with gastroesophageal reflux. Chest 99:1330–1335, 1991.

26. Allan CJ, Anvari M: Gastro-oesophageal reflux–related cough and its response to laparoscopic fundoplication. Thorax 53:963–968, 1998.

27. Kavuru MS, Richter JE. Medical treatment of gastroesophageal reflux disease and airway disease. In Stein MR (ed): Gastroesophageal Reflux Disease and Airway Disease. New York: Marcel Dekker, 1999, pp 179–207.

28. Simpson WG: Gastroesophageal reflux disease and asthma: Diagnosis and management. Arch Intern Med 155:798–803, 1995.

29. Ing AJ, Ngu MC: Cough and gastro-oesophageal reflux. Lancet 353:944–946, 1999.

30. Ayres JG, Miles JF: Oesophageal reflux and asthma. Eur Respir J 9:1073–1078, 1996.

31. Rogers BHG, Clark L, Kirsher JP: The epidemiologic and demographic characteristics of inflammatory bowel disease: An analysis of a computerized file of 1400 patients. J Chronic Dis 24:743–773, 1971.

32. Eade OE, Smith CL, Alexander JR: Pulmonary function in patients with inflammatory bowel disease. Am J Gastroenterol 73:154–156, 1980.

33. Heatley RV, Thomas V, Prokipchuk EJ, et al: Pulmonary function abnormalities in patients with inflammatory bowel disease. Q J Med 51:241–250, 1982.

34. Munck A, Murciano D, Pariente R, et al: Latent pulmonary function abnormalities in children with Crohn's disease. Eur Respir J 8:377–380, 1995.

35. Tzanakis N, Samiou M, Bouros D, et al: Small airways function in patients with inflammatory bowel disease. Am J Respir Crit Care Med 157:382–386, 1998.

36. Storch I, Sachar D, Katz S: Pulmonary manifestations of inflammatory bowel disease. Inflamm Bowel Dis 9:104–115, 2003.

37. Camus P, Piard F, Ashcroft T, et al: The lung in inflammatory bowel disease. Medicine (Baltimore) 72:151–183, 1993.

38. Kraft SC, Earle RH, Roesler M, et al: Unexplained bronchopulmonary disease with inflammatory bowel disease. Arch Intern Med 136:454–459, 1976.

39. Butland RJ, Cole P, Citron KM, et al: Chronic bronchial suppuration and inflammatory bowel disease. Q J Med 50:63–75, 1981.

40. Higenbottam T, Cochrane GM, Clark TJH, et al: Bronchial disease in ulcerative colitis. Thorax 35:581–585, 1980.

41. Rickli H, Fretz M, Hoffman A, et al: Severe inflammatory upper airway stenosis in ulcerative colitis. Eur Respir J 7:1899–1902, 1994.

42. Kuzela L, Vavrecka A, Prikazska M, et al: Pulmonary complications in patients with inflammatory bowel disorders. Hepatogastroenterology 46:1714–1719, 1999.

43. Alberts WM, Salem AJ, Solomon DA, et al: Hepatic hydrothorax: Cause and management. Arch Intern Med 151:2383–2388, 1991.

44. Agusti AG, Cardus J, Roca J, et al: Ventilation-perfusion mismatch in patients with pleural effusion: Effects of thoracentesis. Am J Respir Crit Care Med 156:1205–1209, 1997.

45. Krowka MJ: Recent pulmonary observations in alpha$_1$-antitrypsin deficiency, primary biliary cirrhosis, chronic hepatitis C, and other hepatic problems. Clin Chest Med 17:67–82, 1996.

46. Hourani M, Bellamy PE, Tashkin DP, et al: Pulmonary dysfunction in advanced liver disease: Frequent occurrence of an abnormal diffusing capacity. Am J Med 90:693–700, 1991.

47. Agusti AG, Roca J, Bosch J, et al: The lung in patients with cirrhosis. J Hepatol 10:251–257, 1990.

48. Krowka MJ, Dickson ER, Wiesner RH, et al: A prospective study of pulmonary function and gas exchange following liver transplantation. Chest 102:1161–1166, 1992.

49. Martinez-Palli G, Barbera JA, Visa J, et al: Hepatopulmonary syndrome in candidates for liver transplantation. J Hepatol 34:651–657, 2001.

50. Rodriguez-Roisin R, Roca J: Hepatopulmonary syndrome: The paradigm of liver-induced hypoxaemia. Ballieres Clin Gastroenterol 11:387–406, 1997.

51. Rodriguez-Roisin R, Agustí AGN, Roca J: The hepatopulmonary syndrome: New name, old complexities. Thorax 47:897–902, 1992.

52. Rodriguez-Roisin R, Krowka MJ, Hervé P, et al, for the ERS Task Force Pulmonary-Hepatic Vascular Disorders (PHD) Scientific Committee: Pulmonary-Hepatic vascular Disorders (PHD). Eur Respir J 24:861–880, 2004.

53. De BK, Sen S, Biswas PK, et al: Occurrence of hepatopulmonary syndrome in Budd-Chiari syndrome and the role of venous decompression. Gastroenterology 122:897–903, 2002.

54. Berthelot P, Walker JG, Sherlock S, et al: Arterial changes in the lungs in cirrhosis of the liver—lung spider nevi. N Engl J Med 274:291–298, 1966.

55. Vanhoutte PM: The endothelium—moderator of vascular smooth muscle tone. N Engl J Med 319:512–513, 1998.

56. Groszmann RJ: Vasodilatation and hyperdynamic circulatory state in chronic liver disease. In Bosch J, Groszmann RJ (eds): Portal Hypertension: Pathophysiology and Treatment. Oxford: Blackwell Scientific, 1994, pp 17–26.

57. Sikuler E, Groszmann RJ: Hemodynamic studies in long and short term portal hypertensive rats: The relation to systemic glucagon levels. Hepatology 6:414–418, 1986.

58. Moncada S, Higgs A: The L-arginine–nitric oxide pathway. N Engl J Med 329:2002–2012, 1993.

59. Vallance P, Moncada S: Hyperdynamic circulation in cirrhosis: A role for nitric oxide? Lancet 337:776–778, 1991.

60. Sogni P, Moreau R, Gadano A, et al: The role of nitric oxide in the hyperdynamic circulatory syndrome associated with portal hypertension. J Hepatol 23:218–224, 1995.

61. Fallon MB, Abrams GA, Ifou Z, et al: The role of endothelial nitric oxide synthase in the pathogenesis of a rat model of hepatopulmonary syndrome. Gastroenterology 113:606–614, 1997.

62. Matsumoto A, Ogura K, Hirata Y, et al: Increased nitric oxide in the exhaled air of patients with decompensated liver cirrhosis. Ann Intern Med 123:110–113, 1995.

63. Sogni P, Garnier P, Adano A, et al: Endogenous pulmonary nitric oxide production measured from exhaled air is increased in patients with hepatic cirrhosis. J Hepatol 23:471–473, 1995.

64. Schenk P, Madl C, Rezale-Majd S, et al: Methylene blue improves the hepatopulmonary syndrome. Ann Intern Med 133:701–708, 2000.

65. Cremona G, Higenbottam T, Mayoral V, et al: Elevated exhaled nitric oxide in patients with hepatopulmonary syndrome. Eur Respir J 8:1883–1885, 1995.

66. Rolla G, Brussino L, Colagrande P, et al: Exhaled nitric oxide and impaired oxygenation in cirrhotic patients before and after liver transplantation. Ann Intern Med 129:375–378, 2001.

66a. Luo B, Liu L, Tang L, et al: ET-1 and TNF-α in HPS: analysis in prehepatic portal hypertension and biliary and nonbiliary cirrhosis in rats. Am J Physiol Gastrointest Liver Physiol 286:G294–G303, 2004.

66b. Dinh-Xuan AT, Naeije R: The hepatopulmonary syndrome: NO way out? Eur Respir J 23:661–662, 2004.

67. Rodriguez-Roisin R, Roca J, Agustí AGN, et al: Gas exchange and pulmonary vascular reactivity in patients with liver cirrhosis. Am Rev Respir Dis 135:1085–1092, 1987.

68. Vachiery F, Moreau R, Hadengue A, et al: Hypoxemia in patients with cirrhosis: Relationship with liver failure and hemodynamic alterations. J Hepatol 27:492–495, 1997.

69. Molleston JP, Kaufman BA, Cohen A, et al: Brain abscess in hepatopulmonary syndrome. J Pediatr Gastroenterol Nutr 29:225–226, 1999.

70. Martinez G, Barbera JA, Navasa M, et al: Hepatopulmonary syndrome associated with cardiorespiratory disease. J Hepatol 30:882–889, 1999.

71. Castro M, Krowka MJ: Hepatopulmonary syndrome: A pulmonary vascular complication of liver disease. Clin Chest Med 17:35–48, 1996.

72. Hopkins WE, Waggoner AD, Barzilai B: Frequency and significance of intrapulmonary right-to-left shunting in end-stage hepatic disease. Am J Cardiol 70:516–519, 1992.

73. Schenk P, Schöniger-Hekele M, Furrman V, et al: Prognostic significance of the hepatopulmonary syndrome in patients with cirrhosis. Gastroenterology 125:1042–1052, 2003.

74. Melot C, Naeije R, Dechamps P, et al: Pulmonary and extrapulmonary factors to hypoxemia in liver cirrhosis. Am Rev Respir Dis 139:632–640, 1989.

75. Hedenstierna G, Soderman C, Eriksson LS, et al: Ventilation-perfusion inequality in patients with non-alcoholic liver cirrhosis. Eur Respir J 4:711–717, 1991.

76. Edell ES, Cortese DE, Krowka MJ, et al: Severe hypoxemia and liver disease. Am Rev Respir Dis 140:1631–1635, 1989.

77. Castaing Y, Manier G: Hemodynamic disturbances and $\dot{V}A/\dot{Q}$ matching in hypoxemic cirrhotic patients. Chest 96:1064–1069, 1989.

78. Agusti AG, Roca J, Rodriguez-Roisin R, et al: Pulmonary hemodynamics and gas exchange during exercise in liver cirrhosis. Am Rev Respir Dis 139:485–491, 1989.

79. Daoud FS, Reeves JT, Schaefer JW: Failure of hypoxic pulmonary vasoconstriction in patients with liver cirrhosis. J Clin Invest 51:1076–1080, 1973.

80. Naeije R, Hallemans R, Mols P, et al: Hypoxic pulmonary vasoconstriction in liver cirrhosis. Chest 80:570–574, 1981.

80a. Gómez FP, Martínez-Pallí G, Barberà JA, et al: Gas exchange mechanism of orthodeoxia in hepatopulmonary syndrome. Hepatology 40:660–666, 2004.

81. Genovesi MG, Tierney DF, Taplin GV, et al: An intravenous radionuclide method to evaluate hypoxemia caused by abnormal alveolar vessels. Am Rev Respir Dis 114:59–65, 1976.

82. Wagner PD: Impairment of gas exchange in liver cirrhosis. Eur Respir J 8:1993–1995, 1995.

83. Riegler JL, Lang KA, Johnson SP, et al: Transjugular intrahepatic portosystemic shunt improves oxygenation in hepatopulmonary syndrome. Gastroenterology 109:978–983, 1995.

84. Eriksson LS: Is intrapulmonary arteriovenous shunting and hypoxemia a contraindication for liver transplantation? Hepatology 14:575–576, 1991.

85. Krowka MJ, Cortese DA: Hepatopulmonary syndrome: Current concepts in diagnostic and therapeutic considerations. Chest 105:1528–1537, 1994.

86. Rodriguez-Roisin R, Krowka MJ: Is arterial hypoxaemia due to hepatic disease a contraindication for liver transplantation? Eur Respir J 7:839–842, 1994.

87. Hoeper M, Krowka MJ, Strassbourg CP: Portopulmonary hypertension and hepatopulmonary syndrome. Lancet 363:1461–1468, 2004.

88. Torregrossa M, Genesca J, Gonzalez A, et al: Role of Doppler echocardiography in the assessment of portopulmonary hypertension in liver transplantation candidates. Transplantation 71:572–574, 2001.

89. Arguedas MR, Abrams GA, Krowka MJ et al: Prospective evaluation of outcomes and predictors of mortality in patients with hepatopulmonary syndrome. Hepatology 37:192–197, 2003.

90. Krowka MJ: Hepatopulmonary syndrome versus portopulmonary hypertension: Distinctions and dilemmas. Hepatology 25:1282–1284, 1997.

91. Rich S, Dantzker DR, Ayres SM: Primary pulmonary hypertension: A national prospective study. Ann Intern Med 107:216–223, 1987.

92. Hervé P, Lebrec D, Brenot F, et al: Pulmonary vascular disorders in portal hypertension. Eur Respir J 11:1153–1166, 1998.

93. Castro M, Krowka MJ, Schroeder D et al: Frequency and clinical implications of increased pulmonary artery pressures in liver transplantation. Mayo Clin Proc 71:543–551, 1996.

94. Chemla D, Castelain V, Hervé P, et al: Haemodynamic evaluation of pulmonary hypertension. Eur Respir J 20:1314–1331, 2002.

95. McDonnell PJ, Toye PA, Hutchins GM: Primary pulmonary hypertension and cirrhosis: Are they related? Am Rev Respir Dis 127:437–441, 1983.

96. Naeije R, Hallemans R, Mols P, et al: Pulmonary hemodynamics in liver cirrhosis. Semin Respir Med 7:164–170, 1985.

97. Hadengue A, Benhayoum MK, Lebrec D, et al: Pulmonary hypertension complicating portal hypertension: Prevalence and relation to splanchnic hemodynamics. Gastroenterology 100:520–528, 1991.

98. Taura P, García-Valdecasas JC, Beltran J, et al: Moderate primary pulmonary hypertension in patients undergoing liver transplantation. Anaesth Analg 83:675–680, 1996.

99. Proceedings of the 3rd World Symposium on Pulmonary Artery Hypertension, Venice, Italy, June 23–25, 2003. J Am Coll Cardiol 42(12 Suppl S):1S–90S, 2004.

100. Abenhaim L, Moride Y, Brenot F, et al: Appetite-suppressant drugs and the risk of primary pulmonary hypertension. N Engl J Med 335:609–616, 1996.

101. Mandell MS, Groves BM: Pulmonary hypertension in chronic liver diseases. Clin Chest Med 17:17–33, 1996.

102. Robalino BD, Moodie DS: Association between primary pulmonary hypertension and portal hypertension: Analysis of its pathophysiology and clinical, laboratory and hemodynamic manifestations. J Am Coll Cardiol 17:492–498, 1991.

103. Raffy O, Sleiman C, Vachiery F, et al: Refractory hypoxemia during liver cirrhosis: Hepatopulmonary syndrome or "primary" pulmonary hypertension? Am J Respir Crit Care Med 153:1169–1171, 1996.

104. McLaughlin VV, Genthner DE, Panella MM, et al: Compassionate use of continuous prostacyclin in the management of secondary pulmonary hypertension. Ann Intern Med 130:740–743, 1999.

105. Schott R, Chaouat A, Launoy A, et al: Improvement of pulmonary hypertension after liver transplantation. Chest 115:1748–1749, 1999.

106. Sherlock S, Scheuer PJ: The presentation of and diagnosis of 100 patients with primary biliary cirrhosis. N Engl J Med 289:674–678, 1973.

107. Wallaert B, Bonniere P, Prin L, et al: Primary biliary cirrhosis: Subclinical inflammatory alveolitis in patients with normal chest roentgenograms. Chest 90:842–848, 1986.

108. Maddrey WC: Sarcoidosis and primary biliary cirrhosis: Associated disorders? N Engl J Med 308:472–475, 1983.

109. Izsdebka-Makosa Z, Zielinski U: Primary biliary cirrhosis in a patient with interstitial lung fibrosis. Chest 92:766–767, 1987.

110. Turner-Warwick M: Fibrosing alveolitis and chronic liver disease. Q J Med 37:133–149, 1968.

111. Rodriguez-Roisin R, Parés A, Bruguera M, et al: Pulmonary involvement in primary biliary cirrhosis. Thorax 36:208–212, 1981.

112. Helman CA, Keeton GR, Benatat SR: Lymphoid interstitial pneumonia with associated chronic active hepatitis and renal tubular acidosis. Am Rev Respir Dis 115:161–164, 1977.

113. Kanazawa H, Hirata K, Yoshikawa J: Accelerated decline of lung function in COPD patients with chronic hepatitis C virus infection: A preliminary study based on small number of patients. Chest 123:596–599, 2003.

114. Wiesner RH, LaRusso NF: Clinicopathologic features of the syndrome of primary sclerosing cholangitis. Gastroenterology 79:200–206, 1980.

115. Sveger T: Liver disease in alpha-1 antitrypsin deficiency detected by screening 200,000 infants. N Engl J Med 294:1316–1321, 1976.

116. Eriksson S: Alpha$_1$-antitrypsin deficiency and liver cirrhosis in adults. Acta Med Scand 221:461–467, 1987.

117. Shapiro MS, Dobbins JW, Matthay RA: Pulmonary manifestations of gastrointestinal disease. Clin Chest Med 10:617–643, 1989.

118. Agarwal N, Pitchumoni CS: Assessment of severity in acute pancreatitis. Am J Gastroenterol 86:1385–1391, 1991.

119. Basran GS, Ramasubramanian R, Verma R: Intrathoracic complications of acute pancreatitis. Br J Dis Chest 81:326–331, 1987.

120. Ranson JHC, Turner JW, Roses DF, et al: Respiratory complications in acute pancreatitis. Ann Surg 179:557–566, 1974.

121. Ranson JH, Roses DF, Fink SD: Early respiratory insufficiency in acute pancreatitis. Ann Surg 178:75–79, 1973.

122. Murphy D, Pack AI, Imrie CW: The mechanism of arterial hypoxia occurring in acute pancreatitis. Q J Med 194:151–163, 1980.

123. De Troyer A, Naeije R, Yernault JC, et al: Impairment of pulmonary function in acute pancreatitis. Chest 73:360–363, 1978.

124. Greenberg AG, Terlizzi L, Peskin G: Oxyhemoglobin affinity in acute pancreatitis. J Surg Res 22:561–565, 1977.

125. Imrie CW, Blumgart LH: Acute pancreatitis: A prospective study on some factors in mortality. Bull Int Soc Surg 6:601–605, 1975.

126. Jacobs ML, Daggett WM, Civetta JM, et al: Acute pancreatitis: Analysis of factors influencing survival. Ann Surg 185:43–51, 1977.

127. Lankisch PG, Rahlf G, Koop H: Pulmonary complications in fatal acute hemorrhagic pancreatitis. Dig Dis Sci 28:110–116, 1983.

128. Renner IG, Savage WT, Pantoja JL, et al: Death due to acute pancreatitis: A retrospective analysis of 405 autopsy cases. Dig Dis Sci 30:1005–1018, 1985.

129. Das SK, Scott MT, McCuiston S: Effects of experimental acute pancreatitis in dogs on metabolism of lung surfactant phosphatidylcholine. Biochem Biophys Res Commun 145:612–618, 1987.

130. Guice KS, Oldham KT, Wolfe RR, et al: Lung injury in acute pancreatitis: Primary inhibition of pulmonary phospholipid synthesis. Am J Surg 153:54–61, 1987.

131. Kimura T, Toung JK, Margolis S, et al: Respiratory failure in acute pancreatitis: The role of free fatty acids. Surgery 87:509–513, 1980.

132. Broe PJ, Toung TJ, Margolis S, et al: Pulmonary injury caused by free fatty acids: Evaluation of steroid and albumin therapy. Surgery 89:582–587, 1981.

133. Tahamont AV, Barie PS, Blumenstock FA: Increased lung vascular permeability after pancreatitis and trypsin infusion. Am J Pathol 109:15–26, 1982.

134. Garcia-Szabo RR, Malik AB: Pancreatitis-induced increase in lung vascular permeability: Protective effect of Trasylol. Am Rev Respir Dis 129:580–583, 1984.

135. Guice KS, Oldham KT, Caty MG, et al: Neutrophil-dependent, oxygen-radical mediated lung injury associated with acute pancreatitis. Ann Surg 210:740–747, 1989.

136. Perez HD, Horn JK, Ong R, et al: Complement (C5)–derived chemotactic activity in serum from patients with pancreatitis. J Lab Clin Med 101:123–129, 1983.

137. Steer ML: Relationship between pancreatitis and lung diseases. Respir Physiol 128:13–16, 2001.

138. Donnelly SC, Strieter RM, Kunkel SL, et al: Interleukin-8 and development of adult respiratory distress syndrome in at-risk patient groups. Lancet 341:643–647, 1993.

139. Medical Research Council Working Party: Death from acute pancreatitis: MRC multicentre trial of glucagon and aprotinin. Lancet 2:632–635, 1977.

140. Fiedler F, Jauernig G, Keim V, et al: Octreotide treatment in patients with necrotizing pancreatitis and pulmonary failure. Intensive Care Med 22:909–915, 1996.

141. Paran H, Neufeld D, Mayo A, et al: Preliminary report of a prospective randomized study of octreotide in the treatment of severe acute pancreatitis. J Am Coll Surg 181:121–124, 1995.

142. Light RW: Pleural Diseases (3rd ed). Philadelphia: Lea & Febiger, 1995.

143. Gumaste V, Singh V, Dave P: Significance of pleural effusion in patients with acute pancreatitis. Am J Gastroenterol 87:871–874, 1992.

144. Uchiyama T, Suzuki T, Adachi A, et al: Pancreatic pleural effusion: Case report and review of 113 cases in Japan. Am J Gastroenterol 87:387–391, 1992.

145. Pottmeyer EW, Frey CF, Matsuno S: Pancreaticopleural fistulas. Arch Surg 122:648–654, 1987.

146. McCarthy S, Pellegrini CA, Moss AA, et al: Pleuropancreatic fistula: Endoscopic retrograde cholangiopancreatography and computed tomography. AJR Am J Roentgenol 142:1151–1154, 1984.

147. Chan KL, Lau WY, Sung JY: Octreotide therapy for pancreaticopleural fistula. J Gastroenterol Hepatol 9:530–532, 1994.

148. Hopps HC, Wissler RW: Uremic pneumonitis. Am J Pathol 31:261–273, 1953.

149. Henkin RI, Maxwell MH, Murray JF: Uremic pneumonitis: A clinical, physiological study. Ann Intern Med 57:1001–1008, 1962.

150. Rackow EC, Fein IA, Sprung C, et al: Uremic pulmonary edema. Am J Med 64:1084–1088, 1978.

151. Rocker GM, Morgan AG, Pearson D, et al: Pulmonary vascular permeability to transferrin in the pulmonary oedema of renal failure. Thorax 42:620–623, 1987.

152. Hung J, Harris PJ, Uren RF, et al: Uremic cardiomyopathy: Effect of hemodialysis on left ventricular function in end-stage renal failure. N Engl J Med 302:547–551, 1980.

153. Scharf S, Wexler J, Longnecker RE, et al: Cardiovascular disease in patients on chronic hemodialytic therapy. Prog Cardiovasc Dis 22:343–356, 1980.

154. Burt RK, Gupta-Burk S, Suki WN, et al: Reversal of left ventricular dysfunction after renal transplantation. Ann Intern Med 111:635–640, 1989.

155. Lai KN, Barneden L, Mathew TH: Effect of renal transplantation on left ventricular function in hemodialysis patients. Clin Nephrol 16:74–78, 1982.

156. Zidulka A, Despas PJ, Milic-Emili J, et al: Pulmonary function with acute loss of excess lung water by hemodialysis in patients with chronic uremia. Am J Med 55:134–141, 1973.

157. Zarday Z, Benjamin JJ, Koerner SK, et al: Effects of hemodialysis and renal transplantation on pulmonary function. Chest 63:532–535, 1973.

158. Stanescu DC, Veriter C, de Plaen JF, et al: Lung function in chronic uraemia before and after removal of excess fluid by hemodialysis. Clin Sci Mol Med 47:143–151, 1974.

159. Cabanes LR, Weber SN, Matran R, et al: Bronchial hyperresponsiveness to methacholine in patients with impaired left-ventricular function. N Engl J Med 320:1317–1322, 1989.

160. Ferrer A, Roca J, Rodriguez-Roisin R, et al: Bronchial reactivity in patients with chronic renal failure undergoing haemodialysis. Eur Respir J 3:387–390, 1990.

161. Fairshter RD, Vaziri ND, Mirahmadi MK: Lung pathology in chronic hemodialysis patients. Int J Artif Organs 5:97–100, 1982.

162. Nidus BD, Matalon R, Cantacuzino D, et al: Uremic pleuritis: A clinopathological entity. N Engl J Med 281:255–256, 1969.

163. Berger HW, Rammohan G, Neff MS, et al: Uremic pleural effusion: A study in 14 patients on chronic dialysis. Ann Intern Med 82:362–364, 1975.

164. Gilbert L, Ribot S, Frankel H, et al: Fibrinous uremic pleuritis: A surgical entity. Chest 67:53–56, 1975.

165. Rodelas R, Rakowski TA, Argy WP, et al: Fibrosing uremic pleuritis during hemodialysis. JAMA 243:2424–2425, 1980.

166. Galen MA, Steinberg SM, Lowrie EG, et al: Hemorrhagic pleural effusion in patients undergoing chronic hemodialysis. Ann Intern Med 82:359–361, 1975.

167. Justrabo E, Genin R, Rifle G: Pulmonary metastatic calcification with respiratory insufficiency in patients on maintenance hemodialysis. Thorax 34:384–388, 1979.

168. Conger JD, Hammond WS, Alfrey AC, et al: Pulmonary calcification in chronic dialysis patients. Ann Intern Med 83:330–336, 1975.

169. Faubert PF, Shapiro WB, Porush JG, et al: Pulmonary calcification in hemodialyzed patients detected by technetium-99m diphosphonate scanning. Kidney Int 18:95–102, 1980.

170. Martin KJ, Gonzalez EA: Vitamin D analogues for the management of secondary hyperparathyroidism. Am J Kidney Dis 38:S34–S40, 2001.

171. Kimmel PL, Miller G: Sleep apnea syndrome in chronic renal disease. Am J Med 86:308–314, 1989.

172. Mendelson WB, Wadhwa NK, Greenberg HE, et al: Effects of hemodialysis on sleep apnea syndrome in end stage renal disease. Clin Nephrol 33:247–251, 1990.

173. Fein AM, Niederman MS, Imbriano L, et al: Reversal of sleep apnea in uremia by dialysis. Arch Intern Med 147:1355–1356, 1987.

174. Ingbar DH, Gee BL: Pathophysiology and treatment of sleep apnea. Annu Rev Med 36:365–395, 1985.

175. Anderton J, Harris E, Robson J: The ventilatory response to carbon dioxide and hydrogen ion in renal failure. Clin Sci 28:251–258, 1965.

176. Langevin B, Fouque D, Léger P, et al: Sleep apnea syndrome and end-stage renal disease: Cure after renal transplantation. Chest 103:1330–1335, 1993.

177. Pressman MR, Benz RL, Schleifer CR, et al: Sleep disordered breathing in ESRD: Acute beneficial effects of treatment with nasal continuous positive airway pressure. Kidney Int 43:1134–1139, 1993.

178. Aurigemma NM, Feldman NT, Gottlieb M, et al: Arterial oxygenation during hemodialysis. N Engl J Med 297:871–873, 1977.

179. Sherlock JE, Ledwith J, Letteri J: Hypoventilation and hypoxemia during hemodialysis: Reflex response to removal of CO$_2$ across the dialyzer. Trans Am Soc Artif Intern Organs 23:406–410, 1977.

180. Patterson RW, Nissenson AR, Miller J, et al: Hypoxemia and pulmonary gas exchange during hemodialysis. J Appl Physiol 50:259–264, 1981.

181. De Backer WA, Verpooten GA, Borgongjon DJ, et al: Hypoxemia during hemodialysis: Effects of different membranes and dialysate compositions. Kidney Int 23:738–743, 1983.

182. Munger MA, Ateshkadi A, Cheung AK, et al: Cardiopulmonary events during hemodialysis: Effects of dialysis membranes and dialysate buffers. Am J Kidney Dis 36:130–139, 2000.

183. Craddock PR, Fehr J, Brigham KL, et al: Complement and leukocyte-mediated pulmonary dysfunction in hemodialysis. N Engl J Med 296:769–774, 1977.

184. Ralph DD, Ott SM, Sherrard DJ, et al: Inert gas analysis of ventilation-perfusion matching during hemodialysis. J Clin Invest 73:1385–1391, 1984.

185. Romaldini H, Rodriguez-Roisin R, Lopez FA, et al: The mechanisms of arterial hypoxemia during hemodialysis. Am Rev Respir Dis 129:780–784, 1984.

186. Rodriguez-Roisin R, Wagner PD: Clinical relevance of ventilation-perfusion inequality determined by inert gas elimination. Eur Respir J 3:469–482, 1990.

187. Dumler F, Levin NW: Leukopenia and hypoxemia: Unrelated effects of hemodialysis. Arch Intern Med 139:1103–1106, 1979.

188. Dolan MJ, Whipp BJ, Davidson WD, et al: Hypopnea associated with acetate hemodialysis: Carbon dioxide-

flow-dependent ventilation. N Engl J Med 305:72–75, 1981.

189. Davidson WD, Dolan MJ, Whipp BJ, et al: Pathogenesis of dialysis-induced hypoxemia. Artif Organs 6:406–409, 1982.

190. Cardoso M, Vinay P, Vinet B, et al: Hypoxemia during hemodialysis: A critical review of the facts. Am J Kidney Dis 11:281–297, 1988.

191. Oh MS, Uribarri J, Del Monte ML, et al: A mechanism of hypoxemia during hemodialysis: Consumption of CO_2 in metabolism of acetate. Am J Nephrol 5:366–371, 1985.

192. De Backer WA, Heyrman RM, Wittesaele WM, et al: Ventilation and breathing patterns during hemodialysis-induced carbon dioxide unloading. Am Rev Respir Dis 136:406–410, 1987.

193. Heyrman RM, De Backer WA, Van Waeleghem JP, et al: Effect of oxygen administration on the breathing pattern during hemodialysis in man. Eur Respir J 2:972–976, 1989.

194. Peces-Serrano R, Fernandez-Vega F, Alvarez-Grande A: Hypoxemia during hemodialysis in patients with impairment in pulmonary function. Nephron 42:14–18, 1986.

195. Pitcher WD, Diamond SM, Henrich WL: Pulmonary gas exchange during dialysis in patients with obstructive lung disease. Chest 96:1136–1141, 1989.

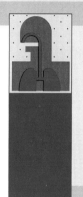

79 Pulmonary Complications of Hematologic Disease

James Hamrick, M.D., M.P.H., Susan Claster, M.D., Elliott Vichinsky, M.D.

INTRODUCTION

Disorders of red blood cells, hemoglobin, white blood cells, and coagulation can upset the homeostasis of respiration by decreasing oxygen-carrying capacity in the blood, impairing blood flow through the pulmonary vasculature, weakening the immunologic defenses of the lungs, and directly damaging lung tissue. Treatment of hematologic conditions may also have adverse consequences for the respiratory system. This chapter details the pathophysiology and treatment of clinical disorders typically requiring joint management by pulmonologists and hematologists. The material is organized by the primary site of the hematologic defect: red blood cells, hemoglobin, white blood cells, and hemostasis/thrombosis. Although convenient, these categorizations belie the complexity of these disorders, as is revealed in the text.

RED BLOOD CELL DISORDERS

ANEMIA

Anemia is defined as a hemoglobin concentration of less than 13.5 g/dL in men and 12 g/dL in women.[1] Resulting from a decrease in red cell mass (RCM) from either increased destruction or decreased production, or both, anemia has multiple causes that are beyond the scope of this chapter. Anemia results in increased levels of 2,3-diphosphoglycerate in red cells, resulting in a right-shifted oxygen-hemoglobin dissociation curve, and an increased ability of the red cell to unload oxygen at lower partial pressures of oxygen. As anemia progresses, exercise capacity is reduced. Severe anemia can compromise gas exchange at the alveolar level because there are fewer red cells available for gas exchange. The diffusion capacity in such individuals may be markedly decreased; however, this measurement is usually reported as corrected for the actual hemoglobin. Interestingly, patients with hemolytic anemias have elevated levels of carbon monoxide, a result of the complete breakdown of heme molecules.[2] Patients who have severe anemia (hemoglobin less than 7 g/dL) may develop high-output cardiac failure as a response to the chronic demands of this state. These individuals may present with pulmonary edema or pulmonary hypertension and may require red cell transfusions.[3-8]

Although red cell transfusions are frequently given in the critical care setting to improve tissue oxygenation in the face of anemia, several recent studies have questioned whether they are immunosuppressive and hasten death.[5-8] In anemic patients in the intensive care unit (ICU), a recent study showed that a "transfusion trigger" of a hemoglobin of 7 g/dL rather than 10 g/dL resulted in improved outcomes for patients with Acute Physiology and Chronic Health Evaluation (APACHE) scores of less or equal to 20 or age less than 55. However, in those patients with myocardial infarction or unstable angina, there was no benefit to the restrictive strategy.[5-8] In contrast to the ICU setting, correcting the anemia improves quality of life and possibly survival in chronically ill patients with end-organ failure. This has led to the increased use of erythropoietin therapy in several populations.[9]

ERYTHROCYTOSIS

Erythrocytosis describes a state of excess number of red blood cells. Patients with this disorder have symptoms related to elevations in whole blood viscosity. Because the viscosity of the blood is dependent on plasma volume as well as the absolute number of red cells, the hematocrit (Hct) is used to define the degree of this problem. Thus, Hct of 54% or greater in men and Hct of 51% in women are considered abnormal. Regardless of the etiology, once the Hct exceeds 55%, whole blood viscosity increases and results in an increase in pulmonary vascular resistance as well as a decrease in cardiac output and cerebral blood flow.[10-12] High Hct levels may inhibit endothelium-dependent vasodilation, possibly through inactivation of nitric oxide (NO) pathways.[13,14] Although ultimately the treatment of the erythrocytosis will depend on the etiology of the problem, phlebotomy should be used initially in all cases to decrease the Hct to acceptable levels and reduce the risk of stroke and other complications.

Before classifying a patient as having true erythrocytosis, one must rule out a decrease in plasma volume as the etiology of the increase in Hct, most conveniently done by measuring the RCM simultaneously. Use of diuretics, alcohol, obesity, hypertension, and renal disease are some of the underlying mechanisms in individuals with mild to moderately reduced plasma volumes and normal RCMs.[15] These patients are classified as having Gaisbock's or stress erythrocytosis.[16] Those patients with true or absolute erythrocytosis have RCMs of greater than 25% of their mean predicted value. Those patients with Hcts of greater than 60% are invariably found to have absolute erythrocytosis; hence, it is not necessary to measure RCM.[15]

Once a true increase in RCM has been determined, the patient must now be classified as having either primary or secondary erythrocytosis. The most common primary cause is polycythemia vera, a myeloproliferative disease characterized by clonal expansion of red cells in an erythropoietin-independent fashion. Erythropoietin-producing tumors, high oxygen-affinity mutant hemoglobins, hypoxia due to chronic lung disease, smoking, renal lesions, congenital cardiac lesions, and drugs such as androgens all can produce increases in Hct. Thus, measurement of erythropoietin levels are very helpful in this workup, with a low level being consistent with inhibition by an autonomous clone as in polycythemia vera, whereas the secondary causes are characterized by elevated erythropoietin levels.[12] The presence of splenomegaly, as well as increased numbers of basophils on a peripheral smear, also point to polycythemia vera. These patients are at higher risk for venous thrombosis due to accompanying thrombocytosis and platelet defects that may increase platelet reactivity.[17] Treatment for polycythemia vera includes phlebotomy, myelosuppression with hydroxyurea, and treatment with aspirin and anagrelide, a specific megakaryocyte inhibitor, to control platelet activity and number, respectively.[12,18-22] Late ("spent") stage polycythemia vera, which is characterized by myelofibrosis, may result in pulmonary and pleural masses that are due to extramedullary hematopoesis.[12]

Those patients with secondary erythrocytosis due to pulmonary disease will benefit from oxygen therapy and smoking cessation. Again, phlebotomy to decrease the Hct to less than 55% to 60% should be used when needed and may easily be performed in an outpatient setting on a weekly basis, if necessary. The usual amount of whole blood withdrawn at one time is 500 mL, which is then replaced with 500 mL of crystalloid, usually normal saline.

HEMOGLOBINOPATHIES

SICKLE CELL DISEASE

Sickle cell disease is characterized by vaso-occlusion by red cells that are abnormally shaped due to the presence of polymerized hemoglobin. A single amino acid substitution of valine for glutamic acid at position 6 of the β chain of the hemoglobin protein is responsible for a cascade of effects starting with this polymerization, followed by red cell membrane damage, adherence to endothelial cells, vascular occlusion, and ultimately widespread organ damage. The life span of a homozygous patient is markedly shortened.[23] In the heterozygous form, this genetic mutation is protective against malaria, hence its widespread prevalence in persons of African, Mediterranean, and Asian ancestry.[23] The homozygous mutation (Hgb SS) affects as many as 120,000 newborns in West Africa, and the total number of patients in the United States approaches 100,000. Clinically, Hgb SS is the most severe form of the disease.[24] Other milder forms of sickle cell disease include hemoglobin SC disease and coinheritance of β-thalassemia with the sickle gene.

The clinical manifestations of this disease are related to two major pathophysiologic mechanisms. The first mechanism, vaso-occlusion, is secondary to the polymerization of the abnormal Hgb S with resultant changes in the red cell membrane and overall red cell function.[23,25,26] Polymerization is promoted by deoxygenation, increases in osmotic tension, and acidosis. Sickle cells are procoagulant[27,28] and have receptors allowing adherence to endothelial cells.[25,29,30] The observation that the steady-state white blood cell count is a strong predictor of morbidity has led to the understanding that chronic inflammation plays an important role in the pathophysiology of sickle cell disease. Repeated vaso-occlusion results in vascular damage of both large and small vessels involving any major organ.[31,32] Vaso-occlusion involving areas of the body with pain receptors, such as the bone or muscle, presents as painful crises. Those in other areas, such as the central nervous system, spleen, or kidneys, may be silent. Often the disease is associated with a progressive small vessel vasculopathy that can result in pulmonary failure and pulmonary hypertension in patients with no history of prior acute pulmonary events.[32-34]

The second pathophysiologic mechanism involves a chronic hemolytic state. This is due both to membrane damage after repeated cycles of sickling as well as to oxidant damage to the cell due to denaturation of hemoglobin in this process. Patients who are the most anemic tend to have less pain from vaso-occlusion due to a lower viscosity, but have a higher incidence of ischemic organ damage and early death.

Most patients with sickle cell disease have significant pulmonary injury on histologic examination of the lung. Although the majority of patients by adulthood have experienced a pulmonary complication, the degree of injury may not correlate with clinical history.[32] Because hypoxia may precipitate vaso-occlusion, the effect of pulmonary disease on the course of sickle cell disease may be profound. Acute chest syndrome (ACS) is the second most common cause, after painful crisis, for hospitalization in these patients and is responsible for a quarter of all deaths.[35-39] Bacterial and viral pneumonias, including infections with *Mycoplasma* and *Chlamydia*, are common in sickle cell patients. Young children are at high risk for pneumococcal disease.[40] Although the use of prophylactic penicillin reduces the incidence of this problem, noncompliance and resistant organisms reduce the effectiveness of this treatment. Chronic lung disease and pulmonary hypertension are increasingly being recognized as a problem in older patients and may affect up to 40% of all patients.[34,40a,40b] Bronchospasm is being studied as a hallmark for respiratory tract damage,[39,40] and newer therapies, including inhaled NO and oral arginine, the nitrogen donor for synthesis of NO, are being considered for patients.[41,42]

Acute Chest Syndrome

Epidemiology. One of the most serious complications of sickle cell disease, ACS has been the subject of many recent studies.[39,40,43] ACS is defined clinically as a new infiltrate on chest radiograph that is accompanied by respiratory symptoms (Fig. 79.1). It is most prevalent in homozygous SS patients (12.8 events per person-year) and patients with S/β[0]-thalassemia (9.4 events per person-year). In the Cooperative Study of Sickle Cell Disease, 29% of the 3751 patients with all types of sickle cell disease who were followed had at least one episode of ACS. The same study also found that the incidence was greater in children than in adults (24.5 events vs. 8.8 events per 100 patient-years, respectively). A subset of patients may have repeated episodes, placing them at increased risk for chronic lung disease and pulmonary hypertension[34,39,40] (see Fig. 79.1).

Risk factors for the development of ACS include elevated white blood cell count, higher hemoglobin, and history of bronchospasm.[39,40] Those patients with baseline high white blood cell counts probably have an associated inflammatory state with elevated levels of cytokines and other mediators, which may promote thrombosis and endothelial adhesion. In children, ACS is most common in the wintertime. This is probably due to the fact that ACS is more commonly associated with an infectious etiology in this age group. Bronchoreactive lung disease is common in sickle cell patients and has been found in 43% of children with this disease in the steady state.[39,40,44] Some patients will progress to obstructive lung disease. Recent studies suggest that airway reactivity may be a sign of subclinical lung injury from sickling.

Some 30% of patients who develop ACS have a painful event within 2 weeks of the diagnosis.[39,45] This phenomenon is more common in adults (Fig. 79.2). A febrile illness often precedes ACS in children. In a large national study of patients with ACS, over half were admitted to the hospital for another diagnosis[39,45] and, of those, most developed ACS within 2.5 days of hospital admission. Nontransfused patients who undergo a major surgical procedure have a 25% risk of developing ACS postoperatively.[46,47] Other clinical parameters that appear to increase the likelihood of developing ACS include the presence of rib infarcts, pregnancy, avascular necrosis of the hips, use of narcotics, acute anemic events, and previous pulmonary events.[39]

Pathophysiology. The etiology of ACS is multifactorial. On the cellular level, it is a complex process involving elaboration of proinflammatory cytokines and proteins, oxidant damage, increases in endothelial cell adherence due to vascular damage, neutrophil activation, and in situ thrombo-

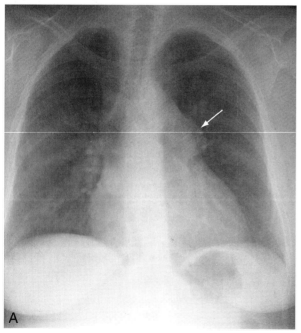
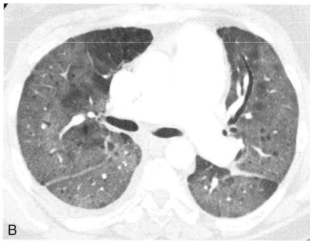

Figure 79.1 Acute chest syndrome. **A,** Chest radiograph in a patient with sickle cell disease who experienced new chest pain and hypoxemia, showing new infiltrates and pulmonary hypertension as evidenced by an enlarged main pulmonary artery segment (*arrow*). **B,** In this patient, infiltrates are well seen on computed tomography scan. (Courtesy of Michael B. Gotway, MD, Department of Radiology, University of California, San Francisco).

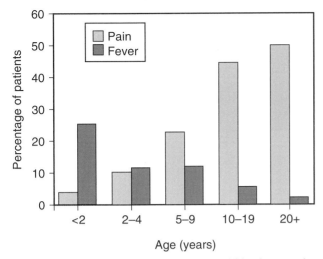

Figure 79.2 Age-specific associated events within the 2 weeks preceding the first episode of acute chest syndrome. (From Vichinsky EP, Styles LA, Colangelo LH, et al: Acute chest syndrome in sickle cell disease: Clinical presentation and course. Cooperative Study of Sickle Cell Disease. Blood 89:1787–1792, 1997.)

sis in the pulmonary vasculature.[26,30,43,48] Early studies by Barrett-Conner found that 50% of cases had an infectious etiology. Later, a study of adults found that less than half of the 34 episodes evaluated had a related infectious cause, and suggested pulmonary infarction as an etiology.[38] Recently, the contribution of fat emboli released during bone marrow infarction has been recognized.[49]

A multicenter study of 671 episodes of ACS shed new light on the etiology of this syndrome, demonstrating that 38% of the episodes were attributable to either infection or pulmonary fat embolism.[40] Nearly half of the patients were admitted to the hospital for another reason, mainly pain. Over 27 unique pathogens were discovered to be causative (Table 79.1), including such atypical organisms as *Mycoplasma*, *Legionella* and *Chlamydia*. This latter organism was the most frequent, accounting for 71 of 249 episodes. Unlike its more benign course in the community, *Chlamydia* was associated with serious outcomes in sickle cell patients. Twenty percent of patients with *Chlamydia pneumoniae* developed respiratory failure and 12% had a neurologic event. Two thirds of these patients had pain.[40] Studies of the incidence of mycoplasmal disease in this same cohort reveal that many of the infected patients had a similar severe course, especially young children.[40] All patients with

Table 79.1 Causes of the Acute Chest Syndrome*

Cause	All Episodes (N = 670)	Age at Episode of Acute Chest Syndrome		
		0–9 yr (N = 329) No. of Episodes (%)	10–19 yr (N = 188)	≥20 yr (N = 153)
Fat embolism, with or without infection[†]	59 (8.8)	24	16	19
Chlamydia[‡]	48 (7.2)	19	15	14
Mycoplasma[§]	44 (6.6)	29	7	8
Virus	43 (6.4)	36	5	2
Bacteria	30 (4.5)	13	5	12
Mixed infections	25 (3.7)	16	6	3
Legionella	4 (0.6)	3	0	1
Miscellaneous infections[¶]	3 (0.4)	0	3	0
Infarction[‖]	108 (16.1)	50	43	15
Unknown**	306 (45.7)	139	88	79

* Data on one episode were excluded because the patient's birth date was not known.
† Nineteen of the episodes of pulmonary fat embolism were associated with infectious pathogens.
‡ This category included episodes in which chlamydia alone was identified but not episodes involving mixed infections or pulmonary fat embolism.
§ This category included episodes in which only *Mycoplasma pneumoniae* or *Mycoplasma hominis* was indentified, but not episodes involving mixed infections, *Mycobacterium tuberculosis*, or pulmonary fat embolism.
¶ This category included two cases of tuberculosis and one case of *Myobacterium avium* complex infection.
‖ A pulmonary infarction was presumed to have occurred during episodes in which the results of the analysis for pulmonary fat embolism, bacterial studies, viral-isolation studies, and serologic tests were complete and were all negative.
** The cause of episodes for which some or all of the diagnostic data were incomplete and no etiologic agent was identified was considered to be unknown.
From Vichinsky EP, Neumayr LD, Earles AN, et al: Causes and outcomes of the acute chest syndrome in sickle cell disease. National Acute Chest Syndrome Study Group. N Engl J Med 342:1855–1865, 2000.

fever and ACS should be given broad-spectrum antibiotics including coverage for these atypical organisms. Viral infections may also play a role in ACS. Parvovirus B19, in particular, has been associated with pulmonary events related to bone marrow necrosis. Other viruses associated with ACS include respiratory syncytial virus, adenovirus, cytomegalovirus, and influenza virus.[39,40]

Pulmonary fat embolus is the second most common etiology of ACS. Definitive diagnosis requires bronchoscopy; however, the classic presentation of severe long bone pain followed several days later by fever, leukocytosis, and a new infiltrate is highly suggestive of pulmonary fat embolus. The amount of fat released from the marrow following sickling and infarction rivals that of a fracture. Once the fat reaches the lung (Figs. 79.3 and 79.4), a host of inflammatory mediators are up-regulated, causing noncardiogenic pulmonary edema.[50] Secretory phospholipase A_2, an enzyme that cleaves phospholipids into highly inflammatory free fatty acids, is elevated early in the course of ACS, even before the chest radiograph becomes abnormal. As a result, phospholipase A_2 has been used to predict the onset of this syndrome.[50]

Other causative factors in ACS are rib infarcts, bronchospasm, sleep apnea, and excessive use of pain medications.[26,30,38] These scenarios result in hypoventilation, which can enhance sickling. A link between ACS and positive thoracic bone scans demonstrating rib or sternal infarcts has been demonstrated. A multicenter ACS study demonstrated that pulmonary infarction was the sole cause of ACS in approximately 20% of cases.[40] These are events for which no other specific cause could be found. A multifactorial hypercoagulable state contributes to many of the problems in sickle cell disease,[26,30] including pulmonary and thrombotic embolism. Thus, pulmonary infarction is assumed to play a role in all ACS events. The increase in activated neutrophils, cytokines, procoagulants, and adhesion proteins found in steady-state sickle cell disease is further accentuated during hypoxia, resulting in widespread lung injury.[26,30] Regional perfusion defects cause shunting and further vasoconstriction, resulting in a vicious cycle of further sickling and infarction. Recent studies have demonstrated that free heme, released from hemolyzed sickle cells, causes consumption of NO as well as generation of free radicals, which further depress NO levels. Lack of NO results in further vasoconstriction and hypoxia in the lung.[42,43,48,51]

Clinical Findings. The most common clinical findings are fever, cough, and chest pain. Adults also may present with hemoptysis and dyspnea. Wheezing is common in children. More than one third of adults initially present with extremity pain without pulmonary symptoms. Although the majority of patients will demonstrate abnormal findings such as rales and dullness on physical examination, 35% of patients will have no findings on lung examination. Radiographic findings are age dependent; children have more upper and middle lobe changes and adults have more lower lobe changes. Pleural effusions and multilobar findings are common. Hematologic changes are also common. Most patients have a significant drop in steady-state hemoglobin, a doubling of the white blood cell count, and a decrease in platelets. Platelet counts of less than $200,000/\mu L$ were found to predict more severe disease, probably reflecting the effect of fat emboli.[40,49] Mean oxygen saturation averages 92% on admission, falling farther with progressive disease during hospitalization. In addition, there was evidence of bronchoconstriction, with an average forced expiratory volume of 53% of the predicted value. A fifth of patients in the multicenter study had improvement in pulmonary function testing with bronchodilators.

Treatment. Despite the recent advances in the understanding of the pathogenesis of ACS, the mortality remains high at 3% for all patients and 9% for adults. Fifteen percent of patients require intubation and 11% (25% of adults) develop multiorgan failure and neurologic events such as seizures, anoxic brain injury, and stroke.[40] Early detection of ACS improves the prognosis and can often be accomplished by close monitoring of all patients with painful crisis, surgery or a febrile illness. The onset of a new fever or pulmonary symptoms should prompt the clinician to obtain a chest radiograph. All patients should have careful monitoring of their respiratory status, including arterial blood gas meas-

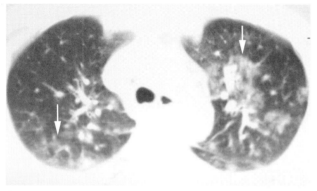

Figure 79.3 Fat embolization. An axial computed tomography image through the upper thorax in a patient with sickle cell disease shows multifocal, bilateral areas of ground-glass opacity (*arrows*). (Courtesy of Michael B. Gotway, MD, Department of Radiology, University of California, San Francisco).

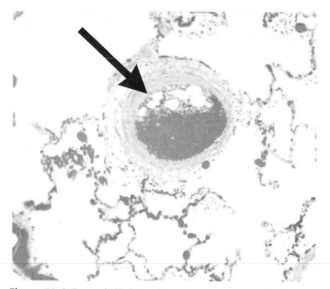

Figure 79.4 Fat emboli (*arrow*) in a pulmonary vessel of a sickle cell patient who died from acute chest syndrome. *See Color Plate*

urements if oxygen saturation falls below 95%. An alveolar-arterial PO_2 gradient of greater than 29 was found to predict clinical severity in children with ACS.[40,52] Use of incentive spirometry has been shown to decrease the incidence of new infiltrates in patients receiving narcotics who were admitted for pain. Oxygen therapy is important for those patients who are hypoxic or have dyspnea. Bronchodilators should be given to all patients with decreased peak flow measurements. Unnecessary oxygen use in the patients without hypoxia or dyspnea may suppress erythropoiesis.[26,38,40,53]

Knowledge of the patient's steady-state laboratory findings, including complete blood count, pulmonary function tests, oxygen saturation, and chest radiograph, are important. Radiographic pulmonary scarring and hypoxia are common at baseline and may be misdiagnosed as a new event. Standard care should also include careful attention to fluid status. Initial replacement with fluids to correct dehydration is important; however, the routine use of large volumes of fluids is not warranted and may result in pulmonary edema, further compromising respiratory status. Sickle cell patients often have biventricular dilation secondary to anemia and may develop transient increases in pulmonary arterial pressures during ACS.

The mainstay of therapy remains blood transfusions. Early studies confirmed that transfusion improves respiratory function and reverses pulmonary deterioration. In the multicenter ACS study, the average PO_2 rose from 63 to 71 mm Hg following transfusion.[40] Although, initially, exchange transfusion was routinely recommended for most patients, simple transfusions are effective and should be tried first with stable patients. Most patients have a significant decrease in hemoglobin, allowing several units of packed cells to be given without an increase in viscosity. All blood should be leukodepleted and matched for Rh, C, E, and Kell antigens. Additionally, the use of sickle-negative blood allows posttransfusion use of hemoglobin electrophoresis as a means of assessing the efficacy of transfusion and assists in making clinical decisions about the need for further transfusions. Deteriorating patients benefit from early transfer to the ICU and exchange transfusion therapy. It is unclear why transfusions produce such an immediate benefit in these patients. Possible mechanisms include changes in cell-cell interactions, correction of ventilation-perfusion mismatches, and decreases in cytokine levels.

New therapies for ACS have been developed in the past several years. Glucocorticoids were recently shown to decrease length of hospital stay in ACS, probably by reducing the inflammatory component of the disease. However, a rebound effect was noted after the steroids were withdrawn, resulting in frequent readmission.[54] This, coupled with concerns about exacerbating avascular necrosis, has limited the use of steroids. Hydroxyurea decreases the incidence of ACS by 50% in adults when used as chronic therapy (and is recommended for all patients with history of pulmonary disease). Use of chronic blood transfusions will also markedly decrease ACS events.[55] Detection and treatment of patients with a bronchoreactive lung component also lowers admission rate. In young patients, recurrent ACS is a common indication for stem-cell transplantation, which has an 85% disease-free survival.[56]

NO is a very exciting new therapy for ACS. NO is a potent vasodilator in the pulmonary circulation. Inhalation of this gas results in a decrease in pulmonary shunting, a decrease in endothelial cell adhesion, an increase in anti-inflammatory effects and bronchodilation, and a decrease in vascular leak.[43,48] Sickle cell patients are deficient in NO secondary to depletion of its precursor (arginine). Because of this deficiency, which worsens during ACS, NO has been used to treat critically ill sickle cell patients with ACS with promising results.[33,42,51] Supplementation with arginine also raises NO levels. The combined use of these two compounds in ACS is currently under study.[43,48]

Chronic Lung Disease

As they age, many patients with sickle cell disease develop chronic pulmonary disease. All patients should be followed with yearly pulmonary function tests. Lung damage in sickle cell disease may present as reactive airway disease or as fibrotic lung disease from scarring. Measurement of diffusion capacity will often demonstrate reduced values, even when corrected for hemoglobin. Pulmonary hypertension, defined as a pulmonary artery systolic pressure of greater than 30 mm Hg on echocardiogram, is common in these patients. The incidence may be as high as 40%.[34] The etiology is multifactorial and includes not only chronic scarring from repeated episodes of ACS, but also the effects of chronic anemia, hypoxia, and the chronic hypercoagulable state of sickle cell disease causing in situ thrombi. Recently, the contribution of decreased levels of NO to the pathophysiology of pulmonary hypertension in sickle cell and other hemolytic states has been elucidated by Gladwin and his colleagues.[43,48] This work shows that free hemoglobin and oxidants, released during the process of hemolysis, consume NO. Arginine, a substrate for NO, when given to patients orally, has been shown to improve echocardiographic measurements of pulmonary artery pressures.[42] Other therapeutic modalities, such as chronic transfusion and hydroxyurea, may also improve the outcome of pulmonary hypertension. Other drugs, such as endothelin-1 inhibitors and sildenafil, have not been studied in sickle cell disease as of yet.[41,57–59] All patients should be screened yearly with echocardiography for the development of pulmonary hypertension.

THALASSEMIA

Thalassemia is a genetic disorder of hemoglobin chain production, which results in a variable degree of anemia depending on the amount and the type of chain that is underproduced. This disease also arose as a protective effect against malaria, thus it is more frequently found in those individuals from the Mediterranean, Asia, and Africa. Most severely ill patients are deficient in β chain production and are classified as having thalassemia major (transfusion dependent) or intermedia (less severe and only intermittently requiring transfusion). Severely affected patients require hypertransfusion from an early age to prevent serious complications arising from expansion of the bone marrow as well as to treat the hemolysis, which can result in hemoglobin concentrations of 4 to 5 g/dL. In addition, thalassemia patients have increased absorption of iron in the gut. Thus, iron overload is the most significant problem facing thalassemia patients. Patients also are commonly splenectomized to decrease transfusion requirements. Just as in other splenectomized individuals, these patients require preoperative vaccinations for protection against *Pneumococcus* and *Haemophilus influenzae*.

The pulmonary complications of this disease relate mainly to the effects of chronic hemolysis and iron overload. Much like those with sickle cell and other hemolytic anemias, patients with thalassemia can develop pulmonary hypertension that is probably related to decreased NO levels. Splenectomy may also contribute to the development of this complication, perhaps by the development of circulating platelet thrombi, which would otherwise be removed by the spleen.[60-64] Even patients with thalassemia intermedia are at risk for pulmonary hypertension,[65] suggesting that all patients be screened yearly with echocardiography and transfused if found to have pulmonary hypertension. Patients who are poorly transfused may have extramedullary hematopoiesis, which can present as lung masses or pleural effusions.

Iron overload causes myocardial toxicity, which may result in pulmonary edema if cardiac failure ensues. Other features of iron overload are discussed next.

PULMONARY COMPLICATIONS OF IRON OVERLOAD AND TRANSFUSION

IRON OVERLOAD

Iron impacts the respiratory system through primary effects on the lung, secondary effects of iron-induced cardiotoxicity, and toxic effects of deferoxamine used in the treatment of iron overload. This section reviews pulmonary manifestations of hematogenous iron overload, as seen in patients on chronic transfusion protocols, in hemochromatosis, and in idiopathic pulmonary hemosiderosis.

Dietary iron is primarily absorbed in the duodenum in the ferrous (Fe^{2+}) state via a carrier protein, but enters the circulation in the ferric (Fe^{3+}) state bound to transferrin. The ability of transferrin and other plasma or cellular proteins to bind or maintain iron in the less reactive ferric state is of great importance in the prevention of the formation of reactive oxygen species, a likely culprit in acute lung injury and acute respiratory distress syndrome (ARDS).[66-68] Most circulating iron enters cells via transferrin receptors on the cell surface and is used by the cell or stored in the intracellular protein, ferritin.

The pathophysiologic role of iron in the lung is not well defined, but it can potentially cause damage through at least two mechanisms: formation of reactive oxygen species and promotion of bacterial growth and virulence. Nonetheless, chelatable iron is present in the lung-lining fluid of the lower lungs of normal individuals.[69] It has been hypothesized that this physiologic pool of iron is necessary for cellular growth and proliferation[69] and serves in an antimicrobial capacity as a oxidative killer, deviating from its usual role as a promoter of bacterial growth.[67]

A growing body of evidence supports iron's role as a direct pulmonary toxin. Oxidative stress and damage have been convincingly implicated in ARDS. Iron's capacity to form free radicals coupled with remarkable disturbances in iron metabolism noted in ARDS suggest that it contributes

to the disorder.[67,70] Elevated serum ferritin levels may predict ARDS in trauma patients.[71] Patients subjected to cardiopulmonary bypass for surgery can develop transient plasma iron overload due to red cell shearing and release of iron from heme.[72] These patients are at increased risk for acute lung injury[73] and ARDS, a complication that occurs in approximately 1.5% of all patients undergoing bypass.[67] Pulmonary edema has been reported as an atypical anaphylactoid reaction to intravenous iron dextran in hemodialysis patients,[74] though the mechanism is unclear. Finally, bronchoalveolar lavage (BAL) fluid from lung transplant recipients has an elevated iron concentration compared to that in normal subjects, perhaps implicating iron in obliterative bronchiolitis, a fibroproliferative disease associated with transplant failure.[75]

The most common clinical iron overload syndromes are hereditary hemochromatosis and hypertransfusion. Hereditary hemochromatosis is an autosomal recessive disorder of iron metabolism. Primary lung involvement is not a common clinical feature, though pulmonary interstitial disease has been reported as a presenting feature.[76] Regular phlebotomy effectively prevents and reverses clinical consequences of iron overload in hereditary hemochromatosis, most notably cardiomyopathy.

Phlebotomy is not an option for patients requiring chronic transfusions for anemia. Patients with thalassemia, aplastic anemia, myelodysplastic syndromes, and sickle cell disease often require regular red blood cell transfusions to control symptoms and end-organ damage. Normal total body iron ranges from 2 to 4 g, with a balanced turnover of approximately 1 mg/day. Physiologic iron excretion occurs via sloughing of skin and mucosal cells; however, this route of excretion has no significant capacity to compensate for exogenous iron overload or increased iron absorption (as occurs in ineffective erythropoiesis). Chronic transfusion regimens vary by patient and disease, but a typical regimen is two units of packed red blood cells per month. Each unit of packed red blood cells contains approximately 250 mg of iron, far exceeding the body's excretional capacity. Clinical iron overload syndromes typically begin after accumulation of 20 g of iron. To ameliorate iron loading, patients on chronic transfusion protocols are treated with burdensome regimens using the parenteral iron chelator deferoxamine. An oral chelator, Deferiprone, is not approved for use in the United States, but is available in other countries. Even with optimal chelation therapy, iron accumulates in the liver, heart, lung, and other tissues, as noted in autopsy series.[77,78]

The relationship of iron overload to pulmonary dysfunction is poorly understood in thalassemic patients. These patients exhibit a variety of pulmonary function abnormalities, including restrictive defects, obstructive defects, and reduced lung diffusion capacity.[78-87] Correction of anemia in thalassemic patients with pulmonary dysfunction and iron overload appears to improve pulmonary function tests. Some investigators[80,88] have noted a relationship between ferritin level or transfusion history and pulmonary dysfunction, whereas others have not.[84,87] Iron-mediated oxidative damage is a potential mechanism for lung damage. Iron chelators have also been associated with lung injury. Continuously infused deferoxamine has been implicated in a pulmonary syndrome comprising severe hypoxemia, radiographic interstitial infiltrates, and inflammation with fibrosis on lung biopsy specimens.[89] In a separate series,[90] four fatal cases of ARDS were attributed to 24-hour deferoxamine infusions. A mouse lung model[91] suggested that deferoxamine induced oxidative damage. The findings of these case series have not been confirmed in prospective studies. The effect of chronic chelation therapy on pulmonary function has not been well studied.

Idiopathic pulmonary hemosiderosis is an uncommon and poorly understood cause of hemoptysis characterized by recurrent pulmonary hemorrhage and hemosiderin accumulation in the lungs. It primarily affects children[92] and young adults, with an estimated incidence of 0.24 to 1.23 cases per million persons.[93] In addition to hemoptysis, presenting features are nonspecific and can include anemia; migratory, patchy parenchymal infiltrates; cough; hypoxemia; clubbing; and fever. Patients frequently have a microcytic, hypochromic anemia resembling an iron deficiency state, but with a blunted response to iron supplementation therapy. Owing to the nonspecific symptoms, the diagnosis may be overlooked or misclassified as pneumonia or reactive airway disease. Other features suggesting IPH are restrictive physiology on pulmonary function testing, hypoxemia with mild exercise, a relapsing and remitting course, and pulmonary hypertension. Associated conditions may include systemic vasculitis and collagen vascular disease. In the appropriate clinical setting, a finding of hemosiderin-laden macrophages in BAL fluid or laryngeal swab specimens is supportive, though other causes of recurrent pulmonary hemorrhage must be excluded. The clinical course is variable, with outcomes ranging from mild hemoptysis to death from acute pulmonary hemorrhage or respiratory failure from chronic hemorrhage. IPH is considered an immune-mediated disorder, though no specific antibodies have been identified for confirmation of the diagnosis. Children with IPH sometimes improve when cow's milk is removed from their diet; the explanation for this is unclear, and treatment is generally supportive.

TRANSFUSION-RELATED ACUTE LUNG INJURY

Epidemiology

Transfusion-related acute lung injury (TRALI) is a complication of blood component transfusion therapy that clinically resembles ARDS but has a much better overall prognosis. The clinical syndrome is characterized by dyspnea, fever, hypoxemia, hypotension, and bilateral pulmonary edema and usually occurs within 1 to 6 hours of transfusion. It is a diagnosis of exclusion and may often be misclassified as ARDS, cardiogenic pulmonary edema, or volume overload. Noncardiogenic pulmonary edema associated with transfusion was first described in 1951,[94] and the term *transfusion-related acute lung injury* was coined in 1983.[95] Case reports have become more frequent since the mid-1980s, most likely due to increased blood component transfusions and increased recognition and reporting of TRALI as a clinical entity. Early case reports of TRALI described severe respiratory distress and hypoxemia. Recent data suggest that subtle (and often undiagnosed) lung injury can occur after transfusion, broadening the case definition of the disorder.

Misclassification, underreporting, and the evolving definition of TRALI make measurement of its frequency difficult. Estimates of incidence based on cohort studies and case series vary considerably. A series of 36 cases at the Mayo Clinic from the early 1980s reported an incidence of 1 case per 5400 units of transfused blood components.[96] Another case series[97] (90 cases from 1991–1995) from one hospital in Edmonton, Alberta, Canada, reported an incidence of 1 case per 1323 units of transfused components. This report stratified the cases by type of blood product, suggesting highest risk with platelets separated from whole blood (1 in 432) and lowest risk with fresh frozen plasma (1 in 19,411). Smaller case series have estimated incidences from 1 case per 7150[98] to 1 case per 28,000[99] transfused units. These are the largest published case series of TRALI, and it is important to note that in each series the investigators' case definition required severe hypoxemia and respiratory distress accompanied by radiographic evidence of pulmonary edema. Mortality in these series ranged from 1% to 66%. Recently published data[100,101] suggest that there are subtle instances of TRALI that may not have met the case definition in these series, so they may have underestimated the true incidence of the disorder.

The risk of TRALI does not seem to vary with sex, and cases have been reported in persons of all ages.[102] Despite variations in estimates of incidence, it is clear that TRALI is an important cause of lung injury and mortality in transfused patients. Recognition of this importance prompted an advisory[103] from the Food and Drug Administration (FDA) to clinicians dated October 19, 2001. Using FDA data, the advisory noted that TRALI is the third leading cause of transfusion-related mortality, accounting for 13% of transfusion-related deaths.

Pathophysiology

The mechanism of lung injury in TRALI is not well defined. Autopsy series report heavy, congested lungs with evidence of diffuse alveolar damage, early fibrosis, hyaline membrane formation, neutrophil infiltration, and alveolar cell hypertrophy.[94,98] Activation of recipient neutrophils, lymphocytes, and complement is a common pathway in two proposed mechanisms of lung injury. In the first proposed mechanism, leukocyte-activating donor antibodies present in the transfused blood component activate recipient leukocytes and complement, causing an inflammatory response in the lungs. Activated neutrophils attach to pulmonary endothelium with resultant injury and capillary leak. Complement activation and neutrophil influx into the lung resembles the pathology seen in ARDS. In support of this theory, Popovsky and Moore[96] documented the presence of nonspecific antigranulocyte antibodies in 89% and antilymphocyte antibodies in 72% of implicated donors' serum in 36 cases at the Mayo Clinic from 1982 to 1984. Sixty-five percent of the antilymphocyte antibodies had human lymphocyte antigen (HLA) specificity corresponding to at least one of their recipient's antigens. Unfortunately, no control group was used for comparison. The authors hypothesized that donor antibodies activate recipient leukocytes, and not vice versa, because the donor antibodies are exposed to a large pool of recipient leukocytes. A reaction of recipient antibodies with donor leukocytes has also been proposed, but the activated donor leukocyte pool would be comparatively small. In further support of this theory, a rabbit lung model demonstrates a TRALI-type reaction when perfused with plasma containing anti-5b antibodies, 5b-positive granulocytes, and rabbit plasma. If 5b-negative granulocytes are substituted or plasma (containing complement) is not perfused, the reaction does not occur.[104] Multiparous women and recipients of granulocyte transfusions are frequently alloimmunized against granulocyte antigens and as such may be more likely than the general population to donate blood that can cause TRALI.[100]

This model fails to explain why TRALI does not always occur when donor antileukocyte antibodies are present and why TRALI has been documented in the absence of antileukocyte antibodies. For example, despite the high frequency of antigranulocyte antibodies noted by Popovsky and Moore,[96] Silliman and colleagues[105] reported no difference in the prevalence of such antibodies in TRALI-implicated donors ($n = 28$) and controls in a nested case-control study, as well as an overall low prevalence of anti-HLA class I and II donor antibodies (3% and 25%, respectively). However, Kao and coworkers[106] suggested that conventional lymphocytotoxicity assays may fail to detect non–complement-binding or low-titer HLA class I antibodies, which may be detected by more sensitive flow cytometry methods.[106] Using flow cytometry, Kopko and colleagues[107] reported a 64% prevalence of anti–HLA II antibodies in implicated donor serum and proposed a role of these antibodies in TRALI. Nonetheless, Kao and coworkers[106] found no staining of HLA class II antigens on vascular endothelial cells or on intravascular leukocytes of either TRALI cases or controls. HLA class II antigen was present on monocyte and macrophage lineage cells in the intra-alveolar space, but antibodies normally do not have access to this area. They concluded that HLA class II antibodies may exacerbate TRALI but do not trigger the lung injury.

In the second proposed mechanism, Silliman and colleagues[108] described an alternative two-event mechanism for TRALI that does not implicate donor antibodies. In their model, the first event is the development of a predisposing clinical situation and the second event is the infusion of biologically active lipids in the plasma fraction of stored blood components. The final pathway is thus activation of host leukocytes and complement, incited in this model by the biologically active lipids in stored blood. They demonstrated that infusion of 5-day-old platelets into the lungs of rats exposed to endotoxin (to simulate sepsis) resulted in a TRALI-type reaction. This reaction did not occur when the rats' lungs were infused with fresh platelets or when rats had not been exposed previously to endotoxin. The results were the same with platelets collected by apheresis or from whole blood, and prestorage white blood cell reduction did not prevent the TRALI-type reaction.[105] Similar results were obtained when plasma from red blood cells was substituted for platelets.[108] According to this model, biologically active lipids accumulate over time during routine storage of all cellular blood components and are capable of activating host neutrophils, complement, pulmonary microvasculature endothelial cells, and cytokines.[105,109] Human case series have demonstrated an association between increased risk

and severity of TRALI and the age of transfused blood components.[105,110]

Diagnosis and Clinical Findings

TRALI is a diagnosis of exclusion based on clinical history and testing as necessary to rule out conditions with similar presentations, most notably congestive heart failure. All plasma-containing blood components have been implicated, including whole blood, red blood cells, fresh frozen plasma, granulocytes from apheresis, platelets from whole blood and apheresis, and cryoprecipitate. Intravenous immune globulin has been implicated in at least one case. Plasma derivatives manufactured from large pools of plasma donors, including albumin and plasma protein fraction, have not been implicated.[102] Timing is an important key to the diagnosis; most cases of TRALI occur within 1 to 2 hours of the transfusion of blood products, and virtually all cases of severe TRALI begin within 6 hours of transfusion. Alternative diagnoses should be sought for severe respiratory problems beginning more than 6 hours after transfusion. The constellation of fever, hypotension, hypoxemia, and bilateral pulmonary edema in a recently transfused patient should alert the clinician to the possibility of TRALI, and any case of respiratory distress occurring within 6 hours should be reported to the transfusion service. Confirmed cases of TRALI should be reported to the FDA. Congestive heart failure can be ruled out on the basis of clinical history, normal jugular venous pressure, absence of an S_3 gallop, and absence of dependent edema. A normal pulmonary capillary wedge pressure on right heart catheterization is helpful but not necessary for the diagnosis. The probability of ARDS, sepsis, or other causes of noncardiogenic pulmonary edema must be considered in the context of clinical history and temporal association with transfusion. Some investigators have noted radiographic findings out of proportion to physical examination in patients with TRALI.

There are no diagnostic laboratory tests shown to affect clinical outcome in TRALI and, as such, management of patients with suspected TRALI should not be delayed for laboratory tests. Popovsky and associates[111] have proposed an algorithm for confirming the diagnosis based on the presence of antileukocyte antibodies in the serum of multiparous donors of implicated blood products. This diagnostic algorithm has not been validated in clinical studies.

The classic clinical course of TRALI is most notable for severe but brief respiratory compromise. Hypoxemia, bilateral pulmonary edema or diffuse infiltrates on chest radiograph, fever, and hypotension herald the onset of the reaction. Hypoxemia can be severe, with arterial PO_2 of 30 to 50 mm Hg in fulminant cases. In 80% of cases the hypoxemia and infiltrates resolve within 96 hours, whereas in approximately 20% they persist more than 7 days. Supplemental oxygen or mechanical ventilation is required in many cases of TRALI, and hypotension can be unresponsive to fluid resuscitation. Mortality is estimated at 5% to 13%. Descriptions of the clinical course of TRALI are evolving as new data suggest that there may be many unrecognized and unreported cases of mild respiratory compromise due to transfusion of blood components. A randomized trial[100] of transfusions from multiparous donors in the ICU showed widespread pulmonary compromise (decreased ratio of arterial PO$_2$ to fraction of oxygen inspired) among recipients, suggesting the existence of subclinical TRALI.

Treatment and Prevention

Treatment of TRALI begins with immediate cessation of transfusion of any implicated blood product and continues with supportive care. Traditionally, patients have been treated with steroids, epinephrine, and diuretics. There are no randomized clinical trials to guide therapy. Steroids have not been shown to result in convincing benefit and are not recommended in the management of TRALI. Epinephrine has also not been convincingly demonstrated to improve clinical outcomes. Diuretics may be harmful; case reports exist of patients dying after the administration of diuretics led to volume depletion and circulatory collapse.[94] Diuretics should be avoided in euvolemic patients. Ventilatory support is the mainstay of care.

TRALI is potentially amenable to both primary and secondary prevention. Avoidance of unnecessary transfusions should reduce the frequency of TRALI. A requirement for hematology consult approval for all nonemergent transfusions has reduced unnecessary transfusions in some scenarios, notably in sickle cell disease, but has not been tested in TRALI prevention. Identifying patients at risk for TRALI may allow clinicians and blood banks to tailor transfusion protocols for at-risk patients, for instance, by preventing blood products from multiparous donors from being given to those at highest risk. Hematologic malignancy, cardiac disease, older age, infection, cytokine administration, recent surgery, and massive transfusion have all been suggested as risk factors for TRALI.[94,97] A randomized clinical trial[100] assessed the risk of TRALI from multiparous (at least three live births) donors in the ICU and found that transfusion of blood from multiparous donors was associated with significantly lower oxygen saturation and higher tumor necrosis factor-α concentrations in recipients compared to non-multiparous controls. No difference in mortality or length of ICU stay was reported. On the basis of this randomized trial and observational studies revealing an association between multiparous donors and previously implicated donors and TRALI, some investigators have recommended removing multiparous women and implicated donors from the donor pool entirely or diverting their donations to plasma protein derivatives.[94,100,112] The risk-benefit impact of these interventions on the already scarce donor pool is controversial. For example, leukodepletion during bypass for elective cardiac surgery has been shown in a randomized trial[113] to enhance oxygenation, but had no impact on mortality or length of ICU stay or hospitalization. Enhanced recognition and reporting of TRALI, as endorsed by the FDA, may lead to identification of high-risk blood donors and restrictions on use of their donations.

Finally, there are no prospective data to guide management of patients who have experienced TRALI and require further transfusions. Preventing reexposure to an implicated donor is a common sense intervention, even in the absence of donor antibody identification. There are no data to support routinely testing patients for antileukocyte antibodies. No other measures apart from the usual prudence in choosing to transfuse are required for secondary prevention.

WHITE BLOOD CELL DISORDERS

LEUKEMIA

The leukemias are a diverse group of neoplasms characterized by quantitative and qualitative white blood cell abnormalities that begin with malignant transformation of leukocyte precursors in the bone marrow that disseminate to peripheral blood and other organs, including the lungs. In addition to direct infiltration of malignant cells in the pulmonary vasculature and parenchyma, leukemia affects the respiratory system through its secondary effects (immunocompromise, anemia) and adverse consequences of its treatment. The effects of radiation therapy, chemotherapy, and stem-cell transplantation on the respiratory system are discussed elsewhere.

Leukemic infiltrates represent direct invasion of the alveoli and interstitium by leukemic cells and frequently are accompanied by infectious pneumonia. As such, fever, cough, hypoxemia, and pleuritic chest pain are common presenting symptoms. Chest radiography typically reveals focal or multifocal infiltrates. Exudative parapneumonic or leukemic pleural effusions may be present. The diagnosis of leukemic infiltration is made by demonstration of leukemic cells in pleural fluid, BAL fluid, or tissue biopsy. Tissue biopsy is usually not necessary; a clinical diagnosis can be made in patients with leukemia and pulmonary infiltrates without evidence of infection, in patients with persistent pulmonary infiltrates despite appropriate antibiotic therapy, and in patients whose infiltrate resolves with antileukemic therapy. Apart from treatment of the underlying leukemia, management is supportive.

When the peripheral white blood cell count is greater than 50,000/μL, as often occurs in acute leukemia, patients are at risk for the hyperleukocytic syndrome. In this disorder, the massive proliferation of neoplastic cells increases the viscosity of blood to the point of stasis and thrombosis in the microvasculature of the lung and other organs. Lung involvement is characterized by dyspnea, hypoxemia, diffuse radiographic infiltrates, and a high risk of intrapulmonary thrombosis. Leukapheresis should be initiated promptly if the extent of pulmonary involvement is severe enough to cause profound dyspnea or hypoxemia.

Neutropenia, a serious consequence of leukemia and its treatment, also occurs in nonmalignant diseases and is discussed next.

NEUTROPENIA

Neutrophils are white blood cells of myeloid lineage that are found in peripheral blood, bone marrow, and tissues. Their central role in the immune system, particularly in phagocytosis and oxidative killing of bacteria, has long been recognized. They also perform other immunomodulatory tasks and contribute to acute lung injury.

Neutropenia is defined as an absolute neutrophil count (ANC) of fewer than 1500 cells/μL, though 1200 cells/μL may be the lower limit of normal in African Americans and a few other smaller select populations. The ANC may be calculated by the following equation:

$$ANC = \frac{[\text{white blood cell count} \times (\%\text{neutrophils} + \%\text{bands})]}{100}$$

Neutropenia is commonly stratified by ANC as mild (1000 to 1500/μL), moderate (500 to 999/μL), or severe (<500/μL). These strata correlate somewhat with the risk of infection but fail to take into account etiology and duration of neutropenia, factors that impact risk significantly. For instance, a patient recently given myeloablative chemotherapy for leukemia with an ANC of 300/μL is at considerably higher risk for infection than an otherwise similar non-leukemic patient with long-standing autoimmune neutropenia and the same ANC. In 1966, Bodey and colleagues[114] published the first cohort study addressing infection risk in neutropenic patients with acute leukemia. These patients are at extremely high risk of infection owing to both quantitative and qualitative neutrophil defects. In that study, the risk of any infection began to increase when the ANC was less than 1000/μL and continued to increase as ANC declined. In patients with an ANC of less than 100/μL, infection occurred in 80% within 2 weeks and 100% within 3 weeks. Neutropenic patients infected with the human immunodeficiency virus (HIV) are at increased risk for bacterial infection compared to non-neutropenic controls with a similar CD4 cell count,[115,116] but their risk is less than that of neutropenic cancer patients.[116] In general, neutropenia due to hypoproliferative marrow poses a higher risk of infection than neutropenia in the setting of functioning marrow. This is not surprising considering that patients with functional marrow continue to release normal neutrophils into their peripheral blood, even if those are quickly sequestered or destroyed. Leukemic patients with protracted (>2 weeks), severe neutropenia, such as high-dose chemotherapy recipients with ANCs of less than 200/μL, are at highest risk owing to quantitative and qualitative neutrophil defects.

The causes of neutropenia can be classified by residual marrow function (Table 79.2). Hypoproliferative marrow states include aplastic anemia, myelodysplasia, pure white cell aplasia, hematologic malignancies, exposure to cytotoxic chemotherapy, congenital neutropenias, infectious infiltration of the marrow, alcoholism, and nutritional (vitamin B_{12} or folate) deficiency. Neutropenia with preserved marrow function occurs in conditions causing peripheral destruction, redistribution, or segregation of neutrophils. These include postinfectious, drug-induced, and primary immune-mediated neutropenias, as well as hypersplenism.

Pulmonary infiltrates and infections are common in neutropenic patients and pose considerable challenges to clinicians. Pulmonary infiltrates occur in up to one third of neutropenic cancer patients, and mortality can approach 50%.[117-121] Infection is the presumed culprit in most cases, though a pathogen is identified less than half of the time. Noninfectious causes of pulmonary infiltrates include alveolar hemorrhage, aspiration or hypersensitivity pneumonitis, radiation injury, leukemic infiltration, pulmonary leukostasis, diffuse alveolar damage, and ARDS.

Staphylococcus aureus and gram-negative rods, often in combination, are typical bacterial organisms identified in neutropenic cancer patients with pneumonia. Among the gram-negative rods, *Escherichia coli* and *Pseudomonas aeruginosa* are the most common offenders (Table 79.3).[122] The gram-negative infectious flora shifts later in the course of neutropenia under selective pressure from broad-spectrum antibiotics, with antibiotic-resistant organisms becoming a serious problem. In pneumonia occurring more than 2 weeks after onset of neutropenia, *Acinetobacter* species, *Citrobacter* species, *Enterobacter* species, *Flavobacterium*

Table 79.2 Classification of Neutropenia by Bone Marrow Function

Hypoproliferative
Aplastic anemia
Myelodysplasia
Pure white cell aplasia
Fanconi's anemia
Hematologic malignancies
Cytotoxic chemotherapy
Congenital neutropenias
Infection/infectious marrow infiltration: parvovirus B19, HIV, hepatitis B and C, CMV, EBV, mycobacteria, fungi
Liver disease
Drug-mediated idiosyncratic agranulocytosis: clozapine, TMP-SMX, antithyroid agents, ticlopidine, dapsone
Alcoholism (direct marrow toxicity and nutritional deficiency)
Nutritional deficiency: vitamin B_{12}, folate

Normal or Hyperproliferative
Direct infection: rickettsiae, malaria, kala azar
Immune mediated
Drugs (direct neutrophil toxicity or immune mediated)
Autoimmune diseases: Felty's syndrome, SLE
Hypersplenism

CMV, cytomegalovirus; EBV, Epstein-Barr virus; HIV, human immunodeficiency virus; SLE, systemic lupus erythematosus; TMP-SMX, trimethoprim-sulfamethoxazole.

Table 79.3 Selected Organisms Causing Pulmonary Infection in Neutropenic Cancer Patients

Bacteria		Fungi
Gram-positive	Gram-negative	
Coagulase-negative staphylococci	*Escherichia coli**	*Aspergillus* species*
*Staphylococcus aureus**	*Pseudomonas aeruginosa**	*Zygomycetes*
Viridans streptococci	*Klebsiella* species*	*Fusarium* species
Enterococcus species (incl. VRE)	*Enterobacter* species	
Beta-hemolytic streptococci	*Citrobacter* species	
Corynebacterium jeikeium	*Acinetobacter* species	
Bacillus species	*Proteus* species	
	Stenotrophomonas maltophilia	
	Pseudomonas species	

* Most common species causing pneumonia.
From Rolston KV: The spectrum of pulmonary infections in cancer patients. Curr Opin Oncol 13:218–223, 2001.

meningosepticum, Pseudomonas species, and *Stenotrophomonas maltophilia* are frequently identified[122,123] and necessitate yet broader antibiotic coverage. The predominance of gram-negative organisms has persisted in neutropenic pneumonia despite shifts in the infectious flora of neutropenic bacteremia to more gram-positive organisms over the past 15 years.[122,124] The increased incidence of gram-positive bacteria is likely due to frequent use of indwelling venous and arterial catheters.

Fungal pneumonia is common among neutropenic patients, especially those with severe neutropenia lasting at least 2 weeks who are on broad-spectrum antibiotics. Fungal infection should be suspected in any neutropenic patient with persistent fever despite broad-spectrum antibiotics. Empirical coverage for fungal organisms is necessary in stem-cell transplant recipients and patients with hematologic neoplasia, as mortality rates approach 90%[125] when invasive fungal infection strikes these populations. Invasive aspergillosis is the most common fungal infection in neutropenic cancer patients, and the lung is the most frequent site of infection by *Aspergillus* species. Other important causes of fungal pneumonia are *Zygomycetes* and *Fusarium* species. *Candida* species rarely cause pneumonia, though they are frequently implicated in neutropenic bacteremia. Distinguishing between the various subtypes of fungal pneumonia by clinical presentation is very difficult.

Diagnosing pulmonary processes in neutropenic patients is a challenging endeavor. Impaired immunity frequently blunts the clinical findings commonly associated with pneumonia, such as fever, cough, and radiographic infiltrates, and cultures of blood and sputum are frequently nondiagnostic. Most of the available data on diagnostic strategies has been obtained in cancer patients, and caution must be used in generalizing these to non–cancer patients, who often merit a less aggressive approach. Computed tomography of the chest is superior to radiography in terms of diagnostic yield and should be obtained immediately upon suspicion of pulmonary pathology in a neutropenic patient[126-130] and serially during the course of the illness. Computed tomography scans are useful for radiographic diagnosis and to guide invasive diagnostic procedures such as fiberoptic bronchoscopy, BAL, fine-needle aspiration, transbronchial biopsy, and open-lung biopsy. Invasive procedures are reasonable in some cases but offer frustratingly low diagnostic yields. They have not been shown to improve mortality, and their impact on clinical outcome and treatment is controversial. The yields of BAL fluid and tissue cultures are reduced by broad-spectrum antibiotics. BAL is reported to provide a diagnosis in 31% to 66% of cases of neutropenic pneumonia.[131] A recent prospective study[131] of BAL in neutropenic cancer patients in the ICU demonstrated an overall diagnostic yield of 49% (38% in bone marrow transplant recipients and 63% in nontransplanted patients). Fiberoptic bronchoscopy is generally safe in neutropenic patients; complication rates are reported in up to 27% in uncontrolled series of neutropenic patients with respiratory dysfunction,[132-134] but controlled studies are required to distinguish procedural complications from the high morbidity of neutropenia itself. Reported complications include fever, mildly decreased oxygenation (rarely requiring intubation), mild to moderate bleeding, and moderate hypotension. A recent prospective study[135] of bronchoscopy in neutropenic cancer patients without respiratory compromise showed no difference in complication rates between subjects and controls. A platelet count of less than 50,000/μL has been suggested as a relative contraindication to bronchoscopy, but a prospective study[60,136] of bronchoscopies with BAL in thrombocytopenic patients (platelets < 100,000/μL, including 13 cases with < 20,000/μL) reported only mild bleeding in 8% of patients, even by the transnasal route. As always, the risks of invasive procedures must be carefully weighed against potential benefits.

Various strategies have been proposed for the prevention of pneumonia and other infections in patients with or at risk for neutropenia. Prophylactic antibiotics, especially fluoroquinolones, have reduced fever and gram-negative bacteremia in clinical trials in leukemia patients, but they have shown no significant effect on pneumonia or mortality.[137,138] Based on clinical trials data, granulocyte-colony stimulating factor (G-CSF) was approved by the FDA for the primary prevention of neutropenia and neutropenic fever and for decreasing length of hospital stay in patients with cancer. However, these promising clinical end points have not been coupled with any reduction in mortality in controlled clinical trials. Furthermore, they are offset by the high cost of hematopoietic growth factors and the risk of side effects. The American Society of Clinical Oncology guidelines recommend reserving G-CSF for use in only the patients at highest (>40%) risk of febrile neutropenia and a prolonged (>10 to 14 days) hospital course.[139] G-CSF is commonly used for the treatment of neutropenic fever, but no convincing benefit for any clinical end point beyond shortening the duration of neutropenia has been demonstrated despite multiple clinical trials. The same lack of mortality or cost benefit is true for patients with HIV infection,[140] though the clinical trial experience is smaller. The theoretical benefit of G-CSF on neutrophil function, supported by preclinical data, has prompted clinical trials of its use in non-neutropenic patients with pneumonia and sepsis. Once again, these trials have not resulted in convincing clinical benefit.[141]

NEUTROPHILS AND ACUTE LUNG INJURY

Mucociliary clearance and immunoglobulin A secretion are the main defenses of the upper airways. Neutrophils and alveolar macrophages police the alveolar space, which is sterile under physiologic conditions. Neutrophils become activated and migrate into lung tissue through a complex process of chemoattraction, adhesion to endothelium, and signaling. During infection or inflammation, neutrophils in the peripheral circulation are exposed to a variety of stimulating factors or cytokines and become increasingly rigid.[142] This enhanced rigidity affects their ability to navigate the pulmonary microvasculature, where endothelial adhesion molecules, selectins, and integrin receptors[143] slow their transit time through alveolar capillaries. This results in a relative sequestration of neutrophils in the pulmonary vasculature, a phenomenon that has been observed in inflammation,[144] sepsis,[142] and acute lung injury.[145] As they slowly roll across the endothelial surface of alveolar capillaries, neutrophils are exposed to a variety of endothelial chemokines, resulting in further adhesion and activation.

From the endothelium, neutrophils migrate into the alveolar space in a process that may be dependent on the p38 mitogen-activated protein kinase.[146] In the alveolar space, neutrophils secrete a variety of pro- and anti-inflammatory cytokines and participate in antimicrobial oxidative destruction and phagocytosis, with acute lung injury as a consequence. The degree of lung injury varies widely by individual and inciting cofactor, as do in vitro responses of neutrophils to activating factors. These observations have led some investigators to hypothesize that a genetic predisposition to neutrophil-mediated lung injury may exist,[145] but as yet no such predisposition or underlying neutrophil disorder has been identified. The existence of ARDS in neutropenic patients[147] suggests that large numbers of neutrophils are not necessary for acute lung injury to occur. Some investigators have observed exacerbations of acute lung injury with recovery from neutropenia,[148] but others have not.[149]

DISORDERS OF THROMBOSIS AND HEMOSTASIS

THROMBOPHILIA

Thrombophilia, a predisposition to form intravascular clots, affects the lungs through its role in pulmonary thromboembolism, pulmonary hypertension, and pulmonary hemorrhage. Thrombophilic conditions include inherited and acquired disorders (Table 79.4); often multiple predisposing factors are present in patients with clinically significant clots. An underlying inherited or acquired predisposing factor can be identified in the majority of cases of venous thromboembolism.[150]

A thorough history and physical examination is appropriate to identify predisposing conditions in patients with documented pulmonary embolism (PE) or deep venous thrombosis (DVT). The history should focus on age at first clot, family history of thrombosis, recurrence of disease and common predisposing clinical circumstances (surgery, pregnancy, trauma, hormone therapy, or malignancy) in order to classify the DVT/PE as "provoked" or "unprovoked" to guide duration of anticoagulation. Unprovoked DVT/PEs (those not associated with pregnancy, cancer, recent limb fracture/immobilization, or recent hospitalization) are associated with a higher risk of recurrence and merit consideration of long-term anticoagulation, whereas provoked DVT/PEs may require as little as 3 months of anticoagulation,[151] with the exception of cancer patients, in whom prolonged therapy may be necessary. Anticoagulation greatly decreases recurrences of clots, but in most patients with unprovoked clots the protective effect is lost when anticoagulation is stopped, regardless of its duration. Identification of those at highest risk of recurrence is thus important for management. Recent studies suggest persistently elevated D-dimers or factor VIII levels 6 months after acute thrombosis may help predict increased recurrence risk. Evidence of persistent thrombosis on ultrasound after completion of therapy may also have predictive value.[152-154] Of note, promising clinical trials of new oral direct thrombin inhibitors not requiring routine laboratory monitoring may revolutionize outpatient anticoagulation practice.

Table 79.4 Causes of Venous Thrombosis

Inherited Thrombophilia
Factor V Leiden mutation
Prothrombin mutation
Protein S deficiency
Protein C deficiency
Antithrombin deficiency
Rare disorders
    Heparin cofactor II deficiency
    Plasminogen deficiency
    Dysfibrogenemia
    Factor XII deficiency
    Increased factor VIII coagulant activity
Congenital venous anomalies

Acquired Disorders
Malignancy
    Tissue factor
    Cancer procoagulant
Surgery, especially orthopedic
Trauma
Pregnancy
Oral contraceptives
Hormone replacement therapy
Tamoxifen
Immobilization
Congestive heart failure
Hyperhomocysteinemia
Antiphospholipid syndrome
Myeloproliferative disorders
    Polycythemia vera
    Essential thrombocythemia
Paroxysmal nocturnal hemoglobinuria
Inflammatory bowel disease
Nephrotic syndrome
Hyperviscosity
    Waldenström's macroglobulinemia
    Multiple myeloma
    Polycythemia vera
Leukocytosis in acute leukemia
Sickle cell anemia

Adapted from Bauer KA, Lip GYH: Evaluation of the patient with established venous thrombosis. *In* Rose BD (ed): Up To Date. Wellesley, MA: Up To Date, 2003.

The utility of a laboratory hypercoagulable evaluation to identify predisposing genetic mutations or coagulation factor abnormalities is controversial. Functional, serologic or genetic assays are available for the factor V Leiden mutation, prothrombin mutations, antithrombin deficiency, protein C or S deficiency, hyperhomocystinemia, antiphospholipid antibodies, and other less common mutations or deficiencies. The prevalence of these defects is well defined in the white population; data are lacking in nonwhites. To date, no prospective studies have demonstrated a significant impact of such a laboratory evaluation on thrombosis recurrence or related morbidity and mortality. In a recent prospective cohort study,[155] 85% of 570 patients (those with the antiphospholipid syndrome or malignancy were excluded) with a first episode of DVT were screened for heritable thrombophilias. The overall DVT recurrence rate was 11%, with no statistically significant difference between patients with and without inherited thrombophilic conditions. In large randomized clinical trials[156,157] of the use of warfarin for the prevention of recurrent DVT/PE, subgroups of patients with heterozygous factor V Leiden or prothrombin mutation were not at higher risk for clot recurrence than patients without these defects.

Despite unproven effects on morbidity and mortality, laboratory evaluation for thrombophilia has some theoretical benefits and is reasonable in high-risk patients. Persons with an unprovoked clot prior to age 50, a history of clotting in first-degree relatives, or recurrent clots may have more than one genetic or factor-related predisposition. A few provoked scenarios may also warrant limited hypercoagulability evaluation. Patients who develop thrombosis on oral contraceptive pills have a high prevalence of factor V Leiden. Patients on oral contraceptive pills with a heterozygous defect for factor V Leiden have a 35-fold increased risk of thrombosis. Pregnancy will often uncover thrombophilia in patients with underlying factor V Leiden, hyperhomocystinemia, prothrombin gene mutation, antiphospholipid syndrome, or protein C or S deficiency. Identification of a defect in this population is important for determining duration and type of anticoagulation as well as predicting pregnancy complications. Because coumadin is teratogenic, heparin must be used in pregnancy (see Chapter 81). Identification of predisposing factors can shift the balance of the risk-benefit decision in favor of indefinite anticoagulation. It may also change management in high-risk clinical scenarios, for instance surgery, pregnancy, or use of hormone therapy. Finally, the first-degree relatives of patients with inherited predispositions may benefit from screening, though this has not been prospectively studied. In choosing to embark on a laboratory hypercoagulability evaluation, careful timing is required. Acute clots and anticoagulation therapy can affect many of the assays, and hematology or laboratory medicine consultation is advised.

ANTIPHOSPHOLIPID SYNDROME AND THE LUNG

The antiphospholipid syndrome is a clinical and laboratory diagnosis based on thrombosis or recurrent miscarriage in a patient with evidence of lupus anticoagulant or anticardiolipin antibodies that are present on two or more occasions measured at least 6 weeks apart. It is often associated with systemic lupus erythematosus. As with other thrombophilic states, the optimal use of anticoagulation is not known for the antiphospholipid syndrome,[158] though a recent randomized clinical trial[159] showed no benefit to the long-held belief that high-intensity anticoagulation (International Normalized Ratio [INR] of 3.1 to 4.0) is superior to moderate-intensity anticoagulation (INR of 2.0 to 3.0).

Pulmonary embolism is the most common lung-associated complication of the antiphospholipid syndrome and may be the initial clinical event. Chronic pulmonary thromboembolism may contribute to pulmonary hypertension, a condition associated with the syndrome. Anticoagulation and vena cava filter placement may prevent worsening of pulmonary hypertension in this scenario. In situ thrombosis in large and small arteries and arterioles has been noted in case reports.[160] Alveolar hemorrhage is a severe complication and has responded to high-dose steroids in case reports.[161] The catastrophic antiphospholipid syndrome is a severe and rare condition involving multiorgan failure, rapid deterioration, and high mortality (over 50%). The lung is frequently involved, and death may result from hypoxic respiratory failure. Treatment strategies are based on anecdotal evidence and include anticoagulation, plasmapheresis, intravenous immune globulin, and steroids.[162]

COAGULOPATHIES AND PLATELET DISORDERS

Hemophilia and von Willebrand's disease are the most common inherited coagulation disorders. Hemophilia A and B are X-linked recessive disorders affecting males (females may rarely exhibit mild disease). Hemophilia A is caused by a deficiency of factor VIII and occurs in one of every 5000 live male births. Hemophilia B, or Christmas disease, is due to a deficiency of factor IX and occurs in one of every 30,000 live male births. Bleeding in hemophilia often results from trauma but may occur spontaneously into tissues or joints. Patients with hemophilia A or B experience massive pulmonary hemorrhage only rarely, and hemoptysis should prompt the clinician to search for an underlying bleeding source in the aerodigestive tract. Most of the lung problems in older hemophiliacs are due to the high prevalence of HIV infection and related pneumonia. Prior to the HIV epidemic, pneumonia accounted for 6.5% of deaths in hemophiliacs.[163] Centers for Disease Control and Prevention data indicate that respiratory disease accounted for 14.4% of adult male hemophilia deaths from 1993 to 1995[164]; HIV infection may have contributed to this increase. Although massive pulmonary hemorrhage is rare, recurrent small hemorrhages or hemothoraces may lead to scarring, fibrosis, or pleural thickening evident on chest radiography.[165] Management of hemophilia is complex and requires purified or recombinant factor replacement. Aminocaproic acid and vasopressin (DDAVP)[166] are useful in certain bleeding episodes. Cryoprecipitate and fresh frozen plasma should only be used in an acute bleeding situation when purified products are unavailable.

Von Willebrand's disease is a common (incidence 1:1,000) autosomal dominant disorder resulting from deficiency or dysfunction of the von Willebrand's factor glycoprotein. Von Willebrand's factor plays two key roles in coagulation: stabilization of factor VIII in plasma and mediation of platelet adhesion to vascular endothelium. Clinical sequelae range from mild to severe and usually manifest as postoperative oozing, menorrhagia, epistaxis, or mucosal bleeding. As with hemophilia, massive pulmonary hemorrhage is rare. DDAVP, factor replacement, and aminocaproic acid are used to control significant bleeding in these patients.

Thrombocytopenia (platelet count less than 150,000/μL) has a broad differential diagnosis that can usually be narrowed by assessment of the patient's medication history and severity of illness. In a healthy outpatient, medications and idiopathic thrombocytopenic purpura are common causes of isolated thrombocytopenia. Severely ill hospitalized patients often have thrombocytopenia due to sepsis, medications, bone marrow toxicity or infiltration, or thrombotic thrombocytopenic purpura. In addition to thrombocytopenia, qualitative platelet defects are frequently seen with aspirin therapy, glycoprotein IIb/IIIa therapy, and uremia. The lung is not frequently a source of clinically significant bleeding in patients with quantitative or qualitative platelet defects. The risk of any clinically significant bleeding begins to increase when the platelet count drops below 20,000/μL, and most experts agree that, in the absence of bleeding, a platelet count of 10,000/μL is a reasonable transfusion threshold.

Patients with coagulation or platelet defects frequently require diagnostic bronchoscopy with or without BAL or biopsy. Concern over bleeding risk has prompted investigation of safe thresholds in platelet count and INR for performance of these procedures. As described earlier, Weiss and colleagues[136] prospectively followed 47 bone marrow transplant patients undergoing fiberoptic bronchoscopy with BAL to assess the complication rate. Sixty-six procedures were performed in this group, and the rate of complications (epistaxis, hemoptysis, bradycardia, or bronchospasm) among the 58 procedures in thrombocytopenic patients was 12%. All but one of these complications were minor and self-limited without worsening fever, oxygenation, or radiographic infiltrates within 4 hours. One patient with a platelet count of 18,000/μL had "life-threatening" epistaxis. Historically, a count of 50,000/μL had been considered a reasonable threshold for performing bronchoscopy. In light of this study, the procedure may be safely performed at counts as low as 20,000/μL, but 20,000 to 50,000/μL ml is an acceptable transfusion range for non-bleeding patients preparing for bronchoscopy.[167] Kozak and Brath[168] performed a retrospective review of 305 episodes of bronchoscopy with biopsy to determine the utility of screening coagulation tests for prediction of bleeding. Of the 35 patients who bled, only 3 were coagulopathic (elevated prothrombin time or activated partial thromboplastin time), and there was no statistically significant difference between bleeding rates in coagulopathic and noncoagulopathic patients. There are no prospective studies of bleeding risk in coagulopathic humans. Brickey and Lawlor[169] prospectively studied bronchoscopy with transbronchial biopsy in a pig model and found no association between INR elevation and bleeding risk, even at profoundly elevated INR levels. These studies suggest that bronchoscopy with BAL and biopsy is safe in thrombocytopenic and coagulopathic patients, but the absence of clinical trial data in humans necessitates experienced clinical judgment on a case-by-case basis. The discontinuation of aspirin prior to bronchoscopy is also controversial. One study recently demonstrated no increased risk of bleeding postprocedure in patients on aspirin.[170] Nonsteroidal antiinflammatory medications inhibit platelets in a reversible manner. Discontinuation of these drugs within 24 hours or less of a procedure should be adequate for prevention of bleeding complications.

SUMMARY

Pulmonologists frequently direct or assist with the care of patients with primary hematologic disorders. This chapter addresses the underlying pathophysiology and management of disorders of red blood cells, hemoglobin, white blood cells, and thrombosis/hemostasis. Special focus is on the current understanding of the pulmonary complications of sickle cell disease. Although ACS has long been recognized

as a cause of death in sickle cell disease, chronic lung disease and pulmonary hypertension in sickle cell disease patients have only recently received the investigation they merit. Pulmonary complications of thalassemia, iron overload, and blood transfusions are explored. Neutropenia is discussed as a complication of malignancy and other disorders. Finally, the impact of thrombosis and coagulopathy on the respiratory system are addressed. When available, randomized clinical trials are cited to support treatment recommendations. Unfortunately, many of these disorders have not been studied in randomized prospective trials. Until and unless they are, clinicians must make the best decisions possible for their patients given the understanding of pathophysiology and the critical review of observational studies.

REFERENCES

1. Marks PW, Glader B: Approach to anemia in the adult and child. *In* Hoffman R (ed): Hematology (4th ed). Philadelphia: Elsevier, 2005, p 457.
2. Sears D, Udden M, Thomas L: Carboxyhemoglobin levels in patients with sickle-cell anemia: Relationship to hemolytic severity. Am J Med Sci 322:345–348, 2001.
3. Levine E, Rosen A, Sehgal L, et al: Physiologic effects of acute anemia: Implications for a reduced transfusion trigger. Transfusion 30:11–14, 1990.
4. Crosby E: Re-evaluating the transfusion trigger: How low is safe? Am J Ther 9:411–416, 2002.
5. Hebert P, Yetisir E, Martin C, et al: Is a low transfusion threshold safe in critically ill patients with cardiovascular diseases? Crit Care Med 29:227–234, 2001.
6. Hebert P, Wells G, Tweeddale M, et al: Does transfusion practice affect mortality in critically ill patients? Transfusion Requirements in Critical Care (TRICC) Investigators and the Canadian Critical Care Trials Group. Am J Respir Crit Care Med 155:1618–1623, 1997.
7. Hebert P, Blajchman M, Cook D, et al: Do blood transfusions improve outcomes related to mechanical ventilation? Chest 119:1850–1857, 2001.
8. Vincent JL, Baron J, Reinhart K, et al: Anemia and blood transfusion in critically ill patients. JAMA 288:1499–1507, 2002.
9. Marsh JT, Brown W, Wolcott D, et al: rHuEPO treatment improves brain and cognitive function of anemic dialysis patients. Kidney Int 39:155–163, 1991.
10. Finch C, Lenfant C: Oxygen transport in man. N Engl J Med 286:407–415, 1972.
11. Van De Pette JE, Guthrie DL, Pearson TC: Whole blood viscosity in polycythaemia: The effect of iron deficiency at a range of haemoglobin and packed cell volumes. Br J Haematol 63:369–375, 1986.
12. Hocking WG, Golde DN: Polycythemia: Evaluation and management. Blood Rev 3:59–65, 1989.
13. Girgis R, Li D, Zhan X, et al: Attenuation of chronic hypoxic pulmonary hypertension by simvastatin. Am J Physiol Heart Circ Physiol 285:H938–H945, 2003.
14. Jernigan N, Resta T: Chronic hypoxia attenuates cGMP-dependent pulmonary vasodilation. Am J Physiol Lung Cell Mol Physiol 282:L1366–L1375, 2002.
15. Fairbanks V, Klee G, Wiseman G, et al: Measurement of blood volume and red cell mass: Re-examination of ^{51}Cr and ^{125}I methods. Blood Cells Mol Dis 22:169–186, 1996.
16. El-Yousef MK, Bakewell WE Jr: The Gaisbock syndrome. JAMA 220:864, 1972.
17. Shibata J, Hasegawa J, Siemens H, et al: Hemostasis and coagulation at a hematocrit level of 0.85: Functional

consequences of erythrocytosis. Blood 101:4416–4422, 2003.

18. Petitt RM, Silverstein MN, Petrone ME: Anagrelide for control of thrombocythemia in polycythemia and other myeloproliferative disorders. Semin Hematol 34:51–54, 1997.

19. Willoughby S, Pearson TC: The use of aspirin in polycythaemia vera and primary thrombocythaemia. Blood Rev 12:12–22, 1998.

20. Piccirillo G, Fimognari F, Valdivia JL, Marigliano V: Effects of phlebotomy on a patient with secondary polycythemia and angina pectoris. Int J Cardiol 44:175–177, 1994.

21. Tartaglia AP, Goldberg JD, Berk PD, Wasserman LR: Adverse effects of antiaggregating platelet therapy in the treatment of polycythemia vera. Semin Hematol 23:172–176, 1986.

22. Najean Y, Rain JD: Treatment of polycythemia vera: The use of hydroxyurea and pipobroman in 292 patients under the age of 65 years. Blood 90:3370–3377, 1997.

23. Hagar RW, Vichinsky EP: Major changes in sickle cell disease. Adv Pediatr 47:249–272, 2000.

24. Vichinsky E, Hurst D, Earles A, et al: Newborn screening for sickle cell disease: Effect on mortality. Pediatrics 81:749–755, 1988.

25. Hebbel RP, Boogaerts MA, Eaton JW, et al: Erythrocyte adherence to endothelium in sickle-cell anemia: A possible determinant of disease severity. N Engl J Med 302:992–995, 1980.

26. Stuart MJ, Setty BN: Acute chest syndrome of sickle cell disease: New light on an old problem. Curr Opin Hematol 8:111–122, 2001.

27. Nagel RL: The challenge of painful crisis in sickle cell disease. JAMA 286:2152–2153, 2001.

28. Tomer A, Harker LA, Kasey S, et al: Thrombogenesis in sickle cell disease. J Lab Clin Med 137:398–407, 2001.

29. Solovey AA, Solovey AN, Harkness J, et al: Modulation of endothelial cell activation in sickle cell disease: A pilot study. Blood 97:1937–1941, 2001.

30. Stuart MJ, Setty BN: Sickle cell acute chest syndrome: Pathogenesis and rationale for treatment. Blood 94:1555–1560, 1999.

31. Cheung AT, Harmatz P, Wun T, et al: Correlation of abnormal intracranial vessel velocity, measured by transcranial Doppler ultrasonography, with abnormal conjunctival vessel velocity, measured by computer-assisted intravital microscopy, in sickle cell disease. Blood 97:3401–3404, 2001.

32. Adedeji MO, Cespedes J, Allen K, et al: Pulmonary thrombotic arteriopathy in patients with sickle cell disease. Arch Pathol Lab Med 125:1436–1441, 2001.

33. Morris CR, Kuypers FA, Larkin S, et al: Arginine therapy: A novel strategy to induce nitric oxide production in sickle cell disease. Br J Haematol 111:498–500, 2000.

34. Castro O, Hoque M, Brown B: Pulmonary hypertension in sickle cell disease: Cardiac catheterization results and survival. Blood 101:1257–1261, 2003.

35. Vichinsky E, McDonald C: Contraceptive use in the chronically ill adolescent female. J Adolesc Health Care 9:87, 1988.

36. Vichinsky EP, Earles A, Johnson R, et al: Alloimmunization in sickle cell anemia and transfusion of racially unmatched blood. N Engl J Med 322:1617–1621, 1990.

37. Vichinsky EP: Comprehensive care in sickle cell disease: Its impact on morbidity and mortality. Semin Hematol 28:220–226, 1991.

38. Vichinsky E, Styles L: Pulmonary complications. Hematol Oncol Clin North Am 10:1275–1287, 1996.

39. Vichinsky EP, Styles LA, Colangelo LH, et al: Acute chest syndrome in sickle cell disease: Clinical presentation and course. Cooperative Study of Sickle Cell Disease. Blood 89:1787–1792, 1997.

40. Vichinsky EP, Neumayr LD, Earles AN, et al: Causes and outcomes of the acute chest syndrome in sickle cell disease. National Acute Chest Syndrome Study Group. N Engl J Med 342:1855–1865, 2000.

40a. Ataga KI, Sood N, De Gent G, et al: Pulmonary hypertension in sickle cell disease. Am J Med 117:665–669, 2004.

40b. Gladwin MT, Sachdev V, Jison ML, et al: Pulmonary hypertension as a risk factor for death in patients with sickle cell disease. N Engl J Med 350:886–895, 2004.

41. Vichinsky E: New therapies in sickle cell disease. Lancet 360:629–631, 2002.

42. Morris CR, Morris S, Hagar W, et al: Arginine therapy: A new treatment for pulmonary hypertension in sickle cell disease. Am J Respir Crit Care Med 168:63–69, 2003.

43. Gladwin MT, Schechter AN, Shelhamer JH, et al: The acute chest syndrome in sickle cell disease: Possible role of nitric oxide in its pathophysiology and treatment. Am J Respir Crit Care Med 159:1368–1376, 1999.

44. Koumbourlis AC, Zar HJ, Hurlet-Jensen A, et al: Prevalence and reversibility of lower airway obstruction in children with sickle cell disease. J Pediatr 138:188–192, 2001.

45. Vichinsky E: A possible disparity between standards of care and delivery of care in sickle cell disease, as assessed from sickle cell centers. Int J Pediatr Hematol Oncol 6:189–197, 1999.

46. Vichinsky EP, Haberkern CM, Neumayr L, et al: A comparison of conservative and aggressive transfusion regimens in the perioperative management of sickle cell disease. The Preoperative Transfusion in Sickle Cell Disease Study Group. N Engl J Med 333:206–213, 1995.

47. Haberkern CM, Neumayr LD, Orringer EP, et al: Cholecystectomy in sickle cell anemia patients: Perioperative outcome of 364 cases from the National Preoperative Transfusion Study. Preoperative Transfusion in Sickle Cell Disease Study Group. Blood 89:1533–1542, 1997.

48. Gladwin MT, Rodgers GP: Pathogenesis and treatment of acute chest syndrome of sickle-cell anaemia. Lancet 355:1476–1478, 2000.

49. Vichinsky E, Williams R, Das M, et al: Pulmonary fat embolism: A distinct cause of severe acute chest syndrome in sickle cell anemia. Blood 83:3107–3112, 1994.

50. Styles LA, Schalkwijk CG, Aarsman AJ, et al: Phospholipase A$_2$ levels in acute chest syndrome of sickle cell disease. Blood 87:2573–2578, 1996.

51. Morris CR, Kuypers FA, Larkin S, et al: Patterns of arginine and nitric oxide in patients with sickle cell disease with vaso-occlusive crisis and acute chest syndrome. J Pediatr Hematol Oncol 22:515–520, 2000.

52. Emre U, Miller S, Rao S, et al: Alveolar-arterial oxygen gradient in acute chest syndrome of sickle cell disease. J Pediatr 123:272–275, 1993.

53. Sherwin BB: Mild cognitive impairment: Potential pharmacological treatment options. J Am Geriatr Soc 48:431–441, 2000.

54. Bernini JC, Rogers ZR, Sandler ES, et al: Beneficial effect of intravenous dexamethasone in children with mild to moderately severe acute chest syndrome complicating sickle cell disease. Blood 92:3082–3089, 1998.

55. Styles LA: Hemoglobin H-Constant Spring disease: An under recognized, severe form of a thalassemia. J Pediatr Hematol Oncol 4:69–74, 1997.

56. Walters MC, Nienhuis AW, Vichinsky E: Novel therapeutic approaches in sickle cell disease. Hematology (Am Soc Hematol Educ Program) 2002:10–34, 2002.

57. Hammerman SI, Klings ES, Hendra KP, et al: Endothelial cell nitric oxide production in acute chest syndrome. Am J Physiol 277:H1579–H1592, 1999.

58. Hammerman SI, Kourembanas S, Conca TJ, et al: Endothelin-1 production during the acute chest syndrome in sickle cell disease. Am J Respir Crit Care Med 156:280–285, 1997.

59. Guidot DM, Hybertson BM, Kitlowski RP, et al: Inhaled NO prevents IL-1-induced neutrophil accumulation and associated acute edema in isolated rat lungs. Am J Physiol 271:L225–L229, 1996.

60. Du ZD, Roguin N, Milgram E, et al: Pulmonary hypertension in patients with thalassemia major. Am Heart J 134:532–537, 1997.

61. Hirsh J, Dacie JV: Persistent post-splenectomy thrombocytosis and thrombo-embolism: A consequence of continuing anaemia. Br J Haematol 12:44–53, 1966.

62. Shebl SS, el-Sharkawy HM, el-Fadaly NH: Haemostatic disorders in nonsplenectomized and splenectomized thalassaemic children. East Mediterr Health J 5:1171–1177, 1999.

63. Tso SC, Chan TK, Todd D: Venous thrombosis in haemoglobin H disease after splenectomy. Aust N Z J Med 12:635–638, 1982.

64. Harlan JM: Introduction: Anti-adhesion therapy in sickle cell disease. Blood 95:365–367, 2000.

65. Beattie KM, Shafer AW: Broadening the base of a rare donor program by targeting minority populations. Transfusion 26:401–404, 1986.

66. Ghio AJ, Carter JD, Richards JH, et al: Iron and iron-related proteins in the lower respiratory tract of patients with acute respiratory distress syndrome. Crit Care Med 31:395–400, 2003.

67. Quinlan GJ, Evans TW, Gutteridge JM: Iron and the redox status of the lungs. Free Radic Biol Med 33:1306–1313, 2002.

68. Upton RL, Chen Y, Mumby S, et al: Variable tissue expression of transferrin receptors: Relevance to acute respiratory distress syndrome. Eur Respir J 22:335–341, 2003.

69. Gutteridge JM, Mumby S, Quinlan GJ, et al: Pro-oxidant iron is present in human pulmonary epithelial lining fluid: Implications for oxidative stress in the lung. Biochem Biophys Res Commun 220:1024–1027, 1996.

70. Lamb NJ, Gutteridge JM, Baker C, et al: Oxidative damage to proteins of bronchoalveolar lavage fluid in patients with acute respiratory distress syndrome: Evidence for neutrophil-mediated hydroxylation, nitration, and chlorination. Crit Care Med 27:1738–1744, 1999.

71. Sharkey RA, Donnelly SC, Connelly KG, et al: Initial serum ferritin levels in patients with multiple trauma and the subsequent development of acute respiratory distress syndrome. Am J Respir Crit Care Med 159:1506–1509, 1999.

72. Pepper JR, Mumby S, Gutteridge JM: Blood cardioplegia increases plasma iron overload and thiol levels during cardiopulmonary bypass. Ann Thorac Surg 60:1735–1740, 1995.

73. Messent M, Sinclair DG, Quinlan GJ, et al: Pulmonary vascular permeability after cardiopulmonary bypass and its relationship to oxidative stress. Crit Care Med 25:425–429, 1997.

74. Freter S, Davidman M, Lipman M, et al: Pulmonary edema: Atypical anaphylactoid reaction to intravenous iron dextran. Am J Nephrol 17:477–479, 1997.

75. Baz MA, Ghio AJ, Roggli VL, et al: Iron accumulation in lung allografts after transplantation. Chest 112:435–439, 1997.

76. Pereiro Alonso ME, Garcia Garcia JM, Martinez Muniz MA, et al: Pulmonary interstitial disease due to hemochromatosis as a presenting sign of disease (in Spanish). Arch Bronconeumol 31:37–39, 1995.

77. Ooi GC, Khong PL, Lam WK, et al: Pulmonary iron overload in thalassemia major presenting as small airway disease. Acta Haematol 108:43–46, 2002.

78. Carnelli V, D'Angelo E, Pecchiari M, et al: Pulmonary dysfunction in transfusion-dependent patients with thalassemia major. Am J Respir Crit Care Med 168:180–184, 2003.

79. Cooper DM, Mansell AL, Weiner MA, et al: Low lung capacity and hypoxemia in children with thalassemia major. Am Rev Respir Dis 121:639–646, 1980.

80. Factor JM, Pottipati SR, Rappoport I, et al: Pulmonary function abnormalities in thalassemia major and the role of iron overload. Am J Respir Crit Care Med 149:1570–1574, 1994.

81. Grisaru D, Rachmilewitz EA, Mosseri M, et al: Cardiopulmonary assessment in beta-thalassemia major. Chest 98:1138–1142, 1990.

82. Keens TG, O'Neal MH, Ortega JA, et al: Pulmonary function abnormalities in thalassemia patients on a hypertransfusion program. Pediatrics 65:1013–1017, 1980.

83. Hoyt RW, Scarpa N, Wilmott RW, et al: Pulmonary function abnormalities in homozygous beta-thalassemia. J Pediatr 109:452–455, 1986.

84. Li AM, Chan D, Li CK, et al: Respiratory function in patients with thalassaemia major: Relation with iron overload. Arch Dis Child 87:328–330, 2002.

85. Santamaria F, Villa MP, Ronchetti R: Pulmonary function abnormalities in thalassemia major. Am J Respir Crit Care Med 151(3 Pt 1):919, 1995.

86. Piatti G, Allegra L, Ambrosetti U, et al: Beta-thalassemia and pulmonary function. Haematologica 84:804–808, 1999.

87. Tai DY, Wang YT, Lou J, et al: Lungs in thalassaemia major patients receiving regular transfusion. Eur Respir J 9:1389–1394, 1996.

88. Filosa A, Esposito V, Meoli I, et al: Evidence of lymphocyte alveolitis by bronchoalveolar lavage in thalassemic patients with pulmonary dysfunction. Acta Haematol 103:90–95, 2000.

89. Freedman MH, Grisaru D, Olivieri N, et al: Pulmonary syndrome in patients with thalassemia major receiving intravenous deferoxamine infusions. Am J Dis Child 144:565–569, 1990.

90. Tenenbein M, Kowalski S, Sienko A, et al: Pulmonary toxic effects of continuous desferrioxamine administration in acute iron poisoning. Lancet 339:699–701, 1992.

91. Adamson IY, Sienko A, Tenenbein M: Pulmonary toxicity of deferoxamine in iron-poisoned mice. Toxicol Appl Pharmacol 120:13–19, 1993.

92. Le Clainche L, Le Bourgeois M, Fauroux B, et al: Long-term outcome of idiopathic pulmonary hemosiderosis in children. Medicine (Baltimore) 79:318–326, 2000.

93. Saeed MM, Woo MS, MacLaughlin EF, et al: Prognosis in pediatric idiopathic pulmonary hemosiderosis. Chest 116:721–725, 1999.

94. Kopko PM, Holland PV: Transfusion-related acute lung injury. Br J Haematol 105:322–329, 1999.

95. Popovsky MA, Abel MD, Moore SB: Transfusion-related acute lung injury associated with passive transfer of antileukocyte antibodies. Am Rev Respir Dis 128:185–189, 1983.

96. Popovsky MA, Moore SB: Diagnostic and pathogenetic considerations in transfusion-related acute lung injury. Transfusion 25:573–577, 1985.

97. Silliman CC, Boshkov LK, Mehdizadehkashi Z, et al: Transfusion-related acute lung injury: Epidemiology and a prospective analysis of etiologic factors. Blood 101:454–462, 2003.

98. Ausley MB Jr: Fatal transfusion reactions caused by donor antibodies to recipient leukocytes. Am J Forensic Med Pathol 8:287–290, 1987.

99. Wallis JP, Lubenko A, Wells AW, et al: Single hospital experience of TRALI. Transfusion 43:1053–1059, 2003.

100. Palfi M, Berg S, Ernerudh J, et al: A randomized controlled trial of transfusion-related acute lung injury: Is plasma from multiparous blood donors dangerous? Transfusion 41:317–322, 2001.

101. Kopko PM, Marshall CS, MacKenzie MR, et al: Transfusion-related acute lung injury: Report of a clinical look-back investigation. JAMA 287:1968–1971, 2002.

102. Popovsky MA: Transfusion and lung injury. Transfus Clin Biol 8:272–277, 2001.

103. Zoon K: Transfusion related acute lung injury (Letter). Accessed Jan. 11, 2005 www.fda.gov/cber/Hr/trali101901.htm.

104. Seeger W, Schneider U, Kreusler B, et al: Reproduction of transfusion-related acute lung injury in an ex vivo lung model. Blood 76:1438–1444, 1990.

105. Silliman CC, Bjornsen AJ, Wyman TH, et al: Plasma and lipids from stored platelets cause acute lung injury in an animal model. Transfusion 43:633–640, 2003.

106. Kao GS, Wood IG, Dorfman DM, et al: Investigations into the role of anti-HLA class II antibodies in TRALI. Transfusion 43:185–191, 2003.

107. Kopko PM, Popovsky MA, MacKenzie MR, et al: HLA class II antibodies in transfusion-related acute lung injury. Transfusion 41:1244–1248, 2001.

108. Silliman CC, Voelkel NF, Allard JD, et al: Plasma and lipids from stored packed red blood cells cause acute lung injury in an animal model. J Clin Invest 101:1458–1467, 1998.

109. Wyman TH, Bjornsen AJ, Elzi DJ, et al: A two-insult in vitro model of PMN-mediated pulmonary endothelial damage: Requirements for adherence and chemokine release. Am J Physiol Cell Physiol 283:C1592–C1603, 2002.

110. Clarke G, Podlosky L, Petrie L, Boshkov L: Severe respiratory reactions to random donor platelets. Blood 84(Suppl 1):465, 1994.

111. Popovsky MA, Chaplin HC Jr, Moore SB: Transfusion-related acute lung injury: A neglected, serious complication of hemotherapy. Transfusion 32:589–592, 1992.

112. Ramanathan RK, Triulzi DJ, Logan TF: Transfusion-related acute lung injury following random donor platelet transfusion: A report of two cases. Vox Sang 73:43–45, 1997.

113. Efstathiou A, Vlachveis M, Tsonis G, et al: Does leukodepletion during elective cardiac surgery really influence the overall clinical outcome? J Cardiovasc Surg (Torino) 44:197–204, 2003.

114. Bodey GP, Buckley M, Sathe YS, et al: Quantitative relationships between circulating leukocytes and infection in patients with acute leukemia. Ann Intern Med 64:328–340, 1966.

115. Jacobson MA, Liu RC, Davies D, et al: Human immunodeficiency virus disease-related neutropenia and the risk of hospitalization for bacterial infection. Arch Intern Med 157:1825–1831, 1997.

116. Moore RD, Keruly JC, Chaisson RE: Neutropenia and bacterial infection in acquired immunodeficiency syndrome. Arch Intern Med 155:1965–1970, 1995.

117. Rossini F, Verga M, Pioltelli P, et al: Incidence and outcome of pneumonia in patients with acute leukemia receiving first induction therapy with anthracycline-containing regimens. Haematologica 85:1255–1260, 2000.

118. Wilson WR, Cockerill FR 3rd, Rosenow EC 3rd: Pulmonary disease in the immunocompromised host (2). Mayo Clin Proc 60:610–631, 1985.

119. Wardman AG, Milligan DW, Child JA, et al: Pulmonary infiltrates and adult acute leukaemia: Empirical treatment and survival related to the extent of pulmonary radiological disease. Thorax 39:568–571, 1984.

120. Poe RH, Wahl GW, Qazi R, et al: Predictors of mortality in the immunocompromised patient with pulmonary infiltrates. Arch Intern Med 146:1304–1308, 1986.

121. Ewig S, Glasmacher A, Ulrich B, et al: Pulmonary infiltrates in neutropenic patients with acute leukemia during chemotherapy: Outcome and prognostic factors. Chest 114:444–451, 1998.

122. Rolston KV: The spectrum of pulmonary infections in cancer patients. Curr Opin Oncol 13:218–223, 2001.

123. Labarca JA, Leber AL, Kern VL, et al: Outbreak of Stenotrophomonas maltophilia bacteremia in allogenic bone marrow transplant patients: Role of severe neutropenia and mucositis. Clin Infect Dis 30:195–197, 2000.

124. Zinner SH: Changing epidemiology of infections in patients with neutropenia and cancer: Emphasis on gram-positive and resistant bacteria. Clin Infect Dis 29:490–494, 1999.

125. Jantunen E, Ruutu P, Piilonen A, et al: Treatment and outcome of invasive Aspergillus infections in allogeneic BMT recipients. Bone Marrow Transplant 26:759–762, 2000.

126. Heussel CP, Kauczor HU, Heussel GE, et al: Pneumonia in febrile neutropenic patients and in bone marrow and blood stem-cell transplant recipients: Use of high-resolution computed tomography. J Clin Oncol 17:796–805, 1999.

127. Heussel CP, Kauczor HU, Heussel G, et al: Early detection of pneumonia in febrile neutropenic patients: Use of thin-section CT. AJR Am J Roentgenol 169:1347–1353, 1997.

128. Caillot D, Couaillier JF, Bernard A, et al: Increasing volume and changing characteristics of invasive pulmonary aspergillosis on sequential thoracic computed tomography scans in patients with neutropenia. J Clin Oncol 19:253–259, 2001.

129. Caillot D, Casasnovas O, Bernard A, et al: Improved management of invasive pulmonary aspergillosis in neutropenic patients using early thoracic computed tomographic scan and surgery. J Clin Oncol 15:139–147, 1997.

130. Maschmeyer G: Pneumonia in febrile neutropenic patients: Radiologic diagnosis. Curr Opin Oncol 13:229–235, 2001.

131. Gruson D, Hilbert G, Valentino R, et al: Utility of fiberoptic bronchoscopy in neutropenic patients admitted to the intensive care unit with pulmonary infiltrates. Crit Care Med 28:2224–2230, 2000.

132. White P, Bonacum JT, Miller CB: Utility of fiberoptic bronchoscopy in bone marrow transplant patients. Bone Marrow Transplant 20:681–687, 1997.

133. Dunagan DP, Baker AM, Hurd DD, et al: Bronchoscopic evaluation of pulmonary infiltrates following bone marrow transplantation. Chest 111:135–141, 1997.

134. Cordonnier C, Escudier E, Verra F, et al: Bronchoalveolar lavage during neutropenic episodes: Diagnostic yield and cellular pattern. Eur Respir J 7:114–120, 1994.

135. Whittle AT, Davis M, Johnson PR, et al: The safety and usefulness of routine bronchoscopy before stem cell

transplantation and during neutropenia. Bone Marrow Transplant 24:63–67, 1999.

136. Weiss SM, Hert RC, Gianola FJ, et al: Complications of fiberoptic bronchoscopy in thrombocytopenic patients. Chest 104:1025–1028, 1993.

137. Cruciani M, Rampazzo R, Malena M, et al: Prophylaxis with fluoroquinolones for bacterial infections in neutropenic patients: A meta-analysis. Clin Infect Dis 23:795–805, 1996.

138. Engels EA, Lau J, Barza M: Efficacy of quinolone prophylaxis in neutropenic cancer patients: A meta-analysis. J Clin Oncol 16:1179–1187, 1998.

139. Ozer H, Armitage JO, Bennett CL, et al: 2000 update of recommendations for the use of hematopoietic colony-stimulating factors: Evidence-based, clinical practice guidelines. American Society of Clinical Oncology Growth Factors Expert Panel. J Clin Oncol 18:3558–3585, 2000.

140. Kuritzkes DR, Parenti D, Ward DJ, et al: Filgrastim prevents severe neutropenia and reduces infective morbidity in patients with advanced HIV infection: Results of a randomized, multicenter, controlled trial. G-CSF 930101 Study Group. AIDS 12:65–74, 1998.

141. Root RK, Lodato RF, Patrick W, et al: Multicenter, double-blind, placebo-controlled study of the use of filgrastim in patients hospitalized with pneumonia and severe sepsis. Crit Care Med 31:367–373, 2003.

142. Drost EM, Kassabian G, Meiselman HJ, et al: Increased rigidity and priming of polymorphonuclear leukocytes in sepsis. Am J Respir Crit Care Med 159:1696–1702, 1999.

143. Poletti V, Salvucci M, Zanchini R, et al: The lung as a target organ in patients with hematologic disorders. Haematologica 85:855–864, 2000.

144. Downey GP, Worthen GS, Henson PM, et al: Neutrophil sequestration and migration in localized pulmonary inflammation: Capillary localization and migration across the interalveolar septum. Am Rev Respir Dis 147:168–176, 1993.

145. Abraham E: Neutrophils and acute lung injury. Crit Care Med 31:S195–S199, 2003.

146. Nick JA, Young SK, Arndt PG, et al: Selective suppression of neutrophil accumulation in ongoing pulmonary inflammation by systemic inhibition of p38 mitogen-activated protein kinase. J Immunol 169:5260–5269, 2002.

147. Laufe MD, Simon RH, Flint A, et al: Adult respiratory distress syndrome in neutropenic patients. Am J Med 80:1022–1026, 1986.

148. Azoulay E, Darmon M, Delclaux C, et al: Deterioration of previous acute lung injury during neutropenia recovery. Crit Care Med 30:781–786, 2002.

149. Nelson S, Belknap SM, Carlson RW, et al: A randomized controlled trial of filgrastim as an adjunct to antibiotics for treatment of hospitalized patients with community-acquired pneumonia. CAP Study Group. J Infect Dis 178:1075–1080, 1998.

150. Bauer KA: Management of thrombophilia. J Thromb Haemost 1:1429–1434, 2003.

151. Kearon C, Gent M, Hirsh J, et al: A comparison of three months of anticoagulation with extended anticoagulation for a first episode of idiopathic venous thromboembolism. N Engl J Med 340:901–907, 1999.

152. Kyrle PA, Minar E, Hirschl M, et al: High plasma levels of factor VIII and the risk of recurrent venous thromboembolism. N Engl J Med 343:457–462, 2000.

153. Palareti G, Legnani C, Cosmi B, et al: Predictive value of D-dimer test for recurrent venous thromboembolism after anticoagulation withdrawal in subjects with a previous idiopathic event and in carriers of congenital thrombophilia. Circulation 108:313–318, 2003.

154. Prandoni P, Lensing AW, Prins MH, et al: Residual venous thrombosis as a predictive factor of recurrent venous thromboembolism. Ann Intern Med 137:955–960, 2002.

155. Baglin T, Luddington R, Brown K, et al: Incidence of recurrent venous thromboembolism in relation to clinical and thrombophilic risk factors: Prospective cohort study. Lancet 362:523–526, 2003.

156. Kearon C, Ginsberg JS, Kovacs MJ, et al: Comparison of low-intensity warfarin therapy with conventional-intensity warfarin therapy for long-term prevention of recurrent venous thromboembolism. N Engl J Med 349:631–639, 2003.

157. Ridker PM, Goldhaber SZ, Danielson E, et al: Long-term, low-intensity warfarin therapy for the prevention of recurrent venous thromboembolism. N Engl J Med 348:1425–1434, 2003.

158. Lockshin MD, Erkan D: Treatment of the antiphospholipid syndrome. N Engl J Med 349:1177–1179, 2003.

159. Crowther MA, Ginsberg JS, Julian J, et al: A comparison of two intensities of warfarin for the prevention of recurrent thrombosis in patients with the antiphospholipid antibody syndrome. N Engl J Med 349:1133–1138, 2003.

160. Espinosa G, Cervera R, Font J, et al: The lung in the antiphospholipid syndrome. Ann Rheum Dis 61:195–198, 2002.

161. Gertner E: Diffuse alveolar hemorrhage in the antiphospholipid syndrome: Spectrum of disease and treatment. J Rheumatol 26:805–807, 1999.

162. Asherson RA, Cervera R: Catastrophic antiphospholipid syndrome. Curr Rheumatol Rep 5:395–400, 2003.

163. Aronson DL: Cause of death in hemophilia A patients in the United States from 1968 to 1979. Am J Hematol 27:7–12, 1988.

164. Soucie JM, Nuss R, Evatt B, et al: Mortality among males with hemophilia: Relations with source of medical care. The Hemophilia Surveillance System Project Investigators. Blood 96:437–442, 2000.

165. Putman CE, Gamsu G, Zinn D, et al: Radiographic chest abnormalities in adult hemophilia. Radiology 118:41–43, 1976.

166. Le Clainche L, Le Bourgeois M, Fauroux B, et al: Long-term outcome of idiopathic pulmonary hemosiderosis in children. Medicine 79:318–326, 2000.

167. Rebulla P: Platelet transfusion trigger in difficult patients. Transfus Clin Biol 8:249–254, 2001.

168. Kozak EA, Brath LK: Do "screening" coagulation tests predict bleeding in patients undergoing fiberoptic bronchoscopy with biopsy? Chest 106:703–705, 1994.

169. Brickey DA, Lawlor DP: Transbronchial biopsy in the presence of profound elevation of the international normalized ratio. Chest 115:1667–1671, 1999.

170. Herth J, Becker H, Ernst A: Aspirin does not increase bleeding complications after transbronchial biopsy. Chest 122:1461–1464, 2002.

80

Pulmonary Complications of Endocrine Diseases

Martha Cavazos, M.D., Leslie Zimmerman, M.D.

INTRODUCTION

Common endocrine disorders can affect the respiratory system in a variety of ways, from an increased risk of specific infections in patients with diabetes to upper airway compression in patients with goiter. Many studies of pulmonary physiology have been done on patients with endocrine disorders, some of which have revealed clinically significant abnormalities. In other studies, however, physiologic abnormalities do not translate into clinical dysfunction, but they help add to our understanding of lung parenchymal growth and development, response to extrathoracic influences, and perhaps even aging. This chapter reviews the effects of various endocrine abnormalities on the pulmonary system.

DIABETES MELLITUS

Diabetes mellitus is the most common of all endocrine disorders and affects 150 million people worldwide. Because of the chronic metabolic derangements, many patients with diabetes develop cardiovascular and end-organ dysfunction. The effects of diabetes on the respiratory system are numerous (Table 80.1), but data are mixed with regard to the effect of diabetes on pulmonary function. Some studies have revealed lower than predicted vital capacity,[1] total lung capacity,[1,2] diffusion capacity for carbon monoxide,[1] maximal oxygen uptake,[1] and inspiratory muscle strength.[3] These mild functional abnormalities have been ascribed to premature aging of the lungs in a fashion similar to the microangiopathic changes that occur in other affected organs in patients with diabetes.[4] However, the results of other studies showed no significant impairment in total lung capacity,[5–10] diffusion capacity for carbon monoxide,[7,8,10] vital capacity,[5–9] pulmonary distensibility,[7] or maximal inspiratory pressure.[11] Results of the Offspring Cohort of the Framington Heart Study[12] found that patients with diabetes had a lower forced vital capacity, with the greatest effect seen in current smokers. There did not seem to be an association between the diagnosis of diabetes and chronic obstructive pulmonary disease, nor did diabetes seem to accelerate chronic obstructive pulmonary disease in smokers. In a study[13] of patients with cystic fibrosis, the presence of cystic fibrosis–related diabetes was associated with a higher rate of decline of FEV_1 and forced vital capacity than in those without diabetes. Compared to patients without diabetes, patients with cystic fibrosis–related diabetes had a higher rate of airway colonization with *Pseudomonas,* which might contribute to the accelerated decline in lung function. In summary, diabetes mellitus (in the absence of cystic fibrosis) does not appear to cause clinically significant pulmonary impairment, and routine pulmonary function testing in patients with diabetes is not warranted.

Cardiovascular factors appear to contribute more than pulmonary factors to impaired physical performance in patients with diabetes. In addition to the increased risk of cardiovascular events in patients with diabetes, there may be an increased frequency of heart failure not explained by coronary artery disease or hypertension. Left ventricular systolic and diastolic dysfunction with exercise appears to be more common in patients with insulin-dependent diabetes than in those without diabetes.[14,15] In addition, when compared with patients with similar degrees of left ventricular dysfunction, exercise limitation and pleural effusions are more common in patients with diabetes.[16,17] There have been reports of peripheral and pulmonary edema in heart failure patients with diabetes treated with the class of oral hypoglycemic drugs known as the thiazolidinediones.[18,19] The mechanism remains undefined and appears to reverse upon withdrawal of the drug.

Acute respiratory distress syndrome has been reported as a complication of diabetic ketoacidosis.[20,21] Interestingly, in patients with septic shock, the presence of diabetes has been associated with a lower risk of developing acute respiratory distress syndrome compared to patients without diabetes, although without a difference in mortality.[22] The presence of diabetes has been associated with a higher mortality in patients with severe acute respiratory syndrome.[23] Diabetes has also been associated with a higher risk of developing idiopathic pulmonary fibrosis.[24]

Table 80.1 Pulmonary Complications of Diabetes Mellitus

Pulmonary function abnormalities (typically minor)
  ↓ Vital capacity
  ↓ Total lung capacity
  ↓ Diffusion capacity for carbon monoxide
  ↓ Carbon monoxide transfer factor
  ↓ Maximal oxygen uptake
  ↓ Inspiratory muscle strength

Left-ventricular dysfunction

Pleural effusions

Obstructive sleep apnea

Infections
  Poorer outcome with
    Community-acquired pneumonia
    Legionella pneumonia
  Increased risk of
    Aspiration pneumonia
    Mucormycosis infection
    Tuberculosis

In previous decades, newborn babies of diabetic mothers were at increased risk for neonatal respiratory distress syndrome. Now, with better metabolic control and more accurate estimations of gestational age, most pregnant diabetic mothers deliver at or near term; this may account for the current low rate of respiratory distress syndrome in this population.[25,26]

Because obesity is a risk factor both for diabetes mellitus type 2 and for obstructive sleep apnea, prevalence of obstructive sleep apnea may be higher in patients with diabetes.[27,28,28a] In addition, obstructive sleep apnea may impose a stress that increases sympathetic output during sleep, which in turn contributes to insulin resistance.[29]

Patients with diabetes are at greater risk for some upper and lower airway infections. Patients with diabetes are particularly predisposed to mucormycosis, a group of infections caused by fungi in the *Mucor* or *Rhizopus* genera. These ubiquitous, saprophytic fungi are found in soil and decaying food. Infection typically occurs during or after an episode of diabetic ketoacidosis, perhaps because the fungus grows best in an acidic, hyperglycemic environment. Five infectious manifestations have been described: rhinocerebral, pulmonary, disseminated, cutaneous, and gastrointestinal.[30] Rhinocerebral infection is the most common form, especially in patients with diabetes. Presentation includes sudden periorbital or paranasal swelling and pain, bloody nasal discharge, and black necrotic nasal mucosa. Characteristic findings on computed tomography are helpful in suggesting the diagnosis.[31] Treatment requires control of the diabetes, antifungal therapy, and often aggressive surgical débridement. Mortality remains high, especially in patients with intracranial involvement. Pulmonary infection mimics invasive aspergillosis and occurs mostly in patients with diabetes or neutropenia. Inhaled mold spores penetrate bronchiole walls, invade arterioles, and cause thrombosis and ischemia. Patients develop nonspecific cough, fever, and pleuritic chest pain. Hemoptysis occurs in one fourth of cases and can be massive.[32] The most common chest radiographic pattern is consolidation; cavitation occurs in about one third of patients.[33] Adenopathy and pleural effusions may also be present, but are less common. Patients with diabetes appear to have a predilection for endobronchial disease; however, sputum culture appears to have a very low yield for diagnosis. For bronchoscopy, histopathologic examination appears to be more sensitive than fungal cultures.[32,33] Treatment requires antifungal therapy (see Chapter 34) and, if localized, surgical resection. Bronchial stenosis is a potential sequela.

Diabetes mellitus is an independent risk factor for tuberculosis,[34–36] and for multidrug-resistant tuberculosis.[36] Treatment of latent tuberculosis in patients with diabetes with a positive purified protein derivative test of greater than 10 mm induration is currently recommended.[37] The radiographic location of tuberculosis in diabetes (i.e., upper or lower lobe predilection) depends on the case series.[36,38] Patients with diabetes and tuberculosis appear to have a higher rate of cavitation.[36,38]

Bacterial pneumonia may or may not be more frequent in patients with diabetes. In a study[39] of over 4000 elderly inhabitants in one township, diabetes mellitus was not an independent risk factor for community-acquired pneumonia. In a separate study,[40] diabetes was not an independent risk factor for nosocomial pneumonia. Nonetheless, diabetes may be a risk factor for poorer outcome in those persons who develop pneumonia. In a meta-analysis,[41] diabetes was found to be a risk factor for higher mortality in community-acquired pneumonia. Given the high prevalence of and mortality from pneumococcal pneumonia, the demonstrated efficacy of the pneumococcal vaccine, and the increasing prevalence of penicillin resistance in pneumococcal strains, pneumococcal vaccination is indicated to reduce invasive disease from pneumococcus in people with diabetes. Diabetes appears to be a risk factor for mortality for critically ill patients with *Legionella* pneumonia.[42] Diabetes may also predispose patients to aspiration pneumonia because of pharyngeal dysfunction and diabetic gastroparesis.[43]

THYROID DISORDERS

Although most patients with goiter are asymptomatic, goiter can cause airway compression with symptoms of dyspnea, stridor, wheezing, hoarseness, and cough (Fig. 80.1).[44–47] Depending on the location and extent, the obstruction may be extra- or intrathoracic. Intrathoracic goiter may cause orthopnea, because of increased airflow limitation in the supine position. In these patients, flow-volume loops produced in a recumbent position may illustrate upper airway obstruction not demonstrated in upright testing.[47] Surgical resection usually relieves compressive symptoms.[44] Iodine-131 is an alternative therapy for some patients with large goiters who may not be surgical candidates because of comorbid illnesses.[48] For patients with baseline tracheal compression, there is often some temporary goiter enlargement from edema and additional airway compromise in the week following ^{131}I treatment. Despite this, with glucocorticoid prophylaxis, most patients do well, and have subsequent goiter shrinkage.[49]

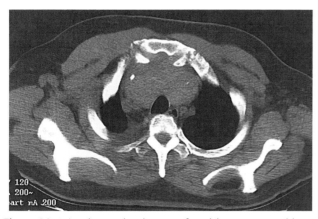

Figure 80.1 A substernal goiter was found in a 69-year-old man who presented with nonproductive cough and mild dyspnea on exertion. The chest radiograph revealed a superior mediastinal mass. A computed tomography scan revealed a large substernal goiter, confirmed to be thyroid by nuclear medicine scan. (Courtesy of Marcia McCowin, MD.)

Table 80.2 Etiologies of Pleural Effusions in Hypothyroid Patients (*n* = 28)

Etiology	No.
Non–hypothyroid-associated pleural effusions	22
Pneumonia	7
Congestive heart failure	7
Malignancy	4
Atelectasis	2
Pancreatitis	1
Cirrhosis with ascites	1
Hypothyroid pleural effusion	5
Hypothyroid-associated effusion due to pericardial involvement	1

Modified from Gottehrer A, Roa J, Stanford GG, et al: Hypothyroidism and pleural effusions. Chest 98:1130–1132, 1990.

HYPERTHYROIDISM

Many patients with hyperthyroidism complain of rest and exertional dyspnea, despite elevated resting cardiac output. Hyperthyroid patients may have decreased vital capacity,[50,51] decreased respiratory muscle strength,[50-53] and an elevated resting minute ventilation[53] (perhaps due to increased central ventilatory drive) that becomes excessive with exercise.[53] Anaerobic thresholds are typically lower than those of age-matched controls.[53,54] With treatment, vital capacity and respiratory muscle strength improve,[50-52] although some patients have persistent dyspnea.[52,53] Hyperthyroidism may also lead to cardiomyopathy and congestive heart failure, thereby contributing to dyspnea and exercise limitation.[55]

Although a case series of five patients suggested an association between hyperthyroidism and worsening of asthma control,[56] bronchial hyperreactivity in response to methacholine challenge is not present in most patients with hyperthyroidism.[53] However, patients with coincident asthma and thyrotoxicosis may have worsening of asthma control if β-blocker agents are used to control hyperthyroid manifestations.

In recent years, there have been a number of reports[57-59] suggesting an association between hyperthyroidism and pulmonary hypertension that can improve with normalization of the hyperthyroid state. The explanation for this association is not clear, but may be due to a generalized autoimmune state, a direct influence of thyroid hormone on pulmonary vasculature, changes in metabolism of pulmonary vasculature vasodilators/vasoconstrictors, or excess cardiovascular stimulation by the sympathoadrenal system. Interestingly, there may also be a high prevalence of hypothyroidism in patients with primary pulmonary hypertension.[60]

HYPOTHYROIDISM

Hypothyroidism has been associated with dyspnea on exertion, respiratory muscle weakness, alveolar hypoventilation, respiratory failure, obstructive and central sleep apnea, and pleural effusions. Lung volumes are generally normal or mildly decreased in mixed populations of obese and nonobese hypothyroid patients.[61-63] Lung volumes typically, though not uniformly, improve with thyroid replacement. In one case series,[64] a subset of hypothyroid, nonobese patients had normal lung volumes and arterial blood gases. However, the diffusion capacities for carbon monoxide were significantly reduced at baseline and improved to near-normal after therapy. In the same series,[63] moderate pulmonary restriction was found in hypothyroid, obese patients, which normalized with weight loss. The most consistent finding in both nonobese and obese hypothyroid patients is that some have a markedly blunted ventilatory response to hypoxia,[63-65] which improves often within weeks of initiation of thyroid hormone replacement. This improvement is not associated with changes in spirometric function or maximal voluntary ventilation, thus suggesting a central nervous system cause for the abnormal ventilatory response. Hypercapnic ventilatory response is also blunted in some, but not all, patients with hypothyroidism.[64,65] Both obese and nonobese hypothyroid patients may develop diaphragmatic muscle weakness that can range from mild impairment, which limits exercise tolerance, to severe dysfunction, with marked resting dyspnea and chronic hypercarbia.[61] Respiratory failure from hypothyroidism has been reported.[66]

Although up to 25% of patients with hypothyroidism have radiographic evidence of a pleural effusion, most patients also have underlying congestive heart failure (Table 80.2).[67] A small percentage of hypothyroid patients do not have another disease process that would explain the effusion. In these patients, the hypothyroid-related effusions tend to be small, less than one third of the chest cavity; unilateral or bilateral; serous or serosanguinous; and transudates or exudates, although generally noninflammatory.[67] Hypothyroid-related effusions typically resolve with treatment of the hypothyroidism.[67]

Hypothyroidism can predispose patients to sleep apnea,[68-70] possibly from narrowing of the upper airway from mucopolysaccharide and protein deposition in the tongue and oropharynx[71] or from abnormalities in ventilatory control.[64] In a case series,[70] only 3.1% of patients with obstructive sleep apnea were found to have hypothyroidism; however, 25% of newly diagnosed hypothyroid patients were found to have obstructive sleep apnea (see Chapter 74 for full discussion of sleep apnea). In this series, the hypothyroid patients with obstructive sleep apnea had blunted ventilatory responses to hypoxia and hypercapnia. Age and body weight were the best predictors of associated obstructive sleep apnea. All the hypothyroid patients with obstructive sleep apnea had improvement in their sleep respiratory disturbance index and their awake ventilatory response to hypoxia and hypercapnia with thyroid replacement. However, in another study,[69] investigators found less than full improvement with thyroid replacement. Central sleep apnea also occurs in hypothyroid patients, and the blunted ventilatory response to hypoxia can improve with thyroid replacement.[68]

Thyroid hormones play an important role in the growth and development of the lung and in the maturation of the lung's surfactant system.[72,73] Although previous studies[74,75] suggested that thyroid hormone levels are decreased in premature infants who develop respiratory distress syndrome, this may be due to decreased thyroxine protein binding, in a manner similar to the euthyroid sick syndrome seen in other acute illnesses.[76] The addition of maternal antenatal thyrotropin-releasing hormone, which increases fetal thyroid hormone levels, did not decrease the frequency or severity of respiratory distress syndrome in premature babies in a large multicenter trial.[77]

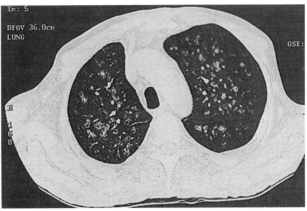

Figure 80.2 Metastatic calcification occurred in the lungs because of chronic renal failure. A 59-year-old man with end-stage renal disease for 5 years complained of chronic progressive shortness of breath. The serum calcium level was 9.9 mg/dL (normal range, 8.5 to 10.5 mg/dL) and the parathyroid hormone level was 271 pg/mL (normal for the laboratory, 11 to 54 pg/mL). High-resolution computed tomography scan revealed numerous nodular ground-glass densities in a peribronchial pattern, most prominently in the upper lobes. (Courtesy of Marcia McCowin, MD.)

PARATHYROID DISEASES

Hyperparathyroidism, typically secondary hyperparathyroidism in patients with end-stage renal disease, may cause diffuse metastatic calcification in the lungs. Metastatic calcification is the deposition of calcium salts in previously normal tissue. This is in contrast to dystrophic calcification, in which there is calcification of diseased or abnormal tissue, as in granulomatous processes. Despite dietary phosphate restriction, administration of phosphate binders, and hemodialysis, renal failure patients are at risk for metastatic calcification, especially if the calcium-phosphorus product increases above 70 mg^2/dL^2. Pulmonary metastatic calcific nodules occur predominantly in the alveolar septa and are associated with varying degrees of fibrosis and septal thickening. Calcification may also occur in pulmonary arterial and bronchial walls. This phenomenon appears to be quite common; up to 60% of chronic dialysis patients have autopsy evidence of pulmonary metastatic calcification.[78,79] Most patients are asymptomatic and have normal chest radiographs and pulmonary function; the presence of pulmonary calcification is detected only at autopsy. However, patients with heavy deposition of calcific nodules may complain of dyspnea and nonproductive cough. Pulmonary function tests in patients with extensive metastatic calcification may show ventilatory restriction with hypoxemia and low diffusion capacity for carbon monoxide.[78,80] Calcium salts tend to precipitate in alkaline conditions. Indeed, metastatic calcification has a predilection for the apical portions of the lungs, the stomach, and the kidneys—all tissues with a relative alkalinity, either because of carbon dioxide removal or hydrogen ion excretion. Due to the higher ventilation-perfusion ratio and lower carbon dioxide concentration at the lung apex, it is estimated that the pH at the apex is 7.5 compared to a pH of 7.3 at the base.[80,81] Other

common sites of deposition include soft tissues and the skin. Radiographically, patients with more extensive calcification typically have numerous nodules about 3 to 10 mm in size which are better visualized on computed tomography scans than on plain chest radiographs (Fig. 80.2).[82] In addition to the nodular densities, patchy consolidation and ground-glass attenuation may be seen that may mimic pneumonia or pulmonary edema. The calcific nature of the nodules may not be apparent on plain radiographic or even computed tomography images, perhaps due to the small size of the calcium deposits. However, radionuclide bone scans usually reveal intense uptake in the lungs and other affected organs (Fig. 80.3).[83,84] Parathyroidectomy or treatment with vitamin D analogues[85] can decrease the calcium-phosphorus double product, reverse bone scan abnormalities and organ deposition, and presumably improve pulmonary function. Metastatic calcification can also rarely occur in primary hyperparathyroidism.[86-88]

Rarely, enlarged mediastinal parathyroid cysts can cause tracheal compression with stridor or vocal cord impingement and hoarseness, or both. Surgical excision is the treatment of choice.[89]

ADRENAL DISEASES

Endogenous Cushing's syndrome (i.e., not from glucocorticoid administration) may be caused by pituitary Cushing's disease, ectopic adrenocorticotropic hormone production such as from small cell lung cancer, bronchial carcinoid, thymic carcinoid, islet cell carcinoma of the pancreas, and adrenal neoplasia. Cortisol levels tend to be much higher with ectopic adrenocorticotropic hormone production and adrenal neoplasia than with pituitary Cushing's disease and pose a greater risk for infection. Hypercortisolism particularly predisposes patients to mucocutaneous fungal

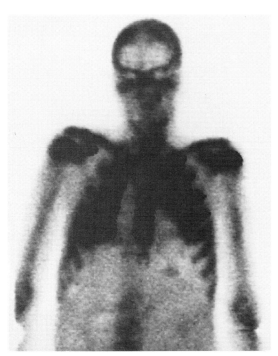

Figure 80.3 Metastatic calcification in the lungs was caused by chronic renal failure. This is the same patient as in Figure 80.2. Whole-body bone imaging revealed diffuse soft-tissue avidity in both lungs.

infections and opportunistic pulmonary infections. The most common pulmonary infections are caused by *Cryptococcus, Aspergillus, Nocardia, Pneumocystis,* and *Mycobacterium tuberculosis.*[90–93] *Pneumocystis carinii* pneumonia tends to occur in patients with the highest morning cortisol levels.[93] Correction of hypercortisolism is an important adjunct to antimicrobial therapy. Cushing's syndrome is also associated with a hypercoagulable state and fourfold increase in thromboembolic disease.[94,95] The risk may be due to an increase in various coagulation factors.

Adrenal insufficiency may be due to either primary adrenal failure (Addison's disease) or secondary adrenal insufficiency. Secondary adrenal insufficiency is most commonly iatrogenic as a result of exogenous glucocorticoid therapy, or may also result from disease of the hypothalamic-pituitary axis. In industrialized countries, 70% to 80% of cases of Addison's disease are autoimmune in origin; in contrast, in resource-poor countries, tuberculosis remains the most common cause.[96] Computed tomography scanning can be somewhat helpful in determining the cause of Addison's disease, because tuberculosis and histoplasmosis can cause adrenal calcification.[97] Adrenal insufficiency via the hypothalamic-pituitary axis may be seen in stressed, very-low-birth-weight infants and may render them more susceptible to bronchopulmonary dysplasia.[98,99]

ACROMEGALY

Acromegaly is a disorder of excess growth hormone secretion in adults, most commonly from a pituitary adenoma. It is characterized by excessive bone growth, soft-tissue hypertrophy, and coarsening of facial features. Total lung capacity and vital capacity are typically increased in patients with acromegaly compared with controls.[100–104] In one study,[102] the increase of the total lung capacity correlated with the duration of acromegaly. Possible causes for the increased lung volumes in these patients include hypertrophy or enlargement of individual alveoli, or an increase in the number of alveoli.[100,103,104] Diffusion capacity for carbon monoxide may be within normal limits[100,103] or elevated.[101]

Macroglossia, nasal polyps, oropharyngeal airway narrowing, and vocal cord restriction and edema may occur in patients with acromegaly. These changes appear to be due to high levels of growth hormone and particularly of insulin-like growth factor-I, which is generated by the action of growth hormone. In addition, coincidental goiter is common in patients with acromegaly and may add to upper airway narrowing.[105,106] Clinical respiratory manifestations of acromegaly include sleep apnea, extrathoracic airway obstruction, vocal cord dysfunction, and an increased risk of difficult intubation. Patients with acromegaly have an increased prevalence of heavy snoring, obstructive sleep apnea, and central sleep apnea.[107,108] Obstructive sleep apnea may be more prevalent in patients with acromegaly because of a narrowed upper airway from osseous enlargement, swelling and hyperplasia of tissues in the oropharynx, and macroglossia. The circumference of neck and fingers, but not body mass index, are predictive of the development of sleep apnea in these patients.[109] Obstructive sleep apnea may improve with treatment of acromegaly with pituitary ablation[110] or with octreotide, a somatostatin analogue.[105,111] Central sleep apnea is also seen in patients with acromegaly. In one study of patients with acromegaly and sleep apnea, 33% had central sleep apnea; interestingly, these patients had higher growth hormone and insulin-like growth factor-I levels than those with obstructive sleep apnea.[107] Patients with acromegaly and central sleep apnea also had a higher ventilatory responses to carbon dioxide than those with acromegaly and obstructive sleep apnea or normal controls.[112] Central sleep apnea may therefore be due to altered ventilatory control.

Evidence of a variable extrathoracic airway obstruction on flow-volume loops in seen in 30% to 50% of patients with acromegaly.[102,113] Intubation may be more difficult in patients with acromegaly because of vocal cord fixation, vocal cord edema, prolapse of an enlarged tongue, and soft-tissue thickening of the oropharynx.[105,114] Preoperative treatment of patients with somatostatin analogues may decrease soft-tissue swelling and enable easier intubation.[105]

SUMMARY

Hypothyroidism and diabetes mellitus are very common medical conditions that can also affect the respiratory system. Manifestations range from respiratory muscle weakness in hypothyroidism to fulminant, life-threatening infection with mucormycosis in poorly controlled diabetes. Other less common endocrine disorders also have specific, common, and fascinating effects on the lung.

REFERENCES

1. Niranjan V, McBrayer DG, Ramirez LC, et al: Glycemic control and cardiopulmonary function in patients with

insulin-dependent diabetes mellitus. Am J Med 103:504–513, 1997.

2. Schnapf BM, Banks RA, Silverstein JH, et al: Pulmonary function in insulin-dependent diabetes mellitus with limited joint mobility. Am Rev Respir Dis 130:930–932, 1984.

3. Wanke T, Formanek D, Auinger M, et al: Inspiratory muscle performance and pulmonary function changes in insulin-dependent diabetes mellitus. Am Rev Respir Dis 143:97–100, 1991.

4. Sandler M: Is the lung a "target organ" in diabetes mellitus? Arch Intern Med 150:1385–1388, 1990.

5. Weir DC, Jennings PE, Hendy MS, et al: Transfer factor for carbon monoxide in patients with diabetes with and without microangiopathy. Thorax 43:725–726, 1988.

6. Sandler M, Bunn AE, Stewart RI: Pulmonary function in young diabetic patients. Chest 90:670–675, 1986.

7. Maccioni FJ, Colebatch HJH: Lung volume and distensibility in insulin-dependent diabetes mellitus. Am Rev Respir Dis 143:1253–1256, 1991.

8. Fuso L, Cotroneo P, Basso S, et al: Postural variations of pulmonary diffusing capacity in insulin-dependent diabetes mellitus. Chest 110:1009–1013, 1996.

9. Sandler M, Bunn AE, Stewart RI: Cross-section study of pulmonary function in patients with insulin-dependent diabetes mellitus. Am Rev Respir Dis 135:223–229, 1987.

10. Benbasssat CA, Stern E, Kramer M, et al: Pulmonary function in patients with diabetes mellitus. Am J Med Sci 322:127–132, 2001.

11. Enright PL, Kronmal RA, Manolio TA, et al: Respiratory muscle strength in the elderly. Am J Respir Crit Care Med 149:430–438, 1994.

12. Walter RE, Beiser A, Givelber RJ, et al: Association between glycemic state and lung function: The Framingham Heart Study. Am J Respir Crit Care Med 167:911–916, 2003.

13. Milla CE, Warwick WJ, Moran A: Trends in pulmonary function in patients with cystic fibrosis correlate with the degree of glucose intolerance at baseline. Am J Respir Crit Care Med 162:891–895, 2000.

14. Mustonen JN, Uusitupa MIJ, Tahvanainen K, et al: Impaired left ventricular systolic function during exercise in middle-aged insulin-dependent and noninsulin-dependent diabetic subjects without clinically evident cardiovascular disease. Am J Cardiol 62:1273–1279, 1988.

15. Jermendy G, Khoor S, Koltai MZ, et al: Left ventricular diastolic dysfunction in type 1 (insulin dependent) diabetic patients during exercise. Cardiology 77:9–16, 1990.

16. Guazzi M, Brambilla R, Pontone G, et al: Effect of non-insulin-dependent diabetes mellitus on pulmonary function and exercise tolerance in chronic congestive heart failure. Am J Cardiol 89:191–197, 2002.

17. Chertow BS, Kadzielawa R, Burger AJ: Benign pleural effusions in long standing diabetes. Chest 99:1108–1111, 1991.

18. Tang WHW, Francis GS, Hoogwerf BJ, Young JB: Fluid retention after initiation of thiazolidinedione therapy in diabetic patients with established chronic heart failure. J Am Coll Cardiol 41:1394–1398, 2003.

19. Hirsch IB, Kelly J, Cooper S: Pulmonary edema associated with troglitazone therapy. Arch Intern Med 159:1811, 1999.

20. Russel J, Follansbee S, Matthay MA: Adult respiratory distress syndrome complicating diabetic ketoacidosis. West J Med 135:148–150, 1981.

21. Powner D, Synder JV, Grenwich A: Altered pulmonary capillary permeability recovering from diabetic ketoacidosis. Chest 68:253–256, 1975.

22. Moss M, Guidot DM, Steinberg KP, et al: Diabetic patients have a decreased incidence of acute respiratory distress syndrome. Crit Care Med 28:2187–2192, 2000.

23. Fowler RA, Lapinsky SE, Hallett D, et al: Critically ill patients with severe acute respiratory syndrome. JAMA 290:367–373, 2003.

24. Enomoto T, Usuki J, Azuma A, et al: Diabetes mellitus may increase risk for idiopathic pulmonary fibrosis. Chest 123:2007–2011, 2003.

25. Livingston EG, Herbert WNP, Hage ML, et al: Use of the TDx-FLM assay in evaluating fetal lung maturity in an insulin-dependent diabetic population. Obstet Gynecol 86:826–829, 1995.

26. Tanasijevic MJ, Winkelman JW, Wybenga DR, et al: Prediction of fetal lung maturity in infants of diabetic mothers using the FLM S/A and desaturated phosphatidylcholine tests. Am J Clin Pathol 105:17–22, 1996.

27. Katsumata K, Okada T, Miyao M, et al: High incidence of sleep apnea syndrome in a male diabetic population. Diabetes Res Clin Pract 13:45–51, 1991.

28. Brooks B, Cistulli PA, Borkman M, et al: Obstructive sleep apnea in obese noninsulin-dependent diabetic patients: Effects of continuous positive airway pressure treatment on insulin responsiveness. J Clin Endocrinol Metab 79:1681–1685, 1994.

28a. Gidding SS, Nehgme R, Heise C, et al: Severe obesity associated with cardiovascular deconditioning, high prevalence of cardiovascular risk factors, diabetes mellitus/hyperinsulinemia, and respiratory compromise. J Pediatr 144:766–769, 2004.

29. Ip MSM, Ng MMT, Lam WK, et al: Obstructive sleep apnea is independently associated with insulin resistance. Am J Respir Crit Care Med 165:670–676, 2002.

30. Tedder M, Spratt JA, Anstadt MP, et al: Pulmonary mucormycosis: Results of medical and surgical therapy. Ann Thorac Surg 57:1044–1050, 1994.

31. Kim KH, Choi YW, Jeon SC, et al: Mucormycosis of the central airway: CT findings in three patients. J Thorac Imaging 14:210–214, 1999.

32. Lee FYW, Mossad SB, Adal KA: Pulmonary mucormycosis: The last 30 years. Arch Intern Med 159:1301–1309, 1999.

33. McAdams HP, Rosado de Christenson M, Strollo DC, Patz EF Jr: Pulmonary mucormycosis: Radiographic findings in 32 cases. AJR Am J Roentgenol 186:1541–1548, 1997.

34. Pablos-Mendez A, Blustein J, Knirsch CA: The role of diabetes mellitus in the higher prevalence of tuberculosis among Hispanics. Am J Public Health 87:574–579, 1997.

35. Kim SJ, Hong YP, Lew WJ, et al: Incidence of pulmonary tuberculosis among diabetics. Tuber Lung Dis 76:529–533, 1995.

36. Bashar M, Alcabes P, Rom WN, Condos R: Increased incidence of multidrug-resistant tuberculosis in diabetic patients on the Bellevue Chest Service, 1987–1997. Chest 129:1514–1519, 2001.

37. Jasmer RM, Nahid P, Hopewell PC: Clinical practice: Latent tuberculosis infection. N Engl J Med 347:1860–1866, 2002.

38. Perez-Guzman C, Torres-Cruz A, Villareal-Velarde H, Vargas MH: Progressive age-related changes in pulmonary tuberculosis images and the effect of diabetes. Am J Respir Crit Care Med 162:1738–1740, 2000.

39. Koivula I, Sten M, Makela PH: Risk factors for pneumonia in the elderly. Am J Med 96:313–320, 1994.

40. Hanson LC, Weber DJ, Rutala WA: Risk factors for nosocomial pneumonia in the elderly. Am J Med 92:161–166, 1992.

41. Fine MJ, Smith MA, Carson CA, et al: Prognosis and outcomes of patients with community-acquired pneumonia: A meta-analysis. JAMA 274:134–141, 1995.

42. El-Ebiary M, Sarmiento X, Torres A, et al: Prognostic factors of severe *Legionella* pneumonia requiring admission to ICU. Am J Respir Crit Care Med 156:1467–1472, 1997.

43. Harrington OB, Duckworth JK, Starnes CL, et al: Silent aspiration after coronary artery bypass grafting. Ann Thorac Surg 65:1599–1603, 1998.

44. McHenry CR, Piorowski JJ: Thyroidectomy in patients with marked thyroid enlargement: Airway management, morbidity, and outcome. Am Surg 60:586–591, 1994.

44a. Shen WT, Kebebew E, Duh QY, Clark OH: Predictors of airway complications after thyroidectomy for substernal goiter. Arch Surg 139:656–659, 2004.

45. Melliere D, Saada F, Etienne G, et al: Goiter with severe respiratory compromise: Evaluation and treatment. Surgery 103:367–373, 1988.

46. Torchio R, Gulotta C, Perboni A, et al: Orthopnea and tidal expiratory flow limitation in patients with euthyroid goiter. Chest 124:133–140, 2003.

47. Meysman M, Noppen M, Vincken W: Effect of posture on the flow-volume loop in two patients with euthyroid goiter. Chest 110:1615–1618, 1996.

48. Huysmans D, Hermus A, Corstens F, et al: Large, compressive goiters treated with radioiodine. Ann Intern Med 121:757–762, 1994.

49. Bonnema SJ, Bertelsen H, Mortensen J, et al: The feasibility of high dose iodine 131 treatment as an alternative to surgery in patients with a very large goiter: Effect on thyroid function and size and pulmonary function. J Clin Endocrinol Metab 84:3636–3641, 1999.

50. Mier A, Brophy C, Wass JAH, et al: Reversible respiratory muscle weakness in hyperthyroidism. Am Rev Respir Dis 139:529–533, 1989.

51. Siafakas NM, Milona I, Salesiotou V, et al: Respiratory muscle strength in hyperthyroidism before and after treatment. Am Rev Respir Dis 146:1025–1029, 1992.

52. McElvaney GN, Wilcox PG, Fairbarn MS, et al: Respiratory muscle weakness and dyspnea in thyrotoxic patients. Am Rev Respir Dis 141:1221–1227, 1990.

53. Kendrick AH, O'Reilly JF, Laszlo G: Lung function and exercise performance in hyperthyroidism before and after treatment. Q J Med 68:615–627, 1988.

54. Kahaly G, Hellermann J, Mohr-Kahaly S, et al: Impaired cardiopulmonary exercise capacity in patients with hyperthyroidism. Chest 109:57–61, 1996.

55. Forfar JC, Muir AL, Sawers SA, et al: Abnormal left ventricular function in hyperthyroidism: Evidence for a possible reversible cardiomyopathy. N Engl J Med 307:1165–1170, 1982.

56. Settipane GA, Schoenfeld E, Hamolsky MW: Asthma and hyperthyroidism. J Allergy Clin Immunol 49:348–355, 1972.

57. Nakchbandi IA, Wirth JA, Inzucchi SE: Pulmonary hypertension caused by Graves' thyrotoxicosis. Chest 116:1483–1485, 1999.

58. Chu JW, Kao PN, Faul JL, Doyle RL: High prevalence of autoimmune thyroid disease in pulmonary arterial hypertension. Chest 122:1668–1673, 2002.

59. Marvsis M, Brianti M, Marani G, et al: Hyperthyroidism and pulmonary hypertension. Respir Med 96:215–220, 2002.

60. Curnock AL, Dweik RA, Higgins BH, et al: High prevalence of hypothyroidism in patients with primary pulmonary hypertension. Am J Med Sci 318:289–292, 1999.

61. Martinez FJ, Bermudez-Gomez M, Celli BR: Hypothyroidism: A reversible cause of diaphragmatic dysfunction. Chest 96:1059–1063, 1989.

62. Freedman S: Lung volumes and distensibility, and maximum respiratory pressures in thyroid disease before and after treatment. Thorax 33:785–790, 1978.

63. Wilson WR, Bedell GN: The pulmonary abnormalities in myxedema. J Clin Invest 39:42–55, 1960.

64. Zwillich CW, Pierson DJ, Hofeldt FD, et al: Ventilatory control in myxedema and hypothyroidism. N Engl J Med 292:662–665, 1975.

65. Ladenson PW, Goldenheim PD, Ridgway EC: Prediction and reversal of blunted ventilatory responsiveness in patients with hypothyroidism. Am J Med 84:877–883, 1988.

66. Pandya K, Lal C, Scheinhorn D, et al: Hypothyroidism and ventilator dependency. Arch Intern Med 149:2115–2116, 1989.

67. Gottehrer A, Roa J, Stanford GG, et al: Hypothyroidism and pleural effusions. Chest 98:1130–1132, 1990.

68. Millman RP, Bevilacqua J, Peterson DD, Pack AI: Central sleep apnea in hypothyroidism. Am Rev Respir Dis 127:504–507, 1983.

69. Grunstein RR, Sullivan CE: Sleep apnea and hypothyroidism: Mechanisms and management. Am J Med 85:775–779, 1988.

70. Lin CC, Tsan KW, Chen PJ: The relationship between sleep apnea syndrome and hypothyroidism. Chest 102:1663–1667, 1992.

71. Orr WC, Males JL, Imes NK: Myxedema and obstructive sleep apnea. Am J Med 70:1061–1066, 1981.

72. Ballard PL, Hovey ML, Gonzales LK: Thyroid hormone stimulation of phosphatidylcholine synthesis in cultured fetal rabbit lung. J Clin Invest 74:898–905, 1984.

73. Gonzales LW, Ballard PL, Ertsey R, et al: Glucocorticoids and thyroid hormones stimulate biochemical and morphological differentiation of human fetal lung in organ culture. J Clin Endocrinol Metab 62:678–691, 1986.

74. Redding RA, Pereira C: Thyroid function in respiratory distress syndrome (RDS) of the newborn. Pediatrics 54:423–428, 1974.

75. Klein AH, Foley B, Kenny FM, et al: Thyroid hormone and thyrotropin responses to parturition in premature infants with and without respiratory distress syndrome. Pediatrics 63:380–385, 1979.

76. Job L, Emery JR, Hopper AO, et al: Serum free thyroxine concentration is not reduced in premature infants with respiratory distress syndrome. J Pediatr 131:489–492, 1997.

77. Collaborative Santiago Surfactant Group: Collaborative trial of prenatal thyrotropin-releasing hormone and corticosteroids for prevention of respiratory distress syndrome. Am J Obstet Gynecol 178:33–39, 1998.

78. Conger JD, Hammond WS, Alfrey AC, et al: Pulmonary calcification in chronic dialysis patients: Clinical and pathological studies. Ann Intern Med 83:330–336, 1975.

79. Ullmer E, Borer H, Sandoz P, et al: Diffuse pulmonary nodular infiltrates in a renal transplant recipient: Metastatic pulmonary calcification. Chest 120:1394–1398, 2001.

80. Murris-Espin M, Lacassagne L, Didier A, et al: Metastatic pulmonary calcification after renal transplantation. Eur Respir J 10:1925–1927, 1997.

81. Chan ED, Morales DV, Welsh CH, et al: Calcium deposition with or without bone formation in the lung. Am J Respir Crit Care Med 1165:1654–1669, 2002.

82. Hartman TE, Muller NL, Primack SL, et al: Metastatic pulmonary calcification in patients with hypercalcemia: Findings on chest radiographs and CT scans. AJR Am J Roentgenol 162:799–802, 1994.

83. Hwang GJ, Lee JD, Park CY, et al: Reversible extraskeletal uptake of bone scanning in primary hyperparathyroidism. J Nucl Med 37:469–471, 1996.

84. Brodeur FJ, Kazerooni EA: Metastatic pulmonary calcification mimicking airspace disease: Technetium-99m-MDP SPECT imaging. Chest 106:620–622, 1994.

85. Martin KJ, Gonzalez EA, Gellens ME, et al: Therapy of secondary hyperparathyroidism with 19-Nor-1a,25-dihydroxyvitamin D2. Am J Kidney Dis 32:S61–S66, 1998.

86. Cohen AM, Maxon HR, Goldsmith RE, et al: Metastatic pulmonary calcification in primary hyperparathyroidism. Arch Intern Med 137:520–522, 1977.

87. De Nardi P, Gini P, Molteni B, et al: Metastatic pulmonary and rectal calcification secondary to primary hyperparathyroidism. Eur J Surg 162:735–738, 1996.

88. Poddar B, Bharti S, Parmar VR, et al: Respiratory failure due to pulmonary calcification in primary hyperparathyroidism. Arch Dis Child 87:257, 2002.

89. Landau O, Chamberlain DW, Kennedy RS, et al: Mediastinal parathyroid cysts. Ann Thorac Surg 63:951–953, 1997.

90. Drew PA, Takezawa K: Pulmonary cryptococcosis and pituitary Cushing's disease. Diagn Cytopathol 18:365–367, 1998.

91. Anthony LB, Greco FA: *Pneumocystis carinii* pneumonia: A complication of Cushing's syndrome. Ann Intern Med 94:488–489, 1981.

92. Hill AT, Stewart PM, Hughes EA, et al: Cushing's disease and tuberculosis. Respir Med 92:604–606, 1998.

93. Graham BS, Tucker WS: Opportunistic infections in endogenous Cushing's syndrome. Ann Intern Med 101:334–338, 1984.

94. Jacoby RC, Owings JT, Ortega T, et al: Biochemical basis for the hypercoagulable state seen in Cushing syndrome. Arch Surg 136:1003–1007, 2001.

95. Small M, Lowe GD, Forbes CD, Thomson JA: Thromboembolic complications in Cushing's syndrome. Clin Endocrinol (Oxf) 19:503–511, 1983.

96. Bhatia E, Jain SK, Gupta RK, et al: Tuberculous Addison's disease: Lack of normalization of adrenocortical function after anti-tuberculous chemotherapy. Clin Endocrinol (Oxf) 48:355–359, 1998.

97. Vita JA, Silverberg SJ, Goland RS, et al: Clinical clues to the cause of Addison's disease. Am J Med 78:461–466,1985.

98. Watterberg KL, Scott SM: Evidence of adrenal insufficiency in babies who develop bronchopulmonary dysplasia. Pediatrics 95:120–125, 1995.

99. Korte C, Styne D, Merritt A, et al: Adrenocortical function in the very low birth weight infant: Improved testing sensitivity and association with neonatal outcome. J Pediatr 128:257–263, 1996.

100. Donnelly PM, Grunstein RR, Peat JK, et al: Large lungs and growth hormone: An increased alveolar number? Eur Respir J 8:938–947, 1995.

101. Trotman-Dickenson B, Weetman AP, Hughes JMB: Upper airflow obstruction and pulmonary function in acromegaly: Relationship to disease activity. Q J Med 79:527–538, 1991.

102. Harrison BDW, Millhouse KA, Harrington M, et al: Lung function in acromegaly. Q J Med 47:517–532, 1978.

103. Brody JS, Fisher AB, Gocmen A, et al: Acromegalic pneumonomegaly: Lung growth in the adult. J Clin Invest 49:1051–1060, 1970.

104. Garcia-Rio F, Pino JM, Diez JJ, et al: Reduction of lung distensibility in acromegaly after suppression of growth hormone hypersecretion. Am J Respir Crit Care Med 164:852–857, 2001.

105. Ben-Shlomo A, Melmed S: The role of pharmacotherapy in perioperative management of patients with acromegaly. J Clin Endocrinol Metab 83:2730–2734, 2003.

106. Gasperi M, Martino E, Manetti L, et al: Prevalence of thyroid diseases in patients with acromegaly: Results of an Italian multi-center study. J Endocrinol Invest 25:240–245, 2002.

107. Grunstein RR, Ho KH, Sullivan CE: Sleep apnea in acromegaly. Ann Intern Med 115:527–532, 1991.

108. Pelttari L, Polo O, Rauhala E, et al: Nocturnal breathing abnormalities in acromegaly after adenomectomy. Clin Endocrinol (Oxf) 43:175–182, 1995.

109. Fatti LM, Scacchi M, Pincelli AI, et al: Prevalence and pathogenesis of sleep apnea and lung disease in acromegaly. Pituitary 4:259–262, 2001.

110. Mickelson SA, Rosenthal LD, Rock JP, et al: Obstructive sleep apnea syndrome and acromegaly. Otolaryngol Head Neck Surg 111:25–30, 1994.

111. Bayse B, Michiels E, Bouillon R, et al: Relief of sleep apnoea after treatment of acromegaly: Report of three cases and review of the literature. Eur Respir J 10:401–404, 1997.

112. Grunstein RR, Ho KY, Berthon-Jones M, et al: Central sleep apnea is associated with increased ventilatory response to carbon dioxide and hypersecretion of growth hormone in patients with acromegaly. Am J Respir Crit Care Med 150:496–502, 1994.

113. Evans CC, Hipkin JL, Murray GM: Pulmonary function in acromegaly. Thorax 32:322–327, 1977.

114. Kitahata LM: Airway difficulties associated with anaesthesia in acromegaly. Br J Anaesth 43:1187–1190, 1971.

81

The Lungs in Obstetric and Gynecologic Disease

Norman W. Rizk, M.D., **Stephen E. Lapinsky,** M.B., B.Ch.

INTRODUCTION

Both respiratory physiology and the respiratory tract's susceptibility to disease are uniquely altered in gynecologic and obstetric conditions, including normal pregnancy. This chapter summarizes normal physiologic alterations during pregnancy and then considers pathologic diseases and disorders that arise during pregnancy. Airway disorders, infectious diseases, pulmonary vascular and embolic disorders, and acute lung injury are considered in turn. Finally, pleural and parenchymal diseases that arise as a consequence of gynecologic conditions are addressed.

PHYSIOLOGIC ALTERATIONS DURING NORMAL PREGNANCY

Profound alterations of respiratory function and cardiovascular physiology accompany pregnancy; these conditions contribute to many of the disorders of the lung during pregnancy. The adaptive changes during the gravid period are designed to support maternal and fetal well-being during the special stresses of fetal growth and parturition, but they exacerbate some disorders and confuse interpretation of laboratory and imaging studies used to assess many other common conditions.

ALTERATIONS IN RESPIRATORY PHYSIOLOGY

Upper airway, particularly nasal, mucosal edema is a common finding in normal pregnancy. About 20% to 30% of gravid women complain of rhinitis symptoms,[1] conventionally attributed to the effects of estrogen on mucosal congestion. Animal studies appear to support this attribution.[1] The symptoms begin in the first trimester and persist throughout gestation. Many patients thought to have rhinitis of pregnancy may actually have other or coincident causes of rhinitis.[2] An important implication of nasal mucosal edema in pregnancy is that it predisposes to nosebleeds from nasal intubations, so an oral approach is favored at the time of delivery.

Chest wall configuration is also altered, partially due to a 50% increase in the average costal angle[3] and partially due to an increase in the circumference of the lower chest wall. Diaphragmatic position is elevated 4 to 5 cm, but excursion does not diminish.[3] Muscle strength, as measured by maximum transdiaphragmatic pressure, does not appear to be diminished from its usual mean value of about 95 cm H_2O,[4] allowing reserve for both the augmented minute ventilation of pregnancy and the stresses of delivery.

Important changes occur in lung function and lung volumes. Because the loss of lung volume resulting from elevation of the diaphragm is only partially offset by the smaller increase in chest wall diameter, functional residual capacity (FRC) is usually diminished by about 18%, or 300 to 500 mL.[5] The FRC diminution is partitioned almost equally between the expiratory reserve volume and the residual volume.[3,5] The loss of FRC at term is made worse by recumbency, when diaphragm elevation is greatest because of the higher intra-abdominal pressure. Increased pulmonary blood volume in pregnancy may also serve to lower the FRC.[6] This reduction in FRC is associated clinically with increased uptake and elimination of inhalational anesthetics and with rapid desaturation during hypopnea, as a result of the loss of the oxygen reservoir function of end-expiratory lung volume. Endotracheal intubation at term is thus substantially more hazardous than in nongravid patients.

Although the FRC is lower, total lung capacity decreases only marginally, and vital capacity does not change.[5] Inspiratory capacity actually increases slightly due to the decrease in FRC, so incentive spirometry is effective in preventing postpartum atelectasis.

Airway function is also largely unchanged during pregnancy.[3] Airway resistance may actually slightly decrease. Routine measurements of air flow, such as the FEV_1 and flow rates at mid-expiratory lung volume (forced expiratory flow, or FEF_{25-75}) are thus valuable in assessing dyspnea during pregnancy.

The most striking changes are in respiratory drive and minute ventilation. Central drive, as assessed by the inspiratory pressure measured 100 msec after airway occlusion at the onset of inspiration ($P_{0.1}$), has been measured during pregnancy.[4] $P_{0.1}$ is increased by 13 weeks and continues to increase to week 37 of gestation, returning to normal by 24 weeks after delivery. These serial changes in respiratory drive appear to correlate with changes in serum progesterone levels,[4,7] which either stimulate respiration directly or increase the sensitivity of the respiratory center to PCO_2.[4,7] Carbon dioxide production itself increases one third to one half by the last trimester, but this is more than made up for by the greatly augmented minute ventilation, so primary respiratory alkalosis with renal bicarbonate wasting as compensation is normal.[8] Arterial blood gas measurements typically show the pH ranging from 7.40 to 7.47, with PCO_2 reaching as low as 28 to 32 mm Hg. PO_2 rises slightly as a result of an increase in alveolar ventilation.

Most of the increase in minute ventilation is due to a 30% to 35% increase in tidal volume. Respiratory rate is unchanged early and rises only about 10% later in pregnancy. Oxygen consumption increases 20% to 33% in pregnancy, owing to both maternal and fetal metabolic demands. Changes in some of these parameters are shown in Figure 81.1.

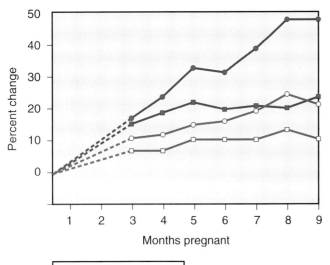

Figure 81.1 Changes in minute ventilation, oxygen uptake, basal metabolism, and the ventilatory equivalent for oxygen at monthly intervals throughout pregnancy. (From Prowse CM, Gaensler EA: Respiratory and acid-base changes during pregnancy. Anesthesiology 26:381, 1965.)

ALTERATIONS IN CARDIOVASCULAR PHYSIOLOGY

Adaptive cardiovascular changes are designed to support dual circulations but contribute to the risk for hydrostatic pulmonary edema, so cardiac disorders during pregnancy often present as respiratory failure. During normal pregnancy, maternal blood volume increases by about 2 liters, or 40%.[9,10] Red blood cell mass increases as well, but only by 20% to 30%, accounting for the normal 10% to 12% drop in hematocrit.[10,11] Plasma oncotic pressure also drops as intravascular volume expands, increasing the risk for pulmonary edema at lower intravascular hydrostatic pressures. During the 24 hours after parturition, oncotic pressure falls further because of blood loss and mobilization of extravascular fluid.

The enlarged intravascular volume of pregnancy is accommodated chiefly by venous capacitance vessels. Central venous pressure and pulmonary capillary occlusion ("wedge") pressure are unchanged, reflecting an increase in left ventricular compliance, as evidenced by the enlarged cardiac silhouette seen on chest radiograph. The increased left ventricular end-diastolic volume results in an augmented stroke volume (ejection fraction is little changed), but systemic vascular resistance (SVR) diminishes.[11,12] These changes account for the 30% to 45% increase in cardiac output reached by 25 to 32 weeks of gestation. After 5 weeks, heart rate increases as well,[13] but less so than stroke volume. The time frame of these changes is depicted in Figure 81.2, which also illustrates the profound effect of vena caval and aortic compression by the gravid uterus when the supine position is assumed.

OBSTETRIC DISORDERS AND THE LUNGS

Gravid and newly postpartum patients may acquire disorders and diseases unique to pregnancy but also continue to experience common disorders that occur outside of pregnancy; the natural history or frequency of the disorder is sometimes altered by the gravid state. Even for diseases not altered by pregnancy, management requires special knowledge of the safety of therapies.[14] Specific diseases are considered here with these principles in mind.

OBSTRUCTIVE AIRWAY DISEASE

Asthma

Asthma affects 4% to 8% of the general population and is the most common pulmonary disorder in pregnancy.[14a] The Working Group on Asthma and Pregnancy of the National Asthma Education Program (NAEP) estimated that 1% to 4% of pregnancies are complicated by asthma[15]; about 10% of pregnant asthmatic patients have an attack of asthma during labor, and status asthmaticus has been shown to complicate about 0.2% of pregnancies.[16]

Investigations of the interaction of asthma and pregnancy have been of two types: natural history and outcome studies. Studies examining the hormonal milieu have suggested that progesterone might diminish smooth muscle contractility in the lung, as it does in the uterus and the gut. Juniper and colleagues[17] performed serial measurements of bronchial

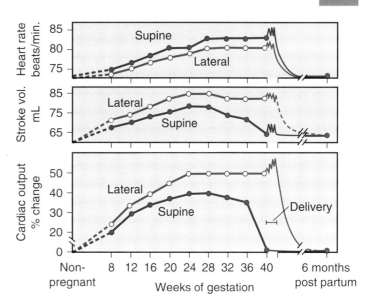

Figure 81.2 Changes in maternal heart rate, stroke volume, and output during pregnancy with the gravida in the supine and lateral positions. (From Cheek TG, Gutsche BB: Maternal physiologic alterations during pregnancy. *In* Shnider SM, Levinson G [eds]: Anesthesia for Obstetrics. Baltimore: Williams & Wilkins, 1993, p 8.)

reactivity to methacholine challenge in 16 women before and during pregnancy and found that airway responsiveness improved. Clinical and epidemiologic studies, however, have failed to provide convincing evidence of any consistent change in the natural history of asthma during pregnancy. Turner and coworkers,[18] for example, compiled the results of nine studies of asthma symptoms reported by pregnant women. Among them, 22% reported worsening, 29% reported improvement, and 22% reported no change. Other studies have reported similar figures, with about 23% to 42% worsening, 18% to 36% improving, and 40% to 41% exhibiting no change.[19,20] The differences reported in the natural history probably reflect differences in study populations, smoking history, ethnicity, or other variables.[21] The NAEP Working Group concluded that the symptomatic course of asthma in pregnancy is probably better in approximately one third, worse in one third, and unchanged in one third.[15]

Fetal and maternal outcome for asthma and pregnancy have also been examined in a variety of studies since 1980. Adverse outcomes, including an increased incidence of preterm labor, low neonatal birth weight, increased perinatal mortality, preeclampsia, vaginal hemorrhage, chronic hypertension, and complicated labor, have been reported.[15,21] A prospective case-control study performed over 12 years in one institution demonstrated no differences in the rates of preeclampsia, perinatal mortality, low birth weight, or congenital malformations,[22] whereas a large epidemiologic study from Sweden did suggest an association with perinatal mortality and low birth weight.[22]

Therapy of asthma in pregnancy should be individualized according to severity of disease, as outlined by the NAEP.[15] Objective measurement of lung volumes and flow should be part of the regimen; initial office spirometry is recommended, and home peak flow monitoring should be considered for patients taking medication daily. Fetal monitoring should include ultrasonography between 12 and 20 weeks of gestation, and serial ultrasonography and fetal heart rate monitoring may be needed in the third trimester. Patients can supplement this with recordings of fetal activity using "kick counts."[15] For women who have asthma

attacks during labor, fetal monitoring is considered essential by the NAEP.

Environmental control measures are also important to reduce exposure to stimuli that exacerbate the disease.[15,21] Avoidance of cigarette smoke is particularly important. Other specific triggers in individual patients should be identified and controlled; but because of the small risk for anaphylaxis, immunotherapy should be deferred until after delivery.

Asthma that causes more than occasional symptoms should be treated daily with anti-inflammatory therapy, using either an inhaled corticosteroid or sodium cromolyn.[15] The former is more consistently effective. Inhaled short-acting beta2-agonists should be prescribed for symptomatic relief in all grades of asthma and are sufficient as the sole therapy for mild episodic asthma. Frequent need for beta2-agonists should prompt institution of, or an increase in, the use of anti-inflammatory agents to treat, rather than mask, a deteriorating clinical course. A stepwise approach encompasses the use of beta2-agonists for only mild occasional asthma, moving on to inhaled anti-inflammatory agents (corticosteroids or cromolyn) for chronic asthma.[23] Use of sustained-release theophylline or long-acting beta-agonists is appropriate for persistent asthma in patients already taking the first two agents.[23] Finally, addition of rapidly tapered courses of oral corticosteroids for active symptoms occurring in patients already taking the first three drugs should be considered. Daily or alternate-day oral steroid administration should be reserved for patients for whom burst therapy fails to control the asthma for more than 10 to 24 days or for whom frequent treatments are required.[15] Extensive practice algorithms have been made available by the NAEP Working Group on Asthma and Pregnancy.[15]

A large body of literature has examined the topic of possible teratogenicity of agents used in the pharmacotherapy of asthma in pregnancy. In general, the risks of poorly controlled asthma far outweigh the possible hazards of drug therapy.[24] Both animal and human studies of beta2-agonists, administered either by inhalation or systemically, have indicated an acceptable safety profile for the fetus. They are also safe for use during lactation. Nonselective beta-agonists, such as epinephrine, carry a risk of uterine vasoconstriction[25] and are probably best avoided. Acceptable beta₂-agonists in pregnancy include metaproterenol, albuterol, pirbuterol, bitolterol, and terbutaline. The safety of long-acting beta-agonists (e.g., salmeterol and formoterol) is unknown, but these drugs have been recommended in patients with poor control on a combination of inhaled corticosteroids and short-acting beta-agonists.[23]

Theophylline has a long history of use during pregnancy and is considered safe, but the therapeutic range in plasma should be adjusted to 8 to 12 µg/mL because of diminished protein binding during pregnancy. Theophylline passes freely to the fetus, and newborns occasionally show signs of theophylline toxicity, particularly when maternal blood levels are high. Theophylline is also transmitted to breast milk, with a milk-to-serum ratio of about 0.70; but, in general, less than 1% of the maternal dose is transferred to the infant. Animal studies suggest that the leukotriene inhibitors montelukast and zafirlukast are safe in pregnancy, and they can be continued in patients who have previously responded.[24,26] Zileuton should be avoided, as animal studies have raised questions about its safety in pregnancy.

Although animal studies have shown an increased incidence of cleft palate with use of corticosteroids, no human data support this association. Systemic corticosteroids have been reported to cause intrauterine growth retardation but of a relatively modest degree. Halogenated corticosteroids do not cross the placenta easily, and so fetal and neonatal adrenal suppression is not a major concern with these compounds.[15] Among the inhaled steroids, beclomethasone and budesonide are preferred because of their long history of use in pregnancy and the absence of any demonstrated toxicity to the fetus.[24] Table 81.1 summarizes the U.S. Food and Drug Administration safety classification for agents useful for the treatment of asthma in pregnancy.

Labor and delivery can be especially hazardous for asthmatic patients, partly because of the drugs commonly administered. Narcotics other than fentanyl release histamine, which may worsen bronchospasm. Lumbar epidural analgesia is generally preferred; but if general anesthesia is to be used, pretreatment with atropine or glycopyrrolate assists bronchodilation. Ketamine is the preferred anesthetic, although halogenated anesthetics at low concentrations may provide bronchodilatation as well.[15] Preterm labor may be safely treated with nifedipine or magnesium sulfate.[16] Oxytocin is the optimal labor induction agent and is useful for postpartum hemorrhage, but 15-methyl prostaglandin F₂ₐ, methylergonovine, and ergonovine may cause bronchospasm and should be avoided if possible.

Cystic Fibrosis

Cystic fibrosis (CF), occurring in about 1 in 1500 whites and 1 in 17,000 blacks, is a common genetic disease. With improved therapy, median survival has now increased to 32 years,[27] and the Cystic Fibrosis Foundation found that 4% of female CF patients between the ages of 17 and 37 were pregnant in 1990.[28] This occurs despite the frequent infertility of women due to delayed sexual development. Pregnancy in CF patients, as might be anticipated, has been associated

Table 81.1 Potential Fetal Risk of Drug Therapy in Pregnancy According to the FDA Classification for Safety in Pregnancy

Drug	FDA Classification*
Asthma Therapy	
Inhaled Bronchodilators	
Albuterol (salbutamol)	C
Terbutaline	B
Ipratropium	B
Salmeterol	C
Formoterol	B
Inhaled Corticosteroids	
Beclomethasone	C
Budesonide	B
Fluticasone	C
Leukotriene Antagonists	
Zafirlukast	B
Montelukast	B
Zileuton	C
Other Agents for Asthma	
Theophylline	C
Cromolyn	B
Systemic corticosteroids	B
Anticoagulants	
Heparin	C
Low-molecular-weight heparin	B
Warfarin	X
Antibiotics	
Penicillins	B
Cephalosporins	B
Macrolides	B/C
Quinolones	C
Clindamycin	B
Tetracyclines	D

Although the Food and Drug Administration (FDA) classification provides an overview of fetal risk, detailed information should be consulted for individual drugs. Classification of individual drugs may change as the literature evolves.

* Class A: Controlled studies in women fail to demonstrate a risk to the fetus in the first trimester, and the possibility of fetal harm seems remote. Class B: Animal studies do not indicate a risk to the fetus, and there are no controlled human studies; or animal studies do show an adverse effect on the fetus, but well controlled studies in pregnant women have failed to demonstrate a risk to the fetus. Class C: Studies in animals have shown the drug to have teratogenic or embryocidal effects, but there are no controlled studies in women; or no studies are available in either animals or women. Class D: Positive evidence of human fetal risk exists, but benefits in certain situations (e.g., life-threatening situations or diseases for which safer drugs cannot be used or are ineffective) may make use of the drug acceptable despite its risks. Class X: Studies in animals or humans have demonstrated fetal abnormalities, or there is evidence of fetal risk based on human experience, and the risk of the drug clearly outweighs any possible benefit. These drugs are contraindicated in pregnancy.

with adverse fetal and maternal outcomes.[29,29a] In a review of 215 pregnancies reported between 1960 and 1991, Kent and Farquharson[30] showed that although more than 80% progressed to at least 20 weeks one fourth of them delivered preterm, and the perinatal death rate was 14%. In this study, there were three maternal deaths, and by 2 years after delivery 14% of mothers had died.[30] More recent studies suggest that risk stratifies according to severity of illness.[29,31] In one case-control study, pregnancy had little effect on patients with stable CF, although poor outcomes were seen in those with severe disease.[32] Prepregnancy counseling, particularly for women with more severe disease, is essential in limiting excessive maternal and fetal risk. In this regard, it has been suggested that FEV_1 below 60% of predicted and the presence of pulmonary hypertension are poor prognostic factors for both mother and infant.[28,30]

INFECTIOUS DISEASES

Bacterial Pneumonia

Pneumonia is a leading cause of maternal and fetal morbidity and mortality.[33-37] Maternal mortality from pneumonia in nonimmunocompromised hosts ranged from 0% to 4% in series published since 1980.[33-35] The reported incidence varies widely, from 1 per 367 to 1 per 2388 deliveries[33-36] but may not be higher than that in the general population. One report, however, indicated that pneumonia may be increasing in incidence, with human immunodeficiency virus (HIV) and chronic disease the major risk factors.[33]

Pregnancy increases the risk for major complications of pneumonia. In the series by Madinger and colleagues,[35] of 25 patients culled from 25,000 deliveries, 40% suffered major complications, including five intubations, two empyemas, one pneumothorax, and one pericardial tamponade. Similarly, in the series by Briggs and associates[38] of 34 patients, 7 required mechanical ventilation, and 2 died. Gestation is also threatened; preterm labor occurs in 4% to 44%.[33-36] The small-for-gestational-age rate is as high as 12%,[33] and intrauterine and neonatal death rates have ranged from 2.6% to 12.0%.[34,35] In all series, underlying chronic illness in the mother has been a powerful predictor of adverse outcome in both fetus and mother.

Pneumonia in pregnancy is most commonly bacterial in origin; the microbiologic spectrum mirrors community-acquired pneumonia, with *Streptococcus pneumoniae* and *Haemophilus influenzae* the most common organisms.[33-35] Other common organisms include *Mycoplasma pneumoniae* and *Chlamydia pneumoniae*. As in other community-acquired pneumonias, the causative agent is identified in only about half the cases. Unfortunately, the diagnosis of pneumonia is frequently delayed because of reluctance to obtain a chest radiograph; a posteroanterior radiograph performed with a grid and a peak voltage of 90 to 120 kV exposes the mother to 5–30 mrad but the fetus to 100 times less or about 300 μrad.[39] A lateral chest radiograph produces greater maternal exposure (150–250 mrad) and is usually not required.[39] The hazard to both fetus and mother of delaying the diagnosis greatly exceeds the risk of this very small dose. Antibacterial therapy is similar to treatment in the nonpregnant patient, although tetracyclines, quinolones, and metronidazole should be avoided if possible.[39]

Viral Pneumonia

Viral pneumonia remains a serious concern in pregnancy. In the influenza pandemic of 1918 to 1919, the maternal rate of mortality from pneumonia was as high as 50%. In the more recent epidemic of 1957 to 1958, pregnant women accounted for 10% of fatalities, and about half of the women of childbearing age who died were pregnant.[40] Since the epidemic of 1957 to 1958, the maternal mortality rate from influenza A and B has been relatively low but still higher than that in the general population. Because of this, the Centers for Disease Control and Prevention (CDC) recommend trivalent inactivated influenza vaccine in otherwise healthy women during the second and third trimesters of pregnancy.[41] Although influenza virus does cross the placenta, current opinion holds that it is not likely to be teratogenic to the fetus, despite isolated reports that link influenza with neural tube and other malformations. Amantadine has been used in pregnancy successfully, both as treatment and as prophylaxis, although the newer neuraminidase inhibitor zanamirir, given by inhalation, is increasingly a treatment option. The chief risk of influenza in the modern era probably resides in its dreaded complication of superimposed staphylococcal or gram-negative bacillary pneumonia.

Varicella pneumonia, caused by a virus of the DNA herpesvirus group, has also been linked to particularly adverse outcomes during pregnancy. In one review, Haake and coworkers[42] reported a 35% mortality rate in pregnant subjects, compared with 10% in other adults. Data are conflicting, and not all prospective studies have confirmed an increased incidence or mortality in pregnancy.[39] Treatment with acyclovir does appear to reduce mortality in gravid patients and probably should be used as therapy for active disease.[43] Use of varicella-zoster immunoglobulin (VZIG) should be considered for susceptible pregnant women who have been exposed to varicella, optimally within 72 hours of exposure. Administration of VZIG reduces but does not abolish risk for fetal infection or congenital varicella syndrome, and it is effective in preventing complications of varicella in the mother. Patients should be evaluated similarly to other adults and a decision made to administer the immunoglobulin based on immune status, type of exposure, and health status.[44] The currently licensed attenuated live virus against varicella is contraindicated in pregnancy.

Rubeola viral infection, often complicated by viral and then superimposed bacterial pneumonia, has also been associated with adverse outcomes, including preterm labor, spontaneous abortion, and perinatal mortality.[45] Fetal malformation, however, does not appear to be a consequence of the disease. Nonimmune, exposed pregnant patients can receive passive immunoprophylaxis with immunoglobulin within 6 days of exposure; the live viral vaccine is contraindicated during pregnancy.

Hantavirus, which usually presents as a hemorrhagic fever and renal syndrome, can be accompanied by pneumonitis and acute respiratory distress syndrome (ARDS). It has been reported to have a similar presentation and course in pregnancy; outcomes of pregnant patients with hantavirus appear similar to those for nonpregnant patients with hantavirus and to those of pregnant patients with other causes of ARDS.[46]

Severe acute respiratory syndrome (SARS), due to a novel coronavirus, causes pneumonia and ARDS, with respiratory failure occurring in 15% of patients and a mortality rate of 8% to 30%.[47,47a] Although data are limited, pregnant women appear to do worse than nonpregnant patients, with four of seven patients requiring ventilatory support in one series.[48] SARS adversely affects the pregnancy, with miscarriage, fetal distress, and intrauterine death reported, likely related to hypoxemia.

Fungal Pneumonias

Fungal pneumonias are uncommon in pregnancy. Although there is no evidence that blastomycosis and histoplasmosis are more severe during pregnancy, it does appear that coccidiomycosis is more likely to disseminate in pregnancy.[49] In the southwestern United States, about 1 in 5000 pregnancies is complicated by this deep mycosis.[50] Dissemination is most likely in the third trimester and has been related both to subtle impairment of cell-mediated immunity and to a stimulatory effect of progesterone and 17-beta-estradiols on fungal proliferation.[51] Amphotericin is the accepted therapy for disseminated coccidiomycosis.

Tuberculosis

Tuberculosis does not appear to be more common or severe in pregnancy. Isoniazid, rifampin, and ethambutol have acceptable safety profiles in pregnancy and are part of the standard treatment regimens advised by the CDC and the American Thoracic Society for pregnant women.[52] There is less collective experience with pyrazinamide, but this drug is recommended for use in pregnancy by the World Health Organization.[52] Worldwide data are accumulating, and pyrazinamide appears to be emerging as a drug that can be considered for treating multidrug-resistant tuberculosis. Streptomycin, by contrast, is clearly associated with congenital deafness and is contraindicated during pregnancy.

PULMONARY EDEMA AND PULMONARY VASCULAR DISEASE

Gravid women are at special risk for pulmonary edema for a variety of reasons, including the hypervolemia and high cardiac output of pregnancy, the occasional need for tocolytic drugs that affect the vascular bed, and unique vascular and endothelial disorders of pregnancy. Among these effects, it is noteworthy that colloid osmotic pressure diminishes during pregnancy, although the effect on transcapillary pressure gradients is partially offset by a decrease in interstitial fluid colloid osmotic pressure.[53] Etiologically, underlying cardiac disease, use of tocolytic drugs, fluid overload, and preeclampsia are the most common causes for acute pulmonary edema in pregnancy.[53]

Hydrostatic (Cardiogenic) Pulmonary Edema

The cardiovascular adaptations to pregnancy have already been summarized. Their effects on underlying cardiac disorders are predictable. Stenotic lesions are particularly poorly tolerated.[54] Of these, mitral stenosis is the most common symptomatic valvular disease in pregnancy and frequently presents with pulmonary edema, not only during gestation but also immediately postpartum, because of the large shifts in intravascular volume associated with delivery. The gradient across a stenotic mitral valve is augmented by the increases in blood volume, cardiac output, and heart rate that occur during gestation and the puerperium. In aortic stenosis, the increase in cardiac output required for pregnancy worsens the gradient across the valve. As a compensatory mechanism, the end-diastolic volume increases, but the low SVR in aortic stenosis impairs diastolic coronary artery filling and can precipitate ischemic syndromes. The reduction in SVR of pregnancy mitigates the consequences of mitral and aortic regurgitation and of the left-to-right intracardiac shunts of endocardial cushion defects but worsens the consequences of Eisenmenger's syndrome and uncorrected tetralogy of Fallot. Depending on the cardiac disorder, perturbations induced by pregnancy can alter fractional shunts, induce hypoxemia, and precipitate pulmonary edema.

A special problem of pregnancy is peripartum cardiomyopathy, a disorder that occurs in 1 of 1300 to 15,000 deliveries, may present with congestive heart failure, and is associated with a special propensity for pulmonary and systemic embolization during the last month of pregnancy and for up to 5 months thereafter.[55] An inflammatory subset of this disorder that may respond to immunosuppressive therapy can be identified by endomyocardial biopsy.[56]

Tocolysis-Associated Pulmonary Edema

The systemic administration of beta$_2$-sympathomimetic agents to retard premature labor has been associated with a 0% to 4.4% incidence of pulmonary edema.[57] The etiology of this disorder is controversial.[58] One speculation is that it is due to myocardial dysfunction from prolonged sympathetic stimulation, but descriptions of cases in which hemodynamic parameters were measured report normal pulmonary capillary wedge pressures. The idea that increased vascular permeability may contribute to the syndrome is given weight by its association with maternal infection.[59] Some authors have speculated that the development of the disorder requires a coexisting condition, such as volume overload, sepsis, or preeclampsia.[60] It usually presents after at least 24 hours of beta-adrenergic therapy, with relatively acute onset of dyspnea and pulmonary edema seen on chest radiographs (Fig. 81.3).

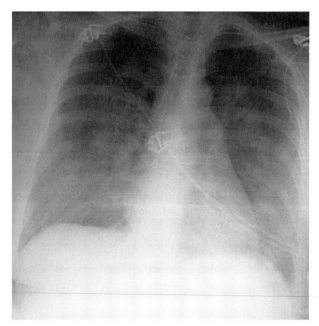

Figure 81.3 Tocolysis-associated pulmonary edema in a 38-year-old woman in premature labor.

Simple discontinuation of beta-adrenergic therapy often results in rapid improvement; whether diuretics need to be given is unresolved, but furosemide is usually administered.

Pulmonary Edema Associated with Preeclampsia

About 2.9% of patients with preeclampsia or eclampsia develop pulmonary edema.[61] The spectrum of hemodynamic findings associated with pregnancy-induced hypertension and preeclampsia is wide; but, in general, left ventricular preload is normal or low, afterload is high, and cardiac output is normal or low (Fig. 81.4). Systolic and diastolic function may also be impaired.[62] The pulmonary edema commonly first presents in the postpartum period,[61,62] reflecting fluid administration at delivery. Low colloid oncotic pressure and abnormal vascular permeability likely contribute as well. Hemodynamic monitoring of these patients is probably warranted if oliguria complicates the picture.

Pulmonary Embolism

Pulmonary embolism is a leading cause of maternal mortality,[63] accounting for 19.6% of 4200 pregnancy-related deaths in the United States between 1991 and 1999.[64] Even though the risk for venous thromboembolism in pregnant women is about five times as great as in age-matched and sex-matched nongravid controls, it is still relatively infrequent. A Danish population-based study of 63,000 deliveries found a cumulative incidence of 0.85 in 1000 deliveries

from 1984 to 1994.[65] In this study, the incidence of detected venous thromboembolism increased to 1.23 in 1000 deliveries after the introduction of ultrasonography, demonstrating that its reported incidence may depend on the adequacy of diagnostic procedures employed. Other studies have reported rates of 0.5 to 1.3 per 1000, with a lower incidence in younger patients and higher incidence in those over 35 years of age.[66,67]

The risk for thrombosis is increased in pregnancy, partly because of the increase in the coagulation factors, particularly V, VIII, X, and von Willebrand factor Ag, and partly because of a marked fall in protein S.[68] Venous stasis, an important contributor to thrombosis, is caused by uterine compression of the inferior vena cava and the left iliac vein. Local trauma to pelvic veins at the time of delivery probably accounts for the peak incidence of thromboembolism in the postpartum period, especially after cesarean section. Specific risk factors for thromboembolism include previous thromboembolism during pregnancy or while taking oral contraceptives, prolonged bed rest, a complicated or cesarean delivery, age, and inherited coagulation defects. The latter include deficiencies of factor S, factor C, and antithrombin III or the presence of antiphospholipid antibodies, factor V Leiden, and prothrombin G20210A.[66,68] The first two risk factors probably warrant prophylactic subcutaneous heparin administration throughout pregnancy, now more commonly accomplished with low-molecular-weight heparins due to their safety and decreased risk of heparin-induced osteopenia and thrombocytopenia.

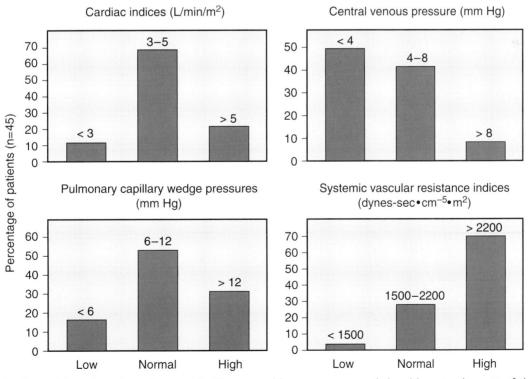

Figure 81.4 Spectrum of hemodynamic profiles seen in 45 women with severe pregnancy-induced hypertension, one of the disorders sometimes complicated by pulmonary edema. Pulmonary edema in pregnancy-induced hypertension usually does not reflect simple volume overload. (From Cotton DB, Lee W, Huhta JC, et al: Hemodynamic profile of severe pregnancy-induced hypertension. Am J Obstet Gynecol 158:523–529, 1988.)

Clinical diagnosis of deep vein thrombosis during pregnancy and the puerperium is exceptionally difficult because of the peripheral edema associated with pregnancy and the asymmetrical compression of the left-sided common iliac vein by the gravid uterus. The initial diagnostic test should be duplex ultrasonography (combined real-time B-mode compression ultrasonography plus Doppler venous ultrasonography). In the patient with high clinical suspicion but a negative test, a repeat examination at 5 to 7 days may be valuable. The gold standard for detecting lower extremity thrombosis remains venography, but in pregnancy thrombosis is typically confined to the iliac veins and may be difficult to visualize, even by this technique. When venous thrombosis of the lower extremity is documented, it is usually left-sided, as it was in 58 of 60 cases reported by Ginsberg and colleagues.[69]

The diagnosis of pulmonary embolism in pregnant women is relatively straightforward. Both ventilation-perfusion scanning and pulmonary angiography can be performed during pregnancy in a modified fashion. Estimated fetal radiation exposure for a standard technetium-labeled macroaggregated albumin perfusion scan is about 0.018 cGy (18 mrad),[70] which can be reduced further by simply halving the dose without greatly impairing resolution. There is no need for the ventilation portion of the study if perfusion is normal. Computed tomographic (CT) angiography is an acceptable imaging modality and is associated with similarly low radiation doses to the fetus.[71] Pulmonary angiography, when performed by the brachial route, exposes the fetus to only about 0.050 cGy (50 mrad).[72] Such levels of exposure are not believed to cause teratogenicity, which is associated with exposure of greater than 5 to 10 cGy (5–10 rad). However, an increased incidence of childhood leukemia has been documented with lower fetal radiation exposure, in the range of 1 to 5 cGy (1–5 rad). Magnetic resonance imaging (MRI) with gadolinium contrast also has promise because it can image pelvic and lower extremity veins as well as the pulmonary arteries, and it has no contrast-associated toxicity. Its widespread use requires availability of ultrafast scanners and more evaluation of its accuracy.

Embolism in pregnancy is treated with heparin because warfarin crosses the placenta and causes nasal, ophthalmologic, and central nervous system abnormalities. Low-molecular-weight heparin (LMWH) appears to be safe in pregnancy and compared to unfractionated heparin is associated with fewer adverse effects such as thrombocytopenia and osteoporosis.[73,74] A consensus is emerging that LMWH is preferable in pregnancy, but some authors also advocate titrating the dose to achieve anti-factor X levels of 0.5 to 1.24 U/ml 4 hours after injection.[73,75] Weight gain in pregnancy makes formulaic dosing less reliable.

Standard therapy of thromboembolism antepartum encompasses either continuous intravenous unfractionated heparin or LMWH until 24 hours before elective induced or planned surgical delivery. For spontaneous deliveries, because of the risk of epidermal hematoma formation with regional anesthesia, LMWH should be switched to unfractionated heparin about 2 weeks prior to the anticipated delivery. If labor begins unexpectedly, reversal of the heparin effect with protamine is advisable. Postpartum, warfarin can be given safely during lactation.

Amniotic Fluid Embolism

Small amounts of amniotic fluid may enter the circulation during uncomplicated pregnancy, but in 1 of 20,000 to 80,000 deliveries there is a catastrophic syndrome of amniotic fluid embolism, first described by Steiner and Lushbaugh.[76] The onset is usually during labor and delivery or immediately after uterine manipulation, when severe dyspnea, hypoxemia, and then seizures and cardiovascular collapse or arrest occur. If the patient survives the initial insult, disseminated intravascular coagulation and ARDS usually supervene.[77] Risk factors include older maternal age, high parity, cesarean section, low uterine segment laceration, and meconium staining of amniotic fluid.[60] Abruptio placentae is present in 50% of cases, and fetal demise occurs in 40%.[77] The maternal mortality rate has been as high as 86%[78] but has appeared more recently to be as low as 26%[79]; overall, amniotic fluid embolism may account for 10% of all maternal deaths.

In a U.S. registry of cases, 78% of the patients with amniotic fluid embolism had ruptured membranes, and several had just undergone intrauterine procedures,[80] clearly implicating traumatic opening of uterine vessels in the pathogenesis. The exact quantity or constituent of the amniotic fluid required to initiate the syndrome is unknown. Pathologically, fetal squamous cells are found in the maternal pulmonary circulation at autopsy (Fig. 81.5), but even in symptom-free patients fetal cells may be recovered from pulmonary artery catheters placed for other reasons.[81] Hemodynamically, the process is often biphasic, with pulmonary hypertension initially followed by left ventricular failure.[82] These changes may be caused by leukotrienes and arachidonic acid metabolites, particularly prostaglandin F_2, which appear in amniotic fluid during labor. An immunologic basis for some of the changes seems likely because women with male fetuses are more likely to acquire the disorder.[83] Clark and associates seized on the similarities to anaphylaxis and suggested that the disorder be renamed *anaphylactoid syndrome of pregnancy*.[80] A recent small study did not demonstrate evidence of mast cell degranulation but suggests a role for complement activation.[84]

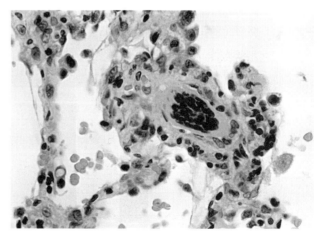

Figure 81.5 Small pulmonary vessel filled and distended by fetal squamous cells from a fatal case of amniotic fluid embolism in a 39-year-old woman who succumbed within 4 hours of delivery. (Keratin stain; original magnification × 400.) (Courtesy of Dr. Gerald Berry.)

Radiographically, the patients usually develop bilateral parenchymal infiltrates consistent with pulmonary edema and then acute lung injury. Treatment consists of supportive care for the associated disseminated intravascular coagulation and left ventricular and respiratory failure. If the fetus survives the initial insult and is intrauterine, it should be promptly delivered. In cases of maternal demise, emergency postmortem or periresuscitative cesarean section is warranted, as in other instances of cardiopulmonary resuscitation in pregnancy.[85]

Arteriovenous Malformations

Pulmonary arteriovenous malformations may expand during pregnancy because of the increase in blood volume and venous distensibility. This increases the likelihood of bleeding. Embolization and surgical management have been utilized successfully during pregnancy.[86]

Air Embolism

Occasionally, venous air embolism occurs during pregnancy, presumably through the subplacental venous sinuses.[87] This disorder has been clearly documented during labor and delivery, during abortions, in patients with placenta previa, and in those engaging in orogenital sex during pregnancy.

ACUTE LUNG INJURY IN PREGNANCY

Aspiration Pneumonitis

Since Mendelson's[88] original report of 66 cases of gastric aspiration in 44,016 deliveries between 1932 and 1945 (an incidence of 0.15%), aspiration has continued to be a major cause of maternal morbidity and mortality. Increased intra-abdominal pressure due to the gravid uterus, the inhibitory effect of progesterone on the tone of the esophageal sphincter, and the assumption of the supine position for delivery all contribute. Eating during labor increases the volume of emesis.[89] Aspiration of gastric contents with pH 2.5 or lower is known to cause chemical pneumonitis and permeability edema. Both in Mendelson's original report and today, about two thirds of cases of aspiration occur in the delivery suite. Emergency intubation of the obstetric airway is particularly difficult,[90] and failed intubation in the delivery suite occurs at a rate eight times that in the general surgical population.[91] To reduce the risk for aspiration and to minimize the chance of acid aspiration at intubation, oral administration of histamine-2 blockers or sodium citrate before intubation, in conjunction with a formal airway assessment, is desirable. Identified risk factors in intubation include a high Mallampati class, indicating poor visibility of the posterior pharynx, a short neck, protruding maxillary incisors, and a receding mandible.[92]

Acute Respiratory Distress Syndrome

Acute respiratory distress syndrome occurs relatively frequently in pregnancy; in one obstetric intensive care unit, it was the leading cause of maternal death during a 6-year period.[93] The three most common nonobstetric causes are pneumonia, sepsis, and aspiration. Common obstetric causes include chorioamnionitis, amniotic fluid embolism, and trophoblastic embolism.[94] Ventilator management is unaltered in pregnancy; the prognosis also appears to be the same, with an anticipated 40% to 75% survival rate.[94,95]

OTHER RESPIRATORY DISEASES IN PREGNANCY

Obstructive Sleep Apnea

Pregnancy may be complicated by obstructive sleep apnea (OSA), potentially adversely affecting both mother and fetus.[96] In general, apnea and hypopnea are uncommon in pregnancy because of the respiratory stimulatory effect of progesterone. OSA usually occurs in obese patients, precipitated by the airway mucosal edema and vascular congestion that accompany pregnancy. Nocturnal hypoxemia may produce poor fetal growth, although snoring alone is not associated with fetal risk.[97] Treatment with nasal continuous positive airway pressure (CPAP) is safe and effective.

Interstitial Lung Disease

Most causes of interstitial lung disease occur in patients older than those in their childbearing years, When interstitial disease exists in pregnant women, the reduced diffusing capacity may cause difficulty in meeting the increased oxygen-consumption requirements of pregnancy. Associated pulmonary hypertension carries significant risks, because cardiac output increases during pregnancy. Few data exist on the management and outcome in these patients, but restrictive lung disease appears reasonably well tolerated in pregnancy.[98] Patients who have a vital capacity of less than 1 liter and those who have pulmonary hypertension should consider avoiding pregnancy.[99] Lymphangioleiomyomatosis and systemic lupus erythematosus may worsen as a result of pregnancy.

Pleural Disease

Pleural effusions may accompany obstetric complications such as preeclampsia and choriocarcinoma, but many women with normal pregnancies develop small, asymptomatic pleural effusions in the postpartum period.[100] They occur as a result of the increased blood volume and reduced colloid osmotic pressure that occur in pregnancy, as well as from impaired lymphatic drainage due to the Valsalva maneuver during labor. Moderate-size effusions or the presence of symptoms should prompt a full clinical evaluation. The Valsalva maneuver of labor may also produce spontaneous pneumothorax and pneumomediastinum, particularly in patients with predisposing conditions such as asthma. This diagnosis should be considered in the woman who develops chest discomfort and dyspnea during, or immediately following, delivery.

GYNECOLOGIC DISORDERS AND THE LUNGS

CATAMENIAL PNEUMOTHORAX

Lillington and colleagues[101] introduced in 1972 the term *catamenial pneumothorax* to describe the already reported phenomenon of spontaneous pneumothorax occurring within 24 to 72 hours after onset of menses. More than 100 cases have been reported. It appears to account for about 2.8% to 5.6% of spontaneous pneumothoraces in women,[102,103] most often affecting women in the third or fourth decade of life. About 30% to 60% of cases are attributable to thoracic endometriosis, as judged by inspection at thoracotomy[104]; other cases have a more obscure etiology, however, so a number of theories have been advanced. First, during menstruation, the absence of the normal cervical mucous plug permits an open connection between ambient air and the abdominal cavity through the uterus and fallopian tubes. Air can move transdiaphragmatically through right-sided diaphragmatic fenestrations into the pleural space, as it sometimes does during abdominal laparoscopy.[105] This may account for the condition's 90% to 95% right-sided predominance.[106] A second theory is that high levels of prostaglandin $F_{2\alpha}$ during menstruation cause bronchospasm with attendant air-trapping and pneumothorax, but wheezing is not a common symptom of this disorder. A third theory is that pleural blebs or bullae are more susceptible to rupture during menstruation because of hormonal changes,[104,106] but visceral pleural leaks are rarely found at surgery (see also Chapter 69 for a full discussion).

For cases of endometriosis-associated pneumothorax, a trial of gonadotropin-releasing hormones is warranted if the phenomenon is repetitive but not life-threatening. Oral contraceptives, other progestational agents, and tubal ligation have also been used with some success. For cases not clearly associated with systemic endometriosis, thoracoscopy during menstruation serves to define the etiology and can be used to achieve pleurodesis.[105]

ENDOMETRIOSIS

Endometriosis probably affects about 10% of women, shows no clear ethnic differences in prevalence, and is most commonly diagnosed at 25 to 29 years of age.[107] Although pelvic pain, dysmenorrhea, and infertility are its predominant manifestations, atypical locations, including diaphragmatic, pleural, and endobronchial sites, have been documented. As described previously, endometriosis can result in recurrent catamenial pneumothorax, which is its most common thoracic presentation. It also has been associated with right-sided pleural pain, pleuritic effusions, and hemothorax. Inspection at thoracotomy or thoracoscopy typically reveals blue-brown nodules on the pleural surface, sometimes in a "gunshot" distribution.[108] The absence of known pelvic endometriosis is not helpful in excluding the diagnosis because only 20% to 70% of patients have associated pelvic disease.[109] Rarely, the implants are found in lung parenchyma, accounting for the catamenial hemoptysis. Most pleural and diaphragmatic disease is thought to arise from transdiaphragmatic spread from retrograde menses,[107] even when abdominal disease is not evident. Massive ascites is sometimes related, although only 27 cases have been reported.[110] Pneumothoraces may be attributed to cyclical sloughing of implants on key surfaces, such as the visceral pleura,[104] or to air trapping from airway involvement or compression.[101] Pulmonary parenchymal disease may be embolic in origin, as it is presumed to be in the central nervous system. The diagnosis can be established only by biopsy showing the characteristic ectopic endometrial glands in involved sites. Medical therapy consists of progestational agents or gonadotropin-releasing hormones; surgical approaches include excision, local laser ablation, or pleurodesis.

LYMPHANGIOLEIOMYOMATOSIS

Lymphangioleiomyomatosis (LAM) is a rare disorder, with only about 300 reported cases, that afflicts premenopausal women almost exclusively.[111,112] It is fundamentally a disorder of smooth muscle proliferation that results in functional obstruction of vessels, lymphatics, and airways. (See Chapter 62 for a complete discussion of LAM.) Involvement of pulmonary vascular structures is responsible for the hemoptysis, whereas lymphatic obstruction accounts for the chylous effusions. Mediastinal and retroperitoneal lymphatic proliferation may be a feature of the disease as well. LAM is also associated with renal angiomyolipomas, another hamartomatous disorder. Conventional therapy has included oophorectomy or progestational agents, mainly medroxyprogesterone acetate. Lung transplantation has been performed in more than 60 patients with this disorder, but it has clearly recurred in some of them. Current research focuses on growth factors and genetic factors that have been implicated in the disease's causation.[113]

TROPHOBLASTIC EMBOLIZATION

Trophoblastic embolism is a rare complication of hydatidiform mole. In one series, only 2.6% of 189 patients with hydatidiform mole had an embolic event, so most episodes of respiratory distress in patients with molar gestations are not caused by embolic events but, rather, by pulmonary edema, anemia, or other complicating event.[114] Embolization, when it does occur, is most common at the time of evacuation of the mole. Chorionic neoplasms that arise during gestation are suggested by a large discrepancy between gestational date and uterine size and should be evaluated by transvaginal ultrasonography.[115] Moles can also arise outside of gestation from the gonads of either sex.

OVARIAN HYPERSTIMULATION SYNDROME

The use of exogenous gonadotrophins to stimulate ovulation for in vitro fertilization has been associated with pulmonary complications.[116] This ovarian hyperstimulation syndrome usually manifests with ovarian cysts, bilateral pleural effusions, ascites, and intravascular volume depletion. Hypovolemic shock, renal failure, and ARDS may result. Pulmonary embolism may occur due to the hypercoagulable state induced by estrogens associated with intravascular volume depletion. The mechanism of the effusions is unclear but is related to increased permeability due to release of vasoactive mediators, of which vascular endothelial growth factor appears to be the most important.[117] Recent evidence points to mutations in the follicle-stimulating hormone receptor as etiologic in at least some cases.[118] Treatment is supportive and involves maintaining intravascular volume and thoracentesis if required for respiratory distress.

SUMMARY

Obstetric and gynecologic disorders alter the structure, hormonal milieu, and physiologic function of the lung in ways that determine and condition a variety of pulmonary diseases. Some disorders are unique to pregnancy, such as pulmonary edema associated with tocolytic therapy or amniotic fluid embolism. Other conditions, such as mitral stenosis, pulmonary embolism, and coccidiomycosis, are clearly exacerbated by gestation. Still others, such as obstructive airway disease and acute lung injury, are neither more frequent nor more severe in pregnancy but require expert care to optimize maternal and fetal outcome.

Disorders associated with gynecologic function and disease are rare but distinctive. The causation of many of them, such as catamenial pneumothorax, thoracic endometriosis, and LAM, remains obscure but is linked to gonadal function. Because of their recurrent and sometimes malignant natural history, they require a definitive diagnosis, which is facilitated by awareness of their distinctive features.

REFERENCES

1. Mabry RL: Rhinitis of pregnancy. South Med J 79:965–971, 1986.
2. Blaiss MS, Food and Drug Administration (US), ACAAI-ACOG (American College of Asthma and Immunology and American College of Obstetricians and Gynecologists): Management of rhinitis and asthma in pregnancy. Ann Allergy Asthma Immunol 90(Suppl 3):16–22, 2003.
3. Weinberger SE, Weiss ST, Cohen WR, et al: Pregnancy and the lung: State of the art. Am Rev Respir Dis 121:559–581, 1980.
4. Contreras G, Gutierrez M, Berioza T, et al: Ventilatory drive and respiratory function in pregnancy. Am Rev Respir Dis 144:837–841, 1991.
5. Cugell DW, Frank NR, Gaensler EA: Pulmonary function in pregnancy. I. Serial observations in normal women. Am Rev Tuberc 67:568–597, 1953.
6. Gilroy RJ, Mangura BT, Layietes MH: Ribcage and abdominal volume displacements during breathing in pregnancy. Am Rev Respir Dis 137:668–672, 1988.
7. Skatrud JB, Bempsey JA, Kaiser DG: Ventilatory response to medroxyprogesterone acetate in normal subjects: Time course and mechanism. J Appl Physiol 44:939, 1978.
8. Lucius H, Gahlenbeck HO, Kleine O, et al: Respiratory functions, buffer system, and electrolyte concentrations of blood during human pregnancy. Respir Physiol 9:311–317, 1970.
9. Pritchard JA, Baldwin RM, Dickey JC, et al: Blood volume changes in pregnancy and the puerperium. Am J Obstet Gynecol 84:1271–1281, 1962.
10. Silver HM, Seebeck M, Carlson R: Comparison of total blood volume in normal, preeclamptic and nonproteinuric gestational hypertensive pregnancy by simultaneous measurement of red blood cell and plasma volumes. Am J Obstet Gynecol 179:87–93, 1998.
11. Crapo RO: Normal cardiopulmonary physiology during pregnancy. Clin Obstet Gynecol 39:3–16, 1996.
12. Clark SL, Cotton DB, Lee W, et al: Central hemodynamic assessment of normal near term pregnancy. Am J Obstet Gynecol 161:1439–1442, 1989.
13. Hunter S, Robson SC: Adaptation of the maternal heart in pregnancy. Br Heart J 68:540–543, 1992.
14. Rizk N, Kalassian K, Gilligan T, et al: Obstetric complications in pulmonary and critical care medicine. Chest 110:791–809, 1996.
14a. Namazy JA, Schatz M: Pregnancy and asthma: recent developments. Curr Opin Pulm Med 11:56–60, 2005.
15. National Asthma Education Program. National Heart, Lung, and Blood Institute, National Institutes of Health: Report of the Working Group on Asthma and Pregnancy: Executive Summary; Management of Asthma During Pregnancy. NIH Publication No. 93–3279A, March 1993. Available at http://www.nhlbi.nih.gov/health/prof/lung/asthma/astpreg.txt.
16. Mabie WC, Barton JR, Wasserstrum N, et al: Clinical observations on asthma in pregnancy. J Matern Fetal Med 1:45–50, 1992.
17. Juniper EF, Daniel EE, Roberts RS, et al: Improvement in airway responsiveness and asthma severity during pregnancy. Am Rev Respir Dis 140:924–931, 1989.
18. Turner ES, Greenberger PA, Patterson R: Management of the pregnant asthmatic patient. Ann Intern Med 93:905–918, 1980.
19. Gluck JC, Gluck PA: The effects of pregnancy on asthma: A prospective study. Ann Allergy 37:164–168, 1976.
20. Stenius-Aarniala B, Piirila P, Terampo K: Asthma and pregnancy: A prospective study of 198 pregnancies. Thorax 43:12–18, 1988.
21. Nelson-Piercy C: Asthma in pregnancy. Thorax 56:325–328, 2001.
22. Kallen B, Rydhstroem H, Averg A: Asthma during pregnancy—a population based study. Eur J Epidemiol 16:167–171, 2000.
23. The American College of Obstetricians and Gynecologists (ACOG) and The American College of Allergy, Asthma and Immunology (ACAAI): The use of newer asthma and allergy medications during pregnancy. Ann Allergy Asthma Immunol 84:475–480, 2000.
24. Schatz M: The efficacy and safety of asthma medications during pregnancy. Semin Perinatal 25:145–152, 2001.
25. Briggs GE, Freeman RK, Yaffe SJ: Drugs in Pregnancy and Lactation (6th ed). Philadelphia: Lippincott Williams & Wilkins, 2002, pp 483–484.
26. Spector SL: Antileukotriene Working Group: Safety of antileukotriene agents in asthma management. Ann Allergy Asthma Immunol 86(Suppl 1):18–23, 2001.
27. Cystic Fibrosis Foundation: Cystic Fibrosis Foundation Annual Report 2000. Bethesda, MD: Cystic Fibrosis Foundation, 2001.
28. Kotloff RM, FitzSimmons SC, Fiel SB: Fertility and pregnancy in patients with cystic fibrosis. Clin Chest Med 13:623–635, 1992.
29. Edenborough FP, Stableforth DE, Webb AK, et al: The outcome of pregnancy in cystic fibrosis. Thorax 50:170, 1995.
29a. Boyd JM, Metha A, Murphy DJ: Fertility and pregnancy outcomes in men and women with cystic fibrosis in the United Kingdom. Hum Reprod 19:2238–2243, 2004.
30. Kent NE, Farquharson DF: Cystic fibrosis in pregnancy. Can Med Assoc 149:809, 1993.
31. Canny GJ, Corey M, Livingstone RA, et al: Pregnancy and cystic fibrosis. Obstet Gynecol 77:850, 1991.
32. Frangolias DD, Nakielna EM, Wilcox PG. Pregnancy and cystic fibrosis: A case-controlled study. Chest 111:963–969, 1997.
33. Berkowitz K, LaSala A: Risk factors associated with the increasing prevalence of pneumonia during pregnancy. Am J Obstet Gynecol 163:981985, 1990.
34. Benedetti TJ, Valle R, Ledger WJ: Antepartum pneumonia in pregnancy. Am J Obstet Gyncol 144:413–417, 1982.

35. Madinger NE, Greenspoon JS, Ellrodt AG: Pneumonia during pregnancy: Has modern technology improved maternal and fetal outcome? Am J Obstet Gynecol 161:657–662, 1989.

36. Richey SD, Roberts SW, Ramin KD, et al: Pneumonia complicating pregnancy. Obstet Gynecol 84:525–528, 1994.

37. Rodrigues J, Neiderman MS: Pneumonia complicating pregnancy. Am J Obstet Gynecol 13:678–692, 1992.

38. Briggs RG, Mabie WC, Sibai BM: Community acquired pneumonia in pregnancy. Am J Obstet Gynecol 174:389, 1996.

39. Lim WS, Macfarlane JT, Colthorpe CL: Pneumonia and pregnancy. Thorax 56:398–405, 2001.

40. McKinney P, Volkert P, Kaufman J: Fatal swine influenza pneumonia occurring during late pregnancy. Arch Intern Med 150:213–215, 1990.

41. Centers for Disease Control: Prevention and control of influenza: Recommendation of the Advisory Committee on Immunization. MMWR Morb Mortal Wkly Rep 2002;51 (RR03):1–47.

42. Haake DA, Zakokwski PC, Haake DL, et al: Early treatment with acyclovir for varicella pneumonia in otherwise healthy adults: Retrospective controlled study and review. Rev Infect Dis 12:788, 1990.

43. Broussard RC, Payne K, George RB: Treatment with acyclovir of varicella pneumonia in pregnancy. Chest 99:1045, 1991.

44. Centers for Disease Control and Prevention: Prevention of varicella: Recommendations of the Advisory Committee on Immunization Practices (ACIP). MMWR Recomm Rep 45(RR-11):1–36, 1996.

45. Rosa C: Rubella and rubeola. Semin Perinatol 22:318–322, 1998.

46. Howard MJ, Doyle TJ, Koster FT, et al: Hantavirus pulmonary syndrome in pregnancy. Clin Infect Dis 29:1538–1544, 1999.

47. Fowler R, Lapinsky SE, Hallett D, et al: Critically ill patients with severe acute respiratory syndrome (SARS). JAMA 290:367–373, 2003.

47a. Lam CM, Wong SF, Leung TN, et al: A case-controlled study comparing clinical course and outcomes of pregnant and non-pregnant women with severe acute respiratory syndrome. BJOG 111:771–774, 2004.

48. Wong SF, Chow KM, de Swiet M: Severe acute respiratory syndrome and pregnancy. Br J Obstet Gynaecol 110:641–642, 2003.

49. Stevens DA: Coccidiomycosis. N Engl J Med 332:1077, 1995.

50. Wack EE, Ampel NM, Galgiani JN, et al: Coccidiomycosis during pregnancy: An analysis of ten cases among 47,120 pregnancies. Chest 94:376–379, 1988.

51. Catanzaro A: Pulmonary mycosis in pregnant women. Chest 86:14S–18S, 1984.

52. Blumberg HM, Burman WJ, Chaisson RE, et al: American Thoracic Society/Centers for Disease Control and Prevention/Infection Diseases Society of America: Treatment of tuberculosis. Am J Respir Crit Care Med 167:603–662, 2003.

53. Oian P, Maltari JM, Noddeland H, et al: Oedema preventing mechanisms in subcutaneous tissue of normal pregnant women. Br J Obstet Gynaecol 92:113–119, 1985.

54. Sciscione AC, Ivester T, Largoza M, et al: Acute pulmonary edema in pregnancy. Obstet Gynecol 101:511–515, 2003.

55. Siu SC, Sermer M, Colman JM: Prospective multicenter study of pregnancy outcomes in women with heart disease. Circulation 104:515–521, 2001.

56. Mehta NJ, Mehta RN, Khan IA: Peripartum cardiomyopathy: Clinical and therapeutic aspects. Angiology 52:759–762, 201.

57. Pisani RJ, Rosenow EC: Pulmonary edema associated with tocolytic therapy. Ann Intern Med 110:714–718, 1992.

58. Lapinsky SE, Kruczynski K, Slutsky A: Critical care in the pregnant patient. Am J Respir Crit Care Med 152:427–455, 1995.

59. Hatjos CG, Swain M: Systemic tocolysis for premature labor is associated with an increased incidence of pulmonary edema in the presence of maternal infection. Am J Obstet Gynecol 159:723–728, 1988.

60. Karetzky M, Ramirez M: Acute respiratory failure in pregnancy: An analysis of 19 cases. Medicine (Baltimore) 77:41–49, 1998.

61. Sibai BM, Mabie BC, Harvey CJ, et al: Pulmonary edema in severe preeclampsia-eclampsia: Analysis of thirty-seven consecutive cases. Am J Obstet Gynecol 156:1174–1179, 1987.

62. Benedetti TJ, Kates R, Williams V: Hemodynamic observation of severe preeclampsia complicated by pulmonary edema. Am J Obstet Gynecol 152:33–34, 1985.

63. American College of Gynecology and Obstetrics practice bulletin: Thromboembolism in pregnancy. Int J Gynecol Obstet 75:203–212, 2001.

64. Chang J, Elam-Evans LD, Berg CJ, et al: Pregnancy related mortality surveillance in United States, 1991–1999. MMWR Surveill Summ 32:1–8, 2003.

65. Andersen BS, Steffensen FH, Sorensen HT, et al: The cumulative incidence of venous thromboembolism during pregnancy and puerperium: An 11 year Danish study population-based study of 63,000 pregnancies. Acta Obstet Gynecol Scand 77:170–173, 1998.

66. Brown HL, Hiett AK: Deep venous thrombosis and pulmonary embolism. Clin Obstet Gynecol 39:87–100, 1996.

67. Greer IA. Prevention and management of venous thromboembolism in pregnancy. Clin Chest Med 24:123–137, 2003.

68. McColl MD, Walker ID, Greer IA: Risk factors for venous thromboembolism in pregnancy. Curr Opin Pulm Med 5:227–232, 1999.

69. Ginsberg JS, Brill-Edwards P, Burrows RF, et al: Venous thrombosis during pregnancy: Leg and trimester of presentation. Thromb Haemost 67:519, 1992.

70. Ginsberg JS, Hirsh J, Rainbow AJ, et al: Risks to the fetus of radiologic procedures used in the diagnosis of maternal venous thromboembolic disease. Thromb Haemost 61:189–196, 1989.

71. Parry RA, Glaze SA, Archer BR: The AAPM/RSNA physics tutorial for residents: Typical patient radiation doses in diagnostic radiology. Radiographics 19:1289–1302, 1999.

72. Howie PW: Thromboembolism. Clin Obstet Gynecol 4:397–417, 1977.

73. Ginsberg JS, Greer I, Hirsh J. Use of antithrombotic agents during pregnancy. Chest 119(Suppl 1):122S–131S, 2001.

74. Nelson-Piercy C, Letsky EA, de Swiet M: Low molecular weight heparin for obstetric prophylaxis: Experience of sixty-nine pregnancies in sixty-one women at high risk. Am J Obstet Gynecol 176:1062–1068, 1997.

75. Ginsberg JS, Bates SM: Management of venous thromboembolism during pregnancy. J Thromb Haemost 1:1435–1442, 2003.

76. Steiner PE, Lushbaugh CC: Maternal pulmonary embolus by amniotic fluid. JAMA 117:1245–1254, 1941.

77. Clark SL: Amniotic fluid embolism. Crit Care Clin 7:877–882, 1991.
78. Morgan M: Amniotic fluid embolism. Anesthesia 34:20–32, 1979.
79. Gilbert WM, Danielsen B: Amniotic fluid embolism: Decreased mortality in a population-based study. Obstet Gynecol 93:973–977, 1999.
80. Clark SL, Hankins GD, Dudley DA, et al: Amniotic fluid embolism: Analysis of the national registry. Am J Obstet Gynecol 172:1158–1169, 1995.
81. Clark SL, Pavlova Z, Greenspoon J, et al: Squamous cells in the maternal pulmonary circulation. Am J Obstet Gynecol 154:104–106, 1986.
82. Clark SL: New concepts of amniotic fluid embolism: A review. Obstet Gynecol Surv 45:360–368, 1990.
83. Martin RW: Amniotic fluid embolism. Clin Obstet Gynecol 39:101–106, 1996.
84. Benson MD, Kobayashi H, Silver RK, et al: Immunologic studies in presumed amniotic fluid embolism. Obstet Gynecol 97:510–514, 2001.
85. American Heart Association: Guidelines 2000 for cardiopulmonary resuscitation and emergency cardiovascular care. Part 8: Advanced challenges in resuscitation: Section 3: Special challenges in ECC. Circulation 102(Suppl):I229–I252, 2001.
86. Esplin MS, Varner MW. Progression of pulmonary arteriovenous malformation during pregnancy: Case report and review of the literature. Obstet Gynecol Surv 52:248–253, 1997.
87. Gottlieb JD, Ericsson JA, Sweet RB: Venous air embolism. Anesth Analg 44:773, 1965.
88. Mendelson CJ: The aspiration of stomach contents into the lungs during obstetric anesthesia. Am J Obstet Gynecol 52:191–204, 1946.
89. Scrutton MJ, Metcalfe GA, Lowry C, et al: Eating in labor: A randomised controlled trial assessing the risks and benefits. Anesthesia 54:529–534, 1999.
90. Rasmussen GE, Malinow AM: Toward reducing maternal mortality: The problem airway in obstetrics. Int Anesthesiol Clin 32:83–101, 1994.
91. King TA, Adams AP: Failed tracheal intubation. Br J Anesth 65:400–414, 1990.
92. Rocke DA, Murray WB, Rout CC, et al: Relative risk analysis of factors associated with difficult intubation in obstetric anesthesia. Anesthesiology 77:67–73, 1992.
93. Kirshon BG, Hinkley CM, Cotton DB, et al: Maternal mortality in a maternal-fetal medicine intensive care unit. J Reprod Med 35:25–28, 1990.
94. Hollingsworth HM, Irwin RS: Acute respiratory failure in pregnancy. Clin Chest Med 13:723–740, 1992.
95. Perry KG, Martin RW, Blake PG, et al: Maternal mortality associated with the adult respiratory distress syndrome. South Med J 91:441–444, 1998.
96. Edwards N, Middleton PG, Blyton DM, Sullivan CE: Sleep disordered breathing and pregnancy. Thorax 57:555–558, 2002.
97. Littner MR, Brock BJ. Snoring in pregnancy: Disease or not? Chest 109:859–860, 1996.
98. Boggess KA, Easterling TR, Raghu G: Management and outcome of pregnant women with interstitial and restrictive lung disease. Am J Obstet Gynecol 173:1007–1014, 1995.
99. King TE: Restrictive lung disease in pregnancy. Clin Chest Med 13:607–622, 1992.
100. Heffner JE, Sahn SA: Pleural disease in pregnancy. Clin Chest Med 13:667–668, 1992.
101. Lillington GA, Mitchell SP, Wood GA: Catamenial pneumothorax. JAMA 219:1328–1332, 1972.
102. Nakamura H, Konishiike K, Sugamura A, et al: Epidemiology of spontaneous pneumothorax in women. Chest 89:378–382, 1986.
103. Shearin RPN, Hepper NPG, Payne WS: Recurrent spontaneous pneumothorax concurrent with menses. Mayo Clin Proc 49:98–101, 1974.
104. Blanco S, Hernando F, Gomez A, et al: Catamenial pneumothorax caused by diaphragmatic endometriosis. J Thorac Cardiovasc Surg 116:179–180, 1998.
105. Bagan P, Le Pimpec Barthes F, Assouad J, et al: Catamenial pneumothorax: retrospective study of surgical treatment. Ann Thorac Surg 75:378–381, 2003.
106. Carter EJ, Ettensohn DB: Catamenial pneumothorax. Chest 98:713–716, 1990.
107. Olive DB, Schwartz LB: Endometriosis. N Engl J Med 328:1759–1769, 1993.
108. Van Schil PE, Vercauteren SR, Vermeire PA, et al: Catamenial pneumothorax caused by thoracic endometriosis. Ann Thorac Surg 62:585–586, 1996.
109. Shiraishi T: Catamenial pneumothorax: Report of a case and review of the Japanese and non-Japanese literature. Thorac Cardiovasc Surg 39:304–307, 1991.
110. Muneyyirci-Delale O, Neil G, Serur E, et al: Endometriosis with massive ascites. Gynecol Oncol 69:42–46, 1998.
111. Taylor JR, Ryu J, Colby TV, et al: Lymphangioleiomyomatosis: Clinical course in 32 patients. N Engl J Med 323:1254–1260, 1990.
112. Kalassian K, Doyle R, Kao P, et al: Lymphangioleiomyomatosis: New insights. Am J Respir Crit Care Med 155:1183–1186, 1997.
113. NHLBI Workshop Summary: Report of workshop on lymphangioleiomyomatosis: NHLBI. Am J Respir Crit Care Med 159:679, 1999.
114. Kohorn EI: Clinical management and the neoplastic sequelae of trophoblastic embolization associated with hydatidiform mole. Obstet Gynecol Surv 42:484–488, 1987.
115. Coukos G, Makrigiannakis A, Chung J, et al: Complete hydatidiform mole: A disease with a changing profile. J Reprod Med 44:698–704, 1999.
116. Abramov, Y, Elchalal, U, Schenker, JG: Obstetric outcome of in vitro fertilized pregnancies complicated by severe ovarian hyperstimulation syndrome: A multicenter study. Fertil Steril 70:1070, 1998.
117. Elchalal U, Schenker JG: The pathophysiology of ovarian hyperstimulation syndrome views and ideas. Hum Reprod 12:1129, 1997.
118. Kaiser UB: The pathogenesis of the ovarian hyperstimulation syndrome. N Engl J Med 349:729–732, 2003.

82

The Lungs and Neuromuscular Diseases

Thomas K. Aldrich, M.D., Raymond Tso, M.D.

INTRODUCTION

Respiratory complications, chiefly pneumonia and respiratory failure, are among the most common causes of morbidity and mortality in neuromuscular diseases.[1,2] Few generalized neuromuscular diseases spare the respiratory muscles, and neuromuscular disease is a leading cause of ventilatory failure.

Neuromuscular diseases can affect the respiratory system at multiple sites in the neuromuscular apparatus, from the spinal cord to the peripheral nerves, the neuromuscular junctions, and the muscles themselves. Table 82.1 lists the most commonly encountered neuromuscular diseases that affect respiration; several recent reviews provide more exhaustive coverage.[3,4] This chapter reviews normal neuromuscular function of the respiratory pump, the diseases that weaken or paralyze the respiratory muscles, and their principal respiratory complications. Neurologic diseases that primarily affect the control of breathing are discussed in Chapters 73 and 74.

THE RESPIRATORY MUSCLES

UPPER AIRWAY MUSCLES

The muscles of respiration include not only those muscles in the neck, rib cage, and abdomen that perform the mechanical pumping function but also the muscles that maintain patency of the upper airway to allow airflow to proceed unimpeded.[5] During quiet breathing, this latter task is accomplished primarily by the vocal cord abductor muscles. At higher levels of ventilatory effort, elevators of the palate, dilators of the pharynx, retractors of the tongue, and even the masseters and the dilators of the nares become active. All help to maintain upper airway caliber and to prevent undue obstruction. The upper airway muscles derive their innervation from cranial nerves V, VII, IX, X, XI, and XII.

Table 82.1 Neuromuscular Diseases That Involve the Respiratory Muscles, Classified According to Site of Neurologic or Muscular Involvement

Site	Disease
Spinal cord	Trauma
	Space-occupying lesions
	Tumor
	Syringomyelia
	Anterior horn cell diseases
	Poliomyelitis
	Amyotrophic lateral sclerosis
	Blockade of inhibiting neurons
	Tetanus
	Strychnine poisoning
Motor nerves	Trauma
	Peripheral neuropathy
	Infectious
	Diabetes mellitus
	Chronic alcoholism
	Idiopathic
Neuromuscular junction	Myasthenia gravis
	Botulism
	Organophosphate poisoning
	Antibiotic toxicity
Muscle	Progressive dystrophies
	Myotonia
	Myopathy
	Inflammatory
	With collagen vascular disease
	Congenital
	Nutritional
	Metabolic
	Other

Table 82.2 Innervation of the Respiratory Muscles

Muscle Group	Spinal Cord Level	Nerve(s)
Inspiratory Muscles		
Diaphragm	C3–C5	Phrenic
Parasternal intercostals	T1–T7	Intercostal
Lateral external intercostals	T1–T12	Intercostal
Scalenes	C4–C8	
Sternocleidomastoid	XI, C1, C2	
Expiratory Muscles		
Lateral internal intercostals	T1–T12	Intercostal
Rectus abdominis	T7–L1	Lumbar
External and internal obliques	T7–L1	Lumbar
Transversus abdominis	T7–L1	Lumbar

VENTILATORY MUSCLES

Inspiratory Muscles

The muscles of the ventilatory pump can be divided into inspiratory and expiratory muscles.[6,7] The principal inspiratory muscles are the diaphragm, the parasternal intercostal muscles, and the scalene muscles in the neck (Fig. 82.1, Table 82.2). The sternomastoids and the lateral external intercostals also contribute to the inspiratory effort. Even the trapezius and serratus superior may assist the inspiratory effort under some circumstances.[4] The diaphragm is innervated by the phrenic nerves, which derive from cervical roots 3 to 5 in humans. The high level of innervation of this primary inspiratory muscle accounts for the survival of many victims of cervical spine injuries; if the diaphragm received its innervation from spinal roots closer to its anatomic position, virtually no inspiratory muscle activity would be left to a person who had just suffered a cervical spine transection.

Expiratory Muscles

The principal expiratory muscles are those of the anterolateral wall of the abdomen.[6,7] The external and internal obliques and the transversus abdominus are most important

in terms of ventilation, whereas the rectus abdominus serves primarily to restrain the abdominal contents. The lateral internal intercostals and the transversus thoracis (triangularis sterni) may also assist the expiratory effort.

Muscle Recruitment

Normally, during quiet supine breathing, the diaphragm alone is responsible for most of the inspiratory effort, while the expiratory phase is virtually entirely passive, with the necessary energy for expiratory airflow contributed by inward elastic recoil of the lungs and chest wall.[7] Upon sitting or standing upright, the scalene and parasternal intercostal muscles begin to enhance the generation of inspiratory vacuum, and low-level abdominal muscle activity begins to assist expiratory airflow. As higher levels of ventilatory effort become necessary, either because of a higher minute volume requirement or because of the need to overcome airway obstruction or a stiff respiratory system, additional muscle groups are recruited.

At high levels of ventilatory effort, end-expiratory abdominal muscle contraction actually assists the subsequent inspiration. With abdominal muscle contraction, the diaphragm is pushed higher into the chest and lengthened, improving its position on its length-tension curve and providing a mechanical advantage. Moreover, at the very onset of inspiration, sudden relaxation of the abdominal muscles enhances inspiratory airflow via gravity and recoil pressure.

RESPIRATORY DYSFUNCTION IN NEUROMUSCULAR DISEASE

PULMONARY FUNCTION

The principal respiratory manifestation of neuromuscular disease is a restrictive defect in ventilatory function, coming about because weakened respiratory muscles are unable to generate either the intrathoracic vacuum necessary for full inspiration or the positive pressure needed for full expiration. Furthermore, patients with neuromuscular weakness tend to breathe with a rapid, shallow pattern that compromises their ventilatory function by increasing the ratio of

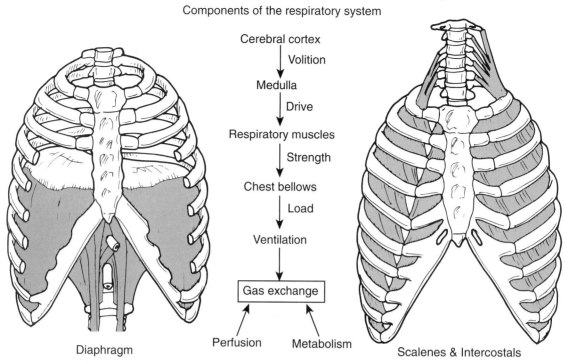

Components of the respiratory system

Figure 82.1 Illustration of the principal respiratory muscles and their position in the respiratory system. (The drawing of the diaphragm is from Rochester DF, Arora NS, Braun NMT: Maximum contractile force of the human diaphragm muscle determined in vivo. Trans Am Clin Climatol Assoc 93:200–208, 1981; and the drawing of the scalene and intercostal muscles is from Osmond DG: Functional anatomy of the chest wall. *In* Roussos C, Macklem PT [eds]: The Thorax. New York: Marcel Dekker, 1985, pp 199–223.) *See Color Plate*

dead space to tidal volume.[8] Rapid, shallow breathing also predisposes to basilar atelectasis and perhaps more generalized microatelectasis. Both children and adults with neuromuscular disease have abnormally low chest wall compliance, possibly due to chronically impaired chest wall mobility.[9]

Paralysis or paresis of some or all of the inspiratory muscles results in a reduced ability to generate intrathoracic vacuum. When severe, inspiratory muscle weakness causes ventilatory failure even in the absence of lung or chest wall dysfunction. When combined with lung or chest wall diseases, even relatively minor inspiratory muscle weakness can result in ventilatory failure.[8,10] Because elastic recoil of the respiratory system provides a driving pressure for expiratory airflow, weakness of the expiratory muscles causes less severe impairments of pulmonary mechanical and ventilatory function.

Stiffness (reduced compliance) of the lungs or chest wall, or both, is another common complication of neuromuscular disease.[11] The reduction in pulmonary compliance appears to be closely linked to the reduction in lung volumes that is characteristic of neuromuscular disease. The cause may be microatelectasis, increased surface tension, alterations in the elastic fibers of the pulmonary interstitium, or a combination of one or more of these factors, each of which may result from habitually low lung volumes. Evidently, lung compliance falls only with relatively long-standing disease; the fact that lung compliance is virtually normal in curarized normal subjects[12] indicates that brief periods of respiratory muscle weakness are not sufficient to stiffen the lungs.

ALTERED VENTILATORY DRIVE

Increased Ventilatory Drive

In most cases of neuromuscular disease, even those complicated by ventilatory failure, respiratory drive is normal or somewhat increased,[13-15] but the mechanical response to neural drive is often depressed.[13,14,16] Respiratory muscle weakness per se or possibly the need to compensate for the concomitant mechanical disadvantages triggers an increase in ventilatory drive, as demonstrated by the finding of reciprocal changes in maximal voluntary inspiratory (PI_{max}) and spontaneous airway occlusion pressure ($P_{0.1}$, the occluded airway pressure measured 100 msec after onset of an inspiratory effort) in curarized normal volunteers.[12]

Decreased Ventilatory Drive

In contrast, patients with quadriplegia[17] and some with congenital myopathy[18,19] or myotonic dystrophy[20] have reduced ventilatory drive, manifested as impaired ventilatory response to hypercapnia, hypoxia, or both. The cause may be abnormalities of carotid body or medullary chemoreceptor function. These patients usually have only mild to moderate respiratory muscle weakness, and their voluntary ventilatory capacity and ventilatory response to exercise are often well preserved. Hypercapnia may be present only during sleep. In addition, patients with chronic ventilatory failure may acquire a blunted response to hypercapnia that reverses when blood gas composition is improved by mechanical ventilation.[21]

Sleep-Related Breathing Disorders

Sleep disorders are common in neuromuscular diseases; 42% of an unselected neuromuscular disease clinic population[22] and 27.5% of a representative sample of patients with chronic quadriplegia[23] had respiratory disturbance indices greater than 15/hr (see Chapter 74 for full discussion of sleep-disordered breathing). High rates of primarily central apneas and hypopneas have been demonstrated in a wide variety of neuromuscular illnesses, including diaphragmatic paralysis,[24] postpolio syndrome,[25] amyotrophic lateral sclerosis,[26] and myotonic dystrophy.[27] Primarily obstructive apneas are common in quadriplegics[23] and in children with many types of neuromuscular disease.[28] Duchenne type muscular dystrophy is characterized by high rates of both obstructive and central apneas.[29]

Hypopnea and oxygen desaturation are most apt to occur during rapid eye movement (REM) sleep, when the neck and rib cage muscles are inhibited.[30] The major consequences of sleep-disordered breathing in neuromuscular disease are hypoxemia and the resulting impairments in right ventricular and cognitive function.[31] Bicarbonate retention, sometimes with associated worsening of daytime hypercapnia, may also result. Probably because obstructive sleep apnea and the consequent frequent arousals from sleep are not common in neuromuscular disease, hypersomnolence is often not present to alert the clinician to the presence of a sleep disturbance.[22]

ASPIRATION AND COUGH

Many patients with neuromuscular diseases are susceptible to recurrent aspiration, especially in conditions with prominent bulbar involvement such as amyotrophic lateral sclerosis, myasthenia gravis, and multiple sclerosis. The consequence can be acute upper airway obstruction, acute pneumonia, or more chronic syndromes of lipoid pneumonia, basilar fibrosis, or bronchiectasis.

The importance of the expiratory muscles in the generation of an effective cough means that expiratory muscle weakness or paralysis seriously impairs clearance of secretions and compromises the defense against pulmonary infection. Effective coughing requires, first, an intact sensory limb of the cough reflex,[32] and, second, functioning inspiratory, laryngeal, and expiratory muscles. An initial deep inspiration is necessary, followed by adduction of the vocal cords, strong contraction of the abdominal muscles to create a strongly positive intrathoracic pressure, and abrupt but narrow opening of the glottis, leading to explosive decompression of the thorax through a small orifice.[33] Thus, weakness of any of the respiratory muscles, including the laryngeal muscles, inspiratory muscles, and especially expiratory muscles, compromises the ability to cough effectively. The physiology of cough and cough-related abnormalities is described further in Chapter 29.

UPPER AIRWAY OBSTRUCTION

Patients with neuromuscular disease are at risk of upper airway obstruction from aspirated food or foreign bodies. In addition, patients with weakness of bulbar muscles are susceptible to a functional type of upper airway obstruction caused by inadequate abduction of upper airway structures during the inspiratory phase of respiration.[34]

KYPHOSCOLIOSIS

Because of critical and unbalanced weakness of postural muscles of the spine, kyphoscoliosis is a common complication of certain neuromuscular diseases, particularly poliomyelitis and Duchenne type muscular dystrophy.[11] When severe, kyphoscoliosis results in major increases in the oxygen cost of breathing; the combination of respiratory muscle weakness and kyphoscoliosis results in particular susceptibility to ventilatory failure (see also full discussion in Chapter 83).

PULMONARY EMBOLISM

Pulmonary embolism is a constant threat to any immobilized patient, including those with neuromuscular disease. Patients with spinal cord injury and resulting paralysis appear to be at particularly high risk; Myllynen and associates[35] found evidence for deep venous thrombosis by ^{125}I-labeled fibrinogen scanning in 23 consecutive patients with spinal cord injury; 9% of these patients had concomitant pulmonary embolism. Prophylactic use of anticoagulation is highly effective and, although associated with significant risk of hemorrhagic complications, reduces overall mortality.[36]

EVALUATION OF RESPIRATORY FUNCTION IN NEUROMUSCULAR DISEASE

PHYSICAL EXAMINATION

The level of consciousness and the pattern of breathing may provide clues regarding the risk of aspiration or to the presence or absence of impending or overt respiratory acidosis. Respiratory distress and tachypnea at rest are signs of severe ventilatory dysfunction. The lung examination may reveal evidence of complicating atelectasis or pneumonia, or it may demonstrate differential expansion of the lungs, as in unilateral diaphragmatic paralysis. The accessible respiratory muscles—the sternomastoids, scalenes, intercostals, and abdominals—may be palpated directly to assess their level of activity and the presence or absence of atrophy. Inspiratory motion of the abdomen, best assessed in the supine position, often provides information regarding the adequacy of diaphragmatic contraction; paradoxical, inward movement of the abdomen with inspiration indicates weak diaphragmatic contraction due to paresis or fatigue.[37]

IMAGING

The chest radiograph provides essential information regarding the presence or absence of complicating pneumonia, atelectasis, kyphoscoliosis, or other conditions. Occasionally, specific neuromuscular problems, such as unilateral phrenic nerve palsy, will be suggested by the finding of an elevated hemidiaphragm. Because apparent or real elevation of a hemidiaphragm may also result from a number of unilateral pulmonary or pleural abnormalities, such as lobar atelectasis, diaphragmatic herniation, or subpulmonic pleural effusion, it is often useful to test the functional status of the phrenic nerve and diaphragm, using fluoroscopic or, preferably, ultrasonic monitoring of diaphragmatic motion.[38] During a sniff, which represents a brief but powerful contraction of the diaphragm, the healthy hemidiaphragm descends sharply while the resulting intrathoracic vacuum causes the paralyzed side to rise.

ARTERIAL BLOOD GAS COMPOSITION

Pulse oximetry is widely used to detect hypoxemia, both in waking states and during sleep. However, oximetric measurements of arterial oxygenation are inadequate to distinguish hypoventilation from other causes of hypoxemia; patients with suspected ventilatory failure also require measurements of arterial pH and P_{CO_2}.

PULMONARY FUNCTION TESTS

Pulmonary function tests are described in detail in Chapter 24. The characteristic finding in most neuromuscular diseases is a restrictive pattern, with well-preserved forced expiratory flow rates,[39] because lung recoil is often above normal and the airways are usually patent. The residual volume (RV) is often well preserved,[9,10] not because of airway obstruction, but because the expiratory muscles cannot overcome the outward recoil of the chest wall below functional residual capacity (FRC). Maximum voluntary ventilation (MVV) is usually reduced as much as or more than vital capacity (VC). In patients with weak bulbar muscles, but relatively well-preserved inspiratory muscle function, the flow-volume loop may show flattening of the inspiratory limb, suggestive of variable extrathoracic upper airway obstruction; however, weak inspiratory flow rates due to inspiratory muscle weakness or poor effort may show much the same pattern.[34] Except when there is accompanying parenchymal or pulmonary vascular disease, the diffusing capacity for carbon monoxide tends to be normal, or at least the ratio of diffusing capacity to lung volume tends to be normal. Fallat and coworkers[40] have pointed out that reductions in forced vital capacity and MVV by as much as 50% are frequently missed by routine clinical evaluation, so all patients with muscular weakness should undergo pulmonary and respiratory muscle function evaluation by objective tests.

TESTS OF RESPIRATORY MUSCLE STRENGTH

The hallmark of most neuromuscular disease is respiratory muscle weakness, for which the simplest tests are measurements of maximal inspiratory and expiratory pressures ($P_{I_{max}}$ and $P_{E_{max}}$). These tests are conducted by measuring airway pressure while requiring the subject to make maximal inspiratory or expiratory efforts against a closed airway at low or high lung volume, respectively (Fig. 82.2).[41] To avoid spuriously strong $P_{I_{max}}$ results due to suction by pharyngeal muscles, a small leak is provided in the apparatus. The results of the tests are strongly influenced by lung volume for several reasons: respiratory system elastic recoil provides additional pressure below and above FRC, translation of intramuscular tension to pressure is affected by lung volume, and muscle tension-generating ability (strength) is

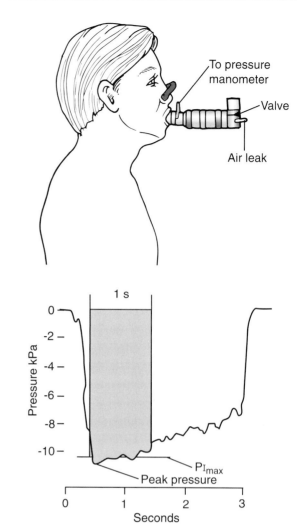

Figure 82.2 Technique for the measurement of maximal inspiratory pressure (MIP or $P_{I_{max}}$). (Adapted from Moxham J, Grassino A [eds]: ATS/ERS Statement on respiratory muscle testing. Am J Respir Crit Care Med 166:518–624, 2002.)

markedly influenced by fiber length, which, in turn, depends on lung volume (inspiratory and expiratory muscles are optimally lengthened at low or high lung volumes, respectively).[42] Thus, when $P_{I_{max}}$ or $P_{E_{max}}$ is measured, lung volume must be controlled for.

To allow comparison of tidal to maximal efforts, intrathoracic pressure can be measured via a balloon catheter advanced transnasally into the esophagus, or, to examine the strength of the diaphragm specifically, a gastric catheter can be added, and transdiaphragmatic pressure (Pdi) can be measured as the difference between gastric and esophageal pressures.[41] In patients who have a urinary catheter present, pressure in the clamped catheter, with a partially full bladder, appears to be a reasonable estimate of gastric pressure.[43] In contrast, although central venous pressure rises and falls along with intrathoracic pressure, the amplitude of the pressure change is variably damped and does not reliably reflect changes in esophageal pressure.[44]

Unfortunately, the maximal respiratory pressure tests are totally dependent on patient effort—even more influenced by poor effort than is spirometry—and reproducibility of maximal pressures does not verify that maximal efforts have been made.[45] Nevertheless, PI_{max} and PE_{max} provide "lower limit" estimates of inspiratory and expiratory muscle strength, which are usually adequate for clinical decision making. When more objective measurements are required, at least for diaphragm strength, the phrenic nerves can be stimulated electrically, using percutaneous or needle electrodes, or magnetically, and the resulting Pdi or $P_{0.1}$ can be measured.[41] The advantage of magnetic stimulation is that it is painless; its disadvantage is that the precise site of phrenic nerve activation cannot be known, making it difficult to standardize phrenic nerve latency measurements.

TESTS OF VENTILATORY DRIVE

Ventilatory drive can be assessed by measuring minute ventilation while the subject is inhaling a gas mixture that contains carbon dioxide (hypercapnic response) or one that contains a subnormal concentration of oxygen (hypoxic response).[41] The problems with these tests are that there is a wide range of normal responses, and that they may be abnormally low due to impaired generation of muscle strength despite well-preserved neural drive. To circumvent this difficulty, the $P_{0.1}$ can be monitored during hypercapnic or hypoxic challenges. Even more direct measurements of respiratory drive can be obtained by measuring the electromyographic activity of the diaphragm.[41]

SLEEP STUDIES

A variety of sleep-related breathing abnormalities occur in neuromuscular disease, often with subtle presentation.[46,47] Patients may be screened by overnight pulse oximetry, but, if there is any reason to suspect sleep-disordered breathing, the optimal test is a full polysomnographic study to identify sleep architecture, the extent of central and obstructive apneas and hypopneas, and the severity of arterial desaturation. Sleep-disordered breathing is discussed in more detail in Chapter 74.

DIAPHRAGMATIC PARALYSIS

ETIOLOGY

Paralysis of one or both hemidiaphragms, often called *eventration* of the diaphragm, is a common clinical finding. A leading cause of unilateral phrenic palsy is open heart surgery; injury to a phrenic nerve occurs in 2% to 20% of such patients[48,49] and in similar percentages of lung transplantation patients.[50] Left-sided involvement is most frequently seen, but right-sided or bilateral phrenic palsies are not uncommon. In most cases, it is thought that the portion of the phrenic nerve that courses along the pericardium is injured by the effects of the cold cardioplegia solution. In other cases, intraoperative stretching of the phrenic nerves may be at fault. Thoracotomy, pleurectomy, and even pneumonectomy are generally not accompanied by the risk of phrenic nerve injury,[51] but mediastinal and esophageal procedures do carry that risk.

Other traumatic causes of partial or complete paralysis of phrenic nerves or their roots include manipulation of the cervical spine,[52] penetrating or occasionally blunt injuries or surgery of the neck or thorax,[53,54] jugular or subclavian venous catheterization,[55] and birth trauma.[56] The phrenic nerves or their roots can also be injured by compression or by destruction by space-occupying lesions. Examples include von Recklinghausen's disease,[57] cervical osteoarthritis,[58] aortic aneurysm, substernal thyroid, and bronchogenic or mediastinal tumors. Although intrathoracic malignancy is the most feared diagnosis when unilateral diaphragmatic paresis is detected, in a series of 142 cases it accounted for only 5%.[59]

Local inflammatory conditions, such as pleurisy and pneumonia, and specific inflammations of the phrenic nerves, as in herpes zoster infection or vasculitis,[60] can also injure one or both phrenic nerves. Phrenic neuropathy has been reported 7 months[61] and 30 years[62] after mediastinal radiotherapy. The phrenic nerves are often involved in peripheral neuropathy, which appears to be particularly common in diabetes.[63] Neuralgic amyotrophy, a relatively common but poorly understood peripheral nerve disorder that usually affects the brachial plexus, may also cause unilateral or bilateral paralysis of the diaphragm.[64] Bilateral diaphragmatic paralysis may be the initial manifestation of neuromuscular diseases that are usually generalized, such as multiple sclerosis,[65] anterior horn cell disease,[66] chronic inflammatory demyelinating polyneuropathy,[67] and myopathies, particularly acid maltase deficiency.[11] In many cases of diaphragmatic paralysis, no definite cause can be established.[59]

CLINICAL FEATURES

The clinical manifestations of diaphragmatic paresis depend on the severity of the weakness, whether it is unilateral or bilateral, the rapidity of its onset, and the presence or absence of other respiratory illness. The features are also markedly different in infants as compared to older children and adults.

Unilateral Paralysis

Over half of adult patients with unilateral hemidiaphragmatic paralysis are entirely asymptomatic,[59] and another quarter experience only mild exertional dyspnea. Others experience generalized muscle fatigue, chest wall pain, cough, or dyspnea at rest.[59] A few have severe exertional dyspnea, often associated with chest pain, and a few experience dyspnea at rest, especially if they lie with the paralyzed side down. Occasionally, a transient episode of dyspnea identifies the onset of phrenic palsy. Not surprisingly, symptoms are more common in patients with preexisting lung disease.[68]

The prognosis of adult patients with unilateral diaphragmatic paralysis is generally good, primarily because of the relatively mild pulmonary function impairment that results from unilateral paralysis. The good prognosis also stems in part from development of compensatory mechanisms and in part from the recovery by the injured phrenic nerve of part or all of its function. Two series of patients have been studied after deliberate ablation of one phrenic nerve by local anesthesia[69] or by surgical transection.[70] The pulmonary function deficit was severe in normal subjects immediately after the phrenic nerve was anesthetized, but less severe over a 6- to 12-month interval after phrenic section. Studies of one patient before, immediately after, and 7 weeks after right phrenic crush demonstrated an adaptive increase in the contraction characteristics of the remaining, unparalyzed inspiratory muscles.[71]

Regional lung function and gas exchange are mildly abnormal when one side of the diaphragm is paralyzed,[66] with reductions in both ventilation and perfusion on the involved side, primarily adjacent to the paralyzed hemidiaphragm. In the supine position, arterial PO_2 generally falls significantly, and regional lung function is more abnormal than in the upright position.[72] Exercise capacity is mildly to moderately reduced,[73] and arterial PO_2 tends to increase with exercise.

Bilateral Paralysis

Unlike unilateral phrenic palsy, bilateral paralysis of the diaphragm almost always causes severe symptoms, abnormalities of pulmonary function, and morbidity in adults and children as well as in infants.[56] Typically, there is severe exertional dyspnea and patients experience marked orthopnea. Most patients develop ventilatory failure, frequently complicated by cor pulmonale, atelectasis, and pneumonia. The manifestations of bilateral diaphragmatic paralysis are much worse in the supine position. In the upright position, the weight of the abdominal contents tends to prevent excessive paradoxic and cephalad motions of the diaphragm; in the supine position, this protective effect is lost. As a result of the exaggerated respiratory dysfunction in the supine position, sleep disturbances are common. Furthermore, during REM sleep, activity of respiratory muscles other than the diaphragm is reduced.[30] Consequently, when the diaphragm is paralyzed, REM sleep is associated with particularly severe ventilatory dysfunction. Nocturnal hypoxia and worsening hypercapnia are common in patients with bilateral diaphragmatic paralysis, leading to anxiety, daytime somnolence, and morning headaches. In severe cases, confusion, memory loss, and motor impairment may occur.

The prognosis of bilateral diaphragmatic paralysis depends on the nature of the underlying disease. Enhanced use of neck and rib cage inspiratory muscles allows for better pulmonary function in the upright position, but as long as the diaphragm is weak, patients still have severe symptoms when lying down. If the nerve injury is not due to a progressive, generalized neuropathic process, phrenic nerve and diaphragm function often recover, albeit slowly, often only after 2 years.[49]

Diaphragmatic Paralysis in Infants

Infants are much more severely affected by either unilateral or bilateral diaphragmatic paralysis than are older children and adults. Because their chest wall is relatively compliant, chest wall inspiratory muscles are needed to stabilize the chest. The inability of infants to sit up accentuates the postural problems of diaphragmatic paralysis, and the relative predominance of REM sleep reduces the ability of the other inspiratory muscles to compensate for the loss of one and especially both hemidiaphragms. Infants are particularly susceptible to atelectasis, pneumonia, and ventilatory failure

even in unilateral paralysis, and they virtually always suffer ventilatory failure when the paralysis is bilateral.[56]

DIAGNOSIS

Physical examination of patients with *unilateral paralysis* of the diaphragm reveals dullness to percussion and absent breath sounds over the lower chest on the involved side. Frequently, the compressed lung will give rise to crackles on auscultation just above the area of dullness. On deep palpation, it may be appreciated that the inspiratory excursions of the abdomen are less on the paralyzed side than on the healthy side. Paradoxically, the excursions of the lower rib cage may be greater on the side of the paralyzed hemidiaphragm (M. H. Williams, Jr., personal communication). When the normal hemidiaphragm contracts, the resultant positive abdominal pressure exerts an outward force, creating an apparently inspiratory effect on the lower rib cage through the zone of apposition. In unilateral diaphragmatic paralysis, this effect is greater on the paralyzed side because the zone of apposition is larger under the elevated paralyzed hemidiaphragm. The diagnosis of unilateral paralysis of the diaphragm is often suggested by the finding of an elevated hemidiaphragm on the chest radiograph, but that is a nonspecific finding (Fig. 82.3). The sniff test, optimally monitored by ultrasound,[38] is usually unequivocally diagnostic.

The detection of *bilateral paralysis* is much easier than of unilateral paralysis by physical examination, but much harder by imaging techniques, because a comparison of the behavior of one side with the other does not help. The hallmark finding on physical examination is paradoxic, inward movement of the abdomen with inspiration. Instead of the normal pattern of synchronized outward inspiratory movement of both chest and abdomen, the abdomen moves inward when the upper chest moves outward. In some cases, recruitment of the abdominal expiratory muscles masks diaphragmatic paralysis by restoring the inward movement of the abdomen on expiration, and permitting a passive outward movement of the abdomen in early inspiration, when the expiratory muscles relax. The chest film shows a totally nonspecific elevation of both hemidiaphragms. Comparisons of inspiratory and expiratory chest films, and even the sniff test, are often equivocal, because the observer cannot rely on a comparison of the two sides, and must accurately identify both the inspiratory phase of respiration and the diaphragm's motion in that phase. Moreover, if the abdominal muscles actively contract during the expiratory phase, the diaphragm will be forced cephalad and its subsequent passive descent during the inspiratory phase may lead to a falsely normal examination. Thus, unless careful observations are made of inspiratory and expiratory timing and the presence or absence of abdominal muscle activity, the sniff test and its variants are often misleading.

Pulmonary and Ventilatory Function

Pulmonary function tests usually show a mild restrictive process in unilateral paralysis (Table 82.3). In bilateral paralysis, severe restriction is the rule, with reductions in VC and MVV averaging 55% and 45%, respectively, owing to inspiratory muscle weakness. In contrast to the findings in unilateral paralysis, the FRC and RV are decreased by 40%

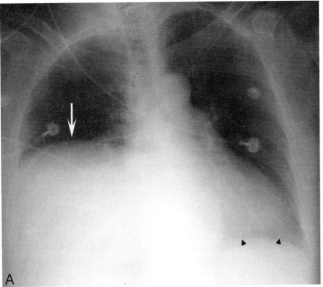 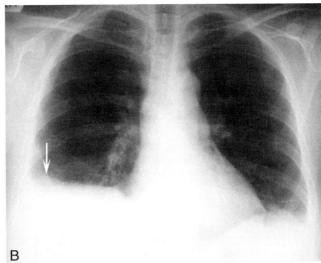

Figure 82.3 **A,** Paralysis of right hemidiaphragm. Frontal radiograph shows elevation of the right diaphragm associated with right basilar atelectasis. Note that the frontal view of the chest shows that the diaphragm has a smooth, rounded contour with its peak (*arrow*) in the center of the right hemithorax. Opposite diaphragm is in normal position (*arrowheads*). **B,** Subpulmonic effusion. In subpulmonic effusion, the elevated right hemidiaphragm has a peak that is more lateral (*arrow*), a feature that helps to distinguish subpulmonic effusion from diaphragmatic paralysis. (Courtesy of Michael B. Gotway, MD, Department of Radiology, University of California, San Francisco).

Table 82.3 Comparison of Pulmonary and Respiratory Muscle Function in Unilateral and Bilateral Paralysis of the Diaphragm*

Variable	Unilateral	Bilateral
VC	75	45
TLC	85	55
FRC	100	60
RV	100	55
FEV$_1$	70	50
PI$_{max}$ (cm H$_2$O)	70	10 to 20
Pdi$_{max}$ (cm H$_2$O)	70	40 to 10

* Values expressed as percentage of predicted normal value unless otherwise specified.
FEV$_1$, forced expiratory volume in 1 second; FRC, functional residual capacity; PI$_{max}$ and Pdi$_{max}$, maximal inspiratory and transdiaphragmatic pressures, respectively; RV, residual volume; TLC, total lung capacity; VC, vital capacity.

and 45%, respectively, because of pulmonary atelectasis. Comparisons of VC measured in the supine and upright position can be striking; supine VC is usually less than 75% of the upright value in severe bilateral diaphragmatic weakness.[72,74]

Phrenic Nerve Stimulation

The most specific tests for diaphragmatic weakness or paralysis are electrophysiologic assessments of phrenic nerve competence and measurements of Pdi.[41] In most patients, either the right or the left phrenic nerve can be stimulated electrically, using percutaneous or needle electrodes, or magnetically, using a single posterior cervical coil or single or dual anterolateral cervical coils. The electromyographic response to phrenic stimulation can be detected as compound action potentials recorded from cutaneous electrodes at the seventh, eighth, or ninth intercostal spaces in the anterior axillary line or from esophageal electrodes. The mechanical response of the diaphragm is measured by the elicited Pdi twitch, usually against a closed airway. In neuropathy, the latency may be prolonged and action potentials and twitch pressures may be markedly reduced or absent. In myopathy, the latency and action potentials may be normal but the mechanical responses are reduced or absent. The sensitivity and specificity of these tests are not established. Although not as specific for diaphragmatic weakness and more effort dependent than twitch Pdi, PI$_{max}$ is reduced in parallel with Pdi in most neuromuscular diseases.

DIFFERENTIAL DIAGNOSIS

Pleural and Pulmonary Disease

Pleural effusions, especially when subpulmonic, may produce radiographic images resembling either unilateral or bilateral diaphragmatic paralysis (see Fig. 82.3); lateral decubitus chest radiograms or ultrasound examination of the chest can resolve this question. Intrapulmonary processes that reduce the compliance of the lung mimic diaphragmatic paralysis because they reduce the inspiratory excursion of the diaphragm. Atelectasis, pneumonia, edema, and fibrosis may be unilateral or bilateral. Usually, such conditions are readily apparent on chest radiographs. In most cases, the diagnosis can be established by careful physical examination, coupled with inspiratory and expiratory radiograms or by fluoroscopic or ultrasonographic imaging of the diaphragm, or both.

Other Neuromuscular Disease

Neuromuscular diseases that may be confused with diaphragmatic paralysis include alveolar hypoventilation caused by brain-stem or high cervical spinal cord disease, and diffuse respiratory muscle weakness consequent to anterior horn cell, neuromuscular junction, or muscle disorders.

The most practical and reliable methods to diagnose bilateral diaphragmatic paralysis are the observation of inward inspiratory movement of the abdomen in the supine position, fluoroscopic or ultrasonographic determination of upward movement of the diaphragm while the patient makes a full inspiration to total lung capacity (TLC), and measurement of Pdi during the same maneuver.

TREATMENT

Unilateral Paralysis

When unilateral diaphragmatic paralysis is detected, a primary goal in management is to exclude serious intrathoracic pathology, such as an infection or a malignant tumor in or adjacent to the mediastinum. In most cases, no such disease will be found, and no practical treatment is available. Fortunately, the relatively mild symptoms and favorable prognosis of such cases do not require aggressive treatment.

In some instances, surgical treatment is indicated. Infants with unilateral paralysis are much more severely compromised than are similarly affected adults, and surgical plication of the paralyzed hemidiaphragm can often ameliorate ventilatory failure by improving ipsilateral lung expansion and preventing excessive inefficient flailing of the paralyzed hemidiaphragm.[56] Recently, a few cases of plication of unilaterally paralyzed hemidiaphragms have been reported in adults.[75,75a] Surgical repair of injured phrenic nerves has been accomplished in at least two cases.[76,77] Autologous nerve transplantation restored phrenic nerve function in a child with phrenic nerve palsy[78] and made diaphragmatic pacing possible in a patient with phrenic motoneuron damage.[79]

Bilateral Paralysis

In bilateral phrenic paralysis, some form of treatment is almost always required. Plication of both hemidiaphragms or of the more severely affected hemidiaphragm is often recommended for infants.[80] The benefits are improved expansion of the lower lobes and prevention of the paradoxical motion, with resulting improved efficiency of the remaining innervated inspiratory muscles. Because many cases of phrenic nerve injury are reversible, especially those induced by trauma, and because it is likely that plication may interfere with the subsequent function of a reinnervated hemidiaphragm, bilateral plication should be reserved for cases of irreversible denervation with substantial paradoxical motion documented by fluoroscopy.

Many patients with bilateral diaphragmatic paralysis will require mechanical support of ventilation. Often, this can be provided without tracheostomy by a rocking bed,[81] a negative-pressure body respirator such as the cuirass respirator,[56] nasal continuous positive airway pressure (CPAP), or intermittent positive-pressure ventilation by nasal mask[82] or oral appliance.[83] These devices are most useful when carbon dioxide retention occurs only at night. For bilateral phrenic nerve paralysis, electrophrenic respiration is not an option, because this form of therapy depends on intact phrenic nerves and diaphragm muscle. A nerve that is stimulated below the site of its transection may respond to pacing for a short period, but it eventually atrophies, and the threshold for activation of the muscle itself by direct stimulation is too high for pacing to be effective.

POSTOPERATIVE DIAPHRAGMATIC DYSFUNCTION

Clinical Features

A relatively mild and temporary form of isolated diaphragmatic dysfunction occurs in patients who undergo upper abdominal surgery[84,85] or thoracotomy.[86] After upper abdominal surgery, the TLC, VC, FEV_1, tidal volume, and tidal and maximal Pdi values fall and respiratory rate increases. Recovery occurs over 2 to 7 days. Postoperative diaphragmatic dysfunction undoubtedly contributes to atelectasis, hypoxemia, and increased risk of surgical morbidity. Thus, measures designed to inflate the lungs and to improve inspiratory effort, such as incentive spirometry, and, in severe cases, CPAP, are indicated.

Pathophysiology

Postoperative diaphragmatic dysfunction does not seem to be mediated by pain, as it has been shown not to be abolished by opiate epidural anesthesia.[85] Animal studies show that anesthesia and lower abdominal surgery do not cause postoperative diaphragmatic dysfunction, whereas thoracotomy and upper abdominal surgery do.[87,88] It may be that local irritation of the diaphragm evokes afferent inhibitory neural activity. Certainly, the phrenic nerves contain plentiful afferent fibers, and stimulation of these fibers may have an inhibitory effect on ventilation.[89] Furthermore, phrenic afferents may be highly selective in their inhibitory effects, reducing only ipsilateral phrenic nerve activity. Local inflammation or pressure may thus activate free nerve endings in the diaphragm, thereby suppressing diaphragmatic activity while preserving the activity of the other inspiratory muscles.

SPINAL CORD INJURY

GENERAL ASPECTS

Serious impairment of spinal cord function can result from any of a number of causes, but approximately three quarters of the injuries are traumatic, from motor vehicle, industrial, or sports accidents, or from gunshot wounds. Other causes include diabetes mellitus, epidural abscesses, tumors (especially metastatic neoplasms), vascular accidents, transverse myelitis, and syringomyelia. Obviously, the onset of the disability is sudden in the case of trauma, whereas it may be subacute or chronic in some of the other conditions.

Nonetheless, the ultimate outcome is similar, and we focus on spinal cord traumatic injury as the primary example of this type of neuromuscular disease.

Spinal cord injury is a catastrophic event with multiple severe consequences. Many manifestations that do not primarily involve the respiratory system nevertheless exert indirect effects on it. Major nonrespiratory problems include the shattering psychological impact of the disease, with severe depression; immobility; loss of bowel, bladder, and sexual functions; decubitus ulcers; and infections of the skin and urinary tract. These conditions, and sometimes the measures used to treat them, predispose to malnutrition, wasting of nonparalyzed muscles, and pulmonary infection, especially pneumonia, which is the most common cause of death.[2,90]

Because the effects of high cervical spinal cord injury differ substantially from injuries at lower levels, we consider them separately.

HIGH CERVICAL SPINAL CORD INJURY

Clinical Features

Injuries above the C3 level produce nearly complete respiratory muscle paralysis. Such patients are virtually unable to breathe or talk, and they cannot cough. Lesions that disrupt the reticulospinal pathways in the ventral aspect of the upper cervical cord eliminate automatic control of breathing, except to the limited extent that the sternomastoid and trapezius muscles receive innervation from the spinal accessory (XIth) nerve. Such injuries therefore produce a syndrome that resembles central alveolar hypoventilation. Lesions that disrupt the more lateral cortical spinal pathways make it impossible to execute voluntary respiratory movements, but automatic control is preserved.[91] In traumatic injury, both sets of pathways are apt to be involved, such that voluntary and involuntary automatic respiratory function is minimal or absent.

The symptoms are dominated by asphyxia, dyspnea that may be aggravated in the sitting position, and difficulty with secretions. The physical examination during brief suspension of mechanical ventilation reveals either apnea or marked inspiratory contraction of the sternomastoid muscle and trapezius muscles, which hypertrophy as other muscles become atrophic. Breath sounds are faint, and there may be basilar rhonchi. There is no diaphragmatic excursion with respiration, but the diaphragm does descend on changing from the supine to the sitting posture. The abdominal muscles are flaccid, and the patient is unable to cough.

Pulmonary Function

Pulmonary function data are sparse for patients with high spinal cord injury. Rapid, shallow breathing is the rule.[92,93] The VC is 20% of normal at best, and expiratory reserve volume (ERV) is nearly zero. FRC is reduced, probably primarily because of underlying atelectasis but also because the absent tone of the chest wall muscles reduces the chest wall recoil pressure. In one patient, PI_{max} was severely impaired at −20 cm H_2O, but PE_{max} was relatively well preserved at 66 cm H_2O.[94] The latter value was primarily due to elastic recoil of lung and chest wall after a large inspira-

tion, achieved by a series of small glossopharyngeal breaths, rather than by expiratory muscle contraction.

Patients with high spinal cord injury recruit the trapezius, platysma, mylohyoid, and sternohyoid muscles to assist the sternomastoid muscles with inspiration.[92] The synchronous contraction of these recruited muscles pulls the sternum cranially, expanding the upper rib cage while the abdominal and lateral rib cage diameters decrease.

MIDDLE AND LOWER CERVICAL SPINAL CORD INJURY

Clinical Features

One of the remarkable features of middle to lower cervical spinal cord injury is the extent to which the inspiratory and expiratory deficits fail to correlate with the level of injury, as assessed from peripheral sensory and motor examination. We hypothesize that several factors account for this discrepancy, not the least of which is the fact that trauma produces anatomically irregular rather than surgically precise lesions of the spinal cord. It would appear that some injuries are complete; whereas others produce only partial interruptions of spinal neural pathways.[95] Other mechanisms include recruitment of muscles not normally having phasic respiratory function, progression or partial recovery from the original injury, variability in the functional status of the nonparalyzed musculature, and injury-induced, or coexistent, pulmonary mechanical abnormalities.[96]

Respiratory Muscle Function

Both PE_{max} and PI_{max} tend to be more severely impaired in midcervical, as opposed to low cervical or thoracic injuries, but the range of values at each injury level is so large that no statistically significant differences have been demonstrated. At all levels of injury, PE_{max} is more severely impaired than is PI_{max}. Consequently, coughing is severely hampered; peak expiratory flow during cough is weakly, but significantly, correlated with the level of injury.[97]

One would expect that quadriplegic patients could not exhale below the resting, end-expiratory position (FRC) because their expiratory muscles are paralyzed. However, ERV is actually moderately well preserved; averaging 0.5 L in the 14 cases described by De Troyer and associates.[98] The mechanism of expiration is contraction of the clavicular portion of the pectoralis major muscle, with some additional help from the cranial portion of the serratus anterior muscle. The latissimus dorsi and teres major muscles assist by fixing the position of the humerus. The abdominal muscles are electrically silent, but the diaphragm contracts during the early expiratory phase of cough much as in normal subjects.[99] The expiratory action of the clavicular portion of the pectoralis major is approximately halved when the shoulders are abducted, because this maneuver lessens the downward pull of the pectoralis on the manubrium. These observations help to explain why cough is partially preserved in patients with C6-level injury.

Pulmonary Function

Patients with C3 to C8 lesions are usually not dependent upon mechanical ventilation, and most have normal levels

Table 82.4 Pulmonary and Respiratory Muscle Function in Quadriplegic Patients with Middle to Lower Cervical Spinal Cord Injury*

Variable	C4–C7 Injury	T3–T12 Injury
FVC	52	69
FEV_1/FVC (%)	85	82
IC	71	—
ERV	21	64
TLC	70	82
FRC	86	86
RV	141	91
MVV	49	61
PI_{max} (cm H_2O)	64	79
PE_{max} (cm H_2O)	41	98

* Values expressed as percentage of predicted normal unless otherwise specified.
ERV, expiratory reserve volume; FVC, forced vital capacity; IC, inspiratory capacity; MVV, maximal voluntary ventilation. Other abbreviations as in Table 82.3.

of arterial PCO_2 when awake. Typical values for pulmonary and respiratory muscle function are summarized in Table 82.4. The overall pattern is that of a restrictive defect, with a normal FEV_1/FVC ratio and with relatively more severe reduction in ERV than in inspiratory capacity. Patients with cervical spine injuries tend to have hyperreactive bronchi; eight of eight chronic quadriplegics without histories of asthma or cigarette smoking were found to be hyperresponsive to methacholine,[100] and similar hyperresponsiveness to distilled water challenge has been reported.[101] Although overt asthma has not been reported as a common complication of spinal cord injury, this finding suggests a susceptibility, probably due to unopposed cholinergic influences.

Lung volumes in quadriplegic patients are more sensitive to changes of posture than in normal subjects. When a quadriplegic patient is upright, gravity causes the abdominal contents to pull the diaphragm down and bulge out the flaccid abdominal wall. In the supine position, gravity causes the abdominal contents to push the diaphragm craniad. Thus, in the supine position, RV and FRC decrease while PI_{max} and VC increase.[102] The increase in VC is usually not enough to counterbalance the reduction in RV, so TLC is slightly smaller in the supine than the upright position.

Because of the loss of intercostal muscle function, the upper rib cage moves paradoxically inward with inspiration in quadriplegic patients, and the relative contribution of the rib cage to the tidal volume is reduced.[103] The extent to which the upper rib cage moves paradoxically depends largely on whether or not scalene muscle function is preserved. Upper rib cage distortion has also been shown to result in part from paralysis of the abdominal muscles, and the degree of distention can be minimized by abdominal compression.[104] Because contraction of the well-preserved diaphragm expands the lower rib cage through its action on

the area of apposition, lower rib cage motion is relatively normal.

Lung compliance is reduced,[95] especially among patients with impaired parasternal inspiratory intercostal muscles, but specific compliance, compliance corrected for lung volume, is normal. Airway resistance is usually normal.[105] The work and oxygen cost of breathing are moderately elevated,[106] mostly due to work done by the diaphragm in displacing the abdominal viscera. The compliance of the abdominal compartment is lower in the sitting than in the supine position.

Quadriplegic patients usually have mild hypoxemia and an increase in the alveolar-arterial PO_2 gradient,[105] usually due to abnormally low ventilation-perfusion ratios in collapsed or partially collapsed areas of lung, although small airway dysfunction may also contribute. There is a mild reduction of ventilation to basilar regions, even though the abdominal contribution to tidal volume that results from diaphragmatic contraction is higher than normal.[107]

Control of Breathing

The control of breathing may or may not be altered. In one series, the ventilatory response to carbon dioxide was normal,[105] but it was half normal in another study.[108] Axen and Bergofsky[109] found that quadriplegic patients show varying responses to added elastic loads; some did and others with equally severe levels of injury did not allow their tidal volumes to fall. The former stiffened their chest walls when presented with the elastic load, and maintained inspiratory efforts for longer periods. The ability to stiffen the chest wall and preserve tidal volume is thought to be due to the influence of preserved thoracic sensory receptors on the control of the inspiratory muscles.

DiMarco and colleagues[110] reported that quadriplegic patients are able to sense the size of an inspired breath in normal fashion during passive, voluntary, and loaded breathing, even after local anesthesia of the upper airways, suggesting that this form of respiratory sensation depends on tension developed by the diaphragm or on the level of central nervous system motor command.

Prognosis

Spontaneous partial recovery of ventilatory function usually occurs in the first few months after the initial injury.[111,112] For example, in patients with C5-6 injuries, VC averaged 31% of predicted initially, 51% at 3 months, and 58% at 5 months. PI_{max} and maximal Pdi improve in parallel with VC, but FRC does not change, suggesting that the improved ventilatory function is due to improved inspiratory muscle strength. Wicks and Menter[111] showed that the majority of quadriplegic patients who initially required mechanical ventilation could be weaned as their pulmonary function improved.

Quadriplegic patients are extremely vulnerable to any insult that worsens pulmonary function. Although there have been vast improvements in prognosis over the last two decades, the mortality from lower cervical spinal cord injury is still 15% to 40% in the first year, mostly from respiratory failure.[2] After the first year, pulmonary complications, especially pneumonia, continue to take a toll, and the risk of fatal pneumonia remains severalfold higher for spinal cord–injured patients than for matched controls.[2,90]

THORACIC SPINAL CORD INJURY

The respiratory problems of paraplegic patients whose injuries are in the thoracic region are usually less prominent than those in quadriplegic patients. The major problem is poor cough. Expiratory muscle weakness is just as severe in midthoracic lesions as in lower cervical injuries, but less in lower thoracic and upper lumbar injuries. Typical values for pulmonary function tests are summarized in Table 82.4. In general, function is better the lower the level of injury, but the mean values obscure a very wide range.

TREATMENT

Spinal cord injury remains a devastating problem, usually with no or limited neurologic recovery. Utilization of high-dose steroids for acute injury is a standard clinical approach to prevent further damage from inflammation and edema.[113] Other neuroprotective agents, such as gangliosides, have shown modest benefits.[114] Several animal studies have demonstrated the potential efficacy of cellular transplantation, which can facilitate growth of new neurons and secretion of neurotropic factors. They have shown promise for cellular repair, axonal growth, alleviating chronic dysesthetic pain, and reversing demyelination, but none is yet in clinical use.[115,116]

Prior to the advent of phrenic nerve pacing, most patients who survived high spinal cord injuries required permanent mechanical ventilatory support. Occasional highly motivated individuals learn to perform glossopharyngeal breathing;[93,94] that is, they use tongue, cheek, pharyngeal, and laryngeal muscles in a coordinated way to inject successive small boluses of air into the trachea, sometimes achieving enough tidal volume to talk and to breathe without support for brief periods. Glossopharyngeal breathing also enables patients to inhale deeply from time to time, so as to prevent atelectasis and to improve the effectiveness of coughing.

Spinal cord injuries above C3 denervate but do not destroy the cell bodies of the phrenic motoneuron pool. These neurons lie at levels C3, C4, and C5 in humans, with the highest concentration at C4. Because the phrenic nerves and their cell bodies in the anterior horn of the spinal cord are intact, they can be stimulated electrically. Details of the procedure for electrophrenic respiration have been summarized by Glenn and associates[117] and are reviewed later (see "Treatment of Ventilatory Failure" section).

Specific treatments to prevent pneumonia include frequent changes in the patient's position in bed, the regular use of deep-breathing exercises and incentive spirometry, and assisted coughing. When secretions are retained, chest percussion, and bronchodilator and possibly mucolytic therapy, are recommended, followed by therapeutic bronchoscopy in refractory cases.

OTHER FOCAL RESPIRATORY MUSCLE PARALYSES

After isolated diaphragmatic paralysis and spinal cord injury, hemiplegia and poliomyelitis are the next most common causes of focal respiratory muscle weakness or paralysis. The major respiratory complications of stroke are due to its effects on the level of consciousness and the ability to swallow. Hemiplegia is not usually associated with significant ventilatory impairment unless the lesion lies in the brain stem.

Large epidemics of acute poliomyelitis no longer occur in developed countries, but sporadic cases still appear in patients who have not been vaccinated. Therefore, one must consider the diagnosis and inquire into the vaccination history when one encounters a patient with an acute syndrome of fever, myalgia, and weakness. The degree of impairment in poliomyelitis varies from mild to severe, but the ventilatory deficit often worsens late in life, owing to postpolio syndrome.

HEMIPLEGIA

Neural Pathways

The paralysis of hemiplegia results from damage to upper motor neurons. Lower motor neurons in the spinal cord remain viable and are subject to stimulation by spinal cord sensorimotor reflex arcs. As a result, the affected muscles do not respond to voluntary motor control, but they are often spastic. The respiratory muscles receive their upper motor neuronal innervation from two anatomically and functionally discrete pathways: the corticospinal tracts, which comprise the pyramidal system, and the reticulospinal tracts, which course from the respiratory centers to the anterior horns of the spinal cord. The corticospinal tracts mediate voluntary respiratory motions, whereas the reticulospinal tracts mediate automatic breathing patterns. Patients with stroke usually have corticospinal tract damage but not reticulospinal tract damage unless the brain stem is infarcted.

Clinical Features

In hemiplegic patients, the anteroposterior excursions of the paralyzed side of the chest are marginally less than on the nonparalyzed side.[118] The position of the diaphragm as seen on ordinary supine chest roentgenograms may be subtly elevated,[119] and the motion of the diaphragm, assessed by fluoroscopy with the patient supine, is mildly limited on the side of the paralysis,[120] an abnormality that is apparent only when breathing is augmented, either voluntarily or by carbon dioxide inhalation. The relatively less severe paralysis of respiratory as compared to limb muscles can be explained by relative prominence of decussating, or crossing, fibers in the upper motor innervation of the respiratory muscles.[121]

POLIOMYELITIS

General Considerations

Poliovirus destroys motoneurons in the anterior horns of the spinal cord. The distribution of muscle paralysis, which involves limb, truncal, and respiratory muscles, depends on the site of anterior horn cell damage. Muscle weakness and paralysis are most severe in the early, febrile stage of the illness. During convalescence, partial recovery is common; it may depend on recovery of some anterior horn cells or on improved function of the nonparalyzed muscles. The mechanism of late deterioration, which is referred to as postpolio syndrome, appears to be denervation of previously reinnervated muscles. Although the number is diminishing, former victims of poliomyelitis constitute an important group of patients receiving long-term ventilatory support.[122]

Clinical Features and Ventilatory Function

In one large series studied after the 1953 polio epidemic, significant respiratory paresis occurred in about 15% of patients,[123] and the degree of disability was quite variable.[124] Data from two series[124,125] show the relationship between dependence on mechanical ventilation, pulmonary function, and respiratory muscle strength (Table 82.5). The mean values do not reflect the wide range of values in individual patients. Moreover, because of the variable distribution of paresis, there are patients whose inspiratory and expiratory muscle weaknesses are roughly equal, others in whom expiratory muscle weakness predominates, and still others in whom inspiratory muscle weakness predominates. The general tendency is for inspiratory weakness to exceed expiratory weakness.[124]

As in other forms of neuromuscular disease, the VC is lower than would be predicted from muscle weakness alone, largely due to the reduction of respiratory system compliance to about half normal.[124] Compliance of the lungs is reduced to a greater extent than chest wall compliance,[124] but both contribute to the reduction in total respiratory system compliance. Respiratory system resistance is normal to slightly reduced in poliomyelitis.[125]

Patients with poliomyelitis often have a low ventilatory response to carbon dioxide inhalation,[123] apparently depending more on the extent of reduction in VC or MVV than on whether the virus involved the medullary respiratory center. For example, Plum and Swanson[126] found that patients with bulbar poliomyelitis without severe muscle weakness had normal ventilatory responses, whereas the responses were less than half normal in patients, irrespective of bulbar disease, who also had spinal cord and respiratory

muscle involvement. The ventilatory response to hypoxia was relatively unimpaired.[123]

Late Complications

Another prominent aspect of poliomyelitis is the propensity for late respiratory complications. Fischer[127] described 114 patients followed since 1958 or before. Ninety-eight (86%) of these patients now require some form of ventilatory assistance, and 52 have had tracheostomies, half for worsening ventilatory failure. In general, postpolio syndrome affects the same muscle groups that were affected during the original onset of the disease; thus, if respiratory insufficiency was not a feature of the initial presentation of polio, it is relatively unlikely to manifest itself during the postpolio syndrome. Sleep-disordered breathing—obstructive sleep apneas, hypoventilation, or a mixed syndrome—is common in postpolio syndrome.[128]

DIFFUSE NEUROMUSCULAR DISEASE

The disorders considered in this section have widely diverse etiologies (see Table 82.1), but their common features are that the entire respiratory musculature is involved and that respiratory muscle weakness is relatively symmetrical. It is convenient to subdivide these disorders into those that have an acute onset and those with a more gradual onset. Detailed descriptions of the general clinical and neurologic characteristics of these disorders are available in several reviews;[3,4] we focus on the respiratory system involvement.

DISEASES OF ACUTE ONSET

Disorders in this category fall into two etiologic groups. Three of the diseases are immunologic in origin: acute inflammatory polyneuropathy (Landry-Guillain-Barré-Strohl syndrome), myasthenia gravis, and Lambert-Eaton syndrome. The other three are toxic in origin: botulism, organophosphate poisoning, and toxicity from aminoglycoside or polymyxin antibiotics. Acute inflammatory polyneuropathy affects transmission of impulses along the nerve, whereas all the other conditions affect transmission across the neuromuscular junction. Botulism, organophosphate poisoning, and antibiotic toxicity typically have acute onset. Acute inflammatory polyneuropathy may present acutely or subacutely. The symptoms of myasthenia gravis and Lambert-Eaton syndrome may be acute, but more often are of gradual onset.

Acute Inflammatory Polyneuropathy

Acute inflammatory polyneuropathy is an acquired demyelinating neuropathy. Potential risk factors include influenza-like infection, some viral exanthems, and other viral or mycoplasmal infections. Although nerve conduction studies are usually abnormal at the time of maximal weakness, early in the clinical course the nerve conduction studies may be normal.

Acute inflammatory polyneuropathy is an excellent model of the effects of acute respiratory muscle weakness, because the ascending nature of the paralysis usually involves the

Table 82.5 Vital Capacity and Its Subdivisions, Maximal Voluntary Ventilation, and Maximal Respiratory Pressures in Three Categories of Patients with Poliomyelitis*

Variable	Group 1	Group 2	Group 3
VC	15	34	56
IC	10	25	43
ERV	1	6	26
MVV	20	35	75
PI_{max}	25	35	47
PE_{max}	26	41	55

* All values are expressed as percentage of predicted normal.
Group 1, dependent on mechanical ventilation greater than 12 hr/day; group 2, dependent on mechanical ventilation less than 12 hr/day; group 3, not dependent on ventilatory support. Abbreviations as in Tables 82.3 and 82.4.

chest wall and abdominal muscles before the laryngeal and pharyngeal muscles, and because other complications characteristic of botulism and organophosphate poisoning are absent. The clinical picture of acute ventilatory failure consequent to muscle weakness is dominated by symptoms of progressive weakness and dyspnea, difficulty in coughing, and, later on, dysphagia and difficulty with speech.[129] Physical examination reveals limb and truncal muscle weakness, but examination of the respiratory system initially reveals only tachypnea. Later, the voice and gag reflex may fail.

The most useful parameters with which to follow the progressive ventilatory deficit are the VC and measurement of PI_{max} and PE_{max}. Early on, arterial blood gas analysis shows hypoxemia with an increased alveolar-arterial PO_2 gradient and a low arterial PCO_2. The arterial PCO_2 values rise back above normal only when VC has fallen to very low levels, usually to less than one third normal. It must be emphasized that the combination of dyspnea, tachypnea, falling VC, and low arterial PCO_2 is a harbinger of ventilatory failure; patients should receive appropriate treatment before overt hypercapnia ensues.

A recent prospective cohort study of 791 patients admitted to hospitals with acute inflammatory polyneuropathy[130] demonstrated that 9% required endotracheal intubation and mechanical ventilation on admission, and a further 40% required intubation and mechanical ventilation during the hospital stay. The most important predictor of the need for mechanical ventilation was inability to cough. Other significant predictors included brief duration of symptoms, VC less than 60% of the predicted value, a number of indices of muscle weakness, and, surprisingly, liver enzyme elevation. The duration of respiratory failure for this condition varies widely, in one study ranging from 10 to 104 days and averaging 58 days.[129]

Major complications during treatment are pulmonary embolism and cerebellar hemorrhage. Others include aspiration, atelectasis, pneumonia, decubitus ulcers, and impaired nutrition.[129] The prolonged course of acute inflammatory polyneuropathy in most afflicted patients is an argument for early tracheostomy.

Myasthenia Gravis

Myasthenia gravis is a disease of the motor end plate. It produces muscle weakness that is aggravated by repetitive muscular contraction. The disease may be limited to ocular or bulbar muscles, but it often affects limb and respiratory muscles, and ventilatory failure is one of its most severe complications. In untreated states, the weakness can be severe, but it improves when anticholinesterase therapy with drugs such as neostigmine or pyridostigmine is instituted.

In mild disease, there is subtle respiratory muscle weakness, with expiratory muscles affected more than inspiratory muscles.[131] Pulmonary function changes in proportion to respiratory muscle strength, but RV is relatively well preserved. A retrospective review of pulmonary function laboratory records disclosed a flow-volume pattern suggestive of variable extrathoracic upper airway obstruction in 7 of 12 myasthenia gravis patients,[131] probably due to weakness of upper airway abductors, such that they were unable to oppose the airway vacuum generated by relatively strong

contraction of the inspiratory muscles. Respiratory muscles are sometimes more severely affected than other skeletal muscles.[132] Indeed, ventilatory failure may occasionally be the sole clinically apparent manifestation of the disease.[133]

The effects of anticholinesterase treatment are improvements in respiratory muscle strength, lung volumes, and inspiratory and expiratory flow rates, and no effect on the pattern of breathing.[16] The resting lung volume and the transpulmonary pressure at that volume increase, suggesting that, with improved respiratory muscle tonic activity, there is an increase in the outward recoil of the chest wall.[132] Neostigmine therapy increases respiratory muscle strength but has relatively little effect on endurance, so a prolonged static effort, an MVV effort, or, presumably, increased respiratory effort requirements caused by pneumonia, asthma, or the like will reverse the gain produced by prostigmine.

Myasthenia gravis is caused by an immunoglobulin G (IgG) autoantibody that attacks the acetylcholine receptor of skeletal muscle. Treatment with anticholinesterase drugs acts only by temporarily increasing the available acetylcholine concentration. Corticosteroids sometimes have a more prolonged effect, but are not always successful. In such cases, plasmapheresis to remove the IgG autoantibody may be indicated. Three to five exchanges may be required because less than half the IgG antibody is in the intravascular compartment at any one time, and a 70% reduction in concentration of the antibody at the acetylcholine receptor may be needed for remission of disease. Intravenous immune globulin has been reported to be effective in reversing an exacerbation of myasthenia with few side effects; its benefit can persist for several months.[134] Other immunologic approaches such as immunoablation, acetylcholine receptor antigen, and "hot antigen suicide" are currently being evaluated for clinical use.[135]

The major problems in managing myasthenia gravis are complications of surgery (especially thymectomy),[136] myasthenic crisis,[137] and cholinergic crisis, each of which results in ventilatory failure, sometimes for prolonged periods.

Lambert-Eaton Syndrome

Lambert-Eaton syndrome, like myasthenia gravis, is an autoimmune disorder of neuromuscular transmission. In contrast to myasthenia gravis, muscle strength tends to improve with repeated testing.[138] About 50% of cases of Lambert-Eaton syndrome occur in association with small cell carcinoma of the lung (discussed in Chapter 44), in which cases IgG antibodies against presynaptic calcium channels are produced. Diaphragmatic weakness is common, and is occasionally severe enough to produce ventilatory failure. The syndrome often improves with treatment of the underlying carcinoma. Treatment with intravenous immune globulin[139] or the potassium channel–blocking aminopyridine derivatives[140] may be of short-term benefit.

Botulism

Botulism is a serious, potentially fatal disease that is caused by neurotoxin from the anaerobic gram-negative bacterium *Clostridium botulinum*. The potent toxin may be absorbed from the gastrointestinal tract, from wounds, or from the airspaces; recent attention has centered on its potential use in bioterrorism.[141] The neurotoxin causes presynaptic blockade of the neuromuscular junction, thus inhibiting acetylcholine release. The classic symptoms include visual impairment, slurred speech, dysphagia, dry mouth, nausea, vomiting or diarrhea, weakness, dyspnea, and dizziness. Physical signs include ptosis, extraocular muscle paresis, pupillary abnormality, dysarthria, and extreme muscle weakness.

Ventilatory failure is common. Patients who need mechanical ventilation have more dyspnea and gastrointestinal symptoms and are much more apt to have tachypnea, ptosis, and extreme muscle weakness on physical examination than patients who do not need ventilation. The onset of ventilatory failure may be insidious, unless the physician pays careful attention to the severity and progression of dyspnea, tachypnea, reduction in VC, and reduction in maximal respiratory pressures. As with other forms of neuromuscular disease, overt hypercapnia occurs very rapidly once respiratory muscle weakness has progressed far enough.

The course of botulism may be prolonged, and late residual symptoms of exertional fatigue and dyspnea are common. However, with prompt treatment, the mortality has been reduced to 10% by aggressive therapy with trivalent equine antitoxin.[142]

Symptoms of dyspnea and fatigue persist for several years after recovery from botulism, even when pulmonary function tests have returned to normal.[143] Exercise intolerance in patients recovered from botulism is characterized by dyspnea, rapid shallow breathing, and reduced maximal oxygen consumption, and seems to be related to poor cardiovascular fitness, rapid leg fatigue, or poor motivation. In a few cases, inspiratory muscle weakness also contributes.

Organophosphate Poisoning

Highly toxic organophosphates and carbonates such as parathion, malathion, and carbaryl are used in agricultural insecticides; similar quaternary organophosphates are used in nerve gases. These compounds cause muscle paralysis and other side effects because, like the antimyasthenic therapeutic agents edrophonium, physostigmine, neostigmine, and pyridostigmine, they inhibit acetylcholinesterase and lead to excessive concentrations of acetylcholine at the neuromuscular junction and other cholinergic synaptic sites.[144]

Symptoms of acute intoxication reflect muscarinic and nicotinic effects. The former include sweating, excessive salivation, nausea, vomiting, abdominal cramps and diarrhea, bradycardia, and hypotension. Nicotinic effects include weakness, muscle fasciculation, and paralysis. Central nervous system effects include confusion, ataxia, loss of reflexes, convulsions, and coma. Specific respiratory manifestations include laryngospasm, excessive tracheobronchial secretions, bronchoconstriction, respiratory muscle weakness, and central ventilatory depression.

Treatment of organophosphate poisoning requires large doses of atropine to reverse the muscarinic effects, and pralidoxime to reverse the neuromuscular junction paralysis. The initial dose of atropine should be 2 to 4 mg, intravenously if possible, repeated every 5 to 10 minutes until the muscarinic symptoms disappear. Pralidoxime is given to adults in doses of 1 to 2 g intravenously, as soon as possible.

Antibiotic Toxicity

Ventilatory failure may occur following administration of aminoglycoside and polymyxin antibiotics.[145] Again, this is mediated by interference with neuromuscular transmission, and the risk is particularly high in patients with myasthenia gravis and those with renal failure. Symptoms resemble those of botulism, with diplopia, dysphagia, slurred speech, and dyspnea. Spontaneous recovery can occur within a few hours or days after stopping the antibiotic. Anticholinesterase therapy has been used effectively in reversing the effects of aminoglycoside neuromuscular blockade, but it is ineffective against blockade produced by polymyxin B and sodium colistimethate.

A large number of other drugs, including calcium channel blockers, β-blockers, antirheumatics, and diuretics, have the potential to impair respiratory muscle function.[145] For most of these, any muscle dysfunction is usually subclinical. However, it is likely that patients with other causes of mild or subclinical respiratory muscle dysfunction may be more susceptible than healthy persons to the neuropathic or myopathic effects of drugs.

DISEASES OF GRADUAL ONSET

Etiology

Although on occasion the onset may be abrupt, in most cases, the symptoms and signs of diffuse neuromuscular diseases are subacute or chronic. The major categories of diffuse neuromuscular disease are *amyotrophic lateral sclerosis* (ALS), various types of *muscular dystrophy*, and many kinds of *myopathy*. The myopathies that involve the respiratory muscles are highly diverse; they may be congenital; related to infection or diabetes mellitus; induced by steroids, alcohol, or impaired nutritional status; or related to inflammatory autoimmune disease. Many of the last type are associated with collagen vascular diseases.

Clinical Features

The clinical course varies according to the nature of the underlying disease. Patients with ALS have an average life expectancy of 3 to 4 years after the onset of symptoms, and death is usually due to pneumonia or ventilatory failure.[146] Life expectancy in muscular dystrophies is often longer, but, again, death is usually due to respiratory failure.[1] Some congenital myopathies may progress rapidly, but most of those seen in adults are slowly progressive. Acquired myopathies may progress rapidly or slowly, and patients may stabilize or recover, depending on removal of the inciting cause or treatment.

Patients are usually aware of limb muscle weakness before they have respiratory symptoms, but at times the respiratory symptoms appear first. Limb muscle weakness may be proximal, distal, or both. Muscle cramps and fasciculations occur in some of the disorders. In the absence of associated lung disease, the predominant respiratory symptoms are dyspnea on exertion and fatigue. As the disease progresses, dyspnea is present at rest, and difficulty in coughing, speaking, or swallowing becomes more prominent. Some patients have morning headache, disturbed sleep, and daytime somnolence, and others may develop symptoms of heart failure.

Diagnosis

The diagnostic workup of patients suspected of having neuromuscular diseases should include tests of the neuromuscular apparatus. The pattern of muscle weakness, the presence or absence of fasciculations, and the presence or absence of hyperreflexia are important aspects of the physical examination. Electrophysiologic techniques, such as nerve conduction and electromyographic studies, are useful to differentiate among denervation, dystrophies, and myopathic processes. Biopsy of affected muscles helps to identify dystrophies and myopathies. Serum creatine kinase and aldolase levels are often elevated in dystrophies and myopathies. Strength does not improve with administration of edrophonium.

Pulmonary and Respiratory Muscle Function. Respiratory muscle weakness and impaired pulmonary function are readily detectable by objective testing well in advance of overt respiratory symptoms.[10] Because patients with neuromuscular diseases may have coincident obstructive or interstitial lung disease, it is necessary to measure maximal pressures in addition to performing spirometric and lung volume measurements. In diffuse neuromuscular diseases, the inspiratory and expiratory muscles are usually weakened to the same degree.[10] On occasion, the primary manifestation of these diseases is severe diaphragmatic weakness, out of proportion to limb or other respiratory muscle involvement.

Pulmonary function testing of patients with respiratory muscle weakness uncomplicated by coexisting pulmonary disease reveals an apparent restrictive pattern, with reductions in VC and a normal FEV_1/FVC ratio, but with an elevated RV.[10] The forced expiratory flow-volume curve is often truncated near RV when expiratory muscle weakness is severe. MVV is almost always below normal.[10] The diffusing capacity is usually normal, especially if it is corrected for the reduction in TLC.[1] All of the pulmonary function abnormalities worsen as the disease progresses, usually in direct relation to the degree of respiratory muscle weakness.[1,10]

Again, the reduction in VC in patients with respiratory muscle weakness is out of proportion to what would be expected from muscle weakness alone. The most likely reason is decrease in the distensibility of the lungs due to microatelectasis, coupled with a decrease in the outward pull of the chest wall. The reduction in lung compliance is not reversed by intermittent positive-pressure breathing. In addition, the relaxed chest wall is on average almost twice as stiff in patients with neuromuscular disease as it is in normal subjects.

In the early stages of neuromuscular disease, the spirometric tests may be near normal when PI_{max} and PE_{max} are considerably reduced. The data obtained by Braun and colleagues[10] in patients with myopathy are typical for all of the diffuse neuromuscular diseases, and are consistent with data of other investigators. Even in the absence of coexistent lung disease, VC ranges from 50% to 100% of normal when respiratory muscle strength is above 40% of the predicted value, but VC falls when respiratory muscle strength is below 40% of the predicted value (Fig. 82.4). The increase in RV is inversely related to PE_{max} (Fig. 82.5), and MVV is directly related to respiratory muscle strength (Fig. 82.6). The regression lines in the figures are calculated only from patients without coexistent lung disease (closed circles). It

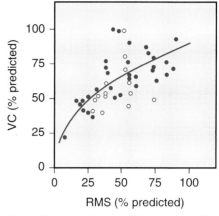

Figure 82.4 Relationship between vital capacity (VC) and respiratory muscle strength (RMS) in patients with proximal myopathies. In Figures 82.4 to 82.8, *closed circles* denote patients without, and *open circles* patients with, coexisting lung disease. The regression lines are calculated from data of patients with myopathy uncomplicated by lung disease. (From Braun NMT, Arora NS, Rochester DF: Respiratory muscle and pulmonary function in polymyositis and other proximal myopathies. Thorax 38:616–623, 1983.)

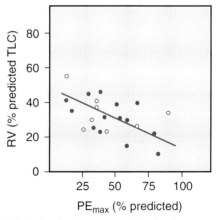

Figure 82.5 Relationship between residual volume (RV) and maximal expiratory pressure (PE$_{max}$) in patients with proximal myopathies. Symbols used as in Figure 82.4; TLC, total lung capacity. (From Braun NMT, Arora NS, Rochester DF: Respiratory muscle and pulmonary function in polymyositis and other proximal myopathies. Thorax 38:616–623, 1983.)

can be seen that patients with associated lung disease (open circles) cannot be distinguished from those without lung disease on the VC and RV graphs (see Figs. 82.5 and 82.6), but most patients with associated lung disease have a lower MVV than could be predicted on the basis of respiratory muscle strength alone (see Fig. 82.6).

In myotonic dystrophy, respiratory muscle dyskinesia may occur, characterized by better performance during rhythmic efforts than with static efforts, abnormal expiratory muscle activity, and prolongation of diaphragmatic activity during expiration elicited by expiratory resistive loads.[147] The latter may represent a form of abnormal control of breathing, but more likely is a manifestation of impaired relaxation of the respiratory muscles.[148]

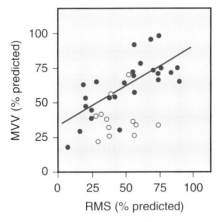

Figure 82.6 Relationship between maximal voluntary ventilation (MVV) and respiratory muscle strength (RMS) in patients with proximal myopathies. Symbols used as in Figure 82.4. (From Braun NMT, Arora NS, Rochester DF: Respiratory muscle and pulmonary function in polymyositis and other proximal myopathies. Thorax 38:616–623, 1983.)

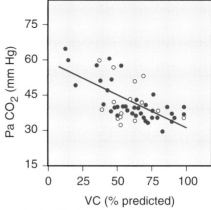

Figure 82.7 Relationship between arterial P_{CO_2} (Pa_{CO_2}) and vital capacity (VC) in patients with proximal myopathies. Symbols used as in Figure 82.4. (From Braun NMT, Arora NS, Rochester DF: Respiratory muscle and pulmonary function in polymyositis and other proximal myopathies. Thorax 38:616–623, 1983.)

VENTILATORY FAILURE

Respiratory Muscle Weakness

Ventilatory failure in patients with diffuse neuromuscular disease does not develop because of respiratory muscle weakness per se. Early in neuromuscular disease, the respiratory rate increases and arterial P_{CO_2} falls.[10] The onset of ventilatory failure is likely to be abrupt, even when it has taken a long time to develop a critical degree of respiratory muscle weakness. Ventilatory failure is often precipitated by a respiratory infection, not only because of the additional respiratory loads associated with consolidation, airway mucus, reactive bronchospasm, edema, and fever-associated tachypnea, but probably also because of cytokine-mediated respiratory muscle weakness.[149] The clinical signs that indicate that ventilatory failure is imminent or in progress are increasing weakness and fatigue, dyspnea at rest, tachypnea, coughing and difficulty clearing secretions, sleep disturbances, and daytime somnolence.

Pattern of Breathing

The cause of the respiratory failure is muscle weakness, but the mechanism is a progressive reduction in tidal volume, leading to an increased dead space–to–tidal volume ratio. Rapid, shallow breathing is characteristic of neuromuscular disease,[15] despite the fact that ventilatory drive is normal or increased. Patients with severe respiratory muscle weakness recruit their neck inspiratory and abdominal expiratory muscles in a fashion highly reminiscent of normal subjects breathing at 50% MVV or higher.[150]

Weakness versus Fatigue

The relative magnitude of the ventilatory load in neuromuscular disease can be quantified by the intrathoracic pressure-time index, the integral over time of the intrathoracic vacuum required for tidal breathing, divided by PI_{max}.[41]

Whenever the respiratory muscles are weak, the pressure-time index is much higher than normal, both because the load is increased and because PI_{max} is reduced. Thus, inspiratory muscle weakness predisposes to fatigue. In patients with myotonic dystrophies, the diaphragm becomes fatigued more rapidly than in normal subjects for the same relative load.[14] It is not yet known whether the diaphragm is more susceptible to fatigue in the other neuromuscular diseases. Observations in patients recovering from acute ventilatory failure caused by myasthenia gravis or acute inflammatory polyneuropathy (Landry-Guillain-Barré-Strohl syndrome) suggest that overt fatigue of the respiratory muscles is uncommon.[151] Despite considerable residual diaphragmatic and inspiratory muscle weakness, the diaphragmatic pressure-time index rarely exceeds the fatigue threshold, even in patients who cannot sustain adequate levels of ventilation. This is because the patients inspire very small tidal volumes.

Harbingers of Ventilatory Failure

It must be emphasized that overt ventilatory failure occurs abruptly and that measurement of arterial blood gas composition is not a reliable indicator of impending respiratory acidosis. We stress the importance of heeding the clinical observations of increasing dyspnea and tachypnea, as well as sleep disturbance, morning headache, and daytime somnolence. We urge physicians to make serial measurements of VC and respiratory muscle strength in patients shown to be at risk by their symptoms. As VC decreases, there is a progressive increase in arterial P_{CO_2} (Fig. 82.7), such that P_{CO_2} values reach respiratory failure levels when VC is less than half normal. As respiratory muscle strength decreases from normal to half normal, arterial P_{CO_2} remains normal or somewhat low (Fig. 82.8). Thereafter, P_{CO_2} values rise progressively, reaching respiratory failure levels when respiratory muscle strength is less than 25% to 30% normal in patients with muscle weakness uncomplicated by lung disease.

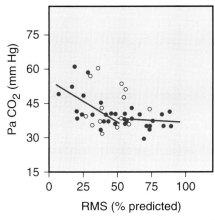

Figure 82.8 Relationship between arterial PCO_2 ($PaCO_2$) and respiratory muscle strength (RMS) in patients with proximal myopathies. Symbols used as in Figure 82.4. (From Braun NMT, Arora NS, Rochester DF: Respiratory muscle and pulmonary function in polymyositis and other proximal myopathies. Thorax 38:616–623, 1983.)

TREATMENT OF VENTILATORY FAILURE

Treatment of Underlying Disease

Treatment of respiratory muscle weakness is specific in a few cases and supportive in most. Examples of diseases that respond to some extent to specific therapy include myasthenia gravis (outlined earlier), polymyositis and dermatomyositis, hyper- and hypothyroidism, malnutrition, and alcoholic and steroid myopathies. By and large, the anterior horn cell diseases, dystrophies and congenital myopathies are relentlessly progressive and specific treatments have been disappointing. The antiglutamate drug riluzole prolongs survival in ALS, but only for a few months.[152] However, enhanced understanding of the roles of oxidative stress, glutamate excitotoxicity, and apoptosis in the pathogenesis and genetic susceptibility to ALS may lead to more effective pharmacotherapy.[153] Similarly, although there is currently no definitive therapy for the muscular dystrophies, preliminary animal experiments demonstrating that the gene coding for dystrophin can be delivered to the diaphragm via an adenovirus vector[154] suggest that specific genetic therapy may be achievable. There is also increasing interest in symptomatic treatment to increase the strength and decrease the rate of muscle necrosis, using corticosteroids,[155] anabolic steroids (see later),[156] and creatine.[157]

Pharmacologic Means to Improve Ventilatory Drive or Respiratory Muscle Strength

Ventilatory stimulants have not met with much success in the treatment or prevention of ventilatory failure in neuromuscular disease. In general, ventilatory drive is more than adequate in neuromuscular diseases, but the presence of denervation, neuropathy, or myopathy prevents an adequate response of the muscle. Thus, use of ventilatory stimulation may lead to overuse of weakened ventilatory muscles, potentially leading to further impairment of muscle function.[158] In the few cases of congenital myopathy or endocrinopathy in which control of breathing is compromised out of proportion to the degree of respiratory muscle weakness, a cautious trial of acetazolamide or progesterone may be warranted.

Anabolic steroids, growth hormone, insulin-like growth factor-I (IGF-I), and other neurotrophic factors have been suggested as pharmacologic approaches to improving respiratory muscle strength in neuromuscular disease and in other wasting conditions.[159–161] Preliminary results in small number of patients with acquired immunodeficiency virus–associated myopathy,[162] spinal cord injury,[163] Duchenne type muscular dystrophy,[156] inclusion body myositis,[164] and ALS[165] have suggested that certain anabolic steroids can effect small but potentially useful improvements in muscle strength. There have been fewer trials of growth hormone and IGF-I. Preliminary trials of growth hormone in acquired immunodeficiency virus–associated myopathy[166] and ALS[167] have demonstrated safety but little benefit. Both growth hormone and IGF-I have shown promise as preventive or treatment agents for steroid myopathy,[168] but IGF-I has been generally disappointing in the treatment of ALS.[169]

Supportive Therapy

Several forms of supportive therapy are available to improve ventilatory and respiratory muscle function,[169a] even when the underlying disease process is progressive, as discussed in Chapters 84 to 86. Supplemental oxygen is indicated in patients with documented hypoxemia at rest, on exercise, or during sleep. Adequate oxygenation can prevent or improve cor pulmonale, polycythemia, hypoxia-related intellectual and cognitive dysfunction,[170] and possibly respiratory muscle dysfunction.[171]

Measures designed to assist coughing and clearances of secretions are often helpful in patients with neuromuscular diseases. A few techniques have been developed to enhance cough capacity in the presence of severe respiratory muscle weakness. For example, the effectiveness of coughing can be augmented by synchronizing coughing attempts with manual compression of the abdomen by an assistant.[93,172] Patients may also use the insufflator/exsufflator, or "cough machine," an instrument that provides a deep insufflation by mask, followed by rapid decompression.[173,173a] In patients with cervical cord injuries, the abdominal expiratory muscles, which remain innervated by intact lower motor neurons that cannot be voluntarily activated, can be stimulated electrically[172,174] or magnetically[175] to enhance cough effectiveness. Stimulation is unlikely to be of benefit for victims of neuropathy or myopathy, because the neuromuscular apparatus is not intact.

Certain types of physical training are also beneficial. With glossopharyngeal breathing, patients who otherwise would be incapable of a deep inspiratory effort can learn to augment their vital capacity by up to 1 L. With the larger inspiration, there is more passive recoil, which promotes a more effective cough.[93] Estenne and colleagues[176] have shown that isometric exercise of the pectoralis muscle, designed to strengthen its clavicular portion, increases the expiratory capacity, and thereby improves cough efficiency of quadriplegic patients.

β-Adrenergic agonists can improve clearance of secretions even in the absence of bronchial obstruction. When secretions are particularly tenacious, mucolytics such as nebulized acetylcysteine may help; however, it should be noted that nebulized acetylcysteine can precipitate severe bronchoconstriction in patients with asthma or hyperreactive airways. Nasotracheal suctioning, percussion, and postural drainage, and even bronchoscopy, are occasionally necessary to remove secretions from large airways.

Inspiratory muscle training (IMT) has been used with some success in selected patients with neuromuscular disease. In lower cervical spinal cord injury, a 6-week regimen of daily forced inspiration and expiration through resistances, coupled with manual insufflation of air to increase TLC above the spontaneously achieved value, approximately doubled PI_{max}, PE_{max}, and VC, increased TLC by about 10%, and lowered RV by about 25%.[177] Four additional studies of 4,[174] 6,[178] 8,[179] or 16[180] weeks of IMT demonstrated smaller, but potentially meaningful, increases in inspiratory muscle strength,[179,180] inspiratory muscle endurance,[178] and VC.[173,179,180] Both VC and PI_{max} tended to return toward baseline after termination of the study,[179] suggesting not only that some level of continuing challenge is required for maintenance of the beneficial effect, but also that the observed IMT-associated improvements were actually due to improved function, not simply improved ability to perform the tests.

The results of IMT are more variable in patients with muscular dystrophy. DiMarco and colleagues[181] reported that respiratory muscle endurance could be significantly improved by 6 to 12 weeks of IMT. The results were best in patients whose baseline PI_{max} was at least 60% normal or higher. Wanke and coworkers[182] showed similar results of 1 to 6 months of IMT, with small improvements in inspiratory muscle strength and endurance, but no improvement in VC, and no improvement in strength among the most severely affected patients (VC < 25% of the predicted value). In contrast, Koessler and associates[183] found substantial improvements in inspiratory muscle strength and vital capacity during and after a prolonged (2-year) training program in a combined group of patients with Duchenne type muscular dystrophy and with spinal muscular atrophy. In two additional studies, IMT was not found to be of benefit.[184,185]

IMT has shown some promise in a single case of adult-onset acid maltase deficiency,[186] in myasthenia gravis,[187] and in a mixed group of patients with neuromuscular disease.[188]

Results of several studies involving small numbers of patients suggest that IMT, by voluntary effort[189,190] or with phrenic nerve stimulation,[191] may help to improve the strength and endurance of mechanically ventilated patients with spinal cord injury,[189–191] muscular dystrophy,[189] or neuropathies,[189] improving their chances to become independent of mechanical ventilation. These favorable results suggest that the reason that severely affected, but spontaneously breathing, patients have been found to be relatively unlikely to respond to IMT[187,188] is that it is relatively easy for such patients to breathe around the resistor, thereby failing to achieve the inspiratory muscle overload necessary for a training effect; in patients on mechanical ventilation, the closed ventilatory circuit, and perhaps the close attention paid by therapists throughout the training sessions, makes it more likely that strong inspiratory efforts will continue throughout the sessions.[189]

Ventilatory Assistance

When neuromuscular disease is far advanced and ventilatory failure is impending or already established, ventilatory support is necessary if patients are to survive. Many such patients do not choose to accept ventilatory support, whether delivered by traditional means, including tracheostomy and volume-cycled ventilators, or by "noninvasive" means.[192] Indeed, it is often argued that the quality of life on chronic mechanical ventilation is unacceptably poor. There is no doubt that the cumbersome nature of ventilatory support equipment, the ever-present risk of death from disconnection or power failure, the problems of maintaining communication, and the expense of equipment and caregivers present major challenges to patients and their families. However, recent advances in respiratory care have made it possible for highly motivated individuals with access to financial support and to creative and resourceful rehabilitation specialists to live long periods of acceptable quality on mechanical ventilation, with or without tracheostomy.[193]

Although tracheostomy facilitates access to large airways for clearance of secretions by suction catheter, it also virtually destroys the patient's ability to generate the strongly positive expiratory pressures and the narrow glottic orifice that are necessary for effective clearance of secretions from smaller airways by coughing.[33] Thus, where possible, avoidance of tracheostomy yields important benefits.

Techniques for Noninvasive Mechanical Ventilatory Support. The principal categories of noninvasive mechanical ventilation are based on utilization of gravity (rocking bed), application of positive pressure to the body (abdominal belt), application of negative pressure to the body (iron lung, cuirass, body wrap), and application of positive pressure to the airway (nose mask or mouthpiece).

Rocking Bed. The rocking bed is a conventional bed mounted on an apparatus that allows it to cycle from 30 degrees head up to 15 degrees head down several times each minute. The resulting shifting of the abdominal organs assists diaphragmatic excursion. The rocking bed is useful for patients who cannot sustain their own ventilatory support indefinitely but who have relatively good ventilatory function when sitting upright. It is particularly useful for patients with diaphragmatic paralysis or quadriplegia.

Abdominal Pneumatic Belt. Similar assistance in diaphragmatic excursion can be provided by an abdominal positive-pressure belt ventilator. This consists of a pneumatic belt that is connected to a cyclic positive-pressure source. As the bladder in the belt is inflated, the abdomen is compressed. This pushes the diaphragm upward and assists expiratory airflow. When the bladder is deflated, the descent of the diaphragm and the passive recoil of the rib cage back to FRC provide the force for inspiration. Unlike the rocking bed, the abdominal ventilators function best when the patient is in a sitting position. Bach and Alba[194] have shown that selected patients can be maintained on abdominal positive-pressure breathing for long periods.

Negative-Pressure Body Ventilators. Negative-pressure ventilators have been extensively used in the support of patients with a variety of neuromuscular diseases.[195] Such ventilators have the advantage that they leave the upper airway free, allowing unimpeded speech. The early versions of negative-pressure ventilators, the iron lungs, are too cumbersome for practical use by most patients at home. The smaller cuirass and body-wrap ventilators are more acceptable to most patients, though they still require considerable skill for successful operation.

A major problem with the use of negative-pressure mechanical ventilation is upper airway obstruction, occurring when the upper airway abductors fail to contract vigorously enough to oppose the intratracheal vacuum generated by the inspiratory cycle of the negative-pressure ventilator.[196] This is a particularly severe problem during sleep in patients with prominent weakness of bulbar muscles. In most cases, the solution to this problem is to switch to positive-pressure ventilation.

Noninvasive Positive-Pressure Ventilation. Noninvasive intermittent positive-pressure ventilation has been used with great success in patients with neuromuscular diseases.[195] In most cases, positive-pressure ventilation has been delivered via a nasal mask, but in some cases oral masks or mouthpieces are used. Patients may use a portable volume-cycled ventilator or a bilevel CPAP device. The tidal volume is adjusted to compensate for small leaks occurring through the mouth; if excessive leakage occurs, the mouth can be loosely held closed with a strap.

Complications of nasal positive-pressure ventilation are common and often troublesome. They include leaks at the mouth or the infraorbital area, chronic nasal congestion, sinusitis, and skin breakdown at sites of contact with the mask. Nevertheless, the majority of patients who start on nasal positive-pressure ventilation are able to tolerate it,[197] and its use often prevents the need for tracheostomy.

Continuous and Bilevel Positive Airway Pressure. In normal subjects, CPAP increases tidal volume by 25% and lowers respiratory rate by over 30%.[198] In patients with neuromuscular and chest wall diseases, nasal CPAP prevents atelectasis.[199] Nasal CPAP also prevents the upper airway collapse and consequent functional inspiratory upper airway obstruction that occasionally complicate neuromuscular diseases. CPAP can prevent the flail action of a paralyzed hemidiaphragm as well,[70] thereby improving the efficiency of the remaining, functioning inspiratory muscles. On the other hand, CPAP often increases FRC and shortens inspiratory muscles, potentially placing them at a mechanical disadvantage. Thus, CPAP has the potential to worsen inspiratory muscle weakness. We think that CPAP is most beneficial in patients with upper airway obstruction due to paresis of the upper airway musculature and in patients with isolated diaphragmatic paralysis. CPAP or bilevel CPAP alone should be used only with caution and close monitoring in other neuromuscular diseases.

Ventilatory Rest. In patients with chronic ventilatory failure, nocturnal mechanical ventilatory support using either negative-pressure or positive-pressure respirators provides at least several hours per day of adequate oxygenation, which can prevent or reverse cor pulmonale, improve intellectual and cognitive function, and provide a margin of safety during the patient's most vulnerable period. A number of studies have also suggested that, perhaps by relieving fatigue, nocturnal ventilation can improve the function of the ventilatory muscles during the remaining hours, during which the patient breathes spontaneously.[197]

Electrophrenic Respiration. Electrophrenic respiration is indicated for patients in whom the neuromuscular apparatus is intact from the nerve to the muscle but in whom ventilatory drive fails or cannot be translated normally into neural impulses.[200] Thus, patients with central alveolar hypoventilation or high cervical spinal cord injuries, in which the phrenic motor neurons remain intact, are appropriate candidates for phrenic pacing. In patients with ventilatory failure due to anterior horn diseases, neuropathies, or myopathies, the muscles are no more likely to respond to electrical stimulation than to voluntary or automatic respiratory effort.

Before initiation of pacing, the phrenic nerve must be tested for viability. This involves percutaneous stimulation of the cervical portion of the nerve and recording the diaphragmatic action potentials using surface electrodes over the anterolateral rib cage. Sometimes it is necessary to expose the phrenic nerve surgically to be sure of its response to stimulation. Pacemaker electrodes are usually implanted on both phrenic nerves so that an alternating pacing schedule can be employed. Cervical implantation is easier and carries lower risk, but it may not fully stimulate the diaphragm. Therefore, in cases in which maximal diaphragmatic response is required (e.g., in patients with underlying lung disease), the thoracic implantation procedure is preferred. After implantation, the performance of each hemidiaphragm is tested fluoroscopically and spirometrically.

The electrical stimulation parameters have been selected to minimize nerve and muscle damage. The pulse waveform is bipolar. The current per pulse is adjusted to the point beyond which further increases in current no longer increase tidal volume. The stimulation frequency is usually 10 to 15 impulses/sec. Higher frequencies, 25 to 35 impulses/sec, may be required initially, when the diaphragm is deconditioned. However, animal experiments show that prolonged use of higher frequencies causes myopathic changes and weakness of the diaphragm, whereas lower frequencies of stimulation do not.[205] The duration of each train of impulses is selected to be about one quarter of t he whole breath duration. At a typical stimulated respiratory rate of 12 breaths/min, the duration of each train of stimuli is 1.3 seconds, and the inspiratory-to-expiratory ratio is 1:3.

Various pacing patterns have been employed. If the diaphragm has atrophied prior to the initiation of pacing, it will rapidly fatigue when stimulated.[201] Therefore, one must start by stimulating the phrenic nerves for only a few minutes per hour, and then progress each day by a few minutes per hour until diaphragmatic endurance time is at least 30 minutes. Thereafter, pacing can be carried out on a schedule of 30 minutes of pacing, alternating with 30 minutes of rest, for several hours at a time. The length of the pacing periods is increased until a single hemidiaphragm can be paced continuously for 6 to 12 hours. Note that the process of retraining an atrophied diaphragm is analogous to weaning patients with weak respiratory muscles from mechanical ventilation. The process will succeed provided that nutritional status is adequate and that complications, especially infections, are absent.

When a full pacing schedule has been achieved, additional variables must be considered. Some patients are more comfortable when both hemidiaphragms are paced simultaneously,[117] but they may need rest periods, during which they use a mechanical ventilator. To sustain patients without ventilators, it is often better to pace one hemidiaphragm for 6 to 12 hours, then switch to the other side. Tidal volumes and Pdi values are about 50% higher when both hemidiaphragms are paced. Diaphragmatic pacing increases the inspiratory excursions of the abdomen and lower rib cage, but the upper rib cage moves paradoxically inward.[202] Diaphragmatic pacing is much more effective when the patient is supine than upright, but the effectiveness of pacing in the sitting position can be enhanced by abdominal compression.[202]

The complications of electrophrenic respiration include nerve damage, infection, and upper airway occlusion.[200] Upper airway occlusion results from failure of the pharyngeal and laryngeal muscles to open the upper airway and is associated with an increase in rib cage paradox. Both tracheostomy and voluntary inspiratory efforts circumvent this problem. Therefore, an alternative solution is to trigger the phrenic pacemaker from the electromyogram of the sternomastoid muscles.[203]

SYNDROMES OF INAPPROPRIATE RESPIRATORY MUSCLE CONTRACTION

In this section, we discuss a number of disorders that we term *syndromes of inappropriate respiratory muscle contraction*. They share some common features in that either the timing of contraction is inappropriate, the synchronization between inspiratory and expiratory muscles is lacking or abnormal, or the intensity of the contraction is excessive (Table 82.6). As a group, these syndromes cause dyspnea

Table 82.6 Syndromes of Inappropriate Respiratory Muscle Contraction

Syndrome	Type of Respiratory Muscle Involvement
Hiccups (singultus)	Spasmodic contraction of diaphragm, other inspiratory muscles Upper airway closure
Respiratory myoclonus (tic, flutter of diaphragm)	Spasmodic contraction of diaphragm (most cases) or of abdominal muscles (one case)
Respiratory dyskinesia	Abnormal asynchronous pattern of breathing, involving all respiratory muscle groups, associated with neurocirculatory asthenia Associated facial and limb muscle dyskinesia (four cases); limited to respiratory muscles (one case)
Convulsive disorders	Status epilepticus, tetanus, strychnine poisoning Severe spasmodic contraction of all respiratory muscle groups causes hypoventilation

and chest discomfort, as well as interfere with speech and swallowing. Unlike other neuromuscular diseases, muscle weakness is generally not a prominent component, and only in extreme cases does inappropriate contraction of the respiratory muscles cause ventilatory failure.

HICCUPS

Etiology

Hiccup is a common phenomenon that is usually innocuous, but that sometimes produces significant morbidity. Hiccups are associated with many conditions that involve the central nervous system, the vagus and phrenic nerves, the mediastinum, the diaphragm, and the gastrointestinal and genitourinary tracts.[204] In some cases no obvious organic disease is present, and the hiccup phenomenon may be psychogenic. Examples of central nervous system conditions associated with hiccups include multiple sclerosis, toxic states such as uremia and alcohol intoxication, dexamethasone therapy, meningitis and encephalitis, vascular lesions and brain tumor, and surgery. Peripheral nerve causes include herpes zoster and irritation of branches of the vagus or phrenic nerves. Visceral causes include stimulation of the gastrointestinal tract by heat, cold, spasm, dilation, and distention, and inflammatory, neoplastic or surgical lesions of the mediastinum, diaphragm, or upper gastrointestinal tract.

Hiccups are usually only a nuisance. However, prolonged hiccups cause discomfort and interfere with speech, eating, and sleep. Hiccups during or after surgery can pose particular problems. In one adult, hiccups were thought to be the cause, rather than the result, of severe esophageal reflux,[205] and in one infant, hiccups were considered to have caused a Mallory-Weiss injury to the esophageal mucosa, with serious bleeding.[206]

Pathophysiology

The spasm of hiccup is not limited to the diaphragm. There are short, sharp contractions of the diaphragm and inspiratory intercostal muscles, coupled with transient closure to the glottis, that can occur 10 to 30 times per minute.[204] In infants, the upper airway closure involves pharyngeal muscles, and it may persist after diaphragmatic spasms have stopped.[207] Thus, in infants, the upper airway closure mechanism bears some resemblance to that occurring in obstructive sleep apnea. The pathogenesis of hiccup is unclear, but seems to be related to supraspinal mechanisms as well as reflex arcs.

Treatment

Numerous treatments for hiccups have been described; many derive from folklore, many are ineffective, and few have been investigated systematically.[204] In one study, swallowing a teaspoonful of dry granulated sugar rapidly stopped hiccups in 19 of 20 patients, 12 of whom had had the hiccups for only a few hours, and 8 of whom had suffered for 1 day to several weeks.[208] In another study, stimulation of the pharynx with a catheter introduced through the nose stopped hiccups in 84 of 85 patients.[209] In our experience, however, this leads to only transient relief. Electrical stimulation of the phrenic nerves has also been reported to be successful.[210] Treatment of the underlying irritative or metabolic cause is sometimes helpful; in one case, hiccups stopped when a hair in contact with the eardrum was removed from the external auditory canal.[204] Isolated successes have occurred with anesthetic or surgical block of phrenic or vagus nerves.[204] Other maneuvers have included hyperventilation, breath-holding, rebreathing or inhaling carbon dioxide, rapidly swallowing water or ice chips, induction of vomiting, carotid massage, and pressure on the eyes.

Many drug treatments have been proposed, including tranquilizers, muscle relaxants, anticonvulsives, and narcotics.[204] Chlorpromazine, carbamazepine, metoclopramide, haloperidol, amitriptyline, ketamine, nifedipine, quinidine, phenytoin, baclofen, and valproic acid have been used, with variable success.[204,211,212] Frequently, the doses must be increased to toxic levels.

On the basis of the preceding observations, we recommend the following: First, have the patient swallow 1 teaspoonful of dry granulated sugar. Next, if need be, proceed to pharyngeal stimulation with a nasogastric tube, and use the tube to decompress the stomach. Also, check for and remove foreign bodies in the external auditory canal. Because phrenic stimulation and nerve block procedures require special skills, we would reserve those interventions for patients in whom all other measures fail.

If mechanical measures fail, and the hiccups persist for more than 12 hours, we would resort to pharmacologic therapy. One may begin with intravenous chlorpromazine, 50 mg, diluted in saline, and follow with oral chlorpromazine for a few days if necessary. Haloperidol in doses up to 5 mg every 8 hours may also be used. One must be cautious about the long-term use of chlorpromazine and haloperidol because they may cause permanent dyskinesia. Baclofen, a centrally acting muscle relaxant, often works; the initial dose is 5 mg three times a day, increasing slowly to a maximum of 20 mg three to four times a day if necessary. Lorazepam may be a useful supplement. Additional or alternative drugs are amitriptyline and nifedipine. Metoclopramide as a treatment for hiccup should probably be reserved for patients who have gastrointestinal disease; the dose is 10 mg every 6 hours. Carbamazepine and valproic acid are potentially very toxic drugs and should be used only as a last resort. Other centrally acting drugs such as baclofen or chlorpromazine should be discontinued if either carbamazepine or valproic acid is given.

RESPIRATORY MYOCLONUS

Myoclonus of the diaphragm and other respiratory muscles, often referred to as "tic," "flutter," or Leeuwenhoek's disease, is a rhythmic repetitive contraction of respiratory muscles, at a frequency of 30 to 300/min.[216] Myoclonus may be limited to the diaphragm or another respiratory muscle group. The duration and intensity of the contractions are less than with hiccup, and upper airway closure does not occur with myoclonus. A single episode of respiratory myoclonus may last for only a few seconds, or it may persist for hours. Repetitive bouts are common in afflicted patients.

The etiology and pathogenesis of respiratory myoclonus are unknown. It is thought that there is some form of central nervous system dysfunction at the level of the brain or spinal cord. Respiratory myoclonus has been likened to palatal myoclonus, and the two may occur together.[213] The list of conditions that are associated with respiratory myoclonus is similar to that for hiccup.

The symptoms of respiratory myoclonus vary to some extent, according to which respiratory muscle groups are involved. In general, there is dyspnea, a sensation of muscular fatigue, and a sense of choking. Speech may be of a staccato nature. Physical examination reveals the repetitive abdominal movements. Spirometric testing and examination of rib cage and abdominal motions using magnetometers or an inductance plethysmograph will show a flutter pattern in inspiration or expiration. Electromyography of the affected muscles demonstrates rhythmic bursts of activity synchronous with the waveforms on the spirogram. These bursts may also show up on the electrocardiogram. In one patient, the ventilatory response to inhaled carbon dioxide was normal, but the patient had posthyperventilation apnea, which indicates central nervous system dysfunction.[213] Because respiratory myoclonus is a rare disorder, there are no systematic evaluations of therapy.

RESPIRATORY DYSKINESIAS

Unclassified Dyskinesia

Respiratory dyskinesia refers to irregular breathing patterns produced by asynchronous and inappropriate respiratory muscle contractions that are variable in timing.[214] In general, the contractions are not as rhythmic as in respiratory myoclonus, and the frequency is lower. Although these patients are dissimilar in many ways, they all had dyspnea in the absence of primary pulmonary disease, and they all had some abnormality of respiratory muscle motion.

In one series of 33 patients, abnormally large contractions of the diaphragm occurred at intervals of every few breaths, causing irregular variations in respiratory rate and tidal volume.[215] These patients had the syndrome of neurocirculatory asthenia, characterized by dyspnea, fatigue, faintness, dizziness, anxiety, and hyperventilation. In another group of four patients, similar symptoms and signs occurred in association with choreiform movement disorders involving facial and limb muscles.[214] Treatment of neurocirculatory asthenia is generally unsatisfactory. Patients with choreiform motion disorders due to extrapyramidal dysfunction may respond to reserpine and to reduction in doses of dopaminergic drugs.[214]

Parkinson's Disease

Parkinson's disease is another form of extrapyramidal disorder that can affect the respiratory muscles. Its respiratory manifestations were described in a well-studied group of 23 patients.[216] The predominant respiratory symptom is dyspnea. Physical examination reveals the typical neurologic findings of rigidity, tremor, and poor performance of alternating movements of limb muscles. Excess salivation is common. Defective coordination of coughing has also been described.[217] Pulmonary function testing reveals mild tachypnea and near-normal VC, but inspiratory and expiratory flow rates are reduced by 35% and 25%, respectively. RV is twice normal, and FRC is about 140% normal. Maximal respiratory pressures are approximately half normal. Lung compliance is slightly reduced, but airway resistance is twice normal. Thus, there is an obstructive component not usually seen in neuromuscular disease per se, which is attributed to abnormally high parasympathetic activity. It appears that the main problems are respiratory muscle weakness and airway obstruction. Part of the airway obstruction may be explained by abnormal contractions of the upper airway musculature,[218] but abnormal contraction of the scalene and parasternal intercostal muscles may also contribute to abnormal oscillations of airflow. Treatment is that for Parkinson's disease.

Myotonia Congenita

Respiratory dyskinesia of a different sort occurs in myotonia congenita (Thomsen's disease), a condition characterized by increased muscle excitability and impaired relaxation. One patient was shown to have respiratory as well as limb muscle involvement.[219] Electromyographic testing of the scalene muscles and diaphragm showed abnormal myotonic discharges in the absence of voluntary contraction and greatly prolonged afterdischarges with voluntary contraction. Abdominal pressure tracings reflected the impaired diaphragmatic relaxation, and pleural pressure tracings made during sustained static inspiratory contraction showed the rapid development of weakness. This patient had a normal chest roentgenogram and normal pulmonary function tests. He experienced dyspnea and chest tightness at the onset of exercise, but these symptoms cleared after a warm-up period and he could then run for several miles. Rhythmic contraction of the muscles produced much less weakness than sustained static contractions.

CONVULSIVE DISORDERS

Respiratory and Metabolic Acidosis

The most life-threatening form of abnormal respiratory muscle contraction is the maximal contractile spasm of all respiratory muscles seen in convulsions arising from the brain (grand mal seizure) or the spinal cord (tetanus, strychnine poisoning). The respiratory effects include alveolar hypoventilation, increased carbon dioxide production, respiratory and metabolic (lactic) acidosis, and hyperthermia.

Grand mal seizures do not pose a serious threat to ventilation unless they are prolonged, as in status epilepticus. Usually, seizures increase blood lactate concentration without causing hypercapnia.[220] In general, the major therapeutic goal is to stop the seizure activity, in which case the respiratory acidosis and metabolic acidosis promptly clear.

Strychnine

Strychnine is a common diluent of street drugs, as well as being a common ingredient of many legitimate compounds. Strychnine blocks inhibitory neurons in the spinal cord.[221] The motor neurons to all muscles are released from inhibitory influences, so motor neuron discharge can be precipitated by even trivial sensory stimuli. The general mechanism of action of picrotoxin and tetanus toxin is similar to the action of strychnine, although the precise nature of inhibitory transmitter blockade differs among the three substances.

The result of strychnine poisoning is global muscle spasm that is somewhat difficult to differentiate clinically from a grand mal seizure. The pattern of the seizure is dominated by the more powerful extensor muscles, so tonic and clonic activity is absent. The symptoms of strychnine poisoning begin within minutes of ingestion and progress over several hours. Patients are usually highly alert, with no postictal mental depression.

Treatment is supportive, and includes measures to minimize muscle spasms. Milder spasms can be controlled with phenobarbital or diazepam, but in severe cases it is necessary to paralyze the patient with pancuronium or *d*-tubocurarine or to use general anesthesia. Detoxification and excretion of strychnine occur within 72 hours, and cumulative toxicity does not occur. Therefore, one can anticipate that paralysis and mechanical ventilatory support need to be maintained for less than 24 hours in the absence of other complications. When the muscle spasms have resolved, temperature, lactic acid concentration, and blood gas composition rapidly return to normal. Severe muscle damage and renal failure are the major complications. The most important aspect of the clinical management of strychnine poisoning is to think of the diagnosis in the first place. The sooner effective treatment is started, the less likelihood there is of complications.

Tetanus

Tetanus produces muscle spasms virtually identical to those of strychnine poisoning, but recovery is delayed. Again, inhibitory neurotransmitter blockade is a prominent effect of tetanus toxin, although by no means the only one. Unlike the abrupt onset of symptoms in strychnine poisoning, the symptoms of tetanus progress more slowly, often over days; consequently, cases that initially appear to be mild may turn out to be extremely severe. The prevalence, underlying causes, and pathophysiology of tetanus have been reviewed by Alfery and Rauscher[222]; these authors also described the various complicating factors and multiple aspects of treatment. Here, we wish to emphasize the life-threatening asphyxia consequent to severe and prolonged spasms of all muscles, including the respiratory muscles.

As with strychnine poisoning, mild cases of tetanus can be managed conservatively with sedation and muscle relaxants. However, severe cases require aggressive treatment with paralytic agents and mechanical ventilation.[223] The ventilatory component of management consists of sedation, muscle relaxants, tracheal intubation, and mechanical ventilation. Because the course of severe tetanus is prolonged, many physicians opt for tracheostomy early on. Patients with tetanus often experience a level of muscle spasm that produces rigidity without an overt convulsive episode. When this occurs, the ventilator pressure gauge will show very high peak inspiratory pressures, not because of abnormal lung compliance or airway resistance, but because of chest wall stiffness. If severe, this is an indication for muscle paralysis, in part to facilitate ventilation and in part to minimize lactic acidosis and muscle necrosis. The principal agents for muscle paralysis are pancuronium and *d*-tubocurarine. Pancuronium is the agent of choice, despite its mild sympathomimetic side effects. *d*-Tubocurarine can cause hypotension, and its effects are to some extent cumulative. The principal pulmonary complications of tetanus and its treatment are related to intubation or tracheostomy, atelectasis, aspiration, and infectious pneumonia. Treatment is as for any patient with prolonged mechanical ventilation. Patients with tetanus frequently have excessive sympathetic nervous system activity, which may be treated with β-adrenergic antagonists.

SUMMARY

Different types of neuromuscular disease produce essentially similar ventilatory dysfunction. Pulmonary function tests typically show a restrictive pattern, with decreases in VC and TLC. RV is often increased. Sometimes there is variable extrathoracic upper airway obstruction. Tachypnea is a common feature of almost all neuromuscular diseases, and tidal volume tends to fall. Other symptoms and signs depend on the specific condition and its severity.

Respiratory complications are common in neuromuscular diseases. The most serious is ventilatory failure; carbon dioxide retention generally occurs when inspiratory muscle strength is less than half normal. The magnitude of hypercapnia is proportional to the severity of the respiratory muscle weakness. Pneumonia is a constant threat because of impaired cough, microatelectasis consequent to shallow breathing, and, in many patients, recurrent aspiration. Some patients with neuromuscular disease are also particularly susceptible to deep venous thrombosis and pulmonary embolism.

Few specific treatments are available for ventilatory insufficiency in neuromuscular disease. Nevertheless, supportive care based on administration of oxygen, assisted coughing, and attention to nutritional status can often prevent or delay the progression to ventilatory failure. Furthermore, recent advances in the noninvasive management of ventilatory failure have greatly improved the quality of life for such patients.

REFERENCES

1. Inkley SR, Oldenburg FC, Vignos PJ Jr: Pulmonary function in Duchenne muscular dystrophy related to stage of disease. Am J Med 56:297–306, 1974.
2. Frankel HL, Coll JR, Charlifue SW, et al: Long-term survival in spinal cord injury: A fifty year investigation. Spinal Cord 36:266–274, 1998.
3. Lieberman SL, Young RR, Shefner JM: Neurological disorders affecting respiration. *In* Roussos C (ed): Lung Biology in Health and Disease (2nd ed). Vol 85: The Thorax. New York: Marcel Dekker, 1995, pp 2135–2175.
4. De Troyer A, Estenne M: The respiratory system in neuromuscular disorders. *In* Roussos C (ed): Lung Biology in Health and Disease (2nd ed). Vol 85: The Thorax. New York: Marcel Dekker, 1995, pp 2177–2212.
5. Cohen MI, Sicca AL, Donnelly DF, et al: Differences between thoracic and airway motoneuron discharge patterns and their significance. *In* Sieck GC, Gandevia SC, Cameron WE (eds): Respiratory Muscles and Their Neuromotor Control: Proceedings of an IUPS Satellite Symposium Held in Los Angeles, California, July 22–24, 1986. New York: Alan R Liss, 1987, pp 175–184.
6. Osmond DG: Functional anatomy of the chest wall. *In* Roussos C (ed): Lung Biology in Health and Disease (2nd ed). Vol 85: The Thorax. New York: Marcel Dekker, 1995, pp 413–444.
7. De Troyer A, Loring SH: Actions of the respiratory muscles. *In* Roussos C (ed): Lung Biology in Health and Disease (2nd ed). Vol 85: The Thorax. New York: Marcel Dekker, 1995, pp 535–563.
8. Misuri G, Lanini B, Gigliotti F, et al: Mechanism of CO_2 retention in patients with neuromuscular disease. Chest 117:447–453, 2000.
9. Papastamelos C, Panitch HB, Allen JL: Chest wall compliance in infants and children with neuromuscular disease. Am J Respir Crit Care Med 154:1045–1048, 1996.
10. Braun NMT, Arora NS, Rochester DF: Respiratory muscle and pulmonary function in polymyositis and other proximal myopathies. Thorax 38:616–623, 1983.
11. Aldrich TK, Aldrich MS: Primary muscle diseases: Respiratory mechanisms and complications. *In* Kamholz SL (ed): Pulmonary Aspects of Neurologic Disease. New York: SP Scientific and Medical Books, 1986.
12. Gal TJ, Arora NS: Respiratory mechanics in supine subjects during progressive partial curarization. J Appl Physiol 52:57–63, 1982.
13. Begin R, Bureau MA, Lupien L, et al: Control of breathing in Duchenne's muscular dystrophy. Am J Med 69:227–234, 1980.
14. Begin P, Mathieu J, Almirall J, et al: Relationship between chronic hypercapnia and inspiratory muscle weakness in myotonic dystrophy. Am J Respir Crit Care Med 156:133–139, 1997.
15. Baydur A: Respiratory muscle strength and control of ventilation in patients with neuromuscular disease. Chest 99:330–338, 1991.
16. Spinelli A, Marconi G, Gorini M, et al: Control of breathing in patients with myasthenia gravis. Am Rev Respir Dis 145:1359–1366, 1992.
17. Manning HL, Brown R, Scharf SM, et al: Ventilatory and $P_{0.1}$ response to hypercapnia in quadriplegia. Respir Physiol 89:97–112, 1992.
18. Weng TR, Schultz GE, Chang CH, et al: Pulmonary function and ventilatory response to chemical stimuli in familial myopathy. Chest 88:488–495, 1985.
19. Wilson DO, Saunders MH, Dauber JH: Abnormal ventilatory chemosensitivity and congenital myopathy. Arch Intern Med 147:1773–1777, 1987.
20. Carroll JE, Zwillich CW, Weil JV: Ventilatory response in myotonic dystrophy. Neurology 27:1125–1128, 1977.
21. Garay SM, Turino GM, Goldring RM: Sustained reversal of chronic hypercapnia in patients with alveolar hypoventilation syndromes: Long-term maintenance with noninvasive nocturnal mechanical ventilation. Am J Med 70:269–274, 1981.
22. Labanowski J, Schmidt-Nowara W, Guilleminault C: Sleep and neuromuscular disease: Frequency of sleep-disordered breathing in a neuromuscular disease clinic population. Neurology 47:1173–1180, 1996.
23. McEvoy RD, Mykytun I, Sajkov D, et al: Sleep apnoea in patients with quadriplegia. Thorax 50:613–619, 1995.
24. Thorpy MJ, Schmidt-Nowara WW, Pollack CP, et al: Sleep-induced non-obstructive hypoventilation associated with diaphragmatic paralysis. Ann Neurol 12:308–311, 1982.

25. Steljes DG, Kryger MH, Kirk BW, et al: Sleep in postpolio syndrome. Chest 98:133–140, 1990.

26. Ferguson KA, Strong MJ, Ahmad D: Sleep-disordered breathing in amyotrophic lateral sclerosis. Chest 110:664–669, 1996.

27. Hansotia P, Frens D: Hypersomnolence associated with alveolar hypoventilation in myotonic dystrophy. Neurology 31:1336–1337, 1981.

28. Marcus CL, Loughlin GM: Obstructive sleep apnea in children. Semin Pediatr Neurol 3:23–38, 1996.

29. Khan Y, Heckmatt JZ: Obstructive apnoeas in Duchenne muscular dystrophy. Thorax 49:157–161, 1994.

30. Skatrud J, Iber C, McHugh W, et al: Determinants of hypoventilation during wakefulness and sleep in diaphragmatic paralysis. Am Rev Respir Dis 121:587–593, 1980.

31. Sajkov D, Marshall R, Walker P, et al: Sleep apnoea related hypoxia is associated with cognitive disturbances in patients with tetraplegia. Spinal Cord 36:231–239, 1998.

32. Dicpinigaitis PV, Grimm DR, Lesser M: Cough reflex sensitivity in subjects with cervical spinal cord injury. Am J Respir Crit Care Med 159:1660–1662, 1999.

33. Arora NS, Gal TJ: Cough dynamics during progressive expiratory muscle weakness in healthy curarized subjects. J Appl Physiol 51:494–498, 1981.

34. Aldrich TK, Shapiro SM, Sherman MS, et al: Alveolar pressure and airway resistance during maximal and submaximal respiratory efforts. Am Rev Respir Dis 140:899–906, 1989.

35. Myllynen P, Kammonen M, Rokkanen P, et al: Deep venous thrombosis and pulmonary embolism in patients with acute spinal cord injury: A comparison with nonparalyzed patients immobilized due to spinal fractures. Trauma 25:541–543, 1985.

36. Hamilton MG, Hull RD, Pineo GF: Venous thromboembolism in neurosurgery and neurology patients: A review. Neurosurgery 34:280–296, 1994.

37. Roussos C, Fixley M, Gross D, et al: Fatigue of inspiratory muscles and their synergistic behavior. J Appl Physiol 46:897–904, 1979.

38. Gerscovich EO, Cronan M, McGahan JP, et al: Ultrasonographic evaluation of diaphragmatic motion. J Ultrasound Med 20:597–604, 2001.

39. Rochester DF, Esau SA: Assessment of ventilatory function in patients with neuromuscular disease. Clin Chest Med 15:751–763, 1994.

40. Fallat RJ, Jewitt B, Bass M, et al: Spirometry in amyotrophic lateral sclerosis. Arch Neurol 36:74–80, 1979.

41. Moxham J, Grassino A (eds): ATS/ERS statement on respiratory muscle testing. Am J Respir Crit Care Med 166:518–624, 2002.

42. Braun NMT, Arora NS, Rochester DF: Force-length relationship of the normal human diaphragm. J Appl Physiol 53:405–412, 1982.

43. Iberti TJ, Lieber CE, Benjamin E: Determination of intra-abdominal pressure using a transurethral bladder catheter: Clinical validation of the technique. Anesthesiology 70:47–50, 1989.

44. Ostrander LE, Schneider AJL, Burma G, et al: A comparison of central venous and pleural pressure in supine dogs. Respir Physiol 31:63–70, 1977.

45. Aldrich TK, Spiro P: Maximal inspiratory pressure: Does reproducibility indicate full effort? Thorax 50:40–43, 1995.

46. Aldrich MS: Central sleep apnea and hypoventilation during sleep. *In* Sleep Medicine. New York: Oxford University Press, 1999, pp 237–259.

47. Ragette R, Mellies U, Schwake C, et al: Patterns and predictors of sleep disordered breathing in primary myopathies. Thorax 57:724–728, 2002.

48. Dimopoulou I, Daganou M, Dafni U, et al: Phrenic nerve dysfunction after cardiac operations: Electrophysiologic evaluation of risk factors. Chest 113:8–14, 1998.

49. Olopade CO, Staats BA: Time course of recovery from frostbitten phrenics after coronary artery bypass graft surgery. Chest 99:1112–1115, 1991.

50. Dorffner R, Eibenberger K, Youssefzadeh S: Diaphragmatic dysfunction after heart or lung transplantation. J Heart Lung Transplant 16:566–569, 1997.

51. De Troyer A, Vanderhoeft P: Phrenic nerve function after pneumonectomy. Chest 81:212–214, 1982.

52. Heffner JE: Diaphragmatic paralysis following chiropractic manipulation of the cervical spine. Arch Intern Med 145:562–563, 1985.

53. Bell D, Siriwardena A: Phrenic nerve injury following blunt trauma. J Accid Emerg Med 17:419–420, 2000.

54. DeJong AA, Manni JJ: Phrenic nerve paralysis following neck dissection. Eur Arch Otorhinolaryngol 248:132–134, 1991.

55. Vest JV, Pereira M, Senior RM: Phrenic nerve injury associated with venipuncture of the internal jugular vein. Chest 78:777–779, 1980.

56. Aldrich TK, Herman JH, Rochester DF: Bilateral diaphragmatic paralysis in the newborn infant. J Pediatr 97:988–991, 1980.

57. Hassoun PM, Celli BR: Bilateral diaphragm paralysis secondary to central von Recklinghausen's disease. Chest 117:1196–1200, 2000.

58. Mellem H, Johansen B, Nakstad P, et al: Unilateral phrenic nerve paralysis caused by osteoarthritis of the cervical spine. Eur J Respir Dis 71:56–58, 1987.

59. Piehler JM, Pairolero PC, Gracey DR, et al: Unexplained diaphragmatic paralysis: A harbinger of malignant disease? J Thorac Cardiovasc Surg 84:861–864, 1982.

60. Stowasser M, Cameron J, Oliver WA: Diaphragmatic paralysis following cervical herpes zoster. Med J Aust 153:555–556, 1990.

61. De Vito EL, Quadrelli SA, Montiel GC, et al: Bilateral diaphragmatic paralysis after mediastinal radiotherapy. Respiration 63:187–190, 1996.

62. Brander PE, Jarvinen V, Lohela P, et al: Bilateral diaphragmatic weakness: A late complication of radiotherapy. Thorax 52:829–831, 1997.

63. Chan CK, Loke J, Virgulto JA, et al: Bilateral diaphragmatic paralysis: Clinical spectrum, prognosis, and diagnostic approach. Arch Phys Med Rehabil 67:161–165, 1988.

64. Mulvey DA, Aquilina RJ, Elliott MW, et al: Diaphragmatic dysfunction in neuralgic amyotrophy: An electrophysiologic evaluation of 16 patients presenting with dyspnea. Am Rev Respir Dis 147:66–71, 1993.

65. Balbierz JM, Ellenberg M, Honet JC: Complete hemidiaphragmatic paralysis in a patient with multiple sclerosis. Am J Phys Med Rehabil 67:161–165, 1988.

66. Haas H, Johnson LR, Gill TH, et al: Diaphragm paralysis and ventilatory failure in proximal spinal muscular atrophy. Am Rev Respir Dis 123:465–467, 1981.

67. Stojkovic T, De Seze J, Hurtevent JF, et al: Phrenic nerve palsy as a feature of chronic inflammatory demyelinating polyradiculoneuropathy. Muscle Nerve 27:497–499, 2003.

68. Lisboa C, Pare PD, Pertuze J, et al: Inspiratory muscle function in unilateral diaphragmatic paralysis. Am Rev Respir Dis 134:488–492, 1986.

69. Gould L, Kaplan S, McElhinney AJ, et al: A method for the production of hemidiaphragmatic paralysis. Am Rev Respir Dis 96:812–814, 1967.

70. Fackler CD, Perret GE, Bedell GN: Effect of unilateral phrenic nerve section on lung function. J Appl Physiol 23:923–926, 1967.

71. Easton PA, Fleetham JA, De La Rocha A, et al: Respiratory function after paralysis of the right hemidiaphragm. Am Rev Respir Dis 127:125–128, 1983.

72. Allen SM, Hunt B, Green M: Fall in vital capacity with posture. Br J Dis Chest 79:267–271, 1985.

73. Hart N, Nickol AH, Cramer D, et al: Effect of severe isolated unilateral and bilateral diaphragm weakness on exercise performance. Am J Respir Crit Care Med 165:1265–1270, 2002.

74. Fromageot C, Lofaso F, Annane D, et al: Supine fall in lung volumes in the assessment of diaphragmatic weakness in neuromuscular disorders. Arch Phys Med Rehabil 82:123–128, 2001.

75. Graham DR, Kaplan D, Evans CC, et al: Diaphragmatic plication for unilateral diaphragmatic paralysis: A 10-year experience. Ann Thorac Surg 49:248–252, 1990.

75a. Kuniyoshi Y, Yamashiro S, Miyagi K, et al: Diaphragmatic plication in adult patients with diaphragm paralysis after cardiac surgery. Ann Thoracic Cardiovasc Surg 10:160–166, 2004.

76. Merav AD, Attai LA, Condit DD: Successful repair of a transected phrenic nerve with restoration of diaphragmatic function. Chest 84:642–644, 1983.

77. Brouillette RT, Hahn YS, Noah ZL, et al: Successful reinnervation of the diaphragm after phrenic nerve transection. J Pediatr Surg 21:63–65, 1986.

78. Zifko U, Hartmann M, Girsch W, et al: Diaphragmatic paresis in newborns due to phrenic nerve injury. Neuropediatrics 26:281–284, 1995.

79. Kreiger AJ, Gropper MR, Adler RJ: Electrophrenic respiration after intercostal to phrenic nerve anastomosis in a patient with anterior spinal artery syndrome: Technical case report. Neurosurgery 35:760–763, 1994.

80. Haller JA, Pickard LR, Trepas JJ, et al: Management of diaphragmatic paralysis in infants with special emphasis on selection of patients for operative plication. J Pediatr Surg 14:779–785, 1979.

81. Abd AG, Braun NMT, Baskin MI, et al: Diaphragmatic dysfunction after open heart surgery: Treatment with a rocking bed. Ann Intern Med 111:881–886, 1989.

82. Bach JR, Alba AS: Management of chronic alveolar hypoventilation by nasal ventilation. Chest 97:52–57, 1990.

83. Bach JR, McDermott IG: Strapless oral-nasal interface for positive-pressure ventilation. Arch Phys Med Rehabil 71:910–913, 1990.

84. Ford GT, Whitelaw WA, Rosenal TW, et al: Diaphragm function after upper abdominal surgery in humans. Am Rev Respir Dis 127:431–436, 1983.

85. Simonneau E, Vivien A, Sartene R, et al: Diaphragm dysfunction induced by upper abdominal surgery. Am Rev Respir Dis 128:899–903, 1983.

86. Melendez JA, Alagesan R, Reinsel R, et al: Postthoracotomy respiratory muscle mechanics during incentive spirometry using respiratory inductance plethysmography. Chest 101:432–436, 1992.

87. Road JD, Burgess KR, Whitelaw WA, et al: Diaphragm function and respiratory response after upper abdominal surgery in dogs. J Appl Physiol 57:576–582, 1984.

88. Torres A, Kimball WR, Qvist J, et al: Sonomicrometric regional diaphragmatic shortening in awake sheep after thoracic surgery. J Appl Physiol 67:2357–2368, 1989.

89. Road J, Vahi R, Del Rio P, et al: In vivo contractile properties of fatigued diaphragm. J Appl Physiol 63:471–478, 1987.

90. Hartkopp A, Bronnum-Hansen H, Seidenschnur A-M, et al: Survival and cause of death after traumatic spinal cord injury: A long-term epidemiological survey from Denmark. Spinal Cord 35:76–85, 1997.

91. Newsom-Davis J: Autonomous breathing. Arch Neurol 30:480–483, 1974.

92. De Troyer A, Estenne M, Vincken W: Rib cage motion and muscle use in high tetraplegics. Am Rev Respir Dis 133:1115–1119, 1986.

93. Bach JR, Alba AS: Noninvasive options for ventilatory support of the traumatic high level quadriplegic patient. Chest 98:613–619, 1990.

94. James WS III, Minh V, Minteer MA, et al: Cervical accessory respiratory muscle function in a patient with a high cervical cord lesion. Chest 71:59–64, 1977.

95. De Troyer A, Heilporn A: Respiratory mechanics in quadriplegia: The respiratory function of the intercostal muscles. Am Rev Respir Dis 122:591–600, 1980.

96. Haas F, Axen K, Pineda H, et al: Temporal pulmonary function changes in cervical cord injury. Arch Phys Med Rehabil 66:139–144, 1985.

97. Wang AY, Jaeger RJ, Yarkony GM, Turba RM: Cough in spinal cord injured patients: The relationship between motor level and peak expiratory flow. Spinal Cord 35:299–302, 1997.

98. De Troyer A, Estenne M, Heilporn A: Mechanism of active expiration in tetraplegic subjects. N Engl J Med 314:740–744, 1986.

99. Estenne M, Gorini M: Action of the diaphragm during cough in tetraplegic subjects. J Appl Physiol 72:1074–1080, 1992.

100. Dicpinigaitis PV, Spungen AM, Bauman WA, et al: Bronchial hyperresponsiveness after cervical spinal cord injury. Chest 105:1073–1076, 1994.

101. Grimm DR, Arias E, Lesser M, et al: Airway hyperresponsiveness to ultrasonically nebulized distilled water in subjects with tetraplegia. J Appl Physiol 86:1165–1169, 1999.

102. Estenne M, De Troyer A: Mechanism of the postural dependence of vital capacity in tetraplegic subjects. Am Rev Respir Dis 135:367–371, 1987.

103. Estenne M, De Troyer A: Relationship between respiratory muscle electromyogram and rib cage motion in tetraplegia. Am Rev Respir Dis 132:53–59, 1985.

104. Urmey W, Loring S, Mead J, et al: Upper and lower rib cage deformation during breathing in quadriplegia. J Appl Physiol 60:618–622, 1986.

105. Stone DJ, Keltz H: The effect of respiratory muscle dysfunction on pulmonary function. Am Rev Respir Dis 88:621–629, 1963.

106. Silver JR: The oxygen cost of breathing in tetraplegic patients. Paraplegia 1:204–214, 1963.

107. Bake B, Fugl-Meyer AR, Grimby G: Breathing patterns and regional ventilation distribution in tetraplegic patients and in normal subjects. Clin Sci 42:117–128, 1972.

108. Schwartzstein R, Leight D, Scharf S, et al: CO_2 response in chronic quadriplegics. Am Rev Respir Dis 131:A337, 1985.

109. Axen K, Bergofsky EH: Thoracic reflexes stabilizing loaded ventilation in normal and cord-injured man. J Appl Physiol 43:339–346, 1977.

110. DiMarco AF, Wolfson DA, Gottfried SB, et al: Sensation of inspired volume in normal subjects and quadriplegic patients. J Appl Physiol 53:1481–1486, 1982.

111. Wicks AB, Menter RR: Long-term outlook in quadriplegic patients with initial ventilator dependency. Chest 90:406–410, 1986.

112. Oo T, Watt JW, Soni BM, Sett PK: Delayed diaphragm recovery in 12 patients after high cervical spinal cord injury: A retrospective review of the diaphragm status of 107 patients ventilated after acute spinal cord injury. Spinal Cord 37:117–122, 1999.

113. Guidelines for the management of acute cervical spine and spinal cord injuries: Guidelines Committee of the Section on Disorders of the Spine and Peripheral Nerves of the American Association of Neurological Surgeons/Congress of Neurological Surgeons. Neurosurgery 50:S1–S99, 2002.

114. Geisler FH, Coleman WP, Grieco G, et al: The Sygen® multicenter acute spinal cord injury study. Spine 26:S87–S98, 2001.

115. Toshiki M, Sakae T, et al: Partial functional recovery of paraplegic rat by adenovirus-mediated gene delivery of constitutively active MEK1. Neurology 166:115–126, 2000.

116. O'Leary MT, Charlton HM: A model for long-term transgene expression in spinal cord regeneration studies. Gene Ther 6:1351–1359, 1999.

117. Glenn WWL, Hogan JF, Phelps ML: Ventilatory support of the quadriplegic patient with respiratory paralysis by diaphragm pacing. Surg Clin North Am 60:1055–1078, 1980.

118. Fluck DC: Chest movements in hemiplegia. Clin Sci 31:383–388, 1966.

119. Santamaria J, Ruiz C: Diaphragm elevation in stroke. Eur Neurol 28:81–83, 1988.

120. Korczyn AD, Leibowitz U, Bruderman I: Involvement of the diaphragm in hemiplegia. Neurology 19:97–100, 1969.

121. De Troyer A, De Beyl DZ, Thirion M: Function of the respiratory muscles in acute hemiplegia. Am Rev Respir Dis 123:631–632, 1981.

122. Adams AB, Whitman J, Marcy T: Surveys of long-term ventilatory support in Minnesota: 1986 and 1992. Chest 103:1463–1469, 1993.

123. Linderholm H, Werneman H: On respiratory regulation in poliomyelitis convalescents. Acta Med Scand Suppl 316:135–157, 1956.

124. Brody AW, O'Halloran PS, Connolly JJ Jr, et al: Ventilatory mechanics and strength in subjects paralyzed after poliomyelitis. Dis Chest 46:263–275, 1964.

125. Ferris BG, Whittenberger JL, Affeldt JE: Pulmonary function in convalescent poliomyelitic patients. N Engl J Med 246:919–923, 1952.

126. Plum F, Swanson AG: Abnormalities in central regulation of respiration in acute and convalescent poliomyelitis. Arch Neurol Psychiatry 80:267–285, 1958.

127. Fischer DA: Poliomyelitis: Late pulmonary complications and management. In Halstead LS, Wiechers DO (eds): Late Effects of Poliomyelitis. Miami: Symposium Foundation, 1985, pp 185–192.

128. Hsu AA, Staats BA: "Postpolio" sequelae and sleep-related disordered breathing. Mayo Clinic Proc 73:216–224, 1998.

129. Gracey DR, McMichan JC, Divertie MB, et al: Respiratory failure in Guillain-Barre syndrome. Mayo Clin Proc 57:742–746, 1982.

130. Sharshar T, Chevret S, Bourdin F, et al: Early predictors of mechanical ventilation in Guillain-Barré syndrome. Crit Care Med 31:278–283, 2003.

131. De Troyer A, Borenstein S: Acute changes in respiratory mechanics after pyridostigmine injection in patients with myasthenia gravis. Am Rev Respir Dis 121:629–638, 1980.

132. Ringqvist I, Ringqvist T: Changes in respiratory mechanics in myasthenia gravis with therapy. Acta Med Scand 190:509–518, 1971.

133. Mier A, Laroche C, Green M: Unsuspected myasthenia gravis presenting as respiratory failure. Thorax 45:422–423, 1990.

134. Gajdos P, Chevret S, Clair B, et al: Clinical trial of plasma exchange and high-dose intravenous immunoglobulin in myasthenia gravis. Myasthenia Gravis Clinical Study Group. Ann Neurol 41:789–796, 1997.

135. Wang ZY, Qiao J, Link H, et al: Suppression of experimental autoimmune myasthenia gravis by oral administration of acetylcholine receptor. J Neuroimmunol 44:209–214, 1993.

136. Gronseth GS: Practice parameter. Thymectomy for autoimmune myasthenia gravis: Report of the Quality Standards Subcommittee of the American Academy of Neurology. Neurology 55:7–15, 2000.

137. Berrouschot J, Baumann I, Kalischewski P, et al: Therapy of myasthenic crisis. Crit Care Med 25:1228–1235, 1997.

138. Wilcox PG, Morrison NJ, Anzarut ARA, et al: Lambert-Eaton myasthenic syndrome involving the diaphragm. Chest 93:604–607, 1988.

139. Bain PG, Motomura M, Newsom-Davis J: Effects of intravenous immunoglobulin on muscle weakness and calcium-channel auto-antibodies in the Lambert-Eaton myasthenic syndrome. Neurology 47:678–683, 1996.

140. Smith AG, Wald J: Acute ventilatory failure in Lambert-Eaton myasthenic syndrome and its response to 3,4-diaminopyridine. Neurology 46:1143–1145, 1996.

141. Atlas RM: Bioterrorism: From threat to reality. Annu Rev Microbiol 56:167–185, 2002.

142. Shapiro RL, Hatheway C, Swerdlow DL: Botulism in the United States. Ann Intern Med 129:2218, 2003.

143. Wilcox P, Andolfatto G, Fairbairn MS, et al: Long-term follow up of symptoms, pulmonary function, respiratory muscle strength, and exercise performance after botulism. Am Rev Respir Dis 139:157–163, 1989.

144. Sungur M, Guven M: Intensive care management of organophosphate insecticide poisoning. Crit Care 5:211–215, 2001.

145. Aldrich TK, Prezant DJ: Adverse effects of drugs on the respiratory muscles. Clin Chest Med 11:177–189, 1990.

146. Ringel SP, Murphy JR, Alderson MK, et al: The natural history of amyotrophic lateral sclerosis. Neurology 43:1316–1322, 1993.

147. Jammes Y, Pouget J, Grimaud C, et al: Pulmonary function and electromyographic study of respiratory muscles in myotonic dystrophy. Muscle Nerve 8:586–594, 1985.

148. Rimmer KP, Golar SD, Lee MA, et al: Myotonia of the respiratory muscles in myotonic dystrophy. Am Rev Respir Dis 148:1018–1022, 1993.

149. Poponick J, Jacobs I, Supinski G, et al: Effect of upper respiratory tract infection in patients with neuromuscular disease. Am J Respir Crit Care Med 156:659–664, 1997.

150. Grinman S, Whitelaw WA: Pattern of breathing in a case of generalized respiratory muscle weakness. Chest 84:770–772, 1983.

151. Borel CO, Tilford C, Nichols DG, et al: Diaphragmatic performance during recovery from acute ventilatory failure in Guillain-Barre syndrome and myasthenia gravis. Chest 99:444–451, 1991.

152. Traynor BJ, Alexander M, Corr B, et al: An outcome study of riluzole in amyotrophic lateral sclerosis—a population-based study in Ireland, 1996–2000. J Neurol 250:473–479, 2003.

153. Festoff B, Suo Z, Citron B: Prospects for the pharmacotherapy of amyotrophic lateral sclerosis: Old strategies and new paradigms for the third millennium. CNS Drugs 17:699–717, 2003.

154. Watchko J, O'Day T, Wang B, et al: Adeno-associated virus vector-mediated minidystrophin gene therapy improves dystrophic muscle contractile function in mdx mice. Hum Gene Ther 13:1451–1460, 2002.

155. Bonifati MD, Ruzza G, Bonometto P, et al: A multicenter, double-blind, randomized trial of deflazacort versus prednisone in Duchenne muscular dystrophy. Muscle Nerve 23:1344–1347, 2000.

156. Fenichel GM, Griggs RC, Kissel J, et al: A randomized efficacy and safety trial of oxandrolone in the treatment of Duchenne dystrophy. Neurology 56:1075–1079, 2001.

157. Ellis AC, Rosenfeld J: The role of creatine in the management of amyotrophic lateral sclerosis and other neurodegenerative disorders. CNS Drugs 18:967–980, 2004.

158. Braun NMT, Faulkner J: When should respiratory muscles be exercised? Chest 84:76–84, 1983.

159. Demling RH: Comparison of the anabolic effects and complications of human growth hormone and the testosterone analog, oxandrolone, after severe burn injury. Burns 25:215–221, 1999.

160. Lynch GS: Therapies for improving muscle function in neuromuscular disorders. Exerc Sport Sci Rev 29:141–148, 2001.

161. Yuen EC: The role of neurotrophic factors in disorders of peripheral nerves and motor neurons. Phys Med Rehabil Clin N Am 12:293–306, 2001.

162. Grinspoon S, Corcoran C, Askari H, et al: Effects of androgen administration in men with the AIDS wasting syndrome: A randomized, double-blind, placebo-controlled trial. Ann Intern Med 129:18–26, 1998.

163. Spungen AM, Grimm DR, Strakhan M, et al: Treatment with an anabolic agent is associated with improvement in respiratory function in persons with tetraplegia: A pilot study. Mt Sinai J Med 66:201–205, 1999.

164. Rutkove SB, Parker RA, Nardin RA, et al: A pilot randomized trial of oxandrolone in inclusion body myositis. Neurology 58:1081–1087, 2002.

165. Rosenfeld J, King RM, Smith JE: Oxandrolone in ALS: Preliminary analysis. Amyotroph Lateral Scler Other Motor Neuron Disord 1(Suppl 4):21–25, 2000.

166. Schambelan M, Mulligan K, Grunfeld C, et al: Recombinant human growth hormone in patients with HIV-associated wasting: A randomized, placebo-controlled trial. Ann Intern Med 125:873–882, 1996.

167. Smith RA, Melmed S, Sherman B, et al: Recombinant growth hormone treatment of amyotrophic lateral sclerosis. Muscle Nerve 16:624–633, 1993.

168. Kanda F, Okuda S, Matsushita T, et al: Steroid myopathy: Pathogenesis and effects of growth hormone and insulin-like growth factor-1 administration. Horm Res 56(Suppl 1):24–28, 2001.

169. Mitchell JD, Wokke JH, Borasio GD: Recombinant human insulin-like growth factor I (rhIGF-1) for amyotrophic lateral sclerosis/motor neuron disease. Cochrane Database Syst Rev 3:CD002064, 2002.

169a. Finder JD, Birnkrandt D, Carl J, et al: Respiratory care of the patient with Duchenne muscular dystrophy: ATS consensus statement. Am J Respir Crit Care Med 170:456–465, 2004.

170. Grant I, Prigatano GP, Heaton RK, et al: Progressive neuropsychologic impairment and hypoxemia. Arch Gen Psychiatry 44:999–1006, 1987.

171. Jardim J, Farkas G, Prefaut C, et al: The failing inspiratory muscles under normoxic and hypoxic conditions. Am Rev Respir Dis 124:274–279, 1981.

172. Jaeger RJ, Turba RM, Yarkony GM, et al: Cough in spinal cord injured patients: Comparison of three methods to produce cough. Arch Phys Med Rehabil 74:1358–1361, 1993.

173. Miske LJ, Hickey EM, Kolb SM, et al: Use of the mechanical in-exsufflator in pediatric patients with neuromuscular disease and impaired cough. Chest 125:1406–1412, 2004.

173a. Winck JC, Goncalves MR, Lourenco C, et al: Effects of mechanical insufflation-exsufflation on respiratory parameters for patients with chronic airway secretion encumbance. Chest 126:774–780, 2004.

174. Zupan A, Savrin R, Erjavec T, et al: Effects of respiratory muscle training and electrical stimulation of abdominal muscles on respiratory capabilities in tetraplegic patients. Spinal Cord 35:540–545, 1997.

175. Lin VW, Singh H, Chitkara RK, et al: Functional magnetic stimulation for restoring cough in patients with tetraplegia. Arch Phys Med Rehabil 79:517–522, 1998.

176. Estenne M, Knoop C, Vanvaerenbergh J, et al: The effect of pectoralis muscle training in tetraplegic subjects. Am Rev Respir Dis 139:1218–1222, 1989.

177. Huldtgren AC, Fugl-Meyer AR, Jonasson E, et al: Ventilatory dysfunction and respiratory rehabilitation in post-traumatic quadriplegia. Eur J Respir Dis 61:347–356, 1980.

178. Uijl SG, Houtman S, Folgering HT, Hepman MT: Training of the respiratory muscles in individuals with tetraplegia. Spinal Cord 37:575–579, 1999.

179. Rutchik A, Issman AR, Almenoff PL, et al: Resistive inspiratory muscle training in subjects with chronic cervical spinal cord injury. Arch Phys Med Rehabil 79:293–297, 1998.

180. Gross D, Ladd HW, Riley EJ, et al: The effect of training on strength and endurance of the diaphragm in quadriplegia. Am J Med 68:27–35, 1980.

181. DiMarco AF, Kelling JS, DiMarco MS, et al: The effects of inspiratory resistive training on respiratory muscle function in patients with muscular dystrophy. Muscle Nerve 8:284–290, 1985.

182. Wanke T, Toifl K, Merkle M, et al: Inspiratory muscle training in patients with Duchenne muscular dystrophy. Chest 105:475–482, 1994.

183. Koessler W, Wanke T, Winkler G, et al: 2 years' experience with inspiratory muscle training in patients with neuromuscular disorders. Chest 120:765–769, 2001.

184. Martin AJ, Stern L, Yeates J, et al: Respiratory muscle training in Duchenne muscular dystrophy. Dev Med Child Neurol 28:314–318, 1986.

185. Smith PEM, Coakley JH, Edwards RHT: Respiratory muscle training in Duchenne muscular dystrophy. Muscle Nerve 11:784, 1988.

186. Martin RJ, Sufit RL, Ringel SP, et al: Respiratory improvement by muscle training in adult-onset acid maltase deficiency. Muscle Nerve 6:201–203, 1983.

187. Weiner P, Gross D, Meiner Z, et al: Respiratory muscle training in patients with moderate to severe myasthenia gravis. Can J Neurol Sci 25:236–241, 1998.

188. Estrup C, Lyager S, Noeraa N, et al: Effect of respiratory muscle training in patients with neuromuscular diseases. Respiration 50:36–43, 1986.

189. Aldrich TK, Karpel JP, Uhrlass RM, et al: Weaning from mechanical ventilation: Adjunctive use of inspiratory muscle resistive training. Crit Care Med 17:143–147, 1989.

190. Lerman RM, Weiss MS: Progressive resistive exercises in weaning high quadriplegics from the ventilator. Paraplegia 25:130–135, 1987.

191. Nochomovitz ML, Hopkins M, Brodkey J, et al: Conditioning of the diaphragm with phrenic nerve stimulation after prolonged disuse. Am Rev Respir Dis 130:685–688, 1984.

192. Sherman MS, Paz HL: Review of respiratory care of the patient with amyotrophic lateral sclerosis. Respiration 61:61–67, 1994.

193. Bach JR, Rajaraman R, Ballanger F, et al: Neuromuscular ventilatory insufficiency: Effect of home mechanical ventilator use v oxygen therapy on pneumonia and hospitalization rates. Am J Phys Med Rehabil 77:8–19, 1998.

194. Bach JR, Alba AS: Intermittent abdominal pressure ventilator in a regimen of noninvasive ventilatory support. Chest 99:630–636, 1991.

195. Bonekat HW: Noninvasive ventilation in neuromuscular disease. Crit Care Clin 14:775–797, 1998.

196. Bach JR, Penek J: Obstructive sleep apnea complicating negative-pressure ventilatory support in patients with chronic paralytic/restrictive ventilatory dysfunction. Chest 99:1386–1393, 1991.

197. Gay PC, Patel AM, Viggiano RW, et al: Nocturnal nasal ventilation for treatment of patients with hypercapnic respiratory failure. Mayo Clin Proc 66:695–703, 1991.

198. Kesten S, Rebuck AS: Ventilatory effects of nasal continuous positive airway pressure. Eur Respir J 3:498–501, 1990.

199. Duncan SR, Negrin RS, Mihm FG, et al: Nasal continuous positive airway pressure in atelectasis. Chest 92:621–624, 1987.

200. Elefteriades JA, Quin JA: Diaphragm pacing. Chest Surg Clin N Am 8:331–357, 1998.

201. Ciesielski TE, Fukuda Y, Glenn WWL, et al: Response of the diaphragm muscle to electrical stimulation of the phrenic nerve. J Neurosurg 58:92–100, 1983.

202. Mead J, Banzett RB, Lehr J, et al: Effect of posture on upper and lower rib cage motion and tidal volume during diaphragm pacing. Am Rev Respir Dis 130:320–321, 1984.

203. Scharf SM, Feldman NT, Goldman MD, et al: Vocal cord closure: A cause of upper airway obstruction during controlled ventilation. Am Rev Respir Dis 117:391–397, 1978.

204. Lewis JH: Hiccups: Causes and cures. J Clin Gastroenterol 7:539–552, 1985.

205. Shay SS, Meyers RL, Johnson LT: Hiccups associated with reflux esophagitis. Gastroenterology 87:204–207, 1984.

206. Cannon RA, Lee G, Cox KL: Gastrointestinal hemorrhage due to Mallory-Weiss syndrome in an infant. J Pediatr Gastroenterol Nutr 4:323–324, 1985.

207. Brouillette RT, Thach BT, Abu-Osba YK, et al: Hiccups in infants: Characteristics and effects on ventilation. J Pediatr 96:219–225, 1980.

208. Engleman EG, Lankton J, Lankton B: Granulated sugar as treatment for hiccups in conscious patients (letter). N Engl J Med 285:1489, 1971.

209. Salem RM, Baraka A, Rattenborg CC, et al: Treatment of hiccups by pharyngeal stimulation in anesthetized and conscious subjects. JAMA 202:126–130, 1967.

210. Fodstad H, Blom S: Phrenic nerve stimulation (diaphragm pacing) in chronic singultus. Neurochirurgia 27:115–116, 1984.

211. Guelaud C, Similowski T, Bizec JL, et al: Baclofen therapy for chronic hiccup. Eur Respir J 8:235–237, 1995.

212. Jacobson PL, Messenheimer JA, Farmer TW: Treatment of intractable hiccups with valproic acid. Neurology 31:1458–1460, 1981.

213. Phillips JR, Eldridge FL: Respiratory myoclonus (Leeuwenhoek's disease). N Engl J Med 289:1390–1395, 1973.

214. Weiner WJ, Goetz CG, Nausieda PA, et al: Respiratory dyskinesias: Extrapyramidal dysfunction and dyspnea. Ann Intern Med 88:327–331, 1978.

215. Kimura E, Ichikawa A, Takahashi K, et al: Abnormal respiration and unusual movements of the diaphragm in patients with neurocirculatory asthenia. Am J Med Sci 265:205–214, 1973.

216. Neu HC, Connolly JJ Jr, Schwertley FW, et al: Obstructive respiratory dysfunction in Parkinsonian patients. Am Rev Respir Dis 95:33–47, 1967.

217. Fontana GA, Pantaleo T, Lavorini F, et al: Defective motor control of coughing in Parkinson's disease. Am J Respir Crit Care Med 158:458–464, 1998.

218. Vincken WG, Gauthier SG, Dollfus RE, et al: Involvement of upper airway muscles in extrapyramidal disorders: A cause of airflow limitation. N Engl J Med 311:438–442, 1984.

219. Estenne M, Borenstein S, De Troyer A: Respiratory muscle dysfunction in myotonia congenita. Am Rev Respir Dis 130:691–684, 1984.

220. Lipka K, Bulow HH: Lactic acidosis following convulsions. Acta Anaesthesiol Scand 47:616–618, 2003.

221. Boyd RE, Brennan PT, Deng JF, et al: Strychnine poisoning. Am J Med 74:507–512, 1983.

222. Alfery DD, Rauscher LA: Tetanus: A review. Crit Care Med 7:176–181, 1979.

223. Trujillo MJ, Castillo A, Espana JV, et al: Tetanus in the adult: Intensive care and management experience with 233 cases. Crit Care Med 8:419–423, 1980.

83

The Lungs and Chest Wall Disease

George E. Tzelepis, M.D., F. Dennis McCool, M.D.

INTRODUCTION

Disorders of the chest wall may involve the respiratory muscles, the bony structure of the rib cage, the spine, the spine's articulations, and the soft tissue comprising the abdomen. These disorders may by themselves or in combination with other diseases interfere with inspiratory pump function and lead to respiratory failure. The diseases of the chest wall that most profoundly embarrass ventilatory function are kyphoscoliosis and restrictive disease resulting from previous thoracoplasty. Flail chest may result in respiratory failure, especially when there is associated pulmonary contusion. Other diseases that involve the bones of the rib cage or the spinal column, such as pectus excavatum, pectus carinatum, and ankylosing spondylitis, have much less effect on ventilatory capacity. Obesity is included in this section because of its profound effects on the mechanical properties of the chest wall. Diseases directly involving the respiratory muscles also depress ventilatory function and are discussed in Chapter 82.

KYPHOSCOLIOSIS

DIAGNOSIS AND ETIOLOGY

Kyphoscoliosis is a disorder of the spine, with its articulations characterized by abnormal curvature in the coronal and sagittal plane as well as spinal rotation. The anteroposterior (AP) angulation is referred to as *kyphosis* and lateral angulation as *scoliosis* (Fig. 83.1). Scoliosis is almost always associated with kyphosis and with the rotation of the spine around its long axis. Spinal rotation may create severe distortion of the ribs, consisting of wide separation of the interspaces posteriorly and crowding of the interspaces anteriorly.[1] Kyphosis may exist as an isolated deformity (e.g., in elderly patients with osteoporosis, following radiation therapy). The estimated prevalence of mild spinal deformities is 1 per 1000 people and that of severe spinal deformities 1 per 10,000 people in the United States.[2]

The causes of kyphoscoliosis are conveniently grouped into three categories: congenital, paralytic or secondary, and idiopathic. Congenital kyphoscoliosis is present at birth, and it may or may not be genetic. There may be isolated malformations of vertebrae during prenatal development, or it may be one manifestation of a more generalized disorder such as muscular dystrophy, Ehlers-Danlos syndrome, or neurofibromatosis. Paralytic, or secondary, kyphoscoliosis is due to diseases that primarily affect the neuromuscular system supporting either the spine, the vertebrae, or the vertebral connective tissue (Table 83.1). The most common causes of paralytic kyphoscoliosis are polio, muscular dystrophy, cerebral palsy, and spina bifida. Other forms of paralytic kyphoscoliosis, such as Marfan's syndrome, osteomalacia, post-thoracoplasty, and Charcot-Marie-Tooth disease, are much less common.[3] Finally, idiopathic kyphoscoliosis often begins in late childhood or early adolescence, has a female predominance of 4 to 1, and may account for as many as 80% of cases of kyphoscoliosis.

Severe kyphoscoliosis is easily identifiable on physical examination. In children and adolescents, however, the changes in spinal curvature may be subtle, and the spine should be carefully inspected for signs of mild scoliosis. Because of the rotation of the vertebrae in scoliosis, the

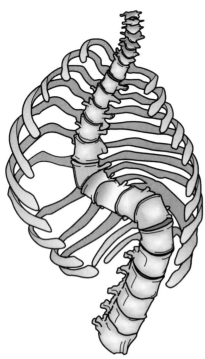

Figure 83.1 Schema showing the rotation of the spine and rib cage in kyphoscoliosis. (From Bergofsky EH, Turino GM, Fishman AP: Cardiorespiratory failure in kyphoscoliosis. Medicine [Baltimore] 38:263, 1959.)

Table 83.1 Causes of Kyphoscoliosis

Congenital
Paralytic or Secondary
Neuromuscular
Poliomyelitis
Muscular dystrophy
Cerebral palsy
Friedreich's ataxia
Charcot-Marie-Tooth disease
Disorders of Connective Tissue
Marfan's syndrome
Ehler's-Danlos syndrome
Morquio's syndrome
Vertebral Disease
Osteoporosis
Osteomalacia
Vitamin D-resistant rickets
Tuberculous spondylitis
Spina bifida
Post-Thoracoplasty
Idiopathic

curvature of the vertebral column is much greater than that of the palpable spinous processes, and only radiographs can reveal the true severity. The dorsal hump seen on examination is due to the angulated ribs rather than to the spine. In severe kyphoscoliosis complicated by both respiratory and right heart failure, clinical examination may reveal cyanosis, distended neck veins, peripheral edema, and hepatomegaly.

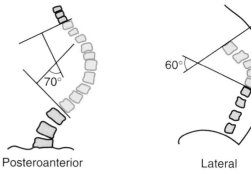

Posteroanterior   Lateral

Figure 83.2 Schematized examples of posteroanterior (PA) and lateral chest radiographs depicting the lines constructed to measure the Cobb angle. The degree of scoliosis can be assessed by the Cobb angle of the PA radiograph, and the degree of kyphosis by the Cobb angle of the lateral radiograph. The angle can be calculated either from the intersection of the lines parallel to the vertebra (as shown for kyphosis, on the right) or from the intersection of lines perpendicular to these lines (as shown for scoliosis, on the left).

The severity of the spinal deformity can be quantified radiographically by measuring the Cobb angle.[4] This angle is formed by the intersection of two lines, each of which is parallel to the top and bottom vertebra of the scoliotic or kyphotic curves (Fig. 83.2). The magnitude of the Cobb angle has been used to predict development of respiratory failure.[5] A Cobb angle greater than 100 degrees is considered a severe deformity and is more likely to be associated with respiratory failure. Chest radiographs are limited in utility when evaluating the mediastinum or lung parenchyma. In these instances, a computed tomography (CT) scan of the chest is more informative.

PATHOPHYSIOLOGY

Pulmonary Function

Among the chest wall diseases, kyphoscoliosis produces the most severe restrictive defect.[1,6] Measurement of pulmonary function characteristically shows a decrease in total lung capacity (TLC) and vital capacity (VC) and normal or increased residual volume (RV).[7] The FEV_1 is typically decreased, but the FEV_1/FVC remains normal. The RV/TLC can be as high as 50%.[8,9]

In adults with idiopathic kyphoscoliosis, the Cobb angle is associated with the degree of restriction. Patients with mild to moderate idiopathic kyphoscoliosis may not be restricted or only have mild restrictive dysfunction. Patients with an angle greater than 60 degrees are more likely to exhibit a restrictive defect,[10] whereas those individuals with angles in the 90- to 100-degree range invariably have pulmonary function impairment[8,10] proportional to the degree of spinal deformity.[11] Although spinal deformity is unquestionably a major determinant of respiratory impairment in idiopathic kyphoscoliosis, the relationship is complex and the severity of pulmonary impairment cannot be inferred from the scoliosis angle alone.[9] Additional contributing factors may include the number of vertebrae involved,[9,10] the location of the curve,[9,10] the patient's age,[10] presence of kyphosis,[9,10] and degree of rotation.[10]

In patients with kyphoscoliosis secondary to paralysis or to neuromuscular weakness, the association between the restrictive process and the degree of spinal deformity is not as strong. In patients with neuromuscular weakness, the spinal deformity starts at an earlier age and progresses faster than that in patients with idiopathic scoliosis. These patients are more likely to have a greater Cobb angle and more pulmonary function impairment.[10] Reductions in vital capacity correlate more closely with muscle weakness than with the degree of spinal curvature.[8] In patients with congenital scoliosis, for any given Cobb angle, the loss in VC is approximately 15% greater than in patients with idiopathic scoliosis. Associated rib deformities or underlying lung abnormalities contribute to the restrictive process.

Airway obstruction is not usually a feature of kyphoscoliosis. Although forced expiratory flow rates (FEV₁) are usually decreased, the reduction in expiratory flow is proportional to the restrictive process and is not related to intrinsic airway disease. Because TLC may be markedly reduced with relative preservation of RV (Table 83.2), the RV/TLC ratio may be elevated. The combination of reduced expiratory flow rates and an increased RV/TLC ratio may at times be mistakenly attributed to a superimposed obstructive process. Specific airway conductance, however, is usually normal or even increased despite the reduction in expiratory flow rates.[12] The increase in airway conductance may be partly explained by increased radial tension on the airways as a result of the increased elastic recoil of the lung. In rare cases, airway obstruction occurs as a consequence of torsion of the central airways[13] or impingement of a mediastinal structure, such as the aorta, on the tracheal wall.[14] Measurements of the diffusing capacity,[15,16] both steady-state and single-breath measurements, are often reduced in proportion to the reduction in TLC. The diffusing capacity in some patients (usually elderly patients with cor pulmonale and Cobb angles of 120 degrees or more) may be reduced disproportionately and may reflect failure of alveolar development[16] or anatomic changes in the pulmonary circulation.[15]

Respiratory Mechanics

Respiratory system compliance is reduced in kyphoscoliosis. This is primarily due to a reduction in chest wall compliance and, to a lesser degree, reductions in lung compliance. The decreased compliance of the chest wall correlates with the angle of scoliosis.[7] In general, scoliotic angles of up to 50 degrees have a minimal effect in decreasing respiratory system compliance, whereas angles of greater than 100 degrees decrease the respiratory system compliance to levels comparable to those seen in patients with adult respiratory distress syndrome[7,15] (Table 83.3). The stiffened chest wall also places the resting position of the respiratory system [functional residual capacity (FRC)] at a lower lung volume. This further reduces respiratory system compliance by shifting tidal breathing to a flatter portion of the volume-pressure curve (Fig. 83.3). Interestingly, in children with

Table 83.2 Pulmonary Function in Chest Wall Diseases

Parameter	KS	Post-Thor	PE	AS
TLC (% predicted)	44	64	90	85
VC (% predicted)	30	49	90	79
RV (% predicted)	94	91	100	97
FEV₁ (% predicted)	40	41	93	81
FEV₁/FVC	80	57	81	74

KS, kyphoscoliosis; Post-Thor, post-thoracoplasty; PE, pectus excavatum; AS, ankylosing spondylitis; TLC, total lung capacity; VC, vital capacity; RV, residual volume; FEV₁, forced expiratory volume in 1 second; FVC, forced vital capacity.

Table 83.3 Respiratory Mechanics in Chest Wall Diseases

Parameter	KS	Post-Thor	PE	AS
CRS % predicted	50	50	—	70
CCW % predicted	30	40	—	60
CL % predicted	60	50	80	80
PImax cm H₂O	37	50	90	56
MVV L/min	37	37	107	80

KS, kyphoscoliosis; Post-Thor, post-thoracoplasty; PE, pectus excavatum; AS, ankylosing spondylitis; CRS, compliance of respiratory system; CCW, compliance of chest wall; CL, compliance of lungs; PImax, maximum inspiratory pressure; MVV, maximum voluntary ventilation.

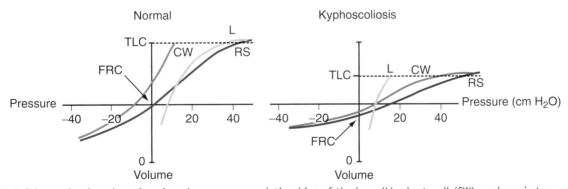

Figure 83.3 Schema showing alterations in volume-pressure relationships of the lung (L), chest wall (CW), and respiratory system (RS) in kyphoscoliosis. The chest wall is less compliant, leading to a reduction in functional residual capacity (FRC) and tidal breathing on a flatter portion of the respiratory system volume-pressure curve. TLC, total lung capacity.

kyphoscoliosis, even in those with severe spinal deformity, chest wall compliance is normal, and impairment in ventilatory function may be due to mechanical inefficiency of the unequal hemithoraces.[17]

The reduction in lung compliance is likely related to microatelectasis due to the relatively immobile chest wall and not to intrinsic lung disease.[17,18] With pneumonia or other infiltrative processes, lung compliance may be as severely reduced as chest wall compliance.[18]

The reduction in respiratory system compliance increases the elastic load placed on the respiratory muscles, thereby increasing the work of breathing. Some estimates of the work per unit of ventilation are twice the normal value to inflate the lung and five times the normal value to inflate the chest wall.[15] To the extent that the work of breathing is positively related to the oxygen cost of breathing, it is not surprising that the oxygen cost of breathing in patients with kyphoscoliosis may be increased three to five times that seen in healthy subjects.[1] Such an increase in the oxygen cost of breathing may place these patients at risk for respiratory muscle fatigue.[19] Intercurrent illnesses, such as pneumonia or sepsis, may pose additional elastic loads, further increasing the work and oxygen cost of breathing.[18]

Respiratory Muscle Strength

In patients with paralytic kyphoscoliosis related to neuromuscular diseases, inspiratory muscle weakness contributes to the restrictive process. In patients with idiopathic kyphoscoliosis, however, the prevalence of respiratory muscle weakness and its role in the development of respiratory failure is unknown. Respiratory muscle strength, as assessed from measurements of maximal static inspiratory and expiratory pressures (PImax and PEmax) is typically normal in young patients with idiopathic scoliosis with Cobb angles of less than 50 degrees.[20] In those with idiopathic kyphoscoliosis and mean scoliosis Cobb angles of more than 50 degrees, both PImax and PEmax are mildly decreased to 70% and 80% of control values, respectively.[8,17] In older patients with somewhat more scoliosis, PImax is about 50% of predicted in eucapnic patients and 25% of predicted in hypercapnic patients (Table 83.3).[6] In contrast, other investigators have found that the reduction of respiratory muscle strength is not a regular feature of scoliosis in adults.[21] If present, inspiratory and expiratory muscle weakness may not be due to intrinsic muscle disease but to changes in geometry of the chest wall affecting the mechanical advantage of the inspiratory muscles. The finding that inspiratory muscle weakness is independent of the degree of spinal curvature, however, argues against this assertion.[17]

Control and Pattern of Breathing

To compensate for the reduced respiratory system compliance and the increased elastic load on the inspiratory muscles, patients with kyphoscoliosis recruit the inspiratory muscles of the rib cage[22] and may adopt a rapid shallow breathing pattern consisting of a low tidal volume and shortened inspiratory time. Both the tidal volume and inspiratory time were found to correlate negatively with the angle of scoliosis.[23] In these patients, the minute ventilation is normal or slightly elevated despite increases in the respiratory frequency. One advantage of breathing with low tidal volumes is a reduction in the work per breath. A second benefit is reducing the ratio of the pressure needed to inhale (Pbreath) to PImax, thereby lowering the risk of developing inspiratory muscle fatigue and reducing dyspnea. Compared to normal tidal volume breathing, the disadvantages of adopting a low tidal volume breathing pattern include the potential for developing microatelectasis and increased dead space ventilation.

Alternatively, individuals with kyphoscoliosis may compensate for the increased elastic load by increasing central neural drive to the muscles.[24] Increasing ventilatory drive, as measured by mouth occlusion pressure ($P_{0.1}$), correlates positively with the degree of scoliotic deformity and may represent a strategy adopted by scoliotic patients.[23] The ventilatory response to carbon dioxide, however, may be normal or reduced. If the response is reduced, the magnitude of the reduction is proportional to the degree of mechanical limitation imposed by the chest wall. Thus, the decrement in the ventilatory response to carbon dioxide resembles that of external resistive loading and can be attributed to the restricted respiratory system rather than to an inherent problem with respiratory control. These findings suggest that the drive to breathe in these patients is normal, but compensatory increases in minute ventilation are limited by mechanical factors. The effects of aging and its influence on central ventilatory control, however, require further clarification in this population.

Gas Exchange

Hypoxemia may be due to ventilation-perfusion mismatch, underlying atelectasis, or alveolar hypoventilation. Because airway and intrinsic lung disease are usually absent in kyphoscoliosis, ventilation-perfusion mismatching is attributed to underventilation of lung regions. The maldistribution of ventilation appears to be independent of the side of the hemithorax relative to the scoliosis. The degree of ventilation-perfusion mismatching is worse in patients with Cobb angles greater than 65 degrees.[25] For normocapnic patients with kyphoscoliosis, the alveolar-arterial PO_2 difference is usually less than that seen in normocapnic patients with chronic obstructive pulmonary disease (COPD) (15 vs. 40 mm Hg). When hypoventilation supervenes, hypoxemia worsens, with little or no increase in the alveolar-arterial PO_2 difference,[1,15] and hypercapnia develops. Hypercapnia initially appears during sleep and with exercise. Eventually, with further disease progression, it occurs at rest. Persistent hypoxemia leads to pulmonary vasoconstriction, right ventricular hypertrophy, and cor pulmonale. Proliferation of pulmonary artery smooth muscle or compression of the pulmonary vascular bed by a deflated lung may further increase pulmonary artery pressure at rest or during exercise. Pulmonary hypertension correlates with the degree of hypoxemia but not with etiology, severity, or age of onset of the scoliosis.[26] Patients with severe kyphoscoliosis may have oxyhemoglobin desaturation with minimal activity.[27]

Exercise Capacity

Exercise capacity can be significantly impaired in patients with severe kyphoscoliosis. Maximum oxygen consumption

Table 83.4 Exercise Capacity in Normal Subjects and in Patients With Thoracic Cage Disorders

Parameter	No.	Age (years)	$\dot{V}o_{2max}$ (mL/kg/min)	$\dot{V}E$ (L/min)
Normal	14	24	45.9	93
KS	15	32	31.6	66
Post-Thor	29	64	14.3	25
PE	12	14	38.5	73
AS	33	47	23.4	—
Obesity	13	23	27.7	82

KS, kyphoscoliosis; Post-Thor, post-thoracoplasty; PE, pectus excavatum; AS, ankylosing spondylitis; $\dot{V}o_{2max}$, maximum oxygen consumption; $\dot{V}E$, expired volume (minute ventilation). Representative values are from Kesten et al.[28]; Fisher et al.[139]; Phillips et al., 1989; Wynn et al.[84]; Dempsey et al., 1966; Kollias et al., 1972; and Dempsey Rankin, 1966.

($\dot{V}o_{2max}$) may be reduced to about 60% to 80% of predicted, with the lower values seen in patients with the lowest forced vital capacity (FVC), FEV_1, and maximum voluntary ventilation (MVV) (Table 83.4).[28] However, the breathing pattern response to exercise in patients with mild to moderate kyphoscoliosis (Cobb angle between 25 and 70 degrees) is similar to that seen in normal subjects. The ratio of tidal volume to vital capacity (VT/VC) is roughly 0.5, and the ratio of maximum exercise ventilation to maximal voluntary ventilation ($\dot{V}Emax/MVV$) can reach 70%.[28] In adolescent scoliotic patients with near-normal respiratory muscle strength, exercise capacity was, on average, 80% to 85% of normal.[29] Supplemental oxygen during exercise may increase oxygen saturation and decrease dyspnea, but it does not affect walking distance[27] in patients with kyphoscoliosis. Corrective surgery such as spinal fusion has not been found to improve exercise capacity in these patients.[30] Deconditioning and lack of regular aerobic exercise may also contribute to poor exercise performance in adolescents and adults with moderate scoliosis.

Sleep-Disordered Breathing

Sleep-related abnormalities may have a significant impact on the clinical course and quality of life of patients with kyphoscoliosis.[31] The most common abnormality during sleep is hypoventilation. When awake, patients with kyphoscoliosis may recruit the intercostal and accessory muscles to assist the diaphragm in displacing the stiff chest wall.[22] When sleeping, these patients may hypoventilate due to hypotonia of the intercostal and accessory muscles, particularly during rapid-eye-movement (REM) sleep.[32,33] Decreased neural drive to the diaphragm during REM sleep and decreased chest wall compliance may also contribute to nocturnal hypoventilation. The degree of oxyhemoglobin desaturation during sleep in these patients appears to be more severe than that seen during sleep in patients with COPD or interstitial lung disease[34] and may not correlate with the degree of thoracic deformity or the severity of the restrictive process.[35] Hypoxemia-related autonomic

dysfunction manifested by pronounced variability of heart rate may also occur in these patients.[36]

Individuals with kyphoscoliosis also may have coexistent obstructive sleep apnea.[37] Distortion of the upper airway anatomy may predispose these individuals to intermittent airway obstruction during REM-induced hypotonia of the pharyngeal muscles; however, the incidence of obstructive sleep apnea in patients with kyphoscoliosis is not increased over that seen in the general population.[32]

Patients with nocturnal desaturation may become hypercapnic during the daytime.[34] Recurrent hypercarbia and hypoxemia during sleep may potentiate the daytime development of hypercarbia, cor pulmonale, and respiratory muscle dysfunction[33] and predispose to cardiorespiratory failure. Because sleep-related disorders represent a potentially treatable or reversible cause of respiratory failure, they should be evaluated in patients with kyphoscoliosis who develop carbon dioxide retention.

CLINICAL COURSE

The natural history of kyphoscoliosis depends on its etiology and the severity of the thoracic deformity. Congenital kyphoscoliosis may progress rapidly, leading to severe deformity with possible spinal cord compression and respiratory impairment.[38] The course of secondary kyphoscoliosis depends largely on the nature of the underlying neuromuscular disease and its age of onset. In general, secondary kyphoscoliosis is characterized by an early onset with rapid progression during growth, continued progression after skeletal maturity, and profound impairment of respiratory function.[39] Idiopathic kyphoscoliosis has a more benign course in individuals with mild thoracic deformity. They have an excellent prognosis with little impairment of breathing or overall lifestyle.[40] Those with moderate or severe idiopathic kyphoscolioisis may have profound respiratory compromise.

Progression of the thoracic deformity from moderate to severe may depend on skeletal immaturity and the degree of deformity at the time of diagnosis. After skeletal maturity, thoracic deformities less than 30 degrees are unlikely to progress, whereas those between 30 to 50 degrees increase slowly by an average total of 10 to 15 degrees during adulthood.[40] Thoracic deformities greater than 50 degrees at skeletal maturity increase steadily at a rate of about 1 degree annually.[41] In general, patients with mild to moderate idiopathic kyphoscoliosis do not require special treatment to prevent ventilatory failure and, with the exception of backache,[40] are not significantly different from the general population with regard to symptoms,[17] loss of lung volume with aging,[41] or life expectancy.[39] Similarly, patients with severe idiopathic kyphoscoliosis who are younger than 35 years of age also tend not to have symptoms. In contrast, middle-aged patients with severe idiopathic kyphoscoliosis and scoliotic curves around 100 degrees tend to develop dyspnea and decreased exercise tolerance, have repeated acute respiratory infections, and are at risk for respiratory failure.[42] The onset of respiratory failure is often insidious, and its incidence is variable. Kyphoscoliosis accounts for less than 5% of chronic ventilatory failure in adults. After cor pulmonale develops, the prognosis is poor; without treatment, death generally occurs within a year.[1] The prognosis is worsened by any associated obstructive lung process.[43] Pregnancy usually

Table 83.5 Factors Predisposing to Ventilatory Failure in Kyphoscoliosis

Spinal deformity of more than 100 degrees
Inspiratory muscle weakness
Underlying neuromuscular disease
Earlier age of onset
Sleep-disordered breathing
Airway compression

Table 83.6 Indications for Instituting Long-Term Noninvasive Ventilation for Kyphoscoliosis (Chest Wall Diseases)

Symptoms (e.g., fatigue, morning headaches, dyspnea) or signs of cor pulmonale and one of the following:
Daytime arterial P_{CO_2} ≥45 mm Hg
Nocturnal oxygen saturation ≤88% for five consecutive minutes
Progressive neuromuscular disease with PImax <60 cm H_2O or FVC <50% of predicted

PImax, maximal static inspiratory pressure; FVC, forced vital capacity.

poses no added risk for respiratory complications,[44] however, with severe degrees of kyphoscoliosis and reductions in VC to less than 1 liter, the risk for respiratory complications during pregnancy may be increased.

The notion that the extent of the spinal deformity is the key predictor of respiratory failure has been challenged. Patients may survive into their seventh decade with minimal or mild cardiorespiratory impairment despite a Cobb angle of greater than 105 degrees.[45] Other investigators have found no correlation between the severity of hypercapnia and the degree of thoracic deformity.[6] Despite these findings, the role of reduced chest wall compliance in the evolution of respiratory dysfunction and its strong relationship to the chest wall deformity implies that the degree of spinal deformity is a key factor in the development of respiratory failure. When respiratory failure occurs and the Cobb angle is less than 100 degrees, the etiology of respiratory failure should not be attributed solely to the skeletal deformity. Other factors that contribute to the development of respiratory failure are summarized in Table 83.5.

TREATMENT

General Measures

Medical therapy for adults with kyphoscoliosis includes both preventive and supportive measures. Immunization, adequate hydration, prompt care of respiratory infections, avoidance of sedatives, and carefully monitored supplemental oxygen are the mainstays of therapy. Abstaining from smoking and maintaining body weight within desirable levels is especially important for individuals with reduced pulmonary function. Physical training is encouraged to improve exercise capacity in sedentary patients. If hypercapnia and cor pulmonale develop, chronic respiratory failure may be treated conservatively with chest physiotherapy, bronchodilators, oxygen therapy, and diuretics if needed. Oxyhemoglobin saturation should be routinely assessed both at rest and during exercise in patients with moderate to severe kyphoscoliosis. Supplemental oxygen administered at rest or with exercise can minimize dyspnea and exercise-induced desaturation in patients with moderately severe kyphoscoliosis and chronic ventilatory failure.[46]

Mechanical Ventilation

Noninvasive nocturnal ventilation has become an effective modality for treating respiratory failure in patients with severe kyphoscoliosis.[47] Over the last two decades, there has been significant progress in understanding noninvasive ventilatory techniques delivered either by negative- or positive-pressure ventilators.

Nocturnal negative-pressure ventilation has been administered primarily with devices such as cuirass and body-wrap ventilators, which are generally preferred to tank ventilators. Negative-pressure ventilation, which is primarily available in the pressure-controlled mode, may lead to patient–ventilator asynchrony. Additional disadvantages of using negative-pressure devices include the induction of upper airway obstruction during sleep, the need to custom-fit a cuirass to the deformed chest wall, and the associated patient discomfort of having to lie supine throughout the night.

Noninvasive positive-pressure ventilation is usually delivered via a nasal mask, a full face mask or less frequently a mouthpiece. A pressure- or volume-preset ventilator can be used with similar efficacy and acceptance by the patients.[48] There is usually no need for supplemental oxygen; the exception is when hypoxemia persists despite correction of alveolar hypoventilation.[49] Because of the rapid, shallow breathing pattern adopted by these patients, the ventilator triggering system should have a short response time to minimize patient–ventilator asynchrony. Tracheostomy may be indicated for patients who fail to respond to or cannot tolerate noninvasive positive-pressure ventilation, or patients requiring airway access to manage excessive secretions.

The indications for instituting noninvasive nocturnal ventilation in patients with kyphoscoliosis are not fully defined.[47] In the absence of randomized controlled clinical studies, there has been continued debate about whether nocturnal ventilation is of any benefit to asymptomatic patients who either belong to a high-risk group or have abnormal diurnal blood gases. Indisputable indications for nocturnal ventilation (Table 83.6) include symptoms suggestive of nocturnal hypoventilation (dyspnea, fatigue, morning headaches), with either arterial P_{CO_2} greater than 45 mm Hg or nocturnal oxygen saturation (≤88%) for five consecutive minutes.[47,49,50] Contraindications to noninvasive ventilation in patients with kyphoscoliosis include the inability to protect the upper airway due to cough impairment or excessive airway secretions.

The benefits of noninvasive nocturnal ventilation in patients with kyphoscoliosis appear to be the same whether a negative-pressure or positive-pressure ventilatory mode is used and include improvements in both physiological measurements and quality of life indices (Table 83.7). Whereas

Table 83.7 Benefits of Noninvasive Nocturnal Ventilation in Chest Wall Diseases

Gas Exchange
Increased PO_2
Decreased PCO_2

Hemodynamics
Decreased pulmonary artery pressure
Increased right ventricular function

Mechanics
Reduced work of breathing
Increased PImax

Sleep Hygiene
Normalized sleep patterns
Fewer apneic episodes

Outcomes
Fewer hospitalizations
Improved quality of life, relief of dyspnea

improvements in sleep architecture and normalization of blood gases may occur within the first few days of treatment, improvements in pulmonary hemodynamics may take longer to evolve.[49,51,52] Small improvements in vital capacity, respiratory muscle strength, and endurance have also been recorded.[49,53] Dyspnea on exertion, daytime somnolence, and early morning headaches can all be alleviated, thus contributing to better overall psychosocial and mental function and an improved ability to carry out activities of daily living.[53,54] Long-term ventilatory support in patients with kyphoscoliosis and respiratory failure significantly reduces the number of days spent in hospital.[48,53,54] Randomized clinical trials demonstrating survival benefit in patients with kyphoscoliosis and respiratory failure treated with noninvasive ventilation are lacking. However, recent data[47,48,54,55] from long-term follow-up studies provide strong evidence that survival of ventilated patients is prolonged in comparison to that of unventilated patients. In these uncontrolled studies,[48,54,55] survival of patients with kyphoscoliosis and respiratory failure receiving noninvasive ventilation was 90% after 1 year and 80% after 5 years.

The outcome appears to be similar whether ventilation is delivered with a positive-pressure or negative-pressure system, but there are fewer data for negative-pressure ventilation.[56,57] The advantages of positive-pressure ventilation over negative-pressure ventilation include the compact and portable features of the equipment and its relative ease of use. In addition, nocturnal positive-pressure ventilation may benefit individuals with kyphoscoliosis by reducing both obstructive and nonobstructive sleep-related events, whereby negative-pressure ventilation may induce upper airway obstruction.[52] As far as the choice of volume-cycled versus pressure-cycled ventilation is concerned, there are currently no firm guidelines.[50] Both types have similar effects on blood gas indices, treatment compliance, and patient survival.[48,50] Advantages of pressure-cycled ventilation include patient comfort related to flow-triggering systems, ability to compensate for leaks, and ability to adjust the time to peak inspiratory positive airway pressure.[48,50] Because of its greater alarm capabilities, volume-cycled ven-

tilation may be a good choice for a ventilator-dependent kyphoscoliotic patient with severe respiratory failure. Nasal proportional assist ventilation has also been used to a limited extent in these patients.[56] In cases of acute respiratory failure refractory to the measures described previously, positive-pressure ventilation with a volume-cycled ventilator delivered by an endotracheal tube may be needed to treat hypoventilation and hypoxemia.[45]

Factors contributing to the improvement in pulmonary function with nocturnal positive-pressure ventilation may include reversing microatelectasis and increasing lung compliance. These benefits have been noted following brief periods (20 minutes) of intermittent positive-pressure breathing (IPPB). Improvements in lung mechanics, resting arterial PCO_2, and oxygenation may last up to 4 hours after a single treatment of IPPB. With daily IPPB therapy, the improvement in vital capacity may persist for up to 9 months.[58] IPPB, however, has not been shown to be as efficacious in other diseases associated with diminished respiratory system compliance and has little effect on improving chest wall compliance.[59]

Surgical Treatment

Operative and nonoperative (brace) orthopedic treatments have been used in immature patients with idiopathic kyphoscoliosis to alter the natural history of the disease and prevent respiratory failure. Treatment with a brace is recommended for growing children with angles between 25 and 40 degrees, whereas surgical correction of the curve with fusion is offered to those with curves greater than 40 degrees.[60] However, there are no randomized clinical trials of either bracing or surgery compared with no treatment, the long-term complications of spinal fusion are numerous, and the need to stabilize the spine surgically to avoid respiratory failure later in life is questionable.[40]

Immediately after surgery, pulmonary function may deteriorate,[57] with reductions of chest wall and respiratory system compliance of 20% to 129%.[61] This deterioration in respiratory mechanics is thought to be due to the extent of rib cage trauma and changes in chest wall caliber.[61] Despite several years of observation, the long-term benefits of spinal surgery on pulmonary function remain controversial. In adults, it is generally accepted that surgical procedures do not improve pulmonary function. Spinal fusion and Harrington rod placement did not significantly improve the FVC, FEV_1, or resting arterial PO_2 in patients over the age of 20, and these procedures had associated complications.[62] In children and adolescents, there may be a role for corrective surgery. After Harrington rod instrumentation and spinal fusion, lung function was improved in children and adolescents 18 months and 3 years after surgery, respectively.[21,30] In women with an average curvature of 58 degrees, VC was improved by 12% after 3 years. In a long-term follow-up study involving patients with idiopathic kyphoscoliosis treated with a brace or posterior spinal surgery, pulmonary function improved in most patients up to 25 years after treatment.[63] In patients with kyphoscoliosis associated with neurologic disorders, early stabilization may help prevent progressive myelopathy.[64] Titanium rib implantation and expansion has met with early success in individuals with congenital kyphoscoliosis.

To summarize, patients with severe kyphoscoliosis have impaired lung function characterized by a reduction in respiratory system compliance, an increased elastic load on the respiratory muscles, and an increase in the work of breathing. As they age, adults with severe spinal deformities are at risk for respiratory failure. Although the degree of spinal distortion certainly plays a significant role in the pathogenesis of respiratory failure, other factors, such as inspiratory muscle weakness and sleep-related dysfunction, should be evaluated in patients with symptoms. After cardiorespiratory failure develops, conservative measures coupled with nocturnal positive-pressure ventilation improve symptoms, reduce hospitalization, and improve prognosis.

THORACOPLASTY

DIAGNOSIS AND ETIOLOGY

Thoracoplasty was one of the most common surgical procedures used to treat tuberculous empyema and cavitary pulmonary tuberculosis prior to the advent of antituberculous chemotherapy. It entailed removal of a number of ribs, up to seven or eight, along with the intercostal muscles in order to collapse the infected lung (Fig. 83.4). Some of the patients who had this procedure performed in the 1940s and 1950s are still alive and often have restrictive disease as a result of distortion of the chest wall, pleural thickening, and secondary scoliosis.[65] Although not entirely abandoned, thoracoplasty is still used to a limited extent to treat postresectional or postinfectious empyema.[66]

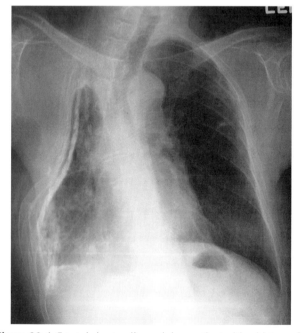

Figure 83.4 Frontal chest radiograph in a patient with a history of prior *M. tuberculosis* infection shows extensive deformity of the right thorax, consistent with prior thoracoplasty. Extensive calcification of the pleura on the right side, consistent with prior tuberculous effusion or empyema, is also evident, and linear opacity related to prior pulmonary inflammation is present within the left upper lobe. Scoliosis of the thoracic spine convex to the right is probably related to the right chest wall deformity. (Courtesy of Michael Gotway, MD, Department of Radiology, University of California, San Francisco.)

The natural history of thoracoplasty typically includes a period of years during which patients are asymptomatic. Eventually, patients develop dyspnea on exertion and may progress to develop acute or chronic respiratory failure. Of 171 patients who were operated on between 1951 and 1953, over one third had died by 1987.[67] Risk factors associated with developing respiratory failure include preoperative tuberculous cavitary disease, advanced age at the time of operation, a preoperative contralateral surgically induced pneumothorax, and male gender.[67] The risk was greater in patients who underwent thoracoplasty than in those who underwent pneumonectomy alone.

PATHOPHYSIOLOGY

Pulmonary Function

Of the chest wall disorders, thoracoplasty is second only to kyphoscoliosis in producing a severe restrictive pattern (Table 83.2). The restrictive pattern is due to a number of factors, including a reduction in respiratory system compliance, fibrothorax, progressive lung fibrosis related to underlying granulomatous disease, previous lung resection, phrenic nerve damage, and scoliosis (Table 83.8). VC and TLC may be reduced to 40% and 70% of predicted, respectively. RV and FRC are reduced to the range of 70% and 90% of predicted, respectively.[68] Progressive scoliosis[65] and the effects of aging on respiratory system compliance worsen the restrictive process. The degree of restriction, however, does not correlate with the extent of thoracoplasty.[68]

Unlike other restrictive diseases of the chest wall, coincident airflow obstruction is common.[68,69] When airflow obstruction is present, the FEV_1 and the FEV_1/FVC ratio are reduced, and the RV/TLC ratio is increased (Table 83.2). Airway obstruction may be due to chronic bronchitis from cigarette smoking or other factors, such as previous tuberculous bronchitis or bronchiectasis.[68] Airway obstruction becomes more prevalent with aging and is associated with carbon dioxide retention, hypoxemia, and complaints of dyspnea.[69] The obstructive process may be reversible.[69a] Determining its presence and severity may help identify those at greater risk for developing respiratory failure.

Respiratory Mechanics

The long-term sequelae of thoracoplasty include a reduction of respiratory system, chest wall, and lung compliance values (Table 83.3). As with kyphoscoliosis, respiratory

Table 83.8 Factors Contributing to Pulmonary Restriction in Thoracoplasty

Reduced respiratory system compliance
Fibrothorax
Pulmonary fibrosis due to underlying granulomatous disease
Previous lung resection
Phrenic nerve injury
Progressive scoliosis
Inspiratory muscle weakness

system compliance may be reduced to 50% of predicted, thus imposing a substantial elastic load on the respiratory muscles. This elastic load, in combination with the resistive load due to airway obstruction, increases the work of breathing. The oxygen cost of breathing is thus three to four times higher in these patients than in controls[70] and may predispose these patients to respiratory failure.

Gas Exchange and Exercise Tolerance

Patients who have undergone thoracoplasty may have hypoxemia and complain of exercise intolerance. The maximal work rate and oxygen consumption are reduced, and there is a ventilatory limit to exercise (Table 83.4). The diminished $\dot{V}O_{2max}$ has been correlated with reductions in FEV_1.[69] Post-thoracoplasty patients may develop severe hypoxemia and hypercarbia during exercise or at rest. The capacity to exercise, as measured by the 6-minute walk test, is roughly equal to that of individuals with COPD of similar age and comparable FEV_1.[71] Diffusion capacity is moderately reduced, but when corrected for lung volume it is within the normal range.[68] During exercise, the diffusion capacity fails to increase appropriately, indicating an irreversibly restricted pulmonary vascular bed. Nocturnal hypoxemia is common in patients with hypercapnia or borderline low arterial PO_2 during daytime.[72] Cor pulmonale may develop as a result of hypoxemia and resultant pulmonary hypertension.

TREATMENT

Treatment is supportive with the use of domiciliary oxygen, antibiotics when appropriate, and noninvasive nocturnal ventilation. In addition, any obstructive component should be vigorously treated. Positive-pressure ventilation delivered by means of an endotracheal tube or tracheostomy has been used to treat acute respiratory failure. Management of chronic respiratory failure often entails the use of positive-pressure or negative-pressure noninvasive ventilation. Noninvasive ventilation reduces the work of breathing, alleviates respiratory muscle fatigue, relieves dyspnea, lessens sleep-induced desaturation, and improves overall prognosis.[73,73a] Improvements in VC, maximal inspiratory pressure, maximal expiratory pressure, and arterial blood gases occur soon after initiation of noninvasive ventilation and can be maintained over the long term. Even with nocturnal ventilatory assistance, however, mortality is still high, with a 55% survival rate 7 years after initiating treatment.[73]

PECTUS EXCAVATUM

DIAGNOSIS AND ETIOLOGY

Pectus excavatum is a chest wall deformity characterized by excessive depression of the sternum. The sternal depression may be minimal or extreme, diffuse or local, symmetrical or asymmetrical. Pectus excavatum is the most common chest wall deformity seen by pediatricians and primary care providers.[74] It affects between 0.5% and 2.0% of the population and occurs in approximately 1 in every 1000 children. Boys are affected about three times more often than girls.[75] The chest deformity is apparent at birth in over 80% of indi-

viduals with pectus excavatum.[76] The natural history of the pectus deformity is variable; but it usually progresses as the child grows, especially during the teenage years.

The etiology of pectus excavatum is unknown. A defect in the connective tissue surrounding the sternum has been implicated because of the frequent association of pectus excavatum with connective tissue disorders such as Marfan's syndrome. A genetic predisposition was suggested by one large series in which a family history of pectus deformity was present in 41% of the members.[77] In another series, however, only 5 of 315 patients had a positive family history of pectus.[78] Scoliosis, congenital heart disease, and functional heart murmurs can be associated with pectus excavatum and were noted in 15%, 4%, and 31% of patients, respectively, in one large series.[77] Pectus carinatum, a disorder in which the sternum is protuberant, is less common than pectus excavatum. It is of unknown etiology and may be associated with congenital heart disease, severe childhood asthma, and rickets.[79]

The most frequent complaints of patients with pectus deformity are cosmetic in nature and arise in patients between the ages of 15 and 20 years.[78] Psychological problems related to the deformity occur in as many as 85% of patients. Dyspnea on exertion also occurs in 30% to 70% of patients. Other symptoms include chest pain, palpitations, and frequent respiratory infections.[77] Although extremely rare, respiratory failure can occur in adults with severe pectus excavatum.[80]

The degree of chest wall deformity can be assessed clinically or radiographically (Table 83.9). A greater than 3 cm distance between the surface of the anterior chest wall and the deepest sternal depression is considered significant. Another bedside determination, which is of historical interest, is the hollow index. This is the ratio between the amount of water contained in the chest depression and the body surface area. An index of greater than 50 mL/m^2 indicates the presence of pectus deformity. Radiographic techniques are most relied upon to assess the degree of pectus deformity. A minimal distance of less than 10 cm between the posterior border of the sternum and the anterior border of the thoracic vertebra on the lateral chest radiograph is considered significant for pectus. This measure, however, does not account for differences in body size. To address this question, the ratio of the AP to transverse diameters of the rib cage (as seen on the posteroanterior and lateral chest radiograph) is calculated. A ratio of less than 0.4 indicates

Table 83.9 Assessment of Severity of Pectus Deformity
A >3 cm distance between anterior chest wall and the sternal depression
A <10 cm distance between the posterior border of the sternum and the anterior border of the thoracic vertebra (as seen on the lateral chest radiograph)
AP/transverse diameters ratio of the rib cage <0.4 (as seen on PA and lateral chest radiographs)
Transverse/AP diameters ratio of the rib cage >3.25 (as seen on a CT scan at the level of the deepest sternal depression)

AP, anteroposterior diameter of the rib cage; PA, posteroanterior; CT, computed tomography.

Pre-OP

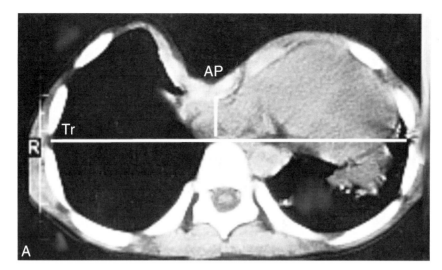

A

Post-OP

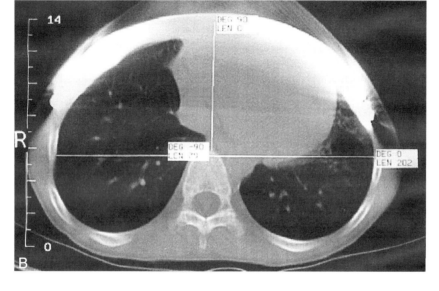

B

Figure 83.5 Preoperative chest CT scan of a patient with pectus excavatum, demonstrating a severely reduced anteroposterior (AP) diameter relative to the transverse rib cage diameter (Tr) (transverse/AP ratio = 8.6). Following the minimally invasive Nuss procedure, there is a greater AP distance.

the presence of pectus, and a ratio less than 0.3 indicates a severe deformity. However, better anatomic definition can be obtained with CT scans. Measurements of transverse and AP chest wall diameters are taken at the level of the deepest sternal depression (Fig. 83.5).[75,81] A ratio of the transverse to AP diameter of the inner chest wall of greater than 3.25 is considered significant for pectus. In some centers, this ratio has been used to select patients for surgical correction.

PATHOPHYSIOLOGY

Pulmonary Function and Respiratory Mechanics

Lung volumes are usually normal or mildly reduced (Table 83.2).[82–85a] If a restrictive impairment is present, it is positively associated with the degree of sternal depression and is more severe if there is associated scoliosis.[85,86] The RV may be normal[85] or slightly elevated.[85a,86] Any increase in RV is unlikely to be related to an obstructive process because the FEV_1/FVC ratio is typically within normal limits.[86] FRC is usually within the normal range.[85] Although deformed, the mobility of the rib cage is not impaired during quiet breathing or exercise.[83] Unlike kyphoscoliosis,

in which lung compliance is reduced because of limited chest wall mobility, lung compliance in pectus excavatum is within normal limits unless these patients develop intrinsic lung disease (Table 83.3).[82]

Exercise Capacity

Despite the high prevalence of subjective complaints of exercise intolerance, cardiopulmonary exercise testing is often normal.[86] In particular, the maximal work rate, oxygen consumption, and heart rate, as well as the oxygen pulse, are similar among patients with pectus excavatum and controls. In patients with more severe deformities, however, there may be a mild reduction in the maximal work rate[84] or a decrease in the oxygen consumption for a given work rate (Table 83.4).[82] The reduced exercise capacity in patients with pectus excavatum has been attributed to decreased venous return to the heart.[87] The association of pectus excavatum with right ventricular dysfunction is uncertain. The depressed sternum may compress the right atrium, reduce cardiac output, and limit exercise. In support of this assertion, cardiac anomalies, such as compression of the right ventricle, narrowing of the right ventricular outflow tract, and sacculations of the right ventricular wall, have been observed using two-dimensional cross-sectional echocardiography.[88] However, the results of the various clinical studies are controversial, and additional studies are needed to define the relationship between pectus excavatum and cardiac function.

TREATMENT

Candidates for surgical repair are patients with a transverse-to-AP diameter ratio of greater than 3.25 as determined by CT of the chest,[89] although patients with lesser degrees of deformity have also undergone repair. The surgical approach to pectus excavatum has evolved over time. The early operation (Ravitch repair) included resection of costal cartilage and sternal osteotomy with or without fixation of the sternum with external or internal supports.[74,90] A drawback of this approach is its invasive nature and the risk of sternal necrosis, infection, or recurrence of the deformity, especially in younger children in whom sternal supports are not used.

Over the last decade, less invasive approaches to pectus excavatum have been developed.[78,91] Of these, the Nuss procedure[91] is widely used as an alternative to the traditional corrective operation (Fig. 83.5). It involves placing a customized, curved metal bar under the sternum at the point of its deepest depression through small incisions made on each side of the chest. There is no need to resect costal cartilages as the sternum is pushed forward and stabilized by the metal bar. The bar is removed after 2 to 4 years when permanent chest wall remodeling has occurred.[92] The advantages of this technique include a minimally invasive approach with immediate cosmetic improvement, shorter operating time, less time to return to regular activities, and excellent long-term results.[91,92] Problems with this approach include bar displacement or rotation requiring reoperation, pneumothorax, pericarditis, and infection.[92] Surgical repair provides cosmetic benefits and may positively affect the psychosocial well-being of the patient.[93] The pathophysiologic benefits of the repair remain controversial. Exercise capacity and dyspnea[75,85] often improve, but pulmonary function typically decreases.[94] Because most studies on pulmonary function included patients who had undergone the more invasive Ravitch operation, the reduction in pulmonary function seen early or several years after surgical repair[84] has been attributed to abnormal chest wall mechanics as a result of articular changes in the sternal and parasternal areas.[95] The less invasive Nuss procedure might have fewer adverse effects on postoperative pulmonary function.[96]

The effects of surgery on exercise tolerance are also controversial. Improvements in exercise tolerance, cardiac output, and $\dot{V}O_{2max}$ after surgical correction have been reported in some[86,94] but not all,[84] studies. Discrepancies among studies regarding the benefits of surgery on pulmonary function and exercise tolerance may be related to differences in patient selection, surgical techniques, the period of time after the operation, and the effects of growth on pulmonary function.

To summarize, pectus deformities are often accompanied by complaints of exercise intolerance but are associated with only mild reductions in TLC and VC. Radiographic techniques used to measure the transverse and AP diameters of the chest wall are used to assist in selecting patients for surgery. After surgery, there is often symptomatic improvement and cosmetic benefit but no change in pulmonary function or aerobic capacity. Most studies have evaluated postoperative changes in pulmonary function in either young adolescents or adults. Whether younger patients may benefit from minimally invasive surgical correction because of the continued growth of the thorax during adolescence is unknown.

FLAIL CHEST

DIAGNOSIS AND ETIOLOGY

Flail chest denotes a condition in which fractures of ribs produce a segment of the rib cage that is disconnected from the rest of the chest wall and deforms markedly with breathing.[97] Usually, double fractures of three or more contiguous ribs or combined sternal and rib fractures are needed to create the flail segment.[98,99] As a result, the detached part of the rib segment is pulled inward with inspiration and bulges outward with expiration (Fig. 83.6), thereby compromising ventilation. Since the late 1980s there has been a renewed interest in flail chest from both a pathophysiological and therapeutic standpoint.[100-104]

In general, flail chest is more common in adults than in children; it is estimated to occur in up to 25% of adults but in only 1% of children following blunt chest trauma. This lower incidence in children may be related to their greater chest wall compliance.[105] The most common cause of flail chest is trauma related to automobile accidents or falls (Table 83.10). Flail chest may also be seen after chest compressions during cardiopulmonary resuscitation, with an estimated incidence of 5% in survivors of cardiopulmonary resuscitation.[106] In this group of patients, flail chest does not

Figure 83.6 Forces producing disordered chest wall motion in flail chest. **A,** During inspiration, the lowering of pleural pressure produces inward motion of the flail segment. **B,** During expiration, the increase in pleural pressure produces an outward displacement of the flail segment.

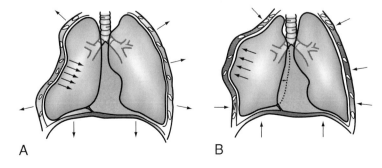

A   B

Table 83.10 Causes of Flail Chest

Trauma
    Automobile accidents, falls
    After cardiopulmonary resuscitation

Pathologic fractures (multiple myeloma, other rib metastases)
Sternectomy and simple rib fractures
Corrective rib resection
Congenital

Table 83.11 Pulmonary Function in Flail Chest Initially and 6 Months Following Injury

Parameter	Flail Chest		Flail Chest + Pulmonary Contusion	
	Initial	6 Months	Initial	6 Months
VC (% predicted)	60	100	50	88
FRC (% predicted)	60	75	45	50
FEV_1/FVC (%)	78	81	83	83

VC, vital capacity; FRC, functional residual capacity; FEV_1, forced expired volume in 1 second; FVC, forced vital capacity.
From Kishikawa M, Yoshioka T, Shimazu T, et al: Pulmonary contusion causes long-term respiratory dysfunction with decreased functional residual capacity. J Trauma 31:1203–1210, 1991.

appear to be related to the duration of resuscitation or age of the patient and does not regularly affect patient mortality or length of hospital stay.[106] Rarely, flail chest occurs with pathologic fractures of ribs, such as those due to multiple myeloma.[107] Total sternectomy by itself does not usually cause clinically significant flail chest. However, sternectomy in conjunction with simple rib fractures can lead to flail chest and respiratory failure.[108] Other rare causes of flail chest include excessive rib resection to correct rib deformities such as in idiopathic scoliosis[109] and abnormal rib development causing congenital flail chest, which may present with life-threatening respiratory failure.[110]

Flail chest is a clinical diagnosis that is usually made by observing the paradoxical motion of the chest wall in the spontaneously breathing patient with blunt trauma and subsequent radiographic documentation of rib or sternal fractures. Chest radiographs occasionally demonstrate the fractured ribs but often underestimate the presence and extent of rib fractures, especially in the presence of hemothorax and pulmonary contusion.[111] Special rib views or oblique films can diagnose many rib fractures missed by plain chest radiographs. Nuclear medicine scans are the most accurate in detecting rib fractures,[112] but this modality may not be needed because the diagnosis is primarily made on clinical grounds. A three-dimensional reconstruction of a thoracic helical-CT scan, which is often performed in the setting of blunt chest trauma to evaluate the extent of thoracic injuries, can also identify rib fractures.[113] The diagnosis may be delayed if the patient is intubated and ventilated with positive-pressure ventilation and become apparent only during weaning from mechanical ventilation.[114]

Traumatic flail chest is a marker of severe chest injury and an independent risk factor for significant respiratory complications, respiratory failure, and death.[115,116,116a] Flail chest promotes atelectasis and impairs effectiveness of cough, which can lead to retention of airway secretions and lung infections. Atelectasis, via its effect on lung compliance, may then increase the severity of flail chest and lead to worsening of respiratory failure. Patients with isolated flail chest developed respiratory failure and required mechanical ventilation almost twice as often (57%) as did patients with isolated pulmonary contusion (31%).[116] Because of an incompetent chest wall in patients with flail chest, external chest compressions during cardiopulmonary resuscitation are ineffective. In such cases, internal cardiac massage may be recommended.[117]

The mortality rate from chest wall trauma alone is high, ranging from 7% to 14%.[118] When chest wall trauma is complicated by flail chest, the mortality rate further increases.[97,98,115,116] In a series of 1026 multiple-trauma patients, the mortality rate for those with flail chest was 68%, compared with a 27% mortality rate for the entire group.[98] This high mortality is in part attributed to other associated injuries, such as fractures of long bones or vertebra, head trauma, rupture of the aortic arch or other arteries, and laceration of the liver or spleen. A significant correlate of survival in patients with traumatic flail chest is the presence or absence of head injury.[111] If the patient survives the initial injury, long-term disability after flail chest is relatively common. Symptoms consist of chest tightness, chest pain, or dyspnea on exertion in as many as half of patients.[119] Operative stabilization of the chronic flail chest can correct the defect and dramatically relieve the symptoms.[120]

The lung may also be injured in patients who sustain chest wall trauma. Pulmonary complications, such as pulmonary contusion, hemothorax, and pneumothorax, can occur in up to 60% of patients with flail chest.[120] Patients with multiple trauma and lung contusion had a mortality rate (56%) almost as high as those with flail chest (67%).[98] Pulmonary contusion is best detected by chest CT scans. If the contusion is seen on the chest radiograph, however, it may be more clinically significant.[121]

PATHOPHYSIOLOGY

Pulmonary Function

Flail chest can severely impair pulmonary function. TLC, VC, and FRC can be reduced to 50% of predicted (Table 83.11). The initial reductions in FRC and VC after flail chest can be attributed to disordered chest wall motion. VC either returns to its baseline value within 6 months[122] or remains mildly reduced.[119] In contrast, patients with pulmonary contusion complicating flail chest may have persistent reductions in FRC for up to 4 years,[122] which may be due to fibrous changes in the contused area. Thus, flail chest with pulmonary contusion may cause more long-term respiratory dysfunction than flail chest without contusion.

Respiratory Mechanics

Flail chest alters the mechanics of breathing. Normally, pleural pressure is reduced during inspiration. This subatmospheric pressure is inflationary to the lung but deflationary to the rib cage. Unlike the changes in pleural pressure, it is the passive outward recoil of the rib cage, the insertional actions of the diaphragm and intercostal muscles, and the rise of abdominal pressure during inspiration that promotes rib cage expansion during inspiration. With flail chest, the multiple rib fractures uncouple the flail segment from the remainder of the chest wall. The usual factors that promote rib cage expansion, therefore, are not operant on the flail segment. Consequently, during inspiration, the sub-atmospheric pleural pressure is unopposed, and the uncoupled segment of chest wall moves paradoxically inward during inspiration. During expiration, pleural pressure becomes less negative, and the flail segment can be seen moving paradoxically outward. A reduction in lung compliance due to pulmonary contusion or microatelectasis or an increase in airway resistance further lowers pleural pressure during inspiration and worsens the flail.

On the basis of rib fractures and anatomic location of flail segment, three types of flail chest have been described: lateral, anterior, and posterior. Lateral flail chest is the most common; in this instance, the flail segment is located posteriorly and laterally. Anterior flail chest occurs when there is separation of the sternum from the ribs. Posterior flail chest is associated with less severe clinical derangement because of splinting provided by the back muscles. However, this anatomic classification is merely descriptive and does not provide any information about the actual degree of chest wall distortion in flail chest. Chest wall distortion is better characterized by recording the respiratory changes in the dimensions of not only the rib cage but also the abdomen. Paradoxical motion may occur between the rib cage and abdomen or within the rib cage itself. Abnormal patterns that have been described[100] include (1) inward displacement of the transverse rib cage as the lower anterior rib cage and abdomen are expanding, (2) inward displacement of the anterior lower rib cage and abdomen as the transverse rib cage is expanding, and (3) inward displacement of the lower rib cage as the transverse rib cage and abdomen are expanding. It should be noted that a given location of flail segment is not necessarily associated with a specific pattern of distortion,[100] and the same anatomic location may be associated with one or more patterns of chest

wall distortion.[100] These different flail patterns may therefore reflect not only differences in the location of the rib cage fractures but also differences in respiratory muscle recruitment patterns. Support for the latter mechanism comes from the observation that external intercostal electromyographic activity is increased by more than threefold in the involved area.[101]

Respiratory Failure

The pathogenesis of respiratory failure in flail chest has intrigued clinicians for many years. Initially, respiratory failure was attributed to *pendelluft*, referring to an abnormal movement of air from the injured to the uninjured side during inspiration and the reverse occurring during expiration.[123] Clinical observations and recent experimental data suggest that the pathogenesis is complex, and that there are several contributing factors including hypoventilation and the flail-induced changes in lung and muscle function (Fig. 83.7). The effects of lung contusion, which frequently accompanies flail chest, are usually additive.

The argument that the flail segment per se is unimportant and does not lead to respiratory failure has been challenged.[124] Current evidence suggests that the flail chest and the pain that invariably accompanies chest trauma lead to cough impairment, regional atelectasis, rib cage muscle spasm, and specific changes in the pattern of muscle activation and recruitment. This altered muscle function may determine, to a large extent, both the magnitude and the pattern of rib cage paradox seen in these patients.[102] Furthermore, the paradoxical motion of the flail segment may also increase the degree of muscle shortening during inspiration. This excess muscle shortening represents "internal work," which is not measured using standard techniques yet has an energetic cost. In addition to the added muscle shortening during inspiration, any associated process, such as pulmonary contusion or pleural restriction, further adds to the work of breathing by increasing the negative pressure needed to inhale. Because the inspiratory muscles become inefficient when operating over shorter lengths,[125] the paradoxical motion of the flail segment may result in diaphragm inefficiency. The added work of breathing, along

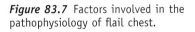

Figure 83.7 Factors involved in the pathophysiology of flail chest.

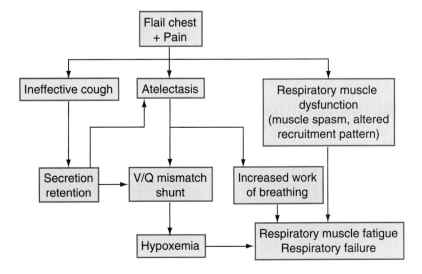

with respiratory muscle inefficiency, increases the oxygen cost of breathing and predisposes these muscles to fatigue (Fig. 83.7). Atelectasis and lung contusion in conjunction with respiratory muscle fatigue result in hypoxemia, hypercapnia, and ultimately respiratory failure. Hypoxemia due to either process would contribute to respiratory muscle dysfunction by reducing energy supplies to the muscles.

TREATMENT

General Aspects

The management of flail chest has undergone significant changes over the last 50 years and is still evolving. The primary goal of treatment is to restore the anatomic and functional integrity of the chest wall by providing stability of the flail segment. This can be accomplished with conservative management, which may or may not include intubation and mechanical ventilation, or with surgical intervention. The most appropriate treatment approach for a given patient can be difficult to determine.

Because of its central role in the development of respiratory failure, pain should be adequately controlled in all patients with flail chest. Chest wall pain may cause patients to adopt a rapid, shallow breathing pattern, which can further worsen atelectasis and lead to arteriovenous shunting and hypoxemia. Adequate pain relief, therefore, is imperative not only for patient comfort but also because it reduces splinting, improves tidal volume, and facilitates cough. Pain control can be accomplished by oral medications, patient-controlled analgesia pumps, intermittent intercostal nerve blocks, or epidural anesthesia. Many patients can be treated successfully with adequate pain relief, supplemental oxygen, tracheobronchial toilet, and cautious fluid replacement.

Mechanical Ventilation

Mechanical ventilation has been used in the treatment of flail chest for more than 40 years.[126] In fact, during the 1950s the advent of positive-pressure ventilation provided a nonsurgical means of stabilizing the flail segment. Such "internal pneumatic stabilization" consisted of tracheostomy with a prolonged 3- to 5-week period of mechanical ventilation. This approach had been the accepted form of treatment for nearly two decades. However, mechanical ventilation failed to improve survival and predisposed patients to several complications such as pneumonia, barotrauma, sepsis, and tracheal stenosis.[124,127] Consequently, continuous prolonged mechanical ventilation is no longer recommended as a primary means of stabilizing the chest wall; rather, it is recommended when there is concomitant central nervous system or intra-abdominal injury, shock, or a need to operate for other injuries.

The role of noninvasive mechanical ventilation in stabilizing the flail segment has not been fully evaluated in patients with flail chest.[103,107,128] Noninvasive ventilation can be delivered via a nasal or face mask to selected patients with spontaneous breathing and intact ability to protect the upper airway. Unlike intubation and invasive ventilation, this ventilatory mode, in conjunction with regional anesthesia, can improve gas exchange, allow physiotherapy and early patient mobilization, and significantly reduce morbidity and length of hospitalization in selected patients with flail chest.[103,129]

When mechanical ventilation is needed to treat respiratory failure, the mode of ventilation chosen should minimize the resistive and elastic loads imposed by the ventilator. Although intermittent mandatory ventilation (IMV) has been frequently used as a mode of ventilating patients with flail chest,[130] spontaneous breaths through the added resistance of the IMV circuit may aggravate chest wall distortion. In contrast, low impedance modes, such as high-flow continuous positive airway pressure (CPAP), are accompanied by less chest wall distortion during inspiration.[100] Low impedance modes of ventilation may therefore reduce the risk for inspiratory muscle fatigue and may be preferred for weaning. This speculation is supported by a randomized controlled trial in which patients treated with mask CPAP alone have fewer complications, fewer hospital and intensive care unit (ICU) days, and less ventilator time than patients with similar degrees of blunt thoracic trauma treated with assist-control ventilation.[103] Pressure support ventilation may be an alternate means of reducing the ventilator-imposed loads, but the effects of this mode on chest wall distortion have not been evaluated.

Surgical Management

The purpose of surgical stabilization is to achieve a mechanically stable chest wall to reduce ventilator time and avoid ventilator-associated complications. Attempts to stabilize the flail segment surgically have been made for decades. Initial attempts consisted of applying tape, strapping, and external devices to the chest wall. These attempts met with limited success. Over the last decade, the role of more invasive surgical techniques to fixate the flail segment externally has been reevaluated. Surgical techniques incorporate the use of wires, steel plates, and staples to approximate the fractured ribs. By externally stabilizing the chest wall, inward displacement of the ribs during the healing phase can be avoided, and the chest wall contour can be restored to normal. In the absence of randomized studies, the overall role and effectiveness of this modality is not defined. In patients with severe flail chest and respiratory failure requiring intubation and mechanical ventilation, a recent randomized study showed surgical stabilization performed during the first week of therapy was superior to mechanical ventilation with respect to the duration of ventilatory support, infection rate, and length of ICU stay.[131] Although the indications of operative chest wall stabilization in flail chest are still evolving, they most likely include ventilator-dependent patients able to protect their upper airways and with no concurrent problems for which they need prolonged mechanical ventilation.[104] Candidates for operative stabilization may also be flail chest patients undergoing thoracotomy for intrathoracic injuries.[104] In addition, young patients with severe chest wall deformation and patients with large, unstable segments ("stove-in chest") and borderline pulmonary function may be candidates for external fixation. Chest wall external fixation in such patients improves respiratory mechanics, reduces the duration of mechanical ventilation, reduces hospital stay, and decreases the incidence of pulmonary infection and barotrauma.[99,104,132]

To summarize, flail chest carries a high risk for acute respiratory failure and is associated with a high mortality rate. Complications that accompany chest trauma, such as ARDS, tracheal injury, and pneumonia, may further increase the mortality in this patient population. Adverse effects of flail chest on the respiratory system include (1) a reduction in VC as a result of inward displacement of the rib cage, (2) an increase in the work of breathing and energy demands of the inspiratory muscles, and (3) hypoxemia due to underlying pulmonary contusion or microatelectasis. The essential components of treatment include pain control and mechanical ventilation for respiratory failure. Surgical fixation of the flail segment may be indicated in some patients and may reduce the duration of mechanical ventilation. When mechanical ventilation is needed to treat respiratory failure, modes of ventilation should be chosen that reduce the elastic and resistive loads on the respiratory system.

ANKYLOSING SPONDYLITIS

DIAGNOSIS AND ETIOLOGY

Ankylosing spondylitis is a rheumatic disease characterized by chronic inflammation of the ligamentous structures of the spine and the sacroiliac and large peripheral joints. It commonly afflicts men and has a genetic predisposition, with 95% of white persons with primary ankylosing spondylitis being positive for the HLA-B27 antigen.[133] Over time, chronic inflammation of the spinal structures and sacroiliac joints results in fibrosis and ossification of these structures, bony ankylosis of the costovertebral and sternoclavicular joints, and ultimately rigidity of the spine and immobility of the rib cage.

Individuals with ankylosing spondylitis typically complain of chronic low back pain and stiffness in the back and other affected joints; symptoms are usually worse in the morning or after rest. Systemic manifestations occur in as many as 10% to 20% of patients and include iritis, aortic insufficiency, heart block, and diastolic dysfunction. Dyspnea and chest wall pain are uncommon. If present, they may be related to chest wall restriction, kyphosis, upper lobe fibrobullous disease, or interstitial lung disease. Occasionally, patients experience mild exercise intolerance. Respiratory failure is uncommon unless the patient has underlying lung disease, diaphragm dysfunction, or cardiac disease. Upper airway obstruction is an infrequent complication of ankylosing spondylitis and is due to involvement of the cricoarytenoid cartilage. When it occurs, patients may present with hoarseness or stridor.[134]

PATHOPHYSIOLOGY

Pulmonary Function and Mechanics

Rib cage expansion is often severely limited in patients with ankylosing spondylitis. Although the direction of rib movement is similar to that in normals, the magnitude of movement is severely restricted.[135] During a VC maneuver, the rib cage may expand by only 2.5 cm, less than half of what is expected.[133] Despite this limited expansion of the rib cage, VC is only mildly reduced to 70% of predicted and the TLC to 80% of predicted (Table 83.2).[136–139b] The reduction in

lung volume, if present, is proportional to the radiographic severity of the spinal ankylosis, the degree of spinal immobility, and the degree of rib cage immobility.[138,139] The reduced lung volume is also positively correlated with disease activity and duration.[137] Because the rib cage is often fixed in an inspiratory position, both FRC and RV may be increased above the predicted levels. Reduced rib cage mobility may also lead to a reduction in chest wall and respiratory system compliance values and to an increase in chest wall resistance.[136] Lung compliance is generally normal unless there is concomitant fibrobullous or interstitial lung disease.[140]

The mild restrictive process seen in ankylosing spondylitis is worsened by concomitant kyphosis. However, there is no correlation between the kyphosis angle and the reduction in vital capacity in ankylosing spondylitis. This lack of correlation may be due to the posterior fusion of the ribs playing a greater role in causing restriction than the degree of kyphosis.[139] Nonetheless, surgical correction of kyphosis in these patients may improve respiratory function.[141]

Respiratory Muscle Function

Modest reductions in PImax and PEmax of 56% and 76% of predicted, respectively, have been reported with ankylosing spondylitis and may contribute to the mild restrictive process (Table 83.3).[138,139a] The reduction in PImax may reflect intercostal muscle weakness rather than diaphragm dysfunction. The severe limitation of rib cage expansion with ankylosing spondylitis may promote intercostal muscle atrophy and increase the diaphragm's contribution to the inhaled volume.[142] It appears that the diaphragm is strong enough to compensate for the impaired rib cage excursion, because these patients have only a mild reduction in vital capacity.

Exercise Capacity

Exercise capacity may be reduced in patients with ankylosing spondylitis.[139] The lack of correlation between the degree of chest wall expansion and $\dot{V}O_{2max}$ or maximal work rate suggests that deconditioning rather than ventilatory impairment contributes to exercise intolerance in these patients (Table 83.4).

Gas Exchange

The arterial PO_2 is either normal or slightly decreased in patients with ankylosing spondylitis. Reductions in diffusion capacity usually can be attributed to reductions in lung volume.[138] However, gas exchange may be severely compromised in those patients who have associated interstitial lung disease. With the exception of apical fibrobullous disease, regional ventilation is normal despite restriction of the rib cage.[143]

Interstitial Lung Disease

About 1% to 4% of patients with ankylosing spondylitis, especially men with chronic disease, develop fibrobullous upper lobe disease.[144,145] The cause of apical fibrobullous disease is unknown. Diminished upper lobe ventilation and apical mechanical stress due to thoracic rigidity, as well as recurrent pulmonary infections due to impaired cough, have been proposed as predisposing factors.[146] The spectrum of fibrobullous disease ranges from minimal upper lobe interstitial infiltrates to marked fibrosis, honeycombing, and cavity formation that may mimic tuberculosis. These patients usually do not have symptoms but are at risk for spontaneous pneumothorax and aspergillosis or mycobacterial infection. Corticosteroids have been used to treat symptoms, but they do not prevent progression of the disease.[144] Because thoracic surgery for fibrobullous disease is complicated by bronchopleural fistula in 50% to 60% of patients, it is recommended only for the treatment of major hemoptysis.[144] Another 10% to 20% of patients with ankylosing spondylitis develop nonapical interstitial lung disease, which can be detected by high-resolution CT scans of the chest.[139b,145]

TREATMENT

Medical therapy for adult patients with ankylosing spondylitis is both preventive and supportive. Tobacco use should be avoided and baseline chest radiography and spirometry performed. Cardiorespiratory fitness and spinal mobility may be enhanced by instituting exercise and physiotherapy programs, but there may be little or no change in pulmonary function despite improved chest wall and spinal mobility.[147] Similarly, specific pulmonary rehabilitation has been tried with varied success. Recently, treatment with TNF antagonists such as infliximab, an antibody to tumor necrosis factor-alpha, and etanercept, a TNF receptor fusion protein, have been found to be effective in reducing the activity of the disease and improving quality of life.[148,148a] These patients are usually managed by a clinician skillful in the treatment of rheumatic disease but are often referred to a pulmonologist for evaluation of abnormal chest radiographs, deteriorating pulmonary function, hypoxemia, or hypercapnia. If intubation is required, it should be performed with caution because these patients are at increased risk for spinal cord injury because of involvement of the cricoarytenoid joint.[149]

To summarize, ankylosing spondylitis is a chronic inflammatory disease that may limit spinal flexion and rib cage expansion and is sometimes associated with interstitial lung disease. The reduced rib cage mobility leads to only mild reductions in VC and TLC and possibly to atrophy of the inspiratory muscles of the rib cage. This mild restrictive disease may contribute to exercise intolerance in these patients.

OBESITY

DIAGNOSIS AND ETIOLOGY

This section focuses mainly on the respiratory effects of obesity uncomplicated by coexistent obstructive airway disease or restrictive disease of the lungs. Even uncomplicated or "simple" obesity exerts substantial effects on pulmonary gas exchange, oxygenation of the blood, and the work of breathing; and it has modest effects on ventilatory drive and the pattern of breathing. Obese patients often complain of exercise intolerance and dyspnea during exertion. In addition, they are at increased risk for complications such as pneumonia, hypoxemia, atelectasis, and pulmonary embolism. Patients with simple obesity do not have ventilatory failure, but some manifestations of the obesity hypoventilation syndrome (OHS) are presented for the sake of comparison. The OHS and its relation to obstructive sleep apnea are covered in Chapters 73 and 74.

Obesity constitutes a significant health problem worldwide, and its prevalence continues to increase in many countries. In the United States, it is estimated that more than half of all adults are overweight or obese,[150] an increase of more than 25% over the last three decades. Also, the number of individuals with severe obesity has tripled over the last decade.[151] It is a leading cause of preventable death in the United States, second only to cigarette smoking.

The severity of obesity can be assessed from several indices that relate weight to height. The most commonly used indicator is the body mass index (BMI), which is calculated as body weight (BW) in kilograms divided by the square of the height (Ht) in meters (BW/Ht^2). The BMI (kg/m^2) can also be calculated as the weight in pounds multiplied by 703 and then divided by the square of the height in inches. Morbidity and mortality associated with obesity seem to increase with increasing BMI. Intra-abdominal fat distribution is also an independent risk for cardiovascular disease and mortality.[152] Both the World Health Organization and the National Institutes of Health have classified obesity as follows: an individual with a BMI between 18.5 and 24.9 kg/m^2 is normal, with a BMI between 25.0 and 29.9 kg/m^2 is overweight, and with a BMI greater than 30.0 kg/m^2 is obese. Obesity is severe when the BMI is greater than 40 kg/m^2.

Body fat usually constitutes 15% to 20% of the body mass in healthy men and 25% to 30% in healthy women. In obesity, the body fat content may increase by as much as 500% in women and 800% in men, and the body fat mass is proportional to the BMI.[153,154] The fat-free mass increases along with the fat mass, so 15% to 30% of the weight gain in obesity results from increased fat-free mass.[154,155] Resting energy expenditure is proportional to the fat-free mass, and the ratio of energy expenditure to the fat-free mass is the same in patients with mild and severe obesity as it is in normal-weight subjects (Table 83.12).[154]

Table 83.12 Body Composition in Obesity			
Parameter	Normal	Mild Obesity	Severe Obesity
Body mass index (kg/m^2)	23	34	50
Body fat (%)	22	35	45
Body weight (kg)	65	96	132
Fat-free mass (kg)	51	63	72
Body cell mass (kg)	27	32	36
Total body water (L)	38	44	49
Resting energy expenditure (watts)	68	86	96

The distribution of obesity also has an effect on the respiratory function, independent of the body fat content per se, and appears to vary with age.[156] Upper body or central fat distribution has a greater effect on pulmonary function than lower body fat distribution. Furthermore, abdominal fat distribution is more often associated with sleep-disordered breathing.[157] Methods to assess the distribution of body fat include measurement of the waist/hip circumference ratio, the abdominal girth/hip breadth ratio, and the thickness of skin folds at multiple sites as well as the use of CT or magnetic resonance imaging to assess the cross-sectional area of the visceral fat/subcutaneous fat ratio. A waist circumference of 35 inches or more for women and 40 inches or more for men indicates upper body fat distribution.[158]

Obesity can be evaluated in three contexts: simple obesity, in which individuals are eucapnic with no pulmonary compromise; morbid obesity, in which pulmonary complications are present; obesity hypoventilation, in which there is morbid obesity with carbon dioxide retention during wakefulness.

PATHOPHYSIOLOGY

Pulmonary Function

Tests of pulmonary function are only minimally affected in simple obesity unless the obesity is severe.[159] The most common abnormality is a decrease in expiratory reserve volume (ERV) and FRC[159] due to the effects of abdominal contents on the position of the diaphragm. The ERV is reduced, on average, to 60% of the predicted normal value and is inversely proportional to the BMI. VC and TLC are usually normal in simple obesity (Table 83.13) but may be reduced by 20% to 30% in morbid obesity.[159–161] In general, RV is not reduced in simple obesity. Consequently, the RV/TLC ratio may be greater than normal when obesity causes restriction.[159] Spirometry is generally normal in simple obesity except for a modest reduction in VC or FVC

when the BMI exceeds 45 kg/m².[160–162] The FEV_1/FVC ratio is usually normal. MVV and peak inspiratory flow rate are also normal, provided respiratory muscle strength is normal.[161] Pulmonary function of obese patients is reviewed in detail in Chapter 24.

Spirometry in individuals with obesity hypoventilation syndrome (OHS) usually reveals a more severe restrictive pattern with reductions in TLC, VC, MVV, and peak inspiratory flow rate.[161,162] This appears to be related to weakness of the respiratory muscles.[161] The ERV may be reduced to 35% of predicted and the FVC to 60% of predicted.[162] It appears that the adverse effects of obesity on pulmonary function cannot be entirely explained by the absolute load of adipose tissue on the chest wall because similar degrees of obesity in simple obesity and OHS result in different patterns of lung volume changes (Table 83.13).

Respiratory Mechanics

Obesity generally lowers compliance of the lung, chest wall, and total respiratory system. These changes are more pronounced with OHS.[160,162] Respiratory system compliance decreases exponentially as a function of increased BMI.[163] In simple obesity, chest wall and total respiratory system compliance values are generally 80% and 90%, respectively, of values obtained in normal subjects even when the body weight/height ratio and BMI are as high as 1.2 kg/cm and 80 kg/m², respectively.[162] In OHS, the chest wall and total respiratory system compliance values are generally less than 45% of normal. The changes in compliance are thought to be due to weight pressing on the thorax and abdomen, thereby imposing an elastic load. In addition, the excess weight may impose a threshold-type load on the chest wall in which pleural pressure must be lowered to a sufficient degree before inspiratory flow can begin.

Obesity is associated with increases in airway and respiratory system resistance, in part because of the reduction in lung volume.[160,164] However, even after correcting for lung volume, specific airway conductance may be reduced to 50% to 70% of normal.[160,162,164] Because the FEV_1/FVC ratio is normal, the source of the increased airway resistance in obesity appears to lie in lung tissue and small airways rather than in the large airways. Chest wall and total respiratory system resistances are increased more in OHS than in simple obesity.[162] Part of the impediment to breathing in obesity results from a two- to threefold increase in intra-abdominal pressure.[165]

The transition from upright to the supine position may alter the respiratory mechanics by further decreasing respiratory system compliance and increasing respiratory resistance in severe obesity.[164,166] This alteration is attributed to a reduction in lung volume due to increased intra-abdominal pressure.[165,167] The same mechanism, especially in the supine position, can promote expiratory flow limitation during tidal breathing and may lead to the development of intrinsic positive end-expiratory pressure (PEEP) and orthopnea in severe obesity.[168,169] The increased elastic and resistive loads imposed by the lung and chest wall, along with the threshold load imposed by the abdominal fat mass, increase the work of breathing in both simple obesity and OHS. When compared with normal, the work of breathing is 60% higher in simple obesity and may be as much as 250% higher in OHS. The

Table 83.13 Respiratory Pathophysiology of Simple Obesity and Obesity Hypoventilation Syndrome

Parameter	Normal	Simple Obesity	Obesity Hypoventilation
BW (% ideal)	105	195	201
BW/Ht (kg/cm)	0.42	0.75	0.78
BMI (kg/m²)	24	45	46
TLC (% Predicted)	100	95	83
CRS (L/cm H₂O)	0.11	0.05	0.06
RRS (cm H₂O·L⁻¹·sec⁻¹)	1.2	4.0	7.8
Work (J/L)	0.43	0.74	1.64
MVV (L/min)	159	129	89
PImax (cm H₂O)	100	95	60

BW, body weight; BMI, body mass index; TLC, total lung capacity; CRS, compliance of the respiratory system; J, joule; RRS, respiratory system resistance; PImax, maximal inspiratory pressure; MVV, maximum ventilatory volume.

increased work is accompanied by an increase in the energy cost of breathing; the oxygen cost of breathing at rest in simple obesity is about five times normal, and that in OHS is nearly 10 times normal.[162,170] This disproportionately high percentage of the total body $\dot{V}O_2$ required for quiet breathing may place obese patients at risk for respiratory failure during conditions characterized by increased ventilatory demands such as an intercurrent illness.[170]

Gas Exchange

Hypoxemia may be mild or absent in simple obesity.[171] However, gas exchange is usually impaired, and severely obese patients tend to have a widened alveolar-arterial oxygen tension gradient.[172] The arterial PO_2 is even lower in OHS.[172] In both simple obesity and OHS, hypoxemia becomes more pronounced when assuming the supine position, which can be a major concern during anesthesia induction.[173] The single-breath diffusion capacity is usually normal or increased in simple obesity[162] and slightly reduced in OHS.[162] The physiologic dead space (VD) and the dead space/tidal volume ratio (VD/VT) are normal.[162]

The mechanism responsible for hypoxemia is primarily a ventilation-perfusion mismatch that results from airway closure,[174] although in OHS venous admixture and hypoventilation may also contribute. With obesity, the lung bases are well perfused but poorly ventilated because of airway closure and alveolar collapse.[175] Weight loss, via its effect on the FRC and prevention of airway closure during tidal breathing, improves oxygen saturation.[176] The practical consequence of a reduced FRC and the increased metabolic rate in obesity is that the rate at which arterial SO_2 falls during apnea is three times faster in obese subjects than in normal-weight subjects.[177]

Control of Breathing

In obese eucapnic individuals, the resting ventilation and the respiratory drive are either normal or increased when compared with those of nonobese subjects,[162,178] as are the ventilatory responses to hypoxia and hypercapnia.[178] The diaphragm electrical (electromyography, or EMG) response to inhalation of carbon dioxide, another index of the central ventilatory drive, is also elevated in simple obesity.[162] Because the work of breathing is increased in obesity, the increase in ventilatory drive appears to be an appropriate compensatory response. This increased chemosensitivity in simple obesity may correlate with the BMI and can decrease following weight loss.[178]

In patients with OHS, the ventilatory drive is inappropriately low. In addition, there is significant depression of the ventilatory response to hypercapnic stimulation with analogous reductions in both the $P_{0.1}$ and the diaphragmatic EMG.[179] The ventilatory response to carbon dioxide is reduced by about 65%, but arterial PCO_2 can be lowered to a normal level by voluntary hyperventilation in OHS.[180] The ventilatory response to hypoxia is also decreased, frequently to a greater extent that the hypercapnic response.[181] The etiology of the attenuated ventilatory drive in patients with OHS is not fully known but may be related to a genetically determined predisposition or other acquired causes (hypoxemia, sleep apnea). The role of leptin in the pathogenesis

of hypoventilation in obesity is currently under investigation. Leptin, a protein produced by adipose tissue, acts within the hypothalamus to suppress appetite. Recent studies have suggested that insufficient central nervous system leptin levels in the presence of severe obesity may contribute to the development of OHS.[182,183]

Pattern of Breathing

Obese patients may also alter their breathing pattern to compensate for the increased load placed on the respiratory system. During quiet breathing, the respiratory rate in subjects with simple obesity is about 40% higher than in normal-weight subjects. The increased rate is accomplished by shortening both inspiratory and expiratory times, and the ratio of inspiratory to total breath time is normal. In contrast to the increase in breathing frequency, VT remains normal in simple obesity both at rest and during maximal exercise.[162] In OHS, however, breathing frequency is 25% higher, and VT is 25% lower than in those with simple obesity; and the rapid, shallow breathing pattern in OHS contributes to carbon dioxide retention.[162]

Respiratory Muscle Function and Dyspnea

Inspiratory and expiratory muscle strength is usually normal in seated patients with simple obesity.[184,185] In severely obese subjects, especially those with dyspnea or OHS,[185] reductions of diaphragmatic function are found more frequently and are perhaps related to overstretching of the diaphragm, especially in the recumbent position.[186] The inspiratory muscles of subjects with simple obesity are strong enough to overcome the reduction in lung and chest wall compliance so that TLC is not reduced, whereas in OHS, respiratory muscle endurance is decreased. In OHS, inspiratory muscle strength may be reduced by 40%,[162] perhaps because of deconditioning or other factors related to chronic disease.

Mild dyspnea at rest is an infrequent complaint of patients with simple obesity[185]; it is associated with greater BMI, mild expiratory muscle weakness, and peripheral airway disease.[185] The latter may indicate that dyspnea in this group of patients results from the interaction of obesity and a minor degree of airway obstruction, not from the obesity per se.[187]

Exercise Capacity

In simple obesity, exercise capacity is near normal. Minute ventilation, respiratory rate, heart rate, and oxygen consumption during treadmill exercise are higher in obese subjects than in normal-weight subjects,[188] but $\dot{V}O_2$ at anaerobic threshold is lower than in normal-weight subjects.[189] With weight loss, the metabolic demands are reduced, and carbon dioxide production and alveolar ventilation during exercise fall by 12% to 22%.[162]

TREATMENT

Weight Reduction

The optimal treatment for obesity is weight loss, but it is difficult for patients to lose weight and even more difficult to remain at the lower weight. The problem is that losing weight decreases total energy expenditure in both normal and obese subjects, whereas the opposite is true with weight gain.[155] With weight loss, the percentage reduction in resting energy expenditure exceeds the percentage reduction in fat-free mass. In other words, the body has a tendency to resist changes in weight.

The effects of weight loss, induced by diet or surgery, on pulmonary function in simple obesity have been well documented.[162,190,191,191a] With a weight loss of 40 kg, there is either no change or a small increase in VC, TLC, and compliance. However, there is a 75% increase in ERV and lesser increases in FRC and RV. These changes are associated with better ventilation to the lung bases, and the arterial PO_2 may be increased by about 4 to 8 mm Hg.[162,171] In OHS, the effects of weight loss on ERV and FRC are even more pronounced, and VC increases as well. The increases in VC and arterial PO_2 and the fall in arterial PCO_2 are positively correlated with weight loss.[162]

In one study of simple obesity, weight loss led to a small decrease in PEmax, suggesting some respiratory muscle weakness, but also a small increase in MVV.[191] Alternatively, respiratory muscle strength and especially endurance may improve, with the improvement in endurance correlated with weight loss. There is a significant reduction in the oxygen consumption needed for a given exercise power output.[190] Respiratory control remains essentially unaltered after weight loss.[162]

Mechanical Ventilation

Bilevel positive airway pressure has been used successfully to treat atelectasis after gastroplasty.[192] Obese patients who experience nocturnal or nocturnal and daytime hypercapnia generally require some form of mechanical ventilation. Negative-pressure ventilation can improve nocturnal oxygenation, but it often aggravates upper airway obstruction during sleep. Positive-pressure ventilation delivered by nose mask improves sleep quality, corrects hypercapnia, and improves daytime oxygenation.[193,194]

SUMMARY

Chest wall diseases, including obesity, exert important effects on the respiratory system. Initially, the lungs may be normal; but when the primary problem is severe, there can be multiple pulmonary complications, including atelectasis, pneumonia, hypoxemia, and hypercapnia. Among the diseases discussed in this chapter, flail chest is the most likely to precipitate acute respiratory failure. Kyphoscoliosis, restrictive disease due to previous thoracoplasty, and severe obesity are the diseases most likely to lead to chronic ventilatory failure, pulmonary hypertension, and cor pulmonale. In these patients, the stiff chest wall imposes a large elastic load on the respiratory muscles, which increases the work of breathing and impairs lung function. Coincident inspiratory muscle weakness in any of these disorders and sleep-related dysfunction also contribute to daytime hypercapnia, cor pulmonale, and pulmonary hypertension. Acute respiratory failure is treated with positive-pressure ventilation. In some patients with flail chest, surgical fixation of the flail segment may reduce the duration of mechanical ventilation. Chronic respiratory failure, which can be seen in kyphoscoliosis, after thoracoplasty, or with severe obesity, can be successfully managed with nocturnal positive-pressure ventilation. This therapy reduces morbidity and mortality from respiratory failure and improves prognosis.

Other diseases of the chest wall, such as ankylosing spondylitis, pectus excavatum, and simple obesity, impair respiratory function only mildly. These patients often have complaints of exercise intolerance but have only mild reductions in lung volumes and in exercise capacity. Surgical repair of pectus is performed in older children or adolescents. After repair of the pectus deformity, there is often symptomatic improvement but no change in aerobic capacity.

More discussion about the pathophysiology and management of pulmonary hypertension and cor pulmonale can be found in Chapter 52. Further information about the pathophysiology and treatment of respiratory failure is provided in Chapters 84 to 86. The role of rehabilitation in management is considered in Chapter 88. The interested reader should consult these chapters for further details about the diagnosis, treatment, and prevention of the pulmonary complications of chest wall disorders.

REFERENCES

1. Bergofsky EH, Turino GM, Fishman AP: Cardiorespiratory failure in kyphoscoliosis. Medicine (Baltimore) 38:263–317, 1959.
2. Kane WJ: Prevalence of scoliosis. Clin Orthop 126:3–46, 1977.
3. Walker JL, Nelson KR, Stevens DB, et al: Spinal deformity in Charcot-Marie-Tooth disease. Spine 19:1044–1047, 1994.
4. Cobb JR: Outline for the study of scoliosis. AAOS Instruct Course Lect 5:261–275, 1948.
5. Bjure J, Grimby G, Kasalicky J, et al: Respiratory impairment and airway closure in patients with untreated idiopathic scoliosis. Thorax 25:451–456, 1970.
6. Lisboa C, Moreno R, Fava M, et al: Inspiratory muscle function in patients with severe kyphoscoliosis. Am Rev Respir Dis 132:48–52, 1985.
7. Kafer ER: Respiratory function in paralytic scoliosis. Am Rev Respir Dis 119:450–457, 1974.
8. Smyth RJ, Chapman KR, Wright TA, et al: Pulmonary function in adolescents with mild idiopathic scoliosis. Thorax 39:901–904, 1984.
9. Kearon C, Viviani GR, Kirkley KJ, et al: Factors determining pulmonary function in adolescent idiopathic thoracic scoliosis. Am Rev Respir Dis 148:288–294, 1993.
10. Lin MC, Liaw MY, Chen WJ, et al: Pulmonary function and spinal characteristics: Their relationships in persons with idiopathic and postpoliomyelitic scoliosis. Arch Phys Med Rehabil 82:335–341, 2001.
11. Jackson RP, Simmons EH, Stripinis D: Coronal and sagittal plane spinal deformities correlating with back pain and pulmonary function in adult idiopathic scoliosis. Spine 14:1391–1397, 1989.
12. Baydur A, Milic-Emili J: Respiratory mechanics in kyphoscoliosis. Monaldi Arch Chest Dis 48:69–79, 1993.
13. Al-Kattan K, Simonds A, Chung KF, et al: Kyphoscoliosis and bronchial torsion. Chest 111:1134–1137, 1997.
14. Wright PM, Alexander JP: Acute airway obstruction, hypertension and kyphoscoliosis. Anaesthesia 46:119–121, 1991.

15. Bergofsky EH: Respiratory failure in disorders of the thoracic cage. Am Rev Respir Dis 119:643–669, 1979.

16. Olgiati R, Levine D, Smith JP, et al: Diffusing capacity in idiopathic scoliosis and its interpretation regarding alveolar development. Am Rev Respir Dis 126:229–234, 1982.

17. Jones RS, Kennedy JD, Hasam F, et al: Mechanical inefficiency of the thoracic cage in scoliosis. Thorax 36:456–461, 1981.

18. Conti G, Rocco M, Antonelli M, et al: Respiratory system mechanics in the early phase of acute respiratory failure due to severe kyphoscoliosis. Intensive Care Med 23:539–544, 1997.

19. McCool FD, Tzelepis GE, Leith DE, et al: Oxygen cost of breathing during fatiguing inspiratory resistive loads. J Appl Physiol 66:2045–2055, 1989.

20. Leech JA, Ernst P, Rogal EJ, et al: Cardiorespiratory status in relation to mild deformity in adolescent idiopathic scoliosis. J Pediatr 106:143–149, 1985.

21. Szeinberg A, Canny GJ, Rashed N, et al: Forced vital capacity and maximal respiratory pressures in patients with mild and moderate scoliosis. Pediatr Pulmonol 4:8–12, 1988.

22. Estenne M, Derom E, De Troyer A: Neck and abdominal muscle activity in patients with severe thoracic scoliosis. Am J Respir Crit Care Med 158:452–457, 1998.

23. Ramonatxo M, Milic-Emili J, Prefaut C: Breathing pattern and load compensatory responses in young scoliotic patients. Eur Respir J 1:421–427, 1988.

24. Tardif C, Sohier B, Derenne JP: Control of breathing in chest wall disease. Monaldi Arch Chest Dis 48:83–86, 1993.

25. Bake B, Bjure J, Kasalichy J, et al: Regional pulmonary ventilation and perfusion distribution in patients with untreated idiopathic scoliosis. Thorax 27:703–712, 1972.

26. Shneerson JM, Venco A, Prime FJ: A study of pulmonary artery pressure, electrocardiography, and mechanocardiography in thoracic scoliosis. Thorax 32:700–705, 1977.

27. Jones DJ, Paul EA, Bell JH, et al: Ambulatory oxygen therapy in stable kyphoscoliosis. Eur Respir J 8:819–823, 1995.

28. Kesten S, Garfinkel SK, Wright T, et al: Impaired exercise capacity in adults with moderate scoliosis. Chest 99:663–666, 1991.

29. Kearon C, Viviani GR, Killian KJ: Factors influencing work capacity in adolescent idiopathic thoracic scoliosis. Am Rev Respir Dis 148:295–303, 1993.

30. Lenke LG, White DK, Kemp JS, et al: Evaluation of ventilatory efficiency during exercise in patients with idiopathic scoliosis undergoing spinal fusion. Spine 27:2041–2045, 2002.

31. Nauffal D, Domenech R, Martizez Garcia MA, et al. Noninvasive positive pressure home ventilation in restrictive disorders: Outcome and impact on health-related quality of life. Respir Med 96:777–783, 2002.

32. Guilleminault C, Kurlan G, Wirkle R: Severe kyphoscoliosis, breathing, and sleep. Chest 79:626–630, 1981.

33. Sawicka EH, Branthwaite MA: Respiration during sleep in kyphoscoliosis. Thorax 42:801–808, 1987.

34. Midgren B: Oxygen desaturation during sleep as a function of the underlying respiratory disease. Am Rev Respir Dis 141:43–46, 1990.

35. Mezon BL, West P, Israels J, et al: Sleep breathing abnormalities in kyphoscoliosis. Am Rev Respir Dis 122:617–621, 1980.

36. Watson JP, Nolan J, Elliott MW: Autonomic dysfunction in patients with nocturnal hypoventilation in extrapulmonary restrictive disease. Eur Respir J 13:1097–1102, 1999.

37. Pehrsson K, Bake JB, Larsson S, et al: Lung function in adult idiopathic scoliosis: A 20-year follow-up. Thorax 46:474–478, 1991.

38. McMaster MJ, Ohtsuka K: The natural history of congenital scoliosis: A study of 251 patients. J Bone Joint Surg [Am] 64:1128–1147, 1982.

39. McCarthy RE: Management of neuromuscular scoliosis. Orthop Clin North Am 30:435–449, 1999.

40. Weistein SL, Dolan LA, Spratt KF, et al: Health and function of patients with untreated idiopathic scoliosis: A 50-year natural history study. JAMA 289:559–567, 2003.

41. Miller NH: Cause and natural history of adolescent idiopathic scoliosis. Orthop Clin North Am 30:343–352, 1999.

42. Branthwaite MR: Cardiorespiratory consequences of unfused idiopathic scoliosis. Br J Dis Chest 80:360–369, 1986.

43. Chailleux E, Fauroux B, Binet F, et al: Predictors of survival in patients receiving domiciliary oxygen therapy or mechanical ventilation: A 10-year analysis of ANTADIR observatory. Chest 109:741–749, 1996.

44. To WW, Wong MN: Kyphoscoliosis complicating pregnancy. Int J Gynaecol Obstet 55:123–128, 1996.

45. Rom WN, Miller A: Unexpected longevity in patients with severe kyphoscoliosis. Thorax 33:106–110, 1978.

46. Strom K, Pehrsson K, Boe J, et al: Survival of patients with severe thoracic spine deformities receiving domiciliary oxygen therapy. Chest 102:164–168, 1992.

47. Mehta S, Hill NS: Noninvasive ventilation: State of the art. Am J Respir Crit Care Med. 163:540–577, 2001.

48. Janseens JP, Derivaz S, Bretitenstein E, et al. Changing pattern in long-term noninvasive ventilation: A 7-year prospective study in the Geneva Lake area. Chest 123:67–79, 2003.

49. Shneerson JM, Simmonds AK: Nonivasive ventilation for chest wall and neuromuscular disorders. Eur Respir J 20:480–487, 2002.

50. Consensus Conference: Clinical indications for noninvasive positive pressure ventilation in chronic respiratory failure due to restrictive lung disease, COPD, and nocturnal hypoventilation: A consensus conference report. Chest 116:521–534, 1999.

51. McNicholas WT: Impact of sleep in respiratory failure. Eur Respir J 10:920–933, 1997.

52. Carrey Z, Gottfried SG, Levy RD: Ventilatory muscle support in respiratory failure with nasal positive-pressure ventilation. Chest 97:150–158, 1990.

53. Ferris G, Servena-Pieras E, Vergata P, et al: Kyphoscoliosis ventilatory insufficiency: Noninvasive management outcomes. Am J Phys Med Rehabil 79:24–29, 2000.

54. Leger P, Bedicam JM, Cornette A, et al: Nasal intermittent positive pressure ventilation: Long-term follow-up in patients with severe chronic respiratory insufficiency. Chest 105:100–105, 1994.

55. Simmonds AK, Elliott MW: Outcome of domiciliary nasal intermittent positive pressure ventilation in restrictive and obstructive disorders. Thorax 50:604–609, 1995.

56. Ambrosino N, Vitacca M, Polease G, et al: Short-term effects of nasal proportional assist ventilation in patients with chronic hypercapnic respiratory insufficiency. Eur Respir J 10:2829–2834, 1997.

57. Lenke LG, Bridwell KH, Blanke K, et al: Analysis of pulmonary function and chest cage dimension changes after thoracoplasty in idiopathic scoliosis. Spine 20:1343–1350, 1995.

58. Simonds AK, Parker RA, Branthwaite MA: The effect of intermittent positive-pressure hyperinflation in restrictive chest wall disease. Respir 55:136–143, 1989.

59. McCool FD, Mayewski RJ, Shayne DS, et al: Intermittent positive pressure breathing in patients with respiratory muscle weakness: Alterations in total respiratory system compliance. Chest 90:546–552, 1986.

60. Roach JW: Adolescent idiopathic scoliosis. Orthop Clin North Am 30:353–365, 1999.

61. Baydur A, Swank SM, Stiles CM, et al: Respiratory mechanics in anesthetized young patients with kyphoscoliosis: Immediate and delayed effects of corrective spinal surgery. Chest 97:1157–1164, 1990.

62. Swank S, Lonstein J, Moe J, et al: Surgical treatment of adult scoliosis. J Bone Joint Surg [Am] 63:268–287, 1981.

63. Pehrsson K, Danielsson A, Nachemson A: Pulmonary function in adolescent idiopathic scoliosis: A 25 year follow up after surgery or start of brace treatment. Thorax 56:388–389, 2001.

64. Vandenbroucke J, van Ooy A, Gfeukers C, et al: Dystrophic kyphoscoliosis in neurofibromatosis type I: A report of two cases and review of the literature. Eur Spine J 6:273–277, 1997.

65. Loynes RD: Scoliosis after thoracoplasty. J Bone Joint Surg Br 54:484–498, 1972.

66. Deslauriers J, Jacques LF, Gregoire J: Role of Eloesser flap and thoracoplasty in the third millennium. Chest Surg Clin N Am 12:605–623, 2002.

67. Phillips MS, Kinnear WJM, Shneerson JM: Late sequelae of pulmonary tuberculosis treated by thoracoplasty. Thorax 42:445–451, 1987.

68. Bredin CP: Pulmonary function in long-term survivors of thoracoplasty. Chest 95:18–20, 1989.

69. Phillips MS, Miller MR, Kinnear WJM, et al: Importance of airflow obstruction after thoracoplasty. Thorax 42:348–352, 1987.

69a. O'Connor TM, O'Riordan DM, Stack M, Bredin CP: Airways obstruction in survivors of thoracoplasty: reversibility is greater in non-smokers. Respirology 9:130–133, 2004.

70. Sridhar MK, Carter R, Lean ME, et al: Resting energy expenditure and nutritional state of patients with increased oxygen cost of breathing due to emphysema, scoliosis and thoracoplasty. Thorax 49:781–785, 1994.

71. Ando M, Mori A, Esaki H, et al: The effect of pulmonary rehabilitation in patients with post-tuberculous lung disorder. Chest 123:1988–1995, 2003.

72. Brander PE, Salmi T, Partinen M, et al: Nocturnal oxygen saturation and sleep quality in long-term survivors of thoracoplasty. Respiration 60:325–331, 1993.

73. Jackson M, Smith I, King M, et al: Long term non-invasive domiciliary assisted ventilation for respiratory failure following thoracoplasty. Thorax 49:915–919, 1994.

73a. Shneerson JM: Respiratory failure in tuberculosis: a modern perspective. Clin Med 4:72–76, 2004.

74. Ravitch MM: Congenital Deformities of the Chest Wall and Their Operative Correction. Philadelphia: WB Saunders, 1977.

75. Haller JA, Scherer LR, Turner CS, et al: Evolving management of pectus excavatum based on a single institutional experience of 664 patients. Ann Surg 209:578–582, 1989.

76. Molic KA, Engum SA, Rescorla FJ, et al: Pectus excavatum repair: Experience with standard and minimal invasive techniques. J Pediatr Surg 36:324–328, 2001.

77. Fonkalsrud EW, Salmon T, Guo W, et al: Repair of pectus deformities with sternal support. J Thorac Cardiovasc Surg 107:37–42, 1994.

78. Dato GMA, DePaulis R, Dato AA, et al: Correction of pectus excavatum with a self-retaining seagull wing prosthesis. Chest 107:303–306, 1995.

79. Chidambaram B, Mehta AV: Currarino-Silverman syndrome (pectus carinatum type 2 deformity) and mitral valve disease. Chest 102:780–782, 1992.

80. Theerthakarai R, El-Halees W, Javadpoor S, et al: Severe pectus excavatum associated with cor pulmonare and chronic respiratory acidosis in a young woman. Chest 119:1957–1961, 2001.

81. Chuang J-H, Wan Y-L: Evaluation of pectus excavatum with repeated CT scans. Pediatr Radiol 25:654–656, 1995.

82. Castile R, Staats B, Westbrook P: Symptomatic pectus deformities of the chest. Am Rev Respir Dis 126:564–568, 1982.

83. Mead J, Sly P, Lesouef P, et al: Rib cage mobility in pectus excavatum. Am Rev Respir Dis 130:1223–1228, 1985.

84. Wynn S, Driscol D, Ostrom N, et al: Exercise cardiorespiratory function in adolescents with pectus excavatum. J Thorac Cardiovasc Surg 99:41–47, 1990.

85. Morshuis W, Folgering H, Barentsz J, et al: Pulmonary function before surgery for pectus excavatum and at long-term follow-up. Chest 105:1646–1652, 1994.

85a. Koumbourlis AC, Stolar CJ: Lung growth and function in children and adolescents with idiopathic pectus excavatum. Pediatr Pulmonol 38:339–343, 2004.

86. Quigley PM, Haller JA, Jelus KL, et al: Cardiorespiratory function before and after corrective surgery in pectus excavatum. J Pediatr 128:638–643, 1996.

87. Zhao L, Feinberg MS, Gaides M, et al: Why is exercise capacity reduced in subjects with pectus excavatum? J Pediatr 136:163–167, 2000.

88. Mocchegiani R, Badano L, Lestuzzi C, et al: Relation of right ventricular morphology and function in pectus excavatum to the severity of the chest wall deformity. Am J Cardiol 76:941–946, 1995.

89. Haller JA Jr, Kramer SS, Lietman SA: Use of CT scans in selection of patients for pectus excavatum surgery: A preliminary report. J Pediatr Surg 22:615–622, 1988.

90. Ravitch MM: The operative repair of pectus excavatum. Ann Surg 129:429–444, 1949.

91. Nuss D, Kelly RE, Croitoru DP, et al: A 10-year review of a minimally invasive technique for the correction of pectus excavatum. J Pediatr Surg 33:545–552, 1998.

92. Croitoru DP, Kelly RE, Goretsky MJ, et al: Experience and modification update for the minimally invasive Nuss technique for pectus excavatum repair in 303 patients. J Pediatr Surg 37:437–445, 2002.

93. Lwason ML, Cash TF, Akers R, et al: A pilot study of the impact of surgical repair on disease-specific quality of life among patients with pectus excavatum. J Pediatr Surg 38:916–918, 2003.

94. Cahill JJ, Lees GM, Roberston HT: A summary of pre-operative and post-operative cardiorespiratory performance in patients undergoing pectus excavatum and carinatum repair. J Pediatr Surg 19:430–433, 1984.

95. Derveaux L, Clarysse I, Ivanoff I, et al: Preoperative and postoperative abnormalities in chest x-ray indices and in lung function in pectus deformities. Chest 95:850–856, 1989.

96. Borowitz D, Cerny F, Zallen G, et al: Pulmonary function and exercise response in patients with pectus excavatum after Nuss repair. J Pediatr Surg 38:543–547, 2003.

97. Todd TRJ, Shamji F: Pathophysiology of chest wall trauma. In Roussos C, Macklem PT (eds): The Thorax. Part B. New York: Marcel Dekker, 1985, pp 979–997.

98. Gaillard M, Herve C, Mandin L, et al: Mortality prognostic factors in chest injury. J Trauma 30:93–96, 1990.

99. Ahmed Z, Mohyuddin Z: Managment of flail chest injury: Internal fixation versus endotracheal intubation and

ventilation. J Thorac Cardiovasc Surg 110:1676–1680, 1995.

100. Tzelepis GE, McCool FD, Hoppin FG Jr: Chest wall distortion in patients with flail chest. Am Rev Respir Dis 140:31–37, 1989.

101. Cappello M, Yuehua C, DeTroyer A: Respiratory muscle response to flail chest. Am J Respir Crit Care Med 153:1897–1901, 1996.

102. Cappello M, Legrand A, DeTroyer A: Determinants of rib motion in flail chest. Am J Respir Crit Care Med 159:886–891, 1999.

103. Bolliger CT, Van Eeden SF: Treatment of multiple rib fractures: Randomized control trial comparing ventilatory and nonventilatory management. Chest 97:943–948, 1990.

104. Voggenreiter G, Neudect F, Aufmkolk M, et al: Operative chest wall stabilization in flail chest: Outcomes of patients with or without pulmonary contusion. J Am Coll Surg 187:130–138, 1998.

105. Nakayama DK, Ramenofsky ML, Rowe MI: Chest injuries in childhood. Ann Surg 210:770–775, 1989.

106. Enarson DA, Didier EP, Gracey DR: Flail chest as a complication of cardiopulmonary resuscitation. Heart Lung 6:1020–1022, 1977.

107. Abisheganaden J, Chee CB, Wang YT: Use of bilevel positive airway pressure ventilatory support for pathological flail chest complicating multiple myeloma. Eur Respir J 12:238–239, 1998.

108. Adams JW, Hazard PB, Gooch JB: Flail chest injury in a patient with surgical absence of the sternum. Chest 92:185–186, 1987.

109. Winter RB: Flail chest secondary to excessive rib resection in idiopathic scoliosis: Case report. Spine 15:668–670, 2002.

110. Cardenas N, Manrique TA, Catlin EA: Flail chest in the newborn. Clin Pediatr (Phila) 27:161–162, 1988.

111. Mayberry JC, Trunkey DD: The fractured rib in chest wall trauma. Chest Surg Clin N Am 7:239–261, 1997.

112. Leban M, Siegel C, Schultz L, et al: Occult radiographic fractures of the chest wall identified by nuclear scan imaging: Report of seven cases. Arch Phys Med Rehabil 75:353–754, 1994.

113. Weyant MJ, Bleier JI, Naama H, et al: Severe crushed chest injury with large flail segment: Computed tomographic three-dimensional reconstruction. J Trauma 52:605, 2002.

114. Landercasper J, Cogbill TH, Strutt PJ: Delayed diagnosis of flail chest. Crit Care Med 18:611–613, 1990.

115. Velmahos GC, Vassiliu P, Chan LS, et al: Influence of flail chest on outcome among patients with severe thoracic cage trauma. Int Surg 87:240–244, 2002.

116. Clark GC, Schecter WP, Trunkey DD: Variables affecting outcome in blunt chest trauma: Flail vs. pulmonary contusion. J Trauma 28:298–304, 1988.

116a. Wanek S, Mayberry JC: Blunt thoracic trauma: flail chest, pulmonary contusion, and blast injury. Crit Care Clin 20:71–81, 2004.

117. Suresh Kumar S, Saith V, Chawla R, et al: Successful transdiaphragmatic cardiac resuscitation through midline abdominal incision in patient with flail chest. Resuscitation 50:239–241, 2001.

118. Moore P, James O, Byth P, et al: Factors affecting outcome after chest injury. Anaesth Intens Care 13:362–369, 1985.

119. Landercasper J, Cogbill TH, Lindesmith LA: Long-term disability after flail chest injury. Trauma 24:410–414, 1984.

120. Slater MS, Mayberry JC, Trunkey DD: Operative stabilization of a flail chest six years after injury. Ann Thorac Surg 72:600–601, 2001.

121. Smejkal R, O'Malley KF, David E, et al: Routine initial computed tomography of the chest in blunt torso trauma. Chest 100:667–669, 1991.

122. Kishikawa M, Yoshioka T, Shimazu T, et al: Pulmonary contusion causes long-term respiratory dysfunction with decreased functional residual capacity. J Trauma 31:1203–1210, 1991.

123. Maloney JV, Schmutzer KJ, Raschke E: Paradoxical respiration and "pendeluft." J Thorac Cardiovasc Surg 41:291–296, 1961.

124. Trinkle JK, Richardson JD, Franz JL, et al: Management of flail chest without mechanical ventilation. Ann Thorac Surg 19:355–363, 1975.

125. Tzelepis GE, McCool FD, Leith DE, et al: Influence of lung volume on inspiratory muscle endurance. J Appl Phys 64:1796–1802, 1988.

126. Avery EE, Morch ET, Benson DW: Critically crushed chest: A new method of treatment with continuous mechanical hyperventilation to produce alkalotic apnea and internal pneumatic stabilization. J Thorac Cardiovasc Surg 32:291–311, 1956.

127. Shackford SR, Smith DE, Zarins CD, et al: The management of flail chest: A comparison of ventilatory and nonventilatory treatment. Am J Surg 132:759–762, 1976.

128. Hartke RH Jr, Block AJ: External stabilization of flail chest using continuous negative extrathoracic pressure. Chest 102:1283–1285, 1992.

129. Tanaka H, Tajimi K, Endoh Y, et al: Pneumatic stabilization for flail chest injury: An 11-year study. Surg Today 31:12–17, 2001.

130. Cullen P, Modell JH, Dirby RR, et al: Treatment of flail chest: Use of intermittent mandatory ventilation and positive end expiratory pressure. Arch Surg 110:1099–1103, 1985.

131. Tanaka H, Yukioka T, Yamaguti Y, et al: Surgical stabilization or internal pneumatic stabilization? A prospective randomized study of management of severe flail chest patients. J Trauma 52:727–732, 2002.

132. Mouton W, Lardinois D, Furrer M, et al: Long-term follow-up of patients with operative stabilization of a flail chest. Thorac Cardiovasc Surg 45:242–244, 1997.

133. Calin A: Ankylosing spondylitis. Clin Rheum Dis 11:41–60, 1985.

134. Libby DM, Schley WS, Smith JP: Cricoarytenoid arthritis in ankylosing spondylitis: A cause of acute respiratory failure and cor pulmonale. Chest 80:641–642, 1981.

135. Jordanoglu J: Rib movement in health, kyphoscoliosis and ankylosing spondylitis. Thorax 24:407–414, 1969.

136. VanNoord JA, Caubergs M, Van de Woestigne KP, et al: Total respiratory system resistance and reactance in ankylosing spondylitis and kyphoscoliosis. Eur Respir J 4:945–951, 1991.

137. Feltelius N, Hedenstrom H, Hillerdal G, et al: Pulmonary involvement in ankylosing spondylitis. Ann Rheum Dis 45:736–740, 1986.

138. Vanderschueren D, Decramer M, Van Den Dael P, et al: Pulmonary function and maximal transrespiratory pressure in ankylosing spondylitis. Ann Rheum Dis 48:632–635, 1989.

139. Fisher LR, Cawley MI, Holgate S: Relation between chest expansion, pulmonary function, and exercise tolerance in patients with ankylosing spondylitis. Ann Rheum Dis 49:921–925, 1990.

139a. Sahin G, Calikoglu M, Ozge C, et al: Respiratory muscle strength but not BASFI score relates to diminished chest expansion in ankylosing spondylitis. Clin Rheumatol 23:199–202, 2004.

139b. El Maghraoui A, Chaouir S, Abid A, et al: Lung findings on thoracic high-resolution computed tomography in patients with ankylosing spondylitis. Correlations with disease duration, clinical findings and pulmonary funcion testing. Clin Rheumatol 23:123–128, 2004.

140. Aggarwal AN, Gupta D, Wanchu A, et al: Use of static lung mechanics to identify early pulmonary involvement in patients with ankylosing spondylitis. J Postgrad Med 47:89–94, 2001.

141. Thiranont N, Netrawichien P: Transpedicular decancellation closed wedge vertebral osteotomy for treatment of fixed flexion deformity of spine in ankylosing spondylitis. Spine 18:2517–2522, 1993.

142. Grimby G, Fugl-Meyer AR, Blomstrand A: Partitioning of the contributions of rib cage and abdomen to ventilation in ankylosing spondylitis. Thorax 29:179–184, 1974.

143. Parkin A, Robinson PJ, Hickling P: Regional lung ventilation in ankylosing spondylitis. Br J Radiol 55:833–836, 1982.

144. Rosenow E, Strimlan C, Muhm J, et al: Pleuropulmonary manifestations of ankylosing spondylitis. Mayo Clin Proc 52:641–649, 1977.

145. Fenlon HM, Casserly I, Sant SM, et al: Plain radiographs and thoracic high-resolution CT in patients with ankylosing spondylitis. AJR Am J Roentgenol 168:1067–1072, 1997.

146. Thai D, Ratani RS, Salama S, et al: Upper lobe fibrocavitary disease in a patient with back pain and stiffness. Chest 118:1814–1816, 2000.

147. Viitanen VJ, Suni J, Kautiainen H, et al: Effect of physiotherapy on spinal mobility in ankylosing spondylitis. Scand J Rheumatol 21:38–41, 1992.

148. Braun J, Brandt J, Listing J, et al: Treatment of active ankylosing spondylitis with infliximab: A randomized controlled multicentre trial. Lancet 359:1187–1193, 2002.

148a. Brandt J, Listing J, Haibel H, et al: Long-term efficacy and safety of etanercept after readministration in patients with active ankylosis spondylitis. Rheumatology (Oxford) 44:342–348, 2005.

149. Sinclair JR, Mason RA: Ankylosing spondylitis: The case for awake intubation. Anaesthesia 39:3–11, 1984.

150. Flegal KM, Carroll MD, Ogden CL, et al: Prevalence and trends in obesity among US adults, 1999–2000. JAMA 288:1723–1727, 2000.

151. Freedman DS, Khan LK, Serdula MK, et al: Trends and correlates of class 3 obesity in the United States from 1990 through 2000. JAMA 288:1758–1761, 2002.

152. Gasteyger C, Tremblay A: Metabolic impact of body fat distribution. J Endocrinol Invest 25:876–883, 2002.

153. Strain GW, Zumoff B: The relationship of weight-height indices of obesity to body fat content. J Am Coll Nutr 6:715–718, 1992.

154. Verga S, Buscemi C, Caimi G: Resting energy expenditure and body composition in morbidly obese, obese and control subjects. Acta Diabetol 31:47–51, 1994.

155. Leibel RL, Rosenbaum M, Hirsch J: Changes in energy expenditure resulting from altered body weight. N Engl J Med 332:621–628, 1995.

156. Lazarus R, Gore CJ, Booth M, et al: Effects of body composition and fat distribution on pulmonary function in adults. Am J Clin Nutr 68:35–41, 1998.

157. Schafer H, Pauleit D, Sudhop T, et al: Body fat distribution, serum leptin and cardiovascular risk factors in men with obstructive sleep apnea. Chest 122:829–839, 2002.

158. Foster GD: Principles and practice in the management of obesity. Am J Respir Crit Care Med 168:274–280, 2003.

159. Ray CS, Sue DH, Bray G, et al: Effects of obesity on respiratory function. Am Rev Respir Dis 128:501–506, 1983.

160. Zerah F, Harf A, Perlemuter L, et al: Effects of obesity on respiratory resistance. Chest 103:1470–1476, 1993.

161. Sahebjami H, Gartside PS: Pulmonary function in obese subjects with a normal FEV_1/FVC ratio. Chest 110:1425–1429, 1996.

162. Rochester DF: Obesity and pulmonary function. *In* Alpert MA, Alexander JK (eds): The Heart and Lung in Obesity (1st ed). Armonk, NY: Futura, 1998, pp 109–131.

163. Pelosi P, Croci M, Ravagnan I, et al: Effects of body mass on lung volumes, respiratory mechanics, and gas exchange during general anesthesia. Anesth Analg 87:654–660, 1998.

164. Yap JCH, Watson RA, Gilbey S, et al: Effects of posture on respiratory mechanics in obesity. J Appl Physiol 79:1199–1205, 1995.

165. Pelosi P, Croci M, Ravagnan I, et al: Respiratory system mechanics in sedated, paralyzed, morbidly obese patients. J Appl Physiol 82:811–818, 1997.

166. Naimark A, Cherniack RM: Compliance of the respiratory system and its components in health and obesity. J Appl Physiol 15:377–382, 1960.

167. Auler JOC, Miyoshi E, Fernandes CR, et al: The effects of abdominal opening on respiratory mechanics during general anesthesia in normal and morbidly obese patients: A comparative study. Anesth Analg 94:741–748, 2002.

168. Pankow W, Podszus T, Gutheil T, et al: Expiratory flow limitation and intrinsic positive end-expiratory pressure in obesity. J Appl Physiol 85:1236–1243, 1998.

169. Ferretti A, Giampiccolo P, Cavalli A, et al: Expiratory flow limitation in massively obese subjects. Chest 119:1401–1408, 2001.

170. Kress JP, Pohlman AS, Alverdy J, et al: The impact of morbid obesity on oxygen cost of breathing (VO(2RESP)) at rest. Am J Respir Crit Care Med 160:883–886, 1999.

171. Thomas PS, Cowen ERT, Hulands G, et al: Respiratory function in the morbidly obese before and after weight loss. Thorax 44:382–386, 1989.

172. Bradley TD, Rutherford R, Lue F, et al: Role of diffuse airway obstruction in the hypercapnia of obstructive sleep apnea. Am Rev Respir Dis 134:920–924, 1986.

173. Brodsky JB: Positioning the morbidly obese patient for anesthesia. Obes Surg 12:751–758, 2002.

174. Farebrother MJ, McHardy GJ, Munro JF: Relation between pulmonary gas exchange and closing volume before and after substantial weight loss in obese subjects. BMJ 3:391–393, 1974.

175. Hurewitz AN, Susskind H, Harold WH: Obesity alters regional ventilation in lateral decubitus position. J Appl Physiol 59:774–783, 1985.

176. Santesson J, Nordenstrom J: Pulmonary function in extreme obesity: Influence of weight loss following intestinal shunt operation. Act Chir Scand Suppl 482:36–40, 1978.

177. Jense HG, Dubin SA, Silverstein PI, et al: Effect of obesity on safe duration of apnea in anesthetized patients. Anesth Analg 72:89–93, 1991.

178. Chapman KR, Himal HS, Rebuck AS: Ventilatory responses to hypercapnia and hypoxia in patients with eucapnic morbid obesity before and after weight loss. Clin Sci 78:541–545, 1990.

179. Sampson MG, Grassino K: Neurochemical properties in obese patients during carbon dioxide rebreathing. Am J Med 75:81–90, 1983.

180. Leech J, Onal E, Aronson R, et al: Voluntary hyperventilation in obesity hypoventilation. Chest 100:1334–1338, 1991.

181. Zwillich CW, Sutton FD, Person DJ, et al: Decreased hypoxic ventilatory drive in the obesity-hypoventilation syndrome. Am J Med 59:343–348, 1975.

182. O'Donnell CP, Tankersley CG, Polotsky VP, et al: Leptin, obesity, and respiratory function. Respir Physiol 119:163–170, 2000.

183. O'Donnell CP, Schaub CD, Haines AS, et al: Leptin prevents respiratory depression in obesity, Am J Respir Crit Care Med 159:1477–1484, 1999.

184. Kelly TM, Jensen RL, Elliott CG, et al: Maximum respiratory pressures in morbidly obese subjects. Respiration 54:73–77, 1988.

185. Sahebjami H: Dyspnea in obese healthy men. Chest 114:1373–1377, 1998.

186. Sharp JT, Druz WS, Kondragunta VR: Diaphragmatic responses to body position changes in obese patients with obstructive sleep apnea. Am Rev Respir Dis 133:32–37, 1986.

187. Gibson GJ: Obesity, respiratory function and breathlessness. Thorax 55:541–544, 2000.

188. Babb TG, Korzick D, Meador M, et al: Ventilatory response of moderately obese women to submaximal exercise. Int J Obes Relat Metab Disord 15:59–65, 1991.

189. Salvadori A, Fanari P, Mazza P, et al: Breathing pattern during and after maximal exercise testing in young untrained subjects and obese patients. Respiration 60:162–169, 1993.

190. Refsum HE, Holter PH, Lovig T, et al: Pulmonary function and energy expenditure after marked weight loss in obese women: Observations before and one year after gastric banding. Int J Obes Relat Metab Disord 14:175–183, 1990.

191. Wadstrom C, Muller-Suur R, Backman L: Influence of excessive weight loss on respiratory function: A study of obese patients following gastroplasty. Eur J Surg 157:341–346, 1991.

191a. Davila-Cervantes A, Dominguez-Cherit G, Borunda D, et al: Impact of surgically-induced weight loss on respiratory function: a prospective analysis. Obes Surg 14:1389–1392, 2004.

192. Ebeo CT, Benotti PN, Byrd RP, et al: The effect of bi-level positive airway pressure on postoperative pulmonary function following gastric surgery for obesity. Respir Med 96: 672–676, 2002.

193. Waldhorn RE: Nocturnal nasal intermittent positive pressure ventilation with bi-level positive airway pressure (BiPAP) in respiratory failure. Chest 101:516–521, 1992.

194. Masa JF, Celli BR, Riesco JA, et al: Noninvasive positive pressure ventilation and not oxygen may prevent overt ventilatory failure in patients with chest wall diseases. Chest 112:207–213, 1997.

MANAGEMENT OF RESPIRATORY FAILURE

84

Principles of Mechanical Ventilation

Neil R. MacIntyre, M.D.

INTRODUCTION

Mechanical ventilation is the process of using devices to provide oxygen and carbon dioxide transport between the environment and the alveolar-pulmonary capillary interface. The desired effect of mechanical ventilation is to maintain appropriate levels of P_{O_2} and P_{CO_2} in arterial blood while also unloading the ventilatory muscles. Although negative-pressure chambers or wraps and extracorporeal circuits might fulfill this definition, this discussion focuses on the use of positive airway pressure to provide mechanical ventilatory support.

The use of positive-pressure mechanical ventilation is widespread. In the United States, estimates range from 1 million to 3 million patients annually requiring mechanical ventilatory support outside the operating room.[1] This is supplied by an installed base of approximately 50,000 positive-pressure ventilators in the United States. Traditionally, this support has been provided in intensive care units, but there are clear trends toward expanding the venues to subacute facilities, long-term care facilities, and the home. As the aged population expands and as more aggressive surgical and immunosuppressive therapies are developed, the need for mechanical ventilation in all of these venues is likely to expand.[1]

POSITIVE-PRESSURE MECHANICAL VENTILATOR DESIGN FEATURES

GAS DELIVERY SYSTEMS

Positive-Pressure Breath Controller

Most modern ventilators utilize piston/bellows systems or controllers of high–pressure gas sources to drive gas flow.[2,3]

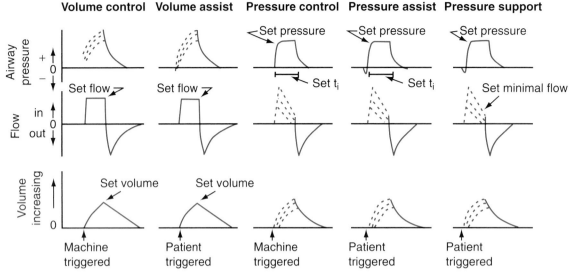

Figure 84.1 Airway pressure, flow, and volume tracings over time depicting the five basic breaths available on most modern mechanical ventilators. Breaths are classified by their trigger (machine timer, patient effort), target/limit (set flow, set pressure), and cycle (set volume, set time, set flow) variables. The *solid lines* represent set responses, the *dashed lines* represent dependent responses. In all of these breaths, pressure is usually a "backup" cycle variable designed to terminate gas delivery if airway pressure rises above an alarm limit. A recent modification of the pressure control/pressure assisted breath provides an additional pressure release mechanism that vents gas if inspiratory pressure rises above the target, thereby allowing spontaneous breathing to occur during the inflation phase (the pressure release breath).

Tidal breaths are generated by this gas flow and can either be controlled entirely by the ventilator or be interactive with patient efforts. The characteristics of these tidal breaths can be classified by the behavior of three variables: (1) the trigger variable (initiates the breath); (2) the target or limit variable (controls gas delivery during the breath); and (3) the cycle variable (terminates the breath).[4,5] Trigger variables are either patient effort (detected by the ventilator as a pressure or flow change; see later) or a set machine timer. Target or limit variables are generally either a set flow or a set inspiratory pressure. Cycle variables are generally a set volume, a set inspiratory time, or a set flow rate. Pressure is often a backup safety cycle variable. Figure 84.1 uses this classification scheme to describe the most common breath types available on the current generation of mechanical ventilators.

Feedback controllers on breath delivery also exist. Early examples of such controllers were synchronized intermittent mandatory ventilation (SIMV), with the machine breath rate adjusted in response to spontaneous efforts, and mandatory minute ventilation (MMV), with the machine breath rate adjusted in response to minute ventilation. Newer microprocessor-based ventilators can also provide more sophisticated feedback controllers on breath delivery. The most common of these provides a basic pressure-targeted breath but also allows a clinician-set tidal volume to drive a feedback controller that continuously adjusts the inspiratory pressure target to achieve this volume.[6] This breath type goes by a variety of proprietary names that include "pressure regulated volume control," "volume control plus," and "autoflow" (all time-cycled) and "volume support" (flow-cycled).

Mode Controller

The availability and delivery logic of different breath types define the "mode" of mechanical ventilatory support.[2,4,5]

The mode controller is an electronic, pneumatic, or microprocessor-based system that is designed to provide the proper combination of breaths according to both set and feedback algorithms. Table 84.1 summarizes many of the commonly available modes. Newer ventilators can also incorporate feedback systems to change modes. A simple example is a system that would shift between assist control and pressure support depending upon patient activity. A more complex system has recently been introduced ("adaptive support ventilation") that incorporates respiratory system mechanics, minute ventilation, and the presence of spontaneous efforts to set and adjust both an "ideal" tidal volume and an "ideal" ventilatory pattern based on the minimal work concept.[6–8]

SUBSYSTEMS OF MECHANICAL VENTILATORS

Effort (Demand) Sensors

Current ventilators allow a number of patient–ventilator interactions.[9,9a] Examples include patient-triggered breaths (ventilator initiates flow in response to patient demand) and pressure-targeted/limited breaths (ventilator adjusts flow in response to patient demand) (see discussion of patient–ventilator interactions, later). Patient effort sensors are needed to allow the ventilator to track patient effort and thereby properly deliver these interactive breaths. These sensors are usually either pressure or flow transducers in the ventilatory circuitry and are characterized by their sensitivity (how much of a circuit pressure or flow change must be generated to initiate a ventilator response) and their responsiveness (the delay in providing this response).[10]

Gas Blenders

Blenders mix air and oxygen to produce a delivered $F_{I_{O_2}}$ from 0.21 to 1.0. On newer systems, blenders are also

Table 84.1 Breath Types Available on Common Modes of Mechanical Ventilation

Mode	VC	VA	PC*	PA*	PS*	PR	Sp
Volume assist-control (VACV)	X	X					
Pressure assist-control (PACV)			X	X			
Synchronized IMV (Volume)	X	X			X		X
Synchronized IMV (Pressure)			X	X	X		X
Pressure support (PSV)					X		
Airway pressure release (APRV)					X	X	X

VC, volume control; VA, volume assist; PC, pressure control; PA, pressure assist; PS, pressure support; PR, pressure release; Sp, spontaneous unassisted; IMV, intermittent mandatory ventilation.
* Volume feedback control based on delivered volume available on some devices.

available for other gases such as helium-oxygen mixtures (heliox), nitric oxide (NO), and anesthetic agents.

Humidifiers

With the upper airway bypassed by tracheal intubation, sufficient heat and moisture must be added to the inspired gas mixtures to avert mucosal desiccation. "Active" humidifiers utilize external water sources and electrical power to adjust blended gas mixtures to near body conditions (tracheal temperature of >35° C, water content >40 mg/L).[11] "Passive" humidifiers use simple heat/moisture exchange devices in the ventilator circuit that reutilize heat and moisture trapped from expired gas. These disposable units can usually supply adequate heat and moisture (i.e., greater than 30°–33° C and greater than 28 to 32 mg/L H_2O) for many patients, particularly those receiving mechanical ventilation for only short periods of time.[11]

Expiratory Pressure Generator

Positive airway pressure can be sustained throughout expiration (positive end-expiratory pressure, or PEEP) to help maintain alveolar patency and improve ventilation-perfusion ($\dot{V}/\dot{Q}$) matching (see discussion of the physiologic effects of mechanical ventilation, later). PEEP is usually applied by regulating pressure in the expiratory valve of the ventilator system, although a continuous flow of source gas during the expiratory phase can provide a similar effect. Note that some expiratory valves, even when fully open, have measurable resistance, which may result in some inadvertently applied PEEP.[12] As discussed in more detail later, PEEP can also be generated in alveoli if the expiratory time is inadequate for the lung to return to its "rest volume" or if significant flow limitation prevents full lung emptying (intrinsic PEEP, sometimes referred to as "auto-PEEP," "occult PEEP," or "air trapping").[13]

Gas Delivery Circuit

The gas delivery circuit usually consists of flexible tubing that often has pressure or flow sensors and an exhalation valve included. It is important to remember that this tubing

has measurable compliance (4 mL/cm H_2O is a representative figure), and significant amounts of delivered gas may serve only to distend this circuitry rather than enter the patient's lungs when high airway pressures are encountered.

Patient–Ventilator Circuit Interface

Positive-pressure ventilation is generally supplied through a tube inserted into the patient's airway (orotracheal or nasotracheal tube or tracheostomy). These tubes generally have air-filled balloons to provide a proper seal in the airway.

An alternative to the tracheal tube is a mask system. Both full face and nasal masks have been utilized with a variety of ventilatory support systems and modes.[14–16] Mask leak can be significant, however, and thus support modes using masks must be able to provide adequate volumes and proper inspiratory timing despite this leak. To this end, special nasal mask ventilators with pressure-targeted and either time-cycled or leak-compensated, flow-cycled capabilities have been developed.[16] Advantages of mask systems are preservation of normal glottic airway protection, less tracheal damage, and the ability to remove the device to eat or speak. Disadvantages of mask systems are lack of total airway control by the clinician and discomfort or skin trauma in some patients.

Aerosol Generators

Therapeutic aerosols (e.g., bronchodilators, steroids, antibiotics) can be delivered through the ventilator circuitry.[17] This can be accomplished by in-line nebulizers or by special chambers designed for metered-dose inhalers. When using an in-line nebulizer, caution must be taken to ensure that the added flow through the nebulizer does not disrupt ventilator operations. Aerosol deposition in the lung of an intubated patient is generally less than that in a nonintubated patient because the endotracheal tube serves as a significant barrier to aerosol delivery.[18] Higher dosing is thus advisable.

Monitors and Graphic Displays

Although electronic and microprocessor-based systems have considerable internal monitoring of electronic and pneumatic function, the three variables generally displayed for clinical use are circuit pressures, flows, and volumes.[19] Most modern positive-pressure ventilators also have oxygen sensors in the circuitry to ensure that the desired FI_{O_2} is being delivered. In addition, some ventilators may also have analyzers for exhaled carbon dioxide and inhaled therapeutic gases such as NO or heliox. The exhaled carbon dioxide analyzer may have particular value as a backup disconnect alarm.

Alarm Systems

Alarms can be utilized on virtually any component of the ventilator or circuitry.[5,20] Alarm strategies should be prioritized based on two factors: the rapidity at which an adverse event develops (either mechanical function of the machine or patient status) and the rapidity at which a clinical response is required. Three levels of monitoring and alarms thus exist: high level—rapidly developing events requiring an immediate response (e.g., patient disconnect, gas supply failure); moderate level—rapidly developing events that require a prompt but not necessarily immediate response (e.g., oxygen blender failure, loss of PEEP); low level—slowly developing events that do not necessarily require a clinical response (e.g., worsening lung compliance). In general, high level monitoring and alarm conditions require redundant, continuous monitoring with high priority alarms (and even automated responses). Moderate and low level monitoring and alarm conditions require less intensive setups. Table 84.2 gives examples of monitoring and alarm priorities.

PHYSIOLOGIC EFFECTS OF POSITIVE-PRESSURE MECHANICAL VENTILATION

MINUTE VENTILATION, ALVEOLAR VENTILATION, AND ALVEOLAR GAS TENSIONS

Minute ventilation is defined as the product of frequency × tidal volume ($MV = f \times VT$). Alveolar ventilation ($\dot{V}A$) is the proportion of MV that actually comes in contact with the alveolar-capillary gas exchange interface:

$$\dot{V}A = MV - \dot{V}D = (f \times VT) - (f \times VD)$$

where $\dot{V}D$ is dead space ventilation, and VD is dead space volume (i.e., the volume of each tidal breath that does not come in contact with the alveolar capillary interface).

Because carbon dioxide transport is primarily dependent on alveolar ventilation (and much less on ventilation-perfusion matching), the Bohr equation can be used to calculate the proportion of VT that is dead space:

$$VD/VT = (Pa_{CO_2} - PE_{CO_2})/Pa_{CO_2}$$

where Pa_{CO_2} is the arterial carbon dioxide tension, and PE_{CO_2} is the mixed expired carbon dioxide tension. Note that end-tidal PCO_2 is often substituted in this equation for arterial PCO_2 in many ventilator monitors.

The relationships between alveolar ventilation provided by mechanical ventilation and alveolar (and arterial) partial pressure of carbon dioxide is depicted in Figure 84.2. In

---

Table 84.2 Levels of Monitoring and Alarms: Clinical Examples and Monitoring/Alarm Sites

Event	Possible Monitoring Site
Level 1	
Power failure (including when battery is in use)	Electrical control system*
Absence of gas delivery (apnea)	Circuit pressures,* circuit flows, timing monitor, CO_2 analysis
Loss of gas source	Pneumatic control system*
Excessive gas delivery	Circuit pressures,* circuit flows, timing monitor
Exhalation valve failure	Circuit pressures, circuit flows, timing monitor
Timing failure	Circuit pressures, circuit flows, timing monitor
Level 2	
Battery power loss (when battery is not in use)	Electrical control system*
Circuit leak	Circuit pressure,* circuit flows
Blender failure	FI_{O_2} sensor
Circuit partially occluded	Circuit pressures, circuit flows
Heater/humidifier failure	Temperature probe in circuit
Loss of/or excessive PEEP	Circuit pressures
Autocycling	Circuit pressures, circuit flows
Other electrical or preventive subsystem out of limits without immediate overt gas delivery effects	Electrical and pneumatic systems monitor
Level 3	
Change in central nervous system drive	Circuit pressures, circuit flows, timing monitor
Change in impedances	Circuit pressures, circuit flows, timing monitor
Intrinsic PEEP (auto) >5 cm H_2O	Circuit pressures, circuit flows

Level 1 events are high priority, requiring an immediate response and thus needing continuous monitoring and redundant alarms. Level 2 events are moderate priority, requiring prompt (but not necessarily immediate) response and thus needing continuous monitoring with some alarm capability. Level 3 events are low priority, requiring clinician alerts and thus needing only intermittent monitoring with optional alarm capability.
* Specifications defined by both the American Society for Testing and Materials F-29.03.0, 1990; and the International Organization for Standardization Technical Standards Committee ISO 5369:1987.
Adapted from American Association for Respiratory Care Consensus Group: Essentials of Mechanical Ventilators. Respir Care 37:1000–1008, 1992.

21. Hess, DR, MacIntyre NR: Tracheal gas insufflation: Overcoming obstacles to clinical implementation. Respir Care 46:198–199, 2001.

22. Truwit JD, Marini JJ: Evaluation of thoracic mechanics in the ventilated patient. Part I. Primary measurements. J Crit Care 3:133–150, 1988.

23. Truwit JD, Marini JJ: Evaluation of thoracic mechanics in the ventilated patient. Part II. Applied mechanics. J Crit Care 3:192–213, 1988.

24. MacIntyre NR, McConnell R, Cheng KC, Sane A: Pressure limited breaths improve flow dys-synchrony during assisted ventilation. Crit Care Med 25:167–171, 1997.

25. Marini JJ, Crooke PS: A general mathematical model for respiratory dynamics relevant to the clinical setting. Am Rev Respir Dis 147:14–24, 1993.

26. Macklen PT: Relationship between lung mechanics and ventilation distribution. Physiology 16:580–588, 1973.

27. Mili-Emili J, Henderson JAN, Dolovich MB, et al: Regional distribution of inhaled gas in the lung. J Appl Physiol 21:749–759, 1966.

28. Abraham, E, Yoshihara G: Cardiorespiratory effects of pressure controlled ventilation in severe respiratory failure. Chest 98:1445–1449, 1990.

29. Pratt PC: Pathology of the adult respiratory distress syndrome. In Thurlbeck WM, Ael MR (eds): The Lung: Structure, Function and Disease. Baltimore: Williams & Wilkins, 1978, pp 43–57.

30. Slutsky AS: ACCP consensus conference: Mechanical ventilation. Chest 104:1833–1859, 1993.

31. Kacmarek RM, Pierson DJ (eds): AARC conference on positive end expiratory pressure. Respir Care 33:419–527, 1988.

32. Gattinoni L, Pesenti A, Baglioni, S, et al: Inflammatory pulmonary edema and PEEP: Correlation between imaging and physiologic studies. J Thorac Imaging 3:59–64, 1988.

33. Kacmarek RM: Strategies to optimize alveolar recruitment. Curr Opin Crit Care 7:15–20, 2001.

34. Gattinoni L, Pelosi P, Crotti S, et al: Effects of positive end expiratory pressure on regional distribution of tidal volume and recruitment in adult respiratory distress syndrome. Am J Respir Crit Care Med 151:1807–1814, 1995.

35. Gattinoni L, Pelosi P, Suter P, et al: ARDS caused by pulmonary and extra pulmonary disease: Different syndromes? Am J Respir Crit Care Med 158:3–11, 1998.

36. Webb HJH, Tierney DF: Experimental pulmonary edema due to intermittent positive pressure ventilation with high inflation pressures: Protection by positive end-expiratory pressure. Am Rev Respir Dis 110:556–565, 1974.

37. Dreyfus D, Soler P, Bassett G, et al: High inflation pressure pulmonary edema. Am Rev Respir Dis 137:1159–1164, 1988.

38. Muscedere JG, Mullen JB, Gan K, Slutsky AS: Tidal ventilation at low airway pressures can augment lung injury. Am J Respir Crit Care Med 149:1327–1334, 1994.

39. Wyszogrodski IK, Kyei-Aboagye HW, Taaeusch JR, Avery ME: Surfactant inactivation by hyperventilation: Conservation by end-expiratory pressure. J Appl Physiol 38:461–466, 1975.

40. Pinsky MR, Guimond JG: The effects of positive end-expiratory pressure on heart-lung interactions. J Crit Care 6:1–15, 1991.

41. Crotti S, Mascheroni D, Caironi P, et al: Recruitment and derecruitment during acute respiratory failure. Am J Respir Crit Care Med 164:131–140, 2001.

42. Hickling KG: Best compliance during a decremental, but not incremental, positive end-expiratory pressure trial is related to open-lung positive end-expiratory pressure: A mathematical model of acute respiratory distress syndrome lungs. Am J Respir Crit Care Med 163:69–78, 2001.

43. Rimensberger PC, Prisine G, Mullen BM, et al: Lung recruitment during small tidal volume ventilation allows minimal positive end expiratory pressure without augmenting lung injury. Crit Care Med 27:1940–1945, 1999.

44. Chumello D, Pristine G, Slutsky AS: Mechanical ventilation affects local and systemic cytokines in an animal model of acute respiratory distress syndrome. Am J Respir Crit Care Med 160:109–116, 1999.

45. Pelosi P, Cadringher P, Bottino N, et al: Sigh in acute respiratory distress syndrome. Am J Respir Crit Care Med 159:872–880, 1999.

46. MacIntyre NR: Respiratory system mechanics. In MacIntyre NR, Branson RD (eds): Mechanical Ventilation. Philadelphia: WB Saunders, 2001.

47. Armstrong BW, MacIntyre NR: Pressure controlled inverse ratio ventilation that avoids air trapping in ARDS. Crit Care Med 23:279–285, 1995.

48. Cole AGH, Weller SF, Sykes MD: Inverse ratio ventilation compared with PEEP in adult respiratory failure. Intensive Care Med 10:227–232, 1984.

49. Tharratt RS, Allen RP, Albertson TE: Pressure controlled inverse ratio ventilation in severe adult respiratory failure. Chest 94:755–762, 1988.

50. Shanholtz C, Brower R: Should inverse ratio ventilation be used in ARDS? Am J Respir Crit Care Med 149:1354–1358, 1994.

51. Stock MC, Downs JB, Frolicher DA: Airway pressure release ventilation. Crit Care Med 15:462–466, 1987.

52. Samuelson WN, Fulkerson WJ: Barotrauma in mechanical ventilation. Probl Respir Care 4:52–67, 1991.

53. Kolobow T, Morentti MP, Fumagalli R, et al: Severe impairment in lung function induced by high peak airway pressure during mechanical ventilation. Am Rev Respir Dis 135:312–315, 1987.

54. Dreyfuss D, Savmon G: Ventilator induced lung injury: Lessons from experimental studies. Am J Respir Crit Care Med 157:294–323, 1998.

55. Slutsky AS, Ranieri VM: Mechanical ventilation: Lessons from the ARDSNet trial. Respir Res 1:73–77, 2000.

56. Trembly L, Valenza F, Ribiero, SP, et al: Injurious ventilatory strategies increase cytokines and C-fos M-RNA expression in an isolated rat lung model. J Clin Invest 99:944–952, 1997.

57. Ranieri VM, Suter PM, Totorella C, et al: Effect of mechanical ventilation on inflammatory mediators in patients with acute respiratory distress syndrome. JAMA 282:54–61, 1999.

58. Nahum A, Hoyt J, Schmitz L, et al: Effect of mechanical ventilation strategy on dissemination of intratracheally instilled E. coli in dogs. Crit Care Med 25:1733–1743, 1997.

59. Benito S, Lemaire F: Pulmonary pressure-volume relationship in acute respiratory distress syndrome in adults: Role of positive and expiratory pressure. J Crit Care 5:27–34, 1990.

60. Gajic O, Lee J, Doerr CH, et al: Ventilator-induced cell wounding and repair in the intact lung. Am J Respir Crit Care Med 167:1057–1063, 2003.

60a. Gajic O, Dara SI, Mendez JL, et al: Ventilator-associated lung injury in patients without acute lung injury at the onset of mechanical ventilation. Crit Care Med 32:1817–1824, 2004.

61. Rich BR, Reickert CA, Sawada S, et al: Effect of rate and inspiratory flow on ventilator induced lung injury. J Trauma 49:903–911, 2000.

62. MacIntyre NR, Leatherman, NE: Mechanical loads on the ventilatory muscles. Am Rev Respir Dis 144:968–973, 1989.

63. McGregor M, Bechlake MR: The relationship of oxygen cost of breathing to mechanical work and respiratory force. J Clin Invest 40:971–980, 1961.

64. Bellemare F, Grassino A: Effect of pressure and timing of contraction on human diaphragm fatigue. J Appl Physiol 53:1190–1195, 1982.

65. Banner MJ, Kirby RR, MacIntyre NR: Patient and ventilator work of breathing and ventilatory muscle loads at different levels of pressure support ventilation. Chest 100:531–533, 1991.

66. MacIntyre NR: Weaning from mechanical ventilatory support: Volume-assisting intermittent breaths versus pressure-assisting every breath. Respir Care 33:121–125, 1988.

67. Marini JJ: Exertion during ventilator support: How much and how important? Respir Care 31:385–387, 1986.

68. MacIntyre N: Of Goldilocks and ventilatory muscle loading. Crit Care Med 28:588–589, 2000.

69. Anzueto A, Peters JI, Tobin MJ, et al: Effects of prolonged controlled mechanical ventilation on diaphragmatic function in healthy adult baboons. Crit Care Med 25:1187–1190, 1997.

70. MacIntyre NR: Patient-ventilator interactions. *In* Grenvik A (ed): Textbook of Critical Care Medicine (4th ed). Philadelphia: WB Saunders, 1999.

71. Hansen-Flaschen J, Brazinsky S, Bassles C, Lanken PV: Use of sedating drugs and neuromuscular blockade in patients requiring mechanical ventilation for respiratory failure. JAMA 266:2870–2875, 1991.

72. Sassoon CSH, Giron AE, Ely E, Light RW: Inspiratory work of breathing on flow-by and demand-flow continuous positive airway pressure. Crit Care Med 17:1108–1114, 1989.

73. Petrof BJ, Legare M, Goldberg P, et al: Continuous positive airway pressure reduces work of breathing and dyspnea during weaning from mechanical ventilation in severe chronic obstructive pulmonary disease. Am Rev Respir Dis 141:281–289, 1990.

74. MacIntyre NR, McConnell R, Cheng KC: Applied PEEP reduces the inspiratory load of intrinsic PEEP during pressure support. Chest 1111:188–193, 1997.

75. Flick GR, Belamy PE, Simmons DH: Diaphragmatic contraction during assisted mechanical ventilation. Chest 96:130–135, 1989.

76. Marini JJ, Smith TC, Lamb VJ: External work output and force generation during synchronized intermittent mechanical ventilation. Am Rev Respir Dis 138:1169–1179, 1988.

77. Imsand C, Feihl F, Perret C, Fitting JW: Regulation of inspiratory neuromuscular output during synchronized intermittent mechanical ventilation. Anesthesiology 80:13–22, 1994.

78. Knebel AR, Janson-Bjerklie SL, Malley JD, et al: Comparison of breathing comfort during weaning with two ventilatory modes. Am J Respir Crit Care Med 149:14–18, 1994.

79. Jubran A, Van de Graaf WB, Tobin MJ: Variability of patient ventilator interactions with pressure support ventilation in patients with chronic obstructive pulmonary disease. Am J Respir Crit Care Med 152:129–136, 1995.

80. AARC Conference: Invasive mechanical ventilation in adults. Respir Care 47:508–518, 2002.

81. Fabry B, Zappe D, Guttman J: Breathing pattern and additional work of breathing in spontaneously breathing patients with different ventilatory demand during inspiratory pressure support and automatic tube compensation. Intensive Care Med 23:545–552, 1997.

82. Ho L, MacIntyre NR: Effects of initial flow rate and breath termination criteria on pressure support ventilation. Chest 99:134–138, 1991.

83. Younes M: Proportional assist ventilation, a new approach to ventilatory support. Am Rev Respir Dis 145:114–120, 1992.

84. Grasso S, Ranieri VM: Proportional assist ventilation. Respir Care Clin North Am 7:465–473, 2001.

85. Marini JJ, Culver BH, Butler J: Mechanical effect of lung inflation with positive pressure on cardiac function. Am Rev Respir Dis 124:382–386, 1979.

86. Scharf SM, Caldini P, Ingram RH Jr: Cardiovascular effects of increasing airway pressure in dogs. Am J Physiol 232:1135–1143, 1977.

87. Pinsky MR, Summer WR, Wise RA, et al: Augmentation of cardiac function by elevation of intrathoracic pressure. J Appl Physiol 54:450–455, 1983.

88. Lemaire F, Teboul JL, Cinotti L, et al: Acute left ventricular dysfunction during unsuccessful weaning from mechanical ventilation. Anesthesiology 69:171–179, 1988.

89. Hughes JM, Glazier JB, Maloney JE, West JB: Effect of lung volume on the distribution of pulmonary blood flow in man. Respir Physiol 4:58–72, 1968.

90. Jenkinson SG: Oxygen toxicity. New Horiz 1:504–511, 1993.

91. Betbese AJ, Perez M, Bak E, et al: A prospective study of unplanned endotracheal extubation in ICU patients. Crit Care Med 26:1180–1186, 1998.

92. Craven DE, Kunches LM, Kilinsky V, et al: Risk factors for pneumonia and fatality in patients receiving continuous mechanical ventilation. Am Rev Respir Dis 133:792–796, 1986.

93. Langer M, Mosconi P, Cigada M, et al: Long-term respiratory support and risk of pneumonia in critically ill patients. Am Rev Respir Dis 140:302–305, 1989.

94. Fagon J, Chastre J, Domart Y, et al: Nosocomial pneumonia in patients receiving continuous mechanical ventilation. Am Rev Respir Dis 139:877–884, 1989.

95. Torres A, Serra-Batlles J, Ros E, et al: Pulmonary aspiration of gastric contents in patients receiving mechanical ventilation: The effect of body position. Ann Intern Med 116:540–543, 1992.

96. Kollef MH, Shapiro SD, Fraser VG, et al: Mechanical ventilation with or without seven day circuit change. Ann Intern Med 123:168–174, 1995.

97. Mahjul P, Auboyer C, Jospe R, et al: Prevention of nosocomial pneuomonia in intubated patients: Respective role of mechanical subglottic secretion drainage and stress ulcer prophylaxis. Intensive Care Med 18:20–25, 1992.

98. Hickling KG, Walsh J, Henderson S, Jackson R: Low mortality rate in adult respiratory distress syndrome using low-volume, pressure-limited ventilation with permissive hypercapnia: A prospective study. Crit Care Med 22:1568–1578, 1994.

98a. Sinclair SE, Kregenow DA, Lamm WJ, et al: Hypercapnic acidosis is protective in an in vivo model of ventilator induced lung injury. Am J Resp Crit Care Med 166:403–408, 2002

99. Amato MB, Barbas CSV, Medievos DM, et al: Effect of a protective ventilation strategy on mortality in ARDS. N Engl J Med 338:347–354, 1998.

100. NIH ARDS Network: Ventilation with lower tidal volumes as compared with traditional tidal volumes for acute lung injury and the acute respiratory distress syndrome. N Engl J Med 342:1301–1308, 2000.

101. Putensen C, Bain M, Hormann C: Selecting ventilator settings according to the variables derived from the quasi static pressure volume relationship in patients with acute lung injury. Anesth Analg 77:436–447, 1993.

102. Suter PM, Fairley HB, Isenberg MD: Optimal end expiratory pressure in patients with acute pulmonary failure. N Engl J Med 292:284–289, 1975.

103. ARDS Clinical Trials Network. A trial of high versus low PEEP in patients with ALI/ARDS. N Engl J Med 351:327–336, 2004.

104. Putensen C, Zech S, Wrigge H, et al: Long term effects of spontaneous breathing during ventilatory support in patients with ALI. Am J Respir Crit Care Med 164:43–49, 2001.

105. Hickling KG: Permissive hypercapnia. Respir Care Clin North Am 8:155–169, 2002.

106. Mehta S, Hill NS: Noninvasive ventilation. Am J Respir Crit Care Med 163:540–577, 2001.

107. ACCP/AARC/SCCM Task Force: Evidence based guidelines for weaning and discontinuing mechanical ventilatory support. Chest 120(Suppl 6):1–128, 2001. Also in: Respir Care 47:20–35, 2002.

108. Brochard L, Rauss A, Benito S, et al: Comparison of three methods of gradual withdrawal from ventilatory support during weaning from mechanical ventilation. Am J Respir Crit Care Med 150:896–903, 1994.

109. Esteban A, Frutos F, Tobin MJ, et al: A comparison of four methods of weaning patients from mechanical ventilation: Spanish Lung Failure Collaborative Group. N Engl J Med 332:345–350, 1995.

110. Dos Santos CC, Slutsky AS: Overview of high-frequency ventilation modes, clinical rationale, and gas transport mechanisms. Respir Care Clin North Am 7:549–575, 2001.

111. Froese AB, Bryan C: High frequency ventilation. Am Rev Respir Dis 135:1363–1374, 1987.

112. Chang HK: Mechanisms of gas transport during high frequency ventilation. J Appl Physiol 56:553–563, 1984.

113. MacIntyre NR: High frequency ventilation. In Tobin M (ed): Mechanical Ventilation: Principles and Practice. New York: McGraw-Hill, 1994.

114. Froese AB: High frequency oscillatory ventilation for ARDS: Let's get it right this time. Crit Care Med 25:906–908, 1998.

115. Keszler M, Donn SM, Bucciarelli RL, et al: Multicenter controlled trial comparing HFJV and conventional mechanical ventilation in newborns with PIE. J Pediatr 119:85–93, 1991.

116. Arnold JH, Anas NG, Luckett P, et al: High-frequency oscillatory ventilation in pediatric respiratory failure: A multicenter experience. Crit Care Med 28:3913–3919, 2000.

117. Clark RH, Gerstmann DR, Null DM Jr, deLemos RA: Prospective randomized comparison of high-frequency oscillatory and conventional ventilation in respiratory distress syndrome. Pediatrics 89:5–12, 1992.

118. Mehta S, Lapinsky SE, Hallett DC, et al: Prospective trial of high frequency oscillation in adults with acute respiratory distress syndrome. Crit Care Med 29:1360–1369, 2001.

119. Derdak S, Mehta S, Stewart TE, et al: High-frequency oscillatory ventilation for acute respiratory distress syndrome in adults: A randomized, controlled trial. Am J Respir Crit Care Med 166:801–808, 2002.

85 Hypoxemic Respiratory Failure, Including Acute Respiratory Distress Syndrome

Warren L. Lee, M.D., F.R.C.P.(C), Arthur S. Slutsky, M.D.

INTRODUCTION

Hypoxemic respiratory failure has classically been defined as an arterial PO_2 of less than 60 mm Hg. It is distinguished from hypercapnic respiratory failure ($PCO_2 > 45$ mm Hg), although the two conditions may coexist. There are a number of important qualifications to this definition that must be made. The threshold of 60 mm Hg reflects the shape of the oxyhemoglobin dissociation curve, marking the arterial PO_2 below which the saturation of hemoglobin with oxygen falls precipitously in most people. That being said, it is obvious that whether hypoxemic respiratory failure is acute (over hours to days) or chronic (over weeks to months) has implications not just for diagnosis and treatment, but also for the physiologic adaptations to hypoxemia that develop over time. For example, an individual living at high altitude may have an arterial PO_2 less than 50 mm Hg because of a low inspired partial pressure of oxygen. Such an individual could well be asymptomatic because of acclimatization to that environment, and would not clinically be in hypoxemic respiratory failure despite the low arterial PO_2. It is also important to realize that this definition of hypoxemic respiratory failure (arterial $PO_2 <$ 60 mm Hg) encompasses a broad spectrum of severity of illness. For example, a patient on a general medical ward with community-acquired pneumonia and a mechanically ventilated patient on 100% oxygen in the critical care unit might both fulfill the definition.

This definition of hypoxemic respiratory failure (based on the arterial PO_2) does not fully address the importance of oxygenation at the level of the tissues. Oxygen delivery to the tissues is the product of cardiac output and oxygen content. Oxygen content is critically dependent on the hemoglobin concentration and its saturation with oxygen; although the oxygen saturation depends on the arterial PO_2 (as described by the oxyhemoglobin dissociation curve), the direct contribution of dissolved oxygen to blood oxygen content is very low under most conditions. In other words, in the anemic patient or in patients with very low cardiac output, tissue hypoxia may occur despite a seemingly adequate arterial PO_2. Finally, as indicated earlier, both hypoxemic and hypercarbic respiratory failure may coexist. A patient may initially present with isolated hypoxemia, yet upon tiring may develop hypercarbia. Analogously, hypoventilation can cause both hypercarbia and hypoxemia.

In this chapter, we focus on *acute* hypoxemic respiratory failure. In particular, much of our discussion pertains to the etiology and management of hypoxemia at the "severe" end of the spectrum. This is not to say that mild hypoxemia is not important; certainly the patient on the medical ward with pneumonia and mild hypoxemia can deteriorate and require intubation and mechanical ventilation.

CLASSIFICATION OF HYPOXEMIA

The traditional approach to the causes of arterial hypoxemia classifies them into five pathophysiologic mechanisms: decreased inspired PO_2, hypoventilation, impaired diffusion, ventilation-perfusion (V/Q) mismatch, and right-to-left shunt. Whereas hypoxemia from V/Q mismatch is responsive to supplemental oxygen, hypoxemia from a right-to-left shunt is not. This physiologic approach is probably most useful in understanding how a particular disease causes hypoxemia, but is not usually very illuminating when trying to make a specific diagnosis. In a hospital setting, a decreased inspired PO_2 can essentially be excluded, as most patients will be placed on supplemental oxygen. Hypoventilation can rapidly be excluded if the patient is not hypercapnic or acidemic. Impaired diffusion by itself is not an important cause of acute hypoxemia, as oxygen transfer across the alveolar-capillary membrane to red blood cells is usually *perfusion-limited*, not diffusion-limited. What this means is that there is usually ample time for diffusion of oxygen, even in the presence of intrinsic lung disease. Most patients in the intensive care unit with acute hypoxemic respiratory failure have some combination of V/Q mismatch and right-to-left shunt.

Another classification of acute hypoxemic respiratory failure is structural-anatomic (Table 85.1). Causes of acute

Table 85.1 Structural Classification of Acute Hypoxemic Respiratory Failure

Structure	Examples of Possible Diagnoses*
Air spaces (alveoli)	Pulmonary edema (cardiogenic)[†] Acute lung injury (ALI)/acute respiratory distress syndrome (ARDS) Pulmonary hemorrhage Pneumonia
Interstitium	Pulmonary fibrosis (e.g., Hamman-Rich syndrome) Extrinsic allergic alveolitis Viral or "atypical" pneumonia
Heart/pulmonary vasculature	Pulmonary embolism Intracardiac or intrapulmonary shunt Congestive heart failure
Airways	Asthma Chronic obstructive pulmonary disease Mucous plugging Right main-stem bronchus intubation
Pleura	Pneumothorax Pleural effusion

* This is by no means an exhaustive list, and is meant for illustrative purposes only.
[†] Also possible in heart/pulmonary vasculature.

arterial hypoxemia can be classified based on whether the primary pathology is located in the air spaces, interstitium, heart and pulmonary vasculature, airways, or pleural space. Such an approach would quickly lead one to consider such causes as pulmonary edema or pneumonia, hypersensitivity pneumonitis, pulmonary embolism, bronchospasm, and pneumothorax. Although disorders involving other structures such as the central nervous system and respiratory muscles can lead to hypoxemia, these causes would be expected to have associated hypercarbia.

CLINICAL FEATURES AND DIAGNOSTIC APPROACH

The clinical features of acute hypoxemic respiratory failure will vary to some degree based on the underlying cause. Assuming an intact drive to breathe and that the patient has not fatigued, the hypoxemic patient will be tachypneic and tachycardic. Cyanosis of the lips or tongue (so-called central cyanosis) can be seen when the concentration of reduced (deoxygenated) hemoglobin is greater than 5 g/100 mL.

Given the extensive differential diagnosis of acute hypoxemic respiratory failure and the often urgent need for therapy, the clinician must be practical yet thoughtful. A basic history should be obtained to identify risk factors for cardiac dysfunction, pulmonary infection or aspiration, venous thromboembolism, or obstructive lung diseases. In the setting of trauma to the chest, pneumothorax, hemothorax, and pulmonary contusion must be considered. Further questions to identify less common causes of acute hypoxemic respiratory failure can be posed as appropriate. A focused physical examination of the cardiac and respiratory systems can often establish the presence or absence of

congestive heart failure or a focal area of consolidation or effusion. Similarly, the diagnosis of a pneumothorax is more satisfying (and prompt) when made on physical examination rather than later only after chest radiography.

Implementation of therapy is *simultaneous* with the diagnostic workup. As always, this starts with the "ABCs" of airway, breathing, and circulation. Once the ABCs are assured, the patient should be given supplemental oxygen (if coexistent hypercapnia is present, care must be taken in the dose of supplemental oxygen) and intravenous access should be obtained. Continuous cardiac monitoring and pulse oximetry should be available.

The initial investigations will be dictated by the findings on history and physical examination. However, all patients should have a chest radiograph, an electrocardiogram, and routine blood work, including a complete blood count and differential and serum chemistry. An arterial blood gas should be obtained and the alveolar-arterial PO_2 gradient should be calculated; a normal alveolar-arterial PO_2 gradient in the setting of arterial hypoxemia suggests hypoventilation as the sole cause of the hypoxemia. The blood gas is also useful for diagnosing other acid-base disturbances. The need for further investigations, including bronchoscopy, computed tomographic angiography of the chest, and echocardiography, will depend on the results of the initial assessment. A completely normal chest radiograph in the setting of hypoxemic respiratory failure narrows the differential diagnosis substantially. In this uncommon circumstance, the clinician should consider pulmonary embolism and right-to-left shunts (i.e., intracardiac or pulmonary arteriovenous malformations) as possibilities. A more common scenario is that the chest radiograph of a patient with pneumonia can appear surprisingly normal (or may show only a "small" infiltrate) due to concomitant intravascular volume depletion. Once intravascular volume has been restored, the true extent of the infiltrate can be appreciated.

CAUSES OF ACUTE HYPOXEMIC RESPIRATORY FAILURE

In a large multicenter international prospective cohort study of patients requiring mechanical ventilation, the most common reported causes of acute respiratory failure were postoperative respiratory failure, pneumonia, congestive heart failure, sepsis, and trauma.[1] In a small prospective cohort study that included 41 patients with hypoxemic respiratory failure, chronic obstructive pulmonary disease and pneumonia were the most common causes.[2] Other data from small, randomized controlled trials of noninvasive ventilation identified congestive heart failure, pneumonia, trauma, acute respiratory distress syndrome (ARDS), and mucous plugging as the most common causes of respiratory failure.[3,4] However, in these studies patients with certain diseases were excluded, including those with chronic obstructive pulmonary disease[3,4] and asthma,[3] limiting the ability to generalize from these findings. Indeed, in the one randomized study that specifically enrolled only patients with acute hypoxemic respiratory failure, patients had to have bilateral lung infiltrates on chest radiography to be included.[4]

For a detailed discussion of many of the specific causes of acute hypoxemic respiratory failure (e.g., pneumonia), the reader is referred to the appropriate chapters in this book. The remainder of this chapter focuses on a particular subtype of acute hypoxemic respiratory failure, known as *acute respiratory distress syndrome.*

ACUTE RESPIRATORY DISTRESS SYNDROME

DIAGNOSIS AND EPIDEMIOLOGY

Diagnosis

ARDS is characterized by noncardiogenic pulmonary edema, lung inflammation, hypoxemia, and decreased lung compliance. Unlike some disorders (e.g., coronary artery disease), ARDS, as its name suggests, is a syndrome, reflecting a constellation of clinical and physiologic observations thought to represent a common pathology. In coronary artery disease, narrowing of the coronary vasculature and disruption of an unstable atherosclerotic plaque are known to underpin the symptoms of angina and unstable angina, respectively. A diagnostic "gold standard," namely coronary angiography, exists. In contrast, the pathogenesis of ARDS remains elusive and there is no gold standard diagnostic test. The heterogeneity of the clinical conditions associated with ARDS (discussed later) would be consistent with the possibility that ARDS is in fact a collection of different diseases that have not yet been separately identified. These problems necessarily permeate any discussion or research into ARDS, and this chapter is no exception.

The first description of ARDS appeared in a remarkable case series reported in 1967.[5] Ashbaugh and colleagues described 12 patients ranging in age from 11 to 48 years, who presented with respiratory distress, hypoxemic respiratory failure, and patchy bilateral infiltrates on chest radiographs (Fig. 85.1). The syndrome was characterized by rapid onset, as most of the patients developed respiratory distress within 48 to 72 hours of the beginning of their illness. Most of the cases were preceded by severe trauma or viral infection. Many patients required positive-pressure

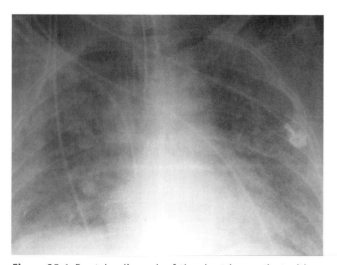

Figure 85.1 Frontal radiograph of the chest in a patient with acute respiratory distress syndrome. Note the presence of bilateral infiltrates. (Courtesy of Michael B. Gotway, MD, Department of Radiology, University of California, San Francisco.)

ventilation and exhibited low respiratory system compliance, and some experienced improvement in oxygenation with the application of positive end-expiratory pressure (PEEP). This syndrome was initially termed the *adult* respiratory distress syndrome, to distinguish it from the respiratory distress syndrome seen in neonates. Subsequently, recognizing that it can occur in children, it was renamed the *acute* respiratory distress syndrome.

The cases described by Ashbaugh and colleagues generated interest and research into ARDS. Unfortunately, the lack of either specific diagnostic criteria or an understanding of the pathogenesis of the disorder made it difficult both to undertake and to compare studies. In 1988, a formalized and expanded definition of ARDS was proposed that consisted of three parts: one part described whether the illness was acute or chronic, and another described any associated risk factors or medical conditions (e.g., sepsis).[6] Another part assigned points based on the severity of pulmonary dysfunction (the Lung Injury Score [LIS]), as measured by the degree of hypoxemia, the level of PEEP required, the respiratory system compliance, and the degree of radiographic abnormality. An average score was calculated and a final value greater than 2.5 was used to diagnose ARDS. One advantage of this system was its description of associated medical conditions, which might be pertinent to the etiology of ARDS. Because ARDS from different etiologies might reflect different pathogeneses and perhaps confer a different response to therapy, knowing the cause of ARDS would be important in the conduct and comparison of studies. However, the definition made no attempt to exclude cardiogenic pulmonary edema, assuming that clinicians would do so automatically.

Subsequently, a consensus conference of American and European investigators published their definition of ARDS, which has since been widely adopted[7] (Table 85.2). Aiming for simplicity, ARDS was defined as a syndrome of acute onset, with bilateral infiltrates on chest radiography consistent with pulmonary edema, pulmonary artery occlusion pressure less than or equal to 18 mm Hg (or absence of clinical evidence of left atrial hypertension), and hypoxemia as measured by the ratio of the arterial partial pressure of oxygen (PaO_2) to the fraction of oxygen inspired (FIO_2). Recognizing the spectrum of severity of the disease, the consensus panel recommended that a PaO_2/FIO_2 ratio of less than or equal to 300 define an entity termed *acute lung injury* (ALI). ARDS was the most severe form of ALI and was defined as occurring if the PaO_2/FIO_2 ratio is less than or equal to 200. The simplicity of the definition led to its general acceptance by clinicians and its incorporation into clinical research. At the same time, such a straightforward definition could take into account neither the heterogeneity of the disease nor the ambiguity of clinical practice.

For example, the requirement for bilateral infiltrates on chest radiograph is open to interpretation. One study presented a random series of chest radiographs from intubated hypoxemic patients (PaO_2/FIO_2 ratio < 300) to an international group of expert clinicians, the majority of whom give lectures and conduct clinical research on ARDS. The clinicians were asked to examine each radiograph and to decide whether it fulfilled the American-European consensus conference (AECC) definition of ARDS (bilateral infiltrates consistent with pulmonary edema). This select group of

Table 85.2 American-European Consensus Conference Criteria for Acute Respiratory Distress Syndrome (ARDS)

	Timing	Oxygenation	Frontal Chest Radiograph	Pulmonary Artery Wedge Pressure
Acute lung injury	Acute	$PaO_2/FIO_2 \leq 300$ m Hg*	Bilateral infiltrates	≤ 18 m Hg if measured, or no clinical evidence of left atrial hypertension
ARDS	Acute	$PaO_2/FIO_2 \leq 200$ mm Hg*	Bilateral infiltrates	≤ 18 mm Hg if measured, or no clinical evidence of left atrial hypertension

* Regardless of positive end-expiratory pressure (PEEP).
FIO_2, fraction of oxygen inspired; PaO_2, arterial PO_2.
Adapted from Bernard GR, Artigas A, Brigham KL, et al: The American-European Consensus Conference on ARDS: Definitions, mechanisms, relevant outcomes, and clinical trial coordination. Am J Respir Crit Care Med 149:818–824, 1994.

physicians demonstrated only moderate agreement (kappa statistic, 0.55) in their classification of the radiographs; when the percentage of radiographs deemed to be consistent with ARDS by each physician was examined, the percentages were evenly distributed from a low of 36% to a high of 71%.[8] Another larger study on the issue also demonstrated only moderate agreement when two physicians were asked to rate radiographs on the presence or absence of diffuse bilateral infiltrates consistent with ARDS. However, with prior training and discussion, the agreement between an intensivist and a radiologist in the rating of the films was excellent.[9]

The AECC definition has also been criticized for not taking the level of PEEP into consideration. Clinicians have long appreciated that applying PEEP can improve oxygenation, an observation that was noted in the first description of ARDS. This implies that the PaO_2/FIO_2 ratio will change as the level of applied PEEP changes; indeed, a patient who meets the AECC criteria for ARDS may no longer meet them once applied PEEP has been increased.[10] Finally, unlike the LIS described earlier, the AECC definition makes no mention of associated risk factors for ARDS.

When the LIS and AECC definitions have been compared, they have been found to identify similar patients with a similar mortality rate.[11,12] In other words, the differences in the definitions of ARDS do not seem to have prognostic importance. This finding is reassuring to clinicians, because it suggests that results from studies that used one or the other definition can still be meaningfully compared.

Incidence

If it is difficult to make a diagnosis of ARDS or ALI, it is not surprising that determining the incidence of the disease is challenging. The reported incidence of ARDS has ranged from 75 per 100,000 population[13] to as low as 1.5 per 100,000.[14] Many studies did not use the AECC definition and did not include ALI. By definition, the incidence of ALI is higher (20 to 50 cases per 100,000) than the incidence of ARDS (3 to 8 cases per 100,000).[15] A recent study calculated an incidence of ARDS and ALI of 22 cases per 100,000 using data from a large prospective trial of ARDS and from the American Hospital Association.[16] One of the methodologic strengths of the study was its inclusion of cases of both ALI and ARDS over a 3-year period, thereby decreasing the impact of seasonal variability. The heterogeneity in the literature of the estimates of incidence may reflect differences in the methodology of the various studies, but may also reflect true variation. Regional differences in genetic or environmental factors and in disease-specific associations such as cardiopulmonary bypass or lung transplantation may account for some of the regional variability in the incidence of ARDS and ALI.[15]

Risk Factors

Data from a number of studies have demonstrated that sepsis, aspiration of gastric contents, and multiple transfusions (>15 units per 24 hours in one study) were associated with the highest risk of developing ARDS. In particular, almost 40% of patients with sepsis went on to develop ARDS. The presence of more than one presumed risk factor for ARDS increased the incidence of ARDS, although the sample sizes of these subsets were quite small.[17] In these studies, over a third of patients receiving massive blood transfusion and a quarter of patients with multiple trauma (one or more of pulmonary contusion, multiple fractures, and multiple transfusions) developed ARDS.[18]

Investigators in Denver conducted a prospective cohort study involving 351 patients admitted to the intensive care unit who had one of seven diagnoses thought to put them at risk for ARDS. The incidence of ARDS was compared between patients with and without a history of chronic alcoholism as determined from medical records. Interestingly, a history of alcohol abuse was associated with a higher incidence of ARDS (relative risk of 1.98; 95% confidence interval, 1.32 to 2.85). This relationship remained significant after adjustment for gender, at-risk diagnosis, and severity of illness. Among those who developed ARDS, patients with a history of alcoholism had a higher mortality rate than those without this history (odds ratio 6.26; 95% confidence interval 2.22 to 20.38).[19] The mechanisms of this association are unknown.

The same researchers examined whether patients with diabetes might be protected against the development of ARDS, the rationale being that hyperglycemia is known to impair neutrophil function, and neutrophils are thought to be central to the pathogenesis of ARDS (see "Etiology and Pathogenesis" section). Over 100 patients admitted to the intensive care unit with septic shock were followed prospectively for the development of ARDS. Over a 2-year period, diabetes was associated with a significantly decreased risk of ARDS (relative risk 0.53; 95% confidence interval 0.28 to 0.98), which persisted after adjustment for the source of

Table 85.3 Conditions Associated with Acute Respiratory Distress Syndrome, by Possible Mechanisms of Injury

Indirect Injury	Direct Injury
Sepsis	Pneumonia
Major trauma	Aspiration
Multiple blood transfusions	Pulmonary contusion
Pancreatitis	Toxic inhalation
Cardiopulmonary bypass	Near drowning
Drug overdose	Reperfusion injury (e.g., post–lung transplantation)
Adverse effect of medication	

sepsis and other potential confounders. Interestingly, there was no difference in mortality between patients with ARDS who had and did not have diabetes.[20]

A systematic overview of studies examining potential risk factors for ARDS concluded that the strongest evidence of a causal relationship was for sepsis, trauma, multiple transfusions, aspiration of gastric contents, pulmonary contusion, pneumonia, and smoke inhalation. It is important to acknowledge that most of the data for these conclusions come from methodologically weak studies, in which risk factors or ARDS itself were not well defined, or from case series rather than true prospective cohort studies. That being said, the relatively low incidence of ARDS would make conducting a prospective cohort study to look at specific potential risk factors quite difficult.[21]

The heterogeneity of risk factors for ARDS is remarkable. At the AECC, investigators divided the known risk factors into those thought to cause *direct* lung injury (e.g., pneumonia), and those in which the mechanism of lung injury was thought to be *indirect* (e.g., pancreatitis) (Table 85.3). Whether this conceptually attractive classification scheme (also known as the *pulmonary* versus *nonpulmonary* risk factor classification) reflects underlying differences in the mechanisms, severity, or outcome of lung injury is still being debated. For example, one group of investigators has documented differences in lung elastance between patients with ARDS in the two groups; in those with a pulmonary cause, lung elastance was significantly higher.[22] In addition, increasing PEEP led to improved recruitment of the lung in the nonpulmonary group, but to decreased recruitment in patients with ARDS from a presumed pulmonary source. Despite these interesting observations, whether these two groups of patients have different prognoses or different responses to therapy is unclear. We discuss this issue in more detail in the section on outcome.

ETIOLOGY AND PATHOGENESIS

Overview of Pathophysiology

In the past, ARDS has also been called noncardiogenic pulmonary edema, a descriptive term that nonetheless reflected what was known of the pathogenesis of the disorder. Unlike congestive heart failure, in which elevated left-sided cardiac

pressures cause hydrostatic pulmonary edema, in ARDS, the edema fluid that fills the alveoli is exudative in origin. In other words, the alveolar-capillary barrier exhibits increased permeability, allowing for the leakage of protein-rich fluid into the air spaces. Alveolar filling leads to decreased respiratory system compliance as well as right-to-left shunting and profound hypoxemia. Although arterial PCO_2 is generally within the normal range, dead space ventilation is significantly increased, as demonstrated by elevated minute ventilation. Pulmonary hypertension is also commonly observed in ARDS, and a number of mechanisms have been proposed; these include hypoxic vasoconstriction, intravascular fibrin deposition in the pulmonary capillaries, and compression of blood vessels by the positive-pressure ventilation used to treat the disorder. In this section, we review the pathology of ARDS and discuss current theories as to its pathogenesis. As we shall see, much of the research into ARDS has focused on determining the basis for the increase in alveolar-capillary permeability. It is important to note that the pathophysiology of ALI is thought to be the same as ARDS, and we will use the terms almost interchangeably for the remainder of this chapter.

Pathology

The pathologic features of ARDS have classically been described using three overlapping and sequential stages.[23] In the first or exudative phase of lung injury, the pathologic findings have been termed *diffuse alveolar damage*. There are hyaline membranes and protein-rich edema fluid in the alveolar spaces, as well as epithelial disruption and infiltration of the interstitium and air spaces with neutrophils. Areas of hemorrhage and macrophages can also be found in the alveoli. This phase, which is thought to last for 5 to 7 days, is followed in some patients by the so-called proliferative phase. At this point, hyaline membranes are reorganized and fibrosis begins to be observed. Obliteration of pulmonary capillaries and deposition of interstitial and alveolar collagen may be observed, along with a decrease in the number of neutrophils and the extent of pulmonary edema. This proliferative stage has traditionally been described as being followed by a fibrotic phase, essentially emphasizing the appearance of pulmonary fibrosis in a subset of patients with persistent (i.e., >2 weeks) ARDS.

More recently, it has been realized that the development of areas of fibrosis may actually occur sooner than usually appreciated—elevated levels of N-terminal procollagen peptide III, thought to represent collagen synthesis, can be detected in bronchoalveolar lavage fluid of patients with ARDS as early as 24 hours into the course of the illness. In addition, the bronchoalveolar lavage fluid from these patients has been shown to stimulate cultured fibroblasts to proliferate.[24] These and other observations have led some investigators to hypothesize that fibroproliferation may be initiated simultaneously with (rather than after) inflammatory lung injury.[25]

The Alveolar-Capillary Membrane

If ARDS is a disorder of increased alveolar-capillary permeability, it stands to reason that the pulmonary microvascular endothelium or the alveolar epithelium (or both) must be involved in its pathophysiology. Damage to the alveolar epithelium is now thought to be a key event in the increased permeability of the alveolar-capillary membrane in ARDS.[26] As an example, in the lung, epithelial cells are normally more resistant than endothelial cells to the injurious effects of circulating endotoxin,[27] and epithelial disruption may therefore be conceptualized as a rate-limiting event in the development of alveolar flooding. The importance of the alveolar epithelium once ARDS has occurred is also clear. Type II pneumocytes differentiate into type I cells to help cover the denuded epithelial surface. Both type I and II cells express the Na^+/K^+-ATPase, which is thought to be important in clearance of edema fluid (discussed in some detail later). Finally, type II pneumocytes produce and metabolize surfactant. How the damage to the alveolar-capillary membrane occurs is not known for certain, although neutrophils are suspected to play a role (see later).

Surfactant

Many researchers have described alterations to surfactant that are associated with ARDS. Surfactant is a complex mixture of phospholipids and surfactant proteins that reduces alveolar surface tension. It is known that there are decreased amounts of surfactant-related protein and decreased dipalmitoylphosphatidylcholine and phosphatidylglycerol, in the surfactant of patients with ARDS. The proportion of large (active) to small (inactive) aggregates of surfactant is diminished, due to both decreased production of surfactant and increased conversion of the large to small forms. In addition, plasma proteins that have leaked through the alveolar-capillary barrier may interfere with surfactant function.[28] For example, damage to surfactant protein A has been demonstrated in patients with ARDS.[29] The impairment in surfactant function observed in ARDS would theoretically predispose to alveolar collapse. In addition, surfactant proteins have been found to have antimicrobial properties,[30,31] although whether the loss of these properties is relevant to the pathogenesis of ARDS is not known. Indeed, despite the litany of abnormalities in surfactant that have been described,[32] the extent to which these alterations contribute to the pathogenesis of ARDS remains controversial: Unlike the neonatal respiratory distress syndrome, in which a deficiency of surfactant underlies the pathophysiology of the disease, it is possible that the abnormalities of surfactant in ARDS are the result rather than the cause of altered physiology. Indeed, four large randomized controlled trials of exogenous surfactant supplementation in ARDS failed to demonstrate any improvement in mortality or in the requirement for mechanical ventilation[28] (see "Therapy" section).

Sodium Ion and Water

Na^+ channels at the apical surface of alveolar epithelial cells mediate Na^+ uptake from the alveoli. This creates an osmotic gradient and causes alveolar fluid to follow, thereby allowing for the clearance of pulmonary edema. Na^+/K^+-ATPases in the basolateral membrane of the epithelial cell exchange intracellular Na^+ for extracellular K^+, maintaining the intracellular sodium concentration low enough for the apical Na^+ resorption to continue. This process allows for the net removal of Na^+ and fluid from the alveolar space, and can be accelerated (at least experimentally) by catecholamines.

Dysfunction of either the apical Na^+ channels or the basolateral Na^+/K^+-ATPases (or both) has been postulated to be involved in the pathogenesis of ARDS. For example, it is known that hypoxia decreases epithelial Na^+ reabsorption by impairing the expression of subunits of the epithelial Na^+ channel.[33] Hypoxia also decreases the activity of both the apical Na^+ channel[34] and the Na^+/K^+-ATPase.[35] In an animal model of hemorrhagic shock–induced ALI, the normal upregulation of alveolar fluid reabsorption in response to catecholamines was absent. This defect was attributed to an increase in nitric oxide (NO) in the lung, which may have impaired β-adrenergic receptor signaling.[36] In a recent retrospective study of patients with ALI, alveolar fluid clearance was measured. When patients were stratified by their rate of fluid clearance, those with the highest rates had the lowest mortality and the shortest duration of mechanical ventilation.[37] Whether alveolar fluid clearance can be manipulated in a clinical setting (e.g., by β-adrenergic agonists) to improve prognosis is an area of ongoing research.

Neutrophils and Other Inflammatory Mediators

Histologically, one of the hallmarks of ALI/ARDS is the accumulation of neutrophils in the microvasculature of the lung.[38] As key players in innate immunity, neutrophils can generate an impressive array of cytotoxic compounds. These include reactive oxygen species, cationic peptides, eicosanoids, and proteolytic enzymes such as leukocyte elastase. In addition, once activated, neutrophils release growth factors and cytokines (such as tumor necrosis factor-α [TNF-α] and interleukin-1β) that may enhance the inflammatory response. Given this destructive potential, it has long been theorized that neutrophils may be central to the pathogenesis of ALI[39] (Fig. 85.2). There is an abundance of clinical and preclinical data to support this hypothesis. For example, in humans with ARDS following sepsis, bronchoalveolar lavage neutrophilia is associated with a poor prognosis.[40] Neutrophil-depleted mice exposed to hyperoxia develop less lung injury than normal mice.[41] Similarly, in a hamster model of ALI induced by endotoxin inhalation, the administration of a specific inhibitor of neutrophil elastase (even hours after administration of endotoxin) prevented the development of lung injury.[42]

If neutrophils are involved in the pathogenesis of ARDS, some defect in their regulation must be invoked. For example, in an uncomplicated bacterial pneumonia, the pulmonary inflammatory response is limited by counterregulatory processes that prevent tissue damage. Why this regulation is ineffective or insufficient in ARDS is a fascinating and unanswered question.[43]

One of the earliest manifestations of ARDS, even before hypoxemia, is a transient leukopenia due to sequestration of neutrophils in the lung microvasculature.[44] The average pulmonary capillary is smaller than the average neutrophil, and neutrophils therefore have to deform to pass through the microvasculature. Activated neutrophils "stiffen" and cannot negotiate narrow capillary segments.[45] Inhibitors of actin polymerization can abrogate this stiffening, implicating a change in the actin cytoskeleton in neutrophil sequestration in the lung.[46] Longer lasting neutrophil sequestration

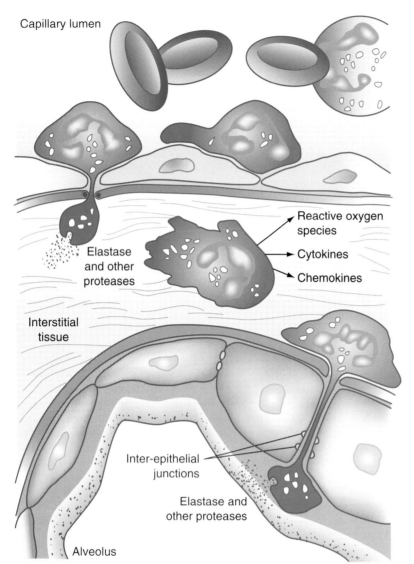

Capillary lumen

Reactive oxygen species

Cytokines

Chemokines

Elastase and other proteases

Interstitial tissue

Inter-epithelial junctions

Elastase and other proteases

Alveolus

Figure 85.2 Role of neutrophils in the pathogenesis of acute lung injury. Activated neutrophils exit the bloodstream and transmigrate across the alveolar-capillary membrane, releasing cytokines, proteases, reactive oxygen species, and other compounds. Although crucial to host defense against pathogens, the compounds secreted or released by the neutrophil have the capacity to damage the tissue of the host. (Adapted from Lee WL, Downey GP: Leukocyte elastase: Physiological functions and role in acute lung injury. A state of the art review. Am J Respir Crit Care Med 164:896–904, 2001.) *See Color Plate*

is thought to involve interactions between molecules on the surface of the neutrophil and the lung capillary endothelium. For example, in rabbits, blocking the adhesion molecule L-selectin on the surface of the neutrophil prevented neutrophil sequestration in alveolar capillaries induced by exposure to endotoxin.[47]

After the initial sequestration, neutrophils must translocate across the alveolar-capillary barrier to access the alveolar space (diapedesis). The determinants of this seemingly simple movement remain incompletely understood. Integrins on the surface of the neutrophil are thought to mediate emigration of neutrophils from the pulmonary circulation in response to some, but not all, inflammatory stimuli.[48] Proteases secreted by the alveolar epithelium, in concert with regional cytokine production and glycosaminoglycans on the epithelial surface, may act together to form a chemotactic gradient for neutrophils to follow.[49]

Many investigators are focusing on the mechanisms of neutrophil activation. Multiple studies have looked at various components of intracellular signal transduction pathways, such as kinases (enzymes that phosphorylate substrates) and transcription factors. For example, one such kinase is the p38 mitogen-activated protein kinase, which is activated when cells are stimulated with lipopolysaccharide (LPS).[50] Activation of this kinase stimulates TNF-α production and macrophage inflammatory protein-2 release (a chemotactic factor for macrophages).[51] Interestingly, inhibition of p38 mitogen-activated protein kinase in mice, even hours after the mice are exposed to aerosolized LPS, attenuates neutrophil chemotaxis and migration from the lung microvasculature into alveoli.[52] Another kinase often discussed in the context of inflammation is phosphatidylinositol 3-kinase (PI3K). This enzyme phosphorylates phosphatidylinositol, a lipid-derived second messenger whose phosphorylated forms have been implicated in a myriad of intracellular signaling events. PI3Kγ is preferentially activated in neutrophils exposed to interleukin-8 or *N*-formyl-methionyl-leucyl-phenylalanine (fMLP, a bacterial-derived peptide).[53] Despite exposure to intraperitoneal endotoxin, PI3Kγ knockout mice displayed decreased neutrophil accumulation, cytokine production, and lung injury compared to control mice. The neutrophils in the lung of the knockout mice also demonstrated diminished activation of nuclear factor-κB, an important transcription factor known to mediate the up-regulation of numerous cytokines and proinflammatory mediators.[54]

There are many potential mechanisms by which activated neutrophils might mediate ALI. In addition to secreting cytokines and growth factors that might stimulate the local and systemic inflammatory response, neutrophils generate reactive oxygen species that can mediate tissue damage.[55] In animal studies, inhibition of the assembly of nicotinamide adenine dinucleotide phosphate oxidase (the major source of reactive oxygen species) by apocynin has been shown to attenuate sepsis-induced lung injury.[56] The NO synthase pathway has also been implicated in mediating lung injury; knockout mice lacking the gene for inducible NO synthase developed less severe lung injury than wild-type animals upon injection with LPS.[57]

Neutrophils contain proteolytic enzymes that may be involved in the pathogenesis of ALI. In particular, both neutrophil elastase and metalloproteinases have been extensively studied.[58] Because of its ability to degrade multiple substrates, including growth factors and cytokines, neutrophil elastase may be involved in regulation of the inflammatory response. It has also been shown to degrade epithelial and endothelial cadherins, proteins that are major components of adherens junctions, which hold cells together. It is possible that elastase-mediated destruction of cadherin could predispose to alveolar flooding. Despite its potential to cause unwanted tissue damage, neutrophil elastase is likely crucial to host defense. In neutrophil elastase–deficient mice, the administration of intraperitoneal *Klebsiella pneumoniae* causes 100% mortality within 48 hours, compared to only 50% mortality in normal mice.[59] However, neutrophil elastase–deficient mice are paradoxically resistant to normally lethal doses of LPS. Furthermore, mice that lack both neutrophil elastase and another neutrophil protease (cathepsin G) are protected against alveolar damage induced by endotoxic shock.[60] These apparently contradictory results suggest that neutrophil elastase, although important in a regulated inflammatory response, may nonetheless participate in inflammatory injury under certain circumstances. Numerous studies in multiple species of animals and using multiple different experimental models suggest that neutrophil elastase plays an important role in the pathogenesis of ALI in animals. Whether it is as important in the development of ALI or ARDS in humans remains unanswered. A clinical trial of a leukocyte elastase inhibitor in ARDS was recently halted because preliminary analysis suggested lack of efficacy.[60a]

Other studies have indicated the importance of metalloproteinases in leukocyte-mediated lung injury. Elevated concentrations of the matrix metalloproteinases gelatinase A and B have been found in the epithelial lining fluid of patients with ARDS.[61] Mice lacking the genes for gelatinase B or stromelysin 1 had less severe injury in an animal model of ALI.[62] As mentioned earlier, matrilysin (matrix metalloproteinase 7) has been shown to regulate the formation of a chemotactic gradient and the transmigration of neutrophils across the alveolar epithelium in a mouse model of ALI.[49] Finally, administration of an inhibitor of elastase and metalloproteinases (chemically modified tetracycline-3) attenuated ALI after cardiopulmonary bypass in pigs.[63]

Another important aspect of the inflammatory response in ARDS is its down-regulation. In the normal host, this process likely involves the removal of neutrophils without release of their cytotoxic armamentarium in order to prevent unnecessary damage to the surrounding tissues. Apoptosis of neutrophils, which does not incite inflammation, may therefore be important in the resolution of lung injury. Indeed, it has been suggested that a delay in apoptosis of neutrophils might be implicated in the development or persistence of ALI. Although this theory has theoretical merit, there is at present little clinical evidence to substantiate it. A randomized controlled trial of granulocyte colony-stimulating factor (which, in addition to stimulating new neutrophil formation, also delays neutrophil apoptosis) in patients with pneumonia found increased blood neutrophils, faster radiologic improvement, and a *decreased* incidence of ARDS in the patients receiving the growth factor.[64] Furthermore, another recent randomized controlled trial administered granulocyte-monocyte colony-stimulating factor or placebo to patients with severe sepsis and respiratory dysfunction; patients who received the drug had an improvement in their PaO_2/FIO_2 ratio and a decrease in alveolar neutrophils. Importantly, there was no evidence of aggravated pulmonary or extrapulmonary organ dysfunction in the group that received granulocyte-monocyte colony-stimulating factor.[65] It is worth pointing out that these results from human clinical trials are in contrast to studies using *animal* models of ALI,[66,67] which suggested that granulocyte colony-stimulating factor might be harmful.

An extension to this line of thinking is that the role of neutrophils themselves in the pathogenesis of ALI may have been overstated. ARDS has certainly been described in patients with profound neutropenia.[68,69] Indeed, it is possible that the neutrophil infiltration observed in some cases of ALI/ARDS is adaptive (i.e., a physiologic response to a primary injury) rather than destructive. At present, however, we believe that the balance of the evidence implicates neutrophils as a causative factor in the development of most cases of ALI. Comparatively little is known about the mechanisms of neutrophil-independent ALI, and this must be a goal of future investigations.

Inflammation and Coagulation: Chicken or Egg?

One of the most common precipitants for ARDS is sepsis, and it is hoped that therapies for sepsis may either prevent or improve the outcome of ARDS. Our current concept of sepsis is of an initial inflammatory state, with up-regulation of inflammatory cytokines such as TNF-α and interleukin-1β and recruitment and activation of inflammatory cells such as neutrophils. This early stage of inflammation is followed by relatively depressed immunity, in which the patient is vulnerable to nosocomial infections.[70] The theory that dysregulation of the inflammatory response is responsible for sepsis has led to the search for agents that would selectively block components of the inflammatory pathway, such as antibodies to TNF-α. More recently, it has been appreciated that there are important connections between the molecular cascades that regulate both inflammation and coagulation; for example, TNF-α causes an increase in thrombin and fibrin formation, and fibrin fragments themselves are known to be chemotactic for neutrophils.[71] TNF-α increases tissue factor expression on endothelium and inhibits fibrinolysis, both of which favor fibrin formation.

Activated protein C, an endogenous anticoagulant, has direct and indirect anti-inflammatory effects, which include decreasing levels of interleukin-6 and attenuating neutrophil activation in sepsis.[72,73] Because sepsis is the most common cause of ARDS and because abnormalities of coagulation are very common in sepsis, investigators have wondered whether altered coagulation is involved in the genesis of ARDS. How this might occur is largely speculative, but intra-alveolar, interstitial, and intravascular fibrin depositions have all been observed in patients with ARDS. Indeed, fibrin is a major component of hyaline membranes. Intra-alveolar fibrin has been postulated to serve as a nidus for fibroblast proliferation and, potentially, as ALI resolves, as a stimulus for pulmonary fibrosis. Fibrin might contribute as well to ongoing lung injury through its chemotactic properties, and intravascular fibrin deposition, as in microthrombi, might contribute to the elevated pulmonary vascular pressures observed in ARDS.

Interest in the role of coagulation in the pathogenesis of ARDS has been buttressed in part by observations in animal studies that anticoagulation can attenuate the severity of sepsis-induced lung injury.[74] In addition, a randomized controlled trial of activated protein C in human sepsis showed a significant reduction in mortality.[75] In this study, because about three quarters of the patients were receiving mechanical ventilation, it is likely that a significant proportion of them had ARDS. A subgroup analysis of the effect of activated protein C in ARDS has not been presented, but this field (the crossover between inflammation and coagulation) is an area of very active research.[75a]

Other molecular determinants of inflammation continue to be elucidated. Recent data have implicated transforming growth factor-β in animal models of ALI. In one study, transforming growth factor-β was postulated to cause increased alveolar epithelial cell permeability by depleting intracellular glutathione levels.[76] Platelet-activating factor (PAF) is another inflammatory mediator receiving a lot of attention in animal models of ARDS.[76a] Other investigators have attempted to improve the endogenous counterinflammatory response; in one recent study, the gene for heat shock protein 70 (HSP-70) was ligated to an adenoviral promoter, and the resultant recombinant construct was administered into the lungs of rats in which ARDS had been induced by cecal ligation and perforation. Administration of the recombinant construct increased heat shock protein 70 expression specifically in the lung; remarkably, this increased expression was associated with a significant reduction in pulmonary edema and inflammation and even mortality.[77] The mechanisms underlying this surprising benefit are not yet clear.

Ventilator-Associated Lung Injury

Although mechanical ventilation for ARDS may be lifesaving, there is abundant preclinical and clinical evidence that it can also be harmful.[78] Although it was quickly recognized that excessive airway pressure could lead to *barotrauma* (Fig. 85.3), including pneumothorax, pneumomediastinum, and subcutaneous emphysema, more recently, attention has turned to subtler but more common manifestations of lung injury related to mechanical ventilation. Mechanical ventilation can induce pulmonary edema by

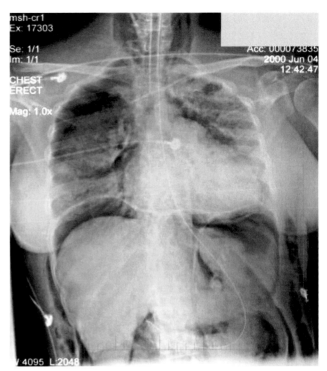

Figure 85.3 Barotrauma as a consequence of acute respiratory distress syndrome. Note the presence of a pneumothorax, pneumomediastinum, pneumoperitoneum, and subcutaneous air in this patient receiving positive-pressure ventilation. (Courtesy of Dr. Thomas E. Stewart.)

causing increases in both epithelial and endothelial permeability.[78] Indeed, almost 15 years ago, investigators noted that mechanical ventilation could produce a form of increased-permeability pulmonary edema remarkably similar to ARDS.[79] Now, the accumulated evidence suggests that inappropriate mechanical ventilation strategies may aggravate if not induce ARDS in some patients.[80]

A major mechanism causing ventilator-induced lung injury is overdistention of lung units, rather than the absolute airway pressure per se. Normal rats ventilated with high airway pressure due to a high tidal volume developed increased permeability, whereas rats ventilated with smaller tidal volumes, but with the same end-inspiratory pressure (obtained by strapping the chest walls of the rats) did not develop increased permeability.[81] Rats were also ventilated with low airway pressure using negative inspiratory pressure (applied at the chest wall) and high tidal volumes. Results demonstrated that the rats ventilated with high tidal volumes had significantly more edema than others. In particular, the negative (low) pressure and high tidal volume group had the worst edema. These important observations, confirmed in other species,[82] led to the appreciation that large tidal volumes, rather than high airway pressures per se, are an important determinant of ventilator-induced pulmonary edema. The term *volutrauma* was created to recognize this fact.

The repetitive opening and closing of terminal lung units associated with mechanical ventilation is also considered to be detrimental. The mechanism of this injury, which has been termed *atelectrauma*,[83] is thought to be the high shear stresses generated at the interface of collapsed and aerated

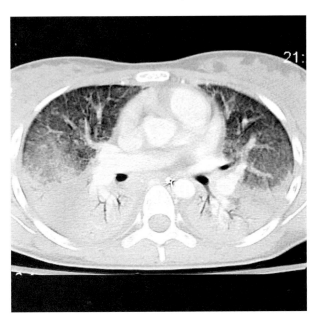

Figure 85.4 Section from a computed tomography scan of the chest in a patient with acute respiratory distress syndrome. Note the presence of dense consolidation with air bronchograms in the dorsal lung, with relative sparing of the ventral lung. (Courtesy of Dr. Thomas E. Stewart.)

tissue when a collapsed airway is reopened.[84] Theoretically, PEEP would be helpful in minimizing this injury by keeping the lung recruited, and promoting greater lung homogeneity.

It is important to point out that patients with ARDS may be especially vulnerable to ventilator-associated lung injury (VALI) because of the heterogeneous nature of the pulmonary parenchymal injury. On computed tomography scans of the lungs, normal-appearing lung and densely consolidated injured lung are both seen; as a consequence, there are marked regional differences in lung compliance[85] (Fig. 85.4). A tidal volume designed to inflate an entire lung would preferentially inflate the normal-appearing areas, potentially leading to overdistention and volutrauma. Patients with ARDS may similarly be more vulnerable to atelectrauma. Although some evidence suggests that normal lungs can tolerate at least short periods of cyclic opening and closing of airways from mechanical ventilation,[86] injured lungs, such as in ARDS, would be exposed to much higher shear stresses and would not be expected to fare as well.[87]

In the last decade, there has been a growing appreciation that VALI not only is a mechanical injury, but also reflects an underlying complex cellular and molecular response. The term *biotrauma* has been coined to emphasize this change in thinking.[88] An in-depth discussion of this area is beyond the scope of this chapter. Nonetheless, we should emphasize that one of the most significant advances made in our understanding of VALI is that mechanical ventilation per se can induce both a local and a systemic inflammatory response. In animal studies, it has been shown that ventilation with either zero PEEP or high tidal volumes causes elevations in lung lavage levels of inflammatory cytokines. Lungs ventilated with *both* high tidal volumes and zero PEEP had a synergistic elevation in cytokine levels.[89] This

inflammatory response to an injurious ventilation strategy has also been shown to extend beyond the lung. In an acid aspiration rat model of lung injury, a ventilatory strategy using high tidal volumes and zero PEEP was associated with an increase in *blood* levels of various cytokines; this was not observed in groups ventilated with a small tidal volume or in the group ventilated with the large tidal volume but higher PEEP levels.[90]

Most importantly, similar observations have been made in humans with ARDS. In one study, patients were randomized to "lung-protective" ventilation, in which the tidal volume was set to avoid overdistention and PEEP was set above the lower inflection point of the pressure-volume curve[91] (the pressure-volume curve is discussed in more detail in the section on mechanical ventilation). The control group received a strategy that would have been considered conventional ventilation at the time. Whereas cytokine levels in bronchoalveolar lavage fluid and plasma declined in the lung-protective group, they rose significantly in the control group. Post hoc analyses revealed a significantly higher number of ventilator-free days in the lung-protective group as compared to controls, and significant correlations between the development of multisystem organ failure and plasma cytokine levels. As we discuss in the section on outcome and complications, patients with ARDS often die of the systemic inflammatory response syndrome and multiorgan dysfunction. Hence, the observation that mechanical ventilation can influence pulmonary and systemic cytokine levels is intriguing. Taken together, these findings suggest that mechanical ventilation has the potential not only to injure the lungs, but to disseminate the pulmonary inflammatory response. Systemic dissemination of this response could be associated with the development of the systemic inflammatory response syndrome and potentially, with multisystem organ failure (Fig. 85.5). In fact, a recent study has shown that injurious mechanical ventilation in rats not only increases elevated plasma and lung cytokine levels, but also induces renal epithelial cell apoptosis and associated renal dysfunction.[92]

Finally, patients with ARDS often require very high levels of FIO_2. The toxic effects of hyperoxia on the lung have been well described,[93] and the histologic appearance mirrors that of human ARDS. Oxygen toxicity is thought to be mediated by the formation of both reactive oxygen and nitrogen species, which can damage tissues by a multitude of mechanisms.[55] Antioxidants have been considered as a potential therapeutic strategy for preventing and treating ARDS, although clinical trials have so far been disappointing (see section on therapy).

Genetic Determinants

To date, little is known about which genes might affect the development or prognosis of ARDS. A small pilot study has reported an association between a polymorphism in the gene for surfactant protein B[94] and ARDS, and a larger study described an association between a polymorphism in angiotensin-converting enzyme[95] and both the incidence and outcome of ARDS. We should emphasize that both these findings remain to be confirmed in larger populations. The heterogeneity of patients with ARDS is likely to make it difficult to identify clinically important genetic associations except in clearly defined subsets of patients.

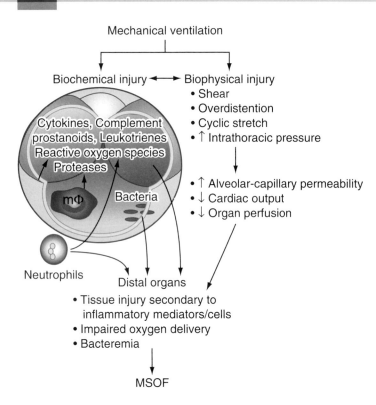

Figure 85.5 Potential mechanisms by which mechanical ventilation might cause or contribute to multisystem organ failure (MSOF). (mΦ, macrophage.) (From Slutsky AS, Tremblay LN: Multiple system organ failure: Is mechanical ventilation a contributing factor? Am J Respir Crit Care Med 157:1721–1725, 1998.)

Conclusion

Our discussion of the pathogenesis of these disorders must conclude with the humble acknowledgment that much remains unknown. Investigators in the field have benefited from the tremendous accrual of knowledge and technology in molecular and cellular biology, as well as the development of the Internet and sophisticated software allowing for the rapid comparison and interpretation of data. Indeed, the torrid pace of research allowed by these technologies presents yet another caveat to the reader: Despite our best efforts, we cannot predict how accurate this presentation on the pathogenesis and pathophysiology of ARDS may seem in just a few years. As in other fields of medicine, the literature on the pathogenesis of ARDS is filled with unanswered questions and unproven theories. Fortunately, in this post-genomics era, investigators have an unprecedented ability to address exciting novel hypotheses.

THERAPY

Supportive Care

One of the first goals of therapy in ARDS is to treat the underlying cause. In particular, patients with sepsis may respond to aggressive source control, including antibiotics and, when appropriate, surgical débridement and drainage. In patients with ARDS and sepsis of unknown origin, both the lung and the abdomen should be considered and excluded as foci of infection.[96,97]

Additional treatment focuses on preventing complications and providing supportive care (e.g., nutrition, ventilation) to allow time for the body to heal. Typically, such treatment should include prophylaxis against gastrointestinal stress ulceration and deep venous thrombosis.

Hemodynamic Management

The optimal approach to hemodynamic management in ARDS remains controversial. On the one hand, the pulmonary edema in ARDS could theoretically be improved by manipulation of Starling forces. For example, decreasing hydrostatic pressure by diuresis might decrease pulmonary edema. Indeed, preliminary data have suggested that a negative fluid balance is correlated with a reduced requirement for mechanical ventilation in ARDS.[98,99] However, the interpretation of such studies must consider that an improved outcome in ARDS might simply reflect a lesser degree of pulmonary injury and capillary permeability, which would by themselves be associated with less fluid gain. Another caveat is that ARDS and its most common precipitant, sepsis, are characterized by impaired arterial or tissue oxygenation (or both). Fluid restriction or diuresis alone might cause hypovolemia and a concomitant decrease in oxygen delivery.

There has been little additional information to guide clinicians on this issue over the last 10 years. A small placebo-controlled study in ARDS demonstrated that a regimen of albumin and furosemide infusions over 5 days caused a substantial and statistically significant improvement in oxygenation accompanied by a decrease in heart rate. However, most of the patients had ARDS as a result of trauma, with less than 5% having sepsis. There were no differences in important clinical outcomes (e.g., mortality), although the study was not designed to address these issues.[100]

Another study that may have tangential relevance to the hemodynamic management of ARDS examined the role of early "goal-directed" therapy in severe sepsis and septic shock.[101] This study did not specifically enroll patients with ARDS or consider ARDS as an outcome, yet, because sepsis is among the most common causes of ARDS, the results of the study are still relevant to this discussion. Patients with severe sepsis or septic shock who arrived in the emergency department were randomized to 6 hours of goal-directed therapy versus standard therapy before admission to the intensive care unit. Goal-directed therapy involved administration of crystalloid, red blood cells, and vasoactive and inotropic agents by protocol to achieve a central venous pressure of 8 to 12 mmHg, a mean arterial pressure of 65 to 90 mm Hg, a central venous saturation of 70% or greater, and a hematocrit of 30% or greater. In the first 6 hours of the study (but not subsequently), patients in the goal-directed group received significantly more blood and crystalloid than control-group patients. In addition, more patients in the goal-directed group received dobutamine. The study found that patients randomized to the goal-directed group had a significantly lower in-hospital mortality rate than those in the control arm. In addition, patients in the goal-directed group were significantly less likely to require mechanical ventilation than patients receiving standard therapy. Although the incidence of ARDS was not discussed in the paper, it is likely that many of the patients who ultimately received mechanical ventilation would have fulfilled the diagnostic criteria for ARDS. That being said, the implications of this study for ARDS relate primarily to prevention rather than to treatment. In addition, because of the multiple interventions in the study, it is difficult to attribute the benefit to any one aspect of fluid management (e.g., crystalloid versus blood versus inotropes).

Outside of these two trials, there are few additional prospective human data to guide the administration of fluids and vasoactive drugs in ARDS. It is likely that the correct therapeutic approach will differ depending on the cause of ARDS, such as septic shock versus aspiration pneumonitis or pulmonary contusion. In the former situation, most clinicians would favor aggressive fluid resuscitation, whereas in the latter, most would likely be more circumspect. In both cases, adequate tissue oxygenation is monitored using a variety of clinical and laboratory parameters, including urine output, arterial pH, serum lactate concentration, cardiac monitoring, and mixed (or central) venous oxygenation, to name just a few. It is important to mention that there is no clear evidence supporting the use of one particular vasopressor or inotrope in ARDS.

In the setting of refractory hypoxemia, the judicious use of sedation is a useful strategy to reduce peripheral oxygen utilization. Although neuromuscular blocking agents have also been used for this purpose (together with sedatives), we make a conscious effort to limit their use because of growing awareness of their association with persistent weakness. Similarly, cooling a febrile patient and administering antipyretics may decrease oxygen consumption.

In summary, the optimal fluid and hemodynamic strategy to use in patients with ARDS remains unclear. The ARDS Network, made up of investigators at multiple North American hospitals, is currently performing a randomized controlled trial of restricted versus liberal fluid management using pulmonary artery catheterization or a central venous catheter for monitoring.

Nutrition

It has been hypothesized that manipulations in diet can favorably affect the immune system and improve the outcome of "inflammatory" diseases such as sepsis and ARDS. Such strategies have involved supplementing enteral feeds with one or more of arginine, glutamine, ω-3 fatty acids, and antioxidants.

One small randomized study examined the effect of a modified enteral feed containing eicosapentaenoic acid, gamma-linolenic acid, and various antioxidants compared to a control enteral feed in patients with ARDS.[102] The authors found that the modified feed improved oxygenation, reduced the number of neutrophils in alveolar lavage fluid, decreased length of stay, and decreased the requirement for mechanical ventilation. These findings have yet to be replicated. Many other studies of modified enteral feeds (often called immunonutrition) have been conducted in less well-defined populations of critically ill patients, with conflicting results. A recent meta-analysis on the topic highlighted the heterogeneity of the studies and suggested that the effect of immunonutrition varied depending on the group of patients being studied.[103] At this point, the role of immunonutrition in the management of ARDS remains unclear.

Pharmacotherapy

Attempts to develop pharmacologic therapies for ARDS have been frustrating and largely unsuccessful, with no pharmacotherapies that unequivocally reduce mortality from ARDS, despite a multitude of randomized controlled trials of dozens of potential agents.[104] Despite the heterogeneity of the agents that have been evaluated, three generalizations can be observed:

1. Despite showing effectiveness in vitro or in animal studies, most potential therapies have failed to reduce mortality or other important clinical outcomes in human clinical trials.
2. A number of agents improve oxygenation but do not affect mortality from ARDS.
3. Post hoc analyses of subsets of patients from a number of studies of various agents suggest benefit, but prospective data are lacking.

In this section, we review the biologic rationale for various potential therapies for ARDS, with an emphasis on evidence from clinical trials when available.

Corticosteroids. Because of the presumed inflammatory pathophysiology underlying ARDS, a number of trials of high-dose corticosteroids have been performed. In some, the goal was the prevention of ARDS in patients at risk (e.g., those with septic shock), whereas in others, steroids were given in established ARDS in an effort to improve the outcome. The usual regimen was methylprednisolone 30 mg/kg every 6 hours for 1 to 2 days. None of the trials using this treatment regimen showed any benefit from the use of steroids,[105,106] and one showed a higher incidence of infection in patients who received steroids.[107] More recently, the use of steroids has been contemplated later in the course of ARDS, during the fibroproliferative phase. Persistently elevated plasma cytokine levels have been shown to correlate with worsened survival from ARDS, prompting some to theorize that late ARDS (>7 days after onset) is characterized by persistent inflammation that might be responsive to treatment with steroids. A small study randomized 24 patients with late ARDS to 2 mg/kg of methylprednisolone (followed by a 32-day taper) or placebo. Patients in the steroid group had lower mortality, improved oxygenation, decreased organ dysfunction, and earlier extubation, but also had a higher (but not statistically significant) rate of infection.[108] However, these data are difficult to interpret because of the small sample size and the number of patients who crossed over to the alternate therapy. Preliminary results from a larger randomized, double-blind trial undertaken by the ARDS Network showed no benefit at 30 days in the group that received corticosteroids.

Vasodilators. Prostaglandin E_1 (PGE_1) is a vasodilator that has been studied as a potential therapy for ARDS, based largely on its putative anti-inflammatory properties. In vitro and preclinical studies in animals suggested that PGE_1 given parenterally, especially when administered in a liposome, had the potential to decrease neutrophil activation. Despite promising early data,[109] a large randomized, double-blind, multicenter trial of liposomal PGE_1 found that, even though the drug improved oxygenation, there was no improvement in survival or in ventilator dependence.[110]

Prostacyclin (prostaglandin I_2) is another vasodilator that, when administered by nebulizer, acts selectively on the pulmonary vasculature. Because the aerosolized solution will tend to go to the better ventilated areas of the lung, vasodilation of the branches of the pulmonary artery that supply these areas will lead to improved V/Q matching and improved oxygenation. Although prostacyclin has been used as rescue therapy for refractory hypoxemia and is well tolerated,[111] there are no large randomized studies and no placebo-controlled studies of its use in ARDS.[112,113]

NO is a highly reactive gas formed endogenously by NO synthase from the amino acid arginine. It stimulates cellular guanylate cyclase, leading to increased cyclic guanosine monophosphate levels. It acts as a potent vasodilator, and, when given by inhalation, it causes vasodilation of the pulmonary circulation. NO is rapidly inactivated in the bloodstream by combining with hemoglobin to form methemoglobin, which is usually rapidly metabolized and does not accumulate to levels that are thought to be toxic (i.e., methemoglobin >5%). Because of this rapid inactivation, NO is a selective vasodilator that does not affect the systemic circulation. Like aerosolized prostacyclin, NO vasodilates most in the areas of the lung that are best ventilated, thereby improving V/Q matching.[114] In addition, NO has both anti-inflammatory and proinflammatory properties, although the contribution of these properties to its clinical effects is unclear.[115] NO can also react with oxygen and water to form toxic metabolites, such as nitrogen dioxide and nitrous and nitric acid, although, at concentrations of NO of less than 40 ppm, this problem is not usually clinically significant. A soda lime absorber can be placed in the inspiratory limb of the NO circuit in order to remove any nitrogen dioxide before the inspired gas reaches the patient.

In one of the largest randomized, double-blind, placebo-controlled study of NO in ARDS to date, over 170 patients were randomized to different doses of NO (from 1.25 up to 80 ppm) or placebo. Although approximately 60% of patients had a significant improvement in oxygenation within 4 hours of NO administration, there was no differ-

ence in survival or in liberation from mechanical ventilation between patients receiving NO and those in the placebo group.[116] In addition, the initial improvement in oxygenation from NO was not sustained over the course of study. There were few adverse effects of NO, and for patients who were administered less than 40 ppm, methemoglobin and nitrogen dioxide levels were the same as in the placebo group. The results of this study confirmed the findings of other smaller unblinded trials of NO in ARDS,[117,118] and were repeated in a recent systematic review.[119] In another large randomized but unblinded study of NO in ARDS, a higher proportion of patients in the NO group than in the control group required renal replacement therapy,[120] although this was not observed in the other studies. Many clinicians continue to use low doses (<10 to 15 ppm) of NO as a "rescue" therapy for refractory hypoxemia, despite the lack of evidence for an improvement in survival.[120a]

Surfactant. As discussed in the section on pathogenesis, a number of abnormalities of surfactant have been described in ARDS. These include an increase in relatively inactive forms, inactivation of surfactant by proteins that have leaked into the alveolar space, damage to type II epithelial cells (which produce surfactant), and destruction of surfactant constituents by the inflammatory process.[32] These changes, along with the efficacy of surfactant supplementation in the neonatal respiratory distress syndrome, led to the hypothesis that surfactant supplementation might be beneficial in ARDS. Data from animal studies and small case series were promising.[121] A small randomized controlled trial administered bovine surfactant through an endotracheal catheter in patients with ARDS and showed (in one subgroup of patients) an improvement in oxygenation and a trend to decreased mortality.[122]

However, enthusiasm for surfactant was greatly dampened by the results of a large multicenter, randomized, blinded, placebo-controlled trial. In this study, investigators administered an aerosolized synthetic (protein-free) surfactant or saline placebo continuously for up to 5 days to patients with new-onset (<48 hours) sepsis-induced ARDS. There was no physiologic or clinical benefit from the surfactant. Despite its methodologic rigor, the study has been criticized because less than 5% of the administered dose of surfactant was thought to have reached the distal lung. In addition, the lack of surfactant proteins in the synthetic surfactant may have diminished its ability to reduce surface tension.[123] Because of these issues, the role of surfactant supplementation continues to be studied.

In a recent Phase I–II trial, 40 patients with new-onset ARDS were randomized to a surfactant protein C–based preparation (given up to four times over 24 hours) or to no drug. The surfactant was administered through a catheter placed in the endotracheal tube. The drug had no effect on oxygenation or on ventilator-free days, which were the primary outcomes of the study. The authors reported a significant decrease in interleukin-6 levels in bronchoalveolar lavage fluid from patients who received the surfactant preparation, although it is unclear whether this was a prespecified end point.[124]

Recently, two Phase III trials of the recombinant surfactant protein C–based preparation have been completed. The studies demonstrated that the surfactant improved oxygenation, but had no impact on mortality or ventilator-free days. Whether surfactant will prove to be useful in well-defined subgroups of patients with ARDS remains an open question.[28] Other large trials assessing different forms of surfactant are currently ongoing.

Antioxidants and Anti-inflammatory Agents (Other Than Steroids). Oxidative stress has long been postulated to be involved in the pathogenesis of ARDS.[55] In fact, lung injury due to hyperoxia is a commonly used model to study ARDS in animals. Reactive oxygen species form as a by-product of activation of neutrophils and macrophages; in addition, the requirement by many patients with ARDS for a high FIO_2 may predispose to oxidative stress. Decreased levels of glutathione, a major endogenous scavenger of reactive oxygen species, have been observed in the alveolar fluid of patients with ARDS. Small clinical trials with N-acetylcysteine and procysteine were promising.[125] Unfortunately, despite this optimistic background, larger clinical trials of antioxidants in ARDS have been disappointing. A multicenter trial of the antioxidant procysteine in ARDS showed no beneficial effect of the drug.[38]

Various agents with putative anti-inflammatory effects have been tested in ARDS. These include ketoconazole, lisofylline, and (in patients with sepsis at risk for ARDS) the nonsteroidal anti-inflammatory drug ibuprofen. In separate, well-conducted, randomized blinded controlled trials, none of these agents demonstrated benefit in ARDS.[126–128] A recent prospective randomized controlled trial evaluated the effect of recombinant platelet-activating factor acetylhydrolase (the major activating enzyme for platelet-activating factor, a phospholipid mediator of inflammation) in preventing ARDS in patients with severe sepsis. This trial of over 100 patients showed no decrease in the development of ARDS in patients who received the drug; however, the mortality rate was lower in patients receiving an intermediate dose of the study drug.[129] Other trials of so-called anti-inflammatory therapies in sepsis have been disappointing.[70]

Discrepancies between Studies in Animals and Humans. Why have the findings from animal studies not been replicated in human clinical trials? In animal studies, the agent being investigated is often administered at the same time as or shortly after the lung is injured (e.g., cecal ligation and perforation followed by administration of the drug within a few hours). In contrast, the onset of lung injury in humans is often much more difficult to define, and potential therapies are given many hours after the diagnosis is made. Thus, agents that might have been effective at preventing or attenuating ARDS may have be given too late. In addition, most "proof of principle" animal studies are of relatively short duration and do not mimic the complicated clinical course of human ARDS. As well, animals in studies are essentially a homogeneous group; in contrast, human patients have multiple comorbidities and have received multiple cointerventions. Finally, the underlying precipitant for ARDS, even in carefully selected subgroups of patients, will differ in severity and duration, unlike the situation in animals, in which a uniform injury is applied. This heterogeneity makes it challenging to identify agents that may be of only modest clinical benefit.

Potential New Pharmacologic Therapies. Any discussion of potential therapies for ARDS runs the real risk of becoming obsolete within months after publication. That being said, many potential therapeutic targets in ARDS have already been discussed in the section on pathogenesis. These include matrix metalloproteinases, transforming growth factor-β1 and intracellular signaling molecules such as PI3K. Other potential agents include keratinocyte growth factor,[130] heat shock protein 70, β-agonists, and activated protein C. As clinical trials accrue and as our understanding of the mechanisms of ARDS increases, this list will undoubtedly change.

Mechanical Ventilation

Mechanical ventilation is lifesaving and is the standard therapy for ARDS. Ventilatory management of ARDS has undergone a dramatic change within the last 15 years, in large part due to increased usage of computed tomography to image the lungs and to advances in our understanding of VALI.

Pressure and Volume Limitation. Mechanical ventilation of patients under anesthesia for surgery traditionally involves large tidal volumes of 10 to 15 mL/kg, with the dual goals of achieving normal arterial oxygenation and arterial pH. A similar approach to ventilating patients with ARDS was followed in the past. This emphasis on achieving normal physiologic parameters in patients with ARDS was understandable at the time: In addition to being characterized by profound hypoxemia and diminished pulmonary compliance, ARDS was thought to involve the lungs diffusely and homogeneously based on plain radiography.[5] A large tidal volume therefore appeared to be the only way to both ventilate patients and maintain oxygenation. Subsequently, studies using computed tomography[131] demonstrated that the lungs of many patients with ARDS appear heterogeneous: Instead of the diffuse involvement suggested by plain radiographs, computed tomography scans often show patchy infiltrates, interspersed with more normal-appearing areas of lung (see Fig. 85.4). The heterogeneous distribution of the injury in ARDS implies that the tidal volume administered to a patient will preferentially inflate the more compliant (or normal) areas of lung. These regions of the lung, exposed to tidal volumes meant for an entire lung, are therefore at risk for overdistention and VALI. As discussed in some detail earlier, mechanical ventilation with excessive tidal volumes can cause pulmonary edema due to increased alveolar-capillary permeability, remarkably similar histologically to ARDS.

Despite the clear physiologic rationale and abundant experimental data to support pressure and volume limitation when ventilating patients with ARDS, it was not until the late 1990s that data from randomized clinical trials in humans began to accrue. Between 1998 and 2000, five randomized controlled trials of ventilation strategies in ARDS were published.[80,132–135] In all of the trials, patients were randomized either to a strategy involving some degree of tidal volume and pressure limitation, or to a "conventional" ventilation strategy with higher tidal volume and pressure limits. Of the five studies, the most recent and the largest was conducted by the ARDS Network, composed of investigators from multiple American hospitals and supported by the National Heart, Lung and Blood Institute of the United

States.[80] This study, which was more than seven times larger than any of the other four, randomized 861 patients to lower tidal volumes or traditional tidal volumes. In the traditional group, plateau pressure was also kept below 50 cm H_2O. In the lower volume group, tidal volume was set at 6 mL/kg of predicted body weight and reduced if necessary to maintain plateau pressure between 25 and 30 cm H_2O. Respiratory acidosis was treated aggressively, with the ventilator rate being set at 6 to 35 breaths/min to achieve a pH of 7.3 to 7.45. Bicarbonate infusions were allowed for acidosis that persisted despite a ventilator rate of 35 breaths/min. Tidal volume was increased for refractory acidemia, until pH was greater than 7.15. Only preset combinations of PEEP and FIO_2 were allowed in the two groups, for a target oxygen saturation of 88% to 95%. Patient-ventilator dyssynchrony was reduced by sedating the patient, when necessary (Table 85.4). The complete protocol used in the study can be reviewed on the Internet at http://hedwig.mgh.harvard.edu/ardsnet/studies.html.

The trial was stopped early because an interim analysis showed benefit in the lower tidal volume group. The mortality rate was 39.8% in the traditional group, compared to 31.0% in the lower tidal volume group ($P = 0.007$). Breathing without assistance at day 28 was also significantly more frequent in the lower volume group, and the number of ventilator-free days was higher. The number of days without organ failure was also higher in the lower volume arm.

The other study to show a survival benefit was much smaller, involving just 53 patients.[135] In this study, unlike the ARDS Network study, static inspiratory pressure-volume curves of the total respiratory system were determined in all patients after their condition was stabilized, but before randomization. Patients were randomized to either conventional ventilation or a "protective" ventilation strategy. Conventional ventilation consisted of tidal volumes of 12 mL/kg, and PEEP was set according to an algorithm to optimize oxygenation with a FIO_2 less than or equal to 0.6. There was no stated limit to airway pressures in the control group. Protective ventilation included a tidal volume of less than or equal to 6 mL/kg and peak pressures of less than 40 cm H_2O. Driving pressures (plateau pressure – PEEP) were kept at less than 20 cm H_2O. PEEP was set at 2 cmH_2O above the lower inflection point of the pressure-volume curve (as measured prior to randomization), and the protective ventilation group also underwent "frequent" recruitment maneuvers, in which continuous positive airway pressure of 35 to 40 cm H_2O was applied for 40 seconds. In the protective group, pressure-controlled inverse-ratio ventilation was used if the FIO_2 exceeded 0.5 (see later discussion of inverse-ratio ventilation).

The study was stopped early because a significant survival difference was detected: 38% of the protective ventilation group had died at 28 days, compared to 71% in the conventional group ($P < 0.001$). There was no significant difference in survival to hospital discharge between the two arms, although there was a very strong trend in favor of the protective group. The rate of barotrauma was also significantly different: 7% in the protective ventilation arm, versus 42% in the conventional ventilation group.

Unfortunately, multiple confounding factors color the interpretation of this small trial. Airway pressure was not limited in the control arm, and mean plateau pressure exceeded 35 cm H_2O in those patients. Although the study showed an impressive 33% absolute reduction in 28-day mortality, the mortality rate in the traditional ventilation group was 71%, much higher than in all of the other trials. In addition, the population studied was substantially younger than patients in other trials, with a mean age of about 35 years (compared to 50 to 60 years in the other studies). Finally, the rate of barotrauma in the traditional group (42%) was approximately four times higher than in other trials. Thus, it is uncertain whether the difference in outcome was related to a true benefit of the intervention arm or to harm in the control arm.

Of the five randomized controlled trials of volume or pressure limitation in ARDS, the two just described were positive and the other three[132-134] were negative. Why these three trials, but not the other two, failed to demonstrate any benefit of pressure and volume limitation in ARDS is unclear, and continues to be a source of speculation and considerable controversy.[136,137] It has been postulated that apparently minor differences in the studies' protocols may have had a larger than expected impact on the outcome. For example, an examination of the plateau pressures in the five studies demonstrates an interesting difference: In the negative trials, the conventional ventilation arms had mean plateau pressures well below 35 cm H_2O, the level originally hypothesized by an early international consensus conference on mechanical ventilation[138] as being safe. In contrast, in

Table 85.4 Ventilation Protocol Used for the Lower Tidal Volume Group in the ARDS Network Study*

Parameter	Protocol
Mode of ventilation	Volume assist-control
Tidal volume	≤6 mL/kg predicted body weight[†]
Plateau pressure	≤30 cm H_2O
Frequency	6–35 breaths/min, titrated for pH 7.30–7.45
I:E ratio	1:1 to 1:3
Oxygenation goal	PaO_2 55–80 mm Hg, or SaO_2 88–95%
FIO_2/PEEP (cm H_2O) combinations allowed	0.3/5, 0.4/5, 0.4/8, 0.5/8, 0.5/10, 0.6/10, 0.7/10, 0.7/12, 0.7/14, 0.8/14, 0.9/14, 0.9/16, 0.9/18, 1.0/18, 1.0/20, 1.0/22, 1.0/24
Weaning	By pressure support, required when FIO_2/PEEP ≤ 0.4/8

* The complete protocol can be reviewed on the Internet at http://hedwig.mgh.harvard.edu
[†] Predicted body weight (in kilograms) can be calculated for male patients as 50 + 0.91(cm of height −152.4), and for female patients as 45.5 + 0.91(cm of height −152.4).[80]
FIO_2, fraction of oxygen inspired; I:E, inspiration-to-expiration; PaO_2, arterial PO_2; PEEP, positive end-expiratory pressure; SaO_2, arterial oxyhemoglobin saturation.
From Ventilation with lower tidal volumes as compared with traditional tidal volumes for acute lung injury and the acute respiratory distress syndrome. The Acute Respiratory Distress Syndrome Network. N Engl J Med 342:1301–1308, 2000.

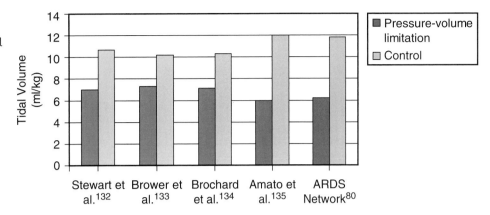

Figure 85.6 Mean tidal volume on day 1 for patients in the lower tidal volume or pressure groups and the conventional groups in five recent studies. Of note, tidal volumes in three of the studies[132,133,80] were calculated based on predicted or ideal body weight, whereas in the others,[134,135] measured body weight was used. The different definitions of body weight make direct comparisons of the tidal volumes difficult (see text for details.)

the studies by Amato and colleagues[135] and the ARDS Network,[80] the conventional ventilation arms had plateau pressures near or above this level. In other words, it is possible that the control arms in the negative trials were already ventilated in a safe manner, such that any further reduction in tidal volume would not yield any additional benefit.

It has also been argued that the tidal volumes achieved in the control (traditional ventilatory strategy) arm of ARDS Network trial were higher than what might have been considered the "standard of care" at that time[136] (Fig. 85.6). Proponents of this view suggest that the difference in mortality between the control arm and the low tidal volume arm was in fact due to a deleterious effect of the ventilation strategy in the control patients, rather than any benefit in the low tidal volume group. However, it is important to point out that the tidal volume in the control group (~10 mL/kg based on measured body weight) was well within the range considered to be routine clinical practice at the time the trial was ongoing. A key factor in comparing trials is to appreciate that the ARDS Network study used predicted body weight, whereas other studies used ideal body weight or measured body weight. The distinction is worth emphasizing, because data from the ARDS Network study demonstrate that measured body weight was approximately 20% higher than predicted body weight; thus a tidal volume of 12 mL/kg predicted body weight would be roughly equivalent to 10 mL/kg based on the actual weight of the patient. Predicted body weight (in kilograms) can be calculated for male patients as $50 + 0.91$ (centimeters of height -152.4), and for female patients as $45.5 + 0.91$(centimeters of height -152.4).[80]

The ARDS Network study adopted an aggressive approach to hypercarbia and acidemia, including tachypnea, bicarbonate infusions, and loosening of ventilatory restrictions. As a result, hypercarbia and subsequent low pH in the treatment arm was less marked than in other studies. This too may have contributed to the lower mortality in the lower tidal volume arm.

Some investigators have proposed that mechanical ventilation of a given patient be set based on the static inspiratory pressure-volume curve of the patient's respiratory system.[135] In ARDS, such curves often have a sigmoidal shape, with a lower inflection point at low lung volumes, and an upper inflection point at high volumes. Initially, it

was thought that the lower inflection point represented the pressure at which collapsed lung units reexpand, explaining the abrupt change in compliance. The upper inflection point was thought to represent the pressure at which alveolar overdistention occurs. On this basis, it was proposed that PEEP should be set higher than the pressure of the lower inflection point, and plateau pressure be kept lower than the upper inflection point. Although conceptually appealing, this interpretation of the static inspiratory pressure-volume curve is likely erroneous. Recruitment of the lung is known to continue even above the lower inflection point,[139] and tidal ventilation in patients with ARDS may take place on the expiratory (rather than the inspiratory) limb of the pressure-volume curve.[140] Because of this, setting ventilatory parameters based on the static inspiratory pressure-volume curve remains controversial.[141]

The Role of Positive End-Expiratory Pressure. As mentioned earlier, the first description of ARDS commented on the apparent utility of PEEP in improving oxygenation. From a theoretical standpoint, PEEP may be beneficial in avoiding damage from cyclic opening and closing of terminal lung units (atelectrauma; see "Etiology and Pathogenesis" section), and in allowing for a reduction in tidal volume (and hence volutrauma). In addition, the improvement in oxygenation that often occurs with PEEP may allow for lowering of the FIO_2, decreasing the risk of oxygen toxicity. On the other hand, PEEP that is too high can itself cause excessive end-inspiratory lung volume and volutrauma. Many clinicians are also familiar with the potential effect of PEEP to depress cardiac output and blood pressure. The optimal level of PEEP to use in patients with ARDS has therefore been a source of controversy.[142]

In the ARDS Network study, in addition to the beneficial effect from lower tidal volumes, the treatment arm may have benefited from higher levels of PEEP. For example, the study used a PEEP algorithm based on FIO_2 that called for high levels of PEEP (14 to 24 cm H_2O) when FIO_2 was greater than 0.7 (see Table 85.4). Respiratory rates were allowed to rise up to 35 breaths/min to maintain pH between 7.3 and 7.45, and it is possible that some patients developed auto-PEEP.[143] Whether the elevated PEEP was beneficial is not known; however, a second trial by the ARDS Network of higher levels of PEEP than used in the original study has recently been reported as showing no reduction in mortality.[144]

Recruitment Maneuvers. The low tidal volumes and pressures advocated for lung-protective ventilation can lead to progressive derecruitment of the lung, which can worsen hypoxemia and potentially aggravate atelectrauma. To counteract derecruitment, so-called recruitment maneuvers have been proposed. These maneuvers involve an increase in airway pressure, although the pressure to be applied and the duration of its application have not been standardized. One example of a recruitment maneuver would be the application of 40 cm H_2O of continuous positive airway pressure for 40 seconds.

The role of recruitment maneuvers in the management of ARDS is controversial, and interpreting the literature is complicated by the widely varying techniques used for recruitment.[145] Many studies report a transient improvement in oxygenation after some form of recruitment, although it is possible that the same degree of recruitment could be achieved by simply raising the level of PEEP.[146,147] As with PEEP, it is not known how much positive pressure should be applied to maximize recruitment of atelectic lung while minimizing overdistention of relatively normal lung. Overdistention of well-perfused lung units could result in diversion of blood to poorly perfused alveoli, with consequent worsening of right-to-left shunt and hypoxemia.[148] Although recruitment maneuvers are generally safe, the patient must be closely monitored for any adverse effects on hemodynamics or oxygenation. The effect of recruitment maneuvers on the outcome of ARDS is only now being measured. One study has suggested that recruitment maneuvers to a relatively low pressure of 35 to 40 cm H_2O do not improve survival in ARDS.[149,149a]

Permissive Hypercapnia and Tracheal Gas Insufflation. The use of lower tidal volumes (to avoid VALI) often results in respiratory acidemia, an effect that has been termed *permissive hypercapnia*. The theoretical detrimental effects of hypercapnia include myocardial depression, increased pulmonary vascular resistance, and decreased renal blood flow. Perhaps the most clinically important adverse effect of hypercapnia is elevated intracranial pressure from increased cerebral blood flow. Nonetheless, the overall effect of permissive hypercapnia on ARDS is controversial: some have proposed that it may actually have protective effects, including attenuation of free radical–mediated lung injury and pulmonary inflammation[150,151]; other studies have reported an injurious effect on alveolar epithelial cells.[152]

Given the uncertainty about permissive hypercapnia, it is worth remembering that the only large randomized controlled trial to show a reduction in mortality in ARDS treated respiratory acidosis fairly aggressively (discussed earlier). In the absence of other data, following the protocol used in that study seems prudent.

One approach that has been used to decrease high levels of arterial P_{CO_2} is tracheal gas insufflation (TGI). TGI is a technique whereby a gas flow is introduced via a small catheter placed in the endotracheal tube, with its tip near the carina. TGI has been proposed as an adjunct to permissive hypercapnia, as the insufflated gas improves carbon dioxide clearance from the anatomic dead space and ventilator tubing. However, the gas flow has the potential to increase alveolar volume and pressure, and may increase PEEP.[153] Although there are many case reports describing the use of TGI,[154] there have been no randomized studies in ARDS. Because of technical and monitoring issues related to TGI, we do not recommend its routine use in ARDS.

Mechanical Ventilation of Patients in the Prone Position (Proning). Placing patients with ARDS in the prone position ("proning") was described almost 30 years ago as a means of improving oxygenation. The mechanisms by which this improvement occurs are multiple, but probably the most important factor is the effect that proning has on chest wall and lung compliance.[155] In the supine position, the most dorsal and caudal regions of lung (along the spine and diaphragm) are the worst affected in many patients with ARDS. Some of this is due to gravity, but the weight of the heart and of the abdominal organs on the lungs also contributes. When a patient is placed in the prone position, the anterior chest wall is fixed (by the bed) and becomes less compliant, thus increasing the proportion of ventilation directed to the dorsal lung. In addition, the volume of lung that is being compressed by the heart due to gravity is substantially decreased. The net result is more homogeneous ventilation of the lung and presumably improved V/Q matching. Data from a study in dogs suggest that ventilation in the prone position can attenuate the severity of VALI.[156]

A relatively large multicenter trial enrolled over 300 patients with ALI or ARDS and randomized them to conventional treatment (supine only) or treatment including proning for 6 or more hours for 10 days. The study found that oxygenation improved in approximately 70% of proning procedures, and that most of the improvement was evident within 1 hour of proning. However, although oxygenation improved significantly in the patients who were proned, there was no difference in mortality between the groups. Retrospective analyses of the quartile of patients with the poorest oxygenation or the highest acuity of illness (or the highest tidal volume) showed a lower mortality rate at 10 days in the patients who had been proned, but this difference did not persist beyond discharge from the intensive care unit.[157] The study has been criticized for the relative short duration of the intervention, and the fact that most patients spent the majority of the day supine.[158] A more recent study of proning for acute hypoxemic respiratory failure showed similar results.[158a]

Proning patients with ARDS requires some attention to detail. Lines and tubes are vulnerable to dislodgment during the process, and sufficient staff should be on hand to assist with the move. Personnel should be ready for and capable of immediate reintubation should the endotracheal tube be displaced. Patients who are proned are more susceptible to the development of pressure sores, and exquisite care must be taken to ensure that no stray objects (e.g., syringes, electrocardiograph leads) are left under the patient, as these will leave impressions and even scars on the body. An unstable spinal injury is an absolute contraindication to proning. Finally, in the event that cardiopulmonary resuscitation is required, the patient will have to be returned to the supine position emergently.

The lack of a mortality benefit in the multicenter trial of proning has decreased its popularity with intensivists. It is possible that, in the most severe subset of patients with ARDS, proning for longer periods (>7 hr/day, >10 days at a time) might be beneficial, although prospective data are lacking. In patients with focal causes of hypoxemia, such as lobar pneumonia, it is useful to remember that oxygenation may improve when the unaffected (or better) side is placed down.

Volume-Control versus Pressure-Control Ventilation. The volume- and pressure-limited protocol used in the ARDS Network study employed volume assist-control as the mode of ventilation. Whether pressure-control ventilation could be used instead is unknown. A number of studies that have examined this issue have found little difference in physiologic parameters or outcome between the two modes of ventilation.[159,160]

High-Frequency Jet Ventilation and High-Frequency Oscillation. In high-frequency jet ventilation, a small-gauge catheter is used to introduce gas under high pressure into the endotracheal tube. The high velocity of the gas entrains additional oxygen and humidified air from side ports in the system. This form of mechanical ventilation achieves a tidal volume of 2 to 5 mL/kg and involves frequencies of 100 to 200 breaths/min.[161] Exhalation is passive, requiring recoil of the lungs and chest wall. There is little evidence that high-frequency jet ventilation is superior to conventional mechanical ventilation for ARDS. In a randomized trial of over 300 oncology patients, conventional ventilation (using volume-cycled ventilation) was compared to high-frequency jet ventilation. The end points of the study were physiologic and were defined differently for the two groups of patients, making it difficult to interpret the data. Nonetheless, the authors found no significant difference in any clinically important outcome.[162]

In high-frequency oscillation (HFO) ventilation, lung recruitment is maintained using a constant mean airway pressure, generated by an inspiratory bias flow and limitation of gas outflow from the circuit. Ventilation is achieved through rapid (e.g., 5 Hz) regular oscillations of a piston or diaphragm. The push-and-pull action of the piston causes oscillations in pressure in the endotracheal tube and proximal airways, creating peak and trough pressures around the set mean airway pressure. The tidal volumes achieved through HFO are small, on the order of 1 to 5 mL/kg. In theory, HFO seems ideally suited for avoiding VALI; atelectrauma is minimized because of the relatively high mean airway pressure, which, along with small tidal volumes, limits derecruitment of the lung, and volutrauma is minimized because the small tidal volumes limit end-inspiratory stretch. Recruitment maneuvers (e.g., application of continuous positive airway pressure for approximately 30 to 40 seconds) should be applied after each patient disconnect from the ventilator (e.g., open suctioning), because loss of pressure from the circuit upon disconnection will lead to portions of the lung becoming atelectatic (derecruited).

In the only randomized trial of HFO in adults to date, 148 patients with ARDS were randomized to conventional ventilation using the pressure-control mode or to HFO.[163] The specific ventilatory parameters for both the conventional group and the HFO group were adjusted to achieve adequate oxygenation at a minimum FIO_2 (i.e., arterial oxygen saturation ≥88% at $FIO_2 ≤ 0.60$), as well as an arterial pH greater than 7.15. To show that HFO is equivalent or superior to the best available ventilation strategy using a conventional ventilator, the study ideally would have randomized patients to HFO or to the lower volume ventilation strategy used in the ARDS Network study, which is essentially the current standard of care (discussed in detail earlier). Unfortunately because the study was begun before the publication of the ARDS Network trial on tidal volume limitation, the conventional ventilation arm of this study targeted tidal volumes of 6 to 10 mL/kg. Although HFO was well tolerated, there was no significant difference in 30- or 90-day mortality, or in any other outcome. The authors performed a retrospective analysis of predictors of mortality, and discovered that being on conventional ventilation for more than 5 days correlated with a poor outcome. This finding has been interpreted by some as suggesting that HFO might be most effective early on in the course of ARDS, rather than as a rescue therapy (which is how it is used most commonly). However, it should be emphasized that, at present, there are no prospective data to support this hypothesis. More importantly, a trial of HFO compared to lower tidal volume ventilation using the protocol of the ARDS Network study has not yet been performed. As such, it is not known whether HFO offers any benefit over the lower tidal volume strategy proven to be efficacious in the ARDS Network trial.

Inverse-Ratio Ventilation. The normal ratio of inspiration to expiration (I:E ratio) ranges from 1:2 to 1:4, varying with the respiratory rate. Inverse-ratio ventilation (IRV) refers to a mode of ventilation in which the duration of inspiration is extended to yield an I:E ratio greater than 1. Clinicians found that IRV could improve oxygenation (by decreasing right-to-left shunt) in ARDS while allowing lower peak inspiratory and end-expiratory airway pressures. However, the mechanism of the improvement in oxygenation is likely due to the increase in mean airway pressure due to the longer inspiratory time or, as I:E is increased, due to the generation of auto-PEEP because of the shortened time available for expiration. This latter mechanism would lead to an increase in end-expiratory alveolar volume. IRV causes an increase in mean airway pressure relative to conventional ventilation, even though peak airway pressure is lower. The same reduction in right-to-left shunt can be achieved using a normal I:E ratio by increasing the applied (extrinsic) PEEP alone. For the same reduction in shunt, the mean alveolar pressure is elevated more by IRV than by simply raising the PEEP. Given the concern over volutrauma, the fact that IRV increases mean alveolar pressure (and hence mean alveolar volume) relative to extrinsic PEEP alone makes it less attractive. In addition, IRV is uncomfortable for patients and often requires the administration of sedatives and neuromuscular blocking agents. For these reasons, the use of IRV in the management of ARDS has largely fallen out of favor.[164]

Liquid Ventilation. Liquid ventilation relies on the oxygen- and carbon dioxide–carrying capacity of organic liquids such as perfluorocarbons. Perfluorocarbons are modified hydrocarbons in which hydrogen atoms are replaced with fluorine, generating inert liquids that are nontoxic and minimally absorbed through the respiratory epithelium. The most widely studied perfluorocarbon, perflubron (perfluorooctylbromide), can dissolve about 17 times more oxygen than saline and almost 4 times more carbon dioxide.[165] Total liquid ventilation is a technique in which the lungs are completely filled with liquid and an extracorporeal exchanger is used to add oxygen and remove carbon dioxide from the liquid. Partial liquid ventilation, which is much easier to use clinically, involves partially filling the lung with liquid and then using a traditional ventilator to deliver gas tidal volumes.[166]

The theoretical benefits of liquid ventilation stem largely from improved lung recruitment, due to the lower surface tension of the perfluorocarbons and because the liquid tends to distribute to the dependent regions of the lung. Deposition of liquid with low surface tension in these areas may enhance alveolar recruitment; in addition, the weight of the liquid is thought to cause diversion of pulmonary blood flow to the nondependent (better ventilated) areas, improving V/Q matching. Clearance of secretions (due to their displacement by the liquid) is also improved. Anti-inflammatory effects of perflubron have been described, although the clinical relevance of these effects is not well understood. To date, only one randomized controlled trial of partial liquid ventilation in adults with ARDS has been published.[167] This study enrolled 90 patients with ARDS to partial liquid ventilation with perflubron or to conventional mechanical ventilation. Other than very general guidelines (such as target arterial oxygen saturation >90%), neither of the two ventilation strategies was guided by protocol. In addition, the inclusion and exclusion criteria were modified slightly during the course of the study. There was no significant difference in the number of ventilator-free days (the primary outcome measure) or in any other predefined outcome. More patients in the liquid ventilation arm experienced hypoxia, bradycardia, and respiratory acidosis, although the increase in the incidence of these adverse events was not statistically significant. A large multicenter trial of liquid ventilation in ARDS, which used a lung-protective control, was recently completed, and no advantage over conventional ventilation was observed.

Extracorporeal Membrane Oxygenation. Extracorporeal membrane oxygenation (ECMO), also referred to as extracorporeal life support or extracorporeal lung assist, refers to the process by which the patient's blood is circulated to an external machine that provides oxygenation or carbon dioxide removal (or both).[168] In theory, ECMO could be used to oxygenate patients with ARDS while minimizing VALI and oxygen toxicity and allowing the lungs time to heal. There are multiple case reports of ECMO being used in ARDS, and it is used routinely in neonates with severe respiratory failure. A randomized controlled trial of ECMO in ARDS was completed 25 years ago and did not show any benefit.[169] It is worth pointing out that the mortality rate in that study was approximately 90% in both the ECMO and the control arm. Subsequently, a variant of ECMO dedicated to carbon dioxide removal (extracorporeal CO_2 removal, or $ECCO_2R$) was developed and showed promise in a case series when compared to a historical control group.[170] However, when concurrent controls were used, a randomized controlled trial comparing pressure-controlled inverse-ratio ventilation and $ECCO_2R$ to conventional mechanical ventilation in ARDS showed no difference in survival.[171]

Patients on ECMO have a high rate of bleeding; in the most recent randomized trial, patients randomized to the device were transfused an average of 1.7 L of blood *per day*.[171] Given its cost and the lack of evidence to support its use, we do not recommend the use of ECMO in the routine management of patients with ARDS.

Summary. The approach to mechanical ventilation of patients with ARDS is remarkably different from what it was only 15 years ago. Most of this change is from the integration of two discoveries: first, that the diffuse lung injury of ARDS is not as diffuse as once thought; and second, that mechanical ventilation can itself cause ALI. In the last few years, data from clinical trials in humans have emerged to help intensivists select the most appropriate ventilation strategy in ARDS.

To date, the only large randomized trial to demonstrate a survival benefit from a ventilatory strategy is the ARDS Network study.[80] Its unique success raises the question of whether the specific ventilatory protocol used in that study should be the standard of care for patients with ARDS, or whether simply avoidance of large volumes and pressures (i.e., >10 mL/kg, plateau pressure >30 cm H_2O) would suffice. We believe that the evidence to date supports the adoption of tidal volume and pressure limitation in patients with ARDS as outlined by the ARDS Network study. Plateau pressure should be maintained at less than 30 cm H_2O, and tidal volume should be limited to 6 mL/kg predicted body weight as much as possible. Further study will be required to determine whether intermediate tidal volumes (<10 mL/kg but >6 mL/kg), which might be easier to implement, are as safe in ARDS.

It is unknown whether it is necessary to use volume assist-control ventilation, or whether pressure-control ventilation with plateau pressures limited to 30 cm H_2O would be equivalent. The optimal level of PEEP in ARDS remains similarly unclear; based on preclinical data, we favor high levels of PEEP in order to prevent atelectrauma, reduce FIO_2, and prevent hyperoxic lung injury, as long as the patient's hemodynamic status remains stable. We use the lowest possible FIO_2 that maintains oxygen saturation above 90%, and empirically adopt a target FIO_2 of less than 0.6. The role of recruitment maneuvers remains controversial. Although proning of patients with ARDS may transiently improve oxygenation, it has not as yet been shown to improve survival. Finally, there are some data that suggest that HFO is an effective and safe alternative to conventional ventilators, although no survival benefit has yet been demonstrated.

OUTCOME AND COMPLICATIONS

Mortality

The mortality rate for ARDS has fallen over the last 10 to 15 years, with a number of studies describing a decline in the rate from over 60% to about 40% since 1993.[172,173] The reasons for this improvement in survival are not known, although some have attributed it to better supportive care in the intensive care unit given the absence of any specific therapy.

As discussed earlier, the AECC distinguished ARDS as the most severe form of ALI, in order to recognize the spectrum of severity of the syndrome. Nonetheless, it is still unclear whether this gradation has any prognostic importance. Despite the more profound oxygenation defect in ARDS, there is conflicting and little evidence to suggest that it is associated with a worse outcome than is ALI.[174–176]

Predictors of Poor Prognosis

Despite the prominence of hypoxemia among the clinical manifestations of ARDS, early trials did not find that the severity of hypoxemia early in the course of the illness was a good predictor of subsequent mortality.[176] Data from a more recent larger trial did find that the PaO_2/FIO_2 ratio was an independent predictor of mortality (R. Brower, personal communication). Pulmonary injury scoring systems like the LIS and the ARDS score have been shown to be useful in predicting a prolonged (>2 weeks) requirement for intubation and ventilation,[177] whereas scoring systems that measure the overall severity of illness, such as the Simplified Acute Physiology Score (SAPS), correlate better with survival.[178] The classic teaching is that patients with ARDS do not usually die of refractory hypoxemia, which may seem paradoxical given that hypoxemia is frequently the focus of resuscitative efforts. In fact, most patients with fatal ARDS die of sepsis and multiorgan failure.[97,96] The explanation for this apparent paradox is unknown, although it has been hypothesized that injurious mechanical ventilation during the course of ARDS may be involved.[179] As discussed earlier, ventilation using excessive tidal volumes has been shown to cause elevations in pulmonary and systemic cytokine levels, and has recently been linked in an animal model to apoptosis of renal cells and renal dysfunction.[92]

Cumulative data from multiple studies have suggested that the mortality rate from ARDS varies depending on the precipitant (Table 85.5). The highest risk of death has consistently been reported to occur in sepsis, whereas ARDS occurring in the setting of major trauma has a much better prognosis.[180] In addition, it is known that chronic liver disease,[176] older age,[181] chronic alcoholism,[19] and nonpulmonary organ dysfunction[176] are associated with higher mortality from ARDS. Other predictors of death from ARDS have included a history of organ transplantation and human immunodeficiency virus infection,[182] and a recent study described a higher mortality rate in men and in African Americans compared to non–African Americans.[183]

As mentioned earlier, risk factors for ARDS have been classified as being pulmonary or nonpulmonary in origin. It remains unclear whether this distinction has prognostic importance. In one prospective cohort study of ARDS patients, investigators found a trend toward higher mortality in patients with a pulmonary precipitant, although the difference was not statistically significant.[184] In contrast, the ARDS Network investigators retrospectively analyzed the data from their large randomized study of low tidal volume ventilation versus traditional tidal volume ventilation. Although this analysis confirmed that the mortality rate for ARDS was highest in patients with sepsis and lowest in patients with trauma, there was no difference in mortality, days off the mechanical ventilator, or the development of organ failure between patients with pulmonary and those with nonpulmonary risk factors. In addition, there was no difference in efficacy of the low tidal volume strategy in any subgroup.[180]

Because hypoxemia is not a reliable predictor of mortality from ARDS, investigators have searched for other lung-specific markers of prognosis. In one prospective study of 179 patients with ARDS, a multiple logistic regression was performed to identify which clinical and physiologic variables predicted mortality.[185] The analysis found that the dead space fraction (as calculated by the Bohr equation) was elevated in ARDS and was an independent predictor of mortality. For every increase of 0.05 in the dead space fraction, the odds of death from ARDS increased by 45%. The mechanism of this association is not known; it is possible that the extent of pulmonary vascular injury in ARDS may be greater than previously suspected and may account for the increase in dead space.

The development of pulmonary fibrosis is also thought to connote a worse prognosis. Elevated procollagen III levels, thought to be indicative of collagen synthesis, have been found in the pulmonary edema fluid of patients with ARDS and have been shown to correlate with increased mortality.[186,187] In another study, 22 of 25 consecutive patients with ARDS underwent transbronchial biopsies of the most abnormal-appearing areas on their chest radiographs. The mortality rate in patients whose biopsies showed fibrosis, regardless of severity, was significantly higher than in patients whose biopsies showed no fibrosis.[188]

Complications

Acute. ARDS is complicated by ventilator-associated pneumonia (VAP) in about 30% to 65% of cases. In this setting, VAP usually occurs more than 5 to 7 days after the onset of mechanical ventilation, and is often preceded by colonization of the lower respiratory tract by potential pathogens.[189] The likely organisms include nonfermenting gram-negative rods, methicillin-resistant *Staphylococcus aureus*, and Enterobacteriaceae.[190] Although the development of VAP prolongs the duration of mechanical ventilation in ARDS, it does not appear to result in increased mortality.[189,191,192] Making a definitive diagnosis of VAP in patients with ARDS can be challenging, because patients

Table 85.5 Factors Associated with a Poor Prognosis from Acute Respiratory Distress Syndrome

Extrapulmonary organ dysfunction[176]
Sepsis[180]
Advanced age[181]
Chronic liver disease[176]
Chronic alcohol abuse[19]
Human immunodeficiency virus infection[182]
Organ transplantation[182]
Active malignancy[182]
Male gender[183]
African American race[183]

with ARDS already have radiographic infiltrates, and not uncommonly have leukocytosis and fever. Two different strategies to diagnose VAP are debated in the literature.[193] In the "noninvasive" approach, clinical criteria (e.g., leukocytosis, new radiographic infiltrate) in combination with the results of semiquantitative cultures of endotracheal aspirates (e.g., light vs. heavy growth of a bacterial isolate) are used to diagnose pneumonia. In contrast, the "invasive" approach recommends sampling the distal lung bronchoscopically either by performing bronchoalveolar lavage or by using a protected specimen brush. With this approach, pneumonia is diagnosed when quantitative cultures from these specimens exceed a predetermined threshold. At present, there is only limited evidence that following the invasive approach is associated with less antibiotic use and decreased mortality.[194] This paucity of data and the added expense of bronchoscopy have prevented the general adoption of the invasive strategy to diagnosing VAP. If diagnostic techniques such as bronchoalveolar lavage or protected specimen brushes are used, the yield is higher when the lung is sampled bilaterally and when the patient is off antibiotics.[195]

Another feared complication of ARDS is barotrauma (pneumothorax, pneumomediastinum, subcutaneous emphysema) due to the effect of positive-pressure ventilation in heterogeneous lungs with diminished compliance. In the supine (rather than erect) patient, diagnosing a pneumothorax requires vigilance because the radiographic appearance of a pneumothorax is different and more subtle (e.g., air in the costophrenic angle, the "deep sulcus" sign; see Fig. 69.4). Data from a number of prospective studies suggest that the incidence of barotrauma in ARDS currently is about 10% or less.[80,132,196]

Long Term. Despite the profound derangement in oxygenation and respiratory system compliance that is characteristic of ARDS, it is remarkable that patients who survive often have near-normal pulmonary function tests 6 to 12 months later. Lung volumes and flows are generally slightly reduced or normal at 6 to 12 months, although the diffusion capacity may remain slightly reduced.[197,198] Follow-up chest radiographs are usually normal, with a minority showing subtle abnormalities, including pleural thickening or small cysts.[198]

Despite this impressive physiologic and radiologic recovery, patients who survive ARDS continue to have important functional limitations and a decreased health-related quality of life. This reduction in quality of life seems attributable to ARDS or to its management or complications. In one parallel cohort study, patients with ARDS were matched to patients with sepsis or trauma with an equivalent severity of illness. The ARDS survivors continued to report significant decrements in health-related quality of life, particularly as related to physical function and pulmonary symptoms.[199] This reduced quality of life (in areas reflecting physical function) has been correlated to the presence of persistent abnormalities in pulmonary function tests.[197] In other patients, a persistent reduction in exercise capacity (as measured by a 6-minute walk test) has been observed, and was ascribed to persistent muscle weakness and wasting.[198] A multivariate analysis in that study found that better functional capacity was associated with lack of systemic corticosteroid administration, absence of illness acquired in the intensive care unit, and rapid resolution of lung injury and multiorgan dysfunction. However, patients who ultimately survive an episode of ARDS do *not* appear to have an increased mortality compared to other similarly ill intensive care unit survivors.[200]

Psychological problems have been described in survivors of ARDS. In a retrospective case-control study, survivors of ARDS were found to have significantly more signs and symptoms of posttraumatic stress disorder than patients who had undergone maxillofacial (and presumably elective) surgery; they also had more signs and symptoms of posttraumatic stress disorder than soldiers who had served for prolonged periods of time in Bosnia.[201] Persistent cognitive impairment has also been observed in survivors of ARDS for as long as 1 year after hospital discharge.[202] Most patients in this study had impairments in at least one of the following: memory, concentration, attention, or mental processing speed. Interestingly, these abnormalities were correlated to the degree and duration of hypoxemia of the patients.

SUMMARY

Acute hypoxemic respiratory failure is a broad category that encompasses an impressive variety of disorders, of which ARDS is but one. Similarly, ARDS is itself a syndrome caused by a heterogeneous group of pulmonary and extrapulmonary insults. Whether a patient is labeled as having acute hypoxemic respiratory failure or ARDS, it is important to remember that neither appellation is a specific diagnosis. In both cases, the clinician must search for an underlying cause in order to begin appropriate therapy. What has changed in the last 15 years is our realization that, in ARDS, regardless of the precipitant, inappropriate mechanical ventilation can do more harm than good. Amid all the heterogeneity that is ARDS, it is perhaps ironic that this potential for iatrogenic injury may turn out to be one of the few common elements.

REFERENCES

1. Esteban A, Anzueto A, Frutos F, et al: Characteristics and outcomes in adult patients receiving mechanical ventilation: A 28-day international study. JAMA 287:345–355, 2002.
2. Meduri GU, Turner RE, Abou-Shala N, et al: Noninvasive positive pressure ventilation via face mask: First-line intervention in patients with acute hypercapnic and hypoxemic respiratory failure. Chest 109:179–193, 1996.
3. Antonelli M, Conti G, Rocco M, et al: A comparison of noninvasive positive-pressure ventilation and conventional mechanical ventilation in patients with acute respiratory failure. N Engl J Med 339:429–435, 1998.
4. Delclaux C, L'Her E, Alberti C, et al: Treatment of acute hypoxemic nonhypercapnic respiratory insufficiency with continuous positive airway pressure delivered by a face mask: A randomized controlled trial. JAMA 284:2352–2360, 2000.
5. Ashbaugh DG, Bigelow DB, Petty TL, et al: Acute respiratory distress in adults. Lancet 2:319–323, 1967.
6. Murray JF, Matthay MA, Luce JM, et al: An expanded definition of the adult respiratory distress syndrome. Am

Rev Respir Dis 138:720–723, 1988 [published erratum appears in Am Rev Respir Dis 139:1065, 1989].

7. Bernard GR, Artigas A, Brigham KL, et al: The American-European Consensus Conference on ARDS: Definitions, mechanisms, relevant outcomes, and clinical trial coordination. Am J Respir Crit Care Med 149:818–824, 1994.

8. Rubenfeld GD, Caldwell E, Granton J, et al: Interobserver variability in applying a radiographic definition for ARDS. Chest 116:1347–1353, 1999.

9. Meade MO, Cook RJ, Guyatt GH, et al: Interobserver variation in interpreting chest radiographs for the diagnosis of acute respiratory distress syndrome. Am J Respir Crit Care Med 161:85–90, 2000.

10. Villar J, Perez-Mendez L, Kacmarek RM: Current definitions of acute lung injury and the acute respiratory distress syndrome do not reflect their true severity and outcome (see comment). Intensive Care Med 25:930–935, 1999.

11. Moss M, Goodman PL, Heinig M, et al: Establishing the relative accuracy of three new definitions of the adult respiratory distress syndrome. Crit Care Med 23:1629–1637, 1995.

12. Meade MO, Guyatt GH, Cook RJ, et al: Agreement between alternative classifications of acute respiratory distress syndrome. Am J Respir Crit Care Med 163:490–493, 2001.

13. Conference report: Mechanisms of acute respiratory failure. Am Rev Respir Dis 115:1071–1078, 1977.

14. Villar J, Slutsky AS: The incidence of the adult respiratory distress syndrome. Am Rev Respir Dis 140:814–816, 1989.

15. Rubenfeld GD: Epidemiology of acute lung injury. Crit Care Med 31:S276–S284, 2003.

16. Goss CH, Brower RG, Hudson LD, et al: Incidence of acute lung injury in the United States. Crit Care Med 31:1607–1611, 2003.

17. Pepe PE, Potkin RT, Reus DH, et al: Clinical predictors of the adult respiratory distress syndrome. Am J Surg 144:124–130, 1982.

18. Hudson LD, Milberg JA, Anardi D, et al: Clinical risks for development of the acute respiratory distress syndrome. Am J Respir Crit Care Med 151:293–301, 1995.

19. Moss M, Bucher B, Moore FA, et al: The role of chronic alcohol abuse in the development of acute respiratory distress syndrome in adults. JAMA 275:50–54, 1996.

20. Moss M, Guidot DM, Steinberg KP, et al: Diabetic patients have a decreased incidence of acute respiratory distress syndrome. Crit Care Med 28:2187–2192, 2000.

21. Garber BG, Hebert PC, Yelle JD, et al: Adult respiratory distress syndrome: A systemic overview of incidence and risk factors. Crit Care Med 24:687–695, 1996.

22. Gattinoni L, Pelosi P, Suter PM, et al: Acute respiratory distress syndrome caused by pulmonary and extrapulmonary disease: Different syndromes? Am J Respir Crit Care Med 158:3–11, 1998.

23. Tomashefski JF Jr: Pulmonary pathology of the adult respiratory distress syndrome. Clin Chest Med 11:593–619, 1990.

24. Marshall RP, Bellingan G, Webb S, et al: Fibroproliferation occurs early in the acute respiratory distress syndrome and impacts on outcome. Am J Respir Crit Care Med 162:1783–1788, 2000.

25. Marshall R, Bellingan G, Laurent G: The acute respiratory distress syndrome: Fibrosis in the fast lane. Thorax 53:815–817, 1998.

26. Matthay MA, Wiener-Kronish JP: Intact epithelial barrier function is critical for the resolution of alveolar edema in humans. Am Rev Respir Dis 142:1250–1257, 1990.

27. Wiener-Kronish JP, Albertine KH, Matthay MA: Differential responses of the endothelial and epithelial barriers of the lung in sheep to *Escherichia coli* endotoxin. J Clin Invest 88:864–875, 1991.

28. Lewis JF, Brackenbury A: Role of exogenous surfactant in acute lung injury. Crit Care Med 31:S324–S328, 2003.

29. Baker CS, Evans TW, Randle BJ, et al: Damage to surfactant-specific protein in acute respiratory distress syndrome. Lancet 353:1232–1237, 1999.

30. Tino MJ, Wright JR: Surfactant protein A stimulates phagocytosis of specific pulmonary pathogens by alveolar macrophages. Am J Physiol 270:L677–L688, 1996.

31. Kuan SF, Rust K, Crouch E: Interactions of surfactant protein D with bacterial lipopolysaccharides: Surfactant protein D is an *Escherichia coli*-binding protein in bronchoalveolar lavage. J Clin Invest 90:97–106, 1992.

32. Lewis JF, Jobe AH: Surfactant and the adult respiratory distress syndrome. Am Rev Respir Dis 147:218–233, 1993 [published erratum appears in Am Rev Respir Dis 147:following 1068, 1993].

33. Planes C, Blot-Chabaud M, Matthay MA, et al: Hypoxia and beta 2-agonists regulate cell surface expression of the epithelial sodium channel in native alveolar epithelial cells. J Biol Chem 277:47318–47324, 2002.

34. Mairbaurl H, Mayer K, Kim KJ, et al: Hypoxia decreases active Na transport across primary rat alveolar epithelial cell monolayers. Am J Physiol Lung Cell Mol Physiol 282:L659–L665, 2002.

35. Dada LA, Chandel NS, Ridge KM, et al: Hypoxia-induced endocytosis of Na,K-ATPase in alveolar epithelial cells is mediated by mitochondrial reactive oxygen species and PKC-zeta. J Clin Invest 111:1057–1064, 2003.

36. Pittet JF, Lu LN, Morris DG, et al: Reactive nitrogen species inhibit alveolar epithelial fluid transport after hemorrhagic shock in rats. J Immunol 166:6301–6310, 2001.

37. Ware LB, Matthay MA: Alveolar fluid clearance is impaired in the majority of patients with acute lung injury and the acute respiratory distress syndrome. Am J Respir Crit Care Med 163:1376–1383, 2001.

38. Ware LB, Matthay MA: The acute respiratory distress syndrome (see comment). N Engl J Med 342:1334–1349, 2000.

39. Rinaldo JE: Mediation of ARDS by leukocytes: Clinical evidence and implications for therapy. Chest 89:590–593, 1986.

40. Steinberg KP, Milberg JA, Martin TR, et al: Evolution of bronchoalveolar cell populations in the adult respiratory distress syndrome. Am J Respir Crit Care Med 150:113–122, 1994.

41. Folz RJ, Abushamaa AM, Suliman HB: Extracellular superoxide dismutase in the airways of transgenic mice reduces inflammation and attenuates lung toxicity following hyperoxia. J Clin Invest 103:1055–1066, 1999.

42. Kawabata K, Hagio T, Matsumoto S, et al: Delayed neutrophil elastase inhibition prevents subsequent progression of acute lung injury induced by endotoxin inhalation in hamsters. Am J Respir Crit Care Med 161:2013–2018, 2000.

43. Lee WL, Downey GP: Neutrophil activation and acute lung injury. Curr Opin Crit Care 7:1–7, 2001.

44. Thommasen HV, Russell JA, Boyko WJ, et al: Transient leucopenia associated with adult respiratory distress syndrome. Lancet 1:809–812, 1984.

45. Worthen GS, Schwab B 3rd, Elson EL, et al: Mechanics of stimulated neutrophils: Cell stiffening induces retention in capillaries. Science 245:183–186, 1989.

46. Skoutelis AT, Kaleridis V, Athanassiou GM, et al: Neutrophil deformability in patients with sepsis, septic

shock, and adult respiratory distress syndrome. Crit Care Med 28:2355–2359, 2000.

47. Kuebler WM, Borges J, Sckell A, et al: Role of L-selectin in leukocyte sequestration in lung capillaries in a rabbit model of endotoxemia. Am J Respir Crit Care Med 161:36–43, 2000.

48. Doerschuk CM, Tasaka S, Wang Q: CD11/CD18-dependent and -independent neutrophil emigration in the lungs: How do neutrophils know which route to take? Am J Respir Cell Mol Biol 23:133–136, 2000.

49. Li Q, Park PW, Wilson CL, et al: Matrilysin shedding of syndecan-1 regulates chemokine mobilization and transepithelial efflux of neutrophils in acute lung injury. Cell 111:635–646, 2002.

50. Nick JA, Avdi NJ, Young SK, et al: Selective activation and functional significance of p38alpha mitogen-activated protein kinase in lipopolysaccharide-stimulated neutrophils. J Clin Invest 103:851–858, 1999.

51. Nick JA, Young SK, Brown KK, et al: Role of p38 mitogen-activated protein kinase in a murine model of pulmonary inflammation. J Immunol 164:2151–2159, 2000.

52. Nick JA, Young SK, Arndt PG, et al: Selective suppression of neutrophil accumulation in ongoing pulmonary inflammation by systemic inhibition of p38 mitogen-activated protein kinase. J Immunol 169:5260–5269, 2002.

53. Naccache PH, Levasseur S, Lachance G, et al: Stimulation of human neutrophils by chemotactic factors is associated with the activation of phosphatidylinositol 3-kinase gamma. J Biol Chem 275:23636–23641, 2000.

54. Yum HK, Arcaroli J, Kupfner J, et al: Involvement of phosphoinositide 3-kinases in neutrophil activation and the development of acute lung injury. J Immunol 167:6601–6608, 2001.

55. Fink MP: Role of reactive oxygen and nitrogen species in acute respiratory distress syndrome. Curr Opin Crit Care 8:6–11, 2002.

56. Wang W, Suzuki Y, Tanigaki T, et al: Effect of the NADPH oxidase inhibitor apocynin on septic lung injury in guinea pigs. Am J Respir Crit Care Med 150:1449–1452, 1994.

57. Kristof AS, Goldberg P, Laubach V, et al: Role of inducible nitric oxide synthase in endotoxin-induced acute lung injury. Am J Respir Crit Care Med 158:1883–1889, 1998.

58. Lee WL, Downey GP: Leukocyte elastase: Physiological functions and role in acute lung injury. Am J Respir Crit Care Med 164:896–904, 2001.

59. Belaaouaj A, McCarthy R, Baumann M, et al: Mice lacking neutrophil elastase reveal impaired host defense against gram negative bacterial sepsis. Nat Med 4:615–618, 1998.

60. Tkalcevic J, Novelli M, Phylactides M, et al: Impaired immunity and enhanced resistance to endotoxin in the absence of neutrophil elastase and cathepsin G. Immunity 12:201–210, 2000.

60a. Zeiher BG, Artigas A, Vincent JL, et al for the STRIVE Study Group: Neutrophil elastase inhibition in acute lung injury: results of the STRIVE study. Crit Care Med 32:1695–1702, 2004.

61. Delclaux C, d'Ortho MP, Delacourt C, et al: Gelatinases in epithelial lining fluid of patients with adult respiratory distress syndrome. Am J Physiol 272:L442–L451, 1997.

62. Warner RL, Beltran L, Younkin EM, et al: Role of stromelysin 1 and gelatinase B in experimental acute lung injury. Am J Respir Cell Mol Biol 24:537–544, 2001.

63. Carney DE, Lutz CJ, Picone AL, et al: Matrix metalloproteinase inhibitor prevents acute lung injury after cardiopulmonary bypass. Circulation 100:400–406, 1999.

64. Nelson S, Belknap SM, Carlson RW, et al: A randomized controlled trial of filgrastim as an adjunct to antibiotics for treatment of hospitalized patients with community-acquired pneumonia. CAP Study Group. J Infect Dis 178:1075–1080, 1998.

65. Presneill JJ, Harris T, Stewart AG, et al: A randomized Phase II trial of granulocyte-macrophage colony-stimulating factor therapy in severe sepsis with respiratory dysfunction. Am J Respir Crit Care Med 166:138–143, 2002.

66. Azoulay E, Attalah H, Yang K, et al: Exacerbation with granulocyte colony-stimulating factor of prior acute lung injury during neutropenia recovery in rats. Crit Care Med 31:157–165, 2003.

67. Azoulay E, Herigault S, Levame M, et al: Effect of granulocyte colony-stimulating factor on bleomycin-induced acute lung injury and pulmonary fibrosis. Crit Care Med 31:1442–1448, 2003.

68. Ognibene FP, Martin SE, Parker MM, et al: Adult respiratory distress syndrome in patients with severe neutropenia. N Engl J Med 315:547–551, 1986.

69. Vansteenkiste JF, Boogaerts MA: Adult respiratory distress syndrome in neutropenic leukemia patients. Blut 58:287–290, 1989.

70. Hotchkiss RS, Karl IE: The pathophysiology and treatment of sepsis. N Engl J Med 348:138–150, 2003.

71. Laterre PF, Wittebole X, Dhainaut JF: Anticoagulant therapy in acute lung injury. Crit Care Med 31:S329–S336, 2003.

72. Marshall JC: Inflammation, coagulopathy, and the pathogenesis of multiple organ dysfunction syndrome. Crit Care Med 29:S99–S106, 2001.

73. Esmon CT: Protein C anticoagulant pathway and its role in controlling microvascular thrombosis and inflammation. Crit Care Med 29:S48–51, 2001 [discussion appears in Crit Care Med 29:51–52, 2001].

74. Welty-Wolf KE, Carraway MS, Miller DL, et al: Coagulation blockade prevents sepsis-induced respiratory and renal failure in baboons. Am J Respir Crit Care Med 164:1988–1996, 2001.

75. Bernard GR, Vincent JL, Laterre PF, et al: Efficacy and safety of recombinant human activated protein C for severe sepsis. N Engl J Med 344:699–709, 2001.

75a. Nick JA, Coldren CD, Geraci MW, et al: Recombinant human activated protein C reduces human endotoxin-induced pulmonary inflammation via inhibition of neutrophil chemotaxis. Blood 104:3878–3885, 2004.

76. Pittet JF, Griffiths MJ, Geiser T, et al: TGF-beta is a critical mediator of acute lung injury. J Clin Invest 107:1537–1544, 2001.

76a. Goggel R, Winoto-Morbach S, Vielhaber G, et al: PAF-mediated pulmonary edema: a new role for acid sphingomyelinase and ceramide. Nat Med 10:155–160, 2004.

77. Weiss YG, Maloyan A, Tazelaar J, et al: Adenoviral transfer of HSP-70 into pulmonary epithelium ameliorates experimental acute respiratory distress syndrome. J Clin Invest 110:801–806, 2002.

78. Dreyfuss D, Saumon G: Ventilator-induced lung injury: Lessons from experimental studies. Am J Respir Crit Care Med 157:294–323, 1998.

79. Tsuno K, Miura K, Takeya M, et al: Histopathologic pulmonary changes from mechanical ventilation at high peak airway pressures. Am Rev Respir Dis 143:1115–1120, 1991.

80. Ventilation with lower tidal volumes as compared with traditional tidal volumes for acute lung injury and the acute respiratory distress syndrome. The Acute Respiratory

Distress Syndrome Network. N Engl J Med 342:1301–1308, 2000.

81. Dreyfuss D, Soler P, Basset G, et al: High inflation pressure pulmonary edema: Respective effects of high airway pressure, high tidal volume, and positive end-expiratory pressure. Am Rev Respir Dis 137:1159–1164, 1988.

82. Hernandez LA, Peevy KJ, Moise AA, et al: Chest wall restriction limits high airway pressure-induced lung injury in young rabbits. J Appl Physiol 66:2364–2368, 1989.

83. Slutsky AS: Lung injury caused by mechanical ventilation. Chest 116:9S–15S, 1999.

84. Mead J, Takishima T, Leith D: Stress distribution in lungs: A model of pulmonary elasticity. J Appl Physiol 28:596–608, 1970.

85. Gattinoni L, D'Andrea L, Pelosi P, et al: Regional effects and mechanism of positive end-expiratory pressure in early adult respiratory distress syndrome. JAMA 269:2122–2127, 1993. [published erratum appears in JAMA 270:1814, 1993].

86. Taskar V, John J, Evander E, et al: Healthy lungs tolerate repetitive collapse and reopening during short periods of mechanical ventilation. Acta Anaesthesiol Scand 39:370–376, 1995.

87. Taskar V, John J, Evander E, et al: Surfactant dysfunction makes lungs vulnerable to repetitive collapse and reexpansion. Am J Respir Crit Care Med 155:313–320, 1997.

88. Tremblay LN, Slutsky AS: Ventilator-induced injury: From barotrauma to biotrauma. Proc Assoc Am Physicians 110:482–488, 1998.

89. Tremblay L, Valenza F, Ribeiro SP, et al: Injurious ventilatory strategies increase cytokines and c-fos m-RNA expression in an isolated rat lung model. J Clin Invest 99:944–952, 1997.

90. Chiumello D, Pristine G, Slutsky AS: Mechanical ventilation affects local and systemic cytokines in an animal model of acute respiratory distress syndrome. Am J Respir Crit Care Med 160:109–116, 1999.

91. Ranieri VM, Suter PM, Tortorella C, et al: Effect of mechanical ventilation on inflammatory mediators in patients with acute respiratory distress syndrome: A randomized controlled trial. JAMA 282:54–61, 1999.

92. Imai Y, Parodo J, Kajikawa O, et al: Injurious mechanical ventilation and end-organ epithelial cell apoptosis and organ dysfunction in an experimental model of acute respiratory distress syndrome. JAMA 289:2104–2112, 2003.

93. de los Santos R, Seidenfeld JJ, Anzueto A, et al: One hundred percent oxygen lung injury in adult baboons. Am Rev Respir Dis 136:657–661, 1987.

94. Lin Z, Pearson C, Chinchilli V, et al: Polymorphisms of human SP-A, SP-B, and SP-D genes: Association of SP-B Thr131Ile with ARDS. Clin Genet 58:181–191, 2000.

95. Marshall RP, Webb S, Bellingan GJ, et al: Angiotensin converting enzyme insertion/deletion polymorphism is associated with susceptibility and outcome in acute respiratory distress syndrome. Am J Respir Crit Care Med 166:646–650, 2002.

96. Bell RC, Coalson JJ, Smith JD, et al: Multiple organ system failure and infection in adult respiratory distress syndrome. Ann Intern Med 99:293–298, 1983.

97. Montgomery AB, Stager MA, Carrico CJ, et al: Causes of mortality in patients with the adult respiratory distress syndrome. Am Rev Respir Dis 132:485–489, 1985.

98. Mitchell JP, Schuller D, Calandrino FS, et al: Improved outcome based on fluid management in critically ill patients requiring pulmonary artery catheterization. Am Rev Respir Dis 145:990–998, 1992.

99. Schuller D, Mitchell JP, Calandrino FS, et al: Fluid balance during pulmonary edema: Is fluid gain a marker or a cause of poor outcome? Chest 100:1068–1075, 1991.

100. Martin GS, Mangialardi RJ, Wheeler AP, et al: Albumin and furosemide therapy in hypoproteinemic patients with acute lung injury. Crit Care Med 30:2175–2182, 2002.

101. Rivers E, Nguyen B, Havstad S, et al: Early goal-directed therapy in the treatment of severe sepsis and septic shock. N Engl J Med 345:1368–1377, 2001.

102. Gadek JE, DeMichele SJ, Karlstad MD, et al: Effect of enteral feeding with eicosapentaenoic acid, gamma-linolenic acid, and antioxidants in patients with acute respiratory distress syndrome. Enteral Nutrition in ARDS Study Group. Crit Care Med 27:1409–1420, 1999.

103. Heyland DK, Novak F, Drover JW, et al: Should immunonutrition become routine in critically ill patients? A systematic review of the evidence. JAMA 286:944–953, 2001.

104. dos Santos C, Chant C, Slutsky AS: Pharmacotherapy of acute respiratory distress syndrome (a review). Expert Opin Pharmacother 3:875–888, 2002.

105. Lucas CE, Ledgerwood AM: Pulmonary response of massive steroids in seriously injured patients. Ann Surg 194:256–261, 1981.

106. Bernard GR, Luce JM, Sprung CL, et al: High-dose corticosteroids in patients with the adult respiratory distress syndrome. N Engl J Med 317:1565–1570, 1987.

107. Weigelt JA, Norcross JF, Borman KR, et al: Early steroid therapy for respiratory failure. Arch Surg 120:536–540, 1985.

108. Meduri GU, Headley AS, Golden E, et al: Effect of prolonged methylprednisolone therapy in unresolving acute respiratory distress syndrome: A randomized controlled trial. JAMA 280:159–165, 1998.

109. Abraham E, Park YC, Covington P, et al: Liposomal prostaglandin E_1 in acute respiratory distress syndrome: A placebo-controlled, randomized, double-blind, multicenter clinical trial. Crit Care Med 24:10–15, 1996.

110. Abraham E, Fletcher E, Heard S, et al: Liposomal prostaglandin E_1 (TLC C-53) in acute respiratory distress syndrome: A controlled, randomized, double-blind, multicenter clinical trial. Crit Care Med 27:1478–1485, 1999.

111. Walmrath D, Schneider T, Pilch J, et al: Aerosolised prostacyclin in adult respiratory distress syndrome. Lancet 342:961–962, 1993.

112. Walmrath D, Schneider T, Schermuly R, et al: Direct comparison of inhaled nitric oxide and aerosolized prostacyclin in acute respiratory distress syndrome. Am J Respir Crit Care Med 153:991–996, 1996.

113. Zwissler B, Kemming G, Habler O, et al: Inhaled prostacyclin (PGI_2) versus inhaled nitric oxide in adult respiratory distress syndrome. Am J Respir Crit Care Med 154:1671–1677, 1996.

114. Rossaint R, Falke KJ, Lopez F, et al: Inhaled nitric oxide for the adult respiratory distress syndrome. N Engl J Med 328:399–405, 1993.

115. van der Vliet A, Eiserich JP, Cross CE: Nitric oxide: A pro-inflammatory mediator in lung disease? Respir Res 1:67–72, 2000.

116. Dellinger RP, Zimmerman JL, Taylor RW, et al: Effects of inhaled nitric oxide in patients with acute respiratory distress syndrome: Results of a randomized Phase II trial. Inhaled Nitric Oxide in ARDS Study Group. Crit Care Med 26:15–23, 1998.

117. Troncy E, Collet JP, Shapiro S, et al: Inhaled nitric oxide in acute respiratory distress syndrome: A pilot randomized controlled study. Am J Respir Crit Care Med 157:1483–1488, 1998.

118. Michael JR, Barton RG, Saffle JR, et al: Inhaled nitric oxide versus conventional therapy: Effect on oxygenation in ARDS. Am J Respir Crit Care Med 157:1372–1380, 1998.

119. Sokol J, Jacobs SE, Bohn D: Inhaled nitric oxide for acute hypoxemic respiratory failure in children and adults (Cochrane Review). *In* The Cochrane Library. Oxford: Update Software, Issue 1, 2003.

120. Lundin S, Mang H, Smithies M, et al: Inhalation of nitric oxide in acute lung injury: Results of a European multicentre study. The European Study Group of Inhaled Nitric Oxide. Intensive Care Med 25:911–919, 1999.

120a. Taylor RW, Zimmerman JL, Dellinger RP, et al: Low-dose inhaled nitric oxide in patients with acute lung injury: a randomized controlled trial. JAMA 291:1603–1609, 2004.

121. Spragg RG, Gilliard N, Richman P, et al: Acute effects of a single dose of porcine surfactant on patients with the adult respiratory distress syndrome. Chest 105:195–202, 1994.

122. Gregory TJ, Steinberg KP, Spragg R, et al: Bovine surfactant therapy for patients with acute respiratory distress syndrome. Am J Respir Crit Care Med 155:1309–1315, 1997.

123. Anzueto A, Baughman RP, Guntupalli KK, et al: Aerosolized surfactant in adults with sepsis-induced acute respiratory distress syndrome. Exosurf Acute Respiratory Distress Syndrome Sepsis Study Group. N Engl J Med 334:1417–1421, 1996.

124. Spragg RG, Lewis JF, Wurst W, et al: Treatment of acute respiratory distress syndrome with recombinant surfactant protein C surfactant. Am J Respir Crit Care Med 167:1562–1566, 2003.

125. Bernard GR, Wheeler AP, Arons MM, et al: A trial of antioxidants *N*-acetylcysteine and procysteine in ARDS. The Antioxidant in ARDS Study Group. Chest 112:164–172, 1997.

126. Randomized, placebo-controlled trial of lisofylline for early treatment of acute lung injury and acute respiratory distress syndrome. Crit Care Med 30:1–6, 2002.

127. Ketoconazole for early treatment of acute lung injury and acute respiratory distress syndrome: A randomized controlled trial. The ARDS Network. JAMA 283:1995–2002, 2000 [published erratum appears in JAMA 284:2450, 2000].

128. Bernard GR, Wheeler AP, Russell JA, et al: The effects of ibuprofen on the physiology and survival of patients with sepsis. The Ibuprofen in Sepsis Study Group. N Engl J Med 336:912–918, 1997.

129. Schuster DP, Metzler M, Opal S, et al: Recombinant platelet-activating factor acetylhydrolase to prevent acute respiratory distress syndrome and mortality in severe sepsis: Phase IIb, multicenter, randomized, placebo-controlled, clinical trial. Crit Care Med 31:1612–1619, 2003.

130. Panos RJ, Bak PM, Simonet WS, et al: Intratracheal instillation of keratinocyte growth factor decreases hyperoxia-induced mortality in rats. J Clin Invest 96:2026–2033, 1995.

131. Maunder RJ, Shuman WP, McHugh JW, et al: Preservation of normal lung regions in the adult respiratory distress syndrome—analysis by computer tomography. JAMA 255:2463–2465, 1986.

132. Stewart TE, Meade MO, Cook DJ, et al: Evaluation of a ventilation strategy to prevent barotrauma in patients at high risk for acute respiratory distress syndrome. Pressure- and Volume-Limited Ventilation Strategy Group. N Engl J Med 338:355–361, 1998.

133. Brower RG, Shanholtz CB, Fessler HE, et al: Prospective, randomized, controlled clinical trial comparing traditional versus reduced tidal volume ventilation in acute respiratory distress syndrome patients. Crit Care Med 27:1492–1498, 1999.

134. Brochard L, Roudot-Thoraval F, Roupie E, et al: Tidal volume reduction for prevention of ventilator-induced lung injury in acute respiratory distress syndrome. The Multicenter Trial Group on Tidal Volume Reduction in ARDS. Am J Respir Crit Care Med 158:1831–1838, 1998.

135. Amato MB, Barbas CS, Medeiros DM, et al: Effect of a protective-ventilation strategy on mortality in the acute respiratory distress syndrome. N Engl J Med 338:347–354, 1998.

136. Eichacker PQ, Gerstenberger EP, Banks SM, et al: Meta-analysis of acute lung injury and acute respiratory distress syndrome trials testing low tidal volumes. Am J Respir Crit Care Med 166:1510–1514, 2002.

137. Steinbrook R: How best to ventilate? Trial design and patient safety in studies of the acute respiratory distress syndrome. N Engl J Med 348:1393–1401, 2003.

138. Slutsky AS: Mechanical ventilation. American College of Chest Physicians' Consensus Conference. Chest 104:1833–1859, 1993 [erratum appears in Chest 106:656, 1994].

139. Jonson B, Richard JC, Straus C, et al: Pressure-volume curves and compliance in acute lung injury: Evidence of recruitment above the lower inflection point. Am J Respir Crit Care Med 159:1172–1178, 1999.

140. Rimensberger PC, Cox PN, Frndova H, et al: The open lung during small tidal volume ventilation: Concepts of recruitment and "optimal" positive end-expiratory pressure. Crit Care Med 27:1946–1952, 1999.

141. Pelosi P, Gattinoni L: Respiratory mechanics in ARDS: A siren for physicians? Intensive Care Med 26:653–656, 2000.

142. Rouby JJ, Lu Q, Goldstein I: Selecting the right level of positive end-expiratory pressure in patients with acute respiratory distress syndrome. Am J Respir Crit Care Med 165:1182–1186, 2002.

143. de Durante G, del Turco M, Rustichini L, et al: ARDSNet lower tidal volume ventilatory strategy may generate intrinsic positive end-expiratory pressure in patients with acute respiratory distress syndrome. Am J Respir Crit Care Med 165:1271–1274, 2002.

144. Brower RG, Lanken PN, MacIntyre N, et al for the National Heart, Lung, and Blood Institute ARDS Clinical Trials Network: Higher versus lower positive end-expiratory pressures in patients with the acute respiratory distress syndrome. N Engl J Med 351:327–336, 2004.

145. Barbas CSV: Lung recruitment maneuvers in acute respiratory distress syndrome and facilitating resolution. Crit Care Med 31(Suppl):S265–S271, 2003.

146. Richard JC, Maggiore SM, Jonson B, et al: Influence of tidal volume on alveolar recruitment: Respective role of PEEP and a recruitment maneuver. Am J Respir Crit Care Med 163:1609–1613, 2001.

147. Foti G, Cereda M, Sparacino ME, et al: Effects of periodic lung recruitment maneuvers on gas exchange and respiratory mechanics in mechanically ventilated acute respiratory distress syndrome (ARDS) patients. Intensive Care Med 26:501–507, 2000.

148. Villagra A, Ochagavia A, Vatua S, et al: Recruitment maneuvers during lung protective ventilation in acute respiratory distress syndrome. Am J Respir Crit Care Med 165:165–170, 2002.

149. Brower RG, Clemmer T, Lanken P, et al: Effects of recruitment maneuvers in acute lung injury patients ventilated with lower tidal volumes and higher positive end-expiratory pressures (abstract). Am J Respir Crit Care Med:163A, 2001.

149a. Brower RG, Morris A, MacIntyre N, et al for the ARDS Clinical Trials Network, National Heart, Lung, and Blood Institute, National Institutes of Health: Effects of recruitment maneuvers in patients with acute lung injury and acute respiratory distress syndrome ventilated with high positive end-expiratory pressure. Crit Care Med 31:2592–2597, 2003.

150. Laffey JG, Tanaka M, Engelberts D, et al: Therapeutic hypercapnia reduces pulmonary and systemic injury following in vivo lung reperfusion. Am J Respir Crit Care Med 162:2287–2294, 2000.

151. Takeshita K, Suzuki Y, Nishio K, et al: Hypercapnic acidosis attenuates endotoxin-induced nuclear factor-κB activation. Am J Respir Cell Mol Biol 29:124–132, 2003.

152. Lang JD Jr, Chumley P, Eiserich JP, et al: Hypercapnia induces injury to alveolar epithelial cells via a nitric oxide-dependent pathway. Am J Physiol Lung Cell Mol Physiol 279:L994–L1002, 2000.

153. Kacmarek RM: A workable alternative to the problems with tracheal gas insufflation? Intensive Care Med 28:1009–1011, 2002.

154. Kalfon P, Rao GS, Gallart L, et al: Permissive hypercapnia with and without expiratory washout in patients with severe acute respiratory distress syndrome. Anesthesiology 87:6–17, 1997 [discussion appears in Anesthesiology 87:25A–26A, 1997].

155. Pelosi P, Tubiolo D, Mascheroni D, et al: Effects of the prone position on respiratory mechanics and gas exchange during acute lung injury. Am J Respir Crit Care Med 157:387–393, 1998.

156. Broccard AF, Shapiro RS, Schmitz LL, et al: Influence of prone position on the extent and distribution of lung injury in a high tidal volume oleic acid model of acute respiratory distress syndrome. Crit Care Med 25:16–27, 1997.

157. Gattinoni L, Tognoni G, Pesenti A, et al: Effect of prone positioning on the survival of patients with acute respiratory failure. N Engl J Med 345:568–573, 2001.

158. Slutsky AS: The acute respiratory distress syndrome, mechanical ventilation, and the prone position. N Engl J Med 345:610–612, 2001.

158a. Guerin C, Gaillard S, Lemasson S, et al: Effects of systematic prone positioning in hypoxemic acute respiratory failure: a randomized controlled trial. JAMA 292:2379–2387, 2004.

159. Prella M, Feihl F, Domenighetti G: Effects of short-term pressure-controlled ventilation on gas exchange, airway pressures, and gas distribution in patients with acute lung injury/ARDS: Comparison with volume-controlled ventilation. Chest 122:1382–1388, 2002 [published erratum appears in Chest 123:315, 2003].

160. Esteban A, Alia I, Gordo F, et al, for the Spanish Lung Failure Collaborative Group: Prospective randomized trial comparing pressure-controlled ventilation and volume-controlled ventilation in ARDS. Chest 117:1690–1696, 2000.

161. Krishnan JA, Brower RG: High-frequency ventilation for acute lung injury and ARDS. Chest 118:795–807, 2000.

162. Carlon GC, Howland WS, Ray C, et al: High-frequency jet ventilation: A prospective randomized evaluation. Chest 84:551–559, 1983.

163. Derdak S, Mehta S, Stewart TE, et al: High-frequency oscillatory ventilation for acute respiratory distress syndrome in adults: A randomized, controlled trial. Am J Respir Crit Care Med 166:801–808, 2002.

164. Shanholtz C, Brower R: Should inverse ratio ventilation be used in adult respiratory distress syndrome? Am J Respir Crit Care Med 149:1354–1358, 1994.

165. Hirschl RB, Conrad S, Kaiser R, et al: Partial liquid ventilation in adult patients with ARDS: A multicenter Phase I-II trial. Adult PLV Study Group. Ann Surg 228:692–700, 1998.

166. Fuhrman BP, Hernan LJ, Holm BA, et al: Perfluorocarbon associated gas exchange (PAGE): Gas ventilation of the perfluorocarbon filled lung. Artif Cells Blood Substit Immobil Biotechnol 22:1133–1139, 1994.

167. Hirschl RB, Croce M, Gore D, et al: Prospective, randomized, controlled pilot study of partial liquid ventilation in adult acute respiratory distress syndrome. Am J Respir Crit Care Med 165:781–787, 2002.

168. Wassermann J, Mazer CD: ECMO in adults: What is its role? Can J Anaesth 45:1044–1048, 1998.

169. Zapol WM, Snider MT, Hill JD, et al: Extracorporeal membrane oxygenation in severe acute respiratory failure: A randomized prospective study. JAMA 242:2193–2196, 1979.

170. Gattinoni L, Pesenti A, Mascheroni D, et al: Low-frequency positive-pressure ventilation with extracorporeal CO_2 removal in severe acute respiratory failure. JAMA 256:881–886, 1986.

171. Morris AH, Wallace CJ, Menlove RL, et al: Randomized clinical trial of pressure-controlled inverse ratio ventilation and extracorporeal CO_2 removal for adult respiratory distress syndrome. Am J Respir Crit Care Med 149:295–305, 1994 [published erratum appears in Am J Respir Crit Care Med 149(3 Pt 1):838, 1994].

172. Milberg JA, Davis DR, Steinberg KP, et al: Improved survival of patients with acute respiratory distress syndrome (ARDS): 1983–1993. JAMA 273:306–309, 1995.

173. Abel SJ, Finney SJ, Brett SJ, et al: Reduced mortality in association with the acute respiratory distress syndrome (ARDS). Thorax 53:292–294, 1998.

174. Luhr OR, Antonsen K, Karlsson M, et al: Incidence and mortality after acute respiratory failure and acute respiratory distress syndrome in Sweden, Denmark, and Iceland. The ARF Study Group. Am J Respir Crit Care Med 159:1849–1861, 1999.

175. Bersten AD, Edibam C, Hunt T, et al: Incidence and mortality of acute lung injury and the acute respiratory distress syndrome in three Australian states. Am J Respir Crit Care Med 165:443–448, 2002.

176. Doyle RL, Szaflarski N, Modin GW, et al: Identification of patients with acute lung injury: Predictors of mortality. Am J Respir Crit Care Med 152:1818–1824, 1995.

177. Heffner JE, Brown LK, Barbieri CA, et al: Prospective validation of an acute respiratory distress syndrome predictive score. Am J Respir Crit Care Med 152:1518–1526, 1995.

178. Roupie E, Lepage E, Wysocki M, et al: Prevalence, etiologies and outcome of the acute respiratory distress syndrome among hypoxemic ventilated patients. Intensive Care Med 25:920–929, 1999.

179. Slutsky AS, Tremblay LN: Multiple system organ failure: Is mechanical ventilation a contributing factor? Am J Respir Crit Care Med 157:1721–1725, 1998.

180. Eisner MD, Thompson T, Hudson LD, et al: Efficacy of low tidal volume ventilation in patients with different clinical risk factors for acute lung injury and the acute respiratory distress syndrome. Am J Respir Crit Care Med 164:231–236, 2001.

181. Sloane PJ, Gee MH, Gottlieb JE, et al: A multicenter registry of patients with acute respiratory distress syndrome—physiology and outcome. Am Rev Respir Dis 146:419–425, 1992.

182. Zilberberg MD, Epstein SK: Acute lung injury in the medical ICU: Comorbid conditions, age, etiology, and

hospital outcome. Am J Respir Crit Care Med 157:1159–1164, 1998.

183. Moss M, Mannino DM: Race and gender differences in acute respiratory distress syndrome deaths in the United States: An analysis of multiple-cause mortality data (1979–1996). Crit Care Med 30:1679–1685, 2002.

184. Suntharalingam G, Regan K, Keogh BF, et al: Influence of direct and indirect etiology on acute outcome and 6-month functional recovery in acute respiratory distress syndrome. Crit Care Med 29:562–566, 2001.

185. Nuckton TJ, Alonso JA, Kallet RH, et al: Pulmonary dead-space fraction as a risk factor for death in the acute respiratory distress syndrome. N Engl J Med 346:1281–1286, 2002.

186. Clark JG, Milberg JA, Steinberg KP, et al: Type III procollagen peptide in the adult respiratory distress syndrome: Association of increased peptide levels in bronchoalveolar lavage fluid with increased risk for death. Ann Intern Med 122:17–23, 1995.

187. Chesnutt AN, Matthay MA, Tibayan FA, et al: Early detection of type III procollagen peptide in acute lung injury: Pathogenetic and prognostic significance. Am J Respir Crit Care Med 156:840–845, 1997.

188. Martin C, Papazian L, Payan MJ, et al: Pulmonary fibrosis correlates with outcome in adult respiratory distress syndrome: A study in mechanically ventilated patients. Chest 107:196–200, 1995.

189. Delclaux C, Roupie E, Blot F, et al: Lower respiratory tract colonization and infection during severe acute respiratory distress syndrome: Incidence and diagnosis. Am J Respir Crit Care Med 156:1092–1098, 1997.

190. Chastre J, Trouillet JL, Vuagnat A, et al: Nosocomial pneumonia in patients with acute respiratory distress syndrome. Am J Respir Crit Care Med 157:1165–1172, 1998.

191. Markowicz P, Wolff M, Djedaini K, et al: Multicenter prospective study of ventilator-associated pneumonia during acute respiratory distress syndrome: Incidence, prognosis, and risk factors. ARDS Study Group. Am J Respir Crit Care Med 161:1942–1948, 2000.

192. Sutherland KR, Steinberg KP, Maunder RJ, et al: Pulmonary infection during the acute respiratory distress syndrome. Am J Respir Crit Care Med 152:550–556, 1995.

193. Chastre J, Fagon JY: Ventilator-associated pneumonia. Am J Respir Crit Care Med 165:867–903, 2002.

194. Fagon JY, Chastre J, Wolff M, et al: Invasive and noninvasive strategies for management of suspected ventilator-associated pneumonia: A randomized trial. Ann Intern Med 132:621–630, 2000.

195. Meduri GU, Reddy RC, Stanley T, et al: Pneumonia in acute respiratory distress syndrome: A prospective evaluation of bilateral bronchoscopic sampling. Am J Respir Crit Care Med 158:870–875, 1998.

196. Weg JG, Anzueto A, Balk RA, et al: The relation of pneumothorax and other air leaks to mortality in the acute respiratory distress syndrome. N Engl J Med 338:341–346, 1998.

197. Orme J Jr, Romney JS, Hopkins RO, et al: Pulmonary function and health-related quality of life in survivors of acute respiratory distress syndrome. Am J Respir Crit Care Med 167:690–694, 2003.

198. Herridge MS, Cheung AM, Tansey CM, et al: One-year outcomes in survivors of the acute respiratory distress syndrome. N Engl J Med 348:683–693, 2003.

199. Davidson TA, Caldwell ES, Curtis JR, et al: Reduced quality of life in survivors of acute respiratory distress syndrome compared with critically ill control patients. JAMA 281:354–360, 1999.

200. Davidson TA, Rubenfeld GD, Caldwell ES, et al: The effect of acute respiratory distress syndrome on long-term survival. Am J Respir Crit Care Med 160:1838–1842, 1999.

201. Schelling G, Stoll C, Haller M, et al: Health-related quality of life and posttraumatic stress disorder in survivors of the acute respiratory distress syndrome. Crit Care Med 26:651–659, 1998.

202. Hopkins RO, Weaver LK, Pope D, et al: Neuropsychological sequelae and impaired health status in survivors of severe acute respiratory distress syndrome. Am J Respir Crit Care Med 160:50–56, 1999.

86 Acute Ventilatory Failure

David J. Pierson, M.D., Nicholas S. Hill, M.D.

INTRODUCTION AND DEFINITIONS

Respiratory failure exists when the function of the respiratory system is sufficiently impaired to cause severe dysfunction in other organs or to threaten life. Such impairment can affect either the gas exchange function of the lung, in which case the problem is primarily one of hypoxemia, or the ventilatory pump, manifested by hypercapnia and respiratory acidosis. This chapter deals with this latter circumstance, commonly called ventilatory failure.

Carbon dioxide tension in the arterial blood ($PaCO_2$) is a function of alveolar ventilation ($\dot{V}A$) and carbon dioxide production ($\dot{V}CO_2$), according to the following relationship.

$$PaCO_2 = (\dot{V}CO_2 \times k)/\dot{V}A \qquad (1)$$

Total minute ventilation is made up of both $\dot{V}A$ and dead space ventilation. Either a decrease in total minute ventilation or an increase in dead space ventilation can thus decrease $\dot{V}A$. Any decrease in $\dot{V}A$, or increase in $\dot{V}CO_2$ relative to $\dot{V}A$, results in an increase in arterial PCO_2. Because bicarbonate retention by the kidney in response to hypercapnia occurs slowly, a sudden increase in arterial PCO_2 abruptly lowers arterial pH. Ventilatory failure exists whenever arterial PCO_2 is substantially elevated, and acute ventilatory failure is present when the change from the patient's baseline state develops rapidly enough to produce a clinically important drop in arterial pH. Because patients with severe chronic obstructive pulmonary disease (COPD), chronic neuromuscular disease, and other disorders may already have hypercapnia at baseline, the presence of acute ventilatory failure is determined not so much by the arterial PCO_2 value as by the presence of acidemia, typically to an arterial pH of less than 7.30. The presence of acute ventilatory failure cannot be determined accurately by physical examination, pulse oximetry, exhaled carbon dioxide, or other noninvasive tests. Thus, making the diagnosis requires arterial blood gas analysis.[1]

PATHOPHYSIOLOGY OF ACUTE VENTILATORY FAILURE

Alveolar ventilation becomes inadequate in relation to carbon dioxide production either because ventilatory demand exceeds the patient's capability (pump failure) or because the patient's ventilatory effort is insufficient (drive failure)[2-4] (Fig. 86.1). These two mechanisms are distinct in their clinical presentation. Patients with acute failure of the ventilatory pump are dyspneic and tachypneic with other signs of distress and sympathetic nervous system activation, whereas patients with failure of ventilatory drive are not short of breath and typically demonstrate bradypnea or apnea.

Although acute ventilatory failure is primarily a disorder of alveolar ventilation, hypoxemia is also usually present. Alveolar hypoventilation causes a proportional fall in alveolar PO_2 (PA_{O_2}), according to the alveolar gas equation.

$$PA_{O_2} = PI_{O_2} - (PaCO_2/R) \qquad (2)$$

where arterial PCO_2 can be assumed to be the same as alveolar PCO_2, PI_{O_2} is the inspired PO_2, [i.e., the inspired oxygen fraction multiplied by the quotient of barometric pressure

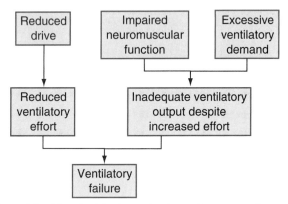

Figure 86.1 The physiologic mechanisms of acute ventilatory failure.

minus 47 (water vapor pressure at body temperature)], and R is the respiratory exchange ratio. This relationship explains the fall in arterial PO_2 that accompanies alveolar hypoventilation, as shown in Figure 86.2.[2] Calculating alveolar PO_2 using Equation 2 permits determination of the alveolar-arterial PO_2 difference $[P(A-a)O_2]$ (commonly but imprecisely called the "A-a gradient" and more precisely called the "A-a oxygen tension difference"). This calculation distinguishes between pure hypoventilation as an explanation for hypoxemia (in which case $[P(A-a)O_2]$ is normal) and the presence of other mechanisms such as low ventilation-perfusion ratios and right-to-left shunt (in which case $[P(A-a)O_2]$ is increased).

Finally, hypercapnia can be a feature of hypoxemic respiratory failure if the derangement in gas exchange is sufficiently severe. Both right-to-left shunt and low ventilation-perfusion ratios are present in the acute respiratory distress syndrome (ARDS) and can increase dead space (VD/VT) as determined by the Bohr equation,[5,6] thus impairing carbon dioxide elimination and contributing to hypercapnia.

Table 86.1 classifies the typical clinical presentations of acute ventilatory failure according to the site or type of defect and the physiologic mechanism or category of disorder responsible. Not every listed example is discussed in this chapter.

More than one mechanism may coexist in a given patient, producing a life-threatening condition even when the individual processes are only moderate in severity. For example, in decompensated obesity hypoventilation syndrome, a patient whose underlying respiratory drive is reduced and whose obesity poses an increased elastic load on the ventilatory pump may develop acute-on-chronic ventilatory failure in the presence of a relatively modest increase in the work of breathing from the additional restrictive effects of cardiomegaly and pleural effusions. Another common example is the combination of narcotic administration and phrenic nerve dysfunction following coronary artery bypass grafting in a patient with COPD, in whom blunted drive and impaired bellows function in the presence of increased resistive work from airway obstruction lead to acute ventilatory decompensation.

ACUTE VENTILATORY FAILURE DUE TO INSUFFICIENT VENTILATORY DRIVE

PHARMACOLOGIC CAUSES

Depression of the drive to breathe by drugs is by far the most common circumstance in which this form of acute ventilatory failure occurs and, it may be argued, the only one in which it is the primary mechanism. In the conditions discussed below, and even in acute drug overdose, an inability to protect the airway and the increased work of breathing usually play a major role in the genesis of acute respiratory acidosis.[7] The opioids are the most potent depressors of both hypoxic and hypercapnic ventilatory drive,[8] but any sedative, hypnotic, or anxiolytic agent causes respiratory depression if administered in sufficient quantity.[9-11]

Respiratory depression resolves as the drug is cleared from the body, as signaled by the return of spontaneous breathing efforts. Because the central nervous system effects of some agents may wax and wane due to the enterohepatic circulation, lipid storage, or other mechanisms, patients should be observed until it is clear that the ventilatory drive has been reestablished before they are weaned from ventilatory support. In the case of drug overdoses and other poisoning, identifying the specific agent or agents involved and the use of any specific therapies available, such as antidotes or dialysis, is important to expedite the weaning process from ventilatory support.[12]

Patients who fail to wean from mechanical ventilation because of inadequate drive from depressant drugs breathe slowly or not at all when ventilatory support is briefly discontinued. The much more common reason for difficulty weaning after drug overdose is that other mechanisms intervene (e.g., aspiration pneumonia or sepsis). In these circumstances, with a return of respiratory drive, patients become tachypneic and manifest signs of respiratory distress when ventilatory support is discontinued.[13,14]

DISEASE (CONGENITAL, ACQUIRED)

Decreased ventilatory drive is a frequent contributor to the development of chronic ventilatory insufficiency, but it is typically not the sole mechanism for acute ventilatory failure, except for those presenting with drug-induced suppression. When patients with underlying abnormalities of ventilatory drive develop respiratory infections, congestive heart failure,

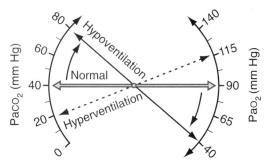

Figure 86.2 The relationship between arterial PO_2 (PaO_2) and arterial PCO_2 ($PaCO_2$) as ventilation increases or decreases, assuming that the alveolar-arterial PO_2 difference does not change and the respiratory exchange ratio is 0.8. (From Pierson DJ, Kacmarek RM [eds]: Foundations of Respiratory Care. New York: Churchill Livingstone, 1992, p 298.)

Table 86.1 Clinical Classification of Ventilatory Failure

Site or Type of Defect	Mechanism or Category	Clinical Examples
Ventilatory drive	Pharmacologic Congenital Acquired Combination	Drug overdose (opioids, sedatives, alcohol); general anesthesia Primary alveolar ventilation (Ondine's curse) Cerebrovascular accident; neoplasm; carotid body resection Obesity hypoventilation syndrome
Neural transmission to ventilatory muscles	Cervical spinal cord injury Demyelinating peripheral neuropathy Anterior horn cell disease Phrenic nerve lesion	Trauma; tumor; vascular accident Guillain-Barré syndrome Poliomyelitis; amyotrophic lateral sclerosis Trauma; cardiac surgery; neoplasm; idiopathic
Ventilatory muscles	Pharmacologic Primary muscle disorder Disorders of the neuromuscular junction Electrolyte and metabolic disturbances	Neuromuscular blocking agents Muscular dystrophy; polymyositis; dermatomyositis Myasthenia gravis; botulism; tetanus; tick paralysis Hypophosphatemia; hypokalemia; hypomagnesemia; myxedema
Chest wall	Decreased mobility	Kyphoscoliosis; traumatic asphyxia; tight casts or bandages; severe obesity
Pleural disorders	Extrapulmonary restriction	Pneumothorax; pleural effusion; pleural thickening or malignancy
Airway obstruction	Upper airway obstruction Lower airway obstruction	Epiglottitis; foreign body; tumor; vocal cord paralysis; tracheomalacia COPD; acute severe asthma
Increased dead space ventilation	Very high $\dot{V}/\dot{Q}$ Very low $\dot{V}/\dot{Q}$; right-to-left shunt Generalized pulmonary hypoperfusion Localized pulmonary hypoperfusion	COPD Severe ARDS Hypovolemic or cardiogenic shock; during CPR; pulmonary hyperinflation (excessive applied PEEP; intrinsic PEEP) Pulmonary thromboembolism*; venous air embolism
Increased CO_2 production*	Inflammation; hypermetabolism Muscle activity Excessive caloric intake	Fever; sepsis; burns; severe trauma Shivering; tetany; seizures; malignant hyperthermia Increased overall caloric intake (especially carbohydrate calories)
Exogenous CO_2 inhalation	Increased inspired PCO_2	Laboratory or industrial accident; therapeutic use

ARDS, acute respiratory distress syndrome; COPD, chronic obstructive pulmonary disease; CPR, cardiopulmonary resuscitation; PEEP, positive end-expiratory pressure; $\dot{V}/\dot{Q}$, ventilation-to-perfusion ratio.
* In the absence of ability to compensate with increased overall ventilation.

or other acute illness, they are more likely than individuals without such defects to develop acute ventilatory failure.

The obesity hypoventilation syndrome, discussed in Chapter 73, is characterized by blunted responses to hypoxia and hypercapnia[15] and is one disorder in which patients may first present in acute ventilatory failure. Typically, such patients have a history of recent weight gain and are found to be markedly fluid-overloaded, with features of cor pulmonale. The increased work of breathing from decreased chest wall compliance, cardiomegaly, and often large pleural effusions, as well as worsening hypoxemia, all contribute to respiratory muscle fatigue and the development of severe hypercapnia and respiratory acidosis. Hypoventilation is more common among hospitalized patients with severe obesity than has previously been appreciated.[16] As the prevalence of obesity increases, ventilatory failure from decompensation of the obesity hypoventilation syndrome is likely to be encountered more frequently.

Disorders in addition to the obesity hypoventilation syndrome that may be associated with diminished hypoxic and/or hypercapnic ventilatory drive include myxedema,[17] the Prader-Willi syndrome,[18] and hypogonadism treated with exogenous testosterone.[19] These disorders may con-

tribute to the development of acute ventilatory failure in susceptible individuals.

Acute stroke is another setting in which disordered ventilatory drive may contribute to acute ventilatory failure. The prognosis of patients with strokes who require intubation and mechanical ventilation is poor.[20–22] Outcomes in patients with ischemic and hemorrhagic strokes were equally poor in one study.[23] Other reports have found an especially unfavorable prognosis after basilar artery occlusion.[24] However, acute ventilatory failure in the setting of acute stroke does not preclude survival; and in one series of 124 patients with hemispheric stroke requiring mechanical ventilation, one-third of the patients were alive after 1 year.[25] Although impaired ventilatory drive may contribute to acute ventilatory failure following acute stroke, other processes, especially the inability to protect the lower airway and adequately clear respiratory tract secretions, are usually present.[22,26]

PRINCIPLES OF MANAGEMENT

Because the underlying physiologic defect is inadequate drive for ventilation with a presumably normal ventilatory pump, management focuses on restoring normal alveolar ventilation. Although noninvasive ventilation is being applied in an increasing number of clinical settings to augment alveolar ventilation, its utility lies mainly in maintaining respiration in patients with failure of the ventilatory pump, whereas endotracheal intubation is generally necessary following failure of respiratory drive. This is not only because restoration of alveolar ventilation can be attained more rapidly and reliably with invasive mechanical ventilation but also because the concomitant problems with airway protection and secretion clearance in most patients with acute depression of ventilatory drive are relative contraindications to noninvasive ventilation.

Because of the patient's impaired ventilatory drive, a ventilator mode should initially be chosen that provides full support, such as volume-targeted assist-control ventilation.[27] In the absence of acute lung injury or severe airflow obstruction, the tidal volume chosen should be 10 to 12 mL/kg predicted body weight in order to help prevent atelectasis. Target values for arterial pH and PCO_2 should be in the normal range, and supplemental oxygen should be supplied (with positive end-expiratory pressure if necessary) to maintain normal arterial PO_2. Unless there are serious coexisting pulmonary conditions, weaning should be carried out as soon as there is evidence that ventilatory drive is restored (see Chapter 84). Extubation is probably safe if the patient has a spontaneous cough, does not require frequent suctioning, and is judged able to protect the airway, even if alertness remains impaired.[28]

ACUTE VENTILATORY FAILURE DUE TO NEUROMUSCULAR IMPAIRMENT

CERVICAL SPINAL CORD INJURY

Injury to the upper cervical spinal cord may interrupt transmission of the stimulus to breathe from the respiratory centers in the brain stem to the diaphragm and other ventilatory muscles. Because the phrenic nerve roots that supply the diaphragm arise from spinal segments C3 to C5, patients with acute injury at this level or above usually require mechanical ventilation. Patients with C1-2 spinal injury levels are permanently ventilator-dependent, whereas those with C3-4 injuries may eventually achieve at least partial ventilator independence. Lesions below C4 are usually compatible with unassisted ventilation unless there are complicating processes such as intrinsic lung disease or impaired mental status (see also Chapter 82).

Adverse physiologic effects of cervical spinal cord injury in the initial days or weeks include loss of lung volumes and inability to take deep breaths (which predispose to atelectasis), inability to cough normally (which predisposes to the development of pneumonia and complicates its management), and impaired hypoxic pulmonary vasoconstriction (which predisposes to severe and often refractory hypoxemia when atelectasis or pneumonia occurs). Although it is accurate to say that the short-term prognosis is generally related to the level of the injury,[29–31] retrospective studies have shown that both mortality[32] and intensive care unit (ICU) length of stay[31] for patients with cervical spinal cord injury are more strongly influenced by the development of

pneumonia and other respiratory complications than by the specific cord injury level.

Although there are reports of patients with high cervical spinal cord injury being managed from the time of injury with noninvasive ventilation,[33] great expertise is required to manage such patients without aspiration and other complications; and in most centers invasive ventilatory support is preferable, at least initially. Successful phrenic nerve pacing,[34,35] permitting extubation or decannulation from tracheostomy, has also been reported but not in the early period following injury. The eventual ability to wean from ventilatory support[29,30] and undergo tracheostomy decannulation are major determinants not only of survival but also of quality of life for patients with cervical spinal cord injury.[30]

INJURY OR DISEASE AFFECTING THE PHRENIC NERVE

Although loss of diaphragm function after spinal cord injury is the major determinant of the need for mechanical ventilation in that condition, phrenic nerve injury resulting in paralysis of the diaphragm also occurs in other settings. The most common setting is phrenic nerve injury, which is almost always unilateral, following cardiac surgery. Both cold cardioplegia and physical injury during internal mammary artery harvesting or other surgical manipulations may be important mechanisms. The presentation ranges from an incidentally discovered radiographic abnormality without clinical impact (most common) to ventilatory failure requiring long-term mechanical ventilation.[36]

Diehl and associates[37] demonstrated that post-cardiac surgery phrenic nerve injury can be a severe problem. They retrospectively evaluated 13 patients encountered during a 2-year period who could not be weaned from ventilatory support for several weeks after cardiac surgery and were found to have severely impaired respiratory muscle function. Diehl and associates estimated the prevalence of clinically relevant diaphragmatic dysfunction to be 0.5% when no topical cooling was used and 2.1% when iced slush with no insulation pad was added for myocardial protection.[37]

Although it is a rare cause of acute ventilatory failure, bilateral diaphragmatic paralysis can present unassociated with trauma or surgical manipulation. In some patients, no systemic disease or specific cause could be found.[38,39] One case of bilateral diaphragm paralysis complicating von Recklinghausen's neurofibromatosis has been reported.[40] Isolated ventilatory muscle weakness can also be the initial manifestation of generalized neuromuscular disorders such as myasthenia gravis[41] and amyotrophic lateral sclerosis.[42,43]

NEUROMUSCULAR DISEASE

The most common cause of acute paralysis and neuromuscular ventilatory failure is Guillain-Barré syndrome,[44] in which one third of patients may develop acute ventilatory failure.[45–47] Therapy with plasma exchange and immune globulins has improved the outlook for patients who develop Guillain-Barré syndrome, although 3% to 8% die, and 5% to 10% of individuals who survive remain seriously disabled.[44,48] Theoretically, death should be preventable in most if not all patients with this disease, as mortality is primarily from potentially avoidable respiratory complications. (See also the discussion in Chapter 82.)

In one retrospective study of patients with Guillain-Barré syndrome, 60 patients who required intubation and mechanical ventilation had more rapid disease progression, prominent bulbar dysfunction, bilateral facial weakness, or dysautonomia, whereas 54 patients who did not require intubation had a significantly lower incidence and severity of these findings.[46] As noted later, it remains unclear whether the need for mechanical ventilation can be predicted prior to the onset of frank ventilatory failure in this condition.

Myasthenia gravis is a relatively infrequent cause of acute ventilatory failure.[49] Investigators at one large regional neuromuscular disease center reported 18 patients with 24 episodes of ventilatory failure requiring mechanical ventilation during a 9-year period.[50] Acute ventilatory failure usually occurs in patients with an established diagnosis of myasthenia gravis, although isolated ventilatory muscle weakness requiring mechanical ventilation has been reported as the initial manifestation of the disorder.[41]

Amyotrophic lateral sclerosis and other motor neuron diseases may demonstrate progressive weakness of the bulbar and ventilatory muscles that is variable both in presentation and in the rate of progression.[51,52] Typically, ventilatory muscle weakness develops in patients in whom the diagnosis of amyotrophic lateral sclerosis is well established.[51–55] Repeated assessment can usually detect the onset of ventilatory muscle dysfunction during outpatient management.[52,54,55] However, dyspnea or even acute ventilatory failure can be the initial clinical manifestation of motor neuron disease.[42,43,56–58] Elective initiation of noninvasive ventilation is becoming more common in patients with gradually progressive ventilatory insufficiency.[54,55] Its successful use has also been reported in acute ventilatory failure complicating amyotrophic lateral sclerosis,[59] although bulbar weakness and a high risk of aspiration make invasive mechanical ventilation a safer choice for most patients, at least initially.[27]

Botulism remains an important cause of acute ventilatory failure worldwide, although only about 25 cases of food-borne illness and 3 cases of wound botulism have been reported annually in the United States since the 1970s.[60] A high proportion of patients with both forms of botulism develop clinically important respiratory muscle weakness. In one food-borne outbreak, 81% of patients developed pulmonary involvement, and 11 of 34 patients required mechanical ventilation for acute ventilatory failure.[61]

Because it is infrequent and does not occur in outbreaks, wound botulism poses a challenge in both diagnosis and appropriate early management. Historically associated with dirty traumatic wounds, especially those sustained in rural areas,[62] wound botulism has also been encountered in recent years as a complication of injecting "black tar" heroin.[63,64] In a series of 20 consecutive patients with black tar heroin-associated wound botulism,[63] acute ventilatory failure developed in 15 (75%) and was more frequent in those patients in whom the administration of antitoxin and/or antibiotics was delayed beyond 12 hours of initial presentation. Ventilatory failure in wound botulism may be prolonged. Two patients with trauma-associated disease required 77 and 78 days of mechanical ventilation, respectively,[62] and 12 of 15 patients with black tar heroin-associated botulism needed ventilatory support for more than 30 days.[63] Recovery may likewise be prolonged, with residual ventilatory muscle weakness detectable as long as 2 years after presentation.[65]

Dermatomyositis may also cause respiratory muscle weakness severe enough to cause acute ventilatory failure,[66,67] although not as an initial manifestation in the absence of other typical symptoms and signs of this condition. In these reported cases, ventilatory function recovered as the disease was brought under control with immunosuppressive therapy.

NEUROMUSCULAR WEAKNESS ASSOCIATED WITH CRITICAL ILLNESS

Neuromuscular dysfunction associated with critical illness commonly contributes to the subsequent inability to wean such patients from mechanical ventilation.[68] Several forms of critical illness-associated neuromuscular dysfunction are recognized.

Prolonged Neuromuscular Blockade

Neuromuscular blocking drugs are sometimes administered to ventilated patients, in conjunction with sedation, to facilitate mechanical ventilation, to reduce oxygen consumption, or to control intracranial pressure. The clinical kinetics of these agents have been determined mainly in the context of short-term general anesthesia, and their effects on ventilatory muscle function in critically ill patients is much more variable. Most neuromuscular blocking drugs are cleared more slowly in the presence of hepatic—and especially renal—insufficiency. This is particularly true for pancuronium and vecuronium, and the effects of these drugs can last days or even weeks in the presence of renal failure.[69] Because they are metabolized in plasma and thus do not depend on renal or hepatic function for clearance, atracurium and cisatracurium are not associated with prolonged muscle weakness as a result of delayed clearance.[68]

"Train-of-four" stimulation can be used to monitor the depth of neuromuscular blockade, avoiding excessive paralysis and reducing the quantity of drug used as well as the recovery time of neuromuscular function in critically ill patients.[70] Minimizing the use of neuromuscular blocking drugs in ventilator management and using train-of-four stimulation to monitor the degree of muscle relaxation as well as daily "sedation vacations" can prevent unsuspected prolonged paralysis.[71]

Critical Illness Polyneuropathy and Myopathy

Although the mechanism is unknown, about half of all patients who require more than 7 days of ICU care and the majority of patients who develop the systemic inflammatory response syndrome can be shown by neurophysiologic testing to have critical illness neuropathy and/or myopathy.[68] Prospective studies have shown that about one third of critically ill patients exhibit weakness on clinical evaluation.[68,72] Clinically, this disorder can produce severe neuromuscular weakness and greatly prolong the need for ventilatory support. The increased incidence of this phenomenon with sepsis and dysfunction of multiple organ systems suggests that the neuromuscular system (by whatever mechanism) is another organ system affected by inflammation and other processes that lead to multiple organ failure. Critical illness polyneuropathy/myopathy is also more frequent in patients with uncontrolled hyperglycemia.[68,73]

The diagnosis of this syndrome should be considered in patients who are weak in the context of critical illness. Confirmation is either by nerve conduction studies or by electromyography. The only interventional study published at the time of this writing that prospectively used critical illness polyneuropathy/myopathy as an outcome measure showed that the incidence of this disorder by neurophysiologic testing was reduced from 52% in patients managed by usual measures to 29% when an intensive insulin protocol was used to prevent or correct hyperglycemia.[74] No other specific preventive measures have been identified. Because critical illness polyneuropathy/myopathy is so strongly associated with severity of illness, length of ICU stay, and the presence of multiple organ system dysfunction, prevention at present focuses on scrupulous attention to good general ICU care and avoidance of sepsis.[68]

Acute Quadriplegic Myopathy

Development of acute myopathy, with severe weakness and requirement for prolonged ventilatory support, was first reported in patients with status asthmaticus who were treated with corticosteroids concurrently with neuromuscular blocking drugs.[75,76] Although usually seen in patients who have received high-dose systemic corticosteroids or neuromuscular blocking drugs, this syndrome can occur without exposure to these agents.[68] Both proximal and distal muscles are affected, including the diaphragm. Electromyography reveals reduced muscle membrane excitability, and skeletal muscle biopsy shows a variable combination of thick (myosin) filament loss and frank myonecrosis.[77] Clinically evident rhabdomyolysis can occur. There appears to be some degree of overlap between acute quadriplegic myopathy and critical illness polyneuropathy/myopathy. Because of the strong association of this disorder with the administration of corticosteroids and neuromuscular blocking drugs, using these agents as sparingly as possible in critically ill patients is reasonable; at present, it is the only recommended approach to prevention.

Ventilator-Induced Diaphragmatic Dysfunction

Indirect and inferential evidence supports the notion that mechanical ventilation itself can induce diaphragmatic dysfunction.[78] Data from experiments on animals shows that controlled mechanical ventilation leads to diminished diaphragmatic endurance as well as to a time-dependent decrease in diaphragmatic force-generating capacity, with reductions of 40% to 50% after 3 to 10 days without spontaneous breathing. Using phrenic nerve stimulation, one study demonstrated a reduction in maximal transdiaphragmatic pressure in a group of ventilated patients in comparison to findings in normal volunteers.[79] The relevance of these findings to ventilatory muscle function and the ability to breathe unassisted in critically ill patients is unknown. It is still not known whether some ventilatory muscle activity should be maintained in all ventilated patients through partial rather than full ventilatory support, as was recommended 30 years ago by the proponents of intermittent mandatory ventilation and is urged today by some authors.[27,78,80]

ASSESSMENT OF NEED FOR MECHANICAL VENTILATION IN NEUROMUSCULAR WEAKNESS

Early clinical indicators of the need for mechanical ventilation in patients with neuromuscular weakness remain controversial. In addition to symptoms of dyspnea and the subjective assessment of respiratory distress, repeated measurements of vital capacity and maximum inspiratory pressure are the more objective assessments of ventilatory muscle capability that have generally been used. In one retrospective study, 60 patients with Guillain-Barré syndrome who were intubated and ventilated were compared with 54 similar patients who were not. Clinical evidence of rapid disease progression, development of bulbar weakness, bilateral facial weakness, and dysautonomia were highly correlated with intubation and mechanical ventilation.[46] Other findings associated with intubation were a vital capacity of less than 20 mL/kg, a maximum inspiratory pressure that failed to reach -30 cm H_2O, a maximum expiratory pressure of less than 40 cm H_2O, or a decrease in one or more of these functions by at least 30% of the initial value.[46] However, without prospective randomized studies, the predictive value of these thresholds cannot be confirmed.

A prospective study of electromyography in 60 patients with Guillain-Barré syndrome, in which the managing clinicians were unaware of the test results, showed that electrophysiological evidence of demyelination was highly correlated with the need for intubation and mechanical ventilation.[81] In another recent study of patients with Guillain-Barré syndrome, 44 patients who required mechanical ventilation were more likely to have cranial nerve involvement and immunoglobulin G (IgG) anti-GQ1b antibodies than were 87 unventilated patients.[82]

A study of patients with myasthenia gravis did not find bedside tests of pulmonary function to be predictive of the need for intubation and mechanical ventilation.[83] Nonetheless, most authors recommend serial assessments such as vital capacity in patients hospitalized with acute neuromuscular disease in order to detect as early as possible the need for ventilatory assistance.[84] Although the optimal means for monitoring respiratory muscle function remain uncertain, it is clear that intubation and mechanical ventilation should be undertaken prior to the development of severe respiratory acidosis or respiratory arrest. For this reason, patients with acute neuromuscular disease who show signs of pulmonary compromise should be monitored in the ICU. Although the rate of progression may vary, serial measurements of vital capacity and maximal inspiratory pressure along with repeated physical examinations focusing on bulbar function and ability to cough are advisable to avoid emergent intubations (Fig. 86.3).[85]

PRINCIPLES OF VENTILATOR MANAGEMENT

Patients with acute ventilatory failure complicating neuromuscular disease usually have normal underlying lung function. Because atelectasis is especially common,[86,87] it has

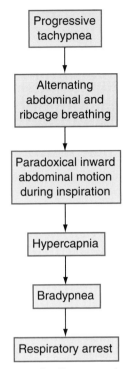

Figure 86.3 The sequence leading to respiratory arrest with failure of the ventilatory pump. Individual patients proceed through the steps shown at variable rates and may skip one or more stages. However, except for sudden events affecting the central nervous system or the administration of paralyzing drugs, respiratory arrest does not occur abruptly without preceding physical manifestations. (Adapted in part from Cohen CA, Zagelbaum G, Gross D, et al: Clinical manifestations of inspiratory muscle fatigue. Am J Med 73:308–316, 1982.)

been common practice to use larger than usual tidal volumes in such patients, typically 12 to 15 mL/kg or more.[27] Anecdotally, many patients with neuromuscular disease seem to prefer large tidal volumes, but this has not been subjected to prospective evaluation. As a result of the use of large tidal volumes, such patients commonly manifest respiratory alkalosis, although there is no physiologic reason why arterial Pco_2 and pH should not be maintained in the normal range. Patients incapable of breathing unassisted should be ventilated in a manner that makes them comfortable; as mentioned earlier, there is no convincing evidence that their respiratory muscles need to be "exercised" in order to speed recovery. No evidence supports the use of weaning approaches other than those currently recommended for other patients with acute ventilatory failure,[88] although special attention should be paid to the patient's ability to protect the airway and clear secretions once the patient can breathe unassisted.

ACUTE VENTILATORY FAILURE DUE TO RESTRICTIVE MECHANISMS

CHEST WALL AND PLEURAL DISEASE

Pulmonary restriction and ventilatory muscle dysfunction due to severe kyphoscoliosis typically lead to gradually

progressive ventilatory insufficiency, and patients with this disorder can present with acute or acute-on-chronic ventilatory failure and require intensive care. Physiologic studies have shown that both lung and chest wall mechanics are impaired during acute respiratory failure in patients with kyphoscoliosis.[89] Primary disease of the pleura, such as asbestos-related diffuse pleural thickening or post-inflammatory fibrothorax, could potentially present in similar fashion; but dyspnea and hyperventilation are more common with these diseases, and respiratory acidosis occurs late in the course unless ventilatory drive is depressed or there is concomitant lung involvement. Pleural effusion or pneumothorax can likewise precipitate acute ventilatory failure but usually in the presence of underlying obstructive or restrictive pulmonary disease.

Obesity hypoventilation syndrome with decompensated cor pulmonale, discussed earlier, is another example of acute-on-chronic ventilatory failure involving pulmonary restriction. The fact that the majority of severely obese individuals do not have hypercapnia or develop acute ventilatory failure emphasizes the fact that these phenomena are multifactorial.

Long-term noninvasive ventilation appears to be beneficial in selected patients with kyphoscoliosis and other chest wall diseases,[90] and the successful application of this modality has been reported in acute-on-chronic ventilatory failure.[91,92] However, patients with acute ventilatory failure due to restrictive mechanisms pose difficulties in noninvasive ventilation that are different from those in obstructive lung disease, including the need for higher inflation pressures, impaired cough, and retention of secretions; thus, invasive ventilation is generally preferred in the context of currently available data.[27] Some authors have reported success using continuous noninvasive ventilation and aggressive use of coughing aids to prevent the occurrence of acute deterioration when neuromuscular patients get respiratory infections; but if these measures fail, intubation is necessary unless the patient has refused.

PARENCHYMAL LUNG DISEASE

Idiopathic pulmonary fibrosis and other pulmonary parenchymal restrictive diseases are usually associated with hyperventilation rather than hypoventilation. However, acute ventilatory failure can occur in the late stages of these conditions, either as a manifestation of the primary disease process[93,94] or in conjunction with pneumonia, surgery, or other intercurrent illness.[95-98] Physiologic assessment has demonstrated markedly increased lung stiffness and resistance in patients with end-stage idiopathic pulmonary fibrosis requiring mechanical ventilation,[99] explaining the development of hypercapnia and acute ventilatory failure in such individuals.

Several series have documented the poor prognosis of patients who present with acute respiratory failure in the setting of advanced interstitial fibrosis.[94,95,97,98] In one report, of 15 consecutive patients with idiopathic pulmonary fibrosis admitted to the ICU with acute respiratory failure, 11 died in the unit and 2 others shortly after discharge.[95] In a second report, of 23 similar patients, 22 patients died, the single survivor having received a lung transplant shortly after admission.[98] In a third series of 19 patients with pulmonary fibrosis who received mechanical ventilation mostly for acute respiratory failure complicating the underlying disease, 13 died.[97]

PRINCIPLES OF VENTILATOR MANAGEMENT

The best way to ventilate patients with acute respiratory failure in the setting of underlying restrictive lung disease has not been determined by clinical trials. However, because of the physiologic similarity to acute lung injury and the potential for both hemodynamic compromise and barotrauma with the use of high ventilating volumes and pressures, it is reasonable to apply similar principles and management targets (see Chapters 84 and 85). The need for higher airway pressures than are required in COPD, and thus the difficulty in achieving a seal at the interface and in avoiding gastric insufflation, makes it less likely that noninvasive ventilation can be applied successfully in this setting. Because the work of breathing is high, full ventilatory support (as with volume-targeted assist-control ventilation) is generally required. Low tidal volumes (e.g., 6 mL/kg predicted body weight) should be applied, attempting to keep the end-inspiratory plateau pressure at less than 30 cm H_2O if possible. Patients with restrictive lung disease typically breathe rapidly and shallowly, so tachypnea may not be avoidable during the weaning process and should not be used as the sole reason for delaying extubation if gas exchange and other assessments are satisfactory.

ACUTE VENTILATORY FAILURE DUE TO AIRWAY OBSTRUCTION

UPPER AIRWAY OBSTRUCTION

Upper airway obstruction is an occasional cause of acute ventilatory failure. The onset can be precipitous, as with occlusion of the glottis by an aspirated foreign body (i.e., "café coronary") or a swollen and edematous epiglottis with acute epiglottitis. The onset can also be insidious, occurring over months, as with a tracheal tumor. The severity and length of narrowing and air flow determine the additional work of breathing imposed by the obstruction. Gradually progressive upper airway narrowing may be well tolerated, at least during breathing at rest, until a critical limit is reached, often when the airway diameter drops to the range of 5 to 6 mm.

The location and variability of the narrowing are also important in determining clinical manifestations. Extrathoracic variable upper airway narrowing affects mainly inspiratory flow because the negative intraluminal pressure exacerbates the narrowing during inspiration. During expiration, the positive intraluminal pressure tends to push variable extrathoracic obstructions open. Vocal cord paralysis is an excellent example of a variable extrathoracic upper airway obstruction, producing stridor and severe airway obstruction during inspiration but no significant obstruction during expiration. The opposite pertains to variable intrathoracic obstructions, with narrowing becoming less severe during inspiration as pressure gradients favor airway widening. During expiration the airways narrow, and the severity of the obstruction worsens. Tracheomalacia can cause variable intrathoracic airway obstruction. Fixed obstructions affect both inspiration and expiration regardless of their location.

Pathophysiologically, upper airway obstruction causes ventilatory failure by increasing airway resistance to the point where respiratory muscles can no longer maintain minute volume at a level adequate to maintain carbon dioxide homeostasis. Conceptually, the therapeutic aim is to relieve the obstruction. This may be achieved by removal of a foreign body, laser therapy of an endotracheal tumor, placement of a stent in an area of tracheomalacia or stenosis, or tracheostomy to bypass an area of obstruction. Inhalation of heliox and/or noninvasive ventilation can be useful to reduce work of breathing and avoid intubation in patients who have reversible causes of their upper airway obstruction, such as post-extubation stridor.

CHRONIC OBSTRUCTIVE PULMONARY DISEASE

Chronic obstructive pulmonary disease is the fourth leading cause of death among adults aged 65 to 84 in the United States[100,101] and poses enormous costs to the U.S. health care system. Exacerbation of COPD is the most common cause of acute ventilatory failure in the U.S. adult population. Although COPD exacerbations are most commonly infectious in etiology, either viral or bacterial, a number of other etiologies should be considered when patients with COPD have respiratory deterioration, including acute pneumonia, congestive heart failure, pulmonary embolism, pneumothorax, and/or environmental exposure.

Pathophysiology

Exacerbations of COPD lead to acute ventilatory failure in perhaps one third of patients. Those with severe COPD (Stage 2 or 3, $FEV_1 < 50\%$) are at the highest risk. Severe COPD places the respiratory muscles at a mechanical disadvantage.[102] As depicted in Figure 86.4 for a patient with emphysema, hyperinflation flattens the diaphragm, increasing its radius of curvature. According to LaPlace's law, this increases muscle tension and the impedance to blood flow. Even at residual volume, the diaphragm remains flat with a relatively short sarcomere length, and inspiratory-force generation is compromised by the diaphragm's inability to reach a sufficient length on its length-tension curve. Also, because of the horizontal orientation of the diaphragm and the loss of the zone of apposition between the visceral and parietal pleurae, the force vector on the lower rib cage becomes inward rather than cephalad, so lower rib cage motion during inspiration becomes paradoxical, moving inward on inspiration instead of outward, a movement referred to as the "Hoover sign." Accessory muscles are recruited to maintain ventilation at the hyperinflated lung volumes, contributing to the already increased oxygen cost of breathing. Finally, incomplete emptying leading to positive pressure in alveoli at end-expiration (auto-PEEP) poses an inspiratory threshold load requiring that the inspiratory muscles work to reduce this pressure to atmospheric pressure before the muscles can further lower the pressure to the subatmospheric level necessary to begin inspiration.

During an exacerbation of COPD, a precarious situation becomes potentially catastrophic. Usually related to a

Figure 86.4 Schema depicting the chest wall configuration at functional residual capacity of a normal individual (left hemithorax) and a patient with severe COPD (right hemithorax). The COPD patient has a flattened diaphragm, which increases the radius of curvature and increases the tension for a given pressure. The COPD patient's ribs are horizontal, and the zone of apposition between the pleural surfaces is reduced, greatly reducing the diaphragm's efficiency in expanding the chest wall. Also, intrinsic positive end-expiratory pressure (PEEP) poses an inspiratory load, adding further to the inspiratory work. Exhalation is slowed by airway collapse and the loss of elastic recoil. (From Hill NS: Current concepts in mechanical ventilation for chronic obstructive pulmonary disease. Semin Respir Crit Care Med 20:375–395, 1999.)

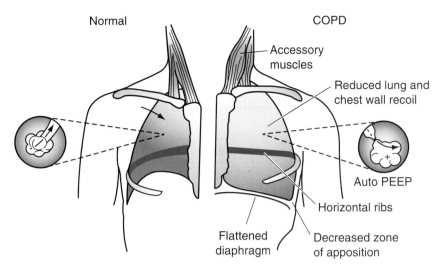

combination of swelling, secretions, and bronchospasm caused by the acute inflammation, airway resistance increases, adding to the work of breathing. As depicted in Figure 86.5, patients with severe COPD often reach their expiratory flow limitation, even during resting breathing, and a small increase in airway resistance lowers airflow further at any given lung volume. The patient's only workable strategy, if airflow is to be maintained, is to breathe at even higher lung volumes, a futile compensatory response that adds further to the work of breathing. Patients adopt a rapid, shallow breathing pattern, thus shortening the time for expiration and aggravating auto-PEEP. The diaphragm flattens more and increases tension, augmenting impedance to blood flow. The resulting limitation in the supply of substrate to the muscle is aggravated by progressive hypoxemia, caused by worsening hypoventilation and ventilation-perfusion imbalance related to secretion retention. Thus, as the demand for breathing work increases, the capacity to supply the work becomes further compromised. Despite the worsening alveolar hypoventilation, the drive to breathe is increased and the diaphragm becomes fatigued, characterized by reduced muscular performance despite a steady or increased neural drive. A vicious cycle ensues, leading inexorably to worsening respiratory muscle fatigue, ventilatory failure, and death unless therapeutic interventions interrupt the cycle.

Clinical Assessment

Patients with exacerbations of COPD must be carefully evaluated to identify those at risk of developing respiratory failure and to exclude other causes of respiratory failure. Historical and physical features are very useful. Although Borg or visual analogue scales help gauge the level of dyspnea in clinical studies, a subjective assessment that dyspnea is worse than baseline and of at least moderate severity places the patient at risk for respiratory failure. Physical findings seen with severe exacerbations include tachypnea, accessory muscle use, abdominal paradox, cyanosis, and mental status alterations.

In addition to a sputum examination for purulence, a white blood cell count, an electrocardiogram, a chest

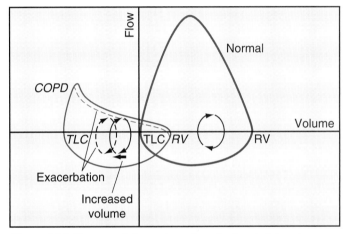

Figure 86.5 The normal flow-volume loop (outer circle) and tidal breathing (smaller inner circle) are indicated by *heavy lines* on the right. The flow-volume loop and tidal breathing for a COPD patient are depicted by *thinner lines* on the left. Note that the expiratory flow during tidal breathing in the COPD patient reaches maximal expiratory flow. During an exacerbation (*interrupted lines*), expiratory flow drops slightly; and because the flow during tidal breathing is already maximal, the only mechanism available for maintaining flow is to increase lung volume during tidal breathing (leftward shift of tidal breathing loop, shown by *thick arrow*). Although this strategy maintains expiratory flow, it increases the work of breathing and oxygen consumption, predisposing to inspiratory muscle fatigue and eventual respiratory failure. (From Hill NS: Current concepts in mechanical ventilation for chronic obstructive pulmonary disease. Semin Respir Crit Care Med 20:375–393, 1999.)

radiograph, and arterial blood gases should be obtained to assess the severity of an exacerbation. The widespread use of continuous oximetry has decreased, but not eliminated, the need for arterial blood gases. Arterial blood gases provide a rapid assessment of arterial PCO_2 and pH, information that is critical in deciding when to place COPD patients in critical care units or initiate mechanical ventilation. During severe exacerbations, chronic carbon dioxide retainers develop acute-on-chronic carbon dioxide retention, manifested by a drop in pH indicative of retained carbon dioxide uncompensated by bicarbonate.

Medical Therapy

When patients with severe exacerbations come to medical attention, they are promptly begun on medical therapy, including bronchodilators, corticosteroids, and antibiotics. Additional therapies, such as diuretics and nitrates, are used if congestive heart failure is thought to be a contributing factor. Oxygen supplementation is routine but must be administered with caution in patients with carbon dioxide retention. Overzealous oxygen supplementation in such patients has long been known to aggravate carbon dioxide retention, either by blunting the hypoxic ventilatory drive, increasing physiologic dead space, or both. Because hypoxemia in COPD patients is usually due mainly to the hypoventilation and is easily reversed, initial supplementation with nasal oxygen at 2 L/min is often adequate. In patients with severe exacerbations, arterial blood gases should be repeated periodically to assess the effect of oxygen supplementation on arterial P_{CO_2}.

Noninvasive Mechanical Ventilation

Medical therapy alone is often effective and is the therapy of choice for mild COPD exacerbations. However, failure of medical therapy, manifested by persisting or worsening tachypnea and dyspnea as well as carbon dioxide retention, is not uncommon, partly because the physiologic defects associated with COPD exacerbations reverse gradually and respiratory muscles may begin to fatigue before medical therapy is effective. In the past, patients who failed medical therapy were endotracheally intubated and mechanically ventilated; or if they declined intubation, they were kept comfortable and usually died. Invasive mechanical ventilation was successful in the majority of cases, but hospital mortality rates were substantial, averaging 30% in several studies.[103] Complications of invasive mechanical ventilation were common, including upper airway trauma, pneumothorax, and nosocomial infection, and they contribted to patient mortality.[104]

Beginning approximately a dozen years ago, noninvasive positive-pressure ventilation (NPPV) began to be used increasingly to treat COPD exacerbations. Consisting of a mask (or interface) that conducts pressurized air into the lungs from a positive-pressure ventilator, NPPV has appeal for the therapy of COPD exacerbations because it is an effective way of providing partial ventilatory assistance.[105] Because it avoids airway invasion, it also has the potential to avoid many of the complications of invasive mechanical ventilation, such as upper airway trauma, nosocomial infection, and prolonged intubation.[104]

NPPV has the potential to reverse the vicious cycle leading to respiratory failure in patients with severe exacerbations of COPD. Continuous positive airway pressure (CPAP) alone reduces the work of breathing during COPD exacerbations by counterbalancing the effects of intrinsic positive end-expiratory pressure (PEEP), effectively reducing or even eliminating the inspiratory threshold load.[106] Pressure support alone also reduces the work of breathing in COPD patients, assisting each breath by increasing airway pressure during inspiration.[106] However, when PEEP and pressure support are combined, noninvasive ventilation reduces the transdiaphragmatic pressure more than with either PEEP or pressure support alone.[106] Thereby, NPPV has the potential to serve as a "crutch," reducing the work of breathing and halting the progression of respiratory muscle fatigue while medical therapies are given time to work.

Acute Exacerbations. Noninvasive positive-pressure ventilation has been shown to be effective in treating acute respiratory failure due to COPD exacerbations. Starting with the trial by Brochard and associates[105] that used historically matched controls and subsequent randomized controlled trials,[107–112] a number of benefits have been attributed to NPPV in these patients. They include more rapid improvements in arterial P_{CO_2},[107,108] heart and respiratory rates,[108,109] and dyspnea scores[107–109] within the first hour in noninvasively treated patients compared to randomized conventionally treated controls. Encephalopathy scores also improve more rapidly,[109] intubation rates drop precipitously (from roughly 75% in controls to 25% in NPPV-treated patients),[108,109] and the mortality rate is lowered (from 30% in controls to approximately 10% with NPPV).[107,109] In addition, complication rates and hospital lengths of stay fall significantly compared to those of controls.[109,110]

In the largest study reported to date,[111] 236 patients with exacerbations of COPD were randomized to receive NPPV or standard therapy administered by nurses in general medical respiratory wards at 14 medical centers in England. Intubation and mortality rates were significantly lower in the NPPV group compared to controls (15% vs. 27%, $P = 0.02$ and 10% vs. 20%, $P = 0.05$, respectively), and the study confirmed the earlier findings of more rapid improvements in arterial pH, respiratory rate, and breathlessness in the NPPV group compared to the control group. Notably, the mortality benefit was not apparent in patients with pH less than 7.30, suggesting that this more severely ill subgroup should be monitored in an ICU.

In the only study with negative findings,[112] NPPV failed to lower intubation or mortality rates or hospital lengths of stay in patients admitted consecutively to the hospital with COPD exacerbations, but it is notable that no intubations or mortality occurred in the control group. The most important finding of this study was that patients with relatively mild COPD exacerbations are not likely to benefit from NPPV, inferring that NPPV should be applied to selected patients who have a demonstrable need for ventilatory assistance.

Several meta-analyses have combined the results of the above studies.[113–116] These analyses concluded that NPPV is effective in avoiding intubation (relative risk 0.42 and absolute risk reduction 28%, respectively), reducing mortality (relative risk 0.41 and absolute risk reduction 10%, respectively), and shortening hospital length of stay (by roughly 4 days). In addition, one analysis calculated $3200 (1996 Canadian) savings per hospitalization.[113] Based on this evidence, the authors of these meta-analyses and consensus groups[117,118] have advised that NPPV should be used early in the course of COPD exacerbations.

COPD Complicated by Pneumonia. Pneumonia has been associated with a poor outcome in patients treated with

NPPV.[119] However, in one randomized trial of patients with "severe community-acquired pneumonia," defined as patients with severe hypoxemia ($PaO_2/FIO_2 < 200$) and respiratory distress (respiratory rate > 35/min), NPPV reduced the need for intubation (21% vs. 50%, $P = 0.03$), shortened the ICU length of stay (1.8 vs. 6.0 days, $P = 0.04$), and reduced the mortality rate among the COPD subgroup of patients 2 months after hospital discharge (11% vs. 63%).[120] Thus, although the presence of pneumonia is a risk factor for poorer outcome with NPPV, these patients can still benefit from NPPV. Moreover, a COPD exacerbation complicated by pneumonia is an appropriate indication for NPPV.

Postoperative COPD Patients. A randomized trial of NPPV in post-lung resection patients with acute respiratory insufficiency showed significant reductions in the need for intubation, ICU length of stay, and mortality rate compared to conventionally treated controls.[121] Although only a portion of these patients had COPD, accumulating evidence now supports the use of NPPV in selected postoperative (including COPD) patients to maintain improved gas exchange and avoid reintubation and its attendant complications.

To Facilitate Extubation. NPPV has been used to facilitate early extubation after bouts of acute respiratory failure in patients who fail to meet standard extubation criteria, with the aim of shortening the duration and thereby avoiding the complications of invasive mechanical ventilation. In the first controlled trial to test this idea, 56 COPD patients who had been intubated for 48 hours and failed a T-piece trial[122] were randomized either to early extubation with NPPV or to continued intubation and standard weaning. Compared to the standard weaning group, the extubation/NPPV group had higher overall weaning rates after 60 days (88% vs. 68%), a shorter duration of mechanical ventilation (10.2 vs. 16.6 days), briefer stays in the ICU (15 vs. 24 days) and improved 60-day survival rates (92% vs. 72%) (all $P < 0.05$). In addition, no NPPV-treated patient had a nosocomial pneumonia compared to seven in the standard group. In a subsequent trial of 33 patients randomized to early extubation and NPPV or to standard weaning, the NPPV group experienced a shorter duration of invasive mechanical ventilation (4.6 vs. 7.7 days for NPPV vs. controls, $P < 0.05$) but a longer duration of overall mechanical ventilation; there were no other significant benefits attributable to NPPV.[123]

More recently, a randomized controlled trial on the use of NPPV to facilitate weaning in patients with "persistent weaning failure" (failure of spontaneous weaning trials on three consecutive days) showed that the NPPV group had significant reductions in ICU and hospital days, a lower incidence of nosocomial pneumonia (from 59% to 24%, $P < 0.05$), diminished hospital and 90-day mortality (odds ratio 3.5), and fewer complications.[124] Thus, randomized controlled trials testing the idea that early extubation to NPPV can improve outcomes of COPD patients have yielded generally favorable results: two studies showing significant benefit and the other showing no attributable harm. If early extubation is contemplated for intubated COPD patients, careful patient selection is advised. Patients should be supportable on less than 15 to 20 cm H_2O pressure support, be able to sustain 5 to 10 minutes of unassisted breathing,

have an adequate cough without excessive secretions, be easy to intubate, and have few if any comorbidities.

Extubation Failure. NPPV can be used to avoid reintubation in patients who fail extubation by developing tachypnea, respiratory distress, and rising arterial carbon dioxide following extubation. Extubation failure occurs after 5% to 20% of planned[125] and 40% to 50% of unplanned extubations[126] and has been associated with a mortality of 43% compared to only 12% in those who succeed after extubation.[125] In a historically controlled study of 30 COPD patients with extubation failure,[127] NPPV lowered the reintubation rate (20% vs. 67%, $P < 0.05$) and ICU length of stay. In a subsequent randomized trial of patients at high risk for extubation failure and who developed respiratory distress within 48 hours of extubation, however, NPPV did not reduce the need for intubation, duration of mechanical ventilation, length of hospital stay, or mortality.[128] However, COPD patients were excluded from this study after the first year because of ethical concerns. In a more recent international randomized trial of 221 patients at high risk for extubation failure, those randomized to NPPV showed an increased mortality rate compared to the standard treatment group, most likely related to a significantly longer delay before proceeding with reintubation.[129]

In summary, the use of NPPV to treat extubation failure in COPD patients is supported by a historically controlled study, but not by randomized controlled trials. This is partly related to the reluctance of many investigators to enroll COPD patients in such a trial because of ethical concerns about subjecting them to the risk of reintubation, which might add to their morbidity or even mortality. The likelihood is that if NPPV is effective in de novo COPD exacerbations leading to respiratory failure, it will be effective in the post-extubation setting. Thus, the best current recommendation is to use NPPV for COPD patients with extubation failure but to avoid delays in needed intubation should NPPV fail.

Do-Not-Intubate Patients. The use of NPPV to treat respiratory failure in patients who have declined intubation accounted for 10% of acute applications in a recent survey.[130] This application has been controversial, with some arguing that there is little to lose because it may reverse the acute deterioration or, at least, provide relief of dyspnea and a few extra hours to finalize affairs.[131] Others have argued that this merely prolongs the dying process, consumes resources inappropriately, and may add to discomfort or counter patients' wishes about avoiding life-prolonging measures.[132] In one study of 30 patients, mostly with COPD in whom endotracheal intubation was "contraindicated or postponed," 18 (60%) patients were successfully supported with NPPV and weaned.[133] In a more recent prospective survey of 113 "do-not-intubate" (DNI) patients treated with NPPV, survival to hospital discharge was 52% for COPD patients, whereas it was less than 25% for those with a diagnosis of pneumonia or cancer.[130] Thus, NPPV use is sensible in DNI patients with acutely reversible processes that are known to respond well, including COPD exacerbations. However, patients and/or their families should be informed that NPPV is being used as a form of life support that may be uncomfortable and can be removed at any time.

Heliox Combined with Noninvasive Ventilation. By virtue of its lower density compared to nitrogen, helium can be combined with oxygen to lower the airway resistance attributable to turbulent flow. The $F_{I_{O_2}}$ can be increased up to 40% in the helium and oxygen mixture but not higher without losing the density advantage of the added helium. Heliox has been combined with NPPV to treat patients with COPD exacerbations, with beneficial physiologic responses including reduced airway resistance and more rapid improvements in gas exchange.[134] However, a randomized prospective trial found that the addition of heliox to NPPV offered no significant advantages compared to NPPV alone in terms of intubation or mortality rates or hospital lengths of stay.[135]

Patient Selection. Selection of appropriate patients is key to the successful application of NPPV. The selection process takes into account a number of factors, including the patient's clinical characteristics and risk of failure on NPPV. Ultimately, it becomes a clinical judgment depending largely on physician experience. Predictors of success of NPPV have been identified[119,136,137] (Table 86.2) and include a better neurologic status (and hence more cooperativeness), ability to protect the airway, and no more than moderate acid-base or gas exchange derangement. Several studies have also found that improvements in pH, arterial P_{CO_2}, and level of consciousness within the first hour or two of NPPV initiation are strong predictors of success.[136,137] These studies indicate that there is a "window of opportunity" when initiating NPPV that opens when patients need ventilatory assistance but closes if they progress too far and become severely acidemic. Thus, early initiation of NPPV is recommended so patients have time to adapt and respiratory crises can be averted. On the other hand, NPPV begun too early might be unhelpful and wasteful of resources if treated patients would have done well without any ventilatory assistance. For this reason, selection guidelines suggest first establishing the need for ventilatory assistance according to clinical and blood gas criteria (indicating that the window of opportunity has opened) and exclusion of patients in whom NPPV is contraindicated or likely to fail (indicating that the window of opportunity has closed)[138] (Table 86.3).

Practical Application of NPPV. A thorough discussion of the application of NPPV is beyond the scope of this chapter, and the reader is referred elsewhere for a more complete description.[101,139] The following sections focus on aspects relevant to applications in COPD patients with acute respiratory failure.

Mask Selection. The full face (oronasal) mask is usually the preferred initial mask choice for the acute setting because, compared to the situation with nose masks, there is less leaking of air through the mouth.[140] Patients rate nasal masks as more comfortable for long-term applications,[141] so transitioning from a full face mask to a nasal mask should be contemplated after the first few days if NPPV is to be continued. Masks should fit optimally; a mask that is too small is uncomfortable, and one that is too large may necessitate excessive tightening of the straps to minimize air leakage, predisposing to ulceration over the nose. Within each mask category (nasal and oronasal), many types of masks are now available. Practitioners should have a current knowledge of available masks in order to maximize the likelihood of success.

Ventilator Selection. In the acute setting, both "critical care" and "bilevel" ventilators (portable pressure-limited

---

Table 86.2 Predictors of Success for NPPV in the Acute Setting

Cooperative
  Synchronous breathing with NPPV
  Good neurologic status
  Better "compliance"*

Able to protect airway
  Lower volume of secretions
  Minimal air leaking
  Dentate (dentition corresponds with minimal air leak)

Not too acutely ill
  No pneumonia
  Low APACHE score
  Initial arterial P_{CO_2} < 92 mm Hg
  Initial pH > 7.10

Good initial response to NPPV (within first hour or two)
  Improvement in pH
  Reduction in respiratory rate
  Reduction in arterial P_{CO_2}

APACHE, Acute Physiology, Age, and Chronic Health Evaluation; NPPV, noninvasive positive-pressure ventilation.
* "Compliance" refers to the clinician's assessment of the patient's acceptance of the technique.
Adapted from Ambrosino N, Foglio K, Rubini F, et al: Non-invasive mechanical ventilation in acute respiratory failure due to chronic obstructive pulmonary disease: Correlates for success. Thorax 50:755–757, 1995; and Soo Hoo GW, Santiago S, Williams AJ; Nasal mechanical ventilation for hypercapnic respiratory failure in chronic obstructive pulmonary disease: Determinants of success and failure. Crit Care Med 22:1253–1261, 1994.

Table 86.3 Selection Criteria for NPPV in Acute COPD Exacerbations

Establish Need for Ventilatory Assistance
Moderate to severe respiratory distress
Tachypnea (RR > 24 breaths/min)
Accessory muscle use or abdominal paradox
Blood gas derangement
  pH < 7.35, arterial P_{CO_2} > 45 mmHg *or*
  Arterial $P_{O_2}/F_{I_{O_2}}$ < 200

Exclude Patients with Contraindications to NPPV
Respiratory arrest
Medically unstable (septic or cardiogenic shock, uncontrolled upper gastrointestinal bleeding, acute myocardial infarction with planned intervention, uncontrolled arrhythmias)
Unable to protect airway
Excessive secretions
Uncooperative or agitated
Unable to fit mask
Recent upper airway or upper gastrointestinal surgery

NPPV, noninvasive positive-pressure ventilation.
Adapted from Lieschling T, Kwok H, Hill NS: Acute applications of noninvasive positive pressure ventilation. Chest 124:699–713, 2003.

devices designed especially for the administration of NPPV) have been used with similar success rates. A "bilevel" device designed for use in the acute care setting that includes an oxygen blender and displays waveforms is gaining popularity.

Ventilator Initiation. To begin NPPV, the properly fit mask is placed on the patient's face and attached to the ventilator. Patients often feel more comfortable if they can hold the mask themselves. Initial ventilator pressures are usually low to enhance patient comfort and acceptance, but inspiratory pressure or tidal volume should be adjusted upward as tolerated to provide adequate ventilatory assistance. Typical initial settings on pressure-limited ventilators are 8 to 12 cm H_2O for inspiratory pressures (IPAP) and 4 to 5 cm H_2O for expiratory pressures (EPAP or PEEP), with subsequent adjustments as needed to alleviate respiratory distress (inspiratory pressure up to 20 cm H_2O) or to counterbalance auto-PEEP or treat hypoxemia (expiratory pressure up to 8 cm H_2O). The difference between IPAP and EPAP is the level of pressure support and should be adequate to alleviate inspiratory effort while avoiding excessive discomfort.

Coaching is usually necessary to enhance synchrony between the patient and ventilator. Some ventilators permit adjustments in airflow to enhance synchrony, such as the "rise time," which determines the time to reach the target inspiratory pressure, and the adjustable inspiratory time. These may be helpful in optimizing comfort in COPD patients who prefer relatively high inspiratory flows[142] (and hence short rise times, often 0.1 second) and short inspiratory times (often <1 second) to avoid prolongation of delivered inspiratory pressure during patient expiration.

Oxygenation and Humidification. Most patients with COPD exacerbations do not have severe oxygenation defects and can be managed successfully with "bilevel" ventilators lacking oxygen blenders. With these ventilators, oxygen is administered at rates up to 15 L/min into ports in the mask or via a T-connector at the proximal end of the ventilator tubing, adjusted to maintain the desired level of oxygenation (usually oxygen saturation >90–92%). Because FI_{O_2} using this arrangement cannot exceed 45% to 50%, ventilators with oxygen blenders are necessary when the oxygen defect is more severe, such as may occur when COPD is complicated by pneumonia. Humidification should be used routinely because it may reduce the work of breathing and enhance comfort and tolerance during NPPV.[143]

Adaptation and Monitoring. The first few hours are critical in achieving successful adaptation. Coaching and encouragement are usually required to assist the patient in synchronizing with the ventilator and reducing their breathing effort. Instructions such as "try to take slow deep breaths" and "let the machine breathe for you" may be helpful. Also, judicious administration of low doses of sedatives may enhance patient acceptance.

Close bedside monitoring is essential until the patient's respiratory status stabilizes. Although NPPV can easily be administered on general medical wards, the acuteness of the patient's illness and need for close monitoring should dictate the site of administration. Acutely ill patients should be treated in an ICU or step-down unit until their condition stabilizes, regardless of whether they are treated with

Table 86.4 Monitoring NPPV in COPD Patients

Acute Setting
Patient comfort
Mask fit and leak
Patient–ventilator synchrony
Sternocleidomastoid muscle activity
Vital signs (heart and respiratory rate; systemic blood pressure)
Continuous oximetry (until stabilized)
Occasional blood gases (initial and after 30–120 minutes, then as clinically indicated)

Chronic Setting
Patient comfort
Mask fit and leak
Hours of use
Problems with adaptation (e.g., nasal congestion, dryness, gastric insufflation, conjunctival irritation, inability to sleep)
Symptoms (e.g., dyspnea, fatigue, morning headache, hypersomnolence)
Gas exchange (daytime, nocturnal oximetry, blood gases periodically to assess arterial P_{CO_2})
Polysomnography (If symptoms of sleep disturbance persist or nocturnal desaturation persists without clear explanation)

COPD, chronic obstructive pulmonary disease; NPPV, noninvasive positive-pressure ventilation.

invasive or noninvasive ventilation. As shown in Table 86.4, patient comfort and tolerance are key initial goals. In COPD patients, a drop in respiratory rate and reduction in sternocleidomastoid muscle activity are important salutary signs that should be apparent early. They are usually accompanied by good patient–ventilator synchrony, and upward adjustments in inspiratory pressure may enhance these effects. Oxygen saturation is monitored continuously, and blood gases are obtained as is clinically indicated, usually at least once during the first hour or two.

Commonly Encountered Problems and Possible Remedies. Noninvasive ventilation is safe and well tolerated in most properly selected patients. The most commonly encountered problems in COPD patients are similar to those in other patients and are related to the mask, air pressure, or airflow (Table 86.4). Patients often complain of mask discomfort, which can be alleviated by minimizing strap tension or by trying different mask sizes or types. Patients may be anxious and experience difficulty synchronizing their breathing efforts with the ventilator. Adjustments in ventilator settings (increasing or lowering inspiratory pressure or titrating expiratory pressure to counterbalance auto-PEEP) and judicious use of sedation often improves synchrony.

Excessive air pressure leading to sinus or ear pain is another common complaint, alleviated by lowering the pressure temporarily and then gradually raising it again as tolerance improves. Other commonly encountered problems include erythema, pain, or ulceration on the bridge of the nose related to pressure from the mask seal. Minimizing strap tension, using artificial skin, or switching to alternative masks such as nasal "pillows" can alleviate this problem. Gastric insufflation occurs frequently but is usually not severe, probably because inflation pressures are low.

Air leaking through the mouth (with nasal masks) or around the mask (with all interfaces) is inevitable during

NPPV. Nasal and oronasal masks, particularly if too large, may leak air onto the eyes causing conjunctival irritation. Refitting or reseating the mask usually addresses this problem. Pressure-limited devices compensate for air leaks by maintaining inspiratory airflow during leaking, but during nasal ventilation patients should keep their mouths shut, try chin straps to assist in mouth closure, or, failing these measures, try an oronasal mask.

Invasive Mechanical Ventilation

Indications and Patient Selection. The increasing use of NPPV has reduced the need for invasive mechanical ventilation. However, there remain patients who are too ill and are not candidates for NPPV upon arrival to the hospital or who subsequently fail a trial of NPPV. Indications for the use of invasive mechanical ventilation for COPD are listed in Table 86.5.[144]

Invasive mechanical ventilation in COPD must be administered with caution to minimize the risk of complications. Excessive tidal volumes and rates must be avoided, and the urge to normalize arterial PCO_2 must be repressed in an effort to minimize intrinsic PEEP and excessive hyperinflation. Excessive respiratory rates reduce the respiratory cycle, shorten expiratory time, and prevent complete exhalation. This problem is aggravated by large tidal volumes. The consequence is air trapping and the potential for adverse consequences of intrinsic PEEP. With intrinsic PEEP, increased intrathoracic pressure reduces venous return and lowers cardiac output. Patients with severe intrinsic PEEP may be hypotensive with low cardiac output and elevated pulmonary artery wedge pressure due to transmission of the intrathoracic pressure. In their clinical presentation, they

may therefore mimic those with cardiac shock. Temporary disconnection from the ventilator can differentiate hemodynamic compromise due to intrinsic PEEP from true cardiogenic shock because the release of intrathoracic pressure permits rapid resolution of the former but not the latter. Intrinsic PEEP may also cause patient–ventilator asynchrony related to missed triggering due to the delay needed to lower the inspiratory threshold load.

Recommended Ventilator Settings. Volume-limited or pressure-limited modes can be used, but volume-limited assist/control is the most frequent choice initially and provides control over the tidal volume, which is important in avoiding dynamic hyperinflation. A small tidal volume (e.g., 5–7 mL/kg predicted body weight) should be used. Care should be taken to avoid overventilation and alkalemia.[27] The need for sedation varies among patients, although muscle relaxants are seldom necessary. The backup respiratory rate for COPD patients receiving invasive mechanical ventilation should be set between 10 and 14/min. If the inspiratory time is 1 second and the respiratory rate is 20/min, the expiratory time is only 2 seconds; at a rate of 15/min, it is 3 seconds. Thus, relatively small changes in rate can effect large changes in expiratory time. Another way to maximize expiratory time is to raise the inspiratory flow rate and shorten the inspiratory time. However, this strategy is not as fruitful because substantial increases in flow rate result in only minor increases in expiratory time. For example, if the inspiratory time is 1 second and inspiratory flow is 60 L/min, an increase in the inspiratory flow rate to 100 L/min decreases the inspiratory time to 0.6 second (if tidal volume is maintained constant); thus, expiratory time only increases from 2.0 to 2.4 seconds. Furthermore, rapid flow rates may increase the spontaneous respiratory rate[145] as well as respiratory distress. COPD patients prefer flow rates in the 60 L/min range, with faster or slower rates being sensed as less comfortable.[142]

Weaning COPD Patients from Invasive Mechanical Ventilation. Minimizing the duration of mechanical ventilation is desirable to minimize potential complications such as ventilator-associated pneumonia. When patients no longer require high levels of oxygen [arterial oxygen saturation (SaO_2) > 89% on FI_{O_2} ≤ 40%] and the patient is hemodynamically stable and not excessively sedated, spontaneous breathing trials should be initiated.[88] If the patient can comfortably tolerate a trial of 30 to 120 minutes without excessive tachypnea, hemodynamic instability, or oxygen desaturation, extubation should be undertaken so long as the patient has an adequate cough without excessive airway secretions. If the patient fails to meet extubation criteria but is otherwise a good candidate for noninvasive ventilation, extubation to noninvasive ventilation should be considered with the caveats discussed earlier.

ASTHMA

Acute ventilatory failure due to acute asthma should be unusual if patients adhere to a medical regimen including corticosteroid inhalers, monitor their peak flows, and alter their medical regimen (with the addition of enteral steroids) when peak flows begin to drop. Unfortunately, some patients are not treated with optimal regimens, some do not

---

Table 86.5 Indications for Invasive Mechanical Ventilation in COPD

Severe dyspnea with the use of accessory muscles and paradoxical abdominal motion
Respiratory frequency > 35 breaths/min
Life-threatening hypoxemia (arterial PO_2 < 40 mm Hg or arterial PO_2/FI_{O_2} < 200 mm Hg)
Severe acidosis (pH < 7.25) and hypercapnia (arterial PCO_2 > 60 mm Hg)
Respiratory arrest
Somnolence; impaired mental status
Cardiovascular complications (hypotension; shock; heart failure)
Other complications (metabolic abnormalities; sepsis; pneumonia; pulmonary embolism; barotrauma; massive pleural effusion)
Failure of noninvasive positive-pressure ventilation

From Pauwels RA, Buist AS, Calverley PM, et al: Global strategy for the diagnosis, management, and prevention of chronic obstructive pulmonary disease; NHLBI/WHO Global Initiative for Chronic Obstructive Lung Disease (GOLD) workshop summary. Am J Respir Crit Care Med 163:1256–1276, 2001.

adhere to the regimen, and some have severe exacerbations even with optimal regimens, so acute ventilatory failure in asthmatics remains a problem in acute care hospitals. Studies on near-fatal asthma have identified several risk factors for exacerbation including poor access to health care, substance abuse, nonadherence with therapy, underuse of corticosteroids, and underestimation of the severity of attacks.[146]

Medical Management of Acute Asthma

Patients presenting with severe asthma should be promptly treated with systemic as well as inhaled corticosteroids and bronchodilators. Rapidly acting beta$_2$-agonists are administered by inhalation, although no optimal route of administration or dose has been established metered-dose inhalers with spacers or nebulizers may be used, usually every 20 minutes for the first hour. Some centers use continuous nebulization for severe acute asthma. Magnesium, either intravenous or inhaled, has been administered, but evidence that it abets aggressive beta$_2$-agonist therapy is inconclusive.

Mixtures of helium and oxygen have been used since the 1930s to lower resistance to flow related to turbulence in the airways of asthma patients, just as they have in COPD patients. Four randomized controlled trials of heliox have been performed on patients with acute asthma, but the results are inconclusive.[147] Two demonstrated more rapid improvements in dyspnea and airflow with heliox than with oxygen alone,[148,149] but another showed no improvement in airflow rates (although dyspnea was reduced more)[150]; the fourth revealed no significant benefit over oxygen alone.[151] The two studies showing little or no improvement with heliox enrolled less severely obstructed patients than the favorable studies, but a subgroup analysis of sicker patients in the negative study showed no benefit in that subgroup, either. A Cochrane analysis concluded that there is no defined role for heliox in treating severe acute asthma,[152] but many centers use it when patients are not responding promptly to standard therapy.

Ventilatory Management

Assessment of Ventilatory Status.
In patients with acute asthma exacerbations, frank ventilatory failure is unusual. Signs of severe respiratory distress, such as excessive use of accessory muscles, extreme tachypnea, or abdominal paradox, warrant the initiation of ventilatory assistance. Arterial blood gases showing normocapnia in a patient with severe respiratory distress should also cause alarm because patients reach a "crossover" point as they fail, when they can no longer sustain hyperventilation but have not become sufficiently fatigued to retain carbon dioxide. These patients should be monitored closely so intervention with noninvasive ventilatory aids can be initiated promptly in order to avert the need for invasive ventilation with its attendant potential complications.

Continuous Positive Airway Pressure.
CPAP alone may ameliorate respiratory distress in asthmatics by stenting airways open, reducing atelectasis, and offsetting auto-PEEP. However, caution should be exercised because the unequal distribution of airways resistance, in contrast to the simultaneous closure of airways in COPD, creates areas with very different expiratory time constants, so CPAP could promote overdistention of some regions. Thus, caution should be exercised when applying CPAP to these patients, at least at levels exceeding 5 cm H_2O.

Noninvasive Ventilation.
Despite the success of noninvasive ventilation in COPD exacerbations, its role in treating asthma exacerbations has not been clearly defined. An early cohort study observed substantial improvements in blood gases (arterial PCO_2 dropping from 65 to 52 mm Hg in the first 2 hours) among 17 patients treated with noninvasive ventilation, only 2 of whom required intubation.[153] In a subsequent retrospective report, only 3 of 22 patients treated with noninvasive ventilation required intubation, although arterial PCO_2 levels tended to fall less rapidly than in an invasively ventilated group. The ICU and hospital lengths of stay were shorter in the noninvasive ventilation group.[154]

Two randomized controlled trials have also been performed. In one, only 35 patients were enrolled despite a power analysis calling for 10 times as many. No significant differences were found, but clinicians were reluctant to enter patients who were good candidates for noninvasive ventilation into the trial because they feared the patients would be intubated if randomized to the control group.[155] In the other randomized trial,[156] patients treated with noninvasive ventilation had significantly greater improvements in FEV$_1$ in the first hour compared to sham-treated patients (53.5% vs. 28.5%), and the need for hospitalization was significantly reduced. These results are encouraging but not compelling because there has been no evidence for reduced need for intubation or mortality. Nonetheless, a trial of noninvasive ventilation seems reasonable when patients fail to respond promptly to initial bronchodilator therapy, particularly if they manifest signs of respiratory muscle fatigue including a respiratory rate of more than 30 breaths/min, accessory muscle use, abdominal paradox, normocapnia in patients with respiratory distress, hypercapnia, or hypoxemia.

Invasive Mechanical Ventilation.
Invasive mechanical ventilation in patients with acute ventilatory failure due to asthma should be used as a last resort but is necessary when patents present with coma, delirium, or medical instability. Hemodynamic or cardiac instability is also a clear indication, as is failure of noninvasive ventilation. Although about one third of patients admitted to the ICU because of acute severe asthma have been managed with invasive mechanical ventilation in recently reported series,[146,157] the proportion of patients who require intubation when its avoidance is a specific goal of therapy has not been determined. Invasive mechanical ventilation is best avoided because of the frequency and severity of the potential complications. These include clinical barotrauma such as pneumothorax and pneumomediastinum, which occurred in 6.5% of patients in one series,[158] the need for sedation and possible paralysis with the risk of post-paralysis myopathy, ventilator-associated pneumonia, and mortality rates in the 5% to 10% range in some series.[159,160]

If invasive mechanical ventilation is necessary, great care must be exercised to minimize the risk of complications, and the approach is similar to that used for COPD patients. Excessive respiratory rates and tidal volumes should be avoided, and plateau pressures should be kept under 30 to

35 cm H_2O. "Permissive hypercapnia,"[161,162] first described in invasively ventilated asthma patients,[163] remains a sensible approach in severely obstructed patients. Bicarbonate can be administered if the pH drops too low (<7.0–7.1). Because of the variability of resistance between airways, some of which may be entirely obstructed, measurement of auto-PEEP using the expiratory hold technique may underestimate the severity of regional hyperinflation.[164] When ventilation remains difficult, even with use of lung-protective ventilation and permissive hypercapnia, the addition of heliox to the ventilator circuit may help (although heliox may alter ventilator performance and not all ventilators can accommodate heliox). As a last resort, extreme measures such as general anesthesia with bronchodilator anesthetics (e.g., halothane)[165] or induced hypothermia may be helpful.

ACUTE VENTILATORY FAILURE DUE TO VASCULAR IMPAIRMENT

By increasing the physiologic dead space, disorders affecting the pulmonary vasculature reduce alveolar ventilation in relation to overall minute ventilation. Although hypercapnia might be expected in such a circumstance, it is typically prevented by a modest increase in overall ventilation, and acute ventilatory failure is seldom seen in primary pulmonary vascular disease. In pulmonary thromboembolism, for example, hypercapnia is unusual in the absence of a comorbid condition such as severe COPD or drug-induced ventilatory drive depression that impairs the function of the ventilatory pump. An exception is when pulmonary thromboembolism occurs during controlled mechanical ventilation, when the patient is incapable of increasing minute ventilation because of conditions such as high cervical spinal cord injury or pharmacologic paralysis. In such a setting, acute respiratory acidosis, with or without concomitant worsening in oxygenation, may be the initial manifestation of pulmonary thromboembolism.

Another rare circumstance in which acute ventilatory failure may develop as a result of a disorder of the pulmonary circulation is venous air embolism,[166,167] in which hypercapnia and a marked discrepancy between arterial and end-tidal exhaled carbon dioxide levels may be observed.[168] Hypercapnia may also complicate the acute chest syndrome in patients with sickle cell disease; one series documented respiratory acidosis in 42% of patients who developed this syndrome.[169]

As discussed earlier, intrapulmonary right-to-left shunting and very low ventilation-perfusion ratios in ARDS can cause hypercapnia. Although the term "permissive hypercapnia" is often applied to the respiratory acidosis that occurs with low-tidal-volume, lung-protective ventilatory strategies, hypercapnia can be a manifestation of the underlying disease process rather than of the management strategy.

SUMMARY

Acute ventilatory failure develops because of insufficient ventilatory effort due to reduced drive, inadequate ventilatory output despite increased effort (because of either impaired neuromuscular function or excessive ventilatory demand), or a combination of these factors. It cannot be diagnosed or its severity adequately assessed without arterial blood gas measurements. Impairment of ventilatory drive severe enough to cause acute ventilatory failure can occur because of disease, but most often it is due to drugs. Acute ventilatory failure due to neuromuscular disorders is commonly encountered in cervical spinal cord injury or primary neurologic or neuromuscular disease such as Guillain-Barré syndrome, acute stroke, or amyotrophic lateral sclerosis. With each of these mechanisms the lungs and airways are usually normal, so management focuses on providing adequate alveolar ventilation, with or without supplemental oxygen. When ventilatory failure occurs in the setting of restrictive disease, whether pulmonary or extrapulmonary, effective management must overcome the increased work of breathing caused by severely reduced lung and/or chest wall compliance; invasive mechanical ventilation is the mainstay of management. The outlook for acute ventilatory failure complicating idiopathic pulmonary fibrosis is poor. The most challenging form of acute ventilatory failure is that seen in severe obstructive disease, most often COPD or asthma. Here, management focuses on decreasing airway obstruction through the use of intensive medical therapy and avoiding intubation with its attendant complications through the use of noninvasive ventilation. Noninvasive ventilation has become the standard of care in severe COPD exacerbations, whereas its role in status asthmaticus, acute hypoxemic respiratory failure, extubation failure, and other circumstances is unclear. Proper patient selection is the key to successful noninvasive positive-pressure ventilation along with skilled application of the right apparatus and appropriate monitoring. Pulmonary vascular disease is an unusual primary cause of acute ventilatory failure but can contribute to increased ventilatory requirements in ARDS and some other conditions.

REFERENCES

1. Epstein SK, Singh N: Respiratory acidosis. Respir Care 46:366–383, 2001.
2. Pierson DJ: Respiratory failure: Introduction and overview. *In* Pierson DJ, Kacmarek RM (eds): Foundations of Respiratory Care. New York: Churchill Livingstone, 1992, pp 295–302.
3. Roussos C, Macklem PT: The respiratory muscles. N Engl J Med 307:786–797, 1982.
4. Roussos C, Koutsoukou A: Respiratory failure. Eur Respir J Suppl;47:3s–14s, 2003.
5. Coffey RL, Albert RK, Robertson HT: Mechanisms of physiological dead space: Response to PEEP after oleic acid injury. J Appl Physiol 55:1550–1557, 1983.
6. Swenson E, Robertson HT: What do dead-space measurements tell us about the lung with acute respiratory distress syndrome. Respir Care 49:1006–1007, 2004.
7. Henson LC, Ward DS: Effects of anaesthetics and sedatives on the control of breathing. Ann Acad Med Singapore 23(Suppl):125–129, 1994.
8. Weil JV, McCullough RE, Kline JS, Sodal IE: Diminished ventilatory response to hypoxia and hypercapnia after morphine in normal man. N Engl J Med 292:1103–1106, 1975.
9. Sahn SA, Lakshminarayan S, Pierson DJ, et al: Effect of ethanol on the ventilatory responses to oxygen and carbon dioxide in man. Clin Sci Mol Med 49:33–38, 1975.

10. Forster A, Gardaz JP, Suter PM, et al: Respiratory depression by midazolam and diazepam. Anesthesiology 53:494–497, 1980.

11. Kafer ER, Marsh HM: The effects of anesthetic drugs and disease on the chemical regulation of ventilation. Int Anesthesiol Clin 15(2):1–38, 1977.

12. Zimmerman JL: Poisonings and overdoses in the intensive care unit: General and specific management issues. Crit Care Med 31:2794–2801, 2003.

13. Aubier M, Murciano D, Fournier M, et al. Central respiratory drive in acute respiratory failure of patients with chronic obstructive pulmonary disease. Am Rev Respir Dis 122:191–199, 1980.

14. Montgomery AB, Holle RHO, Neagley SR, et al: Prediction of successful ventilator weaning using airway occlusion pressure and hypercapnic challenge. Chest 91:496–499, 1987.

15. Zwillich CW, Sutton FD Jr, Pierson DJ, et al: Decreased hypoxic ventilatory drive in the obesity-hypoventilation syndrome. Am J Med 59:343–348, 1975.

16. Nowbar S, Burkart KM, Gonzales R, et al: Obesity-associated hypoventilation in hospitalized patients: Prevalence, effects, and outcome. Am J Med 116:1–7, 2004.

17. Zwillich CW, Pierson DJ, Hofeldt FD, et al: Ventilatory control in myxedema and hypothyroidism. N Engl J Med 292:662–665, 1975.

18. Orenstein DM, Boat TF, Owens RP, et al: The obesity hypoventilation syndrome in children with the Prader-Willi syndrome: A possible role for familial decreased response to carbon dioxide. J Pediatr 97:765–767, 1980.

19. Sandblom RE, Matsumoto AM, Schoene RB, et al: Obstructive sleep apnea syndrome induced by testosterone administration. N Engl J Med 308:508–510, 1983.

20. Burtin P, Bollaert PE, Feldmann L, et al: Prognosis of stroke patients undergoing mechanical ventilation. Intensive Care Med 20:32–36, 1994.

21. El-Ad B, Bornstein NM, Fuchs P, Korczyn AD: Mechanical ventilation in stroke patients—is it worthwhile? Neurology 47:657–659, 1996.

22. Wijdicks EF, Scott JP: Stroke in the medical intensive-care unit. Mayo Clin Proc 73:642–646, 1998.

23. Gujjar AR, Deibert E, Manno EM, et al: Mechanical ventilation for ischemic stroke and intracerebral hemorrhage: Indications, timing, and outcome. Neurology 51:447–451, 1998.

24. Wijdicks EF, Scott JP: Outcome in patients with acute basilar artery occlusion requiring mechanical ventilation. Stroke 27:1301–1303, 1996.

25. Steiner T, Mendoza G, De Georgia M, et al: Prognosis of stroke patients requiring mechanical ventilation in a neurological critical care unit. Stroke 28:711–715, 1997.

26. Berrouschot J, Rossler A, Koster J, et al: Mechanical ventilation in patients with hemispheric ischemic stroke. Crit Care Med 28:2956–2961, 2000.

27. Pierson DJ: Invasive mechanical ventilation. In Albert RK, Spiro SG, Jett JR (eds): Clinical Respiratory medicine (2nd ed). London/Philadelphia: Saunders, 2004, pp 189–209.

28. Coplin WM, Pierson DJ, Cooley KD, et al: Implications of extubation delay in brain-injured patients meeting standard weaning criteria. Am J Respir Crit Care Med 161:1530–1536, 2000.

29. Slack RS, Shucart W: Respiratory dysfunction associated with traumatic injury to the central nervous system. Clin Chest Med 15:739–749, 1994.

30. Viroslav J, Rosenblatt R, Tomazevic SM: Respiratory management, survival, and quality of life for high-level traumatic tetraplegics. Respir Care Clin North Am 2:313–322, 1996.

31. Winslow C, Bode RK, Felton D, et al: Impact of respiratory complications on length of stay and hospital costs in acute cervical spine injury. Chest 121:1548–1554, 2002.

32. Claxton AR, Wong DT, Chung F, et al: Predictors of hospital mortality and mechanical ventilation in patients with cervical spinal cord injury. Can J Anaesth 45:144–149, 1998.

33. Bach JR, Hunt D, Horton JA III: Traumatic tetraplegia: Noninvasive respiratory management in the acute setting. Am J Phys Med Rehabil 81:792–797, 2002.

34. Chervin RD, Guilleminault C: Diaphragm pacing for respiratory insufficiency. J Clin Neurophysiol 14:369–377, 1997

35. DiMarco AF, Onders RP, Kowalski KE, et al: Phrenic nerve pacing in a tetraplegic patient via intramuscular diaphragm electrodes. Am J Respir Crit Care Med 166(12 Pt 1):1604–1606, 2002.

36. Tripp HF, Bolton JW: Phrenic nerve injury following cardiac surgery: A review. J Card Surg 13:218–223, 1998.

37. Diehl JL, Lofaso F, Deleuze P, et al: Clinically relevant diaphragmatic dysfunction after cardiac operations. J Thorac Cardiovasc Surg 107:487–498, 1994.

38. Lin MC, Liaw MY, Huang CC, et al: Bilateral diaphragmatic paralysis—a rare cause of acute respiratory failure managed with nasal mask bilevel positive airway pressure (BiPAP) ventilation. Eur Respir J 10:1922–1924, 1997.

39. Valls-Sole J, Solans M: Idiopathic bilateral diaphragmatic paralysis. Muscle Nerve 25:619–623, 2002.

40. Hassoun PM, Celli BR: Bilateral diaphragm paralysis secondary to central von Recklinghausen's disease. Chest 117:1196–1200, 2000.

41. Dushay KM, Zibrak JD, Jensen WA: Myasthenia gravis presenting as isolated respiratory failure. Chest 97:232–234, 1990.

42. Fromm GB, Wisdom PJ, Block AJ: Amyotrophic lateral sclerosis presenting with respiratory failure: Diaphragmatic paralysis and dependence on mechanical ventilation in two patients. Chest 71:612–614, 1977.

43. Czaplinski A, Strobel W, Gobbi C, et al: Respiratory failure due to bilateral diaphragm palsy as an early manifestation of ALS. Med Sci Monit 9:CS34–CS36, 2003.

44. Teitelbaum JS, Borel CO: Respiratory dysfunction in Guillain-Barre syndrome. Clin Chest Med 15:705–714, 1994.

45. Chalela JA: Pearls and pitfalls in the intensive care management of Guillain-Barre syndrome. Semin Neurol 21:399–405, 2001.

46. Lawn ND, Fletcher DD, Henderson RD, et al: Anticipating mechanical ventilation in Guillain-Barre syndrome. Arch Neurol 58:893–898, 2001.

47. Sharshar T, Chevret S, Bourdain F, et al: French Cooperative Group on Plasma Exchange in Guillain-Barre syndrome: Early predictors of mechanical ventilation in Guillain-Barre syndrome. Crit Care Med 31:278–283, 2003.

48. Hund EF, Borel CO, Cornblath DR, et al: Intensive management and treatment of severe Guillain-Barre syndrome. Crit Care Med 21:433–446, 1993.

49. Zulueta JJ, Fanburg BL: Respiratory dysfunction in myasthenia gravis. Clin Chest Med 15:683–691, 1994.

50. Varelas PN, Chua HC, Natterman J, et al: Ventilatory care in myasthenia gravis crisis: Assessing the baseline adverse event rate. Crit Care Med 30:2663–2668, 2002.

51. Lechtzin N, Rothstein J, Clawson L, et al: Amyotrophic lateral sclerosis: Evaluation and treatment of respiratory impairment. Amyotroph Lateral Scler Other Motor Neuron Disord 3:5–13, 2002.

52. Kaplan LM, Hollander D: Respiratory dysfunction in amyotrophic lateral sclerosis. Clin Chest Med 15:675–681, 1994.
53. Bonekat HW: Noninvasive ventilation in neuromuscular disease. Crit Care Clin 14:775–797, 1998.
54. Benditt JO: Management of pulmonary complications in neuromuscular disease. Phys Med Rehabil Clin N Am 9:167–185, 1998.
55. Perrin C, Unterborn JN, Ambrosio CD, et al: Pulmonary complications of chronic neuromuscular diseases and their management. Muscle Nerve 29:5–27, 2004.
56. De Carvalho M, Matias T, Coelho F, et al: Motor neuron disease presenting with respiratory failure. J Neurol Sci 139(Suppl):117–122, 1996.
57. Massey EW, Harrell LE: Motor neuron disease presenting with respiratory failure: Report of two cases. Postgrad Med 76:216–218, 1984.
58. Meyrignac C, Poirier J, Degos JD: Amyotrophic lateral sclerosis presenting with respiratory insufficiency as the primary complaint: Clinicopathological study of a case. Eur Neurol 24:115–120, 1985.
59. Vianello A, Bevilacqua M, Arcaro G, et al: Non-invasive ventilatory approach to treatment of acute respiratory failure in neuromuscular disorders: A comparison with endotracheal intubation. Intensive Care Med 26:384–390, 2000.
60. Shapiro RL, Hatheway C, Swerdlow DL: Botulism in the United States: A clinical and epidemiologic review. Ann Intern Med 129:221–228, 1998.
61. Schmidt-Nowara WW, Samet JM, Rosario PA: Early and late pulmonary complications of botulism. Arch Intern Med 143:451–456, 1983.
62. Lewis SW, Pierson DJ, Cary JM, Hudson LD: Prolonged respiratory paralysis in wound botulism. Chest 75:59–61, 1979.
63. Sandrock CE, Murin S: Clinical predictors of respiratory failure and long-term outcome in black tar heroin-associated wound botulism. Chest 120:562–566, 2001.
64. Mitchell PA, Pons PT: Wound botulism associated with black tar heroin and lower extremity cellulitis. J Emerg Med 20:371–375, 2001.
65. Wilcox P, Andolfatto G, Fairbarn MS, Pardy RL: Long-term follow-up of symptoms, pulmonary function, respiratory muscle strength, and exercise performance after botulism. Am Rev Respir Dis 139:157–163, 1989.
66. Astudillo LM, Carreiro M, Sailler L, et al: Hypercapnic coma due to diaphragmatic involvement in a patient with dermatomyositis. Clin Exp Rheumatol 19:456–458, 2001.
67. Haskard DO: Successful treatment of dermatomyositis complicated by ventilatory failure. Ann Rheum Dis 42:460–461, 1983.
68. Deem S, Lee CM, Curtis JR: Acquired neuromuscular disorders in the intensive care unit. Am J Respir Crit Care Med 168:735–739, 2003.
69. Segredo V, Caldwell JE, Matthay MA, et al: Persistent paralysis in critically ill patients after long-term administration of vecuronium. N Engl J Med 327:524–528, 1992.
70. Rudis MI, Sikora CA, Angus E: A prospective, randomized, controlled evaluation of peripheral nerve stimulation versus standard clinical dosing of neuromuscular blocking agents in critically ill patients. Crit Care Med 25:575–583, 1997.
71. Murray MJ, Cowen J, DeBlock H, et al: Clinical practice guidelines for sustained neuromuscular blockade in the adult critically ill patient. Crit Care Med 30:142–156, 2002.
72. De Jonghe B, Sharshar T, Lefaucheur JP, et al: Paresis acquired in the intensive care unit: A prospective multicenter study. JAMA 288:2859–2867, 2002.
73. Van den Berghe G, Wouters PJ, Bouillon R, et al: Outcome benefit of intensive insulin therapy in the critically ill: Insulin dose versus glycemic control. Crit Care Med 31:359–366, 2003.
74. Van den Berghe G, Wouters PJ, Weekers F, et al: Intensive insulin therapy in the critically ill patient. N Engl J Med 345:1359–1367, 2001.
75. Hansen-Flaschen J, Cowen J, Raps EC: Neuromuscular blockade in the intensive care unit: More than we bargained for. Am Rev Respir Dis 147:234–236, 1993.
76. Leatherman JW, Fluegel WL, David WS, et al: Muscle weakness in mechanically ventilated patients with severe asthma. Am J Respir Crit Care Med 153:1686–1690, 1996.
77. Hund E: Myopathy in critically ill patients. Crit Care Med 27:2544–2547, 1999.
78. Vassilakopoulos T, Petrof BJ: Ventilator-induced diaphragmatic dysfunction. Am J Respir Crit Care Med 169:336–341, 2004.
79. Watson AC, Hughes PD, Louise Harris M, et al: Measurement of twitch transdiaphragmatic, esophageal, and endotracheal tube pressure with bilateral anterolateral magnetic phrenic nerve stimulation in patients in the intensive care unit. Crit Care Med 29:1325–1331, 2001.
80. Luce JM, Pierson DJ, Hudson LD: Intermittent mandatory ventilation: A critical review. Chest 79:678–685, 1981.
81. Durand MC, Lofaso F, Lefaucheur JP, et al: Electrophysiology to predict mechanical ventilation in Guillain-Barre syndrome. Eur J Neurol 10:39–44, 2003.
82. Kaida K, Kusunoki S, Kanzaki M, et al: Anti-GQ1b antibody as a factor predictive of mechanical ventilation in Guillain-Barre syndrome. Neurology 62:821–824, 2004.
83. Rieder P, Louis M, Jolliet P, Chevrolet JC: The repeated measurement of vital capacity is a poor predictor of the need for mechanical ventilation in myasthenia gravis. Intensive Care Med 21:663–668, 1995.
84. Rabinstein AA, Wijdicks EF: Warning signs of imminent respiratory failure in neurological patients. Semin Neurol 23:97–104, 2003.
85. Cohen CA, Zagelbaum G, Gross D, et al: Clinical manifestations of inspiratory muscle fatigue. Am J Med 73:308–316, 1982.
86. Schmidt-Nowara WW, Altman AR: Atelectasis and neuromuscular respiratory failure. Chest 85:792–795, 1984.
87. Henderson RD, Lawn ND, Fletcher DD, et al: The morbidity of Guillain-Barre syndrome admitted to the intensive care unit. Neurology 60:17–21, 2003.
88. ACCP-AARC-SCCM Collective Weaning Task Force: Evidence-based guidelines for weaning and discontinuing ventilatory support. I. Guidelines. Chest 120(Suppl):375s–395s, 2001.
89. Conti G, Rocco M, Antonelli M, et al: Respiratory system mechanics in the early phase of acute respiratory failure due to severe kyphoscoliosis. Intensive Care Med 23:539–544, 1997.
90. Annane D, Chevrolet JC, Chevret S, et al: Nocturnal mechanical ventilation for chronic hypoventilation in patients with neuromuscular and chest wall disorders. Cochrane Database Syst Rev 2000;(2):CD001941.
91. Finlay G, Concannon D, McDonnell TJ: Treatment of respiratory failure due to kyphoscoliosis with nasal intermittent positive pressure ventilation (NIPPV). Ir J Med Sci 164:28–30, 1995.
92. Masa JF, Celli BR, Riesco JA, et al: The obesity hypoventilation syndrome can be treated with noninvasive mechanical ventilation. Chest 119:1102–1107, 2001.

93. Ambrosini V, Cancellieri A, Chilosi M, et al: Acute exacerbation of idiopathic pulmonary fibrosis: Report of a series. Eur Respir J 22:821–826, 2003.

94. Al-Hameed FM, Sharma S: Outcome of patients admitted to the intensive care unit for acute exacerbation of idiopathic pulmonary fibrosis. Can Respir J 11:117–122, 2004.

95. Blivet S, Philit F, Sab JM, et al: Outcome of patients with idiopathic pulmonary fibrosis admitted to the ICU for respiratory failure. Chest 120:209–212, 2001.

96. Fumeaux T, Rothmeier C, Jolliet P: Outcome of mechanical ventilation for acute respiratory failure in patients with pulmonary fibrosis. Intensive Care Med 27:1868–1874, 2001.

97. Saydain G, Islam A, Afessa B, et al: Outcome of patients with idiopathic pulmonary fibrosis admitted to the intensive care unit. Am J Respir Crit Care Med 166:839–842, 2002.

98. Stern JB, Mal H, Groussard O, et al: Prognosis of patients with advanced idiopathic pulmonary fibrosis requiring mechanical ventilation for acute respiratory failure. Chest 120:213–219, 2001.

99. Nava S, Rubini F: Lung and chest wall mechanics in ventilated patients with end stage idiopathic pulmonary fibrosis. Thorax 54:390–395, 1999.

100. Carlucci A, Richard JC, Wysocki M, et al: Noninvasive versus conventional mechanical ventilation: An epidemiologic survey. Am J Respir Crit Care Med 163:874–880, 2001.

101. Mehta S, Hill NS: Noninvasive ventilation; state of the art. Am J Respir Crit Care Med 163:540–577, 2001.

102. Rochester DF, Braun NMT, Arora NS: Respiratory muscle strength in chronic obstructive pulmonary disease. Am Rev Respir Dis 119:151–154, 1979.

103. Groenewegen KH, Schols AM, Wouters EF: Mortality and mortality-related factors after hospitalization for acute exacerbation of COPD. Chest 124:459–467, 2003.

104. Pingleton SK: Complications of acute respiratory failure. Am Rev Respir Dis 137:1463–1493, 1988.

105. Brochard L, Isabey D, Piquet J, et al: Reversal of acute exacerbations of chronic obstructive lung disease by inspiratory assistance with a face mask. N Engl J Med 323:1523–1530, 1990.

106. Appendini L, Palessio A, Zanaboni S, et al: Physiologic effects of positive end-expiratory pressure and mask pressure support during exacerbations of chronic obstructive pulmonary disease. Am J Respir Crit Care Med 149:1069–1076, 1994.

107. Bott J, Carroll MP, Conway JH, et al: Randomized controlled trial of nasal ventilation in acute ventilatory failure due to chronic obstructive airways disease. Lancet 341:1555–1557, 1993.

108. Kramer N, Meyer TJ, Meharg J, et al: Randomized, prospective trial of noninvasive positive pressure ventilation in acute respiratory failure. Am J Respir Crit Care Med 151:1799–1806, 1995.

109. Brochard L, Mancebo J, Wysocki M, et al: Noninvasive ventilation for acute exacerbations of chronic obstructive pulmonary disease. N Engl J Med 333:817–822, 1995.

110. Celikel T, Sungur M, Ceyhan B, et al: Comparison of noninvasive positive pressure ventilation with standard medical therapy in hypercapnic acute respiratory failure. Chest 114:1636–1642, 1998.

111. Plant PK, Owen JL, Elliott MW: Early use of non-invasive ventilation for acute exacerbations of chronic obstructive pulmonary disease on general respiratory wards: A multicenter randomized controlled trial. Lancet 355:1931–1935, 2000.

112. Barbe F, Togores B, Rubi M, et al: Noninvasive ventilatory support does not facilitate recovery from acute respiratory failure in chronic obstructive pulmonary disease. Eur Respir J 9:1240–1245, 1996.

113. Keenan SP, Kernerman PD, Cook DJ, et al: Effect of noninvasive positive pressure ventilation on mortality in patients admitted with acute respiratory failure: A meta-analysis. Crit Care Med 25:1685–1692, 1997.

114. Peter JV, Moran JL, Phillips-Hughes J, et al: Noninvasive ventilation in acute respiratory failure: A meta-analysis update. Crit Care Med 30:555–562, 2002.

115. Lightowler JV, Wedjicha JA, Elliot MW, et al: Non-invasive positive pressure ventilation to treat respiratory failure resulting from exacerbations of chronic obstructive pulmonary disease: Cochrane systematic review and meta-analysis. BMJ 326:185–189, 2003.

116. Keenan SP, Sinuff T, Cook DJ, et al: Which patients with exacerbation of chronic obstructive pulmonary disease benefit from noninvasive positive pressure ventilation? A systematic review of the literature. Ann Intern Med 138:861–870, 2003.

117. International consensus conferences in intensive care medicine: Noninvasive positive pressure ventilation in acute respiratory failure. Am J Respir Crit Care Med 163:283–291, 2001.

118. Hill NS: Noninvasive positive pressure ventilation for respiratory failure caused by exacerbations of chronic obstructive pulmonary disease: A standard of care? Crit Care 7:400–401, 2003.

119. Ambrosino N, Foglio K, Rubini F, et al: Non-invasive mechanical ventilation in acute respiratory failure due to chronic obstructive pulmonary disease: Correlates for success. Thorax 50:755–757, 1995.

120. Confalonieri M, Potena A, Carbone G, et al: Acute respiratory failure in patients with severe community-acquired pneumonia: A prospective randomized evaluation of noninvasive ventilation. Am J Respir Crit Care Med 160:1585–1591, 1999.

121. Auriant I, Jallot A, Herve P, et al: Noninvasive ventilation reduces mortality in acute respiratory failure following lung resection. Am J Respir Crit Care Med 164:1231–1235, 2001.

122. Nava S, Ambrosino N, Clini E, et al: Noninvasive mechanical ventilation in the weaning of patients with respiratory failure due to chronic obstructive pulmonary disease: A randomized, controlled trial. Ann Intern Med 128:721–728, 1998.

123. Girault C, Daudenthun I, Chevron V, et al: Noninvasive ventilation as a systematic extubation and weaning technique in acute-on-chronic respiratory failure: A prospective, randomized controlled study. Am J Respir Crit Care Med 160:86–92, 1999.

124. Ferrer M, Esquinas A, Arancibia F, et al: Noninvasive ventilation during persistent weaning failure. Am J Respir Crit Care Med 168:70–76, 2003.

125. Epstein SK, Ciubotaru RL, Wong JB: Effect of failed extubation on the outcome of mechanical ventilation. Chest 112:186–192, 1997.

126. Chevron V, Menard JF, Richard JC, et al: Unplanned extubation: Risk factors of development and predictive criteria for reintubation. Crit Care Med 26:1049–1053, 1998.

127. Hilbert G, Gruson D, Portel L, et al: Noninvasive pressure support ventilation in COPD patients with post-extubation hypercapnic respiratory insufficiency. Eur Respir J 11:1349–1353, 1998.

128. Keenan SP, Powers C, McCormack DG, et al: Noninvasive positive pressure ventilation for postextubation respiratory

distress: a randomized controlled trial. JAMA 287:3238–3244, 2002.

129. Esteban A, Frutos-Vivar F, Ferguson ND, et al: Noninvasive positive-pressure ventilation for respiratory failure after extubation. N Engl J Med 350:2452–2460, 2004.

130. Levy M, Tanios MA, Nelson D, et al: Outcomes of patients with do-not-intubate orders treated with noninvasive ventilation. Crit Care Med 32:2002–2007, 2004.

131. Freichels TA. Palliative ventilatory support: Use of noninvasive positive pressure ventilation in terminal respiratory insufficiency. Am J Crit Care 3:6–10, 1994.

132. Clarke DE, Vaughan L, Raffin TA: Noninvasive positive pressure ventilation for patients with terminal respiratory failure: The ethical and economic costs of delaying the inevitable are too great. Am J Crit Care 3:4–5, 1994.

133. Benhamou D, Girault C, Faure C, et al: Nasal mask ventilation in acute respiratory failure: Experience in elderly patients. Chest 102:912–917, 1992.

134. Jaber S, Fodil R, Carlucci A, et al: Noninvasive ventilation with helium-oxygen in acute exacerbations of chronic obstructive pulmonary disease. Am J Respir Crit Care Med 161:1191–1200, 2000.

135. Jolliet P, Tassaux D, Roeseler J, et al: Helium-oxygen versus air-oxygen noninvasive pressure support in decompensated chronic obstructive disease: A prospective, multicenter study. Crit Care Med 31:878–884, 2003.

136. Soo Hoo GW, Santiago S, Williams AJ: Nasal mechanical ventilation for hypercapnic respiratory failure in chronic obstructive pulmonary disease: determinants of success and failure. Crit Care Med 22:1253–1261, 1994.

137. Anton A, Guell R, Gomez J, et al: Predicting the result of noninvasive ventilation in severe acute exacerbations of patients with chronic airflow limitation. Chest 117:828–833, 2000.

138. Liesching T, Kwok H, Hill NS: Acute applications of noninvasive positive pressure ventilation. Chest 124:699–713, 2003.

139. Hill NS (ed): Noninvasive Positive Pressure Ventilation: Principles and Applications. Armonk, NY: Futura, 2001.

140. Kwok H, McCormack J, Cece R, et al: Controlled trial of nasal versus oronasal masks in patients with acute respiratory failure. Crit Care Med (in press).

141. Navalesi P, Fanfulla F, Frigerio P, et al: Physiologic evaluation of noninvasive mechanical ventilation delivered with three types of masks in patients with chronic hypercapnic respiratory failure. Crit Care Med 28:1785–1790, 2000.

142. Bonmarchand G, Chevron V, Chopin C, et al: Increased initial flow rate reduces inspiratory work of breathing during pressure support ventilation in patients with exacerbation of chronic obstructive pulmonary disease. Intensive Care Med 22:1147–1154, 1996.

143. Lellouche F, Maggiore SM, Deye N, et al: Effect of the humidification device on the work of breathing during noninvasive ventilation. Intensive Care Med 28:1582–1589, 2002.

144. Pauwels RA, Buist AS, Calverley PM, et al: Global strategy for the diagnosis, management, and prevention of chronic obstructive pulmonary disease; NHLBI/WHO Global Initiative for Chronic Obstructive Lung Disease (GOLD) workshop summary. Am J Respir Crit Care Med 163:1256–1276, 2001.

145. Laghi F: Effect of inspiratory time and flow settings during assist-control ventilation. Curr Opin Crit Care 9:39–44, 2003.

146. McFadden ER Jr: Acute severe asthma. Am J Respir Crit Care Med 168:740–759, 2003.

147. Reuben AD, Harris AR: Heliox for asthma in the emergency department: A review of the literature. Emerg Med J 21:131–135, 2004.

148. Kass JE, Terregino CA: The effect of heliox in acute severe asthma: A randomized controlled trial. Chest 116:296–300, 1999.

149. Kress JP, Noth I, Gehlbach BK, et al: The utility of albuterol nebulized with heliox during acute asthma exacerbations. Am J Respir Crit Care Med 165:1317–1321, 2002.

150. Rose JS, Panacek EA, Miller P: Prospective randomized trial of heliox-driven continuous nebulizers in the treatment of asthma in the emergency department. J Emerg Med 22:133–137, 2002.

151. Henderson SO, Acharya P, Kilaghbian T, et al: Use of heliox-driven nebulizer therapy in the treatment of acute asthma. Ann Emerg Med 33:141–146, 1999.

152. Rodrigo G, Pollack C, Rodrigo C, et al: Heliox for nonintubated acute asthma patients. Cochrane Database Syst Rev. 2003;(4):CD002884.

153. Meduri GU, Cook TR, Turner RE, et al: Noninvasive positive pressure ventilation in status asthmaticus. Chest 110:767–774, 1996.

154. Fernandez MM, Villagra A, Blanch L, et al: Non-invasive mechanical ventilation in status asthmaticus. Intensive Care Med 27:486–492, 2001.

155. Holley MT, Morrissey TK, Seaberg DC, et al: Ethical dilemmas in a randomized trial of asthma treatment: Can bayesian statistical analysis explain the results? Acad Emerg Med 8:1128–1135, 2001.

156. Soroksky A, Stav D, Shpirer I: A pilot prospective, randomized, placebo-controlled trial of bilevel positive airway pressure in acute asthmatic attack. Chest 123:1018–1025, 2003.

157. Afessa B, Morales I, Cury JD: Clinical course and outcome of patients admitted to an ICU for status asthmaticus. Chest 120:1616–1621, 2001.

158. Anzueto A, Frutos-Vivar F, Esteban A, et al: Incidence, risk factors and outcome of barotrauma in mechanically ventilated patients. Intensive Care Med 30:612–619, 2004.

159. Zimmerman JL, Dellinger RP, Shah AN, et al: Endotracheal intubation and mechanical ventilation in severe asthma. Crit Care Med 21:1727–1730, 1993.

160. Levy BD, Kitch B, Fanta CH: Medical and ventilatory management of status asthmaticus. Intensive Care Med 24:105–117, 1998.

161. Bigatello LM, Patroniti N, Sangalli F: Permissive hypercapnia. Curr Opin Crit Care 7:34–40, 2001.

162. Hickling KG: Permissive hypercapnia. Respir Care Clin North Am 8:155–169, 2002.

163. Darioli R, Perret C: Mechanical controlled hypoventilation in status asthmaticus. Am Rev Respir Dis 129:385–387, 1984.

164. Leatherman JW, Ravenscraft SA: Low measured auto-positive end-expiratory pressure during mechanical ventilation of patients with severe asthma: Hidden auto-positive end-expiratory pressure. Crit Care Med 24:541–546, 1996.

165. Mutlu GM, Factor P, Schwartz DE, et al: Severe status asthmaticus: Management with permissive hypercapnia and inhalation anesthesia. Crit Care Med 30:477–480, 2002.

166. O'Quin RJ, Lakshminarayan S: Venous air embolism. Arch Intern Med 142:2173–2176, 1982.

167. Souders JE: Pulmonary air embolism. J Clin Monit Comput 16:375–383, 2000.

168. Russell GB, Graybeal JM: Detection of venous air embolism: Comparison of oxygenation and ventilation monitoring methods in dogs. Neurosurg Anesthesiol 4:36–40, 1992.

169. Maitre B, Habibi A, Roudot-Thoraval F, et al: Acute chest syndrome in adults with sickle cell disease. Chest 117:1386–1392, 2000.

87 Care at the End of Life for Patients with Respiratory Failure

John M. Luce, M.D.

INTRODUCTION

Patients with acute, chronic, and acute-on-chronic respiratory failure often suffer from symptoms such as pain and dyspnea, and they manifest a high mortality. These patients may be aggressively treated when they, their families, and their physicians believe that the patients' health and quality of life can be restored. Nevertheless, treatment goals at the end of life generally should be more palliative than restorative. In keeping with this approach, therapies such as mechanical ventilation, which can reverse respiratory failure in patients with acute decompensation, may be forgone for the terminally ill. When clinically appropriate, the withholding and withdrawal of life-sustaining therapy is supported by ethical and legal principles. These principles, along with the process of medical decision-making and the desirable components of end-of-life care, are discussed in detail in this chapter.

THE BURDEN OF RESPIRATORY FAILURE

Respiratory failure is characterized by inadequate ventilation, inadequate oxygenation, or both (see Chapter 84). These inadequacies are reflected in increased systemic arterial carbon dioxide tension (PCO_2), decreased systemic arterial oxygen tension (PO_2), or a combination of the two. Acute respiratory failure may be caused by conditions such as pneumonia and the acute respiratory distress syndrome (ARDS). Chronic respiratory failure may be due to chronic obstructive pulmonary disease (COPD), lung cancer, and other disorders. Many patients are healthy and feel well before they develop acute respiratory failure. In contrast, most patients with chronic respiratory failure experience progressively more severe symptoms as their pulmonary function declines.[1-3] Their downhill course often is punctuated by acute exacerbations (acute-on-chronic respiratory failure) caused either by worsening of their primary disorder or by superimposed secondary illnesses such as pneumonia.[4]

Respiratory failure and the diseases responsible for it are a major cause of death throughout the world. For example, of the 2,337,256 people who were known to have died during 1998 in the United States, 154,972 (6.6%) did so because of malignant neoplasms of the lungs, trachea, bronchi, or pleura. Another 117,966 people (5.1%) died because of COPD and related conditions; and 64,144 (2.7%) did so because of pneumonia or influenza. These data from the Division of Vital Statistics of the Department of Health and Human Services were derived from death certificates containing International Classification of Diseases, Ninth Revision (ICD-9) codes for the underlying cause of death.[5,6] Deaths attributable to ARDS are more difficult to identify because a specific ICD-9 code is lacking for this condition, and death due to ARDS may be attributed to pneumonia or other disorders. Nevertheless, ARDS probably accounted for approximately 25,000 deaths in the United States in 1998.[7]

Respiratory failure and the diseases that cause it are associated with considerable morbidity as well as mortality. This association was demonstrated by the Study to Understand Prognoses and Preferences for Seriously Ill Hospitalized Patients (SUPPORT).[8] The SUPPORT study was based on a large cohort of hospitalized adult patients with at least one of nine conditions, including pneumonia, ARDS, COPD, and stage III or stage IV non-small cell lung cancer. Many SUPPORT patients with acute respiratory failure due to pneumonia or ARDS had normal physiologic function and enjoyed a good quality of life before hospitalization. Yet they had an in-hospital death rate of 42%, and another 11% died within 1 year after discharge. Dying patients who were in an intensive care unit (ICU) spent an average of 9 days on a mechanical ventilator, most with severe pain and confusion, according to their families.[9] Of the ventilated patients who survived hospitalization and lived to 6 months, 29% rated their quality of life as only fair or poor.[10]

Regarding the impact of chronic respiratory failure on morbidity and mortality, SUPPORT demonstrated that an exacerbation of COPD among patients with an arterial PCO_2 of 50 mm Hg or more on hospital admission was associated with an in-hospital death rate of 11% and a 1-year mortality rate of 43%.[11] The families of patients who died in the hospital reported that their relatives generally experienced intense pain and dyspnea. Most of the patients who survived hospitalization were dyspneic for the rest of their lives, and their quality of life generally was poor.[12] Of SUPPORT patients with advanced non-small cell lung cancer, 16% died during hospitalization, and an additional 42% did so in the following year. Suffering was commonplace among lung cancer patients during death in the hospital; those patients who were discharged demonstrated a progressive loss of function and an increase in symptoms as death approached.[13]

PREDICTING THE OUTCOME OF RESPIRATORY FAILURE

The prevalence of diseases that cause respiratory failure, coupled with the morbidity and mortality they produce, has prompted clinicians and investigators alike to seek prognostic information about patients with these disorders. Some of this prognostic information has been derived from single- or multi-institutional studies of specific conditions such as COPD,[14] *Pneumocystis* pneumonia in patients with the acquired immunodeficiency syndrome (AIDS),[15] and ARDS.[16,17] Other information has come from studies of certain age groups, such as the elderly,[18] or from studies of interventions, such as mechanical ventilation.[19,20] These studies in turn have been used to develop tools to predict not only patient outcome but also the need for admission to the ICU for diseases such as pneumonia.[21,22]

Additional information has been obtained from the use of prognostic scoring systems based largely on physiological variables such as arterial PCO_2 and arterial PO_2 recorded on hospital admission or other occasions. Although many of these systems were developed specifically for patients in ICUs, where physiological variables are routinely measured, they also have been applied to patients elsewhere. Perhaps the best known prognostic scoring system is the Acute

Physiology and Chronic Health Evaluation (APACHE), which has gone through three iterations, the most recent of which is proprietary.[23–25] The prognostic system developed for SUPPORT is similar to APACHE. It was based on patient diagnosis, age, number of days in the hospital before study entry, presence of cancer, neurologic function, and 11 physiological variables recorded on day 3 of study entry.[26]

Prognosis based on the experience of individual clinicians or institutions is necessarily limited; and despite wide use, it has never been subjected to rigorous evaluation. Although prognostication based on broader investigations of specific diseases should be more accurate, the changing outcome from *Pneumocystis* pneumonia,[27] ARDS,[28] and other conditions over time limits the use of these investigations in predicting outcome unless they are frequently repeated. Furthermore, the tools based on these studies that may be used to determine the need for intensive care for pneumonia and other diseases have limited predictive value, presumably in part because the outcome from these conditions has changed.[29,30]

Physiologically based prognostic scoring systems have been shown to be as accurate (or inaccurate) as clinical assessment by physicians and nurses.[31] They also have demonstrated good calibration in that the overall hospital mortality predicted by the systems is comparable to that actually observed in research studies. Nevertheless, the systems have not discriminated well between individual survivors and nonsurvivors.[32] For example, recommended prediction criteria were not effective in identifying a SUPPORT population with a survival prognosis of 6 months or less, limiting their use in determining which patients might generally meet hospice eligibility requirements.[33] Furthermore, the median predicted likelihood of survival for 2 months on the day before actual death was 17%, and it was 51% one week before death among patients using the SUPPORT prognostic system, indicating how poorly the system could predict death shortly before it occurred.[34]

Prognostic scoring systems have contributed greatly to our understanding of the general outcomes of patients with respiratory failure and other conditions. Furthermore, the calibration and discriminatory power of the systems may improve as more studies of the systems are performed and more patients are entered into their databases. Yet at present the systems are imperfect in predicting outcome in individual patients. For the foreseeable future, therefore, the use of prognostic scoring systems should continue to be adjunctive in that they provide information for medical decision-making but cannot be used by themselves to decide who is destined to die despite intensive care.[35]

TREATMENT GOALS AT THE END OF LIFE

The limitations of prognostication are unfortunate because patients' and their families' predictions of prognosis largely determine their treatment preferences, just as physicians often base their recommendations to patients and families on how long they expect the patients to live. Presumably because their quality of life was good and their deaths were not anticipated prior to becoming ill, SUPPORT patients with acute respiratory failure due to pneumonia and ARDS and their families and physicians generally preferred life-sustaining therapies until death appeared imminent.[9] In contrast, SUPPORT patients with advanced COPD and lung cancer usually preferred care that was focused on their comfort rather than extending their lives when they were hospitalized.[36] These preferences were related primarily to the patients' perceptions of how far advanced their underlying conditions were. For example, patients with lung cancer who thought they were going to live at least 6 months after being hospitalized were more likely to favor life-sustaining treatment over comfort care than patients who thought they had at least a 10% chance of dying within the next 6 months.[37]

The SUPPORT data suggest that as patients with respiratory failure become more symptomatic and perceive that death is near, they, their families, and their physicians become interested less in therapies that improve physiological function and prolong life than in those that ease suffering and provide a peaceful and dignified death. Of course, these treatment goals are neither distinctly different nor mutually exclusive: Life support and symptom relief often are sought simultaneously. Nevertheless, inside and outside the ICU, the emphasis often changes from restorative to palliative care among patients at the end of life. This change was described as "the transition from cure to comfort" in the title of the first published textbook on end-of-life care in the ICU.[38]

The term *end-of-life care* is meant to encompass two processes. One, the withholding and withdrawal of life support, represents the tapering of life-sustaining interventions such as pulmonary rehabilitation in the outpatient setting and mechanical ventilation in the ICU.[39–42] The other, the administration of palliative treatment, applies, among other things, to improving patient comfort through the giving of sedatives and analgesics. Combining these two processes signifies that end-of-life care involves more than removing something—in this case, life-saving treatments—from patients. It also means giving something to them: proper medical decision-making; thoughtful communication; an appreciation of their needs and those of their families, physicians, and other caregivers; the use of an appropriate setting for death; and the management of pain, dyspnea, and other symptoms. This comprehensive and compassionate approach is what is meant by the expression, "intensive caring at the end of life."[43]

WHERE AND HOW DEATH OCCURS

Most patients with respiratory failure who die in undeveloped countries do so at home largely because they have limited access to hospitals and other institutional settings. In the United States and other developed nations, however, death increasingly occurs outside the home. For example, of the large cohort of hospitalized patients in SUPPORT, 46% died within 6 months of study enrollment, and 55% of these deaths occurred during the enrollment hospitalization. Of the patients who survived the enrollment hospitalization, 46% died during hospitalization later that year, and only a minority died in a nursing home or hospice, let alone at home.[44] Similarly, in a recent investigation[45] of all the deaths recorded in six states during 1999, 38% occurred in hospitals and 22% occurred following ICU admission. Using

these data to project national estimates, the investigators concluded that 540,000—fully one fifth—of all patients who die in the United States do so in ICUs each year.

Many factors account for the prevalence of in-hospital and in-ICU deaths in the United States and presumably other developed countries. Among them are the availability of these facilities and the physicians who admit patients to them and the fact that increasingly fewer elderly persons still reside with their families. In the United States, patients must be determined to have fewer than 6 months to live to qualify for hospice placement, but it is difficult to predict with accuracy which patients have such a limited life expectancy. Most patients want to live as long as possible unless life is a burden to them and their families, and most physicians want to use all the means at their disposal to prolong life. Given these factors and the limits of prognostication, it is understandable that many patients with respiratory failure die in hospitals and ICUs, not in hospices or at home.

When ICUs were first developed during the 1950s and 1960s in the United States and Europe, patients who died in them did so despite full support, including attempted cardiopulmonary resuscitation (CPR). The wishes of patients and their surrogates regarding such support rarely were solicited, and do-not-attempt-resuscitation (DNAR) orders rarely were written for the patients because most hospitals felt obligated to perform CPR on everyone. Indeed, a host of potentially restorative treatments were automatically provided with little concern about their effectiveness or desirability. This approach was based on the belief, held by both health professionals and the public, that technologies should be used to preserve life whenever possible regardless of the human and economic costs.[46]

In recent years, however, the "technologic imperative" has been challenged, just as the expenses of the ICU have been scrutinized.[47] CPR has been shown to be ineffective in hospitalized patients in several studies.[48,49] Similarly, SUPPORT[8] has demonstrated that many seriously ill patients never leave the hospital alive or do so only after prolonged pain and suffering. Patients have been found not to prefer attempted restorative therapy in all instances, and courts in the United States have declared that these patients have a "right to die."[50] The ethical, legal, and economic consensus that has resulted from these developments has been reflected in a series of statements[51–54] from professional societies on the appropriateness of forgoing life-sustaining therapies at the end of life. As a result, although hospitalized patients once died despite attempted restorative treatment, they are more likely to die today during the withholding and withdrawal of life support and the administration of palliative care, especially in the ICU.[40–42,55]

ETHICAL AND LEGAL JUSTIFICATION FOR END-OF-LIFE CARE

JUSTIFICATION FOR WITHHOLDING AND WITHDRAWING LIFE-SUSTAINING THERAPY

The withholding and withdrawal of life support is justified by three ethical principles. The first principle is beneficence: the physicians' obligation to do good for patients. The

Table 87.1 Ethical (Worldwide) and Legal (United States) Principles For Withholding and Withdrawing Life-Sustaining Therapy

Ethical Principles
Beneficence
Nonmaleficence
Autonomy

Legal Principle: Right of Informed Consent and Refusal

Exercised by Patients With Decision-Making Capacity

Exercised by Family Members for Incapacitated Patients
   As authorized under proxy directives
   Using a substituted judgment standard (facilitated by instructional directives)
   Using a best interests standard

Exercised by a Court-Appointed Conservator
   Using a substituted judgment standard (facilitated by instructional directives)
   Using a best interests standard

Exercised by Physicians, Ideally After Ethics Committee Review
   Using a substituted judgment standard (facilitated by instructional directives) (legal justification in a few states)
   Using a best interests standard (no legal justification)
   Based on physiologic or medical futility (no legal justification)

From Beauchamp TL, Childress JF: Principles of Biomedical Ethics (4th ed). Oxford: Oxford University Press, 1994 and Luce JM, Alpers A: End-of-life care: What do the American courts say? Crit Care Med 29:N40–N45, 2001.

second is nonmaleficence: the physicians' obligation to avoid harm. The third principle is autonomy: respect for the patients' right of self-determination[56] (Table 87.1). These principles are the basis of the fiduciary relationship through which physicians serve their patients' interests above their own and hold these interests in trust.[57] Although the relative importance of the three ethical principles varies from country to country, the fiduciary relationship remains much the same.

In the United States, the withholding and withdrawal of life-sustaining therapies is justified legally by the principles of informed consent and refusal, which have strong roots in common law.[58,59] The right of adults who are capable of making medical decisions either to consent to or to refuse treatment was first established in *Schloendorff v. Society of New York Hospitals* in 1914.[60] In this case, the Court of Appeal of New York declared that "Every being of adult years and sound mind has the right to determine what should be done with his own body; and a surgeon who performs an operation without his patient's consent commits an assault, for which he is liable in damages, except in cases of emergency when the patient is unconscious or when it is necessary to operate before consent can be obtained."

The right of adults with decision-making capacity to refuse treatment was furthered in cases such as *Bartling v. Superior Court*[61] and *Bouvia v. Superior Court*[62] in California. In the first of these cases, the Court of Appeals allowed a man with advanced COPD to have a mechanical ventilator removed against the wishes of his physicians and the hospital where he was being treated. In the second, the appeals court ordered a hospital to stop force-feeding a quadriple-

gic woman against her will even though she might die in the process. Most states have dealt with similar cases, and the principle that adults with capacity can refuse unwanted therapies is now widely accepted.

As SUPPORT[8] and other studies[40,41] have shown, many critically ill patients cannot make medical decisions because they are sick and sedated. In this circumstance, family members and other surrogates, if available, may consent to or refuse treatment for them. Parents have a long-standing right, indeed obligation, to speak for their dependent children. The legal right of surrogates to act for incapacitated adult patients was established in *In re Quinlan*[63] in which the Supreme Court of New Jersey allowed the parents of a vegetative patient to refuse mechanical ventilation for their daughter under the principle of substituted judgment. Under this principle, family members also were allowed to make life-determining decisions for their adult relative in *Barber v. Superior Court*[64] in California. In this case, the court determined not only that mechanical ventilation but also that nutrition and hydration—indeed, any therapy that was not clearly benefiting the patient—could be forgone.

The U.S. Supreme Court dealt with the issue of substituted judgment in the case of *Cruzan v. Director, Missouri Department of Health*.[65] In this case, a family argued that it was unconstitutional for a chronic care facility in Missouri to deny their request to remove a feeding tube from their vegetative adult daughter. The facility argued that the daughter had not specified her wishes not to be fed artificially in advance of incapacity. The Supreme Court allowed Missouri and other states to require "clear and convincing evidence" of patients' prior wishes before care was forgone for them in its *Cruzan* decision. Nevertheless, it did not demand this requirement of other states, and it accepted the argument that the right of adult patients with decision-making capacity to refuse any and all therapies was protected under the Constitution.

Although substituted judgment is the highest standard under which surrogates may make medical decisions for incapacitated patients, surrogates also may consider the patients' best interests. One delineation of a best interests standard is that of the New Jersey Supreme Court relative to *In re Conroy*.[66] In this case, a nephew asked that a feeding tube be withdrawn from his elderly aunt, who had not declared her wishes before becoming demented, on the grounds that forgoing nutrition and hydration was in her best interests. The court would allow the best interests standard in this case only because the burdens of the patients' life with treatment outweighed the benefits of continuing life, and because the recurring, unavoidable pain of life with treatment was such that administering therapies such as nutrition and hydration was inhumane.

Another legal perspective on the best interests standard came in the case of *Wendland v. Wendland*.[67] This case involved a middle-aged man who was conscious but hemiplegic, uncommunicative, and unable to feed himself after a motor vehicle accident. After his feeding tube repeatedly became dislodged, his wife, who was his conservator, refused to authorize its reinsertion. In support of her decision, she cited her husband's statements prior to his accident that he would not want to live in a severely debilitated condition. At this point, his mother went to court to block the plan not to reinsert the feeding tube, and it was reinserted. Mr. Wendland subsequently died, but the California Supreme Court deliberated on the issue of whether a conservator could withhold or withdraw life support from a patient who was conscious but incapable of articulating his current wishes. The Court ultimately ruled that feedings could be discontinued only if there was clear and convincing evidence that "the patient wished to refuse life-sustaining treatment or that to withhold such treatment would have been in his best interest," which was not thought to be true of Mr. Wendland. The decision in his case suggests that the courts are unlikely to allow surrogates to limit treatment in patients who are neither terminally ill nor severely neurologically impaired on the basis of a best interests standard unless the patients have specified what they would want done in such a situation.[68]

Legal guidelines are less clear when incapacitated patients lack family members or other surrogates. Some states (e.g., Hawaii, Connecticut) allow physicians to make decisions for such patients based on wishes expressed to the physicians when the patients had decision-making capacity. However, no state explicitly allows physicians to make decisions based on a best interests standard. Be that as it may, some physicians do make decisions to withhold or withdraw life-sustaining therapy from incapacitated patients, usually after consultation with their colleagues or with a hospital ethics committee, on the basis of best interests.[69] Others ask the probate court to appoint conservators or other advocates for the patients, presumably under the unproven assumption that such advocates can determine what is in the patients' interests better than physicians can.

The U.S. Congress supported patient autonomy and the substituted judgment standard by passing the Patient Self-Determination Act. This statute mandates that patients be asked on admission to medical facilities whether they have advance directives and that they be assisted in drawing up directives if they do not already have them.[70] Advance directives are of two types: instructional directives that articulate what patients want done in a given situation (e.g., living wills) and proxy directives that appoint surrogates to make decisions for them in these situations (e.g., the durable power of attorney for health care). SUPPORT has shown that most hospitalized patients have not filled out advance directives, that many physicians are not aware of the directives when they have been filled out, and that the directives have little impact on decision-making or the use of hospital resources.[71–73] Nevertheless, advance directives remain potential ways of reinforcing patient autonomy, even though this potential has not been realized.[74]

Before leaving the subject of justification for withholding and withdrawing life support, it is important to mention that decisions regarding this process are different in brain-dead patients than they are in patients who have lesser degrees of neurologic impairment. In the United States, death is defined as the total and irreversible loss either of cardiopulmonary function or of the function of the entire brain.[75] The determination of death by whole-brain criteria requires the demonstration of coma indicating the loss of cerebral hemispheric function; and the documentation of absent corneal, oculovestibular, and ventilatory reflexes, indicating loss of function of the brain stem. Absence of ventilatory reflexes is demonstrated by apnea testing, in which intubated patients are given oxygen through anesthesia bags and then observed for respiratory muscle efforts while they are not mechanically ventilated and their arterial PCO_2 rises to at least 60 mm Hg.

Formal declaration of brain death is not required when life-sustaining therapy is forgone for most patients because patients do not need to be dead before such therapy is forgone. On the other hand, some surrogates may insist that therapy be continued until patients die, in which case determining death by whole-brain criteria may be desirable. That said, the only patients in whom brain death must be determined are those who seem to be dead and whose organs will be transplanted after life support is withheld or withdrawn. Regarding the latter patients, one might argue that withdrawing life support from someone who is dead is an oxymoron. Because of this argument, and because brain-dead patients usually receive mechanical ventilation and other interventions only until their organs can be harvested, "life support" for them has been likened to "organ support."

The ethical and legal justification for removing therapies from brain-dead patients is not just that the therapies generally are unwanted by patients and surrogates in this situation but also that the patients are dead and cannot benefit from them. Inasmuch as the patients are dead, physicians have no obligation to treat them, and they do not need to obtain consent from surrogates before withholding or withdrawing treatment. Nevertheless, consent is required for organ retrieval and transplantation. Furthermore, the families of brain-dead patients frequently do not understand the concept of brain death and consider the patients to be alive because their chests rise and fall as the ventilator cycles and a tracing of their cardiac rhythms is displayed on the bedside monitor.

Motivated by consideration for such families and by a desire to gain their consent for organ donation, many physicians are appropriately nonconfrontational in addressing the issue of brain death. They take time to explain what death means in a biologic and legal sense, how brain death is determined, and how valuable transplantation may be not only to organ recipients but also to the families of patients who serve as organ donors, if not to the patients themselves. This approach generally is helpful to families, regardless of whether it ends in their approving transplantation. It also is useful in maintaining emotional equilibrium during a difficult time for all parties in the ICU.[76]

MEDICAL FUTILITY

Although the ethical principle of autonomy and the legal principles of informed consent and refusal are the most compelling justifications for withholding and withdrawing life support, the concept of futility also has been used as a justification. This concept is invoked on the relatively rare occasions when patients or their surrogates request interventions (particularly those that are costly, scarce, or both) that physicians object to because they believe the patients cannot benefit from them.[77] Some treatments, such as brain transplantation for patients who are brain-dead, are physiologically futile in that they cannot be accomplished. Other treatments, such as the administration of vasopressors to raise blood pressure, can succeed physiologically, but some physicians may consider them medically futile because they cannot prolong life indefinitely or improve its quality in patients whose life expectancy is short and whose quality of life is poor.

One group of investigators[78] sought to define medical futility as an intervention that has been useless in the last 100 cases or that "merely preserves unconsciousness and cannot end dependence on intensive medical care." In a similar vein, the American Thoracic Society[54] argued that "a life-sustaining intervention may be withheld or withdrawn from a patient without the consent of the patient or surrogate if the intervention is judged to be futile. A life-sustaining intervention is futile if reasoning and experience indicate that the intervention would be highly unlikely to result in a meaningful survival for that patient. Here, meaningful survival specifically refers to a quality or duration of survival that would have value to that patient as an individual. Survival in a state with permanent lack of consciousness (i.e., completely lacking cognitive and sentient capacity) may be generally regarded as having no value for such a patient."

Despite what has been called the "futility movement," a broad concept of futility has never achieved consensus within the medical community in the United States or elsewhere.[79] As one group of investigators[80] noted, "Rather than being a discrete and definable entity, futile therapy is merely the end of the spectrum of therapies with very low efficacy." In some ways, the development of prognostic scoring systems can be seen as an attempt to predict which patients cannot benefit from therapies with very low efficacy, especially those that are expensive, and thereby provide a rationale for denying such therapies to them.[81] Yet most patients and families are quite willing to forgo such therapies even when physicians are not, as indicated by SUPPORT.[8] Furthermore, a study[82] of the theoretical implementation of a strict futility guideline among over 4000 SUPPORT patients demonstrated that only minimal cost savings could be realized by not treating patients who were predicted to have a 1% or less 2-month survival. Nearly 75% of the savings in hospital days would have resulted from stopping treatment for 12 patients, one half of whom were under 51 years of age and one of whom lived 10 months when treatment was continued.

The emphasis on cost savings in the aforementioned study speaks to the fact that arguments about futility often have economic overtones. At one time it appeared that American society could transition from a "rule of rescue," in which large sums of money were spent on therapies providing only marginal benefit, to a "rule of reason," in which this money could be used for primary and preventive care.[83] Yet health care reform failed in the United States, and managed care has become identified as a tool for increasing corporate profits by denying medical services.[84] Arguments based on futility seem to provide a rationale for forgoing treatment on the grounds that it is not worthwhile, apart from the matter of cost. Yet these arguments conceal value-laden assumptions, and they obscure the underlying issue of rationing.[85] American physicians lack a social mandate to perform such rationing, a fact that is overlooked when they invoke futility.

Thus, the greatest problem with medical futility is not how it is defined but who defines it.[86] In this regard, the debate over futility pits physicians, who believe that their training and experience enables them to know what therapies are truly useful and cost-effective, against patients and families, who feel entitled to such therapies regardless of whether they pay for them directly. Physicians certainly are able to identify physiological futility, and they are not legally or ethically required to perform procedures they consider nonbeneficial and below professional standards. Benefit, however, seems often to be in the eyes of the beholder: Although physicians may regard mere prolongation of life as undesirable in certain circumstances, patients and families may consider it valuable. When these persons want treatments that physicians consider futile in more than a physiological sense, which party should decide?

The American Medical Association Council on Ethical and Judicial Affairs has stated that, "Since definitions of futile care are value laden, universal consensus on futile care is unlikely to be achieved."[87] At the same time, the Council has recommended a process-based approach to futility determinations whereby patients or families who insisted on therapies physicians considered futile would be required to undergo a dispute resolution process. Central to this process would be mediation by a hospital ethics committee. If resolution was not reached through mediation, the patients would be transferred to another institution, or care would be terminated if transfer were impossible. So-called futility policies based on this model have been developed in Houston, Texas and other cities.[88]

Recently, the State of Texas adopted a law providing an extrajudicial due process mechanism for resolving medical futility disputes based on the Houston experience.[89] Although this mechanism apparently has been workable at one hospital, where few futility disputes actually have occurred, no study of the Texas law's statewide impact has been conducted. Furthermore, the constitutionality of the Texas statute has not been determined at the appellate or U.S. Supreme Court level. As a result, the implications of the Texas statute for that state and for the rest of the United States are unclear.

To date, legal cases such as *In re Helen Wanglie*[90] and *In the Matter of Baby K*[91] suggest that judges are unwilling to allow physicians to withhold or withdraw support from patients when the physicians ask to do so in advance and the patients or families object. In the first of these cases, a court in Minneapolis refused to replace a husband who was seeking continued life support for his wife, which her physicians considered nonbeneficial, with another conservator who might allow support to be forgone. In the second, a Virginia court required that physicians repeatedly resuscitate an anencephalic infant at the request of its mother but against their own wishes, reasoning that to do otherwise would violate the Emergency Medical Treatment and Active Labor Act.

In contrast, the case of *Gilgunn v. Massachusetts General Hospital*[92] indicates that physicians are likely to obtain legal results more to their liking when they refuse to provide care they consider futile and defend their decisions in court as consistent with professional standards. In this case, a jury in Boston exonerated physicians at Massachusetts General Hospital for removing a patient from life support and writing a DNAR order for her over the objections of her daughter. The patient's husband and other children did not protest the physicians' actions, and the jury apparently believed that the physicians acted within the standard of care. This case does not set legal precedent because a written judgment was not rendered. Nevertheless, the jury decision in *Gilgunn* suggests some public support for the concept of futility.

How the debate over futility will be resolved is uncertain. Because patient autonomy is so widely accepted in the United States, because national health insurance does not exist there, and because patients and families are suspicious of managed care organizations, it seems unlikely that American physicians will soon be granted a mandate to restrict services on the basis of futility. This is not the case in other countries, however, where resources are limited, national health insurance exists, and physicians implicitly and explicitly are allowed to ration care.[93] Whether physicians will continue to exercise this and other prerogatives as American-style patient autonomy becomes more prevalent in their countries remains to be seen.

JUSTIFICATION FOR ADMINISTERING PALLIATIVE CARE

One reason that the concept of futility remains unresolved in the United States is that the Supreme Court has not dealt with this issue. Nevertheless, the Court has provided ethical and legal justification for the administration of palliative care at the end of life, as in the cases of *Washington v. Glucksberg*[94] and *Vacco v. Quill*.[95] These cases dealt with the constitutionality of laws prohibiting physician-assisted suicide in the states of Washington and New York. In *Glucksberg*, the Court decided that terminally ill patients do not have a liberty interest in committing suicide or in receiving a physician's assistance in committing suicide because of both the long tradition of prohibiting suicide in the United States and the states' legitimate interest for continuing to make suicide illegal. In *Vacco*, it distinguished between assisted suicide and withholding and withdrawal of life support. "Everyone, regardless of physical condition, is entitled, if competent, to refuse lifesaving medical treatment; no one is permitted to assist a suicide," the Court wrote. "When a patient refuses life-sustaining medical treatment, he dies from an underlying fatal disease or pathology; but if a patient ingests lethal medicine prescribed by a physician, he is killed by that medication."

In *Glucksberg* and *Vacco*, five justices reasoned that Washington and New York could prohibit assisted suicide because these states had no barriers that prevented patients from receiving medications to relieve pain and suffering. However, as Justice Breyer wrote, "Were state laws to prevent the provision of palliative care, including the administration of drugs as needed to avoid pain at the end of life, an action against such law might be called for by the Supreme Court." Through this and other statements, a majority of the justices suggested that being free of pain while dying was a liberty interest protected under the Constitution.[96]

The Supreme Court distinguished assisted suicide from palliative care in *Glucksberg* and *Vacco* by accepting the ethical principle of double effect. Under this rule, acts such as giving sedatives and analgesics that lead to morally good effects, such as the relief of suffering, are permissible even if they produce morally bad effects, such as the hastening of death, provided that only the good effect is intended. The morally bad effect may be forseen in that physicians are aware of its possibility and even its likelihood, but they may not wish that it occur. The bad effect also may not be a means to the good effect, and the good effect must outweigh the bad one; that is, risking death is reasonable in palliating a terminally ill patient only if there are no less risky ways of relieving suffering.[97]

The Supreme Court's approval of palliative care included sanctioning the practice of *terminal sedation*, in which patients are rendered unconscious, after which life-sustaining therapies, including nutrition and hydration, are withdrawn. Under *Vacco*, a state may allow terminal sedation if it is "based on informed consent and the double effect. Just as a state may prohibit assisted suicide while permitting patients to refuse unwanted lifesaving treatment, it may permit palliative care related to that refusal, which may have the foreseen but unintended 'double effect' of hastening the patient's death."

Some[98] have argued that the rule of double effect has many shortcomings as an ethical guideline, in particular because it overlooks the complexity of human intention. Such complexity was demonstrated in a study[99] of the administration of sedatives and analgesics during the withholding and withdrawal of life support in two ICUs. In this study, physicians indicated that they ordered these agents primarily to decrease pain, anxiety, and dyspnea—but also to hasten death—in 39% of critically ill patients. In another investigation,[100] 16% of a sample of ICU nurses reported that they had engaged in assisted suicide or euthanasia while trying to relieve patient suffering, often without physicians' knowledge.

Just as some physicians and nurses have mixed motives in caring for dying patients, so do some family members want to ease suffering and hasten death simultaneously in their relatives. That such motivation is widespread presumably accounts for the fact that few physicians who are suspected of participating in assisted suicide or euthanasia have been punished through the criminal justice system in the United States.[101] In general, physicians and other caregivers are unlikely to be prosecuted or even criticized if they act compassionately in administering sedatives and analgesics to dying patients and do so with informed consent.

The Supreme Court did not judge the laws prohibiting physician-assisted suicide in Washington and New York to be unconstitutional in *Glucksberg* and *Vacco*, but it also did not prevent other states from permitting this practice. Physician-assisted suicide was legalized in Oregon in 1997 under that state's Death with Dignity Act. Experience over the subsequent 2 years indicated that few patients requested lethal medications, that physicians granted few requests, and that palliative interventions led some, but not all, patients to change their minds about assisted suicide.[102] By and large, the decision to request and use a prescription for lethal medication stemmed from patients' concern about loss of autonomy or control of bodily functions, not from fear of intractable pain or financial loss.[103,104]

Although the Death with Dignity Act has not been abused, the U.S. Congress and the Bush administration have tried to overturn it. In 1999, Congress considered a so-called Pain Relief Promotion Act, which would have amended the federal Controlled Substance Act, a law designed to prevent drug abuse and drug trafficking within the United States. This amendment "to promote pain relief and palliative care without permitting assisted suicide and euthanasia" would have interfered with Oregon's law had it not died in Congress. In 2001, Attorney General John Ashcroft ruled that the Death with Dignity Act violated the Controlled Substance Act and authorized the Drug Enforcement Administration to take action against Oregon physicians who prescribe lethal medications. This directive was blocked, however, by a U.S. District Court Judge. As a result, physician-assisted suicide remains legal in Oregon. The U.S. Supreme Court may ultimately decide the fate of that state's Death with Dignity Act.[105]

Physician-assisted suicide and euthanasia are practiced in several European countries.[106] Although none of these countries has legalized the practices, physicians in The Netherlands have not been punished for performing them since 1991, when a national study[107] revealed that assisted suicide and euthanasia were being performed. Instead, Dutch physicians are required to report all cases in which they administered or supplied drugs with the explicit intent of hastening death. Patient requests for assisted suicide or euthanasia rose from 8900 in 1990 to 9700 in 1995 and remained stable at 9700 in 2001, according to a recent study.[108] Assisted suicide was listed as the cause of death on only 0.2% of all death certificates in The Netherlands during the same years. In 1990, 64% of Dutch physicians thought that patients have a right to decide about their own life or death; the percentage of physicians was the same in 1995 but fell to 56% in 2001. These data suggest that, in the Netherlands as in Oregon, the demand for assisted suicide has not increased; in fact, over time, Dutch physicians appear to have grown more reluctant in their attitude toward this practice. How common assisted suicide will become in other European countries and how their laws will deal with these practices is unclear.

MEDICAL DECISION-MAKING AT THE END OF LIFE

TWO MODELS OF THE PHYSICIAN-PATIENT RELATIONSHIP

Medical decisions may be made by physicians, patients, their families, or other surrogates alone or in combination. How decisions are actually made depends in large part on the model of the physician-patient relationship that is used. Perhaps the oldest model is *paternalistic;* this model also has been called parental or priestly. According to it, physicians using superior knowledge and experience act as guardians in defining what their patients' interests are and then serving these interests as they see fit, with little or no input from the patients themselves.[109] With pediatric patients, the families' input similarly might not be sought or might be disregarded. The paternalistic model overlooks patient autonomy and is supported primarily by the ethical principles of beneficence and nonmaleficence: acting to benefit patients and to avoid harm.

Another model of the physician-patient relationship is the *deliberative* one. Under this model, physicians help patients define their best interests, provide treatment alternatives through which the interests can be served, and assist the patients in deciding which alternative is best. With pediatric patients, families decide what the patients' interests are and how best to serve them with the physicians' assistance. This process is more than the mere passing of information: a moral deliberation, based on a mutual understanding of patients' wishes and values, is pursued. Physicians functioning under the deliberative model serve as teachers, not guardians as they do under the paternalistic model.[109] The deliberative model is a model of shared decision-making. It is supported primarily by the ethical principle of autonomy: respect for the patients' right of self-determination.

The paternalistic model is particularly well suited to decision-making in emergency situations wherein time is of the essence, patients may be unable to communicate, and their consent for treatment is considered to be implied because most of them presumably would want to be treated in emergencies. The deliberative model is best suited for situations in which physicians, patients, and families have ample time to discuss alternatives, extensive communication is possible, and consent can be informed. Consent can only be informed if patients or their surrogates are competent to make decisions, are provided with information relevant to their situation, can ask questions, and can act voluntarily.[110]

The paternalistic model once dominated medical decision-making at the end of life in the United States. In fact, the early cases such as *Bartling, Bouvia,* and *Quinlan* were brought because physicians and hospitals were unwilling to let patients or surrogates refuse therapy. The deliberative model is more widely used today because the ethical principle of autonomy and the legal principles of informed consent and refusal are more widely accepted. Nevertheless, paternalism is implicit when physicians argue that therapies they consider futile should be withheld or withdrawn. It is ironic that some physicians today demand that patients and families forgo treatment that other physicians once insisted they accept.

Although the deliberative model is gaining popularity in France, the paternalistic model still is employed at the end-of-life in ICUs there. Physicians are granted decision-making prerogatives in these ICUs that are not permitted their American counterparts. Furthermore, French families have no legal right to make decisions for patients who cannot make decisions for themselves.[111,112] In response to a questionnaire distributed to members of the European Society of Intensive Care Medicine, only 49% of respondents involved patients and families in end-of-life decisions, and physicians differed in implementing the decisions.[113] The paternalistic model also is prevalent in Hong Kong, where people fear that acknowledging impending death is like casting a curse, physicians and families commonly make decisions for patients, and there is no legislation regarding patient autonomy or the status of advanced directives.[114]

These studies indicate that medical decision-making and the attitudes that underlie it vary from country to country. The variations also exist within a given country depending on its ethnic and cultural composition.[115] For example, in one study[116] in the United States, Korean Americans and Mexican Americans were significantly less likely than European Americans and African Americans to believe that a patient should be told the diagnosis of metastatic cancer and that the patient should make the decision about the use of life-sustaining therapy. In another study,[117] African Americans were more likely than European Americans to want to be kept alive on life support. Interviews of these African Americans subjects documented a deep distrust of the health care system and a fear that health care was based on one's ability to pay.

Regardless of their cultural beliefs, patients' preferences regarding life-sustaining treatment can change with their medical condition.[118,119] This finding underscores the limited usefulness of advance directives that are not reviewed and updated periodically. Indeed, when asked if they would want their stated wishes followed if they were no longer able to make decisions, inpatients who were older and had more serious illnesses in SUPPORT said that they would rather have their families and physicians make decisions for them.[120] Even if updated, advance directives can only provide a rough roadmap for the families and physicians to follow.

Given that families are allowed to make decisions for patients and that the highest standard for surrogate decision-making is substituted judgment in the United States, some have questioned whether families would make the same decisions as patients would, especially when the patients are critically ill. This question has been prompted in part by the demonstration that anxiety and depression are prominent among family members visiting patients in French ICUs.[121] To date, studies[122,123] of substituted judgment among the families of terminally ill patients in the United States have shown that family decisions are reasonably concordant with what patients themselves want, particularly if the two parties have discussed end-of-life issues beforehand. Physicians have been no better than family members in predicting patient choices in these investigations.

IMPORTANCE OF PHYSICIAN, PATIENT, AND FAMILY COMMUNICATION

Of course, American families would not need to be so involved in medical decision-making in the ICU setting if physicians facilitated such decision-making when the patients' diseases were not far advanced and they could speak for themselves.[124] Yet SUPPORT[8] and other studies[125] have shown that physicians and patients rarely discuss end-of-life issues in advance of the patients' deterioration, even when they reside in nursing homes. A study[126] of patients with severe COPD enrolled in pulmonary rehabilitation revealed that almost all had health concerns, the most common of which was fear of increasing dyspnea. Although many of the patients had concerns about being intubated, a minority had completed an advance directive describing their choices in regard to that intervention. Furthermore, although the patients generally wanted discussions with their physicians, only 19% had such discussions, only 15% had discussed life support, and only 14% thought that their physicians understood their end-of-life wishes.

Why patients with chronic and terminal diseases do not discuss end-of-life care with their physicians has been the subject of several investigations. In the study of patients with COPD enrolled in pulmonary rehabilitation,[127] those patients who had not had discussions identified their own procrastination and the fact that their physicians had not brought up the topic as the most important reasons. When these patients participated in an end-of-life educational intervention as part of their rehabilitation, they were more likely to have such discussions subsequently with their physicians and to complete durable powers of attorney for health care.

In another study[128] of patients with advanced AIDS, structured interviews of the patients and their physicians were used to identify barriers to communication. Patients who had not had discussions with their physicians about end-of-life care most frequently agreed that, "I don't like talking about getting very sick" and "I would rather concentrate on staying alive than talking about death." Physicians who did not initiate discussions most often agreed that, "There is too little time during our appointments to discuss everything we should" and "I worry that discussing end-of-life with [patient name] will take away his or her hope." Many physicians in this study acknowledged that they felt uncomfortable discussing end-of-life issues, suggesting that their own discomfort was as important as the lack of time for discussions in inhibiting communication.

Limited communication between physicians and patients also was reported in SUPPORT.[8] Furthermore, SUPPORT disclosed that communication was frequently inadequate between physicians and the families of critically ill patients. This finding was corroborated by a study[129] from an ICU in France in which half the families of critically ill patients reported the same inadequacy. A follow-up investigation[130] from that and other ICUs in France indicated that family satisfaction with their relatives' care was due in part to their being of French descent and having a language and cultural values similar to those of the ICU caregivers. Family satisfaction also related to an absence of perceived contradictions in information provided by caregivers, information provided by a junior physician, a patient-to-nurse ratio of 3:1 or less, knowledge of the specific role of each caregiver, help from the family's own physician, and sufficient time spent giving information. Distribution of a family information leaflet in the ICUs improved family understanding of how the units functioned and increased their satisfaction with the care given therein.[131]

The importance of good communication also has been highlighted in a study[132] of the quality of end-of-life care assessed through the responses of family members to a quality of death and dying (QODD) questionnaire after their relatives had died in and outside of hospitals. In this study, higher QODD scores, which reflected a better quality of care at the end of life, were associated with death at home, death in the location the patient wanted, lower symptom burden, and better ratings of symptom treatment. Although the presence of an advance directive was not associated with a higher QODD score, higher scores were associated with communication about treatment preferences, compliance with treatment preferences, and family satisfaction regarding communication with the health care team.

In a study from one U.S. hospital,[133] families were interviewed about their experiences in the ICU and the decision-making process for withholding or withdrawing life support. They reported a high incidence of conflicts, the vast majority of which were between themselves and physicians. The conflicts most often involved problems in communication or perceived unprofessional behavior, such as disregarding the primary caregiver in treatment decisions. These families identified pastoral care and prior discussion of treatment preferences as sources of psychological support. They appreciated lenient visiting hours and the availability of family conference rooms. Most of the families singled out attending physicians as the preferred source of information and reassurance. In this regard, a study from another institution[134] demonstrated that intensive communication achieved through regular family meetings led by attending physicians increased family satisfaction and also decreased ICU length of stay among patients who died. Still another recent study[134a] indicated that allowing family members more opportunity to speak during conferences may increase their satisfaction.

Another investigation[135] looked at priorities and problems in end-of-life care identified by parents of children who had died after withdrawal of life support in three pediatric ICUs. In response to a parental perspectives questionnaire, these parents placed highest priorities on their children's quality of life, likelihood of improvement, and their perceptions of their children's pain when considering withdrawal of support. Twenty percent of parents disagreed that their children were comfortable in their final days, a finding that echoed the SUPPORT study involving adults.[8] Fifty-five percent of parents felt that they had little to no control during their children's final days; and nearly one fourth reported that, if able to do so, they would have made decisions differently. At the same time, the parents generally reported that ICU nurses and physicians were available and helpful to them, and many also had access to their community pediatricians.

Successful conflict resolution at the end of life is a process of negotiation between physicians and patients and families.[135a] This process varies depending on whether the paternalistic or deliberative model of decision-making is used, which in turn depends on the cultural context. In the United States, the process involves educating patients and families about likely prognoses, deferring to requests for seemingly benign treatments, convincing patients or families to forgo potentially harmful interventions, and occasionally refusing requests for therapy that physicians consider nonbeneficial.[136] Proper negotiation requires cross-cultural understanding and the use of communication skills, particularly that of listening to patients and families.[137] Ethics committee consultations appear to be useful in resolving conflicts over treatments said to be futile and also are associated with reductions in ICU hospital days and life-sustaining therapy among patients who ultimately fail to survive until discharge from the hospital.[138-140] Whether such consultations also increase family satisfaction with the dying process of their loved ones is unclear.

UNDERSTANDING WHAT PHYSICIANS, PATIENTS, AND FAMILIES NEED AT THE END OF LIFE

End-of-life care could be optimized if the needs of the parties involved in the dying process were better understood. In this regard, a survey[141] of seriously ill patients, recently bereaved families, and physicians and other caregivers revealed that decisions about treatment preferences, knowing what to expect about one's physical condition, and preparation for death were important to all four groups at the end of life. So were sharing time with family and friends; being kept clean; being free of pain, anxiety, and dyspnea; and being treated as a "whole person." Patients, but not physicians, also rated as important being mentally aware, coming to peace with God, not being a burden to their families, being able to help others, praying, having funeral

Table 87.2 Factors Considered Important by Patients at the End of Life

Being kept clean
Naming a decision-maker
Having a nurse with whom one feels comfortable
Knowing what to expect about one's physical condition
Having someone who will listen
Maintaining one's dignity
Trusting one's physician
Having financial affairs in order
Being free of pain
Maintaining a sense of humor
Saying goodbye to important people
Being free of shortness of breath
Being free of anxiety
Having a physician with whom one can discuss fears

From Steinhauser KE, Christakis NA, Clipp EC, et al: Factors considered important at the end of life by patients, family, physicians, and other care providers. JAMA 284:2476–2482, 2000.

arrangements planned, and gaining a sense of completion in life (Table 87.2).

The needs of families also have been assessed with a survey tool called the Critical Care Family Needs Inventory in several studies. In a recent overview of recommendations for end-of-life care in the ICU, the Ethics Committee of the Society of Critical Care Medicine[142] combined these studies to determine what these needs are. They include being with the dying patient, being helpful to that patient, being informed of the dying patient's changing condition, understanding what is being done to the patient and why, being assured of the patient's comfort, being comforted, having an opportunity to express emotions, being assured that the family's decisions were right, finding meaning in the patient's death, and having personal needs attended to during the dying process.

Unfortunately, the needs of physicians and others who care for dying patients have not been well addressed. Nevertheless, at a minimum, all caregivers probably need to feel comfortable during the dying process, to gain experience from it, to feel supported by their colleagues and by their institutions, and to have opportunities for bereavement themselves. Nurses, respiratory therapists, social workers, and clergy who work alongside physicians want to know that the physicians respect them, provide them with adequate information, take their opinions into account, and engage in proper decision-making practices at the end of life.[143]

PROVIDING APPROPRIATE SETTINGS FOR DYING PATIENTS

Under the deliberative model of the physician-patient relationship, physicians are obligated to help patients understand their conditions, explore their therapeutic options, and decide what is best for them. Essential to this relationship is preparing patients for death when appropriate. Such preparation should include consideration of whether the patients' interests are best served by hospital and ICU admission when death is imminent, assuming that the imminence of death can be identified. Many patients, especially those with COPD and other chronic diseases that allow time for advance planning as death approaches, decide to die in a hospice or at home if given the opportunity.

Terminal patients who prefer a trial of attempted restorative treatment in the hospital or undergo it because their wishes are not known should at least die in an environment that is comfortable for them and their families when the trial fails. A private room with enough space to accommodate visitors might be such an environment. Visiting hours should be relaxed, if necessary, to allow families and friends to spend as much time as they wish with dying patients. Some hospitals have separate palliative care units for this purpose. Others offer palliative care teams or services that consult throughout the hospital.[144]

EMOTIONAL AND SPIRITUAL SUPPORT

Recent reviews[38,43,135a,145,146] of end-of-life care in and outside the ICU have emphasized the importance of providing emotional and spiritual support to dying patients and their families. Physicians contribute to this support, of course, and their regular communications and presence at the bedside are greatly appreciated. Nurses, social workers, clergy, and other members of the health care team deliver most of the support, however. Occasionally, patients or their families request that friends, caregivers, and religious persons from outside a particular institution provide consultations or participate in bedside rituals or observances. These should be allowed, if not encouraged, unless they interfere with patient care.

End-of-life care may extend after death in that physicians, nurses, and others who have cared for the patients' families when the patients were alive have much to offer them thereafter. Advising on the disposition of bodies, reporting the results of autopsy studies, coordinating burials and funeral services, and attending funerals are among the professional responsibilities of caregivers that are greatly appreciated by families. These responsibilities can be assumed by independent bereavement follow-up services, which have been described at one hospital.[147] Alternatively, caregivers who have established personal relationships with families in the ICU and other settings may maintain them after the patients' death.

Physicians, nurses, and other caregivers have their own emotional and spiritual needs, of course, and caring for dying patients and their families exacts an appreciable toll on them. Because of this, caregivers themselves should have opportunities to grieve. Conferences scheduled after patients die provide both an opportunity for bereavement and a mechanism for evaluating the processes of withholding and withdrawal of life support and of administering palliative care to them. Such evaluation may lead to improvements in these processes for future patients.

SYMPTOM MANAGEMENT

WHY SYMPTOMS MAY BE POORLY MANAGED

Management of pain and other symptoms is a traditional role and responsibility of the medical profession. Nevertheless, patients too frequently die with pain and other symptoms. Nearly 50% of SUPPORT patients or their surrogates interviewed after study enrollment reported that the patients experienced pain during hospitalization. Nearly 15% reported extremely or moderately severe pain occurring at least half the time, and many of those patients with pain were dissatisfied with its control. Uncontrolled pain was most common among patients with more dependence on others in activities of daily living and who had more comorbid conditions, more anxiety, more depression, and a poor quality of life.[148]

That pain and other symptoms are poorly managed in some patients probably is due in large part to the strong emphasis restorative care places on the diagnosis and treatment of diseases rather than on the relief of symptoms. Palliative care reverses this emphasis and, when properly applied, should help increase patient comfort at the end of life. Nevertheless, the transition from restorative to palliative care is far from seamless for many patients. In this regard, it is difficult for patients and their families to know when to stop requesting treatment, just as it is for physicians and other caregivers to stop recommending life-sustaining therapies.

Pain and other symptoms also may be poorly managed because they are subjective experiences that are not easily assessed by objective methods. Pain and sedation scales have been developed to quantify the levels of pain and anxiety among patients who can self-report.[142] Nevertheless, some patients cannot adequately communicate these sensations, either because they cannot find the words or because they are intubated and sedated. To detect pain in these patients, physicians and other caregivers must attend to patient grimacing and other admittedly nonspecific manifestations of pain, including tachycardia and hypertension. Although bispectral analysis of the electroencephalogram has been used to assess the level of sedation in ICU patients, the correlation of this technique with sedation scales and, most important, the subjective experiences of patients, is unclear.[149]

A third reason that symptoms are poorly managed at the end of life is that patients differ in their desire to have symptoms relieved. Some patients value symptom relief highly and would prefer to be rendered unconscious rather than to experience pain, anxiety, or dyspnea, especially at the end of life. Others, however, would be willing to tolerate these symptoms or have them mitigated only slightly in order to stay awake. Dying patients may find it difficult to titrate sedatives and analgesics to their desired level of consciousness, although they should be encouraged to do so. Physicians and caregivers may find it even more difficult to achieve the ideal level of sedation and analgesia for patients who cannot communicate or administer drugs to themselves.

Finally, symptoms may be inadequately managed because physicians and other caregivers feel uncomfortable about giving high doses of sedatives, analgesics, and other mood-altering agents. In some instances, this discomfort stems from a reluctance to cause drug addiction in dying patients, a phenomenon irrelevant to the patients' condition. Other discomfort results from awareness that the agents may hasten death by depressing not only consciousness but also respiratory and cardiovascular function. That the U.S. Supreme Court has justified the administration of sedatives and analgesics under the principle of the double effect should help put caregivers at ease. Although one third of physicians who ordered these agents to dying adult patients did so in part to hasten death in one study[99] virtually all the physicians in a comparable study[150] conducted in a pediatric ICU viewed hastening death only as an "acceptable, unintended side effect."

MANAGEMENT OF PAIN

Pain can be managed indirectly by nonpharmacologic means. For example, placing patients in a quiet environment where friends and family can visit may diminish the sense of pain, as may the proper treatment of anxiety and depression. Although respiratory depression due to drugs or underlying disease usually is undesirable in patients with COPD, the encephalopathy that results from the hypercapnia and hypoxia may be tolerated, if not favored, in terminal patients because it attenuates pain. Similarly, patients who forgo nutrition and hydration at the end of life may develop a euphoria that has been attributed to the release of endogenous opioids or the analgesic effects of ketosis.[145]

A direct approach to pain control generally centers on the use of opioids, and morphine is the opioid most commonly used. In addition to causing analgesia, morphine induces some degree of sedation, respiratory depression, constipation, urinary retention, nausea, and euphoria. It also produces vasodilation, which may cause hypotension, in part through the release of histamine. Fentanyl, a synthetic opioid that is approximately 100 times more potent than morphine, does not release histamine and therefore causes less hypotension. Hydromorphone, a semisynthetic morphine derivative, is more sedating than morphine and produces little euphoria.[142,151]

Morphine, fentanyl, and hydromorphone can be administered orally, subcutaneously, rectally, or intravenously. Opioids usually are given by the intravenous route to ICU patients, including those who are dying. These agents may be administered to inpatients and outpatients alike through the technique of patient-controlled analgesia.[152] Long-acting oral preparations of morphine and hydromorphone are available for outpatients. Fentanyl can be administered orally in the form of a lollipop. It can also be given by the transcutaneous route, which makes this agent particularly suitable for patients who have difficulty with oral medications.

Opioids ideally should be administered in anticipation of pain and not after its occurrence. The optimal doses of these drugs given for pain relief are unknown and certainly vary among patients. Nevertheless, opioids generally should be started in relatively low doses if respiratory depression and other side effects are to be avoided and titrated upward until their analgesic effect is realized. In reports of critically ill patients undergoing the withholding and withdrawal of life support in both adult and pediatric ICUs, opioids were used in doses sufficient to achieve pain relief that caregivers considered adequate.[99,150,153] In dying patients, the use of opioids should not be limited by some arbitrary amount but by the balance between analgesia and any undesirable side effects.[154]

MANAGEMENT OF ANXIETY

As in the case of pain, anxiety and its physical manifestation agitation can be managed nonpharmacologically. If drugs are required, benzodiazepines and propofol are preferred. Benzodiazepines cause anterograde amnesia in addition to anxiolysis, and they exert a synergistic sedating effect with opioids. Benzodiazepines also cause hypotension and cardiac depression, especially when administered quickly and in high doses. Lorazepam, an intermediate-acting agent, can be given by the oral, intramuscular, or intravenous route; when given intravenously, it can be done so by bolus or by constant infusion. Midazolam, which is short-acting, usually is administered intravenously by constant infusion, although boluses may be required when therapy is initiated.[142,151,155]

Propofol is an intravenous general anesthetic agent with sedating, amnestic, and anxiolytic properties when administered in subanesthetic doses. In such doses, propofol is similar to midazolam in that it usually is given by constant infusion after bolus injection. The drugs also are comparable in the sedation they produce, although propofol has a greater propensity to cause hypotension.[156] Neither propofol nor midazolam is appropriate for the management of anxiety in outpatients, and in hospitals their continuous use may be restricted to the ICU.

MANAGEMENT OF DELIRIUM

Delirium may be confused with anxiety because it too can cause agitation. The confusion is clinically important both because the conditions are treated pharmacologically with different drugs and because the drugs used to treat anxiety can exacerbate delirium.[142,151] Delirious patients should be helped to obtain regular sleep, should be oriented regularly to their environment, and should avoid benzodiazepines, which cloud consciousness. Haloperidol, a butyrophenone neuroleptic agent, is widely used to treat delirium in critically ill patients. It may be given orally, rectally, intramuscularly, or intravenously. Haloperidol may cause QT prolongation on the electrocardiogram and should be used cautiously with other agents that have a similar effect. Haloperidol also can cause rigidity, restlessness, and other dyskinesias.

MANAGEMENT OF DYSPNEA

Dyspnea should be understood and managed according to its underlying pathophysiology, especially in its earlier stages[4,157] (see Chapter 28). For example, patients with moderate to severe COPD may benefit from oral bronchodilators that decrease airflow resistance,[158] inhaled corticosteroids that decrease airway inflammation,[159] and lung volume reduction surgery that decreases hyperinflation.[160] These patients also may become less dyspneic through exercise training and the emotional support available through pulmonary rehabilitation programs.[161] At the same time, patients with lung cancer may feel less breathless after drainage of malignant pleural effusions or placement of stents to overcome airway obstruction.[4]

In patients with far advanced lung disease, attention to pathophysiological mechanisms is less important, and treatment is more palliative than restorative. Bronchodilators may not reduce breathlessness in such patients; corticosteroids may cause more unwanted side effects than symptom relief; lung reduction surgery may prove fatal. Patients with COPD who are dying, at home or in hospice, do not benefit from exercise training and may be too breathless to attend pulmonary rehabilitation programs; these patients should be encouraged to use wheelchairs and to rest. In most terminal cancer patients, malignant effusions and airway obstruction should not be diagnosed or treated.[4]

Patients with chronic respiratory failure of whatever cause should receive supplemental oxygen, which has been shown to both increase survival and decrease breathlessness.[162] In the United States, Medicare reimbursement for long-term oxygen therapy is based on physiological criteria (e.g., arterial PO_2 of 55 mm Hg or less while breathing room air), not symptomatology. Despite this fact, many patients use oxygen primarily to relieve dyspnea, and hospice patients do not have to meet physiological criteria to receive reimbursement. Supplemental oxygen usually is started in low doses (e.g., 1–3 L/min) and titrated to effect. The results of titration are difficult to predict inasmuch as neither the flow rate nor the route of administration of oxygen determines its impact on breathlessness.[4] Furthermore, air may relieve dyspnea as well as oxygen does in patients with advanced malignancy.[163] In addition, breathless patients frequently are relieved by exposure to fresh air in the outdoors or during automobile rides with the windows down. Those who are bedridden may benefit from using fans to blow air over their faces.[4]

Opioids such as oral morphine have been demonstrated to increase exercise tolerance acutely and to alleviate dyspnea in some patients with COPD.[164] Nevertheless, the long-term administration of sustained-release morphine has not been shown to be superior to placebo in reducing breathlessness in such patients, most of whom reported nausea, constipation, and other adverse effects.[165] Although many patients become tolerant to these effects over time, opioids probably should be used only on a trial or as-needed basis for patients with recalcitrant dyspnea who do not respond to oxygen or air. However, because their analgesic properties are undisputed, these agents may be particularly useful in patients who have pain in addition to breathlessness, such as those with lung cancer.[4] Although the use of morphine and other opioids to relieve dyspnea in patients with ARDS and other causes of acute respiratory failure is widespread and seems reasonable, this practice is not supported by research studies.

Benzodiazepines such as alprazolam have been shown to reduce dyspnea in some patients with COPD.[166] Yet these agents also may cause drowsiness, uncoordination, and dysphoria; and they probably should be used only in outpatients whose dyspnea is not relieved by oxygen and opioids.[4] As is true of opioids, benzodiazepines and propofol are commonly used to reduce dyspnea, in addition to anxiety, among patients with acute respiratory failure, particularly those receiving mechanical ventilation. Again, this practice appears reasonable, especially if the patients are not experiencing unwanted side effects. Nevertheless, benefits of treating dyspnea with sedatives in ICU patients have not been demonstrated scientifically.

MANAGEMENT OF NAUSEA AND VOMITING

Nausea and vomiting may result from systemic illnesses such as diabetes, renal failure, hypercalcemia, adrenal insufficiency, and viral infections. These symptoms also may be caused by central nervous system disorders, including cerebral metastases and other conditions that increase intracranial pressure; primary gastrointestinal diseases such as gastric outlet obstruction; and a variety of drugs, including theophylline, phenytoin, opioids, antibiotics, and chemotherapeutic agents. Nausea and vomiting may remit with treatment of the disorder or discontinuing use of the drugs that cause them. Patients often stop eating when they are nauseated, and they can be placed on a nothing-by-mouth status or undergo gastric decompression. Clear liquid diets may be administered to patients as tolerated. Supplemental oxygen has been shown to reduce the incidence of postoperative nausea and vomiting.[167]

Patients with nausea and vomiting who do not respond to more conservative measures may be candidates for prophylactic or therapeutic antiemetic therapy, which can be given orally, intramuscularly, intravenously, or in suppository form. Among the older antiemetics are dexamethasone and other corticosteroids; butyrophenones such as haloperidol and droperidol; chlorpromazine, promethazine, prochlorperazine, and other phenothiazines; and muscarinic receptor antagonists such as scopolamine, which is particularly helpful in patients with vestibular symptoms. Of these agents, dexamethasone, droperidol, and promethazine are the most widely used.

Newer antiemetics include the serotonin receptor antagonists ondansetron, dolastron, granisetron, and tropisetron. These drugs have been tested primarily in the postoperative period and among patients who have received chemotherapy or radiation therapy. Because of their expense, they probably should be used only after other agents are found to be unsuccessful in preventing or relieving symptoms.[168,169] Cannabinoids, administered either orally or through smoking the *Cannabis sativa* (marijuana) plant, are as effective as older antiemetic agents such as chlorpromazine, prochlorperazine, and metaclopramide in reducing nausea and vomiting caused by chemotherapy. Nevertheless, although some patients welcome the sedation and euphoria they experience with cannabinoids, others complain of dizziness and dysphoria.[170]

MANAGEMENT OF HUNGER AND THIRST

People eat food and drink fluids to relieve hunger and thirst and to sustain metabolic processes. Food and fluids are administered to hospitalized patients under the assumption that they are staples of life and components of routine medical and nursing care. Under this assumption, some[171] have argued that refusal of nutrition and hydration is tantamount to suicide and that food and fluids should be administered to all patients other than those who reject them because of intolerable pain and suffering in the last moments of life. Others[172] have noted that voluntary forgoing of nutrition and hydration by terminal patients represents only a refusal of unwanted treatment that is ethically and legally justified. Still others[173] have argued that force-feeding violates patient autonomy, and that voluntary "terminal dehydration" on the part of patients offers substantial advantages over physician-assisted suicide with respect to self-determination, access, and professional integrity.

Of course, patients may desire food and fluids until they die; alternatively, they may be choose not to eat or drink. In fact, a recent study[174] has documented that in Oregon, where physician-assisted suicide is allowed, many hospice patients forgo eating and drinking, perhaps as an alternative to assisted suicide. As was the case in this study, another investigation[175] conducted in a comfort care unit demonstrated that most cancer patients either never experienced hunger and thirst or did so only initially during their terminal illnesses. In the few patients who were symptomatic, hunger, thirst, and dry mouth usually could be alleviated with small amounts of food and fluids, or by the application of ice chips or lubrication to the lips. Similar measures can be used in other settings, including the ICU.

WITHHOLDING AND WITHDRAWAL OF LIFE-SUSTAINING THERAPY

WHAT THERAPIES ARE WITHHELD AND WITHDRAWN

Life-sustaining therapies are withheld and withdrawn in many settings. Nevertheless, most of the studies of this process have been conducted in ICUs. These studies,[40–41,176–181] from pediatric and adult ICUs around the world, reveal that, although any and all interventions may be withheld or withdrawn, variation exists in the type, number, and sequence of interventions forgone. In one investigation[182] in an adult ICU in the United States, an average of five separate interventions were forgone per patient. CPR, intubation and mechanical ventilation, and dialysis generally were the first interventions withheld; thereafter, vasopressors, transfusions, intravenous fluids, parenteral nutrition, antibiotics, and tube feedings were either withheld or withdrawn. Decisions regarding withdrawing therapy occurred later than decisions regarding withholding it. Whereas a decision not to intubate a patient was made early for patients not already on ventilators, once patients were on ventilators decisions to withdraw ventilatory support were generally made late, after several other interventions were first forgone.

Another study[183] in which physicians were surveyed about the withdrawal process indicated distinct preferences about the form of support withdrawn. From most likely to least likely, the order was blood products, dialysis, vasopressors, parenteral nutrition, antibiotics, mechanical ventilation, tube feedings, and intravenous fluids. Four biases in decision-making also were identified. Physicians preferred to withdraw forms of therapy supporting organs that failed for natural, rather than iatrogenic, reasons and recently instituted, rather than long-standing, interventions. They also preferred to withdraw forms of therapy resulting in an immediate, rather than a delayed, death and to withdraw forms of therapy resulting in a delayed death only when faced with diagnostic uncertainty.

WITHHOLDING AND WITHDRAWAL OF INTUBATION AND MECHANICAL VENTILATION

Intubation and mechanical ventilation are often used in patients with acute, chronic, or acute-on-chronic respiratory failure and are among the therapies most commonly withheld or withdrawn from them. As noted earlier, many patients with advanced COPD and other causes of chronic respiratory failure have concerns about intubation and mechanical ventilation and decide against these therapies in advance of decompensation. Nevertheless, some patients with chronic respiratory failure request intubation and mechanical ventilation or are intubated and ventilated—either in the field, in the emergency department, or in the ICU—without having decided on their wishes or having communicated them. Similarly, patients with acute respiratory failure often end up on ventilators because their conditions are assumed to be reversible. When they and their counterparts with chronic respiratory failure do not improve, intubation and mechanical ventilation may be withdrawn. A recent study[184] revealed that the strongest determinants of the withdrawal of mechanical ventilation in critically ill patients were the physicians' perception that the patients preferred not to use life support, the physicians' prediction of a low likelihood of survival in the ICU and a high likelihood of poor cognitive function, and the use of inotropes or vasopressors.

How intubation and mechanical ventilation are withdrawn varies among institutions. One approach is rapid extubation: the patient is given analgesics and sedatives, and both the endotracheal (or tracheotomy) tube and the ventilator are removed. Patients then are given either supplemental oxygen or, more commonly, room air to breathe. Rapid extubation is direct, and it offers the potential advantage of allowing parents to hold their infants without being encumbered by the ventilator or its tubing. A potential disadvantage is that patients may appear distressed due to upper airway obstruction after the tube is removed.

A second process, called *terminal weaning*, involves decreasing the inspired oxygen fraction, the ventilator rate, the level of positive end-expiratory pressure, or some combination of these variables before the ventilator is removed. Patients are given drugs during this process, and they most often die before extubation. First described in 1983, this technique was developed in order to avoid abruptly discontinuing treatment in such a way that "might be interpreted with intent to kill" and might make patients uncomfortable.[185] The first part of this rationale is not relevant today because the differences between terminal weaning and euthanasia have been delineated by the U.S. Supreme Court. Nevertheless, terminal weaning still may cause less discomfort than rapid extubation by preventing upper airway obstruction.

The relative advantages and disadvantages of rapid extubation and terminal weaning have been debated.[186,187] They have not been compared scientifically, although one study[188] of what was called "rapid terminal weaning" demonstrated that patients could be kept comfortable during the procedure with relatively low doses of opioids and benzodiazepines. A survey[189] of critical care physicians indicated that 15% of respondents almost never withdrew intubation and mechanical ventilation from dying patients. Of physicians who did, 33% preferred terminal weaning, 13% preferred rapid extubation, and the remainder used both methods. Reasons for preferring rapid extubation included the directness of the action, family perceptions, and patient comfort. Reasons for preferring terminal weaning included patient comfort, family perceptions, and the belief that terminal weaning was less abrupt. Most physicians in this study administered sedatives and analgesics during the withdrawal process; 6% also used neuromuscular blocking agents at least occasionally.

Most patients with respiratory failure die from their underlying diseases when intubation and mechanical ventilation are withdrawn. Nevertheless, some survive, and their survival should not be prevented by drugs that hasten death. At the same time, even patients who are too sick to survive should not receive drugs that interfere with observing tachypnea and other signs that may signal the need for symptom relief. For these reasons, although sedatives and analgesics may be given to relieve suffering, neuromuscular blocking agents should not be introduced to patients while intubation and mechanical ventilation are withdrawn. Furthermore, if the patients are already receiving them, a common situation with infants, these agents should be continued only if two requirements are met. First, death is expected to be both rapid and certain after removal of the endotracheal tube, the ventilator, or both. Second, the burdens to patients and families of waiting for neuromuscular blockade to diminish to a reversible level exceed the benefits of allowing better assessment of the patients' comfort and possible interaction with their families.[190]

IMPROVING THE QUALITY OF CARE AT THE END OF LIFE

Palliative care is a robust, well recognized discipline, and it is extensively practiced in the outpatient setting. Yet end-of-life care has been incorporated into inpatient practice only recently, as patients in developed countries increasingly die in hospitals and in ICUs. Despite its fledgling status, however, inpatient end-of-life care is rapidly being improved upon as more physicians and other caregivers participate in it. Such improvement and participation were stimulated in large part by publication of the SUPPORT study[8] and the articles drawn from the SUPPORT database, many of which are cited in this chapter. For the most part, these publications documented the deficiencies of care at the end of life for hospitalized patients with respiratory failure and other critical illnesses.

In response to SUPPORT and its spin-offs have come a number of recent articles recommending possible improvements in end-of-life care; again, many of these articles are referred to in this chapter. Also referenced are a recent international consensus conference on challenges in end-of-life care in the ICU[190a] and the first textbook on end-of-life care in the ICU.[38] Publication of this textbook was accompanied by release of a research agenda that outlines some of the questions about end-of-life care that must be answered before such care can be improved.[191] One strategy noted

Table 87.3 Seven Domains of End-of-Life Care
Patient- and family-centered decision-making
Communication
Continuity of care
Emotional and practical support
Symptom management and comfort care
Spiritual support
Emotional and organizational support for staff

From Clark EB, Curtis JR, Luce JM, et al: Quality indicators for end-of-life care in the intensive care unit. Crit Care Med 31:2255–2262, 2003.

in the agenda is the need for structural changes such as the expansion of family waiting areas in addition to procedural changes such as the development of clinical guidelines for palliative care. Pursuing this strategy has led to the recent articulation of end-of-life care domains and quality indicators[192] (Table 87.3), a content analysis of forms and other materials documenting end-of-life care in ICUs,[193] and the creation of standardized comfort care orders for the withdrawal of life-sustaining therapies[194] (Fig. 87.1). In the future, tools such as these will be used to assess and improve the quality of care at the end of life in ICUs.

Physicians and nurses training today receive more exposure to end-of-life issues than their predecessors did. Nevertheless, the training of tomorrow's practitioners can be improved upon. A recent study[195] indicates that palliative care training for critical care fellows is feasible and that fellows value the incorporation of such training into their regular rotations more than a discrete clinical rotation in palliative care. Similarly, experiential, case-based, patient-centered curricula are associated with resident confidence in withdrawal of life support decisions.[196] A working group in end-of-life care has outlined the requirements for teaching care of the dying in the ICU.[197] Such teaching should emphasize using goals at the end of life to guide the use of technology, understanding prognostication, communicating effectively, respecting cultural differences, and employing palliative techniques. It should not be limited to caregivers in training; acquiring and improving the skills required for end-of-life care is a lifelong learning process.[198]

SUMMARY

End-of-life care usually is a combination of palliative treatment and withholding and withdrawal of life-sustaining therapy provided to patients who are terminally ill, including those with acute, chronic, and acute-on-chronic respiratory failure. Such care represents a change from the restorative treatment that is delivered to patients whose respiratory failure is not far advanced. End-of-life care commonly occurs in the ICU, although other settings may be more desirable. It is justified by the ethical principles of beneficence, nonmaleficence, and autonomy and by the legal right of patients to consent to or refuse any or all therapy, including that which sustains life. This legal right

DATE	TIME	ADMITTING SERVICE/ATTENDING

Complete the following:

- Do Not Attempt Resuscitation (DNAR) order written
- Note written in chart that documents rationale for comfort care, discussions with attending and discussions with family (or attempts to contact family)
- Discontinue all previous orders including routine vital signs, medication, enteral feeding, intravenous drips, radiographs, laboratory tests. See below for new orders.
- Remove devices not necessary for comfort including monitors, blood pressure cuffs, and leg compression sleeves. See below for orders related to the ventilator.
- Remove all devices (cardiac output computer, transfusers, defibrillator, intra-aortic balloon pump, ventricular assist device, temporary pacemaker) from ICU room.
- Liberalize visitation.

SEDATION AND ANALGESIA:

1) <u>Select one:</u>
   - ❏ Morphine drip at current rate (assuming patient comfortable at that dose) <u>or</u> 10 mg/hr <u>or</u> _____mg/hr
     For signs of discomfort, up to Q 15 min, give additional morphine equal to current hourly drip rate and increase drip by 25%
   - ❏ Fentanyl drip at current rate (assuming patient comfortable at that dose) <u>or</u> 100 µg/hr <u>or</u> _____µg/hr
     For signs of discomfort , up to Q 15 min, give additional fentanyl equal to current hourly drip rate and increase drip by 25%
   - ❏ Other narcotic:_____

2) <u>Select one:</u>
   - ❏ Lorazepam drip at current rate (assuming patient comfortable at that dose) or 5 mg/hr or _____mg/hr
     For signs of discomfort, up to Q 15 min, give additional lorazepam equal to current hourly drip rate and increase drip by 25%
   - ❏ Midazolam drip at current rate (assuming patient comfortable at that dose) or 10 mg/hr or _____mg/hr
     For signs of discomfort, up to Q 15 min, give additional midazolam equal to current hourly drip rate and increase drip by 25%
   - ❏ Other benzodiazepine, barbiturate, or propofol:

3) For pediatric patients, $\leq$ 15 years of age, adjust above gtts by 10 mcg/kg/hr until comfort is attained.

VENTILATOR:

4) Initial ventilator setting: IMV rate_____, PS level_____, (choose IMV <u>or</u> PS not a combination), F_iO_2_____, PEEP_____.
5) Reduce apnea, heater, and other ventilator alarms to minimum setting.
6) Reduce F_iO_2 to room air and PEEP to zero over about 5 minutes and titrate sedation as indicated for discomfort.
7) As indicated by level of discomfort, wean IMV to 4 or PS to 5 over 5 to 20 minutes and titrate sedation as indicated for discomfort.
8) <u>When patient is comfortable in IMV rate 4 or PS of 5, select one:</u>
   - ❏ Extubate patient to air
   - ❏ T-piece with air (not CPAP on ventilator)

MD signature:_____   RN signature: _____

Date/Time:_____   Date/Time:_____

| PT.NO.

NAME

D.O.B. | **UNIVERSITY OF WASHINGTON MEDICAL CENTERS**
HARBORVIEW MEDICAL CENTER - UW MEDICAL CENTER
SEATTLE, WASHINGTON
PHYSICIAN ORDERS
COMFORT CARE ORDERS FOR THE WITHDRAWAL OF LIFE SUPPORT IN THE ICU

* H 1 4 5 0 *

PAGE 1 OF 2 | WHITE-MEDICAL RECORD
CANARY-PHARMACY
PINK-NURSING |

Figure 87.1 University of Washington comfort care orders for the withdrawal of life support in the intensive care unit. (From Treece PD, Engelberg RA, Crowley L, et al: Evaluation of a standardized order form for the withdrawal of life support in the intensive care unit. Crit Care Med 32:1141–1148, 2004.)   *Figure continued on opposite page*

PRINCIPLES FOR WITHHOLDING AND WITHDRAWING LIFE SUSTAINING TREATMENT

1) Death occurs as a complication of the underlying disease. The goal of the comfort care outlined on the reverse is to relieve suffering in a dying patient not to hasten death.

2) Withdrawal of life sustaining treatment is a medical procedure that requires the same degree of physician participation and quality as other procedures.

3) Actions solely intended to hasten death (for example, high doses of potassium or paralytic drugs) are morally unacceptable, however, any dose of pain relieving medication can be used when required to provide comfort even if these doses may hasten death.

4) Withholding treatments is morally and legally equivalent to withdrawing them.

5) When one life sustaining treatment is withheld, strong consideration should be given to withdrawing other current life sustaining treatments and changing the goals of care to comfort.

6) Any treatment can be withdrawn including nutrition, fluids, antibiotics, and blood.

7) Assessing pain and discomfort in intubated, critically ill, patients can be difficult. The following should be assessed and documented in the medical record when increasing sedation: tachypnea, tachycardia, diaphoresis, grimacing, accessory muscle use, nasal flaring, and restlessness.

8) Concerns about hastening death by over-sedating patients are understandable. However, clinicians should be extremely sensitive to the difficulties of assessing discomfort in critically ill patients and should know that many patients develop tolerance to sedative medication. Therefore, clinicians should be wary of under-treating discomfort during the withdrawal of life sustaining treatments in the ICU.

9) Brain dead patients do not need sedation during the withdrawal of life sustaining treatment.

10) Patients should not have life support withdrawn while receiving paralytic drugs as these will mask signs of discomfort. Life support can be withdrawn from patients after paralytic drugs have been stopped as long as clinicians feel that the patient has sufficient motor activity to demonstrate discomfort.

PT.NO.

NAME

D.O.B.

UNIVERSITY OF WASHINGTON MEDICAL CENTERS
HARBORVIEW MEDICAL CENTER - UW MEDICAL CENTER
SEATTLE, WASHINGTON
PHYSICIAN ORDERS

COMFORT CARE ORDERS FOR THE WITHDRAWAL OF LIFE SUPPORT IN THE ICU

* H 1 4 5 0 *

PAGE 2 OF 2

WHITE-MEDICAL RECORD
CANARY-PHARMACY
PINK-NURSING

Figure 87.1 cont'd

may be exercised by patients themselves and by their family members and legally appointed surrogates through substituted judgment and best interests standards. It also may be exercised by the patients' physicians using the same standards, although little legal support exists for this practice.

End-of-life care is enhanced by a shared model of medical decision-making and by intensive communication among patients, family members, and caregivers. Such care should attend to the needs of patients, families, and caregivers. Its components include providing appropriate settings for dying patients; supplying emotional and spiritual support; managing such symptoms as pain, anxiety, delerium, dyspnea, nausea and vomiting, and hunger and thirst; and removing unwanted therapies so these symptoms are minimized. Increasingly, physicians and other health care professionals are trying to improve the quality of end-of-life care inside and outside the ICU.

ACKNOWLEDGMENTS

The author thanks Douglas B. White, M.D., Judith A. Luce, M.D., and V. Courtney Broaddus, M.D. for their editorial assistance.

REFERENCES

1. Burrows B, Earle RH: Course and prognosis of chronic obstructive lung disease. N Engl J Med 280:397–404, 1969.
2. Ferrer M, Alonso J, Morera J, et al: Chronic obstructive pulmonary disease stage and health-related quality of life. Ann Intern Med 127:1072–1079, 1997.
3. Mercadante S, Casuccio A, Fulfaro F: The course and symptom frequency and intensity in advanced cancer patients followed at home. J Pain Symptom Manage 20:104–112, 2000.
4. Luce JM, Luce JA: Management of dyspnea in patients with far-advanced lung disease: "Once I lose it, it's kinda hard to catch it. . . ." JAMA 285:1331–1337, 2001.
5. Arias E, Smith BL: Deaths: Preliminary data for 2001. Natl Vital Stat Rep 51:1–44, 2003.
6. Wingo PA, Cardinez CJ, Landis SH, et al: Long-term trends in cancer mortality in the United States, 1930–1998. Cancer 97:3133–3275, 2003.
7. Moss M, Mannino DM: Race and gender differences in acute respiratory distress syndrome deaths in the United States: An analysis of multiple-cause mortality data (1979–1996). Crit Care Med 30:1679–1685, 2002.
8. The SUPPORT Principal Investigators: A controlled trial to improve care for seriously ill hospitalized patients: The study to understand prognoses and preferences for outcomes and risks of treatment (SUPPORT). JAMA 274:1591–1598, 1995.
9. Somogyi-Zalud E, Zhong Z, Lynn J, et al: Dying with acute respiratory failure or multiple organ system failure with sepsis. J Am Geriatr Soc 48:S140–S145, 2000.
10. Hamel MB, Phillips RS, Davis RB, et al: Outcomes and cost-effectiveness of ventilator support and aggressive care for patients with acute respiratory failure due to pneumonia or acute respiratory distress syndrome. Am J Med 109:614–620, 2000.
11. Conners AF, Dawson NV, Thomas C, et al: Outcomes following acute exacerbations of chronic obstructive lung disease. Am J Respir Crit Care Med 154:959–9677, 1996.
12. Lynn J, Ely EW, Zhong Z, et al: Living and dying with chronic obstructive pulmonary disease. J Am Geriatr Soc 48:S91–S100, 2000.
13. McCarthy EP, Phillips RS, Zhong Z, et al: Dying with cancer: Patients' function, symptoms, and care preferences as death approaches. J Am Geriatr Soc 48:S110–S121, 2000.
14. Seneff MG, Wagner DP, Wagner RP, et al: Hospital and 1-year survival of patients admitted to intensive care units with acute exacerbations of chronic obstructive pulmonary disease. JAMA 274:1852–1857, 1995.
15. Wachter RM, Luce JM, Safrin S, et al: Cost and outcome of intensive care for patients with AIDS, Pneumocystis carinii pneumonia, and severe respiratory failure. JAMA 273:230–235, 1995.
16. Fowler AA, Hamman RF, Zerbe GO, et al: Adult respiratory distress syndrome: Prognosis after onset. Am Rev Respir Dis 132:472–478, 1985.
17. Ely EW, Wheeler AP, Thompson BT, et al: Recovery rate and prognosis in older persons who develop acute lung injury and the acute respiratory distress syndrome. Ann Intern Med 136:25–36, 2002.
18. Chelluri L, Pinsky MR, Donahoe MP, et al: Long-term outcome of critically ill elderly patients requiring intensive care. JAMA 269:3119–3123, 1993.
19. Ely EW, Evans GW, Haponik EF: Mechanical ventilation in a cohort of elderly patients admitted to an intensive care unit. Ann Intern Med 131:96–104, 1999.
20. Gillespie DJ, Marsh HMM, Divertie MB, et al: Clinical outcome of respiratory failure in patients requiring prolonged (>24 hours) mechanical ventilation. Chest 90:364–369, 1986.
21. American Thoracic Society: Guidelines for the management of adults with community-acquired pneumonia: Diagnosis, assessment of severity, antimicrobial therapy, and prevention. Am J Respir Care Med 163:1730–1754, 2001.
22. Fine MJ, Auble E, Yealy DM, et al: A prediction rule to identify low-risk patients with community-acquired pneumonia. N Engl J Med 336:243–250, 1997.
23. Knaus WA, Zimmerman JE, Wagner DP, et al: APACHE—acute physiology and chronic health evaluation: A physiologically based classification system. Crit Care Med 9:591–597, 1981.
24. Knaus WA, Draper EA, Wagner DP, et al: APACHE II—a severity of disease classification system. Crit Care Med 13:818–829, 1985.
25. Knaus WA, Wagner DP, Draper EA, et al: The APACHE III prognostic system: Risk prediction of hospital mortality for critically ill hospitalized adults. Chest 100:1619–1636, 1991.
26. Knaus WA, Harrell FE, Lynn J, et al: The SUPPORT prognostic model: Objective estimates of survival for seriously ill hospitalized adults. Ann Intern Med 122:191–203, 1995.
27. Morris A, Creasman J, Turner J, et al: Intensive care of human immunodeficiency virus-infected patients during the era of highly active antiretroviral therapy. Am J Respir Crit Care Med 166:262–267, 2002.
28. Milberg JA, Davis DR, Steinberg KP, et al: Improved survival of patients with acute respiratory distress syndrome (ARDS): 1983–1993. JAMA 273:306–309, 1995.
29. Angus DC, Marrie TJ, Obrosky DS, et al: Severe community-acquired pneumonia: Use of intensive care services and evaluation of American and British Thoracic Society diagnostic criteria. Am J Respir Crit Care Med 166:717–723, 2002.
30. Ewig S, Ruiz M, Mensa J, et al: Severe community-acquired pneumonia: Assessment of severity criteria. Am J Respir Crit Care Med 158:1102–1108, 1998.

31. Kruse JA, Thill-Baharozian MC, Carlson RW: Comparison of clinical assessment with APACHE II for predicting mortality risk in patients admitted to a medical intensive care unit. JAMA 260:1739–1742, 1988.

32. Zimmerman JE, Wagner DP, Draper EA, et al: Evaluation of Acute Physiology and Chronic Healh Evaluation III predictions of hospital mortality in an independent database. Crit Care Med 26:1317–1326, 1998.

33. Fox E, Landrum-McNiff K, Zhong Z, et al: Evaluation of prognostic criteria for determining hospice eligibility in patients with advanced lung, heart, or liver disease. JAMA 282:1638–1645, 1999.

34. Lynn J, Harrell F, Cohn F, et al: Prognoses of seriously ill hospitalized patients on the days before death: Implications for patient care and public policy. New Horiz 5:56–61, 1997.

35. Luce JM, Wachter RM: The ethical appropriateness of using prognostic scoring systems in clinical management. Crit Care Clin 10:229–241, 1994.

36. Claessens MT, Lynn J, Zhong Z, et al: Dying with lung cancer or chronic obstructive pulmonary disease: Insights from SUPPORT. J Am Geriatr Soc 48:S146–S153, 2000.

37. Weeks JC, Cook EF, O'Day SJ, et al: Relationship between cancer patients' predictions of prognosis and their treatment preferences. JAMA 279:1709–1714, 1998.

38. Curtis JR, Rubenfeld GD (eds): Managing Death in the Intensive Care Unit: The Transition from Cure to Comfort. Oxford: Oxford University Press, 2001.

39. Luce JM: Withholding and withdrawal of life support from critically ill patients. West J Med 167:411–416, 1997.

40. Smedira NG, Evans BH, Grais LS, et al: Withholding and withdrawal of life support from the critically ill. N Engl J Med 322:309–315, 1990.

41. Prendergast TJ, Luce JM: Increasing incidence of withholding and withdrawal of life support from the critically ill. Am J Respir Crit Care Med 155:15–20, 1997.

42. Prendergast TJ, Claessens MT, Luce JM: A national survey of end-of-life care for critically ill patients. Am J Respir Crit Care Med 158:1163–1167, 1998.

43. Prendergast TJ, Puntillo KA: Withdrawal of life support: Intensive caring at the end of life. JAMA 288:2732–2740, 2002.

44. Lynn J, Teno JM, Phillips RS, et al: Perceptions by family members of the dying experience of older and seriously ill patients. Ann Intern Med 126:97–106, 1997.

45. Angus DC, Barnato AE, Linde-Zwirble WT, et al: The use of intensive care at the end of life in the United States: An epidemiologic study. Crit Care Med 32:638–643, 2004.

46. Luce JM, Prendergast TJ: The changing nature of death in the ICU. In Curtis JR, Rubenfeld GD (eds): Managing Death in the Intensive Care Unit: The Transition from Cure to Comfort. Oxford: Oxford University Press, 2001, pp 19–29.

47. Fuchs VR: Who Shall Choose? Health, Economics, and Social Choice. New York: Basic Books, 1974.

48. Bedell SE, Delblarco TL, Cook F, et al: Survival after cardiopulmonary resuscitation in the hospital. N Engl J Med 309:569–576, 1983.

49. Taffet GE, Teasdale TA, Luchi RJ: In-hospital cardiopulmonary resuscitation. JAMA 260:2069–2072, 1988.

50. Gostin LO: Deciding life and death in the courtroom: From Quinlan to Cruzan, Glucksberg, and Vacco—a brief history and analysis of constitutional protection of the "right to die." JAMA 278:1523–1528, 1997.

51. Bone RC, Rackow EC, Weg JG, et al: Ethical and moral guidelines for the initiation, continuation, and withdrawal of intensive care. Chest 97:949–958, 1990.

52. Task Force on Ethics of the Society of Critical Care Medicine: Consensus report on the ethics of foregoing life-sustaining treatments in the critically ill. Crit Care Med 18:1435–1439, 1990.

53. Council on Ethics and Judicial affairs, American Medical Association: Decisions near the end of life. JAMA 267:2229–2234, 1992.

54. American Thoracic Society: Withholding and withdrawing life-sustaining therapy. Am Rev Respir Dis 144:726–731, 1991.

55. Karlawish JHT, Hall JB: Managing death and dying in the intensive care unit. Am J Respir Crit Care Med 155:1–2, 1997.

56. Beauchamp TL, Childress JF: Principles of Biomedical Ethics (4th ed). Oxford: Oxford University Press, 1994.

57. Rodwin MA: Strains in the fiduciary relationship: Divided physician loyalties and obligations in a changing health care system. Am J Law Med 21:241–257, 1995.

58. Luce JM, Alpers A: Legal aspects of withholding and withdrawing life support from critically ill patients in the United States and providing palliative care to them. Am J Respir Crit Care Med 162:2029–2032, 2000.

59. Luce JM, Alpers A: End-of-life care: What do the American courts say? Crit Care Med 29:N40–N45, 2001.

60. Schloendorff v. Society of New York Hospitals, 211 NY 125, 105 NE 92, 1914.

61. Bartling v. Superior Court, 163 Cal. App. ed 190, 209 Cal. Rptr. 220 (1984).

62. Bouvia v. Superior Court, 179 Cal. App. ed 190, 225 Cal. Rptr. 297 (1986).

63. In re Quinlan, 755 A2A 647 (NJ), cert. Denied, 429 US 922 (1976).

64. Barber v. Superior Court, 147 Cal. App. 3d 1006 (Cal. App. 1983).

65. Cruzan v. Director, Missouri Department of Health, 497 US 261 (1990).

66. In re Conroy, 486A: 2d 1209 (N.J. 1985).

67. Wendland v. Wendland, 26 Cal. 4th 519, 28 P.3d 151 (2001).

68. Lo B, Dornbrand L, Wolf LE, et al: The Wendland case—withdrawing life support from incompetent patients who are not terminally ill. N Engl J Med 346:1489–1494, 2002.

69. Luce JM: Three patients who asked that life support be withheld or withdrawn in the surgical intensive care unit. Crit Care Med 30:775–780, 2002.

70. Grew PJ, Schulman KA, Lavison MR, et al: The Patient Self-Determination Act and the future of advance directives. Ann Intern Med 115:639–643, 1991.

71. Teno JM, Licks S, Lynn J, et al: Do advance directives provide instructions that direct care? J Am Geriatr Soc 45:508–512, 1997.

72. Covinsky KE, Fuller JD, Yaffe K, et al: Communication and decision-making in seriously ill patients: Findings of the SUPPORT project. J Am Geriatr Soc 48:S187–S193, 2000.

73. Teno J, Lynn J, Conners AF, et al: The illusion of end-of-life resource savings with advance directives. J Am Geriatr Soc 45:513–518, 1997.

74. Quill TE, Brody H: Physician recommendations and patient autonomy: Finding a balance between physician power and patient choice. Ann Intern Med 125:763–769, 1996.

75. President's Commission for the Study of Ethical Problems in Medicine and Biomedical and Behavioral Research: Guidelines for the determination of brain death. JAMA 246:2184–2186, 1981.

76. Luce JM: Ethical principles in critical care. JAMA 263:696–700, 1990.

77. Daar JF: Medical futility and implications for physician autonomy. Am J Law Med 21:221–240, 1995.

78. Schneiderman LJ, Jecker NS, Jonsen AR: Medical futility: Its meaning and ethical implications. Ann Intern Med 112:949–954, 1990.

79. Helft PR, Siegler M, Lantos J: The rise and fall of the futility movement. N Engl J Med 343:293–296, 2000.

80. Lantos JD, Singer PA, Walker RM, et al: The illusion of futility in clinical practice. Am J Med 87:81–84, 1989.

81. Knaus WA, Wagner DP, Lynn J: Short-term mortality predictions for critically ill hospitalized adults: Science and ethics. Science 254:389–394, 1991.

82. Teno JM, Murphy D, Lynn J, et al: Prognosis-based futility guidelines: Does anyone win? J Am Geriatr Soc 42:1202–1207, 1994.

83. Luce JM: The changing physician-patient relationship in critical care medicine under health care reform. Am J Respir Crit Care Med 150:266–270, 1994.

84. Luce JM: Making decisions about the forgoing of life-sustaining therapy. Am J Respir Crit Care Med 156:1715–1718, 1997.

85. Truog RD, Brett AS, Frader J: The problem with futility. N Engl J Med 326:1560–1564, 1992.

86. Younger SJ: Who defines futility? JAMA 260:2094–2095, 1988.

87. Council on Ethical and Judicial Affairs, American Medical Association: Medical futility in end-of-life care. JAMA 281:937–941, 1999.

88. Halevy A, Brody BA: A multi-institutional collaborative policy on medical futility. JAMA 276:571–574, 1996.

89. Fine RJ, Mayo TW: Resolution of futility by due process: Early experience with the Texas Advance Directives Act. Ann Intern Med 138:743–746, 2003.

90. In re Helen Wanglie, Fourth Judicial District (Dist. Ct., Probate Ct. Div.) PX-91-283. Minnesota. Hennipin County.

91. In the Matter of Baby K, 832 F. Supp. 1022 (E.D. Va. 1993).

92. Gilgunn v. Massachusetts General Hospital, Na: 92-4820 (Mass. Super. Ct. Civ. Action Suffolk S. April 22, 1995).

93. Aaron HJ, Schwartz WB: The Painful Prescription: Rationing Hospital Care. Washington, DC: Brookings Institution, 1984.

94. Washington v. Glucksberg, 521 US 702 (1997).

95. Vacco v. Quill, 521 US 797 (1997).

96. Burt RA: The Supreme Court speaks: Not assisted suicide but a constitutional right to palliative care. N Engl J Med 337:1234–1236, 1997.

97. Sulmasy DP: The rule of double effect: Clearing up the double talk. Arch Intern Med 159:545–550, 1999.

98. Quill TE, Dressner R, Brock DW: The rule of double effect: A critique of its role in end-of-life decisdion making. N Engl J Med 337:1768–1772, 1997.

99. Wilson WC, Smedira NG, Fink C, et al: Ordering and administration of sedatives and analgesics during the withholding and withdrawal of life support from critically ill patients. JAMA 267:949–953, 1992.

100. Asch DA: The role of critical care nurses in euthanasia and assisted suicide. N Engl J Med 334:1374–1379, 1996.

101. Alpers A: Criminal act or palliative care? Prosecutions involving the care of the dying. J Law Med Ethics 26:308–331, 1998.

102. Ganzini L, Nelson HD, Schmidt TA, et al: Physicians' experiences with the Oregon Death With Dignity Act. N Engl J Med 342:557–563, 2000.

103. Chin AE, Hedberg K, Higginson GK, et al: Legalized physician-assisted suicide in Oregon: The first year's experience. N Engl J Med 340:577–583, 1999.

104. Sullivan AD, Hedberg K, Fleming DW: Legalized physician-assisted suicide in Oregon: The second year. N Engl J Med 342:598–604, 2000.

105. Steinbrook R: Physician-assisted suicide in Oregon—an uncertain future. N Engl J Med 346:460–464, 2002.

106. Van der Heide A, Dekliens L, Faisst K, et al: End-of-life decision-making in six European countries: Descriptive study. Lancet 361:345–350, 2003.

107. Van der Maas PJ, van der wal G, Haverkate I, et al: Euthanasia, physician assisted suicide, and other medical practices involving the end of life in The Netherlands, 1990–1995. N Engl J Med 335:1699–1705, 1996.

108. Onwuteaka-Phillipsen BD, van der Heide A, Keij-Deerenberg I, et al: Euthanasia and other end-of-life decisions in The Netherlands in 1990, 1995, and 2003. Lancet 362:395–399, 2003.

109. Emanuel EJ, Emanuel LL: Four models of the physician-patient relationship. JAMA 267:2221–2226, 1992.

110. Faden RR, Beauchamp TL: A History and Theory of Informed Consent. Oxford: Oxford University Press, 1986.

111. Luce JM, Lemaire F: Two trans-Atlantic viewpoints on an ethical quandary. Am J Respir Crit Care Med 163:818–821, 2001.

112. Pochard F, Azoulay E, Chevret S, et al: French intensivists do not apply American recommendations regarding decisions to forgo life-sustaining therapy. Crit Care Med 29:1887–1892, 2001.

113. Vincent J-L: Forgoing life support in western European intensive care units: The results of an ethical questionnaire. Crit Care Med 27:1626–1633, 1999.

114. Ip M, Gilligan T, Koenig B, et al: Ethical decision-making in critical care in Hong Kong. Crit Care Med 26:447–451, 1998.

115. Astrow AB, Puchalski CM, Sulmasy DP: Religion, spirituality, and health care: Social, ethical, and practical considerations. Am J Med 110:283–287, 2001.

116. Blackhall LJ, Murphy ST, Frank G, et al: Ethnicity and attitudes toward patient autonomy. JAMA 274:820–825, 1995.

117. Blackhall LJ, Frank G, Murphy ST, et al: Ethnicity and attitudes towards life sustaining technology. Soc Sci Med 48:1779–1789, 1999.

118. Danis M, Garrett J, Harris R, et al: Stability of choices about life-sustaining treatments. Ann Intern Med 120:567–573, 1994.

119. Everhart MA, Pearlman RA: Stability of patient preferences regarding life-sustaining treatments. Chest 97:159–164, 1990.

120. Puchalski CM, Zhong Z, Jacobs MM, et al: Patients who want their family and physician to make resuscitation decisions for them: Observations from SUPPORT and HELP. J Am Geriatr Soc 48:S84–S90, 2000.

121. Pochard F, Azoulay E, Chevret S, et al: Symptoms of anxiety and depression in family members of intensive care unit patients: Ethical hypothesis regarding decision-making capacity. Crit Care Med 29:1893–1897, 2001.

122. Seckler AB, Meier DE, Mulvihill M, et al: Substituted judgment: how accurate are proxy predictions? Ann Intern Med 115:92–98, 1991.

123. Sulmasy DP, Terry PB, Weisman CS, et al: The accuracy of substituted judgments in patients with terminal diagnoses. Ann Intern Med 128:621–629, 1998.

124. Quill TE: Initiating end-of-life discussions with seriously ill patients: Addressing the "elephant in the room." JAMA 284:2502–2507, 2000.

125. O'Brein LA, Grisso JA, Maislin G, et al: Nursing home residents' preferences for life-sustaining treatments. JAMA 274:1775–1779, 1995.

126. Heffner JE, Fahy B, Hilling L, et al: Attitudes regarding advance directives among patients in pulmonary rehabilitation. Am J Respir Crit Care Med 154:1735–1740, 1996.

127. Heffner JE, Fahy B, Hilling L, et al: Outcomes of advance directive education of pulmonary rehabilitation patients. Am J Respir Crit Care Med 155:1055–1059, 1997.

128. Curtis JR, Patrick DL, Caldwell ES, et al: Why don't patients and physicians talk about end-of-life care? Barriers to communication for patients with acquired immunodeficiency syndrome and their primary care clinicians. Arch Intern Med 160:1690–1696, 2000.

129. Azoulay E, Chevret S, Leleu G, et al: Half the families of intensive care unit patients experience inadequate communication with physicians. Crit Care Med 28:3044–3049, 2000.

130. Azoulay E, Pochard F, Chevret S, et al: Meeting the needs of intensive care unit patient families: A multicenter study. Am J Respir Crit Care Med 163:135–139, 2001.

131. Azoulay E, Pochard F, Chevret S, et al: Impact of a family information leaflet on effectiveness of information provided to family members of intensive care unit patients. Am J Respir Crit Care Med 165:438–442, 2002.

132. Curtis JR, Patrick DL, Engelberg RA, et al: A measure of the quality of dying and death: Initial validation using after-death interviews with family members. J Pain Symptom Manage 24:17–31, 2002.

133. Abbott KH, Sago JG, Breen CM, et al: Families looking back: One year after discussion of withdrawal or withholding of life-sustaining support. Crit Care Med 29:197–201, 2001.

134. Lilly CM, DeMeo DL, Sonna LA, et al: An intensive communication intervention for the critically ill. Am J Med 109:469–475, 2000.

134a. McDonagh JR, Elliott TB, Engelberg RA, et al: Family satisfaction with family conferences about end-of-life care in the intensive care unit: increased proportion of family speech is associated with increased satisfaction. Crit Care Med 32:1484–1488, 2004.

135. Meyer EC, Burns JP, Griffith JL, et al: Parental perspectives on end-of-life care in the pediatric intensive care unit. Crit Care Med 30:226–231, 2002.

135a. White DB, Luce JM: Palliative care in the intensive care unit: barriers, advances, and unmet needs. Crit Care Clin 20:329–343, 2004.

136. Fetters MD, Churchill L, Danis M: Conflict resolution at the end of life. Crit Care Med 29:921–925, 2001.

137. Kagawa-Singer M, Blackhall LJ: Negotiating cross-cultural issues at the end of life: "You got to go where he lives." JAMA 286:2993–3001, 2001.

138. Casarett D, Siegler M: Unilateral do-not-attempt-resuscitation orders and ethics consultation: A case series. Crit Care Med 27:1116–1120, 1999.

139. Schneiderman LJ, Gilmer T, Teetzel HD: Impact of ethics consultations in the intensive care setting: A randomized, controlled trial. Crit Care Med 28:3920–3924, 2000.

140. Schneiderman LJ, Gilmer T, Teetzel HD, et al: Effects of ethics consultations on nonbeneficial life-sustaining treatments in the intensive care setting: A randomized controlled trial. JAMA 290:1166–1172, 2003.

141. Steinhauser KE, Christakis NA, Clipp EC, et al: Factors considered important at the end of life by patients, family, physicians, and other care providers. JAMA 284:2476–2482, 2000.

142. Truog RD, Cist EFM, Brackett SE, et al: Recommendations for end-of-life care in the intensive care unit: The ethics committee of the Society of Critical Care Medicine. Crit Care Med 29:2332–2348, 2001.

143. Ferrand E, Lemaire F, Regnier B, et al: Discrepancies between perceptions by physicians and nursing staff of intensive care unit end-of-life decisions. Am J Respir Crit Care Med 167:1310–1315, 2003.

144. Campbell ML, Frank RR: Experience with an end-of-life practice at a university hospital. Crit Care Med 25:197–202, 1997.

145. Brock H, Campbell ML, Faber-Langendoen K, et al: Withdrawing intensive life-sustaining treatment: Recommendations for compassionate clinical management. N Engl J Med 336:652–657, 1997.

146. Faber-Langendoen K, Lanken PN: Dying patients in the intensive care unit: Forgoing treatment, maintaining care. Ann Intern Med 133:886–893, 2000.

147. Cuthbertson SJ, Margetts MA, Streat SJ: Bereavement follow-up after critical illness. Crit Care Med 28:1196–1201, 2000.

148. Desbiens NA, Wu AW, Broste SK, et al: Pain and satisfaction with pain control in seriously ill hospitalized adults: Findings from the SUPPORT research investigations. Crit Care Med 24:1953–1961, 1996.

149. Simmons LE, Riker RR, Prato BS, et al: Assessing sedation during intensive care unit mechanical ventilation with the bispectral index and the sedation-agitation scale. Crit Care Med 27:1499–1504, 1999.

150. Burns JP, Mitchell C, Outwater KM, et al: End-of-life care in the pediatric intensive care unit after the forgoing of life-sustaining treatment. Crit Care Med 28:654–661, 2000.

151. Shapiro BA, Warren J, Egol AB, et al: Practice parameters for intravenous analgesia and sedation in adult patients in the intensive care unit: An executive summary. Crit Care Med 23:1596–1600, 1995.

152. Kerr IG, Sone M, DeAngelis C, et al: Continuous narcotic infusion with patient-controlled analgesia for chronic cancer pain in outpatients. Ann Intern Med 108:554–557, 1988.

153. Hall RI, Rocker GM: End-of-life care in the ICU: Treatments provided when life support was or was not withdrawn. Chest 118:1424–1430, 2000.

154. Jacox A, Carr DB, Payne R: New clinical-practice guidelines for the management of pain in patients with cancer. N Engl J Med 330:651–655, 1994.

155. Kress JP, Pohlman AS, Hall JB: Sedation and analgesia in the intensive care unit. Am J Respir Crit Care Med 166:1024–1028, 2002.

156. Ostermann ME, Keenan SP, Seiferling RA, et al: Sedation in the intensive care unit: A systematic review. JAMA 283:1451–1459, 2000.

157. American Thoracic Society: Dyspnea: Mechanisms, assessment, and management; a consensus statement. Am J Respir Crit Care Med 159:321–340, 1999.

158. Ferguson GT, Cherniack RM: Management of chronic obstructive pulmonary disease. N Engl J Med 328:1017–1022, 1993.

159. The Lung Health Study Research Group: Effect of inhaled triamcinolone on the decline in pulmonary function in chronic obstructive pulmonary disease. N Engl J Med 343:1902–1909, 2000.

160. National Emphysema Treatment Trials Research Group: A randomized trial comparing lung-volume-reduction surgery with medical therapy for severe emphysema. N Engl J Med 348:2059–2074, 2003.

161. American Thoracic Society: Pulmonary rehabilitation—1999. Am J Respir Crit Care Med 159:1666–1682, 1999.

162. Nocturnal Oxygen Therapy Trials Group: Continuous or nocturnal oxygen therapy in hypoxemic chronic obstructive lung disease. Ann Intern Med 93:391–398, 1980.

163. Booth S, Kelly MJ, Cox NP, et al: Does oxygen help dyspnea in patients with cancer? Am J Respir Crit Care Med 153:1515–1518, 1996.

164. Light RW, Muro JR, Sato RI, et al: Effects of oral morphine on breathlessness and exercise tolerance in patients with chronic obstructive pulmonary disease. Am Rev Respir Dis 139:126–133, 1989.

165. Poole PJ, Veale AG, Black PN: The effect of sustained-release morphine on breathlessness and quality of life in severe chronic obstructive pulmonary disease. Am J Respir Crit Care 157:1877–1880, 1998.

166. Man GCW, Hsu K, Sproule BJ: Effect of alprazolam on exercise and dyspnea in patients with chronic obstructive pulmonary disease. Chest 90:832–836, 1986.

167. Greif R, Laciny S, Rapf B, et al: Supplemental oxygen reduces the incidence of postoperative nausea and vomiting. Anesthesiology 91:1246–1252, 1999.

168. Roscoe JA, Morrow GR, Hickok JT, et al: Nausea and vomiting remain a significant clinical problem: Trends over time in controlling chemotherapy-induced nausea and vomiting in 1413 patients treated in community clinical practices. J Pain Symptom Manage 20:113–121, 2000.

169. Gan TJ, Meyer T, Apfel CC, et al: Consensus guidelines for managing postoperative nausea and vomiting. Anesth Analg 97:62–71, 2003.

170. Tramer MR, Carroll D, Campbell FA, et al: Cannabinoids for control of chemotherapy induced nausea and vomiting: Quantitative systematic review. BMJ 323:16–21, 2001.

171. Rosner F: Why nutrition and hydration should not be withheld from patients. Chest 104:1892–1896, 1993.

172. Jansen LA, Sulmasy DP: Sedation, alimentation, hydration, and equivocation: Careful conversation about care at the end of life. Ann Intern Med 136:845–849, 2002.

173. Miller FG, Meier DE: Voluntary death: A comparison of terminal hydration and physician-assisted suicide. Ann Intern Med 128:559–562, 1998.

174. Ganzini L, Goy ER, Miller LL, et al: Nurses' experience with hospice patients who refuse food and fluids to hasten death. N Engl J Med 349:359–365, 2003.

175. McCann RM, Hall WJ, Groth-Juncker A: Comfort care for terminally ill patients: The appropriate use of nutrition and hydration. JAMA 272:1263–1266, 1994.

176. Koch KA, Rodeffer HD, Wears RL: Changing patterns of terminal care management in an intensive care unit. Crit Care Med 22:233–243, 1994.

177. Lee DKP, Swinburne AJ, Fedullo AJ, et al: Withdrawing care: Experience in a medical intensive care unit. JAMA 271:1358–1361, 1994.

178. McLean RF, Tarshis J, Mazer CD, et al: Death in two Canadian intensive care units: Institutional differences and changes over time. Crit Care Med 28:100–103, 2000.

179. Vincent J-L, Parquier J-N, Presier J-C, et al: Terminal events in the intensive care unit: Review of 258 fatal cases in one year. Crit Care Med 17:530–533, 1989.

180. Keenan SP, Busche KD, Chen LM, et al: Withdrawal and withholding of life support in the intensive care unit: A comparison of teaching and community hospitals. Crit Care Med 26:245–251, 1998.

181. Keenan SP, Busche KD, Chen LM, et al: A retrospective review of a large cohort of patients undergoing the process of withholding or withdrawal of life support. Crit Care Med 25:1324–1331, 1997.

182. Faber-Langendoen K, Bartels DM: Process of forgoing life-sustaining treatment in a university hospital: An empiric study. Crit Care Med 20:570–577, 1992.

183. Christakis NA, Asch DA: Biases in how physicians choose to withdraw life support. Lancet 342:642–646, 1993.

184. Cook D, Rocker G, Marshall J, et al: Withdrawal of mechanical ventilation in anticipation of death in the intensive care unit. N Engl J Med 349:1123–1132, 2003.

185. Grenvik A: "Terminal weaning": Discontinuance of life-support therapy in the terminally ill patient. Crit Care Med 11:394–395, 1983.

186. Gianakos D: Terminal weaning. Chest 108:1405–1406, 1995.

187. Gilligan T, Raffin TA: Rapid withdrawal of support. Chest 108:1407–1408, 1995.

188. Campbell ML, Bizek KS, Thill M: Patient responses during rapid terminal weaning from mechanical ventilation: A prospective study. Crit Care Med 27:73–77, 1999.

189. Faber-Langendoen K: The clinical management of dying patients receiving mechanical ventilation. Chest 106:880–888, 1994.

190. Truog RD, Burns JP, Mitchell C, et al: Pharmacologic paralysis and withdrawal of mechanical ventilation at the end of life. N Engl J Med 342:508–512, 2000.

190a. Thompson BT, Cox PN, Antonelli M, et al: Challenges in end-of-life care in the ICU: statement of the 5th International Consensus Conference in Critical Care: Brussels, Belgium, April 2003: executive summary. Crit Care Med 32:1781–1784, 2004.

191. Rubenfeld GD, Curtis JR: End-of-life care in the intensive care unit: A research agenda. Crit Care Med 29:2001–2006, 2001.

192. Clark EB, Curtis JR, Luce JM, et al: Quality indicators for end-of-life care in the intensive care unit. Crit Care Med 31:2255–2262, 2003.

193. Clark EB, Luce JM, Curtis JR, et al: A content analysis of forms, guidelines, and other materials documenting end-of-life care in intensive care units. J Crit Care 19:108–117, 2004.

194. Treece PD, Engelberg RA, Crowley L, et al: Evaluation of a standardized order form for the withdrawal of life support in the intensive care unit. Crit Care Med 32:1141–1148, 2004.

195. DeVita MA, Arnold RM, Barnard D: Teaching palliative care to critical care medicine trainees. Crit Care Med 31:1257–1262, 2003.

196. Stevens L, Cook D, Guyatt G, et al: Education, ethics, and end-of-life decisions in the intensive care unit. Crit Care Med 30:290–296, 2002.

197. Danis M, Federman D, Fins JJ, et al: Incorporating palliative care into critical care education: Principles, challenges, and opportunities. Crit Care Med 27:2005–2013, 1999.

198. Levy MM: End-of-life care in the intensive care unit: Can we do better? Crit Care Med 29:N56–N61, 2001.

88 Pulmonary Rehabilitation

Bartolome R. Celli, M.D., Richard L. ZuWallack, M.D.

INTRODUCTION

Patients with advanced chronic respiratory disease frequently have distressing symptoms, limitations in exercise ability, and reductions in health and functional status that persist despite optimal pharmacologic management. Pulmonary rehabilitation complements standard medical therapy and can provide additional, clinically meaningful benefit in these areas. Indeed, pulmonary rehabilitation has become the standard of care for patients who are motivated to participate in such programs. As is described in this chapter, patients improve their exercise and functional capacity, decrease their dyspnea, improve their health status, and perhaps postpone premature morbidity and mortality. Although pulmonary rehabilitation was designed and is applied primarily to symptomatic patients who are limited due to the burden of chronic obstructive pulmonary disease (COPD), the same fundamental principles appear applicable to other disease states leading to disability.

DEFINITION AND GOALS

Rehabilitation focuses on restoring the individual to the fullest medical, mental, emotional, social, and vocational potential to which he or she is capable. Based on this basic concept, *pulmonary rehabilitation* has been defined as "a multidisciplinary program of care for patients with chronic respiratory impairment that is individually tailored and designed to optimize physical and social performance and autonomy."[1]

From this definition it follows that pulmonary rehabilitation has three major goals.

1. To control, alleviate and, as much as possible, reverse the symptoms and pathophysiologic processes leading to respiratory impairment

2. To improve functional status and participation in daily activities

3. To enhance health-related quality of life and attempt to prolong the patient's life

The concept of pulmonary rehabilitation has two other important elements: its use of a wide array of disciplines to achieve these goals,[1a] and its recognition that the patient has unique medical problems and needs that require an individualized approach.

HISTORY

Pulmonary rehabilitation and its components had been recognized by clinicians as an effective intervention since at least the middle of the 20th century.[2-4] However, in the past 15 years it has risen to prominence as a state-of-the-art, scientifically proven intervention for individuals with chronic lung disease. Its current importance as a therapeutic option is underscored by three recent events.

- Its incorporation as the "best therapy" to which lung volume reduction surgery was compared in the National Emphysema Treatment Trial (NETT)[5]
- A Cochrane report demonstrating the effectiveness of pulmonary rehabilitation in their meta-analyses[6]
- Its endorsement by the Global Initiative for Obstructive Lung disease (GOLD), and its prominent position in their treatment algorithm for COPD[7]

Over time, what was considered a form of therapy reserved only for patients with the most severe impairment is now recommended for patients with symptoms that limit their performance and a moderate severity of disease.

Several recent influential studies prominent in the history of pulmonary rehabilitation are listed in Table 88.1. These studies demonstrate the near-meteoric development of the

Table 88.1 Selected Studies in the Development of the Field of Pulmonary Rehabilitation

Year	Study	Importance in the Field of Pulmonary Rehabilitation
1991	Casaburi[12]	Demonstrates a dose-dependent physiologic benefit from exercise training
1994	Goldstein[13]	First of many randomized controlled trials establishing the effectiveness of pulmonary rehabilitation
1994	Reardon[14]	First study to prove that pulmonary rehabilitation relieves dyspnea
1995	Ries[17]	Landmark study showing the effectiveness of pulmonary rehabilitation in multiple outcome areas
1996	Maltais[18]	Demonstrates the importance of biochemical abnormalities in the muscles of COPD, and their improvement with pulmonary rehabilitation
2000	Griffiths[19]	Large randomized trial showing, among other positive outcomes, a substantial reduction in health care utilization following pulmonary rehabilitation
2003	Bourbeau[21]	Provided strong evidence supporting role of the educational component of pulmonary rehabilitation

COPD, chronic obstructive pulmonary disease.

science behind pulmonary rehabilitation and the effectiveness of this form of treatment.

Prior to 1991, much of the literature supporting pulmonary rehabilitation consisted of descriptions of comprehensive pulmonary rehabilitation and presentations of uncontrolled, preintervention-postintervention studies showing its effectiveness primarily in reducing hospital utilization.[8–11] However, in 1991 Casaburi and colleagues[12] reported on a study of 19 COPD patients who were randomized to either higher or lower levels of exercise training on a cycle ergometer. Training was 5 days per week for a total of 8 weeks. The patients who trained at lower levels exercised longer, so the total amount of work was roughly equivalent in the two groups. Low levels of exercise resulted in lactic acid production, indicating a low aerobic capacity at baseline. Both levels of training led to significant physiologic benefits manifested by reduced lactic acidosis and ventilatory requirement at the same work rate. However, those who trained at higher intensity had more physiologic benefit than those who trained at lower intensity. Prior to this study, it was believed by many that patients with advanced COPD, often being ventilatory-limited during exercise, could not derive true physiologic benefit from this type of intervention. This was the first randomized, controlled trial to prove that a training effect could occur with exercise training, the cornerstone of pulmonary rehabilitation.

In 1994, Goldstein and associates reported a prospective, randomized, controlled trial of pulmonary rehabilitation.[13] Eighty-nine patients with COPD were randomized to either

pulmonary rehabilitation, initially given in an inpatient setting, or conventional medical care. The group who participated in pulmonary rehabilitation had significantly greater increases in the 6-minute walk distance, submaximal cycle endurance time, and health status compared to the group given standard medical care. This was the first of several randomized, controlled trials of pulmonary rehabilitation that unequivocally established the effectiveness of pulmonary rehabilitation as a treatment option for chronic lung disease.

That same year, Reardon and colleagues[14] reported on 20 COPD patients, who were randomized to either comprehensive outpatient pulmonary rehabilitation or to a waiting period, where they were given conventional medical care. Rehabilitation led to significant improvement in exertional dyspnea, measured during incremental treadmill exercise testing and overall questionnaire-rated dyspnea with daily activities. The reduction in exertional dyspnea probably occurred at levels common to activities of daily living, underscoring its clinical meaningfulness. This was the first study to demonstrate the effectiveness of pulmonary rehabilitation on dyspnea, the most important symptom in advanced lung disease. Subsequent studies by O'Donnell and colleagues[15,16] showed that the reduction in post-exercise training dyspnea was associated with decreased ventilatory demand, probably due to improved exercise efficiency.

In 1996, Ries and colleagues[17] reported on 119 patients with COPD who were randomized to either comprehensive outpatient pulmonary rehabilitation or education alone. Compared to education alone, rehabilitation led to significant relief of dyspnea, maximal exercise capacity, exercise endurance, and self-efficacy for walking. Self-efficacy refers to the patient's confidence in successfully managing respiratory symptoms associated with an activity. Positive results declined over time, approaching those of the control group by 18 to 24 months. This was the first large, randomized, controlled study showing the effectiveness of outpatient pulmonary rehabilitation on multiple outcomes. The decline in gains made over time underscored the importance of strategies to improve long-term adherence with rehabilitation.

Maltais and colleagues[18] reported on 11 patients with COPD who were evaluated before and after 36 sessions of high-intensity endurance training. In addition to the expected physiologic training effect (including reduced exercise-induced lactic acidosis), exercise training led to increased levels of oxidative enzymes in muscle biopsy specimens. Of additional importance, the improvement in biochemical markers correlated with reduced lactic acid production during exercise. Along with other work, this study proves that exercise training improves skeletal muscle oxidative capacity in COPD patients, and this improvement has clinical meaningfulness.

In 2000, Griffiths and colleagues[19] presented data on 200 patients with chronic lung disease who were randomized to either 6 weeks of multidisciplinary pulmonary rehabilitation or standard medical management. In addition to showing substantial improvements in exercise performance and health-related quality of life, the pulmonary rehabilitation intervention led to fewer days in the hospital and fewer primary care home visits in the 1-year follow-up period. Thus, this large, randomized trial demonstrated a substantial reduction in health care utilization following pulmonary rehabilitation, confirming conclusions from noncontrolled studies years earlier. A subsequent study from this group[20] provided evidence supporting the cost-effectiveness of pulmonary rehabilitation.

Bourbeau and colleagues[21] demonstrated in 2003 that a self-management program aimed at the home setting led to fewer hospital admissions and other health utilization variables and improvement in health status. Self-management skills are prominent components of comprehensive pulmonary rehabilitation. This study provides scientific evidence supporting this educational component of comprehensive pulmonary rehabilitation.

RATIONALE

Pulmonary rehabilitation has a minimal, if any, effect on the abnormal lung function or respiratory physiology of individuals with chronic lung disease. Despite this, it usually results in clinically meaningful improvement in multiple outcome areas of considerable importance to the patient, including a reduction in exertional dyspnea and dyspnea associated with daily activities, improvement in exercise performance and in health status, and reduction in health care utilization.

The apparent paradox in which functional capacity can improve without major change in pulmonary function is explained by the fact that a considerable portion of the dyspnea and the functional status and health status limitations from chronic lung disease results from extrapulmonary effects of the disease, which do respond to treatment. Some of the associated systemic manifestations include nutritional depletion,[22,23] decrease in lower extremity muscle mass and peripheral muscle weakness and fatigability,[24,25] alterations in peripheral muscle fiber type,[26] and reduction in peripheral muscle oxidative enzymes.[27,28] This, in addition to the classic changes of cardiovascular deconditioning, poor pacing techniques, maladaptive coping skills, and fear and anxiety for dyspnea-producing activities results in a vicious circle of ever further deconditioning and debilitation. The accumulated evidence indicates that pulmonary rehabilitation is highly effective in improving and in some instances reversing many of these systemic abnormalities.[28a]

INDICATIONS

Pulmonary rehabilitation is indicated for individuals with chronic respiratory disease who have persistent symptoms or disability despite standard medical therapy. Figure 88.1 represents the course of patients with lung function limitation over time and the role of pulmonary rehabilitation. Figure 88.2 represents the relative roles of medical therapy and pulmonary rehabilitation during disease progression. Although all individuals with chronic respiratory disease are eligible for consideration for pulmonary rehabilitation, to date COPD is the most common disease for which patients are referred, often for one or more of the following symptoms or conditions.[29]

1. Severe dyspnea and/or fatigue
2. Decreased exercise ability

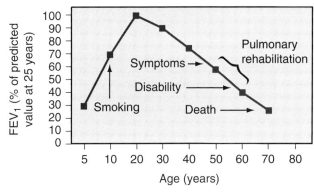

Figure 88.1 Change in forced expiratory volume in 1 second (FEV_1) over time in persons susceptible to the effect of cigarette smoking and who develop chronic obstructive pulmonary disease (COPD). The progressive decline results in functional limitation, poor health status, and eventual death. Pulmonary rehabilitation has a role once persistent symptoms or disabilities develop and for as long as patients benefit.

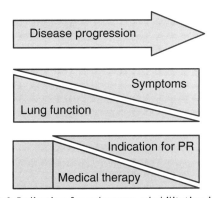

Figure 88.2 Indication for pulmonary rehabilitation in disease progression. Pulmonary rehabilitation is an appropriate therapy in the course of respiratory disease when, after usual medical therapy, physiologic impairment is associated with significant symptoms and functional status limitation.

3. Interference with performing activities of daily living
4. Impaired health status
5. Decreased occupational performance
6. Nutritional depletion
7. Increased medical resource consumption

It should be noted that persistent symptoms and/or limitation in these clinical areas—not just the specific physiologic impairment of the lungs (such as a low FEV_1 or hypoxemia)—dictate the need for this intervention. Furthermore, symptoms, exercise performance, functional status, and health status each individually correlate relatively poorly with pulmonary function abnormalities. Because of this, there are no specific threshold pulmonary function inclusion criteria for pulmonary rehabilitation.

Often the referral to pulmonary rehabilitation has been reserved for advanced lung disease. Although patients in this category can benefit from the intervention,[30] referral at an earlier stage would allow more emphasis on preventive strategies such as smoking cessation and exercise training at higher levels of intensity.

Traditionally, pulmonary rehabilitation has dealt primarily with COPD, and its effectiveness for other pulmonary conditions has received less attention.[31] However, patients with chronic asthma and airways remodeling, bronchiectasis, cystic fibrosis, chest wall disease, or interstitial lung disease may be appropriate candidates. Pulmonary rehabilitation is the standard of care before and after lung transplantation and lung volume reduction surgery. Based on these accepted indications, pulmonary rehabilitation should also be useful to recondition patients for other major surgical procedures.

There are two primary exclusion criteria for pulmonary rehabilitation.

1. An associated condition that might interfere with the rehabilitative process. Examples include disabling arthritis and severe neurologic, cognitive, or psychiatric disease.
2. A comorbid condition that might place the patient at undue risk during exercise training. Examples include severe pulmonary hypertension and unstable cardiovascular disease.

Poor motivation is a relative contraindication to pulmonary rehabilitation. However, the level of motivation might change during therapy, especially if patients perceive demonstrable benefit from the sessions.

SMOKING CESSATION

Cigarette smoking is the cause of COPD in over 90% of affected patients. Furthermore, there is no doubt that smoking cessation is the single most important therapy that can retard the progression of airflow limitation and positively influence survival. The various pharmacologic and behavior modification techniques that are available to assist persons to stop smoking are reviewed in Chapter 90. Although controversy still exists, active cigarette smokers are reasonable candidates for pulmonary rehabilitation provided smoking cessation interventions become an important component of the process. Indeed, frequent contact and reinforcement during the rehabilitation program can influence a patient to adopt a proactive role in cessation.

COMPONENTS OF A COMPREHENSIVE PULMONARY REHABILITATION PROGRAM

EXERCISE TRAINING

Comprehensive exercise training, including upper and lower extremity endurance training and strength training, is an essential component of comprehensive pulmonary rehabilitation. This follows the current knowledge that the peripheral muscles in chronic lung disease are not only wasted but also appear to have alterations in fiber-type distribution and decreased metabolic capacity. Exercise training improves endurance, increases the level of functioning, aids in performance of activities of daily living, helps reduce systemic blood pressure, improves lipid profiles, tends to counteract depression, reduces anxiety associated with dyspnea-producing activities, and facilitates sleep.

Exercise training for individuals with chronic lung disease, similar to that in healthy individuals, is based on general principles of intensity (higher levels of training produce more results), specificity (only those muscles trained show an effect), and reversibility (cessation of regular exercise training leads to loss of training effect).[32]

Ventilatory or gas exchange limitations are common in advanced chronic lung disease and limit the intensity of exercise training. However, many patients are also limited by peripheral muscle and cardiovascular deconditioning, with an early onset of anaerobic metabolism and lactic acidosis during exercise. This is responsive to the exercise training intervention. Additionally, many respiratory patients are often capable of exercising for prolonged periods of time at levels close to their peak exercise capacity.[33] Higher levels of exercise training result in greater improvement in exercise performance.[34] The demonstrated reduction in ventilation and lactate levels at identical submaximal work rates[12] following high-intensity exercise training strongly suggests that a training effect is attainable in many patients with advanced lung disease. A dose-related increase in oxidative enzymes in the peripheral muscles accompanies these physiologic adaptations to training.[33,35] A reduction in lactic acid production has been demonstrated to be associated with improvement in oxidative capacity of the peripheral muscles.[36]

Most pulmonary rehabilitation programs emphasize endurance training of the lower extremities, often advocating sustained exercise for about 20 to 30 minutes two to five times a week. This may include exercise on a stationary cycle ergometer, motorized treadmill, climbing stairs, or walking on a flat surface such as a corridor or auditorium. Training is usually performed at levels at or greater than 50% or 60% of the maximal work rate. For those unable to maintain this intensity for the recommended duration, interval training, consisting of 2 to 3 minutes of high intensity (60–80% maximal exercise capacity) training alternating with equal periods of rest, has similar results with less dyspnea.[37,38]

The total duration of exercise training depends on the individual pulmonary rehabilitation program but should reflect the patient's underlying respiratory disease, his or her level of physical and cardiovascular conditioning, and the progress made during the exercise training sessions. Recent COPD guidelines (GOLD) recommend at least 8 weeks of exercise training as part of a pulmonary rehabilitation program.[7]

Although the strength of the upper extremity muscles is relatively preserved compared to that of the lower extremities in COPD,[39,40] these muscles are very important in many activities of daily living, and their use is associated with considerable dyspnea. Endurance training of the upper extremities is also important[1] because the arms are used in many activities of daily living and the arm muscles are also accessory muscles of respiration. Training can be accomplished using supported arm exercises, such as arm ergometry, or unsupported arm exercises, such as lifting free weights, dowels, or stretching elastic bands.

Because peripheral muscle weakness and/or atrophy contribute to exercise limitation in patients with lung disease,[42] strength training is a rational component of exercise training during pulmonary rehabilitation.[42a] Training in weight-lifting exercises alone, involving the upper and lower extremities, increases muscle strength and endurance performance on a cycle ergometer.[43] Current practice of pulmonary rehabilitation usually adds strength training to standard aerobic training. This combination increases muscle strength and mass, but its additive effect on health status has not been proven.[44]

Inspiratory muscle training increases strength and endurance of the inspiratory muscles.[45,46] However, most studies have not established a link between improvements in respiratory muscle strength or endurance and dyspnea, exercise performance, or health status.[47] Newer approaches emphasizing endurance training of the respiratory muscles at more precise percentages of maximal capacity are promising although not yet proven.

EDUCATION

Education is an integral component of virtually all comprehensive pulmonary rehabilitation programs. In addition to providing the patient and the family important information on the disease process, its comorbidity, and its treatment, it encourages active participation in health care, thereby promoting adherence and self-management skills.[17,48,49] Additionally, it helps the patient and family find ways to cope better with the illness.[50,51] Important components of the educational process include encouraging a healthy lifestyle, incorporating adaptive techniques learned in rehabilitation into the home setting, and promoting long-term adherence with the rehabilitative instructions.

Education is usually provided in both small group settings and in a one-to-one format.[52] Educational needs are determined as part of the initial evaluation and then are reassessed during the course of the program. Advance directive discussions are an important component of pulmonary rehabilitation.[53,54] Generally, a number of standard topics are addressed in the educational sessions,[55] some of which are outlined in Table 88.2.

Education is a component of virtually all pulmonary rehabilitation programs. Consequently, there are few studies evaluating the effectiveness of this single component as isolated therapy. However, a recent study evaluating self-management strategies applied to the home setting showed this form of therapy to be effective in improving health status and reducing utilization of medical resources.[21]

PSYCHOSOCIAL TRAINING AND SUPPORT

Psychosocial problems, such as anxiety, depression, deficiencies with coping, and decreased self-efficacy, contribute to the burden of advanced respiratory disease.[56–58] Psychosocial and behavioral interventions vary widely among comprehensive pulmonary rehabilitation programs but often involve educational sessions or support groups, focusing on areas such as coping strategies or stress management techniques. Techniques of progressive muscle relaxation, stress reduction, and panic control may reduce not only anxiety but dyspnea as well.[59] Educational efforts may also improve coping skills.[60,61] Participation by family members or friends in pulmonary rehabilitation support groups is encouraged. Informal discussions of symptoms frequently present in chronic lung disease and common concerns may provide emotional support to patients and their families. Individuals

Table 88.2 Educational Elements of a Comprehensive Pulmonary Rehabilitation Program

Normal pulmonary anatomy and physiology
Pathophysiology of lung disease
Description and interpretation of medical tests
Breathing retraining
Bronchial hygiene
Medications
Exercise principles
Activities of daily living (ADL) and energy conservation
Respiratory modalities
Self-assessment and symptom management
Nutrition
Psychosocial issues
Ethical issues
Advance directives

Adapted from: Patient training. *In* AACVPR/ACCP Pulmonary Rehabilitation Guidelines. Champaign, IL: AACVPR.

with substantial psychiatric disease should be referred for appropriate professional care outside the program.

A few studies have evaluated the effect of pulmonary rehabilitation on psychological outcomes.[62] A randomized, controlled trial of comprehensive pulmonary rehabilitation failed to demonstrate a significant effect on depression. However, in one noncontrolled study of pulmonary rehabilitation, depression and anxiety levels decreased following 1 month of pulmonary rehabilitation. This program included psychological counseling and stress management sessions twice weekly in addition to standard exercise training and educational topics.[63] Of importance, the feeling of self-efficacy, including self-efficacy for walking, may increase with exercise training.[64,64a]

NUTRITIONAL SUPPORT

Nutritional depletion, including decreased weight and abnormalities in body composition such as decreased lean body mass, is present in 20% to 35% of patients with stable COPD.[65–67] This undoubtedly contributes to the morbidity of this disease. For instance, nutritional depletion is associated with reductions in respiratory muscle strength,[68,69] handgrip strength,[70] and exercise tolerance,[68,71] as well as health status.[72] Nutritional depletion and alteration in body composition are also significant predictors of the mortality of COPD, independent of FEV_1.[73,74] Because of this, nutritional intervention is a recommended component of comprehensive pulmonary rehabilitation.

However, the benefit from simple nutritional supplementation to underweight patients with chronic lung disease has not been substantial, with one recent meta-analysis of nutritional intervention for COPD reporting only a 1.65 kg increase in weight following intervention.[75]

In view of these disappointing results with calorie supplementation alone, consideration is being given to hormonal supplementation with anabolic steroids.[76] This has led to increases in weight, lean body mass, respiratory muscle strength, and arm and thigh muscle circumference.[77] To date, however, improvements in these areas of impairment have not been convincingly demonstrated to be associated with improvements in exercise tolerance or functional status. Of considerable importance is a recent study that demonstrated that therapeutic increases in weight in COPD patients might favorably affect long-term survival. Further studies are needed to determine the optimal approach to treatment of nutritional depletion in chronic lung disease.

BREATHING TRAINING AND CHEST PHYSICAL THERAPY

These modalities have been part of the armamentarium of pulmonary rehabilitation over the years, but conclusive evidence supporting their effectiveness in pulmonary rehabilitation is lacking. They comprise two categories: Controlled breathing techniques (pursed lip breathing, bending forward posture, diaphragmatic breathing exercise) and chest physical therapy (postural drainage, chest percussion and vibration, directed cough). The former are aimed at decreasing dyspnea and the latter at enhancing drainage of secretions. Reputed benefits of these modalities include less dyspnea, a decrement in anxiety and panic attacks, and improvement in sensation of well-being. These modalities require careful instruction by persons familiar with the techniques. It is often necessary to involve relatives, as some of these modalities require the help of another person (e.g., chest percussion).

Breathing training is aimed at controlling the respiratory rate and breathing pattern, possibly resulting in decreased air trapping. It also may decrease the work of breathing by improving the position and function of the respiratory muscles.[78] The easiest of these maneuvers is pursed lip breathing. For this, patients inhale through the nose and exhale over 4 and 6 seconds through lips pursed in a whistling/kissing position. The exact mechanism by which it decreases dyspnea is unknown. It does not seem to change functional residual capacity or oxygen uptake, but it does decrease respiratory frequency, increase tidal volume, and improve blood gases.[79]

Bending forward posture has been shown to result in a decrease in dyspnea in some patients with severe COPD, both at rest and during exercise. These changes can also be seen in the supine and Trendelenberg positions. The best explanation for this improvement is through improved diaphragmatic function, as the increased abdominal pressure in these positions stretches the diaphragm, placing it in a better contracting position.

Diaphragmatic breathing is a technique aimed at changing the breathing pattern from one where the rib cage muscles are the predominant pressure generators to a more normal one where the pressures are generated with the diaphragm. It is usually practiced for at least 20 minutes two or three times daily. The patient should start the training in the supine position and, once familiar with it, perform it in the upright posture. Patients are instructed to breathe in, trying to outwardly displace their own hand placed on the abdomen. The patient then exhales with pursed lips while encouraged to use his or her abdominal muscles in an attempt to return the diaphragm to a more lengthened resting position. Although most patients report improvement in dyspnea, diaphragmatic breathing results in minimal if any changes in oxygen uptake and resting lung volume. Similar to the effects of pursed lip breathing, there is usually a decrease in respiratory rate and minute ventilation and an increase in tidal volume.

Chest physical therapy is used to attempt to remove airways secretions. The techniques include postural drainage, chest percussion and vibration, and directed cough. Postural drainage uses gravity to help drain the individual lung segments. Chest percussion should be performed with care in patients with osteoporosis or bone problems.

Cough is also an effective technique for removing excess mucus from the larger airways. Unfortunately, patients with COPD have impaired cough mechanisms (maximum expiratory flow is reduced, ciliary beat is impaired), and the mucus itself has altered viscoelastic properties. Because spasms of coughing may lead to dyspnea, fatigue, and worsened obstruction, directed cough might be helpful by modulating the beneficial effect and preventing the untoward ones. With directed coughs, patients are instructed to inhale deeply, hold their breath for a few seconds and then cough two or three times with the mouth open. They are also instructed to compress the upper abdomen to assist in the cough.

It seems clear that pulmonary function does not improve with any of these techniques. On the other hand, programs that include a combination of postural drainage, percussion, vibration, and directed cough do increase the clearance of inhaled radiotracers and increase sputum volume and weight. The single most important indication for initiating chest physical therapy is the presence of sputum production.

VACCINATION

The causes of exacerbations of COPD are poorly understood and are probably multifactorial; both influenza virus and *Streptococcus pneumoniae* may play a role; and there is no doubt that, when either of these infections occurs, patients with chronic lung disease have an increased incidence of serious complications, including death.[80] One of the national health objectives in the United States for the year 2000 was to increase influenza and pneumococcal vaccination levels to higher than 60% among persons at high risk for complications and everyone 65 years of age or older.[81] As stated, this includes all patients with COPD and other forms of chronic lung disease, regardless of age. Because the influenza vaccine is type-specific and serotypes are constantly changing, vaccination must be repeated every year, preferably at the beginning of the season in the fall; in contrast, the pneumococcal vaccine is polyvalent, and its benefits should last a lifetime.[82] One of the responsibilities of a rehabilitation program is to educate enrollees about the importance of vaccination against influenza and pneumococcal infections and to ensure that it is carried out and (for influenza) repeated annually.

OXYGEN ASSESSMENT AND THERAPY

Although not in itself a unique component of pulmonary rehabilitation, testing for oxygen needs and/or adjusting

Table 88.3 Guidelines for Prescribing Home Oxygen for Advanced COPD

Patient Selection Criteria

Accepted Indications

Resting arterial Po_2 consistently 55 mm Hg or less, *or* consistently 55 to 59 mm Hg plus cor pulmonale clinically diagnosed and/or hematocrit > 55%

Stable course of disease on optimum medical therapy

Arterial blood gas determinations while breathing room air at rest for a minimum of 20 minutes

Patients with substantial nocturnal hypoxemia (i.e., arterial Po_2 < 55 mm Hg on multiple occasions, *or* patients with hematocrit > 55%, *or* clinical evidence of pulmonary hypertension)

Possible Indications

Normoxic patients in whom less dyspnea and substantially increased exercise capability is demonstrated with oxygen

Supplementation during exercise training

Oxygen Dose

Continuous flow by double or single nasal cannulas (see text) or by demand system with demonstration of adequate oxygen saturation

Lowest liter flow to raise Po_2 to 60–65 mm Hg or oxygen saturation to 90–94%.

Increase baseline liter flow by 1 L/min during exercise and sleep. Consider higher flows if patient traveling by air.

COPD, chronic obstructive pulmonary disease.

the oxygen to achieve its full benefits are part of all rehabilitation programs. Two landmark studies clearly showed improved survival in patients with COPD and hypoxemia (arterial Po_2 < 55 mm Hg) who breathed supplementary oxygen at night compared with those who received no oxygen; there was even better survival in those who breathed oxygen for longer periods through the aid of an ambulatory delivery system.[83,84] Contemporary guidelines for prescribing home oxygen for patients with COPD, based in part on these trials, are shown in Table 88.3. The chief criterion is a significant level of hypoxemia, defined as an arterial Po_2 of 55 mm Hg or less for 3 weeks or more when the patient is in a clinically stable state (i.e., has been free from exacerbation of bronchitis, heart failure, or other intercurrent complications). Additional criteria were also used in the North American multicenter trial to enroll stable patients with COPD whose arterial Po_2 values were between 55 and 59 mm Hg. They included evidence of pulmonary hypertension as judged by radiographic abnormalities (an enlarged pulmonary outflow tract); electrocardiographic findings of elevated right-sided intracardiac pressures (*P* waves in standard leads II, III, and aVF > 2 mm amplitude); clinical evidence of cor pulmonale with heart failure; or secondary polycythemia from chronic hypoxemia. Patients with COPD who have echocardiographic evidence of right ventricular hypertrophy and/or pulmonary hypertension also qualify.

Dosage

The therapeutic goal of administering supplementary oxygen is to raise arterial Po_2 to the range of 60 to 65 mm Hg or, alternatively, to reach an oxygen saturation of 90% to 94%. The results of the NOTT trial established the fact that the great majority of patients with advanced COPD and hypoxemia achieve this goal with oxygen delivered by nasal cannula at 1 to 2 L/min. Less than 10% of the patients require 3 L/min or more while at rest. Additional results obtained during the conduct of the trial indicate that additional oxygen, 1 L/min, was required during the stress of exercise and while sleeping; those extra needs are undoubtedly caused by the increased metabolic demands of exercise and the modest degree of hypoventilation and/or worsening of gas exchange that occurs during sleep.

Thus, if the baseline flow of oxygen is 2 L/min with patients at rest, the flow rate should be turned up to 3 L/min when they are exercising or sleeping. Periodic monitoring of oxygenation is essential to determine who should receive supplementary oxygen in the first place; moreover, in those who are being treated, it is used to evaluate if therapeutic goals are being met or exceeded. Two techniques are available: arterial puncture with direct measurement of Po_2 and pulse oximetry to quantify oxygen saturation. The latter is being increasingly used given the convenience and improved accuracy of the newer oximeters.

Delivery Systems

The oxygen delivery systems available for home use are as follows: compressed gas in high-pressure cylinders; liquid gas in lightweight canisters; and stationary oxygen concentrators. Large compressed gas cylinders are fixed in place, but patients can move short distances while using long (50 foot) tubing; smaller cylinders can be attached to wheelchairs or installed in automobiles to allow journeys out of the home. Ambulatory patients are best served with a small portable, liquid system, which is the only truly practicable way to deliver oxygen to someone who is working or active. Liquid gas-containing canisters are constantly being improved in terms of weight and duration of use. Because the goal of pulmonary rehabilitation is to restore the patients' functional capacity to its optimal level and exercise is a fundamental part of pulmonary rehabilitation, every effort must be made to provide hypoxemic patients with portable devices that help achieve these goals.

LONG-TERM ADHERENCE

Although the short-term effects of pulmonary rehabilitation in multiple outcome areas are firmly established, the long-term effectiveness of this therapy is often disappointing. In controlled trials of pulmonary rehabilitation, gains in exercise performance and health status obtained after 6 to 8 weeks of therapy essentially disappear by 18 to 24 months.[17,19,85,86–88] However, it seems illogical to expect that a therapy that is only applied for 6 to 8 weeks could substantially modify the natural course of the disease. The decline in function is probably greater than what would be expected from progression of the underlying disease process. In all likelihood, two factors are mainly responsible for this drop-off in effectiveness: (1) exacerbations of underlying lung disease, leading to prolonged symptoms and reassuming a more sedentary lifestyle; and (2) a gradual decline in adherence with the post-rehabilitation exercise prescription.

With these factors in mind, the pulmonary rehabilitation program must include strategies to promote long-term adherence. One approach is to incorporate the principles of pulmonary rehabilitation (including exercise training) more actively into the home setting. This is supported by studies of home-based programs, which suggest that gains made in this setting may be longer-lasting[89] than those of hospital-based programs. Additionally, giving a "booster shot" of pulmonary rehabilitation following an exacerbation, emphasizing short periods of supervised exercise training to return the patient to baseline performance appears to be a reasonable intervention in selected cases.

PROGRAM ORGANIZATION

The pulmonary rehabilitation program needs a coordinator to organize the various components into a functioning unit. The coordinator develops the integrated program and monitors its progress and function. The program should have resources available to teach and supervise respiratory therapy techniques (e.g., oxygen, use of inhalers, nebulizers), physical therapy (breathing techniques, chest physical therapy, postural drainage), exercise conditioning (upper and lower extremities), and activities of daily living (work simplification, energy conservation). Also desirable are services to evaluate and advise on nutritional, psychological, and vocational needs.[90]

The decision whether to have an inpatient or an outpatient program depends on the methods of reimbursement, patient population, available personnel, and institutional policy. The ideal system is one that provides an in-hospital component for patients who may benefit from the program while recovering from acute exacerbations and an outpatient component (including home therapy) that could complete the program started in the hospital. This program ensures good continuity of care.

OUTCOMES

Outcome analysis can be defined as the assessment of the "consequences" of an intervention. Pulmonary rehabilitation does not affect the degree of respiratory impairment as measured by tests of physiologic pulmonary function. However, exercise training in rehabilitation increases the content of oxidative enzymes in the trained muscles, which is accompanied by a beneficial delay in the generation of lactate (a marker of muscle performance). This results in improved exercise performance and dyspnea, and it may be responsible, at least in part, for the improved functional capacity of those patients. Therefore, even though pulmonary rehabilitation does not change the impairment (lung function), it profoundly affects the disability and handicap of the patient.

Outcome assessment for pulmonary rehabilitation encompasses three areas: (1) a generalized audit of the effectiveness of the global pulmonary rehabilitation program and its components; (2) evaluation of individual patient response to the intervention; and (3) assessment of the effect of pulmonary rehabilitation on society, especially with respect to its effect on health care utilization and its cost-effectiveness. Some commonly used outcome measures are listed in Table 88.4.

Table 88.4 Examples of Outcome Assessment for Pulmonary Rehabilitation

Measurement	Scales/Tests
Exertional dyspnea	Borg scale or visual analogue scale during exercise testing
Dyspnea with daily activities	Modified Medical Research Council (MRC) questionnaire; Baseline and Transitional Dyspnea Indexes (BDI/TDI); San Diego Shortness of Breath Questionnaire
Functional exercise capacity	Six-minute walk test; incremental and endurance shuttle walk tests
Laboratory measures of exercise performance	Incremental cardiopulmonary exercise testing; endurance testing at constant work rate
Health status	Chronic Respiratory Disease Questionnaire (CRQ); St. George's Respiratory Questionnaire (SGRQ); Medical Outcomes Study Short Form 36 (SF-36)
Functional performance	Pulmonary Functional Status Scale (PFSS); Pulmonary Function Status and Dyspnea Questionnaire (PFSDQ)[2]
Nutritional status/body composition	Body mass index (BMI); body composition using bioelectrical impedance or dual energy x-ray absorption (DEXA)
Psychological variables	Measurement of anxiety and depression using the Hospital Anxiety and Depression (HAD) questionnaire

Evaluating the effectiveness of the pulmonary rehabilitation program is important in continuous quality assessment. Testing can be made in several areas, especially in the measurements of dyspnea, exercise performance, and health status. Dyspnea evaluation falls into two categories: measurement of exertional dyspnea during standardized exercise testing and questionnaire measurement of breathlessness. Exertional dyspnea is usually rated using a Borg scale[91] or visual analogue scale.[14] Questionnaire measurement of dyspnea usually assesses dyspnea associated with daily activities or the effect of exertional dyspnea on limiting activities.[92–94]

Exercise performance can be measured in the laboratory using protocols involving incremental treadmill or stationary bicycle exercise.[15] However, field tests of exercise performance, such as the 6-minute walk test or the shuttle walk test, are more commonly performed. The 6-minute test is easy to perform, relates well to functional status, and is responsive to the pulmonary rehabilitation intervention. For the shuttle walk test,[95,96] the patient is instructed to walk around a 10-meter course at gradually increasing speeds. Speed is determined by an auditory beeping signal that sets the pace. The test is terminated when the patient cannot complete the course in time, usually because of breathlessness. Total distance traveled is the variable assessed.

Health status is often assessed using respiratory-specific questionnaires, such as the Chronic Respiratory Disease Questionnaire (CRQ)[97] or the St. George's Respiratory Questionnaire (SGRQ).[98] Some pulmonary rehabilitation programs may also use a generic instrument, such as the Medical Outcomes Study Short Form 36 (SF-36)[99] to complement information from the respiratory-specific questionnaires.

Assessment in the areas of nutrition/body composition, educational goal achievement, and psychosocial variables (e.g., anxiety, depression, coping skills) is also possible.

In the evaluation of the individual patient response to therapy, exercise tests such as the timed walk or questionnaire assessment of dyspnea, functional status, or health status may provide some useful information. However, to date these outcome measures, which have become routine for program assessment, have not been extensively validated for *individual* patient assessment. Traditional one-on-one clinical assessment remains necessary for the individual patient.

Outcome assessment in health care utilization or cost-effectiveness generally requires participation of several centers in a multicenter study to accrue the necessary number of subjects for this type of analysis.

Despite the short time that has elapsed since the introduction of outcome studies, there is evidence that pulmonary rehabilitation has resulted in important improvement in many outcomes, all of which are important to patients. They include reduced exertional dyspnea,[17] decreased dyspnea with daily activities,[32] increased exercise performance of the lower and upper extremities,[12,30,33,34] increased peripheral muscle strength,[43,44] increased strength and endurance of respiratory muscles,[45] increased self-efficacy for walking,[17] improved health status, and reduced health care utilization and thus increased cost-effectiveness.[19]

RECENT ADJUNCTS

Noninvasive invasive positive-pressure ventilation (NPPV), through its effect in helping unload the respiratory muscles, may improve breathlessness in COPD.[100,101] The use of proportional assist ventilation in pulmonary rehabilitation in patients without hypercapnia had no appreciable added benefits in mild COPD.[102] However, in patients with more severe lung disease, this form of therapy allowed the patient to exercise at a higher intensity, resulting in the achievement of a greater maximum exercise capacity.[103] Similarly, the application of electrical stimulation combined with active limb mobilization in COPD patients on mechanical ventilation significantly improved muscle strength and decreased the time needed to transfer the patient from bed to chair.[104] However, these techniques remain experimental and subjects for research.

SUMMARY

Pulmonary rehabilitation has gradually become the gold standard treatment for patients with severe lung disease, especially COPD. By definition, rehabilitation services are provided to patients with symptoms, most of them with moderate to advanced lung disease. As new therapeutic strategies such as lung volume reduction surgery and lung transplantation require well conditioned patients, pulmonary rehabilitation is becoming a crucial component of the overall treatment strategy of many patients who heretofore were deemed untreatable. The positive results in several randomized trials have documented the effectiveness of pulmonary rehabilitation. Currently, this therapeutic modality should be made available to all patients with symptomatic respiratory disease.

REFERENCES

1. Pulmonary rehabilitation: Official statement of the American Thoracic Society. Am J Respir Crit Care Med 159:1666–1682, 1999.
1a. Ambrosino N: Pulmonary rehabilitation: an interdisciplinary approach. Eur Respir J 24:1076, 2004.
2. Barach AL: Breathing exercises in pulmonary emphysema and allied chronic respiratory disease. Arch Phys Med Rehabil 36:379–390, 1955.
3. Haas A, Cardon H: Rehabilitation in chronic obstructive lung disease: A 5-year study of 252 male patients. Med Clin North Am 53:593–606, 1969.
4. Petty TL, Nett L, Finigan NM, et al: A comprehensive care program for chronic airway obstruction: Methods and preliminary evaluations of symptomatic and functional improvement. Ann Intern Med 70:1109–1120, 1969.
5. National Emphysema Treatment Trial Research Group: A randomized trial comparing lung-volume–reduction surgery with medical therapy for severe emphysema. N Engl J Med 348:2059–2073, 2003.
6. Lacasse Y, Brosseau L, Milne S, et al: Pulmonary rehabilitation for chronic obstructive pulmonary disease (Cochrane Review). In: The Cochrane Library, Issue 4. Chichester, UK: Wiley, 2003.
7. Global Initiative for Chronic Obstructive Pulmonary Disease Workshop Report. Updated July 2003. Available at: http://www.goldcopd.com.
8. Haas A, Cardon H: Rehabilitation in chronic obstructive pulmonary disease: A five-year study of 252 male pateints. Med Clin North Am 53:593, 1969.
9. Petty TL: Ambulatory care for emphysema and chronic bronchitis. Chest 58:441, 1970.
10. Bebout DE, Hodgkin JE, Zorn EG, et al: Clinical and physiological outcomes of a university-hospital pulmonary rehabilitation program. Respir Care 28:1468, 1983.
11. Hodgkin JE, Balchum OJ, Kass I, et al: Chronic obstructive airway disease: Current concepts in diagnosis and comprehensive care. JAMA 232:1243, 1975.
12. Casaburi R, Patessio A, Ioli F, et al: Reductions in exercise lactic acidosis and ventilation as a result of exercise training in patients with obstructive lung disease. Am Rev Respir Dis 143:9–18, 1991.
13. Goldstein RS, Gort EH, Stubbing D, et al: Randomized controlled trial of respiratory rehabilitation. Lancet 344:1394–1397, 1994.
14. Reardon J, Awad E, Normandin E, et al: The effect of comprehensive outpatient pulmonary rehabilitation on dyspnea. Chest 105:1046–1052, 1994.
15. O'Donnell DE, McGuire M, Samis L, Webb KA: The impact of exercise reconditioning on breathlessness in severe airflow limitation. Am J Respir Crit Care Med 152:2005–2013, 1995.

16. O'Donnell DE, McGuire M, Samis L, Webb KA: General exercise training improves ventilatory and peripheral muscle strength and endurance in chronic airflow limitation. Am J Respir Crit Care Med 157:1489–1497, 1998.

17. Ries AL, Moser KM, Bullock PJ, et al (eds): Shortness of Breath: A Guide to Better Living and Breathing. St. Louis: Mosby, 1996.

18. Maltais F, LeBlanc P, Simard C, et al: Skeletal muscle adaptation to endurance training in patients with chronic obstructive pulmonary disease. Am J Respir Crit Care Med 154:442–447, 1996.

19. Griffiths TL, Burr ML, Campbell IA, et al: Results at 1 year of outpatient multidisciplinary pulmonary rehabilitation: A randomised controlled trial. Lancet 355:362–368, 2000.

20. Griffiths TL, Phillips CJ, Davies S, et al: Cost effectiveness of an outpatient multidisciplinary pulmonary rehabilitation programme. Thorax 56:779–784, 2001.

21. Bourbeau J, Julien M, Maltais F, et al: Reduction in hospital utilization in patients with chronic obstructive pulmonary disease. Arch Intern Med 163:585–591, 2003.

22. Wouters EFM, Schols AMWJ: Prevalence and pathophysiology of nutritional depletion in chronic obstructive pulmonary disease. Respir Med 87(Suppl B):45–47, 1993.

23. Schols AMWJ, Soeters PB, Dingemans MC, et al: Prevalence and characteristics of nutritional depletion in patients with stable COPD eligible for pulmonary rehabilitation. Am Rev Respir Dis 147:1151–1156, 1993.

24. Bernard S, LeBlanc P, Whittom F, et al: Peripheral muscle weakness in patients with chronic obstructive pulmonary disease. Am J Respir Crit Care Med 158:629–634, 1998.

25. Mador MJ, Deniz O, Aggarwal A, Kufel TJ: Quadriceps fatigability after single muscle exercise in patients with chronic obstructive pulmonary disease. Am J Respir Crit Care Med 168:102–108, 2003.

26. Whittom F, Jobin J, Simard PM, et al: Histochemical and morphological characteristics of the vastus lateralis muscle in COPD patients: Comparison with normal subjects and effects of exercise training. Med Sci Sports Exerc 30:1467–1474, 1998.

27. Maltais F, Simard AA, Simard C, et al: Oxidative capacity of the skeletal muscle and lactic acid kinetics during exercise in normal subjects and in patients with COPD. Am J Respir Crit Care Med 153:288–293, 1996.

28. Maltais F, Simard AA, Simard C, et al: Oxidative capacity of the skeletal muscle and lactic acid kinetics during exercise in normal subjects and in patients with COPD. Am J Respir Crit Care Med 153:288–293, 1996.

28a. Baltzan MA, Kamel H, Alter A, et al: Pulmonary rehabilitation improves functional capacity in patients 80 years of age or older. Can Respir J 11:407–413, 2004.

29. www.brit-thoracic.org.uk.

30. ZuWallack RL, Patel K, Reardon JZ, et al: Predictors of improvement in the 12-minute walking distance following a six-week outpatient pulmonary rehabilitation program. Chest 99:805–808, 1991.

31. Novitch RS, Thomas HM: Rehabilitation of patients with chronic ventilatory limitation from nonobstructive lung diseases. In Casaburi R, Petty T (eds): Principles and Practice of Pulmonary Rehabilitation. Philadelphia: Saunders, 1993, pp 416–423.

32. American College of Sports Medicine position stand: The recommended quantity and quality of exercise for developing and maintaining cardiorespiratory and muscular fitness in healthy adults. Med Sci Sports Exerc 22:265–274, 1990.

33. Maltais F, LeBlanc P, Jobin J, et al: Intensity of training and physiologic adaptation in patients with chronic obstructive pulmonary disease. Am J Respir Crit Care Med 155:555–561, 1997.

34. Normandin EA, McCusker C, Connors ML, et al: An evaluation of two approaches to exercise conditioning in pulmonary rehabilitation. Chest 121:1085–1091, 2002.

35. Maltais F, Leblanc P, Simard C, et al: Skeletal muscle adaptation to endurance training in patients with chronic obstructive pulmonary disease. Am J Respir Crit Care Med 154:442–447, 1996.

36. Sala E, Roca J, Marrades RM, et al: Effects of endurance training on skeletal muscle bioenergetics in chronic obstructive pulmonary disease. Am J Respir Crit Care Med 159:1726–1734, 1999.

37. Coppoolse R, Schols AMWJ, Baarends EM, et al: Interval versus continuous training in patients with severe COPD: A randomized clinical trial. Eur Respir J 14:258–263, 1999.

38. Vogiatzis I, Nanas S, Roussos C: Interval training as an alternative modality to continuous exercise in patients with COPD. Eur Respir J 20:12–19, 2002.

39. Bernard S, Leblanc P, Whittom F, et al: Peripheral muscle weakness in patients with chronic obstructive pulmonary disease. Am J Respir Crit Care Med 158:629–634, 1998.

40. Gosselink R, Troosters T, Decramer T: Peripheral muscle weakness contributes to exercise limitation in COPD. Am J Respir Crit Care Med 153:976–980, 1996.

41. Celli BR: Physical reconditioning of patients with respiratory disease: Legs, arms, and breathing retraining. Respir Care 39:482–501, 1994.

42. Hamilton N, Killian KJ, Summers E, Jones NL: Muscle strength, symptom intensity, and exercise capacity in patients with cardiorespiratory disorders. Am J Respir Crit Care Med 152:2021–2031, 1995.

42a. Mador MJ, Bozkanat E, Aggarwal A, et al: Endurance and strength training in patients with COPD. Chest 125:2036–2045, 2004.

43. Simpson K, Killian K, McCartney N, et al: Randomised controlled trial of weightlifting exercise inpatients with chronic airflow limitation. Thorax 47:70–75, 1992.

44. Bernard S, Whittom F, LeBlanc P, et al: Aerobic and strength training in patients with chronic obstructive pulmonary disease. Am J Respir Crit Care Med 159:896–901, 1999.

45. Leith DE, Bradley M: Ventilatory muscle strength and endurance training. J Appl Physiol 41:508–516, 1976.

46. Weiner P, Rasmi M, Berar-Yanay R, et al: The cumulative effect of long-acting bronchodilators, exercise, and inspiratory muscle training in patients with advanced COPD. Chest 118:672–678, 2000.

47. Lotters F, van Tol B, Kwakkel G, Gosselink R: Effects of controlled inspiratory muscle training in patients with COPD: A meta-analysis. Eur Respir J 20:570–576, 2002.

48. Ries AL: Pulmonary rehabilitation. In Tierney DF (ed): Current Pulmonology. St. Louis: Mosby, pp 441–467.

49. Von Korff M, J. Gruman J, Schaefer SJ, et al: Collaborative management of chronic illness. Ann Intern Med 127:1097–1102, 1997.

50. Gilmartin ME: Patient and family education. Clin Chest Med 7:619–627. 1986.

51. Neish CM, Hopp JW: The role of education in pulmonary rehabilitation. J Cardiopulm Rehabil 11:439–441, 1988.

52. Hopp JW, Neish CW: Patient and family education. In Hodgkin JE, Connors GL, Bell CW (eds): Pulmonary Rehabilitation: Guidelines to Success. Philadelphia: Lippincott, 1993, pp 72–85.

53. Heffner JE, Fahy B, Barbieri C: Advance directive education during pulmonary rehabilitation. Chest 109:373–379, 1996.
54. Heffner JE, Fahy B, Hilling L, Barbieri C: Outcomes of advance directive education of pulmonary rehabilitation patients. Am J Respir Crit Care Med 155:1055–1059, 1997.
55. Patient Training. In AACVPR Guidelines for Pulmonary Rehabilitation Programs. Champaign, IL: Human Kinetics, 1998.
56. Agle DP, Baum GL: Psychosocial aspects of chronic obstructive pulmonary disease. Med Clin North Am 61:749–758, 1977.
57. McSweeny AJ, Grant I, Heaton RK, et al: Life quality of patients with chronic obstructive pulmonary disease. Arch Intern Med 142:473–478, 1982.
58. Kaplan RM, Ries AL, Prewitt LM, Eakin E: Self-efficacy expectations predict survival for patients with chronic obstructive pulmonary disease. Health Psychol 13:366–368, 1994.
59. Renfroe KL: Effect of progressive relaxation on dyspnea and state anxiety in patients with chronic obstructive pulmonary disease. Heart Lung 17:408–413, 1988.
60. Gilmartin ME: Patient and family education. Clin Chest Med 7:619–627, 1986.
61. Neish CM, Hopp JW: The role of education in pulmonary rehabilitation. J Cardiopulm Rehabil 11:439–441, 1988.
62. Emery CF, Schein RL, Hauck ER, MacIntyre NR: Psychological and cognitive outcomes of a randomized trial of exercise among patients with chronic obstructive pulmonary disease. Health Psychol 17:232–240, 1998.
63. Emery C, Leatherman NE, Burker EJ, MacIntyre NR: Psychological outcomes of a pulmonary rehabilitation program. Chest 100:613–617, 1991.
64. Kaplan R, Atkins C: Specific efficacy expectations mediate exercise compliance in patients with COPD. Health Psychol 3:223–242, 1984.
64a. Emery CF, Shermer RL, Hauck ER, et al: Cognitive and psychological outcomes of exercise in a 1-year follow-up study of patients with chronic obstructive pulmonary disease. Health Psychol 22:598–604, 2003.
65. Wilson DO, Rogers RM, Wright E, Anthonisen NR: Body weight in chronic obstructive pulmonary disease. Am Rev Respir Dis 139:1435–1438, 1989.
66. Gray-Donald K, Gibbons L, Shapiro SH, et al: Nutritional status and mortality in chronic obstructive pulmonary disease. Am J Respir Crit Care Med 153:961–966, 1996.
67. Wouters EFM, Schols AMWJ: Prevalence and pathophysiology of nutritional depletion in chronic obstructive pulmonary disease. Respir Med 87 (Suppl B):45–47, 1993.
68. Schols AMWJ, Mostert R, Soeters PB, Wouters EFM: Body composition and exercise performance in patients with chronic obstructive pulmonary disease. Thorax 46:695–699, 1991.
69. Nishimura Y, Tsutsumi M, Nakata H, et al: Relationship between respiratory muscle strength and lean body mass in men with COPD. Chest 107:1232–1236, 1995.
70. Engelen MPKJ, Schols AMWJ, Baken WC, et al: Nutritional depletion in relation to respiratory and peripheral skeletal muscle function in out-patients with COPD. Eur Respir J 7:1793–1797, 1994.
71. Palange P, Forte S, Felli A, et al: Nutritional status and exercise tolerance in patients with COPD. Chest 107:1206–1212, 1995.
72. Shoup R, Dalsky G, Warner S, et al: Body composition and health-related quality of life in patients with obstructive airways disease. Eur Respir J 10:1576–1580, 1997.
73. Schols AMWJ, Slangen J, Volovics L, Wouters EFM: Weight loss is a reversible factor in the prognosis of chronic obstructive pulmonary disease. Am J Respir Crit Care Med 157:1791–1797, 1998.
74. Marquis K, Debigare R, Lacasse Y, et al: Midthigh muscle cross-sectional area is a better predictor of mortality than body mass index in patients with chronic obstructive pulmonary disease. Am J Respir Crit Care Med 166:809–813, 2002.
75. Ferreira IM, Brooks D, Lacasse Y, Goldstein RS: Nutritional intervention in COPD: A systematic overview. Chest 119:353–363, 2001.
76. Schols AMWJ, Soeters PB, Mostert R, et al: Physiological effects of nutritional support and anabolic steroids in patients with chronic obstructive pulmonary disease. Am J Respir Crit Care Med 152:1268–1174, 1995.
77. Ferreira IM, Verreschi IT, Nery LE, et al: The influence of 6 months of oral anabolic steroids on body mass and respiratory muscles in undernourished COPD patients. Chest 114:19–28, 1998.
78. Faling LJ: Pulmonary rehabilitation: Physical modalities. Clin Chest Med 7:599–603, 1986.
79. Mueller R, Petty T, Filley G: Ventilation and arterial blood gas changes induced by pursed lips breathing. J Appl Physiol 28:784–789, 1970.
80. Gordon A. Vaccines and vaccinations. N Engl J Med 345:1042–1053, 2001.
81. CDC. Centers for Disease Prevention: Influenza and pneumococcal vaccinations levels among adults aged > 65 years. MMWR Morb Mortal Wkly Rep 46:797–802, 1998.
82. Nichol K, Margolis KL, Wuorenma J, Von Sternberg T: The efficacy and cost effectiveness of vaccination against influenza among elderly persons living in the community. N Engl J Med 331:778–784, 1994.
83. Nocturnal Oxygen Therapy Trial Group: Continuous or nocturnal oxygen therapy in hypoxemic chronic obstructive lung disease: A clinical trial. Ann Intern Med 93:391–398, 1980.
84. Report of the Medical Research Council Working Party: Long term domiciliary oxygen therapy in chronic hypoxic cor pulmonale complicating chronic bronchitis and emphysema. Lancet 1:681–686, 1981.
85. Vale F, Reardon JZ, ZuWallack RL: The long-term benefits of outpatient pulmonary rehabilitation on exercise endurance and quality of life. Chest 103:42–45, 1993.
86. Bestall JC, Paul EA, Garrod R, et al: Longitudinal trends in exercise capacity and health status after pulmonary rehabilitation in patients with COPD. Respir Med 97:173–180, 2003.
87. Guell R, Casan P, Belda J, et al: Long-term effects of outpatient rehabilitation of COPD: A randomized trial. Chest 117:976–983, 2000.
88. Troosters T, Gosselink R, Decramer M: Short- and long-term effects of outpatient rehabilitation in patients with chronic obstructive pulmonary disease: A randomized trial. Am J Med 109:207–212, 2000.
89. Wijkstra PJ, Van der Mark TW, Kraan J, et al: Long-term effects of home rehabilitation on physical performance in chronic obstructive pulmonary disease. Am J Respir Crit Care Med 153:1234–1241, 1996.
90. Hodgkin JE, Celli B, Connors GL: Pulmonary Rehabilitation: Guidelines to Success (3rd ed). Philadelphia: Lippincott, 2001.
91. Borg GAV: Psychophysical bases of perceived exertion. Med Sci Sports Exerc 14:377–381, 1982.
92. Mahler DA, Weinberg DH, Wells CK, et al: The measurement of dyspnea: Contents, interobserver

agreement, and physiologic correlations of two new clinical indexes. Chest 85:751–758, 1984.

93. Mahler DA, Tomlinson D, Olmstead EM, et al: Changes in dyspnea, health status, and lung function in chronic airway disease. Am J Respir Crit Care Med 151:61–65, 1995.

94. Eakin EG, Resnikoff PM, Prewitt LM, et al: Validation of a new dyspnea measure: The UCSD shortness of breath questionnaire. Chest 113:619–624, 1998.

95. Singh SJ, Morgan MDL, Scott S, et al: Development of a shuttle walking test of disability in patients with chronic airways obstruction. Thorax 47:1019–1024, 1992.

96. Revill SM, Morgan MDL, Singh SJ, et al: The endurance shuttle walk: A new field test for the assessment of endurance capacity in chronic obstructive pulmonary disease. Thorax 54:213–222, 1999.

97. Guyatt GH, Berman LB, Townsend M, et al: A measure of quality of life for clinical trials in chronic lung disease. Thorax 42:773–778, 1987.

98. Jones PW, Quirk FH, Baveystock CM, Littlejohns P: A self-complete measure of health status for chronic airflow limitation: The St. George's Respiratory Questionnaire. Am Rev Respir Dis 145:1321–1327, 1992.

99. Ware JE: SF-36 Health Survey Manual and Interpretation Guide. Boson: The Health Institute, New England Medical Center, 1978.

100. Keilty SEJ, Ponte J, Fleming TA, Moxham J: Effect of inspiratory pressure support on exercise tolerance and breathlessness in patients with severe stable chronic obstructive pulmonary disease. Thorax 49:990–994, 1994.

101. Maltais F, Reissmann H, Gottfried SB: Pressure support reduces inspiratory effort and dyspnea during exercise in chronic airflow obstruction. Am J Respir Crit Care Med 151:1027–1033, 1995.

102. Bianchi L, Foglio K, Porta R, et al: Lack of additional effect of adjunct of assisted ventilation to pulmonary rehabilitation in mild COPD patients. Respir Med 96:359–367, 2002.

103. Hawkins P, Johnson LP, Nikoletou D, et al: Proportional assist ventilation as an aid to exercise training in severe chronic obstructive pulmonary disease. Thorax 57:853–859, 2002.

104. Zanotti E, Felicetti G, Maini M, Fracchia C: Peripheral muscle strength training in bed-bound patients with COPD receiving mechanical ventilation: Effect of electrical stimulation. Chest 124:292–296, 2003.

89

Lung Transplantation

Janet R. Maurer, M.D., Noe Zamel, M.D.

INTRODUCTION

Successful lung transplantation dates to the early 1980s, although attempts at human lung transplantation had been made since 1963, when Hardy and coworkers[1] first reported a unilateral lung graft. The recipient lived only 18 days, but that report was the stimulus for more than 40 attempts at lung transplantation over the next 20 years. The longest survival during those two decades, however, was less than a year, largely because of technical issues and the lack of adequate immunosuppressive drugs.[2]

The first long-term survivor was reported in 1982. With the aid of the new and revolutionary immunosuppressive drug cyclosporine, a calcineurin inhibitor, the Stanford group, who had been pioneers in both heart and lung transplantation, reported successful heart-lung transplantation in a patient with primary pulmonary hypertension. This patient ultimately survived more than 5 years.[3] Within 4 years of the Stanford report, both isolated unilateral and bilateral lung transplantation were successfully performed at the University of Toronto and subsequently at many other medical centers internationally.[4,5]

A registry of the numbers and types of lung transplantations performed internationally is kept by the International Society of Heart and Lung Transplant in conjunction with the United Network for Organ Sharing (ISHLT/UNOS). Each year an update of the Registry is published in the *Journal of Heart and Lung Transplant.* In 2004 the Registry reported data from 1985 through June 30, 2003. It had recorded an overall total of 3049 heart-lung transplantations from 132 transplantation centers and 17,128 isolated lung transplants from 201 centers worldwide.[6] The number of heart-lung transplantations per year rose rapidly in the late 1980s to a peak of about 240 and then fell as the numbers of isolated lung transplantations increased and competition for donor organs increased. The number per year continues to decrease, and in 2002 it was 71. Isolated lung transplant numbers per year rose slowly until the late 1980s, then increased rapidly until 1995 when the numbers leveled off at approximately 1400 per year as donor limits were reached. However, in 2000 the number per year began to increase again and reached 1655 in 2002. This increase likely reflects a willingness to accept less-than-perfect donors in an attempt to expand the donor pool. Between January 1, 1995, and June 30, 2003, a total of 10,959 isolated lung transplants have been reported. Of those, 5793, or slightly more than half, are unilateral, and slightly less than half are bilateral. Despite the increased use of older donors, living donors, and so-called marginal donors, the demand for transplantable lungs still far exceeds the supply. In January 2005, approximately 4000 patients were listed on the U.S. wait list for isolated lung transplant and approximately 175 for heart-lung transplant.

CLINICAL LUNG TRANSPLANTATION

SURVIVAL DATA

Bilateral and unilateral lung transplants have nearly identical early courses, with approximately 70% and 62% survival at 1 year and 2 years, respectively.[6] This is considerably better than that of the heart-lung recipients, of whom 60% are alive at 1 year and about 50% at 2 years. Despite the isolated transplant recipients' early similar survivals, Registry data suggest that after 3 years the survival curves begin to splay, and the bilateral transplant recipients have a statistically significantly better survival than either the unilateral transplant recipients or the heart-lung recipients. The respective half-lives for bilateral, unilateral, and heart-lung recipients are 5.3, 3.9, and 2.7 years, respectively (Fig.

89.1). Other important factors related to survival that have been identified include the age of the recipient, the diagnosis for which the patient was given a transplant, and the pretransplantation status of the patient. Patients who are older than 45 years, and particularly those older than 65 years, have significantly poorer survival. Diagnosis-related risk factors include higher early mortality for primary pulmonary hypertension, Eisenmenger's syndrome, and idiopathic pulmonary fibrosis patients. The accelerated death rate continues for pulmonary fibrosis patients and for Eisenmenger's patients, who have survival half-lives of only 3.0 years and 2.0 years, respectively; however, primary pulmonary hypertension patients who survive the perioperative period have a half-life of 4.0 years.[6] Obstructive lung disease and cystic fibrosis patients have the longest half-life. When comparing outcomes from unilateral and bilateral transplants for the same diagnoses, the survivals are similar in primary pulmonary hypertension and idiopathic pulmonary fibrosis; however, survival is statistically significantly better for bilateral graft recipients among obstructive lung disease patients. The greatest general risk factor for survival is ventilator-dependent status of a potential recipient [odds ratio (OR) 2.42 (1.65–3.55)]. For this reason, such patients are

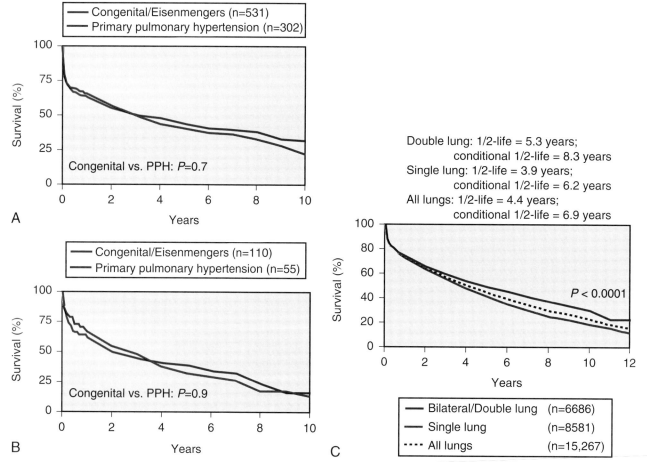

Figure 89.1 **A,** Survival of adult heart-lung transplant patients, 1990–2001. **B,** Survival of pediatric heart-lung transplants, 1990–2001. **C,** Actuarial survival of adult lung transplant recipients, 1990–2001. PPH, primary pulmonary hypertension. (From Trulock EP, Edwards LB, Taylor DO, et al: The Registry of the International Society for Heart and Lung Transplantation: Twenty-first official adult lung and heart-lung transplant report—2004. J Heart Lung Transplant 23:804–815, 2004 [http://www.ishlt.org/registries/quarterlyDataReport.asp]. International Society for Heart and Lung Transplantation official website also holds this material.)

usually not considered for lung transplantation unless they have been ventilated for short periods of time. The OR for 5-year mortality for patients greater than age 45 years rises steadily and approaches 2.1 at age 65. Recently, several articles have addressed the issue of obesity and its impact on outcome. Data from individual centers suggest that high body mass indexes, particularly in the obese range, may negatively affect both short-term and long-term outcomes.[7,8] The registry data has been unable to confirm a negative survival impact.[6]

Unlike the heart transplantation or other solid organ experience, the long-term survivals of lung recipients have not improved greatly over time. There is a statistically significant improvement in survival when comparing the post-1993 time period to the pre-1993 time period; however, in the last decade survivals have improved only slightly. Overall, less than 50% of patients survive more than 4 years. This inability to significantly improve survival reflects a lack of progress in successfully preventing and treating bronchiolitis obliterans (chronic rejection) despite increasing research into the immunologic basis of the process. It also emphasizes the ongoing susceptibility of this population to graft and life-threatening infection, which is a major cause of late death.

TYPES OF LUNG TRANSPLANTATION

Unilateral Lung Transplantation

Unilateral transplantation remains the most commonly performed type of lung transplantation. Early attempts at isolated lung transplantation were most often unilateral, and the major surgical problems in the preclinical and early clinical eras were bronchial anastomotic problems ranging from complete dehiscence to varying degrees of bronchial stenosis.[9] These difficulties were presumed to arise from ischemia of the anastomosed bronchus, and various attempts to "revascularize" the bronchi were made.[10–12] The most successful was the use of omentopexy by the Toronto group, who reported the first long-term survivor of isolated lung transplantation in 1986.[13] Since then, the surgical technique and the medical management complementing the surgery have been much refined. Today omentopexy or other specific revascularization techniques are rarely used, and yet the rate of anastomotic complications has fallen considerably. Surgical technique-related frank dehiscence with death is uncommon.[14,15] Bronchial anastomoses are completed usually by an end-to-end technique. Another approach is the "telescoping" technique in which either the donor or the recipient bronchus is pulled approximately one cartilage ring inside of the other and sutured, resulting in a short area of overlap of the donor and recipient bronchi.[16] Originally, this approach was thought to result in fewer airway complications; however, it is now generally recognized that the rate of complications is similar with either technique and is more related to surgical skill and the individual patient circumstances at the time of the operation. Thus the telescoping technique has been largely abandoned.[17]

Candidates for unilateral transplantation include patients with pulmonary fibrosis, either idiopathic or as a primary manifestation of a systemic illness, emphysema, and in some cases primary or secondary pulmonary hypertension or unusual diseases such as lymphangioleiomyomatosis.[6] To date, the overwhelming majority of unilateral transplants (62%) have been performed in patients with obstructive lung disease and in patients with idiopathic pulmonary fibrosis (23%).

Since the early 1990s, as long-term survivors of isolated lung transplantation have increased in number, several potential issues relating to the native lung have been identified. In patients with obstructive lung disease, the native lung can become excessively hyperinflated, potentially compromising function of the graft. In some cases, this has been managed successfully by volume reduction of the native lung.[18,19] In other cases, hyperinflation seems to develop in the setting of dysfunction (e.g., obliterative bronchiolitis) of the graft.[20] Recently, several reports of bronchogenic carcinoma occurring in the native lung have been published. The largest study reported that 1% of 2168 unilateral transplant recipients from seven lung transplant centers developed cancer in the native lung.[21] All recipients developing cancer had underlying emphysema (n = 18) or pulmonary fibrosis (n = 6). A smaller one-center report confirmed a similar incidence of bronchogenic carcinoma and reported a very rapidly fatal course.[22] In that paper some tumors were discovered at the time of transplant, but others were discovered up to 5 years post-transplant. Finally, several reports of opportunistic infections originating in or progressing relentlessly in the native lung with its poor perfusion, distorted architecture, or both have led some to suggest that the remaining native lung characteristics may be important in choosing potential recipients for unilateral procedures.[23–25] Potential recipients of unilateral grafts should have computed tomographic (CT) scans to evaluate the presence of cystic disease or bronchiectasis, especially if chronic sputum production is present. If cultures show potentially opportunistic organisms (e.g., fungal organisms), consideration should be given to bilateral transplantation. In any case, ongoing surveillance of the native lung in at-risk patients is important in post-transplantation management.

Bilateral Lung Transplantation

Bilateral lung transplantation has evolved through more technical improvements than unilateral lung transplantation. Initially, the approach used was en bloc transplantation with a tracheal anastomosis and vascular anastomoses at the main pulmonary artery and the posterior left atrium.[5] This technique, however, resulted in unacceptable numbers of ischemic dehiscences, and a second iteration of the technique was developed. The airway anastomoses were moved lower into the main bronchi (to leave more airway with native perfusion), and the single vascular anastomosis was retained.[26] This still required all patients to be placed on cardiopulmonary bypass, however, and resulted in significant perioperative bleeding in many cases. The final evolution of bilateral lung transplantation was to transplant each lung individually, essentially sequential unilateral transplantation.[27] This approach allows many bilateral transplant recipients to undergo the surgery without requiring cardiopulmonary bypass, thereby circumventing many of the previous perioperative complications. A final technique-associated change occurred in 1988 when the transverse bilateral submammary thoracotomy, which allows good visualization of nearly the entire chest cavity, replaced median sternotomy as the incision of choice for many transplant surgeons.[27]

Bilateral lung transplantation is the procedure of choice when chronic infection is present, as in patients with bronchiectasis. Cystic fibrosis patients have made up the bulk of the bronchiectasis patients receiving lung transplants. One third of bilateral transplant recipients have been cystic fibrosis patients, and another third have been obstructive lung disease patients.[6] The remaining one third have been patients with pulmonary hypertension, idiopathic pulmonary fibrosis, or a host of rarer diagnoses. Transplant physicians and candidates face a difficult decision in deciding between unilateral and bilateral transplantation. Because the number of potential recipients still far exceeds the available donors, some believe there should be clear justification for bilateral transplantation for a patient with a diagnosis that could be treated with unilateral transplantation. On the other hand, the recent demonstration of statistically better survival for recipients of bilateral transplantation has led some practitioners to favor bilateral transplantation whenever possible.

Heart-Lung Transplantation

As noted above, the number of heart-lung transplantations performed per year has fallen to fewer than 100 worldwide. Because this type of graft uses three donor organs, it is now reserved for patients who have both advanced lung disease and poor left ventricular function or who have complex congenital cardiac anomalies and Eisenmenger's syndrome who are not amenable to unilateral or bilateral isolated lung transplant with intracardiac repair.[28] Patients with severe right ventricular dysfunction secondary to pulmonary hypertension but with preserved left ventricular function almost always do well with isolated bilateral or unilateral lung grafts.[29]

Living Donor Lobe Transplantation

Several transplantation programs now include living donor procedures. In the most common approach, two donors are used. A right lower lobe is removed from one donor and a left lower lobe from the other. The recipient has both diseased lungs removed, and the right lobe is transplanted in the right side and the left in the left side. This approach is intuitively appealing in that relatively good tissue antigen matches should be able to be achieved and ischemic times should be minimized. Ethical issues have been explored but seem to be no greater a barrier than those faced by potential kidney donors.[30] In 2001 the largest living donor program published results in 101 recipients.[31] In this report the majority of patients had cystic fibrosis, and the 1-year survival was a somewhat disappointing 72%. The authors attributed this to the poor pretransplant condition of recipients because more than three fourths of deaths occurred within the first 2 months after transplant. The authors stated that improved selection in the more recent cases has resulted in outcomes comparable to those of cadaveric recipients. Of note, no donor deaths have occurred; however, a 15% to 20% fall in FVC has been

reported,[32,32a] and more than one half of donors have some complications, though most are minor.[33] More recently, a Japanese group has reported excellent early outcomes in 30 living donor patients. With survivals of 1–66 months, this transplant cohort had experienced no deaths at the time of the report.[33a]

SELECTION AND EVALUATION OF CANDIDATES

The single most important aspect of successful outcome in lung or heart-lung transplantation is selection of appropriate candidates for the procedure. The importance of standardized selection criteria has been increasingly recognized by transplant programs throughout the world. In 1998, a unified set of criteria, the International Guidelines for the Selection of Lung Transplant Candidates, was published[34] with the endorsement of five organizations involved in lung transplantation in North America, Europe, Australia, and New Zealand. The Guidelines were the result of collaboration among the organizations with contributors representing each organization. Uniform criteria have the potential benefits of (1) increasing the fairness of organ distribution because candidates worldwide will meet similar selection criteria; (2) providing uniform information to referring physicians who are considering transplantation for potential candidates; and (3) improving the ability to compare outcomes among both different medical centers and different countries. The 1998 Guidelines addressed both general medical criteria and disease-specific criteria indicative of advanced disease. Since the criteria were published, several studies have sought to better define appropriate determinants of "end stage" in the various diagnoses. A revision of criteria is underway. The following discussion includes some of the points that have been made in the newer studies and will be considered in the revised document.

Good general medical health has been recognized as critical to acceptable outcomes in lung transplantation. Approximate age limits suggested in the Guidelines are 55 years for heart-lung transplants, 60 years for bilateral lung transplants, and 65 years for single lung transplants. Although these age limits are relative, data suggest that older patients, especially where the donors are also older, have poorer outcomes. The survival advantage for recipients less than age 50 years compared with those older is statistically significant ($P < 0.0001$).[6] Candidates for lung transplant may have chronic conditions that are able to be managed with medical therapy so long as there has been no significant end-organ damage (other than their lung disease). Acceptable medical conditions include, for example, systemic hypertension, diabetes mellitus, and peptic ulcer disease. Relative contraindications to lung transplantation include symptomatic osteoporosis; severe musculoskeletal disease (e.g., severe kyphoscoliosis; progressive neuromuscular disease is an absolute contraindication); ongoing use of steroids with evidence of significant complications; poor nutritional state, especially morbid obesity; abuse of alcohol, tobacco, or narcotics in the prior 6 months; and psychosocial issues that are unable to be resolved with intervention and are likely to negatively affect the patient's outcome. This includes a documented history of persistent noncompliance with medical care or treatment

Table 89.1 General Medical Selection Criteria

Relative Contraindications

Symptomatic osteoporosis

Severe musculoskeletal disease

Unresponsive psychosocial issues

Suboptimally treated medical comorbidities

Malnutrition

Mechanically ventilated

HIV infection (absolute contraindication in some centers)

Absolute Contraindications

Significant nonpulmonary vital organ dysfunction

Active malignancy within 2 years (except some skin cancers or carcinoma in situ)

HBAg-positive

Hepatitis C with abnormal liver biopsy

Substance abuse within 6 months

HIV, human immunodeficiency virus; HBAg, hepatitis B antigen.

Adapted from International guidelines for the selection of lung transplant candidates: Joint statement of the American Society for Transplant Physicians (ASTP)/American Thoracic Society (ATS)/European Respiratory Society (ERS)/International Society for Heart and Lung Transplantation (ISHLT). Am J Respir Crit Care Med 158:335–339, 1998.

Table 89.2 Disease-Specific Selection Guidelines for Various End-Stage Lung Disease*

Nonbronchiectatic COPD

$FEV_1 < 25\%$ predicted (without reversibility) *and/or*

Arterial $PCO_2 \geq 55$ mm Hg *and/or*

↑ Pulmonary artery pressures (PAPs) especially if cor pulmonale present

Cystic Fibrosis/Bronchiectasis

$FEV_1 \leq 30\%$ predicted *or*

$FEV_1 > 30\%$ predicted *and* any of the following

Rapid fall in FEV_1

Massive hemoptysis

Increase in cachexia

Increase in hospitalizations

Other helpful criteria

Arterial $PCO_2 \geq 50$ mm Hg

Arterial $PO_2 \leq 55$ mm Hg

NOTE: Young children with $FEV_1 < 50\%$ may be suitable candidates[†]

Idiopathic Pulmonary Fibrosis

Symptomatic, progressive disease despite 3 months of medical therapy

Rest or exercise oxygen desaturation

"Symptomatic" often correlates with

VC < 60–70% predicted

$DL_{CO} < 50$–60% predicted

Pulmonary Hypertension

Symptomatic, progressive disease despite optimal medical treatment including epoprostenol or similar drug for minimum of 3 months (usually NYHA III-IV)

Useful hemodynamic predictors

Cardiac index <2 $L/min/m^2$

Right atrial pressure >15 mm Hg

PAP mean > 55 mm Hg

VC, vital capacity; NYHA, New York Heart Association.

* Adapted from International guidelines for the selection of lung transplant candidates: Joint statement of the American Society for Transplant Physicians (ASTP)/American Thoracic Society (ATS)/European Respiratory Society (ERS)/International Society for Heart and Lung Transplantation (ISHLT). Am J Respir Crit Care Med 158:335–339, 1998.

† Adapted from Spray TL, Mallory GB, Cantor CB, et al: Pediatric lung transplantation: Indications, techniques and early results. J Thorac Cardiovasc Surg 107:990–1000, 1994.

plans. The absolute contraindications generally include dysfunction of major organs, particularly renal dysfunction, such that creatinine clearance is less than half normal; infection with human immunodeficiency virus (HIV); active malignancy within the past 2 years, with the exception of basal cell and squamous cell carcinoma of the skin; hepatitis B antigen positivity; and hepatitis C infection with biopsy-proven histologic evidence of liver disease (Table 89.1). At the time these Guidelines were originally published, few data existed to support the suggested weight criteria that had been extrapolated from the literature for other solid organ transplants. Recent data, however, support a limit on excessive body weight.[7,8] Now, a few programs also consider transplants in HIV-infected patients who have been well controlled on highly active antiretroviral therapy (HAART) so long as: (1) HIV has been undetectable for a sustained period of time (usually 6 months); (2) there is no acquired immunodeficiency syndrome (AIDS)-defining criteria or illness; (3) the body weight is near normal; and (4) the T4 cell count is at least 200.[35]

Some groups of patients with systemic disease occasionally have severe pulmonary dysfunction as a major manifestation of that disease. Examples include sarcoidosis and collagen vascular diseases. Lung transplantation is not contraindicated per se for patients with systemic disease, but each candidate should be considered on an individual basis, and a careful assessment of significant nonpulmonary end-organ damage that might affect the long-term outcome should be made.

Much of the candidate's pretransplantation evaluation can be accomplished locally. Recommended studies include full lung function tests; exercise performance measured by a standard test such as a 6-minute walk; electrocardiogram; echocardiogram, including, if applicable, an estimate of right ventricular systolic pressure; high-resolution CT of the chest; stress echocardiogram or coronary angiogram

in patients at high risk for coronary artery disease; a 24-hour creatinine clearance assay; and liver function studies. Recent data have documented a very high rate of severe osteopenia/osteoporosis that may require preventive treatment in many preoperative cystic fibrosis and chronic obstructive pulmonary disease (COPD) patients.[36] Thus, bone densitometry is strongly recommended as part of the preoperative evaluation. Preventive screening studies such as mammography, Papanicolaou smears, colonoscopy, and prostate-specific antigen assay should be completed in patients in appropriate risk groups. Investigations often done at the transplantation center include cytomegalovirus and other serologies, tissue typing, and psychosocial evaluation. Disease-specific criteria are summarized in Table 89.2. Several issues of note in specific diseases are discussed in the following sections.

CYSTIC FIBROSIS

Criteria for referral of patients with cystic fibrosis are based primarily on the longitudinal study of Kerem and coworkers,[37] who evaluated predictors for mortality in a large, single-center population of cystic fibrosis patients. Several new models for selection of appropriate cystic fibrosis candidates have been proposed since the publication of the 1998 Guidelines. The impetus for these models has been the concern that the Kerem criteria are not generalizable to the broader population of cystic fibrosis patients because they are single-center data and might be biased by unique characteristics of patients in that center. Two of the new models are based on data from the U.S. Cystic Fibrosis Foundation Patient Registry, which lists longitudinal data from more than 30,000 cystic fibrosis patients. Each of these models uses several patient parameters to predict either 5-year or 2-year mortality.[38,39] The models require further verification before they can be used to select patients, but they promise to be more specific in identifying those patients who are truly approaching the final stages of the disease. Concerns about the management of resistant organisms in cystic fibrosis patients remain. Patients colonized with fungal or atypical mycobacterial organisms or with multiple resistant bacterial organisms appear to have survival rates comparable with those who are colonized with more sensitive organisms.[40] Even pan-resistance is now considered only a relative contraindication because in vitro sensitivities do not necessarily correspond to in vivo sensitivities. Probably the only absolute contraindication in most medical centers to transplantation in the cystic fibrosis patient that remains is resistant *Burkholderia cepacia* or similar organisms.[41] It is recommended that microbiologic review of sputum be performed on a periodic basis, usually at 3-month intervals during the pretransplantation waiting period.

NON-CYSTIC FIBROSIS BRONCHIECTASIS

Patients with bronchiectasis from other causes, including immunodeficiency syndromes, immotile or dysfunctional cilia syndromes, postinfectious syndromes, or unknown etiologies, are assessed according to the same guidelines as cystic fibrosis patients because adequate independent literature does not exist to determine prognosis in these patients.

NONBRONCHIECTATIC CHRONIC OBSTRUCTIVE LUNG DISEASE

In patients with nonbronchiectatic COPD, those with elevated arterial P_{CO_2}, elevated pulmonary artery pressure, or both and with progressive deterioration (especially cor pulmonale) have the poorest prognosis. This subgroup of patients probably derives a survival benefit from lung transplantation. Candidates who do not fit into this category may, however, experience improved functional capacity without necessarily increased survival[42] because in many cases it is inherently difficult to predict survival in patients with advanced obstructive lung disease. A recently published model, termed the BODE index, purports to determine prognosis more precisely than FEV_1 alone. It uses body mass index, airflow obstruction, dyspnea and exercise capacity as parameters and may prove valuable in assessing patients for transplant.[42a]

IDIOPATHIC PULMONARY FIBROSIS

Idiopathic pulmonary fibrosis patients have by far the highest death rate while waiting for transplantation; in most medical centers, more than 50% of these patients die while waiting.[42,43] It is likely that death occurs both because the disease progresses rapidly and because patients are often referred for transplantation only when they are extremely ill. In addition, because most patients with idiopathic pulmonary fibrosis are in the sixth and seventh decades, they may have comorbid conditions that influence survival or may have significant side effects from extensive steroid or cytotoxic treatment. The Guidelines reflect the need for transplantation centers to access these patients as soon as they are symptomatic or are not improving with medical therapy, or both. A recent attempt to develop a model to predict 2-year survival has identified a diffusing capacity of less than 39% and a high-resolution CT fibrosis score of 2.25 or greater as highly predictive.[44]

PULMONARY HYPERTENSION

The widespread use of continuous intravenous epoprostenol, subcutaneous treprostinil, and oral drugs such as bosentan and off-label sildenafil to treat patients with advanced primary pulmonary hypertension has led to some cautious optimism about the prognosis of this disease.[45,46] It has also made it more difficult to determine when such patients should be listed as transplant candidates. The Guidelines state that patients who are functionally New York Heart Association (NYHA) class III or NYHA class IV despite therapy with epoprostenol should be considered candidates for transplantation. This is consistent with a recent report that confirms a poor prognosis in patients who, after 3 months of epoprostenol therapy, do not have at least a 30% fall in pulmonary vascular resistance and whose NYHA class does not improve.[47] Additional useful hemodynamic parameters in the assessment of failure of medical therapy include a cardiac index of less than 2 L/min/m^2, right atrial pressure more than 15 mm Hg, and mean pulmonary artery pressure more than 55 mm Hg.[48] Such parameters are not well defined for patients with pulmonary hypertension secondary to congenital heart disease. That group of patients appears to have better survival with similar hemodynamic parameters.[49] Nevertheless, in the absence of good data, the criteria used are severe, progressive symptoms with function at an NYHA class III or IV level.

OTHER DIAGNOSES

In a 2001 update of selection criteria for solid organ transplant candidates, the American Society of Transplantation listed selection criteria for two additional lung diseases that occasionally come to transplant: sarcoidosis and lymphangioleiomyomatosis (LAM).[35] The criteria for sarcoidosis included Stage 3 disease on chest radiograph, an FEV_1 of less than 50% or total lung capacity (TLC) of less than 80%, and/or a history of cor pulmonale. For LAM it is noted that the time from diagnosis to transplant averages 11 years in published reports. The criteria listed were an FEV_1/FVC ratio of less than 45% and TLC less than 113%. More data on LAM patients will be forthcoming in the next 2 years as a patient registry sponsored by the National Heart, Lung, and Blood Institute winds down and the information is published.

PEDIATRIC LUNG TRANSPLANTATION

Most pediatric patients presenting with advanced lung disease have either cystic fibrosis or primary or secondary pulmonary hypertension. Guidelines for pediatric cystic fibrosis patients are generally adapted from the guidelines for their adult counterparts, although some data suggest that patients with high FEV_1 values can have poorer prognoses.[50] In cases of pulmonary hypertension, the underlying diagnoses tend to be diverse, and prognostic indicators are difficult to develop. In general, the following criteria are used: the disease is no longer responding to maximal medical and surgical treatment; the patient is functioning in NYHA class III or IV; and the patient has clinical right ventricular failure, severe cyanosis, and low cardiac output.[51]

PREOPERATIVE AND PERIOPERATIVE MANAGEMENT

PREOPERATIVE MANAGEMENT

Patients listed for transplantation have progressive diseases and require careful medical management during the waiting period. Any comorbid issues such as osteoporosis, systemic hypertension, or obesity should be managed aggressively to ensure that the patient remains the best possible candidate for transplantation. Maintaining good functional capacity with pulmonary rehabilitation programs for those patients without severe pulmonary hypertension and frequently measuring and adjusting supplemental oxygen therapy to ensure adequate oxygen saturation at rest and exercise are important aspects of preoperative care.

IMMUNOSUPPRESSION

Induction immunosuppression is used in about 40% of patients reported to the ISHLT/UNOS Registry.[6] Polyclonal antilymphocyte/antithymocyte products and selective interleukin-2 (IL-2) receptor antagonists are the most commonly used agents for induction. Most patients continue to receive intraoperative and perioperative steroid preparations with small doses of oral prednisone continued in nearly all patients indefinitely.[6] Calcineurin inhibitors are used in nearly all patients. Tacrolimus is used in about 55% of patients and cyclosporine in about 45%. The Registry reports that only about 80% of patients receive cell cycle inhibitors at 1 and 5 years, respectively. Those who receive these drugs are nearly evenly split between mycophenolate mofetil and azathioprine. Sirolimus (rapamycin), a new type of immunosuppressive released in 2000 is reported as being used in about 5% of patients. Reports of anastomotic dehiscence when used early in the postoperative period has undoubtedly dampened enthusiasm for the drug.[52] However, its antiproliferative effects may be of value in

maintenance regimens remote from the operative period, and its value in lung transplantation needs to be assessed. Within the next few years several other agents will also be approved by the U.S. Food and Drug Administration, and increasingly the immunosuppressive protocol for individual patients will be tailored to individual needs. Future maintenance regimens may include low doses of prednisone, a drug such as sirolimus, cell cycle inhibitor, and little if any calcineurin inhibitor. Long-term use of calcineurin inhibitors reliably results in significant renal dysfunction and regimens minimizing their dosages will be important in managing this complication.

POSTOPERATIVE PROPHYLAXIS

Early reports of infection in lung transplant recipients emphasized the high rate of bacterial postoperative infections, along with the usual opportunistic agents.[53,54] These observations resulted in many programs using a broad-based prophylaxis regimen directed against not only bacterial but also viral and fungal organisms. Prophylactic regimens are most intense in the first weeks after transplantation but are often continued for months. Because prophylactic regimens are both expensive and potentially toxic, some groups are using close prospective monitoring with preemptive treatment as an alternative approach. Monitoring for cytomegalovirus antigenemia or DNA in peripheral blood, for example, instead of weeks to months of ganciclovir with or without cytomegalovirus gamma globulin is increasingly used.[55,56]

INFECTIOUS COMPLICATIONS

Infections and chronic rejection (bronchiolitis obliterans) remain the two major causes of death.[6] In the first year after transplantation, infections account for about 40% of all deaths; after the first year, bronchiolitis obliterans outstrips infection as a cause of death and accounts for one third of deaths. The two etiologies together account for about one half of all deaths throughout a follow-up of more than 5 years.[6]

BACTERIAL INFECTIONS

Routine postoperative prophylaxis appears to have decreased the frequency of early postoperative bacterial infections. Typically, broad-spectrum antibiotics are used initially and modified when the results of donor and recipient airway cultures are known. In recipients with preoperative diagnoses of bronchiectasis (primarily cystic fibrosis patients), who often harbor one or more species of gram-negative organisms in their airways, the prophylaxis is usually more complex. Typically, the most recently effective antibiotics or those that have shown good activity against the organism(s) are used. Because of this approach, it is important to keep abreast of the sensitivities of the organisms in these patients. For this reason, the International Guidelines detailed earlier recommend that patients with known colonizing organisms have sputum cultures and antibiotic sensitivity studies repeated every 3 months during the preoperative period.[34]

Bacterial pneumonias represent the bulk of the severe bacterial infections. Gram-negative organisms, especially *Pseudomonas* species, account for about 75% of them.[57] Other reported bacteria run the gamut of nosocomial organisms. *Nocardia*, an uncommon infecting organism, was recently reported to occur in 2.1% of lung transplant recipients and tends to occur in the native lung.[58] Legionellosis and mycobacterial infection are rarely reported.[59,60] Bacterial bronchitis, mediastinitis, empyema, and less often sepsis account for most of the remaining bacterial processes. Bronchiectasis commonly occurs in patients who have developed bronchiolitis obliterans.[61] These patients often develop recurrent episodes of bacterial bronchitis and occasionally pneumonia. Pseudomonal species again are the predominant infecting organisms.

VIRAL INFECTIONS

Viral infections are common and often cause more morbidity and mortality than do bacterial infections. Viral infections can be divided into two basic groups: those caused by members of the herpesvirus family and those caused by common respiratory viruses. The second group has been increasingly recognized as a major factor in long-term outcomes.

In the herpesvirus group, cytomegalovirus (CMV) is the most important. In patients who have not had prophylaxis, the peak incidence of CMV infection, which can be either reactivated infection (already present in the recipient) or primary infection (from the donor), occurs between 30 and 100 days after transplantation.[62] Infection rates with this organism vary depending on the serologic status of the donor and recipient but can approach 100% in particularly susceptible groups.[63] All donor-recipient serologic combinations, with the exception of donor-negative, recipient-negative, are at significant risk of developing symptomatic infection. In lung transplant recipients the organism appears to target the graft, and in patients who have received no or only short-term prophylaxis the incidence of pneumonia is very high.[64]

Early detection of CMV infection and prompt institution of antiviral therapy has significantly reduced the morbidity and mortality from this disease. Fortunately, both antiviral and immunoglobulin therapies are now available to treat CMV infections. Most lung transplantation programs routinely provide prophylactic therapy for the most at-risk patients, with ganciclovir or ganciclovir plus CMV immunoglobulin for varying periods postoperatively.[65] Although these drugs may not prevent infection, the course of the infection is modified, resulting in less morbidity.[66] Because of the expense, toxicity of pharmacologic prophylaxis, and recent concern about the emergence of resistant organisms,[67-69] a growing number of institutions are using an alternative approach to the CMV problem. The patient's blood is monitored for genetic evidence of CMV activity as measured by DNA or antigenemia. When the activity levels rise appreciably, therapy is instituted preemptively before a clinical syndrome appears.[55] CMV infection (primarily when pneumonitis has been histologically diagnosed) has been identified by several authors as a risk factor for bronchiolitis obliterans.[70,71] This relationship, however, remains controversial.

Herpes simplex and herpes zoster also occur commonly in lung transplant recipients. Acyclovir is effective prophylaxis against these infections in patients not already receiving ganciclovir prophylaxis. With proper prophylaxis, the morbidity from these viruses can be significantly reduced. Human herpesvirus 6 (HHV-6) infection has also been reported, but the clinical impact is unclear.[72]

Infection with another herpesvirus, Epstein-Barr virus, is intimately related to the development of post-transplant lymphoproliferative disorders (PTLD).[73,74] These usually appear within the first year after transplant in 4% to 10% of lung transplant recipients and often occur initially in the transplanted lung. Pediatric recipients who have never had Epstein-Barr virus have been known to be at high risk of developing this process.[75] It has also recently been shown that adult graft recipients who have never had Epstein-Barr virus have a similar risk of developing PTLD. Serology-negative recipients who receive serology-positive organs have at least an 80% chance of primary infection, and those who develop infection may have a 50% chance of developing PTLD.[76] Because this is ultimately a fatal disease in at least half of the recipients who develop it, strategies to reduce the risk should be devised. Currently, there is no specific treatment for the process; reduction of immunosuppression, administration of ganciclovir and alpha-interferon, the use of anti-CD20 antibody, rituximab,[77] and occasionally chemotherapeutic agents have all been used with varied success.

The common respiratory viruses have emerged as important pathogens in lung transplant recipients. Since 1995, several reports of infections with paramyxoviruses [respiratory syncytial virus (RSV) and parainfluenza virus], adenovirus, and influenza virus have highlighted this problem and suggested that up to 20% of recipients may be affected.[78-82] RSV, usually of minor importance in adults, presents most frequently in the winter with a broad spectrum of respiratory signs and symptoms. Pneumonia is common. Adenoviral infections have been reported mostly in pediatric recipients and appear to have a significant impact on survival.[83] Influenza A also appears frequently as pneumonia and in conjunction with other types of infection.[84] Overall, the death rate in these series is about 20%, with the adenoviral infections reported as having the worst outcomes. It is unclear whether antiviral therapy is of benefit because the data on treatment are scant; however, ribavirin treatment of paramyxoviral infections has been used.[85] It is reported by several groups that respiratory virus infection is associated with a higher rate of chronic rejection relative to the overall lung transplant population.[86,87,87a] This suggests that, whenever possible, prophylactic measures against infection should be used. Influenza vaccine has been studied in this population and has been shown to produce a poor humoral response.[88] It may still have beneficial effects, however, and thus is generally recommended because of the potentially devastating impact of influenza infection. The role of preventive pharmacologic measures for RSV has not been explored, but it is important to advise patients to avoid young children who have symptoms compatible with RSV or other upper respiratory viral infection.

FUNGAL INFECTIONS

The most lethal infections are invasive fungal infections, particularly those caused by *Aspergillus* species. The very high incidence of these infections[89] and increasing recognition of the severe morbidity and high mortality caused by these organisms has led to widespread use of antifungal prophylaxis at least within the first few months postoperatively. Invasive disease is varied and includes ulcerative tracheitis, empyemas, bronchitis, localized parenchymal infection, and disseminated disease.[90-95] *Aspergillus* colonization in these reports varied between 22% and nearly 50% of patients. In one medical center, patients with single-lung transplants were prone to more invasive infections, particularly in the native lung.[96] The relationship between colonization and invasive disease has not been clearly established, although a recent case series suggests that rising antibody titers to *Aspergillus* may be an important marker.[97] Allergic bronchopulmonary aspergillosis has also been noted in a few patients.[98] In patients with complicated post-transplantation courses, fungal infection is a common terminal event. The severity of this disease and its often progressive course in immunosuppressed patients despite aggressive antifungal therapy has led increasingly to surgical approaches to management when disease is localized.[99-101] Important questions as to the best prophylactic regimen remain unanswered; various combinations of intravenous and aerosolized amphotericin B as well as oral drugs have been tried.

Occasional cases of deep fungal infections (e.g., histoplasmosis) have been reported from areas where the fungi are indigenous. It is important to remember that when considering the possibility of such an infection one must take into account the geographic areas from which both the donor and recipient originate or have traveled. Lung transplant patients are also prone to disseminate fungal species that are generally considered only as colonizers. *Scedosporium* species, for example, can be problematic and have been reported in invasive infections.[102]

PNEUMOCYSTIS JIROVECII INFECTIONS

Pneumocystis jirovecii is now rarely seen as a serious pathogen in lung transplant recipients primarily because of universal prophylaxis with trimethoprim-sulfamethoxazole (or an alternative). If no prophylaxis is used, however, this disease occurs in nearly all lung recipients.[103] Most programs continue this prophylaxis indefinitely, although there are no specific data to support this practice.

REJECTION

ACUTE REJECTION

Clinical Signs

Acute rejection is common in the first weeks after lung transplantation. Clinically, it is often difficult to distinguish acute rejection from infection.[104] Symptoms include a general feeling of malaise, dyspnea, and low-grade fever. Signs are also confusing and can include a falling FEV_1, chest radiographs that range from clear to those with ill-defined infiltrates, pleural effusion, elevated white blood cell count, and hypoxemia.[103] Because of these nonspecific findings, a "shotgun" approach to treatment has often been used.[4] A histologic diagnosis, however, is reliably obtained by transbronchial biopsy.[105-110]

Histologic Diagnosis

Transbronchial biopsy is the gold standard for diagnosis of acute rejection (see Fig. 18.37). It is recommended that at least five pieces of tissue be obtained to give the most reliable information.[111] Animal studies have documented the histologic spectrum of rejection and the high sensitivity of detecting this process by transbronchial biopsy.[105,112] It has also been shown in humans that, with adequate tissue, the sensitivity of detecting acute rejection is at least 80%, and the specificity approaches 100% in the absence of complicating infections.[113] Acute rejection is graded universally by a scheme initially set up in 1990 by a study group supported by the International Society for Heart and Lung Transplantation.[111] The group revised this scheme in 1995 to reflect increasing experience with the spectrum of pathologic changes after lung transplantation, and it remains the worldwide standard classification of acute rejection.[114]

Multiple groups have attempted to distinguish between acute rejection and infection based on cytokine milieu, cellular components in bronchoalveolar lavage fluid, or other local factors.[115-118] In general, however, changes in these parameters overlap sufficiently that clear distinctions cannot be made without a histologic diagnosis. Studies of bronchoalveolar lavage cells to assess up-regulation of genes known to be associated with acute rejection are under way.[119] Although gene up-regulation might be a useful biomarker of acute rejection, like the cytokines and chemokines, it is unclear whether acute rejection and infection can be reliably distinguished. This is a continuing area of intense research as a noninvasive means of detecting acute rejection. Detection of, or a propensity to develop, acute rejection could allow preemptive measures or tailored immunosuppressive regimens.

Treatment

Acute rejection is usually treated by bolus intravenous steroid therapy with or without temporary increases in the maintenance immunosuppression. In at least 80% of cases, the acute rejection is adequately treated by this approach. In 15% to 20% of acute rejection episodes, however, the process is either persistent or recurrent and presents a particularly difficult problem for the clinician.[120,121] Intensified immunosuppression with one or more agents, often cytolytic drugs, is usually tried, but it has been shown that persistent or recurrent or late (at least 3 months postoperatively) acute rejection episodes greatly increase the risk of chronic rejection.[122,123]

Surveillance Bronchoscopy

The role of surveillance bronchoscopy—bronchoscopy performed in clinically stable patients after transplantation—to detect asymptomatic rejection or infection remains ambiguous. A recent survey of North American lung transplant centers highlights the ongoing controversy.[123a] At least half report they perform at least one surveillance bronchoscopy with transbronchial biopsies in the post-transplantation period. Several early studies showed that at least 20% of asymptomatic patients had grade II or greater rejection.[124,125] Newer approaches to immunosuppression and improved overall management may have reduced the rate of occult rejection and the potential need for surveillance procedures.[126,127] Although most centers treat patients with grade II or higher histology, no one has shown that this results in better survivals or lower rates of bronchiolitis obliterans.[128]

BRONCHIOLITIS OBLITERANS

Bronchiolitis obliterans, or chronic rejection, is the most feared complication after lung transplantation. It is manifested by a pathologic process centered predominantly in the small airways with the resulting development of varying degrees of obstructive airway disease. It occurs in at least 50% of survivors by 5 years post-transplantation.[129] Described as early as 2 months after transplantation, the onset is more often 6 months or more after surgery, with a mean onset from 1 to 2 years. Over the nearly 20-year history of human lung transplantation, little headway has been made in either preventing or treating this process, and it remains a major cause of mortality.[130]

Clinical Signs

In most cases, the onset of bronchiolitis obliterans is insidious, with the patient complaining of malaise and a vague, nonspecific ill feeling. Initially, this may or may not be accompanied by mild shortness of breath and intermittent nonproductive cough, although eventually the dyspnea becomes a dominant complaint. Even before the onset of vague symptoms, a fall in the forced expiratory flow between 25% and 75% of the forced vital capacity (FEF_{25-75}) may herald the onset of this disease, as may a variety of less commonly available pulmonary function studies.[121-133] Eventually, the FEV_1 falls, and ultimately so does the vital capacity.[131] Chest radiographs are typically normal until very late in the disease when bronchiectasis may develop, but CT scans may show a mottled appearance with peripheral lucency, especially during expiration.[134]

Diagnosis

As with acute rejection, the gold standard for diagnosis of bronchiolitis obliterans is transbronchial biopsy. Diagnosis by transbronchial biopsy is not, however, a sensitive means of detection. For this reason, in 1994 a clinical description was set up to characterize this process in lung transplant recipients.[135] Experience with this schema showed it to be useful in categorizing established disease and, to some degree, prognosis. It is not as useful in detecting early, preclinical changes. Thus, in 2002 a revised schema designed to identify earlier disease was published[136] (Table 89.3). Validation of the new classification is currently in progress.[137,137a] This clinical classification that is widely used in transplantation centers describes bronchiolitis obliterans by the degree of obstructive airway disease present. When defined according to these criteria, the process is called *bronchiolitis obliterans syndrome*, or BOS. Thus, the criteria recognize, but do not require, histologic diagnosis to identify chronic rejection. Although the histologic diagnosis is difficult, bronchoscopy is often performed at least once in patients suspected of having developed bronchiolitis obliterans because it is necessary to eliminate infections as a potential

Table 89.3 Clinical Classification of Bronchiolitis Obliterans Syndrome

Original Classification	New Classification
BOS 0: FEV_1 > 80% of baseline*	BOS 0: FEV_1 > 90% of baseline* and FEF_{25-75} > 75% baseline
	BOS 0-p: FEV_1 81–90% of baseline and/or FEF_{25-75} ≤ 75% baseline
BOS 1: FEV_1 66–79% of baseline	BOS 1: FEV_1 66–79% of baseline
BOS 2: FEV_1 51–65% of baseline	BOS 2: FEV_1 51–65% of baseline
BOS 3: FEV_1 ≤ 50 of baseline	BOS 3: FEV_1 ≤ 50% of baseline

BOS, bronchiolitis obliterans syndrome.
* Baseline FEV_1 is the average of the two highest consecutive measurements post-transplant.
Adapted from Estenne M, Maurer JR, Boehler A, et al: Bronchiolitis obliterans syndrome 2001: An update of the diagnostic criteria. J Heart Lung Transplant 21:297–310, 2002.

cause of the functional loss in these patients. A number of investigators have tried to associate specific cytokines, chemokines, and other substances in bronchoalveolar lavage fluid, neutrophilia, or changes on bronchial biopsies with impending bronchiolitis obliterans.[138-141] None of these surrogate markers is specific enough to distinguish between BOS and other inflammatory processes.

Treatment

Treatment of bronchiolitis obliterans is largely unrewarding. A number of immunosuppressive protocols have been reported in the literature to slow or stabilize the process.[142-146] Macrolides are under investigation.[146a] Reversal of functional loss, however, is rare. Even without treatment, the syndrome appears to have a variable course, with some patients experiencing rapid loss of function resulting in death within a few months and others having a slow loss of function over several years.[147] Many patients who develop advanced disease also develop bronchiectasis or malacia in central airways, complicated by infection with *Pseudomonas* or other gram-negative organisms.[148]

Etiology

Precipitating factors for bronchiolitis obliterans and the events that occur in its pathogenesis have been the subject of much research and debate in the lung transplantation community. Predisposing factors that have most consistently been identified include the number and severity of acute rejection episodes and CMV pneumonitis.[149,150] A number of other factors that have also been identified as important by individual centers include, for example, human leukocyte antigen (HLA) mismatches,[151-153] viral infections,[85,86,154] and the development of anti-HLA antibodies.[155,156] Small animal models of heterotopic tracheal transplantation and some larger animal models of orthotopic whole lung transplants have been developed to study the process by which transplantation bronchiolitis obliterans occurs.[157-159] These models may help to better define the process that initiates this complication and hopefully will provide some help in dealing with this complication in human transplant recipients.

BRONCHIOLITIS OBLITERANS IN PEDIATRIC PATIENTS

Bronchiolitis obliterans probably occurs in children at least as often as in adults. Detecting the process, however, can be difficult especially in young children who have difficulty performing pulmonary function studies.[160]

FUNCTIONAL OUTCOMES

PULMONARY FUNCTION

Despite the many complications that can plague lung transplant recipients, most experience a dramatic improvement in lung function that greatly improves their quality of life.[5,161] Reports from several medical centers suggest that lung volumes in bilateral lung transplant recipients approach normal values,[161-163] whereas the lung function in unilateral recipients depends on the underlying disease.[164] Heart-lung transplant recipients tend to have restrictive pulmonary physiology, which has been attributed to a variety of factors[165] but likely is most influenced by the relationship of donor and recipient size. Diffusing capacity has been reported as remaining slightly below normal in most patients.[166] Chacon and coworkers[167] studied the factors determining respiratory mechanics after heart-lung transplantation and bilateral lung transplantation. They compared the lung volumes post-transplantation with the size of the recipient's lung pre-transplantation and the pre-dicted size of the donor lungs. In addition, they measured pressure-volume curves and maximum respiratory pressures post-transplantation. The results suggest that at high volumes the chest wall adapts to the size of the transplanted lungs, whereas at lower volumes the transplanted lungs adapt to the recipient's chest wall.[167]

Recipients of bilateral living donor lobar transplant have pulmonary function that lies somewhere between that of unilateral and bilateral cadaveric lung transplants. Donors are reported to have a fall in vital capacity of between 15% and 20%.[32]

AIRWAY FUNCTION

The remarkable improvements in pulmonary function after transplantation are accompanied by interesting findings possibly related to the loss of innervation, relative airway ischemia, or loss of lymphatics after the surgery. Increased airway responsiveness to methacholine and histamine has been found after both heart-lung and isolated lung transplantation.[168,169] This is not usually clinically evident, however. Patients with heart-lung grafts do not exhibit airway constriction following exercise challenge as is the case with asthmatic patients,[170] yet they respond with airway dilation to inhaled albuterol and ipratropium bromide.[171] Glanville and coworkers[171] used these findings, along with the observations that the hyperresponsiveness to methacholine was stable over 1 to 4 years and that the maximal

airway narrowing to methacholine was limited (plateau of dose response), to suggest that the post-transplant changes were related to denervation hypersensitivity of muscarinic receptors. Using bronchial rings of lungs undergoing retransplantation, however, Stretton and associates[172] could not confirm this. Ward and coworkers[173] compared the results of methacholine and hypertonic saline challenges to amounts of inflammation in airway biopsies and found very little correlation. Snell and colleagues[174] have shown that even healthy, stable lung recipients have evidence of ongoing inflammation as demonstrated by increased numbers of $CD68^+$ cells on endobronchial biopsy but again were unable to correlate this with hyperresponsiveness. Thus, the mechanism of post-transplantation hyperresponsiveness remains unclear. Healthy individuals have airway dilation following a deep breath while their airways are constricted, but heart-lung transplant recipients fail to show such dilation.[175] This absence of dilation following lung inflation is similar to the findings in asthmatic patients.[176]

EXERCISE CAPACITY

Exercise capacity increases significantly following any type of lung transplantation.[177,178] Maximal exercise testing, as well as 6-minute walk tests, have been used to measure exercise capacity of lung transplant recipients before and after transplantation. Early studies showed that double-lung and single-lung recipients can expect to approximately double the distance covered in 6-minute walk tests after transplantation and that this improvement is maintained over time.[178] Maximal exercise capacity also increases dramatically after transplantation. Various authors have shown, however, that neither single-lung nor double-lung transplants achieve greater than about 60% of predicted maximum oxygen uptakes. Levy and colleagues[164] compared maximal, symptom-limited cycle ergometer exercise performance in 11 heart-lung, 6 double-lung, and 16 single-lung recipients and found that in all cases oxygen uptakes were in the 40% to 60% range; and no significant difference was apparent depending on the type of transplant. Furthermore, subjects were not limited by cardiac or ventilatory capacity; rather, exercise responses were characterized by reduced aerobic capacity (Fig. 89.2).[164] Subsequent studies to further delineate the defect have suggested a role for muscle deconditioning, but of more importance may be abnormalities in systemic oxygen extraction related to skeletal muscle oxidative capacity.[179,180] It has been suggested that immunosuppressive drugs, which have been shown in animal models to impair mitochondrial function,[181] are the cause. Other recent studies evaluating exercise performance in pretransplant patients with advanced disease have also, however, shown impairment of systemic oxygen uptake, the mechanism of which remains unclear.[182]

CONTROL OF BREATHING

Sanders and associates[183] examined the responses to hypercapnia and hypoxia in patients with heart-lung transplants and found that, although hypoxia had no effect, the pulmonary denervation that occurs with transplantation was associated with a reduction of the overall ventilatory response to progressive hypercapnia. Using patients with

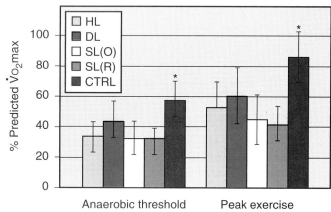

Figure 89.2 Mean values for oxygen uptake ($\dot{V}O_2$) were similar among the various groups of lung transplant recipients at the anaerobic threshold and at peak exercise; however, these values were significantly lower than those observed in the control subjects. CTRL, control; DL, double lung; HL, heart-lung; SL(O), single lung obstructive; SL(R), single lung restrictive; *$P < 0.05$. (From Levy RD, Ernst P, Shennib H, et al: Exercise performance after lung transplantation. J Heart Lung Transplant 12:23–33, 1993.)

Table 89.4 Common Medical Complications in Lung Transplant Recipients
Hypercoagulability
Nephrotoxicity
Hypertension
Osteoporosis
Hyperlipidemia
Diabetes mellitus
Neurotoxicity
Anemia
Pancreatitis
Myopathy
Hemolytic-uremic syndrome
Menstrual irregularities
Lymphoproliferative disorders
Other malignancies
Gastroparesis
Esophagitis/gastroesophageal reflux disease
Diarrhea
Perforated bowel

heart-lung transplants who had normal spirometry, Duncan and colleagues[184] found that the ventilatory response to hypercapnia was normal but the mouth occlusion pressure was increased, and the pattern of breathing during progressive hypercapnia was consistent with the absence of vagally mediated inflation inhibition. In a double-lung transplant population with tracheal anastomoses, Frost and coworkers[185] found that hypercapneic ventilatory responses were low or low normal, and the responses did not correlate with preoperative or postoperative PCO_2 or muscle strength.

FUNCTION IN SOCIETY AND PSYCHOSOCIAL FACTORS

The International Registry reports that more than 80% of patients resume normal activities without any limitations and 17% resume normal activities with some assistance. However, by 3 years post-transplant, only about 40% are working part-time or full-time.[6] The reason for this discrepancy is not clear.

Despite the many concerns and potential complications faced by recipients after lung transplantation, these patients generally report an improved quality of life.[186–188] In the long term, with the onset of complications related to their immunosuppressive regimens, the quality of life falls some but remains better than pretransplant levels.[189] It is important to recognize that many patients with advanced lung disease have significant anxiety, depression, and other psychological diagnoses, and failure to address these issues before transplantation may result in a less than optimal post-transplantation adjustment.[190]

MEDICAL COMPLICATIONS OF LONG-TERM SURVIVORS

As more recipients of lung grafts have achieved long-term survival, the impact of medical complications (Table 89.4) related to immunosuppressive therapy, to the patient's

underlying illness, or to the usual diseases of aging have become of increasing concern to the transplantation pulmonologist. Nearly 10% of lung transplant recipients die of these complications, and many more experience significant morbidity.[191,192] Recognition of the severity of these complications has led to more stringent selection criteria (see earlier discussion) and to aggressive preventive approaches in the hope that the impact of these complications can be lessened.

NEPHROTOXICITY

Nearly all patients receiving cyclosporine or tacrolimus immunosuppression experience a reduction in renal function. A significant fall in creatinine clearance occurs in the first few months after transplantation.[193] Although only a small percentage of patients ultimately develop renal failure requiring dialysis, care should be taken to minimize the use of concomitant nephrotoxic antibiotics and other medications. A new immunosuppressive, sirolimus, does not have nephrotoxic effects like the calcineurin inhibitors. It is sometimes introduced in patients who are developing renal insufficiency, as it allows substantial reduction in dose of the calcineurin inhibitor. It should not be used, however, as an initial part of immunosuppressive regimens, as its antiproliferative effect has been associated with bronchial dehiscence.[52]

HYPERTENSION

Within 1 year about one half of lung transplant patients and within 5 years approximately 85% have systemic hypertension as a result largely of their calcineurin inhibitor drugs.[6]

The hypertension requires aggressive management to protect renal function.

GASTROESOPHAGEAL REFLUX DISEASE

Gastric paresis and gastroesophageal reflux disease has been shown to exist in a significant number of post-transplant patients. Recent data suggest that recurrent reflux may affect pulmonary function, presumably through episodes of occult aspiration.[194] Some patients have undergone fundal plications in an attempt to control the reflux.

HYPERLIPIDEMIA

Hyperlipidemia is present in nearly one half the patients by 5 years post-transplant.[6] Calcineurin inhibitors, steroids, and particularly sirolimus can elevate lipids. The role of aggressive treatment of the hyperlipidemia is unclear because the impact on outcomes is not known.

DIABETES MELLITUS

Diabetes mellitus is a side effect of both steroids and calcineurin inhibitors, tacrolimus in particular. This complication, present in more than 25% of patients by 5 years post-transplant, requires close monitoring and management. High blood glucose levels predispose the patient to infections in addition to the potential impact long term on renal function.

NEUROTOXICITY

A high rate of neurologic complications occurs in patients receiving cyclosporine or tacrolimus. One report noted an incidence of about 25% in a post-lung transplantation population.[195] The complications include seizures, severe headaches, confusion, and strokes, as well as varying levels of delirium; and they do not appear to be reliably related to immunosuppressive levels. In many cases, typical white matter changes can be seen with CT or magnetic resonance imaging techniques.

OSTEOPOROSIS

Between 30% and 50% of patients who come to lung transplantation have osteoporosis by the World Health Organization's definition (−2.5 standard deviations from peak bone mass).[196] More importantly, post-transplantation patients have been found to have rapid bone loss in the first 6 months after surgery,[197] and the fracture rates are excessive,[36] a problem that greatly impairs quality of life. Particularly distressing are vertebral compression fractures, which can impair cough and pulmonary function. Preventive therapy is of paramount importance.

OTHER MEDICAL ISSUES

Table 89.4 shows myriad potential medical issues. Special note should be made of those that are potentially preventable. Thromboembolic phenomena, for example, can be minimized by use of low-dose warfarin in the presence of indwelling catheters. Finally, regular preventive medicine

Table 89.5 Preventive Care Monitoring of Lung Transplant Recipients

Provide preoperative and postoperative patient instruction regarding risks of immunosuppression, high-risk activities (e.g., sun exposure), and worrisome symptoms.
Identify individual patient risks that predispose to postoperative problems, such as the history of smoking, osteoporosis, family history of malignancy, and family history of heart disease.
Perform routine preventive medicine screens (e.g., mammograms, colonoscopy, complete skin inspection) yearly for all patients and more frequently if indicated for high-risk patients.
When possible, institute preoperative or preemptive therapy and education to prevent postoperative problems (e.g., antiresportive therapy for osteopenia or osteoporosis).

Adapted from Maurer JR, Tewari S: Nonpulmonary medical complications in the intermediate and long-term survivor. Clin Chest Med 18:367–378, 1997.

screening should not be forgotten because there is a significantly increased incidence of several types of malignancy, particularly skin malignancies, besides the Epstein-Barr-related lymphocytic disorders noted above (Table 89.5). In fact, the International Registry reports around a 13% incidence of malignancy by 5 years after transplant. The prevalence of this problem increases as the time from transplant increases.

RECURRENT DISEASE

A number of diseases have been reported to recur in the allograft. Recurrent sarcoidosis has been reported by several authors, although it is usually subclinical.[198,199] Other diagnoses with case reports of recurring disease include lymphangioleiomyomatosis,[200] giant cell interstitial pneumonia,[201] panbronchiolitis,[202] eosinophilic granuloma,[203] bronchoalveolar cell carcinoma,[204] and desquamative interstitial pneumonia.[205]

RETRANSPLANTATION

Lung retransplantation is performed less often than in other types of solid organ transplants. Retransplantation after early graft failure is associated with poor outcomes and is rarely considered. Candidates for retransplantation are usually stable intermediate-term or long-term survivors with progressive loss of lung function because of bronchiolitis obliterans. Most programs are very selective in choosing patients for retransplantation because of the overall shortage of organs. Retransplant candidates, in general, must meet the same criteria as candidates for an initial transplant.[206]

SUMMARY

Donor scarcity remains an important limitation to lung transplantation. Despite the use of living-related donors, non-heart-beating donors, and marginal donors, a significant discrepancy between supply and demand exists. Approximately 4000 potential recipients wait for the fewer than 1000 organs that are donated in the U.S. each year. Research continues on transgenic organs and other biotechnologic approaches to lung replacement, but any real options are years away. Major issues that affect the outcomes of lung transplant recipients are organ preservation, management of acute and chronic rejection, infections, and the many medical complications of immunosuppression. Finding solutions to these problems is critical to improving the long-term outcomes and an enhanced quality of life for lung transplant recipients. Our current most viable options are more selective immunosuppressive agents and approaches to the development of allograft tolerance.

REFERENCES

1. Hardy JD, Webb WR, Dalton ML, et al: Lung homotransplantation in man. JAMA 186:1065–1074, 1963.
2. Derom F, Barbier F, Ringoir S, et al: Ten month survival after lung homotransplantation in man. J Thorac Cardiovasc Surg 61:835–846, 1971.
3. Reitz BA, Wallwork JL, Hunt SA, et al: Heart-lung transplantation: Successful therapy for patients with pulmonary vascular disease. N Engl J Med 306:557–564, 1982.
4. Toronto Lung Transplant Group: Unilateral lung transplantation for pulmonary fibrosis. N Engl J Med 314:1140–1145, 1986.
5. Cooper JD, Patterson GA, Grossman R, et al: Double-lung transplant for advanced chronic obstructive lung disease. Am Rev Respir Dis 139:303–307, 1989.
6. Trulock EP, Edwards LB, Taylor DO, et al: The Registry of the International Society for Heart and Lung Transplantation: Twenty-first official adult lung and heart-lung transplant report—2004. J Heart Lung Transplant 23:804–815, 2004. (http://www.ishlt.org/registries/quarterlyDataReport.asp). International Society for Heart and Lung Transplantation official website also holds this material.
7. Madill J, Gutierrez C, Grossman J, et al: Toronto Lung Transplant Program: Nutritional assessment of the lung transplant patient: body mass index as a predictor of 90-day mortality following transplantation. J Heart Lung Transplant 20:288–296, 2001.
8. Kanasky WF Jr, Anton SD, Rodrigue JR, et al: Impact of body weight on long-term survival after lung transplantation. Chest 121:401–406, 2002.
9. Lillihei CW: In discussion of Wildevuur CRH, Benfield JRA: A review of 23 human lung transplantations by 20 surgeons. Ann Thorac Surg 9:489–515, 1970.
10. Mills NL, Boyd AD, Gheranpong C: The significance of the bronchial circulation in lung transplantation. J Thorac Cardiovasc Surg 60:866–878, 1970.
11. Lima O, Cooper JD, Peters WJ, et al: Effects of methylprednisolone and azathioprine on bronchial healing following lung autotransplantation. J Thorac Cardiovasc Surg 82:211–215, 1981.
12. Morgan WE, Lima O, Goldberg M, et al: Improved bronchial healing in canine left lung reimplantation using omental pedicle wrap. J Thorac Cardiovasc Surg 85:134–139, 1983.
13. Miller JD, deHoyos A, Patterson GA, et al: An evaluation of the role of omentopexy and of early corticosteroid administration in clinical lung transplantation. J Thorac Cardiovasc Surg 105:247–252, 1993.
14. Schafers H-J, Haverich A, Wagner TOF, et al: Decreased incidence of bronchial complications following lung transplantation. Eur J Cardiovasc Surg 6:174–179, 1992.
15. Miller JD, deHoyos A: An evaluation of the role of omentopexy and of early perioperative corticosteroid administration in clinical transplantation: The University of Toronto and Washington University lung transplant programs. J Thorac Cardiovasc Surg 105:247–252, 1993.
16. Calhoon JH, Grover FL, Gibbons WJ, et al: Single lung transplantation: Alternative indications and technique. J Thorac Cardiovasc Surg 101:816–825, 1991.
17. Schroder C, Scholl F, Daon E, et al: A modified bronchial anastomosis technique for lung transplantation. Ann Thorac Surg 75:1697–704, 2003.
18. Kroshus TJ, Bolman RM, Kshettry VR: Unilateral volume reduction after single-lung transplantation for emphysema. Ann Thorac Surg 62:363–368, 1996.
19. Anderson MB, Kriet JM, Kapelanski DP, et al: Volume reduction surgery in the native lung after single lung transplantation for emphysema. J Heart Lung Transplant 16:752–757, 1997.
20. Schulman LL, O'Hair DP, Cantu E, et al: Salvage by volume reduction of chronic allograft rejection in emphysema. J Heart Lung Transplant 18:107–112, 1999.
21. Collins J, Kazerooni EA, Lacomis J, et al: Bronchogenic carcinoma after lung transplantation: Frequency, clinical characteristics, and imaging findings. Radiology 224:131–138, 2002.
22. Arcasoy SM, Hersh C, Christie JD, et al: Bronchogenic carcinoma complicating lung transplantation. J Heart Lung Transplant 20:1044–1053, 2001.
23. Horvath J, Dummer S, Loyd J, et al: Infection in the transplanted and native lung after single lung transplant. Chest 104:681–685, 1993.
24. Frost AE, Keller CA, Noon GP, et al: Outcome of the native lung after single lung transplantation: Multiorgan Transplant Group. Chest 107:981–984, 1995.
25. Westney GE, Kesten S, de Hoyos A, et al: *Aspergillus* infection in single and double lung transplant recipients. Transplantation 61:915–919, 1996.
26. Dark JH, Patterson GA, Al-Jilaihawi AN, et al: Experimental en bloc double-lung transplantation. Ann Thorac Surg 42:394–398, 1986.
27. Pasque MK, Cooper JD, Kaiser LR, et al: Improved technique for bilateral lung transplantation: Rationale and initial clinical experience. Ann Thorac Surg 49:785–791, 1990.
28. Spray TL, Mallory GB, Cantor CB, et al: Pediatric lung transplantation: Indications, techniques and early results. J Thorac Cardiovasc Surg 107:990–1000, 1994.
29. Gammie JS, Keenan RJ, Pham SM, et al: Single versus double-lung transplantation for pulmonary hypertension. J Thorac Cardiovasc Surg 115:397–402, 1998.
30. Shaw LR, Miller JD, Slutsky AS, et al: Ethics of lung transplantation with live donors. Lancet 338:678–681, 1991.
31. Cohen RG, Starnes VA: Living donor lung transplantation. World J Surg 25:244–250, 2001.
32. Woo MS, MacLaughlin EF, Horn MV, et al: Living donor lobar lung transplantation: the pediatric experience. Pediatr Transplant 2:185–190, 1998.
32a. Bowdish ME, Barr ML, Starnes VA: Living lobar transplantation. Chest Surg Clin N Am 13:505–524, 2003.
33. Battafarano RJ, Anderson RC, Meyers BF, et al: Perioperative complications after living donor lobectomy. J Thorac Cardiovasc Surg 120:909–915, 2000.

33a. Date H, Aoe M, Sano Y, et al: Improved survival after living-donor lobar lung transplantation. J Thorac Cardiovasc Surg 128:933–940, 2004.

34. International guidelines for the selection of lung transplant candidates: Joint statement of the American Society for Transplant Physicians (ASTP)/American Thoracic Society (ATS)/European Respiratory Society (ERS)/International Society for Heart and Lung Transplantation (ISHLT). Am J Respir Crit Care Med 158:335–339, 1998.

35. Steinman TI, Becker BN, Frost AE, et al: Clinical Practice Committee, American Society of Transplantation. Transplantation 71:1189–1204, 2001.

36. Aris RM, Neuringer IP, Weiner MA, et al: Severe osteoporosis before and after lung transplantation. Chest 109:1176–1183, 1996.

37. Kerem H, Reisman J, Corey M, et al: Prediction of mortality in patients with cystic fibrosis. N Engl J Med 326:1187–1191, 1992.

38. Liou TG, Adler FR, Fitzsimmons SC, et al: Predictive 5-year survivorship model of cystic fibrosis. Am J Epidemiol 153:345–352, 2001.

39. Mayer-Hamblett N, Rosenfeld M, Emerson J, et al: Developing cystic fibrosis lung transplant referral criteria using predictors of 2-year mortality. Am J Respir Crit Care Med 166:1550–1555, 2002.

40. Aris RM, Gilligan PH, Neuringer IP, et al: The effects of panresistant bacteria in cystic fibrosis patients on lung transplant outcome. Am J Respir Crit Care Med 155:1699–1704, 1997.

41. Chaparro C, Maurer, Gutierrez C, et al: Infection with Burkholderia cepacia in cystic fibrosis: Outcome following lung transplantation. Am J Respir Crit Care Med 163:43–48, 2001.

42. Hosenpud JD, Bennett LE, Keck BM, et al: Effect of diagnosis on survival benefit of lung transplantation for end-stage lung disease. Lancet 351:24–27, 1998.

42a. Celli BR, Cote CG, Marin JM, et al: The body-mass index, airflow obstruction, dyspnea, and exercise capacity index in chronic obstructive pulmonary disease. N Engl J Med 350:1005–1012, 2004.

43. Hayden AM, Robert RC, Kriett JM, et al: Primary diagnosis predicts prognosis of lung transplant candidates. Transplantation 55:1048–1050, 1993.

44. Mogulkoc N, Brutsche MH, Bishop PW, et al: Greater Manchester Pulmonary Fibrosis Consortium: Pulmonary function in idiopathic pulmonary fibrosis and referral for lung transplantation. Am J Respir Crit Care Med 164:103–108, 2001.

45. McLaughlin VV, Genthner DE, Panella MM, et al: Reduction in pulmonary vascular resistance with long-term epoprostenol (prostacyclin) therapy in primary pulmonary hypertension. N Engl J Med 338:273–277, 1998.

46. Rosenzweig EB, Kerstein D, Barst RJ: Long-term prostacyclin for pulmonary hypertension with associated congenital heart defects. Circulation 99:1858–1865, 1999.

47. Sitbon O, Humbert M, Nunes H, et al: Long-term intravenous epoprostenol infusion in primary pulmonary hypertension: Prognostic factors and survival. J Am Coll Cardiol 40:780–788, 2002.

48. D'Alonzo GE, Barst RJ, Ayres SM, et al: Survival in patients with primary pulmonary hypertension: Results from a national prospective registry. Ann Intern Med 115:343–349, 1991.

49. Hopkins WE, Ochoa LL, Richardson GW, et al: Comparison of the hemodynamics and survival of adults with severe primary pulmonary hypertension or Eisenmenger syndrome. J Heart Lung Transplant 15:100–105, 1996.

50. Robinson W, Waltz DA: FEV(1) as a guide to lung transplant referral in young patients with cystic fibrosis. Pediatr Pulmonol 30:198–202, 2000.

51. Bridges ND, Clark BJ, Gaynor JW, et al: Outcome of children with pulmonary hypertension referred for lung or heart and lung transplantation. Transplantation 62:1824–1828, 1996.

52. King-Biggs MB, Dunitz JM, Park SJ, et al: Airway anastomotic dehiscence associated with use of sirolimus immediately after lung transplantation. Transplantation 75:1437–1443, 2003.

53. Brooks RG, Hofflin JM, Jamieson SW, et al: Infectious complications in heart-lung transplant recipients. Am J Med 79:412–422, 1985.

54. Maurer JR, Tullis E, Grossman RF, et al: Infectious complications following isolated lung transplantation. Chest 101:1056–1059, 1992.

55. Egan JJ, Lomax J, Barber L, et al: Preemptive treatment for the prevention of cytomegalovirus disease: In lung and heart transplant recipients. Transplantation 65:747–752, 1998.

56. Stephan F, Fajac A, Grenet D, et al: Predictive value of cytomegalovirus DNA detection by polymerase chain reaction in blood and bronchoalveolar lavage in lung transplant patients. Transplantation 63:1430–1435, 1997.

57. Kramer MR, Marshal SE, Starnes VA, et al: Infectious complications in heart-lung transplantation: Analysis of 200 episodes. Arch Intern Med 153:2010–2016, 1993.

58. Husain S, McCurry K, Dauber J, et al: Nocardia infection in lung transplant recipients. J Heart Lung Transplant 21:354–359, 2002.

59. Bangsborg JM, Uldum S, Jensen JS, et al: Nosocomial legionnellosis in three heart-lung transplant patients: Case reports and environmental observations. Eur J Clin Microbiol Infect Dis 14:99–104, 1995.

60. Kesten S, Chaparro C: Mycobacterial infections in lung transplant recipients. Chest 115:741–745, 1999.

61. Loubeye P, Revel D, Delignette A, et al: Bronchiectasis detected with thin-section CT as a predictor of chronic lung allograft rejection. Radiology 194:213–216, 1995.

62. Smyth RL, Scott JP, Borysiewicz LK, et al: Cytomegalovirus infection in heart-lung transplant recipients: Risk factors, clinical associations, and response to treatment. J Infect Dis 164:1045–1050, 1991.

63. Ettinger NA, Bailey TC, Trulock EP, et al: Cytomegalovirus infection and pneumonitis: Impact after isolated lung transplantation; Washington University Lung Transplant Group. Am Rev Respir Dis 147:1017–1023, 1993.

64. Dauber JH, Paradis IL, Dummer JS: Infectious complications in pulmonary allograft recipients. Clin Chest Med 11:291–308, 1990.

65. Zamora MR: Use of cytomegalovirus immune globulin and ganciclovir for the prevention of cytomegalovirus disease in lung transplantation. Transpl Infect Dis 3(Suppl 2):49–56, 2001.

66. Gutierrez CA, Chaparro C, Krajden M, et al: Cytomegalovirus viremia in lung transplant recipients receiving ganciclovir and immune globulin. Chest 113:924–932, 1998.

67. Isada CM, Yen-Liberman B, Lurain NS, et al: Clinical characteristics of 13 solid organ transplant recipients with ganciclovir-resistant cytomegalovirus infection. Transpl Infect Dis 4:189–194, 2002.

68. Lurain NS, Bhorade SM, Pursell KJ, et al: Analysis and characterization of antiviral drug-resistant cytomegalovirus isolates from solid organ transplant recipients. J Infect Dis 186:760–768, 2002.

69. Bhorade SM, Lurain NS, Jordan A, et al: Emergence of ganciclovir-resistant cytomegalovirus in lung transplant recipients. J Heart Lung Transplant 21:1274–1282, 2002.

70. Kroshus TJ, Kshettry VR, Savik K, et al: Risk factors for the development of bronchiolitis obliterans syndrome after lung transplantation. J Thorac Cardiovasc Surg 114:195–202, 1997.

71. Ettinger NA, Bailey TC, Trulock EP, et al: Cytomegalovirus infection and pneumonitis: Impact after isolated lung transplantation; Washington University Lung Transplant Group. Am Rev Respir Dis 147:1017–1023, 1993.

72. Jacobs F, Knoop C, Brancart F, et al: Human herpesvirus-6 infection after lung and heart-lung transplantation: A prospective longitudinal study. Transplantation 75:1996–2001, 2003.

73. Malouf MA, Chhajed PN, Hopkins P, et al: Anti-viral prophylaxis reduces the incidence of lymphoproliferative disease in lung transplant recipients. J Heart Lung Transplant 21:547–554, 2002.

74. Wigle DA, Chaparro C, Humar A, et al: Epstein-Barr virus serology and posttransplant lymphoproliferative disease in lung transplantation. Transplantation 72:1783–1786, 2001.

75. Boyle GJ, Michaels MG, Webber SA, et al: Posttransplantation lymphoproliferative disorders in pediatric thoracic organ recipients. J Pediatr 131:309–313, 1997.

76. Aris RM, Maia DM, Neuringer IP, et al: Posttransplantation lymphoproliferative disorder in the Epstein-Barr virus–naive lung transplant recipient. Am J Respir Crit Care Med 154:1712–1717, 1996.

77. Verschuuren EA, Stevens SJ, van Imhoff GW, et al: Treatment of posttransplant lymphoproliferative disease with rituximab: The remission, the relapse, and the complication. 73:100–104, 2002.

78. Billings JL, Hertz MI, Wendt CH: Community respiratory virus infections following lung transplantation. Transpl Infect Dis 3:138–148, 2001.

79. Palmer SM, Henshaw NG, Howell DN, et al: Community respiratory viral infection in adult lung transplant recipients. Chest 113:944–950, 1998.

80. Krinzman S, Basgoz N, Kradin R, et al: Respiratory syncytial virus-associated infections in adult recipients of solid organ transplants. J Heart Lung Transplant 17:202–210, 1998.

81. Vilchez R, McCurry K, Dauber J, et al: Influenza and parainfluenza respiratory viral infection requiring admission in adult lung transplant recipients. Transplantation 73:1075–1078, 2002.

82. Vilchez RA, McCurry K, Dauber J, et al: The epidemiology of parainfluenza virus infection in lung transplant recipients. Clin Infect Dis 33:2004–2008, 2001.

83. Bridges ND, Spray TL, Collins MH, et al: Adenovirus infection in the lung results in graft failure after lung transplantation. J Thorac Cardiovasc Surg 116:617–623, 1998.

84. Umeh F, Sarodia BD, Haug MT, et al: Influenza A infection in patients after lung transplantation. Chest 114:399S, 1998.

85. McCurdy LH, Milstone A, Dummer S: Clinical features and outcomes of paramyxoviral infection in lung transplant recipients treated with ribavirin. J Heart Lung Transplant 22:745–753, 2003.

86. Billings JL, Hertz MI, Savik K, Wendt CH: Respiratory viruses and chronic rejection in lung transplant recipients. J Heart Lung Transplant 21:559–566, 2002.

87. Vilchez RA, Dauber J, McCurry K, et al: Parainfluenza virus infection in adult lung transplant recipients: An emergent clinical syndrome with implications on allograft function. Am J Transplant 3:116–120, 2003.

87a. Khalifah AP, Hachem RR, Chakinala MM, et al: Respiratory viral infections are a distinct risk for bronchiolitis obliterans syndrome and death. Am J Respir Crit Care Med 170:181–187, 2004.

88. Mazzone PJ, Mossad SB, Mawhorter SD, et al: The humoral immune response to influenza vaccination in lung transplant patients. Eur Respir J 18:971–976, 2001.

89. Minari A, Husni R, Avery RK, et al: The incidence of invasive aspergillosis among solid organ transplant recipients and implications for prophylaxis in lung transplants. Transpl Infect Dis 4:195–200, 2002.

90. Kramer MR, Denning DW, Marshall SE, et al: Ulcerative tracheobronchitis after lung transplantation: A new form of invasive aspergillosis. Am Rev Respir Dis 144:552–556, 1991.

91. Westney G, Kesten S, DeHoyos A, et al: Aspergillus infection in single and double lung transplant recipients. Transplantation 61:915–919, 1996.

92. Helmi M, Love RB, Welter D, et al: Aspergillus infection in lung transplant recipients with cystic fibrosis: Risk factors and outcomes comparison to other types of transplant recipients. Chest 123:800–808, 2003.

93. Cahill BC, Hibbs JR, Savik K, et al: Aspergillus airway colonization and invasive disease after lung transplantation. Chest 112:1160–1164, 1997.

94. Mehrad B, Paciocco G, Martinez FJ, et al: Spectrum of aspergillus infection in lung transplant recipients: Case series and review of the literature. Chest 119:169–175, 2001.

95. Grossi P, Farina C, Fiocchi R, Dalla Gasperina D: Prevalence and outcome of invasive fungal infections in 1,963 thoracic organ transplant recipients: A multicenter retrospective study; Italian Study Group of Fungal Infections in Thoracic Organ Transplant Recipients. Transplantation 70:112–116, 2000.

96. Singh N, Hussain S: Aspergillus infections after lung transplantation: Clinical differences in type of transplant and implications for management. J Heart Lung Transplant 22:258–266, 2003.

97. Tomee JF, Mannes GP, van der Bij W, et al: Serodiagnosis and monitoring of Aspergillus infections after lung transplantation. Ann Intern Med 125:197–201, 1996.

98. Egan JJ, Yonan N, Carroll KB, et al: Allergic bronchopulmonary aspergillosis in a lung allograft recipients. Eur Respir J 9:169–171, 1996.

99. Salerno CT, Ouyang DW, Pederson TS, et al: Surgical therapy for pulmonary aspergillosis in immunocompromised patients. Ann Thorac Surg 65:1415–1419, 1998.

100. Caillot D, Casasnovas O, Bernard A, et al: Improved management of invasive pulmonary aspergillosis in neutropenic patients using early thoracic computed tomographic scan and surgery. J Clin Oncol 15:139–147, 1997.

101. Baron O, Guillaume B, Moreau P, et al: Aggressive surgical management in localized pulmonary mycotic and nonmycotic infections for neutropenic patients with acute leukemia: Report of eighteen cases. J Thorac Cardiovasc Surg 115:63–68, 1998.

102. Tamm M, Malouf M, Glanville A: Pulmonary scedosporium infection following lung transplantation. Transpl Infect Dis 3:189–194, 2001.

103. Gryzan S, Paradis IL, Zeevi A, et al: Unexpectedly high incidence of Pneumocystis carini infection after heart-lung transplantation. Am Rev Respir Dis 137:268–274, 1988.

104. Lawrence EC: Diagnosis and management of lung allograft rejection. Clin Chest Med 11:269–278, 1990.

105. Prop J, Nieuwenhuis P, Wildevuur CRH: Lung allograft rejection in the rat. Transplantation 40:25–29, 1985.

106. Veith FJ, Sinha SBP, Blumcke S, et al: Nature and evolution of lung allograft rejection with and without immunosuppression. J Thorac Cardiovasc Surg 63:509–520, 1972.

107. Koerner SK, Hagstrom JWC, Veith FJ: Transbronchial biopsy for the diagnosis of lung transplant rejection: Comparison with needle and open-lung biopsy techniques in canine lung allografts. Am Rev Respir Dis 114:575–579, 1976.

108. Hutter J, Stewart S, Higenbottam TW, et al: Histological changes in heart-lung transplant recipients during rejection episodes and at routine biopsy. J Heart Transplant 7:440–444, 1988.

109. Higenbottam T, Stewart S, Penketh A, et al: Transbronchial lung biopsy for the diagnosis of rejection in heart-lung transplant patients. Transplantation 46:532–539, 1988.

110. Starnes VA, Theodore J, Oyer PE, et al: Evaluation of heart-lung transplant recipients with prospective serial transbronchial biopsies and pulmonary function studies. J Thorac Cardiovasc Surg 98:683–690, 1989.

111. Yousem SA, Berry GJ, Brunt EM, et al: A working formulation for the standardization of nomenclature in the diagnosis of heart and lung rejection: Lung Rejection Study Group. J Heart Transplant 9:593–601, 1990.

112. Tazelaar HD, Nilsson FN, Rinaldi M, et al: The sensitivity of transbronchial biopsy for the diagnosis of acute lung rejection. J Thorac Cardiovasc Surg 105:674–678, 1993.

113. Higenbottam T, Stewart S, Penketh A, et al: Transbronchial lung biopsy for the diagnosis of rejection in heart-lung transplant patients. Transplantation 46:532–536, 1988.

114. Yousem SA, Berry GJ, Cagle PT, et al: Revision of the 1990 working formulation for the classification of pulmonary allograft rejection: Lung Rejection Study Group. J Heart Lung Transplant 15:1–15, 1996.

115. Sundaresan S, Alevy YG, Steward N, et al: Cytokine gene transcripts for tumor necrosis factor a, interleukin-2, and interferon γ in human pulmonary allografts. J Heart Lung Transplant 14:512–518, 1995.

116. Whitehead BF, Stoehr C, Wu CJ, et al: Cytokine gene expression in human lung transplant recipients. Transplantation 56:956–961, 1993.

117. Schersten H, Aarnio P, Burnett JC Jr, et al: Endothelin-1 in bronchoalveolar lavage during acute rejection of allotransplanted lungs. Transplantation 57:159–161, 1994.

118. Laan M, Linden A, Riise GC: IL-16 in the airways of lung allograft recipients with acute rejection or obliterative bronchiolitis. Clin Exp Immunol 133:290–296, 2003.

119. Gimino VJ, Lande JD, Berryman TR, et al: Gene expression profiling of bronchoalveolar lavage cells in acute lung rejection. Am J Respir Crit Care 168:1237–1242, 2003.

120. Shennib H, Mercado M, Nguyen D, et al: Successful treatment of steroid-resistant double-lung allograft rejection with orthoclone OKT3. Am Rev Respir Dis 144:224–226, 1991.

121. Keenan RJ, Iacono A, Dauber JH, et al: Treatment of refractory acute allograft rejection with aerosolized cyclosporine in lung transplant recipients. J Thorac Cardiovasc Surg 113:335–340, 1997.

122. Cahill B, O'Rourke MK, Strasburg KA, et al: Methotrexate for lung transplant recipients with steroid resistant acute rejection. J Heart Lung Transplant 15:1130–1137, 1996.

123. Valentine VG, Robbins RC, Wehner JH, et al: Total lymphoid irradiation for refractory acute rejection in heart-lung and lung allografts. Chest 109:1184–1189, 1996.

123a. Levine SM, Transplant/Immunology Network of the American College of Chest Physicians: A survey of clinical practice of lung transplantation in North America. Chest 125:1224–1238, 2004.

124. DeHoyos A, Chamberlain D, Schvartzman R, et al: Prospective assessment of a standardized pathological grading system for acute rejection in lung transplantation. Chest 103:1813–1818, 1993.

125. Trulock EP, Ettinger NA, Brunt EM, et al: The role of transbronchial lung biopsy in the treatment of lung transplant recipients: An analysis of 200 consecutive procedures. Chest 102:1049–1054, 1992.

126. Valentine VG, Taylor DE, Dhillon GS, et al: Success of lung transplantation without surveillance bronchoscopy. J Heart Lung Transplant 21:319–326, 2002.

127. Hopkins PM, Aboyoun CL, Chhajed PN, et al: Prospective analysis of 1,235 transbronchial lung biopsies in lung transplant recipients. J Heart Lung Transplant 21:1062–1067, 2002.

128. Chakinala MM, Trulock EP: Acute allograft rejection after lung transplantation: Diagnosis and therapy. Chest Surg Clin N Am 13:525–542, 2003.

129. Boehler A, Kesten S, Weder W, et al: Bronchiolitis obliterans after lung transplantation: A review. Chest 114:1411–1426, 1998.

130. Estenne M, Hertz MI: Bronchiolitis obliterans after human lung transplantation. Am J Respir Crit Care Med 166:440–444, 2002.

131. Patterson GM, Wilson S, Whang JL, et al: Physiologic definitions of obliterative bronchiolitis in heart-lung and double lung transplantation: A comparison of the forced expiratory flow between 25% and 75% of the forced vital capacity and forced expiratory volume in one second. J Heart Lung Transplant 15:175–181, 1996.

132. Bassiri AG, Girgis RE, Doyle RL, et al: Detection of small airway dysfunction using specific airway conductance. Chest 111:1533–1535, 1997.

133. Ikonen T, Harjula AL, Kinnula VL, et al: Assessment of forced expiratory volume in one second-fraction of the engrafted lung with ^{133}Xe radiospirometry improves the diagnosis of bronchiolitis obliterans syndrome in single lung transplant recipients. J Heart Lung Transplant 14:244–250, 1995.

134. Leung AN, Fisher KL, Valentine V, et al: Bronchiolitis obliterans after lung transplantation: Detection using expiratory HRCT. Chest 113:365–370, 1998.

135. Cooper J, Billingham M, Egan T, et al: A working formulation for the standardization of nomenclature and for clinical staging of chronic dysfunction in lung allografts: International Society for Heart and Lung Transplantation. J Heart Lung Transplant 12:713–716, 1993.

136. Estenne M, Maurer JR, Boehler A, et al: Bronchiolitis obliterans syndrome 2001: An update of the diagnostic criteria. J Heart Lung Transplant 21:297–310, 2002.

137. Nathan SD, Barnett SD, Wohlrab J, Burton N: Bronchiolitis obliterans syndrome: Utility of the new guidelines in single lung transplant recipients. J Heart Lung Transplant 22:427–432, 2003.

137a. Hachem RR, Chakinala MM, Yusen RD, et al: The predictive value of bronchiolitis obliterans syndrome stage 0-p. Am J Respir Crit Care Med 169:468–472, 2004.

138. Devouassoux G, Drouet C, Pin I, et al: Alveolar neutrophilia is a predictor for the bronchiolitis obliterans syndrome, and increases with degree of severity. Transpl Immunol 10:303–310, 2002.

139. Elssner A, Vogelmeier C: The role of neutrophils in the pathogenesis of obliterative bronchiolitis after lung transplantation. Transpl Infect Dis 3:168–176, 2001.

140. Reynaud-Gaubert M, Maria V, Thirion X, et al: Upregulation of chemokines in bronchoalveolar lavage fluid as a predictive marker of post transplant airway obliteration. J Heart Lung Transplant 21:721–730, 2002.

141. Lu KC, Jaramillo A, Lecha RL, et al: Interleukin-6 and interferon-gamma gene polymorphisms in the development of bronchiolitis obliterans syndrome after lung transplantation. Transplantation 74:1297–1302, 2002.

142. Kesten S, Chaparro C, Scavuzzo M, et al: Tacrolimus as rescue therapy for bronchiolitis obliterans syndrome. J Heart Lung Transplant 16:905–912, 1997.

143. Dusmet M, Maurer J, Winton T, et al: Methotrexate can halt the progression of bronchiolitis obliterans syndrome in lung transplant recipients. J Heart Lung Transplant 15:948–954, 1996.

144. Snell GI, Esmore DS, Williams TJ: Cytolytic therapy for the bronchiolitis obliterans syndrome complicating lung transplantation. Chest 109:874–878, 1996.

145. Cahill BC, Somerville KT, Crompton JA, et al: Early experience with sirolimus in lung transplant recipients with chronic allograft rejection. J Heart Lung Transplant 22:169–176, 2003.

146. Verleden GM, Dupont LJ, Van Raemdonck D, Vanhaecke J: Effect of switching from cyclosporine to tacrolimus on exhaled nitric oxide and pulmonary function in patients with chronic rejection after lung transplantation. J Heart Lung Transplant 22:908–913, 2003.

146a. Verleden GM, Dupont LJ: Azithromycin therapy for patients with bronchiolitis obliterans syndrome after lung transplantation. Transplantation 77:1465–1467, 2004.

147. Nathan SD, Ross DJ, Belman MJ, et al: Bronchiolitis obliterans in single-lung transplant recipients. Chest 107:967–972, 1995.

148. Yousem SA, Burke CM, Billingham ME: Pathologic pulmonary alterations in long-term human heart-lung transplantation. Hum Pathol 16:911–923, 1985.

149. Clelland C, Higenbottam T, Otulana B, et al: Histologic prognostic indicators for the lung allografts of heart-lung transplants. J Heart Lung Transplant 9:177–186, 1990.

150. Keenan RJ, Lega ME, Dummer JS, et al: Cytomegalovirus serologic status and postoperative infection correlated with risk of developing chronic rejection after pulmonary transplantation. Transplantation 51:433–438, 1991.

151. Schulman LL, Weinberg AD, McGregor C, et al: Mismatches at the HLA-DR and HLA-B loci are risk factors for acute rejection after transplantation. Am J Respir Crit Care Med 157:1833–1837, 1998.

152. Bando K, Paradis IL, Similo S, et al: Obliterative bronchiolitis after lung and heart-lung transplantation: An analysis of risk factors and management. J Thorac Cardiovasc Surg 110:4–13, 1995.

153. Itescu S, Weinberg AD, Burke EM, et al: Risk factors for early onset obliterative bronchiolitis after lung transplantation: Influence of donor HLA-DR4 type (abstract). J Heart Lung Transplant 16:A69, 1997.

154. Hohlfeld J, Niedermeyer J, Hamm H, et al: Seasonal onset of bronchiolitis obliterans syndrome in lung transplant recipients. J Heart Lung Transplant 15:888–894, 1996.

155. Jaramillo A, Smith MA, Phelan D, et al: Development of ELISA-detected anti-HLA antibodies precedes the development of bronchiolitis obliterans syndrome and correlates with progressive decline in pulmonary function after lung transplantation. Transplantation 67:1155–1161, 1999.

156. Palmer SM, Davis RD, Hadjiliadis D, et al: Development of an antibody specific to major histocompatibility antigens detectable by flow cytometry after lung transplant is associated with bonchiolitis obliterans syndrome. Transplantation 74:799–804, 2002.

157. Hertz MI, Jessurun J, King MB, et al: Reproduction of the obliterative bronchiolitis lesion after heterotopic transplantation of mouse airways. Am J Pathol 142:1945–1951, 1993.

158. Koskinen PK, Kallio EA, Krebs R, et al: A dose-dependent inhibitory effect of cyclosporine A on obliterative bronchiolitis of rat tracheal allografts. Am J Respir Crit Care Med 155:303–312, 1997.

159. Boehler A, Chamberlain D, Kesten S, et al: Lymphocytic airway infiltration as a precursor to fibrous obliteration in a rat model of bronchiolitis obliterans. Transplantation 64:311–317, 1997.

160. Sritippayawan S, Keens TG, Horn MV, et al: What are the best pulmonary function test parameters for early detection of post-lung transplant bronchiolitis obliterans syndrome in children? Pediatr Transplant 7:200–203, 2003.

161. Toronto Lung Transplant group: Experience with single lung transplantation for pulmonary fibrosis. JAMA 259:2258–2262, 1988.

162. Williams TJ, Grossman RF, Maurer JR: Long-term functional follow-up of lung transplant recipients. Clin Chest Med 11:347–358, 1990.

163. Gaissert HA, Trulock EP, Cooper JD, et al: Comparison of early functional results after lung volume reduction or lung transplantation for COPD. J Thorac Cardiovasc Surg 111:296–307, 1996.

164. Levy RD, Ernst P, Shennib H, et al: Exercise performance after lung transplantation. J Heart Lung Transplant 12:23–33, 1993.

165. Madden BP, Hodgson ME, Tsang V, et al: Intermediate results of heart-lung transplantation for cystic fibrosis. Lancet 339:1583–1587, 1992.

166. Williams TJ, Johns DP, Side E, et al: DL_{CO} reduction is not associated with altered DM/V_C in heart-lung transplant recipients (abstract). Am Rev Respir Dis 145:A703, 1992.

167. Chacon RA, Corris PA, Dark JH, et al: Respiratory mechanics after heart-lung and bilateral lung transplantation. Thorax 52:718–722, 1997.

168. Glanville AR, Burke CM, Theodore J, et al: Bronchial hyper-responsiveness after human cardiopulmonary transplantation. Clin Sci 73:299–303, 1987.

169. Maurer JR, McClean PA, Cooper JD, et al: Airway hyper-reactivity in patients undergoing lung and heart-lung transplantation. Am Rev Respir Dis 139:1038–1041, 1989.

170. Glanville AR, Gabb GM, Theodore J, et al: Bronchial responsiveness to exercise after human cardiopulmonary transplantation. Chest 96:281–286, 1989.

171. Glanville AR, Theodore J, Baldwin JC, et al: Bronchial responsiveness after human heart-lung transplantation. Chest 97:1360–1366, 1990.

172. Stretton CD, Mak JC, Belvisi MG, et al: Cholinergic control of human airways in vitro following extrinsic denervation of human respiratory tract by heart-lung transplantation. Am Rev Respir Dis 142:1030–1033, 1990.

173. Ward C, Snell GI, Orsida B, et al: Airway versus transbronchial biopsy and BAL in lung transplant recipients: Different but complementary. Eur Respir J 10:2876–2880, 1997.

174. Snell GI, Ward C, Wilson JW, et al: Immunopathological changes in the airways of stable lung transplant recipients. Thorax 52:322–328, 1997.

175. Glanville AR, Yeend RA, Theodore J, et al: Effect of single respiratory manoeuvres on specific airway conductance in

heart-lung transplant recipients. Clin Sci 74:311–317, 1988.

176. Fish JE, Ankin MG, Kelly JF, et al: Regulation of bronchomotor tone by lung inflation in asthmatic and non-asthmatic subjects. J Appl Physiol 50:1079–1086, 1981.

177. Miyoshi S, Trulock EP, Schaefers HJ, et al: Cardio-pulmonary exercise testing after single and double lung transplantation. Chest 97:1130–1136, 1990.

178. Williams TJ, Grossman RF, Maurer JR: Long-term functional follow-up of lung transplant recipients. Clin Chest Med 11:347–358, 1990.

179. Morton JM, McKenna MJ, Carey MF, et al: Reductions in type I fibre proportions and oxidative enzyme activity in skeletal muscle exist pre and post lung transplantation. J Heart Lung Transplant 18:A66, 1999.

180. Evans AB, Al-Himyary AJ, Hrovat MI, et al: Abnormal skeletal muscle oxidative capacity after lung transplantation by ^{31}P-MRS. Am J Respir Crit Care Med 155:615–622, 1997.

181. Mercier JG, Hokanson JF, Brooks GA: Effects of cyclosporine A on skeletal muscle mitochondrial respiration and endurance time in rats. Am J Respir Crit Care Med 151:1532–1536, 1995.

182. Oelberg DA, Medoff BD, Markowitz DH, et al: Systemic oxygen extraction during incremental exercise in patients with severe chronic obstructive pulmonary disease. Eur J Appl Physiol 78:201–207, 1998.

183. Sanders MH, Owens GR, Sciurba FC, et al: Ventilation and breathing pattern during progressive hypercapnia and hypoxia after human heart-lung transplantation. Am Rev Respir Dis 140:38–44, 1989.

184. Duncan SR, Kagawa FT, Starnes VA, et al: Hypercarbic ventilatory responses of human heart-lung transplant recipients. Am Rev Respir Dis 144:126–130, 1991.

185. Frost AE, Zamel N, McClean P, et al: Hypercapnic ventilatory response in recipients of double-lung transplants. Am Rev Respir Dis 146:1610–1612, 1992.

186. Cohen L, Littlefield C, Kelly P, et al: Predictors of quality of life and adjustment after lung transplantation. Chest 113:633–644, 1998.

187. Gross CR, Savik K, Bolman RM III, et al. Long-term health status and quality of life outcomes of lung transplant recipients. Chest 108:1587–1593, 1995.

188. TenVergert EM, Vermeulen KM, Geertsma A, et al: Quality of life before and after lung transplantation in patients with emphysema versus other indications. Psychol Rep 89:707–717, 2001.

189. Vermeulen KM, Ouwens JP, van der Bij W, et al: Long-term quality of life in patients surviving at least 55 months after lung transplantation. Gen J Hosp Psychiatry 25:95–102, 2003.

190. Singer HK, Ruchinskas RA, Riley KC, et al: The psychological impact of end-stage lung disease. Chest 120:1246–1252, 2001.

191. Chaparro C, Kesten S, Chamberlain D, et al: Causes of death in lung transplant recipients. J Heart Lung Transplant 13:758–767, 1994.

192. Maurer JR: Medical complications following lung transplantation. Semin Respir Crit Care Med 17:173–185, 1996.

193. Zaltzman JS, Pei Y, Maurer J, et al: Cyclosporine nephrotoxicity in lung transplant recipients. Transplantation 54:875–878, 1992.

194. Hadjiliadis D, Davis DR, Steele MP, et al: Gastroesophageal reflux disease in lung transplant recipients. Clin Transplant 17:363–368, 2003.

195. Goldstein LS, Haug MT, Perl J, et al: Central nervous system complications after lung transplantation. J Heart Lung Transplant 17:185–191, 1998.

196. Kanis JA, World Health Organization (WHO) Study Group: Assessment of fracture risk and its application to screening for postmenopausal osteoporosis: Synopsis of a WHO report. Osteoporos Int 4:368–381, 1994.

197. Ferrari SL, Nicod LP, Hamacher J, et al: Osteoporosis in patients undergoing lung transplantation. Eur Respir J 9:2378–2382, 1996.

198. Johnson BA, Duncan SR, Ohori NP, et al: Recurrence of sarcoidosis in pulmonary allograft recipients. Am Rev Respir Dis 148:1373–1377, 1993.

199. Muller C, Briegel J, Haller M, et al: Sarcoidosis recurrence following lung transplantation. Transplantation 61:1117–1119, 1996.

200. Nine JS, Yousem SA, Paradis IL, et al: Lymphangioleiomyomatosis: Recurrence after lung transplantation. J Heart Lung Transplant 13:714–719, 1994.

201. Frost AE, Keller CA, Brown RW, et al: Giant cell interstitial pneumonitis: Disease recurrence in the transplanted lung. Am Rev Respir Dis 148:1401–1404, 1993.

202. Baz MA, Kussin PS, Van Trigt P, et al: Recurrence of diffuse panbronchiolitis after lung transplantation. Am J Respir Crit Care Med 151:895–898, 1995.

203. Gabbay E, Dark JH, Ashcroft T, et al: Recurrence of Langerhan's cell granulomatosis following lung transplantation. Thorax 53:326–327, 1998.

204. Garver RI, Zorn GL, Wu X, et al: Recurrence of bronchoalveolar cell carcinoma in transplanted lungs. N Engl J Med 340:1071–1074, 1999.

205. King MB, Jessurun J, Hertz MI: Recurrence of desquamative interstitial pneumonia after lung transplantation. Am J Respir Crit Care Med 157:1349–1350, 1998.

206. Novick RJ, Stitt LW, Al-Kattan K, et al: Pulmonary retransplantation: Predictors of graft function and survival in 230 patients; Pulmonary Retransplant Registry. Ann Thorac Surg 65:227–234, 1998.

90 Smoking Hazards and Cessation

Neal L. Benowitz, M.D., Paul G. Brunetta, M.D.

INTRODUCTION

Cigarette smoking remains the leading cause of preventable premature morbidity and mortality in the United States and in many countries around the world. An average of 435,000 people in the United States die prematurely from tobacco-related disease in a year, which includes one of every three cancers and one in five overall deaths.[1] A lifelong smoker has about a one in three chance of dying prematurely from a complication of smoking.[2]

Smoking is particularly relevant to respiratory medicine, as it is by far the major cause of lung cancer and chronic obstructive pulmonary disease (COPD) in developed countries. Smoking is also a substantial causative factor in respiratory infections, including pneumococcal pneumonia, influenza, and tuberculosis.

EPIDEMIOLOGY OF CIGARETTE SMOKING

Currently about 46 million individuals (23.3% of the adult population) in the United States are cigarette smokers, including 26% of men and 22% of women.[3] People who are less well educated and/or have unskilled occupations are more likely to smoke. For example, 35.6% of people with 9 to 11 years of education are smokers, compared to 16.5% of those with a college degree.

The global tobacco disease burden has been reviewed by the World Health Organization in *World Health Report 2000*.[4] Smoking prevalence continues to rise in many low-income and middle-income countries. Disease burden was estimated using the disability adjusted life-years (DALYs) lost. In 2000, 8.8% of the global total deaths were attributable to tobacco use, a 45% increase from 1990. If the current levels of smoking remain unchanged, the burden from tobacco consumption is estimated to double by 2020. These figures informed the recently negotiated WHO Framework Convention on Tobacco Control, which aims to reduce the demand and supply of tobacco around the world through educational, political, and legislative means.[5]

TOXICOLOGY OF CIGARETTE SMOKE

Tobacco smoke is an aerosol of droplets (particulates) containing water, nicotine and other alkaloids, and tar. Tobacco smoke contains several thousand chemicals, many of which may contribute to human disease.[6] Major toxic chemicals in the particulate phase of tobacco include nicotine, benzo(a)pyrene and other polycyclic hydrocarbons, N'-nitrosonornicotine, beta-naphthylamine, polonium-210, nickel, cadmium, arsenic, and lead. The gaseous phase contains carbon monoxide, acetaldehyde, acetone, methanol, nitrogen oxides, hydrogen cyanide, acrolein, ammonia, benzene, formaldehyde, nitrosamines, and vinyl chloride. Tobacco smoke may produce illness by way of systemic absorption of toxins and/or cause local pulmonary injury by oxidant chemicals.

SMOKING-RELATED DISEASES

Tobacco use is a major cause of death from cancer, cardiovascular disease, and pulmonary disease (Table 90.1). Smoking is also a major risk factor for osteoporosis, reproductive disorders, and fire-related and trauma-related injuries.

CANCER

Smoking, the largest preventable cause of cancer (Table 90.2), is responsible for about 30% of cancer deaths.[7] Many chemicals in tobacco smoke may contribute to carcinogenesis as tumor initiators, cocarcinogens, tumor promoters, or complete carcinogens.[8] Complexes of tobacco smoke carcinogens and DNA are thought to be a crucial step in cancer induction.[9] Cigarette smoking induces specific patterns of $p53$ gene mutations that are associated with squamous cell carcinomas of the lung, head, and neck.[10] Lung cancer is the leading cause of cancer deaths in the United States and is predominantly attributable to cigarette smoking. The risk of lung and other cancers is proportional to how many cigarettes are smoked per day and even more strongly to the duration of smoking. In current smokers, DNA adduct levels in nontumerous lung tissue or blood mononuclear cells are related to cigarette consumption.[11] Of note, however, in former smokers DNA adduct levels were inversely associated with the age at which the person started smoking. This finding suggests that young smokers are more susceptible to DNA damage and persistence of genetic alterations than are those who begin smoking at an older age, which has substantial implications for the need to prevent adolescent smoking.[12]

Workplace exposure to asbestos or alpha radiation (the latter in uranium miners) synergistically increases the risk of lung cancer in cigarette smokers.[13] Alcohol use interacts synergistically with tobacco in causing oral, laryngeal, and esophageal cancer.[14] The mechanism of interaction may involve alcohol solubilizing tobacco carcinogens and/or alcohol-related induction of liver or gastrointestinal enzymes that metabolize and activate tobacco carcinogens. Smoking is associated with 15% of leukemia cases in adults and 20% of colorectal cancers.[15,16]

A detailed description of the pathogenesis and epidemiology of smoking-induced lung cancer is presented elsewhere in this textbook (see Chapters 42 and 43).

Table 90.1 Health Hazards of Tobacco Use (Risks Increased by Smoking)

Cancer (see Table 90.2)

Cardiovascular Disease
Sudden death
Acute myocardial infarction
Unstable angina
Stroke
Peripheral arterial occlusive disease (including thromboangiitis obliterans)
Aortic aneurysm

Pulmonary Disease
Lung cancer
Chronic bronchitis
Emphysema
Asthma
Increased susceptibility to pneumonia and pulmonary tuberculosis
Increased susceptibility to desquamative interstitial pneumonitis
Increased morbidity from viral respiratory infection

Gastrointestinal Disease
Peptic ulcer
Esophageal reflux

Reproductive Disturbances
Reduced fertility
Premature birth
Lower birth weight
Spontaneous abortion
Abruptio placentae
Premature rupture of membranes
Increased perinatal mortality

Oral Disease (Smokeless Tobacco)
Oral cancer
Leukoplakia
Gingivitis
Gingival recession
Tooth staining

Other
Non-insulin-dependent diabetes mellitus
Earlier menopause
Osteoporosis
Cataract
Tobacco amblyopia (loss of vision)
Age-related macular degeneration
Premature skin wrinkling
Aggravation of hypothyroidism
Altered drug metabolism or effects

CHRONIC PULMONARY DISEASE

More than 80% of COPD in the United States is attributable to cigarette smoking. Cigarette smoking also increases the risk of respiratory infection, including pneumonia, and results in greater disability from viral respiratory tract infections.[17,18] Pulmonary disease from smoking includes the overlapping syndromes of chronic bronchitis (cough and mucus secretion), emphysema, and airway obstruction. The lung pathology produced by cigarette smoking includes loss of cilia, mucous gland hyperplasia, increased number of

Table 90.2 Cigarette Smoking and Cancer Risk

Cancer Site	Average Relative Risk
Lung	15.0–30.0
Urinary tract	3.0
Oral cavity	4.0–5.0
Oropharynx and hypopharynx	4.0–5.0*
Esophagus	1.5–5.0*
Larynx	10.0*
Pancreas	2.0–4.0
Nasal cavity, sinuses, nasopharynx	1.5–2.5
Stomach	1.5–2.0
Liver	1.5–2.5
Kidney	1.5–2.0
Uterine cervix	1.5–2.5
Myeloid leukemia	1.5–2.0

Adapted from Vineis P, Alavanja M, Buffler P, et al: Tobacco and cancer: recent epidemiological evidence. J Natl Cancer Inst 96:99–106, 2004; and International Agency for Research on Cancer: Tobacco smoking and involuntary smoking. IARC Monographs on the Evaluation of Carcinogenic Risks to Humans. IARC Scientific Publication 83. Lyon, 2004.
* Synergistic interaction with alcohol use.

goblet cells in the central airways, inflammation, goblet cell metaplasia, squamous metaplasia, mucus plugging of small airways, destruction of alveoli, and a reduced number of small arteries. The mechanism of injury is complex and seems to include inflammation as well as direct injury by oxidant chemicals, increased elastase activity (a protein that breaks down elastin and other connective tissue), and decreased antiprotease activity.[19] A genetic deficiency of alpha$_1$-antiprotease activity produces a similar imbalance between pulmonary protease and antiprotease activity and is a risk factor for early and severe smoking-induced pulmonary disease.[20]

In addition to the effects of cigarette smoke-induced injury, the delivery of carbon monoxide from cigarette smoke serves to worsen the level of functioning in smokers who have significant COPD. Carbon monoxide binds to hemoglobin, reduces the capacity of hemoglobin to carry oxygen, and impairs oxygen release. Thus, carbon monoxide exposure produces a functional anemia. Carboxyhemoglobin levels are typically 5% to 10% in smokers, compared to 1% or less in nonsmokers. In a normal person, carbon monoxide from cigarette smoke causes few symptoms, but in patients with pulmonary disease carbon monoxide has the potential to cause significant impairment. Exposure to carbon monoxide at levels less than that derived from cigarette smoking have been shown to reduce exercise tolerance in patients with COPD.

Cigarette smoking may contribute to the development of asthma, although this potential link could be confounded by the increased rate of pulmonary infections observed in smokers. A longitudinal study of 5800 individuals taking part in a British national study suggested that regular smoking was associated with asthma in people between the ages of 17 to 33 [odds ratio (OR) = 4.42].[21] The relationship between asthma and smoking was further studied in more than 14,000 Finnish adults, and the prevalence of asthma was higher among male smokers than among male nonsmokers [relative risk (RR) = 1.73], although no smoking effect was observed for women.[22] Current smokers, compared to never smokers and ex-smokers, demonstrate higher asthma severity scores, more frequent asthma symptoms, and more frequent asthma attacks (OR = 2.39).[23] Silverman et al. evaluated 1847 emergency room patients presenting with acute asthma and found that 35% were current smokers.[24] Fifty percent of these smoking asthmatics reported that cigarette use worsened their asthma symptoms.

The link between second-hand smoke and asthma supports the hypothesis that bronchial hyperresponsiveness is worsened by tobacco exposure. A study evaluating infants in their first year of life exposed to smoking mothers demonstrated that they were 2.1 times more likely to develop asthma than children of nonsmoking mothers.[25] Likewise, the Swiss Study on Air Pollution and Lung Disease in Adults (SAPALDIA) suggested that second-hand smoke was associated with an increased risk of asthma (OR = 1.39) or reactive airway disease in nonsmoking adults.[26]

Bronchoalveolar lavage fluid in a small cohort of healthy nonasthmatic smokers documented altered macrophage cytokine release, increased cellularity, and depressed levels of interleukin-6.[27] These abnormalities further suggest a plausible link between smoking and an increased incidence and severity of a chronic lung inflammatory condition such as asthma.

Cigarette smoking has been associated with multiple non-neoplastic pulmonary disorders other than emphysema and chronic bronchitis. These include respiratory bronchiolitis-associated interstitial lung disease, desquamative interstitial pneumonitis (DIP), Langerhan's cell histiocytosis, cryptogenic fibrosing alveolitis, and eosinophilic pneumonia.[28] Ninety percent of patients with pulmonary Langerhan's cell histiocytosis are smokers. Respiratory bronchiolitis and DIP have similar histopathologic features and are characterized by the accumulation of pigmented macrophages within the alveoli. Respiratory bronchiolitis ("smoker's bronchiolitis") is most often an asymptomatic finding that can persist after smoking cessation.[29] DIP often affects smokers in their fourth or fifth decade of life, and the symptoms are more frequent in smokers.[28] Smoking may also have an association with idiopathic pulmonary fibrosis.[30]

INFECTION

Cigarette smoking is a major risk factor for respiratory tract and other systemic infections.[31] Both active and passive cigarette smoke exposure increase the risk of infection. The mechanisms by which smoking increases risk are multifactorial and include structural and immunologic alterations. As mentioned previously, cigarette smoking causes structural changes in the respiratory tract. These changes include peribronchiolar inflammation and fibrosis, increased mucosal permeability, impairment of mucociliary clearance, changes in pathogen adherence, and disruption of the

Table 90.3 Cigarette Smoking and Infection

Infection	Odds Ratio (95% CI)
Pneumococcal pneumonia	2.6 (1.9–3.5)
Legionnaire's disease	3.5 (2.1–5.8)
Meningococcal disease	2.4 (0.9–6.6)
Periodontal disease	2.8 (1.9–4.1)
Common cold	1.5 (1.1–1.8)
Influenza	2.4 (1.5–3.8)
HIV	3.4 (1.6–7.5)
Tuberculosis	4.5 (4.0–5.0)

HIV, human immunodeficiency virus; CI, confidence interval.

respiratory epithelium. A number of components of ciga-rette smoke, including acrolein, acetaldehyde, formalde-hyde, free radicals produced from chemical reactions in the cigarette smoke, and nitric oxide, may contribute to the observed structural alterations in airway epithelial cells.

Immunologic mechanisms include alterations in cellular and humoral immune system function. These include a decreased level of circulating immunoglobulins, a depres-sion of antibody response to certain antigens, a decrease in CD4+ lymphocyte counts, an increase in CD8+ lymphocyte counts, depressed phagocyte activity, and decreased release of pro-inflammatory cytokines. Many of the immunologic disturbances in smokers resolve within 6 weeks after smoking cessation, supporting the idea that smoking cessa-tion is highly effective in a relatively short period of time in the prevention of infection.[31]

Cigarette smoking is associated with an increased risk of bacterial and viral infections (Table 90.3). Cigarette smoking is a substantial risk factor for pneumococcal pneumonia, especially in patients with COPD. Smoking is strongly associated with invasive pneumococcal disease in otherwise healthy adults. A population-based case-control study showed that smoking was the strongest independent risk factor for invasive pneumococcal disease among immunocompetent adults.[17] The odds ratio was 4.1 [95% confidence interval (CI) 2.4–7.3] for active smoking and 2.5 (95% CI 1.2–5.1) for passive smoke exposure in non-smokers compared to nonexposed nonsmokers. The attribu-table risk in this population was 51% for cigarette smoking and 17% for passive smoking, and this effect showed a strong dose response. The risk of pneumococcal disease declined to nonsmoker levels 10 years after cessation. Cig-arette smoking has also been shown to be associated with a nearly twofold increased risk of community-acquired pneumonia, with 32% of the risk attributable to cigarette smoking.[32]

Cigarette smoking increases the risk of developing, and the severity of, viral infections including the common cold, influenza, and varicella. Influenza infections are more severe, with more cough, acute and chronic phlegm production, breathlessness, and wheezing in smokers.[18] Influenza infections produce more work loss days in smokers compared to nonsmokers. Influenza vaccination is effective in preventing the disease in smokers. Cigarette smoking should be considered a high priority indication for influenza vaccination. The risk of the development of varicella pneumonitis in adults is substantially greater in smokers compared to nonsmokers.[33]

Tuberculosis is perhaps the most important smoking-associated infection. Cigarette smoking is a risk factor for tuberculin skin test reactivity, skin test conversion, and the development of active tuberculosis. Of note is a recent large case-control study from India that examined smoking and tuberculosis in men between 35 and 69 years of age. The tuberculosis prevalence risk ratio was 2.9 (95% CI 2.6–3.3) for ever smokers compared to never smokers, and the prevalence was higher with a higher level of cigarette consumption.[34] The mortality from tuberculosis among men 25 to 69 years old showed a risk ratio of 4.5 (95% CI 4.0–5.0) and 4.2 (95% CI 3.7–4.8) for urban and rural res-idents, respectively. The authors found that the smoking-attributable proportion of deaths from tuberculosis was 61% greater than the proportion of smoking-attributable deaths from vascular disease or cancer. Thus, it is likely that smoking contributes substantially to the worldwide disease burden of tuberculosis.

Of historical interest is the relationship between tuber-culosis and the risk of cigarette smoking in the early 20th century. Prior to that time, chewing tobacco was the pre-ferred type of tobacco. Public fears that users of chewing tobacco who spit in public places might be spreading tuber-culosis is one of the factors that led to the increase in ciga-rette sales in the United States. This is nicely described by Kluger[35] as follows:

Chewing tobacco was no longer merely messy but socially dis-agreeable in more crowded urban America, and in its inevitable byproduct, spitting, was now identified as a spreader of tubercu-losis and other contagions and, thus, an official health menace. The leisurely pipe all at once seemed a remnant of a slower-temp age, and cigar fumes were newly offensive amid thronged city life. The cigarette by contrast, could be quickly consumed and easily snuffed out on the job as well as to and from work.

CARDIOVASCULAR DISEASE

Although not the focus of this textbook, cardiovascular disease is common in patients with respiratory disease. This relates to the facts that both diseases are common and both increase with age, and that smoking is a major risk factor for both respiratory disease and cardiovascular disease.

Cigarette smoking accounts for about 20% of cardiovas-cular deaths in the United States. Risks are increased for coronary artery disease, sudden death, cerebrovascular disease, and peripheral vascular disease, including aortic aneurysm.[36] Cigarette smoking accelerates atherosclerosis and promotes acute ischemic events. The mechanisms of the effects of cigarette smoking are not fully elucidated but are believed to include (1) hemodynamic stress (nicotine increases the heart rate and transiently increases blood pres-sure); (2) endothelial injury and dysfunction (nitric oxide release and resultant vasodilation are impaired); (3) devel-opment of an atherogenic lipid profile (smokers have on average higher levels of low density lipoprotein, more oxidized low density lipoprotein, and lower levels of high density lipoprotein cholesterol than nonsmokers do); (4) enhanced coagulability; (5) arrhythmogenesis, and (6) relative hypoxemia because of the effects of carbon monoxide.[37] Carbon monoxide reduces the capacity of hemoglobin to carry oxygen and impairs the release of oxygen from hemoglobin to body tissues, both of which combine to result in a state of relative hypoxemia. As compensation for the reduced oxygen-carrying capacity, polycythemia develops in smokers, with the hematocrit often 50% or more. The polycythemia and the increased fibrinogen levels that are found in cigarette smokers also increase blood viscosity, which adds to the risk of thrombotic events. Cigarette smoking also induces a chronic inflammatory state, as evidenced by an increased neutrophil count and increased levels of fibrinogen and C-reactive protein in the blood of smokers. Chronic inflammation is thought to contribute to atherogenesis.

Cigarette smoking acts synergistically with other cardiac risk factors to increase the risk of ischemic heart disease. Although the risk of cardiovascular disease is roughly proportional to cigarette consumption, the risk persists even at low levels of smoking, that is, at one to two cigarettes per day.[38] Cigarette smoking reduces exercise tolerance in patients with angina pectoris and intermittent claudication. Vasospastic angina is more common, and the response to vasodilator medication is impaired in patients who smoke. The number of episodes and total duration of ischemic episodes as assessed by ambulatory electrocardiographic monitoring in patients with coronary heart disease are substantially increased by cigarette smoking.[39] The increase in relative risk of coronary heart disease because of cigarette smoking is greatest in young adults who, in the absence of cigarette smoking, would have a relatively low risk.[36] Women who use oral contraceptives and smoke cigarettes have a synergistically increased risk of both myocardial infarction and stroke.

After acute myocardial infarction, the risk of recurrent myocardial infarction is higher and survival is half over the next 12 years in persistent smokers compared with quitters.[40] Smoking also interferes with revascularization therapy for acute myocardial infarction. After thrombolysis, the reocclusion rate is fourfold higher in smokers who continue than in those who quit.[41] The risk of reocclusion of a coronary artery after angioplasty or occlusion of a bypass graft is increased in smokers.[42] Cigarette smoking is not a risk factor for hypertension per se but does increase the risk of complications, including the development of nephrosclerosis and progression to malignant hypertension.[43] Cigarette smoking has been shown to be a substantial contributor to morbidity and mortality in patients with left ventricular dysfunction. The mortality benefit of stopping smoking in such patients is equal to or greater than the benefit of therapy with angiotensin-converting enzyme inhibitors, beta-blockers, or spironolactone.[44]

WOUND HEALING/POSTOPERATIVE COMPLICATIONS

Cigarette smoking is associated with adverse postoperative events and delayed wound healing. The mechanisms include cutaneous vasoconstriction (reducing skin blood flow), local thrombosis, and reduced oxygen-carrying capacity, all of which can delay wound healing. Impaired clearance of secretions, altered immune function, altered collagen synthesis, as well as the influence of underlying tobacco-related diseases (e.g., COPD and altered cardiovascular function) also contribute to postoperative complications.

Moller and colleagues recently published the results of a randomized, controlled trial of smokers awaiting elective hip or knee surgery at three hospitals in Copenhagen.[45] They compared 56 patients in a smoking cessation intervention arm (83% stopped or reduced smoking) versus 62 patients in a usual-care arm. The overall complication rate was 18% in the intervention arm and 52% in the controls, a highly significant difference. The greatest differences were seen in wound complication rates (5% vs. 31%) and cardiovascular complications (0% vs. 10%), without a significant difference in length of hospital stay.

A study of 489 adult patients undergoing ambulatory surgery demonstrated a significantly higher rate of respiratory complications in smokers compared to nonsmokers (32.8% in smokers vs. 25.9% in nonsmokers) and wound infections (3.6% in smokers vs. 0.6% in nonsmokers).[46] Causes of major pulmonary events after pneumonectomy for lung surgery were sought in a retrospective analysis of 261 patients.[47] Patients who continued to smoke within 1 month of operation were determined to be at an increased risk of pulmonary events, which was associated with increased postoperative mortality. Cigarette smoking is associated with an increased risk of hepatic artery thrombosis after liver transplantation, and cessation 2 years before transplantation was associated with a decreased risk.[48] Similar data exist regarding renal transplantation and allograft survival in smokers compared to nonsmokers.[49]

The optimal window for smoking cessation intervention may be at 8 weeks prior to elective surgery, as suggested by data demonstrating that patients who had stopped smoking at least 2 months preoperatively had nearly maximal reduction in postoperative respiratory complications.[50] Recent data suggest that short-term (2–3 weeks) cessation or reduction in smoking does not substantially alter postoperative wound complications in patients undergoing colorectal surgery.[51]

An important issue related to elective surgery is that patients are often highly motivated to quit smoking just before elective surgery and can benefit from cessation counseling prior to surgery as well as in-hospital cessation counseling and medication in the postoperative setting. Specific issues related to smoking cessation are discussed later in this chapter.

OTHER COMPLICATIONS OF CIGARETTE SMOKING

Cigarette smoking increases the risk of duodenal and gastric ulcers, delays the rate of ulcer healing, and increases the risk of relapse after ulcer treatment.[52] Smoking is also associated with esophageal reflux symptoms. Smoking produces ulcer disease by increasing acid secretion, reducing pancreatic bicarbonate secretion, impairing the gastric mucosal barrier (related to decreased gastric mucosal blood flow and/or inhibition of prostaglandin synthesis), reducing pyloric sphincter tone, and increasing the risk of *Helicobacter pylori* infection.[53]

Cigarette smoking is an independent risk factor for the development of non-insulin-dependent diabetes mellitus, which is a consequence of developing resistance to the effects of insulin.[54] The effects of nicotine seem to contribute at least in part to insulin resistance, and insulin resistance has been described in users of smokeless tobacco, who are not exposed to tobacco combustion products.

Cigarette smoking is a risk factor for osteoporosis in that it reduces the peak bone mass attained in early adulthood and increases the rate of bone loss in later adulthood. Smoking antagonizes the protective effect of estrogen replacement therapy on the risk of osteoporosis in postmenopausal women.[55]

Cigarette smoking is a major cause of reproductive problems and results in approximately 4600 U.S. infant deaths annually. Growth retardation from cigarette smoking has been termed fetal tobacco syndrome. Cigarette smoking causes reproductive complications by causing placental ischemia mediated by the hypoxic effects of chronic carbon monoxide exposure, endothelial dysfunction, and the general increase in coagulability produced by oxidant chemicals in cigarette smoke.[56]

Other adverse effects of cigarette smoking include premature facial wrinkling, an increased risk of cataracts, olfactory dysfunction, and fire-related injuries. The last-mentioned effect contributes significantly to the economic costs of tobacco use. Smoking reduces the secretion of thyroid hormone in women with subclinical hypothyroidism and increases the severity of clinical symptoms of hypothyroidism in women with subclinical or overt hypothyroidism, the latter effect reflecting antagonism of thyroid hormone action.[57] Cigarette smoking also potentially interacts with a variety of drugs by accelerating drug metabolism or by the antagonistic pharmacologic actions that nicotine and/or other constituents of tobacco have with other drugs (Table 90.4).

HEALTH HAZARDS OF SECONDHAND SMOKE

Considerable evidence indicates that exposure to secondhand smoke is harmful to the health of nonsmokers (Table

Table 90.4 Interaction Between Cigarette Smoking and Drugs

Drugs	Interaction (Effects Compared with Nonsmokers)	Significance
Antipyrine Caffeine Chlorpromazine Clozapine Desmethyldiazepam Estradiol Estrone Flecainide Fluvoxamine Haloperidol Imipramine Lidocaine Olanzapine Oxazepam Pentazocine Phenacetin Phenylbutazone Propranolol Tacrine Theophylline	Accelerated metabolism	May require higher doses in smokers; reduced doses after quitting
Oral contraceptives	Enhanced thrombosis, increased risk of stroke and myocardial infarction	Do not prescribe to smokers, especially if >35 years old
Cimetidine and other H_2-blockers	Lower rate of ulcer healing, higher ulcer recurrence rates	Consider using mucosal protective agents
Propranolol	Less antihypertensive effect, less antianginal efficacy; more effective in reducing mortality after myocardial infarction	Consider the use of cardioselective beta-blockers
Nifedipine (and probably other calcium blockers)	Less antianginal effect	May require higher doses and/or multiple-drug antianginal therapy
Diazepam, chlordiazepoxide (and possibly other sedative-hypnotics)	Less sedation	Smokers may need higher doses
Chlorpromazine (and possibly other neuroleptics)	Less sedation; possibly reduced efficacy	Smokers may need higher doses
Propoxyphene	Reduced analgesia	Smokers may need higher doses

Table 90.5 Health Hazards of Environmental Tobacco Smoke in Nonsmokers

Children
Sudden infant death syndrome
Hospitalization for respiratory tract infection in first year of life
Wheezing
Middle ear effusion
Asthma

Adults
Lung cancer
Myocardial infarction
Reduced pulmonary function
Irritation of eyes, nasal congestion, headache
Cough

90.5). The U.S. Environmental Protection Agency classifies secondhand smoke as a class A carcinogen, which means that it has been shown to cause cancer in humans.[58]

Secondhand smoke consists of sidestream smoke that is generated while the cigarette is smoldering and mainstream smoke that has been exhaled by the smoker. Of the total combustion product from a cigarette, 75% or more enters the air. The constituents of environmental tobacco smoke are qualitatively similar to those of mainstream smoke. However, some toxins, such as ammonia, formaldehyde, and nitrosamines, are present in much higher concentrations in environmental tobacco smoke than in mainstream smoke. The Environmental Protection Agency has estimated that secondhand smoke is responsible for approximately 3000 lung cancer deaths annually in nonsmokers in the United States, is causally associated with 150,000 to 300,000 cases of lower respiratory tract infection in infants and young children up to 18 months of age, and is causally associated with the aggravation of asthma in 200,000 to 1 million children. Secondhand smoke exposure is also responsible for 40,000 cardiovascular deaths.[59] An appreciation of the hazards of environmental tobacco smoke is important to the physician because it provides a basis for advising parents not to smoke when children are in the home, for insisting that child care facilities be smoke-free, and for recommending smoking restrictions in work sites and other public places.

NICOTINE ADDICTION

Tobacco use is motivated primarily by the desire for nicotine. Drug addiction is defined as compulsive use of a psychoactive substance, the consequences of which are detrimental to the individual or society. Understanding addiction is useful in providing effective smoking cessation therapy.[60] Nicotine is absorbed rapidly from tobacco smoke into the pulmonary circulation; it then moves quickly to the brain, where it acts on nicotinic cholinergic receptors to produce its gratifying effects, which occur within 10 to 15 seconds after a puff. Smokeless tobacco is absorbed more slowly and results in less intense acute pharmacologic effects. With long-term use of tobacco, physical dependence

develops, associated with an increased number of nicotinic cholinergic receptors in the brain.[61] When tobacco is unavailable, even for only a few hours, withdrawal symptoms often occur, including anxiety, irritability, difficulty concentrating, restlessness, hunger, craving for tobacco, disturbed sleep, and in some people depression.

Addiction to tobacco is multifactorial, including a desire for the direct pharmacologic actions of nicotine, relief of withdrawal symptoms, and learned associations. Smokers report a variety of reasons for smoking, including pleasure, arousal, enhanced vigilance, improved performance, relief of anxiety or depression, reduced hunger, and control of body weight. Environmental cues—such as a meal, a cup of coffee, talking on the phone, an alcoholic beverage, friends who smoke—often trigger an urge to smoke. Smoking and depression are strongly linked. Smokers are more likely to have a history of major depression than nonsmokers are. Smokers with a history of depression are also likely to be more highly dependent on nicotine and have a lower likelihood of quitting. When they do quit, depression is more apt to be a prominent withdrawal symptom.

Most tobacco use begins in childhood or adolescence.[62] Risk factors for youth smoking include peer and parental influences; behavioral problems (e.g., poor school performance); personality characteristics such as rebelliousness or risk taking, depression, and anxiety; and genetic influences. The adolescent's desire to appear older and more sophisticated, such as emulating more mature role models, is another strong motivator. Environmental influences such as advertising and smoking in movies also contribute. Although smoking rates among adults have been declining since the 1970s, initiation rates for youth have remained constant since the mid-1980s. Approaches to preventing tobacco addiction in youth include educational activities in schools, aggressive anti-tobacco media campaigns, taxation of tobacco products, changing the social and environmental norms (restricting indoor smoking, educating parents not to smoke around children), and deglamorizing smoking.

NEUROBIOLOGIC MECHANISMS OF ADDICTION

Nicotine binds stereoselectively to nicotinic cholinergic receptors in the brain, autonomic ganglia, adrenal medulla, and neuromuscular junctions. Most relevant to nicotine addiction are the neuronal nicotinic cholinergic receptors. These are found throughout the brain, with the greatest number of binding sites in the cortex, thalamus, and interpeduncular nucleus as well as substantial binding in the amygdala, septum, brain stem motor nuclei, and locus coeruleus. The nicotinic cholinergic receptor is a ligand-gated ion channel comprised of five subunits. Brain nicotinic cholinergic receptors are comprised of alpha and beta subunits. Usually, there are two alpha subunits and three beta subunits, with the alpha subunits responsible for ligand binding and the beta subunits mediating other aspects of receptor function.[63] There is much diversity of nicotinic cholinergic receptors with nine alpha subunit isoforms (alpha 2 through alpha 10) and three beta subunit isoforms (beta 2 through beta 4) identified in brain tissues. Different nicotinic receptors are found in different parts of the brain and have different chemical conductances for sodium and calcium and different sensitivity to different nicotinic agonists. The different nicotinic receptors are believed to mediate different pharmacologic actions of nicotine, perhaps corresponding to the multiple effects of nicotine experienced by human smokers.[64]

Nicotine receptors appear to be located both on cell bodies and at nerve terminals. All nicotine receptors are permeable to calcium ions. Nicotinic receptor activation works, at least in part and possibly in the main, by facilitating the release of neurotransmitters, including acetylcholine, norepinephrine, dopamine, serotonin, beta-endorphin, gamma-aminobutyric acid, and others.[65] Nicotine enhances fast excitatory synaptic transmission, which may contribute to learning and memory.[66,67] These effects appear to be mediated by nicotine acting on alpha 7 receptors to release glutamate. Nicotine also releases growth hormone, prolactin, vasopressin, and ACTH. Behavioral rewards from nicotine and perhaps nicotine addiction as well appear to be linked to dopamine release.[68]

The two main dopamine systems in the brain are the mesocorticolimbic and the nigrostriatal systems. The mesocorticolimbic system includes the ventral tegmental area projecting to the nucleus accumbens, the cortex, and limbic regions. The nigrostriatal system includes the substantia nigra and the pars compacta projecting to the dorsal striatum. Nicotine causes an increase in burst firing of ventral tegmental area neurons, resulting in release of dopamine in the nucleus accumbens.[68] Dopamine release is potentiated and sustained by nicotine-mediated release of glutamate.[69] Dopamine release in the outer shell of the nucleus accumbens is characteristic of the effects of many addicting drugs (e.g., heroin, cocaine, alcohol) and is thought to be an important site for drug-mediated reinforcement.[70]

Whereas acute exposure to nicotine produces stimulation of dopaminergic neurons in mesolimbic pathways, chronic exposure to nicotine and other drugs of abuse produces other changes in mesolimbic function. Chronic nicotine exposure results in neuroadaptation or the development of tolerance, and the absence of nicotine results in subnormal release of dopamine and other neurotransmitters. Thus, nicotine withdrawal may result in a state of deficient dopamine responses to novel stimuli in general and to a state of malaise and inability to experience pleasure. This has been termed by Koob and LeMoal "hedonic dysregulation."[71] Hedonic dysregulation may explain craving, and sensitivity to drug effects may explain why even a single slip might easily result in a return to compulsive drug use.

The release of various neurotransmitters discussed previously results in behavioral arousal, sympathetic neural activation, and a number of other effects that are believed to be rewarding.[72] The release of specific neurotransmitters has been speculatively linked to the reported reinforcing effects of nicotine (Fig. 90.1). For example, enhanced release of dopamine and norepinephrine may be associated with pleasure as well as appetite suppression, the latter of which may contribute to lower body weight. Release of acetylcholine may be associated with improved performance on behavioral tasks and improvement of memory. Release of beta-endorphin may be associated with reduction of anxiety and tension.

Although smokers give different explanations for their smoking, most agree that smoking produces arousal, particularly with the first cigarettes of the day, and relaxation, particularly in stressful situations. Consistent with reports of arousal, electroencephalographic desynchronization with an upward shift in the dominant alpha frequency and decreased total alpha and theta power follows cigarette smoking or the administration of nicotine.[73]

LOW-YIELD CIGARETTES

That smokers regulate their intake of nicotine has been clearly demonstrated. Smokers change the way they puff a cigarette depending on nicotine yield, as determined by the cigarette smoking machine.[74,75] They puff lower-yield cigarettes more frequently or more intensely than higher yield cigarettes, presumably to obtain more nicotine. Smokers who switch from higher-yield cigarettes to lower-yield cigarettes consume more nicotine from the lower-yield cigarettes than is predicted by smoking machine tests. Conversely, smokers consume less nicotine than predicted from higher-yield cigarettes. The intake of nicotine—with blood cotinine or nicotine concentrations or urine metabolites used as markers of nicotine intake—has been studied

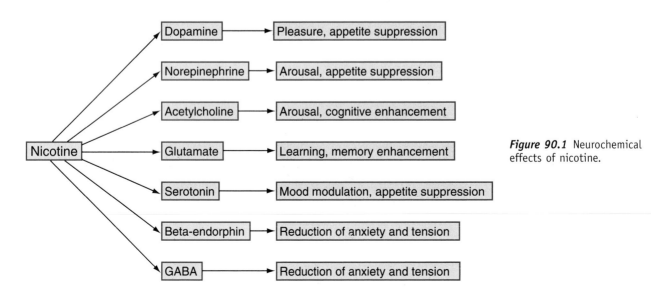

Figure 90.1 Neurochemical effects of nicotine.

in large groups of people smoking their own chosen brand of cigarettes.[74] In such studies, nicotine intake correlates only weakly with the machine-determined yield. Despite smoking cigarettes with widely differing nicotine yields, smokers demonstrate only small differences in nicotine intake. Correspondingly, the health benefits of switching to lower-yield cigarettes rather than higher-yield cigarettes are quite small, if any.[76,77]

The shift over the years from higher- to lower-yield cigarettes may explain the change in the pathology of lung cancer.[78] That is, the percentage of lung cancers that are adenocarcinomas has increased, and the percentage of squamous cell cancers has decreased. The change in tumor type is believed to reflect the higher nitrosamine delivery of lower-yield cigarettes and the increased depth of volume of inhalation of low-yield cigarettes to compensate for lower concentrations of nicotine in the smoke.

SMOKING CESSATION

Among cigarette smokers, 70% would like to quit, and 46% try to quit each year. Spontaneous quit rates are about 1% per year. Simple physician advice to quit increases the quit rate to 3%. Minimal intervention programs increase quit rates to 5% to 10%, whereas more intensive treatments, including smoking cessation clinics, can yield quit rates of 25% to 30%.[79]

The main strategies for cessation are behavioral counseling, pharmacologic intervention, or a combination of the two. Many patients try over-the-counter smoking cessation medications prior to discussing smoking with their health care providers. The efficacy of over-the-counter medications may be limited by improper use of medications and concomitant untreated issues such as depression, alcoholism, or other factors. Assessing stress, exposure to family members or roommates who smoke, or other factors shown to predict relapse are an important part of history-taking before a therapeutic intervention is undertaken.

GUIDELINES

Evidence-based guidelines for the treatment of tobacco addiction emphasize identifying all tobacco users in a physician's practice and ascertaining each patient's intent with respect to quitting smoking (Fig. 90.2).[80] Identification of tobacco use is facilitated by the implementation of an office-based system so patients are queried about tobacco use at every visit. Tobacco use should be treated as a vital sign by using tobacco status stickers on patients' charts, electronic medical records, or computer reminder systems. The practice of routinely recording a patient's tobacco use status increases the odds ratio for quitting by twofold.

Brief strategies to help a patient quit (the "5 A's") (Table 90.6), which can be implemented in as little as 3 minutes, increase cessation rates significantly. In a meta-analysis of 31 trials, brief physician advice increased quit rates by 70%.[79] Intensive behavioral treatment of tobacco dependence produces higher success rates than brief advice does and is cost-effective. However, these intensive programs are less widely available and may be less acceptable to patients than brief interventions. Nevertheless, clinicians with training in intensive smoking cessation therapy should be identified as a referral source for smokers who are interested.

The recent U.S. Public Health Service guideline recommends that all smokers trying to quit should be offered pharmacotherapy (Table 90.7).[80] In brief, two types of medication have been approved by the U.S. Food and Drug Administration (FDA) for smoking cessation: bupropion, which was originally marketed as an antidepressant drug, and nicotine (Table 90.8). Other drugs, such as nortriptyline and clonidine, have been shown in clinical trials to be effective in aiding smoking cessation but have not been approved by the FDA for this purpose.

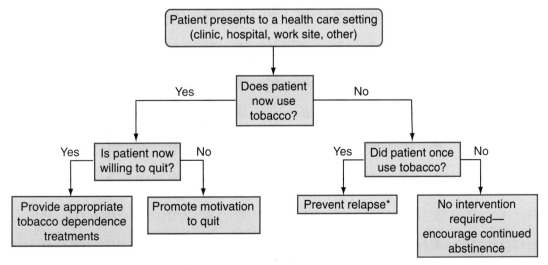

* Relapse prevention interventions are not necessary in the case of the adult who has not used tobacco for many years.

Figure 90.2 An algorithm for treating tobacco use. (Adapted from The Tobacco Use and Dependence Clinical Practice Guideline Panel, Staff, and Consortium Representatives: A clinical practice guideline for treating tobacco use and dependence: A US Public Health Service Report. JAMA 283:3244–3254, 2000.)

Table 90.6 Brief Strategies to Help the Patient Willing to Quit Tobacco Use: The "5 A's"

Strategies for Implementation	Action
Ask—Systematically identify all tobacco users at every visit.	Implement an office-wide system that ensures that at every clinic visit by every patient tobacco-use status is queried and documented.
Advise—Strongly urge all tobacco users to quit.	In a clear, strong, and personalized manner, urge every tobacco user to quit.
Assess—Determine willingness to make a quit attempt.	Ask every tobacco user if he/she is willing to make a quit attempt at this time (e.g., within the next 30 days).
Assist—Aid the patient in quitting.	Help the patient with a quit plan. Provide practical counseling (problem solving/skills training). Provide intratreatment social support. Help patient obtain extratreatment social support. Recommend the use of approved pharmacotherapy except in special circumstances.
Arrange—Schedule follow-up contact.	Schedule follow-up contact, either in person or via telephone.

Adapted from The Tobacco Use and Dependence Clinical Practice Guideline Panel, Staff, and Consortium Representatives: A clinical practice guideline for treating tobacco use and dependence: A US Public Health Service Report. JAMA 283:3244–3254, 2000.

SMOKING CESSATION COUNSELING

Counseling smokers about the dangerous effects of tobacco should be routine medical practice and has been shown to be an effective method to improve cessation rates. Based on a review of 188 randomized trials, personal advice and encouragement to stop smoking provided by a physician during a routine office visit resulted in an estimated 2% of all smokers stopping and not relapsing over 1 year.[81] Although this percentage seems low, it is both cost-effective and important when considering the large population and the risk for disease. Specific patient populations may have better results: 8% of pregnant smokers, 21% of healthy men at risk for cardiovascular disease, and 36% of survivors of myocardial infarction stop smoking when receiving advice and encouragement. This high success rate reflects the patient's inherent motivation once challenged by a condition that has been caused or may be aggravated by cigarettte smoking.

Group counseling is less cost-effective than brief advice but may be necessary for smokers who are having a hard time quitting with less intensive therapy. A recent review of 16 studies comparing group counseling found increased rates of cessation compared to self-help programs (16 studies; OR = 1.97) or no intervention (6 studies; OR = 2.19).[79] There is no evidence that group counseling is more effective than a similar intensity of individual counseling.

Table 90.7 General Clinical Guidelines for Prescribing Pharmacotherapy for Smoking Cessation

- In general, all smokers trying to quit smoking should be offered pharmacotherapy.

- There are five first-line smoking cessation medications: four types of nicotine replacement therapy, and sustained-release bupropion. There are inadequate data to rank these agents in order of efficacy. The choice of first-line therapy should be governed by patient preference, familiarity of the clinician with the medication, contraindications for specific patients, and prior experience of the patient with specific pharmacotherapies.

- Second-line therapies include clonidine and nortriptyline. These agents should be reserved for individuals with contraindications to, or failure of, a response to first-line medications.

- Several pharmacotherapies may delay but not prevent weight gain after smoking cessation. It is recommended that patients start or increase physical activity, but strict dieting is discouraged because this appears to increase the likelihood of relapse to smoking. Patients should be reassured that weight gain after quitting is self-limited and poses much less of a risk to health than smoking.

- Transdermal nicotine (patches) and nicotine gum appear to be safe for patients with chronic cardiovascular disease. Other medications are likely to be much safer than smoking in the presence of medical disease but need further evaluation.

- In smokers with prolonged withdrawal symptoms or in an individual who is unable to quit smoking in the absence of medication, long-term therapy with nicotine replacement medication or bupropion appears to be safe and reasonable therapy.

- Recent research suggests that combining bupropion with nicotine patches or combining nicotine patches with ad libitum use of nicotine gum or nicotine nasal spray increases abstinence rates compared to the rates produced by a single form of therapy.

Adapted from The Tobacco Use and Dependence Clinical Practice Guideline Panel, Staff, and Consortium Representatives: A clinical practice guideline for treating tobacco use and dependence: A US Public Health Service Report. JAMA 283:3244–3254, 2000.

Telephone counseling is effective in promoting cessation. In a large randomly controlled trial of 1973 intensively counseled callers versus 1309 controls, telephone counseling through the California Quitline nearly doubled abstinence rates.[82] The 12-month self-reported cessation rates for those who made one or more cessation attempts was 23.3% in the treatment group and 18.4% in the control group. Telephone hot lines for smoking cessation are available at no cost in many states across the United States. Thus, the busiest physician can easily refer patients to a hotline for cessation if personal counseling time is not readily available.

In-hospital counseling is found to be effective for patients admitted with cardiovascular disease but is not well studied in other populations. Molyneux and associates evaluated 274 patients in a randomized, controlled trial and found that nicotine replacement therapy given with brief

Table 90.8 Suggestions for the Clinical Use of Pharmacotherapies for Smoking Cessation

Pharmacotherapy	Precautions/ Contraindications	Adverse Effects	Dosage	Duration	Availability	Cost per Day*
First-line Drugs						
Sustained-release bupropion hydrochloride	History of seizure History of eating disorders	Insomnia Dry mouth	150 mg every morning for 3 days then 150 mg twice daily (begin treatment 1–2 weeks prequit)	7–12 weeks maintenance up to 6 months	Prescription only	$3.33
Nicotine gum	Temporo-mandibular joint disorder	Mouth soreness Dyspepsia	1–24 cigarettes/day; 2 mg gum (up to 24 pieces/day) ≥25 cigarettes/day; 4 mg gum (up to 24 pieces/day)	Up to 12 weeks	OTC only	$6.25 for ten 2-mg pieces $6.87 for ten 4-mg pieces
Nicotine inhaler		Local irritation of mouth and throat	6–16 cartridges/day	Up to 6 months	Prescription only	$10.94 for 10 cartridges
Nicotine nasal spray	Chronic nasal disorders, including rhinitis, polyps, and sinusitis	Nasal irritation Throat burning	8–40 doses/day	3–6 months	Prescription only	$5.40 for 12 doses
Nicotine patch	Skin diseases, such as atopic or eczematous dermatitis	Local skin reaction Insomnia	21 mg/24 hr 14 mg/24 hr 7 mg/24 hr 15 mg/16 hr	4 weeks, then 2 weeks, then 2 weeks 8 weeks	Prescription and OTC	$4.22 $4.51
Second-line Drugs						
Clonidine	Rebound hypertension	Dry mouth Drowsiness Dizziness Sedation	0.15–0.75 mg/day	3–10 weeks	Prescription only (oral formulation) Prescription only (patch)	$0.24 for 0.2 mg $3.50
Nortriptyline	Risk of arrhythmias	Sedation Dry mouth	75–100 mg/day	12 weeks	Prescription only	$0.74 for 75 mg

* Based on retail prices, Madison, Wisc., April 2000.
OTC, over the counter.
Adapted from The Tobacco Use and Dependence Clinical Practice Guideline Panel, Staff, and Consortium Representatives: A clinical practice guideline for treating tobacco use and dependence: A US Public Health Service Report. JAMA 283:3244–3254, 2000.

counseling is more effective than counseling alone or usual care.[83] Counseling alone was not more effective than usual care, and differences between all groups disappeared at 12 months. These findings underscore the value of cessation medications when given with even brief advice. Longer physician counseling time and more office visits translate into higher cessation rates, independent of pharmacotherapy.

PHARMACOTHERAPY OF SMOKING CESSATION

Nicotine Replacement Therapy

Currently, two medications have been approved for smoking cessation: nicotine and bupropion. All types of smoking cessation medications, if used properly, double the smoking cessation rates compared with placebo treatment.[80] Nicotine replacement medications include 2 mg and 4 mg

nicotine polacrilex gum, transdermal nicotine patches, nicotine nasal spray, nicotine inhaler, and nicotine lozenges. All seem to have comparable efficacy, but in a randomized study compliance was greatest for the patch, lower for gum, and very low for the spray and the inhaler.[84] A smoker should be instructed to quit smoking entirely before beginning nicotine replacement therapies. Optimal use of nicotine gum includes instructions to chew slowly, to chew 8 to 10 pieces per day for 20 to 30 minutes each, and to continue for an adequate period for the smoker to learn a lifestyle without cigarettes, usually 3 months or longer. Side effects of nicotine gum are primarily local and include jaw fatigue, sore mouth and throat, upset stomach, and hiccups.

Several transdermal nicotine preparations are marketed; three deliver 21 or 22 mg over a 24-hour period, and one delivers 15 mg over a period of 16 hours. Most brands have lower-dose patches for tapering. Patches are applied in the morning and removed either the next morning or at bedtime, depending on the patch. Patches intended for 24-hour use can also be removed at bedtime if the patient is experiencing insomnia or disturbing dreams. Full-dose patches are recommended for most smokers for the first 1 to 3 months, followed by one or two tapering doses for 2 to 4 weeks each. Nicotine nasal spray, one spray into each nostril, delivers about 0.5 mg nicotine systemically and can be used every 30 to 60 minutes. Local irritation of the nose commonly produces burning, sneezing, and watery eyes during initial treatment, but tolerance develops to these effects in 1 to 2 days. The nicotine inhaler actually delivers nicotine to the throat and upper airway, from where it is absorbed similarly to nicotine from gum. It is marketed as a cigarette-like plastic device and can be used ad libitum.

Most recently, nicotine lozenges have been marketed over the counter. The lozenges are available in 2 mg and 4 mg strengths and are to be placed in the buccal cavity where they are slowly absorbed over 30 minutes.[85] Smokers are instructed to choose their dose according to how long after awakening in the morning they smoke their first cigarette (a measure of the level of dependence). Those who smoke within 30 minutes are advised to use the 4 mg lozenge, whereas those who smoke their first cigarette at 30 minutes or more are advised to use the 2 mg lozenges. Use is recommended every 1 to 2 hours.

Nicotine medications seem to be safe in patients with cardiovascular disease and should be offered to cardiovascular patients.[86-88] Although smoking cessation medications are recommended by the manufacturer for relatively short-term use (generally 3–6 months), the use of these medications for 6 months or longer is safe and may be helpful in smokers who fear relapse without medication.

Bupropion

Sustained-release bupropion (Zyban) is a dopamine-norepinephrine reuptake inhibitor originally marketed and still widely used as an antidepressant. Bupropion was found to aid smoking cessation independent of whether a smoker is depressed.[89] Hurt and colleagues[89] demonstrated that with a 300 mg sustained-release dose 44% of patients quit at 7 weeks versus 19% of controls. This difference was sustained at 12 months (23% vs. 12%). This study also indicated that when smokers quit they gain less weight while taking bupropion compared to placebo. An additional randomized, placebo-controlled trial demonstrated that the combination of bupropion with the nicotine patch is safe, and that bupropion alone or in combination was as effective or more effective than the patch alone.[90] Bupropion used for 1 year for relapse prevention was demonstrated to be safe and effective and significantly better at promoting cessation (55%) than placebo (42%, point prevalence of smoking abstinence).[91] Given its antidepressant properties, bupropion is a logical choice for depressed smokers but, as mentioned previously, has clear efficacy in smokers without depression as well.

Bupropion is dosed at 150 mg (sustained release) per day for 7 days prior to stopping smoking, then at 300 mg (two 150 mg sustained-release doses) per day for the next 6 to 12 weeks. Bupropion in excessive doses can cause seizures and should not be used in an individual with a history of seizures or with eating disorders (bulemia or anorexia).

Combination Therapy

Combined medications for smoking cessation can be more effective than individual therapies, particularly when combining long-acting medications such as a nicotine patch or bupropion with short-acting nicotine replacement therapy used at times of intense urges or cravings to smoke. Only bupropion and transdermal nicotine in combination have been approved by the FDA. However, a number of studies have looked at various combinations of medications, and there have been no significant safety issues.[91-94] Studies comparing different therapies have found that combinations are two to three times more effective than single medications used alone. A stepwise process that incorporates combination therapies after patients have failed single therapies would be logical and would balance the increased costs associated with additional medications with increased benefit.

MOTIVATING SMOKERS TO QUIT

The well known association between cigarette use and lethal diseases such as lung cancer, myocardial infarction, stroke, and COPD is insufficient to motivate many cigarette smokers to quit. This is due to addiction to nicotine, which includes denial and rationalization (which are a part of all drug addictions). As described previously, many smokers depend on nicotine to cope with stressors encountered in daily life. The perceived stress-reducing effect of nicotine is rapid and readily available. In contrast, quitting for many smokers results in a period of intense dysphoria and dysfunction that can easily be avoided by smoking one more cigarette. A telephone-based survey conducted in 1999 found that only 29% of smokers thought that they were at greater risk of myocardial infarction, and only 40% thought they were at greater risk for developing cancer compared to nonsmokers.[95] This clearly indicates denial of risk and may explain why many smokers only become motivated to quit when they develop a medical condition later in life. Becoming a nonsmoker requires a profound change of self-image and a discovery of personal coping skills that may have not been used previously.

The physician's role in the motivation process can be substantial. The message to the smoker must be consistent and inspirational. Patients clearly respond to physician advice, and hopelessness can by allayed by describing the many options available for cessation medication and counseling. Smoking cessation is the most important health initiative many patients ever undertake, and it is highly cost-effective for the health care system. It is difficult to address smoking in patients when three or four medical issues are being managed in addition to smoking cessation. For this reason, a separate return appointment that focuses solely on smoking cessation is recommended.

Motivating patients to quit needs to be more than steering them away from disease; it must also steer them toward greater self-control, self-expression, independence, and positive role modeling. Exercise during trials of smoking cessation may reduce anxiety, tension, and stress but was not found to be an independent predictor of success in a randomized, controlled trial.[96] Walking on a regular basis is a reasonable initial step and in many cases improves self-esteem and investment in health.

BENEFITS OF QUITTING

The benefits of quitting smoking are substantial for smokers of any age. A person who quits smoking before age 50 has half the risk of dying in the next 15 years compared with a continuing smoker.[97] Smoking cessation reduces the risks of developing lung cancer, with the risk falling to one half that of a continuing smoker by 10 years and one sixth that of a smoker after 15 years' cessation. Quitting smoking in middle age substantially reduces lung cancer risk, with a 50% reduction in risk if a lifelong smoker quits at age 55 compared with age 75.[98] The risk of acute myocardial infarction falls rapidly after quitting smoking and approaches nonsmoking levels within 1 year of abstinence. Cigarette smoking produces a progressive loss of airway function over time that is characterized by an accelerated loss of forced expiratory volume in 1 second (FEV$_1$) with increasing age. Loss of FEV$_1$ due to cigarette smoking cannot be regained by cessation, but the rate of decline slows after smoking cessation and returns to that of nonsmokers.[99] Women who stop smoking during the first 3 to 4 months of pregnancy reduce the risk of having a low-birth-weight infant to that of a woman who has never smoked.

After quitting, smokers gain an average of 5 to 7 pounds, which is perceived by some smokers as undesirable and as a reason not to quit.[100] Smokers tend to be thinner because nicotine increases energy expenditure and suppresses a compensatory increase in food consumption. After they quit smoking, ex-smokers tend to reach the weight expected had they never smoked. On balance, the benefits of quitting far outweigh the risks associated with weight gain, and patients should be counseled accordingly.

RESOURCES FOR PHYSICIANS

Most hospitals have smoking cessation services available that enable referral of smokers if deemed necessary. Many states have toll-free quit lines (e.g., in California: 1-800-7-NO-BUTTS) that can provide additional information or additional counseling, and they appear to be effective.[82] Internet-based programs such as QuitNet (www.quitnet.com) can provide online chat rooms and can give smokers with access to a computer a sense of community with other smokers in a similar position. If patients do not have their own computer, the public library is a smoke-free environment where they can access computers. The American Lung Association (www.lungusa.org/tobacco) has significant information and an online program called "Seven Steps to a Smoke-free Life" to which patients can be referred. The Centers for Disease Control has information that can be downloaded for adults, youth, and Spanish-speaking patients (www.cdc.gov/tobacco/). Patients suspected of having underlying depression, anxiety, or other substance abuse disorders may benefit from psychiatric referral to evaluate these conditions known to reduce the likelihood of smoking cessation.

SUMMARY

Cigarette smoking is the most important preventable cause of respiratory disease. Smoking is responsible for the vast majority of cases of lung cancer and COPD. Smoking is also responsible for many cases of respiratory infections, including pneumococcal pneumonia, influenza, and tuberculosis, as well as for desquamative interstitial pneumonitis and other forms of interstitial lung disease. Smoking is a major risk factor for adverse postoperative events, including respiratory infection, cardiovascular events, and delayed wound healing.

Tobacco use is motivated primarily by a desire for nicotine. Nicotine provides direct effects such as pleasure, stimulation, and stress relief, and it also reverses the unpleasant symptoms of nicotine withdrawal. Nicotine acts on specific cholinergic receptors in the brain, and changes in brain chemistry and structure are found in regular smokers.

Most smokers would like to quit smoking but have difficulty doing so because of nicotine addiction. Both behavioral counseling and pharmacotherapy (nicotine medications and bupropion) enhance quit rates, and the effects of these interventions are generally additive. Office practices should identify all smokers, counsel them to quit, and provide guidance and (if necessary) prescriptions for pharmacotherapy. Telephone quit lines, which are widely available, are a promising way to provide effective pre-cessation and post-cessation counseling.

Quitting smoking results in tremendous benefits in that it reduces respiratory cancer as well as cardiovascular disease risk, and it slows the progression of COPD. Smoking cessation therapy is far more cost-effective than almost any other preventive medicine intervention.

REFERENCES

1. Mokdad AH, Marks JS, Stroup DF, et al: Actual causes of death in the United States, 2000. Jama 291:1238–1245, 2004.
2. Peto R, Lopez AD, Boreham J, et al: Mortality from tobacco in developed countries: indirect estimation from national vital statistics. Lancet 339:1268–1278, 1992.
3. Centers for Disease Control and Prevention: Cigarette smoking among adults—United States, 2000. MMWR Morb Mortal Wkly Rep 51:637–660, 2002.
4. World Health Organization: The World Health Report 2002: Reducing Risks, Extending Healthy Life. Geneva: WHO, 2002.
5. Shibuya K, Ciecierski C, Guindon E, et al: WHO framework convention on tobacco control: development of an evidence based global public health treaty. Bmj 327:154–157, 2003.
6. Hoffmann D, Hoffmann I: The changing cigarette, 1950–1995. J Toxicol Environ Health 50:307–364, 1997.
7. Vineis P, Alavanja M, Buffler P, et al: Tobacco and cancer: recent epidemiological evidence. J Natl Cancer Inst 96:99–106, 2004.
8. Pfeifer GP, Denissenko MF, Olivier M, et al: Tobacco smoke carcinogens, DNA damage and p53 mutations in smoking-associated cancers. Oncogene 21:7435–7451, 2002.
9. Wiencke JK: DNA adduct burden and tobacco carcinogenesis. Oncogene 21:7376–7391, 2002.
10. Hainaut P, Pfeifer GP: Patterns of p53 G→T transversions in lung cancers reflect the primary mutagenic signature of DNA-damage by tobacco smoke. Carcinogenesis 22:367–374, 2001.
11. Wiencke JK, Thurston SW, Kelsey KT, et al: Early age at smoking initiation and tobacco carcinogen DNA damage in the lung. J Natl Cancer Inst 91:614–619, 1999.

12. Flanders WD, Lally CA, Zhu BP, et al: Lung cancer mortality in relation to age, duration of smoking, and daily cigarette consumption: Results from Cancer Prevention Study II. Cancer Res 63:6556–6562, 2003.

13. Department of Health and Human Services, PHS: The Health Consequences of Smoking: Cancer and Chronic Lung Disease in the Workplace; A Report of the Surgeon General. Washington, DC: Government Printing Office, 1985.

14. Thun MJ, Henley SJ, Calle EE: Tobacco use and cancer: an epidemiologic perspective for geneticists. Oncogene 21:7307–7325, 2002.

15. Brownson RC, Novotny TE, Perry MC: Cigarette smoking and adult leukemia: A meta-analysis. Arch Intern Med 153:469–475, 1993.

16. Giovannucci E: An updated review of the epidemiological evidence that cigarette smoking increases risk of colorectal cancer. Cancer Epidemiol Biomarkers Prev 10:725–731, 2001.

17. Nuorti JP, Butler JC, Farley MM, et al: Cigarette smoking and invasive pneumococcal disease: Active Bacterial Core Surveillance Team. N Engl J Med 342:681–689, 2000.

18. Kark JD, Lebiush M, Rannon L: Cigarette smoking as a risk factor for epidemic A(H_1N_1) influenza in young men. N Engl J Med 307:1042–1046, 1982.

19. Barnes PJ, Shapiro SD, Pauwels RA: Chronic obstructive pulmonary disease: Molecular and cellular mechanisms. Eur Respir J 22:672–688, 2003.

20. Walter R, Gottlieb DJ, O'Connor GT: Environmental and genetic risk factors and gene-environment interactions in the pathogenesis of chronic obstructive lung disease. Environ Health Perspect 108(Suppl 4):733–742, 2000.

21. Strachan DP, Butland BK, Anderson HR: Incidence and prognosis of asthma and wheezing illness from early childhood to age 33 in a national British cohort. BMJ 312:1195–1199, 1996.

22. Vesterinen E, Kaprio J, Koskenvuo M: Prospective study of asthma in relation to smoking habits among 14,729 adults. Thorax 43:534–539, 1988.

23. Siroux V, Pin I, Oryszczyn MP, et al: Relationships of active smoking to asthma and asthma severity in the EGEA study: Epidemiological study on the genetics and environment of asthma. Eur Respir J 15:470–477, 2000.

24. Silverman RA, Boudreaux ED, Woodruff PG, et al: Cigarette smoking among asthmatic adults presenting to 64 emergency departments. Chest 123:1472–1479, 2003.

25. Weitzman M, Gortmaker S, Walker DK, et al: Maternal smoking and childhood asthma. Pediatrics 85:505–511, 1990.

26. Leuenberger P, Schwartz J, Ackermann-Liebrich U, et al: Passive smoking exposure in adults and chronic respiratory symptoms (SAPALDIA study): Swiss Study on Air Pollution and Lung Diseases in Adults, SAPALDIA team. Am J Respir Crit Care Med 150:1222–1228, 1994.

27. McCrea KA, Ensor JE, Nall K, et al: Altered cytokine regulation in the lungs of cigarette smokers. Am J Respir Crit Care Med 150:696–703, 1994.

28. Desai SR, Ryan SM, Colby TV: Smoking-related interstitial lung diseases: Histopathological and imaging perspectives. Clin Radiol 58:259–268, 2003.

29. Fraig M, Shreesha U, Savici D, et al: Respiratory bronchiolitis: A clinicopathologic study in current smokers, ex-smokers, and never-smokers. Am J Surg Pathol 26:647–653, 2002.

30. Baumgartner KB, Samet JM, Stidley CA, et al: Cigarette smoking: A risk factor for idiopathic pulmonary fibrosis. Am J Respir Crit Care Med 155:242–248, 1997.

31. Arcavi L, Benowitz NL: Cigarette smoking and infection. Arch Intern Med 164:2206–2216, 2004.

32. Almirall J, Gonzalez CA, Balanzo X, et al: Proportion of community-acquired pneumonia cases attributable to tobacco smoking. Chest 116:375–379, 1999.

33. Mohsen AH, McKendrick MW: Risk factors for pneumonia in adults with chickenpox. J Infect Dis 186:1053–1054, 2002.

34. Gajalakshmi V, Peto R, Kanaka TS, et al: Smoking and mortality from tuberculosis and other diseases in India: Retrospective study of 43,000 adult male deaths and 35,000 controls. Lancet 362:507–515, 2003.

35. Kluger R: Ashes to ashes: America's Hundred-Year Cigarette War, The Public Health, and The Unabashed Triumph of Philip Morris. New York: Alfred A. Knopf, 1996, p 19.

36. Burns DM: Epidemiology of smoking-induced cardiovascular disease. Prog Cardiovasc Dis 46:11–29, 2003.

37. Benowitz NL: Cigarette smoking and cardiovascular disease: Pathophysiology and implications for treatment. Prog Cardiovasc Dis 46:91–111, 2003.

38. Law MR, Wald NJ: Environmental tobacco smoke and ischemic heart disease. Prog Cardiovasc Dis 46:31–38, 2003.

39. Barry J, Mead K, Nabel EG, et al: Effect of smoking on the activity of ischemic heart disease. JAMA 261:398–402, 1989.

40. Mulcahy R: Influence of cigarette smoking on morbidity and mortality after myocardial infarction. BMJ 49:410–415, 1983.

41. Rivers JT, White HD, Cross DB, et al: Reinfarction after thrombolytic therapy for acute myocardial infarction followed by conservative management: Incidence and effect of smoking. J Am Coll Cardiol 16:340–348, 1990.

42. Galan KM, Deligonul U, Kern MJ, et al: Increased frequency of restenosis in patients continuing to smoke cigarettes after percutaneous transluminal coronary angioplasty. Am J Cardiol 61:260–263, 1988.

43. Isles C, Brown JJ, Cumming AM, et al: Excess smoking in malignant-phase hypertension. BMJ 1:579–581, 1979.

44. Suskin N, Sheth T, Negassa A, et al: Relationship of current and past smoking to mortality and morbidity in patients with left ventricular dysfunction. J Am Coll Cardiol 37:1677–1682, 2001.

45. Moller AM, Villebro N, Pedersen T, et al: Effect of preoperative smoking intervention on postoperative complications: A randomised clinical trial. Lancet 359:114–117, 2002.

46. Myles PS, Iacono GA, Hunt JO, et al: Risk of respiratory complications and wound infection in patients undergoing ambulatory surgery: Smokers versus nonsmokers. Anesthesiology 97:842–847, 2002.

47. Vaporciyan AA, Merriman KW, Ece F, et al: Incidence of major pulmonary morbidity after pneumonectomy: Association with timing of smoking cessation. Ann Thorac Surg 73:420–426, 2002.

48. Pungpapong S, Manzarbeitia C, Ortiz J, et al: Cigarette smoking is associated with an increased incidence of vascular complications after liver transplantation. Liver Transpl 8:582–587, 2002.

49. Sung RS, Althoen M, Howell TA, et al: Excess risk of renal allograft loss associated with cigarette smoking. Transplantation 71:1752–1757, 2001.

50. Warner MA, Divertie MB, Tinker JH: Preoperative cessation of smoking and pulmonary complications in coronary artery bypass patients. Anesthesiology 60:380–383, 1984.

51. Sorensen LT, Jorgensen T: Short-term pre-operative smoking cessation intervention does not affect postoperative complications in colorectal surgery: A randomized clinical trial. Colorectal Dis 5:347–352, 2003.

52. Kato I, Nomura AM, Stemmermann GN, et al: A prospective study of gastric and duodenal ulcer and its relation to smoking, alcohol, and diet. Am J Epidemiol 135:521–530, 1992.

53. Maity P, Biswas K, Roy S, et al: Smoking and the pathogenesis of gastroduodenal ulcer—recent mechanistic update. Mol Cell Biochem 253:329–338, 2003.

54. Eliasson B: Cigarette smoking and diabetes. Prog Cardiovasc Dis 45:405–414, 2003.

55. Bjarnason NH, Christiansen C: The influence of thinness and smoking on bone loss and response to hormone replacement therapy in early postmenopausal women. J Clin Endocrinol Metab 85:590–596, 2000.

56. Dempsey DA, Benowitz NL: Risks and benefits of nicotine and other medications to aid smoking cessation in pregnancy. Drug Saf 24:277–322, 2001.

57. Muller B, Zulewski H, Huber P, et al: Impaired action of thyroid hormone associated with smoking in women with hypothyroidism. N Engl J Med 333:964–969, 1995.

58. Environmental Protection Agency: Respiratory Health Effects of Passive Smoking: Lung Cancer and Other Disorders. Washington, DC: Office of Research and Development, U.S. Environmental Protection Agency, 1992.

59. Glantz SA, Parmley WW: Passive smoking and heart disease: Epidemiology, physiology, and biochemistry. Circulation 82:1–12, 1991.

60. Benowitz NL: Nicotine addiction. Primary Care 26:611–631, 1999.

61. Benwell MEM, Balfour DJK, Anderson JM: Evidence that tobacco smoking increases the density of (-)-[³H]nicotine binding sites in human brain. J Neurochem 50:1243–1247, 1988.

62. Institute of Medicine: The nature of nicotine addiction. In Lynch BS, Bonnie RJ (eds): Growing Up Tobacco Free: Preventing Nicotine Addiction in Children and Youths. Washington, DC: National Academy Press, 1994, pp 28–68.

63. Picciotto MR, Caldarone BJ, King SL, et al: Nicotinic receptors in the brain: Links between molecular biology and behavior. Neuropsychopharmacology 22:451–465, 2000.

64. Fattinger K, Verotta D, Benowitz NL: Pharmacodynamics of acute tolerance to multiple nicotinic effects in humans. J Pharmacol Exp Ther 281:1238–1246, 1997.

65. Wonnacott S: Presynaptic nicotinic ACh receptors. Trends Neurosci 20:92–98, 1997.

66. McGehee DS, Heath MJS, Gelber S, et al: Nicotine enhancement of fast excitatory synaptic transmission in CNS by presynaptic receptors. Science 269:1692–1696, 1995.

67. Gray R, Rajan AS, Radcliffe KA, et al: Hippocampal synaptic transmission enhanced by low concentrations of nicotine. BMJ 383:713–716, 1996.

68. Corrigall WA, Coen KM, Adamson KL: Self-administered nicotine activates the mesolimbic dopamine system through the ventral tegmental area. Brain Res 653:278–284, 1994.

69. Mansvelder HD, Lodder JC, Sons MS, et al: Dopamine modulates exocytosis independent of Ca(2+) entry in melanotropic cells. J Neurophysiol 87:793–801, 2002.

70. Pontieri FE, Tanda G, Orzi F, et al: Effects of nicotine on the nucleus accumbens and similarity to those of addictive drugs. BMJ 382:255–257, 1996.

71. Koob GF, LeMoal M: Drug abuse: Hedonic homeostatic dysregulation. Science 278:52–58, 1997.

72. Benowitz NL: Pharmacologic aspects of cigarette smoking and nicotine addiction. N Engl J Med 319:1318–1330, 1988.

73. Pickworth WB, Herning RI, Henningfield JE: Spontaneous EEG changes during tobacco abstinence and nicotine substitution in human volunteers. J Pharmacol Exp Ther 251:976–982, 1989.

74. Benowitz NL: Compensatory smoking of low yield cigarettes. In Shopland DR, Burns DM, Benowitz NL, et al (eds): Risks Associated with Smoking Cigarettes with Low Machine-Measured Yields of Tar and Nicotine. NCI Smoking and Tobacco Control Monograph No. 13. NIH Publication No. 02-5074. Bethesda, MD: U.S. National Institutes of Health, National Cancer Institute, 1991, pp 39–64.

75. Benowitz NL, Jacob P III, Yu L, et al: Reduced tar, nicotine, and carbon monoxide exposure while smoking ultralow- but not low-yield cigarettes. JAMA 256:241–246, 1986.

76. Burns DR, Major JM, Shanks TG, et al: Smoking lower yield cigarettes and disease risks. In Shopland DR, Burns DM, Benowitz NL, et al (eds): Risks Associated with Smoking Cigarettes with Low Machine-Measured Yields of Tar and Nicotine. NCI Smoking and Tobacco Control Monograph No. 13. NIH Publication No. 02-5074. Bethesda, MD: U.S. National Institutes of Health, National Cancer Institute, 1991, pp 65–158.

77. Harris JE, Thun MJ, Mondul AM, et al: Cigarette tar yields in relation to mortality from lung cancer in the cancer prevention study II prospective cohort, 1982–8. BMJ 328:72, 2004.

78. Thun MJ, Lally CA, Flannery JT, et al: Cigarette smoking and changes in the histopathology of lung cancer. J Natl Cancer Inst 89:1580–1586, 1997.

79. Lancaster T, Stead L, Silagy C, et al: Effectiveness of interventions to help people stop smoking: Findings from the Cochrane Library. BMJ 321:355–358, 2000.

80. The Tobacco Use and Dependence Clinical Practice Guideline Panel S and Consortium Representatives: A clinical practice guideline for treating tobacco use and dependence: A US Public Health Service Report. JAMA 283:3244–3254, 2000.

81. Law M, Tang JL: An analysis of the effectiveness of interventions intended to help people stop smoking. Arch Intern Med 155:1933–1941, 1995.

82. Zhu SH, Anderson CM, Tedeschi GJ, et al: Evidence of real-world effectiveness of a telephone quitline for smokers. N Engl J Med 347:1087–1093, 2002.

83. Molyneux A, Lewis S, Leivers U, et al: Clinical trial comparing nicotine replacement therapy (NRT) plus brief counselling, brief counselling alone, and minimal intervention on smoking cessation in hospital inpatients. Thorax 58:484–488, 2003.

84. Hajek P, West R, Foulds J, et al: Randomized comparative trial of nicotine polacrilex, a transdermal patch, nasal spray, and an inhaler. Arch Intern Med 159:2033–2038, 1999.

85. Shiffman S, Dresler CM, Hajek P, et al: Efficacy of a nicotine lozenge for smoking cessation. Arch Intern Med 162:1267–1276, 2002.

86. Miller NH, Smith PM, DeBusk RF, et al: Smoking cessation in hospitalized patients: Results of a randomized trial. Arch Intern Med 157:409–415, 1997.

87. Thomson CC, Rigotti NA: Hospital and clinic-based smoking cessation interventions for smokers with cardiovascular disease. Prog Cardiovasc Dis 45:459–479, 2003.

88. Joseph AM, Fu S: Safety issues in pharmacology for smoking in patients with cardiovascular disease. Prog Cardiovasc Dis 45:429–441, 2003.

89. Hurt RD, Sachs DP, Glover ED, et al: A comparison of sustained-release bupropion and placebo for smoking cessation. N Engl J Med 337:1195–1202, 1997.

90. Jorenby DE, Leischow SJ, Nides MA, et al: A controlled trial of sustained-release bupropion, a nicotine patch, or both for smoking cessation. N Engl J Med 340:685–691, 1999.

91. Hays JT, Hurt RD, Rigotti NA, et al: Sustained-release bupropion for pharmacologic relapse prevention after smoking cessation: a randomized, controlled trial. Ann Intern Med 135:423–433, 2001.

92. Kornitzer M, Boutsen M, Dramaix M, et al: Combined use of nicotine patch and gum in smoking cessation: A placebo-controlled clinical trial. Prev Med 24:41–47, 1995.

93. Puska P, Korhonen HJ, Vartiainen E: Combined use of nicotine patch and gum compared with gum alone in smoking cessation: A clinical trial in North Karelia. Tobacco Control 4:321, 1995.

94. Blondal T, Gudmundsson LJ, Olafsdottis I, et al: Nicotine nasal spray with nicotine patch for smoking cessation: Randomized trial with six years followup. BMJ 318:285–288, 1999.

95. Ayanian JZ, Cleary PD: Perceived risks of heart disease and cancer among cigarette smokers. JAMA 281:1019–1021, 1999.

96. Ussher M, West R, McEwen A, et al: Efficacy of exercise counselling as an aid for smoking cessation: A randomized controlled trial. Addiction 98:523–532, 2003.

97. Department of Health and Human Services PHS: The Health Benefits of Smoking Cessation: A Report of the Surgeon General. DHHS (CDC) Publication No. 90-8406. Washington, DC: Government Printing Office, 1990.

98. Peto R, Darby S, Deo H, et al: Smoking, smoking cessation, and lung cancer in the UK since 1950: Combination of national statistics with two case-control studies. BMJ 321:323–329, 2000.

99. Fletcher C, Peto R: The natural history of chronic airflow obstruction. BMJ 1:1645–1648, 1977.

100. Williamson DF, Madans J, Anda RF, et al: Smoking cessation and severity of weight gain in a national cohort. N Engl J Med 324:739–745, 1991.

101. International Agency for Research on Cancer: Tobacco smoking and involuntary smoking. IARC Monographs on the Evaluation of Carcinogenic Risks to Humans. IARC Scientific Publication 83. Lyon, 2004.

91

Patient Education and Compliance

Susan L. Janson, D.N.Sc., R.N., N.P., FAAN

INTRODUCTION

This chapter focuses on issues in patient education and compliance that influence treatment plans and disease management. Patient education is not limited to the transfer of information but also includes teaching the essential skills needed to self-manage chronic disease outside the usual context of the medical visit. The broader term, self-management education, is considered essential for all patients living with chronic medical conditions, and it requires skills in monitoring, taking medication, rescue actions, and communication. Self-management means patients are actively involved in using strategies to control their disease. Research conducted over the last two decades shows that patients can learn to manage chronic conditions through education in self-management knowledge and skills. A large body of research shows that patients can be taught these skills, thus contributing to the control of their chronic conditions and minimizing the impact of their disease, resulting in improved health status and decreased health care utilization.

The link between patient self-management education and patient adherence to treatment recommendations is the subject of considerable scientific inquiry. The assumption that patient education automatically leads to adherence behavior is not warranted. In this chapter, chronic illness is the model for understanding the links between patient education, self-management, and adherence. Asthma is used as the example of a chronic disease where significant research on patient education and patient adherence to treatment has contributed to our understanding of chronic illness management. Chronic obstructive pulmonary disease (COPD) is an example of a disease where chronic symptoms and acute exacerbations cause significant distress. It is tempting to believe that self-management education would lead to improved patient outcomes, as it does with asthma. Yet,

there is little to no evidence to support similar outcomes resulting from self-management approaches for COPD.

PATIENT EDUCATION

Individuals living with chronic illness have a variety of needs, including expert guidance and care from qualified and interested health professionals, access to a responsive and user-friendly health care system, feedback of relevant health status information, and adequate self-care knowledge and self-management skills. Historically, patient education programs focused on delivering information to people at risk for, or who have developed, health problems. Often the goal of patient education programs is to improve adherence to treatment recommendations and thereby improve health outcomes. Unfortunately, repeated studies of providing information designed to increase knowledge of patients show little or no impact on health outcomes in any chronic disease population.[1] This is not surprising because information-only patient education programs assume that individuals translate information into actions that change outcomes, yet without specific skills training.

Research has shown that specific training in self-management skills is necessary to produce behavior that changes the outcomes of chronic illness. Expert care by health professionals is necessary but not sufficient to improve outcomes. Patients must participate actively in their own care, and the focus of patient education must include self-management skills, including surveillance, self-care actions, adherence, and appraisal of progress in keeping chronic illness under good control. The patient practicing self-management is consciously using strategies and taking actions to manipulate treatments and situations to improve disease control and reduce the impact of the disease on functional ability and the quality of life.

PATIENT SELF-MANAGEMENT EDUCATION

The chronic care model developed by Wagner and associates[2] describes six components that must be present in a health care system to improve chronic illness outcomes: organizational design of health care delivery, community resources and policies, delivery system design, decision support, clinical information systems, and self-management support for patients. These six components identify the changes in the health care delivery system, providers, and patients that are needed to improve outcomes.[3] Because usual medical care is organized to address acute care needs and chronic illness is increasing in prevalence, the chronic care model has received significant attention in the literature. The model provides a framework for integrating new research findings into evidence-based clinical practice within the context of a health care delivery system. Chronic illness care requires a dynamic, responsive delivery system, yet most current health care delivery systems remain rigidly structured for acute illness care.

The self-management dimension of the model emphasizes the patients' active and central role in managing the illness condition. The focus is on attaining sufficient self-management knowledge, skills, confidence, supports, and help with overcoming barriers. Behavior change and maintenance is an essential component of self-management education. Once the patient is armed with the information and skills necessary to manage a chronic illness, direct ongoing interaction with a knowledgeable proactive practice team is hypothesized to produce positive functional and clinical outcomes. Even when some of the components of an effective health care delivery system are lacking, self-management support by a prepared provider can alter the outcomes of chronic illness. The individual health care provider or health care team ensures care planning and assistance with problem-solving in order to reduce morbidity in the patients they care for. A key question not answered by the model is, How does one produce an "informed and activated" patient who can carry out self-management activities? Decades of research on self-management have shed light on the answer to this question.

SELF-MANAGEMENT AND BEHAVIOR CHANGE THEORY

Successful self-management of a chronic illness requires patients to master three activities: (1) gain sufficient knowledge of the illness and its current treatment; (2) perform activities directed toward clinical management of the illness; and (3) apply skills necessary for optimal psychosocial functioning.[4] Each of these areas manifests as behavior aimed at reducing the impact of the disease and is consistent with social cognitive theory.[5] The key concepts of this theory are incentives, outcome expectations, and self-efficacy, which is confidence in one's ability to perform specific tasks. The principles of social learning were delineated by Bandura[6] in the model of a person engaging in a behavior that would produce a certain outcome as a consequence of that behavior—the social cognitive theory. The behavior change is limited to the expectations of outcomes and expectations of self-efficacy for the required task. When applied to self-management of a chronic disease, social cognitive theory uses a number of principles. Cognitive skills are required

for symptom recognition and response. An important determinant of behavior is the amount and type of prior knowledge a person has. Self-efficacy beliefs are strong determinants of behavior and have been shown to be a primary indication of motivation to continue with a specific behavior. Decisional processes are cognitions that enable one to integrate general knowledge and situational information to plan behavior. Self-management programs and interventions are based on these principles.

Expectations of self-efficacy are learned from four sources: (1) personal experience of mastery over a difficult or feared task; (2) vicarious experience obtained from observing events or other people who serve as "models;" (3) verbal persuasion where health care providers encourage patients to persevere in efforts to change behavior; and (4) one's physiological state, which provides information that influences efficacy expectations.[5,6] Self-efficacy is an important influence, but it is specific to the required task and is not the sole factor that determines behavior leading to achievement. Effective self-management behavior depends on knowledge and skills, outcome expectations, and the perceived value of those outcomes.[7] When requisite skills and knowledge are lacking, high self-efficacy does not produce positive performance or outcomes. The perceived value of outcomes is a key factor related to behavior change. That is, people must value the outcome enough to engage in self-management behaviors. This concept is directly applicable to asthma, which requires daily long-term medication compliance and self-monitoring. The sources of efficacy expectations for asthmatic patients involved in a clinical partnership with their clinician are most likely verbal persuasion from the clinician, physiologic information from peak flow monitoring, and self-assessment of symptoms.

PATIENT EDUCATION FOR ADULTS WITH ASTHMA

Chronic respiratory conditions represent a large percentage of chronic illnesses in the U.S population.[8] Asthma and COPD account for the majority of chronic respiratory illnesses. The goal of self-management in chronic diseases is to reduce disability and promote active participation in a normal life. Most patients with asthma, except those with very severe disease, can live normal, active lives. Effective therapeutic treatment with appropriate medications is required to achieve this goal, and patients must be involved in the self-management of their asthma to the highest possible degree.[9] The benefits of educating patients about their disease and instructing them in the skills of self-assessment, use of medications, and self-management actions to control exacerbations have been demonstrated for both asthmatic children and adults in numerous published studies over the last two decades. These benefits include a reduction in health services use, a reduction of asthma-related health care costs, and improvement in health status.[10–16] Cost analysis studies have shown that asthma education can be delivered in a cost-effective manner, and that morbidity is reduced as a result, especially in high-risk subjects.[10,17,18]

Repeated studies of asthma patient education and self-management interventions are so consistent in showing benefit that patient education in self-management is explicitly recommended in national and international asthma guidelines.[9,19] These guidelines specify the essential information that should be provided to all people with asthma. In brief, patients and families need to understand the basic pathophysiology of the disease and the actions of the medications on the airway. They need to know how to use the recommended pharmacotherapy appropriately, control exposure to exacerbating factors, monitor their own disease status, and take appropriate rescue actions when asthma worsens. The key informational messages to be given to patients and families about managing asthma are brief and specific.

- Asthma is a chronic inflammatory disease of the airways that waxes and wanes, with periods of asthma control interrupted by occasional flares.
- Treatment is aimed at controlling airway inflammation with anti-inflammatory medication and reduction or avoidance of exacerbating factors.
- Acute flares of asthma must be treated at the earliest sign to control the disease.

The essential skills patients should be taught are also recommended in asthma guidelines and include self-monitoring of peak flow, self-assessment of symptoms that signal a need for immediate medical attention, and how to follow a written self-management action plan when asthma worsens. Although all of these guidelines specify what patients need to know and the skills they need to be trained in, the evidence on which these recommendations are based used different content and emphasized different components of self-management knowledge. At the time most of these guidelines were written and last revised,[20] it was not known which components of asthma self-management education were most related to producing positive outcomes in asthma control, but in general the guidelines recommended peak flow monitoring, regular physician review at recurring visits, and a written action plan in addition to conveying essential information about asthma.

Asthma education may be most effective when delivered individually in the context where medical care is provided. However, managed care mandates that lower reimbursements for medical care have resulted in shorter primary care visits for follow-up care, a situation making the management of chronic illnesses such as asthma a unique challenge. The proportion of physicians reporting inadequate time to care for patients rose from 28% in 1997 to 34% in 2001.[21] The time constraints imposed on these clinicians limit self-management education in the clinic setting. In addition, even when asthma education programs are funded, many patients do not attend due to busy schedules or their personal beliefs about self-management.

ASTHMA EDUCATION LIMITED TO INFORMATION ONLY

Many researchers have explored the options and methods for imparting knowledge and skills to patients and their families. An important and consistent finding is that focusing on providing information without teaching skills is likely to increase patients' and families' knowledge of facts about asthma but is unlikely to change their ability to self-manage asthma or carry out the treatment plan. At its simplest, education is limited to the transfer of information about asthma, its cause, and its treatment. A scientific review of

12 randomized controlled trials,[10,22–32] showed that limited asthma education increased knowledge of asthma but did not reduce hospitalizations, emergency room visits, unscheduled doctor visits, or lost work days; neither did it improve lung function or medication use.[1] The impact on symptoms was variable, but perceived symptoms improved in just 2 of the 12 studies.[25,32] Overall, asthma education interventions limited to imparting information have little impact on health-related behavior and health outcomes. The findings of these trials, conducted over 20 years, are consistent with educational theory and support guideline recommendations that information alone is insufficient to change patient self-management behavior. However, educational interventions that are limited to giving information may still be useful in specific situations where patients identify the need for more information about their condition. Brief interventions that motivate patients to seek help in acute flares or that increase confidence in accessing the health care system could be very useful in busy medical practices and emergency departments. These brief, specific, and targeted interventions need to be designed and tested.

The health status of the patient and the setting in which care is delivered may influence the success of educational interventions. People with asthma who seek care in emergency departments tend to have more severe asthma and poor self-management skills, and they are at risk for relapse and recurrence of exacerbations. Two early studies of brief asthma education limited to information only, given in the emergency department setting, both showed a reduction in subsequent emergency department visits.[10,26] Further work testing brief interventions that include specific information coupled with targeted self-management skills warrant further exploration to reach patients, who are difficult to capture in regular follow-up care and who are at risk for asthma relapse and recurrences.

Clinic or hospital-based asthma educational interventions designed to target patients who have suffered such acute exacerbations they required admission to the hospital as well as those with high rates of health care utilization also show evidence of an impact on asthma outcomes. Three randomized controlled trials have shown that asthma education can lower asthma morbidity in specific subgroups of patients with high health care utilization.[33–35] Asthma education combined with intensive case management by a nurse practitioner has been recently shown to have an impact on morbidity and asthma relapse rates.[36] Two additional studies showed that relapse rates in patients who have visited the emergency department for asthma exacerbations can be reduced with asthma education[10] and with asthma self-management training,[37] whereas a third study of an at-risk population showed no impact on emergency room recidivism.[38] Although several studies showed that asthma education programs could reduce the use of health care services, the studies emphasized different components of education and training, making it difficult to know which components are essential to produce improved outcomes.

ASTHMA SELF-MANAGEMENT EDUCATION

Over the last two decades, considerable data have been accumulated that demonstrate the positive effects of asthma self-management education on health outcomes for adults with asthma. However, early studies were difficult to interpret due to design flaws such as lack of control groups, failure to control for regression to the mean with appropriate statistical methods, and confounding of the educational intervention with changes in medical therapy. In several randomized controlled trials of adults with asthma, patient self-management education produced significant improvement in asthma knowledge and treatment adherence; but after pharmaceutical treatment was optimized, no further improvements from the educational intervention could be detected.[32,39-41] This finding led to confusion about the true value of self-management education. Nevertheless, structured self-management education programs have been shown to increase knowledge about asthma, increase confidence, improve school and work attendance, and reduce rescue medication use, urgent care visits, and hospitalizations in both children and adults.[42,43] Therefore, research on self-management content and processes continues to be conducted to determine the essential components that are related to positive health outcomes and disease control.

The most effective programs are those that teach self-management skills as well as impart information about asthma. Asthma self-management includes self-monitoring, a written action plan, and regular review of medications by a clinician. The results of a meta-analysis showed that asthma self-management interventions with these components reduced the relative risk of hospitalizations for asthma by 39%, as shown in Figure 91.1.[43] The meta-analysis included six randomized controlled trials,[17,34,37,39,44,45] each

with different modes of delivering the intervention. Self-monitoring of symptoms was shown to produce benefits similar to those seen with self-monitoring of peak flow. Self-monitoring without a written action plan or medication review did not produce consistently improved outcomes. Written self-management plans have been advocated as a method of improving the ability to carry out asthma self-management actions, such as taking daily medications and adjusting the dose when the asthma worsens.

The impact of patient education that included asthma self-management training with self-monitoring of symptoms and peak flow and a written asthma action plan in addition to regular medical review has been studied by several investigators. A recent scientific review compared self-management education to regular clinician review for adults with asthma to evaluate the impact on health outcomes.[46] The review included 36 randomized controlled trials[15,23,32-35,37-41,44-69] comparing self-management education with usual care in 6090 adults with asthma. The intervention trials were conducted in primary care, specialty care, and hospital inpatient or community settings. "Usual care" was defined as a control condition where patients were followed by their clinician and may have received varying amounts of education, regular review, or recommendations for monitoring but no action plan. The interventions included education, self-monitoring of symptoms and/or peak flow, regular review of treatment and asthma severity by a physician or nurse practitioner, and a written action plan. The results of the statistical analysis, including meta-analysis where possible, showed that self-management education significantly reduced hospitalizations for asthma [relative risk (RR) 0.64, 95% confidence interval (CI) 0.50–0.82], emergency department visits (RR 0.82, 95% CI 0.73–0.94), unscheduled doctor visits (RR 0.68, 95% CI 0.56–0.81), nocturnal asthma (RR 0.67, 95% CI 0.56–0.79), missed work days (RR 0.79, 95% CI 0.67–0.93), and improved quality of life (standardized mean difference [SMD] 0.29, 95% CI 0.11–0.47). There was little effect on lung function; FEV_1 did not change, although there was a statistically significant small mean increase (14.5 L/min, $P < 0.05$) in peak flow. Self-management education that included a written action plan had the most effect on reducing hospitalizations. The intensity (number of sessions) of teaching and the number of different components taught had little impact.

The reviewers concluded that education in asthma self-management that includes self-monitoring of either peak flow or symptoms and a written action plan can, when accompanied by regular review of medications and asthma control by a medical practitioner, improve health outcomes for adults with asthma significantly more than does usual care. They further concluded that self-management programs that enable people with asthma to adjust their medication using a written action plan are more effective than other forms of self-management education that do not include this option.

This important review and meta-analysis identified the key components of optimal asthma self-management education (in addition to providing information) that are most efficacious in improving health outcomes for adults with asthma: self-monitoring of symptoms and/or peak flow, regular medical review of treatment and asthma control, and a written action plan for self-adjustment of medication.

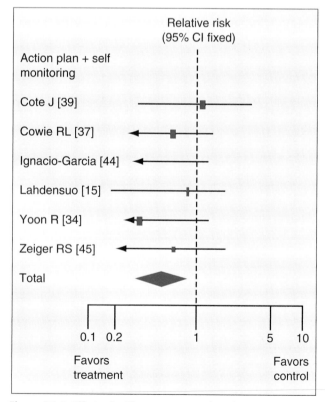

Figure 91.1 Effect of self-management education on hospitalizations for adults with asthma. (From Gibson PG: Monitoring the patient with asthma: An evidence based approach. J Allergy Clin Immunol 106:17–26, 2000.)

Information is the fourth component, but it has no impact on outcomes without the other three.

Optimal self-management education is an important intervention that appears to be as effective in primary care practice settings as in specialty practice. A recent study testing the effectiveness and safety of asthma self-management in 19 primary care general practices in The Netherlands[70] showed that the self-management groups had more weeks without significant symptoms and fewer days of restricted activity than those in usual care. The results of this trial suggest that a detailed asthma action plan directing self-treatment with inhaled and oral corticosteroids can be administered safely in general practice and can reduce the symptom burden of asthma.

The questions that remain unanswered are the duration of self-monitoring that is optimal, the duration of the effect of self-management education, how often reinforcement is needed to maintain effects, the optimal format of a written action plan, and the theoretical underpinnings of successful interventions. Asthma educational interventions based on self-management theory, designed to enhance self-efficacy for adjusting medications and making self-assessments, may be more effective in improving clinical outcomes, as suggested in at least one theoretically derived intervention study.[71]

Other unknowns are whether self-management education must be integrated into the medical care setting or whether community-based programs would produce the same improvements. Despite the success of asthma self-management programs, significant barriers remain that prevent all patients from receiving this training. Time pressure, reimbursement, safety, and standards for quality education are just some of the issues that influence implementation of asthma self-management education for all patients.

Brief asthma self-management education has an appeal for asthmatic patients who recently have sought urgent care for acute asthma. However, the impact of this education may not be observed for up to 6 months, indicating that gaining confidence in self-management takes time.[32,71,72] Brief interventions may lack the intensity necessary to improve self-confidence and task-specific self-efficacy.

Self-management education may have an impact even on novel outcomes. In a recent randomized controlled trial, 65 patients with moderate or severe asthma were randomized to self-management education or monitoring alone.[73] The intervention included asthma facts, inhaler skill training, symptom and peak flow monitoring, environmental strategies, and a written action plan. Intervention patients had significantly improved adherence to inhaled corticosteroid, perceived control of asthma, quality of life, and reduction in sputum eosinophilia. The latter finding presumably reflects a decrease in airway inflammation, a novel outcome of self-management education. Yet the significant changes in outcomes were found to be independent of the improvement in adherence.

SELF-MONITORING

Self-monitoring is often a part of optimal self-management and can include peak-flow monitoring, monitoring of symptoms, or both. Self-monitoring combined with a written action plan is considered optimal. At least six randomized trials compared the effects of a peak flow-based action plan to a symptom-based action plan on asthma outcomes.[37,39,74-77] A meta-analysis of these trials found that these two options for self-monitoring and self-management had equivalent positive effects on hospitalizations, emergency department visits, unscheduled physician visits, and frequency of nocturnal asthma.[46] The implication of this finding is that the choice of peak flow or symptom-based monitoring can be based on the judgment of the individual clinician and the preference of the patient. A mutually acceptable decision should be made after open discussion and shared decision-making.

Peak flow monitoring has several advantages and disadvantages and may not be useful in all patients. If performed correctly, home peak flow monitoring can provide an objective measure of variations in airflow obstruction; and when combined with a written action plan based on critical peak flow cut-off values, it can lead to timely and early self-management intervention by the patient, including self-treatment and early entrance to medical care during an acute exacerbation.

Regular monitoring of peak flow is recommended in national asthma guidelines for patients with moderate persistent and severe persistent asthma.[9] The usefulness of peak flow monitoring for the clinical management of asthma includes assessing exposures and short-term responses to new therapy as well as providing information during periods of clinical instability. However, two problems have been documented with home peak flow monitoring: nonadherence to home measurements and inaccurate measurement technique. The accuracy of patient recordings of peak flow measurements in daily diaries has long been suspect. These suspicions were confirmed by investigators who covertly measured peak flow electronically and compared the electronic data with the subjects' handwritten diary data. They found 44% adherence to monitoring and falsification of 22% of recordings over a 3-month period.[78] Similar studies[79,80] that documented poor adherence to monitoring when the participants were unaware of electronic data storage led many investigators and clinicians to believe that adherence to peak flow monitoring cannot be achieved. To test this assumption, Reddel and colleagues[81] measured long-term adherence to peak flow monitoring when participants were aware that data were being stored and used to guide treatment. Under these conditions, adherence was 89% over 72 weeks. Likewise, another study showed that median adherence was 91% with electronic monitoring alone, compared to 65% when subjects were required to also record the data by hand in a diary.[82] These findings suggest that ease of recording and storing data could influence adherence to peak flow monitoring. Electronic measurement of peak flow eliminates the need for patients to keep a diary and may improve adherence for some patients.

Self-monitoring of asthma status by symptoms is preferred by some patients because it does not require laborious record-keeping. Many patients become adept at monitoring subtle changes in their symptoms by refining skills of self-perception. This process is difficult to teach and seems to occur through long experience with the variations in the illness. However, studies show that symptoms do not correlate closely with changes in pulmonary function in most people.[83]

Despite the problems with long-term adherence, home peak flow monitoring may be the best option for patients who remain asymptomatic[84-86] even during marked drops in lung function because these patients are at risk for life-threatening attacks. For these adults, peak flow monitoring is a necessary choice if they are to benefit from self-monitoring and know when to activate a written action plan. For these patients, termed "poor perceivers," peak flow monitoring may be life-saving. Others, such as those with mild exacerbations who notice symptoms before a decrement in lung function can be detected,[87,88] may benefit more from symptom monitoring.

MONITORING BY CLINICIANS

While self-monitoring by patients with asthma has been shown to be valuable for optimal self-management, it does not obviate the need for monitoring and review by the primary clinician. Under the definition of optimal self-management, such clinician monitoring is often termed "regular medical review." The primary clinician managing asthma needs to monitor asthma severity to optimize therapy and detect changes in disease status. Current asthma status should be evaluated during regular review visits by assessing control as indicated by the frequency of nocturnal symptoms, use of rescue beta-agonist medication, impairment of activity and quality of life, pulmonary function, and recent history of exacerbations. In addition, asthma guidelines recommend that clinicians routinely assess the effectiveness of communication between themselves and their patients and evaluate patient satisfaction with their asthma care and asthma control.[9] These visits also provide an opportunity for the clinician to evaluate the patient's self-assessment and self-management skills as well identify problems in medication adherence.

The primary clinician is aided by a host of other professionals who can support and reinforce the patient's self-management skills. These professionals include pharmacists, nurses, respiratory therapists, and specialists who come in contact with patients and family members. Pharmacists in particular have the opportunity to reinforce self-management skills each time the patient fills prescriptions. Incorporation of pharmacists in system-based care models can facilitate asthma self-management skills.[59] Asthma educators and social workers can help by identifying factors and situations that impair the patients' and families' ability to carry out the treatment plan, intervene by activating community resources, and communicate these problems to the primary clinician. The contributions of the interdisciplinary professionals are maximized when they are organized in a team-care delivery design.[89] Standards for asthma patient education recently have been raised by the increasing availability of professional certification for asthma educators. These trained and certified educators are likely to become key members of the health care team, providing assistance to primary clinicians for asthma education and management.[89a]

OPTIONS FOR SELF-MANAGEMENT EDUCATION

The equivalence and efficacy of different modalities for self-management of asthma were analyzed in another recent scientific review.[90] Optimal self-management, including self-adjustment of medications guided by an asthma action plan, was compared to regular physician review and man-

agement in six studies.[17,41,55,68,91,92] These two methods for achieving asthma control were found to be equivalent. Different outcomes were reported in these studies, but there was no significant difference between these methods of medication adjustment in terms of hospitalizations,[17,55,68] emergency department visits,[68] unscheduled doctor visits,[17,55,93] or frequency of nocturnal asthma symptoms.[41,55,92] Three studies measured days lost from work or school, and two of them reported no significant differences between clinician review and self-management[41,55]; the third study[17] reported a significant impact of peak-flow-based self-management on work or school absenteeism. Lung function as measured by FEV_1 was not significantly different between the two styles of management, but peak flow significantly improved with peak-flow-based self-adjustment of medications compared to physician adjustment. Available evidence indicates that these two methods of adjusting medications for asthma control are equivalent, and the choice depends on the comfort and agreement between the clinician and the patients.

When self-management is the chosen method for maintaining asthma control, peak-flow-based self management is equivalent to symptoms-based self-management so long as either method also includes a written action plan for self-adjustment of medications during asthma exacerbations.[37,39,74-77] Both methods were found to have an equal impact on emergency department visits in three studies,[39,76,77] and peak flow was more effective in reducing emergency visits in one study.[37] One investigator found that when instructions for self-management were given verbally rather than in written form there was no difference in hospitalizations, emergency department visits, or peak flow variability.[93] However, language and cultural differences between patients and their providers were not analyzed in this study and may pose significant barriers to the effectiveness of providing verbal directions.

Optimal self-management including self-monitoring, a written action plan, and asthma education with regular medical review has been found to be more effective than regular medical review alone. However, optimal self-management without regular review has been shown to be associated with greater health care utilization, increased number of sick days, and less improvement in FEV_1.

The intensity of asthma self-management education is of interest because of inordinate time pressures in many care settings. Intensity has been defined by the amount of time spent educating and reinforcing the educational messages. Low-intensity and brief educational interventions have considerable appeal. However, brief, low-intensity interventions may reduce the effectiveness of self-management education unless it is reinforced with more comprehensive self-management education. One study compared a brief intervention, instruction in inhaler technique, and a written action plan to intensive education and found that the brief, low-intensity intervention led to significantly increased unscheduled doctor visits.[71]

TEACHING ASTHMA SELF-MANAGEMENT: MODES OF DELIVERY

The overall goal of self-management education is to provide patients with the knowledge and skills to keep asthma under

Table 91.1 Expected Self-Management Behaviors for Patients With Asthma

Cognitive Behaviors
Able to describe the two components of airflow obstruction in chronic asthma: airway inflammation and bronchoconstriction
Able to state the warning signs of worsening asthma and when to seek urgent medical care
Able to accurately assess symptoms and/or peak flow measurements and recognize significant changes

Affective Behaviors
Able to describe why taking medication consistently is the healthiest approach to controlling asthma
Able to describe why it is important not to delay seeking urgently needed medical care for asthma exacerbations
Able to describe how to follow the steps of an asthma action plan and why each step is important

Psychomotor Behaviors
Able to demonstrate correct use of inhalers
Able to accurately and reliably measure peak expiratory flow and to state when peak flow is indicated

good control and to work in a partnership with a designated clinician who can assist in directing the treatment program. Learning self-management requires behavior change. Behavior change results from three types of learning behavior: cognitive (knowledge and information), affective (attitudes, beliefs, and values), and psychomotor skills and performance. Desirable self-management behaviors for patients with asthma, shown in Table 91.1, allow all patients to participate effectively in the patient-clinician partnership.

Self-management education and training should be appropriate to the age and developmental level of the patients and should be integrated into regular, ongoing medical care whenever possible. Whereas motivation to learn in adults is triggered by the recognition of a gap between what they know and what they want to know, in children the response to learning situations is affected by age and developmental level. Preschool children are attracted to bright colors and pictures. They like to explore and play with dolls but look to parents when confronted with new situations. Their attention span is just 2 to 3 minutes, so messages must be simple. School-age children like to participate in games, videos, computers, and drawing pictures and cartoons; and they respond well to group learning. Attention span in this age group is 10 to 15 minutes. Preadolescents prefer interactive "hands on" learning, including models and computer programs they can manipulate. Adolescents learn best in environments that are not dominated by adults, and they respond well to peers and peer-idols who teach from real experience. They do not respond well to lectures or other formal educational styles but do respond to problem-solving scenarios. Adolescents need and want technical information, and their attention span under these conditions is 20 to 30 minutes.

Older adults may be particularly interested in the details of the disease condition, and they tend to want to understand the rationale for health-related treatment recommendations. Elders may require adaptation of learning materials when visual or auditory impairments interfere with learning. Specific strategies for teaching older patients about asthma include simplified large-print action plans, devices to assist with medication delivery, and reminder dispensing kits. Dry powder inhalers may be easier for older patients to use correctly than metered-dose inhalers. Often, older adults are quite willing to attend and participate in groups because frequently they have more available time than working adults and are motivated by the need for socialization with others. Younger adults are limited by work and child care responsibilities, and they may feel their individual needs are not met in group classes. Providing some structured time for individual questions and advice may help all adults to learn in group settings.

Research directed toward finding the best options for delivery of self-management education has continued, and many modes and settings for asthma education have been explored. Both group and individual educational formats for teaching self-management skills have been tried and found to be equivalent, although one study found that small group education is more effective for teaching certain skills such as metered-dose inhaler use.[32] Self-management skills may develop slowly over time, and the duration of improvement in symptoms and health care use is variable. Little is known about the factors that promote maintenance of self-management skills overtime.

A pitfall for asthma education programs is overreliance on written materials, handouts, and worksheets written in English. Even providing translations of education material cannot solve a low literacy problem for a patient. Low literacy is surprisingly common. Survey data show that nearly 44 million Americans are functionally illiterate in English, and another 50 million have only marginal literacy skills.[94,95]

Literacy in the context of learning and performing health care tasks has been termed functional health literacy. Older patients may be particularly at risk. In a study of 3260 Medicare managed-care enrollees 65 years or older, 40% of English speakers and 54% of Spanish speakers were found to have inadequate or marginal health literacy.[96] Low health literacy creates significant barriers to educating patients with chronic illness in the methods of self-management. In a study of 273 patients visiting the emergency department for acute asthma exacerbation, just 27% read at the high school level, and 33% read at the seventh to eighth grade level.[97] A substantial number of these patients demonstrated poor metered-dose inhaler technique, which correlated with low reading levels.

Clearly, literacy is an important factor in patients' ability to comprehend and apply information and skills required to self-manage asthma, and it can become a significant barrier to achieving asthma control. The Rapid Estimate of Adult Literacy in Medicine shown in Table 91.2 is a screening tool that can provide an approximate grade level of reading ability in less than 3 minutes.[98,99] Simple strategies that may help avoid difficulties include avoiding medical jargon, asking patients to restate what they have learned during teaching sessions using their own words and examples, writing action plans and other important handouts in simple plain words, and using pictures and models whenever possible. Patients who are prescribed more than one medicine should be encouraged to bring all the medicines to their medical appointments to verify the accuracy and understanding of the intended treatment plan.

Table 91.2 Example of the Rapid Estimate of Adult Literacy (REALM) Instrument

Rapid Estimate of Adult Literacy in Medicine*

List 1		List 2		List 3	
Fat	+	Fatigue	+	Allergic	+
Flu	+	Pelvic	+	Menstrual	+
Pill	+	Jaundice	+	Testicle	+
Dose	+	Infection	+	Colitis	+
Eye	+	Exercise	+	Emergency	+
Stress	+	Behavior	+	Medication	+
Smear	+	Prescription	+	Occupation	+
Nerves	+	Notify	+	Sexuality	+

Raw score†	Grade Range Estimates
0–18	**Third grade and below** May not be able to read most low-literacy materials May need repeated oral instructions, materials composed primarily of illustrations or audio/video tapes
19–44	**Fourth to sixth grade** May need low-literacy materials; may not be able to read prescription labels
45–60	**Seventh to eighth grade** May struggle with most currently available patient education materials
61–66	**Ninth grade and above** Should be able to read most patient education materials

* Adapted from Davis T, Long SW, Jackson R, et al: Rapid estimate of adult literacy in medicine: A shortened screening instrument. Fam Med 25:391–395, 1993.
Published in revised form on www.uptodate.com
† Number of correct responses out of a possible 66.

CONCLUSIONS ABOUT ADULT ASTHMA SELF-MANAGEMENT

Patients with asthma need to know facts about asthma (information), and they also need to learn specific skills to assist in the management of their illness to improve and maintain functional ability and quality of life. The components comprising optimal self-management have been identified and tested in numerous studies and verified in scientific reviews and meta-analyses. The four key components are asthma information, self-monitoring, regular clinician review, and a written action plan. Quality asthma care must include these elements, and ways must be found to ensure that every person with asthma is trained in self-management to reduce the burden of the disease.

Asthma action plans are a written set of specific, directed actions to take when asthma worsens. At a minimum, the action plan should state the criteria for worsening asthma, designate the medications and doses to take, specify how to judge response to treatment, and direct when and how to seek help. The action plan can be guided by peak flow parameters or by symptoms with specific action steps to follow for each level of exacerbation severity. The most common plans use a traffic light symbol for identifying the severity of airflow obstruction by zones (green, yellow, red)

and zone-specific instructions about what to do. Figure 91.2 shows an example of an asthma action plan.

Further research in asthma self-management education should be focused in two areas: (1) developing brief, specifically targeted, and cost-effective self-management interventions that can be tested for effectiveness in both acute urgent care and primary care settings; and (2) identifying interventions for supporting and maintaining self-management skills over time. Attention must be given to preparing these interventions in formats usable by populations with low health literacy.

ASTHMA EDUCATION FOR CHILDREN

The prevalence and morbidity of asthma in children has increased over the past two decades, particularly among lower socioeconomic and minority groups. Although many self-management education programs have been developed and tested for children incorporating a wide variety of educational strategies designed for different age groups, clinical settings, and distinct patient groups, the effectiveness of these programs in reducing morbidity in children has not been clearly demonstrated. A meta-analysis based on studies published prior to 1992 found that these programs had no impact on decreasing health care utilization and reducing morbidity.[100]

However, later studies suggested that education might be effective if delivered to children with a recent emergency department visit or hospitalization because they may be more responsive to education and have greater potential for behavior change.[101–103] A systematic analysis[104] of eight studies[38,101,105–110] involving 1407 children recently seen in the emergency department for asthma exacerbation concluded that asthma education did not significantly reduce the number of subsequent emergency department visits, hospital admissions, or unscheduled doctor visits. Asthma education may be effective in other ways not measured in these trials, but there is insufficient evidence to support the belief that asthma education can reduce asthma relapses and recurrences or emergency department visits for children.

When the focus of the analysis is the global impact of self-management education on children with asthma, more positive results are seen. A scientific review and analysis of 32 randomized and controlled studies of asthma self-management education programs in children and adolescents examined the effectiveness of self-management education in modifying clinical outcomes.[111] The 32 trials[11,16,66,72,101,105–109,112–133] included in the analysis studied a total of 3706 children and adolescents with asthma, aged 2 to 18 years, and included outcomes such as pulmonary function, morbidity measures, self-efficacy and self-perceived severity, and health care utilization. These trials tested various forms of self-management education, but a focus on prevention and management of asthma exacerbations was a common element to all the self-management interventions. Overall, asthma self-management education was found to be superior to usual physician care alone in improving lung function, self-efficacy, school absenteeism, days of restricted activity, nocturnal asthma, and decreasing emergency department visits. These effects were statistically significant but modest overall and were stronger in children

My Asthma Plan

ENGLISH

Patient Name: _____

Medical Record #: _____

Physician's name: _____

DOB: _____

Physician's Phone #: _____

Completed by: _____   Date: _____

Controller Medicines	How Much to Take	How Often	Other Instructions
		_____ times per day **EVERYDAY!**	
		_____ times per day **EVERYDAY!**	
		_____ times per day **EVERYDAY!**	
		_____ times per day **EVERYDAY!**	

Quick-Relief Medicines	How Much to Take	How Often	Other Instructions
		Take ONLY as needed	NOTE: If this medicine is needed frequently, call physician to consider increasing controller medications

Special instructions when I feel ● **good**, ○ **not good**, and ◐ **awful**.

GREEN ZONE

I feel **good**.

(My **peak flow** is in the **GREEN** zone.)

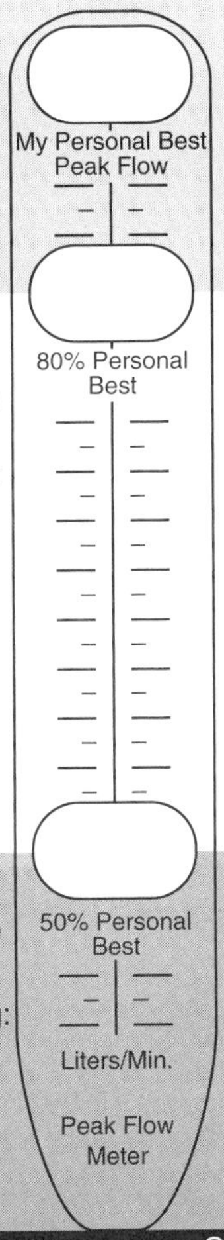

My Personal Best Peak Flow

PREVENT asthma symptoms everyday:

☐ Take my controller medicines (above) everyday.

☐ Before exercise, take _____ puffs of _____

☐ Avoid things that make my asthma worse like:

_____

WHITE ZONE

I do **not** feel **good**.

(My **peak flow** is in the **WHITE** zone.)

My symptoms may include one or more of the following:
- Wheeze
- Tight chest
- Cough
- Shortness of breath
- Waking up at night with asthma symptoms
- Decreased ability to do usual activities
- _____
- _____

80% Personal Best

CAUTION. I should continue taking my everyday controller asthma medicines AND:

☐ Take _____

_____

If I still do not feel good, or my peak flow is not back in the **Green Zone** within one hour, then I should:

☐ Increase _____

☐ Add _____

☐ Call _____

BLACK ZONE

I feel **awful**.

(My **peak flow** is in the **BLACK** zone.)

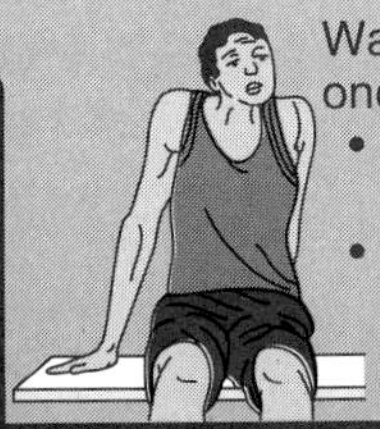

Warning signs may include one or more of the following:
- It's getting harder and harder to breathe
- Unable to sleep or do usual activities because of trouble breathing

50% Personal Best

Liters/Min.

Peak Flow Meter

MEDICAL ALERT! Get help!

☐ Take _____ until I get help immediately.

☐ Take _____

☐ Call _____

Danger! Get help immediately!

Call 911 if trouble walking or talking due to shortness of breath or lips or fingernails are gray or blue

Figure 91.2 Example of an asthma action plan. (From the San Francisco Bay Area Regional Asthma Management Program [www.rampasthma.org].)

with greater asthma severity. Lung function improved within the first 6 months after education, but the morbidity and health care utilization did not improve for nearly 12 months. Educational programs with single sessions had a greater effect on morbidity, whereas those with multiple sessions produced greater improvements in self-efficacy and greater reductions in emergency room visits.

All of the self-management programs produced effects across levels of severity, but the effects were more marked in the more severe samples. Because none of the reported studies included a comparison of the different components of asthma self-management training, it is not known which are most important for producing positive outcomes. Nonetheless, the evidence is strong enough to advocate asthma self-management education for all children with asthma, particularly those with moderate to severe asthma.

Some investigators are testing alternative delivery modes for pediatric asthma education. There are several published trials of interactive computer programs using games or scenarios to teach children about asthma.[134-137a] All of these trials demonstrated an increase in asthma knowledge, and two showed a reduction in emergency room visits,[135,137] one showed a reduction in hospitalizations,[136] and one failed to find differences in health outcomes between children educated through computer games compared to traditional methods.[135] Promising work suggests that self-management education can be accomplished in a busy clinical practice setting without disrupting patient care activities.[137,137a] Further research is needed to explore whether Internet Web-enabled asthma education programs, accessed in the setting where medical care is delivered, help to decrease health disparities by improving access to self-management knowledge and skills.

SELF-MANAGEMENT EDUCATION FOR ADULTS WITH COPD

Chronic obstructive pulmonary disease is another serious respiratory health problem with rising prevalence, morbidity, disability, and mortality. It is estimated that approximately 24 million adults in the United States have evidence of impaired lung function, but many remain undiagnosed.[8] Mortality from COPD has increased dramatically in women, nearly tripling the death rate in 1980; and in 2000 the death rate from COPD for women surpassed that for men.[8] Because the prevalence is rising rapidly worldwide, the disease is expected to place a significant burden on health care delivery systems.

Treatment of COPD is largely directed at symptomatic relief to improve airflow obstruction with inhaled medications and pulmonary rehabilitation. Loss of functional ability and reduction in quality of life are prominent features of the disease in adults. Because the benefits of pharmacologic interventions are limited, patients are often referred to pulmonary rehabilitation programs for education and exercise tolerance training. However, access to these programs is limited to those with certain types of health insurance. In addition, the programs are time-consuming, and the costs are significant. Self-management programs, so successful for asthma, are hoped to be efficacious and affordable options for improving health outcomes

in the COPD population. However, research has not yet shown the efficacy of this approach.

A scientific review[138] of eight trials[53,139-148] involving 1295 patients evaluated the impact of COPD self-management education compared to usual care on health-related outcomes. No effect of self-management education was found for reducing hospitalizations, emergency room visits, or days lost from work or for improving lung function. There was a trend toward improvement in quality of life that favored self-management education, but there was no effect on symptoms. Use of a written self-management action plan by intervention subjects for exacerbations of COPD was associated with significantly more days on oral steroid (15% vs. 9%) and antibiotics (10% vs. 4%) compared to controls.[149] A meta-analysis[138] of three studies[53,146,149] showed a significantly greater likelihood of increased oral steroid use (RR 1.39, 95% CI 1.02–1.91). In two studies,[146,149] self-management education was associated with significantly higher use of antibiotics compared to controls. These findings suggest that patients trained in self-management and with access to medications are more likely to be aware of changes in disease status and take action. However, whether the actions are beneficial in the long-term control of the disease remain unknown.

Overall, self-management education in COPD shows limited effects, but there are many unanswered questions and many limitations to evaluating the published studies. Different outcome measures, wide variations in the length of the trials, and variations in defining the populations make conclusions difficult. The benefits of self-management education in this population warrant further investigation because the legions of patients with COPD are expected to grow. Further studies should focus on improving quality of life and preventing hospitalizations, and they should include long follow-up to fully assess the benefits of self-management education for COPD. In addition, studies should be designed to test the added effect of prescribing a self-management action plan for self-treatment of COPD exacerbations. Just as in asthma, optimal self-management education about COPD will likely involve providing patients with the necessary information and skills for accurate self-assessment and the skills for taking actions when the disease worsens. An example of a COPD action plan[142] is shown in Figure 91.3.

SELF-MANAGEMENT FOR CYSTIC FIBROSIS

Cystic fibrosis is another chronic condition with pulmonary manifestations where self-management education is thought to be useful and relevant. Because children with this disease now often live well into adulthood, the issues of managing chronic symptoms, preventing infections, and facilitating normal development are significant. Health education and self-management programs have been developed to teach patients and their families to manage and cope with the disease. Investigators have found self-efficacy to be the most important factor predicting self-management behavior.[150,151] Knowledge of cystic fibrosis increased as a result of self-management education but was not related to improved patient or caregiver self-management behavior. Application of skills training, reflected by increased monitoring of health

ACTION PLAN FOR PEOPLE WITH CHRONIC OBSTRUCTIVE PULMONARY DISEASE

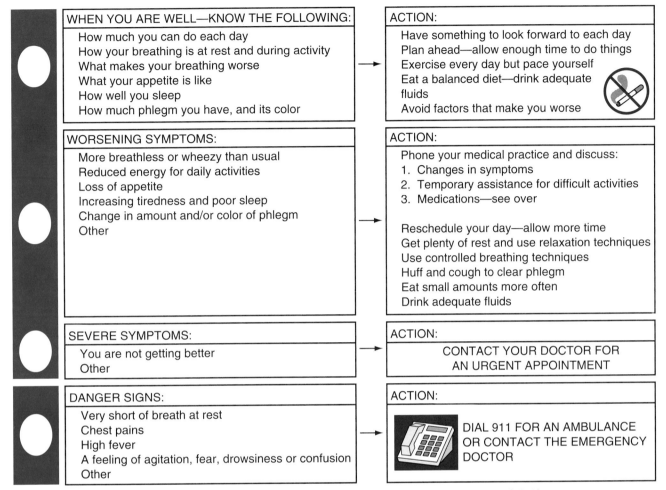

WHEN YOU ARE WELL—KNOW THE FOLLOWING:

How much you can do each day
How your breathing is at rest and during activity
What makes your breathing worse
What your appetite is like
How well you sleep
How much phlegm you have, and its color

ACTION:

Have something to look forward to each day
Plan ahead—allow enough time to do things
Exercise every day but pace yourself
Eat a balanced diet—drink adequate fluids
Avoid factors that make you worse

WORSENING SYMPTOMS:

More breathless or wheezy than usual
Reduced energy for daily activities
Loss of appetite
Increasing tiredness and poor sleep
Change in amount and/or color of phlegm
Other

ACTION:

Phone your medical practice and discuss:
1. Changes in symptoms
2. Temporary assistance for difficult activities
3. Medications—see over

Reschedule your day—allow more time
Get plenty of rest and use relaxation techniques
Use controlled breathing techniques
Huff and cough to clear phlegm
Eat small amounts more often
Drink adequate fluids

SEVERE SYMPTOMS:

You are not getting better
Other

ACTION:

CONTACT YOUR DOCTOR FOR
AN URGENT APPOINTMENT

DANGER SIGNS:

Very short of breath at rest
Chest pains
High fever
A feeling of agitation, fear, drowsiness or confusion
Other

ACTION:

DIAL 911 FOR AN AMBULANCE
OR CONTACT THE EMERGENCY
DOCTOR

Figure 91.3 Example of an action plan for self-management of chronic obstructive pulmonary disease (COPD). (From Watson PB, Town GI, Holbrook N, et al: Evaluation of a self-management plan for chronic obstructive pulmonary disease. Eur Respir J 10:1267–1271, 1997.)

status, resulted in improved self-treatment behavior. These findings are similar to those in asthma and COPD; patients and caregivers must have the opportunity to learn skills and improve self-efficacy (confidence in performing specific behaviors) to improve self-management treatment behaviors. Information alone is not enough to achieve successful self-management behavior.

PATIENT ADHERENCE BEHAVIOR

One of the most challenging areas in clinical management of chronic respiratory conditions is patient adherence to treatment recommendations. Therapeutic compliance, or patient adherence, has been the subject of ongoing discussion and debate for more than four decades. The debate over semantics ignores the evolution of the clinician-patient relationship as a significant factor in trying to understand, predict, and improve therapeutic adherence. The term *compliance* literally means "following orders" and originated in the days when physicians were viewed as unimpeachable authorities who were to be obeyed. The more acceptable term today is *adherence*, which means "sticking to a plan"

for perceived benefit. This concept implies that the patient has adopted and integrated a plan given by a clinician. The notion that an individual will stick to a plan implies a sincere desire for the promised beneficial outcome but ignores the behavior necessary to achieve it. *Concordance* means that two people (clinician and patient) have come to mutual agreement on the best plan for achieving benefit from treatment after exploring the options and potential barriers. Concordance implies give and take, adjustment, tailoring, and individualization of the therapeutic plan with mutual responsibility when the plan succeeds or fails.

The immediate goal of patient education may be to increase adherence to therapy so morbidity outcomes are ultimately reduced. Adherence requires improved self-management behavior as well as knowledge. One report suggested that morbidity and mortality of asthma could be markedly reduced or eliminated with effective education programs that improve adherence.[152] The concept of adherence in current health education literature implies an active, voluntary, collaborative involvement in the therapeutic plan by the patient. Ideally, a mutually acceptable course of behavior designed to produce a desired therapeutic result is agreed to by both the patient and the clinician.

The question of why patients do not follow the treatment plans that health professionals provide is the subject of extensive ongoing research at considerable effort and expense. The effort is justified by the significance of the problem of nonadherence. Estimates suggest that 30% to 60% of patients with chronic illnesses fail to adhere to prescribed therapy. Approximately 10% of all hospital admissions are estimated to be due to medication nonadherence.[152] The consequences of nonadherence are estimated to cost more than $100 billion dollars annually.[153] Poor or low levels of adherence to therapeutic treatments and recommendations are reported across all disease conditions, all treatments, and all ages. Only about one half of the people who are prescribed medications actually take enough doses to achieve a therapeutic effect, a situation that often results in prescription of increased doses and the addition of more medications by clinicians caring for these patients.

Research shows that social factors[154,155] interfering with adherence include multiple life stresses such as poverty, social conflicts, job loss, homelessness; fears and concerns that are not addressed; complex job and family responsibilities; and misunderstanding, language barriers, and literacy factors.[156,157] Similarly, variables such as age, gender, education, race, and ethnic culture may influence learning, communication, and social ability, resulting in problems following a prescribed treatment plan.

Psychological conditions and comorbidities that make adherence difficult, such as depression, anxiety, and panic episodes, interfere with the ability to perform self-management actions. Depression in particular has been shown to be associated with poor adherence in a meta-analysis of 10 studies of adults.[158] Patients who are overwhelmed by depression or anxiety may not be able to apply what they have been taught to do in acute situations where their behavior may be life-saving. Depression is particularly prevalent among patients with COPD, especially as the severity increases. In a study of patients with severe COPD on long-term oxygen therapy, significant depression was present in 57% of the patients, and only 6% were taking an antidepressant medication.[159]

Depression is often not recognized and therefore is undertreated. General medical illnesses, including chronic pulmonary diseases, are thought to be responsible for 10% to 15% of all depression.[160] Depression leads to increased use of health services and increased morbidity and mortality, and it is associated with poor quality of life. When present, it seriously impairs the patient's ability to engage in self-monitoring and self-care. Treatment is usually effective and can include counseling, support groups, and medications. The selective serotonin reuptake inhibitors are especially useful in people with comorbid medical conditions because they are safer than other antidepressants and have a low side-effect profile. Treatment of depression is essential before a self-management education program can be successful. Coping with a chronic disabling pulmonary disease can be extremely difficult and requires ongoing support from clinicians, family, and friends. Local support groups, such as the American Lung Association Better Breather Clubs, are popular among older patients with COPD but are not appropriate for younger patients with asthma. Depression and the need for community support should receive a high priority for recognition and treatment in the setting of chronic pulmonary illness.

Other factors associated with poor treatment adherence include low socioeconomic status and poor literacy skills.[157,161] Lack of literacy is an especially important barrier, as many of the tools of self-management that are found to be important require reading skills. It is estimated that one in four people in the United States are illiterate. Printed materials are by far the most common form of education. A useful screening question for literacy in adults is "How many newspapers or magazines do you read in a typical week?" Videos as teaching formats are not always useful, as people who are illiterate may learn differently and not necessarily understand pictures and diagrams.

MEDICATION ADHERENCE

Medication adherence is the extent to which a patient's medication-taking behavior matches the instructions prescribed by the clinician. Adherence to prescribed complex medication regimens is very difficult even for the most motivated patients. Approximately 50% of patients are unable to achieve full compliance, and nearly 33% never take the prescribed medicine at all.[162] Adherence is higher for short-term, self-administered treatments, estimated at about 65% to 75% but falls to less than 25% for long-term therapies.[162,163] Therapies for asthma are available that can control the disease in most patients, but poor adherence to pharmacotherapy has been identified as a factor contributing to asthma mortality. The benefits of treatment cannot be realized fully if the patient does not use them appropriately. Conversely, improved adherence to an effective pharmacologic regimen can markedly reduce asthma morbidity. Perhaps the common mechanism of improvement initiated by changing self-management behavior is improved adherence to the treatment plan.

Medication-specific factors that interfere with adherence include duration of treatment, frequency of dosing, complexity of medication administration, number and cost of medications, and lack of belief in the efficacy of the treatment. Increased dosing frequency has been associated with decreased adherence to treatment regimens across a wide range of diseases and therapies. One study showed that actual compliance with twice-, three-, and four-times daily dosing was 71%, 34%, and 18%, respectively.[164] Twice-daily dosing significantly improves adherence over four-times daily dosing.[165,166]

Other important causes of nonadherence are lack of confidence in the treatment plan, lack of self-efficacy for adjusting medications, lack of skills in using inhalers and devices, lack of awareness of deteriorating lung function, poor skills in self-assessment, forgetting, misunderstanding, health beliefs, and attitudes toward disease and treatment.[167]

Adherence to prescribed inhaled corticosteroids is notoriously poor; and even in observational studies where patients were aware of being monitored, average adherence was only 63% to 65%.[157,168] Nonadherence to long-term inhaled corticosteroids is thought to be a major reason for treatment failure. In a large HMO-based survey of 5580 people with asthma, 14 to 65 years old, only 54% used inhaled corticosteroid medication as prescribed.[169] Medication adherence in children with asthma is estimated to be even lower.

Factors found to be independently associated with poor adherence to inhaled corticosteroids are less than 12 years of education and poor patient-clinician communication.[157] This finding suggests that educational level and clinician communication are important predictors of adherence to inhaled corticosteroid therapy. In a subsequent study of patients with asthma, poor adherence was associated with sociocultural factors, such as being African American ($P = 0.001$) or having a lower educational level ($P = 0.01$) or a lower income ($P = 0.003$), whereas better adherence was associated with a positive attitude toward inhaled steroids.[168] These findings suggest potential reasons for health disparities and at least one one area where targeted interventions may modify adherence and treatment outcomes. Assessing the patient's understanding, perception of potential benefits, and fears about treatment is essential so educational information and training can be individualized for the best therapeutic outcomes.

EFFECTIVE INTERVENTIONS FOR MEDICATION ADHERENCE

Behavioral techniques are often used to improve medication adherence in patients with asthma. These techniques include shaping, negotiating and contracting, modeling, monitoring, and self-management. Monitoring with interpretation of trends over time may reinforce adherence behavior and promote self-management. Monitoring techniques can include medication diaries or electronic monitors, telephone contacts, periodic medication review by health care providers, feedback of test results or other relevant data, and observation of behavior. Providing patients with feedback of relevant monitoring data and test results may reward high adherence and stimulate adherence when it is low. Subjects with asthma who received feedback about their actual medication-taking behavior adhered significantly more to the prescribed dose than control subjects who did not receive feedback.[170]

A comprehensive review[171] of strategies to help patients adhere to prescribed medications for chronic disease conditions analyzed 33 trials covering a range of chronic conditions. Only one in three interventions for short-term treatment and 16 in 30 long-term interventions produced improvement in both adherence and disease outcomes, providing little evidence for improving medication adherence consistently. Even the effective interventions led to only modest improvements. There were five adherence trials for long-term treatment of asthma and/or COPD[18,39,53,61,172] using similar educational interventions, including education by health professionals, instruction in self-monitoring, and self-adjustment of medications using a plan. These educational interventions produced conflicting results. Educational sessions have been associated with improved adherence among asthmatic patients in some randomized controlled trials[18,40,61,73] but showed no impact on adherence in other trials involving adults, adolescents, and children.[28,39,53,172,173] Improvements in adherence to therapy and psychological well-being have been demonstrated in patients with COPD as the result of psychoeducational interventions delivered as a part of pulmonary rehabilitation.[174]

Individual self-management education may be a powerful way to create behavior change. In a randomized controlled trial, adherence to inhaled corticosteroid medication, perceived control of asthma, and sputum eosinophila all improved significantly after individual self-management training in adults with asthma compared to controls who did monitoring only.[73] The reduction in sputum eosinophils and the improvement in perceived control were statistically significant even when the effect of adherence was removed, showing independent effects of self-management training.

In summary, educational approaches seem to be effective when they include specific help in achieving the behaviors necessary for adherence. The most successful strategies are combinations of education, skills training, feedback and reinforcement, direct involvement of patients in self-management, and enhancement of the patient-clinician relationship. Ways must be found to develop combination strategies that can be implemented in clinical settings in a cost-effective manner. Whether patient education can influence adherence to daily prescribed medications is not clear. The studies with positive outcomes were more likely to include the critical components of self-management training. The negative studies suffered from being underpowered for detecting significant effects of patient education, were confounded by changing medical therapy at the time of education, or were conducted in patients already exposed to high levels of education in specialty practices. Ultimately, the effects of well designed, theoretically sound self-management interventions on medication-taking behavior will be resolved with attention to the requirements of rigorous study design.

PATIENT-CLINICIAN RELATIONSHIP

The quality of the doctor-patient relationship may be the most important factor in whether a patient complies with the medication regimen. Strong, trusting relationships between the patient and health care provider seem to improve patient adherence when the communication is open and a patient-centered, negotiation-based framework is used that promotes direct involvement in decision-making. Medical outcomes studies show that when people with chronic disease learn better disease management (i.e., when to seek medical care, how to decide when treatment is not working, and how to communicate with the doctor) the results are a skilled patient with better adherence to therapy.[175] Collaboration between the clinician and the patient is considered essential in defining health care issues, treatment approaches, and behavioral change on the part of the patient. Chronic illnesses such as asthma require an ongoing partnership between doctor and patient to adjust and individualize the treatment plan. Poor communication between doctor and patient is thought to be a major contributor to nonadherence to treatment. Possibly, cultural, racial, and ethnic differences between clinician and patient may influence therapeutic communication. In chronic illness, adherence is directly related to the degree of autonomy and sense of partnership the patient has with the clinician. Considerably more research is needed to identify methods for improving the communication and therapeutic relationships between clinicians and their patients.

Interventions that target this relationship and/or patient attitude toward inhaled corticosteroids may ultimately prove to be the most successful in improving adherence to the therapeutic plan for patients with chronic illnesses.

SUMMARY

Much has been learned about successful educational interventions for chronic illnesses such as asthma. The components of an optimal self-management asthma educational program include knowledge of the illness and current therapy, means of monitoring therapy, psychosocial skills for dealing with a chronic illness, and action plans. Methods of delivering optimal self-management must be refined and tested for use in busy clinical settings. Clinicians are faced with trying to provide asthma education to patients within the limited time frame of the appointment. Many clinicians find this an impossible task and omit it entirely. Some clinicians are committed to teaching their asthmatic patients but find it easier to accomplish in the context of specialty care. Changes in health policy and reimbursement are needed to ensure that optimal self-management education occurs.

Options for management approaches can be selected based on individual and clinician preferences, as many approaches produce similar results. Patients with more severe asthma may benefit more from certain types of monitoring strategies than those with mild or intermittent disease. Modifications for these subgroups of asthmatic patients need to be developed and tested. Methods of imparting the critical information and skills for people with low literacy skills must be developed. Research is needed to illuminate the links between education, optimal treatment regimens, patient-clinician relationships, adherence, and outcomes.

In contrast to asthma, the benefits of teaching self-management to patients with COPD have not been demonstrated. Much more attention must be paid to this growing group of chronically ill individuals. New and more refined interventions for self-management of COPD exacerbations should focus on symptom pattern recognition and specific symptom management strategies rather than just antibiotics and prednisone.

The current literature on adherence interventions is notably weak. Only a handful of rigorous trials have been published with evidence for selecting strategies to improve treatment adherence among populations of patients or individuals. Many of these reported interventions are too complex, time-consuming, and expensive to realistically transfer to clinical settings. The specific components of these successful interventions that are most associated with improvement in adherence need to be identified.

The recent finding that adherence is linked to social, economic, and health disparities among African Americans calls for intensive focus on developing new approaches to these social problems. Until the disparity in access to health care and distribution of health resources across racial and socioeconomic groups are resolved, poor adherence and poor treatment outcomes will remain significant among these specific populations. Investigating ways to modify the attitudes of patients toward efficacious treatments is an area for increased research because perceptions of benefit and adverse effects are potentially modifiable.

REFERENCES

1. Gibson PG, Powell H, Coughlan J, et al: Limited (information only) patient education programs for adults with asthma (Cochrane Review). *In* The Cochrane Library, Issue 3, 2001. Oxford: Update Software.
2. Wagner EH, Glasgow RE, Davis C, et al: Quality improvement in chronic illness care: A collaborative approach. J Qual Improv 27:63–80, 2001.
3. Wagner EH, Austin BT, Davis C, et al: Improving chronic illness care: Translating evidence into action. Health Affairs 20:64–78, 2001.
4. Clark NM, Janz NK, Becker MH, et al: Impact of self-management education on the functional health status of older adults with heart disease. Gerontologist 32:438–443, 1992.
5. Bandura A: Social Foundations of Thought and Action: A Social Cognitive Theory. Englewood Cliffs, NJ: Prentice-Hall, 1986.
6. Bandura A: Self-Efficacy: The Exercise of Control. New York: WH Freeman, 1977.
7. Schunck DJ: Self-efficacy and cognitive achievement: Implications for students with learning problems. J Learn Disabil 22:14–22, 1989.
8. Mannino DM, Homa DM, Akinbami LG, et al: Chronic obstructive pulmonary disease surveillance—United States, 1971–2000. Respir Care 47:1184–1199, 2000.
9. National Asthma Education and Prevention Program, National Heart, Lung, and Blood Institute: Expert Panel Report 2: Guidelines for the Diagnosis and Management of Asthma, National Institutes of Health Publication No. 97–4051. Bethesda, MD: NHLBI, 1997.
10. Bolton MB, Tilley BC, Kuder J, et al: The cost and effectiveness of an education program for adults who have asthma. J Gen Intern Med 6:401–407, 1991.
11. Clark NM, Feldman CH, Evans D, et al: The impact of health education on frequency and cost of health care use by low income children with asthma. J Allerg Clin Immunol 78:108–115, 1986.
12. Gallefoss F, Bakke PS: Cost-effectiveness of self-management in asthmatics: A 1 year follow-up randomized, controlled trial. Eur Respir J 17:206–213, 2001.
13. Kauppinen R, Sintonene H, Tukiainen H: One-year economic evaluation of intensive vs conventional patient education and supervision for self-management of new asthmatic patients. Respir Med 92:300–307, 1998.
14. Kauppinen R, Sintonen H, Vilkka V, et al: Long-term (3-year) economic evaluation of intensive patient education for self-management during the first year in new asthmatics. Respir Med 93:283–289, 1999.
15. Lahdensuo A, Haahtela T, Herrala J, et al: Randomised comparison of guided self management and traditional treatment of asthma over one year. BMJ 312:748–752, 1996.
16. Carswell F, Robinson EJ, Hek G, et al: A Bristol experience: Benefits and cost of an 'asthma nurse' visiting the homes of asthmatic children. Bristol Med Chir J 104:11–12, 1989.
17. Lahdensuo A, Haahtela T, Herrala J, et al: Randomised comparison of cost effectiveness of guided self management and traditional treatment of asthma in Finland. BMJ 316:1138–1139, 1998.
18. Bailey WC, Richards JM, Brooks CM, et al: A randomised trial to improve self-management practice of adults with asthma. Arch Intern Med 150:1664–1668, 1990.
19. National Heart, Lung, and Blood Institute: Global Initative for Asthma—Revised. National Institutes of Health Publication No. 02–3659. Bethesda, MD: NHLBI, 2002.
20. National Heart, Lung and Blood Institute: National Asthma Education and Prevention Program: Guidelines for

the diagnosis and management of asthma—update 2002. J Allerg Clin Immunol 110:S141–S219, 2002.

21. Center for Studying Health System Change (HSC): Community Tracking Study Physician Survey: Tracking Report No. 8, 2001 (www.hschange.org).

22. Aiolfi S, Confalonieri M, Scartabellati A, et al: International guidelines and educational experiences in an out-patient clinic for asthma. Monaldi Arch Chest Dis 50:477–481, 1995.

23. Hilton S, Sibbald B, Anderson HR, et al: Controlled evaluation of the effects of patient education on asthma morbidity in general practice. Lancet 1:26–29, 1986.

24. Huss K, Huss RW, Squire EN, et al: Computer education for asthmatics: What effects? J Nurs Care Qual 6:57–66, 1992.

25. Jenkinson D, Davison J, Jones S, et al: Comparison of effects of a self management booklet and audio cassette for patients with asthma. BMJ 297:267–270, 1988.

26. Maiman LA, Green LW, Gibson G, et al: Education for self-treatment by adult asthmatics. JAMA 241:1919–1922, 1979.

27. Moldofsky H, Broder I, Davies G, et al: Videotape educational program for people with asthma. Can Med Assoc J 120:669–672, 1979.

28. Osman LM, Abdalla MI, Beattie JA, et al: Reducing hospital admission through computer supported education for asthma patients: Grampian Asthma Study of Integrated Care (GRASSIC). BMJ 308:568–571, 1994.

29. Ringsberg KC, Wiklund I, Wilhelmsen L: Education of adult patients at an "asthma school": Effects on quality of life, knowledge and need for nursing. Eur Respir J 3:33–37, 1990.

30. Sondergaard B, Davidsen F, Kirkeby B, et al: The economics of an intensive education programme for asthmatic patients. Pharmacoeconomics 1:207–212, 1992.

31. Thapar A: Educating asthmatic patients in primary care: A pilot study of small group education. Fam Pract 11:39–43, 1994.

32. Wilson SR, Scamagas P, German OF, et al: A controlled trial of two forms of self-management education for adults with asthma. Am J Med 94:564–576, 1993.

33. Mayo PH, Richman J, Harris HW: Results of a program to reduce admissions for adult asthma. Ann Intern Med 112:864–871, 1990.

34. Yoon R, McKenzie DK, Bauman A, et al: Controlled trial evaluation of an asthma education program for adults. Thorax 48:1110–1116, 1993.

35. George MR, O'Dowd LC, Martin I, et al: A comprehensive educational program improves clinical outcome measures in inner-city patients with asthma. Arch Intern Med 159:1710–1716, 1999.

36. Castro M, Zimmermann NA, Crocker S, et al: Asthma intervention program prevents readmissions in high healthcare utilizers. Am J Respir Crit Care Med 168:1095–1099, 2003.

37. Cowie RL, Revitt SG, Underwood MF, et al: The effect of a peak flow-based action plan in the prevention of exacerbations of asthma. Chest 112:1534–1538, 1997.

38. Garrett J, Fenwick JM, Taylor G, et al: Prospective controlled evaluation of the effect of a community based asthma education center in a multiracial working class neighborhood. Thorax 49:976–983, 1994.

39. Cote J, Cartier A, Robichaud P, et al: Influence on asthma morbidity of asthma education programs based on self-management plans following treatment optimization. Am J Respir Crit Care Med 155:1509–1514, 1997.

40. Allen RM, Jones MP, Oldenburg B: Randomized trial of an asthma self-management programme for adults. Thorax 50:731–738, 1995.

41. Jones KP, Mullee MA, Middleton M, et al: Peak flow based asthma self management: A randomised controlled study in general practice. Thorax 50:851–857, 1995.

42. Guevara JP, Wolf FM, Grum CM, et al: Effects of educational interventions for self management of asthma in children and adolescents: Systematic review and meta-analysis. BMJ 326:1–6, 2003 (bmj.com).

43. Gibson PG: Monitoring the patient with asthma: An evidence-based approach. J Allergy Clin Immunol 106:17–26, 2000.

44. Ignacio-Garcia JM, Gonzalez-Santos P: Asthma self-management education program by home monitoring of peak expiratory flow. Am J Respir Crit Care Med 151:353–359, 1995.

45. Zeiger RS, Heller S, Mellon MH, et al: Facilitated referral to asthma specialist reduces relapses in asthma emergency room visits. J Allergy Clin Immunol 87:1160–1168, 1991.

46. Gibson PG, Powell H, Coughlan J, et al: Self-management and regular practitioner review for adults with asthma (Cochrane Review). In The Cochrane Library, Issue 2, 2003. Oxford: Updated Software.

47. Abdulwadud O, Abramson M, Forbes A, et al: Evaluation of a randomised controlled trial of adult asthma education in a hospital setting. Thorax 54:493–500, 1999.

48. Bailey WC. Richards JM, Manzella BA, et al: Promoting self management in adults with asthma: An overview of the UAB program. Health Educ Q 14:345–355, 1987.

49. Bailey WC, Kohler CL, Richards JM, et al: Asthma self-management (through patient education). Arch Intern Med 59:2422–2428, 1999.

50. Berg J, Dunbar-Jacob J, Serelka SM: An evaluation of a self-management program for adults with asthma. Clin Nurs Res 6:225–238, 1997.

51. Blixen CE, Hammel JP, Murphy D, et al: Feasibility of a nurse-run asthma education program for urban African-Americans: A pilot study. J Asthma 38:23–32, 2001.

52. Brewin AM, Hughes JA: Effect of patient education on asthma management. Br J Nurs 4:81–101, 1995.

53. Gallefoss F, Bakke PS: How does patient education and self-management among asthmatics and patients with chronic obstructive pulmonary disease affect medication? Am J Respir Crit Care Med 160:2000–2005, 1999.

54. Ghosh CS, Ravindran P, Joshi M, et al: Reductions in hospital use from self-management training for chronic asthmatics. Soc Sci Med 46:1087–1093, 1998.

55. Grampian Asthma Study of Integrated Care (GRASSIC): Effectiveness of routine self monitoring of peak flow in patients with asthma. BMJ 308:564–567, 1994.

56. Hayward SA, Jorden M, Golden G, et al: A randomized controlled evaluation of asthma self management in general practice. Asthma Gen Pract 4:11, 1996.

57. Heard AR, Richards D, Alpers JH, et al: Randomized controlled trial of general practice based asthma clinics. Med J Aust 171:68–71, 1999.

58. Knoell DL, Pierson JF, Marsh CB, et al: Measurement of outcomes in adults receiving pharmaceutical care in a comprehensive asthma outpatient clinic. Pharmacotherapy 18:365–374, 1998.

59. Kotses H, Bernstein IL, Bernstein DI, et al: A self-management program for adult asthma. Part I. Development and evaluation. J Allergy Clin Immunol 95:529–540, 1995.

60. Kotses H, Stout C, McConnaughy K, et al: Evaluation of individualized asthma self-management programs. J Asthma 33:113–118, 1996.

61. Levy ML, Robb M, Allen J, et al: A randomized controlled evaluation of specialist nurse education following accident and emergency attendance for acute asthma. Respir Med 94:900–908, 2000.

62. Moudgil H, Marshall T, Honeybourne D: Asthma education and quality of life in the community: A randomised controlled study to evaluate the impact on white European and Indian subcontinent ethnic groups from socioeconomically deprived areas in Birmingham, UK. Thorax 55:177–183, 2000.

63. Mulloy E, Donaghy D, Quigley C, et al: A one-year prospective audit of an asthma education programme in an out-patient setting. Ir Med J 89:226–228, 1996.

64. Neri M, Migllori GB, Spanevello A, et al: Economic analysis of two structured treatment and teaching programs on asthma. Allergy 51:313–319, 1996.

65. Schott-Baer D, Christensen M: Research for practice: A pilot programme to increase self-care of adult asthma patients. Med Surg Nurs 8:78–83, 1999.

66. Shields MC, Griffin KW, McNabb WL: The effect of a patient education program on emergency room use for inner-city children with asthma. Am J Public Health 80:36–38, 1990.

67. Snyder S, Winder JA, Creer TL: Development and evaluation of an adult asthma self-management program: Wheelers anonymous. J Asthma 11:39–43, 1987.

68. Sommaruga M, Spanevello A, Migliori GB, et al: The effects of a cognitive behavioral intervention in asthmatic patients. Monaldi Arch Chest Dis 50:398–402, 1995.

69. De Oliveira MA, Faresin SM, Bruno VF, et al: Evaluation of an educational programme for socially deprived asthma patients. Eur Respir J 14:908–914, 1999.

70. Thoonen BPA, Schermer TRJ, van den Boom G, et al: Self-management of asthma in general practice, asthma control and quality of life: A randomized controlled trial. Thorax 58:30–36, 2003.

71. Cote J, Bowie DM, Robichaud P, et al: Evaluation of two different educational interventions for adult patients consulting with an acute asthma exacerbation. Am J Respir Crit Care Med 163:1415–1419, 2001.

72. Toelle BG, Peat JK, Salome CM, et al: Evaluation of a community-based asthma management program in a population sample of school children. Med J Aust 158:742–746, 1993.

73. Janson SL, Fahy JV, Covington JK, et al: Effects of individual self-management education on clinical, biological and adherence outcomes in asthma. Am J Med 115:620–626, 2003.

74. Charlton I, Charlton G, Broomfield J, Mullee MA: Evaluation of peak flow and symptoms only self-management plans for control of asthma in general practice. BMJ 301:1355–1359, 1990.

75. Turner MO, Taylor D, Bennett R, Fitzgerald JM: A randomized trial comparing peak expiratory flow and symptom self-management plans for patients with asthma attending a primary care clinic. Am J Respir Crit Care Med 157:540–546, 1998.

76. Lopez-Vina A, del Castillo-Arevalo F: Influence of peak expiratory flow monitoring on an asthma self-management education programme. Respir Med 94:760–766, 2000.

77. Adams RJ, Boath K, Homan S, et al: A randomized trial of peak-flow and symptom-based plans in adults with moderate-to-severe asthma. Respirology 6:297–304, 2001.

78. Verschelden P, Cartier A, L'Acheveque J, et al: Compliance with and accuracy of daily self-assessment of peak expiratory flows (PEF) in asthmatic subjects over a three month period. Eur Respir J 9:880–885, 1996.

79. Cote J, Carier A, Malo JL, et al: Compliance with peak expiratory flow monitoring in home management of asthma. Chest 113:968–972, 1998.

80. Kamps AW, Roorda RJ, Brand PL: Peak flow diaries in childhood asthma are unreliable. Thorax 56:180–182, 2001.

81. Reddel HK, Toelle BG, Marks GB, et al: Analysis of adherence to peak flow monitoring when recording of data is electronic. BMJ 324:146–147, 2002.

82. Chowienczyk PJ, Parkin ED, Lawson CP, et al: Do asthmatic patients correctly record home spirometry measurements? BMJ 309:1618, 1994.

83. Teeter JG, Bleecker ER: Relationship between airway obstruction and respiratory symptoms in adult asthmatics. Chest 113:272–277, 1998.

84. Rubinfeld AR, Pain MC: Perception of asthma. Lancet 1:882–884, 1976.

85. Burdon JG, Juniper EF, Kilhan KJ: The perception of breathlessness in asthma. Am Rev Respir Dis 126:825–828, 1982.

86. Kikuchi Y, Okabe S, Tamura G: Chemosensitivity and perception of dyspnoea in patients with a history of near-fatal asthma. N Engl J Med 330:329–334, 1994.

87. Gibson PG, Wang PJO, Hepperle MJG, et al: A research method to induce and examine a mild exacerbation of asthma. Clin Exp Allergy 22:525–532, 1992.

88. Chan-Yeung M, Chang JH, Manfreda J, et al: Changes in peak flow, symptom score, and the use of medications during acute exacerbations of asthma. Am J Respir Crit Care Med 154:889–893, 1996.

89. Wagner EH: The role of patient care teams in chronic disease management. BMJ 320:569–571, 2000.

89a. Griffiths C, Foster G, Barnes N, et al: Specialist nurse intervention to reduce unscheduled asthma care in a deprived multiethnic area: the east London randomized controlled trial for high risk asthma (ELECTRA). BMJ 328:144, 2004.

90. Powell H, Gibson PG: Options for self-management education for adults with asthma (Cochrane Review). *In* The Cochrane Library, Issue 2. Oxford: Update Software, 2003.

91. Ayres JG, Campbell LM: A controlled assessment of an asthma self-management plan involving a budesonide dose regimen. Eur Respir J 9:886–892, 1996.

92. Klein JJ, van der Palen J, Uil SM, et al: Benefit from the inclusion of self-treatment guidelines to a self-management program for adults with asthma. Eur Respir J 17:386–394, 2001.

93. Baldwin DR, Pathak UA, King R, et al: Outcome of asthmatics attending asthma clinics utilizing self-management plans in general practice. Asthma Gen Pract 5:31–32, 1997.

94. Kauppinen R, Vilkka V, Sintonen H, et al: Long term economic evaluation of intensive patient education during the first treatment year in newly diagnosed asthma. Respir Med 95:56–63, 2001.

95. National Center for Education Statistics: National Adult Literacy Survey—1992. (http://nces.ed.gov/nadlits/naal92/overview.html).

96. Gazmararian JA, Baker DW, Williams MV, et al: Health literacy among Medicare enrollees in a managed care organization. JAMA 281:545–551, 1999.

97. Williams MV, Baker DW, Honig EG, et al: Inadequate literacy is a barrier to asthma knowledge and self-care. Chest 114:1008–1015, 1998.

98. Davis T, Long S, Jackson R, et al: Rapid estimate of adult literacy in medicine: A shortened screening instrument. Fam Med 25:391–395, 1993.

99. Davis TC, Michielutte R, Askov EN, et al: Practical assessment of adult literacy in health care. Health Educ Behav 25:613–624, 1998.

100. Bernard-Bonnin A, Stachenko S. Bonin D, et al: Self-management teaching programs and morbidity of pediatric asthma: A meta-analysis. J Allergy Clin Immunol 95:34–41, 1995.

101. Madge P, McColl J, Paton J: Impact of nurse-led home management training programme in children admitted to hospital with acute asthma: A randomised controlled study. Thorax 52:223–228, 1997.

102. Gibson PG, Talbot PI, Hancock J, et al: A prospective audit of asthma management following emergency asthma treatment at a teaching hospital. Med J Aust 158:775–778, 1993.

103. Ordonez GA, Phelan PD, Olinsky A, et al: Preventable factors in hospital admission for asthma. Arch Dis Child 78:143–147, 1998.

104. Haby MM, Waters E, Robertson CF, et al: Interventions for educating children who have attended the emergency room for asthma (Cochrane Review). In The Cochrane Library, Issue 3. Oxford: Update Software, 2003.

105. Alexander JS, Younger RE, Cohen RM, Crawford LV: Effectiveness of a nurse-managed program for children with chronic asthma. J Pediatr Nurs 3:312–317, 1988.

106. Charlton I, Antonio AG, Atkinson J, et al: Asthma at the interface: Bridging the gap between general practice and a district general hospital. Arch Dis Child 70:313–318, 1994.

107. McNabb WL, Wilson-Pessano SR, Hughes GW, Scamagas P: Self-management education of children with asthma: AIR WISE. Am J Public Health 75:1219–1220, 1985.

108. Mitchell EA, Ferguson V, Norwood M: Asthma education by community child health nurses. Arch Dis Child 61:1184–1189, 1986.

109. Talabere LR: In Funk SG (ed): Aspects of Caring for the Chronically Ill: Hospital and Home. New York: Springer, 1993, pp 319–330.

110. Wesseldine LJ, McCarthy P, Silverman M: Structure discharge procedure for children admitted to the hospital with acute asthma: A randomized controlled trial of nursing practice. Arch Dis Child 80:110–114, 1999.

111. Wolf FM, Guevara JP, Grum CM, et al: Educational interventions for asthma in children (Cochrane Review). In The Cochrane Library, Issue 2. Oxford: Update Software, 2003.

112. Christiansen SC, Martin SB, Schleicher NC, et al: Evaluation of a school-based asthma education program for inner-city children. J Allergy Clin Immunol 100:613–617, 1997.

113. Colland VT: Learning to cope with asthma: a behavioral self-management program for children. Patient Educ Couns 22:141–152, 1993.

114. Dahl J, Gustafsson D, Melin L: Effects of a behavioral treatment program on children with asthma. J Asthma 27:41–46, 1990.

115. Deaves DM: An assessment of the value of health education in the prevention of childhood asthma. J Advanced Nurs 18:354–363, 1993.

116. Evans D, Clark NM, Feldman CH, et al: A school health education program for children with asthma aged 8–11 years. Health Educ Q 14:267–279, 1987.

117. Fireman P, Friday GA, Gira C, et al: Teaching self-management skills to asthmatic children and their parents in an ambulatory care setting. Pediatrics 68:341–348, 1981.

118. Hill R, Williams J, Britton J, et al: Can morbidity associated with untreated asthma in primary school children be reduced? A controlled intervention study. BMJ 303:1169–1174, 1991.

119. Holzheimer L, Mohay H, Masters IB: Educating young children about asthma: Comparing the effectiveness of a developmentally appropriate asthma education videotape and picture book. Child Care Health Dev 24:85–99, 1998.

120. Hughes DM, McLeod M, Garner B, et al: Controlled trial of a home and ambulatory program for asthmatic children. Pediatrics 87:54–61, 1991.

121. Kubly LS, McClellan MS: Effects of self-care instruction on asthmatic children. Issues Comprehensive Pediatr Nurs 7:121–130, 1984.

122. LeBaron S, Zeltzer LK, Ratner P, et al: A controlled study of education for improving compliance with cromolyn sodium: The importance of physician-patient communication. Ann Allergy 55:811–818, 1985.

123. Lewis CE, Rachelefsky G, Lewis MA, et al: A randomized trial of A.C.T. (asthma care training) for kids. Pediatrics 74:478–486, 1984.

124. Parcel GS, Nader PR, Tiernan K: A health education program for children with asthma. Dev Behav Pediatr 1:128–132, 1980.

125. Perrin JM, MacLean WE, Gortmaker SL, et al: Improving the psychological status of children with asthma: A randomized controlled trial. J Dev Behav Pediatr 13:241–247, 1992.

126. Persaud DI, Barnett SE, Weller SC, et al: An asthma self-management program for children, including instruction in peak flow monitoring by school nurses. J Asthma 33:37–43, 1996.

127. Rakos RF, Grodek MV, Mack KK: The impact of a self-administered behavioral intervention program on pediatric asthma. J Psychiatr Res 29:101–108, 1985.

128. Ronchetti R, Indinnimeo L, Bonci E, et al: Asthma self-management programmes in a population of Italian children: A multicentric study. Eur Respir J 10:1248–1253, 1997.

129. Rubin DH, Leventhal JM, Sadock RT, et al: Educational intervention by computer in childhood asthma: A randomized clinical trial testing the use of a new teaching intervention in childhood asthma. Pediatrics 77:1–10, 1986.

130. Szczepanski R, Gebert N, Hummelink R, et al: Outcome of structured asthma education in childhood and adolescence [Ergebnis einer strukturlerten asthmaschulung im kindesund jugendalter]. Pneumologie 50:544–548, 1996.

131. Weingarten MA, Goldberg J, Teperberg Y: A pilot study of the multidisciplinary management of childhood asthma in a family practice. J Asthma 22:261–265, 1985.

132. Whitman N, West D, Brough FK, et al: A study of a self-care rehabilitation program in pediatric asthma. Health Educ Q 12:333–342, 1985.

133. Wilson SR, Latini D, Starr NJ, et al: Education of parents of infants and very young children with asthma: A developmental evaluation of the Wee Wheezers program. J Asthma 33:239–254, 1996.

134. Bartholomew LK, Gold RS, Parcel GS, et al: Watch, discover, think, and act: Evaluation of computer-assisted instruction to improve asthma self-management in inner-city children. Patient Educ Couns 39:269–280, 2000.

135. Homer C, Susskind O, Alpert HR, et al: An evaluation of an innovative multimedia educational software program for asthma management: Report of a randomized, controlled trial. Pediatrics 106:210–215, 2000.

136. Yawn BP, Algatt-Bergstrom PJ, Yawn RA, et al: An in-school CD-ROM asthma education program. J School Health 70:153–159, 2000.

137. Krishna S, Francisco BK, Balas A, et al: Internet-enabled interactive multimedia asthma education program: A randomized trial. Pediatrics 111:503–510, 2003.

137a. Shames RS, Sharek P, Mayer M, et al: Effectiveness of a multicomponent self-management program in at-risk school-aged children with asthma. Ann Allergy Asthma Immunol 92:611–618, 2004.

138. Monninkhof EM, van der Valk PDLPM, van der Palen J, et al: Self-management education for chronic obstructive

pulmonary disease (Cochrane Review). *In* The Cochrane Library, Issue 2. Oxford: Update Software, 2003.

139. Blake RL Jr, Vandiver TA, Braun S, et al: A randomized controlled evaluation of a psychosocial intervention in adults with chronic lung disease. Fam Med 22:365–370, 1990.

140. Cockcroft A, Bagnall P, Heslop A, et al: Controlled trial of respiratory health worker visiting patients with chronic respiratory disability. BMJ 294:225–228, 1987.

141. Emery CF, Schein RL, Hauck ER, et al: Psychological and cognitive outcomes of a randomized trial of exercise among patients with chronic obstructive pulmonary disease. Health Psychol 17:232–240, 1998.

142. Gallefoss R: The effects of patient education in COPD in a 1-year follow-up randomized, controlled trial. Patient Educ Couns 52:259–266, 2004.

143. Gallefoss F, Bakke PS: Impact of patient education and self-management on morbidity in asthmatics and patients with chronic obstructive pulmonary disease. Respir Med 94:279–287, 2000.

144. Gourley GA, Portner TS, Gourley DR, et al: Humanistic outcomes in the hypertension and COPD arms of a multi-center outcomes study. J Am Pharm Assoc 38:586–597, 1998.

145. Howland J, Nelson EC, Barlow PB, et al: Chronic obstructive airway disease: Impact of health education. Chest 90:233–238, 1986.

146. Littlejohns P, Baveystock CM, Parnell H, et al: Randomised controlled trial of the effectiveness of a respiratory health worker in reducing impairment, disability, and handicap due to chronic airflow limitation. Thorax 46:559–564, 1991.

147. Sassi-Dambron DE, Eakin EG, Ries AL, et al: Treatment of dyspnea in COPD: A controlled clinical trial of dyspnea management strategies. Chest 107:724–729, 1995.

148. Solomon DK, Portner TS, Bass GE, et al: Clinical and economic outcomes in the hypertension and COPD arms of a multicenter outcomes study. J Am Pharm Assoc 38:574–585, 1998.

149. Watson PB, Town GI, Holbrook N, et al: Evaluation of a self-management plan for chronic obstructive pulmonary disease. Eur Respir J 10:1267–1271, 1997.

150. Parcel GS, Swank PR, Mariotto MJ, et al: Self-management of cystic fibrosis: A structural model for educational and behavioral variables. Soc Sci Med 38:1307–1315, 1995.

151. Bartholomew LK, Czyzewski DI, Parcel GS, et al: Self-management of cystic fribrosis: Short-term outcomes of the Cystic Fibrosis Family Education Program. Health Educ Behav 24:652–666, 1997.

152. Mannino D, Homa D, Pertowski C, et al: Surveillance for asthma—United States, 1960–1995. MMWR Morb Mortality Wkly Rep 47:1–28, 1998.

153. Lewis A: Non-compliance: A $100 billion problem. Remington Rep 5:14–15, 1997.

154. Griffith SA: A review of the factors associated with patient compliance and the taking of prescribed medicines. Br J Gen Pract 40:114–116, 1990.

155. Bosley CM, Fosbury JA, Cochrane GM: The psychological factors associated with poor compliance with treatment in asthma. Eur Respir J 8:899–904, 1995.

156. Cochrane GM: Compliance and outcomes in patients with asthma. Drugs 52:453–457, 1996.

157. Apter AJ, Reisine ST, Affleck G, et al: Adherence with twice-daily dosing of inhaled steroids: Socioeconomic and health-belief differences. Am J Respir Crit Care Med 157:1810–1817, 1998.

158. DiMatteo MR, Lepper HS, Croghan TW: Depression is a risk factor for noncompliance with medical treatment: Meta-analysis of the effects of anxiety and depression on patient adherence. Arch Intern Med 160:2101–2107, 2000.

159. Lacasse Y, Rousseau L, Maltais F: Prevalence of depressive symptoms and depression in patients with severe oxygen-dependent chronic obstructive pulmonary disease. J Cardiopulm Rehabil 21:80–86, 2001.

160. Cole SA, Christensen JF, Raju MA, et al: Depression. *In* Feldman MD, Christensen JF (eds): Behavioral Medicine in Primary Care. Stamford, CT: Appleton & Lange, 1997.

161. Williams MV, Baker DW, Honig EG, et al: Inadequate literacy is a barrier to asthma knowledge and self-care. Chest 114:1008–1015, 1998.

162. Sackett E, Snow JC: The magnitude of compliance and noncompliance. *In* Sacket E, Hayes RB, Taylor DW (eds): Compliance in Health Care. Baltimore: John Hopkins University Press, 1995.

163. Simmons MS, Nides MA, Rand CS, et al: Trends in compliance with bronchodilator inhaler use between follow-up visits in a clinical trial. Chest 109:963–968, 1996.

164. Coutts JA, Gibson NA, Paton JY: Measuring compliance with inhaled medication in asthma. Arch Dis Child 67:332–333, 1992.

165. Eisen SA, Miller DK, Woodward RS, et al: The effect of prescribed daily dose frequency on patient medication compliance. Arch Intern Med 150:1881–1884, 1990.

166. Mann M, Eliasson O, Patel K, et al: A comparison of the effects of bid and qid dosing on compliance with inhaled flunisolide. Chest 101:496–499, 1992.

167. Bender B, Milgrom H, Rand C, et al: Psychological factors associated with medication nonadherence in asthmatic children. J Asthma 35:347–353, 1998.

168. Apter AJ, Boston RC, George M, et al: Modifiable barriers to adherence to inhaled steroids among adults with asthma: It's not just black and white. J Allergy Clin Immunol 111:1219–1226, 2003.

169. Legorreta AP, Christian-Herman J, O'Connor RD, et al: Compliance with national asthma management guidelines and specialty care: A health maintenance organization experience. Arch Intern Med 58:457–464, 1998.

170. Nides MA, Tashkin DP, Simmons MS, et al: Improving inhaler adherence in a clinical trial through the use of the nebulizer chronology. Chest 104:501–507, 1993.

171. Haynes R, McDonald H, Garg AX, et al: Interventions for helping patients follow prescriptions for medication (Cochrane Review). *In* The Cochrane Library, Issue 1. Oxford: Update Software, 2003.

172. Van Es SM, Colland VT, Nagelkerke AF, et al: An intervention programme using the ASE-model aimed at enhancing adherence in adolescents with asthma. Patient Educ Couns 44:193–203, 2001.

173. Bailey WC, Kohler CL, Richards JM, et al: Asthma self-management (through patient education). Arch Intern Med 59:2422–2428, 1999.

174. Devine EC, Pearcy J: Meta-analysis of the effects of psychoeducational care in adults with chronic obstructive pulmonary disease. Patient Educ Couns 29:167–178, 1996.

175. Kaplan SH, Gandek B, Greenfield S, et al: Patient and visit characteristics related to physicians' participatory decision-making style: Results from the Medical Outcomes Study. Med Care 33:1176–1187, 1995.

Appendix
Glossary of Terms and Standard Symbols

I. PRIMARY AND QUALIFYING SYMBOLS

General

P	*Pressure:* Includes also *partial pressure* of a gas in a mixture of gases or in blood.
L	Lung
W	Chest wall
RS	Respiratory system
Pl	Pleura

Ventilation

V	Volume of gas
$\dot{V}$	Flow of gas
I	Inspired
E	Expired
A	Alveolar
T	Tidal
ET	End-tidal
D	Dead space
STPD	*Standard Conditions:* standard temperature (0° C), barometric pressure (760 mm Hg), and dry.
BTPS	*Body Conditions:* body temperature and ambient pressure, saturated with water vapor at these conditions.
ATPS	*Ambient Conditions:* ambient temperature and pressure, saturated with water vapor at these conditions.

Gas Exchange–Blood Flow

Q	Volume of blood
$\dot{Q}$	Flow of blood
F	Fractional concentration of gas
C	Concentration in blood
S	Saturation in blood
b	Blood, in general
a	Arterial blood
v	Venous blood
$\bar{v}$	Mixed venous blood
c	Capillary blood
c′	Pulmonary end-capillary blood

II. VENTILATION AND LUNG MECHANICS

Static Lung Volumes

VC	*Vital Capacity:* The maximum volume of gas that can be exhaled after fully inflating the lungs.
FRC	*Functional Residual Capacity:* The volume of gas remaining in the lungs at the end of quiet expiration.
TLC	*Total Lung Capacity:* The volume of gas in the lungs after a maximum inspiration.
RV	*Residual Volume:* The volume of gas remaining in the lungs after a maximum exhalation.
IC	*Inspiratory Capacity:* The volume of gas that can be inhaled from resting end-expiration (FRC) to full inflation (TLC).
ERV	*Expiratory Reserve Volume:* The volume of gas that can be exhaled from resting end-expiration (FRC) to full exhalation (RV).
IRV	*Inspiratory Reserve Volume:* The volume of gas that can be inhaled from resting end-inspiration to full inflation (TLC).

Descriptors of Forced Breathing Maneuvers

FVC	*Forced Vital Capacity:* The volume of gas that can be forcibly exhaled after fully inflating the lungs.
FEV_t	*Timed Forced Expiratory Volume:* The volume of gas exhaled at a specified time after beginning the forced vital capacity maneuver. For example, FEV_1 = forced expiratory volume in 1 second.
FEV_t/FVC	*Ratio of Timed Expiratory Volume to Forced Vital Capacity:* For example, FEV_1/FVC, usually expressed as a percentage.
FEF_x	*Specified Forced Expiratory Flow:* The forced expiratory flow rate during a specified portion of the forced vital capacity. For example, $FEF_{200-1200\ mL}$ = forced expiratory flow rate between 200 and 1200 mL of the forced vital capacity; $FEF_{25-75\%}$ = forced expiratory flow rate between 25% and 75% of the forced vital capacity.
$\dot{V}max_{x\%}$	*Specified Maximum Expiratory Flow:* The instantaneous expiratory flow rate when x percent of the forced vital capacity has been exhaled. For example, $\dot{V}max_{50\%}$ = maximum expiratory flow rate at 50% of the forced vital capacity.
MVV	*Maximum Voluntary Ventilation:* Volume of gas exhaled while making maximum breathing efforts during a certain time interval (often 12 seconds).
VR	*Ventilatory Reserve:* The difference between ventilatory capacity during maximum exercise (estimated as MVV or calculated from FEV_1) and minute ventilation at peak exercise; VR, which is also known as *breathing reserve*, represents the potential for further increase in ventilation during maximum (or peak) exercise.
PImax	*Maximum Inspiratory Pressure:* The maximum pressure generated by the respiratory muscles during an attempted inspiration.
PEmax	*Maximum Expiratory Pressure:* The maximum pressure generated by the respiratory muscles during an attempted exhalation.

Descriptors of Ventilation

f	*Respiratory Frequency:* The number of breaths during 1 minute.
V_T	*Tidal Volume:* The volume of gas inspired or expired during each breath.
$\dot{V}_E$	*Expired Volume:* The volume of gas (BTPS), usually measured at the mouth, exhaled during 1 minute.
$\dot{V}_I$	*Inspired Volume:* The volume of gas (BTPS), measured or calculated, inhaled during 1 minute.
$\dot{V}_A$	*Alveolar Ventilation:* The volume of gas (BTPS), exhaled from the lungs during 1 minute, that contributed to gas exchange; calculated as expired volume minus dead space ventilation.
$\dot{V}_D$	*Dead Space Ventilation:* The volume of gas (BTPS), exhaled from the lungs during 1 minute, that did not contribute to gas exchange; also known as *wasted ventilation.* Calculated from the equation

$$\dot{V}_D = \dot{V}_E \frac{Pa_{CO_2} - P_{E_{CO_2}}}{Pa_{CO_2} - P_{I_{CO_2}}}$$

where Pa_{CO_2}, $P_{E_{CO_2}}$, and $P_{I_{CO_2}}$ are the partial pressures of CO_2 in arterial blood, mixed expired gas, and inspired gas, respectively.

V_D	*Dead Space Volume:* The volume of the physiologic dead space; calculated as $\dot{V}_D/f$.
V_D/V_T	*Ratio of Dead Space to Tidal Volume:* The proportion, usually expressed as a percentage, of each breath that does not contribute to CO_2 removal (i.e., the proportion of each breath that is wasted).
V_E	*Ventilatory Equivalent:* The minute ventilation required for each liter of gas exchanged, either O_2 or CO_2, used as a measure of the efficiency of the lungs as a gas exchanger. For O_2:

$$V_{E_{O_2}} = \frac{\dot{V}_E(BTPS)}{\dot{V}_{O_2}(STPD)}$$

Volume-Pressure Relationships

C	*Compliance:* General symbol for compliance, or the ratio of volume change of the structure per unit change in applied pressure across the structure.
C_L	*Lung Compliance:* The volume change divided by the difference between alveolar pressure (Palv) and pleural pressure (Ppl), which is also known as the transpulmonary pressure (PL).
C_W	*Chest Wall Compliance:* The volume change divided by the difference between pleural pressure (Ppl) and body surface pressure (Pbs), which is also known as the transthoracic pressure (PW).
C_{RS}	*Respiratory System Compliance:* The volume change divided by the difference between alveolar pressure (Palv) and body surface pressure (Pbs), or transpulmonary pressure (PL) plus transthoracic pressure (PW).
Cdyn	*Dynamic Compliance:* Value for compliance based on measurements made during uninterrupted breathing.
Cst	*Static Compliance:* Value for compliance based on measurements made during periods of no airflow.
C/V_L	*Specific Compliance:* Value for compliance divided by the lung volume at which it was measured, usually functional residual capacity.

Flow-Pressure Relationships

R	*Resistance:* General symbol for frictional resistance, or the pressure difference divided by flow.
RAW	*Airway Resistance:* Resistance calculated from pressure difference between airway opening (Pao) and alveoli (Palv) divided by the airflow.
RL	*Total Pulmonary Resistance:* Resistance calculated by dividing flow-dependent transpulmonary pressure by airflow at the mouth.
GAW	*Airway Conductance:* The reciprocal of RAW.
GAW/V_L	*Specific Conductance:* Value for airway conductance divided by the lung volume at which it was measured.

III. GAS EXCHANGE

Blood

Examples shown are for O_2; other gases (e.g., CO_2, N_2, CO) or other sites (e.g., $\bar{v}$, c') can be substituted when appropriate.

PO_2	*Partial Pressure of O_2:* General designation (expressed in mm Hg); source usually specified (e.g., arterial PO_2 or Pa_{O_2}).
SO_2	*Blood Saturation:* General designation (expressed as a percentage); source usually specified (e.g., arterial SO_2 or Sa_{O_2}).
CO_2	*Oxygen Content:* General designation (expressed in mL/dL); source usually specified (e.g., arterial CO_2).
$\dot{V}_{O_2}$	*Oxygen Consumption:* The volume of O_2 (STPD) utilized by the body during 1 minute; usually calculated as the amount of O_2 extracted from inspired gas.
$\dot{V}_{O_2}max$	*Maximum Oxygen Consumption:* The maximal volume of O_2 (STPD) that can be utilized by the body during 1 minute of maximally attainable exercise.
$\dot{V}_{CO_2}$	*Carbon Dioxide Output:* The volume of CO_2 (STPD) produced by the body during 1 minute; usually calculated as the amount of CO_2 added to exhaled gas.
RQ	*Respiratory Quotient:* The ratio of $\dot{V}_{CO_2}$ to $\dot{V}_{O_2}$ during steady-state metabolic activity.
RER	*Respiratory Exchange Ratio:* The ratio of $\dot{V}_{CO_2}$ to $\dot{V}_{O_2}$, as in RQ, but also including the influence of transient changes in body stores of respiratory gases.

Gas to Blood

$(A-a)PO_2$	*Alveolar-Arterial PO_2 Difference:* The difference in PO_2 between mean alveolar gas and arterial blood (expressed in mm Hg).
	Alveolar Air Equation: Often used to calculate mean alveolar PO_2 (PA_{O_2}):

$$PA_{O_2} = PI_{O_2} - PA_{CO_2}\left[FI_{O_2} + \frac{1 - FI_{O_2}}{R}\right]$$

where PI_{O_2} is the PO_2 of inspired gas; PA_{CO_2} is the alveolar PCO_2 (usually assumed to equal arterial PCO_2); FI_{O_2} is the fractional concentration of O_2 in inspired gas; and R is the respiratory exchange ratio.

DL	*Diffusing Capacity of the Lung:* Expressed as the volume of gas transferred per minute per unit of alveolar-capillary pressure difference for the gas used, which is usually specified (e.g., DL_{CO} or DL_{O_2}).
DM	*Diffusing Capacity of the Alveolocapillary Membrane.*

1/DL   *Total Resistance to Diffusion:* The sum of the resistance to diffusion of the test gas across the alveolo-capillary membrane (1/DM) and the resistance to diffusion within the red blood cells attributable to the chemical reaction between the test gas and hemoglobin (1/θVC). These relationships are expressed by the Roughton-Forster equation:

$$\frac{1}{DL} = \frac{1}{DM} + \frac{1}{\theta VC}$$

DL/VA   *Diffusion per Unit of Alveolar Volume:* The value of DL (STPD) divided by VA (BTPS), both measured in the same breathing maneuver.

IV. HEMODYNAMIC DESCRIPTORS

$\dot{Q}T$ *Cardiac Output:* The total output of the left ventricle.

$\dot{Q}s$ *Pulmonary Shunt:* The total amount of blood perfusing completely nonventilated gas-exchange units; hence, blood that does not come in contact with inspired gas and contribute to oxygen uptake. Often called the *right-to-left shunt,* but this term also includes intracardiac shunts.

$\dot{Q}s/\dot{Q}T$ *Pulmonary Shunt Flow:* The total pulmonary shunt ($\dot{Q}s$), or venous admixture, expressed as a percentage of total cardiac output ($\dot{Q}T$) according to the equation

$$\frac{\dot{Q}s}{\dot{Q}T} = \frac{Cc'_{O_2} - Ca_{O_2}}{Cc'_{O_2} - C\bar{v}_{O_2}} \times 100$$

where Cc'_{O_2} is the O_2 content of end-capillary blood; Ca_{O_2} is the O_2 content of arterial blood; and $C\bar{v}_{O_2}$ is the O_2 content of mixed venous blood. When determined from specimens obtained while breathing 100% O_2, $\dot{Q}s/\dot{Q}T$ is a measure of right-to-left shunting of blood.

PPA   *Pulmonary Artery Pressure:* The pressure—systolic, diastolic, or mean—measured in the pulmonary artery.

PLA   *Left Atrial Pressure:* The pressure, usually mean, measured in the left atrium.

Pcap   *Pulmonary Capillary Pressure:* The mean pressure in the pulmonary capillaries, sometimes abbreviated Pc, which cannot be measured directly in humans but is frequently estimated by the equation

$$Pcap = PLA + 0.4(PPA - PLA)$$

PPW   *Pulmonary Wedge Pressure:* The mean pressure measured by the pulmonary artery occlusion technique, which provides an estimate of the postcapillary, or pulmonary venous, pressure.

PVR   *Pulmonary Vascular Resistance:* The resistance to blood flow through the lungs; a calculated value from the equation

$$PVR = \frac{PPA - PLA}{\dot{Q}T}$$

in which PPW is often used to approximate PLA.

V. OTHER USEFUL TERMS AND EQUATIONS

PEEP   *Positive End-Expiratory Pressure:* The condition in which the pressure in the lungs at the end of expiration is positive (i.e., higher than atmospheric). Usually applied externally by ventilator adjustments; when PEEP results from failure to exhale fully at the end of expiration, it is called *intrinsic* in origin (PEEPi).

P0.1   *Mouth Occlusion Pressure:* The pressure measured in the mouth during the first 0.1 second of attempted inspiration after the airway is temporarily occluded while the subject is breathing. An estimate of the central drive to breathe.

TI/TTOT   *Duty Cycle:* The ratio of the duration of inspiration (TI) to the duration of inspiration and expiration (TTOT), a reflection of respiratory timing.

Henderson-Hasselbalch Equation: Useful for calculating any one of three variables, pH, HCO_3^-, or H_2CO_3, when two of them are known:

$$pH = pK + \log \frac{\left[HCO_3^-\right]}{\left[H_2CO_3\right]}$$

where pK, the dissociation constant, is 6.10 for plasma at 37° C; $[HCO_3^-]$ is the concentration of bicarbonate in plasma; and $[H_2CO_3]$ is the concentration of carbonic acid in plasma (both in mol/L). The equation can be rearranged by using PCO_2 (in mm Hg) and its solubility in plasma so that

$$pH = pK + \log \frac{\left[HCO_3^-\right]}{\left[PCO_2 \times 0.0301\right]}$$

Starling Equation: Net fluid exchange (Jv) across the microvascular barrier in the lungs:

$$Jv = LpS[(Pc - Pi) - \sigma d(\pi c - \pi i)]$$

where Lp is the hydraulic conductivity ("permeability"); S is the surface area; Pc is the microvascular hydrostatic pressure; Pi is the perimicrovascular hydrostatic pressure; σd is the osmotic reflection coefficient; πc is the microvascular colloid osmotic pressure; and πi is the perimicrovascular colloid osmotic pressure.

Index

Note: Page numbers followed by the letter f refer to figures and those followed by t refer to tables.

P